Encyclopedia of
Food Technology

other AVI books

Encyclopedia of Food Technology

ARNOLD H. JOHNSON, Ph.D.

Consultant and Retired President,
Research & Development Division,
Kraftco Corporation,
Glenview, Illinois

MARTIN S. PETERSON, Ph.D.

Editorial Consultant,
Science and Technology,
Natick, Massachusetts

THE AVI PUBLISHING COMPANY, INC.

Westport, Connecticut

1974

Library of Congress Catalog Card Number: 74-14129
ISBN-0-87055-157-4

Printed in the United States of America

Contributors

J. P. ACCOLAS, Station Centrale de Recherches Laitères et de Technologie des Produits Animaux, Jouy-en-Josas, 78 Yvelines, France

RICHARD M. AHLGREN, Aqua-Chem, Inc., 225 N. Grand Ave., Waukesha, Wisconsin 53186

JUSTIN J. ALIKONIS, Director, Research & Development, Paul F. Beich Company, P.O. Box 754, Bloomington, Illinois 61701

R. R. ALLEN, Exploratory Research Department, Anderson Clayton Foods, 333 North Central Expressway, Richardson, Texas 75080

JOSEPH ALLERTON, The Nestlé Company, 555 South 4th St., Fulton, New York 13069

M. A. AMERINE, Professor of Enology and Enologist, Agricultural Experiment Station, University of California, Davis, California 95616

ANDY ANDARMANI, Chief Chemist, Sunsweet Growers, Inc., P.O. Box 670, San Jose, California 95106

EDWARD E. ANDERSON, Special Assistant for the DOD Program, U.S. Army Natick Laboratories, Natick, Massachusetts 01760

J. G. ARMSTRONG, Department of Food Science, University of Alberta, Edmonton, Canada

CAROL LEE ASHIMINE, Norwegian Canning Industry, 114 Sansome St., San Francisco, California 94104

LAWRENCE ATKIN, Arthur D. Little, Inc., A4 Venture Out Park, Jensen Beach, Florida 33457

J. AUCLAIR, Station Centrale de Recherches Laitères et de Technologie des Produits Animaux, Jouy-en-Josas, 78 Yvelines, France

VIGEN K. BABAYAN, Stokely Van Camp. Inc., P.O. Box 1113, Indianapolis, Indiana 46206

B. P. BALIGA, Tata Oil Mills Co., Ltd., Sevrie, Bombay 33, India

C. OLIN BALL, Consultant, P.O. Box 802, New Brunswick, New Jersey 08903

HERBERT I. BARNES, Director, Research & Development, Betty Crocker Division, General Mills, Inc., James Ford Bell Technical Center, 9000 Plymouth Ave. North, Minneapolis, Minnesota 55414

JOHN A. BARNES, Burger King Corp., P.O. Box 338, Miami, Florida 33156

J. C. BAUERNFEIND, Nutrition Research Coordinator, Chemical Research Department, Hoffmann-La Roche, Inc., Nutley, New Jersey 07110

ARNOLD W. BAUMANN, Professional Consulting Engineer, 3215 Thayer Avenue, Evanston, Illinois 60201

F. C. BAWDEN, Director, Rothamsted Experiment Station, Harpenden, Herts, England

KARL M. BECK, Manager, New Product Research, Scientific Division, Abbott Laboratories, North Chicago, Illinois 60064

C. L. BEDFORD, Department of Food Science and Human Nutrition, 139 Food Science Building, Michigan State University, East Lansing, Michigan 48823

DWIGHT H. BERGQUIST, Vice President, Engineering Research, Henningsen Research and Development Center, 810 Farnum St., Omaha, Nebraska 68102

ROBERT E. BERRY, U.S. Fruit and Vegetable Products Laboratory, Agricultural Research Service, U.S. Department of Agriculture, P.O. Box 1909, Winter Haven, Florida 33880

GEORG A. BORGSTROM, Professor, Department of Food Science and Nutrition, Michigan State University, East Lansing, Michigan 48823

FRANK P. BOYLE, Western Regional Research Laboratory, Agricultural Research Service, U.S. Department of Agriculture, Berkeley, California 94710

WILLIAM B. BRADLEY (retired). Formerly, President, American Institute of Baking, 400 East Ontario St., Chicago, Illinois 60611

A. L. BRANEN, Department of Food Science, Washington State University, Pullman, Washington 99163

JAMES G. BRENNAN, Lecturer, National College of Food Technology, University of Reading, St. George's Ave., Weybridge, Surrey, England

JOHN E. BREKKE, U.S. Department of Agriculture Fruit Laboratory, University of Hawaii, 1920 Edmondson Road, Honolulu, Hawaii 96827

MAXWELL C. BROCKMANN, Chief, Animal Products Division, Food Laboratory, U.S. Army Natick Laboratories, Natick, Massachusetts 01760

E. E. BURNS, Department of Soil and Crop Sciences, Texas A&M University, College Station, Texas 77843

FELIX A. BURROWS, JR., 3260 Dato Avenue, Highland Park, Illinois 60035

WILLIAM B. CAMPBELL, B. L. Thomas Associates, P.O. Box 15177, Cincinnati, Ohio 45215

JEAN F. CAUL, Department of Foods and Nutrition, Justin Hall, Kansas State University, Manhattan, Kansas 66502

STANLEY E. CHARM, Scientific Director, New England Enzyme Center, Tufts University School of Medicine, 130 Harrison Ave., Boston, Massachusetts 02111

ROBERT G. CHRISTIE, Breakstone Sugar Creek Foods Division, Kraftco Corp., 810 Seventh Ave., New York, New York 10019

WARREN S. CLARK, JR., in charge of Research and Technical Services, American Dry Milk Institute, 130 N. Franklin St., Chicago, Illinois 60606

F. M. CLYDESDALE, Department of Food Science and Nutrition, University of Massachusetts, Amherst, Massachusetts 01002

HAROLD T. COOK, Director, Market Quality Research Division, U.S. Department of Agriculture, Federal Center Bldg., Hyattsville, Maryland 20782

W. M. CORT, Product Development Department, Hoffmann-La Roche, Inc., Nutley, New Jersey 07110

J. C. COWAN (retired). Formerly, Northern Regional Research Laboratory, Agricultural Research Service, U.S. Department of Agriculture, Peoria, Illinois 61604

LOUIS F. CREMERS, Research & Development Division, Kraftco Corp., 801 Waukegan Road, Glenview, Illinois 60025

RANDY DAHLING, Information Director, Sunsweet Growers, Inc., P.O. Box 670, San Jose, California 95106

ROBERT V. DECAREAU, General Equipment and Packaging Laboratory, U.S. Army Natick Laboratories, Natick, Massachusetts 01760, and Editor, *Microwave Energy Applications Newsletter*

J. E. DESPAUL (retired). Formerly, Defense Subsistence Testing Laboratory, Defense Supply Agency, U.S. Department of Defense, 1819 W. Pershing Road, Chicago, Illinois 60609

NIEL DINESEN, Chr. Hansens Laboratory, 9015 West Maple St., Milwaukee, Wisconsin 53214

L. C. DUGAL, Freshwater Institute, Fisheries Research Board of Canada, 501 University Crescent, Winnipeg, Manitoba, Canada

RALPH C. DOWNING, Research Associate, DuPont de Nemours & Company, 1007 Market St., Wilmington, Delaware 19898

BRUCE A. DREW, Research Associate, The Pillsbury Company, 311 Second St., S.E., Minneapolis, Minnesota 55414

E. DREWS, Federal Research Institute of Cereal Industry, 473 Detmold am Schützenberg 9, Berlin and Detmold, Germany

DAVID A. FELLERS, Chief, Cereals Laboratory, Western Regional Research Laboratory, Agricultural Research Service, U.S. Department of Agriculture, Berkeley, California 94710

GEORGE E. FELTON (retired). Formerly, Dole Company Division, Castle & Cooke, Inc., P.O. Drawer 3380, Honolulu, Hawaii 96801

RAYMOND T. FOULDS, JR., Extension Forrester, Extension Division, University of Vermont, Burlington, Vermont 05401

HARVEY FRAM, B. Manischewitz Company, 9 Clinton St., Newark, New Jersey 07102

F. J. FRANCIS, Head, Department of Food Science and Nutrition, University of Massachusetts, Amherst, Massachusetts 01003

CHARLES N. FREY (deceased). Formerly, Director of Research, Standard Brands, Inc., New York, N.Y.

N. C. GANGULI, National Dairy Research Institute, Karnal, Haryana, India

F. GUNNER GIDLOW, Consultant, 4473 Olson Lake Trail West, St. Paul, Minnesota 55109

J. WALTER GIFFEE, Chief, Food Chemistry Division, Food Laboratory, U.S. Army Natick Laboratories, Natick, Massachusetts 01760

K. A. GILLES, Vice President for Agriculture, Department of Cereal Chemistry and Technology, North Dakota State University, Fargo, N. Dakota 58102

BEN GILLESPIE, Browning Ferris Industries, P.O. Box 3151, Houston, Texas 77001

JOSEPH P. GILLIS, Systems Engineering Manager, Protection Systems Division, Fenwal, Inc., Ashland, Massachusetts 01721

LEO A. GOLDBLATT, Chief, Oilseeds Crops Laboratory, Southern Regional Research Laboratories, Agricultural Research Service, U.S. Department of Agriculture, P.O. Box 19687, New Orleans, Louisiana 70179

SAMUEL A. GOLDBLITH, Professor and Deputy Department Head, Department of Nutrition and Food Science, Massachusetts Institute of Technology, 77 Massachusetts Ave., Cambridge, Massachusetts 02139

DEE M. GRAHAM, Department of Food Science and Nutrition, University of Missouri, Columbia, Missouri 65201

W. R. GRAHAM, JR., Senior Research Fellow, The Quaker Oats Company, 617 West Main St., Barrington, Illinois 60010

GEORGE R. GRANGE, Deputy Administrator, Consumer and Marketing Service, U.S. Department of Agriculture, Washington, D.C. 20250

WILLIAM D. GRAY, Professor Emeritus, Northern Illinois University, DeKalb, Illinois

BERNARD W. GREENWALD, Merck Chemical Division, Merck & Company, Rahway, New Jersey 07065

WILLIAM C. GRIFFIN, Associate Director, Product Development Department, Specialty Chemicals Division, ICI America, Inc., Wilmington, Delaware 19899

DAVID R. GROSS, Research Director, The J. M. Smucker Company, Orrville, Ohio 44667

CARL W. HALL, Dean, College of Engineering, Washington State University, Pullman, Washington 99163

H. GORDON HARDING, Consultant, 1410 Central, Evanston, Illinois 60201. Formerly, Research & Development Division, Kraftco Corp., Glenview, Illinois

ROBERT W. HARKINS, Director, Scientific Affairs, Grocery Manufacturers of America, Inc., 1425 K St., N.W., Washington, D.C. 20005

W. O. HARRINGTON, Eastern Marketing and Nutrition Research Division, Agricultural Research Service, U.S. Department of Agriculture, 600 E. Mermaid Lane, Philadelphia, Pennsylvania 19118

HENRY B. HEATH, Manager, Technical Services, Bush, Boake, Allen, Ltd., Ash Grove, Hackney, London EB4RH, England

A. C. HERRO (retired). Formerly, Research & Development Division, Kraftco Corp., Glenview, Illinois

W. M. HIGBY (retired). Formerly, Chemist, Horlicks, Inc., 1450 Summit Ave., Racine, Wisconsin 53404

C. H. HILLS, Head, Fruit Investigations, Eastern Marketing and Nutrition Research Division, Agricultural Research Service, U.S. Department of Agriculture, 6 E. Mermaid Lane, Philadelphia, Pennsylvania 19118

J. T. HOGAN, Southern Regional Research Laboratory, Agricultural Research Service, U.S. Department of Agriculture, New Orleans, Louisiana

S. D. HOLDSWORTH, The Campden Food Preservation Research Association, Chipping Campden, Glos., England

JOHN L. HOLOHAN, James Ford Bell Technical Center, General Mills, Inc., 9000 Plymouth Ave., North, Minneapolis, Minnesota 55427

IRWIN HORNSTEIN, Science Research Officer, Agency for International Development, U.S. Department of State, Washington, D.C. 20250

BERNARD S. HORTON, Director of Marketing International, Abcor, Inc., 341 Vassar St., Cambridge, Massachusetts 02139

GORDON A. HOURAN, Vice President, Milk and Food Equipment Division, De Laval Separator Company, Poughkeepsie, New York 12602

PETER X. HOYNAK (retired). Formerly, CPC International, International Plaza, Englewood Cliffs, New Jersey 07632

R. S. HUNTER, President, Hunter Associates Laboratory, Inc., 9529 Lee Highway, Fairfax, Virginia 22030

DAVID C. IREDALE, Freshwater Institute, Fisheries Research Board of Canada, 501 University Crescent, Winnipeg, Manitoba, Canada

COL. ROHLAND A. ISKER (retired), U.S. Army, Indian Lake, Florida 33855

J. M. JACKSON, Director, Technical Relations, Green Giant Company, Le Sueur, Minnesota 56058

DANIEL H. JACOBSEN (retired). Formerly, American Dairy Association, 321 Stratford, Des Plaines, Illinois 60016

P. M. JANGAARD, Scientific Liaison Officer, Atlantic Regional Research and Development Office, Fisheries Research Board of Canada, P.O. Box 159, Halifax, Nova Scotia, Canada

E. F. JANSEN (retired). Formerly, Western Regional Research Laboratory, Agricultural Research Service, U.S. Department of Agriculture, Berkeley, California 94710

J. A. JAYNES, President, Borden Foods Division, Beverage Products, 50 West Broad St., 8th Floor, Columbus, Ohio 43215

OTTO G. JENSEN, Consultant, 111 East Allendale Road, Saddle River, New Jersey 07458. Formerly, Research Associate, Nabisco, Inc.

ARNOLD H. JOHNSON, Consultant. Formerly, Director, Research & Development Division, Kraftco Corp., Glenview, Illinois 60025

JOHN J. JONAS, Research & Development Division, Kraftco Corp., 801 Waukegan Road, Glenview, Illinois 60025

EDWARD S. JOSEPHSON, Deputy Technical Director/Food Service Systems Program, Food Laboratory, U.S. Army Natick Laboratories, Natick, Massachusetts 01760

ENDEL KARMAS, Department of Food Science, Rutgers—The State University, New Brunswick, New Jersey 08903

D. A. KAUTER, Deputy Chief, Food Microbiology Branch, Division of Microbiology, Food and Drug Administration, U.S. Department of Health, Education, and Welfare, 200 C St., West, Washington, D.C. 20204

CLAYTON A. KEMPF, Foremost Foods Company, 6393 Clark Ave., Dublin, California 94566

MARY V. KLICKA, Food Laboratory, U.S. Army Natick Laboratories, Natick, Massachusetts 01760

PHILIP E. KOEHLER, Department of Food Science, University of Georgia, College of Agriculture, Athens, Georgia 30601

HERIBERT KOHLHAAS, Kraft, GMBH, 6236 Eschborn Bei, Hauptstrasse 185, Germany

A. P. KOULOHERIS, Superintendent, Process Engineering, Gardinier, Inc., Tampa, Florida 33601

AMIHUD KRAMER, Department of Horticulture, University of Maryland, College Park, Maryland 20742

DAVID KRITCHEVSKY, The Wistar Institute of Anatomy and Biology, 36th Street at Spruce, Philadelphia, Pennsylvania 19104

PAUL A. LACHANCE, Department of Food Science, Rutgers—The State University, New Brunswick, New Jersey 08540

ALFRED LACHMANN, Technical Director, Prodett Company, Wynnewood, Pennsylvania 19096

WILLARD L. LANGHUS, Research & Development Division, Kraftco Corp., 801 Waukegan Road, Glenview, Illinois 60025

FRANK L. LA QUE, Consultant, Claridge Drive, Verona, New Jersey 07044. Formerly, Vice President, The International Nickel Company.

ELIZABETH LARMOND, Central Experimental Farm, Food Research Institute, Canada Department of Agriculture, Ottawa, Canada KIA066

R. J. LEARSON, Technological Laboratory, U.S. Bureau of Commercial Fisheries, Emerson Ave., Gloucester, Massachusetts 01930

S. LEONARD, Department of Food Science and Technology, University of California, Davis, California 95616

ALBERT LEVIE, President, Elgee Meats, 5735 W. Adams Blvd., Los Angeles, California 90016

K. H. LEWIS, Director, Office of Food and Nutrition Sciences, Bureau of Foods, Pesticides and Product Safety, Food and Drug Administration, U.S. Department of Health, Education, and Welfare, Washington, D.C. 20204

IVAN L. LINDAHL, Leader, Sheep Nutrition, Animal Science Research Division, Agricultural Research Service, U.S. Department of Agriculture, Beltsville, Maryland 20708. Also Director, American Dairy Goat Association.

G. E. LIVINGSTON, Director, Food Science Associates, P.O. Box 265, Rye, New York 10580

HENRY LONG, Research & Development Division, Kraftco Corp., 801 Waukegan Road, Glenview, Illinois 60025

ERICH LÜCK, Farbwerke Hoechst, Postfach 80 03 20, Frankfurt am. 6230, Germany

WALTER O. LUNDBERG, Director, The Hormel Institute, 801 16th Ave., N.E., Austin, Minnesota 55912

HERBERT G. LUTHER, Consultant, The Mill Head of the River, Smithtown, New York 11787. Formerly, Research Associate, Pfizer, Inc., New York, N.Y.

MATTHEW J. LYNCH, Development Manager, Product Development Department, Specialty Chemicals Division, ICI America, Inc., Wilmington, Delaware 19899

R. K. LYNT, Food and Drug Administration, U.S. Department of Health, Education, and Welfare, 200 C St., West, Washington, D.C. 20204

P. MARKAKIS, Department of Food Science, Michigan State University, East Lansing, Michigan 48823

ELMER H. MARTH, Department of Food Science, University of Wisconsin, Madison, Wisconsin 53706

KARL F. MATTIL, Food Protein Research and Development Center, Texas A&M University, College Station, Texas 77843

DONALD L. MAXWELL, James Ford Bell Technical Center, General Mills, Inc., 9000 Plymouth Ave., North, Minneapolis, Minnesota 55427

PACKIE McFARLAND, Vice President, Marketing, United Salt Corporation, 2000 West Loop 5, Houston, Texas 70027

DALE K. MECHAM, Western Regional Research Laboratory, Agricultural Research Service, U.S. Department of Agriculture, Berkeley, California 94710

DONALD F. MEISNER, Research & Development Division, Kraftco Corp., 801 Waukegan Road, Glenview, Illinois 60025

F. P. MEHRLICH, Director, Food Laboratory, U.S. Army Natick Laboratories, Natick, Massachusetts 01760

J. M. MENDELSOHN, U.S. Bureau of Commercial Fisheries, Emerson Ave., Gloucester, Massachusetts 01930

H. V. MILES, Central Technology, Dorr-Oliver, Inc., Stamford, Connecticut 06904

ARTHUR I. MORGAN, JR., Director, Western Regional Research Division, Agricultural Research Service, U.S. Department of Agriculture, Berkeley, California 94710

ROY E. MORSE, Department of Food Science, Rutgers—The State University, P.O. Box 231, New Brunswick, New Jersey 08903

GEORGE J. MOUNTNEY, Research Management Specialist, Cooperative State Research Service, U.S. Department of Agriculture, Washington, D.C. 20250

GERALD D. NEU, Senior Technologist, DPI Division, Eastman Chemical Products, Inc., Kingsport, Tennessee 37662

C. NIEMAN, Director, IFT, 172 Joh. Verhulststraat, Amsterdam (Oud-Zuid), The Netherlands

R. S. NORTH, Vice President, Sethness Products Company, P.O. Box 190, Clinton, Iowa 52732

JAMES R. O'CONNOR, Carr Fastener Division, TRW, Inc., 31 Ames, Cambridge, Massachusetts 02142

RALPH P. OFCARIK, Department of Soil and Crop Sciences, Texas A&M University, College Station, Texas 77843

MASAMI O'HARA, Ajinomoto Company, Inc., 7, 1-Chome, Takara-Cho, Chuo-Ku, Japan

MARTIN OTTESON, Director, Chemical Department, Carlsberg Laboratory, Gammel Carlsbergvej 10, Copenhagen, Valby, Denmark

GEORGE W. PACKOWSKI, Assistant to the Vice President, Joseph Seagram & Sons, 375 Park Ave., New York, New York 10022

H. A. B. PARPIA, Food and Agriculture Organization, United Nations, Rome, Italy

D. E. PARRISH, Department of Biochemistry, Kansas State University, Manhattan, Kansas 66506

EUGENE F. PASCHALL, Moffett Technical Center, CPC International, Argo, Illinois 60501

JENS K. PEDERSEN, Kobenhavns Pektinfabrik, 4823 Lille Skensved, Copenhagen, Denmark

C. S. PEDERSON, Professor Emeritus of Bacteriology, New York State Agricultural Experiment Station, Cornell University, Geneva, New York 14456

JOHN A. PETERS, Atlantic Fishery Products Technology Center, U.S. Bureau of Commercial Fisheries, Emerson Ave., Gloucester, Massachusetts 01930

MARTIN S. PETERSON, Consultant, 15 Lakeview Gardens, Natick, Massachusetts 01760

D. M. PINKERT, Chemical Research Department, Hoffmann-La Roche, Inc., Nutley, New Jersey 07110

Y. POMERANZ, Director, U.S. Grain Marketing Research Center, 1515 College Ave., Manhattan, Kansas 66502

NORMAN N. POTTER, Department of Food Science, Cornell University, Ithaca, New York 14850

S. D. POULSEN, Manager, Technical Services, Sun-Maid Raisin Growers of California, 13525 South Bethel Ave., Kingsburg, California 93631

JOHN J. POWERS, Department of Food Science, University of Georgia, College of Agriculture, Athens, Georgia 30601

WALTER PRITCHETT, Consultant, 1220 Crane Blvd., Libertyville, Illinois 60048. Formerly, Laboratory Manager, Fats and Oils, Kraftco Corp., Glenview, Illinois

JERRY F. PROCTOR, Manager, Nutrition Research Laboratory, Research & Development Division, Kraftco Corp., 801 Waukegan Road, Glenveiw, Illinois 60025

R. H. PURDY, Associate Director of Research, Pacific Vegetable Oil Corp., World Trade Center, San Francisco, California 94111

ABDUL R. RAHMAN, Head, Research & Development, Plant Products Division, Food Laboratory, U.S. Army Natick Laboratories, Natick, Massachusetts 01760

JACK W. RALLS, Research Manager, National Canners Association, 6 Highgate Road, Kensington, California 94707

G. RAMA RAO, Central Food Technological Research Institute, Cheluvamba Mansion, Mysore 2-A, India

SUTTON REDFERN, Director of Research, Standard Brands, Inc., Betts Avenue, Stamford, Connecticut 06904

GERALD REED, Vice President, Research, Universal Foods Corp., 433 East Michigan St., Milwaukee, Wisconsin 53201

PIERCE M. REED, Sheffield Chemical Division, Kraftco Corp., 2400 Morris Ave., Union, New Jersey 07083

L. H. REES, Vice President for Research, Gaulin Corporation, Garden St., Everett, Massachusetts 02149

F. H. REUTER (retired). Formerly, Department of Food Technology, University of New South Wales, Sydney, Australia

M. L. RILEY, Division of Animal Science, University of Wyoming, Box 3354, University Station, Laramie, Wyoming 82070

GEORGE C. RIMNAC, Consultant, 1930 Harrison St., Glenview, Illinois 60025

JAMES A. ROGERS, JR., Vice President and Director, Research & Development, Fritzsche, Dodge and Olcott, Inc., 76 9th Ave., New York, New York 10011

L. W. ROONEY, Associate Professor, Department of Soil and Crop Sciences, Texas A&M University, College Station, Texas 77843

EDWARD W. ROSENBAUM, President, David Michael & Company, Inc., 10801 Decatur Road, Philadelphia, Pennsylvania 19154

DANIEL ROSENFIELD, Director, Nutrition Research, Miles Laboratories, Elkhart, Indiana 46514

HOWARD ROTH, DCA Food Industries, Inc., 45 West 36th St., New York, New York 10036

MAX RUEHRMUND, Walter Baker Division, General Foods Corp., P.O. Box 600, Dover, Delaware 19901

J. J. RYAN, U.S. Bureau of Commercial Fisheries, Emerson Ave., Gloucester, Massachusetts 01930

W. WALLACE RYAN, Vice President, Lea and Perrin, Inc., Fair Lawn Industrial Park, Fair Lawn, New Jersey 07410

STANLEY SACHAROW, Regional Packaging Products Supervisor, Reynolds Metals Company, 19 East 47th Street, New York, New York

LOUIS SAIR, Griffith Laboratories, 1415 West 37th St., Chicago, Illinois 60609

ZDENKA SAMISH, Faculty of Agriculture, Hebrew University of Jerusalem, Rehovot, Israel

D. F. SAMPSON, Professor Emeritus, Food Industries Department, California State Polytechnic College, San Luis Obispo, California 93401

TOWNSEND J. SAUSVILLE, District Manager, Flavors and Fragrances, William M. Bell Company, 3312 Bloomingdale Ave., Melrose Park, Illinois 60160

JANE R. SAVAGE, College of Home Economics, University of Tennessee, Knoxville, Tennessee 37916

W. F. SCHROEDER (deceased). Formerly, Carnation Research Laboratories, 8015 Van Nuys Blvd., Van Nuys, California 91412

L. J. SCHUDDEBOOM, Ministry of Social Affairs and Public Health, Austerlitzseweg 42, Doorn, The Netherlands

W. SEIBEL, Federal Research Institute of Cereal Industry, 473 Detmold am Schützenberg 9, Berlin and Detmold, Germany

K. M. SHAHANI, Department of Food Science, University of Nebraska, Lincoln, Nebraska 68503

R. S. SHALLENBERGER, Department of Food Science and Technology, New York Agricultural Experiment Station, Cornell University, Geneva, New York 14456

J. A. SHELLENBERGER, Professor Emeritus, Department of Grain Science and Industry, Kansas State University, Manhattan, Kansas 66502

MIMI SHERATON, Food Editor, 248 West 12th St., New York, New York 10014

LEE SHIPMAN, General Foods Corp., P.O. Box 600, Dover, Delaware 19901

WALTER SILVA, Ministry of Health, Rio de Janeiro 1, Brazil

EDWARD M. SIMMONS, Vice President, McIlhenny Company, Avery Island, Louisiana 70513

PAUL SIMONART, Station de Recherches Laitières, Université Catholique de Louvain, Institut Agronomique, Kardinaal Merceierlaan, 92, 3030 Hèverlee, Belgium

M. SIVETZ, Consultant, 3635 N.W. Elmwood Drive, Corvallis, Oregon 97330

ORA SMITH, Professor Emeritus, Department of Vegetable Crops, Plant Science Bldg., Cornell University, Ithaca, New York 14850

B. SOLOMAN, Chemical Engineer, Institut des Corp Gras, 5 Boul de Letour-Maubourg, Paris, France

NORMAN V. O. SONNTAG, Director of Research, Glyco Chemicals, Inc., P.O. Box 330, Williamsport, Pennsylvania 17701

W. E. L. SPIESS, Federal Research Center for Food Preservation, Engesserstrasse 20, 74 Karlsruhe 1, Germany

JOACHIM M. STAACKMANN, Research & Development Division, Kraftco Corp., 801 Waukegan Road, Glenview, Illinois 60025

MAURICE E. STANSBY, Director, Environmental Conservation Division, Northwest Fisheries Center, National Marine Fisheries Service, 2725 Montlake Blvd. East, Seattle, Washington 98112

J. BRYAN STINE, Vice President, Kraft Foods Division, Kraftco Corp., 500 Peshtigo Court, Chicago, Illinois 60609

J. P. SWEENEY, Research Chemist, Human Nutrition Research Division, Agricultural Research Service, U.S. Department of Agriculture, Beltsville, Maryland 20708

J. SWIFT, Food Laboratory, U.S. Army Natick Laboratories, Natick, Massachusetts 01760

HIROKADZU TAIRA, Food Research Institute, Hamazono-Cho Fukagawa Koto-Ku, Tokyo, Japan

NORMAN W. TAPE, Product Research Advisor, Department of Industry, Trade, and Commerce, Ottawa 4, Canada

H. L. A. TARR (retired). Formerly, Fisheries Research Board of Canada, 4160 Marine Drive, West Vancouver, British Columbia, Canada

F. WARREN TAUBER, Union Carbide Company, 6733 West 65 St., Chicago, Illinois 60638

WELTON I. TAYLOR, Consulting Microbiologist, 7621 S. Prairie, Chicago, Illinois 60119

J. G. TEER, Department of Soil and Crop Sciences, Texas A&M University, College Station, Texas 77843

B. L. THOMAS, B. L. Thomas Associates, P.O. Box 15177, Cincinnati, Ohio 45215

MIRIAM H. THOMAS, Food Laboratory, U.S. Army Natick Laboratories, Natick, Massachusetts 01760

JOHN E. THOMPSON, Thompson Farms, 908 Burns Ave., Flossmoor, Illinois 60422

MARVIN E. THORNER, Consultant, 3 Vanad Drive, East Hills, New York 11576. Also Visiting Professor, The Culinary Institute of America, Hyde Park, N.Y.

DEE TOURTELLOTTE (retired). Formerly, President, Kind and Knox Gelatin Company, Head of North and Fifth St., Camden, New Jersey 08102

DONALD K. TRESSLER, President, Avi Publishing Company, Westport, Connecticut 06880

LEON TUMERMAN, Research & Development Division, Kraftco Corp., 801 Waukegan Road, Glenview, Illinois 60025

MATTHEW K. VELDHUIS (retired). Formerly, Laboratory Chief, Citrus and Subtropical Products Laboratory, Southeastern Marketing and Nutritional Research Division, Agricultural Research Service, U.S. Department of Agriculture, Winter Haven, Florida 33880

H. S. VILLARS, Food Ingredients, Inc., 1411 Peterson Ave., Park Ridge, Illinois 60068

D. E. WALSH, Department of Cereal Chemistry and Technology, North Dakota State University, Fargo, North Dakota 58102

M. E. WATERS, Acting Laboratory Director, Fishery Products Technology Laboratory, U.S. Department of the Interior, P.O. Box 1207, Pascagoula, Mississippi 39567

BETTY M. WATTS, Professor Emeritus, University of Florida, Tallahassee, Florida 32306

BYRON H. WEBB (retired). Formerly, Chief, Dairy Products Laboratory, U.S. Department of Agriculture, Washington, D.C. 20250

K. G. WECKEL, Department of Food Science, University of Wisconsin, Madison, Wisconsin 53706

SAMUEL M. WEISBERG, League for International Food Education, 1155 Sixteenth St., N.W., Washington, D.C. 20036

THEODORE J. WEISS, Hunt-Wesson Foods, 1645 W. Valencia Drive, Fullerton, California 92634

R. L. WHISTLER, Department of Biochemistry, Purdue University, Lafayette, Indiana 47907

JONATHAN W. WHITE, JR., Chief, Plant Products Laboratory, Eastern Regional Research Laboratory, Agricultural Research Service, U.S. Department of Agriculture, 600 E. Mermaid Lane, Philadelphia, Pennsylvania 19118

A. WOHL, Technical Sales Manager, Spices and Botanical Products, Ltd., 450 Lebau Blvd., Montreal, Canada

W. J. WOLF, Northern Regional Research Laboratory, Agricultural Research Service, U.S. Department of Agriculture, 1815 N. University St., Peoria, Illinois 61604

EVERETT R. WOLFORD, Fruit and Vegetable Products Laboratory, Agricultural Research Service, U.S. Department of Agriculture, Puyallup, Washington 93871

BERNARD WOLNAK, Bernard Wolnak & Associates, 75 East Wacker Drive, Room 1400, Chicago, Illinois 60601

JASPER G. WOODROOF, Professor Emeritus of Food Science, University of Georgia, Experiment, Georgia 30212

HAROLD YOUNG, Kraft Foods Division, Kraftco Corp., 500 Peshtigo Court, Chicago, Illinois 60690

Foreword

The field of Food Science and Technology is a new one insofar as scientific disciplines are concerned—and, in fact, even the scientific treatment of foods.

Prior to World War I, the handling, treatment, and consideration of foods were more in the terms of an art rather than a science. Some changes, therefore, even took place during that war, but they were few indeed. The greatest advances in the field of food science have occurred since World War II.

During World War II, there was great emphasis on the development of highly acceptable rations that could be used easily, were high in nutritive value, and could be stored for a considerable period of time with a minimal loss of eating quality and nutritional value. Furthermore it was essential that they be foods that were safe and remained safe. These needs of the armed forces resulted in the development of a large and effective food laboratory by the Quartermaster in Chicago. As a result of this, there developed the philosophy of considering needs and wants of the consumer and especially with respect to acceptability, utility, or ease of use, stability or shelf-life, nutritive value and safety. This was important to the consumer of those days (the soldier) but it is more important to the peacetime consumer—all of us.

As a result of the continuation of this development, specialists have evolved who think scientifically in terms of foods. There has evolved a real need for these specialists. Consequently, universities have developed curricula and laboratories concerned with Food Science and Technology and, of course, more and more people trained in the field have been moving into industry and other teaching institutions.

The food industries have accepted the new philosophy in terms of consumer needs and desires, and this has been a motivating force. In addition to the factors already mentioned, it has been necessary to consider the economics of food production and distribution to the consumer. Curricula and interests have broadened and the field advanced over a period of years to a point where a number of universities are granting the Ph.D. degree in Food Science and Technology.

Prior to World War II there were relatively few books in the field, but since that time, many have appeared covering the field in general, popular books, textbooks, highly specialized and technical books, and even a review series concerned with advances in Food Science and Technology. Several journals have appeared, not only in the United States, but in a number of countries throughout the world.

All this resulted in a new outlook or point-of-view and, one might say, too, a whole new language, old words with new meanings as well as new words and terms.

The field, therefore, has reached the point where a treatise on the meaning of these terms is not only in order, but is direly needed, as a useful tool for students and scientists in the field, teachers, other scientists, writers, and laymen in general.

This new compendium by Arnold H. Johnson and Martin S. Peterson serves well to fill this need—the Encyclopedia of Food Technology. It fits well into the advance of the new and dynamic field of food science.

Drs. Johnson and Peterson have been heavily involved in food science, intensively and extensively for many years. They are the logical ones to prepare a comprehensive summary of knowledge, or in other words an *Encyclopedia of Food Technology*—a first in this field. It will indeed be a useful source of information.

Johnson and Peterson must be congratulated for undertaking this astronomical task and in so doing for helping to advance the field of Food Science and Technology toward full maturity and establishing it as an extremely important field of science in these days when food is foremost in the minds of so many throughout the world.

EMIL M. MRAK
Chancellor Emeritus
University of California,
Davis, California

July 1974

Preface

From "Acidulants" to "Zero Milk," the *Encyclopedia of Food Technology* contains more than 1000 pages on 275 subjects pertinent to food technology plus biographical coverage of men and women of historical importance in this field, awards to individuals in recognition of achievement in food technology, and information which the editors felt would be of general interest to all.

Over two years were spent in planning and amassing contributions from 235 individuals outstanding in the many fields and disciplines in and related to food technology: agriculture, chemistry, microbiology, engineering, quality control, processing and preservation, crops and animal products, fabricated foods, space foods, food service, nutrition and nutritional labeling, sensory evaluation, the ecology of waste handling and disposal . . . to name a portion of the topics covered in this work.

The editors are indeed grateful to these contributors who are acknowledged in the previous pages. A cursory examination of this roster of prominent people will show their high standing in their respective fields of endeavor and the international character of their activity in food technology.

It is on the basis of this expert knowledge that the detailed compilation of "A to Z" articles will be invaluable to students and professors alike in food technology and related fields, and professional people and others engaged in the food industry including those in production, marketing, and merchandising. The editors also trust that the work will be useful to the non-professional, and be available in public and general libraries in the United States and throughout the world.

The *Encyclopedia of Food Technology* represents Volume 2 in The AVI Publishing Company's Encyclopedia of Food Technology and Food Science Series. The *Encyclopedia of Food Engineering* (Hall, Farrall and Rippen) was published in 1971 as Volume 1 and has had wide success. Your editors have already started work on Volume 3 in this series: *Encyclopedia of Food Science*.

It has been a rewarding personal experience to the editors to deal worldwide with so many contributors and to have their good wishes and encouraging comments in the course of the enterprise. Also, thanks are overdue to many others who helped in the various stages of preparation of the *Encyclopedia of Food Technology* and without whom this job could never have been completed.

ARNOLD H. JOHNSON
MARTIN S. PETERSON

October 1973

A

ACIDULANTS

The modern supermarket is a living tribute to the progress of food technology. This technology involves the use of many food additives which ensure the safety and palatability of the vast array of processed foods available today. Among these food additives, the acidulants play a very important role.

Functions

Food acidulants serve many functions. They aid in sterilization, in food preservation, and in chelation. They are important adjuncts in product standardization, in modifying sweetness, in enhancement of flavors, as well as other functions.

Sterilization.—Probably the major contribution of the acidulants to processed food products is as an aid in sterilization. Sterilization of canned food products, in particular, depends on the thermal kill efficiency of the heat applied in retorts and other processing equipment. Many bacteria are highly resistant to heat and in some instances revert to a spore form which can survive high temperatures for a long period of time. Incomplete sterilization can result in instances of botulism or food spoilage. This is a serious public health hazard. Fortunately, bacteria and other deleterious microorganisms are more susceptible to thermal kill in a low pH environment. Therefore, acidification to lower the pH to a safe level is necessary. Many food products, which formerly could not have been adequately sterilized, are now safely processed and maintained for long periods of time through the technique of acidification. Governmental agencies have recognized this need and have promulgated regulations and guidelines on this subject in order to ensure the availability of food products which are safe for general consumption.

Preservation.—In addition to ensuring a more efficient bactericidal effect in the heat sterilization of foods, the acidulant also performs a bacteriostatic function in processed foods such as salad dressings and syrups, among others. The reproduction and growth of bacteria and other microorganisms are inhibited in an acidified medium. This helps improve the shelflife of foods which otherwise would have spoiled in a short period of time. In addition to the acidulants' ability to retard spoilage, they are frequently used as a fixative for flavors.

Chelation.—Certain acidulants have the ability to chelate stray metal ions, especially iron and copper, and thus can be used to retard and inhibit undesirable chemical reactions, such as rancidity in lipids and the browning of fruit. The objectionable metal ion, which could catalyze these reactions, is effectively tied up by the acidulant. Ascorbic acid is frequently used in conjunction with other acidulants such as citric or malic acid in these applications. Partially through their chelating function, the acidulants are also useful in retarding the enzymatic browning of fruits and vegetables.

Product Standardization.—A century ago, most food was consumed in the area in which it grew. Today, modern transportation methods plus large-scale buying practices of major supermarkets have brought about change. Agricultural products may be grown in the south, the midwest, the far west, or elsewhere and, following canning, are transported long distances before they reach the consumer. There are variations in the acid content of fruits and vegetables grown in different parts of the country. In addition, there are annual variations in the acid content of produce grown in the same area; and there is a variation in acid content between early and late crops.

As a result of these variations in product acid, coupled with block buying, warehousing, and large-scale distribution of products, it may be possible to have two cans of "Brand A" tomatoes on a supermarket shelf that have completely different origins. To cite an extreme example, one can could be packed with an early crop of midwestern tomatoes and the other can packed with a late crop of California tomatoes. Thus, seasonal and geographic differences in acid content could make

1

TABLE A-1

PROPERTIES OF SOME COMMON FOOD ACIDULANTS

Property	POMALUS® Malic Acid	Fumaric Acid	Adipic Acid	Succinic Acid	Succinic Anhydride	Citric Acid	Tartaric Acid
	HOCHCOOH — CH_2COOH	HOOCCH ‖ HCCOOH	CH_2CH_2COOH — CH_2CH_2COOH	CH_2COOH — CH_2COOH	CH_2CO O CH_2CO	CH_2COOH — HOCCOOH — CH_2COOH	HOCHCOOH — HOCHCOOH
Appearance	White crystal. powder	White crystal. powder	White crystal. powder	White crystal. powder	White crystals	White crystals	White crystals
Crystal system	Triclinic crystal	Monoclinic prisms	Monoclinic prisms	Monoclinic prisms	Ortho-rhombic prisms	Monoclinic holohedra	Monoclinic sphenoidal prisms
Taste	Smooth tart	Tart	Tart	Tart	Burning tart	Tart	Bitter tart
Empirical formula Melting point, °C	$C_4H_6O_5$ 130°–132°	$C_4H_4O_4$ 286°–287°	$C_6H_{10}O_4$ 153°	$C_4H_6O_4$ 188°	$C_4H_4O_3$ 118.3°–119°[1]	$C_6H_8O_7$ 153°	$C_4H_6O_6$ 168°–170°
Specific gravity	1.601 (20°/4°)	1.635 (20°/4°)	1.380 (25°/4°)	1.564 (15°/4°)	1.503 (20°/4°)	1.542 (18°/4°)	1.7598 (20°/4°)
Bulk density, lb/ft³	57.3	32.6	40.5	55.0	47.2	56.2	50.2
Solubility in ethanol gm/100 ml @ 25°C	39.16	4.3	16.10	9.0	2.56	58.9	19.6
Solubility in ether gm/100 ml @ 25°C	1.41	0.56	0.92	0.66	0.64	1.84	0.59
Solubility in chloroform gm/100 ml @ 25°C	0.04	0.02	<0.01	0.02	0.87	<0.01	0.04
Ionization constant K_1 K_2 K_3	4×10^{-4} 9×10^{-6} —	1×10^{-3} 3×10^{-5}	3.7×10^{-5} 2.4×10^{-6}	6.5×10^{-5} 2.3×10^{-6} —	(See succinic acid)	8.2×10^{-4} 1.8×10^{-5} 3.9×10^{-6}	1.04×10^{-3} 4.55×10^{-5} —
Heat of combustion, kcal/mole, 20°C	-320.1	-320.0	-669.0	-357.1	-369.6	-474.5	-257.1
Heat of solution, kcal/mole solute	4.9	—	—	—	—	3.9	3.3
Viscosity 50% aqueous solutions, cps, @ 25°C	6.5	2	2	2	2	6.5	6.5
Standard free energy of anion formation, ΔF°_f, kcal, @ 25°C, aqueous solutions	-201.98	-144.41	—	-164.97	(See succinic acid)	-278.8	—
Sp gr saturated aqueous solutions, @ 5°	1.210	1.000	1.002	1.012		1.24	1.26
25°	1.250	1.000	1.005	1.024	"	1.28	1.27
75°	1.310	0.989	1.032	1.076	"	1.31	1.31

[1] Solidification point.

these two cans of "Brand A" tomatoes taste different to the consumer. In order to preclude this situation the industry is depending, more and more, upon standardization of products wherein acidulants are added to optimize processing safety and uniform taste acceptability.

In that manner, a late crop California tomato or an early crop Indiana tomato will contain an equivalent amount of acidity and be equally acceptable from a taste standpoint. The influences of origin and differential harvesting time are then nullified and the consumer can purchase a product which is uniform in taste, regardless of origin or time of harvesting. Thus, the acidification of tomatoes and other canned vegetable products helps ensure the availability of food products which have been safely processed and are consistently good.

Modifying Sweetness and Flavor Enhancement.—Another important role of food acidulants is the enhancement of food flavors. Without food acidulants, hard candies, gelatine desserts, carbonated and noncarbonated beverages, jellies, preserves, toppings and many other products would taste flat or sickeningly sweet. The acidulants add the tartness required to balance the excessive sweetness of these products. Until the proper balance of tartness and sweetness is achieved, the flavor cannot develop to its fullest potential. Even near the balance point, the ratio of sweetness to tartness can be fine-tuned to pronounce the primary flavor and enhance the secondary flavor notes which otherwise may be masked by excessive sweetness or tartness. The ratio of sweetness to tartness is commonly called the brix acid ratio. This ratio, contrary to some older beliefs, need not be a rigid rule applied arbitrarily across the board. In order to achieve the optimum of flavor enhancement, it can be varied to suit the product. For example, a lemonade should be more tart than a punch. A hard candy will require a higher level of acidification to compensate for the excessive sweetness of the product.

The effect of acidulants on flavor and taste can also vary, but none has a characteristic flavor per se. The taste of all acidulants is usually described as tart. However, each individual acidulant has a slightly different tartness. Among the organic acids, the tartness of citric has been described as clean; that of malic as smooth; fumaric as metallic; adipic as chalky; vinegar (acetic) as astringent; tartaric as sharp or bitter; and lactic as sour. Phosphoric, which is inorganic, tends to have a flat sourness. The acidulants also vary in their effects on aftertaste. The acidic taste of some acids is retained and stimulates the taste buds for a longer period of

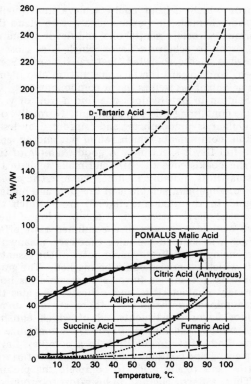

FIG. A-1. SOLUBILITIES IN WATER AT DIFFERENT TEMPERATURES

time. The chalky character of adipic is retained for a while, as is the metallic note of fumaric. The proper selection of flavors and flavor ingredients can usually minimize and mask any undesirable aftertaste. Phosphoric tends to be retained in the taste buds, however. In the case of cola formulations, the resultant overall flavor rendition is highly desirable. Malic stimulates the taste buds for a long duration and the flavor of the product is also carried with it. This helps to disguise the undesirable aftertaste characteristics of artificial sweeteners and medicines. In addition to its ability to mask aftertaste, malic is also utilized to blend combination flavors such as orange/pineapple and apple/raspberry, wherein the end result is a harmonious blend rather than two distinct flavor sensations.

In view of the slightly different taste characteristics of the various acidulants it follows that some are more complementary to certain flavors than others. Moreover, a blend of acidulants, as frequently found in nature, will result in a superior flavor which neither could achieve individually. Flavor chemists, in particular, strive to blend the various extracts, essential oils, and flavor aromatics in order to achieve a flavor which is as close as possible to the so-called "natural flavor." Some seem to disregard the fact that nature also blends its acidulants as well as flavor components.

Seldom in nature does one find a fruit or vegetable containing only one acidulant. Normally, one acidulant is predominant and reinforced by lesser acidic components which round out and enhance the full flavor spectrum. A good example of this is the coexistence of citric and malic acids in the citrus fruits, notably in lime, where citric acid is the predominant acidulant of the juice and malic is found in the rind and flavedo from which the essential oils are extracted. A combination of these two acidulants results in a combined taste effect which will sharpen the juice character, meanwhile enhancing the delicate flavor notes of the essential oils which otherwise could be masked. The grape contains a complex flavor system which is both strongly characteristic and delicate. Besides the predominant anthranilates, there are also many minor flavor constituents, all of which enhance and modify the natural flavor as we recognize it. One finds that, in addition to a complex flavor system, grape contains a mixture of malic, tartaric, citric, and oxalic acids to complete the picture.

Thus, a flavor chemist, in his effort to produce a flavor which is similar to that of nature, should consider the proper use of acidulants as well as the other flavor-imparting raw materials which are available to him.

Substituting One Acid for Another

At equal concentrations, the acidulants vary in their ability to depress pH and in the degree of acidic taste, or intensity of tartness, produced.

However, it has been demonstrated many times that equal amounts of each acidulant, at the same concentration, produce different levels of tartness. Although this physiological difference is not fully understood, it is theorized that the difference may be due to the effect of free anions, in the various acidulants, on the taste buds. Therefore, one acid cannot be substituted for another on an equal weight or concentration basis. Also, the amount of detectable tartness will vary for products because of the differences in overall flavor.

There is no set rule for the replacement of one acidulant by another to achieve the same degree of tartness. The following replacement percentages using anhydrous citric acid as equal to 100% tartness are relative and only rough guides, based on experience; they should be used only as a starting point. The approximate percentages of other acids required to approach anhydrous citric acid are:

Acid	%
Citric	100
Fumaric	67–72
Tartaric	80–85
Malic (citrus flavors)	89–94
Malic (fruit flavors)	78–83
Adipic	110–115
Phosphoric (85%)	55–60

When replacing a single acidulant with a blend of acidulants, some care should be exercised. Occasionally, the acids in the blend will synergize one another and produce a higher degree of tartness than anticipated. They may also enhance various flavor ingredients in a different manner.

In developing an artificial flavor, or in formulating a new consumer product, the best guide is still the reaction of the human taste buds.

Many sophisticated analytical instruments have been developed and are in use in food laboratories and plants throughout the country. However, no instrument can replace the human being when it comes to judging taste.

It has been proven that some people are more discriminating than others when it comes to discerning differences in taste. Tests were run at Allied Chemical's Buffalo Research Center to test the ability of people to detect acid level concentrations in weak water solutions of 0.000%, 0.015%, 0.030%, and 0.040% malic acid. A group of 142 people, chosen at random, participated in the tests. At these threshold levels, only 17% could distinguish between the different acid levels.

Further tests were run on 42 of these people using the following higher levels of acidity: 0.079%, 0.106%, and 0.132% malic acid. These tests were run in sugar solutions having 2 levels of sucrose, 12.5° and 8° Brix, respectively. Results of these tests showed that the ability to detect small differences in acid level decreased proportionally with an increase in sucrose concentration. These results are plotted in Figure A-2. At the high, 12.5% sucrose level, error was about ±10%. At the lower, 8% sucrose level, the error was reduced to ±2.5%.

Thus, to match equivalent acid taste levels and determine acid replacement factors for beverages, it is desirable to evaluate the taste of a product containing the normal amount of acid but with reduced sucrose levels. Using this technique, a selected panel of trained tasters can usually match the equivalent degree of tartness with close to ± 2% accuracy.

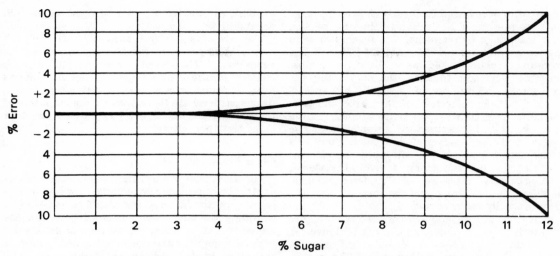

FIG. A-2. ABILITY OF A PANEL TO DETECT ACIDITY IN THE PRESENCE OF SUGAR IN CARBONATED BEVERAGES

Changing Pattern of Consumer Taste Preference and the AM/PM Effect

For years it has been common knowledge in the food and beverage industry that regional taste preferences exist. Therefore, a product designed for consumption in one section of the country may not be the most preferred in another geographic area. Examples of this are the southerners' preference for a sweeter drink, the westerners' liking of a spicy and hot flavor, and the midwesterners' preference for blander tasting products. However, there has been some change in these historic assumptions. Recently a consumer taste center was set up by a large chemical company at their headquarters on Times Square in New York City. During the years of 1968–69 consumer preference tests were run at this location. Testing was restricted to beverages in order to simplify logistics and to handle a large number of people as rapidly as possible. This test panel was located in a center designed to exhibit some of the company's products and, consequently, was open to the general public.

During the 2-yr period of its operation, about 100,000 people participated in taste tests at the center. Because of its location at the so-called "Crossroads of the World," the people who participated in these tests were from every walk of life, covered all age groups, all races, creeds, both sexes, all nationalities, all sections or regions of the country, and many foreign countries. The group included smokers and nonsmokers. In short, it was an excellent cross section of the world population and, in particular, the population of the United States.

Some interesting general results came out of these tests, which should be of interest to food processors. They will be of particular interest to those involved in formulating or merchandising food products.

The test results indicate that so-called regional preferences are diminishing and more universal taste preferences are emerging.

Expected regional differences in taste did not appear. For instance, the southerner showed no preference for a sweeter drink, nor did the westerner show any preference for a spicy drink. There was an amazing agreement in taste preferences of young and old, male and female, black and white, smokers and nonsmokers.

Since the tests were made only with respect to beverages, these results cannot be applied to all food products; nevertheless, they show an interesting trend.

This trend is not so surprising if we consider that the population of the United States became very mobile in the period after World War II. Up to that point, people tended to stay in the areas where they were born. The war itself caused many people to move or travel, either because of military service or defense jobs. This modified the eating habits of many people. Since then, of course, people have traveled extensively and moved frequently as they changed jobs.

Besides demonstrating a shift from regional to a more universal taste preference (for beverage products), the tests came up with one startling result.

Those who were tested frequently showed a change in taste preference in relation to the time of day. For want of a better name, this reversal of taste preference was dubbed "The AM/PM Effect." The consumers being tested were given two almost identical beverages to taste, the only difference being that one product had a slightly higher level of acidity than the other. Flavor, Brix, and temperature were constant for both samples. In the AM, or morning hours, the product with the higher acidic taste was preferred, many times to a significant degree. In the afternoon, or PM, the preference of the consumer switched to the sweeter tasting beverage. This reversal of preference usually nullified the AM trend and the total of the day's results usually averaged out.

Since this phenomenon was noticed at the Times Square location, repeated testings of a 500-member consumer panel in New Jersey have confirmed the original observations. The groups differ in that the New Jersey panel was composed of adults, 50% men and 50% women. This group was tested under controlled conditions in a sophisticated taste panel center.

This AM/PM effect is unique and, to the author's knowledge, little attention has been paid to it in the literature. It can be theorized that this preference is based on the physiological needs of the body. The body may be slightly tired by afternoon and needs extra calories, whereas in the morning it may need vitamin C.

The Food Technologist should take the AM/PM effect into account when formulating a beverage product. A breakfast drink should be slightly on the tart side, while a drink normally consumed in the afternoon can be a bit sweeter.

Use of Buffer Salts in Conjunction With Food Acidulants

Buffer systems are frequently used in food products. The classical purpose of a buffer system is to establish an equilibrium between an acid and an acid salt, which is pH stable and will resist changes in pH when other ingredients are added to the system. This is often used to protect certain ingredients which may become unstable in too high an acid environment. Milk and milk products will curdle in a strongly acidic medium. Protein is subject to degradation and some gums and gelatins are acid sensitive. Pectin sets at 3.2 pH and its rate of setting is also related to pH. Below 3.2 it will set too fast and the ensuing network will be tough and rubbery. Much above 3.2 will create a soft jell with a tendency for syneresis. Erythrosine, FD & C Red #3, is highly sensitive to acidity and will precipitate out as soon as the acidity of the medium approaches 3.5 or gets much below 3.8, depending upon viscosity.

The use of a buffer system will "tie up" the excess hydrogen ions which otherwise could be deleterious. The use of buffer not only ensures stability in acid-sensitive systems, but also imparts a higher acidic taste without lowering the pH to a dangerous level. In this manner, a higher degree of tartness can be imparted to excessively sweet or bland tasting products.

Other Functions

The acidulants act synergistically with antioxidants. They provide the hydrogen ion required to set the pectin in jams and jellies in addition to providing the tart taste required to enhance the flavor of such products. They are also functional in developing the brown pigments in meat products and assist in the preservation of the meat. The USDA permits the use of vinegar and either citric or malic acids to be used in a solution which is sprayed on frankfurters prior to, or after, smoking to improve peelability. Untreated frankfurters could not be deskinned at the rate demanded by recently developed high speed deskinning machines. Effervescent powders and tablets for beverages or pharmaceutical preparations depend upon an acidulant to generate carbon dioxide through its reaction with sodium bicarbonate or similar chemicals.

From the preceding, it is apparent that the food acidulants perform many valuable functions in foods and related products which otherwise would not now be available for general consumption.

TOWNSEND J. SAUSVILLE

ACORNS

Historians contend that most of the human race has depended more upon acorns as a source of nourishment than wheat. Wheat has been a basic food of the European-North American people. The Orientals, Indians (Asiatic), and the tropical peoples utilize little wheat in their diets; many are unaware of its existence.

Ancient people who lived in or near the oak forests in the middle latitudes—areas now known as Japan, China, the Himalaya mountains, West Asia, Europe, North America—subsisted in part on acorns. The earliest inhabitants of Greece and Southern Europe were supported by acorns. These people were described by writers of the period as "fat of person" and were called "balanophagi" (acorn eaters). Acorns, utilized for bread, cake, and as a coffee substitute, have furnished up to

25% of the diets of the poorer classes of Italy and Spain.

Unlike other native North American foods such as turkey, squash, and Indian corn, acorns never became popular with the white settlers. In aboriginal central California, the acorn was a true staple, being eaten in greater quantity than the product of any other genus, animal or vegetable. The Indians of Massachusetts parched fresh acorns, stored them, and utilized them principally in cake preparation. The Indians of the Great Lakes region and California, however, boiled acorns into a mush, often adding maple sugar and venison.

Typically, acorns were prepared by first cracking them open with the aid of a small elongated stone for a hammer and a heavy flat stone for an anvil. Rocks resembling a mortar and pestle were then utilized to grind the nut meats. Tannin and other bitter materials were removed by water-ash soaks or boiling water. Acorn oil removed by boiling water was saved and subsequently utilized either as a meat condiment or skin ointment. Frequently the leached meal was employed in the preparation of unleavened bread, baked beside a fire on a hot stone or in an earth oven.

Laboratory analyses have demonstrated acorns to be similar to chaffy cereals in chemical composition. Except for the presence of thin-walled cells between the epicarp and hypoderm, the microscopic structure is analogous to the chestnut. Starch is the main acorn component, composing over 50% of the kernel.

Food researchers at Texas A & M University have performed an extensive survey of chemical, physical, and organoleptic properties of several species of acorns from the red and black, and white oaks groups. Variability was found between trees within species, between species within subgenera, and between *Lepidobalanus* and *Eyrthrobalanus* subgenera.[1] Quantitative measurements of kernel moisture, ether extract, crude fiber, ash, crude protein, tannin, size, shape, color, and texture established the range in composition and could provide a basis for objective selection for quality as has been done with other tree crops.

Difficulty can be encountered in attempting to evaluate organoleptic properties because of the bitter masking effect of the tannins. This is particularly true in the red and black oak group where tannins constituted up to 9% of the dry kernel. Conversely, tree samples of the white oak group are often sweet, bitter-free, and palatable without leaching.

---

[1] The subgenus *Lepidobalanus* refers to the white oak group, *Erythrobalanus* the red and black oak group.

"Taste panels" of captive wild animals have proven more selective than human panels. Fox squirrels, for example, have demonstrated highly significant preferences for acorns from single trees within a species. There are indications that tannin content, lipid content, shell color, and previous food experience of the animal are involved in selection.

Documentation of past human consumption and optimistic laboratory findings indicate the potential value of acorns as human food. A program involving selection based upon nutritional and organoleptic attributes is desirable, particularly in view of some world food shortages.

RALPH P. OFCARCIK
J. G. TEER
E. E. BURNS

References

Of Technological Significance

OFCARCIK, R. P. 1969. Chemical, physical, and organoleptic properties of acorns of selected species. MS Thesis, Texas A&M Univ.

OFCARIK, R. P., and BURNS, E. E. 1971. Chemical and physical properties of selected acorns. J. Food Sci. *36*, 576–578.

OFCARIK, R. P., BURNS, E. E., and TEER, J. G. 1971. Acorns for human food. League for International Food Education Newsletter, November.

Of Historical Significance

BAUSKETT, F. N. 1908. Acorns as food for man. Tech. World *10*, 78–82, Sept.

CARR, L. G. 1943. Survival foods of the American Aborigine. J. Am. Diet. Assoc. *19*, 845–847.

DRIVER, H. 1952. The acorn in the North American Indian diet. Proc. Indiana Acad. Sci. *62*, 56–62.

LEA, F. T. 1914. Indian bread makers of the Yosemite. Overland Monthly *64*, 24–26, July.

MERRIAM, C. H. 1918. The acorn, a possibly neglected source of food. Ntal. Geographic *34*, 129–137, Aug.

ADDITIVES

The legal definition for a food additive developed in the 1958 Food Additive Amendment to the Food, Drug and Cosmetic Act contains the following: "Any substance, the intended use of which, results or may reasonably be expected to result directly or indirectly in its becoming a component or otherwise affecting the characteristics of any food." Legally GRAS (Generally Regarded As Safe) additives are not considered additives. This exclusion also pertains to condiments, spices, and herbs.

In 1959, the Food Protection Committee of the National Academy of Sciences—National Research Council came up with an all-encompassing definition. It defined a food additive as a "substance or mixture of substances, other than a basic food stuff, which is present in food as a result of any aspect of production, processing, storage, and packaging. The term does not include chance contaminants. An additive may be either nutritive or non-nutritive; it may be physiologically active or inert; it may be present intentionally, to achieve some modification in the foods, or incidentally and serving no useful purpose in the final product."

There appear to be two questions asked most often by the consumer about additives: (1) "Are they safe?" and (2) "Why use an additive at all?"

This article does not address the many chemical and biological tests conducted by the additive manufacturer to assure the safety of additives required to obtain the approval of the Food and Drug Administration.

In general, there are seven major reasons for the use of additives: taste, appearance, texture and eating quality, processing, stability or preservation, nutritional benefit, and for special or dietary foods.

A more detailed look will be taken at each of these reasons to find out how additives are useful.

Taste

Among the oldest food additives are flavorings. Cinnamon, cloves, pepper, and fruit extracts have long been used. The continually-growing use of food flavorings reflects a lively interest on the part of the American public in more varied and more flavorful foods. This interest probably started to grow upon the return of World War II service men. Currently, the increase in foreign travel and spread of world cultures has kept this interest alive and growing. Food companies have become increasingly conscious of the vital importance of high-quality flavors in the public acceptance of foods.

The trend in past years has been to replace many natural flavors with synthetic equivalents. Matching of flavors for traditional foodstuffs has reached a high level of expertise. Among the reasons for these replacements have been the increasing cost of many natural flavors, their nonuniform composition, their instability, their fluctuating availability, and their limited supply. An example often used to illustrate the scarcity of natural flavors is natural vanilla. This flavor is widely used in ice cream, baked goods, candy, and beverages. It is estimated that the world supply of natural vanilla would be insufficient to flavor the vanilla ice cream eaten in the United States alone.

Use of the flavors themselves have brought along need for other additives. Encapsulation is widely used to protect food flavors against loss of volatile components and to minimize oxidative attack. This encapsulation also can control the time or temperature release of the flavor.

In this discussion of taste as a reason for food additives, mention should also be made of the flavor enhancers. Salt and sugar are probably the oldest of the enhancers. Many times these enhancers will be used at levels at which they themselves cannot be tasted, but at which they bring out the natural flavor. For example, a small amount of salt brings out more chocolate flavor from cocoa. Another enhancer is the well-known monosodium glutamate. Other examples include the nucleotides (the inosinates and guanylates) and maltol. Maltol is used quite successfully to intensify strawberry and raspberry flavors.

The use of food additives for flavor development is certainly valid and valuable.

Appearance

Color is another product characteristic to be improved by use of food additives. There is no question that color sells. Foods are made more attractive and appetizing by the use of color. Colors are used to give more uniformity to certain natural products. The readers are all familiar with the seasonal variations in butter and cheese.

More frequently are heard the questions: "Why synthetic or artificial colors?" "Why not the natural ones?" Before the middle of the last century, all colors added to foods were of natural origin. These included annatto, saffron, turmeric, and caramel. These colors are still being used today. Since the synthesis of mauve in 1856, the use of artificial colors has been on the increase. Today about 90% of all colors used in foods are synthetic.

Synthetic colors have marked advantages over natural colors. They have greater coloring power, are more uniform, are more stable, and are usually cheaper. Where natural colors still prevail it is often because no approved synthetic has been found as an acceptable replacement.

It should be noted that the synthetic color field has been in a constant stage of activity in the past few years. Several of the colors available for food use in the early 1950's have since been delisted by the federal government. Replacements are being developed.

Texture and Eating Quality

The category of food additives used to improve texture and eating quality of food products is probably the largest. This group would include emulsifiers, stabilizers, thickeners, anticaking agents, and their opposite, humectants.

Emulsifiers.—In terms of pounds used in U.S. food production, the top-selling additives are emulsifiers. Emulsifiers or surface active agents are commonly used to disperse one liquid in another, usually oil in water or water in oil. They are used in such varied foods as ice cream, margarine, candy, cakes, frostings, and dessert toppings.

Aerated or whipped toppings would have little foam or whip stability without the added emulsifier, usually propylene glycol monostearate. Emulsifiers are used in nondairy creamers to increase dispersion in coffee. Confectionery coatings use emulsifiers to disperse the fat and prevent it from migrating to the surface. The unappetizing grayish color of chocolates improperly emulsified is not uncommon. A natural emulsifier widely used today is eggs, the major emulsifier of mayonnaise. The active component of the egg is lecithin.

Mono- and diglycerides are the largest selling food emulsifiers. They are used in shortenings, ice cream, baked goods. Another widely used emulsifier is sorbitol monostearate. All these emulsifiers are lipophilic. Another class, introduced in the early 1940's, is hydrophilic, the polysorbates or polyoxyethylene sorbitan monoesters (stearates or oleates).

In many instances emulsification is accomplished through a blend of surfacants—a hydrophilic-lipophilic balance.

Thickeners and Stabilizers.—Thickeners and stabilizers constitute another important area of food additives which contribute to texture and eating quality. The role of starches in pie fillings is well known. Both natural and modified starches are used extensively as thickeners. Suppliers have done an excellent job in providing literally custom-made starches. Acid-stable, heat-stable, freeze-thaw stable starches are examples of products where a desired functionality has been "built in."

Stabilizers can also serve as thickeners. Many of these products are vegetable gums and include CMC, carrageenan, sodium alginate, guar, xanthan, methyl cellulose. A fractional percentage of an alginate will retard the settling of cocoa in chocolate milk as well as give it some body. The ice creams enjoyed by all are smooth because of the presence of a vegetable gum to prevent the water from freezing into large ice crystals.

Anticaking Agents.—Various silicates and phosphates are added to salt, baking powder, nondairy creamers to prevent moisture pickup and caking.

Humectants.—At the opposite end of the moisture scale, such humectants as sorbitol, glycerol, or propylene glycol are used to prevent moisture loss from such food items as marshmallows, candy, coconut, and, more recently, the toaster items. These agents also help control the water activity level.

Processing

Processing additives make possible many ingredients to the food processor and to the consumer not otherwise available with the desired quality. For example, a number of years ago the USDA Western Regional Laboratory developed a foam-mat process for dehydration. A high melting monoglyceride was added to tomato paste, the combination whipped into a stable foam. This foam was cast onto a belt moving through a hot air tunnel where the moisture was essentially removed. The foaming created a large surface area resulting in more rapid removal of moisture.

Instant mashed potatoes are another example using a process additive. Without the use of monoglycerides, instant mashed potatoes would resemble library paste as they come from the various types of dryers used by the industry today.

Stability or Preservation

One of the oldest uses of food additives is in the preservation of foods. In the early periods of civilization, wood smoke was used to preserve meats. Today, additives preserve foods against bacteria, molds, yeasts. Calcium propionate or sodium propionate control mold growth as well as rope bacteria in baked products. Other antimycotic agents are sodium benzoate and ethyl formate. Sorbic acid and potassium sorbate inhibit mold growth on cheese, in chocolate syrup, on dried fruits. It might be of interest to note that some mold inhibitors are naturally occurring. For example, propionic acid is naturally present in Swiss cheese where it acts as an effective preservative.

In the many convenience foods today, antioxidants play an important role in helping to preserve the original quality of the food item. They function mainly in preventing the oxidative breakdown of fats and oils. The objectionable flavor and aroma of a rancid potato chip are well known. Beyond the organoleptic function, antioxidants are often used to minimize the oxidative breakdown of vitamins.

Again, the naturally occurring antioxidants have in most instances been replaced by more effective synthetic compounds. Years ago, gum guiac and lecithin were used as antioxidants. Because of their low stabilizing power and poor heat stability, they have been replaced. The most widely used synthetic ones today are butylated hydroxyanisole (BHA) and butylated hydroxytoluene (BHT).

An antioxidant will act as a preferential oxygen acceptor and thus delay rancidity. Other compounds known as sequestrants actually inhibit oxidation by acting as scavengers or chelating agents to tie up trace metals which can be prooxidants. Examples of these are salts of ethylenediaminetetraacetic acid, citric acid, and sodium hexametaphosphate.

Nutritional Benefit

Probably the most widely discussed phase of the subject of food today is that of nutrition. The original White House Conference on Food and Nutrition, held in December, 1969, was widely reported. On February 5, 1971 a day-long session was held in Williamsburg, Virginia as a progress report to the original conference.

As the food industry spokesman, Mr. James P. McFarland, Chairman of the Board, General Mills, Inc., expressed his keen "awareness of the dedication, the social consciousness, the practicality and the determination with which our industry's people are addressing themselves to the vitally important task before us." He was referring to the first of four basic responsibilities of government and the food industry defined by the original conference: "to enhance the nutritional well-being of all Americans."

Nutritional additives are most often vitamins, minerals, and proteins. Vitamins and minerals may be added at restoration levels or at the fortification or supplemental levels. As far back as 1941, the U.S. flour milling industry began enriching flour to replace vitamins and minerals lost during milling. These included thiamin (B_1), riboflavin (B_2), nicotinic acid, and iron. The marked decline in the incidence of nutrition-related disease has been well documented. Corn grits and rice are two other cereals which have been enriched. Enriched flour is being used in many convenience and ready-to-eat foods.

Protein supplementation is currently receiving much attention by the food manufacturer. Plant protein products, primarily from soybeans, are being added to both new products as well as those already in the market place. Meat replacements with balanced nutrition are being created. The instant breakfasts offer 25% of the recommended daily requirement for protein. These same products have recently been reformulated to include higher amounts of iron. Another new product in the form of a cake will, when served with 8 oz of milk, provide 25% of the recommended daily allowance of all nutrients for a 12-yr-old boy. This product is being served in inner city schools since no utensils or special personnel are required.

All progressive food processors and manufacturers should believe in the principle of addition of nutrients to food but should not advocate indiscriminate fortification of food. In an appearance before the Democratic Study Group Conference in September, 1971, Mr. McFarland stated that the government should establish and publish voluntary nutritional guidelines. A research contract has been given by FDA to the National Academy of Sciences—National Research Council to study and recommend such guidelines.

Special and Dietary Foods

The many reasons for special diets make it quite difficult to define what dietary foods are. Attempts are made to match the regular food in taste, appearance, and eating quality. Salt-free diets and sugar-free diets are common medical requirements. When salt or sugar are used solely for flavor reasons, simpler demands are made upon the food technologist to develop a special formulation. When sugar serves as a functional ingredient, the problems are much greater. An example of such a problem would be the use of sugar in a cake mix. Here the sugar relates to the physical structure of the cake.

Additives have resulted in improved food products to the consumer. The food additive manufacturer certainly should continue a search for new and improved ones which will provide the consumer with better products.

JOHN A. BARNES

Cross-references: *Antioxidants; Chemical Preservatives; Food Preservation; Synthetic Sweeteners; Enrichment, Restoration and Fortification.*

ADULTERANTS

An adulterant, whether added to a food or drug, is properly defined as a substance that makes a product inferior or impure. An adulterant differs from an additive in that it does not improve a food and is often added with the intention to defraud. Some adulterants cause a food to look deceptively bulky, others add weight to a food, and yet others substitute a cheaper substance for one more expensive. In the past, before regulatory laws were passed, powdered cocoa could be sold as cocoa even when it was adulterated with starch, butter could be labelled butter though composed of a high percentage of margarine, and mixing wine, milk and other products with water was a common practice. Labeling requirements thwart such practices today; and there are other safeguards. For example, there are laws requiring that foods comply with standards of identity that specify permissible ingredients and quantities of ingredients to be present in a number of foods. Standards have been prescribed for cereal flours, cocoa products, cheeses, dressings, tomato products, and many, many others.

Use of adulterants goes far back into ancient history, both the Greeks and the Romans had laws against their incorporation in foods, particularly the use of water in wine. In 19th century America, dishonest practices with regard to adulteration were fairly common; e.g., farina was used to extend mustard, nontea leaves were added to tea, starch was used not only to stretch out cocoa, as mentioned, but also to increase the bulk of baking powder, flour, and, curiously enough, of lard.

Although adulteration in its strict interpretation is the use of cheaper, inferior, and, for the most part, extrinsic substances, the term has now come to include microbial and chemical contaminants and filth. The FDA together with State agricultural and health departments maintain a constant surveillance over the foods of commerce, both domestic and foreign, to assure compliance with the law.

MARTIN S. PETERSON

AEROSOLS

In scientific usage the word "aerosol" means a suspension of small particles in air or gas and the first aerosol products were of this nature. In recent years, however, the terms "aerosol," "aerosol product," "pressurized product," etc., have come to mean any mixture of liquid, solid, or gas discharged by a self-contained propellant from a disposable type of dispenser. The term "food aerosols" is in common use to describe any kind of food product dispensed in this way.

Aerosol products in general have been commercially successful for several reasons. In some cases they offer convenience in use, in other cases they may be more economical than other methods of achieving the same result, and in other instances it has been possible to offer products that have no counterpart in other methods of dispensing. Hundreds of different aerosol products have been developed but have not been commercially successful unless they could satisfy one of these requirements. Food aerosols are no exception. They must offer utility or exceptional convenience in order to attract users.

Almost every conceivable type of food product has been formulated as an aerosol in the laboratory. These formulations range from whipped toppings, sauces, and flavorings, etc., to cheese preparations, juice concentrates, meats and vegetables, pancake batter, and other similar products. Many of this vast array of possible food aerosols have appeared useful and practical but have not been able to win a place on the grocer's shelf or on the consumer's table. Reasons for the failure of

food aerosols to share in the spectacular growth of the aerosol industry in general are complex. Some products such as an aerosol cocktail vermouth spray were little more than novelties and after a brief flurry of sales vanished from the market. A more basic reason is probably economic. Factors cited for the poor record of food aerosols have been improperly formulated recipes, mechanical failures in packaging, poor package design, unsuitable valves, lack of asceptic filling equipment, and ineffective marketing programs.

Whatever the reasons, the only major food aerosol products today are whipped cream and assorted cheese spreads.

A food aerosol unit or package is made up of four separate parts: the food material, the propellant, the container, and the dispensing valve. Each part must be carefully studied and modified or adapted to give the desired properties to the product. As a rule each formulation must be studied separately in order to arrive at the optimum result. However, various classes of food aerosols have similar problems and similar solutions and technology. Since whipped products have been the most successful, they will be discussed in more detail using whipped cream as a typical example.

The idea of dispensing foods from self-pressurized containers has been around for a long time, but the first commercially available product was whipped cream for institutional use (about 1937). The home market was first reached about 1947 and the number of units produced each year has grown slowly but steadily to the present level. It offers a good product with a considerable factor of convenience over other methods of preparing and serving whipped cream.

A typical whipped cream formulation would include about 75 parts by weight of heavy cream (25% butterfat) and 22 parts of various additives including sugar, emulsifying and stabilizing agents, and flavorings. Emulsifying agents are necessary to encourage the formation of an emulsion between the food concentrate and the propellant. Stabilizing agents are added to help preserve the emulsion after it is formed and to stabilize the foam structure after the food product has been dispensed. The quality of the final product can be changed by varying the proportions of the various ingredients in the concentrate. Using less cream would tend to give a lighter product and one that would have a greater tendency to collapse on standing. With less cream, a higher concentration of emulsifying and stabilizing agents would be needed.

For many years the propellant used with aerosol whipped cream was nitrous oxide or nitrous oxide mixed with a small amount of carbon dioxide.

The propellant is used as a compressed gas; that is, no liquid phase is present. The formulation is put in a container and charged with propellant to a pressure of about 90 psig. The container is shaken to dissolve as much gas in the liquid as possible. The physical properties of a compressed gas propellant lead to the following two problems.

(1) An appreciable amount of time is required for charging the propellant into the container since it is important for as much gas to dissolve in the liquid phase as possible.

(2) The whipped cream is pressurized with the gaseous propellant at a certain pressure level. As the contents of the container are expelled, the vapor space in the can is enlarged and the pressure of the gas is reduced. Toward the end of the discharge the pressure is quite low. In order to provide enough propellant, the container is filled about $1/2$ full with concentrate. As a rule, a small amount of the whipped cream remains in the container when the pressure is exhausted.

These two problems are essentially eliminated by the use of a liquefied gas as a propellant. The liquid provides a reservoir of propellant with a high vapor pressure that occupies a small volume, permitting more concentrate to be used in the container and providing a steady source of pressure that remains constant throughout the use of the product. Two such products have been certified by the FDA for use with foods. They are Propellant 115, chloropentafluoroethane, and Propellant C-318, octafluorocyclobutane. In addition to solving the above problems, the use of liquefied gas propellant improves the quality of the discharged whipped cream. It has a much finer, more appetizing appearance and remains in that condition for a longer period of time. With the compressed gases, the whipped cream begins to collapse and visible liquid is formed shortly after it is discharged.

While the liquefied compressed gas propellants give an improved product, they are too expensive to use alone and in the case of Propellant 115, the vapor pressure is too high. A compromise has been worked out, using a mixture of Propellant 115 and nitrous oxide that retains a good many of the desirable properties of each propellant by itself. On a weight basis, the propellant used with each container amounts to about 4% of the total weight of the contents.

Aerosol whipped cream as well as other types of food aerosols is packaged in light-weight tin-plated cans with volumes ranging from 6 to 12 oz. The cans are lined with a lacquer to prevent any reaction between the can metal and the food product. They comply with Department of Transportation regulations governing the interstate shipment of food products in one-trip containers.

The valves used with food aerosols depend on the type of product to be dispensed. Special valves have been developed for use with whipped toppings and other types are available for dispensing foods in other physical forms. In general, the valves are made with a steel body and spring, plastic dispensing tube, and neoprene or Buna N gaskets.

At present nearly all of the commercial food aerosols are similar to whipped cream. A few, such as some cheese preparations, are dispensed as a paste. With this type the propellant does not influence the nature of the dispensed product but merely serves as a force, much like a piston in a cylinder, to expel it from the container.

The future of aerosol foods is uncertain. A firm market exists for a few products but further development work is necessary for it to grow and expand. Studies to improve formulation, packaging, and marketing are continuing with some success and may soon lead to new products and interest in the aerosol food industry.

RALPH C. DOWNING

References

SANDERS, P. A. 1970. Principles of Aerosol Technology. Van Nostrand Reinhold Co., New York.

SHEPARD, H. R. 1961. Aerosols: Science and Technology. Interscience Publishers, New York.

Recommended Journals

Aerosol Age, P. O. Box 31, Caldwell, N.J.

Chemical and Engineering News, American Chemical Society, 1155 Sixteenth St., N.W., Washington, D.C.

Soap and Chemical Specialties, 254 West 31 St., New York, N.Y.

AFLATOXIN

The toxic metabolic product of the fungus, *Aspergillus flavus*, found to be the causative agent in the death of a large number of turkey poults in England in 1960, was given the name aflatoxin for *A*spergillus *FLA*vus *TOXIN*. The toxin fluoresced intensely when exposed to ultraviolet light. This characteristic was used to recognize the toxin and follow its purification. The toxin can be purified chromatographically and two crystalline products thus obtained were named aflatoxin B, because of its blue fluorescence, and G, because of its greenish fluorescence. When it was recognized that each of these was composed of two compounds, subscripts were assigned to distinguish them. Thus evolved the terminology aflatoxin B_1, B_2, G_1, and G_2 for the four principal aflatoxins. Aflatoxins M_1 and M_2 are hydroxylated derivatives that were originally found in milk (milk toxins) of dairy cattle fed rations containing aflatoxins B_1 and B_2. To date (1971) at least 12 closely related compounds designated aflatoxins have been characterized (Fig. A-3). The latest addition, P_1, a phenol, is the principal urinary metabolite of aflatoxin B_1 in rhesus monkeys but has not been identified from mold cultures.

Production and Occurrence of Aflatoxins

A. parasiticus as well as *A. flavus* produces aflatoxins. Other fungi have also been reported to produce aflatoxins but the reports have been disputed or lack confirmation. No aflatoxin was obtained from cultures of strains of *A. oryzae* used as starters in the manufacture of shoyu, miso, and other fermented food products. *A. flavus* is ubiquitous but all strains do not necessarily pro-

duce aflatoxin. Some produce none, some only B, others B and G or B and M, and some B, G, and M. None has been found to produce G without B. *A. parasiticus* appears to be restricted primarily to the tropics but all strains are toxigenic and generally produce aflatoxins in larger amounts than does *A. flavus*.

Under controlled laboratory conditions *A. flavus* produces good yields of aflatoxin on many commodities, including cereals, legumes, oilseeds, meats, fruits and fruit juices, and tree nuts. Preferred substrates are rice and wheat. Liquid media may also be used. The amounts and proportions of the various aflatoxins produced depend upon the strain of mold, the substrate, and environmental conditions, especially temperature and humidity. Usually the substrates are moistened, sterilized, inoculated with a toxigenic strain of fungus, and incubated at 25°–30°C for 5–15 days.

Aflatoxin has been found, usually at low levels, as a natural contaminant in many agricultural commodities including barley, Brazil nuts, cassava,

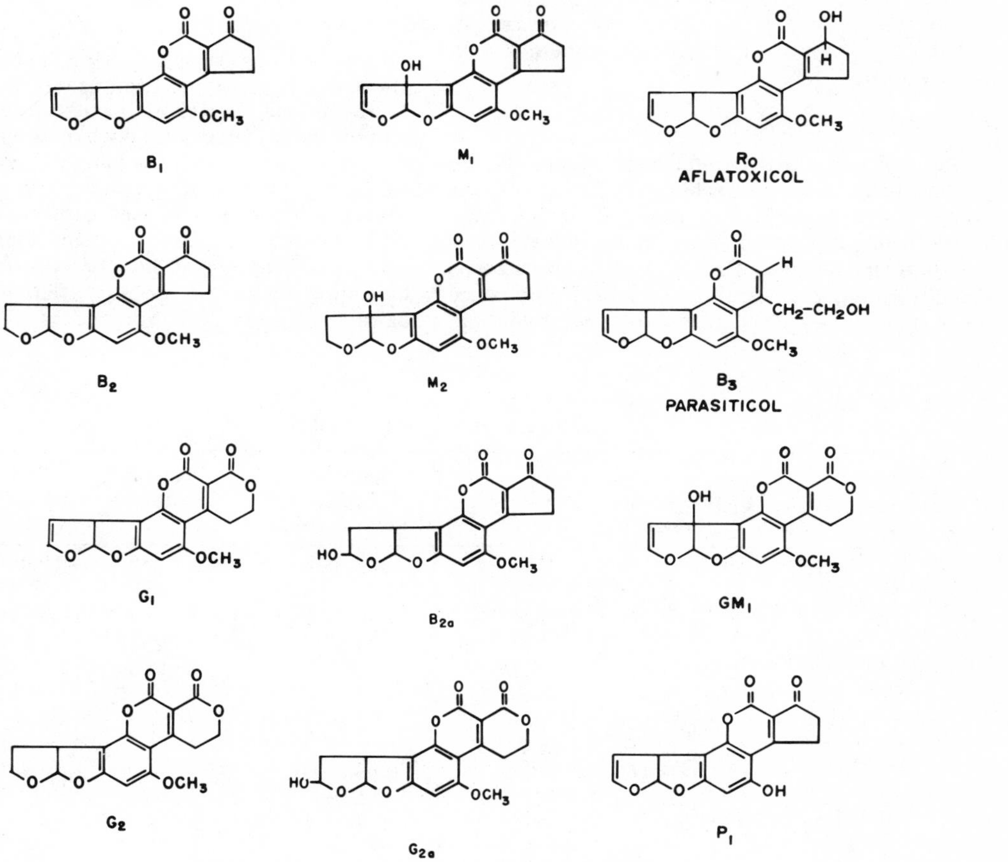

FIG. A-3. STRUCTURES OF THE AFLATOXINS

copra, corn, cottonseed, cottonseed meal, millet, oats, peanuts, peanut meal, pecans, pistachios, sesame, sorghum, and sweet potatoes in various parts of the world. The extent of the growth of fungal flora, and production of aflatoxins, is dependent upon many factors including temperature and moisture content, the commodity, and whether it is sound or damaged.

Cultural, harvesting, and handling methods that prevent mechanical and insect damage and keep commodities in good condition are important. The main requirement for safe storage is to maintain moisture and temperature levels that prevent mold growth. Optimum temperature for production of aflatoxin is 20°-30°C; the limiting lower and upper temperatures are about 10° and 40°C, respectively. The minimum moisture requirement for growth and sporulation by *A. flavus* corresponds to 80–85% relative humidity (RH). Moisture content of natural substrates in equilibrium with such RH depends upon the commodity and the temperature. A moisture content of 13% or less is recommended for storage of grain in the midwest but the moisture level should be 1–2% less in warmer areas. For commodities high in oil content, e.g., peanuts, the moisture content should be below about 8%.

Properties and Analysis

Some physical and chemical properties of the aflatoxins are shown in Table A-2. The aflatoxins are soluble in methanol, acetone, acetonitrile, chloroform, and some other polar solvents but are sparingly soluble in water and hydrocarbons. All the aflatoxins exhibit intense fluorescence when excited by 365 nm ultraviolet radiation.

This permits detection of less than 10^{-9} gm and quantitation at levels of a few ppb (μg per kg) or even less in various commodities.

Several types of methods of analysis have been developed based upon successive stages of extraction, purification, and thin-layer chromatography. Final quantitation is achieved by comparison (visually or densitometrically) of fluorescence with a known standard or by dilution to extinction. Quantitation may also be accomplished by determination of absorbance in the ultraviolet (absorption maxima at about 220, 265, and 360 nm) but this is relatively insensitive. These methods are not specific for aflatoxins and verification is usually achieved by a chemical confirmatory test or biologically. Chemical confirmation is by addition to the vinyl-ether system of the bifuran moiety or by reaction with carbonyl reagents. Confirmation by thin-layer chromatography-mass spectrometry permits positive identification at levels below 50 ng (5×10^{-8} gm). Biological confirmation is usually obtained by assay with 1-day-old ducklings or with chicken egg embryos.

Biological Effects

All living things so far reported are susceptible to aflatoxin. Toxicity has been demonstrated in such diverse animal species as protozoa, brine shrimp, rainbow trout, chickens, pheasants, cattle, guinea pigs, and swine. Some bacteria are inhibited, albinism (chlorophyll deficiency) is produced in some green plants, and seed germination is inhibited. Aflatoxin is toxic to many mammals, fish, and birds. Toxicity of the aflatoxins varies greatly depending upon the specific aflatoxin, the biological test system (microorganisms, plants, various

TABLE A-2

PROPERTIES OF AFLATOXINS

Aflatoxin	Empirical Formula	Mol Wt	Melting Point (°C decomposition)	Specific Rotation $^{\alpha}$D	LD_{50}[1] μg
B_1	$C_{17}H_{12}O_6$	312	268–269	-558	12–50
B_2	$C_{17}H_{14}O_6$	314	286–289	-492	85
G_1	$C_{17}H_{12}O_7$	328	244–246	-556	39
G_2	$C_{17}H_{14}O_7$	330	237–240	-473	172
M_1	$C_{17}H_{12}O_7$	328	299	-280	17
M_2	$C_{17}H_{14}O_7$	330	293	—	62
B_{2a}	$C_{17}H_{14}O_7$	330	240	—	>1200
G_{2a}	$C_{17}H_{14}O_8$	346	190	—	>1600
R_0	$C_{17}H_{14}O_6$	314	188–194	—	900
GM_1	$C_{17}H_{12}O_8$	344	276	—	—
B_3	$C_{16}H_{14}O_6$	302	217(233)	—	—
P_1	$C_{16}H_{10}O_6$	298	—	—	—

[1] For 1-day-old ducklings.

animal systems), the species tested, age, sex, nutritional status, the dose applied and mode of administration, and the length of exposure. The toxic activity may be genetic or nongenetic in nature. Aflatoxin B_1 is carcinogenic, teratogenic, and mutagenic to some animal species.

Nongenetic Effects.—Lethality of aflatoxin B_1 (the most toxic) has been studied in numerous laboratory and farm animals. LD_{50} values range from less than 0.5 to more than 20 mg per kg of body weight. There are marked differences between the animal species but in all species sensitivity decreases with age. The relative lethality patterns of nine aflatoxins in the 1-day-old duckling test are listed in Table A-2. Susceptibility may vary within species; Barred Rock chicks are almost unaffected but New Hampshire chicks are nearly as sensitive as turkey poults. Some species such as sheep are highly resistant. In many farm animals ingestion of feed containing aflatoxin in levels below the LD_{50} causes significant growth inhibition, decreased feed efficiency, and increased internal organ weights (liver and kidney). Most ingested aflatoxin is excreted in urine and feces but lactating cattle excrete as milk toxins (M_1 + M_2) a small proportion of ingested B_1. Aflatoxin B_1 inhibits protein synthesis *in vitro* but not *in vivo*. Bile duct hyperplasia is the most characteristic and easily identified early pathological effect in most species. The comparative pathology may include necrosis and hemorrhage, chronic fibrosis, enlarged hepatic cells, and finally liver tumors.

Genetic Effects.—Aflatoxin B_1 inhibits DNA synthesis and impairs synthesis of nuclear RNA. The carcinogenic activity of three aflatoxins, (B_1, G_1, and M_1) has been demonstrated in several animal species. B_1 is the most potent. The rainbow trout is the most sensitive test species; less than 1 ppb in the diet has caused liver cancer after 20 months of feeding. The rainbow trout is also highly sensitive to aflatoxin M_1. B_1 is also a carcinogen for rats, mice, ducks, and ferrets. In hamsters, B_1 administered during pregnancy has a strong teratogenic effect. This effect is not observed in rats and mice and, therefore, is species specific.

Protection of Food and Feed and Precautions

The United Nations-World Health Organization Expert Committee on Nutrition has recommended that the level of aflatoxin in protein supplements should not exceed 30 ppb although a lower limit would have been preferred if protein needs were not so critical. For feedstuffs, manufacturers in many countries follow the Code of Practice prepared by the Compound Animal Feeding Stuff Manufacturers National Association, Ltd. (England). This code recommends limitation on usage of contaminated protein supplements in mixed animal feeds depending upon age and species. Suggested levels range from none for even weakly positive aflatoxin-contaminated peanut meals for duck foods, turkey starter foods, and baby chick foods, to a maximum of $2^{1}/_{2}\%$ for cattle and 5% for sheep where the reaction is very strong, i.e., more than 5 ppm aflatoxin.

In the United States, the FDA has authority to regulate aflatoxin-contaminated commodities. As aflatoxin is carcinogenic there is no tolerance for aflatoxin in any food or feed. However, the FDA has set a guideline of 20 ppb for routine examination below which action is not taken. Dilution to attain low levels is not condoned and the guideline does not bar regulatory action below 20 ppb.

Prevention of mold growth is the best approach to avoid aflatoxin contamination. Techniques have been developed to detoxify various food and feed products. These include removal of the toxin by physical, chemical, or biological means and inactivation by physical or chemical means. Aflatoxin is relatively stable to heat and cannot be destroyed by heat without excessive damage to nutritive value, nor is extraction by solvents of whole kernels feasible. Physical separation is highly effective for peanuts. This is accomplished by handpicking, photoelectric sorting, and mechanical sorting. Contaminated Brazil nuts are removed by sizing and air aspiration. Solutions of aflatoxin-contaminated milk and corn oil are completely detoxified by cells of *Flavobacterium aurantiacum*. Aflatoxin in crude vegetable oils is removed during refining. Meals made from aflatoxin-contaminated oilseeds contain aflatoxin and this may be removed by extraction with solvents such as aqueous acetone or isopropanol. Aflatoxin may also be destroyed by treatment with chemicals such as ammonia, lime, formaldehyde, and hydrogen peroxide.

Precautions should be taken to protect personnel working with aflatoxin. Use of disposable paper masks and coats which can be burned, cleaning glassware and contaminated surfaces with bleach (NaOCl) solution, and monitoring possible contamination of work areas by means of a portable long-wave ultraviolet lamp are recommended. *A. flavus* cultures should be handled with caution.

LEO A. GOLDBLATT

References

ANON. 1968. Preventing mycotoxins in farm commodities. U.S. Dept. Agr., Agr. Res. Serv. *ARS-20-16.*

GOLDBLATT, L. A. (Editor) 1969. Aflatoxin, Scientific Background, Control, and Implications. Academic Press, New York.

Cross-reference: *Peanuts.*

AGGLOMERATION (INSTANTIZING)

Food products in dry form requiring hydration or dispersion in an aqueous media are abundant in today's markets. Additionally, many products are available as paste or liquid concentrates as an alternative to a powdered or granular form due to unacceptable hydration properties or unstable storage characteristics of the dried products. "Instantizing" is a generic term encompassing a variety of treatments, chemical or physical, that will improve the hydration characteristics of powdered or granular products. Chemical treatment by addition to the powder of surface active compounds or coating them with fatty materials is well known and will not be dealt with here.

Physical treatment to alter the size, shape, and surface structure of solid particles to increase their hydration rate, thus rendering them more "instant," has evolved from a number of basic processes and has become an attractive approach to improve a product's performance, acceptance, and utility. The criteria for an "instant" product are that it can be added to a liquid and dissolved or suspended uniformly with a minimum of agitation, such as stirring with a spoon.

When a quantity of a powdered material is added to a liquid, the initial obstacle to wetting is the liquid surface which by virtue of its surface tension and the interfacial relationship with the powder may present a near impenetrable barrier to the submergence of the powder mass. The particles adjacent to the liquid surface attain an orientation which exposes the largest possible surface to the liquid interface resulting in a buoyant effect. The smaller the individual particles are, the greater this effect becomes as the individual particles do not have sufficient mass to overcome the repelling forces at the interface. A hydrophobic powder, such as one containing proteinaceous components, can remain afloat and unwetted for long periods of time. A powder with great affinity for water often exhibits similar difficulties with respect to initial wetting but there the retarding factor is the formation of a concentrated, often viscous, solution layer at the liquid-solid interface. This layer is of low diffusivity and acts as an effective barrier to hydraulic and capillary flow into the powder mass, leaving much slower diffusion as the only mechanism for fluid transfer.

By increasing the size of the particles in a product, the problem of surface penetration and initial wetting may be overcome. This is accomplished in some spray-dried products by adjusting the spray pattern in the dryer so that a coarser product is obtained and by screening out the finer particles, which may be recycled or disposed of as a different grade product.

Increasing the particle size of a product reaches practical limits as manifested by reduced efficiencies of spray dryers or other process equipment. The rate of solubility of the product after initial wetting may, in itself, be a limiting factor as regards the particle size. Granulated sugar, for instance, dissolves very slowly in ice water due to its relatively small specific surface. The powdered counterpart with its large specific surface exhibits poor initial wetting characteristics. To circumvent the two problems of poor wetting and slow dissolution, it is desirable to provide particles combining relatively large mass with large specific surface. Products of this nature are termed "instant" and their attendant processes "instantizing" or agglomeration.

The physical form of instant products vary depending on the nature of the product and the process for producing them. Typically, they are clusters or agglomerates with varying degrees of void volume or open cell foams.

The process of assembling small particles into clusters or large masses can take many different forms and the mechanisms for bonding the individual particles together varies accordingly. Terms such as "briquetting," "nodulizing," "pelletizing," "sintering," "granulating," "tableting," "spheronizing," "extrusion," "compaction," and many others denote processes for producing agglomerates of varied characteristics to improve bulk flow characteristics, reduce dusting, reduce bulk, etc. In general, however, products of these types, due to their compact nature, have solution rates which are too slow to be termed "instant."

Improved rate of solution of an agglomerate can be accomplished by assembling the particles in such a manner as to leave considerable void space between the component particles and bonding the particles together at "initial point of contact." The void fraction in such an open-structured solid with the individual particles being unit spheres has been calculated to be about 0.80, which is in good agreement with practice.

The void spaces in an open-structured agglomerate attract the liquid by capillary action, as in a sponge, resulting in rapid penetration of liquid to the interior. The "point of contact" bonds rapidly dissolve and the agglomerate virtually disintegrates into a fully wetted mass of component particles which, by virtue of their large specific surfaces, quickly dissolve. In systems containing an insoluble component in conjunction with a soluble material such as a cocoa-sugar mixture, the cocoa particles are individually entrained in the sugar particle matrix and each cocoa particle becomes entirely wetted prior to its release from the agglomerate as the sugar matrix disintegrates.

Products of strong hydrophobic character may

resist wetting and dissolution even in the form of a porous agglomerate. Treating the hydrophobic component to increase its affinity for water then becomes desirable. Cocoa is routinely lecithinated for this purpose and spray-dried milk solids are produced with minimum heat damage and under conditions promoting formation of desired lactose crystal structure. The latter may be accomplished alternatively in the treatment of the wet agglomerates in the drying step.

Agglomeration equipment can be categorized according to the type and shape of the zone where agglomeration takes place. The more common types are: chamber-spray dryer, tube, cascading, fluidized bed, and blender.

Chamber Spray Dryer

The need for improved dispersibility of dried milk products and milk additives was recognized in the dairy industry at a time when spray drying had become the common method for dehydration of milk products. Consequently, several agglomeration processes emerged based on a large chamber as the central unit for the agglomeration step and often for some initial drying. D. D. Peebles patented a process in which a fluidized stream of skim milk powder is dispersed into a vertical spray dryer chamber where it is wetted by condensing water vapor and atomized liquid water, and agglomerated as a result of the turbulent flow pattern within the chamber. To prevent condensation of moisture on the chamber walls, heated air is circulated in a jacket surrounding the chamber to maintain its surface temperature above the dew point of the chamber atmosphere. The aggregated milk product discharging from the chamber cone is allowed to equilibrate on a moving belt prior to drying, sizing, and cooling. In another patent by Peebles, alternate locations and methods for the moisture supply are employed to suit different product requirements.

H. B. Bishop, in his patent, discloses agglomeration of recycled fines onto the primary moist particles in a vertical spray drier processing molasses, fishmeal, and yeast products. Similarly, P. F. Sharp and C. A. Kempf, in their patent, combine the spray drying and agglomeration step in a chamber by causing aggregation to occur when milk particles have been partially dried, thus eliminating the rewetting step.

The patent by J. T. Hutton et al. utilizes separate spray drying and agglomeration chambers. The spray dryer is operated as in Sharp's process with the exception that the milk powder discharges partially dried (6–14% moisture) and partially aggregated and is directly air conveyed into a rewetting chamber where additional moisture is added in the form of a mixture of atomized water

and steam. To facilitate product removal from the rewetting chamber, the cone portion is made of canvas or other flexible material.

N. E. Spiess, Jr., and Neil E. Sullivan patented a process quite similar to Peebles, directing the moistening spray upward directly against the downward flowing stream of fluidized powder feed with the impingement of the two streams causing the turbulent contact required for agglomeration.

A. M. Swanson and C. H. Amundson, in their patent, produce an agglomerated dried milk product from a liquid concentrate in a single spray drying chamber by using two distinctly separate locations for the introduction and atomization of the liquid concentrate. The bulk of the feed is delivered through four nozzles located concentrically at about half the radius of the dryer with relatively confined downward spray pattern. Centrally located inside the spray pattern and some distance below the primary nozzles, a centrifugal atomizer projects a horizontal spray of concentrate onto the downwardly flowing, partially dried particles causing rewetting and agglomeration.

Using a chamber configuration, but without provision for atomized liquid addition, the patents of E. A. Louder and A. Z. Hodson, of H. L. Griffin, and of F. E. Reimers et al., cause agglomeration to occur by directing a falling powder stream through jets of steam or humid air. Of these, the Griffin process is most widely used, particularly in the recovery of fines from spray- and freeze-dried products where the fines are agglomerated with the primary product such as instant coffee and instant tea.

The greatest problem associated with chamber type processes is the sanitation requirements of frequent cleaning due to buildup of sticky material on equipment surfaces.

Tube Type

Agglomeration can be accomplished in tubes or ducts by introducing the powder into a humidified air stream in the tube. The turbulent flow pattern within the tube causes frequent particle-to-particle contact which results in rapid cluster formation. The stream is discharged into a cyclone type collector where further agglomeration usually takes place.

In their patent, E. A. Louder and A. Z. Hodson perform all the steps of wetting, agglomeration, and redrying in one tube, discharging a dried agglomerated product from the cyclone collector.

G. H. Hartman et al., in their patent, use a separate tube dryer after the moistening and agglomerating of the powder in a system similar to Louder's. Hartman's arrangement permits recycling of the humid air and fine particles from the cyclone collector on the agglomerating section.

Spray drying, combined with agglomeration, is practiced in a tube or jet type spray dryer by P. Bradford in his Canadian patent. After initially atomizing and drying the liquid in a hot air stream, additional liquid spray is added in a venturi constriction downstream and further drying takes place in a divergent tube section discharging into a cyclone.

As with chamber-type processes, sanitation is the greatest problem associated with tube-type processes. Material build-up in the tube, collector, and recycle ducts require frequent disassembly and cleaning. As an alternative, elaborate CIP systems are used.

Cascading Type

In a cascading type agglomeration process, the powder in the form of a free falling curtain is contacted with steam or humid air which is directed at and through the powder curtain at specific angles. The wet agglomerated material is projected onto a drying belt prior to sizing. R. H. Bissell, in his patent, delivers a thin layer of powder from an upper belt onto a lower belt while projecting steam from a perforated pipe horizontally through the thin dimension of the falling powder curtain between the belts.

The patent of B. Sienkiewicz et al., in a slight departure from Bissell, delivers the steam from a nozzle directed horizontally against the edge of the falling curtain projecting the particles across the width of the curtain in a confined stream onto a drying belt.

Fluidized Bed

In fluidized bed agglomeration processes, the powder particles are suspended in the fluidizing gas, normally air, in such a way that the particles are in very close proximity to one another, yet in a highly mobile state. The close proximity of the particles promotes rapid and complete agglomeration in a very small space. After the powder particles have initially fused together into agglomerates, the gas velocities and the bed depth often are not sufficient to maintain a fluidized condition and the drying and cooling steps may be conducted under nonfluidized conditions.

The patent of R. G. Gidlow and A. D. Mills moves a layer of powdered material over a permeable support deck while passing humid gas, normally air, through the support and the powder layer. Movement of the powder is imparted by vibratory motion, by having the permeable support in the form of a conveyor belt or in the form of a stationary sloped air-slide type conveyor. To prevent moisture deposition and subsequent fouling on the permeable support, the humid air is heated above its dewpoint prior to entering the bed. This superheat is dissipated as sensible heat to the lower layers of powder in the bed until the air reaches its dewpoint, at which time moisture deposition on the particles occurs in an amount proportional to the difference between the particle temperature and the dewpoint of the air surrounding them. Where fouling occurs due to the deliquescent or thermoplastic nature of the powder, two patents by R. G. Gidlow provide a permeable belt which is continuously moved through a cleaning station prior to re-entering the processing zones.

The subsequent drying, cooling and sizing steps are most generally conducted on a vibratory type processing unit which may or may not be an integral part of the agglomeration unit.

R. J. Patrick and P. M. Sautier, in a similar patented process, form an expanded foam-like mat from the wetted particles in a moving fluidized bed by letting the entire mass fuse together. After drying, the mat is subdivided into agglomerates of desired size and shape.

Atomized liquid in the fluidizing gas stream is used by the patent of D. E. Wurster in a batch process for simultaneous granulation and coating of the powder.

I. Galsmar and J. P. Hansen (Nordisk Mejeri-Tidskrift 5, 1036, 1965) claim to agglomerate partially dried milk powder directly from a spray dryer in a vibrating fluidized bed by maintaining the sticky particles in a nondrying condition in the agglomerating section. This is accomplished by passing a warm air stream through the bed at a temperature that does not result in appreciable drying while the powder particles aggregate. In subsequent sections of the vibrating conveyor, hot and cool air streams are forced through the bed to accomplish drying and cooling of the product.

Blender Type

Blenders of various types are used to agglomerate a wide range of materials. Humid air, atomized liquids and melted solids (ice) are used to provide the adhesive for agglomeration. The use of gentle tumbling in relatively slow moving blenders is the most common practice, with relatively fewer applications of high speed mixers.

In general, the products from blender type processes are denser and more compact than those from the preceding processes and approach in character products produced by granulation, pelletizing, and compaction processes which are considered outside the scope of instantizing and not dealt with here.

Trends in the convenience food market predict an increased demand for instant products. Instantizing equipment has in the past, with minor exceptions, been developed by the food companies rather than the food equipment manufacturers. With the expiration of many of the basic patents in the next few years, expectations are that the equipment manufacturers will take greater interest in developing and providing testing and processing facilities for the growing "instant" food market.

R. GUNNAR GIDLOW

Patents Issued on Agglomeration Processes

BISHOP, H. B. 1955. Drying method and apparatus. U.S. Pat. 2,698,815.

BISSELL, R. H. 1960. Process for increasing the solubility of powdered milk. U.S. Pat. 2,949,363.

BOND, R. W., and SNYDER, E. C. 1960. Process for agglomerating dextrose. U.S. Pat. 2,954,306.

BRADFORD, P. 1961. Agglomeration of spray-dried materials. Can. Pat. 618,970.

CARLSON, E. E., PLAGGE, I. F., and SWANSON, A. M. 1961. Manufacture of dry chocolate drink product. U.S. Pat. 3,013,881.

CARNATION COMPANY. 1963. Process of making a wettable and dispersible flour-containing food product. Brit. Pat. 928,570.

FRITZBERG, E. L. 1966. Method of agglomerating solid particulate material. U.S. Pat. 3,275,449.

GALLE, E. L., WEISS, R. M., OLSON, J. C., and GIDLOW, R. G. 1968. Process and apparatus for agglomerating and drying flour. U.S. Pat. 3,360,865.

GIDLOW, R. G. 1965. Agglomerating apparatus. U.S. Pat. 3,220,054.

GIDLOW, R. G. 1967. Agglomerating process. U.S. Pat. 3,306,958.

GIDLOW, R. G., and MILLS, A. D. 1961. Process and apparatus for agglomerating pulverulent materials. U.S. Pat. 2,995,773.

GIDLOW, R. G., and STEIN, J. A. 1966. Method of agglomerating a dry pulverulent flour base material. U.S. Pat. 3,251,695.

GIDLOW, R. G., STEIN, J. A., GANSKE, W. L., and ZENZES, A. M. 1970. Agglomerated sugar products and method. U.S. Pat. 3,506,457.

GIDLOW, R. G., and TEDERS, R. L. 1966. Method of agglomerating a dry powdery flour base material. U.S. Pat. 3,248,228.

GILLETT, E. G., and PRINCE, R. N. 1958. Fondant and dry fondant sugar product and method of manufacture. U.S. Pat. 2,824,808.

GRIFFIN, H. L. 1959. Agglomeration process and apparatus. U.S. Pat. 2,893,871.

GRÜN, G. 1972. Method of treating powder or granulate substances. U.S. Pat. 3,697,286.

HAGER, J. L. 1970. Agglomerating process and apparatus. U.S. Pat. 3,527,647.

HAIR, E. R., and LAWRENCE, B. 1964. Process for agglomerating culinary mixes. U.S. Pat. 3,135,612.

HARTMAN, G. H., HARDER, H. F., REZBA, A. J., and REEVE, R. K. 1960. Method and apparatus for producing clusters of lacteal material. U.S. Pat. 2,934,434.

HUBBARD, F. E., and McCULLOUGH, C. R. 1946. Water-treating composition. U.S. Pat. 2,396,918.

HUTTON, J. T., NAVA, L. J., SHIELDS, J. B., and KEMPF, C. A. 1966. Process for producing instantized products. U.S. Pat. 3,231,386.

KOMAREK, G., and KOMAREK, K. R. 1961. Method and apparatus for agglomerating particulate materials. U.S. Pat. 2,977,631.

LESLIE, E. H., and CROCKIN, J. M. 1956. System for the agglomeration of solvent-extracted fine solid organic particles. U.S. Pat. 2,751,301.

LINN, S. 1973. Apparatus for agglomeration. U.S. Pat. 3,729,327.

LOUDER, E. A., and HODSON, A. Z. 1958. Instantly soluble milk powder and process for making same. U.S. Pat. 2,832,686.

LUSHBOUGH, C. H. 1955. Method for producing malted milk balls and the resulting product. U.S. Pat. 2,726,959.

MARCY, W., and NETSCH, R. 1961. Method of producing a dry sugar-cocoa mix. U.S. Pat. 3,006,763.

MILTON, C. H. 1967. Method of preparing an agglomerated food product. U.S. Pat. 3,359,119.

MOLLENBRUCK, W. 1964. Mixing and agglomerating device for thermoplastic material. U.S. Pat. 3,155,376.

PATRICK, R. J., and SAUTIER, P. M. 1969. Agglomerating process. U.S. Pat. 3,471,603.

PEEBLES, D. D. 1958. Gelatin product and process of manufacture. U.S. Pat. 2,851,364.

PEEBLES, D. D. 1958. Dried milk product and method of making same. U.S. Pat. 2,835,586.

PEEBLES, D. D. 1958. Lactose product and process of manufacture. U.S. Pat. 2,856,318.

PEEBLES, D. D. 1959. Milk manufacturing method and product. U.S. Pat. 2,911,300.

PEEBLES, D. D. 1960. Dried egg product and process of manufacture. U.S. Pat. 2,950,204.

PEEBLES, D. D. 1961. Sweetening product and method of manufacture. U.S. Pat. 3,014,803.

PEEBLES, D. D. 1963. Apparatus for the treatment of dry powdered materials. U.S. Pat. 3,085,492.

REIMERS, F. E., MILLER, M. D., and NABORNEY, E. 1964. Method and apparatus for agglomeration. U.S. Pat. 3,143,428.

SCHAPIRO, A. 1963. Agglomerated food product and method for making same. U.S. Pat. 3,100,909.

SCHWER, F. W., and BAILEY, G. S. 1966. Method of making sugar. U.S. Pat. 3,257,236.

SEGAL, S. 1965. Method of preparing free-flowing dry flour and other particles. U.S. Pat. 3,221,338.

SHARP, P. F., and KEMPF, C. A. 1960. Method for the preparation of a powdered milk product. U.S. Pat. 2,921,857.

SHENKENBERG, D. R. 1962. Process for the manufacture of a chocolate flavored product. U.S. Pat. 3,027,257.

SHIELDS, J. B. 1962. Method of manufacturing an instantized product. U.S. Pat. 3,057,727.

SIENKIEWICZ, B., and BAGLEY, F. A. 1972. Process and apparatus for agglomeration. U.S. Pat. 3,695,165.

SIENKIEWICZ, B., KOHLER, R. B., and SCHULMAN, M. 1961. Agglomeration process. U.S. Pat. 2,977,203.

SPIESS, N. E., JR., and SULLIVAN, NEIL E. 1962. Powder agglomerating method and apparatus. U.S. Pat. 3,042,526.

SWANSON, A. M., and AMUNDSON, C. H. 1963. Agglomeration process. U.S. Pat. 3,083,099.

SWANSON, A. M., and FENSKE, D. J. 1966. Process for aggregating difficult to aggregate particles and the product thereof. U.S. Pat. 3,262,788.

WURSTER, D. E. 1963. Granulating and coating process for uniform granules. U.S. Pat. 3,089,824.

Cross-reference: *Convenience Foods.*

ALCOHOLIC BEVERAGES

See Distilled Beverage Spirits.

AMINO ACIDS

Amino acids, in their strictest chemical meaning, are compounds which possess carboxyl- and amino-groups. In this article, however, amino acids will be restricted to mean those which compose natural proteins. Among some 20 kinds of α-amino acids and two imino acids, which compose natural proteins, the monosodium salt of glutamic acid was the first to be isolated and used in food technology. The finding goes as far back as 1908. It was made by Japanese researchers.

Hydrolysis by hydrochloric acid was the usual procedure to obtain glutamic acid from such proteinaceous raw materials as wheat gluten or soybean meal. Neutralized hydrolysate itself, a mixture of amino acids and salt, was similarly used after some refining. Isolation of individual amino acid from the hydrolysate was achieved by utilizing ion exchange resins after World War II, which made it possible for food technologists to use amino acids in a number of ways not previously possible.

In the United States, glutamic acid for use in monosodium glutamate (MSG) was also extracted from beet sugar waste, in which it is contained as pyrrolidone carboxylic acid. Production of MSG by the fermentation process began in 1957. The industrial production by chemical synthesis began in 1963 in Japan. These three processes are also applied to other amino acids according to their respective characteristics.

Technical information on amino acids is to be found in the *Food Chemicals Codex*, a publication of the National Academy of Sciences—National Research Council. The Codex was prepared by the Food Protection Committee of the Academy. The first edition of the Codex, published in 1966, contains the description, identifications, specifications, and tests for L-cystine, L-glutamic acid, L-glutamic acid hydrochloride, L-leucine, L-lysine monohydrochloride, DL-methionine, L-methionine, monopotassium L-glutamate, monosodium L-glutamate, and L-tyrosine.

The second edition of *Food Chemicals Codex*, published in 1972, contains data on DL-alanine, L-alanine, L-arginine, L-arginine monohydrochloride, DL-aspartic acid, L-cysteine hydrochloride, DL-isoleucine, L-isoleucine, DL-leucine, L-phenylalanine, L-proline, DL-serine, L-serine, L-threonine, L-tryptophan, and L-valine.

Biochemical Aspects

Amino acids of varying type are present in different proportions in proteins of every organism, not only as tissue constituents but also as the major portion of all enzymes. Molecules of the protein are thought to be polypeptides in which amino acids are linked by peptide bond. The arrangement of amino acids determines the characteristics and physiological properties of the proteins.

Peptide bond

$$NH_2 - \underset{H}{\overset{R}{C}} - CO - NH - \underset{H}{\overset{R'}{C}} - COOH \leftarrow$$

$$NH_2 - \underset{H}{\overset{R}{C}} - CO \; \boxed{OH + H} \; NH - \underset{H}{\overset{R'}{C}} - COOH$$

Ingested dietary proteins are digested to constituent amino acids, and only in this form are they absorbed by the intestine wall.

Nutritional Aspects

Dietary protein is the only source of animal body and functional proteins in which amino

TABLE A-3

AMINO ACIDS OF BIOLOGICAL IMPORTANCE

Class	Name	Abbreviation	Formula	Discoverer from Protein Hydrolysate	
			Neutral Amino Acids		
Aliphatic	Glycine	Gly	NH_2-CH_2-COOH	Braconnot	1820
	L-Alanine	Ala	$CH_3-CH-COOH$ $\quad\quad\ \ |$ $\quad\quad\ \ NH_2$	Weyl Schuetzenberger	1888 1879
	L-Valine	Val	$(CH_3)_2CH-CH-COOH$ $\quad\quad\quad\quad\ |$ $\quad\quad\quad\quad\ NH_2$	Fischer	1901
	L-Leucine	Leu	$(CH_3)_2CH-CH_2-CH-COOH$ $\quad\quad\quad\quad\quad\quad\ |$ $\quad\quad\quad\quad\quad\quad\ NH_2$	Braconnot	1820
	L-Isoleucine	Ile	$C_2H_5-CH-CH-COOH$ $\quad\quad\ \ | \quad |$ $\quad\quad\ CH_3\ NH_2$	Ehrlich	1904
Hydroxy-	L-Serine	Ser	$HO-CH_2-CH-COOH$ $\quad\quad\quad\quad |$ $\quad\quad\quad\quad NH_2$	Cramer	1865
	L-Threonine	Thr	$CH_3-CH-CH-COOH$ $\quad\quad\ |\quad |$ $\quad\quad OH\ NH_2$	Schryver and Buston Cortner and Hoffmann	1925
S-containing	L-Cysteine	Cys	$HS-CH_2-CH-COOH$ $\quad\quad\quad\quad |$ $\quad\quad\quad\quad NH_2$	Neuberg and Friedman	1902
	L-Cystine	Cys Cys	$(-S-CH_2-CH-COOH)_2$ $\quad\quad\quad\quad |$ $\quad\quad\quad\quad NH_2$	Mörner, Emden	1899
	L-Methionine	Met	$CH_3-S-CH_2-CH_2-CH-COOH$ $\quad\quad\quad\quad\quad\quad\quad\ |$ $\quad\quad\quad\quad\quad\quad\quad\ NH_2$	Mueller	1922

TABLE A-3 (*Continued*)

Class	Name	Abbreviation	Formula	Discoverer from Protein Hydrolysate	
Amide	L-Asparagine	Asn	$H_2NOC-CH_2-CH-COOH$ with NH_2	Damodaran	1932
	L-Glutamine	Gln	$H_2NOC-CH_2-CH_2-CH-COOH$ with NH_2	Damodaran, Jaaback and Chibnall	1932
Aromatic	L-Phenylalanine	Phe	$\bigcirc-CH_2-CH-COOH$ with NH_2	Schulze and Barbieri	1881
	L-Tyrosine	Tyr	$HO-\bigcirc-CH_2-CH-COOH$ with NH_2	Bopp	1849
	L-Tryptophan	Trp	indole$-CH_2-CH-COOH$ with NH_2	Hopkins and Cole	1902
	Acidic Amino Acids				
	L-Aspartic acid	Asp	$HOOC-CH_2-CH-COOH$ with NH_2	Ritthausen	1868
	L-Glutamic acid	Glu	$HOOC-CH_2-CH_2-CH-COOH$ with NH_2	Ritthausen	1866
	Basic Amino Acids				
	L-Histidine	His	imidazole$-CH_2-CH-COOH$ with NH_2	Kossel / Hedin	1896 / 1896
	L-Lysine	Lys	$H_2N-(CH_2)_4-CH-COOH$ with NH_2	Drechsel	1889

Name	Abbr.	Structure	Discoverer	Year
L-Arginine	Arg	$H_2N-C-NH(CH_2)_3-CH-COOH$ (=NH, NH₂)	Hedin	1895
Imino Acids				
L-Proline	Pro	(pyrrolidine ring)—COOH, N—H	Fischer	1901
L-Hydroxyproline	Hyp	HO—(pyrrolidine ring)—COOH, N—H	Fischer	1902

acid composition determines the biological nutritional value of the protein. Experiments to substitute dietary proteins by an artificial mixture of amino acids led to the conclusion that amino acids can be classified into essential and nonessential amino acids. Further studies showed that the kinds and quantitative ratio of essential amino acids differ somewhat among experimental animal species. Shown in Table A-5 are the essential amino acids for man in terms of proportionate requirements.

As for nonessential amino acids, biosynthesis and metabolic consequences are cleared in connection with the TCA cycle, etc. It should be noted that though they are nutritionally nonessential, they should be present in proper proportion at the site where their own protein is synthesized.

Uses of Amino Acids

Grain Fortification.—Supplementation of grains with limiting amino acid(s) is a technological advance of great benefit to all, but especially to the peoples of the developing countries. In those parts of the world, people depend for their nutrition upon one or at most a few kind(s) of grain. Malnutrition, due to deficiencies in the protein, therefore becomes one of the most serious of problems. For the solution of this problem, fortification with amino acid(s) is considered feasible both technologically and economically, and this without changing the eating habits of the population.

A fundamental study of fortification was conducted in Japan in 1967, utilizing bread and rolls fortified with L-lysine for school children. Favorable results were obtained, and more than half of the total school children in Japan now have L-lysine-fortified rolls in their school lunch every day.

Several field tests are under way in cooperation with United Nations (FAO/WHO and UNICEF) or by means of United States A.I.D. funds. Among these at present are Rice Fortification Granules, artificial rice-shaped grains containing 20% L-lysine and 10% L-threonine, mixed with bulk rice and tested for the rice-eating population in Thailand. In Tunisia, a field test for wheat flour fortified with L-lysine, vitamin B_1, B_2, and some minerals began in 1971.

The same idea is considered effectively applicable in improving foods for weaning babies in the developing countries. Unutilized oil meals, fortified with limiting amino acid(s) were proposed by the Institute of Nutrition for Central America and Panama (INCAP) some 10 yr ago, but apparently have not been followed up. INCAPARINA and other similar preparations are now being revived

TABLE A-4

SOME PHYSICAL PROPERTIES AND MAIN INDUSTRIAL MANUFACTURING PROCESSES OF AMINO ACIDS

Amino Acid	Mol Wt	Isoelectric Point	Solubility (Gm in 100 Gm of H$_2$O at 20°C)	$[\alpha]_D^{20}$	Specific Optical Rotation Condition Concentration (Gm/100 Ml)	Solvent	Manufacturing Process
Glycine	75.07	6.0	22.5				Synthesis
L-Alanine	89.09	6.0	15.8	+14.7°	10	6 N HCl	Fermentation
L-Valine	117.15	6.0	8.9 (25°)	+28.1°	8	6 N HCl	Fermentation Synthesis
L-Leucine	131.17	6.0	2.4	+15.2°	4	6 N HCl	Extraction
L-Isoleucine	131.17	6.0	4	+41.1°	4	6 N HCl	Fermentation
L-Serine	105.09	5.7	38	+15.2°	10	2 N HCl	Fermentation Synthesis
L-Threonine	119.12	5.6	9	−28.5°	6	H$_2$O	Fermentation Synthesis
L-Cysteine	121.15	5.1	8.0 (25°)	+8.1°	8	1 N HCl	Extraction (Synthesis)[1]
L-Cystine	240.29	5.0	0.009	−220°	2	1 N HCl	Extraction
L-Methionine	149.21	5.7	5.6 (30°)	+23.8°	2	6 N HCl	Synthesis
L-Asparagine	132.12	5.4	3.0 (25°)	+35.0°	10	3 N HCl	Synthesis
L-Glutamine	146.15	5.7	4	+6.8°	4	H$_2$O	Fermentation Synthesis
L-Phenylalanine	165.19	5.5	2.7	−34.4°	2	H$_2$O	Synthesis
L-Tyrosine	181.19	5.7	0.03	−12.0°	5	1 N HCl	Extraction
L-Tryptophan	204.23	5.9	1	−31.5°	1	H$_2$O	Synthesis
L-Aspartic acid	133.10	2.8	0.4	+26.0°	10	2 N HCl	Fermentation
L-Glutamic acid	147.13	3.2	0.7	+32.0°	10	2 N HCl	Fermentation Synthesis
L-Histidine	155.16	7.6	3.8	+12.5°	11	6 N HCl	Fermentation Extraction
L-Lysine	146.19	9.7	70[2]	+21.1°[2]	8	6 N HCl	Fermentation
L-Arginine	174.20	11.2	14	+27.3°	8	6 N HCl	Extraction Fermentation Synthesis
L-Proline	115.13	6.3	154.5	−85.1°	4	H$_2$O	Fermentation
L-Hydroxyproline	131.13	5.8	34.5	−75.5°	4	H$_2$O	Extraction

[1] By chemical reduction of extracted L-cystine.
[2] Values for anhydrous HCl salt.

for consideration. There are difficulties, however, mainly resulting from parents' having very little knowledge of nutrition during the weaning stage.

Feed Supplementation.—With regard to feedstuffs for cattle or poultry, supplementation by amino acids has been used to improve the nutritional value of proteins. DL-Methionine was the first amino acid to be used in the supplementation of soybean meals. This was more than 10 yr ago, and it came about because it was known that D-methionine was converted into L-form when ingested by animals. Favorable results and eco-nomic feasibility shown for DL-methionine fortification opened the way to supplement grains with L-lysine, not only for cattle or poultry but also for human foods.

Taste Characteristics

Free amino acid(s) contained in natural food have been the subject of research by food chemists for several decades. It dates back to the time when monosodium glutamate was industrialized in 1908. At this time L-glutamic acid was found to be the flavorful component of Laminarias, a

TABLE A-5

IDEAL ESSENTIAL AMINO ACID REQUIREMENTS
FOR MAN
(Provisionally Proposed by FAO, 1957)

	Gm/100 Gm Protein
L-Isoleucine	4.2
L-Leucine	4.8
L-Lysine	4.2
Aromatic amino acids	
L-Phenylalanine	2.8
L-Tyrosine	2.8
Total aromatic amino acids	5.6
S-containing amino acids	
L-Methionine	2.2
L-Cystine	2.0
Total S-containing amino acids	4.2
L-Threonine	2.8
L-Tryptophan	1.4
L-Valine	4.2
Total essential amino acids	31.4

TABLE A-6

LIMITING ESSENTIAL AMINO ACIDS OF THE
MAIN GRAIN PROTEINS

	First Limiting Amino Acid	Second Limiting Amino Acid
Rice	L-Lysine	L-Threonine
Wheat	L-Lysine	L-Threonine
Maize	L-Lysine	L-Tryptophan
Sorghum	L-Lysine	L-Threonine
Millet	L-Lysine	L-Threonine
Teff	L-Lysine	L-Threonine

traditional soup stock material used in Japan.
Though the taste of glutamate ion is difficult to
designate by conventional taste descriptives, Dr.
K. Ikeda (1912), inventor of monosodium glutamate, named the taste "glutamate taste" in his
original paper. Later, aspartate was found to
show the same kind of taste, but much less intense. The intensity of the glutamate taste was
found synergistically enhanced when glutamate or
aspartate combined with 5′-ribonucleotides (e.g.,
5′-inosinate and/or 5′-guanylate).

The same but very strong taste effect was found
in the glutamic acid derivatives tricolomic acid

and ibotenic acid, components of wild mushrooms
that are found in the northern part of Japan.
These substances, though without industrial application until today, show taste synergism with
5′-ribonucleotides.

$$H_2C\text{---}CH\text{---}CH\text{---}COOH$$
$$O{=}C \quad O \quad NH_2$$
$$N$$
$$H$$

Tricolomic acid

$$HC\text{---}C\text{---}CH\text{---}COOH$$
$$O{=}C \quad O \quad NH_2$$
$$N$$
$$H$$

Ibotenic acid

Descriptions of tastes of individual amino acids
were proposed as in Table A-7. In this analysis
of taste, results of organoleptic determination by
mass-panel were statistically treated, and the taste
of each amino acid was shown in the percentage
of taste elements: sweet, saline, sour, bitter,
glutamate, and others.

Aside from the use of individual amino acids,
the idea of combining several amino acids and
other food chemicals to imitate some food extracts was also studied in Japan. "Ajimate" is one
product developed to replace beef meat extract,
and "Neri-Aji" is another. The latter is intended
to give a specific fishy taste to kamaboko
(Japanese-style fish gels).

Aromas Released by Heating Amino Acids
Combined with Carbohydrates

Maillard reaction products are known to develop
specific aromas or odors. Examples are shown in
Table A-8.

These phenomena have been exploited in improving rice crackers, and are expected to be
further used in cookies and other baking products.

Salts Between Acidic and Basic Amino Acids

Some basic amino acid salts of acidic amino
acids are also available, among which are: L-
arginine L-glutamate, used as a flavor enhancer
for people who wish to exclude sodium from
their diet. L-Lysine L-glutamate and L-lysine L-
aspartate, both used, if desired, to fortify protein
of vegetable origin, without administering chloride
ions, which always accompany basic amino acids.

TABLE A-7

ANALYTICAL DESCRIPTION OF TASTE OF INDIVIDUAL AMINO ACIDS

| Amino Acid | Concentration | | Taste Intensity | Taste | | | | | |
	Gm/Deciliter	Mol		Sweet (%)	Saline (%)	Sour (%)	Bitter (%)	Glutamate (%)	Others (%)
Glycine	1.0	0.133	2.28	69.8	0.6	9.6	12.2	7.0	0.8
	4.0	0.533	4.32	85.8	0.8	3.6	3.2	5.2	1.4
L-Alanine	0.5	0.056	2.34	83.4	2.0	1.0	7.4	6.2	0
	5.0	0.561	4.71	68.3	0.6	6.8	5.2	17.1	2.0
L-Valine	0.3	0.026	2.33	22.0	1.8	5.6	56.8	10.4	3.4
	3.0	0.256	6.49	23.4	0	2.2	72.0	1.4	1.0
L-Leucine	1.0	0.076	4.08	3.2	1.0	3.2	88.8	2.4	1.4
	2.0	0.152	5.46	1.4	0.6	2.0	92.0	2.4	1.6
L-Isoleucine	0.6	0.046	4.00	1.2	0	1.4	93.0	1.2	3.2
	3.0	0.229	7.00	2.4	0.4	1.2	95.4	0	0.6
L-Serine	1.5	0.143	2.48	63.0	0.4	22.0	8.0	2.6	4.0
	15.0	1.427	5.43	55.4	1.8	15.6	5.2	18.6	3.4
L-Threonine	2.0	0.168	2.58	67.8	0	12.6	16.2	2.0	1.4
	7.0	0.588	3.96	56.9	0.6	30.3	6.0	5.8	0.4
L-Cysteine									
L-Cystine									
L-Methionine	0.3	0.020	2.14	8.8	1.0	4.0	53.0	14.0	19.2
	3.0	0.201	5.71	8.8	6.0	2.7	68.5	3.2	10.8
L-Asparagine monohydrate	1.0	0.067	2.59	8.1	0.6	60.3	20.4	4.6	6.0
	3.0	0.200	4.15	5.6	1.0	62.1	17.2	12.9	1.2
L-Glutamine	1.0	0.068	1.83	3.8	5.4	21.0	56.8	4.4	8.6
	3.0	0.205	2.97	27.5	1.2	23.0	18.0	23.3	7.0
L-Phenylalanine	0.3	0.018	3.92	2.6	0	1.4	90.6	0.8	4.6
	1.5	0.091	7.22	0.4	0.6	1.0	97.8	0	0.4
L-Tyrosine									
L-Tryptophan	0.3	0.015	4.28	1.4	0.6	5.6	87.6	1.2	3.6
	0.7	0.034	6.82	1.4	0.2	0	97.8	0.4	0.2
L-Aspartic acid	0.01	0.001	2.56	3.8	0.6	67.7	24.2	1.4	2.3
	0.3	0.023	7.24	0.6	1.8	80.9	7.0	1.0	8.7
L-Glutamic acid	0.025	0.002	3.74	5.0	0.2	72.2	15.0	6.6	1.0
	0.2	0.014	6.21	0.8	2.2	64.2	5.0	25.1	2.7
L-Histidine	1.0	0.064	3.35	6.4	0.6	14.8	73.0	1.6	3.6
	3.0	0.193	5.13	14.1	0.8	6.8	75.7	2.0	0.6
L-Lysine mono-hydrochloride	0.4	0.022	2.35	31.0	3.4	8.4	48.2	7.2	1.8
	3.0	0.164	5.23	32.3	2.6	5.3	47.4	7.4	5.0
L-Arginine	0.2	0.011	2.66	30.0	1.6	5.2	55.2	5.0	3.0
	1.0	0.057	4.93	5.6	0.4	2.2	87.3	2.7	1.8
L-Proline	2.5	0.217	4.00	44.6	2.2	2.0	43.8	6.0	1.4
	14.0	1.216	6.72	52.4	0.4	0.8	45.4	0.6	0.4
L-Hydroxyproline	0.5	0.038	2.66	60.5	0.8	5.4	24.5	7.4	1.4
	3.0	0.229	5.69	63.0	0.4	1.8	30.1	3.7	1.0

L-Lysine L-glutamate is also used to enhance flavor in deference to sodium-conscious people.

Glycine

Glycine has a pleasant, sweet taste, and can be used as a sweetener replacing sugar when the Maillard reaction is a problem.

Addition of 0.5-2% of glycine to a nutrient broth innoculated with bacteria, especially spore-forming *B. subtilis*, inhibited the growth of these bacteria. This finding led to the use of this natural substance as a rope-retarding agent for some kinds of sausage, boiled noodles, and fish gels. It also has a preservative action. Recently, lysozyme susceptibility of Gram-active bacteria has been demonstrated to be enhanced markedly by the addition of glycine. Glycine is believed to participate in the enhancement action.

Addition of under 0.02% of glycine to mono- or diglyceride as an antioxidant has been approved in the United States.

TABLE A-8

AROMAS DEVELOPED BY HEATING MIXTURES
OF AMINO ACID WITH GLUCOSE TO 180°C

Amino Acid	Aroma
Glycine	Caramel
Alanine	Caramel
Valine	Chocolate
Leucine	Roasted cheese
Isoleucine	Roasted cheese
Proline	Bread
Hydroxyproline	Cracker
Methionine	Potato
Phenylalanine	Violet flower
Tyrosine	Caramel
Aspartic acid	Caramel
Glutamic acid	Butter ball
Histidine	Corn bread
Lysine	Bread
Arginine	Broiled sugar

L-Cysteine Hydrochloride

Because of the reductive characteristics of L-cysteine hydrochloride, this amino acid compound is used in ascorbic acid fortified foods to retard autoxidation.

L-Cysteine has an active -SH group in its chemical structure. This compound is used as a dough conditioner in the baking industry.

When L-cysteine is heated with sugar, especially pentose, a broiled beef aroma is developed. There are several patents utilizing this phenomenon in products imitating beef meat extract.

MASAMI O'HARA

Reference

IKEDA, K. 1912. Original communications. Proc. 8th Intern. Congr. Appl. Chem. Washington, New York, Section VIIIc.

ANNATTO

The annatto plant (*Bixa orellana*) is a small tree that grows in the tropics. For centuries, the red-orange color from the surface of the seed has been used for cosmetics, textile dyeing, lacquers, pottery, and direct addition to edible fats.

The industrial countries in Europe and North America have processed annatto seed for a century, primarily for use in foods.

Chemistry

The main color compound is bixin:

$$CH_3-OOC-C_{22}H_{26}-COOH$$

a monomethylester of a dicarboxylic acid. It is a long chain with many double bonds like other carotenoids. Many steric forms are possible, but only two are important.

The all-*trans*-form is more stable toward oxidation and heat than the naturally-occurring mono-*cis* form, but has lower solubility. The mono-*cis* form is prevalent in all annatto preparations.

Bixin (B) is oil soluble. Saponification leads to the dimeric acid Norbixin (NB), the salt of which is water soluble. The B and NB molecules can split in nature or during processing to form yellow and brown compounds. The yellow ones (Orellin, etc.) are valuable in modifying the color hue of annatto preparations.

B and NB are fairly soluble in alcohols, ketones, chloroform, acetic acid.

Potency

B is one of the most potent color compounds. Its visual strength is $1\frac{1}{2}$ times that of beta-carotene and 6–7 times that of the most common synthetic certified colors, yellow No. 5 and No. 6. From 0.5 to 10 ppm of B/NB suffice in applying a normal color level to foods.

Stability Ratings

Acid and alkali: Very good
Microbiological action: Very good
Oxidation: Good
Light: Fair to good
Temperature: Very good below 100°C
Fair at 100°–125°C
Poor above 125°C, depending on processing time

Toxicology

Annatto has permanent approval according to the U.S. color additive law of 1960. Very comprehensive dog-feeding tests were conducted at that time and no adverse effects were found.

Other investigations, most notably the one by the Pharmacology Institute in Holland, gave the same results.

Annatto is approved as a food color without restrictions in all countries which have food laws.

Commercial Annatto Preparations

Water-Soluble Annatto (Cheese Color).—This is a solution of the di-potassium (sodium or ammonium) salt of norbixin. pH is always high, 11 to 14.

Maximum concentration is 7% NB. Under neutral or acid conditions, the solubility in water is very low. If color is added to milk, cream, cheese curd, or dough mix, however, NB will blend with the solids to form a uniformly-colored product.

Oil-Soluble Annatto (Butter Color).—(1) B-solution in vegetable oil, pH 5–7, maximum 0.75% B. (2) B-suspension in vegetable oil, pH 5–7, maximum 30% B. (3) B and/or NB solution in alkaline propylene glycol and monoglycerides, pH 8–11, maximum 5% B/NB.

(1) will dissolve directly in vegetable oils. (2) needs gentle heat and agitation. Maximum solubility in salad oil is approximately 0.025% B. Both (1) and (2) can also be used in emulsion-type foods. (3) is used primarily in emulsion-type foods, but some preparations are adaptable to vegetable oils.

Insoluble Annatto.—Color acts as a pigment.

How to Use

The colors can normally be added directly to food at the most convenient stage, but because of today's more complex food technology and annatto's high versatility, it is advisable to obtain recommendations from a reliable supplier of the colors.

Annatto alone varies from cheddar cheese orange to butter yellow, depending on use level, color preparation, and product.

Turmeric and paprika can be used to further modify the hue in yellow or red directions.

NIEL DINESEN

References

KARRER, P., and JUCKER, E. 1950. Carotenoids. Elsevier Publishing Co., New York.

McKEOWN, G. G. 1961. Paper chromatography of bixin and related compounds. J. Assoc. Offic. Agr. Chemists 44, 347.

McKEOWN, G. G. and MARK, E. 1962. The composition of oil soluble annatto. J. Assoc. Offic. Agr. Chemists 45, 761.

ZECHMEISTER, L. 1962. Cis-Trans Isomeric Carotenoids. Academic Press, New York.

ANTHOCYANINS

The term "anthocyanin" originates from the Greek words for flower and blue, and was introduced by L. C. Marquart in 1835 to designate the blue pigments of flowers. Later it was realized that not only the blue colors, but also the purple, violet, mauve, magenta, and nearly all the red colors that appear in many flowers and fruits and some leaves, stems, and roots of plants are due to pigments chemically similar to Marquart's anthocyanins. R. Willstätter and co-workers laid the foundation of the chemistry of these pigments, and their work was later supplemented by that of R. Robinson, P. Karrer, K. Hayashi, J. B. Harborne, and others.

Constitution

The anthocyanins are glycosides of the anthocyanidins, the latter being polyhydroxy and methoxy derivatives of a basic structure, the 2-phenyl-benzopyrylium or flavylium.

Some anthocyanins contain an organic acid as a third component of their molecule. Recently, metals (Fe, Al, Mg) and organic residues yet unidentified have been found in certain blue anthocyanins.

Sixteen anthocyanidins have been identified in nature: apigeninidin, aurantinidin, capensinidin, columnidin, cyanidin, delphinidin, europinidin, hirsutidin, luteolinidin, malvidin, pelargonidin, peonidin, petunidin, pulchellidin, rosinidin, and tricetinidin. Six of these appear far more frequently than the others: pelargonidin, cyanidin, delphinidin, peonidin, malvidin and petunidin.

Cyanidin is the most common anthocyanidin, being present in about 80% of permanently anthocyanin-pigmented leaves, 70% of fruits, and 50% of flowers. The number of anthocyanins is much larger than that of anthocyanidins, which is understandable since one or more of several sugars (and acids) can be attached to the same anthocyanidin. Depending on the glycosylation and acylation pattern, the anthocyanins may be grouped into the following classes:

3-Monosides
3-Biosides
3-Triosides
3-Monosides-5-monosides
3-Biosides-5-monosides
3-Monosides-7-monosides
3-Biosides-7-monosides
Complex anthocyanins containing chiefly an organic acid in ester combination with a hydroxyl of the anthocyanidin or the sugar moiety

From surveys of the plant kingdom, more is known about the aglycons than the sugar residues of anthocyanins. The simple sugars most frequently present in anthocyanins are glucose, galactose, and rhamnose.

Properties

The anthocyanins are soluble in water; the anthocyanidins are generally less so. The type of glycosylation significantly affects the solubility of anthocyanins in certain alcohols; and the distribution between 0.5% aqueous hydrochloric acid and isoamyl alcohol (or n-butanol) has been used in differentiating anthocyanin groups from each other. The anthocyanins are insoluble in non-hydroxylic solvents (benzene, ether, chloroform, acetone) and precipitation by these solvents has been used in purifying anthocyanins. The tendency of anthocyanins to form crystalline picrate salts has also been used in the purification of these pigments.

The color of anthocyanins is due to the extensive conjugated double-bond system of the aglycon and is modified by several factors. Increase in the number of hydroxyl groups tends to deepen the color (red to violet), whereas methoxylation has a slight hypsochromic (reddening) effect. The pH of the solution has a profound influence on the color of anthocyanins when they are in a purified state. They are red in acidic and blue in alkaline solutions. Their color fades at in-between pH levels.

The pH alone, however, cannot explain the color differences of anthocyanins in intact plant tissues. Metal chelation, especially of anthocyanins containing an o-diphenol group, and copigmentation, that is, the rather loose combination of anthocyanins chiefly with other flavonoids and tannins, contribute significantly to the creation of deep shades of anthocyanins *in vivo*. The type of anthocyanins and other pigments which may be present as well as their concentration will affect the color of anthocyanin-pigmented plant tissue. The concentration of anthocyanins varies widely, ranging from 0.1 to 1.0% on a dry basis for most fruits and vegetables.

Among the chemical reactions useful in determining the structure of anthocyanins are acid hydrolysis, after which the sugar and the aglycon can be determined qualitatively and quantitatively; mild oxidation with hydrogen peroxide for the elucidation of the position of sugar attachment to the anthocyanidin; and fusion of the anthocyanidin with caustic alkali, allowing the identification of the A and B rings.

A reaction which is technologically important is the reversible decolorization of anthocyanins by sulfur dioxide.

Metabolism

The biogenesis of anthocyanins is not fully understood. There is little doubt that ring A is formed by a head-to-tail condensation of three acetyl units, while ring B and carbon atoms 2, 3, and 4 originate from a phenylpropane unit, such as cinnamic acid, p-coumaric acid, or phenylanine. It appears that an important $C_6C_3C_6$ intermediate

is a chalcone, the heterocyclic ring of which is subsequently closed and a flavonoid is formed. The biogenetic relationships between the various flavonoids, as a result of which anthocyanins would appear, have not been elucidated. Glycosylation appears to occur late in the biosynthetic sequence.

Light promotes anthocyanin production in all cases investigated, although formation of this pigment may begin in the dark. Two photoreactions control this synthesis; one is a low-energy reaction governed by the phytochrome system, and the other is a high-energy reaction the action spectrum of which lies in the blue and red regions.

Anthocyanins may be destroyed by a number of enzymes. Glycosidases remove the sugar moiety and the freed anthocyanidin fades due to its instability. Phenol oxidases decolorize anthocyanins, especially in the presence of other phenolic substrates of these enzymes. Peroxidase also oxidizes these pigments. There is some evidence that specific oxidative anthocyanases may exist.

The metabolic function of anthocyanins is not clear. In the economy of nature they are assumed to contribute in attracting insects to flowers and animals to fruits, thereby facilitating flower fertilization and seed dissemination.

Anthocyanins in Foods

Many fruits and vegetables owe their attractive color to anthocyanins. Chromatographic techniques have improved and facilitated the separation and identification of anthocyanin pigments, and have helped to clarify some of the species and variety differences in anthocyanin composition of certain food crops. It is now known that grapes may contain from 6 to 17 different anthocyanins. According to one report, American Concord grapes contain 14 anthocyanins. The literature, however, is not always unequivocal on the number and full identify of the anthocyanins of fruits. This is understandable since authors do not always use the same variety of a plant and the same method of analysis. Because the anthocyanidin moiety of the anthocyanin molecule is mainly responsible for the color, and the ambiguity of characterization usually refers to the glycosidic moiety, only the identity of anthocyanidins is given in Table A-9.

The red color of tomatoes is due to lycopene and that of red beets to betanin, the glycoside of betanidin, neither of which is an anthocyanin pigment.

Fruits and vegetables also vary quantitatively in their anthocyanin content. Different varieties of the same species may contain different quantities of anthocyanin, or none. The same variety may

TABLE A-9

ANTHOCYANIDINS OCCURRING IN SOME FRUITS AND VEGETABLES

Fruit or Vegetable	Anthocyanidin
Apple (*Malus pumila.* Mill.)	Cyanidin
Blackcurrant (*Ribes nigrum* Linn.)	Cyanidin and delphinidin
Blueberry (*Vaccinium angustifolium* Ait.)	Cyanidin, delphinidin, malvidin, petunidin and peonidin
Cabbage (red, *Brassica oleracea*, var. *capitata* Linn.)	Cyanidin
Cherry (sour, Montmorency, *Prunus cerasus* Linn.)	Cyanidin
Cherry (sweet, Bing, *Prunus avium* Linn.)	Cyanidin and peonidin
Cranberry (*Vaccinium macrocarpon* Ait.)	Peonidin and cyanidin
Eggplant (*Solanum melanogena* Linn.)	Delphinidin
Fig (*Ficus carica* Linn.)	Cyanidin
Grape (*Vitis vinifera* Linn.)	Malvidin, peonidin, delphinidin, cyanidin, petunidin, and pelargonidin
Grape (Concord, *Vitis labrusca* Linn.)	Cyanidin, delphinidin, peonidin, malvidin, and petunidin
Mulberry (*Morus nigra* Linn.)	Cyanidin
Onion (*Allum cepa* Linn.)	Cyanidin and peonidin
Orange (ruby, *Citrus sinensis* (Linn.) Osbeck)	Cyanidin and delphinidin
Peach (*Prunus persica* (Linn.) Sieb. O Zuce.)	Cyanidin
Plum (*Prunus domestica* Linn.)	Cyanidin and peonidin
Pomegranate (*Punica granatum* Linn.)	Delphinidin
Radish (red, *Raphanus sativus* Linn.)	Pelargonidin
Raspberry (*Rubus idaeus* Linn.)	Cyanidin
Strawberry (wild, *Fragaria vesca* Linn.)	Pelargonidin and cyanidin
Strawberry (cultivated, *F. chiloensis* Duchesne and *F. virginiaka* Duchesne)	Pelargonidin and a little cyanidin

display varying intensity of anthocyanin coloration in different years, in different locations, and under different growing practices. Often, low nitrogen supply in the soil results in richer anthocyanin pigmentation. Of course, the same fruit changes color as it ripens and anthocyanin accumulates in it.

The anthocyanin pigments are not very stable. During the handling of fresh fruits and vegetables or during their long-term preservation (canning, dehydration, freezing, etc.), anthocyanin degradation may occur. Enzymes naturally present in the tissue may catalyze this discoloration, especially when the fresh tissue has been bruised or crushed. In red tart cherries surface discoloration (scald) is always preceded by bruising and enhanced by high temperature. It is now known that transportation and holding in cold water minimizes bruising and scald.

Even when the enzymes have been inactivated, the anthocyanins may be altered or destroyed through other mechanisms. In canning, tin complexes with anthocyanins may be formed, resulting in purplish or slate-gray pigments designated as lakes. This reaction also appears to accelerate can corrosion. For these reasons anthocyanin-pig-mented commodities must be packed in cans that are fully lined with special enamels or lacquers developed for this purpose. In addition to complexation, metals also act as catalysts of the degradation of anthocyanins. Temperature and oxygen are two other factors affecting the stability of anthocyanins in foods. Removal of oxygen and use of the lowest possible temperatures during processing and storage of the food will minimize the loss of color due to the destruction of anthocyanins. A decrease of the pH also tends to stabilize these pigments. Since it is practically impossible to avoid some degradation of anthocyanin pigments in processed products, it is advisable to start with raw materials rich in anthocyanin. It is also common practice to enrich the color of foods with artificial dyes, when permissible.

There are instances when anthocyanin coloration is undesirable. Some types of pears, for example, turn reddish on processing, due to conversion of leucoanthocyanin to anthocyanin by the combined effects of heat and acidity, and the anthocyanin-pigmented tissue around the pit cavity of certain peaches may turn brown upon processing. At times, fruit juices are excessively colored with

anthocyanins. In such cases, the enzyme antho-
cyanase, which is now available commercially, may
be used to lower their concentration.

The determination of the anthocyanin content
of a fruit product is simple when only one anthocyanin is present or dominant. The pH of an
aqueous extract of the pigment is adjusted to 2
levels, such as pH 1.0 and 5.0, in the case of the
anthocyanin pigment of strawberries, and the difference of absorbance at these pH levels is related
to the concentration of anthocyanin by means of a
reference curve prepared with pure pigment. In
the presence of more than one anthocyanin, first
separation of the pigments is necessary, which
complicates the determination.

PERICLES MARKAKIS

ANTIBIOTICS IN FOODS

The use of antibiotics in foods, and their applications in food technology have been known and
studied for many years. Antiobiotics may occur
in foods (a) naturally; (b) through direct addition
as a food additive to aid in production and keeping
quality of the food; or (c) as an unintentional
food additive resulting from the carryover of the
antibiotic in milk, meat, or eggs as a result of the
addition of antibiotics to the feed of animals for
growth promotion, or from animal medication for
the prevention or treatment of animal diseases.

Naturally-occurring nisin, for example, is an
antibiotic which is known to occur naturally,
although not frequently, in normal milk. Nisin
may also be added directly to the food as an
intentional food additive. Gassy fermentations in
raw cheese, made with milk containing Clostridia,
are controlled, for example, by the use of nisin-
producing starter cultures. Such nisin-producing
streptococci in milk have been used with success
in France for the commercial manufacture of
processed cheese. The use of such cultures can
result in production of from 50 to 100 units of
nisin per gram of cheese.

Nisin

Nisin is one of the antibiotics which is permitted
in many countries as a direct food additive. It is a
member of a group of closely related polypeptide
antibiotics, produced by some strains of *Streptococcus lactis* of the Lancefield group N.

Antibiotic Spectrum.—Some species of Gram-
positive bacteria, including bacilli, clostridia lactobacilli, streptococci and staphlococci are sensitive

to nisin; however, all enterobacteria and other
Gram-negative organisms are not sensitive. Molds
and yeasts are insensitive to nisin. The importance
of nisin in food preservation is its ability to prevent the outgrowth of bacterial spores in heat-
treated foods. The international reference preparation of nisin is defined as 0.001 mg of the pure
nisin.

Biological Data.—Nisin was reviewed by the
joint FAO/WHO Committee on Food Additives in
July 1968, and on the basis of its toxicological
evaluation was considered as an acceptable additive, the unconditional acceptable daily intake
(ADI) being 0–33,000 units of nisin per kilogram
of bodyweight. Nisin is destroyed by digestive
enzymes and no nisin was detected in human
saliva 10 min after consumption of a chocolate
milk containing 200 units of nisin per milliliter.
It is readily inactivated by pancreatin at a pH of 8.
Nisin has a LD_{50} of over 1,000,000 units per
kilogram of body weight of both oral and intraperitoneal (IP) administration in the rat. In the
rabbit it has an intramuscular (IM) LD_{50} of
800,000 units, and a subcutaneous LD_{50} of
1,000,000 units.

Two-year chronic toxicity studies are summarized in the FAO/WHO report as well as short-
term and other biologic effects including allergy
and microbial resistance. Extensive microbiological studies have not shown any cross resistance in
organisms which might affect the therapeutic dose
of antibiotics. No effect could be demonstrated
on the intestinal flora. The antibiotic is destroyed
rapidly by proteolytic digestion in the upper part
of the GI tract.

Analytical.—The assay of residual nisin in foods
can be determined by reverse phase disc assay.
The method is sensitive to the presence of 1 unit
of nisin per milliliter of supernatant, equivalent to
the presence of 5 units per gram of foodstuff in
this assay, which employs heat-shocked spores of
Bacillus stearothermophilus.

Use in Food Technology.—Nisin was first used
to control bacterial spoilage of processed cheese
spread in the United Kingdom about 1953; since
then, its use has been adopted in many countries
for use in cheese and certain other foods. The
usual recommended level is 20 units per gram.
Nisin may occur naturally in milk and milk
products.

Its use in cheese and cheese products is to prevent putrefaction caused by relatively heat-stable
clostridia. Its use in other foods has been studied,
such as in canned vegetables, fruit, fish, meat,
milk puddings, etc., as a means of increasing
shelf-life, and/or reducing the temperatures or the

time of heat processing required to give the protection obtained in the absence of nisin.

It has been shown that heat-damaged spores have an increased sensitivity to nisin. Information on the mode of action of nisin is presented by several workers and there seems to be general agreement that nisin is sporocidal rather than sporostatic.

The major use of nisin in foods is in cheese and processed cheese products. The principal reason for the use of nisin in these products is to prevent the growth of clostridia and consequent "blowing" caused by clostridia carried through from the original cheese. For this type of use, nisin at levels of 100–400 units per gram of cheese mix has been satisfactory. Nisin can be simply dispersed in water and added to the mix at the same time as the melting salts.

Its use in chocolate milk has been practiced as cocoa powder may be a potential source of spore-forming bacteria. The use of nisin apparently allows for the use of less drastic sterilizing conditions. In this type application, nisin addition can reduce the spoilage at any given processing condition or will allow for some reduction in the severity of processing without increasing the normal spoilage.

In certain countries, nisin is employed as a processing aid in the production of canned milk puddings, such as rice, semolina, and tapioca puddings, to reduce the heat treatment required. In normal production, the heat required for adequate penetration may cause production difficulties and excessive thickening of the pudding. The addition of 50–100 units of nisin per gram has been shown to be an aid in preservation at lower processing temperatures.

Interest is being shown in the possible use of nisin in recombined and reconstituted evaporated milk to control surviving bacterial spores, when less drastic heating is employed in order to produce a more acceptable product.

TABLE A-10

RETENTION OF NISIN IN SKIM MILK HEATED FOR VARIOUS TIMES AND AT VARIOUS TEMPERATURES

| Temp °C | Percentage of Retention | | |
	3 Min (%)	11 Min (%)	40 Min (%)
110.0	84	57	19
115.6	67	38	7
121.1	60	34	4

SOURCE: Fowler and McCann (1971).

TABLE A-11

RETENTION OF NISIN IN FRESHLY PROCESSED FOODS TREATED WITH 100 UNITS OF NISIN PER GRAM

Product	Temp (°C)	Time (Min)	Retention (%)
Canned garden peas	115.6	40	22.0
Canned tomatoes	100	40	72.4
Canned mushrooms	121.1	18	32.7
Processed cheese	93	12	82.0

SOURCE: Fowler and McCann (1971).

Stability.—The stability of nisin in the presence of heat, is largely a function of the pH of the medium. It is quite stable to autoclaving at a pH of 2, but relatively unstable to autoclaving at a pH of 5. The stability is enhanced by the presence of large molecules such as are found in milk solids and broth.

Nisin has a bacteriostatic action, and therefore residual quantities must be present in order to maintain effective preservation. Data on stability during processing is given in Tables A-10 and A-11.

The stability of nisin in a solution during storage at various temperatures, is characterized by the data on stored chocolate milk in Table A-12.

Approved Use.—The FAO/WHO Expert Committee on Food Additives has favorably considered the use of nisin as a direct additive to foods. In the United Kingdom, the use of nisin has been approved for inclusion in cheese, clotted cream, or any canned food. Additionally, any food may contain nisin introduced in the preparation of that food by the use of cheese, clotted cream or canned food containing nisin. In the case of the canned food, the product is defined as contained in a hermetically sealed container which has been sufficiently heat processed to destroy *Clostridium botulinum* in that food or container or which has a pH of less than 4.5. The background for nisin inclusion in cheeses and canned foods is given in the U.K. Food Standard committee 1959 report, paragraph 270 and 278. The use of nisin in canned foods consumed in the United Kingdom is not very extensive, although it is included for technological reasons for some foods exported to tropical countries.

The U.K. Food Additive and Contaminant Committee has just reviewed the use of preservatives in foods and in their report of July 7, 1972 has recommended that these previously approved uses of nisin be allowed to continue. They also reviewed the proposed application of nisin to cream

TABLE A-12

RESIDUAL NISIN ACTIVITY AND ITS STABILITY DURING STORAGE OF CANNED
HEAT-PROCESSED CHOCOLATE MILK[1]

Storage Time Months	Residual U/Ml at 4°C	% Storage Loss at 4°C	Residual U/Ml at 22°C	% Storage Loss at 22°C	Residual U/Ml at 37°C	% Storage Loss at 37°C
0	17.5	0	17.5	0	17.5	0
3	14.0	20	13.5	23	9.0	49
6	13.5	23	12.5	23	6.0	66
9	13.5	23	11.0	37	3.5	80
12	12.5	29	8.0	54	3.0	83
15	12.0	31	7.5	57	3.0	83
18	12.0	31	6.5	63	2.0	89
24	12.0	31	5.0	71	1.0	94

SOURCE: Fowler and McCann (1971).

[1] Initial content prior to heating: 100 U/ml; potency loss in initial processing: 82.7%.

in flour confectionery, but have recommended against such use. Cream, other than clotted cream, may not contain any preservative, based on the U.K. Cream Regulations of 1970.

In New South Wales, Australia, nisin may be added to cheese, canned tomato pulp, canned tomato juice, canned tomato paste, tomato purée, and canned fruit, provided that in all cases the pH of these items is below 4.5. Addition to canned soups is permitted, provided the product is submitted to heat treatment sufficient to destroy *Clostridium botulinum*.

Its use in cheese has been approved in Belgium (2.5 ppm), Czechoslovakia (200 ppm), Finland (100 ppm), Italy (500 ppm), Uruguay (100 ppm), and India at 1000 ppm in cheese and processed cheese. It is also approved in France, Israel (exception of soft white cheese), Jamaica, Mexico, New Zealand (export), Norway (export), South Africa, and Spain. Sweden permits nisin in sterile condensed milk and cream (Group le) and cheese (Group lf) with no limits.

In vegetables, it is approved in Italy in canned vegetables at 100 ppm, and in Russia in certain canned foods. It is also approved in Russia for certain canned fruits. In Italy it is allowed at 100 ppm in creamed desserts.

In Lebanon, Mozambique, Nigeria, Zambia, and Sudan, nisin is acceptable on the basis of existing legislation elsewhere; there are no specific laws covering food additives in these countries.

Pimaricin

Pimaricin is another antibiotic which is permitted by several countries as a direct food additive for certain foods. It is a fungicidal antibiotic, belonging to the group of polyenic macrolides,

more specifically to the tetraenes. It has the following structure:

Pimaricin therefore is closely related to, but not identical with, the other antifungal antibiotics—nystatin, rimocidin, and amphotericin. It is produced by *Streptomyces natalensis Nov. sp.*

Antibiotic Spectrum.—Pimaricin is active against a large number of molds and yeasts, but has no activity against bacteria or viruses. Pimaricin, which is predominantly fungicidal, is effective over a fairly broad pH range. It is also active against fungal spores. Its greatest activity is against actively-multiplying cells, as considerably higher concentrations are required for the destruction of resting cells. For most microorganisms which are sensitive to pimaricin, minimum inhibitory concentration (MIC) ranges from 1 to 15 μg per ml.

The activity of pimaricin against yeasts and molds occurring in foods is considerably greater than that of sorbic acid, pimaricin having MIC of 1–10 μg per ml, while sorbic acid requires approximately 500 μg per ml in most cases.

Biological Data.—Pimaricin is reversibly bound to serum proteins, having a binding strength similar to that of penicillin. There is no evidence of development of resistance to pimaricin, with the exception of the experimental isolation of two strains of *Candida albicans*, which apparently became partially resistant as a result of adaptation. In one of these strains 35 transfers were required to raise the MIC from 1.7 to 15 μg per ml. In this case there was a return from normal sensitivity on withdrawal of pimaricin from the medium. Organisms that become resistant to ampotericin B were also resistant to nystatin, but retained their normal sensitivity to pimaricin. When pimaricin was included in the media it caused no change in sensitivity to erythromycin after 10 transplants different bacterial strains, all sensitive to erythromycin.

Toxicity.—In acute toxicity studies, pimaricin on oral administration showed an LD_{50} of 1500 mg per kilo body weight for rat and mouse, and greater than 1000 for the dog. In additional studies, LD_{50} values of 2730 were found for the female rat and 4670 for the male rat. The LD_{50} for oral dosage yielded in the guinea pig 450 and for the rabbit 1420. Intraperitoneal (IP) dosage yielded an LD_{50} of 250, and intravenous (IV) dosage an LD_{50} of 16.2 for the rat.

In 2-yr chronic toxicity studies, employing dosages of 125, 250, 500, and 1000 ppm of pimaricin in rats, the minimum dosage showing noticeable effect was 1000 ppm which caused a slight inhibition of growth, probably due to diminished appetite.

In 2-year studies with dogs at feeding levels of 125, 250, and 500 ppm, no effects were noticed other than a slight depression in growth in the male dogs at 500 ppm. There were no adverse effects on survival organ weights, or blood, or tissues.

No undesirable allergic effects have been reported, and skin and eye studies reveal no irritant or sensitizing effect of pimaricin. The FAO/WHO Expert Committee on Food additives established a conditional Average Daily Intake (ADI) of 0–0.25 mg of pimaricin per kilo of body weight. On this basis 15 ppm in cheese would be acceptable, assuming a consumption of no more than 1 kilo of cheese a day.

Analytical.—Pimaricin solution in methanol shows ultraviolet absorption spectrogram with minima at 250, 290, and 313 mμ and maxima at 220, 290, 304, and 318 mμ, the latter 3 being used for spectrophotometric assay. The optical density vs. concentration plot for concentrations of 1 to 12 μm per ml yields a straight line; however, with a different slope for each wavelength.

The E 1%/1 cm values are 758 at 290 mμ and 1100 at 318 mμ.

Pimaricin has an isoelectric point at a pH of 6.5, and an R_f value of approximately 0.45 when chromatographed on paper (Whatman #1) for 15 hrs at 23° using a 7 to 1 n-propanol: water mixture as an eluant.

Assay.—A microbiological assay procedure allowing for the quantitative determination of pimaricin is available employing an agar diffusion test. Small discs of the test material are placed onto the surface of solid Whiffen agar, which has been previously inoculated with *Saccharomyces cerevisiae* ATCC 9763, which is sensitive to approximately 0.5 μg per ml of pimaricin. The clear zones of inhibition found around the discs may represent pimaricin or another fungicide. Other fungicides are differentiated from pimaricin by repeating the test with the inclusion of pimaricinase in the agar.

Pimaricin has been shown to be adsorbed or bound to orange juice pulp; recovery from orange juice depends upon proper sample dilution.

Stability.—In the dry state, pimaricin is an extremely stable compound, provided it is not exposed to sunlight and moisture. In solutions, pimaricin may be relatively unstable particularly when exposed to light. It is more unstable at at high and low pHs, showing greatest stability at a pH of 5 to 7. The unsaturated nature of pimaricin probably accounts for its relative instability in solution and when exposed to light.

When incorporated in food, instability due to light can be effectively reduced through opacity, color, and possibly chemical stabilization. Orange juice, for example, stored for 12 weeks at 2.5°C in the dark showed 77, 74, 70, and 68% retention of pimaricin for pimaricin additions of 20, 10, 5, and 2.5 μg/ml. Chlorophyll addition increases stability twofold. The presence of oxygen increases the decomposition rate, and antioxidants therefore retard the oxidation of pimaricin. It is incompatible with oxidants and rapid destruction results from the presence of peroxide, iodates, bromates, hypochlorates, sulfates, etc.

In stability studies with pimaricin added to cottage cheese through soaking in the wash water, the initial concentrations of pimaricin were from 5 to 10 ppm. At storage temperatures of 40°, 50°, and 60°F, there was a rapid initial loss of residual pimaricin, and no activity could be demonstrated after 3 to 16 days.

In U.K. studies on retention of pimaricin in stored apples dipped with 100 or 200 ppm pimaricin, there were very low residues. In 23 tests of apples stored at 4°C for 51 to 156 days variable results were obtained showing an average

TABLE A-13

EFFECT OF ANTIFUNGAL TREATMENT ON KEEPING QUALITY OF COTTAGE CHEESE

Antibiotic[1] Treatment	Level of Antibiotic in Wash (Ppm)	Average Keeping Time in Days					
		At 40°C		At 50°C		At 60°C	
		No. of Days	Improvement (%)	No. of Days	Improvement (%)	No. of Days	Improvement (%)
None	0	12.3		6.6		4.3	
Pimaricin	25	16.3	+33	8.3	+26	4.3	0
None	0	16.8		10.0		7.3	
Pimaricin	50	26.8	+60	22.0	+220	15.0	+105
None	0	16.5		6.0			
Mycostatin	10	19.0	+15	10.0	+67		
None	0	12.5				6.0	
Mycostatin	20	21.0	+68			6.0	0

SOURCE: Shahani *et al.* (1959).

[1] Antibiotics added to wash water.

residue of 0.89 ppm of pimaricin. Hand-dipping gave higher residues than machine-dipping.

In pears dipped in 100 ppm of pimaricin, a residue of less than 0.25 ppm was found after 85 days storage at 4°C.

Applications.—*Cheese.*—Pimaricin is employed in some countries in cheese rind to control undesired fungal growth. It does not penetrate into the cheese but is retained on the outer 1 mm of the rind, which is usually not eaten. After a period of 5–10 weeks, the pimaricin essentially disappears; however, during this time the rind hardens and becomes much less susceptible to fungal invasion.

In work conducted at the Netherlands Dairy Research Institute at Ede, four applications methods of pimaricin to hard cheese were studied. These included: (1) pimaricin addition to the brine bath, (2) immersion in an aqueous suspension of pimaricin for 2–4 min after the brine bath, (3) spraying the cheeses with a pimaricin suspension, and (4) covering the cheese with a coating agent containing pimaricin. In all cases a good fungicidal effect was observed.

The recommended application rate for pimaricin in cheese, when applied in cheese coating is 0.005–0.1%, by weight of the coating, 0.005–0.2% of the dipping liquid when applied by dipping, and 0.1–0.2% by weight of the treating liquid for spraying the cheese or for application with a sponge.

Studies have been conducted on the effect of antifungal agents on cottage cheese. By adding antifungal antibiotics (pimaricin and mycostatin) to the second wash water for cheese curd, and holding 5 min before draining, results were obtained as shown in Table A-13. The antibiotics retarded spoilage by yeasts and molds but had little or no effect on microbial spoilage.

Tests were also run (Table A-14) on retardation of cottage cheese spoilage in conjunction with antibiotic retention studies. Cheese washed with antibiotic suspensions of 20 to 100 μg per ml contained 5–10 μg of antibiotic per gram of cheese. In stability testing, the antibiotics lost their activity completely in 3 to 16 days. The rate of loss was greatest in the initial period, and at the higher temperature of 60°F. The improvements due to antifungal agents were greatest at the lowest storage temperature (40°F) and poorest at the highest storage temperature (60°F).

TABLE A-14

EFFECT OF DIFFERENT ANTIFUNGAL TREATMENTS UPON KEEPING QUALITY OF COTTAGE CHEESE

Treatment Method	Average[1] Increase in Keeping Time in Days	
	Pimaricin	Mycostatin
Added through wash water[2]	+5 to 30	+1 to 28
Added through cheese dressing	+up to 39	+up to 20
Mold-infected cheese	+1 to 30	+1 to 17
Yeast-infected cheese	+1 to 16	+1 to 25

SOURCE: Nilson *et al.* (1960).

[1] Average of all treatments and storage temperatures of 40°, 50°, and 60°F.
[2] Antibiotic added to wash water at 20 to 100 μg per ml.

Beverages.—In the case of grape juice, yeast fermentation is prevented by 20 ppm of pimaricin; however, 100 ppm is required to stop active fermentation completely. In wines rich in yeast, 2 ppm kills $1/2$ of the yeast in 1 hr, with practical sterilization being obtained with 10 ppm. In a study of 12 fungicides in the treatment of apple juice, in which the materials were titrated at 10, 20, and 30 ppm, stored at 40°F, and analyzed at periods of 4, 6, 8 and 10 weeks, 30 ppm of pimaricin prevented fermentation for a period of up to 6 weeks. No off-flavor was observed.

In studies with orange juice, it was shown that juice inoculated with natural contaminant spoiled after 1 week of storage, whereas with pimaricin additions as low as 1.25 ppm, it did not spoil in 8 weeks of storage at 2.5–4°C. There were no undesirable effects reported in the pimaricin treatments, even at additions as high as 20 ppm. Pimaricin reduced the yeast population rapidly and the number of viable cells further decreased with storage time. There was a correlation of viable yeast and the pimaricin level used, higher quantities of pimaricin being more fungicidal, particularly with increased storage time. The low levels of 1.25 and 2.5 ppm were judged as having only borderline utility for practical purposes at the temperature employed.

In testing of orange juice concentrates, 10 and 20 ppm of pimaricin held yeast in check at various temperatures for concentrates of 65° and 42° Brix respectively. For periods of testing of 100 days, the inclusion of 10 ppm of pimaricin prevented growth at 10°C, whereas 20 ppm was required to severely retard growth at room temperature.

Fruit.—In the case of whole apples, a 1–2 min immersion in aqueous suspensions of pimaricin containing 500 ppm resulted in a considerable reduction of discards after 8 months' storage. While gloesporium rot in apples is sensitive to pimaricin, if the infection is deep and has penetrated several layers of cells, pimaricin will naturally be unable to control subsequent spoilage.

In evaluation of the effect of dipping apples in a lecithin-pimaricin dipping bath, it was shown that the spots encountered during extended storage, can be materially reduced by such treatment, as illustrated in Table A-15.

Similar results have been reported on dipping of several varieties of apples in studies in the Netherlands. In the United Kingdom, some 56 trials have been conducted in which apples were dipped either by hand or machine in a lecithin-pimaricin mixture for 30–45 sec within 7 days after picking. The test apples were stored under barn storage, cold storage (37–39°F), and storage at 37–39°F with controlled percentage of O_2 and CO_2 in the air.

The recommended amount of pimaricin for the dipping of fruit is 0.02–0.04% by weight of the dipping liquid.

Soft Fruit.—The shelf-life of soft fruits such as currants, plums, strawberries, and raspberries, has been increased by brief immersions of the fruit in aqueous solutions of 50 ppm pimaricin. Pimaricin has been shown to be effective against yeast and mold growth in strawberries, raspberries, cranberries, and cherries.

Other Applications.—Pimaricin has been studied in various baking operations. Rye and white breads were well protected when their surfaces were sprayed with a solution of 100–500 ppm pimaricin. Uncooked doughs were also improved when their surfaces were protected by surface treatment with pimaricin. The keeping time of

TABLE A-15

EFFECT OF DIPPING APPLES IN A LECITHIN-PIMARICIN SUSPENSION ON INCIDENCE AND SEVERITY OF SPOTS IN STORED WHOLE APPLES

Lecithin-Pimaricin Treatment Level		Number of Spots		
Lecithin-Pimaricin Mix[1] (%)	Equiv of Pimaricin (Ppm)	Test No. 1 177 Days @ 4°C 7 Days @ 15°C	Test No. 2 188 Days @ 4°C 13 Days @ 15°C	Test No. 3 179 Days @ 4°C 13 Days @ 15°C
0	0	37	82	55
0.5	20	8	—	17
1.0	40	—	30	13
1.5	60	—	19	14
2.0	80	—	15	9
2.5	100	8	4	9

SOURCE: Stoll (1969).

[1] Soya lecithin, 20% w/v; pimaricin, 0.4% w/v.

fillings for cakes and pies was more than doubled by the addition of 25-50 ppm of pimaricin. Many other foods have also been studied and utility has been demonstrated in the case of margarines, fruit syrups, jams and jellies, pickled products, meat, fish, and poultry.

In the case of sausage, studies have been conducted in the Netherlands which have demonstrated the value of pimaricin. In sausage manufacture, pimaricin has been added as a suspension in one of several steps such as prior to fermentation, by soaking the casing, or dipping the filled sausage, or spraying the filled sausage. Other application methods included pimaricin addition to the brine bath during fermentation, or dipping or spraying the sausages after fermentation, etc. All methods gave improvement in prevention of the mold growth on the surface. No pimaricin could be detected in the sausage meat with the exception of long-term immersion in the brine bath containing pimaricin in which case only traces of pimaricin could be detected in the sausage at a depth of 1-2 mm.

The recommended levels of pimaricin for treatment of hard sausage is 0.05-0.2% by weight of the dipping liquid used for dipping the sausage casing.

Approvals.—Pimaricin has been approved by FAO/WHO for the external application to hard cheese, provided it does not result in a daily intake by humans exceeding 0.25 mg per kilo of body weight, a figure suggested as a conditional ADI. The recommended applications to the rind of cheese are well below such daily intake.

Approval for the use of pimaricin in hard cheese has been given in the Netherlands, Belgium, France, Italy, Sweden, Norway, Spain, and Luxembourg.

The use of pimaricin in hard sausages has been granted in Netherlands Belgium and Spain. Additionally the Netherlands has approved the application of pimaricin to apples and pears.

Nystatin

Nystatin (mycostatin, fungicidin) is another polyene antifungal antibiotic which has some very limited use as a direct food additive. It is used for surface applications on the skin of the banana, and under special circumstances on the surface of meat.

Nystatin is derived from *Streptomyces noursei*, and is closely related to, but not identical with, the other antifungal antibiotics—pimaricin, ramocidin and amphotericin.

Biological Properties.—Nystatin has a fairly broad antifungal spectrum but has no significant activity against bacteria or viruses. Nystatin inhibits endo-genous respiration in fungi and their utilization of glucose, whether aerobic or anaerobic. It is used medically for prophylaxis and treatment of monilial infections, both superficial and intestinal. Nystatin is very poorly absorbed from GI tract of man, even when administered in doses as high as 16 gm per day. It has an IP LD_{50} in mice of of about 200 mg per kilo.

Applications.—The use of nystatin as an antifungal for use as a direct food additive has been studied for several applications, such as against fungal spoilage, and in prevention of the decay of peaches thru postharvest treatment.

It has also been studied for possible application in improving the keeping quality of cottage cheese. In these studies direct comparisons were made against pimaricin and details are reported in that section (Tables A-13 and A-14). Nystatin (mycostatin) gave a significant improvement in keeping quality of cottage cheese, but was slightly less effective than pimaricin.

Nystatin finds application in treatment of the skin of bananas. In practice the bananas are dipped in a solution containing up to 400 ppm of nystatin. Residues could be demonstrated on the skin but not in the flesh of the banana. Such use has been approved in Great Britain.

The U.K. Food Additive and Contaminant Committee has just reviewed the use of preservatives in food, and in their report of July 7, 1972 they recommend that this use of nystatin should be abandoned, unless it can be shown to be efficacious and necessary. (No satisfactory alternate method of treatment exists.) Previous antibiotic panels had considered that the use of nystatin on the skin of bananas to control rot was without hazard to the consumer. The present panel concluded that, from a toxicological standpoint, there was no significant danger to health unless the whole banana was used. In the particular circumstances of use, they felt the only persons at risk were those carrying out the dipping or handling of the treated bananas in that they might eventually acquire resistance to nystatin.

The use of nystatin has been reported in the USSR as a surface treatment for certain meats.

The FAO/WHO Expert Committee on Food Additives recommended that the existing restricted external use of nystatin should be permitted but not extended until more adequate studies on its breakdown and toxicology have been reported. No ADI was given.

Tylosin

Tylosin is a macrolide antibiotic which has been proposed and evaluated as a direct food additive. It was proposed as an aid in processing in view of its activity against clostridia and other spore-forming bacteria. It is produced by *Streptomyces fradiae*, an actinomycete.

Biological Properties.—Its antimicrobial spectrum is essentially Gram positive. It is very active against avian and swine mycoplasma, and finds application in veterinary medicine. It is not used in human medicine.

Tylosin base has an oral LD_{50} of greater than 5000 in the mouse and rat and greater than 800 in the dog.

Application and Approval.—The FAO/WHO Expert Committee on Food Additives in reviewing this antibiotic and its proposed application as a direct food additive, recommended against its use for any purpose which might result in detectable residues in human foods, unless it was necessary to solve an extremely important problem.

In view of the fact that Tylosin shows cross-resistance to some of the therapeutically important macrolide antibiotics used in human medicine, the FAO/WHO Committee felt this would preclude the use of tylosin as a direct food additive, unless required to solve an extremely important problem.

In the United States, several uses of tylosin have been proposed, all relating to destruction of the spores of *Clostridium botulinum*. The use of tylosin lactate as an additive in conjunction with less severe heat processing resulted in a lighter colored and more attractive mushroom product; however, the FDA reported that there may be a delayed spoilage.

In the case of the proposed use in canned dog food of tylosin to permit less vigorous temperature and time processing conditions to avoid caramelization of the buttermilk in a particular type dog food, this use was also found unacceptable by the Committee on Veterinary Medical and Non-Medical Uses of Antibiotics in 1966. The decision was based on the fact that antibiotic use involved a possibility of the appearance in dogs of resistant strains of pathogenic bacteria which could be transmitted to man. In the proposed application in smoked fish, which can be a serious *Cl. botulinum* peril if not properly processed, the Committee suggested that adequate heat processing could suffice together with adequate plant sanitation and management. The Committee's general rejection of the use of tylosin as a feed additive was similar to that of FAO/WHO, and based on data showing such use doses cause the emergence of some resistant organisms and such organisms are frequently cross-resistant to erythromycin and oleandomycin, both therapeutically important antibiotics in human clinical medicine.

Tetracyclines

Tetracyclines have been studied for many years as direct additives to a wide variety of foodstuffs as preservatives in delaying decomposition during transportation, storage, and marketing. This use has been explored for possible application in those countries where adequate refrigeration is not available.

In Milk.—Early studies showed that penicillin, streptomycin, and other narrow spectrums could reduce lactic acid production in stored milk; however, they were of little value against putrefaction. The broad spectrum tetracyclines, when added at 1 ppm, however, could delay the onset of spoilage for 1 day at 98°F. Utility was also demonstrated in pasteurized milk.

In Fresh Fruits and Vegetables.—In fresh fruits and vegetables, bacterial soft-rot has been materially retarded by the use of the tetracyclines or combinations of streptomycin and oxytetracycline.

In Fish and Sea Food.—In view of the rapid decomposition rate of fish, extensive evaluations have been made of the use of the tetracyclines in aiding in the storage and transportation of this perishable foodstuff. Since many of the bacteria involved in fish storage are psychrophilic and can proliferate at refrigerated conditions, the need for preserving aids is great. The tetracycline antibiotics have been shown to be valuable in conjunction with refrigeration as preservatives in fish. The antibiotics are added by addition to the ice used in packing the fish, at levels of 5 ppm, or by dipping or spraying the fish in concentrations of from 10 to 200 ppm of tetracycline. The addition of tetracyclines at a level of 1 ppm to the refrigeration brine is an effective approach. These additions of tetracyclines approximately double the shelf-life of the treated fish.

In dipping fish filets in oxytetracycline solutions for 30 sec, a 10 ppm dip doubled the keeping period, 25 ppm tripled it, and a 50 ppm dip quadrupled the allowable storage period. The tetracyclines have also been employed when fish are caught for the production of fishmeal. Antibiotics have been used in whale fishing. In its early use, the antibiotic was introduced into the meat by delivering it in the exploding head of the harpoon used. This method of application was replaced by pumping the antibiotic into the abdominal and chest cavity during the period the whale was being inflated.

The use of chlortetracyclines in fish preservation was approved in the United States in 1959. Approval included a tolerance of 5 ppm for residues in or on fish, scallops, and shrimp for retardation of spoilage of these sea foods when each is in fresh, uncooked, unfrozen form. This approval was withdrawn by the FDA in August, 1967 in light of the criteria established by the Committee on Veterinary Medical and Non-Medical Uses of Antibiotics, May 1966. The FDA concluded there was no serious problem in fish handling that would justify this food additive use of chlortetracycline and cited possible public health problems involved if its use continued.

The approval for the use of tetracyclines for the preservation of fish was rather widespread but its use in many countries has been subsequently rescinded in view of the reports of recent advisory committees which have studied such use of antibiotics in foods. In the United Kingdom, the use of tetracyclines in fish was approved in 1960, and a permissible residue level of 5 ppm of the tetracycline in fish flesh was established. In July 1972, the U.K. Food Additive and Contaminant Committee reviewed this use of tetracyclines in fish and recommended its discontinuance. The U.K. Committee indicated that this use of tetracycline did not significantly retard the early stage of fish spoilage, and frequently only extended the storage life by 3 days. In addition, its use had been very slight in the United Kingdom, in view of the increasing use of modern fishing trawlers with freezing facilities. In other countries, such as Japan, and reportedly in USSR, the use of tetracycline in fish still persists. The FAO/WHO Expert Committee on Food Additives recommended against the use of tetracyclines as intentional food additives.

In Meats.—Several workers have shown the value of the use of the tetracyclines in meats. Methods of application of the antibiotic have included surface sprays, infusion into the tissue, both ante- and postmortem. In the case of antemortem treatment, distribution of the antibiotic is accomplished by the action of blood and lymph. Tissue levels of as low as 1 ppm of oxytetracycline were shown to delay internal spoilage, processed meats such as hamburger and sausage having a materially extended shelf-life with a tetracycline treatment. Fresh pork sausage, for example, showed a 50–100% longer shelf-life as a result of adding 3–5 ppm of oxytetracycline.

In Poultry.—In poultry processing, chilled chickens remained salable for only approximately one week at commercial storage temperature. This lead to the investigation of the use of tetracyclines to increase storage life. The addition of 10 ppm to the slush ice reportedly increased the storage time 50–100%.

The FDA approved such use of oxytetracycline and chlortetracycline in the processing of poultry in 1960. As in the case of chlortetracycline with treated fish, the FDA reversed its approval for such direct food addition of the tetracyclines to poultry and rescinded the tolerance for a residue of 7 ppm of the oxytetracycline and chlortetracycline in the edible tissue of uncooked poultry. (This 7 ppm residue was reportedly destroyed during normal cooking.) The revocation of approval and tolerance for tetracyclines was made effective at the same time the FDA rescinded approval for the use of chlortetracycline in fish.

The basis for rescinding both was the same: The FDA no longer felt that such processing aids were essential; and the use of tetracyclines could result in the selection of naturally resistant organisms, and the emergence of resistant strains, as well as an increase in the mold and yeast development.

Subtilin

Subtilin has been the subject of considerable investigation as a direct food additive aid in canning of foods in light of its activity against spores of Clostridium botulinum. This investigational food additive activity was terminated when it was discovered that the combination of subtilin and mild heat was not always effective in killing spores of Clostridium botulinum.

Streptomycin

In the present climate of the restricted regulatory attitude towards the use of antibiotics as direct food additives, as recommended by the several scientific advisory groups studying the problem, many of the previous direct food additive uses of antibiotics have been revised or rescinded. In the case of pome fruits, however, this was not the case. The U.S. Secretary of Agriculture advised that certain commercial varities of apples or pears are highly susceptible and are severely damaged by fire blight; he indicated that streptomycin was the only nonphytotoxic chemical giving effective control.

It was therefore concluded that the serious fire-blight problem justified the use of streptomycin on pome fruits and a tolerance of 0.25 ppm (negligible residue) in or on pome fruit was established when streptomycin was used for controlling fire blight. Streptomycin had been widely used for 15 yr in the control of fire blight on the basis of no residues being present at harvest as determined by the analytical procedure available which was sensitive to 0.25 ppm. The residue tolerance of 0.25 ppm was established in 1968 as a "negligible residue" and was determined by the sensitivity of the assay employed.

Unintentional Food Additives

Antibiotics may enter human food channels from unintentional carryover in meat, eggs, and milk from the agricultural and veterinary use of antibiotics which have been added to animal feeds for the purposes of stimulating the animal's growth and for the prevention and treatment of animal diseases. Additionally, they may enter human food as unintentional residues from oral or parenteral medication of animals for disease treatment.

In the case of all antibiotics used in animals, either a zero tolerance or a "negligible residue" in the tissue has been established. The negligible residue is based upon assay sensitivity. The general philosophy of the regulations and the specific allowances are detailed in the U.S. Code of Federal Regulations, Title 21, Food and Drugs, Part 135-G: .1 General Considerations; .4 Bacitracin; .6 Oleandomycin; .8 Chlortetracycline; .10 Hygromycin; .11 Streptomycin; .12 Penicillin; .13 Novobiocin; .14 Oxytetracycline; .15 Tylosin; .17 Nystatin; .18 Dihydrostreptomycin; .24 Spectinomycin; .25 Neomycin; .35 Erythromycin; .54 Carbomycin; .65 Lincomycin; .66 Polymixin B; .72 Tetracycline. It is published by the Office of the Federal Register and available from the U.S. Government Printing Office, Washington, D.C.

These U.S. regulations also establish specific tolerances for chlortetracycline and oxytetracycline in certain uncooked edible tissue. The permissible tolerance for oxytetracycline for the uncooked tissue of chicken and turkey is 3 ppm for the kidney and 1 ppm for the muscle, liver, fat, and skin. In the case of oxytetracycline, the permissible residue in the uncooked tissue of chicken and turkey is 4 ppm in the kidney, and 1 ppm for muscle, liver, skin, and fat.

In uncooked swine tissue, allowable chlortetracycline residues are 4 ppm in the kidney, 2 ppm in the liver, 1 ppm in muscle, and 0.2 ppm in the fat. In calves, allowable chlortetracycline residues are 4 ppm in the kidney and 1 ppm in muscle and fat. In beef and nonlactating dairy cows, the residues allowed are 0.1 ppm in muscle, kidney, and liver.

These specific tolerances for oxytetracycline and chlortetracycline have been granted after extensive toxicological testing establishing safety and on proof that these residues permitted in the uncooked tissues are destroyed in normal cooking. Examples of established negative residues are: bacitracin at 0.5 ppm in uncooked edible tissue of cattle, swine, chickens, turkeys, pheasants, quail, milk, and eggs; oleandomycin at 0.15 ppm in uncooked edible tissue of chickens, turkeys, and swine; penicillin at 0.05 ppm in uncooked edible tissue of cattle; oxytetracycline at 0.1 ppm in uncooked edible tissue of salmonids and catfish.

In granting approval for the use of antibiotics in animal feeds or in animal medication, the FDA rigorously establishes, on the basis of assay data at variable withdrawal periods, the required legal withdrawal period for the antibiotic between the time of last addition and the animal's slaughter. Occasionally, these required withdrawal periods are not always respected in practice and tissue residues are ocassionally found in the uncooked edible foodstuff.

It is the requirement of USDA to monitor the possible tissue residues in edible foodstuffs; accordingly, USDA maintains such a surveillance program.

Recently, it has been established that, besides assaying tissue for residues, it is possible to effectively monitor withdrawal periods. By assaying urine samples it is possible to determine if proper withdrawal periods have been followed. In those instances where illegal residues are found, the product is removed from food channels.

There is a continuing review of the approval of antibiotics used in livestock production, and a National Academy of Sciences—National Research Council review of efficacy for existing products was recently completed which resulted in modification of some of the claims and requirements for additional documentation.

Considerable attention had been addressed to a review of combinations of antibiotics and drugs for animal use and the indication was that additional documentation must be generated to support their use. Eighteen hundred previously approved combinations, including at least one antibiotic were on file; however, in response to the FDA's requirement of additional supporting data required to satisfy the efficacy documentation, over 1000 products have been dropped as the sponsor indicated he did not intend to supply the required information. On approximately 750 remaining combination products, a commitment was made by the sponsoring organization to supply the required data to support the continued approval of the product.

The widespread use of antibiotics for growth promotion and disease control has been common practice in the United States for many years and to a somewhat smaller extent than in many other countries. In general, the large-scale use of antibiotics is related to the more concentrated animal production practices commonly found in the United States. At the present time there are 16 antibiotics which may be administered to animals through the feed; 12 of these are widely used. These include chlortetracycline, oxytetracycline, penicillin, bacitracin, streptomycin, tylosin, neomycin, tetracycline, erythromycin, oleandomycin, hygromycin, novobiocin, lincomycin, spectinomycin, nystatin, and griseofulvin.

The range of allowable antibiotic application to feed varies from 0.6 gm per ton with procaine to 1000 gm per ton with tylosin. The usual levels for growth promotion are 1 to 50 gm per ton; for disease prevention levels are 50 to 200 gm per ton, and for treatment, 100 to 500 gm per ton.

Most of these antibiotics also find use in human clinical medicine. When all routes of administration are considered as well as all microbial agents, there is a total of 30 microbial agents presently used for improvement of growth rate or disease control and 23 of these are also used in human clinical medicine.

In the United States, virtually all chickens and turkeys receive antibiotics for growth promotion and/or disease prevention and treatment. Low levels for growth, for example, may be 0.6–4.0 gm of penicillin per ton or 4–6 gm of bacitracin per ton of feed for chickens. In the case of turkeys, 3–15 gm of penicillin or 10–50 gm of bacitracin per ton may be used for growth promotion. It is quite common to orally administer fairly high levels of tetracyclines or tetracyclines plus neomycin, or tylosin, etc., through the feed or water as a prophylactic or therapeutic treatment for poultry during periods of stress or anticipated disease outbreak. This short-term high level prophylactic treatment represents a significant portion of the current use of antibiotics.

In the case of swine, approximately 90% of the animals in the United States receive antibiotics for growth promotion and/or the prevention of disease. If baby pigs receive artificial sow's milk, such milk contains a high level of a tetracycline in most instances; also, the baby pig usually receives fairly high levels of tetracycline in the creep feed. It is common, for example, for weaned pigs to receive 250 gm per ton of a tetracycline-penicillin-sulfamethazine combination or a 200-gm combination of tylosin and sulfamethazine per ton of feed until the pig reaches a weight of 75 lb. Lower levels, usually of single antibiotics, are fed from 75 lb to the time the animal almost reaches market weight.

Milk fed calves, for example, usually receive a high level of tetracycline in their milk replacers. Feeder calves, when transported or exposed to stress, commonly receive an injection of 1 million units of penicillin and 1 gm of streptomycin or an injection of 500 mg of oxytetracycline. This is usually followed by antibiotic additions to the feed. Beef cattle, commonly receive a high level regimen of a tetracycline, or a tetracycline and a

sulfa for 10 days upon shipment or receipt in a feed lot, and subsequently receive approximately 75 mg per head per day of tetracycline until marketing period for control of liver abscess and improvement in performance.

In the case of antibiotics used for animal medication, specific directions for use and prescribed withdrawal periods are required whether the product is distributed through a veterinarian only or whether a product is available to the farmer or rancher. For example, in mastitis products, which are used for intramammary application, discarding of the milk is required for a period of 48–96 hr depending upon the excretion pattern of the antibiotic in the vehicle employed. The FDA also assists in minimizing undesirable milk residues by limiting the amount of penicillin that may be contained in an intramammary treatment form to 100,000 units per infusion, a dosage limitation not existing in most other countries.

Previously in the United States, penicillin doses for intramammary infusion of several million units had been employed. Such high levels contributed materially to undesired carryover of penicillin in the milk without materially improving the therapeutic efficacy of the medication. Through this restriction and better medication practices and surveillance, penicillin residues now are found in only 0.25–0.50% of the milk in the United States, whereas 15 yr ago, as high as 12–14% of the milk samples were contaminated with undesirable residues of penicillin.

These residues obviously have undesirable public health implications. Additionally, it has been shown that metabolites of penicillin, having at least as great a sensitizing action as penicillin itself, were formed but not detected by the normal penicillin assay; and they may persist even slightly longer than the penicillin itself.

In 1971, FDA set forth provisions stipulating the allowable use of certain penicillin, streptomycin, dihydrostreptomycin and neomycin products in intramammary infusions, as well as other veterinary drugs allowable in these combinations.

Considerable controversy has recently arisen regarding the use of antibiotics in feeds for growth promotion and for the treatment of animal diseases. Particular focus has been directed to the real or imagined public health hazard associated with the use of the same drugs in animal feeding and medication that are employed in human medicine. The cited potential hazards relate to the possible indirect toxic effects, including hypersensitivity to allergy should the consumer be sensitized to the drug. The potential hazardous bacteriological and epidemiological effects have received more attention as hazards to human health in that animals receiving antibiotics are reported to significantly increase their reservoir of Gram negative bacilli capable of causing human disease, and which may be capable of being transmitted to man.

In a recent epidemiological survey on farms in the United States, which had various programs of antibiotic feeding including some which fed antibiotics continuously in the feed and others who employed the antibiotic for therapeutic and prophylactic purposes, the characteristics and frequency of antimicrobial resistance to *E. coli* was studied in relationship to the veterinary and management use of antimicrobial agents. Multiple resistance in the *E. coli* isolates was found to occur in 84.8% of the herd exposed to continuous feeding of antimicrobial agents, compared to 15.7% in the herds not receiving antimicrobials.

Resistance patterns to 3–4 agents were the most commonly observed. The frequency of transfer factors was much higher in multiple-resistant organisms from the herds exposed to antimicrobial medication. The *E. coli* isolated were relatively efficient in fostering and transferring heterologous resistance factors.

This entire complex area of real or imagined public health hazards associated with the use of antibiotics and determination of the actual risk-benefit ratio involved, has received much attention in many countries. In the United Kingdom, the Swann Committee studied the problem and their conclusions have resulted in legislation in the United Kingdom which prohibits the continuous feeding of the tetracyclines, penicillin and sulfas without the specific prescription of an attending veterinarian.

In the United States, the same subject has been the object of an 18-month study by a special FDA Antibiotic Task Force. It was the Task Force majority recommendation that the tetracyclines, streptomycin, dihydrostreptomycin, sulfonamides, and penicillin be prohibited from use for growth-promoting and any subtherapeutic application in animals. They recommended that these antibiotics be reserved for therapy unless they meet the criteria established for safety and efficacy for growth promotion or subtherapeutic use.

The FDA Antibiotic Task Force also recommended that therapeutic application be restricted to short-term treatment and then only by decision of a veterinarian or on the authority of a veterinarian's prescription. They further recommended that those antibiotics which select for bacterial resistance to the antibiotics most critically needed for man and animals be prohibited for use in animal feed. At the present time, this category includes chloramphenicol, semisynthetic penicillin, gentamycin, and kanamycin. They recommended

that those antibiotics effective and essential for the therapy of certain animal diseases and which select for R-factor mediated multiple resistance should be available for short-term use, only at therapeutic levels and by a veterinarian or on his prescription.

The FDA Antibiotic Task Force recommendations were based on their conclusions that the use of certain antibiotics and sulfonamide drugs, particularly when used at the growth-promotant and subtherapeutic levels, favored the selection and development of single- and multiple-resistant and R-factor-bearing bacteria in food animals which may serve as a reservoir for antibiotic-resistant pathogens and nonpathogens which could produce human infection.

These observations, together with the fact that the prevalence of multiresistant R-factor in animals has been related to the use of certain antibiotics and sulfonamide drugs, and the finding of resistant organisms on meat and meat products, gave rise to the logical conclusions, although not fully documented, that such medication practices may be hazardous to human health.

In their review of the use of antibiotics, a risk-benefit relationship had to be explored in establishing a balance between the value of antibiotic use in agriculture and the potential hazards associated with such use. In their economic evaluation of the use of antibiotics in animal feeds, the Task Force estimated the following economic value for such use in meat animals. Their breakdown for the year 1970 was as follows:

Broilers	$ 33,419,000
Turkeys	13,920,000
Beef	148,890,000
Veal	14,431,000
Swine	202,489,000
	$413,149,000

These data, however, are not intended as an accurate estimate of the economic impact of restricting antibiotics in feeds as all antibiotic use would not cease; undoubtedly some antibiotics would continue to be available for growth-promotant purposes.

The Task Force also estimated the economic value of the use of antibiotics to the pharmaceutical industry. Their estimates for the year 1968–1969, were as follows:

Broilers	$ 2,172,800
Turkeys	583,923
Hogs	46,400,000
Cattle	14,112,000
Calves	761,600
	$64,030,323

The proper regulated use of antibiotics is presently under active discussion and review. Modified regulations have recently been issued in the United States and are in preparation and partial implementation in the European Common Market and other areas of the world.

In the United States, an ad hoc committee of the National Academy of Sciences—National Research Council has reviewed the FDA Antibiotic Task Force recommendations. On April 30, 1973, the FDA ordered regulations that essentially start to implement some of the antibiotic recommendations, in that all approved subtherapeutic use of the antibiotics and sulfonamides will be revoked unless data are submitted which conclusively resolve their safety and efficacy according to the newer and more rigorous standards which have been recommended. These regulations are outlined in *Statement of Policy and Interpretation Regarding Animal Drugs and Medicated Feeds*, Title 21, Part 135-B, Federal Register, *38*, No. 76, 7811–7814.

In the case of tetracyclines, streptomycin, dihydrostreptomycin, penicillin, and sulfonamides, the effect of subtherapeutic feed use of these drugs on the *Salmonella* reservoir of target animals must be concluded by April 20, 1974.

The importance from a public health standpoint of transferrable drug resistance in *Salmonella* is reviewed, together, with other aspects in the FDA Antibiotic Task Force report and its detailed appendices and in other related literature (Baldwin 1970).

In general, the philosophy of antibiotic use for animals in the United States has been that, in those specific conditions where the antibiotic administration is safe and effective under the prescribed restrictions of application, dosage, withdrawal period, etc., and where adequate directions can be written, a particular antibiotic may be so administered in the feed or other route by the farmer or rancher. In all other cases, veterinary application is required.

In most of the rest of the world, there is a greater tendency towards restricting the use of antibiotics for animals through a veterinarian, or on his prescription, without detailing the same degree of specificity of approved application, level of use, withdrawal period, etc.

In the United States, the FDA Antibiotic Task Force, as well as other advisory groups, recommend that the same antibiotic should preferably not be used for human and animal applications, and an antibiotic should not be used which is cross-resistant with important antibiotics used in humans. The Task Force suggested research for the development of new chemotherapeutic agents for animal applications not used in human medi-

cine. Research is addressed to this ideal goal and the first example of success in this area is the recent approval of a new quinoxaline-*N*-oxide, Carbadox, which has recently been developed and approved in the United States and several countries for use in animals.

HERBERT G. LUTHER

References

BALDWIN, R. A. 1970. The development of transferrable drug resistance in Salmonella and its public health implications. J. Am. Vet. Med. Assoc. *157*, No. 11, 1841–1853.

FAO/WHO. 1969. Twelfth report of Joint FAO/WHO Expert Committee on Food Additives. WHO Tech. Rept. Ser. *430*.

FDA Antibiotic Task Force. (Undated) Report to the Commissioner of FDA on the use of antibiotics in animal feeds and Appendices on economic value of human and animal health hazards. FDA Bur. Vet. Med.

FOWLER, G. G., and McCANN, B. 1971. The growing use of nisin in the dairy industry. Australian J. Dairy Technol. *26*, 44–46.

HUBER, W. C. 1973. Antibiotic tissue residues in animals. Symp. Antibiotics in Animal Feeds, American Society of Microbiologists, Atlantic City, Sept. 28.

MERCER, H. D. *et al.* 1971. Characteristics of antimicrobial resistance of *Escherichia coli* from animals: Relationship to veterinary and management uses of antimicrobial agents. Appl. Microbiol 22, no. 4, 700–705.

NILSON, K. M., CARRANCEDO, M., and SHAHANI, K. M. 1960. The use of antifungal antibiotics on the retardation of cottage cheese spoilage. J. Dairy Sci. *43*, 842–843.

SHAHANI, K. M., NILSON, K. M., and DOWNS, P. A. 1959. Effect of anti-fungal antibiotics on keeping quality of cottage cheese. Proc. 15th Intern. Dairy Congr. *2*, Sect. 3, 926–932.

STOLL, VON K. 1969. Method for prevention of Johnathan spot. Swiss J. Fruit Wine Growing *16*, 65. (Swiss)

U.S. Dept. Health, Education, and Welfare. 1973. Preslaughter withdrawal times for drugs. For chickens: HEW Publ. *73-6011*, Bur. Vet. Med. Publ. *73-6012*. For turkeys: Publ. *73-6013*. For sheep and goats: Publ. *74-6008*. For cattle and calves: Publ. *74-6006*.

ANTIOXIDANTS

Oxidation is the major problem in the spoilage of fats and fatty foods. Oxidative changes are manifest as changes in flavor, odor, color or, on occasion, texture as viscosity. While the portion of the fat undergoing such changes may be small the resulting off-odors are potent, pervading, and

TABLE A-16

LIPID ANTIOXIDANTS ACCEPTABLE FOR USE IN HUMAN FOOD IN THE UNITED STATES

Name	Use Limit	Structure
Butylated hydroxyanisole	0.02% of fat content	(BHA structure: phenol ring with OH, $C(CH_3)_3$, and OCH_3 substituents)
Butylated hydroxytoluene	0.02% of fat content	(BHT structure: phenol ring with OH, $(CH_3)_3C$, $C(CH_3)_3$, and CH_3 substituents)
Dilauryl thiodipropionate	0.02% of fat content	$CH_2-CH_2-COO-CH_2-(CH_2)_{10}-CH_3$ S $CH_2-CH_2-COO-CH_2-(CH_2)_{10}-CH_3$
Thiodipropionic acid	0.02% of fat content	CH_2-CH_2-COOH S CH_2-CH_2-COOH
Propyl gallate	0.02% of fat content	(gallate structure: benzene ring with three OH and $COOC_3H_7$)

Gum guaiacol 0.1% in fat

Tocopherols GMP[1]

Ethoxyquin 100 ppm in paprika and chili

2,4,5 Trihydroxy butyrophenone 0.02% of fat content

4 hydroxy methyl-2, 6-di tert-butylphenone 0.02% of fat content

[1] In accordance with good manufacturing practices.

very much out of proportion to the volume of spoiled oil involved.

Fat breakdown falls into four general categories: (1) Rancidity—autoxidation of fatty acids at the double bond leading to offensive off-odors. (2) Hydrolysis—splitting of the fatty acid or acids from the glyceryl backbone leading to "soapy" flavors. (3) Reversion—a "painty" or "grassy" flavor commonly associated with soy oil; the mechanism is still controversial. (4) Polymerization—cross-linking of unsaturated fatty acids, usually in fats highly heated for prolonged periods.

The common antioxidants are helpful in heading off rancidity and to a much lesser extent polymerization, but are not useful in hydrolysis, frequently enzymatic, and reversion.

Mechanism of Food Fat Oxidation

In general, autocatalytic oxidation may be defined as a self-generating reaction between a food lipid and molecular oxygen. These reactions are accompanied by many secondary reactions. The most accepted mechanism is that proposed by Farmer and Sandralingam (1942) and subsequently expanded upon (Farmer and Sutton 1943; Farmer 1946). In brief, he postulates a free radical mechanism leading to an attack upon the carbon alpha to the carbon of the double bond in an unsaturated fatty acid. This, in turn, leads to the formation of a hydroperoxide, or peroxide

bridge at the double bond $\begin{matrix} O-O \\ | \;\; | \\ -C=C- \end{matrix}$ which ultimately leads to cleavage at that site with the subsequent formation in the secondary reaction of aldehydes, ketones, polymers, and lipoperoxides which, in turn, lead to further free radicals, hence the term autocatalytic.

The self-generating nature of the reaction is best illustrated by a typical fat oxidation curve (Fig. A-4).

Several factors influence the rate of this reaction. Among the first must rank the degree of unsaturation; the rate of the reaction rises exponentially with increasing level of unsaturation. Other factors include oxygen tension, light, temperature, pro-oxidants and oxidation catalysts such as traces of heavy metals including copper and iron. Some materials, on the other hand, inhibit this reaction; they include metal scavengers and oxygen interceptors or antioxidants.

Antioxidant Mechanism

It is now apparent that antioxidants operate in diverse ways depending on the substrate and the surrounding conditions. Shelton (1959) has grouped these mechanisms into four categories: (1) Hydrogen donation by the antioxidant. (2) Electron donation by the antioxidant. (3) Addition reaction—lipid to antioxidant. (4) Formation of lipid—antioxidant complex.

Stuckey (1968) believes it is probably a mixture of all of the above factors operating to yield antioxidant reaction. One theory (Privett et al. 1954) postulates that autoxidation is initiated by a yet unelucidated mechanism prior to the formation of a stable hydroperoxide. Further, antioxidants are ineffective in inhibiting this reaction.

Lipid Food Antioxidants

The antioxidants approved for use are shown together with their structural formulae in Table A-16. A perusal of these structures will show that they exhibit certain structural similarities. An unsaturated phenolic structure is common to the most commonly-used compounds except for the thiodipropionates. All have a common "chain-breaking" propensity resulting from ability to transfer a hydrogen atom or an electron, this interfering with the free radical transfer mechanism.

There are several other classes of antioxidants, some, in fact, more active than food-use antioxidants; but usually they exhibit toxic and discoloration properties or, on occasion, odoriferous tendencies. They are commonly used in petroleum products. They include amines, amino phenols, and phenylene diamines. It should be noted that in the list given (Table A-16), tocopherols, are a widespread natural constituent of plant and animal fat and can have extremely good antioxidant properties in unprocessed fatty materials. They are, however, readily degraded by heat and do not survive many heat-based food processing operations, especially refining and high heat rendering.

Synergism and Catalysis

It is now quite well established that certain other additives greatly enhance the effectiveness of antioxidants, and that synergism between antioxidants

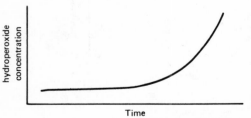

Time

After Lundberg (1962)

FIG. A-4. A TYPICAL FAT OXIDATION CURVE

TABLE A-17

SOME TYPICAL COMMERCIAL ANTIOXIDANT PREPARATIONS

	BHA[1] (%)	BHT[2] (%)	Propyl Gallate (%)	TBHQ[3] (%)	Propylene Glycol (%)	Citric Acid (%)	Vegetable Oil (%)	Glyceryl Mono-oleate (%)	Sorbitan Mono-stearate (%)	Water (%)	Ethyl Alcohol (%)	Citrate Mono-glyceride (%)
Eastman Tenox BHT		X										
Eastman Tenox BHA	X											
Eastman Tenox 2	20	20	6		70	4						
Eastman Tenox 4	20	10					60					
Eastman Tenox 6	10		6	20	12	6	28	20				
Eastman Tenox 7	28		12	6	34	6		20	8			
Eastman Tenox 20				6	70	10						
Eastman Tenox 22	20				70	4						
Eastman Tenox 26	10	10			12	6						
Eastman Tenox R	20		20		60	20	28	28				
Eastman Tenox S-1					70	10						
UOP-BHA	X	X										
UOP Sustane		X										
UOP-Sustane 3F	66.7		20			13.3						
UOP-Sustane 6	18	22					60					
UOP-Sustane E	10	10	6				40			47.5		
UOP-Sustane W	10	20			8	6	28	30	2.5		60	
UOP-Sustane P	20	X										
Shell Ionol		X			X	2						X
Griffiths G-16	6	13.5	5.5									

[1] Butylated Hydroxy Anisole.
[2] Butylated Hydroxy Toluene.
[3] Tertiary Butylated Hydroquinone.

NOTE: Monotertiary butylhydroquinone has recently been introduced as a food grade antioxidant. Its advantages are claimed to be low odor, good fat solubility, and no discoloration in the presence of iron.

is exhibited.　Of particular interest are metal scavengers or chelating agents which serve to tie up the trace heavy metals and thus greatly reduce their catalytic activity.　Most prominent among these are citric acid and citrates, which are included in most commercial antioxidant proprietary mixes.　Some typical commercial mixes are shown in Table A-17.

Commercial mixes take advantage not only of the synergistic effect of mixed antioxidants but of the differences in performance during food processing operations.　Thus propyl gallate is probably the most effective of the antioxidants where no heating is involved in the processing, but because of its ready volatility it is easily lost during heating. BHA and BHT are relatively stable through heating and are commonly called "carry through" antioxidants.　If a product is to be heated it is common to use a mixture containing propyl gallate and BHA and/or BHT.　For example, in Table A-17 Tenox 4 and 5 are recommended for "carry through" use, while Tenox S-1 is not.

Uses and Problems of Usage

Obviously, the major area of application of food lipid antioxidants is in areas where fat spoilage is apt to be a problem.　This includes not only high fat foods but those even of low fat content where fat changes are highly noticeable.　The products of interest with potential antioxidant usage are shown in Table A-18.

of the antioxidant but higher temperatures must be avoided because of the tendency of antioxidants to distill off.

Because of the previously indicated phenolic structures, reaction products of most antioxidants with heavy metals produce colored reaction products, particularly if the metals are introduced in an aqueous phase.　Thus, not only for their catalysis but because of this color reaction, heavy metals must be avoided.　This detail must be scrupulously observed even down to the presence of one bronze valve.　To forestall a temporary metal problem, additional chelater, citric acid, may be added. An additional caution is directed toward the use of metal equipment immediately after a thorough caustic cleaning.　Such equipment is usually newly exposed and may give trouble where it previously performed satisfactorily.　Covering the newly exposed surfaces with oil followed by heating generally results in metal passivation and it is then safe for use.

On another tack, a quick study of Fig. A-4 will show that fat undergoing oxidation has a longish incubation period followed by a meteoric rise.　It should be obvious that attempts to employ antioxidants when oxidation has reached the rise phase are fruitless.　Antioxidant must be employed as early in the life of the oil as possible.

An illustration of the effective inhibition of rancidity in edible oils by antioxidants is shown in Fig. A-5.

As the food industry in the United States moves

TABLE A-18

POTENTIAL FOOD PRODUCT APPLICATIONS OF
LIPID ANTIOXIDANTS

Animal Origin Foods	Cereals	Miscellaneous
Bacon	Breakfast foods	Chewing gum
Chicken fat	Fried snacks	Citrus oils
Dog food	Germ meals	Cosmetics
Fish	Premixes	Essential oils
Ham	Starter feeds	Packaging materials
Lard		

In the application to animal and vegetable oils an extremely important consideration is thorough mixing and dispersion.　A preferred technique calls for proportionate mixing into a stream of the hot (145°–175°F) fat.　Continued agitation is helpful, but care must be taken to ensure against incorporation of air.　Use of an oil-antioxidant premix is also extremely helpful.　Temperatures approaching 200°F in the premix are helpful for solution

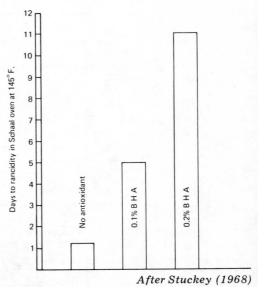

After Stuckey (1968)

FIG. A-5.　INHIBITION OF RANCIDITY IN LARD
BY BHA

further into processed foods and into prolonged shelf-life marketing, the prediction of a projected storage life of a fatty food becomes extremely important. There are many techniques employed, most of which employ stress techniques to the oil, such as heating or bubbling oxygen through it. Spoilage observations may be made by "sniffing"— a surprisingly accurate tool when the "sniffer" is sensitized and trained. Other techniques measure the chemical by products of oxidation such as peroxides, free fatty acids, aldehydes, or oxygen uptake.

The simplest test is the "shelf storage test" in which samples under test are stored under actual shelf conditions and perodically examined organoleptically for spoilage. Peroxide titrations are often employed along with the organoleptic panel. In this test, scrupulous attention must be paid to glassware cleanliness and rinsing.

Shelf storage, however, is very time-consuming and on occasion the results may be shortened by storing test samples at elevated temperatures. One version of this technique, generally known as the Schaal Oven Test, employs 140°C. Although the time is shortened in this technique it can lead to confusing results in some fats due to new reaction mechanism routes. This test is frequently used for cereal-fat foods such as cookies, pie crust, and potato chips.

Another common technique, requiring a bit more equipment and sophistication is the Active Oxygen Method (AOM) or Swift Stability Test. In this technique the test oil is immersed in a bath at 210°F and purified air or oxygen is bubbled through it at a fixed rate. Periodically, peroxides are measured by back titrating liberated iodine from added potassium iodide against sodium thiosulfate employing a starch indicator. In general, this technique is best applied to refined, liquid oils and is less suitable for food mixtures.

For complex food products the thiobarbituric acid test (TBA) finds its best application. This test is in essence a simple colorimetric measurement of a developed red color after addition of TBA.

Further specific details of fat stability testing can be found in the methods of the Association of Official Agricultural Chemists.

ROY E. MORSE

References

FARMER, E. H., and SANDRALINGAM, A. 1942. The cause of autoxidation reactions in polyisoprenes and allied compounds. Part I. The structure and reactive tendencies of the peroxides of simple olefins. J. Chem. Soc. *1942*, 121–139.

FARMER, E. H., and SUTTON, D. A. 1943. The course of autoxidations in polyisoprenes and allied compounds. Part IV. The isolation and constitution of photo-chemically formed methyl oleate peroxides. J. Chem. Soc. *1943*, 119–122.

FARMER, E. H. 1946. Peroxidation in relation to olefinic structure. Trans. Faraday Soc. *42*, 228–236.

LUNDBERG, W. O. 1962. Mechanisms of lipid oxidation. *In* Lipids and Their Oxidation. W. W. Schultz, E. A. Day, and R. O. Sinnhuber (Editors) Avi Publishing Co., Westport, Conn.

PRIVETT, O. S. *et al.* 1954. Evidence for hydroperoxide formation in the autoxidation of methyl linolenate. J. Am. Oil. Chemists Soc. *31*, 23–27.

SHELTON, J. R. 1959. Mechanisms of antioxidant action in the stability of hydrocarbon systems. J. Appl. Polymer Sci. *2*, 345–350.

STUCKEY, B. N. 1968. Antioxidants as food stabilizers. *In* Handbook of Food Additives. Chemical Rubber Co., Cleveland.

Cross-reference: *Food Additives.*

APPERT AWARD

See Awards.

APPERT, NICOLAS (1752–1841)

Nicolas Appert was born at Chalons-sur-Marne in France in 1752. He holds an honored place in the history of food technology as the inventor of canning, a method of food preservation that over the decades has grown into one of the major branches of the food industry. Napoleon was responsible for Appert's work that resulted in this new food process. In 1795, the French Directorate offered a prize of 12,000 francs, a substantial sum, for a food preservation process that would not seriously impair the natural flavor of fresh food. Appert, a confectioner, winemaker, and chef, was no novice in the food arts and set to work at once on the project, which in the course of time won him the coveted prize. The basic principle of Appert's method was to heat the food in closed containers, a principle, which, despite the refinements over Appert's pioneer efforts, remains the central one in the canning process. It is possible that Appert was indebted in some small degree to Papin's invention of the pressure cooker in 1681, but by far the greatest input into the new process was that of Appert. For almost 10 yr, that is, until 1804, Appert struggled unsuccessfully with the method, but in the next few years he made good progress and in 1809 was awarded the prize.

He published his epochal book, *Le Livre de tous les Menages ou l'Art de Conserver pendant Plusieurs Annees Toutes les Substances Animales et Vegetales*, in 1810. A direct translation of the French publication, *The Book for All Households or the Art of Preserving Animal and Vegetable Substances for Many Years*, was published in London in the following year; and a second edition in English was published in 1812 in both England and America.

Although it remained for Pasteur to answer scientifically the *why* of the successful preservation of food by canning, Appert knew quite well what he was seeking, technologically. He knew that other methods of preservation such as drying or soaking in brine injured the flavor, changing it materially; that they hardened the fibres of vegetables; and that, in the case of salted food such as herring, the flavor was often unpleasantly bitter. Canning, he recognized, was also injurious to flavor in some degree, and it would appear that a part of his endeavor in the years of his experimentation was to determine what amount of heat treatment was optimal for preservation and flavor retention, a parametric approach, as it were, without, one presumes, functional values.

It would be gratifying to report that canning took hold immediately and quickly became a major method of preservation. Such was not the case, as is well known, and not until well after the American Civil War—during which some canned foods were used—was canning a commercial enterprise of any size. However, as early as 1814 Appert was preserving fish and a few other products for use by the French Government, and many people in France and a few in England saw the possibilities of the new method. Containers were one of the obstacles to progress. Appert used glass containers and ceramic jars. It is curious that, although the "tin box" was known as early as 1810 (patented by Peter Durand) it was many years before it came into wide use in canning.

M. Raymond Chevallier-Appert, a descendant of Nicolas, brought autoclaving to the canning process in 1851 and the technology of canning, though not perfected, was well on its way toward complete industrial acceptance.

MARTIN S. PETERSON

Cross-reference: *Canning; Food Preservation.*

APPLE PROCESSING

Apples are the most versatile of all deciduous fruits. They possess a unique combination of crisp texture and pleasing flavor that makes them well suited to a wide variety of uses, both fresh and processed. Most apples are grown for the fresh market. A few varieties are grown primarily for processing and some dual-purpose varieties are well suited for both.

The apple processing industry is a natural outgrowth of the specialization and concentration of apple growing areas. The transition from farm industry to a large-scale industry is well advanced in the United States, Canada, and many European countries.

Prior to 1900, apple growing and processing in the United States was largely a farm-and-home operation. The commercial manufacture of canned slices and dried slices began about 1900. This was followed by canned applesauce in 1925, canned apple juice in 1935, and frozen slices around 1938. By 1935 about 18% of the U.S. apple crop was processed. This percentage increased to 43% by the late 1960's.

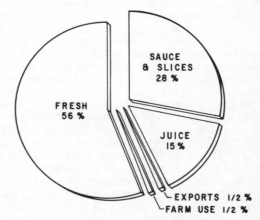

FIG. A-6. UTILIZATION OF APPLE CROP IN THE UNITED STATES, 1965–1969

Total consumption of apples and apple products in the United States is about 29 lb per capita per year. Apple consumption in Central Europe is much higher: France 135, Switzerland 112, Austria 98, and West Germany 83 lb per capita. In Europe, special cider varieties are grown exclusively for the manufacture of fresh or fermented cider. In the United States, apples are grown primarily for fresh market. The culls from the fresh market and dual-purpose varieties plus a few varieties grown for processing, constitute the raw materials for a steadily expanding processing industry.

The major apple varieties grown in the United States may be grouped into three categories according to use: (1) fresh market, 39% of total

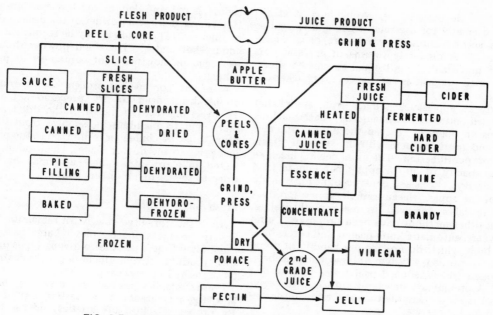

FIG. A-7. PRINCIPAL PROCESSED PRODUCTS FROM APPLES

crop: Red Delicious, Jonathan, Winesap, and Grimes Golden; (2) dual-purpose, 47%: McIntosh, Golden Delicious, Rome, Stayman, Yellow Newtown, Cortland, and Wealthy; (3) processing, 14%: York Imperial, Rhode Island Greening, Northern Spy, Baldwin, and Gravenstein.

Apple products may be divided into two broad groups: flesh products which include sauce, various slice products, and baked apples; and juice products. Flesh products are usually peeled and cored. The peels and cores may be utilized in the manufacture of various by-products. Juice products are prepared by first grinding and pressing the fruit. The press cake may be dried for use as cattle feed or for pectin manufacture.

The sale of apple products is regulated by the general provisions of the Food and Drug laws. In addition, the USDA has established grades for apples for fresh market, for apples for processing, and for various apple products as an aid in establishing quality.

Sauce and Slice Products

Apples to be used in the manufacture of sauce or slices must have good texture, a minimum of defects requiring trimming, and sufficient size to be peeled economically. The following relation of size to yield of slices shows the importance of size in the processing operation:

Size (In.)	Yield of Slices (%)
3	78
2.75	73
2.50	66
2.25	53

Size also affects the volume of fruit that can be peeled per machine per hour, and, in turn, the output of a factory and the labor cost. Apples smaller than 2.25 in. diameter are not economical to peel but may be used in juice products or apple butter. In these latter products the entire apple is used, hence size is not a factor.

The importance of size is also reflected in prices paid to growers. The following prices were paid for processing grade apples in New York State in the late 1960's: 2.75 in. diameter and up, $3.00 per cwt; 2.50-2.75 in., $2.50; 2.25-2.50 in., $1.50; and culls $0.75 per cwt.

Applesauce

Applesauce is by far the most important apple product in the United States. It surpasses apple juice by 2 to 1 and outranks canned slices in volume by nearly 9 to 1. Over 27 million cases of sauce, including some 733,000 cases of baby food applesauce, were packed in the United States in 1969. The sauce pack has nearly doubled in volume in the last 10 yr. Applesauce is manufactured chiefly for the retail trade and is used as a meat accompaniment, as a dessert, or as a cake ingredient. A moderate volume of applesauce is packed in Canada, about equal to canned slices. Only small quantities of sauce are packed in Europe.

Nearly all applesauce is made from apples that are peeled and cored mechanically. Each machine requires an operator to feed the apples, one at a time, and position them with the stem-calyx axis in the proper direction. The usual peeling machine has a capacity of 50–75 apples per minute (2–4 tons per day). Peels and cores account for roughly 30% of the apple. Because of the loss of product and the labor involved in mechanical peeling, several other methods have been proposed. In recent years, automatic knife peelers and corers have been built which do not require hand-positioning of the fruit. Also, a system of lye-peeling has been developed which reduced peel losses to less than 10%. A preliminary dewaxing with hot isopropyl alcohol vapor reduces the time and temperature required for lye-peeling.

The peeled and cored apples are trimmed by hand to remove bits of skin, bruises, and other defects. The fruit is then chopped, cooked with steam, mixed with sugar, and run through a pulper which forces the sauce through a screen with numerous small openings (0.30–0.75 in. in diameter). The pulper removes defects (peel, seeds, and carpel tissue) and produces the desired particle size or "grain." Canned applesauce is packed in hermetically sealed glass or metal containers and sterilized by heat.

A few companies in the United States and Canada presently manufacture applesauce without peeling, using the pulper and screen to eliminate the peel and seeds. Only green or yellow varieties are used. Red varieties are not suitable because of the instability of the red pigment.

Canned Sauce.—The standard applesauce pack is prepared from a blend of several varieties. This permits the use of dessert varieties, which contribute flavor, and cooking varieties to maintain texture or "grain." On the other hand, some single variety sauces have been successful.

In the middle 1950's, blends of applesauce with other fruits were introduced. Other specialty sauces have included "chunky" applesauce and a spiced applesauce. A gelled sauce has been marketed in Canada and the United States.

Frozen Sauce.—Applesauce preserved by freezing is prepared in the same manner as canned applesauce, but packed in frozen food containers and stored at $-15°C$.

Dehydrated Sauce.—Dehydrated applesauce may be prepared by several methods. The simplest procedure is to grind dehydrated low-moisture (2.5% H_2O) apple slices to a powder of the desired degree of fineness. The product may be reconstituted by adding hot water. The dried powder should be packaged in moisture tight containers to prevent caking.

A recent commercial process uses a modified double-drum drier to dry prepared applesauce. To overcome the stickiness of the dried film of sauce and to facilitate its removal from the hot drum, a jet of chilled air is directed at the product just prior to the doctor blade. The product is collected in a dry atmosphere and may be finish-dried to the desired moisture content.

Fresh Slices

Apple slices are used chiefly for remanufacture in bakery products, mostly pies. Large bakeries in the United States use the following types of apple slice product: frozen (including dehydrofrozen), 54%; fresh, 38%; and canned, 8%.

Fresh apple slices are used extensively by bakeries and large restaurants in the Eastern United States. By proper selection of varieties and use of cold storage, the season can be extended to 9–10 months. The apples are peeled, cored, trimmed, dipped in salt brine (with or without a trace of sulfite) and delivered on a daily basis.

Apple tissue contains oxidase enzymes and polyphenols which react to cause a brown discoloration when apple slices are exposed to air or when slices are frozen and thawed. Fresh slices may be protected against browning for periods up to 24 hr by dipping them in a 1–2% salt brine. Improved color and longer protection is obtained by adding 500 to 1500 ppm of sulfite to the brine. Apple slices to be frozen or dehydrated require a much more extensive treatment to prevent enzymatic browning.

Over-mature apples and some of the softer varieties tend to mush when cooked. This may be prevented by dipping or impregnating the slices with calcium salts which combine with the pectin and hemicellulose components of apple tissue to provide a firm, three-dimensional network. This treatment is used extensively to improve the texture and firmness of fresh, canned, or frozen slices.

Canned Slices

Canned apple slices are usually packed without syrup and are sufficiently processed by heat to assure preservation in hermetically sealed containers. The U.S. pack in recent years (1965–1967) has averaged nearly 4 million cases.

Canned apples are prepared from sound, firm, properly ripened fruit by peeling, coring, trimming, and slicing. Apple slices are inspected to remove defects such as pieces of peel, calyx, and carpel tissue. This requires considerable hand labor and expense. A recent innovation, called a "hydro-sorter," uses an electronic eye to detect and eliminate defective apple pieces suspended in a stream of water.

One of the special problems encountered in canning apple slices is the presence of 5–25% of air in the tissues. If this air is not removed, it will cause mushing of the slices during cooking and extensive can corrosion during storage. Steam or hot water blanching will remove intercellular gases but often causes softening of the slices and leaching of flavor and nutrients.

There are several procedures using mechanical vacuum to remove the intercellular gases from apple slices. The fruit may be submerged in a liquid or syrup while being subjected to a vacuum of 24–28 in. (Hg). When the vacuum is released the liquid tends to flow into the spaces previously occupied by the gas.

A process used by many large manufacturers in the United States consists of releasing the vacuum with steam, so that the gas spaces are filled with condensate. This effectively preheats the slices prior to filling into the cans and very little further heat processing is required. Canned slices are heat-sterilized by heating to a center can temperature of 85°C.

Pie Filling.—Apple pie filling is made by canning a mixture of apple slices, sugar, starch thickener, and citric acid. The U.S. pack in 1967 was 1.3 million cases valued at $5.8 million.

Spiced Rings.—Apples are also canned as spiced rings. They are usually colored red or green.

Canned Baked Apples.—There are two types of canned baked apples. The more common type consists of whole apples, cored but not peeled, cooked by baking, and sufficiently heat-processed to be packed in hermetically sealed containers. Spice is added during baking and the apples are packed 2–3 to a container.

The other product is canned baked slices. The apples are peeled, cored, and quartered. The pieces are usually deaerated by vacuum to reduce mushing during baking. The baked slices are packed in glass, and given a further heat processing.

Frozen Slices

Between 3 and 4% of the U.S. apple crop is used in the manufacture of frozen slices. The U.S. pack in 1969 was over 100 million pounds. The principal problem in the preparation of frozen apple slices is the prevention of enzymatic browning during storage and especially after thawing. Sufficient treatment must be provided so that the sulfite penetrates to the center of the largest pieces. A simple rapid test for penetration of sulfite consists of treating a freshly cut section of fruit with a 1% solution of catechol. Any portions of fruit still containing oxidase activity will turn black.

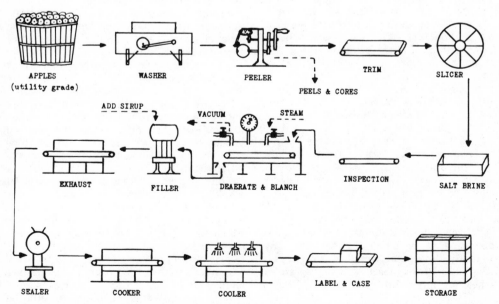

FIG. A-8. FLOW DIAGRAM OF PRODUCTION OF CANNED APPLE SLICES BY VACUUM AND STEAM PROCESS

The penetration of oxidase inhibitors is improved by removing the air from the apple slices by vacuum and then impregnating the slices with the desired solution. Some vacuum-impregnation procedures use sulfite solutions, others use sugar syrups, and others use mixtures of sugar syrup and ascorbic acid. It is claimed that sugar syrup impregnation exerts a slight firming action and improves the flavor.

Apple slices to be frozen are usually packed in metal containers holding 30 lb. The slices are packed with dry sugar or in a sugar syrup. The ratio of fruit to sugar is usually specified by the buyer. Common ratios are 5 plus 1 or 9 plus 1.

Dehydrated Apples

Nearly 4% of the U.S. apple crop is used in the production of dehydrated apple products. Dehydration involves the use of artificial heat to vaporize most of the water from apple pieces. The concentration of soluble solids (sugars, acids, etc.) is increased to the point that the fruit will resist microbial spoilage. Experience has shown that in the case of apples the moisture content must be 24% or lower. For some uses, an extremely low moisture content (2–3%) is desired.

The principal technical problem in the preparation of dehydrated apple products is the prevention of browning. This is generally accomplished by sulfiting. Dried products require more sulfite during preparation and storage than do frozen products.

The yield of dried apples will depend on the soluble solids of the original fruit and the size of apples. The average ratio of fresh to dried (24% moisture) is about 8:1. There are many types of dehydrators suitable for the primary drying stage but a vacuum dehydrator is required for the second stage.

Types of Dehydrators.—Kiln dryers and tunnel dryers are of historical interest. They were used prior to 1950 but have been replaced by more efficient dryers requiring less labor.

Belt dryers consist of long continuous belts of wire or perforated metal plates. Heated air may be drawn horizontally across the belt or directed vertically through the layer of fruit. The dryers are usually divided into stages, using hotter air in the initial stage. These dryers are efficient, easy to regulate, and widely used commercially.

The belt trough dryer is a new, efficient type of dryer operating at relatively high temperatures. The belt passes through a "trough." This stirs or rotates the bed of fruit pieces so that they are exposed to heat for only a short portion of the drying cycle.

Vacuum dryers are used to produce dehydrated apples with 3.5% or less moisture. Apple slices, previously dried to about 24% moisture, are chopped or diced in order to increase the surface area. The fruit is dried on trays in a vacuum chamber by a batch process. The product is hygroscopic and must be packaged so as to exclude moisture.

Explosion puffing is a new method of preparing dehydrated apple pieces with a porous structure. Dried apple pieces of (20–30% moisture) are placed in a closed vessel or "gun," heated to 20–30 lb pressure, and the pressure released suddenly through a quick-opening lid. The flashing of water vapor causes the apple pieces to expand to their original volume. This creates a porous structure that permits a more rapid final dehydration. Because of its porous structure it also rehydrates rapidly. Explosion-puffed apples may be ground to produce an "instant" dried apple sauce.

Dehydrated Products.—The principal dehydrated apple products are dried apples and dehydrated (low-moisture) apples. USDA grades are based on moisture content and quality as judged by flavor, odor, color, texture, uniformity of size, and freedom from defects.

Dried apples consist of slices, rings, or pieces that have been sulfured sufficiently to retain a characteristic color, and dried to a moisture content of not more than 24%.

Dehydrated (low-moisture) apples are similar but must have not more than 2.5% moisture for Grade A, and not more than 3.5% moisture for Grade B.

"Apple Chops" consist of whole apples which are sliced and dried, frequently without treatment to prevent darkening. Small fruit, unsuitable for use in products requiring peeling, may be used. Apple chops are used in preparing apple butter and other products where color and blemishes such as bruises are not a factor in quality.

Dried applesauce may be prepared by grinding "low-moisture" apples to the desired particle size or by drum drying a prepared apple sauce.

Dehydrocanned apples is a potential new product not yet in commercial production. Slices are dried to a 50% weight reduction and then canned. The savings in container, storage, and shipping costs more than offset the cost of dehydration.

Dehydrofrozen slices are prepared by a combination of two processes: drying and freezing. Apple slices are sulfited, dried to a 50% weight reduction, and then frozen without added sugar. The product may be packed in cardboard cartons, which are less expensive than the usual metal containers used for single-strength frozen slices. The frozen pieces are free-flowing, easy to handle, and rehydrate rapidly. The product has been in commercial production in the United States since 1956. It is estimated that the 1965 production was more than 20 million pounds on a rehydrated weight basis.

Apple Juice Products

On a worldwide basis, apple juice products, fresh and fermented, exceed all other apple products combined. Only in the United States do sauce and slice products exceed juices in volume of production. The apple juice pack in the United States, for the period 1965–1969 averaged about 35 million gallons per year. There are no reliable statistics on the volume of fresh cider sold per year but estimates place the volume at 20–25 million gallons.

There is considerable confusion over the terms used for apple juice products. In Europe, "cider" refers to fermented apple juice. The unfermented product is called "apple juice" or "apple must." In this section, for the sake of clarity, we will use the nomenclature commonly used in the United States. "Apple juice" refers to the product preserved by heat and packed in hermetically sealed containers. The unfermented juice from apples is called "cider" or "fresh cider." The fermented product is called "hard cider." There is one notable exception to the above nomenclature: some manufacturers sell pasteurized apple juice in the fall in 1 gal. or ½ gal. glass jugs labelled "cider." This is to take advantage of the seasonal sales appeal of "cider."

Fresh Cider.—Fresh cider is usually prepared in small-scale operations using less expensive equipment than required for the manufacture of pasteurized apple juice. In both operations the manufacturer is limited to those apple varieties available, usually the small sizes which cannot be peeled economically, second grade or surplus fruit from the fresh market, and some windfalls or drops. Blending of varieties is a common practice and provides a more uniform product throughout the season as well as permitting the use of some varieties that are unsuitable when used alone.

The apples are washed, inspected, and trimmed to remove any decay which would affect the flavor. Small cider mills have a grinder or grater mounted above the press. The ground pulp falls into a frame lined with a press cloth. A 2–3 in. layer of apple pulp is wrapped in the press cloth to form a "cheese." Successive layers of "cheeses" are separated by thin slatted wooden racks and built one on top of the other. The juice is expressed by a hydraulic press which exerts a pressure of about 75 lb psi. A pressing cycle requires 20–30 min and the yield is about 160–170 gal. of juice per ton of apples. The juice, or fresh cider, is usually allowed to settle overnight to remove the coarser suspended material.

Courtesy of M. A. Audsley, USDA

FIG. A-9. RACK AND FRAME APPLE JUICE PRESS

Fresh cider contains yeasts, molds, and bacteria which cause spoilage within 1–2 days at room temperature. There are several methods used to delay or prevent fermentation. Refrigeration at 0°–10°C retards the growth of yeasts and molds, and especially bacteria, and extends storage life to 1–2 weeks. Some fresh cider is stored in a frozen condition and thawed for use later in the year.

Until recently most apple cider was preserved by the addition of benzoate of soda. State and federal laws permit the use of amounts up to 0.1%. This will prevent spoilage for about one week at room temperature and several weeks at lower temperatures. Benzoate imparts a noticeably sharp, disagreeable after-taste to apple cider. In the past 10 yr, potassium sorbate has largely replaced benzoate as a chemical preservative for apple cider. Sorbate has little, if any, taste and is nearly as effective as benzoate. Both chemicals are very effective preservatives when used in combination with storage temperatures below 10°C.

Ultraviolet (UV) irradiation is a new procedure for preserving apple cider without affecting the flavor. A few seconds exposure to UV destroys 90–99% of the microorganisms present. Regrowth occurs at a normal rate unless a small quantity of chemical preservative is added, or the cider is stored at 10°C or below.

Fresh cider is gaining rapidly in popularity in the United States. Although most cider is sold at roadside markets, there is an increasing quantity distributed through dairies and supermarkets.

Pasteurized Apple Juice.—Large volumes of pasteurized apple juice are sold in the United States and Canada and in most European countries. Apple juice is manufactured in large installations and somewhat more care is taken to ensure uniform quality and maximum economy than in the manufacture of cider. The USDA has established Grades for Canned Apple Juice. Grade A (Fancy) apple juice shall have a soluble solids content not less than 11.5° Brix and an acid content (calculated as malic) between 0.25 and 0.70%. The requirements for Grade B are 10.5° Brix and between 0.20 and 0.80% acid. The flavor and tartness of apple juice are related to the Brix:acid ratio.

Apple juice should be prepared from sound, properly ripened fruit. The apples are washed, inspected, and trimmed prior to grinding. Hammer mills with dull or serrated blades give maximum disintegration of the tissues and high yields of juice. Until recently, the rack and frame press was commonly used for the manufacture of apple juice. Today it has been largely replaced by semi-automatic presses or continuous presses, with a saving in labor and improved sanitation.

The Willmes press is widely used in the United States and Canada. It consists of a large horizontal cylinder with heavy perforated walls, which may be lined with press cloths. In the center of the cylinder is a heavy rubber innertube. Ground apple pulp is

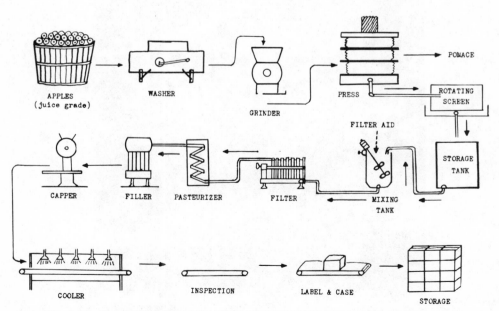

FIG. A-10. FLOW DIAGRAM FOR PRODUCTION OF PASTEURIZED APPLE JUICE

loaded into the cylinder, the doors are closed and the innertube is inflated using pressures up to 80 lb psi. Although it is a batch process, it requires a minimum of labor and produces excellent yields of juice.

There are several types of continuous presses. One type uses a mechanical screw to force the apple pulp against a pressure plate. Another type uses a long, continuous cloth belt which is·folded and pressed between a series of converging rolls. A third type uses a large basket centrifuge followed by a vertical screw press.

Freshly pressed juice contains a large amount of colloidal material and coarse suspended solids. The suspended solids may be removed by filtration or centrifugation to yield a "cloudy" apple juice. Approximately 25% of the apple juice produced in the United States is "cloudy" and the rest is "clarified."

Historically, the earliest processes for clarifying apple juice used heat clarification, gelatin-tannin precipitation, or treatment with bentonite. These procedures were slow, inefficient, and unreliable. Today most apple juice is clarified by using pectolytic enzymes. The juice is then filtered and sterilized by heating to approximately 85°C for 15–30 sec. The hot juice is filled into either metal or glass containers, sealed, cooled, and labelled.

Other Juices and Blends.—Natural apple juice is prepared by adding sufficient ascorbic acid (vitamin C) to the apples at the time of grinding to prevent oxidation. The juice is strained, not filtered, and retains the flavor of fresh apples even after heat sterilization. This juice is very popular in Canada but has not sold well in the United States.

Crushed-apple juice is a pulpy juice containing 3–10% of finely ground, suspended apple pulp. Special grinding mills pulverize the apple and force the juice through a screen with 1600–3600 holes per square inch. The juice is then deaerated, homogenized, and heat sterilized.

Blends of apple juice with other fruit juices such as cherry, grape, cranberry, and raspberry have been marketed in small to moderate volumes. The proportion of apple juice in the blend is usually 60–85%. Apple juice "drinks" are similar to blends but contain such added ingredients as sugar, acid, coloring, and water. There are no standards at present for such products.

Syrups, Concentrates, and Essence

The manufacture of apple sauce and slice products results in large quantities of peels and cores— approximately 30% of the fruit. It is estimated that the juice from grinding and pressing this volume of material would be equivalent to 40 million gallons per year in the United States. This juice is not suitable for sale as apple cider or canned juice but is used in the manufacture of vinegar and various concentrates and syrups. Concentrates for beverage use are prepared from juice grade whole apples.

Boiled cider was one of the first apple products prepared on the farm. Small quantities are still made for use in home-made apple butter. It is made by boiling cider at atmospheric pressure until it reaches a syrupy consistency. It has a dark brown color and a caramelized flavor.

Apple concentrate: Prior to concentration, the apple juice is depectinized by pectolytic enzymes. If this is not done, gelation would result. Water is removed by vacuum evaporators at a temperature below 60°C to prevent heat damage to the product. Apple concentrate (68°–72° Brix) is an item of international trade. It is used in the manufacture of jellies and apple butter.

Apple essence: In the manufacture of apple concentrate the aroma, characteristic of fresh apple juice, is volatilized during the early stages of evaporation. A commercial process, developed in 1944, retains the volatile constituents and concentrates them by fractional distillation. The usual product is a 150-fold "essence." It is used to fortify the flavor of apple jellies and "full-flavored" apple juice concentrates.

Apple syrup for table use is commonly prepared by concentrating apple juice to 20°–30° Brix and then adding sugar to the desired concentration, usually 65° Brix.

Full-flavored concentrates for beverage use are prepared by concentrating apple juice and adding back apple essence. They are marketed either as a 4:1 frozen concentrate or a 7:1 heat-sterilized, canned product.

Semiconcentrates: In Switzerland and other European countries in recent years a process has been developed for the bulk storage of 4-fold apple juice concentrate. The product is stored at 0°C in large metal tanks under carbon dioxide. It is used for the remanufacture of single-strength apple juice.

Apple juice powder is an experimental product which reconstitutes with water to give a full-flavored apple juice. A 60°–80° Brix concentrate is dehydrated on a thin-film cone to a moisture content of 1–4%. The hot molten mass is mixed with a highly concentrated apple essence (700- to 1000-fold), chilled on cooling rolls, ground, and packaged with a desiccant.

Fermented Juice Products

In Europe, large quantities of apples are used in the production of fermented beverages. Products such as hard cider, wine, and brandy are common throughout Europe but are relatively unimportant in the United States. On the other hand, large quantities of cider vinegar are produced in the United States and Canada, yet this product is scarcely known in Europe.

Terminology: The confusion over the meaning of the term "cider" was mentioned in the section on apple juice products. Common usage in the United States and Canada refers to cider as the fresh, unfermented juice from apples. The product of normal alcoholic fermentation, containing between 0.5 and 8.0% alcohol by volume, is called "hard cider" or "fermented cider."

Fermented Cider.—Fermented apple juice products are prepared from apples that are washed, sorted, ground, and pressed in the same manner as outlined for apple juice products. Fermentation may be accomplished by naturally occurring yeasts or by adding a desirable strain of yeast. During fermentation, the yeast converts sugars to alcohol and carbon dioxide.

$$C_6 H_{12} O_6 \xrightarrow{\text{yeast}} 2 C_2 H_5 OH + 2 CO_2$$

$$\underset{(180)}{\text{sugar}} \qquad \underset{(92)}{\text{ethyl alcohol}} \quad \underset{(88)}{\text{carbon dioxide}}$$

Theoretically, 180 gm of a hexose sugar would be converted to 92 gm of alcohol and 88 gm of CO_2. These yields are never achieved in practice because the yeast utilizes some of the sugar and alcohol for growth and energy.

Dry (hard) cider: Fully fermented apple juice with little or no residual sugar is called a "dry" or "hard" cider. Sugar may be added before fermentation to raise the alcohol content of the final product to 6–7%. The product may be heat-sterilized by heating to $65°C$.

Sparkling cider: This product is produced by allowing fermentation to proceed to about 3.5% alcohol. An effervescence is produced by allowing a portion of the carbon dioxide to be retained in the finished product.

Carbonated cider: This term is applied to any fermented apple cider that has been charged with commercial carbon dioxide to produce effervescence.

Champagne type cider: Champagne type cider is produced in a manner similar to that employed in preparing champagne. Effervescence is produced in the final product by a secondary fermentation of the dry cider after it is bottled.

Apple Wine.—Apple wine is the most common fermented apple beverage in the United States and Canada. The annual production in the United States for 1970 was about 770,000 gal. Apple wine is less common in Europe where the principal alcoholic beverages from apples are hard cider and brandy.

Apple wine is a fermented product containing 8% or more of alcohol. Natural apple juice when fully fermented usually contains less than 7% alcohol, since about 2% sugar is required in the juice for each 1% of alcohol produced. Therefore, in the manufacture of apple wine, it is necessary to add more sugar. The highest alcohol content reached by natural fermentation is approximately 13%. Wines of higher alcohol content require fortification.

Apple wine is aged in tanks or casks, preferably of oak, for 2–3 months. This eliminates the yeasty taste and produces a mellow flavor and aroma. It is then filtered and pasteurized at $65°C$.

For purposes of taxation, the United States Government recognizes 3 classes of wines based on their alcohol content: (1) 8–14% alcohol, by volume, produced by natural fermentation in the presence of adequate sugar; (2) 14–21% alcohol, fortified by adding apple brandy; and (3) 21–24% alcohol, also by fortification. Apple wines are further classified on the basis of their sugar content as sweet, semisweet, or dry (low in sugar). Effervescent apple wines, in which the carbon dioxide charge is produced either by natural fermentation or by artificial carbonation, constitute additional types which are subject to special tax rates.

Apple Brandy.—The term "apple brandy" is derived from "burnt wine." Actually, it is a distillation product of fermented apple juice or hard cider. Apple brandy is also known in the United States as "Applejack" and in Europe as "Calvados."

France, the principal apple brandy producing country in Europe, produced 7 million gallons (100% alcohol equivalent) annually in the late 1930s, but in recent years the production has been only 2 million gallons per year. The United States produced nearly 1.4 million gallons of apple brandy in 1945 but in 1970 the production was only 430,000 gallons.

Beverage brandies contain 55–65% alcohol. They are preferably aged in oak casks until suitably mellowed. High proof brandy, rectified to as high as 95% alcohol ($190°$ proof), is commonly used to fortify wines.

Industrial alcohol: Sporadic attempts have been made to produce alcohol from apples for industrial purposes. On a commercial basis about 80% of the total sugar equivalent of apples is converted to alcohol. Thus, a ton of apples (11% sugar) would yield about 12.8 gal. of 100% alcohol. The cost of raw materials and cost of production would not make this an economical source of industrial alcohol.

Cider Vinegar.—Vinegar (sour wine) is a self-preserving product resulting from the oxidation of alcohol to acetic acid by Acetobacter fermentation.

Approximately 30 million gallons of cider vinegar is manufactured in the United States per year. Cider vinegar is widely used in North America as a flavoring and preserving agent. In Europe, vinegar is prepared from a wide variety of materials, including apples, other fruits, and cereal grains.

The conversion of alcohol to acetic acid by Acetobacter may be represented by the following equation:

$$CH_3CH_2OH + O_2 \xrightarrow{Acetobacter}$$

$$\underset{(46)}{alcohol} \quad \underset{(32)}{oxygen}$$

$$CH_3COOH + H_2O$$

$$\underset{(60)}{acetic\ acid} \quad \underset{(18)}{water}$$

Theoretically, 46 gm of alcohol yields 60 gm of acetic acid. Large quantities of oxygen are required and provision must be made to remove the heat produced by fermentation, which is equivalent to 2550 gm calories per gram (4600 BTUs per lb) of alcohol.

History of vinegar production: vinegar-making is a very old art. The oldest method consisted of exposing fermented fruit juice in open vats to the action of airborne vinegar bacteria. The method is called the "Orleans process," after Orleans, France. A slime of bacteria, called "mother of vinegar," converts the alcohol to acetic acid. The process is slow and the efficiency is around 50%.

In 1824, a German chemist named Schutzenbach developed a process of trickling vinegar stock over wood shavings supported in an upright tank or generator. The increased surface speeded up acetification and gave conversion efficiencies of 60–80%. This method with some improvements was used until the late 1940s.

Today, most vinegar is manufactured by submerged culture methods, similar to procedures developed during World War II for the production of antibiotics. The Frings Acetator was developed in Germany in 1955. It consists of a 2000 gal. stainless steel tank equipped with a rotor to pump finely dispersed air through the liquid. Cooling coils maintain the temperature at 30°C. The efficiency of this method is 95–98%.

Preparation of vinegar: Cider vinegar is usually prepared from cull and surplus apples and from the peels and cores of apples used for sauce and slice products. The pressings, containing approximately 11% sugars, are stored several months in large tanks to allow the sugar to ferment to alcohol. The fermented mash, or vinegar stock, is placed in the generator tank together with a culture of Acetobacter from the previous batch. The operation requires about 24 hr per batch. This system can be operated on a continuous automatic basis by the careful adjustment of incoming alcoholic mash and outflow of vinegar. The fermentation is allowed to proceed until the alcohol content falls to 0.2–0.3%.

After acetification, vinegar is aged to develop flavor and to assist in clarification. The vinegar is filtered in the same manner as used for apple juice. Some cider vinegar is delivered in bulk without pasteurization, but most of it is pasteurized at 65°C and bottled.

Cider vinegar usually contains 4–5% acetic acid. The concentration is often expressed as grains, in which case 10 grains is equivalent to 1%. Thus a 40-grain vinegar would contain 4% acetic acid.

Apple Jelly, Butter, and Other Confections

The home preparation of fruit jellies, jams, and butters was the forerunner of the giant modern preserving industry in the United States which produces over 800 million pounds of these items per year. Although there are no accurate data on the quantities of items prepared from apples, it is estimated that the 1967 production of apple and apple-base jellies was about 100 million pounds and apple butter was about 30 million pounds.

Apple Jelly.—Three substances are essential to the preparation of a fruit jelly: pectin, acid, and sugar. Sufficient pectin is added to give a jelly of the desired texture. Acid is necessary to aid in the formation of a hydrogen-bonded, three-dimensional network of sugar and pectin. The usual sugar concentration for jellies and preserves is 65% or higher. This concentration is necessary for gel formation and is sufficient to make the product self-preserving under normal conditions. The FDA has developed Standards of Identity for various food products including fruit jellies, jams, preserves, and butters.

Jellies differ from jams and preserves in that they are clear, free of insoluble solids, and have a definite gel structure rather than a semisolid consistency. By definition, apple jelly contains not less than 45 parts by weight of apple juice (or equivalent amount of concentrate) to each 55 parts of sugar. Apple-base jellies are made from a mixture of apple and other fruit juices. They usually contain 80% apple and 20% of the minor, more expensive fruit.

In commercial practice apple jelly is prepared from concentrate rather than single-strength apple juice. Calculated quantities of concentrate, sugar, pectin, and citric acid are heated in a vacuum pan to remove sufficient water to achieve a soluble solids content of at least 65%. The jelly is hot filled at 85°C into glasses, cooled, allowed to set, and then packaged.

Apple Butter.—Apple butter is a smooth, semi-solid mixture of apple pulp and sugar. Apple juice (or concentrate) may be added to provide more apple flavor. The soluble solids requirement is only 43%. Apple butter is usually prepared by cooking 5 parts apple pulp and 2 parts dry sugar, or 2 parts apple pulp and 1 part apple juice. The mixture is cooked several hours to develop a brown color and a caramelized flavor.

Other Confections.—Candied apples are prepared by impregnating pieces of apple with sugar syrup and then drying and glacéing to overcome stickiness.

Apple candies are specialty confections and their method of preparation depends on the ingenuity of the individual candy maker.

Pomace and Pectin

Apple Pomace.—Apple pomace consists of the press cake resulting from pressing apples for juice. The principal uses for apple pomace are (a) as feed for livestock, and (b) for manufacture of pectin.

Fresh apple pomace has about 75% of the feeding value of corn (maize) silage when fed to dairy cattle. Preservation by fermentation to produce ensilage is a common procedure when the pomace is to be used as a stock feed.

Apple pomace is often dried and mixed with other feeds. In recent years dried apple pomace has been little used for stock feed in the United States because of the restrictions on spray residues.

Apple Pectin.—Commercial pectin manufacture began in Germany and Italy around 1908, with dried apple pomace as a source of material. Pectin production in the United States reached a peak during World War II when large quantities were exported to Europe. During 1943–1946, over 6 million pounds of pectin were produced annually in the United States. About 30% of this quantity was derived from apples. In 1967 only 10% of the U.S. production was from apple and the remainder was from citrus.

Pectin is extracted from dried apple pomace by mild acid hydrolysis. A mixture of pomace, water, and sufficient acid to give a pH of 3.0 is heated to 90°C for 1 hr. The extract is removed by pressing, then clarified and filtered. Pectin is sold either as a liquid concentrate or as a dried powder.

Pectin is marketed on the basis of "grade," which is defined as the number of units (grams or pounds) of sugar that can be made into a 65% sugar jelly of standard firmness by one unit (grams or pounds) of pectin. Dried apple pectin may vary from 150 to 180 grade but is usually standardized at 100 grade by diluting with sugar.

CLAUDE H. HILLS
W. O. HARRINGTON

References

DALRYMPLE, D. G., and FEUSTEL, I. C. 1964. Recent Developments in the Production and Marketing of Apple Juice and Cider. U.S. Dept. Agri. Fed. Ext. Serv., Washington, D.C.

DALRYMPLE, D. G., and FEUSTEL, I. C. 1965. Recent Developments in the Production and Marketing of Apple Sauce and Slices. U.S. Department of Agriculture Federal Ext. Service, Washington, D.C.

JUDGE, E. E. (Editor and Publisher) 1971. The Almanac of the Canning, Freezing, Preserving Industries, 56th Edition. Westminster, Maryland.

ROBINSON, J. F. et al. 1971. Making and preserving apple cider. U.S. Dept. Agri. Farmers' Bull. 2125 (revised).

SMOCK, R. M., and NEUBERT, A. M. 1950. Apples and Apple Products. Interscience Publishers, New York.

Cross-reference: *Dried Fruit; Pectin; Vinegar.*

APRICOTS AND APRICOT PROCESSING

Three species of plum genus *Prunus* are known as apricots. They are: *P. armeniaca*, the common apricot, *P. mume*, the Japanese apricot, and *P. dasycarpa*, the black apricot. The apricot-plum, *P. simonii*, is more closely allied to the plums and is usually classified as a plum.

The apricot is an intermediate between the peach and the plum. The three fruits may be readily intergrafted, and the apricot and plum have been hybridized, the hybrid being called the plumcot, while a supposed hybrid between the peach and apricot is called the peach-apricot.

The common apricot grows spontaneously over a wide area in western and central Asia and as far eastward as Peking, China. Alexander the Great is said to have brought the apricot from Asia to Greece. From there, it was carried to Italy, being first mentioned as a Roman fruit by Pliny in the time of Christ. From Italy, its culture spread slowly northward in Europe, reaching England about the middle of the 14th Century. There seems to be no mention of the apricot in North America until 1720, when it was said to be growing in the mission orchards of California. However, commercial plantations were not started in California until the latter half of the 19th Century. The Blenheim apricot is grown extensively in counties near San Francisco Bay. It is the most sought after for canning purposes. The Tilton, also an important variety for canning, although not as desirable as the Blenheim, is grown in the hot interior valleys of California.

Because of the early harvest maturity and desirable fresh shipping characteristics, the Royal is also grown in the interior valleys. Some plant breeders claim that the Royal and Blenheim are identical and that differences that exist are due to differences in cultural practice and climatic conditions.

At one time, the Moorpark and the Hemskirk had limited plantings in California. These were grown for size and were desirable for fresh shipment and dehydration. They are no longer of commercial significance, however.

The Russian apricot is a strain of the common apricot, although it is thought by some to be a distinct species to which the name *P. sibirica* has been given. This strain differs from the common type of apricot in having a narrower and darker-colored fruit, and in bearing smaller fruits of relatively poor quality. However, the trees are supposed to be hardier. This race was introduced into the Middle West of the United States by the Russian Mennonites soon after the middle of the last century.

The Japanese apricot (*P. mume*, Sieb. & Zucc.) is grown at times as an ornamental. The Japanese grow many varieties, gathering the fruits while green for pickling in a salt solution. Pickled apricots are a common relish used with the morning rice bowl. Two or three varieties are cultivated in the United States for their small yellow fruits, which are so poor in quality, however, that they have little commercial value.

The black apricot (*P. dasycarpa* L.) is cultivated in Manchuria, Kashmir, Afghanistan, and Beluchistan. The tree has long been cultivated in Europe and the United States, but the fruit is small, unattractive in color, and poor in quality. The species is grown only in horticultural collections. In tree and fruit, the black apricot shows close relationship to the plum, its fruits being easily mistaken for dark-colored, round plums. The tree is rather hardier than that of the peach. There are no named varieties.

In the United States, the common apricot (*P. armeniaca* L.) is cultivated mainly in California, and in a few favored areas in the Rocky Mountains and westward. Farther east, apricot-growing is an uncertain venture. The crop is too susceptible to cold weather and frequently is destroyed by spring frosts.

The curulio-beetle also takes too great a toll in the east, unless it is combated by rather expensive treatments.

California leads the world in commercial apricot-growing. The fruits are well suited for canning as well as for drying. The California apricot industry is based on more than three million trees.

Utilization Patterns

In the Mediterranean countries a portion of the annual production was for many years processed into a product called "apricot leather" or "apricot cheese." This product was made from ripe apricot pulp dried on smooth boards in the sun. The strips were rolled up and stored for future distribution. This practice persists in the Middle East today in the making of apricot sheets (qumarddean).

Drying the apricots is, of course, one means of widening and extending the market. The apricot has a very short harvest period of 10–12 days. The ripe apricot, one of our most desirable dessert fruits, has a very full flavor but does not withstand handling and shipment.

Marketing practices for apricots today follow the ancient pattern of the Middle East. A large proportion of our annual crop of apricots is processed even though modern methods of controlling postharvest deterioration have extended the shelf-life of the fresh fruit.

While the United States is the largest single producer of apricots (Table A-19), Europe as a continent produces 52% of the world's supply of apricots; Spain, France, Hungary, Turkey and Italy being the principal producers.

TABLE A-19

WORLDWIDE APRICOT PRODUCTION

	1963	1964	1965
	(Production in 1000 Short Tons)		
Country			
United States	201	224	227
Spain	119	131	214
France	180	40	123
Hungary	115	108	76
Turkey	84	112	97
Italy	66	72	78
Australia	39	47	51
Bulgaria	52	31	25
Iran	22	39	44
S. Africa	29	40	32
Romania	33	44	23
Continent			
Europe	703	545	624
North America	203	234	227
Latin America	26	25	26
Near East	158	215	184
Africa	80	87	93
Oceania	45	52	57
World Total	1216	1158	1211

SOURCE: FAO Production Yearbook, Vol. 20, 1966, Table 54.

TABLE A-20

APRICOT PRODUCTION IN THE UNITED STATES AND CALIFORNIA (1909–1965)

	Total Tons[1]		% Dried		% Canned		% Fresh		% Frozen	
	U.S.	Calif.	U.S.	Calif.	U.S.	Calif.	U.S.	Calif.	U.S.	Calif.
1909	[2]	100,700	[2]	76.5	[2]	15.3	[2]	8.2	0.0	0.0
1913		82,700		69.9		21.2		8.9	0.0	0.0
1917		137,700		61.9		30.2		7.9	0.0	0.0
1921		95,600		69.0		21.0		9.9	0.0	0.0
1925		147,400		67.2		25.5		7.3	0.0	0.0
1929	218,015	210,100	55.8	57.9	34.1	34.8	10.1	7.3	0.0	0.0
1933	268,810	266,100	76.6	77.4	16.4	16.5	7.0	6.1	0.0	0.0
1937	321,870	309,300	58.7	61.1	32.0	32.7	9.2	6.2	0.0	0.0
1941	211,110	196,300	51.3	55.2	35.9	36.8	12.6	8.0	0.1	0.0
1945	187,850	157,300	22.8	27.3	36.1	40.9	23.7	15.0	17.4	16.8
1949	180,500	158,300	43.4	49.5	34.5	37.7	21.8	12.6	0.2	0.2
1953	240,840	228,300	36.6	38.6	50.8	52.7	11.7	7.8	0.8	0.9
1957	182,070	167,000	23.2	25.3	62.4	65.3	12.8	7.7	1.6	1.7
1961	170,690	158,500	19.0	20.5	66.9	71.1	10.9	5.2	3.1	3.3
1965	210,755	204,500	14.6	15.1	74.0	76.3	7.1	4.3	4.3	4.4

SOURCE: USDA and State of California.

[1] Farm disposition (total sold).
[2] Early U.S. statistics not available.

In the United States, most of the apricots are produced in California. The crop is largely marketed as a processed product—either canned, dried, or frozen—with only a very small proportion shipped fresh. With the development of canning and technology, an ever-increasing proportion of annual production has been marketed as a canned product, and smaller percentages have been dried (Table A-20). In 1909, 76% of the apricots in California were dried and 15% were canned; today those proportions are reversed. During this same period, fresh shipments remained static and have even declined since 1950. Since the introduction of frozen apricots, in 1940, there has been a small but steady increase in the freezing of apricots for confections and the baking trade.

Canning

Apricots have been canned commercially in California since before the turn of the century. More recently, some apricots have been canned in other states, but the quantity is small when compared with California production figures (Table A-20).

Apricots may be canned as unpeeled halves, or as whole peeled, or whole unpeeled. Since World War II there has also been a significant development of apricot nectar, fruit juice drinks made with apricots, blended juices of apricots and other fruits, apricot purée, and apricot concentrate.

Blenheim and Tilton apricots are used in canning. Other varieties do not have flavor, color, and tex-

ture characteristics for a satisfactory canned product with present processing methods. Firm, mature apricots are harvested for canning. The fruit is sorted for maturity by color, and the defective apricots are removed.

The fruit may be sized as whole fruit or sized after pitting. If the apricots are sized whole, they are usually sized on a divergent type of belt grader; the fruit is carried on two belts that gradually diverge, dropping smaller fruit first and then progressively larger fruit as the belts move farther apart.

Apricots are still sometimes hand-pitted, but most are halved and the pits removed by automatic or semiautomatic pitting machines. The fruit is rinsed with chlorinated water sprays after the halving and pitting operation.

If sizing is done after pitting, the fruit is graded on a shaker-type screen grader fitted with a progression of screens, the first of which has larger openings which pass all of the smaller fruit and retain only the very large fruit. The second screen is fitted with slightly smaller holes to remove the next-largest fruit, etc. Such a shaker-type grader may have from 3 to as many as 7 steps, depending on the wishes and desires of the processor and the demands of the trade. Apricot sizes are based on count per pound, in which a 10 count (10 apricots to the pound) is large fruit and a 20 count (20 apricots per pound) is small fruit.

Fruit processors, particularly canners, may refer to a count per can, which would mean the number of halves in a particular size of can. Apricot contracts which specify size as a factor of quality may pay a premium for large fruit.

The halved, pitted apricots may be sorted a second time for maturity and/or defects and then filled into cans. Normally, 19½ oz of halved, pitted apricots are filled into a No. 2½ can (401 × 411). The percentage of retention is determined by the relation of fill weight of fresh apricot halves to the drained weight after canning. The drained weight of apricots is an important factor since it must conform to USDA grades, federal specifications, and the requirements for fill of container. The percentage retention of apricots may be influenced by many factors, including growing area, storage time, sugar concentration, and ripeness level. The percentage retention 60 days after canning may range from 90 to 97%.

Immediately after 19½ oz of apricot halves are filled into a No. 2½ can, an aliquot of 10½ oz of syrup is added. The syrup added for choice fruit is made of sucrose sugar and water, or it may be made from a combination of water, sucrose, and corn syrup. The concentration of this syrup is normally 40°–50° Brix or even higher.

Consumers associate apricot flavor intensity with sweetness, and acceptance is directly related to the ratio of soluble solids to total acid in the canned product.

After filling and syruping, air may be removed from the can by exhausting in an exhaust box or in a steam-flow closing machine. In a conventional exhaust box the canned apricots are usually exhausted to a center can temperature of 175°F and then closed.

The exhaust box is being rapidly replaced by the vacuum syruper and the steam-flow closing machine, which removes air and at the same time controls head space efficiently. In this procedure the air is removed from the can by vacuum and the syrup is then filled into the can to an exact head space. This vacuum-syruped can is then transferred to a steam-flow closer, where the air in the head space of the can is replaced with steam immediately prior to lid placement and seaming. This combined system is more efficient than conventional syruping, exhausting, and closing.

Canned apricots are sterilized commercially in an atmospheric rotary agitating cooker operating at 210°–212°F. Canned apricots are normally cooked to a center can temperature of 195°F, depending on the pH of the final product and the textural qualities desired by the manufacturer. This would mean that canned apricots in a No. 2½ can (401 × 411) would be cooked from 8 to possibly 22 min in an atmospheric rotary agitating cooker. The amount of heat treatment is, first, to acquire commercial sterilization, and, second, to acquire quality in terms of both texture and color. Overcooking may soften the fruit too much; so care and experience must be exercised to combine the factors which influence cooking time: maturity, variety, growing area, syrup composition and concentration, fill weight, speed of agitation, and sterilization temperature.

The canned apricots are cooled in an atmospheric rotary agitating cooler in which chlorinated water is used as a cooling medium. Cooling is usually continued to acquire a center can temperature of 110°F. This is sufficient to dry off any excess water on the outside of the can, and yet cool enough not to harm the textural qualities of the fruit.

Textural Properties.—As indicated, the texture of canned apricots is influenced by many factors, including conditions of sterilization and cooking, maturity of the fresh apricot, and storage period of the canned apricots.

Normal softening of canned apricots can be explained, at least in part, by the conversion of protopectins to water-soluble pectins. This occurs enzymatically during ripening. The methoxyl content of the pectin in the fruit gradually decreases as ripening proceeds. During canning, pectic materials gradually move from cell wall into the syrup, causing a gradual softening of texture.

An unusual softening of canned apricots has been observed in recent years. In some cases, fruit tissue may break down completely, yielding an apricot purée instead of a canned apricot. This product, of course, is unacceptable to the trade. One of the factors related to this unusual textural breakdown was a higher acidity and a low pH of the fresh fruit. The higher concentration of hydrogen ions present in the higher-acid fruit may accelerate breakdown of the binding materials between cell walls during heat processing.

Apricots for canning normally have a pH value of 3.6–4.0 and a total acidity of 0.8–1.3 when calculated as citric acid. In certain instances and growing areas, however, apricots have a pH value as low as 3.4 or as high as 4.6.

Other Canned Products.—Successful procedures for the canning of apricot purée and whole apricots were developed as early as 1929 (Marsh and Cruess 1932). Later a process for steam inactivation of the enzymes of whole apricots was introduced (Shallah and Creuss, 1934). The pits were removed with a brush finisher. Apricot nectar and apricot blends have been a popular beverage since that time.

These two original contributions had a marked effect on the development of the canned apricot industry, and these products have taken an important place in the industry.

Subsequent work on the flavor of fruit nectars indicated the nature of the relations between fruit flavors, sweetness, and acidity. There is a level at which added sucrose ceased to enhance flavor and the relation between sweetness and flavor is influenced by acidity. The desirable flavor of apricot nectar, however, is enhanced even further when certain organic acids are added to the sweetened nectar. The most desirable ratio of soluble solids to total acid for apricot nectar is 30.

The canned pickled apricot, as it was first called, led to the use of whole apricots in a 40° Brix spiced syrup, closed and cooked in a rotary atmospheric cooker.

Dehydrated

Dehydration is one of the cheapest, simplest, most effective methods of food preservation. Moisture becomes the limiting factor in preventing microbial and deteriorative changes. Dehydrated foods have an added advantage in that final shipping weight is only a fraction of that of the fresh product (drying ratio approximately 5:1). In proper air-tight, insect-proof packages stored at cool temperatures (50°–60°F), dried apricots can be stored safely for long periods. Antioxidants such as sulfur dioxide extend the shelf-life considerably.

The quality of dried apricots, sun-dried or dehydrated, depends on many factors, first of which is the quality of the fresh fruit. The apricots when harvested must be fully mature. Immature fruits do not produce a quality product but are rather pale in color and lack flavor. Overmature fruit, on the other hand, tends to produce slabs (flat pieces), which have a low market value.

Apricots are given a series of pretreatments before sun drying or dehydrating. The fruit is first washed, and with whole fruit the pit may be removed; whereas, cut fruit is cut in half to remove the pit. With apricot leather, the whole fruit is washed and the enzymes inactivated by a steam blanch, after which the pits are removed by a brush finisher using a $1/8$–$1/4$ in. stainless steel screen. The macerate is then finished to remove coarse fiber material. This finished apricot purée is then evaporated in a thin-film evaporator, after which it is formed into sheets or a thin wide belt for dehydration.

Whole dried apricots or cut fruit must also be submitted to enzyme inactivation to achieve quality and storage stability. Apricot halves are sulfured or sometimes blanched and then sulfured. Steam blanching of cut fruits alone may be adequate as well as boiling sugar solutions. This was developed into a dehydration procedure in testing steam blanch prior to sulfuring.

The industry was in this way able to produce a dried apricot that was higher in nutritional value, free from dry-yard contamination (dirt, insects, etc.) and yet had the translucent appearance of the sun-dried product; in other words, a superior product and the drying time was reduced as much as 20–50%. Such dehydration required the extra step of blanching, otherwise the final apricot was opaque rather than translucent.

Ascorbic acid retention is higher in dehydrated than in sun-dried apricots.

The most practical way of retarding enzymatic degradation of dried apricots is to expose the apricot halves to the fumes of burning sulfur.

As apricots of optimum maturity are cut and the pits removed, the halves are placed on a wooden tray, pit cavity up. These wooden trays usually 3 by 6 ft, are made of $1/4$-in. or $3/8$-in. pine boards with 2-in. sides. They hold approximately 35 lb of cut fruit, depending on fruit size.

These trays are normally stacked 24–28 trays high with longitudinal staggering to permit the circulation of gases (SO_2) during sulfuring, and dry air during dehydration.

The sulfur house is a tight box large enough to hold 1 or perhaps 3 stacks of trays of cut fruit. These stacks of trays of cut fruit are normally called "cars" of fruit. Since the sulfur house should be air-tight, venting must be arranged to allow proper combustion of the sulfur (Phaff and Mrak 1948).

The sulfur is burned in a pan 10–12 in. in diameter with 3-in. sides. A 4–5 lb charge of sulfur for each car (stack of 26 trays, equivalent to 1000 lb of cut fruit) is sufficient. Sulfur should be high-grade refined sulfur leaving only 2–3 oz of residue in a clean burning pan after combustion is complete. Burning sulfur under these conditions in a tight house will usually create about a 2% concentration of SO_2 gas.

Sulfuring at a high temperature (120°F) for 180–200 min causes the apricots to absorb less sulfur dioxide but to retain more of the sulfur after drying. Sulfur dioxide absorption increases with the concentration of SO_2 in the compartment, but not in direct proportion. Retention of sulfur dioxide in the dried product is not markedly or consistently increased when the SO_2 concentration is increased during sulfuring. High temperatures, along with high SO_2 concentrations during sulfuring tend to cause the apricots to become mushy or to bleed badly.

Blanching: In a continuous blancher the tray

of cut fruit are carried through a blanching box on a conveyor. The temperature treatment and the time are uniform for each tray if the steam in the chamber is distributed properly and control is adequate. In a continuous blancher, good performance will be achieved if the temperature is above 200°F within the first $1/4$ of the length of the blanching box.

With cabinet blanchers, a car of trays, staggered in a longitudinal fashion, will take 1 min to acquire a temperature of 200°F and 3 min more to blanch the fruit. In a cabinet blancher, some consideration must be given to the efficiency of bringing the temperature to 200°F and also of removing this temperature after blanching is complete. For this reason, a 3-min blanching time needs to be altered somewhat to allow for a come-up time and to allow at the close of the blanching period for removal of the car. A troublesome feature of cabinet blanchers is steam condensation dripping from tray to tray.

Sun Drying.—In practice, most growers sulfur apricots 2–4 hr in a tight sulfur box using a sulfur charge of 4–5 lb for each car containing 1000 lb of cut apricots. In a farmer-grower yard the cut fruit is quite frequently put on trays, which would then be stacked, using longitudinal staggering, and held until the evening, at which time the cars are placed in the sulfur house to start the sulfuring operation. When the cars are left all night, the sulfur will burn out in 2 hr, at which time the SO₂ content in the sulfur house will decrease. With this decrease the absorbed sulfur in the apricots may also start to decrease. In addition, exposure to this excessive heat in most sulfur houses will cause the apricots to "bleed."

Whole apricots take about twice as long (4–6 hr) as the halves (3 hr) to absorb the SO_2. As a rule, apricots treated in this fashion should have 3000–5000 ppm of SO_2 after sulfuring. When these apricots are dehydrated for export, steps should be taken to be certain that excessive amounts of SO_2 are avoided, for certain foreign governments regulate the permissible residual amount of sulfur dioxide in the dried product.

Soon after sulfuring, or blanching and sulfuring, or simple blanching, the trays of apricots should be placed in the dry-yard. The trays should be arranged as to receive maximum exposure to the sun and minimum contamination from dirt, insects, etc.

It is desirable to spread the fruit as soon as possible after the enzyme inactivation (sulfuring) in order to dry the pit cavity. This is necessary, for cut, sulfured, or blanched apricots often bleed. This liquid contains soluble solids, organic acids, and flavoring compounds of the apricot and should not be lost. Then, too, the bleeding will create a

liquid in the pit cavity of the fruit which is easily spilled onto the trays. This spillage not only soils the tray but causes the dehydrated apricots to stick to the tray. This results in a loss in yield and a poor drying ratio.

When the apricots are at the desired moisture content (15–20%), the sun drying is complete. The apricots may be variable in moisture content from tray to tray and even within trays. This depends on the sugar content of the fruit, the position of the trays in the dry-yard, etc. Over-drying is costly, for the weight of apricots is reduced. On the other hand, the drying of apricots to the moisture content proper for future packaging has an influence on the storage stability of the finished product.

After sun drying, the apricots are removed from the trays by shaking, agitation, and scraping with a broad knife similar to a putty knife. They are then placed in large wooden tubs to cure or "sweat." In this process the moisture content equalizes by transmission of moisture, and to some extent by evaporation. After the curing period (2–3 weeks, or perhaps longer), the apricots are size-graded on a grader screen and slabs and other defective fruit are removed.

The grader is a shaker-type series of screens with circular holes. Grades and corresponding screen size in $1/32$'s of an inch, which is in conformation with the language of the trade, are the following:

Grade	Size (In.)
Standard	$28/32$
Choice	$32/32$
Fancy	$36/32$
Extra Fancy	$40/32$
Extra Fancy	$44/32$

The sorted, sized fruit is then processed by washing in a rotating cylindrical screen equipped with water sprays to clean the dried fruit and rehydrate it for better platability. This mild rinsing process also facilitates subsequent absorption of SO_2.

The rinsed, sorted, and sized apricots are placed on trays 2 in. deep which are stacked on cars in in the usual staggered manner, and the fruit is then resulfured for 1–2 hr. This fruit is then ready to be tightly packed into wooden boxes, cardboard cartons, or plastic bags for storage and/or shipment.

Dehydration.—The term "dehydration" refers to removal of water from a product under controlled conditions of air flow, temperature, and humidity.

There are many types of forced-draft dehydrators available today, including cross-flow, conveyor dehydrator, cabinet dehydrator, vacuum dehydrator, and many more. A countercurrent tunnel dehydrator is the type used most commonly in dehydrating apricots and other fruits.

As the name implies, air flows opposite to the direction of movement of the cars in the tunnel. The tunnel is about $6\frac{1}{2}$ ft wide, 7 ft high, and 40–60 ft long. An average tunnel should be long enough for 12–14 cars, each with 24–28 trays (3 ft wide and 6 ft long). These tunnels have a door at each end, for entrance and discharge of the product.

The cars of fresh, sulfured, cut fruit enter the cool and moist air exhaust end of the tunnel and move forward to the hot end. Depending on the conditions of the dehydrator, a fresh car may be introduced every 1–2 hr, and a dried car removed at the hot end.

Rate of air flow should be 600–1000 fpm if the finished apricot is to have 17–20% moisture. The finishing temperature should be at a maximum of 145°–150°F. If, however, the cut fruit is to be dried to a content of not lower than 25% moisture, a finishing temperature of 155°F may be used.

Humidity control on the wet end of a countercurrent dehydrator is a wet-bulb depression from a minimum of 15° to an average of 25°F.

A typical dehydrator system for apricots in a countercurrent dehydrator would have a starting temperature of 130°F dry bulb and a finished temperature of 150°F dry bulb. This would be approximately 5:1 (pounds of prepared fruit to pounds of dried fruit).

Storage Stability.—Dried apricots naturally undergo deterioration in storage. This deterioration can be traced by changes in color of the finished product.

Moisture, sulfur dioxide, and oxygen affect the rate of deterioration of dried apricots. The edible storage life of the apricot has been described as the time required for the fruit to darken so much that it is no longer generally acceptable. The increase in shelf-life of dried apricots by sulfur dioxide treatment is directly proportional to the initial sulfur dioxide content of the dried product over a range of 1500–8000 ppm. It is approximately doubled by increasing sulfur dioxide content from 2000 to 7000 ppm. (Stadtman *et al.* 1946).

Although sulfur dioxide retards deterioration, it does not prevent it. Apricots can deteriorate to the point of inedibility even when the SO_2 level never falls below 5000 ppm.

During storage at moderate or high temperatures, the SO_2 content of apricots declines steadily until approximately 65% of the initial sulfur dioxide is lost, by which time the fruit has reached the limit of edibility. This effect is independent of moisture and temperature between 36.7°C (96.8°F)

and 49°C (120.2°F). It is possible, therefore, to have apricots darken even though the SO_2 content is still high.

Oxygen increases the rate of darkening. The fruit takes up oxygen and produces carbon dioxide. The rate of oxygen uptake is independent of SO_2 content, but decreases as the moisture content of the fruit is lowered. The rate of deterioration of apricots stored at 120°F decreases almost linearly with the increase of moisture content of 10–32% under anaerobic conditions. With each 10°F rise in storage temperature, the rate of darkening doubles.

The most desirable pack of dried apricots would be at about 25% moisture, with a high sulfur dioxide content of 5000–8000 ppm (exceeds FDA limits), in a tight pack, and in an air-tight container.

Frozen

Freezing technology has never involved a very large proportion of the total production of apricots; but there has been a small pack of frozen apricots since 1940. In 1945, 17% of total U.S. apricot production was frozen. Since that time, the percentage of apricots frozen has been somewhat lower.

Apricots are more difficult to freeze successfully than other fruits such as berries, due to their high susceptibility to browning and oxidation on exposure to air. During freezing at 0°F, enzymatic oxidation is very rapid (Joslyn 1942).

The texture is markedly softened through freezing, and the skin toughened. Blanching was proposed to inactivate the enzyme system, and sulfurous acid treatment because of its antioxidant properties. Ascorbic acid was also utilized as an antioxidant, using a 0.1% concentration of ascorbic acid in 45° Brix syrup (Hohl and Swanburg, 1946).

Blanching was very effective in inactivating enzymes but presented practical difficulties when put into practice. The dipping treatment, using sodium bisulfite with 4000 ppm of SO_2 for 4 min, yields a satisfactory product, but the finished product will have 50–75 ppm of SO_2.

Apricots to be frozen were best when covered with 40° Brix sucrose solution containing 0.1% ascorbic acid. Impregnation of apricots with syrup by deaeration greatly improved the results.

The skins of frozen apricots do not actually toughen as a result of freezing, although they appear so. In canned apricots, this effect is precluded by tenderization of the epidermis and hypodermis through the heat processing.

SHERMAN LEONARD

References

CRUESS, W. V. 1942. Experimental drying of unsulfured fruits. Fruit Prod. J. *21*, No. 5, 135, 157.

HOHL, L. A., and SWANBERG, J. 1946. Freezing of California fruits—apricots. Food Packer *27*, No. 3, 37–38, 68, 70, 72.

JOSLYN, M. A. 1942. Preservation freezing of apricots for subsequent processing by bakers, baby food firms, and others. Frozen Food Recorder, Western Canner Packer *34*, No. 88, 45–50.

MARSH, G. L., and CRUESS, W. V. 1932. Experiments on utilization of surplus apricots Fruit Prod. J. *11*, No. 11, 334, 349.

PHAFF, H. J., and MRAK, E. M. 1948. Sulfur house operation. Calif. Agr. Expt. Sta. Bull. *382.*

SHALLAH, A., and CRUESS, W. V. 1934. Canning of apricot juice. Fruit Prod. J. *13*, No. 7, 205.

STADTMAN, E. R., BARKER, H. A., MRAK, E. M., and MACKINNEY, G. 1945. Storage of dried fruit: The influence of moisture and SO_2 on deterioration of dried apricots. Ind. Eng. Chem. *38*, 99–104, 324, 541–543.

Cross-reference: *Dried Fruit.*

L-ASCORBIC ACID AND FOOD TECHNOLOGY

L-Ascorbic acid, a six-carbon, water-soluble white crystalline compound is commonly called vitamin C or the antiscorbutic vitamin (also referred to as L-xyloascorbic acid, hexuronic acid or cevitamic acid). L-Ascorbic acid resembles the sugars in structure and does react like sugars under some chemical conditions. The unusual properties of the molecule are due to the enediol grouping. Other properties are: melting point of 190°–192°C with decomposition; $[\alpha]_D^{20} + 23°$ in water; a pK_1 of 4.17 and a pK_2 of 11.57. It is a moderately strong reducing agent and is sufficiently acidic to form neutral salts with bases. L-Ascorbic acid (1-gm) dissolves in about 3 ml of water, or 50 ml of absolute ethanol, or 100 ml of glycerol. It is oxidized in aqueous solution by oxygen under the influence of catalytic oxidases and/or traces of some metals. Oxidation proceeds in stages, its rate increasing as the pH is raised, to first form physiologically active dehydroascorbic acid, a reversible stage; continuing oxidation results in the irreversible stage, 2, 3 diketo-gulonic acid, a form without vitamin activity. L-Ascorbic acid is extensively used as a food additive during the processing of foods and beverages to enhance nutritional value; or to replace vitamin C lost during harvesting, processing, storage, or home preparation; or as an oxygen acceptor or water-soluble antioxidant, whose role in the oxidation-reduction phenomena inherently results in improved keeping quality, color, flavor, and texture, or improved processing procedures in the food product. It is a unique compound when comparing it with the fat-soluble antioxidants.

Source and Biogenesis

Vitamin C is found in nature in all living tissue in two forms: reduced (L-ascorbic acid) and oxidized (dehydroascorbic acid). The chemical name is L-threo-2,3,4,5,6-pentahydroxy-2-hexonic acid-4-lactone; the empirical formula is $C_6H_6O_6$; and the structural formula is

It is present in mammalian tissue, for example, in the adrenal cortex, eye lens, suprarenal medulla, etc. It is also abundantly present in some plant tissue (Table A-21) such as broccoli, brussels sprouts, cabbage, paprika, parsley, spinach, tomatoes, and in fruits such as grapefruit, lemons, oranges, strawberries, and tangerines. Citrus fruits are best known as a natural source of ascorbic acid. The content of vitamin C from food is variable due to fluctuations and losses incurred during harvesting, storage, and preparation.

In plants, L-ascorbic acid appears to be formed from D-glucose by a series of related pathways. According to Burns (1970), L-ascorbic acid arises from D-glucose in the rat, through the intermediate stages of D-glucuronic acid, L-gulonic acid and L-gulono-lactone. With the exception of man, monkey, guinea pig, the Indian fruit bat, the prairie dog, the flying fox, the kalabulbul, and possibly some species of fish, most animals have the inborn physiological capacity to synthesize L-ascorbic acid and hence it is not necessary to provide a source in their diet. Deprivation of L-ascorbic acid in humans causes the deterioration of a number of physiological functions of which the deficiency disease of scurvy is best known.

Synthesis

For 40 yr crystalline L-ascorbic acid has been industrially produced by chemical synthesis. This was the first crystalline vitamin to be produced commercially. Commercial synthesis largely fol-

TABLE A-21

ASCORBIC ACID CONTENT OF FOODS

Fruits	Ascorbic Acid (Mg/100 Gm) (A)	(B)	Vegetables	Ascorbic Acid (Mg/100 Gm) (A)	(B)
Apples (raw)	4	6	Asparagus (boiled)	26	25
Apricots (raw)	10	8	Beans, French (boiled)	7	12
Apricot nectar (canned)	3	3	Beet greens (boiled)	15	—
Apricots, dried (raw)	12	10	Broccoli (boiled)	90	92
Apricots, dried (stewed)	3	2	Brussels sprouts (boiled)	87	83
Avocados (raw)	14	13	Cabbage	33	42
Bananas (raw)	10	11	Carrots (canned)	2	3
Blackberries (raw)	21	22	Cauliflower (boiled)	55	52
Cherries (raw)	10	8	Celery (raw)	9	7
Cherries, sour (canned)	10	—	Chicory greens (raw)	22	—
Currents, black (raw)	200	209	Chives (raw)	56	—
Gooseberries (raw)	33	35	Collards (boiled)	51	—
Grapefriut and juice	38	40	Corn, yellow (boiled)	7	7
Lemons and juice (raw)	45	38–47	Dandelion greens (boiled)	18	—
Limes and juice (raw)	35	37	Endive (raw)	10	—
Mangos (raw)	35	41	Kale (boiled)	93	51
Melons (raw)	33	—	Lettuce (raw)	6–18	13
Nectarines (raw)	13	19	Mustard greens (raw)	65	—
Oranges and juice (raw)	45	50	Okra (boiled)	20	20
Peaches (raw)	7	7	Parsley (raw)	172	178
Peaches, dried (raw)	18	16	Peas (boiled)	20	20
Pears (raw)	4	4	Potatoes (boiled)	16	11
Pineapples (raw)	17	26	Spinach (boiled)	28	33
Plums (raw)	5	4	Squash, summer (boiled)	10	11
Prunes, dried (raw)	4	3	Squash, winter (boiled)	8	6
Prunes, dried (stewed)	1	1	Sweet potatoes (boiled)	17	18
Raspberries (raw)	22	23	Tomatoes or juice (raw)	16	17
Rhubarb (raw)	9	10	Tomatoes (canned)	16	18
Strawberries (raw)	59	58	Turnip greens (boiled)	69	—
Tangerines and juice (raw)	31	—	Water cress (raw)	79	—

SOURCE: (A) values from *Composition of Foods*, USDA Agr. Handbook 8 (1963); (B) values from *Tables of Composition of Australian Foods*, Australian Govt. Publishing Serv. (1970).

lows the L-sorbose process (Fig. A-11) of Reichstein. Continuous improvements in the various steps starting with D-glucose have made this approach the commercially feasible process. L-Ascorbic acid and sodium L-ascorbate are available in a variety of mesh sizes to meet the requirements of various kinds of food products. Where greater oil solubility is desired, L-ascorbyl palmitate, also produced commercially, can be considered. These crystalline compounds are stable for years when stored under cool, dry conditions in closed hermetically-sealed containers. Solutions of L-ascorbic acid are fairly heat-stable in the absence of oxygen.

In 1971, in the Roche laboratories, analytically pure L-ascorbic acid was isolated from freshly squeezed lemon juice and compared to the pure L-ascorbic acid prepared by chemical synthesis. By classical examination of physical and chemical properties as well as comparative studies using the most modern instrumentation, no difference could be detected between the samples of L-ascorbic acid from the two sources.

Method of Addition to Food

The four basic methods developed for adding L-ascorbic acid to foods are:

(1) Pure Compound—Crystalline L-ascorbic acid or sodium ascorbate are widely added directly to food in predetermined quantities often in the form of preweighed or packaged packets for convenience. Addition is accompanied by mixing to ensure uniformity.

(2) Premixes—A uniform mixture of a known amount of L-ascorbic acid and a dry carrier, usually a constituent of the food, such as salt. A premix blended with a prescribed quantity of dry food product gives greater assurance of product

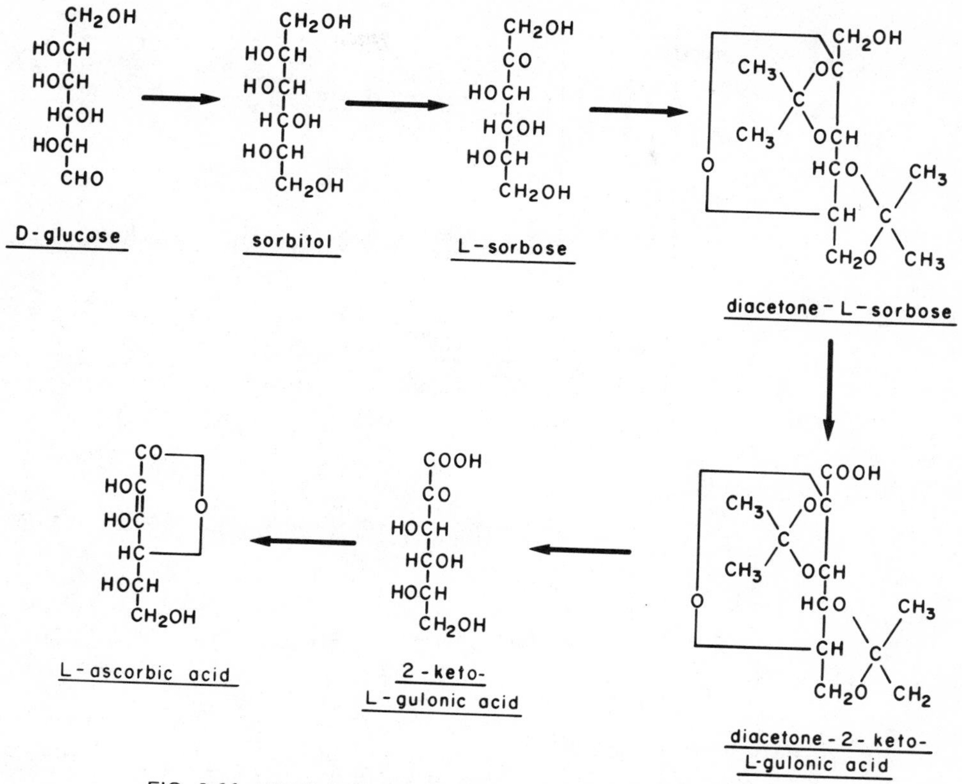

FIG. A-11. THE L-SORBOSE SYNTHESIS OF L-ASCORBIC ACID

uniformity when the added quantity of the pure vitamin is very small.

(3) Liquid Solutions—Sprays of L-ascorbic acid solutions or suspensions which may be considered liquid premixes. The sprays are directed onto the surface of a food or injected into liquid food products in order to circumvent difficult or continuous processing conditions.

(4) Wafers or Tablets—Compressed soluble discs containing inert, edible carriers and sufficient L-ascorbic acid to meet the L-ascorbic acid regulatory and (or) processing requirements of a given quantity of food. The tablet added to the container prior to filling and sealing of liquid foods dissolves immediately, or may be dissolved and added to semisolid foods or dry foods at a late stage of food preparation.

Precautions and Stability

The point in food processing at which ascorbic acid is added is important. The ideal stage at which L-ascorbic acid is introduced is usually as close to the end of the terminal processing stage as possible without loss of uniform distribution or compound decomposition. The stability of L-ascorbic acid is influenced by atmospheric oxygen, oxidative enzymes, pasteurization methods, metal contamination, and sulfur dioxide content. L-Ascorbic acid is not an antimicrobial agent unless used at very high levels. It will not upgrade the initial quality of food prior to processing or mask processing techniques.

In order to maximize the stability and efficacy of L-ascorbic acid added to foodstuffs, the following precautions are recommended: (1) stainless steel, aluminum, or plastic equipment should be used; (2) bronze, brass, copper, monel, cold rolled steel, and black iron equipment should be avoided; (3) deaeration (vacuum) procedures and inert gas treatment are recommended where feasible; (4) containers should be filled at a uniform rate to maximum capacity; and (5) when employed, flash heat processing should be used quickly and the containers cooled promptly.

Table A-22, compiled by Bauernfeind, summarizes commercial trial runs on a number of food products with added L-ascorbic acid. It must be recognized that these were run with the prevailing equipment and under the processing variables in

TABLE A-22

STABILITY OF ADDED ASCORBIC ACID IN FOOD PRODUCTS

Product	Type of Packaging	Goal	After Processing		Storage, 70°–75°F (23°C) 6 Months		12 Months	
			Ascorbic Acid	Vitamin C[1]	Ascorbic Acid	Vitamin C[1]	Ascorbic Acid	Vitamin C[1]
Apple juice	glass, 1 qt	30 mg/10 fl oz	38	49	31	34 (72)[2]	25	37 (76)[2]
Apple juice	glass, 24 oz	30 mg/8 fl oz	35	47	35	—	28	32 (68)
Apple juice	can, 20 oz	35 mg/100 ml	35	41	46	—	26	31 (76)
Apple-orange juice	glass, amber	40 mg/100 ml	62	63	49	48 (76)	37	40 (64)
Apple-orange juice	can	40 mg/100 ml	61	62	59	53 (85)	39	48 (77)
Apple sauce	can, 1 lb	30 mg/100 gm	69	74	61	62 (84)	45	56 (76)
Apricot nectar	can, 4 oz	30 mg/4 fl oz	57	59	40	46 (95)	29	50 (84)
Apricot drink	can, 6 oz	30 mg/6 fl oz	47	48	48	49 (92)	37	40 (83)
Apricot drink	can, 12 oz	30 mg/4 fl oz	49	53				41 (77)
Cereals, dry	box, liner	10 mg/oz	10.3	—	8.3 (80)[2]	9.7	7.2 (70)	9.9
Cocoa powders	foil bags	120 mg/lb	180	214	166	194 (90)	137	171 (80)
Cocoa powders	box, 1 lb	75 mg/20 gm	78	80	76	87 (100)	77	82 (100)
Cranberry juice	glass, 16 oz	30 mg/6 fl oz	38	41	33	35 (86)	32	34 (83)
Cranberry-apricot juice	glass, 1 qt	30 mg/6 fl oz	38	49	35	40 (82)	38	40 (82)
Fruit carbonated beverages								
Grape	can, 12 oz	30 mg/12 fl oz	42	46	30	35 (76)	26	28 (61)
Orange	can, 12 oz	30 mg/12 fl oz	44	46	30	35 (76)	22	25 (54)
Root beer	can, 12 oz	30 mg/12 fl oz	40	50	31	41 (82)	28	32 (64)
Fruit powder mixes	package, 3 oz	30 mg/3 oz	82	87	75	80 (92)	73	79 (91)
Orange	can, 4 oz	75 mg/4 fl oz	144	122	144	121 (99)	106	119 (97)
Fruit gelatin	can, 24 oz	15 mg/3 oz	17.5	18.2	16.8	17.9 (98)	15.5	16.6 (91)
Fruit gelatin	can, 24 oz	15 mg/4 oz	63	68	62	68 (100)	61	66 (97)
Fruit lollipops								
Lemon	lollipop	30 mg/lollipop	29	—		—	30 (100)	—
Pineapple	lollipop	30 mg/lollipop	30	—		—	30 (100)	—

Product								
Milk products								
Liquid formula	can, 13 oz	50 mg/can	99	—	49 (50)	—	49 (50)	—
Evaporated milk	can, 13 oz	50 mg/can	94	—	62 (64)	—	—	—
Dry formula	can/g gas	60 mg/112 gm	57	63	—	—	58	61 (97)
Dry formula	can/g vacuum	60 mg/112 gm	63	79	—	—	63	76 (96)
Dry milk whole	can, air	100 mg/lb	157	188	115	158 (84)	133	122 (65)
Dry milk whole	can, gas	100 mg/lb	184	200	184	189 (95)	188	186 (93)
Orange drink	glass, 1 qt	30 mg/8 fl oz	53	56	50	54 (96)	32	46 (82)
Orange drink	can, 46 oz	30 mg/8 fl oz	37	44	31	37 (84)	27	34 (77)
Orange drink	glass, 1/2 gal.	30 mg/10 fl oz	79	82	71	73 (89)	66	68 (83)
Orange drink, concentrated frozen	can, 6 oz	30 mg/4 fl oz	68	71	62	66 (94)	61	65 (91)
Pineapple juice	can, 6 oz	30 mg/8 fl oz	39	51	40	47 (92)	41	46 (90)
Pineapple juice	can, 11 oz	30 mg/4 fl oz	47	48	43	43 (90)	38 (81)	38 (81)
Pineapple juice	can, 18 oz	30 mg/4 fl oz	44	44	38	45 (100)	35	36 (82)
Pineapple juice, con-centrated frozen	can, 6 oz	30 mg/4 fl oz	79	88	78	82 (93)	—	—
Potato flakes	can	60 mg/3 oz	48	59	30	43 (73)	—	—
Potato flakes	can, air	60 mg/100 gm	51	65	40	60 (92)	—	—
Potato flakes	can, gas	60 mg/100 gm	70	79	68	71 (90)	—	—
Potato sticks, frozen	frozen film pack	60 mg/100 gm	84	—	61 (73)	—	—	—
Soybean products								
Liquid formula	can, 13 oz	50 mg/can	45	—	47 (100)	—	43 (95)	61 (98)
Dry powder	can, 1 lb	60 mg/4 oz	62	62	49	60 (97)	48	44 (81)
Tomato juice	can, 18 oz	30 mg/100 ml	52	54	45	45 (83)	44	30 (77)
Tomato juice	can, 46 oz	30 mg/100 ml	39	—	35 (90)	—	27 (70)	—
Tomato juice	can, 18 oz	30 mg/4 fl oz	40	41	37 (93)	—	34	37 (93)
Tomato juice	can, 46 oz	30 mg/4 fl oz	41	44	41	50 (100)	32	35 (80)
Tomato juice	glass jar	30 mg/6 fl oz	55	59	51	56 (95)	39	47 (80)
Vegetable juice	can, 46 oz	30 mg/6 fl oz	53	58	40	43 (74)	32	38 (66)
Vegetable juice	can, 6 oz	30 mg/4 fl oz	36	42	32	34 (81)	29	29 (69)
Vegetable juice	glass jar	30 mg/4 fl oz	45	—	42 (93)	—	41 (91)	—

[1] Vitamin C includes both ascorbic acid plus dehydroascorbic acid values.
[2] Values in ( ) are percentage of retention during storage.

TABLE A-23

U.S. STANDARDS OR REGULATIONS[1] OF FOODS TO WHICH ASCORBIC ACID MAY BE ADDED

Food	Purpose of Ascorbic Acid	Quantity Permitted
Food for Which an FDA Standard Has Been Established		
Artifically sweetened fruit jelly	Preservative	Not more than 0.1% by weight
Artifically sweetened fruit preserves	Preservative	Not more than 0.1% by weight
Canned applesauce	Preservative	Not more than 150 ppm
	Nutrient	30–60 mg/4 fl oz
Canned artichokes (packed in glass)	Preservative	Not more than 32 mgs/100 gms of finished food
Canned fruit nectars	Antioxidant or nutrient	150 ppm or 30–60 mg/4 fl oz
Canned mushrooms	Preservative	Not more than 37.5 mg/oz of drained weight of mushrooms
Canned fruit cocktail	Color preservative	Approximately 700 ppm by weight of ascorbic acid, but not more than 850 ppm in any individual can (temporary permit expired Oct. 15, 1970)
Canned peaches	Color preservative	Not more than 390 ppm
Canned pineapple juice	Nutrient	30–60 mg/4 fl oz
Canned pineapple-grapefruit juice drink	Nutrient	30–60 mg/6 fl oz
Canned prune juice	Nutrient	30–50 mg/4 fl oz
Cranberry juice cocktail	Nutrient	30–60 mg/6 fl oz
Diluted orange juice drink	Nutrient	30–60 mg/4 fl oz
Flour (white, wheat, plain)	Dough conditioner	Not more than 200 ppm
Frozen raw breaded shrimp	Preservative	Sufficient to retard development of dark spots
Fruit sherbets	Acidulant	Such quantity as seasons the finished food
Nonfruit sherbets	Acidulant	Such quantity as seasons the finished product
Ice cream (the fruit therein)	Acidulant	Such quantity as seasons the finished product and meets the standards for ice cream
Soda water	Preservative	
Water ices (the fruit therein)	Acidulant	Such quantity as seasons the finished product
Nonfruit water ices	Acidulant	Such quantity as seasons the finished product
USDA Regulations Permitting Use		
Ascorbic acid in: cured pork and beef cuts, cured comminuted meat food product	To accelerate color fixing	70 oz per 100 gal. pickle at 10% pump level; 3/4 oz per 100 lb meat or meat byproduct; 10% solution to surfaces of cured cuts prior to packaging (the use of such solution shall not result in the addition of a significant amount of moisture to the product)
Sodium ascorbate in: cured pork and beef cuts, cured comminuted meat food product	To accelerate color fixing	87.5 oz per 100 gal. pickle at 10% pump level; 7/8 oz per 100 lb meat or meat byproduct; 10% solution to surfaces of cured cuts prior to packaging (the use of such solution shall not result in the addition of a significant amount of moisture to the product)

TABLE A-23 (*Continued*)

Food	Purpose of Ascorbic Acid	Quantity Permitted
Alcohol and Tobacco Tax Div., U.S. Dept. of Treasury Regulations		
Wine	To prevent darkening of color and deterioration of flavor, and overoxidation	Within limitations which do not alter the class or type of the wine (use need not be declared on the label)
Beer	Antioxidant and biological stabilization	To be used only by agreement between U.S. Dept. of Treasury and the brewer

[1] Consult regulations for current status. For countries other than United States, governmental authority should be contacted for current regulations.

the particular plant at the time and, hence, can only serve as a guide to expected performance. Meticulous attention to control of processing details is imperative for good performance. Experience in plant trial runs with the particular food dictates the overages needed in commercial practice which are necessary to meet label claim after processing and storage.

Added L-Ascorbic Acid as a Nutrient

L-Ascorbic acid, an important water-soluble vitamin for man, may be added as a nutrient (a) to fortify natural foods having little or no vitamin C, (b) to restore losses, (c) to produce food products having a standardized quantity, or (d) to endow replacement or enrichment of fabricated foods with nutritional value. In the United States, these objectives must be accomplished in conformity with regulations pertaining to "added L-ascorbic acid" as promulgated by the U.S. Food and Drug Administration under authority of the Food, Drug and Cosmetic Act, or regulations of other federal organizations. The numerous applications in this review have worldwide technological and nutritional use and this utility must be considered in terms of application and current regulations of the particular country. Current U.S. governmental regulations regarding the addition of L-ascorbic acid are presented in Table A-23.

In the United States, the populace is obtaining more vitamin C from frozen and canned fruits and vegetables than previously. Juices, especially, are consumed at breakfast, and as between-meal snacks rather than fresh fruit. These juices and fruit drinks are used interchangeably for variety, regardless of the amount of L-ascorbic acid occurring naturally in the original fruit. Therefore, a standardized amount of vitamin C is desirable in these products to ensure a relatively uniform intake of vitamin C by the consumer.

In the United States, L-ascorbic acid is added to a number, but not all, of commercially produced juices and fruit juice drinks. Generally, sufficient L-ascorbic acid is added to provide 30 mg of vitamin C per 4 or 8 fl oz, depending on the consumption pattern. In the case of carbonated beverages, L-ascorbic acid not only provides nutrient fortification, but additionally acts as an antioxidant; thus protecting against color and flavor loss attributable to dissolved and headspace atmospheric oxygen.

In order to protect against scorbutic conditions, especially among infants, the Food and Drug Directorate of Canada established a minimal level of 40 mg vitamin C per quart of reconsituted evaporated milk. Several evaporated milk-base infant foods in the United States contain 50 mg of added L-ascorbic acid per 13 fl oz can designed for dilution before use. Japanese and other workers have reported that yogurt is another excellent dairy product medium for fortification.

The losses of vitamin C occurring in the potato due to storage and processing into dehydrated flakes, granulars, chips, frozen sticks, etc., can be replaced with synthetic L-ascorbic acid during processing to ensure that the potato will continue to contribute significant amounts of the essential nutrient to the consumer. For maximum vitamin and flavor retention, moisture must be kept to a minimum during dry blending and packaging operations.

It has been suggested that the vitamin C variation in canned sauerkraut, attributable to tank storage and canning process losses, can be remedied by adding L-ascorbic acid to produce a uniform product. Among other products mentioned in the literature for vitamin C fortification throughout the world are breakfast cereals; cocoa powder; instant, reconstitutable chocolate drink powders; condensed soybean milk and dried milk products; chocolate bars; icing in cookies; dehydrated and canned soups; sugar; salt; and tea.

Added L-Ascorbic Acid as an Antioxidant

The function of L-ascorbic acid as an antioxidant in food systems is (1) to scavenge oxygen and thereby prevent oxidation of oxygen-sensitive food constituents, (2) to shift the redox potential of the system to a reducing range, (3) to keep iron (ferric and ferrous) in a reduced state, (4) to maintain sulfhydryl groups in SH form, (5) to act synergistically with chelating agents, and/or (6) to reduce undesirable oxidation products.

The role of L-ascorbic acid in the retardation of rancidity of animal fats is as a synergist in conjunction with the role of another antioxidant, tocopherol, for example, whose concentration in animal fat is variable. The addition of L-ascorbic acid to a fat containing prooxidants such as copper may accelerate oxidation; whereas, raising the concentration of tocopherol, or other phenolic antioxidant, in the presence of L-ascorbic acid usually retards oxidative rancidity. Experimentalists have studied the synergistic effect of L-ascorbic acid in the presence of other chemical or radiation reactants such as, citric acid, hematins, γ-rays, butylated hydroxyanisole, nordihydroguaiaretic acid, propyl gallate and pyro-, tripoly- and hexametaphosphates, on the keeping qualities of lard, goose fat, hydrogenated almond oil, hydrogenated whale oil, cacao butter, margarine, etc., and reports exist in the literature.

Vegetable oils usually contain some natural tocopherols; thus, the addition of L-ascorbic acid in the form of L-ascorbyl palmitate has been shown to inhibit oxidation in corn oil, sunflower oil, peanut oil, butterfat, polyunsaturated fatty acid-enriched margarine, and cottonseed and olive oils.

The fruit varieties that discolor upon cutting and exposure to air, such as the apple and banana, do so because they are low in naturally-occurring L-ascorbic acid and relatively high in active phenolases which react on the orthophenolic substrates in the presence of oxygen to produce orthoquinone-type compounds. The presence of L-ascorbic acid reduces the orthoquinones thereby preventing browning. Thus, L-ascorbic acid is used to control browning in frozen and/or canned fruit or juices, e.g., peaches, apricots, pears, plums, nectarines, bananas, apples, apple juice, apple sauce, and a few vegetable products such as frozen French-fried potatoes, refrigerated sauerkraut, canned mushrooms, canned cauliflower, and canned carrots. It does prevent or retard undesireable enzymatic browning oxidation, is claimable as a source of vitamin C if a sufficiently high and uniform level of vitamin C results, and minimizes or eliminates the quantity of sulfur dioxide needed (when used) if adequate heat processing is used to control bacterial growth.

L-Ascorbic acid, applied to fish by dipping in or spraying on a solution (0.5-2.0%) retards enzymatic oxidation which results in rancidity evidenced by "rusting" or yellowing of fresh and marine water species. Thickness or coating agents are frequently added to the solution. Each species of fish or crustacean is unique with respect to fat content and enzyme systems. Therefore, the most beneficial L-ascorbic acid treatment must be ascertained for each species and processing method, e.g., individual or pack treatment, freezing whole organism or filleted treatment, etc.

The discoloration of fresh and canned meat is attributable to the brown ferric oxidation pigment, metmyoglobin, whose formation is accelerated by heat, freezing, salt, certain chemicals or metals, and ultraviolet light. Under appropriate limited conditions, metmyoglobin can be reduced, or its formation retarded by addition of L-ascorbic acid. In the case of cured meat, the myoglobin content reacts with gaseous nitric oxide, resulting from the addition of nitrites during processing, to form the ferrous pigment, nitrosomyoglobin, which is converted during heat denaturation to nitrosomyochrome. L-Ascorbic acid can (1) catalyze the production of nitric oxide hemoglobin, (2) regenerate or stabilize the nitrosomyoglobin on the meat surface when residual nitrite is present, (3) inhibit or reduce the formation of nitrosamines, and (4) delay oxidative flavor change and fading by light exposure. Since nitrites and L-ascorbic acid react vigorously with each other, they should not be mixed together in solution at room temperature. They are usually introduced into the meat at separate stages, or introduced in dry form or as a freshly prepared cold solution. L-Ascorbic acid and sodium L-ascorbate are used on a large scale to improve color of cured meats or speed up the curing action in the smoke house and to retard the development of off-flavor due to fat oxidation.

The participation of L-ascorbic acid in oxidation-reduction reactions has been used to improve the quality of bread with respect to dough handling, texture, and loaf volume. The practical result of adding L-ascorbic acid is strengthening of the gluten to form a stable dough which is better able to retain gases liberated by yeast fermentation prior to and during the baking stage. There is a dual action of L-ascorbic acid in bread, namely (1) for improved sulfhydryl interaction and (2) to reduce the rpm requirements of high speed mixing of the dough.

The versatility of L-ascorbic acid in dynamic oxidation-reduction environments has led to its utilization by the brewing industry. Its addition to beer (³/₄-1 lb per 100 barrels) reduces chill and oxidation haze, gushing and color darkening, and increases shelf-life while retarding flavor change. It improves colloidal stability by protecting proteins, tannins, and their mutual absorbates from oxidation. To minimize the amount of L-ascorbic acid needed, air in the brew should be kept as low as possible by mechanical means, and dissolved metals, e.g., copper and iron, are to be avoided.

L-Ascorbic acid may be added to any stage after fermentation.

Wines, too, benefit from the addition of L-Ascorbic acid which favorably affects taste, flavor, clarity, and stabilization of oxidation-reduction potential in quantities of 25 to 100 mg per liter of wine. Variations inherent in wine making, such as growing region, type of grape, kind of wine, and degree of maturity of the wine determine whether or not L-ascorbic acid should be used or not and in what quantity. It is recommended, generally, that L-ascorbic acid be considered in conjunction with sulfur dioxide and not as a replacement for it since sulfur dioxide has antiseptic, fungicidal, and antidiastase properties as well as antioxidant characteristics.

Ascorbic acid also inhibits oxidation, if adequate natural tocopherols are present, in dairy products: milk, butter, and cheese. It has been reported that its addition to milk delays the development of oxidized flavor, and loss of vitamin A. During the drying of milk it has been shown to have a beneficial effect by exerting an antioxidant action on the lipids. If additions are to be made during the butter making process for an antioxidant effect, the L-ascorbyl esters such as L-ascorbyl palmitate with tocopherol would be a preferred form.

J. C. BAUERNFEIND

D. M. PINKERT

References

BAUERNFEIND, J. C. 1953. The use of Ascorbic acid in processing foods. *In* Advances in Food Research, Vol. 4. Academic Press, New York.

BAUERNFEIND, J. C., and PINKERT, D. M. 1970. Food processing with added ascorbic acid. *In* Advances in Food Research, Vol. 18. Academic Press, New York.

BURNS, J. J. 1970. Ascorbic acid. *In* The Pharmacological Basis of Therapeutics, 4th Edition. L. Goodman and A. Gilman (Editors). Macmillan Co., New York.

KING, C. G. 1967. Ascorbic acid. *In* Present Knowledge in Nutrition, 3rd Edition. The Nutrition Foundation, New York.

SEBRELL, H. W., Jr., and HARRIS, R. S. (Editors) 1967. Ascorbic acid. *In* The Vitamins, Vol. 1. Academic Press, New York.

Cross-reference: *Nutrition.*

AWARDS

Appert Award

The Nicholas Appert Award, established in 1942 by the Chicago Section of the Institute of Food Technology, consists of a Bronze Medal, furnished by the Chicago Section, and an honorarium of $1000 from the Institute. The Award recognizes pre-eminence in and contributions to the field of food technology. It is given annually to a person deemed by a committee of nine jurors to meet this stipulation. The Medal bears a likeness of Appert, the French confectioner, chef, and winemaker, credited with the invention of canning. Appert won fame by winning the prize, offered by the French Directorate in 1795, for a food preservation process that would not seriously impair the flavor of a food. Appert was awarded the prize (12,000 francs) in 1809 after demonstrating the practicality of his preservation method, the prototype of modern canning.

Awardees are:

1942—WILLIAM V. CRUESS
1943—SAMUEL C. PRESCOTT
1944—C. A. BROWNE
1945—A. W. BITTING
1946—C. H. BAILEY
1947—C. OLIN BALL
1948—C. A. ELVEHJEM
1949—ROY C. NEWTON
1950—THOMAS M. RECTOR
1951—A. E. STEVENSON
1952—EDWARD M. CHACE
1953—VICTOR CONQUEST
1954—CHARLES N. FREY
1955—CHARLES G. KING
1956—BERNARD E. PROCTOR
1957—EMIL M. MRAK
1958—WILLIAM F. GEDDES
1959—BERTON S. CLARK
1960—ERNEST H. WIEGAND
1961—HELMUT C. DIEHL
1962—ARNOLD KENT BALLS
1963—KARL F. MEYER
1964—GAIL M. DACK
1965—HAROLD W. SCHULTZ
1966—MAYNARD A. JOSLYN
1967—MICHAEL J. COPLEY
1968—DONALD K. TRESSLER
1969—EDWIN M. FOSTER
1970—SAMUEL A. GOLDBLITH
1971—REID T. MILNER
1972—JOHN C. AYRES
1973—HANS LINEWEAVER

Babcock-Hart Award

One of the several Awards administered by the Institute of Food Technologists, the Babcock-Hart Award was established in 1948 and at that time called the Stephen M. Babcock Award. The title of the Award was changed in 1954 to include the name of Hart, a distinguished co-worker in the field of nutrition.

The Award, sponsored by the Nutrition Foundation, Inc., carries with it an honorarium of $1000 and an engraved certificate. It is awarded annually to a person who has made an outstanding contribution to food technology, specifically a contribution that has resulted in improved public health through some aspect of nutrition; for example, the development of a more nutritious food. The Award can be given only for a technological development or a scientific contribution that leads to a technological development.

The awardees are:

1948—FRED C. BLANCK
1949—CLARENCE BIRDSEYE
1950—CARL R. FELLERS
1951—SAMUEL C. PRESCOTT
1952—FRED W. TANNER
1953—CHARLES N. FREY
1954—EDWIN J. CAMERON
1955—WILLIAM V. CRUESS
1956—GAIL M. DACK
1957—ELMER M. NELSON
1958—BERNARD L. OSER
1959—SAMUEL LEPKOVSKY
1960—ARNOLD H. JOHNSON
1961—EMIL M. MRAK
1962—V. SUBRAHMANYAN
1963—MAYNARD A. JOSLYN
1964—ROBERT R. WILLIAMS
1965—TETSUJIRO OBARA
1966—RODERICK K. ESKEW
1967—WALLACE B. VAN ARSDEL
1968—ARTHUR I. MORGAN JR.
1969—SAMUEL A. GOLDBLITH
1970—RICHARD BRESSANI
1971—HISATERU MITSUDA
1972—JAMES W. PENCE
1973—CLINTON O. CHICHESTER

William V. Cruess Award for Excellence in Teaching

This Award, which consists of a medal and an honorarium of $1000 donated by the Northern California Section of IFT, honors a teacher of food science and technology who has distinguished himself in his profession. The Award was established in 1970.

Awardees are:

1970—MARCUS KAREL
1971—CLIFFORD E. SAMUELS
1972—EDWARD E. BURNS
1973—JOHN R. WHITAKER

IFT Industrial Achievement Award

The IFT Industrial Achievement Award is given in recognition of a significant advance in the application of food technology to food production. The Award consists of a suitably inscribed plaque and a citation at the Annual Meeting of the Institute of Food Technologists.

Awardees are:

1959—Eastern Utilization Research & Development Div., ARS, USDA
1960—Merck & Company and The American Meat Institute Foundation
1961—Swift & Company
1962—Sunkist Growers, Inc.

1963—Swift & Company
1964—Whirlpool Corporation
1965—C. J. Patterson Company
1966—Swift & Company and Trenton Foods, Inc.
1967—Foremost Dairies
1968—Hoffmann-La Roche
1969—Thomas J. Lipton, Inc.
1970—General Foods Corp.
1971—Central Food Technological Research Institute (India)
1972—Western Regional Research Laboratory ARS, USDA
1973—Armour & Company, Food Research Division

IFT International Award

The IFT International Award, administered by the Institute of Food Technologists, is presented annually to a member of the Institute of Food Technologists who has made outstanding efforts to promote international exchange of ideas in food science.

The award consists of an engraved silver salver furnished by the Australian Institute of Food Science and Technology and a $1000 honorarium from the Institute of Food Technologists.

Awardees since its founding in 1956 are:

1956—ROBERT S. SCULL
1957—LAURENCE V. BURTON
1958—HENRI CHEFTEL
1959—ROSS A. CHAPMAN
1960—JAMES R. VICKERY
1961—MAYNARD A. JOSLYN
1962—LAWRENCE J. LYNCH
1963—EMIL M. MRAK
1964—E. C. BATE-SMITH
1965—MORTIMER L. ANSON
1966—GEORGE F. STEWART
1967—ZOLTAN I. KERTESZ
1968—MAX MILNER
1969—NEVIN S. SCRIMSHAW
1970—DAVID B. HAND
1971—AARON M. ALTSCHUL
1972—FRITZ H. REUTER
1973—FRANCIS AYLWARD

Rohland A. Isker Award

The Rohland A. Isker Award was established by the Research and Development Associates for Military Food and Packaging Systems, Inc., in 1959 to recognize outstanding contributions to food and packaging progress in the areas of Armed Forces concern. Personnel of the Department of Defense and other government departments are eligible for the Award, which consists of (1) a bronze plaque on which is engraved the name or names of the awardees and a brief description of their contribution; and (2) an appropriately engraved watch.

Award winners are:

1960—JOSEPH P. AKREP, SAMUEL A. MATZ,
    C. S. MCWILLIAMS, JASON MILLER
1962—HAROLD SALWIN, D. C. HASCALL,
    C. M. SCHOMAN, JR.
1963—WALLACE B. VAN ARSDEL
1966—ROBERT ABERCROMBIE and
    CHARLES MERRITT, JR.
1967—DANIEL J. PALESE
1968—CLARENCE K. WADSWORTH
1969—RAUNO A. LAMPI
1970—ARTHUR I. MORGAN
1971—JAMES W. PENCE
1972—MALCOLM C. SMITH
1973—FRANK J. RUBINATE

Samuel Cate Prescott Award for Research

This Award, established in 1964, named in honor of the famous food scientist, college teacher, and administrator (MIT), is given to honor the achievements of a young research scientist 35 years of age or younger who has displayed outstanding ability for research in food science and technology. The Award consists of an engraved plaque and an honorarium of $1000 given by the Institute of Food Technologists.

Awardees are:

1964—EDGAR ALLAN DAY
1965—ERNEST J. BRISKEY
1967—ROBERT G. CASSENS
1968—HERBERT O. HULTIN
1969—HARRY Y. YAMAMOTO
1970—STEVEN R. TANNENBAUM
1971—DARREL E. GOLL
1972—THEODORE P. LABUSA
1973—NORMAN F. HAARD

MARTIN S. PETERSON

B

BABASSU

The babassu palm, *Orbignya speciosa* (Mart. and Barb. Rodr.) is an Embryophyta Siphonogama, of the Monocotyledonea class, of the Princeps order, of the Palmacae family and the Ceroxylinaceae subfamily. Its trunk is more or less cylindrical, with a diameter between 20 and 40 cm, and can reach up to 20 meters in height.

Its fruits come in bunches of 100 each, and each palm generally produces not more than 1 bunch a year. The fruits have different forms, cylindroidal, long and thin, and round; but the most common one is oval. The size and weight of each fruit also vary, the latter being from 150 to 250 gm and the former from 40 to 75 mm. The epicarp is fibrous (11% of the gross weight); the mesocarp (28% of the gross weight) has a layer rich in starch; the endocarp (57% of the weight) is very hard, with cavities (alveolus) where the nuts numbering 3–4, and sometimes up to 8 (9% of the weight), are lodged.

The nuts are white, covered with a brown skin. Their sizes vary between 2.5 and 6 cm long and 1 to 2 cm wide; their average weight is 3–4 gm and they contain between 60 and 68% and even up to 72% of oil.

The botanical denominations for the babassu palm are the following: *Attalea speciosa*, *Orbignya martiana*, *Orbignya oleira busset*, *Orbignya lydiae*, *Orbignya speciosa*, and *Attalea orbignya speciosa*.

Areas and Conditions of Growth

The babassu palm is native to the mid-North of Brazil, but can be found all over the interior of the country. The babassu palms cover an estimated area of 14 million hectares, being distributed mainly in the states of Maranhão (8.5 million hectares), Piauí (1.2 million), Goiás (1 million) and Mato Grosso (0.8 million hectares). The average concentration is around 200 palms per hectare but it can reach 1000 per hectare.

The alluvial areas, of sandy soil and hot and humid climate, are their "habitat." Babassu char-acterizes a whole geo-economic region, located between the dry Northeast and the super-humid Amazon region, where its extraction, directed to exportation and subsistence agriculture, is the prevailing economic activity. The State of Maranhão is the largest producer, the production of babassu representing 60% of the state income.

Utilization

Babassu offers rich raw material from which more than 50 products can be obtained for a wide range of purposes: from the nuts one can extract edible oils which can replace lard; the refined oil, total or partially hydrogenated, is used in the manufacture of margarine and fats called "compound"; the oil is also used in the manufacture of laundry soap, toilet soap, and shaving creams; from the residues resulting from the pressing of the nuts for the extraction of the oil, one can get oleaginous meal, regular meal, and the middlings which can contain from 19 to 27% protein and from 1 to 15% fat, providing good feed for cattle; from these residues one can also get flour for human consumption. The dry distillation of the endocarp provides activated charcoal and metallurgical cokes (pelotizados), tar, phenol, and derivatives, besides other chemical products of commercial interest. The epicarp (shell) can be used to manufacture cellulose, brushes, tar, acetones, etc. The starchy pulp of the mesocarp can be used in animal feeding.

However, the main products of babassu, with economic significance up to the present, are the oil for food and industrial purposes found in the nuts at the rate of approximately 67%, and the meal for animal rations. Tables B-1 and B-2 show the composition of the oil and the oleaginous meal.

Production

The production of babassu oil for food and industrial purposes has increased considerably; in 1967 it was 51,479 tons at a value of

78

TABLE B-1

INDEX NUMBERS OF THE ALMOND OILS OF THE Orbignya martiana

Specification	Typical Value	Min	Max
Number of experiments	123		
Fat rate of the dry nut in the air (%)		63	70
Index numbers			
Iodine rate	16.1	10	18
Saponification rate	249.0	245	255
Acidity rate	8.0	1.8	8.5
Reichert-Meissl rate	—	5.8	6.2
Polenske rate	—	10.0	12.0
Unsaponifiable (%)	—	0.2	0.8
Solidification point ($^\circ$C)	—	22.0	25.0
Fusion point ($^\circ$C)	24.0	22.0	26.0
Titulação ($^\circ$C) (Titer)	—	22.0	24.0
Specific gravity (25/25)	—	0.916	0.918
Refraction rate N^{40}_D	—	1.449	1.451
Fatty acids: weight in % of the gross weight of the fatty acids	[1]	[2]	
Caprioc Acid	0.2	0.0	0.2
(Caprílico) Acid (caprylic)	4.8	4.0	6.5
(Caprínico) Acid (capric)	6.6	2.7	7.6
Lauric Acid	44.1	44.0	46.0
(Mirístico) Acid (myristic)	15.4	15.0	20.0
Palmitic Acid	8.5	6.0	9.0
Stearic Acid	2.7	3.0	6.0
(Araquídico) Acid (arachidic)	0.2	0.2	0.7
Oleic Acid	16.1	12.0	18.0
(Linoteico) Acid) (linoleic)	1.4	1.4	2.8

SOURCE: *Babassu, Richness Unexplored* (in Spanish) by Christian Wilhelms, Rio de Janeiro.

[1] Analysis by means of the cleavage of the lead salt and the fraction of methylester.
[2] Analysis by means of the fraction of methylester.

Cr$38,777,061.00; in 1968, 65,393 tons, corresponding to Cr$68,893,280.00; in 1969, 100,678 tons, at a value of Cr$104,993,076.00.[1]

Export

The export of babassu oil from Brazil to other countries is still small, but is progressively increasing. In 1967, 4198 tons were exported, in the amount of Cr$3,241,000.00; in 1968, 8985 tons, in the amount of Cr$9,448,000.00; in 1969, 15,497 tons in the amount of Cr$15,128,000.00.
The babassu meal is also exported. For the period of 1967–1969 we have the following data: in 1967 we exported 35,708 tons in the amount of Cr$4,589,000.00; in 1968, 32,935 tons in the amount of Cr$6,041,000.00; in 1969, 46,129 tons in the amount of Cr$8,362,000.00.

WALTER SILVA

Cross-reference: *Fats and Oils.*

[1] 1 Cr = 0.163¢.

BABCOCK, STEPHEN MOULTON (1843–1931)

Stephen Moulton Babcock was regarded by his colleagues as a born inquisitor, and somewhat of a skeptic of man's written interpretation of nature, according to H. L. Russell (then Director) of the Wisconsin Alumni Research Foundation.[2]
Born on a farm in New York in 1843, he graduated from Tuft's College, and then entered a technical institute hoping to become an engineer. Circumstances required he return to the farm, but he worked part time in the laboratory of Professor G. C. Caldwell at Cornell University who urged him to go to the University of Göttingen, Germany, where he completed requirements for a doctorate degree, received in 1879. On his return, he served

[2] Russell, H. L. 1943. *Stephen Moulton Babcock, The Man of Science.* Proceedings of the Centenary Memorial, Wisconsin Alumni Research Foundation.

TABLE B-2

ANALYSES OF OLEAGINOUS MEAL/REGULAR BABASSU MEAL

A Chemical Composition

Elements	Stahlin (%)	Bolton (%)	In Accordance with Honcamp/Petermann (%)	Moebius (%)
Water	9.3	10.4	—	9.5
Gross protein	23.2	22.6	24.9	23.1
Gross fat	6.2	6.1	6.8	7.5
Volatile substances or exempt from N	41.5	43.7	47.4	41.9
Gross fiber	15.2	12.3	15.0	13.1
Ash	5.3	4.9	5.9	4.9

B Ash Composition (in Accordance with Moebius)

Elements	Chemical Formula	%
Potassium	K_2O	1.02
Calcium	CaO	0.36
Magnesium	MgO	0.72
Phosphoric acid	P_2O_5	2.46
Sulphuric acid	SO_3	0.14
Sodium	Na_2O	0.09
Silicon	SiO_2	0.19
Total		4.98

SOURCE: *Babassu, Richness Unexplored* (in Spanish) by Christian Wilhelms, Rio de Janeiro.

as an instructor in chemistry at Cornell University, and as a chemist at the New York Geneva Experiment Station. In 1888, he went to the University of Wisconsin where he worked for 43 yr.

At Geneva, Babcock was assigned to accumulating data to determine the relative feed value of feeds predicated on the basis of the number of calories per quantity. The nutritional value of foods for animals and humans was measured then by respiration calorimeters. Babcock lost faith in the procedures. He found that if he omitted consideration of the mineral ingredients in the rations, the chemical analyses of the intakes closely corresponded with that in the wastes. He thus questioned the caloric premise of adequacy of foods and suggested that if it were valid, he could devise a ration from soft coal and similar materials that would have the same nutritive value. Later at Wisconsin, using two "borrowed" cows, he found that one fed a balanced ration made from the corn plant prospered and grew, while the other fed an equally nutritious ration, as determined by chemical analyses, made from oats pined away and died. Six years later, with the young chemist, Edwin Hart, and animal husbandman, George Humphrey, he tested the then chemical concept of adequacy of equivalent rations made from either corn, wheat, or oats and a mixture of the 3 or 4 lots of 4 calves each. At an early stage, physiological differences in the calves began to show. Ultimately the calves fed solely from the ration of the wheat plant were weak and undersized, and later yielded low milk production. Those on corn produced large vigorous cows and high milk flow; the oat group lay between. Animals on the corn ration when switched to the wheat ration soon died; cows on the wheat ration when switched to the corn ration showed marked improvement. "Hidden hunger" was the difference. Later, E. V. McCollum, who went to Wisconsin from the laboratory of Osborne and Mendel at Yale, repeated the experiments with a less costly procedure using rats. He proceeded to establish beneficial effects of small quantities of butter added to the rations, subsequently identified as the effect of vitamin A. It is acknowledged that the inquisitiveness and doubts of Babcock led to further and very fruitful research in nutrition science by a host of students who followed at the University of Wisconsin. His observation of the regular habit of cows in winter to lick salt while crossing street car tracks near adjacent barns led to early studies on mineral metabolism in animals.

More widely recognized is Babcock's develop

ment of a simple means for measuring the concentration of butterfat in milk, an essential factor in factory rather than farm production of dairy products. The test also led to organization of educational facilities to teach principles of this test, manufacture of dairy products, and dairy factory management. In Hiram Smith Hall, believed to be the first dairy building in the western hemisphere for such instruction, Babcock cooperated with Dean Russell, who studied bacteriology in Pasteur's laboratory, in studies in cheese ripening. This led to the development of the cold curing process for cheese widely used throughout the world.

Among those who knew him well, Babcock is much recognized for his classic investigations in the processes of respiration in either plants or animals. Babcock, a chemist, became interested in the problem of how a clothes moth gets its necessary water supply when forced to live on dry wool fiber which it consumes in the larval stage of development; analyses showed over ten times as much water in the tissue of the animal as in the wool fiber or fur on which the larva fed. For over 6 yr, he watched moths breed generation after generation, living on cloth and fur. He studied the bee moth living on the empty honeycomb, weevils which infest dry seeds such as peas and beans, and flour moths; all of these studies indicated the water needed (metabolic water) to enable metabolism to proceed is dependent not so much on imbibed water as on water produced through respiration processes. These studies led to others on germination of seed, ripening of fruit, and similar phenomena.

More than 20 yr of Babcock's later scientific career was spent in fundamental work in physics, especially on the constitution of matter. With apparatus he had built, he measured variations in weight of water in the solid and liquid state. From this work, in which he persisted even to the age of 87, he postulated on the relation of energy and matter.

A great sports fan, a hearty storyteller, a great lover of flowers in his garden, he was a friend to all who knew him, and a stimulating person in science.

K. G. WECKEL

Cross-reference: *Butter.*

BABCOCK-HART AWARD

See Awards.

BACTERIOLOGY

In the world of living things microorganisms play an important part. The microorganisms of concern in food processing are molds, yeasts, and bacteria, the latter being the subject of the science of bacteriology.

Bacteria are unicellular organisms surrounded by a cell wall. In shape, generally speaking, they are spherical, rod-like, or spiral. Many bacteria have flagella, thin whip-like appendages that act as propellants. Bacteria multiply by simple division, 1 cell divides into 2 cells, 2 into 4, 4 into 8, and in a matter of hours by geometric progression a million or more bacteria are generated from a single bacterium.

The species differ from one another in many ways other than form. A principal difference lies in the chemical changes they can effect in the media into which by accident or design they are introduced. Bacteria differ substantially with regard to their preferences; many prefer a relatively nonacid environment such as meat or vegetables and very few can tolerate an acid environment such as is true of tomatoes, gooseberries, and, in fact, most fruits. A number of species thrive on protein foods; others prefer sugar. The great majority of bacteria are aerobic; that is, they require oxygen for their existence. But a few are anaerobic and thrive inside sealed cans or for that matter in plastic bags. Unfortunately, the anaerobes, *Clostridium botulinum* and *Clostridium perfringens* are dangerous, *C. botulinum* producing a potent poison which is often fatal.

The evolutionary history of bacteria is not yet known and there is no assurance that it ever will be. It has been suggested that they belong to the first stages of the origin of life, this on the assumption that as single-cell organisms they represent a more primitive stage of evolution than cells with a well-defined nucleus. Bacteria do not have a well-defined nucleus, the chromatin being dispersed throughout the cell.

Our systematized knowledge of bacteria begins with the microscope. In fact, advances in bacteriology in some degree parallel the advances in that instrument. Recent advances have been truly remarkable. Van Leeuwenhoek, the Dutch naturalist and one of the first to see bacteria, used a lens with a magnification of only 150 diameters, perhaps even less. By the time Louis Pasteur had begun his classic experiments in the third quarter of the Nineteenth Century, microscopes were capable of a magnification factor of 1000 diameters and more. High resolution electron microscopy today can reach a magnification of 500,000 diameters!

With the introduction of stains in 1871 and the separation of mixtures of organisms by means of plates of nutrient media in 1881, bacteriology took two giant steps forward and rapidly reached the important position among the life sciences that it occupies today. Vast amounts of new knowledge have accumulated down the years. The literature supporting medical bacteriology and immunology has grown from small beginnings in the last century to an imposing body of knowledge. Numerous journals and treatises are devoted to this branch of bacteriology. The same phenomenal growth of knowledge has occurred in industrial bacteriology, one part of which, food bacteriology, holds a commanding position in this general field.

Bacteriology in Relation to Food

Everyone in our day is aware of the fact that bacteria affect food adversely but also beneficially. This fact offers a convenient means of organizing the subject, food bacteriology.

Bacteria enter a food during handling, processing, or serving. Since bacteria require nutrients, moisture, and temperatures conducive to their growth, not all bacteria will grow in food and one species may thrive whereas another may not. Some bacteria like temperatures below freezing, others the higher temperatures. The minimum temperature for most bacteria is $10°F$, the maximum $140°-190°F$. Bacteria are more difficult to destroy than molds and yeasts, a fact that processors have long been aware of.

Bacteria are involved in many but not in all types of food spoilage. Some types of food spoilage are caused by enzymes, some by other microorganisms, and a few by chemical reactions, for example, by nonenzymatic browning. The bacteria which cause food poisoning are of great interest but they will receive only passing mention here since the topic is treated in detail elsewhere in this volume.

The bacteria responsible for food poisoning outbreaks include three groups, the staphylococci, the clostridia, and the salmonellae. The first mentioned, staphylococcus, specifically *Staphylococcus aureus*, is not fatal but the cramps, nausea, and diarrhea that accompany this food intoxication can cause extreme physical distress. The clostridia, *C. botulinum* and *C. perfringens*, represent opposite poles, as it were, of danger. *C. botulinum* is almost always fatal whereas *C. perfringens* is not fatal although anything but mild in its attack on the gastrointestinal tract. *C. perfringens* has been associated with food-borne diseases only since 1959. It is a spore-forming anaerobe widely distributed in soil, sewage, and unsanitary food processing plants. Foods most frequently affected

are meats and the gravies made therefrom. The potential hazard lies in the fact that meats on many occasions are allowed to cool slowly after cooking. Between the temperatures of $158°$ and $176°F$, *C. perfringens* germinates rapidly and at temperatures in the $110°-116°F$ range the growth is extremely rapid. Salmonella bacteria also infect foods, particularly meats and meat products, eggs, poultry, and fish. Salmonellae produce an endotoxin that survives cooking. The result is severe gastroenteritis.

The bacteria that benefit foods present a more cheerful story. Useful industrial applications are many. Butter and cheese, for example, depend on bacteria in the development of their characteristic flavors. The lactic acid bacteria ferment sugars to lactic acid and are indispensable in making cheese, pickles, sauerkraut, and olives. They are also employed in the manufacture of corned beef and rye bread. Bacteria are used to enhance the flavor of coffee, being introduced just prior to the roast. Familiar to all is the use of acetic bacteria in changing alcohol to vinegar.

In recent years, the exciting possibility that bacteria may be employed to produce a high quality protein has attracted wide attention. Grown on petroleum-based raw materials—heavy oils, long chain paraffins, etc.—these bacteria may eventually have outstanding industrial importance. Good progress has been made in petroprotein production to supplement animal foods. Product purity, nutritive quality, and gastrointestinal tolerance stand in the way, at present, of the use of petroproteins as human food.

The control of bacterial spoilage has received a tremendous amount of research attention beginning with Pasteur. Although the principal agents of control are chemicals, there is a group of organisms called phages that attack bacteria. They are capable of destroying disease-producing bacteria in living organisms and have specific effects on bacteria in food, sometimes good, sometimes not. They can cause trouble when they infect culture suspensions. Bacteriophages appear to be viruses composed of nucleoproteins and their capability for multiplying is not contested. They pass through bacterial filters readily.

Chemicals, as mentioned, are the chief source of control agents. The list of such agents begins with salt, its use as a preservative for fish and meat dating far back into antiquity. Sugar in high concentrations inhibits the growth of bacteria (and also yeasts and molds). Sugar in solution apparently dehydrates the bacteria as a result of osmosis. Acetic acid acts as a preservative although it is seldom used alone as is true of other acids. Sorbic acid has been shown to be a most effective fungistat. Sulfur dioxide is another agent with distinct fungistatic effect. Benzoates and nitrates have long been used as preservatives. Their effect is bacteriostatic.

Control by physical means comprises another category of control. Heat, of course, is the chief control method. Freezing retards proliferation. The preservation of food by radiation has received much study and as a pasteurizing agent has been shown to be effective; efforts to use the process in the sterilization of foods continue.

MARTIN S. PETERSON

Cross-reference: *Leeuwenhoek, Antoni Van; Chemical Preservatives.*

BACTOFUGATION

Centrifugal force provides an efficient means of improving the bacteriological quality of liquid foodstuffs; in fact, it can eliminate a very high proportion of the bacteria contained in such foodstuffs. The process which applies this principle is known as "bacterial supercentrifugation." When it is carried out under pasteurization heat conditions it is called "bactofugation." There is a tendency, however, to use the latter term irrespective of the process temperature.

The improvement of bacteriological quality thus obtained is fundamentally different from that obtained by the microbicidal heat treatments. These kill the bacteria and leave them in the food, whereas bactofuging removes both the living and the dead bacterial cells from the treated substance. This can be very important where foodstuffs are infected with bacteria containing thermostable endotoxins. Bactofugation is particularly indicated where an exceptionally high degree of bacteriological purity is sought, where it is desired to avoid heat-resistant bacteria without resorting to excessive heating, and where the aim is to improve the hygienic quality of the product.

Bacterial supercentrifugation is based on Stokes' law:

$$V = \frac{2r^2 (d_1 - d_2) g}{9v}$$

which expresses the velocity "S" at which a solid or semisolid particle of density d_1 is separated from the liquid of density d_2 containing it. This velocity is proportional to the difference $d_1 - d_2$ and to the centrifugal force g corresponding to n times the gravitational force; and it is inversely proportional to the viscosity v of the liquid.

Assuming that the bacteria have a dimension of 1-2 μ and that their density varies from 1.070 to

1.120, the above formula shows that a high centrifugal force will have to be employed.

Furthermore, it is obvious that, depending on their size and their density, certain species of bacteria will be removed more easily than others by centrifugal force. This is notably true of sporulated bacteria—a fact of special interest in view of their resistance to heat.

While bacterial supercentrifugation is not applicable to products that contain sedimenting substances, it can be used for liquids that have a colloidal structure, such as milk, and for certain true solutions such as wines and pulp-free fruit juices.

The first experiments aimed at improving the microbiological quality of a foodstuff by centrifugation were carried out in Belgium, on milk. As a result of those tests, bactofugation was applied on an industrial scale in 1962.

In removing bacteria from milk by supercentrifugation, allowance has to be made for the colloidal structure of milk which contains casein micella measuring up to 200 and even 300 mμ, with a density close to 1.3. One must also bear in mind its viscosity which, at ordinary temperature, is equal to 2.12 centipoises.

Considering these facts one can, on the semi-industrial scale, eliminate 90–95% of the bacteria contained in milk by subjecting it to a gravitational field of 8,000–12,000 g for 8 sec at 50°C. With 2 bactofuges placed in series, about 99% of the bacteria contained in the milk are removed. When applied at a temperature of 72°C this treatment has a twofold effect, as the milk is pasteurized at the same time. Under these conditions one obtains, by comparison with raw milk, a cell-count reduction of the order of 99% and a colony-count reduction of about 99.9%.

Similar results are obtained with the industrial bactofuges (Alfa-Laval, type D 3187M) which, with a 25 hp motor develop a centrifugal, force of 9000 g. The bowl of these machines, which originally had two 0.4-mm nozzles, is now of the self-opening type. This allows an escape of liquid, called "bactofugate," at the rate of about 180 liters an hour. Industrial machines have a capacity of 6000–7000 liters an hour. The capacity has so far been limited by the strength of the steels available, and only a new material stronger than the present-day steels would allow higher hourly throughputs.

The double-effect bactofugation is used on an industrial scale in several countries to process liquid milk, which, under these conditions, has only 1/100 of the bacterial content of the equivalent pasteurized milk.

In cheesemaking, both single- and double-effect bactofugation are used. The process offers many advantages. First, it prevents the swelling caused in certain types of cheese by butyric acid bacteria which are heat-resistant. Secondly, by improving the bacteriological quality of the milk without pasteurizing it, it enables a Cheddar to be produced which has more typical cheese flavor than that from the pasteurized milk cheese. Thirdly, it is useful for the removal of food-poisoning types of bacteria. In the preparation of milk powders, bactofugation is used not merely to obtain a low cell- and colony-count, but also to achieve a significant removal of the heat-resistant bacteria. If bactofugation is applied in the manufacture of sterilized milk, the thermal conditions for sterilization can be reduced. In cream, bactofugation prevents the "floc" caused by the heat-resistant *Bacillus cereus*.

Bactofugation is also useful in other sectors of the food industry: gelatin manufacture, preparation of pulpless fruit juices, and wine processing. Bactofugation has recently been suggested for use in the processing of liquid egg white, as a means of preventing contamination by enterobacteria.

Bacterial supercentrifugation is not a substitute for pasteurization or for sterilization, but used in conjunction with these it can improve their efficacy. Bactofugation, whether single- or double-effect or, again, in combination with a heat process, can be variously fitted into the manufacturing flowsheet for numerous foodstuffs, for the purpose of improving their bacteriological qualities.

PAUL SIMONART

References

KOSIKOWSKI, F. V., and O'SULLIVAN, A. C. 1966. Bacterial centrifugation of low grade milk for Cheddar cheese. Intern. Dairy Congr. D, 25–32.

LANGEVELD, L. P. M., and GALESLOOT, TH. E. 1967. Removal of spores of *Bacillus cereus* from milk with a Alfa-Laval bactofuge and influence on the keeping quality of pasteurized milk. Neth. Milk Dairy J. *21*, 13–28. (Dutch)

MORENO, V., and KOSIKOWSKI, F. V. 1970. Removal of food-poisoning types of bacteria from milk by bacterial centrifugation. Milchwissenschaft *25*, 545–547.

SIMONART, P. and DEBEER, G. 1953. Experiments in view of improving the microbiological quality of milk by ultracentrifugation. Neth. Milk Dairy J. 7, 117–128. (French)

SIMONART, P., POFFE, R., and WECKX, M. 1967. Microbiological quality of bactofuged milk. Neth. Milk Dairy J. *21*, 139–149.

BAKING INDUSTRY: BREAD

The origin of bread baking is lost in antiquity. Bread was first baked and eaten in some crude form long before man learned to record the event. For centuries, religions have used bread as a sacred symbol. The Egyptians and Babylonians had knowledge of baking and brewing more than 1000 yr before the Christian era; the knowledge of both baking and fermenting was conveyed to the Greeks and Romans.

During the height of the Roman Empire bread was baked in ovens, and large complexes developed that included mills to grind grain and breweries to provide the leaven. Roman bakers, at the time of Caesar, were members of trade unions; weights and prices of bread were regulated, and several types of bread were produced.

During the Middle Ages bakeries became numerous in the larger cities and bakers' guilds were formed. Gradually, as industrialization developed, especially in the western and eastern countries, the process of bread manufacturing became mechanized. Today, an ultramodern bakery bears little resemblance to the common concept of a bakery operation. The process is now completely mechanized, so a baker, in the traditional sense, is no longer needed.

Ingredients

Ingredients for bread can be divided into two categories, essential and optional. Essential ingredients are flour, yeast, salt, and water. Optional ingredients include sugar, malt, milk, shortening, enzymes, vitamins, chemical dough improvers, mold inhibitors, and minerals.

Flour.—Flour is the most important and most basic ingredient in bread-making. On the basis of suitability to produce yeast-leavened bread, the common wheats, when milled into flour, are classified as hard or soft, and strong or weak. Strong flours have a high protein content and thus, when mixed with water, form elastic gluten that will retain gas during fermentation and bake into a well-risen, shapely loaf of bread. Such flours have a high water-retention capacity and hence are more suitable for bread production than weak flours; however, some excellent bread is produced from soft wheat flours. Baked products other than bread and rolls, such as cakes, crackers, biscuits, and cookies, are made from soft wheat flours.

Salt.—Apparently, salt has always been an ingredient in breadmaking and has been added mainly for taste, but it also improves dough-handling properties and increases loaf volume. Based on flour weight, the amount of salt added is from 1 to 2%.

Yeast.—Leavened bread was prepared for centuries by mixing a portion of leftover dough with the new dough batch and permitting the mix to ferment. A more recent development was to obtain yeast from a brewery or distillery and mix it with the dough. Today, baker's yeast is a carefully cultured and standardized ingredient used in the amount of 2-5% in yeast-leavened baked products. Dough fermentation is hastened by adding sugar, malt, and diastatic enzymes.

The Baking Procedure

Straight-dough fermentations involve mixing all ingredients—flour, liquid, malt, sugar, salt, and other optional ingredients—together in one operation. A sponge fermentation, with several modifications, is made by mixing a part of the flour and certain other ingredients, such as the yeast, shortening, and sugar, into a stiff dough which is allowed to ferment for several hours. The sponge dough thus formed is then remixed with additions of the total liquid and all other ingredients into a dough that ferments for a brief period before being divided to form loaves.

The sponge- and straight-dough methods of breadmaking thus described are conventional baking procedures, but a continuous baking process has recently been developed. By this process, dough ingredients are fed continuously to a high speed mixer where the homogeneous mass is passed through a dough pump to a developing apparatus. After proper development, the dough is extruded continuously into dough pans. In the continuous process, a preferment produces the required leavening action. Preferments can be developed by blending various ingredients to obtain desired properties and tastes in baked bread.

Following fermentation, the usual baking procedure involves a dough divider, rounder, intermediate proofer, molder, proofer, oven, cooler, slicer, and wrapping machines. In a modern bakery, all of these steps are essentially automated and synchronized; but in many places in the world, baking remains a small shop operation where almost all operations are performed by hand.

The production of buns and rolls follows the same general principle as bread production. Sweet, yeast-raised products are produced by modifying the raised dough process. These products are richer in sugar and shortening, and usually contain eggs.

In contrast to the complexities involved in the breadmaking process, the baking of cakes is, in principle, rather simple. In place of yeast fermentation, chemical leavening agents are used to supply the necessary amounts of carbon dioxide gas. Cakes and pies are usually made from soft wheat flour. Other ingredients can include shortening, milk, sugar, egg yolks and/or whites, and flavoring agents, which are mixed together to form a batter that is poured into cake pans and placed in the oven.

Bread Types Around the World

It is not possible to generalize about the kinds of bread produced throughout the world, because in some countries several hundred types of bread are manufactured. On a worldwide basis, breads vary from those produced in the same manner as they were centuries ago, to the products of ultramodern, completely-automated, continuous-baking procedures. There have been held five international bread conferences where extensive bread displays were prepared; the displays and conference discussions dramatized the extent and diversity of bread types throughout the world.

In major cities everywhere, similar bread types are available such as hearth breads, pan breads, and various soft and hard crust rolls and buns. Also, sweet rolls, cakes, and cookies are generally everywhere similar in appearance and in composition. The types of equipment and baking procedures for production of most sweet goods are similar. Differences occur when specialty breads are produced in a traditional manner, as required by certain races, regions, or religions.

Economic Importance of the Baking Industry

In industrial nations the baking industry is among the top ten in value of product produced. Investment in baking operations varies from modest to huge. In hand-operated shops the investment can be limited to a crude dough mixer and an oven; however, in a modern automatic bakery the investment in building, storage facilities, and equipment is substantial.

Traditionally, the baking industry is a major employer of labor, but as bakeries have become more automated the work force for unit production has decreased.

Bread as Food

Nutritionists and other food authorities have long recognized the important nutritional attributes of bread. In addition to the energy value of bread, it is also an important supplier of protein, fat, minerals, and vitamins. To supplement the nutritional value of bread made only of flour, yeast, salt, and water, much bread is made with additions of shortening and milk. Also, a large amount of bread is made from enriched flour or dough. Enrichment is accomplished by adding specific amounts of certain nutrients such as thiamin, niacin, riboflavin, iron, and calcium and sometimes vitamin D. Special bread can be made even more nutritious than it normally is by adding amino acids such as lysine or by adding protein concentrates such as soy flour.

Future Changes in the Baking Industry

With the population movement from rural to urban centers, small baking operations tend to become uncommon and large bakeries tend to supply the needs for baked products. This trend seems likely to continue with the baking industry becoming more and more completely mechanized. For developing countries, efforts will continue, with limited success, to produce breads from non-wheat flours to better utilize readily available ingredients. This development is based on the use of composite flours from high starch crops, such as cassava, supplemented with soya, cottonseed, peanut, or bean flour as a protein source.

Further integration of the baking industry will take place whereby the bakery will become only one step in the continuous operation of providing the basic ingredients, producing the product, distributing it, and selling it. New products will be convenience type in new forms, marketed by new methods. Nutritional value of baked products, as well as freshness, taste, and aroma will be improved. Consumption of sweet goods will increase competition with many other food items, and in all probability, will cause bread consumption per capita to decrease; however, total bread consumption, because of increased world population, will increase.

J. A. SHELLENBERGER

References

ANON. 1958. From Flour to Bread. Wheat Flour Institute, Chicago.
MATZ, S. A. 1972. Bakery Technology and Engineering, 2nd Edition. Avi Publishing Co., Westport, Conn.
PELSHENKE, P. F. 1966. Evolution of bread technology in the history of man. Cereal Sci. Today 11, 192–199.
POMERANZ, Y., and SHELLENBERGER, J. A. 1971. Bread Science and Technology. Avi Publishing Co., Westport, Conn.
PYLER, E. J. 1958. Our Daily Bread. Siebel Publishing Co., Chicago.

Cross-reference: *Flour Milling Industry.*

BAKING INDUSTRY: CAKES AND PIES

Cakes

It is believed that the oldest example of an aerated batter type cake might be the old-fashioned pound cake, so named because the recipe called for 1 lb each of the four basic ingredients—flour, butter, whole eggs, and sugar. Butter was the preferred shortening because of its superior creaming (aerating) power when mixed with sugar. The lecithin of eggs provided the emulsifying power which stabilized the batter.

Pound cake, by its manner of aeration, tends to be a rather dense, heavy cake. Attempts to leaven bakery foods by other than the fermentation process probably dates from the attempt to "sweeten" sour milk with sodium bicarbonate, a common household ingredient. More properly, the leavening by chemical means dates from about 1842 when Abel Conant patented the first baking powder, a combination of sodium bicarbonate and an acid or acidic salt with flour. This development enabled the production of lighter cakes of superior quality.

The discovery of catalytic hydrogenation of vegetable oils about 1910 enabled the production of shortenings which rivaled butter in creaming power. About 1933, the laboratories of the Procter & Gamble Company found that the superior creaming power of certain hydrogenated shortenings was due to the presence of small amounts of monoglycerides (rather than triglycerides characteristic of fat). This enabled the development of the superior emulsifying (the term "Hi Ratio" is a trademark of Procter & Gamble Company) shortenings which have largely replaced butter as the preferred shortening in fine bakery foods and has enabled the development of modern cake-baking technology.

From rather humble beginnings, cake baking has grown into a major business. In a staff report, Baking Industry has estimated that commercial cake production, including that of retail bakeries, totaled about 1.9 billion pounds in 1971. The manufacturers of cake mixes produce about 760 million pounds of home-type cake mixes which might be equivalent to an additional 1.4 billion pounds of cake. There is no reliable method of estimating the portion of the 2.7 billion pounds of white flour sold to consumers that is used for home baking of cakes.

The Evolution of a Cake Formula and Formula Balance by P. J. Coughlin published by Procter & Gamble Company in 1947 constitutes the first comprehensive attempt to enumerate the functions of the basic ingredients and provide a basic system of determining formula balance for batter type cakes. Coughlin designates five functions as follows: (1) tougheners, (2) tenderizers, (3) moisteners, (4) dryers, and (5) flavorers.

Among the toughening ingredients may be included the flour, milk solids, and egg whites; among the tenderizers, the sugar, shortening, chocolate, and fat in egg yolk; among the moisteners, water, the fluid in milk and eggs; among the dryers, the flour, sugar, dry milk, and cocoa; and among the flavorers, sugar, cocoa, chocolate, added flavor, and the flavor contributed by each of the major ingredients. To procure cake of top quality it is necessary to proportion the various ingredients from their functional viewpoint so that the counter action of the ingredients is in balance.

The formula for the old-fashioned pound cake, 1 lb each of the four basic ingredients, has served as the starting point for a great number of cake variations, some of which bear only a slight resemblance to the original formula.

In studying methods to improve volume and decrease cost, it was found that formulas of any desired degree of richness in terms of fat and eggs could be made by following three basic rules: (1) The weight of the shortening should equal the weight of the whole eggs. (2) The weight of the sugar should equal the weight of the flour. (3) The combined weight of eggs and milk should equal the weight of sugar or flour.

The use of leavening in the form of baking powder was an aid in improving volume and lightness of the cake. Using these principles, it is possible to formulate a wide degree of richness in finished cake limited only by the individual baker's concept of what constitutes a palatable cake.

Modern batter type cake formulations are based on the use of shortenings containing monoglycerides or edible emulsifying agents. These shortenings improve the aerating properties of cake batters and enable the incorporation of high ratios (in relation to flour) of liquid and sugar. Using this concept the rules for balancing high liquid cakes may be generalized: (1) The weight of sugar should exceed the weight of the flour. (2) The weight of liquid eggs should exceed the weight of the shortening. (3) The combined weight of the liquid in the eggs, milk and added water should equal or slightly exceed the weight of the sugar.

Whereas by these rules cakes of almost any sugar to flour ratio could be formulated, the practical limits are 100–150 parts of sugar for 100 parts of flour. In formulas containing cocoa or chocolate this ratio may be extended to 180 parts of sugar.

When hydrogenated shortenings first came into general use it was common practice to use equal amounts of eggs and shortening to balance the toughening effect of eggs against the tenderizing effect of shortening. However, the tenderizing effect of emulsifying type shortenings is more efficient so that in modern formulas egg content may exceed shortening content by some 15–20 parts. The primary function of egg yolk is that of an aerating-emulsifying agent so that in modern formulas the importance of egg yolks is somewhat diminished.

By the third rule above, the weight of combined liquids must exceed the weight of the sugar. Sufficient liquid must be present to dissolve the sugar without depriving the starch (of the flour) of adequate moisture for gelatinization. The ability to carry high ratios of liquids is one of the characteristics of modern cake flours and emulsifying type shortenings. The proper ratio of liquid to flour is essential to cake quality. If too little liquid is used, the cake may be dry, coarse, and harsh. Excessive liquids will weaken the structure of the baked cake to the point that it may collapse on baking.

It has been found that soluble film-forming proteins are responsible for the rheological characteristics of a well formulated cake batter (Howard *et al.* 1968). This structure may have sufficient stability while the cake is baking to hold the leavening gases until the structure is set by the gelation of the flour starch. Failure of structure at this transition temperature results in the phenomenon of "dipping" or collapse of the structure.

Miller and Trimbo (1965) in studies evaluating various cake flours in baking white cakes, observed that conditions which changed the transition temperature from a protein structure to a gelatinized starch structure could be used to overcome certain deficiencies of cake flour. These include: (1) Varying the water-to-sugar ratios, thus altering the amount of water available for starch gelation, hence gelation temperature. (2) Varying the amount of leavening, thus altering the stress on structure at transition temperature. (3) Replacing a portion of cake flour with starches of gelatinization characteristics differing from those of wheat starch. (4) Addition of chemical agents, known to alter gelatinization characteristics of starch, to the batter system.

To prevent dipping of cakes, it is necessary to stabilize the fluid batter until the starch has gelatinized sufficiently to maintain the structure of the cake.

This discussion has been concerned with batter type cakes as their formula balance is more complex. Foam type cakes, such as angel food and sponge cakes, also require proper proportioning of their ingredients. In these cakes the aerated structure is developed by whipping egg whites or whole eggs to develop an aerated foam structure, followed by careful blending of the flour in this foam to avoid a break in structure.

Angel food cake is based upon a relatively simple formula of 1 part of flour to each 3 parts of egg whites and 3 parts of sugar. Thus, the general rules for formulating angel food cakes are: (1) The weight of sugar should equal or slightly exceed the weight of egg whites. (2) The weight of flour should approximate $1/3$ the weight of either the sugar or egg whites.

Sponge cakes depend upon the whipping quality of whole eggs. In balancing their formulas it is necessary to decrease the toughening effect of eggs by inclusion of sufficient sugar and liquid. The general rules are as follow: (1) The amount of sugar should slightly exceed the weight of liquid whole eggs. (2) The combined weight of liquid in whole eggs, milk, and water should exceed the weight of the sugar. (3) The weight of the sugar should exceed the weight of the flour. (4) The combined weight of liquid egg and flour should exceed the combined weight of sugar and liquids other than whole egg.

In baking sponge cakes, the use of certain emulsifiers may be used to improve the whipping quality of whole egg, particularly when dry egg solids are used as the egg component. It is also common practice to use whole egg fortified with additional egg yolk as the egg component.

The methods by which the ingredients of the formula are incorporated into a batter may be as important as formula balance in determining cake quality. The purpose of mixing is: (1) To uniformly incorporate the ingredients of the formula. (2) To develop a film protein structure to hold the leavening gases. (3) To incorporate air and build the proper emulsion structure.

With shortenings that are low in emulsifying power, the creaming method is preferred. In this method, the sugar and shortening are mixed (creamed) until light. The eggs are then added and creaming is continued to build the proper emulsion. The flour, baking powder, salt, and other dry ingredients are sifted together and added alternately with the remaining liquids (water or milk), mixing smooth after each addition. This method is most suitable for sugar-to-flour ratios of 1:1 or less. It does not give satisfactory results with high sugar formulas.

In the second method, the flour mixture and shortening are creamed light in one mixing bowl and in a second bowl the eggs and sugar are whipped to a foam. They are then carefully combined and the remaining liquids are carefully added. This method assures uniform dispersion of shortening in the batter, incorporates more air, results in a cake of fine grain, and is suitable for high sugar formulas. It is somewhat cumbersome for a manufacturing operation.

With emulsifying shortenings of good quality, a single-stage mixing procedure is generally employed. In this procedure, all of the ingredients are combined in the bowl at low speed followed by a mixing period at an intermediate speed. The mixing bowl is then scraped down and the mix finished by a short period of low speed mixing.

A variation of the single-stage procedure may be preferred. In this procedure, $1/3$-$2/3$ of the total liquid is added in the first stage of mixing and the remaining liquid added during the final low speed mix. If liquid eggs are used as the egg component of the formula, this method is preferred and the egg component added as the second-stage liquid. This method of mixing incorporates sufficient air to give relatively low batter specific gravities.

In the so-called continuous mix procedure, the ingredients of the formula are slurried together and then pumped through a high speed, high shear mixing head. Air under pressure is added directly to the batter in the mixing head producing batters of low specific gravity maximizing the cake volume per ounce of batter. This procedure also minimizes the need for baking powder. There is considerable mechanical work done in the mixing head resulting in an increase in batter temperature. To minimize this temperature effect, the temperature of the prepared slurry should be relatively cold, not over $60°F$, and preferably in the $40°$-$50°F$ range. This method is particularly satisfactory for single-stage foam cakes such as angel food or sponge.

There are, of course, many variations of these mixing procedures depending upon richness of formula, size of the baked unit, and type of oven. For commercial baking, solid hearth ovens, rather than open grid, are generally preferred. Temperatures are low to moderate varying from $300°F$ for pound and fruit cakes to $425°F$ for lean sponge cakes. The generally preferred baking temperature is $350°$-$360°F$. Baking time is also variable, ranging from 10 to 14 min for cupcakes to 2–3 hr for 3–5 lb fruit and pound cakes.

Pies

By definition, a pie may be considered as a baked dish consisting of a filling with either a lower or an upper crust, or both. The nature of the filling varies widely and may consist of fruit, custards, puddings, Bavarian creames, meats, etc. Because it is not possible in this brief review to describe the multitude of fillings used in pies, this discussion will be limited to the crust portion only.

Pie might be considered as the typical American dessert. There are not any reliable statistics available upon which to base the volume of homemade pies but it has been reliably estimated that commercial bakers (including retail bakers) produce well over a billion pounds of pie annually. Frozen pies constitute the greatest volume of frozen bakery foods, and, at 400 million pounds annually, is nearly double the combined volume of other frozen bakery foods.

The dough making process for making the crust is comparatively simple as yeast fermentation or chemical leavening are not required. The basic ingredients are flour, shortening, salt, and water.

Almost any type of flour may be used for making pie crust but unbleached flour milled from soft wheat varieties is generally preferred. The preferred flour, on the basis of both economics and function, is the unbleached clear flour remaining after separation of high quality cake flours in the milling of soft wheats. Hard wheat flours may be used, but their higher protein content may result in a toughening effect, making necessary the use of more shortening to produce a tender crust.

Flours bleached with chlorine tend to produce sticky doughs and a soft baked crust. Good pastry flours should possess a pH value of about 6.0, lower values indicating chlorine treatment.

Shortening is the most expensive ingredient in the pie crust formulation. Lard has long been the preferred shortening because of its excellent shortening power, its desirable plastic range, its flavor, and its tendency to spread when the dough is rolled to a sheet. Hydrogenated vegetable shortenings, whose uniformity with respect to such properties as plasticity, shortening power, and freedom of flavor, is more readily maintained, are finding increasing application in pie production. Edible oils may be used as the shortening, but oils (and soft shortenings) tend to produce a mealy rather than a flaky crust. Depending upon flour quality and desired degree of tenderness, the shortenings may be used at levels ranging from 40 to 75% of flour weight.

Water is generally accepted as a constant ingredient although there may be variations in pH, organic, and mineral content of such a range as to cause dough make-up problems. Cold or ice water is preferred as it tends to maintain the plasticity of the shortening. Normal water absorption is approximately 20–25% of flour weight.

Salt is used to accentuate the flavor of the crust. Although salt may exert a small effect on dough consistency, the variable is so small that it is of no practical significance.

As optional ingredients, sugar (particularly dextrose), milk or whey solids may be incorporated in the dough. The reducing sugars in these materials promote crust browning to produce a more pleasing color. These ingredients are particularly helpful in unbaked frozen pies, packaged in bright foil pans as they promote pan crust browning. The level may vary from 2–5% (solids basis) depending upon the degree of color desired.

Baking powder may be used, especially in the baking of unfilled pie shells, to reduce crust shrinkage. Levels in excess of 1% of the flour weight produce a leavening effect that is atypical of pie crust. To assure uniformity of distribution, the baking powder must be blended with the flour, preferably by sifting, before attempting to mix the dough.

Perhaps the secret of good crust quality is the manner in which the dough is mixed. To produce a flaky crust the shortening is lightly blended with the flour. Lumps of shortening as well as uncoated flour should be apparent in the blend. Cold water is then added and the blend is mixed just enough so that the dough holds together. Overmixing must be avoided. Many bakers prefer to refrigerate the dough for several hours (overnight) before rolling out.

To produce a mealy type crust, the flour and shortening are thoroughly blended so that the flour particles are completely enrobed with fat before the water is added. Because soft shortenings and oils blend more readily with flour, these shortenings are used to produce this type of crust. Warm water, because it tends to soften the shortening, is also an aid in producing mealy type crusts. To assure flakiness, some bakers use a hard flaked shortening as a portion (approximately 5%) of the total shortening. This hard fat remains as discreet particles after mixing and is pressed to a flat thin flake when the dough is rolled. Overmixing and the use of too much water tends to develop the flour glutens producing excessive shrinkage on baking and a tough crust.

To form the pie shell, a piece of dough just sufficient to form the desired size crust is scaled and rolled to approximately $1/8$ in. thick, and of round diameter just slightly larger than the pie pan. The sheet of dough is transferred to the pie pan and shaped to conform, trimming off the the excessive dough. The shell may be baked empty or filled with the desired filling.

For two crust pies the top crust is added and the edges crimped to seal before the excess dough is trimmed. Automatic machines are available for shaping, filling, crimping, and trimming. Reworking the pie dough tends to toughen the crust hence trimmings must be held to a minimum.

Fillings must be thoroughly chilled before adding to the formed dough as warm fillings melt the shortening destroying the flaky character of the crust.

The preferred pie oven is a solid hearth, with solid bottom heat and medium top heat although ovens with an open grid hearth may be used sucessfully. Baking time and temperature are usually determined by the filling. Fruit and meat pies are generally baked at temperatures ranging from 400° to 500°F. Custard and pumpkin pies (a type of custard), because of the tendency of these fillings to boil, are baked at lower temperatures ranging from 325° to 400°F.

For many types of cream, Bavarian creme, and other types of cold set fillings, a crumb crust rather than a pastry crust may be preferred. The formulation of most crumb crusts is based upon the use of graham cracker crumbs; almost any type of crumb such as vanilla wafers, base cake for sandwich cookies, gingersnaps, sugar cookies or even crumbed breakfast cereal may be used. For best results the crumb moisture should approximate 4%. The crumb is mixed with sugar, butter, margarine, or shortening (occasionally a small amount of water) and this blend formed into a crust to fit a pie pan. The crust may be hand formed by spreading the crumbs uniformly in the pie tin and patting to compact them, by using a spinning mandrel to distribute and compact the crumb, or by using heated dies and pressure to flow the crumbs and compact them. The rigidity of the formed crust may be varied by the size of the crumb granules, the amount and type of shortening and the amount of water used in the formulation, and the pressure with which the crumb is compacted. This type crust is preferred for many types of frozen cream pies.

DONALD F. MEISNER

References

HOWARD, N. B., HUGHES, D. H., and STROBEL, R. G. K. 1968. Function of the starch granule in the formation of layer cake structure. Cereal Chem. *45*, 329–338.

MATZ, S. A. 1959. Chemistry and Technology of Cereals as Food and Feed. Avi Publishing Co., Westport, Conn. (Out of print.)

MILLER, B. S., and TRIMBO, H. B. 1965. Gelatinization of starch and white layer cake quality. Food Technol. *19*, 640–648.

PYLER, E. J. 1952. Baking Science and Technology, Vol. 2. Siebel Publishing Co., Chicago.

WOODRUFF, S., and NICOLI, L. 1931. Starch gels. Cereal Chem. *8*, 243–251.

Cross-reference: *Flour Milling Industry.*

BAKING INDUSTRY: ETHNIC U.S. BREADS

Bread was first baked in Egypt over 6000 yr ago and from that time and place, traveled west, varying in ingredients, flavor, texture, and form. European and Middle Eastern immigrants to this country brought recipes for their native breads and these have been handed down to second and third generations. As a result, the United States has become the repository of the entire history and geography of the world's breads. While most Americans seem content with a choice of the packaged breads found on supermarket shelves, anyone in a large city with ethnic neighborhoods can find excellent and fascinatingly beautiful breads always available. Although a city of a million or more population, might well offer several types of foreign breads—Italian, Jewish-Eastern European, German, Greek, Scandinavian, and Latin-American—even a small town with a cohesive ethnic enclave (such as Provincetown, Mass. with its Portuguese descendants) will have a few interesting foreign-style bakeries.

Perhaps the most readily available of all foreign breads is the Italian, based on the classic loaves of Naples and Sicily, the areas from which most of our Italian immigrants came. The only northern Italian bread usually found here is Milan's panettone, a high-domed cylinder of sweet yeast dough, golden with saffron and studded with citron and almonds, and sold the year 'round, although it is primarily a Christmas specialty. This same dough, shaped into rings and braids, is entwined around pastel-colored, hard-cooked eggs at Eastertime. For the most part, Italian breads are made of three doughs: A white, similar to but coarser than the French; a light, golden whole-wheat flecked mixture; and Sicilian bread which is plaster white and dry with a fine texture and, when baked, has a pale, golden, very smooth crust. All of these doughs are worked into an enormous variety of shapes: large and small rounds, long slim loaves as small as individual rolls or up to 4 ft in length, braids and twists, rings and crescents. Sicilian bakers, inspired by the seaforms that abound in their island province, shape starfish, shells, and seahorses. Sesame seeds and, less frequently, poppy seeds, top Italian breads and crusts may be scored in criss-cross patterns or have finials of crisp dough "artichokes." Handmade breadsticks, long and uneven, can still be found in a few older Italian bakeshops, and have a far more interesting texture than their machine-extruded counterparts. Flat bread rings flavored with crisp bits of lard or proscuitto ham and coarse black pepper; large, crisp whole-wheat biscuits; and small light golden fluted crowns (tarralucci), are all favorites with cheese and wine. And around lunchtime, in many Italian bakeries, one can still buy squares of "baker's pizza," a spongy bread dough rolled flat, and spread with tomato paste, pepper, oregano, and basil, and then baked.

There is, an even more staggering array of breads among Jewish-Eastern European-Russian groups, for all of these share the same varieties with only minor differences. Challah, the long, oval braids of egg dough served on the Jewish Sabbath, is Ukrainian in origin, both in name and form. In that Republic of the Soviet Union, is is shaped in high rings sometimes stacked one atop the other or into braids decorated with dough pine cones

Sour dough rye breads, seasoned with caraway seeds or flecks of crisp onion are popular; as is corned bread, which derives its name from the very piquant dough which is strongly soured or "corned." Pumpernickels range from sand-colored loaves to others so dark and moist they seem more like Devil's Food cake, and, in fact, many do contain chocolate or coffee for color and flavor; they may also be enriched with raisins. Potato flour is sometimes added to rye or wheat yeast doughs to produce a bland, fragrant, somewhat heavy bread. Marbelized breads, of combined pumpernickel and rye doughs are shaped into loaves or braids. Salt sticks range in size from finger-size to 2–3 ft. And all of these doughs are made into rolls as well. Two specialties thought of as primarily Jewish, but which are really Polish and Russian in origin, are "bialys" and bagels. The first is a round, flat, chewy roll topped with poppy seeds and bits of onion and is named for the Polish town of Bialystock, where it originated. Bagels are made of a gray, heavy, moist dough, shaped into rings, boiled, and then baked. So-called bagels made of pumpernickel and other doughs, are merely ring-shaped rolls, and never beguile true bagel aficionados.

German delicatessens, groceries, and bakeries offer many of the breads described above, and, in addition, always the farmers' bread, Bauernbröt. At its most traditional, this is a gigantic round bread, from which pieces are cut and are sold by weight, the entire round weighing from 7 to 9 lb. Bauernbröt is a sour dough rye with a thick, tough crust that forms a hard, protective natural "wrapping" until it is cut. Many German breads are extremely moist and keep well and are traditionally sold in small squares, thinly sliced and cellophane-wrapped. Among these are, again, a range of pumpernickels, from the palest sand color to the dark malt-flavored Westphalian classic. Vollkornbröt, a rye bread with whole, nut-like kernels of grain, and Kommisbröt, flavored with cumin seeds, are two standard favorites, as are a variety of rye, ranging in sourness. Graubröt is a mixture of rye and wheat flours, and Roggensmichbröt is a similar mix, shaped in rounds or ovals and dusted with flour to give the crust a snowy texture. Germans are especially fond of rolls, and among their regulars are the small, round poppyseeded Mohnbrötchen, a fluted round roll called Kaisersemmel, and a simple breakfast egg roll, Eiernsemmel. Salt sticks are popular as are tangy, chewy rye rolls featured in Bavarian bakeries where they are known as brick-layers' loaves, Mauerloauerlei. Fruited, sweet yeast breads such as Christmas Stollen and the pear bread, Hutzelbröt, and Easter osterfladen, are also prepared by German bakers throughout this country.

Although Scandinavians' most distinctive bread specialties are the crisp-breads which we think of as crackers, there are some other distinctive loaves available in their bakeries as well. Danish rugbrød is a nutty, sweet-smelling blend of whole wheat and rye meals, baked in a small, tight, heavy and savory loaf that looks like a large cobblestone; thinly sliced and buttered, this bread is the base for most of Denmark's famed open sandwiches. French type white breads in various shapes are popular with Scandinavians also. Sweden's Limpa bread is made of rye meal, and is flavored with molasses, fennel and anise and, at Christmas when it is known as Vortlimpa, juice of the whortleberry is added and the bread is used to dip into the drippings from the holiday ham.

Courtesy of Ben Somoroff

FIG. B-1. THIS SHOWS THE UNUSUALLY WIDE VARIETY OF ETHNIC BREADS AVAILABLE IN THE UNITED STATES

Another seasonal specialty available at Swedish bakeries in this country are Lucia buns, small twists and curls and braids, that are really sweet saffron-scented rolls, dotted with currants and served for breakfast on Dec. 12th, St. Lucia's Day. Norway, Finland, Sweden, and Denmark all have variations on sweet yeast Christmas breads, rich with dried fruits and nuts and perfumed with cardamom, anise, and nutmeg, and varying mainly in shape.

Cuban and Porto Rican breads are somewhat similar to each other and to Sicilian bread. They are white, dry, light, and bland and keep better than more moist loaves would in their hot and humid native climates.

While Mexicans also bake this dry white bread, they have more variety in coarser, slightly soured breads as well. The greatest interest is in the shapes: Picones, which are small, light rolls glazed on top; Picones Retrendes, a yellow egg dough, oval shaped with elaborately decorated crusts; Picones Mediones, a round cushion of a bread with sugar and spice flavor; and a variety of twists, crescents, horns, and swirls in rolls and larger loaves.

Egg-enriched, golden sweet bread, flavored with orange or lemon is a Greek specialty, done up in rounds or braids and sprinkled with sesame seeds. at New Year's, (St. Basil's Day), the numbers of the new year are arranged in dough on top of the loaf which is known as Vasilopeta (St. Basil's bread). And at Easter the same dough is braided around red eggs and is called Lambropsomo.

Colored eggs, are, in fact, braided into sweet yeast breads in all of the Catholic Mediterranean countries and the custom continues here, not only with Italians and Greeks but with Portuguese who bake these Easter specialties along with their Christmas bread, Bolo Rei, and their light, bland, white table bread.

Latvian loaves are made of whole wheat and are slightly sweet; their crusts are as black as tar.

In an Irish neighborhood, one will surely come across the soda bread, risen with soda instead of yeast and studded with currants. This soda bread, as well as the Irish oatmeal bread, are always shaped into round cushiony loaves that are scored in quarters to suggest, vaguely, a four-leaf clover.

Scotch bakers feature bannocks, somewhat like pancakes and cut in wedges, to be eaten cold or reheated on a griddle, and scones, very much like what we call English muffins.

Armenian and Middle Eastern breads, sold at Syrian bakeshops, are simple—thin, flat, wafel-like rounds which may be had limp or crisp, topped with sesame seeds or a thick herb and spice paste.

Oddly enough, the famed French bread is harder to find in this country than any other—at least the authentic version. But in larger cities there are usually 3 or 4 bakeries that turn out the incomparable sour dough white breads in long loaves that may be thin and crusty or thick with more inside bread to be used with gravies and sauces. Pain d'epis is made in the shape of a wheat stalk and the "kernels" break off into individual rolls. And of course wherever there is a French bakery there is certain to be the flaky breakfast crescents, croissants, and the golden puffs that are brioches.

Certainly the world of bread is much larger and more interesting than our own poor mass-produced packaged loaves suggest, and the availability of them is one compensation for living in large cities these days.

MIMI SHERATON

BARLEY

Ancient records show that cultivated barley was used by Neolithic cultures in Egypt between 5000 and 6000 B.C. Major gene centers of barley where cultivated varieties may have developed include Abyssinia and the highlands of Sikkim and and Southern Tibet. Barley is a winter-hardy and drought-resistant grain. It matures more rapidly than wheat, oats, or rye and is widely distributed.

Production

World production of barley in 1965–1966 was 86.4 million tons (compared to 236.7 of wheat, 196.6 of corn, and 35.0 of rye). Annual per capita consumption of barley, as food, in the United States is only 1.1 lb (compared to 111 of wheat, 7.8 rice, and 1.2 rye).

The Plant

Barley is a grass that belongs taxonomically to the family Gramineae, subfamily Festucoideae, tribe Hordeae, and genus *Hordeum*. Practically all cultivated barleys are covered. However, in some primitive mountainous areas where barley is used for human food, naked (hull-less) barleys are frequently found (Fig. B-2). The two main types of cultivated covered barleys, depending on the arrangement of grains in the ear, are two-row and six-row. The former predominates in Europe, in parts of Australia, and in the Western United States. The latter is more resistant to extremes of temperature and is grown in North America, India, and the Middle East.

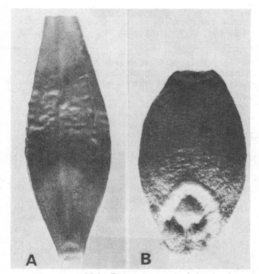

FIG. B-2. TYPES OF BARLEY: A—COVERED;
B—NAKED

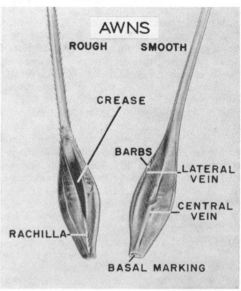

FIG. B-4. VENTRAL (LEFT) AND DORSAL
(RIGHT) VIEWS OF BARLEY KERNELS WITH
GLUMES AND AWNS

The Kernel

The kernel of covered barleys consists of the caryopsis, the flowering glumes (or husks) and the rachilla (Fig. B-3 and B-4). The husks consist of two membraneous sheaths that completely enclose the caryopsis. One of the husks (the lemma) is drawn out into a long awn. The color of the grain in covered barleys depends on the color of the caryopsis and the other husk (the palea). Color in the caryopsis is due to anthocyanin pigment or to a black melanin-like compound. Anthocyanin, when present, is red in the pericarp and blue in the aleurone layer.

The caryopsis is a one-seeded fruit in which the outer pericarp layers enclose the two endosperm layers, aleurone and starchy endosperm, and the embryo. The starchy endosperm is the main storage tissue; the aleurone layer is at least two cells thick and forms the peripheral layer of the endosperm. The caryopsis has a furrow (crease) in the side opposite to the embryo.

Barley Standards

In the United States, barley is divided into three classes (barley, western barley, and mixed barley) and three subclasses (malting barley, blue malting barley, and barley) on the basis of areas of production and color.

Composition

On a dry matter basis, barley contains 63–65% starch, 1–2% sucrose, about 1% of other sugars, 1–1.5% soluble gums, 8–10% hemicellulose, 4–5% cellulose, 2–3% lipids, 8–13% protein (N × 6.25), 2–2.5% ash, and 5–6% other components. In regular barley, the linear starch component comprises 24% of the total starch. A high amylose

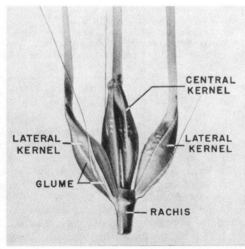

FIG. B-3. ARRANGEMENT OF ONE TRIPLET
OF KERNELS IN 6-ROW BARLEY

(47% of the total starch) barley with small starch granules was recently developed. The proteins in barley are composed of four groups varying in solubility. The albumin fraction comprises less than 10% of the proteins; the globulins are about 20%, the hordeins (soluble in 70% alcohol) are 30%, and the remaining 40% of the proteins are glutelins. About $1/2$ of the amino acid residues in hordeins are either glutamine or proline; the amounts of aspartic acid, glycine, and lysine are small. The amino acid composition of the glutelins resembles that of hordeins but is less extreme. A naked barley that is rich in protein and lysine (Hiproly) was reported by Swedish plant breeders. Barley lipids are concentrated in the embryo and the aleurone layer. Although the whole grain has only 2% petroleum-ether extractable material, isolated embryos contain 15%. The predominant constituent fatty acids are linoleic, oleic, and palmitic, with the unsaturated components accounting for nearly 80% of the total.

Mature barley may contain over 2% of fructosans and unlike starch, which is restricted to the endosperm, the fructosans are distributed throughout the grain. Sucrose is virtually restricted to the embryo and aleurone; it represents 12–15% of the embryo but only 1–2% of the whole grain. Raffinose is also a major embryo constituent, about 5% of the dry weight. The husks contain over $2/3$ of the grains cellulose; the cell walls of the central starchy endosperm lack true cellulose.

Processing and Uses

The most important uses of barley are as grain feed; as malt for manufacturing beverages or malt-enriched food products; as seed; and as human food in the form of parched grain, pearled grain for soup, flour for flat bread, and ground or partly ground grain to be cooked and eaten as porridge (Table B-3).

Most barley that goes directly into human food is consumed as pot or pearl barley; barley flour is a secondary product. Both pot and pearl barley are manufactured by gradually removing the hull and outer portion of the barley kernel by abrasive action; the pearling or decortication process is carried out further in the manufacture of pearl barley. High quality pot and pearl barley are made from clean and sound barley, that has a white endosperm. Well-filled plump kernels of two-row barley are preferred. Grain subjected to 5–6 pearling operations gives small, round, and white pearl barley. The products of pearling are sized by means of a grading wheel. From 100 lb of barley, about 65 lb pot or 35 lb pearl barley are produced. It has been estimated that 6 pearlings remove 74% protein, 85% fat, 97% fiber, and 88%

TABLE B-3

USES OF BARLEY AND BARLEY PRODUCTS

Feed
  Livestock
  Poultry
Export
  Feed
  Malting
Pearling
  Pot barley for soups and dressings
  Pearled barley for soups and dressings
  Flour
  Feed
Milling
  Flour for baby foods and food specialties
  Grits
  Feed
Malting
  Brewers' beverages
  Brewers' grains for dairy feeds
  Brewer's yeast for animal feed, human food, and fine chemicals
  Distillers' alcohol
  Distillers' spirits
  Distillers' solubles for livestock and poultry feeds
  Distillers' grains for livestock and poultry feeds
  Specialty malts
    High dried
    Dextrin for breakfast cereals, sugar colorings, dark beers, and coffee substitutes
    Caramel for breakfast cereals, sugar colorings, dark beers, and coffee substitutes
    Black for breakfast cereals, sugar colorings, dark beers, and coffee substitutes
  Export
  Malt flour for wheat flour supplements, human and animal food products
  Malted milk concentrates for malted milk, malted milk beverages, and infant food
  Malted syrups for medicinal, textile, baking uses, and for breakfast cereals and candies
  Malt sprouts for dairy feeds, vinegar manufacture, and industrial fermentations

SOURCE: U.S. Department of Agriculture, Bureau of Agricultural Economics.

of the mineral ingredients of the original barley. The pearl barley may be ground and sifted to produce barley grits and/or barley flour. The highly refined flour is known as patent barley flour. Barley grits and a less highly refined barley flour may also be made by a process of milling, bolting, and purification similar to that in wheat flour milling. In the larger mills, most hulls are removed before milling by passing the barley through a pearler or a hulling machine, and then sifting and aspirating.

Y. POMERANZ

BARLEY: MALT AND MALTING

Malting

Malting involves controlled wetting (by steeping) and germination of cleaned and graded barley under conditions conducive to production of desired physical and chemical changes associated with the germination process, while holding weight losses due to respiration to a minimum. The germinated grain is dried to halt growth and stop enzyme activity and to develop a storable product of desired color and flavor. Drying is followed by removing malt sprouts. The malting process is given in the form of a flowsheet in Fig. B-5.

Barley in Malting

Barley occupies a unique position in malting and brewing. The prominent position stems from the fact that barley produces relatively large amounts of alpha- and beta-amylases, and the combination of both amylolytic enzymes results in a more complete and rapid degradation of starch than in malts from other cereal grains. This degradation of starch is accompanied by breakdown of other grain components (mainly proteins and nonstarchy polysaccharides) and yields an optimally modified malt. In barley, the husks are cemented to the kernel and remain attached after threshing. The husks protect the kernel from mechanical injury during commercial malting, strengthen the texture of steeped barley, and contribute to a more uniform germination of all kernels. They are also important as a filtration aid in the separation of extract components during mashing and contribute to the flavor of the malt and the beer.

The Malting Process

In steeping, barley may be completely submerged in water or may undergo a combined air and water treatment until a desirable kernel moisture is reached. The moist barley germinates; roots and acrospires start to form, and enzyme modification of the starchy endosperm begins. As a rule of thumb, modification has reached the desired level when the acrospire reaches $2/3$–$3/4$ the length of the kernel, and the roots are $1\frac{1}{2}$ times as long as the kernel. To slow growth and reduce malting loss, germination is controlled by temperature, moisture, and air-composition.

To produce malt in North America, barleys with smaller kernels and higher nitrogen content than in Europe are employed. The Manchurian type and the smooth-awned varieties derived from it are used almost exclusively.

Two general types of malts are produced commercially, brewer's and distillers' malts. Brewer's malts are made from barleys of plumper, heavier kernels, with a mellow or friable starch mass, that is, barleys produced in the more humid sections of the spring barley area. They are steeped and germinated at moisture contents ranging from 43 to 46%; the final temperatures used in drying the malts range from 160° to 180°F. The malts are

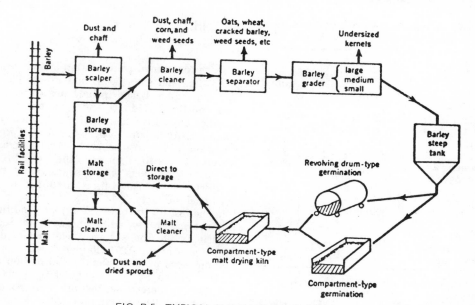

FIG. B-5. TYPICAL MALT HOUSE FLOWSHEET

dried to about 4% moisture. The final moisture and drying temperature vary with the type of barley malted, the malting procedure, and the character of malt desired. The high final drying temperatures used and the low moisture content of the malt tend to reduce the diastatic power of the malt, darken it and the wort made from it, and increase malt flavor and aroma. The distillers' (or high-diastatic) malts are made from barleys high in nitrogen and enzymic potentialities. Varieties grown in less humid areas and capable of producing a high diastatic power, as well as varieties having smaller kernels, are generally used to produce such malt. The barleys are steeped and malted at higher moistures (45–49%) and dried at lower temperatures (120°–140°F) to higher finished moisture contents (5–7%) than the brewer's type of malt. Gibberellic acid stimulating enzymic processes associated with germination of barley has led to the suggestion that activating enzymes and modifying barley should be possible with gibberellic acid and without germ development. Using gibberellic acid to steep water or spraying it during germination (0.5–3.0 ppm) accelerates germination and increases yields. Potassium bromate added to the steep water increases yields by depressing respiration and rootlet development. New malting techniques, including a continuous-flow system, have been described. Comparative ranges in composition of barley and malt are given in Table B-4.

Uses of Malt

The three main types of malt are brewer's malt, distillers' malt, and specialty malts (high dried, dextrin, caramel, black) for breakfast cereals, sugar colorings, dark beers, and coffee substitutes. Malted cereals are also used in malted beverages and infant foods; and as supplements in breadmaking, breakfast foods, candies, and medicinal syrups. Nonfood uses of malts include animal feeds and textile desizing.

By-Products

The main by-product of malting is called malt sprouts; about 3–5% of malt sprouts are obtained in malt cleaning. They are easily separated from the kilned malt by passing the malt through revolving reels of wire screen. The sprouts have a yellow-brown color and a slight bitter taste. They include mainly rootlets, 5–8 mm long and 0.3–0.4 mm thick. They contain, on an "as is" basis, 25–34% protein, about 2% fat, 8–12% fiber, 6–7% ash, and 35–44% N-free extract. The by-product sprouts are well-established as a nutritious feed component. Numerous studies have also shown their high enzymatic activities. On the other hand, excessive amounts of rootlets are an economic loss. Consequently, the maltster is interested in optimally modified malts with smallest amounts of malt sprouts.

Y. POMERANZ

TABLE B-4

COMPARATIVE RANGES IN COMPOSITION OF BARLEY AND MALT

Property	Barley	Malt, Brewer's and Distillers'
Kernel weight (mg)	32–36	29–33
Moisture (%)	10–14	4–6
Starch (%)	55–60	50–55
Sugars (%)	0.5–1.0	8–10
Total nitrogen (%)	1.8–2.3	1.8–2.3
Soluble nitrogen (% of total)	10–12	35–50
Diastatic power (degrees[1])	50–60	100–250
Alpha-amylase (20° units[2])	[3]	30–60
Proteolytic activity (arbitrary units)	[3]	15–30

SOURCE: U.S. Dept. Agr. Handbook 338.

[1] Degrees, a unit of amylase activity.
[2] 20 Degree C dextrinizing units, a unit of alpha-amylase activity.
[3] Trace.

BEANS

Production

Beans for human consumption include primarily green lima and snap beans and dry edible beans. The dry edible beans include pea (navy), pinto, great northern, kidney, and lima beans. These varieties are native to America and make up the commercially important bean-based food products. Soybeans, native to Asia, are becoming increasingly important as a food source. The United States is the largest producer of soybeans. Soy flour, a product of soybean oil, is used for food and industrial products.

In the last 25 yr, both the acreage and the total production of dry edible beans have decreased slightly, while the average yield increased about 50% (now about 1275 lb per acre). Thus, 1.4 million acres produce about 1800 million pounds in the United States. Geographic, climatic, and soil factors determine the areas of commercial production. The major production areas of dry edible beans are as follows:

		Million Pounds
Pea (navy)	Michigan	462
Pinto	Colorado Idaho	380
Great northern	Nebraska Wyoming Idaho	203
Red kidney		112
Small red		104
Large lima	California Delaware	108
Plus others of less volume		—
Total		1730

Dry edible beans are usually handled and marketed in 100-lb bags.

About 20% of the acres devoted to the production of edible beans is used for commercial production of green lima and snap beans. The intensity and value of production is greater for green beans than for dry edible beans. Of the total value of all edible beans, 45% is made up of green lima and snap beans. The major areas for production of edible nondry beans are Oregon and New York for snap beans, and California and Delaware for green lima beans. There is a greater tonnage of snap beans (810,000) produced as compared to shelled lima beans (128,000). In the last 25 yr, the acreage of green beans has doubled and the yield tripled, with the increase being used primarily for processed products.

Transportation

Centers of production are not often next to the centers of population. The harvested beans must be moved to centers of consumption. Fresh green, wax, and lima beans, obviously must be kept cool and moist and be quickly transported to market for sale and consumption. Because of seasonal production, long distances to market, and year-round demand, preservation methods such as freezing, canning, and drying are used. Products can then be stored for extended periods until consumed, processed and/or transported.

Utilization

The commercial production of edible beans are canned, frozen, or stored. The leading beans for canning are the green and wax beans which make up 40–50 million cases of 24 No. 303 cans (1 lb each) per year. Lima beans, as canned products, make only $\frac{1}{10}$ of the total.

Green beans, wax beans and lima beans are frozen. The total green and wax beans frozen each year make up about 150 million pounds.

About the same quantity of various lima beans are frozen.

Dry edible beans may go directly into storage and used throughout the year for processing. Export of beans accounts for 10–15% of the total production.

Consumption

The civilian per capita consumption of dry edible beans has decreased from 8.4 lb in 1940 to about 7.3 lb in 1955 and since then has been between 7 to 8 lb per yr. The civilian per capita consumption of frozen beans is about 2 lb per yr; canned beans, 5–6 lb per yr. In general, as with most vegetables, the per capita consumption of frozen beans (green, wax, and lima) has increased. Canned bean consumption has also increased. The per capita consumption of fresh vegetables has decreased.

Nutrition

The nutritive value of edible beans varies greatly. For example, the nutritive value varies with geographical area of production, and the nutritive value also changes with increasing maturity. In lima beans the ascorbic acid, thiamin, and riboflavin decrease with increasing maturity. The bean as consumed may include additional components (tomato, pork, etc.) which greatly alter the nutritive value of the served portion. Table B-5 summarizes nutritive value of various types of bean.

Beans are also sources of vitamins, particularly vitamin A (except red beans), thiamin, riboflavin, niacin, and ascorbic acid. Dry beans are particularly rich in some of the minerals such as magnesium, manganese, copper, sulfur, calcium, phosphorus, and potassium.

Canning

Canning is done to preserve the product for extended periods. A heat treatment is given to the product to kill microorganisms and to inactivate enzymes. The can serves as a container to hold small portions of the product for the heat treatment and to protect the product from contamination after heat treatment. The container helps in handling and storing the product after the heat treatment.

Canning is carried out under closely-controlled heating conditions. The initial quality of the product can not be improved by canning. Minimum deterioration is maintained by rapid handling from field to can without excessive heating of the product. The beans are washed, sorted, some are hulled, some are cut or diced, and placed into the container. Metal or glass containers are most commonly used; plastic is used to a limited ex-

TABLE B-5

MAJOR NUTRIENT CONTENT OF 1 CUP OF EDIBLE BEANS (½ LB OR 225 GM)

Type of Bean	Water (%)	Calories	Protein (Gm)	Fat (Gm)	Carbohydrate (Gm)	Calcium (Mg)	Iron (Mg)
Lima							
Immature, cooked	75	150	8	1	29	46	2.9
Mature, cooked	64	260	16	1	48	56	5.6
Snap							
Green, canned	94	45	2	Tr	10	65	3.3
Green, cooked	92	25	2	Tr	6	45	0.9
Pea (navy)							
Great northern and red	76	230	15	1	42	74	4.6
With pork, cooked	69	330	16	7	54	172	4.4

tent. *Clostridium botulinum*, which can produce a lethal toxin, must be killed in the heat treatment during processing.

The heat or thermal processes for canning beans must be carefully controlled to assure that adequate heat is provided to accomplish the objectives without greatly damaging the product. Convection heating in the can in retorts or continuous cookers is used.

The extent of the heat treatment is represented by an F_O-value (zero live organisms) which is the number of minutes required to destroy the organisms or to accomplish enzyme inactivation at 250°F. A higher or lower temperature can be used, but the time of treatment must be appropriately decreased or increased. The z-value, which is generally considered to be 18°F for canning, gives the slope of the time-temperature relationship such that if the F_O-value is 15 min (for 250°F), then the time of treatment at 268°F ($+18° = z$) is 1.5 min (1 log cycle). For *Clostridium botulinum*, $F_O = 3$ at 250°F.

Industry values for canning are as follows:

	F_O-values	
Type of Bean	No. 2 Can (Min)	No. 10 Can (Min)
Green and wax, brine packed	3.5	6.0
Shelled type, succulent	11.0	18.0

Sterilization is usually done at a temperature of 240°–250°F for less than 1 hr. Minerals in the water can have a tremendous effect on the quality of canned beans. Soft water is preferred for cooking. Calcium chloride in the water for canning causes beans to become tough; sodium carbonate causes a softening of the tissues.

Blanching

Blanching is a heat treatment employing hot air, steam, or hot water. Blanching is a thermal process short of sterilization which precedes freezing of fresh beans. Blanching whitens beans for drying, and inactivates enzymes, provides a surface treatment and removes volatile odors so that the product will keep better in frozen storage. Other chemical and biological relationships must often be considered when heat treating particular products; for example, the temperature at which the starch in beans is gelatinized is at a higher temperature than that at which the enzyme amylase is inactivated. Pumping the products in liquid to the blancher often fits into the handling system of a production line. Blanching is usually carried out quite quickly. Lima beans are blanched in hot water at 200°–210°F for 1–2 min, depending on the size and maturity of the bean; in steam, 3–4 min are required. Separation of specific gravity fractions in a brine solution and removal of splits may be done after blanching.

Freezing

Freezing may be done in the package or on a continuous belt in a freezing chamber or tunnel. When bulk frozen, packaging usually follows storage after freezing. Packaging keeps in moisture; keeps out organisms. A wide variety of temperature and time combinations may be used for freezing. In general, rapid freezing is preferred so that small instead of large ice crystals form, thus minimizing the product change. Although the temperature at which these products freeze is a little less than 32°F (0°C), products are placed in an environment of much lower temperature for freezing, such as −0°, −20°, −40°F. The frozen product is commonly stored at 0°F or lower.

Drying

Beans may be dried to below 4% in a tunnel, kiln, cabinet, or vacuum drier. These dry products will keep in storage for an extended period. The products are then used for processing or consumption. Blanching precedes drying. Chemical solutions may be used to minimize discoloration during or following dehydration. These chemicals are removed during cooking.

Processing may precede dehydration. Pea beans can be processed and puréed; then dried on a drum drier. Precooked beans, particularly the dry edible beans, are particularly desirable because of the long soaking and cooking required by the housewife to prepare these for the table. Soaking of beans should be in soft water. More rapid water uptake results with heated water. After soaking, the housewife can cook beans in 3-10 min in a pressure cooker at 15 psi (1 atm). The dry product can be used for the manufacture of other foods: cookies, breads, soups, etc.

Soybeans

Soybeans are not normally considered as dry edible beans. Soybeans are dry, but generally not edible until after processed. About 30% of the soybean production in the United States is used for food and industry products. Soybean oil meal is used for livestock feed; soybean oil is used for food and industrial purposes.

There are two basic processing methods: continuous screw press process and solvent extraction process. The solvent extraction process is most widely used—almost exclusively—because of the higher recovery of oil from the soybean (about 11 lb per bu as compared with 9 lb per bu for the screw process). A petroleum solvent is used to remove the oil from the bean. The oil is distilled and the solvent reused. The process is done continuously.

Soy flour is produced from the solvent extraction, followed by grinding, screening, etc. Soy flour is 18-20% protein and 5-9% fat. Soy flour utilizes 1-2% of the soybean production in the United States. Soy flour is used for bakery goods, ice cream, infant foods, dietary foods; as a whipping agent; as a partial replacement ingredient for shortening in margarine and salad dressing; and as spun protein fibers to make analogs with meat-like flavors—bacon, pork, beef, chicken, turkey—used to extend protein values in comminuted meat dishes, as a partial replacement for meat in ground meats such as hamburger, and as a meat substitute for flavoring dishes such as salads and scrambled eggs.

CARL W. HALL

Cross-reference: *Protein Foods from Plant Sources.*

BEEF

Beef is more universally accepted than any other red meat. Of all the red meats consumed in the United States, approximately 60% is beef. The United States far exceeds all other nations in the total production and consumption of beef. Beef is one of the major commodities with which food technology is concerned.

Beef is not native to the Americas. There is evidence that the first cattle were brought to America by the Norsemen in the beginning of the second millennium A.D. Records indicate that Columbus brought cattle with him on his second voyage to America in 1493. In the later centuries, cattle were landed by the American and Mexican settlers and the present American cattle herds have substantially descended by selective breeding from these ancestors. The magnitude of the beef industry operations today constitute an important part of the United States economy.

Beef Consumption

In the first half of the 20th Century, beef consumption in the United States averaged 61 lb of carcass weight per person each year. The standard deviation from this mean value was about 7 lb. This rather low statistical deviation was considerably influenced by the relatively high levels of beef consumption in the period from 1900 to 1910 and low levels in the late 1920's and early 1930's. Since 1953, the per capita beef consumption increased sharply and has steadily increased in the 1960's reaching a record high of 116.0 lb per person in 1972. During the last two decades, the United States has become a prevalently beef-eating nation. The people here eat about $1/3$ of all the beef produced in the world. High levels of beef consumption have become a status symbol and a sign of affluence.

Beef is the principal meat in most of the heavy meat-eating nations. It is exceptionally high in Argentina, Uruguay, New Zealand, and Australia. The two former nations exceed the United States in per capita beef consumption.

Beef Production

Abundant feed resources, coupled with efficient breeding and feeding practices, have made possible a high rate of beef production in the United States. Of equal importance has been the strong domestic demand for beef that has made livestock raising profitable. In spite of all this, the United States is a beef importing country.

The USDA estimated that on January 1, 1972, there were 118 million cattle in the United States, the largest number ever recorded. In 1945, 55% of the cattle were for beef production; today beef cattle make up 81% and only 19% are dairy animals.

The principal breeds of beef cattle raised in this country are Herefords, Angus, and Shorthorns—the so-called English breeds. The use of crossbreeding in commercial beef herds is increasing at a rapid rate and, at the present time, about 30% of market cattle are crossbred to some degree. The trend is based on research that indicates up to 20% improvement in feed-use efficiency over pure line breeding.

In volume of liveweight production, the nation's most important beef cattle producing state is Texas (12.8 million head in 1971), followed by Iowa (7.8), Nebraska (6.8), and Kansas (6.8). These four states also ranked first in the sale of cattle. The annual slaughter of cattle in 1971 was 36 million head.

As was true a century ago, likewise today, most of the nation's beef cattle are raised west of the Mississippi River, while most of the beef consumers live east of the Mississippi River. At the time of the Civil War there was great difficulty in spanning these miles between the beef producer and the beef consumer. It was not until 1876 when the first ammonia compressor was invented that commercial refrigeration and freezing started. The introduction of refrigerated railcars changed the beef production from a local into a long-distance business.

To meet the demand for fresh beef, the meat packing industry is geared to slaughter, process, and distribute beef on a high-speed rate. On the average, beef travels about 1000 miles from the producer to the consumer.

A dressed beef carcass is chilled at 32°-34°F and is usually ready for local sale or movement to distant markets within 2 days after slaughter. About 4-5 days are usually needed to move the beef from North Central meat packing plants to distant wholesale outlets. Another few days are required to sell the meat to the retailer who, in turn, prepares it for the consumer. Thus within 12-14 days after slaughter, the beef has reached the distant consumer. During this time, the beef has gone through an aging process which makes it more tender. Kosher beef is processed in three days: slaughter and chilling on the first day, cutting the second day, and selling the third day.

Feedlots and Marketing

In a maze of cattle trails crossing the continent in the old days, the cattlemen found a profitable market in what is now called the Central Corn Belt States. These states became a stopping-off place for cattle, a place where they could be fattened on locally grown surplus grain before going on to the market. This practice of feeding the cattle as a separate enterprise has been important on farms throughout the Corn Belt and in other areas where abundant quantities of feed grain have been produced. Feedlots could be filled with western cattle at a lower cost than raising native cattle at home. In addition, improved breeding stock throughout the range country resulted in cattle that would fatten and finish out at an early age. Since these cattle proved highly satisfactory for feeding purposes, the beef cattle business in the North Central States became largely a finishing operation. Nearly $2/3$ of all cattle that are fattened in feedlots are fed in the 12 North Central States, Iowa and Nebraska having the largest number of cattle on feed of any state.

In recent years the picture is changing and the trend is moving southwest and west. Large feedlots are located in the west where they make up only 1% of the total number of feedlots in the country, but are currently feeding a large number of cattle. Here feedlots of 50,000 head capacity or more are not uncommon. Most commercial feedlots use completely automated systems in which feed is processed, mixed, and distributed mechanically; therefore, handling large numbers of cattle is facilitated.

Chicago was the traditional terminal livestock market. It is now closed and new terminal markets, such as Omaha, Nebraska, and Sioux City, Iowa, have taken its place and at present are the largest terminal markets in the nation. With this change, the large meat packing companies which were located near the old terminal markets moved to new locations. Today more and more large packing companies are located in the country, near the feedlots, away from the central locations.

Although the feeding and finishing of beef cattle is the principal service performed by commercial feedlots, they perform additional functions including marketing services. Feedlots changed the historical relation that had existed between the producer and the packer. In buying, packers formerly were faced with many thousands of small-volume producers. Presently, feedlots are places where cattle are bought and sold; they are places of both production and markets—markets for feeder cattle and market sources for slaughter cattle. The cattle are either owned by the feedlot operator, or they may be fed on contract for someone else—for the rancher who raised the animals or for the packer who intends to slaughter them.

Fed cattle from feedlots usually move directly to packers. Customarily, the feedlot operator acts as his own agent in selling cattle. Three of the marketing methods—terminal, auction, and direct—account for virtually all of the fed cattle marketed in the United States. These large-scale operations are run on a continuous basis with a turnover of 2–3 times a year.

Quality Standards

Grade, class, and yield, all are important considerations in the determination of beef carcass quality. However, quality in beef is ultimately measured by its palatability. Official grades as well as official classes have been established by the USDA to classify beef according to quality and palatability characteristics. The first quality standards were published in 1923.

The USDA Official Quality Grades of beef are: Prime, Choice, Good, Standard, Commercial, Utility, Cutter, and Canner. Estimates are that about 75% of all beef is sold fresh, including practically all that falls into the USDA Grades Prime, Choice, Good, Standard, Commercial, and about half of Utility. The grades Cutter, Canner and the other half of Utility are used for canning and sausage making. Generally, the fat content decreases from the Prime grade to the Canner, the latter being practically devoid of fat.

The quality grades are determined by visually evaluating certain carcass characteristics. Quality grading is a complex process. The characteristics evaluated are: maturity (general meat and bone characteristics); and marbling, texture, firmness, and color of the rib eye muscle between the 12th and 13th rib. Quality grades are arrived at by a composite evaluation of these factors.

Beef is obtained from full-grown cattle. The USDA Official Classes of beef are: steer, heifer, cow, bull, and stag. The class of the beef animal ultimately determines beef quality. The best grade, U.S. Prime, is produced only by steers and heifers. Usually only hotels and the best restaurants use Prime beef. U.S. Commercial grade is the highest grade possible from cattle more than 4 yr old. Beef of highest quality comes from animals with an average age of $2^{1}/_{2}$ yr.

Beef production is changing in terms of grades. In 1959, 37% of the beef produced in this country was of the Choice grade; in 1969 it was over 56%; presently it is about $^2/_3$. This trend is growing steadily because the large feedlots are gearing themselves to produce only Choice grade beef for economic considerations.

Beef carcass yield is important from the economic standpoint. It is estimated by five USDA Yield Grades numbered 1 through 5. Yield Grade 1 carcasses have the highest yield of retail cuts, Yield Grade 5 the lowest. The yield grades can be expressed either in whole numbers or in tenths of the grade. The USDA Yield Grades are based on four factors: hot carcass weight, rib-eye area and fat thickness at the 12th rib, and estimated percentage of kidney, pelvic, and heart fat.

Composition

A beef animal yields an average of 55% carcass beef, 9% various by-products, 6% hide, and 30% valueless material to the beef packer.

For statistical purposes, beef is measured at slaughter level in terms of dressed or on-the-rail carcass weight. The carcass weight of beef commonly refers only to the muscle tissue and bones to which it is attached.

The average composition of a beef carcass is: muscle tissue 57% (ranging from 49 to 68% depending on the breed), adipose tissue 25%, bone 12%, and a residue which includes mainly tendon and other connective tissue. Thus $^1/_3$ of a beef animal is red muscle tissue. The proportion of muscle tissue varies in a roughly inverse manner with that of the adipose tissue. The latter is determined by such factors as age, breed, and feed. For example, carcasses from grain-fed cattle contain substantially more adipose tissue than do carcasses from grass-fed cattle.

The average chemical composition of beef muscle tissue is: water 75%, protein 20%, fat 2%, carbohydrates (mainly as lactic acid) 1%, nonprotein nitrogeneous substances 1%, and inorganic salts 1%. The average chemical composition of beef adipose tissue is: fat 85%, water 12%, and connective tissue proteins 3%.

Beef Retail Cuts

Beef carcasses may be divided into two groups. Butcher beef is intended for final use in the form of fresh primal cuts while boning beef is used in the manufacture of sausage, canned beef, corned beef, and hamburgers. For ease of handling, each side of beef carcass is usually divided into fore and hind quarters for shipping.

From a Choice grade beef carcass, the retailer can expect an average of 76% beef and 24% suet and bone. The beef portion of a carcass comprises: loins 9%; ribs and rib roasts 7%; rounds, slow-cooking steaks, and roasts 19%; chuck roasts 18%; plate, briskets, and short ribs 6%; flank steaks 2%; and shank-stew, soup, and ground beef 15%.

The less-used muscles along the backbone yield tender primal cuts. For example, the cuts from the thick end of a beef loin, such as filet mignon and porterhouse steak, are the most tender and thus most desirable beef. On the other hand, brisket and short plate belong to the least tender cuts.

Palatability Characteristics

Beef palatability depends on such qualities as tenderness, flavor, and color. Tenderness and flavor are ultimately evaluated in the cooked state, while color is an important factor at the time of purchase. Studies have shown that tenderness is by far the most important palatability characteristic in the acceptance of primal cuts of beef and it appears to be sought at the expense of flavor and color.

Tenderness.—There are several factors that influence the tenderness of beef. The ante-mortem factors include genetic background, physiological aspects, and feeding practices. The post-mortem factors include the storage time and temperature after slaughter, the addition of tenderizing agents, and methods of cooking.

A wide range of tenderness occurs from breed to breed, from animal to animal, among muscles of any one animal, and even within a single muscle. Beef from young animals is usually more tender than beef from old animals. Moderate amounts of finely and uniformly dispersed fat or marbling within the muscle are also associated with tenderness and are dependent to a large extent upon heritability. In general, muscles containing the least connective tissue are more tender.

Naturally-occurring beef proteolytic enzymes may be utilized under controlled conditions to tenderize or age beef. Usually only higher grade carcasses or cuts are aged because of a desirable flavor development and higher selling price. In the normal aging process, beef is stored in a refrigerated space at temperatures of $32°-35°F$ for a time sufficient to permit the natural enzymes to carry out their tenderizing process. At such low temperatures, the activity of enzymes is retarded and tenderization may take from 10 to 40 days to achieve a desired tenderizing effect. Typical aged beef flavor overtones are fully developed after at least one week of aging. Lower grades of beef seldom reach proper tenderness by aging. The limiting factors of the natural aging process are microbial deterioration of the meat surface as well as the large amount of space tied up for extended periods of time; it is a slow and wasteful process. Natural enzymatic tenderization can be accelerated by elevated storage temperatures. It has been found that 2 days at $68°F$ gives the same degree of tenderness as 2 weeks at $32°F$.

Recent findings indicate that prerigor mortis muscle shortening, and hence development of muscle toughness, can considerably be decreased by storing beef at the temperatures of about $68°F$ in the prerigor mortis period. The contractile proteins are thereby "locked" into a relatively relaxed stretched-out configuration and such muscles are more tender than muscles in contracted configuration which occurs in a considerably greater extent at lower or higher temperatures than $68°F$.

Various tenderizing agents are used to increase beef tenderness. Sodium chloride in the concentration levels used in modern curing processes (about 2%) has an appreciable tenderizing effect. For this reason, tough brisket cuts are more tender when processed as cured corned beef. Phosphates, which increase the water binding of meat, also indirectly influence tenderness.

Proteolytic enzymes of plant origin, commonly papain, sometimes also ficin and bromelin, are used as beef tenderizers. Although ficin is reported to be the most active enzyme, its price is relatively high.

Preslaughter injection of a 5–10% aqueous enzyme solution into a live beef animal (about 0.5 mg per lb of liveweight) is a most effective method to obtain tender beef. The animal's own circulatory system distributes the enzyme uniformly throughout the muscle tissues. The more active muscles, which are tougher, also have a greater vascularity and therefore receive more enzyme. The animal is slaughtered within $1/2$ hr. In refrigerated or frozen storage, the enzyme in the meat is inactive, but performs its tenderizing action while the meat is cooked.

Proteolytic enzymes or their mixtures may be applied, in aqueous solution or pulverulent form, to less tender steaks either by the processor or the consumer. These enzyme preparations are effective tenderizers; however, uniform distribution and appropriate amounts are important, otherwise uneven or overtenderization results. Enzymes do not penetrate meat readily, thus relatively thin steaks have to be used.

In muscles with very little connective tissue, such as tenderloin, the main factor contributing to tenderness is the nature of the muscle fibers. A sufficiently short cooking time of these cuts is preferable because overcooking toughens the muscle fibers and results in tough, stringy meat. Connective tissue collagen, which makes the raw meat tough, becomes soft upon cooking; it gelatinizes between $175°$ and $250°F$ and becomes water-soluble. In muscles containing large quantities of collagen, such as in beef chuck, the improvement in tenderness is due to gelatinization of collagen at high-temperature cooking; however, longer cooking time offsets the tenderization effect by toughening muscle fiber. Total cooked meat tenderness, therefore, is the sum of the two effects: toughening of the muscle fibers and gelatinization of collagen.

Flavor.—Flavor (composite taste and odor) is an important property of cooked beef but the chemistry is extremely complex. True beef flavor develops during cooking and, in the case of roast beef, for example, it appears that the bulk of the flavor constituents is produced in the surface portion of the meat, while the inner portions contribute little to the roast beef flavor. Researchers have met with only limited success in capturing the complex and elusive beef flavor essence which seems to be unstable and present in minute concentrations.

Color.—The consumer equates the color of fresh beef with freshness and wholesomeness. The color of fresh raw meat is due almost entirely to myoglobin, only traces of hemoglobin remain after slaughter. Freshly cut beef is purplish-red and becomes bright red in color minutes after exposure to air and the formation of oxymyoglobin.

When beef has substantially depleted stores of glycogen prior to slaughter, the muscles appear very dark and are classified as dark-cutting beef. A high ultimate pH in the muscles causes this aesthetically unpleasant phenomenon. Dark-cutting beef, although otherwise a wholesome and tender meat, is discounted at the retail level because it is difficult for the consumer to distinguish between dark-cutting beef and beef from old animals or beef held under adverse conditions. There is no practical technological solution to prevent the occurrence of the dark-cutting beef.

Beef color changes gradually during cooking from a bright red appearance to a grey or brown. The color change that occurs during cooking is roughly related to cooking temperature which causes denaturation phenomena in the muscle tissue but no noticeable change in the fat color. The following degrees of cooking may be observed: rare beef, no visual color change—below $60°C$; medium rare, decreasing redness—up to $70°C$; medium, reddish-brown—up to $75°C$; well-done beef, complete loss of red color—above $75°C$.

Nutritional Aspects

Beef is an important dietary source of high quality protein, B-group vitamins, and minerals. Beef proteins contain all essential amino acids for balanced nutrition. Upon digestion, proteins are split into elemental units or amino acids in proper proportion, which are then reassembled by the human body for growth and maintenance. About 9 oz of lean beef is enough to provide the daily protein requirement for an adult.

Preservation and Processing

As was mentioned above, about 75% of beef is consumed as fresh meat, including hamburger meat.

Fresh meat may be frozen for preservation. The recommended frozen storage time at $0°F$ is 6-12 months for beef cuts and 3-4 months for ground beef.

The remaining 25% of beef is used in the manufacture of various meat products. The most popular sausage product, either all-beef or containing beef, is the frankfurter. Beef is processed into many other types of sausages, such as bologna, salami, kosher sausages, cervelat, etc. Also various beef loaves may be classified in the sausage group. Typical and popular beef products are corned beef, pastrami, and beef bacon. Many canned products are manufactured containing beef; beef stew may be considered as the most popular.

Future Trends

The beef industry is the fastest expanding segment in the food industry. In recent years there has been considerable interest in the development of more efficient and more economical methods of distributing meats, particularly fresh primal beef cuts. Central processing has been suggested as one of the approaches which offers the greatest opportunity for reducing processing and distribution costs. The term "central packaging" presently means processing of retail cuts of fresh beef in a central plant for a group of retail stores. Instead of moving carcasses to the retail store, retail cuts are delivered to the store in boxes in prepackaged form. This development is considered an intermediate step. Ultimately this operation may be expanded from freezing the packaged cuts to the most elaborate central meat processing operations.

ENDEL KARMAS

Cross-Reference: *Meat and Meat Packing.*

BEEKEEPING: HONEY AND HONEY PRODUCTS

Honeybees were brought to the United States from Europe in the early 17th Century, but beekeeping never became rationalized until the movable-frame hive emerged in the middle of the last century through the discovery by Langstroth of the "bee space," the $3/8$ in. spacing between parts which the bees would not seal. The new hive allowed inspection for disease, manipulation to prevent swarming, and removal of honey without destruction of the colony. Beekeeping acquired its present form between 1850 and 1914. Two major developments, wax comb foundation in 1857 and the centrifugal honey extractor, commercialized in 1870, made large-scale production of liquid honey practical. The bee smoker, the bee escape, and queen excluder were developed in that period and are still in use with only slight change.

Popular demand for liquid honey in the latter part of the 19th Century led to its widespread adulteration. Honey was one of the commodities studied by Harvey Wiley, whose efforts led to the Pure Food and Drug Act in 1906. Honey is not now adulterated in the United States; modern testing methods make detection certain.

Space is not available here to describe modern beekeeping methods. Massive changes in U.S. agriculture in the past four decades have greatly reduced the widespread nature of apiaries. Formerly, nearly every farm had a few beehives, which, together with wild bees in hedgerows and woodlots, ensured adequate pollination of the fruit, vegetable, and seed crops. Today, few family farms have beehives; farming practices have eliminated wild bees and escaped bee colonies. The professional beekeeper now provides much of the pollination needed either as a service for a fee, or as a by-product of his acquisition of high-yielding locations for his bee-yards, ever more difficult to find.

Beekeeping is a highly specialized farm enterprise. The full-time beekeeper maintains at least 400 hives, averaging perhaps 1200. They are dispersed over many locations, each holding 20–200 colonies; the bees in a yard normally cover 4000–5000 acres in searching for nectar and pollen. Colony yield varies between 20 and 200 lb per yr depending upon season, location, and climate. Optimal hive density for good honey yield is usually too dispersed for efficient crop pollination. Growers requiring pollination must therefore compensate the beekeeper for reduced honey crop resulting from relatively high hive density and also for costs of moving colonies and providing strong colonies when required before normal colony build-up.

The literature contains many examples of profitable increase in yield and quality of fruit, vegetable, and seed crops brought about by intelligent cooperation between producers and beekeepers.

Beekeeping is practiced in all States and at all scales from the hobbyist with 1 hive to the professional with more than 20,000. About $1/2$ of the average annual honey production of 250 million pounds comes from the 1200–1500 full-time beekeepers who operate about $1/3$ of the nation's 4.7 million bee colonies. The continuing 25-yr decline in honeybee population, due in part to the complexity and unprofitability of the business, is raising questions about the adequacy of the national pollination force of bees, which is largely responsible for pollinating over $1 billion in crops annually.

Honey

Honey is the sweet, aromatic, viscous syrup produced by the honeybee (*Apis mellifera* L.) from the nectar of flowers. A combined evaporation and sucrose inversion is brought about by the addition of bee enzymes and physical manipulation of the nectar in the hive. As the ripened nectar reaches a solids content of 80–82%, the cells of the comb in which it is deposited are sealed over with beeswax and the honey thus preserved is stored for maintenance of the colony during the winter. Excess over this amount is appropriated by the beekeeper. The color and flavor of honey is closely related to the flower from which it originates. Agricultural practices of large-scale planting of single crops, the differing seasons of bloom, the "constancy" of bees in terms of the flowers they work, and the control exercised by the beekeeper make large amounts of honey of relatively constant floral type available. About 25 floral types of honey are commercially important, and they range in color from nearly water-white (sweet clover) to dark amber (aster-goldenrod) and in flavor from very mild (fireweed, clovers) to pronounced (buckwheat, tulip poplar). The bulk of commercial honey originates from the various legumes (clovers, vetches, alfalfa) with lesser quantities of citrus, tupelo, sage, basswood, cotton, gallberry, and other regional honey types making the balance.

Composition and Properties

The obvious physical aspects of honey—its high viscosity, "stickiness," great sweetness, high density, hygroscopicity, and relative immunity from spoilage—all rise from its nature as a highly concentrated solution of simple sugars. The data below show the gross composition and physical properties of the average U.S. honey.

Composition

Component	%
Water	17.2
Fructose	38.19
Glucose	31.28
Sucrose	1.31
Reducing disaccharides	7.31
Higher sugars	1.50
Organic acids	0.57
Proteins	0.26
Ash	0.17

Physical Properties

	Value
Sp gr 20/20°C	1.4225
RI (20°C)	1.4935
Equilibrium RH at 68°C	60%
Sp ht (20°C)	0.54
Thermal conductivity (21°C)	12.7×10^{-4} cal/cm sec °C
Viscosity	ca 70 poises
Wt per gal.	11 lb 13.2 oz
Caloric value	1380 cal/lb

Exact values for the properties will depend upon moisture content and floral type. Unheated honey also contains variable levels of enzymes added by the bees, including invertase, α-amylase, glucose oxidase, catalase, and others. Vitamin levels are too low to have nutritional significance.

Nearly all honey is liquid as stored by the bees. After it is extracted from the comb by the bee-keeper, much of it will granulate within a few days or weeks. As a rule of thumb, glucose (dextrose hydrate) will crystallize from honey analyzing more than 30% glucose unless appropriate process-ing is applied.

Water content of honey is a most important characteristic. A maximum limit of 18.6% is per-mitted for U.S. Grade A (U.S. Fancy) and Grade B (U.S. Choice) honey. Grade C (U.S. Standard) honey for reprocessing may contain up to 20% water; any higher amount places it in Grade D (Substandard). These limiting values do not represent preferred or proper moisture content for honey. Honey with less than 17.1% water will not ferment within a year regardless of its yeast count. However, fermentation may take place in a honey with 17.1-18% water if it has a yeast content of over 1000 per gm, and between 18.1-19% even though the inoculum is as little as 10 cells per gram. Sugar-tolerant yeasts are a natural contaminant of raw honey. When honey granu-lates, the water content of the liquid phase may in-crease as much as 1%. This increases its liability to fermentation at a given yeast content; this granu-lation is a cause of spring fermentation of origi-nally sound honey held over winter. Unprocessed honey is susceptible to fermentation and this must be kept in mind when any long-term storage of raw honey is undertaken. Honey ferments only be-tween 50° and about 100°F, but storage above 80° is not recommended. Fermenting honey is usually at least partly granulated and has a foam or froth on the surface. It will foam considerably when heated. An odor and flavor of sweet wine or fer-menting fruit may be apparent; gas production may be vigorous enough to burst the container. Fermenting honey can sometimes be reclaimed by heating it to 150°F for a short time to kill the yeasts and expel volatile off-flavors.

Commercial Forms of Honey and Their Processing

The two principal forms in which honey is marketed (other than in the comb) are liquid and solid. Processing of each has the common objec-tive: to stabilize against fermentation and change in state with minimal damage to the fine organo-leptic qualities of the honey.

Liquid Honey.—This appears to be the preferred U.S. market form, judging by the relative amounts sold. Honey is removed from the combs by the beekeeper using large centrifugal extractors after the wax capping is removed by cutting or mechan-ical disintegration. Further treatment may be done by the producer or a packer or both. Coarse contaminants are removed by straining of warm (80°-100°F) honey with or without subsequent settling in a series of large tanks. Honey intended by the producer for retail sale may be pasteurized with or without fine straining or filtration and packed in small containers. Honey for the whole-sale market is largely handled in 55-gal. full-open-ing drums, though the older 5-gal. (60 lb) tinned square can is still in use. Some tank-truck handling has been recently noted.

Wholesale marketing is usually based on samples, so that care is required that the sample be repre-sentative. Packers of honey may be producer co-operatives, independents, producer-packers, or part of a multiple food packing operation.

The retail honey buyer appears to demand a sparkling clear, light-colored jar of liquid honey that will not granulate while in use. To attain this consistently, honey is blended in bulk by the packer to a color and flavor standard, and to a desired moisture content.

Honey is tested for color, flavor, and moisture when received by the packer and warehoused in bulk containers. Containers are selected for the desired blend, and the honey, usually granulated, is removed by inverting the open container in a warm air room (120°-140°F) or oven, with provi-sion for liquefied material to flow away from the heated area, to reduce undesired heat exposure. Honey at 115°-130°F is gently mixed until lique-faction and blending is complete. It is pumped into one of several holding tanks and held for a few hours to allow air, beeswax, and other impurities to rise to the top.

Honey is heated to destroy yeasts and filtered to remove pollen, impurities, and crystal residues.

The two operations are often combined in a closed system wherein honey is pumped by a positive-displacement pump into the heating section of a plate-type heat exchanger. It rapidly reaches 150°–170°F and is passed through a plate-and-frame or horizontal leaf filter using diatomaceous filter-aid. If needed to extend holding time, a variable-speed pump or a pipeline holding section may be used; the honey temperature is then reduced to 120°F in the cooling section of the heat exchanger. It then moves to holding tanks from which it proceeds to jar or can fillers. Common sizes are 8- and 12-oz, 1-, 1½- and 2-lb jars, and 5-lb cans. Plastic "squeeze-bottles" and novelty shapes are popular containers for liquid honey. The sensitivity of honey to darkening from heat exposure requires care to avoid "stack burn" arising from closing and stacking cases of honey before sufficient cooling has taken place. Water-cooling is generally not used.

Controlled heating is the key to a quality commercial honey pack. Honey, having an aromatic but rather delicate flavor, can be damaged by improper handling. It must be warmed to allow efficient pumping, but for this purpose temperatures of 110°–120°F are adequate. Heating for pasteurization must be only to the required exposure, followed by prompt cooling. One recommendation is 170°F for 3 min. Another description of a large commercial operation states that the pasteurization-filtration operation is done at 150°F for 30 sec. Removal of yeast spores by filtration must be implied here, since actual time needed for yeast destruction in honey is reported as 22 min at 140°F, 2.8 min at 150°F, or 0.4 min at 160°F. Honeys vary in the effects of heating upon their color and flavor. Amber or golden types of more definite flavor cannot withstand as much heating without damage as lighter types because they usually contain higher levels of nitrogenous materials that can participate in the Maillard reaction, generating color and off-flavor.

Difficulty with premature regranulation of processed honey may usually be traced to inadvertant seeding of the treated honey, by contact with partly granulated honey in pipeline joints, tanks, pumps, etc. Air in honey packing houses can contain minute "seed" crystals. Examination of freshly processed honey in the retail container by polarized light is quite effective in revealing the presence of traces of introduced crystals.

Crystallized Honey.—Although most honey is sold in the liquid state, the crystallized form is natural for most types of honey produced in the United States and Canada and is the preferred commercial form in Canada. The extent of granulation at equilibrium for a honey is, of course, governed by its degree of glucose (dextrose) supersaturation. This can most easily be expressed by the dextrose:water ratio. Values of 1.7 and less are associated with nongranulating honeys; values of 2.1 and higher predict that a honey will rapidly granulate to a solid unless preventive measures are taken. It must be emphasized that dextrose value for this ratio must be determined by a specific method. Examples of nongranulating honey types are gallberry, the sages, tupelo.

Honey as extracted from the comb is naturally well-seeded with fine dextrose crystals and will usually solidify with a relatively fine grain. After heat processing, without seeding, granulation is delayed for 6–18 months but eventually coarse crystals will accumulate; these require much more severe heating to redissolve than do the natural, fine crystals.

Processing has been developed reproducibly to attain a very fine-grained, fondant-like, relatively soft honey granulation which has several advantages over the liquid form for use as a spread. Methods in commercial use today are primarily based on the Dyce patent (U.S. pat. 1,987,893). Honey is pasteurized, cooled to less than 80°F and 5–15% of a suitably-textured starter honey is mixed in. After filling, the final containers are held for at least 4 days at 57°F, the optimum for crystallization. They may be held thereafter at temperatures not exceeding 80°F, preferably lower. Above this level, softening and phase separation is likely. The starter is a granulated honey with the desired texture, usually with the crystals impalpable to the tongue. This may be from a previous batch or produced by fine grinding of crystallized honey. The most important requirement affecting product quality is the temperature during seeding. If excessive, the most desirable, finest crystals may dissolve and only the largest survive the initial mixing, producing a sandy or grainy product. Commercially, two types of equipment are used: a Canadian cooperative uses the Votator scraped-surface heat transfer equipment to reduce honey temperature in 2 stages from 110° to 83°F and from 83° to 57°F, with seed injection between the stages. Production rate is reported to be about 4000 lb per hr.

The system more commonly used in the United States comprises a batch creamer, capacity 1200–15000 lb, in which a chilled coil immersed in the honey is rotated on a horizontal axis. Starter (10–12%) is added at 80°F and mixing continues until homogeneous. The product is filled into wide-mouth glass jars or bowls, or plastic or waxed-paper tubs of 8-, 12-, 16-oz capacity and held at 57°F at least a week. Because the product is exposed to higher temperatures during summer months, it may be produced at 17½% moisture for that season, and 18% for cold-weather distribution and use.

Comb Honey.—Honey is sold in the original comb in several market forms. These are minor in sales volume in comparison with liquid or granulated honey, but will be described here since honey sold in the comb represents the closest approach to its natural state, and therefore the most nearly perfect embodiment of true honey flavor. All honey in combs, of course, is placed therein by the bees who cap the cells containing the fully ripened honey with thin wax covers.

Section comb honey is that placed by bees in combs they have drawn from thin surplus foundation supplied by the beekeeper in 4¼ in. × 4¼ in × 1⅞ in. wood frames. Specially thin foundation is used to minimize the amount of wax eaten with the honey. This form of honey is costly to produce and is considered the aristocrat of comb honey. Sections are removed from the hive when finished, prepared for market by cleaning, weighing, and grading, and are packaged in window boxes or in clear plastic film.

Cut-comb honey is prepared by the beekeeper by cutting full-size (ca 5 in. × 16½ in.) combs into appropriate sizes. After draining to eliminate liquid honey from cut cells, the pieces may be marketed in plastic film wrap or in shallow plastic boxes.

Chunk or bulk comb honey is the name given to cut comb honey immersed in liquid honey. This is also a premium product and is hand packed. The principal marketing problem is premature granulation initiated in the liquid portion by seed crystals on the surface of the comb. Since beeswax softens above 130°F, heat sufficient to destroy seed crystals cannot be applied. A solution to this problem is the use of nongranulating honey as the liquid portion; gallberry honey is a typical choice.

Grades of Honey

There is no FDA standard of identity for honey, though the old (1906) definition still has advisory status. The USDA has established optional grades for extracted (liquid and crystallized) honey and for the comb honey forms described above. There are seven USDA color classes of honey, but color is not a factor in grading. Honey is graded with respect to its moisture content (18.6% maximum), flavor, clarity, and freedom from extraneous material. Copies of USDA grade standards for these products, as well as the color standards, may be obtained from processed products Standardization and Inspection Branch, Fruit and Vegetable Division, Consumer and Marketing Service, USDA, Washington, D.C. 20250.

Storage and Export

Honey can be stored under appropriate conditions for years, but unless at a temperature of below about 75°F, gradual darkening and flavor deterioration takes place over a period of many months. Honey, being hygroscopic, must be protected from atmospheric moisture. Storage conditions must not favor fermentation, granulation, or heat damage. Fermentation is strongly retarded below 50°F and above 100°F. Granulation is accelerated between 55° and 60°F. The best condition for storing unpasteurized honey is below 50°F. Temperatures above about 80°–85°F should be avoided for long-term storage because heat damage can be appreciable in and above this range.

Honey can be kept indefinitely at refrigerator or especially freezer temperatures; granulation is retarded under the latter condition. Finely-granulated honey spread should not be held at temperatures over 80°F for appreciable periods. At refrigerator temperature it is usually too stiff to spread. During long (9–18 months) storage at moderate room temperatures, a chemical reversion of some of the dextrose will bring about a softening of texture, leading in longer periods to partial liquefaction.

Honey for export to countries using the Codex Alimentarius Standards for honey must meet quality standards not used in U.S. domestic trade. Working from a premise that excessive heating damages the health-giving properties of honey, the Codex Standard specifies honey to have a minimum value of 8 for diastase number and a maximum hydroxymethylfurfural content of 40 mg per kg, except that for certain floral types of naturally low enzyme content, values of 3 and 15, respectively, are specified. There are limits on other aspects, such as moisture, reducing sugar, sucrose, ash, acidity, which are not generally restricting to quality honey. It must be realized, however, that natural unheated U.S. honey can pass beyond the limits named by storage for a few months under not unusual conditions. It is of great importance for honey exporters to be aware of the implications of these standards (FAO/WHO Ref. No. CAC/RS-12-1969) and be prepared to meet them by suitable analytical testing and control of storage conditions.

Honey in Food Products

The baking industry probably is the largest user of honey. Use of honey imparts moisture retention due to its high fructose level, a desirable degree of browning, and a flavor unobtainable elsewhere. Breads, cakes, yeast-raised sweet goods, and cookies, all are improved by honey. A spread consisting of blended butter and honey is available. Several breakfast cereal products use honey in their formulas and several pharmaceutical preparations have honey as a useful adjunct.

Honey has long been used in confections, especially nougats, but its invert sugar content limits its applicability. It is an optional sweetener in jellies, jams, and preserves. It has long been recommended in infant formulas, but no such products are presently available. Honey as a food ingredient deserves serious consideration, with its combination of interesting physical properties, fine flavor, and connotation of old-fashioned goodness.

JONATHAN W. WHITE, JR.

Recommended USDA Publications

Beekeeping in the United States, Agr. Handbook 335. Agr. Res. Serv., USDA, Washington, D.C.
Composition of American Honeys, Tech. Bull. 1261. Agr. Res. Serv. USDA, Washington, D.C.
Honey Market News, Monthly Rept. Fruit and Vegetable Div., Consumer and Marketing Serv., USDA, Washington, D.C.
An Appraisal of the Beekeeping Industry, ARS 42-150. Agr. Res. Serv., USDA, Washington, D.C.

Cross-reference: *Sugars and Sweeteners.*

BERRIES AND BERRY PROCESSING

Botanically speaking a berry is a fruit which comes from a single many-seeded pistil in which all parts become fleshy. In food fields the word "berry" means any pulpy and usually edible small soft fruit irrespective of its structure. In this article the latter definition will be intended whenever the word "berry" is used.

Strawberries

The strawberry, the most widely-grown berry of the world, is not a true berry as the seeds grow on the outside, rather than on the inside of the receptacle of the flower. Some varieties produce well at sea level, while others are known which are adapted to 12,000-ft elevations. The strawberry is grown commercially in every state of the United States and is widely used as fresh fruit. Its main uses as processed fruit are for freezing, preserving, ice cream, and bakery goods. It is a good source of ascorbic acid or vitamin C, some varieties regularly assaying out at 60 mg%.

The varietal picture is slowly, but constantly changing. Between 1900 and 1950 there were nine notable strawberry varieties grown in North America (Darrow 1966). These were: Marshall, Klondike, Missionary, Dunlap, Premier, Aberdeen, Blakemore, Fairfax, and Aroma. In 1966, Blakemore was the only one of these accounting for more than 3% of the acreage grown in the United States (Darrow and Scott 1967). In 1970, the most important varieties, based on tonnage, were Northwest, Tioga, Shasta, Midway, Tennessee Beauty, Fresno, Surecrop, Florida 90, Blakemore and Siletz. Northwest in Western United States and Surecrop in Eastern United States accounted for the greatest acreage in their parts of the country. Two hardy winter varieties, Shuksan and Totem, appear to be well-adapted to the Pacific Northwest (Barritt *et al.* 1972), while Raritan has taken on well in New Jersey, Maryland, and Ohio. Earlibelle was highly rated by Sistrunk and Moore (1971) in Arkansas. The leading California varieties in 1970 were Tioga, Shasta and Fresno according to the California Department of Agriculture.

For processing, a strawberry variety must be productive enough that the grower can afford to produce it. It must have a bright red color which does not appear to be "washed out" or too dark in the product, have a good balance between sweetness, acidity, and aromatic character in its flavor and maintain a texture which gives pleasing mouth feel when eaten. At present, most of the processed berries are frozen while only small amounts are canned. The frozen pack is divided fairly evenly between retail pack and the industrial pack for remanufacture into jams, jellies, ice cream, bakery, and other products.

Processing.—The berries, upon delivery to the freezing plant, are washed, dewatered, and inspected for rots and other defective fruit which is discarded. In some plants the berries are size graded and the very small fruit is diverted to juice or purée lines. Berries packed for retail trade are normally sliced, either into 3/8 -in. slices or cut into half. The cut fruit is mixed with sugar at the ratio of 1 lb of sugar for every 4 lb of fruit (4 + 1). The sugared fruit is then packaged, usually in metal-end, fiber-bodied containers. The filled containers may be tray frozen and then cased for storage; they may be cased and frozen by individual case, or palleted and frozen by the pallet. Some chain store buyers specify pallet freezing, because the slower freeze allows more time for the sugar to equilibrate with the berries. However, investigations have shown that as much as a week's time may be required to completely freeze some of the strawberries in the pallet loads (Durkee *et al.* 1961). Subjective appraisal showed the slowest frozen berries to have lost as much quality during freezing as would happen during more rapid freezing and 1 yr of 0°F storage (Guadagni *et al.* 1961).

Individual quick frozen (IQF) strawberries are retailed in plastic pouches and either slip-cover metal containers or plastic-lined fiber-board cartons. IQF berries are uniform size fruit which is normally tray or belt frozen in subzero air blasts.

Cryogenic freezing is also used in the production of IQF berries. Liquid nitrogen freezing (LNF) is done by immersion in the LN for sufficient time to crust freeze to 50–60% of the radius of the fruit and finishing the freezing in mechanical freezers at $-10°$F or by spraying the liquidfied gas on the berries. LNF berries do not collapse as badly nor leak as much after thawing as do conventionally frozen berries (Wolford 1965). While technically not cryogenic frozen, strawberries can be frozen in Freon 12 at a rate approaching that of LNF. Freon frozen strawberries behave similarly to LNF berries after thawing (Wolford *et al.* 1971).

For the Jam and Preserve Trade.—Strawberries are usually sugared at the 4:1 ratio, by weight of berries to sugar. The sugared fruit is filled into 30-lb containers, or into plastic-lined steel drums and are frozen at $0°$F or lower with minimum delay elapsing between packing and start of freezing. Storage is at $0°$F to $-10°$F.

For the Bakery and Ice Cream Trade.—Strawberries for the ice cream trade are packed in drums, 30-lb tins, $6\frac{1}{2}$-lb cans (No. 10 can, double seamed), and 10-lb tins. Most of the sugaring is at the 4 + 1 level, although some 3 + 1 pack is put up for the ice cream trade. As in strawberries packed for the ice cream trade, the fruit and sugar are layered alternately into the container, although some packers mechanically mix berries and sugar and fill containers with the mixture.

Raspberries

Most commercial red raspberry varieties have come from either of two species, *Rubus idaeus* L. indigenous to Europe and *R. strigosus* Michx, native to North America.

In the United States, the red raspberry is second only to the strawberry in the amount commercially frozen. Small quantities of this fruit are canned and it is a popular fruit for jam. Most red raspberry preserves are remanufactured from frozen berries. One of the reasons for the popularity of frozen raspberries is that they retain fresh fruit flavor better than do many other fruits. For freezing, good sound fruit of firm ripe maturity is needed.

The desired varietal characteristics of red raspberries include full red color, small seeds, rich flavor, and resistance to bruising, crumbliness, and collapse of drupelets after thawing. In 1969, over 90% of the U.S. frozen raspberry production was in Washington and Oregon. The leading Pacific Northwest varieties include Willamette, Sumner, Puyallup, Canby, Fairview, and Washington. Willamette presently accounts for nearly 60% of the raspberry production (Dodge 1971).

Two recent introductions in the Pacific Northwest are Meeker and Matsqui. Both these varieties have some desirable characteristics but were too new for an accurate appraisal of their commercial potential at the time of this writing.

East and Midwest varieties include Chief, Latham, Melton, Newbergh, Sunrise, and Taylor. In 1954, Lee and Slate listed Willamette, Melton, Taylor, and Newbergh to be the best suited for freezing under New York conditions.

Harvesting.—Red raspberries are picked into hallocks in flats as are strawberries. In areas short of harvest labor the berries are mechanically harvested. Mechanical harvesting leads to inclusion of much debris, such as leaves, twigs, and shriveled fruit as well as spiders, thrips, and other insects. Because of an increasing incidence of such foreign material in berries packed for remanufacture, the leading industrial buyers of frozen berries put stringent tolerances for extraneous material in the fruit they purchase. In order to comply with these requirements, many packers found it necessary to install air cleaners in their processing lines. The air cleaner effected a more complete removal of the extraneous material than was previously possible. The removal of a high percentage of thrips by air cleaners was much better than by any earlier method used. Prior to the use of air cleaners, the most satisfactory method was to remove these insects by detergent washing (Brekke *et al.* 1956).

Processing.—The berries are air cleaned and washed, dewatered, and inspected. From the air cleaner the berries go to the berry washer and then go over the belt. For retail trade, 6 oz of sound berries are packed with 4 oz of 60% sucrose syrup.

Freezing may be done by traying the sealed containers and placing the filled trays on buggies which are placed in the freezing tunnel. As each cart is placed into the tunnel the carts preceding it are moved along through the tunnel. In some plants, especially those plants not physically tied in with the freezing facilities, the berries may be cased, palleted, and frozen by the pallet load.

Raspberries for the ice cream, baking, and preserving trades are packed in 10- or 30-lb slip-covered cans, or in plastic-lined steel drums of 55 gal. capacity.

Washed raspberries are filled into these larger containers without added sugar, unless the purchaser specifies sugar added. Between 1960 and 1965 the percentage of red raspberries going into steel drums increased from 1.7 to 12.3%, reflecting the effect of increase in cost of 30-lb size metal containers.

Firm ripe berries dry-cleaned, washed, dewatered, and inspected in the same manner as for freezing, are desired for canning. They should be of deep uniform color and should not be subject to collapse or crumbliness. Cans should be fully enameled with dark fruit enamel. The cans are filled with berries and syruped with water or syrup at 190°–200°F. Number 10 cans are packed with water and smaller cans with syrup up to 40° "put in" density. The cans are exhausted, sealed, and cooked in boiling water. The cook time is based upon the time to raise the center temperature of the cans to 180°F, or 190°F if heavy syrup is used.

Cooling should follow immediately after processing. Water-cooling to average product temperatures to 95°–105°F is desired. Lower temperatures may result in incomplete drying of the can, and rusting may occur. Too high a temperature may result in stack burn. Storage of the canned product at 50°F will materially lengthen the shelf-life of red raspberries. High storage temperatures for canned red raspberries should be avoided.

Black Raspberries

The black raspberry varieties have all been derived from the North American wild black raspberry (*Rubus occidentalis* L.). Desirable varieties have minimum seediness; large, plump, juicy, fleshed berries; and deep dark color. The first named varieties were probably the Doolittle, introduced about 1850, and the Ohio Everbearing, found at Cincinnati in 1852.

In latter years some breeding has been done with black raspberries, particularly at the New York State Agricultural Experiment Station, at Geneva, providing better varieties, and also more resistant against anthracnose, than those available earlier and which largely originated in selections from chance seedlings.

The black raspberry (blackcap) pack is about 1/4 as large as the red raspberry pack. Between 2 and 3% of the U.S. pack is put up in the Northeast, about 45% in Oregon and Washington, and the balance in the Midwest.

Under New York conditions, Bristol is claimed to be the best blackcap for freezing, while in the Pacific Northwest the Munger is the principal variety grown as it is superior to other varieties in yield, fruit quality, and plant characteristics.

Black raspberries are handled in the same manner as are red raspberries. Blackcaps are packed in 30-lb cans or larger containers for the bakery, confectionery, preserve, and other remanufacturing trades.

Black raspberries are also used as a food dye source. Much of the blue-black marking ink used to stamp the grade on meat contains black raspberry pigment. The berries are allowed to dry on the bush before harvesting and dried berries are used for the food dye.

Brambleberries

Blackberries, Boysenberries, Loganberries and Youngberries all belong to the brambleberry group. Like the raspberries the brambleberries are members of the genus *Rubus*.

Varieties of brambleberries grown for processing include Lucretia in the Eastern and Midwestern States, and Young, Boysen, Logan, Himalaya and Evergreen in the Pacific Coast states. In western Oregon and Washington the bulk of the freezing and over half the canning of these berries take place. Evergreen and Himalaya make up a large portion of the processed berries, although several small-seeded, high-flavored varieties such as Chehalen, Cascade, Olympia, and Marion blackberries are grown for processing. Boysenberries, Loganberries and Youngberries are important varieties grown in California.

Berries should be picked when firm-ripe and processed as soon as possible after harvesting. Cool preprocessing storage is desirable if there must be undue delay between harvest and processing.

The brambleberries are frozen largely for remanufacture, although some IQF berries are retailed in plastic pouches, with a small syrup pack being put up for retailing. When packed for preserve or wine trades, the berries are packed in 30-lb containers or in plastic-lined, steel drums. Recently, many pie bakers have switched to IQF berries from those bulk frozen in 30-lb or larger containers. This came about because of differences in the way the berries "juiced out" when thawed and made it difficult for the bakers to get the same weight of fruit in each pie. IQF berries are weighed into each pie shell while still frozen assuring a definite weight of whole fruit in each pie.

In 1970, the U.S. frozen brambleberry pack was 41.7 million pounds. In addition, there was a canned black and other brambleberry pack of 189,000 cases (24 2½ cans per case equivalent). Of the canned berries, about 62% were packed in No. 303 cans and 33% in No. 10 cans. (Anon 1971). The remainder of the pack is in 8-oz or other sizes.

Blueberries and Cranberries

Blueberries and cranberries belong to the genus *Vaccinium* the fruit of which is characterized by nearly spherical berries containing many small seeds.

Blueberries.—There are many commercial varieties of blueberries. The varieties vary greatly in size, color, stem-scars, firmness, and flavor. Leading varieties in the United States during the late 1960's included Jersey, Rubel, Stanley, Concord, and Bluecrop. The varietal picture changes more slowly than does that of strawberries because of the long productive life of the blueberry plant which may bear fruit for several decades. When new plantings are put in, however, due consideration is given to machine harvestability of the varieties. This is necessary because of high and rising harvest costs and increasing scarcity of dependable harvest labor.

In the 1960's, about 60% of the blueberries processed were frozen with only about 1% of the frozen pack going into retail size packages. Of the canned blueberry pack in 1967, the tonnage of berries into No. 10 cans was about 55% of the total blueberries canned. These data indicate that the majority of frozen blueberries are packed for remanufacture by the preserving, bakery, and ice cream trades. While less than half the canned tonnage went into retail size containers the number of 303 containers was much greater than the number of No. 10 cans, attesting to the popularity of canned blueberries in the home.

Cranberries.—The American cranberry (*Vaccinium macrocarpus* A.t.) along with its varieties is one of the few fruits that normally grow in wet places. In five major producing states, Massachusetts, New Jersey, Wisconsin, Washington, and Oregon, the cranberry farms are known as cranberry bogs. They must have ample water during the growing season. The bogs may be flooded at blossom time or at harvest to combat frost, although the bogs may be drained and allowed to dry off 1–2 weeks before harvest. Hand harvesting is done with cranberry scoops, specialized devices with long wooden teeth. Mechanical harvesting may be done with vacuum pickers or by beaters which loosen the fruit from the vines. The beating is followed by flooding the bogs and floating the berries so that they can be scooped up to harvest them.

At one time cranberries were mostly sold fresh, but now processed berries account for much of the consumption. The berries are frozen and held in freezing storage before being converted into whole cranberry or jellied cranberry sauce or the various diluted juice drinks such as cranberry juice cocktail, or the cranberry and apple blend. By using frozen fruit it is possible to extend the processing season to a year-round basis, if necessary. Also freezing facilitates the extraction of juice by pressing as the freezing ruptures the berry tissue. Cranberry juice cocktail and similar cranberry juice products are among the most successful of recently-developed fruit products. More than $1/2$ the processed cranberries go into juice products.

Currents, Black

Although products made from black currents are very popular in Europe, they are not widely-known in the United States. The fact that the black current is an alternate host for white pine blister rust has led to many states banning the cultivation of this crop. In Ontario, Baldwin, Kenny, and Saunders varieties of the fruit are grown.

Black currents are cleaned, washed, sorted, stemmed, and frozen without sugar or syrup. The frozen berries are used for subsequent manufacture into other products.

Currents, Red

Most of the red currents are frozen for conversion into Jelly and jam. Leading varieties include Red Lake, Wilder, Perfection, Red Cross, and Stevens No. 9. Red currents are handled in the same manner as black currents for freezing.

Gooseberries

A small canned pack of gooseberries is put up in the United States (less than a million pounds in 1967). The fruit is also frozen for subsequent use in jams and pies. In the Pacific Northwest, Downing, Poorman, and Oregon have been the leading varieties.

EVERETT R. WOLFORD

References

Strawberries

BARRITT, B. H., TORRE, L., and LOO, H. 1972. Performance of strawberry cultivars and selections throughout the Pacific Northwest. Proc. Western Washington Hort. Assoc., Jan. 1972.

DARROW G. M., and SCOTT, D. H. 1967. Strawberry varieties in the United States. USDA Farmers' Bull. *1043*.

DURKEE, E. L., ELSKEN, R. L., and BARTA, E. J. 1961. Latest research boosts pallet freezing efficiency. Part I. Time-temperature data. Food Eng. *33*, No. 1, 85–86.

GUADAGNI, D. G., HARRIS, JEAN, and SANSUCK, D. 1961. Latest research boosts pallet freezing efficiency. Part II. Effect on quality. Food Eng. *33*, No. 2, 84–86.

SISTRUNK, W. A., and MOORE, J. N. 1971. Strawberry quality studies in relation to new variety development. Univ. Arkansas Agr. Expt. Sta. Bull. *761*.

WOLFORD, E. R. 1965. Freezing at −320°F. Proc. Western Washington Hort. Assoc., Puyallup, Washington.
WOLFORD, E. R., JACKSON, R., and BOYLE, F. P. 1971. Quality evaluation of stone fruits and berries frozen in liquid nitrogen and in Freezant-12. Chem. Eng. Symp. *67*, No. 108, 131–136.

Raspberries

BREKKE, J. E. *et al.* 1956. New washing technique ups berry throughput. Food Eng. *28*, No. 9, 845, 154–155.
DODGE, J. C. 1971. Growing raspberries in Washington. Washington State Univ. Ext. Bull. *401*.
LEE, F. A., and SLATE, G. L. 1954. Chemical composition and freezing adaptability of raspberries. N.Y. Agr. Expt. Sta. Bull. *761*.

Brambleberries

ANON. 1971. Canned fruit pack. Canner/Packer 1971–1972 Yearbook *140*, No. 9, 82.

BIOASSAY

Bioassay refers to the procedure by which the effect of a substance on a living organism can be determined. With regard to food, the substance might be a vitamin, a mineral, an amino acid or acids, a food additive, in fact any substance that might impair or improve a food or feed. The effect of the substance on the growth or the proliferation of the test organism is commonly the basic interest of the assay. The bioassay method among other applications has been used to determine the amino acids essential to animal growth, the human requirements for each of the various vitamins, to assay the effects of trace elements in foods and feeds, and to determine the physiological effects, if any, of food additives.

Procedures in bioassay begin with the formulation of a basal diet or medium suitable in all respects to the requirements of the test organism. To this diet the substance under study (for example, a food additive) is added. If the substance under study inhibits growth, it is suspect. If growth is unimpaired, other things being equal, the substance is not harmful. Bioassay is often used to determine the potential of a substance for stimulating growth, in which case growth is measured in terms of weight increase and other criteria as compared with that of controls.

Although bacteria, molds, and yeasts are widely used in assaying the effect of vitamins, minerals, and amino acids on nutrition, test animals are used in determining the effect of substances that may be harmful to man. Results of such studies must be subjected to statistical analysis since differences in response as between animals might cause a miscalculation.

Bioassay is a time-consuming and a rather expensive analytic method but for the study of the effect of specific substances on living organisms there is no substitute.

MARTIN S. PETERSON

Cross-reference: *Nutrition.*

BIRDSEYE, CLARENCE (1886–1956)

Clarence Birdseye was born in Brooklyn, N.Y. in 1886. He attended Amherst College for 2 yr but left without completing his course to become a field naturalist for the U.S. Biological Survey which position he held from 1910 to 1912. Then he went to Labrador where for 5 yr he was a fur trader. While there, he noted that the freshly caught fish, frozen at low Labrador temperatures and stored in unheated rooms in the winter retained their quality amazingly well.

At the beginning of World War I, he became purchasing agent for the U.S. Housing Corporation. At the end of the war, he took a position as assistant to the president of the U.S. Fisheries Association which he retained until 1922. Then he entered business as a distributor of fresh fishery products in Long Island. In 1924, he went to Gloucester, Mass. where he began experimenting on a pilot plant scale in the "quick freezing" of all kinds of fishery products. He invented the double-belt freezer which consisted of two endless, stainless steel belts, one superimposed over the other. The upper belt was somewhat wider than the lower belt and very cold (−40°F) on which calcium chloride brine was sprayed. The belts were enclosed in an insulated tunnel and the brine, flowing off of the upper belt, fell into a tank. Then it was again refrigerated and recirculated.

In cooperation with Wetmore Hodges, Bassett Jones, I. L. Rice, and others, he formed the General Foods Corporation and began the commercial "quick freezing" of fish fillets and steaks, packaged in rectangular paraffined cartons lined with moisture-proof Cellophane. He also began experimenting with the freezing of meat and other foods.

In 1929, this company was sold to the Postum Company for somewhat more than 22 million dollars. The Postum Company preferred the name of General Foods and took that name for the parent company and called the commercial Birdseye organization "the General Seafoods Corporation."

The General Foods Corporation established the Birdseye Laboratory to study the quick freezing by the Birdseye system of all kinds of food products. That laboratory, directed by Clarence Birdseye, also acted as the quality control organization for the various subsidiary companies set up by General Foods Corporation for the freezing of all kinds of foods. In the Birdseye Laboratories, the methods of preparing for freezing all kinds of vegetables, fruits, meats, poultry, fish, and shellfish were perfected. Of equal importance, the procedures of preparing for freezing and freezing a large variety of prepared and precooked foods, baked goods, etc., were perfected. However, only a few of the precooked foods (squash, corn-on-the-cob, lobster, and one or two others) were actually put into commercial production at that time.

Clarence Birdseye with the aid of Bicknell Hall invented the Birdseye multiplate froster which became the standard equipment for "quick freezing" packaged foods in all of the food freezing plants of the General Foods Corporation. This freezer is still in general use in many food freezing plants.

Because of his leadership in food freezing, Clarence Birdseye became famous. The food frozen by the equipment and processes perfected in the Birdseye Laboratories was given the name of "Birdseye Frosted Foods." The General Foods Corporation has been highly successful in merchandising all kinds of packaged frozen foods.

In 1935, Mr. Birdseye left the Birdseye Laboratories and organized the Birdseye Electric Company which manufactured highly efficient electric lights. Later, he invented a process of making paper of good quality from sugar cane bagasse. He was engaged in this work at the time of his death in 1956.

DONALD K. TRESSLER

Cross-reference: *Frozen Foods.*

BISCUIT[3] AND CRACKER TECHNOLOGY

Major products produced by the biscuit and cracker industry may be classified as: sponge goods, chemically leavened crackers, and sweet goods.

Sponge Goods

The soda cracker, often called a saltine, appears to have originated in the 1850's in America. The first cracker bakery in the United States was established at Newburyport, Mass. in 1792. However, crackers made before 1850 were unleavened. At present, soda crackers represent about 50% of the total biscuit and cracker production in the United States. The evolution from empiricism to a science has not been completed, but the industry has become standardized in the use of spindle mixers; an 18–20 hr sponge fermentation; a 4–5 hr dough proof; automatic lamination of the dough; a short bake (1.5–3.0 min, depending on the thickness of the crackers); and the use of a band oven equipped with a woven wire mesh band.

Important factors in the production of a superior soda cracker are the choice of flours for the sponge and dough, the selection of the fermentation environment, and the baking conditions. For the sponge a standard patent or straight milled flour is commonly employed, usually milled from soft red winter wheat, possibly blended with some hard red winter wheat. A slightly softer flour is used for the dough-up. Specifications for these flours are given in Table B-6. A basic formula for soda crackers is shown in Table B-7.

The production of superior crackers requires the use of uniform and high quality raw materials, and the adoption of, and adherence to, precise production procedures. The setting temperature for sponges is usually about 75°F, but varies from 70° to 80°F depending upon several factors, chiefly the flour available. Flour and water are the basic ingredients of a cracker sponge. Yeast and bacteria are the fermentation agents. Bacteria originate in the yeast, the flour, the surfaces of the trough and, when employed, an inoculum added as a few pounds of sponge from the previous day. During the 19-hr proofing period profound chemical and physical changes occur by virtue of the simultaneous fermentation by yeast and bacteria. Amylases convert starch to dextrins and fermentable sugars. Deficiencies in flour amylase may be corrected by adding diastatically active malt flour or a fungal diastase. As the sugars are produced by the amylases the yeast produces carbon dioxide and alcohol. The bacteria convert the sugars to organic acids. The acids increase the activity of the amylases, accelerating the production of sugars, thus speeding up the entire process.

Significant physical changes occur in the sponge during fermentation. Immediately after mixing, the flour and water form a very stiff mass. During fermentation, the sponge becomes elastic and pliable. Several factors are responsible for the development of these changes: (1) the hydration of the gluten, which prepares it for the following

---

[3] The terms "biscuit" and "cookie" are synonymous. Biscuit means twiced cooked: baking at high temperatures, followed by drying at lower temperatures.

TABLE B-6

FLOUR STANDARDS FOR COOKIES AND CRACKERS
(Figures Apply Only to Unbleached, Standard Patent Flours)

Use of Flour	Ash (%)	Protein (%)	No-Time Viscosity	Spread (%)
Soft cooky, for general sweet goods	0.38–0.42	7.0–8.0	20–40	90–100
Medium, for cracker dough-up, grahams, and rich cookies	0.39–0.42	8.0–9.0	40–60	80–90
Strong, for cracker sponge	0.39–0.42	8.5–10.0	50–100	70–80

SOURCE: *Biscuit and Cracker Handbook*, Biscuit and Cracker Manufacturers Assoc., Chicago.

TABLE B-7

A BASIC FORMULA FOR SODA CRACKERS
(Based on Six Barrels of Flour)

	Lb
Sponge	
Flour	800
Water (variable)	350
Shortening	60
Yeast	2
Yeast food (optional)	1
Ferment (optional)	20
Dough	
Flour	400
Shortening	60
Sugar of malt (optional)	10
Salt	18
Soda (variable)	7
Diammonium phosphate (optional)	2

SOURCE: Bohn (1957).

steps; (2) a slight enzymatic hydrolysis of the flour proteins; and (3) a mechanical development of the gluten. The carbon dioxide produced during the fermentation forms cells which expand and contract, stretching the gluten network, producing an effect similar to mechanical mixing. Sponge temperatures will have increased 10°–15°F. There has been a marked increase in acidity: as measured by pH, a change from near 6.0 to about 4.5. This is shown graphically in Chap. 4 of *Biscuit and Cracker Handbook* (1970). Neutralization of the acids is an important element in the preparation of the dough, involving an estimate of the amount of sodium bicarbonate required to produce the desired pH in the baked cracker. Bohn (1957) states that the optimum pH lies between 7.2 and 8.0. He suggests the addition of diammonium phosphate at the dough-up stage to aid in achieving uniformity of cracker pH.

Sensory properties of a superior cracker are readily defined. Symmetry, with uniform brown blisters on top and smaller lighter blisters on the bottom provide visual appeal. Crispness gives a cracker snap or "crunch." Tenderness provides a pleasant mouth feel and a quick get-away. A superior flavor derives from a blend of yeasty, nutty, buttery, and toasted grainy notes. A raw starchy note is deleterious.

In recent years there has been a shift towards a thinner cracker. At present several of the larger manufacturers are producing the 2-in.-sq cracker at a "count" of 160 per lb. Further increase in the number of crackers per pound does not appear to be advantageous.

Chemically Leavened Crackers

Many cracker varieties which were formerly yeast-leavened and classified as sponge goods are now chemically-leavened. The most popular crackers in this category are the familiar round crackers, about 2 in. in diameter with 7 docker holes. In the production of these crackers a medium soft flour is commonly used. On the basis of 100 lb of flour, the average cracker is made with about 10 lb shortening, 5 lb sugar, 2 lb invert syrup, 2 lb nonfat dry milk, malt extract, salt, and leavening. Many varieties of this cracker are being produced by the addition of other materials, some of which are: whole wheat flour, poppy seeds, sesame seeds, soya grits, and meaty flavors plus spices, onion powders, and cheese. Although some advantages accrue from the use of the sponge and dough method, most cheese cracker doughs are chemically leavened. Matz (1968) states that "the flavor elaborated during fermentation is complementary to the cheese flavor and provides an inexpensive way of getting the desired strength and character." Cheddar cheese, also called American cheese, is used almost exclusively, usually at levels ranging from 10 to 35 lb per 100 lb of flour. Color, paprika, and red pepper are common additives. It is important to adjust the leavening components so that the cracker will be slightly acidic. An alkaline reaction obscures the cheese flavor.

Many of the numerous varieties of chemically-leavened crackers are sprayed with hot oil as they emerge from the band oven. For many years, 76° coconut oil was used almost exclusively. At present several lightly hydrogenated domestic vegetable oils are being employed. Levels of use range between 5 and 20%.

Graham crackers are a special case of chemically-leavened crackers. These, too, were originally made by the sponge and dough procedure. They are unique in that they are much sweeter than other crackers and are alkaline in reaction (pH about 8.0). A considerable degree of expertise is required to produce an excellent graham cracker. Usually, the flour will consist of 70–80 parts of a straight milled medium soft flour and 20–30 parts of whole wheat flour. On the basis of 100 lb of flour, the typical dough is composed of 13 lb shortening, 25 lb sugar, 5 lb invert syrup, 5 lb molasses, salt, ammonium bicarbonate, and water. Some bakers may include one or more of the following: brown sugar, dextrose, and dried whey. Prevailing mixing procedures entail a long mix and a hot dough. Providing that the formulation, mixing, and sheeting are satisfactory, the proper bake should produce a cracker characterized by an open texture with no evidence of shelliness on top, a tender but crisp bite, and an attractive appearance. Ideally, the flavor is a well-balanced blend of sweet, floury, caramel, and branny notes.

In the production of honey graham crackers, honey replaces the molasses, usually with the addition of some more sugar.

Sweet Goods

Discussed here are several types of biscuits, characterized chiefly by their high sugar content. Included are plain cookies, fig bars, soft cookies, sandwiches, and enrobed varieties. Categorically, these varieties require a soft flour and are sweeter than crackers, except graham crackers. For discussion purposes, it is convenient to classify sweet goods according to the equipment used in their production.

Cutters.—In order to use a cutter, it is necessary that the physical properties of the dough permit the formation of a well-knit sheet, resistant to tearing and permitting the removal of scrap. The individual pieces are cut from this sheet by means of a reciprocating cutter or a rotary cutter. A variant of the former is the embossing cutter which simultaneously stamps a design into the top. However its use appears to be diminishing. Representative varieties produced with cutting equipment are: arrowroot, social tea, and Marie biscuits, all known as hard sweet biscuits. Several versions of snaps and sugar cookies are made with cutters, as well as some base cakes.

Rotary Molding Machines.—These are well adapted to forming cookies from doughs containing high levels of shortening. The use of this method is increasing due to several advantages: baking time is short because water content of doughs is low, high rate of production, dimensions of pieces can be well controlled, no scrap dough to rework and it provides a means for producing a fine embossing. Typical of the varieties produced are: shortbreads (the rotary molder was devised specifically for the production of shortbread), chocolate flavored base cakes for sandwiches and butter cookies.

Extruding Devices.—Included in this category are wire cut, deposit, and bar machines. In wire cut machines, the dough is extruded through a series of holes, is cut off with a wire, and drops directly onto the oven band. The size of the holes and the fluidity of the dough during baking determine the size of the cookie. In general, production rates are lower than for cutters and rotary molders. However, the cookies are finely textured and as a consequence have a pleasing "bite." Additionally, less shortening is required to produce a tender cookie. A stringy dough can not be tolerated. Another advantage is the capability of producing a wide variety of cookies, such as vanilla wafers, brown edge wafers, chocolate chip, macaroons, snaps, and sugar cookies.

With a deposit machine, it is possible to produce a cookie with a top design; the spritz is typical. No cut-off device is used, the dough being pulled apart by the movement of the machine relative to the oven band.

Simple bar goods are formed by pressing the dough through a slit, frequently with a notched edge to produce a serrated top. The pieces are cut before baking. Coconut bars and brownie bars are commonly made this way. The formation of fig bars involves the simultaneous extrusion of the envelope dough and the fig jam through two concentric orifices. Continuous strips are deposited on the oven band and cut as they emerge from the oven. Efficient cooling is required following the cutting to permit in-line packaging. The adoption of continuous band oven production has improved the product and the efficiency markedly.

Soft Cookies.—The term "soft cookies" is subject to considerable variation in interpretation.

McGee (1955) prefers to recognize four types: (1) drop cookies, (2) "garden variety" (sugar, molasses, coconut, raisin, date, honey, etc.), (3) shortbread, and (4) macaroon. Several of these have been considered earlier. This discussion is concerned with the technology involved in producing high moisture soft cookies. Flick (1964) has emphasized that in producing the soft type cookies more tenderizing and moisture-retaining ingredients are used than in the usual hard type cookie. He suggests that there are many leaner type cake formulations which would yield excellent soft cookies by adjustment of the liquid and leavening. Flour, sugar, shortening, and eggs are critical ingredients in soft cookies. Unbleached soft winter wheat flour, about 9.5% protein, is satisfactory in most instances. However, a chlorine bleached medium strong soft red winter wheat flour, about 9.0% protein, is often preferred. Fine granulated sugar will produce better structured cookies than powdered sugar. Flick states that from 18 to 27% invert sugar, based on the flour, is required. Honey and molasses, also, are effective hygroscopic agents. Not only does invert syrup provide moisture-retaining properties, but its reducing sugars aid in producing an attractive color. A creamable shortening is required. Flick states that the percentage of whole eggs should be at least 14%.

Sandwiching.—Undoubtedly the most popular sandwiches are those composed of chocolate-flavored base cakes and vanilla-flavored fillers. Substantial amounts of dutched cocoa are used in formulating the base cake in order to achieve a dark color and a flavor which complements the filler. A formula given by Bohn (1957) is representative of most of these fillers: 62% sugar, 33% fat, and 5% nonfat dry milk, plus salt and flavor. The sugar must be sufficiently fine to avoid grittiness but not so fine as to require excessive amount of fat. The characteristics of the fat are of paramount importance: strict conformation to a specific solid fat index being essential to permit high speed sandwiching and quick solidification of the filler.

Enrobing.—Enrobed varieties constitute a significant part of the total production of most biscuit manufacturers. Most of the coatings are either chocolate or chocolate-flavored. It is essential to differentiate clearly between the two types of "chocolate" coatings: (A) the true chocolate coating and (B) the compound coating, also called a confectioner's coating.

For a discussion of the manufacture and application of these coatings refer to Cook (1963) and Minifie (1970). Shown in Table B-8 are typical formulations for chocolate and compound coatings. These will emphasize the differences between the two types. Federal Standards of Identity exist for both. No cocoa, nor any fat other than cocoa butter may be used in chocolate coatings. At times small amounts of chocolate liquor are added to compound coatings to enhance the flavor, but cost and the incompatibility of the cocoa butter and the hard butter limit the amount to a level which is often insignificant flavor-wise. However, recently a hard butter has been developed from domestic oils which is compatible with the cocoa butter in chocolate liquor to the extent that significant levels of chocolate liquor may be included in compound coatings (Ryberg 1970).

The flavor of chocolate coatings is superior to that of compound coatings. The quality of flavor is largely dependent upon the type of beans from which the chocolate liquor is derived. Liquor for chocolate coatings is usually produced from a blend of choice or flavor beans (Criollo) and base beans (Forastero), whereas the cocoa used in compound coatings is often derived entirely from

TABLE B-8

COMPOSITION OF TYPICAL CHOCOLATE AND COMPOUND COATINGS USED BY BISCUIT AND CRACKER MANUFACTURERS

| Ingredients | Chocolate Coating | | Compound Coating | |
	Dark Sweet (%)	Milk (%)	Dark Sweet (%)	Light Sweet (%)
Chocolate liquor	35	16	None	None
Cocoa butter	15	21	None	None
Cocoa (10–12% fat)	None	None	20	10
Hard butter	None	None	31	32
Sugar	50	48	49	53
Whole milk powder	None	15	None	None
Skim milk powder	None	None	None	5
Lecithin, salt, vanillin				

base beans. Additionally, the unique melting characteristics of cocoa butter make it ideally suited for coatings. It remains hard through 80°F, but melts at 90°–94°F, which is below mouth temperatures, thus affording a sudden release of flavor.

Compound coatings provide two advantages over chocolate coatings: they are less expensive and may be tailored to meet seasonal temperatures. For winter, a hard butter melting at 98°F (Wiley melting point) is commonly used, while for summer a melting point of 108°F has been found to be satisfactory for most areas of the United States. At present, most of the hard butters are prepared from imported oils, such as coconut, palm kernel, and babassu, all of which contain high percentages of lauric acid. From these oils, suppliers are able to make hard butters which produce palatable coatings which set quickly and exhibit excellent gloss retention. In using these hard butters in their coatings, biscuit manufacturers did occasionally encounter the development of an exceedingly disagreeable flavor, usually characterized as soapy. Its origin: a slight hydrolysis of the fat by lipase from the cocoa, producing highly flavored free fatty acids. Adequate processing of the cocoa has eliminated this defect. Babayan (1970) discusses advances made by the edible fat and oil industry in producing hard butters as well as other products for the biscuit manufacturer.

Flour

What constitutes quality in biscuit and cracker flours has not been clearly identified. With the exception of reports from the Soft Wheat Quality Laboratory at Wooster, Ohio very little fundamental work has been published. However, some generalizations are admissible. Protein content is the first and perhaps most significant analytical reference mark. Bakers producing a complete line of biscuits and crackers find that they require three types of flour characterized primarily by their protein content: from 7.0–8.0% for the softest flour to 8.5–10.0% for the strongest (Table B-6). Cookie flours are usually milled from blends of soft red winter and soft white wheats. The advent of flour fractionation by fine grinding and air classifications has given the miller much greater latitude than he had. Perhaps the greatest advantage lies in the ability to maintain desirable characteristics in a flour for a specific use with less dependence on wheat varieties and growing conditions.

For cookies, the water-binding capacity of the flour appears to be a significant property. By fractionating soft flours into gluten, prime starch, starch tailings, and water solubles, Yamazaki (1962, 1969) has shown that the hydration capacity of the starch tailings is important in determining cookie flour quality. Better cookies are made with flour in which the starch tailings have a lower affinity for water. On the basis of observed differences in flour hydration properties, Yamazaki (1953) developed the alkaline water-retention capacity test. This has proven to be a reliable guide to cookie spread. Evidently, water binding capacity is the decisive characteristic of flour in determining cookie quality. Certainly, this property is also related to flour particle size, extent of starch damage, protein, and starch gelatinization during baking. Milling is responsible for the first two factors, while starch gelatinization is influenced by other constituents of the dough, especially sugar. Making adjustments in the amount of sugar in the dough is a common expedient used by bakers to control the size of cookies.

The AACC cookie flour test (Method 10-50) has been studied collaboratively for many years and is widely accepted (AACC 1962). Results are reported as the "spread factor." Recognizing the limitations of the AACC test for biscuits containing low levels of sugar, British cereal scientists have studied test-baking procedures for semisweet biscuits. They have concluded that: (1) the best method of evaluating a biscuit flour is a baking test based on the conditions under which the flour is to be used in production; (2) when amount of water and final dough temperature are closely controlled, the effect of flour properties on biscuit weight and dimensions are relatively small, although high-protein flours give hard biscuits of poor appearance; and (3) the use of sodium metabisulfite as a dough-softening agent reduces still further the effect of flour properties on biscuit weight and dimensions, but does not overcome the deleterious effects of high-protein flours on appearance and texture (Wade and Elton 1967).

Cracker flours are milled from the hardest soft wheat. For cracker sponges it is usually necessary to blend in some low protein hard wheat to obtain flour of optimum characteristics. Dough-up flour is of medium strength. Chemically-leavened crackers require medium to medium-soft flours. Satisfactory performance can not be guaranteed even though a flour complies with the well-accepted biscuit and cracker flour standards as well as additional specifications, such as mixogram area and gassing power. Two flours may satisfy all of the requirements, yet one may produce excellent crackers and the other fail. Often, additional background information will reveal why the flours differ (Desrosier 1969). Are the wheat mixes from the same growing area and have both been properly stored, blended, and turned? Have both been produced by the same mill unit? Non-uniformity in biscuit and cracker flour makes it virtually impossible to produce a uniformly excellent product. Uniformity throughout a crop year is of overriding importance. Even though a flour may be judged to be deficient in one or more criteria, satisfactory compensations can usually be made by adjustments in formulation and oven settings. The larger biscuit and cracker producers have resolved most of their problems arising from nonuniformity by acquiring captive mills with adequate storage and blending facilities for their wheat.

The writer gratefully acknowledges the helpful advice of Dr. Norman W. Desrosier.

OTTO G. JENSEN

References

AACC. 1962. Cereal Laboratory Methods, 7th Edition. American Association of Cereal Chemists, St. Paul.

BABAYAN, V. K. 1970. "Tailor Made" fats and oils for bakery, confectionery and cereal uses. Cereal Sci. Today 15, No. 7, 214-217, 225.

BOHN, R. M. 1957. Biscuit and Cracker Production. American Trade Publishing Co., New York.

COOK, L. R. 1963. Chocolate Production and Use. Magazines For Industry, New York.

DESROSIER, N. W. 1969. Cracker flour specifications. Paper presented at Biscuit Bakers Technical Conference, Mar. 1969, Chicago.

FLICK, H. 1964. Fundamentals of cookie production including soft type cookies. Proc. Soc. Bakery Engrs. 286-295.

MATZ, S. A. 1968. Cookie and Cracker Technology. Avi Publishing Co., Westport, Conn.

McGEE, O. 1955. Soft cookies. Proc. Soc. Bakery Engrs. 250-258.

MINIFIE, B. W. 1970. Chocolate, Cocoa and Confectionery, Science and Technology. Avi Publishing Co., Westport, Conn.

RYBERG, J. R. 1970. Domestic hard butters. Cereal Sci. Today 15, No. 1, 16-19.

WADE, P., and ELTON, G. A. H. 1967. Flour properties relating to the manufacture of semi-sweet biscuits. Cereal Sci. Today 12, No. 1, 8-9, 15-16.

YAMAZAKI, W. T. 1953. An alkaline water retention capacity test for the evaluation of cookie baking potentialities of soft winter wheat flours. Cereal Chem. 30, No. 3, 242-246.

YAMAZAKI, W. T. 1962. Laboratory testing of flours and cookie quality research. Cereal Sci. Today 7, No. 4, 98-104, 125.

YAMAZAKI, W. T. 1969. Soft wheat flour evaluation. Bakers Dig. Febr. 30-32, 63.

Cross-references: *Baking Industry, Bread; Pretzels; Hardtack.*

BORDEN, GAIL (1801-1874)

Gail Borden, a remarkably versatile man, holds his place in food technology history by virtue of his invention of canned condensed milk, but his career had many other facets. He was, curiously enough, one of that company of town builders that did much to settle the west in the first half of the Nineteenth Century.

Born in Norwich, N.Y., in 1801, he moved with his family to Kentucky in 1815, and a little later to Indiana. The year 1821 found him in Mississippi and in 1829, for the sake of his health, he moved to Texas where he became a stock raiser.

Somewhere along the way, Gail Borden learned the art of surveying—probably in Indiana. He practiced surveying in Texas, along with stock-raising, and was selected to survey and design the town of Galveston, Texas.

A religious man and a man of deep sympathies, Gail Borden was early imbued with a desire to contribute something of lasting merit to humanity. One of his early ventures, the development of dehydrated meat in what he called "biscuit" form, was undertaken with this thought in mind. It won a prize for him in the London exposition of 1851 but otherwise was not accorded much notice.

From Texas, Borden moved to Lebanon, N.Y., and it is here that he conceived the idea of condensed milk, an idea inspired, it is said, by his observing the results of heating sugar juice in an air-tight pan. Although Borden did not solve the technical problem of the flavor change occasioned by the heat-sensitive nature of milk, he did, without question, start the condensed milk industry on its way in 1857.

Borden felt that his invention of condensed milk was truly a benefaction. It was used by the Union troops in 1861-1865, and during the years after the Civil War it found an important place in the subsistence of laborers operating far from the normal channels of supply. Borden, following his success with condensed milk, also experimented with condensed fruit juice.

In 1861, Gail Borden returned to Texas, this time with the object of educating dairymen in sanitary practices, a need he had observed in connection with his manufacturing enterprise in New York. He continued to live in Texas until his death at Borden, Texas in 1874.

MARTIN S. PETERSON

Cross-reference: *Evaporated Milk History.*

BOTULISM

Botulism is a severe type of food poisoning caused by the ingestion of foods containing a potent neurotoxin formed during growth of *Clostridium botulinum*, a spore-forming bacterium for which molecular oxygen is toxic. The incidence of the disease is low, but it has received much publicity because of the extremely high mortality rate. The majority of the 10–20 outbreaks reported annually in the United States are associated with inadequately processed home-canned foods. Botulinal toxin, the most potent poison known to man, is produced by the growth of the organism in the food material before it is consumed and, thus, the disease is an intoxication and not a food-borne infection. The organism is widely distributed in nature and occurs in both cultivated and virgin forest soils, bottom sediments of streams, lakes and coastal waters, the intestinal tract of fish and mammals, and the gills and viscera of crabs and other shellfish. Sausages, meat products, canned vegetables and fruits, and seafood products have been the most frequent vehicles for human botulism. Six antigenic types of toxin are produced by different members of the species and these form the basis of classification of the organism into types A through F. Types A, B, E, and F have been responsible for human outbreaks, whereas, types C and D are associated with botulism in animals.

History

Although botulism has been known since ancient times, only in the last 200 yr has there been sufficient knowledge to recognize it as a food-borne disease. It was first accurately described and made a reportable disease in southern Germany in the early Nineteenth Century after a study of more than 200 cases of sausage poisoning. The term "botulism" (botulus, Latin meaning sausage) was first applied to this syndrome in 1870 and the causative agent was first isolated and described by Van Ermengem in 1895. The symptoms and severity of the disease in the outbreak from which the organism was isolated led Van Ermengem to name the organism *Bacillus botulinus* (now *Clostridium botulinum*). He also noted the similarity of this disease to the "ichthyism" of Russia and regarded it as probably identical.

Until the causative agent was identified, botulism was thought to be associated exclusively with sausages or meat products, but shortly afterwards one outbreak in Germany and another in California were traced to bean salads. However, the toxin produced by the strains isolated in both cases was immunologically distinct from that of Van Ermengem's strain. These incidents were followed in the United States by an increasing series of outbreaks which were traced to canned vegetables and fruits. Statistics for 1918 through 1922 show 83 outbreaks with 297 cases and 185 deaths. Since then, the occurrence of botulinal toxin in commercially canned foods has been reduced to a negligible level by improved canning methods that resulted from research sponsored by the canning industry and public health authorities.

All of the outbreaks reported through 1922 were due to organisms producing one or the other of the above two types of toxin, later designated types A and B. Both of the type C subtypes (C_α and C_β) and type D were reported in 1922. Although types C and D have caused heavy losses of chickens, ducks, aquatic wildfowl, cattle, horses, and mink, there is little evidence that they have ever been responsible for human botulism but there is no evidence to indicate man is not susceptible.

Type E was first identified as a toxigenic type in 1935. This strain, isolated from Russian sturgeon, was found to be identical to two others previously isolated in New York. One strain had been isolated from an outbreak in 1932 involving salmon caught and smoked in Labrador and the other from imported canned sprats responsible for an outbreak in 1934. Although one type E outbreak was due to commercially canned mushrooms in 1941, the majority of outbreaks in the United States have been associated with fish and seafood. Since 1960, outbreaks traced to fish caught and commercially smoked in the Great Lakes area have been responsible for 21 cases and 9 deaths, but one outbreak responsible for two deaths in 1963 involved canned tuna fish. This organism is an important public health hazard in areas of Japan where "Izushi" is a popular food. This dish is prepared from raw fish which is allowed to ferment in the presence of rice, koji, and chopped vegetables for several days to two months. It has given rise to morbidity rates from type E botulism of about 50% with fatality rates of 20 to 100%.

Type F was first isolated in 1960 from an outbreak in Denmark in which a liver paste was the vehicle. The only other type F outbreak on record occurred in California in 1966 and was traced to contaminated deer jerky.

Geographic Distribution

The disease, botulism, occurs throughout the world. Of the 659 outbreaks recorded in the United States from 1899 through 1969, 21.8% were due to type A, 5.6% to type B, 2.6% to type E and 0.3% to type F. In 69.5% of the outbreaks the type was not determined. Outbreaks have been reported in 44 states, but 5 Western States account for over $1/2$ of all reported outbreaks.

Of the 144 type A outbreaks, 92% were in states west of the Mississippi River, whereas 25 of 37 type B outbreaks, or 67%, occurred in Eastern States from 1899 through 1969. Type E outbreaks have been reported in ten states. The geographic association of this type with Alaska and the Great Lakes area may be more apparent than real.

The regional distribution of outbreaks by toxin type is in keeping with the results of a spore survey of soil samples by Meyer and Dubovsky. These investigators found a predominance of type A in soil specimens from the west and of type B in soils of the northeast and central states. Other investigators have shown that type E is the predominant type in fish and sediments from the Great Lakes, in estuarine and coastal waters and sediments, and in fish and shellfish from the Atlantic, Pacific, and Gulf coasts of North America.

Type B is the predominant type both in soils and in outbreaks in Europe. However, type E has accounted for 46% of outbreaks of botulism in Japan, Canada, and Scandinavia in the Twentieth Century.

Types of Food Involved in Outbreaks

The types of foods involved in botulism vary according to food preservation and eating habits in different regions. Almost any type of food with a pH above 4.5 can support growth and toxin formation. Table B-9 summarizes the types of food which have been involved in outbreaks of botulism in the United States. The majority of these outbreaks were identified on the basis of clinical symptoms and not by the isolation and typing of the toxin.

TABLE B-9

FOODS INVOLVED IN OUTBREAKS OF BOTULISM
IN THE UNITED STATES BETWEEN
1899 AND 1969

Food	Total No. of Times That the Food Was Involved	No. of Times That Home-preserved Food Was Involved
Vegetables	395	362
Meat	44	36
Milk and milk products	7	5
Fish and seafood	48	33
Fruit and pickles	35	34

Most of the outbreaks have been traced to home-canned vegetables, fruits, fish and meat products with a smaller number involving commercially processed foods. Although many outbreaks were caused by commercially canned products during the 1920's and 1930's, home-canned string beans, corn, beans, spinach, and asparagus accounted for over $1/2$ the total number.

Botulism is usually associated with foods which have been given a preserving treatment, stored for some time and consumed without appropriate heating. The growth of C. botulinum in foods frequently, but not always, gives rise to a foul, rancid odor, which serves as a warning for the consumer. However, signs of spoilage have not prevented botulism because the degree of tolerance to disagreeable odors or off-flavors varies among individuals. Moreover, in foods which are smoked, heavily spiced, or fermented, the off-odor may be difficult to recognize.

Symptoms

Botulinal toxin causes paralysis by blocking motor nerve terminals at the myoneural junction. Paralysis progresses downward, usually starting with the eyes and face, to the throat, chest, and extremities. When the diaphragm and chest muscles become fully involved, respiration no longer is possible and death from asphyxia results.

Early signs are marked lassitude, weakness, and vertigo, usually followed by diplopia and progressive difficulty in speaking and swallowing. Difficulty in breathing, weakness of other muscles, abdominal distension and constipation are common symptoms also. Type E, in addition, also may cause severe nausea and vomiting in the early stages, and pharyngeal erythema and urinary retention later. The interval between onset of symptoms and death in a series of cases analyzed in Japan varied from 8 to 28 hr, but in those who recovered, some symptoms such as thirst, weakness, pharyngeal pain, and abdominal swelling persisted for some time.

Although botulism can be diagnosed on clinical symptoms alone, differentiation from a variety of other diseases often is difficult. Initial misdiagnosis as other central nervous system disorders, such as bulbar poliomyelitis, is not uncommon.

Clostridium botulinum

Clostridium botulinum is a large, motile, Gram-positive, anaerobic, spore-forming bacillus. Spores are subterminal and cause swelling of the cell wall, giving the characteristic spindle shape of a typical Clostridium during sporulation. The Gram-positive character is lost in older cultures which become variable or Gram-negative and often exhibit irregular staining and pleomorphic forms. This is especially true of type E which becomes Gram-negative in relatively young cultures and quite pleomorphic in older ones. Flagella are peritrichous and all types are motile. There is considerable variation in the size of the rods of both proteolytic and nonproteolytic strains so that size, though often helpful, is not a reliable criterion for distinction between them.

Although the primary classification of strains of *C. botulinum* is based on the immunological type of toxin produced, the types can also be divided into two physiological groups (proteolytic and nonproteolytic), irrespective of toxin. The proteolytic group includes all type A strains and some of the type B and type F strains. The nonproteolytic, or saccharolytic, strains include all type C, D, and E strains and the remainder of the type B and F strains. The type C and D strains, however, differ somewhat from the other nonproteolytic strains.

Both the proteolytic and nonproteolytic strains produce lipase as evidenced by a precipitate in the medium and a pearly or iridescent layer covering the colony and extending beyond it, when grown on eggyolk agar. They also produce β hemolysis on blood agar. Neither group, on the other hand, reduces nitrates to nitrite, produces indole, reduces urea, nor ferments lactose.

Toxin production is variable and with some strains, notably proteolytic type B, may be barely detectable in enrichment cultures containing other contaminating bacteria. The absence of readily detectable toxin, therefore, does not necessarily mean the absence of *C. botulinum*.

Detection

Since botulism is food-borne and results from ingestion of toxin formed in the food following growth of the organism, determination of the source of an outbreak is based on detection and identification of the toxin or cultivation of *C. botulinum* from the food involved.

Currently the most widely used method for detecting toxin in suspect food is the injection of extracts of the food into passively immunized mice, and the first objective in an epidemiological investigation is usually the detection of toxin in the suspected food by such a test. Rapid identification of the toxin is important for proper treatment of the victims, and in ascertaining the source so that the implicated food can be removed from further distribution as quickly as possible. This analysis is followed by culturing all suspect foods in an enrichment medium for the detection and isolation of the causative organism.

The details of these procedures will vary somewhat with the nature of the material to be examined. Products such as meat or fish are mascerated with gel-phosphate buffer to extract toxin, whereas liquid portions of some products can be injected directly into mice. Suspect foods are cultured for the bacillus because, on occasion, the food is no longer toxic at the time the mouse test is performed. Human illness with symptoms of botulism and isolation of a toxic strain of *C. botulinum* from the food involved is considered a positive laboratory confirmation of the diagnosis even in the absence of positive toxicity tests on the food product itself.

There are many enrichment media used for the cultivation of the different types of *C. botulinum*. The most common enrichment media all contain reducing agents to maintain anaerobic conditions as well as buffering agents.

The usual incubation conditions for maximum toxin production and growth of proteolytic types A, B, and F, types C_α and C_β, and type D are $35°$–$37°C$ for 5–7 days, whereas for the nonproteolytic types B, E, and F, they are $25°$–$28°C$ for 3–5 days.

Elimination of nonspore-forming contaminants from enrichment cultures by heating at $80°C$ for 30 min, which has been used in the isolation of *C. botulinum*, is not possible for nonproteolytic types B, E, and F, since their spores are almost as heat-sensitive as vegetative cells of many of the common contaminants. Therefore, enrichment cultures are treated with alcohol for this purpose. Cultures are then streaked on plating media for the selection of typical colonies of *C. botulinum*.

Plating media frequently employed are blood agar, liver veal egg agar, brain heart infusion agar, a variety of beef infusion agars, and modifications of the egg yolk medium of McClung and Toabe.

Control

The majority of the known outbreaks of botulism have been traced to foods given inadequate or minimal processing such as home canning, smoking, or pickling and eaten after little or no cooking or after holding for periods of time under inadequate refrigeration. Government agencies continue to urge home processors to use safe processes, and the serving of home-preserved foods in public eating places is generally prohibited. However, the chief concern is with the safe processing of commercial products, which, if toxic, could affect large numbers of consumers in diverse areas.

Fresh food whether eaten raw or cooked has not been implicated in an outbreak of botulism. Food preservation methods must, therefore, be designed to prevent the development of botulinal toxin unless the food is, in itself, inhibitory to the growth of the organism. Adequate methods must, in order of preference, either destroy all spores, prevent their germination and the outgrowth of vegetative cells, prevent the development of toxin, or provide conditions under which any toxin that might be formed will be inactivated.

The toxins of *C. botulinum* are heat labile and are therefore readily destroyed by normal cooking. Type A toxin is inactivated at $80°C$ in 6–10 min and type B in 15 min, whereas type E requires 40 min of heating at $60°C$. Boiling for 10 min provides a reasonable margin of safety against all types.

The real safety problem in food preservation, however, is the destruction of spores in processed foods. If they are not destroyed, type A and B spores will readily germinate, grow, and produce toxin between the temperatures of 15°C and 42°C, and the minimum temperature for growth and toxin production by type E is approximately 3°C. Vegetative cells, but not spores, on the other hand, die rapidly at temperatures above 50°C.

The heat resistance of proteolytic C. botulinum varies, but in general 5 hr at 100°C, 120 min at 105°C and 10 min at 120°C can be depended upon to kill most suspensions of C. botulinum spores. Their heat-resistance, however, may be influenced considerably by pH and substrate. For example, it has been shown that spores requiring over 5 hr to be destroyed by 100°C at pH 7.0 could be killed in 10 min at pH 3.7. The spores of the non-proteolytic types have a very low heat-resistance compared to the proteolytic types.

Freezing will not destroy either toxin or spores, but will prevent the germination and outgrowth of spores which would lead to toxin production at higher temperatures. It is most important that nonsterile frozen products be kept frozen until cooked.

The toxin of C. botulinum is very resistant to acid. It is not destroyed by 1–3% HCl in 36 hr at 35°C but is readily inactivated by alkali. Germination and outgrowth of spores are inhibited in most products below pH 4.5, but pH inhibition may also depend on other factors. For example, a pH of 5.7 was found to be inhibitory in baby banana purée whereas in pineapple rice pudding the inhibitory pH was 4.8, and in some canned foods in which yeast was also present as a contaminant, toxin was produced at a pH as low as 4.0.

C. botulinum is an obligate anaerobe, and atmospheric oxygen has a toxic effect on vegetative cells. Growth in food is related to the oxidation-reduction (O-R) potential. Such potentials are established in many foods by reducing systems present, such as S-H groups in meats, ascorbic acid, and other microorganisms. No special conditions of incubation, therefore, are required since frequently the food itself produces a sufficiently low O-R potential to permit outgrowth.

The resistance of C. botulinum spores to chemical agents is quite high. For complete inhibition of spore germination and outgrowth, 5–10% NaCl is required. The inhibitory effect of NaCl as a preservative is enhanced in the presence of sodium nitrite and mild heat. Twenty-five to 200 ppm of sodium nitrite may inhibit the organism for more than a month at optimum temperatures and pH ranges.

Commercial canning procedures have been designed to provide for the destruction of all spores with a sufficient margin of safety to make the possibility of any survivors extremely remote. In the event that there is a question regarding the safety of a product, cans showing even slightly bulging ends are discarded as well as any giving other evidence of spoilage such as souring, gas formation, discoloration, or leaks. All such cans should be suspected as potentially botulogenic and examined for toxicity and the presence of C. botulinum. Never under any circumstances should the contents of such products be tasted, let alone eaten, without thorough cooking.

The canning industry, using the information provided by the research carried out in the 1920's and 1930's, has adopted the "12 D" process for treating low-acid foods so that the probability of C. botulinum spores surviving is very remote. The spores of C. botulinum, although very resistant, are not the most heat-resistant known, and other more resistant spore-formers are frequently used in time-temperature studies. However, canning processes must be of such lethality that the likelihood of C. botulinum spores surviving is negligible. The concentration of spores in a food product is very important because the greater the number of spores there are in the product, the greater are the processing time and temperature required to ensure complete destruction of them. Therefore, the "12 D" process was designed to reduce a bacterial load of a billion spores in each of 1000 cans to the level of 1 spore in 1000 cans. These processes, which take into account among other things the consistency and chemical nature of the product and the size of the can, are now standardized and controlled to the point that only through recontamination after heating is it likely that a significant degree of spoilage or hazard from C. botulinum could occur. In fact, all outbreaks of botulism from canned food in the United States in recent years have been the result of mechanical failure or operator errors and not of the inadequacy of the required time-temperature process itself. An additional safety factor is provided by proper sanitary control, which reduces the original bacterial load to be inactivated during the canning cycle.

The knowledge concerning the effects of chemicals, such as salt, nitrite, and organic acids, on the germination and outgrowth of C. botulinum spores has been utilized by the meat-curing industry to produce safe and acceptable products without subjecting them to the "12 D" canning process. Ham, bacon, sausages, and similar foods have not appeared on the lists of commercially produced foods associated with botulism in the United States in recent years.

The preservation of food by drying, or smoking and drying, goes back beyond recorded history. Modern commercial drying processes are superior to the crude smoking-drying combinations of the past that were sometimes responsible for botulism. Freeze-dehydration and conventional air drying are commercially attractive because of increased shelf-life, weight reduction, and packaging ease. Some type of pretreatment is usually required so that rapid freezing and dehydration can occur.

Vacuum packaging provides special hazards when foods with sufficient moisture content to allow bacterial growth are placed in an environment that will discourage growth of normal spoilage organisms on the surface, but will support the growth of anaerobes. Concomitant growth of facultative organisms may well be an enhancing factor to the outgrowth of anaerobic species. Such growth uses up trace amounts of oxygen and may provide growth-promoting substances. On the other hand, heavy overgrowth by aerobes may prevent the germination and outgrowth of anaerobic species due to the accumulation of toxic metabolites. In vacuum-packaged foods, growth of aerobic organisms is considerably curtailed, and the shelf-life appears, therefore, to be extended because visible spoilage has not occurred. This additional shelf-life may be sufficient for anaerobes, such as *C. botulinum*, to grow and produce toxin. Since it is now known that type E can grow and produce toxin at refrigerator temperatures, this longer storage time may constitute a significant hazard. With vacuum-packaged foods, as with so many others, every attempt must be made to establish high levels of sanitation in the processing plant so that contamination levels with *C. botulinum* will be held to a minimum.

The radiation of foods has been subjected to intensive study in recent years. If the radiation were at a level (4–5 megarads) that produced a sterile product, there would be no hazard from botulism. Processes designed to pasteurize food by irradiation, however, would have little or no effect upon the spores of *C. botulinum* which are resistant to radiation damage. The extended shelf-life obtained by low-dose irradiation might allow outgrowth and toxin production. On the other hand, toxin can be readily inactivated by irradiation but the presence of amino acids offers considerable protection against its effects.

In any commercial operation for the preservation of foods, plant sanitation has an important bearing on the effectiveness of processing in the elimination of the hazard from *C. botulinum*. If the spores are present in the plant they may gain access to the product through handling at any stage of the operation.

The use of germicidal solutions can be of great value in plant sanitation, for example, in sanitizing equipment, work surfaces, etc. The sporicidal capacity of germicides, particularly chlorine, is greatly influenced by the method of application and the environment in which the germicide is used. When used with care, with consideration for pH, water temperature, and assurance of a sufficient free residual concentration, hypochlorite or other germicidal solutions can effectively be used to reduce spore populations of *C. botulinum*.

The ubiquity of *C. botulinum*, the resistance of its spores to physical and chemical agents, and the lethality of its toxin call for careful attention in the preparation of commercial food products. Thorough cleaning of all raw products in preparation for processing, scrupulous attention to sanitation in all phases of plant operation, and meticulous attention to processing conditions and handling of the finished product are required. Although certain types of products have been more frequently incriminated than others, it is probable that almost any food may become contaminated. As new types of processing and packaging are contemplated it is especially important that they be designed to eliminate the hazard presented by contamination with *C. botulinum*.

DONALD A. KAUTTER
RICHARD K. LYNT, JR.
KEITH H. LEWIS

BREADS

See Baking Industry: Ethnic U.S. Breads.

BREAKFAST CEREALS

In the United States, the word "cereal" in current usage refers to an array of products nearly ready for consumption and usually eaten at breakfast, as well as to the grains from which they are largely derived. Cereal products can be classified in part according to their methods of processing: puffed, flaked, shredded, and a few products prepared as granules. "Hot" cereals are milled grain products intended to be heated just before consumption. Some of the products in the above classes are also presweetened, that is, sweetened to a level appropriate for use without further addition of sugar.

About $1\frac{1}{2}$ billion pounds of cereal were produced in the United States in 1971. This total included roughly $\frac{1}{2}$ billion pounds of puffed, $\frac{1}{2}$ billion pounds of flaked, and 100 million pounds of shredded cereals. Some 300 million pounds of hot cereals were produced. The principal producers included Kellogg Co., General Mills, Inc., Post Division of General Foods Corp., Quaker Oats Co., Nabisco, and Ralston Purina Co.

Grain ingredients used in cereals in 1971 included (approximately): 500 million pounds of wheat, bran, or farina, (mostly soft Michigan white winter wheat), 400 million pounds of oatmeal or oat flour, 300 million pounds of corn grits (maize), and 150 million pounds of rice.

Puffed Cereals

Puffed cereal products may be "gun" puffed, oven puffed, or extrusion puffed. Gun puffing is so called because equipment used for expansion of the cooked grain somewhat resembles an old cannon. Technology for puffing of cereals was developed by A. P. Anderson in the early 1900's and his patents led to the marketing of puffed rice and wheat. In Anderson's process, still used today, these grains are cooked, generally without other ingredients, adjusted to proper moisture content, and sealed in the puffing gun. This consists of a horizontal cylinder rotated about its axis, with gas burners or other heaters placed to heat the outside of the cylinder, and means to tip the cylinder for loading and unloading. One end of the cylinder is permanently closed, the other has a closure equipped for instant release. The mass of grain tumbles in the rotating cylinder, becomes heated within a few minutes, and is pressurized by the heated air and by vapor of its own moisture. When the appropriate pressure (in the range of 90–250 psig) is obtained, the closure is released; the contents erupt with a loud report and the cereal pieces are expanded by the sudden volatilization of internal moisture. With proper control of gelatinization and moisture content prior to puffing, the grain remains expanded during cooling and final drying. The exact conditions of the puffing step have important effects on flavor and stability of the product; surface temperatures of 350°F or more inside the gun are likely, and the product temperature is increasing very rapidly in the last few moments of the gun cycle. Firing time must be controlled within a few seconds to avoid either underexpansion or burning of the product.

In 1939, F. A. Collatz developed and patented methods for making puffed cereals from flour rather than whole grain or grits. This technology made possible puffed products based on oats,

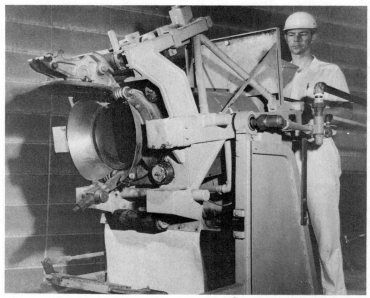

Courtesy of General Mills

FIG. B-6. BATCH PUFFING GUN SHOWING THE QUICK-RELEASE LID IN OPEN POSITION which could not be puffed as whole grains. It also provided for the use of mixtures of grains and the incorporation of additional ingredients for flavor and nutritive purposes. The process involves extrusion of a viscous dough to form pellets which are then puffed as above. The extrusion step allows the product to be made in various shapes. In 1942, T. R. James patented a continuous means for the cooking and extrusion into pellets of milled grain products. These techniques are still of commercial importance.

Several methods for semicontinuous puffing have been developed. These generally involve chambers or cylinders with screw conveyors to move the product through, and rotary or intermittent valves for inlet and outlet. Other workers later developed fully continuous means for carrying out the puffing step, using continuous expansion through a nozzle at the outlet.

Oven puffing is used for some products, principally rice. The grains are pressure cooked at a moisture content of about 30% with sugar, salt, and other ingredients. After drying to about 15% moisture and "tempering" or holding, the grains are subjected to hot air. Temperatures of 350°–600°F and either tumbling of product or air flow at or near fluidization velocities are necessary: heat transfer rates must be high enough to bring about puffing rather than simply drying. Ovens in the form of a perforated rotating horizontal drum have been used. Puffing takes place within seconds, but the product is left in the oven longer to complete drying and flavor development. Accurate control of residence time is important because browning occurs rapidly as the cessation of evaporative cooling allows product temperature to rise.

Cooked pellets or grains being prepared for gun or oven puffing may be impacted by passage between rolls prior to puffing. The partial flattening appears to modify the puffing behavior, presumably by partial disruption of the starch structure. For some formulations, coating of the pellets with 0.2–2% of a lipid such as coconut oil or a monoglyceride is necessary to keep the pellets from agglomerating in the puffing step.

Several puffed cereal products are made by a process closely related to oven puffing. Granular or floury ingredients are continuously mixed and moistened in a steam atmosphere under pressure, extruded to form a strand, surface dried, cut to appropriate piece size, and dropped into a stream of heated air to be puffed under air conveying conditions.

Processes have been developed for extruding and puffing cereals in a single step. A high-powered extruder is used. With input of sufficient mechanical energy, pressure and temperature of the dough are raised enough so that it puffs upon release of pressure at the extrusion die outlet. The dough may be cut at the die face or the strand conveyed for cooling and drying before being cut.

Flaked Cereals

The principal flaked cereals are made of corn and wheat. Corn flakes are made from grits—pieces of corn endosperm with hull and germ completely removed. Wheat flakes are made from whole grain. Bran flakes are made from chunks of the wheat kernel from which part of the endosperm has been removed. Most flaked cereals are made by cooking whole grain or pieces with various flavorings such as sugar, salt, and malt; drying to a firm but slightly plastic state; flaking by passage between rolls; and toasting or drying to final moisture.

Cooking is usually done batchwise. The cooker used is a rotating horizontal cylinder with provision for direct steam injection. A syrup containing flavoring ingredients is charged to the cooker with the grain and absorbed by the grain as it tumbles under steam pressure. (Cooking may alternatively be carried out as a continuous process by conveying the grain through a steam pressure vessel with pressure-lock ports.) Steam pressures used are usually 10–30 psig. After cooking, the grain is cooled and dried with agitation to separate the particles in preparation for further processing.

In some cases, a pelleting step is carried out at this point in the process. Pelleting allows the manufacturer to obtain a larger and more uniform flake size than the original grit or kernel would provide. It also allows the mixing of different cooked grains into a single flake, or the incorporation of ingredients not stable under cooking conditions. Pelleting may be carried out by extruding and cutting to form pellets at the extrusion die face. An auger-type extruder similar to those used for extruding macaroni or plastics is used.

In a few cases, flaked products are prepared from flour or other milled grain products by forming a dough, cooking, and extruding to form pellets.

Properties of the finished flake can be modified by a heating or roasting step immediately before flaking. This can be done by spreading the pellets or grits in a thin layer, for example on a conveyor belt or vibratory pan, using radiative heaters for rapid heating with a minimum of drying. The heated particle apparently deforms with less rupture of starch cells and yields a flake that is slower to absorb liquid (such as milk) and soften.

Courtesy of Kellogg Company

FIG. B-7. BATCH COOKERS IN CEREAL FLAKE PROCESS SYSTEM

Toasting or finish drying of flaked cereals is done in a reel oven or belt oven, with sufficient air velocity through the bed of flakes to provide rapid heat transfer. The conditions used are closely related to those for oven puffing. Corn flakes can be observed to expand, or bubble, after some seconds of exposure to oven conditions; this bubbling appears to be necessary if the product is to have a crisp and tender, rather than flinty, texture. Toasting is carried out at temperatures of 300–600°F and times of about 1–5 min. Toasting time must be accurately controlled to achieve the proper degree of flavor development and sufficiently low moisture.

Shredded Cereals

Shredded wheat, the oldest mass-produced cereal, is still of commercial importance. The original process was described by Henry Perky in a remarkably detailed series of patents from 1893 to 1901 which described the entire shredded wheat factory, including packaging and conveying equipment.

Wheat with no added ingredient is still the most important shredded cereal. Whole grain wheat is cooked, partially dried, and tempered. Then it is passed between rolls, one of which is smooth, the other circumferentially grooved. Heavy forces—of the order of magnitude of 1000 lb per in. of roll length in some cases—are required to maintain the rolls in tight contact. The moist grain becomes plasticized in the nip of the rolls and flows into the roll grooves, issuing as a set of strands roughly 1 mm in diameter. These strands are accumulated in multiple layers and formed by pinch cutting into biscuits of desired size. The biscuits are then baked. Oven conditions would tend toward those used in bakeries, with elevated humidity and low air velocity; the vigorous heating conditions used for oven puffing or toasting are not appropriate for the larger shred biscuits.

A refinement of the shred process added cross grooves to the shred roll to provide lateral strands of dough which tie the shreds together into a coherent perforated sheet; the sheets are layered and cut as described above. The shred sheet allows more precise forming of smaller cereal pieces of only a few layers thickness. This form has been used for corn, wheat, and rice. These grains are flavored with sugar, salt, malt, or other ingredients and cooked approximately the same as they would be for making flakes. The shred sheet is also utilized for raw or lightly cooked mixtures of flours with proteins or other ingredients.

Presweetened Cereals

Some cereals have sugar added prior to cooking to influence the development of desirable flavors during processing. The amount of sugar added for this purpose is generally 12% or less. Most users will add sweetener to such a product at time of use. At some higher level of sugar, depending on type of product and age of users, the product will be consumed by most users without additional sweetening. This presweetening is most often achieved with an enrobed sugar coating.

Sugar, sometimes with corn syrup or other ingredients, is heated with a minor amount of water to make a sugar syrup. The heated syrup is sprayed or dribbled on a rolling mass of cereal particles in a rotating drum called an enrober or coating reel; heat may be applied to the reel. If necessary, the coated particles are then further dried in a belt dryer.

By variation of formulation and mechanical treatment, a range of coating characteristics can be obtained, from glazed or shiny to highly crystalline or frosty. Glazed coatings can be obtained by the addition of invert sugar, honey, and other nonsucrose sugars. Rather than the addition of invert sugar, some of the sucrose present may be inverted by heating the sugar syrup with an acid such as citric acid present. Crystallization can be minimized by avoiding mechanical movement or disturbance of the product during critical parts of the drying and hardening of the coating. More frosty or crystalline coatings are obtained by using all or mostly sucrose and by providing tumbling or other agitation during the cooling and drying of the coating. Flavoring materials such as citrus oils or spices are sometimes incorporated into the sugar coating.

Other additives to cereals are also used as sweeteners. A simple physical mixture of raisins with bran flakes has been commercially important for many years. The products usually contain about 25% raisins; the raisins have about $1/2$% honey or invert sugar syrup and 10–15% granular sugar added during their preparation, to add sweetening and to prevent them from sticking together.

Several cereal products are sold in mixture with dried grained marshmallow pieces; these pieces contribute texture and flavor effects and also constitute a presweetening means. Other sweetening additives such as freeze-dried fruits have been used from time to time without significant commercial success.

Hot Cereals

Hot cereals are those designed to be heated just before use or prepared by adding hot water or other liquid. They are usually milled products of a single grain or a simple mixture. The principal product of this type, rolled oats ("regular" rolled oats), consists of dehulled, steamed, flattened, and dried oats. "Quick" oatmeal uses oat groats that are steel-cut into several fragments after dehulling,

then flattened a little thinner than for regular rolled oats, to reduce the time of preparation.

Instant or "cook in the bowl" oatmeal is prepared in such a way that the user need only add hot water and stir to make the product ready for consumption. Based on quick oatmeal, it is given some additional treatment—such as the incorporation of 0.1–1.0% of an edible gum on the surface of the oat particles—to improve its hydration.

Wheat farina, alone or mixed with wheat germ, bran, malted barley, cocoa, or other flavoring materials, is packaged for use as a hot cereal. Milled rye is also used. Such products are normally steamed and dried or toasted to enhance stability toward enzymatic or other degradative changes.

Stability of Cereals

Although the amounts of fats present in most cereals are quite low—about 0.5–6%—the stability of the fats present is critically important to the product. Most cereals can be expected to deteriorate by oxidative rancidity at low moistures, or by related staling reactions at higher moistures. The naturally-occurring antioxidants present are not entirely known, and subtleties in processing conditions can drastically affect resistance to rancidity. Proper degree of browning in toasting or puffing processes is generally regarded as necessary for adequate stability of cereals. Unexpected failure of natural antioxidant systems has had disastrous effects on some products in the marketplace. A stable shelf-life of six months at moderate to high temperatures is a minimum requirement for cereals in ordinary distribution in the United States at this time, and the absence of obnoxious odors or flavors for several more months is highly desirable.

Nearly all cereals in the U.S. market are now protected by the antioxidants BHA or BHT, applied either directly to the product or dissolved in wax used for packing materials, whence a portion of it diffuses into the product after packaging.

Cereals also go out of condition due to loss of texture (crispness) at a moisture characteristic for the product, generally in the range 5–10%. Cereal packages are designed as moisture barriers so the product, initially at about 1–4% moisture, will remain crisp until consumed.

Nutritional Characteristics

Breakfast cereals are regarded as having origins in the "granola," parched grain mixtures, of the Nineteenth Century. The growth of the present industry was catalyzed by the work of Dr. John Kellogg, a vegetarian and health food advocate, who developed grain food products as replacements for the heavy breakfasts of the day, which were likely to be fat pork and fried foods. Entrepreneurs such as Kellogg's brother Will and competitors C. W. Post and Henry Perky soon found markets for their products. The markets expanded as the population made its transition from a largely agricultural society highly dependent on manual labor, to a largely urban, machine-aided one. (Gerald Carson interestingly described the beginnings of the industry in *Cornflake Crusade*, published in 1957 by Rinehart & Co., New York.)

The early patent literature of the industry abounds with references to nutritional aspects of the products. The state of knowledge of nutrition was at that time rudimentary. As new knowledge of nutrition was gained, more use could be made of breakfast cereals as carriers of nutritional entities. After the decrease of vitamins and minerals values by milling or heat processing of grains had been identified and the nutritional significance understood, a practice of "restoration" was adopted: certain nutrients which had been present in the whole grain in significant amounts were added to the processed product to bring it to raw whole-grain levels. Accordingly, niacin, iron, thiamin, and to a minor extent, riboflavin, were added to many breakfast cereals beginning in the 1940's.

Cereals have become regarded as useful carriers of vitamins and minerals, including some that are not present in consequential amounts in the original grains. The relatively regular pattern of consumption of cereals—both as to quantity and frequency—provides a rationale for such efforts. Various cereals now on the market contain as much as $1/4$ or more of the Recommended Daily Allowances of some vitamins and minerals per ounce of cereal. Depending on their stabilities under processing conditions, various vitamins may be incorporated by inclusion in the cooking step, by inclusion at an intermediate step such as extrusion, by spray application to the cereal surface after processing, or by inclusion in a sugar coating.

Various methods for incorporating additional protein into breakfast cereals have been attempted. The protein supplementation results in significantly altered product flavor and texture properties; in a few cases, such products have been well-accepted by consumers. One product is made by coating oven-puffed rice with a batter of wheat gluten. Another method is the inclusion of dry protein supplement in the extrusion step for forming pellets for a flaked cereal. Another product is obtained by incorporating protein into a moist dough which is then formed into a shred

sheet. All these methods avoid exposing the protein material to the cooking of the grain base. Cereal products without protein supplementation contain about 5–15% protein; the supplemented products are formulated to contain up to about 20% protein.

DONALD L. MAXWELL
JOHN L. HOLAHAN

BRILLAT-SAVARIN, JEAN ANTHELME (1755–1826)

Brillat-Savarin, one of the greatest of the renowned connoisseurs of history, is chiefly known for his *Physiologie du goût* or *Physiology of Taste* (1825) in its translated form. This work, now a classic, was the product of an avocation; Brillat-Savarin was a lawyer by profession and occupied a number of posts of medium importance in France. He was, successively, a magistrate, a parliamentary deputy, and mayor of Belley, the town where he was born in 1755. His father before him was a lawyer, and it may be surmised that the family was one of some importance in Bourbon, France—and perhaps under some suspicion just prior to and during the French Revolution. As a country lawyer, Jean Anthelme was probably not a prime target for persecution by the revolutionaries although the fact that he fled to Switzerland and later to America suggests that he was not without his qualms as to his fate at the hands of the revolutionaries. In any event it is said that he was apprehensive as to the course the Revolution was taking, and one day in 1793 he left hurriedly for nearby Switzerland.

Within the same year, it appears, he set sail for the United States, landed in New York City, and found employment as a violinist in a small New York theatre located on the Battery and also eked out his existence by giving French lessons. Returning to France in 1796, purged apparently of any Bourbon taint, he was accepted by the Directorate and appointed to various government posts including that of member of the Court of Cassation.

Whatever brilliance he may have shown in the legal profession was greatly overshadowed by the fame he gained (after his death it must be recorded) by his book, the *Physiology of Taste*. This book, sophisticated, genial, lively, humorous, often cogent, was written over many years. It contains speculations, meditations, anecdotes, and social commentaries relevant to the art of good eating. Since Brillat-Savarin was an Eighteenth Century man it is not surprising that he added a number of sections to his book that can properly be described as scientific speculation, modestly backed by experimental evidence. It is rather remarkable that he quizzed at great length a man who had had his tongue cut out, this in order to find out whether the sense organs of taste had thereby been removed. They were not, he concluded.

Brillat-Savarin believed that over the generations all of the human senses have been brought to the aid of each other for the use, happiness, and survival of the individual. Taste, he stated, is greatly aided by the sense of smell and sight. "The tongue tastes sapid substances," he said, "and the nose gases." Later on, he makes the point that the sense of smell *explores*, the sense of taste *decides*. These, of course, are observations generated by what the Eighteenth Century philosophic scientists would call common sense. A more surprising example of Brillat-Savarin's scientific speculation is the following: "The sensation of taste is a chemical operation made in the humid way, as we called it formerly. That is to say, that it is necessary for the molecules to be dissolved by some fluid to be finally absorbed by the nervous ganglia, papillae, or suckers which cover the interior of the organ of taste."

These are serious comments and show Brillat-Savarin to have been well acquainted with the physiology of the day. Elsewhere in the book he writes with mock seriousness.

Brillat-Savarin was an amiable, likable, and on occasion, a somewhat eccentric man. He was known, for instance, to carry dead game in the capacious pockets of his cloak in order to let it get high. This habit, according to a biographer, Charles Monselet, greatly upset his colleages on the Court of Cassation.

MARTIN S. PETERSON

BROMINATED VEGETABLE OILS

Brominated Vegetable Oils (BVO) are made by the 1,2-addition of bromine to the olefinic bonds of the unsaturated fatty acid moieties of vegetable oils. The addition preferably is run at low temperatures to prevent α-bromination.

Brominated oils have a high specific gravity and their uses depend upon this property. Specific gravity of a brominated oil is the function of the amount of bromine incorporated into the molecule. Commercial brominated oils have been standardized at two specific gravity values. Vegetable oils with an iodine number 80–90, such as olive oil, yield BVO with a specific gravity about 1.24. Vegetable oils with an iodine number 105–115, such as sesame oil, corn oil, or cottonseed oil, yield BVO with a specific gravity about 1.33.

The principle use of BVO is in the production of flavor emulsions for use in citrus-flavored soft drinks. Therefore, it is important that they be bland in taste and odor. Other important properties are constant or standardized specific gravity, low acidity, and low residual iodine number.

Peel oil is an important source of flavor for citrus-flavored soft drinks. These may be cold pressed oils, concentrated (folded) oils, and terpeneless oils. It is quite common for a soft drink flavor to consist of mixtures of these different types of oils.

Flavoring oils have a low specific gravity, usually around 0.85, and are insoluble in water. Since they are used as a source of flavor in aqueous beverages with a specific gravity around 1.05, it is important that the specific gravity of the flavoring oils be adjusted in order to make emulsions with long-term physical stability. A brominated oil can be used to accomplish this. BVO is miscile with flavoring oils. A blend of BVO and flavoring oils, or oil mix, can be made with a specific gravity balanced with respect to the finished beverage. This oil mix then can be made into an oil-in-water emulsion, using a suspending agent such as gum acacia, and the resulting emulsion will stay suspended homogeneously in a beverage for periods of several months.

In addition to balancing specific gravity of flavoring oils in order to make stable emulsions, BVO provides an important contribution to "cloud." Consumers prefer citrus-flavored beverages with a cloudy appearance resembling the appearance of fruit juices. By using an oil emulsion for flavoring, the beverage does have a desirable opacity or cloudiness.

The amount of BVO required to make a stable citrus oil emulsion for flavoring soft drinks is from 120 to 160 ppm based on the finished beverage. Some countries do not allow BVO at concentrations above 15 ppm. In these situations sucrose acetate isobutyrate (SAIB) or abietic acid esters (rosin ester gum) often are added as supplementary suspending agents for the flavoring oils. It is also possible to make stable emulsions using surfactants, although this results in loss of cloudy appearance. In these cases separate clouding agents may be added to contribute the desired opacity.

KARL M. BECK

Cross-reference: *Fats and Oils.*

BROWNING, ENZYMIC

The enzyme responsible for the browning of cut surfaces of certain fruits and vegetables is phenolase. "Phenolase" is a generic term used to include all terminology describing the enzyme which catalyzes the oxidation of mono- and orthodiphenolic substances. Thus, phenolase covers phenoloxidase, tyrosinase, polyphenoloxidase, catecholase, cresolase, dopa oxidase, potato oxidase, sweet potato oxidase, phenolase complex, phenolase system, etc. This bewildering variety of names will here be simplified to phenolase since where the enzyme has been studied in its purified or isolated form the two diverse reactions are catalyzed by the same enzyme. These reactions are (a) the oxidation of the o-dihydroxyphenols to o-quinones, and (b) the hydroxylation of certain monohydroxyphenols to dihydroxyphenols. An example of (a) is the oxidation of catechol (I) to the o-benzoquinone (II)

An example of (b) is the hydroxylation of p-cresol (III) to 3,4-dihydroxytoluene (IV)

The 3,4-dihydroxytoluene can then be oxidized to the corresponding quinone. The development of the brown color on the cut surfaces of fruits and vegetables is due to reactions of the o-quinones consisting of nonenzymatically catalyzed oxidation and polymerization of the oxidation products.

Phenolase was discovered by G. Bertrand just before the turn of the century; he demonstrated that the darkening of mushrooms was due to the enzymatic oxidation of tyrosine, a phenolic amino acid. F. Kubowitz was the first to purify phenolase, using potatoes as the source of the enzyme. He found copper to be an essential part of the enzyme which helped to establish a function for the copper in plant and animal tissue. Copper had previously been thought to be an accidental contaminant of tissues.

Phenolase is widely distributed in plants and animals. Among the plants containing the enzyme are the squashes, citrus fruit, roots, bananas, plums, peaches, pears, apples, avocados, sweet and white potatoes, mushrooms, eggplant, melons, wheat, spinach, tomatoes, olives, tea, and others.

Phenolase is distinct from laccase. The latter enzyme, first observed in the latex of the Japanese lacquer tree by H. Yoshida in 1883, oxidized only polyhydric phenols and related compounds such as guaiacol, hydroquinone, catechol, pyrogallol, and p-phenylene diamine, but it does not oxidize monophenols, while phenolase oxidizes both mono- and polyhydric phenols. Presence of laccase in many plants, e.g., potatoes, sugar beets, apples, and cabbage, has been reported. However, other than that in the wild mushroom, *Russula foetens* and the latex of lacquer trees this enzyme has not received the attention it deserves.

Assay

Four procedures and variations thereof have been used for the assay of phenolase: (a) measurement of the rate of oxygen uptake in the oxidation of catechol; (b) colorimetric measurement of the amount of purpurogallin formed from pyrogallol in 5 min; (c) chronometric measurement of rate of loss in ascorbic acid due to its oxidation by o-benzoquinone formed from catechol; and (d) measurement of rate of color formed from leuco-2,6-dichlorobenzenoneindo-3'-chlorophenol by its oxidation with the formed o-benzoquinone. All of the methods suffer from the fact that phenolase is reaction inactivated and during that inactivation varies during purification and from preparation to preparation. Therefore, the measurement of the initial rate of phenolase activity is obligatory. The first method, when used with care, is perhaps the most direct and meaningful method. The second suffers from the fact that no rate of reaction is measured. The third procedure will not distinguish between phenolase and ascorbic acid oxidase in crude extracts of plant tissue. The last method, although not a direct one, has convenience to recommend it.

Preparation of the Enzyme

Two facts contribute to the difficulty of the isolation of pure phenolase. The amount of the enzyme in plant sources is extremely low. Even mushrooms, one of the richest sources of phenolase, contain only about 0.03% of the enzyme on a dry-weight basis. The low concentration of the enzyme requires working with large volumes of liquids, especially during the first stages of the preparation. The second difficulty lies in the fact that plant sources of the enzyme also contain natural substrates. Because of reaction inactivation, the oxidation of the natural substrates must be minimized during the extraction, concentration, purification, and ultimate isolation of phenolase.

Kubowitz was the first to attempt the preparation of pure phenolase on a large-scale basis. His method consisted of 12 steps and includes extraction of the enzyme from potato peelings with water, followed by 4 fractionations with acetone and 4 fractionations with ammonium sulfate, 2 selective heat denaturations, decoloration with silver acetate, and adsorption on and elution from aluminum hydroxide. His yield was approximately 0.5% of that present in the original extract.

At about the same time, Keilin and Mann purified mushroom phenolase by an 8-step procedure and obtained 15 mg of enzyme from 15 kg of mushrooms. Subsequently, Mallette and his colleagues developed an improved procedure for purifying the mushroom enzyme. The principal improvement was the removal of most of the natural substrate with cold acetone prior to water extraction. Recently, Kertesz and Zito (1962) isolated mushroom phenolase by a ten-step procedure which involved keeping the solutions of the enzyme cold and under an atmosphere of argon. Their yield was 18%.

Physicochemical Properties

Phenolase, prepared by the last of the methods described above, is a homogeneous enzyme with a molecular weight of 128,000 calculated from the sedimentation constant and partial specific volume. The value obtained from light scattering data is 133,000.

The copper content of phenolase is 0.2%. This value is in accord with four molecules of copper per molecule of enzyme. The copper in freshly prepared enzyme is principally in the cuprous form but on aging is gradually changed to the cupric form without any significant loss in activity. The best evidence indicates that the copper is bound to certain histidine residues of the enzyme. The apoenzyme, i.e., the protein free of copper, is inactive and can be prepared by dialysis of aqueous solutions of the enzyme against dilute potassium cyanide solution. On ultracentrifugation, the apoenzyme has the same sedimentation constant as does the active enzyme. The activity of the apoenzyme can be restored by the addition of copper in the cupric form.

Pure phenolase is colorless and its absorption spectrum in the visible and ultraviolet regions is simply that of a protein. In contrast, purified laccase is blue.

Phenolase in solution is most stable at pH values near neutrality. Concentrated solutions are more stable than dilute ones. Like most enzymes, the application of heat (60°C, 140°F) for a short period, or vigorous shaking of the protein in air cause a rapid inactivation of phenolase. Concentrated solutions of the enzyme in dilute phosphate buffer of a pH near neutrality at 1°C (34°F) or frozen at -25°C (-13°F) can be kept without loss of activity for several months. However, on prolonged storage the enzyme slowly loses activity even in the frozen state. This loss is irreversible and is accompanied by a contemporaneous oxidation of the cuprous copper to cupric copper. The inactivation is not due to the oxidation of the cuprous copper since the apoenzyme can be activated with cupric ions.

During the oxidation of substrates by phenolase, the enzyme is irreversibly inactivated. Since the inactivation appears to be a direct result of the catalytic function of the enzyme, it has been named "reaction inactivation." In spite of the great effort devoted to study of the mechanism of the inactivation reaction, it is not clearly understood. The inactivation is not due to the formation of a product such as hydrogen peroxide during the oxidation reaction. A subtle change in the configuration of the enzyme protein is probably responsible. Support of this explanation is given by the fact that as a consequence of preparative procedures the enzyme may possess a significantly lower specific activity but yet be homogeneous as determined by physical methods. Furthermore, the ability of the enzyme to oxidize monophenols as compared with o-diphenolic substrates may be decreased during purification procedures due to a similar subtle change. This change was first thought to be due to the separation of two enzymes but was later shown to be due to a change in the enzyme molecule. The extreme example of the change is shown by sweet potato phenolase. Oxidation of monophenols by sweet potato tissue slices can be demonstrated in situ. The slices have only slight activity toward o-diphenolic compounds. Treatment of the tissue slices with sodium chloride or the preparation of tissue extracts destroys the ability of the enzyme to oxidize monophenols but apparently increases its action on diphenolic compounds.

Substances which form stable complexes with copper inhibit phenolase. Amongst such inhibitors are potassium cyanide, hydrogen sulfide, carbon monoxide, diethyldithiocarbamate, potassium ethyl xanthate, sodium azide, p-aminobenzoic acid, and sulfathiazole. Reagents reacting with sulfhydryl groups, e.g., iodoacetamide and p-chloromercuribenzoate, do not inhibit the enzyme. 4-Nitro-catechol and 4-nitrophenol are competitive inhibitors of phenolase.

Oxidation of Polyphenols to o-Quinones

Plants contain an array of o-diphenolic substances, all of which are to a greater or lesser extent oxidizable by phenolase. Among the naturally occurring substrates are 3,4-dihydroxyphenylalanine, adrenaline, the chlorogenic acids, protocatechnic, caffeic and gallic acids, and flavonoids such as aesculetin, daphnetin, and fraxetin. Many other non-naturally occurring substrates have been found for the enzyme.

The mechanism of the phenolase action on o-diphenolic substances is indeed complicated. Copper is the prosthetic group of the enzyme. This has led to the postulate that the catalytic activity of the phenolase is based on the cupric-cuprous valency change. On isolation of the enzyme the copper is in the cuprous state. In the presence of o-dihydroxyphenols the copper would be oxidized to cupric copper. The two-state reaction may be represented thus:

$$4Cu^{++}(enzyme) + 2 \text{ catechol} \longrightarrow$$
$$4Cu^{+}(enzyme) + 2 \text{ } o\text{-quinone} + 4H^{+}$$

$$4Cu^{+}(enzyme) + 4H^{+} + O_2 \longrightarrow$$
$$4Cu^{++}(enzyme) + 2H_2O$$

The substrate is oxidized by losing 2 electrons and 2 protons. The two electrons are taken up by the copper of the enzyme which thus passes into the cuprous state. The cuprous enzyme rapidly transfers the 2 electrons to oxygen which immediately forms water with the 2 protons liberated and the enzyme thus returns to the cupric state, ready to recommence the catalytic cycle.

The indirect oxidation of a reducing agent by phenolase plus an o-dihydroxyphenol has been the phenolase reaction most extensively studied. It may be represented as follows:

$$o\text{-dihydroxyphenol} + 1/2 \text{ } O_2 \xrightarrow{\text{phenolase}}$$
$$o\text{-quinone} + H_2O$$

$$\underline{o\text{-quinone} + (RH_2) \longrightarrow o\text{-dihydroxyphenol} + R}$$
$$(RH_2) + 1/2 \text{ } O_2 \longrightarrow R + H_2O$$

RH_2 represents the reducing agent, e.g., ascorbic acid, hydroquinone, or a reduced phosphopyridine nucleotide and R its oxidized form (dehydroascorbic acid, p-quinone or oxidized phosphopyridine nucleotides). Using catalytic amounts of o-dihydroxyphenol, the oxidation of 1 μmole of it in the presence of ascorbic acid corresponds to the consumption of 0.5 μmoles of O_2. Thus, the above reaction applies under these specialized conditions, at least for a reasonable period of time. With higher concentrations of the dihydroxyphenol reaction inactivation occurs rapidly and the linearity of reaction is soon lost. Further, with hydroquinone as the reducing agent and catalytic amounts of o-dihydroxyphenol, the oxidation of 1 μmole of substrate corresponds to the consumption of 0.82 μmoles of O_2. Thus, under these conditions the reaction is more complex than represented.

The enzymatic oxidation of o-dihydroxyphenol in the absence of a reducing reagent is more complex than in the presence of such reagents. In the complete oxidation of catechol by phenolase 2 atoms of oxygen are consumed although only 1 atom is required, stoichiometrically, for the formation of o-benzoquinone. In a study of the mechanism of phenolase reaction, H. Wagreich and J. M. Nelson found: (a) under conditions of low concentration of substrate and high concentration of enzyme, catechol is enzymatically oxidized to o-benzoquinone with the consumption of 1 atom of oxygen per mole of catechol; (b) the consumption of the second atom of oxygen per mole of catechol oxidized is catalyzed by phenolase; (c) a substance is formed when chemically prepared o-benzoquinone disappears in aqueous solution at pH 4.5–6.5, which can be aerobically oxidized to a quinone by phenolase; and (d) the amount of such substance formed corresponds to $1/2$ of the o-benzoquinone which has disappeared.

Oxidation of Monophenols

The second reaction catalyzed by phenolase, i.e., the hydroxylation of certain monophenols to o-dihydroxyphenols, undoubtedly resides in the same enzyme molecule responsible for the oxidation of o-dihydroxyphenols. However, the enzymatic hydroxylation reaction possesses certain characteristics unparalleled in enzymology.

The oxidation of monophenols is preceded by a relatively long induction period and this period increases with the degree of purification of the enzyme. The induction period may last many minutes. Normally, where an enzymatic reaction possesses an induction period, the time of such an induction will consist of a fraction of a second.

The period of induction can be reduced or eliminated by the addition of a small amount of o-dihydroxyphenol and the rate of oxidation after the induction period becomes linear. Phenolase oxidizes the o-dihydroxyphenols at a more rapid rate than the corresponding monohydroxyphenol. However, there is always a certain amount of *o*-dihydroxyphenol present during the oxidation of monophenols by phenolase.

Two hypotheses have been proposed to explain these peculiar properties of phenolase in its oxidation of monophenols. One is called the direct or enzymic hypothesis. Here the enzyme, after the elimination of the induction period, is presumed responsible for the hydroxylation of the monophenol. The other is the indirect or nonenzymic hypothesis. According to this hypothesis it is the *o*-quinone produced by the oxidation of the dihydroxyphenol which is presumed to be the agent responsible for the hydroxylation reaction. Proof of the actual mechanism of action of phenolase on monophenols must await further experimentation. Regardless of which hypothesis is correct, monophenols can be oxidized to the same potential browning substances as can *o*-dihydroxyphenols.

Reaction of *o*-Quinones

The *o*-quinones catalytically formed by phenolase are the precursors of the brown color of certain cut fruits and vegetables. The *o*-quinones themselves possess little color, e.g., *o*-benzoquinone is slightly red in color. However, they are among the most reactive metabolic intermediates occurring in living matter, and among a host of reactions are the browning reaction.

The principal reaction of *o*-quinones in the browning reaction is that leading to the formation of the unstable hydroxyquinone. The hydroxyquinones polymerize readily and are easily further oxidized to a dark-brown, sparingly soluble polymer. This latter oxidation is rapid and nonenzymic.

Quinones react readily with simple amines. The reaction of *o*-benzoquinone with aniline proceeds as follows:

o-benzoquinone + 2 aniline $\longrightarrow$

4,5-dianilino-1,2-benzoquinone

Benzoquinone reacts with amino acids. The reaction with glycine is as follows:

o-benzoquinone + glycine $\longrightarrow$

4-N-glycyl-*o*-benzoquinone

This reaction product is the intermediate responsible for the deamination of glycine with the concomitant formation of deeply colored pigments.

Naturally-occurring sulfhydryl compounds such as cysteine and glutathione react rapidly with *o*-quinones generated from *o*-dihydroxyphenols in the presence of phenolase and characteristic pigments are formed. These reactions occur in addition to the expected oxidation-reduction reactions.

Since proteins contain amino and frequently sulfhydryl groups, it is not surprising that they readily react with *o*-quinones and form dark insoluble products. This reaction constitutes one of the difficulties encountered in the isolation of phenolase or any other protein from a plant source rich in this enzyme. This reaction may be responsible for the reaction inactivation of phenolase.

Role in Plants

In spite of the fact that phenolase has been known to occur in plants for over 70 yr and in spite of the large amount of research effort devoted to this enzyme, its role in plant respiration remains obscure. It is one of the plant enzymes of unknown physiological role which presents a challenge to future investigators in the field of plant metabolism.

Because of the widespread distribution of phenolase in the plant world, many attempts have been made to implicate the enzyme as a catalyst mediating the final reaction with oxygen in cellular respiration. However, there are several facts which are counter to this concept. First, in spite of the widespread nature of phenolase, only $2/3$ of the plants examined contained the enzyme. Certain actively respiring plant tissues have been found to be void of the enzyme, thus necessitating the occurrence of at least two different "terminal oxidase" systems in plants.

In the beginning of the intensified research on phenolase, the enzyme was thought to be a "soluble" oxidase. However, more recently it has been demonstrated that phenolase is present in the mitochondria of certain plant tissue which suggests the enzyme may function in electron transport within the mitochondria.

The basic supposition in implicating phenolase as a catalyst mediating the final reaction with oxygen in cellular respiration is based on the reduction of *o*-quinone formed from an *o*-dihydroxyphenol by reduced coenzymes, ascorbic acid or quinone reductase. The *o*-diphenolic complex would then act as a couple, transporting electrons from reduced coenzyme to copper and finally to oxygen. It has been possible to set up artificial systems which are capable of oxidizing various organic acids in the presence of suitable dehydrogenase, coenzyme, catechol, and phenolase. On the basis of such experiments various investigators have proposed that the main portion, if not all, of the respiration of a variety of plant tissues proceeds through such a system.

However, all efforts to demonstrate that phenolase catalyzes the transfer of electrons to oxygen in tissue respiration have failed to consider two essential points, namely, (a) the low affinity of phenolase for oxygen as compared to that of the tissues themselves, and (b) that cytochromes have been demonstrated in all plant tissues examined whose function is undoubtedly that of the transfer of electrons to oxygen. Accordingly, there is a need for further investigation with respect to the role of phenolase in plants, particularly as to how it functions in the mitochondria.

Control of Phenolase Browning in Foods

The enzymatic browning of foods generally is an adverse change with respect to the acceptability of the foods. The lowered acceptability results not only from the development of an off-color in a product but also from the off-flavor formation accompanying the browning. The practical control of enzymatic browning in foods has been done by five different methods. The method of choice is dependent upon the food product and the intended use of the product. These five methods of phenolase control are heat inactivation, chemical inhibition, addition of reducing reagents, the exclusion of oxygen and the *in situ* alteration of the natural browning substrates. Combinations of two methods have also been employed.

Phenolase, like most proteins, may be denatured (inactivated) by heat. For products like vegetables, which will ultimately end up in a cooked form, heat inactivation by steam blanching is the most straightforward method of inactivating phenolase. Overblanching is, of course, to be avoided. The optimum conditions for blanching the individual products have been established. The process must be specially tailored to each type of raw material and product desired.

Heat-inactivation of the phenolase in fruit may produce a cooked flavor, a destruction of the natural flavor, and/or a softening of texture. For the most part, heat-inactivation of phenolase in fruit products has been applied to fruit juices and purées or fruit intended for such products. The enzyme is very labile to heat at $185°F$ $(85°C)$ and above—the higher the temperature, the shorter the time for complete inactivation. Temperatures of $212°F$ $(100°C)$ are not necessary for complete inactivation. Therefore, for each fruit product the minimum time-temperature requirement for phenolase inactivation must be maintained so as to minimize the undesirable changes accompanying the heating. Rapid cooling after enzyme inactivation is a necessity for best quality retention.

Sulfur dioxide is a very effective inhibitor of phenolase and has been used for this purpose for many years, particularly as applied to the drying of fruit. The use of SO_2 has certain disadvantages, i.e., its obnoxious odor during processing, the undesirable flavor it imparts to the product if used in excess, and the feeling by some that it may be deleterious to health in spite of its long use in food processing. Conversely, SO_2 is very inexpensive and an extremely potent inhibitor of phenolase. The inhibition is not reversible since the removal of the excess SO_2 after inhibition causes no regeneration of phenolase.

Sulfur dioxide forms addition compounds with aldehydes and other carbonyl-containing compounds. In this form it appears to be ineffective in the inhibition of phenolase, free SO_2 being required for this purpose. Therefore, sufficient SO_2 must be added above the level which will react with the carbonyl-containing compounds. Furthermore, SO_2 must be added to the cut tissue or juice before any appreciable phenolase reaction has occurred. The formed o-quinones oxidize the SO_2 and make it ineffective as a phenolase inhibitor.

The difference in the internal atmosphere of fruit in the piece-form dictates the extent of penetration of SO_2 into the respective pieces. Apple segments contain considerable oxygen in their internal tissue so that internal browning can occur. To be effective in apple segments, SO_2 must penetrate throughout the whole segment. Better penetration is obtained with SO_2 in the form of sulfurous acid than in the form of sodium bisulfite. Commercially, for the best control of the amount of SO_2 introduced and its penetration into the apple segment interior, the segments are subjected to a vacuum in a solution of SO_2 in 2–3% sodium chloride with subsequent release of the vacuum. In other fruits, such as apricots and peaches, there is not enough tissue oxygen to cause internal browning. Therefore, complete penetration by SO_2 of the whole fruit piece is not necessary, phenolase inhibition at the surface is sufficient.

Ascorbic acid is a very effective reducing agent and as such reduces the o-quinones formed by phenolase action to the original o-dihydroxy-phenolic compounds. Thus, the reactions of o-quinones which lead to the formation of brown substances can be prevented with ascorbic acid. The prevention of the browning lasts as long as any residual ascorbic acid remains. Thus, frozen peach slices are packed in syrup containing this vitamin. However, after extended periods of storage or at adverse temperatures in nonhermetically sealed containers, the peach slices adjoining the head space will brown due to the localized depletion of ascorbic acid. Treatment of apple segments with ascorbic acid is of little use to prevent browning because of the oxygen in the internal atmosphere of the apple.

Adenosine triphosphate (ATP) prevents or diminishes the enzymatic browning of slices of potatoes, apples, avocados, mushrooms, and peaches without inhibiting the enzyme *per se*. Its effect is similar to that of ascorbic acid. The ATP is presumably stimulating the formation of a reducing agent which reduces the formed *o*-quinone. Because of the cost of ATP, no commercial application of these observations has been made.

The exclusion of oxygen as a means of controlling enzymatic browning is generally used in combination with other methods. For example, retail pack of frozen peach slices maintains its high quality when packaged in ascorbic acid-containing syrup and in hermetically sealed containers wherein the oxygen has been removed from the head space. Bulk pack peach slices intended for remanufacturing purposes are frequently packed in tightly sealed containers and in ascorbic acid syrup. The use of an oxygen barrier such as a layer of dextrins covering the upper surface of bulk pack peaches in friction-tight containers is sometimes employed to prevent darkening. Apricot halves may be frozen in 30-lb friction-top cans by applying ascorbic acid only to the upper surface to prevent browning since the interior of the apricot does not contain sufficient oxygen to be of serious consequence.

Two methods for the control of enzymatic browning have been developed recently. The first of these consists in the *in situ* alteration of the natural phenolase substrates. The enzyme catechol *o*-methyltransferase transfers an S-methyl group to a phenolic group *meta* to the side chain of natural substrates. Thus, caffeic acid (V) is converted to ferulic acid (VI)

V

VI

The monophenolic ferulic acid is oxidized little if at all by phenolase. Accordingly, the *in situ* conversion of all the natural substrates (including the dihydroxyphenolic compounds formed from monophenols as catalyzed by phenolase) would constitute a method of prevention of enzymatic browning. Nelson and Finkle found that an anaerobic methylation treatment with a catechol *o*-methyltransferase system at pH 8 permanently prevented oxidative darkening of apple juice and fruit sections by modifying their phenolase substrates. Simple treatment of fruit sections anaerobically at

pH 8 produced a similar effect, suggesting the intervention of inherent fruit *o*-methyltransferase. These same authors demonstrated the occurrence of *o*-methyltransferase in plant tissue. An improved process for the preservation of fresh peeled apples was developed, based upon the action of inherent *o*-methyltransferase in combination with small amounts of SO_2.

The second recently developed method for the control of enzymatic browning is that of Ponting and his colleagues (Ponting 1960). The fruit is partially dehydrated (reduced to 50% of its original weight) by osmosis in sugar or syrup. After draining, the fruit is either frozen or dried further in an air or vacuum dryer. The sugar or syrup inhibits enzymatic browning through the complete dehydration and also has a protective effect on flavor. The syrups resulting from the dehydration may be evaporated for further use as the dehydration agent or may be used directly as sweetening and flavoring agent in other food products.

EUGENE F. JANSEN

References

BENDALL, D. S., and GREGORY, R. P. F. 1963. Purification of phenol oxidases. *In* Enzyme Chemistry of Phenolic Compounds, J. B. Pridham (Editor). Macmillan Co., New York.

BONNER, W. D., JR. 1957. Soluble oxidases and their functions. Ann. Rev. Plant Physiol. 8, 427–452.

BOSWELL, J. G. 1963. Plant polyphenol oxidases and their relation to other oxidase systems in plants. *In* Enzyme Chemistry of Phenolic Compounds, J. B. Pridham (Editor). Macmillan Co., New York.

BURGES, N. A. 1963. Enzymes associated with phenols. *In* Enzyme Chemistry of Phenolic Compounds, J. B. Pridham (Editor). Macmillan Co., New York.

DAWSON, C. R., and TARPLEY, W. B. 1951. Copper oxidases. *In* The Enzymes. Vol II. J. B. Sumner and K. Myrbäck (Editors). Academic Press, New York.

KERTESZ, D., and ZITO, R. 1962. Phenolase. *In* Oxygenases. O. Hayaishi (Editor). Academic Press, New York.

LAVOLLAY, J., LEGRAND, G., LEHONGRE, G., and NEUMANN, J. 1963. Enzyme-substrate specificity in potato polyphenol oxidase. *In* Enzyme Chemistry of Phenolic Compounds. J. B. Pridham (Editor). Macmillan Co., New York.

MASON, H. S. 1955. Comparative biochemistry of the phenolase complex. Advan. Enzymol. 16, 105–184.

PONTING, J. D. 1960. The control of enzymatic browning in fruit. *In* Food Enzymes. H. W.

Schultz (Editor). Avi Publishing Co., Westport, Conn.

Cross-reference: *Enzymes.*

BROWNING REACTIONS, NONENZYMIC

Nearly all foods processed are subject to non-enzymic "browning" reactions. The nonenzymic browning reactions are heat-induced dehydration, degradation, and condensation reactions which are accompanied with the development of yellow to brown color, and characteristic flavor. When browning reactions occur, food nutritive value is invariably altered.

Many foods are produced that have, as their main attribute, characteristic color and flavor generated by purposefully initiated browning reactions. These are relatively high-temperature reactions such as those used in the roasting of coffee beans, peanuts, and cocoa, the production of sugar caramel and dry breakfast cereals, the deep fat frying of potato chips, and the baking of bread and pastry products.

Many other foods that are processed by dehydration or concentration are subject to browning reactions wherein color and flavor develop which are not particularly desirable since the accepted color and flavor standard of identity is altered. The development of color and flavor in many foods upon storage, and the "stack burn" found in warehoused but undercooled canned products, is also due to these reactions.

Although the browning reactions are numerous and variable, and their chemistry and kinetics have never been fully described, not even for a single case, sufficient knowledge is at hand to permit control, inhibit, or even eliminate the reactions.

Classification of Nonenzymic Browning Reactions

A nonenzymatic browning reaction is either a caramelization or a carbonyl-amine reaction, but the classification is admittedly arbitrary, since the course of both reactions, the intermediates, and the end products are similar.

Caramelization is the heat degradation, fragmentation, and polymerization of carbon compounds. In its popular connotation, caramelization signifies the production of caramel from sugar. For example, when sucrose is melted and heated to about 200°C, water is liberated and the reaction mass becomes viscous and progressively darker. With time, a sequence of distinct endothermic events occur, as shown in Fig. B-8. After the first period of foaming has subsided, the weight loss due to

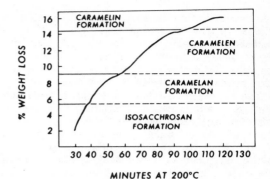

FIG. B-8. WATER LOSS AT VARIOUS ENDO-THERMIC STAGES OF SUCROSE CARAMELI-ZATION

sugar dehydration is 5.5% and the average molecular weight of the product corresponds to the molecular formula $C_{12}H_{20}O_{10}$, and is termed the "isosacchrosan" stage. Soon, the mass begins to foam again, and the 9% weight loss corresponds to the average molecular formula $C_{24}H_{36}O_{18}$ indicating the loss of 2 molecules of water from the sugar molecule, and condensation of the 2 molecules of dehydro sugar. The pigment is water-soluble at this stage, and dialyzable, and is called caramelan. The third phase of the process is termed caramelen formation, and corresponds to a 13.6% weight loss. The average molecular weight of the products corresponds to the condensation of 3 molecules of sucrose with the loss of 8 molecules of water, or $C_{36}H_{50}O_{25}$. Continued heating leads to the formation of humins, which are dark, insoluble, infusible substances with high but variable carbon content (caramelin).

In water solution, the course of events which the caramelization reaction follows depends upon sugar concentration, pH, and temperature. At high sugar concentrations, or in solution at low pH, the initial stages of sugar caramelization are characterized by the formation of sugar anhydrides, such as 1,6-anhydro-β-D-glucose (levoglucosan).

"Reversion" products such as kojibiose, sophorose and nigerose may also be generated. With the continued application of heat, the dehydro sugars and the reversion products polymerize and brown.

Fructose generates a series of dianhydrides, followed by browning. A concomitant reaction is the formation of a deoxyaldosulose as an intermediate to the formation of 5-(hydroxymethyl)-2-furaldehyde.

At neutrality, or alkaline pH, the initial stages of the reaction are characterized by sugar enolization.

$$
\begin{array}{ccc}
HC{=}O & & HCOH \\
| & & \| \\
HCOH & & HC \\
| & \rightleftharpoons & | \\
HCOH & & HCOH \\
| & & |
\end{array}
$$

Subsequently, the intermediate deoxyaldosulose is again produced as an intermediate to the formation of saccharinic acids, rather than furaldehydes. Further heating results in condensation and the development of brown pigments. In either case, sugar fragmentation and dehydration leads to the formation of ketones, furanes, acetals, acids, and esters which are responsible for the flavor, and upon polymerization, are also responsible for the development of brown color. The mechanism for the polymerization reaction is probably analogous to aldol condensation

$$
\begin{array}{cc}
\quad H & \quad H \\
CH_3{-}C{=}O + CH_3C{=}O \longrightarrow \\
\text{acetaldehyde}
\end{array}
$$

$$
CH_3{-}CHOH{-}CH_2 CH{=}O \\
\text{aldol}
$$

and the color developed is probably due to conjugate unsaturation.

Caramelization reactions are known to be "catalyzed" by ammonia, or amines, but the catalysis is indeed an initial addition reaction of the sugar with the ammonia, or an amine, to produce a glycosylamine. Such reactions are known as the nonenzymic carbonyl-amine or Maillard reactions. They are more rapid, and have lower temperatures of activation than the caramelization reactions. For this reason, when a biological system is subjected to conditions conducive to browning, the initial course of events is due to this type of reaction.

Whereas the aroma and flavor of caramelization reactions is usually described as "caramel-like," the flavor produced through the carbonyl-amine reactions is quite variable and depends, in part, upon the identity of the amines which react with the carbonyl compounds. The pigments of the caramelization reactions contain only carbon, hydrogen, and oxygen, and are known as caramels, but the pigments produced by the carbonyl-amine

reaction also contain nitrogen, and are known as melanoidins.

At the outset, the addition of the amine to a carbonyl compound is a mole per mole reaction and the product undergoes rearrangement. Ammonia reacts with glucose to give glucosylamine, which upon rearrangement, yields 1-amino-1-deoxy-D-fructose.

$$
\begin{array}{ccccc}
HC{=}O & & H_2CNH_2 & & CH_2NH_2 \\
| & & | & & | \\
HCOH + NH_3 \longrightarrow & HCOH & \rightleftharpoons & C{=}O \\
| & & | & & | \\
HOCH & & HOCH & & HOCH \\
| & & | & & |
\end{array}
$$

The rearrangement, analogous to the enolization of the sugars is known as the Amadori rearrangement. With the formation of N-substituted 1-amino-1-deoxy ketoses, several alternative pathways are available for the generation of carbonyl compounds, reductones, deoxyhexosones and furaldehydes. Among the host of compounds generated are pyrazines and imidazoles which appear to be at least partly responsible for the flavor of roasted products. Many of the intermediates of the reaction are either the same as those produced in caramelization reactions, or they are N-substituted derivatives.

In foods, free ammonia first probably reacts with carbonyl compounds, but other sources of amines are the amino acids, peptides, proteins, and even thiamin.

As with caramelization, the reaction between an amino acid and a sugar at a relatively high temperature, progresses with the appearance of dark brown products, which appear one after another as though they correspond to successive stages of an overall reaction. After the system has become quite dark, a copious evolution of carbon dioxide occurs, and the resulting pigments are insoluble. Water is also liberated, and apparently several molecules of sugar are dehydrated for every molecule of amino acid decarboxylated.

One mechanism for the production of CO_2 from the amino acids is Strecker degradation. An amino acid will react with a dicarbonyl compound, perhaps produced through sugar dehydration and fragmentation, to yield CO_2 and an aldehyde having one carbon atom less than that of the amino acid carbon chain.

$$
\begin{array}{ccc}
{-}C{=}O & & {-}CNH_2 \\
| \quad + & NH_2 \longrightarrow RCHO + CO_2 + & \| \\
{-}C{=}O & | & {-}COH \\
& RCHCOOH
\end{array}
$$

The Strecker aldehydes have a contributory role in the flavor of foods, but other browning reaction products may be equally important.

Generally, the more labile carbonyl compounds and amines are capable of browning under mild conditions, such as prolonged storage at room temperature. Nonreducing sugars are relatively inert in browning reactions unless conditions are sufficient for hydrolysis to reducing sugars. Among the reducing sugars, reactivity is related to conformational stability. Thus, galactose is more reactive than glucose. Fructose is considered to be a highly reactive sugar.

The basic amino acids are more reactive than the neutral, or acidic amino acids, and the two half-amides asparagine and glutamine readily react.

Model systems have been extensively studied in order to deduce the probable course of browning events in food products, and glucose and glycine are invariably chosen as a representative sugar and amino acid. The use of glycine is perhaps unfortunate since, upon Strecker degradation, the formaldehyde produced binds strongly with residual glycine to inhibit the very reaction being studied.

The rate of nonenzymic browning reactions increases markedly with temperature. Indeed, at high concentrations of reactants, and at a high temperature, the reaction is autocatalytic, and may have explosive tendencies. Depending upon other factors, the browning reaction rate may increase 3-5 times with each 10° increase in temperature. A second effect of increasing temperature is to bring substances into the reactive system that are inert at lower temperatures, i.e., browning reactions are qualitatively different at different temperatures.

Carbonyl-amine reactions are generally inhibited at low pH. The sugars themselves are most stable in the pyranose hemiacetal ring structure at a pH of about 3. At higher pH, a greater proportion of the reactive acyclic aldehydo form is available for the initial sugar amine condensation.

At varying water concentrations, the browning reactions are again qualitatively different. Dry glucose and glycine will not brown when stored at $50^\circ C$, but the addition of small amounts of water soon initiate browning. The significance of this point is that lower temperature browning depends upon the ability of the sugar to transform to the reactive aldehydo form. At higher temperatures dehydration of the sugar itself will supply the moisture to accelerate the reaction. At lower temperatures, the air humidity is an important factor. At a given temperature, increasing the water concentration will accelerate browning until, by virtue of dilution of reactants, the rate decreases. The optimum water concentration for browning seems to be about 30%.

Oxygen is not necessary for nonenzymic browning reactions unless the major substrates need to be oxidized to reactive forms. As with temperature and pH, browning reactions under anaerobic conditions are qualitatively different from those which take place under aerobic conditions.

Various metal ions such as those of copper, iron, and zinc have variable effect on browning reactions. They can apparently catalyze certain reactions, and inhibit others. The phosphate ion, however, has definite color-intensifying ability.

Measurement of Browning Reactions

The diverse nature of the phenomena which occur during nonenzymic browning, and the abundance of different reactants has led to development of a plethora of methods to monitor the reactions. Various methods have been used to study the different stages of the reaction, and the selection of a particular method depends upon that stage of the reactions which are significant in each particular food product, or which browning attribute, such as color development or flavor development, is of particular interest.

The initial reaction between a sugar and an amino acid can be measured by following the change in optical rotatory power of the solution. Another method is to follow the change in pH since the basic amino group disappears in the reaction. Potentiometric titration, cryoscopy, and polarography have also been used. At somewhat later stages of the reaction, specific methods which follow the disappearance of individual sugars and amino acids may be employed. Monitoring the generation of hydroxymethyl furfural may yield important data on the intermediate stage of browning. Later stages of the reaction may be followed by measuring the development of color by absorption or reflectance techniques. After extraction, which may not completely remove the color, however, the optical density of the solution is recorded. Usually this is done at 420–490 mμ, but the selection of wavelength is arbitrary. Browning pigments do not have characteristic absorption bands.

At the later stages of the reaction, the production of CO_2 can be measured since its generation appears to parallel the development of color. Many of the intermediates in browning have fluorescent properties, and fluorescent procedures have been used to follow the reaction.

Control of Browning

The most effective control of browning reactions is brought about by removal of part or all of the reactants, once these have been identified. Glucose has been rendered relatively inert in certain products by oxidizing it to gluconic acid by the use of glucose oxidase. Leaching the most reactive and water-soluble sugars and amino acids from a food prior to processing is successful if flavor is not altered too drastically. Certain foods, in the unprocessed or raw form, lend themselves to metabolic manipulation of the browning reactants. At certain storage temperatures, free sugars in potatoes are converted to starch to minimize browning during processing, or upon storage of the processed product.

Processing and storage of susceptible products at the lowest possible temperature aids in preventing browning. Adjustment of the moisture content, either to low moisture in some cases, or to dilute solutions in others, may inhibit browning. At times, lowering the pH of the system may effectively inhibit browning during processing, after which the pH can be readjusted to the desired value.

Any chemical that will block the free carbonyl function of reducing sugars or another carbonyl compound will inhibit nonenzymatic browning. Sodium and potassium bisulfite are capable of blocking the carbonyl-amine reaction in this sense, but their greatest action appears to be the formation of sulfonated addition compounds produced at later stages of the reaction. Of all the chemical inhibitors of browning studied, none seem to be as universally applicable as the bisulfites.

In special browning cases, the source of the carbonyl compounds may be due to lipid oxidation. Here, browning may be controlled by the use of an antioxidant. Ironically, one of the best inhibitors of enzymic browning in foods during processing is ascorbic acid but upon storage of the processed product, a serious nonenzymic browning problem may develop due to the high reactivity of ascorbic acid in nonenzymic browning reaction systems.

R. S. SHALLENBERGER

Cross-reference: *Maillard, Louis C.*

BUCKWHEAT

Buckwheat is a native of Central Asia and Northeast Asia. The wild species are grown in Siberia and Northeast of China. Common buckwheat was cultivated widely in China during the 10th and 13th Centuries. The crop was introduced to Europe through Turkey and Russia during the 14th and 15th Centuries and to Great Britain and the United States during 17th Century. Tartary buckwheat was cultivated in Europe 3 or 4 centuries after introduction of common buckwheat.

Common buckwheat (*Fagopyrum esculentum*), Tartary buckwheat (*F. tartaricum*), and winged buckwheat (*F. emarginatum*) belong to Poligonaceae (buckwheat family). Buckwheat is a small branching annual with smooth succulent stems. It is a fast growing plant and grows well in cool, moist, temperate regions, and on sandy, well-drained soil. The fruit is a 3-cornered achene which is gray-brown to brown or black in color. Tartary buckwheat fruit has rounded angles.

In buckwheat production, Russia leads all other countries, followed by Poland, Canada, Japan, France, and the United States.

The proximate chemical composition of buckwheat and some its milled products are given in Table B-10.

TABLE B-10

PROXIMATE COMPOSITION OF BUCKWHEAT AND ITS MILLED PRODUCTS

Product	Moisture (%)	Protein (%)	Fat (%)	Fiber (%)	N-Free Extract (%)	Ash (%)
Whole grain	10.0	11.2	2.4	10.7	64.0	1.7
Flour, light	12.1	7.8	1.5	0.7	76.7	1.2
Flour, dark	11.7	15.0	2.8	1.1	67.7	1.7
Groats	10.6	11.2	2.4	0.6	73.7	1.5
Hulls	8.0	4.5	0.9	47.6	36.8	2.2
Middlings	10.7	27.2	7.0	11.4	39.1	4.6
Farina	12.0	3.7	0.4	0.4	83.0	0.5

The principal protein of buckwheat is globulin. The essential amino acid analysis of buckwheat shows that it is high in lysine and low in methionine as compared with cereals belonging to Gramineae. The carbohydrate is mostly starch the granules of which are about $4-15\mu$ in diameter and lend to saccarification easily.

Buckwheat is used as human food and also for livestock and poultry feed. Buckwheat is made into flour by a roller milling process similar to that used in wheat flour production. The buckwheat is cleaned, dried to about 12–15% moisture and then scoured and aspirated to remove dust, fuzz, and calyx that adhere to the fruit. The grain is then passed through break rolls. After sifting out the hulls, the broken grain is further ground and sifted. The flour yield ranges from 60 to 80%. The flour is mostly used for making griddle cakes. In Japan, however, the flour is used for making Soba (buckwheat noodles) which is prepared along with 10–50% wheat flour at home and at the Soba shop.

To get groats, the medium-sized kernels which are obtained by classifying the cleaned and scoured buckwheat over sieves are passed between two mill stones adjusted to crack the hull without a grinding action. The whole groats, and both roasted kernel and farina made from the groats are used as breakfast food and also in soups. In Japan, Soba-mai is cooked with cereals similar to rice cooking. The processing of Soba-mai is similar to that of parboiled rice, i.e., the grain is soaked, steamed, dried, and then milled for removing the hulls.

HIROKADZU TAIRA

BUFFALO MILK

The domestic buffalo (*Bos bubalis*) is distributed over a wide region of the world extending from Brazil to South America to Italy and the Balkan countries of Europe, Southern tracts of USSR, Egypt, all the countries of the Middle East, Pakistan, Bangla Desh, India, Nepal, Ceylon, Burma, South China, Taiwan, Thailand, Laos, Vietnam, Malayasia, the Philippines, Indonesia, Australia and Trinidad. The buffalo serves as a source of milk, meat, and work power. The importance of the buffalo as a milk animal varies from country to country. The largest production of milk is in India and Pakistan where buffalo milk accounts for 50-60% of market milk supply. The world population of buffaloes was estimated to be 118,638 thousands and the total annual milk production at 19.403 million tons in 1969, according to FAO statistics.

The general milk productivity, date of first calving, lactation length and calving interval among buffaloes in different countries do not show any outstanding differences. Age of first calving is longer in buffalo and milk production is seasonal.

The average composition of buffalo milk in India is: fat, 6.80%; milk-solids-not-fat (msnf), 9.61%; total protein, 3.91%; and lactose, 5.48%. The corresponding values for cow milk are 4.14, 9.25, 3.58 and 4.96%. There exists a distinct relationship between fat and msnf with the lactometer reading from milk; Richmond's formula: $TS = 0.27 \ G/D + 1.191 \ F$ where TS is total solids, G is lactometer reading, D is specific gravity, and F is fat. However, these constituents vary in composition with stage of lactation, season, and age of the animal.

The fat globule size is larger in buffalo milk (4-10 μ diam.) compared to cow milk (3-8 μ). Buffalo milk fat contains 98-99% of mixed glycerides having C_4 to C_{19} chain length fatty acids. It has traces of C_4 and C_6 acids, lower concentrations of C_8, C_{10}, and C_{12}, stearic, oleic, and linoleic acids, higher amounts of tridecanoic, myristic, palmetic and linolenic acids. For buffaloes' milkfat, the $C_{14:0}:C_{12:0}$ and linolenic:linoleic acids ratios are about 60 and 6, respectively, compared with values of 0.5 and 1 for cows' milkfat. The polyunsaturated fatty acids level in buffalo milkfat is lower than that for cow milkfat. Phospholipids also present in buffalo milk, do not vary much more in their level than in cow milk. Phosphatidyl ethanolamine, phosphatidyl choline, phosphatidyl serine, phosphatidyl inositol, sphingomyelin, lysophosphatidyl ethanolamine and choline are the phospholipids present.

The average protein content of buffalo milk is 3.80%. The average casein and whey protein contents are 3.2% and 0.59%, respectively. The albumin and globulin in buffalo milk are 0.30-0.36 and 0.158-0.177%, respectively. Casein of buffalo milk has relatively more of the β-casein fraction than other milks and exhibits no genetic variants in κ-casein. It has a lower content of sialic acid than cow milk casein. These fractions vary in their electrophoretic mobilities more than do the cow milk fractions. α-Lactalbumin of buffalo milk shows greater mobility than that in cow's milk. The amino acid pattern of casein from buffalo milk is more or less similar to that of cow milk. Among minor proteins in milk, buffalo milk has less proteose-peptone and contains fewer milk enzymes (lower alkaline phosphatase and lipase activities).

The average values for different mineral constituents in buffalo milk are Ca, 0.220%; P, 0.083%; and Mg, 0.013%; which are higher than in cow milk. Buffalo milk contains a higher amount of colloidal calcium and lower inorganic phosphate. Traces of iron, copper, aluminium, boron, zinc, manganese, cobalt, iodine, fluorine, molybdenum, nickel, lithium, barium, strontium, and silica are also present. The chloride content is 61 mg %. Buffalo milk has more lactose and less chloride, compared to cow milk.

Buffalo milk is richer in Vitamin A than cow milk, but has no carotenoids and hence has an absolute white color; cow milk on the other hand has a golden tint due to the β-carotene in it. Among the B-vitamins, buffalo milk contains riboflavin (2.48 mg per liter) pantothenic acid (3.2 μg per ml), thiamin (0.8 μg per ml), nicotinic acid (0.82 μg per ml), Vitamin B_6 (0.25 μg per ml), biotin (0.08 μg per ml), and Vitamin B_{12} (0.004 μg per ml).

While the viscosity of buffalo milk is higher (2.04 cp) than for cow milk (1.86 cp), the refractive index, surface tension, and pH are similar in the two milks. Curd tension of buffalo milk is higher whereas rennet clotting time is less than for cow milk. The heat stability is also less in buffalo milk due to high salt concentration.

The microbial population of buffalo milk is comprised of staphylococci; micrococci; streptococci; psychrophilic, spore-forming aerobes; and Gram-negative bacteria. Buffalo milk also exhibits bacteriostatic property due to the presence of lactenin. It can be stored for 36 hr using hydrogen peroxide as a preservative.

Different milk products such as condensed milk, cheese, milk powder, and butter are being successfully prepared from buffalo milk. Several indigenous milk products like ghee, khoa, paneer channa, srikhand, dahi, and rosgolla are made from buffalo milk in India.

The current production of infant milk foods in India from buffalo milk is estimated at about 6,000 tons per annum which will likely be increased to 10,000 tons in the near future.

N. C. GANGULI

BUTTER

Butter is a spread made by churning cream separated from milk; it contains 80% by weight of milkfat or slightly more, and may be made with or without salt. It is known and used worldwide and the art of buttermaking has been practiced for centuries.

Standards

With worldwide acceptance of the product there are also variations in standards. In the United States, butter must contain 80% by weight of milkfat and there are no further limits on moisture or other milk solids. Australia, however, has a 16% maximum water standard, Belgium an 82% minimum fat content, Canada a 1.5% maximum milk-solids-not-fat, etc. Such standards complicate world trade and the FAO/WHO has attempted to reach agreement among the different countries on a standard for butter. They define butter as the fatty product exclusively derived from milk, and whey butter as the fatty product derived from whey containing no other fat than milkfat. The designations and standards for these products are as follows: "Butter and whey butter shall contain no less than 80% milkfat by weight and not more than 2% milk-solids-not-fat by weight. If the water content according to national legislation may exceed 16% by weight, it must not exceed 18% by weight." The permitted additions are sodium chloride, lactic acid cultures, and vegetable coloring matter. Forty-six countries have accepted this standard as a minimum standard.

Production

Butter production in 1969 in 35 major producing countries totaled 10.7 billion pounds, a decline of 2% from 1968. Production in the USSR, the world's largest producer of butter, was estimated at 2.5 billion pounds followed by France with 1,190,000,000 lb. Production by other leading countries was as follows:

	Lb
West Germany	1,151,000,000
United States	1,128,000,000
New Zealand	586,000,000
East Germany	494,000,000
Australia	476,000,000
Canada	359,000,000
Denmark	319,000,000

Consumption

New Zealand leads all other countries in per capita consumption of butter with a rate of 40.6 lb per person. Other selected leading countries are as follows:

	Lb		Lb
Finland	35.0	Switzerland	16.4
Ireland	29.6	Sweden	16.3
Australia	22.9	Canada	16.2
Denmark	20.8	Austria	13.2
France	19.9	Norway	13.1
United Kingdom	19.7	Netherland	5.7
Belgium	18.7	United States	4.7
West Germany	18.7	Italy	4.0

Grades

In the United States a considerable portion of the butter production is graded by USDA and retail packages frequently bear the USDA shield stating the grade designated. Many factors are considered in arriving at the grade, flavor being the most important. Sour cream butter is generally given one of two grades, 89 (C) or 90 (B). Sweet cream butter is generally graded 92 (A) or 93 (AA), the latter being considered the best of the four allowable grades.

Sources of Butter Flavor

The good flavor of butter is its most important asset and is derived from two sources, the milk constituents and the products of bacterial growth or added flavor concentrates. Butter churned from fresh sweet cream in which there has been no significant bacterial growth has a definite butter flavor that is pleasing and desired in certain markets, but it lacks the high flavor, preferred by some customers, which is present in butter made so that it contains products formed by certain bacteria or which are added as butter flavor concentrates such as starter distillates. A high flavor in unsalted butter for table use is essential in many markets. The cultures usually used in making butter are lactic cultures and impart a desirable flavor through the production of volatile acids, diacetyl and possibly other compounds.

Use Designation

Butter given one of the above grades may be salted (generally 1.6-1.8% for sweet cream and 2.0% for sour cream butter) or it may be unsalted. Unsalted butter is normally uncolored and is divided into two classes (1) unsalted for manufacturing purposes such as ice cream making and (2) unsalted for retail trade. The former has a nearly neutral pH value and bland flavor while the latter has a pH approximating 5.0 and an acid and diacetyl flavor. Unsalted butter, especially unacidified is often frozen as soon as manufactured to enhance keeping quality.

Packaging

When manufactured, butter normally is put into bulk packages of approximately 64-68 lb weight. It is placed at usual refrigerating temperatures for short holding or below zero for long storage. In either case, the product is finally converted to small units for consumption. A favorite unit for home consumption in the United States is the 1-lb size, consisting of 4 $1/4$-lb prints in a carton. For restaurant or institutional use, a different type package may be employed in which individual portions are served as patties or on a small cardboard tray. Unsalted butter for retail consumption is frequently whipped before packaging in a cup.

Manufacturing

Formerly, much of the butter manufactured in the United States was made from cream separated on the farm and shipped to central points for churning. This practice is being discontinued in favor of shipping milk to a central point where it is separated in power centrifugal separators and the cream churned. Before churning, the cream is subjected to an approved pasteurization process during which the acidity is reduced with alkaline salts if the cream is sour; sweet cream requires no neutralization. With lower grades of cream, pasteurization is sometimes combined with vacuum treatment to remove objectionable off-flavors. After cooling to the churning temperatures, the cream is held a minimum of 2 hr to allow the fat to harden.

Conventional Churning

Metal churns are used to agitate the cream until the fat globules coalesce, yielding butter granules. At this point, the buttermilk is drained and if the butter is to be washed it is done at this time. However, the tendency is to discontinue washing, both to save time and avoid contamination. Salt is added and the butter worked enough to incorpo-

rate the salt before testing and adjusting moisture to yield a product with the proper fat content. If unflavored, unsalted butter is being made the granules are simply worked together and the fat is adjusted to the desired level by the addition of water.

When flavored, unsalted butter is desired it may be made in one of two ways. If the flavor is derived from starter (milk cultured with a combination of *Streptococcus lactis* and citric acid fermenting bacteria) the granules are thoroughly drained of buttermilk and the moisture level is raised by the addition of as much starter as possible consistent with the required amount of fat in the final product. If cultured starter is not used, starter distillate is added to the granules, thoroughly mixed in and moisture added to give the desired final fat concentration. In either case, the pH of the finished butter should be approximately 5.0 and a decided flavor of acid and diacetyl should be present in order to satisfy market requirements.

The final step in conventional churning is to package the butter either in bulk for later conversion to consumer-sized units or directly into consumer units by means of a soft butter packaging machine.

Butter was formerly removed from churns by hand, but mechanical means are available today for this purpose. In the DDMM butter transport system, for example, churns are elevated so that the finished butter can be discharged into a hopper placed under the churn. The hopper or butter trolley is then pulled away from the churn and the butter fed to a pump by a system of augers in the bottom of the hopper. The pump, in turn, sends the product to the bulk butter packer or soft butter printer.

Continuous Churning

Continuous buttermaking, as compared to the conventional or batch process, is a relatively recent development, but one that accounts for a significant amount of the total butter production. Two different concepts are involved in this type of manufacture, one examplified by the Cherry Burrell Gold'n Flow Method and the other by the various machines employing the Fritz process.

In the Gold'n Flow Method, cream is agitated while hot to break the emulsion and separated centrifugally to yield an 85-90% fat concentrate. The concentrate is vacuum pasteurized, after which water, color, salt (if desired), and flavor are added to bring the composition in line with that of butter. The temperature is reduced and the mix solidified by passing through a chiller. The product is further "worked" by passing through a "texturator." At this point, the butter may be printed for consumption or put in bulk packages for storage. Equipment is also available for directly converting the final product to whipped butter.

Machines employing the Fritz process are Contimab, Silkeborg, and Westfalia. In the Fritz process, cream is converted to butter by the same general method as in the conventional process but the construction of the machine allows continuous rather than batch production. In the churning section of each of the above machines, a high speed beater rotates in a horizontal cylinder to churn the cream to granule stage. In the next section, buttermilk is drained off and the granules worked together. Augers push the butter forward into the working section where a salting slurry is injected and final body and composition of the butter is attained. The butter as extruded from the machine is ready for packing by conventional means.

Butter Defects

Spoilage of butter by microorganisms depends first of all upon whether the butter has been contaminated with organisms capable of causing defects and second whether the physical state of the butter allows them to grow sufficiently to bring about changes.

Foster *et al.* (1957) discussed the various factors affecting growth of organisms in butter and resulting spoilage. They pointed out that the number of water droplets in butter is very large, ranging from about 10–18 billion per gram and since the number of bacteria is much less, many of the droplets must be sterile. In butter having finely dispersed moisture (dry butter) nutrients available for growth of bacteria are limited as compared to butter in which the droplets are large and tend to run together (leaky butter). Furthermore, printing bulk chilled butter results in aggregation of moisture into larger droplets than existed in the bulk butter and therefore allows more bacterial growth in prints than in the bulk. This effect of reworking during printing explains the development of defects in printed butter while unprinted butter from the same churning left in boxes remains unchanged.

Theoretically, the amount of salt added to salted butter is sufficient to give a brine concentration inhibitory to most active spoilage organisms. Actually, salt is added late in the churning process with the result that many of the water droplets formed inside the butter granules receive little or no salt. With the resulting incomplete salt distribution, salt-sensitive species of bacteria may develop and cause spoilage.

When butter is properly made and properly handled, the keeping quality normally is excellent. Printed samples will keep satisfactorily for 7 days at 70°F (keeping quality test) or 30 days in commercial channels. On extended holding at refrigerator temperatures, butter prints may sometimes develop mold (with rancid or Roquefort-like flavors) which is often due to contamination during the printing process. Development of a cheesy or putrid odor is another common bacteriological defect; contaminated water supplies, defective equipment, inadequate sanitation, and poor manufacturing procedures are generally involved. Whipped butter rarely shows bacteriological spoilage presumably because the excellent moisture dispersion limits the growth of microorganisms.

Chemical Defects

Rancidity, fishiness, and tallowiness are the chemical defects normally encountered in nonbacterial spoilage. Development of a rancid condition is often caused by lipase action in the raw cream before pasteurization. Fishiness is primarily a defect of salted butter that has been stored, and is much less common now than formerly because of relatively low churning acidities and the elimination of copper from the product by the widespread use of stainless steel equipment. Oxidation, tallowiness, and bleaching may occur in butter held long periods of time. Factors tending to accelerate the above are sunlight, temperature, and metal contamination such as copper. For detailed explanations of butter defects, the reader is referred to *Dairy Bacteriology* by Hammer and Babel (1957).

HENRY LONG

References

ANON. 1970. How Americans Use Their Dairy Foods. National Dairy Council, Chicago.

BAKER, B. C. 1969. Continuous buttermaking. 1. Machine construction and operation. Australian J. Dairy Technol. 159–164.

FOSTER, E. M. *et al.* 1957. Dairy Microbiology. Prentice-Hall, Englewood Cliffs, N.J.

HAMMER, B. W., and BABEL, F. J. 1957. Dairy Bacteriology, 4th Edition. John Wiley & Sons, New York.

Cross-reference: *Babcock, Stephen Moulton.*

C

CABBAGE

Cabbage is a nutritious, inexpensive, convenient food that can be served raw or cooked in a surprising number of ways. Cabbage is a temperate climate crop, native to England, France, and other areas of Europe and Asia. As ordinarily grown commercially, cabbage is a biennial, i.e., the plants are grown one year and stored during winter and replanted in the spring to produce seeds. The seeds may be planted directly or started in greenhouses and replanted. Cabbage plants are subject to attack by various insects and disease-causing organisms.

The crucifers, or members of the mustard family include a number of important crops, such as cabbage, cauliflower, broccoli, brussels sprouts, turnip, radish, mustard, and others. Although there are numerous strains, most of the cabbages grown in the United States may be included in about 9 varieties, 4 of which are fresh market types and 5 are used for sauerkraut, for storage or for fresh market. Cabbage is not only inexpensive but since it keeps well it is available throughout most of the year.

Vegetables are complex substances that show a great diversity in chemical composition. The major constituent of cabbage is water. Carbohydrates, crude fiber, proteins, lipids, and ash comprise the other constituents that occur in relatively high porportions. Numerous other components, primarily cellular, have also been identified. They include the vitamins and related compounds, ascorbic acid, thiamin, riboflavin, pantothenic acid, pyridoxine, nicotinic acid, vitamin K, folic acid, inositol, and pro-vitamin A. Certain lipid components, hormones, and numerous sulfur-containing substances are also present. Cabbage has been recognized for centuries as one of the most valuable, inexpensive antiscorbutics. Numerous studies have shown ascorbic acid values between 30 and 50 mg per 100 gm and some have shown values as high as 200 mg.

The characteristic flavor of cabbage is associated with the sulfur-containing constituents, particularly the glucosides. Flavor and sulfur content vary considerably with variety, maturity, and growing conditions. The sulfur components have been variously associated with the odors developed during cooking, with disease resistance, with the heat-labile bactericidal principle, the antiulcer factor, with goitrogenic properties, and with abnormal sauerkraut fermentations. The lipid components of cabbage, the phospholipids, fats, waxes, pigments, and other minor chloroform-soluble components, are important even though they are present only in small amounts.

Cabbage is consumed raw in salads and cole slaw, as the fermented product, sauerkraut, and in mixed vegetable blends, cooked soups or stews with meats and other vegetables, and in processed relishes alone or with other vegetables. Cabbage is dehydrated for use in some of these products and it may sometimes be frozen.

Cole slaw is ordinarily prepared immediately before use. Some cole slaw, however, is a partially fermented product, prepared by the same methods used for making sauerkraut except for a decreased amount of salt; the product is consumed before a high acidity has developed.

Numerous relishes are prepared with mixtures of vegetables and pickles. These are usually prepared with vinegar, salt, sugar, and spices in concentrations sufficiently high so that the relish may be safely processed at 165°F.

Canned red cabbage is a favorite in some homes. The cabbage is trimmed, cored, and sliced and either vinegar or citric acid in solution, salt, and often sugar and spice are added. The blends are heated to 170°–180°F, filled hot into containers, and given a short cook before cooling. The product is consumed as a relish or eaten with meats.

A small quantity of shredded cabbage is preserved by freezing; however, the product does not retain its crisp character. Shredded cabbage for freezing should be given a short blanch of 2–3 min in steam or hot water before packaging and freezing.

Cabbage juice has a limited use in the treatment of stomach ulcers. Since the antiulcer factor is heat-labile, it is essential that the cabbage and its juice be held at low temperature to avoid chemical, enzymatic, and microbial deterioration. The juice may be frozen. In order to extract the juice, the cleaned or trimmed cabbage may be cut or minced in any one of several types of mills. The juice can be separated from the coarse fibrous material by straining, by pressing, or by centrifuging. Yields of 70% or more based upon the weight of milled cabbage may be obtained.

A considerable quantity of dehydrated cabbage was used by the armed forces during World War II. Much of this was prepared for dehydration, employing machinery used for making sauerkraut. Following blanching in solutions containing sulfur dioxide in various forms, the shredded cabbage was dehydrated to about 7% moisture in tunnel dryers, followed by drying in bins to about 4% moisture. Uniform loading on trays is essential to uniform drying. Excessive change in the shreds from pale green to yellow or brown is undesirable. Bin-drying is essential to equalize the moisture content, since it is so difficult to attain uniform drying in the dryer. The dried product was ordinarily stored in tin containers in a nitrogen atmosphere.

Government specifications have been revised since World War II, particularly in regard to acceptance of diced as well as sliced cabbage. A moisture content of 2% is desired since such a dehydrated product will have a better storage life. Sulfiting procedures have been improved in that a mixture of sulfite and bisulfite is used to obtain a solution with a pH of approximately 7.0–7.5. The solution is now sprayed over the cabbage at a later stage during the drying in order to obtain more uniform sulfiting and to avoid loss of sulfur dioxide. The blanched cabbage is used primarily for cooking, whereas an unblanched product is considered more desirable for relishes and salads. A green type of cabbage is popular with soup manufacturers.

CARL S. PEDERSON

Cross-reference: *Sauerkraut.*

CAFFEINE

Pure caffeine is a white powder. Sublimed crystals are hexagonal prisms. Crystals from saturated aqueous solutions are long silky white needles, which mat together readily. Table C-1 shows the solubility of caffeine in water at various temperatures. It crystallizes from water solutions with one molecule of water. This molecule of water effloresces in air at ambient temperatures gradually, rapidly at 80°C and completely at 100°C. When caffeine crystallizes from nonaqueous solvents, it

is anhydrous, melts at 235°–237.5°C and sublimes without decomposition at 176°C at atmospheric pressure. It sublimes at lower temperatures when held at lower pressures. Considerable caffeine is recovered from sublimed product collected in the chimneys of coffee bean roasters.

TABLE C-1

SOLUBILITY OF CAFFEINE IN WATER FROM 0° TO 100°C

Weight % Caffeine	Temperature	
	°C	°F
0.6	0	32
1.0	15	59
2.1	25	77
2.7	30	86
4.3	40	104
6.3	50	122
8.9	60	140
12.0	70	158
16.0	80	176
33.3	100	212

Caffeine is odorless, has a bitter taste, and its aqueous solutions are neutral to litmus. However, it is considered a weak mono acidic base; its salts dissociate when aqueous solutions are evaporated. The salts with acids are not stable. It does form relatively stable combinations with sodium benzoate and sodium salicylate which are used in oral and intramuscular medicinal applications. Caffeine is decomposed by hot alkalies and reacts with

TABLE C-2

SOLUBILITY OF CAFFEINE IN VARIOUS SOLVENTS

Solvent	Weight % Caffeine	Temperature	
		°C	°F
Tri-chlor ethylene C_2HCl_3	1.5	29	84
	3.0	67	153
	3.6	85	185
Methylene chloride CH_2Cl_2	9.0	33	91
Chloroform $CHCl_3$	15.0	25	77
Di-chlor ethylene $C_2H_2Cl_2$	1.8	25	77
Benzene C_6H_6	1.0	25	77
	4.8	100	212
Acetone $(CH_3)_2CHO$	2.0	25	77
Ethyl alcohol	1.5	25	77
	4.8	60	140
Ethyl acetate	4.0	77	171
Ethyl ether	0.2	20	68

chlorine. Lime water does not affect caffeine, and so it is used in some extraction processes.

Even though the solubility of caffeine is less in tri-chlor ethylene (TCE) than in water, TCE is used as an industrial solvent in caffeine recovery. Table C-2 shows the solubilities of caffeine in various solvents at varying temperatures while Table C-3 shows the distribution of caffeine between water and TCE.

Caffeine is taken up by cation exchange resins, and can be separated from theobromine on columns of fine granule Fuller's earth.

TABLE C-3

DISTRIBUTION OF CAFFEINE BETWEEN WATER AND TCE AT 180°F

Weight % Caffeine	
In Water Phase	In TCE Phase
0.6	0.4
1.2	0.8
1.6	1.0
2.8	1.4
3.6	1.6
4.4	2.0
5.8	2.4

History

Caffeine was isolated in pure form by Runge and others in 1820. In 1861, Strecker prepared caffeine by methylating theobromine.

Natural Sources

Name of Plant	Part of Plant Used	Weight %
Coffee (bean)	seed of *Arabica*	1.1
	seed of *Robusta*	2.0
Tea	leaf	2–4
Guarana (Brazil)		
paste	seed	>4
Cola or kola nut	seed	1.5
Cocoa pod	seed	0.1

Commercial Sources

Primary source is methylation of theobromine from cocoa wastes. Secondary source is solvent or water extraction from coffee beans and tea leaf waste (97% removed).

General Foods Corporation has large decaffeination facilities in Hoboken, N.J. and Houston, Texas. TENCO Division of The Coca-Cola Company has a plant in Linden, N.J. Nestlé has plants in the United States, Germany, and Switzerland. Kaffee HAG has plants in Bremen, Germany, and several other places about the world.

Commercial Disposition

From $^2/_3$ to $^3/_4$ is used in cola-type soft beverages and the balance is used for medicinal purposes.

In 1945, production in the United States amounted to 725,000 lb; in 1969, 2 million pounds. In 1945, imports into the United States (mostly from Germany) amounted to 300,000 lb; in 1969, 2 million pounds. Truck load prices in the United States were from $3.75 to $7.00 per lb in 1945; in 1969, $2.10 per lb.

Medicinal Uses and Functions

Double salts increase caffeine solubility in water. Oral dosages range from 100 to 300 mg caffeine; intramuscular administration, from 250 to 500 mg per 2 ml solution. Solutions prepared as follows: (a) $^{50}/_{50}$ by weight with citric acid—soluble in 4 parts water; (b) $^{50}/_{50}$ by weight with sodium benzoate—soluble in own weight of water; (c) $^{55}/_{45}$ by weight of sodium salicylate and caffeine.

Caffeine decomposes in the body tissues and is excreted from the body as uric acid within 24 hr.

Functions.—1. As a stimulant of the central nervous system it induces faster pulse with accelerated heart action and sometimes higher blood pressure. Caffeine can contribute to insomnia, stimulate gastric intestinal secretion, and contribute to loss of appetite. Since caffeine may interfere with the normal consumption of food, tea and coffee usually are not offered to growing children. Caffeine stimulates the brain and is useful in cases of nervous exhaustion. Caffeine activates the respiratory center in cases of collapse, narcotic or alcoholic poisoning (with falling respiration), and in severe attacks of asthma.

2. Caffeine provides relief from physical and mental fatigue and increases work capacity.

3. Caffeine sometimes gives relief from headaches, including migraine.

4. Caffeine helps prolong wakefulness with alert intellectual facilities.

5. Caffeine is a mild diuretic. It stimulates kidney activity and urine flow. It is not much used for this since theobromine is more effective.

Caffeine Content

A psychic dependence (habit) on coffee and tea no doubt exists for most users. Following is the content of common foods and beverages:

Beverage or Food Item	(Mg Caffeine 5 Fl Oz)
Brewed Coffee	60–100
Instant coffee	40–75
Cola-type carbonated beverages	24–40
Guarana carbonated soft drinks (Brazil)	40–80
Tea	60–75
Hot cocoa (55 mg theobromine)	1–2
Milk chocolate (1.5 oz)	60–80

Properties

Methylation of theobromine forms caffeine. This is done commercially by the Monsanto Chemical Company from the theobromine in cocoa. Chemical compounds related to caffeine and theobromine are called xanthates, purine, and uric acid. Caffeine is 1,3,7-trimethylzanthine; 1,3,7-trimethyl-2,6-dihydroxypurine; theine; $C_8H_{10}N_4O_2$. Molecular weight of anhydrous caffeine is 194.2; of hydrous, 212.2. See chemical structure and related compounds in Fig. C-1.

Decaffeination Processes

(1) Tea dust plus lime, slurried in water to effect caffeine extraction, followed by filtration; filtrate concentration by evaporation, cooling, and caffeine crystallization. The filtered crystals are redissolved in water, treated with carbon and the caffeine is

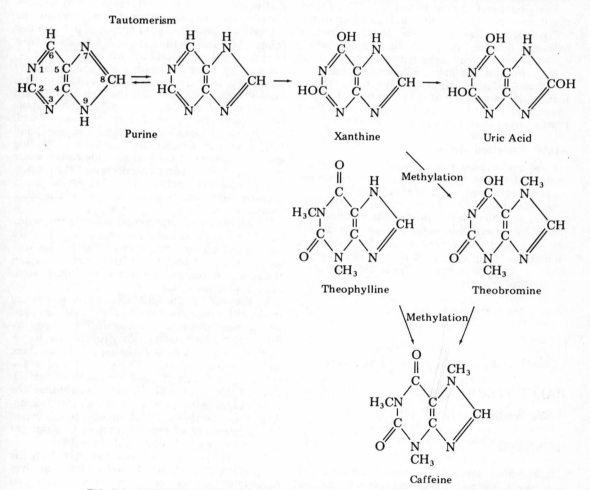

FIG. C-1. CHEMICAL STRUCTURE OF CAFFEINE AND RELATED COMPOUNDS

Each atom is numbered. The molecule can exist in two readily convertible forms.

recrystallized by cooling a saturated solution. Or, the alkaline filtrate can be liquid/liquid extracted with chloroform. Or, lime water-moistened leaves can be contacted with chloroform.

(2) Green coffee beans at 12% moisture are moistened with wet steam (also warmed) to 18% moisture. The warm, moistened beans are directly extracted with benzene or chlorinated solvents. The solvent with caffeine phase is concentrated by evaporation. The solvent phase is contacted with water to transfer the caffeine to the water phase.

The hot water solution with caffeine is cooled to crystallize out crude caffeine. Resolution of the crude caffeine crystals in water, carbon treatment, filtration, and recrystallization produces purified caffeine crystals.

The free water is contrifuged off. The centrifuged crystals are dried in a hot air rotary drier.

(3) Green coffee beans are counter-currently extracted in a percolation column battery with a caffeine-depleted but saturated water solution of green coffee solubles (about 25% solubles) solution. After the caffeine enriched solution leaves the battery, it is liquid/liquid GATX extracted with a chlorinated solvent. The caffeine is recovered and purified from the solvent as described above.

AOAC Analytical Method

Phosphomolybdic acid is used to remove impurities, followed by chloroform drip extraction, evaporating solvent, and taking dry weight.

Unofficial method is more popular: MgO is used to remove impurities from aqueous solution, followed by spectrophotometric absorption at 273 mμ wavelength vs a standard caffeine solution. Aluminum amalgam is used to remove impurities when chicory is present. There are also other methods of analysis.

M. SIVETZ

Cross-reference: *Coffee; Tea.*

CAKES

See Baking Industry: Cakes and Pies.

CALCIUM SORBATE

See Sorbic Acid.

CANNING

Unlike other methods of food preservation, canning was an invention. Man had preserved his food for centuries by naturally-occurring processes such as dehydration, fermentation, freezing, and a high concentration of such preservation agents as salt. When Napoleon offered a prize for a new and better method of food preservation for use by his armies, Nicolas Appert offered his invention—food heated in flasks—as a candidate for the prize. He was awarded the prize and from that time to our own day, canning has been improved upon constantly. Appert ascribed his success to the exclusion of air and it was not until Pasteur conducted his classic experiments, a half century later, that the true reason was discovered; namely, that the success of canning depends on the exclusion of bacteria from a sealed container in which bacteria have been killed by lethal temperatures.

Canning may be described as the sealing of food in an hermetic container, one that is airtight and impervious to the entrance of microorganisms. The destruction of microorganisms within the container that could grow in the food is achieved by heating. Usually, the thermal process that will destroy the bacteria will also inactivate enzymes, but in a few foods additional heating is needed to assure freedom from decomposition by enzymes.

For many years the heating was done in boiling water at a temperature of 212°F (100°C). This method was successful for the sour-tasting acid foods such as fruits because the highly heat resistant bacteria did not grow in the presence of acid. The low acid foods such as vegetables, meat, and fish were not successfully sterilized in boiling water. Addition of calcium chloride to the water raised the boiling point and decreased the proportion of cans that spoiled. Later the closed, steam pressure vessel known as an "autoclave" and more commonly as a "retort" was invented.

By admission of high pressure steam the retort could be maintained at a pressure of 10–15 lb psi providing temperatures of 240°-250°F. By trial and error experimentation with various times and temperatures canners approximated adequate sterilization of many foods.

At the end of the 19th Century, a pioneering investigation was conducted for the canning industry at Massachusetts Institute of Technology by Prescott and Underwood. They isolated the bacteria that commonly caused spoilage and found them to be very heat-resistant. This was followed in due course by research at the laboratories of the National Canners Association which established the time and temperature relationship for sterilization. A plot of the logarithm of minutes to kill versus the temperature of heating resulted in a straight line for which an equation could be written.

Concurrently, other workers were measuring the temperature inside cans of food by inserting thermocouples into the containers. It was found that the plot of the logarithm of the retort temperature minus the can temperature versus minutes of heating usually gave a straight line. An equation could be written describing the temperature changes inside the can. In 1923, Bigelow and Ball reported a graphical method for calculating the time required for sterilization at a selected retort temperature. As the temperature of the can increased the rate of destruction of bacterial spores increased. A summation of the fraction of the spores destroyed at each temperature through which the can passed would equal one when all of the spores had been destroyed. Later Ball extended the method by application of calculus to more exact calculations. Other laboratories in the industry accumulated a mass of data on bacterial destruction times and heat penetration into cans for a great number of foods. These data were reviewed and used to prepare National Canners Bulletin *26L*, *Processes for Low Acid Canned Foods*, which established safe sterilizing processes for commercial canners.

In the earlier years of canning a number of deaths were caused by a toxin produced by growth of *Clostridium botulinum* in low acid canned foods. This virulent toxin is produced only in low acid food from which oxygen has been excluded. Research by Meyer and Esty in California demonstrated that the spores of this microorganism were quite heat-resistant. They determined the time and temperature relationship for its destruction. By application of these data and the process calculation methods, commercial canners consistently produce canned food with assurance that the spores of *Clostridium botulinum* have been destroyed.

In reporting the sterilizing effect of a thermal process, it is customary to quote the "*F*" value. Thus an *F* value of 6.0 can be interpreted as "the process is sufficient to destroy spores that have a thermal death time of 6.0 min if held at a uniform temperature of 250°F. Determination of the *F* value permits calculation of equivalent processes under other conditions such as retort temperature, size of can, or starting temperature of the can of food. This permits calculation of adequate sterilizing processes without explicit knowledge of the bacteria to be destroyed.

The greater the number of bacterial spores, the longer the time required to destroy them. Some of the organisms that may cause either gaseous or sour spoilage in canned foods are more heat-resistant than *Cl. botulinum*. The thermal processes are designed to sterilize the maximum number of *Cl. botulinum* spores, but may not be sufficient to sterilize excessive numbers of the more heat-resistant spoilage organisms. Good sanitation is essential to keep the bacterial contamination of the food as low as possible to avoid excessively long heating and damage to the food.

The sour-tasting acid foods (pH below 4.5), can usually be sterilized by heating to 190°F. This rule is followed by canners of fruits, tomatoes, and other acid foods. The low acid vegetables, meat, and fish require steam pressure sterilization to produce *F* values of 3.0 to 10.0, depending on the food. There are a few exceptions to these generalizations.

Containers

The first containers used for canning were glass flasks that could be sealed with a cork. Soon the commercial canners adapted the canister made of tinplate that later became known as a "can." The cans were made by tinsmiths by hand at the rate of a few hundred a day. Subsequently, machines for soldering the body cylinder were developed and the ends were sealed to the body by immersion in a bath of molten solder. This method of manufacture is still used for cans for evaporated milk.

The food was filled into the can through a hole in the center of one end. A tinplate disc was then soldered over the hole to effect the final sealing. About 1910 the present day "sanitary" can was introduced. The ends were attached to the body by a double seam enclosing a ring of paper as a sealing gasket. The sanitary feature of this can was the fully open end for washing the can and filling and sealing without solder and flux contamination of the food. The paper gasket was later replaced by a rubber-based sealing compound and the use of the paper gasket ended about 1930.

The tinning of steel by immersion in a bath of molten tin had been practiced for centuries before the invention of canning. Although there had been research on the effects of thickness of tin coatings and some of the steel composition in relation to internal corrosion by food acids, the loss of a large volume of canned peaches in 1930 initiated intensive research on the composition of steel for tinplate for canned fruits. The result of this research was the preparation of specifications for the chemical composition of the steel. In general, silicon was prohibited and phosphorous was limited. For the more corrosive fruits, other metallic elements were limited. Thus, today there are several basic chemical composition specifications for the steel for tinplate for cans. Adherence to these specifications for a particular food is more important than the amount of tin coating.

Prior to 1942, the molten tin bath method of coating tin was used exclusively. The extreme shortage of tin in the United States during World War II led to the electroplating of tin developed in the late 1930's. Electroplating permitted thinner coatings of tin than could be produced by the hot dipping method. For many foods, particularly the low acid foods, the electroplated tin coating was reduced to 40% of the minimum coating that could be applied by hot dipping. Later developments resulted in a reduction to 20% of the older coatings.

Some reduction in coating thickness was later made for fruit products. Electroplated tin coatings have become the standard for the industry. The thickness varies from 15 to 60 millionths of an inch thick. The industry designates tin coating in terms of pounds per base box, an area of 31,360 sq in. of plate. Electrolytic coatings range from 0.25 to 1.00 lb per base box, usually less than 1% of the weight of the base steel.

It might be expected that the acids of food would attack the iron of the steel and produce hydrogen gas as the steel dissolved. Fortunately, in the absence of oxygen as is true in sealed cans of food, the acids dissolve tin instead of iron. The tin becomes anodic to steel of the right chemical composition and the rate of solution of tin is very slow. When all of the tin has dissolved, the acid dissolves iron with the production of hydrogen gas. Foods vary in the rate of attack on the tin, consequently the length of time the food may be kept before pressure of the hydrogen distends the ends of the can will vary. In general, the industry selects tin coatings that will provide a service time of at least 3 yr. Canned foods are rarely kept more than 2 yr. The low acid foods such as vegetables, meat, and fish, however, last for many years.

Colored fruits such as strawberries and plums could not be canned successfully in the old style can due to reaction of metal of the can with the color pigments resulting in bleaching or discoloration. With the advent of the sanitary can it became possible to coat the inside of the can with a lacquer which became known as "enamel." Most of the enamels for the inside of cans are oleoresinous types consisting of a hard resin in a drying oil that polymerizes and oxidizes to a hard film when baked in an oven. Currently there are a great many enamel formulations utilizing different synthetic resins, oils, and solvents. One that is widely used for beverage cans consists of a vinyl resin dissolved in a solvent. When the solvent is evaporated, the resin remains as a tough, elastic, taste-free film that effectively covers the inside of the can to prevent solution of metal from the can by the beverage.

Some low acid foods developed black iron sulphide discoloration when canned in sanitary cans. The old style can contributed zinc from the flux that formed white zinc sulphide instead of the black iron compound. About 1925, a method was devised to incorporate zinc oxide in oleoresinous enamels with the result that the formation of black discoloration in vegetables, meat, and fish could be prevented. The first use was for corn so the enamel became known as "C enamel."

The use of enamel coatings has been an important factor in allowing reductions in the thickness and cost of tin coatings. Most of the low acid vegetables, meat, marine, and specialty products are now packed in cans which are fully enameled on the inside. Some of the light colored fruits require plain tinplate to maintain the light color and minimize corrosion.

Substantial quantities of canned foods are packed in glass jars with metal caps. For many years the use of glass jars for home canning was popular. The outstanding commercial use is for canned baby foods. Recent developments have provided convenient twist off caps for the jars.

Canned Foods

In 1929, it was discovered that cured meat sealed in cans in a vacuum chamber to exclude oxygen, then cooked ready to eat, but not fully sterilized, could be stored in refrigeration and kept for a long time. Today there are a large number of cured meats composed of mixtures or cuts of beef and pork available for sandwich and entree consumption. Later research developed safe sterilization for small cans of cured meat that could be kept on the open shelf.

The trend of the industry is to introduce new canned foods that have not previously been canned or to prepare blends and mixes of foods for various purposes. There are such tender vegetables as Italian squash, stewed tomato mixtures, and combinations of vegetable juices. Specialties such as soups, stews, spaghetti, and baby food constitute a substantial part of the canned food pack.

Packaging beer and other carbonated beverages in metal cans rather than glass bottles has developed to a tremendous industry in recent decades and is usually called canning. The beer and beverage cans are specially designed to hold the high pressure of carbonation.

Newer Sterilization Processes

Although cooking is desirable for most of the food products that are preserved by canning, the degree of heating required to sterilize some of the products may impart a flavor which is less desirable than that of the product which is merely cooked for serving. This effect is especially pronounced in products of thick consistency which require a great deal of time for penetration of the sterilizing heat to the center of the can. The industry has expended a great deal of effort toward developing means of obtaining rapid heat penetration in order to permit high temperature-short time (HTST) sterilizing processes. Heat penetration in the food in the sealed can may be substantially accelerated by spinning the can, either about its long axis or end over end, thus stirring the food to mix the hot and cold portions until the entire contents reach sterilizing temperature. Steam pressure retorts, with mechanisms to effect the agitation, are in wide use in the industry and have effected a substantial improvement in the quality of canned foods. Some of these retorts convey the cans through the steam chamber to provide a continuous operation in contrast to the batch operation of the still retorts. The cans are conveyed in and out of the steam pressure chamber and a water cooling chamber through revolving valves. This type of operation offers significant labor saving in comparison with the batch retort process.

Another process called aseptic canning depends on sterilizing the food as it is pumped through a steam jacket for heating followed by a water jacket for cooling the sterilized food. The sterilized and cooled food is then filled and sealed in presterilized containers under aseptic conditions, usually in a chamber where the filling and closing mechanisms are surrounded by superheated steam. The process is particularly applicable to dairy products which are heat-sensitive and can be sterilized in a few seconds at high temperature prior to aseptic filling.

It has been well established that foods may be sterilized by ionizing radiation, such as x-rays or gamma rays from radioactive materials. Sterilization may thus be effected with little or no heating although some heat treatment may be required to inactivate enzymes in the food. A great deal of effort has been devoted to attempting to perfect this process and establish the safety of the foods for human consumption. Much of the effort has been supported by the armed forces in the United States in the hope of developing high quality foods for military use. Many of the results have been favorable, but research continues as a number of products have yet to be approved by FDA.

Regulations and Standards

Foods sold in the United States are generally regulated under the Food, Drug and Cosmetic Act to prevent adulteration of addition of deleterious substances. Many of the canned food commodities are also regulated by Standards of Identity, Quality and Fill established under the Act. These Standards define the principal ingredient such as specific fruits, vegetables, marine products, or milk. The addition of water and certain defined optional ingredients such as salt, sugar, seasoning, flavoring, etc., are also permitted under the Standards. The Standards of Quality give minimum requirements in regard to blemishes, extraneous vegetable matter, etc. The Standards of Fill generally require that the product must fill at least 90% of the internal volume of the container. Products with discrete particles such as peas and corn must fill the container when poured into the container and the remaining space may be filled with liquid packing medium, e.g., brine or syrup, to provide at least a 90% fill. The vegetable or fruit products settle in the container during shipping and handling to give an appearance of less than complete fill. The weight of contents must be stated on the label; this generally includes the liquid packing medium.

The USDA provides an optional system of quality grades and inspection service for food products. Some canners use this system so that they may label their products as Fancy, Choice, or Standard. Those not meeting the standard must be labeled substandard but may be sold as wholesome food if they meet the other requirements. Many canners prefer to have the quality of their products identified with their brand image rather than an arbitrary grading system.

Magnitude of the Industry

The industry has undergone tremendous growth during the 20th century, especially in the United States and Europe, and is a major factor in the food supply of the developed countries. There are numerous impressive statistics, such as the use of 25 billion food cans in the United States during 1965. This does not include the tremendous number of cans used for beer and carbonated beverages. Census figures approach 20 billion pounds of canned foods packed in 1967 at a value exceeding 6 billion dollars. In 1967, there were over 1200 establishments canning fruits and vegetables and nearly 200 canning specialities in the United States. During recent years the number of fruit and vegetable canneries has decreased due to consolidation and more efficient operation of large plants. Per capita consumption of canned fruits and vegetables has remained nearly static for a number of years in spite of the growing use of frozen fruits and vegetables. Growth of the combined industries has been favored by the shift of population to urban centers and the increased use of processed foods instead of fresh foods.

Future of the Industry

The canning industry supplies foods that are basic to an adequate diet at reasonable cost. As population grows in the United States, the consumption of these foods grows apace. The newly introduced foods add variety and convenience, thus expanding the market for canners' products.

Canning is progressing in developing countries where refrigeration is lacking. The sterile, long-keeping canned foods supply a source of needed nutrients that may be lacking in the restricted diets of nations whose food supply is based on cereals. Growth of canning may be anticipated with economic development in the developing countries.

D. F. SAMPSON
J. M. JACKSON

Reference

ANON. 1971. The Canning Industry. National Canners Association. Washington, D.C.

Cross-references: *Appert, Nicholas; Sterilization of Canned Food by Heat; Food Preservation.*

CARAMEL COLORING

The first caramel coloring in this country was probably made accidentally by the American Indians dropping red hot stones into maple sap or maple syrup to concentrate it. To some degree, caramel is obtained whenever sugars are heated alone, or when proteins and sugars are heated together. Research and development has led to improved raw materials, improved manufacturing plants, and much improved processes for producing caramel coloring on a commercial basis. Because of these facts, caramel for many years has been a widely used and approved ingredient for use in the food and beverage industry.

Definition

Caramel coloring, sometimes called "burnt sugar caramel" is defined as "the amorphous, dark brown material resulting from the carefully controlled heat treatment of the food-grade carbohydrates. Food-grade acids, alkalies, and salts may be employed to assist caramelization, in amounts consistent with good manufacturing practice." The above, and more detailed information on caramel coloring may be found in the Color Additives Regulations promulgated under the Federal Food, Drug, and Cosmetic Act published in part 8, Title 21 of the Code of Federal Regulations. This information in Part 8, Subpart D, Section 8.303 of the Color Additives Regulations was published in the "Federal Register" of June 25, 1963, page 6497 (Amended July 11, 1967). Certification of caramel coloring is not necessary for the protection of the public health, and therefore batches are exempt from the certification requirement of the regulations.

Commercial caramel coloring is a dark brown syrup which is freely soluble in water and insoluble in most organic solvents. A water solution of Caramel is sparkling clear and brilliant, with the distinctly lively color observed in cola beverages.

In the concentrated form, caramel color has a distinctive burnt taste, but when diluted to the low concentrations required for most coloring applications, it is without taste.

Raw Materials

The usual raw material for caramel coloring is a liquid corn sugar with a reducing sugar content, expressed as dextrose on a dry basis, above 75%. Cane sugar is not normally used as a raw material because of its higher cost and because the resulting caramel color is generally inferior to the product made from corn sugar. During the burning process, while the color bodies are being formed, the reducing sugar content drops to the vicinity of 25%, and in the case of "double strength" caramel, the reducing sugar content drops to as low as 10%. Different acids, alkalies, and salts are employed in small quantitites to speed up the sugar burning reaction and to obtain certain desired characteristics for different end uses.

Applications

There are several different types of caramel coloring available to the food technologist and a general classification is:

1. Acid Proof: single strength, double strength, foaming, and powdered, or dried.
2. Baker's: regular, positive type, chocolate brown, burnt sugar flavor, and powdered or dried.
3. Miscellaneous: beer, soy sauce, and distillers'.

A large portion of the caramel coloring manufactured today goes into soft drinks, with the majority going into the colas and root beer. Caramel coloring used in soft drinks is usually designated as "Acid Proof," indicating it is quite compatible with phosphoric acid, an important ingredient in cola beverages. Acid proof caramels can be either single-strength or double-strength. As the name implies, the double-strength caramel has twice as much coloring power per unit weight.

Another large volume caramel user is the baking industry. The dark breads are colored with caramel at rates of $1/2$ to 5 lb per 100 lb of flour. Cookie manufacturers also use considerable quantities of the coloring, particularly in sandwich creme types.

In the modern bakery there is an ever-present need for caramel color to maintain a uniform shade of coloring in baked goods. For flavoring reasons, a baker might want to use light colored cocoa or light rye flour, but his trade may be partial to dark-colored baked goods. In this case the caramel color darkens his goods and pleases the consumer's eye as well as his palate. Caramel is also extensively used by cookie and cracker bakers. In fact, it is employed in practically every instance when the manufacturer wishes to darken his baked products.

Caramel for baking uses must have good coloring power, must be free flowing to be easily used, and should be tasteless in the final product. Viscosity, or thickness, should not be confused with coloring strength. In most instances, free flowing, low viscosity caramels are much stronger than the viscous grades. Low viscosity is important in a baker's caramel as it facilitates solution in water or dispersion in dough, which is essential for uniformity of shade in the finished goods. A water solution of a quality baker's caramel should be clear and have the natural caramel shade. It should have a pH near 4.0, which is close to the normal fermentation pH of bakery goods.

There are some products in which it is impractical to use a liquid caramel, products such as cake mixes, spices, etc. Dehydrated or powdered caramel is available for this use. Caramel coloring can be dehydrated by either drum dryers or spray dryers. Powdered caramel is a very stable product, but is hygroscopic and should be protected in storage from a humid atmosphere.

Other products using caramel coloring are blended whiskies, condiments, flavoring extracts, coffee products, soy sauces, gravy and gravy bases, barbecue sauces, smoke sauces, steak sauces, canned meat products, pork and beans, soups, vinegar, licorice candy, dark sugars, table syrups, cough syrups, beer, and dog foods.

The coloring is soluble in solutions varying from 50 to 70% ethyl alcohol content, depending upon the type caramel used. This alcohol solubility characteristic is important to distillers and those manufacturers preparing alcoholic extracts.

Malt colors, or beer caramels, are somewhat weaker in coloring power than most other caramels, and they have a pH of approximately 4.5. Caramels which give higher or lower pH when added to the fermenting wort can alter the pH sufficiently to change the flavor of the resulting beer. Beer caramels must be compatible with hops and all other materials used in brewing, carry a positive charge, and be able to withstand the fermentation process. Beer caramels must be chill-proof and not cause a haze in the beer.

Physical Properties

The specific gravity of caramel coloring, depending upon the type, ranges from 1.25 to 1.38, corresponding to a range of 10.4 to 11.5 lb per gal. The dry substance content, again depending upon the type, varies from 53 to 74%.

The viscosity of caramel coloring can vary from as low as 50 cps at 80°F to as high as 5,000 cps. Most caramels fall in the lower range, and most beverage caramels have a viscosity of less than 300 cps.

Most caramel coloring manufactured today is carefully filtered, and the insoluble content is generally less than 3 mg per 100 gm.

Chemical Properties

The formation of caramel coloring, with the many possible reactions, plus a large number of controlling variables, such as temperature, pH, and concentration of chemical reactants, makes the chemistry of browning an intricate subject. Thus, the exact chemical composition of caramel coloring is not known although some general reactions are apparent.

The caramelization process ends in large molecular-sized polymers, but continues after the manufacturing process is finished, although the reaction rate is very slow at room temperatures. After prolonged storage under adverse conditions, caramel coloring can polymerize into an amorphous irreversible gel, which is not usable. Since the reaction rate varies directly with the temperature, it is wise for the user to avoid storing caramel color in an abnormally warm location. High quality caramel colors can be stored 2 yr or longer at room temperature without adverse effects. However, it is a good policy for a user to use his oldest stocks of caramel first, and not store caramel at temperatures above normal room temperatures.

Caramel color in aqueous solution exhibits colloidal properties. The coloring bodies carry small electrical charges, which may be either positive or negative depending upon the method of manufacture and the pH of the product in which it is used. Most flavoring extracts also contain large organic molecules, such as tannins, which are negatively charged when in slightly acid products. If we introduce caramel particles with positive charges into solutions containing negative charges, mutual attraction will occur causing flocculation or coprecipitation.

The isoelectric point, as defined in the caramel industry, is the pH at which the ionic charge on the coloring bodies is electrically neutral. At a pH above the isoelectric point, caramel is negatively charged in solution, while at a pH below the isoelectric point, it is positively charged. A good soft drink caramel must carry a strong negative charge, with its isoelectric point at a pH of 1.5 or less. Beer caramel, and some other specialty caramels, carry positive charges.

The following simple test may be used to determine the colloid character of a caramel coloring:

Prepare a 1.0% USP tannic acid solution and filter until clear. Make up a 1.0% caramel solution in distilled water. To 13 ml of caramel solution add 12 ml of tannic acid solution and mix well. If the caramel is negatively charged, the solution will remain clear and brilliant for at least 24 hours. A positively charged caramel will cause a precipitation from the solution.

Tinctorial Power

Although no standard method for determining tinctorial power, or coloring strength, has been agreed upon, the most accurate and consistent readings are determined on a high quality spectrophotometer.

It is important to note that dilute solutions (up to 0.2%) of caramel coloring follow Beer's Law. Also, a plot of wavelength vs log absorbance produces a straight line. The method for tinctorial power by Linner (1970) is appropriate. Summarized, his method is:

$$K_{.56} = A_{0.1\% \text{ sol'n (wt/vol)}} @ 560 \text{ m}\mu$$

Hue Index (HI) $= 10 \log (A_{510 \text{ m}\mu} / A_{610 \text{ m}\mu})$

where $K_{.56}$ = tinctorial power

A = absorbance

The Hue Index is actually the slope of the line referred to above, and is a numerical measure of the "redness" of a caramel. The Hue Index increases with increasing "redness."

For many caramel users, quality spectrophotometers are not available, but there are many filter type colorimeters on the market which would be useful in checking caramel coloring shipments for uniformity of tinctorial power, and as a quality control instrument for color in products containing caramel coloring.

R. S. NORTH

References

LINNER, R. T. 1970. Caramel coloring—a new method of defining its color hue and tinctorial power. Proc. 17th Ann. Meeting Soc. Soft Drink Technologists, Orlando, Florida, May 6.

CARBOHYDRATES

Carbohydrates may be defined in a general way as compounds of carbon, hydrogen, and oxygen which contain the saccharose group, $-\overset{\overset{\text{H}}{|}}{\underset{\overset{|}{\text{OH}}}{\text{C}}}-\overset{\overset{\text{O}}{\|}}{\text{C}}-$, or its first reaction product and which usually have the hydrogen and oxygen in the ratio found in water. Thus, most carbohydrates have the empirical formula $C_x(H_2O)_y$. Carbohydrates are the most abundant class of organic compounds. They constitute $3/4$ of the dry weight of the plant world and are widely distributed, often as important physiological components, in plants, animals, and lower forms of life. In plants and animals they serve mainly as structural elements or as food reserves. Plant carbohydrates, in particular, represent a great storehouse of energy as food for man and animals. Large industries process such carbohydrates as sucrose, starch, pectin, plant gums, and cellulose.

D-Glucose

D-Glucose is the central metabolic component in the energy supply of plants and animals. Its most stable conformation is the chair in which all hydroxyl groups are equatorial in the β-D-form. It crystallizes from solution in the chair form but with the C_1, anomeric, hydroxyl group in the axial-position as α-D-glucose. The sugar is called dextrose in the food industry.

D-Glucose occurs in honey, fruits, and berries and is 50% of inverted sucrose. Its main commercial source is cornstarch which on gelatinization in water is hydrolyzed completely to D-glucose by the enzyme glucoamylase often with the aid of diastase for starch thinning. Hydrolyzed this far, the hydrolyzate, on concentration, yields crystals of α-D-glucose monohydrate, the principal crystalline form of dextrose sold commercially. Crystallization at 60°–65° gives anhydrous α-dextrose, α-D-glucose, while crystallization at higher temperature gives β-D-glucose, important because it dissolved rapidly even in cold water. Incompletely hydrolyzed starch and starches hydrolyzed incompletely with alpha and beta amylases produce a series of syrups with different D-glucose contents mixed with different proportions of maltooligo-saccharides, which are low molecular weight fragments of the starch molecules. Since a broad mixture is present, the syrup does not crystallize. It is normally evaluated by its sugar reducing value with the calculation being made as if all reducing groups were those of dextrose, D-glucose. The syrup most used industrially has a dextrose equivalent of 42 (42 DE) indicating the reducing value is equivalent in reducing action to a syrup containing 42% dextrose. The actual content of dextrose is much lower since maltose and higher maltooligosaccharides also are reducing sugars, although of less activity per unit weight than dextrose.

Sucrose

Sucrose $(C_{12}H_{22}O_{11})$ is ordinary table sugar. It is the principal carbohydrate of translocation in plants and the principal sweetening agent to all peoples of the world.

About 65 million tons are produced each year of which about 58% is cane sugar and the remainder beet sugar. The United States consumes about 95 lb per person. Cane sugar is produced by shredding and crushing sugar cane. The juice is neutralized with lime, filtered, concentrated, crystallized, and centrifuged to produce raw sugar. The raw sugar is refined by washing, dissolving, passing over bone char, filtering, concentrating, crystallizing, and centrifuging. The result is refined white sugar which contains 99.96% sucrose. Brown sugar is sucrose where all the coloring materials have not been removed or is finely powdered sucrose crystals coated with layers of colored molasses. Beet sugar is produced by extraction from beet slices called cossettes. The extract is treated with lime, filtered, concentrated, passed over bone char, crystallized, and centrifuged to produce pure sugar.

Sucrose is easily hydrolyzed by acid to produce invert sugar which consists of equal proportions of D-glucose and D-fructose. The process is called inversion since the optical rotation changes from positive to minus during the hydrolysis. The inversion may also be effected by the enzyme sucrase. Inversion decreases the tendency of sugar to crystallize in candy, ice cream, baked goods, and soft drinks.

Lactose, or milk sugar, is present to the extent of 2–8% in the milk of all mammals. It is produced from cow's milk which has had the fat removed. The whey is treated with acid and heat to remove proteins and the filtrate decolorized and concentrated to produce the monohydrate of lactose which crystallizes in the alpha form.

Starches

Carbohydrates are stored as food reserves by all plants, but by far the most abundant and widely distributed carbohydrate reserves are starches. These reserve polysaccharides are stored principally in seeds, fruits, tubers, roots, and stem pith. Starches occur as discrete particles or granules 2 to 150 μ in diameter. The physical appearance and properties of granules vary widely from one plant to another, and may be used to classify starches as to origin. Some are round, some elliptical, and some polygonal. Most have a center of origin, termed a hilum, which is often the center of two or more lines or creases and often is surrounded by concentric laminar rings, which resemble growth rings in a tree. The granules are anisotropic and show strong birefrigence as a maltese cross with two dark extinction lines extending from edge to edge of the granule with their intersection at the hilum. Granual diameters in microns of some food starches are: corn, 4–26; white potato, 15–100;

sweet potato, 15–55; tapioca, 5–36; rice, 3–9; and wheat, 2–36. The latter has a bimodal distribution of small granules and large granules with few of intermediate diameters.

When placed in water, starch granules do not swell noticeably. However, when a suspension is heated to a particular temperature, which is different for different starches but 62°–70°C for cornstarch, a rapid and extensive swelling and gelatinization occurs with loss of granular birefringence and with an increase in clarity of the suspension. The starch paste formed, consists of highly swollen granules which by occupying great volumes of space give the paste its high viscous characteristics. Swelling may be induced at room temperature by numerous chemicals including strong bases. Salts, such as sodium sulfate, impede gelatinization. Pastes of potato starch are much clearer and much less rigid than pastes produced from equivalent concentrations of cornstarch. In many starch-containing foods, suspended particles of protein or other substances mask the clarity of the starch paste. In others, clarity contributes greatly to the eye appeal of the food. Cherry and berry pie fillings are more tempting when the fruit is clearly seen through a transparent thickened juice. Rapid stirring of starch paste causes the granules to be disrupted and the viscosity of the paste to drop progressively toward that of the amylose and amylopectin polysaccharides.

When an aqueous starch suspension is allowed to stand under aseptic conditions, it becomes opalescent and finally undergoes precipitation known as retrogradation. Retrogradation preceeds faster as the starch concentration is increased and as the temperature is decreased toward 0°C. This effect is produced by an attempt at crystallization on the part of the starch molecules and is the prime reaction in the staling of bread.

Cornstarch is the most important of the starches manufactured in the United States. Approximately 220 million bushels of corn are processed annually for starch.

Most starches found in the world are a mixture of two polysaccharides. One, termed amylose, is a linear chain of α-D-glucopyranosyl units joined by 1 → 4 linkages. A two-unit section of the amylose chain is shown structurally. If there were

hydrogen atoms at each of the bonds shown on this segment, the resulting structure would be maltose, which is producible from starch by the action of β-amylase. The second polysaccharide component of starch is amylopectin, a bush-shaped molecule in which most of the α-D-glucopyranosyl units are held together by $1 \rightarrow 4$ linkages as in amylose but with branches attached by $1 \rightarrow 6$ linkages on the average of 1 branch per every 25–27 D-glucopyranosyl units.

Most starches found in the world contain 22–26% amylose and 74–78% amylopectin. Amylose may be selectively precipitated from a hot starch dispersion by the addition of substances such as butanol, fatty acids, various phenols, and nitro compounds such as nitropropane and nitrobenzene. On cooling slowly, the amylose combines with the fractionating agent to form a complex which separates as microscopic crystals. Disruption of the complex with hot water or with ethanol leaves pure linear molecules. A commercial process for the separation of amylose from starch depends on the complete molecular dispersion of starch at high temperature in a jet-cooker and slow cooling to cause preferential crystallization of the linear molecules which are separated by centrifugation. The purity of the amylose is not high and further purification is needed for some potential applications.

Amylose complexes with iodine and is colored blue whereas amylopectin is colored blue but does not complex with iodine. Consequently, a quantitative determination of the amylose content in starch depends upon electrometric titration of a starch dispersion with iodine solution, or upon determining the absorption of the iodine complex at a particular wavelength where the amylose iodine complex absorbs at 680 mμ. Amylose has a molecular weight of 100,000–210,000 and amylopectin 1–6 million.

A waxy starch consisting only of amylopectin is grown commercially in the United States for use in the food industry. The corn is not waxy but the grain has a vitreous sheen when cut with a knife. Through work done by USDA, Purdue University and by private companies, a high amylose corn has been developed whose starch contains 85% or more amylose. Such starch granules do not easily gelatinize because of the strong intermolecular bonding. Amylose is capable of being formed into fibers and continuous, transparent, flexible sheets.

Many enzymes systems hydrolyze starch. β-Amylase splits maltose units sequentially from the nonreducing end of an amylose chain converting it almost completely to the disaccharide. α-Amylase attacks starch molecules randomly and brings about a rapid reduction in the viscosity. Glucoamylase converts starch completely to D-glucose.

Many modified starches are produced commercially for food and nonfood applications. Of these, starch phosphates are the most important in the food industry. Commercial products have low phosphorous contents ranging from 0.01 to 0.20 DS (degree of substitution). DS is the number of phosphate groups per D-glucopyranosyl unit. Monoesters, starch disodium phosphates, are prepared by heating a dry mixture of starch and an acid salt of ortho-, pyro-, or tripolyphosphoric acid. The esters are cold water-soluble and possess high viscosity and thickening power. They do not require cooking. Another phosphate is the diester wherein the phosphate group bridges two starch molecules. Such cross-bonded starches are produced by reacting starch with phosphoryl chloride or by heating starch with trimetaphosphate salts. Starch phosphates are used in a variety of food products such as gravies, creamed soups, sauces, oriental foods, Harvard beets, salad dressings, prepared mustards, creamed pie fillings, fruit pie fillings, creamed style corn, and baby foods. They give good freeze-thaw stability. Cross-bonded starches are particularly useful in pie fillings.

Starch dextrins are made from starch by the action of heat with or without the presence of added chemicals, by acid hydrolysis in aqueous media, or by partial hydrolysis with enzymes.

About $1/3$ of the total cornstarch and 95% of the total corn syrup is sold for food purposes. Other applications of starches and modified starches include adhesives, sizes for textiles, paper and leather industries, binders for sand molding, manufacture of asbestos products, and as a depressant in the flotation process of ore separation.

Gums

Gums, in the form of naturally-occurring polysaccharides or modified polysaccharides, are widely consumed in industry. In the United States more than a billion pounds are used each year. These are polysaccharides which disperse in either cold or hot water to produce viscous solutions. Modern usage includes the water-soluble and water-swellable derivatives of cellulose and derivatives or modification of other polysaccharides that in the natural form are insoluble. Gums may have a variety of properties ranging from tackiness to sliminess or mucilaginousness. The principal quality of gums which leads to their wide application is their ability to give high viscosity even when dissolved at low concentrations. They are used for their viscosity-producing characteristics, their ability to produce suspension stabilization, emulsification, sometimes their ability to complex with other micromolecules such as proteins, and often for their ability to produce gels of controlled rigidity.

Gums of the ancient world were largely plant exudates and many of these, such as gum arabic, gum ghatti, and gum karaya, are still used in large quantities. Seaweed gums such as carrageenan and algin are widely used in the food industry. Seed gums are mainly guar and locust bean gum with some quince, psyllium, and flax gums still employed. Microbial polysaccharides produced by fermentation procedures can supply gums and may represent an important source of these polysaccharides in the future. At present a gum from *Xanthonomas* called xanthan gum is the only one used in food products. Polysaccharide derivatives such as those from starch and cellulose are important gums in the food industry.

Hemicelluloses may be important gums. These are a class of compounds which constitute about $1/4$ of perennial plants and about $1/2$ of annual plants. They are the cell wall polysaccharides in plants except cellulose and pectin. Mainly, they are composed of D-xylopyranosyl units joined in either straight or branched chains with L-arabinosyl and galactosyl units attached. D-Mannosyl units may also be attached or occur in polymers consisting mainly of this sugar with or without small amounts of other sugars attached.

Algin is isolated from the giant kelps growing abundantly from Point Conception, California south to distant Mexican waters. These kelps, *Macrocystis pyrifera* are harvested by large barges and brought to processing plants where the algin is extracted with alkaline solution. Algin and algin derivatives are used widely in food applications where stabilization and suspending power or viscosity control are important. They are also used for these characteristics in the pharmaceutical and cosmetic industries.

Carrageenan is a mixture of two sulfated galactan polysaccharides found in various seaweeds but particularly *Chondrus crispus* and *Gigartina stellata;* plants commonly known as Irish moss. These plants are found along the North Atlantic shores from Rhode Island northward to Newfoundland and from Norway south to the coast of North Africa. Large stands have been reported near the Chilian coast in the South Pacific. After collection, the plants are washed with water and carrageenan extracted with boiling water. Carrageenan may be removed from the water by drying on hot rolls or by precipitation with 2-propanol. Carrageenan has the ability to alter the degree of agglomeration of casein particles in milk. It is widely used to suspend the chocolate in chocolate milk and is used in making milk puddings, pie fillings, and in the dairy industry. Mixed with algin or other stabilizers such as guar or carboxyl-

methylcellulose it prevents syneresis in ice cream and causes the ice cream to have a smooth soft texture.

Agar, obtained from the seaweed *Gelidium* and sometimes from *Gigartina*, is produced in smaller quantities mainly for use in the pharmaceutical industry.

Gum arabic, obtained as a natural exudate from *Acacia* trees primarily in the semiarid regions of Africa, India, Australia, Central America, and most importantly in the Republic of the Sudan, is a slighlty acidic, highly branched polysaccharide producing solutions of comparatively low viscosity. About 55% of the total gum brought into the United States is used in the food industry; the main purpose being to influence viscosity, body, and texture of foods. It is used extensively in confectionary to prevent crystallization of sugar; because of its thickening power, it is used as a glaze in candy products; and it is a component in chewing gum, cough drops, and candy lozenges.

Gum ghatti, obtained from the *Anogeissus latifolia*, is found abundantly in the dry deciduous forests of India and Ceylon. It is a highly branched polysaccharide used mainly in the food industry. Gum karaya, obtained as an exudate from the Indian *Sterculia urens* tree, also is a branched, slighlty acidic polysaccharide. It is used in French dressings, ice pops, sherbets, cheese spreads, ground meat preparations, and meringue products.

Guar and locust bean gums are two seed gums used industrially for many centuries. Guar gum is derived from the seeds of *Cyamopsis tetragonolobus*. The gums, obtained from the endosperms of the seeds, are galactomannans composed of a straight chain of D-mannopyranosyl units joined by β-D-$(1 \rightarrow 4)$-linkages having α-D-galactopyranosyl units attached by $(1 \rightarrow 6)$-linkages. In guar the ratio of D-galactose to D-mannose is 1:2 while in locust bean gum the ratio varies from 1:3 to 1:6. Both gums form colloidal dispersions and find wide use as suspending agents and as thickeners in foods. They are used to stabilize ice cream to prevent graininess.

Pectin

Pectin is a polysaccharide triad occurring in higher plants. Pectins are important because of their immense gelling power in concentrations of less than 1% by weight. Pectins can bring about gelation in fruit juices to form jellies. This action, coupled with the ability to act as an emulsifying agent, has led to large-scale commercial production of pectin. It is produced from low cost food or vegetable by-products such as citrus peel, apple pumice, and beet pulp. High quality pectins are obtained from lemon peel by extraction with a hot solution of dilute acid and are precipitated from solution with 2-propanol. The principal component of pectin is a chain of D-galacturonic acid units, most of which are in the form of the methyl ester. Pectin is sold on the bases of jelly grade, which is defined as the number of pounds of sucrose with which 1 lb of pectin will form, under suitable conditions of acidity, a standard jelly containing 65% sugar. A good jelly may be made which contains as little as 0.2% pectin. Good commercial pectins may have jelly grades ranging from 150 to 300. Pectins containing 10–12% methoxyl are recommended for jelly production.

Cellulose

Cellulose is a linear polymer of $(1 \rightarrow 4)$-linked β-D-glucopyranosyl units and is the most abundant naturally-occurring organic substance. It constitutes approximately $1/3$ of all vegetable matter and exists in far greater quantity than any other polysaccharide. It is the main constituent of the cell walls of land plants and serves therein as the primary structural element. Like starch, it is composed only of D-glucose units; but whereas starch amylose molecules tend to be helical in structure, cellulose molecules tend to be more stretched in a ribbon structure of some 1000–3000 units in length. Wood contains approximately 40–50% cellulose, 20–30% lignin, 10–30% hemicelluloses while annual plants contain 35–40% cellulose, 18–22% lignin, and 30–40% hemicellulose. The purest natural cellulose is cotton fiber which, on a dried basis, consists of about 98% cellulose, 1% protein, 0.45% wax, 0.65% pectic substances, and 0.15% mineral matter. Pure cellulose may be obtained from cotton by simple defatting with a mixture of ethanol and benzene followed by boiling in 1% sodium hydroxide solution to remove other components. The cellulose remains insoluble.

Cellulose in the form of wood pulp is made from forest timber after debarking and cutting into chips. The latter are cooked at elevated temperatures in pressure vessels or digestors. Sulfite pulp is obtained by digesting the chips with calcium or magnesium bisulfite. Kraft or sulfate pulp is obtained by digesting the chips with sodium hydroxide solution containing sodium sulfide.

Cellulose molecules as found in the plant cell walls have some of their segments in perfect crystalline arrangement while other portions wander aimlessly through amorphous regions. On treatment with chemical reagents the segments of chain in amorphous regions are more readily derivatized or reacted than the less accessible chain segments composing the crystalline regions. Thus, for example, on partial acid hydrolysis the amorphous segments of the chains are hydrolized leaving behind fringed crystalline regions which are isolated commercially and termed "avicel." This product is a zero calorie food additive used to thicken ice creams, produce sauces, and other low calorie products.

Cellulose can be dissolved by reacting it with sodium hydroxide and carbon disulfide to produce a xanthate derivative soluble in alkali. When acidified the derivative splits off the carbon disulfide and regenerates insoluble cellulose. Thus, squirting xanthate from an alkaline solution through fine holes in a spinnerette into an acid bath produces rayon fibers. Alternately, if the alkaline xanthate solution is extruded through a slit into an acid bath, cellulose is regenerated in the form of a clear transparent sheet known as Cellophane. If the cellulose is converted into the the acetic acid ester by reacting it with acetic acid, acetic anhydride, and sulfuric acid, the resulting cellulose acetate is soluble in organic solvents such as acetone and dichlorodifluromethane and can be forced under pressure through a spinnerette into warm air where the solvent is quickly evaporated and rayon acetate fibers produced.

Commercial cellulose may be rated according to its solubility in alkaline solution. High molecular weight cellulose is insoluble in 18% sodium hydroxide solution and is known alpha cellulose. If degraded cellulose molecules are present they may be dissolved. If the alkaline solution is neutralized the cellulose which precipitates is known as beta cellulose, while that remaining in the neutral solution with a degree of polymerization of ten or less is called gamma cellulose. Therefore, cellulose of the highest alpha content is the highest quality.

Carboxymethylcellulose is produced by reacting cellulose and sodium hydroxide with chloroacetic acid. It is used in the food industry as a thickening, suspending, and stabilizing agent. It is placed in washing powders to keep the removed soil particles in suspension and prevent their redeposition on the textiles.

ROY L. WHISTLER

Cross-references: *Starches; Sugars and Sweeteners; Photosynthesis; Chlorophyll.*

CARBON DIOXIDE

Carbon dioxide (CO_2) is "a colorless, odorless gas; or a heavy, volatile, colorless liquid; or, in the form of Dry Ice, a white, snow-like solid"—a definition that appears in the *Condensed Chemical Dictionary* (Reinhold) edited by Arthur and Elizabeth Rose. CO_2 was recognized early in the 17th Century by J. B. Van Helmont.

Carbon dioxide is obtainable from several sources: from carbonaceous fuels during combustion, from chemical synthesis, from natural springs, from the fermentation of carbohydrates, and by other processes. Carbon dioxide was reported in the earth's atmosphere (globally) at levels of 0.033 ± 0.01% in 1959. City air may now contain 10 ppm and depending on atmospheric conditions may be several times that much.

Carbon dioxide is used in food preservation, in the carbonation of beverages, and in controlling the storage quality of fresh fruits. It is not particularly efficient as a refrigerant in mechanical systems, but since it is safe from the standpoint of flammability and toxicity it has found considerable use as a refrigerant where safety is a prime consideration and temperatures far lower than those of cold storage rooms are desired. In its solid state as Dry Ice, it can be used effectively as a refrigerant, but close control of temperature is not possible. Dry Ice evaporates slowly and as a consequence finds much use as a refrigerant in refrigerated trucks, where is has the added advantage of leaving no residual water as in the case of water ice.

By far the largest use of gaseous carbon dioxide is in the manufacture of carbonated beverages. Carbonation is applied today to many more products than formerly since the bubbling effect adds attractiveness to the appearance of a beverage as it is poured from the container and comes into contact with the air.

MARTIN S. PETERSON

Cross-reference: *Carbonated Beverages.*

CARBONATED BEVERAGES

The beginnings of the carbonated beverage industry date back to the closing years of the 18th Century. Joseph Priestley, and Englishman, trained as a theologian, but better known for his discovery of oxygen, became interested in the "fixed air" that lay over the liquids in fermentation vats in the brewery near his home. Continuing his studies, he produced this fixed air (CO_2) by pouring acid over chalk. Upon introducing the gas, usually produced by fermentation, into water, he obtained a pleasant-tasting, sparkling water which he described in a publication in 1772. American scientists became interested in the effervescent qualities of mineral water and Dr. Benjamin Rush in Philadelphia undertook the study of "gas" which was a new word at that time.

Benjamin Franklin, who had met Priestley in England, also took an interest in the subject.

By 1807, Benjamin Silliman operated an establishment in New Haven for producing and selling "soda water." By 1860, the census reported 123 plants producing carbonated drinks, and during the Civil War the following flavors for soda water were promoted: pineapple, black cherry, orange, apple, strawberry, raspberry, gooseberry, pear, melon, lemon, cherry, plum, grape, apricot, and peach. At the present time the flavors rank according to popularity as follows: cola, lemon-lime, orange, ginger ale, root beer, and grape. However, every conceivable type of flavor has been produced. Cola outranks, by far, in preference to all the other flavors.

In 1949, there were about 6400 plants producing carbonated beverages; by now, however, this industry numbers about 3000 plants as the production facilities have become larger with distribution over larger areas. The soft drink industry remains basically a local business largely owned and operated by residents of their respective cities. The business, however, is also largely based on a franchise or contract between manufacturer and the franchise company in which both parties agree to certain obligations of product composition and quality as well as of plant specification and of marketing effort. At the present time there are about 200 nationally franchised brands, as well as hundreds of nonfranchised operations.

Soft drink consumption has steadily increased over the years from about 36 million 8-oz servings in 1850 to about 72 billion servings in 1970. Per capita consumption increased over the same period from about 2 to about 350 8-oz servings per year. This is due, in part certainly, to its general availability in almost every place where people gather for work or recreation. The product is also offered in many types of containers and container sizes.

The U.S. Department of Health, Education, and Welfare (Food and Drug Administration) states the standard identity for soda water as "the class of beverages made by absorbing carbon dioxide in potable water." The amount of carbon dioxide used is not less than that which will be absorbed by the beverage at 1 atm pressure and at a temperature of 60°F. The standard of identity also describes other ingredients which may be added to the soda water. These include sweetening agents, acids, flavors, colors, preservatives, and numerous optional ingredients.

Nutrient sweeteners may consist of dry or liquid forms of sugar, invert sugar, dextrose, fructose, corn syrup, glucose syrups, sorbitol, or any combination of two or more of them.

Natural flavoring ingredients in a carrier of ethyl alcohol, glycerin, or propylene glycol may be added as follows: fruit juices (including concentrates) and natural flavoring derived from fruits, vegetables, bark, roots, leaves, and similar plant materials. Artificial flavoring may also be used, as well as natural or artificial color.

Acidifying agents, singly or in combination, from the following may be used: acetic, adipic, citric, fumaric, gluconic, lactic, malic, tartaric, and phosphoric acids.

Soda water may contain other optional ingredients but if any such ingredient is a food or color additive within the meaning of the Federal Food, Drug and Cosmetic Act, it is to be used only in conformity with a regulation established persuant therewith. Such optional ingredients as given above and as follows may be used in soda water in such proportions as are reasonably required to accomplish their intended effects. Buffer agents; emulsifying, stabilizing or viscosity-producing agents; foaming or defoaming agents; preservatives; caffeine (not to exceed 0.02%); and quinine (not to exceed 8.3 ppm) identify other functions without indicating the large number of materials that may be used in a particular carbonated beverage. The definition and standard of identity for soda water give additional information on these optional ingredients.

The ingredient contained in greatest quantity in a carbonated beverage is water. It is not enough that such water be potable municipal drinking water. It is usually necessary to subject the water to a sequence of treatments including chlorination, treatment with lime, coagulation, sedimentation, and sand filtration, followed by treatment with activated carbon, with some adaptation to the properties of the particular water.

The complete mixture of all ingredients required to make up a carbonated beverage with the exception of the carbonated water is referred to as the syrup; with the solution of the sugar in water designated as the simple syrup; and when it contains the acid, as the acidified simple syrup. The following general procedure may be used for preparing the syrup:

(1) Make the simple syrup by dissolving the selected sugars using most of the water required in the formula.

(2) Filter to remove any sediment.

(3) Dissolve preservative and color in a small amount of hot water and add to the simple syrup. Many carbonated beverages are sufficiently preserved by the acid and the carbon dioxide content in the beverage. However, with some beverages, especially those using fruit juices, 0.05% of sodium benzoate may be used.

(4) Add acid and mix well.

(5) Add flavor. Sometimes flavor, color, and preservatives may have been mixed which, if so, should be added before the acid.

(6) Complete the formulation by adding the necessary water.

Correct carbonation is very important because of the pungent taste it gives the beverage. Carbonation involves dissolving the carbon dioxide gas in water under controlled condition of temperature and pressure. The liquefied gas from pressurized tanks is delivered through a valve to the carbonator where the gas is absorbed at a controlled rate. Depending on the specific beverage being produced, the carbonator is regulated so that the water will contain 1 to 5 volumes of the gas. A volume is equivalent to 15 lb per sq in. at sea level and at 60°F. Soft drinks may, accordingly, contain 15 to 75 lb of gas pressure per square inch, designated as 1 to 5 volumes of gas.

The beverages themselves are produced either by the presyrup process or by the premix process. In the presyrup bottling process, a measured amount of the beverage syrup is placed in the freshly washed bottle as it passes through the syruper, following which the bottles are carried to the filler where the carbonated water is added. A constant counter-pressure is maintained as the bottle moves to the crowner, in order to prevent loss of carbon dioxide. A whirling and mixing step followed by inspection completes the process.

In the premix system of filling, the proper volumes of syrup and water for each bottle are automatically measured by a continuous metering system. These volumes are mixed, cooled, and carbonated simultaneously by insertion into a specific type of carbonator. The carbonated beverage obtained in this manner is piped to the filler machine where it is fed into bottles which are carried to the crowner. The mixing step is not required by this procedure.

Table C-4 gives the ingredients of various carbonated beverages.

Until relatively recently, carbonated beverages have been packaged predominantly in returnable glass bottles ranging in size from 6 to 32 oz. Within recent years there has been an increase in the use of nonreturnable bottles. The use of such bottles eliminates the need for the washing operation since new bottles require no washing before use. However, resource-saving and pollution control may influence the ultimate glass packaging operations. At the present time, bottle washing is practiced in all carbonated beverage operations with the use of either hydro- or soaker-type washers. The cleansing and sterilization operation

TABLE C-4

CARBONATED BEVERAGE INGREDIENTS

Beverage	Flavors	Color	Sugar (%)	Acid	Amount of Acid, Oz/Gal. Syrup	CO_2, Volumes of Gas
Sparkling water	Sodium bicarbonate or sodium sulfate 300–400 ppm[1]	None	None	None	None	4–5
Cream soda	Vanillin or ethyl vanillin	Caramel or Amaranth[2]	11–13	Citric	¼	2½
Cola	Extract of cola nut, lime oil, and spice oils, caffeine	Caramel	11–13	Phosphoric	0.6	3½
Ginger ale	Ginger root, oil of ginger, and lime oil	Caramel	7–11	Citric	1	4–4½
Root beer	Oil of wintergreen, vanilla, nutmeg, cloves, or anise	Caramel	11–13	Citric	¼	3
Orange	Oil of orange and orange juice	Sunset Yellow FCF some Tartrazine	12–14	Citric	1	1½–2½
Strawberry	"Aldehyde C_{16}" (ethyl β-methyl-β-phenyl-glycidate, ethyl, α, β-epoxy-β-methyl-hydro-cinnamate)	Amaranth	11–13	Tartaric or citric	1	2½
Grape	Methyl anthranilate and oil of cognac, grape juice sometimes added	Amaranth and Brilliant Blue FCF	11–13	Tartaric	¾	1–2½
Peach	"Aldehyde C_{14}" (γ-heptyl-butyrolacetone)	Tartrazine	11–13	Citric	1	2½
Tonic	Lemon oil, lime oil, quinine hydrochloride	None	9–11	Citric	4	4½
Cherry	Benzaldehyde or oil of bitter almond	Amaranth	11–13	Tartaric or citric	1	2½
Lemon	Oil of lemon	None	11	Citric	1	3½
	Lemon juice and oil of lemon	Tartrazine (optional)	11–13	Citric[3]	1	1½
Tom collins	Lemon juice	None	7–9	Citric[3]	2½	4–4½
Lime rickey	Lime juice	None	8–12	Citric[3]	1	4–4½

SOURCE: Courtesy of Martha B. Jones.

[1] Either sodium bicarbonate or sodium sulfate is added in an effort to simulate the natural mineral waters.
[2] Food Colors are in regular review by FDA FD & C Red No. 2 has only temporary approval for use at 30 ppm in foods.
[3] This acidity is not due to the addition of acid to the other ingredients, but to the natural acid in the lemon or lime juice that is used as the flavor.

is done by a warm alkaline solution followed by rinsing with potable water. The National Association of American Bottlers of Carbonated Beverages has made extensive studies of bottle-washing processes. These studies have shown that the most widely recognized minimum conditions for complete and thorough cleaning and sterilizing of bottles for this industry are as follows: (a) the solution should contain 3% of total alkali of which not less than 60% is caustic soda; (b) the bottles should be soaked not less than 5 min in the sterilizing and cleansing solution; and (c) the minimum temperature of the wash solution must be at least 130°F. A combination of several alkaline materials may be used in achieving these results.

Since the early 1950's, there has been a rapid increase in cans for carbonated beverages. Cans are received sterile from the manufacturer, and are carefully made of special steel plate which is coated with two or more coats of can-lining material to protect taste, appearance, and wholesomeness of the contents. The can has the advantage of complete protection of the product from light and, in addition, permits a very low air content in the canned product. These advantages improve keeping quality. On the other hand, the can may be subject to corrosion due to the acidity of the contents.

Systems control is an integral part of operations in the carbonated beverage plant. Water must be routinely checked for any possible deviation from quality standards. Beverage syrup requires regular Baumé readings to ascertain uniformity. The finished products must be tested by determining carbonation as related to gas pressure and temperature. Sterilizing solutions and conditions must be controlled and bottles checked visually and for sanitary aspects. Possible chemical and microbiological changes in product must be understood and proper means taken to prevent them. Chemical changes taking place in beverages include oxidation, enzyme action, reaction with free chlorine, saponification of esters, hydrolysis and other chemical reactions of flavoring materials, and breakdown of complex molecules in caramel by reaction of acid and minerals.

Microorganisms of importance in carbonated beverages are protozoa, algae, molds, bacteria, and yeast. While typical acidified, carbonated beverages do not readily support the growth of microorganisms, care must be taken all along the line to prevent contamination.

The soft drink plant is subject to both state and federal laws and regulations, the best-known law being the Federal Food, Drug, and Cosmetic Act passed in 1938. These laws and regulations are designed to protect the consumer as well as to serve as an operational guide for the manufacturer.

ARNOLD H. JOHNSON

Cross-reference: *Carbon Dioxide.*

CARLSBERG LABORATORIUM

The Carlsberg Laboratory was founded in 1875 by the Danish brewer, J. C. Jacobsen, who had started the Carlsberg Brewery in 1847 and introduced bottom-fermented beer into Denmark. The new company expanded repeatedly and Jacobsen became very prosperous, but his main interests were centered around continuous efforts aimed at improving the quality of his beer. To further these studies, he established the Carlsberg Labora-

tory which would have as its purpose "independent investigations to test the doctrines already furnished by science, and, by constant studies, to provide as fully a scientific basis as possible for the operations of malting, brewing, and fermentation." In 1876, the laboratory was incorporated into the Carlsberg Foundation, and after Jacobsen's death this foundation also inherited the breweries. It is directed by a board of five members elected by and among the members of the Royal Danish Academy of Sciences and Letters.

The Carlsberg Laboratory is divided into the physiological and the chemical departments. The heads of these departments have always been permitted great freedom to choose the subjects for their scientific investigations within their own fields of interests. The heads of the physiological department have been Emil Chr. Hansen (1879–1909), Johannes Schmidt (1910–1933), Øjvind Winge (1933–1956), and Heinz Holter since 1956.

The first head of the chemical department was Johan Kjeldahl, born in 1849, graduated as chemical engineer in 1873, and appointed by Jacobsen to the new Carlsberg Laboratory in 1875. Kjeldahl focussed his attention on the proteins, especially on the complicated transformations these substances were undergoing during malting and fermentation processes. He realized that studies of these transformations would require better methods for nitrogen determinations than those available at the time. In his attempts to find such a method, he concentrated his efforts on the wet combustion of organic matter in hot, concentrated sulphuric acid in the presence of an oxidizing substance. He arrived at accurate and rapid analytical procedures, and analyses based on his principles are still among the most widely used analyses in biochemical laboratories. In addition to these studies, Kjeldahl's scientific work included methods for determination of carbohydrates and of alcohol, and he also initiated a study of the function of enzymes. Unfortunately, he never found time to complete the protein fractionation studies he had started, before his death in the year 1900 at the age of 51. Kjeldahl was an unusually talented and imaginative research worker. His work was recognized both by Danish and foreign scientific societies, and he received an honorary doctorate from the University of Copenhagen. In private life, Kjeldahl was a very modest man, liked by everybody and deeply interested in literature and art.

In 1901, S. P. L. Sørensen was appointed head of the chemical department as Kjeldahl's successor. He was born in 1868, was graduated from the University of Copenhagen in 1891, and for 10 yr worked with inorganic-chemical problems at the chemical laboratory of the university. Consequently, it was a great change for Sørensen to come to the Carlsberg Laboratory where he had to concentrate on problems which could further the understanding of the processes which were of significance for the production of beer. Like Kjeldahl, Sørensen focussed his interest on the proteins, but he started from the chemical angle by preparing amino acids through a new synthetic procedure based on the use of phthalimide malonic acid esters. The protein-chemical knowledge acquired from this work facilitated his development of the formol titration. This was the first really quantitative method for determination of the amino groups liberated during proteolytic degradations, but Sørensen did not stop at this stage. Like all other enzymatic reactions, the enzymatic splitting of proteins was strongly influenced by the acidity or basicity of the solutions, but the methods available for determining these parameters were still very primitive. In a brilliant series of papers, Sørensen first introduced the now universally adopted pH scale and improved both the electrometric and the colorimetric methods for determining pH. He developed a buffer system of great precision which made it a simple matter to prepare reference solutions of any desired pH value, and he initiated the quantitative studies of the enzyme activities as functions of pH. Many scientists came to his laboratory to learn the new methods, and the use of pH rapidly spread to biochemical laboratories all over the world. Sørensen's own interest went back to the proteins. He improved the methods for preparing crystalline egg albumin and determined the binding of acids and bases to this protein. Sørensen did not believe that proteins were unspecific "colloids," and demonstrated that the solubility of proteins followed Gibb's phase rules and that the osmotic pressure of various egg albumin fractions were consistent with a single molecular weight, thus supporting his idea that the proteins are well-defined chemical entities.

Outside the laboratory, Sørensen was involved in many practical problems and he developed close connections with several Danish industrial companies. Sørensen's main interest in life was his work; he enjoyed making experiments. He had an outstanding critical ability. He received the many honors showered upon him with great pleasure, but honors did not change him from being the just, unselfish and warm-hearted man he had been all his life. Sørensen retired in 1938 at the age of 70. He died a year later in 1939.

His successor as head of the chemical section was K. U. Linderstrøm-Lang. He was born in 1896, graduated as chemical engineer in 1919, and in the same year became assistant to Professor S. P. L. Sørensen. In the beginning he helped Sørensen with the many thousands of Kjeldahl analyses which were the principal analytical tool in Sørensen's research, but besides being a skilled experimentalist he was also an outstanding theoretician. As early as 1925 he could formulate the fundamental theoretical treatment of protein titration curves which are still being used today. During a stay in Munich he learned to work with proteolytic enzymes, and after his return to Denmark he introduced improvements in the techniques which permitted him to work with smaller and smaller amounts of material. In collaboration with Dr. Heinz Holter, he developed a tremendous array of sensitive micro methods for determination of the localization of enzymes in tissues or even within single cells. The laboratory again became a center for new methodology and young scientists came as guests to learn the basic principles in order to apply them to their own fields of interests. When in 1938 Linderstrøm-Lang was appointed head of the chemical department after Sørensen, he remained faithful to the traditions of his predecessors and turned his attention to the proteins. He introduced the concepts of primary, secondary, and tertiary protein structures and devised new tools to study the internal structure of protein molecules such as the volume contractions upon denaturation and hydrogen isotope exchange rates of peptide hydrogens.

In collaboration with Dr. Martin Ottesen he discovered the transformation of ovalbumin into plakalbumin, the first case of a limited proteolysis outside the field of zymogen-enzyme conversions. The enzyme responsible for this transformation, subtilisin, was isolated. This enzyme is now being produced industrially as an additive to detergent mixtures for laundry machines.

Linderstrøm-Lang's scientific talents in combination with his warm and understanding personality brought him early and frequent recognition from many sides. He received numerous honorary degrees and memberships in scientific societies. For some years he was president of the Danish Academy of Technical Sciences and in 1958 he was elected president of the International Union of Biochemistry.

Linderstrøm-Lang died in 1959, at the age of 62. He was unique as a scientist, but he also had talents in the fields of art, music, and literature. His warm personality left a deep impression on everybody who knew him.

M. OTTESON

CAROTENOIDS AND FOOD TECHNOLOGY

Nature has so liberally endowed plant and animal life with color that the association of color with food is inseparable. The rich yellow of an egg yolk and the bright red of a ripe tomato bring about the appetizing appeal of these foods. Except for the red of myoglobin in meat and the green of chlorophyll in plants, most food colors fall in a range from pale yellow through orange to red and purple reds, because of two classes of natural compounds, flavanoids and the carotenoids. When carotenoids are complexed with protein, green and blue colorations can be achieved.

Carotenoids are aliphatic or aliphatic-alicyclic, fat-soluble structures, (Fig. C-2) composed of 5-

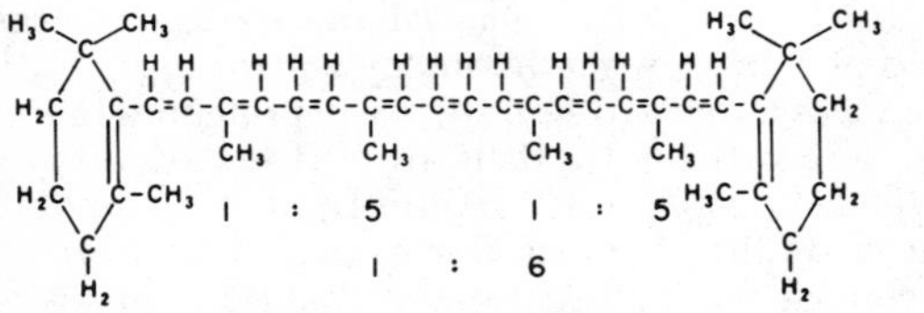

FIG. C-2. STRUCTURAL FORMULA OF β-CAROTENE

carbon isoprene groups, usually 8, so linked that the two methyl groups nearest the center of the molecule are in positions 1:6 and all other lateral methyl groups are in positions 1:5; a series of conjugated C-C double bonds constitute the chromophoric system. Chemically, they may be divided (Fig. C-3) into (a) carotenes, made up of carbon and hydrogen only, and (b) oxycarotenoids containing oxygen in addition to carbon and hydrogen. In addition to their prime purpose as light yellow to dark red food colorings, their varied functions include provitamin A activity, absorbers of light energy, oxygen transporters, quenchers of singlet oxygen, and probably other functions unknown at this time.

Carotenoids exist in nature primarily in their all-*trans* isomeric form, however, *cis* isomeric forms do exist and may even be abundant, as in the case of pro-γcarotene. They occur in plants and animals in solution in the fat depots, in colloidal dispersion in lipoid media, or combined with protein in the aqueous phase.

Source

A variety of foods, yellow vegetables, tomatoes, apricots, oranges, egg yolk, chicken, butter, shrimp, lobsters, salmon, trout, yellow corn, etc., owe their color principally to carotenoids, as do certain food coloring preparations from palm oil, paprika, and annatto. Of the yellow carotenoids, β-carotene, cryptoxanthin, lutein, and zeaxanthin; of the orange carotenoids, β-apo-8'-carotenal; and of the red carotenoids, canthaxanthin, torularhodin, and astaxanthin are the better known pigments. The

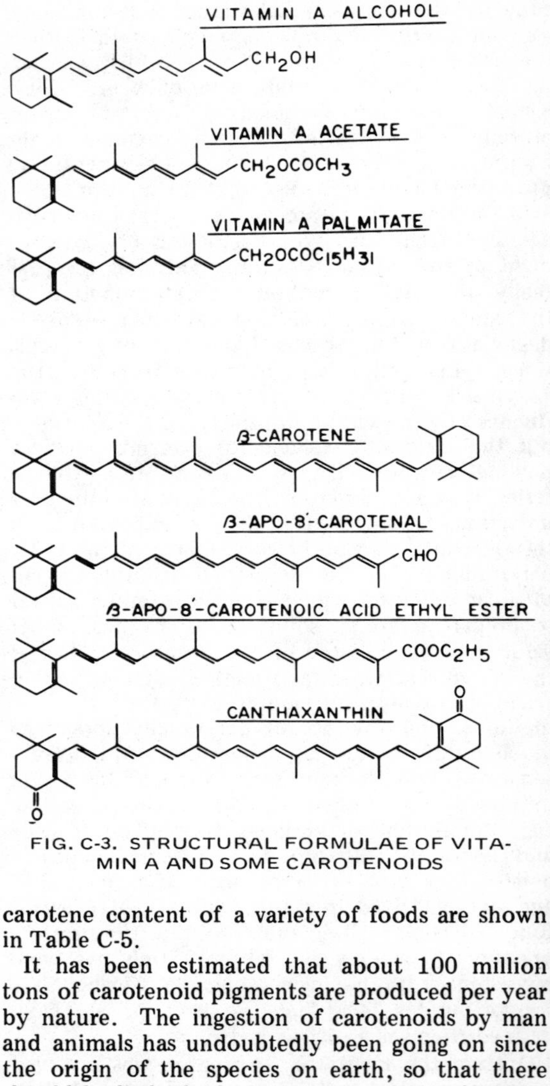

FIG. C-3. STRUCTURAL FORMULAE OF VITAMIN A AND SOME CAROTENOIDS

carotene content of a variety of foods are shown in Table C-5.

It has been estimated that about 100 million tons of carotenoid pigments are produced per year by nature. The ingestion of carotenoids by man and animals has undoubtedly been going on since the origin of the species on earth, so that there should be little doubt as to their relative freedom from toxicity.

Biogenesis

Goodwin (1954) has concluded that carotenoids are manufactured *de novo* only in the plant world. Biosynthetic investigations on plant and microbial preparations, using radioactive tracers over the past several decades, have revealed the starting compounds such as acetate and many of the reactions in carotenoid formation involving enzyme systems present in cellular and/or subcellular components, thus helping to establish biogenetic pathways in understanding the formation of phytoene, the basic 40-carbon acyclic carotenoid structure. By further

TABLE C-5

CAROTENE CONTENT OF FOODS

Food	Carotene (Mg/Kg) (A)[1]	Vitamin A Equivalent (IU/Gm) (B)[2]	(C)[3]
Apples (raw)	0.3	0.5	0.9
Apricots (raw)	15	25	27
Apricot nectar (canned)	—	—	9.5
Apricots, dried (raw)	36	60	109
Apricots, dried (stewed)	12	20	—
Avocados (raw)	1	1.7	2.9
Bananas (raw)	2	3.3	1.9
Blackberries (raw)	1	1.7	2
Cherries (raw)	1.2	2	1.1
Cherries, sour (canned)	5.0	8.3	6.6
Currants, black (raw)	2	3.3	2.3
Gooseberries (raw)	1.8	3	2.9
Melons, yellow (raw)	20	33	34
Mangos, (raw)	—	—	48
Nectarines (raw)	—	—	16.5
Olives, green (canned)	1.5	2.5	3
Oranges and juice (raw)	0.5	0.8	2
Peaches (raw)	5	8.3	13.3
Peaches, dried (raw)	20	33	39
Pears (raw)	0.1	0.2	0.2
Pineapples	0.6	1	0.7
Plums (raw)	2.2	3.7	3
Prunes, dried (raw)	10	17	21.7
Prunes, dried (stewed)	5	8.3	7.6
Raspberries (raw)	0.8	1.3	0.3
Rhubarb (raw)	0.6	1	0.8
Strawberries (raw)	0.3	0.5	0.6
Tangerines (raw)	1	1.7	4.2
Asparagus (boiled)	5	8.3	9
Beans, french (boiled)	5	8.3	5.4

Food	Carotene (MG/Kg) (A)[1]	Vitamin A Equivalent (IU/Gm) (B)[2]	(C)[3]
Beans, runner (boiled)	3	—	—
Beet greens (boiled)	50	83	51
Broccoli (boiled)	25	42	25
Brussels sprouts (boiled)	4	6.7	5.2
Cabbage	3	5	1.3
Carrots (canned)	70	116	105
Cauliflower (boiled)	0.3	0.5	0.6
Celery (raw)	20	33	33
Chicory greens (raw)	—	—	40
Chives (raw)	—	—	58
Collards (boiled)	—	—	78
Corn, yellow (boiled)	—	—	4
Cornmeal, yellow	—	—	5
Dandelion greens (boiled)	—	—	117
Endive (raw)	20	33	33
Kale (boiled)	50	83	83
Lettuce (raw)	10	17	83
Mint (raw)	110	183	3.3–19
Mustard greens (raw)	50	83	58
Okra (boiled)	—	—	4.9
Parsley (raw)	80	133	85
Peas (boiled)	3	5	5.4
Peas, dried (boiled)	0.8	1.3	0.4
Spinach (boiled)	60	100	81
Squash, summer (boiled)	—	—	3.9
Squash, winter (boiled)	—	—	35
Sweet potatoes (boiled)	—	—	79
Tomatoes or juice (raw)	7	11.7	8–10
Tomatoes (canned)	5	8.3	9
Turnip greens (boiled)	60	100	63
Watercress (raw)	30	50	49

[1] Source: McCance and Widdowson (1960).
[2] Vitamin A values calculated from McCance and Widdowson (1960) on basis of 1 mg ⇔ 1667 IU.
[3] Source: Watt and Merrill (1963).

chemical changes, such as cyclization, double bond migration, introduction of the hydroxyl, keto, or alkoxyl groups, partial hydrogenization, oxidative degradation, rearrangement, or isomerization, etc., a wide range of pigments, hydrocarbons, alcohols, aldehydes, ketones, acids, esters, oxides, etc., may be derived from the basic carotenoid.

The naturally synthesized carotenoids as components principally of plants are ingested by mammals, birds, amphibia, and fish; and are metabolized by one or more pathways: (a) unselectively absorbed, (b) selectively absorbed, or (c) chemically altered enroute through the digestive tract or during the absorption process, prior to tissue storage or *in vivo* function. One transformation of practical significance is the conversion of special structure carotenoids into vitamin A (Fig. C-2), exclusively an animal compound present in practically all animal species.

Until the advent of plentiful supplies of pure synthetic vitamin A at low cost, the carotenoids were the most important source of vitamin A in the diet of man and animals. Even today, several dozen naturally-occurring carotenoid vitamin A precursors are known and, *in toto*, they contribute significantly in supplying vitamin A value. Some, because of their rarity in distribution or their low concentration, are of minor significance. β-Carotene is the most important. The more frequently recognized and the more valuable ones are probably the carotenes (α, β, γ), the apo-carotenals, the mono-hydroxy carotenes (cryptoxanthin), the epoxy β-carotenes, and the mono-keto β-carotenes (echinenone).

Synthesis

The brightly colored carotenoid pigments aroused the curiosity of scientists since the beginning of organic chemistry according to Isler (1971). During the 19th Century, emphasis was on isolation of the pigments and their characterization by measurements of light absorption maxima. The second period (1900–1927) centered on the determination of empirical formulae and on tentative efforts to discover a role in photosynthesis. The third period (1928–1959) was dominated by the provitamin A concept, by establishing structural formulae and developing synthetic methods. The latest period (1960 to the present) has seen an exponential increase in the number of known carotenoids, whereby the number of individual carotenoids has increased from about 80 in 1948 to the present total of more than 300, accompanied by notable advances in total synthesis and in demonstrating absolute configurations, in part due to new separation methods (e.g., thin-layer chromatography) and the introduction of modern techniques of structure determination.

A number of carotenoids are produced by chemical syntheses on a commercial scale (Fig. C-4). Crystalline synthetic β-carotene was introduced commercially by Roche in 1954 as a food coloring. In 1960, synthetic β-apo-8'-carotenal; in 1962, β-apo-8'-carotenoic acid ester; and in 1964, canthaxanthin were introduced for the direct coloring of foods and use as pigmenters in poultry feeds. In 1968, the Badische Anilin- & Soda-Fabrik brought citranaxanthin onto the market as a feed additive.

Crystalline carotenoids produced by chemical synthesis are of high purity and uniform color. The melting points of crystalline carotenoids are, in general, fairly high and quite sharp for the pure compounds. There is no problem of admixture of other carotenoids or other substances, as is often the case with natural extracts. Physiochemical data assembled by Klaüi are shown in Table C-6.

Stability

Although the carotenoids are sensitive to light this sensitivity is dependent on the presence of oxygen, the light usually being a catalyst to induce oxidation. In the complete absence of air, light has little effect on β-carotene. Apo-carotenal, like β-carotene is not affected by pH changes, by metal salts or exposed metals, or by reducing conditions It is affected by oxidation which is catalyzed by heat and light; however, this effect can be minimized or eliminated by the exclusion of air or the use of suitable stabilizers. Canthaxanthin is chemically stable in the pH range normally encountered in foods, and the hue is not affected by pH. While oxidation of canthaxanthin is accelerated by light, it is not as sensitive to light as are many other colorants. Canthaxanthin is stable to heat in systems with a minimal oxygen content Conditions conducive to pro-oxidation and/or isomerization of carotenoids have been minimized by the development of special forms for food coloring uses.

In nature, carotenoid content in natural foods is influenced by climatic and environmental conditions, stage of maturity of the crop, harvesting methods, storage and transportation conditions processing of the food, etc. Plants at maturity can have $1/2$ maximum carotenoid value or less Drought reduces the carotene content of plants Destruction of carotenoids result from enzymic and photochemical processes in harvesting and exposure to weathering. Milling and processing of seeds for grains for flour may destroy or remove a considerable portion of the carotenoid content Furthermore, the bleaching stage in flour processing

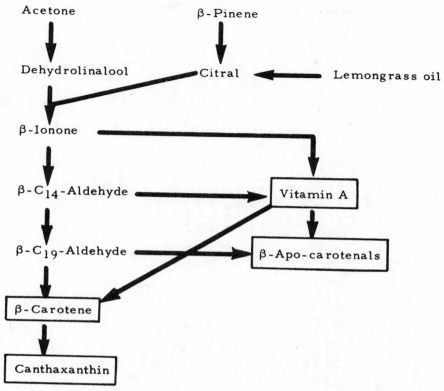

FIG. C-4. SURVEY OF THE INDUSTRIAL SYNTHETIC PROCESSES BY ISLER

destroys the residual carotenes so that white bread may be produced. Where the significant yellow color from carotenoids is desired, such as in pasta products like macaroni, special wheats (durum) are grown and are carefully processed to produce the semolina and farina. The blanching, retorting, and freezing processes of foods generally cause little loss of carotenoid content in vegetables and fruits. Heat, however, does isomerize the all-*trans* carotenoids to *cis* forms. Frozen foods and heat-sterilized foods exhibit excellent carotenoid stability throughout their normal temperature shelf-life with few exceptions. In general, dehydrated and powdered fruits and vegetables have poor carotenoid stability unless carefully processed and promptly placed in a hermetically sealed, inert atmosphere for storage.

Indirect Coloring of Food Products

The term "pigmenters" is used to refer to carotenoids which when present in, or added to an animal ration, will color body tissues such as skin and fat or animal products such as eggs, broilers, butter, cheese, etc. This *indirect* method of coloring food is as old as the animal kingdom.

β-Carotene, in addition to its role as a potent vitamin A precursor, is also a pigmenter for the dairy cow. Ingested β-carotene, not converted to vitamin A in the animal's body, is stored in the fatty deposits in the tissue and in the butterfat as well. Some α-carotene, cryptoxanthin and lutein is also usually present. A great animal breed and species specificity exists in the metabolism of β-carotene.

Avian species convert ingested carotene to vitamin A like mammals but differ from mammals in preferentially storing ingested oxycarotenoids in liver, eggs, body fat, skin, feathers, and shanks. Pigmentation in the poultry field is concerned both with the skin color of meat birds and the degree of yolk color. Moderately colored yolks are preferred for table use in many parts of the world, but in certain areas consumers want dark yolks. Highly colored yolks are desired for the commercial production of bakery products, noodles, mayonnaise, prepared cake mixes and other egg products. Under natural conditions of barnyard feeding of poultry in the past, the chicken obtained the oxycarotenoids from grass and green plants. In modern practices with commercial poultry

TABLE C-6

PHYSICOCHEMICAL DATA ON CAROTENOIDS

Item	β-Carotene	β-Apo-8'-Carotenal (C$_{30}$)	β-Apo-8'-Carotenoic Acid Ethyl Ester (C$_{30}$)	Canthaxanthin
Color of oily solution	Yellow to orange	Orange to orange-red	Yellow to orange	Red
Melting point, crystalline compounds	176°–182°C	136°–140°C	134°–138°C	approx 210°C
Solubility (gm/100 ml solution, 20°C)				
Fats, oils	0.05–0.08	0.07–1.5	Approx 0.7	Approx 0.005
Orange oil	0.2–1.0	Approx 3.1	3.4–4.4	Approx 0.04
Water	Insoluble	Insoluble	Insoluble	Insoluble
Glycerol	Insoluble	Insoluble	Insoluble	Insoluble
Ethanol	Below 0.01	Approx 0.1	Below 0.1	Below 0.01
Cyclohexane	Approx 0.1	Approx 0.8	Approx 2	Below 0.01
Petrol ether (80°–105°C)	Approx 0.1	Approx 0.4	Approx 0.7	Below 0.01
Ether	Approx 0.1	Approx 1.5	Approx 2.5	Approx 0.03
Benzene	Approx 2	Approx 12	Approx 16	Approx 0.2
Chloroform	Approx 3	Approx 20	Approx 30	Approx 10
Acetone	Approx 0.1	Approx 1.8	Approx 1.2	Approx 0.03
Spectrophotometric data[1]				
Mμ max (in cyclohexane)	455–456 mμ	460–462 mμ	448–450 mμ	468–472 mμ
E$^{1\%}_{1cm}$ (in cyclohexane)	456 mμ 2400	461 mμ 2530	449 mμ 2440	470 mμ 2110
	485 mμ 2030	388 mμ 2030	475 mμ 2000	
Biological acitvity				
Vitamin A value	1667 IU/mg	1200 IU/mg	Active	No vitamin A value

[1] Of commercial products, the carotenoids isomerize in solution during storage or on heating; the predominant isomer in the equilibrium mixture is the *trans* compound. The values given correspond to the *trans* isomer.

feeds, the pigmenting ingredients must be supplied by natural oxycarotenoid-containing ingredients or oxycarotenoids of chemical synthesis origin.

In a laying ration for hens of a white grain or a yellow corn formulation, added β-apo-8'-carotenoic acid ethyl ester or β-apo-8'-carotenal can provide the desired range of yellow to orange yolk hue. Added β-apo-8'-carotenoic acid ethyl ester, like added natural oxycarotenoid-bearing ingredients, can serve to give broilers the yellow skin color desired in the market place. Apo-carotenal is not an efficient skin and shank pigmenter for broilers. Canthaxanthin will pigment both yolks and skin but must be used in combination with other oxycarotenoids and not as a sole dietary source. Canthaxanthin is an effective feed additive for the pigmentation of certain species of salmonids (trout and salmon) and crustaceans. The choice of oxycarotenoid pigmenter or pigmenter combinations in feeds is governed by the desired objective, economics, and current availability of the products.

Direct Coloring of Foods

The first carotenoids available for use in food coloring were produced by extraction from natural sources, primarily as concentrated extracts and this method is still in limited commercial use today. Solubility and stability difficulties encountered in handling crystalline carotenoids have been solved by the development of special forms. Two approaches have been primarily employed, namely (a) production of oil suspensions of micropulverized crystals and (b) development of emulsions or beadlet forms containing the carotenoid in supersaturated solution or in colloidal form. These forms make possible the coloring of both fat-base and water-base foods. Table C-7 is a tabulation of results compiled by Bauernfeind of small commercial or pilot-type trial runs made with the prevailing equipment on a number of food products containing added carotenoids as food colors. In general, added carotenoids in the direct coloring of food products are quite stable when prepared under current food technology practices.

Employing the different market forms of β-carotene, it is technically possible to color butter, margarine, shortening, cheese, ice cream, macaroni products, breadings, frozen french fried potatoes, vegetable oils, salad dressing, whipped cream, cream toppings, coffee whiteners, popcorn oil, cocktail tidbits, dried or frozen yolks and whole eggs, eggnog, baked goods, cake mixes, candy, dietetic foods, puddings, creamed foods, soups, gelatin desserts, fruit juices, and beverages.

β-Apo-8'-carotenal finds use in the food industry for coloring either water- or oil-base foods where an orange to reddish-orange shade is desired.

Foods in which apo-carotenal can be used are expanded snack products, baked goods, toppings, frostings, candies, confections, pastry fillings, cheese sauces, cheese spreads, cake mixes, soups, salad dressings, etc.

Canthaxanthin has unusually high tinctorial potency and is a useful food colorant in the red range. It has particular promise in tomato products, soups, barbecue sauce, spaghetti sauce, fruit drinks, salad dressings, simulated meat products, and shrimp, salmon, and lobster products.

The natural color of butter varies with dairy feeding practices. If no butter color were added during butter-making, butter would be quite white in midwinter and very yellow in summer during the weeks of fresh, green luxuriant pastures. Winter butter can be successfully colored with β-carotene special forms both by the continuous and batch methods although the butter industry still clings to the addition of nonnutrient yellow dyes, a practice initiated years ago. β-Carotene is considered an ideal added color for margarine and shortening or lard. The shade of color desired in French dressing is deeper than can be supplied by a practical level of β-carotene, but the more intense color of β-apo-8'-carotenal produces the typical color of the French dressings while canthaxanthin provides a desirable color range for dressings of the Russian type.

Singly or in combination with β-carotene, β-apo-8'-carotenal provides an interesting range for primary and process cheese. Also, since apo-carotenal is produced in pure form, it gives a uniformity of color from batch to batch that is difficult to obtain with colors extracted from variable natural sources. Canthaxanthin produces an attractive process cheese color, resembling the hue of cheese colored with a high-annatto paprika mixture. Vanilla ice cream colored with β-carotene produces a French vanilla type of ice cream. Apo-carotenal gives a very appetizing peach color to ice cream and a desirable orange color to sherbets. In the case of mellorine (vegetable fat imitation ice cream), β-carotene and apo-carotenal, when used as colors in this product will also replace some vitamin A activity normally supplied by butterfat.

In a low heme pigment frankfurter formulation, canthaxanthin produces an attractive cured beef color and simulates cured beef color in sausage products. Added canthaxanthin can be used to color simulated meats, fresh shrimp, and opaque starch-type dressings. The resulting hues depend on the fat content of the products and their intrinsic color. In tomato-based product, such as soup, pizza sauce, barbecue sauce, spaghetti sauce, etc., canthaxanthin can standardize or amplify color, as required.

TABLE C-7

STABILITY OF ADDED CAROTENOID FOOD COLORS IN FOOD PRODUCTS

Product	Packaging	Added Carotenoid	Method of Addition	After Processing	Carotenoid Level After Storage at 70°–75°F (23°C)				
					2 Mo	3 Mo	4 Mo	6 Mo	12 Mo
Apricot drink	Metal can	β-Carotene	Prior to canning	1.21 mg/6 fl oz	—	1.21	—	1.21(100)[1]	1.16(96)[1]
Apricot-orange drink	Metal can	Apo-carotenal (beadlets)	Prior to canning	0.44 mg/6 fl oz	—	0.42	—	0.43(98)	—
Butter	Paper, waxed carton	β-Carotene (emulsion)	At salting stage	4.7 mg/lb	—	4.2[2]	—	4.2[2](89)	—
Butter	Paper, waxed carton	β-Carotene (beadlets)	At salting stage	5.2 mg/lb	—	4.4[2]	—	4.6[2](89)	—
Cheese, primary	Waxed Wedge	β-Carotene (beadlets)	To the milk	5.4 mg/lb	—	5.6[2]	—	—	5.7[3](100)
	Waxed Wedge	Apo-carotenal (beadlets)	To the milk	6.5 mg/lb	—	6.7[2]	—	—	7.8[3](100)
Cheese, primary	Waxed Wedge	β-Carotene (A)	To the milk	(A) 2.4 mg/lb	—	—	—	—	2.2[2](92)
				(B) 1.7 mg/lb	—	—	—	—	1.6[2](99)
		Apo-carotenal (beadlets) (B)		(A) 4.3 mg/lb	—	—	—	—	4.2[2](98)
				(B) 1.7 mg/lb	—	—	—	—	1.6[2](94)
Cheese, processed	Film	Apo-carotenal	To warm cheese	1.09 mg/lb	1.03[2]	—	—	1.06[2](97)	1.03[2](94)
Cheese, processed	Film	Canthaxanthin	To warm cheese	3.1 mg/lb	—	2.44[2]	—	—	2.33[2,4](75)
Cheese, processed	Film	β-Carotene (A)	To warm cheese	(A) 2.1 mg/lb	—	—	—	—	2.0[2](95)
				(B) 1.4 mg/lb	—	—	—	—	1.3[2](93)
		Apo-carotenal (beadlets) (B)		(A) 3.9 mg/lb	—	—	—	—	3.8[2](97)
				(B) 1.6 mg/lb	—	—	—	—	1.4[2](88)
Cheese, processed	Paper and box	Apo-carotenal (suspension)	To warm cheese	4.9 mg/lb	—	5.0[2]	—	5.1[2](100)	—
Fruit juice drink	Metal can	β-Carotene (emulsion)	Prior to canning	1.32 mg/fl oz	—	1.38	—	1.32(100)	—
Fruit juice base, chilled	Metal can	β-Carotene (emulsion)	Prior to canning	2.9 mg/8 fl oz	—	2.98[2]	—	2.86[2](96)	2.90[2](98)
Gelatin powder	Film	Canthaxanthin	To dry powder	55.6 mg/kg	49.4	49.6	—	50.0(90)	—

Product	Container	Colorant	Added	Amount								
Margarine	Waxed paper carton	β-Carotene (suspension)	To warm oil prior to churning	3.24 mg/lb	—	—	—	—	—	—	3.25(100)	—
Margarine	Waxed paper carton	β-Carotene	To warm oil prior to churning	3.84 mg/lb	3.60	—	—	—	3.30(86)	—	3.66[2](95)	—
Margarine	Waxed paper carton	β-Carotene	To warm oil prior to churning	3.51 mg/lb	3.48	—	—	—	3.30(94)	—	3.54[2](100)	—
Margarine	Waxed paper carton	β-Carotene	To warm oil prior to churning	3.63 mg/lb	3.54	—	—	—	3.12(86)	—	3.42[2](94)	—
Orange beverage, carbonated	Glass bottle	Apo-carotenal alone	Prior to bottling	3.5 mg/29 fl oz	—	—	2.73	—	—	—	—	—
	Glass bottle	With added ascorbic acid	Prior to bottling	3.70 mg/29 fl oz	—	—	3.31	—	—	—	—	—
Orange beverage, carbonated	Glass bottle	β-Carotene alone	Prior to bottling	5.87 mg/29 fl oz	—	—	5.00	—	—	—	—	—
	Glass bottle	With added ascorbic acid	Prior to bottling	5.62 mg/29 fl oz	—	—	5.32	—	—	—	—	—
Orange drink, low calorie	Glass bottle	β-Carotene	Prior to canning	0.96 mg/10 fl oz	0.93	—	0.96	—	0.94(98)	—	0.92(96)	—
Orange drink	Metal can	β-Carotene and apo-carotenal (3:1)	Prior to canning	2.75 mg/12 fl oz	—	—	2.71	—	2.64(97)	—	—	—
Orange drink	Enamel lined can	β-Carotene (beadlets)	Prior to canning	1.73 mg/12 fl oz	—	—	—	—	1.67(97)	—	1.60[5](92)	—
Orange juice, concentrated	Metal can	β-Carotene (beadlets)	Prior to canning	2.51 mg/16 fl oz	—	—	2.64	—	2.60(100)	—	2.88(100)	—
Orangeade base	Metal can	β-Carotene (beadlets)	Prior to canning	5.90 mg/6 fl oz	—	—	5.30	—	5.46(93)	—	—	—
Pie filling	Metal can	Apo-carotenal (beadlets)	Prior to canning	2.24 mg/kg	—	—	2.07	—	2.10(94)	—	2.00(89)	—
Pineapple-orange drink	Metal can	β-Carotene	Prior to canning	0.92 mg/6 fl oz	—	—	0.85	—	0.85(92)	—	—	—
Popcorn oil	Pint bottles	β-Carotene (suspension)	To warm oil	13.6 mg/lb	12.7	—	—	—	13.1(96)	—	12.9(95)	—

TABLE C-7 (Continued)

Product	Packaging	Added Carotenoid	Method of Addition	After Processing	Carotenoid Level After Storage at 70°–75° F (23° C)				
					2 Mo	3 Mo	4 Mo	6 Mo	12 Mo
Salad dressing	Glass bottle	Canthaxanthin (beadlets)	To the emulsion	14.6 mg/lb	—	14.4	—	13.6(93)	—
Shortening	Sealed can	β-Carotene	To warm fat	3.80 mg/lb	—	—	—	3.71[2](98)	—
Spaghetti sauce	Metal can	Canthaxanthin (beadlets)	To tomato paste	9.2 mg/kg	9.1	—	—	9.3(100)	—
				18.1 mg/kg	17.7	—	—	18.1	18.1[6](100)
Tomato soup	Metal can	Canthaxanthin (beadlets)	To the soup	6.1 mg/kg	5.5	—	—	5.7(93)	—
Whole yolk, dry	Film	β-Carotene (beadlets)	In liquid yolk	5.5 mg/100 gm	5.0	—	4.7	4.7(85)	—
Whole yolk, dry	Film	β-Carotene (suspension)	In liquid yolk	7.7 mg/100 gm	7.5	—	7.5	6.8(88)	—
Whole yolk, dry	Film	β-Carotene (emulsion)	In liquid yolk	14.1 mg/100 gm	12.8	—	12.1	11.3(80)	—
Whole yolk, frozen	Sealed containers	β-Carotene (beadlets)	In liquid yolk prior to freezing	16.9 mg/100 gm	—	16.5[7]	—	—	15.0[7](89)

[1] Values in parentheses are percentages of retention during storage.
[2] Storage temperature 40° F.
[3] Storage period 24 months.
[4] Storage period 9 months.
[5] Storage period 18 months.
[6] Storage period 14 months.
[7] Storage temperature –5° F.

β-Carotene imparts a color to beverages that simulates natural orange juice whereas β-apo-8'-carotenal, and especially combinations of the latter with β-carotene, give a deeper reddish-orange. β-apo-8'-carotenal gives the deep "artificial" type orange color often desired by carbonated and artificial orange-drink manufacturers. Ascorbic acid has a stabilizing effect on β-carotene and β-apo-8'-carotenal in these beverages contrasted to the instability of FD&C colors which show fading in the presence of ascorbic acid in light.

While the above carotenoids have been primarily discussed as individual additives to food, their utility is considerably broadened in providing a range of hue when they are used in combination with other carotenoids or with other acceptable food colorants such as the FD&C colors, the flavanoids, or natural color concentrates.

β-Carotene, β-apo-8'-carotenal and canthaxanthin are accepted FDA color additives for use in or on foods and are exempted from certification. The quantity of β-apo-8'-carotenal may not exceed 15 mg per lb of solid or semisolid food or per pint of liquid food. Canthaxanthin is also an accepted color additive in the United States and quantities may not exceed 30 mg per lb of solid or semisolid food or per pint of liquid food.

The Joint FAO/WHO Expert Committee on Food Additives, based on the chronic toxicity data and specifications available, has classified β-carotene, β-apo-8'-carotenal, β-apo-8'-carotenoic acid ethyl ester and canthaxanthin in class A, a class found acceptable for use in foods. Only three other coloring agents are in this class. As of 1970, 50 countries permit β-carotene for the coloration of foods, 36 countries permit β-apo-8'-carotenal, 23 countries permit ethyl ester of β-apo-carotenoic acid and 36 countries permit canthaxanthin, thus illustrating the growing world-wide approval of carotenoids as food colors. The contribution of carotenoids produced by the chemical industry and their value as *direct* food colorants, added to processed and fabricated foods, and their *indirect* role, as ingredients of poultry, fish and dairy products, demonstrate the extension of nature's coloring theme.

J. C. BAUERNFEIND

References

BAUERNFEIND, J. C. 1972. Carotenoid vitamin A precursors and analogs in foods and feed. J. Agr. Food Chem. *20*, 456–473.

BAUERNFEIND, J. C. 1973. Direct and indirect coloring with carotenoid food colors. IFT World Directory and Guide, 96–109.

BAUERNFEIND, J. C. 1974. Carotenoid Technology. Academic Press, New York.

BORENSTEIN, B., and BUNNELL, R. H. 1967. Carotenoids, properties, occurrences and utilization. *In* Advances in Food Research, Vol. 15, 195–276. Academic Press, New York.

BUNNELL, R. H., and BAUERNFEIND, J. C. 1962. Chemistry, uses and properties of carotenoids in foods. Food Technol. *16*, 36–38, 40, 42–43.

GOODWIN, T. W. 1954. Carotenoids, Their Comparative Biochemistry. Chemical Publishing Co., New York.

ISLER, O. 1971. Carotenoids. Birkhäuser Verlag Basel, Switzerland.

ISLER, O., RÜEGG, R., and SCHWIETER, U. 1967. Carotenoids as food colorants. Pure Appl. Chem. *14*, 245–263.

KLAÜI, H. M. 1963. Carotene and carotenoids. Wiss. Veröffentl. Deut. Ges. Ernährung *9*, 390–400.

KLAÜI, H. M. 1971. Carotenoids in Foods. Proc. Agr. Chem. Inst., Federal Technischen Hochschule in collaboration with Swiss Soc. Food. Sci. Technol., Sept. 30, Zürich, Switzerland.

MARUSICH, W. L., and BAUERNFEIND, J. C. 1970. Oxycarotenoids in poultry pigmentation. Poultry Sci. *49*, 1555–1579.

McCANCE, R. A., and WIDDOWSON, E. M. 1960. The composition of foods. Med. Res. Council (England) Spec. Rept. Ser. *297*.

WATT, B. K., and MERRILL, A. L. 1963. Composition of Foods. USDA Agr. Res. Serv. Agr. Handbook *8*.

Cross-reference: *Xanthophyll.*

CARROTS

Carrots (*Daucus carota*) are a biennial native to the Middle East. The carrot on the markets today was developed by a seed company in France early in the last century. Over the years it has become a popular vegetable, almost a million tons of the fresh product being consumed in the United States alone each year.

Carrots are grown in many parts of the nation but the principal production is in the states of California, Texas, Michigan, and Wisconsin. The varieties most commonly grown are Chantenay and Imperator. These varieties are well suited to preservation by the major methods—canning, dehydration, and freezing. For the canning operation the procedure follows the general line used for vegetables: washing (usually spray washing), blanching, peeling (using the mechanical potato peeler or steam pressure), filling, brining, and exhausting. All preservation processes yield a product of good quality.

Crop production is a mechanized operation in the major growing areas. Precision seeders are used for planting the crop, weeding is achieved by chemicals, and harvesting is accomplished by mechanical harvesters.

Carrots are rich in carotene, which is converted into vitamin A in the body. It is evident that the discovery of this fact had much to do with the accelerated demand for this product after 1923, the year when the role of carotene was defined.

MARTIN S. PETERSON

CASEIN AND CASEINATES

Casein

Casein in some form is doubtless one of man's oldest manufactured products. It is the major protein fraction of cow milk and along with other milk components has been one of man's most nutritious foods for thousands of years in the form of cheese. The housewife is most familiar with the product in its purest dairy food form, not as casein, but as "low fat" cottage cheese.

Casein comprises approximately 3% by weight of whole milk as shown by the following analysis of whole milk:

	%
Water	87.0
Milk sugar (lactose)	4.9
Fat	3.8
Casein	3.0
Albumin	0.6
Ash	0.7
Total	100.0

In its commercial form, casein is isolated from the skim fraction of cow milk by any one of several methods. Although in appearance it is a homogenous material, casein is composed of at least four different fractions designated alpha, beta, gamma, and kappa and is one of the few proteins containing both sulfur and phosphorous. Casein in its natural form in milk helps to provide stability to the colloidal milk system in the form of calcium caseinate and probably calcium phosphocaseinate.

Recovery of casein by coagulation involves counteraction of one or more of the factors responsible for its stability.

In commercial practice this can be accomplished by the use of mineral acids such as muriatic (hydrochloric) or sulfuric acids, by lactic acid precipitation, and by the use of rennet. Desired properties of the finished product help determine the precipitating agent.

When acids are used precipitation occurs at pH 4.5–4.7 and this is referred to as the isoelectric point of casein.

Originally, all casein was produced by the vat or batch method whether produced from self-soured milk (lactic acid) or mineral acid use.

Later, however, continuous methods were devised. Among the first and most successful of these was the continuous method embodied in a U.S. Patent issued to Chappel (1932). This method is described in detail by Kastens and Baldauski (1952). The most improved lactic casein process can best be described as a very large cottage cheese operation to which was added final pH adjustment to 4.6 with lactic or hydrochloric acid or sodium hydroxide as required, heating to 130°F to set the curd, separation from the whey, washing with warm water to remove salts and acid, separating again from the wash water, dewatering, drying, and sizing.

Rennet casein is produced by the enzyme action of the rennet on the milk casein and this product is subjected to the same separation, washing, drying, and sizing steps as used in the acid casein production.

Almost all casein produced until the late 1940's was for industrial applications such as glue and paper coating.

However, with improved processing equipment, sanitation, research, and imagination this changed. Now edible casein and caseinates have become important products. Today, an estimated 60–70% of the casein produced is for edible use in the form of casein or caseinates.

Casein is comparable in food value to the protein in meat and superior to vegetable proteins because of the better balance of its essential amino acids. A typical analysis for food grade casein is shown below:

Physical
  Color: light cream
  Odor: essentially none
  Water: 8–12%
  Particle size: coarse granular, 30 mesh
                 fine granular, 80 mesh
  Sediment and extraneous matter:
    ADMI Standards
Chemical
  Protein (N × 6.38): 83–84% (as is)
                      95–96% (dry basis)
  Total ash (phosphorus fixed): 2.1%
  Reducing substance (as lactose) 0.1–0.2%
  Ether extractives: 1.5%
  Acidity (as lactic acid): 0.1%
Microbiological
  Standard Plate Count: 6000/gm
  Coliform: negative
  Salmonella: negative

Amino Acid Composition	Gm/100 gm Protein
Glycine	2.7
Alanine	3.0

Valine	7.2
Leucine	9.2
Isoleucine	6.1
Proline	11.3
Phenylalanine	5.0
Cystine	0.34
Methionine	2.8
Tryptophan	1.2
Arginine	4.1
Histidine	3.1
Lysine	8.2
Aspartic acid	7.1
Glutamic acid	22.4
Serine	6.3
Threonine	4.9
Tyrosine	6.3
Amide N	1.6

The use of edible casein, per se, is almost entirely nutritional. The fine mesh form (80 mesh) has been used successfully in fortifying bread and cereals.

Casein supplementation of wheat flour for bread at levels above 3% gives a coarse texture. A 1.1% supplementation gives the same protein and nutritional improvement to white bread as 3% supplementation with nonfat dry milk and creates no problems with either batch or continuous mix breads as shown below:

	Bread Protein %	PER (protein efficiency ratio)	Improvement %
Water bread	7.8	0.7–0.8	
3% nonfat dry milk supplementation	8.3	1.0–1.1	40
1.1% casein or sodium caseinate	8.3	1.0–1.1	40

Caseinates

Because of its amphoteric properties casein reacts with acids or bases to form salts which dissociate in aqueous solutions.

Casein solublized with alkalies is known as caseinate. The two most widely used forms are sodium and calcium caseinate. These products are very useful because they are capable of providing both nutritional and functional roles in their use.

Water solutions of caseinates, 15–18% solids, with a pH of 6.6–7.2, are usually spray dried but they can also be roll dried.

The caseinates are used nutritionally to fortify and give texture to breakfast foods, breads, infant foods, and high protein diets. Functional as well nutritional uses include usage in nondairy coffee creamers, nondairy whip toppings, confections, icings, firming the consistency of yogurt, and many other applications where smoothness and texture improvement are desired.

Sodium caseinate has been approved for use in imitation meat loaves, stews, and soups by the Meat Inspection Division of USDA. Certain states allow its use as a binder and emulsifier in comminuted meats, such as frankfurters, bolognas, and liverwurst. Caseinate, used at 1–3% level, prevents fat capping, shrinkage, and enhances the taste appeal of the product by promoting the retention of natural juices to provide a firm but succulent produce when cooked. In addition, it provides an additional quantity of protein of a quality equal to the meat itself.

In the years ahead it is believed that the superior nutritional and functional properties of casein and the caseinates will channel more and more of the world production into the edible market with industrial uses finding substitutes wherever possible.

The major casein-producing countries at present are New Zealand and Australia with smaller amounts being manufactured in Canada, Argentina, France, Germany, and Holland. Total estimated production is 200–250 million pounds per year.

PIERCE M. REED

References

CHAPPELL, F. L. 1932. Drying and curing casein curd. U.S. Pat. 1,892,233, Dec. 27.
GORDON, W. G., SEMMETT, W. F., CABLE, R. S., and MORRIS, M. 1949. Amino acid composition of α-casein and β-casein. J. Am. Chem. Soc. 71, 3293.
KARSTENS, K. A., and BALDAUSKI, F. A. 1952. Chemicals from milk. Ind. Eng. Chem. 44, 1257.

Cross-reference: *Cheese.*

CAVIAR

Caviar, or caviare, an alternate spelling, goes back originally to the Turkish word, khāvyār. This suggests that the Turks may have originated the delicacy. At any rate, the fish from which caviar comes are caught in the rivers that flow into the Caspian, which as the map shows, is a sea not far from the borders of Turkey.

During the Middle Ages and later there appears to have been considerable trade in fish between Russia and several other nations of Europe, notably, England, The Netherlands, France, and Italy. In 1588, Giles Fletcher, ambassador from Queen Elizabeth to the Court of the Russian Emperor, Theodor, noted that a great quantity of "cavery" was bought, presumably at Astrakhan at the mouth of the Volga, and shipped to Spain and Italy by French and Dutch merchants. Hamlet's phrase " 'twas caviare to the general" suggests that it was known in England at an early date.

Caviar may be described as the roe of various species of sturgeon. It is prepared by a process that combines maturation and salting. When properly controlled the process can produce exquisite flavors, the best being that obtained from the Beluga variety of sturgeon. Sevruga and Ostetrova are next in favor but other members of the *Acipensserides* (sturgeon) family furnish roe which though smaller, are of excellent quality. Caviar looks like a mass of small pellets and is black or grey in color. The roe of salmon, specifically from salmon caught in Siberia and Canada, is also made into caviar. Less expensive than caviar derived from sturgeon, it is also less flavorful. Caviar keeps well in cans but deteriorates rather rapidly if left to stand.

The composition of sturgeon caviar is of interest: (per 100 gm of the edible portion) 57 gm, water; 26.9 gm, protein; 15 gm, fat; 30 mg, calcium; 300 mg, phosphorus; 0.7 mg, iron. Caviar has no carbohydrates and no vitamins; these are 70 cal per oz.

MARTIN S. PETERSON

Cross-references: *Gourmet Foods; Nationality Foods.*

CENTRIFUGAL FORCE

Centrifuges are of two basic types; namely, screening and sedimentation. In each case centrifugal force is used to accelerate the natural force of gravity. In screening centrifuges the centrifugal force increases the drainage rate through the screen and produces a drier product than is possible under normal gravity. In sedimentation centrifuges the centrifugal force increases the sedimentation rate thereby greatly reducing the holding time or size vessel required for a given separator.

Centrifuge design can take many different forms. The basic concept is a bowl or rotating device which is enclosed in a frame and mounted on a spindle and/or bearings. The spindle is driven by gears or belts affixed to a motor.

The bowl does the work and can take many different forms depending on the product to be processed. A list of the major types and some of their characteristics follow:

Centrifuge Designs

Pusher—Particularly suited for crystalline or fibrous solids, drying to a low as 1%. Models to 75 tons per hr.

Peeler—Batch type. Good for fine, difficult-to-dry particles. Can have either solid or filter-type basket. Well suited for abrasive solids.

Basket—Batch type. Models may be either manual or automatic. Available with perforate and imperforate bowls. Similar to Peeler.

Decanter—Extremely versatile design that can handle a broad range of particle sizes and solids content.

Solids-discharging—Nozzles continuously discharge solids as a concentrated slurry.

Solids-ejecting—The bowl stores solids while separating and automatically ejects them at predetermined intervals.

Solids-retaining—Best suited for liquid/liquid applications or for feeds with a low solids content.

The factors that determine the selection of a centrifuge to process a specific food product are: (1) The temperature to which the product can be heated without degradation. (2) The amount of the solids in the feed. (3) The density of the products to be separated. (4) The size and size distribution of the particles to be separated. (5) The efficiency of separation desired. (6) The capacity, lb per hour, desired.

In applying centrifugal separators to a new food product or process, even if all of the foregoing information is available, it is desirable to run a "bench test" with a small laboratory centrifuge to prove feasibility. This can be done in the processor's plant.

Specific Applications

Centrifugal separation and clarification has been applied to food products ever since the centrifugal separator was invented by De Laval nearly 100 yr ago. Designed originally as a farm cream separator, separating butterfat from skim milk the original design has been modified to meet other product requirements and increased in size to meet capacity requirements.

Thus, it is impossible, in the space allocated, to list all such applications to food processing. Listed below are some of the most common and a few of the unusual applications.

Milk and Whey.—Milkfat is separated from skim milk at capacities up to 55,000 lb per hr feed with an efficiency of 0.01 of 1% and at a temperature of 110°F; or separated cold at 40°F with a capacity up to 20,000 lb per hr.

Cheese whey is separated at capacities up to 60,000 lb per hr with efficiency of 0.01 of 1%. Either a solids-ejecting or a solids-retaining separator may be used.

Milk Albumin.—Cheese whey contains approximately 0.9 to 1.0% protein. This can be recovered by a centrifuge of the solids-ejecting type after heat and acid treatment of the whey. The protein discharge is in slurry form with approximately 20% dry solids.

Clarification of Liquid Eggs.—De Laval Air Tight clarifiers are used to continuously remove egg shell dust and shell fragments, chalaze, and protein strands and fibers from liquid eggs. This not only improves the quality and appearance of the product but also permits more effective spray drying of egg products as this material, unless removed, tends to plug spray nozzles.

Vegetable Oil.—Crude vegetable oils containing between 0.8 and 10% impurities in the form of fatty acids, phosphatides, and color bodies, are pretreated with heat and caustic prior to centrifugation. The impurities form a viscous soup-like mass which is separated from the oil in specially-designed, hermetically sealed, solids-retaining centrifuges at capacities up to 35,000 lb per hr.

Starch Processing.—In starch processing, a large number of centrifuges are being used. They replace the old-fashioned settling systems. Centrifugals speed up the process and increase separating efficiencies for higher plant yield; also, sanitation is greatly improved, which is a main consideration for a good processing plant.

Typical application is the selective separation between the starch and protein fractions. The protein fraction consisting mainly of protein combined with fine starch or fine fibers is referred to as gluten, and is insoluble.

The starch fraction is further concentrated by washing and dewatering with a variety of different types of centrifuges. The gluten fraction is also concentrated and dewatered, utilizing centrifugal separators.

Processing streams for corn and wheat starches have similar characteristics, but differ enough to require different processing techniques.

Potato or manioc starch processes are more similar to each other, but differ greatly from the first two in that the protein fraction is all soluble in water. The type of starch plants depends very much on economic conditions in different countries.

Prevalent is the processing of cornstarch in the United States, potato starch in Europe, wheat starch in Australia, and manioc or tapioca starch in the far eastern countries.

Yeast Manufacturing.—Centrifuges have been used for many years in the recovery of yeast cultures from fermenters. Typical are baker's yeast, grown on molasses; Torula yeast, also grown on molasses; or spent sulfate liquor from paper mills.

In pharmaceutical fermentation, centrifuges are used extensively. The main reason is faster processing to maintain product quality, higher yields, and more sanitary operations. In pharmaceutical application, sterilization of the equipment before separation is not an unusual requirement.

Fruit Juice Processing.—In fruit juices and wines, centrifuges are used in various stages of the process. In these fields, the application is dependent on the preference of the local processor. A more general use is the application in the citrus industry for pulp control and for the recovery of peel oil or essential oils from the peels.

New Vegetable Protein Sources.—Centrifuges, having the inherent advantage of fast, efficient separation under good sanitary conditions, are now being used commercially in extracting high grade protein from vegetable sources, such as soy bean and cottonseed.

Breweries.—In the United States, breweries are beginning to adopt centrifugal separators. Centrifugals have been used extensively in breweries in Europe and Japan. However, capacity requirements in those countries are considerably smaller than in the United States. It was not until the introduction of the larger size centrifuges in the mid-1960's that U.S. breweries became interested in this type of equipment. Typical uses are continuous mashing, clarification of wort heels to establish higher wort recovery, separation of freshly fermented beer after the fermenter to increase beer yield, and preclarification of beer before polishing to reduce load on filters. Centrifuges, because of their compact and sanitary design, will enhance any brewery operation in existing, expanding, or new breweries.

Meat Plants.—Any successful modern meat packing company must recover by-products efficiently in order to be profitable.

Here, again, centrifuges have been used extensively to recover and up-grade fats, to recover edible meat protein fractions, and to recover valuable blood solids in an efficient way.

Simple protein fractions are subject to spoilage, under time and temperature influences. Centrifugal recovery processes have been developed to meet this requirement; thereby, in many cases, up-grading the various fractions as compared to the usual practices prevalent during the past 50 yr. The meat industry is also a high labor industry, and centrifugal processes are designed to save labor. Equipment is of all stainless steel and with CIP (cleaning in place) capabilities to meet sanitary requirements and to reduce labor.

Centrifuging Cheese Curd.—In the application of centrifuges for cheese curd, two types of centrifuges are employed. For the harvesting of fines from the whey as it is drawn from the vat, a high speed centrifuge with a desludging self-opening bowl is used. For actual harvesting of cheese curd, the conveyor type centrifuge is used. In the latter case, curd is made in the vat, and both curd and whey are pumped into a horizontal bowl. The whey is discharged from the large diameter end of bowl and the curd conveyed thru the bowl by the scroll discharging it from the small diameter end.

Lactose Crystals.—In the application of centrifugation to harvesting lactose crystals, two types of centrifuges can be employed. One is the basket centrifuge and the other is the conveyor type centrifuge. The basket type is operated in batch. As the basket spins the lactose-carrying solution is fed into the basket at a predetermined volume. This spins for a given number of minutes, followed by a rinse of a given number of minutes, followed by emptying the lactose crystal cake out of the basket. The cycle then starts over with each cycle consuming approximately 8 min.

The process using the conveyor centrifuge is continuous. The centrifuge is of horizontal bowl design with the bowl of conical shape. It is hollow with a scroll traveling in the same direction of rotation but at a slightly lower rpm. The lactose crystals solution is fed into the end of the bowl and effluent is discharged through ports in the larger diameter of the bowl and crystals conveyed to the opposite end of the bowl by the scroll and discharged at the smaller diameter. Crystals can also be washed while passing through the bowl.

Separation of Chicken Broth.—Fat, insoluble solids, and soluble solids are present in water in which chicken has been cooked. This solution with fat and solids is known as broth. Fat is separated from the mixture and discharged; insoluble solids are collected in the periphery of the bowl and discharged on command. Soluble solids are retained in the liquid. The separator used is of solids-ejecting design.

Dewatering Leafy Vegetables.—Some leafy vegetables require washing prior to packaging. This is especially true of spinach which carries sand in the stem area. A basket type centrifuge is used to centrifugally remove the water after washing.

Separation of Fresh Cider.—Fresh cider, before enzyme treatment, is subjected to centrifugal force in a solids-ejecting centrifuge to which nozzles have been added in the periphery of the bowl. Insoluble solids, bacteria, yeast, and mold are continuously discharged from the nozzles with periodic opening of the bowl to discharge excessive solids. The solids-ejecting bowl also lends itself to sanitizing procedures.

G. A. HOURAN

CHEESE

Cheese is a food manufactured from milk. Its early history of development is not known but according to ancient records, cheese has been used as a food for over 4000 yr. It was made during Biblical times and it is believed that the knowledge of cheese making was brought originally from Asia to Europe and was introduced into many parts of Europe when the Roman Empire flourished. During the Middle Ages, important contributions to cheese manufacture were made by monks in the monasteries and mention of cheese is made in the monastery records.

Until about the middle of the 19th Century, cheese was a farm industry wherein cheese was made from the surplus milk produced on the farm. The first cheese factory in the United States was built by Jesse Williams near Rome, N.Y. in 1851.

It is difficult to classify or group cheeses into meaningful categories. In the broadest classification, cheese can be grouped as natural cheese or as process cheese. The cheese made directly from milk is classified as natural cheese and a limited number are also made from whey and combinations of whey and milk. Process cheeses are made by blending and heating one or more varieties of natural cheeses. Process cheeses are further grouped or subdivided into pasteurized process cheese, cheese food, and cheese spread. In these products certain other ingredients may be added. The composition of natural and process cheeses and most cheese-based products is specified in the "Definitions and Standards of Identity" under the Federal Food, Drug and Cosmetic Act of the U.S. Department of Health, Education, and Welfare. These Federal Definitions and Standards of Identity specify the ingredients that may be used, in some instances the processes that must be followed, and the composition of the product with respect to the maximum moisture content and the minimum percentage of fat in the solids. The Regulations also prescribe that, if the milk from which the cheese is made is not pasteurized, the cheese must be cured at a temperature of not less than 35°F for not less than 60 days.

There are several hundred known varieties of cheese. The USDA Handbook 54 contains the description of more than 400 cheeses. Many of these are named after the town, community, or region where they are made and, though known by different names, many of them have very similar characteristics. On the other hand, several different cheeses have the same name. The publication has over 800 names indexed.

Manufacture

The basic processes involved in the manufacture of most cheeses are quite similar. Milk, either raw, heated, hydrogen peroxide treated (where permitted), or pasteurized is placed in a suitable vessel or vat holding up to about 35,000 lb of milk. The temperature of the milk is adjusted to a temperature generally in the range of 86°–96°F and suitable starter culture or cultures are added. These cultures generally consist of lactic acid-producing streptococci or lactobacilli, and for cheeses such as Blue cheese and Swiss cheese additional cultures are used to contribute specific characteristics.

Cheese color may be added to the milk to impart additional color to the cheese or to maintain color uniformity throughout the year. Annatto, an extract from annatto seed, is added at a rate of from $\frac{1}{2}$ to 3 oz per 1000 lb of milk depending upon the demand of the market and the season of the year. In some cheeses where it is desirable to have a white product, it is permissible to remove the natural color contributed by the milk by a bleaching process. Bleaching can be effected by the use of benzoyl peroxide or by masking the natural color by the addition of substances such as chlorophyll or a blue color.

When the proper amount of acidity has been developed in the milk by the starters, rennet is added. This period of time of culturing is commonly referred to as ripening and may range from 0 to several hours, but is usually from 15 to 90 min. Sufficient rennet extract to coagulate the milk in the desired time is diluted approximately 20 times its volume in cold water and added to the milk. After the rennet has been added and thoroughly distributed, the milk is left in a quiescent state until it coagulates. After 20–30 min, the curd is normally ready to be cut. The coagulated milk is cut into cubes ranging in size from $\frac{1}{4}$ to $\frac{1}{2}$ in. The curd knives used to cut the coagulum consist of metal frames across which are stretched parallel stainless steel wires that are spaced to give the desired sized cubes of curd. One of the knives has the cutting wires in a horizontal position and the other in a vertical position. In some of the newer mechanized installations, cutting of the curd is accomplished mechanically by knives attached to the stirring mechanism of the vat. The end result by either method is the same and facilitates the removal of whey from the curd. After the curd has been cut, free whey appears between the cubes of curd and a slight film or skin forms on the outer surface of the cubes. At this stage of curd making, conditions are designed to control the expulsion of whey and to develop a uniform firmness in the cubes. The rate and degree of whey expulsion is controlled by the rate of acid development, by the temperature to which the curd and whey are heated or "cooked," and the time of exposure.

About 5–10 min after the curd is cut, slow agitation or stirring is started. The speed of agitation is gradually increased so that the curd particles do not mat together. Agitation, however, should not be so vigorous that the curd particles are shattered. Depending upon the type of cheese being made, the curd is subjected to heating or "cooking." The heating is generally started within 15 min after the curd is cut by applying steam in the jacket of the vat. The temperature to which the curd is heated depends upon the type of cheese being made and upon the types of cultures used.

As a general rule, the high moisture, soft type cheeses receive a relatively mild heat treatment while some other cheeses such as Swiss cheese may be heated to temperatures approaching 130°F. Cheddar cheese is heated to temperatures ranging from about 100° to 106°F and in some instances as high as 110°F. After the desired temperature has been reached, it is maintained until the curd is removed from the whey.

Up to this stage of curd making, the basic procedures of manufacture are quite similar for most varieties of cheese. There are variations in the degree and manner in which the various steps are accomplished all of which prepare the curd for subsequent steps in the manufacture of the particular type of cheese being made.

Cheddar Cheese

In the manufacture of Cheddar cheese these general basic steps of cheese making are followed until heating the curd or "cooking" is completed. The curd is cooked to a temperature of about 98°–106°F and held at that temperature until the required amount of acid has been developed and the curd has acquired the desired degree of firmness. The moisture content of the finished cheese is largely controlled during this phase of manufacture.

At this point in the manufacture of Cheddar cheese, the curd is allowed to settle to the bottom of the vat and is pushed back and towards the sides of the vat to permit whey drainage down the center of the vat. The curd particles at this stage readily mat together into a solid slab. This is the beginning of the "cheddaring" operation which is a distinguishing feature of Cheddar cheese manufacture. The slab of curd formed on each side of the vat is cut into smaller slabs for ease of handling. The slabs of curd are turned several times and stacked to compress and flatten them. During the cheddaring, the curds acquire a fibrous texture and the acidity develops rapidly, increasing to a titratable acidity of the whey of from 0.4 to 0.6% or higher. When the cheddaring process is completed the slabs of curd are put through a curd mill which cuts the curd into pieces of approximately $\frac{1}{2} \times \frac{1}{2} \times 1$ in.

Salt is added to the milled curd to give a salt content in the finished cheese of from about 1.5 to 2.0%. After the salt has been thoroughly incorporated, the curd is placed into forms or cheese hoops lined with cloth and the filled hoops are placed in a press. In the press, the curd forms a solid mass of a size and shape conforming to the hoop used. The pressing is normally of 15–20 hr duration and the cheese is generally removed from the hoops on the day following manufacture. The hoops may be cylindrical forms such as represented by longhorns, daisies, flats, twins, midgets, cheddars, and barrels or rectangular such as the 40- and 60-lb blocks. Cheeses that are to be paraffined or waxed, such as the round styles (longhorns, Cheddars, etc.) are dried and given a wax coating by submerging the cheese completely in a wax bath maintained at 220°–250°F for about 5 sec. After waxing, the cheese is placed in boxes for storage and curing. Cheeses made into the rectangular shapes or block form are not generally dried but instead are taken from the hoops and immediately wrapped in a flexible wrapper that is coated on the inside with a material that forms a seal. In this method, no rind is formed on the cheese and there is a minimum waste during storage and curing.

Uncured Cheddar cheese has a mild acid taste and aroma and no real cheese flavor. The body is quite firm, elastic, and somewhat tough and rubbery; and though it is eaten and enjoyed by some people in this form, most Cheddar cheese is given some degree of ripening before it is consumed. Cheddar cheese is generally cured at temperatures between 35° and 55°F and the length of the period of ripening largely determines the degree of flavor level that develops. Sharp flavors may require 9–12 months or more to develop. Cheddar cheese is considered to be cured for commercial purposes when it possesses the consistency and flavor desired by the trade or consumer and this has resulted in the selling of cheeses of all ages, flavors, and consistencies. If the cheese is sold at less than 60 days age, it must have been made from pasteurized milk.

The agents responsible for the changes that occur in the cheese during ripening include the enzymes and the microorganisms originating in the milk, starter, and rennet. The chemical and bacteriological changes that take place and their relationship to curing are not very well understood. The rate of ripening of cheese is influenced by several factors among which the most important are temperature, the pH, salt content, water content, and season of the year as it effects the composition of the milk.

The components of cheese that are chiefly affected during curing are fat, protein, and lactose.

Most of the lactose is removed with the whey fraction and the amount retained in the curd is largely fermented into lactic acid during the manufacture of the curd and during the early stages of ripening. Casein is the principal protein in cheese. The water-soluble proteins, albumins, and globulins are normally not coagulated in cheese making and are largely removed in the whey. During ripening, the protein fraction is subjected to the action of microorganisms and enzymes and is partially hydrolyzed. The extent of the protein breakdown and the resulting compounds formed influence the characteristics and quality of the cheese. Cheddar cheese undergoes relatively slight hydrolysis of the proteins in comparison to some of the soft varieties and generally less than $1/3$ of the protein is made soluble. Some of the products resulting from the protein degradation have been associated with desirable cheese flavors while other contribute to flavor defects.

The fat content of Cheddar cheese is specified by Federal Standards, requiring 50% butterfat in the solids or a minimum of 30.5% fat in the cheese. The fat portion of Cheddar cheese undergoes only slight change during ripening but contributes significantly to the flavor. The fat in cheese remains in a finely divided state, is easily digested and much of the satiety value of cheese is attributed to the fat content. Excessive breakdown of the fat may produce rancid and oxidized flavors. The cholesterol content of Cheddar cheese varies with the fat content and will normally be approximately 28 mg per oz of cheese.

Other Cheddar Type Cheeses.—In addition to Cheddar cheese, the family of cheeses usually included in the Cheddar family include Stirred or Granular Curd, Colby, Washed Curd, and Monterey Jack. All of these are sometimes referred to as American cheeses.

Granular or Stirred Curd is made similarly to Cheddar except that the curd particles are stirred and not permitted to mat together after the whey is removed. The resulting cheese has more open texture than Cheddar cheese.

Colby cheese is similar to Granular or Stirred Curd cheese except that the drained curd is washed with cool water. The resulting cheese has a slightly softer body, open texture, and a mild flavor as compared to Cheddar cheese.

Washed Curd cheese is similar in all respects in manufacture to Cheddar cheese except the milled curd is washed or soaked in water. The resulting cheese has a slightly higher moisture content and a more bland flavor than Cheddar.

Monterey Jack or Monterey cheese was developed by monks in Southern California. This white cheese is similar to Colby although it has a higher moisture, softer consistency, and a more open texture.

Swiss Cheese

Next to Cheddar, Swiss cheese is the most popular single variety of cheese in the United States. In Switzerland, Swiss cheese is called Emmentaler which is also an alternate name in the United States. This type of cheese was first made in the Canton of Bern in the Emmental valley from which its native name of Emmentaler originated. The most distinguishing characteristic of this cheese is the eye formation or holes that develop throughout the cheese as it ripens. In its manufacture, three different bacterial cultures are usually used as starters. These are *Streptococcus thermophilus*, *Lactobacillus bulgaricus* or *L. lactis*, and *Propionibacterium shermanii*. The thermophilus and bulgaricus cultures are primarily the lactic acid-producing starters and probably also contribute to flavor and breakdown of the curd during ripening. The propionic acid bacteria are largely responsible for the typical Swiss flavor and for the eye formation. Traditionally, Swiss cheese was made in the form of wheels weighing from about 175 to 250 lb. Milk for Swiss is normally clarified and standardized to contain sufficient butterfat to produce a cheese containing not less than 43% of milkfat in its solids.

Swiss cheese differs from the basic processes described for the Cheddar varieties in that different cultures are used and the curd-whey mixture is cooked to a higher temperature in the range of 125°-130°F. When the curd has firmed sufficiently, it is removed from the whey and pressed into its final form. After pressing, the cheese is salted in a brine solution. If it is made into the wheel form, the cheese is brined for 2-3 days after which it is placed on shelves in a cold room for 1 week or 10 days during which time it is washed, turned, and sprinkled with dry salt daily. If it is made into block form, it is taken from the brine, dried, and wrapped in a suitable flexible film and placed in the cold room. After the cold room treatment, the cheese is transferred to a warm room at 65°-75°F and held until the desired degree of eye formation develops, usually requiring 3-6 weeks, after which the cheese is returned to the cold room for further curing.

Cheeses similar to Swiss cheese are made in many countries. Local names for these cheeses include Allguar Emmentaler, Bellunese, Formaggio Dolce, Fontina, Fontine d' Aosta, Traanen, Gruyere, and Samso. These cheeses have the general basic characteristics of Swiss with respect to eyes, flavor, and body but may differ in size, size of eyes and some such as Gruyere are cured under conditons which permit some degree of surface ripening and the development of a somewhat sharper flavor.

Blue Cheese

Blue cheese is characterized by the distribution of a blue-green mold throughout the cheese which results in a sharp, piquant flavor. Blue cheese is made from cow milk which may be pasteurized, or homogenized and may be bleached with benzoyl peroxide. A lactic starter is used to ripen the milk and the milk is coagulated with rennet similar to the procedure used for Cheddar except that spores of the mold *Penicillium roquefortii* are added either to the milk or to the curd before hooping.

When the curd is sufficiently firm, the whey is drained off and the curd is placed into perforated metal hoops that are about 7½ in. in diameter and 6 in. deep. The hoops are turned frequently and after 18-24 hr, the cheese is removed from the hoops and salted either by submersion in a brine solution or by dry salting to obtain a salt content in the cheese of about 3.5-4.5%. After salting, the cheese is punctured with 50 or more holes to admit air thereby permitting mold development throughout the interior of the cheese. The cheese is then placed on its edge in a curing room maintained at 48°-50°F with high humidity. A satisfactory mold development is obtained in 3-4 weeks after which the cheese is cleaned and wrapped either in foil or other suitable plastic film and stored at 40°F or lower for 2-6 months or longer depending upon sharpness of flavor desired. Some manufacturers prefer to wax or paraffin the cheese before puncturing to reduce drying during the molding period.

Other blue-veined cheeses include Gorgonzola made in Italy, Stilton from England, Danablu from Denmark and Roquefort from France. Roquefort is made from ewe's milk in southeastern France and is cured in the caves in the same area. A French regulation limits the use of the name Roquefort to cheese made in the Roquefort area from ewe's milk.

Parmesan Cheese

Parmesan is a member of the family of "hard grating" type cheeses which were originally developed in Italy in the vicinity of Parma and is closely related to a group of cheeses differing in size, shape, composition, and to some extent, in the method of manufacture. These cheeses are characterized by the hard brittle body which make them suitable for grating.

In the United States, Parmesan is made from partially skimmed milk by much the same basic procedures used for Swiss cheese including the use of *Streptococcus thermophilus* and *Lactobacillus bulgaricus* or *L. lactis* as starters. The curd is normally cooked to 115°-125°F and when the curd is properly firmed, it is placed into cloth lined metal hoops and pressed. After pressing, the cheese is salted either in brine or by dry salting. The period of salting will vary depending upon the size of the cheese, but will normally be from 10 to 20 days. The cheese is cured on shelves for a minimum of 10 months during which time the cheese may be frequently cleaned and rubbed with oil. During the curing at temperatures ranging from 54° to 60°F, there is a gradual loss of moisture so that when it is fully cured, its moisture content is less than 32% and the characteristic hard brittle body has developed.

Other cheeses commonly included in this group of cheeses are Reggiano, Veneto, Parmigiano, Lodigiano, Lombardy, Emiliano, Venezza, and Bagozzo or Bresciano.

The Romano type cheeses are also closely related to the Parmesan group but have a much more sharp piquant flavor and in the United States must contain not less than 38% fat in the solids.

Surface Ripened Cheeses

Surface ripened cheeses, as the name implies, are ripened by the growth of bacterial cultures or mold cultures on the surface of the cheese. The enzymes produced by the growth of these organisms penetrate into the cheese and produce the typical characteristic flavor and texture of these cheeses. The two basic subfamilies within this large family of cheeses are determined by the type of organism used for ripening.

The best known of the mold ripened varieties are Camembert and Brie, both of which originated in France but have become popular all over the world. Among the bacterial ripened cheeses are Brick, Meunster, Limburger, Bel Paese of Italy, and Port du Salut of France. Brick and Muenster can no longer be considered true surface ripened cheeses because as presently made and handled have little or no surface ripening.

The surface ripened cheeses are generally made from pasteurized milk by a method similar to Cheddar except that the process is modified to retain more moisture in the curd which is dipped from the whey into hoops and is not pressed. The cheeses are usually brine salted but may be dry salted. After salting, the cheeses are shelf cured under suitable conditions of temperature and humidity that permit the surface growth to develop in about 2-3 weeks. After the surface growth has developed, the cheese is wrapped in paper, parchment, or Cellophane and may be covered with foil. Depending upon the type of cheese, the ripening of the cheese may be continued for several months but usually at a lower temperature than the temperature at which the surface growth was developed. The surface ripened cheeses are also generally classified as semisoft cheeses.

Provolone

Provolone is a cheese typical of the family known as Pasta Filata cheeses which, in addition to Provolone, includes Mozzarella and Scamorza. Provolone is made by a procedure basically similar to Cheddar cheese until the curd is separated from the whey. At that time, the curd is placed in either hot whey or hot water which changes it into a stringy, plastic-like mass. The hot stringy curd is then stretched and molded into the desired shape and sizes and salted by brining. The cheese may be smoked.

Another Pasta Filata type cheese is Mozzarella, a soft, plastic curd cheese originating in southern Italy. The cheese was originally made from buffalo milk. Mozzarella is made by methods similar to that used for Provolone but modified to produce a cheese containing higher moisture. It is common practice to produce the curd at one facility and, after draining off the whey, shipping the curd to a dealer who completes the manufacturing process when he is ready to market the cheese. He completes the manufacture by heating the curd in hot water and stretching and molding it into irregular spherical shapes weighing approximately $1/2$-1 lb. The cheese is eaten fresh with little or no ripening.

Scamorza is another Pasta Filata cheese, originating in Italy and is similar in characteristics to Mozzarella and is made by a similar process. Mozzarella and Scamorza are both eaten fresh and are used extensively in cooking.

Dutch Cheeses

A group of cheeses originating in Holland are sometimes referred to as Dutch cheeses. The best known and popular of these are Edam and Gouda. Both are semisoft to hard cheeses having a characteristic mild flavor that varies in intensity with age. The basic manufacturing procedure is similar to Cheddar with modifications to obtain a higher moisture content and the curd is not generally salted prior to hooping. The Edam cheese is made into round ball-shaped cheeses weighing from about $1/2-4^1/2$ lb in the United States and is covered with a red wax.

Gouda is made into the shape of a flattened sphere and may weigh from less than 1 lb to 50 lb. Most common are the smaller sizes of less than 1 lb and having the red wax coating similar to Edam.

Fresh, Uncured Cheeses

The cheeses referred to as the fresh, uncured cheeses do not follow the conventional basic manufacturing steps described for the various other cheese varieties. Coagulation of the milk is accomplished principally by the acid produced by the addition of lactic starter with or without the aid of a very small amount of rennet. As the name implies, these cheeses are not cured but are consumed fresh and have a mild acid flavor. The principal varieties in this group are Cream cheese, Neufchatel, and Cottage cheese.

Cream cheese originated in the United States and is made from a mixture of milk and cream which is pasteurized, usually homogenized, and coagulated by culturing with a lactic starter. Originally, the manufacturing process consisted of breaking up the coagulated curd by stirring until its consistency was smooth and homogenous and then draining in muslin bags. These bags permitted the whey to drain off and retained the curd. After sufficient whey had drained off, the bags of curd were piled up in the vat with alternate layers of chipped ice to complete the draining operation and to cool the curd. Draining was considered completed when the moisture level had been reduced to the desired level. Salt was mixed with the curd to obtain 0.8–1.0% of salt in the cheese prior to packaging. Presently most Cream cheese is made by a centrifugation process that separates the curd from the whey.

Neufchatel cheese is a product very similar to Cream cheese except that its fat content is lower. It is usually made by the same processes as Cream cheese.

Cottage cheese is an acid precipitated cheese made from skim milk. When the lactic acid starter has produced sufficient acid to coagulate the milk, the coagulum is cut with curd knives. The curd is cooked to a temperature ranging from $115°$ to $130°F$ after which the whey is drained off and the curd is washed and cooled with cold water. The curd is usually creamed by the addition of cream to obtain a fat content of 4.0% to improve its flavor and texture.

Other unripened cheeses are Baker's cheese, Ricotta which can be made either from whey or milk, and the whey cheeses such as the Scandi-

navian Gjetost and Primost, the latter being basically concentrated whey.

Pasteurized Process Cheese

The second broad classification of cheeses is the category known as process cheeses. Pasteurized process cheese is prepared by comminuting and mixing, with the aid of heat, one or more cheeses of the same or two or more varieties of cheese, and certain emulsifying salts. Water, seasoning, and color may be added. Cheddar cheese is the variety most commonly processed but Swiss, Limburger, Brick, and other similar varieties are also used. Process cheese has certain characteristics which make it popular. It can be attractively packaged and is less subject to spoilage and shrinkage in weight than natural cheese. To the consumer, it has a more uniform flavor, has no waste, and has excellent keeping quality.

When certain optional dairy ingredients such as cream, skim milk, whey, or their solids are added to the cheese blend and processed, the product is called a pasteurized process cheese food or a pasteurized process cheese spread. Both products may contain less fat and more moisture than process cheese as prescribed in the Federal Definitions and Standards of Identity. In addition, the pasteurized process cheese is spreadable at $70°F$.

WILLARD L. LANGHUS

Cross-references: *Casein and Caseinates; Goat Foods.*

CHEMICAL PRESERVATIVES

Most food is preserved through thermal processing, freezing, drying, fermentation, or refrigeration (above freezing). Chemical preservatives are sometimes used: (a) when the product cannot be given a suitable terminal treatment or (b) as a supplement to another method of preservation to reduce the intensity of treatment with a resultant improvement in textural, organoleptic, or other quality. Common chemical preservatives include salt, sugar, and acids which have been used since antiquity. Many others have been suggested and some are acceptable for use. As with other food additives, chemical preservatives cannot be employed in the United States unless the proposed application and level of usage are approved by FDA.

Salt (NaCl)

Small amounts of salt are commonly added to many foods directly or through brines to improve their flavor and enhance their keeping quality.

Salt thus added is in the aqueous phase of the food and hence, if the water content of the product is low, the additive may exert a preservative action way out of proportion to that expected when one considers the concentration of salt on the basis of total product. If the water content of the product is higher, then more salt must be added to achieve the same effect. Preservative activity of salt, then, is determined not by the concentration in the food but by the concentration in the water phase or the "brine concentration" which can be calculated as follows:

$$\frac{\text{grams salt}}{\text{grams salt} + \text{grams water}} \times 100$$

Salt can act in several ways to inhibit microbial growth and thus preserve the food. Perhaps most important, it reduces the amount of water available to microorganisms for growth processes. "Water activity" (a_w) is a term used to express numerically the degree to which water in foods is available to microorganisms and is applicable when salt (or other solutes) are present and serve to "dry" the food. The sodium and chloride ions, especially the latter, when present in sufficient concentration also inhibit some microorganisms, independent of changes in the a_w of the food. Furthermore, the increased osmotic pressure produced by salt causes plasmolysis of cells. Other detrimental effects of salt on microorganisms include: reduces solubility of oxygen in water, sensitizes cells to carbon dioxide, and interferes with the action of proteolytic enzymes.

The kind and number of microorganisms that salt will inhibit are largely related to the concentration of the chemical. The effectiveness of salt as a preservative can be enhanced by reducing the pH of the food and/or storing it at low refrigerator temperatures. Of the food-poisoning microorganisms, *Staphylococcus aureus* is most resistant to deleterious effects of salt and can grow at brine concentrations of 14-15% when the pH value is between 5 and 7. Except for some halophilic bacteria and yeasts that can grow in saturated (or nearly so) salt solutions, other microorganisms are generally more sensitive to salt than is *S. aureus*. It has been demonstrated that low (1-3%) NaCl enhances production of aflatoxin as well as its release by the mycelium of toxigenic aspergilli.

Sugars

Sugars such as glucose, sucrose, lactose, and others are added to some foods as sweeteners. If the concentration of such materials is high enough, as in candy, syrups, condensed milk, jellies, jams, and honey, they act as a preservative. The preservative effect of sugars results because they: (a) reduce the water activity of the food to the point where microbial growth is impossible, and (b) raise the osmotic pressure of the solution and thus cause plasmolysis of microbial cells. Although growth is impossible, some microorganisms or their spores can survive for long periods in high concentrations of sugars, especially if little or no water is present. Some microorganisms, particularly osmophilic yeasts and molds can grow on the surfaces of highly sugared foods, especially when temperature cycling results in accumulation of surface moisture which may have a lower sugar content than the product.

Nitrites and Nitrates

Nitrites (up to 200 ppm permitted in the United States) are added to curing mixtures largely to fix color in cured meats. Nitrites decompose to NO which reacts with heme pigments to form nitrosomyoglobin. Nitrates are believed to serve as a reservoir of nitrite for liberation through microbial reduction.

The concentration of nitrite used in cured meats, when the chemical acts in concert with salt and possibly other ingredients in the product, inhibits outgrowth of spores of such anaerobic bacteria as *Clostridium botulinum* and *Clostridium perfringens*. However, the inhibitory effect is related to the number of spores present in the product; inhibition is complete when meat contains <1 spore per gram but outgrowth occurs when 20-50 spores per gram are present.

The undissociated nitrite molecule is especially effective as an inhibitory substance. Several reasons have been given for this detrimental effect on bacteria: (a) production of sulfhydryl complexes which cannot be metabolized, (b) action on α-amino groups of amino acids at low pH, and (c) reaction with monophenols and heme pigments. The exact reason(s) why nitrites inhibit microbial growth must still be determined.

It has been found that potentially carcinogenic nitrosamines can be formed from food-borne nitrites, particularly in acid conditions. To preclude formation of nitrosamines in meat curing premixes, the Food and Drug Administration has ordered that nitrite and the seasoning mix be packaged separately. Future use of nitrites may be restricted further or the chemical may even be eliminated from the list of acceptable food additives.

Sulfur Dioxide and Sulfites

Sulfur dioxide has a long history of use in the food industry, especially as a sanitizing agent in wine making. In the United States, sulfiting (use of SO_2 or sulfites) continues in the wine industry and the process is also used to treat dehydrated fruits and vegetables, often to preserve color and flavor rather than to interfere with microbial activity.

Sulfite salts offer the convenience of a dry chemical. When dissolved in water, the sulfites form sulfurous acid, the bisulfite ion, and the sulfite ion. The relative proportion of each form depends on the pH of the solution.

Sulfurous acid inhibits yeasts, molds, and bacteria. However, some yeasts are more resistant to the chemical than are the lactic and acetic acid bacteria; this property makes sulfurous acid particularly useful in the wine industry.

The sulfur compounds are believed to inactivate or inhibit microorganisms through: (a) reaction with carbohydrates so they cannot be used as a source of energy, (b) reduction of S-S linkages in enzyme proteins thus preventing the enzymatic action essential for cell metabolism, and (c) interaction of SO_2 and ketone groups to produce hydroxysulfonates which inhibit steps in the respiratory mechanism which involve nicotinamide dinucleotide.

Acetic Acid and Acetates

Acetic acid is most commonly added to foods in the form of vinegar which contains 4% or more of the acid. Vinegar serves to reduce the pH of the product and also contributes to its flavor. Besides vinegar and purified acetic acid, the following compounds which yield acetic acid are available for food use: sodium acetate, sodium diacetate, calcium acetate, and potassium acetate.

Vinegar is widely used in products such as catsup, salad dressings, and cucumber pickles. It is also used in some pickled meat products and in pickled fish. Some of the acetates may be used in bread to control rope formation.

Acetic acid at pH values of 5.0 or below is inhibitory to most bacteria including such foodborne pathogens as salmonellae and staphylococci. Lower pH values are required before yeasts and molds are inhibited. Acetic acid is more detrimental to most bacteria than are many other organic acids. Its antibacterial activity is associated with the undissociated acid molecule.

Sorbic Acid and Sorbates

Sorbic acid, an α-β-unsaturated fatty acid, has fungistatic properties which were first recognized in 1945. Since then sorbic acid and its salts (potassium sorbate and sodium sorbate) have been widely used to protect many acidic foods from spoilage by molds. Included are products such as cheese, orange juice, fruit and fruit syrups, margarine, pickles, and yogurt. Sorbic acid is generally effective at a concentration of 3,000 ppm (maximum permitted in some foods by US federal regulations) provided the pH is below 6.5 (effectiveness increases as the pH decreases). However, some molds can grow in the presence of at least 5300 ppm sorbic acid and then can degrade the acid to form 1,3-pentadiene which imparts a hydrocarbon-like odor to the substrate.

Since sorbic acid has been used largely as an antifungal agent, little attention has been given to its effect on bacteria. Some evidence suggests that bacteria such as salmonellae, staphylococci, *Streptococcus thermophilus*, *Lactobacillus bulgaricus*, and *Escherichia coli* are inhibited or inactivated, depending on concentration of the acid and environmental conditions. Sorbic acid is discussed in more detail elsewhere in this book.

Propionic Acid and Propionates

Propionic acid and its salts (calcium and sodium propionate) are active against molds and some bacteria but are ineffective against yeasts. The salts and the acid have a slight cheese-like flavor which blends well with the flavor of many foods. The salts are readily soluble in water with the sodium salt being more soluble (150 gm per 100 ml water at $100°C$) than the calcium salt (55.8 gm under similar conditions). Optimal antimicrobial activity results when propionates are at pH 5.0, although some activity will be evident at pH values up to or slightly above 6.0.

Propionates are most commonly used to prevent mold growth and ropiness in bread and other baked goods and to prevent mold growth on cheese products. When used in baked goods, propionates can be added in amounts up to 0.32% of the weight of flour in white bread and rolls and 0.38% in similar whole wheat products. Usage in cheese products is limited to 0.3%. In addition to the baked goods already mentioned, propionates have been suggested for use in different types of cakes, pie crust, and pie fillings. Uses for cheese products include dipping of cuts of natural cheese and addition to process cheese and cold pack cheese foods. Other uses proposed for propionates include: treatment of wrappers to protect butter from mold spoilage, and addition to malt extract, syrup, blanched apple slices, figs, cherries, blackberries, peas, and lima beans to prevent mold spoilage of these foods. Propionates may be used as antifungal agents in artificially sweetened jams, jellies, and preserves.

Benzoic Acid and Benzoates

Benzoic acid is usually employed as the sodium salt and has been used for years as an antimicrobial food additive. The optimal pH for antimicrobial activity by benzoic acid is in the range of 2.5–4.0. Thus, the acid is most useful to preserve such products as carbonated beverages, fruit juices, cider, pickles, and sauerkraut. Benzoic acid does occur naturally in cranberries, prunes, greengage plums, cinnamon, and ripe olives.

Sodium benzoate is more active against yeasts and bacteria than against molds. Sodium chloride is believed to have a synergistic effect with sodium benzoate. Benzoate does not accumulate in the human body but is detoxified by conjugating with glycine to form hippuric acid which is excreted. Permitted levels are 0.2 and 0.3% but in practice often only 0.05–0.1% sodium benzoate is added to foods and beverages.

The alkyl esters of p-hydroxybenzoic acid (parabens) have found application as food preservatives because they are active at pH values higher than those for benzoic acid. Methyl and propyl esters are most commonly used in the United States at a concentration of 0.1% or less. These compounds are active antimicrobials at pH 7 or above as well as at lower pH values. Parabens are most active against molds and yeasts and are less effective against bacteria, especially the Gram-negative types. Products which can be preserved with parabens include: baked goods, soft drinks, beer, creams and pastes, flavor extracts, fruit products, jams, jellies, preserves, olives, pickles, and syrups.

Other Acids

Numerous other acids are used as acidulants in the processing of certain foods. If sufficient of the acid is added to reduce the pH of the product to 5.0–5.5 or below, some inhibition or inactivation of microorganisms will occur. Acids useful in food processing besides those already mentioned include: succinic, adipic, fumaric, lactic, malic, tartaric, citric, and phosphoric.

Lactic acid is produced during fermentations used to produce such foods as cucumber pickles, sauerkraut, green olives, cheese, buttermilk, and yogurt. Besides imparting flavor, the acid acts to preserve the products.

Phosphoric acid is the only inorganic acid that is widely used as a food acidulant and accounts for 25% of all acids used in foods. Most of the phosphoric acid is used in soft drinks and many of its salts are ingredients of baking powder or other leavening agents.

Alcohols

Ethanol is commonly used to preserve flavoring extracts, vanilla, and lemon extracts. It serves the same purpose in fortified wine, whiskey, brandy, rum, gin, liquors, and similar alcoholic beverages. The content of ethanol in beer, ale, and unfortified wine is too low to prevent growth of all microorganisms but sufficient alcohol is present to limit the kinds that can cause spoilage.

Recently, propylene glycol has been used to produce certain pet foods. It serves to reduce the water activity of the product below that at which microbial growth is possible and imparts a moist characteristic to the pet food.

Hydrogen Peroxide

Hydrogen peroxide is used as a preservative for milk, particularly in some tropical or subtropical areas. In the United States, use of hydrogen peroxide is limited to treatment of raw milk which is to be made into Swiss or Cheddar cheese. Use of hydrogen peroxide is not intended as a substitute for pasteurization since cheese made from milk treated with the chemical must be handled as if it were made from raw milk. Hydrogen peroxide also has been suggested for treatment of whey and egg albumin.

In practice, hydrogen peroxide (0.05% or less) is added to milk at 37°–54°C, allowed to act for 15 sec to 10 min, and then is destroyed with a catalase preparation (not to exceed 20 ppm in milk) before cheese making. The bactericidal effectiveness of hydrogen peroxide is related to concentration, duration of treatment, and kinds and numbers of microorganisms. Spores of aerobic bacteria are very resistant to inactivation by hydrogen peroxide, whereas Gram-negative bacteria in general and coliform bacteria in particular are very sensitive to the chemical. Resistance of staphylococci is somewhere in between although under some circumstances this can increase, probably because more resistant cells have more catalase activity.

Relatively little US Cheddar cheese is made from milk treated with hydrogen peroxide. In contrast, the chemical is widely used to treat milk intended for manufacture of Swiss cheese. Benefits claimed for the peroxide-catalase treatment include: (a) selective destruction of microorganisms (coliforms, vegetative cells of clostridia, and other defect-causing bacteria are largely destroyed, whereas lactobacilli and streptococci survive), (b) milk proteins are softened by the peroxide and this gives the cheese a medium-firm elastic body, and (c) cheese made from milk treated with peroxide ripens faster and usually is of higher quality than is cheese made from pasteurized milk.

Spices

Spices are not chemical preservatives in the true sense of the term. Many spices do contain antibacterial substances; however, their efficacy may be questioned since spices are generally used at low concentrations. Nevertheless, foods are often preserved by a combination of additives and environmental conditions and under such circumstances spices may contribute to the total preservative effect operating in a given system.

Terpenes obtained from nutmeg, and oils from cinnamon, sweet marjoram, thyme, laurel, pimiento, citrus, clove, peppermint, and coriander do exhibit marked antimicrobial properties. Oils from other spices possess some inhibitory properties but they are less evident. Extracts derived from such spices as caraway, cardamom, coriander, cumin, fennel, sabadilla, wormwood, anise, celery, dill, and mustard also have been found to inhibit some bacteria and fungi.

Although not truly spices, onion and garlic also possess antimicrobial activity. Thiosulfinate compounds are responsible for the activity in both instances. When proper drying procedures are used, antibacterial activity is retained by garlic powder.

Wood Smoke

Smoking of food serves to add desired flavors, aid in preservation, add desired color both inside and on the surface, and sometimes to tenderize the product. Preservation is accomplished jointly by heat, drying of the surface of the food, and impregnating the surface with compounds present in the smoke. Smoke may be obtained from burning such woods as hickory, oak, maple, beech, birch, walnut, or mahogany.

Of the compounds in wood smoke, formaldehyde is considered as the most effective antimicrobial material which is followed in order of effectiveness by phenols and cresols. Other compounds in wood smoke include: aliphatic acids from formic through caproic, primary and secondary alcohols, ketones, acetaldehyde and other aldehydes, waxes, resins, guaiacol, catechol, methyl catechol, and pyrogallol. Wood smoke is more effective against vegetative cells of bacteria than spores and generally is more effective against bacteria than molds. "Liquid smoke," when applied to the surface of foods, has little if any preservative effect.

Ethylene Oxide and Propylene Oxide

Two gaseous chemicals, ethylene oxide and propylene oxide, have found limited application in the food industry for sterilizing certain products. When used to treat some foods, ethylene and propylene glycol and ethylene and propylene chlorohydrin can be formed. The safety of some of these derivatives has been questioned and hence gaseous sterilization of food products is limited.

In 1973, ethylene oxide was approved for treating ground and whole spices, other processed natural seasoning materials except mixtures that contain salt, black walnut meats, and copra. Residual ethylene oxide in the treated products cannot exceed 50 ppm.

At the same time propylene oxide could be used as a fumigant for packaged dry prunes and glacéd fruit. It was also acceptable to treat the following bulk products provided they were to receive further processing: cocoa, gums, processed spices, starch, and processed nut meats except peanuts. Treatment with propylene oxide was further limited to a single exposure in a retort for no longer than 4 hr at a temperature not in excess of 125°F. Residual propylene oxide should not exceed 300 ppm in all products except prunes and glaced fruit where it should not exceed 700 ppm as propylene glycol. Treated products need to be labeled appropriately.

The gaseous sterilants can inactivate a wide variety of molds, yeasts, and bacteria. Data suggest that viruses also are inactivated by these chemicals. Inactivation of microorganisms by these gases is irreversible.

Antibiotics

Direct addition of antibiotics to foods is not permitted in the United States. In the past, limited use of tetracyclines to extend the shelf-life of poultry and fish was permitted. Questions about development of antibiotic-resistant pathogenic and other microorganisms in consumers who were repeatedly exposed to low concentrations of antibiotics led to withdrawal by regulatory agencies of permission for even the limited usage of these preservatives in poultry and fish.

Some antibiotic-like substances are produced naturally during fermentations used to manufacture certain foods. The best-known example is nisin which is elaborated by certain strains of *Streptococcus lactis*, a bacterium commonly used to produce some kinds of cheese and buttermilk. Other examples of antibacterial substances produced by lactic acid bacteria include diplococcin, lactocidin, and bulgarican elaborated by *Streptococcus cremoris*, *Lactobacillus acidophilus*, and *Lactobacillus bulgaricus*, respectively. Production of inhibitory substances also has been associated with other lactobacilli, heterofermantative lactic streptococci, and propionibacteria.

Nisin consists of at least four active polypeptides, designated as fractions A, B, C, and D. Numerous bacteria appear to be susceptible to nisin but its use, either as a pure compound or as produced during fermentation, has been largely restricted to inhibiting spoilage of cheese by clostridia. The pure compound is unacceptable for use in the United States.

Diethyl Pyrocarbonate

The diethyl ester of pyrocarbonic acid has been found suitable for "cold sterilization" of fruit juices, wines, and beers. On hydrolysis, diethyl pyrocarbonate yields ethyl alcohol and carbon dioxide. For this reason and because the compound is lethal to yeasts and bacteria likely to spoil wines and beers, the chemical was thought to be an ideal sterilant for these products. Recently, it was noted that urethane is formed when diethyl pyrocarbonate is used. Since urethane compounds are carcinogenic, the safety of diethyl pyrocarbonate has been questioned and regulatory agencies have banned its use in the United States.

Chlorine and Iodine Compounds

These compounds are not chemical preservatives in the usual sense since they are not added to foods. They are, however, used to reduce the level of microbial contamination on surfaces of food processing equipment and so by reducing the numbers of microorganisms in food, these chemicals serve to enhance its shelf-life.

The most common chlorine-based sanitizers are the hypochlorites and chloramines. Hypochlorites include the sodium and calcium salts; both are rapid in action because they completely dissociate in water. Optimal activity by hypochlorites is obtained when the solution is hot and in the acid pH range and when surfaces of equipment are free of residual organic matter. Complex organic chloramines release chlorine gradually and hence the rate of disinfection is slower than that of the hypochlorites. This characteristic makes the chloramines less suitable than hypochlorites for many disinfectant needs in the food industry.

Iodine by itself is an effective disinfectant but is unsuitable for use because it is toxic, corrodes metal, irritates skin and mucous membranes, stains cloth, and is only slightly soluble in water. To overcome these difficulties, iodine is complexed with an anionic, cationic, or nonionic wetting agent. Such compounds are designated as iodophors and may be combined with certain acids to enhance their germicidal properties.

Both chlorine and iodine compounds have a wide antibacterial spectrum; in practice 100–200 ppm of available chlorine is necessary for adequate sanitization but only 12–25 ppm of iodine is needed to do the same job. Use of hot solutions will not enhance the activity of iodine compounds.

Detergents

As with chlorine and iodine compounds, detergents are not chemical preservatives in the usual sense because they are not added to foods. Instead, they serve to reduce microbial contamination of foods during processing and hence the shelf-life of the products may be extended.

Detergents commonly used include: (a) strong alkalies (sodium hydroxide plus ortho- and sesqui-silicates), (b) mild alkalies (mixtures of sodium metasilicate, sodium carbonate, trisodium phosphate, a wetting agent, and a water conditioner), (c) neutral detergents (organic compounds designed to replace soap or to be used as a wetting agent in a mixture), and (d) acids (these can be organic or inorganic acids).

ELMER H. MARTH

References

BRUCH, C. W., and BRUCH, M. K. 1970. Gaseous disinfection. In Disinfection. M. A. Benarde (Editor). Marcel Dekker, New York.

CHICHESTER, D. F., and TANNER, JR., F. W. 1972. Antimicrobial food additives. In Handbook of Food Additives, 2nd Edition. T. E. Furia (Editor). CRC Press, Cleveland.

CLEGG, L. F. L. 1970. Disinfection in the dairy industry. In Disinfection. M. A. Benarde (Editor). Marcel Dekker, New York.

DUNN, C. G. 1968. Food preservatives. In Disinfection, Sterilization, and Preservation. C. A. Lawrence and S. S. Block (Editors). Lea & Febiger, Philadelphia.

FRAZIER, W. C. 1967. Food Microbiology, 2nd Edition. McGraw-Hill Book Co., New York.

GARDNER, W. H. 1972. Acidulants in food processing. In Handbook of Food Additives, 2nd Edition. T. E. Furia (Editor). CRC Press, Cleveland.

HURST, A. 1972. Interactions of food starter cultures and food-borne pathogens: The antagonism between Streptococcus lactis and spore-forming microbes. J. Milk Food Technol. 35, 418–423.

MARTH, E. H. 1966. Antibiotics in foods—Naturally occurring, developed, and added. Residue Rev. 12, 65–161.

MARTH, E. H. et al. 1966. Degradation of potassium sorbate by Penicillium species. J. Dairy Sci. 49, 1197–1205.

NICKERSON, J. T., and SINSKEY, A. J. 1972. Microbiology of Foods and Food Processing. American Elsevier Publishing Co., New York.

OLIVANT, D. J., and SHAPTON, D. A. 1970. Disinfection in the food processing industry. In Disinfection. M. A. Benarde (Editor). Marcel Dekker, New York.

PARK, H. S., and MARTH, E. H. 1972. Inactivation of Salmonella typhimurium by sorbic acid. J. Milk Food Technol. 35, 532–539.

REINBOLD, G. W. 1972. Swiss Cheese Varieties. Pfizer, Inc., New York.

RIEMANN, H., LEE, W. H. and GENIGEORGIS, C. 1972. Control of Clostridium botulinum and Staphylococcus aureus in semi-preserved meat products. J. Milk Food Technol. 35, 514–523.

SHIH, C. N., and MARTH, E. H. 1972. Production of aflatoxin in a medium fortified with sodium chloride. J. Dairy Sci. *55*, 1415-1419.

Cross-references: *Additives; Food Preservation.*

CHERRIES AND CHERRY PROCESSING

The cherry belongs to the genus *Prunus*, family Rosaceae. The genus *Prunus* also includes other well-known stone or drupaceous fruits, as the almond, apricot, nectarine, peach, and plum.

The sweet cherry, *Prunus avium*, probably came from the region between the Caspian and Black Seas and was widely disseminated by birds and animals over a widely extended territory and may have been domesticated in widely separate regions.

The red or sour cherry, *Prunus cerasus*, also designated as pie, red sour or red tart cherry, is believed to have originated in the same area and, in general, pomologists are inclined to assume that it may have been derived from the sweet cherry.

The Duke cherries, formerly regarded as the botanical variety, are hybrids between *Prunus avium* and *Prunus cerasus*.

Earliest records indicate that the cherry was first domesticated in Greece. Theophrastus described the cherry in 300 B.C., but it probably was cultivated several centuries earlier, possibly more for the wood than for the fruit. Little was accomplished in improving it until the 17th Century. Since then progress has been rather rapid.

The Red Cherry.—There are 270 named varieties but only a few are grown commercially and are well known. Montmorency is the leading and most profitable one grown for processing. Few Early Richmond and English Morello are produced commercially.

The Sweet Cherry.—Some 549 varieties have been named but only about 15 are planted commercially. The dominant varieties are Bing, Black Tartarian, Black Republican, Lambert, Schmidt, Windsor, and Napoleon (Royal Ann).

World Production

The average production of all types of cherries by continents and countries and for the world is presented in Table C-8. The total world production of cherries is over 1.3 million short tons. Of this total approximately 20% are produced in North America, 71% in Europe, 7% in Asia, 1.5% in South America and 0.5% in Oceania. With the exception of the seven countries listed in Table C-9, most of the cherries produced are sweet cherries. Since 1968 the tart cherry production in Canada and the United States has become greater than that of the sweet cherries.

Utilization

Red (Tart) Cherries.—About 94% produced in the United States are processed, 2% are home used, and 4% sold fresh. The canned pack accounts for about 34%, and the frozen pack 60%.

Sweet Cherries.—Fresh fruit sales account for 38% of the total production, 2% are home used and 60% are processed. About 25% of the processed are canned and 75% brined. Frozen pack is negligible.

Harvesting and Handling Red Cherries for Processing

Historically, the harvesting and handling of fruit has been done by hand and has been considered one of the most expensive operations associated with the production of cherries. The cherries are picked without stems to facilitate both harvesting operations and handling in the factory. Until about 1959, all cherries were picked into picking containers, transferred to lugs, holding 25-28 lb and transported to the processing plant. However, with harvest labor costs steadily increasing, interest in and research on mechanical harvesting increased. Rapid progress was made and at present most of the cherries are mechanically harvested by one of several types of tree shakers. The cherries are collected on a catching frame, transferred by conveyor to chilled water in large metal tanks, and transported to the processing plant.

Bruising of cherries occurs in every harvesting and handling operation whether done by hand or machine. Bruising has 2 significant aspects in that it initiates 2 physiological processes, namely, firming and color destruction and oxidation. Physiological firming resulting from the repair and strengthening of the bruised tissue is desirable as it permits pitting with less flesh tearing and loss of juice.

The initial color change due to bruising has been referred to as "scald." This involves the migration of the red pigment from the skin layer into the bruised flesh. Scalded areas initially are light pink in color. The slower oxidation process or browning usually follows in the same damaged tissue and affects cherry quality more seriously. Scalding and oxidation as well as firming rates are governed by temperature and time. Firming and scald are promoted by high temperatures, but since scald and oxidation are more damaging, cooling of the fruit in cold water has become standard practice.

The generally accepted practice of soaking and cooling red cherries in tanks of cold running water for several hours was developed by W. R. Kappler in 1918. His data indicated 6-16 hr soaking was satisfactory for washing the fruit, removing spray residue, replacing moisture lost during transportation, and firming. Subsequent studies have indi-

TABLE C-8

PRODUCTION OF ALL FRESH CHERRIES IN SPECIFIED COUNTRIES, AVG 1955-1959 AND 1960-1967, ANNUAL 1968-1970

Continent and Country	Avg 1955-1959	Avg 1960-1967	1968	1969	1970
			1000 Short Tons		
North America					
Canada	15.0	21.2	14.9	18.9	18.0
United States	216.4	196.8	228.7	285.6	244.9
Total	231.4	218.0	243.6	304.5	262.9
South America					
Argentina	2.9	2.6	1.5	2.1	2.2
Chile	2.8	3.8	4.0	3.9	3.9
Total	5.7	6.4	5.5	6.0	6.1
Europe					
Austria	27.3	38.9	35.7	32.0	31.4
Belgium-Luxembourg	26.6	19.2	22.0	19.8	27.0
Denmark	7.2	1.7	2.0	2.2	2.8
France	82.6	120.4	145.5	120.1	121.3
Germany, West	175.8	241.9	366.6	278.7	350.9
Greece	11.6	17.9	27.2	26.8	37.7
Italy	162.3	235.6	216.2	188.7	209.4
Netherlands	10.2	6.4	8.2	6.0	5.5
Norway	4.8	4.1	5.3	5.0	4.6
Spain	47.5	53.5	60.2	55.3	48.3
Sweden	10.8	8.4	0.4	0.3	0.6
Switzerland	51.1	55.1	56.2	49.6	54.0
United Kingdom	24.7	15.5	6.7	4.8	12.2
Yugoslavia	83.3	90.5	89.0	95.3	102.0
Total	725.5	909.1	1041.2	884.6	1007.7
Asia					
Japan	5.7	8.1	9.4	12.3	14.3
Syria	1.0				
Turkey	55.6	74.0	87.1	88.2	88.2
Total	62.3	82.1	96.5	100.5	102.5
Oceania					
Australia	6.3	8.0	7.6	8.4	7.8
New Zealand	0.3				
Total	6.6	8.0	7.6	8.4	7.8
Total	1031.5	1217.6	1394.4	1304.0	1387.0

SOURCE: USDA World Agr. Production Trade Statist. Rept., August 1971.

cated that soaking the cherries in running cold water is not essential for firming and reducing pitter losses. This can be accomplished by either hydrocooling or air cooling, although not as efficiently for large volumes of fruit. The holding of cherries in cold water for 4-8 hr between harvest and pitting is adequate to permit most of the firming to occur and is short enough to prevent excessive development of scald. Tanking the fruit at the catching frame accomplishes this quite well. Rebruising of the fruit between initial soaking and pitting (postharvest handling) should be minimized since this bruising negates the value of the initial firming.

Grading, Sorting, Pitting Red Cherries

Cherries received at the processing plants are graded for defective, undersized, and immature fruit. The processors pay the growers on a sliding scale determined by grade.

Until 1963, most of the cherries were moved forward over a rubber inspection belt, 12-16 ft long, traveling at a speed of 20 ft per min or less

TABLE C-9

ANNUAL PRODUCTION OF SWEET AND TART CHERRIES IN SPECIFIED COUNTRIES, 1967–1970

Continent and Country	1967 Sweet	1967 Tart	1968 Sweet	1968 Tart	1969 Sweet	1969 Tart	1970 Sweet	1970 Tart
				1000 Short Tons				
North America								
Canada	13.3	11.4	7.1	7.8	8.3	10.6	9.2	8.8
United States	110.0	88.3	91.2	137.5	127.6	158.0	117.3	127.6
Europe								
Austria	23.6	3.0	31.8	3.9	28.3	3.7	27.7	3.7
Germany, West	136.9	89.8	239.4	127.2	175.8	102.9	229.5	121.4
Greece	18.5	4.6	22.1	5.1	18.9	7.9	22.6	15.1
Yugoslavia	52.3	29.9	54.7	34.3	55.1	40.2	59.3	42.7
Asia								
Turkey	55.1	27.6	59.5	27.6	59.5	28.7	60.6	27.6

SOURCE: USDA World Agr. Production Trade Statist. Rept., August 1971.

for sorting. The sorters removed fruit that did not have typical red cherry color and those that showed blemishes as scar tissue, fungus and insect injury, hail injury, limb rubs, and excessive bruises. At present, most cherries are sorted by automatic electronic machines. These sorters are effective in eliminating severely blemished cherries but do not eliminate undercolored fruit.

Sorted cherries are pitted with automatic pitting machines. The pits constitute 6.5–8.5% of the weight of the cherries. A loss of juice also occurs during the pitting operation and varies from 5–8%. From the pitters, the cherries move over a sorting belt to the filling equipment.

Canning Red Cherries

Pitted red cherries are packed in No. 303 and No. 10 cherry enamel cans. Mechanical fillers are used. Most of the pitted red cherries are water-packed since they are packed as pie stock. Water is added and the cans are given sufficient exhaust in hot water to eliminate the air from the can and thereby reduce corrosion of the tinplate and to produce a good vacuum in the sealed can. After exhausting, the cans are closed in automatic closing machines and processed. The processing time varies from 8–12 min for No. 303 cans and 14–20 min for No. 10 cans in boiling water. After processing the cans should be well cooled by passing through tanks or canals of cold water before casing or stacking.

Canned Red Cherry Pie Filling.—Canned, ready-to-use cherry pie filling was introduced in 1946 as an additional item in the canner's list of products. Fresh or frozen red cherries may be used and the fillings can be prepared either by a batch or continuous process. The formula for red cherry pie filling is approximately 60% pitted cherries, 24% sugar, 2% starch, 0.1% salt, 0.017% red color, and 14% cherry juice or water.

Canned Cherry Sauce and Jellied Cherry Sauce.— These may be made either from fresh or frozen pitted cherries. The formula for these are similar to those for pie filling except for the addition of spices such as allspice and cloves.

Freezing Red Cherries

Pitted red cherry is one of the most satisfactory fruits for freezing. There is no record of the first pack of pitted red cherries but it is indicated that freezing on a commercial scale began around 1920. Initially, the fruit was packed in 50 gal. paraffin-coated fir barrels. In 1928, the 30 lb enameled slip-covered can came into usage and at present is the most popular for institutional use.

The methods for harvesting and handling red cherries for freezing are the same as for canning. Careful and rapid handling of cherries for freezing is of great importance since bruises, scalding, and oxidation are easily detected in the frozen pack.

Packing Medium.—Red tart cherries are frozen with or without sugar. Most of the sugar packs are put up as 5 + 1 pack, 5 lb of fruit plus 1 lb of dry sugar in 30-lb containers, although some are packed in the ratio of 4 + 1 or 7 + 1. Freezing of pitted Montmorency cherries as individually quick frozen (IQF) fruit was revived in 1963 for manufacturing and export trade.

Red Cherry Juice

Cherry juice has a pleasing flavor and an attractive color.   Montmorency is the leading juice variety. It may be prepared by either hot or cold pressing of fresh cherries or cold pressing of frozen cherries.

Sweet Cherries

Canning.—Napoleon (Royal Ann) is the most important variety for canning. In fact, this variety is grown almost exclusively for canning and brining. Bing, Lambert, and Schmidt are the most popular of the dark colored fruit.

The cherries should be picked at full maturity to obtain a good quality canned product. Sweet cherries may be canned with or without pitting. They are canned in syrup, the concentrations ranging from 10° to 40° Brix with the highest grade receiving the 40° Brix syrup.

The cans for sweet cherries are filled as full as possible and syruped at 120°–140°F. Adding of syrup at higher temperatures tends to shrink and toughen the fruit. A thorough exhaust is necessary to eliminate gases and to prevent pinholing. The length of processing is from 12 to 25 min at 212°F depending upon the variety and maturity of the cherries, size of the can, and method of processing.

Freezing.—Frozen sweet cherries, have never been as popular as the canned product and the amount frozen is very limited.

Brined Cherries

Substantial quantities of cherries are preserved by brining. The brined fruit is used for preparing Maraschino cherries and for candied and glacéd cherries. Prior to the enactment of the U.S. Tariff Act of 1930, an average of about 7500 tons of cherries were imported annually into the United States, of which 80–85% were brined. At present, the imports of brined cherries are about 2000 tons, mainly from Italy and Spain. Brining accounts for 45–50% of the total production of sweet cherries in the United States.

Practically all of the white or light-colored sweet cherry varieties may be used. Napoleon is the leading and most ideal variety. Bing, and Windsor are the leading red varieties with some Lambert and Black Republican. Relatively few tart cherries are brined.

Brining and Bleaching.—Cherries to be brined are harvested at a maturity that is slightly less than desirable for fresh shipment. The objectives are to bleach the fruits to a uniform white or yellowish-white color and to firm or toughen the fruit. Bleaching is accomplished by the use of sulfur dioxide and firming by the use of calcium, either as lime or some calcium salt. The brine contains from 0.7 to 1.5% sulfur dioxide and 0.4 to 1% of lime. The pH range of the brine should be between 2.5 and 3.5. Cracking or splitting of the cherries will occur if the pH is too low or the SO_2 content is too high. Sufficient free SO_2 must be present in the brine to prevent microbial spoilage.

Initially, all cherries were brined in paraffin-lined spruce, fir, or oak barrels. Brining is now being done in plastic containers and in large tanks of 500–15,000 gal. The curing of the fruit usually requires 4–6 weeks. The cherries may be held indefinitely if the storage is cool and if the brine contains sufficient SO_2 (0.3–0.4%) to prevent spoilage.

Complete color removal from the SO_2-bleached cherries may be accomplished by leaching the cherries in water and bleaching in a 0.75% solution of sodium chlorite adjusted to pH 4.0. After the chlorite bleach, the cherries should be returned to the sulfur dioxide—calcium oxide brine at pH 3.0–3.5 for 2 weeks before leaching and manufacturing into the finished product.

Maraschino Cherries

Brined cherries usually contain in excess of 300 ppm SO_2. This must be reduced to less than 20 ppm in the cherries. The cherries are pitted and then freshened by leaching out the SO_2 with water. Cherries may be leached in cold running water for 24–48 hr or brought to a boil in water with 4–6 changes of water.

Cherries that are to be used in canned fruit cocktails or fruit salads are dyed with FD & C Red No. 3 (erythrosin). The leached, pitted, cherries are boiled for several minutes in a 0.05% dye solution, and then allowed to stand in this solution until desired dye penetration occurs. The cherries are then washed well in boiling water to remove residual dye, brought to boil in a 0.5% citric acid solution and held near boiling point for 15–20 min. The fruit is then rinsed in cold water to remove excess acid. The boiling in citric acid reduces the tendency of the cherries to bleed and stain other fruit.

Preparation of cherries for use in cocktails, desserts, and other household and restaurant uses are sweetened and flavored. Sweetness is restored to the fruit by soaking in sugar syrup, done slowly and progressively to avoid shriveling the fruit. The cherries are heated to boiling in a 20°–30° Brix sugar syrup containing the dye (FD & C No. 4 or 40) and then allowed to stand for 24 hr or overnight. This is repeated daily, increasing the syrup density about 5° Brix by the addition of sugar until a 40° Brix syrup is used. The cherries may then be heated in the syrup to which the artificial flavoring and 0.1% sodium benzoate are added. If the cherries and syrup are packed at or above

190°F in small containers that will be used immediately after opening, the preservative sodium benzoate may be omitted. In large containers the drained fruit may be packed in the containers, and the containers filled with the syrup containing the flavoring and preservative heated to 140°-150°F. The sealed containers are pasteurized at 180°F for 20 min.

Maraschino flavoring.—The original maraschino flavoring was obtained from the fruits and leaves of Marasca cherry trees grown in Yugoslavia. However, today, most maraschino flavoring is made from bitter almond oil, neroli oil, and vanilla extract.

Candied and Glacéd Cherries

The candying process consists essentially of slowly impregnating the fruit with syrup until the sugar concentration in the fruit is high enough to prevent growth of spoilage microorganisms. Following impregnation, the fruit is washed and dried and sold as candied fruit. For glacéd fruit, the washed and dried candied fruit is coated with a thin transparent layer of heavy syrup that dries to a more or less firm texture.

C. L. BEDFORD

CHLORINE

Chlorine, a greenish yellow gas, 2.5 times as heavy as air, was first produced in the late 17th Century. The first liquid chlorine was prepared in 1805 by Northmore. The odor of chlorine is pungent and irritating and for most people decidely unpleasant.

There are a number of methods of production. Examples are the electrolysis of sodium chloride brine whereby chlorine is released at the positive electrode, the electrolysis of other fused chlorides, and by such chemical methods as reacting sodium chloride and nitric acid.

The uses of chlorine in the food industry are several: in the purification of processing water, as a sanitizing agent, as a refrigerant, as a propellant, and, referring now to the chloride of sodium or common salt, as a condiment.

Chlorine is associated for many technologists with "in-plant chlorination," the chlorination of water beyond the "break-point." Break-point chlorination means adding chlorine to water beyond the point where chloramines are oxidized and where adding more chlorine will only result in a proportional increase of chlorine residual. In-plant chlorination does not assure adequate plant sanitation but is a decided aid. When the water used in processing contains 10–20 ppm of chlorine,

the reduction in basterial counts at the stations commonly chosen for test is substantial. Chlorinators are widely used in freezing plants.

Chlorine is a poison and caution must be used in its manufacture, handling, and use.

MARTIN S. PETERSON

Cross-reference: *Sanitation.*

CHLOROPHYLL

Chemical Identity

Chlorophylls are magnesium complexes derived from phorbin. In nature they occur in combination with protein, chiefly as chlorophyll a or chlorophyll b (Fig. C-5). In higher plants the ratio of chlorophyll a to b is about 2.5 to 1. They are of importance in food science because of their photosynthetic role and because of their part in the green coloration of vegetables and fruits.

Function in Photosynthesis

Photosynthesis involves the photoreduction of carbon dioxide to an organic form such as a carbohydrate. In green plants there is also liberation of oxygen from water. $CO_2 + H_2O \rightarrow [CHOH] + O_2 (\Delta F + 112 \text{ kcal})$. The pigment which photosensitizes the reaction in the case of green plants is chlorophyll.

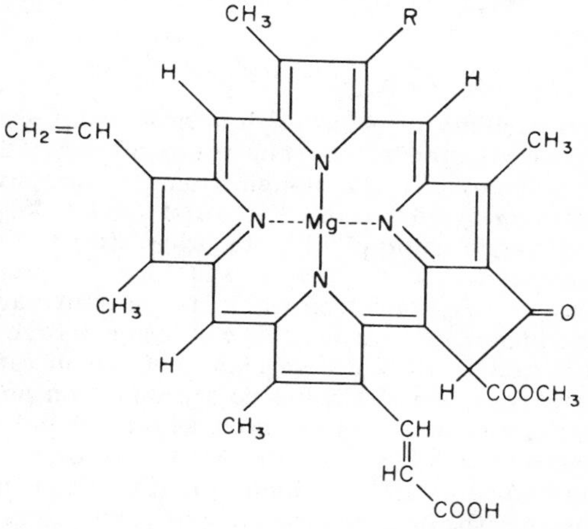

(a) R = $-CH = CH_2$

($C_{35}H_{28}N_4O_5Mg$)

(b) R = $-CH_2-CH_3$

($C_{35}H_{30}N_4O_5Mg$)

FIG. C-5. MOLECULAR STRUCTURE OF CHLOROPHYLL

The exact mechanism of the photosynthetic process has not yet been clearly defined. It is believed that light absorbed by a large number of chlorophylls and accessory pigments is trapped by a small number of chlorophylls in reaction centers which convert quanta to chemical potential. Several of these reaction centers have been identified. However, they constitute only a small portion of the total chlorophyll.

Changes During Senescence

During senescence of a plant, the chlorophyll content decreases and finally disappears. The rate of destruction of chlorophyll a is more rapid than that of chlorophyll b. The overall ultimate fate of the chlorophyll molecule appears to be oxidation. The oxidative destruction appears to be influenced by enzymes, heat, or light as well as other factors.

Physiological changes in stored plant tissue can be slowed or halted by blanching, or drying, or other treatments. The rate of senescence can be slowed by control of the environment by treatments such as cold storage of the plant tissue, or by use of various additives. Kinetin or benzimidazole will delay the normal yellowing and loss of protein in detached leaves. Spraying deciduous leaves with gibberellic acid will delay their yellowing. Formulations of either 2,4-D or 2,4,5-T will delay senescence in both attached and detached leaves. Red light can also retard senescence, apparently through an enhancement of RNA and inhibition of protein decomposition. $N(6)$ benzyladenine delays senescence of many harvested crops.

Stability in Postharvest Vegetables

The stability of chlorophyll in postharvest vegetables is affected by the temperature of storage, the atmosphere, and the illumination. Chlorophyll losses are greater at $85°F$ than at $35°F$. Vegetables retain chlorophyll better when stored in an atmosphere low in oxygen and high in carbon dioxide. Vegetables stored in transparent packages, under fluorescent light, will lose chlorophyll more rapidly than will vegetables stored in cardboard containers. Greater color stability in postharvest vegetables has also been achieved by use of senescence inhibitors such as $N(6)$ benzyladenine. The influence of this kinin on respiration and senescence has been reported to have some practical value in prolonging the fresh quality and chlorophyll retention of certain vegetables throughout the storage and transit periods.

Color Stability in Processed Foods

When green vegetables are cooked, some of the magnesium in the chlorophyll is replaced by hydrogen to form pheophytin, and the characteristic green color of the vegetable is changed to brown-olive green. If the pH is acid, this takes place rapidly during processing.

Color changes during processing of green vegetables can be retarded by increasing the pH by the addition of alkaline substances. There is danger that use of alkaline substances will cause texture deterioration. However, an increase in pH of 0.3 of a unit will result in a 20% increase of unconverted chlorophyll in green beans held 30 min on a steam table. This pH increase can be accomplished, with no significant texture deterioration, by addition of small amounts of magnesium carbonate and calcium acetate.

In canned vegetables there is almost complete loss of chlorophyll. Pheophytin is the principal conversion product. Attempts to prevent this conversion by addition of alkaline substances to the vegetables have not been successful.

Loss of green color in frozen vegetables can be retarded by blanching. Blanching inactivates enzymes responsible for chlorophyll changes. These changes include chlorophyll oxidation, loss of the phytyl group, resulting in chlorophyllide, and loss of both magnesium and phytyl group, producing pheophorbide.

When green beans are blanched at $200°-212°F$ for 1-2 min they have less conversion of chlorophyll during blanching and also during subsequent storage at $20°F$ than do green beans blanched for longer periods of time at any temperature. If an optimum blanch time is used, color deterioration during storage can be measured as chlorophyll conversion to pheophytin. With shorter or longer blanch times, however, chlorophyll oxidation will become a significant factor in the overall assessment of color.

Some of the factors affecting chlorophyll retention in dehydrated vegetables are: variety of vegetable, chemical pretreatment, type of blanch, moisture content of dehydrated vegetables, type of packaging, and atmosphere of storage.

Investigations have revealed wide variety differences in suitability for dehydration of several vegetables including green beans, cabbage, celery, kale, okra, green peas, and spinach. Chemical treatments of the vegetables before blanching have generally resulted in better chlorophyll retention in the dehydrated vegetable. Treatments by immersion in dilute solutions of sulfites, or sodium bicarbonates have been used.

Vegetables must be blanched before dehydration. Steam blanching has been reported to be more effective than water blanching for several vegetables. It is generally advisable to reduce moisture content of vegetables to 4% or less. The moisture content of some vegetables such as green beans can be reduced more readily if the beans are first blanched and then frozen before dehydration.

It is known that dehydrated vegetables stored in sealed containers retain color better than do those stored in containers that are not air tight. Storage in an atmosphere of CO_2 or N_2 has been reported to have a beneficial effect on color of dehydrated vegetables.

Greening and Degreening of Citrus Fruits—Ethylene Effects

In general, as citrus fruit matures, there are losses in chlorophyll and increases in ethylene. It has been demonstrated that ethylene is responsible for change in color of the fruit from green to orange. Green color can be removed from the rind of citrus fruits by use of 4–200 ppm of ethylene. In a study of the chlorophyll and carotenoid content of Valencia oranges, it was found that in late spring, May to July, when the trees began making new growth, there were decreases in carotenoid content while the chlorophyll during that period remained relatively constant. As a consequence a regreening of the fruit occurred.

It has been demonstrated that oxygen is a substrate for the ripening reaction activated by ethylene, and that carbon dioxide inhibits the action of ethylene by competing with it for the receptor site. A carbon dioxide-enriched atmosphere, therefore, suppresses chlorophyll destruction.

Potato Greening

Potatoes exposed to light either before or after harvest, gradually turn green at the surface as chlorophyll develops. Postharvest greening is usually caused by exposure to artificial light. Displays of potatoes in retail stores are usually exposed to a light intensity within a range of 20 to 70 ft candles, an intensity that readily causes greening.

The greening effect is cumulative. Potatoes that have received some light before reaching the retail market may green rapidly in the market. The greening of potatoes is also affected by variety, maturity, temperature of storage, and duration of light. Smooth, white-skinned potatoes green more rapidly than do other varieties. Immature potatoes green rapidly. Postharvest age appears to retard greening. Potatoes exposed to light green faster at warm temperature than in the cold.

Research on potatoes exposed to the same intensity of various wavelengths of light revealed the least chlorophyll formation induced by green light (5000–6000 A), more by blue (4000–5000 A) and red (6000–7000 A), and most by daylight fluorescence (3500–7500 A). It has been reported that dipping potatoes in 0.0084 M 3-amino-1,2,4 triazole reduced chlorophyll formation. However, packaging in opaque materials is considered the most effective method of preventing greening of potatoes.

Potatoes can also become green because of the alkaloid, solanine. However the processes of chlorophyll and solanine synthesis are independent. Light from the blue end of the spectrum is most effective for solanine formation while the yellow and red lights, which were most effective for chlorophyll formation, do not increase solanine.

JAMES P. SWEENEY

Cross-reference: *Photosynthesis.*

CHOCOLATE AND COCOA PRODUCTS

In his classic book, *Cocoa and Chocolate, Their Chemistry and Manufacture*, R. Whymper quotes Brillat Savarin's (qv), *Physiologie du Goût* as follows: "The persons who habitually take chocolate are those who enjoy the most equable and constant health and are least liable to a multitude of illnesses which spoil the enjoyment of life." It is a measure of the times that we must hesitate to introduce a brief chapter on chocolate with that enthusiastic quotation today. Nevertheless, the chocolate industry is making progress in improving the quality of its products and in improving the effectiveness, efficiency, and cleanliness of its processes.

There follows a summary of some present thinking on the origins, processing, use, and technical aspects of chocolate and cocoa products.

History

The Aztecs were using "chocolatl" as a beverage when they were invaded by the Spaniards in 1519. The beverage was made by removing the shell from cocoa beans, grinding the resulting nibs and mixing the fluid mass that came from grinding with corn, spices, and water. The Spaniards added sugar to the beverage and introduced cocoa beans to Spain. With time, cocoa beans were grown in Central and South America and later in Africa.

From Spain, chocolate is believed to have been introduced into Italy, France, and Europe. Gradually, more and more factories were built in Europe generally producing at first the rich drinking chocolate. The first chocolate factories in Switzerland were built in the French part. By the 17th Century, chocolate houses were the places to go to. In 1828, VanHouton of Holland introduced a press to produce cocoa butter and cocoa powder and towards 1875 Daniel Peter of Vevey, Switzerland, in an attempt to meet competition, was manufacturing the first milk chocolate. Dr. James Baker of Dorchester, Mass., U.S.A., founded a chocolate factory in 1765.

Botany

Linnaeus, the Swedish botanist gave the cacao tree the name *Theobroma Cacao* or Food of the Gods. The varieties of the cacao tree among many others include Criollo, Forastero, and a cross between the two, Trinitario; the latter is now the most important type commercially.

The cacao tree has a distinctive gray-brown bark and grows to a height of from 15 to 25 ft. The tree must have conditions just right for good growth. It needs a warm and humid environment. Temperatures of 65°–95°F are adequate, but the tree does very well at temperatures of 105°F and at relative humidities approaching 100%. Good growth requires shade and an annual rainfall of at least 50 in. While more is desirable, too much can result in water logging and the development of fungus diseases.

The flowers are about 1/2 in. in diameter; many are produced but relatively few are pollinated, apparently by a small midge. Flowers are produced all year long so that the flowers and the resulting cocoa pods are found on the same tree. The fully grown pod will usually be 6–10 in. in length and 3–4 in. thick at the center. Yields vary tremendously from as low as 200 lb per acre to 500 lb per acre and as high as 1000 lb per acre.

Diseases and Pests

The cacao tree is not now native to the countries where the major part of the world crop is produced. Because of this and the use of large numbers of plants in relatively compact areas, the tree is very prone to attack by diseases and pests. Between 25 and 40% of each year's crop, it is estimated, is destroyed by disease.

Of the fungus diseases, black pod occurs in every cacao-producing country and causes considerable damage in wet weather. Monilia pot rot causes much damage in Ecuador, Columbia, and other countries especially under humid conditions. Witches broom started in the Amazon and spread to the West Indies. The infected shoot becomes thickened at the base and underdeveloped pods result.

Of the virus diseases, "swollen shoot" is so-called because of a swelling in young shoots, but in time the tree is almost leafless and the upper branches are dead. Red Mottle virus is found in Trinidad.

Capsids cause considerable damage by injecting toxins at the time of feeding. The damage of thrips is done by nymphs and the leaves then become yellow and fall. Repeated attacks result in the death of the tree.

Fermentation and Drying

When the cocoa pods are mature, they are removed from the tree by machetes or by a similar knife attached to a long pole for the higher branches. Then, after a day or two, the pods are split open with the machete and the beans and pulp removed by hand or by hand implements. The beans are then fermented to assist in removing the adhering pulp and to prepare the beans for drying. However, the chemical and biological changes that take place during fermentation are essential to the proper development of chocolate flavor later in the roasting step. The fermentation first takes place in the pulp with yeast fermentation, enzymatic action, with oxidation and condensation resulting in the elimination of much of the original bitterness. Bracco *et al.* (1969) discuss hydrolytic phenomena which may explain variations in the contents of nitrogen compounds, phenolic substances, and carbohydrates.

Drying of fermented beans is best accomplished by natural sun drying but rain, or the season, or the climate may require use of mechanical drying. Products of combustion must not come in contact with the drying beans and contact with smoke can result in objectionable smoky-flavored beans.

Cocoa Bean Commerce

Data covering this subject can best be given in tables prepared by Gil & Duffus in their Cocoa Market Report (London). Table C-10 shows production has steadily increased over the years. As can be seen, the per capita consumption in pounds increased from 0.69 in 1955/56 to 0.84 in 1967/68 and world production from 843,000 to 1,341,000 long tons. Included in this table are the exports for each of the cocoa producing countries as well as total imports for the consuming countries. As can be seen, in the same time period given above, exports and imports increased from over 700,000 to over 1,000,000 long tons.

Gil & Duffus also give world production of raw cocoa, showing statistics for those producing countries which combine into four general areas; Africa, America, West Indies, and Asia plus Oceania, together with world totals. These data cover the period from 1959/60 to 1970/71 during which world production increased from 1,039,000 to 1,432,000 long tons.

Similarly are given grindings of raw cocoa over approximately the same time, representing an estimate of the amounts of cocoa beans that were

TABLE C-10

WORLD PRODUCTION OF COCOA BEANS
(With Summary of World Imports and Exports)

	1955/56	1956/57	1957/58	1958/59	1959/60	1960/61	1961/62	1962/63	1963/64	1964/65	1965/66	1966/67	1967/68
World production (1000 long tons)	843	898	773	908	1039	1173	1124	1158	1220	1218	1484	1337	1341
World population (millions)	2737	2799	2903	2971	3003	3076	3141	3201	3220	3285	3353	3420	3584
Per capita consumption (lb)	0.69	0.72	0.60	0.68	0.78	0.86	0.80	0.81	0.84	0.85	1.01	0.88	0.84
	1956	1957	1958	1959	1960	1961	1962	1963	1964	1965	1966	1967	1968
						Units in 1000 Long Tons							
Total world exports	750	774	628	737	882	999	1019	1024	1016	1285	1092	1065	1027
Africa	516	562	428	556	646	795	845	821	833	1067	839	823	795
Central & South America	194	166	152	133	183	162	122	144	126	159	172	182	166
West Indies	31	36	37	35	41	26	31	36	34	32	35	32	34
Asia and Oceania	9	10	11	13	12	16	21	23	23	27	25	28	32
Total world imports	719	786	650	740	856	979	1005	1012	1024	1200	1151	1075	1049
Western Europe	377	440	371	411	458	499	544	536	522	563	571	524	518
EEC Bloc	247	278	233	267	292	337	354	346	357	398	380	353	345
EFTA Bloc	107	131	116	115	134	134	151	151	121	128	147	128	119
Eastern Europe[1]	43	73	43	69	95	65	95	115	132	171	136	164	200
North America[2]	254	230	198	217	253	352	295	290	278	371	328	293	240
Africa, Asia, Australia, Central and South America	45	43	38	43	50	63	71	71	92	96	116	94	91

SOURCE: Cocoa Market Report, Gil & Duffus, London.

[1] Includes U.S.S.R.
[2] United States and Canada.

TABLE C-11

MISCELLANEOUS COCOA STATISTICS

Year	Gil & Duffus Cocoa Price Index Avg	Financial Times Commodity Price Index Avg	U.S.A. Unit Value Imports ¢ per Lb FOB	Prime English Cocoa Butter £ per Ton Avg
1938	—	—	4.4	79.33
1939	—	—	4.2	79.33
1940	—	—	4.4	130.67
1941	—	—	5.6	163.33
1942	—	—	7.7	163.33
1943	—	—	6.8	163.33
1944	—	—	6.8	163.33
1945	—	—	7.4	163.33
1946	—	—	9.5	163.33
1947	—	—	25.4	326.67
1948	—	—	34.7	555.33
1949	—	—	19.8	492.33
1950	—	—	25.4	532.00
1951	—	—	32.5	618.33
1952	88.90	96.20	31.2	700.00
1953	98.11	88.56	29.6	709.33
1954	152.56	92.27	48.8	914.67
1955	98.66	90.62	37.0	525.00
1956	71.91	88.91	25.9	438.67
1957	80.48	84.91	26.4	592.67
1958	116.59	80.33	38.9	742.00
1959	96.32	82.13	34.1	564.67
1960	74.63	80.74	26.0	457.33
1961	59.46	78.36	20.8	436.33
1962	55.28	77.09	20.5	422.33
1963	66.65	82.24	21.4	471.33
1964	61.66	88.63	21.9	424.67
1965	45.48	86.60	15.2	345.33
1966	64.29	88.55	17.1	443.33
1967	76.49	80.10	23.3	518.00
1968	90.52	83.64	26.7	723.33
1969	120.22	89.64	34.4	889.34
1970 Avg to Dec. 1970	90.32	89.62	32.7	625.77

NOTES:
(1) The Gil & Duffus Cocoa Price Index is based on the Spot Price of Main Crop Ghana Cocoa in New York. Base: 1st July, 1952 = 100. The Financial Times Index of Sensitive Commodity Prices is a geometric average of 12 primary commodities selected from the U.S. and U.K. markets. Base: 1st July, 1952 = 100.
(2) The price of cocoa in the U.K. was controlled by the Ministry of Food from 1st October, 1940 to 1st November, 1950.
(3) From 1942–45 there was a fixed ceiling price in New York for Ghana and Bahia Cocoas of 8.9 and 8.7¢ per lb, respectively. Spot prices remained at these levels during this period.
(4) The unit import value is obtained by dividing the tonnage of gross imports into their value. Annual totals are in some cases amended.
(5) Prime English Cocoa Butter prices are for nearest forward delivery and basis duty paid (where applicable) free delivered. Prices from 1940 to 1950 are the Ministry of Food controlled prices and are basis duty paid ex store. From 1951 onwards prices are the average for the periods shown.

processed in the world. The estimate is made by considering exports and imports and changes in stocks. The data show the world total of grindings increasing from 927,000 long tons in 1960 to 1,323,000 long tons in 1970.

World exports of raw cocoa from producing countries increased steadily from 1940 (605,000 long tons) through 1965 (1,285,000 long tons) with a slight decline thereafter.

World net imports of raw cocoa, points up the continuous growth in world imports by showing the increase in world totals from 630,000 long tons in 1940 to 1,049,000 long tons in 1968.

Table C-11 is a compilation showing average price indices, average U.S. import value, and average English cocoa butter prices for the period since 1938. Price relationships fluctuate from season to season. Due to good crops in Equador, for example, and less demand for Rio Caribe cocoa, the prices for these types can be less than for Ghana, Lagos, and Ivory Coast in nearby positions; and Ghana cocoa can be more expensive in distant positions.

Cocoa Manufacture

There has recently been described (Anon. 1970) what is said to be the most advanced cocoa processing plant and the largest self-contained cocoa plant in the world capable of processing nearly 80,000 tons of cocoa beans per year. It has 150,000 sq ft of floor space and the factory consists of a main process building and administration block, a solvent extraction plant, boiler house, and storage silos. Fig. C-6 is a flow sheet of the manufacturing process.

A simplified block diagram flow sheet is shown in Fig. C-7 for Dutch processed cocoa and milk chocolate manufacture. It indicates cocoa manufacture consists essentially of bean cleaning, roasting, winnowing, nib grinding, dutching, pressing, and cocoa grinding. When dutching is not used, natural cocoa is manufactured. Prior to any manufacture, the proper beans must be selected for use.

Bean Selection.—Beans are generally considered to be in two categories, basic beans and flavor beans.

Basic beans have a strong flavor and even some harshness. They are the commonest and least expensive and include Accra beans from Ghana, Bahia beans from Brazil, Lagos beans from Nigeria, Sanchez from the Dominican Republic and also Ivory Coast, Fernando Po and Cameron beans. Bean types are usually named after major shipping ports or country of origin. The flavor of Ivory Coast, Accra, Lagos, and Bahia beans runs from mild to strong in that order and the color of chocolate liquor from Ivory Coast, Accra, Bahia, and Lagos beans runs from light to dark in that order.

Flavor beans, besides having a good basic chocolate character, have aromatic properties important to the overall chocolate flavor. These beans are not so common, are more expensive, and include Arriba from Ecuador, those from Trinidad, and those from Caracas, Puerto Cabello, Maracaibo, and Rio Caribe in Venezuela.

There are, of course, beans of intermediate types. The selection of beans depends upon the quality of the flavor desired and whether milk chocolate, dark chocolate, cocoa or another product is being made. The beans are usually roasted separately to a degree depending upon the kind of bean and the ultimate use; and then the beans are blended.

Jay C. Musser of Klein Chocolate Company, Elizabethtown, Penn., has compiled characteristics and uses of principal varieties of cocoa beans as shown in Table C-12.

Bean Cleaning.—Cocoa beans coming into a factory are cleaned to remove extraneous matter such as stones, string, chaff, broken beans, shell, and hollow beans. This is done by the use of air streams to carry away relatively light matter, by allowing heavy matter to settle in such air streams, by screening away unwanted materials larger than the beans, and by screening away small matter such as sand.

Roasting.—The roasting process develops the flavor in the cocoa beans in a most important way affecting the flavor and color characteristics of the ultimate chocolate product. At the same time, the moisture content of the cocoa bean is lowered, the shell is made more susceptible for removal from the nib (cotyledon), and the nib made friable so it can be ground.

The range of the degree of roasting is quite wide with a very light roast being called a "fondant" roast, and a very high roast called a "coffee" roast, a "coating" roast, or other such term. There are many degrees of roasts in between, but the most common are "full" roast, "low" roast, and an intermediate roast. In choosing a roast, attention must be given to the ultimate product being made, its use, and the kind of beans being used.

Roasting temperatures can be confusing as they depend upon the type of roaster used and the location of the measuring instrument. Roasters traditionally were of batch design but modern manufacturing practice calls more and more for the continuous roaster.

Winnowing.—Having roasted the cocoa beans, it is necessary to separate the shell from the cotyledon which actually breaks up into segments called nibs. First, however, the roasted beans are passed through a cracker which can consist of two corrugated rolls rotating close enough to squeeze or press the beans cracking or breaking the shell which is then mixed with the nibs.

To separate the shell pieces and the nib pieces, a winnower is used which depends for its operation upon screening and air elutriation. In the United States, it is necessary legally to clean nibs so that they contain less than 1.75% shell. In accomplishing this the manufacturer must operate his winnowers in such a manner to keep the amount of nibs in the discarded shell to a minimum. In Europe, it is often reported that the germ is removed but in the United States that practice is not usually followed.

Nib Grinding.—By grinding, cocoa nibs are converted to chocolate liquor. The nibs have a cellular structure with cocoa butter dispersed throughout, and upon milling, the cell walls are disrupted and the heat of friction developed from the grinding melts the fat globules. The fat content varies from about 51 to 56% depending upon the type of bean. The changes taking place are largely physical in-

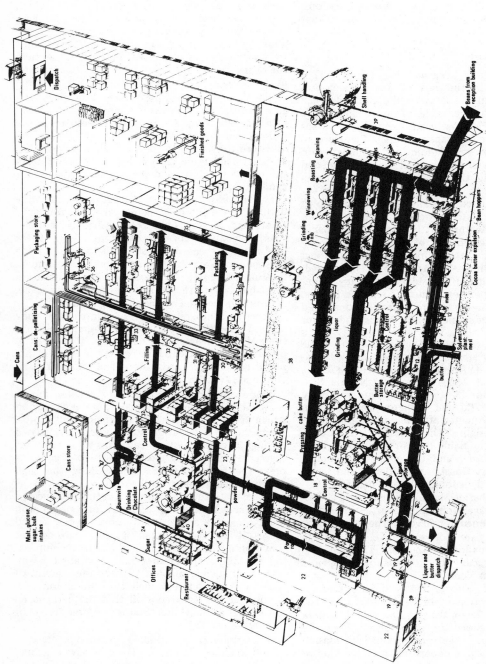

FIG. C-6. FLOW SHEET OF THE MANUFACTURING PROCESS OF NEW CADBURY SCHWEPPES FACTORY

1. Slat conveyors. 2. Belt conveyors. 3. Bucket conveyors. 4. Seven screw-type conveyors. 5. Four gas-fired roasters. 6. Four vibratory winnowers. 7. Four turbo-mills. 8. Twenty liquor-mills. 9. Alkalizing plant and tanks. 10. Tote bins. 11. Substation. 12. Centrifuges (butter). 13. Butter melting facility. 14. Butter deodorizing tower. 15. Liquor-hold tanks. 16. Four 7000 psi liquor presses. 17. Hydraulic pumps for presses. 18. Cake-breaking plant in powder room. 19. Butter molding and store. 20. Powder-hold silo. 21. Powder-feed silo. 22. Vehicle and plant maintenance. 23. Plant services. 24. Shift manager. 25. Drinking chocolate instantizer. 26. Bournvita mixer. 27. Glucose tanks. 28. Malt tank. 29. Vacuum dryer. 30. Cocoa. 31. Can-filling machines. 32. Drinking chocolate. 33. Bournvita. 34. Reject/reclaim. 35. Office. 36. Tote bins. 37. ... 38. ... 39. ... 40. Asbestos panels and ...

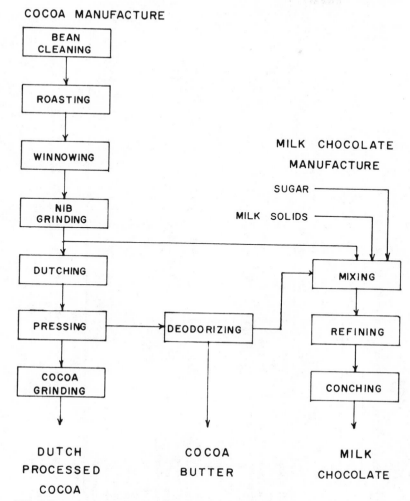

COCOA MANUFACTURE

MILK CHOCOLATE MANUFACTURE

FIG. C-7. FLOW SHEET FOR MANUFACTURE OF MILK CHOCOLATE AND DUTCH PROCESSED COCOA

cluding the removal of water. Chemical and flavor changes depend upon the degree of heating.

Traditionally, nibs have been ground on stone mills with each piece of equipment usually consisting of three pairs. Each pair consists of a stationary base stone with another stone revolving upon it, each stone with grooves to facilitate grinding. The nibs which may be preground are fed to a hole in the center of the top stone and pass between the two stones. The liquor must be ground fine enough to release the fat, coarse enough not to cause difficulties in pressing, and of a fineness consistent with the ultimate use. Following the stone mills, steel rolls have been used to obtain the necessary fineness. For grinding nibs, attrition mills are finding increasing use because of their high output and relatively sanitary nature.

They, in turn, must be followed by stone mills, steel rolls, or disc mills to obtain the necessary fineness.

Chocolate liquor is primarily used to make other chocolate products, but it can be molded and sold for use in other foods, particularly as a baking chocolate.

Dutching.—Dutching or alkalizing is carried out to modify the color and flavor of cocoa. The color becomes darker depending upon the degree of alkalization and the flavor becomes somewhat milder being less harsh than that of natural cocoa. There is no increase in solubility, but the miscibility and dispersibility of the dutched cocoa improves.

Dutching is carried out on chocolate liquor by adding an alkaline solution, agitating, and removing any added water usually by heating. When nibs are

TABLE C-12

CHARACTERISTICS AND USES OF PRINCIPAL VARIETIES OF CACAO BEANS

| Variety[1] | Use | Physical Characteristics | | | Average Chemical Composition of the Nib (Raw) | | | | | | | | Shell |
		Size Gm/100 Beans	Color	Flavor	Moisture (%)	Fat (%)	Starch (%)	Cellulose Fiber (%)	Protein[5] (%)	Ash (%)	Theobromine (%)	Other Components[4] (%)	Wt of Total Bean (%)
Ghana	2	111.6	Red-brown	Ordinary to harsh	4.59	54.80	8.4	2.8	19.2	3.2	1.0	6.2	10.7
Lagos	2	112.3	Medium brown	Ordinary but aromatic	4.39	54.10	8.6	3.1	19.3	2.5	1.1	6.4	10.5
Ivory Coast	2	111.2	Brown to brown-violet	Ordinary to slightly harsh	4.93	54.65	8.7	2.7	19.4	2.8	1.1	6.1	11.0
West Cameroon	1	128.2	Medium brown	Ordinary to mild	5.35	55.75	8.5	2.8	19.0	3.0	1.2	6.4	12.3
Bahia	2	111.1	Red-brown	Ordinary to slightly smoky	4.76	53.7	8.0	2.2	19.1	2.6	1.3	7.6	12.5
Sanchez	3	108.5	Dark maroon	Sharp, distinctive chocolate	3.4	52.85	8.1	2.5	20.4	3.1	1.4	8.1	10.5
Rio Caribe	3	113.4	Red-brown	Excellent chocolate	4.56	52.84	8.8	2.3	20.1	3.2	1.1	6.8	10.9
Trinidad (Plantation)	1	123.0	Red-violet	Superior non-aromatic	5.1	53.65	8.8	2.7	20.5	2.7	1.1	6.3	12.1
Arriba	3	109.7	Very dark red-brown	Fine, strong aromatic	5.9	51.21	6.5	2.2	20.1	3.1	1.7	7.9	12.6
Samoan	3	114.4	Very light brown	Very mild and aromatic	2.92	54.27	7.6	2.8	21.2	3.9	1.2	6.7	10.8

SOURCE: Jay C. Musser, Klein Chocolate Company, Elizabethtown, Penn.

[1] These data are on all superior quality grades of each variety.
[2] These beans are the "ordinary" or basic beans of commerce. The bulk of all chocolate commodities are produced from these beans alone or in a blend with the flavor varieties.
[3] These beans are the flavor varieties. They are superior in flavor and aroma. There are only a small proportion of these beans available in the world. In general, these beans are blended with ordinary beans, or used alone in the production of premium quality products.
[4] Includes: higher sugars, food acids, tannins, phlobaphenes, and similar complex food components (determined by difference).
[5] Total nitrogen minus nitrogen of theobromine times 6.25 = protein.

dutched, it is more difficult to remove the water and additional drying equipment is necessary.

The dutching of cocoa powder has the advantage of not producing a dutched butter. The cocoa resulting from the dutching of nibs is usually milder than that resulting from the dutching of liquor and the choice of which to use depends upon the product qualities desired.

Pressing.—In pressing, cocoa butter is separated from cocoa powder. The presses are large, hydraulic, expensive, and contain steel filter screens. The first part of the press cycle separates the butter from the solids as in normal filtration. The second part, however, begins when the press is filled with solids and a hydraulic ram exerting pressures up to 6000 psi squeezes still more fat from the remaining cocoa solids. The lower the desired fat content in the cocoa, the longer is the pressing time so that it is usually uneconomical to press to cocoa fat contents less than 10–12%. A small amount of cocoa solids remains with the cocoa butter and that is removed usually by a small conventional filter press.

Cocoa Grinding.—As cocoa loaves drop from the presses, they are passed through breakers to form a "kibbled cake" of less than 1 in. in size. The higher fat cocoas break down to a smaller size than do the lower fat cocoas because of the presence of the extra cocoa butter. The cocoa then requires further grinding or pulverizing to be used commercially. Traditionally, pulverized cocoa has been passed over screens to obtain the proper size. The screening method has had the disadvantages of low capacity, high maintenance, and large space requirements. Consequently, air classification is proving more satisfactory with its high throughputs, sanitary features, and flexibility in producing cocoas of different size specifications.

It is very necessary in producing cocoas to control carefully the temperature of the cocoa while it is being heated during grinding and while it is subsequently being cooled. This is in order to produce a cocoa powder containing properly tempered cocoa butter to have a powder of satisfactory color which will not fade.

Chocolate Manufacture

The simplified block diagram of Fig. C-7 indicates milk chocolate manufacturing's relationship to cocoa and cocoa butter manufacturing and that it consists essentially of mixing, refining, and conching. If milk is not an ingredient, then sweet chocolate or semisweet chocolate is manufactured.

Mixing.—The mixing operation prepares the mass for refining by (1) producing a homogeneous mass; (2) coating all of the particles with fat; and (3) mixing in the right amount of fat. If too much fat is added the feed rolls of the refiner will take

the fat first and later the dry solids. If too little fat is added the refiner will overheat due to too much friction and produce a very nonuniform grade product. At this point the chocolate manufacturer wants a soft, plastic, pliable, nonflowable mass. Its cocoa butter content is about 25–30%. Flavorings are not added in the mixer if the mass is later to be conched or heat-treated.

The melangeur could be used when starting with nibs in order to grind and mix in one operation. When this is done the chocolate does have a very distinctive characteristic chocolate flavor highly desired in some quarters.

The mixing operation can be carried out by batchwise weighing ingredients, or continuously by automatic metering of the ingredients.

Refining.—The purpose of refining is to obtain a chocolate mass having the proper particle size. Ordinarily a five-roll refiner is used in which the rolls are water cooled and have a convex surface. Each roll rotates faster than the prior one thus wiping up the mass and passing it, in turn, to the next roll. The rolls cannot be tight together; the operator must adjust the clearance to obtain the desired particle size in the resulting product.

The quality of chocolate depends upon its particle size distribution. A wide range of chocolate quality is produced within the following range of particle sizes as determined by microscope and projector.

Maximum Particle Size of Sugar in Microns	Maximum Particle Size of Chocolate Liquor in Microns
25–57	50–114

For a good eating chocolate, Rostagno (1969) has advised that no more than 20% of the mass should have a particle size greater than 22 μ.

Conching.—Conching (1) develops chocolate flavor; (2) darkens the color; (3) stabilizes the viscosity of the chocolate mass by covering all interfaces with cocoa butter; and (4) lowers the moisture content. The flavor development results from volatizing undesirable flavors (the pH increases as the conching proceeds), oxidation occurs and a "cooking" or browning reaction takes place in milk types of chocolate between the sugar and amino acid substances. No appreciable particle size reduction or change in shape occurs.

Conching is a balance of temperature, time, agitation, and aeration. Dry conching is utilized when the feed material to the conche cannot be pumped and the heat generated by the agitation must be dissipated either by atmospheric conditions or by water-jacketed equipment. Wet conching is utilized when the feed material can be pumped to the conche and in this case the heat for conching is supplied, for instance, by hot water to the jacket of the conche. Either milk or dark chocolate is conched at 120°–180°F for from 1 to 4 days.

The longitudinal conche has been traditionally used in the industry but is being replaced by rotary conches which handle larger quantities of chocolate and require much less labor.

In producing a fondant chocolate, the cocoa beans are given a very light roast, just enough to permit clean separation of the shell and the nib. The chocolate liquor from these nibs is mixed with sugar but with no milk solids, and refined. Conching is carried out at a sufficiently high temperature and long enough time to cause a flavor development characteristic of this process.

Deodorization of Cocoa Butter

If cocoa butter is pressed from chocolate liquor which has been treated with alkali, the cocoa butter will have a strong flavor with bitter after notes. In order to use such a cocoa butter in milk chocolate products, it is necessary to deodorize it. The deodorization is carried out as a steam distillation under vacuum. Live steam is bubbled through the liquid cocoa butter and the steam strips out the undesirable flavors.

It has been found (Rostagno et al. 1970) that the deodorization process does not alter the composition of cocoa butter or its stability to oxidation in any significant manner. The volatile aroma of cocoa butter is determined by the quality of the initial cocoa, and by the deodorization conditions. The measurement of the optical density of cocoa butter at 278 nm of a steam distillate gives an aroma index which is reproducible and a correlation has been found to exist between the value of this index and an organoleptic evaluation. The volatile substances are mainly nitrogenous heterocyclic compounds.

Manufacturing Practices

Sanitation and Infestation Control.—Criteria for good manufacturing practice of food products are being developed in the United States that affect the manufacturer of chocolate products. Some specific considerations are the following:

> Even small amounts of water are microbiologically deleterious in processing such high fat, low moisture products. Water must be avoided unless a known contaminant exists which requires special chemical sanitization. Good sanitation is routinely accomplished by methods not involving washing.
>
> Because of the absence of water, stainless steel is not used as it is in other food processes. Some particular points of practice are: winnow-

ing of roasted cocoa beans is carried out to minimize microbiological contaminations of nibs by the shell which has a relatively high bacteria count; and dust from cocoa bean shells, cracking, and other operations is handled and stored so as not to contaminate other ingredients or chocolate products.

The following is an excellent statement taken from *Infestation Control in the Cocoa, Chocolate, and Confectionary Industry* by The Cocoa, Chocolate and Confectionery Alliance, London:

> Hygiene . . . is not simply a matter of cleanliness in the handling of food. It requires a cooperative and conscious approach by all the diverse personnel concerned with the making of confectionary. The architect must design the building with the maintenance of hygienic conditions in mind, and the buildings must be maintained free from cracks and crevices and holes where rodents may enter. The engineers must install a plant that can be kept clean. Buyers should seek to purchase ingredients as free from infestation as possible. Care must be taken to prevent infestation reaching ingredients, packing materials, or products during transport or storage. Production personnel obviously have a big part to play in maintaining hygiene. Methods of manufacture should be adjusted wherever practicable to facilitate the maintenance of hygienic conditions. Packaging design should aim to prevent as far as possible the entry of insects.

Packaging of Chocolate.—Packaging materials when received in the plant must be inspected to see that they meet specifications including that of not having any off-odors that could be transmitted to chocolate. Foil makes a very satisfactory wrapping because it keeps its fold about the bar. Cost and inability to use metal detectors leads to the use of other materials that will provide moisture, flavor, and infestation protection. The packaging material must also have good machinability properties in wrapping machines.

Storage of Finished Goods.—Finished goods in warehouses should be stored as shown in Table C-13.

Bulk Shipments.—It has been customary to mold chocolate coating into 10-lb cakes wrapped in 30-40-lb kraft paper. The user has to tear off the paper and remelt the cakes before using the chocolate. Today, bulk shipments are used whenever possible in an effort to reduce cost of molding and remelting cakes. Tank trucks are often used which are well insulated and which, especially in winter, have a gasoline heating system from which hot air maintains the temperature of the chocolate by means of a jacket. Before loading, the temperature of the truck should be at least

TABLE C-13

RECOMMENDED STORAGE TEMPERATURES FOR
FINISHED CHOCOLATE GOODS

Type of Material	Maximum Temperature °F	% RH	Minimum Temperature °F	% RH
Chocolate coatings, cocoa butter, chocolate liquor, cocoa beverage powders	70	50	60	60
Syrups and fudges	75	—	60	—
Bulk cocoa	70	50	60	65

75°F and preferably 90°–105°F. The chocolate
should be loaded at 105°–110°F.

Nutrition of Chocolate

The nutrition of chocolate is due largely to its
high energy value. The USDA Agriculture Handbook 8, *Composition of Foods*, lists plain chocolate with 520 cal per 100 gm. Milk chocolate with
almonds has 532 and with peanuts has 543 cal per
100 gm.

The high fat breakfast cocoa (23.7% fat) has 299
cal per 100 gm and a low-medium fat cocoa (12.7%
fat), processed with alkali, has 215 cal per 100 gm.
Chocolate syrup has 245 and chocolate fudge topping has 330 cal per 100 gm.

Technical Properties

Composition of Cocoa.—Table C-14 gives the
average analysis of the fat and moisture-free
components of natural and of dutch process
(slightly alkalized) cocoa powder.

Physical Properties of Chocolate.—A physical
property of chocolate, aside from those relating to
cyrstallizing and tempering, of prime importance
is its rheology. Presently in the United States, the
viscosity of chocolate is measured by the
MacMichael viscometer as recommended by the
NCA (National Confectioners Association). However, the measurement of Casson plastic viscosity
and yield value is much more definitive for knowing
the true flow properties. Plastic viscosity is the
viscosity for a plastic substance calculated as the
ratio of shear stress to shear rate. The yield value
is a measure of the initial shear stress that must be
imposed before flow commences. The Haake
viscometer measures such properties very well because of its wide range of shear rates. Fig. C-8
shows the range of viscometers. It shows that the
Brookfield viscometer provides more information

TABLE C-14

AVERAGE ANALYSIS OF FAT AND
MOISTURE-FREE COMPONENTS OF NATURAL
AND DUTCH PROCESS COCOA POWDER

	Natural %	Dutched %
Ash	6.3	10.3
Theobromine } (purines)	2.9	2.8
Caffeine	0.5	0.5
Polyhydroxyphenols (tannins)	14.6	14.0
Proteins	28.1	27.0
Sugar	2.4	2.3
Starch	14.6	14.0
Cellulose } (carbohydrates)	22.0	21.2
Pentosans	3.7	3.4
Acids	3.7	3.4
Other substances (up to 100%)	1.2	1.1
	100.0	100.0

SOURCE: *Handbook for Cocoa Production*, 2nd Edition
(German) by H. Fincke, published by Springer-Verlag,
Berlin, Heidelberg, New York (1965).

than the MacMichael and that the Haake viscometer
provides still more information.

Generally, when a coating is rheologically unstable, its viscosity decreases upon agitation as is
reflected by the MacMichael viscosity. Also, however, the Casson values decrease with a much
greater decrease in the yield value than in the
plastic viscosity.

The viscosity of chocolate can be decreased by
adding cocoa butter or lecithin. The flow properties are also controlled by the particle size of the
chocolate, by moisture control, and by the presence of emulsifiers.

When molding, a viscosity is wanted that will
permit the chocolate to flow easily into all corners
of the mold quickly and release air bubbles. When
decorating, a chocolate with a high yield value is
wanted. When enrobing, either kind of property
may be desired.

The differential scanning calorimeter has proven
very useful in chocolate work and with it the
following values have been obtained (Chevalley
et al. 1970):

Heat of Fusion in Cal/Gm

Cocoa butter	37.6 ± 1.9
Dark chocolate	11.1 ± 0.4
Milk chocolate	10.6 ± 0.3

Specific Heat in Cal/Gm(°C)

°C	Cocoa Butter	Dark Chocolate	Milk Chocolate
−40	0.31	0.24	0.26
−30	0.34	0.25	0.28

				Pentosan	1.5
-20	0.37	0.26	0.30	Organic Acids	1.5
-10	0.41	0.29	0.32		
0	0.50	0.31	0.37		(Mg/100 Gm)
+10	0.57	0.32	0.40	Vitamin A	0.022

					(µg/100 Gm)
+40	0.48	0.33	0.37	Vitamin D	2.5
+50	0.48	0.35	0.39		
+60	0.49	0.36	0.40		(Mg/100 Gm)

Chemical Properties of Chocolate.—The composition of the milk and sugar used in chocolate is well known and Lange (1969) has given the following composition of cocoa beans:

Vitamin E	4.4
Thiamin	0.18
Lactoflavine (riboflavin)	0.18
Nicotinic acid amide	1.5
Biotin	0.015
Pantothenic acid	0.77
Pyridoxine	0.08

	(%)
H_2O	2.0
Fat	55.7
Ash	2.7
Purine	1.4
Polyhydroxyphenols	6.2
Protein	11.8
Sugars	1.0
Starch	6.2
Cellulose	9.3

	(Cal/100 Gm)
Calories	
Fat	520
Protein	48
Carbohydrate	42
Total	610

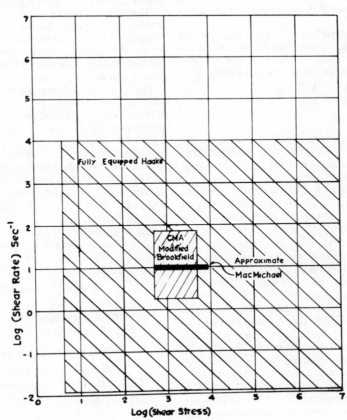

FIG. C-8. RANGE OF VISCOMETERS

J. P. Marion *et al.* (1967) list 126 substances found in cocoa aroma either by themselves or others. B. van der Wal *et al.* (1971) identify 181 compounds.

Physical and Chemical Properties of Cocoa Butter.—Cocoa butter consists primarily of triglycerides of palmitic, stearic, and oleic acids. Because it is a mixture of triglycerides it does not have a sharp melting point but rather a melting range. Minifie (1970) has gathered together analytical values as shown in Table C-15

Cocoa butter, because of its melting range being close to body temperature, has been used in cosmetic formulas for making suntan products, toilet soaps, suppositories, ointments, creams, lotions, and for lipsticks.

Replacement Fats for Cocoa Butter.—There is always some demand for less expensive fats to replace cocoa butter in chocolate. Such replacement fats may be either partial or total substitutes for cocoa butter. Partial replacement requires the use of a fat which being compatible with cocoa butter will not change its physical properties such as bloom resistance, gloss, snap, melting point, and

storage life. Total substitution requires a fat that will provide good eating qualities and hardness as well as the other qualities mentioned above. Usually tempering conditions are not as critical as they are for cocoa butter. It is very important in the manufacture or use of a total substitute not to contaminate it or cocoa butter with each other.

Product Uses

Uses of Cocoa.—Although it is recognized that bean selection, roasting, fineness, and fat content greatly influence the final cocoa product, cocoas are usually classified as to fat content and type of process used, i.e., natural or dutch. The fat percentage can vary from 45% in nuggets to less than 0.5% in the solvent extracted cocoas. The dutch process or alkali-treated cocoas are darker in color and a little milder in flavor. The dutching process, which generally raises the pH to above 7.0, is quite often preferred for cocoas to be used in less sweet foods such as chocolate beverages, cooking, baking, and ice cream. The natural process liquors and cocoas are usually preferred in very

TABLE C-15

ANALYTICAL VALUES OF COCOA BUTTER

Data	Minifie (24)	Fincke (12)	Jensen (15)
Specific gravity	0.8957 (40°/15.5°C)	0.910–0.912 (15°/15°C) liquid 0.976–0.978 (15°/15°C) solid	—
Refractive Index	1.4560–1.4580 (40°C)	1.4565–1.4578 (40°C)	1.4565–1.4575 (40°C)
Iodine Value	35.4 (35–40)	33.5–37.5	33–39
Saponification Value	195 (188–198)	192–197	191–198
Unsaponifiable matter	0.8%	0.3–0.4%	0.5–1.1%
Iodine Value of unsaponifiable matter	80–96	—	—
Melting point			
Complete fusion	33.0°C (32.0°–34.0°C)	32.8°–35.0°C	32.5°–34.5°C
Incipient fusion	32.0°C (31.2°–32.7°C)	31.8°–33.5°C (flow point)	30.0°–32.5°C
Free fatty acids (as oleic acid)	1.5% (maximum permitted)	0.8–3.0% Fatty acids—complete fusion	0.4–1.05%
Titer point	49.0°C	51.5°–53.5°C Fatty acids—flow point 49.0°–51.0°C	49°–50°C
Reichert Meissl value	0.65	0.1–0.5	—
Polenske value	0.3	0.5–1.0	—

SOURCE: Minifie (1970).

sweet foods such as candies and icings. Blends of dutch and natural process cocoas are quite often used for syrups and toppings.

Sometimes known as chocolate flavors, cocoa nuggets, cocoa crumbles, and cocoa chips contain from 34 to 45% fat and usually exhibit a strong chocolaty flavor. Their main use is in fine quality ice cream and fancy icings.

High fat cocoas contain not less than 19% fat and include the breakfast cocoas which contain a minimum of 22% cocoa fat by federal standards. The natural and light dutched cocoas in this class are used for drinking, syrups, and general household use. The dutched cocoas are used for chocolate biscuits and crackers, devil food cakes, and hard candy making and confectionary such as chocolate fudge.

Medium fat cocoas contain from 14 to 18% fat. The natural and light dutched are used for malted milk mixtures, cocoa milk drinks, chocolate flavored desserts, chocolate pies, and chocolate flavored syrups.

Low fat cocoas contain from 11 to 13% cocoa fat. The natural cocoas in this group are used for milk drinks, cocoa skim milk mixtures, sweet cocoas, and icings while the dutch process cocoas are used for cocoa extracts, baking, and devil food mixtures. Where low cost is of importance, these cocoas are commonly used. Microbiological specifications for a dutched cocoa might be as follows:

Per Gm

Bacteria count	25,000 maximum
Yeast	<50
Mold	<50
E. Coli	Negative

Cocoas in the range of $1/2$ to 3% fat are solvent extracted. They have practically no chocolate flavor and are used as dusting powders in confectionery, imitation chocolate, cattle feed, and fertilizer. Table C-16 summarizes the general uses of cocoas and Table C-17 is a summary of U.S. Standards of Identity for cocoas.

Cocoa Beverages.—Chocolate has too much cocoa fat in it to make an acceptable beverage so cocoa has been used. The use of cocoa in the home results in a very satisfactory beverage, but requires quite a bit of care and time. So the use of cocoa beverage mixtures containing all the ingredients and which disperse quickly in hot or cold liquids has had considerable growth. Such beverage mixtures either do or do not contain milk solids. Those which do not contain milk solids contain cocoa, sugar, and other flavoring agents. They are added to either hot or cold milk; lecithin is usually added but too much will affect the flavor of the beverage. The beverage is usually instantized by several processes the most common of which is agglomeration. The composition would be in the range:

	(%)
Cocoa	20–30
Sugar	70–80
Lecithin	Minimum
Salt and flavorings	Trace

Beverages which do contain milk are usually added only to hot water but can be added also to hot milk. With the proper balance of cocoa, sugar, and milk solids, a very satisfactory drink can be obtained. Nonfat milk solids are usually used as whole milk solids do not have as long a storage life. As the cost of milk solids increases, the use of suitable vegetable fats to give "body" to the drink and of milk substitutes increases. The final composition would be in the following range depending upon the ultimate use requirements:

	(%)
Cocoa	10–60
Sugar	25–60
Nonfat dry milk solids	10–30
Salt and flavorings	Trace

Chocolate Products.—There are many kinds of chocolate. Chocolate liquor ground and refined is sold as bitter or baking chocolate. Its fat content is a little over 50%, depending on the beans from which it was made. In the United States, semisweet chocolate, or bittersweet chocolate, has a minimum chocolate liquor content of 35%, while sweet chocolate has a minimum chocolate liquor content of 15%. Both semisweet and sweet chocolate must be sweetened with ingredients such as sugar, dextrose, or corn syrup solids and may contain up to less than 12% milk solids from many different optional dairy products. Certain flavoring ingredients such as vanilla beans, vanillin, ethyl vanillin, spices, natural flavoring oils and ground nut meats, and emulsifiers may also be added. The term dark chocolate usually refers to nonmilk chocolates.

Milk chocolate must have not less than 10% liquor and not less than 12% milk solids. To it, also, certain flavoring ingredients and emulsifiers may be added. Milk chocolate was first made by adding sweetened condensed milk to cocoa nibs or chocolate liquor and mixing in a melangeur until a uniform dry product resulted. Today, a chocolate factory may purchase fresh milk, evaporated milk, condensed milk, dried milk solids or crumb for a source of its milk solids. Crumb is a dried mixture of milk and sugar which may or may not contain chocolate liquor. It has been found to have a good

TABLE C-16

SUMMARY OF USES OF COCOAS

Uses	Chocolate Flavors		High Fat Cocoas, Not Less Than 19% Fat		Medium Fat Cocoas, 14–18% Fat		Low Fat Cocoas, 11–13% Fat		Defatted or Solvent-Extracted Cocoas ½–3% Fat
	Natural	Dutched	Natural and Light Dutched	Dutched	Natural and Light Dutched	Dutched	Natural	Dutched	
Baking			x	x	x	x	x	x	
Beverages									
Cake fillers									
Cattle feed									
Chocolate biscuits				x		x		x	
Chocolate crackers				x		x		x	
Chocolate flavored desserts			x	x	x	x	x	x	
Chocolate pies			x	x	x	x	x	x	
Cocoa-malt, sugar Mixture					x	x	x	x	
Cocoa milks					x	x	x	x	
Confectionery, fudge			x	x	x	x	x	x	
Devil's food cake				x	x	x	x	x	
Dusting powder									
Fertilizers									x
Household use			x	x			x	x	
Ice cream	x	x							
Icings	x	x							
Imitation chocolate coatings									
Medicinal powders or tablets			x	x	x	x	x	x	
Sweet cocoas			x	x	x	x	x	x	
Syrups			x	x	x	x	x	x	
Theobromine									x
Thin syrups							x	x	
Tobacco			x	x	x	x	x	x	

SOURCE: Adapted from Blumenthal (1942).

TABLE C-17

SUMMARY OF U.S. STANDARDS OF IDENTITY FOR COCOAS

Description	Cocoa is food prepared by pulverizing the residual material remaining after part of the cocoa fat has been removed from ground cocoa nibs.
Basis of sale	Fat content and optional ingredients.
Cocoa types	
Breakfast, high-fat cocoas	Contain not less than 22% fat.
Medium-fat cocoas	Contain less than 22% fat, but not less than 10% fat.
Low-fat cocoas	Contain less than 10% fat.
Optional ingredients	(1) Ground spice.
	(2) Ground vanilla beans.
	(3) Vanillin, ethyl vanillin.
	(4) Salt.
	(5) Any natural or artificial flavor oil or flavoring which does not impart a chocolate, milk, or butter flavor.
	(6) Alkali—not greater in neutralizing value than 3 parts by weight of anhydrous potassium carbonate per 100 parts cocoa nibs.

Any combination of:

Sodium	Bicarbonate
Potassium	Carbonate
Ammonium	Hydroxide
Magnesium	Carbonate / Oxide

shelf-life and so it is possible to make crumb at a different location from that of the chocolate factory.

Table C-18 is a summary of U.S. Standards of Identity for chocolate.

Almonds, peanuts, hazelnuts, raisins, and crisp rice are very common additions to chocolate and add appreciably to its acceptance. So-called "white chocolate" is milk chocolate without cocoa and so legally cannot be called chocolate in the United States.

A proposed draft for the Codex international standards (qv) would define chocolate as the homogeneous product obtained by an adequate process of manufacture from a mixture of one or more of the following: cocoa nib, cocoa mass, cocoa press cake, cocoa powder including fat-reduced cocoa powder, with sugars, with or without the addition of cocoa butter. Milk chocolate is defined the same except for the inclusion of milk solids.

Heat Resistant Chocolate.—In 1970, Dr. J. Kleinert made an excellent review of heat resistant chocolates in *der Bauermeister* (German) which is summarized as follows:

    Cocoa butter can be hardened by hydrogenation or fractionation. However, aside from the legal aspects of using such fats, chocolate containing them is usually not satisfactory to the consumer, it not melting well in the mouth.

Chocolate may be made heat resistant by physical means. Extruded chocolate can be worked at lower fat contents than normal, usually not more than 28%, and so some heat-resistant properties result. Chocolate can be processed by introducing moisture in such a form that the normal lubricating effect of the cocoa butter is disrupted.

The nonfatty ingredients mesh with one another frequently by a hydro-colloidal swelling action. Kleinert reports chocolate can be tempered so that the fat phase is "precrystallized" in such a way to increase the chocolate's normal working temperature.

Compound or confectioner's coatings are made heat resistant by replacing at least part of the cocoa butter with another fat of higher melting point.

Uses of Chocolate.—Chocolate is used in large quantities in bars both plain and enrobed. The U.S. Department of Commerce, Business and Defense Services Administration reports in their publication, *Confectionery Manufacturers' Sales & Distribution, 1969* an average annual growth of 4% in value of shipments of bar goods in the 1960–1969 period. Sales were $370,000,000 in

TABLE C-18

SUMMARY OF U.S. STANDARDS OF IDENTITY FOR CHOCOLATE

Description	Chocolate is the solid or semiplastic food, the ingredients of which are intimately mixed and ground, prepared from chocolate liquor and sweetened with one of the optional saccharine ingredients, and may be flavored with one of the optional flavor ingredients. Optional emulsifiers may be added.
Basis of sale	Liquor content and optional ingredients.
Ingredients (3 types)	
Bittersweet (Semisweet)	Not less than 35% liquor + less than 12% milk solids from optional dairy ingredients + must be sweetened with one of the optional saccharine ingredients + optional flavoring ingredients + optional emulsifier.
Sweet	Not less than 15% liquor + less than 12% milk solids from optional dairy ingredients + must be sweetened with one of the optional saccharine ingredients + optional flavoring ingredient + optional emulsifier.
Milk	Not less than 10% liquor + must contain $\geqslant 3.66\%$ milkfat and $\geqslant 12.0\%$ milk solids + must be sweetened with one of the optional saccharine ingredients + optional flavoring ingredient + optional emulsifier.

1960 and $525,000,000 in 1969. Poundage shipments increased from 906,000,000 to 1,065,000,-000 in that period. In the same period, the greatest gain in bar goods sales was in bars selling for 10¢ and which, in 1969, represented 58% of candy bar sales.

The above publication also estimates that 310,307,000 lb of milk chocolate, 65,876,000 lb of other chocolate, and 69,074,000 lb of cocoa powder composition coatings were consumed by confectionery manufacturers in the 1968–1969 period.

Shell molding is employed when the mold, having been filled with tempered chocolate, is inverted so that the chocolate spills out except for a thin shell of solid chocolate that remains in the mold. After cooling, the mold is turned right side up and then usually filled with a center confectionery product, such as caramel, and cooled again. Finally a bottom is put on the mold by overflowing it with tempered chocolate and scraping off all excess chocolate. A final cooling is necessary.

Enrobing with chocolate is carried out in an enrober through which the centers are moved usually on a wire mesh belt in such a way that the centers pass through a curtain of chocolate. Usually a stream of air is used to aid in controlling the amount of chocolate that adheres to the center. There may be a separate section for applying a bottom of chocolate to the center. The chocolate used must be in good temper as in all applications.

Morsels or chips are made by feeding tempered chocolate to a hopper which is connected to a set of pistons which deposit drops of chocolate onto a metal belt. Either the depositor will move (back and forth) to keep pace with the belt while it is depositing, or the belt will stop intermittently to receive the drops.

Baked goods use chocolate products especially in icings. Cocoa, however, is usually used to flavor baked goods themselves.

Ice cream is flavored with chocolate liquor to provide a high quality flavor. Because of cost, however, cocoa is often used.

Ice cream coatings solidify on an ice cream bar after it has been dipped and removed from a container of the molten coating. They usually consist of vegetable oil, sugar, chocolate liquor, milk solids, and flavorings.

Uses for Chocolate Coatings

Chocolate coatings are probably most easily classified as to the percentage of liquor contained. Generally speaking, the more bitter coatings are used for the sweeter centers to produce a balancing effect. The following shows a general classification and usage information for various coatings as adapted from Blumenthal (1942):

Chocolate Liquor—Bitter Chocolate

(1) Natural Process: pH 5.1–6.0;
fat = 50–58%
Use: Coating very sweet centers, butter creams, candy, culinary products, chocolate syrup.
(2) Dutch Process: pH 6.0–7.8;
fat = 50–58%
Use: Coating very sweet centers, flavoring tobacco, or, in general, where a darker milder product is desired. Replaces cocoa when a richer, creamier product is desired.

Bittersweet Coatings

44–49% chocolate liquor
32–42% sugar
36–38% fat
Dark in color, usually low in viscosity
Use: Coating for cordials, peppermint creams, fudge, whipped cream, Italian creams, hand rolls, butter creams, and marshmallow centers and crackers.

Dark Sweet

39–43% chocolate liquor
41–46% sugar
36–39% fat
Use: Enrobing nougats, cordials, peppermints, fudges, and nut-flavored cream fondants.

Medium Dark Sweet

34–38% chocolate liquor
43–49% sugar
33–37% fat
Use: For molding chocolate bars and solid chocolate items for retail trade. Also for enrobing caramels, nougats, fruit-flavored creams, fondants, jelly centers, coconut cream fondants, vanilla cream fondants, nut clusters, raisin clusters, dates, figs, marshmallows, nut-flavored cream fondants, coconut sponge, chip, and marshmallow crackers.

Milk Chocolate

Not less than 10% liquor or 12% milk solids with 43–55% sugar and 28–40% fat
Use: Milk chocolate coatings should generally be avoided on strong-flavored centers, but are good with mild centers low in sweetness and with nuts and fruits. A stronger milk chocolate is used on caramel, nougat, marshmallow, and similar centers.

Ice Cream Coating

50–60% fat for thin running chocolate; may be dark sweet, medium dark sweet, or milk chocolate
Use: Ice cream pops, eskimo pies. Lecithin is often added to ice cream coatings to combat thickening due to moisture absorption from melting ice cream. A full rich chocolate flavor is important here because of diminished flavor due to low temperature.

Table C-19 shows the approximate composition of chocolate coatings and Table C-20 summarizes uses of coatings.

TABLE C-19

APPROXIMATE COMPOSITION OF
CHOCOLATE COATINGS

Classification	Chocolate Liquor (%)	Total Fat (%)	Sugar (%)	Milk Solids (%)
Bitter	100	50–58	0	0
Bittersweet	35 and over	33–39	32–49	0
Light sweet	15–35	34–36	50–60	0
Milk chocolate	10–16	28–40	43–55	12+
Ice cream bar	9–29	50–60	29–39	12+
Imitation	Less than 10% cocoa	30–35	40–50	0

SOURCE: Adapted from Blumenthal (1942).

Compound or Confectioner's Coatings

Compound or confectioner's coatings are made using a mixture of cocoa and vegetable fat in place of chocolate liquor and cocoa butter. The ingredients, cocoa, vegetable fat, sugar, and milk solids in some form, are mixed thoroughly together, refined, and conched.

Alternatively for certain qualities of compound coatings, the cocoa, sugar, and milk solids may be ground in a pulverizer-classifier mill to a fineness it is claimed of 30 μ. This is then mixed with the vegetable fat until the final viscosity is reached.

Compound coatings contain usually less than 10% cocoa (no chocolate liquor), 40–50% sugar,

TABLE C-20

SUMMARY OF USES OF COATINGS

	Chocolate Liquor	Bittersweet	Dark Sweet	Medium Dark Sweet	Light Sweet	Milk Chocolate	Ice Cream Coating	Imitation Coating	Cocoa Butter
Butter creams	x	x							
Candy bars				x	x	x			
Caramels			x	x	x				
Chocolate bars	x			x	x	x			
Chocolate ice cream				x	x				
Chocolate pops							x	x	
Chocolate syrup	x								
Coconut creams				x				x	
Cordials	x	x	x						
Culinary products	x							x	
Frappé		x						x	
Fruit-flavored creams			x	x	x			x	
Fudge	x	x			x				
Hand rolls	x	x							
Ice cream bars									
Italian creams		x					x	x	
Jelly centers									
Lotions				x				x	
Marshmallow, marshmallow crackers		x							x
Nougats			x	x	x				
Nuts, nut clusters, and rolls			x	x	x	x		x	
Nut-flavored creams				x	x	x			
Ointments			x	x				x	
Peppermint creams	x	x	x						x
Raisins, dates, figs				x		x			
Sponge centers				x					
Suppositories								x	x
Tobacco	x							x	
Vanilla creams				x		x		x	

SOURCE: Adapted from Blumenthal (1942).

and 30–35% fat. These coatings are often used as a cheaper substitute for chocolate and can be especially useful in the summertime if the cocoa butter is substituted with higher temperature melting vegetable fats and similar lipids. Although the coatings usually lack the true taste of chocolate, they are often used for enrobing cheap centers, medicated products, and ice cream products. Some coatings do not use higher melting vegetable fats, but vegetable fats having melting points close to that of cocoa butter and they have a very high quality.

Pastel Coatings

Pastel coatings, sometimes called summer coatings, have somewhat the same composition as compound coatings but contain no cocoa solids. Instead, pastel colors are added to the product which may be made using either vegetable fat or cocoa butter.

Chocolate Syrup and Fudges

Chocolate syrup is composed of cocoa, sugar, corn syrup and/or invert syrup, water, salt, vanilla and other flavorings. The cocoa, if dutched, results in a mild product with a relatively low viscosity; if natural cocoa is used, it results in a lighter, more astringent product having a somewhat higher viscosity. Corn syrup gives body to the product and invert sugar gives sweetness. Both serve as anticrystallizing agents.

The product may contain up to about 40% water if completely sanitary conditions are used. It must be canned at 190°–200°F, steam purged at the seamer and then cooled immediately to prevent further flavor changes due to high temperatures.

A range of typical chemical analysis would be

	(%)
Water	25–40
Sucrose	12–45
Reducing sugars	7–40
Cocoa	6–10

Chocolate fudges are composed of a wide range of amounts of water, sugar, corn syrup solids, either chocolate liquor or cocoa, either whole milk solids or nonfat milk solids, starch, flavorings, and possibly at times invert sugar and vegetable oils. They are of heavier consistency than syrup and usually used warm. When whole milk solids are used, the fudge might be called a milk fudge topping and when nonfat milk solids are used might be called a fudge topping.

Tempering of Chocolate

Four different forms in which cocoa butter

crystallizes are $\gamma, \alpha, \beta', \beta$. The latter is the stable form and the purpose of tempering is to crystallize chocolate in essentially that stable form. Otherwise the chocolate will be unstable and in reverting gradually and finally upon storage to the stable form will contract resulting in stresses in the chocolate. Possibly also a temperature rise will result as heats of recrystallization are given off. Thus, poor tempering very likely will conclude in a product with poor appearance due to bloom.

Before tempering, the chocolate should be warmed to completely melt all crystal forms. The stable crystal is formed during tempering either after a preliminary cooling by heating to melt the unstable but not the stable crystals and then cooling again to solidify, or by adding seed of the stable form when cooling to solidify. Some commercial enrobers operate by cooling, heating, and cooling the chocolate and others by only cooling but by returning a small portion of cooled chocolate as seed. Vaeck has basic publications (1961) on tempering, and Korfhage (1967) and Mitchell (1968) have published very practical articles on tempering.

Defects of Chocolate

Chocolate can show, particularly after a long storage period, a grayish cast on the surface which gives an old and stale appearance to the product. The nature of such fat bloom appears to be related to polymorphic transformations and other physical chemical properties of cocoa butter. The bloom can be caused by using improperly tempered chocolate, improper cooling methods, contamination with incompatible fats, and fluctuating storage temperatures.

To avoid fat bloom, proper tempering, cooling and storage is necessary but, also, the addition of chemicals can be helpful. Butter oil (Kleinert 1961) and hydrogenated butter oil (Campbell *et al.* 1969) have been found effective. Span 60 and Tween 60 have been suggested for this purpose and may be added in the United States.

Chocolate can also show a grayish appearance due to the formation of tiny sugar crystals. This can occur if the temperature of the chocolate reaches below the dew point of surrounding air. Dew condenses on the surface and dissolves sugar from the coating. The surface moisture, when it can, then evaporates to leave sugar bloom. Cold packaged chocolate should not be opened until it reaches room temperature.

Cook (1963) devotes a chapter in his book to "Problems in Handling" chocolate and offers many useful suggestions.

JOSEPH ALLERTON

References

ANON. 1970. Designing and engineering the Cadbury Schweppes new factory. Food Manuf. Mar., 40.

BLUMENTHAL, S. 1942. Food Manufacturing. Chemical Publishing Co., Brooklyn, N.Y.

BRACCO, U., GRAILHE, N., ROSTAGNO, W., and EGLI, R. H. 1969. Analytical evaluation of cocoa curing in the Ivory Coast. J. Sci. Food Agr. 20, Dec., 713.

CAMPBELL, L. B., ANDERSON, D. A., and KEENEY, P. G. 1969. Hydrogenated milkfat as an inhibitor of the fat bloom defect in dark chocolate. J. Dairy Sci. 52, No. 7, 976.

CHEVALLEY, J., ROSTAGNO, W., and EGLI, R. H. 1970. A study of the physical properties of chocolate. (Part V) Rev. Intern. Chocolat. (RIC) 25, No. 1, 3.

COOK, L. R. 1963. Chocolate Production and Use. Magazines for Industry, New York.

KLEINERT, J. 1961. Studies on the formation of fat bloom and methods of delaying it. Intern. Chocolate Rev. May, 201–219.

KORFHAGE, R. F. 1967. Scientific reasons for tempering chocolate. Proc. AACT. Atlanta Sect., Febr. 24, 1967, Atlanta, Georgia.

LANGE, H. 1969. Components of cocoa beans and their physiological properties. Swisswaren 13, No. 1, 8.

MARION, J. P. et al. 1967. About the composition of the aroma of cacao. Helv. Chim. Acta 3 VI67. (Swedish)

MEURSING, E. H., and TERINK, J. L. 1969. Cocoa Powders for Industrial Processing: Specifications of Quality Characteristics. N.V. Cacaofabriek De Zaan, Koog-Zaandijk-Holland.

MINIFIE, B. W. 1970. Chocolate, Cocoa and Confectionery: Science and Technology. Avi Publishing Co., Westport, Conn.

MITCHELL, D. G. 1968. Practical chocolate tempering. Proc. 22nd Ann. Production Conf., Penn. Manufacturing Confectioners Assoc., Drexel Hill, Penn.

ROSTAGNO, W. 1969. Chocolate particle size and its organoleptic influence. Proc. 23rd Ann. Production Conf., Penn. Manufacturing Confectioners Assoc., Drexel Hill, Penn.

ROSTAGNO, W., REYMOND, D., and VIANI, R. 1970. Characterization of deodorised cocoa butter. Rev. Intern. Chocolat. (RIC) 25, Oct. 10, 352.

VAECK, S. V. 1961. Periodical circular. Intern. Office Cocoa Chocolate XI, No. 108, 34.

VAN DER WAL, B., et al. 1971. New volatile components of roasted cocoa. Agr. Food Chem. 19, No. 2, 276.

Cross-reference: *Confections.*

CHOLESTEROL

Cholesterol is a steroid alcohol ($C_{27}H_{46}O$) which is ubiquitous in the animal body. It is a component of cells and cell membranes. Cholesterol comprises about 0.2% of the total body weight. The distribution of cholesterol in the body of a hypothetical man weighing 70 kg is:

	(Gm)
Skin	32
Brain and nervous tissue	30
Muscle	24
Adipose and connective tissue	12
Liver	5
Serum	5
Red blood cells	4
Arteries	2
Intestinal lumen	1
Other	15

Cholesterol may be synthesized by most tissues, but the two most active sites of cholesterogenesis are the liver and intestine. Using liver enzymes, the pathway of cholesterol biosynthesis has been elucidated. All 27 carbon atoms of cholesterol are derived from the 2 carbon atoms of acetic acid (as active acetate). The methyl group of acetic acid contributes 15 carbon atoms (10 in the ring and 5 in the side chain) and the carboxyl group contributes 12 carbon atoms (9 in the ring and 3 in the side chain). The biosynthesis pathway is outlined below (number of carbon atoms are in parentheses):

acetate (2C) → hydroxymethylglutarate (6C) → mevalonate (6C) → isopentenylpyrophosphate (5C) → geranylpyrophosphate (10C) → farnesylpyrophosphate (15C) → squalene (30C) → lanosterol (30C) → zymosterol (27C) → desmosterol (27C) → cholesterol (27C).

The site of physiological control of cholesterol synthesis is at the conversion of hydroxymethylglutarate to mevalonate. Physiologically, cholesterol synthesis can be inhibited by cholesterol feeding or starvation. There are pharmacological agents which inhibit cholesterol synthesis, but these appear to exert their effect toward the end of the biosynthetic sequence.

Absorbed cholesterol is mixed with endogenously synthesized cholesterol and delivered to the plasma via the intestinal lymph. The liver is the major source of cholesterol degradation (to bile acids) and also contributes cholesterol to the bile. Some of this cholesterol is reabsorbed and some is excreted. The intestine also excretes cholesterol into its lumen from which it is excreted as cholesterol or hydrogenated by the intestinal flora and excreted in the feces as coprostanol.

Cholesterol is also the precursor of the male and female sex hormones, and of the adrenocortical hormones. These transformations take place in the gonads and adrenals, respectively.

The cholesterol of the blood is in contact with, and in equilibrium with, all other tissues of the body. The exchange between serum cholesterol and erythrocyte or liver cholesterol is rapid and extensive; with other tissues, such as brain or muscle, exchange is slow and often barely detectable.

The cholesterol of the serum is transported as part of large lipid-protein complexes known as lipoproteins. The lipoproteins may be classified in several ways. The broadest classification based on electrophoretic mobility is into alpha- and beta-lipoproteins. Within the alpha- and beta-lipoproteins there is further subclassification based upon density. The alpha-lipoproteins are those of highest density and their average concentration is 350 mg per 100 ml of serum. About 17% of the alpha-lipoprotein is cholesterol. The beta-lipoproteins comprise 550 mg per 100 ml of the serum and about 39% of the beta-lipoprotein is cholesterol. After a fatty meal, very light lipid-containing particles may appear in the serum (50 mg per 100 ml) and these particles contain about 4% cholesterol.

The cholesterol of the serum may occur as free or esterified cholesterol, and generally about $2/3$ of the serum cholesterol is present as esterified cholesterol. The fatty acids with which the serum cholesterol is esterified are primarily linoleic and oleic. Esterified cholesterol is also present in appreciable quantity in the adrenals and liver, but in most other normal tissues there is very little ester cholesterol.

To the nonscientific public, cholesterol is known principally for its connection with the development of human atherosclerotic heart disease. Scientific views on the importance of cholesterol in the etiology of heart disease range from full implication to a minor facet.

The views of most workers in the field fall somewhere in between these extremes, but most attach some degree of importance to cholesterol.

There are compelling reasons for the belief that cholesterol plays an important role in the development of coronary disease. These are: (1) the increase in cholesterol content of aging and atherosclerotic aortas; (2) the strong statistical evidence (available from many countries) that elevated blood cholesterol levels increase the risk of developing coronary disease; and (3) atherosclerotic lesions, especially resembling those seen in early stages of human disease, can be produced in a number of animals by feeding cholesterol or by other means which elevate the levels of the blood beta-lipoproteins. Unfortunately, only risk factors have been identified and no unequivocal antemortem test to determine development of heart disease is available.

On the other hand, it is recognized that the serum cholesterol level is only one of several factors which influence the risk of developing heart disease. Other prime factors are blood pressure and cigarette smoking. Also important are physical activity, emotional stress, gender, and other predisposing diseases, such as nephritis and diabetes. Other areas now being explored include genetic disposition (which may be detected by specific lipoprotein patterns), arterial metabolism, and other dietary components (at this writing the influence of simple sugars, such as sucrose, is under vigorous investigation).

The one aspect of the involvement of cholesterol in the etiology of heart disease most amenable to investigation and manipulation is the serum cholesterol. The hypothesis that lowering blood cholesterol levels will reduce the risk of coronary disease is under intensive study. No clear-cut proof of this hypothesis is yet available, but both dietary and pharmacologic approaches to hypocholesteremia are being explored.

The problem is probably more complex than simple manipulation of cholesterol levels. More has to be learned about individual variations in metabolism of cholesterol, and how cholesterol metabolism is affected by the total diet (quantity and type of fat—carbohydrate and protein—as well as possible roles of vitamins and undigested fiber). The elucidation of all aspects of cholesterol utilization, as well as better identification of persons who are susceptible to coronary disease, will eventually be forthcoming and then we will have a better understanding of the exact position of cholesterol (a compound which is essential to the physiologic economy) in the constellation of factors which determine the course of development of coronary disease.

DAVID KRITCHEVSKY

CITRUS INDUSTRY

Citrus juices are the most common, natural fruit drinks and many would feel that breakfast would be incomplete without them—and with good reason because citrus flavors are among the most popular and the citrus juice products satisfy an important place in the diet. The natural tart taste of citric acid with a reasonable amount of sugars for balance, flavored with a combination of natural essential oils, esters, aldehydes, and ketones make a refreshing drink that is hard to beat. Even most soft drinks are based on citrus flavors.

The citrus industry is very important to the food supply of the United States. According to the 1971 September issue of the USDA *The Fruit Situation*, the value of citrus fruit is approximately equal to that of noncitrus fruit (apples, apricots, avocados, cherries, cranberries, dates, figs, grapes, nectarines, olives, peaches, pears, persimmons, plums, pomegranates, prunes, Florida pineapples, and strawberries). The production during 1968, 1969, and 1970 of citrus fruits averaged 10,950,000 tons and of noncitrus fruits the average was 10,400,000 tons. While most fruit was sold fresh a number of years ago, processed products have increased until 68% of the citrus fruit and 65% of noncitrus fruit were processed during the 1968–1970 period. Of the predominate citrus fruits, 75% of the oranges, 55% of the grapefruit, 43% of the lemons, and 29% of the tangerines were processed.

The annual production averages for the 1968, 1969, 1970 seasons and percentages used for processing follow:

	Million Tons	%
Oranges		
Florida	5.6	88.2
California-Arizona	1.4	37.7
Texas	0.16	38.0
Grapefruit		
Florida	1.5	61.1
California-Arizona	0.30	43.7
Texas	0.2	31.4
Lemons		
California-Arizona	0.5	42.8
Tangerines		
Florida	0.15	25.0

Fresh fruit marketing is favored in California to take advantage of the deeper red and yellow colors which give a more pleasing fruit appearance and culls are used for processing. In Florida, the preference is for processing because the sweeter product is of advantage in juices and concentrates, particularly for oranges, and the production costs are lower. About $1/4$ of the citrus production of the world is in the United States.

One of the factors which has encouraged processing is that citrus fruit production is concentrated in rather limited areas in Florida, California, Arizona, and Texas. Also, the harvesting extends over about six months in each area. The availability of large quantities of fruit over these long periods of time in these areas has permitted the establishment of rather sophisticated and efficient citrus processing plants.

Commercial Citrus Varieties

Citrus species are small trees and shrubs 10–40 ft in height. The leaves are dark green and glossy, are simple, and have a joint between the leaf and petiols. Flowers are abundant, single, mostly white, and fragrant. Trees are covered with leaves the year around and are replaced after the bloom. Bloom occurs mainly in February, March, and April, and the period between bloom and harvest varies from 8 to 17 months, depending on variety and climate. Fruit matures more rapidly in Florida than in California, due to difference in temperature and rainfall.

Citrus trees are subtropical and damaged by freezing, the extent depending on condition of plant dormancy, maturity, and severity of freeze. Progressively, freezes affect leaves, small twigs, fruit, small branches, large branches, and finally the main trunk. If damage reaches large branches, chances of tree survival are small. Freezing causes rapid loss of foliage and replacement by new leaves which are highly sensitive to further freeze damage.

Citrus cultivars and related citroid cultivars form a large group. The general classification is family Rutaceae, subfamily Aurantioideae, tribe *Citreae*, subtribe *Citrinae*, and genus *Citrus*. Sweet oranges belong to the species *Citrus Sinensus* (L) Osbeck, of which the chief cultivars are the early season Hamlin and Parson Brown, the midseason Pineapple oranges, the late season Valencia and the Washington Navel. *C. reticulata* includes the loose skinned Dancy tangerine and King orange. Grapefruit cultivars come under *C. paradisi* Macfayden and include Duncan (common, seeded), Marsh (seedless), Foster Pink (a bud sport of Walters), Thompson (a pink sport of Marsh) and Ruby (a Red sport of Thompson). Lemons are in species *C. Limon* Burmann (Eureka and Villafranca). The Meyer lemon is likely a hybrid between the lemon and some other species of *Citrus*. Lime cultivars (*C. Aurantifolia* Swingle) include the small Mexican or Key limes and the larger oval Tahiti lime. There are a number of crosses including Temple oranges (tangerine × sweet orange) and Tangelo (*C. paradisi* × *C. reticulata*). Commercial cultivars are "budded" onto rootstocks selected to provide optimum yield, tree vigor, and freedom from disease.

Anatomy of Citrus Fruit

Citrus fruit are quite complex, more so than most deciduous fruit such as apples and peaches as

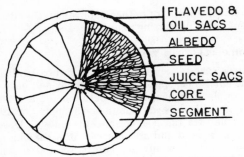

FLAVEDO &
OIL SACS
ALBEDO
SEED
JUICE SACS
CORE
SEGMENT

FIG. C-9. CROSS SECTION OF AN ORANGE

seen in Fig. C-9. The thick rind provides a considerable degree of protection against injury. The outside surface is designated as the pericarp or flavedo and contains the peel oil and pigments. Next is the white spongy layer called the mesocarp or albedo which is rich in pectin. The interior juice containing endocarp is divided into several locules or segments containing individual juice sacs and the seeds, if any. Finally, there is the central, spongy core or placenta. Each of these parts present special problems and opportunities in processing.

Marketing of Fresh Fruit

Fresh citrus fruits have long been popular and are available the year around from one or another of the growing areas. If needed, the fruit is placed in warm coloring rooms where a very small amount of ethylene is added to the air to cause the disappearance of green chlorophyll. The fruit is washed to remove debris and then waxed to decrease the rate of moisture loss. In Florida and Texas certified dyes may be added to the outer peel to improve appearance. The fruit must meet special requirements before color may be added and the degree of coloration is limited. The fruit may also be treated to decrease the rate of microbial spoilage. The fruit is then placed in cardboard cartons, mesh bags, or wooden wire-bound boxes. Fruit is shipped to market in refrigerated cars. It should reach the consumer in 1–2 weeks.

Harvesting

Fruit is sampled periodically to see if it has reached the proper maturity as judged by the sugar content, acid content (Brix/acid ratio), and juice yield. Each State has a distinct set of values in accordance with the type of fruit that can be produced. A higher Brix/acid (sweetness) ratio is specified in Florida and Texas. The traditional method of harvesting is for the picker to lean a tall ladder against the tree, climb to the top with a special picking bag and pick from the top down. After a few fruit are in the bag, the bag can be anchored on a rung and the fruit is picked with both hands. Upon reaching the bottom the fruit is dumped into a box. This is the most rapid method of hand picking and is used exclusively for fruit to be shipped as such. In California the fruit is usually clipped from the tree, but in Florida it is harvested by twisting the fruit and pulling. Skilled pickers are hard to get and different methods of picking have been tried, especially if the fruit is to be processed. The usual procedure now is for one person to climb the tree, pick the fruit, and drop it to the ground, while another person picks it up and transfers it to a box capable of holding about 900 lb of fruit. The big box is picked up by a special lift truck and dumped into a trailer capable of handling about 40,000 lb of fruit. Progress is being made on mechanical harvesting. The trees may be shaken by a mechanical device which grabs a limb at a time; or wind blasts may be used. Citrus fruits are firmly attached and the shaking must be quite severe. Experiments are in progress on chemicals which could enhance the formation of abscission layer; cycloheximide for example. It appears that a material which is effective in loosening the fruit also increases ethylene formation. Fruit falls directly to the ground and is picked up by hand or by mechanical sweeps.

Processing Citrus Fruit

Citrus fruit is received at the cannery in trucks which are unloaded by tilting and opening the tail gates. Fruit is elevated into bins and a sample is taken automatically for use by the official inspector in the determination of juice yield, soluble solids (°Brix) and acid content. The inspector determines whether the fruit meets maturity requirements and is suited for the purpose intended. Maturity regulations are usually more stringent for processing than for fresh fruit. The processor also uses the data to help in deciding whether to use the fruit for canned juice, chilled juice, frozen concentrate, or for sectionizing and in determining the price paid for the fruit. The fruit is collected in bins and labeled with the proper number and analytical results. To improve uniformity of product, the fruit from two or more bins is drawn simultaneously and sent to the plant. For example, more acid fruit may be blended with low-acid fruit. Before the fruit enters the bins it passes over tables where blemished or bruised fruit is removed, and conveyors return it to the truck. When fruit is harvested mechanically, or even dropped to the ground, care must be taken to remove the pieces of tree branches attached to the fruit or these will get stuck in extractors or finishers and stop the plant.

Fruit is usually washed by soaking in water briefly and passing over rotating brushes to remove dirt, sand, and insect fragments. During storage in bins or trucks, oranges will decrease significantly in acid content and show a small increase in Brix/ acid ratio. Grapefruit change much more slowly. Otherwise, the quality of the fruit deteriorates in storage and it must be used without delay.

Canned and Chilled Citrus Sections.—Large fruit are selected for uniformity in size and suitability for use in peeling and ease of separation of sections. Grapefruit, because of larger size, handle much more easily than oranges but there has been an increased demand for a mixture of both fruits in chilled salads, so the volume of oranges used is increasing.

The first step is to immerse the fruit in hot water (1–2 min) to soften the peel so it can be removed readily by machines. After heating, the fruit is cooled in cold water so that it can be handled. The machines remove the flavedo and albedo, but the outer segment or locule membrane remains. This is removed by immersing in hot 1–2% lye solution for 1–2 min, cold water sprays follow to remove the lye and disintegrated tissue.

The sections are usually removed by hand with a dull aluminum knife with a blade about 4 in. long, tapering from 1 $\frac{1}{2}$ in. to $\frac{1}{2}$ in. Some automatic machines are in use for removing sections and have been improved greatly in the past few years. The sections are packed into cans for heat processing in hot water or they are packed in glass, usually with a little sodium benzoate, refrigerated, and sold as a chilled product. There is some pectin esterase enzyme present in chilled sections which assists in the conversion of the pectin to low-methoxyl pectin. There is sufficient calcium present to react and form a gel; so sections of improved firmness result. The pack of canned and chilled sections was at about four million cases for many years, but the pack has decreased somewhat because of increased labor costs even with automatic equipment.

Canned Juices.—Fruit is blended from several bins to aid in the production of a uniform product and washed as mentioned previously. Before going to the juice extractors the fruit is separated into 3 to 5 sizes mechanically. This promotes the removal of an optimum amount of juice without excessive pressure on the peel or deforming the fruit more than necessary during extraction.

The juice is removed from the fruit in automatic machines which handle from 300 to 700 fruit per minute. One operator can handle up to a dozen extractors with ease and his main function is to corret jams in the fruit conveyor or extractor and to clean the extractors periodically. There are two machines which dominate the market. One is the FMC "In-Line" in which the fruit is received in a row of serrated cups and then squeezed by a similar cup which descends and meshes with the stationary one. The juice, seeds, and interior membranes of the fruit pass through a 1-in. hole cut in the bottom of the fruit by the sharpened end of a tube while the shredded peel passes between the fingers of the cups. An extension of the sharpened 1-in. tube serves as a perforated screen to separate the juice from the coarse pulp. Figure C-10

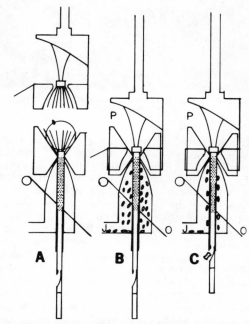

FIG. C-10. SKETCH SHOWING OPERATION OF AN FMC "IN-LINE" CITRUS JUICE EXTRACTOR

illustrates how the fruit is placed in position (A) and squeezed to give the main flow of juice (B), and how the inner tube rises to give the pulp a final squeeze (C). The shredded peel is ejected at P and an emulsion of cold-pressed peel oil is collected from an inclined plane at 0. The Brown juice extractor simulates hand reaming of halved fruit. The fruit is cut in halves by a sharp blade and each half is caught between the halves of a rubber cup while rubber burrs remove the juice, seeds, and membrane. An example of a Brown juice extractor is shown in Fig. C-11. The juice from either the FMC or Brown machine passes to a screw type finisher with a screen of 0.027–0.040-in. openings. Since most of the pulp was removed in the FMC extractor the finisher can be smaller than that for a comparable Brown machine. A citrus juice finisher is illustrated in Fig. C-12.

FIG. C-11. BROWN MODEL 400 CITRUS JUICE
EXTRACTOR

FIG. C-12. SCREW-TYPE CITRUS JUICE FIN-
ISHER DISASSEMBLED TO SHOW CONSTRUC-
TION OF SCREW, SCREEN, HOPPER, AND
RELATED PARTS

The extracted juice is pumped to temporary holding tanks where it is checked for °Brix, and titratable acidity. If the juice is not in the proper range, it may be blended with the next tank of juice. The juice then passes through a pasteurizer to inactivate the pectinesterase enzymes and destroy microorganisms. About 165°F would be sufficient to destroy normal microbial population but about 195°F is needed to destroy the pectinesterase enzymes which would otherwise cause coagulation of the suspended matter and clarification of the juice. The hot juice is pumped to automatic fillers for cans ranging from 6-oz to 46-oz capacity. The lids are put on with a double seamer, the cans are inverted briefly to sterilize the lid and cooled under sprays of cold water. The cooling water should be chlorinated to reduce the microbial population to a low figure to eliminate the possibility of fermentation of canned juice during storage. Canned juice is usually stored at room temperature. Certain changes in flavor may take place, typical of the product; but the food value and vitamin content are conveyed to the consumer to a satisfactory degree. Canned grapefruit juice does not change much in flavor during storage.

Chilled Juices.—Chilled juices are packed in much the same manner as canned juices except that glass jars are used instead of cans and the product is kept under refrigeration at 50°F or below. The low-temperature storage provides a flavor which resembles fresh juice as the flavor changes little under these conditions over a period of several months. Much of the chilled juice is packed aseptically. The jars and caps are sterilized with steam, hot water, or with chemicals and filled with juice which has been sterilized by heating rapidly to about 240°F for a few seconds, and cooled rapidly to about 40°F for filling. Filling is done in an aseptic chamber. The usual container is a 2-qt jar. Frozen concentrate may be reconstituted for this product but not for canned juice.

Frozen Concentrated Orange Juice.—This "Cinderella" product has captured the imagination of many food scientists as well as a substantial part of the food market. It was the first concentrated juice to be widely accepted as the equivalent of single-strength juice. The market for it continues to expand.

Oranges for frozen concentrated orange juice (FCOJ) are handled much like those for canned juice as far as juice extraction and finishing are concerned. Juice is heated briefly before concentrating to inactivate enzymes which would otherwise cause solid gels to form in the container and clarification of the juice after reconstitution. Formerly, low-temperature (80°F or below) evaporators were used but these have been replaced with high speed multistage units having as many as 7 stages and 4 effects. The juice passes through each stage once, so the time the juice is in the evaporator is only minutes instead of hours. The juice is heated to about 210°F in an early stage and this accomplishes enzyme inactivation. The vapors from each effect provide energy for stages at lower temperatures. A pound of steam will vaporize from 3 to 4 lb of water in one of these evaporators (Fig. C-13). The concentrate is removed at 50°–65° Brix and is diluted to the final concentration of 45° Brix with fresh juice called cut-back juice.

time lacks somewhat in sweetness, some barrel stock that was a little too sweet could be used to blend to get exactly the Brix/acid ratio wanted. Citrus fruit, like other agricultural commodities vary in composition and blending can improve overall quality and uniformity.

The blended concentrate is chilled to about $30°F$ in a jacketed tank with refrigerant in the wall, then filled into containers and frozen in tunnels in a blast of air at about $-40°F$, and packed into cartons. The favorite container has been of 6-oz size which reconstitutes to make 24 oz of $12.8°$ Brix juice. Larger cans are becoming popular and a more concentrated product is used in hospitals, restaurants, and other institutions. Some think that all citrus concentrates should be marketed at 5- to 6-fold instead of conventional 4-fold concentration. Technology is available and it is strictly a marketing problem.

Tin-coated steel with soldered side seams were the original containers for frozen citrus concentrates but technology of manufacturing has changed so most containers have bodies of spirally-wound fiberboard coated with aluminum or polyethylene and crimped-on ends.

Citrus By-Products

Only 55–60% of the fruit is used for juice or sections and the remainder must be utilized or it will become a nuisance. Cold-pressed peel oil may be recovered and used for flavoring juice or sold for use in manufacturing carbonated beverages, candy, baked goods, soap, or in any other products where a citrus flavor or aroma is desired. The remaining peel is ground and treated with lime so it is no longer sticky and the juice can be removed by pressing. The pressed pulp is dried in rotary driers of the recycle type to about 8% moisture and sold for cattle feed. The pressed liquor is usually concentrated and added back to the pulp before drying to improve the food value. Sometimes the concentrated liquid of about $72°$ Brix is sold as citrus molasses.

There are a number of other products which are prepared in lesser quantities including distilled peel oils, flavonoids from peel, finisher pulp, washed finisher pulp, brined and candied peel, gelled salad, concentrated essence, pectin, citric acid, and seed oil.

Composition of Citrus Products

The proximate composition of grapefruit juice is 11.8% solids, 0.32% ash, 0.04% ether extract, 0.56% protein, 0.04% crude fiber, and 10.9% carbohydrates. It contains 41 cal per 100 gm. Orange juice contains 11.8% solids, 0.38% ash,

FIG. C-13. HIGH TEMPERATURE-SHORT TIME CITRUS JUICE EVAPORATOR AT BORDO CITRUS PRODUCTS COOPERATIVE, WINTER HAVEN, FLORIDA, WITH EVAPORATION CAPACITY OF 60,000 LB OF WATER VAPOR PER HOUR

Aqueous essence is recovered from the vapors from the first stage of the evaporator and concentrated in a fractionating column for addition to the final concentrate to improve "fresh" flavor. Cold-pressed peel oil is also added to about 0.025% v/v to balance the flavor. Advantage is taken of the opportunity to store concentrate in 55-gal. polyethylene-lined barrels at about $60°$ Brix for blending later to improve quality and standardize the product. So if the fruit available at a particular

0.06% ether extract, 0.65% protein, 0.05% crude fiber, and 10.7% carbohydrates. It also contains 41 cal per 100 gm. Thus, citrus juices are primarily carbohydrate foods with minor amounts of ether extract and protein, and, comparatively speaking, a fair amount of ash. It is high in vitamin C and folic acid and contains significant quantities of other vitamins, pectin, and bioflavonoids, all of interest. Each group of compounds will be discussed separately.

Vitamin Content.—There are a number of vitamins in citrus fruit and fruit products, but Vitamin C (ascorbic acid) is the most important. While the compound had not been isolated, the structure proven, and its effectiveness shown until about 1932, the value of citrus fruit in alleviating scurvey was known in the early 1700's. Citrus juices, generally, contain from 30 to 50 mg ascorbic acid per 100 ml juice. Losses are negligible during manufacture into juice, concentrates, or sections (less than 5%). At room temperature there is a gradual loss in Vitamin C, but even here the retention is over 83% for 6 months at room temperature (78°F). Virtually no losses are experienced in chilled juice provided it is kept in a sealed glass jar or other hermetically sealed container to keep oxygen from the product. Frozen concentrated orange juice had excellent retention of ascorbic acid, even in containers allowing some penetration of oxygen. Vitamin C is quite abundant and once it was considered that no special problem was presented with a reasonably good diet; however, recent surveys have shown more frequent cases of deficiency than anticipated. This has been explained on the premise that people perform less manual labor and consume less fruit and vegetables. Citrus fruit present an opportunity to easily close this gap. Florida frozen concentrated orange juice should be particularly valuable since the concentration was raised recently so it will reconstitute to 12.8° instead of 12° Brix.

Other vitamins in citrus juices include 0.005 mg per 100 gm β-carotene, 0.2 mg per 100 gm niacin, 0.013 mg per 100 gm riboflavin, 0.033 mg per 100 gm B$_6$, 200 mg per 100 gm inositol, and 0.160 mg per 100 gm pantothenic acid.

Recently, improved methods of assay for folic acid have been developed and these indicate a value of about 0.036 mg per 100 gm or nearly 10 times that reported earlier. This makes orange juice interesting for supplementing the diet with this vitamin.

Inorganic Materials.—Citrus juices are interesting as a source of minerals. Approximate mineral contents as milligrams per 100 gm are: calcium, 9; iron, 0.2; phosphorus, 15; magnesium, 10; potassium, 170; sodium, 0.5; sulfur, 6; and chlorine, 3. Normally, grapefruit sections receive a treatment in hot dilute caustic which will increase the sodium content several fold. Grapefruit sections can be prepared by trimming the peel off with a knife thus lowering sodium content, but the cost is high because of lower yield and higher labor costs.

Sugars.—About ²/₃ of the soluble solids in citrus products are composed of sugars and of these ¹/₂ is sucrose and the remainder is ¹/₂ glucose and ¹/₂ levulose. In grapefruit juice the percentage of sucrose is a little lower and that of the reducing sugars a little higher. By paper chromatography, these are the only sugars noted. There is no starch in normal citrus juice, as in maturing there is no conversion from starch to sugars as in some fruits. There is some starch in citrus seeds.

Volatile Flavor Components.—Essential oils from citrus fruit have long been an item of trade and much attention has been given to the chemical composition of distilled and cold-pressed peel oil. Like most essential oils, the principal component is d-limonene and this component comprises over 90% of most citrus peel oils. This serves as a solvent and has no distinct citrus flavor of its own. The unique flavor and aroma of lemon oil is due to citral and it is present to the extent of about 3%. Nootkatone contributes materially to the distinctive flavor of grapefruit and the pure compound reminds one of the aroma over a bin or box of fresh grapefruit. In juice, nootkatone contributes to the distinctive flavor at a level of 2-4 ppm, but at about 8 ppm it begins to impart an objectionable bitter flavor. No single compound stands out as being distinctive of orange flavor and it is likely that a dozen or more compounds are important to full orange flavor.

Other compounds besides nootkatone and citral are necessary for full flavor of grapefruit and lemon oils. The compounds that have been identified in citrus oils are over 100 in number. The principal classes are terpenes, sesquiterpenes, aldehydes, ketones, alcohols, coumarins, and hydrocarbon waxes. Most components are present in very small quantities, but some have potent flavors and only small amounts are needed.

Essences.—These differ from essential oils in that they are collected and concentrated as an aqueous phase. Many of the same compounds are present as in cold-pressed oils. Essences are obtained from the volatiles distilling from citrus juices in the early stages of evaporation and are concentrated in fractionating columns. They may also be obtained from the waste aqueous discharges from citrus peel oil centrifuges. Essences differ from peel oil in composition in that they contain much larger quantities of the more volatile compounds such as hydrogen sulfide, ethyl butyrate, or acetaldehyde and, especially, the more water-soluble components such as alcohols, aldehydes, and ketones. Terpenes and sesquiterpenes are found in higher proportions in the oil. A list is now maintained in the author's laboratory of compounds isolated from orange essence by all workers which number 124 compounds of which 13 are noted as possible artifacts (i.e., xylene and toluene).

Flavonoids.—Flavonoids and related bitter compounds form a small but important group of compounds in citrus juices. Naringin is found in grapefruit to the extent of 200–500 ppm and is the principal component which contributes to the natural bitterness of the product. In oranges the principal flavonoid is hesperidin, but it is quite insoluble and not noticeably bitter. Other flavonoids include neohesperidin, poncirin, eriocitrin, citronin, diosmin, rhoifolin, and rutin and the flavonones, tangeretin, nobiletin, auranetin, 3,5,6,7,8,3′,4′-heptamethoxy flavone, and 5,6,7,-3′,4′-pentamethoxy flavone. The total of the flavones is about 5 ppm in citrus juices.

Limonin.—This complex dilactone has long been known to be the bitter principle in citrus seeds and Washington Naval oranges. It is present in fresh fruit as a nonbitter monolactone but when dissolved in the acid juice is converted to the bitter dilactone. It is very potent and most people object to levels over 5 ppm, so it is roughly 100 times as bitter as naringin. Little was known about the distribution of this compound until recently when methods of quantitative analysis began to be developed. It is now found in most citrus juices and at times at objectionable levels; particularly early in the harvesting season. As the fruit matures, the limonin precursor content suddenly increases being followed by a gradual decrease.

Amino Acids.—Nitrogenous compounds are present to the extent of 0.05–0.1% or comprise from 5 to 10% of the total solids in orange juice. Most of this nitrogen is present as free amino acids, of which the following have been reported: asparagine, alanine, γ-aminobutyric acid, arginine, aspartic acid, betaine, choline, cysteine, glutamic acid, glutamine, glutathione, histidine, proline, putrescine, serene, and stachydrin. Some nitrogenous compounds are present in the suspended matter which give a test for protein. Other nitrogenous compounds in citrus juices include octopamine, synephrine, tryamine, n-methyl tryamine, hordenine and feruloylputrescine. The most abundant is synephrine in tangerine and mandarin juices (125–280 ppm). Unfortunately, synephrine is not effective as a nasal decongestant if one drinks it in juice.

Organic Acids.—Citrus juices are known for their pleasant acid taste, buffered and blended with sugars to the proper Brix/acid ratio. The approximate ranges of acidity for orange juice are 0.5 to 1.5% acid; grapefruit juice, 0.9 to 1.5%; tangerine juice, 0.7 to 1.4%; lemon juice, 3 to 6%; and lime juice, 5 to 8%. The principal acid in the mature fruit is citric and it constitutes from 80 to 90% of the organic acids. Malic acid is next. Trace amounts of tartaric, benzoic, succinic, quinic, oxalic, and formic acids have been reported.

Lipids.—Lipids are substances which are insoluble in water and soluble in fat solvents. The general classes include neutral fats, usually esters of glycerol and fatty acids. Phospholipids are also important. Citrus seed oils are examples and citrus juices contain about 0.05% lipids. The more abundant fatty acids obtained by hydrolysis are linoleic, oleic, palmitic, stearic, and linolenic acids. Recently, it has been shown that many more fatty acids are present in lipid hydrolysates including saturated, mono, di, and tri acids of 12 to 26 carbons in patterns characteristic of each variety. It is thought that the breakdown and oxidation of these acids into those of shorter chain length may be responsible for part of the change in flavor of canned orange juice after extended storage at room temperature.

Pectic Substances.—Pectin is widely distributed in nature and citrus fruits are no exception as it is found to greater or lesser degree in all parts. Protopectin is to be found in the peel, especially in the flavedo, and citrus peels are a major source of commercial pectin. Lemon peel is used because it yields a pectin capable of forming a firm jelly. The insoluble forms are designated as protopectin and are readily converted to soluble pectin or pectinic acids upon mild acid hydrolysis. Soluble pectin can be further broken down into shorter chain pectic acids.

Pigments.—Pigments in citrus fruit are concentrated in the peel and lesser amounts are distributed throughout the fruit. The usual orange and yellow colors are due to carotenoids of which β-carotene is typical; but there are many others such as phytoene, phytofluoene, γ-carotene, cryptoxanthin, and violaxanthin to name only a few. The yellow and orange pigments in the peel are enchanced when the night temperatures in the grove drop to the 40°–50°F range. These temperatures also favor a decrease in the green chlorophyll. Thus, exterior color is not an indication of maturity in citrus fruit but rather of the minimum night temperatures during the month before harvest. Chlorophyll can be decreased by temporary storage in warm "degreening" rooms while a small amount of ethylene is admitted. The pink color of some grapefruit is due to a combination of lycopene and β-carotene. The color of blood oranges is quite different and is due to anthocyanin and is soluble in the juice while the carotenoids are not.

Enzymes.—The principal enzyme of interest in citrus products is pectinesterase. If allowed to remain inactivated, it will cause coagulation of the suspended matter in citrus juices and rapid sedimentation to form a layer at the bottom of the container. The clear supernatent liquid then lacks a characteristic citrus flavor due to the loss of lipids and dissolved essential oils. Shaking to resuspend the sediment is only a partial, temporary measure. The usual remedy is to inactivate the enzymes in the original juice by heating to 190°F or higher. Pectin contains numerous —OCH_3 groups and the pectinesterase replaces them with mildly acidic —OH groups which react with divalent ions such as calcium to form insoluble pectates which precipitate. If unpasteurized 4-fold orange concentrate is held at refrigerator temperature (40°F) for about a month or at room temperature for 1-2 days, a solid gel will form. In the intact fruit there is a residue of complex enzyme systems which regulate the formation of the various portions of the fruit, but most of these are inactivated in the course of juice extraction.

There is continuing research of citrus products and by-products in the following federal and state laboratories located in the citrus-producing areas:

USDA Agricultural Research Service

Citrus and Subtropical Products Laboratory, Winter Haven, Florida.

Food Crops Utilization Research Laboratory, Weslaco, Texas.

Laboratory of Fruit and Vegetable Chemistry, Pasadena, Calif.

State Experiment Stations

California Agricultural Experiment Station, Riverside, Calif.

Agricultural Research and Education Center, Lake Alfred, Florida.

Texas A&M Agricultural Research and Extension Center, Weslaco, Texas.

MATTHEW K. VELDHUIS

References

ANON. 1962. Chemistry and technology of citrus, citrus products and by-products. USDA Agr. Handbook 98.

HENDRICKSON, R., and KESTERSON, J. W. 1964. Hesperiden in Florida oranges. Univ. Florida Agr. Expt. Sta. Tech. Bull. 684.

HENDRICKSON, R., and KESTERSON, J. W. 1965. By-products of Florida citrus: Composition, technology and utilization. Univ. Florida Agr. Expt. Sta. Bull. 698.

HENDRICKSON, R., and KESTERSON, J. W. 1971. Citrus molasses. Univ. Florida Agr. Expt. Sta. Tech. Bull. 677.

KESTERSON, J. W., and HENDRICKSON, R. 1953. Naringin, a bitter principle of grapefruit. Univ. Florida Agr. Expt. Sta. Bull. 511.

PATRICK, R., and HILL, E. C. 1959. Microbiology of citrus fruit processing. Univ. Florida Agr. Expt. Sta. Bull. 618.

REUTER, W., BATCHELOR, L. D., and WEBBER, H. J. 1968. The Citrus Industry, Vol. II, Anatomy, Physiology, Genetics and Reproduction. Univ. Calif. Div. Agr. Sci., Berkeley.

REUTER, W., WEBBER, H. J., and BATCHELOR, L. D. 1967. The Citrus Industry, Vol. I, History, World Distribution, Botany and Varieties, Revised Edition. Univ. Calif. Div. Agr. Sci., Berkeley.

TRESSLER, D. K., and JOSLYN, M. A. 1971. Fruit and Vegetable Juice Processing Technology, 2nd Edition. Avi Publishing Co., Westport, Conn.

WINSTON, J. R. 1950. Harvesting and handling citrus fruits in the Gulf States. USDA Farmers' Bull. 1763.

Cross-reference: *Tropical Fruit.*

CLAMS OF COMMERCIAL IMPORTANCE

Clams are widely distributed and inhabit coastal areas throughout the world. Their natural habitat is from the tide line to many miles off shore. Clam surveys are continually discovering new beds and defining older ones.

The total world landing of clams, one of the more important of marine mollusks, between 1964 and 1969 increased from 384 to 429 thousand metric tons in an irregular pattern reaching a peak of 432 thousand metric tons in 1966. The United States and Japan harvest the largest yields of clams.

There are many known species of clams, but very few are commercially exploited because of the large sustainable yield necessary for commercial utilization. Some of the commercially important species are the hard shell clam or quahog (Mercenaria mercenaria), the surf clam (Spisula solidissima), the soft shell clam (Mya arenaria), the ocean quahog (Arctica islandica), the razor clam (Siliqua patula), the little neck clam (Protothaca staminea), and the butter clam (Saxidomus nuttalli). The most widely eaten is the hard shell clam or quahog, although the dollar value of the soft shell clam products, processed mainly in the United States, is almost equal to that of the hard clam.

Clams belong to the mollusk family having a soft body protected by two shells or valves. Sometimes they are referred to as bivalves. The shells are joined along the back by a hinge which tends to spring apart when the clam is removed from the shell. The shells are held together by two adductor muscles, one at each end of the body. On the shell is a series of concentric lines which occur on nearly all species while only a few species have radiating lines.

All clams have siphons by which they feed. The siphon is extended and a current of water is drawn in. This water not only aerates the gills but also furnishes the plankton or microscopic animals and plants on which they feed. They are found on sandy, muddy, and gravel bottoms. Also they can grow suspended similar to the artificial way used by oyster farmers.

The growth rate is largely governed by two factors—water temperature and food abundance. These factors are interrelated for the temperature regulates what fauna and flora grow to be eaten by the clams. Although water circulation pattern, tidal exposure, crowding, and sediment type can influence growth, clams grow faster in warm water and usually are mature or spawn in 2 yr. The average annual growth rate is 1 in. and the size, rather than the age, determines the maturity of the individual clam. Since growth rate varies with location, the age of the clam is difficult to determine. It can be estimated by the weight of the shell, the frequency of growth lines, and the signs of external wear.

The movements of a clam may be of two types—burrowing of the adult and the migratory activities of the young. Up until the clam reaches about 1 in. in length, it does not imbed itself deep enough to prevent washing out and, therefore, migrates frequently. Once it has grown large enough to burrow deeply, it does not move very far.

Both the adult clam and especially the young have many natural enemies. To list only a few: water fowl, fish (mostly to the young), crabs, starfish, oyster drills, cockles, and man. Man has caused extensive damage to clam flats by over-catching and pollution, but through conservation and antipollution efforts, the clam resource is being improved. Clams are being successfully transferred or transplanted; with good resource management, this resource is being increased. Also, clam farming has proven very successful.

There are essentially three techniques for harvesting clams. The first and most efficient is with the use of a dredge. Most clams are harvested using this method with hydraulic water pumps to loosen the bottom for easier insertion of the teeth of the dredge. The second is with the use of hand tongs of the same type used for gathering oysters. The tonging method is quite slow and costly compared to dredging. The third and least efficient, most costly method is by hand digging at low tide.

Where the clams are taken from uncontaminated areas, they are stored in the cold for shipping or are shucked (meats removed) for further pro-

cessing. Where taken from polluted or restricted areas, they must be put through a depuration or purification process to remove pathogens. In the depuration process, the contaminated shellfish are placed in bacteria-free salt water for 48 hr. Up until recently, a small amount of chlorine was added to the water, but chlorine was found to irritate the clam so that he would not feed and thereby clean himself. The water temperature is kept constant at slightly above 50°F (depending on the species), for at lower temperatures clams will not feed. After depuration they can be handled similarly to clams harvested from acceptable areas. Some species of clams which feed on the dinoflagellate, *Gonyaulax*, become poisonous to humans. These clam areas are very carefully monitored and the clams are not harvested when contaminated with this poison.

Dredged clams are transported to the processing plants in the hold of the dredge boats. Clams taken by other gear are placed in wooden boxes or sacks and brought to the plant, usually not more than a few miles away, by truck or boat.

At the plant the clams are washed and graded for size. Next the meats are removed, except for the soft shell clams eaten raw on the half shell.

Although each species of clams is handled somewhat differently, the two most commonly used techniques for removing the clam meat from the shell are by hand shucking and by heating. Hand shucking is slow, costly, and can result in hand injuries; whereas heating is rapid and less costly, but produces a cooked product. Other more sophisticated methods to remove meats such as localized heating, microwave energy heating, or by other mechanical methods are in various stages of development and are not used widely although some appear to have commercial potential. During removal of the meat a large amount of liquid from within the shell is collected. This liquor is cleaned and concentrated. It is sold as clam juice or broth to be added back to processed clam products or to various products to give them a clam flavor.

Fresh clam meats vary in color from white to dark gray depending on the species. If the clams are large, the visceral contents are removed to lighten the color of the product and to reduce the strong flavor that usually is concentrated in the liver. Large siphons or necks are snipped off. The clam meats are handled quickly to discourage bacterial buildup which can occur during processing. Most clam meats are packed whole in cans; however, some are minced for chowders and stuffings. They are transported and held under refrigeration until ready for use.

Although most clams are used in chowders, there are a variety of other products that can be prepared. Soft shell clams are excellent steamed, deep-fat fried, or made into soufflés, dips, pies, cakes, and loaves. The hard clam can be used for similar products but is usually served in products requiring chopping, grinding, or slicing due to its slightly tough texture.

Clams are a good healthful food, low in calories but high in protein, iodine, iron, and other minerals. An average serving of 3–4 oz of hard shell clam meats is high in useable protein, contains only about 70 cal, and has about the same amount of iron as an equal serving of good grade liver. Even though clams are nutritious, most people purchase them because they can be made into a wide variety of taste-tempting dishes.

JOSEPH M. MENDELSOHN

Cross-reference: *Shellfish.*

CLEAN ROOMS

Clean rooms are controlled environment areas where air-borne and surface contamination is kept down to levels which satisfy established requirements. Air-borne contamination is usually controlled by means of absolute filters which remove 99.97% of particulate material 0.03 μ and larger in size. Surface contamination is controlled by frequent cleaning with detergents and sanitizing agents.

Facilities of this type are used to fabricate structural components for space craft, electronic equipment, miniature mechanical assemblies, and, to a limited extent, for the preparation of food products. Their use is indicated for applications where dust particles and/or microbial contamination cannot be tolerated and where the product is adversely affected by thermal processing.

The shape and nature of the product determines the air-flow pattern and the size of the facility. The flow may be horizontal with the air being introduced through a filter wall on one side of the room or the flow may be vertical with the clean air entering through a bank of filters in the ceiling. Another arrangement for handling products of limited size is the use of clean work stations in ordinary surroundings. Clean work stations are essentially miniature clean rooms. Air velocities are usually within the laminar flow domain, ranging from about 80 to 120 fpm.

Food products can be processed in a clean room facility with minimal risk of microbiological contamination. Foods so processed require less drastic thermal treatment than those prepared under conventional conditions. Thus, flavor and other quality characteristics can be expected to be superior.

The structural configurations and layouts of a clean room are almost limitless. At the U.S. Army Natick Laboratories, where a clean room was designed for the preparation of food products, the air is cleaned by means of absolute filters in the ductwork of the air-conditioning system and by 13 2-by-4 ft horizontal laminar flow work stations. The clean work stations consist of a shelf-type filter unit, a plastic shroud to form a reach-in work area, and separate stainless steel work tables.

JOHN SWIFT

Cross-reference: *Sanitation.*

Clostridium perfringens FOOD POISONING

During the first six months of 1968 the most frequent cause of food poisoning was not one of the familiar organisms that causes enteric distress such as Salmonellae or Staphylococci, but it was the less well-known microbe, *Clostridium perfringens.* In this record 6-month period, 2761 cases of food poisoning caused by this organism, were reported to the U.S. Public Health Service. It was the offender in 36% of all the cases of food poisoning reported, including bacterial, parasitic, viral, chemical, and others. In the like period in 1969, food poisoning by this organism was the second most commonly reported type, representing 40% of all cases. But for the entire year, it was by far the greatest cause of food poisoning reported, affecting 18,527 persons. This accounted for 65% of all cases. The 1969 figure was so high (higher than food poisoning due to all causes in 1968) because of one large outbreak which involved over 13,000 school children. Discounting the large outbreak, the number of cases of food poisoning caused by this organism in 1970 was higher than in the previous year, and higher than that caused by any other organism. It continued to be a common cause of food poisoning in 1971.

Although botulism was a known clinical disease more than 200 yr ago, *C. perfringens* was not recognized as a common cause of food poisoning until relatively recently. The delay is attributed to the odd and many-sided characteristics of this organism. Its varied traits obscured the toxic effect it can have on food, and distracted scientists from observing its capacity to make food unfit to eat. Inasmuch as food poisoning is one of the troublesome diseases that does not respond to immunization or antibiotics, control must come from prevention. This calls for understanding from food consumers and producers, as well as training from public health officials. The purpose of this article is to provide some of the required understanding.

Paradoxical Nature Thwarts Concept of Food Poisoning Role

An enigma is encountered with the bacterium *C. perfringens*.[1] This situation stems from the natural, though inocuous, presence of great numbers of this organism—as with *Escherichia coli*—in the human intestines. Yet, under suitable conditions, certain strains may cause food poisoning. By ingesting food in which *C. perfringens* has multiplied to a high count, varying degrees of distress may affect human subjects. These range in intensity from moderate gastroenteritis caused by type A, to haemorrhagic enteritis necroticans from type F, the latter capable of causing death.

C. perfringens may well be the most widespread and multifarious microorganism in existence. It is perhaps best known for its insidious attack on the deeper wounds in animals and man developing gangrene. Besides gangrene, it is associated with several other critical, often fatal infections. *C. perfringens* is a constant contaminant of soils, water, foods, waste products, and dust everywhere; and it is carried by all animals in contact with the soil. Factors contributing to its ubiquity are the resistance of its spores to drying, heat, irradiation, and survival in chlorinated water. Because it is a normal inhabitant of the healthy human intestine, it is of historic interest that *C. perfringens* has been used as an index of fecal pollution in water. The organism passes readily "through the intestinal wall into the livers" of germ-free mice. As it passes through the alimentary tract, the heat resistance of its spores increases. As a result of its gas-producing capability, it was formerly used in commercial starters for leavening salt-rising bread and for the fermentation of Niszler cheese. Since it possesses critical nutritional requirements, *C. perfringens* was once used in the microbiologic assay of amino acids. Spores of its most heat-resistant strains survive the temperature of boiling water more than 6 hr. They also survive meat curing and smoking processes, and storage in frozen beef for at least six months. Phospholipase C from *C. perfringens* is in wide use as a tool for studying biological membrane structure and function.

In view of these divers attributes, uses, and possible consequences, and because food contaminated with it has little or no off-odor or off-taste, *C. perfringens* was scarcely considered a food poisoner until well into the 20th Century. Furthermore, since most food poisoning outbreaks are caused by aerobes, and because of the relative difficulty in diagnosing an anerobe such as *C. perfringens* as a food poisoner, no real progress was made in the half century following Klein's observation in 1895 and Andrewes' in 1899 to show that it can be the causative agent in food poisoning. Although Larner, in 1922, warned of the possible cause of enteritis by this organism, McClung, in 1945, for the first time in the United States, reported human food poisoning caused by *C. perfringens*. Referring to McClung's report, J. W. Howie in Scotland remarked, "We had a lot of difficulty in persuading our American friends that it was a food-poisoner at all, although one of the most effective demonstrations that *C. welchii* caused food poisoning came from America."

In Sweden, in 1952, Osterling determined that the food poisoning characteristic of *C. perfringens* is limited to human beings. He produced food poisoning symptoms in several persons who had eaten food that was experimentally contaminated with it. However, none of his tests with apes, cats, dogs, or pigs gave positive results. Howie, too, after a number of feeding studies, concluded that domestic and experimental animals are immune to the *C. perfringens* strains known to cause food poisoning in man. In London, Betty Hobbs (1953) sparked great interest in safety from *C. perfringens* food poisoning upon publication of her classic study of this organism in 1953. Dische and Elek, in 1957, produced symptoms of *C. perfringens* food poisoning in 42 volunteers, similar to those in naturally-occurring outbreaks. They stressed that a proper, heat-resistant, food poisoning strain of *C. perfringens* was required. If indefinite or negative results were obtained, as was the case with some researchers, they suggested that the virulence of the strain may have been lost. However, in repeated outbreaks of food poisoning among groups of humans, the failure to find other species in significant numbers, the persistence of high counts of heat-resistant *C. perfringens* in food, and the same serotype in excrement has intensified interest in the subject. Because of the high count (10^8 cells minimum) of this organism required to cause food poisoning, an infection is generally believed to be induced. Baird-Parker (1971), however, cites several researchers whose findings indicate that the illness is likely due to a toxin. Yet, the specific cause of distress is unknown.

---

[1] Called *Clostridium welchii* overseas, after W. H. Welch, its discoverer.

Increase in Number of Reported Outbreaks Overseas Spurs Domestic Insight

Official recognition of *C. perfringens* food poisoning has come about slowly in the United States. In 1959, a confirmed case of food poisoning caused by this organism was published for the first time by the U.S. Public Health Service. However, in Britain, about 250 such reports were disclosed that year, which was a 10-fold rise since Betty Hobbs concluded her far reaching investigation of this organism only 6 yr earlier. In England and Wales, where food poisoning surveillance is developed to a high degree, 3744 food poisoning incidents were registered in 1966. Only 181 such occurences were made known to the U.S. Public Health Service, National Center for Disease Control in that period. Inasmuch as foodborne diseases are reported voluntarily to the NCDC, only 25 states responded in 1966. Since then this optional accounting has increased substantially, leveling off to 45 states in 1970. Even so, food poisoning in the United States is grossly under-reported. Available data represent only an estimated $^1/_{10}$ of the number of outbreaks that occur. This estimate is based on projections from figures supplied by areas such as the states of Washington and California where food-borne disease investigation is highly developed. Often the cause of food poisoning is not given, as was the case in 1970 when the reason was not specified for 27.2% of the food-borne disease outbreaks. Nevertheless, trends and causative factors become apparent.

Public health officials, reflecting increased concern with characterizing food-borne diseases heretofore categorized "etiology unknown," lately have taken to more intensive probing into these cases. While some improvement in surveillance has taken place (366 reported outbreaks in the United States in 1970), the need for a higher priority in the resolution of food-borne health problems is reflected. F. L. Bryan, NCDC Training Collaborator, emphasizes that more definitive identification of strains of *C. perfringens* through laboratory data and serotyping must be accomplished to develop constructive control measures in view of the numerous known varieites of this organism. Nevertheless, the finding of a significant proportion of all bacterial food poisoning outbreaks as being caused by *C. perfringens* is evident from the data in Table C-21, establishing it as a common offender. Taking the average outbreak, roughly $^1/_3$ of the persons ingesting the suspect food are affected. A great many of those affected are school children. Beef and turkey, because of poor heat transfer throughout their bulk, are most often involved. Nearly all outbreaks that materialize from improper food handling occur at places where the food is served, usually in public facilities, rather than at the processing establishment where the food is manufactured.

Survival of Spores in Cooking Provides Means of Food Contamination

Strains of *C. perfringens* that can cause food poisoning may be heat resistant, or not. But, the strains encountered most often in food poisoning outbreaks that cause the greatest difficulty in this respect are the ones possessing *extreme* heat resistance. Our investigation of the heat resistance of spores of this organism isolated from several food poisoning outbreaks offers an insight into the most important situation permitting multiplication of *C. perfringens* in food, namely, the ability of spores of certain of these strains to survive heat at 212°F for long periods of time. This observation is illustrated in Fig. C-14, showing that 6 food poisoning strains survived heating in meat broth at 212°F from 15 min to 6 hr. The survival curve for the most heat-resistant of these strains, F 2985/50, given in Fig. C-15, reveals that it survived heating at 212°F for 6$^2/_3$ hr and that the number of spores was decimated for each hour of boiling. Heat resistance of this capability is

TABLE C-21

REPORTED FOOD POISONING OUTBREAKS ATTRIBUTED TO Clostridium perfringens

Year	Outbreaks No.[1]	% [2]	Persons Affected No.[3]	% [4]	Persons Affected Per Outbreak Range	Median
1967	28	13.7	3,492	15.8	2–495	125
1968	56	16.2	5,966	34.0	2–560	107
1969	65	17.5	18,527[5]	64.9	2–13,500	23
1970	54	14.8	6,952	29.7	2–689	35

[1] Due to *C. perfringens* food poisoning.
[2] Percentage of total outbreaks of bacterial origin.
[3] By *C. perfringens* food poisoning.
[4] Percentage of all persons affected by bacterial food poisoning.
[5] The figures for 1969 are skewed because of one large outbreak involving 13,000 school children.

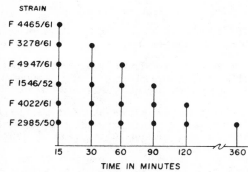

FIG. C-14. GROWTH OF SPORES OF FOOD POISONING STRAINS OF Clostridium perfringens AFTER HEATING AT 212°F IN MEAT MEDIUM FOR THE INDICATED PERIODS

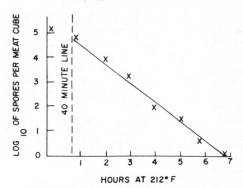

FIG. C-15. SURVIVAL OF SPORES OF Clostridium perfringens STRAIN F 2985/50 IN MEAT STEAMED AT 212°F

The period up to the 40-min line is the time taken for the meat to reach 212°F.

tantamount to survival during most cooking processes.

Inasmuch as *C. perfringens* is universally prevalent, there is little hope of foods being free from it because of the impossibility of avoiding contact with it. Since common cooking methods may be inadequate to destroy the heat-resistant spores, it is presupposed that normally cooked food will contain them. Consequently, one must cope with these spores as having survived cooking. If, after cooking, the food is not eaten promptly but it unwittingly is allowed to reach, and remain at intermediate temperatures that support the growth of the organisms, the spores will germinate and the cells will multiply to the point where the count is very high and may cause illness when ingested. Contaminated meat and fowl cooked in large portions for serving the next day are the greatest cause of trouble. If the huge bulk is left unrefrigerated, or is cooled slowly, heat-resistant spores that survive the cooking germinate and multiply in the tepid product. Survival of the less heat-resistant spores is favored due to poor heat penetration into the center of the mass. Growth is enhanced because air cannot penetrate into these large portions and oxygen is driven off, thus providing the required anaerobic conditions for the spores to flourish. Most other organisms are destroyed, for they cannot survive the heat tolerated by *C. perfringens.* When the temperature becomes favorable, ideal conditions for growth of *C. perfringens* ensue due to anaerobiosis, lack of competition from other microbes, and the rich protein nutrients. A clue to prevention of food poisoning by *C. perfringens* immediately suggests itself in the concept of not permitting survivor spores to thrive.

Temperature Control in Food Handling Affords Key to Safety

L. DS. Smith (1971) observed that the nutri-

tional factors, pH, and redox potential in meat and other high protein dishes are suitable for the demanding and massive growth of *C. perfringens.* He noted also that growth is not inhibited by the salt concentration in food. At 113°F and pH 7.0 he found the generation time to be only 10 min. In a few hours of doubling and redoubling at this prolific rate the organisms would increase in number to an enormous magnitude, easily reaching the high concentration required to cause enteric distress. Consequently, besides adequate hygienic measures, proper temperature precautions must be taken to inhibit proliferation of the probably harmless initial low numbers of the cells of this organism in food, or spores that have survived cooking. Most outbreaks of *C. perfringens* food poisoning are associated with the consumption of beef, poultry, or other suitable high protein food which inadvertently has been subjected to incubation temperatures that make it possible for its spores to germinate and ensuing cells to multiply. Inasmuch as we found the temperature range for supporting the growth of germinated spores to be rather wide (65° to 122°F), a temperature for the propagation of *C. perfringens* could unintentionally be provided at any stage of preparation preceding consumption of the food.

Bryan and Kilpatrick (1971) made a comprehensive time-temperature survey which revealed the vulnerability of roast beef to growth of *C. perfringens* during refrigeration, hot holding serving, and reheating. They also found surprisingly low internal temperatures during roasting, none of which were over 185°F. Thawing was an exception. Their finding that *C. perfringens* cannot multiply during the thawing of frozen beef is predictable from the observation of Kafel and Ayers (1971) that vegetative cells of this organism die in 8 hr at 46°F. Our own studies show that, at higher temperatures, as a result of heat shock, a high proportion of spores of *C. perfringens* germinate after beef is heated to 185°F, but only about 3% germinate without heat activation. In roasting, and in other cooking methods, this temperature is often attained and held sufficiently long to stimulate germination of the spores. If germination and multiplication is allowed to occur, cooking must be continued sufficiently long and held at a high enough temperature (165°F minimum) to kill the vegetative cells that have been generated. Otherwise, it can be concluded that insufficient cooking actually contributes to food poisoning, not only by heat activation of spores and destruction of competing organisms, but also by the removal of oxygen which enhances anaerobiosis. Similarly, these factors combine to establish ideal conditions for growth of *C. perfringens* during hot holding in an oven set at an insufficiently high temperature, throughout serving from an inadequately heated steam table, while cooling unused bulky cooked food at room temperature or during the initial stages of refrigeration, and in reheating leftovers inadequately by not reaching and holding 165°F minimum internally (the lethal temperature for vegetative cells) for at least 15 min. In these processes the food may pass through temperatures near optimum for the active growth of this organism. It follows, therefore, that safety from *C. perfringens* food poisoning lies in avoiding situations that create temperatures favorable for the germination of its spores and multiplication of its cells.

In roasting meat, the internal temperature will destroy vegetative cells but cannot kill the spores, for it rarely rises above 185°F in the center of the cut; because, as determined by H. L. Miller, meat is a poor conductor of heat. Therefore, pieces should not be larger than 6 lb so that sufficient heat can penetrate quickly for destruction of cells; and, cooling for refrigeration can be rapid to prevent surviving spores from germinating. This is especially important for rolled meat, as the center was exposed to contamination before rolling. Food should not be prepared several hours or longer before consumption unless it can be maintained continuously hot at a minimum of of 140°F until served; or, if it is to be served during a subsequent meal, it can be cooled quickly and kept continuously cold below 45°F. If, in addition to proper sanitation, these temperature precautions were conscientiously practiced, food poisoning by *C. perfringens* could be completely averted.

JOHN E. DESPAUL

References

BAIRD-PARKER, A. C. 1971. *C. perfringens* food poisoning—a likely toxin. J. Appl. Bacteriol. *34*, 191-192.

BARNES, E. M., DESPAUL, J. E., and INGRAM, M. 1963. The behavior of food poisoning . . . *C. welchii* in beef. J. Appl. Bacteriol. *26*, 415-427.

BRYAN, F. L., and KILPATRICK, E. G. 1971. *C. perfringens* related to roast beef cooking, storage, and contamination. Am. J. Public Health *32*, 1869-1885.

DESPAUL, J. E. 1966. The gangrene organism—a food poisoning agent. J. Am. Dietetic Assoc. *49*, 185-190.

DUNCAN, C. L., LABBE, R. G., and REICH, R. R. 1972. Germination of spores of *C. perfringens*. J. Bacteriol. *109*, 550-559.

HOBBS, B. C. *et al.* 1953, 1968. Food poisoning: By heat resistant *C. welchii*. J. Hyg. *51*, 75-101. By heat sensitive *C. welchii*. J. Hyg. *66*, 135-146.

KAFEL, S., and AYRES, J. C. 1971. Importance of *C. perfringens* in foods. Proc. 3rd Intern. Cong. Food Sci. and Technol., Inst. Food Technologists.

MCILWAIN, D. L., and RAPPORT, M. M. 1971. The effects of phospholipase C (*C. perfringens*) on purified myelin. Biochim. Biophys. Acta *239*, 71-80.

NAKAMURA, M., and SCHULZE, J. A. 1970. *C. perfringens* food poisoning. Ann. Rev. Microbiol. *24*, 359-372.

National Center for Disease Control. 1967, 1968, 1969, 1970. Foodborne outbreaks. Annual Summaries. U.S. Public Health Service, Atlanta, Ga.

ROBERT, T. A. 1968. Heat and radiation resistance and activation of spores of *C. welchii*. J. Appl. Bacteriol. *31*, 133-144.

SMITH, L. DS. 1971. Factors affecting the growth of *C. perfringens*. Proc. 3rd Intern. Cong. Food Sci. and Technol., Inst. Food Technologists.

COCONUTS

Coconuts (*Cocus nucifera* L.) are by far the most extensively grown and used nuts in the world. The coconut crop of the world, estimated at 16.9 billion nuts, comes from an area of 8.7 million acres distributed over tropical coasts of India, Indonesia, the Philippines, Ceylon, Malaysia, and South Pacific Islands. The native habitant is unknown but through the centuries coconuts were distributed by water and man from continent to continent and island to island around the world where they would grow, and became the

FIG. C-16. NATURAL COCONUT GROVE WITH BANANA UNDERGROWTH IN THE PHILIPPINES

FIG. C-17. GREEN COCONUTS PILED BESIDE THE ROAD READY TO BE CARRIED TO MARKET IN THE PHILIPPINES

"staff of life" to the natives. Most of the coconuts of commerce today are from natural groves, of seedling trees, harvested and processed in a crude, laborious fashion. A great deal of the subsistence of the natives—food, shelter, feed for animals, facilities, and clothing—come from coconuts.

Coconuts grow at elevations up to 1000 ft; within 15° of the equator; at a mean temperature of 77°F (25°C) and above; and with 60 in. of rainfall and above (evenly distributed). They thrive best on rich, sandy soil near the coast; and brackish water is tolerated provided the water table fluctuates to give the roots aeration.

Propagation is only by seed. Well matured nuts are collected from selected trees and laid in trenches, tilted towards the stem, and covered about half with soil. Thousands of nuts germinate by lying on damp soil beneath coconut trees.

Germination of the coconut takes place in 1-2 months after planting. The radicle (root) and plumule (stem) emerge through an "eye," from the swollen cotyledon "apple." The food reserves in the nut support the seedling for at least 1 yr. In several years the basal crown builds up to full size of the mature trunk. Fresh roots appear at each node of the bulbous base of the stem to anchor the tree firmly with from 4000 to 7000 roots.

The coconut palm begins fruiting in 6-9 yr. An inflorescence consists of male and female flowers in separate clusters that develop in the axil of every leaf. Up to 8000 male flowers appear at the apex with about 30 female flowers at the base. The pollen is usually shed before the pistils are receptive on an individual infloresence. Thus, cross pollination by insects and the wind is the rule in varieties of tall coconuts. In the Malay dwarf varieties the male and female flowers develop at the same time and are self pollinated.

The coconut tree flowers and fruits during the entire year, and productivity depends more on the nutritional status of the soil and tree than on the number of flowers formed. The average annual production per tree of a native stand is about 50 fruit per year or 23 lb of copra. The usual spacing of trees in a plantation is about 32 × 32 ft, to give a density of 43 trees per acre (100 trees per hectare), which produce about 2200 lb of copra.

Selection of coconut trees has barely begun in most parts of the world and there are indications that production can be increased 7-fold by improving breeding and cultural practices. The economy may be further improved by growing crops of peanuts, soybeans, sweet potatoes, pineapples, or grass for grazing on the ground level; or by growing bananas, papayas, or coffee trees on a second level. When "weeds" are controlled commercial fertilizers are used to advantage. It is important to keep the soil moist, shaded, and cool to promote abundant root growth.

Uses

There are more than 360 uses of coconuts and coconut products, of which about 200 are in foods which have been extolled for centuries. Six of these are important in world trade. They are (a) whole coconuts (tender, green as well as dry, mature); (b) copra (the dried kernel of the nuts used for shredding and pressing oil); (c) coconut oil (extracted from copra and directly from the meat); (d) coconut oil cake (residue left after extracting oil from copra); (e) coir (fiber of the husks); and (f) desiccated coconut.

Whole Coconuts

Coconuts are of two kinds—green and mature. Green coconuts are harvested while the meat is still soft and rubbery, and can be easily scooped out of the shell with a spoon. At this stage the husk and shell can be cut with a heavy knife. For eating, the whole coconut is cut crosswise with a knife or saw, allowing the water to waste, and the halves are served on a dish with a spoon. No seasoning is added except possibly a scoop of ice cream. The rubbery meat is often removed, chipped, and used in ice cream, pies, cake or cookies to impart a wonderful flavor and texture. The use of green coconuts is restricted to areas that can maintain a supply within one week of the time they are harvested.

Mature coconuts are harvested after the shell is fully hard and the meat is firm. Since they may be stored for more than two months in a dry, cool place, they can be shipped anywhere in the world. Due to the large amount of labor required for shelling, peeling and grinding the meat, fresh coconuts are not used in restaurants and their use in homes is declining.

To use: The "eyes" are punched out and the liquid (called coconut milk) drained off for adding later to the ground product; the shell is broken by striking the side; the meat is removed and hand peeled; it is then ground in a food chopper. The ground meat, moistened by adding the liquid that was drained off, has a delicious aroma, flavor, and texture; and has dozens of kitchen uses in salads, desserts, pudding, candies, toppings, cakes, pies, ices, and ice cream.

Copra

Copra is the meat of coconuts dried from a moisture content of about 45 to 6%, with about 64% oil. The purpose of drying is to prevent spoilage during transportation and storage for oil extraction. The husked nuts are halved and partially dried, allowing the meat to be easily removed and further dried. Drying is in the sun, in an oven, over a fire from burning the shells, or a combination of these.

Copra is made continuously in small or large sheds in areas where coconuts are grown; and is a way of utilizing labor by all members of the family. The finished product is put in bags or baskets and delivered to assembly points by carts, trucks, or on the backs of horses or cacabaus. Here it is graded for maturity of nuts, color, decay, and moisture content. It is then delivered to oil mills where it is further graded and stored in huge quantities for oil extraction.

In general, 1000 coconuts will yield 500 lb of copra and 25 gal. of oil. Copra is fairly resistant to mold, rancidity, and putrifaction, and when protected from insects and rodents by packing it can be stored for many months or shipped to remote sections of the world.

Coconut Oil

Coconut oil is a nondrying oil of 0.91–0.92 sp gr and solidifies at 67°F. The high degree of saturation and long stability of coconut oil makes it one of the world's most desirable oils for confections, bakery goods, deep fat frying, and candles. The chief fatty acids are lauric (45%), myristic (18%), palmitic (9.5%), oleic (8.2%), capryic (7.8%), capric (7.6%), and stearic (5%).

There are three kinds of coconut oil available: (a) oil pressed from copra by expeller or hydraulic pressing, which constitutes most of the commercial coconut oil, is solid at room temperature, is saturated, and very stable alone or in products; (b) oil pressed from peelings (paring oil) and fragments of fresh coconut in the manufacture of desiccated coconut is slightly less saturated, and more suitable for filled milk than regular coconut oil; and (c) oil concentrated from coconut liquid, and available in limited quantities.

Major uses of coconut oil are in toilet soap, laundry soap, shortening and oleomargarine, detergents, and deep fat frying. In each of these it excels. Minor uses of coconut oil are in filled milk, imitation milk, lotions, rubbing creams, prepared flours and cake mixes, and in pressurized toppings. The increased use of fat-free detergents and of hydrogenated oil of other vegetable origins, has decreased the world demand for coconut oil.

Coconut Oil Cake or Copra Meal

This is the ground cake following oil extraction of copra. It contains about 4.8% moisture, 22.89% crude protein, 7.74% fat, 8.53% crude fiber, and 29.15% nitroge-free extract. It is available from oil mills throughout the year, and is used almost entirely for feed to pigs, poultry, cattle, and other animals. It is an incomplete protein and is supplemented with fish meal, peanut meal, chickpea flour, minerals, and vitamins A and D. Only a small portion of the copra meal is fed to animals in coconut growing countries, but rather it is exported to Germany, United States, and other countries for feed.

FIG. C-18. REAR VIEW OF PETER PAUL'S PROCESSING PLANT IN THE PHILIPPINES WHERE 500,000 COCONUTS ARE SHREDDED AND DESICCATED DAILY THROUGHOUT THE YEAR

Coir

Coir (coconut husk fiber) is a major coconut product in Ceylon and certain areas of the Philippines, where the husks (23% of the nuts) are retted, separated, graded, and made into many products. The fibers are separated according to length, dried, twisted to give them a "kink," and woven into mats, ropes, boards, panels, mattresses, cushions for automobile seats, hats, and dozens of other commercial and household objects. The best coir is made from slightly immature nuts. The husks are retted in streams or large tanks of water for 3 days (older husks require retting 4 days). The higher grade "mattress fiber" is 8 in. long, and when woven into braids or mats it has no equal among synthetic fibers. It can be impregnated with mold inhibitors, insect proofed and stiffened to give at a resistance equal to metal wires. The weathering and wearing qualities are extremely good.

Desiccated Coconut

This is the form in which more coconut meat (protein) is used than all other forms combined. It is packed asceptically, is free of mold and bacteria, has a very low moisture content and can be shipped over the world. While refrigeration is recommended, it is not necessary for one month's storage.

This method of preservation is highly developed in the Philippines with three companies (Peter Paul, Baker's Coconut, and Red V) processing more than 1.2 million coconuts daily throughout the year.

JASPER GUY WOODROOF

References

OCHSE, J. J., SOULE, M. J., JR., DIJKMAN, M. J., and WEHLBURG, C. 1961. Tropical and Subtropical Agriculture, Vol. II. Macmillan Co., New York.

WOODROFF, J. G. 1970. Coconuts: Production, Processing, Products. Avi Publishing Co., Westport, Conn.

COCONUT, SHREDDED

Commercial coconut is the shredded, dried, and sometimes sweetened or toasted meat of the coconut palm. Coconut palms (*Cocos nucifera*) are the most important of cultured palms and the most widely distributed of all palms. They are widespread in warm regions, being most abundant in America and Asia—and a few in Africa. They are particularly conspicuous in the Pacific Islands.

There are two major varieties of coconut palms, the tall and the dwarf. At the present time, the tall variety is the best and the most consistent producer and is the most widely used.

Fruit is produced on coconut trees in about 5 yr, and the trees bear in full in about 10 yr. Production continues with some fruit on the palm every month in the year for about 50–60 yr. After that, yield decreases. In any given year, the harvest producing season will be from June through October with yield declining sharply in the November through May period.

The most important products from the coconut palm are copra, desiccated coconut, fresh coconut, and coir. Almost every part of the coconut palm tree is utilized by the natives in the growing areas.

After copra, desiccated or shredded coconut is the second most important commercial product from the coconut palm. In international coconut trade, copra and copra by-products (coconut oil and copra meat) constitute probably better than 90% of the volume. Desiccated or shredded coconut is nevertheless a substantial source of income in the principal producing areas.

The principal producing areas for desiccated or shredded coconut and the estimated annual export for that area are as follows:

Country	Annual Export, 1970 (1000 Lb)
Philippines	129,335
Ceylon	98,070
Polynesia	10,000[1]
Total	237,405

[1] Estimate

At harvest time, field workers cut down the ripe coconuts using knives attached to long poles, some reaching 60–80 ft in the air. Once on the ground, the whole, fresh coconuts—still in the husks—are collected by sweepers into piles. Next, other workers remove the husk from the coconut, using a sharp knife mounted vertically on the ground. The husked coconuts are then transported quickly to one of the roadside collection stations for truck shipment to processing plants. It requires approximately 1 ton of fresh coconuts in the shells to produce 336 lb of desiccated or shredded coconut.

The processing of desiccated coconut is accomplished in seven main steps: shelling, paring, shredding, blanching, drying, sieving, and packing.

The hard shell and tough brown skin of the nut are removed by hand. After shelling and paring, the broken nutmeats are passed through a water bath on their way to the shredding or deviling machines where they are reduced to the desired size in 2–3 sec. From the shredder, the coconut is taken to endless belts where the freshly shredded meat is first blanched with live steam and then dried.

In drying, the moisture content is reduced from 52 to 2.5%. After drying, the coconut is graded to size in a double sieving operation. Finally, the desiccated coconut is packed, according to grade, in a 4-ply natural kraft bag fitted with independent heat-sealed polyethylene liner. The major portion of desiccated or shredded coconut is packed in 100-lb units of a specific grade.

Of the roughly 100,000,000 lb of desiccated coconut imported into the United States, primarily from the Philippines, 70% of it is sold directly to bakery or confectionery manufacturers in the original bags—just as it comes from the producing factories.

The other 30% is reprocessed in tumbling mixers with powdered sugar, propylene glycol, salt, and added moisture to produce white sweetened coconut.

To produce the toasted variety, desiccated coconut is treated with powdered sugar, dextrose and salt and passed through endless belt toasting ovens.

Creamed coconut is made by grinding, aerating, chilling, and whipping desiccated coconut to a smooth shortening-like consistency.

The basic uses for desiccated coconut or the reprocessed varieties are as follows: topping agent, bulking agent, nutmeat, or flavoring. These uses apply to industrial as well as grocery applications.

High grade desiccated coconut for food purposes will have a pure white color; be free of dirt or paring specks; have a clean, fresh taste and odor; be of uniform granulation or cut; and have low bacteria, yeast, and mold counts.

MAX E. RUEHRMUND

COD, ATLANTIC

Total supplies of cod (edible weight) during 1970 were 113,800,000 lb, an 85% jump over the 1965–1969 averages. U.S. landings of cod in 1970 were only 17,200,000 lb (edible weight).

One factor that has led to the increased consumption of cod in recent years has been the rise of fish and chips restaurant chains. By 1970, the total number of such restaurants had risen to close to 1150 and they may have used as much as 56,000,000 lb of cod fillets.

The cod is an important part of our fishery resources of the northeast coast. The term Atlantic cod (*Gadus morhua*) is used to distinguish it from the Pacific cod (*Gadus macrocephalus*). The cod family, the Gadidae, includes the haddock, the pollock, the hakes, and cusk. It is at home on both

sides of the North Atlantic Ocean from the northern Barents Sea south to the Bay of Biscay, around Iceland and the southern tip of Greenland, all the way down to North Carolina. It is found near the ocean floor over rough bottom. The Grand Banks of Newfoundland, Georges Bank off Massachusetts, Iceland, and the Faroe Islands are the most important fishing grounds.

Cod are prolific. A good sized female cod will produce about 5 million eggs. They are buoyant. The adult cod is carniverous and when hungry will eat almost any marine animal. As fry, they eat copepods, barnacles, and other crustaceans. As young adults they continue to eat crustaceans. As they become larger they concentrate on other fish such as herrings, capelin, and sand lance.

The largest percentage of cod is captured in a trawl towed on the bottom by large steel vessels; a small percentage is caught with hand lines, jiggers, trap nets, pair trawls, gill nets, and seine nets.

The shape of the cod is roughly cylindrical with 3 large dorsal fins above and 2 large anal fins below; a prominent chin whisker (barbel); and a wide, nearly square tail. The principal color may vary from gray, green, brown, or red to almost black. The upper portion of the cod is usually olive green marked with spots with the lower portion white. A cod measuring over 6 ft in length and weighing $211^1/_4$ lb is the largest on record. Average weight is about 5 lb and usually the cod does not exceed 60 lb. The usual market classifications in this country are snapper up to $1^1/_2$ lb, scrod $1^1/_2$–$2^1/_2$ lb, market $2^1/_2$–10 lb, large 10–25 lb, and whale over 25 lb.

The Atlantic cod is used fresh, frozen, smoked, dried, salted, and canned. By-products include fish meal, cod liver oil, and glue made from the skin. Frozen blocks of cod fillets form the backbone of the fish stick and portion industry.

As a food fish, the cod is very adaptable; its flesh is rich and gelatinous without being fatty. It adapts to practically every form of fish cookery with its meat white and delicately flavored.

A yield of 41–45% is typical for machine filleted cod, with an average of 43%. On an average, the chemical composition of the Atlantic cod is as follows: Total solids, 17.4%; fat, 0.4%; protein, 16.5%; ash, 1.2%; calories, 315 per lb.

JOHN J. RYAN

Cross-reference: *Fish and Fishery Products.*

CODEX ALIMENTARIUS

For several years prior to 1962, several programs were under way aimed at standardizing foods on an international basis. The two most prominent of these programs were the International Dairy Federation (IDF) program of milk product standards and the Codex Alimentarius of Europe program. The IDF procedure of milk product standardization has been taken over and made a program of the Food and Agriculture Organization (FAO), a unit of the United Nations.

A joint FAO/WHO Conference on Food Standards was held in Geneva, Switzerland, Oct. 1 through 5, 1962. This first meeting had representatives from 44 member nations and observers from 24 international organizations. Any country which participated in either the FAO or WHO was invited to attend this conference. It considered the following points: (1) the proposal of a joint FAO/WHO program on food standards having as its principal organ the Codex Alimentarius Commission; (2) guidelines for the work of the Codex Alimentarius Commission; (3) the date for the first Codex Alimentarius Commission meeting; and (4) the method of financing a joint FAO/WHO program on food standards.

The conference reviewed and endorsed the need for international food standards both on a worldwide and regional basis, and also drew attention to the fact that many problems are involved in setting up such standards and they should be studied and implemented with the following points in mind: health, science, technology, economics, and administration. Only when all of these subjects are covered and applied to a food standard would it be possible to make any real progress in the field.

To begin with, the Codex Alimentarius work was to be financed by a trust fund to which member countries of FAO and WHO were invited to contribute; and then at some later date it would seem desirable to include the Codex Alimentarius work in the budget of FAO and WHO.

This first conference on food standards set up recommended guidelines for the Codex Alimentarius Commission. These guidelines were to lead the Codex Alimentarius Commission to the development of standards which would be of value in international trade. This first conference directed the Commission to take into consideration the aims of the European Council of Codex Alimentarius which was founded by Dr. Hans Frenzel of Austria, as well as the Codigo Latino-Americano de Alimentos which was launched a few years before in the Latin American countries by Dr. Carlos C. Grau of Argentina. The food standards group meeting in Geneva suggested that these two pieces of work be continued and they would then be adopted and brought into the Codex Alimentarius at some later date. A date was set for the first meeting of the Codex Alimentarius Commission

to be held June 1963. The purposes of Codex Alimentarius, as outlined by the food standards meeting in 1962, were as follows:

> The Codex Alimentarius is to be a collection of internationally adopted food standards presented in a unified form. These food standards aim at protecting consumers' health and ensuring fair practices in the food trade. Their publication is intended to promote the standardization of foodstuffs in the various parts of the world, to facilitate harmonization of standards and in so doing to further the development of international food trade. (Report of the Joint FAO/WHO Conference on Food Standards, Oct. 1962, p. 5.)

Scope of Codex Alimentarius

The conference recommended that Codex should, in time, include all of the principal foods whether processed, semiprocessed, or raw for direct sale to the consumer, or, where appropriate, for manufacturing purposes. Codex should, in particular, take in the whole range of food additives and contaminants since these highly complicated problems affect practically all processed foods as well as an ever-increasing number of raw foods. Codex should not include any products other than those ingested for nutritional purposes; in other words, drugs and cosmetics were not to be included. Codex work was to include food hygiene or sanitation associated with the production of foods. It was pointed out that in many legislative organizations food hygiene is handled in a different manner by a different department from food standards work; however, it was specifically brought out that food hygiene should become part of Codex Alimentarius. This would be particularly true and valuable for the developing countries as they look toward Codex Alimentarius for guidance.

After a discussion of the nature of the food standards to be drawn up by the Codex Commission, it was pointed out that the food standards aim at ensuring the marketing of a wholesome product correctly labeled and presented. It was not intended to affect the consumer's preference. The conference considered two kinds of standards: a "platform" (minimum) standard; and what is generally referred to as a "trading standard" (similar to our USDA grading standards). Quite some discussion was held as to the value of the platform standard and the trading standard, and consideration was given as to just how these would be handled. This subject was discussed for several years at subsequent Commission meetings and a final form of standard was later drawn up.

It was pointed out at the first food standards conference that the FAO program of the FAO Committee of Government Experts on the Code of Principles Concerning Milk and Milk Products had worked toward the establishment of platform standards and they had been published under the name of "Code of Principles Concerning Milk and Milk Products" and at the time of the first meeting this Code of Principles had been accepted by no less than 50 governments. Minimum platform standards could be of real use for trading purposes to countries where national standards are usually rigorous as well as developing countries.

The conference recommended that Codex, in due course, cover all of the principal foods and their components in international trade. The type of standard to be included in the same long-term view should aim at covering all facets of the problem; especially, definitions, composition, quality designation, labeling, sampling, analysis, and hygiene. These facets should be studied in their scientific, technical, economic, administrative, and legal aspects in order to ensure that the products to which they apply were in all respects suitable for consumption from both the hygienic and commercial point of view and were correctly described.

Some priorities were set up for study by this first conference on food standards, and these priorities called for study of the following points: food additives, method of sampling and analysis, basic food hygiene, and standards of composition. Certain foods were then listed which should be considered as early as possible, such as fats and oils, preserved fruits including jams, canned fruits, jellies and marmalades, fruit juices, cocoa beans, cocoa and chocolate, honey, and sugar. Also, a further list of priorities was drawn up which included many more foods than those mentioned above.

This first meeting, which as mentioned before was held in October 1962, was really the organizational meeting calling for and setting up the first meeting of the Codex Alimentarius Commission to be held in 1963. The first session of the joint FAO/WHO Codex Alimentarius Commission was held in June 1963 and since that time 8 additional sessions have been held at approximately 1 yr intervals, the last session having been held Nov. 6, 1972. As reported at the Eighth Commission Meeting, the Codex Alimentarius Commission consisted of a membership of 89 countries: 28 from Europe, 2 from North America, 19 from Latin America, 19 from Africa, 2 from Southwest Pacific, and 19 from Asia.

Organization

The exact organization of the Commission consists of a chairman and three vice chairmen. There is an Executive Committee composed of the chairman and the vice chairmen as well as elected members from each of the geographical regions, namely, Africa, Asia, Europe, Latin America, North Amer-

ica, and Australasia. The Executive Committee is the ruling body of the Commission. The work is divided into various forms of committees. In general the committees are set up as follows:

A. Under Rule IX.1. (a)
   Joint FAO/WHO Committee of Government Experts on the Code of Principles Concerning Milk and Milk Products.
B. Under Rule IX.1. (b).1
   Worldwide General Subject Codex Committees:
   1. Food Additives (The Netherlands)[2]
   2. Pesticide Residues (The Netherlands)
   3. Analysis and Sampling (Hungary)
   4. General Principles (France)
   5. Food Labeling (Canada)
   6. Food Hygiene (U.S.A.)

   Worldwide Commodity Codex Committees:
   1. Cocoa Products and Chocolate (Switzerland)
   2. Sugars (United Kingdom)
   3. Processed Fruits and Vegetables (U.S.A.)
   4. Fats and Oils (United Kingdom)
   5. Dietetic Foods (Federal Republic of Germany)
   6. Fish and Fish Products (Norway)
   7. Meat and Meat Products (Federal Republic of Germany)
         Subcommittee on Meat Products (Denmark)
   8. Meat Hygiene (New Zealand)
   9. Frozen Desserts (Sweden)
   Regional Codex Committees:
   1. Mineral Waters (Switzerland)
C. Under Rule IX.1.(b).2
   FAO/WHO Coordinating Committee for Europe
D. In addition to the above committees the Codex Alimentarius Commission also cooperates with the United Nations Economic Commission for Europe through E.C.E./Codex Alimentarius Groups of Experts on the development of standards for:
   1. Fruit juices
   2. Quick frozen foods

The Committee under Rule IX.1.(a) is a joint FAO/WHO Committee of Government Experts on the Code of Principles Concerning Milk and Milk Products. As the name indicates, this is a joint FAO/WHO Committee and it meets regularly, almost once a year, at FAO headquarters in Rome. This Committee has full responsibility for the development of standards for all milk and milk products. Originally formed by the International

---

[2] Country chairing the committee indicated in parentheses.

Dairy Federation, its work was later adopted by the FAO and the work was continued under FAO sponsorship. At the time the Commission was founded, the Joint Committee of Government Experts on the Code of Principles Concerning Milk and Milk Products had already met approximately five times and had certain standards, as well as the "Code of Principles," pretty well developed and adopted by the various countries under a procedure which this Committee had elaborated itself. Since this method was already functioning, the Committee remained intact as a subsidiary to the Codex Alimentarius Commission, but, according to the rules of procedure, having full authority to develop and elaborate standards for milk and milk products.

The standards and codes drawn up by the worldwide general subject committees, as listed above, were to cover all food products. As examples: any additives listed under a standard elaborated by a commodity committee must be approved for that use by the Food Additives Committee chaired by The Netherlands. Also, the labeling of a food standardized by a commodity committee must meet the minimum labeling requirements of the Labeling Committee chaired by Canada. In addition, the commodity committee may require additional labeling particularly required by the product involved.

As could be expected, considerable time was consumed in the various Commission meetings in the first few years to determine the type, the format, the method of elaboration, the mode of acceptance, and the many other problems involved in such a program as international food standards.

Much discussion was had on the relative merits of the platform standard versus a trading standard, and in general it was decided that the Codex Alimentarius, to begin with, would have only one form of standard. This standard was to include a definition of the product, the chemical composition standard, permissible additives, required ingredients, labeling, method of analysis, etc., in connection with the product. It will be noted that the proposed product standards were to cover about the same subject matter as the definitions and standards of our U.S. Food and Drug Administration.

Procedure for Worldwide Elaboration of Standards

After many years, a procedure for the elaboration of worldwide Codex standards has been drawn up consisting of a total of ten steps. These steps are as shown below:

Step 1

The Commission decides on the elaboration of a worldwide Codex standard and decides which subsidiary body or other body should undertake the work.

Step 2

The subsidiary body or other body so designated prepares a proposed draft standard, taking into account the work accomplished by the appropriate international organizations. The draft is sent to the Commission's Secretariat by the Chairman of the subsidiary body or other body.

Step 3

The proposed draft standard is sent by the Commission's Secretariat to Member States and Associate Members of FAO and/or WHO and to the international organizations concerned in order to obtain their comments.

Step 4

The Commission's Secretariat sends the comments received from governments and from the international organizations concerned to the subsidiary body or other body concerned, which has the power to consider such comments and to amend the proposed draft standard, if appropriate.

Step 5

The proposed draft standard is submitted through the Secretariat to the Commission with a view to its adoption as a draft standard. The Commission may, however, refer it to a special subsidiary body, set up under Rule IX.1 (a) of the Rules of Procedure, before adopting it as a draft standard or may entrust the special subsidiary body with the responsibility for undertaking Steps 5, 7 and 8 of this Procedure or any part thereof.

Step 6

The draft standard is sent by the Commission's Secretariat for comment to all Member States and Associate Members of FAO and/or WHO and to the international organizations concerned.

Step 7

The comments received from governments and from the international organizations concerned are sent by the Secretariat to the subsidiary body or other body concerned, which has the power to consider such comments and amend the draft standard, if appropriate.

Step 8

The draft standard is submitted through the Secretariat to the Commission with a view to adoption as a recommended standard.

Step 9

The recommended standard is sent to all Member States and Associate Members of FAO and/or WHO and to the international organizations concerned. Members of the Commission notify the Secretariat of their acceptance of the recommended standard in accordance with the acceptance procedure laid down in paragraph 4 or in paragraph 5 of the General Principles of the Codex Alimentarius, whichever is appropriate. Member States and

Associate Members of FAO and/or WHO that are not Members of the Commission are invited to notify the Secretariat if they wish to accept the recommended standard.

Step 10

The recommended standard will be published in the Codex Alimentarius as a worldwide Codex standard when the Commission determines that it is appropriate to do so in the light of the acceptances received.

In general, regional standards are drawn up following the same procedures as mentioned above for worldwide standards with modifications which would be particularly applicable to regions. One of the most difficult matters for the Commission to handle was the method of acceptance and the meaning of acceptance of Codex standards. After long discussions, Codex commodity standards may be accepted as defined below:

A. A Codex standard may be accepted by a country in accordance with its established legal and Administrative procedures in respect of distribution of the product concerned, whether imported or home-produced, within its territorial jurisdiction in the following ways:
  (i) Full acceptance
    (a) Full acceptance means that the country concerned will ensure that a product to which the standard applies will be permitted to be distributed freely, in accordance with (c) below, within its territorial jurisdiction under the name and description laid down in the standard, provided that it complies with all the relevant requirements of the standard.
    (b) The country will also ensure that products not complying with the standard will not be permitted to be distributed under the name and description laid down in the standard.
    (c) The distribution of any sound products conforming with the standards will not be hindered by any legal or administrative provisions in the country concerned relating to the health of the consumer or to other food standard matters except for considerations of human, plant or animal health which are not specifically dealt with in the standard.
  (ii) Target acceptance
    Target acceptance means that the country concerned indicates its intention to accept the standard after a stated number of years and will meanwhile not hinder within its territorial jurisdiction the distribution of any sound products conforming with the standard by any legal or administrative provisions relating to the health of the consumer or to other food standard matters except for considerations of human, plant or animal health which are not specifically dealt with in the standard.
  (iii) Acceptance with minor deviations
    Acceptance with minor deviations means that the country concerned gives full acceptance as defined in paragraph A(i) to the standard with the exception of minor deviations which are recognized as such by the Codex Alimentarius Commission; it being understood that a product complying with the standard as qualified by such minor deviations will be permitted to be distributed freely within the territorial jurisdiction of the country concerned. The country concerned will further include in its declaration of acceptance a statement of such deviations, the reasons for them, and also indicate:
    (a) whether products fully conforming to the standard may be distributed freely within its territorial jurisdiction in accordance with paragraph A(i);
    (b) whether it expects to be able to give full acceptance to the standard and, if so, when.

B. A country which considers that it cannot accept the standard in any of the ways mentioned above should indicate:
  (i) whether products conforming to the standard may be distributed freely within its territorial jurisdiction;
  (ii) in what ways its present or proposed requirements differ from the standard, and, if possible, the reasons for these differences.

C. (i) A country which accepts a Codex standard according to one of the provisions of A is responsible for the uniform and impartial application of the provisions of the standard as they apply to all home-produced and imported products distributed within its territorial jurisdiction. In addition, the country should be prepared to offer advice and guidance to exporters and processors of products for export to promote understanding of and compliance with the requirements of importing countries which have accepted a Codex standard according to one of the provisions of A.
  (ii) Where, in an importing country, a product claimed to be in compliance with a Codex standard is found not to be in compliance with that standard, whether in respect of the label accompanying the product or otherwise, the importing country should inform the competent authorities in the

exporting country of all the relevent facts and in particular the details of the origin of the product in question (name and address of the exporter), if it is thought that a person in the exporting country is responsible for such noncompliance.

From the beginning, the dairy products standards elaborated by the Committee of Government Experts Concerning the Code of Principles on Milk and Milk Products varied slightly from the procedures set forth by the Codex Alimentarius Commission because the milk products method of acceptance and meaning of acceptance were both drawn up and in use before Codex came up with corresponding procedures, therefore many of the dairy products commodity standards have been accepted by a slightly different procedure, and hence have to go back for acceptance under the Codex Alimentarius procedure of acceptance. The elaboration of standards for milk products does not vary greatly from the Codex Alimentarius standard procedure. The primary difference lies in the fact that the first draft of dairy products standards is drawn up by the International Dairy Federation and sent to the Committee of Codex Alimentarius for discussion and subsequent modification and acceptance by the Committee of Government Experts. Although deviating somewhat, in general the method of elaborating standards is quite comparable to the Codex Alimentarius standard procedure.

How Codex Alimentarius Operates

Having seen the organization of the Committee of Codex Alimentarius, let's consider the manner in which Codex Alimentarius operates.

As stated in the procedures for the adoption of a standard, a decision is made by the Commission to the effect that a standard is needed for a given product and the writing of this standard is assigned to one of the existing committees or, if need be, an additional committee may be set up. It is in these product committees that the real discussion of the relative merits of the technical points appearing in a standard are thoroughly reviewed.

The committee representation consists of representatives of the governments involved, along with technical advisers from industry and trade associations. In the case of the United States, the official representative is a government employee usually from the Food and Drug Administration or the Department of Agriculture. This delegation is assisted by advisers from industry and trade associations. It is in these technical committees that input from industry into the actual standard itself is invited and if the input does not go into the committee activities, it is too late to do much about an error at the Commission level. When the committee has drawn up a stan-

dard and has gone through the procedures of presenting it through the Commission to governments for comment, reworked the comments, and sent the standard back to the Commission for approval, the Commission looks at the standard and examines it for format and content to ascertain that everything is covered that should be covered, and approves the standard for sending out to governments for acceptance.

Under the means of acceptance mentioned above, when a government accepts a standard as presented by Codex Alimentarius that government agrees to apply the standard both to imported and domestically-produced products. As far as the United States is concerned, in order for the United States to accept a standard it becomes necessary for our government to go through the process of standard writing or standard modification so as to make our standard compatible with that of Codex Alimentarius since our Food and Drug Administration does not have authority to promulgate a standard without the usual formalities of regulation writing. At the present time, approximately 50 standards have come out of the Commission for acceptance by governments. Many of these are for products for which the United States does not currently have standards; however, the Food and Drug Administration has gone on record to the effect that they intend to make U.S. standards conform as nearly as possible to those of Codex Alimentarius. Steps are currently under way to establish standards based on Codex standardized items where we have none; and studies are being made as to the advisability of modifying our existing standards to make them conform as nearly as possible to those of Codex. Obviously, the Food and Drug Administration has no intention of modifying our standards to conform to the Codex standards unless these changes would be in the best interest of the consumer. Hence, it is almost inevitable that where we currently have standards for products, any acceptance coming out of the U.S. Government will in all probability include many minor deviations from the Codax Alimentarius standard.

One can readily see that so long as the Food and Drug Administration is of the opinion that our standards should be modified wherever possible to conform to those of Codex Alimentarius, that the Codex Alimentarius standards are of extreme interest to the food industry of the United States even though an individual company may not be involved in international trade. It is urged that individual companies and trade associations become involved in those product committee activities covering products in which they have an interest, otherwise the U.S. food industry will have no input into the U.S. position in the respective Codex Alimentarius committees.

J. BRYAN STINE

COFFEE

Coffee is a beverage made from the hot water extraction of solubles from the ground roasted beans (seeds) of a tropical evergreen shrub that mostly grows between the Tropic of Cancer and Capricorn at elevations of between 2000 and 6000 ft above sea level, at near 70°F, and with annual rains near 50 in. per year. Annual international commerce is about 55 million bags (60 kg) green coffee per year, and its value is second only to petroleum products, being about $2.5 billion per year. Currently, Brazil supplies $^1/_3$, Africa $^1/_3$, and all other countries $^1/_3$. The United States and Europe consume 85% of world exports almost equally. Coffee beverage has no nutritious value and is consumed for its stimulating effects, primarily due to its 1.1% caffein in Arabica varieties and 2.2% caffein in Robusta types.

History

The coffee shrub is native to Ethiopia (Arabica) where it grows wild in rain forests and its seeds have been used by natives since before recorded time. The Robusta shrub, which grows taller (to 30 ft), is more productive and more hardy, grows in warmer climates, and is native to the Congo areas south of Ethiopia. About 900 A.D., Arabs planted the Ethiopian coffee shrub in Yemen and for 700 years coffee propagation was limited to this area with consumption primarily in Arabia, with shipments out of the Red Sea port of Mocha. Pilgrims to Mecca returned with the coffee beans to their native lands, e.g., India and Ceylon. One of the first uses of coffee was medicinal and to keep worshippers awake in mosques. Coffee fulfilled the need for a useful stimulant since Moslems are not to imbibe alcohol. During the 17th Century, coffee was introduced into European countries and was sold in coffee houses which were popular meeting places for merchants and artists. The Dutch started commercial plantings in Java and Ceylon about 1696. The French, English, and Spanish started coffee cultivation in the West Indies from 1715 to 1750. Mexico and Central America did not start to cultivate until after 1800 to 1850, as did Hawaii in 1825. Colombia did not start cultivation until almost 1900. Commercial coffee cultivation was not carried out in Africa until after World War II. Brazil became a dominant supplier in the early 1800's, but in the past decade its dominance has receded and African production has taken its place. Brazil, however, in the past 5 yr has become a large soluble coffee producer, exporting almost 40 million lb of instant coffee per year to the United States and 60 million lb altogether around the world. There are 20 million people engaged in all phases of coffee cultivation and processing in the growing countries, some of which highly depend on coffee sales income. There are over 1 million persons in the consuming countries that are engaged in various phases of coffee processing, sales, etc.

Cultivation

The botanical genus is *Caffea Arabica* and *Caffea Robusta*. *Caffea Liberica* is not commercially important. Before World War I Robusta coffees were not allowed to be dealt with on the N.Y. Coffee Exchange; then washed Robustas were permitted in 1925. Robustas, in general, have a heavy, less agreeable flavor than Arabicas; and it is their cheaper price that has made their presence felt in world markets. Like most evergreens, the coffee shrub requires shade usually, adequate moisture, a rich loamy soil, and freedom from severe winds. It cannot survive frost, nor prolonged periods of drought such as have occurred in Brazil. The seeds are planted in parchment and after leafing out, are transplanted into individual "pots," usually kept under slatted roofed areas. After 1 yr they are about 12–18 in. high and are transplanted to their final field location. In the second or third year some flowering and fruit occur, but the plant does not produce fully until about the fifth year. Production is about 1 $^1/_2$ lb of green dried coffee beans per tree.

Although there are many varieties of Arabicas, only several are for commercial use. The evergreen shrubs are pruned to keep them below 15 ft in height to facilitate berry picking. It has a laurel-like shiny, deep green leaf that is about 5 in. long and 2 in. wide (elliptical) with prominent veining. In dry areas, like Central America, flowering is triggered by the first rains, and each shrub shows several thousand fragrant flowers. Almost exactly six months later, in about November, the ripe red berries will be ready to pick. The berry or cherry resembles very much the American cranberry in appearance. Picking is done by hand. The berries very often occur in clusters. Robusta trees usually are larger and heavier bearing. In Colombia where there is much rain and moisture all year round, flowering, immature berries, and mature berries all occur simultaneously on a single tree and branch. Consequently the harvest seasons in Colombia are almost continuous. Weeding of the shrub lanes and protection from insects and diseases constitute the main part of the agricultural work after planting. In Ceylon, a leaf rust disease brought coffee production to a halt in 1870. In 1970, Brazil had a wide-spread occurence of the same rust disease called *Hemileia Vastatrix*. Most coffee shrub diseases are attributed to the planting of the coffee shrub in environments less than ideal for the plant. Higher altitudes for growth are preferred up to a oint, because height is accompanied by cooler emperatures, more moisture and more cloudiness vith fewer insects, and a more loamy soil. The lower growth of the coffee plant at these higher levations of 4000–6000 ft produces the best asting coffees. but production per tree is less and beans are smaller and more dense. Hence, the best asting and the highest priced coffees come from the high altitudes of Colombia, Venezuela, Costa Rica, Guatemala, Mexico, etc.

All Arabica coffees are mountain grown, usually bove 2000 ft over sea level, including Brazilian offees which are not grown under the shade of other trees as they are in Central America. Trees re planted at about 8-ft intervals, and the 6 illion coffee trees in the world occupy a space of 00,000 square miles equivalent to the area of 'exas or France. The trees can produce for 40 yr, ut peak productivity is up to 20 yr depending on are and variety. In Africa, Robustas propagation is done in some places with branches. Most Robusta coffees in Africa are not picked when ripe, ut are allowed to dry and shrivel on the trees or round before gathering. In Brazil, trees are lanted in clusters of four, and the ripe berries are ully dried on patios. This is called a "natural" or aturally-dried fruit as opposed to most mild coffees that have their outer fruit skin removed and he fruity pulp fermented prior to drying the beans seed) on patios in the sun. These latter washed offees have better and richer flavor than seeds ried within their fruit. Five pounds of fruit or herries results in 1 lb of dried green beans with 1% moisture.

Processing Green Beans

The dry or natural processing of the beans is one in Brazil because it uses less labor and machinery as well as less water. Wet processing, o produce washed coffees as in Central America nd Colombia, produces better quality coffees; and vater is plentiful in these countries. Patio drying n the sun takes 2–4 weeks depending on the

Outer Skin (Deep Red)
Silver Skin (Silver)
Pulp (Buff)
Parchment (Buff/Brown)
Bean (Green)

Courtesy of Squier Corporation

FIG. C-19. CROSS SECTION SHOWING STRUCTURE OF COFFEE CHERRY

weather, and is supplemented by hot air driers especially in the latter stages of drying.

Each bean is made up of two elliptical hemispheres inside of a fiber endocarp, called the "parchment." If the parchment is broken, the bean loses its ability to grow, and is not virile. Covering each hemisphere is a spermaderm or silver skin. When one spherical bean occurs instead of two hemispherical parts, it is called a "peaberry" or "caracol," and often brings a premium price. The seeds are dried in the parchment and are often stored better in the parchment, until prepared for use or export. Then the parchment, whether from dry or wet processing, is removed in a helical auger.

The usually blue-green hemispheric beans are graded by size, weight, color, and density into uniform-appearing and -tasting lots preferably of 250-lb bags or larger "chops." Foreign matter like sticks and stones, and immature, discolored, and decayed beans are removed. "Soft" tasting clean, sweet, mild coffees bring premium prices over "hard" or "harsh" tasting, dirty, fermented and contaminated lots. Trade names are characteristic of origin; for example: Medellins, Armenias, or Manizales (MAM's) for Colombia; Santos, Paranas, and Minas from Brazil; Coatepecs, Oaxacas, and Tapachulas from Mexico; Antiguas from Guatemala; Copans from Honduras; Djimmas or Harrars from Ethiopia, Oicru from the Congo; Ambriz from Angola (Portuguese West Africa). Kona variety comes from Hawaii.

Roasting

Usually the green coffee beans are commercially roasted in 15-min, 4-bag batch roasts or in continuous 10,000 lb per hr (5 min) roasters using hot air at $800°F$ in batch units and $600°F$ in the continuous units. The roasted beans are promptly cooled. Stones or metals are separated by levitating the roast beans into overhead bins.

Until the green beans are roasted, coffee has no characteristic aroma and taste. Roasting is a process whereby the 10–12% moisture is driven off, followed by caramelization of sucrose and finally pyrolysis of the carbohydrates and proteins within the $40-\mu$ cells at internal pressures of several hundred pounds per square inch. Depending on the end temperature of the roast beans, usually near $400°F$, there is a 16% weight loss from green to roast beans. Moisture, oils, aromas, carbon dioxide, chaff, and some caffeine are driven off. Time and temperature but mostly roast bean color is used to establish the end point of the roast corresponding to the taste desired. Abrupt cooling is essential to stop the pyrolysis quickly, and often a water spray is used prior to air cooling.

TABLE C-22

U.S. INDUSTRY STANDARD FOR COFFEE GRANULATIONS

Grind Designation	Amount of Coffee Retained on		Amount of Coffee Passing Through Control Sieve, 28-Mesh (%)	Tolerances on Amount of Coffee Passing Through Control Sieve, 28-Mesh	
	10 and 14 Mesh Sieves (%)	20 and 28 Mesh Sieves (%)		Not Less Than (%)	Not More Tha (%)
Regular	33	55	12	9	15
Drip	7	73	20	16	24
Fine	0	70	30	25	40

SOURCE: U.S. Department of Commerce R 231-48.

Grinding

In order to facilitate later water extraction of the roast bean, it is necessary to reduce the bean size. In the United States, a 1948 industry standard was adopted for three granulations as shown in Table C-22.

Granulations used in soluble coffee extractors are considerably coarser than regular grind, approximating cracked beans. In recent years, a domestic electric percolator grind has supplemented an "all purpose" grind for which there is no industry standard; these grinds vary greatly, often being the same as regular grind. In the mid-1960's, the Pan-American Coffee Bureau helped establish a finer grind standard for the single cup vending brewing machines, which is less than 10% on 28 mesh, 35% on 35 mesh and 35% on 48 mesh with the balance through the 48-mesh screen. This is much finer than retail fine grind coffee. Most of the vacuum commercial can-packed coffee is regular grind and very little fine grind is sold. Regular grind obviates plugging the domestic pumping percolator, but is too coarse for efficient extraction.

Packaging

Roast coffee beans will stale in air at room temperature within 10–14 days. Ground coffee noticeably stales within a few days but is tolerable to consume up to one week depending on ambient temperature, humidity, air exposure, and the drinker's tolerance to stale taste. Staling is primarily due to oxidation of aldehydes and other chemicals in coffee and is accentuated by the loss of aromatics.

In Europe most of the coffee is purchased by consumers in the whole roast bean condition and they have full knowledge of the origin, variety, and caffeine content; whereas in the United States, the consumer buys by brand name which obscures

the origin, grade, variety, and caffeine content The main, but not the only, reason for this is tha vacuum packaging in cans in mass production re quires "uniformizing" the coffee. Additiona sacrifice in quality is made in vacuum packagin; because there is a loss of desirable aromatics; ther is at least a 1% oxygen residue left in the sealed ca which reacts in a few weeks with the ground coffee Hence, vacuum packed coffee never delivers the best in freshness or quality, but is commerciall tolerable. The first vacuum packaging was don about 1905 in San Francisco by Hills Bros. fo shipments to Alaska. Today about 85% of all re tail roast coffee sold in the United States is i evacuated cans, with the 1-, 2-, and 3-lb sizes mos prevalent. Inert gas (nitrogen) packaging of frac tional pound, 1, and 2 lb flexible bags has becom common in the late 1960's for institutional use where protection in freshness is offered for abou 3 months.

Soluble (Instant) Coffee

Soluble coffee was manufactured during the Civil War, WWI, and WWII, but did not achieve large commercial use until just before and mostly after World War II. Since 1957, about $\frac{1}{3}$ of al cups of coffee consumed in the United States ar instants although they only represent about $\frac{1}{5}$ o all green coffee imports. There are about 20 million lb of instant coffee manufactured in th United States each year and over 100,000,000 l per year produced abroad, mostly in Brazi General Foods sells 100 million lb and Nestlé abou 65 million lb of instants per year in the world General Foods sells 53% of the U.S. instant coffee

Soluble coffee is made in a series of 6 or 7 ex traction columns operated in series with 350°) water flowing countercurrently to the roast an ground coffee within the columns. Overall hol time on the coffee is about 3–4 hr, yielding 25–30^c solubles concentration extracts and 40–50% solu

TABLE C-23

PARTICLE SIZE VERSUS NUMBER OF PARTICLES PER UNIT WEIGHT AND AREA

	Size (Mm)	No. Particles Per Gram	Increase Particles/Gm	Ratio of Increase	Total Area (Sq Cm/Gm)
Whole bean	6.0	6	—	—	8
Cracked bean	3.0	48	42	1	16
Instant R & G for					
percolation	1.5	384	336	8	32
Regular	1.0	1,296	912	22	48
Drip	0.75	3,072	1,776	42	64
Fine	0.38	24,572	21,500	512	128

bles yield from roast beans.[3] The extracts may be spray dried directly in 20-ft diameter by 100-ft high stainless steel towers to make a free-flowing powder at rates of 1200 lb per hr; or the extracts may be freeze dried in batch or continuous drying systems. Freeze drying represented almost 40% of all U.S. instant coffee production in 1973. Imports of spray-dried instant coffee into the United States represented 20% of all U.S. usage,

[3] Water extraction at 212°F only solubilizes 22% of roast coffee; commercial instants hydrolyze over 100% more than in the home brewing.

i.e., 40 million pounds per year. Since 1957, most spray-dried instant coffee has been aromatized by adding 0.2%/wt of expelled coffee oil back onto the powder and using inert gas packaging to preserve the freshness of the aromatic oil addition. Since 1969, a major portion of spray-dried instant coffees have been agglomerated, and then aromatized. Agglomeration facilitates solubility without foam, and gives a chunkier, darker color approximating roast and ground coffee. In the United States, the major sales of freeze-dried instant coffee are almost equally shared by MAXIM and Taster's Choice (respectively, General Foods and Nestlé)

TABLE C-24

CHEMICAL COMPOSITION OF GREEN COFFEE
(Approximate Dry Basis)

Classes and Components	Water Solubility	Percentage of Green Coffee Item	Total	Soluble
Carbohydrates				
Reducing sugars	Soluble	1.0		
Sucrose	Soluble	7.0		
Pectins	Soluble	2.0		
Starch	Easily solubilized	10.0		
Pentosans	Easily solubilized	5.0		
Hemicelluloses	Hydrolyzable	15.0		
Holocellulose	Nonhydrolyzable fiber	18.0		
Lignin	Nonhydrolyzable fiber	2.0 ⟶	60	10
Oils	Insoluble		13	
Protein ($N \times 6.25$)	Depends on percentage denatured		13	4
Ash as oxide	Depends on percentage hydrolyzed		4	2
Nonvolatile acids				
Chlorogenic	Soluble	7.0		
Oxalic	Soluble	0.2		
Malic	Soluble	0.3		
Citric	Soluble	0.3		
Tartaric	Soluble	0.4 ⟶	8	8
Trigonelline	Soluble		1	1
Caffeine	Soluble		1	1
(Arabicas 1.0%, Robusta 2.0%)				
			100	26

TABLE C-25

CHEMICAL COMPOSITION OF SOLUBLE AND
INSOLUBLE PORTIONS OF ROAST COFFEE
(Approximate Dry Basis)

	Solubles (%)	Insolubles (%)
Carbohydrates (53%)		
Reducing sugars	2	—
Caramelized sugars	17	—
Hemicellulose (hydrolyzable)	10	4
Fiber (not hydrolyzable)	—	22
Oils	—	15
Proteins ($N \times 6.25$); amino acids are soluble	2	11
Ash (oxide)	3	1
Acids, nonvolatile		
Chlorogenic	4.5	—
Caffeic	0.5	—
Quinic	0.5	—
Oxalic, malic, citric, tartaric	1.0	—
Volatile acids	0.35	—
Trigonelline	1.0	—
Caffeine (Arabicas 1.0%, Robustas 2.0%)	1.2	—
Phenolics (estimated)	2.0	—
Volatiles		
Carbon dioxide	Trace	2
Essence of aroma and flavor	0.04	—
Total	45	55

with very little for TenCo. and miscellaneous producers. Freeze-dried coffees are aromatized either after drying or by incorporation of a coffee oil emulsion into the extract before drying. Freeze drying is usually preceded by freeze concentration by slush freezing in two stages and followed by basket centrifuging off the concentrated extract. This leaves the tiny ice crystals behind in the centrifuge basket. Freeze-dried instant coffee loses most of its advantage in flavor if it is packaged in air. Freeze drying costs about $0.40 per lb dry solubles.

Physical Properties

Picked fruit has a bulk density of near 50 lb per cu ft. Green beans, after fermentation and washing, have a 50% moisture. The dried (12% moisture) parchment-free beans have a bulk density of about 40 lb per cu ft depending on quality and age. Roast bean coffee has a bulk density of near 20 lb per cu ft, while ground coffee can vary from 18 to 24 lb per cu ft with the finer vibrated grinds being more dense. Robusta and high grown coffees are more dense; and this must be considered in equipment design. Coffee beans normally swell 100% in volume during roasting. Table C-23 illustrates the surface exposed with different granulations which is important when considering staling or extraction.

The color of green coffee frequently indicates age, quality, and imperfections. Color of roast coffee is used as a roast/flavor control. Spray-dried powder densities are about 200 gm per liter and must be rigorously controlled for jar packaging. Reflectance colors of roast coffee and spray-dried coffees are common controls. Screen analyses of green beans, ground roast coffee, spray- and agglomerated- as well as freeze-dried coffees are essential in production controls, as are moisture measured by toluene reflux, infrared or lamp balances, and Karl Fisher analyses. Instant coffee moistures in finished products must be below 3%. Solubles must be free of insolubles as measured by a milk test filter disc. This is usually achieved by centrifuging the extract prior to drying. Light transmission through standard solubles concentration solutions are useful controls on either a Beckmann or Klett instrument.

Light refraction through coffee extracts is used as well as specific gravity to relate to soluble concentrations. For example, a Brix refractometer reads about 20% higher in sucrose value than there are coffee solubles. The specific gravity of coffee solubles is about 15% higher than for sucrose. For example, a 25% coffee solubles solution has 30° Brix and a 1.106 sp gr at 60°F. The viscosity of coffee extracts rises appreciably with increased concentrations and reduced temperatures. Coffee extracts foam considerably when mixed with gases. At a beverage strength of 1.0–1.5% solubles most Arabica beverages have a pH near 5.10 ± 0.10 but Robustas are 5.25 and as high as 5.75. Commercial instant coffee beverages have a pH range from 4.7 to 5.0 and are usually near 4.90. A 35% soluble coffee extract may have a pH of 5.20, but the 1% solution will have a pH of 4.85; the dried soluble at 1% will give a pH of 4.95. There is almost 1% acetic acid based on solubles in the coffee. Acidities below 4.75 pH can and do cause curdling of milk and cream.

Chemical Properties

Tables C-24 to C-28 summarize average chemical compositions of green coffee beans, roast bean solubles with hydrolysis products as obtained in commercial instant coffee extractions and the spent coffee grounds. Table C-27 shows that most of the ash goes into the soluble coffee, while Table C-28 shows mineral type distribution in solubles and spent grounds, which is of interest in terms of

TABLE C-26

CHEMICAL COMPOSITION OF COFFEE SOLUBLES AND
SPENT GROUNDS (INSOLUBLES)
(Approximate Dry Basis)

Chemical Compound or Class	Solubles (%)	Spent Grounds (%)
Carbohydrates (3–5% reducing sugars)	35.0	65
(browning complexes)	15.0	—
Oils (and fatty acids)	0.2	18
Proteins (amino acids and complexes)	4.0	15
Ash (oxide)	14.0	Fraction of 1%
Acids nonvolatile		
Chlorogenic	13.0	—
Caffeic	1.4	—
Quinic	1.4	—
Others	3.0	—
Trigonelline	3.5	Few tenths percent
Caffeine		
Arabicas	3.5	Few tenths percent
(Robustas)	(7.0)	—
Phenols (estimated)	5.0	Few tenths percent
Volatiles		
Before drying—acids and essence	(1.1)	Nil
After drying	Nil	Nil
Total	100	98+

fertilizer additions to shrubs. Table C-29 gives an analysis of the 0.1%/wt or less of the very volatile/ aromatic portion of the roast coffee. The 22 items listed are major chemicals isolated and identified but other workers like Gianturco of TenCo have identified dozens more of the lesser volatile components. TenCo has also connected a computer system to the analytical results of gas chromatographical analyses to present a more graphic presentation of the magnitude of components. Of more importance, it is claimed, is the relative magnitude of key components.

The coffee mucilage of the fruit is 85% water and the rest is 9% protein, 4% sugars, 1% pectic acid, and 0.6% ash. Coffee oil composition varies with coffee types. For example, for aromatizing instants good quality beans are used for expressing the oil. Robusta beans have a bad-tasting oil.

Coffee oils are about 3% myristic, 28% palmitic, 10% stearic, 21% oleic, and 28% linoleic (latter two are unsaturated). In addition there is 3% arachidic and 7% unsaponifiables. Coffee oil is not as a rule recovered, although it is readily extracted with hexane and can be used to make soap. Spent coffee grounds from instant coffee processing are usually dried to 25% moisture and burned to recover their heat value (8000 Btu per lb); others dump the grounds as waste, or use them in cattle feed.

Physiological Effects

Coffee beverage is a potent source of caffeine, a stimulant, plus the aromatics and other roast chemical products. A cup of average coffee has 150 mg of caffeine, which is about what a doctor might give to a patient to gain a stimulating effect.

TABLE C-27

ESTIMATED COFFEE ASH DISTRIBUTION

	Green Coffee	Roast Coffee	Soluble Powder	Dry Spent Grounds
Dry weight relations[1]	1.176	1.000	0.380	0.620
Percentage ash content, dry basis	4.00	4.71	10.00	1.47

[1] Assuming 15% weight loss on roasting.

TABLE C-28

PERCENTAGE DISTRIBUTION OF ASH COMPONENTS

Mineral Oxide	Green, Roast (%)	Solubles Ash (%)	(%)	Spent Grounds Ash (%)	(%)
K_2O	62.5	52.0	75.59	10.5	33.65
P_2O_5	13.0	3.0	4.36	10.0	32.05
CaO	5.0	2.0	2.90	3.0	9.62
MgO	11.0	8.0	11.63	3.0	9.62
Fe_2O_3	1.0	0.4	0.58	0.6	1.92
Na_2O	0.5	0.4	0.58	0.1	0.32
SiO_2	1.0	—	—	1.0	3.21
SO_3	5.0	2.0	2.90	3.0	9.61
Cl	1.0	1.0	1.46	—	—
	100.0	68.8	100.0	31.2	100.0

A cup of Robusta coffee or a strong cup of Arabica coffee can have 250 mg caffeine. Caffeine has been studied extensively with regard to its influence on humans. In these doses it causes a stimulation of the central nervous system, increased blood circulation, and increased respiration. Caffeine is prescribed in treatment of alcohol and drug poisoning, and selectively in angina, asthma, dropsy, headaches, and in cases of exposure. Coffee, in fact, is habituating, since it does not have an initially desirable taste, but rather is an acquired taste.

There is a great range in the reactions of the body to caffeine and coffee. Few people under 20 yr of age drink coffee. The hard core of drinkers is in the 30- to 50-yr range, with older people also gaining from its stimulation. A tolerance to caffeine and coffee is developed so that habitual drinkers need more to gain effect. So 2–3 cups

TABLE C-29

ANALYSIS OF A COFFEE AROMA ESSENCE

	Mol Wt	%	Boiling Point °C	°F	Relative Flavor Importance[1]
Acetaldehyde	44	19.9	21	70	1
Acetone	58	18.7	56	133	2
Diacetyl	86	7.5	88	190	1
n-Valeraldehyde	86	7.3	102	216	2
2-Methylbutyraldehyde	86	6.8	91	196	2
3-Methylbutyraldehyde	86	5.0	91	196	2
Methylfuran	82	4.7	63	145	2
Propionaldehyde	58	4.5	49	120	2
Methylformate	60	4.0	32	90	2
Carbon dioxide	44	3.8	−78	−108	—
Furan	68	3.2	32	90	1
Isobutyraldehyde	72	3.0	63	145	1
Pentadiene (isoprene)	68	3.0	30	86	2
Methylethyl ketone	72	2.3	80	176	2
C_4—C_7 paraffins and olefins	—	2.0	35	95	2
Methyl acetate	74	1.7	57	135	2
Dimethyl sulfide	62	1.0	38	100	1
n-Butyraldehyde	72	0.7	75	167	1
Ethyl formate	74	0.3	54	129	2
Carbon disulfide	76	0.2	46	115	2
Methyl alcohol	32	0.2	65	149	3
Methyl mercaptan	48	0.1	6	43	1
		100.0			

[1] Rating: 1, large; 2, medium; and 3, small.

per day may not be felt by some persons, yet cause sleeplessness, body discomfort, intestinal pain, headaches, etc., in other persons. Drinking more than 5-6 cups per day can cause nervousness and irritability.

It is for these reasons that decaffeinated coffee has become more popular; in the United States it represents $1/6$ of all instant coffee sales and 6% of all regular roast coffee sales. There is also the use of coffee substitutes, products like coffee-flavored Postum.

About 1900, Ludwig Roselius devised a method to remove caffeine from coffee. He was motivated to do this because his father was a coffee taster and Ludwig believed his father's early death was caused by caffeine. The German firm, Kaffee HAG, in Bremen used a process of steaming green coffee beans, followed by benzene; later, chlorinated solvent extraction was used in a series of tumbling drums. The solvent was then removed several times from the beans, and finally steam distilled off. The green coffee beans were dried and roasted in the normal manner. In 1943, General Foods Corp. devised a method of decaffeination using a saturated solution of green coffee solubles in a battery of percolators as the means for removing caffeine without direct solvent contact of the coffee beans (U.S. Patent 2,309,092). This patent was issued to N. E. Berry and R. H. Walters; it has now expired. This is the basis for the manufacture of SANKA with 97% of the caffeine removed.

M. SIVETZ

References

NAIR, J. H., and SIVETZ, M. 1973. Coffee and tea. *In* Food Dehydration, Vol. 2. W. B. Van Arsdel *et al.* (Editors). Avi Publishing Co., Westport, Conn.

SIVETZ, M., and FOOTE, E. H. 1963. Coffee Processing Technology, Vol. 1 and 2. Avi Publishing Co., Westport, Conn.

Cross-reference: *Caffeine.*

COLLOID MILLS

See Homogenizers and Colloid Mills.

COLOR[4]

Appearance is an important aspect of food quality, and is normally perceived as an integral

[4] Reprinted from *Proceedings: Symposium on Feeding the Military Man*, Oct. 20-22, 1969, sponsored by U.S. Army Natick Laboratories, Natick, Mass.

part of quality, not as a separate aspect. Normally, in speaking of visual quality of foods, the term color is used rather than appearance. Color is certainly the most important aspect of food appearance, but texture, gloss, haze, and the like are also significant features of overall appearance quality.

Appearance is the aspect of food quality which we know most about and in which great progress has been made towards objective measurements. Techniques for color and gloss measurement have been in use perhaps 40-50 yr. Lovibond glasses were and are still used in the United States for the quality assessment of cottonseed oil by color.

The Physical Aspect

The physical sources of color and appearance of foods are spectral absorption and the projection of light by product surface and structure.

Color as it normally occurs in food products is the result of the absorption of more light at some wavelengths than at others. If one were to project a spectrum on a screen and then put a red filter into the light beam, you would see that it is not what is happening to the red part of the spectrum that makes the light appear red. The red light is unchanged. It is the other parts of the spectrum that are being changed. They are absorbed. The red light remains, and this is what causes the screen to appear red.

In foods, the components which absorb light are called pigments. Yellow carotene in vegetables, green chlorophyll in leaves, and red hemoglobin in

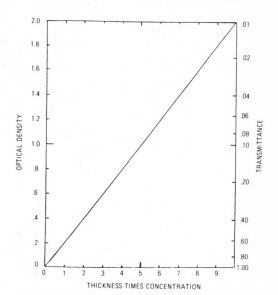

FIG. C-20. BEER'S LAW CURVES OF OPTICAL DENSITY AND TRANSMITTANCE AS A FUNCTION OF RELATIVE THICKNESS, OR CONCENTRATION

red meat are three typical pigments, each of which has more than one form. The relationships between fraction of light absorbed and quantity of pigment are defined by Beer's law. An example of Beer's law is shown in Fig. C-20.

Surface structure (smoothness, texture, granularity, etc.) and product internal structure (degree of homogenization, particle size, etc.) are all responsible for the appearance attributes which are called geometric. Some of the attributes associated with geometric appearance are gloss, turbidity or haze, texture, and luster. The term "geometric" is used to distinguish these appearance attributes, which are associated with the different ways in which the material distributes the light reflected or transmitted by it, from the color attributes. In general, one never attempts to analyze the specific structures of materials as they relate to product appearance. Such analysis would be too complex to be practical. Instead, specific techniques are developed to measure specific geometric and color attributes of importance.

Appearance Dimensions

Specific appearance dimensions are three for color and an indeterminate number for geometric attributes. Just as there are several coordinate systems in mathematics for locating points in three-dimensional space, so there are several "coordinate systems" for describing the locations of colors. They have come into use in response to the particular needs of different industries.

One of the most familiar coordinate systems for the colors of surfaces is the *Munsell Color System*, which is shown in Fig. C-21. The three dimensions of this system are called *hue, value,* and *chroma.* Notice that around the vertical axis of achromatic colors are arranged the hues, and the more saturated colors with higher chroma are on the outside of the solid.

Another type of color scales is called an "opponent-colors system." Here the attributes of importance are yellowness-blueness and redness-greenness, rather than hue and saturation. (The

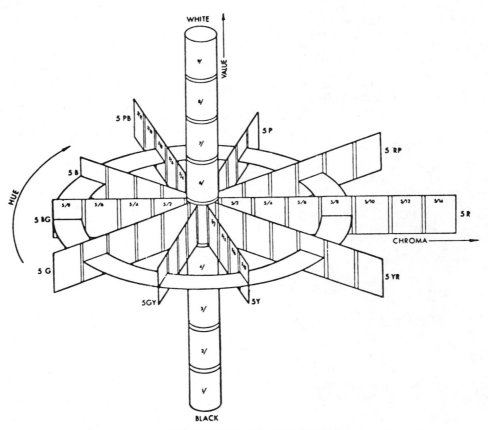

FIG. C-21. DRAWING OF THE MUNSELL COLOR SOLID SHOWING ITS THREE DIMENSIONS OF HUE, VALUE (LIGHTNESS), AND CHROMA (SATURATION)

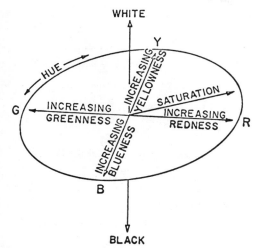

FIG. C-22. COLOR DIMENSIONS: YELLOW-BLUENESS, REDNESS-GREENNESS, AND LIGHTNESS

luminous attribute of lightness is the same as value in the Munsell system.) The paired opposites,

lightness-darkness, yellowness-blueness, and redness-greenness, are measured in an ordinary rectangular coordinate system such as Fig. C-22 shows. These are the L,a,b dimensions, *the only visually meaningful dimensions of color that can be read directly from an instrument.* Figure C-23 shows a digital version of the Hunterlab Color Difference Meter used for these measurements.

Appearance and Food Quality

Relationships between appearance and food quality are developed empirically by one of several approaches:

(A) Investigation of spectral absorption by food pigment.
(B) Simple correlation with color appearance scale.
(C) Multiple correlation with some combination of color appearance scales.
(D) Correlation with some geometric attribute.

Table C-30 gives examples of at least two food products rated for quality by each of these four approaches.

(A) Quality measured by the absorption of light at a specific wavelength. Scales of this type are used where one is primarily concerned with concentration of a single pigment in a food product.

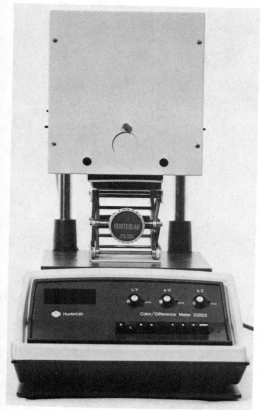

FIG. C-23. THE DIGITAL VERSION OF THE HUNTERLAB COLOR DIFFERENCE METER USED FOR THESE MEASUREMENTS

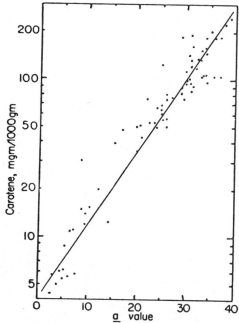

FIG. C-24. GRAPH DEMONSTRATING USE OF THE INSTRUMENT TO MEASURE A CHEMICAL ATTRIBUTE RELATED TO COLOR (CAROTENE IN SWEET POTATO SEEDLINGS)

Graph courtesy of Department of Horticulture, University of Maryland, College Park, Maryland.

TABLE C-30

FOUR TYPES OF SCALES USED FOR THE QUALITY ASSESSMENT OF FOODS

Type of Scale	Product	Scale for Quality
(A) Spectral absorption by food pigment	Beets	Absorption of pigment in solution at 525 nm Absorption of reflected light at 670 nm
(B) Specific single tristimulus color scale	Sweet potato seedlings	Hunter a (redness-greenness)
	Peanut butter degree of roast	Hunter a (redness-greenness)
	Coffee roast	Luminous reflectance, Y
(C) Complex function of 2 or 3 tristimulus color scales	Reconstituted Florida orange juice	$ECS = 22.510 + 0.165CR + 0.11CY$ where ECS = equivalent color scale CR (citrus redness) = $200\,(A/Y - 1)$ CY (citrus yellowness) = $100\,(1 - 0.8472/Y)$ A, Y, Z refers to CIE tristimulus values with substitution of A (amber) for X.
	Raw tomatoes, puréed to form specimen	$TC = \dfrac{21.6}{L} - \dfrac{7.5b}{La}$ where TC = tomato color L = lightness a = redness-greenness b = yellowness-blueness
(D) Specific geometric attribute	Applesauce	Contrast gloss used to measure maturity of fruit used
	Instant iced tea	Haze (is undesirable)
	Wine	Haze (is undesirable)

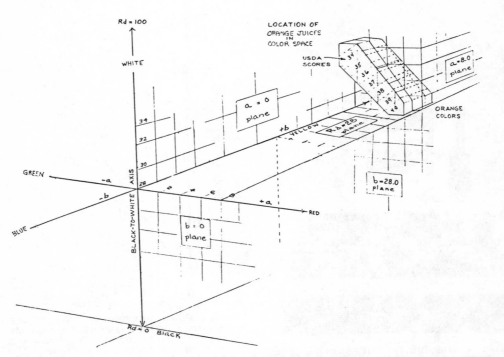

FIG. C-25. DRAWING SHOWING HOW THE COLORS OF ORANGE JUICES OF DIFFERENT USDA COLOR SCORE FIT INTO THE YELLOW-ORANGE REGION OF COLOR SPACE

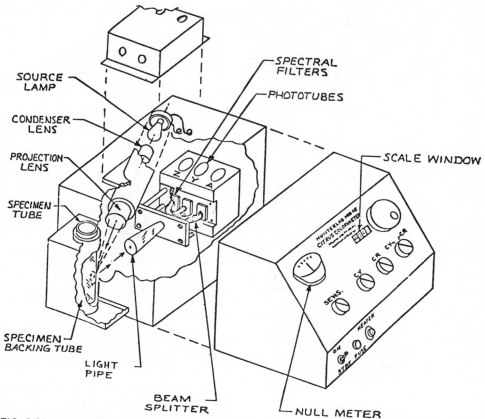

FIG. C-26. DRAWING OF D45 CITRUS COLORIMETER OPTICAL SYSTEM AND MEASUREMENT UNIT

Beets can be evaluated for color quality by measurement of the absorption of light at a wavelength of 525 nm. Loss of chlorophyll in the processing of green vegetables, such as spinach and string beans, can be evaluated by loss of spectral reflectance at 670 nm where absorption of chlorophyll is at a maximum. These scales are designed to measure physical absorption rather than color appearance and they give an indication of the physical concentration of a single specific pigment.

(B) Use of a single color scale for quality assessment. Sometimes one of the specific color coordinate scales described above will correlate directly with the food quality factor of interest. An example of this type is described by Kramer who found that for frozen lima beans, a measurement of Hunter L (lightness) gave good correlation.

In a breeding program designed to improve sweet potato varieties, measurements of a values of smears from the seedling rubbed out on white glass proved to give a quick and effective method for assessing Vitamin A (carotene) content of the plants and of the potatoes they would produce after growth to maturity (Fig. C-24).

(C) Use of composite three-dimensional color scales for quality. Normally, one finds that best correlation of color with food quality is given by a composite of all three dimensions of color. Figure C-25 shows the gamut of colors one encounters in Florida orange juices as they go from the poorest color at the top of the series of stair steps down to best, darkest, and most orange color at the bottom. To convert measurements of the colors of products such as these to visual color scores, composite scales developed from regression equations are used. The equation for Florida orange juice scale which was adopted for the Hunterlab Citrus Colorimeter is:

$$ECS = 22.510 + 0.165CR + 0.11CY$$

in which,

ECS = Equivalent Color Scale
CR (citrus redness) = 200 (A/Y-1)
CY (citrus yellowness) = 100 (1-0.8472/Y)

A,Y,Z refers to CIE tristimulus values, with substitution of A (amber) for X. Figure C-26 shows the Hunterlab D45 Citrus Colorimeter.

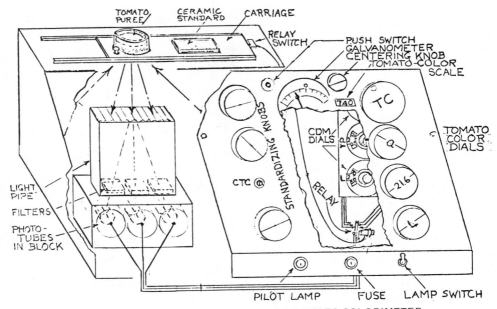

FIG. C-27. DIAGRAM OF HUNTERLAB D6 TOMATO COLORIMETER

A similar empirically-developed color scale is used to assess the color quality of raw tomatoes as they are received at the processing plant. This equation developed by J. N. Yeatman, A. P. Sidwell and K. N. Norris is:

$$TC = \frac{21.6}{L} - \frac{7.5b}{La}$$

where TC stands for tomato color, L is lightness, a is redness-greenness and b is yellowness-blueness. Figure C-27 shows the first Hunterlab Tomato Colorimeter designed to measure TC directly from purées of raw tomato in glass cups.

(D) Geometric attributes of quality. To date there has been relatively little use of measurements of geometric attributes for the appearance quality of food. A few measurements of gloss of apple sauce and gloss of tomato paste have been attempted. In both these cases the problem was the same; sauce made from immature fruit had a spongy low gloss characteristic. The preferred product was definitely more glossy. There has been little experience with this type of product and its quality assessment by appearance.

Standards

Standards are essential for accurate repeatable ratings of food appearance quality.

Instrument standards must be stable. Permanent standards of ceramic tile or porcelain enamel are normally used with instruments to assure stability of their numerical scales. These standards do not have to simulate the appearances of the products measured. Fortunately the instrument ignores the optical differences between sample and standard (such as in gloss and texture) to which it is not responsive.

Visual-comparison standards must be stable and visually similar to the products tested. They must be made to simulate product appearance in almost all characteristics. Plastic is the material most widely used for these standards. Color photographs of products are probably second in frequency of use as color standards for the assessment of product appearance. The Agtron Company in California is perhaps the major supplier of plastic standards of food appearance. The Munsell Color Company in Baltimore has also been active in this field. Some of the government agencies responsible for quality assessment of food have been frequent users of color photographs and color printings for use in grading food products. It can be appreciated that the more nearly identical in overall appearance of standards and food products graded, the more effective will be their use for assessment of appearance quality.

It has been shown that instrumental measurements of food appearance quality must be individually tailored to each specific food product measured for quality. The eye is extremely versatile and agile. In this assessment of food quality we are merely attempting to partially duplicate with an instrument what the eye does everyday with great speed and agility.

RICHARD S. HUNTER

References

HUGGART, R. L., and WENZEL, F. W. 1969. Interim report on the precision and accuracy of the Hunterlab Citrus Colorimeter. Florida Citrus Comm. and Florida Citrus Expt. Sta., Lake Alfred.

HUNTER, R. S. 1967. Development of the Citrus Colorimeter. Food Technol. *21*, No. 6, 100–105.

HUNTER, R. S., and YEATMAN, J. N. 1961. Direct reading Tomato Colorimeter. J. Opt. Soc. Am. *51*, No. 5, 552–554.

KELLY, K. L., GIBSON, K. S., and NICKERSON, D. 1943. Specification of the Munsell Book of Color from spectrophotometric measurements. J. Opt. Soc. Am. *33*, No. 7, 355–376.

KRAMER, A., and SMITH, H. R. 1946. Preliminary investigation and measurement of color in canned foods. Food Res. *11*, No. 1, 14–31.

KRAMER, A., and TWIGG, B. A. 1959. Principles and instrumentation for the physical measurement of food quality with special reference to fruit and vegetable products. *In* Advances in Food Research, Vol. 9. Academic Press, New York.

YEATMAN, J. N., SIDWELL, A. P., and NORRIS, R. H. 1961. Derivation of a new formula for computing raw tomato juice color from objective color measurement. Food Technol. *14*, 16–20.

CONFECTIONS

Product-wise, the growing candy industry, the ninth largest in the food industries, is perhaps also the most diversified. That is because there are close to 2000 varieties of confections being produced by about 1200 candy companies in the United States. Add to this the fact that most of these 2000 varieties are broken down into hundreds of formula variations and modifications. For instance, as many as 500 different formulas go into making of the many kinds of nougats. And there are double that number for the many different types of marshmallows.

Moreover, systematic development, and also modification, of the many confectionery ingredients and additives are further stepping up the pace of formula changes. In most cases, these changes have been made for economic, functional, and quality reasons.

Annual candy production tops 3.90 billion lb with a value close to $2 billion. These figures add up to an approximate daily production of some 100 million bars, pieces, and sticks for an approximate per capita consumption of almost 20 lb. To produce this ever-growing amount of sweets, candy makers are spending an estimated $625 million for over 80 different kinds of ingredients and additives.

Sweeteners, by far, represent the major candy-making ingredient. Approximately 2.5 billion lb of corn, cane, and beet sweeteners go into candies. The $\frac{1}{2}$ billion lb of cocoa and chocolate products come next. This is followed by some 200 million lb of shelled peanuts, 875 million lb of fluid milk, 73 million lb of eggs, 43 million lb of dried coconut, 30 million lb of almond kernels, and 23 million lb of fruit products.

The continuing introduction of an increasing variety of new candies is expected to have a favorable effect upon the industry's sales and profits in the years ahead. New items will include candy bars, taffy confections, and hard candies having new and better flavors and longer keeping qualities (shelf-life).

Packaged goods are the biggest sellers. They amount to some 42% of total dollar sales and 39% of the poundage. They include those candies ranging from carton-packed chocolates to bagged confections. Next come the many different types of candy bars, which garner 32% of sales and 31% of poundage. About 12% of dollar sales and poundage goes to 10- and 15¢-specialties. Bulk goods account for 10% of sales and 13% of poundage. And penny items represent only 4% of sales and 5% of poundage.

Problems Facing the Industry

Ever-rising prices and short supplies are prompting candy makers to produce fewer chocolate confections and to use more cocoa substitutes. The development of more efficient methods of harvesting cocoa beans is being sought, in order to increase yields.

As chocolate continues to rise in cost, candy makers will be forced to use less when making filled molded bars and coated centers. Normally, about 60% of the chocolate goes into molded bars and 40% into coated centers. But if prices increase chocolate may have to be reduced to 45% for bars and 23–30% for centers.

Compound coatings are the lower cost substitutes for chocolate coatings; they are constantly being improved. Despite their excellent stand-up qualities under adverse conditions, better mouth palatability must be built into them with special types of fats, fat fractions, and emulsifiers. All the desirable properties of cocoa butter will be retained in tomorrow's confectioner's coatings; undesirable ones will be eliminated.

Better ways and equipment are needed for milling cocoa beans and, thereby, speeding up operations and increasing yields. Although considerable advances have been made, chocolate bloom continues to be a problem with these coatings.

Not too long ago, FDA sanctioned the use of sorbitan esters as an optional ingredient in chocolate standards. The approval came from the discovery that as little as a 1% combination of sorbitan monostearate and polysorbate 60 increased the number of temperature cycles chocolate could withstand without showing evidence of bloom or discoloration.

With the aid of suppliers, candy technologists are getting corn syrups with increased sweetening properties and more specialized "built-in" functional properties. Properties of future sweeteners must vary even more widely in response to qualities wanted in the different candies yet to be modified, and new ones yet to be developed.

A wider spectrum of corn syrups and blends will be sought to pinpoint sweetness, control graining, improve textures, and extend keeping qualities. Cohesive- and adhesive-imparting properties will be better fingerprinted through basic research directed to higher (poly) saccharide-containing syrups.

Blends containing various amounts of liquid sugar, invert, dextrose, and corn syrups will be formulated according to the candy maker's specifications and requirements. These will offer many added functional properties.

There is an acid-enzyme converted 42 DE corn syrup with a high maltose content and an extra-high acid-enzyme converted 68 to 72 DE syrup. Each provides interesting combinations of properties. The high-maltose syrup, for example, gives hard candies better quality, stability, and shelf-life.

Solutions to certain candy-making problems involving cost and processing are being sought with the development of new kinds of modified starches. These will do things to candies that have never been done before.

Take for example, a modified high-amylose starch that is now speeding up and greatly simplifying the production of cast cream centers for enrobing. It is also replacing higher priced nonfat milk solids in the manufacture of imitation caramels and fudges. The new starch also cuts costs of cream-center finished goods up to 2¢ per lb and up to 6¢ per lb on caramel-coated candy and bar goods with caramel centers.

This new modified starch together with sugar, 65 DE corn syrup and jet cooking produces centers having a smooth consistency. Moreover, it binds up to 8% more water than conventionally-produced centers. But what is significant in the new process for cream centers is the elimination of microcrystal sugar formation and application of invertase technology for breaking down the sugar.

Different modified starches will be needed for yet-to-be-specified viscosity-stability pastes. Such pastes will be important for pressure cooking, cooking for extended periods, or subjecting to mechanical shear actions. Such starches would be less apt to break down and lose their thickening and emulsifying properties.

Candy chemists will want still better "tailored" fats, those with improved and added functional properties. Certain solvent-fractionated fats, and even those to be synthesized from petroleum, should offer many major and fringe benefits to candy makers. They will be less expensive, too.

Newer fats will do a better job of shortening textures of caramels, fudges, and toffees. They will offer even better stand-up body to these candies. Improved for better eating and wrapping will be a more demanding specification. Resistance to rancidity (oxidative and hydrolytic), coupled with inhibition to moisture absorption leading to crystallization, will be emphasized. Better flavors will be modified into fats being researched.

Emphasis will be directed toward improving nutritional properties of candies. Protein levels will be increased, especially in those candies lacking them. Vitamins and minerals are already being incorporated in certain dietetic candies. Sorbitol and manitol sweeteners are in still others. Presently available for protein fortification are less-costly blends, e.g., whey solids-soy protein, caseinates-whey solids, and caseinates-whey solids-soy protein.

There is a continuing search for better stabilizers and combinations of them. They must do a better job of stabilizing and structuring jellies, creams, marshmallows, nougats, hard candies, etc. High-sugar products like creams, fudges, nougats, etc., are in want of smoother mouth-feel, more uniform structure, and longer shelf-life under adverse conditions.

Whipping agents that will give candies a more uniform and stabilized air structure are greatly needed. Fractionated or molecularly-sieved proteins—or combinations of them—may play a significant role in this area.

Already great strides have been made through the extended applications of soy albumen. It is an excellent whipping agent for aqueous systems. Hence, it is being used more and more for aerating syrups for candies. Its ready solubility permits its direct addition to water and syrups without the need of troublesome and time-consuming soaking.

Soy albumen will set the example for future development of even better "whippers." When whipping candy syrups, for instance, soy albumen is a faster whipper. It produces small, uniform air cells; it differs from egg albumen in that it does not "break down" or lose volume. Moreover, it greatly accelerates egg albumen's rate of whip when as little as 5% egg white is mixed with the same amount of soy albumen. Whipping time in this case is cut in half.

Candy makers may eventually get into the production of snack cakes. A few already have. This type of production is ideal because candies are snacks and snack cakes are nothing more than a modification of candies. Individually-wrapped brownies resemble candy bars. Small chocolate-coated cup cakes with cherries inside are made to resemble cherry cordials.

Snack cakes, like certain candies, are small and finished with a wide range and combination of coatings and fillings. Coatings are of the confectioner's type. Fillings are basically of the cream and butter types. And some of the same equipment, like chocolate coaters, are used in making snack cakes.

Kinds of Candies

Confections are broken down into three major groups: hard candies (high-boiled sweets); chewy confections; and aerated or whipped items. Chewy and aerated confections are further classified into two subgroups, grained and nongrained candies. Grained items are made from supersaturated sugar solutions, nongrained ones from unsaturated sugar solutions.

Grained candies possess a crystalline structure. Within this subgroup are fondant-type candies such as fudges, cream centers, pulled grained mints, rigid grained marshmallows, and panned centers (soft and hard). Those of nongrained makeup are marshmallows, taffies, and chewy candies (nougats, caramels, jellies, gums, etc.).

And then there are the hybrid confections. These combine the physical characteristics of grained and nongrained candies.

Hard Candies.—Essentially, hard candies represent a highly saturated, supercooled sugar solution with less than 1% moisture. When making them, invert sugar and corn syrup (or both) are employed to prevent sugar crystal formation. Corn syrup controls sweetness. It also reduces a hard candy's friability, thus preventing the candy from fracturing upon unequal cooling conditions. High-dextrin syrups—with low dextrose and maltose fractions—also control a hard candy's hygroscopicity. With formula and process modifications, hard candies are made to withstand adverse moisture pickup and to possess varying degrees of sweetness, densities, textures, etc.

Chewy Confections.—Nongrain caramels, kisses, gums, and jellies are made from sugar, corn syrup, fat, and milk solids. They are cooked to 12–15% moisture levels. Corn syrups (42 DE) contribute to their chewability. Fats, usually those of the vegetable types, give them body and

lubricity. Emulsifiers (lecithin, mono- and di-glycerides, Spans and Tweens) make them more palatable.

Gums and jellies in this group are of two types: those that use starch and those that use pectin as gelling agents. Starch gum candies are made from 10% thin-boiling starch that is gelatinized when cooked in a combination sugar-corn syrup solution. Cooking is to about 75% solids when casting into starch molds.

Pectin jellies are also cooked to 75% solids from solutions containing sugar, corn syrup, pectin, citric acid, and a buffer salt. Generally, a 50:50 sugar-corn syrup blend avoids graining and moisture pickup.

Frappés and marshmallows are manufactured from unsaturated solutions. These are not necessarily chewy. However, tough marshmallow bars are chewy. They are created from solutions containing sugar (55%), corn syrup (45%) and a whipping agent. Egg or soy albumen is used for whipping frappés and gelatin for marshmallows.

Aerated Confections.—From supersaturated solutions are formed grained confections like creams, fondants, fudges, nougats, and marshmallows (grained). Fondants and creams are concentrated at 238°–242°F to a solids level of about 85%. More sugar than corn syrup is used to induce precipitation when seeding for crystallization. Seeding or agitation (with incorporation of air) is conducted at about 110°F when sugar crystals are formed.

Fondant is used to seed creams. A small amount of egg or soy albumen (in the form of mazetta) imparts some air into the creams. Corn syrup serves as an humectant and keeps the creams soft and pliable.

Fudges, e.g., caramels, contain sugar, corn syrup, milk solids, and vegetable fats. However, they are slightly aerated with the aid of egg or soy protein frappés and mechanical agitation.

In addition to sugar and corn syrup, grained marshmallows contain gelatin or albumen as whipping agents. Corn syrup and invert sugar retain softness within such marshmallows.

History of Candies

Candy making attained the pace of an industry giant with the increased availability of sugar in volume in the 18th Century. This permitted the enjoyment of candies by the average person where formerly it was a luxury made at high cost for only a few people. Today, it is a relatively low-cost food available to millions.

Another breakthrough was the introduction of another candy-making ingredient—chocolate. Chocolate was ushered in with C. J. Van Houten's development of a way of extracting $2/3$ of the cocoa bean's fat, cocoa butter, as a by-product. When this fat is blended with cocoa and finely ground sugar, it is then molded into chocolate bars.

Solid milk chocolate was another significant development that followed. Making smooth-textured fondant was still another important development. Manufacture of former coarse-grained chocolate was discontinued because of the availability of this much-improved fondant.

Because of all these developments, along with recent introduction of high-speed, high-volume automatic equipment, there is almost no end to the many types of chocolate candies that are now being manufactured. Everything from chocolate bars and pieces to chocolate-coated creams, nuts, fruits, caramels, and marshmallows are now made.

Individually-wrapped candies made their appearance in this country some 60 yr ago. They represented mixtures such as almond nougats and chocolate-coated marshmallows and peanuts. These wrapped candy bars were not mass produced until shortly after World War I.

However, the biggest strides in candy making really began about 25 yr ago. This was the time when a few candy technologists and chemists began taking some of the "art" out of candy making by putting some basic technologies into candy manufacture. This was the time, too, when engineers and technologists began developing continuous, high-speed and high-capacity cookers, whippers, etc.

In the early days of candy making, a plant's output ranged from 5000–8000 lb per day. Shelf-life was a matter of only a few months. Today, candy plants are pouring out as much as 50,000 lb of jellies or nougats during an 8-hr day. Shelf-life has been extended to as long as 12 months. And sales have been extended to heretofore undeveloped market areas.

Today's candy-making machines are continuous, highly sophisticated, and automated. For example: (1) For making marshmallows and nougats there are nonstop units like the Cherry-Burrell, Oakes, Votator, and Whizolator machines. (2) For straight-through, high-volume production of caramels, there are the Cherry-Burrell, Blaw-Knox, Groen, Rodney-Hunt, and Votator units. (3) For high-volume production of starch-based candies, there are the Farley, Staley, Votator, and Whizolator machines. (4) Hard candies are continuously cooked with Baker-Perkins, Cherry-Burrell, Groen, Hansella, and Rodney-Hunt units.

During this rapidly growing period, instrumentation became the growth factor in modern candy making. It brought striking rewards of uniformity—ever higher product quality and ever lower costs—to pacemaking operators of candy factories. And, above all, rapid progress has been characterized by one general and far-reaching goal—the trend from batch to continuous flow.

Engineers worked feverishly making obsolete the inefficient batch and semicontinuous methods of yesteryear. For them, they substituted striking new processes that provide indisputable gains in quality and production.

Early in the development of continuous cooking and whipping systems, candy plant engineers and technologists drew from experiences of other industries, such as the chemical industry. They adopted carefully engineered systems of automatic instrumentation. Temperatures, vacuums, humidities, pHs, viscosities, colors, etc., are now being instrument-controlled to speed up production and make better quality candies.

Some operations are even being computer-controlled through instrument sensing and data feedback.

Continuous Candy-Making Machines

Continuous Atmospheric Cookers.—Continuous cookers are of the falling-film type. They are doing an excellent job of concentrating candy syrups within a short time. Units are of the Baker-Perkins (Microfilm), Groen, and Buflovak types.

Earliest of these was the Baker-Perkins cooker, originally used for making hard candies. It consists of an agitator-equipped kettle, steam pressure jacketed evaporator tube, and a conical water-jacketed cooler. It cooks syrups to 320°F and brings moisture levels down to $1\frac{1}{2}\%$. It produces up to 2250 lb of candy per hour—and with product uniformity.

Groen's concentrator is of the falling-film type. It is similar to the Baker-Perkins unit. The only exception is that agitation is not used. Syrup is fed at one end. It then falls along the inner surfaces of the concentrator tube and discharges at the opposite end at temperatures up to 320°F and moisture of $1\frac{1}{2}\%$.

Groen has recently introduced a new continuous cooker of novel design. It is a rising film, scraped surface atmospheric cooker designed so that no shaft seals are required. By using a variable speed rotor, the cooker is very versatile, capable of concentrating a wide range of products from a simple syrup solution to a milk caramel with capacities up to about 3000 lb per hr for a low-cooked caramel on the standard unit. The cookers are custom built, however, and capacity can be built in to suit the user. Since the dwell time is very short, Groen makes a separate unit for caramelizing when required.

The Buflovak concentrator differs from the Baker-Perkins and Groen units in that it has a series of smaller-diameter concentrator tubes for superior heat-transfer efficiencies. Syrup in this case is also top-fed and flows downward in the form of a film inside these small steam-jacketed tubes. Cooked syrup then continues to a unit that separates it from the cooker.

Continuous Vacuum Cookers.—The Mueller cooker was introduced right after World War II. It is a vacuum-type, thin-film concentrator with a vertical evaporator tube surrounded by a steam jacket. A separator is mounted above the tube, with a rotor passing between both. Concentrated, highly turbulent product is discharged from unit's bottom conical outlet.

The Turba-Film Processor uses essentially the same thin-film cooking technique as the Mueller. It is being used for making caramels (with a continuous caramelizer ahead of the unit) and gum jellies. When making caramels, feed rates vary from 4000 to 8000 lb per hr.

The Roto-Vak Cooker is also of the thin-film type with a rotor running throughout its evaporator tube. Downward-traveling syrup and vapors are separated in an internal vat. Vapors go to a vacuum chamber and condensor. Concentrated syrup is pumped out of the cooker.

Pressure Cooking.—The continuous Farley cooker pressure-cooks starch jelly candies at capacities of 1500–1700 lb per hr. The cooker has one or more steam jets through which a slurry of starch, sugar, and corn syrup flows. The slurry is continuously cooked at 280°F at pressures up to 60 psi. Cooked candy then flashes off the water vapor and is discharged to starch depositors.

The Staley unit is also a jet cooker. It utilizes high-amylose starches in the manufacture of these jelly candies. A preheated slurry (180°F) is continuously steam-injection cooked to 300°F and concentrated to about 82% solids.

Scraped-surface heat-exchangers have been used with great versatility in the continuous cooking of starch gum jellies, fudges, caramels, creams, etc. Cherry-Burrell's 3-way system for producing a wide variety of candies consists of a vacuum chamber, metering pumps, premix tanks, accessories, and sophisticated instrumentation.

When making fondant creams, for instance, batches are alternately pumped from a premix tank to the heat-exchanger's first tube for a vacuum cook. Then, from the vacuum chamber, it is pumped through the heat-exchanger's second tube for cooling and controlled crystallization. Simultaneously, metering pumps introduce flavor, color, invertase, and whipping agent. Cooled candy then goes through the heat-exchanger's third tube for reheating. Operations vary with fondants, caramels, and fudges.

The Votator system operates in a somewhat similar manner. It is used alone or in combination with the Votator Turba-Film Processor. Versatile setups provide the hookup of:

(1) Two of three heat-exchange tubes with a premix tank for cooking slurries to finished candies having moisture contents of 12% and above.

(2) Three tubes for pressure-cooking, holding, and then cooling when continuously producing fondants, creams, fudges, etc.

(3) Two tubes (without holding tube) where caramelization is not required, as in fudges, starch gum jellies, etc.

Making Whipped Candies

Candies like nougats and marshmallows are made batchwise or continuously whipped (or aerated). Batch systems employ the older type of horizontal beaters or vertical, planetary mixers. The Morton Pressure Whisk combines the versatility of the batch process with facilities of continuous mixing.

The Oaks, Votator, and Cherry-Burrell units are employed for continuous aeration. These units use mechanical means for finely dispersing a gas (or air) within a foam. On the other hand, the Whizolator uses shear that is created by high-pressure forcing a candy-mix slurry through specially designed impact units. Under all conditions, air or gas (nitrogen) is incorporated under controlled pressures.

Extruding and Forming Candies

Great strides have been made in the development of continuous methods for producing extruded candies. Take, for instance, the continuous extrusion in making marshmallows. Specially developed formulas are used, with the continuously whipped candies extrusion-cut and the cut pieces deposited on a continuous belt. Bypassed this way are the multiple handlings involved in batch-casting the whipped product into starch molds for subsequent setting and removal from trays.

Creamed coconut candies are also continuously extruded through multiple dies. Cut-off extruded pieces are similarly deposited onto a travel belt going to chocolate bottomers and enrobers.

Starch molding machines have been designed for high-efficiency performance—all the way from unstacking trays for automatic feeding to depositor to the stacking of trays filled with deposited candies.

These machines are now more uniformly accelerated and decelerated during the start-stop handling of trays. Operation of these machines is conducted in several staggered rows at a time for making different flavored and kinds of candies at the same time. Depositors are also being used in series to cast alternate banks or rows of candies.

Hard candies are also being automatically deposited. A machine now automatically deposits center-filled goods with toffee or hard candy jackets. A plunger-cylinder pump deposits premeasured amounts of syrup from a Baker-Perkins Vacuum Microfilm unit into molds containing predeposited centers. Another deposit seals opening for complete coverage of the candy centers. Deposited pieces are discharged through a spring-actuated ejector device.

For molding chocolate candies with various types of fillings, there is the continuous and versatile Jensen system. It comprises a continuously traveling conveyor with molds inserted into the conveyor's chains. During the conveyor's travel, sequenced operations are carried out: mold heating, depositing (bottom chocolate layer, center, and top chocolate layer), vibrating (the molds), cooling, and demolding. Capacities are rates at 250 lb per hr and up.

JUSTIN J. ALIKONIS

Cross-reference: *Chocolate and Cocoa Products.*

CONVENIENCE FOODS

Convenience when applied to preprepared food service or to home consumption defines only one segment of a broad spectrum of food forms and products. It is difficult to formulate an exact definition of foods falling into this category. Basically, a preprepared food is convenient in that it can be served and consumed with little or no preliminary preparation other than heating or cooling.

Although "convenience" has become the accepted word for all preprepared frozen foods, many in the industry are referring to the entire concept as efficiency products, with "built-in chef service." Other forms of preprepared or semiprepared edibles cannot be ignored since they complement the fundamental aspect of the overall convenience food service scene. These are the adjunct items necessary to complete a menu that is based on an efficiency program. Freeze dried, artificially dried, fabricated, canned, natural, fermented, intermediate or semimoist, sugar concentrated, convenient, and convenient packaged items are categories of adjunct efficiency foods which complement convenience products to form the full spectrum of the prepared or semiprepared food industry.

Historical Background

Nature provided man with edibles that could be consumed without prior preparation since the beginning of time. These are supplied by nature in the form of nuts, fruits, some vegetables, and

varieties of marine life. The preservation of a number of foods dates back to Biblical times. Preservation by means of salting, smoking, and cheese and bread making are traced back some 4000 yr.

During the latter part of the 18th Century, techniques were discovered to preserve fruits and vegetables by crude methods of canning and bottling. Nicolas Appert, a French confectioner, in the year 1795, while working in a simple kitchen, observed that food heated in sealed containers was preserved if the container was not reopened or the seal did not leak. Some 30 yr later, Appert had developed formulas for processing some 50 different canned foods. In the 1820's, canning plants appeared in the United States in Boston and New York and by 1840 canneries were in operation throughout America.

With the advent of canning, the variety of preserved prepared foods in every conceivable category became available. A complete line of fruits, vegetables, meats, gravies, macaroni and spaghetti mixtures, fish, condiments, jams, pickles, salads, soup, and a myriad of other items were offered to the consumer. Presently, the canning industry has an annual output of about 20,000,000,000 cans. During World War I advancements in packaging and preservation methods continued as a means to feed our armies in Europe. However, major strides were recorded during World War II. The period from 1941 to 1946 not only signalled a dramatic need for prepared packaged foods, but it ushered into being a concerted trend towards convenience food capabilities, fast food serving establishments, and assembly line commissaries.

The Birdseye Era

The "father" of the frozen food industry, Clarence Birdseye, in his Gloucester, Mass., laboratories experimented on a wide range of prepared products. His experiments started during 1923. In this research he was assisted by Dr. Donald K. Tressler, Clifford F. Evers, Bertha E. Nettleton, Lucy Kimball, James Powers, Stuart MacDonald, Karl B. Norton, and Gerald A. Fitzgerald. The results of the work of these pioneers revolutionized the eating habits of the Western world. This was in truth, the beginning of the "convenience food" age.

In 1930, Birdseye began to market frozen vegetables, fruits, meats, and fish in the New England area under his trade name. His ideas were considered premature however, and the program did not meet with popular appeal. In addition, the primitive state of distribution, poor freezing control, scarcity of suitable storage facilities, and the economic severity of the depression exerted a deterring effect on his program. Fortunately, World War II rescued the infant frozen food industry and it began to flourish. Frozen orange juice concentrate made its appearance in 1945 and became an immediate success and was followed by other frozen items. It was clear that the public was ready to accept frozen foods.

The Age of Convenience Foods

From these humble beginnings in the Birdseye laboratories, convenience foods, featuring preprepared frozen entrées, started their meteoric rise during 1950. French fried potatoes spearheaded the surge in the popularity of prepared frozen foods. Sales at first were mainly in retail stores, but as labor costs continued to rise, the food service industry realized the economies of this product and began to use it. Other items soon followed. C. A. Swanson & Sons, Omaha, Neb., introduced Chicken Pot Pie and Chicken a la King. The latter was first prepared and marketed by Birdseye. These were followed by complete dinners packaged on aluminum trays. During 1958 Swanson merchandised these dinners under the "T.V." trade name. The original concept underlying this idea was to take advantage of the television craze sweeping the country and to help feed those people "glued" to their sets.

During the early part of the last decade the plastics industry developed film that served a dual purpose. This film not only protected the contents of the package, but the entire package could be placed in boiling water for heating. The advent of the boilable pouch led to many other novel types of packaging materials and disposable products. These include aluminum containers, tab-pull cans, new light-weight steel cans, paper and foil combinations, flexible laminated films, and plastic containers.

With advances in packaging and methods of freezing, nearly every conceivable food item appeared on the market. Networks of freezer facilities and storage areas were constructed to accommodate the needs of the frozen food industry. Specially designed trucks and freight cars were constructed to move the vast amounts of frozen food products. As the last decade drew to a close, the space allocated to frozen products of all kinds commanded about 1/5 of the shelf space in an average supermarket. The food service industry, because of economic factors and the growth of fast food systems, realized the merits of convenience items so that feeding facilities were designed and planned encompassing their use. Equipment manufacturers and frozen food processors pooled their resources in the form of research grants to foster means to handle and reconstitute prepared frozen items

properly and efficiently. These efforts brought about the development of microwave and convection ovens, high speed steam cookers, infrared ovens, automatic deep fryers, char-broilers, thawing refrigerators, and new concepts of freezer design.

Advances in food technology and commercial production techniques, employing foods that are harvested at the peak of maturity and rapidly and uniformly processed, provide the consumer with flavorful and nutritious foods, superior in many respects to those items prepared at home or in the restaurant. About 80% of all feeding establishments are presently using some form of convenience or efficiency food.

Many operators have become disenchanted with preprepared frozen items, but their numbers are dwindling, chiefly because proper equipment is being installed and methods of handling, heating, garnishing, and plating are improving.

Advantages

The many advantages of preprepared foods are contributing to an increased and accelerated interest in convenience foods. They are: (1) Food costs have decreased due to waste reduction, less shrinkage, easier inventory and portion control. (2) Service has improved and service flexibility increased. (3) Sales have increased since more time and effort are spent on merchandising and customer relations. (4) Food and beverages are more uniform—provided the art of handling and preparation has been mastered. (5) Reliance on skilled chefs and cooks has diminished. (6) Menu versatility, especially by the addition of nationality foods, has increased. (7) Systematic production and a straight orderly flow plan require less preparation space and fewer employees.

Although the foregoing sets forth the many advantages of convenience foods, two other factors are responsible in substantial degree for their growth: (1) The demand of the younger generation and young couples for quick service and a stereotyped menu. (2) It could be said that the quick service market is a direct outgrowth of our modern life style.

Disadvantages

Presently, although disadvantages exist, in many instances they are being corrected by education, improved products and handling methods. The disadvantages are: (1) Little or no product standardization, size or type of packaging. (2) Poor and inadequate training. (3) Packages lacking full instructions for proper reconstitution. (4) National distribution limited to major cities, so that many outlying or remote areas cannot obtain a steady flow of products. (5) High investment in new equipment to fully complement existing kitchen facilities. Lack of it creates production problems when an attempt is made to use traditional preparation devices for reconstitution purposes. (6) Initial phases and introduction of convenience food systems require cautious and careful planning. Guidance towards this end is fragmented. (7) Equipment requires standardization with easily operating controls. (8) Lack of highly skilled mechanics to furnish repairs often means "bottle necks" and excessive "down time." (9) Improper handling of frozen foods such as wrong storage temperatures, intermittent thawing, and faulty reconstitution may result in spoilage and off-flavors. (10) Lack of appreciation for proper plating and garnishing result in unappetizing and unappealing food.

The "Kitchenless" Kitchen

The fast or automated food facility in which the entire activity is based solely on the use of efficiency foods is sometimes referred to as the "kitchenless" restaurant. The expression is a fallacy, since fully appointed or conventional kitchens and those for the fast food operation are both necessary centers for the preparation and portioning of food. The conventional kitchen is equipped to perform the complete cooking process, so that a variety of raw or semiprocessed foods can be prepared, portioned, and served. Fast food centers also employ foods that require heating, garnishing, and portioning. However, the difference between the two is mainly in the techniques employed and equipment involved.

The "Garnish Chef"

The sole use of preprepared frozen foods within a feeding establishment has engendered new methods of food handling and serving. If an organization is to achieve success in this field, special emphasis must be given to proper preparation in order that the food may have high appeal and is appetizing when compared to comparable items cooked in the traditional manner.

To implement these concepts, garnishing and plating have been established as new arts within the field of preprepared food service. Garnishing and plating provide opportunities for imagination, creativeness, and showmanship. To provide the customer with an effective, palatable menu, void of blandness and stereotyping is the aim of every good restaurant. To accomplish this goal a new food profession has emerged. The person responsible for methods of garnishing and plating is referred to as the "garnish chef." The garnish chef is responsible for the preparation and adaptation of sauces, gravies, dressings, addition of spices, and the eventual arrangement of food items on the plate or platter to make them more appealing and appetizing.

Entrées

The focal point of convenience food service is the entrée. An entrée is a main course, usually meat, but it can also be macaroni and cheese or eggplant parmigiana. A main course with no more than one vegetable is still considered an entrée; with two or more vegetables, it then becomes a dinner.

Table C-31 shows the types of prepackaged prepared foods used by various institutions in their convenience food service operation.

Adjunct Efficiency Foods

To round out a menu which has been designed around convenience foods, it becomes necessary to employ various forms of semiprepared or prepared products. The following is a survey of those adjunct items commonly used in both the home and food service establishment to complement preprepared frozen entrées. A number of these products have been in use for many years, others are of recent origin, and some are provided by nature.

Dehydrated Foods.—These are foods in which the free water content is reduced sufficiently to con-

TABLE C-31

TYPES OF PACKAGED PREPARED FOODS USED BY INSTITUTIONS

	Restaurants (%)	Hotels and Motels (%)	Hospitals, Nursing Homes (%)	Colleges and Universities (%)	Schools (%)	Employee Feeding (%)
Disposable tray-packed	12.8	13.0	23.3	28.9	21.5	18.1
Pouch-packed	12.8	19.6	15.5	16.6	5.6	10.6
Individual portion-packed	8.0	9.3	10.3	16.6	7.9	13.6

SOURCE: *Institutions and Volume Feeding Magazine.*

trol microbial growth. Two methods are available: dehydration by nature, such as sun drying, and dehydration by artificial means.

Naturally dried foods have been consumed since Biblical times. These include grains, legumes, nuts, many varieties of dried fruit, fish, and meat.

Artificially dried foods are produced by hot air, superheated steam, under vacuum, in inert gas, and by direct application of heat. Examples of food in this segment are potato chips; spaghetti products; fruits such as apples, pears, grapes (raisins), figs, cherries, and bananas; vegetables like potatoes, onions, celery, parsley and cabbage; meats such as bacon, beef, and pork; fish and fish products; milk products, either whole milk or nonfat skim milk; whole eggs, yolks, and egg whites; instant coffee and tea. In addition, many combinations of food products are obtained by employing dried components; these include dry mixes for milk shakes, salad dressings, soups, lemonade and other soft drinks.

Semimoist or Intermediate Moisture Products.— Semimoist or intermediate moisture products are partially dehydrated foods that have a suitable concentration of dissolved solids to bind the remaining water sufficiently to inhibit the growth of bacteria, mold, and yeasts. Foods in this category can be precooked or raw and are stable at room temperature. Examples of products treated by this process are diced white chicken meat, diced carrots, beef stew, barbecued pork, apple pie filling, beef cubes, and coarse ground hamburger beef. Figs and dates, both of which are air dried, fit into this category. Soft candies, marshmallows, fig newtons, jams and jellies, fruit cake, peperoni, and dry sausage are other products within this group.

Freeze-Dried Foods.—Freeze-dried foods are products that have undergone high vacuum processing while in a frozen state and under the influence of specific conditions of temperature and pressure. Under certain controlled conditions water can exist as a liquid, a solid, and a vapor. These simultaneous properties are referred to as the three-point or triple stage. At $32°F$ and at a pressure of 4.7 mm of mercury, water enters the triple point stage. Below 4.7 mm of mercury the ice sublimes from the frozen product and is emitted in the gaseous form as water vapor. Successful freeze dehydration is performed at a pressure of 4 mm or below to bring about a rapid process of sublimation.

Freeze drying is increasing in popularity because of the many advantageous characteristics these products possess. Flavor, odor, color, texture, and nutrients are practically unaffected which makes freeze-dried foods superior to those obtained by other means of dehydration. Storage stability is excellent and they rehydrate quickly. Bacteria, molds, and yeasts have little chance to multiply. However, a major drawback is the higher processing costs which are four times more than conventional dehydration. Other disadvantages are the expensive air-tight packages required to prevent moisture from impregnating the product, and the cautious handling needed, since freeze-dried items are easily damaged.

Canned Foods.—The category of canned foods refers to those items which are packed in hermetically sealed containers, and are then subjected to a heat processing treatment. The heating process destroys microorganisms that cause spoilage. The amount and length of heat varies with the product being processed and the size of the container.

Canned products also are adjunct efficiency foods and are used in many ways to speed up food preparation in restaurant and institution kitchens. Many are processed in can sizes suitable for quantity food preparation. They are used for cooked vegetables and vegetable dishes, sauces and gravies, pie fillings, and other dessert dishes.

Fermented Foods.—Preservation by fermentation is an old art dating back almost 4000 yr. This method of preservation makes use of microorganisms under controlled conditions. Wine production, beer brewing, bread baking, cheese production, salting, and pickling of various products are all derived from this type of preservation.

Fermented foods preserved by salting or brining are preserved by the beneficial effects that salt has in inhibiting growth of unfavorable organisms which, in turn, promotes the growth of favorable organisms and thus controls the fermentation process. Sauerkraut, olives, and salt stock for pickle manufacture are typical examples of this kind of fermented food.

Cured and Pickled Foods.—The preservation action of salt plays an important role in cured, corned, and pickled meats. Salt and other chemicals are incorporated in either a dry cure or a pickling solution. Cure is effected at $35°-38°F$ temperature for the required length of time to develop the typically pink color of cured meat products: ham, bacon, sausage, corned beef, etc.

Pickled vegetables and fruits are preserved by the combined action of a heavy concentration of sweetening (sugar) and acid (vinegar) agents. These products include all kinds of cucumber pickles (except dill pickles), combinations of vegetable pickles (carrots, cauliflower, cucumbers, etc.), vegetable relishes, and pickled beets, peaches, pears, and plums.

Concentrated Sugared Foods.—Products in this category include jelly, jam, fruit preserves and butters, candied and glacéed fruit, sweetened condensed milk, etc. These products are preserved through concentration by evaporation to a high solids content which together with a high sugar content prevents microbial spoilage. Mild heat is applied to products containing 65% or more of soluble solids and a high acid content. With more than 70% solids, the high acid content is not required for preservation.

Irradiated Foods.—Irradiated foods are those that have been subjected to ionizing radiation at low intensities as a means of food preservation. The process of irradiation results in a sterilized, packaged food with an extended shelf and storage life over that of the fresh counterpart.

When properly packaged, food undergoing this preservation process can be held in a chilled or frozen state during the period of exposure to radiation. However, with some foods, enzymes are first inactivated by heat at 165°F.

Experimental work has satisfactorily preserved foods such as bacon, ham, pork, beef, chicken, fish and seafood, vegetables, and fruit. On the whole, they are as nutritious as their heat-processed counterparts. While irradiation does destroy various amounts of certain nutrients, losses generally are of the same degree as from heat processing. Sterilizing doses of irradiation can deteriorate organoleptic properties of various foods.

For some foods, storage life has been found to be 2 yr or more at room temperature; and storage life can be prolonged by refrigerated temperatures of 32°-34°F to as long as 5 yr. In some cases of lower doses of irradiation, prolonged storage life under refrigeration is proving technically and economically feasible.

Although the food laboratories at the U.S. Army Natick Laboratories, Natick Mass., have done intensive research and development work on radiation preservation, FDA is not yet convinced that irradiated foods are safe for human beings. Production under the auspices of private enterprise has ceased to function in the United States pending further FDA action.

Convenient Foods.—Convenient foods—to use the term in its dictionary sense—are those items that are precut, preportioned, or are basic combinations of prepared products that require additional preparation or mixing with other components. Examples of convenient foods are: preportioned fresh or frozen meat, seafood and poultry, frozen blanched vegetables; cleaned and packaged fresh vegetables; baking mixes, and soup and gravy bases.

Additional convenient foods are chopped celery for salads, shredded cabbage for cole slaw, chopped fresh parsley, caesar salad, tossed salads, peeled and sliced or diced fresh onions, fresh hard boiled eggs for salads or garnishes; and peeled, diced, rissole and French-cut fresh or frozen potatoes. Cold pack fresh fruit (such as orange, grapefruit and pineapple segments), and canteloup, honeydew and watermelon balls are available for fruit salads and garnishes or sold as premixed fruit cocktail.

Convenient Packaged Foods.—Convenient packaged foods constitute a subcategory of preprepared products. The majority of these products are individual portions of ready-to-eat or ready-to-use foods. Examples are sugar packets, tea bags, butter patties, individually portioned coffee cream or nondairy whitener, packets of salad dressing, mustard, salt, pepper and ketchup, and one-cup portions for making instant coffee.

Convenience foods have grown to their present important position in the food industry because they meet the modern need for doing things faster and easier. It is also evident that a tremendous amount of research and development has gone into preserving, and in enhancing the appeal, the nutritional qualities, and the wholesomeness of the long and increasing list of convenience foods.

MARVIN EDWARD THORNER

Cross-reference: *Food Preservation*.

CORN AND ITS PRODUCTS

Corn, known botanically as *Zea mays* Linnaeus, is generally believed to have its origin in the Western Hemisphere. It was the predominant food staple of early civilizations and was prepared by boiling, parching, and laboriously grinding the kernels. Modern technology has simplified corn processing, making it consumer-ready with little effort.

There are three classifications of corn refining: wet milling, dry milling, and fermentation.

Of each year's total corn harvest, about 5% is used by the wet millers for starches, corn sugars, and corn oil; 3.5% by the dry millers for corn flour, cereals, and corn oil; and 1% by the fermentation processors for neutral spirits and alcoholic beverages. About 77% of the harvest is used as livestock feed, and about 13.5% is exported as grain.

Corn Wet Milling

With a process developed by Orlando Jones in 1841 (U.S. Patent No. 2000), the modern corn wet milling industry had its inception.

The process was functional for starch extraction from any appropriate plant source. However, corn at that time, as now, was the best available source of starch.

Thomas Kingsford founded the corn refining industry in 1842. By about 1880 corn starch consumption had reached more than 210 million

TABLE C-32

TYPICAL CHEMICAL ANALYSIS OF AMERICAN
YELLOW HYBRID DENT CORN, GRADE NO. 2

Component	Average (%)	Typical Range (%)
Dry matter	89	87–91
Starch	72	64–78
Protein	10	9.3–10.7
Lipid	4.4	4.0–4.8
Crude fiber	2.2	2.1–2.3
Ash	1.2	0.9–1.5

pounds. Now, almost 100 yr later, production has multiplied over 30 times.

An appreciation of the net worth of the corn refining industry can be noted from the components of the corn: germ, 12%; endosperm, 82%; pericarp, 5%; and tip cap, 1%. A typical chemical analysis is shown in Table C-32;

Wet Milling Process

The processing of the corn may best be illustrated by following the process from beginning to end.

Cleaning.—As the corn is received it is cleaned before storage at the plant. Screening and vacuuming remove all unwanted material such as dust, chaff, cobs, stones, and insects.

Steeping.—Corn with about 16% moisture content is ideal for steeping. If corn is too hard to process for starch separation, a softening process is needed to condition the kernel. For this a 28- to 48-hr sulfurous acid steep at about 125°F best prepares corn for grinding. This accomplishes protein disintegration, which, in turn, is responsible for holding the starch and removal of undesirable solubles which interfere with separation.

Physically the steeping is carried out in a series of tanks in which the steep is controlled by a countercurrent flow of steep water. At regular intervals the sulfurous acid water is recirculated over each steep. The oldest corn is soaked with water containing the smallest amount of solubles, and the newest corn with water containing the largest amount of solubles. The corn is completely covered during steeping. At the end of the steep process period, the steep water is drained off the corn. This steep water contains about 6% solids, comprised of 35–45% protein. Concentrated, the steep water at 35–55% solids is used in animal feeds or as nutrient material in biochemical processes.

Germ Separating.—The steeping process softened the corn kernel to the desirable point (about 45% moisture). Degerming can now be accomplished by a course grind which tears the kernel apart freeing the germ without damaging it. The course grind produces a pulpy material containing germ, hull, starch, and gluten which is passed through a liquid cyclone separator where the germ is recovered.

This shows an example of the use of modern equipment for a process which stays the same.

Older methods involved a system of flotation separators. The new method uses hydroclones to separate particles of different densities. The hulls and endosperm, the heavier particles, are discharged from the bottom of the hydroclone tube, as the germs, which are lighter, are drawn off the top of the vortex.

The cyclone method of germ recovery has several advantages over the flotation method. Equipment takes less space and is less costly to maintain, and, above all, cleaner germ can be recovered.

The recovered germ, washed free of starch and dried in a rotary steam-tube dryer, at this point is ready for oil recovery and refining.

Milling.—After germ separation, the horny endosperm and hulls are ground to release the rest of the starch.

The early buhrstone mills of tough limestone impregnated with silica have now been replaced by either attrition or impact mills.

The attrition mill, Bauer Double Revolving Disc Refiner, uses counter rotating grooved discs with each disc driven by its own motor.

The alternate method, impact milling, is done usually in the Entoleter Impact Mill. The material to be ground enters the machine's spinning rotor and is thrown with great force against the impactors at the periphery of the rotor and also against a stationary impactor.

Both attrition and impact milling easily release starch.

The resulting milled slurry, containing starch, gluten, and hulls, is passed through a series of reels fitted with 18–20 mesh screens where the coarser hulls or the coarse fibers are removed. Thorough washing removes more starch from the screened fibers.

Fine fibers are separated from the starch and gluten slurry by nylon cloth fitted on gyrating shakers.

Screens are available from Dorr-Oliver, Inc. (developed by the Dutch State mines), and from Bauer Bros. Co.

The fiber fractions are then channeled to the animal feed products processing area where, as steepwater, germ meal, and gluten, they are mixed and dried.

Starch-Gluten Separating.—The starch slurry containing from 5 to 8% gluten is passed through high speed centrifuges such as the Merco centrifugal separator.

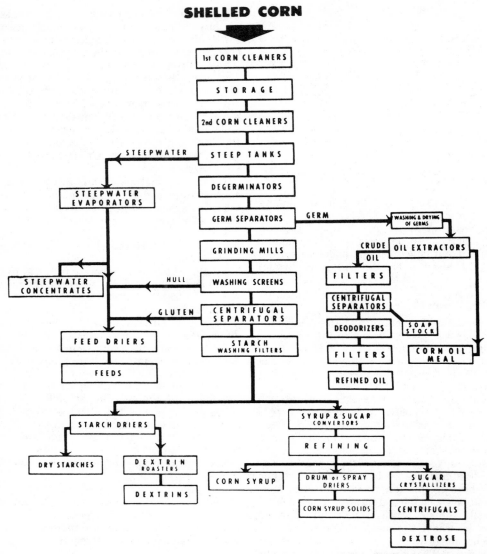

Courtesy of Corn Refiners Association

FIG. C-28. THE CORN REFINING PROCESS

First the good quality gluten is separated from the starch and concentrated by another centrifuge. It is then filtered and dried in rotary or flash driers. This gluten becomes a major part of the feed products.

The starch from the first centrifugation, still containing 2-2½% gluten protein, is further centrifuged with hydroclones.

The hydroclone equipment used for the starch-gluten separation consists of several hundred small hydroclone tubes in a partitioned housing. By using multiple stages of the hydroclone units and countercurrent washing, it is possible to obtain distinct starch-gluten separation.

Much of the water left in the refined starch slurry is filtered; however, any remaining water is removed by tray drying in kilns or ovens, or in tunnel driers or flash driers.

Zein Separating.—Further fractionation of the gluten portion seems worthwhile by certain companies other than the corn starch millers to obtain the important zein protein. The alcohol soluble zein (prolamine) present in corn gluten at about 50% is separated from the gluten by solvent extraction and precipitation. Its prime use in the food industry is as a water protective coating material for nut meats and candy. It also has importance as a binder in drug preparation.

Starch Conversion Products.—Because of the basic chemical nature of starch, other products may be derived from it through certain chemical treatments.

Syrups and Sugars.—About $1/2$ of the starch produced is used for syrup and sugar conversion. Many types of corn sweeteners can be made, depending on the extent of conversion and the degree of purity desired.

The starch conversion to corn sugar can be accomplished by acid and/or enzyme hydrolysis. The syrups are made by partial hydrolysis of starch and the dextrose sugar by complete hydrolysis.

The acid process involves the cooking of a starch slurry with the required amount of dilute acid, usually hydrochloric acid, until the desired degree of conversion is reached. The reaction is then stopped by neutralization with soda ash (sodium carbonate). Impurities and solids are filtered off and the syrup bleached and concentrated to the desired specific gravity.

Dextrose is produced by allowing the reaction to go to completion. The liquor is neutralized, filtered, clarified, and concentrated and finally the entire mass is allowed to crystallize to form the sugar.

The degree of conversion is expressed as dextrose equivalent (DE). The lower the DE, the less hydrolysis has occurred; the higher the DE, the more hydrolysis has occurred.

Enzyme hydrolysis is accomplished by heating starch slurries above the gelatinization temperature of starch while at the same time partially converting the cooked starch with acid or alpha-amylase enzyme to a DE of 15–20. At this point the enzyme is inactivated and the mass is adjusted to pH 4.0–4.5. Addition of another enzyme, glucoamylase, will bring about further conversion to higher degrees of hydrolysis. At the end of the conversion the syrups are finished in the same manner as the acid-treated products.

Dextrins.—Dextrins are degraded starch products produced from dry starch heated with various conversion chemicals such as mineral acids, usually hydrochloric acid.

Dextrins are used mainly as adhesives, sizings, and binders.

Wet Milling of Other Corns

Two types of corn, waxy and high-amylose, also are being commercially wet-milled by conventional procedures. These corns have different starch applications and starch chemistry.

The waxy corn produces starch consisting solely of branched molecules (amylopectin). Regular corn contains about 73% branched molecules and about 27% straight-chain molecules (amylose). The waxy corn starch, referred to as "amioca," has clear, fluid, and cohesive properties. Amioca paste is nongelling and offers stabilizing effects to other starches by reducing their tendency to gel.

The high amylose corns contain from 50 to 70% amylose and yield a starch which has film forming properties resembling those of cellophane. Food application of high amylose starch thus far has been limited. Although work has been done on edible films, long-lasting success of such films has not been demonstrated

A corn especially bred for more nutrition, high-lysine corn, has received significant attention since 1966. Its greatest value apparently would be as a direct food or feed. However, experimental millings have shown an interesting result: Higher starch recovery was possible with high-lysine corn than with dent corn.

Starch modification

Starches can be modified chemically by various means; however, only a few of the resulting modifications are offered for food use.

Pregelatinized starches produced by heating and drying starch-water slurries offer the user instant starches which thicken in cold water.

Starch phosphate monoesters exhibit additional thickening without cooking and have certain emulsifying properties. These monoesters are prepared by heating a dry starch and an acid salt of ortho-, pyro-, or tripolyphosphoric acid to 120°–140°C for 1 hr.

Corn Dry Milling

Two basic processes dominate the dry corn milling industry, degerming and nondegerming methods.

The degerming process separates the basic components, hull, germ, and endosperm, before milling. Resulting products include corn grits, flakes, meal, flour, oil, and feeds, all used in the manufacture of breakfast cereals, baked products, brewed beverages such as beer and malt, snack foods, and animal feeds.

The nondegerming method simply grinds whole corn, usually white dent, into a rich oily corn flour used in baked products.

Nondegermed Corn Meal

Nonremoval of the germ results in high oil content. Some germ and hull, however, can be removed by sifting, which catches the coarse particles of hulls and germ.

The high oil content flour processed by this method does not have good shelf-life because of rancidity tendencies caused by oxidation of the oil. Because of this fact, nondegerming milling is done mostly on a local basis.

The method is simple enough so that the miller, usually located by a stream, drives his stone mill by water power. The method was used even by our colonial settlers.

Now larger mills use more modern roller mills, sifters, and aspirators to process nondegermed meal.

Processors of degermed corn meal can make whole corn meal by adding back germ to the degermed meal.

Degermed Corn Meal

Two degerming methods are used in dry corn milling: tempering-degerming, introduced at the turn of the 20th Century, and a "dry" process made possible later in the mid-1960's by two European equipment manufacturers.

Tempering-Degerming Method.—In tempering-degerming, moisture in controlled amounts is added to the corn before milling.

Cleaning.—The process begins with the cleaning of corn, by a system much like that used in wet milling. Scourers, disc separators, vibrating screens, aspirators, destoners, and indented surface cylinders are used to ensure the removal of metals, over and undersized material, dust, and insects. A wet cleaning often is included to rid the corn of surface dirt and microorganism spores. Basically the wet cleaning equipment consists of a washing-destoning unit and a mechanical dewatering unit.

Tempering.—Moisture is added to the corn in controlled amounts as cold or hot water or steam in 1, 2, or 3 stages with appropriate holding times for each stage. This moisture addition tempers the corn to toughen the germ and hull, making them pliable and resilient and facilitating their release from the endosperm.

Tempering conditions vary considerably, depending upon the characteristics desired in the end products, yield, and equipment available. Normally, a temper time of 3 hr with the addition of 3–8% moisture as cold or warm water brings the corn moisture level to 21–25%, with the germ absorbing moisture faster than the endosperm. For good hull removal 1–4% moisture is added 3 to 15 min before degerming. The final moisture content now ranges from 18 to 27%. A little direct steam may be used to control temperature and thus govern the holding time. The warmer the temper, the shorter the time required.

Moisture is added to the corn in screw conveyors or other mixing equipment. During rest periods,

the corn is held in vertical cylindrical bins about 4 ft in diameter. The bins are built with inverted cone bottoms for better piston-type flow and for uniform holding time under continuous flow conditions.

Degerming.—The majority of the mills in the United States use the Beall degermer and corn huller. This unit is essentially an attrition device consisting of a cast iron, cone-shaped rotor mounted on a rotating, horizontal shaft in a conical cage. Part of the cage is fitted with perforated screens and the remainder with plates having conical protrusions on their inner surface. The cone, which has similar protrusions over most of its surface, also is designed to favor the forward movement of the corn with some sections designed to control rate of flow. The product exits in 2 streams, one, through the perforated screens, which include released germ, hull, degermed fines, and some grits, and the other, the large grits, through the end plate.

Drying.—The degermed product is dried to 15–18% moisture by rotary steam-tube dryers at temperatures of 140°–160°F. The degermed dried stock is cooled by counter-flow or cross-flow rotary, vertical gravity louvers, or fluid bed type coolers.

Rolling and Grading.—The dried, cooled degermed product is now ready for gradual size reduction to the various primary end products by corrugated roller mills. Further release of germ and hull from the endosperm may occur during the rolling.

Each stage of refinement consists of use of an aspirator, a roller mill, and a sifter. Moisture content of stock again is controlled to keep both germ and hull tough and pliable, which allows the germ to be rolled out into platelets as the stock passes between the rollers. At the same time the hull is scraped for further removal of endosperm, germ, and tip cap and the endosperm chunks are broken smaller. The germ, hull, and endosperm fragments then are separated by means of sifters, aspirators, specific gravity table separators, or purifiers.

Sifting is an important operation and is referred to also as scalping, grading, classifying, or bolting, depending upon the means used and the purpose intended for the end product: sifting is separating by particle size on sieves; scalping is coarse separation; grading or classifying is separation of a single stock into two or more groups; bolting is the removal of hull fragments from a corn meal or flour.

Aspirators are used to separate and recover hull fragments from the mill stream.

Purifiers separate small hull and germ fragments from good endosperm stock and also grade the endosperm fractions by particle size.

Finished products are classified as coarse grits, regular grits, coarse meal, fine meal, dusted meal, flour and 100% flour, all graded and controlled by particle size.

Dry Degerming Method.—The most recent (mid 1960's) development in dry milling of corn was the introduction of dry degerming equipment by two companies, Miag of Braunschweig, Germany, and Ocrim of Cremona, Italy.

This new method eliminates the need for drying, as no moisture-tempering is necessary.

Miag Process.—The Miag vertical unit subjects the corn kernels to repeated impact by beater vanes and a spring steel wire cylinder. The fines, and such pieces of hull, germ, and broken kernels as make their way through the woven wire screen, are removed either by gravity or by aspiration through one bottom outlet, while the remainder of the grain leaves through a second conical outlet extending up to the bottom of the woven wire cylinder. From the degermer the stock moves on by a pressure lift to a pneumatic grain separator and cleaner where degermed fines are removed and sent to a cyclone collector for recovery. The stock continues to sifters, separators, rollers, and graders as in the finishing steps of the tempering method.

Ocrim Process.—This process is also an impact breaker type, using 2 horizontal units operating in parallel on 1 housing. Each unit has a paddle type rotor and an enclosing cylinder made of impact bars or perforated steel plates. Reports indicate recovery of higher yields of low fat grits is possible with the Ocrim process than with the Miag process. With low fat grits oil recovery also is higher.

JOACHIM W. STAACKMANN

References

ANON. 1964. Corn Starch. Corn Industries Research Foundation, Washington, D.C.
INGLETT, G. E. 1970. Corn: Culture, Processing, Products. Avi Publishing Co., Westport, Conn.

CORROSION: FOOD INDUSTRY EQUIPMENT MATERIALS

This discussion is confined to materials for equipment for food processing and bulk transportation and is not concerned with containers such as tin cans or the aluminum trays used so extensively for the distribution of frozen foods.

Materials to be used for food processing, transportation, and handling equipment, must have the following characteristics:

(1) Resistance to corrosion at the level required to prevent any harmful contamination of foods by products of corrosion. This will extend to resistance to attack by cleaning and sterilizing agents. Alloy constituents should be nontoxic in even minute concentrations and should be free from harmful effects on vitamins or on color, flavor, odor, and keeping qualities of foods and beverages.

(2) Surface characteristics that will facilitate cleaning and sterilization.

(3) High enough strength and ductility to provide adequate resistance to mechanical damage and abrasion likely to be associated with processing, cleaning, and maintenance operations.

(4) High enough strength to permit the use of sections, thin enough to present no problems in heat transfer.

(5) Amenability to fabrication and repair by common methods and without the need for unusual skills.

(6) Availability in all the forms required ranging from flat rolled plates, sheets and strips, to rods and wires, pipes, tubing, and castings.

All of these necessary characteristics are being provided by the austenitic grades of stainless steel, which are by far the most commonly used materials for food handling equipment. The most frequently used is the AISI Type 304 grade, containing about 18% chromium and 8% nickel. The Type 316 grade is chosen to deal with unusually corrosive conditions, especially where a higher level of resistance to localized attack by chlorides is required.

The stainless steels are used so extensively and almost so exclusively for processing and handling equipment in the food industry as to justify concentration on their properties and applications in this discussion. This is in line with the following statement quoted from the USDA Technical Service Division Handbook *191*, prepared for the guidance of meat inspectors:

> With few exceptions, good quality, smooth surfaced stainless steel is the best readily available material for fabricating food handling equipment. It is durable, highly rust resistant, nonporous, and resistant to most agents encountered in food handling plants. It can be kept clean with minimum effort. Some plastics have most of these qualities, but seldom match the durability of stainless steel.

In studies carried out by the University of Michigan, covered in a report under the title *Bacterial Cleanability of Various Types of Eating Surfaces* and reported in the American Journal of Public Health, Febr. 1953, it was found that in terms of percentage of removal by a detergent wash of *M. aureus* from various worn surfaces when deposited under a protein soil film, stainless steel was rated as high as glass and china, and very much superior to plastics included in the same tests. Supplementary tests at Michigan State University covered in a report entitled *Relative Cleanability of Various Stainless Steel Finishes Used in Dairy Equipment* showed no difference in bacterial cleanability among finishes No. 2B, No. 3, No. 4, and the smoothest, No. 7, finish.

The advantages of stainless steel extend to the handling of prepackaged meats in retail stores as described in a study at the University of Missouri, entitled *Guidelines for Handling Prepackaged Meats in Retail Stores.*

The National Sanitation Foundation has set up standards for the design and fabrication of food handling equipment and a mechanism for certifying compliance with these standards.

Prior to the advent of the stainless steels, the necessary corrosion resistance and food protection qualities were most commonly provided by tin used as a coating on steel, as in milk cans, or on copper for food processing vessels and pipes, etc. These relatively thin tin coatings had a limited life, being subject to some attack by corrosive foods and being even more vulnerable to destruction by abrasion and other mechanical damage during cleaning operations.

Bare copper found use in vessels for processing beverages such as beer, not adversely affected by the small concentrations of copper that might be taken into solution in the usual processing operations. Currently, copper is being replaced for these purposes by stainless steel. Copper with or without tin coatings was used for cooking coils and milk evaporators.

There has been some use of aluminum for food processing, transportation, and distribution purposes. Aluminum is inferior to stainless steels in resistance to corrosion and abrasion by cleaning and sterilizing operations and agents and in resistance to corrosion by the foods themselves. This has restricted its general application except, of course, as a substitute for tin or plastic-coated steel for cans and for frozen food trays which do not come within the scope of this chapter. Coated aluminum barrels have been used for transporting beer and ale but are being displaced in this service by stainless steel barrels which are less susceptible to mechanical damage and do not require initial or periodic application of a protective coating or "pitching."

Pure nickel and the monel nickel copper alloy were used extensively in preference to bare and tinned copper before stainless steel came into such extensive use for purposes for which the latter was found to be at least as satisfactory and more economical. An early use of pure nickel was for milk pasteurizing equipment. It was satisfactory for the transportation and storage of cold milk, and for heating milk to the pasteurizing temperature, but was found to be subject to severe corrosion by milk when it was being cooled from this temperature (Trebler *et al.* 1932). Another early use of nickel was for steam-jacketted kettles used for the processing of soups. Several of these were imported from Austria to the United States over 50 yr ago, and remained in successful use decades later.

A principal advantage of nickel for steam kettles is its relatively high heat transfer capability as compared with stainless steel. In a particular test with 250-gal. kettles made of $1/8$-in. thick stainless steel and $3/16$-in. thick nickel, water was brought to the boiling point in the nickel kettle in about 11 min as compared with 19 min for the stainless steel kettle. Tests with kettles have shown an average overall rate of heat transfer for nickel of about 350 BTU per sq ft per °F per hr during heating and about 675 during boiling. Comparable figures for type 304 stainless steel were 245 during heating and 500 during boiling. Similar figures for heating coils for nickel were 475 during heating and 900 during boiling, and for type 304 stainless steel, 375 during heating and 650 during boiling.

A disadvantage of nickel is its susceptibility to severe tarnishing by foods containing sulfur compounds, very much like the tarnishing of silver by eggs. Kettles have been made using nickel for the steam-jacketed sections supplemented by stainless steel for the upper sections above the liquid level where tarnishing of nickel is most severe.

The monel nickel copper alloy has been used for some applications including ice cream processing equipment, but has been replaced by stainless steel in this service. The monel alloy was for many years the favorite material for table tops, ice cream cabinet tops, soda fountains, refrigerator linings, and other food handling equipment in large hotel and institution kitchens. The monel alloy displaced nickel silver, an alloy of copper, nickel, and zinc, for the application just mentioned, but has since been displaced by stainless steel for the same purposes.

The copper nickel zinc silver type alloys have been used in cast forms for valves and plug cocks where their nongalling characteristics give them a mechanical advantage over nickel and the monel alloy, and over the stainless steels where galling may be a problem as in plug cocks. While the nickel copper zinc alloys are less resistant to corrosion than the stainless steels they are not subject to severe attack by foods. The relatively small areas exposed in relation to the volume of the product with which they come into contact, as in the case of valves and fittings, does not lead to significantly harmful contamination by corrosion products.

The monel nickel copper alloy is the preferred material for equipment used in the processing of common salt. Rates of corrosion observed on specimens exposed for long periods of time under actual operating conditions in salt plants are shown in Table C-33. The monel alloy is superior to

TABLE C-33

RESULTS OF CORROSION TESTS ON MONEL
NICKEL COPPER ALLOY IN SALT
PROCESSING EQUIPMENT

Test Location	Duration Days	Indicated Rate of Corrosion in Inch Penetration per Year
Vapor section of evaporator	210	0.0002
Salt grainer	60	0.0002
Beneath grid of Oliver Filter	145	0.0002
Chute of Oliver Filter	90	0.006
In brine from well	35	0.0005
In oil-fired rotary dryer	—	0.01
In steam-heated rotary dryer	—	0.001

stainless steels in salt processing applications because of its much greater resistance to pitting and crevice corrosion and freedom from stress corrosion cracking.

The susceptibility of the austenitic stainless steels to stress corrosion cracking by chlorides has been observed in steam kettles used for the processing of sauces containing substantial amounts of salt. This danger can be reduced by delaying the addition of salt until as late in the heating and boiling process as practical.

Results of corrosion tests in pickling brines for herring, olives, onions, and sauerkraut showed the type 304 stainless steel to be substantially free from corrosion, with indicated rates of attack less than 0.0001 in. per yr. The greatest danger is for pitting attack that might occur under solid particles that should not be allowed to remain on the alloy surface for extended periods after exposure to products containing substantial amounts of salt.

Limitations of space will not permit an extended discussion of the resistance of stainless steel to corrosion by all the food products and under all the conditions in which stainless steel is used for their processing. A comprehensive compilation of results of tests in more than 100 food handling operations was provided by Technical Bulletin *T-28* issued several years ago by the International Nickel Company, Inc. Food handling operations covered by the tests recorded in this bulletin included the following: Salt refining, refrigerating brines, pickling brines, seafood, sugar refining, corn products, pectin, fruit juices and syrups, carbonated water and beverages, gelatin, condiments, mayonnaise and salad dressing, vanilla extracts, tartaric acid,

breakfast cereals, meat products, vegetables and juices, coffee, and dairy products.

It will suffice to note that in practically all of these tests the losses in weight of stainless steel specimens were less than 0.5 mg per sq dm per day equivalent to penetration at a rate less than 0.0001 in. per yr.

Reference was made previously to the necessity of using metals that will not contaminate foods with toxic corrosion products. H. O. Calvery (1942), then associated with FDA, presented a paper before the American Health Association in which he divided metals into three classes: Nutritive; Nonnutritive and Nontoxic; and Nonnutritive and Toxic. His classification is shown in Table C-34. A great deal of additional pertinent information is provided in the Monograph by Monier-Williams (1949).

In view of the preponderance of use of austenitic stainless steels for food processing and distribution, the results of studies by Titus *et al.* (1930) at Harvard School of Public Health are important. Their tests involved cooking foods in austenitic stainless steel vessels and subsequently analyzing the foods for traces of the alloy constituents. They

TABLE C-34

CLASSIFICATION OF TRACE ELEMENTS IN FOODS

Metal	Nutritive	Nonnutritive, Nontoxic	Toxic
Cobalt	X		
Copper	X		
Iron	X		
Manganese	X		
Zinc	X		
Aluminum		X	
Beryllium		X	
Chromium		X	
Silicon		X	
Strontium		X	
Tin		X	
Titanium		X	
Nickel		X	
Silver			X
Bismuth			X
Cadmium			X
Mercury			X
Lead			X
Arsenic			X
Antimony			X
Barium			X
Silenium			X
Tillurium			X
Molybdenum			X
Vanadium			X
Thallium			X

SOURCE: Calvery (1942).

TABLE C-35

EFFECTS OF METAL ADDITIONS ON QUALITIES OF SOME FOODS AND BEVERAGES

Food	Quality Affected	Concentration of Metal Having a Harmful Effect (Parts per Million)					
		Chromium	Copper	Iron	Nickel	Tin	Zinc
Canned peas	Color	>80	2	50	>80	>80	>80
	Flavor	>80	>80	>80	>80	>80	>80
Canned corn	Color	50	2	6	30	20	20
	Flavor	>80	>80	>80	>80	>80	>80
Tomato juice	Color	>80	16	>80	>80	>80	>80
	Flavor	>80	16	>80	>80	>80	>80
Aged rye whiskey	Color and turbidity	6–15	6	0.5–1	>200	1–3	[1]
	Flavor	6–15	6	0.5–1	>200	1–3	[1]
Aged bourbon whiskey	Color and turbidity	15	15–30	0.5–1	>200	3–6	[1]
	Flavor	15	15–30	0.5–1	>200	3–6	[1]
Beer	Color and turbidity	30	1–3	1	3	1	[1]
	Flavor		1	1		1	[1]
Ale	Color and turbidity	30–60	6	6	6	1	[1]
	Flavor		1	1		1	[1]
Port wine	Brilliance and color	>200	100–200	15–30	>200	6–15	[1]
	Flavor and bouquet	>200	100–200	15–30	>200	6–15	[1]
Claret	Brilliance and color			3–6	>200		[1]
	Flavor and bouquet			3–6	>200		[1]
Sauterne	Brilliance and color	15–30	100–200	1–3	>200	1–3	[1]
	Flavor and bouquet	15–30	100–200	1–3	>200	1–3	[1]
Concord grape juice	Flavor		5–10				[1]
Orange juice	Flavor	30	5	5	100	15–60	[1]

[1] Not tested.

concluded that "the amounts of metal are so minute that these quantities have no hygienic importance."

Many foods and beverages are subject to harmful effects of dissolved metals on their flavor, color, clarity, and keeping qualities. This is ordinarily of no more than academic importance with respect to stainless steel equipment, which is so resistant to corrosion that no significant amount of metal reaches the food as a result of corrosion. However, results of studies of the effects of additions of metal salts to some foods and beverages are appropriate to this general discussion. These are provided in Table C-35.

The alkaline compounds used for cleaning food handling equipment are not significantly corrosive to the stainless steels and other metals ordinarily used. The most corrosive agents are the sterilizing solutions such as hypochlorites containing chlorine.

None of the alloys are likely to be affected adversely by the chlorine sterilizing solutions in the concentrations and for the durations of contact used in sterilization operations. They are subject to severe localized attack by the concentrated chlorine solutions and should not be used for the preparation or storage of these solutions.

FRANK L. LA QUE

References

CALVERY, H. O. 1942. Trace elements in foods. Food Res. 7, No. 4, 313–331.
MONIER-WILLIAMS, G. W. 1949. Trace Elements in Foods. John Wiley & Sons, New York.
TITUS, A. C. et al. 1930. Contamination of food cooked or stored in contact with nickel-chromium-iron alloys. J. Ind. Hygiene 12, No. 8.
TREBLER, H. A., WESLEY, W. A., and LA QUE, F. L. 1932. Corrosion of metals by milk. Ind. Eng. Chem. 24, 330.

COTTONSEED

Of the world's many plant products the cottonseed is one of the most, if not the most, versatile in its usefulness. When mature, the cottonseed is enrobed in a cushion of fibers of varying length within the cotton boll. The many uses of cotton fiber are well known. Historians and archeologists date the use of cotton in fabrics back at least 5000–7000 yr. Not so well known is that in more recent times other products derived from the cottonseed have been important sources of food for man and feed for animals.

With each 100 lb of fiber, the cotton plant yields 170 lb of cottonseed. Seed production averages

TABLE C-36

COTTONSEED PRODUCTION IN MAJOR PRODUCING COUNTRIES

	1966	1967	1968	1969	1970	1971
			(1,000 Metric Tons)			
United States	3592	2912	4209	3690	3713	4031
U.S.S.R.	3755	3755	3755	3600	4365	3960
China (Mainland)	2750	2960	2875	2875	2915	2915
India	2008	2312	2138	2225	1963	2095
Brazil	905	1193	1458	1370	994	1281
Pakistan	928	1056	1073	1093	1071	1171
U.A.R.	820	758	758	921	884	910
Turkey	611	634	696	640	640	750
Mexico	980	871	1067	762	627	679
Sudan	343	334	426	442	453	455
Iran	230	233	305	314	305	288
Syria	288	256	311	303	303	265
Colombia	177	205	283	260	239	256
Argentina	177	148	228	294	177	254
Greece	187	204	155	236	234	249
Peru	200	197	180	165	167	169
Uganda	154	126	154	172	154	168
Nicaragua	243	206	188	143	160	161
Tanzania	159	142	103	143	128	161
Guatemala	122	148	142	102	105	110
Spain	181	132	154	117	106	88

SOURCE: USDA Agr. Res. Serv. Statist. Rept. *World Agriculture Production and Trade,* Oct. 1971.

around 850 lb per acre. Not more than 5% of the seed is required to plant the following year's crop. The remaining 95% is the basis for the cottonseed processing industry. Although the produced weight of cottonseed exceeds that of the fiber, the relative market values are such that cottonseed on the average represents about 10–15% of the total value of the cotton crop. Because of this, the world's supply of cottonseed and the supply in any producing country depend upon the markets for cotton fiber.

The world production of cottonseed was estimated to be 22.5 million metric tons in 1971. This represented a 10% increase over the 1960–1964 average world production. This restricted growth is the direct result of increased popularity of synthetic fibers. In considering the future food potential of cottonseed it is important to note that in spite of the vigorous competition of synthetic fibers, cotton consumption did continue to increase during the past decade. Until a synthetic fiber can be developed that has the comfort characteristics of cotton fiber, it is not an unreasonable presumption that the market volume for cotton will be maintained and perhaps even increased.

The world production of cottonseed in 1971 contained 4.7 billion kilograms of good quality protein. At the present time only an infinitesimal proportion of this is being used directly as human food.

The world production of cottonseed by major producing countries is shown in Table C-36. It is noteworthy that cottonseed is a significant agricultural crop in many countries where there is a marked deficiency of protein foods. In many of those countries cottonseed is presently being used wastefully.

Characteristics and Composition

The gross structural characteristics of cottonseed can be seen in Fig. C-29. The kernel or embryo is contained within the hull to which is attached the cotton linters. The oil and the protein of cottonseed are contained in the kernel.

The cross-sections of two cottonseeds in Fig. C-30 show a glanded and a glandless seed. Note that the glanded seed contains a large number of dark specks. These are called pigment glands and are distinct morphological structures. Most of the deeply colored pigments of the seed are concentrated in the pigment glands. The walls of the pigment glands are sufficiently tough that they can withstand a considerable amount of mechanical abuse without rupturing. Contact of the pigment glands with water causes an immediate discharge of their contents. However, solvents such as hydro-

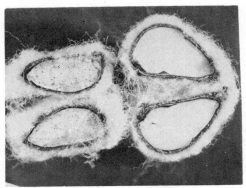

FIG. C-29. STRUCTURAL CHARACTERISTICS OF COTTONSEED

carbons do not rupture the glands. As will be seen later, this is an important property that has led to a new process.

The principal pigments in the glands are gossypol and related compounds. The chemical structure of gossypol was first characterized in 1938 by Dr. Roger Adams and his co-workers:

$$\text{Gossypol structure}$$

Gossypol and its related compounds have constituted a major problem for the processors of cottonseed products. These pigments are dark, bitter, and have been demonstrated to be toxic to monogastric animals and therefore presumably to man.

The pigment glands have been a focal point of research attention for over four decades. In a major scientific breakthrough, it was discovered in 1954 that there were glandless varieties of cottonseed. These were found in wild plants with poor agronomic properties. However, it opened the door to intensive genetic, breeding, and selection research in several agricultural research stations. More recently, major seed breeders have begun to introduce the glandless character into their commercial varieties, so that now most or all of them have glandless varieties ready or nearly ready for release. One of these is shown in Fig. C-30. While the differences in the two seeds in Fig. C-30 are quite dramatic, the differences in the quality of the oil and protein flour obtained from them, as shown in Fig. C-31, are even more striking. Essentially, all of the commercial cottonseed grown in the world today is still the glanded varieties. Without massive government intervention, it normally requires many years to decades for important new crop developments to be widely adopted by farmers. Presently, glandless varieties are being grown on limited acreage, principally in Texas. The rate of transition from glanded to glandless varieties in the United States and other cotton producing countries will be determined in part by economic considerations and by government policies. As will be seen later, the glandless varieties could serve a major human need; but farmers' planting decisions are based on anticipated cash returns.

Referring again to Fig. C-29, the 4 major products recovered from cottonseed are linters, hulls, oil, and meal, the latter 2 being separated from the kernels. Of these, the oil is the most valuable, accounting for over $\frac{1}{2}$ the total value of all 4 products. Typically, cottonseed is comprised of about 10% linters, 35% hull, and 55% kernels (meats). The kernels contain about 7% moisture, 30% crude protein, 30% oil, 24% nitrogen-free extract, 4.8% crude fiber, and 4.4% ash. This composition can vary rather widely depending upon variety, environment, and agronomic conditions.

Processing

As it is harvested, cotton consists of clusters of

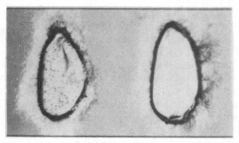

FIG. C-30. CROSS-SECTIONS OF GLANDED (LEFT) AND GLANDLESS (RIGHT) COTTON-SEEDS

FIG. C-31. DRAMATIC DIFFERENCES ARE EVIDENT IN FLOUR AND UNREFINED OIL FROM GLANDED AND GLANDLESS COTTON-SEEDS

lint or fibers in which the seed is tightly embedded. It is first delivered to a cotton gin, where the cottonseeds are separated from the long fibers that are used in the textile industries.

The cottonseed is separated into its components in what is called a crushing mill or an oil mill. The first step in the processing is to clean the seed, using a combination of revolving screens, shaker screens, and penumatic equipment. Next, the linters are removed in either 1 or 2 sequential passes through delinting machines employing the principle of the cotton gin and consisting of a series of circular saws on a horizontal revolving shaft. In the case of the sequential delinting, the first cut removes the longer linters and the second cut, the shorter. Depending upon the length and quality of the linters, they are used in automotive upholstery, furniture, mattresses, cushions, yarns, absorbent cottons, or simply as chemical celluose.

The hull which surrounds the kernel of the cottonseed is relatively tough. Dehulling is accomplished by a machine that employs a series of knives, which cut the hulls and thereby loosen them from the kernels. Seeds are then passed through a series of shakers, beaters, and separators, which effect a qualitative separation of hulls and kernels. The hulls are used principally in feeds for ruminant animals. The latter can convert a substantial proportion of the hulls to energy.

Oil is recovered from the kernels by three major processes: screw pressing, direct solvent extraction, or prepress solvent extraction, which is a combination of the first two. In all three processes the kernels are first passed through a series of rollers to reduce them to thin flakes. For screw pressing the flakes are heated and then passed through the press which has a screw revolving inside a horizontal steel barrel. The pressure created by the screw may be as great as 20,000 psi. Oil is forced from the flaked kernels and flows through small openings in the barrel of the press. Frictional heat can raise the temperature inside the barrel high enough to cause undesirable darkening of the products and a reduction in the protein quality of the meal.

Direct solvent extraction with hexane avoids the heat damage that occurs in screw pressing. Because cottonseed flakes require careful handling for direct solvent extraction, it is the practice in many oil mills to remove part of the oil by a pass through a screw press at reduced pressure, followed by solvent extraction of the press cake. This is referred to as the prepress solvent extraction process.

The defatted material resulting from any of the three processes is referred to as cottonseed meal. When the meal is finely ground, it is called cottonseed flour. The composition and characteristics of cottonseed meal and flour will depend upon the process used. Those from screw pressing will retain 3-5% residual oil, while those from solvent extraction will normally be at 1% or less. The color, nitrogen solubility, and nutritive quality will all vary according to the processing conditions used in the oil recovery. These interrelationships are quite complex and beyond the scope of this presentation.

Cottonseed Oil

Cottonseed oil has been used as food by man for many centuries. In the last century it became and has remained one of the most important food oils, both in the United States and elsewhere. Although its production and consumption in the United States have trended downward, particularly in the past decade as a result of cotton acreage restrictions, it remains the second most widely consumed vegetable oil, with a U.S. domestic disappearance of 925 million pounds in 1970.

Crude cottonseed oil derived from glanded seed has a strong characteristic flavor and odor and a dark reddish brown color from the presence of the highly colored pigments extracted from the seed. It is the only vegetable oil produced on a commercial scale that contains gossypol, and this has caused the oil processors a number of technological problems. On the other hand, cottonseed oil has some favorable characteristics which have caused it to be popular with processors. In particular, it has good flavor stability properties and has a crystalline characteristic which makes it a preferred component both in shortening and margarine. However, because of its relatively higher price, it has gradually been replaced by soybean oil in these two applications. The principal market that has been retained by cottonseed oil in the United States is in salad and cooking oils. Thus in 1970, 550 million pounds of cottonseed oil were used in salad and cooking oils, 315 million pounds in shortening, 68 million pounds in margarine and 55 million pounds in other edible products.

Cottonseed oil is classified among the polyunsaturated vegetable oils. Its principal fatty acid is linoleic, which comprises about 47-50% of the total fatty acids. Its unique crystalline properties result from its containing about 26% of palmitic acid, principally attached to the alpha carbon of the glycerol moiety. Its good flavor qualities are generally ascribed to an absence of linolenic acid. Among the common vegetable oils it is unique in containing 1-3% of fatty acids having a cyclopropene ring, specifically malvalic and sterculic. It is now recognized that these cyclopropene acids were responsible for the positive Halphen test, which has been used to detect cottonseed oil for many years. Under experimental conditions cyclopropene fatty acids have been shown to have some undesirable physiological effects in a variety of experimental animals. There has been no demonstration that the quantities consumed in cottonseed oil have any adverse effect in human diets. Normal oil processing operations effect substantial reduction in the amount of cyclopropene fatty acids in cottonseed oil and with slight alterations could effect a total elimination if this proved to be necessary.

In order to convert crude cottonseed oil into margarine, shortening, and salad oil, a number of processes are necessary, chiefly to eliminate some of the natural materials that are extracted with the oil, but which have undesirable organoleptic and physiological properties. Principal among these are the pigments. Alkali refining techniques have been evolved which remove the pigments quite effectively from all except the most badly damaged oils. Alkali refining is followed by a further removal of pigments by adsorption on activated earths or carbons. After this adsorptive decolorization, traditionally called bleaching, the oil should be a clear light yellow color.

Refined cottonseed oil becomes cloudy at $40°-50°F$ and solid at a little below $32°F$. This is due to crystallization of the more saturated glycerides and is an unacceptable condition in salad oil and salad dressings, particularly mayonnaise. Therefore cottonseed oil intended for these purposes is subjected to a process called "winterizing." That is, the temperature of the oil is reduced to $38°-40°F$ and the glycerides which crystallize are separated from the liquid fraction. The crystalline fraction is referred to as stearine and the liquid fraction as winterized cottonseed salad oil. After steam stripping, called deodorization, the oil is ready for use in salad oils and salad dressings. Deodorization is commonly carried out by blowing steam through the oil at a temperature near $450°F$ under high vacuum. This removes odor and flavor-bearing substances which are present in very minute quantities and results in an oil which is essentially devoid of odor or flavor.

For use in shortening or margarine, cottonseed oil may be partly or completely hydrogenated. Chemically this involves addition of hydrogen to the double bonds of the unsaturated fatty acids. Commercially this requires highly purified hydrogen, an elevated temperature, and the presence of a catalyst, commonly reduced nickel. The catalyst is removed from the hydrogenated oil is an excel- Partially hydrogenated cottonseed oil is an excellent crystal stabilizer in margarine. Wholly hydrogenated cottonseed oil is a preferred crystal stabilizer for shortening and peanut butter. After hydrogenation the oil is deodorized.

Cottonseed Meal

Presently, cottonseed meal is the second most valuable product of cottonseed, accounting for 30-35% of the total product value. It is used principally as a feed for livestock as a source of protein supplement. When hulls are completely removed in the dehulling operation, cottonseed meal will contain substantially in excess of 50% protein. It is common practice to leave sufficient hulls with the kernels to produce a cottonseed meal containing 41% protein, principally for ruminant feeds.

Food Products

It has long been recognized that cottonseed meal is a potential source of a variety of nutritious, low cost protein food products. The presence of gossypol has been a major deterrent in this direct food utilization.

A food grade cottonseed flour has been marketed for several decades. This has been specially processed to minimize the toxicological properties of the gossypol. The necessary processing has darkened the cottonseed flour substantially which has restricted its range of usefulness. More recently similar gossypol-inactivated cottonseed flours have been used in blended food mixtures for infants, the most notable of which is Incaparina. Even with rather extensive support from national and international nutrition agencies, these products have enjoyed rather limited commercial success.

Two major technological breakthroughs have now largely eliminated gossypol as a barrier to the future success of cottonseed products in food. The first of these is the development of glandless cottonseed referred to above. The second is the mechanical separation of the pigment glands from the other components of cottonseed by gravity separation in a hexane dispersion. As noted previously, the pigment glands are able to remain intact under rather vigorous mechanical abuse and are not ruptured by hexane. Taking advantage of these properties and the fact that the pigment glands differ in density from the major protein bodies, a process has been developed by the Southern Regional Research Laboratory of USDA in which cottonseed kernels are disintegrated mechanically in hexane and the components fractionated by centrifugal action in a liquid cyclone. While the fractionation is not quantitative, over $1/2$ of the nonoil solids are recovered as a protein concentrate. This product, which is referred to as LCP flour, is a light cream color, contains about 65% protein, and less than 0.05% free gossypol.

Plants have been constructed for the production of LCP flour in Hubli, India and in Lubbock, Texas. Intensive investigations are under way in university, government, and industry laboratories on a wide variety of potential uses of LCP flour.

Glandless cottonseed kernels have been shown to have properties characteristic of nutmeats. When toasted, roasted, or fried, they have a pleasant flavor and texture and can be used either as a snack or as an ingredient in cookies, candies, etc.

The flour produced from glandless cottonseed has a very light cream color and contains in excess of 50% protein. It can be processed by solvent extraction to retain all of its inherent protein solubility and functional properties.

A number of protein products, including concentrates and isolates, have been produced experimentally from both LCP flour and from glandless cottonseed flour. These have exhibited properties which suggest they might find commercial use as whipping or gelling agents and as protein supplements in meat and bakery products as well as in carbonated beverages.

Scientists and technologists who have worked with cottonseed protein products are convinced that, because of their unique solubility properties, functional properties, and flavor quality, they will be used widely in foods in the future. During the next decade these convictions will be tested in the marketplace.

KARL F. MATTIL

References

ALTSCHUL, A. M. 1958. Processed Plant Protein Foodstuffs. Academic Press, New York.

ANON. 1966. Cottonseed and Its Products, 7th Edition. National Cottonseed Products Association, Memphis.

SWERN, D. 1964. Bailey's Industrial Oil and Fat Products, 3rd Edition. Interscience Publishers Div., John Wiley & Sons, New York.

U.S. Dept. of Agr. 1965. Proc. Conf. Cottonseed Protein Concentrates. USDA Agr. Res. Serv. ARS-72-38, Apr.

U.S. Dept. of Agr. 1969. Proc. Conf. Protein-Rich Food Products from Oilseeds. USDA Agr. Res. Serv. ARS-72-71, May.

U.S. Dept. of Agr. 1971. Proc. Twentieth Oilseed Processing Clinic. USDA Agr. Res. Serv. ARS-72-93, Nov.

Cross-reference: *Fats and Oils.*

CRAB PROCESSING

In general, there are four major crab fisheries in the United States. These are the Blue Crab fishery of the Middle and Southern Atlantic, the King crab fishery of Alaska, the Dungeness crab fishery in the Northern Pacific, and the Tanner crab fishery in the Northern Pacific and Canadian Maritimes.

Other minor crab fisheries include the Jonah and Rock crab fisheries in New England and the Stone crab fishery in the South Atlantic. Although there are many similarities, the catching, handling, and processing of crabs all vary with the different species. For this reason each species will be treated separately.

Blue Crab

The blue crab (*Callinectes sapidus*) represents the largest and oldest crab fishery in the United States. As early as 1635, blue crabs were fished commercially in Chesapeake Bay. In 1970, blue crab landings totaled 142 million pounds valued at 10 million dollars with the 4 states of Maryland, Virginia, North Carolina, and Florida accounting for about 80% of the landings.

The blue crab, a shallow water species, is harvested by means of wire pots and baited trot lines during the summer months and with dredges during the winter when the crabs are dormant. The crabs are handled in barrels or bushel baskets alive.

During unloading the crabs are sorted according to size and the "peeler" crabs are set aside. The "peelers" are crabs ready to molt. These crabs are held in live tanks under close supervision until they shed, after which time they are immediately removed from the tanks, killed, and eviscerated. The crabs are then washed and packed in seaweed for fresh shipment, or individually wrapped in cellophane or parchment for the frozen market.

The larger "hard" crabs are usually sold as live shell stock and the smaller crabs processed for meat.

For meat removal, the crabs must be cooked prior to the picking operation. Although cooking is somewhat variable throughout the industry, in recent years all the larger producers cook crabs in large vertical or horizontal retorts under 15 lb pressure for 10–15 min. After cooking, the retort baskets are sprayed with cold water and placed in refrigerated rooms overnight.

Blue crab meat processing is primarily a hand picking operation. A few picking machines have been developed, but none are in wide-spread use. The only automation widely used in the industry is the "Harris Extractor" which is primarily a hammer mill joined to a brine flotation system. This machine is almost exclusively used for claw meat production.

Meat yield from blue crabs can vary considerably. The physical condition of the crabs and seasonal variations are important considerations. As a whole, the industry averages about 12% meat yield on a live weight basis; however, yields as low as 10% and as high as 16% are possible.

The picked meat is divided into three basic categories: lump meat, broken lump meat, and regular or flake meat. This division is carried out by the pickers as they pick the meat directly into the labeled can. The lump meat, which is the large muscle controlling the swimming legs of the crab, represents about 25% of the yield and is the most valued product. Broken lump meat which is next in value represents lump meat which was not removed intact and larger sections of muscle that can be removed from the body. The regular or flake meat is the remainder of the body meat. Claw meat, which is picked separately either by hand or machine is the least valuable product.

Most meat is sold fresh in cans with snap-on lids. A heat-pasteurization process is being successfully used by the industry to extend shelf-life (Bird 1951; Tatro 1970). In this process, the meat, in hermetically sealed cans, is processed in hot water to an internal temperature of 180°F for 3 min. A shelf-life of up to 6 months at 33°F is possible with this process. Because of the seasonality of the raw material, pasteurization is being used to a much greater degree in the past few years.

Blue crab meat frozen by conventional means does not freeze and store well. After a few weeks of frozen storage the meat becomes fibrous, watery, and loses much of its natural flavor. For this reason only very small amounts are frozen and most of this meat is for institutional use in crab specialty products. Recent work on freezing, however, has shown that a reduced precook combined with cryogenic freezing produces a highly acceptable product through six months of storage (Ampola 1971; Strasser 1971).

King Crab

King crabs (*Paralithodes camtschatica*) were first fished commercially just prior to World War II and shortly thereafter became one of the most rapidly expanding fisheries in the United States. From a catch of 1.5 million pounds in 1950, the Alaska fishery peaked at an average annual catch of 117.5 million between 1964 and 1968. Since then the catch has declined from the results of overfishing. To conserve the resource, 1970 regulations required a six-month closure of certain grounds and severe quotas in most areas. As a result, the 1970 catch was 51.9 million pounds valued at 13.8 million dollars.

During the early years of the U.S. king crab fishery, trawls and tangle nets were the principal gear employed. Tangle nets were outlawed in 1955 and trawls were restricted to offshore waters. As a result, the primary method of catching is by means of large pots. After catching, the crabs are held live on the vessel in sea water tanks. At dockside the crabs are transferred to live holding tanks to await processing.

The king crab is butchered before cooking. The operators break the crab over a stationary iron blade which removes the carapace and cuts the crab into two sections. The viscera and blood are removed from the sections by means of rotating brushes and the sections are thoroughly washed prior to cooking.

Two cooking methods are employed in the industry. The first is a 1-stage cook of about 20 min in seawater at 212°F. The second method consists of a 2-stage cook of 10 min in fresh water at 165°F, followed by meat removal, and a second cook of about 10 min in dilute brine (approx 3%) (Dassow 1968). After cooking, the sections are cooled in chilled water and inspected. At this point the large leg sections suitable for freezing are culled out and the remainder are processed for meat removal.

The meat from the shoulders and claws is removed either by shaking or by water jets. The legs are separated at the joints and the meat is squeezed out by passing them through rubber rollers much like the old washing machine wringers. Total meat yield averages about 20% on a live weight basis.

After picking, the meats are washed and inspected for cartilage and shell material. The meat is then packed in block molds and plate frozen, usually with 10% added water for glazing and to eliminate air pockets.

After the blocks are completely frozen they are cut by means of band saws and packaged for sale. Cooked legs and whole cooked crabs with the viscera removed are blast frozen and glazed for both institutional and retail markets.

Dungeness Crab

The Dungeness crab (*Cancer magister*) fishery is primarily in the area between Southeastern Alaska and San Francisco. This crab is one of the largest edible crabs in the United States, reaching widths up to 9 in. across the back. With the decline of the king crab fishery, the Dungeness crab industry is expanding. In 1970, landings of Dungeness were 58.7 million pounds valued at 13.9 million dollars, a record catch.

Dungeness crabs are harvested primarily by means of circular iron pots. The crabs are held live on the vessel in sea water wells.

Both whole crabs and butchered crab sections are cooked. The butchering operation is essentially similar to the method described previously for king crab. The crab sections are cooked for 10–15 min in either fresh or salt water at 212°F. Whole uneviscerated crabs require a slightly longer cook of 20–25 min. After cooking, the crabs are rapidly chilled in either fresh or salt water (Dassow 1968).

The meat is removed by hand operation. The body sections and the upper leg sections are vigorously struck against the side of a stainless steel tray. Care is taken to avoid breaking the meat in the upper leg sections since these large pieces demand a premium price. After picking, the meat is treated by brine flotation to remove shell and cartilage. This is carried out by placing the meat in a tank of saturated brine and stirring slightly to allow the shell pieces to sink to the bottom. The meat, which floats to the top of the tank, is washed with a fresh water spray to reduce the salt content and inspected. Prior to packing, many processors treat the crab meat in a citric acid dip to help retain quality during storage.

The meats are packaged in cans or formed into blocks and blast or plate frozen. Cooked whole eviscerated crabs are both blast frozen and brine frozen for institutional and retail use. Brine freezing is carried out by dipping the crabs into circulating brine at −15°F for about 45 min. After freezing takes place, the crabs are removed from the brine and dipped into fresh water to remove excess salt and to provide a glaze on the surface of the crab. These products are packaged in flexible film bags for the retail market.

Tanner Crab

The Tanner crab (*Chionoectes tanneri*) fishery is a relatively new fishery established because of the decline in the king crab industry. This crab, marketed as "snow" crab, is harvested in both North Atlantic and North Pacific waters by the same methods used for king crab. The total U.S. catch in 1961 was only 7000 lb valued at $1000. In 1970, a record catch of 15.5 million pounds valued at 1.7 million dollars was landed at Alaskan ports. All North Atlantic landings are in the Canadian Maritime provinces, primarily New Brunswick.

The tanner crab is butchered and cleaned using the same procedures as in the king crab industry. The cooked sections are picked by shaking, and brine flotation is used to remove cartilage and shell. Most of the meat is formed into blocks for freezing. The remainder is canned in 6- to 8-oz units for the retail market. Most canners use dilute brine and citric acid as additives in the can in order to improve the color and flavor of the end product.

Rock Crab and Jonah Crab

The Rock crab (*Cancer Irroratus*) called the sand crab by the local industry is a minor fishery located only in New England, although the species ranges from Nova Scotia to the South Atlantic. The Jonah crab (*Cancer borealis*) is found along the same range in slightly deeper water. These crabs have not been exploited commercially and are only landed incidental to the lobster fishery, primarily in Maine. Maine landings of these species combined in 1970 were 1.6 million pounds valued at $90,000. Because of the high value of lobsters, most fishermen and dealers feel that handling the lesser-valued crabs is not worth the time and effort. However, both species appear to be abundant, and recently there has been much more interest in this fishery as a potential industry.

Most of the catch of these species is marketed locally alive or fresh whole cooked. There are only 3 or 4 plants in Maine producing meat from these species, and most of the meat available in markets or local stores is picked and packed by the families of the lobstermen. Usually, the crabs are boiled live for about 20 min. The pickers separate the upper leg segments and scrape some meat out of the body where the legs connect. The upper leg sections are picked by striking the leg with a mallet to crack the shell along the length of the section. The meat from this section is then removed intact. The body meat and the leg meat are held separately and packed with whole leg pieces on the top and bottom of the package with body meat in the center.

Stone Crab

The Stone crab (*Menippe mercenaria*) is found all along the South Atlantic and Gulf coasts although the industry is located primarily in Florida. Total U.S. landings of stone crab in 1970 were 1.6 million pounds valued at $839,000. The meat yield from the body of this crab is small; however, the two large claws are highly prized. For this reason, the usual practice of the fisherman is to break off the claws and then return the crab to the water. Not much is known about the survival rate of crabs treated in this manner, but it is well-known that crabs are able to grow new claws.

Red Crab

Although at present there is no commercial fishery for deep sea red crab (*Geryon quinquedens*), its commercial potential makes it worthy of mention (Holmsen 1968). The red crab is relatively large and has been found in abundant quantities from Maine to South America in deep water ranging from 600 to 3000 ft deep. Exploratory fishing carried out by National Marine Fisheries Service using king crab and lobster pots has shown commercial quantities of this species ranging between 1200 and 3000 ft. At present, the major obstacle to commercial fishing for red crab is the high capital cost for boats and equipment. Large refrigerated trawlers with specialized deep water potting gear would be a requirement for this fishery.

ROBERT J. LEARSON

References

AMPOLA, V. G. and LEARSON, R. J. 1971. A new approach to the freezing preservation of blue crab. Presented at 13th Congr. Refrig., Intern. Inst. Refrig., Washington, D.C.

BIRD, C. J. 1951. Method of keeping the meat of shellfish in a fresh condition. U.S. Pat. 2,546,428, March.

DASSOW, J. A. 1968. Crabs and lobsters. In The Freezing Preservation of Foods, 4th Edition, Vol. 3. D. K. Tressler, W. B. Van Arsdel, and M. J. Copley (Editors). Avi Publishing Co., Westport, Conn.

HOLMSEN, A. 1968. The commercial potential of the deep sea red crab. In Commercial Fisheries Research and Development Act Project Investigation of the Deep Sea Red Crab. Ann. Rept. U.S. Dept. Interior, Bur. Commercial Fisheries, June 28.

STRASSER, J. H., LENNON, J. S., and KING, F. J. 1971. Blue crab meat. 1. Preservation by freezing. II. Effect of chemical treatments on acceptability. U.S. Dept. Com. Natl. Marine Fisheries Serv. Sci. Rept. 630.

TATRO, M. C. 1970. Guidelines for pasteurizing meat from the blue crab. 1. Water bath method. Natural Resources Inst., Univ. Maryland, Contribution 419.

Cross-reference: Shellfish.

CRACKER TECHNOLOGY

See Biscuit and Cracker Technology.

CRANBERRIES

Cranberries (Vaccinium macrocarpum L.) were one of the native North American fruits in use by Indians at the time of the first contacts by European explorers. The traditional cranberry sauce is as old as the first celebration of Thanksgiving by the Indians and Pilgrims in Massachusetts. Since the bushes grow in acid bogs, the major production is situated in Massachusetts, New Jersey, Wisconsin, Oregon, and Washington. The total production has risen in the past 15 yr from 50,000 tons to about 70,000–80,000 tons. By improved cultivation practices and selection of varieties, the yields per acre have improved from an average of 2 tons to about 5 tons. Something over 20,000 acres are planted to cultivated cranberries. In Massachusetts the principal variety is Early Black, with Howes a poor second. In Wisconsin and the Pacific Northwest, McFarlin dominates the market; the Searls variety is grown in Wisconsin and the Stevens is a new variety showing promise in the West. About 30% of the crop is marketed fresh and the remainder is processed by freezing or canning as sauce or juice.

The price to growers has risen from about $8.00 per barrel (100 lb) in the mid-1950's to $16.00 in the late 1960's. The total value of the U.S. crop has increased from $12,000,000 to $30,000,000 over the same time period.

Some cranberries are still picked by hand, but in most areas the harvest is accelerated by use of hand scoops or rakes. A number of completely mechanical devices have been used, including a vacuum suction device, a dry scooping machine, and a water-reel or "egg beater" machine. The dry harvesting machines tend to damage the vines more than the equipment used in flooded bogs. If harvested wet, the berries must be dried to prevent spoilage in storage. Upon reaching the warehouse, the berries must be cleaned and sorted. From here they may be held in controlled temperature storage for future processing or may go directly to the canning or freezing operations.

Cranberries for freezing may undergo additional inspections to remove debris, defects, or spoiled fruit. Large quantities are frozen in bulk for later processing into sauce, juice, or jelly. They maintain quality in frozen storage at $0°F$ ($-18°C$) better than most fruits.

Although canned sauce or jelly was the principal preserved product for many years, the growth in sales of cranberry juice, blends with other juices, and "cocktails" has been steadily upward in recent years. Sauce production has leveled off at about 3.5 million cases (24 No. 2 1/2 cans). The attractive color, their tartness to pep up bland juices, and the nutritive contents of vitamins A and C are attributes which have helped to increase consumption.

FRANK P. BOYLE

CRUESS, WILLIAM V., AWARD

See Awards.

CURRANTS (BLACK, RED, WHITE) AND GOOSEBERRIES

Most all types of currants are used for making jams and jellies. All of them, as well as the gooseberry, belong to the genus *Ribes* of the rose family. Some varieties, such as Zante, are dried like raisins and have a rather small market in the United States; the total world production of dried currants is a little over 100,000 tons, most of which come from Greece. Black currant juice and beverages are very popular in Europe, because of flavor and high ascorbic acid content. However, the European black currant, and to a lesser extent other currants and gooseberries, are restricted by federal or state regulations which prohibit planting because these species are alternate hosts for white pine blister rust.

For jam and jelly products, the fruit is cleaned, washed, sorted, and stemmed, and then frozen in bulk containers for subsequent processing. Baldwin, Kenny, and Saunders varieties of black currants are recommended; Red Lake, Wilder, London Market, Perfection, Red Cross, and Stephen's No. 9 are good red currant varieties; White Imperial and White Grape have possibilities among the white currants; Downing, Poorman, and Oregon are major commercial varieties of gooseberries. In recent years about 1,500,000 lb of currants of all types have been frozen, and gooseberries have varied from 300,000 to 1,000,000 lb.

For those interested in preparing currants and gooseberries for freezing, a detailed description is to be found in Boyle and Wolford (1968).

FRANK P. BOYLE

Reference

BOYLE, F. P., and WOLFORD, E. R. 1968. The preparation for freezing and freezing of fruits. *In* The Freezing Preservation of Foods, Vol. 3, 4th Edition. Avi Publishing Co., Westport, Conn.

D

DATES

The date palm (*Phoenix dactylifera L.*) is one of the oldest of cultivated tree fruits, with its origin in prehistoric times and records indicating culture as early as 3000 B.C. in the Near East and North Africa. The first commercial plantings in the United States occurred about 1900 when offshoots of superior varieties from North Africa were planted in the Salt River Valley of Arizona and the Coachella Valley of California. At present there are something over 4500 acres of date gardens in California and about 200 acres in Arizona. The production of dates (dry basis) varies from year to year due to climate, culture, and pollination, but has remained in the 15,000- to 26,000-ton range for the past 15 yr. Imports mainly from the Near East have averaged around 16,000 tons annually over the same period. The value of the U.S. crop ranges from $2,000,000 to $4,000,000 depending on production, carryover, exports, etc. More than 75% of the dates grown in the United States are the Deglet Noor variety, followed by Zahidi, Halawy, and Khadrawy which, together, make up another 10% of the production.

Since date palms are dioecious, the female trees must be dusted with pollen collected from male trees. This can be done by hand, by blowers from the ground, or by helicopters. The pollinated flowers are covered by paper bags to protect the developing fruit from rain; and, for optimum size and yield, most bunches are thinned by cutting out some of the strands of the female clusters. Several pickings per year by hand has been practiced for many years, so that the majority of the fruit picked is in a "natural" condition and does not require further drying or hydrating. Mechanical aids to picking consist of hydraulically operated towers to raise men to the level of the bunches (sometimes 50 ft or more in older gardens) so that entire bunches may be cut and lowered to the ground. Shakers on the ground separate the individual fruits from the bunches and these are packed in boxes or bins for transport to the packinghouse.

At the packinghouse the dates are fumigated immediately to kill insects and microorganisms, usually with about 1 lb of methyl bromide per 1000 cu ft of volume in the fumigation house. Next the dates are cleaned either by dry methods using shaker screens, blowers, and vacuum or by rinsing with water followed by drying. Grading consists of sorting out culls, sizing, and separating into lots of uniform maturity or moisture content. Most of this is done by hand, but a few of the operations such as sizing and moisture classification can be done with mechanical equipment if the operation is large enough. Artificial ripening at higher temperatures (80°-120°F) with controlled humidity can be used to upgrade the immature fruit which has been separated. For fruit that is too high in moisture content, dehydration may be used to prevent spoilage and to prolong shelf-life. Hydration to higher moisture levels is used for those dates which are too hard or too dry. Dates at more than 25% moisture are subject to spoilage by microorganisms unless some kind of preservative is added. Storage at low temperatures extends the shelf-life of most dates.

Although dates are mainly sold as dried fruit, they may be canned or frozen. Date paste, diced dates, and other forms are used in the manufacture of baked goods, confections, ice cream, and similar products. A great amount of research on quality, composition, browning, sugar inversion, and processing has been published by the Pasadena Laboratory, Western Marketing and Nutrition Research Division, U.S. Department of Agriculture, at 263 So. Chester Avenue, Pasadena, Calif.

Since the dry flesh of ripe dates is composed of 75-80% sugar, the principal flavor is sweetness. In the dry varieties such as Deglet Noor the sugar is mostly sucrose, while the moist varieties contain invert sugar (glucose and fructose). The natural tannins of dates and the enzymatic and Maillard browning which take place during normal storage

280

impart a brown color and a somewhat caramelized flavor. At 140°F or so a reddish-brown color as well as astringency and off-flavors occur in Deglet Noor dates (Maier *et al.* 1964). The same workers had developed earlier a process for optimum color, flavor, and texture by controlling the moisture content and temperature (Maier and Metzler 1961). Dates are classified as a good source of iron and potassium, a fair source of calcium, a good source of nicotinic acid, and a fair source of vitamins A, B_1, and B_2.

FRANK P. BOYLE

References

BOLIN, H. R., FORREY, R., and BOYLE, F. P. 1972. Effectiveness and stability of various antimicrobial agents on dates. (Unpublished).

COGGINS, C., and KNAPP, J. 1969. Growth, development, and softening of Deglet Noor date fruit. Date Growers Inst. Rept. *46*, 11–14.

HASEGAWA, S., and SMOLENSKY, DORA C. 1970. Date invertase: Properties and activity associated with maturation. Agr. Food Chem. *18*, 902–904.

HUXSOLL, C., and REZNICK, D. 1969. Sorting and processing mechanically harvested dates. Date Growers Inst. Rept. *46*, 8–10.

MAIER, V. P., and METZLER, D. M. 1961. Sucrose inversion in Deglet Noor dates and its processing applications. Date Growers Inst. Rept. *38*, 5–8.

MAIER, V. P., and METZLER, D. M. 1969. Phenolic constituents of the date (*Phoenix dactylifera*) and their relation to browning. Proc. 1st Intern. Cong. Food Sci. Technol.

MAIER, V. P., METZLER, D. M., and HUBER, A. M. 1964. Effects of heat processing on the properties of dates. Date Growers Inst. Rept. *41*, 8–9.

NIXON, R. W. 1959. Growing dates in the United States. USDA Agr. Res. Serv. Agr. Inform. Bull. *207*.

DDT

DDT (1,1,1-trichloro-2,2-bis(*p*-chlorophenyl) ethane) was the first synthetic organic compound to be used on a large scale for insect control. DDT was first synthesized in 1874 by the reaction of chloral hydrate with chlorobenzene in the presence of fuming sulfuric acid. This reaction produces about 85% of the *o,p'*-isomer with about 10% of the *o,p*-isomer and 5% of the *o,o'*-isomer as side products. The purified *p,p'*-isomer of DDT is a crystalline solid melting at 108.5°–109°C. *p,p'*-DDT is readily soluble in acetone, benzene, cyclohexanone, ethyl ether, and carbon tetrachloride. It has a water solubility at 25°C of 1.7 parts per billion. The vapor pressure of *p,p'*-DDT is 3.7×10^{-7} mm of Hg at 25°C.

Since 1945, DDT has been used as an insecticide on agricultural crops. During the period 1945–1970, almost 4 billion pounds of DDT isomers have been used for insect control. DDT is relatively stable in the environment and can be found by sensitive analytical methods, such as gas chromatography and mass spectrometry, in almost any material sampled (including most foods). There has been no demonstrable effect related to the accumulation of DDT residues in human body fat (where the DDT residue content averages 12 ppm in the fatty tissues of persons living in economically developed countries), but evidence is well documented for the harmful effects of DDT residues on wildlife. The untoward effect of residues derived from DDT [occurring largely as DDE (1,1-dichloro-2,2-bis-(*p*-chlorophenyl) ethene) and TDE, also known as DDD, (1,1-dichloro-2,2-bis-(*p*-chlorophenyl) ethane)], on algae, marine life, salt and fresh water fish, and birds has led to a general recommendation to eliminate within 2 yr (from 1970) all uses of DDT and DDD in the United States, excepting those uses essential to the preservation of human health and welfare and approved unanimously by the Secretaries of the Departments of Health, Education, and Welfare, Agriculture, and Interior. Presently, approval comes from the Administrator of the U.S. Environmental Protection Agency.

For many years DDT and DDD were registered for use by USDA on a large number of fiber, fruit, and vegetable commodities. The FDA established tolerances for residues of DDT of 7 ppm on the raw agricultural commodity for many food crops. In 1970 many of the tolerance levels were reduced to 1 ppm on or in vegetables. The tolerance levels are based on studies of the toxicology of DDT in experimental animals (the acute LD_{50} for orally administered DDT in male rats is 217 mg per kg of body weight; the corresponding values reported for DDE and DDD are 880 and 4000, respectively). Long-term feeding studies are also required before tolerances can be established. The feeding tests are continued through several generations of test animals and part of the experimental group are sacrificed for histological examination to exclude possible carcinogenic, mutagenic, or teratogenic activity due to the compound under test.

In 1968 and 1969 DDT residue in excess of 10 ppm were found in samples of fresh water fish, especially in coho salmon taken from Lake Michigan. The DDT residues found their way into the fish tissue through various organisms in the food chain. It was necessary for FDA to establish an interim tolerance of 5 ppm for DDT residues in fish used in commercial channels as fresh market, frozen, or canned material. Almost all reports of DDT residue levels in ocean-derived seafood have been below the 5 ppm tolerance.

DDT residue tolerances established by FDA apply to the raw agricultural commodity. Food products preserved by canning, freezing, dehydration, or irradiation are not specifically mentioned in the regulations listing the tolerances. The Federal Food, Drug and Cosmetic Act provides that no action will be taken against a processed food if the residues are within tolerance and if the pesticide compounds have been removed to the extent possible in good manufacturing practice.

Considerable research has been conducted to determine the effect of various unit operations in food preparation and preservation on reduction of DDT residue levels below the permitted tolerances. For example, water washing of tomatoes and spinach removes 91 and 48% of DDT, respectively. Use of surface active agents during water washing increases the extent of DDT residue removal from spinach to 73%. Water washing, followed by blanching, removes 60% of DDT residues from spinach; blanching alone removes 50% of DDT residues from green beans. Chemical peeling (using 3–15% sodium hydroxide solutions) of fruits and vegetables accomplishes extensive reduction of DDT residue levels, e.g., 99% for tomatoes and 90–94% for potatoes. The thermal process used for canned, low acid, foods results in a partial conversion of DDT to DDD and DDE (as well as other, as yet, unidentified products).

The methodology for the determination of DDT residues in foods in complex and requires special equipment. The recognized method of analysis is that given in the *Guide to the Analysis of Pesticide Residues*, U.S. Department of Health, Education and Welfare, Washington, D.C., Vol. I and II, 1965. The two principal methods used for the final analysis of extracts prepared from food samples suspected of containing DDT residues are microcoulometric detection gas chromatography and electron capture detection gas chromatography.

The great effectiveness of DDT against the body louse, the vector of typhus, led to an announcement by Prime Minister Winston Churchill in 1944 which stated "the excellent DDT powder, which has been fully experimented with and found to yield astonishing results, will henceforth be used on a great scale by the British forces in Burma and by the American and Australian forces in the Pacific and Indian theaters . . ." It now seems that Sir Winston's statement about the excellence of DDT (for the discovery of which Paul Muller of Switzerland received the Nobel Prize in Medicine and Physiology in 1948) was not based on full experimentation and its future use must be carefully controlled. The major place in history for DDT may be as the first synthetic material of unquestioned utility which caused unexpected problems in the total environment and made scientists aware that every new chemical must be evaluated on a total systems basis.

JACK W. RALLS

DEHYDRATION

Dehydration or drying is the process of reversibly removing water from a material so that the storage life is extended by the prevention of microbial growth. Although the two terms are often used synonomously, drying usually refers to the removal of water by natural agencies such as sun or dry wind, and dehydration to mechanical methods. The major exception to this is the term "freeze drying." In this review only dehydration processes carried out under controlled conditions will be discussed.

The preservation of foodstuffs involves not only the inhibition of microbial growth, but also the preservation of color, texture, flavor, and nutrient value, so that it is necessary to control the processes carefully in order to prevent thermal degradation of the product. The level of moisture required to prevent microbial growth is usually less than 10% whereas that for prevention of biochemical deterioration is much lower, less than 5%. The main advantages of dehydrated food products are (1) they can be stored at ambient temperature when suitably packed; (2) there is a considerable saving in storage space, which affects transport and packaging; and (3) they are convenient to use, since the preparation and cooking has already been achieved.

Although, historically, dehydration is probably the oldest form of preservation, considerable research is at present being carried out to improve the reconstitution properties of dried products as well as to formulate new products.

Physical Principles

Scientifically, dehydration involves simultaneous heat transfer and moisture diffusion (mass trans fer). The conversion of liquid (or solid in the case of freeze drying) to vapor demands the supply of latent heat to the product; this can be achieved by a variety of methods: conduction by contact with a heated metal plate, convection from a heated gas (usually air), radiation from an infrared source, or by microwave energy. The process may be accelerated by the application of vacuum.

Factors Affecting the Rate of Drying.—The most important requirement for the food processor is that the rate of drying be as rapid as possible provided that the product quality is maintained at a high level. A study of the basic mechanisms involved in any dehydration process is invaluable, since this knowledge often leads to advantageous redesign of the process or suitable alteration of the processing conditions. Similarly, the study of the rate of drying on a small scale employing widely varying conditions is essential before the design of large-scale plants can be undertaken.

The main factors which affect the rate of drying and the time of the drying cycle are: (a) physical properties of the product; (b) geometrical arrangement of product in relation to heat transfer surface or medium; (c) physical properties of drying environment; and (d) characteristics of the drying equipment.

Physical Properties of the Product.—The main aspects to be considered here are particle size and geometry. Any theoretical formula for drying time must incorporate a term expressing the fact that the thicker the product the longer the time it will take for moisture to be removed. The migration of moisture from inside a particle to the surroundings is controlled either by internal migration of moisture to the surface or diffusion of moisture from the surface to the atmosphere. In general the chief factor controlling the rate of mass transfer is the migration of the water within the sample and through the dried surface. The diffusion away from the surface is usually rapid and may be accelerated by either applying vacuum (i.e., increasing the water vapor pressure differential) or by blowing dry air over the surface. It is, however, restricted by excessive loading on the drying trays, when the diffusion and movement of water vapor between particles becomes restricted. With solid food products the size and shape are predetermined by the product requirements and it is often not possible to reduce the drying time—whole carrots, for example. However, with liquid products rapid rates of drying may be obtained by using sprays of fine droplets as in spray drying. The effect of temperature and heat transfer within the products must also be taken into account.

It is generally observed with many products that initial rate of drying is constant and then the rate decreases, sometimes at two different rates (see Fig. D-1). The drying curve is divided into the constant rate period and falling rate period areas as these represent different mechanisms of drying. The constant rate period indicates that excess surface moisture is being removed and the falling rate periods indicate the progressive receding of the interface between dry material and wet material.

Several internal mechanisms of moisture transfer have been suggested: (a) laminar viscous flow of water vapor (Poiseuille flow) would be expected to cause the permeability to vary inversely with temperature; (b) capillary flow processes in which surface tension, density, and viscosity are im-

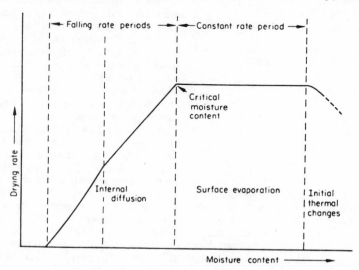

FIG. D-1. IDEALIZED CURVE FOR DRYING RATE

portant; (c) thermal diffusion which requires large temperature gradients to be effective; (d) vapor diffusion would be expected to cause the diffusion coefficient to vary with square root of the temperature cubed; (e) surface diffusion; and (f) molecular diffusion (Knudsen flow) would be expected to cause the diffusion coefficient to vary with square root of the temperature. However, most results are interpreted either in terms of a capillary flow process or, alternatively, vapor diffusion process. The former is obviously applicable to the drying of particles and granules and the latter most appropriate to the drying of foodstuffs.

For food products, the second falling rate period is longer than the first and has the greater effect on the overall rate. The constant rate period is usually very short unless there is an excessive amount of surface water or, alternatively, the drying capacity of the air is very low.

For the falling rate period, when liquid diffusion is controlling, equation (1) applies to a slab of thickness $2L$ with diffusion from the opposite faces.

$$\frac{W - W_e}{W_o - W_e} = \frac{8}{\pi^2} \left[e^{-b} + \frac{e^{-9b}}{9} + \frac{e^{-25b}}{25} + \cdots \right]$$

$$(1)$$

where W = average moisture content (dry basis) at any time θ

W_o = average moisture content at start of the diffusional period $\theta = O$

W_e = the average moisture content when the sample is in equilibrium with the surroundings

$b = D\theta\pi^2/4L^2$

where D = is the liquid diffusivity

L = the half thickness of the sample

The equation also applies to an initially uniform moisture distribution. If θ is large then

$$\frac{W - W_e}{W_o - W_e} = \frac{8}{\pi^2} e^{-D\theta\pi^2/4L^2}$$

and the drying rate

$$\frac{dW}{d\theta} = -\frac{\pi^2 D(W_e - W)}{4L^2}$$

Thus the drying rate for materials requiring large drying times is proportional to the square of the thickness of sample when diffusion controls.

The falling rate equation for coarse or granular materials in which migration of water between particles is occurring has been shown to give a linear relationship between rate of drying and thickness

of product. Thus, a relatively easy test can be applied to determine the broad differences in mechanism.

Geometrical Arrangement of Product.—The important factor here is to determine the effect of tray loading (i.e., of the depth of particles in a layer) on the time for drying. The lower the tray loading and the greater distances between the particles the shorter the drying time and the more uniform the product. However, to achieve reasonable throughputs in practice it is necessary to load the trays on the conveyor to a reasonable depth. In practice it is usual to attempt to have the same weight of material on each tray and to have a uniform thickness of particles. The nature of the product also has to be considered, since there is always a possibility of damage or adhesion with softer products. With granular materials which are themselves porous it is necessary to consider the restriction to flow of water from the particles by the bulk packing.

Physical Properties of the Drying Environment.— Temperature, humidity, and velocity of the air being used for drying have a predominant effect on the rate of drying and on the economics of the process. The combined effect of humidity and temperature of air is determined by the psychrometric relationship and is obtained by measuring the wet bulb temperature (adiabatic saturation temperature for water). The drying rate has been shown to be proportional to the wet bulb depression for a number of food products. However, when the relative humidity of the air is less than about 40% the rate of drying is often independent of wet bulb depression.

The dry bulb temperature of the air has considerable effect on the rate of drying at low moistures but not at high, that is, below 0.1% moisture content measured as pounds of water per pound of dry product. At these low moisture levels the cooling effect of evaporation is very small and consequently the heat is utilized in the internal redistribution of moisture. The limiting temperatures are determined by the biochemical changes which will cause the development of off-flavors and discoloration.

The effect of air velocity on the rate of drying is complex. For individual particles the rate of initial drying period is proportional to $v^{0.7} - v^{0.8}$, where v is the velocity. This corresponds to evaporation from a free water surface; but as the drying proceeds the effect is reduced. This assumes that radiation and conduction are absent, since these processes reduce the effect of varying the air velocity. The rate of drying for air flow (a) parallel to the surface of the product is proportional to $G^{0.8}$ and (b) perpendicular to the surface is proportional to $G^{0.27}$ and the constants of proportionality 0.01 and 0.37, respectively where G is the mass velocity of the gas in pounds of total gas per hour per square foot. These are applicable for the range of G = 500–6000 lb/hr/ft^2 and H = 800–4000 lb/hr/ft^2 respectively.

There are, of course, limitations to the gas velocity which can conveniently be used. The rate of heat transfer is controlled by the thickness of the laminar boundary layer. This decreases with increasing velocity until a point is reached when increasing the velocity further produces no significant increase in heat transfer. Consequently, there is a limitation on the velocity of the air used for drying. A second limitation is an economic one, since power requirements for blowers are proportional to the cube of the velocity. Thus, there is little incentive to use velocities which are higher than necessary.

By increasing the velocity, however, the average humidity in the drying area is substantially reduced and consequently there is a higher moisture gradient between the product and the drying atmosphere which accelerates the drying operation.

Dry heated air is not the only fluid medium that can be used for dehydration; superheated steam is also a possibility. It has been shown that greater drying rates and thermal efficiencies are possible when drying with superheated steam than with air. Although the temperatures involved are very high it is claimed that potato slices have been successfully dried.

The use of solvents, e.g., ethyl acetate, which produced azeotropic mixtures with water, has also been reported for dehydrating fruit as well as osmotic methods involving high concentration solutions of sugar.

Characteristics of Drying Equipment.—The rate of drying is also affected by the geometrical arrangement of the equipment and in particular by the method of containing or supporting the product. These aspects will be considered individually.

Dehydration Processes

Tunnel Dryers.—The tunnel dehydrator is by far one of the most flexible systems which is in commercial use. In its simplest form it consists of a rectangular tunnel that will accommodate trucks containing the trays on which the product to be dried is uniformly spread. The dimensions of these systems vary greatly, depending on the capacity of the plant, but a typical plant for dehydrating carrots at a rate of 75 tons per day would consist of 4 single-stage tunnels about 54 ft in length, 6¼ ft wide and 7 ft high which would contain 14 trucks. The air would be directed in a counterflow direction and would reach a temperature of 160°F (approx), 90°F wet bulb at the unloading end. The air velocities vary in practice from 600 to 1200 linear feet per minute.

The tunnel system is essentially a continuous one in which the trucks gradually enter one by one and are similarly removed at a constant rate when equilibrium conditions are established.

Tunnel driers are usually classified by the direction in which the air traverses the product and several arrangements will now be mentioned.

Single-Stage Parallel Flow.—The 'wet' material encounters initially the driest and warmest air and leaves the dryer at the coolest end. This means that high rates of evaporation are achieved initially and there is little danger of overheating the product, since the surface temperature of the food is below the dry bulb temperature. This results from the fact that during the process of moisture loss heat is removed by the evaporation process. The product is also protected in the latter stages of drying since it comes into contact with progressively cooler air and this is accompanied by a decrease in the drying rate. However, this has the ultimate disadvantage that very low moisture contents cannot be achieved irrespective of length of tunnel. Commercial plants based on single-stage parallel flow are operated mainly for drying grapes; however, they are usually used in combination with counterflow principles.

Single-Stage Countercurrent Flow.—The alternative method of circulating the air is to direct it in the opposite direction to the movement of the product so that the dry product leaving the drier encounters the hot and dry air entering the system. Thus the 'wet' product is initially exposed to very slow drying conditions. However, provided precautions are taken not to overheat the product, ultimately it has a lower moisture content. Countercurrent processes are generally recognized to be more economical to operate and they are widely used for commercial production, especially with dried vegetables. A particularly important problem involves the shrinkage of the product using countercurrent rather than parallel flow. The result is that the former gives a material of relatively high density and slow reconstitution properties whereas the latter gives a product with much less shrinkage and lower density.

Double-Stage.—Several methods of operating double-stage plants are known and, in particular, the two stages may be arranged as separate tunnels or, alternatively, together in the same tunnel.

(1) Countercurrent/parallel system. In this system the product first encounters air flowing in a countercurrent direction and then in a parallel direction, the air being fed in at a central point.

(2) Parallel/countercurrent flow system. The bulk of two-stage plants in commercial operation are of this type so that advantage may be taken

initially of the high rate of evaporation available in parallel flow. The advantages compared with single stage units are more uniform drying, increased output from starter drying time and good overall quality.

It is often found in practice that the first stage is shorter in length than the second to compensate for low drying rate in the latter. However, equal length tunnels are widely used and it is possible by placing them side by side to arrange for loading and unloading to be carried out at the same end. In many systems the air from the secondary tunnel is used to supply the primary parallel flow system.

This system enables the temperature of the air in either system to be adjusted to desired values; it is usual to have the air of higher temperature in the parallel flow system and air of a lower temperature in the countercurrent. It is also important that maximum recirculation be carried out to economize on the heating load.

Multistage Driers.—The chief advantages of multistage driers are that they are more flexible and can achieve under nearly optimum conditions the drying of a wide range of products. However, relatively few are in operation, mainly 3 and 5 stages using countercurrent flow of air.

Conveyor-Type Dryers.—This type of drying system is very similar to the tunnel system except that the material is conveyed through the hot air system on a continuous moving belt. The system has the advantage that the high cost of handling products both before and after drying using trays is substantially reduced. The wet material is loaded uniformly (6–8 in. deep) onto the belt (either a woven metal mesh or interlocking perforated plates) and dried initially by air blowing through the bed and finally by air passing down through the bed. The latter prevents material being lost from the system due to changes in density during drying. The belts vary in length from 30 to 60 ft and in width from 6 to 100 ft. The process conditions are primarily controlled by sectionalizing the system; thus it is possible to control independently flow rates, humidities, and temperatures and thereby give optimum output and quality. Air recirculation is also important in the initial stages. This type of drier is essentially for high capacity water removal and it is necessary to remove the material at a moisture level of about 15% to avoid the use of excessively long belts and waste of evaporative capacity.

A typical drying operation would involve 35 tons per hour of raw material infeed onto a 75 ft long 8 ft wide conveyor belt loaded at a rate of 10 lb per sq ft and allowing $2\frac{1}{2}$ hr for travel through the system.

These dryers are widely used for fruit and vegetables as well as meat products. Each product requires careful control of the temperature at each stage.

Bin-Type Finishing Dryers.—Bin-type finishing driers are widely used for the equilibration and storage prior to packaging of dried products and also for obtaining final moisture levels. Basically, they are cylindrical containers through which warm air is blown at a velocity not greater than 100 ft^3 per min per ft^2. These bins provide a low cost method of removing moisture from particular products during the slowest stages of drying. Both static and portable units are available. The drying time required to reduce the moisture content of vegetables from 10 to 5% is 24–36 hr. For onion dehydration, for which a final moisture content not in excess of 4% is required, an air temperature of 120°F, absolute humidity above 0.003 lb per lb dry air and an air velocity between 80 and 100 ft^3 per min per ft^2 at bin cross-section were required.

Explosion Puffing.—In explosion puffing, partially dehydrated pieces from a preliminary stage drying are heated in a closed rotating cylindrical container known as a "gun" until the internal pressure has reached a predetermined value. When this point has been reached the gun is discharged instantly to atmospheric pressure. During this process a certain amount of water is vaporized but, more important, the explosive or flashing conditions cause a highly porous network of capillaries to be developed within the particles. This porosity enables the final dehydration to be achieved much more rapidly (approximately twice) than would have been the case with conventionally dried products. It also bestows on the product the ability to reconstitute extremely rapidly.

The gun described above was externally heated but it was subsequently redesigned. The heating cycle in the modified process was shortened by introducing superheated steam 500°F at 55 psig into the gun after the charge of partially dehydrated particles had been prewarmed by tumbling in the preheated (gas burners) gun. The latter procedure prevents steam condensation and also ensures that the particles are exposed to heat on all surfaces rather than the less efficient and more random contact with the heated walls alone. The modified gun was constructed of thin wall stainless steel being 10 in. in diameter and 30 in. long. The interior of the gun was furnished with integral fins to increase the area for heat transfer. A particularly important feature in the design is the rapid release mechanism for the lid together with a low inertia arrester for smooth absorption of lid impact. The gun is supported in a horizontal position by a swivel pivot and a mechanism for tilting into either filling or discharging position is incorporated. The capacity of the machine is quoted as being 9 20-lb charges per hour of $^3/_8$-in. vegetable dice containing 22% moisture which is approximately 1 $^1/_2$ ton per day of finished product.

The process has been successfully used on fruits and vegetables and the products have many of the desirable attributes of freeze-dried products. In particular, the porous structure confers rapid reconstitution properties; for example, strips of carrot $^3/_8 \times ^1/_2 \times ^1/_4$ in. when explosion puffed required only 7 min for reconstitution in boiling water compared with 30 min for the conventional air-dried product.

Dispersion Drying.—*Spray Drying.*—This technique, involving the fine dispersion of droplets in a hot gas, is widely used for liquid food products. The process has considerable advantages over batch and roller drying methods since the high surface area obtained by a fine dispersion of droplets facilitates low drying times when coupled with high heat transfer rates. The temperature of the droplets remains below the wet bulk temperature of the drying gas until almost all the water has been removed, due to the high evaporation rate, and consequently high temperatures can be utilized. The particle shape produced is unique, being spherical but hollow, the solids being concentrated in the wall.

The design of spray driers has advanced rapidly during the last 20 yr, the main aim having been to achieve high overall thermal efficiencies with high throughput. This has involved careful consideration of the dynamics of atomization together with methods of bringing the hot gas and atomized particle into contact. The essential stages of any spray drier are (a) an atomizing system, (b) a hot gas producing unit, (c) a chamber to contact the sprayed particles with hot gas, and (d) a recovery system. Spray driers may be classified as follows, according to the nature of the air flow: (1) horizontal cocurrent driers; (2) vertical cocurrent driers: upward and downward, and simple and complex; (3) vertical countercurrent driers.

The importance of the correct atomizing system can be seen when the rate-controlling stages are considered—namely, heat transfer to the droplets, mass transfer by vapor diffusion from the material surface to the surrounding gas, and diffusion of residual moisture through the dried layer of product. The main problems with the spraying operation are that the distribution of particle size is uneven, interaction and coalescence of droplets occurs, and gas dynamics are complex.

However, many designs of atomizer nozzle have been developed to attempt to overcome these problems. The first type consists of those in which pressure is used to develop a droplet system; these include fan spray, impact, swirl, and divergent pintle nozzles. The second class of atomizers involve the use of centrifugal energy and include spinning discs of various geometries (operating speeds between 100 and 600 ft per sec). The third class utilize gaseous energy with twin fluid or blast atomizers using fans, rotary blowers, and reciprocating compressors. It is generally recognized that the method of forming droplets depends upon the production of a very thick sheet of liquid which then breaks down into droplets, the size, shape and nature of which depend on the surface tension and viscosity of the liquid product. Thus, the primary action with pressure nozzles is the production of a conical sheet which subsequently disrupts to give a fine spray of droplets. Basically this follows from the fact that a column or sheet of liquid becomes unstable when its length is greater than its circumference; a uniform thread will in fact produce uniform size droplets. However, when most atomization processes are considered, the threads of liquid tend to be uneven with resulting lack of uniformity in droplets.

Although the processes of disruption of sheets of liquid using a high speed cinecamera technique have been studied, very little information appears to be available on the behavior of liquid food products; however, it is well known that droplet formation is resisted by highly viscous and non-Newtonian food products. Once the droplet is formed it falls at a relatively high velocity until it reaches the terminal velocity which remains constant for the remainder of the journey. The amount of drying which the particle undergoes depends upon the distance of fall and rate of heat transfer. Thus, there are two stages in the evaporation—during the retardation, and during the constant fall period. An important aspect prior to the final stage of surface hardening is the loss of volatiles that impart flavor to food products; this is governed by the relative volatilities of the components.

Among the products which are spray dried, the most important commercially are milk, eggs, beverages, and tomato paste.

Pneumatic or Flash Drying.—In this type of dryer the finely divided solid is fed into a stream of air and in some of the techniques can be recycled, e.g., ring dryers. The term "flash dryer" is used to describe the very rapid vaporization of moisture and extremely short residence time, viz 2–10 sec. Because of the simultaneous flash-cooling effect it is possible to dry heat-sensitive materials using this technique. In general, high thermal efficiencies can be achieved.

The simplest design of pneumatic dryer involves a single pass system with cyclones to separate the dried material from the air. The residence time may be extended by recycling or use of a double tube with counterflow down the inner column. Some systems also include classifiers.

The average evaporative rate for pneumatic dryers is of the order of 150 lb per sq ft per hr compared with 26 lb per sq ft per hr for fluidized beds and 20 lb per sq ft per hr for spray driers.

Agitated- and Fluidized-Bed Dryers.—These driers are an extension of the through-flow type of air dryer, the air velocities through the bed of food particles being such that the particles are suspended in the upward blast of hot air.

The distinction between agitated-bed and fluidized-bed driers is that in the former the bed is less vigorously stirred than in the latter. It is necessary with driers of this type to decrease the air velocity as the particle dries in order to prevent the particles being lost from the system.

The conditions for stable fluidization of food particles (size 3–20 mm) correspond to a range of Reynolds numbers ($VD \rho/\mu$) from 500 to 10,000 and velocities of air vary from 3 m per sec to 6 m per sec. The data quoted here are for fluidized freezing of food particles but can be used if consideration is given to the change in density of the product and air.

An interesting point with fluidized bed processing is the variation in the residence time of the food particles. This has been studied by injecting a known number of dyed peas and shows that a typical sigmoid curve is obtained indicating a wide spread of residence times. In this respect the fluidized bed technique differs from all other types since the particles are mobile.

A further extension of the fluidized bed technique has been described which employs a centrifugal force to allow the velocity of fluidization, and hence the heat transfer, to be improved. Using $3/8$-in. diced carrot it was found that the pressure drop increased linearly with increasing centrifugal force. Heat transfer coefficients and rates of drying have not yet been reported for food products.

An extension of the principle of the agitated bed is incorporated in the belt-trough drier in which air is passed through a moving bed of particles. This drier consists of an endless wire mesh belt arranged in such a way as to form an inclined trough such that the product travels in a spiral path. Partial fluidization is produced by an upward blast of air usually of the order of 400 ft per min and temperature up to 300°F. Experimental work on diced carrot ($1/4 \times 1/4 \times 1/8$ in.) indicated that about 20 min was required to remove half the initial water.

Foam Drying.—*Vacuum Puff Drying.*—The development of this process for drying liquids under vacuum came from the observations made on the freeze drying of orange juice concentrate. It was found that the rate of drying of that product in the liquid state was double that in the frozen state (freeze drying) and the dried product had highly porous structure which exhibited good rehydration properties. This was due to the fact that under vacuum conditions the liquid tends to foam and produce a film structure which dries to give a highly porous solid. The drying characteristics of a two-phase system, air + water vapour/liquid, differ appreciably from those of single-phase liquid. Foaming imparts a more rigid structure to the product and increases the surface area for moisture diffusion. With regard to heat transfer, however, such a system is initially less efficient since foams have an inherent low thermal conductivity. This is subsequently offset by the fact that the latter stages are mass transfer controlled. However, when all aspects are considered, foam drying is a relatively rapid process that does not require high temperatures. With regard to product quality the foamed structure is particularly useful because it confers the property of rapid reconstitution. However, like all food products with high surface areas, these products present a storage problem in relation to moisture uptake and oxidation. Aroma retention also presents a problem, and add-back techniques are required with some processes, e.g., orange oil on sorbitol is added to the dry powder.

The vacuum puff process has also been developed as a continuous drying operation. The type of equipment used for this consists essentially of a belt up to 60 ft long driven by drum rolls, which can be heated or cooled, contained in a vacuum shell.

Foam-Mat Drying.—This process is a development of the former, but, instead of employing a vacuum to foam the material, it is initially foamed by suitable agents and then subjected to drying under atmospheric pressure. The equipment required for this is similar to the continuous band drier described previously, without the vacuum facilities.

The success of the process is dependent upon producing foam of suitable structure. The most desirable characteristics are that it should consist of a large number of small uniform stable bubbles and should retain its structure during drying. In order to facilitate stability it is often necessary to use a film-forming additive, such as solubilized soy protein, glycerol monostearate, propylene glycol monostearate, or sucrose palmitate. The density of foams varies from 0.1 gm per ml to about 0.8 gm per ml with a preference for the more dense. Pseudoplastic and compressible behavior are observed in varying degrees with foams and this affects their flow properties; however, it is possible to handle them with ease either under shear or pressure conditions. The mechanism of the drying process has been studied and it is considered that the drying rate is governed by heat transfer to the foam in the early stages coupled with a rate determining mass transfer operation. It was also shown in connection with the rate of evaporation that this was only 30% of that expected from a free water surface. Although the initial work was based on tomato paste, a range of products was examined including milk products, coffee, pineapple, lemonade, grape and orange juice, apricot purée, and a prune product containing egg albumen.

The success of foam-mat drying depends upon the production of a stable, uniform foam. Although some foods—e.g., egg white, beef extract concentrate, and whole milk concentrate—foam easily and do not require additives, the bulk of food products require some form of stabilizing agent.

Microflake® Dehydration.—This technique involves the drying of a continuous sheet of foam 20 mm thick on a continuous stainless steel belt. The latter is heated from below by steam and above by a high velocity air stream; drying times are reported to be about $1/10$ of the standard processes. The temperature required is of the order of $170°$F and care has to be taken to produce a very uniform film since the rate of dehydration is proportional to the square of the thickness. The rate-controlling factor is the internal diffusion of moisture.

Foam-Spray Drying.—This is an extension of spray drying and involves the use of gases dissolved under pressure prior to spraying. The main advantage is that the density of the product is reduced by $1/2$ and, whereas spray-dried particles are hollow spheres surrounded by thick walls of dried material, the foam process produces particles having many internal spaces and relatively thin walls. The pressures which have been used for this process are considerable—e.g., 4025 psig carbon dioxide for tea and coffee and 2000 psig air for acid-whey.

Drum Drying.—One of the more important techniques for drying liquid food products is the drum drier. The high rate of heat transfer is obtained by direct contact with the hot surface and the equipment may be used either under atmospheric or vacuum conditions. The success of drum drying depends on the application of a uniform film of maximum thickness. This is controlled by the temperature of the surface of the drum and the speed of rotation. The thickness tends to increase with increasing temperature and higher temperatures permit an increase in drum speed and hence capacity. Published data on heat transfer coefficients are very limited, but figures of the order of 200–220 Btu/hr (ft^2) $(°F)$ are considered reasonable. The heat transfer coefficient varies

around the circumference and heat transfer tends to be uneven. The nature of the surface also affects the rate of drying. The final moisture contents are often not as low as required and a final drying operation involving a fluidized bed is required.

Drum drying is extensively used for the manufacture of instant potato products, potato flakes, and also for all liquid food products including infant foods, fruit products, eggs, milk, and beverages.

Infrared Radiation Drying.—The mechanism of heat transfer with thermal radiation involves direct impingement of the radiation on the surface followed by conduction of heat into the food product. The amount of heat absorbed by the surface depends very much on the surface properties; those products which behave as "black bodies" absorb the most heat. Infrared radiation may be generated by heating objects to high temperature by gas flames or by electrical methods. The latter include reflector type incandescent lamps (100–5000 watts), quartz tubes, and resistance elements. The technique can be applied either to a batch process or more easily to continuous band drying. Most of the experimental work has been carried out in U.S.S.R.

Radiation heating is widely used in freeze drying to accelerate the sublimation process. The heat radiation is produced from oil-heated platens arranged above the trays of material.

Microwave Drying.—High frequency radio waves up to 30,000 MH_2 can be used for dehydration. When energy of this frequency impinges on a material, the energy is absorbed and converted into heat inside the product. It is necessary to select the correct wavelength so that the maximum penetration is obtained into the food. The penetration is, in fact, inversely proportional to the frequency.

Microwave devices involve a high frequency generator, e.g., a magnetron from which energy is transported by a hollow rectangular wave guide to an oven or tunnel which is designed to prevent leakage of microwave energy. Considerable care has to be taken when using this type of drier in order to prevent damage to the operator. One of the most important commercial applications is in finish drying of potato chips where considerable quality advantages, especially color, can be obtained.

Freeze Drying.—In this method of removal of water the product is frozen and the temperature maintained below the triple point of the constituent aqueous solutions so that the water vapor can be sublimed from the frozen solution. There is, therefore, a direct transfer from solid to vapor without the ice melting and passing through the liquid phase. The process is carried out under vacuum to provide a high vapor diffusion potential and is accelerated by supplying heat in some convenient form, either radiant, conductive, or from microwaves. It is generally considered that, as a means of dehydration, it produces a dried product of the highest quality and therefore is potentially an extremely attractive method. As a developing technique it provides a good example of the contention that successful commercial exploitation of a competitive technique results from a study of the fundamental processes involved.

Considerable attention has been directed towards the effect of freezing rate on the reconstitution of freeze-dried products since it is well known that the porous nature of the product is controlled by this factor. The basic process of vapor removal is governed by the size, shape, and tortuosity of the pores and, in general, the faster the freezing rate the smaller the voids and the slower the freeze-drying rate.

The major aspects of the mechanism of freeze drying are (a) the removal of vapor from the subliming ice front within the material, (b) the removal of vapor from between the food particles, (c) the supply of heat to the food particles, and (d) the supply of heat to the ice within the food particles. Of these, the removal of vapor from the dried particle and supply of heat to ice within the particle to accelerate the sublimation are the most important.

With regard to vapor transport, the sharpness of the frozen front has been subject to much speculation and it is generally thought that at some stage the front is diffuse rather than sharp. This means that a proportion of water molecules remain on the surface of the pores after the ice has retreated and these are removed during secondary drying. The sharp transition model is, however, considered to be reasonable for mathematical treatment.

Equipment and Processes.—The conventional freeze-drying unit consists of a vacuum chamber into which trays of the material to be dried can be placed, and a method of supplying heat to the material so that the sublimation process can be accelerated. The usual method is to arrange the trays on or between the heated plates which are either electrically heated or internally heated with steam, pressurized hot water, or oil. The vacuum is produced either with a mechanical pump, suitable steam ejectors, or refrigerated condensers. Various arrangements of the last are used depending on the method of defrosting.

Although the majority of freeze-drying plants are batch in nature, several continuous systems have been designed and many are operative on food products. The main problems involve the development of suitable vapor locks for introducing the food into and removing food from the drying chamber, and obtaining uniform distribution of particles of the foodstuff.

With regard to methods of accelerating vapor removal, liquid and solid desiccants have been proposed and used. With liquid desiccants these would continuously remove moisture from the vapor and require low temperatures for absorption. This is usually operated by allowing a thin film of refrigerant to fall down the condenser surface, or alternatively to spray the cold liquid into the absorption chamber. Solid desiccants, such as molecular sieves, have also been investigated.

A considerable amount of work has been devoted to improving heat transfer during freeze drying. In the early techniques heat was supplied by conduction from plates by clamping the food between them. This, however, restricted the vapor flow and also provided uneven contact. In order to overcome this, expanded metal inserts were used between the plates and the product. This process is referred to as AFD (Accelerated Freeze Drying). A method of accelerated heat transfer into meat steaks involves the use of spikes on the trays. A further development in the design of trays, aimed at improving heat transfer, has been the use of longitudinally ribbed trays. This method affords a way in which the surface area may be considerably increased for both conduction and radiation. The trays are made of aluminium which has a relatively high thermal conductivity and the design is such that the trays have a high mechanical strength which makes them suitable for mechanical handling.

A technique which has evolved directly from the basic study of heat and mass transfer phenomena is that of using cyclic pressure variation. It was briefly mentioned earlier that the requirements for maximum thermal conductivity of the porous dried layer and also for moisture diffusion were not the same. Thus, it was considered that it might be advantageous to vary the pressure such that one cycle favored heat transfer while the other favored vapor diffusion. Several workers have investigated this process and indicated that some reduction in overall process time may be achieved. This improvement is probably associated with other factors, such as inert gases used.

Several workers have investigated the use of much higher pressures, such as atmospheric, for freeze drying. The only requirement necessary to achieve this in practice is to maintain the partial pressure of water vapor in the chamber at the equilibrium value of that in the frozen food and this can be done by the presence of another gas (Dalton's Law). Recirculation of the gases to remove water vapor is the method usually adopted. The only drawback is the length of time required for the process, namely, 30–40 hr to dry 8-mm-thick discs of carrot.

S. D. HOLDSWORTH

References

General Books

ANON. 1958. Fundamental Aspects of the Dehydration of Foodstuffs. Society of Chemical Industry, London, England.

CHARM, S. E. 1971. Dehydration of foods. *In* The Fundamentals of Food Engineering, 2nd Edition. Avi Publishing Co., Westport, Conn.

GREENSMITH, M. 1971. Practical Dehydration. Food Trade Press, London, England.

VAN ARSDEL, W. B., COPLEY, M. J., and MORGAN, A. I., JR. 1973. Food Dehydration, 2nd Edition, Vol. 1, Drying Methods and Phenomena. Avi Publishing Co., Westport, Conn.

VAN ARSDEL, W. B., COPLEY, M. J., and MORGAN, A. I., JR. 1973. Food Dehydration, 2nd Edition, Vol. 2, Practices and Applications. Avi Publishing Co., Westport, Conn.

WEBB, F. C. 1964. Biochemical Engineering. Van Nostrand Reinhold Publishing Co., London, England.

WILLIAMS-GARDNER, A. 1971. Industrial Drying. Leonard Hill Publishing Co., London, England.

General Reviews

HERTZENDORF, M. S. 1967. Comparison of food dehydration techniques. Chem. Ind. Jan. 23, 173. Also ASHRAE J. Febr., 65.

HOLDSWORTH, S. D. 1971. Dehydration of food products. J. Food Technol. 6, No. 4, 331.

HOLDSWORTH, S. D. 1971. Bibliographical guide to food dehydration and dehydrated products. Res. Sta., Chipping Campden, Gloucester, England.

TAPE, N. W. 1970. The dehydration of foods and some new methods of drying. Can. Food Ind. *41*, No. 8, 29.

Cross-references: *Freeze Drying; Foam-Mat Drying; Food Preservation.*

de LAVAL, CARL GUSTAV PATRICK (1845–1913)

On the evening of May 12, 1877, at the mansion of the Kloster works in Dalecarlia in Central Sweden, the maid had brought in coffee and cognac for the gentlemen of the factory who were having their usual discussion of the news and the day's events as they might be related to the Kloster enterprise. The works manager, Mr. Logerman, read aloud from a paper about a German inventor regarding the skimming of milk by means of centrifugal force. The Kloster engineer, Gustav de Laval, commented that "no doubt centrifugal force should act the same way

in Sweden as in Germany." Gustav pondered the matter during a sleepless night and during his morning coffee, still absorbed in thought, he suddenly awoke from his pondering and exclaimed, "Gentlemen, a restless night has given me the key to the problem of milk skimming," and added, "my cream separator works continuously." This is how the cream separator was invented.

It has been said that three technical developments were largely responsible for launching dairying from the cottage cheese industry of those days to the great specialized industry of the present. These were: (1) the concept of pasteurization (Pasteur, 1865), which markedly delayed souring and other spoilage phenomena by heat treatment; (2) the development of a rapid fat test by Babcock (1890), which made it possible to arrive at a basis of payment for the milk; and (3) the invention of the centrifugal cream separator (de Laval, 1877), which provided an industrial means of producing cream for butter making. At that time, butterfat was regarded as the most, if not the only valuable constituent of milk.

De Laval kept a diary or sketch book always at hand so that he could record meticulously ideas and items of interest. Thus, there is his nightly sketch (Cream Separator, 1877). Also the notations: 21/12/1885. 4:30 P.M. Found 5 öre at Slussen; 18/10/1886. 7:15 A.M. Became father of a son.

In his notes he emphasized accuracy of thinking and exactitude of converting an idea to a machine, especially important where high speeds were involved. His notebooks show more than 200 ideas with which he was concerned, always several simultaneously. His inventions involve exploitation by 37 companies. His successful constructions were based on ingenious solutions of specific problems. Science was left to others. His collection of ideas under the title "Something to Ponder About for the Future" contains such items as oil from shale, a baking machine, an artificial rain maker, gold from sea water, a herring-scaler, and many others. Some of the items in his list are still being worked on by the company which bears his name. To food technologists, Alfa Laval AB is probably the best known, still operating on the basic de Laval ideas. However, there are seven other companies bearing the de Laval name as well as others not so identified which derive their origins from de Laval concepts.

Not all of de Laval's projects succeeded. A favorite expression of his was, "Tis over the scrapheaps the path of progress lies"; and he himself climbed over huge heaps in his day. There was the bottle manufacturing machine which went out of control, giving a 40,000 kroner deficit against his next idea. Then, in another heap lay the remnants of the "air-greased" boats built to make

40 knots an hour which were scrapped after a few unsuccessful voyages in 6 of them.

De Laval's special interest dealt with high speeds of rotation. In 1889, he introduced the first practical impulse steam turbine. He also introduced the De Laval Nozzle, a device of basic importance in the operation of turbines and ram jets, as well as in rockets.

De Laval was a member of the Lower and Upper Houses of the Swedish Parliament, the Association of Swedish Inventors (founder), the Swedish Society for the Rewarding of Impeccable and Faithful Domestic Servants, and other organizations. He was also honored by the awarding of such decorations as Knight of the Northern Star and Knight Commander of the order of Wasa. He died in 1913.

ARNOLD H. JOHNSON

DENATURATION OF PROTEINS

The proteins are a remarkably versatile group of complex biopolymers with unique physicochemical and biological properties. In the original plant or animal tissue from which all foods are derived, the native proteins perform the most diverse functions essential to the life processes. They function as biocatalytic enzymes and hormones, as oxygen transport agents, and as the genetic encoders. The proteins afford protective capacity as disease antibodies, and stem blood loss through the clotting mechanism. As metabolic enzymes, the proteins regulate the energy resources of the living organism, and as contractile muscle proteins they translate chemical into mechanical energy. The proteins also comprise the basic food depot essential to the cyclic regeneration of all the biofunctional proteins.

In the conversion of crude biological raw materials to refined processed foods, the proteins exert a dominant influence on the choice of process conditions, and on the rheologic, organoleptic, and nutritive qualities of the finished product. As uniquely structured amphoteric macromolecules, the proteins present distinctive physical properties of great consequence in food technology. Through their capacity to interact, they may form molecular aggregates, colloidal micelles, fibers, coagula, gels, and viscoelastic systems. The proteins bind water, may coagulate with heat or acidification and, as surface active molecules, promote foaming and emulsification. The physical and biological properties of the proteins are profoundly affected by temperature, pH, electrolyte environment, and physical stresses which may lead to their denaturation.

On denaturation, the proteins lose their biological activity and frequently sustain important physical changes. Protein denaturation, and its concomitant effects may prove an asset or a liability to the food processor. Blanching, pasteurization, and sterilization treatments used for the inactivation of enzymes and the destruction of microorganisms and spores are, intrinsically, denaturation processes. Denaturation provides the structural foam and heat-set properties required in the production of meringues, souffles, custards, and baked goods. Denaturation improves the tenderness of cooked foods, and the digestibility of proteins. Control of denaturation is necessary in the manufacture of evaporated and sweetened condensed milk, ice cream, and dried milk products. Serum protein denaturation in milk is detrimental to rennet curd formation in cheese manufacture, but it is essential to optimum loaf volume in bread baking. In some food products, differential denaturation requirements may impose severe process restrictions. Thermal destruction of Salmonellae pathogens in egg white, for example, overlaps the denaturation of ovalbumin, and carefully prescribed heat treatments must be abided for the preservation of whip functionality in heat pasteurized egg whites.

Structural Aspects of Denaturation

Denaturation is generally defined as any structural modification of the native protein molecule exclusive of primary covalent bond hydrolysis. The term is restricted to changes in the secondary noncovalent bonds that maintain the unique molecular conformation of native protein, and does not therefore, include proteolysis or disulfide bond rupture.

Denaturation is, essentially, a process of disorganization which leads to the formation of randomized molecules from the highly ordered molecular structure that characterizes the native state. Denaturation has been likened to a "melting" process.

The molecular disorganization, attendant to denaturation, may effect profound changes in the biological, chemical, and physical properties of native proteins. The enzymic, hormonal, and viral proteins generally lose their specific biological activities on denaturation. Nearly all the physicochemical attributes of proteins may be affected by denaturation, either as the result of a direct change in the molecule, or through secondary solvent effects or intermolecular reactions leading to changes in size dispersion through aggregation. Molecular weight change is not an intrinsic consequence of denaturation, but a secondary association of the denatured protein molecules may lead to varying degrees of polymerization, flocculation, and coagulation or gel formation, depending on pH, electrolyte, protein concentration, and other environmental factors.

Denaturation is frequently manifested by a reduction in protein solubility, a loss of crystallizability, increase in solution viscosity, and increased susceptibility to proteolysis. Changes in optical rotatory dispersion, circular dichroism, light absorption, and electrolyte sensitivity are common but highly variable consequences of denaturation, dependent on the protein species and conditions of denaturation.

The alterations in a large number of molecular parameters, including electrophoretic mobility, acid-base binding capacity, intrinsic viscosity, sedimentation coefficient, etc., have been used to delineate the effects of denaturation. Denaturation frequently leads to the exposure of certain inaccessible, functional substituents of the native protein such as amino groups, the sulfhydryl groups of cysteine, the disulfide of cystine, or the phenolic group of tyrosine. The increased chemical reactivity of such groups and the aforementioned changes may be used to quantify the denaturation process for kinetic studies.

The structural conformation of protein molecules, accountable for their diversity, unique functionality, and denaturability, is predicated on the content and linear sequence of their amino acid monomers. The proteins are ampholytic macromolecules containing from several hundred to several thousand amino acid residues per molecule, representing a molecular weight range of from 10,000 to over 200,000. The primary structural elements are some 20 amino acids, linked through peptide bonds into linear polypeptide chains. Constraints on the degree of flexibility of the polypeptide chains are imposed by the *trans*, planar structure of the amido peptide linkage, and steric limitations of the bulky side chain substituents of the amino acid monomers. The substituents on the carbon atom vary in size from the hydrogen atom on glycine to the heterocyclic indole ring of tryptophan. Their relative polarity and chemical reactivity are also highly variable. In a great many proteins, notably the globulins, the polypeptide chain assumes a three dimensional, ordered structure.

Several orders of structural level are recognized in the conformation of the native protein molecule. The primary structure simply represents the linear sequence of the amino acids in the polypeptide chain, maintained by strong covalent bonds. The higher orders, superimposed on the primary linear polypeptide chain, are maintained by relatively weak noncovalent bonds between the carbonyl oxygens and amide hydrogens of the peptide chain backbone. The polypeptide chains appear to assume configurations that maximize such hydrogen bonding potential. Portions of the polypeptide chain may assume a coiled, helical structure, while other sections may be randomly coiled, or in pleated sheet arrangement. This constitutes a secondary structure. The helical content for some of the globular proteins varies from 88 to 94% of the residues in tropomyosin, and 31 to 50% in ovalbumin, to 26 to 31% for pepsin. The coiled polypeptide chains, through additional folding, assume a three dimensional, or tertiary structure, stabilized through hydrogen bonding and hydrophobic interactions. The covalent disulfide bond, in a number of proteins, forms a highly stable linkage of considerable importance in maintaining tertiary structural integrity. However, noncovalent bonding is the dominant form of dimensional structuring of the protein molecule, and the type of primary concern in denaturation. Where proteins consist of two or more polypeptide chains, their association constitutes a structural level that has been designated quaternary.

The molecular conformation and complete amino acid sequence, for a growing number of proteins, have been resolved through the application of highly sophisticated X-ray crystallographic and sequential analyses techniques.

The proteolytic enzyme papain, derived from the latex of the tropical papaya tree and used in tenderizing meat, is one of the proteins for which the molecular structure has been recently resolved. The papain molecule contains 1 folded polypeptide chain, with a total of 212 amino acid residues, whose complete amino acid sequence is illustrated in Fig. D-2. The conformational structure of papain, as shown in Fig. D-3, reveals that the molecule contains two lobes in which the folding of the polypeptide chain varies. Lobe L, is distinguished by a hydrophobic core surrounded by 3 α-helices, while lobe R contains 2 α-helices and a pleated sheet structure.

Since each protein presents a unique native conformation, whose structural elements may be variously modified by a multitude of denaturing conditions, it follows that denaturation is an extraordinarily complex, diverse process. The structural changes for each specific case of denaturation cannot be defined, nor is it currently possible to correlate effectively, structural changes that occur at the molecular level, with the macroscopic properties of the denatured proteins. In fact, denaturation of any one protein may, depending on the type and intensity of the denaturation treatment, evolve variously randomized structures. Thus, under mild denaturing conditions, where only the tertiary molecular structure is altered,

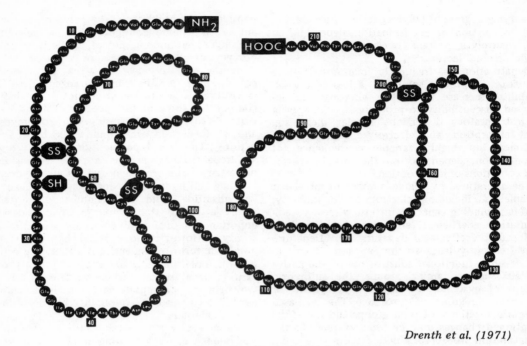

Drenth et al. (1971)

FIG. D-2. THE AMINO ACID SEQUENCE IN PAPAIN

Reprinted with permission of Academic Press.

the process in some instances is reversible. The alkaline phosphatase of milk, for example, is completely inactivated when milk is heat pasteurized at 63°C for 30 min, or 72° for 15 sec. However at very short high temperature treatments, the phosphatase shows gradual reactivation on cool aging.

Under specific conditions, denatured β-lactoglobulin, insulin, and chymotrypsinogen show recovery of native properties with respect to crystallizability, biological activity, reactivity of amino acid substituents, and a number of molecular parameters. Frequently, renaturation of denatured protein is only partial, and the rate and extent of recovery of the various native properties may vary considerably. Reversible denaturation is generally ascribed to the more superficial changes occurring at the tertiary structural level, while irreversible denaturation appears to be predicated on secondary structural changes. Whether the course of denaturation is a stepwise, or an "all or none" process has not been resolved. Denaturation of egg albumin by urea is recognized as a stepwise process, with no discernible intermediate forms, but studies on other systems suggest that denaturation follows a progressive course.

The relative resistance of native proteins to denaturation has, in some instances, been ascribed to certain structural properties. Thus, various fish collagens, with decreasing hydroxyproline and proline content show progressively greater susceptibility to thermal denaturation. This has been related to the capacity of the hydroxyl group for hydrogen bonding, and the steric influence of the pyrollidine ring N–C bond on the polypeptide chain of collagen. The stabilizing influence of the disulfide bonds, thiol, and amino groups on protein structure is well documented. Acetylation of the amino groups of ovalbumin, trypsin, and chymotrypsin sharply reduces denaturation resistance.

Egg white lysozyme, containing four disulfide bonds is extremely heat stable, while bacteriophage lysozyme, devoid of such sulfur bonds, is readily denatured at 45°C. The globin component of native hemoglobin is effectively stabilized by the protoporphyrin ring and heme group.

The important effect that water has on protein structure and denaturation bears emphasis, particularly since all food proteins occur in an aqueous environment. The nonpolar side chains of the amino acids possess a low affinity for water and tend to exclude and minimize their contact with water by hydrophobic interaction. Amino acids with nonpolar side chains, such as phenylalanine, leucine, tryptophan, etc., constitute from

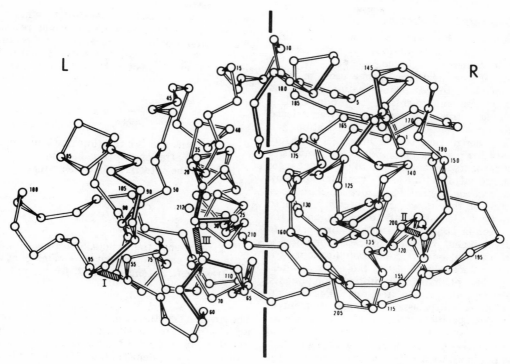

L   R

Drenth et al. (1971)

FIG. D-3. THE CONFORMATIONAL STRUCTURE OF THE PAPAIN MOLECULE

Reprinted with permission of Academic Press.

35 to 50% of the total amino acids in proteins. In an aqueous environment, therefore, protein molecules assume configurations that encourage a minimum exposure of the nonpolar side chains with water, and a high level of hydrophobic interaction, for maximum stability. The water molecules, surrounding exposed hydrophobic protein side chains are believed to assume an ice-like structure. Generally, proteins that contain a higher content of hydrophillic groups exhibit greater solubility in water. Chemical agents such as urea and guanidine, which are strong hydrogen bonding, are well-known protein denaturants. Urea denaturation is ascribed to the reduction of intramolecular hydrophobic forces in the native protein, by creating a less favorable environment than water, for the nonpolar groups. The competitive hydrogen bonding capacity of water, for the internal hydrogen bonded structures in protein, may, for marginally stable proteins, facilitate their denaturation.

The differential orientation of the polar-apolar protein side chains at air-water, and oil-water interfaces is a further expression of the functional role of water in denaturation. The denaturing action of nonaqueous solvents such as alcohol depends on the relative contribution of the hydrogen and hydrophobic protein bonds to its total structural cohesiveness. Intramolecular hydrophobic bonding is generally less stable in ethanol, for example, than in pure water due to the greater solvation of the apolar substituents by alcohol. Reduction of the water content in water-alcohol mixtures lowers the solvents capacity to disrupt hydrogen bonding.

Finally, it should be noted that dried proteins exhibit a far greater resistance to denature than their aqueous solutions. Enzymes show remarkable retention of biological activity in the dried state. The residual moisture level is a critical factor in denaturation resistance of dried proteins. The rate of thermal denaturation of dried ovalbumin is an exponential function of the relative humidity, and the denaturation temperature for 50% insolubilization of the ovalbumin, is a linear function of relative humidity. Egg white proteins, dried to a maximum of 3% moisture, will withstand prolonged hold at 60°–70°C without denaturation, whereas, heat tolerance is reduced to 50°C at 5% moisture. The serum proteins in dried milk products show a comparably increased stability to heat denaturation.

Heat Denaturation of Proteins

Denaturation by heat treatment is the most prevalent type of denaturation, and of the greatest consequence in food technology.

Many of the heat treatments used in food processing lead to complete denaturation of the diverse protein components of the products. This is particularly true of in-can terminally autoclaved products, where total enzyme inactivation and complete destruction of the microbial flora are necessary for preservation. Indeed, such intensive heat treatments frequently lead to protein changes that transcend denaturation. Blanching, pasteurization, and the newer HTST process technologies, by virtue of their lower heat intensity, lead to intermediate and differential denaturation of the varied protein components in food products. In the development of food process technologies, and in practical quality control applications, it is frequently necessary to assess the extent of heat denaturation of individual protein components, or of composite protein fractions. Enzymic denaturation is widely assayed by measurement of the loss of specific catalytic capacity. Loss of solubility is one of the most readily measured changes in the properties of denatured proteins, and is a widely used criterion, particularly in the case of the globular proteins. Increased chemical reactivity of certain protein substituents, such as the sulfhydryl group, is also a useful quantitative reference for denaturation level in some food systems. Secondary effects of denaturation, such as turbidity changes, coagulation, gel formation, and degree of functional loss, as in egg white whip volume, serve as practical guides to denaturation measurement.

Differences in the susceptibility of proteins to heat denature are ascribed to the relative strength of the noncovalent bonds that maintain the structured conformation of the native molecules. Hydrogen bonding strength is known to weaken with increasing temperature, while that of hydrophobic bonding increases at temperatures up to about 60°C. In aqueous solution, the hydrogen bonds of numerous proteins are only of marginal stability, due to the competitive hydrogen bonding properties of the water molecules. With increasing heat energy, such weak internal hydrogen bonds rupture and are displaced by hydrogen bonds with water molecules.

Kinetics and Thermodynamics of Denaturation

In a random distribution of protein molecules, the number having sufficient above average energy to overcome critical intramolecular bonding and to denature at any given temperature should, according to the Maxwell-Boltzmann distribution law, be proportional to the total number of protein molecules. As a unimolecular reaction, denaturation would, therefore, follow, first order kinetics, with a reaction rate proportional to the concentration of unaltered protein (or enzyme), according to

$$-\frac{dc}{dt} = k'c$$

where k, is the specific reaction rate constant and c is the concentration of native protein.

This may be integrated between times $t_1 t_2$ to give

$$\ln \frac{c_1}{c_2} = k'(t_2 - t_1)$$

If x represents the residual fraction of native protein, or enzymic activity, remaining after a heat treatment, at temperature T, for t minutes

$$2.3 \log x = k't$$

The specific denaturation rate constant, or enzyme inactivation rate constant, k, may be obtained, therefore, from a plot of $\log x$ versus t.

In many cases, denaturation does appear to be a first order process, and at least the initial rate of heat denaturation is linearly related to protein concentration. First order kinetics are evident in the denaturation of such proteins as ovalbumin, egg white lysozyme, chymotrypsinogen, lobster hemocyanin, oxyhemoglobin and β-lactoglobulin among others. However, the kinetics are highly dependent on the measurement criteria, and particularly on such environmental factors as pH and electrolyte composition. The apparent first order velocity constant, furthermore, will often decrease with increasing heating time, and such deviations from first order kinetics have been ascribed to the occurrence of sequential first order denaturation steps, branched denaturation mechanisms, and competitive processes. The specific rate constants for the denaturation of a number of proteins and enzymes, at specified conditions, are illustrated in Table D-1.

As seen in Table D-1, the rate of protein denaturation is highly dependent on temperature, and is characterized by the rapidity of its increase over a small temperature rise. At a temperature increment of less than 5°C, above the initiation temperature of thermal denaturation, the rate may be too rapid to measure. A temperature increment of 10°C will normally accelerate conventional chemical reactions by a factor of only 2–3, but for protein denaturation, and enzyme inactivation, the magnitude of the thermal coefficient, Q_{10}, may

TABLE D-1

SPECIFIC RATE CONSTANTS FOR THE DENATURATION OF
PROTEINS AND ENZYMES AT SPECIFIED CONDITIONS

Protein	Denaturation Conditions ($^{\circ}$C)	(At pH)	k' (Sec$^{-1} \times 10^5$)
Soybean trypsin inhibitor	45	3	4.15
	50		16.9
	55		73.4
	60		285.0
	65		970.0
	70		2700.0
Pancreatic carboxy-peptidase A (0.02M Veronal)	45	7.5	46.0
	50		152.0
	52.5		303.0
	55		525.0
Peroxidase (horseradish)	85		26.9
Peroxidase (sweet corn)	85		349.0
Catalase (spinach)	60		145.0
Lipoxygenase (soybean)	65		87.1
o-Diphenol oxidase (pear)	80		591.0
β-lactoglobulin	64.3	6.6	4.6
β-lactoglobulin, phosphate buffer	69.8		26.9
β-lactoglobulin, phosphate buffer	74.6		145.9
Hemoglobin	60	5.7	43.0
Hemoglobulin	60	6.8	10.5

exceed several hundred. The relationship between chemical reaction velocity and temperature is expressed by the Arrhenius equation

$$\frac{d \ln k'}{dT} = \frac{E}{RT^2}$$

For a temperature interval T_1, T_2, integration of the Arrhenius equation yields

$$E = \frac{RT_2 T_1}{T_2 - T_1} \ln \frac{k_2'}{k_1'}$$

where E is the energy of activation (calories per mole), and k_1', k_2' are the respective velocity constants. R is the molar gas constant.

The energy of activation and the temperature coefficient are seen to be logarithmically related and, for a Q_{10} value of 2.6 for normal chemical reactions, the activation energy is about 20,000 cal. For protein denaturation, activation energies generally range from 40,000 to over 100,000 per mole.

. According to Eyring's theory of absolute rate processes, the rate of reaction is related more closely to the free energy of activation, $\Delta F^{\ddagger}$, than to the energy of activation E, and the ex-

perimental activation energy only approximates the heat of activation. In terms of the thermodynamic functions, $\Delta F^{\ddagger}$, $\Delta H^{\ddagger}$, and $\Delta S^{\ddagger}$ (free energies of activation, enthalpy, and entropy respectively), the absolute rate of denaturation as an activation process can be defined by the following relationships

$$k' = \frac{kT}{h} e^{-AF^{\ddagger}/RT}$$

where $\Delta F^{\ddagger} = \Delta H^{\ddagger} - T\Delta S^{\ddagger}$, k' is the specific rate (in sec^{-1}), h is the Planck constant (6.62×10^{-27} erg sec), k the Boltzmann constant (1.38×10^{-16} erg deg^{-1}) R the gas constant, and T the absolute temperature.

The respective free energy values of activation, for the protein denaturation process are then

$$\Delta F^{\ddagger} = RT \ln \frac{kT}{hk'}$$

$$\Delta H^{\ddagger} = RT^2 \frac{d \ln k'}{dt} - RT$$

$$\Delta S^{\ddagger} = -R \left(\ln \frac{kT}{hk'} - T \frac{d \ln k'}{dT} + 1 \right)$$

TABLE D-2

ACTIVATION PARAMETERS FOR HEAT DENATURATION OF A NUMBER OF PROTEINS

Protein	Conditions	$\Delta H^{\ddagger}$ (Cal/Mole)	$\Delta F^{\ddagger}$ (Cal/Mole)	$\Delta S^{\ddagger}$ (Cal/Mole°K)
β-lactoglobulin	Phosphate buffer, pH 6.9			
	u = 0.1, 69.3°C	58,000	19,300	113
	u = 0.1, 79.7°C	58,000	18,200	113
Trypsin	pH 6.5, 44°–60°C	40,200	25,700	45
Carboxypeptidase A	50°C	49,000	23,100	81
Soybean trypsin inhibitor	pH 3, 50°C	55,350	24,600	·95.4
Chymotrypsinogen	pH 3, 45.5°C	80,200	21,500	178.0
Catalase (spinach)	60°C	60,900	23,900	111
Lipoxygenase (soybean)	65°C	101,000	22,900	242
o-Diphenol oxidase (pear)	80°C	100,000	24,320	212
Hemoglobin	pH 6-8, 60°C	76,300	25,500	152

It is evident, from these equations, that the free energy of activation is decisive in establishing the protein denaturation rate. The large increase in entropy of protein denaturation, without an increase in the number of molecular units, is consistent with the view that denaturation involves rupture of structural bonds resulting in an increased freedom of movement of randomized molecular components.

Activation parameters for the heat denaturation of a number of proteins are presented in Table D-2.

Effect of pH on Denaturation

All proteins are polyelectrolytes, due to their ionizable basic and acidic amino acid side chains, with PK values ranging from 3 to 12. The net charge of a protein molecule in solution is a function of pH, and its relative content of basic and acidic amino acids. The native structural conformation of protein molecules may be substantially altered by pH change due to the resultant electrostatic effects. Depending on the protein species, pH change may induce swelling, reversible molecular association-dissociation, or rapid denaturation. Pepsin is readily denatured at pH values above 6. β-lactoglobulin, at pH 8.3, denatures rapidly at temperatures as low as 0°C, exhibiting both reversible and irreversible denaturation changes. Lysozyme is one of the few proteins whose thermal denaturation is but slightly affected by pH. The thermal denaturation of proteins is profoundly altered by pH, and the solubility of of the denatured protein is further influenced by pH, leading to a lowered solubility and, fre-

quently, coagulation in the isoelectric range. This is of particular importance in food processing since enzyme inactivation, bacterial destruction, and the rheological properties of many food products are pH-dependent denaturation phenomena. The curd tension properties, for example, of cottage cheese processed from high heat milk, is sharply reduced by the coprecipitation of the heat-denatured whey proteins with the casein clot in the isoelectric pH range. Reduction of the alkaline pH of liquid egg white allows heat pasteurization without damage to the denaturable proteins.

Heat Denaturation of Enzymes

The inactivation of enzymes, and the thermal destruction of microorganisms in foods, by blanching, pasteurization, and sterilization are, intrinsically, heat denaturation processes. Enzymes catalyze innumerable reactions in food products, often with adverse effect on palatability, color, and texture. Lipase induced rancidity in milk, lipoxygenase derived beaniness in soybean, and discoloration of fruits and vegetables by polyphenol oxidases are but a few prominent examples of the large and growing catalog of such quality defects. However, the heat treatment of food products, required to inactivate such enzymes and for thermal destruction of the microflora, frequently leads to serious deterioration of the natural flavor, color, nutritional value, and textural qualities. Such heat-induced quality deterioration may evolve from caramelization and browning reactions, hydrolytic cleavage, and thermally activated chemical degradations. The unremitting search for improved quality in processed foods has led to the development of shorter heat process treatments, culminating in ultra high temperature-

TABLE D-3

THERMAL INACTIVATION OF ENZYMES

Enzyme	Source	Experimental Temp ($^\circ$F)	Z ($^\circ$F)	D (Min)	Temp for Determination of D Value ($^\circ$F)
Catalase	Purified from spinach (in buffer)	140	—	ca 2	140
	Spinach extract	140	37	22–31	140
		149	15	ca 1	149
Lipoxygenase	20% pea solids	158	15.7	85	154
		171	6.1	12	163
	Values Extrapolated to				
Peroxidase	Horseradish	176	49.8	232	
	Green beans	176	47.0	15	
	Turnips	176	46.0	73	
	Sweet corn	176	54.0	30	
Catalase	Spinach extract	176	15.0	0.02	
Lipoxygenase	Pea Solids	176	15.7	0.09	
o-Diphenol oxidase	Pear	176	10.0	0.82	
Polygalacturonase	Papaya	176	11.0	23	

SOURCE: Aylward and Haisman (1969).

short time, or flash sterilization technology, and ancillary aseptic packaging methods. Such developments are predicated on the much greater magnitude of the thermal coefficients for protein denaturation, as compared to those that characterize chemical decomposition. For a 10°C increase in process temperature, the rate of enzyme inactivation or bacterial kill may rise by a factor much greater than 10, whereas, browning or cooked flavor intensity may only double within this interval.

Thermal destruction of bacteria is a first order reaction, and it appears plausible that the death of a bacterial cell be ascribed to the denaturation of its most critical, life-supporting protein component. Bacterial kill by heat is logarithmic, and the thermal destruction rate constant, K, may be defined by

$$K = 1/t \log \frac{\text{initial population}}{\text{number of survivors}}$$

The thermal denaturation of enzymes is analogous to the thermal destruction of microorganisms, and a number of the pragmatic terms that had been developed for describing the kinetics of bacterial kill, have been adapted by food technologists to define enzyme inactivation. These include D, F_T and Z values. The D value, or

decimal reduction time, represents the heating period required for a 90% reduction in enzymic activity, where

$$D = 2.3/k'$$

This is more widely applied in the form of an F_T value, the heating time required to reduce enzymic activity to a specified residual level, generally 1% of original, at a particular temperature. Over limited temperature ranges, for both enzymes and bacteria, their rates of thermal destruction are logarithmically, linear functions of the temperature, or of the reciprocal of the absolute temperature, according to

$$\log D = a - (t^\circ F/Z) \text{ and}$$

$$\log D = (M/T^\circ K) - b$$

where a, Z, M and b are constants.

The temperature coefficient Q_{10} is a frequently used expression, representing the factor by which the thermal denaturation rate constant increases for a 10°C increment

$$Q_{10} = \frac{K_T + 10}{K_T}$$

The temperature change in degrees Fahrenheit that will effect a tenfold change in the rate of enzyme activation is expressed in the widely-used Z factor, where

$$Z = \frac{18}{\log Q_{10}}$$

A compilation of such values, from the literature on thermal inactivation of various enzymes, is summarized in Table D-3.

Such data illustrate the large diversity in heat lability of enzymes. The peroxidases are by far the most heat stable enzymes in vegetables. Under the more acid conditions in fruits, peroxidases are substantially less stable to heat, but are still most difficult to inactivate. The uniquely high heat stability of the peroxidases indicates a negative entropy of activation, which remains largely unexplained. Pectolytic enzymes generally appear to be relatively thermolabile, with rapid inactivation at temperatures above 70°C. Polygalacturonase is more heat stable than pectinesterase, but one isolated from tomatoes shows some activity retention after 60 min boiling.

A comparable dispersion of thermal inactivation rates of enzymes native to milk is recognized. The acid phosphatase of milk is quite heat stable, requiring 30 min at 80°C for inactivation. The α-amylase in bovine milk is inactivated, at pH 6.4, in the temperature range 45°–52°C. Milk lysozyme is stable at low pH values and is unaffected by heat treatment at 100°C for 3 min. At pH 7.5, however, it sustains a 30% loss of activity in 1 min at 100°C. Bovine milk ribonuclease, at pH 7.0, is completely inactivated at 90°C for 20 min, but is stable at pH 3.5. Xanthine oxidase is moderately stable to heat, retaining 75% of its activity at 76°C for 18 sec. Aldolase is the most thermally labile enzyme in milk and is completely inactivated in 20 min at 45°C. The milk lipases, fairly labile to heat, are inactivated below pasteurization temperatures losing 50% activity in 15 min at 50°C. Alkaline phosphatase is completely inactivated under pasteurization conditions at 62°C for 30 min, or 16 sec at 80°C. The coincidence of alkaline phosphatase inactivation with pasteurization treatment is the basis for its widespread use as a confirmatory test for pasteurization compliance. As previously noted, under ultra high temperature-short time heat treatments alkaline phosphatase shows reversibility of denaturation on cool aging.

Heat Denaturation in Food Systems

Milk Proteins.—Food proteins frequently occur in cellular or tissue structures of great complexity. The course of denaturation, and resulting secondary effects on rheological properties of the food product, are influenced by a variety of environmental factors including pH, electrolyte characteristics, and interspecies reactions of protein with protein, lipid, and carbohydrate components. Simultaneous heat-induced changes in the hydrogen ion activity and electrolyte equilibria frequently exert a profound influence on the denaturation properties. Therefore, studies on heat denaturation of proteins in their natural environment tend to be more empirical and extrapolation from model systems of isolated, discrete proteins must be done with reservation. Milk, as a secretory fluid, is essentially devoid of the cellular and tissue structures that so complicate the study of protein denaturation in meat and fish products. Nevertheless, the denaturation of milk proteins affords an excellent example of the multiple problems encountered in the study of heat denaturation and its effects on the processing of a natural food product.

The several casein components of milk, which together comprise about 80% of the total milk protein, are by many criteria nonheat denaturable. The whey proteins, however, which account for only 20% of the total milk protein are all heat denaturable to varying degrees, a fact of great significance in diary product technology. The process and storage stability of condensed milk and frozen milk products, as well as the functional performance of milk products in the manufacture of cheese, bread and ice cream, are profoundly affected by the extent of heat denaturation of the whey protein fraction.

The milk serum, or whey, proteins comprise β-lactoglobulin, α-lactalbumin, immune globulins, and serum albumin of varying content. The β-lactoglobulin component shows genetically derived compositional variation. The total serum protein content of milk also varies with breed of cow, lactation stage, season, etc. While commercial bulked milk tends to average out such variations, sufficient differences persist to affect the heat processing characteristics of commercial milk. The mean value for the heat denaturable serum protein nitrogen content of commercially pooled milk is 66 mg % with a range of 55–85 mg % N, as determined by the Harland-Ashworth method. β-lactoglobulin represents 40–60% of the total serum protein fraction of milk, and, therefore, dominates the net course of denaturation. The relative heat denaturability, in order of increasing stability of the serum protein components is: immune globulins, serum albumin, β-lactoglobulin and α-lactalbumin. As shown in Fig. D-4, the heat treatment of milk at 70°C for 30 min may denature only 6% of the α-lactalbumin, 32% of the β-lactoglobulin, 52% of the serum albumin, and 89% of the immune globulins, representing a cumulative 29% denaturation level of the total serum proteins.

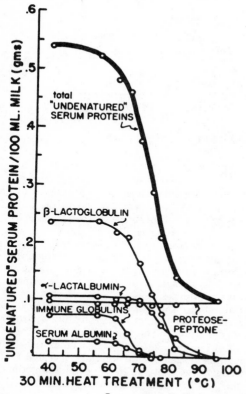

Larson and Rolleri (1955)

FIG. D-4. THERMAL DENATURATION OF THE INDIVIDUAL AND TOTAL SERUM PROTEIN COMPONENTS OF MILK

Reprinted with permission of *Journal of Dairy Science.*

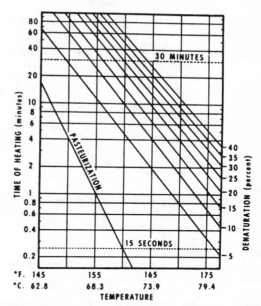

FIG. D-5. THERMAL DENATURATION OF THE TOTAL SERUM PROTEINS IN MILK AS A FUNCTION OF TIME-TERMPERATURE VARIABLES

Reprinted with permission of *Journal of Dairy Science.*

The molecular size dispersion of the serum proteins in milk is not appreciably altered by heat denaturation, but the denatured proteins precipitate on the addition of salt, or acidification to the isoelectric pH range of 4.5–4.8. Such loss of solubility on denaturation is the basis for the Harland-Ashworth assay method which has been widely used in kinetic studies on the denaturation of the composite milk serum proteins, and in the development and quality control of sterile milk products, dried milks, cheese, and dairy by-products.

In the temperature range 62°–80°C, the denaturation rate for the total serum protein fraction of milk is logarithmically related to temperature, as shown in Fig. D-5.

A temperature increase of 7.5°C reduces the time required for a specified level of denaturation to increase tenfold, equivalent to a Z value of 13.5. In the HTST range, the relationship for equivalent denaturation departs from linearity, and at 80°–90°C, the Z value increases to about 19. Temperatures required for pasteurization of milk, and denaturation of the alkaline phosphatase, fall distinctly below that of serum protein denaturation. The first evidence of cooked flavor in heated milk coincides with an albumin-globulin denaturation level of about 58%.

The denaturation of β-lactoglobulin has been more intensively researched than that of the other serum proteins because it can be readily recovered in a highly purified, crystalline state. Several polymorphic genetic variants of β-lactoglobulin have been identified and designated A, B, and C types. β-lactoglobulin is a dimer of 36,000 molecular weight, dissociating into 2 monomers of 18,000 molecular weight at low solution concentration, over a pH range of 2–9. Attempts to characterize the molecular conformation of β-lactoglobulin by a number of physicochemical criteria have led to contradictory results, relative to helical form and content. Definitive measurements on the kinetics of β-lactoglobulin denaturation have been based on the rate of activation of sulfhydryl groups, among other criteria. The denaturation, based on o-iodosobenzoate reactivity of the -SH groups follows first order kinetics to an activation of 60% SH, in the temperature range 64°–75°C.

TABLE D-4

THERMODYNAMIC PARAMETERS FOR THERMAL DENATURATION
OF β-LACTOGLOBULIN

Temp (°C)	k' (Sec^{-1} × 10^5)	$\Delta H^{\ddagger}$ (Cal/Mole)	$\Delta F^{\ddagger}$ (Cal/Mole)	$\Delta S^{\ddagger}$ (Cal/Degree-Mole)
64.3	4.6	79,930	26,517	158.5
67.2	11.1	79,924	26,164	158.0
69.8	26.9	79,919	25,763	158.0
72.0	73.0	79,914	25,271	158.5
74.6	145.9	79,909	24,982	158.0

The activation energy for the denaturation process is 80,000 cal per mole. The velocity constants and calculated thermodynamic functions for heat denaturation of β-lactoglobulin in phosphate buffer, pH 6.6, are given in Table D-4.

The course of β-lactoglobulin denaturation measured by other criteria, suggests that several heat denaturation processes may be involved. Two phases of heat denaturation are distinguishable, the first of which is initiated above 65°C, leading to molecular aggregation but without effect on electromobility. This is followed by a marked increase in electrophoretic mobility as a second order process, with a maximum rate at 75°-80°C. Isoelectric precipitation and light scattering methods also suggest second order kinetics of the formula $1/c - 1/c_o = k''t$. At pH 6.9, phosphate buffer, the k'' value for the rate constant increases from 0.1 to 1.30 cm^3 per gm per sec, for a temperature increase of 69.3° to 79.7°C, when denaturation is assessed by isoelectric precipitation.

Egg Protein Denaturation.—Ovalbumin.—Egg white, which represents about 65% of the whole egg content, contains 11% protein. The heat denaturable ovalbumin is a glycoprotein, with molecular weight 45,000, and constitutes about 63% of the egg white protein. Its isoelectric point is 4.6-4.8. It is readily denatured by heat, and at air-liquid interfaces during whipping. Acetylation of the amino groups of ovalbumin appreciably reduces its stability to denaturation. The volume of the denatured ovalbumin molecule, due to its distension, is approximately twice that of the native molecule.

Thermal denaturation of ovalbumin in the neutral range is minimal at pH 6.76, with an activation energy of 130,000 cal per mole. In acid denaturation, activation energy at pH 3.4 is 97,000 cal, and at pH 2.3 it decreases to 48,000 cal. For the thermal denaturation of ovalbumin in the alkaline region, the activation parameters are for $\Delta H^{\ddagger}$ (74.7 kcal per mole), $\Delta S^{\ddagger}$ (145 eu), and $\Delta F^{\ddagger}$ (25.6 kcal per mole). Heat denaturation of ovalbumin induces formation of an absorption band at 6.15

M in the infrared, increasing with intensity of heat treatment. Its heat denaturation in the presence of 7.5 m urea will occur at temperatures as low as 37°C. The thermal lability of ovalbumin is also amplified by treatment with short waves, 3-30 m, and by pre-exposure to X-rays. The water sorption isotherm of dried denatured ovalbumin is about 20% lower than that of the native protein at all relative humidities.

Ovalbumin, which is quite resistant to tryptic hydrolysis in the native state, is readily hydrolyzed when denatured. The thiol groups in native ovalbumin are undetectable by iodoacetate or N-ethylmaleimide reagents, but are fully revealed in the heat denatured protein. Native ovalbumin contains virtually all the thiol groups of egg white.

Ovomucoid.—A glycoprotein in the molecular weight range 27,000-29,000, ovomucoid constitutes about 12% of the total protein of egg white. Its isoelectric point is pH 3.8-4.5. Ovomucoid is exceptionally heat stable, and exhibits negligible change in viscosity or solubility on heat treatments up to 1 hr at 100°C. It has been identified as an inhibitor of tryptic proteolysis.

Globulins.—The three globulins constitute about 8% of the egg white protein. The lysozyme component, a protein of 17,000 mole weight exhibits lytic action against bacteria and may protect the intact egg from bacterial intrusion. Lysozyme, with an isoelectric point of about 11.0, is unusually resistant to heat denaturation at temperatures up to 100°. Its rate of heat denaturation shows unusually small changes in the pH range 1-6.3. Its pH of maximum heat stability is 5.5. It is largely an α-helical protein with 29-39% of its residues in helical configuration. Its heat denaturation is a first order process. The surface denaturation of lysozyme is also a first order process, with an activation energy of 15 kcal per mole. The globulins contribute to the foaming capability and heat coagulation of egg white.

The heat denaturability of isolated egg yolk proteins has not been researched adequately. The opacity changes and coagulation attendant to the denaturation of egg white become apparent at about 60°C, and increase as a function of time and temperature of heating, while egg yolk thickens at around 65°C and acquires a heat set at 70°C.

The heat treatment required for the pasteurization of liquid whole eggs, 60°–61°C for 3.5 min, is without an adverse effect on functional performance. However, the pasteurization of liquid egg whites under these conditions, tends to impair the whipping rate of meringue and reduces the volume of angel cake. Milder heat pasteurization treatments that retain greater functionality have been developed for liquid egg white. Egg whites can be pasteurized after drying to eliminate recontamination, particularly with Salmonellae. At a moisture level not exceeding 5%, dried whites can be held at 50°C without functional impairment. Lower moisture imparts greater stability to protein denaturation in dried egg white and, therefore, at 3% residual moisture, a holding temperature of 60°–70°C is possible. A hot hold treatment in excess of 7 days may be required for pasteurization of dried egg white at 6% moisture.

Heat Denaturation of Meat Proteins

The heat denaturation of meat proteins during processing and cooking has profound effect on its water holding capacity, shrink characteristics, tenderness and overall textural quality. The denaturation properties of the meat proteins, organized as fibers and filaments in a complex tissue environment, may be expected to depart from that of meat protein isolates. Broadly, the denaturation of meat proteins occurs in the range of 57°–75°C.

In general, most of the soluble proteins of the sarcoplasm and actomyosin system of the fibrils will have denatured on heating meat to about 62°C, and cross-linking of the randomized, denatured protein molecules imparts the characteristic coagulated structure and appearance of cooked meats. The denaturation rate of the sarcoplasmic proteins of pork muscle is greatest in the pH range 5.5–5.8. The myoglobins and myoalbumins show significant heat denaturation only on protracted heating at 60°C, and uncoagulated water-soluble proteins are still evident after 6 hr heating at 60°C.

Collagen is the main connective tissue protein of meat. Its triple helix molecules, $15A \times 2800A$, are arranged in parallel fibrils, intermolecularly cross-linked. About 22% of the collagen residues are proline and hydroxyproline, whose imido group seems to strongly influence the unique structural conformation of collagen. A thermal contraction of the collagen fibers is induced by heat treatment due to unravelling and randomization of the helical regions of the collagen molecule. This thermal contraction, in which the collagen fibers may shrink to $1/3$ their length, occurs at sharply defined

temperatures, known as the shrinkage temperature and designated T_S. For fish collagen the T_S value is 45° and for beef muscle collagen, 65°C. The shrinkage temperature appears analogous to the melting of ordinary crystalline polymers, and presumably represents the point at which "crystalline" regions, near the imido residues of the collagen molecule, randomize. The thermal denaturation of soluble collagen, isolated from collagen fibers, occurs at considerably lower temperature.

The heat resistance of collagen is variable for different muscles, and is lower in the longissimus dorsi than in the semitendinous muscle.

During thermal shrinkage, collagen loses its high elastic modulus and acquires greater susceptibility to stress breakage. The initial increase in meat tenderness, on heat treatment as measured by shear force, is ascribed to collagen shrinkage in the 50°–60°C range, with negligible change noted up to 50°C. Above the shrink temperature, denaturation of the myofibrillar proteins tends to toughen meat, while a competitive softening effect is produced by collagen solubilization. The degradation of collagen to gelatin occurs at temperatures well above the T_S, and involves a more extensive rupture of the collagen cross-links. The collagen protein content in beefsteak cooked to an internal temperature of 80°C is only 40% of that in steak cooked to 61°C. The heat stability of collagen is variable with the animal and its age, as well as its muscle source.

Elastin is quite heat stable to normal process temperatures, and appears to be randomly oriented polypeptide chains, undenaturable at 100°C. The water-soluble myoglobin, on binding oxygen, forms the red pigment oxymyoglobin. It is present in beef muscle in the range of 200–400 mg% of wet tissue. Its denaturation in the presence of O_2, leads to oxidation of its heme iron content and the formation of the brown metmyoglobin. Myoglobin is relatively heat stable up to 60°C, which accounts for the retention of the pink color in rare cooked beef.

Physical Denaturation of Proteins

Proteins are susceptible to denaturation by a number of physical treatments including exposure to high pressure, ultrasonic waves, irradiation, surface denaturation, and freezing.

Surface Denaturation.—Many water-soluble proteins will denature and form insoluble protein films when spread as a monomolecular film at an air-water or liquid-liquid interface. This denaturation is generally completely irreversible. The surface denaturation of globular proteins, at a constant surface pressure, increases with time in a first order process, with an activation energy of 15 kcal per mole. For many proteins such as ovalbumin, pepsin, and gliadin, there is no detectable change in molecular weight on surface denaturation. However, hemoglobin, zein, and β-lactoglobulin show varying degrees of molecular dissociation on interfacial spreading. Enzymes show variable loss of biological activity on surface denaturation. Urease sustains a loss of 98% of its enzymic activity, while pepsin retains its proteolytic potency.

The foaming of egg white by whipping is one of the most important applications of surface denaturation in food technology. The foaming competence of egg white is derived principally from the ovalbumin fraction, with significant contribution from the globulin, lysozyme, and ovomucin. Isolated ovalbumin will, itself, produce a foam, but at a slower whipping rate, and angel cake baked with ovalbumin is of deficient quality.

Duck egg white, which contains less than $1/3$ the lysozyme of chicken egg white exhibits poor whipping properties, attributable to this deficiency.

Ultrasonic and Pressure Denaturation.—Many enzymes are inactivated by ultrasonic denaturation including milk reductase, peroxidase and alkaline phosphatase, trypsin, pepsin, lysozyme, and diastase. Ultrasonic treatment for 30 min at 3 Mc per sec, 1.5 w/cm^2, will reduce diastase activity from 9.9×10^{-4} to 2.7×10^{-4} Willstetter units. Oxyhemoglobin in dilute aqueous solution, under ultrasonic treatment will convert rapidly to methemoglobin and in more concentrated solutions will dissociate from the heme moiety. Homogenization, presumably through comparable cavitation effects, may also denature proteins. The homogenization of egg whites reduces whip functionality in proportion to homogenization pressure. The deterioration in egg white whip performance, as a result of mechanical stress, is attributable to changes in the mucin component.

The enzymic activity of rennin and pepsin is reduced with increasing hydrostatic pressure, as a function of exposure time, and total loss of activity is incurred in the pressure range 5000–6000 kg per cm^2. However, this pressure denaturation effect is not evident at pH values lower than 4. At pH 5.0–5.2, 50% enzymic activity is lost in 5 min at 7750 kg per cm^2. Generally, increased denaturation results from increasing protein concentration at a fixed pressure treatment.

The rate of pressure denaturation of ovalbumin is at a maximum at the isoelectric pH 4.8, by solubility measurement. Pressures in excess of 4000 kg per cm for 1 hr are required to induce turbidity changes in ovalbumin solutions.

Pressure denaturation of carboxyhemoglobin follows first order kinetics. The effect of pressure appears to relate to the equilibrium displacement laws of Le-Chatelier, involving the molecular volume change attendant to denaturation. The denaturation volume changes are ascribed to electrostriction effects resulting from the protein ionization changes produced by denaturation. A volume constriction of 2.5 ml per mole is produced per peptide hydrogen bond broken.

Irradiation.—Ionization radiations induce profound changes in the molecular organization of proteins. Following the disruption of secondary molecular structure, covalent chemical changes and fragmentation may also occur. Intensive X-radiation of deoxyribonuclease causes large, linear increases in ultraviolet absorption at 250 mμ and exponential reduction in enzymic activity. Catalase and egg albumin solutions, 0.1%, when irradiated at 0.6–2McV (10^5 to 5×10^7 rads dosage) undergo molecular fragmentation and aggregation changes. Progressive gel formation is induced in irradiated fibrinogen, and is complete at a dosage of 5×10^5 rads.

Enzymic denaturation is dependent on composition of the medium, oxygen tension, and temperature. Proteins are denatured primarily through indirect action of the radiation on the surrounding medium, and the resultant changes in protein ionization. Radiation effects vary inversely with protein concentration. Radiation effects on milk, with respect to rennet clot time, are comparable to that of heat, both reducing the clot rate.

Aqueous egg albumin solutions show viscosity loss of radiation, while liquid egg white thins due to a probable effect on the ovomucin fraction. Sulfhydryl groups are elaborated under radiation treatment of egg white protein.

The forms of radiation utilized in food processing research include beta radiation from resonant transformers (Van de Graff or linear accelerator), and gamma radiation from spent fuel elements, Co^{60} and fission products. The complete inactivation of enzymes, for the preservation of foods by radiation, requires from 5 to 10 times the radiation dose required for the destruction of the microflora. This is reverse to the relative thermal lability of enzymes and bacteria. For a food product with a D value of 5 million rads, required for a 90% bacterial kill, 20 million rads may be necessary for enzymic denaturation. A radiation dosage of such intensity causes profound deterioration in food quality. Consequently, supplemental methods are required for enzyme inactivation in radiation processing of foods.

Proteins are comparably denatured by ultraviolet (UV) radiation. Denaturation of ovalbumin by UV is a unimolecular reaction, apparently independent of pH and temperature, and leads to isoelectric insolubility. Enzyme inactivation by UV radiation depends on intensity and radiation time. The primary effect of *UV* radiation inactivation of enzymes appears to be a photolysis of aromatic residues such as tryptophan, and of disulfide bonds. The cystyl and tryptophanyl residues of lysozyme, trypsin, and ribonuclease are the principal foci of UV radiation damage.

Freezing.—Freezing, and frozen storage, frequently lead to substantial changes in protein solubility and in the dispersion stability of protein colloids in a variety of food products. In the thawed product such changes, in the case of fish, may be evidenced by an increased tendency to lose moisture on cooking, increased toughness or rubberiness, and a loss of succulence. In frozen milk, a progressive loss of casein dispersion stability is incurred culminating in complete coagulation of the calcium phosphocaseinate phase, and the separation of whey in the thawed product.

It is difficult to differentiate denaturation by freezing, as a direct effect, from secondary changes caused by the increased concentration of electrolytes, hydrogen ion, etc., in the unfrozen matrix. In fish, the textural defects are due solely to alteration of the myofibrillar proteins whose solubility shows progressive, gradual loss in frozen storage. Neither sarcoplasmic, nor connective tissue proteins evidence deterioration during frozen storage, as measured by protein extractability in neutral salt solution, or by electrophoretic criteria. For various fish species, over a wide range of storage temperature and time, protein solubility depreciates exponentially with time of frozen storage down to $-24°C$. This decline in protein solubility closely approximates objective assessment of textural deterioration. However, such protein solubility losses are not accompanied by modification in SH reactivity or protein ionization as criteria of denaturation.

It has been proposed that the formation of intracellular ice crystals generate localized high salt concentrations that, in effect, denature the actomyosin in frozen fish. The dominant source of textural changes, and loss of water-holding capacity in frozen fish, is apparently due to increased bonding between the myofibrillar proteins, but whether this constitutes a true denaturation is at present unresolved.

Mammalian meat generally suffers significantly less damage on freezing than does fish. Changes in tenderness, water-holding capacity, and drip exudation appear to derive from changes at the cellular and fiber level due to ice crystal formation, rather than from protein denaturation.

Fluid egg yolk, on freezing to $-6°C$, becomes pasty on thawing. This viscosity change, termed gelation, increases progressively with decreasing storage temperature and with storage time. Although the gelation is evident, within a few hours at $-10°C$ and below, further viscosity changes occur over protracted frozen storage periods. The mechanism of frozen egg yolk gelation is unresolved. Irreversible precipitation of the lecithovitellin component occurs at $-6°C$ or below possibly as a result of yolk salt concentration. Electrophoretic evidence indicates that the lipoprotein L_2, the major lipoprotein fraction in the plasma, is altered during freezing and thawing of yolk.

The freezing of fluid or concentrated milk leads to extensive destabilization of the colloidally dispersed calcium phosphocaseinate. The loss of casein stability is progressive with storage time but is delayed at lower storage temperatures.

The casein coagulum is initially redispersible with applied heat and agitation, but becomes progressively irreversible with continued storage. Depending on the prefreezing process conditions, 35% solids concentrated whole milk may resist coagulation for a period of 12 weeks at $-20°C$ storage, coagulating more rapidly at higher frozen storage temperature. It has been established that casein coagulation in frozen milk concentrates is "triggered" by nucleation and massive crystallization of the milk serum lactose. A commercial process has been developed for producing a stable frozen milk concentrate based on partial lactase enzyme hydrolysis of the lactose to reduce its supersaturation level and suppress crystallization.

The coagulation of the caseinate dispersion, as a consequence of lactose crystallization indicates that soluble lactose functions as an effective stabilizing component for the casein micelle colloid. The coagulation of casein in frozen milk is, therefore, a colloidal micelle destabilization by the high electrolyte concentration, developed under freezing conditions, and is not attributable to a denaturation process. The denaturation of the serum proteins in milk, however, has an adverse effect on the casein micelle stability in the frozen product, possibly through interaction of the denatured lactogolbulin with casein. Prefreezing process heat treatment should, therefore, be held below 75°C.

The casein in frozen milk may also be stabilized by the addition of polyhydric compounds such as sugars, glycerol, etc., as well as small amounts of monovalent salts, which act as freezing point depressants. The parallel function of polyhydric compounds in the preservation of frozen egg yolk, milk, and red blood cells indicates that such compounds, in addition to their colligative contribution to depression of the freezing point, may perform a specific protein stabilizing role through hydrogen bonding.

Many sugars in concentrated solution are also known to prevent thermal coagulation of proteins. Butyrate and caprylate ions stabilize proteins toward urea and heat denaturation. Glycogen, amino acids, fluoride ion, and DNA, among many other additives, are known to function as specific inhibitors of denaturation.

LEON TUMERMAN

References

ANFINSEN, C. B., and REDFIELD, R. R. 1956. Protein structure in relation to function and biosynthesis. *In* Advances in Protein Chemistry, Vol. 11, Academic Press, New York.

AYLWARD, F., and HAISMAN, D. R. 1969. Oxidation systems in fruits and vegetables—their relation to the quality of preserved products. *In* Advances in Food Research, Vol. 17, Academic Press, New York.

BENDALL, J. R. 1964. Meat proteins. *In* Symposium on Foods: Proteins and Their Reactions. H. W. Schultz and A. F. Anglemier (Editors). Avi Publishing Co., Wesport, Conn.

BRAY, G. H., and WHITE, K. 1957. Kinetics and Thermodynamics in Biochemistry. Academic Press, New York.

BUTLER, L. 1970. Protein structure and properties. J. Am. Oil Chemists' Soc. 48, 101.

CONNELL, J. J. 1964. Fish muscle proteins and some effects on them of processing. *In* Symposium on Foods: Proteins and Their Reactions. H. W. Schultz and A. F. Anglemier (Editors). Avi Publishing Co., Westport, Conn.

DESROSIER, N. W. 1970. The Technology of Food Preservation, 3rd Edition. Avi Publishing Co., Westport, Conn.

DRENTH, J., JANSONIUS, J. N., KOEKOEK, R., and WOLTHERS, B. G. 1971. The study of papain. *In* Advances in Protein Chemistry, Vol. 25, Academic Press, New York.

FEENY, R. E., and HILL, R. M. 1960. Protein chemistry and food research. *In* Advances in Food Research, Vol. 10, Academic Press, New York.

FENNEMA, O., and POWRIE, W. D. 1964. Fundamentals of low temperature food preservation. *In* Advances in Food Research, Vol. 13, Academic Press, New York.

HARLAND, H. A., COULTER, S. T., and JENNESS, R. 1952. The effect of the various steps in the manufacture on the extent of serum protein denaturation in nonfat dry milk solids. J. Dairy Sci. 35, 363.

JENNESS, R., and PATTON, S. 1959. Principles of Dairy Chemistry. John Wiley & Sons, New York.

JOLY, M. 1965. A Physico-Chemical Approach to the Denaturation of Proteins. Academic Press, New York.

LARSON, B. L., and JENNESS, R. 1952. Characterization of the sulfhydryl groups and the ki-netics of heat denaturation of Crystalline β-lacto-globulin. J. Am. Chemical Soc. 74, 3090.

LARSON, B. L., and ROLLERI, G. D. 1955. Heat denaturation of the specific serum proteins in milk. J. Dairy Sci. 38, 351.

McKENZIE, H. A. 1967. Milk proteins. *In* Advances in Protein Chemistry, Academic Press, New York.

McKENZIE, H. A. 1971. Milk proteins. *In* Chemistry and Molecular Biology, Vol. 2. Academic Press, New York.

NEURATH, H. 1963. The Proteins. Academic Press, New York.

PARRY, R. M., JR. 1974. Milk coagulation and protein denaturation. *In* Fundamentals of Dairy Chemistry, 2nd Edition. B. H. Webb, A. H. Johnson, and J. A. Alford (Editors). Avi Publishing Co., Westport, Conn.

PAUL, P. C., and PALMER, H. H. 1972. Food Theory and Applications, John Wiley & Sons, New York.

TUMERMAN, L., FRAM, H., and CORNELY, K. W. 1954. The effect of lactose crystallization on protein stability in frozen concentrated milk. J. Dairy Sci. 37, 830.

TUMERMAN, L., and WEBB, B. H. 1965. Coagulation of milk and protein denaturation. *In* Fundamentals of Dairy Chemistry. B. H. Webb and A. H. Johnson (Editors). Avi Publishing Co., Westport, Conn. (Out of Print)

DETERGENTS

A detergent is any substance that aids in the removal of dirt. For use in a food plant a detergent should be capable of removing food residues, water hardness deposits, and other matter from equipment and other surfaces. Recent actions by the Environmental Protection Agency, the Food and Drug Administration, and similar state and local agencies have limited the choice of detergents, the detergent processes, and the disposal of used detergent solutions.

The removal of foreign matter should be achieved (a) with a minimum possibility of contamination of the food product with residual particulates or chemicals; (b) with minimum overall cost of labor, materials, and power for the cleaning process itself; (c) without injury to the worker, the surface being cleaned, and the surrounding (floors, walls, ceilings, and sewers); and (d) with minimum cost for protection of air and for disposal of waste water in accordance with environmental standards.

Abrasives, such as pumice, sandpaper, metallic and plastic sponges, and spatulas have been effective in the removal of heavy or baked-on deposits but their use has been discontinued in most food plants due to damage to equipment surfaces and the possibility of residual particulate matter reaching the food product.

Water under high pressure—up to 1500 psi—emerging from a narrow orifice exerts excellent soil removal when properly directed, but power and labor costs are relatively high.

Alkaline aqueous solutions are effective in dissolving food product residues. In general, the higher the pH and the temperature the more effective the soil removal. The common alkalies used are caustic soda; ortho-, sesqui-, and metasilicate; trisodium phosphate; and sodium carbonate. For manual cleaning, metasilicate and/or sodium carbonate may be buffered with sodium bicarbonate for lower pH solutions.

Alkaline solutions in bicarbonate hardness waters form precipitates of calcium either as the carbonate or as the orthophosphate if sufficient phosphate is present. These hardness precipitates can be controlled in the following several ways:

(1) The most satisfactory method is usually to soften all waters used in cleaning solutions and in rinsing. This reduces the calcium and magnesium so that little or no hardness precipitation will occur unless the food residue itself is high in hardness.

(2) Sequestering agents such as the polyphosphates—sodium hexametaphosphate, sodium tripolyphosphate, and tetrasodium pyrophosphate—or chelating agents such as salts of ethylene diamine tetra acetic acid, or of nitrilo triacetic acid form soluble complex ions with calcium, magnesium, and other metal ions and so reduce the concentration of free ions below that at which precipitation will occur. In high pH solutions, sugar acid salts such as gluconate, lactobionate, and others tend to form similar complexes. While effective in alkaline-use solutions, there may be a problem of precipitation on dilution with the rinse water.

(3) Certain surfactants readily adsorb on the surface of hardness precipitates, cause dispersion of the precipitate, and so may prevent the growth of larger than submicroscopic particles. A somewhat similar mechanism has been proposed to account for the "threshold" treatment effect of very small concentrations of sodium hexametaphosphate in preventing precipitation of calcium in cooling waters.

(4) While not a preventative of hardness precipitation, the build-up of precipitate on equipment can be eliminated by dissolving the freshly formed deposit in a weak acid solution and using a slightly acid rinse water (about pH 5.5) to prevent hardness precipitation from rinse water.

Detergent solutions of straight acids or alkalies show no significant reduction in surface tension and usually have little penetrating and wetting power for most soils, particularly fats and oils. Surfactants are surface-active organic compounds of relatively large molecular weight—several hundred to several thousand—which tend to concentrate at the liquid interfaces. In varying degree, surfactants reduce surface and interfacial tension and aid in wetting, penetration, emulsification, and dispersion of the soil. Under some circumstances water only and surfactant may give excellent cleaning, particularly with some fatty soils.

Surfactants include several hundred organic compounds which have been classified in three main groups as anionic, cationic, and nonionic on the basis of the charge on the large organic portion of the molecule. The anionics are mainly sodium salts and are commonly used in alkaline, neutral, and acid solutions. The nonionics do not ionize in solution and are being used to a greater extent for their compatibility, especially with cationic materials, and for their detergent characteristics. The cationics are little used in food plant cleaning except for the cationic quaternary ammonium compounds, some of which have excellent germicidal power especially in suitably compounded alkaline cleaner-sanitizer mixtures. Most surfactants used until the early 1960's were resistant to biological degradation and were the cause of persistent foam problems in sewage treatment plants, rivers, and in some cases ground water supplies. Since then, surfactants in all three groups have been produced that are acceptably biodegradable. Foam is a good measure of the residual soap in a cleaning solution but in a synthetic surfactant solution it has no direct relation to detergency. Foam in food plant cleaning is actually a disadvantage and low foam is desirable in a surfactant. The nonionics usually are less soluble at higher temperatures and begin to precipitate at the cloud point temperature. For many food plant procedures, a high cloud point is desirable. Most surfactants are salted out by a high concentration of ions in a strong detergent solution. However, surfactants are available that are soluble even in 50% caustic solution.

Acids are usually not economically effective in removing food residues. Acids are used for water conditioning to prevent hardness precipitation and to dissolve hardness precipitates. Phosphoric acid has been widely used in food plants, is an effective source of acidity, and its residue is nontoxic. However, regulations against phosphates now restrict their use. Hydrochloric acid is effective and of low cost, but is potentially corrosive, particularly for stainless steel. Sulfuric acid is effective but is somewhat hazardous to handle and is corrosive. Sodium acid sulfate (niter cake) is less hazardous, less expensive, and has been widely used. Nitric acid reportedly is widely used in Europe but is little used in this country due to the hazards and corrosiveness to metals other than stainless steel. Organic acids such as hydroxyacetic and gluconic have been used to a limited extent and are biodegradable but are a relatively expensive source of hydrogen ions. Organic compounds are available which greatly reduce the attack of acids on metals.

One system of economical, efficient detergent solutions for food equipment is based on having adequate sequestering power from polyphosphate (such as sodium tripolyphosphate) for the total hardness from soil and water supply; adequate alkalinity (from soda ash, sodium metasilicate, and/or caustic soda) to dissolve the organic soil; and biodegradable, low-foaming, nonionic surfactant (30–200 ppm) to wet, penetrate, and disperse the soil. This solution is daily flushed to the sewer and the surfaces adequately rinsed. Such a system was used for manual cleaning and for recirculation cleaning of pipelines and storage vats. Hardness in the rinse water may result in light mineral deposits which may be removed with periodic treatment with acid solutions. This system does discharge phosphates.

Another approach has been to recirculate a caustic soda solution at a high enough concentration and temperature to be germicidal and so be satisfactory for continued use with makeup of volume and strength daily or more often if required. Preferably this solution contains a small concentration of low-foaming, caustic-stable surfactant and, in hard water, adequate chelating agent (such as gluconate or lactobionate). The caustic solution is drained and returned to its storage tank with its volume made up with the first of the rinse water. The rest of the rinse water is discharged to the sewer with the rinsing continued until the alkalinity is reduced to a satisfactory level. After draining the system, a low concentration of food-grade acid is recirculated to dissolve any hardness precipitates due to interaction of heat with the food product, or alkali with water hardness. This acid solution is drained and returned to its storage tank. The system is then rinsed with slightly acidified rinse water (about pH 5.5) which is drained to the sewer. When properly automated, such a system has given excellent and economical cleaning. Even better results would be expected with softened water for cleaning solutions and rinsing. Considerable savings in acid should then be possible.

The food plant management should know the composition of the proprietary detergent mixtures it uses or intends to use and may compare their costs with those of similar or superior specification mixtures.

H. GORDON HARDING

Cross-reference: *Emulsifiers, Food.*

DIALYTIC MEMBRANE PROCESSES

During the last two decades membrane processes have been developed to a high degree and have found many applications in the food processing industries. The types of separations which can be accomplished through membranes have long been sought but it has not been until the development of specific polymer films that this goal could be practically realized.

In broad terms, membrane processes can achieve three unique useful results. These are:

(1) The removal or modification of ionized components in food products. These processes, often related to classic ion exchange phenomena, are applied for the removal of inorganic salts or ash or for the changing of ionic species.

(2) The removal of water from aqueous food substances for the purpose of collecting a more concentrated product. In this application the ideal goal is the passage of only water through a membrane with the retention of as much as possible of the original dissolved substances in a form as closely as possible resembling their original state. This process would be comparable to evaporation methods for the removal of water with the advantage of better operating economy and less alteration or deterioration of the desired food substances.

(3) The fractionation of food substances or the separation of particular constituents within an aqueous system. In these operations separations are typically made on the basis of differential molecular size, differential substance mobility, diffusity, or concentration difference across a membrane.

The processes of dialysis and electrodialysis are examples of the first and third separation methods mentioned above. In the case of normal dialysis a concentration difference between two substances separated by a permeable membrane is the basis for the separation. The diffusion of a particular solute across the membrane phase is a common operation found in many natural and biological systems. The process of electrodialysis is more specific in that the movement of the solute through the membrane phase is accomplished under the influence of a direct current electrical field. Logically, the only diffusion which can occur is that of ionized materials such as inorganic salts.

The basic constraints and parameters of control are similar in both processes. In either dialysis or electrodialysis the permeability characteristics of the membrane is one of the key design parameters. The second major parameter of control is the rate of flow of the desired component(s) being transported between various streams. With dialysis this control is maintained through the adjustment of concentration differential or, in other words, of the rate of water flow in the compartments into which the specific component is streaming. The control of component removal in electrodialysis is a function of the intensity of electrical current passed through the cells. A secondary mode of control, the adjustment of concentration differential, in electrodialysis is precisely as in dialysis and is an important consideration. The classical methods of component flow or counterflow by dialysis apply to either process. In the case of electrodialysis an added driving force, electrical current flow, enhances the removal or transfer of ionized components. From the practical standpoint, the control of electrodialysis is more intentionally alterable than in dialysis where the control lies with the basic physical nature of the permeable membrane. In either case, the complete removal or separation of any one component from the stream is not practical since motivating forces approach zero as component concentrations approach zero.

Electrodialysis

Electrodialysis is the newer of the 2 dialytic processes and has been in practical existence for only slightly more than 20 yr. The process was conceived several decades before anyone succeeded in the production of viable membrane films which exhibited ion selective properties. Since the discovery of ion exchange phenomena, it has been theorized that if ion exchangers could be constructed into a film form they could be used as selective barriers or passages to the movement of salts in a solution through which direct electric current was being passed. The first preparation of practical ion exchange membranes was accomplished in Holland in the late 1940's. Ironically enough, the functional goal then sought was the development of these membranes for the purpose of removing salt from whey in cheese making operations. Because of world food shortages at that time it was felt that the many latent values of whey could be recovered if salt concentrations

could be reduced. The first membrane specimens were either natural or synthetic films into which were grafted or encapsulated ion exchange sites.

Membranes of two distinct types were conceived, cation or anion permeable. Historically, cation exchange materials have been more readily available and easier to manufacture than those substances which would have the property of exchanging anions. However, viable membrane films were developed with the property of permitting the passage of one type of ion with the exclusion to a major degree of the other type. Obviously, for these membranes to be workable and practical, their chemical properties had to be such that they would resist the agressive nature of the environments in which they were used as well as retain their functional properties over a practical operating life. The first criterion is relatively easily met since the development of polymer chemistry and chemically-resistant films has been rapid during the past several years. However, the development of membranes which would retain their functional properties and not foul or otherwise irreversibly exchange ionized materials was a more difficult problem. The initial development of electrodialysis with ion selective membranes was generally impractical because of the last consideration. Anion membrane materials were strongly subject to irreversible fouling by some of the anionic proteinaceous constituents found in whey. Thus, although it was demonstrated that electro-membrane ion exchange could be accomplished in suitable equipment the economic practicality of the process was not achieved until several years later when techniques were developed to either circumvent or recover from the typical fouling properties of many food solutions.

The physical configuration used in electro-membrane processing follows a generalized pattern. Stacks are constructed of thin cell separators through which process streams flow. Interspersed between the cells or separators are the membranes. Typical cell thicknesses range from $1/2$ up to about 4 mm. Thinner cells are more desirable from the electro-chemical and processing standpoint but often pose problems with greater danger of physical fouling. When relatively clear or filtered solutions are being processed, these separators are often filled with support material which also acts as a turbulence promoter. Separators which would be operating on slurries or high viscosity materials frequently have open-channels for flow. Membrane or cell areas range from approximately 1×2 ft up to 2×5 ft in size. Stacks can be constructed with as many as 500 individual cells between electrode pairs. The electrodes themselves are usually mounted in plastic end blocks or end frames. In most common operations, cathode materials are stainless steel while anodes are either graphite or platinum coated titanium or tantalum.

Membranes used in electro-membrane processing equipment fall into various categories. The main types are homogenous and heterogenous membranes and the physical configuration varies between reinforced and unreinforced forms. The definition of a homogenous membrane is one in which the ion exchange sites or selective capability is polymerized *in situ* directly onto the basic membrane structure. In contrast, a heterogenous membrane uses ion exchange media or resins which have been manufactured outside the membrane phase and then dispersed into the membrane with suitable binders. The difference between reinforced and unreinforced membranes is self-evident in that neutral woven sheeting material is often used to give a membrane more physical stability and reinforcing support. Typically, unreinforced membranes have lower electrical resistances and sometimes superior electrochemical properties but often are lacking in physical stability and handling features.

The heart of any electro-membrane processing plant is the membrane stacks. However, in addition to this basic component, several auxiliary pieces of equipment are needed. One of the primary items in electro-membrane processing systems in the DC power supply. Most commonly, these devices rectify three-phase alternating current into low ripple DC current. Typical units may be of the saturable reactor or solid state semiconductor types. Conventional piping, pumping, and circulating systems are also used. In most cases the product systems are constructed in accordance with sanitary piping standards. Auxiliary streams are frequently fabricated with plastic piping materials and pumps. Common instrumentation and controls include pH monitoring, conductivity measurement, temperature control and measurement, and selected safety devices. In general, safety devices would shut the plant down in the event of the excursion of any key parameters outside of design standards.

Electro-membrane systems currently used in the food processing industries are commonly divided into two modes of operation. One is the classical electrodialysis approach in which both cation and anion selective membranes are utilized. This means that any product treatment cell is bounded on each side by a membrane which is selectively permeable to either positive or negatively charged ionized materials. The result of this is that the flow of ionized material is carefully controlled and if nonfouling conditions are realized high current efficiencies can be achieved. Since many food processing systems involve materials which can potentially foul ion selective membranes a modified electro-membrane approach called Transport Depletion is many times used. Transport Depletion makes use of the fact that the one membrane (anion selective) which is most subject to fouling can be replaced by a nonfouling film. Transport Depletion uses a cation selective membrane to completely control the movement of positively charged ions and a neutral or nonselective membrane film which passes anions as well as some cations. Because basic electrochemical neutrality is maintained within the stack, the net result is the desired removal of ionized materials from the food substance. A small sacrifice is paid through the fact that the theoretical current efficiency of a cation-neutral system is not as high as cation-anion system, however, the net operating efficiency is frequently higher since losses due to membrane fouling are much less.

One of the most common uses of electro-membrane processing is the deashing of whey from cheese making operations. Normal wheys contain approximately 0.5–0.8% ionized materials or ash. It is easily and economically possible to remove as much as 90% of this ash through electro-membrane processing techniques. With either cation-anion or cation-neutral systems cheese whey can be desalted with a total power consumption well under $1/2$ kw hr per lb of dry solids processed. At typical industrial power figures this would mean that the cost of electrical power would be under $1/2$¢ per lb of finished product. Cleaning and sanitation chemicals account for another phase of the total costs and, once again, these typically are well under $1/2$¢ per lb of finished product. The two major cost considerations in electro-membrane processing of cheese whey are the burdens imposed by membrane replacement and operating labor. Based on typical labor charges and membrane replacement costs at this writing, these two factors together may account for anywhere between 1 and 5¢ per lb of finished product. Typically, the lower operating costs would be associated with large production plants where net labor per pound of finished product is less. Direct operating expenses for electro-membrane deashing of whey may vary from 2 to 10¢ per lb. A typical large plant producing 3–4 million pounds per year of dry solids at an ash removal level of about 60% would have net deashing operating costs in the range of 3–4¢ per lb of finished product.

A major consideration not included in the above cost figures would be the amortization or write-off of capital equipment investment. This figure can vary widely with accounting methods and standards but it is not uncommon for this portion of the cost to be about equal to the costs incurred from out-of-pocket expenses such as labor, chemicals, membranes, and electrical power. In total then, with all expenses considered realistic whey deashing costs range between 5 and 15¢ per lb of finished product.

Many speciality operations can be accomplished with electro-membrane deashing of whey. For example, it is economically feasible to deacidify cottage cheese or other acid wheys by electro-membrane techniques. The removal of $1/2$ or more of the acidity of the cottage cheese whey can be accomplished at a total cost of only a few cents per pound of finished product.

In addition to cheese whey, there are several other applications for electro-membrane processing in the food processing industries. The removal of traces of salt from sugar solutions can be readily accomplished by electro-membrane techniques. Applications such as this in a clearly defined system can be very efficient. Such systems as ash removal from beet sugar solution, ash removal from lactose solutions generated as ultrafiltration permeate, and other similar processes removing salts from carbohydrate solutions are quite feasible. Electro-membrane operations can also be used in the removal of ionized materials from soy protein solutions. The modification of sugar-acids ratios in citrus juices can be readily accomplished by electro-membrane techniques. In general, almost any operation in which classical ion exchange techniques could function, electro-membrane processes can also be considered.

There are several important variations and comparisons between electro-membrane ion exchange and fixed bed ion exchange. Some of these comparisons and contrasts are:

(1) Since membrane processes use electrical current as the driving force rather than auxiliary chemicals for regeneration, no salty waste streams are produced.

(2) The cost of electrical power for stack operation is substantially less than the comparable cost of acid or base that must be used for resin regeneration. Electrical power costs are normally less than 20% of the costs of chemicals.

(3) Electro-membrane techniques cannot completely remove ionized materials such as can be accomplished with fixed bed resins.

(4) Electro-membrane techniques are truly continuous and cyclical operations with outage times for regeneration are not required.

(5) Little or no dilution of products occurs with electro-membrane processing techniques.

(6) Electro-membrane techniques can operate on substantially higher salt or ash concentrations than can classical resinous techniques.

Dialysis

The process of dialysis has been known for many years and has been applied on only a limited scale to food processing operations. The physical equipment used for dialysis in many cases resembles plate and frame filter presses or the typical stacks used for electro-membrane work. Feed or product compartments are bounded on either side by the semipermeable membrane. On the other side of these membranes is water or any other fluid which has a lower concentration of the constituents to be removed from the feed material. Because of the concentration differential of the particular solute component in the two streams separated by the membrane, normal diffusion from the feed stream into the dilute or waste water stream will occur. The rate of this passage or diffusion will depend upon the concentration difference, permeability of the membrane, and other physical characteristics of the system. As in mass transfer operations, boundary layer conditions tend to control to a strong degree the rate of passage of any component. Consequently, flowing streams of either the feed or water phase help to avoid concentration polarization at membrane boundary interfaces.

The mathematical description of a dialysis operation is a fairly straightforward relationship between diffusion coefficient, concentration differential, and total area of membrane in the system. The physical equipment utilized for dialysis operations are specially designed plate and frame stacks with components held in place in a typical press type assembly. Both feed and diffusion water streams are pumped into the stacks at controlled pressures and rates. Automation or special controls are seldom incorporated in dialysis systems.

Diffusivities of various materials in water solution vary widely. Acids and bases typically have the highest diffusivity coefficients with neutral salts commonly having diffusivities about $1/2$ that of their corresponding acids or bases. Common alcohols have diffusion coefficients frequently ranging from $1/2$ up to approximately equal to the coefficients of neutral salts. Alkaloids and simple carbohydrates have diffusivities about $1/2$ that of most neutral salts. Higher sugars, starches, proteins, and other more complex molecular species typically diffuse at rates varying between $1/10$ and $1/20$ of that of neutral salts.

Because of the relatively low productivity of dialysis operations and the fact that the complete removal of any specific constituent is not practical, dialysis has had limited use in the food processing industries. Applications such as acid reduction, flavor or essence modifications, and moderate deashing can use dialysis techniques. When applied, dialysis is most commonly used in relatively small scale, often proprietary separations and purifications since it does not offer the efficiency and economy that would make it attractive for large-scale use.

RICHARD M. AHLGREN

DISTILLATION

The separation of components of a solution on the basis of their volatilities is known as distillation. Consider the boiling point diagram of various mixtures of alcohol and water as shown in Fig. D-6. It can be seen that each mixture of alcohol and water boils at a different temperature. The vapor in equilibrium with the boiling liquid is richer in the more volatile component.

Let x refer to mole fraction of the more volatile component in the liquid phase and y to the mole fraction in the vapor phase. If x_1 is the mole fraction of alcohol in an alcohol-water mixture then $1 - x_1$ = mole fraction of water.

At 1 atm total pressure the boiling point of the solution will be at a temperature such that the sum of the partial pressure exerted by each component in the solution equals 1 atm. In this case

$$P_{alc} + P_w = 1 \qquad [1]$$

where

P_{alc} = partial pressure of alcohol
P_w = partial pressure of water

The partial pressure exerted by a component in the solution as related to the mole fraction by

$$\gamma_1 X_1 P_{alc} = P_{alc} \qquad [2a]$$

and

$$\gamma_2 X_2 P_w = \gamma_2 (1 - x_1) P_w = P_w \qquad [2b]$$

where

γ_1 = activity coefficient of volatile component
γ_2 = activity coefficient of less volatile component
P_{alc} = vapor pressure of alcohol
P_w = vapor pressure of water

When γ_1 and γ_2 are equal to 1, the solutions are known as ideal solutions and Equations (2a) and (2b) express what is known as Raoult's Law.

The number of molecules of each component is related to its partial pressure by

$$\frac{P_1}{P_T} = \frac{N_1}{N_T} = y_1 \qquad [3]$$

where

N_T = total number of moles of vapor
P_T = total pressure
N_1 = number of moles of component 1 in the vapor
P_1 = partial pressure of component 1

Batch Distillation

In a batch distillation, the liquid is boiled and condensed in a single step as shown in Fig. D-7.

The composition of the condensate varies because the composition of the distilling liquid varies. The condensate is also always richer in the more volatile component than the distilling liquid.

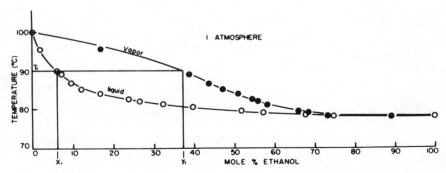

FIG. D-6. BOILING POINT DIAGRAM OF VARIOUS MIXTURES OF ALCOHOL AND WATER

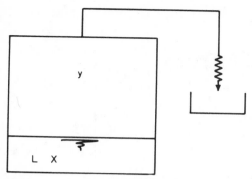

FIG. D-7. DIAGRAM OF BATCH DISTILLATION

Continuous Batch Distillation

It is possible to operate a batch distillation and maintain a constant composition of condensate or distillate. This is done by continuously introducing a feed flow through the still allowing some vaporization. As long as feed composition, flow rate, and rate of vaporization are constant, the distillate composition is constant.

Steam Distillation

In steam distillation, water forms one component of the system and the other an immiscible component such as oil.

The partial pressure exerted by each component is equal to the vapor pressure of each component. Thus, at 1 atm the temperature at which the mixture distills or boils is such that

$$P_w + P_{oil} = 1 \text{ atm} \qquad [4]$$

This equation assumes a water phase is present.

The distilling temperature is found by referring to the vapor pressure-temperature curves of water and oil.

It is possible to have a steam distillation under conditions where the steam does not condense and no water phase is present. This may be done by supplying the heat of vaporization from an external source. The temperature of the system is maintained so that the partial pressure of the steam is less than its saturation pressure at the particular temperature. The saturation pressure of the steam is also equal to the vapor pressure of water at the same temperature. When the partial pressure of steam equals its saturation pressure, the steam condenses. The partial pressure of steam would be

$$P_s = P_T - P_{oil} \qquad [5]$$

In a condensed steam distillation system, the composition of the vapor is related to the vapor pressure of the components by

$$\frac{P_{oil}}{P_w} = \frac{N_{oil}}{N_w} \qquad [6]$$

The composition of the vapor is fixed by the temperature as long as two immiscible liquid phases are present. The temperature of distillation is fixed by the total pressure and the vapor pressure curves. Thus, in the condensed system there is a fixed distillation temperature and a fixed composition,

$$\frac{P_s}{P_{oil}} = \frac{P_T - P_{oil}}{P_{oil}} = \frac{N_w}{N_{oil}} \qquad [7]$$

In this case, the temperature of distillation is not fixed since the vapor pressure of the oil will vary with temperature. Actually it is possible to employ air or any noncondensible gas in this type of distillation. The bubbling of air through water may be thought of in terms of a distillation and the vapor composition equation would be governed by this equation.

The foregoing discussion applies in practice to the steam distillation of a volatile component from a relatively small amount of dissolved nonvolatile component.

Fractionation of Components

Previously, it was noted that by continuously vaporizing and partially condensing the resulting vapor, it was possible to enrich the vapor with the more volatile component and enrich the liquid phase with the less volatile component.

Mechanically, this may be done by employing a fractionating column. One type of fractionating column consists of a tower with a series of plates. The plates are constructed in a manner that permits vapor to rise into the plate and liquid to flow down from the plate (see Fig. D-8). The liquid falling from the plate above comes in contact with the vapor rising from the plate below and tends to condense out the less volatile components. As the vapor rises into a plate it tends to condense the less volatile and vaporize the more volatile. Thus, the liquid on the plates becomes richer in the more volatile component as it proceeds up the column.

It is possible to devise a continuous process employing the fractionating column which permits obtaining a distillate richer in the more volatile components than could be achieved from simple distillation and equilibrium considerations.

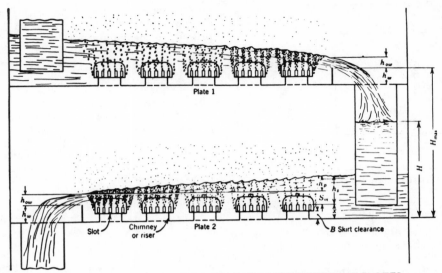

FIG. D-8. SECTION OF FRACTIONATING COLUMN SHOWING PLATES

In this method, a feed (F) is introduced at a particular point in the column. A waste stream (W) containing a high concentration of less volatile is removed at the bottom of the still. A distillate (D) is removed at the top of the still and part of the distillate is returned to the column as a reflux (L). Heat is supplied at the bottom of the column to provide the heat of vaporization.

The composition of the various streams leaving the fractionating column may be related by material balances:

$$F = D + W \qquad [8]$$

$$FX_F = DX_D + WX_W \qquad [9]$$

where

W = waste stream flow rate
X_F = mole fraction of volatile compound in feed
X_D = mole fraction of volatile component in distillate
X_W = mole fraction of more volatile component in the waste

The relationship between vapor rising from a plate and the liquid falling onto the plate may be determined from material balances on the upper and lower portions of the distillation column.

By means of the material balance and the equilibrium diagram it is possible to determine the composition at any point in the column as well as the streams leaving the column. The equilibrium diagram is a plot of liquid composition against equilibrium vapor composition as determined from Fig. D-6.

The composition of the distillate stream and waste stream may be varied by the number of plates in the column, the amount of reflux returned to the column, and the temperature of the entering feed.

As the reflux ratio (amount of distillate returned to column to amount of distillate removed from column) becomes less, the height or number of plates of the column required to obtain the desired stream compositions becomes greater. However, the amount of heat required in the boiler to produce a mole of product becomes less, since less of the condensed vapor is returned to the column to again be vaporized.

In determining the optimum reflux ratio for operating the distillation column, it is necessary to consider the cost of building a tall column against the cost of steam for operating the column.

Essence Recovery

One method of essence recovery employs a distillation column to separate the volatile water. In this case the juice is preheated by condensing vapors from the distillation column in the preheating condensing heat exchanger, and is superheated ($250°$-$275°F$) by injection of steam. The superheated juice is flashed through an orifice into the flash evaporator where the desired degree of evaporation takes place. Separated juice is ordinarily flashed into a vacuum evaporation system. The separated vapors enter the column maintained under partial reflux where water collects at the bottom and volatile flavors concentrate at the top, and in the condensing systems the concentrated volatile flavors (essence) are continually drawn off as a fraction of the condensate flowing back to the head of the column (reflux). The ratio of concentrate withdrawn to feed is 1 to 50.

STANLEY E. CHARM

Cross-references: *Distilled Beverage Spirits; Molecular Distillation.*

DISTILLED BEVERAGE SPIRITS

Distilled beverage spirits are characterized by their geographical origin, type of material used in production, and standard of quality as evaluated by organoleptic analysis (taste and bouquet).

Since secretiveness was a way of life for most ancient distillers and this philosophy has continued to prevail, each producer today operates according to his own methods in the way he feels will be best for his own product.

Legends, traditions, and, to some extent, political influences were great factors in the production and identification of potable distilled liquors. Since most governments were involved economically because of the great source of revenue realized, it was not too surprising to have these same governments establish standards for distilled beverage spirits, generally in keeping with the historic customs prevailing in their country. As a result, geographical identification has become accepted, and each country respects the identity and exclusiveness of the other's products.

Within each category of product there can be wide variations in the flavor which can be caused by: (1) types of materials and their proportions; (2) methods of material preparation; (3) selection of yeast types; (4) fermenter conditions; (5) distillation processes; (6) maturation techniques; and (7) blending experience.

The alcohol and water components are relatively insignificant factors in flavor intensity or palatability. Distillers are primarily interested in the more flavorful constituents—the so-called "congeners" (substances that are generated with the alcohol during the fermentation process and, also, in the course of maturation). It follows, therefore, that in order to produce a palatable product, it is necessary to select the proper configuration of these constituents (congeners). In consideration of items listed above, it is quite impossible to accomplish this by production techniques alone and for that reason the majority of alcoholic beverages offered in world markets are blended to provide uniformity, balanced bouquet, and palatability. To illustrate the variations in flavor constituents an analysis of the leading brand in each category is given in Table D-5.

Although brandy, rum, gin, and vodka are substantial items in world markets, whiskies are the leading distilled beverage spirits, with those from Canada, Scotland, and the United States accounting for most of the sales. Irish whiskey, a distinctive product of Ireland, while not enjoying a large volume of sales, does have good distribution and remains a specialty item among the world's whiskies. Incidentally, the Irish use the spelling "whiskey," the Scotch and Canadians "whisky," and the Americans use both, although U.S. regulations use the spelling "whisky."

Whiskies

Canadian.—Canadian whisky is a distinctive product of Canada, manufactured in Canada in compliance with the laws of Canada regulating the manufacture of whisky for consumption in Canada and containing no distilled spirits less than 2 yr old. Actually, Canadian whiskies are premium products usually bottled at 6 yr of age or more, and, since they are blended, they are not designated as straight whiskies. They are light-bodied and, though delicate in flavor, nevertheless retain a distinct positive character. The Canadian government exercises the customary rigid controls in matters pertaining to labeling of products and in collection of the excise tax. However, it sets no limitations as to grain formulas, distilling proofs, or special types of cooperage for the maturation of whisky. Its policy is to rely on its distillers to be the judges of what their home and world markets require, and the record in terms of worldwide consumer acceptance attests to the wisdom of this policy.

The major cereal grains, corn, rye, and barley malt, are used in the production of Canadian whiskies. The proportions of each grain in the mashing formula remains a distiller's trade secret; otherwise, the process is substantially the same as is found in the major distilleries of the United States. Since Canadian distillers are not faced with artificial proof restrictions in their distillation procedures, they are able to operate batch and continuous distillation systems under conditions optimum for the separation and selection of desirable congeners. With such techniques it is possible to take advantage of the physical relationships that exist between the beverage spirits and the congeners that are in solution in the fermented mash.

White oak casks (50 U.S. gal.) are used in the maturation process. A substantial amount of Canadian whiskies is stored in matured cooperage, which offers a unique compatibility for the

TABLE D-5

CONGENERIC CONTENT OF MAJOR TYPES OF DISTILLED ALCOHOLIC BEVERAGES[1]

Component[2]	American Blended Whisky	Canadian Blended Whisky	Scotch Blended Whisky	Straight Bourbon Whisky	Bonded Bourbon Whisky	Cognac Brandy
Fusel oil	83	58	143	203	195	193
Total acids (as acetic acid)	30	20	15	69	63	36
Esters (as ethyl acetate)	17	14	17	56	43	41
Aldehydes (as acetaldehyde)	2.7	2.9	4.5	6.8	5.4	7.6
Furfural	0.33	0.11	0.11	0.45	0.90	0.67
Total solids	112	97	127	180	159	698
Tannins	21	18	8	52	48	25
Total congeners, wt/vol %	0.116	0.085	0.160	0.292	0.309	0.239

[1] The above determinations were made according to the official methods of analysis of the Association of Official Agricultural Chemists. Fusel oil was determined by the Komarowsky colorimetric method. Foster D. Snell, Inc.
[2] Grams per 100 liters at 100° proof.

whiskies produced for delicacy of flavor. Again, the proportions of new and matured cooperage used for maturation is each distiller's trade secret.

Scotch.—Although Scotch whisky has enjoyed a worldwide reputation for its unique "smoky" flavor and high standard of quality, consumers have very little knowledge about this product. Not much information is revealed by government regulations, which only specify the use of cereal grains and a minimum requirement for aging in oak casks. Little can be garnered from the British definition: "Spirits described as Scotch Whisky shall not be deemed to correspond to that description unless they have been obtained by distillation in Scotland from a mash of cereal grain saccharified by the diastase of malt and have been matured in warehouse in cask for a period of at least three years." Or, from the U.S. definition: "Scotch Whisky is a distinctive product of Scotland, manufactured in Scotland in compliance with the laws of Great Britain regulating the manufacture of Scotch Whisky for consumption in Great Britain, and containing no distilled spirits less than three years old."

No one can be certain when the first spirit was distilled in Scotland, but it is accepted that it occurred centuries prior to the entry found in the Scottish Exchequer Rolls for 1494: "eight bolls of malt to Friar John Cor wherewith to make aqua vitae." "Aqua vitae" was the legal and official term for beverage spirits and also that used by learned people. It took almost three centuries—until nearly the end of the 18th Century—for the term "whisky" to come into being. The Irish

"usquebagh," the Gaelic "usiguebaugh," "uisge," and perhaps "uiskie" (as one reference of 1618 records it) finally became Anglicized as whisky. In George Smith's Compleat Body of Distilling (1738) the word whisky is not used, although, there is frequent reference to malt spirits and spirits of wine, which were rectified malt spirits. Burns, who goes back to 1790, used three terms in his writings: aqua vitae, usquebagh, and whisky.

In 1821, there were 114 distilleries in Scotland, of which only 5 manufactured for the English market. The other 109, scattered over the Highlands, Lowlands, and the Islands, manufactured for Scotch consumption. Surely, at this point in time, "no Scotsman would have been bewildered had he been asked 'What is Whisky' "?

The basic materials used were malted and unmalted barley. The separation of the whisky from the "wash" was done in a pot still—a copper kettle with a "worm," a coiled copper tube enclosed in a cold water jacket, which condensed the vapors within the worm. From 1837 to 1907, pot still distillation was almost exclusively devoted to malt whiskies for home consumption while the product of the continuous patent still invented by Aeneas Coffey in Dublin in 1830 was exported. Such a still was worked by London distillers as early as 1834, and it was undoubtedly used in Scotland and Ireland somewhat prior to 1837. Grain only was used for mashing until about 1847. Some corn (maize) was in use in 1846, but even as late as 1860, the amount was small. When sugar and molasses were introduced this still was also utilized to process these materials to produce other spirits. There is a good deal of controversy as to when the product of the Coffey still was first sold as grain whisky and used to make blends. Up to 1860, most of this production was exported, especially spirits not produced from grain. However, after this date, blends of pot and patent still grain whiskies were available for consumption.

By combining the pungent malt whiskies with the delicate flavors found in grain whiskies, the Scotch distillers were now able to produce a more palatable product, with a worldwide appeal. So today, whereas the materials, geographic location, and the production processes are responsible for the uniqueness of Scotch Whisky, it is the skill of the blenders that makes possible the final achievement—a uniform, pleasant product with a unique taste and aroma. As many as 25 and sometimes more, different malt and grain whiskies are harmoniously "married" to produce a Scotch whisky brand.

There are at present about 100 malt pot still distilleries and 12 grain, or patent still, distilleries producing whisky. The malt whisky distilling season is from autumn through late spring when climatic conditions are most suitable and water supplies are adequate. Malt whiskies are characterized by their geographic location: (1) Highland malt whiskies, made north of a line from Greenock on the west to Dundee in the east, are noted for their individual, distinctive characteristics. They are medium to heavy bodied in flavor intensity. (2) The Lowland malt whiskies, made south of this line, are sometimes called "silent" because of their light flavor intensity. (3) Islay malt whiskies, from the island of the same name. (4) The Campbelltowns, from the town in the Mull of Kintyre—both high in flavor intensity and robust in character.

Even though there are many distilleries and no doubt slight variations in their production methods (that is how single whiskies acquire the characteristics attributable to each specific plant) there are definite processes generally used. A general knowledge of these historic methods, still in use today, will enable one to fully appreciate the quality concept inherent in Scotch whisky. Since a few terms used by the Scotch distillers are unfamiliar to most Americans, these are listed here and defined:

Wort—The liquid drained off the mash tun and containing maltose, a grain sugar derived from the conversion of starch during the mashing process by the action of the organic enzyme, maltase, found in barley malt.

Wash—The liquid obtained by fermenting wort with yeast. It contains the beverage spirits and congeners developed during fermentation.

Low Wines—The term for the initial product obtained by separating (in a pot still) the beverage spirits and congeners from the wash. Low wines are subjected to at least one more pot still distillation to attain a greater degree of refinement in the malt whisky.

Single Whisky—The whisky, either grain or malt, produced by one particular distillery. Blended Scotch whisky is not a single whisky.

Malt Whisky—An alcoholic distillate made from a fermented wort derived from malted barley only, and distilled in pot stills. It is the second fraction (heart of the run) of the distillation process.

Grain Whisky—An alcoholic distillate from a fermented wort derived from malted and unmalted barley and maize (corn), in varying proportions, and distilled in a continuous patent (Coffey) still.

Spirits—Distilled spirits including all whiskies, gin, brandy, rum, cordials and others made by a distillation process for nonindustrial use.

Foreshots—The first fraction of the distillation cycle derived from the distillation of Low Wines in a pot still.

Feints—The third fraction of the distillation cycle derived from the distillation of low wines in a pot still. This term is also used to describe the undesirable constituents of the wash which are removed during the distillation of grain whisky in a continuous patent still (Coffey). These are mostly aldehydes and fusel oils.

Barley Malt.—Clean good quality barley is "steeped" in water for 2–3 days and then allowed to germinate on malt floors for 8–12 days. At the end of this time the sprouting barley has developed the proper level of diastatic power necessary for conversion of starch to grain sugar (maltose) during the mashing process. Germination is stopped by drying the "green malt" over a peat fire. Peat is substantially heather, fern, and evergreen that have been subjected to nature's aging and compression processes over the centuries. The aroma of the burning peat, known as "peat reek," is absorbed by the barley malt. This "smoky flavor" is carried through to the final distillate and becomes a characteristic of single malt whisky. The dried malt is then ground to a meal (grist) and used in the mashing process where the diastase of the malted barley changes starch to grain sugar.

Mashing.—Mashing involves the mixing of malted barley meal with hot water at a temperature (less than 160°F) compatible with the optimum enzyme activity. After the starch is converted to grain sugar (maltose) by the enzyme (maltase) the liquid (wort) is drawn off leaving the grain particles behind. The cooled wort is pumped to the fermenters (washbacks). Mashing is done in a cast iron vessel called a mash tun.

Fermentation.—The fermenters (washbacks) are wooden vessels, about 12 ft in diameter and up to 18 ft in height; their capacity varies from 2,000 to 12,000 gal. The size, of course, is determined by the design capacity of the plant. Larch, a native deciduous tree related to the pine, has been the source of the wood from which the fermenter staves were made. However, in more recent times, this source being limited, Scotch distillers have had to resort to related woods for their fermenter materials.

The wort (mash without grain particles) has a grain sugar concentration of approximately 12%. The setting temperature is about 70°F. After the yeast is added, fermentation begins and continues for 48 hr, reaching a temperature of 90°F. The fermented mash (wash) now contains about 7.5% beverage spirits and a small amount of organic acids, esters, aldehydes, and fusel oils—congeners that result from the action of the yeast.

Distillation.—Distillation involves the separation of the beverage spirits and some congeners from the wash. It can be done in a batch or a continuous system. Scotch malt whisky distillation is a batch process carried out in a pot still, in two steps. First, the wash is distilled into low wines and then the low wines are redistilled at least once to produce malt whisky ready for barreling. Pot stills are made of copper, and are either direct fired by furnaces below the stills or steam heated by means of jackets, coils, or doughnut type heat exchangers within the still. The body or kettle is usually spherical in shape or it may resemble two cones joined at their wider ends. Attached to the body is the head, which is joined by a neck which conveys the alcoholic vapors to the worm, where they are condensed. The method of heating, the size and shape of the still and neck, the condensing arrangements, and the number of distillations of the low wines determine to a great extent the quality of the distillate. Most distilleries will have two pot stills—a "wash still" for handling the wash and a "spirits still" for redistilling the low wines. Since the wash contains only 7.5% beverage spirits, the wash still is the larger and may have a capacity of 4,000–8,000 gal.; a few even exceed 12,000 gal. The low wines still is generally $\frac{1}{2}$ the size of the wash still. The low wines are 35°–45° proof and the final product of the low wine still, malt whisky, ranges from 120° to 150° proof (British).

When only one pot still is available, the non-alcoholic residue in the still called "pot ale," is re-moved, the still is cleaned and recharged with low wines and distillation begins again. The "foreshots" come off the low wine still first. When, in the judgement of the distiller, the distillate measures up to his standard of quality, it is collected in the spirits receiver as the product. Again, when the "heart of the run" has been distilled, the remaining alcoholic content is recovered as "feints." The foreshots and feints are held back for further distillation with the next batch of low wines.

Maturation and Blending.—After distillation and organoleptic (taste and odor) evaluation, the malt whisky is reduced with distilled water to about 111° proof (British) and entered into oak casks for storage in Government Bonded Warehouses. These warehouses are generally one-story stone, brick, or concrete buildings. Since most distilleries are independently owned, their new production is marketed to distillers who have Scotch whisky brand names. The latter rely on a number of these distilleries to supply the unique whiskies that characterize their brands in taste and aroma.

The Scotch distillers use many sizes of oak casks, identified as follows:

	Approx Content (Imperial Gal.)
Butt	110
Hogshead	55–65
Barrel	38–42
Quarter	28–35
Octave	10–15

For malt whisky, the sherry casks (butts and the hogsheads) are most frequently used. For grain whisky, the barrel, similar to its American counterpart, is used. The length of storage, of course, depends on the whisky—the heavier (in body) the new whisky, the longer the time necessary to fully develop its flavor and aroma to maturity. The climate in Scotland differs substantially from that prevailing in the whisky-producing areas of the United States. Although the winters are milder, the summers are cooler and the relative humidity is higher. Under such climatic conditions, maturation proceeds at a slower pace. Maturation is also influenced by the size of the cask and the proof at which the whisky is stored. Each single whisky, in its own time, reaches maturity—the point in time when its flavor potential has been fully developed.

The part of the whisky-making process that science can never replace is the fine art of blending. It all hinges on the creative qualities of the master blender. Blending is the "marriage" of many types of complementary single malt and grain whiskies, according to a formula to produce a blended whisky with a more pleasing taste than that of any individual component. Blending involves two steps—"vatting" and "marrying." Vatting is combining in proper proportions, malts with malts, and grain whiskies with grain whiskies, in large oak vats. When the blend is completed (combining the malts and grains according to formula) it is drawn off into casks and stored for a period of months before it is ready for bottling. This process is known as "marrying." It allows the constituents of the blend to become intimately united. Some distillers deviate from this procedure by letting the malts and the grain whiskies "marry" separately and only combining the two prior to bottling.

Grain Whisky.—This process is distinctly different from the pot still process in the following areas of manufacture:

(1) The mash is composed primarily of maize (corn) with a small proportion of barley malt for conversion. Other cereal grains such as barley may be included.

(2) The cooking of the unmalted cereals, after grinding, is done under steam pressure in converters. The cooked mash after cooling is converted by the barley malt to maltose in the mash tun.

(3) The Coffey still is a two column continuous distillation system capable of removing such flavor constituents as fusel oil and aldehydes from the distillate. Thus the product of the Coffey still, grain whisky, distilled at 180°–186° proof, will have a flavor intensity that is substantially less than that of malt whisky.

(4) Grain whiskies are matured in oak barrels. Since they are lighter, they do not require the extended period of aging to reach maturity as is necessary for the aging of malt whisky.

The care that is given to the production of malt whisky is also given by Scotch distillers to the production of grain whisky.

Irish.—Irish whisky is a distinctive product of Ireland, manufactured either in the Irish Free State or in Northern Ireland, in compliance with their laws regulating the manufacture of Irish whiskey for home consumption, and containing no distilled spirits less than 3 yr old. Like Scotch, Irish whiskies are premium blends of grain and malt whiskies. Unlike Scotch, Irish whisky does not have the unique smokey taste because the barley malt is not dried over peat fires. Since whisky has been known in Ireland as long as in Scotland, it is not surprising that production techniques are very closely related to those used in Scotland. One variation, however, is the use of some small grain in addition to barley malt in the production of malt whiskey. Irish whiskey brands are generally considered to be more flavorful and heavier-bodied than Scotch whiskies.

American.—The first recorded beverage spirits made from grains in the United States of America

were distilled on Staten Island in 1640 by William Kieft, the Director General of the Dutch Colony of New Netherland. Wilhelm Hendricksen, in charge of the still, utilized both corn and rye as basic materials.

Rum was made in Barbados as early as 1650. In America, the earliest reference is in the records of the General Court of Massachusetts in May, 1657. By 1750, there were 63 distilleries. Brandy, which had been made in America as early as 1650, and gin, which was very popular with the poorer classes in England, never had the popular appeal of rum in this country.

With the decline of the "three-cornered" trade, the advent of revolution, and the movement of settlers from the coastal areas into the hinterland, the rum industry slowly declined. To replace molasses, it was natural for the Americans to turn to rye, which was a successful crop in Pennsylvania and Maryland, and to corn, which flourished in the South and West. George Washington is credited with the making of rye whisky in America. His distillery had an excellent reputation for making fine liquor under the supervision of James Anderson, a Scotsman.

Canada's first distillery was started at Quebec City in 1769 producing rum from molasses. The making of whisky did not develop until the 19th Century. By 1850, there were some 200 distilleries operating in Ontario alone.

It is generally agreed that the first bourbon whisky—"genuine, old-fashioned, handmade, sour-mash bourbon"—was made by a Baptist minister, the Reverend Elijah Craig, in 1789 at Georgetown in Scott County. At that time Scott County was part of Bourbon County, from which Elijah Craig's corn whisky got its name. Bourbon, Lincoln, and Jefferson Counties were the original Virginia counties that made up the Kentucky territory. In order to distinguish this corn whisky from Pennsylvania rye, the whisky of the West was called Kentucky bourbon. Up to 1865, few Kentucky distilleries produced more than 1000 barrels per year. Most of them were small, producing only 50 to 500 barrels of whisky.

The method of making whisky, with the exception of malt preparation, was in most respects similar to that used in Scotland and Ireland for hundreds of years. Ground corn and rye meal were scalded in tubs somewhat larger than barrels, stirred with paddles, and allowed to cool and sour overnight. Then malt made from rye or corn was added for conversion of the starch to a fermentable grain sugar. Yeast was added and the mash allowed to ferment from 72 to 96 hr. A simple, single-chambered copper still was used to separate the spirits from the mash. When redistilled, the product was called "double distilled." In 1819,

New Orleans received some 200,000 gal. per month of this type of Kentucky product.

Before the Civil War, not much attention was paid to aging, even though it was recognized that whisky left in charred oak barrels took on a golden color and some mellowness. Originally, whisky was sold in its natural white state or artificially colored to resemble the amber glint of brandy. No one bothered with brand names—whisky was whisky, as everyone knew—and not too much was made of the wide variation in palatability. The hunter or riverman who indulged himself with raw white whisky was not particular about quality.

After the Civil War, the rise in taxes made storage in bond desirable. Many family names, always important in Kentucky lore, now became associated with distinctive whiskies. As the industry grew, it engaged in bitter controversy over what was whisky. As a result, in 1909 during President Taft's administration, whisky was finally defined as any volatile liquor distilled from grain, and standards of identity based upon current manufacturing process for various whisky types—rye, bourbon, etc.—were established. Before the Taft decision few brands were nationally known. The incentive to advertise quality was destroyed by the flagrant exploitation of markets by local labels making fantastic claims which were left unchecked until the passage of the Pure Food and Drug Act of 1906. The new regulations also required labels to tell the process and materials of manufacture. The 18th Amendment to the constitution of the United States which went into effect January 16, 1920, halted the growth of a powerful industry.

Prohibition brought with it evils that were greater than those it was designed to prevent. During Prohibition, consumption of spirits increased from 140 million to 200 million gallons annually. In 1930, the Director of Prohibition Enforcement Bureau estimated that the production of moonshine was more than 800 million gallons a year, most of which went into synthetic gins and semilethal cocktails. On December 5, 1933, the 21st Amendment to the Constitution was ratified by the 36th state, Utah, and the great industry, which had been paralyzed by years of inaction, slowly awoke to the new developments in technology.

The advent of World War II again disrupted the industry, which offered its facilities to the Government for war alcohol production, even before the United States entry into the war. From Pearl Harbor to V-J Day, 750 million gallons of 190° proof alcohol were produced for the war program by registered distillers, who, during peak production in 1944, utilized 127 normal beverage plants.

Distilled spirits for beverage purposes in the United States are characterized specifically as to type, materials, composition, distillation proofs, maturation proofs, storage containers, and the extent of the aging period. The Federal Government also requires that a detailed statement of the production process be filed for each type, and any subsequent improvements or changes must be filed and approved before being placed into operation. In addition, a generalized application of the regulations is made to establish the identity of products where the intensity of flavor may not conform to an arbitrary organoleptic evaluation based on a chemical analysis of the product. As a result, in spite of extensive manufacturing facilities and know-how available for the production of a wide range of whiskies for the improvement of palatability, the distiller is restrained within narrow limits and does not enjoy the wide degree of latitude available to Canadian and Scotch distillers.

American regulations, although specific in detail, reflect a wide divergence of opinion that has prevailed in past years in some geographical areas of the United States as to what product represents the consumer's choice.

Title 27, Code of Federal Regulations, Subpart C, lists several types of American whiskies. Only the types that are major factors in the American market will be identified, other than a general description of whisky and grain neutral spirits.

Whisky.—An alcoholic distillate from a fermented mash of grain distilled at less than 190° proof in such a manner that the distillate possesses the taste, aroma, and characteristics generally attributed to whisky. Any cereal grain qualifies as the raw material. Since this product does not qualify as a straight whisky, it has very little application, and consequently almost none is produced.

Light Whisky.—Light whisky is whisky which has been distilled in the United States at more than 160° proof and less than 190° proof and is stored in used or uncharred new oak containers. This whisky is permitted to be entered for storage at proofs higher than 125°. If light whisky is mixed with less than 20% by volume of 100° proof straight whisky, the mixture shall be designated "Blended Light Whisky." This new standard of identity was adopted on January 26, 1968, and made effective July 1, 1972.

The primary purpose for this category was to permit the production of light distillates that could be aged in seasoned oak casks which are more compatible in developing the lower flavor intensities found in this type of whisky.

In general, the production techniques described under the American Manufacturing Process for the production of straight whisky and grain neutral spirits is followed in making light whisky. The proportions and types of cereal grains used in the formula are left entirely to the discretion of the distiller. However, most distillers will use corn (up to 90%) as the major portion of their formula. The main emphasis in this process will be on distillation techniques. The higher proof requirements will permit the use of more sophisticated distillation systems, such as those used in distilling grain neutral spirits.

Whisky—Rye, Bourbon.—"Rye whisky," "bourbon whisky," "wheat whisky," "malt whisky," or "rye malt whisky" is whisky which has been distilled at not exceeding 160° proof from a fermented mash of not less than 51% rye grain, corn grain, wheat grain, malted barley grain, or malted rye grain, respectively, and stored in charred new oak containers. They also include mixtures of such whiskies where the mixture consists exclusively of whiskies of the same type. Corn whisky has the same distillation proof limitation (160°). However, it must be produced from a fermented mash of not less than 80% corn grain and stored in uncharred oak containers or reused charred oak containers.

In producing bourbon whisky, for example, the mashing formula must contain at least 51% corn and the remaining ingredients (49%) generally are proportioned between rye grains and barley malt. Each distiller selects the formula that he feels will produce his type bourbon. Very little bourbon with 49% small grains is produced. The most popular proportions are 60% corn, 28% rye, 12% barley malt, (referred to as 40% small grains), 70-18-12 (30% small grains), and 75-13-12 (25% small grains). While some bourbons use as much as 15% barley malt, the general practice in the industry is to use 12% barley malt for all bourbon production.

Since rye and barley malt produce more intensive flavors than corn, the formula with the greater small-grains proportion will produce a bourbon with more body, provided, of course, that the same distillation techniques are used.

Straight Whisky.—Any of the whisky types mentioned above further qualify as "straight whisky" by complying with the following: (1) withdrawn from the distillery at not more than 125° and not less than 80° proof (for maturation purposes); (2) aged for not less than 24 calendar months.

The regulations permit the mixing of straight whiskies provided they are homogeneous and, further, provided that the age of this mixture be identified with the age of the youngest whisky in the mixture. Most straight whiskies on the market greatly exceed the minimum age requirement because each distiller attempts to age his product until he feels his whisky has reached the ripeness or maturity which is ideal for that particular whisky. Most authorities agree that the average bourbon attains this organoleptic stage in about 6 yr.

A straight whisky may be further identified as bottled-in-bond provided it is at least 4 yr of age, bottled at 100° proof, and distilled at one plant by the same proprietor. A bottled-in-bond whisky may contain homogeneous mixtures of whiskies, provided they represent one season, or if consolidated with other seasons, the mixture ". . . shall be the distilling season of the youngest spirits contained therein, and shall consist of not less than 10% of spirits of each such season," according to federal regulations. January through June is designated as Spring, and July through December is designated as the Fall season. The federal regulations allow the federal excise tax payment to be delayed until after bottling and removal from bonded case storage. All other American-type whiskies must pay the tax upon withdrawal of the whisky from maturation storage in bonded warehouses.

Blended Whisky.—Blended whisky is a mixture which contains at least 20% by volume of 100° proof straight whisky and, separately or in combination, whisky or grain neutral spirits. In addition, like all American-type whiskies, the bottling proof must be at least 80° proof. When a blended whisky contains at least 51% by volume of straight whisky (bourbon, for example) it may be identified as blended bourbon whisky or bourbon whisky—a blend.

Just as the minimum age requirements are exceeded by distillers on their straight whisky brands, those distillers that market popular brands of blends greatly exceed the minimum requirements set forth by the regulations. As a result, as many as 40 whiskies and matured grain neutral spirits may be utilized harmoniously to achieve a blended whisky. As with the Canadian and Scotch distillers, the final achievement in producing a well-balanced blend, of exceedingly consistent uniformity, and with a high degree of organoleptic attainment depends on the experience and skill of the blender.

Grain Neutral Spirits.—" 'Neutral spirits' or 'alcohol' are distilled spirits distilled from any material at or above 190° proof, whether or not the proof is subsequently reduced." Another section of the same regulations requires "the name of the commodity from which such neutral spirits have been distilled." Thus, grain neutral spirits is an alcoholic distillate from a fermented mash of grain distilled at or above 190° proof.

The requirement of distilling above 190° makes available to a distiller an opportunity to take advantage of the physical relationship that exists between water, alcohol, and congeners that are produced during fermentation. The sophisticated equipment utilized by progressive distillers permits the distiller to include in his distillation system a technique known as selective distillation. The distiller can remove all congeners or retain those congeners which he deems desirable.

Grain Spirits.—While grain neutral spirits have been and continue to be stored in oak containers by some distillers, no acknowledgement of this practice was permitted by regulations. Grain neutral spirits when stored in reused cooperage possess a distinctive character developed during storage, analogous to that which occurs when whisky is stored in reused cooperage.

In order to let the consuming public know about this quality improvement, a new Standard of Grain Spirits, was adopted on June 26, 1968 and became effective July 1, 1972. Thus, "Grain Spirits" are neutral spirits distilled from a fermented mash of grain stored in oak containers and bottled at not less than 80° proof. The period of aging in oak barrels may be stated as "stored _____ (years and/or months) in oak containers."

Since grain spirits have flavors that are very delicate in nature, they must be stored in oak barrels previously seasoned through the storage of whisky or grain neutral spirits. It is important that the barrel is compatible with the flavor intensity of the grain neutral spirits; otherwise, the woody character of the barrel would overwhelm the light flavor of the grain neutral spirits and thus prevent its proper development during aging. They are produced on two basic distillation systems, continuous and batch. Each system produces a number of distillates having a low flavor intensity which when stored in barrels develop in flavor in the same manner as whisky (Baldwin *et al.* 1967).

The continuous complex distillation system for the production of grain neutral spirits is described in detail under Distillation. The batch system while more simple in concept (it is related to the pot still) offers an opportunity to use the heart-of-the-run principle for the production of grain neutral spirits. It is sometimes referred to as a time-cycle distillation system and involves three steps: (1) during the first portion the heads (aldehydes) are removed; (2) during the second, the product is removed; and (3) the residual distillate (tails) remaining in the kettle is removed for subsequent redistillation in the continuous system. The batch system is composed of a large kettle with a capacity of up to 50,000 wine gallons with a vapor pipe leading to a product concentrating column having as many as 55 bubble cap plates. The large capacity of the kettle is important in maintaining product uniformity. Straight whisky produced in the normal manner in the whisky column provides the raw material for this system. It is pumped into the kettle, indirect steam heat is applied through a coil within the kettle, and the alcoholic vapors rise into the product column. The column performs the refinement function and produces the grain neutral spirits which are reduced in proof with deionized water to between 110°–160°, put in oak barrels, and placed in government bonded warehouses for storage.

Gin

Francis de La Boe, a 17th Century professor of medicine at Leyden University, Holland, is credited with being the originator of the botanical-flavored beverage spirits, known as gin. Since his product's primary flavor was due to the essential oils extracted from juniper berries, he gave it the French name "genievre," which appeared later as the Dutch "geneva" and finally was abridged to the English "gin." Distilled gin is a distillate obtained by original distillation from mash, or by the redistillation of distilled spirits, over or with juniper berries and other aromatics customarily used in the production of gin. Gin derives its main characteristic flavor from juniper berries. In addition to juniper berries, other botanicals may be used including angelica root; anise; coriander; caraway seeds; lime, lemon, and orange peel; licorice; calamus; cardamom; cassia bark; orris root; and bitter almonds. The use and proportion of any of these botanicals in the gin formula is left to the producer, and the character and quality of the gin will depend to a great extent on the skill of the craftsman in formulating his recipe. The more discerning producers formulate their aromatic ingredients on the basis of the essential oil content in the raw materials to assure a greater degree of product uniformity.

London dry gin, by far the most popular, is produced by the redistillation of grain neutral spirits with juniper berries and other botanicals. To expose the essential oils, the ingredients are reduced to a granular form and then immersed directly into the kettle (pot) which is filled with grain neutral spirits at approximately 100° proof. It is important that the grain spirits be as neutral as possible (devoid of congeners) to ensure that no undesirable flavors be imparted to the gin. A vapor phase extraction may also be used. In this case the botanical mixture is placed on trays or in baskets in the head of the kettle where the alcoholic vapors, in passing through, extract the essential oils and rise to the condenser. In addition to the kettle, some gin stills have a refinement section (as many as six plates) above the kettle for flavor stability and enrichment. Indirect steam heat is applied and the various essential oils are distilled over during the entire distillation cycle. The first portion (heads) and the last portion of the cycle (tails) are not included in the product. Only the heart of the run is used and it represents approximately an 85% recovery of the original alcohol concentration in the kettle. This, of course, varies with the type of product that is desired by the producer. Some distillers, to avoid thermal decomposition of the delicate flavors and to acquire a degree of softness, conduct distillation under reduced pressure at a temperature of about 135°F.

In Great Britain and Canada the regulations permit and recognize the use of maturation techniques for gin. Gins stored in special oak casks acquire a pale golden hue and a unique "dryness" of flavor. Although distillers are permitted to mature gins in the United States for further flavor development, the Federal Government does not permit an age claim or any reference to aging to appear on the label.

Holland gin, characterized by its high flavor intensity derived mostly from juniper berries and cereal grains (corn, rye, barley malt), is produced by immersing the botanical mixture directly into the grain mash prior to distillation or by extracting the essential oils from the botanical mixture with the heavy distillate (high wines) from a fermented mash of grain, consisting of corn, rye, and barley malt. As a consequence, the flavors produced during fermentation become flavor components of the final product.

Compound gin is a mixture of grain neutral spirits and proportions of essential oil extracts from botanicals. It does not undergo any distillation procedure.

Brandy

Brandy is a distillate or a mixture of distillates obtained solely from the ferment juice, mash, or wine of fruit, or from the residue thereof, distilled at less than 190° proof in such manner as to possess the taste, aroma, and characteristics generally attributed to the product. The most important category of brandy is fruit brandy, distilled solely from the juice or mash of whole, sound, ripe fruit or from standard grape, citrus, or other fruit wine. When brandy is derived exclusively from one variety of fruit it is designated by the name of such fruit. However, a fruit brandy derived exclusively from grapes may be designated as "brandy" without further qualification. Unless the product is specifically identified, the term brandy always means grape brandy and is, therefore, a distillate obtained from grape wine. Brandy is subject to a distillation limitation of 170° proof. If distilled over 170° proof, it must be further identified as "neutral brandy." A minimum maturation of 2 yr in oak casks is required or otherwise the term "immature" must be included in the designation of the brandy. While the age is not carried on the label, brandies are normally aged from 3 to 8 yr.

Brandies are produced in batch or continuous distillation systems. The pot still or its variation is universally utilized in France. In the United States, brandies are produced in both systems. The batch system produces a more flavorful product; the continuous system produces a lighter, more delicate flavor.

The history of brandy can be said to be the history of distillation, because in the dim past it was the distillation of wine in crude stills that gave "aqua vitae" to the world. In the ensuing evolution, many geographical areas of Europe and of the United States became renowned for their brandies. Perhaps the best known and most popular brandy in the world comes from the Cognac region of France, the Department of Charente and Charente Inferieure. As such, it enjoys an exclusive identity, Cognac, under which no other brandy may be labeled. Cognac is produced on the traditional pot stills by small farmer-distillers for sale to the bottlers who age the brandies in limousin oak casks, made of oak from the forest of Limoges. When the brandies reach maturity, they are skillfully blended for marketing under their own brand name.

Cognac is a blend of some Grande Champagne, Petite Champagne, Borderies, and Fins Bois—the proportions of each a well-kept secret and in accordance with the desire of each individual distiller to produce a quality product. To further characterize Cognac, the bottle labels carry letters having the following meanings; E, Especial; F, Fine; V, Very; O, Old; S, Superior; P, Pale; X, Extra; C, Cognac. For example, VSOP means Very Superior Old Pale, and is therefore considered to be a particular shipper's better quality product.

Another well-known brandy of France is Armagnac which is produced near Concon, in the Department of Gers in southern France. Armagnac is distilled from wines made from the Piquepoul, the Colombard, Jurancon, and Meslier grape varieties on a continuous system using two pot stills in series. The black oaks of Gascony provide the wood for the casks which are used for aging Armagnac. It is not uncommon to find Armagnac bottled as a vintage brandy, i.e., the distillation from 1 yr. Armagnac is considered to be more heavy-bodied and drier than Cognac.

There are brandies distilled in almost every wine region of France; they are called eau de vie, and when exported are simply referred to as French Brandy, never as Cognac.

In the United States, California produces almost all of the grape brandy. Generally, it is a well-integrated operation: the cultivation of the grapes; the making of the wine; the distilling, aging, bottling; and the marketing of the brandy being done by the same firm. Distillation is usually accomplished on a continuous, multicolumn distillation system. Of the total brandy consumption in the United States (approximately 12.5 million gallons), California brandies account for over 65%.

Other geographic areas in Europe and in South America are well known for their specialty brandies. Among these are earthy-flavored Spanish brandies, distilled from Jerez sherry wine; the fragrant, fruity Portuguese brandies, distilled from port wine; the pleasant and flowery muscat bouquet of Pisco brandy from Peru; kirschwasser brandy, with its almond undertone flavor, distilled from a fermented mash of small black cherries which grow along the Rhine Valley in Germany and Switzerland; and slivovitz, the plum brandy which is produced in Hungary and in the Balkan countries.

Rum

Rum is any alcoholic distillate or mixture of distillates from the fermented juice of sugarcane, sugarcane syrup, sugarcane molasses, or other sugarcane by-products, distilled at less than 190° proof in such a manner that the distillate possesses the taste, aroma, and characteristics generally attributed to rum. Blackstrap molasses, a by-product of sugar production, is by far the most common raw material used in the manufacture of rum. Otherwise the same basic factors which produce different whiskies are responsible for the varieties of flavors of rums. The type of yeast, fermentation environment, distillation techniques and systems, the maturation conditions, and, not least, the blending skill are important in determining the final character and quality of rum.

Rums are characterized as light-bodied, of which the rums of Puerto Rico are the best known, and as full-bodied, rums which come from Jamaica and certain other islands of the West Indies. Light rums are distilled on multicolumn continuous distillation systems over a proof range of 160°–180°. They are matured in oak casks which are reused for rum storage.

Jamaica and other full-bodied rums are distilled between 140° and 160° proof in pot stills. They are matured in large casks (111.6 gal.) called "puncheons." Unlike the light-bodied rums which use cultured yeast for inoculation, the Jamaica rum relies on natural fermentation, sometimes referred to as "wild" fermentation. In this method the mash is inoculated by the yeast present in the air and in the raw material.

Puerto Rican rums are generally labeled either as white or as gold label. The latter is a little more amber in color and has a more pronounced flavor intensity. Although the rums produced in various geographic areas are not considered distinctive types, they do retain their geographic significance and such names may not be applied to rum produced in any other place than the particular region indicated in the name.

Cordials and Liqueurs

Cordials and liqueurs are synonymous terms, with the former ascribed to American origin and the latter of European extraction. They are products obtained by mixing or redistilling neutral spirits, brandy, gin, or other distilled spirits with or over fruits, flowers, plants, or pure juices therefrom, or other natural flavoring materials. Cordials must contain a minimum of $2\frac{1}{2}\%$, by weight of the finished product, of sugar or dextrose or a combination of both. However, if the added sugar and dextrose are less than 10% by weight of the cordial, then its designation may include the term "dry." Synthetic or imitation flavoring materials cannot be included in United States cordials, nor can they be designated as "distilled" or "compound."

Cordials were known to be in existence during the days of the Pharaohs and the ancient Athenians; and commercial production of cordials dates back to the Middle Ages when the alchemists, physicians, and the mystical monks were all searching for an elixir of life. From all this activity there developed many well-known cordials, such as Benedictine and Chartreuse, both aromatic plant-flavor derivatives and both bearing the name of the fraternal orders by whom they were prepared.

The variety of cordials is very great, simply because of the wide spectrum of flavors that are available from the fruits, peels, leaves, roots, herbs, and seeds flourishing on this earth. Organoleptic attainment, however, becomes a matter of experience and skill in the selection of botanicals and in the extraction and formulation of flavors. Although these elements are carefully guarded secrets, the producer must rely on three well-known basic methods of production; viz, maceration, percolation, and distillation, or any combination thereof.

Maceration involves the steeping of the raw materials in the beverage spirits, usually in a vat, until the beverage spirits have acquired the desired aroma, flavor, and color. The liquid is then drawn off and provides the base for further processing.

Percolation is accomplished by recirculating the beverage spirits through a percolator which contains the raw materials. As the beverage spirit seeps down through the raw materials, it extracts and removes the desired constituents which will give the proper aroma, flavor intensity, and color.

The distillation method is similar to that used in gin production. The ingredients are either immersed in the beverage spirits or placed in trays or pans in the head of the still. The rising vapors extract the essential flavors, which are then condensed and discharged as a colorless liquid. This distillate contains the basic flavor which is used for further processing.

Cordials are characterized and marketed according to their generic names; for example, Anisette (aniseed), Creme de Menthe (peppermint), Triple Sec (citrus fruit peel), Sloe Gin (sloe berries), and by their trade names (propriety brands) of which Benedictine and Chartreuse are well-known examples.

Vodka

Since 1950, the drinking pattern of the United States consumer has become more widely diversified. Vodka, United States variety, has moved up in sales from practically nothing in 1949 to 14% of the beverage spirits sales in 1972. The fact that it can be mixed with any flavorful substance that might appeal to the consumer seems to be the motivating factor for its wide acceptance. Vodka produced on a multicolumn distillation system from a fermented mash of grain at or above 190° proof, must be further treated with charcoal or activated carbon or further refined by distillation in such a manner as to be without character, aroma, or taste. If any flavoring material is added to the distillate, the vodka is characterized with the name of the flavoring material used.

Tequila

Columbus reported an Indian drink made from the marrow of maguey, a species of agave (cactus). The fermented sap of maguey makes pulque and distilled pulque becomes mescal. Whether or not Columbus tasted mescal is conjecture. However, with the Spanish colonization came the still, and, subsequently, the development of Mexico's most popular distilled alcoholic beverage drink, Tequila. Tequila, a distinctive product of Mexico, is an alcoholic distillate obtained from the fermented juice of the heads of Agave Tequilana Weber (mezcal), of the Amarillydaceae family, grown in the State of Jalisco, Mexico, preferably in the county of Tequila. The fermented juice is distilled in pot stills to about 160° proof (American).

Agave ("admirable" in Greek), a natural and common cactus in Mexico, is also found in the southwest regions of the United States, Central America, and in Tropical South America. Agave species (there are about 300) require many years before blooming and hence are called "Century Plants." The "Mezcal Azul" (blue mezcal), the primary source for Tequila, is cultivated. It is usually propagated from 2-yr-old sprouts obtained from 7-yr-old mezcal plants. The sprouts are planted in May to June, in rows 3.3 meters apart,

about 2500 plants per hectacre (2.5 acres). During the first 3 yr, corn, beans or peanuts are grown between the furrows to keep the soil loose. Thereafter, until maturity (8–12 yr) it is necessary to till to prevent weed growth. When mature, the trimmed heads, referred to as "pine apples" because of their physical appearance, and weighing 80–130 lb each, are cut in half and transported to the distillery. In the State of Jalisco up to 20,000 metric tons of mezcal heads are harvested annually.

Juice from the mezcal heads is first extracted by steaming and then the residual juice is removed by shredding the steamed heads, compressing the strips between roller mills and finally washing the strips (bagasse) to recover all of the sugary syrup. The steaming is done in masonry ovens with a capacity of approximately 40 metric tons for 9–24 hr at approximately 200°F. The length of the steaming period is critical. It is during this period that inulin $(C_6H_{10}O_5)_x$, a starch-like substance, is converted into monosaccharides by acid hydrolysis—the action of hot water and a low acid medium. It is desirable to produce as much juice as possible without breaking down other constituents which could have a detrimental effect on the fermentation process. During the steaming, a small amount of "Mieles Amargas," bitter molasses, is drained off and discarded by some producers because it imparts an undesirable flavor to the final product. While mezcal heads are allowed to cool for 12 hr, some additional juice ("Mieles de escurrido"—drained molasses) is recovered. The mezcal heads are now dark brown, soft in texture, with a taste similar to maple syrup.

Analysis of Mezcal Head (Not Steamed)

	%
Moisture	62
Total solids	38
Fiber	11
Inulin	20.0
Ash	2.5
pH	5.5

The mezcal juice from the steaming ovens, the roller mills, and the bagasse washes is pumped into fermenters made of masonry or of local pine wood. The capacity of the fermenters is from 1000 to 2000 U.S. gal. To facilitate fermentation, nitrogen nutrients are added. The Mexican Government also permits the addition of "piloncillo," a brown sugar, up to 30% by weight of the fermentable sugar in the mezcal heads after steaming.

Yeast for fermentation is produced separately in a medium of pure mezcal juice supplemented by "piloncillo." After 6–8 hr of progapation, the yeast has developed sufficiently to be used for inoculating the mash. The mash has a sugar concentration of approximately 9.5° Brix (% sugar) and the yeast mash will amount to 6.5% by volume of the total liquid in the fermenters. The fermentation period is about 42 hr and the final alcoholic concentration is 4.5% by volume of the fermenter mash. When "piloncillo" is not used, the alcoholic yield is lower and the fermentation takes longer.

The fermented mash is pumped to a pot still, capacity around 300 U.S. gal., made of copper and provided with a steam coil within the kettle for heating and a condenser for cooling the vapors. The intermediate of the first distillation called "ordinario" is collected at 28° proof (American) and redistilled in a slightly larger pot still. This distillation cycle can be controlled to yield a product of approximately 106° proof (American). The residual distillate from this process is combined with the fermented mash, starting a new cycle in the primary distillation system.

Tequila, as consumed in Mexico, is unaged and usually bottled at 80°–86° proof (American). However, some producers do age Tequila in seasoned 50-gal. (U.S.) white oak casks imported from the United States. In aging, Tequila becomes golden in color and acquires a pleasant mellowness without altering its inherent taste characteristic. Tequila aged 1 yr is identified as "Añejo;" if it is aged as much as 2–4 yr, it can acquire a further identification as "Muy Añejo." The annual production of Tequila in Mexico is around 20 million liters (4.2 million U.S. gallons), the major portion of which, is produced by 28 plants located in the county of Tequila.

American Manufacturing Process

Any material rich in carbohydrates is a potential source of ethyl alcohol, which, for industrial purposes, is obtained by the fermentation of materials containing sugar (molasses), or a substance convertible into sugar, such as the starch in grains, and also from other sources such as petrochemical processes. In the production of distilled spirits for beverage purposes, however, cereal grains are the principal types of raw material used. Any reference to "alcohol" in beverages is always to ethyl alcohol, C_2H_5OH. Although other alcohols may be present, they are referred to as "higher alcohols," "fusel oils," or are termed specifically as amyl, isoamyl, etc.

The chemical composition of grain varies considerably and depends to a large extent on environmental factors, such as climatic conditions and the nature of the soil upon which it is grown. Another variable is introduced in the use of malt (sprouted or germinated grain). Malt is generally understood to be germinated barley, unless it is further qualified as rye malt, wheat malt, etc. The purpose of malting is the development of the amylases, the active ingredients in malt. Amylases are enzymes of organic origin, and change grain starch into the sugar, maltose. Besides providing the means of converting the grain starch into sugar, the malt is also a contributing factor to the final flavor and aroma of the distillate. The malting techniques may produce a malt of such unusual character that it may indeed furnish the outstanding characteristics of the final product, as in Scotch whisky.

Definitions

Bushels   A "distiller's bushel" of any cereal grain is 56 lb.

Proof   In Canada, Great Britain, and the United States, the alcoholic concentration of beverage spirits is expressed in terms of "proof." The U.S. statutes define this standard as follows: "Proof spirit shall be held to be that alcoholic liquor which contains one-half its volume of alcohol of a specific gravity of 0.7939 at 60°F." More simply, the figure for proof is always twice the alcoholic content by volume. For example, 100° proof means 50% alcohol by volume. In Great Britain as well as Canada "proof spirit is such that at 51°F it weighs exactly $^{12}/_{13}$ of the weight of an equal bulk of distilled water." A proof of 87.7° would indicate an alcohol concentration of 50%. A conversion factor of 1.14 can be used to change British proof to U.S. proof.

Proof gallon   A U.S. gallon of proof spirits or the alcoholic equivalent thereof; i.e., a U.S. gallon of 231 cu in. containing 50% ethyl alcohol by volume. Thus, 1 gal. of liquor at 120° proof is 1.2 proof gallons; 1 gal. at 86° proof is 0.86 proof gallon.

A British and Canadian proof gallon is an imperial gallon of 277.4 cu in. at 100° proof (57.1% of ethyl alcohol by volume). An imperial gallon is equivalent to 1.2 U.S. gallons. To convert British proof gallons to U.S. proof gallons, multiply by the factor 1.37. Since excise taxes are paid on the basis of proof gallons, this term is synonymous with tax gallons.

Congeners   The flavor constituents in beverage spirits which are responsible for its flavor and aroma and which result from the fermentation, distillation, and maturation processes.

Balling   A measure of the sugar concentration in a grain mash, expressed in degrees and approximating percentage by weight of the sugar in solution.

Fusel oil   An inclusive term for heavier, pungent-tasting alcohols produced during fermentation. Fusel oil is composed of approximately 80% amyl alcohols, 15% butyl alcohols, and 5% other alcohols.

Heads   A distillate containing a high percentage of low-boiling components such as aldehydes.

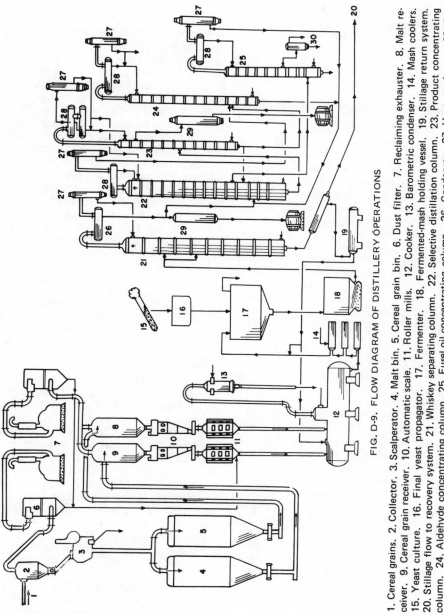

FIG. D-9. FLOW DIAGRAM OF DISTILLERY OPERATIONS

1. Cereal grains. 2. Collector. 3. Scalperator. 4. Malt bin. 5. Cereal grain bin. 6. Dust filter. 7. Reclaiming exhauster. 8. Malt receiver. 9. Cereal grain receiver. 10. Automatic scale. 11. Roller mills. 12. Cooker. 13. Barometric condenser. 14. Mash coolers. 15. Yeast culture. 16. Final yeast propagator. 17. Fermenter. 18. Fermented-mash holding vessel. 19. Stillage return system. 20. Stillage flow to recovery system. 21. Whiskey separating column. 22. Selective distillation column. 23. Product concentrating column. 24. Aldehyde concentrating column. 25. Fusel oil concentrating column. 26. Condenser. 27. Vent condenser. 28. Dephlegmator. 29. Product cooler. 30. Fusel oil decanter.

High wines   An all-inclusive term for beverage spirit distillates which have undergone complete distillation.

Low wines   Products of simple distillation units requiring further refinement.

Tails   A residual alcoholic distillate.

Wine gallon   Measure of actual volume; U.S. gallon contains 231 cu in.; British (Imperial) gallon contains 277.4 cu in.

Grain Handling and Milling

The beverage distilling industry utilizes premium cereal grains. Each distiller supplements government grain standards with his own specifications, especially in the elimination of grain with objectionable odors, which may have developed during storage or kiln drying at the elevators. Hybrid corn, usually of the dent variety because it is readily available, and plump rye, developed from Polish strains (Rosen), are used for beverage alcohol production. The modern distilleries use airveyor unloading systems. Others use the traditional power shovel in conjunction with screw conveyors and bucket elevators. Even though the grain has been subjected to a cleaning process at the elevators, it is passed over receiving separators, a series of vibrating screens which sift out foreign materials. Air jets and dust collectors remove any light material and magnetic separators remove metallic substances.

Milling the grain breaks the outer cellulose protective wall around the kernel and exposes more starch surface to the action of the cooking and conversion process. Distillers require an even, coarse meal without flour.

Two most common methods of accomplishing the milling process are: (1) in roller mills, using pairs of corrugated rolls (breaks) run "sharp to sharp" (projections facing projections) at differential speeds of $2\frac{1}{2}$ to 1 with approximately $3\frac{1}{2}$ bu per inch of roll length at a fast roll speed of 500 rpm for a 9-in. diameter roll; (2) in hammer mills, where a series of revolving hammers within a close-fitting casing and rotating at 1800–3600 rpm shear the grain to a meal; the meal is removed by suction through a screen, with perforations $3/16$-$5/16$ in. in diameter, in the bottom half of the casing; screens are changed for each type of grain.

Mashing

Mashing is a mechanically simple process, involving cooking (gelatinization of starch) and conversion (saccharification), changing starch to grain sugar (maltose). The chemical and biological changes taking place are complex and for best

results must be performed at optimum conditions of time and temperature. Cooking can be carried on atmospherically or under pressure in a batch or a continuous system. For whisky production, batch atmospheric cooking is more widely used although some batch pressure cooking is practiced. For grain neutral spirits production, both batch and continuous pressure systems are used. After cooling, conversion is accomplished in the cooking vessel by the addition of barley malt meal to the cooked grain. Some distillers pump the mash immediately to a converter for the necessary holding time and thus make the cooking vessel available for the next cook. The converted mash is cooled and pumped to the fermenters.

Each individual distiller varies his mashing procedures to suit himself, but generally all of them conform to basic principles, especially in the maintenance of sanitary conditions in the plant, in order to avoid bacterial contamination. The cooking and conversion equipment is provided with direct or indirect steam, propeller or rake-type agitation, and cooling coils or a barometric condenser. Mashing procedures for rye and corn grains are described below.

For Rye.—In the preparation of a bourbon mash, rye may be cooked with the corn and, in that case, it generally is subjected to the corn-cooking process. However, many distillers mash rye separately. Rye undergoes liquefication at a much lower temperature than corn, and, according to some, this avoids thermal decomposition of critical grain constituents which will adversely affect the final flavor of the distillate.

Water at 100°F is drawn at the rate of 29 gal. per bu, and rye and malt meal are added. The mash is slowly heated to 130°F and held for approximately 30 min. Proteolytic enzymes, active at 110°–115°F, aid in reducing the viscosity, and the optimum temperature for beta amylase is 130°F. The mash is then heated to 145°–152°F and held for 30–45 min to ensure maximum conversion. The mash (pH 6.0) is then cooled to the fermenting temperature (68°–72°F). This process of simultaneously cooking and converting small grains is called infusion mashing.

For Corn.—Although the starch in corn grains converts rather easily, higher cooking temperatures are necessary to make the starch available. Usually malt is not added at the beginning, but to reduce viscosity, "premalt" of $\frac{1}{2}\%$ may be added before cooking, preferably at around 150°F. The addition of thin stillage (the residual dealcoholized fermented mash from the whisky distillation process) to adjust pH to 5.2–5.4 is practiced by some. For cookers operating at atmospheric pressure, a mashing ratio of 25–30 gal. of slurry (grain, water, and stillage mixture) per bushel and a holding time of 30 min at 212°F are preferable. The mash is cooled to 152°F and malt is added. Primary conversion, the saccharification taking place during conversion, is in the order of 70–80% of the available starches. The remainder of the conversion to fermentable sugar takes place during the fermentation process and is referred to as secondary conversion. For batch cooking under pressure, only 17–22 gal. of water are drawn, and the maximum temperature is 250°–305°F. In continuous pressure cooking, water is drawn at a ratio of 24 gal. per bu of meal and sufficient thin stillage is added to give a pH of 5.2–5.4. The mash is pumped through the continuous pressure cooker, where it is exposed to temperatures of 340°–360°F for 2–6 min, and then into a flash chamber where it is cooled immediately by vacuum to the malting (conversion) temperature of 145°F. A malt slurry is continuously introduced and the mixture proceeds through the water cooling system to the fermenters.

Fermentation

Beverage alcohol fermentation involves the conversion of fermentable grain sugars (largely maltose), produced by the action of malt enzymes (amylases) on gelatinized starch, into nearly equal parts of ethyl alcohol and carbon dioxide. This is accomplished by an enzyme complex, zymase, which is made available by yeasts, microscopic organisms belonging to the plant kingdom. Yeast multiplies by budding; a new cell is produced about every 70 min. Although yeasts of several genera are capable of some degree of fermentation, *Saccharomyces cerevisiae* is almost exclusively used by the distilling industry. It has the ability to reproduce prolifically under normal growth conditions found in distilleries, it has a high fermentation rate and efficiency, and it can tolerate relatively high alcohol concentrations (up to 15–16% by volume). A great variety of strains exist and the characteristics of each strain are evidenced by the type and amount of congeners the yeast is capable of producing. The strain most suitable for a specific purpose can be selected.

Alcoholic fermentation represents a chain of complicated reactions, which can be indicated by the equation.

$$C_{12}H_{22}O_{11} \xrightarrow{\text{maltase}} (2)\ C_6H_{12}O_6 \xrightarrow{\text{zymase}}$$

maltose   dextrose

$$2\ C_2H_5OH + 2\ CO_2$$

ethyl alcohol

A fermentation efficiency of 95% is obtained based on the sugar available. Of the starch converted to grain sugar and subsequently subjected to fermentation, 5–6% is consumed in side reactions. The extent and type of these reactions depend on (1) yeast strain characteristics; (2) the composition of the wort; and (3) fermentation conditions such as the oxidation-reduction potential, the temperature, and the degree of interference by bacterial contaminants.

Secondary products formed by these side reactions largely determine the characteristics and organoleptic qualities of the final product. In the production of whisky, the secondary products formed and retained during the subsequent operations include a number of aldehydes, esters (such as ethyl acetate), higher alcohols collectively designated "fusel oils," some fatty acids, phenolics or "aromatics," and a great many unidentified trace substances. The secondary products retained in the final distillate are known as "congeners." In the production of grain neutral spirits, the congeners are removed from the distillate in a complex multicolumn distillation system. Some distillers, however, retain a small portion of the low-boiling esters in the distillate when the grain neutral spirits are to be matured.

Fermentation of grain mashes is initiated by the inoculation of the set mash with 2–3% by volume of ripe yeast prepared separately (see below) and is characterized by the following three distinct phases:

(1) Prefermentation. Rapid multiplication of yeast from an initial 4–8 million per milliliter to a maximum of 125–130 million per milliliter of the liquid and an increasing rate of fermentation.

(2) Primary Fermentation. A rapid rate of fermentation, as indicated by the vigorous "boiling" of the fermenting mash, caused by escaping carbon dioxide. During this phase secondary conversion takes place—the changing of dextrins to fermentable substances.

(3) Secondary Fermentation. A slow and decreasing rate of fermentation. Conversion of the remaining dextrins which are difficult to hydrolyze takes place.

The degree of conversion, agitation of the mash, and the temperature directly affect the fermentation rate. Fermenter mash set at a concentration of 38 gal. of mash per bushel of grain (56 lb) will be fermented to completion in 2–5 days, depending on the set and control temperatures. The set temperature (temperature of the mash at the time of inoculation) is largely determined by the available facilities for cooling the fermenting mash. If cooling facilities are adequate, temperatures of 80°–85°F may be employed; otherwise, the set temperature must be low enough to ensure that the temperature will not exceed 90°F during fermentation. When no cooling facilities are provided, the inoculation temperature must be below 70°F. Excessive temperatures during the prefermentation phase retard yeast growth and stimulate the development of bacterial contaminants which are likely to produce undesirable flavors.

In the production of "sour mash" whisky, U.S. federal regulations require that a minimum of 25% of the volume of the fermenting mash must be stillage (cooled, screened liquid recovered from the base discharge of the whisky separating column—pH 3.8-4.1). In addition to producing a heavier-bodied whisky, this procedure provides the distiller with an economical means of adjusting the setting pH (4.8-5.2) to inhibit bacterial development. It also provides buffering action during the fermentation cycle, which is important since secondary conversion will not take place if the fermenting pH drops below 4.1 in the immediate stages. Thin stillage also provides a means of diluting the "cooker" mash to the proper fermenter mash concentration, 30-36 gal. of mash per bushel of grain for the production of spirits, and 38-45 gal. for making whisky.

Preparation of the yeast involves a stepwise propagation; first, on a laboratory scale and then, on a plant scale to produce a sufficient quantity of yeast for stocking the main mash in the fermenters. A strain of yeast is usually carried in a test tube containing a solid medium (agar slant). A series of daily transfers, beginning with the removal of some yeast from the solid medium, are made into successively larger flasks containing liquid media—diamalt (commercial malt extract) diluted to 15°-20° balling, malt extract, or strained sour yeast mash—until the required amount of inoculum is available for the starter yeast mash, called a "dona." After 1 day's fermentation, the dona is added to a yeast mash normally composed of barley malt and rye grains, and representing approximately 2-3½% by weight of the total grain mashed for each fermenter.

The yeast mash is generally prepared by the "infusion mashing" method and then "soured" (acidified) to a pH of 3.9-4.1 by a 4-8 hr fermentation with *Lactobacillus delbrueckii* at a temperature of 120°-130°F. Lactobacillus ferments carbohydrates to lactic acid. Satisfactory souring can be induced with an inoculum of approximately 0.25% of culture per volume of mash. The water to mash ratio of 24-28 gal. per bu attains a yeast mash balling of approximately 21°. Prior to inoculation with yeast, the soured mash is pasteurized to 160°-190°F to curtail bacterial activity, then cooled to the setting temperature, 68°-72°F.

The sour mash media offers an optimum condition for yeast growth and also has an inhibitory effect on contamination by bacteria. In 16 hr the yeast cell count reaches 150-250 million per milliliter.

Some distillers use the "sweet yeast" method for yeast development. In this instance the lactic acid souring is not included and the inoculation temperature is usually above 80°F to ensure rapid yeast growth.

Distillation

Distillation involves the separation, selection, and concentration of the alcoholic products of yeast fermentation from the fermented grain mash, sometimes referred to as "fermented wort" or "distillers' beer." In addition to the alcohol and the desirable secondary products (congeners), the fermented mash contains solid grain particles, yeast cells, water-soluble proteins, some mineral salts, lactic acid, fatty acids, and traces of glycerol and succinic acid. Although a great number of varieties and degrees of distillation are possible, the most common systems used in the United States are: the continuous whisky separating column with or without an auxiliary doubler unit for the production of straight whiskies; the continuous multicolumn, complex system used for the production of grain neutral spirits; and the batch rectifying column and kettle unit, used primarily in the production of grain neutral spirits which are subsequently stored in barrels for maturation purposes. In the batch system, the heads and tails fractions are separated from the product resulting from the middle portion of the distillation cycle.

Even though most modern plants have various capacity whisky stills available, they find it convenient and flexible to incorporate a whisky separating column into the multicolumn system, thus acquiring a greater range of distillation selectivity—the removal or retention of certain congeners. In the beverage distillation industry, stills and auxiliary piping are generally fabricated of copper, although some stainless steel is used for these purposes. All piping that conveys finished products is tin-lined copper, stainless steel, or glass.

The whisky column, a cylindrical shell which is divided into sections, may contain from 14 to 21 perforated plates, normally spaced 22-24 in. apart. The perforations are usually $3/8$-$1/2$ in. in diameter and take up about 10% of the plate area. The vapors from the bottom of the still pass through the perforations with a velocity of 20-40 ft per sec. The fermented mash is introduced near the top of the still, and passes from plate to plate through down pipes until it reaches the base where the residual mash is discharged. The vapor leaving the top of the still is condensed and forms the product. Some whisky stills are fitted with entrainment removal chambers and also with bubble-cap plate sections—sometimes called "wine" plates—at the top to permit operation at higher distillation proofs. The average whisky still uses approximately 12–15 lb of steam per proof gallon of beverage spirits distilled. Steam is introduced at the base of the column through a sparger. Where economy is an important factor, a calandria is utilized as the source of indirect heat. The diameter of the still, the number of perforated and bubble-cap plates, the capacity of the doubler, and the proof of distillation are the critical factors that will largely determine the characteristics of a whisky.

The basic continuous complex distillation system for the production of grain neutral spirits usually consists of a whisky separating column, an aldehyde column (selective distillation column), a product concentrating column (sometimes referred to as an "alcohol" or "rectifying" column, from which the product is drawn), and a fusel oil concentrating column. In addition, some distillers in order to secure a greater degree of refinement and flexibility may include one or more of the following: an aldehyde concentrating column (heads concentrating column) and a fusel oil stripping column. Bubble-cap plates are used throughout the system (except in the whisky column, which may have some bubble-cap plates).

This distillation system offers a wide range of flexibility for the refinement of distilled beverage spirits. A fermented mash (generally composed of 90% corn and 10% barley malt) with an alcohol concentration of approximately 7% by volume is pumped into the whisky column somewhere between the thirteenth and nineteenth perforated plate for stripping. The residual mash is discharged at the base and is pumped to the feed recovery plant; the overhead distillate (ranging in proof from 105°–135°) is fed to the selective distillation column (also called the "aldehyde" column) which has over 75 bubble-cap plates. The main stream (20°–40° proof) from the base of the selective distillation column is pumped to the product concentrating column. A heads draw (containing aldehydes and esters) from the condenser is pumped to the heads concentrating column (also called the "aldehyde concentrating" column), and a fusel oil and ester draw is pumped to the fusel oil concentrating column. The product is withdrawn from the product concentrating column.

Some accumulation of heads, at the top of the product concentrating column, are removed at the condenser, and transferred to the aldehyde concentrating column. The function of the aldehyde concentrating colunm is to remove the heads from the system for disposal. The fusel oil concentrating column removes the fusel oil from the system.

Maturation

In the United States, the final phase of the whisky production process is called maturation and involves the storage of beverage spirits (which at this point are colorless and rather pungent in taste) in new, white oak barrels, whose staves and heading are charred. The duration (years) of storage in the barrel depends on the time it takes a particular whisky to attain the desirable ripeness or maturity. The staves of the barrel may vary in thickness from $3/4$–$1 1/8$ in. The outside dimensions of a barrel that will hold approximately 50 U.S. gallons are: height, approx $34 1/2$ in.; diameter at the head, approx $21 1/4$ in. Storage facilities for barrels of whisky are called warehouses. They vary in construction from brick and mortar types, single and multiple floors (as many as 6) having capacities up to 100,000 barrels, to wooden sheet-metal-covered buildings (called "iron clads"), generally not exceeding 30,000 barrels capacity. It is customary in the industry to provide some means of natural ventilation. As the whisky reposes in the barrel it is subject to critical factors which will largely determine its course of change and its final outcome. The thickness of the stave, the depth of the char (controlled by regulating the duration of the firing, 30–50 sec), the atmospheric conditions of temperature and humidity, the entry proof, and, finally, the length of storage impart definite and intended changes in the aromatic and taste characteristics of a whisky. Where warehousing conditions are not controlled, the maturing process is subject to the natural variations resulting from changes in climatic conditions. It is generally agreed that the changes in the maturing whisky are caused by three principal types of reactions occurring simultaneously and continually in the barrel: (1) extraction of complex wood constituents by the liquid; (2) oxidation of the original components in the liquid and other material extracted from the wood; and (3) reaction between the various organic substances present in the liquid, resulting in the formation of new congeners. The maturation process is responsible for a loss of product due to evaporation and initial soakage; approximately a $3 1/2$% loss per year is experienced.

Comprehensive studies involving the changes occurring during the maturation of whisky have been published (Crampton and Tolman 1908). Although these reports contain detailed information on the concentration of various congeners throughout the course of the maturation period, little is revealed of the interrelationships between various congeners except for the nonvolatile groups, such as solids, nonvolatile acids, tannin, and color. Notable among the observed changes are increases in the concentrations of acids, esters, and solids. Based on the average data in the summary Tables of each study, it is revealed that there exists throughout the maturation period a linear relationship between the increase in acids and esters and the increase in dissolved solids; this suggests that

TABLE D-6

CHANGES TAKING PLACE IN BOURBON WHISKY STORED IN WOOD

Age, Years	Range	Proof	Extract[1]	Acids[1]	Esters[1]	Aldehydes[1]	Furfural[1]	Fusel Oil[1]	Color
New	Avg	101.0	26.5	10.0	18.4	3.2	0.7	100.9	0.0
	Max	104.0	161.0	29.1	53.2	7.9	2.0	171.3	0.0
	Min	100.0	4.0	1.2	13.0	1.0	trace	71.3	0.0
								42.0	
1	Avg	101.8	99.4	41.1	28.6	5.8	1.6	110.1	7.1
	Max	103.0	193.0	55.3	55.9	8.6	7.9	173.4	10.9
	Min	100.0	61.0	24.7	17.2	2.7	trace	58.0	5.4
			54.0	10.4	10.4			42.8	4.6
2	Avg	102.2	126.8	45.6	40.0	8.4	1.6	110.1	8.6
	Max	104.0	214.0	61.7	59.8	12.0	9.1	197.1	11.8
	Min	100.0	81.0	25.5	24.4	5.9	0.4	86.2	6.9
			78.0	23.5	11.2			42.8	5.7
4	Avg	104.3	151.9	58.4	53.5	11.0	1.9	123.9	10.8
	Max	108.0	249.0	73.0	80.6	22.0	9.6	237.1	14.8
	Min	100.0	101.0	40.0	28.2	6.9	0.8	95.0	8.6
			92.0	40.0	40.0	13.8		43.5	7.4
6	Avg	107.9	185.1	67.1	64.0	11.9	1.8	135.3	13.1
	Max	116.0	287.0	81.0	83.9	23.3	9.5	240.0	17.5
	Min	102.0	132.0	53.6	36.4	7.7	0.9	98.1	12.0
			127.0	45.0	17.9				9.8
8	Avg	111.1	210.3	76.4	65.6	12.9	2.1	143.5	14.2
	Max	124.0	326.0	91.4	93.6	28.8	10.0	241.8	20.9
	Min	102.0	152.0	64.1	37.7	8.7	1.0	110.0	12.3
			141.0	53.7	22.1			47.6	10.5

SOURCE: Crampton and Tolman (1908).

[1] Grams per 100 liters (100° proof).

the formation of acids and esters is directly dependent upon some precursor which is extracted from the barrel at the same rate as the bulk of the solid fraction. The progress of maturing of a type of bourbon as measured by the principal ingredients is illustrated in Table D-6. It is evident that the congeners amount to only about $\frac{1}{2}$–$\frac{3}{4}$% of the total weight. Yet, it is this small fraction which determines the quality of the final product. Consequently, there can be a wide variation in the taste and aroma of matured whiskies, simply because of the wide variation in the concentration of their congeners. For example, esters may vary from 8.0–18.0 gm per 100 liters, and aldehydes from 0.7–7.6 gm per 100 liters. Nevertheless, there is no correlation between chemical analysis and quality; i.e., taste and aroma. It is necessary to rely on human senses of smell and taste to detect the fine variations and thus evaluate the quality of whiskies.

Present analytical results are expressed in terms of one component for each chemical class; i.e., acetic acid for acids, acetaldehyde for aldehydes, etc. However, more refined techniques of analysis are being applied to a systematic breakdown of the congener groups to their individual components. Until the advent of gas chromatography, long and tedious chemical procedures were generally required for separation of the congeners. Distillation, countercurrent distribution, and other physical methods were utilized to effect concentration of various congener groups. These concentrates were reacted to form chemical derivatives which were then subjected to further separation. Paper and column chromatography have been used extensively for this work. After separation of components, identification is possible by infrared and mass spectrometry.

It is now possible with the high sensitivity (flame and β-ray ionization detection) and efficiency available with gas chromatographic techniques to present a qualitative profile of alcoholic distillates without prior treatment of sample. One technique, flame ionization, involves the use of a hydrogen flame, for the combustion of organic substances to produce electrons and negative ions which are collected on an anode. The resulting electrical current is proportional to the amount of material burned. The other, β-ray ionization, involves the use of beta particles emitted from a source such as strontium 90 to ionize the carrier gas and components in it. The measure of the electrical current, resulting from the collection of electrons on the anode, is used in the determination or detection of the substance. This may augment sensory evaluations. A positive identification of the separated congeners can be made by infrared and mass spectrometers.

Another field of microanalysis, Nuclear Magnetic Resonance (NMR), offers the organic chemists new methods in the identification of organic substances. It makes use of a number of physical methods which measure nuclear properties, such as spin numbers and nuclear magnetic moments, to identify the structure of an organic compound. This technique may offer possibilities in the identification of congeners present in alcoholic beverages.

Packaging

The focus in the distilling industry's packaging operations is the glass bottle which has a much longer recorded history than the product it was ordained to hold. The art of bottle blowing, discovered about 300 B.C., made it possible to make larger and cheaper bottles, suitable for transporting and storing wine. With the invention of the Coffey still in 1830, blended Scotch whisky came into being, and the use of glass bottles for packaging whisky became widespread.

In the United States, brand names spurred the use of glass bottles for packaging whisky. In 1889, 144 million bottles were used. This increased to 388 million in 1914, and dropped to 144 million in 1919, as the distilling industry faced the specter of Prohibition. In 1972, over 2 billion bottles were used to package distilled beverage spirits sold in the United States.

Since the packaging of distilled spirits is done under Federal Government supervision and the product then distributed to the various states in compliance with their laws and regulations, the packaging operation must consider many factors normally not involved in ordinary glass packaging. First, the product represents a high value, because it does include the federal tax at the time of bottling. In the United States, a bottle of whisky that retails at $4.75, carries a tax burden of $2.85. Obviously, extreme care must be taken to avoid losses of product during the packaging operation. Second, in addition to the problems involved in dealing with cases, bottles, cartons, closures, and labels, the distiller must apply to each bottle a fed-

eral strip stamp indicating that the $10.50 per proof gallon excise tax has been paid and, also apply bottle stamps of the decalcomania type to indicate identification or tax payment in the 10 States that require these in their system of control. With the heavy investment in product taxes and the necessity of applying State stamps, the distiller is not able to build up a substantial case goods inventory to provide immediate service to his customers in those States having this requirement. Third, since this is a licensed industry, in addition to the normal record-keeping necessary for efficient operations and control, federal and individual States require many records which are incorporated into their system of control.

Federal regulations prescribe and limit the standards of fill (size of containers) to the following; 1 gal., $\frac{1}{2}$ gal., 1 qt, $\frac{4}{5}$ qt, 1 pt, $\frac{1}{2}$ pt, $\frac{1}{8}$ pt, and $\frac{1}{10}$ pt. Individual States likewise limit the number of sizes that can be distributed within their borders; for example, some States will not permit the distribution of 1 gal. or $\frac{1}{2}$ gal. sizes.

The most common packaging operation utilized in the industry is the straight line system with a line speed from 120 to 200 bottles per minute. Along with the general progress in packaging, the distilling industry is moving in the direction of automatic line operation with variable frequency control systems keyed to the fill and labeling operations. This is only possible, however, when volume on certain sizes is substantial. Most distillers are faced with some mechanical equipment changes, requiring approximately 4 hr per line, to handle various sizes of bottles. In addition to material specifications for quality control on all supplies, "built in" quality control inspection systems are included on the bottling lines. Likewise, the quality control department, independent of bottling operations, takes random samples for evaluation purposes.

Briefly, the entire operation involves:

(1) The removal of matured beverage spirits from bonded warehouses.

(2) The emptying of the barrels and the tax determination based on a proof gallon basis.

(3) The filtering and reduction in proof of the product with distilled or deionized water prior to its transfer to the glass lined or stainless steel bottling tanks.

(4) The preparation of blended whisky involves an additional operation where the straight whiskies and the grain neutral spirits are combined, according to formula, and permitted to "marry" prior to its transfer to the bottling tank.

(5) New, empty bottles are uncased at the beginning of the line. The sterile bottles then proceed through a pneumatic cleaner to remove any foreign particles that might be present, and continue

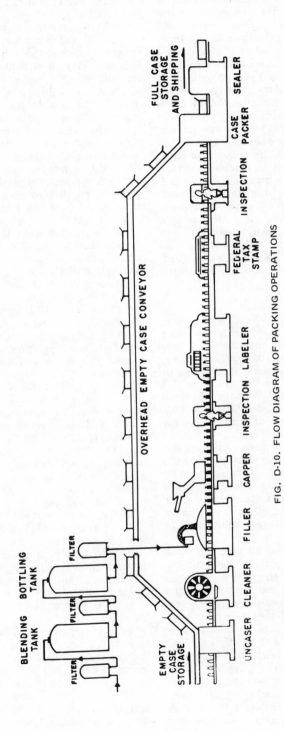

FIG. D-10. FLOW DIAGRAM OF PACKING OPERATIONS

on through a gravity-vacuum type filler, capper, labeler, strip stamp machine, a case packer, and a case sealer.

(6) Each case is registered, dated, and the consignee's name stamped, before the case proceeds to the truck or rail car. Few other consumer products demand as much care and skill in packaging as those of the distilled spirits industry.

Taxation, Government Regulations

The history of liquor taxation is not a pleasant one. No industry has been taxed as heavily as the legal distillers, not only in the United States, but throughout the world. On the one hand, governments have laid an unduly heavy burden on the legal producers of distilled beverage spirits. On the other hand, dishonest men have evaded legal obligations and brought the industry into disrepute. Moreover, in many instances, dry interests have attempted to further their cause of prohibition by advocating confiscatory high taxes. For example, by 1730 in England, the laws were so complicated and onerous that they all but destroyed the industry; and Parliament, realizing that the higher the taxes, the less the income, completely revised regulations in 1743. Whenever legislators forgot the law of diminishing returns, illicit distilling flourished.

Government regulations pertaining to alcoholic beverages find their beginning in one of the very earliest bodies of law, the Babylonian Code of Hammurabi, nearly 2000 years before Christ, which contained provisions for the quality, sale, and use of fermented liquors. In the Magna Carta a clause provided a standard of measurement for the sale of ale and wine. Parliament, in 1643, set the first tax on distilled spirits at eight pence per gallon. After the Restoration, on December 25, 1661, a tax of four pence was placed on every gallon of "aqua vitae" distilled. A few years later, Charles II lowered the tax to two pence a gallon. From that time to the present the tax has been increased—with many fluctuations, of course.

The first liquor tax in the United States (2 guilders on each 1/2 vat of beer) was imposed in 1640 by William Kieft, Director General of New Netherland. The Molasses Act of 1733 and the Sugar Act of 1763, overtaxing the import of French and Dutch rum and molasses and leaving the more expensive British products free, provoked united protest and action against its enforcement.

In 1791, Alexander Hamilton, imposed an excise tax of 7¢ for each gallon produced and 54¢ per gal. of still capacity to be collected by revenue officers assigned to each district. This was repealed in 1800 during Jefferson's administration, and except for the years between 1812-1817, as a war measure, there was no further excise tax on domestic beverage spirits until 1862.

In 1972, the combined federal excise tax and the average state tax amounted to $13.09 per proof gallon (federal tax—$10.50 per proof gallon). Table D-7 lists the federal excise tax rates for various years.

In the United States, the revenue from excise taxes on distilled spirits has become a substantial part of income realized by the three levels of government; federal, state, and local. In 1863, with a $0.20 rate, the Federal Government collected over $5 million, while in 1972 the total revenue amounted to $5,608 million, 66% of which represented the Federal Government's share. From Repeal through 1972, over $100 billion has been paid into the treasuries of the 3 levels of government by the beverage distilling industry. This does not include the normal federal, state, and local corporate taxes of all types generally paid by industry.

Supervision over the production of distilled beverage spirits is maintained by the Bureau of Alcohol, Tobacco, and Firearms of the U.S. Treasury Department which succeeded the Alcohol, Tobacco, and Firearms Division, Internal Revenue Service, on July 1, 1972.

Prior to Prohibition, revenue agents and deputy collectors investigated illegal liquor operations, made arrests, seizures, etc., along with income tax and other miscellaneous work. On January 16, 1920, the effective date of Prohibition, federal prohibition agents took over the duties. An Act of Congress created the Bureau of Prohibition in the Treasury Department on April 1, 1927. During Prohibition in 1928, agents seized 16,220 illicit distilleries, 18,920 stills, 9,133 still worms, 217,278

TABLE D-7

FEDERAL EXCISE TAX RATES
ON DISTILLED SPIRITS

Year	Rate[1] ($)	Year	Rate[1] ($)
1791 (July)	0.09–0.25	1894 (Aug.)	1.10
1792 (July)	0.07–0.18	World War I	2.30
1802 (July)	No tax	1919 (Febr.)	6.40
1815 (Jan.)	0.09	1933 (Dec.)	1.10
1818 (Jan.)	No tax	1934 (Jan.)	2.00
1862 (Sept.)	0.20	1938 (July)	2.25
1864 (March)	0.60	1940 (July)	3.00
1864 (July)	1.50	1941 (Oct.)	4.00
1864 (Dec.)	2.00	1942 (Nov.)	6.00
1868 (July)	0.50	1944 (April)	9.00
1872 (Aug.)	0.70	1951 (Nov.)	10.50
1875 (March)	0.90		

[1] Per tax gallon.

fermenters, 1,048,636 gal. of distilled spirits, 28 million gallons of malt, wine, etc., over $13 million in property, and made 75,307 arrests. This awesome total does not include state and local seizures. The Prohibition Reorganization Act, effective July 1, 1930, created the Bureau of Industrial Alcohol in the Treasury Department, responsible for the permissive provisions of the Act, and the Bureau of Prohibition was transferred to the Department of Justice, responsible for the enforcement of the penal provisions of the National Prohibition Act. These two were merged on December 6, 1933, as the Alcohol Tax Unit, Internal Revenue Department, and subsequently on March 15, 1952, it became the Alcohol and Tobacco Tax Division, Internal Revenue Service. On December 30, 1968, the Alcohol, Tobacco and Firearms Division, Internal Revenue Service, was established.

The 21st Amendment to the Constitution of the United States repealed the 18th Amendment and empowered each state to regulate the use, sale, distribution, and taxing of alcoholic beverages within its jurisdiction. Each state, under this authority has established an agency to administer the laws enacted by its legislature.

With some variations, distribution in 32 states is controlled by the license (open) system, and in 18 states by the control (monopoly) system, wherein the state is in the wholesale and retail alcoholic beverage business. In a license state, under strict control of the administration agency, the distribution and sale of alcoholic beverages is done by licensed wholesalers and retailers.

Manufacture and Consumption

The production of distilled beverage spirits has generally kept pace with consumption. In 1810, according to government records, Pennsylvania produced $6\frac{1}{2}$ million gallons; Indiana, 22,000 gal.; and Kentucky over 2 million gallons. Apparently, in anticipation of Prohibition, 300 million gallons of beverage spirits was produced in 1917, of which 60 million gallons was whisky. In the year 1930, the Prohibition Enforcement Bureau estimated that illicit production amounted to 800 million gallons.

After Repeal, the industry, literally starting again from the beginning, produced almost 108 million gallons of whisky in 1934 and reached an all-time high of 245 million gallons in 1936. Since then, with the exception of 1950 and 1951, most production has been on an inventory replacement basis in line with the expected increase in total consumption due to the steady increase in population. Some apprehension over the Korean police action caused a substantial increase in production in 1950 to 174 million gallons. However, only 68 million gallons were produced in 1952.

In 1972, 183 million gallons of beverage spirits were produced, including 116 million gallons of whisky.

While per capita consumption continued to decline (it was 2.71 gal. in 1864, 1.74 gal. in 1922–1930, and 1.88 gal. in 1972), the growth in population accounted for an increase in total consumption from 145 million wine gallons of distilled beverage spirits in 1940, to 190 million in 1950, to 234 million in 1960, and reached 392.5 million wine gallons in 1972. Since 1961 whisky consumption decreased from 73.1% to 62.1% in 1972 of the total liquor consumption. At the same time, American whiskies decreased from 59.2% in 1956 to 38.3% in 1972. Most of this can be accounted for by the growing popularity of Canadian and Scotch whiskies, gin, and vodka, all of which show a substantial increase.

GEORGE W. PACKOWSKI

References

AOAC. 1970. Methods of Analysis, 11th Edition. Assoc. Offic. Agr. Chemists.

BALDWIN, S., BLACK, R. A., ANDREASEN, A. A., and ADAMS, S. L. 1967. J. Agr. Food Chem. *15*, 381.

BROCKMANN, M. C. 1950. J. Assoc. Offic. Agr. Chemists *33*, 127.

CRAMPTON, C. A., and TOLMAN, L. M. 1908. J. Am. Chem. Soc. *30*, 97.

DISTILLED SPIRITS INSTITUTE. 1972. Summary of State Laws and Regulations Relating to Distilled Spirits, 20th Edition. Distilled Spirits Inst., Washington, D.C.

DISTILLED SPIRITS INSTITUTE. 1973. Annual Statistical Review. Distilled Spirits Inst., Washington, D.C.

Government Regulations

CANADA DEPT. OF NATIONAL REVENUE. 1947. The Excise Act, 1934. Chap. 52, 24–25. Dept. Natl. Revenue, Ottawa, Canada.

CANADA DEPT. OF NATIONAL REVENUE. 1961. Regulations, Distilleries and Their Products. Circ. *ED 203*, Mar. 30. Dept. Natl. Revenue, Ottawa, Canada.

U.S. DEPT. INTERNAL REVENUE. 1970. Title 27, Code of Federal Regulations. Federal Register *27 CFR* 1.1 (1–70). U.S. Govt. Printing Office, Washington, D.C.

Cross-reference: *Wine.*

DOUGHNUTS

The doughnut, or fried cake, was known to man apparently as early as the 5th Century B.C. Leviticus records that the rites of sacrifice entail the offering of cakes mixed of fine flour and dipped in oil as a symbol of thanksgiving. There is no great body of literature describing the rise of the doughnut's popularity but there are occasional references indicating that it was known, made, and eaten in most countries of Europe from antiquity. It was brought to this country by the early settlers and remained a minor pastry delicacy until 1920 when the first automatic doughnut machine was sold. Today, doughnuts account for approximately 18% of the total pastry market or 1 billion pounds worth over $450 million dollars in sales.

Types

Actually doughnuts are of two main varieties or families, and many subvarieties which include crust and crumb textural differences and shape differences. Doughnuts are made as twists, sticks, rings, balls, half moons, and various other shapes.

The two families of product are characterized by the leavening used to make them; thus, one type is called yeast-raised doughnuts while the other is known as the cake doughnut, signifying that chemical leavening is used. Both varieties are deep fat fried and are made, with the exception of the leavening, from similar ingredients. Yet these products are distinctly different in everything from the physical characteristics of crust to shelf-life. These differences are the result of varying the proportion of the ingredients used, the wheat variety from which the flour used is derived, and the method of preparation. Yeast-raised doughnuts have bread-like crumb appearance and texture, while cake doughnuts are more like cake, having a finer cell structure and a more tender crumb.

Essential ingredients for any type of doughnut include water, flour, sugar, shortening, and some form of leavening. All other ingredients used are included to produce a specific quality characteristic such as a specific shape, flavor or shelf-life, or to improve eating quality, etc. Hard spring wheat varieties are used in yeast-raised doughnuts just as they are used in bread, while cake doughnuts use the soft red winter varieties that are used in cakes.

In both families of doughnut, a variety of other structure builders are used to fortify or modify the base wheat flour to give such things as machineability, mixing tolerance, or floor time tolerance. Therefore, some doughnut formulas will be found to contain flours made from soybean, cottonseed, rye, potato, corn and rice, as well as quantities of egg yolk, sodium caseinate, milk solids, guar gum, and carboxymethyl cellulose.

A major difference between yeast-raised and chemically-leavened doughnut formulations is the reliance on sugar as the primary tenderizer in the case of cake doughnuts while shortening serves that purpose in yeast-raised product. Sugar constitutes less than 3% of yeast-raised dough, while cake doughnut doughs contain up to 15%. On the other hand, yeast-raised dough consists of about 5% of shortening while cake doughnut doughs generally have less than 2%.

Years ago it was hard to think of the product as a doughnut if it did not contain lard. Today's doughnut formulator not only compounds his own shortening but selects from a wide variety of processed fats and oils and commercially available emulsifiers.

Leavening

Yeast, of course, is the source of the leavening of yeast-raised doughnuts but the system includes supporting substances, such as malt and ammonium salts, as in other yeast-raised products; and occasionally small amounts of chemical leavening will be used to increase the fat absorption or create a particular crumb texture.

Leavening systems for cake doughnuts can be quite sophisticated. The carbon dioxide leavening gas is always derived from sodium bicarbonate but as many as five different acid sources may be used to liberate it at different times during the dough or frying processes. Common acid sources include specially manufactured varieties of sodium acid pyrophosphate, monocalcium phosphate, sodium aluminum phosphate, and the delta lactone form of gluconic acid.

Production

Before the advent of automatic machinery, the doughnut baker purchased and scaled each of the ingredients in his formula separately, adding them 1 by 1 to the bowl during the mixing. Mixing times and speeds varied widely depending upon the quality of the ingredients the baker was able to get. In order to get any sort of consistency from batch to batch, a highly skilled baker was a necessary ingredient. Today almost all doughnuts are made from prepared doughnut mixes which are made in batches of 3000 lb or more by specialists in this field. In most cases the baker adds nothing but water or water and yeast to a whole bag of prepared mix and mixes the dough following simple directions on the bag.

By far the largest portion of doughnuts of both varieties are made by automatic machinery. In the case of cake doughnuts, the dough is dumped into hoppers from which it is forced mechanically or by air pressure through extruder nozzles that shape and cut individual rings, balls, sticks, etc., directly into the fryer. Cake doughnut machines of this type are available with from 1 to 10 extruder nozzles and production capacities of from 40 to 2000 doz per hr. Size of the product emanating from machines can be varied from 4 oz to 26 oz per doz by changing the size of the extruder nozzle. Yeast-raised doughnuts, similarly, are extruded from pressurized hoppers after the fermentation stage and are shaped and cut onto screens for transfer to the proofer before frying.

The frying process is similar for both varieties. Average frying time is about 90 sec, 45 sec on a side at temperatures of 375°–390°F. There are a few varieties that are fried submerged and are not turned; but most doughnuts are allowed to float so that one side fries while the other is permitted free expansion; then the doughnut is flipped to fry the other side. Frying fats used are hydrogenated vegetable oils or hydrogenated lard with good heat stability. Since large amounts of the frying fat become part of the doughnut it must be bland or have good flavor initially and should not develop off-flavors during the heating. Cake doughnuts contain about 18% frying fat while yeast-raised average about 25% for machine-made product and 15% for hand cut.

Doughnuts must be cooled after frying and before coating or boxing. This is a necessity because the doughnut has a great deal of sensible heat which accounts for the continued loss of moisture almost equal to that lost during the frying. In addition, the frying fat in the skin of the doughnut must be permitted to cool and at least partially set up or it will be absorbed by the coating or the box. Coatings used on doughnuts include powdered sugar, granulated sugar, glaze, icings, and chocolate.

HOWARD ROTH

DRIED FRUIT

Except for a small tonnage of dried prunes produced in the Pacific Northwest, virtually all of the commercial production of dried tree fruits in the United States comes from California.

Historically, prunes have been the most valuable deciduous fruit crop produced in California, and the industry has experienced a resurgence of growth in recent years. This is in sharp contrast to the production of cut dried fruits—i.e., apricots, peaches, and pears—as the production of these commodities has trended steadily downward since the late 1940's. The declining production of cut dried fruits is due to two major factors: (1) rapid growth of canning and freezing outlets, and (2) exorbitant production costs resulting from the large amount of hand labor involved in cutting and

drying operations. Still, each of these commodities has a commercial production of several thousand tons annually and is an important companion product for the major dried fruit crop, prunes.

Prunes

The first dried prunes were produced and sold in California in 1868. Realizing the market potential for this delectable and nutritious fruit, growers quickly expanded their plantings. Bearing acreage increased from less than 1000 acres in 1868 to 90,000 acres in 1890. Today, the State has 96,250 bearing acres of prunes and 14,000 nonbearing acres. Annual production of dried prunes in recent years has averaged 158,000 tons. The value of commercial prune production in California ranges from $40 to $60 million annually. In recent years, dried prune shipments to domestic markets, including Canada, have averaged 108,000 tons annually. Export shipments, principally to Europe, have averaged 36,000 tons.

What is the difference between a plum and a prune? Botanically speaking, a prune is a plum that can be satisfactorily dried whole without fermentation at the pit. Technically, only dried plums are properly called prunes, though the term is commonly applied to fresh plums that can be dried successfully. These are varieties that will dry on the pits without fermentation, remaining sweet, firm, and full-flavored, with thick amber-colored flesh.

The principal prune variety in California, accounting for nearly 97% of the total production, is the French prune, "La Petite Prune d'Agen." This is the variety which Louis Pellier introduced in 1856. The French prune is a medium-sized prune, very sweet and juicy, and a dependable bearer. Other California varieties, including the Imperial, Robe de Sergeant, and Sugar prune, are larger and of excellent quality, but rather erratic bearers.

Over the years, the methods of harvesting and drying have gradually changed. Today, the prune harvest is highly mechanized. Prunes are shaken from the tree by means of mechanical shakers and are caught on canvas frames or tarps and by self-propelled catching frames. Harvested fruit is generally put into large bins. These harvest bins are then hauled to nearby modern dehydraters where the fruit is dried in 12–24 hr, depending on the size of the fruit and the drying method used. These dehydraters have replaced the old method of sun-drying, which took as long as 10 days.

Each dehydrater plant has a number of drying tunnels. In addition to the drying tunnels, dehydration facilities include an office, a receiving station, bin dumping and washing facilities, an automatic tray handling system, and a warehouse for storing dried fruit until it is delivered to packing plants.

Upon receipt of a grower's delivery, the bins are weighed and then mechanically dumped into a hopper where they are washed. They are then elevated to the automatic traying equipment which fills empty trays with fresh fruit in a continuous operation. This equipment spreads the fruit in one even layer which is essential to the production of quality dried fruit. As the trays are filled with fresh fruit, they are automatically stacked on dehydrater cars, then moved to the drying tunnels on steel tracks. The trays of fresh fruit are then placed in the dehydrater and dried down to about 18% moisture, with an approximate drying ratio of 3 to 1.

When the trays of dried prunes are removed from the tunnels, they are moved on tracks to the automatic tray scraping equipment where the fruit is scraped from the trays and put into bins for curing in the warehouses.

When dried fruit is received at packing plants, it is sorted for removal of defects, mechanically size graded, and then stored in cool warehouses in portable bins.

All dried fruit is processed and packed on order. When an order is received, the prunes are blended for uniform size and quality. All dried prunes go through a processing procedure by which they are thoroughly washed, rehydrated, tenderized, and pasteurized prior to packing. Exceptionally high moisture processed prunes are treated with potassium sorbate (preservative) to prevent spoilage by yeast and mold organisms.

Modern harvesting, drying, processing and packaging methods have earned California prunes a reputation for unsurpassed quality in markets throughout the world.

Prunes are a favorite source of quick energy and good nutrition. They are rich in natural fruit sugars and are an excellent source of three vitamins: A, B_1, and B_2. Prunes also provide a special diet bonus for persons requiring a high potassium diet.

Useful in many ways and adaptable for many purposes, prunes are at home in almost any course of any meal. They are used in baked goods, confections, desserts, salads, and meat dishes. However, the first and foremost way of using prunes is as a breakfast or dessert fruit, stewed and served with or without cream. Pitted prunes, a relatively new product, have stimulated the use of prunes as a ready-to-eat snack. Other important prune products are prune juice (a water extract of dried prunes), canned prunes, and diced prunes.

Apricots and Peaches

Apricots.—California accounts for more than 90% of all commercial apricots produced in the United States. Apricot acreage, which reached an all time high of 83,000 bearing acres in 1928, has stabilized at about 35,000 bearing acres in recent years.

The apricot tree tends to be more sensitive to climatic conditions than most other deciduous fruits produced in the State, and heavy rain, frost, or dry weather can drastically affect production. As a result, apricot production in the State in the last 10 yr has ranged from a low of 143,000 tons to a high of 230,000 tons.

California apricots have four principal marketing outlets. Approximately 19% of the crop is dried, 70% is canned, 4% is frozen, and 7% is shipped fresh. Dried apricot tonnage has fallen off sharply since the 1930's, due largely to the growth of canning outlets. The increasing demand for canned apricots has been at the expense of dried production, particularly in the years when production is small and cannery prices are high. In recent years, the dried fruit industry has been making a concerted effort to stimulate dried apricot production.

The Moorpark, Royal, Blenheim, and Tilton are the principal varieties used for drying in California. The Moorpark variety is used almost exclusively for drying. It takes 6–8 lb of fresh apricots to make 1 lb of dried fruit. Dried apricots are high in natural fruit sugars and Vitamins A, B_1, and B_2.

Peaches.—Commercial peach production in California is confined to the warm interior valleys that lie between the mountains of the Coast Range and the Sierra Nevada. The California peach industry has two distinct varietal types—the clingstone (which is used entirely for canning) and the freestone (which is dried, canned, frozen, and shipped fresh). Approximately 12% of the freestone peach crop is dried, 40% is canned, 10% is frozen, and the remainder is shipped fresh. Dried peach production has dropped off sharply in recent years, as canners and freezers have been utilizing a larger portion of the crop.

At present there are about 23,000 bearing acres of freestone peaches in the State, and production in recent years has averaged 250,000 tons.

The Muir, Lovell, and Elberta are the principal varieties that are dried. It takes 6–7 lb of fresh peaches to make 1 lb of dried fruit.

Harvesting and Processing.—Apricots and peaches are carefully picked by hand when they are fully ripened and their sugar content is at its highest. The harvesting season for apricots is from June 15 to Aug. 1; for peaches, from July 15 to Sept. 15.

Peaches and apricots are sorted, halved, pitted and placed cup side up on large flat trays. Most cut fruit is sun dried, but if artificially dehydrated it is first blanched in water or steam and dried several minutes to remove surface moisture. All peaches and apricots, whether sun-dried or dehydrated, are treated with sulfur dioxide to preserve their rich color and aid in the retention of their nutritional qualities.

Sun drying has been used to preserve fruit since the dawn of history, and is still the principal method used for apricots and peaches. After the preparation described above, the fruit is placed in the dry yards for exposure to the direct rays of the sun. Apricots are dried in the sun from 1 to 2 days in the interior valleys or from 2 to 7 days in the coastal area depending on the weather. Peaches usually require 2 days longer in the sun than apricots. After drying, the trays of fruit are stacked in the shade to complete the curing. While sun-drying is the accepted way of curing peaches and apricots, there has been some limited testing of curing by dehydration. This method, however, is not commercially important at the present time. Soon after they are received at the packing plant, dried apricots are graded and placed in cold storage.

Dried apricots and peaches are packed in consumer-size cartons and visible bags, and bulk cases. The trend is steadily toward the small unit packages because of their handiness and the extra protection they provide for the fruit.

The size of dried apricots and peaches is determined by the diameter of the individual piece. The most common grade (size) requirements are as follows, ranging from Standard (small) to Jumbo (largest): Standard, Choice, Extra Choice, Fancy, Jumbo.

Before packing, dried cut fruits are put through a revolving power washer equipped with brushes which thoroughly clean the fruit and make it softer and more pliable. They are then put on trays and resulfured to ensure a good shelf-life in storage. After this, the fruit is exposed to the air for several hours and finally passed on to a long sorting belt, where operators remove any pieces that do not measure up to the standard required for each grade or quality. Dried apricots and peaches are cooled before they go into the cartons and boxes.

Pears

California has about 36,000 acres of Bartlett pears—the variety that is utilized for drying—and in recent years total production has run about 300,000 tons. However, drying accounts for only a very small percentage of the total Bartlett pear crop. Most of the production is either canned or shipped in fresh form.

Dried pear production in recent years has usually been less than 1000 tons. Dried pears generally are used only for mixed fruit packs. Very few pears are marketed separately.

Pears for all uses are generally picked when they have reached full size but still are hard and green. However, the part of the crop that is to be dried may be left on the tree a little longer than the fruit that is to be canned or shipped fresh. All pears are hand-picked from the tree.

Green pears are kept in lug boxes at room temperature until they ripen. Pears are ready for drying when they are eating-ripe.

The fruit is then taken to the cutting shed where workers cut the fruit in half, removing the calyxes and cores. The halved fruit is then spread out on wooden trays, cut surface upward. These trays, loaded with cut pears, are then stacked one on top of another. Each tray is separated by 1-in strips to keep them apart and thus ensure aeration. The entire stack of trays is then placed in the sulfur house where it is exposed for a time to light sulfur fumes.

The trays of fruit are then removed and each tray exposed to the warm sun to permit drying. They are left in the sun but a short time—1 or 2 days—after which the trays are again stacked and properly spaced as to permit the air to circulate, thus completing the drying and curing in the stack. It takes approximately 6 lb of fresh pears to yield 1 lb of dried pears.

When properly dried, the fruit is taken to the packing house where all defective pieces are removed. The sound fruit is then run over a grader which sorts it according to size, namely, Standard, Choice, Extra Choice, Fancy, and Extra Fancy. In the case of Lake County Pears there is an additional grade which is called Jumbo, and as the name signifies, it is an exceptionally large fruit.

Following the grading, pears are then placed in boxes and portable bins, and stored in their natural condition until such time as they are required for packing orders.

Before packing, the fruit is put through a washer, where it is carefully washed in clear, cold water. It is then run over a shaker to remove the moisture. Following this, the fruit is given a light sulfur treatment to help retain the natural bright color. The packing process from this point is the same as for other cut fruits.

Apples

Unlike apricots and peaches, dried apple production in the United States is not confined to California. In recent years, total U.S. dried apple production has ranged from 10,000 to 14,000 tons. California and Washington States are the major producers, each accounting for about 5000–6000 tons annually. New York State accounts for 500–700 tons annually and other States account for about 100 tons.

Evaporated or dried apples are the product resulting from the drying or removal of moisture from fresh apples that have been trimmed, peeled, cored, and sliced.

Two principal styles of dried apples are produced

in California: (1) sliced or ring apples, prepared from peeled and cored apples that are sliced, usually at right angles to the core; (2) quartered apples or apple wedges, prepared form peeled and cored apples that are cut radially from the core. Apples are packed in the same manner as apricots, peaches, and pears, using quality classifications of Fancy, Select, Extra Choice, Extra Choice-Manufacturing Grade, Choice, and Standard.

ANDY ANDARMANI
RANDY DAHLING

DRY MILKS

A study of the history and development of the dry milk industry brings a realism far from our modern times since it dates back to the 13th Century and the days of Marco Polo. It is reported that in his travels through Mongolia, Marco Polo recorded his experience with "sun dried milk."

From this beginning—through pioneering scientists such as Nicholas Appert and Gail Borden—emerged, at the turn of the 20th Century, the accomplishments of Martin Ekenberg and Lewis Merrill, to whom are attributed the first commercially feasible roller- and spray-process operations, respectively, for dry milk production in the United States.

While much transpired in the seven centuries from Marco Polo's "sun dried milk" to the first commercial dry milk production, even more has happened since then and it is evident that early dry milk processing operations triggered technological developments and engineering sophistication up to the present time when "Instant Nonfat Dry Milk Fortified with Vitamins A and D" became universally known and demanded by consumers in today's market places.

A detailed, interesting account of the development of the dry milk industry has been prepared by Beardslee (1948). For an economic overview of the early U.S. dry milk industry, the reader may wish to consult the text of Cook and Day (1947).

Dry Milk Processing

Fluid milk typically undergoes the following handling and processing steps before being dried (Fig. D-11):

(A) Receipt of good quality fluid milk by the processing plant.

(B) Separation of fluid milk, if nonfat dry milk is to be produced, with the resulting cream processed into butter. For the manufacture of dry whole milk, separation is omitted but often it is replaced by clarification.

(C) Pasteurization by high temperature-short time processes which heat the milk to 161°F and maintain it at that temperature continuously for 15 sec.

(D) Dependent upon intended use of the final dry milk product, especially nonfat dry milk, an additional heat treatment may be utilized to obtain product with a specific undenatured whey protein nitrogen content.

(E) Condensing of the milk in an evaporator or vacuum pan. Because moisture is removed more efficiently by this process than by heated air within the dryer, the total solids content of the condensed milk is increased to at least 40%.

Complete and detailed discussions of the techniques utilized in processing fluid milks into dry milk products have been presented by Hall and Hedrick (1971) and Webb and Whittier (1971).

Since the first commercial applications, dry milks have been produced by basically two processes—roller (drum) and spray techniques. Many advances in engineering design and equipment fabrication have been noted since 1900 until the present milk drying processes which can best be described as follows:

Roller Process.—Two large rollers, usually steam heated internally and located adjacent and parallel to each other, revolve at a desired speed (see Fig. D-12 and D-13). The rollers revolve in opposite directions, contacting a reservoir of either pasteurized fluid or condensed milk. During rotation, the fluid milk product dries on the hot roller surface; after approximately 3/4 of a revolution, a carefully positioned, sharp stationary knife detaches the milk product, now in the form of a thin dry sheet. The dry milk next is conveyed by an auger to a hammermill where it undergoes a physical treatment to convert it into uniformly fine particles which then are packaged, usually in 50- or 100-lb bulk packages.

Spray Process.—Two basic configurations of spray dryers presently are in use, these being horizontal (box) and vertical (tower) dryers. In both, pasteurized fluid milk which has been condensed to a total solids of 40% or above is fed under pressure to a spray nozzle, or atomizer, where the dispersed liquid comes into contact with a current of filtered, heated air. The droplets of condensed milk are dried almost immediately and fall to the bottom of the fully enclosed, stainless steel drying chamber. The dry milk product is removed continuously from the drying chamber, transported through a cooling and collecting system, and finally conveyed into a hopper for packaging in 50- or 100-lb bags, or in Tote bins. Collecting systems most commonly used in conjunction with spray dryers are either (a) cyclones or (b) bag units. Figures D-14 and D-15 depict these different dryer styles and collection units.

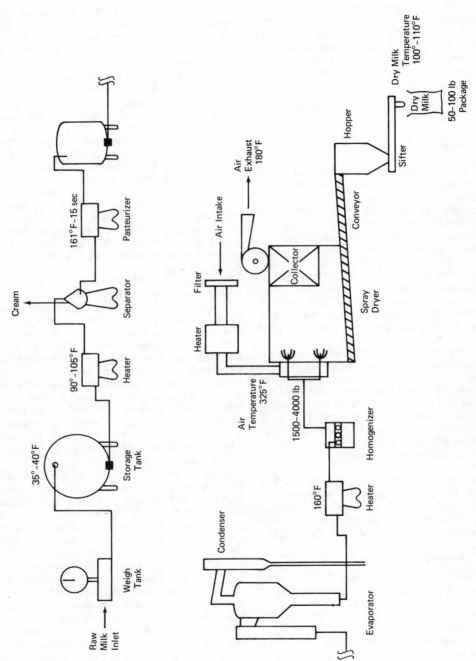

FIG. D-11. FLOW DIAGRAM FOR DRY MILK PROCESSING

*Courtesy of Blaw-Knox Food and
Chemical Equipment, Inc.*

FIG. D-12. A ROLLER DRYER

Recently, sanitary standards have been formulated for milk products spray drying systems (3-A Sanitary Standards Committees 1971). These standards relate to the sanitary aspects of equipment and establish specific criteria for design, material, fabrication, and air supply and quality.

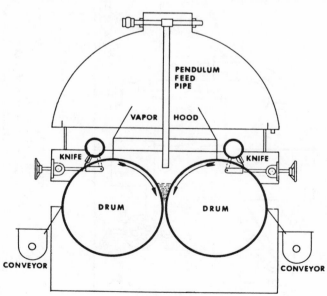

*Courtesy of Blaw-Knox Food and
Chemical Equipment, Inc.*

FIG. D-13. OPERATION OF DRYING DRUMS IN A ROLLER
DRYER

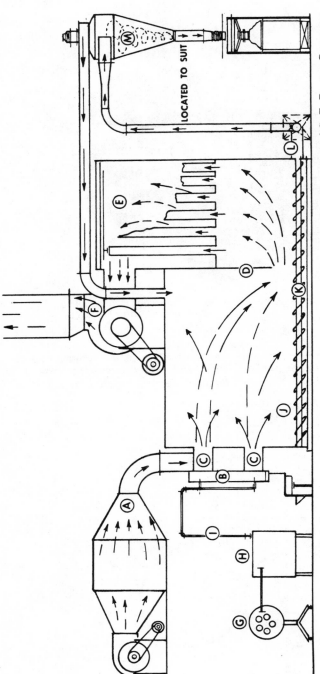

Courtesy of C. E. Rogers Company

FIG. D-14. HORIZONTAL SPRAY DRYING SYSTEM WITH BAG COLLECTION UNIT

Air, properly filtered, preheated with steam or gas is blown into ductwork A and then into the specially proportioned distributing head B, passing through air inlets to the drying chamber C. The hot air absorbs the moisture from the finely atomized liquid spray and passes under air baffle D to air filter bags E where 100% of any remaining powder is trapped from the air passing through the specially designed cloth bags. Filter bags are automatically shaken at intervals to release any adhering powder which then drops to the floor and blends in with the remaining powder. The clean air, freed of powder, is then exhausted to the atmosphere through exhaust fan and exhaust stack F. Liquid to be dried is preheated in heater G, passing to high pressure pump H, through high pressure line I, to spray nozzles located in air inlets C. The atomized liquid spray is instantly dried and the powder falls to the drier floor where it is conveyed by reciprocating conveyor J to screw conveyor K and moved to chamber outlet L. Here it is picked up by pneumatic system M which cools the powder with properly filtered air in the process of conveying it to the sifter. Alternate conveying and sifting arrangements may be used.

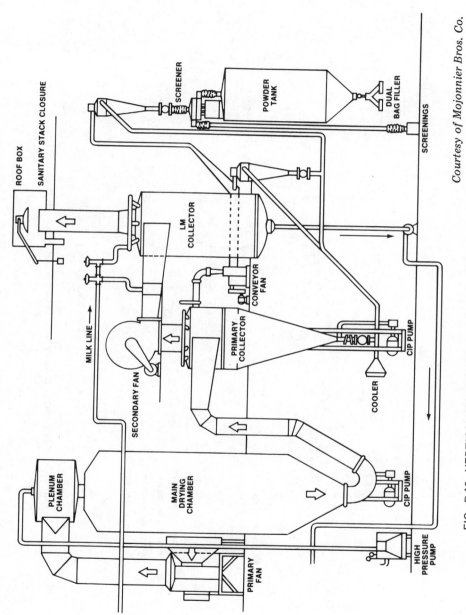

Courtesy of Mojonnier Bros. Co.

FIG. D-15. VERTICAL SPRAY DRYING SYSTEM WITH CYCLONE COLLECTION UNIT

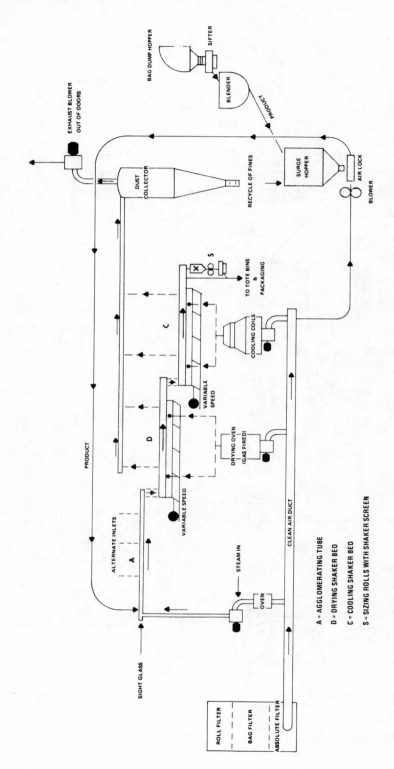

A.D.C.S. AGGLOMERATOR

Courtesy of Cherry-Burell Corp.

FIG. D-16. SCHEMATIC DIAGRAM OF A DRY MILK INSTANTIZING SYSTEM

TABLE D-8

APPROXIMATE COMPOSITION AND FOOD VALUE OF DRY MILKS

Constituents	Nonfat Dry Milk	Dry Whole Milk	Dry Buttermilk
Protein ($N \times 6.38$) (%)	36.0	26.0	34.0
Lactose (Milk Sugar) (%)	51.0	38.0	48.0
Fat (%)	0.7	26.75	5.0
Moisture (%)	3.0	2.25	3.0
Minerals (ash) (%)	8.2	6.0	7.9
Calcium (%)	(1.31)	(0.97)	(1.3)
Phosphorus (%)	(1.02)	(0.75)	(1.0)
Vitamin A (IU/lb)	165.0	4950.0	2300.0
Riboflavin (mg/lb)	9.2	6.7	14.0
Thiamin (mg/lb)	1.6	1.2	1.2
Niacin (mg/lb)	4.2	3.1	4.5
Niacin equivalents[1] (mg/lb)	42.2	30.6	40.6
Pantothenic acid (mg/lb)	15.0	13.0	14.0
Pyridoxine (mg/lb)	2.0	1.5	2.0
Biotin (mg/lb)	0.2	0.185	0.2
Choline (mg/lb)	500.0	400.0	500.0
Energy (cal/lb)	1630.0	2260.0	1700.0

SOURCE: American Dry Milk Institute.

[1] Includes contribution of tryptophan.

TABLE D-9

YEARLY WORLD PRODUCTION OF DRY MILKS[1] IN PRINCIPAL PRODUCING COUNTRIES
(in million pounds)

Year	Belgium	France	West Germany	Netherlands	Sweden	United Kingdom	Canada	United States	Australia	New Zealand
1950	9.4	15.4	—[2]	91.1	19.8	83.5	68.5	884.2	62.6	—
1951	17.3	—	—	75.4	17.8	50.1	70.2	841.1	57.0	—
1952	21.9	—	—	109.6	28.0	57.6	99.2	965.1	70.5	—
1953	34.6	—	—	129.7	25.5	95.4	99.9	1317.3	84.0	—
1954	34.5	35.3	—	130.7	25.9	110.4	100.3	1379.0	84.2	—
1955	34.9	22.0	83.2	117.8	23.2	99.9	108.0	1499.5	96.6	—
1956	41.5	22.0	102.8	136.9	31.7	154.8	98.8	1625.5	100.2	—
1957	55.5	33.1	127.7	149.7	39.1	154.1	142.9	1755.0	102.0	—
1958	66.5	79.4	121.0	181.9	39.8	126.6	205.3	1819.2	103.2	—
1959	62.5	111.0	163.7	173.4	37.7	108.2	197.1	1834.8	135.2	104.7
1960	90.3	210.6	202.7	233.5	55.8	187.9	217.8	1942.5	128.0	106.5
1961	148.1	239.6	224.8	229.1	62.1	204.7	238.7	2122.2	132.7	98.2
1962	120.2	313.1	258.3	255.5	75.2	220.6	215.6	2335.2	126.5	97.7
1963	127.2	441.4	320.1	236.9	77.5	168.0	198.0	2210.7	121.5	123.9
1964	139.2	525.8	375.4	236.8	74.3	125.4	225.4	2286.4	141.0	160.4
1965	190.9	727.3	493.5	263.2	94.1	207.6	244.1	2106.0	135.1	183.2
1966	231.2	901.5	600.6	279.6	97.9	179.0	271.2	1698.8	190.0	255.3
1967	207.9	1163.6	743.8	142.9	68.6	162.4	316.4	1678.0	198.6	324.5
1968	265.0	1496.9	875.4	229.3	83.8	211.9	346.6	1604.0	133.3	298.8
1969	238.3	1474.8	772.7	191.6	93.4	197.6	378.8	1450.8	173.4	287.7
1970	233.7	1393.3	758.6	212.3	76.7	206.3	361.6	1528.4	185.2	252.0
1971	197.1	1333.8	749.6	193.2	72.9	210.4	294.0	1590.0	180.1	267.2

SOURCE: D. R. Strobel, Foreign Agr. Serv., USDA.

[1] Includes nonfat dry milk and dry whole milk.
[2] Data not available.

Instant Dry Milks

Instant dry milks are dry milk products that have been produced in such a manner as to substantially improve their dispersing and reliquefication characteristics. In the United States, both single-pass and agglomerated instant dry milks are manufactured, the latter comprising the majority of instant dry milk. In the process of manufacturing agglomerated instant, the surface of warm dry milk particles is rewetted permitting particles to coalesce upon contact with each other, thus forming large particles or clusters. Following the agglomeration step, the dry milk is redried and recooled, perhaps sized, and packaged.

Detailed information about instantizing systems may be found elsewhere in this publication as well as in that of Hall and Hedrick (1971). Figure D-16 shows one type of instantizer for agglomerating dry milks.

Composition of Dry Milk Products

The average composition and food value of nonfat dry milk, dry whole milk and dry buttermilk are shown in Table D-8. In addition to the nutrients shown in this Table, dry milks contain many other vitamins and minerals. Fat-soluble vitamins are known to be present in appreciable amounts in dry whole milk, in smaller amounts in dry buttermilk, and in only minor quantities in nonfat dry milk. Among the water-soluble vitamins, B_{12} is furnished in significant amounts by dry milks, and approximately 27 mg of vitamin C (ascorbic acid) are furnished per pound of dry whole milk. Important amounts of minerals such as sodium, potassium, and magnesium also are supplied by dry milks.

Dry Milk Standards and Grades

Industry Standards were developed initially in 1929 for nonfat dry milk, 1946 for dry whole milk, 1952 for dry buttermilk, 1963 for instant nonfat dry milk and 1969 for instant nonfat dry milk fortified with vitamins A and D. These Standards served as the basis for grade requirements, based upon various general and specific product characteristics, which determine the overall quality of dry milks. If the raw fluid milk, its handling and processing, and the subsequent storage of dry milk all are in accordance with accepted practices and procedures, the final dry milk product offered for sale should meet grade requirements.

Complete information about general and specific grading requirements for dry milks are contained in Bulletin *916* American Dry Milk Institute and in government publications defining Grades and Standards of Identity for dry milk products (see references).

TABLE D-10

YEARLY U.S. PRODUCTION OF DRY MILKS
(in million pounds)

Year	Nonfat Dry Milk	Dry Whole Milk	Dry Buttermilk
1950	881.5	125.0	48.8
1951	702.5	131.0	45.5
1952	863.2	102.3	47.1
1953	1213.8	101.2	57.4
1954	1334.0	92.7	56.3
1955	1365.8	108.3	58.3
1956	1489.9	110.3	64.3
1957	1623.9	103.2	70.4
1958	1709.7	87.7	77.2
1959	1723.2	90.4	81.5
1960	1818.6	98.0	86.4
1961	2019.8	81.7	89.0
1962	2230.3	86.1	86.4
1963	2106.1	91.0	87.5
1964	2177.2	87.6	92.0
1965	1988.5	88.6	87.4
1966	1579.8	94.4	76.2
1967	1678.7	74.3	72.6
1968	1594.4	79.8	70.4
1969	1452.3	70.2	66.5
1970	1442.8	68.7	59.5
1971[1]	1473.6[1]	77.8[1]	55.9[1]

SOURCE: American Dry Milk Institute.

[1] Preliminary.

Dry Milk Production and Utilization

Total world production of dry milks in 1971 was estimated to be 5,611,100,000 lb. Table D-9 lists the yearly production of dry milks (nonfat dry milk and dry whole milk) in leading countries during the period 1950–1971. U.S. production of nonfat dry milk, dry whole milk, and dry buttermilk during this same period is shown in Table D-10.

Data on the utilization of dry milks in the United States are tabulated annually by the American Dry Milk Institute. In the past, the five largest end-use markets for nonfat dry milk have been: bakery, dairy, packaged for home use, prepared dry mixes, and meat processing. Between 1950 and 1965, and again in 1967, bakery markets ranked first for total domestic nonfat dry milk sales. More recently, dairy and packaged-for-home-use markets have utilized larger quantities of nonfat dry milk than bakery markets. In 1971, 32.6% of domestic nonfat dry milk sales were for dairy use and 24.8% were in the packaged for home use category.

The primary domestic market for dry whole milk is to candy and chocolate coating manufacturers. Other important users are bakers, baby food manufacturers, and institutions. Total U.S. dry whole milk production was 77.8 million pounds in 1971. Human food dry buttermilk production of 55.9 million pounds in 1971 was used in decreasing quantities by the following markets: dairy, bakery, prepared dry mixes, and candy.

WARREN S. CLARK, JR.

References

Standards for Dry Milks

AMERICAN DRY MILK INSTITUTE. 1971. Standards for grades of dry milks including methods of analysis. Bull. *916.*

FDA, DEPT. HEALTH, EDUCATION, and WELFARE. 1968. Nonfat dry milk fortified with vitamins A and D; order establishing definition and Standard of Identity. Federal Register *33,* No. 149, 10926.

U.S. DEPT. OF AGRICULTURE. United States Standards for Grades of Nonfat Dry Milk (Roller Process). Federal Register *23,* 3565 (1958). As amended: Federal Register *24,* 1363 (1959); Federal Register *29,* 11192 (1964); Federal Register *34,* No. 48, 5099 (1969).

U.S. DEPT. OF AGRICULTURE. United States Standards for Grades of Nonfat Dry Milk (Spray Process). Federal Register *23,* 3568 (1958). As amended: Federal Register *24,* 1363 (1959); Federal Register *27,* 6187 (1962); Federal Register *29,* 11192 (1964); Federal Register *34,* No. 48, 5099 (1969).

U.S. DEPT. OF AGRICULTURE. 1970. United States Standards for Instant Nonfat Dry Milk. Federal Register *35,* No. 146, 12097.

U.S. DEPT. OF AGRICULTURE. 1970. United States Standards for Grades of Dry Buttermilk. Federal Register *35,* No. 250, 19629.

U.S. DEPT. OF AGRICULTURE. 1970. United States Standards for Grades of Dry Whole Milk. Federal Register *35,* No. 250, 19630.

General References

AMERICAN DRY MILK INSTITUTE. 1972. Census of dry milk distribution and production trends. Bull. *1000.*

BEARDSLEE, C. E. 1948. Dry Milks—The Story of an Industry. American Dry Milk Institute, Chicago.

COOK, H. L., and DAY, G. H. 1947. The Dry Milk Industry. American Dry Milk Institute, Chicago.

HALL, C. W., and HEDRICK, T. I. 1971. Drying of Milk and Milk Products, 2nd Edition. Avi Publishing Co., Westport, Conn.

3-A SANITARY STANDARDS COMMITTEES. 1971. 3-A accepted practices for milk and milk products spray drying systems. J. Milk Food Technol. *34,* No. 12, 607.

WEBB, B. H., and WHITTIER, E. O. 1971. By-products from Milk, 2nd Edition. Avi Publishing Co., Westport, Conn.

Cross-reference: *Dehydration.*

DUST EXPLOSIONS

Many food products present an explosion hazard when they exist in the form of finely divided solid particles suspended in air in a confined space. Explosions of such clouds of food products have caused many severe industrial accidents resulting in loss of life and extensive plant damage.

When a cloud of flammable dust is subjected to an ignition source, the resulting combustion is extremely rapid because of the large surface area of the material which is exposed to the oxygen in the air. The energy liberated in the form of heat causes expansion of the air and this, together with the large volume of gases evolved by the oxidation reaction itself, produces a pressure rise. When this reaction occurs in a confined volume such as is normally found in food product processing plants, the pressure development can exceed the structural capability of the equipment resulting in failure of the equipment and flames, hot gases, and burning dust will be ejected into the surrounding area.

The probability of an explosion occurring in any given material handling process is a function of the inherent explosive characteristics of the material being processed and the design of the process itself.

Process design should eliminate potential ignition sources such as buildup of static charges, localized hot spots and the presence of tramp metals. This can be accomplished by proper electrical bonding and grounding of process equipment, by preventive maintenance of grinding and milling devices, by the installation of magnetic traps, and adequate inspection of feed materials. Ideally, explosions can be prevented by maintaining the dust-to-air ratio below the lower flammable limit but this usually requires an exceptionally large air handling plant or a product flow too low to be economically practicable.

The explosive characteristics of a dust which determine its sensitivity to ignition are the minimum explosive concentration, minimum ignition energy, and the ignition temperature of the dust cloud. These characteristics vary greatly not only from material to material but within a given material depending on such parameters as particle size, particle configuration, and moisture content. The following illustrates the explosive characteristics of three common food products. All are through 200 mesh samples with less than 5% moisture content.

	Ignition Temp (°F)	Minimum Ignition Energy (Joules)	Minimum Explosive Conc (Oz/Ft^3)
Coffee bean	650	0.32	0.15
Cornstarch	420	0.03	0.05
Soy flour	540	0.46	0.14

Three common methods are employed to minimize or eliminate the potential destruction of an explosion. One involves creating a process atmosphere which lacks sufficient oxygen to support combustion. This is accomplished by the introduction of an inert gas such as nitrogen into the process. The second method of protection is by venting of the process. This is accomplished by installing relief vents of the proper size on the process equipment and directing the pressure build-up to the outside atmosphere. The third method of protection is provided by explosion protection systems in which the explosion is detected and suppressed before destructive pressures can be generated.

Electrostatic Precipitator Function

The function of an electrostatic precipitator is similar to that of a bag filter—namely to remove particulate matter or dust from an airstream before it is exhausted to the atmosphere. It does this by imposing an electrical charge on the flowing particles which are then attracted to plates bearing an opposite charge. A magnetic trap, on the other hand, is normally installed in a hopper feeding a pulverizer or grinder. Its purpose is to attract, trap, and therefore prevent ferrous materials from entering the grinding or pulverizing machinery.

A precipitator removes dust from the exhaust air for ecological reasons. A magnetic trap removes ferrous materials from a process to prevent the creation of ignition sources within the process.

JOSEPH P. GILLIS

E

EGGS AND EGG PRODUCTS

The egg is important as a food and food ingredient. It is one of the most nutritious foods we consume and can be prepared in many different ways by itself, such as scrambled eggs. It is also a major ingredient in dishes, such as souffles, and is an essential part of many baked goods, candies, and other foods. The egg functions in many different ways to give food products in which it is used certain desirable characteristics. It leavens, binds, thickens, emulsifies, tenderizes, retains moisture, adds flavor and color, and improves nutrition.

Eggs are consumed as shell eggs and as further processed egg products. Use of eggs for hatching will not be considered here. Table E-1 shows the

TABLE E-1

PER CAPITA CONSUMPTION OF SHELL AND PROCESSED EGGS, 1954–1968

Year	Egg Consumption			Proportion of Eggs Processed (%)
	Shell (No.)	Processed[1] (No.)	Total (No.)	
1954	351	25	376	6.6
1955	346	25	371	6.7
1956	345	24	369	6.5
1957	335	27	362	7.5
1958	328	26	354	7.3
1959	319	33	352	9.4
1960	306	28	334	8.4
1961	298	30	328	9.1
1962	296	30	326	9.2
1963	290	27	317	8.5
1964	287	31	318	9.7
1965	285	29	314	9.2
1966	283	30	313	9.6
1967	289	35	324	10.8
1968	284	34	318	10.7

SOURCE: Jones (1969).

[1] Shell-egg equivalent.

per capita consumption of eggs and egg products from 1954 to 1968, and indicates the gradual increase of egg products. Though total per capita consumption of eggs has decreased through the years, overall production has increased because of population growth. The annual production of eggs is now approximately 70 billion.

Egg production has changed through the years, from small farm flocks of less than 100 to larger and larger flocks producing eggs under more closely controlled conditions. Now flocks of 100,000 birds are common. There is one operation in California having as many as 2,000,000 birds.

The egg and the component parts of the egg are very unique materials. Table E-2 gives the composition of the basic parts and the mixture of these parts: egg white, egg yolk, and whole egg. Whole egg is actually the mixture of the white and yolk in natural proportions. There are 60 parts by weight of liquid white to 40 parts by weight of liquid yolk. The commercial yolk shown here is not actually pure yolk but has about 10% egg white which stays with the yolk during breaking and separating. Pure yolk with the adhering white removed would have 51% solids, of which 16% is protein and 31% lipids.

Egg white is made up of mostly proteins which have rather unusual properties. The important proteins of egg white are listed in Table E-3, giving their percentages of the total protein and important characteristics.

Egg yolk is a very complex mixture of essentially lipids and proteins. It is further complicated by the inclusion of whites. Half of the water in egg yolk is distributed as free water and the rest is bound to three fractions: the water-soluble protein, the high-density lipoprotein, and the low-density lipoprotein (Schultz and Forsythe 1967). Most of the lipids are in the low-density lipoprotein fraction which, in unaltered egg yolk liquid, is in a finely dispersed state. It has been postulated that the triglycerides make up the inner core of the highly emulsified low-density lipoproteins. This is surrounded by a phospholipid shell and then protein molecules are wrapped

351

TABLE E-2

PERCENTAGE COMPOSITION OF RAW LIQUID EGG PRODUCTS

	Whole Liquid	Whites	Yolks[1]	Yolks (Commercially Separated)
Water (%)	73.7	87.6	51.1	55.5
Protein (%)	12.9	10.9	16.0	15.4
Fat (%)	11.5	Trace	30.6	26.9
Carbohydrate (%)[2]	1.1	1.1	1.0	1.0
Free carbohydrate (%)[3]	0.3	0.4	0.2	0.2

SOURCE: Anon. (1969A).

[1] Yolks separated under laboratory conditions include only a small proportion of white; commercially separated yolks include considerable white.
[2] Unpublished results.
[3] From Mitchell (1932).

TABLE E-3

EGG WHITE PROTEINS

Egg White Consists of Seven Main Proteins	Total Egg White Solids (%)	Heat Stability of Isolated Proteins
Ovomucin	1.5	Very stable
Globulins (two)	7	
Lysozyme	3.5	
Ovalbumin	58	Unstable at pH 9; stability much greater at pH 7
Ovomucoid	10	
Conalbumin	12	Very unstable; metal complexes are much more stable than conalbumin
Conalbumin, Fe_2[1]		
Conalbumin, Al_2		

SOURCE: Anon. (1969A).

[1] This is the form in which conalbumin exists in liquid whole egg due to iron provided by the yolk.

around this shell. The high-density lipoproteins are contained in granules which can be removed by centrifuging. All of the lipids of unaltered egg yolk are associated with lipoproteins.

Functional properties of the egg are briefly considered below.

Leavening Power

This is sometimes called the aerating, foaming, or whipping property of eggs. It means the ability to incorporate air by itself or in a mixture with other ingredients and to hold the aerated structure long enough so that it can be set by heat, drying, or other means. Foams created by egg white are somewhat different from those created by whole egg and yolk.

Egg white protein has the ability to form very stable foams. When egg white is whipped by mechanical means and air is incorporated, large areas of new surfaces are formed and the proteins will unfold and spread as a monomolecular layer over the surfaces. The proteins that spread are actually denatured similar to heat denatured proteins. This surface denaturation is irreversible; thus, a strong network of denatured protein is formed to produce a stable foam, though this denatured protein is only a small percentage of the total. Other types of proteins may foam but will not denature on the surface enough to produce the same results as egg white protein.

The foaming of whole egg and yolk is similar to but more complex than the foaming of egg white. There is a large amount of lipids present and these lipids must be in a highly emulsified state in order for the product to develop a stable foam. Unemulsified or free fat tends to retard foaming. The emulsifying ability of whole egg and yolk is also tied into its foaming ability.

Binding and Thickening

Proteins of egg coagulate during heating and thus give to eggs the ability to bind pieces of food together or to thicken foods, such as custard and puddings. Coagulation is sometimes referred to as denaturation or gelation. Eggs go through the following stages during heat coagulation: denaturation, flocculation, and insolubility.

The ability to coagulate by heat is one of the most important properties of eggs. Egg proteins denature and coagulate over a wide range of temperatures, from 135°F to 180°F (Payawal et al. 1946), which is the reason why egg whites can hold the very delicate structure of an angel cake. When the cake is baked, some of the egg proteins will begin to coagulate at a relatively low temperature, about 135°F, to set the foam batter structure; but this is elastic and all of the proteins will not completely coagulate until the angel cake structure has expanded and developed into its final form at about 180°F.

Emulsifying Power

Egg yolk, whole egg, and egg white are all good emulsifiers. Actually, egg yolk is rated as four times as effective an emulsifier as egg white, and whole egg is intermediate between the two (Lowe 1955). The very excellent emulsifying properties of egg yolk are attributed to the lecithoproteins. However, it has been observed that the ether-insoluble portion of whole egg is the most important emulsifying substance (Chapin 1951). This same study demonstrated that drying enhances the emulsifying properties of whole egg. Proof of the excellent emulsifying properties of egg is given when making mayonnaise which contains a minimum of 65% oil, and which has egg as the only emulsifying ingredient. Emulsifying properties of eggs are important wherever they are used together with other fats and oils.

Tenderizing

Eggs contribute to smoothness, moistness, and a desirable texture in baked products. One reason for this is that they are known to retard crystallization of sugar.

Moisture Retention

In baked goods, eggs help to retain moisture during baking and also during storage. Eggs bind the ingredients together and offer a barrier through which it is difficult for moisture to escape.

Flavor

Eggs are, of course, good eating by themselves. They have a distinct flavor which affects baked products. They also help flavor by imparting better mouth feel to these products.

Nutrition

Eggs have the highest quality protein of any food and they have most of the essential vitamins. The lipids are easily digested, and there are more unsaturated fats than in any other animal product. Table E-4 gives the nutrients found in egg products on a solids basis.

Color

Eggs add color to products in which they are used, though this color can be easily substituted by use of other coloring materials. There are some products, however, in which Federal Standards of Identity will not permit other coloring added and where color of the eggs is essential to indicate richness of the product. An example is egg noodles.

Shell Eggs

Eggs are graded and classified on the basis of apparent interior quality, as well as external appearance. The grade can be established by twisting the egg in front of a candling light and also by knowing how the eggs are handled from specific flocks of hens. Most States have grading laws and USDA has an egg grading program using federal inspectors, usually run in cooperation with the States. A summary of U.S. Standards for quality of individual shell eggs is given in Table E-5.

Eggs are classified as dirty if "the shell is unbroken and has adhering dirt or foreign material, prominent stains or moderate stains covering more than $1/4$ of the shell surface." They are classified as checks if "the individual egg has a broken shell or crack in the shell but with its shell membrane intact and its contents do not leak." A check is considered to be lower in quality than a dirty. Leakers have the shell and membrane broken so that the contents are leaking. Recent regulations prohibit the use of this type of egg for human consumption.

Eggs are also classified as to size, but this is independent of the quality factors above. The U.S. weight classes for consumer grades for shell eggs are as follows:

Size or Weight Class	Minimum Net Weight Per Dozen (Oz)
Jumbo	30
Extra large	27
Large	24
Medium	21
Small	18
Peewee	15

Eggs for frying and poaching should be of Grade A or AA quality, where the whites are firm and the yolks upstanding. Lower grades, such as B and C, are usually suitable for almost all cooking purposes.

Handling of shell eggs from the time of lay to packing can now be mechanized. Candling, grading, and packing are still done by hand at small operations, but most large operations use automatic or semiautomatic equipment. Eggs are

PROXIMATE COMPOSITION OF SOLIDS IN WHOLE EGG, EGG WHITE, AND EGG YOLK

	Whole Egg	Egg White (per 100 Gm)	Egg Yolk (Free of Egg White)
Protein (gm)	49.3	88.6	32.9
Fat (gm)	44.3	—	64.4
Carbohydrate (gm)	2.7	6.6	1.4
Calorie	624	410	729
Minerals			
Calcium (mg)	208	49	297
Phosphorus (mg)	809	139	1,184
Iron (mg)	8.1	2.5	11.3
Iodine (μg)	46.2	55.8	32.3
Sodium (mg)	427	1,435	158
Potassium (mg)	574	1,222	222
Chloride (mg)	385	1,074	135
Magnesium (mg)	35	90	26
Fluorine (mg)	0.23	0.16	0.24
Copper (mg)	0.66	0.33	0.51
Sulphur (mg)	897	1,730	432
Manganese (mg)	0.15	Trace	0.22
Zinc (mg)	5.0	0.08	7.7
Ash (gm)	3.9	4.9	3.4
Vitamins			
Vitamin A (IU)	4,389	—	6,484
Vitamin D (IU)	193	—	303
Vitamin E (mg)	7.7	—	12.1
Vitamin K	+	—	+
Thiamin (mg)	0.39	—	0.55
Riboflavin (mg)	1.12	2.13	0.71
Niacin (mg)	0.39	—	Trace
Pantothenic acid (mg)	10.4	1.07	12.1
Folic acid (μg)	36.2	13.1	46.9
Biotin (μg)	86.6	57	105
Pyridoxine (mg)	0.970	1.780	0.622
Choline chloride (gm)	2.048	Trace	3.01
Vitamin B_{12} (μg)	1.086	0.074	1.669
Inositol (mg)	146	—	—
Lipids and their hydrolysis products			
Total saturated fatty acids (gm)	11.70	—	16.16
Total unsaturated fatty acids (gm)	25.53	—	35.23
Linoleic acid (gm)	8.47	—	11.70
Linolenic acid (gm)	1.16	—	1.58
Arachidonic acid (gm)	0.92	—	1.27
Cholesterol (gm)	2.93	—	4.04
		Percentage of Protein	
Amino Acids			
Arginine	6.7	6.3	7.2
Aspartic acid	5.8	6.0	5.5
Cystine	2.2	2.5	1.7
Glutamic acid	12.3	12.4	12.1
Glycine	3.7	4.0	3.5
Histidine	2.7	2.7	2.9
Isoleucine	7.0	7.2	6.9
Leucine	8.5	8.5	8.5
Lysine	6.8	6.6	7.2
Methionine	3.3	4.1	2.4
Phenylalanine	5.4	6.1	4.6
Serine	7.7	6.9	8.9
Threonine	5.5	5.2	6.1
Tryptophan	1.9	2.0	1.8
Tyrosine	4.6	4.6	4.6
Valine	8.2	8.8	7.3

SOURCE: Calculated from data given by Everson and Souders (1957).

TABLE E-5

SUMMARY OF UNITED STATES STANDARDS FOR QUALITY OF INDIVIDUAL SHELL EGGS GIVING SPECIFICATIONS FOR EACH QUALITY FACTOR

Quality Factor	AA Quality	A Quality	B Quality	C Quality
Shell	Clean	Clean	Clean; to slightly stained	Clean; to moderately stained
	Unbroken	Unbroken	Unbroken	Unbroken
	Practically normal	Practically normal	May be slightly abnormal	May be abnormal
Air cell	1/8-in. or less in depth	3/16-in. or less in depth	3/8-in. or less in depth	May be over 3/8-in. in depth
	Practically regular	Practically regular	May be free or bubbly	May be free or bubbly
White	Clear	Clear	Clear	May be weak and watery
	Firm	May be reasonably firm	May be slightly weak	Small blood clots or spots may be present[1]
Yolk	Outline slightly defined	Outline may be fairly well defined	Outline may be well defined	Outline may be plainly visible
	Practically free from defects	Practically free from defects	May be slightly enlarged and flattened	May be enlarged and flattened
			May show definite but not serious defects	May show clearly visible germ development but no blood
				May show other serious defects

SOURCE: Anon. (1969B).

[1] If they are small (aggregating not more than 1/8-in. in diameter).

transferred from plastic flats on which they are gathered to a conveyor which carries them through washing, drying, spray coating with mineral oil, candling, grading, classifying by weight, and packing. Although most eggs are gathered by hand, automatic egg gathering equipment is becoming common in large commercial operations.

Changes in the quality of eggs during storage can be caused by either chemical or microbiological reactions. Odors can also be absorbed under adverse storage conditions.

As the egg ages, the firmness of the white decreases, and, when broken, the yolk flattens and the contents spread. Loss of carbon dioxide from the egg is associated with quality loss. This loss can be reduced by preventing the escape of carbon dioxide. The common method for doing this is by applying a thin coating of mineral oil.

Sound, clean, fresh eggs are seldom contaminated with microorganisms internally. Eggs may become contaminated through faulty handling procedures. Improper cleaning of eggs is the most common cause for shell egg contamination and bacterial spoilage. It is now common practice to wash all eggs in continuous egg washing machines. Wash solutions must be at least 90°F and at least 20°F warmer than the eggs, and changed frequently. After washing, eggs are rinsed with water containing 100–200 ppm chlorine and are dried as rapidly as possible.

Eggs are packed in cartons, 1 doz per carton, for retail sale or are packed in cases, 30 doz per case, for commercial use. Shell eggs are usually held under refrigeration at about 50°F until they are sold or used. Lower temperatures are seldom necessary today because storage periods are generally very short. Also, there is a problem with moisture condensation when removing eggs from the cooler at too low a temperature. At one time, when egg production was more seasonal, large numbers of eggs were stored for periods up to several months. Now, egg production is rather uniform throughout the year, and long storage periods are not necessary.

Shell eggs are consumed in homes and also in institutions, such as restaurants and hospitals. In recent years, the trend has been away from shell eggs in institutions to the use of egg products. In the early 1900's, each bake shop and candy plant, both large and small, broke their own shell eggs.

This was a laborious and time consuming operation and switchover to egg products came as soon as they became available in a suitable form.

Egg Products

There are basically three types of egg products: dried, frozen, and liquid.

Dried Products

Egg white
  Spray-dried egg white solids
  Flake albumen
  Instant egg white
Plain whole egg and yolk
  Standard whole egg solids
  Stabilized (glucose-free) whole egg solids
  Standard egg yolk solids
  Stabilized (glucose-free) egg yolk solids
  Free-flowing whole egg solids
  Free-flowing egg yolk solids
Blends of whole egg and yolk with carbohydrates
  With sugar
  With corn syrup

Frozen Products

Egg white
Whole egg
Whole egg with yolk added (fortified)
Plain egg yolk
Fortified whole egg with corn syrup
Sugared egg yolk
Salted egg yolk
Salted whole egg

Liquid Products

Egg white
Egg yolk
Whole egg

It is surprising that dried egg products were actually the first to be developed (in the late 1800's), although they may not have been too acceptable at that time. Next came frozen eggs and, finally, liquid egg products.

Early records of egg dehydration in this country date back to about 1880, when a U.S. patent was issued. In 1879, a St. Louis firm started to dry eggs on a drum-type dryer, and commercial production of dried eggs had its beginning. In the early 1900's, China had a very large supply of low cost eggs. Both Americans and Germans developed processes to produce dried eggs and they set up plants in China. The pan drying of egg whites was developed using an egg white that had been naturally fermented. Stability of this product was excellent and it also had good foaming properties. It was not known until many years later that this product was stable because the

natural glucose had been removed by fermentation (Kline and Stewart 1948). Belt dryers were developed, and whole egg and yolk products were dried in a flake form in this type of equipment, as well as on pan dryers. Prior to 1930, the low cost egg products out of China gave little incentive for drying elsewhere. However, tariffs on eggs coming into the country from China were increased during the 1920's, and drying of eggs in the United States began again about 1930, and the industry has expanded since that time. There was a great surge during World War II, when there was a tremendous need for dried eggs by the military and for the Lend-Lease Program. At one time, in 1944, there were 135 spray dryers producing dried whole egg. Total production in that year was over 30,000,000 lb (Koudele and Heinsohn 1960).

The frozen egg business began around 1900. There were many problems encountered with high bacteria counts and spoilage because of poor sanitation and also because of slow freezing and relatively high freezer temperatures. With better sanitation and improvement in refrigeration equipment these problems were overcome. In early days, the slow freezing problem was solved to a certain extent by pouring only 2–3 in. of product each day into a container and placing it in the freezer each day until the can was full. Now egg containers are filled to usually 30 lb per container and placed in a blast freezer at $-20°$ to $-40°F$. Prior to 1930, as in the case of dried egg products, a considerable amount of frozen eggs were imported from China.

The frozen egg has been the principal type of egg product used by the baking industry, but dried egg products have been gaining rapidly. Also, the use of liquid eggs has increased, particularly in large bakeries close to an egg breaking facility. This has been made possible by the introduction of large sanitary stainless steel handling equipment. Table E-6 compares the total production of the three types of egg products in 1968. The proportions of processed eggs used by different food industries are shown in Table E-7. The latter data were determined from a survey taken of the industry in 1960. The proportions would be somewhat different today with dried and liquid eggs at a higher percentage of the industry usage.

Reviews covering the subject of egg products are Lightbody and Fevold (1948), Forsythe (1964, 1968), Bergquist (1973), Matz (1972), Anon. (1969B).

Egg Products Processing

Because more and more eggs are being produced in large commercial operations where the shell egg

TABLE E-6

PRODUCTION OF PROCESSED EGG PRODUCTS BY TYPE OF PRODUCT, 1968

Type of Product	Whole Egg and Blends	Albumen	Plain Yolk and Blends		Share of Production
		(In 1000 lb)		Total	(%)
Frozen	203,757	67,263	89,586	360,606	53
Dried[1]	125,364	99,699	28,116	253,179	38
Liquid	37,608	11,661	13,697	62,966	9
Total	366,729	178,623	131,399	676,751	100
(Percentage of Total Production)					
	54	26	20		100

SOURCE: Jones (1969); USDA Statist. Reporting Serv. Jan. 29, 1969.

[1] On a liquid equivalent basis, ingredients added.

TABLE E-7

PROPORTIONS OF PROCESSED EGG PRODUCTS USED BY SELECTED FOOD MANUFACTURING INDUSTRIES, 1960[1]

Type of Product	Bakeries	Premix Manu-facturers	Confec-tionery Firms	Misc Food Manu-facturers[2]
Frozen	80	—	27	60
Dried	13	100	4	3
Liquid	5	—	63	3
Shell	2	—	6	34

SOURCE: Jones (1969).

[1] Based on survey of food manufacturing industries, *Present and Potential Use of Egg Products in the Food Manufacturing Industry*, USDA, ERS MRR-608, June 1963.
[2] Includes manufacturers of noodles, macaroni, and ravioli; salad dressing and mayonnaise; meat and fish products; baby foods; and specialty items.

for table use has been of prime consideration, the color of egg yolks is becoming uniformly light in color and dark eggs are rather scarce. Only a few egg producers are feeding for color and this must be with the natural color additive. Much of the feeding for color has been experimental. Because of Federal Standards, color cannot be added directly to egg products.

Eggs are received in cases at the breaking plant and are held under refrigeration until they are broken. Before breaking, they are washed and flash candled. The eggs are either separated into yolk and white or are broken out as whole egg. Today, most egg breaking is done by machine. One machine is capable of breaking and separating 20–40 cases of eggs per hour, using 1 person to feed the machine and another to operate and inspect. With the hand separator, which was invented in 1912, 1 person could break and separate from $1\frac{1}{2}$ to $3\frac{1}{2}$ cases per hour. This device is still used in very small operations. Automatic egg breaking and separating equipment started to be developed in the late 1940's.

The egg contents—whites, yolks, and mix or whole egg—go from the breaking and separating operation to churns and mixing devices and then are chilled to usually below 40°F as soon as possible. Passing the liquid through cooling plates of a heat exchanger is one method used for cooling. The liquid is usually held under 40°F until it is processed and then frozen or dried.

Yields in egg production are generally based on the case which has 30 doz eggs. The total amount of liquid obtained from a case varies according to the size and quality of the shell eggs. Yields generally fall in the range of 32–42 lb total liquid per case.

Pasteurization of Egg Products.—The objective in pasteurization of egg products is to reduce the hazard of potential pathogenic microorganisms and still retain the physical and functional properties of the raw liquid eggs. In addition to microbiological properties, one must be concerned about functional properties. In heating eggs for pasteurization, we attempt to use the highest possible temperature without impairing these very delicate and sensitive properties which make eggs so very useful. There is thus a relatively low limit as to how high eggs can be heated. Natural egg white liquid, for example, begins to coagulate at 136°F, whole egg at 143°F, and yolk at 135°F (Payawal *et al.* 1946).

There are a number of egg products, all of which are different in their sensitivity to heat and the

TABLE E-8

USDA PASTEURIZATION REQUIREMENTS

Liquid Egg Product	Minimum Temp Requirements (°F)	Minimum Holding Time Requirements	
		Fastest Particle (Min)	Average Particle (Min)
Albumen (without use of chemicals)	134	1.75	3.5
	132	3.1	6.2
Whole egg	140	1.75	3.5
Whole egg blends (less than 2% added nonegg ingredients)	142	1.75	3.5
	140	3.1	6.2
Fortified whole egg and blends (24–38% egg solids, 2–12% added nonegg ingredients)	144	1.75	3.5
	142	3.1	6.2
Salt whole egg (with 2% or more salt added)	146	1.75	3.5
	144	3.1	6.2
Sugar whole egg (2–12% sugar added)	142	1.75	3.5
	140	3.1	6.2
Plain yolk	142	1.75	3.5
	140	3.1	6.2
Sugar yolk (2% or more sugar added)	146	1.75	3.5
	144	3.1	6.2
Salt yolk (2–12% salt added)	146	1.75	3.5
	144	3.1	6.2

SOURCE: Anon. (1969C).

ease with which bacteria are destroyed within them. Three basic processing methods, alone or in combination, are used commercially to pasteurize egg products. These are: (1) heating the liquid egg, (2) heating the dried egg product, and (3) exposure of the liquid to hydrogen peroxide.

Other methods have been studied but are not now used commercially. Examples are the treatment of dried products with epoxide, such as ethylene oxide or propylene oxide, and radiation of the liquid or dried product with ultraviolet light or ionizing radiation. All of these methods have proven to be effective but have not received clearance by federal agencies.

Since 1966, regulations of USDA and FDA have required pasteurization of eggs. USDA has specified the conditions under which eggs must be pasteurized, while FDA has taken the position that they must be pasteurized by a method which renders the egg products *Salmonella* negative.

Liquid whole egg can be pasteurized at 140°F with 3½ min holding time with good destruction of bacteria (Winter *et al.* 1946; Sugihara *et al.* 1966). All of the pasteurization methods approved by USDA give a bacterial kill equivalent to that obtained when heating whole egg liquid to 140°F and holding at this temperature for 3½ min. The temperatures and holding times specified are actually minimum. For almost all strains of

Salmonella, the kill is good under these conditions. For example, if 1,000,000 *Salmonellae* per gram are present in the raw liquid egg, there would probably be none found in the pasteurized product. Table E-8 shows the most recently published pasteurization requirements by USDA. For minimum holding time, there is a specification for the average time the liquid is held and also for the time of the fastest particle going through the system (which is indicated as ½ the average time). The purpose of this is to take care of pure laminar flow in which the particles at the center of the tube travel twice as fast as the average particle.

There are actually several methods for pasteurizing egg whites. These include:

(1) Heat treatment of the plain liquid egg white above 134°F for at least 3½ min (Kline *et al.* 1966). Plain white is natural unprocessed egg white liquid without additives. Commercially broken egg whites will consistently have a pH of 9.0 ± 0.1. This relatively high pH allows greater destruction of bacteria at a lower temperature than is possible with other natural egg products.

(2) Heat treatment of heat stabilized egg white above 140°F for at least 3½ min (Cunningham and Lineweaver 1965). Heat stabilization is accomplished by adjusting pH to 7.0 with lactic acid and adding aluminum sulfate. The pH adjustment increases the stability of the proteins oval-

bumen, lysozyme, ovomucoid, and ovomucin. The aluminum sulfate stabilizes conalbumin which would otherwise not be stable at pH 7.0. The aluminum ion forms a complex with the conalbumin that is heat stable.

(3) Heat treatment of plain egg white above 125°F in the presence of hydrogen peroxide (Lloyd and Harriman 1957). Heating of the liquid serves to inactivate the natural catalase and also to make the bacterial killing power of hydrogen peroxide more effective. After treatment, catalase is added to decompose the hydrogen peroxide.

(4) Heat treatment of the dried egg white product often in combination with one of the liquid pasteurization procedures (Bergquist 1961). Dry heat treatment of egg white powder is effective in destroying *Salmonella* at temperatures above 120°F. USDA now specifies 130°F for 7 days. Dry heat treatment is often accomplished by placing the container of dried egg white in a room at the desired temperature. Dried egg white with natural glucose removed is very stable and can be heated for extended periods without noticeable effect on functional properties.

Liquid whole egg and yolk products have better natural heat stability than liquid egg white and can be pasteurized above 140°F without stabilization. The British requirement for pasteurizing whole egg is 148°F for 2½ min. This condition inactivates the natural α-amylase of egg and thus the fact that eggs have been pasteurized can be determined by testing for this enzyme. However, more functional damage is noted with the higher pasteurization temperatures.

Equipment used for pasteurizing liquid eggs is the standard high temperature-short time pasteurizing equipment with all of its component parts. This is a continuous process in which the liquid is heated to a specified temperature and held for a specified period of time before it is cooled and either frozen or dried. Safety features are provided to make sure that these requirements are met.

Batch pasteurization was one of the first methods to be applied to egg products, particularly whole egg (Brant *et al.* 1968). This method is again being considered by the industry, especially for small egg processing operations. Temperatures of 132°F for 35 min and 135°F for 15 min are considered to be equivalent to 140°F for 3½ min.

Freezing.—The common container for frozen eggs is a metal can which holds 30 lb of the product. The can is filled with the chilled liquid egg to be frozen and is then placed in a blast freezer at −20° to −40°F for up to 72 hr. After freezing, the frozen products are usually held at 0° to −10°F.

Plastic-coated fiber containers have also been used for packing frozen egg products, with capacities ranging from 5 to 30 lb. Mechanical refrigeration has proven to be the most economical method for freezing eggs. However, some work has been done with liquid nitrogen and carbon dioxide.

Drying.—Spray drying is used for the production of most dried egg products. Products produced by spray drying are in the powder form. Some egg whites are dried by the pan or tray drying method in an air oven. These products are in a granular or flake form, but they can also be milled to a powder form. Freeze drying has been employed to a limited extent for egg products and egg-containing products. A belt drying method was once employed in China but is no longer used. However, a form of belt drying called fluff, or foam drying, has been used successfully for the commercial production of egg whites and experimentally for the drying of whole egg and yolk products.

In addition to pasteurizing, some dried egg products require processing of the liquid prior to drying to improve storage stability of the finished dried product and to assure good functional properties in the dried material.

The stability of dried egg white is assured by removing the glucose by fermentation (Kline and Stewart 1948) or by use of the enzyme glucose oxidase (Baldwin *et al.* 1953). Egg whites with glucose removed will keep almost indefinitely under any storage conditions. Removal of glucose also improves the storage stability of whole egg and yolk products (Kline *et al.* 1951) and this is usually done if long storage is required at room temperature. Other ways of improving storage stability are by reducing pH and by adding carbohydrates (Brooks and Hawthorne 1943). The carbohydrates will also improve whipping ability of dried whole egg and yolk products (Kline *et al.* 1964).

Whipping aids are added to egg white products in order to give to them more uniformity and compensate for any changes that might occur during processing and drying. The selection of the whipping aid depends on the type of egg white product and its use. For liquid and frozen egg whites that have been pasteurized, the ester-type whipping aids, such as triethyl citrate, seem to be preferred. Sodium lauryl sulfate does not work well for frozen egg white but is the most commonly used additive for dried egg white. It is added at a level of less than 0.1% on a solids basis. This is the additive specified by cake manufacturers who prefer to standardize on one whipping aid for egg white.

Types of Products

There are a number of different types of egg products under each of the categories: dried, frozen, and liquid described below. U.S. Standards of Identity are in existence for whole egg, egg white, and egg yolk in liquid, frozen, and dried forms. These standards require pasteurization to ensure that the products are negative *Salmonella*. They also allow for the addition of monosodium phosphate to preserve color in frozen eggs and the use of sodium silicoaluminate to give free-flowing properties to dried egg products.

Dried Products.—(1) Spray-dried egg white. There are a number of different types of dried egg white products, depending upon their end use. All of these have the natural glucose removed to give them extremely good stability when stored by themselves or mixed with other ingredients.

(2) Pan-dried egg albumen. This comes in flake, granular, or milled powder forms. It is used mainly by the candy industry.

(3) Plain spray-dried whole egg and yolk products. These products have excellent functional properties, such as binding, thickening, emulsifying, texturizing, and moistening; but they do not usually whip well under regular conditions. They will work in almost all baked products, even in sponge cakes where emulsifiers are used. Glucose may be removed in order to improve stability. Also, a free-flowing agent, such as sodium silicoaluminate, can be added up to 2% to improve flow properties. Products in this category include standard dried whole egg, stabilized (glucose-free) dried whole egg, standard dried egg yolk, stabilized (glucose-free) dried egg yolk, free-flowing dried whole egg, and free-flowing dried egg yolk.

(4) Blends of whole egg, yolk and fortified whole egg with carbohydrates. Sugar or corn syrups are added to liquid eggs before drying in order to preserve whipping properties and give other desirable physical characteristics.

(5) Blends of eggs with other ingredients, such as skim milk and shortening. Recently, the U.S. Government purchased fairly large quantities of a scrambled egg mix which consists, on a solids basis, of 51% whole egg, 30% skim milk solids, 15% vegetable oil, $1\frac{1}{2}$% salt, and $2\frac{1}{2}$% moisture.

Frozen Products.—(1) Frozen egg white. Egg whites for freezing are pasteurized by 1 of 3 methods which were indicated above. Pasteurized frozen whites are usually somewhat thinner in consistency than the unpasteurized counterpart, which is no longer available, and may have some loose clumps of opaque white material present. The reduced viscosity is apparently caused by mechanical treatment during pasteurizing, rather than by heating itself. Sometimes stabilizers are added to increase the viscosity, and a whipping aid, such as triethyl citrate, is added to improve beating properties.

(2) Frozen whole egg. The viscosity of whole egg increases when it is frozen because of gelation. However, pasteurized frozen whole egg is usually lower in viscosity when thawed than the unpasteurized product. Again, this is apparently due to mechanical treatment.

(3) Frozen fortified whole egg.

(4) Frozen plain egg yolk. The consistency of egg yolk changes considerably during freezing. In fact, frozen egg yolk, when thawed, will not flow. The freezing point of egg yolk is 30.8°F, and gelation occurs at temperatures below 21°F. Storage and the rate of thaw has some effect on the degree of gelation. Physical treatment, which occurs during pasteurizing and also during homogenizing, can reduce the amount of gelation. Mixing in of other ingredients, such as sugar and salt at a 10% level or higher, as in products given below, will virtually eliminate gelation.

(5) Frozen fortified whole egg with corn syrup. This is usually a mixture of approximately 70% whole egg with 30% yolk and 5% corn syrup. This product generally has a high viscosity when thawed because some gelation does occur at this carbohydrate level. At a higher carbohydrate level, viscosity would be lower.

(6) Frozen sugared egg yolk. This is generally 10% sugar (sucrose) and the product is fluid when thawed.

(7) Frozen salted egg yolk. Salt may be added from 2 to 12%. This type of product is used mostly in the mayonnaise and salad dressing industry.

(8) Frozen salted whole egg. This product is also used in the mayonnaise industry.

Liquid Products.—The common liquid egg products are plain egg white, egg yolk, and whole egg. These are pasteurized at the breaking plant before being shipped to the user. They are usually transported in tank trucks but can also be transferred in other suitable containers, such as 55-gal. drums. Egg whites must be held below 45°F, whole egg and yolks below 40°F, and the products must be used within a specified period of time.

DWIGHT H. BERGQUIST

References

ANON. 1969A. Egg Pasteurization Manual. USDA *ARS 74-48*, Mar.

ANON. 1969B. Regulations governing the grading of shell eggs and United States standards, grades, and weight classes for shell eggs. USDA *7 CFR*, Part 56, July 1.

ANON. 1969C. Federal Register *34*, No. 192, 15562.

BALDWIN, R. R., CAMPBELL, H. A., THIESSEN, R., and LORANT, G. J. 1953. The use of glucose oxidase in the processing of food with special emphasis on the desugaring of egg white. Food Technol. 7, 275-282.

BERGQUIST, D. H. 1961. Method of producing egg albumen solids with low bacteria count. U.S. Pat. 2,982,663.

BERGQUIST, D. H. 1973. Eggs. In Food Dehydration, 2nd Edition, Vol. 2, Practices and Applications. W. B. Van Arsdel, M. J. Copley, and A. I. Morgan, Jr. (Editors). Avi Publishing Co., Westport, Conn.

BRANT, A. W., PATTERSON, G. W., and WALTERS, R. E. 1968. Batch pasteurization of liquid whole egg. Poultry Sci. 47, 878,885.

BROOKS, J., and HAWTHORNE, J. R. 1943. Dried egg. IV. Addition of carbohydrates to egg pulp before drying. J. Soc. Chem. Ind. 62, 165-167.

CHAPIN, R. B. 1951. Some factors affecting the emulsifying properties of hen's egg. Ph.D. Dissertation, Iowa State College, Ames, Iowa.

CUNNINGHAM, F. E., and LINEWEAVER, H. 1965. Stabilization of egg white proteins to pasteurizing temperatures above 60°C. Food Technol. 19, 1442-1447.

EVERSON, G. J., and SOUDERS, H. J. 1957. Composition and nutritive importance of eggs. J. Am. Dietet. Assoc. 33, 1244-1254.

FORSYTHE, R. H. 1964. Egg processing technology and egg products. Baker's Dig. 38, 52-59.

FORSYTHE, R. H. 1968. The science and technology of egg products manufacture in the United States. In Egg Quality: A study of the Hen's Egg. T. C. Carter, (Editor). Oliver and Boyd, Ltd., Edinburgh, Scotland.

JONES, H. B. 1969. Processed egg products: a marketing opportunity. USDA, ERS-405, Febr.

KLINE, L., GEGG, J. E., and SONODA, T. T. 1951. Role of glucose in the storage deterioration of whole egg powder. II. A browning reaction involving glucose and cephalin in dried whole egg. Food Technol. 5, 181-187.

KLINE, L., SUGIHARA, T. F., and IJICHI, K. 1966. Further studies on heat pasteurization of raw liquid egg white. Food Technol. 20, 1604-1606.

KLINE, L., SUGIHARA, T. F., and MEEHAN, J. J. 1964. Properties of yolk-containing solids with added carbohydrates. J. Food Sci. 29, 693-709.

KLINE, R. W., and STEWART, G. F. 1948. Glucose-protein reaction in dried egg albumen. Ind. Eng. Chem. 40, 919-922.

KOUDELE, J. W., and HEINSOHN, E. C. 1960. The egg products industry of the United States. Part I. Historical highlights, 1900-59. Kansas State Univ. Agr. Expt. Sta. Bull. 423. Also North Central Regional Publ. 108, Manhattan, Kans.

LIGHTBODY, H. D., and FEVOLD, H. L. 1948.

Biochemical factors influencing the shelf life of dried whole egg and means for their control. In Advances in Food Research, Vol. 1. Academic Press, New York.

LLOYD, W. E., and HARRIMAN, L. A. 1957. Method of treating egg whites. U.S. Pat. 2,776,214. Jan. 1.

LOWE, B. 1955. Experimental Cookery, 4th Edition. John Wiley & Sons, New York.

MATZ, S. A. 1972. Eggs. In Bakery Technology and Engineering, 2nd Edition. Avi Publishing Co., Westport, Conn.

MITCHELL, L. C. 1932. A study of the composition of shell eggs. J. Assoc. Offic. Agr. Chemists 15, 310.

PAYAWAL, S. R., LOWE, B., and STEWART, G. F. 1946. Pasteurization of liquid-egg products. II. Effect of heat treatment on appearance and viscosity. Food Res. 11, 246-260.

SCHULTZ, J. R., and FORSYTHE, R. H. 1967. The influence of egg yolk lipoprotein—carbohydrate interaction on baking performance. Baker's Dig. 41, No. 1, 56-57, 60-62.

SUGIHARA, T. F., IJICHI, K., and KLINE, L. 1966. Heat pasteurization of liquid whole egg. Food Technol. 20, 1076-1083.

WINTER, A. R., GRECO, P. A., and STEWART, G. F. 1946. Pasteurization of liquid-egg products. I. Bacteria reduction in liquid whole egg and improvement in keeping quality. Food Res. 11, 229-245.

Cross-reference: *Poultry Industry in the United States.*

EMULSIFICATION, MECHANICAL PROCEDURES

"Emulsification may be defined as that operation in which two normally immiscible liquids are intimately mixed, one liquid becoming dispersed in the form of small droplets or globules in the other" (Brennan *et al.* 1969).

In food emulsions the liquids involved are water and oil. The water may be present in the form of solutions of salts, sugars, or other organic materials or may be part of a colloidal suspension, i.e., hydrophilic materials. The oil phase may contain fats, oils, hydrocarbons, waxes, and other hydrophobic materials. In addition to the two main phases, a small quantity, usually less than 3% of a third substance, known as an emulsifying agent is necessary to form a stable emulsion system.

Two types of emulsion are possible depending on which phase becomes dispersed in the other. In an oil-in-water (O/W) emulsion the oil is dispersed in the form of droplets throughout a continuous water phase. The reverse is true of a water-in-oil

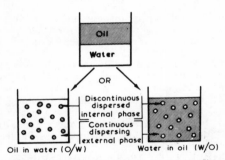

FIG. E-1. ALTERNATIVE TYPES OF EMULSION

(W/O) system as shown in Fig. E-1. In general, an emulsion tends to have characteristics similar to those of the external phase. For example, it can only be successfully diluted by adding external phase material and colored by the use of dyestuffs soluble in the external phase. The type of emulsifying agent used largely determines the type of emulsion formed, but the method of preparation and the proportion of the phases also influences this. The phase present in the largest proportion tends to become the external phase. As a general rule the method of preparation should be such that the external phase is at all stages present in the largest proportion (Brennan *et al.* 1969).

Interfacial Phenomena

As a result of the imbalance in the cohesive forces of the 2 materials, free energy is available at the interface between 2 immiscible liquids. The interface has a tendency to contract which accounts for the spherical shape normally assumed by the droplets of the internal phase of an emulsion and the tendency for those droplets to coalesce, leading, in an unstable system, to separation of the phases. This pattern of breakdown represents a progressive reduction in the interfacial area.

To form an emulsion, this tendency for the interface to contract must be counteracted and this requires energy to be applied to the system. An essential step in emulsion formation is to reduce this tendency to contract or interfacial tension. Raising the temperature of the liquids, within limits which avoid undesirable changes in the materials, has the effect of reducing interfacial tension. However this objective is mainly achieved by the use of emulsifying agents.

Most common emulsifying agents have molecular structures containing both polar and nonpolar groups. If these groups are slightly out of balance (i.e., if the agent exhibits a slightly greater affinity for water than oil or vice versa) then, as a rule, the phase for which the agent shows the greater affinity tends to become the external phase. If a small quantity of such an agent is added to the two immiscible liquids, under favorable conditions, it will become positively adsorbed at the interface between the phases, reducing the interfacial tension. Further, the layer of emulsifying agent, formed around the droplets of the dispersed phase, prevents them from coalescing and stabilizes the emulsion.

Substances which act as emulsifying agents in food applications include naturally occurring proteins, sterols, and phospholipids, and a very large number of synthetic compounds. Apart from exhibiting good emulsifying powers of the appropriate type (i.e., preferentially O/W or W/O promoting), agents for food applications should be nontoxic, relatively odorless, tasteless and colorless compatible with the food, stable under all the conditions to which the food is subjected, and comply with legislative requirements (Brennan *et al.* 1969; Sutheim 1947; Sumner 1954). A more detailed treatment of the subject of emulsifying agents is given elsewhere in this volume.

Methods and Equipment

The energy necessary for emulsification, together with additional energy required to overcome frictional resistances in the system, is normally applied by subjecting the liquids to vigorous agitation. If the type of agitation is such that the large droplets of the internal phase are subjected to shear then these will be distorted from their stable spherical shape and progressively broken into smaller units. The emulsifying agent will become adsorbed at the new interfaces formed and a stable emulsion will result.

The main tools of general use for emulsification in the food industry include: mixers of various types, pressure homogenizers, colloid mills, and ultrasonic devices.

Mixers.—Slow speed agitators have a mild mixing action and in themselves develop little or no shear or turbulence. Their application in emulsification is confined to materials of high viscosity or consistency. In such materials the kneading and folding action of these mixers can cause shear to develop within the mass of the material and thus lead to emulsification. Examples of the application of slow speed agitation to emulsification include dough mixing, butter working, butter and margarine blending.

The agitation produced by higher speed turbine and propeller mixers is more vigorous and often shear and turbulence develop near the impeller. Such mixers are more effective for premixing emulsion ingredients or for producing emulsions from low viscosity materials (Brennan *et al.* 1969; Brennan 1970).

Pressure Homogenizers.—In a pressure homogenizer the emulsion ingredients are pumped under high pressure (500 to 10,000 psig) through a small adjustable opening, of the order of a few thousandths of an inch. Many factors contribute to the disruption of the droplets of the internal phase. Within the opening, provided between a spring loaded valve and valve seat, the droplets accelerate to high velocity, shear against each other and become unstable. As they leave the valve in this unstable condition they strike a hard surface set normal to their direction of travel. This impact promotes break-up of the droplets. Additionally, the sudden pressure drop and cavitational effects have an influence on the dispersion of the internal phase. The simplest type of homogenizer valve consists of a conical or frustrum-shaped valve on a matching seat. The liquids are pumped between the valve and its seat and the pressure is adjusted by means of a heavy spring acting on the valve. Many other, more intricate, valve designs are available. For best results the feed should be supplied to the valve at a constant rate and, of course, high pressure. The most common pumping system in use is a multiple cylinder plunger pump. Pressure homogenizers are very effective emulsifiers for low viscosity materials and droplet sizes of the order of 0.1–0.2 μ are readily attainable.

With certain materials, particularly where proteins act as emulsifying agents, one single pass through an homogenizer valve results in clumping of the droplets of the internal phase and poor dispersion. To overcome this, two-stage homogenization is practiced. The feed is pumped successively through two homogenizer valves, the first operating at a relatively high pressure (1500–7000 psig) and the second at lower pressure (300–500 psig). The second operation has the effect of breaking up the clumps of globules (Brennan et al. 1969; Brennan 1970; Farrall 1963; Clarke 1957; Rees 1967).

Colloid Mills.—In a colloid mill, shear and turbulence are created within the liquids by passing them between two closely spaced surfaces one of

which is stationary and the other rotating. The clearance between the rotor and stator is adjustable, usually in the range 0.002–0.05 in. The feed usually enters near the center of rotation and the product, with the internal phase finely dispersed, is discharged from the perimeter of the rotor and out through an outlet in the casing surrounding the working head. Rotors may rotate about horizontal axes. Such "high speed" machines are applicable to low viscosity materials. Machines with rotors mounted on vertical axes called "paste mills" are used for more viscous materials (Fig. E-2). Rotor speeds range from 3000 to 15,000 rpm. Droplet sizes obtainable are about 1–2 μ. As a general rule, colloid mills are more suited to the treatment of higher viscosity materials than are pressure homogenizers (Brennan et al. 1969; Brennan 1970; Clarke 1957; Rees 1967).

Ultrasonic Equipment.—When high energy ultrasonic waves are applied to a liquid each small region is alternately under tension and compression. When under tension, bubbles present in the liquid will expand. In the positive half of the cycle these bubbles will contract. With small bubbles and at high pressure amplitudes, bubble collapse is quite violent and energy is released. If this phenomenon of cavitation occurs at the interface between two immiscible liquids it can cause the droplets of the internal phase to be disrupted and dispersed. As a general rule, cavitation intensity increases as frequency is reduced. Most ultrasonic devices used for emulsification or cleaning applications operate in the frequency range 18–50 kHz.

Three basic methods are used to produce ultrasonic waves for industrial purposes, namely, mechanical systems, systems employing magnetostrictive oscillators, and piezoelectric oscillators. Only mechanical generators have found wide application for food emulsification duties. The principle of the wedge resonator, the common form of mechanical generator, is shown in Fig. E-3. A blade with wedge shaped edges and clamped at one or more nodal points is positioned in front of a rectangular slit. Liquid is pumped through the slit at relatively low pressure, 50–200 psig. A jet is formed and directed onto the blade, causing it to vibrate. The frequency is normally in the range 18–30 kHz. The intensity, although low, is sufficient to cause cavitation in the vicinity of the blade and dispersion of the internal phase of an

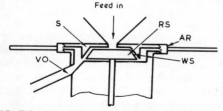

FIG. E-2. TOP-FEED "PASTE" COLLOID MILL

RS—rotor. S—stator. WS—working surfaces. VO—volute (outlet). AR—adjusting ring.

emulsion. The performance, in terms of the droplet sizes produced is of the same order as that of a colloid mill. Such generators are also employed for dispersing solids in liquids, producing homogeneous fruit and vegetable purées and other similar duties (Brennan *et al.* 1969; Brennan 1970; Blitz 1963; Smith 1958).

Ultrasonic Cleaning.[1]—If cavitation occurs in a liquid containing an article to be cleaned, an intense scrubbing action is produced at its surface, loosening soil. Chemical reactions are also accelerated and surface films more quickly dissolved. The emulsification action of the ultrasound also assists in the cleaning action. Streaming is set up in the liquid which assists in dispersing loosened soil and bringing fresh liquid into contact with the surface. Magnetostrictive or piezoelectric transducers are used to produce the waves and these are fixed externally to the sides or bottom of the cleaning tank or they may be fitted into hermetically sealed cases and immersed in the cleaning liquid in the tank. For small articles a single tank, fitted with transducers, is all that is required. The tank is drained, cleaned, and refilled at intervals. For larger operations multitank systems are used. These incorporate an initial soaking stage, with or without the application of ultrasound, to remove gross soil, followed by a second cleaning stage, with ultrasound to complete the soil removal. Rinsing and drying stages may follow. Most ultrasonic cleaning is done in water with the aid of detergents or special additives. For some applications, nonaqueous solvents are used.

Ultrasonic cleaning has, as yet, only found limited application in the food industry mainly for cleaning fish trays, used in kiln smoking and other processes (Anon. 1969), and baking trays. It has been considered for other applications such as bottle washing. Its application to the cleaning of food materials such as eggs, fruit, and vegetables is also a source of study (Anon. 1962), but to date it has not been applied commercially mainly because of unsolved problems relating to product damage.

In addition to the equipment used for general emulsification duties, discussed above, many other types of equipment bring about or contribute to emulsification in particular products. For example churns, various mixers, and scraped surface heat exchangers are used in butter and margarine manufacture. Mincers, bowl choppers, and emulsitators cause emulsification of the fat in meat products

such as sausage meat and meat paste (Brennan 1970).

Applications in Food Processing

Emulsification is applied widely in the food industry. Milk is a naturally occurring oil-in-water emulsion containing 3–5% of fat as the internal phase. Milk is often subjected to two-stage pressure homogenization to reduce the fat globule size and minimize creaming. Homogenized milk is also said to be more digestible and have a smoother appearance than unhomogenized milk. Sterilized milk, low-fat cream, evaporated milk, and sterilized cream are also homogenized to improve their stability. Ice cream mix is basically an oil-in-water emulsion containing typically 10–12% fat. It needs to be a very stable emulsion to withstand the rigors of freezing and whipping. In addition to emulsifying agents, stabilizers such as gelatin, alginates, or gums are added to the mix. Again two-stage pressure homogenization is the main method employed to produce the emulsion but colloid mills and ultrasonic whistles have also been applied to this task (Brennan 1970; Davis 1955).

Salad cream is also an oil-in-water emulsion containing some 30–40% oil. Lecithin contained in the egg ingredients usually acts as the emulsifying agent and gum tragacanth is a commonly-used stabilizer. Pressure homogenizers, colloid mills and liquid whistles are used to disperse the internal phase. Mayonnaise is another oil-in-water emulsion but contains more than 70% oil. It is a potentially unstable system because of this high internal phase content and is usually prepared by careful mixing at relatively low temperatures. In some cases a colloid mill is employed to refine the mix (Brennan 1970; Woollen 1956).

Margarine is classified as a water-in-oil emulsion containing about 16% water. The oil phase consists of a blend of vegetable and fish oils and the aqueous phase is based on skim milk or reconstituted skim milk powder, ripened to an appropriate degree. These, plus additional ingredients, including oil-soluble emulsifying agents are premixed and then simultaneously agitated and cooled in some form of scraped surface heat exchanger. A final kneading or "working" stage produces an appropriate texture (Brennan 1970; Schwitzer 1956; Anderson and Williams 1965). Butter is also a water-in-oil system and is made by complete or partial breakdown of the oil-in-water emulsion structure of cream, followed by the production of the water-in-oil system from the fat phase. The latter is effected by similar means as that used in margarine production or by conventional batch

---

[1] Grateful acknowledgement is hereby made for information received on ultrasonic cleaning from Dawe Instruments, Ltd., London, England.

churning and working procedures (Brennan *et al.* 1969; Brennan 1970; Davis 1955).

Emulsification plays an important role in the production of meat products such as sausage meats and meat pastes. Emulsification influences fat separation, the texture of the product, and its behavior on cooking (Brennan 1970; Saffle 1968).

Efficient emulsification of the fat in cake and bread making is necessary to ensure a good crumb structure and cake or loaf shape and volume (Brennan 1970; Knightly 1969).

JAMES G. BRENNAN

References

ANDERSEN, A. J. C., and WILLIAMS, P. N. 1965. Margarine, 2nd Edition. Pergamon Press, London, England.

ANON. 1962. Ultrasonics in food processing. Food Process. Packaging *31*, No. 12, 456.

ANON. 1969. New ultrasonic washing plant for Findus Aberdeen factory. Food Trade Rev. *39*, No. 10, 57.

BLITZ, J. 1963. Fundamentals of Ultrasonics. Butterworths, London, England.

BRENNAN, J. G. 1970. Emulsions in food technology. Process. Biochem. *5*, No. 7, 33–37.

BRENNAN, J. G., BUTTERS, J. R., COWELL, N. D., and LILLY, A. E. V. 1969. Food Engineering Operations. Elsevier Publishing Co., London, England.

CLARKE, R. J. 1957. Process Engineering in the Food Industries. Heywood & Co., London, England.

DAVIS, J. G. 1955. A Dictionary of Dairying, 2nd Edition. Leonard Hill Publishing Co., London, England.

FARRALL, A. W. 1963. Engineering for Dairy and Food Products. John Wiley & Sons, New York.

KNIGHTLY, W. H. 1969. The use of emulsifiers in bakery foods. Proc. 45th Ann. Meeting Am. Soc. Bakery Engrs.

REES, L. H. 1967. What to know about homogenizers. Food Eng. *39*, No. 8, 69–71.

SAFFLE, R. L. 1968. Meat emulsions. *In* Advances in Food Research, Vol. 16. Academic Press, New York.

SCHWITZER, M. K. 1956. Margarine and Other Food Fats. Leonard Hill Publishing Co., London, England.

SMITH, J. S. 1958. Ultrasonics in food manufacture. Food Manuf. *33*, No. 9, 358–361.

SUMNER, C. G. 1954. Clayton's The Theory of Emulsions and Their Technical Treatment, 5th Edition. J. & A. Churchill, London, England.

SUTHEIM, G. M. 1947. Introduction to Emulsions. Chapman and Hall, London, England.

WOOLLEN, A. H. (Editor) 1956. Food Industries Manual, 20th Edition. Leonard Hill Publishing Co., London, England.

Cross-reference: *Emulsifiers, Food.*

EMULSIFIERS, FOOD

Mono- and Diglycerides

More than 200,000,000 lb of surface-active agents per year are used for food processing in the United States. Of these, 75% are mono- and diglycerides which include mixtures ranging from less than 20% to over 90% monoglycerides. The monoglyceride esters are the more active in most applications and these mixtures are often called "monoglycerides" in the food trade. They are nonionic emulsifiers and may exist as liquids, plastic solids, or hard fats, depending on the type and distribution of fatty acids in the molecule.

Structurally, monoglycerides are the condensation products of 1 molecule of glycerol with either 1 or 2 molecules of fatty acid. These products occur in nature in fats which have undergone partial hydrolysis, for example, in the intestinal tract of man and animals. They are "generally recognized as safe" (GRAS) by FDA and have Meat Inspection Division acceptance by USDA. Commercially, monoglycerides are prepared by esterification of glycerol with fatty acids or by the alcoholysis of triglyceride with glycerol. Both reactions are catalyzed by acidic or, more commonly, alkaline materials. The diagrams in Fig. E-4 represent the two reactions using stearic acid and tristearin.

By selection of optimum amounts of reactants, the reaction mixture after removal of the excess glycerine, fatty acid, and water will usually contain 30–50% monoglycerides and 40–50% diglycerides, and the balance will be mostly triglycerides. The catalyst is generally neutralized and removed. Where the catalyst is neutralized and not removed, the alkaline soaps thus formed in the product can make the monoglycerides self-emulsifying.

Monoglycerides are separated from di- and triglycerides by molecular distillation. Commercial products free of catalyst, fatty acid, and glycerine, and having over 90% monoglyceride, are in wide use in the food-processing industry. These contain from 90 to 96% monoglyceride, with the balance being primarily diglycerides. There are two isomers for the monoglyceride and the diglyceride. The 1-monoglyceride is more stable than the 2-monoglyceride. They exist in an equilibrium concentration which depends upon the temperature. Normally the concentration of 2-monoglyceride does

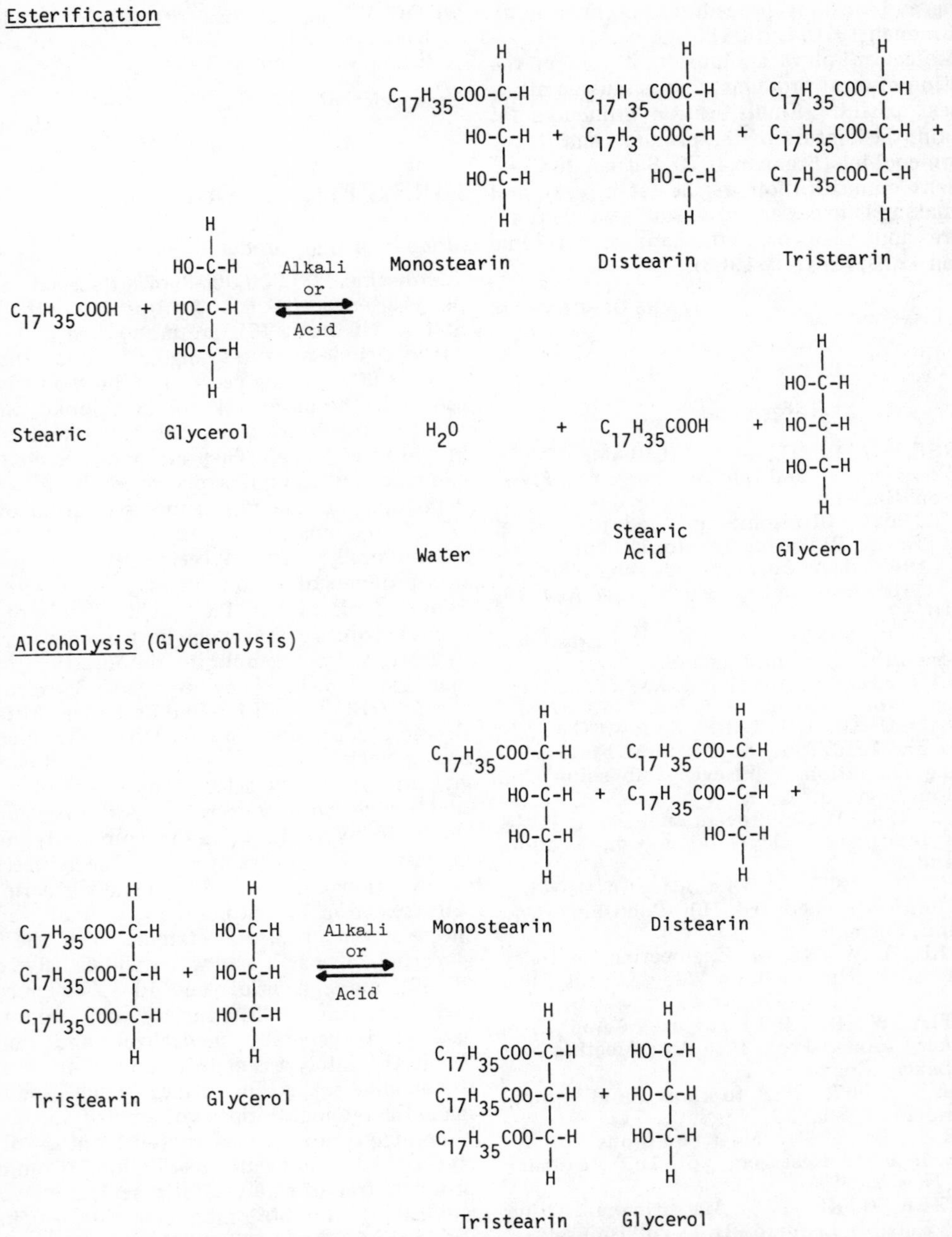

Esterification

$$C_{17}H_{35}COOH + \begin{array}{c} H \\ | \\ HO-C-H \\ | \\ HO-C-H \\ | \\ HO-C-H \\ | \\ H \end{array} \underset{Acid}{\overset{Alkali\ or}{\rightleftharpoons}}$$

Stearic   Glycerol

$$\begin{array}{c} H \\ | \\ C_{17}H_{35}COO-C-H \\ | \\ HO-C-H \\ | \\ HO-C-H \\ | \\ H \end{array} + \begin{array}{c} H \\ | \\ C_{17}H_{35}COOC-H \\ | \\ C_{17}H_{3}COOC-H \\ | \\ HO-C-H \\ | \\ H \end{array} + \begin{array}{c} H \\ | \\ C_{17}H_{35}COO-C-H \\ | \\ C_{17}H_{35}COO-C-H \\ | \\ C_{17}H_{35}COO-C-H \\ | \\ H \end{array} +$$

Monostearin   Distearin   Tristearin

$$H_2O \quad + \quad C_{17}H_{35}COOH \quad + \quad \begin{array}{c} H \\ | \\ HO-C-H \\ | \\ HO-C-H \\ | \\ HO-C-H \\ | \\ H \end{array}$$

Water   Stearic Acid   Glycerol

Alcoholysis (Glycerolysis)

$$\begin{array}{c} H \\ | \\ C_{17}H_{35}COO-C-H \\ | \\ C_{17}H_{35}COO-C-H \\ | \\ C_{17}H_{35}COO-C-H \\ | \\ H \end{array} + \begin{array}{c} H \\ | \\ HO-C-H \\ | \\ HO-C-H \\ | \\ HO-C-H \\ | \\ H \end{array} \underset{Acid}{\overset{Alkali\ or}{\rightleftharpoons}}$$

Tristearin   Glycerol

$$\begin{array}{c} H \\ | \\ C_{17}H_{35}COO-C-H \\ | \\ HO-C-H \\ | \\ HO-C-H \\ | \\ H \end{array} + \begin{array}{c} H \\ | \\ C_{17}H_{35}COO-C-H \\ | \\ C_{17}H_{35}COO-C-H \\ | \\ HO-C-H \\ | \\ H \end{array} +$$

Monostearin   Distearin

$$\begin{array}{c} H \\ | \\ C_{17}H_{35}COO-C-H \\ | \\ C_{17}H_{35}COO-C-H \\ | \\ C_{17}H_{35}COO-C-H \\ | \\ H \end{array} + \begin{array}{c} H \\ | \\ HO-C-H \\ | \\ HO-C-H \\ | \\ HO-C-H \\ | \\ H \end{array}$$

Tristearin   Glycerol

FIG. E-4. REACTIONS SHOWING PREPARATION OF MONOGLYCERIDES BY ESTERIFICATION AND ALCOHOLYSIS

not exceed 10% of the total. Similarly, the 1,2-diglyceride predominates over the 1,3-diglyceride.

Normally, mono- and diglycerides solidify in the α-crystalline polymorphic form and then revert to the β form. Reversion is much slower with the dis-tilled monoglycerides and can be delayed for long periods of time by storage at $2°C$.

While monoglycerides are considered as emulsi-fiers, their important function in foods is to im-prove smoothness, firmness, and stability, and to preserve or modify natural consistency—they are food-texturizing agents. As food additives, monoglycerdies function as emulsifiers, dispersants, solubilizers, bread softeners to retard crumb firming, bread dough conditioners, starch-complexing agents, oil stabilizers, release agents, lubricants, emulsion stabilizers, and viscosity-reducing agents.

Yeast-Raised Baked Goods.—Bread and other yeast-raised baked goods represent a major use for monoglycerides. Bread containing monoglycerides is initially softer after baking and remains softer during storage as compared with bread that does not contain monoglycerides. When starch in bread is gelatinized during the baking process, the amylose fraction diffuses from the swollen starch molecule and sets up a gel network between the granules. Meanwhile the branched amylopectin fraction begins to crystallize slowly. Association of these branched polymers within the starch granule leads to firming and staleness. While the exact mechanism of antistaling is not understood, monoglycerides appear to form insoluble helical clathrates with the amylose fraction within the starch granule. This prevents diffusion of the amylose fraction and no gel structure forms between the granules. Therefore, the fresh bread with monoglyceride additive is softer initially than a control. Furthermore, the complex appears to interfere with association of the branched amylopectin to inhibit the formation of crystalline micelles. As a result, the bread firms more slowly when stored.

Starch Complexing.—Monoglycerides complex with the amylose in other starchy foods to reduce stickiness and improve texture. The helical complex prevents the loss of amylose and consequently the diffusion of gel-like material from the starch granule.

As little as 0.5% of distilled monoglycerides added to dehydrated potatoes during processing helps produce a product which when reconstituted has a fresh-cooked mealy potato texture. Macaroni products containing 1.5% of monoglycerides are firm, nonsticky and very resistant to overcooking. Similarly, cooked cereals containing monoglyceride retain their fresh-cooked texture during steam table storage or even after cooling.

Emulsification.—In cakes and other nonyeast leavened baked goods, monoglycerides serve as an emulsifier for the fat-water-protein system. They enhance the formation of uniform oil droplets and gas bubbles within the batter system and improve the ability of the protein film to coat and entrap these particles. This results in fine, uniform-textured cake of good volume and eating quality.

Monoglycerides are the most widely used emulsifiers for ice cream. They help disperse and stabilize the fat emulsion during processing of the ice cream mix. Furthermore, they aid in air incorporation and promote controlled emulsion inversion (fat agglomeration) of the mix during freezing. The result is a dry ice cream with good body and texture and smooth meltdown. A similar system exists with whipped toppings, margarine, and coffee whiteners. Monoglycerides help to produce and maintain a homogeneous topping mix and promote whipping. By the proper selection of saturated and unsaturated monoglycerides, aeration can be controlled to the desired consistency. In margarine, monoglycerides promote stable emulsions during processing and help maintain emulsion stability during storage. In coffee whiteners, reduction of the size of the fat globules with the aid of monoglycerides improves the whitening ability of the product.

Baker's shortenings for icings and cream fillings, baker's cake shortenings, and household shortenings are other specific formulations in which monoglycerides are widely used. In these types of products, emulsifiers disperse the fat, aerate the ingredients, and stabilize water emulsions.

Monoglycerides are especially effective for preventing oil separation in peanut butter. They also improve palatability, gloss appearance, spreadability, and manufacturing flexibility. The monoglycerides are ground with the peanuts, salt, and sugar, in a mill which raises the temperature sufficiently to melt the stabilizer. Given the same processing treatment, 90% monoglycerides are more effective on a weight basis than those mono- and diglycerides containing larger proportions of diglycerides. Diglycerides are more easily solubilized in the peanut oil and more susceptible to melting if stored at warm temperatures; therefore, they are not as effective as stabilizers.

There are other miscellaneous applications for monoglycerides. For example, up to 1% of monoglycerides serve as emulsifiers and, in addition, reduce the stickiness of caramels and toffees to teeth, equipment, and wrappers. For this latter purpose they function as a lubricant. Emulsification or solubilization of flavors, essential oils, and antioxidants is another use for monoglycerides. In baker's yeast, a small amount of monoglyceride whitens the grey-colored yeast and lubricates the normally granular, crumbly product so that it can be cut into suitable sizes.

Lecithin

The second largest group of food emulsifiers in use today is the phosphatides. These materials represent approximately 10% of the total food emulsifiers market.

Phosphatides consist of a polyhydric alcohol, usually glycerol, which is esterifed with fatty acids and with phosphoric acid. The phosphoric acid is also combined with a nitrogen-containing compound such as choline, ethanolamine, or betaine. Two common phosphatides are lecithin and cephalin.

Lecithin   Cephalin

Phosphatides occur as part of the nonglyceride content of most fats and oils and are removed during refining of these oils. The commercial mixture of phosphatides known as lecithin is prepared almost exclusively from soybean oil. Commercial lecithin is available in phosphatide contents from 50% to over 90% and may vary from viscous fluids to plastic solids or dry free-flowing granular solid materials. The phosphatides content of commercial lecithin is usually indicated as "percent acetone insolubles."

Lecithin functions in a number of valuable ways: it produces lower surface tension, acts as an emulsifier, is an antioxidant, and promotes small crystal formation in food products. It is one of the most active emulsifiers; however, its characteristic flavor is often a limiting factor in the level of use.

Confections.—Large amounts of lecithin are used in candy and especially in cacao products. The addition of 1% or less of lecithin to melted chocolate greatly reduces its viscosity, apparently by reducing the surface tension of the solid fat and fibrous particles in the chocolate. Therefore, less cocoa butter is required to obtain the desired fluidity. This, in turn, improves the flavor and keeping quality of the chocolate. It also imparts a more flexible temperature range and better gloss to enrobing chocolate. In blends containing other fats, lecithin is added to form a stable emulsion. In fudge and creams, lecithin promotes a finer and hence smoother crystal structure.

Bakery Products.—Lecithin appears to improve the shortening effect of fats in bakery doughs by spreading or emulsifying the fat on the hydrophilic dough components. It serves as a release agent,

making rich sweet doughs appear drier thus improving their machinability. In cookies, lecithin is about the only emulsifier currently in use today. While its principal effect is on the dough, cookies with high shortening levels and containing lecithin appear less greasy. In bread doughs, lecithin is usually used in combination with other emulsifiers since its optimum effective level is very low and its effect is almost entirely on the dough-handling characteristics, with some slight crumb-softening action.

Small amounts of lecithin are used as emulsifiers in specialty and frozen doughs and as stabilizers for peanut butter.

Other Emulsifiers

The remaining market for food emulsifiers is satisfied by a variety of products. They are, in order of importance:

Sorbitan esters: sorbitan fatty acid esters
                   ethoxylated sorbitan esters
Propylene glycol monoesters
Miscellaneous: acetylated monoglycerides
                succinylated monoglycerides
                acetylated tartrated mono-
                  gylcerides
                glycerol-lacto esters
                polyglycerol esters

Generally, their specificity has limited their performance to highly specialized applications because they are more hydrophilic than monoglycerides or lecithins. For example, sorbitan esters such as sorbitan monostearate, together with polyoxyethylene sorbitan monostearate, have found use as cake mix emulsifiers. They are also used in combination with monoglycerides in whipped toppings, ice cream, and icing and cream-filling shortenings. Other applications include specialized confection coatings, condiments, and a variety of foods in which emulsifiers having greater hydrophilic activity are needed. For many uses they function as coemulsifiers, thus enabling the monoglycerides to do a better job.

Propylene glycol esters are used primarily as fat and emulsifier crystal modifiers in dry topping mix and as a part of the aerating emulsifier system in dry cake mix. For these purposes, they are inexpensive and effective emulsifiers which allow the use of lower levels of shortening. The glycerol lacto esters are used for these same purposes.

Acetylated tartrated monoglycerides have been used as emulsifiers for bread, cookies, and cakes for a number of years. Due to their poor flavors, they are gradually being replaced by monoglycerides and the specialty emulsifiers.

Acetylated monoglycerides, succinylated monoglycerides and polyglycerol esters are more recent arrivals in the food-emulsifier area. The acetylated monoglycerides are essentially "tailored fats" having sharp melting points, bland flavors, and the ability to form flexible films. Hence, they are useful as edible food coatings, emulsifiers, lubricants and release agents, and fat and emulsifier crystal stabilizers. Raisins and nuts can be protected from moisture transfer and oxidative rancidity by the application of transparent coatings of acetylated monoglycerides. In dry topping mix, acetylated monoglycerides function as emulsifier stabilizers to extend emulsifier activity.

Polyglycerol esters have shown excellent application as emulsifiers for icing and cream-filling shortenings. They have also found limited use in toppings and as cake emulsifiers. Succinylated monoglycerides have been used as dough strengtheners for bread and as shortening emulsifiers.

GERALD D. NEU

References

BECKTEL, W. G. 1961. Progress in the study of the staling phenomenon. Baker's Dig. *35*, No. 5, 48–50, 172.
ENDRES, J. G. 1967. Emulsifiers, a review of their applications in baking. Baker's Dig. *42*, No. 5, 96–98.
FURIA, T. E. (Editor) 1968. Handbook of Food Additives. The Chemical Rubber Co., Cleveland.
MacMASTERS, M. M. 1961. Starch research and baking. Baker's Dig. *35*, No. 5, 42–46.
MONCRIEFF, J. 1966. Emulsifiers in food products. Baker's Dig. *40*, No. 6, 54–56.
OSMAN, E. M., LEITH, S. J., and FLES, M. 1961. Complexes of amylose with surfactants. Cereal Chem. *38*, No. 5, 449–463.
PELSHENKE, P. F., and HAMPEL, G. 1962. Starch retrogradation in various bread products. Baker's Dig. *36*, No. 3, 48–56.
PYLER, E. J. 1952. Baking Science and Technology, Vol. 1 and 2. Siebel Publishing Co., Chicago.
SWERN, D. (Editor) 1964. Bailey's Industrial Oil and Fat Products, 3rd Edition. Interscience Publishers, New York.

Cross-references: *Detergents; Emulsification, Mechanical Procedures.*

ENERGY

Energy in its simplest definition is the capacity to do work. It is somewhat surprising that the food industry uses energy in many forms—thermal, chemical, mechanical, and radiant. There are few operations in the food industries that are not dependent in some degree on thermal energy. If one thinks of the mechanism of heat exchange, the transfer of heat from one substance to another, canning, drying, freezing, and even fermentation depend on thermal energy. The rate of transfer is of much importance not only with regard to the economics of the food process used but also to the product itself. The rate of heat transfer can be determined for general purposes by dividing the driving force by the resistance.

Chemical energy, a form of potential energy, is due to the attraction of one element for those of another. A food preservation method which involves chemical energy is curing, as in the curing of meats which is a large segment of the meat industry. The curing process includes the treatment of meat with salt and other agents—sugar, sodium nitrate, vinegar, and, for some products such as bacon, flavoring agents. In the injection cure process the curing solution is pumped into the arteries and veins of the carcass. Although smoking involves some heat exchange, its principal effect is derived from the components of the smoke, some of which are bactericidal. The chief effect, however, is the enhancement of the natural flavor of the meat.

Mechanical energy is applied to food processing in a variety of ways: by stirring, compressing, agitating, rolling (as in milling), comminuting, and by the application of expanding forces as occurs in vacuum drying of foods.

Last to be considered is radiant energy. The application of ionizing radiations to food is a striking example of the innovative thinking on the part of food scientists, engineers, and technologists in the second half of the 20th Century. Briefly, the use of radiant energy in this instance consists of the bombardment of a food to be sterilized or "pasteurized" by high energy particles (beta, cathode, or gamma rays) for a sufficiently long time to kill or incapacitate the microorganisms associated with food spoilage. The energy sources are of two types—accelerators or cathode ray machines and fission products, for example, Cobalt 60.

Ultraviolet and infrared radiations have also been used to extend the storage life of food, and in the case of infrared, much experimentation has been undertaken in recent years.

The action of sunlight on chlorophyll can be regarded as a form of radiant energy of fundamental interest in connection with food. The formation of carbohydrates in plants is the result of such action, and sun drying as a method of food preservation utilizes the sun as the unique source of energy.

MARTIN S. PETERSON

Cross-reference: *Ultrasonic Energy.*

ENRICHMENT, RESTORATION, AND FORTIFICATION

The addition of isolated nutrients to conventional foods has been widely practiced in this country since the late 1930's for prophylaxis of nutritional deficiencies. There is general agreement that these enrichment programs have substantially reduced the incidence of a host of nutrient deficiency diseases including beriberi, ariboflavinosis, pellagra, and endemic goiter.

Although there is overlap in the use of the terms restoration, enrichment, and fortification, each term does have a unique meaning. Restoration is the process of enriching processed foods with nutrients in amounts sufficient to replenish those nutrients lost during processing. An example of restoration would be the addition of ascorbic acid to instant mashed potatoes. In restoration, nutrient addition is pegged at a level similar to that found in the raw commodity or as traditionally eaten. There is no attempt to set the restoration level at a level calculated to prevent a deficiency syndrome.

In contrast, enrichment and fortification policies are formulated to deliver sufficient amounts of nutrients in widely consumed foods to avert nutritional deficiency diseases. The level of addition of the nutrient is based on the quantity necessary to prevent disease without regard to the amount naturally present in the food. Enrichment and fortification are frequently used interchangeably; however, the term enrichment should be used when a nutrient is added to a food which supplies the nutrient, but whose level is variable or less than the desired goal, as for example, addition of vitamin A to butter. Fortification should be used to speak of the addition of a nutrient to a food which, without the addition, would not be a source of the nutrient, as for example, addition of vitamin A to margarine or of iodide to table salt. In both enrichment and fortification, the level of addition is based on the nutrient needs of the population at risk and is set so that the usual serving of the food will supply sufficient total nutrient to ensure the nutritional adequacy of the population.

Addition of vitamins and iron to white flour and bread arose from the support of the Council on Foods and Nutrition of the American Medical Association. Hearings were held by the Food and Drug Administration and a policy was established in May of 1941 which permitted the addition of thiamin, riboflavin, niacin, and iron. The hearings established the clinical evidence of the prevalence of these nutrients in the American diet, the estimated dietary deficits, and the estimations of the use of white flour and bread in the diet. The enrichment policy was designed to add sufficient

amounts of the stated nutrients to alleviate deficiency without altering the taste and hence the acceptance of bread and products made with white flour. The ability to add these nutrients at low cost meant that the public health goals of prophylaxis could be achieved economically in foods ingested by all Americans.

Nutrient addition programs over the years include the use of iodine in table salt; fortification of margarine with vitamin A concentrates; fortification of milk with vitamin D; enrichment of white bread, flour, and corn meal with thiamin, riboflavin, niacin, and iron; addition of vitamins A and D to nonfat dry milk, and of vitamin C to beverages. Each of these programs has been sanctioned either by the Congress or in regulations promulgated by FDA. Furthermore, each of these programs has been carefully considered before enactment and has had the support of the medical and nutrition communities.

Indeed, the momentum for change in fortification policies has traditionally arisen from the medical and nutrition communities. The early efforts of the Council on Foods and Nutrition of AMA established guidelines for the rationale for nutrient addition to foods (J. Am. Med. Assoc. (1939) 113, 681). In 1941, the Food and Nutrition Board of the National Research Council announced its policy on the addition of synthetic nutrients to foods. The Council's statement was revised in 1945 (J. Am. Med. Assoc. (1945) 129, 348) and issued as a joint statement of the Council and the Board in 1954 (J. Am. Med. Assoc. (1954) 154, 145), in 1961 (J. Am. Med. Assoc. (1961) 178, 1024), and in 1968 (J. Am. Med. Assoc. (1968) 205, 160). The following principles for nutrient fortification are found in the current joint statement:

(1) The intake of the nutrient(s) is below the desirable level in the diets of a significant number of people.

(2) The food(s) used to supply the nutrient(s) is likely to be consumed in quantities that will make a significant contribution to the diet of the population in need.

(3) The addition of the nutrient(s) is not likely to create an imbalance of essential nutrients.

(4) The nutrient(s) added is stable under proper conditions of storage and use.

(5) The nutrient(s) is physiologically available from the food.

(6) There is reasonable assurance against excessive intake to a level of toxicity.

In 1966, FDA attempted to codify and limit foods to which nutrients could be added. FDA's publication (Federal Register 31, 15730, Dec. 14, 1966) precipitated a lengthy hearing between the agency, industry, and consumers. Although there were many side issues, the central theme promoted by the agency was that fortification of foods should be limited to those which have a diminished nutritive content as a result of loss in refining or other processing or to those where there was assurance that the food item would be an effective vehicle of distribution. While it is true that vitamins and minerals are widely distributed and that a diet well chosen will meet the nutritional needs, it has become clear that many consumers are not choosing nutritionally adequate diets. There are many contributing factors which result in the ingestion of inadequate diets including (a) nutritional disinterest, (b) the ever-increasing proportion of meals eaten away from home, (c) increased tendency toward snacking and the disappearance in many families of the three-meal-a-day eating pattern, (d) poverty, (e) reduced energy expenditures and and hence reduced caloric requirements, (f) difficulty in knowing what nutrients are present in foods (g) profound concern with weight control and fad diets, (h) selection of foods with diminished nutrient content as compared to the raw commodities, and (i) constraints placed on industry concerning addition of nutrients to foods and subsequent labeling of such nutrient-enhanced foods.

The White House Conference on Food, Nutrition and Health in December of 1969 was a major milestone in reawakening interest in nutrition. While there was genuine concern about hunger arising from economic deprivation, it became clear that many more people were poorly nourished because of lack of interest in nutrition and inadequate information about the role of foods. Following the Conference, FDA assumed responsibility to devise ways to inform consumers about the nutritional value of foods.

FDA entered into a contract with the National Academy of Sciences to obtain recommendations from the Academy on what classes of foods should have nutritional guidelines and what nutrients should be expected from a class of foods. At this writing, the first recommendation from a special committee of the Food and Nutrition Board of the Academy has been published by FDA in the Federal Register Dec. 23, 1971: "Nutritional Quality Guidelines" for "precooked frozen convenience 'heat and serve' dinners." These guidelines would establish nutritional criteria for this class of foods based on (a) a minimum caloric value for the product, (b) nutrient levels geared to calories, as 0.05 mg of thiamin per 100 Kcal, and (c) establishment of minimum nutrient levels for protein, thiamin, riboflavin, niacin, vitamin A, and iron. Other guidelines are expected in the months and years to come as a means of providing a new nutritional identity for processed foods.

In cultures where dietary patterns are simple and based on a limited number of commodities, one is able to identify which food could be a carrier for an enrichment or fortification program. However, as consumers have access to a broader selection of foods, it becomes extremely difficult, if not impossible, to select a single food which can serve as a nutrient vehicle for all consumers. Viewed in the context of the changes which have occurred in this century—as consumers' ties to agricultural production and knowledge about food composition have weakened—industry and government have been required to undertake programs to inform consumers about food composition and to consider how and when food should be fortified. The design of nutritional guidelines, coupled with informative labeling, will, hopefully, result in new programs of enrichment and fortification by industry.

Heretofore, man has had to adapt to his food supply; today, we are entering an era where the food supply may be tailored to man's needs.

ROBERT W. HARKINS

Cross-reference: *Vitamins.*

ENZYMES

General Properties

Enzymes are soluble organic catalysts which govern, initiate, and control biological reactions for life processes. They are elaborated by living plant as well as animal cells, but can act independently of the cells, if appropriate conditions are prevalent. Enzymes are proteins, and some of the enzymes contain several nonprotein fractions which are generally termed prosthetic groups. Some enzymes, on the other hand, require coenzymes or need activators for their full activity. Like most proteins, enzymes are complex in structure, and little is known concerning the relationship between their structure and enzymic activity. Although much knowledge has been gained during the past 2–3 decades concerning the production of enzymes, their properties, and their applications, enzyme reactions have been utilized by man through the ages. The production of wine, cheese, and bread, utilizing enzyme reactions, predates biblical times. Although the mechanisms of chemical reactions were not known, means were found to exert a general control over these fermentation processes. Buchner was perhaps the first to separate enzymes from living cells of yeast and utilize them for alcoholic fermentation.

Enzymes are characteristically specific in that each enzyme attacks specific types of compounds, called substrates. Due to enzyme action, substrates are either converted into other compounds or are broken down in smaller pieces. Thus, enzymic activity is determined by measuring either the disappearance of the substrate or the production of the end product(s). Furthermore, most of the enzymes depict optimal activity at a specific temperature and pH, which are respectively called "Optimum Temperature" and "Optimum pH." However, some enzymes show low levels of activity even at freezing temperatures. At high temperatures and pH most enzymes are inactivated, but sometimes they show reactivation.

Classification

Several enzyme classification systems have been proposed or used. Most enzymes can be broadly classified according to their substrates. For example, carbohydrases act upon carbohydrates; proteases act upon proteins; lipases act upon lipids, and so forth. The classification proposed by the Commission on Enzymes of the International Union of Biochemistry appears to be the one most widely used, according to which enzymes are divided among six major classes: oxidoreductases, which catalyze oxidation or reduction reactions; transferases which catalyze the transfer of specific chemical moieties; hydrolases which hydrolyze substrates with concomitant uptake of water molecules; lyases which remove or add specific chemical moieties to their substrates; isomerases which catalyze isomerization; and ligases which catalyze the synthesis or bonding together of substrate units. However, most enzymes present in foods or used for technological purposes belong to the classes of oxidoreductases, such as peroxidase or catalase, and hydrolases, such as amylase, protease, or phosphatase.

Applications

With the advances in the field of food technology, advances in the application of food enzymology have occurred. Firstly, the measurement of inherent enzymes in foods has been mainly used as an indicator of the condition of the foods. Many preservatives, antibiotics, inhibitors, poisons, and insecticides inhibit certain enzymes. The presence of such chemicals and possibly their nature and concentrations can be revealed by the extent of enzymic inhibition. Also, one of the oldest methods used for examining various aspects of the state of foods lies in the estimation of the activity of certain inherent enzymes. Enzymes are generally heat sensitive, providing a means to determine the efficacy of processing procedures; e.g., the use of phosphatase test is made to check the efficacy of milk pasteurization; diastase test is used to determine the heat process applied to honey; and peroxidase test used as an indicator of proper blanching of vegetables.

In regard to the applications and uses of external enzymes during the manufacture of foods, it has been estimated that approximately 20–30 million dollars' worth of enzymes are used per year in the food industry. They are used mainly to modify the textural, flavor, and compositional qualities of foods. Generally, after the added enzymes have performed their desired function, they are inactivated during the processing procedures to prevent further modification, leading to possible spoilage. Following are the enzymes most commonly used in the food industry:

Carbohydrases.—A wide variety of carbohydrases are used extensively in the food industry to modify saccharides (sugars) and related compounds. In the baking industry, amylases are used to achieve partial hydrolysis or breakdown of sugars, amylose, starch, and other such compounds, since such enzymic hydrolysis is essential for improving the loaf volume and other qualities of baked goods. Glucamylase and other amylases are used for glucose production. Combined with acid hydrolysis, amylases are used for the conversion of starch into sweet syrups. Invertase is used to effect sugar hydrolysis in confectionery to improve sweetness. In the fruit, vegetable, and wine industries, pectinases are used widely to facilitate and improve the extraction of juices and their clarification. Also pectinases are employed in green coffee processing to enhance the hydrolysis of the mucilage. Lactase can be used effectively to prevent lactose crystallization in products like ice cream. Cellulases are employed in the cereal industry for partial hydrolysis of cellulose and in the juice industry to prevent haze formation due to cellulose. Hemicellulases are used to degrade the gums in the coffee concentrates in order to prevent gelling.

Proteases.—Several different proteases are used in a variety of industrial applications. These enzymes hydrolyze peptide bonds and thus cause the degradation of the protein molecules in foods. In the baking industry proteases are employed to degrade the protein gluten and reduce the mixing time of dough. In the meat industry, such proteases as papain, ficin, and bromelin, are used for meat tenderization. Proteases are also used for chill-proofing of beer to eliminate haze. In the dairy industry, rennin, a protease, is used extensively in the manufacture of cheese. However, pepsin and some microbial milk-clotting proteases have also been used with some success.

Lipases.—These enzymes hydrolyze fats, fatty acid esters, and other lipids. The free fatty acids and their derivatives thus produced give rise to specific flavors. Lipases, such as kid, calf, and lamb pregastric esterases, are the ones most commonly used in the manufacture of Italian cheeses in which they hydrolyze milkfat and give rise to typical Italian cheese flavor. Lipases are used to accentuate flavor in chocolate and confectionery, and they are also used in digestive aids.

Oxidoreductases.—These enzymes catalyze the oxidation or reduction of the substrate by either gaining oxygen atoms or losing hydrogen atoms. In the food industry, the enzymes belonging to this class involve the following: Glucose oxidase which is used to remove traces of glucose or oxygen from eggs, beer, wines, fruit juices, and other products. Since hydrogen peroxide is produced as a by-product of glucose oxidase, catalase is normally used in conjunction (with glucose oxidase) to eliminate hydrogen peroxide. Catalase together with hydrogen peroxide is used for pasteurization of milk intended for cheese manufacture. Lipoxidase is used in the baking industry for bleaching out the natural pigments of flour.

Newer Enzyme Applications

During recent years "continuous" enzyme reactions have been carried out which involve modification of the substrate and removal of the by-products by ultrafiltration membranes. Thus, enzymes can be separated from the reaction mixtures and reused. Another advance has been in the area of binding enzymes on solid support and making them "bound" or "insoluble" enzymes. These bound enzymes can then be held in a column and the food to be treated by the enzymes can be "filtered" through such columns. These newer techniques involving ultrafiltration and insoluble enzymes should find rapid applications in chill-proofing of beer, clarification of juices and wines, and manufacture of syrup. However, such procedures have not yet been perfected for industrial usage.

KHEM M. SHAHANI

References

ESKIN, N. A. M., HENDERSON, H. M., and TOWNSEND, R. J. 1971. Biochemistry of Foods. Academic Press, New York.
UNDERKOFLER, L. A. 1968. Handbook of Food Additives. Chemical Rubber Co., Cleveland.
REED, G. 1966. Enzymes in Food Processing. Academic Press, New York.

Cross-reference: *Browning, Enzymic.*

ESSENCES

See Flavorings and Essences.

ESSENTIAL OILS

The uses of natural products such as drugs and spices predate the recorded history of every culture. When technology and demand had progressed sufficiently, essential oils were developed, appearing originally in the Orient of that time, namely Egypt, Persia and India. Based on the alchemic Paracelsian theory of *Quinta Essentia* or *quintessence*, the *essential* oil of a useful natural substance was considered the most significant characteristic and descriptive isolate or concentrate of that substance. Ground spices were applied to foods for the purposes of flavor, food preservation, and appearance, and it followed naturally that the quintessence of the spice, the essential oil, was applied to foods as well. The first reference to essential oils of food spices appears in the latter 13th Century. Arnald de Villanova steam-distilled rosemary and sage leaves, but it is not certain that he separated the oils from the waters. Since these early times, essential oil technology has been closely bound to advances in organic chemistry. The application of essential oils to food products has expanded accordingly as new oils were produced and technical methods improved.

It is not difficult to define an essential oil which has been steam-distilled directly from the spice; however, other products have been labeled as essential oils, which complicates such a description; therefore, a precise, yet succinct definition is not possible. Most essential oils are steam-distilled from specific parts of plants, some from the whole plant. Such parts as flowers (oil of neroli), buds (oil of clove buds), seeds (oil of coriander), fruit (oils of limes expressed and distilled), leaves (oil of spearmint), twiggs (oil of petitgrain), bark (oil Cinnamon Ceylon), wood (oil of bois de rose), heart wood (oil of cedarwood) and roots (oil of ginger) yield their distinct products which are bound up with the metabolism of the individual plant part and plant itself.

Other essential oils are dry-distilled, vacuum-distilled, or expressed. Most expressed oils (citrus oils), such as lemon, orange, limes, grapefruit, mandarin, and tangerine are now processed by machine, whereas in former times they were pressed by hand. Some delicate flower oils are extracted with purified solvents (oil orris root concrete) or selectively extracted with a series of solvents (oil orris root absolute). The extraction has replaced almost completely the process called "enfleurage," an ancient process consisting of pressing the flower petals into a purified fat with subsequent extraction. Some oils are distilled or rectified several times to remove color (oil bergamot twice rectified), objectionable by-notes (oil peppermint twice rectified), or to increase the concentration of vital compounds (oil eucalyptus double distilled).

There are several oils, mainly citrus, which are cooled to precipitate the natural waxes to improve clarity. At normal temperatures, most oils are liquid, some are semisolid (Oil Mentha Arvensis Natural) and few are solid (oil guaiac wood). Most essential oils are volatile or ethereal, since they must evaporate to affect the senses of smell and taste, but many do contain nonvolatile components. Such things as natural waxes or high molecular weight natural organic components (coumarins, psoralens, and flavanoids) do not evaporate. It is apparent that most steam-distilled oils are likewise fairly volatile.

The plant materials used as sources for essential oils are grown throughout the world, often similar spices are grown in several parts of the world (nutmegs, East Indian and West Indian). It is becoming more prevailent that the oils are distilled close to the area where the plant material is harvested. There are many plant raw materials, however, that are shipped as such for specialized distillation or processing in the more modern distilleries of the highly technical countries. At least 50 important essential oils are distilled in the United States in this manner.

The production yields of oils vary individually as the raw material; dry onions, after fermentation and steam-distillation, would yield 0.09% essential oil; nutmegs yield approximately 12% of oil. The other oils vary within such limits, thus the reason for their particular value. The flavor intensity of the essential oil should be at least as strong as the reciprocal of the yield based on the dried spice.

Advances in investigative analysis using modern electronic instruments have disclosed the quantitative complexity of the essential oils. Some oils are 99% of 1 organic component (oil of bitter almond is composed mainly of benzaldehyde). Individual oils have shown at least 150 components with many more yet to be identified. Mass spectroscopy, nuclear magnetic resonance, infrared and ultraviolet spectrophotometry, thin layer chromatography, and particularly gas chromatography have added greatly to the limited component analyses of these products, which the older, tedious wet method investigations have disclosed.

Preinstrumental analyses have described with good accuracy the major components of most important essential oils. The modern chemists are at work identifying the more complicated, less concentrated organic molecules and, accordingly, determining the specific structure and concentration (not the generalized functional group) which wet methods would allow. In all cases of evaluation, however, subjective odor and flavor analyses are still vital to the quality and acceptance of any essential oil product for food use.

The essential oils are composed of organic compounds with various molecular weight ranges, chain branching, functional groups, oxidative stages, and degrees of unsaturation. The general classes of compounds encountered in essential oil analysis are aliphatic, alicyclic, cyclic, bicyclic, tricyclic, aromatic, alkylaromatic, and the like. Included in these general classes are hydrocarbons, ketones, aldehydes, alcohols, acids, esters, lactones, oxides, phenols, and phenol ethers; and, in rare cases, amines, cyanides, sulfides, nitro compounds, and quinones. As a group, terpenes (C-10 hydrocarbons) and derivatives are the major components of essential oils, with sesquiterpenes (C-15 hydrocarbons) and their derivatives also important.

The remainder of the component mix is extremely complex and many new structures and derivatives are continually brought to light.

Essential oils are used in many food products; singly, as in flavor extracts (orange extract), in combination with other essential oils, fixed oils, oleoresins, extracts or fruit juices, and concentrates, to flavor products such as sausage and meat products, soft drinks, bakery goods, confectionery items, cheese, tobacco, condiments, salad dressings, sauces, cordials, syrups, wines, chewing gum, and innumerable others.

JAMES A. ROGERS, JR.

Reference

GUENTHER, E. 1948 (Reprinted 1955). The Essential Oils, Vols. 1, 2, 3, 4, 5, and 6. Van Nostrand Reinhold Co., New York.

ESTERIFICATION AND INTERESTERIFICATION

Esterification is the reversible reaction between carboxylic acids and alcohols to give esters with the elimination of water

$$R'COOH + R''OH \rightleftharpoons R'COOR'' + H_2O$$

Applied to the food industry, the esterification reactions of primary interest are those between aliphatic fatty acids and di- or polyfunctional alcohols, such as, for example, certain glycols and glycerol. Generally, ester-producing reactions of the direct type (esterification) are speeded up in velocity by (a) increasing the temperature of the reaction, (b) facilitating the removal of the water of reaction by both the use of heat and the careful application of vacuum, and (c) use of an esterification catalyst, most frequently but not exclusively, one of acidic nature.

Monohydric alcohols react with monobasic acids to form so-called simple esters. Methyl stearate, used as an animal growth promoter in feeds, is prepared by the reaction of commercial stearic acid with excess methanol, followed by the removal of the excess alcohol. It may be used as a stripped crude, or may be refined or distilled. Glycols (difunctional alcohols) react with 1 mole of fatty acids to form monoesters; with 2 moles of fatty acids to form diesters. An example of the former is propyleneglycol monostearate, from propylene glycol and stearic acid (one mole), which finds extensive use as a food emulsifier for the preparation of whipped toppings.

Glycerol, $CH_2OHCHOHCH_2OH$, which contains 3 hydroxyl groups capable of esterification (1 of which is *secondary* and 2 of which are *primary* hydroxyls), may be esterified at 1, 2, or 3 of the hydroxyl positions. The resulting directly-esterified glyceride esters are so-called mono-, di- or triglycerides, depending upon the number of moles of fatty acids employed to prepare them. Chemically pure mono- or diglyceride esters cannot be prepared by direct esterification; the products are always mixtures. When the fatty acid employed is homolog-free, triglycerides of high purity may be prepared by direct esterification. Natural triglycerides, which are the mixed triglyceride esters derived from fatty acids of variable but diverse composition, are components of fat foodstuffs. They offer a wide range of predictable physical properties of great utility in food manufacture, and, indeed, after hardening by hydrogenation, may be even more widely used. Synthetic triglycerides, produced by direct esterification with fatty acids of homolog composition not found in nature, offer "tailor-made" performance characteristics uniquely different from natural fats. Coconut oil, the natural triglyceride fat which is composed of mixed esters of C-8, -10, -12, -14, -16 and -18 saturated fatty acids, together with a small amount of C-18 unsaturated fatty acid, after refining and hydrogenation, offers the well-known physical characteristics which make it especially useful in cream fillings, confectionery coatings, coffee whiteners, whipped toppings, margarine, filled milk, and other uses. The synthetic triglyceride ester product prepared by direct esterification of glycerol with a fractionated coconut-derived fatty acid containing less of the C-8 and C-10 as well as less of the C-16 and C-18 homolog fatty acids than is present in the natural fat, has

entirely different physical characteristics than refined coconut oil; in fact, its properties are so unique and unusual that the synthetic product is suited as a substitute for rare and expensive coco butter.

Various so-called synthetic mono- and diglyceride esters have some utility in foodstuffs, but these products, prepared directly from glycerol and fatty acids, do not compete in overall volume or importance with the mono- and diglyceride esters prepared from natural fats by indirect esterification methods (interchange).

Interesterification is the interchange or "acyl migration" which occurs between an ester and a hydroxyl-containing component, such as a monohydric alcohol, a glycol, glycerol, etc., which results in the formation of a new or "interchanged" ester and a new alcohol. In the simple case, the chemical reaction can be represented as

$$R'COOR'' + R'''OH \rightleftharpoons R'COOR''' + R''OH$$

The interchange is reversible and is generally carried out with the aid of a catalyst, most frequently, but not exclusively, one of alkaline character.

One application of interchange esterification of great value in the food industry is the glycerolysis of natural fats, which results in a large series of mono- and diglyceride products of value as food emulsifiers in such products as ice cream, margarine, candy, cakes, cake icings, and dessert toppings. The end use determines the ratio of mono- and diglyceride products required.

The glycerolysis of natural fats has a practical limitation when the reaction is carried out commercially somewhere in the area of 70% total monoglyceride content. Although ester mixtures containing about 40% total "mono-" are readily prepared by glycerolysis, and, indeed, have large application in food emulsification, the monoglyceride products of about 90% total monoglyceride content—also very valuable as balanced hydrophilic-hydrophobic food emulsifiers—are produced by glycerolysis of natural fats like tallow, lard, cottonseed oil, hydrogenated soybean oil, etc., to form a crude reaction mixture of about 65–70% total mono content, followed by molecular distillation of the neutralized crude to afford monoglyceride emulsifiers of 90% total monoglyceride content. These products are especially valuable as water-in-oil dispersants and have a large utility in many foodstuffs.

Another type of water-in-oil food emulsifier is sorbitan monostearate, first introduced into the food industry in the early 1940's. Sorbitan, a complex polyhydric alcohol, does not lend itself well to interchange reactions; consequently, the ester is prepared by direct esterification from sorbitan and stearic acid.

One series of oil-in-water food emulsifiers with different and yet valuable applications in foodstuffs are modified esters. These are the polysorbates, prepared by direct esterification of sorbitan with fatty acid followed by the ethoxylation of the ester to yield polyoxyethylene sorbitan fatty acid esters. Unlike the mono- and diglycerides and sorbitan esters, these compounds are hydrophilic, tend to dissolve more in water and not in oil, and, hence, tend to emulsify oil in water. Polysorbates are used to disperse flavor oils in sherbet, dill oil in pickles, flavorings in soft drinks, etc.

NORMAN O. V. SONNTAG

EVANS, OLIVER (1755–1819)

Oliver Evans, born at Newport, Delaware in 1755, was an able engineer with an inventive mind. Evans' great contribution lay in his hooking up milling operations in a completely mechanized series. By means of gears, elevators, and conveyors, Evans' system made it possible to move grain from one stage to the next, and thus to grind flour in a continuous operation. In barest outline, the system worked as follows: In a bucket conveyor, the grain was lifted to the top floor of a three-story mill where it was moved by a screw conveyor to a hopper fitted with chutes that carried the grain to the room below where the grinders were located. After milling, the flour was conveyed to the first floor where it flowed into a bin and was stored until sacked. This concept quickly took hold and was widely used in the United States and Europe. Within a generation it was universally adopted. Evans' system was one of the very early examples of a continuous production line—and not too far from being the first example of an automated system.

Oliver Evans came from a family of millers and early in life developed an interest in mechanics. He had access to important books on mathematics and mechanical principles. The product of this reading and practical experience in the milling business owned by his brothers and himself was a book entitled: *The Young Mill-Wright and Miller's Guide.* The book was published in many editions.

Oliver Evans had other notable achievements. Intensely interested in the steam engine, he experimented with a steam carriage. Although he did not bring his design to completion, he did develop a steam-powered dredge that could move over the roads under its own power, the first steam-powered vehicle to travel on land.

MARTIN S. PETERSON

Cross-reference: *Flour Milling Industry.*

EVAPORATED MILK HISTORY

This great industry was created in the first half of the 20th Century. It came of age, prospered, and placed an indelible imprint on the history of America. The golden years of the evaporated milk industry were 1920 to 1950. This era covered all the drama of human life: service, crises, defect, intrigue, triumph, success, fortune, growth, and advancing age. At mid-century, there were 124 evaporated milk plants, commonly called condenseries, and 148 receiving stations operating in 31 States. The Carnation Company and Pet Milk Company operated $2/3$ of them; the balance were operated by a number of smaller companies and independents. The production of evaporated milk in 1950 exceeded 40 million cases (2 billion pounds) worth some $240,000,000, making it the largest single canned product in the food industry and a major factor in the U.S. economy.

The Evaporated Milk Association (EMA) was founded in 1923 by many dynamic and visionary leaders of this vigorous new industry; and EMA has played an exemplary role for 50 yr. Its archives at present are probably the best source of detailed information about the early years, industrial development, public responsibility, nutritional research, statistical data, and other details about the evaporated milk industry.

An excellent review of the developing industry was published in the 50th Anniversary Issue of the Journal of Dairy Science and provides further background on the growth years.

The Founders

Countless numbers of dedicated men and women played out their roles in bringing the evaporated milk industry into fruition. The roles of three pioneers stand out. They are Louis Latzer, E. A. Stuart, and John Meyenberg. Louis Latzer, scientist and businessman, was President of Pet Milk Company from 1887 to 1924. Elbridge Amos Stuart, practical businessman and marketeer, was President of Carnation Company from 1899 to 1923. John Meyenberg, a Swiss inventor who knew about evaporating and sterilizing, worked for both—first, for Louis Latzer at Highland, Ill., in 1887, and later for E. A. Stuart at Kent, Wash., in 1899. Meyenberg did not remain long with either Latzer or Stuart; but each was able to glean from Meyenberg's process the seeds of successful business enterprises that surpassed the fondest dreams of any of the three. The Meyenberg Milk Company still operates in California but never became a major factor in the national marketing of evaporated milk.

A host of other dedicated leaders who contributed greatly to the success of the evaporated milk industry includes personalities such as W. C. Cross, Vice President of Carnation Company, a very strong manager and highly respected; Mr. Marhofke of Nestlé, Inc.; Gail Borden and John B. Hunt, of Borden, Inc.; Sam Dean, founder of Dean Milk Company (now Dean Foods); and Walter Page, founder of the Midland Cooperative Association, a group of small canners who joined together to better compete against "The Big Four"—Carnation, Pet, Borden, and Nestlé.

The books *A Portrait of Progress—A Business History of Pet Milk Company from 1885 to 1960* by Martin Bell and *Elbridge A. Stuart—Founder of Carnation Company* by James Marshall detail the invaluable contributions of numerous other leaders whose lives and works were so vital to the fulfillment of the evaporated milk industry.

Milestones of Discovery

The need for safe, transportable food was recognized keenly by the French armies fighting under Napoleon about 1775. Nicholas Appert responded to the need and the incentive of a prize of 12,000 francs offered by the French Government to any one who could find a satisfactory method of preserving food. Appert began a series of experiments which led to success after 15 yr of patient toil in a tiny kitchen back of his confectionery shop. On Jan. 30, 1810, Appert was awarded the prize for his discovery of a process for cooking foods, sealing them air tight, heating them again, and thus providing food which would keep for long periods of time.

Other major milestones in the development of evaporated milk include:

1813 The vacuum pan was patented in England by Edward Howard.
1840 Canning in a "tin canister" was first accomplished in the United States.
1856 Gail Borden learned to preserve condensed milk by adding sugar.
1885 First commercial production of evaporated milk at the Helvetia Milk Condensing Co., Highland, Ill. (later to become Pet Milk Company).

1899 First commercial production of evaporated milk at the Pacific Coast Condensed Milk Plant, Kent, Wash. (later to become Carnation Company).
1901 Machine-made cans replaced hand-made cans increasing production to 60 cans per minute.
1905 John Meyenberg filed U.S. patent No. 207912 covering the processing of evaporated milk.
1909 Homogenization found to prevent cream from separating rapidly.
1923 The Evaporated Milk Association formed and voluntary product standard of 7.8% fat, 25.5% total solids adopted.
1924 The Anderson-Barngrover Continuous Milk Sterilizer marketed by Food Machinery Company (now FMC Corporation).
1937 Irradiation using a carbon arc to develop vitamin D potency began in some plants.
1940 FDA promulgated the standard of identity 7.9% fat, 25.9% total solids, and optionally 22.4 USP units of vitamin D per avoirdupois ounce.
1944 Vitamin D fortification at 400 units per pint (325 units per tall can) adopted on an industry-wide basis to combat rickets.
1958 HTST process for improved evaporated milk introduced by FMC Corporation; aseptic canning process for fresher-tasting evaporated milk pioneered by Foremost Dairies and further developed by Dole Engineering Company.
1961 Postwar decline in evaporated milk usage confirmed despite improvements in quality of product.
1967 Standard of Identity modified to allow use of carrageenan to keep product smooth and creamy during storage.

Documentation of these milestones in the published literature is a tedious if not impossible task. Many of these events, when they occurred, were closely guarded trade secrets within the highly competitive industry. Personal communication with Mr. Herman Grether, Mr. A. E. Peck, and Dr. Harold Adams of FMC Corporation, San Jose, Calif.; Mr. L. G. Leutwiler of Pet Incorporated, St. Louis; Dr. E. B. Oberg of Carnation Company, Los Angeles; Dr. Hartley Howard of The Borden Company, New York; Dr. Byron Webb of the United States Department of Agriculture, Washington, D.C.; and Mr. Fred Greiner of the EMA provided much of the necessary background data, based upon their files and in many cases their direct involvement along with the writer in the events described.

The Process and Equipment

Whole cows' milk is first standardized so that the ratio of fat to solids-not-fat is approximately the same as is required in the finished product (1 to 2.2). In practice with the continuous process, this was done by estimating an average test at the forewarmer and, based on previous records, separating or adding the necessary amount of cream to give the desired ratio. Then it is "forewarmed" to reduce the bacterial count and to stabilize the milk so that it will not coagulate or "break" in the sterilizer. Also, improperly forewarmed milk may gel within a few months after sterilization. Variations of atmospheric or "hot well" and pressure forewarming are most often used. In hot well forewarming, typically the cold milk is heated to 100°F, fed into a 180°F forewarmer with enough capacity to provide 20–30 min holding time, then overflowed into a smaller "hot well" kept at about 200°F and providing 10 min holding time. The hot milk then is drawn typically into a double-effect evaporator where about $1/2$ of the water is removed. The 2 to 1 concentrated milk is homogenized, cooled, restandardized by adding water or condensed skim milk, filled into cans, and sterilized.

An improved forewarming method more suitable for continuous processing involves similar preheating, rapid heating to about 250°F under pressure, holding at this temperature for 2–3 min and then evaporating, etc., as already described.

The precise times and temperatures necessary to produce the best, most stable product are very critical, require experience, exact control, and vary depending on the season and other factors related to the milk supply. Small amounts of disodium phosphate, sodium citrate, or calcium chloride may be used to control the natural variations of these constituents of milk and have profound effects on the stability of the product.

Sterilization typically requires an F_0 of at least 4.7. This may be accomplished by various methods, to give a lethality equivalent to heating for 4.7 min at 250°F.

The crude sterilizers developed by John Meyenberg at Highland, Ill., and Kent, Wash., were improved upon over the years. Most can-making, filling, sterilizing, and handling equipment initially was developed and fabricated on an in-company basis. In 1924, the Food Machinery Company introduced the first Anderson-Barngrover continuous sterilizer which proved difficult to promote.

One of the problems was that the viscosity of the product from the continuous sterilizers was usually thinner than was obtainable in the batch sterilizers. The Carnation and Libby plants were using Berlin-Chapman sterilizers. Many other plants were using Fort Wayne sterilizers in which some of the operators stopped the reel after the milk was up to sterilizing heat to build up a "liver or clabber" in the product. This made the milk appear very stiff, but the "liver" was worked out by the time the product was delivered to the user. Pet was using their own Leutwiler sterilizers which were set into pits in the floor and required special overhead rigging to handle the full length inside and outside lids and baskets.

Can Size Changes.—In 1929 and 1930 the industry changed from 16- to 14.5-oz cans for the family size container. All can handling equipment had to be changed very quickly to reduce loss of production. The intended purpose of the change was to enable canners to reduce their costs to permit a retail price of 10¢ per can. However, major economic changes during the depression made forecasting difficult, and in 1931 prices generally were 11¢ and up.

Some of the sterilizer lines were modified only at the transfer points to permit handling the shorter cans. In others the sterilizers were modified by removing the spiral, resetting it to a narrower spacing, and adding 3 turns or 141 cans to the holding capacity.

Sterilizer Line Sizes, 1931.—The usual tall line units and capacities were

	No. Cans
Standard preheater	1656
Variable preheater	1548
Sterilizer	1833
Cooler	1316
Total	6353

At 15 min sterilizing time this allowed a sterilizer speed of 122 cans per minute. Probably $2/3$ of the sterilizers were converted to 1974 can capacity sterilizer shells during the change from 16- to 14.5-oz cans. This enabled the line to run 132 cpm. This, at the time, matched the capacity of the 48 cell Dickerson fillers which were then standard.

The variable preheater had a conveyor system and 4 inlets permitting the operator to use $1/4$, $1/2$, $3/4$, or the full length of the shell depending upon the stability of the milk and the length of preheat desired.

Speed Increase.—The Borden Company pioneered the 60 cell filler to increase production and was using Fort Wayne sterilizers around 1932. In 1937, a new continuous sterilizer was built by FMC Corporation for the Borden Company in Modesto, Calif., with can capacities as follows: preheater 3300, sterilizer 2585, cooler 1739.

This provided 15 min of sterilizing time at 172 cpm and soon became the standard line, except for some small plants which did not need this higher production rate.

Some new lines were installed every year until all plants for evaporated milk, excepting 1 or 2 very small ones, were using the continuous sterilizers for their 14.5-oz cans. Many of the plants also installed lines for 6-oz cans to eliminate their batch systems.

There was a gradual increase in sterilizer speeds to 258 cpm for 2585-can capacity lines at 10 min sterilizing time, and to 300 cpm for 3854-can capacity lines at 12.85 min sterilizing time. Many of the lines have been fitted with coolers of larger capacity, up to 3008-can capacity, to provide better cooling and to save water.

Advantages of Continuous Lines.—Many of the plant managers resisted the change to continuous sterilizers. Some felt that they could make a better product with the equipment they had. Others may have feared mechanical trouble and the loss of product in case a continuous sterilizer were stalled for any reason. Others felt the cost for installation and continuing lease rentals was too high. Some may have hesitated to make their production figures known to the supplier of the continuous lines, as was necessary to design the equipment.

The continuous lines placed much less dependence on the operators for uniform product. Temperatures, air pressure, and water level were mechanically regulated. In a plant well-equipped with can conveyors and take-away machinery 1 operator could run 3 lines.

A unique system of leak detectors located at the preheater and cooler outlets comprised the main basis of the Anderson-Barngrover patents, and was practicable because of the special design of the soldered evaporated milk can. These leak detectors avoided the need to incubate all of the product before shipment except in isolated cases where there was trouble with can quality. This greatly reduced the cost of labor and supervision, and contributed to an outstanding record of quality and safety for evaporated milk.

World War II Era

The production levels of the evaporated milk industry reveal the major impact of World War II on the use of canned milk. Evaporated milk also was used extensively for relief in war-devastated areas for about 2 yr after the end of World War II, bringing production to an all-time high.

This proved to be a bad time for many milk canners. The wages in these plants had been considerably below those in other industries and then were frozen by the federal government. Better employees were encouraged to leave the the milk plants for better paying jobs making shells and other war goods. This left the milk plants with a shortage of help much of which was unreliable. It was common to see foremen, chief engineers, and other salaried men help push baskets into and out of the Fort Wayne sterilizers because help that had been assigned to that job the day before did not appear.

This labor problem encouraged the change to continuous sterilizers during and just after World War II and, also, in the installation of much other labor-saving equipment. Many of the plants were still using heating equipment with milk contact surfaces made of copper and piping which was not satisfactory for milk on government orders. Because of war orders the plants were able to get priorities for stainless steel equipment, and this resulted in extensive modernization of plants.

One of the problems the industry had to wrestle with during the war was the restriction on the amount of tin that could be used in can manufacture. Tin usage had to be reduced. This led to the use of electrolytic plate rather than hot dipped plate, which proved to be a better product. Bismuth and silver were added to improve the solder, yet there was considerable trouble making the cans as sound as they had been before.

The Double-Effect Evaporator

One of the men who had considerable impact on the milk industry was Roy Henszey who was chief engineer for the Carnation Company when the headquarters were in Oconomowoc, Wisc. He was especially versed in the application of steam. He experimented with adding heat exchanger units to existing copper vacuum pans to provide double effect. This cut the use of steam and water roughly in $1/2$. He went on from that to set up the Henszey Company with an office in the building of the Otto Biefeld Co. in Watertown, Wisc., where this company ran a heavy machine and fabricating shop. The Henszey Company developed all stainless steel triple-effect evaporators. This type of evaporator became widely used in the industry. The fabrication, at least at first, was done by the Biefeld Company.

Mr. Henszey also had ideas for building a continuous sterilizer, but this did not materialize.

Location of Plants

Prior to 1931, plants for evaporated milk were located mainly in Wisconsin and California. There were some in Michigan, Northwestern Ohio, Illinois, Oregon, Washington, Tennessee, Virginia, Maryland, Missouri, and Kansas.

In 1971, there was only one small plant in Wisconsin, the Page Milk Company in Merrill. The large cities, especially in the east, south, and southeast comprized the major markets. Freight rates on the product, as well as on coal and other supplies, made it difficult for canners in Wisconsin to compete. Also, a high proportion of the milk produced in Wisconsin is Grade A and priced too high for the manufacturing market.

With the advent of the tanker trucks making it feasible to transport milk long distances, the need to have the plants close to the milk sources decreased. In the early 1930's milk was hauled in 10-gal. cans and in winter, west of Wausau, Wisc., milk was still hauled to the plant on sleds having a small shack built on the front end in which the driver had a small stove to help him survive the subzero winds.

Originally, the plants for evaporation were not very large and were located in small towns with often only one 14.5-oz sterilizer running all the required production in the forenoon, except during the flush of milk production in June. Other plants had 2 small capacity sterilizers and a 6-oz sterilizer. Exceptions were the plants at Manitowoc and West Bend, Wisc., which had 4 and 3 14.5-oz lines, respectively. The same pattern applied in nearby states. As longer distance hauling became feasible and labor costs increased plants became larger, hours of operation were increased, and the number of plants was reduced. In 1972, all plants ran at least two 14.5-oz and one 6-oz line, except for a few small plants.

Much experimentation was done from about 1955 to 1965 with high temperature-short time (HTST) sterilizing processes in an effort to produce a product with less evidence of caramelization (browning) and "heated flavor." High speed sterilizers requiring only about 3 min in the sterilizer shell at about 265°F were tested, as well as "aseptic canning" in which the milk was sterilized within a few seconds, and then filled into sterile cans in a sterile environment. The desired product improvements were attained, but in extensive market tests had little or no impact on the declining use of evaporated milk during the postwar years.

The Infant Feeding Story

E. A. Stuart's first contact with evaporated milk came when as a Texas grocer in about 1889, he purchased a case of Helvetia Evaporated Cream to see if it might help his ailing infant. Within a few months the child became healthy and strong, growing normally on the formula made with evaporated milk. No doubt this early favorable experience with evaporated milk encouraged Stuart

to accept John Meyenberg's proposition in 1899. Throughout the years, infant feeding has played a major role in the use of evaporated milk.

Early in the 1920's, pediatricians around the country were prescribing evaporated milk for infant formulas in difficult feeding cases.

Leaders in the industry felt the need for a controlled study of the use of evaporated milk in formulas fed to a substantial number of babies. The EMA inaugurated such a program under the direction of Dr. Frank E. Rice.

Two pediatricians of international reputations, Dr. Marriott of St. Louis and Dr. Brennemann of Chicago undertook the massive feeding study. Publications of their work in leading medical journals appeared in 1929, confirming the utility of evaporated milk formulas in infant feeding. For 2 decades, from 1930 to 1950, evaporated milk was used extensively for infant feeding, accounting for 75-80% of the formula feedings during much of this period.

Thus, research became an important EMA activity.

Research and Education

The Administrative Technologists Committee of EMA rose to the research challenge in response to a letter written Sept. 17, 1938 by James T. Jardine, then Chief of Experiment Stations for USDA. Over the ensuing years, the evaporated milk industry maintained close liaison through its technical specialists with the USDA. This resulted in much fundamental research on milk proteins, lipids, and milk derivatives.

The education phase of the EMA program was directed to leaders in food science and nutrition, editors, physicians, home economists, etc. The EMA staff included specialists who traveled the "circuit" of home economics schools giving lectures and demonstrations. Personal contacts were made at annual conventions, and educational materials were provided for use in classrooms all over the country. Although some consumer advertising was done in women's journals, the major thrust of the EMA educational program followed the "educate the educators" theme.

The Product and Its Life Cycle

Originally the product was marketed as "evaporated cream" because of its rich, cream-like consistency. The name was changed to "evaporated milk" in 1906. Federal Standards for its composition were established in 1923, with slight modification in 1940. This U.S. Standard required that all evaporated milk contain 7.9% fat, 25.9% total milk solids, and provided for the optional addition of 22.4 USP units of Vitamin D per avoirdupois ounce. In 1944, the nutritional signif-icance of Vitamin D fortification in preventing rickets was fully recognized. Through prompt, voluntary industry action the addition of 400 USP units of Vitamin D per pint, the level considered optimum for infants, was inaugurated on an in-dustry-wide basis. The striking effectiveness of the Vitamin D program was confirmed by the practical eradication of infantile rickets by 1955.

In 1967, a further optional ingredient was ad-mitted in the Standard of Identity. A colloidal food stabilizer called "carrageenan" was permitted as an optional ingredient to help assure the creamy consistency and uniformity of the product as poured from the can, especially after long periods on the shelf without periodically inverting the cases to prevent separation.

Evaporated skim milk, a companion product except that the cream has been removed, was marketed in most States in the late 1960's.

A modified product containing vegetable fat instead of milkfat was marketed successfully in a few States but was never marketed on a nation-wide basis. The Filled Milk Act of 1923 pro-hibited the interstate shipment of this modified product. A unique result of this law developed in the Milnot plant at Senaca, Missouri. The plant was built exactly on the line dividing Missouri and Oklahoma. The sterilizer was built on wheels, and was moved across the line into the appropriate State during processing so that 1 plant could produce for 2 States.

Originally, evaporated milk was sold in a 1-lb tin. Later the industry adopted the $13^1/_2$-oz "tall" can which when mixed with water in usual pro-portions for infant formula yielded a day's supply. Also, a 6-oz "baby" can gained in popularity and the 2 sizes, "tall" and "baby," have been the standards of the industry for over 50 yr.

Exact production data for the industry are not available prior. to 1925. This was a period of market exploration and technical development requiring about 25 yr to provide the necessary sound basis for the nationwide production and marketing of a major new food commodity on the American scene.

With the exception of the war years (1941–1945), the evaporated milk industry has ex-perienced the classical growth curve: from 1890 to 1900, years of experimentation; from 1900 to 1925, years of innovation; from 1925 to 1940, years of growth, from 1940 to 1955, years of maturity; with 1955–1970, years of decline. This latter period closely parallels the gradual growth of many other basic commodities: combination, processed products in the form of convenience foods; service-ready foods; the development of

liquid dietary food products such as Metrecal (Mead-Johnson), Sego (Pet), and Slender (Carna-tion); and the trend toward commercially-prepared, proprietary infant formulas.

A unique feature of the product life cycle for evaporated milk is its remarkably long time-span exceeding 80 yr. Further, the 1970 volume of 27,714,000 cases of 48 cans substantially exceeds the volume of many exciting new products which are considered highly successful when their annual volume exceeds 2 or 3 million cases with a typical life cycle of 5–7 yr. Intimately interwoven within these changes in production volume are concurrent innovations in social structures, life styles, food habits, employment and income levels, govern-ment distribution to needy families, food prepara-tion and distribution methods, and a host of related, fascinating, and continuing trends which lie far outside the scope of this history of an industry.

DEE M. GRAHAM

Reference

PARFITT, E. H. 1956. The development of the evaporated milk industry in the United States. J. Dairy Sci. *39*, 838–842.

Cross-reference: *Borden, Gail.*

EVAPORATION

Evaporation is used to remove water from such products as milk, citrus juices, soups, glucose, whey, and other liquid foods. This operation is also referred to as condensing and the products are designated as concentrates.

To preserve the original organoleptic charac-teristics of taste, flavor, color, and vitamins, evaporation is accomplished under a partial vacuum permitting reduced temperatures. This process was first used by Nicholas Appert in France in 1796. Later, in 1856, Gail Borden in the United States and Henry Nestlé in Switzerland used the process to produce condensed milk. Several types of equipment are used for the evaporative process.

Single-Effect Batch-Type Evaporators

The earliest evaporators were known as vacuum pans and were made of copper. They consisted of an air-tight cylindrical vessel 3 to 7 ft in diameter. The lower portion housed the heating coils and jacket which were supplied with low pressure steam. The space above the liquid level (e.g., milk) was the vapor separator which was con-nected to a condenser.

To produce and maintain a vacuum during the condensing operation a steam driven vacuum pump was used. Evaporation was carried out at temperatures between 130° and 140°F. The steam to the heating surfaces was supplied at a pressure of from 1 to 10 lb. Most condensing operations were carried out in batches. These early operations were applied to sweetened condensed milk.

Modern single-effect evaporators are now made of stainless steel and heating surfaces usually consist of a vertical tube bundle or tube chest through which the product circulates at high velocity. For high product concentrations and viscosities, coils and jacketed surfaces are still in use.

A steam separator and flash chamber are used to reduce entrainment losses (Fig. E-5). Evaporation temperatures vary from 110° to 135°F. To evaporate 1 lb of water from the product, a single-effect evaporator requires ap-proximately 1 lb of steam and 16–30 lb of condenser water, depending on the available water temperature. Because of the relatively high steam and water requirements, the use of the single-effect evaporator is limited to small capacity operations; and for high solids concentrations.

Continuous operation of single-effect evaporators is possible by using two or more in series, each with its own independent steam supply, condenser, and vacuum pump. Such a system is used where boiling temperatures must be kept at a minimum. Compared with single unit operations, the total required heat transfer surface can be materially reduced by using two or more units in series. This system is employed for processing such highly viscous products as sweetened condensed milk and lactose.

Other types of single-effect evaporators vary in the design and location of the heating surface. Mechanically rotated thin-film or swept-wall evaporators lend themselves to the high concentration of viscous products at low temperatures. Such equipment may also be used for the final con-

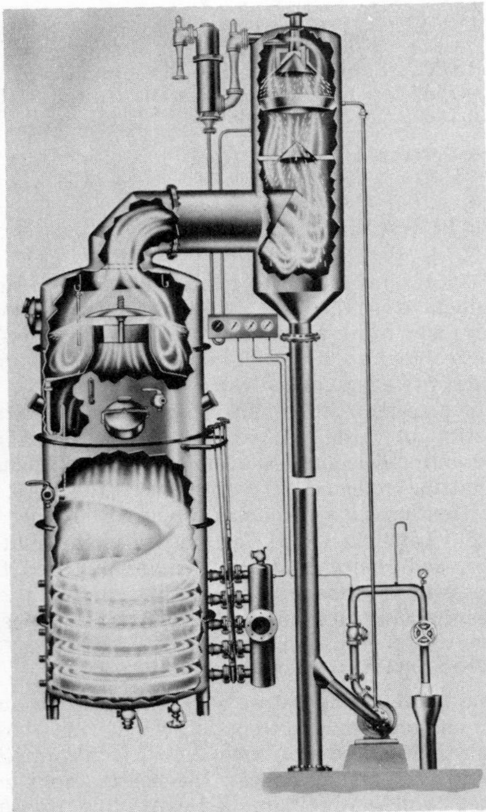

Courtesy of Arthur Harris & Co.

FIG. E-5. VACUUM PAN WITH ENTRAINMENT SEPARATOR AND JET CONDENSER WITH 2-STAGE STEAM EJECTOR

Courtesy of Arthur Harris & Co.

FIG. E-6. DOUBLE-EFFECT UP-FLOW EVAPO-RATOR

Courtesy of A. W. Baumann

FIG. E-7. A CONTINUOUS OPERATION DOUBLE-EFFECT RECOMPRESSION WHEY EVAPO-
RATOR CONDENSING FROM 6 to 50% TOTAL SOLIDS; FEED CAPACITY 55,000 LB PER HR

centration of a product discharged from a multiple-effect evaporator.

Evaporators with plate-type heating surfaces, both falling and rising film types, are used for small and medium capacities, particularly in buildings with limited ceiling heights.

Multiple-Effect Evaporators

Double-Effect.—This system consists of two single effects operating in series as far as the product flow is concerned (Fig. E-6 and E-7). The vapors originating from the first effect are conducted into the tube chest of the second effect, thus supplying the heat required for evaporation in the second effect. In comparison with a single-effect operation, only $1/2$ of the steam and water are required. One pound of steam now does double duty and will evaporate approximately 2 lb of water from the product.

Triple-Effect and Quadruple-Effect.—Three or four evaporators may operate in series. Vapor originating from the preceding effect supplies the heat to operate the following effect. In comparison with a single-effect operation, steam and water requirements are about $1/3$ in the triple effect and $1/4$ in the quadruple effect. Each effect carries the same evaporation load. The heat transmission from one unit to another is made possible by lowering the boiling temperature (higher vacuum) in each successive stage; approximately 170°F in the first effect and approximately 115°F in the last effect.

Such evaporators operate continuously. Raw product is preheated to at least the operating temperature of the first effect. The final concentrate is discharged from the last stage. Evaporator tubes $1 \frac{1}{2}$ in. in diameter varying in length from 10 to 14 ft are used. Steam and water flow, temperatures, pressures, product levels, and concentrations are automatically controlled. Such evaporators are usually equipped with in-place cleaning devices. Jet-type condensers are used where the condenser water comes in direct contact with the vapors. Because of steam pollution problems, surface condensers of the shell and tube types are now used.

To produce and maintain a vacuum in these evaporator stages, air and non-condensible gases are removed by multistage steam ejectors or water ring vacuum pumps where high pressure steam is not available.

Falling-Film Evaporators

Such evaporators were used in the food industry in Europe soon after World War II long before they were introduced in the United States. For most products and applications, this evaporation offers advantages that cannot be realized with other types (Fig. E-8). The heating surfaces of such evaporators consist of vertical tube bundles, the tubes being usually $1 \frac{1}{2}$ in. in diameter by 14 to 20 ft long standing above a centrifugal steam separator. The preheated product enters on top of the tube chest where it is uniformly distributed into the evaporator tubes. As it flows by gravity in a thin film over the tubular surfaces, its velocity is further accelerated by the increasing vapor volumes also traveling in a downward direction.

While a minimum temperature difference of 20° to 50°F (steam to product) is required in a tubular, up-flow recirculation evaporator to maintain product circulation, the falling-film type evaporator operates with much lower temperature

Courtesy of Arthur Harris & Co.

FIG. E-8. TWO SINGLE-STAGE FALLING-FILM
EVAPORATORS OPERATING IN SERIES

a higher temperature than is maintained in that effect.

Many features of the falling-film evaporator are superior to any other type: (1) Minimum heat exposure time with the product—3-4 min flow-through time for a triple-effect evaporator. (2) Lower temperatures of heating surfaces. (3) Single pass or controlled recirculation. (4) Better heat transfer rates resulting in reduced heating surfaces. (5) Absence of product level controls and simplicity of operation. (6) Operation with very small temperature differences (steam and product) resulting in higher steam economy when used with thermo compression.

For condensing heat-sensitive products such as citrus juices, milk, tomato juice, etc., the falling-film evaporator produces fresh-tasting concentrates without discoloration. This type of evaporator is at present the most widely-used in the condensing industry.

Steam-Jet Vapor Compression

A thermo compressor may be used to reduce the steam and water requirements of an evaporator.

Courtesy of Wiegand Karlsruhe, West Germany

FIG. E-9. A QUADRUPLE EFFECT FALLING-FILM
EVAPORATOR FOR THE DAIRY INDUSTRY

Features a built-in degassing and finishing stage, high-heating by direct steam injection, surface condensation for cooling tower operation. Evaporative capacity: 14,400 kg per hr of skim milk from 9 to 50% total solids.

differences. To sustain the product film velocity, no heat energy is required. Product flow through the evaporator can be controlled for single pass or recirculation, depending on concentration requirements. Most falling-film evaporators are used as multiple-effect units, with single-pass flow in all but the last stage where recirculation for higher concentrations is indicated. Steam and water economies are the same as with the up-flow type recirculation evaporators. The most important part of a falling-film evaporator is the method of product distribution over the tube chest. Full cone distribution nozzles, rotating spray arms, and perforated plates are used. If the distribution requires flash evaporation, the entering product to the first effect must be preheated to

Under normal operating conditions, the steam and water requirements of a single-effect evaporator are cut $1/2$ by the use of thermo compression. Its economy is that of a double-effect evaporator: 1 lb of steam will evaporate 2 lb of water. Attached to a multiple-effect evaporator, the thermo compressor adds the economy of an additional effect. In a steam-jet vapor compressor, the high-pressure, motive steam is converted into velocity energy. The steam jet draws product vapors from the flash chamber by impingement, or suction, and discharges the mixture of steam and vapor at a higher temperature into the evaporator tube chest.

Vapor compression of $14°$-$30°$F above the evaporator boiling temperature is used. Normally, 1 lb of motive, high-pressure steam at 90–140 psig will compress 1 lb of product vapor approximately $25°$F.

The falling-film evaporator usually operates with steam temperatures about 14 degrees higher than evaporator boiling temperatures, which will further increase the economy of operation.

The possible disadvantages of thermo compression are reduced flexibility of evaporator temperatures and capacities, and mandatory use of high-pressure steam.

Vacuum Cooling.—Product cooling by evaporation under vacuum to temperatures as low as $60°$F is economical for high solids and viscous concentrates such as sweetened condensed milk, soup stock, ice cream mix, whey, and honey. The

Courtesy of C. P. Division, St. Regis

FIG. E-11. FLASH CHAMBER FOR THE REMOVAL OF VOLATILE FLAVORS FROM MILK

equipment used in this process is similar to that of a single-effect vacuum pan with condenser and steam jets, but without any heating surface. The establishment of a high vacuum over the warm product level in the flash chamber lowers the boiling temperature and causes the product to dissipate its superheat, the temperature being reduced by evaporation. Depending on the cooling range and the specific heat of the product, a relatively small amount of water is evaporated in this process. Where cold condenser water is not available, a thermo compressor is used to deliver the vapors into the condenser at elevated temperatures which will make possible the use of cooling tower water.

Vacuum Cooling/Deodorizing.—The flash deodorizer process for removal of volatile off-flavors (taints) from liquid products usually consists of a vacuum vessel, condenser, vacuum pump, and product removal pump. The heated product enters near the top of the vacuum vessel, flows in a thin film down the inside and is pumped out of the bottom. Due to the vacuum maintained in the vessel, a portion of the water evaporates, or vaporizes, and the water vapor carries with it the objectionable volatile flavor and odor components. Turbulence resulting from the boiling promotes the removal of these volatile flavors and

Courtesy of Arthur Harris & Co.

FIG. E-10. VACUUM-FLASH COOLER WITH SHELL AND TUBE CONDENSER AND VAPOR COMPRESSOR odors. The water vapor is removed by condensation, and air and the noncondensible gases are discharged through the vacuum pump or steam ejector.

There are two types of flash deodorizers: (1) vacuum treatment and (2) vacuum treatment preceded by direct-contact steam heating.

Vacuum treatment alone will remove most of the volatile off-flavors associated with weeds and feed, but will also remove a small amount of moisture from the product through vaporization. The amount of moisture loss depends upon the temperature drop in the product, produced by the evaporation, which, in turn, is controlled by the vacuum level maintained in the vessel.

If the water content of the product needs to be maintained, steam can be injected into the product ahead of the cooler deodorizer and by the use of proper controls, the water added by the steam will balance the water removed by vaporization. In some products, direct steam heating will aid in the removal of off-flavors.

For viscous products or for volatile flavors difficult to remove, many variations of this equipment are available.

ARNOLD W. BAUMANN

EXTRACTION

In its simplest definition, extraction is the art of separating into its component parts, two liquids, or two solids, or a liquid and a solid. One of the component parts must be chemically reactive or soluble. Extraction is employed in the food industry where one or both of the parts extracted have value as food. Since the engineering details of expression and extraction are dealt with in detail elsewhere, some uses of extraction in the food industry will be the chief emphasis here.

Extraction is used to separate *edible oil* from nuts and seeds. The first step is to release the oil from within the cell wall. This is achieved by presses, crushers and/or cookers specifically designed for the edible oil industry. The next step is solvent extraction. The solvents in use are several, one of the most common (except for water) being trichloroethylene, a low-boiling, colorless, mobile liquid. Since it is toxic, its complete removal from the extracted oil is mandatory.

Solvent extraction methods are used to extract sugar from beets. The solvent used in this instance is water. The initial operation is slicing the beets, this in order that extraction may be more efficiently accomplished. The extract is then limed, filtered, concentrated, passed over bone char (a decolorizing agent and filtering medium), crystal-ized, centrifuged, and then dried—the resulting product being refined sugar.

One of the major uses of extraction today is that employed in the soluble coffee industry. It has been estimated that over 300,000,000 lb of soluble (instant) coffee is manufactured each year, $2/3$ of it in the United States.

Extraction is accomplished by means of a series of extraction columns. The solvent is water, heated to 350°F. It flows countercurrently to the roast and the ground coffee. The extract is either spray dried or freeze dried. Coffee aroma is incorporated in the extract by means of a coffee oil emulsion.

Solvent extraction is also used in the decaffeination of coffee, the solvent being trichloroethylene, a nonflammable solvent.

Soluble tea is prepared both from the fresh tea leaf and from processed black tea. In extraction from the fresh leaf, the leaf is macerated and allowed to ferment. The soluble solids are separated by water extraction. The extract, as in the manufacture of soluble coffee, is either spray dried or freeze dried. Extracting the water solubles from black tea begins with an infusion which is then concentrated and dried.

Meat extracts have been used for years to impart a better or stronger meat flavor to foods. They are manufactured by cooking or soaking in hot water and then concentrating the meat liquor thus obtained. The yield is low and the product is therefore rather costly. It is of interest that the great German chemist, Justus von Leibig, formulated an extract of beef as a by-product of his studies of animal physiology. The purpose was not to improve flavor but to provide a highly nutritious food for invalids.

The basic types of equipment for extraction are open percolation tanks, extraction batteries, and continuous moving-bed extractors, all of which are used with solid-liquid mixtures. Open mixing tanks, packed or plate columns, centrifuge contactors such as Podbielniak machines are used for continuous extraction. Percolation tanks are vessels with bottom outlets and valves. The solvent percolates, i.e., passes through the solids, by force of gravity. Percolation extraction batteries are tanks or vessels joined in series. These vessels have the same features as the percolation tanks (bottom outlet, valve, etc.). The control valves are so arranged that a given vessel can be separated from the others in order that it may be emptied and refilled.

Continuous extractors are varied in design but the tower type with (a) traveling elements that contain the solids, (b) sprays to deliver the solvent to the solid, and (c) a feeder and discharger for the solids is representative. Continuous liquid-

liquid extraction towers are designed as vertical towers, equipped with feed inlet, outlet fittings and packing, that is, wetted solid surfaces. Liquid-liquid extractions require an agitation device, either a paddle or a propeller type of mixer, this in order to assure a more uniform contacting of the liquids. In some instances where the contactor is also used as the separator, mixing is undesirable.

MARTIN S. PETERSON

F

FABRICATED FOODS

Interest in fabricated foods has been heightened by the threat of critical food shortages in the foreseeable future and the need to alleviate these shortages by advanced engineering and technological techniques. A brief summary of the problem will be useful.

United Nations experts estimate that the population will reach 3.8 billion by 1975 and 6.3 billion by 2000. So far, the major source of food is agricultural products. The United States, through extensive research in plant and animal breeding, from equipment technology, soil, environmental and nutritional requirements was able to produce food in abundance. Yearly surplus of foods is a common phenomenon; thus, the United States citizens spend the lowest percentage of their income on foods as compared to many countries around the world. However, this trend may not continue forever as indicated by recent increases in food prices.

The increase in food production cannot keep ahead of the increase in population for many years. New crop lands and increases in yield have definite limits; under the law of diminishing returns, the production of food by agriculture will approach a limit asymptotically. Therefore, to continue to depend only on agriculture, even with maximum production, the inevitable shortage of food can lead only to major war, mass starvation, or both. The other alternative is to mobilize the world's scientific and engineering resources for the synthesis of foods by utilizing the talents of chemists, biologists, physicists, and engineers. Chemistry can make a great contribution to civilization in the next 100 yr, perhaps as agriculture did in the preceeding 9000 yr. In general, any substance that can be grown by plant or animal can be synthesized. All 22 amino acids and most vitamins, fatty acids and many simple carbohydrates, food colors and flavors have been successfully synthesized.

Raw materials derived by chemical means may be called "synthetic"; those derived from agricultural raw materials as "fabricated"; and foods which are prepared and processed to improve nutrition, reduce cost, increase convenience in meal preparation, and improve acceptability as "engineered foods."

The trend to consume fabricated, synthetic, or engineered foods has grown slowly but steadily over the past two decades. Recently, however, a sudden acceleration of consumer demand took place due to new advances in processing and technology. This trend should not alarm farmers since most of the ingredients of such new foods come from agricultural sources.

The following data on current and estimated fabricated food markets were published by *Food Technology*, Dec. 1973:

	1972	1976	1980
		(Millions of $)	
Dairy substitutes	847.4	994.2	2527.4
Beverages	157.3	211.8	273.9
Snack foods	2001.8	2467.3	3066.1
Prepared desserts	60.0	82.0	111.0
Salad dressings			
Spoonable	313.6	370.9	439.2
Pourable	122.6	172.0	238.1
Vegetable protein			
products	82.0	316.5	1531.9
Dietetic foods	39.5	47.7	96.0
Prepared cereals	670.0	753.0	848.0
Cookies and crackers	1558.0	1686.0	1825.0
Cake and roll mixes	230.5	240.6	250.4
Pop tart products	68	86	109.0
Soft drinks	5450.0	7412.0	10100.0
Pet foods	1304.0	1648.0	2081.0
	12904.4	15588.0	23497.0

USDA economists made the following tentative assessments relative to several families of food products.

Dairy Products

In 1940, per capita consumption of butter was 17.2 lb vs 2.4 lb for margarine, whereas in 1969 butter decreased to 5.4 lb and margarine increased to 10.8 lb. Most experts expect the ratio to stabilize. Nondairy coffee whiteners amount to 35% of the market for light cream and nondairy toppings now have ½ the market for whipped toppings. For filled milk (a mixture of nonfat milk solids and vegetable fat) and imitation milk (containing no milk components) the future is less promising.

Citrus

Synthetic orange drink containing no citrus derivatives claims 12.5% of the retail citrus beverage market. Future increase may not be very significant by 1980 due to citrus industry's fight back with research to develop new and improved products.

Sweeteners

Synthetic sweeteners since the ban on cyclamates have been adversely affected. Other than starch sweeteners (such as corn syrup, dextrose) no major new synthetic sweetener appears on the horizon. Sugar is likely to receive growing demands in the future.

Meat, Poultry and Fish

Production of meat, poultry, and sea food substitutes is already a big business and will probably get much bigger. Soy bean is the principal raw material for the vast majority of meat substitutes. Soy grits or soy flour contains about 50% protein; soy protein concentrates, 70% protein; and isolated soy protein, about 90% protein. These proteins can be used as substitutes for meat in two ways: (1) They constitute a minor part of the finished product where small amounts of soy protein are added to meat as an extender to reduce cost or help the product's quality and stability. Products fortified with soy protein include, but are not limited to, sausage mixtures, patties, meatballs, chilies, and others. (2) Soy protein constitutes the bulk of the product to simulate meat items in appearance, taste, and texture. These meat analogs are manufactured by spinning isolated soy proteins into fibers which can be colored, flavored, and formed into slices, chunks, cubes, chips, or any desired form and size.

Other sources of relatively inexpensive protein to be used in fabricated foods have been investigated. With optimum control of production, significantly higher yields of protein per day can be obtained from yeast and algae than that obtained from plant products or farm animals.

The chemical and biological production of new unconventional foods is but a small aspect of what is to come. Problems which today appear overwhelming will be solved and appear passe in 1980.

ABDUL R. RAHMAN

References

BIRD, K. 1971. The food processing front of the seventies. J. Am. Dietet. Assoc. 58, 103–107.

McPHERSON, T. A. 1962. The synthesis of food. Food Technol. 16, No. 11, 34–40.

MATTHERN, R. O. 1966. The potential of algae as a food. Activities Rept. Fall Issue, 18, No. 2, 101–109.

SANZO, R. 1973. Fabricated food market to exceed $23 billion by 1980. Food Technol. 27, No. 12, 46.

SOLLENBERGER, G. F. 1972. Fabricated foods and fibers. Furrow Jan.–Febr. 2–4.

FATS AND OILS

Fats and oils have been one of the main food sources for man from the time he was a hunter. Later when he became a farmer or a city dweller, fats and oils remained one of his preferred foods. Fats and oils, whether the source is animal, vegetable, or marine in origin, represent the highest source of energy per unit weight that man can consume. In many societies, even today, the fatty food is still considered the choice morsel and offered to the honored guest.

Fats and oils are essentially triglycerides, the esterification product of 1 molecule of glycerine with 3 molecules of fatty acids. The type of fatty acid and its structural position in the triglyceride molecule determines to a great extent, the physical and chemical properties of the resulting triglycerides. For example, a solid fat may differ from a liquid oil merely in the type of fatty acid present in the triglyceride, even though both products may be 18 carbon chain fatty acids. Stearines, for example, are essentially C_{18} saturated fatty acid triglycerides while vegetable oils are essentially C_{18} unsaturated fatty acid triglycerides. The degree of saturation or unsaturation can alter the physical form of the triglycerides into a solid fat or a liquid oil. An example illustrating the structural position in the triglyceride dictating specific properties may be shown in a comparison of tallow and cocoa butter. Although each fat is a combination of C_{16} and C_{18} fatty acids in about the same percentage ratios, cocoa butter has C_{18} monounsaturated fatty acid (oleic acid) in the 2 position in the triglyceride while tallow has a C_{18} saturated fatty acid (stearic acid) in the 2 position of the triglyceride. This one structural difference accounts for the unique property of cocoa butter vs tallow.

Although such fatty acid type and structural position account for specific and unique variations between fats and oils, they still share many properties in common. Most fats and oils are insoluble in water but soluble in most organic solvents. They have lower densities than water even though at room temperature they may vary from liquid to solid-appearing substances. Generally, liquid products are called oils while solid products are referred to as fats. Both terms, fats and oils, however, refer to triglycerides and represent about 95% of all fatty components in consumed foods. A broader term, lipid, is used to embrace a variety of chemical substances such as mono- and diglycerides, phosphotides, cerebrosides, sterols, terpenes, fatty alcohols, fatty acids, fat-soluble vitamins and other substances. These, however, are considered the minor components of the fatty compounds found in consumed foods.

The term, triglyceride, which identifies fats and oils and constitutes the major component of consumed foods, may be defined in various ways. When all of the fatty acids in the triglyceride are identical, it is termed a simple triglyceride. Most fats and oils, however, are mixed triglycerides in which 2 or 3 kinds of fatty acid radicals are present in the triglyceride molecule. Illustrations of each structure are

Simple Triglyceride	Mixed Triglyceride
R—COO—CH$_2$	R$_1$—COO—CH$_2$
R—COO—CH	R$_2$—COO—CH
R—COO—CH$_2$	R$_3$—COO—CH$_2$
(Where R is common to each fatty acid)	(Where R is different for each fatty acid)

Fatty acids are by far the greatest single class of the components of fats and oils. When a triglyceride is hydrolyzed, 100 gm of a fat yields approximately 95 gm of fatty acids. Fats and oils as found in nature may have fatty acids of carbon chain length of 2–24 with the predominant use of fatty acids of C_{12}–C_{18}. With modern analytical techniques and methodology, we can now establish that some 68 components are present in butter even though the predominant fatty acids are C_{16}–C_{18}. Other fats and oils such as olive oil, soybean oil, and other vegetable oils have relatively few components even when they are mixed glycerides and of essentially the C_{16}–C_{18} composition of fatty acids.

The fatty acids of most general interest are the straight aliphatic chains with the even number of carbon atoms and a single carboxyl group. The general structure formula for a saturated fatty acid is

$$\underset{\text{Aliphatic Chain}}{\underline{CH_3(CH_2) \times CH_2}}\underset{\text{Carboxyl Chain}}{\underline{-COOH}}$$

Although branched chain, cyclic chain, and odd number straight chain acids have been isolated, the fatty acids found naturally and in abundance in animal or vegetable sources are predominantly the straight chain type having even number of carbons.

These fatty acids may be further classified as saturated or unsaturated. The unsaturated fatty acids may be further classified as mono-, di- or polyunsaturated depending on the number of double bonds found in the fatty acid radical. The double bonds of the polyunsaturated fatty acids may be further classified as conjugated or nonconjugated. Typical structural diagramatical formula are

Saturated Bond	Monounsaturated Bond

Diunsaturated Bond (nonconjugated)	Diunsaturated Bond (conjugated)

Polyunsaturated Bond

Table F-1 lists the saturated fatty acids of practical interest which are found in fats and oils and the fat source in which they may be found. Table F-2 lists some of the unsaturated fatty acids found in natural fats and oils and typical sources of each.

Oleic acid is the fatty acid that occurs most frequently in nature.

Fatty acids of greater unsaturation are more chemically reactive. The activity increases as the number of double bonds increase. Polyunsaturated oils are subject to polymerization and the unsaturated oils, having conjugated double bonds, polymerize more rapidly than those of isolated double bonds. Vegetable oils are the principal sources of such polyunsaturated oils. Fish oils contain larger quantities of a variety of longer chain fatty acids than C_{18} with three or more double bonds.

Among the unsaturated fatty acids which make up the triglycerides, we also encounter the phenomenon of isomerism. Two or more structures that are composed of the same elements are united in the same proportion but differ in molecular structure. The two important types of isomerism

TABLE F-1

SATURATED FATTY ACIDS

Chemical Description	Common Name	No. of Carbon Atoms	Typical Fat Source
Ethanoic	Acetic	2	—
Butanoic	Butyric	4	Butterfat
Hexanoic	Caproic	6	Butterfat
Octanoic	Caprylic	8	Butterfat, coconut oil
Decanoic	Capric	10	Butterfat, coconut oil
Dodecanoic	Lauric	12	Coconut oil
Tetradecanoic	Myristic	14	Butterfat, coconut oil
Hexadecanoic	Palmitic	16	Most fats and oils
Octadecanoic	Stearic	18	Most fats and oils
Eicosanoic	Arachidic	20	Peanut oil
Docosanoic	Behenic	22	Rapeseed oil

encountered in such fatty acids are positional and geometric. In positional isomerism, the location of the double bond differs in the isomers. For example, linolenic acid has 3 double bonds at positions 9, 12, and 15. Its positional isomer, elaeostearic, has 3 double bonds at positions 9, 11, and 13. In geometric isomerism, the unsaturated fatty acid can exist in either *cis* or *trans* form depending on the confirmation of the hydrogen atoms attached to the carbon atoms joined by the double bonds. If the hydrogen atoms are on the same side of the carbon chain, the arrangement is called *cis*. If the hydrogen atoms are on opposite side of the carbon chain, the arrangement is *trans*. A simplified schematic diagram illustrates *cis* and *trans* configurations

Cis   *Trans*

Oleic acid and elaidic acid are isomers. Oleic acid is *cis* configuration while elaidic is *trans* configuration. When more than one double bond is present in a fatty acid molecule, a greater number of combinations is possible. One would have to determine whether the isomers are *cis-cis*, *cis-trans*, *trans-cis* or *trans-trans*. Generally, the geometric configuration of the atoms at the double bond has an appreciable effect on the melting point of the fatty acid. *Cis-cis* isomers are generally found in naturally-occurring food fats and oils. *Trans* isomers are more commonly found in fats and oils which have been subjected to hydrogenation processes.

The physical characteristics of fats and oils are dependent essentially upon four factors: (1) The degree of unsaturation. (2) The length of the carbon chain of the fatty acids. (3) The isomeric forms of the fatty acids. (4) The molecular configuration of the triglyceride.

The types of fatty acid combined in the molecule determine the classification of the triglyceride into mono-, di- and trisaturated and triunsaturated as illustrated

Monosaturated   Disaturated

Trisaturated   Triunsaturated

The various fats and oils will fall into one or another of the above four categories, even though under each category there may exist numerous variations and forms.

In general, fats and oils which are solid at room temperature tend to be high in saturated fatty acids while those oils which are liquid at room temperature tend to be more unsaturated. It is not true, however, to make a blanket rule and

TABLE F-2

SOME UNSATURATED FATTY ACIDS IN NATURAL FATS

Chemical Description	Common Name	No. of Double Bonds	No. of Carbon Atoms	Typical Fat Source
9-Decenoic	Caproleic	1	10	Butterfat
9-Dodecenoic	Lauroleic	1	12	Butterfat
9-Tetradecenoic	Myristoleic	1	14	Butterfat
9-Hexadecenoic	Palmitoleic	1	16	Animal fats, seed oils
9-Octadecenoic	Oleic	1	18	Most fats and oils
6-Octadecenoic	Petroselinic	1	18	Parsley seed oil
11-Octadecenoic	Vaccenic	1	18	Butterfat, beef fat
9,12-Octadecadienoic	Linoleic	2	18	Most seed fats
9,12,15-Octadecatrienoic	Linolenic	3	18	Soybean oil, linseed oil
9,11,13-Octadecatrienoic	Elaeostearic	3	18	Tung oil
9-Eicosenoic	Gadoleic	1	20	Fish oils
5,8,11,14-Eicosatetraenoic	Arachidonic	4	20	Lard
13-Docosenoic	Erucic	1	22	Rapeseed oil

judge the saturation-unsaturation of fats and oils merely from their physical state at room temperature. The saturation-unsaturation relationship is but one factor. Other factors must also be considered. The degree of unsaturation and its structural position can greatly influence the physical form of the triglyceride.

The chain length of the fatty acid may well play a role in the physical form of the triglyceride. As the chain length of the fatty acid increases, the melting point also increases. A short chain triglyceride may be a liquid oil but the long chain triglyceride (if saturated) will be a solid fat. Triacetin, tributyrin, tricaproin are liquids at room temperature. Trimyristin, tripalmatin, tristearin are solid at room temperature. If it were not for other factors, this chain length identification could well serve as a yardstick in fat and oil physical form identification.

The isomeric forms of the fatty acids in the triglyceride very definitely influence the physical form of the triglyceride. Particularly in shortening and margarine compositions, the isomeric form of the fatty acid contributes materially to the plastic to solid form desired in packaging and marketing such consumer products. Geometric isomers and their ratio to one another is one of the processing techniques used by the manufacturer to produce the physical forms desired.

Along with the other factors described above, we cannot overlook the contribution of the molecular configuration of the triglycerides. The structural form has definite influence on the physical properties of the fats and oils. Whether the triglyceride is a simple or mixed one having few or many chemical entities in its structure, the manner or way in which such fatty acids are structured in the triglyceride can make a very important difference in the form of the final triglyceride. We referred to cocoa butter earlier as a typical unique fat where the molecular structure is the predominant factor in this unique physical behavior.

It is also worthy of note to refer to the phenomenon of polymorphism of fats. Solid fats as a class tend to exhibit polymorphism. Polymorphism is generally described as the state in which the solid can exist in several different crystalline forms depending on the manner in which the molecules orient themselves in the solid state. Temperature and time, as well as physical sheer appear to be factors which influence the polymorphic form of the solid fat when it is going from a liquid state to the solid form. Such crystalline forms of the fat also have a marked effect on the melting point of the fat as well as its application and use.

As our technology and methodology have improved, we have learned to build, alter, redesign, and tailor-make molecules to suit our specific needs and requirements. With such unit operations as splitting (hydrolysis) of fats, distilling, fractionating, hydrogenating, and esterifying, we have really broadened the possibilities of structuring just about any order and sequence of fatty acids in a triglyceride. With alcoholysis, rearrangement, and modification of such triglycerides, we have developed an even greater specialization for tailor-made molecules. By altering the physical-chemical properties of fats by such processing innovations, we are able to adapt different raw materials for specific industrial and consumer uses. Hydrogenation and molecular rearrangement are by far the most versatile unit operations.

U.S. CONSUMPTION OF FOOD FATS AND OILS PER PERSON

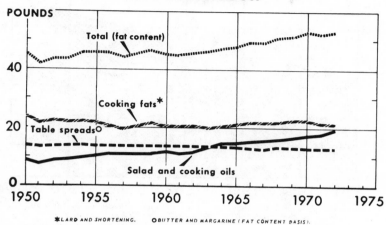

*LARD AND SHORTENING.   OBUTTER AND MARGARINE (FAT CONTENT BASIS).

Courtesy of USDA Econ. Res. Serv.

FIG. F-1.   U.S. CONSUMPTION OF FOOD FATS AND OILS PER PERSON

Hydrogenation controls the degree of saturation to unsaturation and the ratio of *cis* to *trans* isomers. Molecular rearrangement controls the specific or random distribution of the fatty acids in the triglyceride.

Lard by itself is not an ideal shortening, but a combination of lard and rearranged lard brings about ideal physical-chemical properties for a general all-purpose adaptable shortening base. Soybean oil per se is not suitable for an all-purpose shortening base but a selectively hydrogenated soybean oil with a balanced saturate-unsaturate ratio and a *cis-trans* isomer balance, makes a very versatile shortening base.

Lauric fats such as coconut and palm kernel, per se, are not suitable as cocoa butter substitutes or

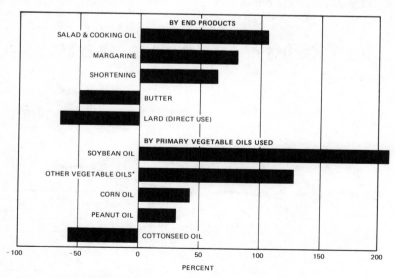

*Includes coconut oil, palm oil, palm kernel oil, safflower oil and sesame oil.

Courtesy of USDA Econ. Res. Serv.

FIG. F-2. FOOD FAT USAGE CHANGES 1950 TO 1970 IN PER PERSON CONSUMPTION

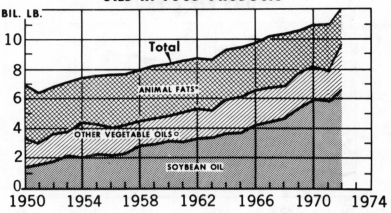

FIG. F-3. U.S. DISAPPEARANCE OF FATS AND OILS IN FOOD PRODUCTS

as coating fats. But, by a combination of hydrogenation and molecular rearrangement, some very good and economical hard butters have been prepared and used extensively for coating fats for biscuit, cracker, and confectionery coatings.

The modern refinery for edible products is set up to do all of the unit processes which give the plant the flexibility and latitude to tailor-make the various fats and oils products. Shortening, margarine, salad oils, frying oils, and coating fats constitute the major areas of consumer use. Such products utilize any number of these unit operations. The predominant, consistent needs, however, still remain refining, bleaching, hydrogenation, rearranging, and deodorizing. From such edible oil operations has emerged, not only the huge edible oil industry, but its companion industry, the fatty acid and fatty derivatives industry, which utilizes a great deal of the raw materials of the fats and oils produced in commerce.

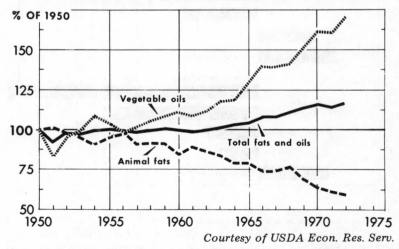

FIG. F-4. U.S. FOOD USE OF FATS AND OILS PER PERSON

TABLE F-3

FOOD FATS AND OILS CONSUMPTION, YEAR 1971[1]
(In Million Pounds)

| | | | Amount Processed as[2] | | | |
| | | | Salad and Cooking Oils for | | | |
	Shortening	Margarine	Salad Dressings and Mayonnaise[4]	All Others[5]	Misc and Direct Use[6]	Total Edible Usage
Vegetable oils[3]						
Soybean	1,708	1,234	718	736	51	4,447
Cottonseed	267	77	109	486	25	964
Corn	12	167	16	215	5	415
Peanut	24	5	—	132	9	170
Safflower	8	35	—	30	10	83
Olive	—	—	—	50	—	50
Coconut	40	16	—	—	305	361
Palm Kernel	2	2	—	—	82	86
Palm	61	—	—	—	8	69
Other	3	2	—	—	—	5
Animal fats						
Lard	568	125	—	—	1,078	1,771
Tallow	497	10	—	—	10	517
Butter (Prod.)[7]	—	—	—	—	1,102	1,102
Total	3,190	1,673	843	1,649	2,685	10,040

SOURCE: Based on U.S. Dept. of Commerce (Bureau of the Census) data for processing less exports and on USDA data for butter supplies.

[1] Excludes fats and oils used in manufacture of products for export and overseas donation.
[2] Includes retail trade, food manufacturing usage, caterers, USDA Welfare Programs, etc.
[3] Use of refined and further processed oil in manufacture of edible products.
[4] Commercial usage.
[5] Includes retail trade, use of oil in commercial frying, roasting and other products.
[6] Vegetable oil usage consists mainly of confectionery fats, toppings, milk fillings, and other specialty fats; lard and butter are mainly direct distribution and used as such.
[7] Contains approximately 80% fat.

The economic impact on our national income is a major factor for consideration in any economic forecast.

By planned, organized efforts in both genetic and technological operations and innovations, government and industry have achieved an agricultural balance and abundance never before seen in the history of man. Now with the world food problem becoming a factor for consideration, we are proceeding even further in maintaining nutrition considerations as well as oil and protein production and availability. Such planned economy on the part of the USDA has been a determining factor in the international position of the United States as a supplier not only of grain and vegetable oilseeds, but fats and oils as well.

The main sources of fats and oils are pretty much covered by about a dozen vegetable oils and several animal fats. In the United States over the last 20 yr, we have seen the gradual decrease of the consumption of butter and lard which are of animal source. In the same period, the vegetable oils, notably soybean oil, have steadily increased in usage. The USDA Economic Research Reports for 1971 clearly indicate these trends which appear to be continuing and perhaps will be even more pronounced in the years to come. Table F-3 and Fig. F-1, F-2, F-3, and F-4 illustrate this 20-yr trend for the various fats and oils which are one of the major products of consumption in the diet of the American public.

VIGEN K. BABAYAN

References

DEUEL, H. J., JR. 1951, 1955, 1957. The Lipids, Their Chemistry and Biochemistry, Vol. 1, 2, and 3. Interscience Division, John Wiley & Sons, New York.

ECKEY, E. W. 1954. Vegetable Fats and Oils. Van Nostrand Reinhold Publishing Co., New York.

HILDITCH, T. P. 1956. The Chemical Constitution of Natural Fats, 3rd Edition. John Wiley & Sons, New York.

SWERN, D. (Editor) 1964. Bailey's Industrial Oil and Fat Products, 3rd Edition. Interscience Division, John Wiley & Sons, New York.

U.S. DEPT. OF AGRICULTURE. 1968. Fats and Oils Situation. USDA Econ. Res. Serv. FOS-244.

Cross-references: *Antioxidants; Brominated Vegetable Oils; Cottonseed; Salad Oil; Rapeseed Technology; Shortenings; Soybeans.*

FERMENTATION

Fermentation is a chemical change brought about by enzymes or living organisms such as bacteria or as microorganisms existing as unicellular plants including yeasts, molds, and fungi. The chemical changes are chiefly three—the acidulation of milk, the oxidation of nitrogenous organic compounds, and the decomposition of sugars and starches to ethyl alcohol and carbon dioxide. Fermentations that result in such alcoholic beverages as wine, beer, and, after distillation, rum and the so-called hard liquors are the first in industrial importance but added to these are many other fermentations: bread making, the manufacture of cheeses, pickles, and sauerkraut being a few of the many.

The art of fermentation was well known to ancient civilizations. The ancients were not ignorant, moreover, of methods of control. Both the Romans and the Greeks, for instance, applied preservatives to their wines and also knew that heating could arrest fermentation and prevent deterioration. The ancients knew virtually nothing about the nature of fermentation—not surprising since prior to the invention of the microscope there were no means by which the fermentatives could be recognized and studied.

Although the chemical changes induced by fermentation were studied in some depth in the 18th Century, the nature of such ferments as yeast were not observed until the 19th Century. One of the classic disputes of the last century revolved around the question: Is fermentation caused by a living organism or by a chemical? There were two powerful antagonists, von Liebig who held it to be a chemical, and Pasteur, who insisted that fermentation was the product of a living organism. Pasteur's view prevailed in the end, the evidence being provided by E. Fischer who found that a soluble ferment, or enzyme, could be extracted from yeast, namely, invertase, and that this was the causative agent that set the fermentation process in motion. The fermentative microorganisms have a high capacity for producing enzymes, the reactive substances that catalyze reactions in fermentations and control them.

Today, as would be expected as a result of the vast amount of research that has gone into the fermentation process, much more is known about control then formerly. It is known that microorganisms vary in their sensitivity to acids, one type being able to inhibit the proliferation of another. By this means the growth of proteolytic, lypolytic, and other spoilage organisms can be controlled. Other means of control, heating and the use of chemicals, are not new, as mentioned, but great progress has been made in defining the limits of their applicability. Generally speaking, the limits are set by adverse effects on quality.

Fermentation changes the quality of both plant and animal products in marked degree. A number of food products are more edible in the fermented state than in their original, others are made more nutritious, and yet others, more flavorful. The flavors of some fermentation products meet with mixed reception by certain consumers, the reaction of the uninitiated to the flavor of olives being a case in point. Once acquired, however, the taste for olives and other distinctive flavors produced by fermentation becomes for many not only tolerable but highly prized.

Carl S. Pederson, a pre-eminent authority on fermentation, has provided a convenient list of industrial fermentations based on the three primary types: (1) Bacterial fermentation of carbohydrates. (2) Bacterial fermentation of alcohol to the acetic acid of vinegar. (3) Yeast fermentation, resulting in the production of alcohol.

Lactic acid-producing organisms acting on fruits and vegetables are prominently involved in the following fermentations:

Cucumbers: dill pickles, sour pickles
Olives: green olives, ripe olives
Cabbage: sauerkraut
Vegetables and rice: Sajur asin
Taro: poi, the well-known Hawaiian dish

Their action on meats produce:

Salami sausage	Thuringer
Lebanon bologna	Cervelat

Their action on dairy products produce:

Cheeses: Schmierkase	Milk:	Yoghurt
Ricotta		Acidophilus
Cheddar		Buttermilk
Edam		Bulgarian

Lactic acid bacteria with other organisms can produce such products as Limburger, Roquefort, and Stilton Cheeses, soy sauce, etc.

Acetic acid bacteria can convert cider, wine, honey, and any other product high in sugar or starch to vinegar.

Yeasts, acting alone, can produce wines from fruits, rum from molasses, whiskey from grain mashes, and bread from dough. Yeasts in combination with other organisms can produce such familiar products as ginger beer, citron, soy sauce, and many Oriental dishes.

General requirements for fermentation: The media, temperature, salt, acidity, the culture, the receptacle in which fermentation takes place, control of the process with respect to the time factor, environmental conditions, etc., are the factors of greatest importance in fermentation. Since each of the three main types of fermentation has its specific requirements, the requirements for a given product should be sought under its appropriate title.

MARTIN S. PETERSON

Cross-references: *Pickles; Olives; Sauerkraut; Food Preservation.*

FIGS

In ancient times the fig tree was considered to be sacred. The belief goes back into Greek, Roman, and Egyptian mythology and is to be found in early Hebrew and Christian literature. The fig tree was cultivated first in Arabia and later spread to surrounding areas where the climate was suitable. The commercially important figs are derived from *Ficus carica L.* of the Near East region, but Hedrick (1919) lists 20 species which are edible and are native to tropical America, Asia, and Africa. The story of how figs are pollinated and grow into edible fruits is fascinating, but too complicated to describe in a short space. Condit in *The Fig*, published by Chronica Botanica Co., Waltham, Mass., gives all the details of the history and development of this most interesting fruit.

California has become the third or fourth most important fig-producing area in the world, planted mostly to Calimyrna (Lob Injir), White Adriatic, Kadota (Dottato), and Mission varieties. The total annual dried tonnage from California has decreased from about 25,000 tons in the middle 1950's to about 18,000 tons in the late 1960's. Yields vary from 2 to 8 tons per acre on a fresh weight basis. Since there may be from 1 to 5 crops per year, depending on the climate and the variety, accurate yield data are difficult to obtain. In California,

two crops may be harvested, with the late summer or early fall crop (Mammoni) being the most important.

Since figs do not ripen after picking, the stage of maturity must be selected carefully whether they are intended for the fresh market, the dried fruit market, or the canning industry. Usually the figs fall from the tree or are picked by hand and then are swept into hedge rows and picked up by mechanical equipment. Upon arrival at a packing or processing facility, the figs are fumigated to kill insects; then they may be placed on trays and dried in the sun to about 16% moisture. Next they are washed thoroughly and dried, after which they are sorted and graded for size. For the fresh market the fruit is usually packed in bulk cartons and held under refrigeration. Dried figs may be slit and pressed together in either bulk or retail size packages. For canning, the fruit is filled into metal cans, covered with syrup, and processed like any other canned fruit. Statistics show that about $1/8 - 1/10$ of the annual crop is sold as fresh or canned and the remainder sold as dried fruit. In the 1940's, up to one million cases of Kadota figs were canned. A major processed product is fig paste or dried fig jam which is used to fill the familiar fig Newton bar. High moisture fruit can be treated with potassium sorbate dips to prevent microbial spoilage.

Figs have been made into an acceptable wine and brandy, but no commercial production has developed. A proteolytic enzyme, ficin, is found in the milky latex and has been used to tenderize meat or break down protein haze in beverages. The Black Mission fig makes an excellent frozen product but is not on the market at present. Nutritionists consider the fig to be a good source of calcium, iron, and copper, and a fair source of some of the B-vitamins.

FRANK P. BOYLE

References

HEDRICK, U. P. (Editor) 1919. Sturtevant's Notes on Edible Plants. J. B. Lyon Company State Printers, Albany, N.Y.
CONDIT, I. J. 1947. The Fig. Chronica Botanica Co., Waltham, Mass.

FILTRATION

Filtration is a unit operation designed to separate solids from liquids or liquids from liquids. Filtration is involved in many branches of the food industry: in the making of fruit juices, vegetable oils, olive oil, wine, beer, sugar syrups, and vinegar, and the list could be extended.

Filtration equipment in a properly designed plant layout is positioned in accord with the flow of the work. In consequence, the location varies with the commodity being manufactured and with the stage or stages at which filtration is required. Where preliminary filtration of a product is required, as in the vegetable oil industry, the filtration facility is placed early in the production line. In the manufacture of wine there may be a preliminary filtration station and, later in the line, a final station.

Filtration is accomplished by a filter medium through which, by means of gravity, pressure, or vacuum, a slurry is separated into solids and a liquid. In the food industry the liquid is usually the valued constituent and the solids are the unwanted or at least the less important constituent. That constituent which passes through the filter medium is called the filtrate, that which remains on the surface or within the pores of the filter medium is termed the residue.

The gravity filter has been known for centuries. As a sieve, it was probably a common household utensil used by those earliest of food technologists, the Egyptians. No doubt a rudimentary form of pressure to hurry the filtration process was also developed early. The use of vacuum to draw the filtrate through the medium is by contrast a modern innovation.

Filtration Equipment

Filter media, of first concern in any type of filtration, can be of metal, plant, or animal fiber. The materials used include metals such as brass, Monel, aluminum, stainless steel; fibers such as cotton, wool, paper, and synthetic fibers; and substances not easily classified such as sand or sponge. Regardless of the material the basic requirements of a filter medium are that they be temperature tolerant and resistive to the degradative effects of the slurry, e.g., the corrosive effect of moisture or acid. It goes without saying that the filter medium should not impede the filtration process. In this connection the weave pattern of the mesh of the filter material is important. A weave pattern should allow the passage of the filtrate and not block up, that is not become clogged, thus defeating the purpose of the filtration function.

The factors to be considered in the purchase of filter equipment, in addition to its appropriateness for the purpose intended, are flow rate, the length of the filtration cycle, and the method of cleaning. Closed circuit filtration is a desirable feature in many applications and so also is continuous operation.

The main types of filtration equipment include leaf filters, pressure filter, vacuum filters, and drum filters. Continuous centrifugals are used for liquid-liquid separation and also for solids-liquid separation, especially in those instances where the solids are extremely fine and might cause plugging in a filter medium.

Leaf filters utilize leaves contained in a pressure shell. The liquid is introduced into a feed inlet, distributed through the shell, and discharged at the outlet. Plate and open frame filters are of the pressure type, each plate and frame constituting one filter unit. Filtration is accomplished by the plates which are covered with the filter media. The hollow frames collect and consolidate the cake. Drum types of filter equipment can be described as cylindrical drums rotating on their own axes. The drums are placed in troughs containing the slurry to be filtered. Rotary vacuum filters are available in various forms and are used to separate solids from liquids and liquids from liquids. Centrifugal machines for separating the constituents of a material are used in a number of branches of the food industry, notably the sugar industry. De Laval's cream separator was perhaps the earliest of the centrifugal separators and the general principal remains the same, the heavy phase of a material moves along spinning discs under the influence of centrifugal force to the outside of the bowl where it is collected and retained until removed. The light phase of the liquid moves inward and is discharged through its outlet.

MARTIN S. PETERSON

Reference

SLADE, F. M. 1967. Food Processing Plant, Vol. 1. CRC Press, Cleveland.

Cross-references: *Ultrafiltration; Reverse Osmosis.*

FISH AND FISHERY PRODUCTS

Composition, Deterioration, and Nutritive Value

Most fish contain 13–22% protein (usually about 18%), 1.5–30% lipid (oil), and the balance largely water. The moisture and oil content are inversely proportional, the sum of the 2 approximating 80%. Carbohydrate, except for a very small amount of glycogen, is absent. Small, but nutritionally important, amounts of vitamins and minerals are present.

Fish proteins resemble those in mammalian muscle and contain amino acids in similar proportions. There is little difference in the type of protein from one species to another and in most species the amount is close to 18%. Fish lipids, on the other hand, are quite different from those in other foods; they vary widely both in amount and type from one species to another. All fish contain lipid bound in two ways: (1) largely as phospholipid in an intracellular form in an amount somewhat under 1% of the muscle; and (2) quantities of additional oil more loosely bound throughout the muscle or in fat depots and which may vary from almost none to amounts up to 20% of the flesh, occasionally even more. Where the principal fatty acids of animal and vegetable fats and oils ordinarily contain 2, at the most 3, double bonds per molecule, in fish oils considerable fatty acids with 5 and 6 double bonds are present, making them highly susceptible to oxidation. Unusual lipids such as alkoxydiglycerides and wax esters occur in a few species. The triglycerides of fish occur in light and dark muscle, the latter containing hemeprotein (myoglobin). The oil in the latter type tissue, because of the presence of the strongly prooxidant heme pigment, is especially vulnerable to oxidation.

Because microorganisms associated with fish are predominantly psychrophilic, bacterial decomposition occurs much more readily at relatively low temperatures (i.e., just above $32°F$) than is the case with meat from warm-blooded animals or poultry. The microorganisms during spoilage invade the fish largely from the surface. During immediate post mortem stages and while the acidity associated with *rigor mortis* is still high, growth of bacteria is slow. As the pH of the flesh rises (within a few hours or days), the microorganisms grow at an exponential pace, resulting first in conversion of trimethylamine oxide (a natural fish component) to trimethylamine, then in hydrolysis of protein to give ammonia, and, later, obnoxious sulfur-containing and other compounds resulting in complete spoilage. Modern food technology has provided means, particularly with regard to temperature control, which permits fish to be held without serious microbiological spoilage. Control of oxidation of the oil of fish leading to rancidity has not found any satisfactory solution, especially when the oil remains in the flesh of the fish.

The wide range of oil content in different species of fish provides a means of supplying protein with varying calorie contents. Thus, a serving of lean cod may contain less than $1/3$ the calories of an equivalent sized serving of an oily species such as mackerel or king salmon. The highly polyunsaturated fatty acids of fish oil have been shown to possess marked cholesterol depressant activity which, even when making up only a small part of the diet, drastically and rapidly lowers serum cholesterol. Canned fish containing softened bone, such as salmon, is an extremely rich source of calcium as well as of other important trace minerals and vitamins.

TABLE F-4

LANDINGS OF FISH BY COUNTRIES IN 1968

Rank	Country	Landings in Millions of Pounds
1	Peru	23,520
2	Japan	21,488
3	China	15,456
4	USSR	13,660
5	Norway	6,272
6	United States	5,380
7	India	3,405
8	Spain	3,360
9	Canada	3,338
10	Denmark	3,293
11	Chile	3,091
12	Indonesia	2,643
13	South Africa	2,531
14	Thailand	2,442
15	United Kingdom	2,330
16	Namumbia (SW Africa)	2,195

SOURCE: Data from FAO yearbook of fishery statistics, Rome (1968).

Geographical Pattern of Fisheries

Peru today is the leading nation in fishery landings (Table F-4) even though only a few short years ago it was not even among the 25 leading countries. Its exploitation of anchovy for fish meal and oil has caused its rapid rise in fish production and is an example of the complete change taking place in fishing distribution among nations. The ability to fish in waters far removed from the homeland by use of factory or freezer ships is another factor in changing traditional landing patterns. The United States which for many years ranked second in landings, not far behind Japan, is today sixth—behind Peru, Japan, China, USSR, and Norway. Table F-5 summarizes several features of the United States fishing industry. It must be remembered that information concerning species of fish landed in this country is not synonymous with fish consumed. Nearly 60% of the fish consumed in this country in 1969 was imported so that figures on domestic production are misleading if taken as an indication of fish consumption. Species in Table F-5 are arranged in descending order of the value of the leading species by pounds landed; however, menhaden, because it is used exclusively for industrial purposes and thus brings a very low price per pound, ranks only eighth on a value basis in spite of the fact that nearly five times as much of it is produced as that of any other species. Recent trends in the relative importance of different species in the United States are affected by the public's desire to obtain fishery products having

TABLE F-5

U.S. LANDINGS IN 1969 OF 20 LEADING SPECIES BY VALUE OF CATCH

Species[1]	Value (Millions of Dollars)	Rank by Value	Volume (Millions of Pounds)	Rank by Volume	New England	Middle Atlantic	Chesapeake	South Atlantic	Gulf of Mexico	California	Oreg. and Wash.	Alaska	Inland Waters	Record Prod. Year	Record Prod. Wt	Seine	Trawl	Lines	Gill Net	Traps	Other
Shrimp	122.9	1	317.0	3				*[2]	X[3]	+[4]	+	*		1969	317	X	X				
Salmon	54.7	2	246.0	4						*	X	X		1936	791	X			X	+	+
Tuna	54.3	3	323.0	2		+				X	*	*		1950	391	X		*		+	+
Crab	39.4	4	235.0	5	+	+	X	X	X	X	*	*		1966	33		*	*		X	X
Lobster	32.4	5	39.5	16	X	*	+							1889	31		+			X	X
Oyster	28.2	6	51.9	12	+	+	X	*	*	+	*			1908	152						X
Clam	23.9	7	75.5	10	*	X	*	+	+	+	+	+		1969	75	X					+
Menhaden	22.9	8	1548.0	1		X	X	X	X					1962	2348	X					
Flounder	16.1	9	117.5	7	X	+	+	+		*	X	+		1965	180		X				
Scallop	9.8	10	9.7	30	+	*								1961	27		X			+	
Halibut	8.5	11	33.4	17						+	X	X		1915	66		X	X			
Haddock	7.7	12	46.2	15	X	+								1929	294		X	+			
Catfish, Bullheads	7.0	13	32.9	18									X	1963	39	+		X		*	
Red Snapper	4.0	14	9.5	31				*	X					1902	23			X	+		
Cod	3.5	15	49.0	13	X	+					*			1880	294		X	X	+		
Whiting	2.7	16	46.3	14	X	+								1957	133		X		X		
Mullet	2.6	17	31.4	20				*	X					1902	43	X					
Ocean perch Atlantic	2.4	18	9.3	32	X									1951	258		X				
Scup	2.2	19	12.4	25	*	X	*	*	+					1960	49	*	X			*	
Striped bass	2.2	20	11.3	27	*	*	X	*		+				1969	11		*	+	X	*	

[1] Species of fish high in volume of landing but too low in value to be included in this table are: anchovies, ranking sixth by volume of catch; herring, eighth; alewives, ninth; and jack mackerel, eleventh.
[2] Minor, 5–25%.
[3] Major, 25% or more.
[4] Very minor, under 5%.

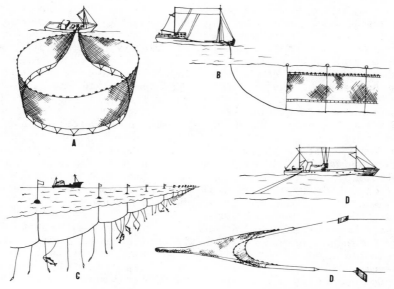

Courtesy of D. L. Alverson

FIG. F-5. FOUR METHODS OF HIGH SEA FISHING GEAR: A—PURSE SEINING; B—DRIFT OR GILL NETTING; C—LONG LINING; D—OTTER TRAWLING

high keeping qualities and presenting uniform high palatability at all times. Thus, today 6 of the 10 leading species are shellfish or crustacea, species of low oil content where maximum keeping quality is assured. Failure to develop adequate means for controlling deterioration, especially oxidation with resulting rancidity, has lead to the increased production of species like shrimp or canned tuna while species for which high quality cannot always be maintained (e.g., mackerel) have declined drastically in popularity and production. Some desired species, where production costs are much less in foreign countries, are no longer produced in quantity in this country but are imported instead.

The New England and Middle Atlantic areas have been especially hard hit from foreign competition and from changing public preference. The bottom fish industry for cod, haddock, and ocean perch has drastically declined; much of the raw material of this type used today primarily for fish stick production is being imported. More than half the value of the fish production of New England and Middle Atlantic areas now comes from shellfish with lobster, clams, and scallops being of major importance. States bordering Chesapeake Bay produce predominantly oysters and clams although considerable menhaden is also processed into meal and oil. The rapidly growing shrimp industry provides the major dollar value fishery in the South Atlantic and Gulf States with menhaden production the largest volume fishery, especially in

the Gulf States. On the Pacific Coast, the steadily increasing tuna industry is the major one in California; in Oregon, both the salmon and tuna fisheries are important; while in Washington and Alaska, the salmon fisheries predominate. King crab production is also of considerable importance in Alaska.

Gear and Vessels

Principal Methods for Catching Fish

Varieties of Nets.—(1) Those maneuvered around the fish such as purse seines. (2) Those left more or less stationary in the water including traps, gill nets, and drift nets. (3) Nets such as otter trawls which are dragged along the bottom to capture bottom dwelling fish like cod.

Hook and Line Gear.—(1) Trolling gear in which multiple pole, multiple line gear is towed through the water to catch such fish as salmon. (2) Multiple hook long line gear floated from the surface such as long lines that are used to take halibut, and pole and line gear such as that formerly widely used for taking tuna, but now becoming superseded by American fishermen in favor of use of purse seines.

Special Gear.—Special gear used especially for taking shellfish and crustaceans includes pots used for lobster and crab, dredges for oysters and scallops, and hydraulic dredges for clams in which water jets are used in front of the dredge to loosen the clams from the bottom.

Lights are frequently used with various types of gear to attract the fish. Electrical waves sent through the water have sometimes been used especially in fresh water, and in the menhaden fishery experimental work has been carried out to guide, by such electrical means, fish already in nets to pumps where they can be lifted into the vessel.

An example of how combination of modern techniques can revolutionize a fishery is the change-over from hook and line to purse seining by the American tuna industry. Prior to 1959, the preponderant tuna fishing method employed hooks and lines operated from huge tuna clippers which first caught their own live bait, then used it for a hand-operated hook and line fishery. Because of cheaper labor abroad, the cost of tuna fishing soon became of marginal efficiency in the United States so that tuna canners began importing frozen tuna loins from Japan for canning. In 1958, more than $1/3$ of the tuna canned in this country was processed from foreign-caught fish. In 1959, the American tuna fleet began converting to a purse seine operation which resulted in more rapid and efficient catching and hence shorter trips to the distant fishing grounds such as off the South American Coast. This conversion was made possible by the combination of the then relatively new power blocks and the use of nylon netting. This purse seining operation is now by far the main harvesting method used by the American tuna vessels. It not only has reversed the trend away from large-scale use of foreign-caught tuna but also, by increasing harvesting efficiency, has been an important factor in increasing tuna landings by a factor of almost 2 since the new fishing method was adopted.

In recent years there has been a considerable increase in the use of factory ships for processing fish at sea. Such ships frequently employ a fleet of smaller fishing vessels to supply them with fish. The factory ship may freeze whole or dressed fish, machine fillet and package fishery products, can fish, or even produce fish meal and oil. Use of such factory ships has had moderate success by several Western European nations, and has been used very extensively by the USSR. Efforts to introduce use of such factory ship operation into the U.S. fishing industry shortly after the end of World War II indicated that the high labor cost which had to be paid for process workers aboard ship in this country, at least at that time, made such an operation infeasible.

Handling of Fresh and Preserved Fish

Fresh fish is largely iced aboard fishing vessels in pens for preservation until it can be landed. Because of need to keep in good condition fish which are caught at great distances from the processing port, several variations may occur. Fish may be chilled in refrigerated sea water and held in it. This permits more rapid chilling; and by careful control, the fish may be held at their freezing point or about 30°F, only a few degrees colder than iced fish, yet this difference increases satisfactory holding time by several days. A recent variant is to chill and hold the fish at about 27°F, a temperature at which a small part of the water is frozen. Past theories on freezing of fish had indicated that such practice would ruin the texture of the fish flesh, yet experience has shown that such treatment is not harmful, and the several degrees lower temperature achieved can be very helpful in holding fish destined for fresh (unfrozen) markets for maximum time without spoilage.

In several fisheries, notably the U.S. tuna industry, where fish must be kept for several months before landing, brine freezing followed by dry frozen storage is employed. Tuna handled in this way is thawed or partially thawed at sea just before reaching port to facilitate unloading and to make possible immediate canning.

Icing of fish aboard the fishing vessel is the most general method of preservation, and this method is also the principal one used for transhipment in wooden boxes after the fish is landed. Use of adequate quantity of ice applied in the proper manner will make the difference between first-grade fresh fish and partially spoiled fish of marginal marketability. The proper ratio of ice to fish varies widely with such conditions as temperature, holding time, and presence or absence of insulation around the icing areas. For average conditions aboard a wooden vessel (uninsulated) in northern waters, a ratio of 1 part ice to 2 parts fish is often adequate. Eviscerated fish should be packed so that the gut and gill cavities are filled with crushed ice, and that ice surrounds the fish such that during melting, bare fish does not become exposed. Preservative ices containing such substances as benzoates or hypochlorites have been used so that the melting ice trickles a weak preservative solution over the fish to enhance keeping quality. Use of such preservative ice must be used only as an adjunct to the more important factors involving use of sufficient ice, properly applied. At best, the use of preservative ice adds only 2–3 days to storage life of commercially handled fish. Fillets are most commonly cut by hand although several successful filleting machines are available for a variety of sizes and shapes of fish. Fillets to be frozen, especially from lean, nonoily species, are often given a short dip in a weak brine solution to minimize escape of "drip" formed during freezing and subsequent processing.

Experimental work has shown that fish, especially fish fillets, can be given a greatly extended storage

Courtesy of J. W. Greer

FIG. F-6. FISH PORTIONS BEING BREADED

life by first irradiating them at about a 100,000 rad level ordinarily employing Cobalt-60 as a radiation source. Such fish are pasteurized, not sterilized by this treatment. The different flora of microorganisms present on fish are affected to differing extents by such irradiation. The surviving flora are quite different from those normally present, resulting in a quite different spoilage pattern. The storage life of most lean species of fillets can be about doubled when such radiation pasteurization treatment precedes iced storage. Such a process has not yet been cleared for use in the United States by FDA. Complete sterilization can be achieved by use of several million rad dosages, but results in objectionable off-flavor development. Most fatty fish when given low dosage irradiation rapidly develop rancidity during subsequent iced storage making this process infeasible. The radiation also bleaches pigments in the highly colored flesh of species like salmon.

Blast freezing (use of a high velocity stream of cold air) is used in most freezing of whole fish or packaged products commercially produced in the United States. Whole or gutted fish, after freezing, are given a protective coating of ice by dipping the frozen fish several times in cold water. This ice glaze is surprisingly effective in protecting the fish both against dehydration and oxidation. The glaze may be lost by sublimation, but as long as it remains intact (or is replaced before being lost), little or no moisture loss occurs from the fish, and almost no oxygen penetrates through the glaze.

Various packaging materials are available, some involving several ply of moisture vapor and oxygen resistant materials. Some can be used with either an inert gas or a vacuum within. All such materials will sooner or later permit oxygen to penetrate, resulting in oxidative rancidity and sometimes discoloration. Use of plate freezing under pressure results in much better storage life of packaged fish by squeezing out much residual air, but this freezing method is no longer much used in the United States. None of these treatments are as satisfactory for protecting fish during cold storage as an ice glaze. Sometimes fillets or especially steaks of fish are given an ice glaze before packaging, an efficient means to reduce oxidation, but such treatment results in undesirable addition of water and complicates proper net weight labeling. Highly satisfactory long-term storage life can be achieved by freezing fish in metal cans, but this method of packaging has not yet been adopted for commercial use.

Within recent years a greatly preponderant portion of frozen packaged fishery products in the United States is put up as breaded fish sticks or portions. As a source of raw material for such products, lean species such as cod are largely imported as fillets frozen in glazed block form usually of a size of 14–15 lb. The blocks are cut into strips

Courtesy of Fish Boat, H. L. Peace Publications
FIG. F-7. PEELING AND DEVEINING SHRIMP

or pieces by band or gang saws while still frozen. These are machine coated with a batter usually containing corn or wheat cereal flours and other components. Dry breading compound is then added to the surfaces of the breaded product. Some sticks or portions are packed and frozen raw to be cooked by the ultimate consumer. Most production, however, is of a cooked item in which the fish stick or other shaped piece passes through a continuous oil cooker, often about 30 ft long and

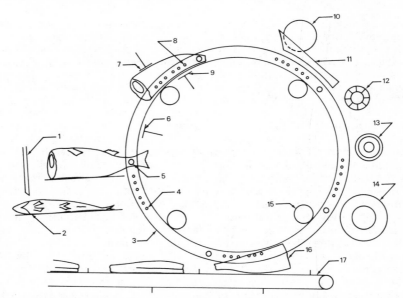

FIG. F-8. "IRON CHINK" USED FOR CLEANING SALMON FOR CANNING

1. Header knife. 2. Fish in position for heading. 3. Bull ring which carries fish through machine. 4. Back pincers. 5. Tail pincers advanced and grasping fish. 6. Tail cut-off saw. 7. Belly finning knife. 8. Back pincers advanced and grasping fish. 9. Back finning knife. 10. Belly slitting saw. 11. Guide to open belly flaps for gutting reel. 12. Gutting reel to remove viscera. 13. Knife and reel to slit kidney membrane and to remove kidney. 14. Brush to remove blood and membranes. 15. Roller to support bull ring. 16. Fish released as back and tail pincers retract. 17. Conveyor to remove butchered fish.

Courtesy of Starkist Foods, Inc., subsidiary of H. J. Heinz Co.
FIG. F-9. CLEANING PRECOOKED LOINS PRIOR TO CANNING

4 ft wide and containing about 250 gal. of hydrogenated fat or liquid vegetable oil held at about 400°F. The product is air cooled to 90°F before packaging and freezing. In 1969, 360 million pounds of such product was produced in the United States.

Shellfish and crustaceans are handled very differently from fin fishes. Because of great susceptibility to spoilage, such species are often kept alive during a part of their commercial handling. Oysters and clams should be alive until shucked and crab and lobster until cooked. A considerable portion of the U.S. shrimp is beheaded (usually at sea), washed and graded ashore, and packaged and frozen in the shell usually in institution-sized packages. For the ultimate consumer's use, shrimp is peeled and deveined often by machine, and then packaged and frozen. A considerable portion (104 million pounds in 1969) is breaded after peeling and then packaged and frozen. Crab are cooked in the shell and the meat picked by hand. Some-

times, especially in the Chesapeake Bay area, the picked meat is pasteurized by raising the temperature of the meat to 170°F for 1 min, thereby greatly extending the storage life of the refrigerated (unfrozen) product. Much of both the East Coast blue crab and of the Pacific Coast dungeness crab is marketed unfrozen, but a considerable portion of the more recently developed Alaskan king crab is sold as a frozen product. The crab is cooked in the shell and the meat removed from the shell by passing through rubber rollers. The meat is then usually frozen in large blocks which are iced glazed and later sawed into consumer sized units. Some king crab is cut in sections and frozen in the shell.

Very few major changes have been made in the technology of canned fish in the past 4–5 decades. Canned salmon processing represents the least complex type of operation in which the fish are merely cleaned (an intricate butchering machine, the "iron chink," is used to remove head, fins, and viscera), cut into can-sized pieces, and filled into

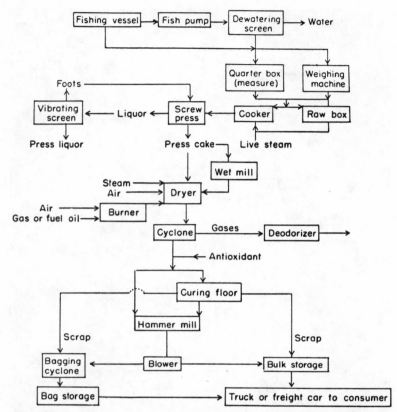

FIG. F-10. FLOW DIAGRAM OF PRODUCTION OF FISH MEAL BY THE
WET-RENDERING PROCESS

cans. Salt and sometimes salmon oil are added, and the cans are then seamed and retorted.

Tuna represents a more complex operation in which the fish are first precooked to facilitate separation of meat to be canned. The light, skin-free loins are separated by hand from dark meat and introduced into the filling machine. For solid packs, a relatively simple machine, replacing former hand-packing, molds the loins into an endless cylinder which is chopped into can-sized pieces. Vegetable oil, salt, and sometimes other substances are added before seaming and processing.

Sardines, actually usually small herring, are generally machine eviscerated, generally cooked by steaming, baking, or frying—sometimes also smoked—and put into cans with salt and occasionally with added sauce such as tomato or mustard, and then seamed and retorted.

Crustaceans are almost always given a precook and sometimes an acidification, brining, blanching, or some combination thereof.

Vacuum, always required in canned seafood, is usually obtained by vacuum closing machines but in some cases the older exhaust box or the steam-vac closing methods are employed. Heat processing times and temperatures necessary for sterilization have been worked out for all the various fishery products and are carefully applied often with state inspection to ensure invariable compliance.

Fish are cured by salting, smoking, or pickling processes devised before the more modern techniques such as freezing or canning had been developed. Cured fish production has drastically declined in countries such as the United States (annual production about 25 million pounds of smoked, and 20 million pounds each of salted and pickled fish). Some lesser developed countries still produce sizable quantities of salt fish. Although most salt fish has almost indefinite keeping quality at room temperature, the modern types of smoked fish are often so mildly smoked and so little salted and dried as to be almost as perishable as fresh fish, and sometimes they have presented a botulism hazard. In the United States, drastic pasteurizing treatment which considerably alters texture has been imposed recently on some hot-smoked products. In some cases, use of nitrite as a preservative has been permitted to allow lower pasteurizing temperatures.

Fish Protein Concentrate (FPC), formerly called fish flour is a form of edible, relatively moisture- and oil-free fish consisting mostly of protein with a little ash and moisture, and usually only a few tenths percent oil. It is generally prepared by a solvent extraction process using, most frequently, isopropanol to extract both moisture and oil. A similar product was made in Norway from cod with very limited use about 1870 and another, made from salmon, had been produced by solvent extraction in the United States as early as 1900, but no markets were then available and commercial production never was initiated. Because of recent urgent need for a product for supplementing the protein in a number of undeveloped countries, much research was carried out on further refinements in production methods for FPC in the 1960's, and its use has been attempted in several areas. It has the advantage of high nutritive value equivalent to that of the best animal protein in a form which can be kept for long periods of time without refrigeration. The principal difficulty toward its large-scale use has been consumer resistance to use of such an unfamiliar product.

Fishery Industrial Products

Tremendous quantities of whole fish go into the production of fish meal, used largely as a poultry feed supplement, and fish oil, used both for margarine and shortening after hydrogenation, and for numerous industrial applications. Nearly all of Peru's annual twenty-odd billion pounds of anchovy, much herring throughout the world, and 1–2 billion pounds per year of menhaden in the United States are used in this way. Considerable quantities of trimmings from cannery or fish fillet operations also go into fish meal and oil production. The method most generally used for this production is known as the wet reduction process. It consists of cooking the fish with steam, pressing the cooked fish, centrifuging the press fluid into crude oil and "stickwater," and drying the press cake by use of steam or flame rotary dryers. The stickwater contains dissolved protein and vitamins and is often concentrated in multiple effect vacuum evaporators either to be used as condensed fish solubles of about 50% solids content for animal or poultry feed, or to be added back to the meal as it is being dried to produce what is termed as "full meal." The oil is freed of moisture and suspended protein particles by high speed centrifuging. The wet process production requires huge quantities of raw material and is a continuous process. Smaller quantities may be processed by the dry, batch process in which the fish is cooked and dried as a single operation in a vacuum rotary, steam-jacketed dryer, and then the oil is pressed out. Solvent extraction using azeotropic solvent to remove both oil and water (such as in the Viobin process which employes a chlorinated hydrocarbon as solvent) has had limited application. At least 95% of fish meal and oil production, however, uses the wet process.

Frozen whole fish or fish waste is often used as animal feed especially for feeding fur-bearing animals. Oyster and clam shells are ground for use as grits in poultry feed. Fish are used for a wide variety of industrial purposes such as the making from fish scales of "pearl essence," a guanine crystalline material which by reflecting the light gives a pearlescent appearance and can be applied to give a decorative appearance to countless objects; fish glue and isinglass, the latter a filter aid for wine clarification are made from fish skins; leather for decorative purposes is made from fish, particularly shark skins; and buttons are made from clam shells.

MAURICE E. STANSBY

References

BORGSTROM, G. (Editor) 1961–1965. Fish as Food, Vol. 1, 2, 3, and 4. Academic Press, New York.

BRODY, J. 1965. Fishery By-Products Technology. Avi Publishing Co., Westport, Conn.

STANSBY, M. E. 1963. Industry Fishery Technology. Reinhold Publishing Corp., New York.

TRESSLER, D. K., and LEMON, J. M. 1951. Marine Products of Commerce, 2nd Edition. Reinhold Publishing Corp., New York.

Cross-reference: *Cod, Atlantic.*

FLAVORINGS AND ESSENCES

The importance of flavor in determining the acceptability of what we eat and drink is established beyond dispute. The mere ingestion of the correct balance of proteins, carbohydrates, fats, salts, and vitamins, if not adequately flavorful, does not for long satisfy the human appetite, for food has both a social and a nutritional function in which flavor plays a major part. The components of our diet may be classified into one of two main categories: (A) Items which are highly nutritious but lacking in intrinsic flavor until cooked (e.g., meat, fish, cereals, etc.). (B) Items which have little or no nutritional value but possess strong flavoring properties (e.g., aromatic fruits, vegetables, herbs, and spices).

The culinary art is aimed at blending these components into a dish which is at once attractive to the eye and appetizing to the palate.

Added Flavorings

Two basic flavoring additives are widely used—salt and sugar. If these are used correctly, as appropriate, each can enhance the other complementary flavors present. Food may be divided into one of two categories: it is either sweet or savory, the nature of the product being determined largely by the main food components present. Sweet foods are usually flavored by the addition of sugar together with fruit juices or fruit-flavored essences. In savory goods the most important flavoring materials, after salt, are the culinary herbs and spices.

Flavorings are added to food and beverage products for several reasons: (a) to give flavor to a flavorless base (e.g., strawberry in jelly, peppermint in fondant cream, etc.); (b) to impart a different flavor character to the basic product (e.g., fruit flavors in yoghurt); (c) to boost intrinsic flavors which would otherwise be too weak (e.g., mushroom flavor in mushroom soup); and (d) to disguise objectionable intrinsic flavors (e.g., flavors to cover the unpleasant taste of carboxymethyl cellulose in dietetic products).

Generalization in the use of flavorings is of little value for usage is determined by the nature of the product, the manufacturing process, the anticipated shelf-life of the product, and the demands of the consumer.

Nature of Flavorings

Flavorings may be entirely natural in composition, or they may be a blend of natural extractives with synthetic components, or they may be composed entirely of synthetic chemicals dissolved in a suitable solvent or carried on an appropriate dry base. Liquid products of natural origin are normally called essences (e.g., essence of vanilla), whereas fortified or entirely synthetic products are called flavors (e.g., vanilla flavor). Whatever their nature, the aim of the flavorist is to provide in the end-product a flavor having a high level of acceptability. Food flavorings, irrespective of their actual composition, are available as pastes, liquids, or dry powders which, in turn, may be simple dispersions or encapsulated—the choice of which to use depending upon the nature of the end-product into which it is to be incorporated.

Any flavoring must be quite harmless in use; it must fit the end-product both technically and aesthetically; it must comply with any legislative requirements prevailing in the country in which the end-product is to be sold; it must be convenient to handle; it must be stable before, during, and after incorporation into the product; it must resist adverse storage conditions; and it must be economical in use.

Natural versus Synthetic

Many factors have to be considered in deciding whether to use a natural flavor or one based wholly, or in part, upon synthetic chemicals. Although widely acceptable under current legislation, natural flavorings, particularly those based on fruits, do have several marked disadvantages: (a) they are, in many cases, very costly to use due to their relatively low flavor intensity; (b) even when concentrated, the amount necessary to give a desirable flavor level is high and may pose insuperable manufacturing difficulties, often resulting in the product having an unacceptable texture or shortened shelf-life; (c) most natural flavors exhibit marked variation in both flavor strength and character although, in the case of herbs and spices, further processing can result in products having standardized flavoring effect; (d) increasingly, the supply of natural flavoring materials is falling short of demand, and, hence, a pattern of increasing costs; (e) many natural flavors, although highly acceptable when raw, change their aromatic character when processed, particularly when heat is involved; (f) natural flavors may continue to change as they mature, and, hence, may give rise to an unacceptable flavor in the end-product during storage or may result in off-odors and off-flavors; and (g) the toxicity of many widely-accepted natural flavorings has yet to be studied.

Flavors based on synthetic chemicals are being increasingly used but these, too, have certain disadvantages: (a) the original natural flavor is often, but not always, more acceptable; (b) the synthetic flavor may pose difficulties in labeling and, in any event, must comply with current legislation; (c) synthetic flavorings are composed of powerful aromatic chemicals which must be dissolved or dispersed in a suitable solvent or carrier which may, again, pose problems of legality. On the other hand, the synthetic flavors have many advantages: (a) much cheaper than the equivalent natural product and are less sensitive to price changes; (b) stable and have a long shelf-life; (c) designed to withstand severe processing conditions; (d) highly concentrated; (e) may be produced in different forms, tailor-made to suit specific processes or products; (f) of unlimited availability, independent of seasons, shipping delays, etc; and (g) consistent in quality and flavoring effect. In addition, synthetic flavorings can be designed to achieve any desired flavor effect in the end-product. This flexibility leads to an ability to create product distinctiveness.

Materials Used in Flavorings

Flavorings are composed of highly aromatic materials specifically selected to contribute some particular nuance to the overall blend. The raw materials available to the creative flavorist may be classified as: (A) Naturally-occurring herbs, spices, vanilla, aromatic vegetables, and fruits. (B) Prepared directly from natural sources by processes such as extraction, distillation, expression, etc., which include essential oils, oleoresins, extracts, fruit juices. (C) Isolates prepared from naturally-occurring substances, e.g., eugenol from clove leaf oil. (D) Synthetics prepared from isolates or from natural raw materials such as vanillin. (E) Synthetics identical with those known to exist in nature, e.g., allyl isothiocynate in mustard oil. (F) Synthetics having no natural counterparts, e.g., gamma undecalactone. (G) Natural flavor potentiators such as monosodium glutamate, ribonucleotides. (H) Inorganic salts.

Natural Flavorings

The herbs and spices, either whole or, more usually, ground, have been used in the seasoning of foods since time immemorial. Herbs are generally classified as soft-stemmed plants, the whole herbaceous tops of which are gathered and may be used either fresh or dried. In the latter case, they are usually rubbed or screened to remove the harder stem portions which lack flavor. The herbs have only low volatile oil content and are derived from the temperate regions of the world.

The spices are all the other dried aromatic vegetable products used in food seasonings. They are usually of tropical or semitropical origin and include: barks (cinnamon), roots or rhizomes (ginger), flower buds (clove), fruits and seeds (pepper, cardamom). In most cases, spices are very aromatic and may contain large percentages of essential oil from which they derive their main flavoring character. In certain pungent spices (capsicum, pepper, ginger), the nonvolatile components are of greater importance to the flavoring effect.

The use of herbs and spices in food processing is well documented. They are classified as shown below.

Culinary Herbs

Group 1: herbs containing cineol (eucalyptol)
Bay, Bay Laurel or Sweet Bay (*Laurus nobilis*)
Rosemary (*Rosmarinus officinalis*)
Spanish Sage (*Salvia lavandulaefolia*)
Group 2: herbs containing eugenol
West Indian Bay (*Pimenta acris*)
Group 3: herbs containing thymol or carvacrol
Thyme (*Thymus vulgaris*)
Wild Marjoram (*Origanum majorana*)
Origanum (*Origanum vulgare*)
Mexican Sage (*Origanum vulgare*)
Sweet Savory (*Saturea hortensis*)
Group 4: herbs which are characteristically sweet
Basil (*Ocimum basilicum*)
Sweet Marjoram (*Majorana sativum*)
Parsley Herb (*Petrosilinum sativum*)
English Sage (*Salvia officinalis*)
Tarragon or Estragon (*Artemisia dracunculus*)
Group 5: herbs containing thujone
Dalmatian Sage (*Salvia officinalis*)
Group 6: the mints
Applemint (*Mentha rotundifolia*)
Corn mint (*Mentha arvensis*)
Garden mint (*Mentha sps*)
Peppermint (*Mentha piperita*)
Spearmint (*Mentha spicata* or *M. viridis*)

Spices

Group 1: the pungent spices
Capsicum, Chillies, Red Pepper, Tobasco (*Capsicum annuum* and sps)
Black and White Pepper (*Piper nigrum*)
Mustard (*Brassica nigra* and other sps)
Ginger (*Zingiber officinale*)
Horseradish (*Cochlearia armoracia*)
Group 2: the aromatic fruits and seeds
Nutmeg and Mace (*Mynstica fragrans*)
Cardamom (*Elettaria cardamomum*)
Fenugreek (*Trigonella foenum-graecum*)
Group 3: the umbelliferous fruits
Anise (*Pimpinella anisum*)
Caraway (*Carum carvi*)
Celery (*Apium graveolens*)
Coriander (*Coriandrum sativum*)
Cumin (*Cuminum vulgare*)
Dill (*Anethum graveolens*)
Fennel (*Foeniculum vulgare*)
Parsley (*Petroselinum sativum*)
Group 4: the aromatic barks
Cinnamon (*Cinnamomum zeylanicum*)
Cassia (*C. cassia* and other sps)
Group 5: the phenolic spices
Clove Buds (*Eugenia caryophylata*)
Cinnamon Leaves (*Cinnamomum zeylanicum*)
Pimento or Allspice (*Pimenta dioica*)
Group 6: the colored spices
Paprika (*Capsicum annuum*)
Saffron (*Crocus sativus*)
False Saffron (*Carmathus tinctorius*)
Turmeric (*Curcuma longa*)

Flavorings Prepared from Natural Raw Materials

With the exception of ground herbs and spices, few natural flavoring materials can be used directly in food processing, due to their comparatively low flavor intensity. For this reason, numerous processes have been devised to separate out the flavoring from the nonflavoring components. The resulting products include: (a) essential (or volatile) oils; (b) alcoholic tinctures and extracts; (c) oleoresins; (d) absolutes; (e) fruit pastes; (f) fruit juices and concentrates; and (g) distillates. Of these, the following are worthy of additional comment.

Essential Oils.—An essential (or volatile) oil is the mixture of organic compounds derived by some physical process, usually steam or water distillation, from odorous plant materials. A specific oil is derived from one botanical source with which it agrees in both name and odor. Essential oils are found in varying amounts in different parts of plants. They generally constitute the odorous principles by which the material is recognized, the amount present being an index of the flavoring strength. The quality, composition and, hence, flavoring characters of an essential oil vary not only with the type of plant but also, in particular, with the conditions prevailing during its growth, harvest, and postharvest treatment.

The essential oils are specified by the Essential Oil Association of the U.S.A. (EOA) and are fully treated in standard works.

Essential oils may be further processed to give concentrated, terpeneless and sesquiterpeneless oils which have specific uses in flavorings. They have the advantages of increased solubility and stability, resulting from the removal of terpenes which are low in flavor character, less soluble, and more subject to oxidation.

Extracts.—Extracts are obtained from comminuted plant material by maceration or percolation with a solvent, usually ethanol. The solution of flavoring constituents may be used directly (tincture) or be subsequently concentrated by wholly or partially removing the solvent under vacuum. Great care is necessary to ensure the minimum of damage to heat-labile flavor components.

Oleoresins.—Oleoresins are prepared from comminuted herbs and spices by extraction with a suitable solvent which may be either polar (acetone, methanol), nonpolar (hexane), or chlorinated (methylene dichloride). The solvent used in the extraction is completely removed from the product by distillation under vacuum, special treatment being required to attain the very low levels set by U.S. regulations. The nature of the oleoresins depends upon the solvent used.

These products are difficult to handle directly in food flavors and they are usually diluted to an acceptable level as (a) emulsions, or (b) dispersed onto a dry edible character, or (c) encapsulated in gelatin or an edible gum.

Fruit Products.—For use as flavorings it is necessary to process fruit to separate the juice from the nonflavorful cellular pulp. Such juices must be preserved and are usually held in cold storage to ensure retention of their fresh character. In general, single-strength juices are weak in flavoring and can only be used in products which do not involve high processing temperatures or where large volumes of liquor can be tolerated. The following concentrated products are available to the flavorist: (a) concentrated juices, usually 60°–70° Brix, suitably preserved; (b) depectinized juices; (c) fortified juices based on (i) with not more than 5% of added bouquet which consists mainly of natural aromatics. In the United States, reinforced products called WONF flavorings are available. These consist of not less than 51% extract of the named fruit and up to 49% of flavoring from other natural sources.

Fruit Powder—Spray-Dried Juice.—The manufacturer's literature should be consulted for details of concentration, preservatives, and relative usage rates of these products.

Synthetics

Synthetics used in flavorings may either be identical with those found in nature or they may not yet have been identified as naturally occurring but, nevertheless, have valuable flavoring characteristics. They represent the whole spectrum of organic chemistry and any classification is impracticable. The extent of the materials available can be judged by consulting the literature specific to this subject.

The Blending of Flavorings and Seasonings

The blending of materials to create an acceptable flavoring is a highly skilled process, based on the long, practical experience of the flavorist in handling these products. The proper blending of such physically dissimilar components as fruit juices, tinctures, extracts, essential oils, aromatic chemicals, and solvents demands a high level of technical proficiency both in the selection of the individual components and in the establishment of the optimum conditions of usage. The aim of the flavorist is to produce a flavor which will contribute a high level of acceptability to the end-product. Often, the use of the most appropriate constituents is far from straightforward. Not least of the problems encountered is the need for complaince with the ever-increasing load of restrictive legislation governing the use of synthetics in food flavorings which differs between countries. To the flavorist, these restrictions are at times inhibiting and frequently prevent the attainment of the best flavoring effect. To achieve the desired flavoring effect, the flavorist—using his imagination and experience—may select any combination of ingredients having simple or complex quality attributes, so long as the ultimate blend is balanced, having an acceptable top-note which gives an odor identity, a rounded "body" carrying the main flavor characteristics smoothly blended so that no one note predominates unless specifically required, an acceptable "after-taste," all in an appropriate solvent. Many flavors require a period of maturation before they can be used in food processing.

There are few occasions when only one herb or spice is sufficient to achieve the desired flavor in a product and, hence, it is necessary to create blends or seasonings. Being natural products, the herbs and spices display wide variations in both flavor strength and quality so that the creation of seasonings is not so predictable as that of blending aromatic chemicals. Seasonings are designed to enhance the natural flavors present, modifying them as little as necessary, but certainly not swamping them. In a seasoning, the various aromas and flavors contributed by the individual spices used, together with those of the basic food constituents, will all intermingle to give one overall impression in which no one constituent should predominate. In this respect it is necessary to realize that spices do not all have the same flavoring power. Some are excessively strong and override other flavors readily; others are weak and just as easily suppressed. The preparation of a well-balanced seasoning, therefore, requires considerable skill.

Solvents

In the creation of liquid flavorings, the component aromatic chemicals are far too powerful for use and, in addition, exist in various forms ranging from light fluids to crystalline solids. It is necessary, therefore, to use appropriate solvents to (a) dilute the flavorings down to an acceptable level for use, and (b) act as a blender for the component chemicals. The nature of the solvent will be determined by cost, toxicity, volatility, solvent power, intrinsic flavor or mouth effects, potential chemical reactivity, and viscosity. In addition, the solvent selected must be legally acceptable in the country in which the product is to be sold. The solvents most commonly used include water, ethanol, glycerol, diacetin, triacetin, isopropyl alcohol, and propylene glycol.

H. B. HEATH

References

ARCTANDER, S.   1960.   Flavor Materials of Natural Origin. Published by author, Elizabeth, N.J.

ARCTANDER, S.   1969.   Perfume and Flavor Chemicals, Vol. 1 and 2. Published by author, Montclair, N.J.

BINSTED, R., and DEWEY, J. D.   1970.   Soup Manufacture, 3rd Edition. Food Trade Press, London, England.

BINSTED, R. and DEWEY, J. D.   1971.   Pickle and Sauce Making, 3rd Edition. Food Trade Press, London, England.

ESSENTIAL OIL ASSOC. OF THE U.S.A. 1967. E.O.A. Specifications and Standards. Essential Oil Assoc. U.S.A., New York.

FURIA, T. E., and BELLANCA, N. (Editors) 1971.   CRC Fernaroli's Handbook of Flavor Ingredients, International Edition.   Chemical Rubber Co., Cleveland.

GUENTHER, E. 1948. The Essential Oils. Van Nostrand Reinhold Co., New York.

HEATH, H. B. 1964. Standardized spices. *In* Proc. Intern. Food Ind. Congr., London, England.

HEID, J. L., and JOSLYN, M. A. 1963. Food Processing Operations, Vol. 2. Avi Publishing Co., Westport, Conn.

JACOBS, M. B. 1947. Synthetic Food Adjuncts. Van Nostrand Reinhold Co., New York.

MERORY, J. 1968. Food Flavorings, Composition, Manufacture, and Use, 2nd Edition. Avi Publishing Co., Westport, Conn.

PARRY, J. W. 1969. The story of spices. *In* Spices, Vol. 1. Food Trade Press, London, England.

PARRY, J. W. 1969. Morphology, histology, chemistry. *In* Spices, Vol. 2, 2nd Edition. Food Trade Press, London, England.

PENDLETON, G. 1970. Solvents used in the flavor industry. Flavor Ind. *1*, No. 4, 220–222.

Cross-references: *Spices; Vanilla Extract and Synthetic Vanillin; Worcestershire Sauce.*

FLOCCULATION

Flocculation is the process of agglomerating the dispersed solids in a liquid phase to facilitate separation by sedimentation, filtration, flotation, or centrifugation. The process is dependent upon the use of chemicals that promote flocculating action, ranging from soluble neutral salts (e.g., certain chlorides and sulfates) and precipitating salts (lime, aluminum and iron sulfates, and chlorides) to organic polymers (polyelectrolytes) of high molecular weight. The flocculating mechanism depends on physical and chemical factors involving either neutralization of particle charges causing interparticle repulsive forces, a physical entrapment by a precipitating floc, chemical bridging by means of long chain polymer, or some combination of these.

Flocculation plays a significant role in the liquid/ solids separation process. Without this agglomerating step, the basic separation processes (sedimentation, filtration, etc.) in many instances would be either too inefficient or impractical. This is primarily due to the adverse effect of fine particles, especially colloids where particle sizes are less than 1 μ. Surface charges on these particles often result in a repelling force that prevents agglomeration; without agglomeration, free settling of individual colloids is so slow as to be impractical. As a result, the performance of sedimentation equipment is adversely affected. Likewise in filtration operations, fine particles greatly reduce cake permeability and may lead to premature media blinding. With proper flocculation, filtration rates may be increased many-fold, often quite dramatically.

In the food industry, flocculation has significance in certain types of processing (such as beet and cane juice clarification) as well as for treatment of water before use in various products such as carbonated beverages, fruit drinks, beer, etc., where undesirable characteristics (such as alkalinity, taste, odor, and suspended matter) must be eliminated. With the increasing emphasis on waste treatment, flocculation can play an important role for the food industry. It is often an essential step in the waste treatment process that must provide for effective removal of color, suspended solids, and organic matter.

Suspended Solids Systems

Raw water, wastes or plant process streams represent the various suspended solids systems where flocculation generally is one of the key steps in the preconditioning of the solids to facilitate liquid/solids separation by conventional means (sedimentation, filtration, etc.). The liquid/solids system may be either a simple or complex inorganic-organic mixture with various chemical and biological components. Thus, the flocculation step may be complicated by the presence of various inorganic salts, soluble organic matter, or emulsified organics due to their hindering effect on the process. The various chemical and physical properties of the liquid/solids system such as pH, alkalinity, colloid stability, particle size distribution, particle hydration, etc., have an important bearing on the response to specific types of flocculents. To achieve adequate flocculation, it is usually necessary to determine experimentally what particular conditions (such as pH adjustment, coagulant addition, increased alkalinity, type of coagulant, coagulant dosage, etc.) are necessary for the desired results. Thus, each liquid/solids system more than likely presents a particular problem whether the application applies to industrial processing use, water quality up-grading, or pollution abatement.

Suspended Solids Characteristics

Suspended solids in raw water, wastes, or plant process streams cover a range of particle sizes from a fraction of a micron to several hundred or more. Particles 1 μ or less in diameter are generally classified as colloidal; those from 1 to 100 μ sometimes as supra-colloidal; and those over 100 microns as coarse. Since the latter settle quite rapidly, it is only the colloidal and supracolloidal particles that flocculation may substantially benefit insofar as subsequent liquid/solids separation processes are concerned.

Theory

Flocculation is the process of attaining a cluster of particles, referred to as a floc, from the suspended solids dispersed in the liquid. It is thus a process of agglomeration resulting in irregular clumps with the particles either tightly or loosely bound. Flocculation is also referred to as coagulation though some authorities (La Mer 1964; La Mer and Healey 1966) insist that a sharp distinction should apply. Others use the terms interchangeably to describe the process. La Mer on the other hand states that coagulation is appropriate only when related to neutralizing the repulsive forces stemming from colloidal particle charges and the subsequent agglomeration due to interionic attractions. Gregory (1969), however, points out that such a differentiation cannot be made in practice when polyelectrolytes are involved as both charge neutralization and chemical bridging occur almost simultaneously. Even the agglomerating mechanism of the common alum floc appears to involve both charge neutralization and a chemical bridging by positively charged microflocs (Black 1948).

It is questionable that any rigid distinction is likely to be accepted. Both terms undoubtedly will continue to be used interchangeably. A more practical way of distinguishing between two major categories of flocculation and avoiding the difficulty of applying a term to one specific mechanism (charge neutralization and particle cohesion) is to use the terms "microfloc" and "macrofloc" as proposed by Butler (1969) and Black (1948). The former term is proposed to apply to flocs formed from colloidal particles (1 μ or less) in the primary flocculent stage. Macroflocs then form the floc-building process when the preformed colloid aggregate (microflocs) combine to form large agglomerates that settle rapidly. In this discussion, the term coagulant when used will be considered to have the same meaning as flocculent.

Since flocculation embraces more than a single phenomenon, theoretical studies have been concerned with the specific mechanisms as well as the overall process. One of the significant earlier contributions was that by Smoluchowski (1917) in 1917 who published a mathematical theory applying to the coagulation kinetics of colloids. He presented kinetic equations to describe the rate of change in total particle concentration after the repulsive forces between similarly charged particles were reduced sufficiently so interparticle collisions could occur. In recent years, Swift and Friedlander (1964) experimentally verified his first and second order equations that related to shear and Brownian motion controlled flocculation although the rate constants were considerably less than predicted by Smoluchowski's theory. Higuchi et al. (1963, 1965) also studied the kinetics of aggregation and suspensions about the same time and reported similar results (low rate constants). Many others (such as La Mer and co-workers) have studied the major flocculation reactions as well as the fundamentals involving charge (Zeta potential) and chemical bridging as occurs with polyelectrolytes.

Colloidal Stability

Particles in the colloidal size range (1 μ and below) usually do not settle but remain dispersed in the aqueous media. This colloidal stability is attributed to hydration and surface charges, either positive or negative. Particles having an affinity for water (lyophilic) and with unshared or resonating electrons at the surface will adsorb oppositely oriented water dipoles (hydration). By the preferential adsorption of ions in a concentration gradient, an electrostatic potential gradient is established. In somewhat similar fashion, a lyophobic particle with an existing surface charge will likewise result in a concentration gradient of oppositely charged ions with a corresponding electrostatic potential. This is commonly referred to as the electric double layer—a characteristic of colloidal particles that accounts for their stability due to the repulsive forces from like charges (positive or negative).

Zeta Potential

The potential gradient across the diffuse double layer (called the Gouy-Chapman layer) is known as the Zeta potential—a measure of the extent of

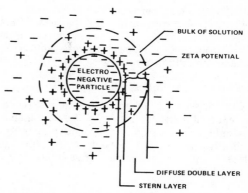

FIG. F-11. CONCEPT OF ZETA POTENTIAL

the repelling force and, hence, the stability of the colloidal system. This diffuse layer extends beyond the rigid compact double layer of ions attached to the particle surface, known as the Stern layer as illustrated in Fig. F-11. Due to Brownian motion and induced velocity gradients, the Stern layer cannot establish electroneutrality within itself. The fluid motion diffuses the counterions out into the bulk of the solution and this establishes electroneutrality at some distance from the particle surface (Hunter and Henkelekian 1961).

The actual potential depends on the surface charge density and the thickness of the double layer. The nature and extent of the charge can be determined by imposing a direct current

TABLE F-6

RELATIONSHIP OF PRACTICAL COLLOID STABILITY TO ZETA POTENTIAL

Stability Characteristics	Avg ZP in Millivolts
Maximum agglomeration and precipitation	+3 to zero
Excellent agglomeration and precipitation	−1 to −4
Fair agglomeration and precipitation	−5 to −10
Threshold of agglomeration (agglomerates of 2–10 colloids)	−11 to −20
Plateau of slight stability (few agglomerates)	−21 to −30
Moderate stability (no agglomerates)	−31 to −40
Good stability	−41 to −50
Very good stability	−51 to −60
Excellent stability	−61 to −80
Maximum stability	−81 to −100

potential gradient between two electrodes in the suspension and measuring the particle velocity toward the electrode of opposite sign (the process of electrophoresis). Electrophoretic apparatus is available for laboratory use.

Zeta Potential vs Colloid Stability

With increasing Zeta potential, the resistance of the charged particles to agglomeration increases as would be expected. The relative stability in qualitative terms with respect to Zeta potential values is shown in Table F-6 as classified by Butler (1969).

Flocculation Process

Flocculation may be considered to basically comprise three steps: (1) Charge neutralization of colloids (reducing Zeta potential close to zero). (2) Agglomeration of neutral colloids to form microflocs. (3) Agglomeration of microflocs into large macroflocs with good settling and/or filtration characteristics. The latter cannot always be realized practically due to the collapse of the microflocs, the resulting consolidation substantially reducing permeability.

Flocculation Mechanisms

To achieve flocculation, the first step is to remove the one primary resistance to agglomeration—particle surface charge. This is effected by neutralizing the Zeta potential, accomplished in any one of several ways: (1) Adjusting pH to the isoelectric point. (2) Addition of neutral electrolytes (salts). (3) Addition of oppositely charged colloids (mutual coagulation). (4) Addition of inorganic flocculents (alum, ferrous or ferric salts, sodium aluminate). (5) Addition of an organic flocculent (polyelectrolytes—natural or synthetic).

Since the ions responsible for the charge on colloidal particles are often hydroxyl (OH^-) or hydrogen (H^+), changes in the pH can reduce the Zeta potential. The zero value is referred to as the isoelectric point. Other ions represented by the neutral electrolyte salts (Na^+, Al^+, Cl^-, SO_4^-, Ca^+, etc.) in similar fashion can reduce the Zeta potential. Valence is of particular importance. According to Shulze-Hardy (1952), divalent ions are roughly 10 times as effective as monovalent ions and trivalent ions are 1000 times more effective when applied to hydrophobic sols. While applicable to hydrophobic sols, the lyotropic series (Cs^+, Rb^+, NH_4^+, K^+, Na^+, and Li^+; F^-, IO_3^-, $H_2PO_4^-$, BrO_3^-, Cl^-, ClO_3^-, Br^-, NO_3^-, ClO_4^-, I^-, CNS^- in order of their decreasing flocculating effect according to Priesing) (1962), also play a lesser understood part.

The addition of another colloid of opposite charge can also result in coagulation. In addition, certain amphoteric materials such as clay or protein (having a negative Zeta potential) can reduce the Zeta potential of the colloid system. On the other hand, mutual coagulation can occur with the interaction between certain hydrophobic sols and hydrophilic sols (such as polymers) forming a new colloid floc particle having greater stability. Instead of flocculation, the process is one of stabilization (Priesing 1962).

With the neutralization of the Zeta potential, the particles come under the influence of the van der Waal-London forces. Agglomeration occurs as the individual particles come into close contact (the attractive force varying as the sixth power of the distance between particles). This is often referred to as microfloc formation. With continuing agglomeration, floc buildup (macrofloc formation) takes place, resulting in larger, more settleable flocs.

Agglomeration may be facilitated by the proper mixing action to promote particle contact and floc-building. On the other hand, too much shear will tend to disperse flocs already formed. In such cases, they may not reform so the flocculating mixing action is critical.

With the inorganic and organic flocculents, other mechanisms are involved aside from charge neutralization as will be discussed later on. In the case of polyelectrolytes, the basic flocculation steps (charge neutralization, floc formation, and building) occur instantaneously under the proper conditions.

Inorganic flocculents such as alum and ferric chloride provide ions of high charge capacity for neutralizing negatively charged colloids (characteristic of most of the natural occurring colloids). At the same time, these coagulants react with the alkalinity when present to form hydrate flocs that serve to physically enmesh the colloidal and larger particles to form larger flocs. Lime hydrate also has flocculating ability and is commonly used in a number of ways either alone or in conjunction with alum or ferric salts. In water treatment, lime reacts with carbonate hardness to form a calcium carbonate precipitate as part of the water softening process. The calcium carbonate, in turn, is flocculated with alum and sometimes other flocculent-assisting materials such as sodium aluminate, activated silica, bentonite, etc.

Organic flocculents (known as polyelectrolytes) are natural or synthetic polymers of high molecular weight and are extensively employed in many flocculating applications. They may be cationic, anionic, or nonionic. Thus, the appropriately selected polymer can provide the desired charge neutralization and, at the same time, produce a large floc by reason of the unique capacity of the single long chain polymer to be adsorbed on many particle surfaces almost instantaneously.

Polyelectrolyte Flocculents

Polyelectrolytes are organic polymers (either natural or synthetic) that exhibit exceptional flocculating power on a unit weight basis. Due to their unique floc forming and floc building capabilities, they are widely used in many applications in the chemical process industries when their superior performance and/or the better economics over other flocculents are demonstrated.

Such polymers are of high molecular weight, characterized by a long chain with many active sites for adsorption on particle surfaces. They are classified as either cationic, anionic, or non-ionic though the latter become negative in solution. Molecular weights are on the order of several million, usually 1–15 although precise methods for molecular weight determination are yet to be developed. The chain length may reach into colloidal ranges (20–300 angstroms).

In solution, the polymer assumes a random coil configuration since the presence of even a small amount of salt prevents its complete extension like a rigid rod such as would normally be expected due to the mutual repulsive forces from the multi-charge sites. With increasing salt content, the random coil contracts due to shielding of the charges by the counterions according to the Donnan equilibria theory (Edelson and Fuoss 1950; Kotin and Nagasawa 1961). Thus, the size and shape of the polyelectrolyte in solution depends on the net polymer charge—a consequence of ionic strength, ionic valences (per Shulze-Hardy 1952), and pH (depending on the nature of the polymer).

Polyelectrolytes apparently function according to the principles of mutual coagulation of sols (Pilipovitch *et al.* 1958; Black 1961; Cohen *et al.* 1958). The polymer with its charged sites (either positive or negative) rapidly diffuses among the dispersed particles with active sites attaching to the surface. The process is considered to be one of ion exchange (Ruehrwein 1952; Swanson *et al.* 1959) involving dehydration and neutralization at the interface of the two charged surfaces. By means of its extended surface, active sites tend to adsorb on adjacent particles simultaneously. Thus, the process of flocculation is referred to as chemical bridging. At the same time, the polymer may undergo contraction, bringing the particles closer together as often can be visually observed. This process of chemical bridging short-circuits, in effect, the classical flocculation process of floc-building through van der Waal's forces as particles come into close contact after charge neutralization. The chemical floc-building results in a strong floc, more rapidly formed than in the classical interparticle process. While the actual mechanism of this chemical bridging has been in dispute, some recent work (e.g., Ries and Meyers 1968) indicates that simultaneous charge neutralization and bridging appears likely.

The optimum polymer dose (minimum for effective flocculation) depends primarily on the surface charge density of the colloid. Since the surface charge density is determined as an average quantity, the dosage can be expressed as a percentage of the solids weight.

Method of Applying

The effectiveness of any given polyelectrolyte polymer is specific to the particular solids/liquid system but is also greatly dependent upon its proper application. This arises from the special characteristics of these long chain polymers. Due to the multiplicity of active (adsorptive) sites, individual molecules will tend to rapidly attach to adjacent particles, leading to excessive polymer consumption at the point of addition. Obviously,

TABLE F-7

MAXIMUM DOSAGES SPECIFIED FOR SPECIFIC APPLICATIONS

Application	Type of Flocculent	Max Dosage (Ppm)	Code of Federal Regulation
Raw cane or beet juice	Anionic (polyacrylamide and copolymers)	5	CFR 121.1092
Raw cane or beet juice	Cationic (acrylamide—MTMMS copolymer)	5	CFR 121.1192
Washing fruits and vegetables	Polyacrylamide	10	CFR 121.1091

SOURCE: Federal Register.

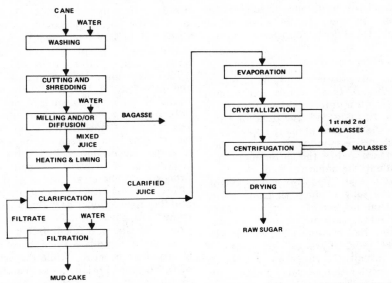

FIG. F-12. CANE JUICE PURIFICATION AND RAW SUGAR MANUFACTURE

the more dilute the polymer solution feed, the lower the probability of excessive consumption. Further, a rapid initial mixing action aids dispersion of the polymer before adsorptive action on particle surfaces begins to any great extent. On the other hand, excessive mixing action involving high shear is harmful, causing the breakup of large flocs already formed. Almost invariably reforming into large flocks does not occur. High shear action can also cause degradation of the polymer into shorter chain lengths of correspondingly lower flocculating power. The most efficient use of the polymer is thus achieved by employing the following practice:

(1) Feeding polymer solution at maximum practical dilution (usually less than 0.10% and preferably 0.02% or lower).

(2) Multipoint addition of solution.

(3) Providing gentle, rolling-type mixing action at point of addition (avoiding high shear).

In preparing polyelectrolyte solutions, high shear mixing should also be avoided to prevent degradation, as previously mentioned. Also, dilute solutions should be used within probably 24 hr to avoid degradation as may occur with some polymers, resulting in an increase in the monomer content. In general, supplier's recommendations should be followed for solution preparation.

Polyelectrolytes are subject to restrictions imposed by the FDA relating to food additives. Maximum dosages have been specified for specific applications and published in the Federal Register (Table F-7).

Similarly, polyelectrolytes employed as coagulants in producing potable water have been subject to approval of the U.S. Public Health Service and now the Division of Water Hygiene in the Environmental Protection Agency (EPA). Approval is granted for the use of specific polymers either as coagulants or coagulant aids at specific dosages (usual maximum 1 ppm).

Cost of Polymer Flocculents

Food grade or potable water type polyelectrolytes range in cost from $1.00–$2.00 per lb on a solids basis. These products are premium grade with low monomer content as required by federal regulations.

Process Applications

Raw Sugar Production

In the food industry, flocculents are most widely used in raw sugar manufacture from both cane and beets. Their principal function is to improve clarification and thickening, increase settling rates, and improve filtration performance through higher capacities and better filtrate clarity. In both cane and beet operations, the primary objective is to extract the maximum amount of sugar at the highest purity. This means separating the impurities (soluble nonsugars and suspended solids) from the raw juice with a minimum loss of sugar. While both types of processing involve clarification and filtration steps after extraction

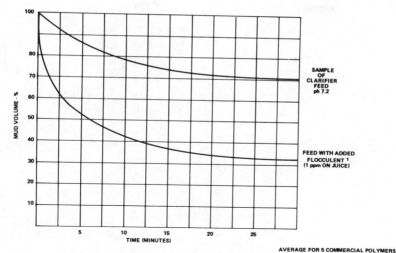

FIG. F-13. EFFECT OF POLYELECTROLYTE ADDITION ON SETTLING
RATE OF CANE JUICE (AFTER LIMING)

of the juice from the cane or sugar beets, there are basic technical differences in the chemistry involved as well as in the impurities (primarily organic for beets but inorganic for cane).

In producing raw sugar from cane, the first part of the process involves extraction of the sugar and subsequent treatment of the raw juice with lime for separating the bulk of the impurities. The process is referred to as lime defecation and is the one predominantly employed in the industry. A typical flowsheet is shown in Fig. F-12.

Two other processes (sulphitation and carbonatation) are also in use but to a limited extent and usually when direct consumption white sugar is being produced. They are simply extensions of lime defecation. In sulphitation, SO_2 gas is added after liming to produce a calcium sulphite. In the carbonatation process, gassing with CO_2 converts the residual lime to calcium carbonate to reduce the pH and minimize the formation of color bodies from the invert sugar.

In the lime separation process, the mixed juice, after heating and liming to a pH around 7.0, contains suspended solids ranging in size from 1 to 10 μ as well as colloidal particles. The solids comprise field soil, bagasse, wax, and other impurities. Although the dispersed particles are negatively charged (as generally characteristic of most naturally-occuring suspensions) lime treatment prior to sedimentation apparently results in positively charged particles (Butler 1969) as the juice pH is raised to around 7.0 (the approximate isoelectric point) or slightly higher. By reducing the Zeta potential to near zero (isoelectric point), lime conditioning along with heating of the juice

promotes flocculation of the dispersed solids. In addition, lime reacts with soluble phosphates to precipitate one or more of the calcium phosphates that assist materially in the flocculation of the colloidal particles. Such preconditioning is essential for effective clarification in the subsequent sedimentation unit, usually a multitray type clarifier. Under ideal conditions, the clarified juice has excellent clarity (less than 10 ppm suspended solids). Thickened solids in the underflow range from 5 to 10% by weight though normally nearer 5%. Sucrose in this thickened slurry is largely recovered by washing and dewatering on a rotary vacuum filter. The conventional perforated screens employed on rotary vacuum filters produce a highly turbid filtrate that must be recycled to the clarifier. Although adding to the clarifier load, it only aggravates clarification problems when overload conditions prevail due to increased operating rates or high mud loads during rainy periods. As a consequence, the clarified juice has a high turbidity, causing objectionable scaling in the evaporator and an increase in impurities.

In the mid 1950's, the possibility of employing polyelectrolyte flocculents to improve clarifier and filter performance through improved flocculation was realized and experimentation was undertaken by both flocculent suppliers and equipment manufacturers. The most successful and widely-adopted flocculent was the high molecular weight, anionic, polyacrylamide introduced by Dow Chemical (Separan AP-30). It was employed for improving clarifier performance especially under high mud loads by addition to the mixed juice ahead of the clarifier at dosages of 1–4 ppm (on juice feed). The

TABLE F-8

TYPICAL COMMERCIAL POLYELECTROLYTE POLYMERS FOR FOOD INDUSTRY APPLICATION

Application	Supplier	Trade Name and Type	Ionic Classification	Molecular Weight[1]	Chemical Character
Cane or beet juice Clarification & filtration and Sugar refinery liquors	American Cyanamid	Magnifloc 845A	Anionic	Very high	Polyacrylamide-sodium acrylate copolymer
	Betz Laboratories	1420 & 1430	Anionic	High	Polyacrylamide-sodium acrylate copolymer
	Calgon, Inc.	CA-243	Anionic	Very high	Polyacrylamide-sodium acrylate copolymer
	Dow Chemical	Separan AP-30	Anionic	Medium	Polyacrylamide
		Separan AP-273 Premium	Anionic	Very high	Polyacrylamide
	Fabcon, Inc.	Zuclar 110	Anionic	Very high	Polyacrylamide
		Fab-Floc M & H	Anionic	Medium-high	Polyacrylamide
	Hodag Chemical	Flocs 433	Anionic	Medium	Polyacrylamide
		Flocs 411	Anionic	Medium	Polyacrylamide
	Hercules, Inc.	Hercofloc 820	Anionic (strongly)	High	Polyacrylamide-sodium acrylate copolymer
		Hercofloc 839	Anionic (medium)	High	Polyacrylamide-sodium acrylate copolymer
		Hercofloc 811	Cationic	Medium	Acrylamide—MTMMS copolymer
	Nalco	Nalcolyte 746	Anionic	High	Polyacrylamide-sodium acrylate copolymer

Application	Manufacturer	Trade name	Type	Molecular weight	Chemical nature
Potable water (for product use) and Product washing (Fruits & vegetables)	American Cyanamid	Magnifloc 845C Series	Anionic	Very high	Polyacrylamide-sodium acrylate copolymer
		Magnifloc 573C Series	Cationic	Low	Polyamine
		Magnifloc 971 Series	Nonionic	High	Polyacrylamide
	Betz Laboratories	1150 & 1160	Cationic	Very high	Quaternary ammonium copolymer of polyacrylamide
		1100-P	Anionic	Very high	Polyacrylamide-sodium acrylate copolymer
	Calgon, Inc.	Cat-Floc	Cationic	Low	Quaternary ammonium homopolymer
		Cat-Floc B	Cationic	Low	Quaternary ammonium homopolymer
	Drew Chemical	Drew-Floc 21	Cationic		Chemical modified natural polymer
	Dow Chemical	Separan NP-10 PWG	Anionic (slightly)	Medium	Polyacrylamide
		Separan AP-30	Anionic	Medium	Polyacrylamide
		Separan AP-273 Premium	Anionic	Very high	Polyacrylamide
	General Mills	Supercol GF	Nonionic	Low	Guar gum (galactomannan)
	Hercules, Inc.	Hercofloc 818	Anionic (slightly)	High	Polyacrylamide-sodium acrylate copolymer
		Hercofloc 821	Anionic (highly)	Very high	Polyacrylamide-sodium acrylate copolymer
		Hercofloc 827	Nonionic	Low to medium	Polyacrylamide

[1] As classified by supplier. Molecular weights range from 1 to 10 million except for natural gum and cationics that generally are less than 1 million.

FIG. F-14. LOUISIANA CANE MUD BEFORE AND AFTER FLOCCULATION (ANIONIC TYPE POLYELECTROLYTE)

substantial effect polyelectrolyte addition has on juice sedimentation rates is illustrated in Fig. F-13. Various commercial products are available for this application (see Table F-8).

During the same period, the problem of handling heavy mud loads on the filter and reducing the cycling of filtrate solids to the clarifier led to the development of a mud coagulating and filtration process (Rapi-Floc[1]) using a high molecular weight, anionic, polyacrylamide product (such as Separan AP-30) coupled with lime pretreatment for enhancing floc formation. While the physico-chemical mechanism has not been established, coagulation studies indicated that the enhanced flocculation was dependent upon a minimum juice phosphate level that would provide further calcium phosphate precipitation. The increased lime would also increase the Zeta potential of the positively charged particles, thus promoting floc-building with the anionic polyelectrolyte. The effectiveness of this floc forming procedure is illustrated by the photomicrographs in Fig. F-14.

When the rotary drum filter is employed with a fabric filter media of medium porosity, a clear juice suitable for evaporator feed can be produced. At the same time, filtration rates are increased 2- to 4-fold with coagulant dosages in the range of 10–20 ppm (based on feed). However, few filters today are operated with fabric media attached to the drum as mill operators prefer to eliminate cloth changing and maintenance. Instead, the polyelectrolyte flocculents are used for improving the performance of the conventional rotary filter equipped with perforated screens. Due to the effective flocculation, a substantial reduction in filtrate solids is obtained along with high mud capacity. With the substantial reduction in filtrate solids, recycling to the clarifiers has little if any adverse effect.

Traveling media or belt filters where the filter fabric is continually washed off the drum are also used to a limited extent although cloth blinding

---

[1] Dorr-Oliver, Inc.

TABLE F-9

POLYELECTROLYTE CONSUMPTION IN VARIOUS CANE MILLS

Mill Location	Application Clarification	Application Filtration	Avg Dosage % on Cane	Avg Dosage Ppm[1]
Venezuela			—	5.8
Mexico	x		—	2.0[2]
Florida		x	0.006	60
Mexico	x		0.00025	2.5
Louisiana			0.0012	12
Columbia	x	x	—	3.5[3]
Florida	x		0.00015	1.5
Florida[4]			0.00078	7.8
Florida			0.00032	3.2

SOURCE: Sugar Y Asucar. Aug. 1967, p. 28, 30 (Coagulent—Dow *AP-30*).
[1] Based on yearly consumption and total cane ground.
[2] Intermittent use.
[3] Clarification dosage.
[4] Dow *AP-273*.

is still a problem. Flocculation of the mud prior to filtration is almost always necessary for satisfactory operation.

It is estimated that 20–25% of the mills today employ polyelectrolyte flocculents to improve clarification and/or filtration. Although applied primarily in mills using the lime defecation process, similar flocculation benefits with these polyelectrolytes have been demonstrated for the sulphitation process.

Typical coagulant dosages are 1–5 ppm for clarification and 10–40 ppm for filter feed. Consumption figures reported by a number of mills are given in Table F-9.

While lime predominates throughout the industry for juice purification, its scaling characteristics led to field trials (in Hawaii) of magnesium oxide in the late 1950's. It was subsequently shown to reduce overall costs by increasing capacity of heaters, clarifiers, mud filters, and evaporators despite higher costs for the MgO. Some mills also used MgO along with lime (Madrazzo 1968) but its use has largely been discontinued.

Polyelectrolyte flocculents have been found to be effective also when MgO is employed for juice purification. Dosages on the order of 1 ppm allow the MgO consumption to be reduced by as much as 10–20% according to Studnicky (1969). MgO also has been added to filter muds (Studnicky 1970) from lime defecation to improve filterability, reduce lime salts, and filtrate color.

Economics

Polyelectrolytes cost on the order of $1.00–$2.00 per lb depending on type, grade, and

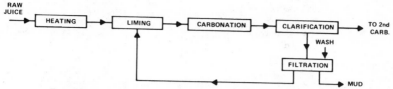

FIG. F-15. DORR CONTINUOUS CARBONATION SYSTEM

quantity purchased.   Thus, for a $1.50 per lb cost at a dosage of 1 ppm the polymer cost would be $3.00 per 1000 tons of cane (assuming 1 ton of cane equates to 1 ton of juice). Related costs (labor, dosing equipment, freight, etc.) must also be taken into consideration. The economics of employing a synthetic polyelectrolyte are dependent entirely on the individual situation for each mill. Where heavy mud loads or undercapacity equipment necessitates a cut-back in production or excessive maintenance costs arising from poor clarification, the net savings can be appreciable. Where improved clarification on a continuous basis reduces evaporator maintenance and improves purity, the extent of the savings must be determined for each situation.

Beet Sugar Manufacture

The purification of raw juice from beets requires a somewhat different process than that for cane due to the nature of the nonsugars that are largely organic. As pointed out by Honig (1953), a large amount of lime is required to precipitate these nonsugars. The excess lime, however, results in an increase in the ash content of the raw sugar and also a higher viscosity in the molasses. To overcome this, the juice is gassed with CO_2 after liming to convert the excess lime to carbonate. The process is known as carbonation (or carbonatation). Following carbonation, the treated juice is sent to a sedimentation unit for clarification along with thickening of the solids. The calcium carbonate sludge is subsequently deliquored on rotary vacuum filters where wash is applied in the "sweetening-off" process to remove most of the sucrose before discarding the solids or calcining to produce lime. A typical flowsheet is shown in Fig. F-15.

There are numerous variations involving two-stage liming, recirculation of solids, sedimentation before carbonation, etc. All are directed to the process objective of maximizing the removal of nonsugars and minimizing color formation while, at the same time, producing a well-flocculated carbonate with the best sedimentation and filtration characteristics. The two objectives are somewhat incompatible since fine carbonate has increased purification ability (due to greater surface area) but, on the other hand, adversely effects sedimentation and filtration. By progressive liming and other process techniques involving the principal process steps of heating, liming, carbonation, and sedimentation (McGinnis 1971), it is possible to obtain compact flocs that settle rapidly and filter well. Further, by recirculating a portion of the carbonate prior to liming, seed is provided for accumulation of the colloidal floc, thus enhancing settling as agglomerates are formed. Recent work (Vandewijer and Pieck 1968) has also shown that if the liming is carried out so that pH is raised gradually, a more compact floc is obtained especially in the presence of recycled carbonatation mud. In two-stage liming with carbonate recycling, a typical process (Wiklund) is illustrated in Fig. F-16.

Polyelectrolyte flocculents are employed to a limited extent in beet sugar purification primarily to improve clarification on existing clarifiers and, in a few cases, to reduce the size of the clarifier on a new installation. With existing clarifiers of the three-compartment type, some factories (e.g., in England particularly) prefer to operate with only two compartments in order to reduce detention time and thereby possibly achieve lower color and lime salts. When following this practice, the addition of a polyelectrolyte flocculent is neces-

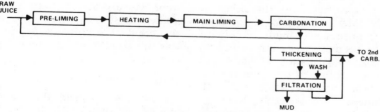

FIG. F-16. TWO-STAGE LIMING WITH CARBONATE RECYCLE

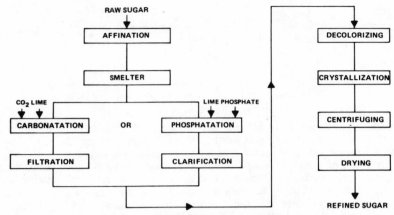

FIG. F-17. SUGAR REFINING PROCESS

sary to obtain a clear overflow with the increased rates.

Anionic polyacrylamide polymers, as employed for cane juice purification, are similarly effective for beet juice clarification. The trend is toward the higher molecular weight polymers requiring lower dosages. Depending on the application and the polymer selected, the dosage ranges from 0.5 to 2.0 ppm on juice (typical dosage, 0.2 lb polymer per 100 tons of beets).

Polyelectrolyte flocculents are particularly beneficial when a cloudy overflow condition develops whether due to an overload on the clarifier or a process problem (e.g., deteriorated beets). Experience has shown that polyacrylamide flocculents are capable of improving settling rates when adversely affected by frost-damaged beets.

Sugar Refining

In the refining of raw sugar, further impurities are removed and color reduced so a white sugar may be produced on recrystallization. The process steps involved are shown in Fig. F-17.

Clarification

The clarification process involves chemical treatment to produce a flocculent by precipitation to aid in coagulating suspended solids and colloidal color bodies. There are two principal processes. One is known as carbonatation; the other as phosphatation (the oldest). In the former, milk of lime and CO_2 are introduced simultaneously to the melt liquor to produce a calcium carbonate precipitate. Effective coagulation of impurities occurs along with adsorption of the color bodies. The removal of these impurities reduces the ash content of the liquor. This is accomplished by filtering the liquor following the calcium carbonate precipitation.

The classical method of clarifying raw sugar liquor involves the addition of lime and phosphoric acid to form a tricalcium phosphate precipitate. While excellent removal of color and suspended solids is obtained, the tricalcium phosphate precipitate is difficult to filter. This has been largely overcome in recent years by the adoption of the Williamson frothing clarifier and subsequent modifications (e.g., Jacobs, multiple compartment flotation clarifier, etc.) (Saranin 1970). By aerating the liquor and producing fine bubbles, the flocculent phosphate precipitate is floated to the surface, forming a scum that is removed by a suitable scraper. Sucrose in the scum (around 5%) is recovered by filtering and washing. The clarified liquor is drawn off at the bottom. It is generally of high clarity so a filtration step is not required. Any remaining turbidity, however, is subsequently removed by the char in the decolorizing step following. Clarification, however, is sensitive to the variations in the quality of the raw sugar so a brilliantly clarified juice is not always obtained.

Supplementary Flocculents

Where juice clarity from the frothing clarifier is not satisfactory due to lower quality raw sugar or an overloaded clarifier, supplementary flocculents such as polyelectrolytes may be employed. The dilute (0.1-0.2%) solution of a polyelectrolyte coagulant is added continuously to the sugar liquor at dosages of 5-10 ppm ahead of the clarifier. Best results are said to be obtained when the coagulant solution is fed to an inline mixer after the addition of the lime sucrate but before aeration.

Fruits and Vegetables

In the processing of fruits and vegetables for canning, the character of the water may adversely affect product quality during blanching or cooking, or in the preparation of the brine. Calcium and magnesium hardness have a toughening effect and can lower quality, particularly in the case of certain vegetables such as peas, beans, tomatoes, lentils, etc. (as little as 45 ppm hardness is reported to have a toughening effect on peas).

Alkalinity reduction by treatment of the water with lime and a coagulant such as alum is readily accomplished in standard water treatment units. The alum floc effectively coagulates the calcium carbonate precipitate so there is rapid settling and a clear overflow of low turbidity for final clarification by filtration.

Beverages

Water quality plays a profound role in beverages where consumer acceptance rests on taste appeal. Consumers are not only responsive to the unique flavor but to subtle flavor variances as well. The quality of the water, as would be expected, can well be the source of such variances. The soft drink industry is a good example of the importance of water quality to the final product. Obviously, any degree of taste or odor could adversely effect the special taste appeal carefully developed by the bottling company. However, excess alkalinity is of much greater significance to final taste since most soft drinks owe a good deal of their tang and zest to acid syrups containing phosphoric or citric acid. Neutralization of these acids results in a flat taste. While most bottling plants use municipal water, the problem still exists in most areas as alkalinities usually exceed the maximum that can be tolerated (less than 100 ppm as $CaCO_3$). Consequently, most bottlers install water treating equipment to reduce alkalinity (and/or total solids if excessive) along with any taste, odor, organic matter, and turbidity in order to have a sparkling, clear water for their product.

Alkalinity reduction is accomplished by lime treatment to precipitate the so-called carbonate hardness as calcium carbonate. Alum is introduced to provide the necessary flocculent $(Al(OH)_3)$ for agglomerating and settling the carbonate while a relatively clear effluent is produced for final clarification by filters, activated carbon units, and sometimes a polishing filter.

Other beverages such as beer and fruit drinks adhere to high standards of water quality specific for their requirements. Depending on the source of the water and its characteristics, treatment may range from simple filtration to alkalinity or dissolved solids reduction. Even with filtration (as with sand filters), a flocculent (almost always alum) plays an important role. The flocculent aluminum hydroxide acts to enmesh fine particles on the surface of the sand bed. The filtered water is sparkling clear with less than 1 ppm turbidity.

Water for Product Use

When the available water supply is unsuited for product use, water treatment for removal of suspended solids, color, excessive alkalinity or dissolved solids, organic matter, taste or odor is necessary. Clarification and color removal may require coagulation employing flocculents (lime, alum, polyelectrolytes) or coagulant aids (sodium aluminates, polyelectrolytes). When polyelectrolytes are used, the potable grades (see Table F-7) as approved by the Division of Water Hygiene (EPA) must be employed. The type of treatment and choice of flocculents including dosages to achieve the desired water quality must be determined for each situation.

Alum and ferric salts are normally the primary coagulants employed but polyelectrolytes have been making inroads in the potable market. For example, a cationic polyelectrolyte may be employed as a primary flocculent in water clarification at dosages on the order of a few tenths to 7.0 ppm, replacing 50-60 ppm alum. Lesser dosages (0.1-2.0 ppm) can serve as coagulant aids, reducing the alum requirement by 70-80%. The economics in such cases determine the optimum coagulant combination.

H. V. MILES

References

Theory

BLACK, A. P. 1948. The chemistry of water coagulation. Water Sewage Works 95, 142.

BLACK, A. P. 1961. Swimming pool disinfection with iodine. Water Sewage Works 108, 286-289.

COHEN, J. M., ROURKE, G. A., and WOODWARD, R. L. 1958. Natural and synthetic polyelectrolytes as coagulant aids. J. Am. Water Works Assoc. 50, 463.

EDELSON, S., and FUOSS, R. A. 1950. A contrast between polyelectrolytes and electrolytes. J. Am. Chem. Soc. 72, 306.

GREGORY, J. 1969. Flocculation of polystyrene particles with cationic polyelectrolytes. Discussions Faraday Soc. 1969, 2260.

HIGUCHI, W. I. et al. 1963. Kinetics of rapid aggregation in suspensions. J. Pharm. Sci. 52, 49.

HIGUCHI, W. I. et al. 1965. Kinetics of rapid aggregation in suspensions. J. Pharm. Sci. 54, 510.

HUNTER, J. V., and HENKELEKIAN, H. 1960. Separation and materials balance of solid fractions in sewage. Purdue Univ. Eng. Bull. Ext. Ser. 106, 150.

KOTIN, L., and NAGASAWA, M. 1961. A study of the ionization of polystyrene sulfonic acid by proton magnetic resonance. J. Am. Chem. Soc. *83*, 1026.

LA MER, V. L. 1964. Coagulation Symposium. J. Colloid Sci. *19*, 291–293.

LA MER, V. K., and HEALEY, T. W. 1966. Nature of the flocculation reaction in solid liquid separation. *In* Solid-Liquid Separation. HM Stationery Office, London, England.

PILIPOVICH, J. N., BLACK, A. P., EIDSNESS, F. A., and STEARNS, T. W. 1958. Electrophoretic studies in water coagulation. J. Am. Water Works Assoc. *50*, 1467.

PRIESING, C. P. 1962. A theory of coagulation useful for design. Ind. Eng. Chem. *54*, No. 8, 38–45.

RIES, H. E., Jr., and MEYERS, B. L. 1968. Flocculation mechanism: charge neutralization and bridging. Science *160*, 1449–1450.

RUEHRWEIN, R. A., and WARD, D. W. Mechanism of clay aggregation by polyelectrolytes. 1952. Soil Sci. *73*, 485.

SMOLUCHOWSKI, M. 1917. Mathematical theory of the kenetics of the coagulation of colloidal solutions. Z. Physik. Chem. (Frankfort) *92*, 129. (German)

SWIFT, D. L., and FRIEDLANDER, S. K. 1964. The coagulation of hydrosols by Brownian motion and laminar shear flow. J. Colloid Sci. *19*, 621.

THODE, E. F., SWANSON, J. W., KURATH, S. F., and HOFFMAN, G. R. 1959. Mechanism of retention of wet-strength resins. Tappi *42*, 170–174.

Process Applications

BUTLER, B. P. 1969. Some guidelines for flocculation and clarification in the sugar industry. Proc. Queensland Soc. Sugar Cane Technologists, 36th Conf., Apr. 16–22.

HONIG, P. 1953. Principles of Sugar Technology. Elsevier Publishing Co., New York.

MADRAZZO, C. M. 1968. Use of magnesium oxide in cane juice clarification. Proc. Philippines Sugar Technologists 16th Ann. Conv., 246–258.

McGINNIS, R. A. 1971. Beet-Sugar Technology. Van Nostrand Reinhold Publishing Corp., New York.

SARANIN, A. P. 1970. Multicell flotation clarifier. Sugar J. *32* Aug., 18–20.

SCHULZE, H., and HARDY, W. B. 1952. Colloid Science, Vol. 1. H. R. Krugt (Editor). Elsevier Publishing Co., New York.

STUDNICKY, J. 1969. Use of flocculents to improve filterability of juice purified with MgO. Sobre Derivados Cana Azucar, ISJ *3*, No. 3, 3–20.

STUDNICKY, J. 1970. Use of flocculents to improve filterability of juice purified with MgO. Sovre Derivados Cana Azucar, ISJ *4*, No. 1, 3–14.

VANDEWIJER, R., and PIECK, R. 1968. Development of a modified RT process for beet juice purification. Sucr. Belge *87*, 651–656.

Cross-reference: *Water Treatment (Liquid).*

FLOUR MILLING INDUSTRY

Milling of cereal grains is often described as the earliest application of mechanical arts by prehistoric man. When primitive man began to eat seeds of the grass family, Gramineae (poaceae), it was evident that the interior of the kernel was more edible than the branny outer husk. To assist in breaking through the outer protective cellulose layers of the kernel to reach the softer endosperm portion, man learned to shatter seeds between two stones. No doubt flat stones were used first with the grain pounded between them, but later a slightly hollowed stone was used below and a rounded one above, which led to a grinding action. Through the centuries, that evolved to the saddle stone, a type of grinding and pounding action, dating from at least 4000 yr before the Christian era but still used in some places in the world today.

In prehistoric times man could not permit himself the luxury of being choosy about the kinds of seeds he ate. As the art of cereal crop production became known, first in the Syrian-Palestine area, wheat became the preferred grain. There is evidence of its cultivation dating from at least 6000 yr. Once the cultivation of grain developed, it became possible for more persons to dwell permanently in a restricted area because searching for food over extended areas was no longer necessary. Permanency of population led to the development of the wheat-flour milling industry.

Milling in Greece, the Roman Empire, and During the Middle Ages

The English word "milling" is derived from the Greek word "myle," which became "myln" in Old English and finally "mill." Greek mythology abounds with references to milling wheat and barley. Reference to grinding grain while others sleep, indicates that milling, from the beginning, may have been an around-the-clock occupation.

The rise of the Roman Empire brought several important improvements in the art of milling. Use of such power as mules, oxen, and water wheels to operate rotary millstones became widespread. Also, animal hair was used to make sieves to remove straw, chaff, bran, and coarse particles during grinding operations. The coarse material could be reground and the bran removed, thus initiating the steps that comprise modern milling. Commerce, too, became a part of the milling industry because wheat was imported from Africa and the Middle East to help feed Roman citizens.

Following the fall of the Roman Empire, little change occurred in milling except the introduction of the windmill for power. The use of the windmill probably originated in the Middle East, from whence it was taken to Europe by Crusaders.

The Beginning of Modern Milling

James Watt's invention of the steam engine made it practical in 1783 to construct on the Thames River in London a flour mill with 20 pairs of grinding stones. In North America, wind and water-powered mills were constructed in New England beginning about 1632. Wheat began to be produced in New York and New Jersey. Soon several mills were established and flour became an export commodity.

The construction of flour mills spread across the United States as population moved westward and wheat production became more widespread. The same situation prevailed in Canada. Various cities became, for a time, renowned as milling centers. In the United States, they included Baltimore, Richmond, Rochester, Buffalo, St. Louis, Minneapolis, and Kansas City.

Flour milling developed along similar technical lines, using millstones and various sources of power, wherever in the world wheat was grown or imported in large quantities. Milling was done throughout all of Europe, parts of Asia and Africa, and in Argentina, Chile, and Peru in South America. The person most responsible for the beginning of complete automation of the milling process was Oliver Evans, a Pennsylvania miller. Inventions attributed to Mr. Evans made possible a continuous milling operation; and thus milling became the first entirely automated food processing operation. Soon after 1770 the roller mill replaced stone burrs for grinding; and somewhat later the middling purifier laid the basis for the gradual reduction systems of milling. Those events established flour milling principles as practiced today.

The Milling Process

There are three main wheat types, namely, hard, soft, and durum. The type of flour manufactured from wheats of different properties varies and the baked products made from different flours vary widely. However, the milling operations remain basically the same.

Although wheat milling is an extremely complicated operation in practice, it is quite simple in theory. The objectives are to remove foreign material from wheat, clean it, add a small amount of moisture to decrease the tendency of the outer cellulose structure of the kernel to pulverize, disintegrate the kernel between steel rolls, sift out the germ and bran, and leave the endosperm or flour for food use. To accomplish those steps successfully requires a complex array of machinery, considerable power, and competent technical knowledge and supervision.

Briefly, the steps involved in the milling operation follow.

Wheat is removed from storage elevators, blended as desired to produce a specific type of flour, then sent in sequence to grain separators, aspirators, and destoners to remove foreign material and other seed types. It then may go to wheat washers, dryers, and scourer machines to remove wheat hairs and any loosened bran material. A slight amount of water is accurately added to the wheat and it is then placed in tempering bins for several hours after which it again is scoured, aspirated, and placed in grinding bins. The wheat is then ready to start the actual milling operation that is designed to separate outer layers or bran and germ from the inner portion or endosperm.

The first operation is to crush the tempered wheat slightly between steel corrugated rolls rotating at high speed, with one roll revolving faster than the other. The differential speeds cause a shearing action on the wheat kernels that fractures them into chunks. The partially ground material is then separated into different portions by sifting. The larger particles are subject to recrushing on another set of corrugated rolls; intermediate sized particles are sent to machines called purifiers that separate particles on the basis of both size and specific gravity, using sieving action and air suction. The fine flour produced will require no further grinding and is conveyed to storage bins for blending with other flour streams. However, the purified endosperm particles that are essentially free from germ and bran are spouted to smooth rolls and ground into flour. Branny particles, being lighter than endosperm particles, are removed by sieves and air currents and become animal feed as does the bran and other fibrous material.

In the process of the gradual reduction of chunks of wheat kernels to the fineness of flour, a number of sets of smooth rolls are used. It is thus evident that there are a tremendous number of possible combinations for blending flour fractions obtained during the normal milling process. Flour brands are manufactured to exacting and uniform specifications; but to do this requires control of wheat type and the milling operation along with proper blending of flour streams. To bring about beneficial improvements in flour quality, chemical agents can be added to reduce the content of yellow pigments to make flour whiter. This is known as bleaching. Other compounds called maturing agents bring about desirable changes in the physio-chemical properties of flour similar to what occurs when natural aging takes place. Many countries prohibit such treatments by law.

Flour milling usually is a 24-hr-a-day operation; therefore, bulk flour storage is often used in order that blending, packing, and shipping can be done during 1 work shift. Bulk flour and feed shipments are common and generally lower delivery costs.

New Developments

The basic concept of converting wheat to flour has remained unchanged for many centuries but modifications of milling operations have undergone profound changes. The milling industry has initiated or adopted every modern innovation pertaining to methods of measuring, metering, weighing, conveying, blending materials, applying power, maintaining sanitation, improving efficiencies, overall scientific control, and improved nutrition.

Among more recent developments in the industry are fine grinding and air classification whereby a flour can be separated into higher protein or higher starch fractions. It is thus possible to custom blend flour over a wider property range than previously. Also, flour can be made more free flowing by causing particles to agglomerate into clusters by means of moisture and spray drying. Bulk handling of flour by truck, railroad car, and barge as well as in-plant operations have seen great change and improvements in equipment in recent years.

Manufacture of ready-mixed flours for the production of cakes, pie crust, doughnuts, biscuits, muffins, pancakes, and waffles (where the preparation contains all the required ingredients other than liquid in the proportions necessary to make the final product) is a large and expanding development. Phosphated, self-rising, and bromated flours have long been manufactured for certain markets.

Although not a part of the flour milling operation, enrichment is a most important development, because vitamins and minerals added to flour can greatly improve the nutritive value of by-products. At the present time, enriched flour has additions of thiamin (B_1), niacin, and riboflavin (B_2). Iron, Vitamin D, and calcium are sometimes added, also.

Wheat Flour Utilization in Human Food

The nutritional value of wheat and wheat products has been recognized for centuries and has provided a main source of food for a large portion of the human race; however, because wheat has been and remains an abundant and economical food and feed, its value is sometimes depreciated. On the average, wheat flour is composed of about 74% carbohydrate, 11% protein, 1.25% lipids, 0.4% mineral matter, and varying amounts of several B vitamins. The protein-amino acid balance of wheat and wheat products is good. The most limiting amino acid is lysine, but the ingestion of 228 gm of flour per day would satisfy this lysine deficiency in the average diet. The full nutritional value of feed products from the processing of wheat such as bran, shorts, and red dog for various animals and fowls has only recently been investigated thoroughly. They constitute important ingredients for the formula feed industry.

The Economic Importance of the Milling Industry

In industrial countries the flour milling industry is among the top ten industries in economic importance. In less developed countries flour mills often represent one of the major industries. Although flour milling requires large investment in buildings and equipment, it is not an important employer of labor; however, employment is substantial, is year-round, and is full-time.

Originally, flour mills were constructed near areas of wheat production but in the past quarter century especially, mills have been built throughout the earth. Location is based on the potential demand for flour for human consumption because wheat supplies may be received from many exporting countries.

Corn, Rice, Rye, and Sorghum Milling

In principle, the basic concept for milling wheat is applicable to other cereal grains when the objective is to produce flour or meal. The steps consist of cleaning the grain, tempering (slight addition of moisture), grinding, and sieving. Seldom are the processes as complicated for other grains as for wheat.

Corn

In several countries like Mexico, for example, corn is a main food product and most processing is done with food use as the main objective. In the United States, however, only a small part of the total corn production is processed for food use. Animal feed and industrial uses of corn predominate.

Probably the first milling of corn occurred somewhere in Central America, because corn is indigenous to the Americas. Corn has been milled for food for at least 1500 yr. At present, there are two distinct systems used, namely, dry milling and wet milling. Most corn for food use is dry milled.

The following steps are involved in corn milling: cleaning, tempering, degerming, drying, cooling, grading, grinding, sifting, purifying, aspirating, packing, and extracting oil.

The floury endosperm portion of the corn kernel constitutes about 82%, the bran coat 5%, germ 12%, and top cap 1%. About 80% of the oil is concentrated in the germ. The usual products of corn milling are: grits, coarse meal, flour, germ, and hominy feeds. The products of dry milling are further processed in various ways by heat, pressure rolling, gelatinization, chemical treatment, and extrusion to provide both food and industrial uses. The main products of wet milling are cornstarch, corn oil, and corn gluten feed.

Rye

Rye is grown mainly in northern Europe. It is hardier than wheat and does well on poor soil or in arid climate. The main uses for rye are livestock feed, the manufacture of whiskey, and production of flour for rye bread. The milling operation is a modification of the one for wheat except that purifying and grinding operations are much simpler for wheat. Rye, being tougher and starchier than wheat, requires more grinding and more bolting surface. Usually all roll surfaces are corrugated. The milling process yields different grades of rye flour such as "light" or "dark" flour, a rye bran, and red dog.

Sorghum

Sorghum is both wet and dry milled. The principal product of wet milling is starch, with edible oil and gluten feed the main by-products. Dry milling of sorghum results in the preparation of flour that can be used in a wide variety of such products as wall board, an ingredient of oil-well-drilling muds, and in fermentation industries. Dry milling is done by a modified system of grinding and sieving similar to that used in the wheat milling industry.

Rice

Rice milling is a considerably different type of operation from those for other cereal grains, although the object is the same; namely, the separation of the outer portions of the kernel from the inner endosperm with a minimum of breakage. Rough or paddy rice is cleaned of foreign material and graded as to kernel size. Rotating vertical cylinders containing indentations and perforations are used to remove certain types of foreign seeds. Shelling machines are used to loosen, and hullers to remove, the hulls, thus producing brown rice. By abrasive action, pearling machines combined with brush machines produce polished rice from brown rice.

Almost all rice is used for human food consumption, although some is used for livestock feed and for the production of alcoholic beverages.

JOHN A. SHELLENBERGER

References

MATZ, S. A. 1970. Cereal Technology. Avi Publishing Co., Westport, Conn.

SHELLENBERGER, J. A. 1965. Fifty years of milling advances. Cereal Sci. Today 10, 260–262.

STORCK, J., and TEAGUE, W. D. 1952. A History of Milling. Flour for Man's Bread. University of Minnesota Press, Minneapolis.

Cross-references: Baking Industry; Evans, Oliver.

FOAM PHENOMENA

An understanding of the principles governing foam phenomena is necessary in present day food technology. From the sparkling and tantalizing foam bubbles of champagne to the "foamy scum" overflowing a reactor, the foam phenomenon and its mechanism might be the same. Otherwise stated, whether foam formation or foam destruction, controlling and maintaining the desired condition is the ultimate goal of a technologist.

Foam Theory and "Mechanism"

Foam is generally defined as gas dispersed in liquid in such ratio that its bulk density approaches that of gas rather than liquid. The fundamental relationships developed by Gibbs in 1878 (Prutton and Maron 1951) still remain the best for interpreting foam formation and destruction. Pure liquids rarely foam when gassed (Gaden and Kevorkian 1956). A "foreign compound" must be added to produce a stable gas-liquid dispersion. Such a compound is usually an existing or added surface-active agent that reduces the surface tension of the liquid and promotes a surface layer of a composition different from the rest of the liquid. This layer, acting as a "buffer," prevents the natural coalescence of gas bubbles dispersed in the liquid. By contrast, a defoaming agent might be regarded as a "negative" surface-active agent that increases the surface tension of the liquid (Kouloheris 1970). It tends to concentrate in the bulk of the liquid. Gibbs' equation qualitatively predicts the foam behavior of solution:

$$q = -(C/RT)\,(d\gamma/dc) \qquad (1)$$

with q the excess of solute in the surface over that in the body of the liquid, C the solute concentration, T the absolute temperature, γ the surface tension of the solution, and R the gas constant. With a surface-active solute, the rate of change of surface tension with concentration $(d\gamma/dc)$ is negative, and foaming takes place. Conversely, with a surface-inactive substance, $d\gamma/dc$ is positive, and foaming is inhibited.

There is more to it, however. A reduction in surface tension is not enough to produce foam. The nature of the adsorbed layer is also important. Foam can, in fact, be produced with a surface-active agent. It is what is called foam stability, or even foam "elasticity" that may ultimately determine the formation or destruction of foam. Usually, foam is stable if the surface tension of the solution is considerably less than that of the pure solvent. According to Gibbs, foam eleasticity is defined as:

$$E = 2A\,(d\gamma/dA) \qquad (2)$$

with A the area of the liquid film, and γ the surface tension of the liquid. It follows from Equation (2) that foam elasticity is "a measure of the changes of the surface tension which result in response to a change in area" (Gaden and Kevorkian 1956). In other words, a stable foam is one whose liquid film has a surface tension capable of enduring rapid local variations.

Foam Formation

Foam is simply a collection of gas or air bubbles. Prolongation of bubble life is therefore essential in foaming if foam formation were desired (Taggart 1953). As stated previously, a surface-active agent already included in the liquid or purposely added, is required to initiate foaming (Schoen 1962). The type and dosage of this agent will effect the degree as well as the life of foaming. It should be noted again that bubbles in pure liquid coalesce immediately on contact. Foaming agents, conversely, decrease this coalescence significantly by the surface tension phenomena described above.

Generally speaking, foaming once initiated will greatly sustain itself through extensive aeration-gasification (i.e., more CFM) or high agitator speed. Production of finely divided bubbles favors foaming resulting in a more stable and persistent foam. The inclusion of finely divided solids or colloids appears to stabilize foam perhaps by increasing the so-called "foam elasticity" factor. Temperature itself may or may not have a significant effect in foaming. Rather, abrupt temperature changes may have a foam destruction effect by weakening the foam stability. The acidity or alkalinity of the solution may affect foaming primarily due to a destruction of one of the active groups of the foaming reagent. In this regard, the chemical structure of the surface-active agents is important and some laboratory tests should be conducted. Some agents (Taggart 1953) may be polar organic compounds type RA (R = hydrocarbon radical normally $> C_6$, and A = polar solubilizing group such as (OH), (COOH), (CO), (NH_2), etc.

In alkyl compounds, the solubilizing effect of the principal polar groups is

$$COOH > NH_2 > OH > CO$$

Generally, the compound containing the more powerful solubilizing group could be the better foaming agent. Quantity of the added agent is critical. Remember, a surface agent can be both a foaming or defoaming chemical. Finally, pressure can have a decisive effect. High pressure depresses foaming. Low pressures—especially below atmospheric—favor foaming.

Typical applications of foam formation as useful industrial unit operations are "foam fractionation," "ion flotation," and "froth flotation" of minerals. The latter has been fully developed as a widely applied method. The former two, while not so well known, have a great future in food technology. Separation and enrichment of fats, soaps, protein, and enzymes (Lemlich 1968; Schoen 1962) are all promising areas of application for either "foam fractionation" or "ion flotation." Both of these methods take advantage of the fact that "surface active" components of a solution are preferentially adsorbed at gas-liquid interfaces, while "surface-inactive" components concentrate in the bulk of the liquid. When metal ions are to be separated or concentrated, a foaming agent is used capable of complexing the metal ion into a surface-active form. This type of foam fractionation is then called "ion flotation."

Thus, from an enrichment point of view, the top foam fraction represents the concentrate while the depleted bottom liquid fraction the tailing.

A number of sophisticated laboratory apparatuses for studying foaming have been reported

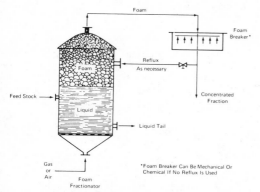

FIG. F-18. SCHEMATIC FLOW DIAGRAM OF A
TYPICAL FOAM FRACTIONATION APPLICA-
TION

in the literature (Reigh *et al.* 1961; Gaden and
Kevorkian 1956; Carpenter and Gellman 1967)
and can be used effectively for laboratory foam
studies. A typical foam fractionation application
has a schematic flow diagram as shown in Fig.
F-18.

Foam Destruction and Inhibition

Among all the foam phenomena, perhaps foam
destruction and inhibition are the ones studied
most.

Foam destruction, or defoaming as is commonly known, should be distinguished from foam
inhibition. Defoaming can be achieved by physical,
mechanical, or chemical means. However, destruction of foam does not prevent it from forming
again under the proper conditions of pumping and
gasification (Kouloheris 1970). Foam inhibition,
through a chemical addition, will be required to
destroy as well as inhibit further foam formation.

In physical or mechanical foam destruction, a
mechanical shock is simply applied to knock down
foam by rupturing the bubble film. This "shock"
may be applied by various devices: rotating foam
breakers that whip the surface foam; spray headers
that shower the foam layer with an umbrella of
finely divided liquid or steam to collapse the
foam; or fluid jets that jettison gas, steam, or air
at high pressure into the foam. Foam may also be
controlled through thermal shock, by rapidly
heating or cooling froth enclosed in a relatively
closed space.

A more recent development is ultrasonic defoaming, in which sonic waves, produced by an
ultrasonic generator ("whistle") at beyond 20,000
cycles per second, are applied onto the surface of
the foam. Foam is believed to be broken by the
rapid, local change in its elasticity (Kouloheris
1970).

Generally speaking, the efficiency of these devices is extremely low. The performance of defoaming is not always consistent. The power
requirements as well as the equipment might not
be justified. A number of mechanical defoamers
in the form of rotating blades or spray jets are
being used in some plants. Some pharmaceutical
or food industries may find the application of
ultrasonic defoaming a necessity to avoid undesired contamination.

In chemical foam destruction, defoaming through
the addition of an agent may be carried out
simultaneously with foam generation. Foam
"knockdown" and formation in a reactor, for
instance, are likely to be in some kind of equilibrium determined by the type and amount of
defoaming agent used, as well as by reaction
conditions. However, in addition to "knockdown"
ability, an agent may also exhibit a foam inhibition ability that can sustain foamless conditions
for a prolonged period. In other words, a good
defoaming agent should destroy foam at its point
of generation; and, in addition, its stability should
be such that it inhibits foam formation should the
condition that produces foam (agitation, aeration,
pumping, etc.) persist.

Preliminary laboratory evaluations (Kouloheris
1970; Carbarino *et al.* 1966) are necessary to
screen out and study the many defoaming agents
now available on the market. Table F-10 shows a
partial list of typical defoamers. A laboratory
set-up for testing defoaming agents is shown
schematically in Fig. F-19 and should be self-
explanatory. Details of the techniques involved
in these tests are given in the literature (Kouloheris
1970; Carbarino *et al.* 1966).

Foam knockdown ability can be studied by
means of this laboratory technique. Figure F-20
presents typical curves of defoaming obtained
(Kouloheris 1970). Without a defoaming agent,

TABLE F-10

PARTIAL LIST OF TYPICAL DEFOAMERS

Trade Name	Manufacturer
Antifoam H-10B	Dow Corning Corporation
OA-5, OA-5U	Cities Service Company
GE 10, 60, 66, 70, 71	General Electric Company
Nopco 8050, 8187	Diamond-Shammrock Chemical Co.
Pluronic L-G1	Wyandotte Chemical Corporation
Unitol	Union Camp Corporation
Ucar L-45	Union Carbide Corporation

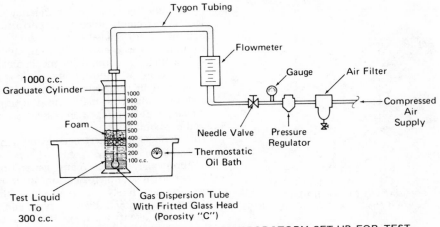

FIG. F-19. SCHEMATIC DIAGRAM OF LABORATORY SET-UP FOR TEST-
ING DEFOAMING AGENTS

foam height reached the top of the graduate cylinder within 1 min. With agent A added at 0.4 gal. per ton of product the foam layer was knocked down from an initial height of 500 cc to 370 cc. However, the knockdown was not sustained; within 4 min the foam exceeded its initial height. Thus, while this defoamer exhibited a good foam knockdown ability, its foam inhibition properties were limited. By contrast, agents B and C exhibited both good foam destruction and inhibition. Agent B inhibited further foaming by creating an equilibrium between the forces of foaming and defoaming.

Foam inhibition may be sustained or temporary depending on the type and dosage of a defoaming agent. It is therefore necessary to know whether or not the selected defoamer inhibits foaming for at least the time duration required by the process.

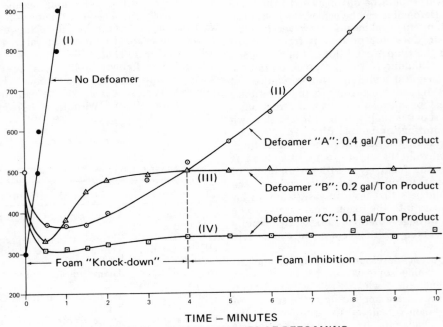

TIME — MINUTES

FIG. F-20. TYPICAL CURVES OF DEFOAMING

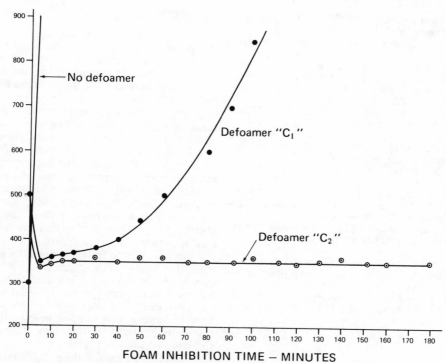

FIG. F-21. TYPICAL LABORATORY CURVES OF A PROLONGED FOAM
INHIBITION VERSUS A LIMITED ONE

Figure F-21 presents typical laboratory curves of a prolonged foam inhibition versus a limited one.

Technical Aspects of Defoaming

In evaluating a specific defoaming problem, it is necessary to thoroughly define the dimensions of the foam problem and from it extract more-or-less the desired defoaming requirements. The following list of questions may help in defining the problem:

Is rapid foam knockdown required?

Is stability of foam inhibition necessary?

Does the temperature, alkalinity or acidity of the process stream change at numerous points? Does this mean that one single or many defoamers will be required?

Does filtration affect defoaming? It is possible that the filtered solids may remove some of the defoaming agent through adsorption?

Is the defoamer compatible with the process pH?

Is addition of defoamer repeatedly required to sustain foam inhibition?

Most of the time, a well-organized laboratory program will answer effectively most of the above questions. The laboratory defoaming technique presented previously should be utilized. Next to the laboratory test, plant test should be in order.

Usually, the volume of agent required is very small in comparison to the process stream. Therefore, an accurate metering pump will be justified.

Point of addition is important, because the agent must be efficiently diffused into the main stream. The feeding point may also be as close as possible to where the foam is formed, such as in the reactor. However, problems may arise if the agent is not compatible with some of the entering reactants. Also, if a minimum effective dosage of defoamer is ascertained at one operating rate of the plant, this may not be applicable at another. The variation may be logarithmic, rather than linear.

Plant testing should cover both normal and abnormal operating conditions. Finally, the nature of the agent must also be considered. Some agents may affect equipment corrosion rate, add undesired or prohibitive toxicity, or change the color or taste of the final product.

A. P. KOULOHERIS

References

CARBARINO, T. T., ENCKE, F. L., and GEORGEHENAN, T. T. 1966. Evaluation of foam control agents for wet process phosphoric acid system. Proc. Fall Soc. Mining Engrs. Meeting (Oct.). Am. Inst. Mining Engrs. Preprint *66B330.*

CARPENTER, W. L., and GELLMAN, I. 1967. Measurement, control and changes in foaming characteristics of pulping wastes during biological treatment. TAPPI *50*, 83A–87A.

GADEN, E. L., and KEVORKIAN, V. 1956. Foams in chemical technology. Chem Eng. *63*, 173–184.

KOULOHERIS, A. P. 1970. Foam destruction and inhibition. Chem Eng., 77, 143–146.

LEMLICH, R. 1968. Foam fractionation. Chem Eng. *75*, 95–102.

PRUTTON, C. F., and MARON, S. H. 1951. Principles of Physical Chemistry, Revised Edition. Macmillan Co., New York.

REIGH, H. E. *et al.* 1961. Detergent foam measurement. Soap Chem. Specialties, *37*, Apr., 55–57.

SCHOEN, H. M. 1962. New Chemical Engineering Separation Techniques. Interscience Publishers, New York.

TAGGART, A. F. 1953. Frothing. *In* Handbook of Mineral Dressing. John Wiley & Sons, New York.

FOAM-MAT DRYING

Foam-mat drying is a method of dehydrating food liquids developed about 1960 at the USDA's Western Regional Research Laboratory. The liquids are first foamed, then spread out in thin mats on some support, and then dried in warm air streams. The foam structure persists during drying so that the dried mats can be easily scraped off the support and readily crumbled up into tiny pieces. The solid pieces so produced also have a foamy fine structure which promotes rapid rehydration by the user. Commercial use has so far been restricted to fruit juices.

Advantages

Foam-mat offers the advantages of air drying—cheapness and accessibility. Foam structure offers peculiar advantages in spreading, in drying, in surface removal, in crumbling up, and in rehydration of the product. The liquid foams are stiff and can be extruded, shaped and placed accurately. High quality dried products are obtained by uniform treatment. Overheating is inevitable when liquid thickness varies significantly, because drying rate is very sensitive to thickness of the layer or piece. Layer thickness must be very small, probably 0.1–0.5 mm, for drying times of a few minutes in 150°F air streams. It seems hopeless to achieve very thin liquid layers with, say, less than 20% variation in an industrial machine. The results had therefore been poor quality in air dryers and high final moisture in vacuum dryers.

Foam is an escape from the dilemma of thickness control. When liquid density is sufficiently reduced, the thickness for any surface loading is so increased as to make practical the desired percentage uniformity. Furthermore, with stiff foams, flow is so slow that surface irregularities do not cause dangerous layer thinnings after application and before complete drying.

A liquid layer usually dries at the rate water can find its way through the previously dried material at or near the free surface where the water is evaporating. A layer of foam dries much more rapidly than the same amount of unfoamed liquid under the same external conditions. This is because liquid moves more easily through a dry foam structure than through a dense layer of the same material. This is due to capillary action along the dry interstices; also, evaporation inside bubble spaces followed by gaseous diffusion through the thin outer dry walls aids rapid drying. A sponge dries more quickly than a potato. Bread dries faster than meat loaf. The foam structure decreases drying time to about $1/3$ what it would be for liquids under con-

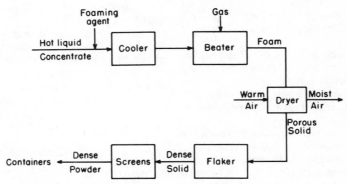

FIG. F-22. SCHEMATIC OF FOAM-MAT DRYING

ditions of interest in food dehydration. To acquire processing efficiency and the product quality and convenience advantages, the liquid must not only be foamed, but the foam must persist through drying to a great extent. Only certain foams have this durability.

Disadvantages

Foam-mat drying is useable only on liquids. Some liquids do not foam readily. Others collapse during drying. In many cases, therefore, it becomes necessary to add a foam stabilizer for foam-mat drying. A number of edible stabilizers have been found useful. This means that such powders cannot be sold as pure substances. Labels include such statements as "vegetable gum added" or "soluble protein added." Only a few foods, such as whole milk, contain enough foam stabilizing solutes naturally.

Another difficulty arises from the thin mats which must be used. Layers thicker than about 3 mm take longer to dry than most foams will remain stable. The result is that much surface must be installed for a practical production. The consequence of this is a higher cost than spray or drum drying, although lower than vacuum or freeze drying.

Processing Factors

Pretreatments.—In order to reduce the load on a dryer, feed should be concentrated in an evapora-tor if possible. Concentrates, furthermore, form stiffer, more stable foams for foam-mat drying. Too highly preconcentrated food, on the other hand, yields solids so dense that the final moisture cannot be easily removed in the dryer. Good feed solids concentrations are 30% for tomato and 55% for orange.

Foaming.—A stabilizer seems to fill either of two needs—bulk stiffening or film forming. Stiffening is needed for feeds of low insoluble-solids content or low bulk viscosity. Methyl cellulose or guar gum can stiffen most foams well when used at about 0.5% DSB. Film forming is needed for feeds poor in surface active solutes. Glyceryl monostearate, soluble soya protein, or egg albumin have usually been satisfactory. In a few cases, only sucrose fatty esters were usable. Continuous foaming consists of adding the stabilizer, injecting the right proportion of gas, subjecting the two-phase mixture to high-shear mixing, and cooling the foam at least enough to remove the heat of mixing. The correct density of foam is the highest consistent with a stable foam. Foam densities of 0.4–0.6 gm per ml are normal. This actually consists of spherical bubbles, averaging 0.1 mm in diameter, dispersed in a continuous liquid. Light froths, which consist of larger gas spaces separated by nearly planar liquid walls, are not suitable. Air foams seem to make as good product as inert gas foams.

Drying.—Foams must be spread into mats 2–3 mm thick. These layers will dry in 10–20 min while

FIG. F-23. THIN LAYER OF CRATERED FOAM SHOWN AS IT IS DRYING

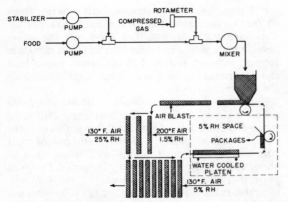

FIG. F-24. SCHEMATIC OF CRATER FOAM-MAT
DRYING

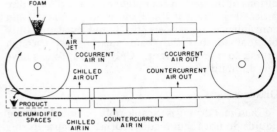

FIG. F-25. SCHEMATIC OF PERFORATED BELT
DRYER OPERATION

keeping the product below 135°F. Thinner layers
dry much faster but contain less material. The
result is a production rate limit of 0.3–0.4 lb
powder per hour per square foot of surface installed.
Drying rate is sensitive to air velocity over or
through the mat only while the foam is still quite
wet. As the product becomes nearly dry, the
drying rate is most sensitive to air relative humidity.
At least two drying stages seem desirable. The first
might use 300 ft per min of 220°F cocurrent flow,
the second using 50 ft per min of 135°F countercurrent flow.

Scraping.—When the product has a low hot-sticky
temperature, such as citrus powders, the mats must
be cooled with dehumidified air before scraping of
the drying surface. Scraping must be sufficiently
complete so that the surface can be reloaded without washing in order to avoid losses of product.

Equipment

Two dryer concepts have been built. Neither
seems to have a clear advantage as yet. In one
case, foam is dried on a belt, in the other it is
dried on trays.

Belts.—Foams are spread or extruded onto stainless steel belts up to 4 ft wide. The belts may be
perforated with $1/8$ in. holes on $3/16$ in. centers.
The foam mat extruded onto this perforated surface
spans the holes without dropping through. The
belt passes over an air jet which pierces the mat
above each hole and heaps up the displaced foam
around the hole like a little crater. The drying air
then flows up through the belt and foam, coming
into good contact with an extended foam surface.
The air is side ducted in such a way that it passes
a number of times through the belt in the dryer—
first cocurrent, then countercurrent to belt
movement.

Another belt foam-mat dryer uses an unperforated belt. This version, known as microflake, uses
thinner mats and shorter residence times. In addition to cross or longitudinal air flows, heat can be
added by condensing atmospheric steam on the
bottom of the belt. The belt acts as top of boxes
into which the steam is admitted, the condensate
being wiped off by the down stream side of the
boxes. This method is said to achieve higher production rates at the cost of a higher percentage of
exposed surface to weight ratio in the product.

Trays.—Foams may be extruded onto perforated
trays up to 4 by 4 ft in size. Both stainless steel
and aluminum have been used. The $1/8$-in. hole on
$3/16$-in. center pattern has been applied to trays as
well as belts. The trays pass continuously end to
end under the foam extruder and over the cratering
air jet. They are then inserted one at a time at the
bottom of a vertical stack of trays inside a duct
which forms the dryer. The trays move up the
dryer and leave the top—dry. Flat trays may be
moved by stubs attached to roller chains, only the
stub extending through a slot in the wall of the
dryer. Alternatively, the trays may have a self-
stacking shape. The trays then rest on each other
in the dryer. The stack can be pushed upward
from below and latched into position. A new
tray is inserted below and the dryest tray is dragged
off at the top. The trays are cooled, scraped, and
returned continuously for reloading. In this version, somewhat better product is obtained through

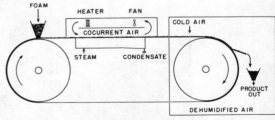

FIG. F-26. SCHEMATIC OF UNPERFORATED BELT
DRYER OPERATION

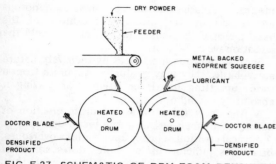

FIG. F-27. SCHEMATIC OF DRY FOAM DENSIFICATION

thicker layers and slower drying. The more complicated apparatus requires more sophisticated, if not more, labor. It has been made fully automatic.

Product Characteristics

Moisture.—A critical moisture content must be reached in drying to permit handling of the product. A somewhat lower moisture, about 1% for citrus powders, is needed for storage stability. About 2% moisture is required by tomato powder. These low moistures can be reached only by using countercurrent drying and good foams. Such low moistures require a dehumidified packing space. The product, once cooled below 100°F, must remain in air below 15% RH. Moisture contents are usually determined by Karl Fischer method.

Densifying.—The dry product often has a bulk density of 0.3 gm per ml. This can be raised as high as 0.8 gm per ml by compacting the powder between strong, warm steel rolls. The extent of densifying is determined by balancing reduced rehydration rates against smaller container costs. Where a foamy rehydrated product, or a floating powder is undesirable, densifying is necessary. Another compacting device used is the pelletizer. For bite-sized doses, or for simulated berries, the pelletizer has proven useful.

Packaging.—Foam-mat dried products have storage requirements equal to the same materials dried other ways. Fruit powders must be protected from humidity, especially if storage temperatures are above 85°F. In addition, tomato powder must be protected against oxygen content above 1%. Aluminum or Saran films, cans or glass have been used.

Present Use

Foam-mat dryers have been sold by four equipment manufacturers: FMC Corp. of San Jose, California; Chemet Engineers of Pasadena, California; AMF of Stamford, Connecticut; and TAG of Berlin. A number of users have constructed their own units, such as Foamat Foods of Corvallis, Oregon; Kikkoman Foods of Tokyo; and Gerber Foods of Fremont, Michigan. At present, orange, grapefruit, pineapple, berry, and tomato powders are being made. Potato mash is foamed by some processors before drying to granules or aggregates. The quantity of fruit powder foam-mat dried is small, probably less than 3 million pounds per year total in 1970.

Prospects

Uses will grow only slowly until new product classes are found. The high raw material value of fruit solids makes sales of these products difficult. The uses in which only dry products can compete are expanding slowly—dry soup mixes, drink powders, bakery ingredients, fruit-cereal mixtures, or dry dessert items. If dry whole milk can become popular, a sudden expansion might occur. If European and Japanese consumers continue to lean toward dry products over frozen, an important penetration of this fruit juice market might take place. The instant coffee and tea trend toward freeze drying may slacken. Producers could reduce charges by foam-mat drying at the cost of mentioning a stabilizer on the label. Any of these events would rocket the method to high use.

ARTHUR I. MORGAN, JR.

Cross-references: *Dehydration; Freeze Drying.*

FOOD ADDITIVES

See Additives, Food.

FOOD AND AGRICULTURE ORGANIZATION OF THE UNITED NATIONS

The Food and Agriculture Organization (FAO) of the United Nations was set up as the first new postwar independent specialized agency in the family of the United Nations. The Conference which took a decision on its establishment met at Quebec, Canada, in October 1945, when 44 countries became founding members. The present membership is 125 governments which pool their efforts to help meet the needs of over 3 billion of their citizens.

FAO is concerned with the development of world agriculture, fisheries and forestry, and the welfare of the people working in these fields. In the area of food science, technology, and nutrition, its main activities as defined in the Constitution are:

(A) Scientific, technological, social and economic research relating to nutrition, food, and agriculture.

(B) The improvement of education and administration relating to nutrition, food, and agriculture; and the spread of public knowledge of nutritional and agricultural science and practice.

(C) The *conservation* of natural resources and the adoption of improved methods of agricultural production.

(D) The improvement of the *processing, marketing and distribution of food* and agricultural products.

In the area of technical assistance, FAO provides, in response to the requests from member governments, technical cooperation on projects in the form of advisory missions and services of specialized personnel, grants for fellowships to carry out studies and provide training, and procurement of essential equipment and supplies.

In the area of postharvest technology, FAO provides assistance for conservation and processing of food and agricultural commodities, specially to the economically less-advanced countries. The primary objective of this program is to retain and enhance the nutritive value of foods, minimize losses, raise the level of employment, ensure better income distribution, and add value to the primary produce.

Assistance in different fields of food and agricultural products processing industries is provided through selection, modification, and transfer of appropriate technologies from advanced as well as developing countries to those countries which need it. Surveys are carried out to assist countries in the formulation of their nutritional policies and implementation of the latter within the resources available. In order to achieve this objective, an integrated approach to production, handling, storage, processing, marketing, and utilization of agricultural produce is pursued. Assistance is also provided to the setting up of institutions in the areas of credit, finance, research, development, and training to help countries achieve a greater degree of self-reliance.

H. A. B. PARPIA

FOOD FLAVORS

The flavor of a food can be lost or damaged as a consequence of physical, chemical, or biological change. Sometimes these same forces can be used to enhance the flavor of a food.

Flavor depends upon two broad classes of substances. Nonvolatile compounds possessing taste attributes are sensed by the taste buds of the mouth. Volatile substances which are odorous are sensed by the olfactory receptors of the nasal passage. Together, the two classes yield the sensation we call flavor.

Because odorous substances by their very nature are volatile, they may gradually evaporate from a food, upsetting its flavor balance or leaving it absolutely devoid of flavor.

A fine food flavor is an exquisite creation of nature or of man just as a fine piano concerto is. A musical creation depends upon various overtones, base notes, judicious use of "hold" notes, shades of softness or vigor, and of course, timing or rhythm. Flavor is akin to a musical creation in many respects. There are certain base notes with overtones; compounds volatilize at different rates and are perceived at different times; and perception is lingering for some and fleeting for others. The fugacity of the odor portion of flavor often leads to the undoing of flavor quality. Through the outright loss or dimunition of certain flavor notes, harmonious combinations may be destroyed, even dissonance may result. If a new odor or taste is added to a food, there is an even greater change of strong dissonance.

Physical Processes

The physical processes will be discussed first as they are relatively simple. Odorous substances are volatile because they have appreciable vapor pressure at room temperature. Lowering of the temperature reduces the vapor pressure and thus the amount of material volatilizing during any given time.

Volatility is not solely dependent on temperature, however. In foods, flavors may be adsorbed on solid surfaces and, of course, they may be dissolved in the aqueous or fat phases of the food, sometimes both, depending upon the partition coefficient of the particular compound. Porosity, the type of surface, and the composition of the food thus affect the rate with which a given compound will volatilize from the food. Furthermore, these same factors may affect the ease with which a food will pick up a foreign odor.

Not in all instances is the volatility of odorous compounds detrimental to flavor. Off-odors caused by weeds or feed are sometimes stripped from fluid milk by subjecting the milk to a vacuumization step as a part of processing. Vegetable oils are deodorized by steam- or vacuum-distillation processes to remove the typical odor of the particular oil so as to make the oil nearly devoid of odor and thus suitable for several uses. Fractional distillation and steam distillation likewise are used to control flavor as witness the degree of rectification to which a brandy may be subjected according to the need to leave out as well as include certain components generated in the parent wine material.

Just as physical forces may be manipulated to remove unwanted odors, as in the vacuumization of oils or the distillation of alcoholic beverages, so too may they be used to hold in wanted odors. Flavoring substances (and perfumes) are dissolved in solvents, in part to adjust strength. The vapor pressure of the solvent is lower than that of the most volatile of the flavor materials, but it does contribute to the vapor pressure; consequently somewhat less of the volatile substances vaporize than would if the flavor substances were the sole source of vapor pressure. Actually, many solvents function in a second way and are sometimes called fixatives on that account. Hydrogen bonding is quite common among organic compounds. Most of the solvents used form hydrogen bonds readily. A substance which is hydrogen bonded to another substance has less of an escaping tendency than the pure substance. Water itself is the best illustration of this principle. Water has an extraordinarily high boiling point considering its molecular weight. This comes about because water molecules tend to hydrogen bond; in other words, they exist as aggregates of water molecules. The molecules are in a constant state of flux, becoming aggregated, then breaking up again; but enough hydrogen bonding is going on at any one time to make water a relatively nonvolatile substance. The foregoing statement is an exaggeration in part because water does evaporate readily, but it does not volatilize as readily as would be expected from knowing its molecular weight only.

Another physical means used to preserve or protect flavor substances is what is known as flavor entrapment. In the last two decades, there has been a great expansion in the development of methods of entrapping flavors. Initially, flavors were entrapped within matrices of such substances as crystalized glucose; but more recently, entrapment within minute gelled spheres or particles has become more common. The basic principle behind entrapment is the formation of an emulsion of the flavor with a gelling material such as pectin, gum arabic, or some similar hydrophilic colloid. The particles are then dried rapidly at first—as by spray drying or some other means—so as to form a "skin" on the particle. In dehydration, drying processes are controlled so as to prevent the development of case hardening. In flavor entrapment, the reverse is sought. Rapid drying at the surface causes a "skin" to form which thereafter acts as a molecular sieve. Water molecules are small enough to pass through the surface layer upon further drying, but the flavor materials being of higher molecular weight (size) cannot pass through the dry film as readily.

Aside from the detrimental loss of flavor from a food, there is the very practical problem of preventing odor transfer. Unpackaged foods often will pick up foreign odors from their surroundings. Even packaged foods may do so if the package is not gas-proof. Some foods cannot be packaged in gas-proof packages because they must be in a package which "breathes." In that case, extra precautions need to be taken to ensure that the food is not stored in an atmosphere or near substances from which odor transfer can take place. This applies to fresh fruits and vegetables, eggs, milk, butter, and, in fact, to most food products. Foods sometimes develop a foreign odor as a result of contamination by odors derived from insecticides or fumigants. Generally, the odor comes from the solvent, but in some cases the active ingredient itself may be the cause of trouble. This applies especially to fumigants.

Food packages themselves may be the cause of trouble. Odors can be picked up from adhesives, coatings, added odorants, printing inks, and the board stock itself. Musty or moldy odors often come from the use of slimy wash water in the manufacture of the paperboard. Packaging materials used for foods thus have to be of high quality.

Chemical Changes

While physical phenomena leading to flavor loss or change are not truly simple they are far less complex than chemical processes. Chemical change in flavor accounts for the greatest number of problems, and it is the most difficult form of deterioration to prevent. The kinds of chemical reactions involved in food deterioration probably encompass every type of reaction known.

A typical food consists of three major categories of constituents. They are: (1) the solid structure; (2) other materials which are present in appreciable amounts such as water, fat, sugars, acids, coloring matters, and several of the plant or animal colloids (proteins, starches, plant gums); and (3) organic compounds which can only be categorized as trace materials. The solid substances, while not dissolved are often important because they provide the surface or the sites which aid in promoting chemical reactions. If the food is packaged, there is a fourth phase, the headspace, consisting of gases and vapors.

Of the components which are normally present in large amounts (grams or milligrams per 100 gm), fats, sugars, and N-containing compound account for much of the trouble in preventing flavor deterioration. Fats may either split hydrolytically or be oxidized. Reducing sugars and amino acids take part in the classical Maillard reaction, leading to browning and the development of new flavor substances. In the case of bread crust or meat this is desirable. In dehydrated fruits, dried eggs, and several other products, the flavor produced is undesirable. Actually, browning today is no longer considered to be confined to the classical Maillard reaction but to include several classes of reactions involving substances other than reducing sugars and amino acids.

The Maillard reaction involves the reaction of the carbonyl groups ($-\overset{\overset{\displaystyle O}{\|}}{C}-$) of sugars with the amino group ($-NH_2$) of amino acids or other substances possessing an amino group. The two compounds react to form a Schiff's base, then rearrange to form a nitrogen-substituted glycosylamine, then ultimately rearrange again to form a nitrogen-substituted 1-amino-1-deoxy-2-ketose. From this stage on, several other reactions then can take place, yielding flavor compounds and brown pigments.

Reducing sugars may also react with other types of compounds containing $-NH_2$ or $-NH$ groups to yield brown pigments. Ascorbic acid upon being oxidized to dehydroascorbic acid and then degraded to furfural also reacts with α-amino acids to produce a reddish-brown complex. A fourth major type of browning involves dehydration of sugars or sugar acids to form furfuraldehyde or related compounds having active aldehyde groups, these products then condense with N-containing compounds or polymerize with themselves to form brown materials.

Initially, browning reactions were studied primarily from the color point of view, but today there is much interest in them as means of generating useful flavor substances. By selecting particular reactants, flavors reminiscent or typical of certain products may be formed. A recent patent, for example, describes the formation of meal-like flavors by heating 2-aminoethane sulfuric acid and thiamin.

The browning reaction is also important from a nutritional or a food satiety point of view. Several years ago, the Quartermaster Food and Container Institute observed that the eating of a food with a slight off-odor is not restricted in its effect to that particular food. Upon feeding soldiers instant potatoes which were stale, there was marked satiety for other foods even when given 1.5 hr later. There is ample evidence that unpleasant odors may affect hunger and appetite. In the case of the browning reaction, there is a considerable body of evidence that microorganisms initiate growth better in media free of browning end products than they do in media containing them.

The whole subject of the relationship between pleasant flavors and appetite stimulation is just beginning to open up. Wines, for example, taken in moderate doses, have been shown to improve the appetite of geriatric patients (and others). Part of this may be mild tranquilization and the suppression of emotional tension. All alcoholic beverages in small doses have this property to some extent, but there are differences among the alcoholic beverages. It is claimed that certain compounds help to maintain olfactory acuity and that as long as olfactory acuity is high the hunger sensation persists. This particular theory is contested, but there probably is substance to the idea that some flavor components have central-nervous-system action and thus affect appetite.

When fats decompose, they also have a profound effect on food acceptability. If the fat is merely hydrolyzed, the resulting sharpness caused by the liberated fatty acid may be beneficial up to a point, as in aged cheese or country-cured hams. If the reaction goes too far, a quality otherwise desirable becomes undesirable. Sometimes hydrolysis of fat leads to the formation of a "soapy" taste instead of a sharp, acidulous taste. This is true when the pH is above 7. The fatty acid then exists as an alkali-earth salt instead of the free acid. At one time this was somewhat of a problem in the formulation of instant cake mixes because of the presence of leavening agents, but the problem has been pretty much overcome through modification of formulas and methods of combining the dry ingredients. However, occasionally a soapy taste is still encountered in foods which have a high pH.

While hydrolysis of fats is important, far worse is oxidative rancidity. Light catalyzes oxidative rancidity, heat accelerates it, and so do traces of metallic catalysts such as iron or copper. Of these agents, light is probably the most harmful. Potato chips exposed to sunlight for $1/2$ hr often will develop a definite off-flavor whereas a considerably greater exposure to heat is necessary to bring about a corresponding degree of deterioration. The two types of off-flavor are, however, different.

Basically, light and heat function by providing energy. Light does so by being absorbed. This "activates" the molecule or, in other words, an active radical is formed. Upon the active radical colliding with another molecule, activated or not, the sum of energy in the two molecules usually is sufficient to permit them to react. At any temperature above absolute zero, molecules are in motion and a certain percentage of them contain sufficient energy to react provided they collide with another molecule. Raising the temperature steps up the rate of reaction because molecules vibrate more vigorously the higher the temperature. Light, by being absorbed, likewise provides energy. An increase of $10°C$ may result in a substantially greater percentage of the molecules containing sufficient energy to react, thus the rate of reaction goes up. The rate at different temperatures is normally expressed as a

Q_{10} value, i.e., a Q_{10} value of 3, for example, means that a reaction will go on 3 times faster $10°C$ higher than at some given temperature and $1/3$ as fast $10°C$ below that same temperature. Chemical reactions involving flavor often have Q_{10} values of 5–7. They may however be quite low.

In the case of fats, light leads to the production of an active hydroperoxide, the active radical ultimately cleaves, and the breakdown products in turn decompose again, leading ultimately to the formation of low molecular-weight carbonyls. Most of these are quite odorous, and some are distinctly unpleasant. Fats which are thermally oxidized decompose by different pathways in many instances, but off-flavors develop for the same reason, because the carbonyls produced are malodorous. If traces of metal are present to act as catalysts, the reactions usually go on even faster.

Fats are not the only compounds which may be changed by light. Riboflavin in milk acts as a photosensitizer. While paperboard cartons are generally looked upon as being opaque materials by the average person, some of them do pass sufficient light to permit light-activated reactions to occur. In a supermarket lighted to 100 foot-candles with fluorescent light as much as 10% of the light may pass through the carton. This is an appreciable amount of light. The riboflavin content will be decreased (also ascorbic acid, if present) and a form of off-flavor known as light-struck flavor develops.

A similar thing occurs in beer. The off-flavor is then called skunky or sunlight off-flavor. It is due to the formation of methyl-2-butene-1-thiol which is a reaction product of H_2S and 3-methyl-2-butenyl. The H_2S and the 3-methyl-2-butenyl originate from degradation of a sulfur-containing amino acid and isohumulones. The riboflavin is the compound which absorbs the energy of the light and sets off the reaction.

Antioxidants are widely used to control oxidative rancidity. Primary antioxidants are usually o- or p-substituted phenols or aromatic amines. They function by reacting with free radicals, particularly the hydroperoxide radical which is the chief propagator of the chain oxidation of fats. In breaking the chain, the antioxidant itself is usually oxidized. Butylated hydroxyanisole, butylated hydroxytoluene, and propyl gallate are antioxidants of this type. Citric, ascorbic, other hydroxy acids, and phosphoric acid are also used as antioxidants but they function as metal deactivators rather than as primary antioxidants. Flavonols function in both fashions. When suitably substituted, they are powerful primary antioxidants. They also chelate metals and deactivate them as does citric acid.

Antioxidants have enabled remarkable advances to be made in the food industry. Antioxidants are not completely effective, but often they extend the shelf-life of a food from an unacceptably short time to a time well within the range of economic suitability.

Browning and rancidification were discussed first among the chemical reactions because they are so pervasive in their action and the number of foods they affect. Often the cause of flavor differences in foods is not known. This is especially so of the compounds which are present in only trace amounts.

Thousands, nay, millions of hours and dollars have been expended merely to identify flavor compounds, but in almost every case after 100, or 200, or 300 compounds have been identified in a given food, attempts to formulate a synthetic flavor approaching that of nature have proved futile. Flavorists who create flavor formulations based upon their keen scent and memory for flavor notes have been far more successful in formulating a given flavor than have scientists. This is because we still do not understand the relationships among compounds. Let us return to the analogy of a piano composition to illustrate this point. Merely knowing the names of the 88 keys of a piano does not make one a composer. The notes must be used in certain combinations, with a certain touch or degree of shading, and with rhythm. The scientist attempting to duplicate a flavor of nature has the added disadvantage that he does not know all the notes. Sometimes instrumental methods are as sensitive as the human nose, but generally we can detect odors in concentrations more dilute than can be detected by instrumental means.

Some success has been attained. There are flavor materials on the market made by first identifying the major components in natural compounds and then combining the identified substances in the right proportion; but nature can invariably top man's best efforts when the natural things are at their best. When good flavors rather than supreme ones are involved, man can often produce flavors equal to authentic products of nature.

In a flavor complex of from 100 to 400 substances, each compound is generally present at a rather low level, often as parts per million or parts per billion. The major component of green bell pepper has recently been identified. It is 2-methoxy-3-isobutylpyrazine. Its odor threshold in water is 2 parts per trillion.

The fact that so many compounds are present in the flavor complex of a food is part of the reason flavors are so difficult to stabilize. With dozens of kinds of compounds present, some in the vapor phase, some in the aqueous phase, and some in the fat phase, there are also dozens of possibilities for different types of reaction to occur because even the same compound may have a different reactivity in the vapor phase and dissolved in water or in fat. Furthermore, a comparatively small amount of energy may be all that is required to bring about a substantial change in the concentration of one compound. As the threshold level for detection of the compound is often in the ppm or ppb range, a change involving only $1/2$ ppm may lead to the loss of a desirable flavor note or to the development of an undesirable flavor. This is the reason traces of light, heat, or metals are often so detrimental to the flavor of a food or the stability of a flavor extract.

Biological Factors

The products of nature are produced by biological processes, and as has already been indicated, some natural flavor substances are incomparable indeed. Even the synthetic chemist often uses nature's molecules as starting materials to build new flavor compounds.

Biological processes can likewise lend to the degradation of flavor or to aberrations in flavor. Mold growing on meat or cheese may decarboxylate and deaminate an amino acid leading to the formation of an aldehyde possessing a strong or unpleasant odor whereas the original amino acid may be quite mild in taste or almost lacking it. Methionine is sometimes converted to methional in this fashion.

Many of our fermented foods depend upon differences in the end products of organisms of the same species but of different strains. Wine and bread yeast illustrate this. Sometimes a given strain which has long proved satisfactory will undergo an aberration and become unsatisfactory. A defect of Cheddar cheese is a fruity flavor. Ethyl butyrate and ethyl hexanoate have been shown to be the primary cause of the fruity note. Sometimes starter cultures go astray because of a mutagenic change in the strain. More common, the strain just changes physiologically because of long culture on an artificial medium or gradual ascendency of a substrain within the strain as a consequence of repeated subculturing.

The fact that microorganisms are nature's most versatile factories is a great problem in holding desired flavors constant, as in fermentation, and in preventing them from bringing about change in food when none is wanted at all. On the other hand, their versatility can sometimes be put to work to produce chemicals used in the flavor industry.

Assessment of Flavor

Modes of flavor assessment vary. They range from quite simple methods, depending upon the ability to pick out an odd sample from among three samples, for example, to ranking or scoring procedures for several samples. Generally, the number of samples should be kept fairly low so as to avoid fatigue. Irrespective of the method used, they all depend upon statistical inference to decide whether the results are within the realm of chance variation or the differences observed are true differences.

Measurement of threshold levels is comparatively simple (though tedious), but attempts to quantify suprathreshold levels are quite difficult; and this is the range within which food flavors come. It is hard to get people to agree on word descriptions as to the character of an odor or flavor and its intensity. Clear-cut cases of off-flavor are easy to recognize. One cannot make the foregoing statement completely catholic. Some people through custom have acquired a taste for certain kinds of flavor which to others is an off-flavor. Examples of this are the acceptability of traces of rancidity by some whose food supply is not of the best or the acquiring of a particular taste—as the metallic- or heat-generated taste of canned tomato juice simply because few of us consume fresh tomato juice.

One thing which sometimes needs to be taken into consideration is that anosmics exist for odor as well as for taste. Some geneticists maintain anosmia does not exist at all, that such people merely have extraordinarily high threshold requirements. Irrespective of there being a genetic difference or merely a physiological one, there are wide differences in the ability of people to sense and to quantify particular flavors; and there is an even greater difference in the kind of word descriptions they will attach to the substances they perceive.

Not only is greater knowledge of flavor compounds needed from an analytical point of view, but we are grossly short of basic physiological knowledge regarding them. Some flavors possess trigeminal qualities as well as odorous ones. The manner by which they are perceived, the effects they have upon the body such as the central-nervous-system, and the role pleasant or unpleasant flavors play in appetite stimulation and satiety from both the physiological and psychological points of view are indeed challenging tasks for the investigator, as are the problems of bringing semantic order to the field.

The food technologist or the marketing man is not, of course, concerned with flavor in the abstract. Just as the qualities of a fine painting may be enhanced or detracted from by the frame within which it is put, so too does flavor play a key role in motivating people to accept, reject, or be indifferent to a particular food. This is important in marketing. It is important from a nutritional point of view, too. A substance can hardly be called a food until it is ingested. Flavor plays a critical role in determining whether a substance will be included at all among food items and the extent to which it will be used.

JOHN J. POWERS

Cross-reference: *Flavorings and Essences.*

FOOD PRESERVATION

Food preservation involves the application of scientific and engineering principles to the practical control of food deterioration. Practical control is complicated by the interactions of numerous deteriorative factors that lead to unique spoilage patterns of specific foods.

From the moment food is harvested, gathered, caught, or slaughtered it undergoes progressive deterioration, which, depending upon the food, may be very slow or so rapid as to render the food virtually useless in a matter of hours. Bacteria, yeasts, molds, insects, and rodents are in constant competition with man for his food supply. Further, the highly sensitive organic compounds of food, and the biochemical balance of these compounds, are subject to destruction by nearly every variable in man's natural environment. Heat, cold, light, oxygen, moisture, dryness, the natural food enzymes themselves, and time—all tend to deteriorate foods.

This has immediate significance in underdeveloped areas of the world as well as in the most highly advanced and organized societies. In less developed areas, starvation has occurred in villages only a few miles from locations of a lush harvest because of spoilage. In highly advanced societies, food production generally is centralized where food can be most efficiently grown or processed. These areas in the United States can be 2 or 3 thousand miles distant from a population center where the food will be consumed. Unless the deteriorative factors are controlled, there would be no food for these population centers and indeed there could be no highly advanced society.

The essence of food science and technology may be said to be an understanding of the deteriorative factors and their control through preservation processes. Commonly, various degrees of preservation were accomplished long before an understanding of the principles involved were known; and many of the foods prized today developed out of attempts to prolong storage life. One might not ordinarily think of butter as a means of preserving food, but it was long ago discovered that while milk deteriorated in a day or two, clumps of butter fat that formed when milk was agitated could be removed from the milk and would store for weeks or months. Similarly, cheese, wine, sauerkraut, smoked fish, dried fruits, and other valued foods had their beginnings in attempts to slow down the deteriorative processes.

Total food preservation that would encompass absolute food safety, complete retention of nutritional value, and prolonged stability of all of a food's natural organoleptic properties is an idealized goal that for many foods may never become technically or economically feasible. However, modern food processing is based on preservation methods that for all practical purposes ensure food safety, minimize nutrient destruction, and are constantly being improved to yield products of superior appearance, texture, flavor, and keeping qualities.

Such processes must eliminate or minimize all of the deteriorative factors that may operate against a given food. Thus, for example, in the case of canned meats the canned product is retorted to kill microorganisms and to destroy natural meat enzymes. The metal can subsequently protects the product from insects and rodents, as well as from light which could deteriorate color and possibly nutritive value. Vacuum is applied or the can is flushed with nitrogen or carbon dioxide before closure to remove oxygen that could promote randicity. The hermetically sealed can also protects the meat from drying out, reabsorbing oxygen, or becoming recontaminated by microorganisms. The cans are stored at a moderate temperature and the length of time the cans are held in supermarkets is limited. In this case, the preservation method, which is relatively simple, is quite adequate for the product being preserved. A very different sequence of operations is employed in the preservation of orange juice in the form of frozen juice concentrate. Juice squeezed from the fruit contains air. Oxygen will cause destruction of vitamin C, loss of color, and impairment of flavor so the juice is first passed through a vacuum deaerator to remove oxygen. The deaerated juice is still highly perishable due to microorganisms and natural fruit enzymes. Therefore it is next pasteurized prior to concentration. Pasteurization and subsequent vacuum evaporation to yield a concentrate are carried out at relatively mild time-temperature exposures to minimize vitamin destruction and flavor change. The concentrate is then slush frozen, canned, hard frozen, and maintained in frozen condition until reconstituted for consumption.

Modern food processes to achieve preservation thus generally involve multiple operations directed against a complex of spoilage factors unique to a specific product. Preservation technology is concerned with the optimization of these operations from the standpoints of product quality, storage life, and cost.

Principles and Applications

Generally, preservation processes are primarily directed at controlling the growth of microorganisms. The most important means of controlling microorganisms include heat, cold, drying, acid, sugar, salt, smoke, air, chemicals, and radiations. Fortunately, several of these means, such as heat, cold, drying, certain chemicals, and to some extent radiations, also are useful in destroying or limiting the activities of a variety of undesirable food enzymes. Additionally, cold temperatures and the removal of moisture markedly decrease the rates of nonenzymatic chemical reactions that contribute to a wide range of adverse changes in foods.

Heat

Most bacteria, yeasts, and molds grow best in the temperature range of about $60°$-$100°$F. Thermophiles will grow in the range of $150°$-$180°$F. Most bacteria are killed in the range of $180°$-$200°$F. But many bacterial spores are not destroyed even by boiling water at $212°$F for 30 min. To ensure sterility, that is *total* destruction of microorganisms, a temperature of about $250°$F (wet heat) must be maintained for 15 min or longer. This generally is done with steam under pressure. When foods are high in acid, such as tomatoes or orange juice, one need not heat as severely because acid increases the lethal effects of heat. A temperature of $200°$F for 15 min may be sufficient to gain sterility if sufficient acid is present.

Fortunately, it is not always necessary to kill all microorganisms and very few food products are truly sterile. Our canned foods are "commercially sterile," which means that they are safe from a public health standpoint and the few organisms that do survive the heat treatment normally will not multiply and spoil the food over a period of 2 yrs or more. More heat to ensure sterility would have adverse effects on food quality. Many foods receive still less severe heating and are only pasteurized. Such products are made free of pathogenic organisms but because of relatively high numbers of surviving bacteria would rapidly spoil if not refrigerated. Heat blanching is a kind of pasteurization generally applied to vegetables to inactivate natural food enzymes. This is common practice when such products are to be frozen, since frozen storage in itself does not completely arrest enzyme activity.

While temperature and time are required to destroy microorganisms, different temperature-time combinations that are equally effective in microbial destruction can be far different with regard to their damaging effect upon foods. This is of the greatest practical importance in modern heat processing and is the basis for several of the more advanced heat preservation methods. The higher the temperature the shorter will be the time that is required for microbial destruction. However, the more important factor in damaging foods with respect to color, flavor, texture, and nutritional value is long time rather than high temperature. Thus, while time-temperature combinations of 10 min at $240°$F and 0.78 min at $260°$F are equally effective in destroying spores of the toxin-producing bacterium *Clostridium botulinum* in low-acid media, the higher temperature, shorter time exposure is far less damaging to food quality. This principle underlies the use of high temperature-short time (HTST) pasteurization and commercial sterilization processes where foods are especially sensitive to heat. In the latter case, foods cannot be rapidly heated within a can due to excessive times required for heat penetration. This is solved by exposing thin layers of the food to HTST treatment in special heat exchangers and then sealing the food under aseptic conditions in previously sterilized containers, as in the process of aseptic canning.

Cold

Although most bacteria, yeasts, and molds grow best in the temperature range of $60°$-$100°$F, psychrophiles will grow down to $32°$F and below if free water exists. At temperatures below $50°$F, however, growth is slow and becomes progressively slower with decreased temperature. The rates of enzymatic and nonenzymatic reactions in foods also decrease with temperature, although enzymes not inactivated by other means such as blanching or chemical treatment continue to function at slow rates in frozen foods. Even the severest cold is not a sterilizing process; and commonly, large numbers of bacteria survive food freezing and then proceed to grow rapidly if the food is permitted to thaw and incubate.

In preservation by cold a distinction must be made between refrigeration and cool storage on the one hand and freezing and frozen storage on the other. Refrigeration and cool storage generally cover a range of about $60°$F down to $30°$F. Commercial and household refrigerators are usually run at $40°$-$45°$F but this is too cold for some fruit and vegetable products which exhibit optimum storage properties at temperatures of about $50°$F. For all foods that can withstand freezing, good frozen storage means $0°$F or below without intermittant fluctuations that would lead to partial thawing.

Highest quality frozen foods, especially with respect to retention of natural texture, depend upon fast freezing. Slow freezing leads to growth of large ice crystals and prolonged time for food constituents to be in contact with solutes that become concentrated as freezing progresses. Both ice crystal damage and solute concentration effects are greatly minimized, and frozen food quality improved by very rapid freezing. This has been the motivation behind the development of advanced rapid freezing equipment and processes.

Commercial freezing methods generally are classified under the headings of air freezing, indirect contact freezing, and immersion freezing. Air freezing may utilize still air, high velocity air which is more efficient, and high velocity air applied to particulate foods to suspend them as in a fluidized-bed freezer. Indirect contact freezing generally utilizes chilled plates to freeze solid foods, or refrigerated tubular heat exchangers to slush freeze liquid foods in a continuous fashion. Immersion freezing involves direct contact of the food or its container with the refrigerant which may be cold brine, propylene glycol, or a cryogenic liquid (or gas) such as carbon dioxide, liquid nitrogen, or a food approved Freon.

Drying

Free water is required for microbial growth and for many enzymatic and nonenzymatic chemical reactions. Water may be partially removed from liquid foods and juices by atmospheric and vacuum evaporation processes and by the newer membrane processes such as reverse osmosis. More complete drying to the range of about 95-98% solids involves the use of dehydration equipment of varying design often optimized for the specific product to be dried.

Grains dry naturally under the sun and sun drying of certain fruits continues to be of economic importance. In underdeveloped areas sun drying often is a most important method of preservation of animal as well as vegetable foodstuffs. Far greater control of drying variables and product quality can be obtained, however, with mechanical dehydration equipment designed to maximize transfer of heat into the product and mass transfer (of water) out under economical operating conditions.

Dehydration methods and equipment may be roughly divided according to whether liquid or solid food materials are being dried. Liquid foods and purées commonly are atomized into a heated chamber as in spray drying, spread over the surface of a revolving heated drum from which they are continuously scraped as in drum drying, and sometimes thickened or foamed and cast on belts that move through an oven chamber. Solid foods of varying piece size commonly are air dried in heated cabinets, on belts moving through tunnel

ovens, in rotating cylinders that give the food a tumbling motion, or in fluidized-bed driers where high velocity heated air suspends particulates for more efficient heat and mass transfer.

Foods that are especially heat sensitive may be processed in vacuum driers at relatively low temperatures since the boiling point of water decreases with reduced pressure. A special kind of vacuum drying is freeze drying in which the food that may be a solid or a liquid is frozen and then placed in a high vacuum chamber. Temperature and vacuum are so controlled that the frozen food is prevented from melting and the moisture goes directly from the frozen ice state to the gaseous vapor state without passing through the liquid state—a condition of sublimation. This results in a gently dehydrated porous structure with minimum shape distortion, flavor or color loss, and excellent rehydration properties. Many products, however, cannot justify the generally greater costs of freeze drying compared with other dehydration methods. Dehydrated food products differ greatly in their hygroscopic properties and in their sensitivity to oxidative deterioration and these properties, to a large extent, determine packaging requirements.

Acid

Microorganisms are sensitive to acid in varying degrees, and the acid produced by one type of organism often will inhibit multiplication of another type. This is one of the principles behind controlled fermentation as a means of preserving foods against growth of proteolytic, lipolytic and other types of spoilage organisms.

Acid may be produced in a food by fermentation, added directly as a chemical, or be present as a natural food component. Much of the preservative effect from acid is due directly to the hydrogen ion concentration and its destabilizing influence on proteins, but acids producing the same pH may not be equally effective since the anions of certain acids also exert an effect.

As previously mentioned, acid enhances the lethality of heat. Further, foods can be divided on the basis of pH with respect to their ability to support growth of *Clostridium botulinum*. This organism will not grow in acidic foods with a pH below 4.5. As a result, such acid foods need not be heated as severely as more alkaline products that must be rendered free of this spore-forming pathogen.

It is well to recognize that the degree of acidity tolerable in foods from the standpoint of palatability is never sufficient in itself to ensure food sterility. Thus, even vinegar frequently is pasteurized for prolonged shelf-life. As a preservative, acid generally must be combined with some other treatment for long-term food stability.

Sugar, Salt

Microorganisms are contained within cell membranes which regulate the flow of water and solutes in and out of the cells. Normal growing cells may contain in excess of 80% water. When such cells are placed in a heavy sugar syrup or salt brine, water in the cells moves out through the membranes into the concentrated syrup or brine by the process of osmosis and microbial growth is adversely affected. Another effect of sugar and salt has to do with lowering the "water activity" or "free water content" of foods. In this case the sugar and salt in concentrated solution binds water so that it is not available to support microbial processes.

Organisms differ with respect to their sensitivity to sugar and salt but usually 70% of sucrose or 20% of salt dissolved in the water phase of foods is highly preservative. Lesser amounts are effective for shorter times. Jellies, sugared fruits, and brined meats are preserved in this way.

Smoke

As with many preservative methods, smoke was used long before the reasons for its effectiveness were understood. When smoke is effective several factors generally are responsible. Smoke from the burning of wood contains traces of formaldehyde and other chemicals unfavorable to microorganisms. But in addition, smoke generally is associated with heat and the drying out of animal tissue which contribute to preservation. In underdeveloped lands where expensive processing equipment and electric power are unavailable, smoking of meat and fish is an important preservation method. In technically advanced societies, however, where more effective preservation methods are available smoke is more commonly used for flavor than for preservation. Further, today smoke may be efficiently generated in one room and conveyed to another where the food is to be treated. Such smoke is cool and by itself only a poor preservative.

Chemicals

Many chemicals will kill microorganisms and inhibit enzymes but most of these are not permitted in foods. A few that are include sodium benzoate, sorbic acid, sodium and calcium propionate, ethyl formate, sulfur dioxide, and sodium nitrate or nitrite; all in prescribed low levels, and only in certain foods. The use of chemicals as preservatives, or for other purposes in foods, is part of the broader consideration of permissible food additives. The Pure Food Law, administered by the Secretary of Health, Education, and Welfare through the Food and Drug Administration regulates what chemicals may be used in foods, and the conditions of their use. New chemicals to be approved must undergo rigorous testing. The FDA also retains the right to reverse former decisions and prohibit use of approved chemicals if new knowledge relative to safety warrants such action. In recent years, several antibiotics previously approved for food use were thus disapproved as preservatives for food consumed directly by humans. However, certain antibiotics may still be added to animal feeds and this is common practice.

Radiations

Microorganisms, enzymes, and insects are inactivated to various degrees by different kinds of radiations. X-rays, microwaves, ultraviolet light, and ionizing radiations are all kinds of electromagnetic radiations differing in wavelength and other properties that have been studied to preserve food. It can be said of all of these radiations that the doses required to *sterilize* most foods, and inactivate their enzymes, are generally excessive or borderline from the standpoint of food quality. Less than sterilization doses appear more generally useful to "radiopasteurize" and thus extend product storage life for a limited time.

By irradiated foods today is usually meant foods treated with ionizing radiations, as may be obtained from radioactive isotopes such as Co^{60}, or electron accelerators. These radiations penetrate food materials and appear to exert their major effects by producing free radicals from water and other substrates, which then interact causing lethality or sublethal changes in living cells and alteration of food constituents. There is no significant temperature rise from this form of irradiation and so the term "cold sterilization" has been used.

Since World War II an enormous amount of study has gone into food irradiation preservation from the standpoints of food safety, food quality, equipment design, and process control. By 1968 in the United States, specific irradiation doses capable of sterilization had been approved for several foods, and petitions to clear additional irradiated foods were being considered by the Food and Drug Administration. In this same year, after further consideration of accumulated data, the FDA rescinded prior approval of radiosterilized bacon and thereby created a climate of doubt with regard to irradiated food safety. Additional studies are now in progress and their findings will greatly influence the future of irradiation as an important food preservation method. At the present time in the United States low level doses of irradiation are permitted for such applications as deinfestation of grain and prevention of sprouting of stored potatoes.

NORMAN N. POTTER

Cross-references: *Canning; Dehydration; Radiation Processing of Food; Fermentation; Microwave Food Processing.*

FOOD RADIATION

See Radiation Processing of Foods.

FOOD RESEARCH AND DEVELOPMENT PROGRAM, DEPARTMENT OF DEFENSE

The Department of Defense (DOD) food research and development program embraces both basic and applied research on foods and feeding; testing and engineering studies on food, packaging, service equipment and systems; and the numerous subdivisions of these broad areas. The program is assigned to the U.S. Army Natick Laboratories, Natick, Massachusetts. The Department of Defense program is the culmination of an evolutionary process that began with the very limited investigative program of the Quartermaster in World War I, expanded greatly in the late 1930's and during the World War II years, continued to grow and widen its influence in the years following, first, at the Quartermaster Food and Container Institute in Chicago and, later, at the Food Laboratory of the Army Natick Laboratories. The Department of Defense program is, in essence, a conversion of the Army program to a joint effort in which all the Services participate.

The DOD program is formulated annually, the military services and defense agencies forwarding to the Natick Laboratories detailed descriptions of their requirements. The Natick Laboratories, more specifically the Food Laboratory, the General Equipment and Packaging Laboratory, and the Pioneering Research Laboratory, evaluate and review the requirements of the services and after further evaluation and approval by the Joint Formulation Board, which represents each of the services and the Surgeon General, an integrated program is established and funded.

A perspective on the DOD food research and development program is provided by the titles of the projects currently established. They are:

Food and food service research
Systems studies in military feeding
Radiation preservation of food
Military food service and subsistence technology
Packaging technology
Military subsistence systems
Wholesomeness test of irradiated food

Food and food service research will be responsive to the requirements of the services. Systems studies in military feeding will utilize operations research systems analysis methods, this in order to define the nature and scope of the DOD feeding system, and identify its components and the areas where improvements and innovations may be made. A consumer study of garrison feeding, under way at Fort Lewis, Washington, is searching out the reasons why Army personnel choose to eat many of their meals in outside establishments despite the fact that they can eat in Army dining halls free of charge. Along with other studies that will analyze cost and performance factors, this study will provide criteria for the design of new feeding systems better adapted to the eating patterns of today's youth. Investigations in the area of military food service and subsistence technology will, in the course of time, streamline food service operations. Specific tasks under this project look toward the future. Examples are tasks devoted to the equipment to be used for central food preparation, mobile field kitchens that can prepare meals in minutes possibly by use of microwave energy, and an automated food dispensing operation. Among the many tasks in the area of packaging is a most interesting one—the design of flexible packaging for heat processed foods.

In the military subsistence systems project, the tasks run largely to development, with attendant research, of rations for combat feeding. The studies in progress are related directly or indirectly to the four elements of quality that must be present in field rations: optimum stability, the ultimate in nutritional values, high acceptability, and, within the special conditions of combat, convenience of use. From the beginning of warfare, efforts to reduce the weight and volume of rations have doubtless been made. These efforts continue and it is noteworthy that in the years since the close of World War II weight reductions of more than 50% have been made. Recent work on compression of dehydrated components has substantially reduced volume, and this accomplished without impairing the reconstitution properties of a dried food.

The DOD Food Research and Development Program is staffed by an able group of military and civilian experts in the food and food service areas; and it can draw upon the expertise of food scientists, engineers, and technologists in Government, academic, and industrial laboratories throughout the nation and, for that matter, beyond our borders.

The objective of the program: to provide the military man at home and overseas and in whatever type of operation he is engaged with food that will benefit his health, add pleasure and satisfaction to his meals, increase his mobility, and to accomplish all this at the lowest possible cost.

EDWARD E. ANDERSON

Cross-reference: *Military Foods.*

FOOD SERVICE SYSTEMS

The term "food service industry" refers to all the activities related to the serving of food away from home. While terms such as "institutional feeding," "catering," or "food management" are sometimes used in its place, "food service" is now preferred since it clearly includes all the types of public feeding situations encountered. The food service industry is very important in the United States, ranking as the fourth largest industry in terms of sales and the largest in number of workers employed. According to the National Restaurant Association (1970) report, commercial feeding establishments (i.e., restaurants, hotels, cafeterias, etc.) purchased an estimated $9.4 billion of food and drinks in 1968 and enjoyed sales estimated at $29.1 billion. During the same year, other sectors of the food service industry showed the following estimated purchases and sales: semi-commercial feeding establishments (i.e., schools, colleges, clubs, ships, airlines, railroads, etc.) $2.3 billion purchases and $3.4 billion sales; institutional and charitable feeding establishments (hospitals, nursing homes, prisons, etc.) $2.3 billion purchases and $4.3 billion sales or "commercial equivalent"; and government feeding (military and civilian employees) $1.2 billion purchases. Since much of the food and beverages supplied to individuals through semicommercial, institutional, charitable, and government feeding establishments is not, in fact, sold, the purchase figure is more significant than the sales figure. The National Restaurant Association's analysis for 1968 indicates total food and drink purchases of $16,020,294,000 for all categories of the food service industry and total estimated sales (or commercial equivalent) of $36,781,762,000 for the commercial, semicommercial, institutional, and charitable feeding establishments.

While the food processing industry has consistently taken advantage of technological advances to increase its productivity and reduce its costs, the food service industry, by and large, has continued to operate using the methods employed since the earliest days of its existence. Until now, each food service operation has continued to remain, in effect, an on-site food factory and retail sales establishment. While other industries adopted the concepts of mass production engendered by the industrial revolution, the food service industry did not begin to undergo its own industrial revolution until after World War II. Even today, in the United States as well as in other countries, the majority of food service operations continue to produce food from raw ingredients and sell the finished product on the same location. Consequently, modernization of food service operations requires, as a first step, a two-dimensional separation of food preparation from its service to the ultimate consumers, i.e., in time and in place.

As endeavors were made to develop new methods of food service which would take full advantage of the technological advances in the food processing industry and in the equipment and packaging fields, it became evident that on-site food production could be reduced or eliminated only through the use of partially or fully prepared foods: canned, dried, chilled, or frozen. It also became evident that food packaging and the equipment for handling and preparing "convenience foods" for service, as well as the management of the total operation itself, had to be planned on a "systems" basis. The development of the concept of "food service systems" is based on the realization that food, packaging, and equipment procurement, the utilization and training of personnel, and the development of management controls are inexorably interrelated if the success of a food service operation based on convenience foods is to be ensured.

A "food service systems" has been defined as "an integrated program in which the procurement, storage, preparation, and service of foods and beverages, and the equipment and methods required to accomplish these objectives, are fully coordinated for minimum labor and optimum customer satisfaction, quality, and cost control" (Livingston 1968).

In designing a food service system it is essential to set forth, in quantitative terms insofar as possible, the system requirements relating to costs, menu, and quality.

In institutional systems, raw food cost limits are frequently imposed by external factors, i.e., monies appropriated for the feeding of military personnel, mental hospital patients, prison inmates, etc. In commercial feeding, cost targets are based upon management's profit objectives.

In addition to food cost, profitability is affected by direct and indirect labor costs, overhead and administrative costs, and sales and marketing costs. While conventional food service operators all too rarely consider the direct labor cost involved in the preparation of individual menu items, and food and labor costs therefore tend to be treated as if they were unrelated, the designers of food service systems will usually have a combined food and labor cost target. This is indeed essential since the manufacturer's labor costs for the preparation of convenience foods are incorporated in the food cost of the operations using them. The underlying economic premise of food service systems is that through mass purchasing of raw ingredients at a manufacturing or central kitchen level, combined with the reduced unit labor cost of mass production—automated wherever possible—the ultimate food and labor cost at the point of usage will be significantly lower than if the item had been prepared in the conventional manner.

Menu requirements are set by the food preferences and nutritional needs of the clientele to be served, and are, consequently, affected by a variety of factors including age, dietary needs, regional and ethnic food habits, and economic status.

Quality measurement techniques common to the food processing industry, while useful insofar as they go, fall short of meeting the needs of a food service operation with an elaborate menu cycle. While culinary experts, i.e., trained chefs, continue to offer the best means of controlling food quality at the source, the most reliable judgment of quality is that rendered by the ultimate consumer and can be quantified through measurements of meal attendence or plate waste in institutional or semi-commercial operations or sales analysis in commercial establishments.

The functional development of a food service system must be treated simultaneously, therefore, with the cost and acceptance factors. Both in the study of existing feeding operations and in the design of new systems, electronic data processing techniques are immeasurably valuable. They permit rapid analysis in terms of cost, nutrient content, etc., of existing operations; they serve as a useful tool in the type of market research which will be needed to define achievable objectives for the new system; and they permit rapid computation of costs and nutrient contents of possible system alternatives.

In operating food service systems, computers play a significant role in menu planning, inventory control, and production scheduling, in addition to the usual tasks normally assigned to them in industrial operations. Limited food service systems designed to achieve least-cost menus meeting nutritional goals and food preference constraints have been put into operation by a number of hospitals in the United States. Linear programming methods are entirely suitable to this purpose.

The "make or buy" decision frequently required in designing a system is most often made on the basis of the size of the operation. For operations feeding less than 500 it is usually more economical to buy than to make. Above 500, the investment and operating costs of a central kitchen operation—and importantly, too, the distribution costs—should be carefully weighed against the cost of purchasing fully prepared foods.

The complexity of food service systems varies enormously with the type of operation: from school lunches to a highly diversified menu including foods to which consumers may not have been exposed. School lunch systems are relatively simple, since they usually do not involve more than 2 meals a day, 5 days a week, and youngsters prefer a limited, repetitive menu of common favorites. Hospital systems, on the other hand, with their requirement for various types of modified diets, many of which are used in limited quantities, present a far more formidable challenge to the system designer.

To achieve a quality level at the point of usage comparable with that offered by a conventional food service operation, made-up chilled or frozen foods must be procured and employed for the majority of the menu items. Chilled foods are most suitable for operations in which food can be delivered from a central kitchen to the satellite feeding units within a day after preparation. An exception is the Swedish Nacka Hospital Food System (Bjorkman and Delphin 1966) in which chilled foods are prepared in such a manner as to permit a 2–3 week storage life. In this method, foods are prepared in the ordinary manner by frying, boiling, roasting, or other means of cooking, an effort being made to ensure that all parts of the food reach a temperature of at least $80°C$ ($176°F$). While hot, the foods are packed in plastic bags, which are then evacuated and heat sealed. Pouched foods are then subjected to a brief pasteurization treatment of 3 min in a boiling water bath.

Chilled food systems of various types have gained acceptance in school lunch programs, airline catering, large-scale industrial feeding, and hospital feeding. In airline feeding and usually in school and hospital feeding such systems use preplated individual meals, while most large-scale inplant feeding systems in the United States which utilize chilled foods ship the food in bulk. In Europe, however, there appears to be a preference for individual preplated chilled meals for office and plant feeding, frequently utilizing reusable plates.

Since most food service systems have an inherent requirement for longer holding times than those afforded by chilled systems, frozen foods are gaining rapidly in popularity. Many of the pioneering advances in food service systems based on quick frozen foods were made during and after World War II. For example, Pan American World Airways began its frozen meal program in 1945 in order to be able to supply high quality meals, without regard to local availability of food ingredients or skilled labor, over their far-flung network of stations (Parrott 1963). To supply their 50 London area restaurants with precooked frozen foods out of their central commissary, Lyons, Ltd., introduced the practice of freezing cooked foods in shallow aluminum pans holding about 8 portions each, after which they were removed from the pan and wrapped in waxed paper for storage and shipment. At the point of usage, aluminum pans of the same dimension as used for freezing were used for reheating (Logan 1955). In the early 1950's, experiments were initiated in the Uppsala and Huddinge school districts in Sweden to study the feasibility of employing frozen meals in school feeding (Landry 1961). Since then, the use of precooked or frozen prepared, ready-to-cook, foods has become commonplace in the airline industry. Some major U.S. restaurant chains have fully converted to convenience systems built around frozen precooked or ready-to-cook foods, and important school districts, such as that of New York City have formally adopted frozen food programs (Anon. 1965).

Just as packaging must be subordinated to the requirements of the system, with the result that individual and bulk, reusable and disposable, and plastic and metal packaging are in use, so must reheating equipment decisions be based on such system requirements as type of menu, quantities of meals to be reheated at any particular time and choice of packaging materials or serving dishes. Generally, forced hot air convection ovens, equipped with roll-in racks, are preferred for large institutional operations where many meals must be readied at about the same time. High pressure steamers offer a fast means of heating fairly large quantities of foods and are particularly well-suited to the heating of frozen vegetables or sauce type entrées. Infrared ovens offer speed and are well adapted to the reheating of fried or breaded products. Microwave ovens are the most rapid for heating individual portions or preplated meals and are primarily used in vending operations and in hospital systems in which meals are assembled chilled in a central kitchen (frequently using thawed, prepared, frozen foods purchased commercially) and are heated on the ward just prior to delivery to the patients.

The need for strict microbiological surveillance of mass food preparation and distribution is self-evident. Not only must careful control be exercised over the food production operation, but methods of food delivery, storage, reheating, and service must be carefully audited to eliminate any potential public health hazard. Similarly, in institutional systems (colleges, nursing homes, mental hospitals, etc.) when feeding individuals over extended periods of time, it is imperative that food preparation and service methods be selected which minimize losses of key nutrients, such as thiamin and ascorbic acid.

The design of a successful food service system must, therefore, address itself effectively to all of the factors involved: culinary, economic, functional, psychological, engineering, nutritional, and microbiological.

G. E. LIVINGSTON

References

ANON. 1965. Prepared frozen foods shine in New York City school test. Frozen Food Age 13, No. 6, 16A–16F.

BJORKMAN, A., and DELPHIN, K. A. 1966. Sweden's Nacka Hospital food system centralizes preparation and distribution. Cornell Hotel Restaurant Admin. Quart. 7, No. 3, 84–87.

LANDRY, H. A. 1961. A survey of the experimental program conducted by the Swedish Board of Education on the use of precooked, preportioned, frozen foods and its effect on kitchen design, labor, space and equipment costs as compared with the conventional method of conducting a school lunch program. Rept. in A Study of School Building Types. Board of Education of the City of New York, Mar. 30.

LIVINGSTON, G. E. 1968. The design of a food service system. Food Technol. 22, No. 1, 35–39.

LOGAN, P. P. 1955. Use of precooked frozen food products in hotels, restaurants and railroad dining cars. In Precooked Frozen Foods. M. Bollman and M. S. Peterson (Editors). Natl. Acad. Sci.—Natl. Res. Council, Washington, D.C.

NATIONAL RESTAURANT ASSOCIATION. 1970. The Food Service Industry, 1968. Washington Rept. 13, No. 22. Natl. Restaurant Assoc., Washington, D.C.

PARROTT, P. J. 1963. Trends in airline feeding. Cornell Hotel Restaurant Admin. Quart. 4, No. 1, 83–86.

FOOD STANDARDS

See USDA Grade Standards for Food.

FOOD TECHNOLOGY

Technology is the application of discovery or invention to practical ends.

Man's technological progress started when he fashioned and used his tools for agriculture, weapons, and the crafts. Far into the age of the Industrial Revolution, all technological progress entirely depended on the exploitation of chance discovery and invention by enterprising men. In this manner man developed the technology of food preservation by drying, including freeze drying; chilling and freezing; high salt or high sugar content; alcoholic and lactic acid fermentation; oil pressing; smoking; the conversion of milk to curd, butter and cheese; fat embedding; the use of preservatives; cured meat and fish; sausage making; baked and pasta products from cereals; parboiling of cereals; the milling of grain; ice deserts; leaf fermentation of tea; confectionery and chocolate making and packaging.

Most of these techniques can be traced back to the earliest days of recorded history. The 19th Century contributed canning, margarine making, and concentration. Thus, fat hardening is the only branch of food technology that originated from a scientific discovery.

Until the middle of the 19th Century, science had little, if any, impact on the industrial revolution. Pasteur's work for the wine and beer industries in the 1860's probably is the earliest example of a scientist's impact on food technology when he demonstrated the link between microorganisms and the "diseases" of these beverages. Not until the turn of this century did science begin to intrude itself into the technology of foods and that at a very slow pace. Many food processing industries that have become established without the help of science still are indifferent to present-day science. Indeed it is quite a recent discovery that advances in food technology result from an understanding of scientific principles. *Science* is systematic, formulated knowledge. According to the rules of scientific investigations, the scientist defines his problem, and carries out experiments leading to observations. Their evaluation leads to the formulation of a hypothesis which may need a further experimentation to validate. Though good scientific research has clear objectives, its outcome is of necessity unpredictable. Science is a cultural pursuit akin, indeed, to music and the arts; it has had, and still has, little direct effect on society.

Technology, as we know it today, is the application of science and the results of scientific research to the solution of practical problems. Advancing as it is at ever-increasing speed, the new technology is fed by, and itself is feeding, a similarly advancing science. This feed-back is a novel feature and distinctive from the days when scientists were supposed to be concerned with ideas alone and technologists with the promotion of technical efficiency. Both need analytical and creative or synthetic faculties; indeed the real distinction between pure and applied research lies in the purpose of the work and not in the nature of the work itself.

Compromise has no place in scientific investigations but is an integral part of the technologist's work. When the technologist applies the results of scientific research to the solution of practical problems, he faces many conflicting requirements—technical, commercial and financial, and often personal ones. He works within limitations of materials, men, money, time, and space. More often than not he must form judgment and reach decisions on incomplete data and within an inadequate time scale.

It is the essence of scientific method that the human element must be eliminated. But the technologist is up to his neck in human problems whether he likes it or not. The resolution of the diverse elements in a situation demands good judgment and brings in the art of compromise. It is indeed an intellectual challenge of a high order and calls not only for imagination but for courage.

Food Science by its very nature is interdisciplinary; it gained acceptance as a discipline in its own right by the end of the World War II.

Food Science is concerned with the knowledge of the physical, chemical, and biological, including nutritional, properties of food and their constituents and the changes they undergo when subjected to handling, preservation, processing, storage, and distribution.

In the early days of Food Science, up until World War II, it was the pure scientists, the chemists, botanists, plant physiologists, zoologists, etc., who searched for knowledge on foods. They selected their problems and pursued their investigations without concerning themselves with industrial application. Progress would be ill-served if this attitude were to fall into disfavor because advances in applications depend on an ever-growing body of scientific observation and their evaluation, which, in turn, lead to fresh inquiry. Food Science holds the key to all future development in food technology.

Research on processed, preserved, manufactured, and packaged foods is a very modern development, resulting from the feed-back of problems from the area of food technology and considerations of food quality, behavior in processing and storage, and problems of public health and nutrition. There also have come into focus the interaction of food and package as well as the elucidation of physico-chemical characteristics of foods to serve the chemical-engineer concerned with factory-scale food operations.

Since advances in food science must continue to

depend on advances in the biological and physical sciences, food scientists and food technologists must keep abreast of progress in these sciences. This involves them in the literature of several disciplines, because it is typical for food research that problem solution demands an interdisciplinary and integrated approach, one that brings several scientific disciplines into effective focus. The solution of this problem is seen in team work as reflected in the staffing policies of industrial and governmental research organizations.

In 1964 the Institute of Food Technologists defined food technology as "the application of science and engineering to the production, processing, packaging, distribution, preparation, and utilization of foods. Knowledge of food technology enables its possessor to solve technological problems in one or more of these fields by the application of one or more of the physical or biological sciences, or branches of engineering. It may involve problems in the development of products, processes, or equipment; the selection of raw materials; the fundamental changes of composition or physical condition prior to, during, and subsequent to industrial processing; or the nutritional value and health safety of foods."

The food technologist is concerned with development and operations. Development may involve him in handling or making conventional foods in new and better ways or making new foods. Any one of these pursuits may involve him in design or testing the properties of materials, requirements of maintenance, convenience of operations, and considerations of the nutritional consequences and of food laws. The idea that development merely consists of following a scientific discovery by choosing the right nuts and bolts is quite wrong.

There is a school of thought that looks at food science and food technology not as two separate subjects but merely broad divisions of what is, in truth, a continuous spectrum. Undoubtedly the relations of food science and food technology are subtle and complex. But in Great Britain, the introduction of courses in food science and in food technology at university level and below appear to have consolidated food science and food technology as two separate disciplines. This development has been reinforced by the structure of the British food industry which has enabled two professions to establish themselves. The foundation of the (British) Institute of Food Science and Technology in the 1960's took note of this fact by stating in its official brochure that this professional body was set up "as a necessary step to enable the collective views of those engaged in these professions to be effective in implementing the aims" of the IFST.

In retrospect, it would appear that the founders of IFT in the late 1930's visualized food technology to be essentially concerned with preserved, processed, and manufactured foods; this probably happened because they themselves, the originators of a new profession, were involved in the preservation, processing, and manufacture of foods or worked for public health authorities with responsibilities for these foods. The agricultural produce from which these foods were derived concerned them as raw materials for these industries and not as fresh food for the consumer market. Produce for the fresh food market—meat, fish, eggs, fruit, and vegetables—were the responsibilities of other specialists, including agricultural engineers who, in turn, were less concerned with food processing.

For the same reason, the early food technologists were not involved in beer brewing, dairy and cereal products, enology, fats, sugar, and confectionery. Other groups of professional people were concerned with these commodities who had their own professional organizations and literature that had been in existence for many years before food technologists were ever thought of. Recent years have brought a reversal of this situation and food technology now is considered to embrace all foods. Textbooks of food technology still reflect the earlier attitude of food technologists, food science texts fortunately don't.

Speaking of "fresh food" introduces problems of semantics. In this context, "fresh" signifies plant or animal produce in the original state, though it may have been "processed" by packaging or held in cold storage, i.e., the fruit and vegetable as harvested, animal flesh after slaughter, the egg in shell, fish raw in the round and filleted.

The agencies concerned with the management of fresh foods—sorting, grading, packaging, storage, transportation and marketing—now find that qualified food technologists can render valuable service. Progressive teaching institutions are taking note of this situation and plan their programs accordingly.

Foodstuffs have certain levels of nutrients while in the original state. Some are consumed raw, most of them after some culinary treatment. The latter involves certain nutrient losses, but the public at large is not greatly concerned with them.

Traditional techniques of food preservation such as pickling, curing, smoking, fermentation, and drying as well as the conversion of cereals to baked or paste goods entail significant nutrient losses that do not seem to exercise people's minds since traditional foods rate high in public esteem.

However there is public disquiet about the potential detrimental nutritional consequences of present-day management of foods, a matter of concern to food technologists.

In the years following the isolation of the major

vitamins, the U.S. canned and frozen food industries conducted comprehensive studies of the nutritive quality of their raw materials and the effects of processing and storage on the nutritive quality of their products. Results demonstrated that retention of nutient value runs parallel with desirable flavor, color and physical condition of the products. This work was essentially concerned with ingredients from which cooks or chefs prepare the dish. Since those days, food processors have taken over a great deal of the work of cook and chef by offering foods in a form more convenient to the user, housewife, or caterer than they used to do. Instead of ingredients for meal preparation, they now can buy the makings. Whether or not this development has brought with it nutrient losses to which the consumer had not been exposed previously is not known. Nutritionists have expressed concern that those who develop modern convenience foods and improve the technology of traditional foods or improve storage techniques fail to concern themselves with the nutritional consequences that may ensue.

Food must be of the nature and substance expectable by the consumer and that includes retention of nutrients. Food technologists carry this burden of responsibility.

Since few food technologists have access to laboratories for the evaluation of food quality, they must exercise eternal vigilance of potential nutritional consequences of their actions.

Except where man uses foodstuffs produced for his own immediate use, food technology as the technology involved in conveying food from land and water to man embraces one, or a combination of, the following operations: preparation, processing, storage, packaging, transportation. This holds equally for food that goes from farmer or fisherman to market, as for the produce that is stored or cold-stored before marketing, preserving, processing, or combining with other foods in manufactured foods. Food technology thus embraces the farm and large-scale storage of cereal grain and other produce destined as food for man. The food technologist practices his profession within a legal framework that normally encompasses all foods offered for sale.

Legislation has the prime objective of protecting the consumer from deception and fraud. Food must not offer a health hazard and must be as nutritious (or if it is a low-calorie food, be as little nutritious) as it purports to be. Food technologists now are involved in the framing of food legislation as well as in the policing of food processing practices.

Food law enforcement demands effective food inspection services supported by adequate analytical laboratories. The employment of food technologists in senior positions makes valuable contributions to the operations of food inspection service.

In the more highly developed countries, the achievements of agriculture and food technology in combination with an awareness of the link between nutrition and health have largely eliminated the classical deficiency diseases and protein deficiency, with advances in medicine and sanitary standards of the people and their environment being contributing factors. It is hoped that with a decrease of the poverty of the masses in the developing nations, the wider application of food science and food technology will produce similar effects.

In developing countries a high proportion of the population lives on the land or in small communities, while at the same time the cities are large and grow fast. Assuming that (1) the rural population's diet will change but slowly, (2) each country aims at living on the food it produces, and (3) the number of people living on the land will not diminish in the foreseeable future or even increase in spite of growing city populations, the rural populations can substantially benefit from food technology in three ways: (1) Production of infant foods from indigenous raw materials to combat infant mortality and improve the nutritional status of the very young. (2) Improved techniques of food management in storage, transportation, and distribution. (3) Improved technology of traditional foods processed by drying, salting, smoking, and fermentation.

To bring about these improvements, there is little need for basic research. It is applied research and development that is needed, carried out in the countries or regions by their own people with personnel from the developed countries giving help and guidance for some time. This approach holds high promise that reduced food losses will improve food producers' and processors' incomes and yield more food for the consumer at economical prices. Progress in this direction has so far been unsatisfactory because of the reluctance of the people to change traditional practices of food management. Moreover, the low prestige of applied research has bedeviled such work in these countries. Such advances in food technology only can eventuate if accompanied by rising standards of sanitation and hygiene.

With city populations in developing countries, problems involved are food transportation to the cities, its distribution, and the education of homemakers to bring about changes of dietary habits and acceptance of processed and packaged foods. The replacement of traditional cereal staples by bread is typical for this kind of change. Exposure to advertising will promote greater acceptance of a better dietary pattern.

The practice of food technology, as with all other technologies, needs a limited number of creative scientists and technologists to generate new ideas but many more technicians, a group that U.N. agencies designate as middle-lever personnel whose task it is to apply the scientists' and technologists' ideas to practical use.

In few countries has technician's education received adequate attention in terms of training and clear-cut, socially respectable career structures that follow.

Where technicians are lacking, scientists and technologists have to do the work of technicians and suffer frustration accordingly. This is a real problem in developed nations and to a very much greater extent it will manifest itself in the developing countries as they advance technologically. The situation calls for early remedial action in the system of technical education.

Technicians are needed both for quality control laboratories, for which they require skills in chemical and microbiological techniques, and for positions in plant operations at the foreman and submanagerial levels, both of which need appropriately different forms of training and education.

F. H. REUTER

FOOD TECHNOLOGY INDUSTRIAL ACHIEVEMENT AWARD

See Awards.

FOOD: WHAT MAN EATS

A Japanese breakfast might consist of a fermented bean paste soup, a raw egg beaten with soy sauce and poured over rice, fish cooked in soy sauce, pickles, a salted plum, and green tea. To a European, a hard roll with coffee suffices; whereas to many Americans the day could not start properly without orange juice, fried eggs, bacon, toast, and coffee. The foods man eats are as varied as the physical, social, and cultural environments in which he lives and are, in truth, a mirror reflecting these environments. How the varied food habits of man developed and the factors which influenced their development are fascinating subjects because in reality they are the study of man's history (Trager 1970).

Food was early man's most precious and sacred commodity. The question of survival was of uppermost importance. Oppressed by hunger, he con-

sumed all he could gather at random from his physical environment without much regard to what that food was. His diet consisted primarily of roots, nuts, berries, wild fruits, bee's honey, and eggs of many varieties. By trial and error he determined which of these foods were safe for human consumption. This information painfully learned was carefully transmitted to each new generation and gradually for that group the distinction between what was edible for humans and what was not became established.

As man progressed from a food gatherer to a hunter the variety of foods in his diet increased to include various types of meat, fish and poultry. By 8000 B.C. the early stages of food production of such crops as millet and barley and the domestication of some species of wild animals marked a turning point in history. The area of the world, to be known as the Fertile Crescent, bounded on the east by the Tigris and Euphrates Rivers and on the west by the Indus River had the unique combination of productive soil, adequate rainfall, sufficient sunlight, and favorable temperatures which led to the development of agriculture and the subsequent banding together of people in a cooperative effort for food production. Foods known to be available and consumed in this region at that time were beef, lamb, mutton, and fish. Wheat was to become the predominant grain of the Mediterranean area and North Africa while rice developed in the region of the Indus River and spread throughout Southeast Asia as the staple food. In addition to the cereal grains, onions, lettuce, cucumbers, cabbage, and legumes were available. Flat breads were made from mixtures of barley and sesame seed flours and flavored with onions. A variety of fruits such as apples, dates, figs, apricots, pears, and plums rounded out the food supply. Cheese was thought to have been used as a food about 3000 B.C.; milk by 2000 B.C.

Mesopotamia and Egypt were the first cultures to escape from a primitive survival existence; others have followed but unfortunately, even today, this has not been achieved on a global basis. Centuries of slow development culminating with the industrial revolution, the technological advances in food processing and preservation, coupled with efficient distribution and marketing systems, and a high standard of living have made it possible for many peoples in the developed world to draw their food supply from an environment which encompasses the world itself. In many other parts of our planet, however, man is still a prisoner of his physical environment and eats what is grown locally depending almost completely on the crops he grows for survival.

In the course of the development of civilization as food supply became more plentiful each group of people developed a particular pattern of eating using only certain of the edible plants, animals, fish, and birds of their own environment. This selectivity has continued until today it is estimated that of the 2 million known species of animals only about 50 have been domesticated and make a contribution to man's food. Correspondingly, only 100 species of the known 350 thousand vegetables are widely cultivated and consumed. Thus, the culture of the group dictated not only what was edible to humans but more specifically what was edible to "our group." How, when, and why certain foods were or were not to be eaten were carefully taught to the young members of the group and over the centuries became instilled into the societies' ways of life and in some cases served as an identifying characteristic of the group itself. Jacques May has stated this very simply. "Man eats what he can get from his environment, then, given a chance what his forebearers ate" (May 1957).

Over the centuries of man's history, the foods locally available in one region and consumed by a particular culture group were diffused and blended with those of other groups as man's contacts with others increased through wars, explorations, and migrations of people. The voyages of Marco Polo and other great explorers brought back to Europe the foods and spices of the East. Columbus and later Spanish explorers brought back to Spain from the new world such foods as potatoes, various types of beans, peanut and cashew nuts to name only a few. The returning Crusaders introduced sugar into the diets of Europeans. The Turkish conquest of Hungary in the 16th and 17th Century introduced the Hungarians to Turkish coffee and paprika which today are identifying marks of Hungarian cuisine. The Italian invasion of Libya during World War II left its imprint as evidenced by the popular consumption there today of spaghetti. Many other examples could be cited to illustrate this blending of food habits between different cultural groups.

Cultural and social influences on food habits are remarkably strong and an understanding and appreciation of man's beliefs and attitudes about food are just as important as an understanding of the body's need for certain nutrients and how these nutrients function. Jelliffe (1967) has pointed out that each cultural group has a subconscious classification of foods which is learned in childhood by imitation and is notoriously difficult to change. This classification system usually bears no relation to scientific knowledge about food and is not based on any idea of the relationship between the type and quality of the diet eaten and health and disease. Of course, food habits of individuals within a particular culture group do undergo change and may be different than those dictated by the larger culture. For within any society subcultural groups exist depending on such things as common ancestry, family social status, age, sex, and common religious, social or professional interests which influence the food consumption of an individual.

Five universal classifications have been identified by Jelliffe (1967). In all cultures one can identify a cultural superfood. These foods usually provide the main source of calories and protein in the diet and are foods which, if not consumed in a meal, leaves one with the feeling that he has really not eaten. These foods would be rice for many Southeast Asian peoples, corn or maize for certain Central and South Americans, wheat for the people of Northern Europe and Middle East, cassava or sorghum and millets for many Africans, and teff for Ethiopians to mention only a few. The cultural superfood in the United States is difficult to identify today because of the abundant, varied, and widely-available food supply. Some would suggest that it is meat, based on the 1965 USDA Household Food Consumption Survey which showed the per capita consumption of meat to be 3.4 lb per week.

The important role of these superfoods is well illustrated in the refusal of Europeans following World War I to eat corn which was imported from the United States. To the European, corn was considered a food suitable only for animals and certainly not one to replace their long-standing staple, wheat. Similarly, South Indians who are basically rice eaters refused to accept wheat sent by the United States as a stop-gap measure to relieve a local famine situation. In more recent years, new high-yielding varieties of staple grains have been developed in the struggle to balance the race between food production and human reproduction. However, due to differences in the stickiness of the new varieties of rice or the altered taste of tortillas made from new varieties of corn, these foods did not receive the wide acceptability anticipated.

Another food classification prevalent in all cultures is prestige foods. These are foods mainly served on important or special occasions, and are usually relatively rare or expensive foods. Among many Arab groups such foods are the roasted hump of the camel or the eyes of a sheep. Milk desserts are served as a prestige food in many parts of India and in China a truly honored guest might be served bird's nest soup at a banquet. This soup is made from a jelly-like material secreted by the salivary glands of the swift with which he lines his nest. These nests, built on very steep cliffs, are difficult to obtain and the soup is very expensive. The psychological impact on a Westerner served such a delicacy would doubtless be great, especially if accompanied by shark fin soup and the 100-yr-old duck eggs which in reality are only 100 days old and have been buried in ashes.

Many foods are eaten or rejected by various people because of some assumed magical property of the food. Tomatoes, or "love apples" as they were sometimes called, were for many years a food taboo in the United States because they were considered a sexual stimulant. As late as 1900 many people believed cancer resulted from eating tomatoes. Children in some African cultural groups are not allowed to eat eggs as they are thought to cause bladder disease and sterility after marriage. In other cultures milk is taboo because it causes barrenness in women. Fish has long been proclaimed a brain food in the United States but in early Rome the banana was considered the fruit of the wise man and in Gujerat, India the walnut, whose convolutions resemble those of the brain is considered "the food" for wisdom.

A fourth classification is the body-image foods. These are foods which are reported to have various effects on the workings of the body. In India and various South American countries foods are classified as hot or cold depending not on their actual temperature but on how they affect the body. In China foods are classified as yin or yang foods; yang foods are meat, eggs and fish, whereas yin foods are fruits and dairy products. The grains and vegetables are considered to provide a good balance of yin and yang together. To the Zen Buddhist a proper balance between these two types of foods is necessary to ensure good health and happiness. The balance between hot and cold foods in the diet is also important to Indians and the peoples of many South American countries.

Finally, cultural classifications dictate certain foods for certain physiological groups within the population. Foods acceptable for adults, children, and pregnant and lactating women vary with societies. Fish in some cultures is considered an improper food for children due to the belief that fish produce intestinal worms. Women, especially when pregnant or lactating, often have more dietary restrictions imposed on them than any other segment of the population. A saying of the Chukchee people of Siberia is "Being woman, eat crumbs."

An individual having learned the ways of his culture usually accepts these as the best way and the right way and is conditioned to judge others through this culture screen. People who consume different foods or prepare foods in different ways than those of his own culture are often judged to be inferior and their food habits are often repulsive to him. For example, in Uganda and other African countries a commonly accepted food is ants. Westerners, revolted by the idea of eating ants or other insects, for many years tried to discourage this practice by making fun of it and implying it was degrading. They forgot one rather important point in their ethnocentrism and that was that ants are approximately 20% protein and provide a widely-available and cheap supply of good quality protein to many poor Ugandans.

The revulsion toward the eating habits of others is probably more generally related to the variety of animal foods eaten than to foods of plant origin. The book, *Eat Not This Flesh* by Simoons (1961), gives an excellent account of the various cultural groups in the world which have consumed or abstained from the numerous types of meats. The consumption of organ meats by Americans is limited and, except for liver, is often regarded as degrading and being "poor folk" food. However, a favorite old Scottish dish known as Haggis makes extensive use of organ meats. It is a mixture of oatmeal, onions, beef suet, beef lungs, intestine, pancreas, liver, and heart all cooked in a sheep's large stomach bag. Many an American, even of Scottish ancestry, has ordered this with great trepidation in the restaurants of Edinburgh, and has usually not returned home clutching the recipe. The Southern black's use of chittlings has, in general, been looked down upon by whites. Head cheese served at Scandinavian smörgåsbords or even bought by Americans as cold cuts might not be so widely acceptable if people knew that it contained meat from the cheek, snout, and underlip of a calf or pig, as well as their brain, heart, tongue, and feet. Brain salad, a delight to some from the Middle East, would not be a large seller in a typical American restaurant.

Blood as a food brings varied reactions. To the Jew it is a strict taboo and, as part of the koshering process, very special precautions are observed to remove as much blood as possible from all meats. Many Christians symbolically drink wine in a communion service as the blood of Christ but would react violently to the use of actual blood in this service. Yet, to the Masai of Kenya the blood removed from the jugular vein of their cows and mixed with milk is the mainstay of their diet. Blood sausages are heartily enjoyed by the peoples of many eastern European countries.

It is estimated that about 1% of the world's food comes from the sea but this small percentage is consumed in ways which are exotic to some and eschewed by others. The raw fish consumed by many peoples of Holland and the jellied eel, a favorite of the Scandinavians, would be revolting to many. The Japanese fondness for pickled jellyfish cut up like spaghetti, raw oysters, and seaweed does not meet with exclamations of joy by other population groups. Nor does a plate containing the gonads of the sea urchin excite everyone's appetite and start his digestive juices flowing. The fish market of Athens, Greece is a sight to behold—fish of every imaginable description and color can be found with squid and octopus predominating, but this does not entice every visitor to want to eat them.

Some Americans often wonder why Indians do not use some of the old cows cared for by the Indian Government in special farms, to help meet the reduced food supply of the masses. Indian students in the United States may wonder why very poor Americans do not use dogs to help meet their reduced food supply. Although consumption of dogmeat is an unwritten taboo in the American society, they don't see why Indians shouldn't eat beef even though it is prohibited in the sacred writings of the Hindu religion. Interestingly, at one time many centuries ago beef was consumed in India.

This disdain for someone else's food habits may lead to a strong feeling of prejudice and contempt for people who do not eat as you do. The conflict between Hindus and Moslems in India has been heightened by the Hindu feeling of revulsion toward Moslems because they eat beef. Some have claimed that the Chinese aversion to dairy products originated centuries ago as a result of their hatred of the conquering Tartars and Mongols.

People have a physiological need for food to maintain their body cells and tissues with nutrients needed to provide good health. Except for the air one breathes, food is the most important environmental factor that affects the health of the body. But people also have a psychological want for food to attain their desires and satisfactions of security, belongingness to a group, self-esteem, and creativity. Food has many symbolic and psychological meanings to man which vary from one cultural group to another. These non-nutritive uses of food may be far more important to an individual than his physiological need and are more apt to be the dominant factor in determining food choices in an affluent society. A major problem of nutrition education today is ensuring that man's psychological want for food matches his physiological need for food.

An abundance of a cultural superfood may well give man a sense of security and safety. Milk is often considered a security food especially if it recalls man's early childhood memories of love and affection. The foods one eats with pleasure as a child often remain the best-liked foods. Although one learns to like other foods in later life, they do not usually give one the same sense of satisfaction and pleasure. To many a displaced Bostonian raised on Saturday night baked beans and brown bread, there is still nothing that can quite replace these foods. The same can be said of a Southerner far from home who remembers with nostalgia the

grits, red-eye gravy, and country ham. These foods symbolize home, family, love and security. Lowenberg et al. (1974) discuss these non-nutritive uses of food in considerable detail.

The foods man eats are a kaleidoscope of many complex interacting factors. The picture changes from one cultural group to another depending on the mix of these factors and is vastly different in many areas of the world. Regardless of how different these foods may be, they have supported man throughout history and have provided an exciting adventure in eating to those who have lost their ethnocentrism. Differences amongst people whether it be in food habits, clothing, or any other aspect of human life are to be respected and treasured, for they are truly the spice of life.

JANE R. SAVAGE

References

JELLIFFE, D. B. 1967. Parallel food classifications in developing and industrialized countries. Am. J. Clin. Nutr. 20, 279.

LOWENBERG, M. E. et al. 1974. Food and Man, 2nd Edition. John Wiley & Sons, New York.

MAY, J. 1957. The geography of food and cooking. Intern. Rec. Med. 170, 231.

SIMOONS, F. J. 1961. Eat Not This Flesh. University of Wisconsin Press, Madison, Wisconsin.

TRAGER, J. 1970. The Foodbook. Grossman Publishers, New York.

Cross-reference: *Foods of Primitive Man.*

FOODS OF PRIMITIVE MAN

In a short article on so broad a topic as the foods of primitive man it is necessary to limit the coverage to Homo sapiens, specifically to Stone Age man, and to consider his foods in terms of the food resources of his habitat, the traditional types of food getting, and, insofar as they can be inferred, the attitudes and values that are characteristic of primitive peoples. For a definitive, as opposed to so highly generalized an account such as this, the reader is referred to Jensen (1953).

Food Resources of Primitive Man

There is little evidence to show that agriculture including the domestication of animals existed anywhere in the world prior to the Ice Age. It can be surmised that edible flora and fauna were so plentiful then that hunting and fishing together with some collection of wild plant foods took care of the subsistence needs of nonsapiens man prior to the glacial ages. The Ice Age caused the extinction of many animals that were hunted, killed, and

TABLE F-11

REPRESENTATIVE FOODS OF THREE TYPES OF PRIMITIVE MAN

Types of Early Man	Methods of Obtaining Food	Foods
Peking Man Ca 500,000 B.C. Used fire for cooking.	Hunting; limited gathering of plant foods.	Flesh foods: bison, deer, mammoth, rhinoceros, sheep, camel, hyena, baboon, wolf, among others. Plant foods: berries, particularly sweet hackberries. Other: not identifiable.
Neanderthal Man 400,000 B.C. to ca 40,000 B.C. Used fire for cooking.	Hunting; fishing; gathering wild plant foods.	Flesh foods: horse, dog, hyena, ibex, reindeer, birds, fish, shellfish, others. Plant foods: roots, berries, nuts, tree fruits. Other: honey, eggs, insects, gastropods.
Mesolithic and Neolithic Man (Europe) Ca 20,000 to 7000 B.C. Used fire for cooking and had developed cooking utensils.	Gathering wild plant foods; hunting; fishing and some agriculture.	Flesh foods: dog, horse, cattle, sheep, pig, wolf, fish, shellfish, birds, reptiles, hare, civet. Plant foods: nuts (particularly hazel nuts, acorns, beechnuts), melons, grapes, roots, leaves, cereals. Other: honey, eggs, insects, gastropods.

eaten by ancient man and this, among other reasons, turned man to plant foods as an important part of their subsistence. It has been suggested that with an increased use of plant foods, particularly cereals, the addition of salt to foods became widely practiced.

Of the long list of foods eaten by primitive man, most are not different from those of modern man except in modes of preparation (Table F-11). A few foods, which many contemporary people regard with some distaste, were consumed in some quantity by ancient men. Among these may be listed horse meat, dog meat, lizards, insects, and reptiles. Curiously enough, a number of unconventional foods on the menu of primitive man are now gourmet foods, e.g., locusts, snails, and rattlesnake steaks, the last-mentioned having a considerable gourmet market. Some primitive groups enjoyed putrid meat—for example, the Australian aborigines, who feast on stranded dead whales, and the Eskimo, who prefers fish when well along toward putrefaction. In the main, however, Stone Age man subsisted on much the same food that we do and, depending on the availability of food in his habitat, lived well except when foods were out of season. With the invention of preservation methods—drying, fermenting, salting—his off-season dietary was at least adequate, this on the basis of the analogy between primitive peoples of today and their supposed similarity to primitives of the Stone Age.

Primitive man exploited the food resources of his habitat in terms of what was available, what means he had for capturing the game or harvesting the wild crops of the region where he found himself, and what techniques he had for cooking or preserving the foods he acquired. As to cookery, archaeological evidence shows that he could roast meat, or boil it in vessels into which he placed hot stones onto which he poured water, that he could make bread of a crude sort, malt barley and make beer, and ferment fruit to make wine.

The art of bread making was primitive by our standards but in general it followed the same formula. Flour was made by grinding the grain, usually wheat or barley, between stones, moistening the flour, and baking it in the hot ashes of a spent fire. Leavens were known at an early date, the principal one being yeast, conjectured to have been discovered by the Egyptians. Another method was to add old dough to the new.

Food Types

The structure of primitive groups had much influence on the foods eaten. The American Indian tribes of the Plains were hunters and their chief subsistence was the buffalo or bison. The bison of the Plains were the basis in large degree of the whole economy: the flesh provided food; the hides, raiment and shelter; and the bones, instruments of one kind or another. The Plains Indians traveled in small units, were not tied down to one habitat, and were remarkably self-sufficient. Agricultural groups, such as those found in North Africa and the regions bordering the Mediterranean, were dependent on plant foods, in considerable degree on cereals. Although the early Egyptians had domesticated the pig, it was never eaten. Agricultural groups were not tied to plant foods, however, and their dietary included flesh foods, particularly fish, where available. Agricultural groups tended to establish themselves permanently in an area and as a result, in many instances, developed an intricate system of property rights. Pastoral peoples settled in one locality only reluctantly. Their settlements were chosen in correspondence with the needs of their flocks or herds; thus pastoral villages were often found near a water source, a lush grazing area, or a sheltered area. Pastoral groups derived their food from the animals they tended and from the vegetation of a region. Milk was a principal food in many instances and as a natural consequence, a by-product was cheese. In areas where they grew, dates were a major source of food.

Food Attitudes and Values

In discussing food attitudes and values placed on food by ancient man, one is on shaky ground. No records are available from which to draw inferences as to primitive man's food preferences, his appreciation or lack of appreciation for flavor, or his food idiosyncrasies.

Possible analogies between the primitives that exist today and those of yesterday, suggest that primitive man had taboos with regard to food, that he ascribed special virtues to certain foods, and that he regarded food as of paramount importance in his economy. With regard to taboos, it seems likely that primitive men, like those existing today, placed restrictions on certain foods on the basis of supernatural advice. Proscribed foods were sometimes those that had caused physical distress; but in most cases, presumably, reasons for the taboo came out of the dark otherworld and were not questioned. Special virtues were assigned to foods derived from animals; a brave, or a ferocious, or a cunning animal conveyed with his flesh that quality for which he was distinguished to the consumer. It seems evident, again on the basis of analogy, that the food economy of a group influenced food evaluations; thus, a number of American Indian tribes had sanctions against the wanton waste of food.

Instinct and Selection of Foods

In considering the foods of primitive man, one comes inevitably to the question as to what part instinct played in his selection of foods. Did he choose foods in response to his physiological needs or was he motivated entirely by his caloric requirements? It would seem plausible that his physiologic needs had some influence on his selection of foods. Certainly, he sought, whether knowingly or not, to satisfy his need for protein by placing a high value on animal foods. But the whole matter would seem to come down to the satiety quality of the foods available in a region, the capability of a group to find a variety and an abundance of food, and their ability to preserve foods to tide them over the lean seasons.

MARTIN S. PETERSON

Reference

JENSEN, L. B. 1953. Man's Foods. Garrard Publishing Co., Champaign, Illinois.

Cross-reference: *Food: What Man Eats.*

FREEZE DRYING

Drying is man's oldest and most reliable method of preserving food. Naturally dried grains and fodder are intimately associated with the beginning of agriculture. Throughout recorded history, dried food, either directly or indirectly, accounts for an important part of man's subsistence. Almost all foods can be preserved by drying, generally without significant loss of nutritional quality. Several air-dried fruits, such as raisins, figs, and dates, have been important items of commerce for thousands of years. On the other hand, air drying of meats as well as many fruits and vegetables is generally associated with adverse changes in texture, flavor, and appearance. Vacuum drying, notwithstanding a relatively low temperature, results in collapse of structure (shrink) and consequent damage to texture and appearance. Spray drying is limited to "structureless" products, such as milk or to solid foods which have been comminuted to a fine paste.

Freeze drying, also designated as sublimation drying and lyophilization (German: Gefriertrocknung; French: lyophilisation or cryodesiccation; Russian: сушка сублимацией) results in the least damage to food of all commercial processes for drying. Freeze drying is applicable to all foods, both raw and cooked, which can withstand freezing. Utilizing current technology, freeze-dried foods can be reconstituted in less than 15 min to yield products which are often indistinguishable from their commercially frozen counterparts.

As a prerequisite for freeze drying, food is solidly frozen. In the drying operation water is vaporized from the frozen state without passing through the liquid phase. Under such conditions, shrink is prevented and the resulting product has a dry, highly porous structure, since the spaces formerly occupied by ice crystals become voids. The porous structure favors rapid rehydration. In reality, freezing results in a physical separation of water in the form of ice crystals from the other components of the food. These crystals are vaporized under mild conditions in which heat damage and other adverse changes commonly associated with dehydration of food are minimized.

History

The dissappearance of ice and snow without melting is a timeless observation. The freezing of water under vacuum and the subsequent sublimation of ice were discussed by the Royal Society of London early in the 19th Century. The first application of freeze drying to biological material was reported in 1890 by a German histologist, Altmann, who observed that tissues could be dried without shrink at a temperature of $-20°C$. Flosdorf (1949) reports finding fewer than ten articles dealing with freeze drying and its applications prior to 1930. The major impetus for the development of freeze drying began in the early 1930's with its application to the drying of human blood plasma and immune sera and soon extended to a wide variety of heat-sensitive materials.

While procedures for the freeze drying of blood plasma, antitoxins, viable bacteria, and histological preparations were reported in the 1930's, freeze drying was generally regarded as a laboratory curiosity until World War II. Experience in western Europe during the early years of the war revealed the need for a nonrefrigerated supply of blood plasma for transfusion. The contributions of Flosdorf (1949) in the United States and of Greaves (1964A) in England advanced freeze drying of blood plasma from a laboratory operation to a successful commercial process. Several years later this development played a major role in expediting the production of penicillin, which, in the early

years of its commercial development was stabilized by freeze drying (Brockmann 1970).

The application of freeze drying to food was considered by several investigators prior to World War II. As early as 1935, Flosdorf (1945) experimented with fruit juices and milk and during the decade to follow extended his observations to raw meats, oysters, fish fillets, soups, corned beef, fruits, vegetables, and coffee extract. Also, before the beginning of World War II an experimental program on the freeze drying of food was initiated at the Low Temperature Research Station of Cambridge University (Baker et al. 1946). Except for a renewed study at the latter institution, there was little activity with freeze-dried food from the beginning of World War II until the early 1950's. The few food processors who were knowledgeable of freeze drying regarded it as too expensive to be feasible. Furthermore, foods preserved by freeze drying offered no discernible advantage over the frozen products already in the market. In fact, as a result of wartime experience, there existed widespread prejudice against dried foods which categorically extended to those prepared by freeze drying.

In the late 1940's, a commission of scientists studying the vulnerability of the United Kingdom to a food crisis such as experienced in World War II, expressed alarm that both research and production of dehydrated foods had been abandoned (Hanson 1961). This commission noted that the foods imported each year contained 3 million tons of water. In time of emergency the potential of dried food for savings in transportation, storage, and packaging, and particularly through nonperishability, is not likely to be overestimated. As a result of this study, the British Government started an experimental station in 1951 at Aberdeen to develop processes and to improve dehydrated foods. By converting a vacuum contact plate drier to a freeze drier the Aberdeen group demonstrated a marked improvement in the quality of dried products together with a highly significant reduction in the time required for rehydration. An innovation in the freeze-drying equipment reduced the drying time to about 8 hr, roughly $1/3$ the time previously required to freeze dry food masses of comparable dimensions (Hanson 1961).

In 1954, the Quartermaster Food and Container Institute for the U.S. Armed Forces recognized the unique advantages of freeze-dried foods for operational rations and supported research and development on both raw and precooked products. When properly dried and packaged, freeze-dried items were found to have a storage stability equal or superior to their canned counterparts. Freeze-dried products rehydrated in 15–20 min to yield a food of greater acceptability; this was most noteworthy with meat items. An additional major advantage was seen in the loss of weight equal to 50–90% and the potential for a significant reduction in volume.

The British and U.S. programs did much to promote interest in freeze drying and in the products produced thereby. This expansion of interest in freeze drying of food is illustrated by the references cited in three comprehensive review articles specifically directed to freeze-dried food: Harper and Tapple (1957) cited 65 references; Burke and Decareau (1964) cited 155 references only 24 of which were prior to 1957; and King (1970) cited 238 references, 61 of which were prior to 1964.

The Process

While freezing is a general prerequisite to freeze drying, the operations preliminary to freezing are essentially product oriented. Selection of varieties or grades best suited to a specific freeze-drying regimen must be based on experience. Damage or deterioration, including microbiological, in the starting material will be reflected in the final product. Components, such as bones and seeds which are not eaten, are eliminated. Meat is freed of trimmable fat and superficial connective tissue. As a practical matter, the thickness of all items destined for freeze drying is limited to about 2.0 cm. In adjusting the thickness of fibrous products such as muscle, it is advantageous to cut perpendicular to the fibers. Items with relatively impermeable skins such as peas are scarified to facilitate escape of water vapor. Vegetables are normally blanched to inactivate enzymes. As in air drying, both fruits and vegetables are usually treated with bisulfite. Since the subsequent performance of precooked freeze-dried foods, including compounded items such as beef stew, is dependent upon time, temperature, and method of cooking, suitable conditions must be established experimentally for each product.

Both the rate and completeness of freezing foods destined for freeze drying have been found to influence the drying process and the properties of the dried product. Wide disparities exist among the few reports which identify freezing rate in quantitative terms; on a relative scale, however, there is general recognition that a fast rate produces small crystals which are located preferentially within the cell or, in the case of meat, within the sarcolemma. A slow freezing rate results in large crystals which develop in extra cellular spaces. Most observed differences between high and low freezing rates can be explained on the basis of the size and location of voids resulting from the sublimation of ice crystals (King 1970). Many experimental observations involving fast rates of freezing have no counterpart in commercial practice owing to the large masses of food involved and to the restraints imposed by large-scale operations. Commercial freezing conditions, however, may result in small pores at the surface of the dried product due either to fast freezing of a thin external layer or to surface dehydration during freezing.

In commercial freeze drying, foods are generally frozen to about –20°C by procedures similar to those used for commercially frozen foods. At –20°C, according to Kuprianoff (1964), only about 1–4% of freezable water remains unfrozen. However, most foods contain bound or "unfreezable" water equal to 0.2–0.4 gm per gm of dry material. Incomplete freezing of the freezable water usually results from failure to attain a temperature below the lowest eutectic point, or to eliminate a vitreous metastable phase. Rey and Bastien (1962) demonstrated the use of differential thermal analysis and of electrical resistance measurements to identify insipient melting or incomplete freezing of orange juice.

Both the unfrozen and unfreezable forms of water may have an adverse effect on the dry product. During sublimation the presence of small amounts of aqueous phase, whether due to incomplete freezing or thawing during processing may result in foaming, splattering, protein denaturation, translocation of soluble substances, shrunken products which resist rehydration, excessive loss of volatile flavor, and to slow drying. King (1970) has summarized recent studies which indicate that under the temperature regimen to which food is generally subjected during the final phase of drying the presence of unfreezable, bound, or adsorbed water promotes the browning reaction.

For liquid or "structureless" products, notably coffee extract, the freezing operation is reported to be combined with a freeze concentration process in which ice crystals are removed mechanically from a slush frozen extract. When coffee solids attain a prescribed concentration the extract is solidly frozen for freeze drying.

Evaporative freezing is not widely used in commercial freeze drying although it is seen as the preferred method for freezing cottage cheese prior to drying. On both theoretical and applied grounds, evaporative freezing should be attractive for products which do not foam, are not subject to denaturation, and undergo no adverse effects from the translocation of small amounts of soluble material. Evaporative freezing performed in the freeze drier eliminates the requirement for a separate freezing unit and at least one handling operation. In addition 15–20% of the moisture present is utilized for freezing and hence is not included in the freeze-drying operation.

Evaporative cooling and freezing are based on the fundamental relationship between temperature and

TABLE F-12

RELATIONSHIP BETWEEN TEMPERATURE AND
VAPOR PRESSURE

Temp (C)	Vapor Pressure Torr (= mm Hg)	Phases
30	31.8	water and vapor
20	17.5	water and vapor
10	9.21	water and vapor
5	6.54	water and vapor
0	4.58	ice, water and vapor
-5	3.01	ice and vapor
-10	1.95	ice and vapor
-20	0.776	ice and vapor
-30	0.286	ice and vapor
-50	0.0296	ice and vapor
-90	0.00007	ice and vapor

vapor pressure of both water and ice as shown in Table F-12. Thus, if water at 30°C is subjected to an external pressure of 9.21 torr, it will lose heat through evaporation and cool to 10°C. Further reduction of external pressure to 1.95 torr will result in additional evaporative cooling, conversion to ice, and thence evaporative cooling of the ice to -10°C. The evaporative cooling of ice is designated as sublimative cooling which is an integral component of all freeze-drying mechanisms.

Freeze drying involves a series of heat and vapor transfers which converge at the subliming ice interface. For practical reasons, freeze drying is performed in a closed system favorable to those transfers. Figure F-28 illustrates the essential features of a system widely used in commercial freeze drying. The sublimation of ice requires heat. The minimum requirement is equal to the heat of fusion (80 cal per gram) plus the heat of vaporization

(approximately 595 cal per gm at 0°C). Thus 675 gcal are required to convert 1 gm of ice to vapor. The following example emphasizes the necessity for supplying heat from an external source to the subliming ice. Assume 4 gm of ice are sublimed from an ice mass of 64 gm, initially at 0°C. To sublime 4 gm of ice requires 2700 gcal. Ice has a specific heat of 0.5; thus, withdrawal of 2700 gcal would reduce the temperature of the remaining 60 gm of ice to -90°C. At this temperature, according to Table F-12 the vapor pressure of ice is 0.000070 torr. Under such conditions the rate of freeze drying would have only theoretical interest. For sublimation to progress at a steady rate it is essential to introduce heat at approximately the same rate as heat is required for sublimation.

Theoretically, heat may be supplied to subliming ice by conduction from contact with a heated surface, by infrared radiation, by convection from a circulating gas, and by microwave energy. In Fig. F-28 this requirement is met by supporting the frozen product on a tray between two platens which serve as a controlled source of heat. Under the conditions of commercial freeze drying most of the heat transfer from the platens to the surface of the food is by radiation with an additional contribution from convection.

In addition to supplying heat, provision must be made for the disposition of the vapor produced by sublimation. Theoretically, any mechanism for effectively reducing the concentration of water vapor in the system will favor its diffusion away from the subliming surface. Vapor may be pumped from the system, absorbed by a desiccant, or condensed on a cold surface. In this latter case, the temperature of the condensed ice must be substantially lower than the subliming ice because the

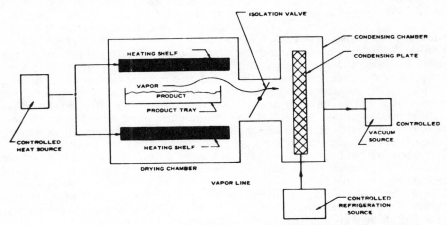

Courtesy of Stokes Division, Pennwalt Corp.

FIG. F-28. SCHEMATIC OF A RADIATION FREEZE DRIER

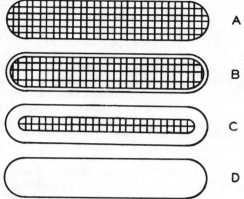

FIG. F-29. SCHEMATIC REPRESENTATION OF RECEDING ICE ZONE AS FREEZE DRYING PROGRESSES

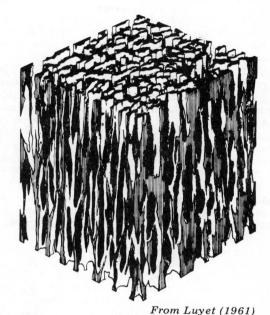

From Luyet (1961)

FIG. F-30. RECONSTRUCTION OF FREEZE-DRIED BEEF MUSCLE SHOWING ORIENTATION AND DISTRIBUTION OF CHANNELS

difference in vapor pressure (see Table F-12) provides the driving force for vapor transfer. Figure F-28 shows a condensing chamber connected with the drying chamber and equipped with a condensing plate connected to a source of refrigeration.

In theory, even at atmospheric pressure, water vapor would diffuse from the frozen food to the cold condenser under the influence of a gradient in vapor pressure. However, at atmospheric pressure the rate of diffusion would be exceedingly slow due to the resistance of the stagnant air between the food and the condenser. By evacuating the system to around 1 torr, the resistance from stagnant gas is largely eliminated thereby accelerating markedly the transfer of water vapor away from the food. In addition, as seen from Table F-12, a reduced pressure at the ice surface prevents the ice from melting. Figure F-28 shows a source of vacuum connected to the condensing chamber. Under the conditions of commercial freeze drying the system is generally maintained at pressures between 0.2 and 1.5 torr.

As freeze drying progresses, the frozen zone recedes and is surrounded by an ever increasing layer of dry food solids. This developing dry layer is illustrated in Fig. F-29. Diagram A represents a slab of frozen food at the start of drying. Owing to superficial ice, the behavior of A is similar to a block of pure ice. Diagrams B and C represent the slab of frozen food after freeze drying has progressed. B and C characterize dry layers of increasing thickness. Whether the receding ice front is sharp or diffuse has not been fully resolved. King (1970) reviews the evidence for each configuration. Likewise, the concentration gradient for moisture in the dry layer remains an item of conjecture. Diagram D represents the slab of freeze-dried food after the ice zone has completely disappeared.

Figure F-30 is a magnified reconstruction of freeze-dried beef and illustrates the complexity of the internal structure which consists of 75% voids. This product resembles a stretched rubber sponge. This porous layer provides a formidable resistance to heat transfer. Many freeze-dried foods have a thermal conductivity of the same order of magnitude as cork. In addition, the dry layer serves as a resistance to vapor diffusion. These resistances within the food mass so profoundly alter the heat and vapor transfer that investigators treat the internal relationships separately from external heat and vapor transfers which mediate between the surface of the food and the relevant components of the freeze-drying system.

Owing to the internal complexity and variability of natural foods and the difficulties inherent in measuring transient temperatures and pressures, a number of investigators have utilized model systems. Others have sought to relate measurable variables of freeze-dried or frozen food to drying behavior. In an extensive investigation on turkey breast muscle, King and his colleagues have described the relationships of a number of internal variables to heat and vapor transfer and to the rate of freeze drying. These studies together with similar reports from other investigators have been summarized in a critical review by King (1970).

At chamber pressures of 0.2–1.5 torr, as commonly used for the freeze drying of food, the rate of drying is controlled by the rate of heat transfer through the dry layer. The driving force for conductive transfer through this dry layer is the temperature gradient between the surface of the food and the ice interface. The extent to which this gradient can be exploited to enhance heat transfer is subject to innate limitations imposed by the susceptibility of the dry surface to thermal damage as well as the sensitivity of the ice zone to incipient melting. The resistance of the dry layer to thermal conduction varies with thickness, with the type of food, its method of freezing, and in many cases with its orientation, and with chamber pressure.

As previously noted, rapid rates of freezing produce smaller ice crystals which, on sublimation leave smaller pores in the food. The smaller pores, as statistically defined, are associated with lower thermal conductivity and hence with a slower rate of freeze drying. In fibrous foods such as meat, there is a marked anisotropic effect with respect to both heat and vapor transfer. Within the usual pressure range of commercial freeze drying, the thermal conductivity parallel to the fibers of dry turkey breast muscle is about three times that in a perpendicular plane. Also, over the pressure range between 0.1 and 100 torr there is a marked increase in thermal conductivity. Even at the extremes of the limited pressure range of commercial operations (0.2–1.5 torr) this pressure effect may account for a doubling of the thermal conductivity of the dry layer. While heat conductivity of the dry layer increases with chamber pressure, the thermal gradient which provides the driving force for heat transfer reacts in the opposite direction. On the basis of theoretical calculations and assuming a maximum permissible surface temperature of $60°C$ for turkey muscle, King (1970) concludes that the maximum rate of freeze drying should occur at a pressure between 8 and 15 torr. While theoretically attractive, operations at pressures so far above the triple point necessitates a degree of control not yet attained in commercial freeze-drying systems.

In commercial freeze-drying operations requiring maximum productivity of the drying equipment, the temperature of the platens is programmed to provide an acceptable cycle time without excessive damage to the final product. Such a compromise must be based on experience with each food processed. Care is exercised to avoid superficial melting during loading and while the chamber is being evacuated to operating pressure, generally 1.5 torr or less. At the beginning there is no definite restriction on the temperature to which the platens may be raised as long as low pressure can be maintained in the chamber. Temperatures above $150°C$ have frequently been used. The high initial temperature is programmed downward as a dry layer is developed. During the greater part of the cycle the platens are held at constant temperature compatible with product quality. For example, with beef and chicken the temperature is maintained below $65°C$, with pork below $55°C$.

When all of the ice has been sublimed, freeze drying is theoretically completed. At this point, however, a portion of the bound or unfreezable moisture still remains in the ice-free food. Depending on the food and the conditions of drying, this residual water may run from 0.3 to 0.04 gm per gm of dry (fat-free) solids. This water is removed at an ever-decreasing rate under the terminal temperature, pressure, and relative humidity in the drying chamber. Under commercial drying conditions the terminal phase of drying is complicated by a great variability in the moisture content of the individual pieces. A number of ingenious mechanisms (see Burke and Decareau 1964), to identify the moisture content of food in the drier during the terminal phase have been examined for the purpose of minimizing prolongation of the drying cycle and reducing exposure of product to the terminal drying temperature. In commercial practice, freeze-dried foods which are designed to be held for 6 months or more are usually dried to a residual moisture of 2% or less.

In view of the sensitivity of freeze-dried products to moisture and oxygen, it is customary to use a dry inert gas, generally nitrogen, to restore the drying chamber to atmospheric pressure before removing the dried product. Likewise, after the freeze-dried product has been removed from the drier, it should be transferred with minimum delay to a package which affords reliable protection against subsequent exposure to oxygen and moisture.

Freeze-Dried Foods

Most foods, either raw or cooked, when freeze dried in accordance with the best commercially feasible procedure rehydrate rapidly to yield products which are equal in acceptability to their frozen counterparts. Time required for rehydration at normal serving temperature, ranges from $1/4$ min for patty items to 15 min for shrimp, steaks, and chops. Representative freeze-dried products undergo no important loss of vitamins as a result of freeze drying (Thomas and Calloway 1961); nor is the nutritive quality of their proteins significantly changed (de Groot 1963). When properly prepared and packaged, freeze-dried products are generally acceptable after 12 months storage at $38°C$—few commercially canned foods can equal this stability. In addition, freeze-dried items are not susceptible to microbial deterioration. The 50–90% reduction in weight from dehydration represents a significant logistic advantage. Thus, freeze-dried foods are acceptable, wholesome, and stable, and are concentrates of unimpaired nutritional quality which can be quickly and conveniently prepared for consumption. Notwithstanding these credentials, freeze-dried products reflect defects in initial quality and often accumulated damage incurred from processing, from storage, and from preparation for consumption.

A number of reports illustrate that prefreezing treatments influence the characteristics of the freeze-dried food. For example, Mellor and Irving (1970) point to the need for treatment with sulfite or other agents for the control of subsequent browning. Other investigators have shown that time-temperature schedules for cooking affect the texture of beef, pork, and poultry. Goldblith *et al.* (1964) noted that cooking for different periods at 100°C had a significant effect on the rehydration of freeze-dried shrimp.

The unfortunate consequences of inadequate freezing or melting during drying have been noted previously. Recognition has also been given to the effect of the rate of freezing on the characteristics and behavior of freeze-dried foods. Application of excessive temperature to the dry layer during the drying operation is undoubtedly a common cause of damage. Immediate manifestations of thermal damage include toasting of the surface, browning with attendant color and flavor changes, protein denaturation, impaired water-binding capacity, vitamin destruction, textural changes, and fat leakage. Evidence is developing which points to insidious damage from excessive temperature which is not revealed at the time of removal from the drier, but which results either in accelerated deterioration during storage or in the eventual development of qualitatively different deteriorative changes. As an example of predisposition to deterioration, Karel (1963) shows that an excessive drying temperature promotes the oxidative deterioration of color of shrimp.

It is generally recognized that many products, notably fruits, undergo a marked loss of volatile flavor during freeze drying. Unfortunately operating schedules have not been developed to control flavor loss. King (1970) has reviewed several widely differing concepts regarding flavor-retaining mechanisms. Flink and Karel (1970) report that adsorption is not an important factor in flavor retention during the freeze drying of essentially carbohydrate systems.

The major loss of acceptability most commonly occurs during storage, particularly at elevated temperatures (35°C and above). A frequent cause of damage is the Maillard or nonenzymic browning reaction involving interaction between carbonyl and amino groups. In the early stages of browning, beef develops a red-brown color and a roast or scorched flavor which progresses to an objection-

able bitter-burnt flavor. Concurrently, beef undergoes loss of its ability to absorb and hold water. In theory, the browning reaction may be controlled by removal of either the carbonyl or amino groups. In practice, reduction of moisture to 2% or less permits storage of most freeze-dried items for 12 months at 38°C. Additional protection of fruits and vegetables is achieved by treatment with bisulfite. In view of the hygroscopic nature of many freeze-dried foods, exposure to humid air must be avoided and packaging materials must provide an effective barrier to moisture.

Oxidative changes are also common. Carotenoid and heme pigments in freeze-dried products are especially vulnerable to gaseous oxygen. Several investigators have noted that freeze-dried meats in the presence of oxygen undergo a decrease in soluble nitrogen, oxidation of $-SH$ groups and an increase in toughness. The oxidation of lipids in freeze-dried foods has been the subject of numerous investigations, frequently as model systems. In commercially freeze-dried products the oxidation of neutral lipids is infrequently encountered. More frequent is the reaction of oxygen with the phospholipid fraction. This reaction has been designated as "lipid browning" by Fishwick and Zmarlicki (1970) and results in discoloration and unpalatability in freeze-dried turkey. Tuomy *et al.* (1970) noted a similar relationship between temperature and oxygen uptake in a number of precooked casserole items. In a related study, Tuomy *et al.* (1969) show a significant relationship between oxygen uptake and loss of acceptability.

Freeze-dried raw meat has been shown to have lipolytic action on triglycerides at moisture levels as low as 4-5%. Enzymic browning, which is oxygen dependent, is troublesome especially during rehydration of sliced fruits such as peaches. Enzymes responsible for deteriorative changes are either heat inactivated by blanching or controlled by addition of citric acid and sulfite.

Most of the observations reported on the rehydration of freeze-dried food are obtained in connection with the routine evaluation of other experimental objectives. In reality, rehydration involves two measurements: (a) total water uptake, and (b) water-holding capacity. Too often such tests are performed under arbitrary conditions without due recognition that water must thoroughly permeate the freeze-dried mass as a prerequisite to imbibition by the cells or other components. Fine channels and minute capillary structures are often occluded by gas or are water repellent. Most studies on rehydration of muscle are difficult to reconcile with Luyet's (1962) observation that isolated fibers rehydrate to the extent of 80% within a few seconds. The rehydration of freeze-dried food, no doubt, reflects

Courtesy of Stokes Division, Pennwalt Corp.

FIG. F-31. PHOTOGRAPH OF A COMMERCIAL FREEZE DRIER

many aspects of damage sustained throughout its history. From the perspective of the taste panel, defects of rehydration are frequently translated into defects of texture, mouth feel, and juiciness.

The current status of freeze-dried foods is summarized by the following statement from Rey and Bastien (1962): "Theoretically, freeze drying could be the best technique for preservation of foods. However, it must be remembered that any industrial process must result from a happy compromise between the operating cost and the quality of the product to be marketed."

Freeze-Drying Systems

Batch freeze-drying equipment commonly used for the commercial drying of food consists of two basic components: (a) drying chamber designed for low pressure, and (b) pumping system for performing the combined functions of developing low pressure and removing water vapor from the chamber. The drying chamber is equipped with fixed horizontal platens stacked with interspaces for trays which support the frozen food. The platens are usually channeled internally for circulation of heating fluid which provides for control of platen temperature over a broad range. Food trays are either supported between platens or rest directly thereon. In this latter case conduction may account for a small part of the heat transfer to the tray. Figure F-31 illustrates the arrangement of platens and trays in a large commercial freeze drier.

With few exceptions the pumping system consists either of multistage steam jets or of a refrigerated condenser plus a mechanical vacuum pump. With this latter system refrigeration equipment is required to cool the condenser for the effective removal of water vapor. Depending on the manufacturer of the equipment, the condenser plates are located either in a separate chamber connected with the drying chamber or within the drying chamber itself. Regardless of whether the system utilizes jets or mechanical pumps for evacuation, provision must be made for a rapid pump-down at the start of a cycle, since it is essential to attain a chamber pressure of about 1 torr to avoid superficial melting of the food.

Modern freeze driers are instrumented for process control and programmed to a predetermined cycle. Ancillary equipment has been developed for efficient material handling and reduction of other labor costs. Burke and Decareau (1964) provide additional insight into the application of such equipment in conjunction with conventional batch equipment.

Burke and Decareau (1964) and King (1970) describe several continuous and semicontinuous systems for freeze drying food which are used in Europe. With few exceptions these systems are semicontinuous in that a double system of pressure locks is provided for incoming and outgoing product. While one system is on-stream; the alternate set is being loaded or unloaded. A report from the Krauss-Maffei organization in Munich (Anon. 1969) mentions an adaptation of a vacuum plate drier in which berries are mechanically moved across a platen then passed to the next. From such contact with heated platens, drying time is said to be reduced from 6 to 10 hr to 1 to 3 hr. In addition to the advantage of maintaining stable operating conditions, continuous or semicontinuous systems permit the dried product to be transferred to a reliable container without exposure to atmospheric moisture and oxygen.

While not used commercially, equipment and procedures have been described for freeze drying at atmospheric pressure, with pulsed pressures, with heat supplied by microwaves or by gas convection, and with a desiccant for removal of vapor from the system. Reviews by Burke and Decareau (1964) and by King (1970) discuss freeze drying at atmospheric pressure. While theoretically feasible, such a system is unattractive for commercial applications from the standpoints of engineering design and of operating requirements. For example, air, if used, must be maintained at a temperature compatible with ice. At such a temperature the amount of water vapor carried is a minute fraction of the total mass of air. As a consequence, an enormous volume of air must be circulated to approach saturation and subsequently be dehydrated.

Mink and Sachsel (1968) describe the use of a fluidized bed for rapid freeze drying of foods of uniform configuration, such as diced beef, ham, haddock, shrimp, whole kernel corn, diced carrots, asparagus segments, and whole blueberries. Since heat is uniformly provided to all surfaces, ice is sublimed within 3–4 hr at a pressure well below the triple point. Secondary drying for removal of bound water is relatively slow, especially at 38°C. As a theoretical extension of freeze drying in a fluidized bed, Greaves (1964B) describes the equipment and the formidable problems encountered in the spray freeze drying of liquids such as milk.

King (1970) has analyzed both the theory and the claims of a number of investigators regarding the application of pulsed or cycled pressures to accelerate the rate of freeze drying. King points to the difficulty of separating the enhancement of conductive heat transfer through the dry layer as achieved at higher operating pressures from the effect of pulsing per se. King's calculations support only a small part of the rate advantage claimed for the use of pulsed pressures.

Observations have been reported by Graham et al. (1959) and by Strasser (1967) on freeze drying of food in an evacuated chamber containing silica gel or other desiccants. King and Clark (1968) analyzed the factors contributing to the rate of freeze drying in mixed beds or in layered configurations involving frozen food and desiccant (silica gel or molecular sieves) and extended the potential of such drying systems by demonstrating the increased effectiveness of circulating a gas, preferably helium, through the bed at a pressure of 8–15 torr. Freeze drying in mixed beds with a desiccant minimizes the requirement for costly and sophisticated equipment.

The use of microwave energy for supplying heat to the ice interface is particularly attractive since it circumvents the resistance of the dry layer to conductive heat transfer. Notwithstanding extensive investigation, formidable physical problems have not been resolved; notably, the dielectric difference between ice and water, control of the glow discharge within the drying chamber, and uniform application of energy. Additional obstacles to the use of microwaves are seen in the outlay for generating equipment, the increased operating cost, and the necessity for major design changes in existing freeze-drying chambers.

Prospectus

Notwithstanding the superior quality of freeze-dried foods compared with canned products and foods dried by other methods, the capitalization requirements and high cost of preparing freeze-dried foods place them at a competitive disadvantage with frozen foods in the civilian market. These economic realities have severely restricted the growth of the freeze-dried food industry in the United States and confined output to specialized products for limited markets. Essentially the same picture prevails in Western Europe where freeze-dried products have developed through their merits in an economically competitive environment. According to Spicer's (1969) analysis, freeze drying requires a sophisticated market for food which is expected to embrace only a small selected portion of the total.

Cost data on freeze drying of food are, of necessity, so extensively qualified that their utility is marginal. Maguire (1967) provides an economic analysis for a plant having 4000 sq ft of shelf space and engaged in drying sliced bananas. Based on operating 24 hr a day for 320 days a year, and with the investment amortized in 10 yr, the cost of removing 1 lb of water is calculated at $0.0325. This cost includes freezing but not protective packaging for the dried product.

The growth of the freeze-dried food industry depends on the interaction among the unique properties of freeze-dried products, their acceptance, their negative features, and the economic realities of their production. None of these parameters is susceptible to meaningful assessment. The combination of reliable preservation without power requirements, rapid rehydration to yield quality foods, and elimination of non-nutritive weight are unique qualifications for a number of military situations as well as for campers, hikers, hunters, and other sportsmen. By reversible compression the volume of freeze-dried products can be reduced to between $1/3$ and $1/20$ of their original volume without significant loss of acceptability. This feature enhances the logistic value of freeze-dried foods for military and civilian applications.

As the demands of future markets become increasingly sophisticated, it is anticipated that numerous applications for freeze-dried foods will emerge. Through such applications, freeze drying has the potential to become prominent among the unit operations of the food industry.

MAXWELL C. BROCKMANN

References

ANON. 1969. Freeze-dries in 1 to 3 hr. Food Eng. *41*, No. 4, 166-167.

BAKER, J., GANE, R., and MAPSON, L. W. 1946. The quality of green peas dried in the frozen state. Food Manuf. *21*, 345-348.

BROCKMANN, M. C. 1970. Freeze drying. Chem. Eng. Progr. Symp. Ser. *66*, No. 100, 51-61.

BURKE, R. F., and DECAREAU, R. V. 1964. Recent advances in the freeze-drying of food products. Advan. Food Res. *13*, 1-88.

DE GROOT, A. P. 1963. The influence of dehydration of foods on the digestibility and biological value of the protein. Food Technol. *17*, 339-343.

FLINK, J. and KAREL, M. 1970. Retention of organic volatiles in freeze-dried solutions of carbohydrates. J. Agr. Food Chem. *18*, 295-297.

FISHWICK, M. J. and ZMARLICKI, S. 1970. Freeze-dried turkey muscle. I. Changes in nitrogenous compounds and lipids of dehydrated turkey during storage. J. Sci. Food Agr. *21*, 155-160.

FLOSDORF, E. W. 1945. Drying by sublimation. Food Ind. *17*, 22-25, 98-108.

FLOSDORF, E. W. 1949. Freeze-drying. Reinhold Publishing Co., New York.

GOLDBLITH, S. A. 1964. Freeze-dehydration of foods. *In* Lyophilisation (pp. 555-572). L. R. Rey (Editor). Hermann, Paris.

GOLDBLITH, S. A., KAREL, M. and LUSK, G. 1964. The role of food science and technology in the freeze dehydration of foods. *In* Lyophilisation (pp 527-553). L. R. Rey (Editor). Hermann, Paris.

GRAHAM, R. P., BROWN, A. H. and RAMAGE, W. D. 1959. Process of dehydrating biological materials. U.S. Pat. 2,897,600. Aug. 4.

GREAVES, R. I. N. 1964A. Historical development of the freeze-drying of human plasma for transfusion. *In* Lyophilisation (pp 323-334). L. R. Rey (Editor). Hermann, Paris.

GREAVES, R. I. N. 1964B. High vacuum spray freeze-drying. *In* Lyophilisation (pp 171-182). L. R. Rey (Editor). Hermann, Paris.

HANSON, S. W. F. (Editor) 1961. The Accelerated Freeze-Drying Method of Food Preservation. HM Stationery Office, London.

HARPER, J. C. and TAPPEL, A. L. 1957. Freeze-drying of food products. Advan. Food Res. 7, 171-234.

KAREL, M. 1963. Physical and chemical considerations in freeze-dehydrated foods. *In* Exploration in Future Food-Processing Techniques. S. A. Goldblith (Editor). MIT Press, Cambridge, Massachusetts.

KING, C. J. 1970. Freeze-drying of foods. Critical Rev. Food Technol. *1*, No. 3, 379-451.

KING, C. J. and CLARK, J. P. 1968. Convective heat transfer for freeze drying of foods. Food Technol. *22*, 1235-1239.

KUPRIANOFF, J. 1964. Fundamental and practical aspects of the freezing of foodstuffs. *In* Lyophilisation (pp 497-517). L. R. Rey (Editor). Hermann, Paris.

LUYET, B. J. 1961. Rehydration of freeze dried meat. Final Report, Contract DA 129-QM-1413. Quartermaster Food & Container Inst.

LUYET, B. J. 1962. Effect of freezing rates on the structure of freeze-dried materials and on the mechanism of rehydration. *In* Freeze-Drying of Foods (pp 194-211). F. R. Fisher (Editor). Natl. Acad. Sci.—Natl. Res. Council, Washington, D.C.

MAGUIRE, J. F. 1967. Vacuum techniques in freeze-drying pilot plants. Vacuum *17*, No. 12, 631-638.

MELLOR, J. D. and IRVING, A. R. 1970. Product quality in freeze drying. CSIRO Food Preserv. *30*, No. 1, 9-14.

MINK, W. H. and SACHSEL, G. F. 1968. Rapid freeze-drying by use of the fluidized bed. Chem. Eng. Progr. Symp. Ser. *64*, No. 86, 54-59.

REY, L. R. and BASTIEN, MARIE-CLAUDE. 1962. Biophysical aspects of freeze drying, importance of the preliminary freezing and and sublimation periods. *In* Freeze-Drying of Foods. F. R. Fisher (Editor). Natl. Acad. Sci.—Natl. Res. Council, Washington, D.C.

SPICER, A. 1969. Freeze drying of foods in Europe. Food Technol. *23*, 1272-1275.

STRASSER, J. and GIFFEE, J. W. 1967. The freeze-desiccation process. Activities Rept. *19* No. 1, 125-132.

THOMAS, MIRIAM HIGGINS, and CALLOWAY, DORIS HOWES. 1961. Nutritional value of dehydrated foods. J. Am. Dietetic Assoc. *39*, No. 2, 105-116.

TUOMY, J. M. HINNERGARDT, L. C. and HELMER, R. L. 1969. Effect of oxygen uptake on quality of cooked, freeze-dried combination foods. Agr. Food Chem. *17*, 1360-1363.

TUOMY, J. M., HINNERGARDT, L. C. and HELMER, R. L. 1970. Effect of storage temperature on the oxygen uptake of cooked, freeze-dried combination foods. Agr. Food Chem. *18*, 899-901.

Cross-reference: *Dehydration.*

FROZEN FOODS

Freezing has long been recognized as an excellent method of preserving meat and fish. Since early times, farmers, fishermen, and trappers residing in regions having cold winters have preserved their meat, game, and fish by freezing and storage in unheated buildings. Even the commercial freezing of fish, meat, and poultry is not a new industry. The artificial freezing of fish on a commercial scale began about 1865. Even before that time, fish caught through the ice in the Great Lakes were frozen by allowing them to remain on the ice for a few hours. This system, called weather freezing, is still occasionally used in the Great Lakes region.

In 1868, prior to the introduction of refrigeration machines using ammonia, ocean fish were artificially frozen by placing them in covered pans surrounded by salt and ice. In about 1880, ammonia refrigeration machines began to be used to freeze fish in the United States. At the end of the 19th Century, fish freezing was already an important industry in this country. The commercial freezing of poultry was also begun nearly a century ago. Even egg freezing in the United States goes back to 1889.

The freezing of small fruits, for later use in making preserves, jams, and jellies, began in 1905 in the eastern part of the United States, and in the Pacific Northwest in 1911.

The freezing of vegetables is of much more recent origin having been started by the Birdseye organization in Hillsboro, Oregon in 1929. The industry started slowly but since World War II has grown to great proportions. In 1969, the U.S. pack of frozen vegetables exceeded 3844 million pounds. Today, the leading product is frozen potatoes. The 1969 pack of this product exceeded 2 billion pounds, approximately 6 times that of the next most-important product, green peas. In 1969, the pack of frozen fruit exceeded 781,681,000 lb, approximately $1/3$ of which was frozen strawberries. Poultry is in second place in quantity frozen. In 1969, 2,578,823,000 lb of poultry was frozen! The quantity of turkey frozen exceeded a billion pounds (ready-to-cook weight). The quantity of chickens frozen was also very great, being about 1,175,000,000.

By comparison, the quantity of seafood frozen in 1969 seems small, being only 358,639,000 lb. The total quantity of shellfish frozen in 1969 was 121,873,000 lb.

The quantity of concentrated orange juice frozen in 1969–1970 was also very great, reaching 124,947,000 gal., prepared from approximately 375,000,000 gal. of orange juice. Relatively small amounts of grapefruit, lemon, lime, and tangerine juice concentrates were also frozen.

Not only is the quantity of food frozen very great, but a large number of kinds of fresh foods, prepared in a great variety of ways, are frozen. For example, there are more than 30 different vegetables frozen on an important commercial scale. Some, e.g., potatoes, are prepared in several different ways.

Thirty-five different fruits are now frozen commercially and if the number of purées, juices, and concentrates is included, the total reaches 52.

Precooked and Convenience Foods

Although a few precooked frozen foods were packed for sale in the 1930's, e.g., squash, corn on the cob, and crab meat, it was not until after World War II that an enormous variety of frozen precooked foods of all kinds were offered. There are now at least 300 different kinds of frozen precooked foods (including baked goods), and if the number of flavors and types of each product is counted, the number is well over 1000.

Many products which were once thought to be unsuited for freezing have been modified in composition or by the method of preparation and/or freezing are now frozen and marketed successfully. As has been pointed out previously, the quantity of prepared and precooked potato products frozen is very great, some of the more important of these are par-fried potatoes (partially fried in deep fat), blanched, hash brown, mashed, whipped, diced and creamed, puffs, rissole, patties, shredded, stuffed, baked, and fried after extrusion.

Nearly all baked products can be frozen and thawed without great change. The list of baked goods includes bread, nearly all kinds of pies (except certain custard pies), tarts, all kinds of cakes, cookies, muffins, shortcakes, waffles, pancakes, pizza, and many others. Most kinds of bread can be rapidly frozen and stored for a year at 0°F or lower and then thawed without serious deterioration, being about as fresh as day-old bread. The baked products which freeze almost perfectly and can be stored for six months or longer without notable change include all kinds of pot pies—chicken, turkey, beef, and other meat pies. These have been very popular for several years, and are still in great demand. The production and sale of pizza and some other nationality foods have increased greatly recently. Perhaps this is not surprising since it is difficult for most housewives to make good pizza, and the commercially frozen product is not only convenient to use but as good or better than the housewife can make.

Packaging

Prior to the advent of "quick frozen foods" (about 1929) most products were packed in large containers for freezing. Chickens were "New York dressed" and packed one dozen to a parchment-paper-lined crate. Cream and also liquid eggs were put into 30-lb, slip-cover tin cans. Berries were usually mixed with sugar and then either put in barrels or 30-lb tin cans for freezing.

Bulk-packing had several disadvantages: (1) freezing even at low temperatures was very slow, resulting in marked loss of quality; (2) many products could not be removed from the container without thawing and this required many hours, and also resulted in marked deterioration; and (3) the market was limited to wholesale establishments, institutions, processors, and certain grocers who were willing to take the trouble of thawing and repackaging the products (this resulted in inferior products).

Birdseye was the first to "quick freeze" foods in small retail size rectangular packages lined with moisture-proof cellophane. Later, other plastic liners were used. Other food freezers introduced many different types of aluminum-foil packages. These small retail-size packages permit both rapid freezing and rapid thawing. Recently, vegetables, fruits and some precooked foods have been frozen in small vacuumized bags in which the food can be cold-stored without notable deterioration from desiccation and/or oxidation. The housewife can thaw and/or reheat the food quickly with little or no deterioration.

Quality Control

Prior to the advent of "quick freezing," foods were frozen as a means of preventing microbial spoilage to save a crop surplus, or to permit transport from agricultural regions to metropolitan centers. Little or no consideration was given to the variety frozen, the method of freezing, or the quality of the product. The fish dealer froze any seafood left at the weekend and usually thawed it for sale the following week.

Today's frozen food packers select the varieties of fruits and vegetables of high quality which yield excellent frozen products that do not deteriorate rapidly during frozen storage, prepare them for the table, and pack them in containers which prevent desiccation and retard oxidation and which permit quick freezing and rapid thawing for later use.

Similarly, strictly fresh fish of high quality are cleaned and filleted, packed in moisture-vapor-proof consumer-size packages, then frozen quickly and stored at $0°F$ or below. Poultry of high quality is cleaned, the feathers rapidly removed, the feet and heads are cut off, then, after thorough washing, the chickens or other fowl are put in packages which prevent desiccation and retard oxidation, and rapidly frozen.

Because of the care now taken in the selection, preparation, packaging, freezing, and thawing of foods, the quality of frozen foods on the market is excellent. Further, as a rule the price is relatively low. Also, since the food has been prepared for the table, the housewife does not need to spend time sorting, cleaning, and washing the frozen products. Consequently, many prefer the frozen to the fresh product.

The Future of Frozen Foods

The food freezing industry will continue to expand for many years to come. One field into which it is entering and in which it will become an important factor is in hospital feeding. The Kaiser hospitals on the West Coast have discontinued operation of most of their kitchens and have the food for their patients frozen in pans made from plastic covered aluminum and plastic bags in which the food can be thawed and reheated in 2–3 min in a microwave oven. Each container has just enough for a serving. This will mean that the food packer will have to prepare a large number of dietetic dishes for patients on special diets. These foods will be kept frozen in the hospital freezer and then prepared for serving without the help of a cook.

More and more chains of hotels and restaurants are preparing, cooking, and freezing their foods in large factory-size kitchens. The entrées are packaged and frozen in individual servings.

Some restaurants thaw and reheat precooked foods in microwave ovens; others use "boil-in-the-bag" techniques. Such a system is far more economical than maintaining a large kitchen and high-salaried chef in each restaurant or hotel. Further, there is far less waste. A menu with many choice entrées can be offered even in locations where there is a wide daily variation in the number of patrons.

The discovery that frozen foods in plastic coated aluminum containers can be thawed and reheated without danger of arcing and causing the food to burn because of uneven heating will do much to further the use of inexpensive aluminum foil containers for precooked frozen foods.

The use of cryogenic methods of freezing foods at very low temperatures which are greatly damaged by slower methods of freezing has made possible the freezing of many additional products, including tomatoes and whole strawberries. These methods, together with storage of the ultra fast frozen foods at very low temperatures, are employed for the freezing of many products which have been thought to be irreparably damaged by freezing.

The horticulturist is perfecting new varieties of fruits (e.g., strawberries) and vegetables (e.g., sweet corn) which when frozen are of far better quality than those now frozen. When these new varieties of sweet corn are grown and harvested at optimum maturity, frozen corn-on-the-cob of such high quality can be obtained that few persons can tell it from fresh corn that has not been frozen.

As the preservation of food by freezing becomes common practice all over the world, we in America will be able to enjoy the great variety of wonderful fruits and vegetables grown in the tropics which will be imported in frozen form. Conversely, we will have a market in tropical countries for vegetables such as peas which we can grow and they cannot.

DONALD K. TRESSLER

FRUIT PRESERVES AND JELLIES

There are many historical references to indicate that products very similar to the preserves and marmalades we know today were made in ancient times. These sweetened fruit items were served as a part of the meal or even as a confection or dessert.

Accounts of meals in Roman times, for example, often indicate the use of preserved fruits as one of the courses of the meal. Although the combining of a large amount of sugar with the fruit has a preservative effect, it is very likely that these sweetened fruits were first developed on the basis of their flavor rather than as a method of keeping fruit from spoiling.

Until the 16th Century these products, at least in Europe, had to be made with honey, which was the universal sweetener at that time. The appearance of sugar made from sugar cane or sugar beets made it possible to preserve fruits on a much wider scale than had been possible in earlier centuries. This became especially important in climates where fruit seasons were brief and where it was a great advantage to be able to eat summer fruits all year long. When sugar became more readily available, marmalades originated in Portugal as a method of preserving quinces. The term came to be used to denote almost any preserved fruit. Marmalades are now usually thought of as being a preserve made with chopped citrus fruits.

Many variations of these products were developed, including jellies which were made the same way except that a strained or clarified fruit juice was used rather than the crushed fruit. Fruit butters normally have a much higher proportion of fruit and are almost deliberately altered by the extensive cooking necessary to reach the desired solids level.

Definitions

Federal Standards and definitions have existed in the United States since 1940 for fruit preserves and jellies. These standards, not too unlike those of other countries, define the products, the minimum quantity of fruit or fruit juice that may be used, as well as permitted optional ingredients. The standard for preserves does not distinguish between preserves and jams but says that a preserve is the semisolid product made by combining at least 45 parts properly-prepared fruit with 55 parts of sugar and cooking until the final soluble solids content is 68% or higher (65% in the case of certain fruits).

Similarly, jellies are to be made by combining 45 parts of a clarified fruit juice with 55 parts of sugar. In both products the current standard permits the use of corn syrup to the extent of 25% of the added sweetner solids. Unlimited amounts of dextrose or invert sugar may be used as the sweetener.

Traditionally, jams are often thought of as the more highly comminuted product while preserves might describe products with whole or distinct pieces of fruit. Legally, however, there is no distinction and the names are used interchangeably.

Both jellies and preserves are permitted to contain reasonable quantities of added pectin, citric, tartaric, malic, or lactic acid, and a buffer salt of the acid used. Sodium benzoate may be used as a preservative (if declared on the label). No added flavor or color is permitted except in mint and cinnamon jellies.

Pectin is a polymer of galacturonic acid molecules and is the adhesive or firming agent in many fruits and vegetables. The albedo of citrus fruits and apples is especially rich in pectin. The peel of these fruits is a commercial source for the powdered, refined pectin used by preservers and jelly makers to achieve a gel or adjust the consistency.

Pectin exists in fruits in a variety of forms. When the fruit is immature, it exists as a large, relatively insoluble molecule containing a maximum number of methyl groups. As the fruit matures, this protopectin becomes more soluble until finally, during senescence, hydrolysis of the pectin has proceeded to a point where the fruit has lost firmness and the pectin has little gelling power.

Citric, tartaric, and malic acids are found in fruits. However, they are largely made synthetically and the choice of which acid is largely a matter of economics. The acid serves to adjust the pH or acidity of the product. This acidity is important to flavor and is essential to promote the formation of a gel by the pectin present.

The buffer compounds, salts of the above-mentioned weak acids, are used in many cases to delay the setting time of the product. Present regulations permit the use of 3 oz of sodium citrate or similar buffer per 100 lb of sweetener.

Principles of Preserve and Jelly Making

Most investigators feel that the thickening or gelling of a pectin-sugar mixture is the result of pectin molecules cross-linking by means of hydrogen bonds. Thus, there must be present sufficient pectin, the correct hydrogen-ion content (pH), and a sugar or solids content of 60% or more. All three of these factors are necessary for the typical high solids preserve or jelly. These principles have been known to housewives for years and home preservers have recognized that pectin-rich fruits with a certain degree of tartness were necessary. If pectin was deficient, it could be made up by blending with another fruit, such as apple, or refined pectin available in retail packages could be used. Lemon juice has been commonly used in the home kitchen to adjust the acidity. The cooking, of course, removed water to a point where gelation would take place and, incidentally, raised the soluble solids content to a preservative level.

As a general rule, the pectin necessary in terms of 150 grade commercial pectin is about 0.5% for preserves and 1.0% for jellies. A pH somewhere between 3.0 and 3.5 is optimum for both flavor and gelling quality.

The end point or finishing point when preparing a preserve or jelly can be determined in many ways. Most simply it was probably first done by observing the viscosity of the hot product as it would drip from the spoon or stirring paddle. Since there is a relationship between soluble solids content and the boiling temperature, a thermometer can be used along the same lines as is done with confectionery products. In fact, much commercial production has been done using an accurate thermometer and cooking to a temperature the proper number of degrees above the boiling temperature of water. However, it is much more accurate and simpler to use a refractometer, the commonly-used method today in commercial production. These refractometers are usually made specifically for this purpose and rather than reading in terms of indices of refraction are scaled to show directly the brix or percentage of soluble solids.

Manufacturing Practices

As with any food manufacturing operation, actual procedures can vary from plant to plant. Certainly, these products could be made in a single steam-jacketed kettle. In actual practice, it has been found more efficient to divide the manufacture into steps. The maintenance of a discrete batch at least until the filling point permits close control of the soluble solids and pH, factors vital to the quality of the product. Probably most preserves and jellies are now cooked (that is, the water removed) in vacuum vessels rather than in open atmospheric kettles. The use of vacuum means lower boiling temperatures; in turn, less damage to the color and flavor of the fruit.

The pectin used can be made up separately either for each batch or in sufficient volume for the day's production. A variety of techniques is available to make the pectin solution. Pectin, like other gums, can be difficult to disperse. A common procedure is to blend the dry pectin with about five times its weight of dry sugar. The mixture is dispersed in water using good agitation. After dispersion is complete, the temperature must be raised to 190° F or higher to ensure solution.

The fruit, sugar, and corn syrup, if used, are blended in a mixing kettle, usually a steam-jacketed kettle equipped with slow speed agitation. If desired, the proper amount of pectin solution can be added at this time. Although this results in a viscous material to be handled through the subsequent steps, it does supply some added water to aid in dissolving the sugar. Sufficient heat and agitation are used to dissolve the sugar and effect some diffusion of the sugar into the fruit. The batch is then drained into the vacuum vessel by vacuum, by pumping or by gravity. These cookers are usually about $1/3$ steam-jacketed and should have a height/diameter ratio of at least three. Vapors are drawn off by a suitable vapor line leading to a condenser and a vacuum pump (steam ejector or mechanical). Boiling is done at a low temperature, about 140°F being customary. Near the conclusion of this cycle, the pectin solution, if not already present, can be added. As pointed out earlier, the end point is determined with a refractometer.

When the desired end point (65° Brix for jellies and 68° Brix for preserves) has been reached, the proper amount of acid must be added to effect the gelling process. There are several procedures that can be used. The pH can be measured while the batch is in the vacuum vessel and the acid added directly at that point, or the batch can be discharged to a holding kettle for the acid incorporation. In either case, the temperature must be raised to a point where the addition of the acid will not cause pregelation. The pectin used for these products is not truly reversible, and too rapid a gelling combined with agitation will result in a product which will never gel properly. Thus, the batch should be at 160°F and even higher if a fast-setting pectin is used. Once the pH has been adjusted, usually somewhere between 3.1 and 3.4, the batch is ready for filling.

Filling

Although preserving itself suggests that these products should resist spoilage by microorganisms because of their high sugar content, there is still a danger of infection. The low pH and low water activity preclude bacterial action. However, even 68% solids is not a guarantee against the growth of certain molds and yeasts, particularly molds. Furthermore, the accumulation of a small amount of moisture on the surface of the product after the jar is capped can dilute the soluble solids content enough to encourage surface mold growth. Contrary to general opinion, molds can grow in low oxygen atmosphere and the usual headspace vacuums (12–16 in.) certainly do not indicate an oxygen-free atmosphere above the product.

Unfortunately, less has been published about fungal spoilage agents than about the bacterial ones and clear-cut processing and sterilization guidelines do not exist as they do for the low acid or neutral food products. The problem is further complicated by the sudden appearance of mold infections often due to organisms that have not been seen before. Many preservers have made and canned products for months or years without any spoilage only to have appear suddenly a rash of product with mold growth. As a result, filling and poststerilization times and temperatures are usually planned to give a large margin of safety.

It might be mentioned that an *Aspergillus glaucus* mold has been found that will grow readily in 68% sugar solutions and which takes 165°F for 20 min to kill that serves as a good organism in planning sterilization procedures.

The manufacturer has several choices as to the procedure to follow, usually dictated by the available equipment. However, regardless of the methods used, plant and equipment sanitation is probably the single most important step. A sanitation expert should be consulted to assure that plant and equipment are kept both visibly and hygienically clean.

Probably most manufacturers handle preserves and jellies by raising the temperature of the product (either in the vacuum kettle or the holding kettle) so that little or no poststerilization is necessary. Certainly, temperatures should be in the 190°F range, and the manufacturer should consult with someone familiar with these products to specify his own individual process.

It is possible to fill at lower temperatures so long as pregelation is avoided. The filled and sealed container must then be conveyed through a hot water or steam sterilizer for 10–20 min depending on the fill temperature.

In either case, the product should be cooled promptly by having the jars pass directly into sprays of cool water. It would certainly be desirable to cool the product to at least 110°F (stirred temperature) before warehousing. Obviously, continued heating of fruit products beyond what is necessary will be destructive to the quality.

Equipment

The steam-jacketed kettles and cookers are of a fairly standard design and are readily available from many equipment manufacturers. Stainless steel should be used for the contact surfaces. Although these fruit products can certainly be processed in copper and aluminum kettles, the corrosion resistance of stainless steel is a great advantage despite the better heat transfer properties of other metals. The more sensitive fruits, such as strawberry, have anthocyanin pigments easily degraded and this breakdown is catalyzed by traces of copper.

Modifications of equipment have been made to suit an individual processor's requirement. Many preservers have added surface condensers to their vacuum equipment so as to collect the distillate from the cooking operation. This condensate is then concentrated in an essence recovery still to give an essence for reincorporation into the product.

One equipment innovation recently made at the Smucker plant in Memphis, Tenn., has been the use of vacuum vessels where the heating surface is a revolving steam coil rather than the conventional equipment. Not only are heat exchange rates increased significantly but less heat damage occurs to the product because of the constant movement of the heating surface through the product.

Both rotary and straight line piston-type fillers are used, depending on the speed desired by the processor.

Sterilization (in jar) and cooling is usually done by conveying the filled and sealed container through a tunnel of which the first portion is for heating by steam or hot water and the remainder for cooling by water sprays.

Quality Aspects

Improvement in processing techniques, more basic knowledge about fruit characteristics, and competitive situations have resulted in a great increase in the overall quality of fruit preserves and jellies.

The quality of the raw material is the single most important factor affecting the quality of the finished products. In the United States, frozen fruits and juices are the usual raw materials and it is essential that varieties, flavor, color, freedom from defects, and handling and storage conditions be carefully controlled to ensure consistently good quality products. The seedless jams and jellies are being made to a greater extent from concentrated fruit and juices. If properly prepared, concentrates are of excellent quality and can usually be obtained along with the volatile essence that normally would be lost.

Obviously, the preserver will want to exercise finished product quality control. The firmness of jellies and the viscosity of preserves can be checked by objective measurement. A variety of methods are available. Jelly strength can be measured by some sort of penetration test. Preserves can be evaluated by a spread or flow test. What is important is that the manufacturer use these tests as a way of maintaining uniformity in his products.

The USDA does have grade standards for preserves and jellies, and it would be wise to use these as a guide.

Specific help regarding these products is available from all of the major suppliers of pectin, gums, and sweeteners.

Related Products

Mention has been made of fruit butters and marmalades. Fruit butters have a Federal definition which differs from preserves in that 5 parts of fruit must be used to every 2 parts of sweetener. There is no standard for marmalades. However, the product is normally made like a preserve.

A standard does exist for an artificially-sweetened product in which no sugar is permitted. In this case, a gum of some sort may be used or a de-methylated pectin which sets in the presence of calcium ion.

Importance of Fruit Preserves and Jellies

These fruit products are widely used in nearly every part of the world. In the United States as well as other countries per capita consumption has slowed, but the overall production of preserves, jellies, and butters still shows a steady increase. The U.S. usage of all items of this type totals about 514,000,000 lb. The usage is about evenly divided between jellies and preserves. Marmalades and butters are not one of the most popular items in the United States and probably account for about 8% of the production. There is, of course, a significant quantity imported (largely marmalades), and this amount would be in addition to the previously quoted figure.

The preference in flavors varies very little from year to year. By far the most popular flavor is grape jelly, which accounts on the average for about 30% of the volume of all the products. Next in popularity is strawberry preserves, followed by apple jelly and other fruit preserves. There is a limited amount of pure jam or jelly used for in-

dustrial purposes (i.e., baking). However, the cost is generally prohibitive except to make very deluxe items. The fillings used for baking purposes are imitation from a legal standpoint and contain no fruit or only a portion of the usual required fruit content. Actually, these products require special characteristics to withstand the usage they receive in filling and processing a pastry item and are specially formulated for this purpose.

Each year many new products appear on retail shelves and represent competition for the traditional fruit spread. Thus, many preservers are looking to related items in an effort to increase the usage of fruit spreads. Preservers have also made great strides in the overall quality of the products until today it is virtually impossible to find a poor quality jam or jelly on the supermarket shelf.

DAVID R. GROSS

FUNGI AS FOOD

In general fungi may be considered to be one of the few remaining relatively unexplored and unexploited sources of food. Although there are several thousand species of fleshy fungi, many of which are quite edible, probably no more than a dozen or so species are collected and eaten in the United States, and these by a very small percentage of the total population. Collecting and eating wild mushrooms is a much more prevalent practice in Europe, and in some countries there a variety of species of wild mushrooms may be offered for sale in the markets.

Man has demonstrated a remarkable lack of initiative in the cultivation of mushrooms for food purposes. Of the several thousands of species of fleshy fungi which are known, only four have been cultivated for food by man to an extent that warrants their being seriously considered as important food items. These are (1) the Common Cultivated Mushroom (*Agaricus bisporus*) of the Occident (and Taiwan since about 1960), (2) the Padi Straw Mushroom (*Volvariella volvacea*) of the Orient, (3) the Shiitake (*Lenzites edodes*) of Japan, and (4) the Truffle (*Tuber melanospermum*) of France.

The Common Cultivated Mushroom was first cultivated by French horticulturalists about 1700, and production of this mushroom has now expanded to a very sizeable industry in the United States and various European countries. Traditionally, *Agaricus bisporus* (Basidiomycetes: Agaricaceae) has been grown on composted horse manure and even today most mushroom compost consists primarily of this waste material. However, recent experimentation in Florida has pointed to the possibility of cultivating *A. bisporus* on a compost made of a mixture of old newspapers and kitchen wastes. Mushrooms have been and still are grown in caves and abandoned mines, but most modern growers produce their crops in specially constructed mushroom houses in which temperature and humidity can be controlled. Houses are also provided with ventilating systems which prevent carbon dioxide concentration from becoming too great, since high concentrations of this gas inhibit or prevent mushroom development. Aside from the composting process which is still conducted empirically, mushroom production is now conducted quite scientifically, and a well-run mushroom production facility may almost be thought of in modern factory terms. Most U.S. housewives, who constitute the major part of the mushroom-buying public, have been conditioned to buy only the "Snow White" variety of *Agaricus bisporus*—picked in the unexpanded (button) stage. Although buttons have a longer shelf-life, this is a most unfortunate practice, because, as a result, most Americans never taste mushrooms in which full flavor development has been allowed to occur. Nearly 200 million pounds of mushrooms are produced annually in the United States (with Pennsylvania being the greatest producing state), but this is still not enough to satisfy the demand, and so very considerable amounts are imported—primarily from Taiwan. Recent analyses have shown that not only is total consumption of mushrooms increasing but that per capita consumption is also markedly increasing. However, in fiscal 1968/69 mushrooms represented less than 0.07% of the food consumed in the United States, since they are used primarily as condiments rather than as a food staple.

The Padi Straw Mushroom (*Volvariella volvacea*—Basidiomycetes: Amanitaceae) has been widely produced in Oriental countries for many centuries, where in some instances it constitutes a staple item of the diet. Oddly enough, it is a member of the same family as *Amanita phalloides*—one of the most poisonous of all fleshy fungi. It is cultivated on soaked bundles of rice straw and picked either in the button or expanded stage. Production figures on this mushroom are not available because many are grown on a small scale by peasant farmers for home consumption or for sale in small local markets. Most production is still conducted on a rather crude basis although in some areas of the Orient efforts are being made to place Padi Straw Mushroom cultivation on a more scientific basis. Although dried Padi Straw Mushrooms have been available for years in American markets, in large cities which have considerable Chinese populations, most Americans have never tasted this type of mushroom. However, in recent years imported canned mushrooms of this type have begun to show up more and more in U.S. markets. Research is currently being conducted in California and Texas to determine if the Padi Straw Mushroom can be grown in those states.

The Shiitake (*Lenzites edodes*—Basidiomycetes: Tricholomataceae) is a highly-prized mushroom in Japan and is produced there in considerable quantity. It is also collected in its natural habitat in various parts of the Orient. The Shiitake is a wood-inhabiting fungus and so it is cultured on small logs. In some instances the logs are inoculated with pure cultures of *Lenzites edodes* but in others the logs are merely laid next to logs in which the Shiitake mycelium is already growing. Methods of inoculating logs vary but in all cases the objective is to have the mycelium growing profusely through the logs. During this period of mycelial growth inoculated logs are placed against low bamboo fences in shaded areas; they may be watered at intervals depending on the amount of rainfall. When the logs are well-permeated with mycelium they are placed against higher fences (in a more nearly upright position) in an even moister situation. Crops of mushrooms appear in the spring and in the fall, and crops may be borne on the same log for several years. Dried, imported Shiitake may be purchased in various cities in the United States, but to many Occidentals the taste of this mushroom is too strong—especially if it has been stored dry in a closed container.

There are several types of edible truffles but the truffle of commerce is usually the Perigord Truffle—*Tuber melanospermum* (Ascomycetes: Tuberaceae). This fungus does not resemble the umbrella-shaped structure that is commonly associated with mushrooms. It is tuberous, black, rough-surfaced, and grows only underground in association with the roots of certain species of oaks. It is produced only in France where large plantings of oaks have been made in order to provide the proper habitat for this particular type of fungus. A considerable folklore has developed around truffles. Theophrastus believed that they were caused by thunder, and in the Middle Ages they were considered evil things which grew from the spit of witches. There have long been legends that truffles have aphrodisiac properties—possibly because Madame Pompadour fed them to Louis XV, and because Napoleon sired his only son after having eaten these fungi. In some rural areas of France trained dogs and pigs are used to hunt truffles, but apparently the knowledgeable truffle hunter does not need help from such animals. Many gourmets consider truffles the most delicious of all mushrooms—certainly they are the most expensive, the wholesale price in May, 1971 being $20.00 per lb. Production of truffles in France seems to be declining, since only about 40 tons were harvested in the 1971 season as compared to 1500–2000 tons annually in the mid-nineteenth century.

A very considerable number of edible mushrooms grow only in the wild state. Some of these are collected and eaten by people who are familiar with them—a practice far more common in Europe and certain parts of the Orient than it is in the United States. Wild mushrooms most commonly collected in the United States as food are species of the Ascomycete genus *Morchella* (morels; spring mushroom). Many people are hesitant about eating wild mushrooms (and properly so unless they know exactly what species they have) because there are some extremely poisonous mushrooms. Some of these are deadly in their effects, but fortunately these represent an extremely small percentage of the total number of species of mushrooms. A very popular fleshy fungus in China is the Ear Fungus (*Auricularia polytricha*—Basidiomycetes: Auriculariaceae). It is a wood-inhabiting species and is mostly collected in the wild state, although there is some deliberate cultivation of the species. Dried Ear Fungus is imported from the Orient and may be purchased in some cities of the United States; however, it does not have wide popularity in this country because of the slimy texture and bland taste.

Fungi of the mold type are used both in the Orient and in the Occident in the processing of foods, but this practice has reached its greatest development in the Orient. While Occident and Orient can be distinguished on geographical and ethnological grounds, there is also possible a separation based on the type of food processed with proper fungi. In the Occident only milk is processed with fungi. In the Orient many foods are processed with fungi although the great preponderance of such material is either soybeans or "soybean milk."

The large-scale use of filamentous fungi in food processing in the Occident is confined entirely to cheesemaking. There are many name brands of fungus-processed cheeses but these can all be grouped into two basic types—Roquefort and Camembert. In the manufacture of a Roquefort-type cheese, spores of *Penicillium roquefortii* are mixed with the curd (or in a long-established factory the curds are allowed to become naturally inoculated). During the aging process which follows, mycelium grows through the curd forming the characteristic blue streaks. During this process the fungus hydrolyzes the milk fats, and various fatty acids are thus released. These are subsequently converted to methyl ketones (presumably by beta-oxidation) and the characteristic odor and flavor of "blue cheese" seems to be due primarily to these methyl ketones but especially to 2-heptanone which is formed from caprylic acid. In recent times, white strains of *Penicillium roquefortii* have been derived by use of ultraviolet radiation, and cheeses ripened by such white strains develop a milder flavor. True Roquefort was originally made only from ewe's milk, but today most blue cheeses are made from cow's milk. There are many Roquefort-type cheeses of which the most common are: Gorgonzola, Stilton, Blue Cheshire, Wensleydale, Blue Vinney, and Dolce Verde.

The Camembert type of cheese and its varieties are also ripened with a *Penicillium*—*P. camemberti*. However, in the preparation of this cheese the mold grows only on the outside during the ripening process. Proteolytic enzymes diffuse inward through the curd, softening the milk proteins with the result that a properly-ripened cheese has a smooth, buttery consistency throughout. Thus, a

TABLE F-13

SOME COMMON ORIENTAL FOODS WHICH ARE PRODUCED BY PROCESSES IN WHICH
FILAMENTOUS FUNGI ARE USED

Food Type	Consistency	Raw Materials	Fungus Employed
Miso	Paste	Soybeans and rice	*Aspergillus oryzae*
Shoyu	Liquid	Soybeans and rice or wheat	*Aspergillus oryzae*
Tempeh	Solid	Soybeans or coconut meat	*Rhizopus oligosporus*
Ang-khak	Solid	Rice	*Monascus purpureus*
Ontjom	Solid	Peanut press cake	*Neurospora sitophila*
Sufu	Moist solid	Soybean "milk"	*Actinomucor elegans*
Meitauza	Solid	Residuum from preparation of soybean "milk"	*Actinomucor elegans*
Ketjap	Liquid	Black soybeans	*Aspergillus oryzae*
Katsuobushi	Solid	Bonito fish	*Aspergillus glaucus*

fungus is used in the ripening of Camembert cheese for an entirely different purpose than in the ripening of Roquefort cheese. In the one instance it is used to develop a desired consistency, in the other to develop desired flavor and odor. Brie, Thenay, Troyes, and Vendome are all Camembert-type cheeses.

Mold type fungi (such as *Thamnidium* spp.) may also be used to age and flavor meat, but in this age of "instant living" this type of aging is not conducted on a commercial basis. Only the occasional connoisseur of good meat would bother to age meat in this fashion.

The use of mold type fungi in food processing has reached its greatest development in the Orient where fungi have been used for many centuries in the preparation of a variety of foods. Unfortunately, it has been only in recent years that information on these important and interesting food types has been made generally available in the Occident. Several of the more widely-produced fungus-fermented Oriental foods are listed in Table F-13.

With an ever-increasing Chinese-American population, certain of the Oriental foods in Table F-13 are becoming better known and somewhat more common in the United States.

It has been suggested by various workers that the growth of fungus mycelium (both of the mushroom and mold type) in pure culture would provide means of making very significant contributions to the world's edible protein pool. Many fungi have the capability of synthesizing their amino acids and subsequently their proteins from inorganic nitrogen compounds and cheap or waste carbohydrates. Such a process could be used to produce immense amounts of additional protein which conceivably could be used as a high protein supplement in the feeding of cattle or poultry. As yet, such a process is not in commercial production but as population continues to increase and edible protein supply does not show a concomitant increase, we may well see many fungi being used in this manner.

It has been known for centuries that certain mushrooms are poisonous, but such mushrooms represent a very small percentage of the total. In recent years a very considerable amount of research has been conducted on the production of toxins by the mold type of fungi, but to date the number of such fungi that produce toxic materials represents a very tiny percentage of the total number of mold species. The toxins which have received the greatest amount of publicity are the aflatoxins which are produced by *Aspergillus flavus*. This was primarily because the feeding of moldy Brazilian peanut meal resulted in the death in 1960 of about 100,000 turkey poults in England. To date there is no evidence that aflatoxins constitute any problem insofar as human health is concerned, although attempts have been made to link liver cancer in Africa and the Orient with mold toxins. It seems reasonable to predict that other mold type fungi will be found to produce toxins of one type or another; however, in such instances the reasonable approach would seem to be to avoid such fungi.

At this point in time fungi may be considered as one of man's few remaining unexploited food resources, but this situation may well change as population pressures create greater and greater demands for protein.

WILLIAM D. GRAY

Reference

GRAY, W. D. 1970. The Use of Fungi as Food and in Food Processing. Chemical Rubber Co., Cleveland.

GRAY, W. D. 1973. The Use of Fungi as Food and in Food Processing. Part II. Chemical Rubber Co., Cleveland.

G

GELATIN

Gelatin is a derived water-soluble protein made by controlled hydrolytic conversion of collagen, the protein constituent of white fibrous connective tissue from animals. It is composed of long chains of amino acids joined through peptide linkages and is rich in both acidic and basic functional groups. White connective tissue is the basis of the protective and structural organs of the mammalian body and the constituent collagen comprises about 60% of the total body protein. Bone, pork skins, hide splits and trimmings are the only raw materials from which gelatin is prepared.

Bone is first degreased then demineralized with acid to yield the ossein or crude collagen. Ossein, hide trimmings, or hide splits are then subjected to a prolonged liming to extract such extraneous materials as albumins and mucopolysaccharides as well as initiating the hydrolysis of the collagen to gelatin. After neutralization and washing, the converted collagen is extracted with hot water to yield dilute 5–6% solutions of gelatin which are filtered, vacuum concentrated to 25–35%, chilled into jellied sheets, and dried to 90% solids followed by crushing and laboratory grading. The gelatin thus produced is Type B, anionic at pH values above its isoionic value of 5.0.

The largest production of food gelatin in the United States is made from hog skins by a process involving soaking and swelling in dilute hydrochloric, sulfuric, or phosphoric acid solutions at low pH values (1.0–3.0) for several hours, followed by water washing to a pH of 3.5–4.0, followed by cooking and finishing as for limed type above. This process yields a gelatin known as Type A, and cationic at pH values below its isoionic value of pH 8.0.

Yields of gelatin from typical raw materials are bone 16%, ossein 65%, dry splits 60%, wet splits 15%, and fresh porkskin 20%. Since gelatin is made by a series of hot water extractions of treated collagen, it appears in different grades varying from the first with the highest test values, to lower values for the latter extractions as

TABLE G-1

SPECIFICATION RANGES FOR GELATIN

Property	Type A	Type B
Gel strength, Bloom gm	75–300	75–275
Viscosity, cp	2.0–7.5	2.0–7.5
Ash, %	0.3–2.0	0.05–2.0
pH	3.8–6.0	5.0–7.4
Isoionic point, pI	9.0–9.2	4.8–5.0

measured by standard tests of gel strength and viscosity. These values are outlined in Table G-1.

Gelatin is tested by a number of laboratory procedures to establish its commercial grade, as well as its suitability for the large number of applications which are based on one or more of the product specific qualities. The tests of gelatin are quite uniformly established and used by producers and customers throughout the world. These include gel strength, viscosity, moisture, ash, trace metals, pH, isoionic range, color, clarity, odor, and sanitary quality. While there is no Federal Food Standard for gelatin, the conditions for its manufacture and import are under control of FDA. Gelatin is typically specified in the United States Pharmacopoeia, The British Pharmacopoeia, and The Canadian Food Standards. The tests are divided into three main categories: (1) Physical. (2) Chemical. (3) Biological. They are described briefly as follows:

The gel strength is determined by the Bloom Gelometer in a procedure which has become standardized throughout the industry and is included in the official methods of analysis 21.012, 10th Edition of the Association of Official Analytical Chemists for gelatin and dessert preparations. The Bloom value is expressed in grams and represents a weight required to impress a 0.5-in. diameter flat plunger 4 mm into the surface of a jelled sample made under prescribed conditions.

Viscosity is tested by an industry procedure using a pipette of special design and calibrated against standard viscosity oils at 60°C. Methods are

TABLE G-2

AMINO ACIDS OBTAINED BY COMPLETE
HYDROLYSIS OF GELATIN

Amino Acid	% by Wt	Amino Acid	% by Wt
Alanine	11.0	Lysine	4.5
Arginine	8.8	Methionine	0.9
Aspartic acid	6.7	Phenylalanine	2.2
Glutamic acid	11.4	Proline	16.4
Glycine	27.5	Serine	4.2
Histidine	0.78	Threonine	2.2
Hydroxyproline	14.1	Tyrosine	0.3
Leucine and iso-		Valine	2.6
leucine	5.1	Cystine	trace

SOURCE: Eastoe (1955).

available from the Gelatin Manufacturers Institute of America Inc. or from a member manufacturer.

The method for ashing is described in the official methods of analysis 21.012, 10th Edition of the Association of Official Analytical Chemists or in the United States Pharmacopoeia. Additional chemical tests are made with standard laboratory procedures. Isoelectric values are determined by cloud range procedure on 1.5% solutions and isoionic pH value is made after passing a 1.5% solution through a mixed exchange resin.

Gelatin must conform to strict sanitary control measures to yield low aerobic bacterial counts and negative counts for coliform and salmonella types. These methods with standards are specified in the United States Pharmacopoeia and are approximately the methods used by the FDA for regulation in the industry.

As a derived protein, gelatin is digestible and contributes to protein nutrition according to its constituent amino acid composition. Extensive studies have shown that the amino acid content of white connective tissue whether from bone, skin, or tendons, or from different species is very uniform and yields gelatins also having uniform amino acid composition (see Table G-2).

Gelatin is lacking in the amino acids methionine and tryptophan which, together with a high concentration of nonessential amino acids, gives it low biological value unless combined with complementary sources of amino acids from other protein rich foods or specific amino acid supplements.

Gelatin is subject to hydrolytic breakdown as a continuation of the process by which it is converted from the insoluble macromolecular collagen. This breakdown is affected by heating in water solution, by acid or alkaline reaction, and by various proteolytic enzymes according to their particular activities. Gelatin then is a mixture of breakdown products having varying molecular weight and which theoretically can include every possible peptide from single amino acid to chains containing only one less residue than the parent molecule. The number average molecular weight of commercial gelatins between 100 and 300 gm Bloom values is approximately 10,000–50,000. The collagen raw material is determined to have a more uniform and average molecular weight of 345,000. Commercially, the first extraction gelatin is relatively more valuable; however, lower grades and even hydrolysates having no jelling properties have useful technical functions.

In addition to its utilization as a food, very extensive applications for gelatin depend on its specific physical qualities of solubility, clarity, gelation, and viscosity. Gelatin desserts, powdered and flavored mixes, and table jellies (Britain) represent the largest single food uses for gelatin. The finished preparation is variously formulated to include gelatin (175–250 Bloom), sugar, acid, and flavor which will dissolve in hot water to give approximately a 2% clear gelatin solution that will jell to an acceptable degree in 3–4 hr at refrigerator temperatures (40°–45°F). The Federal Specification C-D-00221d Type II, gelatin-dessert powder, details the ingredients and proportions of a very satisfactory product. Plain edible gelatin is also well specified in the Federal Specification C-D-00221d.

Many additional food uses for gelatin include confections, such as marshmallows, and candies, meat products, consommes, bakery and dairy products, including ice cream. Gelatin is an important protective material for the preparation of such food additives as vitamins and flavors, including their protective agents such as antioxidants. These applications depend upon one or another of the unique qualities of gelatin to perform a certain function.

In the case of marshmallows, gelatin serves to stabilize a foam of gas (air) in a hot liquid dispersion with sugar syrup. After casting or extruding such a foam, it sets to a characteristic plastic form which is dusted with starch and packaged.

The meat packing industry uses quantities of gelatin as a vehicle for adhering various ingredients into meat loaves and sausages and also for stabilizing the juices and filling the voids in such canned items as ham, tongue, and roast beef. Some of these uses were formerly served by fat which must be discarded in final preparation. Consommes are basically meat broths which in preparation have converted connective tissues to gelatin along with other extractives. Current practice uses gelatin solutions with meat extractives and flavors to give more uniform performance, particularly for serving jelled.

Low strength gelatins are being used extensively alone or in combination with vegetable gums as vehicles for food additives. This is usually accomplished by spray drying the mixture into a form which is self-protected by surface films and easily handled for ingredient uses. Due to the isoionic and amphoteric properties of gelatin, it is being used in microencapsulation procedures where, for example, anionic gelatins are made to co-acervate with cationic vegetable gums (example, gum arabic) and form micelles incorporating various types of food additives. In this area certain flavor constituents may be reactive with food mixtures and result in deterioration of quality. For example, certain flavors are aldehydic and will cause instability and loss of flavor unless protected or added in final preparation. Gelatin can be chemically treated to avoid the typical reaction with aldehydes and thus become useful as a carrier for such flavors.

Stabilizers are used in ice cream manufacture for producing smoothness in body and texture by controlling ice crystal growth during storage and melting. Ice cream is an emulsion and may be made with milk and milk products alone; however, such stabilizers as gelatin and vegetable gums are used to improve smoothness, texture, and volume. The usual amount of gelatin is between 0.25 and 0.5% and may be combined with other stabilizers to give advantages of each.

Exact production figures for edible food gelatin for the United States are not available, but estimations are 60 million pounds of Type A and 20 million pounds of Type B annually. Foreign manufacturers approximately match the quantity of gelatin produced in the United States and it is principally Type B material.

A rather specialized adaptation of the edible quality of gelatin is its film-forming ability for making both hard and soft capsules as a dosage form for the oral administration of drugs and vitamins. Approximately 10 million pounds of edible grades Type A and Type B gelatin are used annually in the United States for this purpose. A nonfood use for gelatin in the technical field of photographic film and paper is significant because the manufacture is usually carried out along with food gelatin processing from the same types of raw material. Most photographic applications are made with Type B gelatin.

D. TOURTELLOTTE

References

BOGUE, R. H. 1922. The Chemistry and Technology of Gelatin and Glue. McGraw-Hill Book Co., New York.

EASTOE, J. E. 1955. The amino acid composition of mammalian collagen and gelatin. Biochem. J. *61*, 589.
IDSON, B., and BRASWELL, E. 1957. Gelatin. *In* Advances in Food Research, Vol. VII. Academic Press, New York.
VEIS, A. 1964. The Macromolecular Chemistry of Gelatin. Academic Press, New York.

GHEE

Clarified butter, essentially butterfat, is prepared by heating and boiling mainly "desi" butter or cream from cow or buffalo milk to deprive it from moisture. A golden yellow liquid oil (in summer) and semisolid fat (in winter) is obtained when made from cow milk (carotene being present); but colorless fat in the case of buffalo milk (carotene being absent). This milk product is mainly used in India in the household as a culinary article. It has a pleasing flavor and aroma and good keeping quality at room temperature.

It has been extensively used from time immemorial both in the diet and in religious functions of Hindus in India. It is admirably suited for handling under tropical conditions and is a most valuable indigenous milk product. A large quantity of milk in India is used for ghee production with ghee being the only source of animal fat for the predominantly vegetarian diet.

About 43% of total milk production is utilized in ghee making, with total annual production being estimated at 480 million kilograms with a value of approximately 2500 million Rupees. Uttar Pradesh, Punjab, and Rajasthan are the major ghee-producing states in India. Ghee is produced more in winter than in summer, being dependent on the seasons of maximum and minimum milk production. The average annual intake of milkfat as ghee is about 1.2 kg per capita, 80% being used for culinary purposes, 18% for confectionery, and 2% for religious ceremonies.

Ghee contains 99–99.5% milkfat, and not more than 0.5% moisture. Among the unsaponifiable matter, ghee has carotene (for cow ghee only), vitamin A (15–40 IU per gm) and tocopherol (18–48 μg per gm). In addition, ghee contains free fatty acids to the extent of 2.8%, traces of charred casein (known as ghee residue), and sometimes salts of copper, iron, etc. Its melting point is 28°–44°C; sp gr, 0.93–0.94; RI, 40–45 at 40°C; RM number not less than 28; P number, nor more than 2; Saponification number, not less than 220, and Iodine number, 26–38.

Ghee is prepared either from butter or cream and is manufactured broadly by two methods: (a) from creamery butter made from mechanically separated and churned cream, and (b) from "desi" butter made by churning "dahi" or cream (accounting for the bulk of the production).

Clarification is accomplished by heating butter or cream at 120°C, the technique of clarification varying from place to place. Yields of ghee also vary according to method. Ghee also is made by the prestratification method and the direct cream method, quality depending on the method of preparation.

Ghee is marketed in tin containers with the bulk of it being packed in 4-gal. units. Tins are filled to the brim with no air gap to prevent oxidative deterioration. Chemical preservatives such as butylhydroxyanisole (BHA) are permitted for long shelf-life. Ghee storage temperature varies from 5° to 38°C depending upon the season of the year.

Agencies engaged in ghee assembling and distribution are (a) producers, (b) village merchants, (c) itinerant traders, (d) cooperative societies, and (e) retailers.

No standard practice exists for grading ghee. Only the Agricultural Marketing Department (AGMARK) of India has a ghee grading program. According to the Prevention of Food Adulteration Rules, 1955, ghee produced in different States of India have different specifications. This is necessary as the properties of ghee are dependent on the feeding pattern of the animal. Cotton-tract ghee (ghee made from milk of animals fed with cotton seeds) has different physical properties than normal ghee, namely a higher melting point.

Ghee is extensively adulterated either by vegetable oil (vanaspati) or with animal body fat. Detection of hydrogenated fat is a compulsory test under the Control Order by the Vegetable Products Controller. According to this Order, hydrogenated oil should contain refined sesame oil so that if added to ghee detection can be made by the Baudouin test.

Ghee is gradually becoming popular in other countries as it stores well and provides a means of preserving surplus fats.

N. C. GANGULI

Cross-reference: *Nationality Foods.*

GIBBERELLINS

The gibberellins are a group of plant growth regulators whose chemistry and effects on plants have been widely studied since 1926. The initial observations on this class of plant chemicals were made by Kurosawa (1926) when he noted that certain soluble extracts of the fungus *Gibberella fujikuroi* induced the same abnormal growth response on rice normally associated with this particular fungus. It was not until 1938 (Yabuta and Sumiki 1938) that significant progress was made on the chemical characterization of the gibberellins. There are now a total of 29 gibberellins (Lang 1970) that have been identified, of which only one (gibberellic acid or gibberellin A_3) has been used extensively in commercial agriculture.

Gibberellic acid ($C_{19}H_{22}O_6$; mol wt 346.37) can be generally described as a diterpene possessing a free carboxylic acid group in the C-10 position. It has been isolated from crude plant extracts and has also been identified as a metabolite of the fungus *Gibberella fujikuroi*. In recent years it has played an important role in the production of such crops as grapes, naval oranges, and rhubarb as well as in the malting process used to produce beer. The widespread natural occurrence of gibberellic acid in plants at levels commensurate with use levels employed in agriculture imply the absence of any hazard resulting from its use (Gould 1961).

The various physiological responses induced in plants by gibberellic acid have been summarized by Wittmer and Bukovac (1958). Its use on grapes includes increasing the berry size as well as to elongate stems in order to loosen each cluster. Use on naval oranges results in a reduction of the aging of this particular fruit. By so doing, the naval orange is less susceptible to physical damage normally a result of fruit aging (i.e., increased storage life). In the case of rhubarb, use of gibberellic acid results in the production of an early crop by virtue of its substitution for all or part of the usual two-month chilling in the field required to break the dormancy of the crop. Another noteworthy use of gibberellic acid evolves from its ability to increase the development of lateral vegatative buds on sour cherry trees. In so doing, the effects of the cherry yellows virus are counteracted. Gibberellic acid has been used successfully to hasten the malting process normally followed in the production of fermented malt beverages (e.g., beer).

BERNARD R. GREENWALD

References

GOULD, R. F. (Editor) 1961. Gibberellins. Advan. Chem. Ser. *28*.

KUROSAWA, E. 1926. Experimental studies on the secretions of Fusarium heterosporum on rice plants. J. Nat. Hist. Soc. Formosa (Japanese) *16*, 213–227; Biol. Abstr. *3*, 11348 (1929).

LANG, A. 1970. Gibberellins: structure and metabolism. Ann. Rev. Plant Physiol. *21*, 537–570.

WITTWER, S. H., and BUKOVAC, M. J. 1958. The effect of gibberellins on economic crops. Econ. Botany *12*, No. 3, July–Sept., 213.

YABUTA, T., and HAYASI, Y. 1939. Biochemical studies on "bakanae" fungus of rice: isolation of gibberellin, the active principle which produces slender rice seedlings. J. Agr. Chem. Soc. Japan 15, 257–266.

GLUTAMINE AND GLUTAMIC ACID

Glutamine has a molecular weight of 146.15 and an elementary composition of C = 41.09%, H = 6.00%, O = 32.84%, and N = 19.17%. It is soluble in water (13.6 parts in 100 parts water at 18°C), slightly soluble in absolute methyl alcohol (0.46 mg per 100 cc at 23°C) and almost insoluble in ethyl acetate, chloroform, ethyl ether, and acetone. It has been reported that glutamine isolated from horse meat melts at 205°C.

Glutamine is known to be capable of ring condensation to form 2-pyrrolidone-5-carboxylic acid (PCA) while severe acid hydrolysis yields glutamic acid. These reactions and the formulas for these compounds are shown in Fig. G-1.

Once glutamine is combined with other amino acid residues, as is the case in protein, its amide group becomes more stable and more closely simulates the properties of other amides. Glutamine, when heated in weak acid, neutral, or alkaline solution is converted to PCA or its salt much more rapidly than is glutamic acid. At pH 6.5, 99% of the glutamine is converted to PCA in $1\frac{1}{2}$ hr at 100°C, and the other 1% is converted to ammonium glutamate.

Glutamine occurs naturally in meat and plant tissue to a varying extent. During the heat processing of certain vegetables such as beets, spinach, and green beans it has been shown that glutamine is hydrolyzed to PCA which produces bitter, phenolic, or medicinal off-flavors in beets. Moreover, in spinach and beans which have been

processed at varying temperatures with the same F_0 it has been found that this reaction occurs mainly at conventional retort temperatures (less than 260°F) and only to a negligible extent with a high-temperature short-time process (HTST); i.e., processes which use temperatures of greater than 260°F. However, it has been shown that during the storage of processed spinach purée which has undergone an HTST process glutamine is hydrolyzed to PCA such that after three months storage HTST-processed packs have approximately the same concentration of PCA as the packs which were conventionally processed. There is also some evidence that glutamine is formed during storage of heat-processed spinach purée.

Glutamic acid is a monoamino-dicarboxylic acid with the structural formula represented in Fig. G-1.

It is a naturally occurring amino acid which was first isolated in 1866 by a German chemist, Ritthausen. Nutritionally, it is recognized as a nonessential or dispensable amino acid.

It has been found that excessive heat, such as that which might be encountered in thermal processing, changed the structure of glutamic acid in such a manner that it became bound by a linkage which is resistant to an enzymatic action. Lysine and aspartic acid were also found to be susceptible to such a change. These amino acids, however, are not actually destroyed since they can be released by acid hydrolysis. Retardation such as this could lead to a decrease in the nutritive value of heated proteins since the essential amino acids need to be liberated from the protein at approximately the same time for their effective incorporation into metabolic pathways. Glutamic acid can also be bound by carbohydrates as may all amino acids.

In the food industry one of the most important roles of glutamic acid is as a flavor potentiator in the form of its sodium salt, monosodium glutamate (MSG).

In 1908, a Japanese chemist at the University of Tokyo, Dr. Kikunae Ikeda, discovered the ability of MSG to enhance or intensify the flavor of high protein foods.

MSG meets several of the criteria that have been set for true flavor potentiators as opposed to seasonings. It acts on one, and possibly two, types of nerve endings, i.e., those of the taste buds and those of the tactile receptors of the mouth. Also, it contributes no flavor of its own when used in normal small quantities, and it seems to affect basic taste as well as producing a feeling of satisfaction.

It is used widely in canned, frozen, and dried foods producing the desirable effects which have been described.

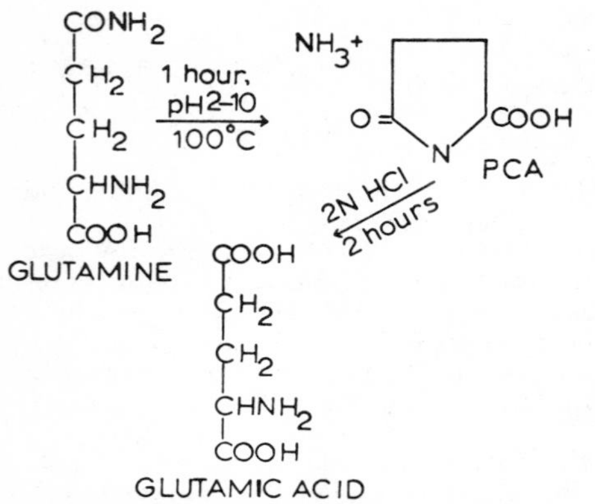

FIG. G-1. CONVERSION OF GLUTAMINE TO PCA AND GLUTAMIC ACID

F. M. CLYDESDALE

GLUTEN

Gluten is the common name for a light cream-to-tan colored, free flowing powder of bland taste and aroma containing 70–80% protein ($N \times 5.7$) (as is). It has sold from 32¢ per lb in 1971 to 50¢ per lb in 1973 in the United States and is obtained as the rubbery residue when starch and solubles are washed out of wheat flour doughs. In the freshly recovered wet form (30% solids) it is known as gum gluten and is characteristically tenacious but elastic. It can be drawn out into a film. These properties are unique to wheat gluten. In bread doughs, the natural flour gluten provides the cohesive factor imparting a plastic sticky character. As yeast fermentation proceeds and liberates carbon dioxide in the bread dough, the gluten extends and traps the gas in an intricate cellular network (proofing). In the oven, these gases further expand (oven spring) until the gluten is denatured and the bread structure is set.

When the word gluten is used to describe protein-rich fractions from other grains, the source is almost always specified, e.g., corn gluten.

Production and Use

In the United States, there are at least 8 gluten plants processing a total of about 320 million pounds of hard wheat, second clear flour each year yielding on the order of 40 million pounds of gluten, 166 million pounds of prime starch and 33 million pounds of low grade starch. Second clear flour has been used in the United States because of the lower cost, higher protein content, and a tax incentive designed to encourage industrial use. The tax or wheat certificate program, however, was ended in 1973. Gluten is usually the primary reason for making the separation. Demand has outstripped domestic production and thus substantial gluten is imported; 27 million pounds in 1972. One projection indicates a total U.S. gluten consumption of 150 million pounds in 1983. The starch tends to be the by-product though several preferred uses exist. Wheat starch is considered superior in laundry work, in some pharmaceuticals, and cosmetics because of its very white color, and in wallpaper paste because of good adhesive properties and a desirable slip-slide property important to paperhangers. It is also prized for its baking quality. Basically, however, corn is by far the primary starch source and usually has an economic edge except on the west coast, where wheat starch is often cheaper because of transportation considerations.

In Australia, wheat is the primary starch source, feeding such large users as glucose, paper, and textile manufacturers. The great demand for starch results in substantial gluten for export. The Australian government encourages the industrial use of flour, including gluten-starch separation, by allowing a lower price for such flour. Gluten and starch are also commercially recovered in Japan, Canada, South America, and many European countries. The Soviet Union had no gluten plants as of 1959.

Current production methods are the Martin process, the batter process, and, beginning in 1974, the Pillsbury Company will be producing gluten from whole kernel wheat by their newly invented Hydro Process. The Martin process was invented in Paris in 1835 and except for the introduction of modern equipment the process today is basically the same. In this process, flour is mixed with about 0.7 parts of water (20°C) to form a dough. After resting for up to 60 min, the dough is kneaded while additional water is added and removed. The starch granules are essentially washed out; a large portion of the solubles are leached out; and the remaining coherent, elastic mass is the gum gluten. Generally, 10–15% of the starting flour is recovered as gluten. The wash water containing the starch is sieved to remove any gluten particles that were broken away and to remove fibrous bran and cell wall material. The starch is then recovered by settling or centrifuging. Soluble and suspended materials will comprise from 10 to 20% of the starting flour and are usually discarded as a dilute effluent. In the batter process, more and warmer (50°C) water is used initially to rapidly produce a well hydrated smooth batter or weak dough. This is fed to a cutting pump with additional cold water and the weak dough is mechanically broken into small pieces from which the starch and solubles are quickly washed out. The suspended gluten curds are separated from the slurry on a gyrating shaker screen and washed to remove residual starch yielding gum gluten. The starch is generally recovered as in the Martin process.

In drying gum gluten, extreme care must be taken to avoid denaturation and loss of the unique and valuable dough-forming properties (vitality). The most common method of drying is to first mix dry vital gluten into the wet gum gluten; the resulting mass is broken into small pieces which are then fed to a flash drier. In another method the gum gluten is dispersed with water and ammonia to yield a dispersion of 10% solids and pH 9–10 which is then spray dried.

Vitality is not important when gluten is used for production of hydrolysates high in monosodium glutamate (gluten contains about 30% of glutamic acid) or for feed and in these cases drum drying or other less expensive methods are often used.

The primary use of gluten in the United States is as vital gluten in bakery products. A recent product innovation has been the enrobing of gluten with about 20% of a monoglyceride-emulsifier system. Improved dispersibility and performance are claimed. The FDA Standards of Identity for white or white enriched bread allows, as an optional ingredient, 2 parts of vital gluten per 100 parts of flour and for white or white enriched buns and rolls and raisin bread, 4 parts of gluten per 100 parts of flour. Some bakers routinely add gluten to their white bread formula, especially for bread to be produced by the continuously mixed process, to improve dough handling tolerance and to ensure high loaf volume (good gas retention), strong side walls, and a more resilient and softer crumb that remains softer longer. Other bakers use vital gluten to overcome problems with occasional poor performing lots of flour. Bread that must carry fruits, nuts, or other inert ingredients are often strengthened through added gluten. A frequent use is in rye bread. Much gluten is used in hamburger and hot dog buns where the added gluten improves hinge strength and produces a crust which is desirable in markets where the buns are placed in a steamer. Yeast raised doughnuts will show greater volume, longer proof tolerance, and more strength during subsequent glazing when fortified with gluten. Bread and rolls produced under the Standards of Identity and that contain gluten do not have to declare the presence of gluten on the label. For nonstandard products using gluten, the ingredients list should contain the words "wheat gluten." Other uses of gluten are: (1) as a protein supplement and binder in such products as ready-to-eat, high-protein breakfast cereals, some baby foods, pet foods, lunch meats, and meat and poultry rolls; (2) as a texturizing protein and meat substitute in all-vegetable, meat-like products; (3) as a protein source for preparation of hydrolyzed vegetable protein (HVP); and (4) as a strengthening agent for pretzels, crackers, and macaroni (increased crispness, less breakage).

Gluten was first produced in the United States about 1900 as a by-product of the production of laundry starch. One of its early uses was as a blend with wheat flour to produce a 41% protein gluten flour used in the manufacture of dietetic gluten bread low in carbohydrate. Some gluten bread is still made. The early glutens were often partially denatured or devitalized. The present form of high quality vital-gluten was introduced to the bakery trade in 1956 and its use has been steadily increasing since then.

In the United States, millers, bakers and other food processors have a wide range of wheat types and protein levels to choose from. This is because of the widely divergent areas where wheat is grown and because domestic food use represents only 30–40% of production. In other countries, especially in Europe, the choice is not so great and the cereal processor must make do with the limited wheat types available, usually lower protein, weaker types. The availability of gluten under these conditions greatly enhances the processor's options with regard to flour strength. In Japan, gluten has been used in soy sauce production, as a meat or fish extender in sausage or paste type products, and in all-vegetable meat-like products.

Chemistry and Functionality

Commercial gluten usually contains 70–75% total protein ($N \times 5.7$) and 5–10% total lipids, with residual starch and moisture governed by the thoroughness of washing and drying. (The Code of Federal Regulations (U.S.) specifies that gluten for use in bakery products shall have a minimum protein content of 75% on a moisture-free basis.) Only a small part of the lipids can be extracted with ether; they can be dissociated from protein by treatment with alcohol or acid and then are ether-soluble. In lab-prepared gluten, more than $1/2$ the lipids are phospholipids and glycolipids; about 60% of the fatty acids are linoleic.

A neutral wet gluten placed in dilute acid gradually becomes more hydrated until most of the protein eventually forms a milky dispersion. Acetic and lactic acids (0.01–0.1 N) have been most often used and are considered more effective than other acids. The dispersed protein is easily precipitated by salt, however. Gluten also can be dispersed in alkali, in concentrated urea and guanidine hydrochloride solutions, and in 10% or higher concentration of sodium salicylate. All of these solvents have limitations for the study of physical properties of the proteins; and lactate buffers, especially aluminum lactate, have been more useful for such measurements.

Half or more of gluten is soluble in aqueous alcohol (e.g., 70% EtOH); this separation was the basis of T. B. Osborne's designation of two classes of proteins—the aqueous alcohol-soluble prolamins (gliadin of wheat gluten) and the insoluble residue of glutelins (glutenin of wheat gluten). Neither gliadin nor glutenin are homogeneous; but each is made up of closely related proteins with certain characteristic properties. By gel electrophoresis, 12 or more gliadin components can be demonstrated; by isoelectric focusing, the number detectable has been reported to be more than 30. All the gliadin components appear to be compact in molecular structure, of limited molecular weight range (ca 30,000 to 80,000) and similar in amino acid composition. Glutenin components are much more heterogeneous, probably derived from several cellular parts. Polypeptide or protein subunits of ca 20,000 mol wt joined by disulfide bonds into extended macromolecules ranging to more than 500,000 mol wt may comprise a major part.

Consistent with these molecular structures, gliadin forms very viscous concentrated aqueous solutions with none of the elasticity of gluten; and glutenin when hydrated does not dissolve but forms relatively tough rubbery particles with little extensibility. Also, gluten and glutenin (and wheat flour doughs) in the presence of reagents able to rupture disulfide bonds lose their elasticity rapidly, becoming fluid and sticky; dispersions rapidly decrease in viscosity. The viscosity of gliadin solutions is little affected by disulfide rupture. However, a major gliadin component is sensitive to shearing stress, forming aggregates and becoming insoluble. Pepsin solubilizes glutens rapidly with rupture of relatively few peptide bonds.

Heat denatures wet glutenin more rapidly than wet gliadin; the rate decreases as pH is lowered.

The sticky, rubbery properties of gum gluten make it difficult to dry, particularly on a commercial scale, without heat damage and loss of some of its baking value. Solubility in acetic acid has been used as a test of heat damage; dough mixing behavior of wet gluten in a recording dough mixer may be a more sensitive test of slight heat damage. The Code of Federal Regulations specifies a test for denaturation based on the agglomeration of 30 gm of dry gluten added to 100 ml water and mixed in a 1-pt capacity sigma-bladed mixer. Agglomeration must occur within 1 hr or the gluten is considered to be denatured. In addition to those uses of gluten based on its water-binding, cohesive and dough-forming properties, gluten, even when wet, also has a considerable capacity for binding added fats and oils.

Representative values for the amino acid composition of gluten and of gliadin and glutenin fractions obtained by separation in aqueous alcohol have been reported as follows:

	Grams Amino Acid Per 16.0 Gm N in		
	Gluten	Gliadin	Glutenin
Arginine	3.2	2.4	3.3
Histidine	2.1	2.2	1.9
Lysine	1.2	0.7	1.9
Threonine	2.3	2.0	3.0
Serine	3.9	3.7	5.0
Aspartic acid	2.7	2.5	2.9
Glutamic acid	39.0	43.3	39.1
Glycine	3.2	1.7	5.6
Alanine	2.5	2.1	2.9
Valine	4.8	4.7	4.6
Leucine	7.1	7.6	7.1
Isoleucine	4.0	4.5	3.5
Proline	14.4	15.8	12.5
Tyrosine	3.3	2.7	4.3
Phenylalanine	4.8	5.8	4.3
Tryptophan	1.1	1.0	1.6
Cystine/2	1.5	1.1	1.2
Methionine	1.6	1.7	1.7
Ammonia	4.6	4.8	3.9

The authors are indebted to Walter A. Carlson, General Mills, Minneapolis, Minn., for his helpful suggestions.

DAVID A. FELLERS
DALE K. MECHAM

References

ANDERSON, R. A. 1967. Manufacture of wheat starch. In Starch: Chemistry and Technology, Vol. 2, Industrial Aspects. R. L. Whistler and E. F. Paschall (Editors). Academic Press, New York.

BLISH, M. J. 1945. Wheat gluten. In Advances in Protein Chemistry, Vol. 2. M. L. Anson and J. T. Edsall (Editors). Academic Press, New York.

DUBOIS, D. K., and COTTLE, F. E. 1969. Vital wheat gluten applications in bakery foods. Am. Soc. Bakery Engrs. Bull. 188.

KNIGHT, J. W. 1965. The Chemistry of Wheat Starch and Gluten and Their Conversion Products. Leonard Hill, London, England.

PENCE, J. W., NIMMO, C. C., and HEPBURN, F. N. 1964. Proteins. In Wheat: Chemistry and Technology. I. Hlynka (Editor). American Association of Cereal Chemists, St. Paul.

SIMMONDS, D. H. 1972. Wheat-grain morphology and its relationship to dough structure. Cereal Chem. 49, 324–335.

Cross-reference: *Baking Industry: Bread.*

GLYCERIN (POLYOLS)

Polyols

Polyols, or polyhydric alcohols, are widely used in the formulation of many types of food products. They are often used at low levels but nevertheless have an important effect on texture or flavor of the food in which they are incorporated.

The polyols are straight chained organic compounds with two or more hydroxyl groups but with no other functional groups present. The sugars, for example, contain an aldehyde or ketone group in addition to the several hydroxyls. Polyols are usually sweet, although not as sweet as sugar. More important, the polyols are hygroscopic, the degree of hygroscopicity being dependent upon the particular compound involved. Except for problems with exposure to excessive moisture, the polyols are quite stable under normal storage conditions.

There are many polyhydric alcohols. Only four are used in food products in any quantity, however. These are glycerin, propylene glycol, mannitol, and sorbitol. Those that are not toxic have not shown sufficient promise commercially to have been developed further for food use. Xylitol is an exception in that it has been approved by FDA as a food additive to some dietary products.

Glycerin

Glycerin is a sweet, viscous, syrupy, water-white, clear liquid. It is soluble in all proportions in water. Glycerin is very hygroscopic and will hold its own weight in water in an atmosphere of about 80% RH. There is a multiplicity of uses for glycerin in many industries. Its particular uses in the food industry are as a modifier for sugar crystals, a humectant, a plasticizer, a solvent, and use in the manufacture of various emulsifiers.

Occurrence

Free glycerin is rarely found in natural products. It is formed during the fermentation of sugar into alcohol. Beer and wine, therefore, contain small amounts of glycerin.

Fats and oils are fatty acid esters of glycerin. Combined glycerin is thus found universally in all living organisms. Hydrolysis of an average triglyceride oil with water would yield about 10% free glycerin and 90% free fatty acids on a weight basis.

Commercial Preparation

Crude glycerin is prepared by splitting animal and vegetable fats and oils during the production of soaps, fatty acids, or fatty alcohols. It may also be produced by the hydrogenolysis of sugar. The crude material is then refined to different degrees of purity and concentration by chemical treatment, distillation, and bleaching with activated carbon.

Synthetic glycerin is manufactured by chlorination or oxidation of propylene gas, a by-product of the petroleum industry. Subsequent hydrolysis of chemical intermediates followed by bleaching and concentration yields a pure glycerin.

USP glycerin is the grade accepted for food use. It is described by the U.S. Pharmacopoeia as a clear, colorless, syrupy liquid having a sweet taste with not more than a slight characteristic odor, being neither harsh nor disagreeable. It is hygroscopic. Its solutions are neutral, i.e., neither acidic nor alkaline. It must pass certain chemical tests for purity including one for arsenic, another for

organic chlorides, etc. The source of the glycerin may be natural fats or propylene. The glycerin content must be not less than 95% although 96% is the normal commercial concentration. The balance of the product is primarily water. CP (chemically pure) glycerin usually meets all USP standards and can therefore be used in foods. It may be obtained in concentrations of 96% and 99% glycerin.

Chemical and Physical Properties

Glycerin is a 3-carbon trihydric alcohol; molecular weight, 92. Chemically, it is referred to as "glycerol" to indicate its relationship to other polyols. As an alcohol, it can be reacted with acids to form esters, with other alcohols to form ethers, with itself to form polyglycerol ethers, with aldehydes to form acetals, and with a number of other types of compounds which, being potentially toxic, have no bearing on food products.

Glycerin is nontoxic and nonirritating. It has about the same food value as sugar, 4.32 cal per gm. It is approximately 65% as sweet as sugar. The FDA has placed glycerin on the list of food additives which are generally recognized as safe (GRAS).

The specific gravity of 96% glycerin is 1.252 at 25°C. Pure glycerin melts at 18.2°C and boils at 290°C (760 Torr). Mixtures of glycerin and water, however, freeze at very low temperatures with a minimum of -46.5°C for a 67% (by weight) glycerin solution. Glycerin is infinitely soluble in water and in alcohol. It is almost insoluble in oils and oil solvents, such as hexane, at ordinary temperatures. On the other hand, glycerin is an excellent solvent for many organic and inorganic compounds.

Food Uses

The primary use for glycerin in foods is for the preparation of monoglycerides and related products. Glycerin in free or unesterified form is still being used to some extent as a solvent, a humectant, and a plasticizer. At one time, glycerin was the only edible polyol available at a sufficiently low cost to be commercially useful. As the other polyols became more available, they tended to supplant glycerin where their functionality or cost warranted it. In many cases, a blend of two or more polyols or a blend of polyol and sugar were found to have superior function to any individual component of the mixture.

Glycerin was once used in fudges, fondants, and similar confections at a level of 2–5% by weight to keep the sugar in a microcrystalline form and thereby retain the desired smooth and creamy texture. Sorbitol has been found to be more effective than glycerin for this purpose. Propylene glycol has replaced glycerin to a great extent as a nonalcoholic (grain alcohol) solvent for food colors and flavors. However, glycerin is still a superior solvent for some individual colors and flavors.

A blend of glycerin and propylene glycol is used at about 4% by weight as a softener and humectant in shredded coconut to retain a moist, soft texture. A mixture of glycerin with corn or invert sugar has similar function in the preparation of candied citrus peel.

Sausage casings, both natural and artificial (regenerated cellulose) would become dry and stiff without the addition of glycerin as a plasticizer. Glycerin is preferred since it is nontoxic and will not be lost by evaporation. Migration of glycerin into the sausage will not affect the flavor of the sausage.

Glycerin is an effective lubricant for food machinery, especially for low temperature applications. It will remain fluid at temperatures at which most normal petroleum lubricants would freeze. Here, too, the absence of toxicity is important.

Glycerin is heated with fats in the presence of a small amount of sodium hydroxide catalyst to produce mono- and diglycerides. These esters are the basic emulsifiers for food products. They may be reacted further with acetic, lactic, or citric acid for specialized purposes. Glycerin is heated with a catalyst, such as sodium acetate, to form a polymer of 2 or more (usually no more than 12) glycerin units. Chemically, these polyglycerols are ethers. They are then esterified with various fatty acids to produce a wide range of food emulsifiers.

THEODORE J. WEISS

Cross-reference: *Food Preservation.*

GLYCOLS AND GLYCOL ESTERS

Glycols are difunctional alcohols which have some application in the food industry. Certain glycol mono- and diesters, or mixtures thereof, have extensive application as food emulsifiers.

Ethylene glycol, CH_2OHCH_2OH, the simplest glycol, has a moderate toxic ingestion rating, and, as such, is not permitted in foodstuffs, although, were it not for this, would certainly find some use. Because of this, few of the mono- and diester derivatives of ethylene glycol have been considered for use in food, or even for use in wrapping or packaging materials which come into contact with food.

Propylene glycol (1,2-dihydroxypropane), $CH_2OHCHOHCH_3$, is substantially less toxic than ethylene glycol and finds utility as a direct food additive. Its principal use is to assist dissolving another material such as a flavor into a product where such flavor is insoluble in water. It is common practice to use as much as 15–30% propylene glycol in flavor concentrates. Other areas of use in foods are as a humectant and preservative. As a solvent, propylene glycol functions also in extract preparations and food colors for soft drinks, baking, and candy products. Propylene glycol is a humectant for baked goods and packaged foods such as shredded coconut, where some moisture content must be preserved to offer a suitable consumer product. Propylene glycol can be used in the manufacture of materials that come into contact with foods. It is used as a plasticizer in cork seals, or crowns for food packages and bottle cap linings and in cellulose coatings for sausage and cheese. The glycol is a preferred solvent for high speed steam-set inks used for printing paper and cloth food wrappers. Since some food products come into contact with wrappers, the inks must be odorless and harmless. Propylene glycol is also a lubricant for machinery used in packaging foodstuffs, pharmaceuticals, and beverages.

"Polyethylene glycols," are ether-linked glycols commonly prepared by the ethoxylation of simple glycols. A few find limited use in the food industry. Those of minimum molecular weight of 1300, for example, find use as a coatings component on pills, tablets, and beads to inhibit the hygroscopic properties of such mixtures.

Propylene glycol mono- and diesters of edible-grade fatty acids may be safely used in food and have numerous applications therein as a consequence of their water-in-oil emulsification properties. Propylene glycol monostearate, for example, is extensively used as a component of whipped toppings, in liquid suspension-type shortenings, and in the preparation of clear liquid shortening products which remain transparent under varied conditions. Although the shortening may solidify at refrigeration temperatures, when it is brought back to ambient conditions for baking it must be clear and homogeneous. Propylene glycol monostearate, properly prepared, has the required solubility in vegetable oils to be used at levels necessary to provide adequate batter aeration.

NORMAN V. O. SONNTAG

GOAT FOODS

According to present information, the goat was the first ruminant to be domesticated by man. This appears to have occurred approximately 7000 to 10,000 years B.C. Goats, therefore, have been a valuable source of milk and meat for human consumption for the past 9000 to 12,000 yr.

The world population of goats was estimated to be 316 million in 1965, with approximately 181 million in the tropic or subtropical regions of the world. The majority of goats in the tropics are used for meat; however, a few breeds have been developed for milk production in the tropics. The goat can thrive as meat-producers under conditions in which it is difficult for other species of domestic livestock to live. The goat has an unsurpassed ability to forage, to consume a wide variety of plants and to withstand the extremes of a tropical climate.

Goats fill a unique role as a major source of meat in the world for reasons other than their adaptability to tropical regions. Official figures indicate that some 11,000–12,000 dwarf goats are slaughtered each month in Ghana. This dwarf goat weighs 30–45 lb when fully grown. Because of the small size of the goat carcass, small butchers, even in villages, are able to dispose of a whole carcass in a day without the problem of unsold meat, where facilities for refrigeration do not exist. There are no religious prejudices against the eating of goat meat in countries such as India and Ceylon so goat meat is held in high esteem. The majority of the population of East and West Pakistan also have a definite preference for goat meat over mutton or beef. Barbecued kid (young goat) is becoming quite popular in the Southwestern United States. A sizeable number of kids are also consumed each year in the Northeastern United States during the Easter season by people of Greek and Middle East origins.

Goats are kept primarily for the production of milk in the nontropical regions of the world. The total annual production of goat milk in the world, with the exception of the USSR, is estimated to be 8 million metric tons. Raising of goats for milk production is actuated by various motives in different parts of the world. Since their maintenance requirement per animal is much less than for cattle, goats have an obvious advantage in localities where feed is restricted in quantity and quality. The dairy goat is often called the "poor man's cow," since people throughout the world can keep 1–2 dairy goats, and thus have a source of fresh milk, where it would be impossible for them to keep a cow or buffalo. Goat milk production also can be rapidly increased to meet emergency needs. During the general food shortage in Japan after World War II, goat milk was considered to be a precious protein source. People were encouraged to keep goats and many volunteered to do so. The number of goats increased rapidly and reached a peak number of 669,200 in 1957. Postwar rehabilitation changed the food supply situation

sharply and the numbers of goats decreased to 245,870 in 1967.

The small fat globules and the soft curd of goat's milk contribute to its ease of digestibility. Some infants and adults who are allergic to cow's milk can consume goat's milk readily. In a great many cases, goat's milk has proved especially valuable for infants and invalids. In many instances, goats are thus kept for the "health benefits" of the milk rather than for supply of milk per se.

In 1965, 95% of the dairy goat owners in the United States were estimated to be family milk suppliers, 2% as small dairymen with 10–19 head of goats, and 3% as medium to large dairymen with average herds running from 50 to 150 head. Goat milk in the United States is sold in a number of different forms. These include bottled, powdered, and evaporated milk; cheese; and speciality products such as yogurt and ice cream. Approximately 650,000 U.S. gal. of goat milk were evaporated, sterilized, and sold in $14\frac{1}{2}$ oz cans in 1965. This product is quite widely available all over the country in supermarkets and drug stores. Most of the evaporated milk is used for infant feeding. The demand for powdered, dry, whole goat milk is increasing since most people prefer the flavor to that of the evaporated product. The amount of goat's milk used to produce powdered milk probably equals or exceeds that used for evaporated milk.

Although there is a large demand for some types of goat's milk cheese in the United States, most of it is imported rather than manufactured in the United States.

The greatest quantity of goat's milk cheese is made in Mediterranean Countries, but it is produced in some quantities throughout the world. Nearly 30% of milk used for cheese making in Greece is goat's milk. Goat milk constitutes about 11% of the total used for cheese making in Spain. Of the 216,200 metric tons of goat milk produced in France in 1954, 45% was used for the production of cheese. Whey cheese is very popular in Norway. The Gjetost or Mysost is manufactured by concentrating the whey resulting from the manufacture of goat's cheese or from casein. "Goat flavor" is very important in the manufacture of Mysost. The goat flavor probably is of genetic character, but can be affected by feeding, the environmental conditions, and the milk yield. The Maltese Rkotta is made equally well from goats' as from ewes' milk; this is also true for Ricotta. Particularly in Corsica, Broccio is preferably made from goats' milk.

Separation of the cream from goats' milk is more difficult than in the case of cows' milk, so very little goat milk butter is made. Greece is an exception where about 11% of the goat milk is used for butter making. Some goat milk butter also is used in the Balkans and in North Africa.

Registration of dairy goats, by the American Dairy Goat Association, more than doubled between 1965 and 1970, so the use of goat products in the United States is increasing.

IVAN L. LINDAHL

Cross-reference: *Cheese.*

GOOSEBERRIES

See Currants and Gooseberries.

GOURMET FOODS

The word "gourmet" means many things to many people. As a descriptive term it is loosely used in our daily conversation and advertising, by the consumer, food retailers, and food service establishment. The original concept of the word when applied to edibles has lost most of its meaning. Commercial usage of the term "gourmet foods" to characterize unusual quality has become a misnomer and has led the consumer and connoisseur alike into a maze of confusion.

Gourmet foods are also being marketed under the following guises: (1) High priced, unadvertized brands to engender prestige purchasing. (2) Fancy and expensive packaging into which are packed ordinary foods. (3) Imported foods from around the world featured as gourmet foods, regardless of the quality. (4) Foods sold as adjunct items by gift shops and department stores.

The True Role of Gourmet Foods

The true role or concept of gourmet foods can best be understood by referring to the basic or fundamental definitions that underlie the principles for this branch of the industry. Current dictionary meanings denote the gourmet as a connoisseur of fine food and drink, an epicure. An epicure is defined as a person who is fastidious and refined in his taste for food and wine. The term "delicacies," which refer to choice edibles, edibles that are rare and delicate, is also to be associated with gourmet foods. Delicacies are the chief objects of a gourmet's interest in foods.

By utilizing these definitions it is possible to categorize the wide range of food and beverages that come under the heading of gourmet foods:

(1) Exotic and specialty foods, such as rattle-snake meat, canned fried hare, chocolate-covered grasshoppers, snails, India curry sauce, chutney, canned wild boar, deer goulash.

(2) Fancy foods and beverages that are choice or of extra fine quality; these can be either imported or domestic such as vintage wines, cheese, Iranian caviar, Belgian carrots, wild rice from Minnesota, petite pois.

(3) Unusual foods, beverages, and concoctions, e.g., brandied pears, peaches, minted tea, Jasmine tea, smoked rainbow trout, canned pheasant, Cornish game hen, Scandinavian Glögg (a beverage mix), candied fruits.

(4) Nationality and regional domestic foods such as Pennsylvania Dutch specialties; items generic to New Orleans, New England or Hawaii; Swedish, Italian, French, Spanish, and other nationality foods.

Imported Gourmet Foods

Gourmet foods and the culinary arts in the Occident are usually associated with a number of European countries such as France, Austria, Switzerland, Belgium, Holland, and the British Isles. The Orient, of course, has given us a number of delicacies. France enjoys the leading role, however, in the area of gourmet foods, both in prestige and in the varieties of items exported to the United States. Leading Haute Cuisine restaurants are, in fact, either all French in style or Continental, that is, restaurants that offer a mixed French and Italian menu. French cooking, wines, cheeses, and desserts are all high on the list of gourmet foods but the list can be extended to include:

Baked products, biscottes, breads, cocktail
    snacks, crackers, cookies
Chestnuts (marrons)
Condiments, gherkins, mustard, oils,
    vinegar (tarragon and wine)
Confections, chocolates, desserts, puddings
Foie gras and patés
Honey (miel)
Jams, jellies, preserves
Sauces
Snails (escargots)
Soups (dehydrated and canned)
Truffles
Vegetables including cultivated, wild, and
    freeze-dried mushrooms
Cheese (fromage) of which there are about
    100 varieties
Wines, sparkling and still

MARVIN EDWARD THORNER

Cross-reference: *Nationality Foods.*

GRAPES

The grape vine is one of the oldest cultivated plants in the world, predating the Christian era by many centuries. The origin of grapes has been traced to Asia Minor and from there the Phoenicians brought the vines to Greece and to Rome. In time the cultivation of the vine spread to the whole Mediterranean area for the primary purpose of making wine. All of these plantings consist of thousands of varieties of the "European" grape, *Vitis vinifera L.* Columbus brought cuttings to the New World in 1494, and eventually the Mission fathers planted wine grapes in California from 1769 on. Two other species of native American grapes are important in the Northwest, Midwest, and in the Southeast—*V. labrusca L.* and *V. rotundifolia Michx.*

Grapes are one of the most important fruit crops in the world, both from the standpoint of acreage planted and the farm value of the harvested fruit. In the United States some 4 million tons of grapes are produced on about 600,000 acres. The total farm value of these grapes exceeds 300 million dollars. When made into finished products—fresh, dried, canned, frozen, or fermented—the retail value is well over one billion dollars. The greatest acreage and production of grapes consists of raisin types in California, most of which are sun dried in normal years into 250,000 to 300,000 tons of raisins. In some years of high production and low prices, a million tons or more of raisin grapes may be crushed for wine. Next in importance as to acreage and production are wine grapes. In California 600,000–700,000 tons of *V. vinifera* varieties are produced on 135,000 acres. In the remainder of the United States the total production for all purposes is around 300,000 tons, practically all of which are *V. labrusca* varieties.

Total wine production in the United States for recent years has been increasing steadily, reaching an all-time high of 270 million gallons in 1969. This total does not include wine used for distilling into beverage brandy, of which an average of 13 million proof gallons is made from grape wine each year, mostly in California.

Grapes classified as table or fresh fruit varieties are crushed for wine also. From an annual crop of table types in California of 500,000–600,000 tons, over 60% are crushed.

Utilization of all 3 types of grapes in California (raisin, wine, table) can be summarized as follows: 63% crushed for wine, 25% dried as raisins, 11% consumed fresh, and 1–2% canned.

Wine

There are hundreds of good books on wine and wine-making, but for a basic introduction to the subject and a lead into additional literature, one could start with *Technology of Wine Making* (Amerine *et al.* 1972).

The fermentation of the sugars in grape "must" into ethyl alcohol and other components of wine depends on the chance inoculation with yeasts. Pasteur helped to put the whole industry on a more scientific basis when he studied the importance of yeasts and bacteria on the process. This led to the development of pure yeast cultures and the control of fermentation. Spoilage of wines by yeasts and bacteria was studied by Pasteur also and resulted in better sanitary practices as well as the use of sulfur dioxide.

Red wines are fermented on the skins after crushing to extract color and flavor constituents, while white wines are fermented after separation from the skins. Free-run wine is drawn off after several days and fermentation continued in the storage tank. The pomace is pressed to recover more wine and the residue fermented again as a source of distilling material. During storage the wine is "racked off" several times in order to separate it from the settlings or "lees." Fine red wines are aged for 1–4 yr in wooden containers to improve the quality. Early in the aging process the red wines are refrigerated or passed through ion exchange resins in order to remove excess bitartrate. A final filtration just before bottling makes the wine brilliantly clear and aging of fine wines in the bottle for a year or so improves the aroma, mouth feel, and taste.

The above discussion on vinification has been extremely brief and general, but details can be found in Amerine *et al.* (1972).

Another classification which is useful in assessing the wine industry is the subdivision into wine types. Table wines are the largest category, followed by dessert wines (fortified), special natural wines (flavored), and sparkling wines; brandy is another grape product made by distilling the wines to increase the alcohol content—some 15–18 million proof gallons (equivalent to 100 proof) of brandy are produced annually in the United States, mostly in California.

Dried Grapes

More than a million tons of fresh grapes are dried in California each year into 200,000–300,000 tons of raisins.

Canned Grapes

From 50,000 to 60,000 tons of grapes are canned each year and consist almost entirely of Thompson Seedless or other seedless varieties which are mixed with peaches, pears, and pineapple in fruit cocktail or fruit salad. The total pack of mixed fruits is around 20 million actual cases annually, and the U.S. Standards for Grade specify that from 6 to 20% by weight of drained fruit must be whole seedless grapes. The preparation, filling, and sterilizing of the canned product is the standard procedure used for most canned fruits. The mixing of the specified quantities of each fruit in the can may be done by hand or by calibrated pockets in the filling machine. A small quantity of whole seedless grapes in syrup is packed each year, but no statistics are available.

Frozen Grapes

Two types of native American grapes are frozen as "grapes-and-pulp." The most important use is for Concord grapes which are made into jam and jelly. The grapes are heated to 140°–150°F (60°–67°C), the seeds are removed in a finisher, and the pulp frozen in 30-lb cans or 55-gal. drums. Altogether, the bulk pack of frozen grapes-and-pulp for remanufacture varies from a low of 5 million pounds to a high of almost 23 million pounds per year.

A small quantity of Muscadine-type American grapes is frozen for dessert products in the Southeast. Woodroof (1946) and Woodroof and Atkinson (1945) have published on the freezing of this product.

Grape Juice

The pack of Concord grape juice for retail sale has been quite steady at 5 million cases per year for the last 10 yr. Although most of this juice goes into 46-oz cans or quart bottles as single-strength juice or grape drink, large quantities are concentrated and stored in bulk containers for later remanufacture. Again, the grape concentrate may be diluted for retail single strength or diluted products, but some also finds its way into the wine and jelly industries. Juice from wine grapes is concentrated in substantial quantities, too; but ends up as blending material to ameliorate ordinary, generic, and special natural wines.

FRANK P. BOYLE

References

AMERINE, M. A., BERG, H. W., and CRUESS, W. V. 1972. Technology of Wine Making, 3rd Edition. Avi Publishing Co., Westport, Conn.

WOODROOF, J. G. 1946. New method of freezing grapes. Ice Cream Field 4, No. 2, 69, 72.

WOODROOF, J. G., and ATKINSON, J. S. 1945. Freezing Muscadine grapes. Fruit Prod. J. 25, 52.

Cross-reference: *Raisins.*

GUMS

Gums, as this term is applied in food technology, are edible polymeric materials which are soluble or dispersible in water and cause a viscous or gelled consistency in food systems. Very often it appears that the food technologically important functionality of a gum resides in its hydrating and colloidal properties. Consequently, these observations become the basis for the synonymous terms "hydrocolloids" or "hydrocolloid gums." The materials falling under the above broad definition of gums, or hydrocolloid gums, are derived from a large variety of natural products such as gelatin, exudates of injured trees, seaweeds, plant seeds, fruits, animal hides or bones, fermentation products, milk by-products, cellulose, chemically modified celluloses, and finally a few totally or partially man-made products which could be classified as "synthetic" hydrocolloid gums.

The present article, however, will restrict the coverage of gums to those obtained from tree exudates, certain nonstarchy plant seeds, seaweeds, wood by-products, cellulose, and a few synthetics. Other hydrocolloids such as starches, pectins, microbial gums, gelatins and caseinates, or other proteinaceous hydrocolloids will be covered in different specific articles.

The most commonly used gums of food technological significance, which are subject of this article, can be classified as follows:

Plant Exudate Gums	Plant Seed Gums
Gum arabic	Guar gum
Gum ghatti	Locust bean gum
Gum karaya	Psyllium seed gum
Gum tragacanth	Tamarind seed gum

Seaweed Gums	Cellulose Gums
Agar	Microcrystalline
Alginates	cellulose
Carrageenans	Carboxymethylcellulose
Furcellarines	Methylethylcellulose
	Hydroxypropylcellulose

Wood By-Products	Fully Synthetic Gums
Arabino galactanes	Polyvinyl pyrrolidone
	Carbopols
	Gantrez AN
	Ethylene oxide polymers

Functionality of Hydrocolloid Gums in Food Systems

The use of hydrocolloid gums as ingredients in food formulations has been developed mostly through empirical observations; in fact, certain regional foods with crude seaweed extracts have been the results of ingenuity of the local housewife (i.e., the blanc mange made of milk and carrageenan-containing seaweeds, Japanese dessert-jellies made of agar-agar). However, with the growing emphasis to produce ready-to-eat foods through industrial means, the last 20–30 yr have encouraged applied food research in the hydrocolloid gum field. It was recognized that the most important contribution of hydrocolloid gums to foods involves textural modification.

One of the basic functionality features of the hydrocolloids is their capability of modifying the behavior of water of the foods. This is effected mainly through the immobilization of a portion of the water molecules. As a result, water will be held more effectively in the food structure, and stabilization of the textural properties will be obtained. Examples of eminently important functionality features resulting in foodstuffs, in the presence of hydrocolloid gums, are the reduction of the evaporation rate of water, alteration in the freezing rates, modifications in the ice crystal formation during frozen storage, regulation of the flow properties, suspension of insoluble particles, resistance against syneresis, stabilization of foams and emulsions, and promotion of encapsulation of oil droplets in aqueous hydrocolloid systems.

Correlation Between Chemical Structures and Functionality Features of Hydrocolloid Gums

The above functionality features are the consequence of distinct structural properties of the hydrocolloid gum molecules. Chemically, hydrocolloids are polymeric substances built of molecular units which contain in a regular, repeating sequence hydrophilic, hydrophobic, and occasionally also ionic groups. These groups serve as the effective sites for the interactions between the gums and water or other food constituents. The chemical linkages within and between the individual repeating building units lend a characteristic shape to the polymeric molecule. We may visualize the hydrocolloid molecules as rather long structures of definite shapes which contain sites with pronounced affinity to other chemical groups.

Using a rather free analogy, certain hydrocolloid gums might be compared to a semirigid spiraling (helical) wire structure which contains hooks and magnets along its length; these structures are capable of interacting by mechanical or magnetic forces with other materials. The actual hydrocolloid molecules in reacting with each other or interacting with responsive reaction sites of other food constituents and water, will tie up the randomly present other molecules in a cross-linked, rigid form. Many of the interacting sites attract, by means of hydrogen bonds, the water molecules and through this mechanism the water immobilizing function of the gums can be explained.

In recent years the interaction capability of the hydrocolloids with water and other food ingredients has been studied by sophisticated physical-chemical methods and, as a result, rational explanations of the gum functionality and its quantitative estimation became possible in certain cases.

Individual Gums

Exudate Gums.—*Gum Arabic.*—Gum arabic, or gum acacia, is obtained from dried exudates of various *Acacia* trees by selection and thorough physical purification. The most significant exporting countries are Sudan and French West Africa. The crude gum arabic is collected by hand and after a preliminary visual sorting is shipped to processors. Here the gum drops are further sorted for color, milled, sieved, and graded.

Chemically, gum arabic is a heterogeneous polysaccharide with slightly acidic characteristics, mainly in the form of its potassium salt. On complete hydrolysis gum arabic yields, as basic building blocks, the following simple carbohydrates: D-galactose, L-arabinose, L-rhamnose, and D-glucuronic acid. These building units form a molecule with a branched basic chain.

The main chain of the molecule is composed of 1, 3-linked β-galactopyranose units, and has branches of 1,6-linked galactopyranose units terminating in glucuronic acid, or 4-O-methyl glucuronic acid residues. Secondary side chains are also attached in C-3 positions on the primary galactose side chains. The molecular weight is between 250,000–1,000,000. The shape of the molecule is coiled, its length about 1000–2000 Angstroms.

The solubility features of gum arabic are unique among the hydrocolloids. It is capable of forming aqueous solutions up to 50% concentration; it is also soluble in aqueous alcohols and to a certain extent in glycerol, but it is insoluble in fats or fat solvents. The aqueous solutions reduce the surface tension of water and lower the interfacial tension between water and oil. This property of the gum is often utilized in the preparation of emulsions. The surface tension-reducing capability of gum arabic and its film-forming tendency on oily surfaces, coupled with its viscosity-building properties, put this gum into the groups of emulsifiers, stabilizers, protective colloids, and emulsion encapsulating agents.

Gum arabic finds a multiplicity of uses in the confectionery industry by its retarding capacity of sugar crystallization; confectioners use it for dispersing oils in the form of fine droplets in caramels and toffees. Oil-soluble flavor additives are also emulsified in the body of the candy by the use of gum arabic. This results in a uniform flavor distribution and the absence of unwanted oil-filled cavities. The bakery trade applies gum arabic for obtaining a softer crumb, and, further, for glazes on buns. Sugar syrup glazes containing the gum adhere better to the surface of baked goods on cooling, and have a controlled flow when still hot. Gum arabic also facilitates the emulsion formation of glazes with fats or fat-containing flavors.

Dairy products make use of gum arabic extensively in ice cream stabilizers; however, this application is declining. The encapsulating and film-forming capability of gum arabic gave rise to the new technology of microencapsulation. By this method, flavors can be sealed in the matrix of of the gum by spray drying. The resulting microscopic flavor packets protect the flavoring principles against deterioration, make them free flowing and blendable into dry formulations. On addition of water, the encapsulating matrix is easily dissolved and the flavors are readily released. Higher concentration gum arabic solutions find application in the preparation of certain dietetic foods.

Gum Ghatti.—The exudate of the *Anogeissus latifolia* tree, which grows in India and Ceylon, is known as gum ghatti (Indian gum). The center of the gum ghatti trade is Bombay. The exact chemical structure of this gum is not known. Essentially it consists of a 1,6-linked linear D-galactopyranose chain, with side chains containing L-arabinose, D-mannose, D-xylose, and D-glucuronic acid. This latter component contributes to the acidic nature of the polymer; the gum ghatti is assumed to be the calcium salt of the complex heterogeneous polysaccharide. Gum ghatti is not used extensively in foods.

Gum Karaya.—Gum karaya is obtained by tapping the *Sterculia urens* tree. The exudate solidifies in the form of lumps. The lumps are hand selected and ground before the product is introduced into the trade under the synonyms of gum karaya, Indian tragacanth, and sterculia gum. Gum karaya, in recent years, found a few food applications with specific advantages and is enjoying a growing market. Several decades ago, karaya was often used as a low-cost adulterant of

the expensive tragacanth. Gum karaya is a partially acetylated polysaccharide with a molecular weight approaching 10,000,000; it is acidic in nature. On hydrolysis it was found to contain L-rhamnose, D-galactose, D-galacturonic acid as carbohydrate entities, and acetic acid.

Gum karaya does not form aqueous solutions, but rather hydrates to a gel-like paste. If gum karaya hydrates and is exposed to heat under pressure, a smooth, translucent colloidal dispersion is obtained.

Its food uses extend to the dairy-type frozen desserts, sherbets, and lollipops. In meat products it serves as a water binder in sausages and bolognas. In the baking trade gum karaya was recommended for dough stabilization and the prevention of bread staling. Several applications involving foam stabilization have been studied in imitation dairy creamers. In cheese foods karaya can be used for the retardation of syneresis and for the increase of spreadability. Salad dressings have been formulated with gum karaya to retard the separation of oil and water.

Gum Tragacanth.—Gum tragacanth is an exudate obtained from various kinds of *Astragalus* plants. The crude gum is in the form of curved, "goat horn"-shaped ribbons. Gum tragacanth is collected in Iran, Syria, and Turkey. Its commercial synonyms are: Syrian gum, bassora gum, goat's horn, and leaf gum.

The chemical structure of the gum tragacanth is not known in full detail. The commercial product is usually composed of two major fractions: the water-insoluble, but hydratable, bassorin and the water-soluble tragacanthin. As carbohydrate building blocks, gum tragacanth contains D-galacturonic acid and D-galactose, L-fucose, D-xylose, and L-arabinose. Its molecular weight is close to 1,000,000.

Gum tragacanth, when brought in contact with small amounts of water, at first forms a gel-like paste. On further water addition the tragacanthin fraction becomes dissolved, while the bassorin remains as a pliable gel. Special precautions and suitable equipment are needed when lump-free preparations of the gum are required for food use. Gum tragacanth yields the highest viscosities at the lowest concentrations among the edible gums. Its unique feature among the commonly-used food gums is its stability in acid systems. Hence, this gum is the preferred additive for salad dressings. The dairy and confectionary industries use gum tragacanth to a limited extent.

Plant Seed Gums.—*Locust Bean Gum.*—The fruit of the locust or carob tree (*Ceratonia siliqua*) is the source of the locust bean gum. The fruit of this tree is similar to the well-known string bean. The pods contain the small brown seeds which, when dehulled and degermed, expose the endosperm portion for the gum production. The finely ground endosperm, after careful separation, is the carob gum of commerce. The purity and quality of the gum depend on the efficiency of the separation of the husks, seed hulls, and germ constituents. Good quality locust bean gum should contain close to 90% galactomannan. Synonyms for locust bean gum are carob gum, St. John's bread, gum gatto, jandagum, gum tragon, and many other regional names.

Chemically, locust bean gum is a galactomannan with a molecular weight of about 300,000. This polymer is basically a C_1–C_4 linked D-mannose chain with regular branching at every fourth or fifth mannose group. The side branches are single units of D-galactose.

Locust bean gum is practically insoluble in cold water, but goes into a complete colloidal dispersion on heating. The hot locust bean gum dispersions on cooling become very viscous and slimy. At 1% concentration levels the aqueous hydrate of the locust bean gum has 3000–4000 cps viscosity.

Locust bean gum finds application in ice cream preparation because of its great water-binding capacity. It imparts increased heat-shock resistance to ice cream. However, locust bean gum causes precipitation of the proteins in milk and, therefore, in order to suspend the flocculated proteins, carrageenan is used in the ice cream mix.

The protein flocculating feature of locust bean gum is used in cheese production. Cheese spreads utilize the gum both for water-binding property and for securing good spreadability. In sausage meat products locust bean gum is a useful moisture binder, which controls the extrusion process. In synthetic, extruded meat products the addition of locust bean gum seems to increase the chewability. Numerous patents have been filed on this use. The bakery trade uses locust bean gum in limited quantities for texture improvement of pie fillings. The salad dressing industry uses locust bean gum for emulsion stabilization and thickening.

Guar Gum.—Guar gum is obtained from the seeds of the leguminous plant *Cyamopsis tetragonolobus*. This plant originated in India and has been adapted to North American growing conditions. It is a commercial crop in Texas, California, and Arizona. The seeds, after harvesting, are processed by dehulling and milling. In this process the gum-containing fractions are enriched by differential milling. The final form of the gum is a fine powder which contains about 80% guar galactomannan.

Chemically, guar gum is a straight chain polymer of D-mannopyranose with one unit length D-galactopyranose substituents on every second mannopyranose unit. The molecular weight of guar gum is about 300,000. Guar gum hydrates easily in cold water and yields highly viscous colloidal solutions. Heating of the aqueous dispersion of guar increases the rate of hydration, but on prolonged exposure to elevated temperatures viscosity may decrease. Guar gum's rate of hydration is also dependent on the pH range of the aqueous dispersion. Guar, being nonionic, is little affected by salt additives; however, polyvalent cations can cause precipitation at certain pH levels. Like most hydrocolloid solutions, guar also is sensitive to molecular degradation; consequently, some precautions are indicated in handling this material. Sugar solutions considerably influence the hydration of guar.

Guar gum is one of the most often-used food additives for water binding. It is commonly used in ice cream, cakes, pie fillings, in cheese spreads, in vegetable fat toppings, in cottage cheese creaming mixtures, in canned goods, baby foods, beverages, and icings. Guar is also an effective emulsion stabilizer and thus finds applications in salad dressings, barbecue sauces, etc.

Psyllium, Quince, and Tamarind Seed Gums.— These gums have undergone less study and are generally not used in food formulations, but each has special properties which would make further investigation worthwhile. Quince seed gum, in certain respects, has properties similar to the seaweed gum carrageenan, and tamarind seed gum forms gels useful in fruit jellies.

Western Larch Gum (Arabinogalactan).—Arabinogalactans are obtained from various larch trees, most commonly from the western larch (*Larix occidentalis*). This water-soluble gum is accumulated under the barks of these deciduous pine-like trees. The gum is recovered by a patented process using continuous countercurrent extraction.

Chemically, the larch gum is a highly branched arabinogalactan polymer which contains L-arabinose and D-galactose in 1 to 6 ratio. The gum contains a wide spectrum of fractions in the molecular weight range of 30,000–100,000.

The arabino galactan gum is easily soluble in water and concentrations up to 60% solids can be reached. The viscosity of the larch gum solutions is low in comparison to the other gum solutions. The food uses of the larch gum are not yet numerous. The purpose of its use in conjunction with artificial sweetening agents is to simulate the bodying properties of the sucrose solutions.

Seaweed Extracts.—The seaweed hydrocolloids are found in various algae, primitive plants, living both in fresh and sea water. The plants are essentially an aggregate of the individual living cells, each of which is a biological functional element in its own right. The material which binds these individual cells together in a flexible manner is the basic source of the seaweed gums. The alginate type seaweed hydrocolloids are obtained from the brown algae and the carrageenan and furcellaran hydrocolloids from the red seaweeds.

Alginates.—Alginates, or alginic acid derivatives, or their salts, are recovered from the giant kelp plant (*Macrocytis pyrifera*) which is most extensively harvested in the coastal waters of California. Other related brown seaweeds are also suitable raw materials for alginic acid recovery, such as the rockweed (*Ascophyllum nodosum*) and the several *Laminaria* species from the coastline of the North Sea. A great number of specific patented processes are applied for the recovery of the alginic hydrocolloids. The extraction processes are based on the solubility of the sodium salts of the alginic acids for the isolation step and the insolubility of the calcium salts of the alginic acids for the purification steps.

Chemically, the alginic acids are linear polymers of beta-D-mannuronic acid units linked to each other in 1-4 positions. Depending on the algae species, L-guluronic acid polymers are also found in the alginic hydrocolloids. In certain respects, the above two kinds of polymers can differ considerably; however, for most applications they are interchangeable.

The alginic acid is essentially insoluble in both cold and hot water. The alkali salts of the alginic acids are soluble in water, whereas the calcium salts are extremely insoluble. Gel formation is brought about by exchanging the sodium ions for calcium ions on the carboxylic groups of the polymer. By esterification of some of the carboxylic groups (derived from the constituent uronic acids) the sensitivity of the alginic acid chain against the insolubilizing effect of the calcium ions can be greatly reduced. By partial esterification it can be regulated to bring about certain desired technical effects. The interaction of the calcium ions with the alginic acid polymers is mediated by the carboxylic groups and the *cis* standing hydroxylic groups of the neighboring polymeric chains. This cross-linking of the chains by the calcium ions may result in three-dimensional molecular aggregates.

Alginic acid salts or esters are widely used in the food industry for their water-binding, gel-forming, and emulsion-stabilizing power. Since the alginic acid polymer is essentially stable against the hydrolytic action of the strong mineral acids—a property rather rare in the edible polymeric carbohydrate group—the alginates and their derivatives are the choice stabilizers in acid foods such as salad dressings. The gradual reaction of algin derivatives with calcium is the basis of their use in instant puddings and in various milk desserts.

Alginates, when blended with cheese foods, effectively reduce the surface hardening of the products. Alginic derivatives are widely used as foam stabilizers in whippable food systems. Alginate gel formed on the surface of sliced fish products has been found to preserve the tenderness and freshness during frozen storage.

Many stabilization problems occurring in beverage technology have been successfully solved with the various alginate products. Suspension of finely chopped pulp particles in fruit drinks can be effectively stabilized with alginates at reasonably low viscosity levels. Flavored, fermented milk products are given spoonable characteristics by esterified alginate derivatives. Elimination of the undesired cloudiness in beer can be achieved by the use of alginic acid derivatives. The propylene glycol ester of alginic acid successfully replaces in salad dressings the expensive and difficult-to-handle gum tragacanth. Alginates find applications in the processing of canned sauces. The thickening properties of alginates have been explored in the design of low-calorie dressings.

Agar.—The agar-agar hydrocolloid and its food use originated in Japan and it spread from there to Indonesia. Dutch colonists trading in this area brought these high gel strength gums to Europe for use in preserved fruit jellies. Agar gained high significance in microbiological research as a culture media base.

Many seaweeds belonging to the *Gracillaria*, *Gelidium*, and *Acanthopeltis* groups yield agar on extraction. The seaweed plants are usually harvested by divers, collected and dried on the shore, and bleached by the sunlight. The crude seaweed is transported to plants, where it is subjected to a hot-water extraction, filtration, and freeze-thaw treatment for the removal of water and impurities. The concentrate remaining in gel form is finally dried and ground to a powder.

The chemical structure of the agar hydrocolloid is known. It is composed of two major fractions: agarose and agaropectin. Agarose is a neutral, straight chain polymeric molecule, built up from the repeating unit of the disaccharide: agarobiose. Agarobiose is a 1,4-connected 3,6-anhydro-L-galactose with 1,3-linked D-galactose. The agaropectin is essentially a partially sulfonated agarose in which the amount of sulfate ester might vary between 5-10%.

Agar is a unique gel-forming agent which has its solidification point about 50°C below its liquefaction point. The agar gels are remarkable for their strength, brilliance, and reversibility. Agars, when used at concentration levels below their massive gelling, are useful protective colloids in food systems.

The food uses of agar are commonly in bakeries for icings, piping jellies, and pie fillings. The confectionery industry applies agar in the preparation of jellied candies and sweet meats. The meat and fish canning industries use agar for imbedding tender textured products in order to prevent their disintegration during shipment. Agars find limited application in frozen dairy desserts and in certain cheese foods. The food applications of agar are declining because of its high price and the development of more abundant hydrocolloids with similar functionalities.

Carrageenan.—The use of carrageenan-containing seaweeds in human foods originated in North European countries where people could gather the marine algae *Chondrus crispus* in the tidal pools of the rocky seacoast. This seaweed slowly became an article of commerce under the name of Irish moss and was exported to the United States also. By the first half of the 19th Century, Americans recognized that Irish moss can be collected on the New England seacoast and development work was started mostly on a home-industry basis for the preparation of an edible extract. Larger-scale commercial processing of the Irish moss algae was started only after World War II in the United States.

Carrageenan occurs in many seaweeds, but the Irish moss is the preferred raw material for its large-scale production. Extracts of unique properties are obtained from *Gigartina*, *Euchema*, *Hypnea*, and *Iridophycus* seamoss types also.

Carrageenan is extracted from the respective seaweeds by hot water and is separated from the insoluble plant debris by filtration. The highly viscous crude extract is carefully purified and, in many cases, subjected to a controlled chemical treatment. Finally it is concentrated in vacuum evaporators and brought to the dry state, either by alcohol precipitation or by roller drying.

The seaweed extracts have been found to contain several fractions which are significantly different in their food technological utility. The most studied fractions are referred to as the kappa, lambda, and iota carrageenans. The basic chemical structure of the kappa carrageenan fraction is 1,3-linked galactose 4-sulfate units connected in 1,4 position with 3,6-anhydro-D-galactose units. The lambda fraction is 1,4-linked galactose 2,6-disulfate units connected in 1,3 position with galactose 2-sulfate. The iota carrageenan fraction is composed of 1,3-linked galactose 4-sulfate units with 1,4-linked 3,6-anhydro-D-galactose 2-sulfate units. In all three carrageenan fractions the 6-sulfate group can be removed by an alkaline treatment which results in a 3,6-anhydro galactose ring. This reaction is often used in commercial production to modify the functionality of the carrageenan extracts.

The gelation of carrageenan can be explained by the formation of a double helix between adjacent chains. This double helical structure is stabilized by potassium ions.

The chemical structure of carrageenan shows that the molecule is a highly negatively charged polyelectrolyte. This property holds the key to its many possible interactions with other compounds which is effected by hydrogen bonding, ionic interactions, and by Van der Waals forces. The results of these interactions usually modify the sol or gel characteristic of the media and represent the basis of its food technological applicability. Particularly, specific functionality is observed when the carrageenan is introduced into food systems containing milk or other colloidally dispersed proteins. Very often the viscosity and gelling properties of the various carrageenan extracts with milk are used for the standardization of their food technological utility ("milk reactivity tests").

The major carrageenan-producing countries are the United States, France, and Denmark. The carrageenan consumption of the food industry nearly doubled in the 1960–1970 period.

Dairy industry pioneered the use of carrageenan among the food processors. Substantial quantities are used for ice cream stabilization; for the suspension of cocoa particles in chocolate milk; and in refrigerated gelled milk desserts (flans). Besides these large-volume, well-established applications, carrageenan gained significant new uses in the water gel desserts, in the milk-based starch puddings, and in instant puddings. With the advent of dairy cream substitutes, coffee whiteners, and whipped toppings, carrageenan gained further markets and applications as bodying agents and foam stabilizers. Frozen fruit concentrates and fruit drink powder bases use carrageenans for viscosity control and mouth feel effects. Carrageenans effectively stabilize milkfat- and vegetable fat-based emulsion systems by reacting both with the caseinate micelles and lecithins which are adsorbed on the fat globule membranes.

Carrageenans have been developed with various cold water and milk solubilities. These found widespread applications in instantly reconstituted flavored milks and instantly dispersible suspensions such as breakfast drinks. Carrageenans are useful in certain sterilized baby foods; and also have found limited applications in the bread baking field. In bread and macaroni products, carrageenans form stable complexes between the cereal and milk proteins, thus aiding in building suitable textures in the intermediate dough stage.

Other Marine Hydrocolloids.—Furcellarin, or Danish agar, is obtained from the *Furcellaria fastigiata* seaweed. Its relatively limited occurrence restricts its broader use. The properties of furcellarin, in many respects, resemble carrageenan and its use areas are also similar.

Hypnean extracts, from certain Mediterranean *Hypnea* seaweeds, form gels very similar to the kappa carrageenan gels and are considered to be promising in pudding and milk flan applications.

Cellulose Hydrocolloids.—Traditionally, the food art used only natural materials for the purpose of conditioning the body, texture, and viscosity characteristics of its products. However, with the advances of organic chemistry and the increased knowledge of polymeric materials, the opportunity developed to consider certain semisynthetic or fully synthetic products for use in foods as the replacements for the natural gums. This new class of gum-like food additives has used the abundant natural cellulose as the raw material. Chemically, cellulose is a long polymeric chain built from cellobiose units. Cellobiose is a disaccharide composed of two glucose molecules, linked in 1-4 positions. In order to obtain such cellulose-based artificial food additives, purified cellulose, usually referred to as α-cellulose, imparted by a particular chemical degradation and fractionation, yielded the "microcrystalline cellulose." When the cellulose is chemically modified by the introduction of certain organic chemical radicals the methoxy-, ethoxy-, carboxymethyl-, or hydroxypropylcellulose derivatives are obtained. These products are tailored for the required functionalities by controlling the chain length (degree of polymerization) of the parent cellulose and by controlling the quantity of the introduced organic radicals (degree of substitution). An additional controlling factor is supplied by the use of celluloses in which the degree of crystallinity is varied.

Carboxymethylcellulose.—Among the cellulose derivatives useful in the food industry the carboxymethylcellulose (CMC) is of the major importance. In CMC the basic polymeric structure of the cellulose is chemically modified by the introduction of the sodium carboxymethyl groups ($-CH_2COONa$). The presence of this group lends ionizable groups and negative ionic charges to the nonionic cellulose chain, and transforms it into a polyelectrolyte. As a result, the water-binding capacity of the modified product (CMC) is greatly increased over that of the parent compound and, depending on the degree of substitution (DS), the CMC will form colloidal solutions. The careful and purposeful control of the degree of polymerization, the degree of substitution, and the uniformity of the substituents are the major technological parameters by which CMC manufacturers develop the properties required by the food applications.

Solutions of CMC in water supply various degrees of viscosities. Depending on the particular combinations of the above listed parameters, a 2% aqueous solution of CMC may have viscosities in the 10 to 50,000 cps range. The flow characteristics of the CMC solutions are mostly non-Newtonian, pseudo-plastic, indicating that the CMC molecules will orient themselves in the direction of the movement of the liquid. By varying the molecular weight of the CMC, the flow behavior can be reduced or increased. The viscosity of CMC will depend on the strength of the shear forces also; this property is referred to as thixotrophy. Heat processing of the CMC solutions temporarily reduces the viscosity, but on cooling the viscosity is regained, unless molecular degradation occurred. Such molecular degradation can happen after prolonged heating, or at pH values below 4. Salts of monovalent cations, such as sodium, potassium or ammonium, have no significant effect on CMC solutions provided oxidative anions are not present. The presence of calcium salts, depending on their concentrations, might cause partial insolubilization; trivalent cations cause precipitation. CMC solutions, when heated with proteins, will display colloidal changes, but this effect is not as pronounced as those observed between carrageenan and proteins. CMC solutions are subject to microbial degradations.

Carboxymethylcellulose finds many food applications: it is often used as an ingredient in ice cream stabilizers, in dairy substitutes, in puddings, frozen foods, in citrus fruit concentrates, sauces and gravies, and in baked items. In food preservation the film-forming capability of CMC solutions is applied in meats and fish products. CMC is also a good encapsulating agent for emulsifying fats and oils.

The carboxymethylcellulose is generally recognized as safe (GRAS) in foods. There are a number of standardized foods which permit the use of CMC without further ingredient declaration. If label statements are made, the terms "cellulose gum" or "sodium carboxymethylcellulose" are appropriate for use.

Methyl Ether of Cellulose (Methylcellulose).— Methylcellulose is the partial methyl ether of cellulose. The introduction of the methyl groups on the cellulose chain facilitates the separation of the chains from each other and thus it increases the solubility of the product over the solubility of the mother compound. The methylcellulose molecules, when dissolved, are enveloped in a partially immobilized hydrate layer and thus a viscous, colloidal solution is formed. However, on heating, the structure of the separating aqueous layer is damaged by the vigorous heat movement and the exposed unhydrated surfaces of the cellulose might approach each other to such extent that hydrogen bond formation results. In this case, molecular aggregation will occur with the increase of viscosity and incipient gelation. This course of events will result in the heat gelation of a hydrated methylcellulose solution.

Methylcellulose has many-fold applications in the food industry as an additive in bakery products and in frozen and dehydrated foods. Methylcellulose is rated GRAS in foods and can be used in a few standardized items also.

Hydroxypropylcellulose. — Hydroxypropylcellulose is the ether formed between cellulose and propylene glycol. Unique features of the hydroxypropylcellulose are its low viscosity and its tendency to precipitate at elevated temperatures, followed by a spontaneous redissolution on cooling. This cellulose gum is acid stable and thus could be used preferentially in acid food systems.

Synthetic Gums.—Completely synthetic gums or hydrocolloids, as far as their food technological use is concerned, are in their infancy. It is believed that the modern polymer technology is capable of producing replicas of the natural hydrocolloids, or creating new ones which might surpass the functionality of the existing gums. However, production costs, toxicological problems due to residual chemicals, and legal clearances for food use may be serious limiting factors of developmental pursuits. In a few cases, where the development of fully synthetic gums was justified by pharmaceutical or other industrial applications, certain manufacturers have conducted food technological evaluation work also, which in some cases resulted in FDA approval of certain products for specific uses. Otherwise, it is assumed that the use and acceptance of fully synthetic gums in the food industry will be slow.

At the present time, polyvinylpyrrolidone (PVP) is cleared for use in the brewing industry, in the clarification of wines, and in the clarification of vinegar.

Other fully synthetic gums which have been subjected to food technological evaluation are: methyl vinylether maleic acid polymers (Gantrez AN), ethylene oxide polymers (Polyox) and carboxyvinyl polymers (Carbopol).

Economical Significance of Hydrocolloid Gums in the U.S. Food Industry

The total yearly consumption in the U.S. food industry of the hydrocolloid gums discussed in the present article was estimated to be approximately 40–50 million pounds in 1970, representing a value 35–40 million dollars.

With the expansion of manufactured foods, the use of hydrocolloid gums is expected to grow; however, the total volume is always subject to the limitations of the legal and actual functionality use levels. For most gums that is about 0.5% and often it might be as slow as 0.01%.

A major expansion for the use of hydrocolloid gums in the food industry could be expected by the development of such edible gum derivatives which when applied to the surface of the foods could offer packaging advantages. For that purpose, moisture-isolating and oxygen-excluding capabilities, sanitation aspects, protection against the penetration of bacteria, structural rigidity, and complete lack of toxicity have to be designed into the candidate products.

JOHN J. JONAS

References

GLICKSMAN, M. 1967. Utilization of synthetic gums in the food industry. *In* Advances in Food Research, Vol. 12. Academic Press, New York.

GLICKSMAN, M. 1969. Gum Technology in the Food Industry. Academic Press, New York.

WHISTLER, R. L. 1959. Industrial Gums. Academic Press, New York.

H

HARDTACK (KNÄCKEBROT)

Hardtack or Knäckebrot takes an exceptional position among the many types of bread that are on the market today. It is a flat-shaped crisp bread made out of whole-meal grain which, due to its low moisture content, belongs to long-life bakery goods.

The home country of Knäckebrot is Scandinavia, where it is possible to retrace the development to the original type of bread, the flat bread. Besides flat bread, Knäckebrot was formerly made by almost every farmer. Today Knäckebrot is produced in factories only.

Even today the Scandinavian countries, in particular Sweden, have the highest production and consumption of Knäckebrot. During the last decades the consumption of Knäckebrot increased in Germany and also other European countries.

For the production of Knäckebrot the whole grain is used. Contrary to other bread types, in the case of Knäckebrot not only normal flour, but also the bran and the germ of the grain are used. There are two different manufacturing procedures. The puffing up of the bread is either by whipping air into the ice-cooled dough or by yeast fermentation.

So-called Ice-bread

This procedure is by far the most common for Knäckebrot. Air is whipped into the dough by special equipment. This requires that the dough have a heavy body in spite of the high moisture. This is achieved by cooling the dough with added ice chips, which is the traditional procedure. Today, in the modern factories the surface cooler is used for cooling the dough. After the whipping and cooling process the dough is formed into thin layered pieces. The layer is perforated by needles, cut into pieces, and conveyed into the oven which is normally a continuous conveyor oven. This procedure differs considerably from that for loaf bread. During a relatively short time of 5–10 min the product passes through the oven starting at a temperature of about 300°C which decreases to about 200°C towards the end of the baking procedure.

Knäckebrot Made According to the Fermentation Procedure

With this procedure the ingredients (ground grain, salt, yeast) are mixed with warm water for about 15 min in a dough blender. The dough is being kept at a constant temperature of about 30°C during this procedure. Then the dough is rolled out by a dough-forming machine into a thin layer of 3–4 mm. The dough layer is then perforated by needles and finally cut into dough pieces of desired sizes. Then the dough cakes are transported through a fermentation tunnel on a screen conveyor. The air in this tunnel is kept at a constant temperature and at a constant moisture. There the final fermentation procedure takes place, the cakes being baked in a continuous conveyor oven.

After the baking procedure, which is about the same as for ice-bread, this Knäckebrot still has a water content of 10–15%. A drying room is connected to the baking oven in which the bread is finally dried to a remaining water content of approx 5–7%. Thereafter the bread cakes are cut in consumer size slices and packaged.

Knäckebrot is an easily digestible whole-meal bread. Because of its low salt content and acid value which are below normal loaf bread, Knäckebrot is used as diet food.

Knäckebrot is mainly produced from rye and only to a small extent made from wheat. Other varieties are on the market, for instance, with added milk or buttermilk solids. Further varieties of Knäckebrot have additions of sesame seed, caraway, poppy, etc., sprinkled on the surface.

General Analysis of Knäckebrot

	%
Moisture	7
Protein	10

Fat	1.4
Carbohydrates	77.2
Roughage	2.0
Minerals	2.3

Vitamins B_1, B_2, B_6, E, nicotinamide
100 gm Knäckebrot contain approx 380 cal

HERIBERT KOHLHAAS

Cross-reference: *Biscuit and Cracker Technology.*

HEAT EXCHANGE

In processing food, heat has many applications, not only in canning, which comes to mind first, but also in pasteurizing, blanching, cooking, and several other processing operations. Heat is applied to products by conduction, convection, compression, radiation, induction, and by vibration as in dielectric heating. The transfer of energy in the form of heat is an important if not the most important operation in converting a raw edible material into a finished product. Heat transfer or exchange occurs when the temperature is increased for purposes of boiling or otherwise cooking a product or when the temperature is decreased for purposes of freezing. Heat exchange, in short, is a part of the operation of preserving foods.

Heat itself is the kinetic energy of molecular motion, which can be transmitted by conduction (from molecule to molecule), by convection (the mass movement of heated molecules), or by radiation (the generation of heat by atoms or molecules as they undergo internal change).

Conduction

In the food industry the most common method of heat transfer is by conduction, i.e., by transferring heat from a source such as a stove to a vessel containing the food to be processed. The thermal conductivity of a food is measured by the number of Btu (British thermal units) transmitted per hour per square foot of area per inch of thickness per degree of difference in temperature between the stove and the pot containing the food. There are, of course, many types of heat exchangers other than a stove and a pot. These include the drum type heat exchangers, the plate type, the screw type, the surface tubular type, the coil type, the flat surface type, and various modifications of these.

Convection

Heat transfer is also accomplished by convection, for example, by transmitting currents of heat through a liquid substance. Circulating currents of heat through a liquid or a liquid mixture will eventually establish an equilibrium. The canning process utilizes convection although conduction is also involved since a metal can has heat transfer surfaces, viz, the tops and sides of the can. Convection heating occurs inside the can. This phenomenon is treated in depth elsewhere in this volume.

Radiation

Radiation is the process whereby energy in the form of rays is sent out by atoms and molecules as they change internally. The sun is the source of radiant energy which reaches the earth and provides directly and indirectly the life force in plants and animals. The radiation energy generated in baking, roasting, thermal drying, etc., includes both radiation and convection. Commercial forms of radiant heaters are infrared lamps, heated silica glass tubes, and heated borosilicate glass panels. The outdoor barbecue is a form of radiant heating known to all. Microwave heating is distinct from radiant heating in that this type of heating is induced by interatomic friction.

Heat Exchange as a Refrigeration Application

Refrigeration is heat loss, i.e., the withdrawal of heat from a food. Heat loss varies with the product. The loss is achieved by conduction alone.

Ionizing Irradiations

Ionizing irradiations used in the preservation of food experimentally is also a form of radiant energy but it needs only passing mention in this article since it is treated in depth elsewhere in this volume.

MARTIN S. PETERSON

Cross-reference: *Sterilization of Canned Food by Heat.*

HEAT STERILIZATION OF CANNED FOODS

See Sterilization of Canned Foods by Heat.

HOMOGENIZER AND COLLOID MILLS

Pressure homogenizers and colloid mills are used in the processing of food products for one or more of the following reasons: (1) Preparation of stable emulsion of fat or oil in water. (2) Control of viscosity or consistency in the product. (3) Provide desired texture and appearance to a product. (4) Enhance flavor or improve mouth feel. (5) Increase product shelf-life.

The homogenizer or colloid mill may be used interchangeably on many food products. In practice, more homogenizers are used due to their greater versatility in meeting the requirements of food processors. There are a few products where, due to the nature of the formulation, only a colloid mill may be used and, conversely, others will require homogenization. For colloid mills these uses include mayonnaise or salad dressings and gravies where the starch component is shear sensitive, or fat emulsions using maximum fat content. On other products, such as frozen whip topping where an extremely small particle size is required, only the homogenizer may be used. For reasons unknown to us, the homogenizer is the only equipment that will produce a satisfactory emulsion on milk and most dairy products.

What are Homogenizers and Colloid Mills?

Homogenizers are positive displacement plunger-type pumps having from 1 to 6 plungers, a common suction manifold, a common high pressure discharge manifold terminating in either a single- or

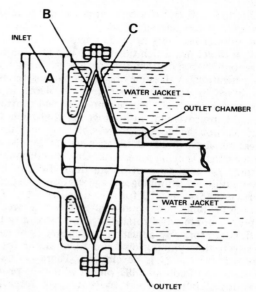

FIG. H-2. CROSS SECTION OF COLLOID MILL IN WHICH PRODUCT FLOWS COUNTERCURRENT TO CENTRIFUGAL FORCE IN THE WORKING AREA

two-stage homogenizing valve assembly. The homogenizing valve is an orifice whose opening may be controlled. The product enters the opening at high pressure and instantaneously changes from pressure to velocity. This extreme change in flow conditions causes high velocity shear, turbulence,

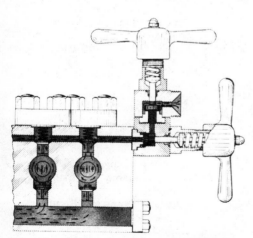

FIG. H-1. CROSS SECTION SHOWING THE FLOW OF MILK THROUGH THE HOMOGENIZER CYLINDER HEAD AND THE HOMOGENIZING VALVES

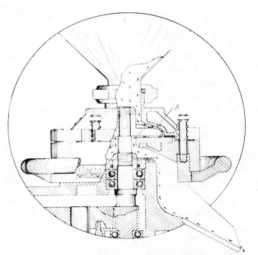

FIG. H-3. CROSS SECTION OF COLLOID MILL IN WHICH PRODUCT FLOWS WITH CENTRIFUGAL FORCE IN THE WORKING AREA

cavitation, and an ultrasonic vibration of the valve system. A ring surrounds the orfice, upon which the product impinges as it immerges. This combination of actions which takes place in a fraction of a second is responsible for the effect called homogenization. Valves may be either single-stage or two-stage in which a second valve is placed in a series with the first. The second valve will provide a slight improvement in homogenizing efficiency, but is not economically feasible at operating pressures above 3000 psi, unless a high fat emulsion or ice cream is being processed. On these products it may be used to control the final viscosity by elimination of clumping or aggregation of small particles. (See Fig. H-1 for flow details.)

Colloid mills are rotational devices where a rapidly spinning disc rotates in close proximity to a fixed stator. By adjusting the clearance or gap between the spinning disc and fixed stator rotational shear energy is developed. There are two basic types of colloid mills, one in which the product flows countercurrent to centrifugal force in the working area. (See Fig. H-2; working area is indicated by C.) In the second type of mill, the product flows with centrifugal force in the working area. (See Fig. H-3 area marked A.)

Both designs have advantages and disadvantages. The type shown in Fig. H-2 is extremely efficient on fluid product and is usually operated so that rotor has peripheral speed of 10,000 ft per min. The combination of high speed and countercurrent to centrifugal force flow permits a small rotor and minimizes the mechanical frictional losses associated with a large body rotating at high speed. Viscosities over 2000 cps show a sharp increase in hp required.

The mill shown in Fig. H-3 is usually operated with a peripheral speed on the rotor of 5000 ft per min or less and is suitable for paste or high viscosity products. It will not produce as fine a particle size on fluid products as will the mill operating at the higher speed and with countercurrent flow.

The following lists some of the parameters that must be met in selecting food processing equipment.

Parameter	Homogenizer	Colloid Mill
Particle size oil emulsion minimum	0.03μ	$1.0\ \mu$ high speed mill $2.0\ \mu$ slow speed mill
Maximum particle size	20μ	50–$100\ \mu$ high and slow speed mill
Viscosity minimum	1 cp	1 cp high speed mill 1000 cp slow speed mill
Viscosity maximum [1]	2000 cp	5000 cp high speed mill 50,000 cp slow speed mill
Maximum shear level available	Equivalent to 10,000 psi through a restricted orfice	Equivalent to homogenizer operating at 1500–2000 psi (high speed mill) Slow speed mill will be less efficient
Temperature rise during processing	$1.5°C/1000$ lb of homogenizing pressure	$1°$ to $50°C$ depending upon mill gap setting
Maximum operating temperature	$140°C$	$140°C$ on special designs only
Suitable for Continuous processing	Yes	Yes
Can be used to pump product to next operation	Yes	No
Suitable for sterile operation	Yes	Requires a special design not available on many mills
Effect of viscosity on capacity	None	Capacity decreases with increasing viscosity
Effect of increasing shear energy level on capacity	None	Reduction

[1] Newtonian may be 20,000 cp in a thixotropic system.

Following is a list of products that may be processed in both the homogenizer and colloid mill together with the homogenizing pressure range. Only those products shown under the low pressure listing (0-3000 psi) would normally be suitable for processing in a colloid mill. It should be remembered that the mill energy level is less than the homogenizer at 3000 psi, hence all products would not meet specifications. The dairy products mentioned earlier are a definite exception, and must be homogenized.

Low Homogenizing Pressure (100-3000 psi)

Milk, ice cream, cream, evaporated milk, cream cheese, soft cheeses, cottage cheese dressing, sour cream, yogurt, eggnog, apricot juice, tropical fruit purées, tomato juice, tomato products, coffee whiteners, toppings, chocolate syrups and fudges, butterscotch syrups, cream replacers, meat and vegetable baby foods, bakery products, candy, mixes, pie fillings, gravies, starches, mayonnaise, puddings, buttered syrups, cream soups, salad dressings, French dressings.

Medium Pressure (3000-5000 psi)

Citrus juices, citrus purées, pear purées, flavor oil emulsions, peanut butter, meat and vegetable baby foods, sauces, starches, chicken products, meat spreads, mustard, soya beverages.

High Pressure Homogenized Products (5000-8000 psi)

Frozen whipped toppings, yeast, chicken products.

L. H. REES

HONEY AND HONEY PRODUCTS

See Beekeeping.

HOT PEPPER SAUCE

See Tabasco Sauce.

HUMECTANTS (POLYHYDRIC ALCOHOLS) IN FOODS

Scope

Polyhydric alcohols or polyols represent a wide spectrum of unique chemical products. They can be defined as straight chain, organic compounds in which the only functional group present is hydroxyl (Benson 1963). Polyols are generally used as (1) vehicles, (2) humectants, and/or (3) chemical reactants. Food applications are frequently based on other effects, such as solvency, crystallization control, and others unique to food processing and handling problems. The polyhydric alcohols used in food products are glycerine, sorbitol, mannitol, and propylene glycol. These materials are used alone and in combination with each other to produce many special effects in fabricated foods. Certain polyols can be blended with sugars to produce very beneficial crystallization effects (DuRoss U.S. Pat. 1969; Atlas Chemical Industries *ILG-91*).

The term polyhydric alcohol or polyol in this discussion will be restricted to those molecules that have two or more hydroxyl groups and have only hydroxyl groups. This will exclude sugars, although they have many hydroxyl groups and, in some instances, exhibit similar properties (Benson 1963). The chief difference noted between polyols and sugars is related to the aldehyde linkage present in the sugars. As a class polyols are more stable chemically and thermally than sugars. They are usually more expensive than sugars; hence, the food industry demands that a polyol contribute a notable desired property to the final product. For these reasons, we shall not treat sugars as polyhydric alcohols.

Polyhydric alcohols for our use then are defined as derivatives of aliphatic hydrocarbons formed by the replacement of 2 or more hydrogen atoms with 2 or more monovalent hydroxyl groups, each being attached to a different carbon atom. While the polyhydric alcohol family continues to challenge the curiosity of the scientist, only a few polyols are of actual commercial importance in the food industry.

Sources and Characteristics of Polyhydric Alcohols

Many polyhydric alcohols are present in natural foods, either in the free state or chemically combined. Of the 4 polyols most often added in food preparation, only 2 occur naturally in the free state, sorbitol and mannitol. Sorbitol is found in many fruits such as apples, pears, and berries. It also has been isolated from certain plants. Mannitol also occurs at levels as high as 90% in the manna of some types of trees as well as in a variety of vegetables and fruits. Mannitol was first isolated by Proust in 1806 from the mountain ash tree. Sorbitol was first isolated by Joseph Boussingault in 1872 (Atlas Chemical Industries *CD-60*).

Propylene glycol does not exist as a natural product in foods. Propylene glycol is made commercially by a three-step procedure; propylene is reacted with chlorine and water as a source of hypochlorous acid to form propylene chlorohydrin which is converted to propylene epoxide in the presence of sodium carbonate. The propylene epoxide is exposed to dilute acids (H_2SO_4) which hydrates the propylene epoxide to propylene glycol.

Propylene glycol has a molecular weight of 76 and exists as a clear, colorless, and practically odorless liquid with a slight acid taste and has a moderate viscosity and volatility. Propylene glycol boils at 190°C. It absorbs moisture from the air and is miscible with water, alcohol, acetone, and chloroform. It is soluble in ether and is used as a solvent for many flavors.

Glycerine is by far the most plentiful polyol present in natural foods; however, it is almost always exclusively in chemical combination as fats (triesters of long chain fatty acids) in meats and some vegetables.

Glycerine has a molecular weight of 92 and is a trihydric alcohol. It is prepared by several methods: (1) The saponification of fats and oils by alkalies where the glycerine is removed from the soap and sold as a by-product. (2) By the hydrolysis of fats and oils through pressure and superheated steam. This is the process most frequently used. (3) The hydrocarbon, propylene is chlorinated to form alkyl chloride which is converted to allyl alcohol. This unsaturated alcohol is treated with hypochlorous acid (HOCl) to yield a chlorohydrin intermediate. Extraction of hydrochloric acid with soda lime followed by hydrolysis yields glycerine.

Glycerine was discovered by K. W. Scheele in 1779 and later more fully investigated by M. E. Chevreul who named it. Glycerine exists as a clear, colorless, syrupy liquid with a slightly sweet taste and slight characteristic odor. When exposed to moist air, it absorbs water and such gases as H_2S and SO_2. Glycerine boils at 290°C under 1 atm pressure with decomposition. It is miscible with water, alcohol, and methanol. It is insoluble in ether, and in mineral, volatile, or vegetable oils.

Sorbitol has a molecular weight of 182. It is a hexahydric alcohol prepared by the reduction (hydrogenation) of certain sugars such as glucose. The reaction consists of the following steps: (1) prepare the reaction slurry by dissolving the refined sugar in water and mixing with nickel catalyst; (2) continuous catalytic reduction of the sugar to sorbitol with hydrogen in a specially designed high pressure reactor system; (3) filtering off the spent catalyst from the solution and reprocessing it to return to the system; (4) purifying the solution by ion exchange and decolorizing it with activated carbon. At this step, it can be crystallized out as crystalline sorbitol powder or concentrated into a pure sorbitol solution in a vacuum evaporator. The concentration is adjusted with demineralized water to yield the product of commerce, Sorbitol Solution 70% w/w.

Crystalline sorbitol melts at 110°C and is isomeric with mannitol. It is very soluble in water and hot alcohol. Sorbitol solution is a water solution containing in each 100 gm not less than 69 gm or more than 71 gm of sorbitol.

Sorbitol solution is a clear, colorless, syrupy liquid, having a sweet taste and is essentially odorless. It is miscible with water, glycerine, and propylene glycol; and is slightly soluble in alcohol and practically insoluble in other common organic solvents.

Mannitol has a molecular weight of 182. It is a hexahydric alcohol and is isomeric with sorbitol. Commercially, mannitol is produced by the catalytic or electrolytic reduction of certain monosaccharides such as mannose and glucose. The manufacture of mannitol is complex due primarily to the need for separation of steroisomers. The following steps are involved in preparing mannitol from a monosaccharide (sugar) catalytically: (1) preparing the reaction slurry by dissolving the refined sugar in water and mixing with catalyst; (2) continuous catalytic reduction of the sugar to a mixture of sorbitol and mannitol with hydrogen in a specially designed high-pressure reaction system; (3) filtering off the spent catalyst and reprocessing it for return to the system; (4) purifying the solution by ion exchange and decolorizing it with activated carbon; (5) separation of the mannitol by crystallizing it from the solution; (6) purifying the mannitol by recrystallization from water solution and drying; and (7) grinding the dry mannitol to a uniform powder.

Mannitol exists as a white crystalline powder, odorless, and has a sweet taste. It melts between 165° and 167°C. One gram dissolves in about 5.5 ml of water, in about 83 ml of alcohol, and about 2.3 ml of pyridine. It is insoluble in ether.

Table H-1 shows a comparison of the properties of the four commercial polyhydric alcohols approved for use in foods.[2] They are all permitted in unstandardized foods, provided the amount used does not exceed that reasonably required to accomplish the intended physical or technical effect. Of course, they are not permitted in

---

[2] In addition (A) 121.1057: Polyethylene glycol 6000 is permitted (1) as a binder in plasticizing agents, (2) as an adjuvant in tablet coatings and (3) as an adjuvant to improve flavor and body work with non-nutritive sweeteners; (B) 121.1114: Xylitol was permitted in some special dietary uses.

TABLE H-1

PROPERTIES OF POLYHYDRIC ALCOHOLS

	Propylene Glycol	Glycerine	Sorbitol	Mannitol
Molecular weight	76	92	182	182
Melting point, °C	Supercools	18.6	Metastable	166
Boiling point, °C 760 mm	187	290°C Decomposes	Decomposes	Decomposes
Density, 25°C	1.036	1.2613	1.49	1.49
Viscosity cp, 25°C	44.0	954	Solid	Solid
Viscosity 70% soln @ 25°C	10	17	110	Insoluble (crystallizes)
Hygroscopicity	High	Med.–High	Med.–Low	Low
Solvency (for oils)	Good	Fair	Poor	Poor
Solubility[1] in water @ 25°C	Infinite	Infinite	71%	22%
High temperature resistance	Stable, volatile	Stable, slightly volatile	Stable	Stable
Taste	Bitter	Slightly sweet	Cool, sweet	Sweet
Refractive Index, 25°C	1.4293	1.4729	1.459 (70% soln)	1.345 (10% soln)

[1] Gm/100 gm water.

standardized foods, unless the Standard of Identity permits their use. Each case for a standardized food must be investigated separately.

Data in Table H-1 show that as the molecular weight increases, the melting points, boiling points, and viscosities generally increase. It has also been observed that with increasing molecular weight hygroscopicity and solvent properties for nonpolar materials decrease. While generalizations of this type are useful, detailed comparative studies have been made and it is now possible to recommend, with some assurance, a specific polyol to contribute a certain function or property to a food. These studies have revealed that polyhydric alcohols act in a special way, each having its own functionality profile.

Most sugars have properties quite similar to that of high molecular weight polyols. However, though they are polyhydric compounds they also contain aldehyde linkages that adversely affect their high temperature stability.

Of the various properties of polyols related to food applications, there are four worthy of special note: (1) viscosity, (2) solvency, (3) taste, and (4) hygroscopicity.

Viscosity.—The viscosity of polyhydric alcohols in aqueous solution is of importance in food applications because of the bodying effect that is conveyed. Viscosity generally increases with increasing molecular weight. Viscosity is, of course, a function of concentration and temperature. Room temperature viscosity versus concentration data for the major polyols are presented in Fig. H-4.

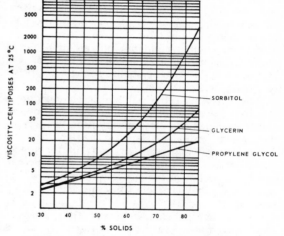

FIG. H-4. COMPARATIVE VISCOSITIES OF POLYOL SOLUTIONS

Source: Atlas Sorbitol and Related Polyols, CD-60. Copyright 1951, Atlas Chemical Industries, Inc.— now ICI America Inc. Revised June 1953.

Solvency and Water Solubility.—It is generally recognized that solvent properties improve with a reduction in molecular weight. The polyhydric alcohol series is no exception and propylene glycol is by far the best solvent of the group used in foods. Table H-2, shows the solvent power of propylene glycol for a variety of essential oils (Lakritz 1946). The water solubility of the typical polyhydric

SOLVENCY OF PROPYLENE
GLYCOL FOR ESSENTIAL OILS AND
FLAVORS (25°C)

Oil or Flavor	V/v%
Amyl acetate	Miscible
Bay oil	9.0
Dill seed	8.2
Ethyl acetate	Miscible
Geranium (rose)	9.9
Lemon	0.8
Peppermint	Over 10
Vanillin	Miscible
Wintergreen	6.9

SOURCE: Lakritz (1946).

RELATIVE SWEETNESS OF POLYOLS AND SUGARS
(SUCROSE = 1)

Polyol or Sugar	Relative Sweetness
Fructose or levulose	1.4–1.7
Invert sugar	1.0–1.3
Sucrose	1
Dextrose, anhydrous	0.7–0.8
Xylitol	
Iditol	0.7
Maltitol	
Dextrose, monohydrate	0.6–0.7
Galactose	
Corn syrup, enzyme converted	0.6
Glucose hydrate	
Sorbitol	0.5–0.6
Mannitol	
Dulcitol	0.5
Inositol	
Erythritol	0.4–0.5
Lactitol	
Xylose	0.4
Corn syrup, unmixed	0.3
Maltose	
Raffinose	0.2
Lactose	0.1–0.2
Erythritan	0

SOURCE: Courtesy of D. R. Ward, Atlas Chemical Industries, Wilmington, Del.

alcohol appears to be correlated with molecular weight as well as with crystalline structure and melting point. For example, propylene glycol and glycerine are infinitely water soluble at room temperature, though glycerine can be crystallized from water at lower temperatures. As the molecular weight increases, the tendency toward crystallization increases and inherent solubility decreases. The food scientist combines polyols of different water solubilities and different viscosities, as well as those with different crystallization characteristics to modify crystallization in foods.

Taste.—Although the polyhydric alcohols are a relatively homogeneous family of compounds, their taste characteristics can vary from the decided harshness of propylene glycol to the semisweetness of sorbitol. Isomers in any one of the higher classifications can show tremendous differences in sweetness, although their overall molecular weight and many other characteristics are similar. However, none of these polyhydric alcohols should be classed as synthetic sweeteners. They range in sweetness from $1/2$ as sweet to essentially $3/4$ as sweet as sugars. The results of a recent study of relative sweetness of polyols and sugars are presented in Table H-3 with a comparison of some earlier published data. This comparative property has been the subject of many studies (Eisenberg 1955; Ulrich 1952).

Hygroscopicity.—The hygroscopicity, or the ability to absorb and retain water under conditions of medium and high relative humidity also varies partially according to molecular weight. Generally, the higher the molecular weight, the less hygroscopic the polyol. A nonhygroscopic material does not imbibe water even at high humidities.

Figure H-5 shows the hygroscopicity for the polyols being considered. The dotted line is invert

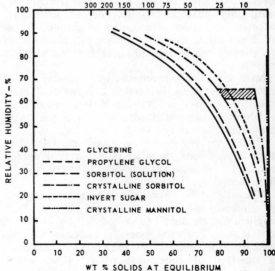

FIG. H-5. COMPARATIVE EQUILIBRIUM HYGROSCOPICITIES OF POLYOLS

sugar, which is only slightly hygroscopic. Cane sugar (sucrose) is even less hygroscopic, because it is relatively more crystalline. The effect of crystallization is shown in Fig. H-5 in the comparison of sorbitol and mannitol. Mannitol, when crystallized (which applies to most of the humidity range), exhibits a very low hygroscopicity, making it useful as a nutritive powder that is stable at high humidity (Atlas Chemical Industries *CD-156*).

For comparison, consider the usual polyols versus a similar food raw material, sugar. Equilibrium data for glycerine, invert sugar, and sorbitol are presented in Fig. H-5.

Proteins, cellulose, and similar products that exhibit a "shelf" in their hygroscopicity at about 13% water actually show a diminution in moisture-holding capacity when small amounts of polyol are added; this is recovered only when the amount of polyol becomes appreciable with relation to the other ingredients.

A further consideration with respect to hygroscopicity is whether static (equilibrium) or dynamic moisture control is the point at issue. Most reported data, as in Fig. H-5, are equilibrium values. Seldom is it practical to add sufficient polyol to achieve adequate moisture levels or protection from evaporation at low humidities, or even moderate humidities. This is true primarily because foods inherently have high moisture levels to provide the desired texture, taste, and mouth feel.

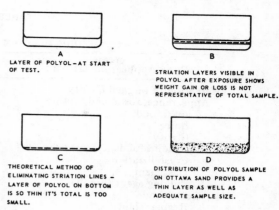

FIG. H-7. HYGROSCOPICITY DETERMINATIONS

On the other hand, polyols in many instances can help control the rate of moisture gain and loss (Atlas Chemical Industries *CD-156*). Generally, the higher the molecular weight, the lower the rate of change (Fig. H-6). Note, though, that these rate change times are short term hours, not days or weeks; and moisture levels over longer periods of time are not controlled by humectants under these circumstances; rather, control is effected by vapor-resistant packaging.

Dynamic hygroscopicity, the rate with which moisture is gained or lost, is far more difficult to measure accurately. Hygroscopicity is often studied by placing a small amount of liquid, unstirred, in a crystallizing dish or beaker and exposing it to a higher or lower humidity (Fig. H-7A). If the sample is carefully examined after this exposure, striation lines will be observed showing that the surface concentration has changed because of either gain or loss (Fig. H-7B). At this point, change in weight of the sample is related not only to the rate of gain or loss of moisture at the surface of the sample but also to the rate of moisture transfer within the bulk of the sample, which is, in many instances, the controlling function. The ideal situation would be to present essentially a layer of polyol only a few molecules thick, as in Fig. H-7C. Since the sample would be too small to note meaningful weight changes, it appears most expedient to disperse a small sample on Ottawa sand and observe the rate of moisture change (Fig. H-7D). Even with this method, it is necessary to take precautions that the samples are exposed to a uniform draft, maintained, of course, at a constant temperature and constant relative humidity. Following these techniques, valid dynamic hygroscopicity information can be obtained. Figure H-6 shows data obtained on sorbitol and glycerine by this technique.

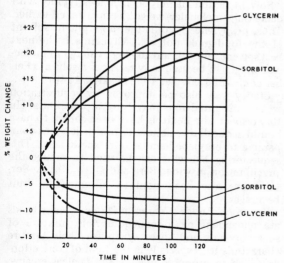

FIG. H-6. COMPARATIVE DYNAMIC HYGRO-
SCOPICITIES OF POLYOLS

Source: Atlas Sorbitol and Related Polyols, CD-60.
Copyright 1951, Atlas Chemical Industries, Inc.—
now ICI America Inc. Revised June 1953.

TABLE H-4

POLYHYDRIC ALCOHOL FOOD APPLICATIONS

Food Application Effects	Achieved by
Retention of original quality:	
Appearance, form, and texture	
Liquid foods	
Body	Viscosity
Clarity	Solvency, sequestration
Semisolid foods, creams or pastes	
Crystallization	Crystallization modification
Plasticizing	Plasticizer-softener
Bulking agent (liquid)	Solubility/viscosity
Solid foods	
Regular solid foods	Humidity resistance
Rehydrated foods	
Taste	
Sweetness control	Sweetness
Flavor stabilization	Antioxidants, sequestration
Preservative (microbiological)	Preservative action, osmotic affect

Food Application Effects

Polyhydric alcohols are added to manufactured foods, either to promote the retention of the original quality of the food on aging and shipment to the consumer, or to gain a texture or product quality that was not present in the original formula. Table H-4 shows a comparison of the most usually desired effects with the polyol properties utilized to achieve the effects.

Appearance, Form and Texture.—The importance of appearance of food can hardly be over-rated. Appetizing food is a combination of appearance and flavor. These are further composed of form, texture, and color, and, relative to taste, flavor, and odor. Of course, texture is a component of taste as well. The problem of proper appearance, and hence acceptability, exists in the entire range of foods, from liquid to solid. Polyol effects vary sufficiently that it is desirable to consider these three classes separately.

Liquid Foods (Beverages).—The major effect of polyols added to foods is one of body. This is related to viscosity.

While the viscosity effect of a dilute polyol is minimal when compared with viscous liquids, it is apparently an effect that the tongue and other sensory receptors of the mouth are able to discern. Relatively small proportions of polyols added to beverages convey an improvement in mouth feel that is described as bodying action. Similar effects are obtained with thickening agents, although frequently their overall characteristics are not as desirable as those of polyols.

Polyols may be employed in some foods to increase their viscosity and in others to effect a reduction. Sorbitol is effective in increasing viscosity because of the inherent high viscosity of its aqueous solution. Propylene glycol represents the other end of the viscosity scale. Often the best control of viscosity can be achieved by a blend of glycerine, sorbitol and sugars.

Clarity of a beverage is often important to its appearance. This may be achieved with polyols by improvement in solubility characteristics of the ingredients and the vehicles.

Solvent action of polyols increases rapidly with decreasing molecular weight as mentioned earlier. Thus, propylene glycol is the most potent solvent of the food-grade polyols. Glycerine is the next best solvent, but it is already high enough in molecular weight to be used only rarely as a solvent (Felber *et al.* 1959; Fiedler 1959; Lakritz 1946).

Clarity may also be improved by sequestration where unwanted ions may form a precipitate. In this respect, the hexitols have been shown to have a mild sequestering action, although it is not comparable to ethylenediamine tetra acetic acid. This sequestering behavior can be used to reduce the precipitation in wine (Berg and Ough 1962). Sorbitol has also been used to advantage in fruit beverages.

Semisolid Foods (Creams or Pastes.)—Many foods are dependent on a semiequilibrium mixture of sugar crystals and sugar syrup for their texture characteristics, especially in the field of confectionery. These products include the typical creams, fondants, and fudge. Because the crystallization continues in storage, this type of product exhibits a limited shelf-life with reference to texture. It has long been standard practice to add invert sugar as a "doctor" to maintain the desired consistency. It has been found that the addition of glycerine and sorbitol, when properly employed, can increase the shelf-life by further complexing the crystalline nature of the confection, thus reducing its tendency to harden. DuRoss (1968) has studied the development of sugar crystals with and without the addition of sorbitol and has shown a beneficial difference (Alikonis 1957; Barnett 1961, 1965; Childs 1961; DuRoss 1968, 1967; Hachtman 1968; Kapeller 1952; Shearon 1952). This reduction in crystallizing tendencies is also of value in the production of marshmallow and nougat where the crystallization inhibitory action provides advantages in processing (Glabau 1956; Anon. 1957; Downey 1962). Polyhydric alcohols are included in military specifications for shelf-life improvement (MIL-C-10928B, Jan. 1956).

The soft consistency of some foods is achieved by the use of polyols and/or sugars for their softening or plasticizing effect. This is at least partially allied with the moisture-holding power of the polyols, especially since water is one of the best plasticizers. However, for shelf stability reasons, a minimum moisture content is often desirable. Polyols no doubt satisfy some of the hydrogen bonding tendencies of the aqueous food systems and at low moisture levels the lower molecular weight polyols exhibit a basic softening effect.

Humectancy, hygroscopicity, or moisture-holding power of a polyol added to a confection has been reported to be of importance in maintaining freshness. It is believed that the effect of crystal modification discussed in the previous section is of far greater importance. This belief is based on the premise that the amounts of polyols that are employed cannot sufficiently influence the moisture-holding power of the confection to create the indicated effect. The loss of moisture has been shown not to be a primary factor in bread or cake staling (Herz 1965). Usually, polyols are added at considerably less than 10% of the weight of the confection; if they were twice as effective at holding moisture, they would tend to raise the moisture-holding power by less than 5%. Humectancy is important in the processing of marshmallows where the rate of moisture loss to the casting starch over a specific time interval is reduced (Anon. 1957; Glabau 1956; Downey 1962).

Polyols are often used as bulking agents in semisolid and solid foods and their concentrates or mixes. The need for bulking agents is usually occasioned by the use of an artificial sweetener. For example, if saccharin is used instead of sugar, one of the immediate problems that is encountered is the reduction in solids content of the food or the change in ratio of solids of sweetener to other ingredients. A few milligrams of artificial sweetener are equivalent to one ounce of sugar. In foods such as ice cream, cakes, cookies, and confections, the problem is pronounced. Elimination of the sugar gives a totally unbalanced formula that does not behave properly and results in an unpalatable end product. Polyols such as sorbitol and mannitol are commonly-used bulking agents, replacing sugar generally on an equivalent basis.

Solid Foods.—There are only a limited number of truly solid foods, for example, hard candy, dry cereals, crackers and chips, and dehydrated foods. In most instances, these products attain and retain their appearance and consistency by virtue of a very low water content. Polyols are used to only a limited extent under these circumstances, the dry condition being attained by proper packaging. However, an example of the application of polyols is the use of mannitol as a moisture-resisting dusting powder for some types of chewing gum. A further advantage here is the cool, sweet taste exhibited by mannitol (Atlas Chemical Industries *CD-156*).

In some solid food concentrates, for example, an imitation orange juice, polyols may be used as flavor carriers. For example, sorbitol and mannitol have been used in various ways: (1) as flavor carriers or flavor-encapsulating agents (Dame 1967; Griffin 1951; Schapiro 1959; Strachun et al. 1958); (2) as flavor enhancers in a wide variety of products, such as coffee concentrates (Epstein 1948), meat-curing compositions (Hall 1954; Hall and Kalchbrenner 1956; Kahn et al. 1960), flavor additives for nuts (Avera 1958, 1960), and pure juice concentrates (Dimick et al. 1960); and (3) in a number of flavor-enhancing compositions (Dame 1967; Schimazono et al. 1967; Anon. 1953, 1956).

The dehydration of foods is of value in preservation and reduction in weight for shipping. Unfortunately, in many instances food dehydration causes difficulty in rehydration, and the reconstituted food is significantly different from the original food. Many years ago, the use of a hexitol to improve the rehydration and terminal characteristics of vegetables was described (Brandner 1947). More recently, the armed services laboratories have determined that the inclusion of a small amount of a polyol blend during dehydration will allow a marked improvement in quality of rehydration characteristics (Brockmann 1969). It is probable that the polyol prevents the total collapse of the cellular structure during dehydration and keeps it in a better form for acceptance of water at the time of rehydration.

Taste.—Taste, to the consumer, is a complex sensation, comprising flavor, texture, temperature, mouth feel, and other factors, both physical and chemical. Taste actually is chemical (salt, sour, bitter, sweet). The taste of polyols is generally of little consequence since they usually constitute a minor additive. When a polyol is a major component, such as in sugar-free candies, it may be the major source of sweetness. Sorbitol and mannitol are especially effective in this application. Relative sweetness levels were discussed earlier (see Table H-3). From this, it is apparent that the polyols, as a class, are not suitable sugar replacements, nor are they synthetic sweeteners.

On the other hand, even in minor amounts, polyols may exert a decided improvement. Polyols have also been used to modify the sweetness of a product rather than to create sweetness. Sorbitol has been reported to cause a taste improvement when used with saccharin (Vincent *et al.* 1955; Walker 1951) by inhibiting the strong bitter characteristic that is correlated with saccharin (Vincent *et al.* 1955; Helgrin *et al.* 1955). In wine, a small amount of sorbitol exhibits a distinct smoothing and bodying action, probably due to a combination of viscosity and sequestrant (or complexing action) (Berg and Ough 1962).

The objectionable off-taste called rancidity may occur as a result of one or both of two chemical reactions. The first is oxidation of double bonds, catalyzed by heavy metals; the second is hydrolytic rancidity.

Hexitols exert a mild sequestering action, as noted in the previous discussion of sequestering; in a few instances, particularly with natural oils present such as in butter, a mild reduction in rate of rancidity formation may be observed.

Polyols may also aid in hydrolytic rancidity, glycerine having been reported to retard free fatty-acid formation and thus reduce the rancidity tendency (Robinson 1956).

Microbiological Preservation

Polyols as well as sugars act as preservatives at high concentrations based generally on osmotic-pressure effects. These concentration levels are usually at greater than 75 weight percent to be effective. An exception to this is the effectiveness of propylene glycol as a preservative. Often propylene glycol is effective at a level as low as 10%. In many instances, combinations of propylene glycol and higher molecular weight polyols are employed (Barr and Tice 1957).

In the same fashion, as one is able to retain original characteristics it is possible to achieve new food properties with the use of polyols in conjunction with modification of standard recipes. This is especially true in the formulation of dietary foods. Polyols are used in dietary foods as replacements for sugars, an application related to bulking. The metabolism of hexitols in comparison with sugars has been studied, although not extensively (Olmsted 1953). Studies have shown that sorbitol is less readily attacked by *Lactobacillus* than sucrose—thus, possibly reducing potential tooth decay (Felber *et al.* 1959; Frostell 1963, 1965). At times, processors have labeled their products "sugar-free" when using the hexitols in place of sugar. This may have some valid basis on the above, but often the inference leads the consumer to believe the product contains fewer or no calories. This is not true, since basically the hexitols have the same caloric value as sugar—and this is true of the polyols in general. Certain polyols (mannitol and dulcitol) actually afford fewer absorbed calories because of the lack of solubility. The major uses in dietetic foods have been in confectionery products (Knetchtel 1964; Kuzio 1964; Langwill 1953; Meyer 1967; Pratt 1953).

How to Select a Polyol

There is no easily followed set of instructions or method in the selection of polyols for food applications. Property improvements that are desired should be considered and compared with the reasons for use presented above. Based on the desired functionality indicated, polyols should be evaluated at probably what initially would appear to be higher than desirable levels. This type of

TABLE H-5

GUIDE FOR CHOOSING POLYHYDRIC ALCOHOLS

	Propylene Glycol	Glycerine	Sorbitol	Mannitol
Crystallization modifier		X	X	
Humectant	X	X	X	
(Moisture resistant dust)				X
Plasticizer		X		
Bodying agent			X	
Solvent	X			
Bulking agent			X	X
Rehydration		X	X	

evaluation will give an indication as to whether or not the inclusion of a polyol will have any effect on the formula. Should a desired effect be observed, retrial at lower levels will allow a choice of concentration that should be suitable.

A brief summarization of behavior characteristics and application data has been assembled in Table H-5 for use as a starting reference to simplify the selection of a polyol to perform a specific task.

Equipment

Most of the polyols above that contain more than a three carbon-chain length are available in either crystalline form or a solution or syrup. The choice of liquid or solid will depend on the economics of handling and the desired moisture content of the final product. Where a low final moisture content is desired, for example, as in some forms of tableted mints, it may be desirable or even necessary to maintain a relatively uniform low humidity in the manufacturing area throughout the year. Seldom is it necessary to go below approximately 40% RH (75°F) to gain excellent processing characteristics.

WILLIAM C. GRIFFIN
MATTHEW J. LYNCH

References

ALIKONIS, J. 1957. Aeration in candy technology. Mfg. Confectioner 37, No. 5, 35–37.

ANON. 1953. Solid odors and flavors have greatly improved stability. Chem. Eng. News 31, No. 20, 2094–2096.

ANON. 1956. Flavor in citrus concentrates. Givauden Flavorits No. 1, 3.

ANON. 1957. Marshmallow and nougat—nonstop. Food Eng. 29, No. 4, 104–107.

BARNETT, C. D. 1961. How to extend shelf-life of candies, Mfg. Confectioner 41, 37–40.

BARNETT, C. D. 1965. Shelf-life can be adjusted by two means. Candy Ind. 124, 31–33.

BARR, M., and TICE, L. F. 1957. The inhibitory concentrations of various sugars and polyols on the growth of microorganisms. J. Am. Pharm. Assoc. 46, 219–221.

BENSON, F. R. 1963. Polyhydric alcohols. In Encyclopedia of Chemical Technology, 2nd Edition, Vol. 1. R. E. Kirk and D. F. Othmer (Editors). John Wiley & Sons, New York.

BERG, H. W., and OUGH, C. S. 1962. Wines and Vines. Hiaring Co., San Francisco.

BROCKMANN, M. C. 1969. Compaction of military foods. Res. Develop. Assoc. Activities Rept. 21, No. 2, 83–87.

CHILDS, W. 1961. Superior fudge and caramel processing time cut to less than four minutes. Candy Ind. 117, 51–52.

DuROSS, J. W. 1967. How sorbitol keeps soft candies in desired state. Candy Ind. Conf. J. 128, No. 1, 34.

DuROSS, J. W. 1968. Functionality and application of sorbitol 70% solution in confectionery products. Proc. 22nd Ann. Production Conf., Penn. Mfg. Confectioners' Assoc.

EISENBERG, S. 1955. Use of sugars and other carbohydrates in the food industry. Advan. Chem. Ser. 12, 78.

FELBER, J. P., RENOLD, A. E., and SAHND, G. R. 1959. The comparative metabolism of glucose, fructose, galactose, and sorbitol in normal subjects and in disease states. Mod. Probl. Pediat. 4, 467–489.

FIEDLER, W. C. 1959. Flavor-masking a new calcium syrup. Am. J. Pharm. 131, 217–223.

FREE, M. 1970. Fructose—the extraordinary natural sweetener. Food Prod. Develop. Febr.–Mar. 38–39.

FROSTELL, G. 1963. A new type of presumably low cariogenic sweets. Sverges Tandlakarforbunds Tidning 55, 529–531.

FROSTELL, G. 1965. The shape of the Stephan-curve after ingestion of different kinds of sweets. Sverges Tendlakarforbunds Tidning 57, 696–704.

GLABAU, C. A. 1956. Formula and handling of the ever popular marshmallow. Baker's Weekly 172, No. 10, 45–47.

HELGREN, F. J., LYNCH, M. J., and KIRCHMEYER, F. J. 1955. A taste panel study of the saccharin "off-taste." J. Am. Pharm. Assoc., Sci. Edition 44, No. 6, 353–355.

HERZ, K. O. 1965. Staling of bread—a review. Food Technol. Dec., 94.

KAPELLER, A. R. 1952. Sorbitol and its application in the confectionery and chocolate industry. Intern. Chocolate Rev., Mar., 74–76.

KNECHTEL, H. 1964. What the candy manufacturer should know about dietetic confectionery. Candy Ind. Conf. J. 123, No. 11, 37–38.

KUZIO, W. 1964. Estee finds dietetic candy a growth field. Candy Ind. Conf. J. 123, No. 11, 8, 26, 35.

LAKRITZ, D. E. 1946. Propylene glycol can become the most important flavor solvent. Flavors 9, No. 6, 11–12.

LANGWILL, K. E. 1953. Chocolate for the diabetic. Candy Ind. Conf. J., June, 16–21.

OLMSTED, W. H. 1953. The metabolism of mannitol and sorbitol, their use as sugar substitutes in diabetic therapy. Diabetes 2, 132–137.

PRATT, C. D. 1953. Special uses for sorbitol and emulsifiers in confectionery products. Candy Ind. 18, 18, 23.

ROBINSON, H. M. 1956. Stabilization of fats in candy. Mfg. Confectioner 36, 21.

SHEARON, W. H., JR. 1952. Chemistry in candy manufacturing. Chem. Eng. News 30, No. 44, 4606–4610.

ULRICH, K. 1952. The sweetness of synthetic and natural products. Zucker 5, 236–239.

VINCENT, H. C. et al. 1955. A taste panel study of cyclamate-saccharin mixture and of its components, J. Am. Pharm. Assoc., Sci. Edition *44*, No. 7, 442–446.

Patents

AVERA, F. L. 1958. Process of manufacturing coated nuts. U.S. Pat. 2,859,121.

AVERA, F. L. 1960. Nut-flavoring additives. U.S. Pat. 2,955,040.

BRANDNER, J. D. 1947. Dehydration of foods by means of hydrophilic liquids. U.S. Pat. 2,420,517.

DAME, C., JR. 1967. Mannitol foxed flavor and method of making. U.S. Pat. 3,314,803.

DIMICK, K. P. *et al.* 1960. Purification of fruit essences and production of solid compositions. U.S. Pat. 2,949,368.

DOWNEY, H. A. 1962. Marshmallow dry mix. U.S. Pat. 3,018,183.

DuROSS, J. W. 1969. Sugarless confection. U.S. Pat. 3,438,787. Apr. 15.

EPSTEIN, A. A. 1948. Coffee concentrate and the process of producing it. U.S. Pat. 2,457,036.

GRIFFIN, W. C. 1951. Solid essential oil concentrate and process of preparing same. U.S. Pat. 2,566,410.

HALL, L. A. 1954. Manufacture of meat-curing composition. U.S. Pat. 2,668,770.

HALL, L. A., and KALCHBRENNER, W. S. 1956. Meat curing salt compositions. U.S. Pat. 2,770,-548.

HACHTMAN, S. J. 1968. Confection manufacture. U.S. Pat. 3,371,626.

KAHN, L. E. *et al.* 1960. Process of curing meat and composition therefore. U.S. Pat. 2,946,692.

MEYER, E. G. 1967. Process for producing a confectionery cream candy center and the resulting product. U.S. Pat. 3,325,293.

SCHAPIRO, A. 1959. Effervescent drink concentrate and method of making same. U.S. Pat. 2,868,646.

SHIMAZONO, H., *et al.* 1967. Liquid flavor enhancers. U.S. Pat. 3,326,697.

STRASHUN, S. I. *et al.* 1958. Full flavored dehydrated food products. U.S. Pat. 2,854,343.

WALKER, H. W. 1951. Synergistically sweetened canned fruits and methods of making the same. U.S. Pat. 2,608,989.

Atlas Chemical Industries Information Booklets

Atlas Chemicals for the Food and Beverage Industry, *ILG-91*.

General Characteristics of Atlas Polyols, *CD-156*.

Sorbitol and Related Polyols, *CD-60*.

HYDROGEN PEROXIDE

While hydrogen peroxide is probably best known for its effect as a chemical preservative (*q.v.*) in food technology, i.e., its bacteriostatic or bacteriocidal effect, it finds other uses in which this effect and some other property combine to produce a desired result. Thus, Reichert and Sparks (1934) describe a process for making bread, cakes, or biscuits without the use of yeast or CO_2-evolving substances in which H_2O_2 equivalent to 0.5–2.0% of the flour is incorporated into the dough. The dough is allowed to stand and the leavening accomplished by reaction between H_2O_2 and flour catalase.

Perhaps the most extensive investigations have involved procedures to "sterilize" milk by the substitution of H_2O_2 treatment for pasteurization. Roundy (1958) reviewed some of the early work on treatment of milk with H_2O_2, in particular on milk destined for cheese making, commenting on the advantages and disadvantages of H_2O_2 treatment of cheese milk and giving details of the processing. Morris (1951) reported on a comparative study on the treatment of milk with H_2O_2 and pasteurization. A series of experiments with 3 classes of milk showed that treatment of milk with 0.2% H_2O_2 followed by addition of a catalase enzyme to remove residual enzyme compared well with pasteurization in all respects. It has been observed generally that the H_2O_2-catalase treatment yields milk of reduced curd tension and cheese of soft body. The use of the H_2O_2-catalase treatment of milk does not find general use except under special conditions. Toma (1967) used the H_2O_2-catalase treatment of high bacterial count milk in the production of Kachkaval cheese and to prevent "blowing" in Edam cheese. Tentoni and associates (1968) used H_2O_2 levels up to 550 ppm for milk to be collected under difficult conditions.

Koop and Westerbeck (1970) noted that the heat stability of concentrated skim milk is increased under certain conditions by small addition of H_2O_2. This phenomenon has been applied in the preparation of sterilized whole milks. Guy and associates (1968) showed that milk preheated at 63°C or 85°C for 30 min and treated with 0.25% H_2O_2 yielded a dried product which, when used in bread making, resulted in the production of bread of greater volume and superior total score as compared to high-heat treatment alone.

Rogers and associates (1972) describe treating whole egg magma with H_2O_2 and heating to 130°–150°F to prepare a pasteurized product free of Salmonella. Sigmund (1969) found that 0.25% of a 30% H_2O_2 solution was sufficient to supply the oxygen for the desaccharification of liquid whole egg.

Considerable application has been made of H_2O_2 in Japanese food technology in treating fish flour, soy protein, and other protein products to improve organoleptic properties. Thus Solomon (1971) describes a process for boiling fish meat in water,

treating with H_2O_2, heating at a temperature of 70°C, converting to a slurry, and dehydrating to yield a product of improved flavor, odor, and color.

Hydrogen peroxide is sometimes employed in Japanese food technology for certain foods which are held in a moist stage during their manufacture, such foods as rice cakes, pasta products, and soybean curd. Kawasaki and associates (1971) have described the use of H_2O_2 in the production of noodles and have discussed the general sterilizing effect of H_2O_2 in food. Another Japanese application (Sigmund 1969) is the immersion of seeds or nuts in aqueous peroxide before wet skinning in order to cause the skin to loosen by generation of oxygen.

There are also many strictly chemical applications of H_2O_2 to food technological processing. Thus Rao (1971) describes the detoxification of defatted castor bean meal with the possibility of yielding a source of protein for man. Mitsyk and co-workers (1972) describe a decolorization system for commercial fats using H_2O_2. A 33% solution of H_2O_2 is introduced into the fat and the batch heated to 65°–70°C for 40–60 min. After washing the fat with hot water, the residual peroxide is removed with catalase. The amount of peroxide required is 2.5–3.0% of the fat weight. The method of decolorization was considered preferable to the use of solid absorbents since the latter retained a part of the fat.

In its function as a bleaching agent decomposing to yield water and oxygen, H_2O_2 finds other applications such as the treatment of tripe in the meat industry, the stabilization of color during heat-degassing of anthocyanin-containing fruit juices, and the preparation of modified starches. In some instances approval by food regulatory agencies may be required.

ARNOLD H. JOHNSON

References

GUY, E. J., VITTEL, H. E., and PALLANSCH, M. J. 1968. Effect of hydrogen peroxide treatment of skim milk for sponge bread baking. Cereal Sci. Today 13, 434.
KAWASAKI, C., NAGANO, H., and KONO, K. 1971. Sterilizing effect of hydrogen peroxide in food. J. Food Hyg. Soc. Japan 11, 139 (1970); cited in Food Sci. Technol. Abstr. 3, 12M1394.
KOOP, J., and WESTERBECK, D. 1970. Some features of the heat stability of concentrated milk. II The effect of hydrogen peroxide. Neth. Milk Dairy J. 24, 52.
MITSYK, V. et al. 1972. Peroxide-catalase method of decolorizing commercial fat. Myasnaya Industriya SSSR 42, No. 9, 21 (1971); cited in Food Sci. Technol. Abstr. 4, 8N391.

MORRIS, A. J. 1951. A comparative study of the treatment of milk with hydrogen peroxide and pasteurization. Proc. Western Div. Am. Dairy Sci. Assoc. (1950). Dairy Sci. Abstr. 13, 8.
RAO, K. H. 1971. Toxic factors and their detoxification in castor. J. Food Sci. Technol. (Mysore) 7, 77 (1970); cited in Food Sci. Technol. Abstr. 3, 10T511.
REICHERT, J. S., and SPARKS, W. J. 1934. Use of hydrogen peroxide as a dough leavening agent. U.S. Pat. 1,953, 567, April 3.
ROGERS, A. B., SEBRING, M., and KLINE, R. W. 1972. Whole egg magma. U.S. Pat. 3,658,558, June 8.
ROUNDY, Z. D. 1958. Treatment of milk for cheese with hydrogen peroxide. J. Dairy Sci. 41, 1460.
SIGMUND, V. 1969. Effect of oxygen on enzymatic desaccharification of liquid whole eggs. Hydinarsky Priemysel 10, 225 (1968); cited in Food Sci. Technol. Abstr. 1, 5Q56.
SOLOMON, A. 1971. Fish meal. Japanese Pat. 16,137/71 (1971); cited in Food Sci. Technol. Abstr. 3, 11R482.
TENTONI, R., PASTORE, M., and OTTOGALLI, G. 1968. Hydrogen peroxide for milk collection under difficult conditions. Ann. Microbiol. Enzimol. 18, 85. Cited in Food Sci. Technol. Abstr. 1, 581 (1969).
TOMA, C. 1967. Utilization of hydrogen peroxide in the milk industry. Ind. Aliment. Agr. 18, No. 11, 516.

HYDROGENATION

Hydrogenation is the process by which elemental hydrogen combines catalytically with unsaturated organic compounds. It is conducted extensively in the edible fats and oils industry to modify the characteristics of natural fats and oils. Hydrogenation raises the melting point and increases the hardness so that it is useful in changing vegetable oils from liquids to solids which make them suitable for shortening and margarine.

Hydrogenation came into use in the 1930's when cottonseed oil became increasingly used for food. After World War II, soybean oil became prevalent, and the use of hydrogenated vegetable oils increasingly replaced the use of animal fats for shortening and cooking. With the removal of restrictions on the use of margarine, much of the butter market was replaced by margarine produced from hydrogenated vegetable oils. Today, hydrogenated soybean, cottonseed, corn, and safflower oils are extensively used for margarine and shortening.

The commonly-used catalyst is finely divided metallic nickel. It is produced by reducing finely ground nickel hydroxide with hydrogen in a heated furnace. The reaction takes place at a temperature of about 600°F. The catalyst is highly pyrophoric and burns violently when exposed to air. To protect it from oxidation, it is commonly suspended in a fat or oil which is compatible with the edible products with which it is used.

In another process, a mixture of nickel and aluminum is cast—in granular form. The aluminum is then removed by treating with a caustic soda solution leaving metallic nickel with large surface area. This catalyst has the advantage that it is easily removed from the product by filtration.

Hydrogen is commonly produced by either electrolysis or the reforming of hydrocarbons.

Electrolysis is used only when small quantities are required or when it is a by-product of another process such as the production of metallic sodium and chlorine or caustic soda and chlorine. Electrolytic hydrogen has the advantage of being extremely pure containing only a small amount of water vapor.

Where large quantities of hydrogen are required, it is usually produced by reacting natural gas (which is mostly methane), or occasionally propane, with steam to form hydrogen and carbon dioxide. Methane is preheated, mixed into an accurately measured amount of steam and passed through tubes heated to 1500°F containing a catalyst. The mixture reacts to form hydrogen and carbon monoxide. It is then partially cooled and additional steam added and passed through a catalyst chamber where most of the carbon monoxide reacts with steam to form hydrogen and carbon dioxide. Steam is again added and the mixture is again catalytically reacted to remove all but a trace of carbon monoxide. The carbon dioxide is then absorbed in a solution of monoethanolamine which is continually regenerated by heating to a temperature where the carbon dioxide escapes to the atmosphere. The last traces of carbon monoxide are removed by passing the gas through another catalyst where hydrogen reacts with carbon monoxide to form methane and water.

The newest method for purifying hydrogen is the swing adsorption process. Hydrogen containing carbon dioxide, carbon monoxide, methane, water vapor, and other impurities is passed through a bed of adsorptive material. The large sized molecules are adsorbed and hydrogen of 99.999% purity leaves the bed. This system operates at approximately 250 psi. When the bed becomes saturated with impurities, the flow is stopped and the pressure reduced to near atmosphere and some pure hydrogen is allowed to flow, thus regenerating the bed. By using multiple beds it is possible to maintain a continuous flow. The gases obtained during regeneration have a low fuel value because of the presence of hydrogen and are burned to heat the reformer tubes.

Hydrogen is usually stored in pressure vessels at 100–150 psi. Some hydrogen plants operate at slightly above atmospheric pressure and the gas is compressed with conventional reciprocating compressors. The most recent hydrogen plants operate at storage pressure and the methane is compressed as it enters the system. The latter method requires only $1/4$ the power for compression, since each volume of methane produces 4 volumes of hydrogen.

Most hydrogenation is accomplished in batches, although equipment for continuous operation is now available. The typical hydrogenator is a carbon steel vertical pressure vessel. It is equipped with coils for heating with steam and for cooling with water. Two or more turbine type agitators are mounted on a central shaft which is driven by a motor mounted on top of the vessel. The agitator speeds are usually 100–125 rpm and are sized to require approximately 2 hp per 1000 lb of product. Stationary baffles are located along the wall of the vessel from the bottom up to the normal product level. Usually 4 baffles are used and their width is $1/12$ the vessel diameter. A sparge pipe for the admission of hydrogen is located near the bottom of the vessel.

It is possible to operate a hydrogenator with a thermometer and a pressure gauge and the necessary manual valves for admitting hydrogen, steam, and water, but this method requires constant operator attention. Most units are now equipped with automatic controls to maintain a constant temperature and hydrogen pressure. These controls admit steam at the start, and shut off the steam and admit water as the temperature rises to the set point.

In operation, the vessel is filled to its operating level with the oil to be processed. Usually the feed has been refined and bleached and is free of water and dissolved gases. The oil is first heated to approximately 200°F and a small amount removed to a catalyst mix tank where catalyst is added. The oil and catalyst are then returned to the hydrogenator. Heating is then continued to 250°–275°F at which point hydrogen is admitted through the sparge pipe at a rate to maintain a predetermined pressure. As the hydrogen reacts the temperature rises due to the exothermic reaction and it is necessary to cool with water to maintain the desired temperature.

Hydrogen produced from natural gas usually contains some nitrogen which remains in the hydrogen. Also, some methane is present from incomplete reaction and from the catalytic reaction of carbon monoxide with hydrogen. The hydrogen also is saturated with water vapor at its storage conditions.

The product also always contains some dissolved gases. During hydrogenation these inert gases accumulate in the head space and must be removed to maintain the reaction. Hydrogenators are equipped with a controlled "bleed" to allow the head space gases to escape. A suitable rate of bleed is considered to be 10 volumes of hydrogen to 1 volume of inert gas.

The degree of hydrogenation is determined by measuring its refractive index. When the desired point is reached, the agitator is stopped and the hydrogen cut off. The product is then cooled to about 200°F and then pumped from the vessel through a filter to remove the catalyst. Traces of catalyst in the filtered product cause instability and a second filtration, termed postbleaching, is usually necessary.

Under proper conditions, hydrogenation of the more unsaturated fats proceeds at a more rapid rate than the less saturated. This property is known as selectivity. Selectivity is increased by hydrogenating at a high temperature and low hydrogen pressure and by the use of active catalyst. It is useful in producing products of varying textures for special shortenings and margarines.

Soybean oil contains considerable fat with the linolenic acid radical which is unstable and causes a short shelf-life and off-flavor. For this reason, unmodified soya oil is unsuitable for an all-purpose household oil. By selective hydrogenation, it is possible to convert the linolenic radical to linoleic and oleic radicals. In so doing, some unsaturated fat becomes saturated which causes the oil to become cloudy when cooled. The saturated fat is removed by chilling and filtering. Large amounts of soya oil are now processed in this manner and sold as all-purpose household oil.

Small amounts of saturated fats are used for adjusting the properties of products to a more precise degree than is possible by commercial hydrogenation. Saturated or hard fats are produced by hydrogenation at 50-60 psi hydrogen pressure and by continuing the process to completion.

The activity of catalysts is reduced by impurities in the oils and in the hydrogen gas. Sulfur compounds, water, soap, and carbon monoxide have deleterious effects on nickel catalysts. Since traces of these compounds are always present, the catalyst gradually looses its activity and must be replaced. After a catalyst has been used 4 or 5 times, it is no longer suitable for selective hydrogenation and must be discarded.

The degree of saturation of fats is determined by measuring its iodine value by a chemical test. The higher the iodine value, the greater the degree of unsaturation. The common edible vegetable oils have iodine values ranging from 100 to 150. Fats for shortening and margarine are hydrogenated to an iodine value of 70-90. These products at ambient temperatures are plastic solids.

WILLIAM B. CAMPBELL
B. L. THOMAS

HYDROLYSATES, PROTEIN

Protein hydrolysates were first commercially made in China and Japan around 1900 and originally were by-products of monosodium glutamate manufacture; that is, after the crystallization of the bulk of the MSG the remaining amino acids were neutralized followed by drying. It was found that this by-product had a pleasant flavor which blended well with many food products. Later, the hydrolysate was made directly from proteins without the separation of the MSG. This led to greatly improved products which developed meat-like or chicken-like flavors. In Germany, during World War I, several liquid hydrolysates were prepared commercially from waste protein materials.

The proteins used for the manufacture of hydrolysates include wheat gluten, casein, fish flour, gelatin, yeast, corn gluten, rice gluten, cottonseed flour, and soy protein. The analysis and particular flavor of a hydrolysate is greatly dependent on the starting material, being related to the amino acid composition of the protein. Thus, the hydrolysate produced from gelatin is relatively sweet due to its high glycine content.

Almost all hydrolysates being manufactured follow essentially the same process which involves the addition of the protein material to a water-hydrochloric acid solution followed by refluxing at boiling temperatures for 9-12 hr which completely hydrolyzes the protein to the amino acids. The humin, formed largely from the tyrosine and tryptophan of the protein, is removed and the batch is then neutralized. The liquor may or may not be decolorized with carbon and the product then spray or pan dried.

Procedures involved in using sulfuric acid, alkali, pressure, or enzymes have been used experimentally but with little commercial application. Enzyme hydrolysis of the protein does not destroy the tyrosine or tryptophan, particularly the latter, in the digest as does acid hydrolysis for which reason enzyme hydrolysates may be preferred in cases where the complete amino acid complement of the intact protein is required. However, enzymes do not usually hydrolyze the protein completely to amino acids which results in a bitter-tasting end product not satisfactory for use in most foods.

A typical composition of a protein hydrolysate is:

	(%)
Total solids	97
Ash including NaCl	45
Organic solids	50
Sodium chloride	35
Total nitrogen	7.0
Monosodium glutamate	19.8
Ammonium chloride	3.5
pH 5.2 (3% solution)	

Hydrolysates contain from 30 to 50% salt depending on the concentration of hydrochloric acid used, the protein content in the starting material, and the degree of neutralization.

The usage of hydrolysates has increased greatly through the development of the prepared food era and hydrolysates are present in many food products including:

Soups	Macaroni with
Stews	Meat Sauce
Broths	Poultry Stuffing
Bouillons	and Basting
Bouillon Cubes	Processed Meat
Fish	Hash
Gravies	Meat Sauces
Scrapple	Hors d'oeuvre Pastes
Sandwich Spreads	Cheese Spreads
Headcheese	Pickle Relishes
Mince Meat	Baked Beans
Sausage Meat	Pancake Flour
Goulash	Cheese Rarebits
Biscuits and Crackers	Chili Sauce
Spice Mixtures	Salad Dressings
Chop Suey Sauce	Mayonnaise
Chow Mein	Dog Foods

Many food manufacturers have found that the protein hydrolysates give a more rounded flavor than the MSG itself and for many applications the hydrolysates have replaced MSG. MSG is more of a flavor accentuator whereas the hydrolysates have definite flavors which they contribute to food products.

Partial protein hydrolysates, using the acid system, have been developed where the finished product is a combination of peptides and amino acids. These products prepared by carefully controlled hydrolysis, have much stronger flavor and are finding useful food flavoring applications.

LOUIS SAIR

References

HALL, L. A. 1946. Protein hydrolysates—flavor ingredients for foods. Food Ind. *18*, 681–684, 808–816.

SAIR, L. 1968. Production of flavorful protein hydrolysates. U.S. Pat. 3,391,001.

HYDROLYSIS

Hydrolysis refers to a nucleophilic displacement reaction brought about by attack of the hydroxyl ion of water on a carbon atom. If the attack occurs at a saturated carbon atom such as in the glycosidic bond of starch, the reaction is termed O-alkylation, and if the attack is at a carbonyl carbon such as in the amides of proteins and the esters of lipids, the reaction is referred to as solvolysis (Roberts and Caserio 1965). In either case, covalently linked compounds are hydrolyzed by reaction with water to yield simpler units.

Hydrolysis is conventionally achieved by chemical means involving the use of an acidic, basic, or other chemical catalyst. However, to gain more selective hydrolysis, enzymes are often used. Processes utilizing hydrolysis are important in the food industry and are used commercially for production of food ingredients such as corn syrups, fatty acids, amino acids, etc., and for *in situ* alteration of the physical, chemical, and nutritional properties of foods.

Carbohydrates Hydrolysis

Chemical Hydrolysis.—Acid is normally used to catalyze carbohydrate hydrolysis. The rate of the reaction depends on the concentration and structure of the carbohydrate, the concentration and type of acid, and the hydrolysis temperature and duration (Whistler and Paschall 1965; Pigman 1957).

Hydrochloric acid is most commonly used as a catalyst and the choice of concentration and hydrolysis temperature and duration are primarily dependent on the carbohydrate structure. In this regard, α-D-glycosidic bonds are more readily hydrolyzed than β-D-glycosidic bonds and polysaccharides with furanoside units are more readily attacked than those with hexopyranoside units. Glycuronans are even more acid-resistant and are only slowly hydrolyzed by normal hydrochloric acid. Apparently glycuronans undergo more extensive hydrolysis elsewhere in the molecule than at the glycuronopyranosidic bond.

Alkaline conditions are only used for hydrolysis of the ester linkages in pectin. Little is known about the alkaline hydrolysis of other carbohydrates and it has thus found little use in the industry.

Starch.—Acid hydrolysis alone or in combination with enzymes is the most common means of starch hydrolysis. Starch is hydrolyzed to produce the regular acid conversion syrup by acidifying a slurry of starch to pH 1.8 and heating at 120°C for 20–30 min. Such a syrup has a dextrose equivalent of 42 and has about the following composition: dextrose 22%, maltose 20%, tri- and tetrasaccharides 20%, and dextrins 38% (Reed 1966). Acid hydrolysis usually yields the same percentage of different sugars at any given dextrose equivalent value.

By increasing the duration of the hydrolysis, starch syrups can be prepared to a dextrose equivalent of 58–60. However, syrups tend to become bitter and glucose has a tendency to crystallize when hydrolysis is carried beyond this point. If hydrolysis is extended for glucose production, about 80% of anhydrous glucose (based on starch) can be crystallized (Whistler and Paschall 1965).

Pectin.—Reaction of pectin with acid proceeds slowly resulting in the removal of ester groups. With prolonged treatment, high concentrations of acid or alkali and high temperatures, the $1 \rightarrow 4$ linkages are also hydrolyzed. To accomplish de-esterification with as little degradation of the macromolecule as possible in most instances, a 3% solution of pectin is adjusted to a pH of 0.3 with hydrochloric acid and kept at temperatures below 50°C (Kertesz 1951). The main advantage of acid hydrolysis is that admixed undesirable hemicellulases are extensively hydrolyzed.

Alkaline de-esterification proceeds at a rate 100 times faster than that of acid de-esterification and the bulk of the ester groups are removed within a few minutes (Kertesz 1951). To avoid further degradation of the pectin chains, most workers recommend careful de-esterification of pectin at pH values below 8.5 and at temperatures not exceeding 35°C (Kertesz 1951). Ammonium hydroxide provides slower catalysis than sodium hydroxide but is used when low-ash pectins are needed.

Cellulose.—Complete acid hydrolysis of cellulose gives 95–96% glucose (Meyer 1960). Essentially the same principles of acid hydrolysis which are used with starch can be applied to cellulose although slightly higher acid concentrations and temperatures and longer reaction times are required because of the greater stability of β linkages towards hydrolysis.

Lactose.—Lactose is somewhat resistant to hydrolysis; however Ramsdell and Webb (1945) reported that a 30% solution of lactose is 93% hydrolyzed in less than 65 min in 0.007 M HCl at 147°C. Pressure is needed for the process and high grade pure lactose must be used to prevent browning reactions.

Sucrose.—Acid hydrolysis of sucrose is most commonly used for invert sugar production. Reducing the pH of the reaction by 1 unit increases the hydrolysis rate 10-fold whereas increasing the temperature by 10°C increases the rate 2.8 times (Honig 1953). It would theoretically take 40 min to achieve 100% inversion at a pH of 3.0 and a temperature of 100°C (Silin 1964).

Enzymatic Hydrolysis.—Specific enzymes are available for hydrolysis of each type of carbohydrate. Enzymatic hydrolysis is usually more costly; however, pure carbohydrate solutions are not necessary and a more specific breakdown can be achieved without the degradation of other food components.

Starch.—α-amylase, β-amylase and glucoamylase are the enzymes commonly used for starch hydrolysis (Knight 1969). Starch gelatinization is required for the action of enzymes and this limits the concentration of starch to about 20% (Reed 1966). On extended hydrolysis α-amylase converts starch to maltose, glucose, and limit dextrins; while β-amylase converts starch to maltose, limit dextrins, and maltotriose. Glucoamylase hydrolyzes the starch directly to glucose.

Acid-enzyme converted syrups are obtained by using acid to convert the starch to a dextrose equivalent of 21 and a combination of starch enzymes to carry the conversion to a dextrose equivalent of 63. The resulting syrup contains approximately 32% dextrose, 44.5% maltose, and 6% dextrin and is better flavored and less viscous than acid converted syrups (Reed 1966). In contrast to acid hydrolyzates, enzyme hydrolyzates may have entirely different compositions at the same dextrose equivalent depending upon the conditions of the hydrolytic reaction.

Enzymes can also be used consecutively in an enzyme-enzyme conversion with the choice of enzymes depending upon the desired composition of the syrup. By using a bacterial amylase followed by a glucoamylose over 90% of the starch can be converted to glucose (Reed 1966).

Pectin.—The enzymes catalyzing pectin hydrolysis are classified into two groups: polygalacturonases, which split the glycosidic linkage between adjoining galacturonic acid molecules, and pectin methyl esterases which split the ester linkage between methyl esters of the galacturonic acid molecules (Reed 1966).

One of the major uses of pectic enzymes is for fruit juice clarification. Several sources of enzymes are available but usually a preparation is selected which has a pH optimum near to that of the fruit juice in question and which contains both a pectin methyl esterase and a polygalacturonase (Reed 1966). In apple juice at a pH of 3 and a temperature of 5°C, 250 min are required for full clarification.

The use of fungal pectin methyl esterase for preparation of low-ester pectins is rapid and easy to control; however, low-ester pectins prepared thus show certain undesirable characteristics in gel preparations due to a nonrandom removal of ester groups.

Cellulose.—The enzyme cellulase breaks the gly-cosidic linkage of cellulose first yielding linear, insoluble glucose chains and eventually soluble low molecular weight products. A powerful cellulase from *Trichoderma köningii* hydrolyzes native cellulose completely to glucose (Reed 1966).

Lactose.—Lactase (β-galactosidase) enzymes obtained from yeast and fungi offer the most feasible means of lactose hydrolysis since browning reactions can be avoided. Commercial yeast preparations hydrolyze from 7 to 10 times their weight of lactose per hour under optimum conditions (Reed 1966). With a concentration of 2% of an enzyme preparation (based on lactose), skim milk or sweet whey shows 30% hydrolysis after 4 hr at 48°C (Reed 1966). Addition of 100 ppm of sodium sulfite increases hydrolysis to 86% in the skim milk and 90% in the whey.

Sucrose.—Sucrose can be hydrolyzed by yeast invertase, a fructosidase, or taka-invertase, a glucosidase. Preparations of these enzymes have a pH optimum between 4.5 and 5.5 and a temperature optimum of 55°C for dilute sucrose solutions and 65°–70°C for concentrated sucrose solutions. Optimum conversion of sucrose is obtained at about 5–8% sucrose, and at 70% sucrose the rate is only $1/4$ that of the maximum rate (Reed 1966).

Protein Hydrolysis

Chemical Hydrolysis.—Acid hydrolysis has classically been used for hydrolysis of proteins both for subsequent amino acid analysis and for commercial production of protein hydrolyzates. For small quantities of proteins, particularly for amino acid analysis, the proteins are heated *in vacuo* to 110°C in 6 N HCl for 24 hrs (Schultz 1964). However, in large-scale hydrolysis, the proteins are often mixed with 6 N hydrochloric acid and heated under pressure, thus yielding the hydrochloride derivatives of the amino acids (Powell 1968). Cation and anion exchange resins also act as catalysts and give the same pattern of amino acids as hydrochloric acid except that there is a low yield of glutamic acid (Joslyn 1970). Acid hydrolysis is disadvantageous since tryptophan, asparagine, glutamine and small quantities of other amino acids are destroyed and extended hydrolysis is necessary to release all of the amino acids. Also acid hydrolysis results in the production of humin or humin-like materials which complicates recovery of amino acids from the hydrolyzate.

Alkaline hydrolysis of proteins is often used where acid hydrolysis is undesirable. It can be achieved using sodium or potassium hydroxide along with heat. In some instances the hydroxides of calcium, barium, and strontium are more desirable since these compounds are easily precipitated and removed from the hydrolyzate. The use of alkali for hydrolysis is limited because of racemization and complete destruction of certain amino acids.

Enzymatic Hydrolysis.—Theoretically the most efficient method of protein hydrolysis is by enzymes. Enzymes give high yields of peptides which are less complex and more easily fractionated and avoid a nonhydrolytic alteration or destruction of products.

There are a number of proteolytic enzymes available for hydrolyzing proteins. The choice of an enzyme for a particular use must be based on the specificity, pH optimum, heat stability, effect of activators and inhibitors, and the price and availability of the enzyme needed (Reed 1966). Papain is the most widely-used proteolytic enzyme in the food industry and has a rather broad specificity producing more extensive hydrolysis than many of the other proteases. Microbial proteases have potentially the widest application because of a wide pH optima, substrate specificity, and high activity.

A substrate-to-enzyme ratio of 100:1 to 360:1 is normally used for protein hydrolysis and the reaction is carried out at room temperature or up to 37°C for 1–6 hr (Joslyn 1970). Hydrolysis is seldom complete, usually only 50–70% hydrolysis is obtained. Complete hydrolysis almost to the extent of acid hydrolysis can be obtained by first digesting with papain and then treating with leucine aminopeptidase and prolidase (Joslyn 1970).

Lipid Hydrolysis

Fat or lipid hydrolysis, often referred to as fat splitting, results in the release of fatty acids from glycerol. The reaction proceeds in stages with the fatty acid radicals being displaced from the triglyceride molecule one at a time, so that an incompletely split fat contains glycerol, fatty acids, and mono-, di-, and triglycerides.

Chemical Hydrolysis.—Chemically catalyzed hydrolysis occurs through the action of water dispersed in the fat phase and the reaction is accelerated by increasing the temperature and by adding mineral acids, certain metal oxides, and organic compounds of the Twitchell type (Bailey 1951). Since fat splitting is reversible, a point of equilibrium is reached between hydrolysis and re-esterification and the maximum obtainable degree of splitting is a function of the concentration of glycerol in the water. There is no considerable difference in the reaction rates of saturated and unsaturated fatty acids except in alkali saponification where more saturated fats are preferred (Bailey 1951).

The selection of a hydrolytic process must be based on the type of raw material, the size of operation, and the number and kinds of raw materials handled (Pattison 1968). The most common process is the Twitchell process which consists of boiling the fat-water mixture with steam in the presence of a Twitchell reagent such as sulfonic acid. A 92-95% split can be obtained by use of relatively simple equipment and low temperatures. The process does, however, require a long reaction time and a high steam consumption (Bailey 1951).

The high pressure or batch autoclave process requires less time and produces lighter color fatty acids than the Twitchell process. Zinc oxide is used as a catalyst and the fat-water mixture heated under 150 lb pressure to 365°F (Pattison 1968). A 95% split can be obtained in 6-10 hr.

Continuous countercurrent splitting offers the most feasible means of fat hydrolysis. The process employs a countercurrent flow of fat and water in a splitting tower. A 96-99% split can be achieved in 2 hr at 250°-260°C and 750 psi (Pattison 1968). A more concentrated glycerine solution is obtained and the process requires less room, process inventory, and labor (Pattison 1968). It does, however, have less flexibility and can polymerize highly unsaturated oils.

A less common method of hydrolysis involves saponification with caustic soda followed by acidification. The process is more expensive but gives close to 100% conversion and avoids high temperatures (Pattison 1968).

Enzymatic Hydrolysis.—The most common enzymes for fat hydrolysis are lipases, enzymes which hydrolyze insoluble fats and fatty acid esters. Lipases show a nonrandom breakdown of fats due to a preference for certain positions and fatty acid lengths. There are many sources of lipases but the microbial lipases have the widest application showing high activity and wide ranges of pH, chain length, and positional specificity. A crystalline lipase from *Aspergillus niger* results in 93% hydrolysis of olive oil, 86% hydrolysis of cottonseed oil and 85% hydrolysis of soybean oil (Reed 1966). Pregastric lipases from animal sources are often used in the confectionery and cheese indus-

try because of their high specificity for butyric acid.

Lipases are seldom used for commercial fat splitting and find the most use for altering the flavor of food products.

A. L. BRANEN

References

BAILEY, A. E. 1951. Industrial Oil and Fat Products. Interscience Publishers, New York.

HONIG, P. (Editor) 1953. Principles of Sugar Technology. Elsevier Publishing Co., Amsterdam.

JOSLYN, M. A. (Editor) 1970. Methods in Food Analysis. Academic Press, New York.

KERTESZ, Z. I. 1951. The Pectic Substances. Interscience Publishers, New York.

KNIGHT, I. W. 1969. The Starch Industry. Pergamon Press, Oxford, England.

MEYER, L. H. 1960. Food Chemistry, Van Nostrand Reinhold Co., New York.

PATTISON, E. S. 1968. Fatty Acids and Their Industrial Applications. Marcel Dekker, New York.

PIGMAN, W. (Editor) 1957. The Carbohydrates: Chemistry, Biochemistry, Physiology. Academic Press, New York.

POWELL, R. 1968. Monosodium Glutamate and Glutamic Acid. Noyes Development Corp., Park Ridge, N.J.

RAMSDELL, G. A., and WEBB, B. H. 1945. The acid hydrolysis of lactose and the preparation of hydrolyzed lactose sirup. J. Dairy Sci. 28, 677.

REED, G. 1966. Enzymes in Food Processing. Academic Press, New York.

ROBERTS, J. D., and CASERIO, M. C. 1965. Basic Principles of Organic Chemistry. W. A. Benjamin, New York.

SILIN, P. M. 1964. Technology of beet-sugar production and refining. Translated from Russian by Lazar Markin, Israel Program for Scientific Translations, Jerusalem.

SCHULTZ, H. W. 1964. Proteins and Their Reactions. Avi Publishing Co., Westport, Conn.

WHISTLER, R. L., and PASCHALL, E. F. (Editors) 1965. Starch: Chemistry and Technology, Vol. 1. Academic Press, New York.

HYSTERESIS

A dictionary definition of hysteresis includes "a lagging or retardation of an effect, when the forces acting upon a body are changed, as if from viscosity or internal friction." One example, frequently offered in the field of physics, is the residual magnetism that remains for a time in an iron bar after the magnetizing force is removed.

In food systems a number of hysteresis effects are commonly observed. Many have to do with rheological changes in plastic systems and in colloidal gels. Others show up as differences in the melting and solidifying temperatures of food constituents. Still others are related to moisture adsorption and desorption phenomena in frozen and dehydrated foods.

To understand the underlying causes of various hysteresis effects it is important to recognize the high order of chemical and physical organization that characterizes major classes of food constituents, and mixtures thereof. This organization in the case of proteins involves ordered sequences of amino acids in protein chains, orientation of chains with respect to one another including parallelism or random tangling, distances between adjacent chains and forces holding them together as affected by hydrogen bonding and cross linking, whether the chains are straight, coiled, or folded, etc. Similar considerations apply to orientation of straight chain amylose or branched chain amylopectin fractions in starch-containing systems, and polymers of sugar derivatives in the case of vegetable gums. A different kind of organization involving crystal size and distribution is of the greatest importance in determining the physical properties of fats, even when chemical composition with respect to kinds and proportions of glycerides is fixed.

Natural and manufactured food systems exhibit a still higher order of organization than indicated above because of the complex mixtures of components normally present, and the states of emulsification, dispersion, crystallization, and general "structure" that characterize a food's optimum state. This organization, however, is never static. Emulsions tend to separate, crystals grow in size, micelles in colloidal suspension may aggregate into larger units, water may be squeezed out of fibrillar structures as fibers contract. In food systems some of these reactions are reversible but seldom are they completely so. Often where there is a degree of reversibility the time factor or the energy involved to return to an original state differs from that of the forward reaction. When this happens a "lag" or "damping" effect, referred to as hysteresis, occurs.

Examples of hysteresis in food systems differ widely. Many gums show a high degree of temperature hysteresis. Thus, liquified gels formed by dissolving agar at about 200°F do not solidify until the temperature is decreased to about 100°F. The gel will then retain its solid form when heated to intermediate temperatures. A similar behavior occurs with gelatin. The melting and setting points do not coincide; the former always occurring at the higher temperature. The mechanical history of a gelatin solution also affects the setting point, which can be depressed by stirring. Apparently, here mechanical energy keeps colloidal micelles from aggregating.

Partially solidified fats at a given temperature may have very different rheological properties depending upon whether the temperature was reached by heating up or cooling down the fat, and depending upon mechanical and other variables in its history which can alter the crystalline state. Starch granules in water swell or gelatinize adding viscosity to suspensions that form pastes and gels. Pastes and gels can revert or retrograde back to the insoluble form on freezing or ageing. This is a contributing factor to the staling of bread. Retrogradation can then be partially reversed by steaming the bread to "refresh" it but this reversal is never complete.

Water exists in food as free moisture capable of exerting vapor pressure. But water also may exist in the same food tightly bound as an adsorbed monomolecular layer, or somewhat less tightly bound to food constituents as multimolecular layers of water molecules. These different states of binding determine the characteristic shapes of water sorption isotherms of different foods. But hysteresis in water sorption is commonly observed when foods are dehydrated and subsequently remoistened. In this case the equilibrium moisture content of the food at a given temperature and humidity frequently will be found to be different depending upon whether the food is dried down from a higher moisture content (desorption), or is rehumidified from a dryer condition (adsorption). Foods that are dehydrated also generally cannot be fully rehydrated to their original moisture content, which often is a contributing factor to impaired texture. Many foods that are frozen exude moisture on thawing. This moisture rarely is completely reabsorbed due to many changes that may occur at the molecular and colloidal levels, although grosser effects, such as cellular rupture from the growth of ice crystals, is also a contributing factor.

Hysteresis phenomena are often imperfectly understood in complex food systems because of the many changes that occur simultaneously. Much that has been learned has come from studies on model systems.

NORMAN N. POTTER

I

ICE CREAM AND RELATED FROZEN DESSERTS

Frozen desserts, known to the Romans, and consumed by French and English Royalties in the 15th Century, came to the American scene in the first half of the 18th Century. It was not until 1851, however, that the first ice cream enterprise was started by Jacob Fussell in Baltimore, Maryland. Developments in dairy technology and merchandising resulted in the production, in 1970, of more than 763 million gallons of ice cream plus an additional 380 million gallons of related products (Milk Ind. Found. 1972). The fact that 9.4% of the total milk produced in the United States is used in frozen desserts compared to 17.7% for cheese making indicates the economic importance of the ice cream industry.

Definitions

Ice Cream, a frozen food product prepared from a mixture of dairy ingredients, sweeteners, stabilizers, emulsifiers, and flavoring materials, is the most important of the frozen desserts. Dietary considerations have, in recent years, prompted consumers to use substantial quantities of ice milk, a product similar to ice cream but containing less milkfat. Other major related products include sherbets, usually a tart product made from the same basic ingredients as ice cream but fortified with fruit and/or fruit juice; and ices, prepared from water, sugar, fruit juices, stabilizer, acid, and color. Products in which a vegetable or animal fat is substituted for butterfat are similar to ice cream, ice milk, or sherbet and are classified as mellorine-type frozen desserts.

Composition and Ingredients

The basic composition of ice cream, ice milk, sherbet, and water ice is fairly uniform due to Federal Standards and State laws regulating the minimum and sometimes maximum percentages of the different ingredients. Although the individual States have their own legal standards, the differ-

ences are only minor, and in time most State laws will conform to the Federal Standards. Table I-1 lists the minimum and maximum levels of the different constituents of frozen desserts as permitted by the Federal Frozen Dessert Standard (Code of Federal Regulation, 21 CFR Part 20).

TABLE I-1

MINIMUM STANDARDS FOR FROZEN DAIRY DESSERTS

	Ice Cream[1]		Ice Milk[2]	Fruit Sherbet[3]	Water Ice
	Plain	Bulky Flavors			
Milkfat					
min (%)	10.0	8.0	2.0	1.0	—
max (%)	—	—	7.0	2.0	—
Milk solids					
min (%)	20.0	16.0	11.0	5.0	—
max (%)	—	—	—	5.0	—
Food solids					
min (lb/gal.)	1.60	1.60	1.30	—	—
Weight					
min (lb/gal.)	4.50	4.50	4.50	6.0	—
Stabilizer					
max (%)	0.50	0.50	0.50	0.50	0.50
Emulsifier					
max (%)	0.30	0.30	0.30	0.30	—
Salts					
max (%)	0.24	0.24	0.24	—	—
Acidity					
min (%)	—	—	—	0.35	0.35

[1] Frozen Custard: Same standards as for ice cream, except plain custard shall have a minimum egg yolk solids content of 1.4% and 1.12% for bulky-flavored frozen custard.
[2] No permitted reduction in standards for bulky-flavored ice milk.
[3] No minimum total foods solids provided. Nonacid sherbet does not require the 0.35% acidity.

The manufacturer can choose from a wide choice of ingredients as specified by the Federal Definitions and Standards for Frozen Desserts. These optional ingredients are grouped as followed: (a) dairy ingredients, (b) sweetening ingredients, (c) flavor ingredients, (d) other optional ingredients, (e) stabilizers and emulsifiers, (f) mineral salts, and (g) coloring. Quality ice cream depends, first, on the selections of good ingredients and, second, on a well-balanced mix. Representative formulas for the various frozen desserts are given in Table I-2.

whey solids may only replace 25% of the MSNF. Sweet cream buttermilk finds only a limited use in

TABLE I-2

REPRESENTATIVE FROZEN DESSERT FORMULAS[1]

| | Ice Cream | | | | | |
	Premium[2] (%)	Average (%)	Ice Milk (%)	Sherbet (%)	Ice (%)	Soft-Serve (%)
Milkfat[3]	16.0	10.5	3.0	1.5	—	6.0
Milk solids not fat	9.0	11.0	12.0	3.5	—	12.0
Sucrose	16.0	12.5	12.0	19.0	23.0	9.0
Corn syrup solids	—	5.5	7.0	9.0	7.0	6.0
Stabilizer[4]	0.1	0.3	0.3	0.5	0.3	0.3
Emulsifier[4]	—	0.1	0.15	—	—	0.2
Total solids	41.1	39.9	34.45	33.5	30.3	33.5
Pounds/Gallon of mix	9.17	9.36	9.46	9.48	9.4	9.30
			Draw From Freezer			
Overrun (%)	65–70	95–100	90–95	50	10	40
Approx lb/gal. finished product	5.4	4.6	4.8	6.25	8.5	6.5

[1] Frozen desserts containing vegetable fat (mellorine type) are permitted in some states. A wide variation of composition exists depending on individual State Standards.
[2] If classified as Custard or French, it must contain not less than 1.4% egg yolk solids.
[3] Milkfat content regulated by individual State.
[4] Usage level as recommended by manufacturer of stabilizer and emulsifier.

Functions and Sources of Ingredients

Milkfat increases richness and creamy flavor and produces a characteristic smooth texture and full body in ice cream; it is, therefore, the most important ingredient. The limitations, however, include its relatively high cost as well as the relatively small amount which can be consumed because of its high caloric value and sustaining power. The usual sources of milkfat are fresh cream, whole milk, frozen cream, plastic cream, and butter.

The milk solids not fat (MSNF) are high in food value and relatively inexpensive. Their influence on flavor is indirect by rounding out the flavor of the finished product. The protein part of the MSNF improves texture, gives body to the frozen products, and is essential for the incorporation of stable air cells. The lactose adds to the sweetness which is, however, derived mainly from sucrose or corn syrup solids. The percentage of lactose limits the total MSNF which can be used. When the free water contains more than 8.7% lactose, the lactose might crystallize and produce a "sandy" ice cream. The usage level of MSNF lies between 9 and 13% dependent upon the product composition. The most common sources for MSNF used in frozen desserts are fresh skim milk, condensed skim milk, nonfat dry milk powder, and condensed whey or whey powder. Legally as well as functionally

ice cream, but has special value because it contains phospholipids which act as an emulsifier.

Sweeteners provide the necessary sweetness, enhance the flavor, and produce a desirable body and texture. They depress the freezing point which, up to a point, is desirable. Sucrose is the most widely-accepted source of sugar. Corn sweeteners can be used to provide up to 40–50% of the total sweetness.

The corn sweeteners (dextrose, corn syrup solids, and corn syrup) are significantly lower in sweetness than sucrose. However, the advantages of their use includes increasing solids without excessive sweetness, imparting a "chewiness" to the body of ice cream, and providing added protection against development of coarse texture in ice cream upon storage.

Stabilizers and emulsifiers are added to the frozen dessert mixes in rather small quantities for a specific purpose. It should, however, first be pointed out that the other ice cream ingredients also possess stabilizing and emulsifying properties. Furthermore, the mechanical processing of the mix has a definite effect upon stabilization and emulsification. Stabilizers function in ice cream through their ability to form gel structures in a water solution or to combine with water as water of hydration. Stabilizers bind water and, by virtue of this function, produce smoothness in body and texture by reducing ice crystal size and retarding ice crystal growth during freezing and storage. They provide uniformity and chewiness of product and resistance to melting. Gelatin was for many years the most widely-used stabilizer. At the present time, many other materials are used; mostly colloids derived from seaweeds or plants; sodium carbomethylcellulose may also be used. Each stabilizer has its advantages and disadvantages and often a combination of two or more is used.

Emulsifiers function in ice cream through their ability to reduce the interfacial tension between the fat-aqueous phases of the emulsion. This results in a finer dispersion of the fat in ice cream and a fine air cell structure, producing a stiff and dry body character as well as an improved apparent richness. Keeney and Josephson (1958), have pointed out that the rate of agglomeration and coalescence of the fat globules involves not only the emulsifier but also a number of other factors important in affecting ice cream quality. The emulsifiers can be divided into the following groups:

(1) Glyceryl or sorbitan compounds of fatty acids, largely stearates.

(2) Polyoxyethylene derivates of fatty acids, or their glyceryl or sorbitan compounds.

The dairy ingredients which contain natural emulsifying constituents include: milk proteins, lecithin, phosphates, and citrates. Egg yolk products are high in lecithin and have long been used in ice cream.

A number of mineral salts are listed under the optional nondairy ingredients which may be used in frozen desserts. Their main function has to do with the heat stability of the milk protein and they may influence some characteristics of the finished product.

Air and water in frozen desserts are necessary ingredients. The air, incorporated as very tiny air cells, and the water, partly frozen into small ice crystals, give the product the palatability, the texture, and body necessary for good quality and pleasant eating characteristics. Both ingredients are important for the physicochemical system which ice cream represents (Arbuckle 1972).

The increase in product volume resulting from air incorporation is referred to as overrun and is defined as the volume of ice cream obtained in excess of the volume of mix.

The "percentage overrun" is calculated as follows:

Overrun

$$= \frac{\text{volume of ice cream} - \text{volume of the mix}}{\text{volume of the mix}} \times 100$$

The Federal Standards or State laws on the weight per gallon of finished product determine the maximum overrun percentage (see Table I-2). The usual range varies from 40% for the hand-filled "bulk" package to 75-100% for the machine-filled product.

Processing and Manufacturing

Processing of the ice cream mix consists of selecting the composition of the mix; calculating and blending the different ingredients; and pasteurizing, homogenizing, and cooling the mix.

The pasteurization of the mix provides a safeguard for the health of the public since undesirable bacteria are destroyed during this process. Pasteurization is universally required by States and cities; however, the temperature and time combination may differ.

The most common temperature and time systems for pasteurization are:

Method	Temp ($^\circ$F)	Time
Batch system	150-160	30 min
High temperature-short time	175	25-30 sec
Ultra high temperature	210-265	0-40 sec
Vacuum pasteurizer	194-205	2 sec

All commercial mixes are homogenized; a process which consists of passing the mix under pressure through a small opening, resulting in a reduction in size of the fat globules to at least 4.0 μ in diameter, with the vast majority smaller than 2.0 μ. The mix is homogenized at a temperature in the range of 120°-165°F and at a pressure between 1500 and 3000 psi. Sommer (1951) discusses in detail the effects of homogenization as applied to ice cream mixes. The most important advantages of homogenization are uniform and permanent suspension of fat globules, smoother texture, improved whipping ability, and diminished danger of churning during freezing.

The engineering and mechanical aspects of the different pasteurization systems and of homogenization are discussed by Hall, Farrell and Rippen (1971).

With the use of improved stabilizers and freezing techniques, storage of white mix for 3-6 hr and of chocolate mix for 12 hr is sufficient to improve freezing; thus making unnecessary the longer time of "aging" the mix, earlier thought necessary to permit hydration and phase equilibria of mix constituents.

Freezing Process

The freezing process consists of a rapid withdrawing of heat from the ice cream mix, thus freezing part of the water into ice crystals and the concurrent incorporation of air under agitation. To produce a smooth quality ice cream, it is essential that the ice crystals and air cells be small; this is accomplished by rapid withdrawal of heat and vigorous agitation. Leighton (1927) published a formula to calculate the percentage of water frozen as ice at any given temperature. The amount of water frozen as ice in the freezer varies between 30 and 60%, depending on drawing temperature and composition of the mix. The size of the ice crystals frozen during mechanical agitation of the mix and the distribution of the water in the unfrozen portion of the mix determine, in part, the smoothness of the finished product.

The second important function of the freezing process is the incorporation of air. Whipping properties of the mix are dependent to a large extent upon its composition, although this is of less importance when the continuous freezer is used. The amount of air incorporated into the mix and the size of the air cells influence the body and texture of the resulting ice cream.

Batch, continuous, and soft-serve freezers are the primary machines used for manufacturing frozen desserts. The batch freezer consists of a cylinder mounted vertically or horizontally. A motor operates a dasher inside the cylinder. The dasher is equipped with scrapers for removing the ice cream as it freezes to the inside of the cylinder, and it serves as a beater, facilitating the incorporation of air. The refrigerant (brine, ammonia, or freon) circulates through the double wall of the freezer cylinder which consists of a steel or copper tube with an inner lining of stainless steel. The mix enters the freezer at approximately 40°F.

As the refrigerant is applied, the temperature drops rapidly to 21-22°F and the flow of refrigerant is discontinued when the mix develops a rather firm body. Operation of the dasher and attached mechanism is continued until the desired overrun (incorporation of air) is obtained. The minimum temperature reached by the ice cream (in the batch freezer) is about 21-25°F. On completion of freezing, the batch of ice cream, as a semifrozen mass, is drawn from the batch freezer into containers and placed in the hardening room.

The continuous freezers, with capacities ranging from 80 to 1000 gal. per hr, have replaced the batch freezer in commercial plants. Ice cream mix and air are pumped into the freezer chamber and continuously agitated by a dasher. A refrigerant cools the inner surface of the chamber where the dasher knives scrape the semifrozen ice cream from the wall while the unfrozen mix takes its place. The Vogt and the Creamery Package continuous freezers are well known and are similar in their operation. In the Vogt freezer, the air is metered into the mix prior to entering the freezing chamber; while in the Creamery Package freezer, air is injected directly into the chamber. An ice cream

pump in the latter case moves the semifrozen ice cream from the chamber. The operation of these freezers is discussed by Hall, Farrell and Rippen (1971).

The low-temperature continuous freezer is capable of delivering the semifrozen product at 16°-17°F compared to 20°-23°F for conventional freezers. This lower temperature is accomplished by a second freezer chamber which has an eccentrical dasher. The finished product has more resistance to adverse handling conditions.

The soft-serve freezer is a combination of a batch and a continuous freezer. After an initial filling of the freezing chamber, mix is automatically fed from a container into the chamber whenever product is withdrawn. The product is kept chilled in the chamber when no soft-serve product is withdrawn.

In the manufacturing of fruit, nut, or candy ice cream when visible particles are desired, the flavor, fruit juices, and color are added to the mix but the fruit, nuts, and candy must be incorporated into the product after it leaves the freezer via a fruit feeder.

Variegated flavors, often called "royaled" or "rippled" ice cream, are very popular. These ice creams are made by injecting one or more fudge or fruit bases into the ice cream as it leaves the freezer. A number of variegator machines are available which can be controlled to inject the desired amount of the flavor base. Some of the most popular variegated flavors are chocolate, caramel, butterscotch, strawberry, raspberry, and orange.

The final step in ice cream manufacturing is the hardening process. When ice cream is drawn from the freezers, it has a semifluid consistency and is not stiff enough to hold its shape. It is, therefore, hardened until it reaches a temperature of 0°F or below. Here, as in the freezer, fast hardening will facilitate the formation of small ice crystals. The hardening takes place in rooms where the temperature is −20° to −30°F or in specially designed hardening tunnels where air at a temperature of −50°F is blown on packages of incoming ice cream. Numerous types of fast hardening devices are in general use for wrapped units, including plate or contact hardeners, blast tunnels, and roller beds. Ice cream may be hardened within 4 hr in any of these systems.

In a modern ice cream plant the processing and manufacturing have become mechanized and automated. A description of such an automated plant is described by Arbuckle (1972).

Flavors of Frozen Desserts

Ice cream owes its variety and popular appeal to many pleasing flavoring materials which can be used in its manufacture. The flavors are added directly into the mix when powders, liquids, or purées are used. With fruits or nuts, a fruit feeder is used which incorporates the particles into the semifrozen ice cream as it leaves the freezer. Although there are over 150 different ice cream flavors, a survey showed that the following flavors account for more than 80%: vanilla 47.5, chocolate 14.0, variegated chocolate 7.3, nut meats 7.10, strawberry 5.5, coffee 1.5 and peach 1.5 percent (Anon. 1972). The Federal Standards of Identity specify the minimum flavor as well as labeling requirement.

Vanilla ice cream is flavored with an extract of the vanilla bean, or combinations of natural vanilla extracts and vanillins. In some areas, ground vanilla beans are added for eye appeal.

Fruits, fruit concentrates and essences are quite extensively used as flavorings in frozen desserts. Fresh frozen fruit is preferred; strawberries, raspberries, pineapple, peaches, banana, and cherries are the most favored. The amount to be added varies according to the particular fruit, from 25% for pineapple to 30% for peaches, calculated on the weight of the finished product.

The most important nut flavors include buttered pecans, buttered almonds, cashews, walnuts, and pistachios. The amount of nuts added to the mix may vary from 5 to 10 lb per 100 lb of mix. Increasingly popular are the variegated ice creams, where 10–15% of a prepared sauce is injected usually into vanilla or chocolate ice cream. The most popular flavors in this category are: chocolate, butterscotch, caramel, marshmallow, and several fruit sauces.

Novelties and Specialties

Novelty ice creams or frozen products come in many flavors, shapes, sizes, and colors. They are individually wrapped and intended for individual servings. The annual production is estimated at close to 10 billion pieces and accounts for approximately 25% of the industry's total gallonage. The most popular novelty items are: chocolate or candy-coated ice cream and ice milk bars usually with a stick, Eskimo Pies (chocolate or candy-coated ice cream bars), ice cream sandwiches (ice cream slice between two wafers), ice cream cups (plain or with a fruit or candy topping), and sherbet and ice-like mixtures frozen on a stick.

Soft ice cream and ice milk have the same ingredients as regular ice cream and ice milk. The major difference between the two is that soft ice cream is dispensed to the consumer in a semifrozen state drawn directly from the freezer and contains from 30 to 50% overrun.

The total soft-serve production products in 1970 was 120.0 million gallons.

Structure of Ice Cream

The internal structure of ice cream is determined by the composition of the mix, the manufacturing procedure, and by the distribution and particle size of the components as they occur in the frozen ice cream. The ingredients in the frozen ice cream are present in a complicated physicochemical system. A large portion of the water is frozen and the resulting ice crystal size greatly affects the crystalline structure of the ice cream. Air cells of different sizes are dispersed throughout the entire structure. Fat globules are in emulsion; milk proteins, insoluble salts, and stabilizers are present as particles of colloid dimensions; the sugars and soluble salts are in true solutions. The size, shape, arrangement, and distribution of all these components determine the internal structure of the ice cream.

Arbuckle (1972) has investigated extensively the average size of the constituents of ice cream in an attempt to relate their characteristics to product quality.

The texture of ice cream is directly related to the structure—the size, shape, number, and arrangement of the air cells, ice crystals, lactose crystals and fat clumps, and the thickness of the foam lamellae. In a quality product a smooth texture is indicative of uniformly small ice crystals and air cells, and no detectable lactose crystals. A coarse and icy texture is caused by relatively large ice crystals; while sandiness is the result of lactose crystallization. A buttery or greasy texture is caused by the presence of butterfat lumps. A snowy texture is the result of large and/or too many air cells.

The body in ice cream is related to the mass of ice cream as a whole and refers to its consistency or firmness, and resistance to melting. An ice cream with a heavy or soggy body has too little air. Too much air results in a fluffy body.

Defects of Ice Cream

Flavor, body, and texture are the principal factors used in judging the quality of the finished ice cream. Flavor defects are imparted by the mix ingredients (oxidized, acid, and cooked; or by the flavoring materials—too strong, unnatural, etc.). Body defects are commonly described as crumbly, soggy, and weak; while the common texture defects are coarse, icy, fluffy, sandy, and buttery. Another defect to which consumers object is a too high or too pale color.

Two defects, although important but not readily noticeable, are bacterial defects and melting defects. States and communities have imposed maximum permissible numbers of bacteria in the product for public health reasons. The most common defects in meltdown characteristics are curdled meltdown, whey-like consistency upon melting, and ice cream which "does not melt."

An unclassified defect is "shrinkage." When this defect occurs, ice cream, after hardening, shrinks away from the top and sides of the packages and gives a "not full" appearance.

Sherbets and Ices

Sherbets and ices are manufactured in a manner similar to ice cream. One of the important factors in making these products involves a well-balanced mix and the choice of stabilizer, since product quality depends on the proper functioning of the stabilizer to give a smooth texture and a firm body and to aid in controlling overrun. Only stabilizers which control the overrun, prevent syrup drainage, and eliminate crumbly body should be selected. One or a combination of the following stabilizers can be used: gelatin, gum tragacanth, pectin, cellulose gum, or algin products.

The kind and amount of sugars used in sherbets and ices are important in relation to properties of the finished product. The use of dextrose or corn syrup to the extent of 25–30% of the amount of sucrose, is advisable as a means of preventing surface crustation.

Tartness differentiates sherbets and ices from ice cream. The amount of acid needed varies with the amount of sugar and the amount of fruit acid contained in the fruits or fruit combinations. The legal minimum is 0.35% calculated as lactic acid.

Citric acid is the most commonly-added acidulant. The more common flavors for ices and sherbets are orange, pineapple, raspberry, lime, and lemon. The amount of fruit required varies with the intensity of flavor and the quality of fruit; it should be from 13 to 20% of the weight of the finished product, except for lemon and lime where 7% is usually sufficient. Recently, "nonacid" sherbets have been permitted. The legal standard is the same as for regular sherbets except for its acidity.

Other Frozen Desserts

There are a number of other frozen desserts which are usually classed with the ices and sherbets.

Granites are made from the same mixes as ices, the main difference being that they are frozen so as to permit little or no whipping. The product is, therefore, hard, has a low overrun and a coarse texture, resulting from a minimum of stirring during freezing.

Punches are essentially ices with alcoholic beverages used in place of, or supplementary to, fruit juices. Rum flavoring or cordials may be used in place of the alcoholic beverages. An ice or sherbet

TABLE I-3

NUTRIENT COMPOSITION PER 100 GRAMS OF VARIOUS
FROZEN DESSERTS

	Vanilla Ice Cream	Vanilla Ice Milk	Orange Sherbet	Orange Ice
Fat (gm)	10.2	12.1	3.1	1.1	Trace
Protein (gm)	3.5	3.8	3.9	1.4	0.1
Carbohydrates (gm)	24.3	24.8	25.7	29.8	35.4
Total Solids (gm)	39.3	42.0	34.1	33.6	37.0
Calcium (mg)	135.0	144.0	150.0	59.0	1.0
Phosphorus (mg)	107.0	115.0	119.0	42.0	2.0
Sodium (mg)	73.0	78.0	82.0	33.0	Trace
Potassium (mg)	216.0	232.0	241.0	71.0	15.0
Iron (mg)	0.1	0.1	0.1	Trace	—
Magnesium (mg)	15.0	16.0	17.0	6	—
Vitamin A (IU)	412.0	486.0	124.0	44.0	14.0
Thiamin (mg)	0.04	0.05	0.05	0.01	0.01
Riboflavin (mg)	0.22	0.24	0.25	0.07	Trace
Niacin (mg Equiv)	0.96	1.02	1.06	0.37	0.02
Vitamin B6 (mg)	0.06	0.07	0.07	0.02	—
Vitamin B12 (mcg)	0.58	0.63	0.65	0.25	—
Vitamin C (mg)	—	—	—	—	—
Vitamin D (IU)	—	—	—	—	—
Vitamin E (IU)	0.3	0.3	0.1	Trace	—
Calories	204.0	223.0	146.0	135.0	142.0

SOURCE: Anon. (1971).

in frozen condition is sometimes added to the fluid punch.

Frappés are made in identically the same manner as sherbets, differing only in that they are served at the consistency of sherbets when the latter leave the freezer. A frappé is, accordingly, a sherbet before it goes to the hardening room.

Soufflés are made from the same mixes as sherbets, but with chilled and beaten whole egg added at the freezer at the rate of about two eggs per gallon of mix. A further difference is that soufflés are usually frozen with a high overrun to obtain a fluffy product.

Bisque ice cream is usually higher in fat than regular ice cream and contains a bread or confection product such as dried macaroons, marshmallows, or sponge cake.

Parfait is also high in fat, containing egg yolks with or without nuts or fruits, or other natural flavors.

Mousse is a frozen whipped cream to which sugar and flavor have been added. Ice cream mix is also usually added to the cream before whipping and freezing.

Ice cream pudding is a high fat ice cream with nuts and fruits, highly flavored or seasoned. Common types of puddings are Manhattan, Nesselrode, plum, and Oriental.

Aufait is a brick ice cream, consisting of layers of one or more kinds of ice cream, alternating with layers of frozen fruit.

Lacto is a frozen product manufactured from cultured skim or whole milk, eggs, and sugar, with or without natural flavoring.

The old-fashioned "home-made" type of ice creams are now commercially produced. These products have a very low overrun and are extremely cold to the taste.

Nutritive Value of Frozen Dessert

Frozen desserts are excellent sources for food energy because of their high sugar content. Furthermore, ice cream and ice milk are excellent food products containing all and often more of the milk solids than milk itself. The digestibility and palatability of these products add to their nutritive value. Table I-3 shows the nutrient content of frozen desserts.

LOUIS F. CREMERS

References

ANON. 1971. Average Composition of Sealtest Food Products. Kraftco Corp., Glenview, Illinois.

ANON. 1972. The 20th annual survey of frozen dessert trends. Dairy Ice Cream Field, *155*, No. 4.

ARBUCKLE, W. S. 1972. Ice Cream, 2nd Edition. Avi Publishing Co., Westport, Conn.

HALL, C. W., FARRALL, A. W., and RIPPEN, A. L. 1971. Encyclopedia of Food Engineering. Avi Publishing Co., Westport, Conn.

KEENEY, P. G., and JOSEPHSON, D. V. 1958. Measure of fat stability in ice cream and its relationship to dryness. Ice Cream Trade J. *54*, No. 5, 32.

LEIGHTON, A. 1927. On the calculation of the freezing point of ice cream mixes and of the quantities of ice separated during the freezing process. J. Dairy Sci. *10*, 300.

MILK IND. FOUND. 1972. Milk Facts, 1972 Edition. Milk Industry Foundation, Washington, D. C.

SOMMER, H. H. 1951. Theory and Practice of Ice Cream Making, 6th Edition. Olson Publishing Co., Milwaukee.

IFT INDUSTRIAL ACHIEVEMENT AWARD

See Awards.

IFT INTERNATIONAL AWARD

See Awards.

INFRARED

The invisible rays just beyond the red in the visible spectrum, designated infrared, have a penetrating heat effect that has been increasingly used by the food industry in recent years. Infrared energy is not in itself a form of heat but rather the cause of heating through the absorption of energy quanta. Natural sources of infrared are any objects with temperatures above absolute zero. Artificial sources include tungsten filament lamps, cesium vapor lamps, quartz tube lamps, carbon filament lamps, nonluminous gas flames, and ceramic rods. Infrared energy is transferred to a material by the acceleration of charged particles within that material. The infrared spectrum lies between wavelengths 0.76 and 35 μ.

Although infrared energy is used in the food industry to effect sanitary conditions in storages and other areas of food plants, it is also utilized in processing foods, three examples of which are its use in cooking, in freeze drying, and in peeling vegetables and fruits. Infrared units are available for cooking, for instance, by means of ovens in which a 1550 infrared heat bulb, set in a reflector and covered with a red glass, generates instant heat. A heat switch provides a means of controlling the amount of heat applied to a material. Infrared energy is also used in freeze drying as a means of speeding up the drying process. The advantage of infrared in freeze drying is that it accelerates the sublimation of ice and by proper control does this without melting the ice. Melting damages the product.

Research on masers and lasers will doubtless have an impact on infrared technology in years to come, adding a new order of magnitude to heat production by artificial infrared sources.

A peeling process, based on the application of infrared radiation to potatoes treated with a caustic, has proved successful and shows promise of being applicable to other vegetables (carrots, beats, onions) and to some fruits, for example, apples. The infrared unit consists of a feeder which aligns the potatoes in rows, delivers them to a conveyor which is designed to turn the potatoes as they pass under the infrared source. Radiation is provided by ceramic burners, operating at 1650°F and the exposure is for 60 sec. The infrared process (a dry method of peeling) reduces the pollution load and hence cuts waste disposal costs.

MARTIN S. PETERSON

INSTANTIZING

See Agglomeration.

ION EXCHANGE

In less than three decades ion exchange has advanced from a poorly-understood phenomenon to a well-understood theory and has become an important unit operation of the chemical industry. Valuable sources of information on the subject include *Ion Exchange* by F. Helfferich (1962) published by McGraw-Hill Book Co., New York; and, commencing in 1948, a series of annual reviews in *Industrial and Engineering Chemistry* by R. Kunin, *et al.* The uses of ion exchange in the food industry are numerous.

An ion exchanger may be pictured as a mass of immobilized ionic charges which attract mobile ions of opposite sign. The mobile ions, known as counter ions, vary in their affinities for the immobile charges, thus affording selective exchange. Exchangers are classified as *cation* or *anion* exchangers according to the type of mobile ions they attract; thus, cation exchangers are used with positively charged ions (Na^+, Ca^{++}, RNH_3^+, etc.)

while anion exchangers are used with negatively charged species (Cl^-, $CO_3^=$, $SO_4^=$, $RCOO^-$, etc.).

The nature of the exchanger determines its value to the user, and this discussion will not address the wide range of ion exchange phenomena that occur in nature. For a given process the man-made forms are the most useful. We mention only in passing such substances as chemically-modified coals and gums, as well as such food wastes as olive pits, nut shells, and spent coffee grounds modified by introduction of sulfonic acid groups to confer cation exchange properties. Some of these materials require chemical cross-linking to stabilize their matrices. The zeolites are crystalline aluminosilicates of sodium, potassium, calcium, and barium and have cation exchange properties; they have been important in softening water by reducing its calcium and magnesium content. The modern zeolites are synthesized with completely regular crystal structures and have major value as molecular sieves. The synthesis of ion exchange *resins* (after 1940) has provided food scientists and technologists with opportunities to perform a variety of difficult tasks. These resin polymers usually contain a large number of benzene rings to which are attached ionogenic groups ranging from strongly acid (e.g., $-SO_3^-$) through weakly acid ($-COO^-$, $-CH_2COO^-$) and weakly basic ($-NH_3^+$) to strongly basic character (quarternary ammonium groups). Early resins are the gel types wherein the polymers are formed into beads which have gel structures when solvated. Two limiting consequences of this physical structure are slow separation rate, because exchanging species must diffuse through the gel, and restricted molecular size range, because the charge sites are shielded. More recently, development of the *macroreticular bead* (1959) with a sponge-like cross section permits much higher diffusion rates as well as separation of high molecular weight ions. This form also exhibits markedly increased resistance to mechanical attrition. Other factors which influence the rate and degree of separation are ionic charge, solvated ion size, ion concentrations, and pH of the medium.

The broad range of ion exchange applications includes separations for both industrial and laboratory analytical purposes, product treatment for quality improvement, and use as acid or base catalysts.

The use of cation exchange to separate amino acids in protein hydrolysates is the most widely-used approach to analysis of protein composition; and large-scale production of amino acids from economical protein sources utilizes the same principles.

Perhaps the broadest application is, and has been, water treatment where the need may vary from the simple removal of calcium, magnesium, iron, lead, mercury, or other unwanted cation to total deionization. The process is economically attractive as an alternative to distillation because of its innate efficiency. Only that capacity which is needed is used because the process is stoichiometric, whereas the energy required for distillation is directly related to the quantity of water and not the concentration of unwanted ion species. High temperature boilers also enjoy economic benefits through pretreatment of the water by ion exchange to remove silica. Not only are other unwanted anions removed, but claims are also made for removal of colloidal silica and colloidal iron. The operation mode may include a tandem arrangement of either cation or anion exchanger in appropriate form or mixed beds containing both types. Factors influencing choice of mode are highest quality effluent from mixed beds and highest resin stability with cation exchangers.

In general, the food products and by-products treated by ion exchange are in liquid form. Apple juice benefits from use of both cationic and anionic resins (also mixed beds). The removal of calcium malate was first performed because of its bitter flavor. Other minerals needed for microbial growth were also removed resulting in higher product stability. Residues of lead and arsenic were also reduced to acceptable levels; lead was also effectively removed from maple syrup by this method. Grape juice is sometimes modified by ion exchange prior to fermentation in wine making; and grape waste has proved a useful source of tartaric, malic, acetic, and other acids. Several wines have even been restored by treatment with anion exchange and readdition of tartaric acid. These resins also serve to reduce the level of undesirable aldehydes by promotion of acetal and ester formation although their use for such purposes is subject to regulation. Pineapple wastes have been treated extensively with anion exchangers for recovery of sugar syrups and citric acid.

Adjustment of calcium in cow's milk to obtain a soft curd milk for infant feeding has made use of cation exchange to make it more like human milk.

When fallout became of concern, methods were developed to remove up to 90% of the radioactive strontium-90. Removal of calcium from whey improved the ease with which lactose could be crystallized.

Ion exchange (together with bone charcoal) has been used increasingly to deionize and decolorize corn and beet syrup. A recent report describes use of a mixed bed of weakly acid and weakly basic ion exchangers to both demineralize and decolorize corn syrup with significantly improved flow rates and lessened inversion of sucrose.

Cation resins have been used to extend shelf-life of olive oil by removal of trace amounts of copper and iron. Such a resin was utilized as a catalyst (H form) in lowering the free fatty acid level in vegetable oil by forming the ethyl esters in the presence of ethyl alcohol. These resins are also useful as catalysts in promoting hydrolysis of sugar syrups of various origins.

Although most applications of ion exchange in the food industry have involved synthetic resins, some of the newer inorganic ion exchangers may work as well, though not possessing equivalent chemical and mechanical stability. The modified celluloses have their primary value in the laboratory.

Recently-developed ion exchange membranes may become increasingly useful, particularly in the field of pollution abatement and treatment of brackish waters. Recognition should be given to the fact that ion exchangers are potentially useful in regulating nutrient levels in hydroponic growth media. Although such application has been limited thus far, the exchange capacity of the resins is many times that of soil and offers desirable control over available levels of both cationic and anionic nutrients.

J. WALTER GIFFEE

Cross-reference: *Water Treatment.*

ISKER, ROHLAND A., AWARD
See Awards.

J

JELLIES, JAMS, AND FRUIT PRESERVES

See Fruit Preserves and Jellies.

JUICES

There has been a rapid rise in the production and consumption of fruit and vegetable juices in the United States since about 1930. This trend increased sharply during the 1940's and has leveled off slightly since that time but has still continued to gradually increase. Total juices consumed in the United States are only exceeded by milk, coffee, malt beverages, tea, and soft drinks. The most commercially important juice is tomato, followed by the citrus juices (including orange, grapefruit, lemon, lime, and novelty citrus juices), pineapple, juices from deciduous fruits such as apples and pears, and followed by juices of smaller fruits and berries such as grapes, cherries, currants, and cranberries, and succeeded by vegetable juices.

The suitability of fruits and vegetables for juice production is greatly affected by cultivar, maturity, and growing conditions. For most fruits and vegetables there are gross differences in the characteristics of juice from different cultivars, some of which are highly satisfactory and desirable for juice production and others of which are rendered entirely unpalatable by juicing. Further changes take place during storage and handling of the fruits and vegetables before they are converted to juice and these postharvest changes may affect the quality and stability of the juice to a great extent. The degree of importance of postharvest changes varies considerably with the type of juice.

In some fruits and vegetables, rate of maturation and development of the fruit for optimum juice characteristics can be controlled to a great extent by controlling storage conditions. This is partic-ularly true of tomatoes, pears, and apples. In other fruits and vegetables such as citrus, pineapples, grapes, celery, and asparagus, they must be harvested when near the optimum point for juicing and relatively little change can be further developed through postharvest treatments.

Extraction and Subsequent Operations

The detailed operations for obtaining juices vary considerably depending upon the types and characteristics of the fruit or vegetable cultivars concerned. However, almost without exception there are separate stages of (1) juice extraction, (2) finishing (separation of juice from pulp or fruit parts), and (3) some kind of stabilization (often pasteurization or heat treatment in some form). Juice extraction is usually carried out by a crushing or squeezing process (or some combination of these) using grinders, disintegrators, or reamers. Finishing the juices then is usually carried out by means of a screening device, usually with a conical or cylindrical screw forcing the juice components through a fine screen. This separates seeds, pulp, fruit and peel pieces, etc., from the juice and may be arranged to allow certain portions of these materials to transfer into the juice depending upon the specific characteristics desired. Usually this phase is followed by a heat or enzymic treatment, or, more recently, ion exchange or dialysis to protect or stabilize flavor, cloud, and other desirable physical factors. Because of wide variations in specific methods applied to different fruits and vegetables, several of those as applied to the more important commodities will be described in general terms.

Tomato Juice

Tomatoes are generally extracted by what may be thought of as a preliminary finishing operation. After being inspected, trimmed, and sorted, the fruit may be chopped into relatively large pieces without preheating (cold-break) or after preheating to about 160°F (hot-break). The tomato pieces are then pressed through a screen usually having

0.040–0.060 in. openings and this may be followed by a similar pressure-screening-finisher type operation using 0.020–0.025 in. openings. The finished material is used as tomato juice and the residue from the finisher may be re-extracted for blending with tomato juice or used in other products such as purée, sauce, or catsup. In some tomato juice operations the juice is presterilized and therefore cold packed. In others it is deaerated, and then pasteurized and canned hot. More recently, it has been found that washing the juice thoroughly to remove water-soluble electrolytes or adding acid during the maceration of the raw tomatoes increases the viscosity of the juice. This increased consistency may also be brought about by adding chemicals to increase pH.

Citrus Fruit Juices

Although there are wide variations in size and shape of different citrus fruits, there are surprisingly few basic differences in types of extraction operations used to remove juice from them. From oranges, juice is usually obtained by cutting the fruit in half, with the cut halves being applied with pressure over rotating reamers, the juice then being transferred in one direction and the spent hulls in another. A second type of industrial juice extractor used for oranges has a slotted, serrated cup that positions the fruit, after which a round steel tube is inserted into the fruit. In the next step pressure is applied upon the entire fruit forcing its contents out through the inserted tube, which may be fitted with specified screens, thus combining a preliminary finishing operation with the extraction step. These two basic extractor types are used throughout the industry for most other kinds of citrus, as well. Smaller cups are used for lemons and limes and larger cups for grapefruit. Some variations in extraction may be followed for fruits such as lemon and lime where oil is of prime importance and juice retention is secondary.

After extraction the juices are generally finished in a conical or paddle type finisher which forces the juice under pressure through screens similar in type to those units described for juice extraction of tomatoes. Citrus juices are nearly always heat treated (pasteurized) at about 140°–190°F. This is partly to assure microbial stability and lessen chances of fermentation but is principally to assure cloud stability by deactivating enzymes which destabilize cloud. In most citrus juices cloud is an important and desirable factor. Specific sizes and types of screens are often used in the finishing operation to ensure optimum cloud. Because of the sensitivity to heat damage, recent production techniques for citrus juices have turned more in favor of cold-pack juices especially for single-strength juice. These may be obtained by immediate chilling after the traditional heat treatment or by using a bacteriocide in the containers and enzymatic treatment or only a very brief and mild heat treatment to stabilize cloud thus avoiding or minimizing heat contact. Until recently, certain types of oranges had not been satisfactory for processed juices because of undesirable bitterness which developed. However, in some cases it has been found possible to wash the separated pulp thoroughly with warm water and thus remove the bitter flavor-forming factors (mostly limonin and naringin) so that such cultivars may now be used for juices. Nevertheless, Naval oranges and Murcotts have still not become very widely accepted for commercial juicing because of excess formation of a bitter principal (limonin) after juicing.

Pineapple Juice

Because of the nature of the fruit, and the fact that much of the crop is used for special products such as slices, chunks, and crushed meat, pineapples are one of the most complex fruits for juices. This is primarily due to the fact that there are so many different types of material resulting from slicing and fruit packing operations which may serve as sources of juice, and because of the great diversity in the shape, size, and character of these materials. Pineapple juice may come from drainage from other operations such as pineapple crushing, slicing, cutting off ends and chunk-cutting operations, or solids which consist of cores cut from the fruit, trimming around the edges of the fruit, ends which have been cut from the fruit (eradicator) and whole small fruit. The liquid juice constituents from these sources are combined and fed into holding tanks to be blended with juice from the solid constituents. The solid materials are passed through some sort of comminuter or grinder which reduces them to pieces of relatively small, uniform size and shape. This may be carried out in two stages rendering a coarse and fine grind. Juice extraction then may be carried out by transmitting these pieces to a pressure screw extractor similar to the type used for extracting tomato juice or the juice finishers used in citrus operations. Another type extractor used almost exclusively in the pineapple industry consists of a pressure filtration device wherein the juice is mixed with a filter aid and passed through a filtering cake under pressure. The spent pulp may be washed from the filter aid and used as a by-product or reblended partially with the juice, and the washed filter aid may be reused in succeeding batches of juice. Juices are then blended to achieve the desired characteristics of sweetness, acid, and flavor and then are heat-processed usually to about 140°-145°F. The hot juices may then be finished by centrifuging to remove excess suspended solids and to retain desirable cloud characteristics. Often the juice is passed through pressure homogenizers to more completely stabilize the cloud. Following these operations and before canning, the juice is heated to about 190°F for pasteurization.

Apple Juice

Apple juice is one of the oldest types of juices produced commercially in the United States. It was originally sold as sweet cider and in the later 1930's when preservative methods were adopted the newly preserved form was termed apple juice. The steps in processing apple juice are not as complex as with some fruits, and the source is almost exclusively whole sound fruit of good quality. For some years bruised and discolored fruits were used but it became obvious that these had highly undesirable influences on the quality of the juice and were not worth the savings which might be brought about through their use. After cleaning and sorting, the fruit is ground to a very fine slush or slurry consistency by passing it through hammer mills or rapidly rotating blade-screen type grinders. Grinding is controlled to give desirable characteristics of suspended solids in the juice, which vary depending upon the type of juice being manufactured.

Juice extraction may be carried out in any of several different ways, most all of which are based upon some kind of pressing action through a screen or filtration device. They may be operated by hydraulic or pneumatic mechanisms and may be pressed through cheese cloth, cider cloth, or filter aid over a pressed cloth. Other more recent extraction systems use a screening centrifuge followed by a press, the centrifuge removing the major portion of pulp and apple pomace, and the press being used as a type of super-finisher. Another recent type of apple juice extractor uses a continuous screw press and a continuous belt type filter. The continuous press is somewhat similar to the screw type screen finishers used in citrus and juice extractors used for tomatoes.

Apple juice may then be further finished to yield the desired amount of suspended solids depending upon the type of juice. The types of juices in order of lessening amounts of suspended solids are: (1) crushed apple juice, (2) unclarified juice, (3) centrifuged juice, and (4) filtered and treated juice.

Apple juice may be treated to remove cloud and produce a brilliantly clear juice by addition of tannins, gelatin, certain types of enzymes, heat treatments, or filtration devices. After the general characteristics of the desired juice have been obtained and juices have been blended to provide desired flavor quality, they are stabilized by pasteurization. This may require heating from 150° to 155°F for 10-20 min. More recently high temperature-short time (HTST) pasteurization methods have been adopted enabling the use of 170°-190°F for times of 25-30 sec. It is generally felt that higher quality juices are obtained through these HTST methods. Prevention of discoloration and further color stabilization of apple juice may be achieved through the addition of malic acid.

Grape Juice

Grape juice, the original processed fruit juice and consequently the juice which has undergone developments in processing over the longest period of time, is still a highly successful commercial product. Begun for the purpose of preparing juices for communion in the Methodist Church in 1869, it has progressed to an industry producing millions of cases of grape juice per year around the world. Processing methods used for grape juice vary considerably depending upon cultivar and the local practice. The two principal methods are referred to as hot and cold pressing, depending upon whether the grapes are heated before pressing the juice. With the darker colored grapes it is almost essential that the grapes be heated in order to assure a good color in the juice. Since Concord grapes are the principle cultivar used in the United States and since most other grapes used for processing are of the dark-colored variety, most commercial juice prepared in the United States is hot pressed. After harvesting, the grapes are usually held for a period of time to permit them to mellow. Then they are conveyed to a hopper from which they are fed into the juice extractor. The extractor is similar in design and general operating principle to the units described above for extracting tomato juice and the finishing of citrus juices except that clearances and hole sizes are different. Generally, these consist of a rapidly rotating worm screw with rotating beater blades which beat the berries and throw them outward against a screen with coarse apertures. The holes in the screen and spacing between blades and screen are so designed that seed and stems will not be crushed but will be retained within the screen. The juice and pulp are forced through the screen and transferred for further processing, while the stems and seeds are transferred to a different stream. The pulp and juice proceed to preheaters (usually of vacuum type) with steam jackets and are then transported to steam-heated stainless steel kettles where the grape mass is mixed and heated. Usually the temperatures will range from 140° to 145°F. Color and body of the juice can be controlled somewhat by the degree of heating as well as the pressure exerted when the juice is pressed. To maintain uniform color, processors may be required to vary these two factors as the season progresses to compensate for dfiferences in natural color and stages of maturity.

The grape mass is then transferred to presses, after a preliminary enzyme treatment. The presses may operate on a paddle or pressure screw principle or, more recently, on compressed air pressure applied to a perforated rotating cylinder with inner rubber sleeves pressing upon the juice cake. The old established, most widely used, method consists of conveying the grape mass into blankets or cloths made of cotton or nylon and supported by wooden racks. Sometimes a filter aid is added as well. Layers of cloth and grape mass are alternated for several layers and then the top rank of the wooden rack is applied and hydraulic pressure is used to squeeze the juice from the grape mass. More recently developed continuous extraction methods depend upon conveying the grape mass into large settling tanks followed by enzyme treatments and slow withdrawal from the tanks or pressure filtration through a rotating filter bed that is continuously being recoated. In another version, cellulose fibers are added to the grape mass followed by pressure filtration through a worm screw and screen arrangement. After extraction the juice is flash heated to 175°-185°F, then rapidly cooled to 22°-28°F and stored in large holding tanks for blending and packaging.

Grapes usually have to receive an additional treatment to remove argols and crude tartrates, insoluble dark-colored crystalline sludge materials which form upon storage of the juice. These may be removed by freezing, thawing, and decanting, filtering, or centrifuging and more recently have been removed by chemical treatment with calcium acid malate, lactate, or phosphate. Other treatments used for this purpose include the addition of tartaric acid, tartrate salts, or treatment with specific enzymes such as pectinol.

Other Juices

Generally, the methods used for cherry, berry (blackberry, blueberry, strawberry, raspberry, and cranberry), and currant juices are similar in most respects to the processes used for grape juices. The juices may be crushed in a screw or paddle type pressure extractor similar in principle to citrus juice finishers, or in some cases merely crushed by mixing with large paddles in holding tanks. They may be either hot or cold pressed as described above and the pressing is usually carried out by hydraulic pressure or, more recently, by pressure filtration or continuous screw expeller presses. Most juices are pasteurized or stabilized at 175°-190°F for a few minutes.

Relatively few vegetables are treated as commercial sources for juices. Of the nonacid vegetables used for this purpose, nearly all are converted to a highly homogeneous suspension of micro-milled purée of the whole vegetable. This is essentially true for asparagus, beet, carrot, celery, onion and garlic, spinach, and rhubarb juices. Most of these juices are sold in blends or in such specialty products as health-food and baby-food items. Usually comminution and pressing may be accompanied by or followed by a pressure screening or filtration step to remove undesirable parts of the vegetables, such as stems, peels, hard pieces, cores, etc. Other vegetable juices may be acidified by blending with highly acid fruits or vegetables, or by blending directly with added organic acids—usually citric, malic, acetic, or lactic. Specific methods used for individual juices depend upon the processor and ultimate use of the product. Certain combinations of acids with vegetable juices may cause coagulation, undue sourness, insufficient buffering effect, or undesirable blending characteristics. About the only juice made commercially from fermented vegetables is sauerkraut juice. It usually is obtained by pressing or simple drainage from fermented cabbage. Although a number of other fermented vegetable juices have been suggested and prepared experimentally, including turnips, celery, tomatoes, and beets, none has received commercial application to any great extent.

ROBERT E. BERRY

K

K-RATION

Probably the best-known ration to come out of World War II was the K-ration. It was designed and developed at the Quartermaster Subsistence Research and Development Laboratory (QMSRDL), Chicago, the prototype laboratory for the food laboratories that succeeded it: the Quartermaster Food and Container Laboratory for the Armed Forces followed by the Food Laboratory of the U.S. Army Natick Laboratories. The Quartermaster Subsistence Research and Development Laboratory, established in 1936, was concerned with setting up a logical system for rationing military men in large groups, in small groups, and individually. In addition, the laboratory performed or sponsored research and development that resulted in rations of the highest possible palatability, stability, and nutritional quality.

A most important part of the mission of the QMRDSL was designing rations to fit special purposes. The "special purposes" were usually specified by the users and it was a request from the Air Force for an easy-to-carry, pocket-size ration that a paratrooper could use that brought into being the K-ration. The K-ration was intended to sustain paratroopers during the first few days of nip-and-tuck assault operations and for this purpose its success was immediate. Later in the war when the K-ration was prescribed for all-service use, it was sometimes used for weeks on end either out of necessity or because of its convenience. As a result, as would be true of any ration repetitively issued, the troops grew weary of it.

This misuse of the K should not obscure the fact that in its day, prior to the remarkable advances in dehydration, nutrition, and compression, the K-ration was a compact, convenient, scientifically formulated, pocket-sized ration meeting the special purpose for which it was designed to fulfill.

The K evolved into a 1-package, 3-meal ration (breakfast, dinner, and supper) that contained a variety of components. Examples are pemmican, canned cheese, veal loaf, a ham spread, malted milk tablets, candy bars, bouillon cubes, and soluble coffee. In 1944, 105 million of the K were procured. They were used in every theatre of World War II.

The K-ration was only one of the numerous advances in ration design made at the Quartermaster Subsistence Research and Development Laboratory in Chicago. The Laboratory was fortunate from the start in being able to obtain outstanding food scientists and technologists, including packaging engineers, for the vital work of modernizing rations to fit the vast changes in warfare that occurred between World War I and World War II. Mobility, firepower, communications, and the personal equipment and supplies of the World War II military forces were far more complex than those of World War I. The speed with which military forces could be moved from one quarter of the world to another had increased by a whole new order of magnitude. It was essential that military feeding systems be designed to fit tactics and complex logistics systems and the needs of the military man wherever he might be—in Europe, in Asia, in the mountains, in the jungle, traveling by air, land vehicles, on or under the sea. The parameters bearing on foods and food service problems made a challenging program. The work of the laboratory embraced four areas—(1) storage stability, (2) palatability, (3) nutritional adequacy, and (4) convenience of use under military conditions. The able staff within the laboratory and distinguished technical people working as consultants opened new avenues of research and pioneered in many areas, for example, in dehydration areas that continue to be explored today.

ROHLAND A. ISKER

Cross-reference: *Military Foods.*

KEFIR (KEFYR, KEPHIR)

The word kefir, of Caucasian origin, designates the best-known fermented milk produced by a double lactic acid-alcohol fermentation. It is made from the milk of the goat, sheep, or cow.

Its origin dates from antiquity to the time when

the peasants of the north Caucasus Mountains prepared empirically a beverage of variable quality, known as "airan." These peasants prepared airan by letting the milk of their animals ferment in goatskin bags reserved for this use. They were rarely, if ever, washed and cleaned. The bags were traditionally hung near the front door of the house, outside or inside, according to the season, so that anyone passing nearby could shake them by kicking or tossing them around with their hands. Fermentation progressed more or less continuously, fresh milk being added as the fermented milk was consumed. The origin of kefir is probably linked with the observation that the whitish grains, disposed in irregular bunches which formed on the inner surface of the skin, were capable, once set apart and added to fresh milk, of producing a fermented beverage of a quality comparable to, if not better than, airan.

Kefir Grains

According to the legend, kefir grains are the gift of the Prophet to his faithful. The kefir grains are the most original of the characteristics of this fermented milk. They contain microorganism conglomerates agglutinated by a complex substrate composed of coagulated casein and of products of microbial metabolism. For instance, it was shown in 1967 that almost half of the material embedding the microbial population of kefir grains consists of kefiran, a polysaccharide consisting of equal amounts of glucose and galactose. This polysaccharide was the capsular material synthesized by rod-shaped lactic acid bacteria which predominated in the grains studied and has the properties of *Lactobacillus brevis*, a heterofermentative lactobacillus of the subgenus *Betabacterium* Orla-Jensen.

When the grains are dried, they appear as little yellowish, mamillated clusters, $1/4$–$3/4$ in. in diameter, resembling popcorn or cauliflower. The kefir grains can be kept dry for several months. Before they are used again, it is advisable to let them macerate a few hours in boiling water, allowing them to swell and become white again, and then to immerse them in milk for about 24 hr to encourage the reactivation of the microorganisms.

From the end of the last century on, the microbiology of kefir grains has roused the interest of eminent microbiologists such as Beijerink, Freudenreich, and Orla-Jensen. Studies concerned with the microbiology of kefir have often led to a good deal of controversy among specialists. This is due to the diversity and the complexity of the present flora, and to the fact that this flora may vary considerably from one sample of grains to another. Now, it is generally considered that the micro-

organisms characteristic of kefir grains—and for different reasons indispensable for the preparation of this fermented milk—constitute a more or less complex symbiotic association composed, on the one hand, of lactic acid bacteria (mesophilic lactic streptococci, heterofermentative streptococci of the *Leuconostoc* genus, various lactobacilli belonging to the subgenera *Thermobacterium, Streptobacterium, Betabacterium* of Orla-Jensen), and, on the other, of various lactose fermenting or nonfermenting yeasts. Moreover, this "normal" microbial flora may be combined with other microorganisms, whose presence is less desirable, for instance, acetic acid bacteria, or even undesirable enterobacteria (sporulated butyric acid bacteria, molds such as *Geotrichum candidum*, etc.).

Industrial Preparation

The kefir grains are used to prepare the milk starter, which constitutes a convenient means of keeping them active and letting them multiply. After incubation, the grains are separated from the starter by sieving.

Today, the actual preparation is made with cow's milk. The milk is first standardized to 3.2% fat, pasteurized ($85°$–$90°C$ during at least 3 min), and homogenized.

The milk thus treated is cooled to $20°$–$25°C$, seeded with the starter, and a first fermentation ensues. This takes place in a tank at the above temperature and lasts 8–10 hr. A soft curd, resulting from the lactic acid fermentation, has then formed. The curd is stirred and cooled in the same tank down to $12°$–$15°C$, the temperature of ripening, which continues for 14–16 hr, lets the alcoholic fermentation develop. After this ripening, the kefir is cooled once more down to a temperature of $5°$–$8°C$. It is packed in glass bottles sealed with aluminium caps, or in Tetra-Pak cartons, and kept at a low temperature until consumed.

In these conditions the kefir acquires its original characteristics of a refreshing fermented milk with an unctuous but not ropy texture, slightly fizzy, and with a moderately sharp and alcoholized acid taste.

According to the degree of ripening, there are two types—the fresh or sweet kefir (slightly acid, fizzy, alcoholized), and the ripe or strong kefir (acid, fizzy, rich in alcohol). As an indication of good kefir, it contains 0.6–1% lactic acid (pH 4.2–4.7), 0.6–0.8% alcohol, and about 50% carbon dioxide by volume.

Countries Where it is Produced

The preparation of kefir in the USSR has changed in the last 30 yr from the home-made to the industrial product. However, the traditional and original use of the natural symbiotic starter prepared from kefir grains is retained. This fermented milk, used as a drink or consumed during meals especially in the morning and evening, is by far the most popular fermented milk prepared in the USSR, particularly in the big cities. In Moscow, for instance, the daily consumption of kefir reached nearly 400 tons in 1970.

The total consumption of kefir in the USSR increases regularly. Over 1,100,000 tons were consumed in 1970, representing about 75% of the total consumption of the various fermented milks made in the USSR.

Outside the USSR, apart from a few countries like Poland where kefir is also very popular, the preparation of kefir is not extensively developed. It has generally been of a sporadic character and limited to household production, the consumers buying kefir grains or dried starters in the form of pills from certain specialized factories.

J.-P. ACCOLAS
J. AUCLAIR

KNÄCKEBROT

See Hardtack.

KOLA NUTS

Kola (cola) nuts (Fig. K-1) are the seeds of a tree of the family *Sterculiaceae* found mostly in tropical Africa and Central America. There are two principal varieties, *Cola nitida* and *Cola acuminata*. Nitida (commonly called "large" nuts) is the more important of the two varieties. It is found wild in the Ivory Coast. *Acuminata* (small nuts) grows, both wild and cultivated, in Angola, Gabon, and Congo, and other tropical areas of Africa.

FIG. K-1. KOLA NUTS

Primary use of the nut in the United States is in the soft drink industry where it is employed in cola-type beverages. Such beverages now dominate the soft drink market constituting over half of the soft drinks sold in the United States. In use, a 60% alcoholic extract is made of macerated cola nuts and this "tincture" is blended into the syrup base such that the final beverage contains about 120 ppm of extract.

Composition of the extract is probably widely known in select circles, but little published. Some early data published in 1884 by Heckel give the analysis as follows·

Chloroform Soluble	%
Caffeine	2.35
Theobromine	0.02
Tannin	0.03
Fats	0.59
Total	2.99

Alcohol Soluble	%
Tannins	1.59
Kola red	1.29
Glucose	2.88
Others	0.07
Total	5.83

Others	%
Starch	33.75
Colors	2.56
Proteids	6.76
Ash	3.33
Cellulose	29.83
Water	14.95
Total	91.38

The history of the origin of cola-type soft drinks is clouded by the passage of time and conflicting claims of origin. But it is certain that the development of such drinks began as an outgrowth of "tonics" dispensed for health by the local druggist. Use of the word "tonic" continues today in New England to describe carbonated soft drinks. The history of one such drink, Coca Cola, is known and its name indicates that at its origin the beverage purported to contain extract of coca leaves and kola nuts as important constitutents.

Undoubtedly, the use of cola nuts in human foods arose in Central Africa where early visitors observed the chewing of such nuts as an important tribal social custom, reserved for high ranking tribesmen and on other occasions to produce a "lift." Seeds made their way out of Africa via Tunis and Tripoli, thence to Portugese seafarers in early 1700. While the Africans had known and prepared a drink from cola nuts, the earliest known usage on the Continent would seem to be about the mid to the late 1800's. Such continental drinks were carbonated early in their development.

There is considerable debate as to the origin of the "kick" resulting from the ingestion of cola nut extract. Early claims indicated the "kick" came only from fresh nuts while the dried nuts were useless for such purposes. Others claim it to be produced by kolanin, an oxidation product found only in dried nuts. Probably both claims are correct since considerable caffeine is not only originally present, but more is generated on drying by hydrolysis of a "red" glucoside.

Cola nut extract is prepared by lengthy maceration of dried, roasted, pulverized nuts, or by percolation using dilute ethanol. The process is similar to that used in the extraction of vanilla beans. In some instances, caffeine is added to replace caffeine lost in processing, though this addition is frowned on. In the United Kingdom some cola nut extract must be used in all cola beverages.

Extract of cola does not of itself make a suitable beverage and must be supplemented by other flavorings such as ginger, lime, bitter orange, and lemon. While this is so, it is equally true that preparation of a beverage substituting caffeine and theobromine for cola extract does not produce the same results.

ROY E. MORSE

References

HALL, R., and OSER, B. 1965. Use of flavoring ingredients: GRAS list. Food Technol. 19, 253.

HECKEL, D. P. 1896. Repertoire De Pharmacie. From G. B. Beattie, 1970. Soft drink flavors, their history and characteristics. Flavor Ind. (Brit.) 390–394.

KOSHER FOOD

It has been suggested that the Jewish Dietary Laws, which regulate the food eating practices of Jews, are basically laws of good health and good sanitation. For example, the restriction against eating pork eliminated the danger of trichninosis among the Jews; the prohibition against eating oysters and other shellfish was a protection against possible typhoid infection. Others have pointed out that the observance of the Laws of Kashruth has been important to the Jews as a means of preventing the Jews—a minority population—from being absorbed into the general population of the countries where they have lived, thereby preserving and perpetuating their identity.

Although both of these factors may be true and important to the continued observance of the kosher food laws, the basis and origin of these laws are to be found in the Bible. The dietary laws are said to have made the Jewish home unique in that religion becomes an important part of each day's meals. Basically the laws are concerned with the taking of animal life to provide human foods. The restriction against predatory birds (beasts of prey) and the prohibition against all blood of animals (with slaughtering requirements that minimize pain to the animal) all indicate a humane and sensitive reverence for life. Maimonides stated that the dietary laws train us to master our appetites and not to consider eating and drinking the end of man's existence. The Bible then regards the observance of the dietary laws as spiritual and holy, and the many references in the Bible to proper food practices have been detailed and consolidated in the Talmud—the Book of Jewish Civil and Religious Law—to form the kosher food laws as we know them today.

Kosher literally means "fit" or "proper" and when applied to foods it has come to mean "ritually proper" or "ritually clean and edible." The opposite of kosher is "T'refah" which literally means "torn by wild beast," and which now has come to include all foods that are considered objectionable by Jewish tradition.

The Jewish Dietary Laws clearly separate foods into three categories: (1) of meat origin, including fowl, called "fleischig"; (2) of milk origin, including all dairy products, called "milchig"; and (3) neutral foods, including vegetables, fruits, eggs, fish, and all other nonmeat and nonmilk foods, called "Pareve." It is prohibited to eat milk and meat food at the same meal, or to mix them together in cooking. Pareve foods, however, may be mixed with either milk or meat foods. In addition, the prohibition against mixing of milk and meat foods also applies to utensils and dishes, so that a pan or utensil once used for meat cannot then be used for a dairy food, and vice versa. Because of this restriction, two sets of dishes and utensils are required in the kosher kitchen. There is a further restriction as to the time interval between eating meat and milk foods. Meat foods may be eaten after milk foods, but after meat has been eaten, one must wait 6 hr before eating milk foods.

In identifying kosher foods, we should remember that the word "kosher" does not refer to a type of cooking or an ethnic type product, but rather describes foods and practices that are specifically permitted by Jewish religious law.

All fruits, vegetables, and mineral products are kosher and are permitted without restriction. They are also "pareve" and may be mixed with or eaten with milk or meat foods.

With respect to the so-called animal foods, the kosher requirements are much more restrictive.

The only fish that are kosher are those with fins and easily removable scales; so that seafood such as eel, shark, shellfish, oysters, crab, and lobster, are not kosher. Kosher fish, however, require no special preparation or handling and, although classified as "pareve," they may be mixed with or eaten with milk products but not with meat products. However, fish may be eaten immediately before or after meat without restriction. For warm-blooded creatures—fowl and animals—there is not only a restriction with respect to allowable species, but there is a further critical restriction as to the method of slaughtering and subsequent handling. For birds or fowl, the Torah lists 24 forbidden birds by name—all others are kosher. Generally, the acceptable fowl are the domesticated fowl such as chickens, ducks, geese, turkeys, pigeons, and squabs. In describing the permissible animals for food use, the Torah is also quite specific saying, "Whatsoever parteth the hoof, and is wholly cloven footed, and cheweth the cud among the beasts, that ye may eat" (Leviticus 11:3). This then restricts kosher meat to the cow, the sheep, and the goat. The deer would qualify as to species, but it is quite unlikely that we could catch a deer unharmed to be slaughtered ritually. Animals or fowl that have died of natural causes, or have been killed by other animals, birds of prey, or hunters are, then, not kosher. The slaughter of animals for food purposes must be accomplished by a specially trained and religious man called a "shochet." Because of the Biblical restriction against the eating of blood—which is regarded as life—the ritual slaughtering of animals is controlled by strictly prescribed regulations which ensure a minimum pain to the animal, and a maximum effusion of blood from the animal. Before taking the life of the animal, a prayer must be pronounced. The knife used for slaughtering must be carefully sharpened to ensure that its edge is perfectly smooth so that no tearing of the flesh will occur. The blade must be drawn across the throat of the animal severing the jugular vein resulting in immediate death to the animal without pain. After the carcass is drained of blood and opened, it must be carefully examined to ensure that all the internal organs are free of disease. After separating the hind quarter from the forequarter of the animal, it is then necessary to remove specific forbidden fats, tendons, and blood vessels from certain parts of the meat. Because the hind quarter of the animal contains such a large number of forbidden veins, fats, and tendons—many of which are difficult to get at—it becomes impractical and too costly to utilize the hind quarter of the animal for kosher meat. To ensure the complete removal of blood before eating, the meat must then be "kashered." This involves detailed and specific procedures of soaking, salting, and wash-

ing of the meat. Meat that is to be broiled does not have to be "kashered" in the usual manner, since the process of broiling is so effective in removing blood. However, the broiling must be done in such a manner which allows the blood to drip freely away from the meat. Because liver contains so much blood, it cannot be "kashered" through the usual salting and soaking method, but must be broiled. Once meat is made kosher, it may then be treated as ordinary fresh meat, and can be frozen or refrigerated as required before processing or other use.

The eggs of kosher fowl are of course kosher but, here again, the prohibition against eating blood applies. If a speck of blood is found in the egg, it is not considered kosher, and may not be used. Eggs are "pareve" and may be mixed with or eaten with either milk or meat dishes; but eggs found inside poultry upon slaughtering—even with the shell intact—must be "kashered" as meat, and these eggs are then not pareve, but considered to be a meat product.

With respect to commercially processed foods, there are many products that are usually accepted as kosher without any special certification or labeling. These might include such items as canned fruits, vegetables, milk, cream, coffee, tea, sugar, salt, spices, etc. However, if a product manufactured under commercial plant conditions is to be designated as kosher, it must conform to all the dietary laws as outlined. Obviously, all the ingredients must be kosher. Meat and poultry products must not only conform to the requirements of the USDA Meat Inspection Division but must also be certified as kosher. Kosher-dressed frozen poultry is readily available on a commercial scale, as is kosher-slaughtered meat, and "kashered" ready-to-use meat. However, most plants will receive beef (lamb or veal) from the slaughterhouse before it is "kashered" so that the detailed procedure of soaking, salting, and washing, must be carried out before use.

The processing equipment in a kosher food plant requires somewhat different handling than the equipment in an ordinary plant. The cleaning and sanitizing of the equipment is handled in the usual manner, except that all soaps, cleaners, and sanitizers, must be kosher—must contain no animal products. In addition, however, all the equipment and utensils must be made kosher by a special cleaning procedure which involves time, boiling water or steam, and, in some instances, the application of an open flame to the surface being koshered. Since all kosher foods fall into one of three categories—meat, milk, and pareve—the equipment used in processing these foods must also be so designated. Obviously, it is not possible or practical to duplicate large equipment like kettles or fillers in a food plant, but fortunately it is possible to "kosher" the equipment between processing the different types of foods. An additional requirement of a kosher food plant, is that no production of the product may take place on the Sabbath or on a religious holiday.

The certification that a food product is kosher is made by a Rabbi or Rabbinical organization, and a symbol or signature will generally appear on the label. This certification is called a "Hechsher." To assure that the kosher food laws are being carefully observed and carried out in the food plant, a "Mashgiah," a learned and religious man, familiar with the Jewish Dietary Laws is present at all times during the manufacture of the kosher product.

The foregoing applies to food that is eaten throughout the year. At Passover however—the Jewish holiday which celebrates the emergence of the Jews from Egyptian slavery and bondage—additional restrictions are placed on the Jewish home. Because the Jews did not have time to properly leaven their bread in their flight from Egypt, they ate Matzo, or unleavened bread during this time. To commemorate this occasion at Passover, all traces of leaven, or "chometz," must be meticulously removed from the home. The prohibition against "chometz" also applies to equipment and utensils, so that only properly koshered and prescribed dishes and equipment may be used during the Passover holiday. Many specific foods are forbidden during Passover, including bread, leavened cakes, biscuits, crackers, all cereals, peas, beans, rice, liquids containing or made from grain alcohol or grain vinegar. Wheat flour carefully and strictly supervised for Passover use, may be used only for the production of Matzos. All other foods for Passover use require the certification of a recognized Rabbi or Rabbinical organization that the foods have been properly supervised and specially prepared and are kosher for Passover.

HARVEY FRAM

Cross-reference: *Nationality Foods.*

KOUMISS (KOUMYSS, COOMYS)

The word "koumiss" is of Tartar origin. It designates a fermented milk traditionally prepared with mare's milk and occasionally with ass's or camel's milk. Koumiss and also kefir are the best known of the fermented milks that have a double lactic and alcoholic fermentation.

The name of this fermented milk probably derives from a nomad tribe which once lived on the banks of the Kuma river. The preparation of koumiss was continued by tribes of Mongol origin who invaded the steppes of central Asia, particu-

TABLE K-1

COMPOSITION OF MARE'S AND COW'S MILK

Milk	Total Dry Matter (%)	Fat (%)	Lactose (%)	Ash (%)	Proteins Whey (%)	Casein (%)
Mare	11.2	1.9	6.2	0.5	1.2	1.3
Cow	12.7	3.7	4.8	0.7	0.6	2.8

SOURCE: Janness and Sloan (1970).

larly the Tartars and the Kalmuds, famous horse breeders.

Traditional Mare's Milk Koumiss

Characteristics.—The koumiss prepared with mare's milk is a milky grey beverage. It is the end product of the combined fermentation of lactic acid microorganisms (lactobacilli of the subgenus *Thermobacterium* Orla-Jensen) and of lactose-fermenting yeasts.

Koumiss has a homogeneous, very fluid consistency without any tendency to flake or to whey-off. Lactic acid, ethylic alcohol, and carbon dioxide are the main products of the double fermentation and give koumiss its essential properties, a drink which is refreshing, light, fizzy, sharp, acid, tasty, and alcoholized. This characteristic of a light and very fluid drink is mainly due to the composition of mare's milk, which distinguishes it from cow's milk (Table K-1) and is nearer human milk.

The percentages of fat, minerals and casein in mare's milk are, in fact, considerably lower than in cow's milk. Mare's milk is also characterized by a high percentage of noncasein nitrogen and richness in lactose and vitamins (the percentage of vitamin C in mare's milk is 5–10 times higher than in cow's milk).

As a result, rennetted mare's milk gives no visible coagulum (unlike cow's milk) and, on the other hand, in acidified mare's milk the precipitation of the casein is hardly perceptible by taste and practically does not alter the fluidity of the milk.

Preparation.—Formerly, koumiss was prepared by letting the mare's milk ferment in smoked horse skin bags, this fermentation developing more or less continuously as fresh milk replaced the fermented milk that was consumed.

This empirical process, difficult to control, has been replaced by more elaborated processes. As an example, one of these processes is described in a report by P. J. Berlin of the USSR (Ann. Bull. Intern. Dairy Federation, 1962, Brussels, Belgium, Part IV, Section A, 4–16): The first stage consists in preparing separately 2 mother cultures with pasteurized cow's milk ($70°C$, 30 min). One of these cultures is inoculated with a pure lactose fermenting yeast culture and incubated at 28°-30°C for 15-18 hr. The other is inoculated with the thermophilic lactobacillus and incubated at 35°-37°C for 6-7 hr until a compact coagulum is obtained.

In a second stage, the actual starter is prepared. The 2 mother cultures are mixed in a starter tank with a small quantity of mare's milk and the incubation is continued at 26°-28°C. At regular intervals during the following days, fresh mare's milk is added in order to reduce the titrable acidity of the mixture to 0.6-0.7% and to increase gradually the volume of the starter. After 3-4 days, when the required volume is reached, the acidity is permitted to rise to 1.4%. The third stage is the preparation of the koumiss. The starter is added to fresh mare's milk, at a level of about 30%, in order to increase the acidity of the mixture to 0.5%.

The mixture is kept at 28°C and vigorously stirred to obtain an aeration favorable to the multiplication of the yeasts, and is then left to settle. When the acidity is about 0.6%, the mixture is stirred once more for about 1 hr, in order to favor aeration and ensure a good homogeneity in the product.

It is then packed in narrow-neck glass bottles, sealed with crown caps. The incubation continues in the bottle at 18°-20°C for about 2 hr. The bottles are then stored at 4°-6°C and kept cold for 12-18 hr or until the milk is consumed.

According to the degree of ripening, the product that is obtained varies between sweet koumiss (0.6-0.8% acidity, 0.7-1% alcohol) and strong koumiss (1-1.2% acidity, 1.8-2.5% alcohol).

Production and Therapeutic Use.—In the USSR, koumiss prepared with mare's milk is not, unlike kefir, a widely-consumed fermented milk produced industrially. In fact, it is only prepared in breeding kolkhozes and sovkhozes, part of it being consumed where it is prepared and the other part being delivered locally. In the early 1960's, koumiss was still quite a popular drink in the Soviet Republics of central Asia, in Bashkiria, and in the southern part of the Volga. At that time, about 225,000 mares were bred for this milk production.

In the USSR, the mare's milk koumiss is not only a pleasant fermented drink, but also thirst quenching and nutritious. It also has been used for a long time in the treatment of various illnesses, particularly tuberculosis, apparently with some success. The combined use of antibiotics and koumiss constitutes a particularly effective treatment. Koumiss was used therapeutically in this manner in the early 1960's, in the steppes region, in the central region of the USSR, on the south coast of the Crimea, in the Ural mountains, and other areas. At that time there were about 50 sanatoria, which could care for 11,000 patients using this treatment. The koumiss was prepared by the establishments themselves, and 35,000 mares were bred for this milk production.

Cow's Milk Koumiss

Because of the rarity of mare's milk, and taking into account the therapeutic, dietetic, and attractive properties of this fermented milk, research has been conducted in the USSR in the last 10 yr to develop a fermented milk with characteristics similar to those of traditional koumiss, but made with cow's milk. One of the major technological difficulties is the fact that cow's milk, unlike mare's milk, forms a firm and thick coagulum after fermentation.

For instance, the Moscow Dairy Research Institute has developed a technology using skimmed cow's milk, with saccharose added (2.5%). A sanatorium in the Moscow region uses with success a koumiss prepared with skimmed cow's milk, sometimes diluted with milk serum (20%) and with saccharose added (2-3%). Various continuous processes, that assure an effective control of the balance of the two fermentations and of the carbon dioxide production, have also been described recently and indicates a desire on the part of Soviet research workers to develop this fermented milk industrially. From a commercial point of view, the various attempts are still too new to judge their reception by Russian consumers.

J. AUCLAIR
J.-P. ACCOLAS

Cross-reference: *Nationality Foods.*

Reference

JENNESS, R., and SLOAN, R. E. 1970. The composition of milks of various species. A. Dairy Sci. Abstr. *32*, 599-612.

L

LACTOSE

Chemical and Physical Characteristics

An extensive review of these characteristics of lactose are found in Nickerson (1974). Lactose is disaccaride that yields D-glucose and D-galactose on hydrolysis. Lactose may be designated as 4-Oβ-D-galactopyranosyl-D-glucopyranose, occurring in both alpha and beta forms. The designation of α is arbitrarily assigned to the form having the greater rotation in the dextro direction. By virtue of the single aldehyde on the glucose portion lactose is reducing sugar. Jenness and Patton (1959) present principal classes of chemical reactions of lactose. Lactose may be hydrolyzed by mineral acids and lactase enzymes, but not by common organic acids. Oxidation of the aldehyde group of lactose produces lactobionic acid. Strong oxidizing agents will decompose lactose to carbon dioxide and water. A variety of different oxidation products may be produced by treatment with intermediate strength oxidizing reagents such as periodate, iodine, and nitric acid. The aldehyde group undergoes reduction to produce lactositol, which possesses the expected chemical structure 4-(β-D-galactosyl)-D-sorbitol.

Heat decomposition of lactose can take place in the processing of foods and the reactions can be categorized as (a) hydrolysis, (b) dealdolization, (c) dehydration, and (d) internal oxidation and reduction rearrangements. The course of decomposition is influenced by the pH of the medium (Jenness and Patton 1959). Lactose enters into browning reactions which can be highly desirable or undesirable depending upon the particular requirements for the product.

Lactose exists commercially in more than one form. Its most common commercial form is crystalline α-monohydrate, $C_{12}H_{22}O_{11}\cdot H_2O$ and is produced by crystallization from supersaturated solutions below 93.5°C. The β anhydride is available commercially also and is produced by crystallization above 93.5°C. Either the α or β modification when placed in water solution will equilibrate at a rate dependent on temperature, pH to a ratio primarily characteristic of the temperature. At 0°C the characteristic ratio is 62.25:37.75 β to α. The solubility behavior of lactose is complex (Nickerson 1974).

Source

The commercial source of lactose is whey resulting from cheese or casein manufacture from cow's milk. The average lactose content is 4.8% accounting for about 5.57 billion pounds of lactose based on the total 1969 U.S. milk supply (116 billion pounds) (Batz 1970). Of this total about 1.23 billion pounds or 22% went into whey. About 183 million pounds of this lactose or about 15% is estimated to have been harvested in the form of crude milk sugar, food grade lactose, and USP lactose, combined. About 338 million pounds were used in dry whey products leaving approximately 700 million pounds of the lactose of whey unused (Batz 1970). This amount constitutes about 12.5% of the total lactose appearing in the total milk supply in 1969. Totally unused whey accounts for approximately 50% of that produced. At the present time the nonuse of potentially available lactose can be explained partly on the basis of excess costs of centralization for processing, and partly upon unfamiliarity with the benefits to be had from the use of this sugar in a wide variety of food and beverage products and in selected dairy products.

Historical Background

Nickerson (1974) outlines the history of lactose and also gives numerous historical references in this work. Bartolettus in Italy is credited with the first isolation of lactose from whey, and the first use of lactose is believed to have been during the 18th Century and was medicinal. Present knowledge of the physical and chemical characteristics of lactose was substantially developed during the 19th Century and developed further in the present century. As recently as 1944, the principal use of lactose was in foods for infants and invalids, supplemented by its use in the pharmaceutical industry as an energy source in fermentation, as excipients, and as carriers for drugs. The major single use of lactose today is as a component of infant foods, being added to cows' milk to approximate the lactose content of human milk. Since 1944, as larger supplies of lactose have developed, lactose has found use in numerous classes of processed foods.

World trade in food grade lactose had grown sufficiently so that promulgation of a Standard for the World Food Codex was begun in 1964, and is now before U.N. member nations for adoption (Nickerson 1970).

Methods of Manufacture

Modern methods of manufacture depend upon crystallization from whey. Generally, such methods still conform closely to the processes described by Whittier and Webb (1970) and Nickerson (1974), starting with either cheese whey or casein whey. Processing of cheese whey for lactose production necessitated innovations in processing to control adverse effects of proteins and salts of whey on crystallization, removal, and purification of the lactose. Generally, the method consists of pretreatment of the whey by pH adjustment, heat treatment, and selected salt additives, then concentrating to 50–65% total solids, followed by crystallization. The crude lactose monohydrate obtained is usually redissolved, decolorized, recrystallized, and dried. Lactose concentrates may be spray dried to produce either α-lactose monohydrate, mixtures of α-lactose monohydrate and lactose glass, or products high in crystalline β-lactose content. Noncrystalline products consisting of mixtures of α- and β-lactose in glass form may be produced. The principal grades of lactose currently being supplied to the U.S. industry are described by Nickerson (1974).

Uses

Food uses of lactose have increased markedly during the last 20 yr. Its use has grown in convenience and variety foods. These have increased in volume and kinds while lactose supplies have increased correspondingly. In 1965 and 1970 Nickerson (1970, 1974) could list uses for lactose in such items as toppings, icings, pie fillings, confections, etc., while pointing out certain unique properties of lactose that modify sugar crystallization, contribute body and viscosity without excessive sweetness, and absorb and stabilize food and beverage flavors and aromas. In the growing instantized food industry, lactose is a useful aid in promoting and strengthening agglomerate structure. As a component in breading mixes, lactose enhances colors and flavors developed in the cooking process. Currently, lactose is being supplied to the dairy industry for use in such products as nonfat milk, buttermilk, cottage cheese starters and dressings, ice cream, and chocolate drink to enhance flavor and body characteristics. Commercial suppliers of lactose provide recommendations for use. Currently, major suppliers of lactose to the food industry are providing varieties of lactose designed for specific food uses with recommendations for levels and methods of use.

Nutritional Characteristics

The most recent reviews are given by Brink (1970) and Nickerson (1974). Lactose stimulates in some manner the absorption of calcium, magnesium, and phosphorus. It is absorbed at a relatively slow rate from the digestive tract. Theories concerning the mechanism of absorption are reviewed by Brink (1970). Factors influencing the absorption of lactose in human subjects are actively being studied. It seems probable that the relationships between lactose and mineral absorption may prove to be reciprocal. Lactose has the property of influencing the nature of intestinal flora, generally lowering the pH of the lower intestinal tract and opposing the proliferation of putrifactive organisms. Current research suggests that lactose improves the digestion coefficients of dietary protein and fat.

Economic Importance

The market value of lactose depends upon the degree to which it is refined; it currently ranges between 16¢ for fermentation grade and 28¢ per lb for USP crystalline lactose. Edible or food grade lactose has a market value of from 20¢ to 21¢ per lb.

A waste product representing a costly pollution control problem is currently being converted to a resource representing a total value of about 30 million dollars annually, with approximately 50% of this going into food applications.

The economic value of the improvement of food products through the judicious use of lactose, while difficult to estimate, is important and must be added to the commercial value of the lactose produced.

CLAYTON A. KEMPF

References

BATZ, W. F. 1970. How Americans Use Their Dairy Foods. National Dairy Council, Chicago.
BRINK, M. F. 1970. Nutritional characteristics of milk components. In Byproducts from Milk, 2nd Edition. B. H. Webb and E. O. Whittier (Editors). Avi Publishing Co., Westport, Conn.

JENNESS, R., and PATTON, S. 1959. Principles of Dairy Chemistry. John Wiley & Sons, New York.

NICKERSON, T. A. 1970. Lactose. *In* Byproducts from Milk, 2nd Edition. B. H. Webb and E. O. Whittier (Editors). Avi Publishing Co., Westport, Conn.

NICKERSON, T. A. 1974. Lactose. *In* Fundamentals of Dairy Chemistry, 2nd Edition. B. H. Webb, A. H. Johnson, and J. A. Alford (Editors). Avi Publishing Co., Westport, Conn.

LAMB (PRODUCTION)

Lamb has been a stable portion of the meat diet since the beginning of recorded time. Religious prejudice against lamb is far less than for any other meat except fish. Lamb has also enjoyed a reputation of being nutritious and easily digestible. The world per capita consumption of lamb and mutton has remained relatively constant over the last 10 yr, although total consumption has risen slightly. The per capita consumption in the United States has declined since 1942, when consumption was 7.2 lb per person. It is estimated that the 1974 consumption will be just over 2.6 lb per person. This decline in U.S. production and consumption of lamb and mutton has been especially sharp since 1961.

Australia and New Zealand are the largest producers of lamb and mutton, and also lead in per capita consumption at 89 and 87 lb per person respectively. New Zealand and Australia are also the largest exporters of lamb and mutton at 1 billion and 404 million lb, respectively, in 1969. The United Kingdom is the largest importer of lamb and mutton. With the steady decrease in sheep numbers in the United States, the importation of lamb and mutton into the United States has increased from an average of 108 million lb of carcass weight in 1961 to 152.3 million pounds in 1969.

Lamb has traditionally been raised in the western part of the United States and consumed on the east and west coasts. Most of the slaughtering plants are in the west, and the wholesale and retail establishments handling lamb are in the east. The majority of the lamb in the United States is handled fresh, being shipped and stored under refrigeration. Lamb imported from New Zealand and Australia is frozen.

The average lamb in the United States weighs just over 100 lb live weight and has a 50% dressing percentage, resulting in a 50-lb carcass. Carcass weights vary considerably with lighter weights in the spring and summer from the milk-fed and grass-fat lambs and heavier weights from the feedlot lambs during the fall and winter months. New Zealand lambs average about 30 lb per carcass and Australian lambs are slightly heavier. There is a small trade in hothouse lambs in the Eastern part of the United States. These carcasses usually weigh around 25 lb and are from lambs born in the middle of the winter and slaughtered at 10–16 weeks of age.

Approximately 94% of the lambs slaughtered in the United States are federally inspected. A smaller percentage of lamb is condemned than either beef or pork. There were 169 plants killing lamb in 1968; 32 fewer than in 1949.

In the United States, lambs may be graded for quality and for cutability by USDA graders. The quality grades are prime, choice, good, utility, and cull. These grades are determined by the maturity, conformation, and quality of lean of the carcass. These factors have been associated with the eating quality of lamb. About 98% of the carcasses grade prime or choice.

The cutability grades are ranked 1, 2, 3, 4, and 5, with 1 being the highest cutability and 5 being the lowest. The amount of fat cover over the rib eye muscle, percentage of internal fat, and conformation of the leg are used to estimate yield grade. Yield grade is the percentage of boneless, closely-trimmed cuts from the shoulder, rib, loin, and leg and should make up 47.3% or more of the carcass weight in yield grade 1 lambs. The expected yield drops 1.7% for each full yield grade. A retail store would expect to sell 70–80% of the carcass as retail cuts.

Lamb carcasses have approximately 50% of their weight in each of the fore- and hind-saddles when separated between the 12th and 13th rib. The closely-trimmed leg, loin, rib, and boneless shoulder comprise 26, 7, 7, and 23% of the carcass, respectively. These four cuts account for most of the lamb carcass value.

An average lamb carcass is approximately 16% protein, 30% fat, 14% bone, and 40% moisture. These figures vary considerably from one carcass to the next, primarily because of the difference in the fat composition between lambs.

Mutton carcasses are produced from sheep 20 months of age or more and are identified by the presence of a spool joint or mutton joint on the front leg. This joint is hard, smooth, and white, with two prominent ridges in contrast to the saw tooth sharp red break joint in lambs situated about $3/8$ of an inch higher up. Most mutton carcasses are boned and used in processed meats, such as luncheon meats, pot pies, baby foods, and soup. Australia exports a large amount of boneless mutton.

Many new ideas and innovations are being investigated to stop the decline of lamb production and consumption in the United States. Mutton flavor has been blamed for part of the decline. Mutton has a strong flavor that has been associated with mutton but often occurs in lamb. Research work is now in progress to identify and eliminate mutton flavor in lamb.

Production of lambs in the United States is seasonal, with peak slaughter of lambs in fall and winter and short supplies in spring and summer. New breeding and management techniques are being introduced to level out the supply and provide retailers and packers with a consistent high quality product year around. This would enable retailers to display lamb during all seasons of the year. Many retailers cannot sell all parts of the carcass, and, in some stores, they sell such a small volume that lamb is not normally displayed. Some packers and wholesalers are now breaking lamb carcasses into boneless or semiboneless primal cuts; this enables a retailer to buy those portions of a carcass which he can readily sell. There is also considerable interest in freezing lamb. With the new improved methods of freezing meat, lamb could be frozen in retail cuts allowing stores selling small amounts of lamb to stock frozen lamb.

M. L. RILEY

Cross-reference: *Meat and Meat Packing.*

LAMB (CLASSES, CUTS, STORAGE)

Three classes generally relating to age have been established for lamb: (1) Lamb: to 14 months of age; young lamb up to 5-6 months is termed "spring lamb" without regard for the time of year it is marketed. (2) Yearling: over 14 months but not fully developed. (3) Mutton: mature lamb.

The muscular and skeletal development provides the age timetable for the meat grader. The break joint on the foreshank matures into a "spool joint"; red, narrow bones become wide and less red; the light red meat color darkens; the fine texture of the lean becomes coarse; and the compact forequarter becomes "spready."

Five grades are applied for each class of lamb, yearling, and mutton starting with the best, Prime, then Choice, Good, Utility, and the lowest, Cull. The grading criteria are conformation which relates to yield along with an intramuscular evaluation of color, texture, firmness, and degree of marbling. The top three grades are most significant commercially. Choice is most widely produced and accepted. Prime commands little if any premium because it is wasty and doubtfully more palatable. Good, which is generally leaner, may bring a premium when marketed as a private brand instead of the official USDA grade.

Lamb is marketed in four main cuts: leg, shoulder, loin, and rack. These cuts from a young lamb are all tender and delicately flavored. The loin and rack are most tender. All may be roasted, broiled, or pan fried. The fell, a parchment-like covering, is best removed from the rack and loins but it is better if left on the leg. Wholesale legs include the loin butt, which is removed in the retail cut. The leg may be roasted—bone-in or boneless, cut into lamb steaks, or cut up for excellent shish kabob.

The shoulder may be used in much the same manner as the leg. It commands a lower price because it is less tender, more wasty, and more irregular in shape making it difficult to portion. Very acceptable lower cost chops may be produced from the shoulder when boned, rolled, tied and held together with a skewer.

The loin (really the short loin) makes chops having the conformation of the T-bone and porterhouse. Sometimes the double unsplit loin is roasted whole, referred to as the saddle. Sometimes it is boned, rolled, tied, and roasted or cut into chops, using a skewer to hold the chop together. Inserting a kidney in the loin roll makes an English Kidney Chop. It is not uncommon to refer to any boneless chop as the Saratoga Chop regardless of the cut.

The rack is the same cut as the rib of beef. It may be "Frenched" by exposing a portion of the rib bones. A Frenched rack is sometimes sewn into a crown and stuffed with ground lamb or variations. The rack may be cut into single or double rib chops. Removing all the cover fat and feather bones from the rack will maximize surface caramelization and flavor when roasting.

The shank and breast are relatively low priced but wasty. They can be attractively braised. Sometimes the breast is stuffed. The raw, stuffed breast may be sliced into mock lamb chops.

The variety meats—heart, liver, tongue, brain, and kidney—are nutritious and inexpensive.

The price of the cut does not relate to nutritional value. An average $3\frac{1}{2}$ oz portion of lamb provides 27 gm of protein along with 2.9 mg of iron, 0.22 mg of thiamin, 0.32 mg of riboflavin, 7.6 mg of niacin, and 258 calories.

Lamb stores well. Ideal temperatures for fresh lamb are 30°-35°F. The carcass stores better than cuts. For protracted shelf-life, freezing is the most satisfactory method of preserving the flavor. Sharp freeze from 0° to -20°F; and for optimum 6 months storage, -10°F consistently maintained is best. A good freezer wrap should be used. Flexible PVC (polyvinyl chloride) films and sheeting provide optimum protection. Defrosting may be accomplished equally well in a cooler or at room temperature. It is practical to defrost during cooking ag but there is more risk of producing an inferior end product. Little palatability change, if any, is apparent if frozen lamb is properly cared or.

ALBERT LEVIE

ross-reference: *Meat and Meat Packing.*

EAGUE FOR INTERNATIONAL OOD EDUCATION

The League for International Food Education .I.F.E.) was organized in 1968 to meet the need om all corners of the world to provide a rapid, dividualized procedure by which American food cientists and technicians could volunteer in the orld's "War on Hunger" and help solve specific roblems.   Six scientific professional societies ith the United States Agency for International evelopment launched the program.   There are ow eight such member societies whose total embership number 160,000 providing volun-ers in specialties from agronomy to zoology. The esent scientific professional society participation cludes: American Chemical Society, American stitute of Nutrition, American Oil Chemists' ciety, Institute of Food Technologists, Ameri-n Society of Agronomy, American Association Cereal Chemists, American Institute of Chemical gineers, and Volunteers for International Tech-cal Assistance.

Although funded by "seed money" from AID, I.F.E. has won recognition and contributions m private interests around the world. Its activ-es include preparation of a *Newsletter* circulated business, research institutes, and universities in 0 countries; direct problem-solving of inquiries esented to it; preparation of reference lists on od and nutrition topics; domestic and inter-tional workshops with international food in-stry leaders; nutrition surveys; status studies on rldwide development of low cost nutritious ods; liaison activity linking government, indus-, university, and international personnel; main-ning special information files on food problem utions; maintaining liaison with United Nations, rld Bank, and voluntary agencies of interna-nal scope; and preparation of digest articles in glish and sometimes in foreign languages.

The *Newsletter* is issued monthly from head-arters in Washington, located in the American emical Society building.   The mailing list cur-tly numbers approximately 5000 and grows at rate of 75-100 per month.   Individuals in vate industry (domestic and overseas) receive 00 copies; universities and colleges, 700 copies;

governments, 500 copies.   The remainder go to voluntary agencies (250), international organiza-tions (100), trade associations (180), publications (100), institutes and foundations (190), and con-sultants (50).

ARNOLD H. JOHNSON

LEAVENERS AND LEAVENING

A rather wide range of foods, predominantly cereal-based, is characterized by being leavened. In food technology terms leavening is the process whereby a portion or mass of food material is expanded (raised) and made lighter (reduced in density).

The origin of the word "leaven" is somewhat obscure but appears to have been derived from a combination of roots meaning "lever" and "light."

Virtually all leavening is brought about by the development of a gas phase within the food material by one or more of several processes whereby the final food product achieves and maintains a characteristic expanded structure.

The classical example of leavening is found in the bread making procedure which is probably also the first leavening process known to man.

The well-known antiquity of leavened bread invites speculation on the discovery of the phenom-enon and the importance attached to it by the ancients.   Zymologists are inclined to infer that, because of the ubiquity of yeasts in nature, the discovery was accidental, much the same way that enologists find it logical to imagine that the wine-making process was discovered accidentally and for the same reasons.

Bread making, however, requires a grinding of the grain, a maceration with water, a waiting period, and a final step of baking.   It is true that macerated grain is a natural and attractive medium for yeast growth and fermentation but the other parts of the process probably involved invention rather than accident.

Ripe but undried grain seeds are succulent and can be eaten with little further processing.   When dry, however, as they must be for storage, they become hard and scarcely palatable.   The second discovery could have been the effect of grinding or cracking on increasing the rate and effectiveness of rehydration. Invention of the final step of cooking or baking could well have been motivated by the fact that some raw seeds are unpleasant to the taste and a few are even toxic.   Heating by sun or fire improves the taste and stabilizes the food so that it can be stored or transported.

Whether or not these speculations reflect the true origin of bread leavening, we know that leavened bread was developed in prehistoric times and was a cherished and persistent element of man's early food technology.

Other kinds of leavening such as chemical leavening do not have such an ancient history but are nevertheless widely used and highly valued.

Leaveners and Leavening Classified

The gas that is characteristic of all leavening processes comes from one of three sources: (1) microbiological, via evolution of fermentation gases, (2) chemical, via reaction of an acidic substance with an alkali carbonate, (3) physical, via the incorporation of a preformed gas as in a whipping or a mixing operation.

Many foods are leavened by processes that involve more than one of these gas sources. Every leavening process, however, has the common feature of a final step of coagulating or fixing the leavened structure, usually by heat, after the gas has been incorporated in the desired form and amount.

The Mechanism of Leavening

The raising and lightening of the food mass that constitutes the leavening process requires the expenditure of energy, i.e., a force must be exerted in opposition to the natural cohesiveness of the dough or other food mass.

An important part of the energy input starts with the mixing of the dough or batter. This is especially true when the gas (air) introduced at this step is to be the main leavening agent. The physical incorporation of air into a heavy dough mass as in chilled puff pastry or the emulsification of air as in cake batters requires a significant input of energy.

The energy source for the expansion of the gas that develops in bread doughs, biscuit doughs, or cake batters after mixing and before baking comes from biochemical or chemical reactions: biochemical, as in the case of yeast fermentation; and chemical, when carbon dioxide is liberated from soda by interaction with an acid substance. The energy for fermentation comes from sugar that is decomposed or consumed by the microorganisms. The decomposition of soda and the neutralization of an acid are energy-liberating reactions.

In nearly all of the leavening processes a very large part of the total energy required is derived from the heat input during baking. The gas, whether it be carbon dioxide or air, absorbs heat energy and expands. The simultaneous expansion of numerous small, even microscopic, bubbles produces the typical internal structure of leavened material.

When the dough or batter is introduced into the oven and the temperature of the mass begins to increase, the biochemical reaction due to yeast accelerates very rapidly for a time until the cell

enzymes are inactivated by heat. Many of th leavening acids undergo their principle reactio with soda during this initial heating period. Lea ening in the oven is terminated by one or more at least three events: (1) The gas reaches a tempera ture at which it is in equilibrium with the heat tha reaches it from the outside. (2) The viscosity cohesiveness of the food mass increases so greatl under the influence of heat that further expansio of the bubbles is prevented. (3) The walls of the g cells become porous and although the gas continu to expand it escapes and consequently no furth leavening is accomplished.

All three of these events occur to some extent practically every example of leavening. In brea for example, the temperature of the interior of t loaf at the end of the baking period never excee the boiling point of the water solution of suga salt, etc., that comprises the liquid phase of t dough although oven temperatures are much high than this.

The sharp increase in cohesiveness which c restrict further leavening is probably best illustrat by the coagulation of so-called egg-leavened cak in which, as the temperature rises, the egg protei change their physical state so markedly that furth expansion or leavening is halted.

The escape of gas due to the developing porosi of the leavened mass is a natural consequence the redistribution of water that occurs in eve baking operation when starch or starch-like su stances are part of the dough. The swelling hydration of the starch granules, induced by he removes a large proportion of the water from t fluid matrix that characterizes a dough or batt As a result the fluidity or extensibility of the cell walls is sharply reduced, the walls rupture, a gas leakage prevents any further leavening. T phenomenon plays a large role in bread baking a is responsible for much of the familiar aroma duri the baking of bread.

The sum of all of the leavening that occurs in t oven has been called "oven spring." This term ser to distinguish leavening in the oven from pr leavening of the dough or batter. As outlin above, oven spring is a complex process includi both physical and chemical events.

Microbiological Leavening

By far the most important microbiological le ener is yeast. The commercial production of co pressed yeast, S. cerevisiae, dates back only to ab 1792 and an Englishman named Mason, bu biochemically equivalent process dates back antiquity.

The microorganism S. cerevisiae and many ot species of the same genus are well adapted survive and multiply in the flour-water-salt mixture that constitutes a dough. This mixture always contains some fermentable sugars, vitamins of the B complex, and other nutrients from the flour, and the yeasts avidly absorb these nutrients to use them for energy and for survival. When sufficient oxygen from the surrounding air is incorporated in the dough during mixing, the yeast metabolizes the sugar in such a fashion that one molecule of carbon dioxide is liberated for each molecule of oxygen absorbed. No leavening occurs during this stage of respiration or aerobic metabolism. When the oxygen is greatly reduced or exhausted and the environment becomes anaerobic, fermentation is initiated. This process has been called "life without oxygen" for yeast cells. If oxygen is reintroduced into the system respiration takes over, a change that is known as the "Pasteur effect."

During fermentation, and also during respiration, the yeast utilizes hexose sugars, preferably glucose if present. Levosin, a mixture of glucofructans naturally present in flour, is converted to hexose sugar by enzymatic action and utilized. The cane sugar that may be added to the dough is rapidly inverted by the yeast enzyme invertase to glucose and levulose. Glucose is converted by a series of coenzymes following a sequence that has been called the Embden-Meyerhof-Parnas cycle. The net result of significance to leavening during the fermentation reaction was summed up in the Gay-Lussac equation

$$C_6H_{12}O_6 \longrightarrow 2C_2H_5OH + 2CO_2$$

Following the exhaustion of the hexoses in the dough by the fermenting yeast, maltose formed by diastatic enzymes in the dough is fermented (after a lag period) at a rate equal to or surpassing that at which glucose is fermented.

The CO_2 formed is at first dissolved in the aqueous environment but soon reaches saturation. Small bubbles of free CO_2 are formed which stretch the gluten fibers of the flour protein and the leavening process is started.

A subportion of such a fermenting dough, if set aside in a cool place, can be used to start another batch of dough the next day. If kept cool enough or if allowed to dry slowly it can be used as a starter weeks or months later. Material like this has been called by many names, "leaven" and "yeast" being two of the most common. This kind of yeast or leaven can be originated by simply exposing a fermentable mixture to the ambient air, including some inevitable dust, and in antiquity many were the favorite recipes passed from family to family and from tribe to tribe. The origin of fermentation was a great mystery even for many years after microorganisms were detected because

the yeast cells seemed to appear spontaneously in the mixture but only, it seemed, if the spirits or demons were favorable.

Although the use of such a primitive leaven probably still survives in some corners of the world and may even have a sophisticated descendent in certain sour dough fermentations currently in use, most yeast leavening today is accomplished by commercial yeast specifically manufactured for the purpose.

Baker's Compressed Yeast

The commercial production of baker's yeast began as a by-product of the brewing and distilling industries only about 100 yr ago. Following the observations of Pasteur there began the development of a specific technology for the production and the use of compressed baker's yeast.

The term "compressed" probably originated with the use of the filter press to separate or harvest the yeast cells from the medium in which it was grown. The filter cake which has a putty- or cheese-like consistency consists of nothing but single cells of Saccharomyces cerevisiae. There are approximately 13 billion cells per gram of ordinary compressed baker's yeast. As distributed to the baker it comes in 1-lb blocks usually wax wrapped, or, more recently, in a curd-like form in 25- or 50-lb units in plastic lined paper bags. In a few instances bakers have employed liquid yeast, i.e., a suspension containing from 14 to 19% yeast solids in water.

The moisture content of the compressed yeast mass generally ranges from 69 to 71%. This is mostly intracellular moisture which accounts for the firmness of the yeast cake. In this form, yeast must be treated as a perishable product and kept under refrigeration at all times during production, transportation, and storage. A temperature of 40°–45°F is desirable. At this temperature very little change in activity is detected after several weeks of storage.

In the bakery, the yeast must be measured out and then "dissolved," i.e., dispersed in water before being added to the dough mixer. The 1-lb blocks facilitate measurement since each is 1-lb and $1/2$ or $1/4$ is readily measured. Bulk yeast does not have this convenience but has other advantages in handling insofar as hand unwrapping of individual pounds is by-passed.

The proportions of yeast to other dough ingredients varies widely according to the type of baked goods being produced and the time schedule required in the individual bakery. Yeast proportion is expressed as percentage of the flour used in the baker's recipe or formula without regard for the other ingredients. Usage levels vary from under 1%

(1 lb per 100 lb of flour) to 10% in sweet doughs. Some commonly used levels are:

	(%)
Bread (wheat)	2-4
Bread (sour rye)	1
Buns and rolls	2-5
Sweet goods	5-10

The higher levels employed in sweet goods are a direct result of the osmotic effect of high sugar concentrations. This high osmotic condition has a retarding effect upon the rate of fermentation as evidenced by gas evolution. This retardation of fermentation would mean lengthy holding times for doughs and lower output by the bakery. Increasing the yeast level helps to bring about the desired leavening in less time.

The effect of acidity on yeast activity should not be overlooked when certain types of doughs are fermented. Baker's yeast is generally most active in the pH range of 4.2-6.4. In addition, important factors which may affect the activity of the yeast are percentage of sugar, type of dough, temperature of dough, amount of alcohol produced, salt concentration, water content of dough, and prefermentation.

In the dough, temperature has a pronounced effect on the rate of leavening. A temperature of 25°C is a relatively cool fermentation temperature. The rate of leavening is about twice as rapid at 35°C and many commercial processes operate at 35°-45°C. Some researchers believe that 44°C represents a peak above which fermentation activity decreases rapidly due to inactivation of the cells so that it is nearly nil at 50°C. However, the time to reach rapid gas production is greatly shortened if the initial temperature is set at 42°C.

For every gram of glucose a theoretical yield of 249 cc of CO_2 gas is produced at standard conditions, but this amount is not realized in dough fermentation because of the formation of by-products.

An important part of modern bakery operation is the scheduling of mixing, fermenting, proofing, and baking. The fermentation and proofing steps depend on the uniform functioning of the living organism yeast. For this reason, one of the major challenges to the yeast manufacturer is the delivery of a uniform product in terms of its functioning in the various dough systems.

Active Dry Yeast (ADY)

Baker's yeast can be dried so as to preserve the viability of a very large proportion of the individual yeast cells. This active dry yeast is available in the form of small frangible rods, small pellets, or as a granular powder. In these forms, the yeast contains only about 8% moisture. It is far more stable than compressed yeast. Under ambient temperature conditions and exposed to air it may lose about 7% of its activity in a month but in an inert gas (N_2 or CO_2) this can be reduced to as little as 1% loss in 3 months and no more than 10% in 1 yr.

Rehydration of Dry Yeast.—Active dry yeast is usually rehydrated in warm water (110°F) or warm sugar solutions before use. Rehydration at cool water temperatures is usually detrimental to cell vitality and is avoided. After rehydration the yeast suspension is used in substantially the same way as compressed yeast.

Dry yeast is not directly interchangeable, cell for cell, with compressed yeast. Some processes require adjustment when shifting from compressed to active dry. The latter tends to reduce mixing time requirements and if not rehydrated properly it may produce sticky doughs which are difficult to handle and process.

The replacement ratio of active dry yeast to compressed yeast is of the order of 40-50%. This means that 0.4-0.5 lb of ADY will replace 1 lb of compressed yeast.

Sour Dough Fermentations

There are sour dough breads that are leavened without any commercial compressed yeast and some others that use very low levels of yeast. Typical of some of these leavening actions is that used in the San Francisco Sour Dough French Bread Process.

The heart of the process is the starter or mother sponge. This sponge is rebuilt about every 8 hr every day of the week. About $1/3$ of the new sponge consists of the previous sponge. The other $2/3$ of the sponge is used for the dough stage at a rate of 20 parts per 100 parts of flour. Fermentation time is at least 8 hr.

The leavening agents in the San Francisco Sour French Bread appear to be two organisms, one a yeast S. exiguus, which does not ferment maltose but ferments sucrose, raffinose, and the monosaccharides glucose and galactose, and the other a lactobacillus of a unique type that requires maltose for growth and acid formation. It also utilizes glucose and galactose. This unusual combination of organisms produces the characteristic sour flavor desired in this type of bread. The exact mechanism of leavening has not been elucidated. Other sour dough processes used here and there around the world may have similar if not identical leavening microorganisms.

Chemical Leaveners

Baking powder is the typical chemical leavener Historically, baking powder is new as compared to yeast leavening. The principle was actually patented in England in 1838. The basic reaction of chemical leaveners may be written as follows:

$$Soda + Acid \longrightarrow Carbon\ dioxide + Salt + Water$$

The alkaline substance used to react with an acid substance to produce CO_2 is nearly always sodium bicarbonate, i.e., soda. Ammonium carbonate and ammonium bicarbonate have been used for many years to generate CO_2 but they are used singly. The use of sour milk, containing as it does lactic acid, $CH_3CHOHCOOH$, plus sodium bicarbonate, $NaHCO_3$, was prevalent in America before baking powders were available. The salt formed in this reaction is sodium lactate.

One of the earliest baking powders consisted of cream of tartar (potassium hydrogen tartrate) and soda. This mixture reacts rapidly in the batter and a small proportion of the mixture remains to react in the oven.

Because the acid component of this early baking powder was known as "cream" of tartar it became the practice to refer to other acid components of baking powders as "creams."

Cream of tartar is a typical fast-acting baking acid. The leavening gas is liberated chiefly during the mixing of the batter. The oven spring, expansion in the oven, is derived mainly from expansion of the preformed bubbles in the batter. The bench tolerance of such leaveners is not suited for commercial bakery operations where machines are involved and there may be delays between mixing the batter and baking. Another fast-acting acid that was introduced very early is monocalcium phosphate monohydrate. This substance, $MCP \cdot H_2O$, is a more efficient leavener on a weight basis than cream of tartar and does not react quite so rapidly in the batter. An acid with improved bench tolerance is anhydrous monocalcium phosphate, AMCP, a portion of which is slow to dissolve in the batter and consequently has more oven spring. The reaction of MCP and AMCP with soda cannot be expressed by a simple chemical equation.

An acid made available many years ago and still widely used in baking powder is sodium aluminum sulfate, SAS. This acid reacts with soda mainly in the oven. When combined with MCP, a baking powder is produced in which one ingredient, MCP, produces gas bubbles in the batter and the other, SAS, accomplishes its leavening entirely in the oven. Mixtures like this are widely used and are known as double-acting powders. The reaction of SAS or alum as it is sometimes called with soda is described by the equation

$$Na_2SO_4 \cdot Al_2(SO_4)_3 + 6NaHCO_3 \longrightarrow$$
$$Al_2O_3 \cdot 3H_2O + 4Na_2SO_4 + 6CO_2$$

For some applications SAS is not without flavor and rancidity problems and other acids with similar functional properties were sought. One of these, sodium acid pyrophosphate, SAPP, has been very successful. This acid can be manufactured so that its function can be controlled via granulation and certain additives to give a desirable rate of reaction both in the batter and in the oven.

With the variety of acids now available baking powders can be designed either for specific applications or for general purpose usage. One powder, for example, combines a specified form of SAPP with some MCP and contains also a calcium salt to help control the rate of reaction. Calcium lactate or calcium sulfate have been employed for this purpose.

The equation describing the reaction of straight SAPP with soda is

$$Na_2H_2P_2O_7 + NaHCO_3 \longrightarrow$$
$$Na_2HPO_4 + CO_2 + H_2O$$

Other acids have been introduced as leaveners in recent years, such as sodium aluminum phosphate. This acid, SALP, reacts slightly before the oven and gives a good oven reaction. Its composition is described by the formula $NaH_{14}Al_3(PO_4)_8 4H_2O$. Glucono delta lactone and dicalcium phosphate dihydrate are two other acids that have been introduced for specific applications.

Federal specifications require that a baking powder yield not less than 12% of carbon dioxide by weight. Most commercial powders yield 14–17%.

The neutralizing value of a leavening acid is defined as the parts by weight of sodium bicarbonate that can be neutralized, i.e., converted to CO_2 and salt by 100 parts of the leavening acid. Because complete knowledge of the details of the reaction is not usually available the neutralizing value is determined empirically. In addition, because the composition of some of the acids is controlled by conditions of manufacture, there are small variations in reported values.

The neutralizing values of the major leavening acids arranged in the order of increasing value are:

Leavening Acids	Neutralizing Value
Dicalcium phosphate dihydrate	33
Cream of tartar	45
Glucono delta lactone	45–47
Sodium acid pyrophosphate (SAPP)	71–74
Monocalcium phosphate monohydrate (MCP)	80
Anhydrous monocalcium phosphate (AMCP)	83–84

Sodium aluminum sulfate
(SAS)   100
Sodium aluminum phos-
phate (SALP)   102

Cornstarch is a very important ingredient in baking powder since it stabilizes the mixed acid and soda preventing interaction during storage and transportation. This stabilizing action is aided by the use of specially dried low moisture starch. The particle size of the soda is also an important factor in determining the stability of the mixed powder. If too fine, the stability of the mixture is poor; and if too coarse, specking of the crust is caused by local excessive alkalinity. The acid ingredients are also carefully standardized for some of the same reasons. All ingredients must, of course, meet FDA regulations in regard to wholesomeness and safety.

Self-rising Flour and Cake Mixes

Baking powder can be premixed with flour and other ingredients to make a convenient product. The stability of the leaveners is usually excellent. The leavening action starts when a batter is formed by addition of water or milk and continues in the oven.

Soda-Leavened Baked Products

Soda itself has some leavening action in the oven but the baked product is on the alkaline side which is not suitable for many items. If sour milk is incorporated in the batter, the acids contained in it will react with soda to produce a leavened product closer to neutrality.

LAWRENCE ATKIN
SUTTON REDFERN
CHARLES N. FREY

Cross-reference: *Yeasts.*

LEEUWENHOEK, ANTONI VAN (1632–1723)

Antoni Van Leeuwenhoek, discoverer of micro-organisms, was born at Delft (The Netherlands) on October 24, 1632, and died there on August 26, 1723. He was the son of a basketmaker. His father died when he was five and he was educated by his uncle, an attorney. In 1648 he went to Amsterdam where he qualified himself as a draper, returning to his native town in 1654. He set up in business there as a draper. In 1660 he was made chamberlain (kamerbewaarder) to the Sheriffs of Delft; in 1669 he was admitted as surveyor (landmeter); and in 1679 he was elected as a wine-gauger (wijnroeier).

In 1673 he was introduced by the Dutch physician Reinier de Graaf to the Royal Society at London because of his observations as a "most ingenious person, who has devised microscopes which far surpass those which we have hitherto seen." Over a 50-yr period he wrote more than 560 letters about his discoveries to the Royal Society, to the College " 't Wilde Swijn" of the University of Louvain, and to others. In 1680 the Royal Society appointed him as a member.

Most of his writings contain observations and discoveries made with the microscope in the (micro)biological field as well as in the field of chemistry and physics. He never learned a foreign language and was not able to read foreign publications. Fascinated by his discoveries, he expressed his observations in an elaborate but not very systematic way, calling the small and moving organisms "kleine dierkens" (little animals). Amazing, however, is the exactitude of his descriptions and the skillful evaluation of the magnitude of his objects. His observations led him to carrying out experiments, e.g., with anaerobic fermentations.

From his microscopes, which were all of the single type and consisted of a pair of brass or silver plates with one small self-ground lens with magnifications up to 500X, a few have been preserved (there is one in the University Museum at Utrecht with a magnification of 270X).

From his discoveries have come, to mention a few, the discovery of the protozoa (1674), the bacteria (1676), the spermatozoa (1677), and the striating of muscle fibers (1682).

His daughter Maria erected for him a memorial in the Old Church at Delft where he was buried.

L. J. SCHUDDEBOOM

Cross-reference: *Bacteriology.*

LETTUCE

Lettuce (*Lactuca sativa*) has been known and used as a salad vegetable for centuries. It is presumed to be native to central Asia or perhaps India. First mention of lettuce appears to have been made in Persia about 550 B.C. with the comment that it was served to kings. It was favored as a salad vegetable by both the Greeks and the Romans. A reference to lettuce occurs in Chinese literature in the 5th Century of our era, but no doubt it had been a familiar vegetable in China and the Orient long before that date. Lettuce was widely used in Europe in the 16th Century but how long before that it was introduced there is unknown. There is a reference to lettuce in 1290 in a southern England legend—"a fair herb that men call lettuce"—and it may be inferred that it had a place in the cuisine of the time. In times past the herb was regarded as having a sedative effect and a pharmaceutical, "lactucarium," made from the milky substance that exudes from the plant on being pressed, had some medicinal standing until late in the last century. Lettuce is a good source of vitamin A but any claim to medicinal powers has long since been abandoned. Gastronomically, it is a prized food, cultivated in all parts of the globe where the climate permits.

There are three main types of lettuce with numerous varieties under each: (1) Head lettuce (Iceberg, Boston, New York Imperial, etc.). (2) Leaf lettuce (Salad Bowl, and many other varieties). (3) Cos or romaine (Paris White, and others).

There are well over 100 varieties of lettuce. New York Imperial and the Iceberg varieties ship well and are the favored head lettuce varieties in many areas of the United States and Canada. The main production areas of the United States vary somewhat with the seasons, as indicated below:

Winter	Early Spring
Florida	North Carolina
Texas	New Mexico
Arizona	Arizona
California	California
Late Spring	Summer
Massachusetts	New York
Connecticut	Ohio
New Jersey	Michigan
Early Fall	Wisconsin
New Jersey	Colorado
Texas	California
California	Oregon
New Mexico	Washington
	Late Fall
	Arizona

Production is heaviest in winter and summer, the winter harvest coming from the Southern part of the United States and the summer harvest from the northern.

The annual U.S. yield amounted to about $230,000,000 in 1971, this from a total area of 234,000 acres. Over 3 billion pounds of lettuce are consumed in the United States each year.

Harvesting is a manual operation at present but there seems to be a good chance that mechanical harvesting will eventually take over. A University of California invention uses a paddle wheel under the harvester which "feels" the heads and, if firm enough to pick up with the paddle fingers, grips the heads and cuts the stems, lifts them on to the conveyor for packing. The University of Arizona also has a patent on a mechanical harvester.

Mechanized harvesting will require genetic improvements before it can be applied to lettuce crops generally; and, no doubt, cultivation practices will have to be changed to accommodate the rather complex harvesters. But, harvesting of other vegetable crops is now mechanized, among the most successful being the mechanical harvest of tomatoes.

Getting lettuce to market is something more of a problem than it is for other vegetables because of the high respiration rate of lettuce and the necessity of maintaining the crispness and other characteristics that the consumer demands.

Formerly, lettuce was packed in crushed ice in crates containing 60 lb of product and 30 lb of ice. This method brought the temperature of the lettuce down to 32°–34°F and the freshness quality was preserved; but a good deal of physical damage was caused by the ice. Later the so-called dry pack was introduced whereby the lettuce was packed in the field without ice but shipped to the users in refrigerated trucks or cars. This method worked fairly well for short distances but could not be used for cross-country shipments. Vacuum cooling solved the problem. By this method packed crates of lettuce are loaded into steel tanks equipped with steam ejector vacuum pumps and condensers. Sufficient vacuum is created in these tanks to lower atmospheric pressure and evaporate the water in the lettuce; as the water is removed the temperature is reduced. The lettuce can then be transferred to refrigerated media (trucks or cars) and shipped to any point in the United States.

Lettuce is packed in paperboard cartons, basket crates, or hampers. The individual units are sometimes wrapped in film. A standard crate contains about 45 lb of lettuce.

Lettuce does not tolerate freezing, dehydration or the canning process since it wilts under excessive temperatures, either hot or cold. This is not to say that lettuce cannot be cooked. Lettuce soup, creamed lettuce, baked lettuce, braised lettuce with bacon and onion are familiar examples of cooked lettuce.

Lettuce has a delicate flavor which together with its crispness accounts for its almost universal use as a salad vegetable.

MARTIN S. PETERSON

References

CRUESS, W. V. 1958. Commercial Fruit and Vegetable Products, 4th Edition. McGraw-Hill Book Co., New York.

FRIEDMAN, B. A. 1951. Vacuum cooling of vegetables and fruits. Ann. Rept. Vegetable Growers' Assoc. Am., 98.

KOTSCHEVAR, L. H. 1965. Quantity Food Purchasing. John Wiley & Sons, New York.

RYALL, A. L., and LIPTON, W. J. 1972. Handling, Transportation and Storage of Fruits and Vegetables, Vol. 1—Vegetables and Melons. Avi Publishing Co., Westport, Conn.

LICORICE CONFECTIONERY

Licorice confections in all probability belong to the oldest sweetmeats popular with the average citizen. Licorice root, native in the Mediterranean area, was put to early use in pharmacy by the Arabs who also prepared the extract. The virtues of the root soon became known north of the Alps, and 13th Century Middle Dutch, Lower German and Middle English manuscripts advocate its use as a medicine for cough, sore throat, and troubles of the chest. Grocer-apothecaries, importing spices and medicinal herbs including licorice root and extract, were probably the first to combine the juice with honey, and later with sugar—still a precious commodity in 13th Century Europe and therefore mainly used in medicinal preparations. The late Middle Ages knew about licorice pastilles cast in crude molds, while according to Dodonaeus "cough of chest cookies" were made from licorice in Dutch monasteries, the latter being similar to the cut licorice lozenges of "trochisci bechici nigri" made popular by French apothecaries. Extruded licorice sweets are said to have been introduced into Holland in the beginning of the 17th Century, whereas salty licorice—known in pharmacy as "trochisci chloreti ammonici" and deriving its saline taste from ammonium chloride—was probably not produced before the 18th Century when Baumé started the first French production of sal-ammoniac, used as an expectorant. Eventually, licorice confections became one of the first lines of the confectionery manufacturer when this industry began to develop toward the middle of the 19th Century.

Types

Today licorice confectionery, in which licorice extract is the characteristic ingredient, exists in a large variety of kinds and types. Since Holland has the highest per capita consumption of licorice sweets (1 kg per year or more, of which an estimated 90% is in the form of salty licorice) and the annual sales volume (approximately 60 million guilders retail worth) constitutes between 25 and 50% of the total volume of sugar confectionery, the variegated types of licorice confections manufactured in that country serve well to illustrate the technological possibilities. Although class names for licorice sweets can be based upon different criteria such as color (black versus brown licorice, the latter without added black coloring), flavor ("salty," laurel or sweet-bay licorice, anise licorice), finishing (panned or dragée licorice), geometrical shape, or intended semi-pharmaceutical use (cough licorice, "stomach" licorice), these classifications are considered subordinate to the 2 or 4 subdivisions that can be based on the method of manufacture.

Leaving aside other categories of confections to which licorice extract may be added in smaller proportions as a mere flavoring material (often in caramels, toffees, and chewing gum; sometimes in taffy, fudge, hard candy, cough drops, or other types of medicated confections), or for technological purposes (halva), or dietetic reasons (glycyrrhizin as a noncaloric sweetener), as well as products that have only the denomination in common without containing any licorice at all ("Chinese" licorice, "white" licorice, or marshmallow paste), the two principal classes of genuine licorice confectionery distinguished according to the manufacturing process are cast (molded) licorice and extruded (pressed) licorice.

The more expensive types of licorice confections, making up the majority of prepackaged articles in Holland and consumed by children and adults alike, are made from a cooked mixture cast in molding starch. Sometimes, however, the warm mixture is simply poured out or ladled (hence the Dutch name "scooped" licorice) into lined trays or onto greased slabs, and after solidification is cut into the required shape; this type of slab licorice is generally slightly more tender, but the formulas do not differ much from the starch molded variety. Cast licorice, as developed originally in Europe, was a genuine gum article if the large group of gums and jellies is tripartitioned into "gums"—hard and sometimes even brittle products containing over 50% of gum arabic. "Pastilles" are more soft and resilient because of a higher moisture content and replacement of part of the gum arabic with gelatin. "Jellies" are soft and tender because of the use of gelling agents resulting in high moisture contents. The original gum or "hard gumdrop" (in the United States sometimes referred to as an "old style druggist gumdrop") was made exclusively with gum arabic as the bodying agent. Since gum arabic does not produce a gel but dissolves to a high concentration, the formula of the products is characterized by a proportion of gum arabic which equals or preferably exceeds the combined amount of carbohydrate sweeteners. From the genuine gum article, other lines developed by partial replacement of the gum arabic, for example, the pastille-like "jujubes" with part gum, part gelatin, often deposited in metal trays, and after stoving cut into simple forms. During recent years the use of gum arabic has declined due to the desire to reduce production costs and because of the gum's inherent variability in quality from season to season. As substitutes, thin-boiling starches and, more recently, other modified starches are being used.

The second main category of licorice goods is made from paste or dough, obtained from low-boiled or cold mixed blends of carbohydrate sweeteners with a suitable binder. One subgroup, usually heavily flavored, is made from a cold mix or stiff dough which is pressed between rollers into a sheet from which small shapes are cut or stamped out. The well-known, cheaper children's items are prepared from a dough made with gelatinized wheat flour, which is extruded in all sorts of finished shapes and designs. Licorice paste, sandwiched between other layers of cream paste with various fillers (e.g., coconut), gives the name to "licorice all-sorts," sometimes called "English licorice" in Holland and other continental European countries.

Licorice Extracts

The characteristic ingredient and dominant flavoring material of licorice confections is the extract or "juice" of the licorice root (*Glycyrrhiza glabra* L. and other Glycyrrhiza species and varieties), either in the form of large solidified blocks ("block licorice") or some sort of smaller and more dried particles (drum-dried granules or flakes, or spray-dried powder). The composition of the extract depends markedly upon the root source, the processing method, and the country of origin of manufacture (See Table L-1).

The glycyrrhizin contents, which are based on traditional gravimetric methods (and therefore sometimes too high), serve as an indication for the purity of the extract, taking into account natural variations as to botanical origin and other data suggesting the possible addition of starchy or sugary materials. Glycyrrhizin is generally stated to have a sweetness 50 times as much as sucrose; however, other constituents of the extract are responsible for the licorice flavor as such. Glycyrrhizin is a glycoside of which the aglycone, glycyrrhetic (glycyrrhetinic) acid, is a pentacyclic triterpene devoid of sweet taste. Various analogs and derivatives of glycyrrhetic acid as well as related pentacyclic triterpenes have been found in licorice. In addition to starch and "gums" (including pectins), reducing sugars and sucrose, other carbohydrate matter includes mannitol and pinitol, whereas also fat is said to be present. Asparagin and canavanin are associated with the protein fraction. In addition to resins and tannins, a bitter principle (sometimes called glycyramarin) is present. Other components found in licorice extract embrace sterols (sitosterol and dihydrostigmasterol), flavonoids (liquiritin, liquiritoside, formononetin), vitamins (biotin, pantothenic acid), metals (copper, manganese, sodium, and numerous trace elements), and enzymes (catalase, peroxidase). Also present are malic acid, methylsalicylate, ferulic acid, and coumarin derivatives. Estrogenic activity has been reported.

Other Ingredients

Other ingredients of licorice confectionery are carbohydrate sweeteners (sucrose or molasses and glucose syrup, sometimes also dextrose), a binding agent (gum arabic, gelatin, thin-boiling starch or modified starch or wheat flour), flavoring materials (sal-ammoniac, anise oil, etc.), coloring (carbon black, caramel), and often a glazing material (paraffin or mineral oil). Whereas exclusive use of gum arabic for the setting of cast licorice produces the traditional hard gum, the softer pastilles mostly contain a low-grade gelatin of medium bloom value as a plasticiser; care should be taken that its use does not result in the introduction of too much sulphur dioxide.

TABLE L-1

AVERAGE COMPOSITION (PERCENTAGE BY WEIGHT) OF BLOCK LICORICE EXTRACT

Country of Manufacture	Moisture	Ash	Insolubles	Gums and Starch	Reducing Sugars	Sucrose	Glycyrrhizin
Italy	15(12–18)	4(3–5)	8(2–14)	42(34–50)	5(2–8)	4(1–7)	12(7–17)
Spain	14(11–17)	—	16(3–29)	36(31–41)	4(2–6)	3(1–5)	13(10–16)
Israel	16	6	4	30	5	6	16
Turkey	13(11–15)	9(6–12)	4(1–7)	26(16–36)	6(3–9)	12(6–18)	16(11–21)
USA	16(13–19)	6(5–7)	3(1–5)	28(24–32)	4(2–6)	6(2–10)	21(16–26)
Syria	15(14–16)	8(6–10)	3(2–4)	21(15–27)	6(4–8)	11(7–15)	21(15–27)
Iran	17	7	3	38	7	5	25
China	13(12–14)	13(12–14)	4(1–7)	25(17–33)	5(3–7)	10(6–14)	26(22–30)
USSR	12(18–16)	8(7–9)	2(1–3)	19(16–22)	9(7–11)	5(2–8)	32(25–39)

Apart from hydrolyzed collagen, starchy materials are being more and more introduced to replace part of the gum arabic in molded licorice. These substitutes should reproduce as much as possible the textural properties of the traditional gumdrop or "arabic drop," namely, a strong and firm body, a clean "bite" without stickiness, and a slow rate of dissolution in the mouth. In extruded licorice, wheat flour is used to produce a dough; if gelatin is added, a low bloom type is preferred. With regard to the use of glucose syrup in licorice confectionery as a bodying agent, to improve cohesiveness, as a stabilizer to produce sheen and as a humectant, its function to prevent sucrose crystallization is particularly important in extruded licorice because of its tendency to dry out.

Cast Licorice

Cast licorice molded in starch is manufactured by blending and cooking the ingredients, depositing the warm fluid or semifluid mixture into forms imprinted in molding starch, drying the cooled pieces in stoves to the desired consistency, and finishing them by steam dampening, polishing, or any other appropriate operation. The actual molding process and its auxiliary operations (filling in and imprinting of the starch, depositing, discharging and refilling the starch) is generally carried out as one synchronized process by means of a molding (or "master") starch machine, the so-called "mogul." One way of preparing the fluid mixture is by dissolving sucrose in water and bringing it to the boil, adding glucose syrup and boiling the batch at a temperature around 125°C. In the meantime, gum arabic—kibbled or crushed if necessary—is dissolved without boiling in approximately the same amount of water by stirring in a steam pan; the solution may be rested for some hours at about 45°C during which period coarse particles and other impurities settle to the bottom of the tank while a foamy crust rises to the top and can be scooped off. The sucrose-glucose blend is poured slowly into the "melted" gum under continuous stirring, and licorice extract is added in the form of a prepared solution. The mixed batch is reheated—flavorings and colorings being added at the last possible moment—to a consistency suitable for depositing in starch, a point that is chosen either by routine skill or more scientifically by measurement of the viscosity or moisture content (for a given formula). The cast licorice in the starch trays is heated in a drying room at approximately 50°C until the moisture content has been reduced to 11-13%. After cooling, the gumdrops are cleaned of starch, placed on screens, steam dampened (to close the pores) and finished by polishing, for example with mineral oil.

Pressed Licorice

Roller shaped and cut licorice is usually manufactured by cold mixing licorice extract and other flavoring materials (menthol, peppermint oil, laurel essence, anise oil, or sal-ammoniac) with dry carbohydrate sweeteners and some starch, with gum arabic and/or gum tragacanth (and sometimes a small proportion of wheat flour or gelatin as the binding agent). The paste is pressed between rollers into a sheet, dried, and cut into small forms; or the dough may be pressed and shaped in one operation by two pairs of rollers, and dried afterwards. Articles belonging to this group, such as pellets, cachous, small rhombic lozenges, etc. generally have a high content of licorice extract and are heavily flavored.

Extruded Licorice

Extruded licorice, in English usually called licorice paste, is actually made from a dough in which gelatinized wheat flour of a soft type is the binding ingredient. The low-boiled mixture, cooked to around 19% moisture by continuous method, is conducted to the extruding machine by pumping through electrically-heated pipes. It comes out in endless strands such as whips, braids, straws, twists, shoestrings, ribbons (often coiled into whirls), strips, sticks, telephone poles, tubes, bars, ropes, rods, etc., which are cut in pieces of the required length, dried, and often coated with a glaze. Extruded centers for licorice comfits or "torpedoes" are covered with a colored coating by panning. These children's items are often flavored with oil of anise to such an extent that this flavor has become virtually synonymous with the licorice taste in the United States. Licorice paste (usually colored with caramel and of a more "short" texture) can be sandwiched between layers of colored cream pastes by means of a layering machine that extrudes layered sheets which are subsequently cut by a guillotine-type machine.

A guide to the formulas used in various types of licorice confectionery is given in Table L-2, showing average proportions of the principal ingredients together with an estimated range within which they can be varied. Coloring and flavoring are not included; these are added at the discretion of the confectioner.

Food Laws

In the food regulations of some European countries, provisions occur with regard to licorice confectionery. The French requirements are somewhat confusing: a licorice sweet, if colored artificially, must contain not less than 4% licorice extract (which itself should contain at least 6% glycyrrhizin), and both the extract and the final

TABLE L-2

FORMULAS FOR LICORICE CONFECTIONERY

Ingredient	Cast (Molded)		Cut Paste		Extruded Dough	
	(Percentage by Weight)					
Gum arabic	50	(40–60)	10	(2–12)	—	
Starch	16[1]	(6–26)	10	(5–15)	—	
Modified starch	8[1]	(6–10)	—		—	
Gelatin	6[1]	(4–8)	—		5	(0–10)
Wheat flour	—		—		32	(25–39)
Sucrose, molasses	30	(20–40)	40	(20–60)	45	(30–60)
Glucose syrup	7	(4–10)	10	(5–15)	15	(5–25)
Licorice extract	4	(3–5)	30	(10–50)	3	(1–5)
Sal-ammoniac	9	(4–14)	—		—	

[1] Alternative ingredients to replace part of the gum arabic.

product may contain gum arabic and sugars (including glucose syrup); the confection may, however, not be designated a gum article if other binding agents (starchy materials) are present, so that as a result all licorice articles containing wheat flour or gum arabic substitutes are to be called "licorice fantasy." In Western Germany, semiofficial provisions published by the confectionery industry require that licorice articles contain a minimum of 5% licorice juice; artificial coloring is prohibited by law and the addition of sal-ammoniac is limited to 2%. The German Democratic Republic requires at least 5% block licorice (or 10% licorice juice with a maximum of 35% moisture) in licorice dragees. Rather unexpectedly, Argentina also has a minimum requirement (4% licorice extract) in licorice pastilles. The EEC Commission has proposed a harmonized regulation for sugar confectionery which requires a minimum of 0.5% glycyrrhizin in confection-designated licorice; the addition of sal-ammoniac is not regulated and, therefore, prohibited according to the proposed text.

Toxicology

During the course of the past 15 yr, there have been many reports on the undesired effects (such as hypertension, pseudoaldosteronism, and hypokalemia) of the characteristic component of licorice—glycyrrhizin. Licorice was put up for toxicological evaluation (as a food color) before the 8th Session (Dec. 1964) of the Joint FAO/WHO Expert Committee on Food Additives. The reports of this meeting show that licorice was classified in category IV: "food colors for which the Committee did not attempt to prepare specifications because the toxicological data were totally lacking or because the colors were found to be harmful and their use in foods was not considered desirable." It appears that in the case of licorice the first reason applies, namely, that "no attempt was made at a toxicological evaluation" because of the lack of biological studies as well as knowledge of composition combined with the variation in composition according to the source and the method of preparation employed. However, licorice may be re-evaluated at a future meeting of JECFA. Similarly, the Council of Europe (Partial Agreement) in a recent survey with toxicological classification of flavoring materials has indicated that for licorice further data on short-term toxicity as well as chronological effects, are required. The toxicological re-evaluation of GRAS substances in the United States also includes licorice.

C. NIEMAN

Cross-reference: *Confections*.

LIEBIG, JUSTUS VON (1803–1873)

Justus von Liebig's influence on food technology was not direct, but this famous German chemist, teacher, and experimentalist made important contributions to both physiology and agriculture, contributions that substantially extended contemporary understanding of the role of oxidation in the growth and repair of the body and of the part mineral constituents of plants, e.g., potash and phosphates, play in plant growth. Liebig's formulation of beef tea resulted in a considerable manufacturing enterprise and thus, as the inventor of a new product, he can by a stretch of the imagination be called an early food technologist. It must be admitted, however, that Liebig belongs primarily to the field of chemistry where he excelled both in teaching and in research.

Liebig briefly attended the University of Bonn, the University of Erlangen, and the University of Paris where he studied under some of the leading chemists of Europe, notably Gay-Lussac, who recognized his exceptional ability. He began his teaching career at Giessen in the School of Chemistry in 1824 and it was there that he established an experimental research program. It was the first of its kind wherein the students worked independently but discussed their results with one another. Liebig supervised their work and taught them how, by experimental study, to gain a command of their subject. In 1852 Liebig left Giessen for an important post at the University of Munich. Liebig's achievements, in addition to those in the field of chemical education, included innovations in analytical methods, the discovery of chloroform, chloral and cyanogen compounds, and, as mentioned, contributions to physiology and agricultural chemistry.

MARTIN S. PETERSON

LIQUID SALAD DRESSING

See Salad Dressing.

LOBSTERS

This article presents certain aspects of the occurrence, biology, catching, live-holding, processing, and marketing of lobsters of the genus *Homarus* which includes the American lobster (*Homarus americanus*) and the European lobster (*Homarus vulgaris* or *Homarus gammarus*).

Not covered are the Norway lobster, *Nephrops norvegicus*, a smaller relative, which is marketed in Europe as scampi or Dublin Bay Prawn, and some other products commonly marketed as "lobsters." These include various species of spiny lobsters, also known as rock lobsters, langusta, or ocean crayfish.

Occurrence and Landings

Lobsters are found on both sides of the North Atlantic Ocean. The American lobster occurs along the east coast of North America from North Carolina to Labrador. It is most abundant in the central part of this range and the largest catches are being taken in the State of Maine, southern Nova Scotia, and the southern Gulf of St. Lawrence. The European lobster is found off the coasts of Europe from Norway to the Mediterranean Sea. The two species are closely related and differ only slightly in shape and color.

Most lobsters live close to shore in water from the low water mark to about 20 fathoms (40 m). Other stocks are found at depths of 50–300 fathoms (90–550 m) on the slope of the Continental Shelf, especially off the coast of the United States from Corsair Canyon off New England to as far south as Norfolk Canyon off Maryland. Lobsters live in waters where temperatures can go as low as 29°F (−1.7°C) in later winter and as high as 75°F (24°C) in summer and where the salinity of the water approximates 3%.

Landings of American lobsters in 1971 totalled 32,620 metric tons (71,851,000 lb) with Canada contributing 17,220 tons and the United States 15,400 tons. Catches of European lobsters are much smaller, about 2000 tons a year with the United Kingdom landing about 1000 tons.

Physical Characteristics

The body of the lobster is divided into two main sections: the combined head and thorax usually known as the body and the tail section. The one-piece shell covering the head and thorax is known as the carapace. The first of the five pairs of walking legs is large and armed with strong claws and, of these, the "crusher" is considerably heavier than the more slender "pincer" claw. The large, greenish, digestive gland in the body is the liver and is commonly referred to as tomalley. The greenish-black roe in mature female lobsters turns bright red when cooked and is then sometimes referred to as "coral." Fresh lobster blood is colorless, but turns white and rather curd-like when cooked.

Growth and Size Limits

The female lays her eggs from early June to September and the fertilized eggs become fastened to the swimmerets under the tail. These so-called "berried" females carry the eggs externally for about a year before hatching. The larvae are free-swimming until they have changed their shells (moulted) three times. They then settle to the bottom.

The growth rate which depends on water temperature and availability of food is quite variable as is the size and age at maturity. In the warmer waters of the southern Gulf of St. Lawrence where lobsters grow faster and mature early, they can be retained legally at a carapace length of $2\frac{1}{2}$ in. (6.4 cm) and a weight of about 7 oz (200 gm). In the colder waters off Nova Scotia and Newfoundland, the lobsters grow slowly and mature later and the size limit is set at $3\frac{3}{16}$ in. (8.1 cm); these lobsters weigh about 15 oz (425 gm). Other Canadian areas have size limits of $2\frac{3}{4}$ and 3 in. In the United States, the minimum size limits range from $3\frac{1}{16}$ to $3\frac{3}{16}$ in. and in Maine there is a maximum or jumbo size limit of $5\frac{3}{16}$ in.

Catching Methods

Practically all lobsters are captured in traps of various shapes and sizes. The only exception is in the offshore fishery on the slope of the Continental Shelf where otter trawls are in use in addition to traps.

FIG. L-1. A "BERRIED" FEMALE LOBSTER

FIG. L-2. INSHORE LOBSTER TRAP OF THE TYPE USED BY NEW ENGLAND AND CANADIAN FISHER-MEN

FIG. L-3. TYPICAL INSHORE LOBSTER BOAT USED IN CANADA

In Canada, gear is restricted by law to the conventional lobster trap. These traps and those used in the United States are usually built in the form of a half cylinder, $2^{1}/_{2}$-4 ft long (75-120 cm), with the wooden frame covered with laths and netting. One to three mesh funnels lead to the bait compartment from which another funnel leads to the "parlour" or "bedroom" section. Traps used in other areas may be square, rectangular, or round, made of metal, wood, or plastic and in the offshore fishery, large steel, wooden, or plastic traps are used.

Most American lobsters are caught by inshore fishermen using open motor boats 25-45 ft (7.5-14 m) in length. Most of these fish within ten miles of their home port and land their catches daily. When each trap is hauled, the lobsters are removed and those found to be egg-bearing or below legal size are released. The claws are immobilized with rubber bands or wooden plugs. The catch is then placed in wooden crates until landed.

Live Holding

Lobster catches are seasonal, especially in countries such as Canada and Norway where closed fishing seasons are enforced. In order to market the lobster in an orderly fashion, and to maximize profits, it is often necessary to hold the animals alive for extended periods. Fishermen usually keep lobsters in floating crates until sold to a dealer, and the dealer may keep them at landing points until enough have accumulated for economic shipment to large depots where storage conditions and shipping facilities are better.

The ideal site for longer-term lobster storage should be protected from storm damage and have good water circulation. The water should be reasonably cool in summer, but should not freeze in winter and the salinity should remain fairly constant at about 3%. For short-term storage, lobsters are held in ordinary crates, floating wooden "cars," or in tank units ashore supplied with running sea water. Long-term storage of up to six months is usually restricted to tidal pounds.

Care must be taken to avoid disease in live-holding installations. A bacterial lobster blood disease, Gaffkaemia, although completely harmless to humans, is transmitted only through wounds and can occasionally cause mortalities, especially when water temperatures are high.

Shipping

Since almost $^{3}/_{4}$ of the Canadian lobster catch is marketed alive, distribution of the lobsters to market is of major importance. Bulk shipments to New England from Canada are usually made by refrigerated or insulated trucks with the lobsters packed in standard 100-lb capacity crates and with the temperatures kept at 35°-40°F (1.7°-4.4°C). Smaller shipments are often made in double compartment wooden boxes or barrels where about 50 lb (23 kg) of lobsters are packed in seaweed and kept cool with 50-70 lb (23-32 kg) of ice placed in the outer compartment.

With the large increase in air cargo traffic in the past few years, shipments of lobsters by air have increased correspondingly. This has opened up new markets in Europe and across North America for lobsters from the Eastern United States and Canada. For air shipments, new, lighter, leak-proof shipping containers have been designed. Cardboard containers with insulation such as styrofoam and with ice in plastic bags are in common use. Lobsters packed in wood shavings with ice packs will stay alive for up to 72-96 hr.

In inland locations, the lobsters are kept in refrigerated units with natural or artificial sea water.

Processing

Fresh Whole Lobsters.—The bulk of the lobster catch is marketed alive and consumed as fresh lobster in the shell.

Lobsters are processed by boiling with a recommended cooking time in salted water (3-4% salt) of 15-20 min for a 1-1$^1/_2$-lb lobster. There are no "poisonous" parts in the lobster, but the stomach, a sac located in the forward part of the body, is sometimes removed before serving.

Frozen Whole Lobsters.—Relatively small quantities are marketed as frozen, whole lobsters. These are prepared by placing the live lobster in hot or boiling water for 1-2 min before cooling and freezing. "Fractional cooking" is also reportedly used. The frozen lobsters are vacuum packed in airtight, tough, nylon bags or foam plastic containers for storage, shipment, and display.

At a temperature of -20°F (-29°C) the useful storage time is reported to be at least 6 months. For preparation, the lobsters are thawed and cooked for 15-20 min, similar to live lobsters. If whole lobsters are frozen without the short precook, the meat sticks to the shell and is reportedly difficult to remove. Fully-cooked lobsters can be frozen in the shell for shorter periods, but preferably not longer than one month if not protected against dehydration and oxidation.

Fresh and Frozen Lobster Meat.—The shucked meat from lobsters handled in processing plants is marketed as fresh or frozen lobster meat. In Canada this represents a sizable proportion of the catch and the annual production of lobster meat is over 3 million pounds (1430 metric tons in 1971). The smaller lobsters or "canners" are often used for this purpose and in the United States a quantity of the large lobsters (jumbos) from the offshore fishery are processed.

The "canners" are cooked in boiling water or by live steam for 7-12 min, depending on size, and cooled by immersing in cold, running water. The tails and claws are broken from the bodies and the meat removed from the tail, claw, and arm shells. The tail meat is usually pulled from the shell by means of a fork or similar instrument. The claw shell is cracked with a heavy cleaver-type instrument on a rubber cracking block and the meat shaken from the shell, preferably into stainless steel containers. Arm meat is removed from the arm shells by means of a "pick." Lobster meat must be well washed in order to remove all traces of gut content, blood, etc. To remove the gut from the tail meat, a cut is made lengthwise in the underside of the tail.

The average yield of meat in a commercial operation is about 25%, although about 40% of the lobster is considered to be edible.

Fresh lobster meat is usually packed in "window-top" hermetically sealed cans or in push-cover cans. The meat is arranged so that both claws and tails can be seen in the top layer. The packaging of fresh meat is carried out throughout the week to take advantage of available transport in order to reach the major markets without delay.

For freezing, the lobster meat is packed in cans with the claws on top, tail meat on the bottom and shoulder and arm meat in the middle. Enough salt brine is added to flavor the meat and the cans are then exhausted to create a vacuum by shooting a jet of steam into the headspace without heating the contents and immediately sealing the cans. Mechanical vacuum chambers are also in use. They are then frozen in blast freezers.

Vacuum packaging and storage at temperatures of -15°F (-26°C) or lower are necessary to maintain the quality of lobster meat in frozen storage. Experiments have shown that vacuum packed meat kept at -10°F (-23°C) was of acceptable quality for at least 6 months, whereas packages from the same lot, stored at higher temperatures, were unacceptable due to off-odors and -flavors and toughening of texture. In nonvacuum packed lobster meat, these undesirable quality changes developed much more rapidly and were also accompanied by a yellow discoloration due to oxidation.

Canned Lobsters.—Although most shucked lobster meat is now marketed fresh or frozen, a considerable quantity is still packed as heat processed canned lobster in Canada. The 1971 production in that country was over 32,000, 30-lb cases, representing almost 970,000 lb (440 metric tons) of lobster meat.

The cooking and shucking operations are similar to those described above. Special care must be taken when washing the meat to make sure all traces of coagulated blood are removed in order to avoid possible blue or black discoloration from developing. The cans are lined with parchment paper and the meat arranged so as to present an attractive appearance upon opening. Hot, salt brine is added and the cans evacuated before sealing by steam-vacuum closer or mechanical vacuum chamber.

The most commonly used can is the so-called $^1/_2$-lb can which contains 5 oz (142 gm) of drained lobster meat. To meet this requirement, about 6-6$^1/_2$ oz (170-185 gm) shucked meat is packed, depending on season and the condition of the lobster. The $^1/_4$-lb can contains 2$^1/_2$ oz (70 gm) drained meat and the 1-lb can contains 10 oz (284 gm).

The heat sterilization of the can contents is carried out with steam in a retort under pressure. The $^1/_4$-lb can should be processed for a minimum of 25 min at 239°F (116°C) and the $^1/_2$-lb can for 28 min at 239°F. The cans are cooled immediately following the process by immersion or in a spray of cold water.

When the cans are cool and dry they must be inspected for defects, such as leaks, "flippers," dented cans, etc., and these are removed.

By-Products

The tomalley and roe are canned as lobster paste or as tomalley. Some lobster meat, cereal fillers, spices, and artificial coloring can be included in the paste, but tomalley is canned as such with no additives.

The picked shells are almost always discarded by the lobster processing plants, although a simple drying and grinding process could produce a meal suitable for poultry feed. Experimental lots of meal have been produced with a crude protein content of 32–40%, fat 4–7% and ash 25–30%. Feeding tests with chickens showed that at least 20% of the protein in the rations could be supplied by the lobster meal without affecting the growth or quality of the chickens.

Chemicals can also be prepared from lobster shells. One of the principal components of the shells is a polysaccharide called chitin which can be isolated in a yield of about 6–12%. The deacetylated form of chitin, chitosan, has found applications in shrink-proofing of wool and also as a very effective chelating agent. As such, it has found use in chromatography, in water purification, and waste water treatment.

By splitting the polymer structure in chitin, N-acetyl-glucosamine can be isolated. This compound has shown promise in medical applications, especially as an aid in wound healing.

The fresh shells and bodies from lobster processing plants can be processed to yield a concentrated lobster flavor extract for use in soups, chowders, etc. Although pilot plant studies appear promising, commercial production is not yet underway.

Composition and Nutritional Value

Analyses of raw lobster meat from lobsters captured in the southern Gulf of St. Lawrence showed considerable variation over the season. In the tail meat the moisture content averaged 77.0%; protein, 19.7%; fat, 2.0%; and ash, 1.5%. In the claw meat the corresponding values were 81.4, 14.2, 1.6, and 1.9%; in the liver, 65.7, 11.5, 21.0, and 1.3%; and in the roe, 59.8, 25.0, 13.4, and 1.5%.

Other studies have shown that the fat (lipid) content of lobster muscle is around 1%. Lobster meat is, therefore, a low fat, high protein food.

P. M. JANGAARD

Cross-reference: *Shellfish*.

M

MACARONI PRODUCTS[1]

According to legend, the famous Italian explorer, Marco Polo, upon his return from China, first introduced pasta products to the royal courts of Italy in the 13th Century. As you can imagine, food storage was a major problem for the sailing vessels of the 13th Century. A major consideration was to carry enough food aboard ship for voyages of several months. To do this, a food was required which could be stored without deterioration for long periods of time. Macaroni products, if kept dry, could be stored without refrigeration for several years, or longer, with little noticeable deterioration in either nutritional or aesthetic quality. Therefore, such products would be useful on voyages. Macaroni products have survived the test of time and remain one of the popular foods of modern day society.

Although macaroni products had their origin in antiquity, only since the beginning of the 20th Century have efficient equipment and high quality ingredients for macaroni been available. Prior to the industrial revolution, most macaroni products were homemade, or produced by hand in small shops where the products could be made and sold in small quantities. The mechanization of the macaroni processing industry began in about 1850 when the first mechanical presses (which were not hand powered) were invented. Shown in Fig. M-1 is one of the early "Gramola" presses. The machine consisted of a mixer, a dough kneading device, and a large, mechanical piston and cylinder for forcing the pasta through the die. While there are still a few of the Gramola machines in operation, they have been replaced largely by continuous, high capacity extruders of the type shown in Fig. M-2. The continuous press works on the auger extrusion principle in which the kneading and extrusion are done in a single

operation. For efficient production, modern presses require uniform raw ingredients so that the continuous equipment may be operated with few adjustments.

Raw Materials for Pasta Products

Three main milled products of durum wheat, semolina, durum granulars, and durum flour, are preferred for use in pasta products. To a lesser extent, farina and flour from common wheat are used also.

Semolina.—Semolina is the raw material of choice for macaroni products. Semolina is a granular product which is milled from the endosperm of amber durum wheat and contains less than 3% flour. Most U.S. macaroni manufacturers prefer semolina which has a uniform fine particle size rather than a coarse ground semolina. With a fine granulation, less trouble is encountered in mixing the semolina and water to form a uniform dough for extrusion. If the semolina is not uniform, but consists of fine as well as coarse particles, the fine particles will tend to absorb water faster than the larger particles. Consequently, the coarse particles remain relatively dry throughout mixing operations and tend to result in white specks in the macaroni. Macaroni made from good quality durum semolina is characterized by a bright clear yellow color. A pale or gray color results if the product is made from other ingredients, such as common wheat flour.

Durum Granular and Flour.—Durum granular is another milled product of durum wheat which, like semolina, is used in macaroni making. While semolina contains less than 3% flour, durum granular may contain as much as 20% flour. Durum flour, which has a particle size less than 140 μ, is generally used in noodles, but also may be used for macaroni. Generally, macaroni made from durum flour has good color, but is less resistant to overcooking than products made from semolina or durum granular.

Water.—Water used for macaroni products should be pure, have no off-flavors, and should be suitable for drinking. Since macaroni is processed below

[1] Published with the approval of the Director of the Agricultural Experiment Station, North Dakota State University, Fargo, North Dakota as Journal Series No. 359.

Courtesy of Werner Lehara, Inc., New York, N.Y.

FIG. M-1. GRAMOLA PRESS FIRST INTRODUCED IN 1840

pasteurization temperatures, the bacterial count of the water is directly related to the bacterial count of the finished product. Consequently, only pure water of low total plate count should be used.

Eggs.—The final ingredient of major importance is eggs. In the United States, egg noodles and egg spaghetti must contain at least $5\frac{1}{2}\%$ egg solids by weight in the finished product. The eggs improve the nutritional quality and richness of the product. Moreover, noodles which do not contain eggs must be specially labeled as "plain noodles" to distinguish them from the egg-containing products.

Eggs may be added either as fresh eggs, frozen eggs, dry eggs, egg yolks, or dried egg solids. A major problem with the use and incorporation of eggs into macaroni products is bacterial contamination. Because eggs provide an excellent medium for bacterial growth, special care and precautions must be taken in storage and handling of eggs and egg products. Only pasteurized egg products which have low bacterial count should be used. Good quality liquid whole egg or egg yolks generally contain a total plate count of less than 5000 bacteria per gram. Moreover, the eggs must show negative Salmonella and should contain less than 10 mold spores, and less than 10 yeast spores and coliforms per gram of egg.

Artificial coloring material is not used in macaroni products. However, eggs may be added to improve the color. Chickens which lay the special

Courtesy of Braibanti, Milan, Italy

FIG. M-2. MODERN CONTINUOUS PRESS FOR LONG SPAGHETTI PRODUCTION

The press is equipped with a rectangular die. A "curtain" of spaghetti is shown being placed on dryer rods.

high yellow eggs are fed a high carotene diet which enhances the color and adds to the cost of the eggs.

Optional Ingredients.—In addition to semolina, eggs, and water, other minor ingredients may be added to macaroni products. These optional ingredients are listed later in the chapter under the Standards of Identity for macaroni products. When optional ingredients are included, they must be declared on the label of the package.

Types of Macaroni Products

One of the reasons for the popularity of macaroni products is the great number of possible shapes and sizes available and numerous methods of preparing macaroni foods. Although most macaroni products consist only of semolina and water, the products can be formed into various shapes which provide an interesting and pleasant variation of the food. Some of the popular shapes of macaroni and their names are shown in Fig. M-3 and M-4. In the United States, the most popular macaroni products are spaghetti, elbow macaroni, and noodles. Grouped by types and consumption, spaghetti is listed as the most popular pasta product with approximately 40.5% of the total consumption; macaroni is second and accounts for 32.5% of the total while noodles represent 27% of the U.S. total.

Consumption

The per capita consumption of macaroni products naturally varies throughout the world. Italy, as expected, leads world consumption with 87 lb per person per year. France has a yearly average of 13 lb per person; the United States has a per capita consumption of $7^{1}/_{2}$ lb per person, while England shows a per capita consumption of 3 lb. In addition, Spain, the South American countries, Japan, and North African countries also consume significant amounts of macaroni products.

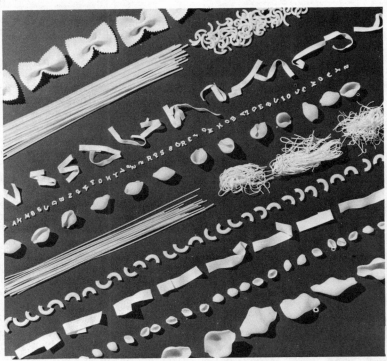

Courtesy of Wheat Flour Institute, Chicago, Ill.

FIG. M-3. POPULAR MACARONI SHAPES

Reading top left to bottom right: noodle bows, long spaghetti, elbow spaghetti, medium noodles, alphabets, shell macaroni, spaghetti or thin spaghetti, fine noodles, elbow macaroni, broad noodles, small macaroni shells, jumbo macaroni shells.

FIG. M-4. UNUSUAL MACARONI SHAPES

Reading clockwise beginning top left: egg cappelletti, mafalde, rigatoni, attup-patelli lisci, fusilli senza buco, shells, mostacciolino, margherite (flat macaroni), egg novelties and green noodles, fusilli bucati, cavatelle, tufoli, cresta di gallo (rooster crest), lasagna, rosetta, long zitoni, rotini, manicotti.

Economic Importance

In the United States, the macaroni industry has shown a steady growth over the past 20 yrs in the total volume as well as in per capita sales. This is unique, since the per capita consumption of wheat products in general has declined in the United States during the same period. Estimated sales for the industry show that in 1967 a total of 434 million dollars worth of macaroni products were sold. In 1968, an increase of 9 million dollars in macaroni sales was noted, and in 1969 an 18 million dollar increase was shown. For 1970, total sales for the industry were approximately 480 million dollars.

Wheat and Milling

Wheat

A primary factor which sets the economic value of durum wheat is the grade. In the United States, there are 21 possible grades for durum wheat. In determining durum wheat grade, physical factors such as test weight, kernel vitreousness, amount of damaged kernels, and extraneous material are used. Each of the factors has a significant effect on the quality as well as the selling price of the durum wheat.

In order to understand durum wheat quality, it is necessary to be familiar with the terms used to describe durum wheat and durum wheat grades. According to the Official Grain Standards of the United States, durum wheat is divided into the following three subclasses: "Hard Amber Durum Wheat" which must contain 75% or more hard vitreous kernels, "Amber Durum Wheat" which must contain more than 60% but less than 75% hard vitreous kernels, "Durum Wheat" which contains less than 60% hard vitreous kernels. Within the three subclasses for durum wheat, there are also numerical grades which are assigned according to Table M-1. In addition, the classification of "heavy" also may be assigned to the grade to indicate that the wheat has a test weight greater than 62 lb per bu. Accordingly, the highest possible grade for durum wheat in the

TABLE M-1

GRADES AND GRADE REQUIREMENTS FOR DURUM WHEAT
(REVISED FEBR. 1970)

U.S. Grade	Minimum Test Weight Per Bushel (Lb)	Maximum Limits of						
		Defects					Wheat of Other Classes	
		Heat Damaged Kernels (%)	Damaged Kernels (Total) (%)	Foreign Material (%)	Shrunken and Broken Kernels (%)	Defects (Total) (%)	Contrasting Classes (%)	Wheat of Other Classes (Total) (%)
1	60.0	0.1	2.0	0.5	3.0	3.0	1.0	3.0
2	58.0	0.2	4.0	1.0	5.0	5.0	2.0	5.0
3	56.0	0.5	7.0	2.0	8.0	8.0	3.0	10.0
4	54.0	1.0	10.0	3.0	12.0	12.0	10.0	10.0
5	51.0	3.0	15.0	5.0	20.0	20.0	10.0	10.0
Sample grade[1]								

SOURCE: U.S. Dept. Agr.

[1] Sample grade shall be wheat which does not meet the requirements for any of the grades from No. 1 to No. 5, inclusive; or which contains stones; or which is musty, or sour, or heating; or which has any commercially objectionable foreign odor except of smut or garlic; or which contains a quantity of smut so great that any one or more of the grade requirements cannot be applied accurately; or which is otherwise of distinctly low quality.

United States is U.S. No. 1 Heavy Hard Amber Durum. It is commonly assumed that high grade wheat will result in high quality macaroni products. However, it should be recognized that the grade does not take into account macaroni processing criteria. Consequently, the grade gives only a rough indication of the quality in terms of macaroni-making criteria.

There are, however, a few generalizations which can be drawn to relate durum wheat grade to quality. For example, top grade durum wheat has a high test weight, contains more than 75% vitreous kernels, and is relatively free of damaged or broken kernels. Durum millers prefer high grades of durum wheat because vitreous kernels give a high yield of semolina when milled. For the upper grades, there will be less wheat lost due to removal of broken and damaged kernels during the cleaning operation. Furthermore, the upper grades are more valuable to the miller because there are more pounds of wheat per bushel than for the lower grades.

Protein content of durum wheat is not a grading factor, and there is no protein premium paid in the United States for high protein durum. However, protein is important from a nutritional standpoint. Furthermore, a minimum of about 11% protein in the semolina is necessary to make macaroni products which have good cooking quality.

Durum wheat grade and quality are influenced by the environment under which the durum is grown. In the United States, the conditions in North Dakota are best suited for the production of good quality durum wheat. Other areas of the world suitable for durum wheat production are North Africa, Russia, Italy, France, Canada, and Argentina.

Wheat diseases often limit the production of quality durum wheat to certain climatic regions. Blight, black point, ergot, and various fungus infections can occur where the growing season is cool and wet. With fungus damage, portions or all of the durum kernel turn black. Black kernels are similar in size and density to normal wheat and, therefore, difficult to remove with conventional wheat cleaning equipment. When inadequately-cleaned, fungus-damaged wheat is milled, the black kernels are ground into black particles which appear as unsightly specks in the semolina and ultimately in the finished product.

A topic of special interest with regard to wheat condition is sprout damage. In the United States, since most of the durum wheat is grown in a fairly small area of North Dakota, sprouting can occur in a large percentage of the total crop in the event of heavy rainfall during the harvest season. Because of sprouting in 1965 and 1968, it was difficult for millers to obtain top grade durum. In many cases, sprouted durum was milled into semolina in order to meet the demands of the pasta processing industry. Although the sprouted durum wheat was used in large quantities by the pasta processors, there was little agreement as to what effect the sprouting had on the quality of the finished product. In recent studies (Dick *et al.* 1970) sprouted durum wheat was tested at a number of levels of germination to determine the effect of field sprouting on durum wheat. The results of the experiment showed that sprouting caused a significant drop in the wheat grade and vitreous kernel content, protein content, test weight, and the number of damaged kernels. On the other hand, semolina milling yield and the speck count were not significantly altered by the sprouting. The results also indicated that spaghetti color, cooked weight, cooking loss, and cooked firmness were not influenced significantly by sprouting.

Durum Wheat Milling Process

Durum wheat usually is milled into either semolina, durum granular, or flour. Milling of durum patent flour is similar to conventional flour milling. Semolina milling is unique in that the objective of the operation is to prepare granular middlings with a minimum of flour production. To mill durum wheat into semolina, several steps are necessary. First, the wheat is cleaned to remove any foreign material and shrunken and broken kernels. Next, the wheat is tempered by applying moisture to the outer portion of the wheat kernel. Tempering the wheat to a moisture content of about 16.5% toughens the seed coat so bran may be scraped from the endosperm during milling. Unlike the conventional flour mill, the semolina mill contains no reduction or smooth rolls; only corrugated "break" rolls are used. The corrugated rolls break the wheat into coarse particles and subsequent rolls crush the wheat and scrape the endosperm portion from the bran. If the wheat has been tempered properly, the inside portion will crumble into granular middlings while the bran and germ remain as flakes which can be easily removed by sifting and air purification. Sifting separates large bran flakes and the flour from the semolina, while purifying pneumatically separates the remaining flour and small particles of bran from the semolina.

Semolina Storage

Unlike bread wheat flour which improves in quality with age, storage of durum milled products is detrimental to quality. The natural pigments of durum wheat, responsible for the characteristic yellow color of macaroni products, are destroyed by oxidation during the storage. Consequently, durum semolina or flour should be shipped to the macaroni manufacturers as soon as possible after milling. To minimize loss of color, even brief storage is best done under cool, dry conditions.

Insects are another problem associated with storing semolina. Since semolina is granular, it cannot be passed through an entolator to destroy insect eggs. As a result, if semolina is held for long periods at temperatures above 50°F, there is a possibility of infestation due to hatching of insect eggs during storage.

Standards of Identity of Milled Products

Durum semolina, durum granular, and durum flour are the three general classes of durum wheat products used for making macaroni and other pasta products. Semolina is defined as the purified middlings of durum wheat which has been ground so that all of the product shall pass through a No. 20 U.S. sieve and not more than 3% shall pass through a No. 100 U.S. sieve. Durum granular is defined as the purified middlings of durum wheat which shall pass through a No. 20 U.S. sieve and not more than 20% shall pass through a No. 100 U.S. sieve. Durum flour is the purified endosperm of durum which is ground fine enough to pass through a No. 100 U.S. sieve. Thus, it is possible to mill durum patent flour, semolina, or granulars and have a wide range of possible combinations of milled products which can be used to make macaroni products.

Macaroni Production

In commercial practice, macaroni products are formed by extrusion on large, automatic machines which perform several processing operations.

Mixing

In the mixing operation, water is added to the semolina or flour so that the moisture content of the dough (pasta) is approximately 31%. To obtain a uniform mixture, water and semolina are usually mixed in a special twin shaft mixing chamber (Fig. M-5).

The shafts of the mixer turn in opposition so that the pasta is simultaneously pulled in two different directions to limit the amount of balling that can occur.

Modern presses are equipped with a vacuum chamber to remove air bubbles from the pasta prior to extruding. A vacuum is applied to the pasta either by enclosing the entire mixer in a vacuum chamber or by drawing a vacuum on the pasta just prior to extrusion. An example of the latter design is shown in Fig. M-5. With this type of press, air is removed as the pasta is transferred to the final extrusion auger. If air is not removed, small bubbles will form and give the finished product a white, chalky appearance. Furthermore, air bubbles can diminish the mechanical strength of the dried product.

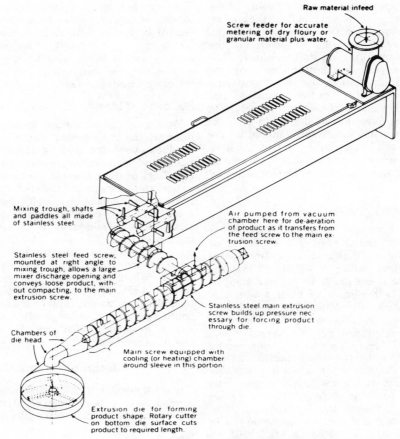

Raw material infeed

Screw feeder for accurate
metering of dry floury or
granular material plus water.

Mixing trough, shafts
and paddles all made
of stainless steel.

Air pumped from vacuum
chamber here for de-aeration
of product as it transfers from
the feed screw to the main extrusion screw.

Stainless steel feed screw,
mounted at right angle to
mixing trough, allows a large
mixer discharge opening and
conveys loose product, without compacting, to the main
extrusion screw.

Stainless steel main extrusion
screw builds up pressure necessary for forcing product
through die.

Chambers of
die head

Main screw equipped with
cooling (or heating) chamber
around sleeve in this portion.

Extrusion die for forming
product shape. Rotary cutter
on bottom die surface cuts
product to required length.

Courtesy of Buhler Corp., Minneapolis, Minn.

FIG. M-5. DIAGRAM SHOWING THE PROCESSING ELEMENTS OF SINGLE-
AUGER EXTRUDER

Extruding

The extrusion auger is the heart of the macaroni press. The auger not only forces the dough through the die, but it also kneads the dough into a homogeneous mass, controls the rate of production and influences the quality of the product. Recent research shows that the auger speed as well as the dough temperature affect the color and the cooking quality of the finished macaroni product (Walsh *et al.* 1971).

Construction and dimension of the extrusion augers vary among equipment manufacturers. However, most modern presses are equipped with sharp edged augers which have a uniform pitch over their entire length rather than an increasing pitch. The auger fits into an extrusion barrel which is grooved. The grooves help the dough move forward and reduce friction between the auger and the inside of the barrel. Actually, when

the press is in operation, there is little wear on the barrel and the auger because the auger floats inside the barrel on a cushion of dough. The auger is in contact with the barrel only when the cylinder is empty; therefore, equipment manufacturers caution that excessive wear will take place on the cylinder walls and auger if the press is run empty.

During the extrusion process, a considerable amount of heat is generated. Extruder barrels should be equipped with a water cooling jacket to dissipate heat and hold a constant extrusion temperature. For best results, the pasta temperature should be held near 125°F during the extrusion process. If the dough becomes too hot (above 165°F), the cooking quality of the finished product will be damaged.

Figure M-6 shows a short goods macaroni die with a rotating knife which sweeps the surface of the die to cut the product. Because variations in the flow rate across the die will cause variation in

Courtesy of Buhler Corp., Minneapolis, Minn.

FIG. M-6. SHORT GOODS MACARONI DIE EQUIPPED WITH ROTATING KNIFE

the lengths of the product, the flow rate of the dough through the die is quite important. In spaghetti making, if dough does not flow uniformly through the die, there will be a variation in length of the spaghetti. When cut to lengths, some spaghetti may be too short to package and must be either discarded or reprocessed. Since waste and reprocessing of material add to the unit production cost of the product, an even flow rate of pasta through the die is very important. To control the extrusion pattern, rotation rate of the auger and the temperature and physical condition of the dough are quite important. Usually these are adjusted by trial and error—to get an even flow rate across the die is considered part of the art of macaroni making.

The inside surface of the die influences the product appearance and the extrusion rate. Until recently, most macaroni dies were made of bronze. A good bronze die which had uniform extrusion characteristics resulted in a fairly good product with acceptable color. However, bronze dies were relatively soft and tended to wear with prolonged use. Consequently, as wear on the die increased, the size and shape of the macaroni products changed accordingly. In order to maintain the proper dimensions, it was necessary periodically to repair or replace dies. Recently, dies have been introduced where the extruding surface of the die is fitted with Teflon inserts to extend the life of the dies and improve the quality of the product.

Macaroni products extruded through Teflon are very smooth and tend to have a much better appearance than similar products extruded through a bronze die. This improved appearance is due to the waxy smooth surface imparted by low friction Teflon dies.

Drying

Drying is without doubt the most difficult and critical step to control in the processing of macaroni products. The objective of the drying is to lower the moisture content of the product from 31 to 12–13% so that the macaroni will be hard, retain its shape, and will store without spoiling. To accomplish this, any number of dryer designs are used. However, the problems in selecting a dryer and setting the proper temperatures and relative humidity increments are similar regardless of the design of the dryer. If dried too slowly, macaroni products will tend to spoil or become moldy during the drying. On the other hand, if they are dried too rapidly, moisture gradients will occur which cause the products to crack or check. Checking can occur either during the drying period or as long as several weeks after the product has left the dryer. In the latter case, the product may check even after the product has been packaged and sold.

Space in this chapter does not allow for a complete description of drying theory. However, some of the factors which influence drying and an example of a drying cycle are presented. Drying of macaroni depends on the hygroscopic equilibrium moisture content (M_1), the free moisture (M_2) and the shape and size of the product to be dried. M_1 is the moisture content of the product at equilibrium with the atmosphere at a specified relative humidity. M_2 is the difference between equilibrium moisture and the actual moisture content (M_3) of the product ($M_2 = M_3 - M_1$). Charts and formulas are available (Hummel 1966) to compute drying rates for macaroni products.

Most macaroni drying operations use a preliminary dryer to quickly dry the product surface immediately after extruding. Predrying casehardens the surface so that the pieces of macaroni will not stick together. The interior of the product remains soft and plastic during this operation. The final dryer is used to remove the bulk of the moisture from the interior of the product. Since the surface of macaroni products dries more rapidly than the inside, a moisture gradient develops across the surface to the interior of the product. As the product dries, the interior shrinks more rapidly than the outer crust. Shrinkage sets up strains inside the product. If the strain becomes greater than the mechanical strength of the macaroni, cracks and checks will develop below the surface of the macaroni product. Cracks give the product a poor appearance and a very low mechanical strength. Cracked products are usually so fragile that they will crumble during the packaging and shipment.

It is essential that products be dried with a drying cycle which is tailored to meet the requirements of each product. The following is an example of the drying cycle which has been successfully used for long spaghetti. The predryer exposes the product to air at 150°F for 1 hr at 65% relative humidity and lowers the product moisture content from 31 to 25%. At this point, the macaroni is still quite pliable so that rapid predrying does not set up stresses which would result in cracking. The product then enters the final dryer, which is usually a continuous dryer having several zones or chambers in which the relative humidity can be varied, with the temperature held constant at 130°F. The first stage of the final dryer holds the product for 1½ hr at 95% RH. This is called the "sweating" or rest period where the product is equilibrated with high humidity air. In the second zone of the dryer, the product is exposed to a relative humidity of 83% for 4 hr after which the moisture content of the product is about 18%. Additional moisture is removed in the third zone of the dryer, where the product is held for 6 hr at a relative humidity of 70%. Finally, the product is removed from the dryer and cooled to room temperature and cut to the proper length for packaging. If the drying cycle is successful, the product will be quite hard and flexible so that it can bend to a considerable degree before breaking. If the product has not been dried properly, it will be rather soft and tend to crumble quite easily. The true test of drying is to find the product free of checks a week after the product has left the dryer.

For best results, automatic controllers are used to hold the relative humidity of the dryer at precise settings. Relative humidity under processing conditions is often difficult to control and at times even the best controllers give erroneous readings. It is often necessary to return to the wet bulb depression method to determine the actual relative humidity in the dryer. The cost, in any case, of measuring the relative humidity at regular intervals and installing reliable automatic controllers can be recovered if uniform drying conditions are achieved and product losses due to improper drying are minimized.

Packaging

There are literally thousands of different sizes, shapes, and types of packages in which macaroni products may be sold. However, they all perform a similar function; that is, to keep the product free from contamination, to protect the product from damage during shipment and storage, and to display the product favorably.

The principal packaging material for noodles is the cellophane bag. The cellophane bag provides moisture-proof protection for the product and is used easily on automatic machines. Macaroni products are packed often in low density poly-etheylene bags, which have the disadvantage of being difficult to stack on grocery store shelves.

Many macaroni manufacturers prefer packaging their products in boxes, although bags are considerably less expensive. Boxes are easy to stack and provide good protection for the fragile macaroni products. There is also an opportunity to print more readable advertising on boxes than on bags.

Whether bags or boxes are used, selecting, ordering, and specifications for packaging materials is one aspect of the macaroni manufacturing business which bears considerable thought. In all cases, it is necessary for the macaroni manufacturer to specify the type of material used in his packaging, the specific information, size, and construction of the packaging material. Every operation from the design to the delivery of packaging material must be tailored to fit the product as well as the available packaging equipment.

Consequently, packaging must be ordered far in advance of when it is needed.

Standards of Identity

The following are excerpts for definitions and standards under the Federal Food, Drug and Cosmetic Act, Part 16.1, Macaroni and Noodle Products:

(a) Macaroni products are the class of food each of which is prepared by drying formed units of dough made from semolina, durum flour, farina, flour, or any combinations of two or more of these with water and with or without one or more of the optional ingredients specified in subparagraphs (1) to (6) inclusive, of this paragraph.

(1) Egg white, frozen egg white, dried egg white, or any two or all of these in such quantity that the solids thereof is not less than 0.5 percent and not more than 2.0 percent of the weight of the finished food.

(2) Disodium phosphate, in a quantity not less than 0.5 percent and not more than 1.0 percent of the weight of the finished food.

(3) Onions, celery, garlic, bay leaf, or any two or more of these in a quantity which seasons food.

(4) Salt, in a quantity which seasons the food.

(5) Gum gluten in such quantity that the protein content of the finished food is not more than 13 percent by weight. The finished macaroni product con-

tains not less than 87 percent of total solids as determined by the method prescribed in "Official and Tentative Methods of Analysis of the Association of Official Agricultural Chemists," Fifth Edition, 1940, page 235, (Ed. note, 9th Edition, 1960, p. 175, sec. 13:112) Under "Vacuum Oven Method—Official."

(6) Concentrated glyceryl monostearate (containing not less than 90 percent monoester) in a quantity not exceeding 2 percent by weight of the finished food.

(b) Macaroni is the macaroni product the units of which are tube shaped and more than 0.11 inches but not more than 0.27 inches in diameter.

(c) Spaghetti is the macaroni product the units of which are tube shaped or cord shaped (not tubular) and more than 0.06 but not more than 0.11 inch in diameter.

(d) Vermicelli is the macaroni product the units of which are cord shaped (not tubular) and not more than 0.06 inches in diameter.

(e) The name of each food for which a definition and standard of identity is prescribed by this section is "macaroni product" or alternately, the name is "Macaroni," "spaghetti," or "Vermicelli" as the case may be when the units of the food are the shapes and sizes specified in paragraph (b) (c) or (d), respectively, of this section.

(f) (1) When disodium phosphate is used, the label shall bear the statement "Disodium phosphate added for quick cooking."

(2) When any ingredients specified in paragraph (a) (3) of this section is used, the label shall bear the statement "Seasoned with _____." The blank being filled in with the common name of the ingredient; or in the case of bay leaves, the statements "spiced" or "spice added" or "spiced with bay leaves."

(3) When the ingredient specified in paragraph (a) (6) of this section is used, the label shall bear the statement "glyceryl monostearate added" or the statement "with added glyceryl monostearate."

(4) Wherever the name of the food appears on the label so conspicuously as to be easily seen under customary conditions of purchase, the words or statements prescribed in this section, showing the optional ingredients used, shall immediately and conspicuously precede or follow, or in part precede and in part follow, such name, without intervening written, printed or graphic matter.

Enrichment

Macaroni products may be enriched by adding vitamins and minerals according to the levels specified in paragraph 16.9 of the FDA Definitions and Standards for Macaroni Products. To be labeled as "Enriched Macaroni" each pound of product must contain not less than 4 mg and not more than 5 mg of thiamin, not less than 1.7 mg and not more than 2.2 mg riboflavin, not less than 27 mg and not more than 34 mg niacin or niacinamide, and not less than 13 mg and not more than 16.5 mg of iron (Fe). As optional enrichment, Vitamin D may be added at levels of not less than 250 USP units and not more than 1000 USP units per pound. Calcium also may be added as an optional ingredient so that a pound of product contains not less than 500 mg and not more than 625 mg of calcium.

Composition

Table M-2 shows the composition of macaroni and noodle products with values given for the cooked as well as dry products. Information in the table was adopted from Bowes and Church (1970) and USDA Handbook No. 8 (Watt and Merrill 1967). The data are expressed for 100 gm of macaroni products which are prepared according to the definition of standards for macaroni and noodle products without optional ingredients. In the case of cooked macaroni or noodles, a considerable variation from the data is possible, since the degree of swelling influences the analysis.

Quality

Since a detailed description of tests for quality of macaroni ingredients and products is beyond the scope of this chapter, only the more common tests are presented. A more complete description of quality tests is described in AACC Approved Methods, 7th Edition, American Association of Cereal Chemists (1962).

Wheat Products

Physical Properties.—*Granulation Test.*—Granulation of semolina can be measured with a series of stacked sieves on a rotary shaker (Rotap). The following example shows granulation data for a typical U.S. commercial semolina.

TABLE M-2

COMPOSITION OF MACARONI AND NOODLES

Food[1]	Energy, Cal/100 Gm	Major Constituents[2]					Minerals, Mg/100 Gm						Vitamins/100 Gm			
		Proteins (%)	Carbohydrates (%)	Crude Fiber (%)	Fat (%)	Moisture (%)	Na	K	Ca	Mg	P	Fe	Thiamin (Mg)	Riboflavin (Mg)	Niacin (Mg)	A (IU)
Macaroni, enriched dry	368	12.5	74.0	0.3	1.2	12.0	2.0	197	27	48	161	2.9	0.88	0.37	6.0	0
Macaroni, enriched cooked	107	3.4	23.0	0.1	0.4	73.1	0.7	60	8	18	50	0.9	0.14	0.08	1.1	0
Macaroni, not enriched dry	386	12.5	74.0	0.3	1.2	12.0	2.0	197	27	48	161	1.3	0.09	0.06	1.7	0
Macaroni, not enriched cooked	107	3.4	23.0	0.1	0.4	73.1	0.7	60	8	18	50	0.4	0.01	0.01	0.3	0
Egg noodles, enriched dry	388	15.5	67.8	0.3	4.4	12.0	6.0	133	33	48	183	2.8	0.89	0.39	6.1	220
Egg noodles, enriched cooked	125	4.1	23.3	0.1	1.5	71.0	2.0	44	10	14	59	0.9	0.14	0.08	1.2	70

[1] All products as defined by FDA Definitions and Standards, no optional ingredients included.
[2] All data reported on an "as is" basis.

U.S. Sieve No.	Sieve Opening (Mm)	Total Semolina (%)
On 20	0.86	0.0
On 40	0.38	28.8
On 60	0.23	51.6
On 80	0.18	14.6
On 100	0.14	3.3
Through 100		1.7

Semolina Speck Test.—Since black specks and bran particles can detract from the appearance of macaroni products, the speck test is a simple but valuable test of semolina quality. To test, a well-blended sample of semolina is poured on a flat surface. A 4 × 5 in. glass plate with a 1-in.-sq window is placed at random on the semolina surface and the visible specks (bran or black particles) within the window are counted. The determination is replicated 3 times, and the average is expressed as specks per 10 sq in. Values of 10–20 specks per 10 sq in. are considered normal for good quality semolina.

Moisture Test.—The moisture test is used to determine the performance of macaroni drying operations as well as to check incoming ingredients. The test is performed by drying 10 gm of ground macaroni, semolina, or flour for 1 hr in an air oven at 130°C. The weight loss by drying is expressed as moisture on a percentage basis. To store macaroni, semolina, or flour, the moisture content of the material should be less than 13.5%.

Chemical Tests.—*Sprout Damage.*—Sprout-damaged wheat, semolina, or flour can be detected with a simple test called the Falling Number test (Medcalf *et al.* 1966; Hagberg 1961). Flour may be tested directly. However, semolina must be ground to flour and sifted through a No. 70 U.S. sieve for the test. In the method, 7.0 gm of flour (15% moisture basis) are mixed and gelatinized in a test tube which is fitted with a special metal plunger. The time in seconds required for the plunger to fall through the gelatinized flour is the "falling number." Falling numbers below 300 are an indication that the semolina or flour has been milled from sprouted wheat.

Macaroni Products

Appearance.—Color and appearance of macaroni products are usually judged visually. However, since this depends on personal bias, the visual test is subject to human error, and color values are difficult to compare among different laboratories.

Recently, a method was developed for accurate measurement of spaghetti color with a reflectance colorimeter (Walsh 1970; Walsh *et al.* 1969). In the method, the color of spaghetti is expressed in

FIG. M-7. THIS SPECIALLY EQUIPPED INSTRON TEST INSTRUMENT, USED TO MEASURE THE FIRMNESS OF COOKED SPAGHETTI, RECORDS THE "WORK" (GM CM) REQUIRED TO SHEAR A SINGLE COOKED STRAND GIVING AN INDICATION OF SPAGHETTI "BITE" OR "FIRMNESS"

terms of lightness, L%, and yellowness, b% values—high values indicate good color. Good agreement between photoelectric readings and visual judgement of the color was reported.

Composition Quality.—The quality of macaroni products is related to the quality of the wheat used in the milling process. Generally, products milled from durum are preferred for pasta. Substitution of lower cost common wheat for durum may occur, particularly when the price differential between these wheat classes becomes excessive. The detection of admixtures of common and durum wheats, while easily accomplished by visual observation of wheat kernels, is relatively difficult after milling.

The chemical composition of the major components, starch and protein, is similar (Sheu *et al.* 1967). However, significant differences are able to be detected in the lipids. Fractionation of the lipids extracted from semolina, granular or flour, by means of thin-layer chromatography (TLC) shows that sitosterol palmitate is present in common wheat but absent in durum wheat (Gilles and Youngs 1964). This TLC technique is useful for quality control purposes as it is more rapid than either the crystallization technique or the infrared procedure.

Cooking Quality.—The quality of cooked macaroni products depends upon several factors: how the product holds up to cooking, how much water

is absorbed, the loss of solids to the cooking water, and especially the final firmness. Water absorbed during cooking can be measured easily by weighing the product before and after cooking. The weight increase is due to water absorption. Cooking loss is usually measured by evaporating the cooking water to dryness. The residue after drying is weighed and reported as a percentage based on the weight of the uncooked product.

Firmness of cooked macaroni products is usually measured with the "bite test" where a judge or panel of judges tastes and scores the product for firmness. However, the "bite test" depends on human judgement and personal preference of the judges who perform the test. Consequently, errors are inherent in the "bite test."

Recently, an instrument method was developed to objectively measure the firmness of cooked spaghetti (Walsh 1971). In the method, an Instron Universal Test Instrument was fitted with a blunt plexiglass tooth, so that a single strand of cooked spaghetti could be sheared. The work (gm cm) required to shear the spaghetti is used as a measure of cooked spaghetti firmness. The test data showed a high positive correlation with the taste panel results (r = 0.812). In addition, the instrumental method appeared more convenient and reproducible than the "bite test."

Nutritional Quality

Macaroni products are a good source of many essential nutrients (Table M-2). However, like any single food source, macaroni does not supply all of the nutrients for a complete human diet.

The proteins of macaroni contain all 8 essential amino acids; thus, $1\frac{1}{2}$ lb of macaroni of 12% protein content *could* supply the required daily amounts of protein for a normal man. However, the protein of macaroni lacks the proper balance of amino acids and is particularly low in lysine. To improve the amino acid balance, optional ingredients like egg solids, milk, dry yeast, and soy proteins which are rich in lysine may be added to macaroni products. Since there are strict rules regulating labeling and enrichment of foods, the FDA must be consulted before any new protein-enriched product is marketed.

When assessing nutritional quality, the combined value of other foods which are consumed with macaroni products should be considered. Most often, when macaroni products are eaten, a cheese or meat sauce is added. The protein in the sauce usually balances the macaroni protein so that the combined nutritional quality of the food is very high.

D. E. WALSH
K. A. GILLES

References

AMERICAN ASSOCIATION OF CEREAL CHEMISTS. 1962. AACC Approved Methods, 7th Edition. American Association of Cereal Chemists, St. Paul.

BOWES, C. F., and CHURCH, H. N. 1970. Bowes' and Church's Food Values of Portions Commonly Used, 11th Edition. J. B. Lippincott Co., Philadelphia.

DICK, J. W., WALSH, D. E., and GILLES, K. A. 1970. Effect of sprout-damaged durum wheat on spaghetti quality. Cereal Sci. Today Abstr. 15, No. 9, 108.

GILLES, K. A., and YOUNGS, V. E. 1964. Evaluation of durum wheat and durum products. Cereal Chem. 41, 502.

HAGBERG, S. 1961. Note on a simplified rapid method for determining alpha-amylase activity. Cereal Chem. 38, 202.

HUMMEL, C. 1966. Macaroni Products. Food Trade Press, London, England.

MEDCALF, D. G., GILLES, K. A., and SIBBITT, L. D. 1966. Detection of sprout damage in wheat. Northwestern Miller 273, No. 5, 16.

SHEU, R.-Y., MEDCALF, D. G., GILLES, K. A., and SIBBITT, L. D. 1967. Effect of biochemical constituents on macaroni quality. I. Differences between hard red spring and durum wheats. J. Sci. Food Agr. 18, 237.

WALSH, D. E. 1971. Measurement of spaghetti firmness. Cereal Sci. Today 16, 202.

WALSH, D. E., EBELING, K. A., and GILLES, K. A. 1971. A linear programming approach to spaghetti processing. Cereal Sci. Today 16, 388.

WALSH, D. E., GILLES, K. A., and SHUEY, W. C. 1969. Color determination of spaghetti by the tristimulus method. Cereal Chem. 46, 7.

WATT, BERNICE K., and MERRILL, ANNABELL L. 1967. Composition of Foods. USDA Agr. Handbook 8.

MAILLARD, LOUIS C. (1878–1936)

The work of the eminent French chemist and physician, Dr. L. C. Maillard, has become classic, and the term the "Maillard reaction" has been used countless times in almost countless papers. Yet, biographical data of substance are hard to come by, and *Comptes rendu*, the noted French scientific journal, contains no obituary nor for that matter a mention of his death. The reason for this neglect is evident. Dr. Maillard's pioneering work on nonenzymatic browning was not intensively followed up for a decade or more after his untimely death in 1936.

L. C. Maillard was born in France in 1878. It is known that he earned a diploma in "Higher Pharmacy" and some years later a doctorate in medicine. It is on record that he became a qualified teacher on the Faculty of Medicine, Paris, in 1904. The year 1910 finds him a Professor of Biological and Medical Chemistry on the faculty of the University of Algiers.

A few years prior to the outbreak of World War I, Dr. Maillard appears to have been on a commission to study the "regular rations of the French Army," *regular* apparently meaning the garrison ration. It is interesting that he found the ration deficient in animal protein, oversupplied with plant protein, and that the carbohydrate components were excessive. He also calculated the calories in the ration and found that the rations averaged about 4000 with the artillerymen getting slightly more calories than the infantrymen. This study suggests that Dr. Maillard had an interest in nutrition, at least in the chemical aspects of nutrition. This is borne out by other studies, for example, those on the nature of the color of urine, the metabolic formation of urea, and the structure of the proteins. His study of the formation of peptides from amino acids in the presence of alcohols, a study which led him to examine the reaction of the sugars and amino acids, is a further example.

Stated in its simplest form, Maillard discovered

that simple amino acids react, on warming, with certain sugars to form brown products (melanoidins). A whole literature has grown up on the basis of this observation. That Maillard recognized the research implications of the phenomenon is evident. He states:

"The brown substances in question—of very great interest for certain natural phenomena and the cycle of organic material on the surface of the globe—are amorphous, insoluble in the usual media, impossible to volatilize without profound decomposition, so resistant to total combustion that even their simple percentage is not easy to establish. The necessary identification can therefore rest only in the assemblage of a rather deep comparative study."

In his first study, Maillard comments that the brown products (melanoidins) are formed by the hydrolysis of any material "yielding simultaneously sugars and amino acids." He reported on a number of reactions using such amino acids as glycine, sarcosine, alanine, valine, leucine, tyrosine, and glutamic acid and such sugars as xylose, arabinose, fructose, galactose, mannose, lactose, and maltose. Sucrose, he noted, does not undergo the reaction. In a later study he undertakes to determine whether or not (1) the action of glycerine in glycine would be duplicated by more complex alcohols, especially with D-glucose, which, like glycerine is widely distributed in nature, and (2) whether or not a reaction of D-glucose can be made to occur parallel to that of the alcoholic functions of glycerine even though the aldehyde group does not react. Both of these papers were summarized (in English) and discussed by Dr. J. H. Looker in the April 1952 issue of the *Activities Report* of the Research and Development Associates, Qm Food and Container Institute, Chicago.

MARTIN S. PETERSON

Cross-reference: *Browning, Nonenzymic.*

MALT AND MALTING

See Barley: Malt and Malting.

MALTED MILK

The origin and early development of the Malted Milk industry was due largely to the efforts of William Horlick with assistance from his brother, James Horlick.

William Horlick, born in England migrated to the United States midwest in 1869. Through contacts with Chicago members of the medical profession in 1870 he became concerned about the sickness and death rate of infants due to infantile diarrhea. His interest was further enhanced by Justus Von Leibig's published formula of an infant food prepared from malt-flour infusion and mixed with liquid whole milk. This preparation, referred to as "Leibig's Malt Soup," was perishable, a factor that greatly limited its use.

James Horlick conducted experiments on the production of a dry maltose-dextrin milk modifier until in 1873 it became a factory-manufactured product. This dried maltose-dextrin milk additive became known as Horlicks Food (U.S. Pat. 163,493, May 18, 1875, issued to James and William Horlick).

The Horlick brothers observed that the favorable results from use of the prepared food were often ruined by unsafe milk. They further experimented on methods of combining milk with the mash from a mixture of barley malt and wheat flour. The culmination of much research was revealed in a patent issued to William Horlick in 1883 (U.S. Pat. 278, 967, June 5).

The development of the process for preparing this desiccated food required several years of experimentation for the selection and assembly of suitable manufacturing equipment. Therefore, it was not until June of 1887 that Malted Milk was formally introduced to the medical profession at their Chicago convention. In the same year, 1887, a registered trademark was issued to James Horlick of Horlick Food Company (U.S. Pat. Office Trade Mark 14,856, Oct. 25) for "Malted Milk, a Food Preparation for Infants and Invalids."

The product qualities of safety, convenience, nutritive value, and ease of digestion soon won recognition of the medical profession. The industry grew rapidly and attracted other manufacturers of dairy products when the patent protection ended.

The dietetic and economic value of malted milk gradually increased until in 1916 the USDA issued a Standard of Purity that sets forth the essential requirements for its preparation and for the purposes of standardization fixes the milkfat and moisture content: "Malted Milk is the product made by combining whole milk with the liquid separated from a mash of ground barley malt and wheat flour, with or without the addition of sodium chloride, sodium bicarbonate, and potassium bicarbonate in such a manner as to secure the full enzymic action of the malt extract and by removing water. The resulting product contains not less than seven and one-half percent (7.5%) of butter fat and not more than three and one-half percent (3.5%) of moisture."

A pleasant malt flavor is the reason for malted milk becoming popular as a favored milk beverage of the soda fountain trade. Retail store trade now accounts for the greatest amount of malted milk type products manufactured. The finished product is packaged in glass bottles or cans that can be resealed for safekeeping.

The manufacturing trade uses malted milk as an ingredient in crackers, cookies, cake mixes, frostings, confections, malted milk balls, and ice cream.

Annual production of malted milk is compiled by the USDA. The increase in production was gradual until it became fairly well stabilized in the range of 20–25 million pounds. Periods of war and postwar were exceptions with production almost double.

Malted milk tablets have played important roles as emergency or survival rations during wars and exploration expeditions. Polar explorers, Rear Admiral Richard Peary, Captain Roald Amundson, and Rear Admiral Richard Byrd were supplied with malted milk tablets as was our first Astronaut, Colonel John Glenn.

Ingredient Materials and Processing Technology

The Federal Standard in its definition of malted milk has established the minimum amount of milkfat and the maximum amount of water. Calculated on a basis of containing 7.5% butterfat, a typical malted milk powder would have 26% milk solids, 73.3% malt-flour solids, and 0.7% salts.

There is no provision in the standards relative to the ratio of malt to flour. The Horlick patent specified equal parts of ground barley malt and wheat flour. This ratio of malt to flour has, through general practice, been gradually increased to the use of a higher ratio of malt.

Barley malt and wheat flour (q.v.) are intermediate products that require specialized equipment and accurate control during processing. It is common practice to purchase these ingredients from reliable suppliers.

Mashing is a term that refers to the conversion and solubilization of all the starch and a portion of the protein materials contained in the dry cereal mixture. Water is added to the crushed malt-wheat flour mixture to effect the conversion through the action of enzyme systems released from the ground barley malt.

The most important enzymic constituents of malt are the starch-splitting enzymes known as amylases. These preform best in the 63°–67°C temperature range. Secondly, the presence of peptases, proteolytic enzymes, are important in the breakdown of high molecular protein complexes into smaller soluble amino acids and dispersible proteins. Proteolytic enzymes perform best in 45°–55°C temperature range.

The mash is prepared by adding ground malt to a gelatinized mixture of wheat flour and water. Gelatinized flour is obtained by heating all of the wheat flour with $1\frac{1}{2}$ times its weight of water to a temperature of 95°C. The combined grains are steeped in approximately five times their weight of water and transferred to a steam-jacketed mash kettle.

The converting of the mash is usually accomplished in stages to allow for protein peptization and complete starch conversion. The mash process usually proceeds by heating to the protein rest stage and then on to the saccharifying temperature of 66°C where it is usually held for 30 min. The temperature is then raised to 77°C and held until all the starch is converted.

Barley malt and wheat flour are biological products subjected to many variables as variety, soil, growing season and storage. The best combination of materials and process will render only slightly more than 40% of the protein soluble.

The malt husks and other insoluble materials are separated from the mash by one or more of the processes that involve settlement, screening, centrifuging, and filter pressing.

The liquid fraction from the mash being acidic in reaction, pH 5.7, is neutralized with sodium or potassium bicarbonate. A small amount of sodium chloride is also added as a flavor stimulus.

The liquid fraction from the mash is combined with fluid milk and the mixture brought to dryness in specially designed vacuum equipment. The temperatures during the drying periods are kept below a maximum of 60°C. The interaction of the milk constituents with the soluble proteins, amino acids, carbohydrates and tannins in the mash liquor produces the typical malted milk flavor. The final stage of drying ends with the production of an expanded, porous-structured dried product that is removed and ground to a granular powder.

Chocolate-flavored malted milk powder is obtained by processing chocolate liquor, cocoa, and sugar with the malted milk food. A recent development has been the addition of lecithin to the finished product for imparting instant wetting characteristics.

When properly packaged to prevent air and moisture absorption, malted milk powder has good keeping qualities.

The composition of malted milk includes a combination of extractives from the barley malt-wheat flour cereal mix with all the solids from cow's milk. A proximate average composition of plain or natural malted milk is moisture, 2.6%; fat, 7.8%; carbohydrates, 70.7%; protein, 14.8%; ash, 3.7%; fiber, 0.3%. For chocolate malted milk the values are moisture, 1.8%; fat, 5.8%; carbohydrates, 80.2%; protein, 9.4%; ash, 2.4%; fiber 0.4%.

Malted milk powder is highly hygroscopic due to the sugars it contains: maltose, dextrin, lactose, and dextrose.

W. M. HIGBY

MAPLE SUGAR

History has not recorded who first made syrup or sugar from the sap of the maple tree. Legend has it that an Indian squaw first discovered the secret when boiling venison in maple sap. Both syrup and sugar were well-established items of barter among the Indians living in the area of the Great Lakes and the St. Lawrence River, even before the arrival of the white man. Later French soldiers made a year's supply of sugar from maple sap and stored it in wooden casks or barrels.

Since early settlers could not afford cane sugar from Cuba, Puerto Rico, or Central America, they made maple sugar. Since it was cheaper than cane sugar it was sold by sugar makers to other settlers. It was produced and processed entirely on the farm, principally in Vermont, New York, and other New England States, but also in Pennsylvania, Wisconsin, Ohio, Michigan, Minnesota, Indiana, West Virginia, and Virginia. In 1860, a record crop of 4,132,000 gal. was produced. In the years that followed production declined as the price of cane sugar became cheaper. During World War I production increased again to a figure slightly higher than in 1860 because of the shortage of cane sugar. Production was also high during World War II. Since then it has declined. In 1970 production was 1,110,000 gal.

In Canada, the province of Quebec is the principal producer, with Ontario second in importance. A small amount of syrup is made in Nova Scotia and New Brunswick. Total Canadian production is about 2,000,000 gal.

Maple sugar is composed of 0–12% hexose sugar; 88–99% sucrose; and minute amounts of raffinose, a glycosyl sucrose; and three oligosaccharides which have not as yet been identified. It also contains organic acids, ash, and protein. Included in the acids are malic, citric, succinic, fumaric, and glycolic, as well as traces of seven other acids. Included in the ash are potassium, calcium, silicon oxide, manganese, sodium, and magnesium.

In recent years attempts have been made by chemists to isolate the materials that cause the unique flavor in pure maple syrup and sugar. If this were achieved, it might be possible to make maple sugar synthetically. One of the three major flavor components has been identified as syringaldehyde. The others have not as yet been isolated and identified.

In most maple areas, maple sugar or syrup must be made during a period of time between Nov. 1 and May 1. The tree is then in a dormant state, and starch manufactured by the leaves during the growing season has been changed to sugar and stored in the cells of the twigs, branches, trunk, and roots. Cold weather has frozen the tissues, and the sap "run" does not occur until the sun warms the air considerably above freezing. As warming occurs in the woody tissues, pressure is developed which is greater than atmospheric—sometimes as much as 20 lb per sq in. This pressure forces sap out through any wound. The "wound" usually made by the sugar maker is with a bit $7/16$ in. in diameter and 3 in. long. The "tapping" is usually done from Febr. 15 to Mar. 25, depending upon the latitude and elevation. A spout, or spile, is hammered into the hole until it fits snugly against the bark. A metal or plastic bucket, or sometimes a plastic bag, is then hung on a hook beneath the spout; or a length of plastic tubing is connected to it. As warm days follow cold nights the sap drips into the buckets or bags or flows through the tubing. A sap run, once started, may last for a few hours, or for as long as 48 hr. During an average season there may be from 6 to 20 runs. The average taphole produces 8–15 gal. of sap. The sap ranges from 1 to 9% in sugar content. The average is 2.5% sugar.

When the sap has run long enough so that a quart or more is present in the bucket or bag, the gathering, or collecting process begins. Large gathering pails are used. The sap is poured into the pail, and when the pail is full it is carried to a gathering tank pulled by a tractor or team of horses. When the gathering tank is full, it is hauled to the sugar house where the sap runs by gravity into a large storage tank.

With the use of plastic tubing the sap runs by gravity through $1/4$- or $5/16$-in. lines; then through $1/2$-in. and larger conduits until it reaches a temporary storage tank or the storage tank at the sugar house. From temporary storage tanks it is picked up by a tank truck and transported to the sugar house. When tubing is used, extra sap storage tanks must be planned.

Recently, vacuum systems have been developed for pumping sap from the tree to the sugar house. The most efficient is a dry vacuum pump pulling a vacuum on a tank into which the sap flows. A water pump then moves the sap from the vacuum tank into the main storage tank at the sugar house.

Processing the sap into syrup is accomplished in the sugar house. It is necessary to boil down sap which contains an average of 2.5% sugar into finished syrup which contains 66.5% sugar. Thus 33 gal. of water must be turned into steam in order to make 1 gal. of syrup. The evaporators used range from 2 ft wide and 6 ft long to 6 ft wide and 20 ft long. The sap first runs into a flue pan, which contains several flues which drop down into the fire box and expose a maximum amount of sap to the heat; it is regulated by a float, and flows gradually into different compartments until it reaches the front pan, which is flat. In the front pan it is finally condensed into standard syrup. A thermometer is used to test the syrup as it comes close to "standard" density. Standard syrup boils at from $7°-7\frac{1}{2}°$ above the boiling point of water. A final test for standard density is made with a thermometer and a hydrometer. The finished syrup at $60°F$ should test $35.75°$ Baumé or $66.5°$Brix.

The evaporator pans are set on arches made of steel and lined with asbestos and fire brick. Heat is provided by wood, oil burners, or gas burners.

The finished syrup is graded as to density, color, and flavor. The light amber color and more delicate flavor is usually considered the best grade. However, the dark amber color with a stronger, caramelized flavor, is preferred by some. Syrups with off-flavors, such as metallic, or moldy, or bitter are usually put in drums and used for commercial processing into blends of cane and maple syrup. Such blends usually contain from 6 to 11% of pure maple syrup.

Standard syrup is usually packed temporarily into 32-gal. drums, milk cans, or 5-gal. containers. Later it is heated to $180°F$ or higher, filtered through wool, orlon, or felt filters, and packed into small containers made of tin, glass, or plastic. However, some sugar makers carry or pump the syrup directly into insulated filter tanks, and then pack the syrup directly from a spigot at the bottom of the filter tank. Good packers take care to fill the container so as to eliminate all air in the container. The container is sealed so as to prevent the entrance of air at a later date. It must be labelled in most states and provinces as to its liquid contents, name and address of the processor, and grade.

For best results pure maple syrup is stored in cool, dry places. The original flavor is kept best if the syrup is stored at temperatures below freezing. The sizes of retail containers usually packed are 1 gal., 2 qt, 1 qt, 1 pt, and $\frac{1}{2}$ pt.

For variety and greater marketability, pure maple syrup is often boiled down to a thicker density and sold as various kinds of sugar.

"Sugar-on-snow" is syrup boiled until it reaches a waxy consistency. At this point the temperature is usually about $22°F$ above the boiling point of water. The syrup is usually ladled onto packed snow or crushed ice. Upon contact with the snow or ice it becomes like taffy and is usually eaten with a fork. At "sugar-on-snow parties" the servings of syrup are accompanied by raised or cake doughnuts, sliced sour pickles, and coffee.

Commercial maple sugar prepared from syrup is "soft sugar," which is made by boiling the syrup to a temperature of $23°$ above the boiling point of water (about $235°F$); "hard sugar," which is made by boiling the syrup to $27°$ above the boiling point of water (usually $239°F$); and Indian, or crumb sugar, which is made by boiling the syrup to $38°-40°$ above the boiling point of water (usually $250°-252°F$).

Maple cotton candy can be made in a cotton candy machine by using a blend of about 25% maple sugar and 75% cane sugar. The maple flavor in the cotton candy is very pleasing.

Maple cream is made by boiling maple syrup to a temperature $20°$ above the boiling point of water (usually $232°F$); cooling it rapidly without stirring to $70°F$; and then scraping into a cream consistency. It is usually packed in glass jars and used as a spread on bread or crackers.

Pure maple syrup and sugar are used in many favorite recipes for cakes, baked beans, fudge, and other foods. Recently, syrup has been used in peanut and walnut brittle and in a sugar coating on popcorn. For maple recipes contact the Extension Service at the State Agricultural College of one of the maple states.

For most farmers with sugar bushes in the maple states the production and sale of maple products is a valuable source of income. The $800-$1,200 of additional income received in the spring months helps to pay taxes, the grain bill, or other costs of the farming operation.

A recent trend in the maple industry is the development of "central evaporation" plants that process sap from as many as 100,000 trees. These are usually operated as a full-time business, rather than as part of a farming enterprise. Some people just produce sap for sale to such plants, and earn from $0.50 to $1.25 per tap each year. Sap is paid for on the basis of sugar content and quality. The average plant makes 3000-5000 gal. of syrup per year and buys from 8 to 10 sap producers. The plant manager usually operates a gift shop or restaurant in connection with his maple sales business.

RAYMOND T. FOULDS, JR.

Cross-reference: *Sugars and Sweeteners.*

MARGARINE

Margarine is an economical, manufactured food resembling butter in appearance, form, and composition except that the fat component consists of vegetable and/or animal fats largely not derived from milk. The great number of available fatty materials and the statutory latitude in product definition and use of other approved ingredients makes possible its production in a variety of esthetically pleasing forms sometimes preferred to the natural prototype product for certain culinary and nutritional properties and advantages. Margarine has become a very important food in a number of countries around the world. At a price substantially less than that of butter, U.S. consumption of margarine equalled that of butter in 1957–1958 and has been steadily increasing since then with a parallel decline in butter usage. In some essentially dairy countries not so well supplied with fats and oils, the price differential may be considerably less than in the United States, but the extensive use of the substitute for cooking and baking, as well as a table spread, often makes butter available for export.

A plastic emulsion, margarine consists usually of an aqueous phase dispersed in a fatty continuous phase comprising a mixture of vegetable and/or animal fats of such nature and composition as to maintain the product in its solid emulsion form at prevailing temperatures, but rapidly and completely meltable in the mouth for good flavor release with no apparent salve-like, hard-fat residue. The aqueous phase is usually either specially prepared skim milk or water, or a mixture of these. Other ingredients such as salt, flavoring and coloring agents, vitamins, emulsifiers, antioxidants, and preservatives are usually contained in either of the two phases.

Invention and Development

H. Mège-Mouriès, a French chemist, invented margarine in 1869 in response to an appeal by Napoleon III for an economical, nutritious butter substitute for his needy peasants and armies. He was awarded a prize by the emperor and patents the same year in France and England; and in Germany and the United States in the ensuing years. Mouriès' product, composed of oleo oil carefully prepared from selected beef fats, milk, salt, and annatto for color, was made by rapidly chilling the partially emulsified mixture in ice water, separating the solidified fatty granules from the watery excess of milk, and kneading the solid emulsion as in butter manufacture to obtain the finished margarine in print form. Thus was established in essence the method by which margarine is made even today. The product was somewhat pearly in appearance and was therefore called "oleomargarine"—oleo from the oleo oil and margarine from the Greek word margarites meaning pearly. Since oleo oil has a pleasant, sweet, animal-like flavor resembling that of butter, Mouriès' product was hardly dis-

tinguishable from the butter of that time. By 1876, Mouriès' invention was being applied in Holland and Austria in addition to the other countries mentioned, initial production in the United States having begun in 1874. The industry expanded rapidly in Europe and the United States, the product satisfying a definite need for an inexpensive spread.

The young margarine business was beset by a host of problems and their resolution has been slow and interdependent, the sophistication of the product to its present state of excellent quality and broad consumer acceptance having been attained largely during the last 40 yr. The development of margarine follows closely the improvements made in producing, processing, and handling animal and vegetable fats and oils. Paralleling and complementing these developments were the advancements made in flavor chemistry, emulsion technology, and nutrition. Employing butter processing methods initially, the industry has gradually developed fully continuous processes specifically for margarine. In addition to the many technical problems to be resolved, competitive pressures of the butter industry resulted in governmental restrictions which have only in recent years been largely eliminated as margarine has gradually established itself as a high-quality, wholesome, nutritious food, acceptable on its own merits, largely free now of any stigma of artificiality. To standardize the product in the consumers' interest, various world governments have defined the product in terms of composition and approved ingredients, and have specified the conditions for its packaging and distribution.

Oil Blend Development

Constituting 75–84% of the finished product, the fat component of margarine is the most important single ingredient because it maintains print form, determines melting properties, and influences flavor quality and oxidative stability. It is generally formulated with sufficient hard fat (usually melting at 40°–44°C) along with softer fats and oils so that the chilled emulsion will be firm enough for efficient processing and packaging, yet plastic over a wide range of prevailing temperatures and melting completely in the mouth for good flavor release. Fats and oils must be processed so that any slight residual flavor shall not adversely affect the delicate butter-like flavor notes from other ingredients. Selection and extent of processing of the fats and oils comprising a margarine oil blend are determined not only by cost, availability, and functionality, but also by shelf-life requirements in the various market areas.

Oleo oil, supplemented as necessary by neutral lard from selected hog fats, provided the early margarines with reasonably good physical and culinary properties but the limited supply of these two fats was inadequate to meet the constantly increasing demand. The manufacturers were therefore soon forced to extend the supply of oleo oil-lard blends by using some of the higher-melting-point tallow (premier jus from which oleo oil was extracted) as well as liquid vegetable oils to offset the hardness imparted by the beef fats. Only a small amount of liquid oil could be used initially due to poor flavor quality; but the introduction of fuller's earth bleaching in the 1880's and of steam deodorization about 1890 provided vegetable oils of reasonably acceptable quality, particularly coconut and palm kernel oils which exhibited superior flavor quality, good resistance to oxidation, and melting properties somewhat similar to those of oleo oil and butter.

By the turn of the century, two types of margarine had evolved, "animal" and "vegetable." The first consisted largely of an oleo oil-lard blend, some oleo stock and liquid oils such as cottonseed, soybean, peanut, sesame, olive, and sunflower seed, and often a small amount of coconut and palm kernel oils. The vegetable-type contained predominantly the latter two oils in combination with lesser amounts of liquid vegetable oils, even some animal fats. Largely dependent on imported fats and oils and their markets being more localized, western Europeans preferred the animal-type product for quality and economy, obtaining substantially all of their requirements of oleo oil, oleo stock, and neutral lard from the United States. The U.S. market being less localized, the vegetable-type product based on coconut oil soon came to be preferred, taking advantage of the good flavor and stability of this oil.

The application of hydrogenation to hardening liquid vegetable oils immediately after its invention in 1903 marked a great forward step in supplying the food industry with a great variety of oils of improved flavor and oxidative stability. It was found, too, that the so-called "isoacids" melting at about $38°C$ made the partially hydrogenated liquid oils particularly useful for margarine. In the period from 1903-1910 in Europe and thereafter in the United States, partially hydrogenated liquid vegetable oils, usually of $30°-34°C$ and $40°-44°C$ melting points, came into increased use as ingredients in blends with the natural fats and oils. Hydrogenation and improvements in refining soon made it possible to use the less expensive whale and other marine oils. During the ensuing years whale oil became one of the most important oils in European margarine oil blends, gradually and almost completely displacing by 1930-1940 the more expensive beef fats and lard imported from the United States. Having good flavor quality and

stability, lightly hydrogenated coconut oil came into extensive use in all-vegetable margarine in the United States.

As the U.S. cotton industry burgeoned during the period 1900-1935, cottonseed oil usage increased steadily until about 1935 when the rapidly expanding soybean industry began to provide U.S. margarine producers with larger supplies of less expensive soybean oil. High import duties on coconut oil, the large supply of domestic vegetable oils, the greater stability of the hydrogenated oils, and the market requirements for margarine with longer shelf-life, all combined to displace coconut oil almost completely by 1935 and the animal fats, also, by the late 1940's.

The supply of soybean oil increased rapidly in the United States after 1930 and, as a result of a succession of technological improvements in oil processing during the period 1930-1960, soybean oil has become the principal oil ingredient of U.S. margarines. European manufacturers, on the other hand, being dependent largely on imported stocks, employed as many as 5 or 6 different fats and oils in their margarine oil blends continuing the animal-type with whale oil, lard, oleo oil, etc., in combination with suitable vegetable oils, the vegetable-type employing coconut, palm, and palm kernel oils for the harder components along with liquid-type oils such as cottonseed, peanut, sunflower, etc., either in liquid or slightly hardened form as desired. The characteristically red palm oils came into extensive use at moderately low levels, in both liquid and moderately hydrogenated form, to provide vitamin A and color in addition to melting point control as a harder ingredient. As world supplies of whale oil have gradually diminished, increased demand for proteins and edible oil in Europe and the Far East has led to the more extensive use of soybeans and the oil in these areas.

To meet the distribution and shelf-life requirements of 90-120 days, U.S. margarines are now refrigerated and during the past 30-35 yr have employed all-hydrogenated oil blends, although nutritional developments of the mid-1950's have dictated the production of margarines containing liquid oils to provide a higher level of the essential fatty acids. In 1957, soybean oil comprised 84% of U.S. margarine oils, but its use has declined to about 70% as corn, safflower, and other polyunsaturated oils came into use in recent years. Russia and the eastern European countries have developed domestic crops providing liquid vegetable oils, particularly sunflower in recent years, and their margarines have probably made use of vegetable oils to a greater extent than has western Europe.

The ability of the margarine industry to produce a variety of margarine types comprising the modern margarines is due not only to refinements in oil processing but also to the development and use of sophisticated laboratory techniques and instrumentation which have enabled the technician to control processing and margarine oil blending more meaningfully than by melting point alone. Dilatometry enables the formulator to blend oils on the basis of the percentage of solid fat fraction in the ingredient oils and blends, thereby permitting the control of the hardness and melting point characteristics of the product during manufacture and use. Spectrophotometry, infrared spectroscopy, and gas liquid chromatography have enabled the analyst for the first time to analyze fats and oils accurately for their content of component fatty acids and isomeric forms. Other analytical methods of importance are differential thermal analysis and nuclear magnetic resonance, but dilatometry is perhaps the most important for practical developmental and control purposes.

Development of Flavors

Since the compounds responsible for the delicate buttery flavor desired in both margarine and butter total only 10–20 ppm, it is readily understandable that the fat component comprising 80% of the finished margarine must be almost flavorless if the desired butter-like flavor notes from the other ingredients are to produce the intended taste sensation. While the early margarines with oleo oil and neutral lard tasted somewhat buttery, they lacked the cultured milk flavor notes of present-day margarines and butter. Fortunately for the new industry, about 1890 Storch and Weikman introduced the practice of inoculating cream with lactic acid-forming bacteria (*Streptococcus lactis*) to obtain butters of uniformly good flavor quality. This practice, applied to pasteurized skim milk somewhat coincidentally with the introduction of steam deodorization of vegetable oils, was immediately responsible for a definite improvement in the aroma, flavor, and acidity of margarine, probably making possible at the same time a substantial reduction in milk usage and increased tolerance of deodorized vegetable oils. During the period 1890–1930, the microorganisms in milk starter cultures were characterized as a variety of Streptococcus types. Other investigations identified acetylmethyl carbinol and diacetyl as the principal sources of flavor and aroma in butter, these two agents immediately coming into use as additives to margarine. As the result of work in the 1940's and 1950's, aliphatic lactones were shown to have butter-like flavorings suitable for margarine. In 1963, investigations demonstrated the presence of volatile carbonyls in butter flavor. While some countries have been more liberal in allowing the direct addition of these and other chemical flavoring agents, the United States permitted only diacetyl until 1966 when less restrictive regulations allowed the use of any approved nontoxic additives, thus giving the manufacturer much more latitude in the development of specific flavor formulations for specific margarines.

The use of artificial flavors in margarines has enabled the manufacturer to reduce the amount of cultured milk necessary for optimum flavor level. This has been beneficial not only in reducing the amount of milk to be pasteurized and cultured, but also in improving margarine flavor quality since cultured milk deteriorates rather rapidly. A few years ago as much as 50% of the milk was cultured as compared with current levels in the range of 5–10%. In recent years, dry starter cultures have become available, making it possible to inoculate the pasteurized milk a day in advance of its use, thus providing cultured milk of uniform, standardized quality while simplifying production and reducing the danger of contamination with undesirable bacteria.

Some factors influencing the development of satisfactory flavor formulations are the stability (or lack of it) of the flavor ingredients, the possible loss of some of the more volatile fractions, the relative solubilities and distributions of the flavor components in the aqueous or fatty phases and the effects of these factors on the taste sensation as functions of the emulsion properties and release rates from the two phases as the margarine melts, and, of course, the compatibility of the flavor formulation with the flavor of salt and cultured milk at different levels.

Emulsification and Processing

Emulsion stabilizers are necessary in margarine production not only to effect uniform, stable distribution of the various ingredients in the liquid emulsion but also to maintain this distribution in the solidified fatty mass without coalescence and extrusion of moisture during subsequent kneading, printing, and packaging. They are also necessary to prevent "leakage" of moisture during distribution and to control the color, form of sedimentation, and spattering in frying.

The earliest margarines were made by several minor variations of Mouriès' process which usually included churning the margarine oil blend and minor ingredients for 1–2 hr with about twice as much fresh or sour milk, cream, or cream and milk mixture in order to obtain a creamy emulsion resulting from the effect of the lecithin-protein complex normally present in butterfat at the level of about 0.3%. Chilling the emulsion by slowly pouring ice water into it caused the formation of fatty granules with moderate development of fatty crystals of pearly appearance. In order to obtain products with indistinguishably small crystals for smoother texture, manufacturers devised a variety of emulsifying techniques depending on the formula and also procedures for spraying the emulsion into ice water or on crushed ice, such plants still being in limited use as late as the 1930's. Fresh egg yolk, which contains a much higher concentration of the lecithin-protein complex than butterfat, came into extensive use during the late 1890's when cultured milk was being introduced for flavor improvement, these two developments both contributing to a gradual reduction in the excessive use of milk. Fresh egg yolks being subject to spoilage, the dried yolk being both expensive and less effective, lecithin of vegetable origin was found to be useful early in this century, soybean lecithin being in almost universal use by 1930. Although milk contains colloidal proteins which exert emulsifying effects, more highly functional emulsifiers and stabilizing agents were developed after about 1920. A partial list of these includes the polymerized glyceride oils; polyglycerol fatty acid esters; aliphatic monohydric esters of polyhydroxy organic acids; the mono- and diglyceride esters of the longer fatty acids and their esters with the polyhydroxy acids, such as succinic and tartaric; propylene glycol fatty acid esters; sorbitan esters of the fatty acids and their polyoxyethylene derivatives; as well as cellulose gum variations. The mono- and diglycerides in combination with lecithin are now in most general use to provide in the churn a w/o emulsion that will be sufficiently stable in the subsequent processing steps to minimize moisture separation and loss.

During the early 1900's the "dry" rotating drum, chilled initially with brine and later by direct expansion of ammonia, was introduced for quick chilling the liquid emulsion in a thin layer that could be scraped off by a doctor blade. More effective equipment was designed for kneading the tempered, flaked emulsion into a continuous mass, some units applying vacuum to reduce air content for improved product stability. In combination, the roll and the new emulsifying systems made it possible to make up the emulsion with about the desired moisture content, then to crystallize and recover it in solid emulsion form. However, some lack of uniformity in the moisture content of the finished product was experienced due to variable moisture losses in kneading and packaging. During the 1930's the introduction of the closed continuous tubular heat exchanger for chilling the emulsion was the first step in the development of entirely closed continuous processes, a major forward step in the development of modern margarines. By 1950, entirely closed systems were operating, the product not being exposed to the atmosphere after leaving the liquid emulsion churn. Initially it was found that closed continuous crystallization

under moderate pressure resulted in a firmer, more closely textured product that was slower to melt and less spreadable; these objections later were overcome by reducing the solid fat content of the oil blend, by modifying the solid fat-temperature curves so as to adapt the product more favorably to processing and culinary requirements, by using in-line mixers and screens to break down the crystalline structure, by gradually reducing the amount of emulsifiers so as to loosen the solid emulsion, and by employing precrystallization techniques. The closed continuous system makes it possible not only to maintain precise formulary control from the churn into the package, but it also permits the manufacturer to process formulations varying widely in solid fat contents; i.e., very soft margarines as well as firmer types.

Nutrition

Although the ingredients of margarine are very similar to those of butter, concern was expressed immediately after its introduction that it might not be as nutritious as butter. Since butter and margarine both contain about 80% fat, interest was focused on the possible nutritional differences between butterfat and other animal fats or vegetable fats and oils. By 1900, it was shown that although the calorific content of both products was the same, digestibility was related to the melting point of the hard fat component and tended to decrease with increases in the melting point and concentration of the hard fat, depending to a considerable extent on whether or not the hard component was completely dissolved in the lower melting fraction at body temperature. Subsequent research demonstrated that digestibility decreases markedly as fully saturated triglycerides harder than tripalmitin are ingested. Also, the position of the saturated acid in a mixed triglyceride is a factor. Although puff pastry margarine—sometimes used in special bakery products—may be only 75–90% digestible, table margarines have long been considered to be as digestible as butter.

During the period 1910–1922, McCollum (q.v.) and others established the presence of fat-soluble, essential accessory food factors in natural unprocessed fats, later identified as vitamins A and D. Since butter was found to contain high levels of vitamin A the margarine industry fortified its product initially in 1946 with 9000 IU per pound and in 1951 with 15,000 IU which compared to maximum levels in butter. After 1953, when irradiation of ergosterol provided a uniform supply of vitamin D, this vitamin was added on a noncompulsory basis at a level of 2000 IU per pound. The fish liver oil concentrates used initially for vitamin A fortification were eventually replaced by a combination of synthetic vitamin A and beta-carotene, precursor of vitamin A. Coloring the margarine as desired, beta-carotene also provides 5000-6000 IU of the required 15,000 IU of vitamin A, the difference being supplied by use of the synthetic vitamin A product. Beta-carotene may be derived from natural products such as carrots, but is usually a synthetic product (q.v.). A third source of coloring employed in some margarines is derived from the tropical annatto plant (q.v.). In recent years, fortification of margarine with vitamin D has been largely discontinued, the supply from other food sources being considered adequate. Vitamin E, commonly referred to as tocopherol, occurs quite generally in vegetable oils and is known to be an antioxidant, but its dietary significance appears to be unclear. Vitamin K, also soluble in fat, does not seem to occur to any appreciable degree in either butter or margarine. During the 1940's it was demonstrated that margarines and butters having the same vitamin contents were nutritionally equivalent in dietetic and reproductive aspects.

Other studies of the nutritional properties and adequacy of various oils, including hydrogenated oils, led to a demonstration in 1929-1930 that linoleic acid is essential to health and general well-being. Other essential acids were subsequently identified, but linoleic is the most prevalent. During the 1950's, there was reported an inverse relationship between linoleic acid content of ingested fats and oils and the cholesterol content of the blood. Some nutritionists and medical researchers associated blood cholesterol with atherosclerosis and coronary heart disease, thus initiating a change in dietary patterns and calling for higher levels of ingested linoleic acid, particularly in the case of middle-aged and elderly people. The margarine industry modified their products accordingly or created new ones to provide margarines with higher levels of linoleic acid. Whereas earlier margarines employing all-hydrogenated oil blends for superior flavor quality and stability had exhibited polyunsaturated to saturated fatty acid ratios as low as 0.5, most regular margarines have been modified so that this ratio complies with the recommended range of 1.0-2.0, with some special margarines employing as much as 50-75% of the so-called polyunsaturated liquid oils; thus P/S ratios of 4-5 have been obtained.

By 1957-1958, U.S. margarine consumption equalled that of butter for the first time, largely because of cost. Since then the steady increase in margarine consumption at the expense of butter has been for reasons of nutrition and economy.

Products and Statistics

Production of margarine was initiated in western Europe and the United States, but it is now quite prevalent in most of the developed countries of the world. Although margarines from the various countries are quite similar in appearance, they differ in a number of details, not only in flavor, salt, and fat composition, etc., but also in texture, spreadability, and, perhaps most significantly, in plastic range. Western European-type margarines containing substantial amounts of coconut, palm kernel and palm oils have excellent melting properties but tend to be hard, brittle, and unspreadable at temperatures below $50°-60°F$ and are apt to slump at $75°-80°F$ due to the melting characteristics of the nut oils. The partially hydrogenated liquid oils, however, comprised of a variety of fatty acids, melt over a wider temperature range; margarines made from them now are readily spreadable at $35°-45°F$, yet firm enough not to slump objectionably in ordinary table use at $80°-85°F$.

With less costly soybean oil in great supply after World War II, with a rising demand for margarine from war-time fat shortages, with sophisticated technology and equipment, with increasing use and availability of refrigeration in distribution and the home, and with the advantage of wide plastic range accruing from the liquid vegetable oils, the U.S. margarine manufacturer had all the essentials necessary for expanding margarine into a line of products. Beginning in the 1950's this is precisely what happened. In 1952, margarine spreadable even "when ice cold" was introduced. In 1956, a softer than normal margarine containing 5-10% butter was introduced nationally, for the first time establishing margarine as a perishable food product requiring refrigerated distribution. About the same time, whipped margarines containing occluded nitrogen provided a diet-type product packaged with six conventionally foil-wrapped sticks per pound, 1 pat containing $1/3$ less calories than regular products. Salt-free margarine was also introduced for those on low-salt diets. Stated previously, in 1955-1960 margarines were gradually changed from polyunsaturated to saturated fatty acid ratios of as low as 0.5 to the recommended range of 1.0-2.0 and higher by the use of more highly polyunsaturated oils. In order to obtain generally higher P/S ratios, the industry, during the 1960's, introduced "soft" margarines employing lower melting point fats and oils, packaging such products in plastic and aluminum cups with slip-top covers. The soft margarines were not only dramatically more spreadable but moisture and oil separation problems such as were experienced with parchment- and foil-wrapped products were largely eliminated by cup packaging. This development also enabled the manufacturer to formulate oil blends more readily complying with the recommended P/S range. Since practically all U.S. margarines are now refrigerated products, the regular products in stick form have also been softened considerably, although not nearly as much as the cup products.

In 1963, the concept of a fluid, pourable product extrudable from a plastic tube was introduced, but marketing has not been extensive. By 1965, margarine without milk solids had been marketed to provide a product that would not stick to the pan while frying. Products employing aliphatic lactones as the butter flavor were market-tested in 1965. These several products represented deviations from statutory limits which required modification to permit their production.

The growth of the margarine industry is an outstanding example of the development of a food product. By 1957–1958, production of margarine in the U.S. had grown to the butter equivalent of 1.5 billion pounds and by 1970 to 2.1 billion pounds annually. World production of margarine in 1967 totaled over 10.2 billion pounds, almost equal to world butter production, the United States accounting for 22% and Russia for 11%. By regions of the world, Western Europe and the United Kingdom produced 4.13 billion, Eastern Europe and the U.S.S.R. 2.28 billion, North America 2.30 billion, Central America 0.10 billion, and the rest of the world including Australia, Japan, India, Pakistan, and Israel 1.60 billion pounds of margarine. U.S. per capita consumption of margarine in 1969 was 10.8 lb and for butter it was 5.3 lb. Elsewhere in the world, per capita consumption of margarine varies widely depending on custom, supply, economics, and other factors. Some western European countries may consume 40–50 lb of margarine in addition to 8–18 lb of butter per capita while in New Zealand, primarily a dairy country, there is practically no use of margarine. In spite of inflation in recent years, the cost of regular U.S. margarines has actually declined; in 1949 margarine cost was 49% of that of butter, whereas now regular margarine cost is about $1/4$–$1/2$ that of butter. The soft margarines in cups, however, demand about $2/3$ the cost of butter.

Although margarine is generally thought of as a table spread, 5–10% of total production is used in the preparation of bakery products. Such margarines are not necessarily vitaminized and are somewhat firmer to adapt them to the preparation of batters, creams, etc. Puff pastry margarines are within statutory controls if they melt under 118°F.

Statutory Definitions and Regulations

Since margarine is a manufactured product competing directly with the natural spread, governments of most countries producing it have defined the product in terms of its ingredients and composition and have established regulations for its manufacture, packaging, and distribution, not only to protect the consumer but to distinguish it from natural dairy butter. Heavy taxes once imposed on margarine in the United States have now largely been eliminated. Government regulations vary considerably from country to country, and even from state to state within a country, and therefore statutory controls vary accordingly. Canada and the Union of South Africa prohibited the manufacture and sale of margarine for many years, but in general legal controls have become more realistic as margarine has become a greater factor in the economy and the food situation of the producing countries.

In general, margarines contain 75–84% fat and not more than about 16% moisture, water and fresh or reconstituted skim milk usually comprising the aqueous phase. In some European countries, essentially 100% fat margarines are made by heating the emulsion in the churn to cause a separation of the aqueous phase. Indian and Pakistani "vanaspati" is a 100% fat-type margarine. Some countries require an "indicator" ingredient such as starch or sesame oil which can be simply determined by colorimetric tests. While butter may generally be employed as an ingredient, legal limitations are imposed in many countries. Salt is generally permitted. Some European countries require the use of a specified amount of rapeseed oil. Most countries permit the use of specified preservatives, coloring and flavoring agents, and emulsifier-stabilizer combinations. Vitamins, especially vitamin A, are required by most countries. Product size and shape as well as labelling are generally controlled to distinguish margarine from butter, U.S. products being designated by law as oleomargarine until 1952 when the term "margarine" was approved. For details of the statutory controls, reference to the literature and government agencies is suggested.

WALTER PRITCHETT

References

ANDERSON, A. J. C., and WILLIAMS, P. N. 1965. Margarine, 2nd Revised Edition. Pergamon Press, London, England.

BAILEY, A. E. 1948. Cottonseed and Cottonseed Products. Interscience Publishers, New York.

BAILEY, A. E. 1951. Industrial Oil and Fat Products, 2nd Revised Edition. Interscience Publishers, New York.

Cross-reference: *Fats and Oils.*

MARKET MILK INDUSTRY

Market Milk

The market milk industry in the United States is involved with the processing and distribution of fluid milk and cream as well as other "fresh products" such as sour cream, buttermilk, and cottage cheese. The other dairy products are generally classified as manufactured dairy products and are dealt with under other subjects. Market milk and cream sales in the United States in 1970 represented 44.1% of all milk produced. The retail value of market milk and cream sold at retail in that year was estimated to be more than $9 billion.

The utilization of milk in other products in 1970 was reported by USDA as follows:

	(%)
Butter, creamery	20.3
Cheese	16.6
Ice cream, etc.	9.3
Evaporated and condensed	2.9
Used on farms where produced	3.5
Other	3.3

Many of the characteristics of the market milk industry are unique in that the milk for retail sales is produced under strict sanitary regulations including cooling and refrigerated transport of the raw milk from the farms to the processing plant. This has led to rather highly organized market milk production areas surrounding the metropolitan centers to supply the daily needs of consumers. Thus, the milk is moved as rapidly as possible from farm to plant and from plant to consumer to maintain its fresh character.

Over the years the milk industry has changed with the trend toward urbanization from a cottage industry to the highly developed systems we have today. In the early days, milk was delivered to consumer in the raw, unprocessed form from the small nearby farms but today this practice has almost totally disappeared. The increasing population and concentration of consumers in cities and towns has required the development of public health and minimum composition standards to assure consumers of the safety and wholesomeness of the products offered on the market. Today, most of the market milk supplies are produced under the Standards of the U.S. Public Health Service Grade A Pasteurized Milk Ordinance. This means that dairy farms and plants are inspected to ensure sanitary operations and the milk itself is subject to chemical and bacteriological testing both in the plants and in government laboratories.

Milk Production on the Farm.—Milk production has become a highly specialized operation. The trend over the years has been toward larger and fewer herds and this is particularly evident in the market milk sheds supplying the large centers of population. Milk production on farms has continued to increase over the years as population

increased. Production reached a high point of nearly 127 billion pounds in 1964, but since that time has decreased due to dairymen going out of business. Production in 1970 was reported by the USDA to be approximately 117 billion pounds.

The requirements for mechanization and special production and handling facilities have made it difficult for small dairy farms to maintain profitable operations. Operations now require mechanical milking machines and refrigerated milk tanks on the farms as well as special milk houses for handling the milk. This is a great change from operations prior to 1940 when hand milking was still a common practice, and cooling of milk on the farm was done in 10-gal. cans immersed in water tanks. Today, milk is cooled and held at the farm in electrically cooled tanks. Transport from the farm to the plant in cans has been replaced by refrigerated tank trucks. These changed operations have accelerated the trend toward fewer and larger herds. Small herds of 10 or fewer cows have gradually disappeared and herds of 30–50 cows have become more common. Herds of 100 milking cows or more are frequently found in high production areas.

The modern dairy farm is a specialized operation and there is a growing movement toward open housing and "milking parlors" which are replacing the old style stanchion barn where milking was done in the stall. The cows are fed and housed in barns or sheds which are open on one side and the cows are allowed free movement. Groups of six or more cows are brought to the "milking parlor" where milking is done under highly sanitary conditions. Cows are washed and fed only the grain concentrate at this point. The mechanical milking machines are attached and the milk flows by pipeline to refrigerated milk tanks in the milk house. Milking is done twice a day and the milk cooled and held below 45°F until the tank truck collects the milk for delivery to the processing plant.

Each farmer's milk is sampled at the farm by the tank truck driver at the time of pickup to provide the sample for composition and bacterial tests. These tests are regularly done at the plant laboratory as quality control measures as well as providing a basis for payment. Excessively high bacterial counts, above the standard set for Grade A milk, are cause for rejection or at least a warning that production conditions must be improved. These tests also provide information needed by the milk fieldman who works with the dairy farmers.

The dairy farm is subject to regular inspection by the local public health department. The inspector is authorized to inspect the equipment and milk handling practices on the farm to make

TABLE M-3

RELATIONSHIP OF FAT TO
SOLIDS-NOT-FAT CONTENT

| Fat Content (%) | Solids-Not-Fat Content | | Total Solids (%) |
	Extremes (%)	Average (%)	
3.0	7.75–8.35	8.05	11.05
3.5	8.20–8.90	8.55	11.60
4.0	8.55–9.25	8.90	12.90
4.5	8.85–9.50	9.2	13.70
5.0	9.05–9.65	9.35	14.35
5.5	9.20–9.80	9.50	15.00
6.0	9.30–9.90	9.60	15.60

SOURCE: Manual for Milk Plant Operators, Milk Industry Foundation.

sure that they are in compliance with the standards set for Grade A milk production. Sanitary methods of milking, milk cooling, and sanitizing of milk-handling equipment are major areas covered. Also included are such related factors as surroundings including barns, yards, and milk houses. Grade A producers operate under a permit and failure to meet standards causes the loss of the permit and exclusion from the Grade A market.

Milk Composition.—The milk produced in the United States comes from cows especially developed for milk production. The breeds of dairy cattle include Holsteins, Guernseys, Jerseys, Ayrshires, Brown Swiss, and Milking Shorthorns. Although milk cows of all these breeds as well as mixed breeds or "grades" are found in most areas, the predominant breed in the market milk areas is the Holstein breed. This trend toward Holsteins has been significant since the richer milk breeds have diminished in numbers, bringing about a lower fat level in market milk supplies.

The relationship between fat and solids-not-fat in raw milk as produced is shown by the data in Table M-3.

These results show that as the fat content increases, the solids-not-fat increases but at a lower rate. It can be roughly stated that a change of 0.40% solids-not-fat goes with a change of 1% fat and in the same direction.

The Holstein, Ayrshire, Milking Shorthorn, and Brown Swiss milks contain 3.0–4.0% fat; and Jersey and Guernsey milk 4.0–5.5% fat. Individual cows in each breed may vary widely in fat content but the composition of milk from a large herd tends to even out within the above ranges.

Milk composition is influenced by season and also by feeding and management practices. Milk-fat content is inversely related to milk yield, and increases in yield in the spring are accompanied by small decreases in fat content. Such changes in composition in pooled milk are usually less than 0.5% fat and the variations in the supply are a basic reason for fat standardization.

The composition of milk as packaged for the consumer is influenced by the almost universal practice of standardization of the fat content. State regulations provide minimum standards for fat and solids-not-fat in milk of each type on the retail market. Standardization of whole milk involves the adjustment of the fat content of the raw milk to make a uniform level at or above the minimum standard set by the respective states. This is accomplished by removing cream or adding skim milk of the same grade.

Homogenized Vitamin D Milk is the major type of milk in all markets as indicated by the product sales report for 1970. The sales of this whole milk product amounted to 76%, which together with flavored whole milk accounted for 78.4% of the fluid milk market. This dominant position of whole milk is changing, however, with the introduction of low-fat and skim milk with or without added milk-solids-not-fat, usually designated MSNF. These lower fat products accounted for 19% of the market milk sold in 1970.

Milk carrying the vitamin D label must contain 400 IU per qt as approved by the U.S. Public Health Association. Vitamin D is added to the milk prior to homogenization and pasteurization. The vitamin D level is subject to test and 400 IU of vitamin D is the minimum standard. There is no federal standard for composition of milk. This is the responsibility of the states. The predominant minimum fat standard in all 50 states is 3.25% with only 12 states at 3.5% or above and 6 states below 3.25% according to the USDA 1971 report on Federal and State Standards for the Composition of Milk Products. These minimum standards have been adjusted downward over the years but they do not necessarily represent the prevailing fat content of the milk in the markets. The average test for whole milk sold at retail in the major marketing areas in 1970 was 3.46%, according to USDA data.

Standardization of non-fat-solids is not practiced with whole milk. The minimum standards for MSNF set by the states vary between 8.0 and 8.5% with the majority of states at 8.25%. It should again be noted that these are minimum standards for regulatory purposes and the market milk sold in each state is influenced by the natural solids content of the raw milk processed.

There is no federal standard for composition of milk in terms of fat and MSNF content. The only federal standard sets minimum vitamin D content of milks labelled as vitamin D fortified milk. Vitamin D is added now as a concentrate and not by irradiation as it was in the early days of vitamin D fortification.

TABLE M-4

REPRESENTATIVE VALUES FOR THE COMPOSITION OF PASTEURIZED WHOLE MILK

Milk Component	Amount per 100 Gm	Milk Component	Amount per 100 Gm	Milk Component	Amount per 100 Gm
Water (gm)	87.4	Macrominerals	(Mg)	Amino acids	(Mg)
Food Energy		Calcium	118	Isoleucine	162
Calories (Kcal)	65	Iron	0.057	Leucine	328
Kilojoules[1]	272	Magnesium	13	Lysine	268
Protein (gm)	3.5	Phosphorus	93	Methionine	86
Fat (gm)	3.5	Potassium	144	Cystine	28
Lactose (gm)	4.9	Sodium	50	Phenylalanine	185
Ash (gm)	0.7			Tyrosine	163
		Microminerals	(Mcg)	Threonine	153
Fat-soluble vitamins		Aluminum	350	Tryptophan	48
Vitamin A (IU)	140	Boron	60	Valine	199
Vitamin D (IU)	41	Bromine	400	Arginine	113
(fortified milk)		Chromium	1.4	Histidine	92
Vitamin E (IU)	0.13	Cobalt	0.13	Alanine	119
Vitamin K (mcg)	6	Copper	32	Aspartic acid	264
		Fluorine	30	Glutamic acid	764
Water-soluble vitamins		Iodine	35	Glycine	68
Ascorbic acid (mg)	1	Manganese	5.5	Proline	314
Biotin (mcg)	3.1	Molybdenum	6	Serine	199
Choline (mg)	20	Nickel	6.5		
Folic acid (mcg)	6	Selenium	2.5	Saturated fatty acids	(Gm)
Inositol (mg)	18	Silicon	82	Butyric (C_4)	0.12
Niacin (mg)	0.1	Vanadium	Trace	Caproic (C_6)	0.05
Niacin equivalents (mg)	0.92	Zinc	450	Caprylic (C_8)	0.06
Pantothenic acid (mg)	0.34			Capric (C_{10})	0.09
Pyridoxine (mg)	0.04			Lauric (C_{12})	0.16
Riboflavin (mg)	0.17			Myristic (C_{14})	0.51
Thiamin (mg)	0.03			Palmitic (C_{16})	1.06
Vitamin B_{12} (mcg)	0.4			Stearic (C_{18})	0.37
				C_{20} and higher	0.06
				Total saturated	2.47
				Unsaturated fatty acids	
				Palmitoleic (C_{16}-2H)	0.20
				Oleic (C_{18}-2H)	0.65
				Linoleic (C_{18}-4H)	0.07
				C_{20} and C_{22} unsaturated fatty acids	0.03
				Total unsaturated	1.03

SOURCE: Composition and Nutritive Value of Dairy Foods, *Dairy Council Digest*, National Dairy Council.

[1] Kilojoules = kilocalories $\times$ 4.184.

The minimum standards for both fat and MSNF in most states assure the consumer of a minimum of 11.5% total food solids in milk (3.25% fat and 8.25% MSNF). The market milk business is a highly competitive business, however, and competition is usually on a quality and price basis.

Another class of milks based on whole milk includes the special milks which are fortified with minerals and vitamins. These products are also subject to state standards on basic milk composition and labelling which includes a statement of the nutrients added. Such products represent only a small fraction of the milk market.

Other whole milk products include the special milks such as Guernsey and Jersey milks which represent the richer milks produced by these breeds of cattle. Also "Certified Milk" is available in certain markets. This product is produced under the stringent regulations of the Association of Medical Milk Commissions. Originally introduced as a certified raw milk, it is now also produced as a pasteurized product.

Flavored milks are available primarily as chocolate flavored milk and chocolate milk drink. Chocolate milk drink is made with skim milk or low-fat milk. Flavored milks are widely available and in 1970 constituted 3.7% of the fluid milk market.

Published milk composition Tables usually represent raw milk analyses based on rather limited sampling. The emphasis has been on sampling and reporting of breed averages and variations among individuals. Such data are not very representative of the market milk composition today since milk is pooled in the milk procurement system and the raw milk supply at the plant represents the blending of milk from many herds. Recent estimates indicate that milk from one breed, Holsteins, provides more than 80% of the market milk supply.

In the absence of a national sampling program, perhaps the best representation of raw milk composition can be derived from the average fat content as reported by the reports from Federal Order Markets (USDA Statistical Reporting Service). These markets represent the major volume of milk marketed as market milk in the United States. They do not include the milk produced for manufactured products such as cheese, condensed milk, and butter which historically have been of higher fat test. The USDA production reports for 1970 show the average fat test for raw milk supplies received in Federal Order Markets in 1970 as 3.67%. The MSNF content can be estimated to be approximately 8.5% since studies over the years have shown a close correlation between fat and solids-not-fat (MSNF) in milk as produced.

The constituents of MSNF include lactose, protein, minerals, and vitamins. The lactose and minerals content of milk supplies is quite uniform and subject to only minor variations. Protein on the other hand is variable and is related to the MSNF content of the milk. Higher MSNF levels mean higher protein levels. The minor components of milk include the vitamins, minerals, and enzymes which make up the balance of this complex food.

Representative values for the nutrient components of pasteurized whole milk are presented in Table M-4.

Additional information on the detailed composition of milk and its nutritional value is available in *Newer Knowledge of Milk*, published by National Dairy Council.

Low-fat and skim milks are also subject to state standards and regulations. They differ from whole milk primarily in that they contain lower fat levels and are usually standardized to a higher level of MSNF by the addition of Grade A condensed skim milk or Grade A nonfat solids.

Low-fat milks as they appear on the market are variable in fat content, ranging between 0.5 and 2.0%. They are sold under many different brand names and the identity of the product can best be determined by examining the label. State regulations require that the label carry the information on MSNF added when solids standardization is practiced. Most of the low-fat milks contain added MSNF as indicated by the USDA market reports

for 1970. Low-fat milks and skim milks have gained a significant share of the fluid milk market and represented nearly $1/5$ of the fluid milk products sold in 1970.

Skim milks, those products with less than 0.5% fat, represent a smaller part of the fluid milk market since the wide introduction of low-fat milks in the 1960's. State standards are variable and it is of interest to note that these standards are in terms of maximum fat and minimum MSNF. Here again, the addition of MSNF is widely practiced and about $3/4$ of the volume of skim milk sold in 1970 contained added solids.

Standards for vitamin A and vitamin fortified skim milk are in effect in most states and uniformly require a minimum of 2000 USP units of vitamin A and 400 IU units of vitamin D per quart. The identity of such fortified milks can be determined from the label since this information is required. Such fortification is not widely practiced and skim milks without vitamin A fortification are low in vitamin A when compared with whole milk. Vitamin A is a fat-soluble vitamin and carried in the fat portion of the milk.

Other special milks such as low sodium milk and enzyme treated milks for special dietary purposes are available to a very limited extent. They are produced by specialized plants which have the processing facilities and special permits for such operations. These products are usually obtainable only on special order and are not regularly carried on milk routes or sold in stores.

Consumption.—Milk consumption in the United States and 16 other countries has been reported by USDA for the years 1960–1969 as shown in Table M-5.

It will be noted that total dairy products consumption in the United States was lower than in 15 other countries in 1969, with only Italy showing a lower annual consumption. Finland, France, Norway, and New Zealand showed almost twice the consumption in terms of whole milk equivalent on a fat-solids basis. Five countries showed an increase over the 10-yr period while the others showed decreases ranging from 0.5 to 20.2%.

Fluid milk and cream consumption in the United States in 1969 was lower than in all but 3 of the 17 countries reported. Consumption has been showing a downward trend in most countries with increases in only 6 of these countries during the 10-yr period.

Many factors are cited as reasons for these declines in consumption including economic and dietary factors and the trend toward industrialization and metropolitan living in many countries. In the United States, the decline has been occurring during a period when fat test or richness of milk products has been reduced and a move

TABLE M-5

MILK AND DAIRY PRODUCTS: PER CAPITA CONSUMPTION IN 17 COUNTRIES, SELECTED YEARS, 1960-1969

Country	Total Dairy Products[1]							Fluid Milk and Cream						
	1960 (Lb)	1962 (Lb)	1964 (Lb)	1966 (Lb)	1968 (Lb)	1969[2] (Lb)	Change 1960-69 (%)	1960 (Lb)	1962 (Lb)	1964 (Lb)	1966 (Lb)	1968 (Lb)	1969[2] (Lb)	Change 1960-69 (%)
Austria	653	715	716	733	748	732	+12.1	337	351	356	349	329	328	-2.7
Belgium	908	896	865	883	823	873	-3.9	233	238	231	242	173	177	-24.0
Denmark	993	990	999	971	968	968	-2.5	380	382	387	384	398	412	+8.4
Finland	1360	1550	1511	1500	1370	1353	-0.5	622	646	651	625	597	574	-7.7
France	850	749	917	914	1027	1081	+27.2	228	237	226	214	244	237	+3.9
West Germany	783	784	766	758	762	764	-2.4	232	221	210	209	209	207	-10.8
Ireland	1506	1428	1406	1341	1276	1247	-17.2	448	492	473	495	472	470	+4.9
Italy	389	388	361	404	400	401	+3.1	121	118	127	139	137	140	+15.7
Netherlands	653	721	812	804	762	796	+21.9	[3]	[3]	328	347	337	342	+4.3[4]
Norway	877	905	894	948	1024	1005	+14.6	503	513	519	530	547	546	+8.5
Sweden	1039	1035	975	936	873	829	-20.2	427	412	394	386	374	364	-14.8
Switzerland	1000	979	967	959	943	947	-5.3	453	431	417	412	370	369	-18.5
United Kingdom	867	906	856	878	878	879	+1.4	360	366	334	344	350	350	-2.8
Australia	975	972	929	915	898	923	-5.3	305	306	304	308	306	308	+1.0
New Zealand[5]	1350	1334	1317	1275	1207	1222	-9.5	470	469	432	416	395	398	-15.3
Canada	887	899	878	848	802	781	-12.0	383	376	314	304	288	280	-26.9
United States	653	642	632	604	577	570	-12.7	322	308	304	297	280	272	-15.5

SOURCE: USDA Dairy Situation *DS-335* (1971).

[1] Fluid milk and dairy products in terms of whole milk equivalent, fat solids basis.
[2] Preliminary
[3] Not available on comparable basis.
[4] 1964 to 1969 change.
[5] Year ending May 31.

toward low-fat milk and cream products has occurred. It would be interesting to know whether consumers drink less milk because it is less appealing or because of other reasons.

Processing and Quality Control.—Milk processing actually begins on the farm where the raw milk must be filtered and cooled. It is kept cold from the time of milking until the refrigerated tank truck collects the milk for transport to the processing plant. The freshly-drawn milk is cooled in electrically refrigerated cooling tanks to lower the temperature to below 45°F to prevent bacterial growth. Grade A raw milk supplies must meet a standard of not more than 100,000 bacteria per milliliter at the farm and not more than 300,000 bacteria per milliliter for the mixed milk at the plant as determined by the standard plate count as prescribed in *Standard Methods for the Examination of Dairy Products* published by the American Public Health Association. These tests are performed by the plant laboratory on samples of the raw milk of the individual farms and comingled milk at the plant, respectively.

Processes normally carried on in the milk plant include the following: cooling and refrigerated storage of raw milk; clarification; separation of a portion for standardizing purposes; standardization of fat content; fortification with vitamin D; homogenization; pasteurization and cooling; packaging or bottling; refrigerated 40°F storage and delivery; cleaning and sanitizing equipment.

On arrival at the plant, milk is transferred from the truck tank to refrigerated storage tanks or silos which are designed to cool the milk and maintain a temperature of 40°F. At this point the raw milk is tested and standardized for fat content and vitamin D is added.

Part of the supply is separated by centrifugal separation to provide cream and skim milk for use in making these products. This step also supplies the cream and skim milk required for standardization of whole milk and low-fat milks.

The standardized whole milk is then ready for processing and packaging. Milk is clarified prior to pasteurization. This is done by large centrifuges which spin out any sediment, primarily the leucocytes which are present in normal milk. The milk then proceeds to the homogenization and pasteurization steps in a continuous process.

Homogenization of market milk is a universal practice today, having been introduced in about 1935. This treatment results in a uniform dispersion of finely divided fat globules in milk and prevents the formation of a cream layer on standing. The process consists of pumping the milk under high pressure through special valves which divide the normal fat globules into many smaller ones. These small fat globules are not able to rise

by gravity and therefore the process provides a uniform or homogeneous product.

Homogenization and pasteurization are always carried out as steps in a continuous process. The earlier method of vat pasteurization which involved heating to at least 143°F and holding for not less than 30 min has been almost completely replaced by the high temperature-short time (HTST) system which heats milk to at least 161°F and holds it for not less than 16 sec. These systems consist of heat exchange equipment automatically controlled by temperature sensing devices and electrically operated valves which ensure the required heat treatment. These enclosed plate systems are engineered to provide continuous processing of 25,000–60,000 lb of milk per hour.

Such installations are subject to inspection and approval by the state public health officials when installed and during subsequent operation. Printed time and temperature charts from the recorder on the operating panel must be dated and maintained for regular inspection.

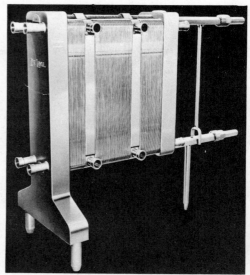

Courtesy of DeLaval Separator Company
FIG. M-8. PLATE PASTEURIZER

Since pasteurization of milk and cream is compulsory in market milk operations, this processing step is of primary importance. The time-temperature requirements have been the subject of exhaustive research since the introduction of the commercial process in 1895. The process is essentially based on the minimum temperature-time combination which will assure destruction of all pathogenic bacteria which may be present in the raw product.

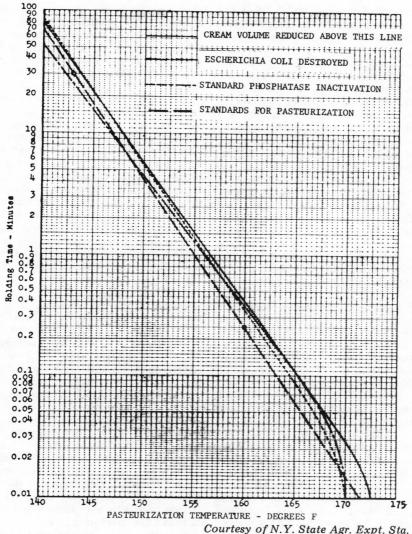

Holding Time – Minutes

CREAM VOLUME REDUCED ABOVE THIS LINE

ESCHERICHIA COLI DESTROYED

STANDARD PHOSPHATASE INACTIVATION

STANDARDS FOR PASTEURIZATION

PASTEURIZATION TEMPERATURE – DEGREES F

Courtesy of N.Y. State Agr. Expt. Sta.

FIG. M-9. TIME-TEMPERATURE PASTEURIZATION CHART

Reprinted from *Manual for Milk Plant Operators*, Milk Industry Foundation, and showing composite of the relationships existing between creaming, phosphatase test, bacterial destruction, and the present standards for pasteurization.

The accompanying chart (Fig. M-9) shows that this can be accomplished at various temperatures provided that the time is adequate. The minimum pasteurization standard of 161°F for 16 sec is safely above the points on the chart and in practice the settings are well above the minimum requirements. Higher temperatures and longer times are used to assure longer shelf-life by reducing the bacterial population to a minimum.

The high temperature-short time pasteurizer is essentially a plate heat exchanger in which the heating medium is hot water in the heating section and chilled water in the cooling section. The use of plate construction exposes thin films of milk which reach the pasteurization temperature in a few seconds. The minimum standard treatment of 161°F for 16 sec or more is assured by a holding tube which retains flow for the required time. It is a fully enclosed system to prevent any contact with air contamination.

Cooling is accomplished by the use of the same principles in these highly engineered systems. Continuous flow of chilled water at 33°-34°F in the cooling section quickly reduces the milk temperature to 40°F or lower and the milk then flows to the packaging machines.

A highly efficient "regeneration" system has been engineered to conserve power and reduce processing cost. In simple terms this feature takes advantage of the incoming cold milk as a cooling medium in part of the cooling plate section and utilizes the hot milk as a heating medium in the preheating section of the plate heat exchanger. Thus, there are several sections of plates each designed to perform a heat exchange function and all engineered into a continuous flow pattern.

The fillers or packaging machines are highly automated units which discharge a measured amount of milk into the carton or bottle. These units are also fully enclosed systems which exclude air contamination during the packaging operation. The fillers are sized and synchronized with the pasteurizing system so that the time from the raw milk inlet to cold milk in the final package is very short.

The packaged products from the fillers are moved by special conveyer systems to the casing machines which prepare the products for delivery. In some high volume operations the milk is transferred to refrigerated trucks for immediate delivery to transfer stations or stores.

Packaging.—Milk packaging has shown two very significant trends since 1940 and both have been influenced primarily by the trend toward store sales in all parts of the country. Milk in glass bottles was the standard package prior to 1940 when home delivery was the most common practice. With the increase in store sales, the paper and plastic containers have gradually replaced glass and a packaging survey of Federal Order Markets in 1969 showed that fluid milk sales in paper and plastic coated containers comprised 77% of the market. An additional 11% was packaged in plastic containers.

The most common container size has become the $1/2$-gal., followed by gallons, quarts, pints and $1/2$-pt. Nearly $1/2$ of the fluid milk sold in 1969 was packaged in $1/2$-gal. containers. An additional 24% was packed in gallon containers.

Store or wholesale volume accounted for more than 80% of the fluid milk sales in the Federal Order Markets in 1969. The home delivery portion of the market continues to decline and in 1969 represented only 20% of total fluid milk sales.

A new development in packaging in Western Europe and Canada has been the plastic pouch. As of 1971 only limited use of this packaging system has occurred in the United States. It offers lower costs per unit and weighs much less than even the coated paper carton. For ease in han-

dling in the home, a pouring pitcher has been developed. This container is designed to hold the plastic pouch and make pouring easy.

In addition to home delivery and store sales, there is a considerable volume of milk sold to eating establishments, schools, and other institutions. Packaging for these outlets may be in $1/2$-pt or in cans or packages of several gallons' capacity. The growing use of vending machines in cafeterias and institutional feeding has, however, reduced the use of the $1/2$-pt package.

Milk cans have been replaced in many markets by a plastic bag in a box. These packages are usually of 5-gal. capacity and are designed for direct use in vending machines. A similar container of 10-qt capacity has been offered for home use.

Filled and Imitation Milk.—Another class of fluid milk products which are classed as "filled or imitation milk" appeared on the market in the 1960's. These products were labelled with various trade names and were packaged in the same type of container as regular milk. They differ from regular milks primarily in that they have the milk-fat replaced by vegetable fat. The two products differ in that filled milk is basically skim milk with vegetable fat substituted for milkfat while the imitation milk also has the milk protein substituted by casein or vegetable protein and has no natural milk content. They also differ from regular milk in that stabilizers, emulsifiers, and other minor ingredients are used in these formulated products.

Sales of filled milk made limited gains during a period up to early 1969 but have declined since that time. The share of market was small as indicated by the peak sales of 5.8 million pounds per month in the Federal Order Markets in early 1969 compared with monthly sales of nearly 5 billion pounds of regular milk. The sales of imitation milk were very limited and it was available only in a few marketing areas.

Factors causing the decline in sales were cited as the competition from low-fat milks and rulings on base milk pricing which reduced the economic advantage of these new product operations.

UHT Sterilization.—Ultra-high-temperature(UHT) sterilization of milk together with asceptic packaging has received much investigation in recent years. This process is designed to produce fluid milk and cream products with a keeping quality of at least several months under refrigerated conditions. In this process, the milk is heated rapidly to temperatures in the range of 96°-153°C (205°-307°F) and held at the given temperature for 3 sec or less.

UHT processing has been much more widely practiced in Western Europe than in the United States. This process has not been extensively used on market milk in the United States but has been used in specialized plants on special products. These products include nondairy creaming products in portion packs, milk-based diet drinks, milk puddings, chocolate-flavored drink, half-and-half, and whipping cream.

Fresh Cream and Related Products

Fresh cream products make up a significant part of the market milk industry. These products are processed, packaged, and distributed in the same manner as described for milk. Cream of all grades is derived from the Grade A raw milk supply by centrifugal separation of whole milk into two portions, cream and skim milk. Assuming a raw milk fat test of 3.7%, the separation of 100 lb of milk yields 10 lb of 37% fat cream and 90 lb of skim milk. The skim milk is almost fat free with a fat content of less than 0.1%. Cream of the different grades is then produced by blending calculated amounts of the rich cream with milk to obtain cream of each grade.

The fresh cream products are listed in the USDA report of Federal and State standards as light, medium, whipping, and heavy whipping creams. Another product used by consumers as cream is half-and-half which is a mixture of milk and cream as suggested by the name of the product. Of the 5 cream type products listed above, 3 are most commonly found in the dairy case in the food store or on the delivery route. They are half-and-half, light or coffee cream, and whipping cream with fat richness of about 11, 18, and 30% fat respectively. Federal standards have been set for light or coffee cream, whipping, and heavy whipping cream which define these products as having not less than 18, 30, and 36% fat respectively. State minimum standards generally follow these Federal Standards.

Both total sales and per capita sales of cream have been declining for many years and sales reports indicate total cream type products volume of about 2% of total milk and cream sold in 1970. Half-and-half has become the largest volume item in this class of products. The addition of nonfat milk solids to half-and-half has become a common practice and many state standards permit this practice with the provision that the added milk solids be shown on the label. The most common addition is $1\frac{1}{2}\%$ which is sufficient to give the product a richer appearance and more coffee whitening power.

Beginning in the late 1960's there has been a trend toward sterilized whipping cream replacing the pasteurized product. Since whipping cream is not used in large volume in the home the problem of keeping quality has been of concern to consumers. The sterilized product overcomes this problem and permits greater flexibility in distribution.

The sterilization process used on cream is an ultra-high-temperature (UHT) treatment which destroys essentially all the bacteria and thereby increases the keeping quality or shelf-life of the product. Such products are still refrigerated to maintain fresh flavor and physical stability and the unopened carton or bottle keeps well for several weeks.

During the 1960's another class of products serving the same purposes as cream has entered the market and achieved considerable acceptance by consumers. These products are generally described as coffee whiteners and whipping cream substitutes. Coffee whiteners are of two types, liquid products sold in frozen state and dried products. These products are characterized by the substitution of vegetable oil for milkfat. The nonfat portion is also a nondairy formulation and consists of proteins and sugars together with stabilizers and emulsifiers and other ingredients needed to produce a stable product.

The substitutes for whipping cream include frozen ready whipped topping and powdered products which can be reconstituted and whipped to produce a whipped topping for desserts. These products are nondairy in composition and are based on vegetable oil, usually coconut oil, vegetable protein, sweeteners, stabilizers, emulsifiers, and flavorings. These products are quite stable and have extended shelf-life as compared with fresh cream products. They are generally produced by the large food companies rather than by milk plants.

Aerosol packaged whipping cream products and also cream substitutes are widely distributed and provide added convenience in use. These products are processed and packaged in dispensing cans which are charged with a gas propellant, either nitrogen or freon. The cream products are of whipping cream composition while the cream toppings are nondairy products similar to those described above.

It should be noted that evaporated milk is rather widely used as a creaming agent in coffee. This sterile product provides very good coffee whitening power and contains less fat than coffee cream, half-and-half, or the substitute coffee whiteners. Evaporated milk is essentially double milk with the added advantage of excellent keeping quality. It is an homogenized, sterilized, and vitamin D-enriched product.

Cream sales, including milk and cream mixtures, were estimated at 1.13 billion pounds in 1970 compared with total fluid milk sales of 57.4 billion pounds. Fluid milk sales include whole milk, low-fat milk, skim milk, buttermilk, and flavored milk drinks. Thus, cream type products represent only about 2% of the volume of fluid milk and cream sold. The continuous decline in per capita and total sales of sweet cream products has been attributed to changes in dietary habits and concern over weight control. Other factors may be the changes in marketing practices with the trend toward store sales and toward cream products of lower fat content. Milk and cream mixtures have replaced the richer products and perhaps the appeal of cream was in its characteristic richness which can now be found only in richer products of coffee cream or whipping cream grades.

Cream products are packaged for the retail market in 1 pt and $\frac{1}{2}$ pt sizes and for restaurant use in larger containers. There has, however, been a growing trend toward "portion pack" creamers in restaurants and other eating establishments. These packages which may be either paper or glass contain a fraction of an ounce of the product and are designed for direct use in coffee. They may be labelled "coffee cream" or half-and-half, or they may be nondairy creamers in liquid or dry form. These nondairy products have made rapid gains in the food service industry in the 1960's. Nondairy creaming agents are made from the milk protein casein, vegetable oil, and sweetener plus stabilizers and emulsifiers.

Buttermilk

Buttermilk, as the name implies, was originally a by-product of butter making. It was the fluid milky product remaining after cream has been churned. This type of buttermilk has had very limited commercial distribution over the years, and buttermilk today is "cultured buttermilk" made by the lactic acid fermentation of pasteurized skim milk. Thus, it is made under controlled conditions and not subject to the variations inherent in butter production from different grades of cream varying from sour to sweet. Since most of the butter today is made from sweet cream, the buttermilk has the flavor character of skim milk and not the acidy, piquant flavor which is typical of cultured buttermilk or at one time from the churning of unneutralized sour cream.

Buttermilk has been on the market over the years without any significant change in per capita consumption. Its use as a beverage is limited largely to adults and primarily male adults. Geographically, its greatest use is in the southeastern states where it is commonly used in baking.

Buttermilk appears on the label of many prepared mixes and prepared foods. The ingredient product used here is sweet buttermilk powder derived from the buttermilk produced from the churning of sweet cream. Thus, this "buttermilk" is not the acidy product available in liquid form as cultured buttermilk on the retail market.

The making of cultured buttermilk is a simple process but the marketing of a uniform, fine-flavored product with good shelf-life requires very careful methods. The process is essentially a lactic acid fermentation process designed to produce the flavor and thick body desired in buttermilk. The special starter or culture used in buttermilk manufacture is a mixture of lactic acid-producing bacteria, *Streptococcus lactis* and a flavor and aroma producer, *Leuconostoc citrovorum*.

The cultures used in making buttermilk as well as in the other fermented milk products, cottage cheese and sour cream, are available from special culture laboratories. These firms are specialists in the propagating and blending of the types and strains of bacteria which are needed to produce each of the fermented milk products. In the early development of the industry, these laboratories provided cultures in liquid and dried form, 2-oz bottles being mailed to plants on a regular basis. The 2-oz culture was then used at the dairy plant for the inoculation of a "mother culture."

The mother culture is made by transferring the laboratory culture to 1 qt of sterilized milk and incubating it in a culture cabinet at 72°F for 14–18 hr. This mother culture is then used in a continuous daily transfer and culturing plan which provides the culture supply for fermented milk products production. Only a few milliliters are required for daily transfers and the remainder is available each day for the inoculation of "bulk starter" or culture tanks which furnish the large inoculations for the vats or tanks of buttermilk, sour cream, or cottage cheese.

This operation requires the ultimate in sanitary conditions because any contamination of the cultures at any stage will destroy the usefulness of the cultures. Sterile glassware and sterilized milk must be used in the mother culture propagation system. Special culture handling rooms with filtered air supply are required to ensure successful operations.

A new development now widely used in production plants is the frozen concentrate cultures which are designed for direct inoculation in the vats. Such cultures or starters are shipped in sealed containers containing liquid nitrogen to maintain extremely low temperatures and maintain maximum viability of the organisms. The introduction of this system has eliminated the need for the culture propagation program in the plant. Both systems are in use but the commercial production of ready-to-use starters is growing.

The vat or tank of buttermilk is made by first pasteurizing the skim milk and cooling to the setting temperature of 70°F. The culture is then added and stirred to mix the culture uniformly throughout the vat. The inoculated milk is held without agitation until the milk has coagulated. A sample is then tested for acidity by titration.

An acidity level of 0.85% as lactic acid indicates that the fermentation is complete and the coagulum is ready for stirring and packaging.

Some brands of buttermilk contain butter granules or flakes and for these products, churned milkfat is added to the buttermilk. In another system, the process starts with low-fat milk rather than skim milk and the fermented buttermilk is actually churned to produce the butter granules.

Buttermilk is packaged in the same manner as milk but with the 1-qt container as the most common size. Buttermilk must be refrigerated; long holding is inadvisable because the culture continues to cause changes which may not be pleasing to the consumer.

The composition and food value of cultured buttermilk is the same as that of the skim milk from which it is made. The addition of butter granules or flakes, of course, raises the fat content slightly when the product is offered in this special form. One cup of regular buttermilk provides about 9 gm of protein, 90 cal, and only traces of fat. It is a good source of all of the nonfat components of milk.

A portion of the lactose or milk sugar is converted to lactic acid in the fermentation process. This does not change its food value significantly and the sour product has certain advantages for the consumer in stimulating the digestive process.

Buttermilk is made for consumption as a fresh product and should be kept cold (40°F) and consumed within 4–6 days. Higher temperatures and prolonged storage cause additional acidity development and the development of flavors which are not desirable. Whey separation may occur under such conditions but the product can be remixed and used for cooking or baking, although it may have lost its appeal as a beverage.

Cottage Cheese and Related Products

Cottage cheese is one of the few dairy products that has its origin in the United States. It is a fresh cheese as contrasted with most cheeses which require curing for the development of the characteristic flavor and texture. It is marketed immediately after manufacture and is associated with the fluid milk and cream products in the retail market.

Most of the cottage cheese in the market is creamed cottage cheese which has a cream dressing added to the curd to improve its flavor and palatability. To be labeled creamed cottage cheese the product must contain not less than 4% milkfat and not more than 80% moisture. This is both a Federal and a State Standard in all the States.

Plain or uncreamed cottage cheese is also offered as the lightly salted, plain skim milk curd. It is very low in fat and is sometimes referred to as dry curd. Federal and State Standards limit the moisture content to 80%.

In addition to these two product types, a low-fat cottage cheese has appeared on the market in many areas. The product cannot be labeled "creamed cottage cheese" since the fat content is set at 2% or lower. It may be labeled as partially creamed or low-fat cottage cheese. These products are made by adding a milk and cream mixture to the curd instead of the cream dressing used in the standard product.

Cottage cheese is made from pasteurized skim milk by a process of lactic acid fermentation under controlled temperature conditions. A culture of lactic acid bacteria, *Streptococcus lactis*, is added at setting time and under favorable temperature conditions this results in a firm coagulum after 5–14 hr, depending on temperature and the amount of starter or culture used. The long set process uses less culture and requires 12–14 hr at 72°F while the short set process requires only 4–5 hr at 90°F with a larger inoculation. Cottage cheese is not a rennet-type cheese but small additions of rennet of 1 ml or less per 1000 lb of milk are used to improve the curd or coagulum.

Cottage cheese is made in large rectangular vats which are water-jacketed to permit constant temperature control during setting and cooking stages. When the curd is properly set as indicated by a firm gel it is ready for cutting. The coagulum is tested at this stage by breaking it and observing whether whey separates at the break. Samples of whey are also titrated in the laboratory to determine the degree of acidity developed. Whey acidity 0.48–0.55% expressed as lactic acid indicates that the curd has reached the proper stage for cutting.

At this stage the semisolid mass of curd in the vat is ready for cutting into cubes of predetermined size. Larger cubes are cut for large curd cottage cheese and smaller cubes are made when the product is to be marketed as small curd or "country style" cottage cheese. Cutting is done with curd knives which are metal frames strung with fine wires which are uniformly spaced at $3/8$ or $1/2$ in. apart. Both vertical and horizontal knives are used. First, the curd is cut horizontally to make thin layers running the length of the vat. This is followed by two vertical cuts lengthwise and crosswise to complete the cubing operation.

The cubes now floating in their own whey are gently stirred by paddles in small vats or by large traveling agitators in larger vats. The temperature is raised slowly during gentle stirring to aid in expressing the whey while at the same time maintaining the cubes in unbroken condition. The goal here is to produce tender but uniformly cooked curds which will maintain their attractive form and texture through the draining, washing, and creaming stages which follow. The success of the operation depends on the judgement and experience of the cottage cheese maker. Slight errors in processing can result in cottage cheese curds which are too firm and gritty at one extreme to a weak fragile curd at the other extreme which appears pasty when finished.

The cooking process is a critical phase of cottage cheese making and the temperature rise from the setting temperature to the final cooking temperature of 120°-130°F usually takes 1-1.5 hr. No water is added at this stage because the acid whey is essential to the proper shrinkage of the curd cubes.

At the end of the cooking process, heating is stopped and the whey is drained. The whey which contains part of the milk sugar, minerals, and proteins is pumped to whey tanks for further use or discarded. The food solids in cottage cheese are primarily the milk protein, casein and significant amounts of all of the other components of skim milk.

The curd is rinsed with cold water and then washed by flooding with chilled water to remove the whey completely from the curd. After draining, the curd is salted and then goes either to the creaming and packaging stage or is placed in large metal cans for later handling.

Creaming is done by adding a standardized milk and cream mixture to the curd mass and gently stirring to obtain a uniform mixture. Small additions of salt, gelatin, lactose, or other ingredients are used in the cream dressing to enhance flavor and improve the appearance of the product.

Another process for cottage cheese making has been developed which utilizes chemical acidulation agents instead of the lactic acid fermentation process for coagulation. The acidulants used are muriatic, lactic, phosphoric, or glucono delta lactone. This process has not yet been widely accepted even though it offers a considerable saving in time and eliminates the use of starter cultures.

Automated processes for producing the curd, handling the whey drainage, and the washing and creaming functions have been developed and are being introduced in larger plant operations.

Packaging of cottage cheese was once a hand filling and capping operation using wide-mouthed glass containers or waxed paper tubs. Recent developments have led to mechanical fillers and lidders which eliminate hand work. Cartons of 8, 12, and 16 oz are common and occasionally the 2-lb carton is offered. Cartons are of plastic or plastic-coated paper construction with reclosable lids. Protection from contamination after opening as well as exclusion of air are important in protecting the flavor of this mild, delicately-flavored product.

The composition of cottage cheese as listed in USDA Agr. Handbook *8, Composition of Foods* is as follows for a 1-cup portion (225 gm):

	Creamed	Uncreamed
Water (%)	78	79
Calories	240	195
Protein (gm)	31	38
Fat (gm)	9	1
Carbohydrate (gm)	7	6
Calcium (mg)	212	202
Vitamin A (IU)	380	20

It will be noted that the uncreamed cottage cheese has about $4/5$ of the calories of the popular creamed cottage cheese. Both products are important primarily for their relatively high protein content and low fat content. The recently-introduced low-fat cottage cheese would be intermediate in fat content and calories as well as in protein content.

Cottage cheese consumption increased in volume rather sharply during the period 1940 to 1960 and reached a level of about 4.6 lb per capita. Since that time this level has remained rather steady in spite of the appeal of this product for low calorie diets. Total production of creamed cottage cheese was estimated by USDA for 1970 at 981.1 million pounds.

Related products which are available in some areas include baker's cheese, pot cheese and farmer's cheese. These products differ from cottage cheese in that no attempt is made to produce cubes but rather a fine-grained curd which resembles homemade cottage cheese. These products are made in much the same way as cottage cheese up to the point of cutting the curd. For these products the curd is stirred to break it up and permit whey separation. Baker's cheese is produced in large quantities for use in the bakery industry. These products are used in the home primarily for cooking purposes. They have a mild, acidy flavor and are similar to uncreamed cottage cheese in composition and food value.

Sour Cream and Related Products

Sour cream is a cultured cream product and is commonly labeled "Cultured Sour Cream" in the market. Sour cream is made by a process very similar to that used in buttermilk manufacture except that coffee grade cream rather than skim milk is used. The addition of culture and the incubation period are much the same. The mixture of acid-producing and flavor-producing bacteria is similar to that described under buttermilk. The cream is pasteurized prior to culturing and then cooled to 70°F before the culture is added. The cream with culture added is held at 70°F until coagulation occurs. At this point the acidity reaches a level of about 0.6%. The incubation period is normally 12–16 hr after which the product is cooled and held at 40°F to prevent further acid development. It is now ready for packaging and is moved into distribution immediately as a fresh product. In some cases the culturing is carried on in the final package under conditions described above.

The body or consistency of sour cream is carefully controlled to produce a smooth rich-appearing product. Homogenization prior to pasteurization aids in producing this desirable physical character. When properly refrigerated, sour cream should maintain its smooth consistency for several days. Exposure to higher temperature or long holding (more than a week) may cause whey separation. The product is still usable after stirring but at this stage it may be somewhat less appealing in flavor.

A lower fat product, sour half-and-half, has been developed and is widely available being made, as the name implies, from half-and-half instead of cream. The process of manufacture is the same as for sour cream. This product has the same composition as half-and-half and differs from sour cream in that it contains about 11.0% fat as compared with sour cream fat content of 18%. There is no federal standard for sour half-and-half but minimum fat standards are being developed by the states. They generally follow the composition standards for half-and-half which require a minimum of 10.5 and 11.5% fat.

A recent development is the "acidified sour cream" which uses cream as a base but produces the flavor and heavy body by the direct addition of organic acids and stabilizers. State standards developed up to this time recognize the same minimum fat level as existing for sour cream.

Another class of products serving the same purposes as the real cream products includes filled or imitation sour creams appearing under various trade names. These products have recently appeared on the market and have in common a vegetable fat base. They contain no milkfat and the states that have developed standards require that these products carry the statement "Imitation" on the label and list the ingredients. These products are of various fat content since minimum standards for fat composition have not been developed by federal or state governments. They are usually made by direct acidulation of a fat emulsion and thus are not closely comparable with the fermentation products such as sour cream which rely on the natural fermentation of lactose to produce a characteristic sour cream flavor.

Little information is available on the composition of the imitation cream products since state or federal composition standards have not yet been developed. They are of variable composition and may be higher or lower in fat content than the comparable sour cream product. The labels list the ingredients but do not indicate the amounts of each component in these products.

Cultured sour cream has the same composition and food value as the cream from which it is made. Fermentation of the cream does not change its basic food value.

Technical Laboratory Control

The processing operations in the milk industry are subject to many external standards set by various government agencies to ensure the safety of the products and also to provide minimum composition standards that ensure the integrity of the product and promote fair dealing. The compliance with standards is of major concern to the quality control staff in the plant and requires the services of a well-staffed and well-equipped modern laboratory. Regular schedules of sampling and testing of both raw materials and the finished products are an important part of the plant operation.

There are also internal standards of operation which require the use of the laboratory. Product specifications are set by management and the modern plant depends upon the laboratory to ensure the day-to-day uniformity of its products. Plant standards are determined by management and each company has its own product standards. Milk plants have the option of making their own decisions on composition provided that they are above the minimum requirements as set forth in federal and state standards.

Bacteriological standards on raw and pasteurized products are set by public health agencies and these indicate the maximum permissible counts which must be met for pasteurized milk and cream products sold at retail.

Routine samples of the incoming raw milk, products at the various stages of processing, and the finished products are taken and sent to the laboratory to provide for the control of composition and bacteriological quality of all products processed. The results are then communicated to the plant operators who supervise the milk processing operations.

Fat tests are made regularly to provide the information required for standardization of the fat content of whole milk, low-fat milk, and the various cream products. These tests are usually made by the Babcock or Gerber methods. For greater precision, tests are made by the Mojonnier method which involves solvent (ether) extraction of the fat and accurate weighing of the extracted fat.

Tests for solids-not-fat content of milk are commonly done by the use of the lactometer, a density measurement instrument. This quick method serves well for control purposes but more precise tests are made by the Mojonnier method which involves drying of an accurately weighed sample.

These tests are made to ensure compliance with the solids-not-fat standards set by the states on market milk. They also serve to measure the solids-not-fat levels of milk used in other milk products where yield and product quality depend on milk composition.

No attempt will be made here to outline the various testing procedures used in the dairy laboratory. These methods are available in the various books describing the testing of dairy products such as *Standard Methods for the Examination of Dairy Products* published by American Public Health Association. Most of the chemical methods have approval of the Association of Official Agricultural Chemists. The general guide for bacterial standards in the United States is the U.S. Public Health Service Grade A Pasteurized Milk Ordinance which has been widely adopted by city health departments which are responsible for the enforcement of standards. Cities and towns not officially operating under the code generally use the code as a guide. The official code sets maximum permissible bacterial counts of 300,000 per ml for the raw milk received for fluid milk as well as maximum limits for the pasteurized products of 20,000 per ml.

The counts are determined by the standard plate count method which requires the culturing of measured samples on nutrient agar plates. Incubation of the agar plates for 48 hr at 32°C develops visible colonies which indicate the number of living organisms in the product. Counting is done with the aid of a low power lens in a lighted counting chamber, specially developed for this purpose.

Additional bacteriological controls are provided by making counts of specific kinds of bacteria such as the thermophilic (heat-loving) and psychrophilic (cold-loving) organisms. These counts require special temperatures and times for culturing the agar plates. The results of these tests are used to detect the causes or sources of high counts which may be indicated by the standard plate count.

Control of coliform organisms in milk also requires special plating methods. These organisms are considered to be indicators of contamination of special public health significance. Maximum permissible counts in milk and cream are very low at 10 per ml. High counts in pasteurized milk indicate gross contamination of the raw milk at the farm and need for improvement in sanitary methods of milking and milk handling on the farm.

It should be pointed out that the pasteurization process is not a process for improving milk but, more importantly, a safeguard against the spread of disease through milk. Pasteurization standards were originally developed on a basis of the minimum times and temperatures which would destroy all pathogenic bacteria which might gain entrance into the product. The improvement in keeping quality is an important reason for pasteurization but is only secondary in importance to the public health reason for this practice.

The test used as a pasteurization check is the phosphatase test. The destruction of the phosphatase enzyme in milk by pasteurization is measured by a color test. This provides a quick test of this important process.

Acidity tests include titration of milk and cream samples to detect developed acidity. A measured sample of milk is mixed with an indicator (phenolphthalein) which changes color with the addition of increments of a standard alkali solution. When the neutral end-point is reached the degree of acidity is determined from the amount of standard alkali solution required. Acidity developed in pasteurized milk and cream usually indicates that the product has been underprocessed or held at higher temperatures than the 40°F required for protection of the freshness of the product.

Viscosity tests are used on cream and yogurt to control the body or resistance to flow in these products. Processing conditions as well as composition influence viscosity and regular testing helps control the uniformity of product from day to day.

Quality control on milk products also includes the checks on flavor and odor of the raw milk supply as well as on the processed products. Observations are made on the samples obtained from the tank trucks to detect feed or weed flavors which would make the milk less palatable to the consumer. When serious off-flavors are detected the milk is rejected as unfit for market milk.

Keeping quality tests are also carried on to check the flavor stability of the processed milk and cream. This may be done by holding random samples from 2 to 7 days at refrigeration temperatures (40°–45°F) and making organoleptic examination of the fresh and stored product. Cottage cheese, buttermilk, sour cream, and yogurt are examined in a similar manner to detect changes in appearance as well as flavor.

Other tests made routinely by the milk plant laboratory include tests on water potability, strength of sterilizing solutions, tests of water hardness, and tests of cleaning solutions.

DANIEL H. JACOBSEN

MATÉ

Maté (*Ilex paraguaariensis*) is an aromatic beverage prepared in South America from the leaves of the Paraguay tea plant. The plant, actually a tree of medium height, grows wild in the temperate regions of South America. The leaves of this tree, after processing, are infused, not brewed, and the result is a beverage pleasant in aroma and pleasing to the taste. The infusion is consumed hot, with or without sugar depending on the preference of the person drinking it, but it is also used as an iced drink just as is true tea. In South America the beverage is usually sucked through a hollow reed from the gourd in which it was steeped. Remarkable digestive and stimulative properties are attributed to maté, and the attributions have in some measure been verified. The drink is most popular in South America, the total production being in the neighborhood of 100,000 tons annually. The production is based on harvests from cultivated plantations as well as from areas where the plant grows wild. The harvested crop consists of prunings from the lower branches of the plant.

Procedures used in preparing maté for market are comparatively uncomplicated. The cut branches are first passed over a fire to reduce the initial moisture. Then the maté is dried in ovens to further reduce the moisture. The next step is milling. The first milling is accomplished at the place where the maté is harvested and is a comparatively primitive operation. After milling the maté is passed through a series of sieves with different meshes, this in order to obtain a rough classification of the product. The roughly milled product is now sent to the maté mills which refine and separate the product into official grades and classifications. Classification is largely a matter of color, flavor quality, the ratio of leaves to twigs, and similar criteria.

In recent years research has been expended on the production of soluble maté.

MARTIN S. PETERSON

MAYONNAISE

See Salad Dressings.

McCOLLUM, E. V. (1879-1967)

Elmer Verner McCollum, born March 3, 1879, was the child of a pioneer family in Kansas who lived on a homestead farm near Fort Scott. Pioneering is also the best word to epitomize his achievements.

Dr. McCollum entered the University of Kansas in September 1900 with the intent to prepare for a medical career. However, during his sophomore year he became deeply interested in organic chemistry as taught by Dr. Edward Bartow. Thereafter he devoted nearly all his attention to chem-

istry courses, graduating with an A.B. degree in 3 yr.

He went on at Kansas to obtain an M.S. degree in chemistry. Guided by Dr. H. P. Cady, he decided that Yale University would offer him the best graduate training in organic chemistry. He applied and was promptly admitted and received a scholarship that paid his tuition. He received his doctorate from Yale in June 1906.

No suitable academic position became available that summer, so he remained at Yale and went to work in Professor L. B. Mendel's biochemistry laboratory. He was exposed to the lectures of Drs. Mendel, Underhill, and Chittendon and thus was guided in a direction that was to determine a lifetime career which had an enormous impact on world nutrition.

On July 1, 1907, through his mentor, Dr. Mendel, he received an appointment as an instructor in agricultural chemistry at the University of Wisconsin. Under the direction of Dr. E. B. Hart, Dr. McCollum participated in a study with heifers restricted to rations derived from single plant sources—wheat, corn, oats. Each ration in terms of accepted chemical analysis methods had the same composition as the others. There was also included a blended ration of the three plant sources. Great and unexpected differences had developed in the nutritional status of the animals on the different diets. The experiments as conducted could not provide an explanation for the nutritional shortcomings of the plants. However, acquaintance with these studies, supplemented by extensive literature reading, led Dr. McCollum to draw inferences which were to shape his researches for the balance of his life. He decided it would be desirable to (1) work with small animals having a short life span, and (2) feed them purified diet components in order to determine exactly which substances were needed for successful nutrition.

After some opposition, he managed to establish the first rat colony in the United States (January 1908) for the study of nutrition. At first he believed that improving palatability would increase food consumption and thus cure the nutritional inadequacy. This conclusion was challenged and proved to be erroneous. But the challenge soon cleared the way for major discoveries.

With the devoted help of Marguerite Davis, he discovered in 1912 the first known fat-soluble vitamin, later designated as vitamin A. He developed with her the "biological method for the analysis of food." Continuing the work with Miss Davis, he showed that if wheat was the basic dietary ingredient, calcium, vitamin A, and supplementary protein would be needed for successful growth and reproduction of his rats.

By 1915, McCollum and Davis had discovered that water extracts of wheat germ or rice polish could greatly improve the nutritive value of polished rice. They showed that the antiberiberi factor which relieved polyneuritis in pigeons was also needed by their rats. They designated this factor as "water soluble B" to distinguish it from "fat soluble A."

Dr. McCollum came to realize that his discoveries with the domesticated rat must surely have a relation to nutritional needs in humans. Starting in 1917, he began to comment adversely about the muscle meat, potatoes, white flour, corn meal, and sugar diets of that era. He recommended diets containing more milk, leafy vegetables, and the glandular organs of animals, such as the liver. Milk and leafy vegetables he designated as the "protective foods"—a phrase still in wide use.

In 1917, after 10 yr at Wisconsin, Dr. McCollum was offered and accepted the first appointment to the faculty of the new School of Hygiene and Public Health at Johns Hopkins University. His post was that of Professor and head of the department which later became known as the department of biochemistry.

The Newer Knowledge of Nutrition, a comprehensive text, was written by him in 1918. It came to fill a unique place in the world literature on nutrition, was republished in many languages, and passed through five editions. This famous text contained fruitful concepts for research and delineated unsolved challenging problems in nutrition.

During these years Dr. McCollum greatly influenced teachers of nutrition, dietetics, and home economics. He served on the Hoover Advisory Committee on Nutrition during World War I. For nearly 20 yr, beginning in 1923, he wrote authoritatively for *McCall's Magazine* on nutrition and food selection. He lectured at major universities, inaugurating a new era in the teaching of better food habits.

His basic nutrition studies were continued at Johns Hopkins with great vigor and insight. Dr. McCollum had observed in 1918 that young rats developed a ricketic condition when restricted to diets composed of cereal grains and containing disproportionate amounts of calcium and phosphorus. He established that small amounts of cod liver oil could alleviate this effect.

There was a congenial atmosphere at Johns Hopkins for pursuing this matter. There followed during the next 3 yr a close collaboration with the faculty in the department of pediatrics in the medical school. More than 300 experimental diets were fed to rats and histological bone sections were examined. It was concluded there existed a fat-soluble antiricketic substance which Dr. McCollum designated as vitamin D.

Now followed classical researches in the nutrition of the inorganic elements, including the so-called trace elements. These studies delineated the specific nutritional functions of sodium, potassium, phosphorus, iron, zinc, magnesium, manganese, calcium, and boron. The domesticated rat was used as the subject. These pioneering studies paved the way for the subsequent unfolding of the role of trace elements in domestic animal and human nutrition.

The contributions to the public good by Dr. McCollum were numerous and effective. He was consultant to the Merrill-Palmer Institute in Detroit for 12 yr. He was consultant for the Bureau of Animal Industry, U.S. Department of Agriculture, for 9 yr. He was a member of the U.S. Pharmacopoeial Revision Board for 17 yr. For 5 yr he was a member of the National Advisory Health Council. He held many offices relating to food and nutrition activities of the scientific societies and the federal government. During World War II, Dr. McCollum rendered valuable service on committees dealing with U.S. emergency food and nutrition needs.

Beginning in 1931, the international community often sought and obtained his services. He contributed in many ways to the nutrition work of the League of Nations and to the Pan American Bureau.

Dr. McCollum had a life-long and fruitful association with the food industry—in particular with the dairy industry. He was a staunch believer in the nutritive value of dairy products (based on his animal studies) and lectured extensively about their merits. He was instrumental in the founding of the National Dairy Council.

In the late 1920's, Dr. McCollum accepted the assignment of establishing in Baltimore the first research laboratory of the National Dairy Products Corporation. He selected the first premises and the initial staff. Subsequently he provided inspiring leadership as a consultant. Under his guidance, homogenized vitamin D milk was developed, the use of stainless steel equipment for handling dairy products was promoted, and effective methods for dairy waste disposal were developed. Major advances in milk sanitation practices for dairy plants were also pioneered here. Eventually, this enterprise became one of the world's great food industry laboratories.

Dr. McCollum's personal relations with people were superb. He was an unassuming, warm-hearted, witty man. He made his associates and friends feel completely comfortable in his presence. He had a great "activist" feeling for the underprivileged. His helping hand, quietly outstretched, started many off toward a distinguished career. Every visit with him was elevating and inspiring. On November 15, 1967, he "joined the angels" to use a phrase he coined. He will, however, live on in the hearts and minds of all who were privileged to know him.

It seems fitting to close with a quotation near the end of Dr. McCollum's autobiography, *From Kansas Farm Boy to Scientist:*

> From all I have written it is clear that I believe in the physiological value of study, thought, and work. In my experience these habits of life have paid off well. My days are still vivid and eventful. I still have abundant energy and a taste for the purposeful use of time and resources. Nothing in my past causes me uneasiness or concern. Through good fortune I have avoided dependency. My friends will attest that I have never appeared as one bearing a heavy burden. I conclude that enthusiasm for something worth while, and not variety, is the spice of life. After the satisfaction from my friendships, my greatest reward comes from the realization that I have participated in a great pageant of human endeavor which has demonstrated the new truth that the provision of a specific nutrient lacking in the diet of people in great numbers in many parts of the world will do more than argument, law, and sermons to create comfort, courage, optimism, and purpose.

SAMUEL M. WEISBERG

MEAT AND MEAT PACKING

The meat industry is a complexity of farming, slaughtering, and distribution, including meat and a host of by-products ranging from pharmaceuticals, sporting goods, and paint brushes to fertilizers. In 1970, it is reliably reported that U.S. meat production reached over 35 billion pounds. A host of people, facilities, and skills, are involved in the ultimate delivery of meat products to the consumer.

Beef farming is a sophisticated three-phase operation of breeding, pasture or range feeding, and final dry lot finish feeding. Some farmers are engaged in all 3 phases; in many cases, 3 operators, remotely located, each perform a single function. Meat production often involves many different steps, e.g., slaughtering, branch house distribution, shipment to specialized fabricators who produce a variety of products from Canadian bacon to corned beef, and shipment to retailers, locker plants, and jobbers (the people who deal directly with the consumer).

In the last 20 yr, 3 significant industry changes have occurred:

(1) Economic obsolescence of packing house facilities caused by city pressures, antiquated plants, and new production techniques. The replacement facilities have moved from former major slaughter centers such as Chicago, Omaha, and Los Angeles, to the country, close to the source of livestock.

(2) Dependable, swift, and economical refriger-

ated trucking. This has expanded marketing areas up to a radius of 3500 miles.

(3) Polyvinyl chloride-Saran packaging in the form of a bag, vacuumized and shrunk. This advance has made it feasible to market primal meat cuts without freezing; a shelf-life up to 4–5 weeks is attainable.

The Meat Inspection Act of 1906 set forth Standards for plant sanitation. Included were ante- and postmortem inspections to detect animal-carried diseases communicable to humans. The authority of the Act extended to interstate and foreign commerce. This Act has been recently updated by the Wholesome Meat Act of 1967 which is an attempt to assure all U.S. consumers on a national basis of inspected wholesome meat and meat products. Jurisdiction is extended to intrastate transactions, formerly exempt. As of Dec. 15, 1970, all meat products sold in the 50 States are under compulsory jurisdiction, either being Federally-inspected or State-inspected.

Federal meat grading was instituted in 1927 to provide an "official yardstick for measuring quality." This service is used by the meat processor on a voluntary basis. The effectiveness of the system is attested by its wide usage for top quality beef. It enables commerce to be conducted nationally on a reasonably objective basis.

Grading standards are used widely for beef (ranging mostly for USDA Good, USDA Choice, and USDA Prime grades) and for most lamb and some veal. Graded beef, versus private brands, is the stated preference of the American consumer. Grading standards are under constant surveillance, and are upgraded through objective evaluations, and adjusted from time to time to better meet changing social needs.

A practical definition of meat can be stated as follows: The carcass of any animal used for food including domestic mammals: (1) bovine (beef and veal); (2) ovine (lamb and mutton); (3) swine (hogs); (4) marginal types (goats, horses, dogs), along with poultry, fish, and game. Meat is composed of muscles, connective tissue, bones, fat, water, organic extractives, enzymes, and pigments. All of these components make some contribution to the palatability of the consumed product. Dietetically, meat is an important source of protein, some vitamin A, a rich source of thiamin, riboflavin, and niacin, as well as all B complex vitamins. Most essential minerals, except calcium, are found in the lean, including phosphorus, iron, copper, and trace elements. Nutrients are equally distributed in both expensive and inexpensive cuts.

Meat is not only significant nutritionally but is also popular as a food because it is attractive, aromatic, flavorful, and satisfying. Cooking generally improves these attributes, contributing to flavor, tenderness, and digestibility. Three basic heat techniques are employed in cooking: dry heat (roasting, broiling), moist heat (braising, stewing), and frying (sautéeing, deep fat frying). Other methods include smoking, barbecuing, and microwaves. Each method has its own special effect on the end product. Dry heat and frying caramelize the surface improving color, texture, and flavor. Generally, the more tender cuts are used for these methods, because dry heat also tends to shorten the muscle fibres, making the product tougher. Oven roasting, with some degree of relative humidity, will deliver a more tender product than broiling. Moist heat cookery partially hydrolyzes the tough collagenous tissues, making the product more tender. The color and flavor produced by moist heat are not as acceptable as dry heat cookery, but less expensive, generally tougher cuts may be used. As a rule, the tenderness of the cut, and the intended finished product, determine the cooking technique.

Palatability of meat dishes is judged by the senses of sight, taste, smell, touch, and, in lesser degree, by hearing. From time to time, the visceral senses—appetite, hunger, thirst, satiety, and peristalsis—have significant roles. Color of the cooked product influences appetite. Internal color reflects the internal cooked temperature. Medium rare is a term that can be defined as a chemical phenomenon reflecting the color that is manifested at $131°F$ through $145°F$, the point of coagulation of oxyhemoglobin. Above $150°F$, heme pigments occur, which account for the brown-gray color of meats cooked at this temperature. With top-of-stove cooking, with high temperatures achieved through dry heat, caramelization produces a very acceptable deep brown color.

A number of methods have been devised to achieve palatability scores on an objective basis. At this writing, methods are not sophisticated to the point where subjective evaluations and market testing can be replaced. Most devices score tenderness because "it is the most sought-after factor." This conclusion is in some degree incorrect. If tenderness is actually that important, most people would prefer ground or boiled meat or fillet steaks to tougher strip loin steaks. This is not borne out, even granting that economic considerations play a part. Acceptability is an eclectic, variable, subjective evaluation. Preferences will vary with region, climate, season, and ethnic groups, as well as a complexity of personal subjective reactions. Preference is best qualified by Adler's phrase—contentious apperception.

Shelf-Life

To protract the shelf-life of meat wholesomeness and palatability, various techniques are employed depending on the desired type of end product. A number of barriers have been devised to block changes caused by bacteria, molds, spores, and enzymes.

Fresh State.—Effective control can be achieved at temperatures ranging above freezing to $40°F$. High relative humidity and minimum velocity of air flow are important. Foreign growth, negative enzymatic action, and fat oxidation are retarded. The "butcher bloom" on fresh cut portions will remain bright for 2–3 days when the product is wrapped in MSAD 80 Cellophane, sucrose coated, which creates hydrostatic surface pressures. Shelf-life up to as much as 4–5 weeks can be achieved with PVC-Saran bags, vacuumized and shrunk over the product. The negative color which occurs on the surface of the product contained in this bag does not penetrate deeply and can be trimmed away. The negative odor is dissipated shortly after removal from the bag. Anaerobic bacteria unfortunately, will grow in the bag and lead ultimately to souring of the product. The bag is almost impervious to gases and moisture and thus precludes an oxygen source which accounts for the destruction of aerobic bacteria, a major shelf-life problem.

Frozen State.—Temperatures ranging from $+5°F$ to as low as $-40°F$ (and lower) effectively extend shelf-life. Enzymatic action is generally retarded below freezing, and bacterial growths are inhibited by changing the state of water to ice. Product may readily be restored for cooking by defrosting. In most cases, under optimum conditions, little or no palatability changes can be detected. Drip loss causes no significant palatability change. Constant temperatures from $-10°F$ to $-20°F$ are the best to achieve maximum shelf-life, especially to retard fat oxidation, the cause of rancid flavor. At $0°F$, beef and lamb can be held up to 6 months; at $-10°F$, it is possible to double this holding period. Veal and pork can be held for 4 months at $0°F$ and 8 months at $-10°F$. Products for freezing should be suitably wrapped, the PVC-Saran bag offering the best protection. Sharp freezing is not imperative and virtually impossible to achieve for almost any thick cut of meat. It is not harmful to refreeze a defrosted product if it is still in wholesome condition.

Curing and Corning.—Salt solutions inhibit the development of bacteria and reduce the water content of the product. Storing at temperatures below $50°F$ increases shelf-life.

Smoking.—Often, cured products are also smoked. This process further increases the shelf-life by retarding the oxidation of fats, reducing the water content of the product, and leaving a deposition of smoke components which have some bacteriostatic effect. Product should be refrigerated for maximum shelf-life.

Cooking and Canning.—Cooking meats to an internal temperature above 140°F halts enzymatic action and sterilizes meat surfaces and will extend product shelf-life, especially when the product is packed in hermetically sealed cans. No refrigeration is necessary.

Freeze Drying.—In this process the product is frozen under extremely low pressures. The ice sublimates leaving a sponge-like almost moistureless mass. The product retains its shape but the total weight is often reduced by over 50%. Final moisture ranges from 1 to 4%. Product can be stored safely at room temperature. Light weight and ambient storage temperatures are the economic advantages. Compared with conventional freezing, this process is much more expensive, and, because of reconstitution with water, less palatable for a number of meat entrées.

Irradiation.—This method of preservation through sterilization is presently being re-evaluated. The ultimate use of the method will be determined by cost, flavor changes, and the FDA's stamp of approval.

It seems logical to conclude that major industry changes will occur in the not-too-distant future as they have in the past. Economists generally predict in the years ahead a worldwide shortage of protein due to population increases. It is thus logical to predict higher prices for meats and other protein foods. Distribution will become more efficient in the future. The disassembly of beef, similar to what happened to pork over 50 yr ago, is an increasing practice. Primal cuts ready for final retail packaging are enjoying an expanding market. The next logical step is retail fabrication at the packer level. The primary concern is shelf-life. This can be achieved when the consumer fully accepts frozen products, for otherwise it becomes economically unrewarding to expand fabrication at the packer level. The retail consumer is presently being "conditioned" to the use of frozen meats by means of the home freezer, even though in many cases that freezer is nothing more than part of a home refrigerator. The institutional buyer is also slowly yielding to the use of frozen meats. Some day fresh meat cuts *may* be as extinct as the bulk pickle barrel.

ALBERT LEVIE

Cross-references: *Beef, Pork, Lamb, Sausage.*

MEAT CURING AND SMOKING

Curing and smoking as a method to preserve meat is documented in ancient Egypt. The Conquistadors found the American Indians drying and smoking meat to preserve it and to improve its flavor. They selected the most tender parts, which they cut into thin strips and hung to dry. Embellishing the flavor with smoke from a camp fire or inside a tepee was also practiced by the Indians. Brine curing of meat was extensively used in the 17th Century to "pack" pork cuts in "Porkpolis" (Cincinnati) and ship them to Eastern markets.

The effect of curing and smoking is relatively simple to define. Both methods have a bacteriostatic effect by reducing the available water, and creating an environment hostile to bacteria. The drying effect of smoke and the smoke components, creosote, acetic acid, and pyroligneous acids inhibit bacteria, and retard fat oxidization. Color and flavor changes that occur are very acceptable.

Modern smokehouses are insulated, hermetically sealed, and thermostatically controlled; smoke is generated with a device which burns sawdust or wood chips. Fruit tree woods as well as hickory, maple, oak, and ash are popular. Resinous woods such as pine should not be used. Slight flavor changes can be achieved with different woods.

Trichinae are destroyed at 137°F and enzymatic activity is halted at about 140°F. Internal temperatures of 140°F must be sustained if the label states, under USDA authorization, "fully-cooked" or "ready to eat." Temperatures of the smokehouse and smoking time are inversely proportional. At temperatures of 80°–90°F, 3–4 days are required; at 90°–100°F, 30–40 hr; at 125°–135°F, 18 hr. Many smoked products are cured before smoking. The cure is basically a matter of adding salt to retard bacterial action. Salt may be applied to the surface (dry curing); the product may be immersed in brine (sweet pickle); or brine may be injected into veins, or "stitch" injected at regular intervals. Garlic, pepper, and spices may be added to enhance the flavor. Sugar and sodium nitrate are generally added to the "sweet pickle" brine. Pit barbecuing essentially combines smoking and oven roasting to produce a flavorful, tender, sterile, and fully-cooked product.

Members of the smoked/cured family of meats include:

Breakfast bacon, made from pork bellies, cured and smoked. It is available in slabs or slices.

Canadian bacon, made from Canadian backs, the sirloin portion of the pork loin. It is cured and smoked, and available in visking, canned, and sometimes ready to eat.

Hams, made from whole or boneless pork legs. They are generally cured and smoked. "Ready-to-eat" ham is a most popular product.

Virginia ham is not smoked but is barrel cured for about 7 weeks in salt, then rubbed with a mixture of molasses, brown sugar, black and cayenne pepper, and sodium nitrate, and cured for 2 more weeks. It is then hung from 1–12 months or more.

Smithfield ham is rubbed with salt and sodium

nitrate and shelf cured for 5 days plus 1 day per pound. After curing, it is washed, rubbed with black pepper, shelved for 30 days, and then aged for 10–12 months.

Prosciutto ham (Italy) and Wesphalian ham (Germany) are hard, ready-to-eat hams of distinctive flavor. Both are outstanding for use as hor d'ouevres.

Sausage denotes, along with fresh ground pork items, a host of items sometimes but not always smoked, including wieners and salamis. Over 100 million pounds of sausage are produced annually in the United States.

ALBERT LEVIE

MELONS

The fruits of this group all belong to the *Cucurbitaceae* family which includes muskmelons, cantaloups, and watermelons as well as cucumbers, pumpkins, and squashes. In general, melons are consumed fresh; but there are a number of processed products. Watermelons make up the greatest tonnage, being around 3 million tons annually in the United States with a total value of over $50 million. Next in tonnage are cantaloups (including Casaba and Persian melons) at 600,000–700,000 tons worth some $78 million. Honeydews are produced at a rate of 75,000 tons per year with a value of $10 million. It would be impossible to list the hundreds of varieties of different melons most suited to various regions of the country. For watermelons the Charleston Gray, Florida Grant, Congo, Dixie Queen, and Blackstone are grown most widely (Doolittle *et al*, 1962). For other melons, varieties have been developed which best suit the local growing conditions. One of the most important factors for selection of all types of melons is resistance to anthracnose and fusarium wilt diseases. County agricultural agents and local growers should be consulted for information on varieties best adapted to specific localities.

Although melons have been canned successfully (Cutin and Samish 1958), the only product of commercial significance is frozen melon balls. The process consists of washing and sorting, cutting into halves, removing the seeds, and scooping out round balls with a spoon. The melon balls are $1\frac{1}{8}$ in. in diameter and may be packed as individual muskmelon, honeydew, or watermelon balls or may be mixed in the same package. A final washing and inspection to remove imperfect pieces precedes filling into retail or institutional packages. The packages are filled with the melon balls and 28° Brix syrup added; and then are put on racks to be placed in an air-blast tunnel for freezing (Anon.

1965). Since melons are very susceptible to microbial spoilage, great precautions must be taken to assure complete sanitation of the cut fruit and the equipment. This is accomplished by thorough washing with chlorinated water at various concentrations for different steps of the operation.

A recent development has been an individually quick frozen (IQF) product as described by Mariani *et al.* (1966).

FRANK P. BOYLE

REFERENCES

ANON. 1965. Product of the month—melon balls. Sterling Ind. Div., Green Giant Co., Sacramento, Calif.

CUTIN, J., and SAMISH, Z. 1958. The suitability of certain melon varieties for canning. Ktavim (Agr. Res. Sta. Israel) 8, 337–341.

DOOLITTLE, S. P., TAYLOR, A. L., DANIELSON, L. L., and REED, L. B. 1962. Commercial watermelon growing. USDA Agr. Inform. Bull. 259.

MARIANI, P. A., JR., de ALCUAZ, L., SNYDER, H. P., and ROBE, K. 1966. Freezes fresh melon texture and flavor. Food Process. 27, No. 12, 35, 38.

MEMBRANE FILTRATION

See Ultrafiltration and Reverse Osmosis.

MICROWAVE FOOD PROCESSING

High frequency electromagnetic energy in the microwave region of the spectrum (300 MHz to 30,000 MHz) has been and is being used in a variety of food processing applications, many of which are rather novel and would not have been possible without the advent of microwave power. Most work is being carried out at two specific frequencies; 915 MHz and 2450 MHz, frequencies which were assigned by the Federal Communications Commission for industrial, scientific and medical uses. The most important characteristic of this form of energy is the ability to penetrate and produce heat deep within food materials rather than just at the surface as is the case with other forms of heat. This characteristic is responsible for the generally much shorter process cycles. Though such deep heating provides speed of processing, it is often accompanied by a lack of surface effects such as browning. In the case of vegetable blanching, evaporative cooling at the surface can result in inadequate inactivation of surface enzymes. These and other deficiencies can be easily overcome by providing simultaneous surface heating by means of other energy sources.

Included among the microwave processes in use today are: finish drying of potato chips; cooking of cut-up poultry parts; precooking of sliced bacon; proofing of doughnuts; gaping of oysters; tempering of frozen meats, fish and poultry; and drying of short goods pasta.

Finish Drying of Potato Chips

In this process, potato slices are fried in the usual manner in hot fat to about 6% moisture, then finish dried by the combined action of microwave energy and heated air to a final moisture content of less than 2%. The process was developed from studies which demonstrated that potatoes high in reducing sugar content, which normally give chips which are too dark in color, could be fried in hot fat to a proper color end point, then finish dried by microwave energy with no further change in color. Potato chips produced in this manner are somewhat lower in fat content than the usual product. Possibly related to this is evidence of a reduced propensity toward rancidity in storage.

Practically all the equipment in use today in this process is operating at a frequency of 915 MHz. There are approximately 20 units each with a total installed microwave power of 50 kw in the United States, a dozen or so at 75 kw in England, and several others on the continent. All of the U.S. installations are of the resonant cavity design, that is, a chamber 2-3 ft sq by about 20 ft long into which microwave energy is introduced along its length by means of a leaky wall waveguide attached to the oven ceiling. The partially dried product is introduced through a wave trap into the microwave cavity onto an open mesh conveyor belt. Heated air at 190°-220°F flows up through the bed of chips to carry off the moisture, and the finish dried chips exit the unit through another wave trap. Residence time in the microwave dryer varies between 2½ and 4 min. Production rate is 1400-2000 lb per hr of finished chips depending on input moisture. Most of the units in England are of the split folded waveguide design in which the belt carrying the chips passes through the center of the guide. Heated air is introduced above the chip bed to carry off moisture. Maximum product rate with this technique is about 1600 lb per hr. Because a solid polypropylene belt is used in this latter design, crumbs from the chips do not accumulate in the equipment, but rather are carried on through. The unit is therefore somewhat easier to keep clean.

Precooking of Poultry Parts

Several installations using a combination of microwave power at 2450 MHz and saturated steam for precooking of poultry are in existence. The process replaces a batch steam system which was heavily labor sensitive with a continuous process requiring far fewer workers. The continuous process also demonstrated a substantial improvement in yield even when compared with a continuous steam cooking process. Processing rates of 2500-3000 lb per hr are claimed and the duration of the process averages about 14 min. In practice, cut-up parts are separated into legs and wings and breasts and thighs. The first 2 are processed together at one rate and the latter 2 at another rate. The reason for this is, of course, the greater weight of the breast and thighs and, therefore, the need for more energy to accomplish the cooking. The two cooking rates are accomplished in parallel units so that the proper mix of finished product is obtained at the end.

Equipment used in this process is of the resonant cavity design; however, two different philosophies of microwave input to the units are in evidence. The first of the installations employed a multiplicity of 2.5 kw microwave power modules. The output of each module is carried by waveguide into the process chamber at regularly spaced locations. Failure of one or more modules does not result in shut-down of the equipment, rather a number of spare modules already in the system can be turned on and the defective modules replaced during normal shutdown. Only minimum maintenance skills are required to change modules. Another advantage claimed for this approach is that the energy is more uniformly distributed along the length of the unit than is possible with higher powered generators. The second design philosophy employs 25-30 kw microwave generators. Obviously, far fewer units are required to provide the same total installed power. The power supplies for these generators are more sophisticated and, therefore, require a higher level of competence on the part of maintenance personnel. Failure of a single source could reduce production by $1/3$ or more.

Bacon Cooking

Bacon cooking has been studied and a precooked product extensively test marketed, with apparent success. In spite of this, only one 50 kw, 915 MHz installation is known to be in operation. Bacon, like potato chips, is a product whose dielectric properties change significantly during the process. Chips change from a high moisture content to a high fat content and in doing so the dielectric properties approach that of pure fat which is an order of magnitude more transparent than the wet chips. Thus, the process is somewhat self-controlling; that is, as the microwave drying approaches completion the chips are less subject to damage from overheating. As bacon is rendered and the moisture of the lean is removed, it too becomes more transparent to microwave energy. This process is less sensitive to differences in the distribution of fat and lean from one end of the bacon belly to the other, as well as to slight differences in thickness of the slices than other cooking processes because of the above reason.

Microwave Proofing of Doughnuts

Continuous microwave doughnut proofers were first installed in 1970 and there are a number of known installations in the United States. The use of microwave power reduces proofing time from 25–30 min down to 4 min. A typical 25 kw unit operating at a frequency of 2450 MHz can proof 350–400 doughnuts per hour. Advantages claimed for the process include a sharp reduction in labor and space requirements, a 6% increase in usable dough by the elimination of misshapen product in this straight line operation, and simplified clean-up and sanitation.

Microwave Seafood Processing

Microwave gaping of oysters to simplify the shucking operation has been studied in considerable detail by the National Fisheries Institute Laboratory in Gloucester, Mass. The technique permits shuckers to handle considerably larger quantities of oysters with much less effort and with far less danger of injury to themselves. A number of commercial-scale pilot studies have been completed and the economics of the process shown to be quite favorable. Relatively low powered equipment at 2450 MHz appears to be adequate to meet commercial requirements.

Another application in this industry uses microwave energy to pasteurize and firm oysters. The oysters are carried on a conveyor belt through a microwave field to raise their temperature to about 170°F. Taste approximates that of freshly shucked oysters and the pasteurization treatment permits quality to be maintained for short periods of time at refrigerated temperatures. A commercial installation at 2450 MHz is in operation at the present time.

Microwave pasteurization of a variety of shellfish meats has been studied by the Seafood Processing Laboratory, Crisfield, Maryland. Rapid in-package processing at 2450 MHz followed by rapid cooling results in a product of high quality. Microwave processing accomplishes this in 3 min as compared to a conventional process of 110 min.

Tempering of Frozen Meats

This process promises to be one of the more important applications of microwave energy in the food field. A commercial 20 kw, 2450 MHz installation in France (see Fig. M-10) is being used to temper frozen pork shoulders to permit salting by arterial pumping. Process uses 60 kg per watt hour of installed power.

The tempering process is one in which the product is raised from its frozen storage temperature to a few degrees below its freezing point. At such temperature, the product is still firm but not solid,

FIG. M-10. A COMMERCIAL INSTALLATION FOR MICROWAVE FOOD PROCESSING IN FRANCE USED TO TEMPER FROZEN PORK SHOULDERS SO AS TO PERMIT SALTING BY ARTERIAL PUMPING

and is, therefore, easy to handle. There is also no drip loss, whereas controls thawed at 8°C showed weight losses of 8–10%. Operating costs including amortization, maintenance, magnetron replacement, and electricity amount to slightly over $\frac{1}{2}$¢ per lb. The same application in the United States is being carried out at 915 MHz with equal success. The major advantage of this process is that it accomplishes in minutes that which takes several days under controlled temperatures. Since the products can be tempered as needed, there is a minimum space requirement.

Miscellaneous Processing Applications

Microwave drying of short goods pasta is being employed on a commercial scale by at least two major manufacturers. The process takes approximately 15 min compared to 14 hr for the conventional drying process. Far less space is required and clean-up is considerably simplified.

Microwave blanching of corn-on-the-cob has been extensively studied by the Western Utilization Research and Development Division of USDA. The studies were carried out in a 915 MHz 25 kw conveyor unit. A 4-min microwave blanch followed by a 12-min steam blanch gave best results.

Microwave finish drying of breakfast cereals, drying of apples, carrots, potatoes and other vegetables, and the puffing of fruits, vegetables, and snack foods have all been studied. Pilot runs on apple drying have been under study in the northwest for some time and the puffing and drying of apple segments and potato dice was reported by USDA. In this latter work, best results were obtained when apple segments were air dried to 20% moisture then exposed to microwave energy under reduced pressure conditions. After a short period of microwave heating, the system pressure is suddenly changed to give a puffed volume of $2\text{-}\frac{1}{2}\text{--}3\text{-}\frac{1}{2}$ times that of air-dried segments. The moisture content of the apple segments is reduced to less than 2% while still under vacuum conditions.

In-package microwave pasteurization of cakes has been carried out in 915 MHz equipment at a rate of one ton per hour. A substantial increase in shelf-life was the major advantage effecting a significant reduction in distribution costs. The application to in-package bread to obviate the need for use of mold inhibitors has also been studied.

Among other processes which have been studied are coffee roasting, nut roasting, doughnut frying, moisture control of grain, boiling of silk cocoons, freeze drying, in-package sterilization of foods, and milk and beer pasteurization.

ROBERT V. DECAREAU

Cross-reference: *Food Preservation.*

MILITARY FOODS

From earliest times, the availability of food in military operations has been recognized to be a prime determinant of the outcome of campaigns. In a message to Congress, April 17, 1818, the Honorable John C. Calhoun, then Secretary of War, said, "Food sustains the immense machinery of war, and gives the impulse to all its operations; and if this essential be withdrawn, even if but for a few days, the whole must cease to act."

The kinds of food used by the military have varied over the years and have depended upon the levels of agriculture, food preservation, and general social development in the areas affected. Early examples are Caesar's grain trains, which supplied his troops with their staple, boiled wheat, or the cattle driven behind Napoleon's armies. Historically, subsistence has varied from a pouch of raw oilseed or parched grain to foods of a high level of sophistication in form, composition, and stability.

Food for the soldier nourishes not only the body, but affords strong psychological reinforcement: Good food provides positive motivation. It contributes significantly to good morale. Nutritionally balanced diets undershore vigorous health, sustain stamina, and, within bounds, sharpen mental acuity requisite to survival in situations of extreme stress and ultimate mental challenge. Amounts and kinds of sustenance essential to or desirable in the melange of military environments differ, obviously, just as military missions do: with respect to environment, duration of commitment, objectives, circumstances of conflict, and relative to succeeding and anticedent situations. Food performs physiologically protective functions, but if "unbalanced" can contribute to extreme malaise and in the absence of adequate water can compromise survival. An array of kinds of foods, meals, and subsistence systems are requisite, therefore, to the fulfillment of military needs, for not only do military personnel partake of the full spectrum of counterpart civilian activities, but frequently are required to operate for short or longer periods in situations quite unique to their calling.

U.S. military food service, worldwide, during recent years has required 100,000 personnel and expenditures estimated variously to range from $5.0 to $7.5 billion. Food purchases, competitively bid, approximate 225,000 procurements per annum and are, in general, accomplished through a central Federal agency, the Defense Supply Agency, located in Alexandria, Virginia. The annual cost of food alone, at point of first delivery to the government, has exceeded $1.0 billion: 60% of purchases (dollar value) are made from small businesses in accordance with Federal directives.

During the period July 1970–July 1971, acquisitions of representative foods for U.S. Armed Forces included (pounds): beef for general issue, 171.3 million; white potatoes, 146.3 million; chicken (fryers), 56.8 million; bacon (sliced), 24.5 million, and eggs (shell), 49.9 million dozen.

A majority of meals eaten by military personnel, worldwide, are those served in dining facilities of various sizes, ashore or afloat. Even in Southeast Asia during recent years, more than 90% of the meals were of this type. They present familiar foods in a wide array of attractive dishes prepared according to technically tested recipes, in an ever-changing variety of menus: meals and dishes are designed to reflect average American tastes.

Army alone has some 4700 of these facilities, most of which accommodate from 200 to 300 customers. Trends are to combine these and to provide central food preparation.

Continuous review and updating of facilities, menus, recipes, and of foods used, are provided for in Department of Defense Directives and Instructions, establishing and/or defining the functions of requisite agencies, boards and committees participating in the coordinated food program: Directives 1138.9, 1138.10, 1138.11 and Instructions 3200.10, 5126.42, 5154.21.

Under general guidance of the Department of Defense (DoD) Directorate for Subsistence Management Policy, the DoD Food Service Facility & Equipment Planning Board, as well as the Armed Forces (A.F.) Menu Planning Committee, A.F. Recipe Service Committee, and A.F. Product Evaluation Committee carry out their separate but related functions. Recent advances include the publication in March, 1970, of a new cook book containing some 800 recipes, the best from the records and efforts of the four Services.

Illustrative of responsiveness of the Defense Food Service to new trends and standards is an impressive record of menu and recipe updating: achieved have been 205 changes in the cook book; 7 deletions; and 232 additions reflecting the availability of new food items, the greater use of partially prepared "convenience" foods, and the introduction of an interesting array of ethnic foods (Soul, Mexican-American, Italian, Southern. etc.).

The flow of newly developed foods through these appraisal agencies and into military usage is nearly continuous: during the 30-month period ending Dec. 1970, 267 new food items were submitted by industry (without Armed Forces solicitation). Incorporated into the Federal Supply Catalogue during this same period, and thus becoming available for recurrent procurement were 116 new items.

Scheduling and pretesting of menus, recipes and instructions for the millions of meals served daily throughout the world, and provision, on site, of foods requisite for these follows a carefully developed pattern established first during the early days of World War II (1942). An Annual Food Plan is prepared by calendar year. It reflects recommendations of the Department of Defense, the separate Armed Services, the Supply Agency, the Surgeons General, and Food Service staffs and serves as the cornerstone planning document of meals, procurements, dispositions, shipments, and other details. Companion to the Food Plan is the Master Menu which spells out: what; how much; how often (Army Regulation 30-1).

The Master Menu distributed to each food service facility worldwide provides recommended menus, reference to recipe and preparation instructions, costing basis, and nutritional information.

Garrison meals of the type now under discussion, are also known as Type A, or simply as "A Rations." Technically, a ration is food for 1 man for 1 day: generally 3 meals (breakfast, dinner, and supper). Garrison meals have traditionally emphasized fresh foods, but during recent years include frozen meats and a number of "convenience" types of commestibles; instant potato granules are an example. Such meals are in contrast to Type B (B Rations) which are based on the nearly complete use of canned, dried, or other preprocessed classes, all of which are less perishable than fresh produce. The Combat Ration (C Ration) of World War II was superseded about the time of the Korean Conflict by ready-to-eat or heat-and-eat types of packaged "meals." Hundreds of millions of these have supported actions in Southeast Asia up to the present date. Some detail relative to these will be found in later paragraphs.

Precise uniformity in U.S. military meals worldwide is not expected. Deviations from the Master Menu may be recommended to Unit Commanders by Food Service or Medical Officers to take advantage of local availability of foods of superior acceptability, freshness, or better nutritional qualities; or to compensate for sex and age of Forces; or in response to climatic situations; or to preclude monotony. The greatest deviation in quality of meals may be attributed to variance in the skills and motivation of unit cooks. Recognition of these and related problems has given rise to current reform and a marked upgrading of the character and quality of meals, food service, and facilities.

During 1971, the Master Menu was updated to provide for a broader daily variety of foods available for selection by the individual customer: a la carte breakfasts; multiple choice, full course dinners replete with fresh fruits in season and tossed green salads; short order, snack type lunches; multiple choice entrées for supper. At Ft. Lewis, Washington, and to a limited extent elsewhere, Central Food Preparation was instituted under the direction

TABLE M-6

FOODS BEST LIKED BY FT. LEWIS ARMY MEN

Food Name	Hedonic Preference
Milk	8.03
Orange juice	7.65
Grilled steak	7.61
Hot rolls and buns	7.46
Fried chicken	7.43
Chocolate milk	7.42
Oranges	7.33
Ice cream	7.32
Corn-on-the-cob	7.29
French fried potatoes	7.28
Eggs to order	7.27
Chicken	7.26
Bacon, lettuce and tomato sandwich	7.23
Fresh apples	7.20
White bread	7.18
Milk shake	7.15
Toast	7.14
Cola	7.14
Strawberry shortcake	7.14
Bacon	7.12
Fried eggs	7.05
Banana split	7.05
Ice cream sundae	7.05
Fresh peaches	7.04

TABLE M-7

FOODS LEAST LIKED BY FT. LEWIS ARMY MEN

Food Name	Hedonic Preference
Pickled beet/onion salad	3.01
Parsnips	3.10
Zucchini squash	3.21
Iced coffee	3.31
Eggplant	3.43
Rutabagas, turnip	3.48
Carrot, raisin and celery salad	3.56
Raisin pie	3.67
Manhattan clam chowder	3.73
Butterscotch sauce	3.77
Cucumber/onion salad	3.80
Canned figs	3.86
Succotash	3.88
Cabbage and sweet peppers	3.88
Yellow squash	3.88
Cheese soup	3.88
Stuffed celery/peanut butter	3.88
Cooked onions	3.88
Mustard greens	3.89
Turnip greens	3.89
Pepper pot soup	3.89
Onion soup	3.89
Kidney bean salad	3.91
Mincemeat pie	3.93
Sukiyaki	3.94

of highly qualified technologists and dieticians. Self-help cafeteria-like service was provided with great success.

The currently-used, 42-day cycle of Type A meals (essentially repeat Day 1 menu on Day 43) makes use of approximately 300 selected food items, in contrast to the 28-day cycle of "simplified" Type A meals served in Southeast Asia, designed around 200 of the more-available and more-easily-handled Type A and B commestibles. Reversion to the 42-day cycle was scheduled in Southeast Asia to begin in July, 1972.

Foods are selected for Type A meals to reflect troop acceptability, nutritional characteristics, relative availability, and cost, within the bounds of appropriated funds.

The content of military garrison meals and menus has been guided by a series of repetitive, large-scale food preference studies, first initiated by the U.S. Armed Forces Food & Container Institute, during 1947. The latest of such efforts, now under the direction of the U.S. Army Natick Laboratories, was conducted during 1971, at Ft. Lewis, Washington, by Herbert L. Meiselman and colleagues.

A variety of troops, ranging in age and experience from the permanent garrison brigade to thousands of raw recruits passing through the Post to training assignments, comprise a majority of the present 70,000 population of the Fort. New troops ate a record 85% of their meals at Post dining facilities, garrison troops only 46%. Total meals served on the Post daily approximated 16,000 during the period of study, highlights of which are reported herein.

A sample group of 689 military personnel were selected to represent a cross-section of Army elements at Ft. Lewis during April, 1971. To each was presented a list of 416 foods tabulated randomly: these included selections from the Master Menu as well as items anticipated to be added thereto within the ensuing months. Format provided rating scales of two types: (1) the 9-point hedonic, food preference scale of Peryam and Pilgrim, and (2) a preference frequency scale (how many times a week the food would be desired; how many weeks per month, by meal). Hedonic is derived from the Greek word "hedonikos," which means pleasurable. The hedonic scale is a simple calibrated continuum upon which the degree of like or dislike is recorded: nine phrases ranging from "Like Extremely" to "Dislike Extremely" are arranged along a line or scale, designed to suggest

TABLE M-8

FOODS SELECTED MOST FREQUENTLY BY FT. LEWIS ARMY MEN
(All Meals)

Food Name	Frequency[1] Servings/Month
Milk	67.54
White bread	46.71
Whole wheat bread	39.22
Chocolate milk	35.72
Fresh coffee	34.05
Beer	29.60
Hot rolls and buns	28.72
Orange juice	26.98
Cola	26.68
Tea	25.78
Toast	23.78
Lettuce and tomato salad	23.09
Iced tea	22.28
Tossed green salad	22.16
Eggs to order	21.01
Bacon	20.00
Fresh apples	19.75
Oranges	19.67
Hot cross buns	19.60
Milk shake	19.36
Ice cream	19.11
Thousand Island Dressing	19.09
French Salad Dressing	18.63
Biscuits	18.37

[1] Highest possible score: 84, indicating selection at every meal, every day, 4 weeks per month.

TABLE M-9

DAILY DIETARY ALLOWANCE
For military personnel moderately active in a temperate climate

		Male	Female
Calories	(Kcal)	3400	2400
Protein	(gm)	100[1]	80[1]
Fat	(gm)		
Calcium	(mg)	800	800
Iron[2]	(mg)	14	18
Thiamin (vitamin B-1)	(mg)	1.7	1.2
Riboflavin (vitamin B-2)	(mg)	2.0	1.7
Niacin	(mg)	22	16
Ascorbic acid (vitamin C)	(mg)	60	60
Vitamin A	(IU)	5000	5000

SOURCE: Army Regulation 40-25.

[1] Not to exceed 40% of calories.
[2] For women a supplement may be required.
It should be noted that nutrients not listed above will be added when appropriate means for determining levels in food are available. Recommended levels of other of the vitamins are: vitamin D, 400 IU; vitamin E, 30 IU; folacin, 0.4 mg; vitamin B-6, 2.0 mg; vitamin B-12, 5 μg.
Nutritional standards noted above are for men and women in age range of 17–25 yr; of average height and weight (men 68–70 in., 146–170 lb; women 63–64 in., 120–130 lb).
Phosophorus: requirements same as calcium. Iodine: all table salt should be iodized. Fluoride: "The maintenance of optimal fluoride concentrations of about 1 mg per liter in water supplies has proved to be safe, economical, and efficient."

a single dimension. The mid-point is "Neither Like Nor Dislike"; numerical values are assigned; the highest, 9, attaches to the condition of "Like Extremely"; the mid-point is a value of 5; the low-point is 1.

The survey form used permitted recording that a food was *never* wanted, or was unknown. A Consumer Attitude Test was also administered, providing information concerning the respondents age, education, attitude to military service, and other background data.

From 100 responses drawn randomly from the final sample of 573 sets, preliminary observations were gleaned. These, it will be noted, represent the preferences of but one military service, on a single Post, during one season only; however, findings do not differ greatly from those of earlier studies. These preferences are shown in Tables M-6, M-7, and M-8.

Main dinner dishes most frequently preferred and rated highest in regular dinners, hedonically, include, Grilled Steak, Chicken, and Fried Chicken in that order; and in sandwiches, Hamburger; Cheeseburger; Grilled Cheese and Ham; Hot Roast Beef with Gravy; Bacon, Lettuce and Tomato; Hot Turkey and Gravy. Salads most frequently desired and rated highest for dinner were ranked, first, Tossed Greens, followed by Jellied Fruit, Lettuce and Tomato, Tossed Vegetables, Lettuce Salad.

It is interesting to note that the old adage seems to hold "that what is one man's poison is another man's nectar." Foods *never* wanted by a majority of the respondents were nevertheless favored highly by minorities.

Highly acceptable meals can be prepared: higher quality thereof appears to stem from carefully supervised Central preparation. The garrison ration is planned so that consumption of average servings of available dishes will provide a nutritionally balanced diet for military personnel performing moderate exercise in pursuit of their professions, in temperate climates. If food is not eaten, the whole complex system has failed.

General recognition is given in official documents to the necessity of providing some 45–50 nutrients in the military dietary, including essential amino acids, essential fatty acids, vitamins and minerals. Emphasis is placed on cooking methods which prevent excessive amounts of fat in foods (fat is not to exceed 40% of calories in planned menus); substitution of a part of saturated fats by polyunsaturated types is recommended.

The per diem allowances as shown in Table M-9 are presently stipulated by the Surgeons General of the Army, Navy, and Air Force.

F. P. MEHRLICH

Cross-references: *Food Research and Development Program, U.S. Department of Defense*; *K-Ration.*

MILLETS

Millets are rapid-growing, warm-weather cereal grasses of several species, whose small grains are used as food. A small part of the grain and much of the forage is fed to animals. Millets are a major part of the diet of 250 million of poorer people living on poorer, drier lands in India, Africa, China, Russia, and elsewhere. Millets were grown in China many centuries ago. Although some species may have originated in Asia, pearl millet probably developed in Africa. In ancient and medieval ages millet was the leading crop of the known world, and until recent centuries was the principal cereal grown in Europe. It lost favor because millet flour was unsuited for making yeast-raised bread.

Millet production data are scarce, and difficult to obtain and evaluate. Annual production is estimated at 35 million metric tons, grown on some 60 million hectares (150 million acres); more than 98% is produced in Asia and Africa. India alone produces some 35% of the world's millets.

The names and principal production areas of the leading species of millets, in order of importance, are: *Pennisetum typhoideum*, pearl millet (bajra in India), India, Africa; *Setaria italica*, foxtail millet, China, Russia; *Panicum miliaceum*, proso, Russia, China (a very small European and U.S. production); *Eleusine coracana*, finger millet (ragi in India), India. Sorghums often are listed with millets and called giant millet in India. Millets, except pearl millet which may grow to 10 ft or more, normally grow 1–4 ft high, and have long, narrow-bladed leaves. The seed head of pearl and foxtail millets is a long, compacted, cylindrical spike; proso seed is in a loose, open panicle; the finger millet head consists of several short "fingers" with seed on each.

Millets have an advantage in growing and producing under adverse conditions of high temperature, poor soil, and scanty rainfall not tolerated by other cereals. Pearl millet has produced a little grain where annual rainfall was 5 in. and soil 6 in. deep. Since they mature quickly, proso, foxtail, and finger millets grow under dry land conditions, but they also thrive in more temperate climates and conditions.

Although under similar favorable conditions the common millets usually yield less than sorghums and other cereals, certain millet strains and hybrids recently developed are capable of responding to fertilizer, irrigation, and improved agronomic practices with yields comparable to those of other cereals. Millets sometimes are planted as a rapid-growing second or catch crop after a first crop (often different) is lost. Proso is the common European millet, grown as a minor food crop there and in the U.S. northern plains for livestock and poultry feed. Pearl millet is one of the best annual forages for beef cattle production on the U.S. southeastern coastal plains. Some quick-growing millets are sown for wildlife food and used in birdseed mixtures.

Millets have received less research attention than most cereals, but the morphological variations of the some 10,000 specimens in the world grain collection offer many possibilities for improvements in yield, quality, and adaptability through breeding programs.

The protein content of millets averages 10–12%, except for finger millet, 5–7%; however, the newer varieties and hybrids of pearl millet have 8–20% protein, and of finger millet, 5–12%. Fat content of millets is 2–5%; fiber, 2–3%, except for foxtail and proso, 7–8%; mineral is 2.0–3.5%; phosphorus, 0.2–0.4%; calcium, 0.02–0.06%, except for finger millet, 0.2–0.4%; iron is 0.002–0.01%; potassium, 0.3–0.4%. Certain species and newer varieties and hybrids may vary more widely in composition. Content of fiber depends on extent of husking and cleaning of seed before it is analyzed. Pearl millet resembles sorghum in composition; finger millet more closely resembles rice, except for lower protein and higher fiber, mineral, and calcium contents. As a source of water-soluble vitamins, millets are as good as, or better than, other cereals.

The protein of pearl millet has essential amino acid contents and balance similar to sorghum protein, but with somewhat more lysine, sulfur-containing amino acids, threonine, and tryptophan. Compared to the FAO essential amino acid reference pattern, pearl millet protein is deficient only in lysine. Finger millet contains less protein than pearl millet, but finger millet protein has larger quantities of essential amino acids; no amino acid is deficient, although lysine is marginal. The higher the protein content of millets, the lower the lysine:protein ratio tends to become. On several protein quality scores, finger millet protein ranks first; pearl millet, second; and both rank considerably above maize and sorghum. Millets also usually outrank wheat and rice in protein quality.

Millets are not important commercial grains; most are used only in the local production area. Some finger and foxtail millets are used alone or mixed with rice in making beer.

Large quantities of millets are hand ground in villages by rubbing stone, stone or wooden mortar and pestle, or ground in small burrstone or hammer mills. Processes are being developed to mill de-branned, whole-millet flours and flours of different extractions, but the processes have had little commercial application. As with other grains, nutritive value of millet depends on milling method and refinement. One reason for the higher nutritive value of millet diets is that less-refined millet products are eaten rather than the more-refined wheat, rice, or sorghum products. Finger millet is recognized for superior staminal value in the diet. Because of higher calcium content, finger millet is recommended for use by pregnant and nursing women where milk is scarce. Millions of poorer people in India, Africa, China, and parts of Russia depend on millets for perhaps 70% or more of their food calories.

Except for yeast-raised breads, millets are consumed much as are other cereals. The principal uses are as meal or flour in simple, flat breads and griddle-type cakes, and in thick or thin boiled gruels. Millets are eaten as whole grains in soups and stews; ground millets are used in puddings, steamed meals, deep-fried doughs, and mixed with pulses, vegetables, milk, cheese, or dates. The grains are popped, roasted, sprouted, and malted.

Millets yield less starch than does corn or sorghum, but the gross physical properties are similar. Ground millets compare favorably with other cereals as poultry or livestock feed. Plant breeders hope to develop millets providing better bread flours, while maintaining or improving their desirable production and nutritive properties.

D. B. PARRISH

References

DEWIT, J. P., and SCHWEIGART, F. 1970. The potential role of pearl millet as a food in South Africa. S. African Med. J. *44*, 364–366; S. African J. Nutr. *6*, 30–32.

FAO. 1969. Production Yearbook, Vol. 23. Food and Agricultural Organization of the United Nations, Rome.

KURIEN, P. P. 1967. Nutritive value of refine ragi (*Eleusine coracana*) flour. 1. The effect of feeding poor diets based on whole, refined and composite ragi flours on the growth and availability of calcium in albino rats. J. Nutr. Dietetics, India *4*, 96–101.

LEONARD, W. H., and MARTIN, J. H. 1963. Cereal Crops, Macmillan Co., New York.

PUSHPAMMA, S., PARRISH, D. B., and DEYOE, C. W. 1972. Improving protein quality of millet, sorghum and maize diets by supplementation. Nutr. Repts. Intern. *5*, 93–100.

STREETER, C. P. 1969. Millets—hope of the dry country. A Partnership to Improve Food Production in India. Spec. Rept. Rockefeller Foundation, New York.

MOLASSES

Molasses was first processed from sugar cane in China or India so many centuries ago that no one really knows how long people have been enjoying it. The word molasses appeared in early forms as melasses and molasses. It comes, too, from the Portuguese melaco, the Spanish melaza, and the French mélasse, as well as the late Latin mellaceum, meaning syrup made from honey (mel).

Sugar cane, and its resulting molasses, was introduced into Santo Domingo by Christopher Columbus in 1493. By the 18th Century, molasses was very important to American colonial commerce. New England imported this commodity mainly for the production of rum. In 1733, the Molasses and Sugar Act was passed in an attempt to restrict the flourishing trade with the West Indies to the British part of the island by overtaxing the import of French and Dutch rum and molasses, leaving the more expensive British products tax free. The colonies refused to obey the law. It was one of the contributing causes of the American Revolution and John Adams wrote, "I know not why we should blush to confess that molasses was an essential ingredient in American independence. Many great events have proceeded from much smaller causes."

Molasses is the syrupy juice of the cane or beet after most of the water and all, or any part, of the commercially crystallizable sugar has been removed. Although the distinction between molasses and syrups is not always exact in the trade, technically, the terms are accurately defined. Syrup is the concentrated juice from the evaporators, whereas molasses is the mother liquor separated from the sugar crystal by mechanical means.

Production of Molasses

Cane Molasses—Raw sugars are usually produced in a succession of three crystallizations. Mother liquors from the first sugar strike are called first molasses. The first molasses is crystallized with additional syrup to form a crop of crystals called second crystals and the resulting mother liquor is designated as second molasses. The mother liquor recovered from the third and, usually, last strike in the manufacture of raw cane sugar is called third molasses, final molasses, and sometimes cane molasses.

Another product, called refiners' molasses, or refiners' final molasses, is the mother liquor recovered from the final crystallization of refined cane sugar.

Blackstrap molasses is the by-product of either raw sugar manufacture or refining. It is the heavy viscous liquid separated from the final low grade massecuite from which no further sugar can be crystallized by the usual methods.

High-test molasses is a product in which a concentrated cane juice has been partially inverted by acids or enzymes.

Edible Molasses—Edible molasses are usually prepared by blending syrups and mother liquors from different varieties of cane in order to produce a flavor profile which is characteristic to a particular processor.

Many of the molasses are manufactured in

Barbados, West Indies, shipped to this country, and blended to strict specifications. Some molasses are produced in Louisiana.

First and second molasses are often considered as blends with other products. Cane is crushed, and the strained cane juice is run through a clarifier and evaporator at a specific pH (in the range of 7.0–7.3). The material is drained after crystallization, to serve as one of the blends for edible molasses.

In another method, clarified cane juice is treated with an acid or enzyme for partial inversion. After neutralization, with alkali if necessary, the juice is concentrated, reclarified, and serves as "fancy" syrup in molasses blends.

In a third method, the strained cane juice is treated with sulfur dioxide, neutralized with lime and separated from the sediment by decantation. The clear juice is evaporated for graining and the mother liquor serves as sulfited raw material for molasses blends.

Evaporation procedures are often performed in open kettles to accentuate the characteristic molas-

TABLE M-10

CANE FINAL MOLASSES CONSTITUENTS

Components	Molasses Origin	Concentration (Solids Content) (%)
Carbohydrates	Louisiana	80.52[1]
	Cuba	78.90[1]
Sucrose	Louisiana	37.39
	Cuba	47.28
"Reducing sugars"	Louisiana	32.72
	Cuba	20.98
D-glucose	Cuba	6.9
D-fructose	Cuba	1.6
myo-Inositol	Cuba	0.261
Phytin	Cuba	0.225
D-mannitol	Cuba	0.6
Uronic acids	Louisiana	2.0
Methoxyl	Louisiana	0.8
Sugar "reaction products"	Louisiana	10.1
	Cuba	10.7
Vitamins		
Biotin	Cuba	17.0×10^{-5}
Folic acid	Cuba	0.43×10^{-5}
Nicotinic acid	Cuba	222×10^{-5}
Pantothenic acid	Cuba	635×10^{-5}
Pyridoxine	Cuba	19.1×10^{-5}
Riboflavin	Cuba	24.4×10^{-5}
Thiamin	Cuba	8.5×10^{-5}
Nitrogen Compounds		
Total nitrogen	Cuba	0.89
	Florida	1.40
	Hawaii	0.71
	Louisiana	0.38
	Puerto Rico	1.16

TABLE M-10 (*Continued*)

Components	Molasses Origin	Concentration (Solids Content) (%)
Amino Acids		
Alanine	Florida	—
γ-Aminobutyric acid	Florida	—
Asparagine	Florida	—
Aspartic acid	Florida, Hawaii	—
Glutamic acid	Florida, Hawaii	—
Glycine	Florida	—
Leucine (or isoleucine)	Florida	—
Lysine	Hawaii	—
Valine	Florida	—
Nucleic acid bases		
Guanine	Hawaii	—
Hypoxanthine	Hawaii	—
5-Methylcytosine	Hawaii	—
Xanthine	Hawaii	—
Non-nitrogenous acids	Cuba	7.59
	Louisiana	7.39
Aconitic	Louisiana	4.95
	Puerto Rico	0.95
Malic	Puerto Rico	—
Citric	Puerto Rico	—
Formic	Puerto Rico	0.12
Lactic	Puerto Rico	0.60
Acetic	Puerto Rico	0.24
Bacteria		
Mesophilic	Louisiana	300–310,000[2]
Thermophilic	Louisiana	1,200–16,500[2]
Pigments		
Chlorophyll a	Cuba	5×10^{-5}
"Browning products"	Louisiana, Cuba	10.1–10.7
Tannins	Louisiana	—
Anthocyanins	Louisiana	—
Waxes, sterols, and lipids	Cuba	0.50
Melissyl alcohol	Cuba	—
Phytosterol	Cuba	—
Stigmasterol	Formosa (?)	—
Syringic acid	Formosa (?)	—
Odorants		
Molasses odor fraction	Cuba, Hawaii	—
Inorganic components	Louisiana	13.46[3]
	Cuba	13.76[3]

SOURCE: Binkley and Wolfrom (1953).

[1] Total solids in the molasses.
[2] Number of bacteria per milliliter of molasses.
[3] Carbonate ash.

ses flavor. Flavor profiles will depend on the severity with which the cane is crushed and milled, the clarification and evaporation procedures used in the process, and curing conditions of the blends in warehouses or plants.

Standards—Four USDA Standards (1959) exist for sugar cane molasses: Grade A (U.S. Fancy), B (U.S. Choice), C (U.S. Standard), and D (Substandard). Factors of quality include required percentage of minimum Brix solids, percentage of minimum total sugar and sulfites, and percentage of maximum ash. The minimum Brix solids for all grades is 79.0%. Total sugar varies from 63.5% for Grade A to under 58% for the Substandard Grade D. Ash increases from a maximum of 5% for Grade A to over 9% for Grade D. Color and flavor are also part of the sugar cane molasses Standards and will affect grading.

Beet Molasses—Juice is extracted from sugar beets by the diffusion process. This results in a

TABLE M-11

COMPOSITION OF CANE AND BEET MOLASSES

Constituents	Normal Beet Molasses (%)	Final Cane Molasses (%)	Cane Refinery Molasses (%)
Dry substance	76–85	77–84	78–85
Total sugar as invert sugar	48–58	52–65	50–58
C	28–34	—	28–33
N	0.2–2.8	0.4–1.5	0.08–0.5
P_2O_5	0.02–0.07	0.6–2.0	0.009–0.07
CaO	0.15–0.7	0.1–1	0.15–0.8
MgO	0.01–0.1	0.03–0.1	0.25–0.8
K_2O	2.2–4.5	2.6–5.0	0.8–2.2
SiO_2	0.1–0.5	—	0.05–0.3
Al_2O_3	0.005–0.06	—	0.01–0.04
Fe_2O_3	0.001–0.02	—	0.001–0.01
Total ash	4–8	7–11	3.5–7.5

SOURCE: Honig (1963).

juice of higher quality than the one crushed from sugar cane. Whereas final blackstrap cane molasses contains about 30% pure sucrose, the sugar amount is much higher in final beet molasses (approximately 60%). It is the absence of reducing sugars in beet which results in the high purity of these molasses. Dilution with water, followed by precipitation with calcium oxide to form the insoluble tricalcium sucrate, permits an almost complete recovery of sucrose. Tricalcium sucrate, which is recycled with the incoming hot beet juice releases sucrose during this process. Certain impurities, however, will accumulate during this process and, thereby, retard sugar crystallization. Therefore, limited quantities of the circulating final molasses must be discarded in order to maintain the sugar yield. These products are called discard molasses and they have a high protein content.

Other Molasses—Hydrol is the mother liquor from the final crystallization of dextrose. In addition to corn starch, other cereal grains can be converted to dextrose. The final mother liquor of successive crystallization of dextrose is then called grain sorghum molasses.

Constituents and Composition of Cane and Beet Molasses

The constituents of cane final molasses are summarized in Table M-10 and the composition of cane and beet molasses is shown in Table M-11. These tables show that great differences exist between the two types of molasses.

Cane molasses is usually slightly acid with a pH between 5.7 and 6.5 due to the presence of free organic acids. It contains invert sugar but no raffinose; and its ash content is different from that of beet due partly to the different refinery processes.

Beet molasses has higher nonsugars than cane, particularly nitrogenous material. There is practically no invert sugar present in this product but some raffinose. Its pH ranges between 7.6 and 8.6.

Vitamins and Minerals—The vitamin content will depend on the beet and cane variety, as well as the processing steps. In general, cane molasses has more vitamins than beet molasses. Some analytical findings are given in Table M-10.

Iron and calcium salts are present in molasses. To a certain extent, their concentrations will also depend on manufacturing practices.

Uses

The major utilization of molasses is in feeds, the second largest group comprises the manufacture of organic chemicals by fermentation and the production of yeast, and the third group includes incorporation of edible molasses into foods.

Food Products—Consumption of edible molasses is continuously decreasing. Whereas about 90 million pounds per year were consumed in 1940, only approximately 65–70 million pounds were incorporated into food products in 1970. The largest consumption of edible molasses is in the baking industry where the flavor imparts a pleasant note to bread, cakes, and cookies.

In addition to flavor, this product will also act as a humectant and maintain freshness in baked goods. Such an effect will depend on formulation and the level of molasses. Chocolate flavors are enhanced when small amounts of molasses are added to baked goods or chocolate drinks.

In addition to baked goods, edible molasses are often incorporated into baked beans and make appetizing glazes for sweet potatoes and meats such as hams.

Toffees and caramels often contain molasses to round out their flavor.

There are many recipes that have been developed by manufacturing companies which extend the list of foods containing this sugar cane product.

Feeds—Molasses is a major raw material for animal feeds. Some of it is mixed with roughage to produce silage and a wide variety of other feeds. Extensive literature on animal feeding indicates that molasses plays an important role as a carbohydrate source to the animal and, for this reason, the molasses buyer is interested in total sugars and solids, in addition to the presence of certain key inorganic ash constituents.

Industrial Uses—*Yeast*—The production of baker's and brewers' yeast requires both cane and beet molasses. Procedures for sterilizing and clarifying molasses became more streamlined to permit larger and faster yeast production.

Alcohol and Fermentation Chemicals—Although large quantities of molasses have been used for alcohol production, its further utilization in this field is gradually declining due to considerable price fluctuations. Other fermentation chemicals using molasses as an energy source are itaconic acid, citric acid, and possibly others.

Future Uses—One of the greatest future potentials for molasses is in the area of feed stuff. A variety of feeds containing blends of ammoniated or urea-treated molasses have been given to ruminants with excellent success.

ALFRED LACHMANN

References

ANON. 1962. Molasses Classics—For Modern Cooks. SuCrest Corp., New York.

BINKLEY, W. W., and WILFROM, M. L. 1953. Composition of Cane Juice and Cane Final Molasses. Sci. Rept. Ser. *15*, Sugar Research Foundation, New York.

HONIG, P. 1963. Principles of Sugar Technology, Vol. 3. American Elsevier Publishing Co., New York.

SPENCER, L. L., and MEADE, G. P. 1955. Cane Sugar Handbook. John Wiley & Sons, New York.

U.S. Dept. of Agr. 1959. U.S. Standards for Grades of Sugarcane Molasses. USDA Agr. Marketing Serv. Nov. 16.

Cross-reference: *Sugars and Sweeteners.*

MOLECULAR DISTILLATION

Like other distillation processes molecular distillation is a separation method based on vapor pressure differences of materials. Its special features include optimization of conditions to encourage free passage of vaporized molecules to a condenser without prior collisions that would tend to reflect molecules back to the evaporating surface. This is generally accomplished with equipment designed to minimize the distance between the evaporating surface and the condenser surface and provide a high degree of vacuum within the space between these surfaces. Ideally, this evacuated space represents a distance equal to or less than the mean free path of vaporized molecules.

The mean free path of vaporized molecules of a substance represents the average distance that these molecules will travel before they collide with one another. Collision causes premature condensation, return to the evaporating surface, and a reduction in general efficiency of the distillation process. The mean free path can be calculated from the kinetic properties of gases. It is directly proportional to temperature and inversely proportional to pressure and the square of molecular diameter.

Besides collisions of molecules of the same species with one another, evaporating molecules of a material being distilled also may collide with molecules of air ahead of the condenser. This is largely eliminated by the high vacuum (of the order of 0.001 mm or less of total pressure) characteristic of molecular distillation. For efficiency, molecules also must be given sufficient energy to reach the condenser in preference to returning to the evaporating surface. This is optimized by maintaining a maximum temperature differential between the evaporator and the condenser and minimizing physical barriers in the path to the condenser.

Molecular distillation is used in the food industry by processors of fats and oils. The principles of molecular distillation also apply in the special case of ice sublimation and therefore have been incorporated in the design of advanced freeze drying systems. Difficult separations in the manufacture of flavor compounds are made possible by molecular distillation but the method has found only limited use here due to the availability of other effective separation procedures.

In the fats and oils industry large-scale molecular distillation is used for the separation of mono glycerides approaching 100% purity from reaction mixtures of mono-, di-, and triglycerides resulting when fats are reacted with excess glycerol. Other commercial separations from bulk oils by molecular distillation include vitamin A from fish oils tocopherols (vitamin E) from vegetable oils, and to a lesser extent separation of sterols including vitamin D. A principal advantage of molecular distillation is its ability to separate heat-sensitive materials at temperatures below those normally required for conventional distillation processes. This is because of the special design features of molecular stills including the use of high vacuum.

In the case of freeze drying, sublimation rate of water vapor from the food's ice front, and thereby drying rate, is increased by several of the conditions that favor efficient molecular distillation. The driving force for sublimation is produced by maintaining a maximum temperature differential between the frozen food and a condenser that is consistent with the prevention of ice melting under high vacuum conditions. Ideally, the condenser is placed as close to the subliming ice front as is possible, which in some equipment designs is achieved by including refrigerated condenser plates or drums within the vacuum drying chamber. Whether the condenser surface is within or outside of the vacuum chamber sublimation rate from the frozen food decreases as ice builds up on the condenser surface and raises its temperature relative to that of the condenser refrigerant. Ice removal may be achieved by a variety of methods including mechanical scraping of the condenser surface, defrosting with an antifreeze spray, or use of duplicate condensing units so that one condenser may be defrosted while the other is in operation. As an alternate to a refrigerated condenser surface some freeze-drying systems employ high efficiency steam ejectors to remove sublimed water vapor from the drying chamber.

NORMAN N. POTTER

Cross-reference: *Distillation.*

MUSHROOMS

See Fungi as Food.

MUSTARD

See Rape and Mustard in India.

MYCOTOXINS

Molds may cause disease either by actual invasion of animal tissue by living fungal cells or through the production of poisonous metabolites. Poisonous compounds produced by molds are called mycotoxins and the resulting disease a mycotoxicosis. Molds growing on foods can produce mycotoxins which may remain in the food product and cause illness even though the mold itself is killed by sterilization.

The majority of raw food materials and animal feeds are susceptible, in various degrees, to growth of mold contaminants at some stage during growth, harvest, processing, or storage. The damage to foods by molds can be of considerable economic importance. In the past, the occurrence of molds on foods and feeds was generally regarded simply as a nuisance rather than as a potential health hazard. Since 1960, increasing attention has been given to the significance of toxic substances produced by mold contaminants to the safety of foods. As research in the mycotoxin area expands, it is becoming evident that a wide assortment of chemical toxins can be produced by a variety of the approximately 100,000 mold species known.

The first mycotoxicosis to be recognized was ergotism, sometimes known in past centuries as "St. Anthony's Fire." The disease is caused by the ingestion of grain, especially rye, infected with the mold *Claviceps purpurea.* Human poisoning by ergot in grains has been recorded for several centuries. The chemical substances produced by the mold which are responsible for the syndrome were isolated and identified in the 1930's. Six alkaloids, all derivatives of lysergic acid, cause the characteristic ergotism symptoms of gangrene of the limbs, convulsions, hallucinations, and abortion. Understanding of the relationship between ergotism and grain contaminated with *Claviceps purpurea* has made it possible to largely eliminate this hazard from the human food supply. Government regulations now stipulate the extent of this contamination that will be tolerated on the market.

Another serious human mycotoxicosis was first reported in Russia in 1913. Outbreaks have been reported occasionally since then. In certain areas, over 10% of the human population was affected and mortality was high. This mycotoxicosis, which has been given the name alimentary toxic aleukia, is associated with the ingestion of millet grain on which molds of the genera Fusarium and Cladosporium have proliferated. Several mycotoxins have been isolated and identified from infected millet. These cryophilic molds grow in temperatures as low as $-10°C$. Toxin production is favored at near freezing temperatures. The alimentary toxic aleukia mycotoxins are not destroyed by cooking.

Species of Fusaria also attack corn, wheat, and barley. *Fusarium nivale, F. poae, F. culmorum,* and *F. moniliforme* have been shown to produce mycotoxins which cause emetic symptoms. Strains of *F. trinctum* are capable of producing several mycotoxins on infected corn. Symptoms typically involve hemorrhage and shedding of the intestinal mucosa. Certain other Fusaria species produce mycotoxins with potent estrogenic activity. One of the best known of these is the mycotoxin zearalenone produced by the mold *Gibberella zeae* (perfect form of *F. graminearum*). One milligram of this substance produces swollen mammary glands and vulvo-vaginitis in swine.

In 1960, scientific interest and public concern with mycotoxins began to develop rapidly. That year, serious outbreaks of high mortality struck poultry flocks in England. Nearly 100,000 birds died within a few months in the initial outbreaks. The cause of the deaths was soon traced to toxic substances in the peanut meal feed. The spectacular reports of thousands of mortalities and the large economic losses involved prompted a great deal of activity among scientists. Within a year, the source of the toxic substances was traced to the mold *Aspergillus flavus* that had grown on the peanut meal feed. The toxic chemicals were called aflatoxins (*A. flavus* toxins).

The aflatoxins are now the most studied mycotoxin of all. Since its discovery in 1960, there have been nearly 1500 scientific papers published concerning the aflatoxin problem. Because of the extensive work which has been done on aflatoxins and their significance in the human food supply, the chemistry, the toxicity, and methodology for determining aflatoxins will be discussed in more length than for other mycotoxins. Similar investigations are underway with many other mycotoxins and many of the techniques learned from the extensive research on aflatoxins can be applied to the new mycotoxins.

The chemistry of the aflatoxins was elucidated by scientists at the Massachusetts Institute of Technology who found four closely related compounds. These substances were termed aflatoxin B_1, B_2, G_1 and G_2. The letter B denoted the compounds with a blue fluorescence and the letter G those with green fluorescence under ultraviolet light.

Two types of toxicity must be considered when evaluating the hazards associated with aflatoxins. The earlier studies on the biological effects of aflatoxin concerned its short term lethal potential. Hemorrhage of the intestinal tract and necrosis of the liver were the symptoms most commonly observed. The toxicity varies with different animals. The LD_{50} for a single oral dose of aflatoxin is between 0.36 and 10 mg per kg body weight for most animals. Aflatoxin B_1 is the most toxic followed by G_1, B_2 and G_2 in decreasing order of potency.

When aflatoxin B_1 is fed to mammals, related toxic compounds, aflatoxin M_1 and M_2, can be recovered from the milk. The M_1 and M_2 aflatoxins are also found in the liver and urine of animals ingesting aflatoxin B_1. Like the other aflatoxins, aflatoxin M_1 and M_2 have both acute toxic and carcinogenic properties.

The carcinogenic properties of aflatoxins ingested over longer periods, first observed in 1961, are now well-established. Tumors of the liver were produced in rainbow trout fed only 2 parts per billion aflatoxin B_1 in their diet. The effective dose of aflatoxin B_1 for liver tumor induction in rats is approximately 10 μg per day. Compare this potency with other well-known liver carcinogens such as butter yellow (9000 μg/day) and dimethylnitrosamine (750 μg/day). Aflatoxin B_1 is one of the most potent chemical carcinogens known.

Aspergillus flavus and *A. parasiticus*, the orga-

Aflatoxins B_1, B_2, G_1, and G_2.

nisms which produce aflatoxins, have an almost universal geographical distribution and are capable of producing toxins on a wide variety of agricultural products. Some agricultural products in which aflatoxin has been reported are:

Barley	Peas
Brazil nut	Peanuts
Bean	Peanut butter
Cassava	Pepper
Cocoa bean	Raisin
Cocoa products	Rice
Coconut presscake	Sesame
Copra	Sorghum
Corn	Soybean meal
Cottonseed	Sweet potato
Cowpea	Wheat
Millet	Wheat flour

A number of techniques have been developed for the detection of aflatoxins in agricultural products. After extraction by suitable organic solvent, such as chloroform, and cleanup of the extract to remove interferring compounds, thin-layer chromatographic separation of the aflatoxins provides the basis for extremely sensitive analytical determination of these mycotoxins. As mentioned previously, the aflatoxins exhibit an intense blue or green fluorescence when exposed to long-wave ultraviolet light. As little as 10^{-10} gm of aflatoxin can be detected on a thin-layer chromatogram. Determination of the intensity of the fluorescence of the aflatoxin spot with a fluorodensitometer permits considerably better quantitative accuracy than visual comparison of sample and standard spots. Analytical procedures applicable to many agricultural products have been developed (J. Assoc. Offic. Anal. Chem., *49*, 229; *50*, 214; *51*, 485; *52*, 405).

Several species of Aspergillus other than *A. flavus* are capable of producing mycotoxins on agricultural products. Although less toxic than aflatoxin B_1, sterigmatocystin, which is also carcinogenic, has been found in foodstuffs. The structure of sterigmatocystin is closely related to that of the

Sterigmatocystin

aflatoxins. It is produced by *A. flavus*, *A. versicolor*, and *A. nidulans*. Ochratoxin A, discovered

in 1965, is a mycotoxin produced in cultures of moldy corn infected by the mold *A. ochraceus*.

The ochratoxins

	R_1	R_2
Ochratoxin A	H	Cl
Ochratoxin B	H	H
Ochratoxin C	Et	Cl

A. ochraceus has been isolated from stored wheat, grain sorghum, and corn and is capable of producing toxin on all of these substrates. The toxicity of ochratoxin A is probably about $1/10$ that of aflatoxin. Its carcinogenic potential is still uncertain. The related metabolites, ochratoxin B and C, are nontoxic. *Aspergillus chevalieri* is often involved in spoilage of rice. A hepatotoxin, xanthocillin, has been isolated from toxic strains

Xanthocillin

Gliotoxin

of *A. chevalieri* and also certain strains of *Penicillium notatum*. Some strains of *A. chevalieri* produce another mycotoxin, gliotoxin. There have been additional reports of toxicity of Aspergillus species in which the toxic factors have not yet been identified. Some cultures of *A. wentii* and *A. amstelodami* were found to be toxic to a number of animals by investigators in South Africa.

The mycotoxin, patulin, is produced by a variety of mold species and is known by numerous synonyms, clavatin, expansin, penicidin, clavacin, mycoin, and tercinin. *Penicillium patulum*, *P. claviforme*, *P. expansum*, *P. cyclopium*, *P. griseofuluum*, *P. uriticae*, *P. melinii*, *P. divergens*, *P. lapidosum*, *P. equinum*, *P. leucopus*, *P. novaezie-*

landiae, Byssochlamys niver, Aspergillus clavatus, A. giganteus, and *A. terreus* are known to produce patulin under proper conditions. Many of these species are known to be present in foods and feeds.

Patulin

P. expansum causes rot in apples during storage and patulin is frequently found in rotted apples, sometimes at fairly high concentrations. Patulin producing strains of *A. clavatus* have been isolated from wheat flour. Although patulin was once considered for treatment of colds and skin infections, it is now known to have decidedly toxic properties to animals as well as being a potent carcinogen.

Species of Penicillia are rather frequently associated with mycotoxin formation. Islanditoxin is a powerful carcinogenic hepatotoxin produced by *Penicillium islandicum.* It can cause hemorrhage,

Islanditoxin

liver damage, and rapid death. Islanditoxin is one of the most potent of several mycotoxins asso-

Luteoskyrin

ciated with the "yellow rice" toxicosis caused by mold-damaged rice. The LD_{50} of islanditoxin for mice is 0.3 mg by intravenous injection and 6.5 mg by oral ingestion. Luteoskyrin is a much less potent toxin also produced by *P. islandicum.* Luteoskyrin can cause extensive liver damage. *P. citrinum* which produces a toxic metabolite, citrinin, also commonly occurs on improperly stored rice. Citrinin causes lesions primarily in the

Citrinin

kidney. *P. citreoviride* produces a mycotoxin, citreoviridin, which has been associated with rice

Citreoviridin

samples that caused fatal nervous disorders. A lethal dose in rats caused paralysis followed by death. Smaller doses caused swelling of the liver and kidney, hemorrhage, and nervous disorders. *P. cyclopium* is a widely distributed mold often found on stored grains. It is the major cause of spoilage in stored garlic. The principal toxic agent isolated from this mold, cyclopiazonic acid has

Cyclopiazonic acid

caused tremors, paralysis, and death in ducklings and rats.

Soviet scientists have isolated a toxic factor produced by the mold *Stachybotrys atra* which produces disease in both animals and man. As little as 8 oz of moldy straw produced an acute response in horses. Blood clotting mechanisms are almost completely impaired and the number of white blood cells is drastically reduced. Widespread necrosis of tissues and general hemorrhaging are observed.

The consumption of millet grains contaminated by certain strains of *Rhizopus nigricans* causes a human disease termed epidemic polyuria. The symptoms of thirst, weakness, and anorexia have occassionally been followed by death.

A somewhat different type of mycotoxicosis is sometimes observed. The invasion of living plants by certain molds may result in the production of toxic substances in the infected plant tissue. The toxin is produced only by the plant-mold association and not by either organism alone. An example of this which has caused medical problems in humans is the growth of the mold *Sclerotinia sclerotiorum* on celery. Workers in celery fields who contact the mold-infected (pink-rot) celery, often suffer rashes and lesions of the skin. The skin disorder is caused by xanthotoxin, a mycotoxin which sensitizes the skin to light. As little as 10 μg per sq in. of this toxin when applied to skin exposed to light will cause a definite dermatitis.

Many other toxic mold metabolites are known. This discussion has been limited to a sampling of those that appear in human food products. When the known mycotoxins affecting livestock are considered the number swells rapidly. In addition, the toxic principals involved in many outbreaks are still unidentified.

This discussion of mold toxins should not be taken to condemn the presence of molds in all food products. The use of molds for food preservation and production of flavor is an ancient practice. Mold-fermented soybean products have been produced in the Orient for thousands of years. Mold-ripened cheese was prized in ancient Rome. Certainly during the trial and error development of many of these traditional mold-produced food products, problems with mycotoxins must have been encountered. Methods and procedures which produced toxicity were noted and rejected as the process evolved. None of the fermented foods in which molds are intentionally utilized has proven to be a hazard.

The solution to mycotoxin problems resides primarily, then, in elimination of unintentional contamination by possibly hazardous molds during harvest, storage, and processing of foods and feeds. The first step in controlling mycotoxin outbreaks is, of course, a recognition and awareness of the problem. When large numbers of animals die, such as in the 1960 aflatoxin outbreak, the problem receives widespread attention of scientists, public health officials, and the general public. Often, however, sublethal poisoning by mycotoxins

may have equal or even greater economic significance. To a large poultry farmer, for example, a 1% or less decrease in growth rate can create a large economic loss. More important, a number of the mycotoxins are potent carcinogens at dosages considerably below their acute toxic level. In many areas of the world, food customs include the consumption of foods that are usually molded because of either poor storage conditions or the preparation of fermented foods under uncontrolled conditions with ill-defined innocula. There has been considerable speculation associating moldy diet components in humans with illness, high incidence of cancer, etc. The importance of mycotoxins in this regard can only be answered through extensive surveys for the presence of mycotoxins in diets of affected populations.

Once the problem is recognized, a program must be initiated to eliminate the mycotoxin from the food supply. The most effective control would be elimination or minimization of the growth of fungal contaminants on the products. Generally, proliferation of molds occurs during conditions of high humidity and temperature. Each mycotoxin-producing mold has a specific temperature and humidity requirement for growth and elaboration of toxin. It should be kept in mind that the optimum conditions for toxin production may not necessarily be those for optimum growth. Toxic strains of Fusaria responsible for the mycotoxicosis alimentary toxic aleukia can produce toxins at or below freezing temperatures. Knowledge of the environmental conditions necessary for growth and toxin production by the mold, when properly established through research, can be valuable in establishing measures for control of the mycotoxicosis. Improved harvest methods followed by rapid drying can do much to minimize mold contamination.

If ideal cultivation, harvest, and storage methods could be followed in every case, there would be no need to develop means for detoxifying food products. However, with the present state of technology, some contamination of agricultural commodities by molds is inevitable. Underdeveloped areas, where there is the greatest shortage of food, generally have the least sophisticated agricultural technologies. Therefore, methods of detoxifying mycotoxin-contaminated crops have been and will continue to be developed.

Physical separation methods are already used successfully in separating aflatoxin-contaminated peanuts and cottonseeds. Photoelectric sorters eliminate aflatoxin-contaminated seeds on the basis of their fluorescence color. Depending on the stability properties of a given mycotoxin, treatment with heat, extraction by suitable solvents, or destruction through chemical reaction may be successful in removal or destruction of the mycotoxin. Mere disappearance of the mycotoxin after treatment is not sufficient to establish that the product has been detoxified. Detoxification methods should be followed by biological assays with the "detoxified" product since there is a possibility that heat or chemical treatment could convert the mycotoxin into a different but still toxic substance. The possibly deleterious effect of the treatments on the nutritional properties of the food must also be considered.

A satisfactory effort at mycotoxin control must include checks on the quality of mycotoxin-susceptible products. This requires suitable rapid and sensitive assay methods for the mycotoxin under consideration. For such well-known mycotoxins as aflatoxin, many methods have been developed for assays from a wide variety of types of agricultural products. The search for accurate, rapid analytical methods for many of the other mycotoxins must be continued.

PHILIP E. KOEHLER

References

BAMBURG, J. R., STRONG, F. M., and SMALLEY, E. P. 1969. Toxins from moldy cereals. J. Agr. Food Chem. *17*, 443–450.

GOLDBLATT, L. A. (Editor) 1969. Aflatoxin. Food Sci. Technol. Ser. 7 Monographs. Academic Press, New York.

SCOTT, P. M., and SOMERS, E. 1969. Biologically active compounds from field fungi. J. Agr. Food Chem. *17*, 430–442.

WOGAN, G. N. 1969. Alimentary mycotoxicosis. *In* Food-Borne Infections and Intoxications. H. Rieman (Editor). Food Sci. Technol. Ser. 5 Monographs. Academic Press, New York.

N

NATIONALITY FOODS

Nationality foods in the context of the American cuisine are distinctive foreign foods that for one reason or another have come into use in the United States and Canada. There are a number of reasons for the success of foreign foods, or perhaps one should say foreign dishes, in America. In the first place, borrowing ideas from other nations is an ancient and universal practice. The early settlers in the Americas borrowed a number of foods and modes of their cookery from the Indians. The Spaniards and the Portugese, the first to come into close contact with the natives, incorporated such indigenous foods as potatoes, tomatoes, and corn into their dietary and, along with the foods, methods of cooking them.

Many foreign dishes were introduced into the United States and Canada by immigrants from Europe who, naturally enough, were accustomed to the cuisine of their native lands. Thus it is that the Dutch, the French, the Germans, the Scandinavians, the Italians, and the Greeks, and Russians in Europe; the Chinese and Japanese in the Far East; the Southeast Asians; the East Indians in Asia; the Australians and the Africans—all have made contributions to the American menu. But although they "naturalized" a number of native dishes, that did not assure their acceptance by the American public. Their acceptance came about by the intrinsic appeal of these foods—their flavor, their novelty, and in some cases their status value. One evidence of this last is the frequent appearance of foreign dishes on the menus of gourmet restaurants.

Foreign dishes are sometimes holiday foods. Smørgås delicacies are widely served during the Christmas and New Year festivities. Pizzas adorn many a teenager party. Numerous other examples could be cited. Foreign foods have been extensively promoted by food processors and, to a very considerable extent, they are now part and parcel of the American diet.

Our ancestors got along with a few basic foods and in the past none but the well-to-do ever ventured to try foreign dishes. The order of things has changed remarkably in this century and dozens of foreign foods have become naturalized, as mentioned. Some, like pizza, have swept the nation in popularity. The simplest explanation for this is that not only are the flavors of these foods novel and appealing but they are readily available and, for the most part, convenient to use. Today, recipes for these nationalized foods may be found in almost every cookbook.

Only limited space can be given here to nationality foods; a selection of representative foods and a brief identification of each is all that can be attempted.

Soups

Bouillabaisse—a chowder of French origin that includes, usually, several kinds of fish (white fish, mullet, sole, etc.).

Minestrone—an Italian soup based on beef, bacon, and ham, several vegetables, Parmesan cheese, and spaghetti, macaroni or rice.

Vichyssoise—a potato soup, originated in France, that owes its flavor not only to the potato component but to chicken broth, leeks, onion, celery, and chopped chives.

Entrées

Beef Stroganoff—as the name indicates the main ingredient is beef, top round or tenderloin, to which is added butter, onion, mushrooms, sour cream, salt, pepper, and Worcestershire sauce.

Chicken Cacciatore—chicken, to which is added chopped onion, garlic, canned tomatoes, white wine, parsley, cooked noodles, olive oil, salt, and pepper. It is cooked in a skillet.

Chinese Chop Suey—chop suey can be prepared from a number of meats—pork, veal, and chicken being perhaps the most common. The meat is cut into narrow strips and to this is added assorted vegetables, soy sauce, rice or noodles. Traditionally, the vegetable-meat mixture is "stir-cooked" in a pan of Chinese origin called a "wok."

Egg Foo Young—this dish, although it contains eggs, is composed of many other ingredients: water chestnuts, onions, tomatoes, bean sprouts, ground beef, mushrooms, monosodium glutamate, soy sauce, and other seasonings.

Gnocchi—a nonmeat main dish, it is composed of baking potatoes, flour, and grated Parmesan cheese.

Hasen Pfeffer—based on rabbit, this dish includes a considerable number of seasonings: vinegar, sugar, salt, cloves, pepper, onion, and sour cream.

Sauerbraten—boneless beef chuck is perhaps the most common beef cut used. Boiling water, to which vinegar, peppers, bay leaf, and salt have been added, is poured over beef and sliced onion and allowed to stand for two days. The meat is then lifted and browned in a skillet, after which the liquid in which the meat was soaked plus sour cream are poured into the skillet and all is simmered for as much as two hours. Traditionally, it is served with potato dumplings.

Entrées Based on Cereals

Lasagne—this dish has achieved great popularity in the United States and elsewhere in the world. It is composed of a filling of several cheeses (Mozzarella, Ricotta, grated Parmesan) and a tomato and meat sauce in which the flavor of tomatoes predominates. It is a baked dish.

Pizza—pizza is almost too well-known to require a definition. It is probably sufficient to describe it as of Italian origin composed of a bread-like crust covered with a spiced tomato sauce topped with one or a combination of foods: cheese, Italian sausage, ground beef, anchovies, onions, green pepper, and perhaps other vegetable concoctions.

Breads and Cakes

Kolachy—a Bohemian bun topped with various fillings, prunes, apricots, and cottage cheese being the most common.

Lebkuchen—a holiday cookie consisting of candied orange peel, candied cherries, honey, blanched almonds, candied citron, cloves, nutmeg, and cinnamon.

Mandel Kakas—a pressed cookie whose major flavor is that of almonds.

Other Delicacies

Crepes Suzette—very thin dessert pancakes, rolled up and sprinkled with powdered sugar; often served with brandy sauce. When rolled up with a creamed meat filling, they are also served as an entrée.

Vol-au-vents—large patty shells filled with a stew of meat, poultry, egg yolks, or other hearty food. A pastry rather than a dessert.

The foregoing is a random sampling of the many foreign foods that have migrated to and been adopted by the United States and other nations of the world during and prior to the 20th Century.

MARTIN S. PETERSON

Cross-references: *Ghee; Food: What Man Eats; Tamale; Koumiss, Kosher Foods.*

NECTARINES

The nectarine is a peach without the hairy fuzz. This smooth, handsome fruit has been known for over 2000 yr and is represented by several dozens of varieties throughout the world, some cling and some freestone, and some white and some yellow-fleshed. In the United States, practically all the commercial production of some 10,000 acres of nectarines is in the San Joaquin Valley of California. More than $1/2$ of this production is grown in Fresno County. Some 30 yr ago the principal varieties were Gower, John Rivers, Staniwick, and Quetta; but these have been replaced in recent years by the Le Grand selections—Early Sun Grand, Late Le Grand, Le Grand, and Sun Grand. From a total production of 65,000–70,000 tons, only 1000 tons are processed. The total return for the crop is about 10 million dollars.

For the fresh market, the fruit must be harvested by hand several times during the season in order to ship them at the proper maturity. The divided, two-layer, egg case has been popular for protecting the fruit from damage during shipment. The packing operations as well as the handling for canning are similar to those used for peaches. Nectarines may be dried or frozen, too, using the criteria and conditions listed for peaches.

FRANK P. BOYLE

Reference

PHILIP, G. L., and DAVIS, L. D. 1946. Peach and nectarine growing in California. Calif. Agr. Ext. Serv. Circ. *98.*

NEW FOOD PRODUCTS: DEFINITIVE DESCRIPTION

New food products have been coming on the market for generations but never in such volume as today. The motivation for the development of new products is a composite of incentives—competition for a share of the market, the consumer's desire for convenience of use, weight-consciousness, improved appearance, a better or a novel flavor, nutritional benefits, and other incentives including an obvious motivation, the simple urge to innovate.

Whether the term "new food products" is definitive or not need not concern us here, a "new" food product has come to mean one that has not existed before in precisely the same form. Some new products are strikingly unusual; others owe their "newness" to a gadget or a contrivance that changes the original form of the food only moderately. Although it is not possible to provide an explicit meaning for the term, a working definition can be developed by considering the things done to foods to change them.

To make his food products more appealing to the consumer is of primary concern to a processor. The incentive here is plain—to capture a share or a larger share of the market. Since there is no single consumer, nor a prototype of all consumers, appeals vary and new products are usually geared to a particular type of consumer. The elderly consumer, for example, has preferences that differ widely from those of athletically inclined youths. New food products appear frequently in the dietetic category. New foods for infants, new foods for the aged, new foods for the overcorpulent, new foods for invalids—the list is long. A governing principle in the development of dietetic foods is to ameliorate the deprivation, whatever it may be, with an acceptable substitute or a compensating ingredient. Thus, since foods high in protein are clearly less fattening than foods high in carbohydrate and/or fat, foods designed for use in reducing diets increase the protein percentage and seek, in addition, to give the food an image that connotes special benefits.

Another "newness" appeal is to change their form in such a way as to make them more easily prepared, or ready to eat without preparation, or more portable, or more stable in storage. Convenience foods have attained such popularity that new food products in this category appear on the market every year. The governing principle here is to complete as much of the preparatory kitchen labor as possible in the food plant. The introduction of instantized foods some years ago started a trend that has not yet run its course. Another factor that enters into convenience foods is packaging, the effort here being characterized by an intent to make the package serve additional purposes beyond that of containing the food. Changing the form of the ingredients, for example, freeze drying the components of a vegetable soup, is yet another factor utilized to give a traditional product an aspect of newness. Dehydrated mixes of all sorts have come onto the market within the last generation, all of them "new" if we define that term as a departure from the traditional.

There are a number of technological innovations in foods that can truly be said to yield new food products. One example of several is imitation ham made from vegetable proteins, fats, and carbohydrates; it is remarkably close to the natural product. The research and development that has gone into deriving edible proteins from petroleum can also be clearly labeled as an effort reaching toward utilizing a new food source.

But with the exception of explorations into areas of the type just mentioned, new food products are pretty much the result of changing the form or the texture, or modifying the flavor of foods, or combining the attributes of a food in a new way. An example of the latter is combining two flavors, e.g., apple and cranberry, in a juice. Processes can also be combined, e.g., partial dehydration and canning.

New product ideas are not accepted without careful inspection and tests of consumer appeal. Market testing is a costly business but a new product must face this trial. Since older, established products do not need to undergo this trial, any product submitted to market testing might be considered to be, implicitly, a new product.

MARTIN S. PETERSON

NOMOGRAPHIC CHARTS

Nomographic charts are used as a rapid means of determining relationships among the properties (or qualities) of materials. In its simplest form it is a chart in which a straight line intersecting two or more scales will indicate the values that satisfy a given equation. The principle involved goes back to Descartes, but it is only within this century that nomographs have gained wide usage. Nomographs contribute in substantial degree to simplifying a fundamental problem in science and technology; namely, to learn precisely how one quantity or quality varies with any other or others on which it depends. One example of scores is the variation in quality, with time and temperature, of a stored food. One of the great advantages of nomographic charts is that they can be used even by those who are not mathematicians.

Although it is simple to use, the construction of a nomograph involves much more than a nodding acquaintance with mathematics. A first requirement is a clear understanding of the equation or set of conditions on which the nomograph is to be founded. A second requirement is a knowledge of the linear range of the variables; and a third, the

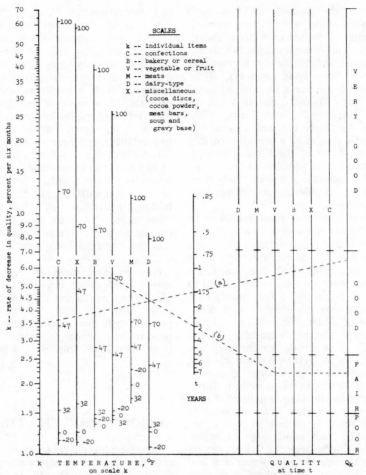

FIG. N-1. NOMOGRAM OF TEMPERATURE, TIME, AND QUALITY FOR THE MILITARY RATION ITEMS USED IN LONG-TERM STORAGE TESTS

Use of the nomogram (as illustrated by dotted lines):

(a) The k values given for storage of individual items may be used with scales k, t, and Q_K. For example, a k value of 3.5% per 6 months resulted in a quality level in the upper range of "good" after 1.5 yr of storage, as shown by the point at which the Q_K scale is intercepted by a straight-edge passing through 3.5 on the k scale and 1.5 on the t scale.

(b) The scales for types of products are used in matched pairs. For example, vegetable or fruit products stored at 70°F (corresponding to an average k value of 5.5 as shown) for 3 yr had an average quality rating in the upper range of "fair," since the V scale for quality is intercepted at this level by the line passing through 70 on the V temperature scale and on 3 on the t scale.

determination of the proper unit intervals for scaling the variables.

In the example given in Fig. N-1, the dependent variable quality is a function of time and temperature. The rate of decrease in the quality of a given food varies with the food.

The authors of the treatise in which this nomograph occurs worked out the rate of decrease for numerous foods. Two examples illustrating how the nomograph works are presented; see dotted lines (a) and (b) in Fig. N-1. It will be noted that there are six vertical lines for the measurement of quality. The reason for this is that dairy, meat, vegetables, baked goods, miscellaneous items, and confections have different rates of deterioration.

MARTIN S. PETERSON

NUTRITION: FOOD COMPOSITION AND NUTRIENT ASPECTS OF FOOD PROCESSING

This review can in no way be comprehensive, but will merely survey the food man eats and nutrients contained therein in relation to the technology of food production. It will further draw attention to many defects in our present knowledge of this field and the need for broad coordinated research. Much of the confusion characterizing the present status of our knowledge is due to either (1) lack of precision in analytical techniques, (2) inadequate data, or (3) poor coordination of the research being conducted in many laboratories. With food processing being broadly defined to include all treatments of a foodstuff from place of production to the point of consumption, then about 95% of our food is processed. This article can only hope to deal briefly with the nutritional effects of the processing of foods as they are prepared for ultimate consumption. Most foods must at least be trimmed and cooked to make them more palatable and nutritious. In addition, some foods involve microbiological and insect hazards and must be treated to make them safe and acceptable. Also, many foods do not keep well and must be milled, pasteurized, canned, refrigerated, frozen, dehydrated, or packaged so that they may be stored and transported to urban areas. Food processing is, accordingly, essential for the feeding of an urbanized population.

The review will begin by briefly discussing the essential nutrients, then by reviewing the nutritive value of major foods as background information to an understanding of the changes that take place during processing, preparation, and storage of raw as well as of processed products. Finally, the significance relative to public health will be discussed in summarizing certain basic principles which are often too little heeded.

Water

Water (moisture) in the strict sense does not contribute to the nutritive value of foods, but is important in describing food composition and therefore, to some extent, in assessing nutritive value. Energy values vary inversely with water content. Obviously, as water content increases, protein, fat, and carbohydrates that contribute to the energy value of foods decrease proportionately.

Moisture content nonetheless is, in marketing terms, a most critical food ingredient. Adulteration

TABLE N-1

MOISTURE CONTENT OF FOODS

	%		%
Lettuce	94–95	Eggs (edible portion)	74
Mushrooms (canned)	93	Broilers	71
Watermelon	92.6	Salmon (canned)	70–65
Cabbage, spinach	92	Turkey (meat)	64
Soups (ready to serve)	92–84	Sausage	62
(condensed)	90–72	Beef	61–65
Green beans	90	Macaroni (cooked)	60.6
Yoghurt	88–89	Tuna (canned)	60–61
Berries	88–83	Hamburger	55
Orange juice	87.5	Corned beef (lean)	54
Milk (cow)	87	Cheddar cheese	37
Apples, pears	83–84	White bread	34
Cod (fillet)	81–82	Biscuits	28
Clams, oysters	81–80	Jams, marmalades	27–28
Peaches, pineapple	80–87	Doughnuts	24
Potatoes	79	Honey	20
Shrimp	78	Butter and margarine	15.5
Cottage cheese	76.5	Peanuts	5.6
Fryers	76–77	Cookies	3.8
Bananas	75	Nuts	3.1–3.5
Halibut	75	Breakfast cereals	2–3
Shrimp	75	Candy	1–2

of foods is most often associated with water—such as the dilution of milk, absorbed water in poultry and other meats, etc.

Moisture is further important in comparing results from different analyses on the same food. Food samples may vary considerably in gross composition, due to varieties, soil, to the amount and kind of fertilizers used, and to rainfall, and, additionally, depending on crop´ years, season, storage condition, and other factors. Comparison of food samples of varying moisture content is not valid unless analyses are expressed on the basis of comparable dry weight of the sample. The moisture content of some representative foods is given in Table N-1.

Protein

Muscle tissues of different animal species commonly consumed differ little as to their protein content. There is a slight preponderance of protein in chicken meat, closely followed by fish, and then by other meats. The biological availability of these proteins is all in the range of 75% or higher. Lysine is in excess in meat proteins but methionine may be the limiting amino acid. Whole milk protein has a slightly higher quality than meat due to

the presence of more sulfur-containing amino acids in lactoglobulin and lactalbumin (about $\frac{1}{5}$–$\frac{1}{4}$ of the total protein in milk). The most prevalent milk protein, casein, by itself is equivalent in protein quality to that of most other animal proteins, and along with lactalbumin is generally considered the standard.

The proteins of eggs are so well-proportioned in their amino acid composition that the whole egg is also often taken as a reference standard for comparing the quality of protein based upon amino acid composition.

Regardless of the species, the amino acid composition of the proteins in muscle tissue foods is relatively constant and of such balance and quality that red meats, fish, and poultry rank only slightly below eggs and milk protein in their ability to effect tissue synthesis. The proteins in legumes and nuts are of somewhat lesser quality than animal proteins because the amounts of methionine and lysine are below optimum levels. Cereal proteins rate generally lower, and certain proteins such as gelatin are significantly inferior (see Fig. N-2).

Tryptophan and methionine are the primary limiting amino acids in beef. Soybean is deficient in sulfur-containing amino acids, whereas corn meal is most limited in tryptophan. The availability

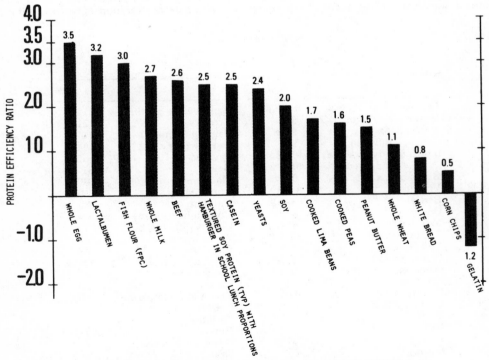

FIG. N-2. PROTEIN QUALITY OF VARIOUS TYPE OF FOODS

of amino acids in food ultimately determines the nutritive value of protein. Thus, the degree to which food proteins are digested and the constituent amino acids absorbed and metabolized are critical factors in determining the biological value of protein foods. Most animal proteins are digested well, while plant proteins, due to being encapsulated by plant fibrous materials principally cellulose, hemicellulose and lignins, are as a consequence less well-digested. This is true even in

TABLE N-2

MILLIGRAMS OF AMINO ACID CONTENT PER 100 GRAMS OF NITROGEN IN EDIBLE PORTION OF FOODS

	Lysine	Tryp-tophan	Threo-nine	Methio-nine	Total S-acids	Leucine	Iso-leucine	Phenyl-alanine	Valine
Milk	49.6	9.0	29.4	15.6	21.3	62.6	40.7	30.9	43.8
Cheese, cheddar	46.8	8.7	23.7	16.6	20.2	62.2	43.0	34.2	45.8
cottage	53.6	6.7	29.8	17.6	23.1	68.5	37.1	34.4	36.7
Casein	50.4	8.4	26.9	19.4	21.8	63.2	41.2	33.9	46.5
Lactalbumin	58.8	14.3	34.0	14.6	36.7	80.1	40.3	28.3	36.9
Eggs	40.0	10.3	31.1	19.6	34.2	55.0	41.5	36.1	46.4
Beef	54.6	7.3	27.6	15.5	23.4	51.2	32.7	25.7	34.7
Lamb	50.6	8.1	28.6	15.0	23.2	48.4	32.4	25.4	30.8
Pork	51.3	8.1	29.0	15.6	22.9	46.0	32.1	24.6	32.5
Chicken	54.9	7.6	26.6	16.3	24.7	45.2	33.0	24.6	30.7
Fish	54.8	6.2	27.1	18.2	26.6	47.2	31.7	23.2	33.3
Shrimp	45.3	5.6	25.2	17.7	31.9	56.3	32.4	29.2	30.7
Beans	46.4	5.8	27.1	6.3	12.5	53.7	35.5	34.5	37.9
Blackeye peas	40.7	6.0	24.6	9.6	17.7	46.8	30.3	32.7	35.3
Peas	45.8	6.6	24.1	7.5	15.6	51.7	35.2	31.5	35.0
Peanuts	22.3	6.9	16.8	8.5	14.9	38.0	25.7	31.6	31.1
Soybeans	39.5	8.6	24.6	8.4	19.5	48.2	33.6	30.9	32.8
Almond	16.2	4.9	17.0	7.2	17.7	40.5	24.3	31.9	31.3
Brazil nuts	16.8	7.1	16.0	35.7	54.8	42.8	22.5	23.4	31.2
Pumpkin seed	24.2	9.6	16.0	9.9		41.8	29.8	30.0	28.8
Sesame seed	16.0	9.1	19.4	17.5	31.1	46.1	26.1	40.0	24.4
Buckwheat	36.7	8.8	24.6	11.0	23.2	36.5	23.5	23.6	32.4
Corn, including meal, grits	18.0	3.8	24.9	11.6	19.7	81.0	28.9	28.4	31.9
Corn flakes	11.9	4.0	21.2	10.4	22.1	80.8	23.6	27.3	29.8
Hominy	25.7	6.0	22.7	7.1	x	58.2	25.1	23.9	28.6
Tortilla	15.6	3.3	25.3	12.0	x	101.2	37.2	27.2	37.8
Zein	—	4.0	19.2	10.9	17.2	123.6	31.9	64.6	25.4
Oats	21.4	7.5	19.3	8.6	21.3	43.7	30.1	31.1	34.7
Rice	23.5	6.4	23.3	10.7	18.8	51.3	27.9	29.9	41.6
Rye	23.8	6.6	21.6	9.2	20.8	39.2	24.8	27.5	30.4
Wheat	16.0	7.2	16.8	8.9	21.7	39.1	25.3	28.8	27.0
Flour	13.0	7.0	16.4	7.5	18.9	43.9	26.2	31.3	24.6
Wheat germ	35.3	6.1	30.9	9.3	15.9	39.3	27.1	20.9	31.4
Gluten	10.9	6.1	15.1	9.9	22.2	42.7	26.2	31.0	27.0
Macaroni, spaghetti	18.4	6.7	22.2	8.6	19.4	37.8	28.6	29.8	32.4
Shredded wheat	19.1	4.9	23.4	8.0	19.8	39.5	25.9	27.8	33.3
Lima beans (frozen)	39.5	8.1	28.2	6.7	13.6	50.4	38.3	32.4	40.4
Peas (canned or frozen)	29.5	5.2	22.9		11.8	39.0	28.7	24.0	25.6
Cassava	25.8	8.1	17.2	3.9	10.8	25.7	17.4	17.5	19.0
Potatoes (white)	33.3	6.7	24.6	7.8	13.8	31.1	27.4	27.6	33.4
Taro	36.3	11.5	29.4	7.0	x	55.6	32.5	32.5	37.5
Sweet potatoes	29.5	10.9	29.4	11.6	21.6	35.8	30.1	34.8	46.8
Yeast	12.2	5.4	15.6	9.6	x	41.0	33.6	30.8	26.8

TABLE N-3

NUTRIENT CONTENT OF RED MEATS, POULTRY, AND FISH

	Chicken	Nonfatty Fish	Herring	Beef	Lamb	Pork
		Per Ounce (28.35 Gm) Raw Meat				
Protein (gm)	5.9	4.5	4.5	4.2	3.7	3.4
Fat (gm)	1.9	0.1	4.0	8.0	8.8	11.4
Calories (kcal)	41	19	54	89	94	116
Calcium (mg)	3	1	28	3	3	3
Iron	0.4	0.3	0.4	1.1	0.6	0.3
Vitamin D (mg)	—	—	6.38	—	—	—
Vitamin A (mg)	—	—	13	—	—	—
Vitamin B_1 (mg)	0.01	0.02	0.01	0.02	0.04	0.28
Vitamin B_2 (mg)	0.05	0.03	0.09	0.06	0.07	0.06
Niacin (mg)	1.7	0.8	1.0	1.4	1.4	1.4
Pantothenic acid (mg)	0.19	0.06	0.28	0.11	0.14	0.17
Vitamin B_6 (mg)	0.28	0.06	0.13	0.08	0.09	0.14
Biotin (mg)	2.83	2.83	x	0.85	0.85	1.1
Folic acid (mg)	0.85	14.1	x	2.83	0.85	0.85
Vitamin B_{12} (mg)	x	0.28	2.83	0.56	0.56	0.56
Vitamin E (mg)	0.06	x	x	0.17	0.23	0.19

cases where the amino acid composition of the protein is somewhat favorable.

Excess lysine to supply its inadequacy in cereals is readily available in animal products and to some degree in pulses (peas, beans, and lentils). Sulfur-containing amino acids are inadequate in most foods with the exception of eggs, whey proteins, sesame seed, and certain nuts.

Table N-2 gives the amino acid content of a wide variety of foods and Table N-3 gives the nutrient content of meats generally regarded as high protein foods.

Fat

The fatty acids in beef, veal, and lamb are more saturated than those in pork, poultry, and fish.

TABLE N-4

FATTY ACID CONTENT OF CERTAIN FATS (WEIGHT PERCENTAGE)

		Milk Fat	Human Milk Fat	Coconut Oil	Soybean Oil	Corn Oil	Cottonseed Oil
Saturated fatty acids							
Butyric	(C_4)	3.5	0.4	—	—	—	—
Caproic	(C_6)	1.4	0.1	0.8	—	—	—
Caprylic	(C_8)	1.7	0.3	5.4	—	—	—
Capric	(C_{10})	2.6	2.2	8.4	—	—	—
Lauric	(C_{12})	4.5	5.5	45.4	—	—	—
Myristic	(C_{14})	14.6	8.5	18.0	0.4	0.2	1.4
Palmitic	(C_{16})	30.2	23.2	10.5	10.6	9.9	23.4
Stearic	(C_{18})	10.5	6.9	2.3	2.4	2.9	1.1
C_{20} and higher		1.6	1.1	0.4	2.4	0.2	1.3
Total saturated		70.6	48.2	91.2	15.8	13.2	27.2
Unsaturated fatty acids							
Palmitoleic	$(C_{16}\text{-}2H)$	5.7	3.0	0.4	1.0	0.5	2.0
Oleic	$(C_{18}\text{-}2H)$	18.7	36.5	7.5	23.5	30.1	22.9
Linoleic	$(C_{18}\text{-}4H)$	2.1	7.8	—	51.2	56.2	47.8
Linolenic	$(C_{18}\text{-}6H)$	—	0.4	—	8.5	0.0	—
C_{20} and C_{22} unsaturated fatty acids		0.9	—	—	—	—	—
Total unsaturated		29.4	48.0	7.9	84.2	86.8	72.8
Iodine value		32.9	—	8.7	132.6	126.0	105.0

Depending upon the diet of the animal, pork and poultry may contain appreciable amounts of linoleic acid which is regarded as an essential dietary constituent. Fatty acids in fish are more highly unsaturated, with a more generous proportion of linoleic and other polyunsaturated fatty acids with quite lengthy carbon chains, up to 24 carbon atoms. Table N-4 gives approximate fatty acid content of various contributors of fat to the diet.

Some legumes, such as peas and beans, are very low in fat, but soybeans and peanuts provide liberal amounts. An important proportion of their fatty acids is polyunsaturated.

The meat group is the principal source of cholesterol in the diet, but this lipid is not uniformly present in all meats. Other animal products such as egg yolk, organ meats, and shellfish are the outstanding sources. Table N-5 gives the cholesterol content of some common foods.

Calcium

Milk in all forms (skimmed, flavored, or cultured) is the outstanding source of calcium in U.S. diets. Most cheeses are good sources of calcium, and to a lesser extent so are cottage cheese and ice cream (Table N-24). Without dairy products, a satisfactory intake of calcium is extremely difficult to attain. They account for 75% of the daily calcium intake, with breads and cereals a distant second (7.5%). The U.S. Recommended Daily Allowance of calcium is 1000 mg. Foods other than dairy products do not generally contribute more than 200 mg calcium daily. Certain green

TABLE N-5

CHOLESTEROL CONTENT OF FOODS

	Food Item (A)	Amount of Cholesterol in		
		100 Gm, Edible Portion (B)[2] (Mg)	Edible Portion of 1 Lb as Purchased (C) (Mg)	Refuse from Item as Purchased (D) (%)
	Beef, raw:			
a[1]	With bone	70	270	15
b[1]	Without bone	70	320	0
	Brains, raw	>2,000	>9,000	0
	Butter	250	1,135	0
	Caviar or fish roe	>300	>1,300	0
	Cheese:			
	Cheddar	100	455	0
	Cottage, creamed	15	70	0
	Cream	120	545	0
	Other (25–30% fat)	85	385	0
	Cheese spread	65	295	0
	Chicken, flesh only, raw	60	—	0
	Crab:			
a	In shell	125	270	52
b	Meat only	125	565	0
	Egg, whole	550	2,200	12
	Egg, white	0	0	0
	Egg yolk:			
	Fresh	1,500	6,800	0
	Frozen	1,280	5,800	0
	Dried	2,950	13,380	0
	Fish:			
a	Steak	70	265	16
b	Fillet	70	320	0
	Heart, raw	150	680	0
	Ice cream	45	205	0
	Kidney, raw	375	1,700	0
	Lamb, raw:			
a	With bone	70	265	16
b	Without bone	70	320	0
	Lard and other animal fat	95	430	0
	Liver, raw	300	1,360	0

TABLE N-5 (*Continued*)

Food Item (A)	100 Gm, Edible Portion (B)[2] (Mg)	Amount of Cholesterol in Edible Portion of 1 Lb as Purchased (C) (Mg)	Refuse from Item as Purchased (D) (%)
Lobster:			
a Whole	200	235	74
b . Meat only	200	900	0
Margarine:			
All-vegetable fat	0	0	0
Two-thirds animal fat, one-third vegetable fat	65	295	0
Milk:			
Fluid, whole	11	50	0
Dried, whole	85	385	0
Fluid, skim	3	15	0
Mutton:			
a With bone	65	250	16
b Without bone	65	295	0
Oysters:			
a In shell	>200	>90	90
b Meat only	>200	>900	0
Pork:			
a With bone	70	260	18
b Without bone	70	320	0
Shrimp:			
a In shell	125	390	31
b Flesh only	125	565	0
Sweetbreads (thymus)	250	1,135	0
Veal:			
a With bone	90	320	21
b Without bone	90	410	0

[1] Letters a and b designate items that have the same chemical composition for the edible portion but differ in the amount of refuse.

[2] Data in column B apply to 100 gm of edible portion of the item, although it may be purchased with the refuse indicated in column D and described or implied in column A.

leafy vegetables are important sources when eaten frequently. Canned salmon or sardines with the bones, clams, oysters, and shrimp are likewise good sources, but they are not eaten with sufficient frequency. Meats and cereal grains are poor in calcium. The use of nonfat dry milk and whey blends in bread enhances its calcium value to the diet. Calcium is also an optional enrichment ingredient in flours and breads.

Two acids (oxalic and phytic) present in some foods restrict the relative availability of calcium. Spinach and rhubarb contain oxalic acid. This acid combines with calcium to form nonabsorbable salts. On the other hand, lactose (milk sugar) enhances calcium absorption.

Cereals contain phytic acid which also binds calcium. Conventional milling removes much of this acid. Through the tendency towards higher flour recovery from the grain by higher extractions levels in milling or even more by grinding whole

kernels, the calcium availability is reduced and sometimes jeopardized.

Magnesium content of foods generally follows calcium and, recently, increasing attention is attached to this mineral element. Tables N-6 and N-7 give the Ca and Mg contents respectively of some common foods.

Trace Elements

An increasing number of trace elements have been established through research as essential to life as well as to normal human nutrition. The previous list of essential trace elements—iron, copper, iodine, and zinc—has in the last 25 yr been lengthened by cobalt, molybdenum, manganese, chromium, fluorine, vanadium, and selenium. Despite much research effort expended upon analyses for such elements in foods, our knowledge in this

TABLE N-6

CALCIUM CONTENT OF SOME TYPICAL FOODS

	Household Measure	Calcium (Mg)	Percentage of Adult Daily Allowance[1]
Milk, fresh	1 cup	288	36
Milk, nonfat dry	3 tblsp	288	36
Cheese (cheddar)	1 oz	219	27
Salmon, canned	3 oz	167[2]	21
Clams or oysters	½ cup	113	14
Shrimp	3 oz	98	12
Ice cream	⅛ qt	87	11
Cottage cheese, uncreamed	3 oz	78	10
Broccoli, cooked	½ cup	66	8
Whole egg	1 medium	27	3
Cabbage, raw, shredded	½ cup	25	3
Carrots, cooked	½ cup	24	3

[1] Recommended Daily Dietary Allowance of calcium for the adult is 800 mg.
[2] Includes bones packed with salmon.

TABLE N-7

MAGNESIUM IN FOOD
(MG PER 100 GM EDIBLE PORTION)

Wheat germ	336	Cheese	45
Brewers' yeast	231	Shrimp	42
Brazil nuts	225	Banana	33
Peanuts	206	Salmon (canned)	27–30
Beans (dry)	170	Peas (frozen)	24
Pecan nuts	142	Beef	21–25
Whey (dried)	130	Asparagus (raw)	20
Dates	58	Bacon	12
Sweet corn	48	Apples (peeled)	5

field is quite rudimentary particularly as to toxic limits, minimum requirements, occurrence in both raw and processed foods, and the amount of these elements as impurities in food additives, flavors, etc. Their role in the predisposition to infections or in sustaining glandular functions and metabolic processes requires much further systematic study. Special interest is currently being attached either to the cancer-protecting effect or conversely the carcinogenic effect of certain trace elements. Requirements of individual trace elements may vary greatly with bodily conditions. Far more attention by way of comparison has been directed towards the area of water and air trace mineral pollutants entering into foods. Examples of such contaminants are lead, nickel, mercury, cadmium, platinum, vanadium, titanium, selenium, etc.

Trace elements remain a major quantitative problem area as to food composition and few meaningful data can be listed. Newer analytical methodology should result in a better knowledge of trace mineral composition and nutrient requirements. The entire field of dietary trace mineral requirements is complicated by the mounting occurrence of trace elements in the drinking water supply. Trace elements may also enter foods as migrants from packaging materials containing such elements as major components, or residues. Most obvious is the transfer of iron, tin, zinc, aluminum, and occasionally cadmium from metal cans. The composition of the water used in processing may also affect the food composition in regard to trace element level.

It is characteristic that attention was first focussed on this major field through trace mineral deficiency diseases in crops, then in livestock, and lastly in man. Trace element supplements (iron, zinc, cobalt, magnesium, and, more recently, selenium), have become common procedure in the feeding of livestock. Goiter was the first disease condition where a trace element, iodine, was early incriminated, first by demonstrating its deficiency in soil, plants, and animals and finally in humans.

Suboptimal effects, though not clinically overt, may be equally significant such as in the case of vitamin deficiencies. The converse might also be true as to concentrations between nutritionally optimum levels and toxic maxima. Fluorine has a very narrow range between the required level and the toxic level. It is essential to bone formation, with drinking water being a principal source. Fluoridation programs aim at guaranteeing a minimal intake to assure sound dental growth. Drinking water containing 1 ppm supplies 1–2 mg per

TABLE N-8

ESSENTIAL TRACE ELEMENTS

Trace Element	Average Intake for Man (μg/Day) and Biological Function(s)	Circumstances Predisposing to a Deficiency in Man
Cobalt (Co)	300(150–600). Essentiality and entire functional significance attributed to its relationship with vitamin B_{12} (cyanocobalamin).	Not evident.
Chromium (Cr)	50–120. Trivalent Cr serves as a cofactor for peripheral action of insulin. Necessary for normal glucose utilization. Complexes with proteins and stimulates several enzyme systems. May stabilize certain nucleic acid structures. Stimulates synthesis of fatty acids and cholesterol in liver.	May be a nutritional problem for the geriatric population and in pregnancy. Unlike most other trace elements, tissue levels of Cr in the U.S. decrease with age. Cr deficiency may be related to the increased incidence of diabetes mellitus in later life. Indirect evidence linking Cr deficiency with atherosclerosis.
Copper (Cu)	2000–5000. Constituent of several enzymes. Aids in absorption and utilization of iron. Role in electron transport, connective tissue metabolism, and nervous system development.	Pure Cu deficiency in man is probably unknown, but it does occur in conjunction with other nutritional deficiencies—kwashiorkor, sprue, nephrotic syndrome.
Iodine (I)	65–529. Integral component of thyroid hormones, thyroxine and triiodothyronine, hormones important in determining rate of basal metabolism.	Insufficient intake of I from diet and water supplies can lead to simple goiter.
Fluorine (F)	710–3400. Probably essential for man. Growth factor in rats. Protection against dental caries. Possibility that dietary F is essential for optimal bone structure and prevention of osteoporosis and aortic calcification in the aged. Known to activate certain enzymes (e.g., adenyl cyclase) and inhibit others.	Insufficient intake from diet and/or especially water supplies.
Manganese (Mn)	2000–3000. Several essential functions in each cell. Specific role in synthesis of mucopolysaccharides of cartilage. Necessary for activation of many enzymes. Can biologically substitute for iron in heme molecule. Involved in melanin formation.	Mn deficiency has not been observed in man. Low Mn intakes and stress conditions (e.g., pregnancy) may lead to a subclinical Mn deficiency. Modern food habits tend to favor foods with low Mn concentrations.
Molybdenum (Mo)	100–400. Constituent of two intracellular flavo-protein enzymes: xanthine oxidase (involved in formation or uric acid) and aldehyde oxidase (necessary for oxidation of aldehydes). These enzymes interact with cytochrome C in the electron transport system. Possible role in iron utilization.	Not evident.
Nickel (Ni)	300–600. Probably essential for man. Essential for chicks. May be involved in the following: hormonal action, structure and metabolism of membranes, nucleic acids and proteins, enzymes (e.g., *in vitro* activation of liver arginase), and skin and hair pigmentation.	Not evident.

TABLE N-8 (*Continued*)

Trace Element	Average Intake for Man (μg/Day) and Biological Function(s)	Circumstances Predisposing to a Deficiency in Man
Selenium (Se)	Unknown. Role linked in some cases with vitamin E and sulfur amino acids. Se acts as an antioxidant protecting cell membranes. Se may be important in red blood cell formation in humans. Implicated, but not proven, as a possible protective agent against human stomach cancer.	May be a complicating factor in certain types of kwashiorkor.
Silicon (Si)	Unknown. Probably essential for man. Essential for chicks and rats. Involved in early stages of bone development and formation of cartilage matrix. Associated with rapidly developing tissue. Chondromucoprotein is high in Si.	Not evident.
Tin (Sn)	1500–3500. Probably essential for man. Essential growth factor for rats. Trivalent Sn forms coordination complexes. May contribute to the tertiary structure of proteins and nucleic acids. May function as active site of metalloenzymes.	Not evident.
Vanadium (V)	1000–4000. Probably essential for man. Essential for chicks and rats. Catalyst in several biological systems. Promotes mineralization of teeth. May exchange with phosphorus in apatite tooth substances. May inhibit cholesterol synthesis.	Not evident.
Zinc (Zn)	10,000–15,000. Integral part of several metalloenzymes (e.g., carbonic anhydrase which is necessary for maintenance of acid-base balance, alkaline phosphatases, alcohol dehydrogenases). Involved in a wide range of cellular activities and the process of RNA, DNA, and protein synthesis. Possibly involved in wound healing as Zn may be essential for synthesis of skin keratin and collagen. Involved in production and function of several hormones. Constituent of insulin. Role in reproduction.	A severe form of Zn deficiency found in Middle East causes dwarfism and delayed sexual development. Inadequate dietary Zn and an intake of phytate which renders Zn unavailable have been incriminated. Conditioned Zn deficiency is a possible feature of a number of clinical syndromes (e.g., alcoholic cirrhosis), stress, geophagia, use of drugs with Zn-chelating properties, and diets limited to vegetable sources of protein.

day. Among food sources, only ocean fish and tea carry this trace element in meaningful dietary amounts.

In contrast, iodine is not present in significant amounts in water or food, generally occurring only in meaningful quantities in ocean fish. By use of fertilizers, iodine can be channelled into grain and vegetables and through animal feed supplements into eggs and milk. Common table salt is used almost exclusively as a vehicle for iodine fortification of food. Some iodine reaches the consumer in the developed countries by the use of iodates in break making, but there is a lack of knowledge as to the adequacy of this input in the iodine deficiency situation in certain segments of the world population.

Table N-8 gives information on essential trace elements found in average diets, and Tables N-9, N-10, N-11, N-12 and N-13 give specific data on Fl, Co, Cu, Mn, and Zn contents of certain foods.

Vitamins

The roles of vitamins in nutrition were dis-

TABLE N-9

FLUORINE CONTENT OF FOODS

Micrograms/100 Gm Edible

Mackerel (fresh)	2690	Honey	100
(canned)	1210	Veal	90
Sardines (canned)	730–1610	Radishes	80
Cod (fresh)	700	Onions	60
Salmon (canned)	450–900	Chocolate	50
Shrimp (canned)	440	Chocolate milk	50–200
Herring (smoked)	350	Rhubarb	40
Crabmeat	200	Filberts	30
Cheese	162	Beef	29–200
Butter	150	Tomato	24
Chicken	140	Bananas	23
Tea (beverage)	120–6200	Milk	10–55
Frankfurters	167	Tuna (canned)	10
Eggs	118	Oranges	7–17

TABLE N-11

COPPER IN FOOD

Micrograms/100 Gm Edible

Liver (beef)	2450	Eggs	230–253
Mushrooms	1790	Bread (white)	205
Oysters	1200–2700	Dates	200–400
Filberts	1350	Bananas	200
Brazil nuts	1300	Cornflakes	200
Chocolate	1100–2700	Spinach	197
Lemon	970	Sweet potato	184
Drybeans	960	Potato (white)	160
Crayfish	700	Almonds	140–1200
Avocados	450–690	Cucumbers	90
Shrimp	430	Beer	70–130
Rainbow trout	330	Milk (whole)	30
Walnuts	300–1000	Sugar	20
Artichokes	300		

covered, not by their presence in the diet but by their absence.

A distinction needs to be made, however, between the metabolic disturbances that occur when a particular vitamin is so minimal in the diet as to cause deficiency disease symptoms and the less dramatic, but nevertheless demonstrable, effects of suboptimal or supraoptimal levels. More and more attention is being devoted to the positive effects of amounts well above minimum requirements (the megavitamin phenomenon).

Niacin.—Establishing niacin requirements is complicated by two facts. This vitamin can be synthesized by bacteria in the intestinal flora, and it can further be derived in the tissues from the amino acid tryptophan. Many bacteria synthesize this and other B vitamins and thus human feces may contain more niacin than was present in the food consumed. Some diets are more favorable for this synthesis than others as, e.g., a vegetable diet in contrast to a meat diet. This relationship may even determine whether or not a deficiency disease such as pellagra occurs.

TABLE N-10

COBALT CONTENT OF FOODS

Micrograms/100 Gm Edible

Lettuce	70–110	Cabbage	7–24
Buckwheat	35	Potato	6
Figs	20	Walnuts	5
Pears	18	Apricots	3
Onions	13	Green peas	3
Liver (beef)	10.5	Rice (white)	0.6
Spinach	10–120	Cherries	0.5
Tomatoes	10	Milk	0.06
Wax beans	10.0		

The amino acid, tryptophan, acts as a precursor substance from which niacin can be formed in the body. If sufficient tryptophan is consumed along with the protein fraction of foods, niacin may no longer be essential in the dietary—all the niacin required is made within the body.

Diets high in corn (maize) increase the incidence of pellagra in man. It was once believed that corn might contain a toxic factor. But, following the discovery that tryptophan was an effective substitute for niacin, it developed that the presence of three conditions was responsible for the detrimental effect of corn: (1) the low amount of niacin, (2) the low amount of tryptophan, and (3) a dietary imbalance caused by the presence of relatively large amounts of other amino acids in proportion to tryptophan making less of this amino acid available for conversion to niacin. Corn is characterized by a low content of both niacin and tryptophan as compared to wheat, as follows:

Per 100 Gm	Niacin (Mg)	Tryptophan (Mg)
Whole wheat	4.3	168
Whole corn	2.0	55

Some foods such as wheat, therefore, have far greater pellagra-preventing potency than would be expected from their niacin content. Other examples are milk and eggs, both of which are low in niacin but contain proteins high in tryptophan. One milligram of niacin may be formed from each 60 mg of tryptophan in the diet. A quart of milk daily, for instance, suffices to prevent pellagra, although its content of niacin is relatively low, as is demonstrated by the following calculations:

TABLE N-12

MANGANESE IN FOOD

Micrograms/100 Gm Edible

Oatmeal	49.5	Spinach	8.3
Avocados	42.0	Bananas	6.4
Filberts	42.0	Beets	5.8
Bread (whole meal)	38.0	Egg solids	5.5
Cacao	31.0	Strawberries	5.1
Blueberries	20.2	Prunes (dried)	4.4
Peas (dry)	19.9	Sweet potato	4.1
Dry beans	15.0	Liver (beef)	3.9
Lettuce	12.4	Snap beans	3.3
Rice (white)	10.1	White bread	3.1

Milk (1 Qt)

	Actual Content (Mg)	Niacin Potency (Mg)
Tryptophan	480	8.0
Niacin	1.0	1.0
	Total	9.0

Ascorbic Acid (Vitamin C).—Ascorbic acid occurs predominantly in its reduced form in most fresh vegetables and fruits, but on storage, varying amounts of dehydroascorbic acid are formed. Food composition Tables frequently recognize only reduced ascorbic acid (given values being then too low). One exception is frozen food, where the figures, due to the original analyses, mostly represent total ascorbic acid.

Reported values for this vitamin therefore, as a rule, show greater variation than those of other vitamins. Under a variety of conditions of food handling, final irreversible oxidation to diketogluconic acid of no nutritive value may occur.

Vitamin A.—Vitamin A values represent both the preformed vitamin and carotene precursors. Evaluation of vitamin A values from plant sources is complicated by the fact that not all of the precursors are biologically active as vitamin A and even those that are active may vary considerably in biological potency.

The International Unit (IU) of vitamin A is the equivalent of 0.30 μ of all *trans*-vitamin A alcohol, 0.344 μ all *trans*-vitamin A acetate, and 0.60 μ β-carotene. Other vitamin A precursors have even a lower potency than β-carotene. The Food and Nutrition Board's Recommended Daily Allowance for adults is 1.5 mg or 5000 IU and is considered to be provided by 1.2 mg (4000 IU) of beta-carotene and 0.3 mg (1000 IU) of preformed vitamin A.

Vitamin D.—Vitamin D occurs in so few foods that analytical values are rarely reported in food

TABLE N-13

ZINC CONTENT OF FOODS

Micrograms/100 Gm Edible

Oysters	160	Peanut butter	2.0
Herring	70–120	Cherries (canned)	1.6–2.2
Egg solids	5.5	Pears (canned)	1.5–1.8
Maple syrup	5.2–10.5	Applesauce	
Nonfat milk		(canned)	1.2–1.4
solids	4.5	Carrots	0.5–3.6
Liver, beef	3.0–8.5	Spinach	0.3–0.9
pork	3.0–15	Butter	0.3
Peas (dry)	3–5	Strawberries	0.28
Beets	2.8	Potato	0.2
Egg yolk	2.6–4.0	Cabbage	0.2–1.5
Bread, wheat		Milk	0.4–3.0
whole wheat	2.4–3.5	Lettuce	0.1–0.7
white	2.4–3.5	Oranges	0.1
Beef	2–5	Mushrooms	0.03
Clams	2.0		

Tables. The few sources as, e.g., eggs, milk, and fish liver oils, vary widely in vitamin D content. There is some question as to whether this compound should be categorized as a vitamin, resembling a hormone in its function and origin.

Tables of Composition

Traditionally, Tables of food composition including data on energy, proximate composition, selected minerals and vitamins are published. The trend has been toward more detailed identification of nutrients present in foods often now including figures on sodium, potassium, magnesium, fatty acids, and cholesterol. Data of this nature, dealing with the composition of raw, processed, and prepared foods, has been published in USDA Agriculture Handbook 8. As new commercially processed foods become available, the task of keeping food composition data up-to-date becomes tremendous. Nevertheless, the USDA is undertaking a revision of Handbook 8. Table N-14 from Harris and Von Loesecke (1971) illustrates the relative stability of nutrients under various conditions. It also illustrates the complexity of considering nutrient composition of processed, stored, and prepared foods.

Nutrient Aspects of Food Processing

Cereals.—The kernel of the cereal grain is divided into three parts, the bran, germ, and endosperm. The aleurone layer just below the bran layer is sometimes identified as a fourth part. Cereal grains vary somewhat in composition yet average 12% protein, 2% fat, and 75% carbohydrate; the remaining 1% is constituted principally by the minerals. Cereals are especially rich in phosphorus and iron, and are a good source of the B-complex vitamins, in some cases particularly of thiamin.

TABLE N-14

STABILITY OF NUTRIENTS

Nutrient	Effect of pH			Air or Oxygen	Light	Heat	Range of Cooking Losses (%)
	Neutral pH 7	Acid <pH 7	Alkaline >pH 7				
Vitamins							
Vitamin A	S	U	S	U	U	U	0–40
Ascorbic acid (C)	U	S	U	U	U	U	0–100
Biotin	S	S	S	S	S	U	0–60
Carotenes (pro-A)	S	U	S	U	U	U	0–30
Choline	S	S	S	U	S	S	0–5
Cobalamin (B$_{12}$)	S	S	S	U	U	S	0–10
Vitamin D	S		U	U	U	U	0–40
Essential fatty acids	S	S	U	U	U	S	0–10
Folic acid	U	U	S	U	U	U	0–100
Inositol	S	S	S	S	S	U	0–95
Vitamin K	S	U	U	S	U	S	0–5
Niacin (PP)	S	S	S	S	S	S	0–75
Pantothenic acid	S	U	U	S	S	U	0–50
p-Amino benzoic acid	S	S	S	U	S	S	0–5
Vitamin B$_6$	S	S	S	S	U	U	0–40
Riboflavin (B$_2$)	S	S	U	S	U	U	0–75
Thiamin (B$_1$)	U	S	U	U	S	U	0–80
Tocopherols (E)	S	S	S	U	U	U	0–55
Essential amino acids							
Isoleucine	S	S	S	S	S	S	0–10
Leucine	S	S	S	S	S	S	0–10
Lysine	S	S	S	S	S	U	0–40
Methionine	S	S	S	S	S	S	0–10
Phenylalanine	S	S	S	S	S	S	0–5
Threonine	S	U	U	S	S	U	0–20
Tryptophan	S	U	S	S	U	S	0–15
Valine	S	S	S	S	S	S	0–10
Mineral salts	S	S	S	S	S	S	0–3

SOURCE: Harris and Von Loesecke (1971).

S = stable (no important destruction).
U = unstable (significant destruction).

Cereal protein is somewhat inferior to that of animal sources because some of the essential amino acids are present in smaller amounts than needed by man. Lysine is the chief limiting amino acid in wheat, rice, and corn, while tryptophan and threonine also are present in insufficient amounts in corn and rice, respectively. The aleurone layer protein is superior to that in the endosperm. The protein of the germ compares favorably with animal protein. These better-quality proteins are removed when cereals are refined. Even small amounts of milk, cheese, eggs, or meat consumed simultaneously with cereal foods, however, readily compensate for this deficiency. Recent knowledge of the amino acid composition of foods is making it feasible to develop mixtures of cereals and other plant foods so that the protein approaches the quality of animal proteins. Lysine has been added to some cereals and breads, although the need for

such supplementation of the U.S. diet has no been demonstrated.

The greater part of the minerals, particularly iron and phosphorus, and of the B-complex vita mins exists in the bran and germ of the grain, an is mostly lost in modern milling of wheat flour.

Cereal foods are the primary source of energy for much of the world's population. Many peopl imply from this fact that cereals per se are fatten ing, and so they attempt to omit or restrict thi group of foods from their diets. By such omissior they also lose the manifold benefits of other nu trients provided by the whole-grain or enriched products. The cereal foods contribute importantl to most nutrient needs except vitamin A, ascorbi acid, and calcium. Bread is, therefore, an im portant dietary constituent contributing to man nutrient requirements.

Cereals, a major source of energy (calories), gen

erally have a protein content of about 10%, with their major constituent being starch. Most cereal proteins are low in lysine and tryptophan, with millets, oats, and rye all slightly better than wheat, rice, or corn. Cereals are generally low in the nutritionally important element, calcium. Its concentration, along with that of other ash and vitamin constituents, is reduced in milling (see the section on Milling and Flour Making).

Fruits and Vegetables.—This food group is unique for its contribution to the ascorbic acid intake. Fruits are also a major source of vitamin A and make significant contributions to the iron level. Fruits are a fair source of certain other minerals and B-complex vitamins.

The composition of vegetables and fruits covers a wide range depending upon the part of the plant represented. Moreover, the handling of the food from farm to table may be so variable that the amounts of vitamins and minerals retained may well be either high or low. The vitamin concentrations of the unprocessed fruit or vegetable is affected by (1) variety, (2) fertilization, (3) season of harvest, (4) degree of maturity, (5) storage conditions, and (6) retail handling.

These foods play a relatively minor role in the total caloric content of the diet; the exception being that when potatoes, sweet potatoes, and bananas are consumed in quantity they may make an appreciable contribution in low-cost diets.

The protein content of most fresh vegetables ranges from 1 to 2% and is even lower in fruits. However, fresh peas, beans, and lentils are considerably higher in protein. All foods of this group are extremely low in fat with the exception of avocados and olives. The calories are conveyed primarily through starch, dextrin, and sugars.

Leafy vegetables are fair sources of calcium and carry fair to good amounts of iron. Apricots, raisins, prunes, dates, figs, peaches, and berries contain significant quantities of iron. Fruits and vegetables are rich sources of potassium, but the sodium content is negligible, except for a few vegetables such as beets, carrots, spinach, and celery.

Oranges, grapefruit, and lemons are good sources of ascorbic acid, as are strawberries, tomatoes, and pineapple. Cantaloupe and honeydew melons are intermediary. Less acid and sweeter fruits such as peaches, pears, apples, and blueberries contribute minor amounts. Exceptionally rich are black currants, rose hips, and cloudberries. These latter hold more ascorbic acid than oranges and serve the tundra Eskimoes as a potent source.

Broccoli, brussels sprouts, spinach, green peppers, and cabbage are good sources. Potatoes and bananas carry little ascorbic acid but when eaten in volume they may add appreciably to the total intake. In the dietaries of certain countries these staples may become a major source of vitamin A.

Dark-green leafy vegetables and deep-yellow vegetables and fruits are outstanding for their carotene content. When lightly colored they are poorer sources, although the outer green leaves of lettuce may contain 30 times as much vitamin A as the inner pale leaves. Most fruits are low in carotene. Exceptions to this are apricots, tomatoes, and peaches.

Meat.—The composition of meat varies from one cut to another within the U.S. Grade of the animal and from one species to another, largely due to the proportion of lean and fat tissue. The proportion of fat is greater in meat from older animals than in young animals; it is also higher in pork than in beef, and in lamb than in veal. Moreover, one cut of meat may be extremely lean, that from another part of the animal may be well marbled with fat—that is, tiny fat streaks are interspersed with the muscle fibers and inseparable from them.

Such considerations as the above do not necessarily modify the nutritive value of meat as consumed since (1) fat may be trimmed off and discarded before meat is cooked, (2) fat lost in drippings may not be used, and (3) surrounding fat on meat may be left as plate waste. Obviously, it is important to know the values for cooked meat as it is actually consumed (see Table N-15).

The mineral element of especial importance in the meat group is iron, all foods of this group being rich in iron. Light meats, including fish and light meat of poultry are somewhat lower in iron content than the red muscle meats of beef, pork, and lamb.

The fatty acids in beef, veal, and lamb are more saturated than those in pork, poultry, and fish. Depending upon the diet of the animal, pork and poultry may contain appreciable amounts of linoleic acid. Fatty acids in fish are more highly unsaturated with more generous proportions of linoleic and other polyunsaturated fatty acids.

TABLE N-15

VALUES OF BROILED T-BONE STEAK AS ACTUALLY CONSUMED

| | Per 100 Gm Broiled T-Bone Steak | | |
	Cal (Kcal)	Protein (Gm)	Fat (Gm)
Choice grade total edible	473	19.5	43.2
Separable lean	223	30.4	10.3
Good grade total edible	442	20.6	39.2
Separable lean	199	31.1	7.3

TABLE N-16

FATTY ACIDS IN FOODS

| | Total Fat | Saturated Fatty Acids | Polyunsaturated Fatty Acids | |
			Oleic	Linoleic
		100 Gm Edible Portions		
Milk				
Whole	3.7	2	1	tr
2% fat	2.0	1	1	tr
Canned, evaporated	7.9	4	3	tr
Dry, whole	27.5	15	9	1
Chicken				
Raw	4.9	2	2	1
Cooked (fried in				
vegetable shortening)	11.8	3	6	2
Eggs	11.5	4	5	1
Turkey	14.7	4	6	3
Hamburger	21.2	10	9	tr
Ham	26.6	10	11	2
Cheese (cheddar)	32.2	18	11	1
Peanuts	47.5	10	20	14
Almonds (shelled)	54.2	4	36	11
Walnuts	59.3	4	21	28
Brazil nuts	66.9	13	32	17

Table N-16 shows fatty acid types in a variety of foods. The meat group is the primary source of cholesterol in the diet, but this is not uniformly present in all flesh foods. Egg yolk, liver, brains, and shellfish are significant sources for persons who commonly consume these foods in considerable quantity. Meats are also rich in phosphorus, sulfur, potassium; moderately high in sodium; and low in calcium. There are surprisingly few differences between different kinds of meat when similar portions are compared. The four kinds of meat—pork, beef, veal, and lamb—may be used interchangeably on a protein, fat, and calorie basis. Some shellfish and salmon canned with the bones are richer in calcium. Saltwater fish also contains an appreciable amount of iodine.

All foods of the meat group are good sources of the B-complex vitamins. Pork, liver, and other organ meats are excellent for their thiamin content; poultry, veal, peas, and peanuts are rich in niacin. Vitamin B_{12} is supplied by organ meats, muscle meats, and all animal products to some extent, but it is not found in vegetable products.

Liver is an outstanding source of vitamin A; other organs such as the kidney contain some vitamin A. Otherwise, meats do not provide vitamin A.

Table N-17 gives comparative data representative of meat dishes with cheese included for comparison.

TABLE N-17

NUTRIENTS OF SOME IMPORTANT STAPLE FOODS IN THE DIETARY (100 GM EDIBLE PORTION)

	Water (%)	Cal	Protein (Gm)	Fat (Gm)	Calcium (Mg)	Vitamin A (IU)	Riboflavin (Mg)	Niacin (Mg)
Cheese (cheddar)	37	398	25	32	725	1,400	0.42	Trace
Beef (cooked)	51	319	24	24	10	—	0.18	4.2
Pork chop (centercut)	50	333	23	26	11	—	0.83	5.0
Tuna, canned (meat)	60	198	29	8	8	80	0.72	12.8
Ham (cooked)	42	400	24	33	11	—	0.24	4.7
Calf Liver (cooked)	51	261	30	13	13	32,700	4.17	16.5

Milk.—Milk is one of the most widely researched of all foods, with more than 100 separate components being identified. Presumably, all have one or another nutritional function.

The exact composition of milk varies with the breed of cattle, the feed used, and the period of lactation. Fluid market milk, however, is standardized, most often to a certain fat percentage although trends may be toward standardization of solids-not-fat. As a rule 1 cup of whole milk contains 8.5 gm of protein, 9 gm of fat, and 12 gm of carbohydrate, and provides 160 cal. Most market milk is now of a composition closer to that of Holstein milk. Skim milk contains the same level of protein and carbohydrate, but there is only a trace of fat, so that the energy value is about 90 cal per cup. Casein accounts for $4/5$ of the protein in milk, while various whey proteins, including albumins and lactoglobulins, constitute the remaining protein components. Whole milk is highly emulsified and easily digested. By homogenization the fat globules are further comminuted to give a more stable emulsion, avoiding the formation of a cream layer. This has had a tremendous impact on the salability of milk, guaranteeing the individual consumer a uniform composition. Milkfat contains a high proportion of short-chain fatty acids. About 60–70% of the fatty acids are saturated, 24–30% monosaturated, and 2–10% polyunsaturated. Lactose is the main sugar occurring in milk. This sugar favors the growth of lactic acid-producing bacteria which retard or prevent the growth of putrifying microorganisms. Lactose also favors the absorption of calcium and phosphorus, and the synthesis of some B-complex vitamins in the small intestine. Milk supplies several mineral elements abundantly. It is the chief dietary source of calcium. Phosphorus is present in correct proportion with calcium to support optimum skeletal growth. Milk contains appreciable amounts of sodium, potassium, and magnesium, but furnishes very little iron and copper so the infant's diet must be supplemented, particularly with iron, to prevent anemia. Milk is an outstanding dietary source of riboflavin and also supplies fair amounts of vitamin A, thiamin, vitamin B_6, and vitamin B_{12}. It is low in preformed niacin, but is an excellent source of tryptophan, which functions as a precursor of niacin. Most market milk is fortified with vitamin D to a level of 400 IU per qt, which is the Recommended Daily Dietary Allowance.

Fish.—Most fish are low in calories due to a low content of fat. Obvious exceptions are fatty fishes, like herring and sardine. A major part of the fat is removed through special processing, as, for example, from tuna, prior to canning. When packed in water, it compares well with red meats.

The chief vitamin asset of fish lies in its high content of biotin. Fatty fishes, like sardine and herring, exceed all meats in riboflavin, pantothenic acid, and vitamin B_{12}, but are lower in thiamin and niacin. Most fishes accumulate vitamins A and D in their livers. Oil pressed from these organs is a potent source of these vitamins. Notable exceptions are herring and, in particular, eels, their flesh being high in these two vitamins. Eels are rather widely consumed in Japan, Europe, and among certain ethnic groups in North America. Few other foods are potent sources of vitamin D—in effect, only eggs. The flesh of fatty fishes (e.g., salmon, tuna, and herring) also carries more calcium than other meats, yet in modest quantities. Dark-fleshed fish contains more iron than the light colored with less red muscle pigment. Ocean fish has the added merit of containing two vital trace elements: iodine and fluorine.

Storage of Raw Products

The retailer, as well as wholesaler, is chiefly interested in the losses taking place in total weight during storage. Plant physiologists and biochemists place more emphasis on the changes in the compositional characteristics of the product. Water losses are, in the latter case, less essential. The nutritionists, on the contrary, want to know changes in the amount of certain nutritive constituents, such as ascorbic acid, thiamin, or carotene and to what degree; e.g., are potatoes or carrots, bought in February, comparable after storage to those harvested and purchased in October? During this period there is a 50–70% loss in ascorbic acid in potatoes, but generally on the other hand an increase in the carotene of carrots of approximately 20–25%.

The handling of harvested vegetables from the field to the can is decisive to nutritive quality. Some products like peas are even iced in the field to slow down metabolic activities and retard any nutritive breakdown. Both canning and freezing, as a rule, are completed within a few hours after harvesting. Thereby, losses of nutrients are negligible. Ascorbic acid and riboflavin are the nutrients which are most vulnerable to losses.

Since the dawn of history, man has been confronted with the problem of survival through alternate periods of glut and famine due to changes of season, pestilence, and the vagaries of climate. Man was forced to store the surplus of good years of providence to nourish himself during the proverbial "seven lean years." Such is reported throughout history from the Middle East, China, the Incas, etc. Storage and preservation of foods remain fundamental features without which advanced civilization cannot exist.

TABLE N-18

RELATIVE NUTRITIVE VALUE AND UTILIZABLE PROTEIN IN PROTEIN SOURCES

	Protein Content (%)	Relative Nutritive Value (%)	Utilizable[1] Protein (%)	FAO Amino Acid Pattern (%)	Milk Protein (%)	Egg Protein (%)	NPU (%)
Lactalbumin	77.60	100	77.6				
Defatted egg	63.00	99	63.0	100	90	100	100
Casein	86.30	75	64.6	80	75	60	7:
Fibrin	87.40	89	77.7				
Fish protein concentrate	81.10	77	62.5	70	70	75	8:
Cottonseed flour I	58.90	66	38.9	70	95	80	6(
Cottonseed flour II	51.60	48	24.8				
Cottonseed flour III	37.70	65	24.5				
Soya flour, heated	51.90	60	31.1	70	85	70	5(
Full fat soya	39.40	58	22.9				
Wheat gluten	71.00	24	17.0	40	40	40	3:
Peanut flour	48.40	54	26.1	60	80	70	4:
Rice flour, high protein	19.10	44	8.4	70	75	75	5:
Sorghum I	9.80	31	3.0	70	60	60	5(
Sorghum II	12.80	26	3.3				
Sorghum III	12.40	34	4.2				
White flour	13.75	28	3.8	50	50	50	5
Rice	8.30	50	4.2	70	75	75	5:
Corn meal	7.95	37	3.0	40	40	45	5:

SOURCE: Hegsted (1969).

[1] RNV X % protein.

The nutritive value of proteinaceous foods, even dry foods, changes progressively with time depending on storage conditions. This depreciation of protein value does not level off to a plateau. The rate of deterioration is accelerated by high humidity and high temperature. Generally the protein value decreases less rapidly when the products are stored at 68°F and 40% RH than when stored at 86°F or 104°F and 50% RH. This impairment is reflected in a reduced growth efficiency as tested on experimental rats. The measurement of protein quality is generally accomplished by biological assay. The protein to be tested is fed to experimental animals, and its capacity to maintain the nitrogen balance or to promote growth measured. The methods employed vary and are accordingly designated as biological value (BV), protein efficiency ratio (PER), net protein retention (NPR), and net protein utilization (NPU). The combined measure of both quality and quantity of the protein in a diet is the net dietary protein value (NDpV) which is defined as

$$\text{Intake of N} \times 6.25 \times \text{NPU}$$

For a complete discussion of protein quality, reports issued by the FAO and WHO should be consulted as well as the works of Munro and Allison (1964).

A newer method being employed is the "Slope Ratio" method, which employs a multidose protein assay. Three or four levels of the test and standard proteins are fed, but only doses falling on the curve-response linear portion are used to compute the assay value. The slope of the response curve for the test protein is expressed as a percentage of the standard protein (lactalbumin). For a discussion of the comparative values of these different techniques, the interested reader should consult Rosenfield (1973) from which Table N-18 was taken.

Modification of Nutritive Value in Processing

Since the conditions of contemporary living demand that foods be transported over long distances and be stored for considerable periods, their limited natural keeping qualities must be improved. Some foods may be safely kept for years without the need for extensive processing. Thus, cereal may be stored almost indefinitely provided they are protected against spoilage through moisture and secured against infestation by insects and vermin. In the case of grains and seeds, natural dehydration serves as the protective process.

The components of food most likely to undergo changes in processing and which might alter their nutritive value are: (1) proteins, (2) fats, or (3) vit

ins. The changes may involve either destruction
r chemical changes that affect availability or
iological properties. Thus, the biological value of
he protein may be changed, the degree of un-
aturation of fatty acids may be altered and they
aay become auto-oxidized, and vitamins may be
estroyed or rendered ineffective as to biological
ctivity. Similar changes also may follow milling,
torage, or cooking. An alteration in the nutritional
roperties of a single foodstuff is not necessarily of
reat significance; the importance of any change
bserved depends upon the contribution that the
oodstuff and the nutrient concerned makes to the
iet as a whole. It must be remembered that the
utrients contained in a particular food are subject
o wide variation according to species, climate,
eason, and many other factors. These differences
re frequently greater than any changes induced
arough processing.

Furthermore, man as a rule depends upon a
aixed diet, to which many foodstuffs normally
ontribute, and the proportions of these foodstuffs
re usually quite varied from day to day. Under
ach circumstances, his nutritional needs can only
e usefully considered in the context of the whole
iet. Finally, processing may cause some reduction
a nutritive value, but yet improve palatability.
he overall effect, therefore, may be better nutri-
on whereby much food may be saved to make
gnificant overall nutritional contributions.

While the manner of agricultural crop fertiliza-
on is not properly a matter of food technology,
is of much interest to the consumer as affecting
ae nutritional value of the processed food. Advo-
ates of organically-grown foods believe that food
rops grown using only barnyard manure, com-
ost, feed lot, and other wastes provide more
ealthful and nutritionally superior diets for ani-
als and man than do crops grown with the
astomary fertilizers composed mainly of inorganic
aemical compounds. These people also believe
aat such plants are more resistant to disease and
asects and hence require no chemical sprays or
rotective treatments. It is claimed, the use of
ods derived from such crops would promote
ouoyant health and longevity." To demonstrate
aat such foods are superior, or even equal to the
rdinary market variety is very difficult, if not
apossible.

Beeson (1972–1973) reviews the findings in his
ablished report. Few scientifically controlled ex-
eriments have been devised to compare quality of
ops grown exclusively with organic fertilizers and
aose grown with inorganic fertilizers. In an ex-
eriment with organic composts in one case, and
ith water culture using soluble inorganic chemicals
the other, the mature crops were fed to guinea
gs for 12 weeks. The animals in both groups
owed equal growth, equal skeletal and muscular

development, good skin condition, and clear eyes.
In another case, two crops, rye and potatoes, were
grown on experimental plots for 25 yr and received, respectively, organic fertilizer (compost or
animal manure) or inorganic fertilizer. No differences were found in vitamin C, carotene, iron,
or copper concentrations of the crops. The value
of organic matter as a source of plant nutrient and
as a soil conditioner is universally recognized. But
extremists would limit or even prohibit the use of
inorganic chemicals. To do so would limit the
output of foods and result in shortages as there are
not sufficient supplies of compost or animal
manures to meet requirements for fertilizers at
present levels of food production. Furthermore,
there is no valid evidence that crops grown solely
with compost, manures, or other organic sources of
plant nutrition are superior.

Canning

In modern commercial usage, great care is taken
to select special varieties of raw material which
lend themselves well to the canning process, to up-
hold meticulous sanitary conditions, and to shorten
the time lag between harvest and process. Fruits
and vegetables canned within 24 hr of picking often
preserve a higher vitamin C content than similar
foods bought "fresh" on the open market after
prolonged shipping, storage, and final cooking in
the home.

In modern canning, less severe but adequate processing is employed to guarantee maximum retention of nutrients in the final products. High-quality
raw products must be employed to produce good
processed foods. Nutritional qualities cannot be
enhanced by processing or by home preparation.
The nutritive content of most canned foods matches
well that of raw foods similarly prepared in the
home. No food can be preserved, or cooked, or
held under refrigeration without some sacrifice in
vitamin content. Costs of canning or freezing may
well be justified in view of the off-season availability and transportability of such nutrient values
accomplished through such processing. New techniques shortening the heating period have reduced
losses considerably.

The thermal processing involved in canning causes
minimal nutritive losses. There is virtually no loss
in protein, fat, or carbohydrate. However, the
vitamin content of canned foods reflects the variations in the nutrient values of the raw materials
used, along with the methods employed in preparation and processing. Exposure to air (oxygen),
contact with hot water, and heating—all conditions
which apply to home kitchen preparation of
foods—induce some reduction in vitamin content
even with modern equipment and methods. These
losses have been reduced by $1/2$-$1/3$ in industrial
manufacturing.

TABLE N-19

AVERAGE PERCENTAGE VITAMIN RETENTION

	Ascorbic Acid	Thiamin	Riboflavin	Niacin	Carotene
Asparagus	92	67	88	96	—
Corn (pressure cooking)	—	90	97	86	97
Green beans	55	71	96	92	87
Peaches	71	76	—	89	85
Tomato juice	67	89	100	98	67

Blanching in hot water or live steam is accorded most vegetables. This process cleanses the product and decreases the volume so that a well-filled can may be obtained; in some cases it may remove undesirable flavors and odors and may or may not aid in retarding the green color of vegetables, depending on the vegetable, the temperatures used in blanching, and the method of preservation after blanching. There is much variation among canners in the temperatures and equipment used in blanching, e.g., blanching in hot water at 170°–212°F, or in live steam. Blanching in hot water can be conducted in such a manner as not to lose more nutrients than are lost by live-steam blanching. Thus, the use of a high temperature-short time (HTST) processing technique results, for example, in retention of 90% of the original thiamin and vitamin C. Present-day methods permit the processing of citrus juices so that they contain practically all the ascorbic acid in the original fruit.

The data in Table N-19 serve to give a general indication of vitamin retention in the canning of several representative fruits and vegetables; and Tables N-20 and N-21 give vitamin content of other canned products.

The retention of ascorbic acid in the processing of acid fruits and berries is of the order of 80–95%. However, due to high oxidase activity, it is difficult

TABLE N-20

AVERAGE PYRIDOXINE, BIOTIN, AND FOLIC ACID CONTENT OF SOME COMMERCIALLY CANNED FOODS

	Pyridoxine	Biotin	Folic Aci
	Mg/100 Gm		
Asparagus, green	30	1.7	5.8–9.0
Beans, green	32	1.3	2.9–7.7
Carrots	22	1.5	1.3–4.1
Corn, yellow	68	2.2	1.7–5.6
Grapefruit juice	14	0.3	0.5–1.2
Peaches	16	0.2	0.5–1.5
Peas	46	2.1	1.7–4.4
Salmon	130	9.9	2.6–6.9
Spinach	60	2.3	7.4–20.7
Tomatoes	71	1.8	2.7–5.4

to retain ascorbic acid during processing of appl juice or apple sauce; but soaking apples in a 2% salt solution prior to processing helps preserve th vitamin C. Exposing peach halves to air for an length of time results in losses of ascorbic acid o the order of 30–40%. Peach slices exposed in similar way show still higher losses (40–60%) Vitamins in canned peaches show a retention withi the range of 70–85%.

TABLE N-21

AVERAGE VITAMIN VALUES FOR CANNED SEAFOOD
(Mg Per 100 Gm)

	Vitamin A	Thiamin Hydrochloride	Riboflavin	Niacin	Calcium Pantothenate
Mackerel	0.029	0.034	0.20	7.65	0.29
Salmon	0.020–0.080	0.021	0.16	7.3–7.8	0.57
Sardines in oil	0.060	0.024	0.14	4.71	0.38
Sardines in tomato sauce	—	0.010	0.22	4.78	0.47
Shrimp	0.017	0.009	0.032	2.23	0.29
Tuna	0.008	0.037	0.14	0.9–10.2	0.17

Hot water blanching is almost universally employed in the preparation of vegetables for processing. Water-soluble vitamins are in this case subject to extraction, usually limited to 15–25% loss. Steam blanching also incurs some losses. In the subsequent heat processing, losses of ascorbic acid are usually directly proportional to the amount of oxygen entrapped in the can. In modern vacuum sealing operations this is greatly diminished, to 5–10% at the most.

Green beans show slightly higher loss figures but on the whole the vitamin content of processed vegetables is not seriously affected.

Freezing

The nutritive losses suffered during preparation for freezing (trimming, washing, blanching) are similar to those experienced in preparation for canning. Actual freezing losses are practically nil. The loss in nutritive value may be smaller than that which takes place during transportation, storage, and aging of "fresh" fruits and vegetables, followed by the preparatory steps toward cooking in the kitchen. Protracted thawing or holding after defrosting may induce nutritive losses due to resumed enzymic activity.

Dehydration

The drying of meat, fish, beans, fruits, and vegetables has been practiced since early days to effect the preservation of fresh foods. Considerable advances have been made in technical procedures, particularly since World War II. Dried milk and dried eggs have a nutritive content practically identical with that of the original products.

Sun drying is destructive to the carotene content of raisins, figs, grapes, and other fruits. On the contrary, dehydration by artificially produced heat, under controlled conditions of humidity and air flow, causes little loss of carotene. Ascorbic acid is easily destroyed by all types of drying.

Dehydrated or dried fruits and vegetables vary in quality and show great varietal differences. In some instances vitamin losses are negligible, in other instances considerable. Special processes, such as sulfuring in the case of fruits and steam blanching in the case of vegetables, tend to prevent losses of vitamin A and ascorbic acid. In general, about $1/3$–$1/2$ of the thiamin in fruits and vegetables is lost during prolonged dehydration. Data are scanty as to the stability of riboflavin and niacin. In theory, both of these B-vitamins are more resistant to heat and oxidation than thiamin.

Blanching preparatory to dehydrating vegetables requires more time than in canning or freezing. This affects the nutrient retention, being somewhat less favorable.

Dry whole milk is a fairly good source of vitamin A, but processing losses of at least $1/4$ have been reported when drying conditions are not properly controlled. Nonfat milk solids contain very little vitamin A, since vitamin A is fat-soluble and is removed in the fat separation process:

Vitamin A Content	IU per 100 Gm
Dry whole milk	1,400
Nonfat milk solids	40

In modern dehydration of milk, water removal is so rapid that the biological value of the milk proteins is little affected.

Spray drying of whole eggs has no significant destructive action on the vitamins contained in the egg—namely vitamin A, vitamin D, thiamin, riboflavin, pantothenic acid, and niacin. There is only a slight loss of riboflavin, even at high storage temperatures. However, thiamin losses are directly related to temperature.

Pasteurization

Pasteurization has no apparent undesirable effect on the protein, fat, carbohydrate, or mineral content of milk, or on most vitamins. Riboflavin, however, may subsequently disappear under the degradative influence of strong daylight. Thiamin may be reduced up to 10% and ascorbic acid up to 25%. Carefully controlled high temperature-short time (HTST) pasteurization permits maximum retention of these two labile vitamins.

Rat studies have revealed that the biological value of the milk proteins is very slightly affected by pasteurizing, even when preheating as high as 190°F for 5 min. The same is true in the pasteurization of eggs.

Pasteurization may also be practiced with citrus juices and is equally lenient to the ascorbic acid and other water-soluble vitamins. The vitamin C content of raw citrus juices varies widely dependent upon several factors. On the average, retention of vitamin C during the canning process is approximately 97%. Subsequent to canning, the loss is on the order of a magnitude of 1–2% per month at room temperature storage. Retention is, of course, inversely related to storage temperature. The vitamin C content of fresh orange juice varies from 35 to 56 mg per 100 ml and that of the hot processed canned juice from 34 to 52 mg per 100 ml. The vitamin C content of fresh grapefruit juice varies between 36 and 45 mg per 100 ml and that of hot processed canned juice from 32 to 45 mg per 100 ml. Studies conducted by the Florida State Horticultural Society over five seasons (1953–1958) show that late-season orange juice concentrate contains less vitamin C than early and mid-season concentrate. Midseason reconstituted frozen orange juice concentrate contained 42–65 mg per 100 ml, while late-season reconstituted juice contained 30–53 mg per 100 ml of vitamin C. Therefore, it is apparent that while there is significant natural variation in vitamin C content, dependent upon variety and season of harvest in particular, there is relatively insignificant loss due to heat processing. Juice packaged in glass and refrigerated has a small initial vitamin C loss due to headspace oxygen, but subsequently remains virtually constant until opened. Vitamin C retention of more than 90% has been reported in juices packed in glass and refrigerated for up to 1 yr.

Cheese Making

The composition of cheese largely depends upon whether it is made from whole or skim milk. This obviously determines the fat and moisture content. The amount of moisture is also affected by the type of cheese made. Cheddar cheese compares with milk as to certain nutrients in the following way:

One Pound of Cheese	Equivalent to Quarts of Milk
Protein	4.0
Fat	2.8
Calcium	3.2
Phosphorus	3.0

The method of production of certain cheeses has variable effects on the amounts of protein, fat, calcium, thiamin, and riboflavin. Some losses of nutrients occur in the making of cheese, as in the case of those nutrients lost in the whey. However, some increased nutrient levels are registered through the microbial activities during cheese ripening.

Cheese may be defined as the concentration of certain components of milk obtained through the coagulation of milk protein (casein) by suitable enzymes and/or microbiologically-produced acid. The curd is comprised of a large proportion of the milk protein, minerals, fat (in case whole milk was used), and the fat-soluble vitamins. Also, significant quantities of the B vitamins remain with the curd. The resulting whey contains lactalbumin and lactoglobulin as well as considerable minerals and water-soluble vitamins, as can be seen in Tables N-22 and N-23. The amount of nutrients retained in the curd following whey separation depends on the type of cheese, as can be seen in Table N-24.

Fats and Oils Processing

When fats and oils are heated they may become oxidized, dependent upon their content of (1) natural antioxidants or (2) impurities which are chiefly

TABLE N-22

PARTITION OF NUTRIENTS IN MILK IN MAKING CHEDDAR CHEESE

Nutrient	Percentage in Curd[1]	Percentage in Whey[1]
Water	6	94
Total solids	48	52
Casein	96	4
Soluble proteins	4	96
Fat	94	6
Lactose	6	94
Calcium	62	38
Vitamin A	94	6
Thiamin	15	85
Riboflavin	26	74
Vitamin C	6	84

SOURCE: Kon (1959).

[1] Percentage of total in original milk at point of separation of curd and whey.

NOTE: The indicated loss of vitamin C, due to the destructive effect of light, is relatively unimportant because the milk itself is not a significant source of vitamin C, particularly pasteurized milk for cheese.

Unaccountable losses usually are observed also with other vitamins, notably riboflavin which also is affected by light. These losses are more noticeable in the whey than in the curd.

trace amounts of metallic ions; other critical factors are: (3) temperature, (4) duration of heating and (5) surface area exposed to oxygen. In the

TABLE N-23

COMPOSITION AND APPROXIMATE VITAMIN CONTENT OF WHEY FROM CHEDDAR CHEESE

Constituent	(%)
Water	93.3
Lactose	4.7
Protein	0.9
Minerals	0.6[1]
Fat	0.3
Lactic acid and other organic substances	0.2
	(Per 100 Ml)
Vitamin A value (IU)	8–16
Vitamin C (mg)	1.5[2]
Pantothenic acid (mg)	0.35
Riboflavin (mg)	0.08[2]
Niacin (mg)	0.07
Thiamin (mg)	0.04
Vitamin B_6 (mg)	0.02
Biotin (mg)	0.0015
Vitamin B_{12} (mcg)	0.15

SOURCE: Kon (1959).

[1] Includes 0.05% calcium.
[2] May be less if much exposure to light; also much less vitamin C if milk is pasteurized for the cheese.

TABLE N-24

MAJOR NUTRIENT CONTENT OF SOME COMMON VARIETIES OF CHEESE (PER 100 GM)

	Water (Gm)	Food Energy (Cal)	Protein (Gm)	Fat (Gm)	Carbohydrate (Gm)	Calcium (Mg)	Phosphorus (Mg)	Iron (Mg)	Sodium (Mg)	Potassium (Mg)	Vitamin A Value (IU)	Thiamin (Mg)	Riboflavin (Mg)	Niacin (Mg)
Cheddar	37.0	398	25.0	32.2	2.1	750	478	1.0	700	82	1310	0.03	0.46	0.1
Pasteurized process														
American cheese	40.0	370	23.2	30.0	1.9	697	771[1]	0.9	1136[1]	80	1220	0.02	0.41	tr
Cheese food	43.2	323	19.8	24.0	7.1	570	754[1]	0.8	—	—	980	0.02	0.58	0.2
Cheese spread	48.6	288	16.0	21.4	8.2	565	875[1]	0.6	1625[1]	240	870	0.01	0.54	0.1
Blue	40.0	368	21.5	30.5	2.0	315	339	0.5	—	—	1240	0.03	0.61	1.2
Brick	41.0	370	22.2	30.5	1.9	730	455	0.9	—	—	1240	—	0.45	0.1
Camembert	52.2	299	17.5	24.7	1.8	105	184	0.5	—	111	1010	0.04	0.75	0.8
Cottage[2]	79.0	86	17.0	0.3	2.7	90	175	0.4	290	72	10	0.03	0.28	0.1
Cottage[3]	78.3	106	13.6	4.2	2.9	94	152	0.3	229	85	170	0.03	0.25	0.1
Cream	51.0	374	8.0	37.7	2.1	62	95	0.2	250	74	1540	0.02	0.24	0.1
Limburger	45.0	345	21.2	28.0	2.2	590	393	0.6	—	—	1140	0.08	0.50	0.2
Parmesan	30.0	393	36.0	26.0	2.9	1140	781	0.4	734	149	1060	0.02	0.73	0.2
Swiss	39.0	370	27.5	28.0	1.7	925	563	0.9	710	104	1140	0.01	0.40	0.1
Pasteurized process														
Swiss cheese	40.0	355	26.4	26.9	1.6	887	867[1]	0.9	1167[1]	100	1100	0.01	0.40	0.1

SOURCE: Watt and Merrill (1963).

[1] If the added emulsifying agent does not contain phosphorus or sodium, the values are respectively: phosphorus, 444, 427, 548, 540 mg; sodium, 650, 1139, 681 mg.
[2] Uncreamed, made of skim milk.
[3] Creamed, 4.2% milkfat.

presence of air, fats may undergo a series of changes affecting their nutritional value. This is due to (a) peroxidation, (b) polymerization, and (c) partial decomposition to free fatty acids. This is a deteriorative sequence, collectively known as autooxidation or oxidative rancidification. When the same fats are heated in the absence (or near-absence) of air, the process is known as thermal polymerization, and under these conditions, undesirable byproducts may be formed.

Because fats constitute a major foodstuff, and development of oxidative rancidity is not always immediately apparent, the ingestion of such fats may be detrimental. Its use may also affect industrial processing of foodstuffs and food preparation in the home.

Deleterious effects of heating on the nutritive value of edible oils have frequently been reported. Diets containing oils which had been heated to about 280°C in an inert atmosphere when fed to laboratory rats depressed growth and the efficiency of food utilization. Such adverse effects on the nutritive value of oils varies in severity with (1) the degree of unsaturation of the oil, (2) the length of time of heating, and (3) the level at which the heated oil is incorporated in the diet.

Refined cottonseed oil, when aerated and heated to 95°C for 50–300 hr, was shown to result in growth depression; diarrhea; enlargement of livers, kidney, and adrenals; and ultimately death. Similar growth depression and other adverse effects have been reported with corn oil, butter oil, and hydrogenated vegetable oil when they are heated in air to 200°C for 24 hr (an abnormally long time) and fed to rats at 20% fat level; although butter oil resisted the deteriorative effects significantly. The thermal oxidation products from the polyunsaturated fatty acids (primarily linoleic an linolenic acid) are responsible for much of the lo of nutritive value.

Milling and Flour-Making

In the milling of cereals, portions of the grai such as the germ, the aleurone layer, and the bra are removed. These parts carry a major share vitamins and minerals contained in the grain see Czerniejewski and coworkers (1964), as well Bradley (1967), determined the effects of millir hard spring wheats on the average mineral and vit min contents of flours and the bread produce from them. The flours milled from the wheats we all of approximately 72% extraction, comparab to patent flours.

The breads were prepared according to a cor mercial U.S. formula using the bread enrichme vitamins and 4% nonfat milk solids. The pate flours contained lower proportions of all minera than the original wheat: Mg, Mn, and Co less tha 20%; P, K, Zn, Fe, Cu, and Na between 20 a 32%; Ca 40%; and Mo 52%. The mineral conte may be somewhat higher in the bread than in t flour due to the presence of some minerals in t nonflour ingredients (Ca in the milk, Fe in t enrichment materials, and Na in the salt).

The data also show the effect of milling to redu the vitamin content of the flour. Milling losses minerals and vitamins may be replaced by enric ment. The enrichment of white flour was intr duced on a major scale in the United Kingdom du ing World War II and in the United States in 19 with a prescribed addition of a mixture of thiami niacin, and iron to wheat flour. Riboflavin was i

TABLE N-25

MINERALS AND VITAMINS IN WHEATS AND THE FLOURS AND BREADS PREPARED FROM THEM
(AVERAGE VALUES ON A DRY BASIS)

| | Minerals | | | | Vitamins | | |
| | | | | | | Mg/100 Gm Dry Weight | |
	Wheat	Flour	Bread		Wheat	Flour	Bread
K (%)	0.454	0.105	0.191	Thiamin	0.40	0.104	0.46
P (%)	0.433	0.126	0.183	Riboflavin	0.16	0.035	0.29
Mg (%)	0.183	0.028	0.034	Niacin	6.95	1.38	4.39
Ca (%)	0.045	0.018	0.129	Biotin	0.016	0.0021	0.00
Na (ppm)	45	9.8	0.858	Choline	216.0	208.0	202.0
Zn (ppm)	35	7.8	9.7	Pantothenic acid	1.37	0.59	0.69
Fe (ppm)	43	10.5	27.3	Folic acid	0.049	0.011	0.04
Mn (ppm)	46	6.5	5.9	Inositol	370.0	47.0	53.0
Cu (ppm)	5.3	1.7	2.3	p-Aminobenzoic acid	0.51	0.050	0.09
Mo (ppm)	0.48	0.25	0.32				
Co (ppm)	0.026	0.003	0.022				

cluded in 1943. Many countries, including Canada, Sweden, Denmark, England, Chile, Brazil, and others permit or have enacted laws making mandatory some type of enrichment of white flour. Bradley (1967) also showed the higher mineral and vitamin contents of the less-refined wheat products.

The nutritive value of cereal protein can certainly be improved by adding lysine. In the manufacture of breakfast cereals by conventional heat processing methods, the protein is impaired by the decreased lysine availability. As breakfast cereals are consumed with milk, this provides sufficient lysine to correct this deficit.

By mixing with milk, the nutritive value of wheat protein is substantially enhanced and the addition of pure lysine does not further improve most breakfast cereals. In other words, the need for additional lysine can be obviated if a mixed cereal diet contains fluid milk, dried milk, evaporated milk, or another protein which is a rich source of lysine.

Processing damage to other cereal foods, not normally consumed with milk, would appear to be a fertile field for lysine fortification. On cooking a cereal dough, there may occur a 10–12% loss of lysine. On toasting, available lysine may decrease by up to 36%.

Experimental evidence suggests that in rice both lysine and threonine may be equally limiting. As a consequence, added lysine is only partially effective, and a significant improvement is only possible when both lysine and threonine are added.

In the post-World War II period the addition of thiamin, riboflavin, niacin, and iron to wheat flour, macaroni and noodle products, farina, rice, corn meal, and corn grits has been introduced and has become a legally-required procedure in several U.S. states and foreign countries.

This principle of enrichment connotes, by definition, a compensatory restoration of the original levels of these nutrients in foods which routinely suffer nutritional losses during the process of milling or refining. Fortification is a term applied to the elevation of the levels of vitamins or minerals above normal. Such fortification has been sanctioned by the American Medical Association and the FDA in cases of specific nutritional deficiencies which exist in the U.S. population. In other countries, more widespread nutritional deficiency diseases may justify further nutrient additions to foods. Dr. Paul La Chance of Rutgers University has coined a new term for this nutrient fortification process which he calls "nutrification."

Both enrichment and fortification have become accepted procedures in the manufacture of certain staple foods. Enriched flour is a good example where the "enrichment" has not been restricted to restoring previous natural values. In setting the legal requirements for enrichment, the human requirement and the general population's dietary status with respect to involved nutrients have been taken into consideration.

The term "bleaching" as used traditionally in the milling industry is an all-inclusive term encompassing both the visible removal of yellow flour pigments by oxidation and the chemical maturation of flour that results from the oxidation of sulphhydryl groups in the dough. Recently, a distinction has been made between reactions that produce only a removal of color without affecting baking quality; those that produce both bleaching and maturation; and those that are solely maturing in their effect. Bleaching or whitening of flour results from the oxidation by selected bleaching agents of the carotenoid pigments of the wheat consisting of xanthophyll and its esters, carotene, flavones, and decomposition products of chlorophyll, with xanthophyll representing the predominant member of the group. The functions of bleaching and maturing agents involve developmental maturing or artificial aging which improve the baking quality of the flour; and a chemical bleaching action resulting in whitening of the flour.

Among permitted chemical oxidants are nitrogen peroxide and benzoyl peroxide, with neither of these compounds producing a maturing effect. Color removal and strong maturing action are obtained by chlorine, nitrosyl chlorine, chlorine dioxide, and acetone peroxide. Chlorine dioxide was introduced as an alternative to chlorine trichloride which latter compound yielded treated flours which caused running fits in dogs and some other animals.

As distinguished from the compounds that have bleaching effects are those that function only as maturing agents, including potassium bromate, azodicarbonamide, and ascorbic acid. These compounds are added to the dough. Pyler (1973) indicates the bread-making characteristics that are effected favorably by bleaching and maturing agents include dough dryness and machineability, and volume, break and shred, grain, texture, and crumb color of the finished bread. Pyler also points out approval of U.S. regulatory agencies for use of bleaching and maturing agents in bread making. Since ascorbic acid has maturing effect in the dough, advantage attends its use because vitamin C increases in the bread. In Germany and in France, ascorbic acid is the only dough improver permitted by law.

Objections have been voiced occasionally by nutritionists on the use of bleaching and maturing agents on the basis that oxidation has a destructive effect on the flour's vitamins and unsaturated fatty acids. Studies have shown that the maturing agents employed in flour treatment do not bring about a

TABLE N-26

AVERAGE NIACIN CONTENT OF SELECTED FOODS (EDIBLE PORTION)

Food (Raw, per 100 Gm)	Niacin (in Mg)	Food (Raw, per 100 Gm)	Niacin (in Mg)
Peanuts (ready to eat)	16.2	Beans, dried	2.4
Peanut butter	14.7	Dried fruits (except raisins)	2.0
Beef liver	13.6	Corn meal	2.0
Pork or calf liver	16.5	Corn, sweet, fresh	1.7
Chicken liver	10.8	Rice, white	1.6
Tuna and swordfish meat (canned)	11.9	Potato	1.5
Broilers	8.8	Lima beans, fresh	1.4
Salmon (canned)	7.3	Broccoli	0.9
Veal	6.5	Nuts (not peanuts)	0.7–0.9
Whole wheat	4.7	Leafy vegetables	0.7
Meat (lean)	4.2–4.6	Raisins	0.5
Corned beef (canned)	3.2–3.5	Fresh fruits	0.3
Bread, whole wheat	2.8	Cheese	0.1–0.2
enriched white	2.4	Eggs, whole, fresh	0.1
unenriched white	1.1	Milk, whole, fresh	0.1

SOURCE: Watt and Merrill (1963).

perceptible reduction in the levels of thiamin, riboflavin, and niacin nor in the amount of unsaturated fatty acid in enriched or nonenriched flour. However, benzoyl peroxide and chlorine dioxide bring about almost complete destruction of tocopherols reducing the daily supply of vitamin E in human nutrition by about 10%: a loss of this magnitude not being considered significant.

Bleaching and maturing effects of flour can be obtained by means other than chemical treatment. Before the turn of the century, millers held flour for several weeks or months to permit whitening and maturing to occur. However, the time and space required, danger of insect infestation, and irregularity of results led to the search for improved methods. Heat treatment of the flour, high-speed mixing of batter-type doughs, and use of lipoxidase-containing soy flour in the dough result in some bleaching-maturing effects. Only the use of soy-lipoxidase has been applied in American practice.

Cereal grains themselves are rather poor sources of calcium, yet are rich in phosphorus. Breakfast cereals and breads, however, may serve as vehicles by which significant calcium is included in the diet. Two chemical additives commonly used by commercial bakers contribute significant amounts of utilizable calcium; namely, certain calcium salts, which are provided as yeast foods or dough conditioners, and calcium propionate, which is a mold inhibitor. Also, many commercial breads contain added nonfat milk solids (4–6%), resulting in a further improvement of the calcium level as well as significantly enhancing the protein quality.

Vitamin Supplementation

Nutritional fortification has gradually become an accepted routine practice, even in products other than cereals, basically with the aim of improving the nutritional status of the population. All brands of margarine in the United States are fortified to contain a minimum of 15,000 IU of vitamin A per pound. Some margarines also contain a minimum of 500 IU of added vitamin D. The latter vitamin is optionally added but vitamin A has a mandatory minimum level. Neither, however, carries a maximum in the newest U.S. standards. Practically all evaporated canned milk in the United States is fortified to contain 400 IU of vitamin D per quart on reconstitution to normal milk solids.

Recognizing the need for a cheap, readily available source of vitamin C (short of citrus), a fortified, standardized apple juice was developed in Canada. This juice contains a minimum of 35 mg of ascorbic acid per 100 ml of juice. Ascorbic acid in the United States has become a commonly added ingredient in fruit juice drinks and dry beverage mixes, and is credited with considerable sales value. Imitation products, both frozen and dried, have become popular as substitutes for citrus juices.

Infant cereals and flour which is used for bread, crackers, pizza dough, spaghetti, and macaroni are now commonly enriched with the standard nutrients. Additional levels above those now employed are being advocated by several outstanding nutritionists. Tables N-26 and N-27 show the niacin and vitamin B_6 content of selected foods.

TABLE N-27

VITAMIN B$_6$ IN SELECTED FOODS

	Mg/100 Gm
Grain	
Wheat germ	1.31
Wheat bran	0.82
Brown rice	0.53
Corn	0.48
Wheat	0.41
Whole wheat	0.40
Barley	0.39
Popcorn	0.37
Whole wheat bread	0.20
Rice crispies	0.14
Oatmeal	0.12
Egg noodles	0.09
Milk	
Canned	7.50
Cow	0.10
Human	0.02
Meat	
Liver	1.42
Ham (cured and cooked)	0.70
Salmon, canned	0.28
Frankfurter	0.16
Beef, ground (cooked)	0.10
Vegetables and fruits	
Lima beans	0.60
Bananas	0.32
Carrots	0.21
Frozen peas	0.11

Effect of Home Preparation

Vitamin losses during cooking are primarily due to the length of cooking time, amount of water added, pH (acidity) of the medium in which food is prepared, and the holding time before serving. The percentage loss of nutrients under good cooking conditions is approximately as shown in Tables N-28 and N-29.

Cooking losses are greatest for thiamin and ascorbic acid, the vitamins most sensitive to destruction by heat; yet considerably less loss occurs in the acid medium provided by fruits and tomatoes.

Preparation of Foods

The processing of fresh foods—trimming, washing, and cooking—in the home or institutional kitchen claims its share of nutrient losses. No matter how carefully preparation and cooking are performed, loss of water-soluble, heat-labile, or oxidation-prone nutrients is inevitable. Excessive losses of vitamins and minerals can be prevented in the same way as in industrial processing; that is, by avoiding prolonged exposure of hot foods to oxygen and by minimizing the leaching of water-soluble constituents through the use of reasonable quantities of wash water, boiling water, or by using, instead of discarding, the cooking water containing water-soluble minerals and vitamins. Cooking under cover and limiting the duration of the cooking period preserves, in particular, the heat-labile vitamins thiamin and ascorbic acid. Pressure or microwave cooking also serves this purpose.

Changes During Storage of Processed Foods

Canned Food.—During warehousing, temperature and duration of storage are important variables affecting losses of labile vitamins in canned foods. Within normal temperature ranges of 45°–75°F, vitamin losses occur at the rate of 2–3% per year, which is indeed negligible. A 15–30% decrease in ascorbic acid occurs, however, during 1 yr of storage at 80°F, whereas only 5–15% is lost at 65°F. Depending on the pH of the food, thiamin losses

TABLE N-28

AVERAGE PERCENTAGE OF NUTRIENTS LOST DURING COOKING

	Thiamin	Riboflavin	Niacin	Ascorbic Acid
Meats	35	20	25	—
Meats plus drippings	25	5	10	—
Eggs	25	10	0	—
Cereals	10	0	10	—
Legumes	20	0	0	—
Vegetables, leafy green and yellow	40	25	25	60
Tomatoes	5	5	5	15
Vegetables, other	25	15	25	60
Potato	40	25	25	60

SOURCE: ICNND (1963).

TABLE N-29

VITAMIN RETENTION DURING MEAT PROCESSING

| | Percentage Retention | | | |
	Thiamin (%)	Riboflavin (%)	Niacin (%)	Pantothenic Acid (%)
Pork				
Cooked	71	107	88	—
Dehydrated	63	104	92	73
Roasted	68	85	94	
Beef				
Cooked	91	109	96	72
Dehydrated	76	105	92	68

are of a similar order of magnitude or very slightly greater. Carotene, riboflavin, and niacin are markedly stable.

Frozen Food.—Frozen foods do, in principle, show a higher level of nutrient retention but this advantage may be nullified by either defective storage or careless thawing (see Fig. N-3).

The nutritive losses of frozen fruits and vegetables are equally modest in storage, as long as prescribed temperatures are maintained. If not, risk prevails of considerable losses, depending on the time and temperature. A rise in the storage temperature to 10°F may triple losses. At 30°F this rate increases about 40 to 50 times. When thawed, the enzymatic breakdown enters into full play—this in contrast to canned products.

Dehydrated Food.—The principle factors affecting the retention of vitamins in dehydrated fruits and vegetables during storage are temperature as well as type and method of packaging. A key factor is the amount of air (oxygen) within the package or its access from outside. Riboflavin is fairly stable under all temperature and packaging conditions. Thiamin is affected principally by storage

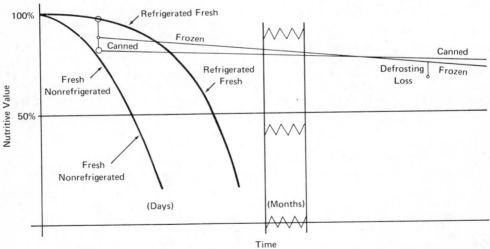

FIG. N-3. RELATIVE NUTRITIVE VALUES OF FRESH AND PROCESSED FOODS ACCORDING TO TIME

Processed foods offer good nutritive values extended over months of storage or distance from growing area, an invaluable asset for the preservation of nutrient value. Time of availability largely determines their relative nutritive values: (a) refrigerated fresh foods are generally superior to nonrefrigerated fresh foods; (b) refrigerated fresh produce is superior to processed (either canned or frozen) only within a brief period; (c) frozen products if thawed rapidly decline slightly compared with canned items, but, as a rule, prior to thawing are superior in nutritive value for many months.

temperatures above 98°F. Ascorbic acid is more stable at low temperatures and when packed in nitrogen. The retention of carotene is somewhat variable and dependent upon the amount of oxygen included in the container.

Whole-grain flours easily become rancid and are more subject to insect infestation if kept for any length of time so that a rapid turnover of this flour is essential. (In some European bakeries using ground whole wheat in baking, the grain is ground in the bakery at time of use.) In view of the loss of nutrients during flour milling and subsequent losses, it is of vast public health significance that refined flour be enriched with thiamin, riboflavin, niacin, and iron. This is equally true for flour to be used for breads, macaroni, spaghetti, crackers, pizza doughs, or other uses.

Milk

Some decrease may occur in the biological value of the protein of nonfat dry milk during storage. The rate of deterioration is determined largely by moisture content, being greater with increased moisture level. This decrease in biological value is due to aminoaldehyde condensation, first investigated by a French chemist, Maillard, during the years 1912–1917. This so-called "Maillard reaction" is accompanied by a physical change (browning) in the product.

While the exact loss in nutritional value of proteins after prolonged storage of nonfat dry milk is unknown, there have been conflicting reports relative to the same. Nevertheless, nonfat dry milk is highly regarded and is generally felt to retain its high nutritive value during storage.

The B-complex vitamins are quite stable to processing conditions encountered in the manufacture of dry milk products. The ascorbic acid content of reconstituted milk made from nonfat dry milk is on the average of 5.0–6.0 mg per liter of such milk. Air-packed, nonfat dry milk stored at room temperature for up to 1 yr retains about 80% of its ascorbic acid content. However, no form of milk can be regarded as an adequate source of ascorbic acid. The product is hygroscopic and it is important that water absorption be prevented in order that nonfat dry milk retain its organoleptic and nutritional value.

The only reported instances of vitamin B_6 deficiency due to inadvertent dietary lack occurred in infants fed a liquid milk formula sterilized by autoclaving and in which palm oil had replaced coconut oil as a source of essential fatty acids. The deficiency symptoms were readily corrected by the administration of vitamin B_6. Subsequent analysis of the formulas revealed that the vitamin B_6 level had been seriously impaired during the processing. New techniques for sterilizing by avoiding excessive heating have circumvented this difficulty.

Infant diarrhea is the result of a change in the intestinal flora when regular saprophytes are replaced by proteolytic organisms which do not require vitamin B_6 as an essential nutrient.

Some loss of vitamin A has been noted on storage of whole milk solids. No loss of carotene or vitamin A occurs when gas-packed, but considerable losses take place in samples stored with access to air.

Insect Infestation

Insect infestations induce several nutrient losses and chemical changes in stored foodstuffs. Primarily there is (1) a loss of thiamin but to some degree also (2) a loss of other B-vitamins, (3) an increase in fat acidity, and finally (4) a contamination through insect excreta and body fragments resulting in further chemical changes.

Consumption of heavily infested cereal grains may cause diarrhea. Such food-grains are obviously inferior in nutritive value and contain appreciable amounts of insect excreta. Continued consumption of such foodstuffs may produce harmful effects.

Naturally Occurring Toxicants

In 1973, the Committee on Food Protection of the Food and Nutrition Board, Natl. Res. Council —Natl. Acad. Sci., published a compilation of articles dealing with "Toxicants Occurring Naturally in Foods." Among the subjects covered are nitrates and nitrites in foods, trace elements, natural radioactivity in the biosphere and foodstuffs, toxic proteins and peptides, potential toxicity of food lipids, natural sulphur compounds, toxicity of the vitamins, antivitamins, enzyme inhibitors in foods, cyanogenic glucosides, plant phenolics, oxalates and phytates, microbial toxins, toxicants occurring naturally in spices and flavors, estrogens, and the toxicity of natural food chemicals. While this subject matter is not truly nutritional, the phenomena involved deserve mention in the overall coverage of food technology.

Differences Between Commercially Processed and Fresh Foods

The general principles involved in comparing processed with fresh or home-prepared foods are quite complex. They nevertheless need to be discussed. Processed foods are often compared to original raw products rather than to identical home-prepared foods, whether based on raw commodities or partially processed items. Many statements, as well as the public debate surrounding these issues, suffer from a lack of precision.

When comparing fresh products with commercially prepared foods, a reasonable basis must be chosen. Sometimes raw, nonprocessed products are directly compared to preserved items, overlooking the fact that the industrial product has been preprepared, and may have been trimmed, sliced, processed, and, in addition, stored for a lengthy period. Any reasonable comparison should naturally be made on identical products—at the moment of consumption. This implies that the preserved product, whether canned, frozen, dehydrated, or salted, should always be prepared ready for eating.

This brings into consideration the inevitable or normal nutrient losses incurred due to storage or in preparation. To obtain the edible portion for each food item, the respective net contents of a package (whether can, glass, or frozen package) has to be multiplied by an appropriate conversion factor. The common denominator for such a comparison consequently is the weighed edible portion of fresh produce.

The second important basis for comparison is the nutritional value. Even when a product seems to be identical as served, its nutrient value may be different when emanating from fresh products, as contrasted to a preserved product. The general opinion is that juice from raw fruits, such as citrus, must be superior to any juice purchased in cans or prepared by reconstituting frozen concentrates or powdered juice. However, such reconstituted items frequently offer the consumer a beverage richer in ascorbic acid and other nutrients than juices prepared from newly purchased fresh oranges which may be weeks removed from harvest, hauled long distances, and held for some time in storage or in supermarkets. Manufacturers who can fruits and vegetables processed at the peak of maturity and who are located near the growing regions are mostly in a position to offer products far superior as to ascorbic acid compared to fresh products shipped from far-removed regions, or grown in less favorable seasons. Processing also allows blending of seasonal batches to attain a more reasonable overall level of nutrients giving all consumers a more stable nutritional benefit.

There is frequently a similar seasonality in the vitamin content of milk, in particular as to vitamins A and E. This might in the future lead to fortification to guarantee a uniform nutritive value. Canned evaporated milk as well as nonfat milk solids manufactured from the surplus production in late spring and summer may provide a product which, when reconstituted, will contain more of certain nutrients than some fresh winter milks.

In some cases processed products will never be exactly comparable to those prepared in the home from fresh or raw counterparts. In other instances the processed item may be slightly modified due to technological necessities. This does not necessarily mean a nutritional deficiency, but sometimes a taste deviation. This, particularly, is in reference to canned items, which in all cases, have to be cooked during the sterilization process. Examples of this are cooked, processed tomatoes and pineapple and the familiar evaporated milk.

Many practices in general food distribution and home cooking impair the nutritive value of product to a far greater degree than commercial canning and freezing procedures which actually conserve certain minimum values of vital nutrients. Even in the case where a product is prepared in the home and is apparently identical with an industrial product, it may not match it from the nutritive point of view.

Another fundamental point in making nutritional comparisons is to ascertain that products being compared are actually in the same stage of preparation. It is only fair to compare a commercially processed product with an identical food prepared in the home in order to render a reasonable basis for comparison. Very few studies give truly comparative figures for the nutrient content of the same food, raw, cooked, canned or frozen—all based on the same original product as produced.

Nutritive evaluations should always indicate whether they refer to the food as harvested, as consumed, or as marketed or purchased (often with delays due to the distribution system). This is important in order to trace the losses of labile nutrients occurring in the various processing steps as well as in the storage and cooking losses of the food. One complicating factor is the degree to which water-soluble nutrients have been transferred to the liquid phases of the pack or, correspondingly, are discarded in home cooking. This explains why in some canned foods advice is given about using such liquids. Such examples are canned fish, meat, and some fruits.

Ascorbic acid is retained to a very considerable degree in the processing of most vegetables and fruits. Such processed foods compare well with similar fresh products purchased in the retail market where the same foods frequently have lost a considerable part of their nutrients in the course of distribution, marketing, and in the ordinary process of preparation in the home.

In a complete balance of comparison between a processed food and the comparable dish prepared in the home from nonprocessed commodities, several additional items frequently are overlooked. These items may include out-of-pocket costs as well as a requirement of more time on the part of the homemaker in the more frequent shopping for fresh products; the additional effort required for preparing raw ingredients for the table and disposing of the kitchen wastes as a result of trimming fresh products; and the capital outlay for specific equipment or appliances required for holding, cooking, and otherwise preparing individual fresh items. Even commercially processed foods require expenditure of time and perhaps monetary expenditure in disposing of glass containers, cans, cartons and other packaging materials. This type of balance helps to indicate the place of processed foods in the household.

Other equally essential considerations frequently neglected in previous research in this field are the changes in nutrient availability and digestibility induced by either processing or food preparation. The chemical composition, whether of raw products or their processed counterparts might, however, be less relevant as to their nutritive significance. Proteins, many vitamins, and minerals in food products are not readily available for efficient uptake. Not only are data on raw foods not accountable for losses in preparation but they may also be grossly misleading as to nutritive value. Frequently, only a fraction of what is contained may be actually digestible. Frequent examples are vitamins in raw vegetables, iron in cereal products, and phosphorus in most cereals. Cooking may also be essential in removing certain antivitamins and antitryptic factors.

This observation indicates a common and dangerous fallacy which frequently ensues from the use of compositional Tables. Excessive content for certain nutrients in some foods needs to be judged in relation to the level of intake as well as to the frequency of their use in each case. One fitting example is parsley. In almost all composition Tables this vegetable shows very high values for ascorbic acid, various trace elements (zinc, etc.), but parsley is actually eaten only in small amounts and is used primarily as a garnish. These highly favorable nutritive values carry little significance in the ordinary diet. Conversely, dietary items like potatoes, although not very potent in ascorbic acid may still account for a considerable daily dietary intake.

Data on food composition also need to be evaluated as to availability and digestibility. There is a fundamental difference between analytical figures and nutritive value. This field of research is complicated by drawing a clear distinction between chemical elements existing as such and the elements which are complexed in organic compounds and thus relatively unavailable. Shrimp, clams, and other foods are examples with organic arsenic compounds seemingly far less toxic, maybe even favorable, as compared to inorganic arsenic.

Food Sanitation

With modern techniques of food processing, the risk for infection and contamination is far greater with raw and home-prepared foods than with processed, packaged foods. After opening cans or defrosting frozen items there naturally exists, no longer, any important differences in this respect.

Recent cases of botulism, given great publicity, contrast drastically with the scant interest shown for the growing number of food poisoning cases primarily due to the expanding sector of mass-feeding. From the public health point of view it is therefore, despite these unfortunate instances, an important asset to rely on processed foods constituting a safer and more reliable way for distributing food and involving far less risk.

The chief advantage of processed foods is the vastly extended shelf-life, being of particular importance to marketing. The extremely long periods over which preserved and packaged foods do remain in good condition is a great asset in food distribution and marketing. Changes in such foods are minimal as compared to the profound and often rapid degradation taking place in the fresh products.

Such lengthened shelf-life and considerably protracted availability—often year round—is invaluable both in public health and to rational food planning on an economic basis.

Food Processing and the Safety of the Food Supply

The supply of food to an urbanized society entails food preservation and the manufacture of easily distributed and prepared food products. The advances of modern food processing and packaging have resulted in a wide array of foods and food products. They are, as a rule, taken for granted. Advances in processing on the whole have resulted in substantial improvements of nutritional standards through removing seasonality and creating dependable availability both in time and space. Even people living far from food producing areas have a wide choice within reach. There is no season of the year when an extensive variety of fresh (through refrigerated and processed foods) in liberal quantities is not available to the smallest community in many parts of the world. Fresh fish and seafoods are available where none were heretofore known; citrus fruits have become commonplace where sources of ascorbic acid had been scarce, and the sometimes monotonous diet of the farm house has become enriched and varied, all with the aid of advances in modern food technology.

Furthermore, the population is no longer exposed to the dangers of moldy or otherwise spoiled foods. The identification of a number of mycotoxins (aflatoxin and others) have revealed the magnitude and nature of this hazard.

Processed food products were initially looked

upon as expensive novelties but have come to occupy prominent places in the general dietary pattern and now serve to enrich the diet and to advance the cause of public health.

Infant nutrition has made particular strides. A whole new field of pediatric nutrition has opened up offering better nourishment and far better sanitary safeguards to this age group.

Morbidity, as well as mortality, in this nation have dropped notably. Essential nutrients are supplied as needed and with guaranteed levels as now expressed on many food labels due to the passage of nutritional labeling regulations by FDA.

A final order for nutritional labeling was issued by FDA in the *Federal Register* on Mar. 14, 1973. This order was synchronized with others pertaining to cholesterol, fat and fatty acid labeling statements, nutritional guidelines for frozen convenience dinners and naming of the dinners, labeling of diluted orange juice beverages, and the labeling of certain standardized foods. The order gives definition of the location of the information that is to be placed on the package and describes the format by which the information is to be displayed. For most foods the location of the nutrition information panel will be immediately contiguous and to the right of the principal display panel.

The information given in nutritional labeling will include the "average serving" of the product, the number of servings per container, the calories and grams of protein, carbohydrate, and fat per serving. In addition, the percentage of the Recommended Dietary Allowance (RDA) for protein and seven key vitamins and minerals will be shown. Optionally, the percentage of RDA for other nutrients may be shown. Also, one can opt to label for fatty-acid composition, cholesterol, and sodium content under the order issued by the FDA pertaining to this. Table N-30 gives an example of how a specific food product, mayonnaise, might be labeled concerning the requirements of these separate orders and comply.

The order further states that the final effective date for labeling for products shipped in interstate commerce is Dec. 31, 1975. A period of 1 yr between Dec. 31, 1974 and 1975 is allowed to make the transition of food manufacturer's labels ordered to comply with the regulations.

Simon and Kuehl (1973) recently reported results of an FDA survey of consumer opinion dealing with public assurance about the safety of foods. Among phases of the study were opinions on the safety of foods which contained pesticide residues, added color, and preservatives; and opinions as to who—government, food processors, consumers, etc. —did the most to make foods safe. Results of the survey were compared with corresponding data obtained from a 1966 survey. The FDA investigators

TABLE N-30

EXAMPLE OF NUTRITION LABEL INFORMATION FOR MAYONNAISE

One Serving (1 Tbsp) (13.5 Gm) Contains:	
Calories	100 Kcal
Protein	0 gm
Carbohydrates	0 gm
Fat	11 gm
Fatty acids:[1]	
Polyunsaturated	6 gm
Saturated	2 gm
Cholesterol (83 mg/100 gm)[1]	11 mg
Sodium (580 mg/100 gm)	80 mg

One serving of this product contains less than 2% U.S. RDA for protein, vitamin A, vitamin C, thiamin, riboflavin, niacin, iron, and calcium.
[1] Information on fat and cholesterol content is provided for individuals who, on the advice of a physician, are modifying their total dietary intake of fat or cholesterol.

were concerned that the survey results indicated that the public believed that food was getting less safe. In the view of FDA, there is no valid evidence to support this opinion. Because of recent advances in science and technology, there can now be identified and measured such minute amounts of substances in food as might have gone undetected in the past. Foods now are also microbiologically cleaner than they have ever been and the quality control systems available to manufacturers are more efficient than ever before.

In addition, FDA finds no evidence of any difference in safety among frozen, canned, or fresh foods when they are prepared, stored, and otherwise handled properly. Before a color or preservative can be added to food, the manufacturer must submit evidence that it is safe in the quantities it is to be used in the food. FDA maintains continuous surveillance of the scientific literature and of ongoing scientific testing and whenever new evidence indicates that any additive may be unsafe, FDA takes the necessary action.

At this writing, the FDA is conducting a comprehensive survey of the over 500 items on the GRAS (Generally Recognized as Safe) list of substances which are permitted as ingredients in food. Items on the present GRAS list are those which, in 1958, had been in use for such a long time that there was no question as to their being safe. When a substance not on the GRAS list is to be added to a food, the manufacturer must file a petition with FDA giving full data about the chemical makeup of the product, how it is to be used, and results of tests showing that the substance can be used safely.

Food manufacturers have the primary responsibility for assuring the safety of the food supply. The FDA monitors the manufacturers to assure that this responsibility is met. Other federal agencies are also involved in the safety of food. The USDA inspects and regulates meat, and the Environmental Protection Agency sets tolerances for pesticides.

GEORG A. BORGSTROM
JERRY F. PROCTOR

References

AMERICAN DRY MILK INSTITUTE. 1972. Census of Dry Milk Distribution and Production Trends, Am. Dry Milk Inst., Chicago, Ill.

BEESON, K. C. 1972-1973. What about the organic way? Plants Gardening, Winter Issue, 58-60.

BORGSTROM, G. A. 1973. Man, Food and Disease. Food and Population—A Critical Appraisal. Stanford Medical School, Palo Alto, Calif.

BRADLEY, W. B. 1967. Wheat foods as sources of nutrients. Baker's Dig. *41*, No. 5, 66-71.

BUNNELL, R. H., et al. 1965. Alpha-tocopherol content of foods. Am. J. Clin. Nutr. *17*, 1-10.

BURTON, B. T. 1965. The Heinz Handbook of Nutrition. McGraw-Hill Book Company, New York.

CLIFCORN, L. F. 1948. Factors influencing the vitamin content of canned foods. Advan. Food Res. *1*, 39-104.

COMMITTEE ON FOOD PROTECTION, FOOD AND NUTRITION BOARD, NATIONAL ACADEMY OF SCIENCES. Second Edition. Printing and Publication Office, 2101 Constitution Avenue, Washington, D. C. 20418.

COONS, CALLIE MAY. 1959. Fats and fatty acids. *In* Food. USDA Agr. Yearbook.

COULTER, S. T., JENNESS, R., and GEDDES, W. F. 1951. Physical and chemical aspects of the production, storage and utility of dry milk products. Advan. Food Res. *3*, 47-118.

CZERNIEJEWSKI, C. P., SHANK, C. W., BECHDEL, W. G., and BRADLEY, W. B. 1964. Minerals of wheat flour and bread. Cereal Chem. *41*, 65-72.

DANIEL, L., and NORRIS, L. C. 1944. Riboflavin content of milk and milk products. Food Res. *9*, 312-318.

DAVIDSON, S., and PASSMORE, R. 1969. Human Nutrition and Dietetics. Williams and Wilkins Co., Baltimore.

FARRER, K. T. J. 1955. The thermal destruction of vitamin B_1 in foods. Advan. Food Res. *6*, 257-311.

HALDEN, W. 1962. Nutritive Value of the Non-Fat, Non-Protein Solids of Milk. Intern. Dairy Federation Ann. Bull. Part II, Brussels, Belgium.

HARDINGE, M. G., and CROOKS, H. 1961. Lesser known vitamins in foods. J. Am. Dietet. Assoc. *38*, 240-245.

HARDINGE, M. G. et al. 1965. Carbohydrates in foods. J. Am. Dietet. Assoc. *46*, 197-204.

HARRIS, R. S., and VON LOESECKE, H. 1971. Nutritional Evaluation of Food Processing.

Now available from Avi Publishing Co., Westport, Conn.

HATHAWAY, M. L., and LEVERTON, R. M. 1959. Calcium and phosphorus. *In* Food. USDA Agr. Yearbook.

HEGSTED, D. M. 1969. Nutrition value of cereal protein in relation to human needs. *In* Protein Enriched Cereal Foods for World Needs. M. Milner (Editor). Am. Assoc. Cereal Chemists, St. Paul.

ICNND. 1963. Manual for Nutrition Surveys, 2nd Edition. Interdepartmental Committee on Nutrition for National Defense, Washington, D. C.

INTERN. DAIRY FEDERATION. 1962. Nutritive Value of Milk and Dairy Products. Ann. Bull. Part II, Brussels, Belgium.

KON, S. K. 1959. Milk and Milk Products in Human Nutrition. FAO Nutritional Studies *17*.

MACY, I. G., KELLY, H. J., and SLOAN, R. E. 1953. Composition of Milks. Natl. Res. Council—Natl. Acad. Sci. Publ. *254*.

MARINE, G., and VAN ALLEN, J. 1972. Food Pollution. The Violation of Our Inner Ecology. Holt, Rinehart, and Winston, New York.

McCANCE, R. A., and WIDDOWSON, E. M. 1960. The Composition of Foods. Privy Council, Med. Res. Council Spec. Rept. Ser. *297*. HM Stationery Office, London, England.

MUNRO, H. N., and ALLISON, J. B. 1964. Mammalian Protein Metabolism, Vol. 2. Academic Press, New York.

NATIONAL DAIRY COUNCIL. 1968. Newer Knowledge of Milk, 3rd Edition. Natl. Dairy Council, Chicago.

NATIONAL DAIRY COUNCIL. 1973. The role of essential trace elements in nutrition. Dairy Council Dig. *44*, July-August.

NATL. RES. COUNCIL—NATL. ACAD. SCI. 1968. A Report of the Food and Nutrition Board, Recommended Dietary Allowances, National Research Council, 7th Revised Edition.

ORR, M. L. 1969. Pantothenic acid, vitamin B_6 and vitamin B_{12} in foods. USDA Home Econ. Res. Rept. *36*.

ORR, M. L., and WATT, B. K. 1957. Amino acid content of foods. USDA Home Econ. Res. Rept. *4*.

POTTER, N. N. 1968. Food Science. Avi Publishing Company, Westport, Conn.

PYLER, E. J. 1973. Bleaching and maturing of flour. *In* Baking Science and Technology, Vol. 1. Siebel Publishing Co., Chicago, Ill.

RAO, M. N. 1972. Trace elements—toward definition of dietary allowances. I. Manganese. Nutr. Newsletter *10*, 1-7.

RICE, E. E., and BEUK, F. J. 1953. The effects of heat upon the nutritive value of protein. Advan. Food Res. *4*, 235-279.

ROBINSON, C. H. 1968. Fundamentals of Normal Nutrition. Macmillan Co., New York.

ROSENFIELD, D. 1973. Utilizable protein: quality and quantity concepts in assessing food. Food Prod. Develop. *7*, 57-62.

RYGG, G. L. 1949. Changes in carotenoid content of harvested carrots. Proc. Am. Soc. Hort. Sci. *54*, 307–309.

SCHÜTTE, K. H. 1964. The Biology of the Trace Elements. Their Role in Nutrition, Crosby Lockwood & Son, London (U.K.).

SIMON, M. E., and KUEHL, P. G. 1973. A survey of consumer opinion about the safety of foods. FDA Consumer 7, No. 5, 15.

SHROEDER, H. A. 1971. Losses of vitamins and trace minerals resulting from processing and preservation of foods. Am. J. Clin. Nutr. *24*, 562–573.

U.S. DEPT. OF AGR. 1959. Fatty acids in animal and plant products. USDA Nutr. Res. Div. (Human), Agr. Res. Serv.

WATT, B. K., and MERRILL, A. L. 1963. Composition of Foods. USDA Agr. Handbook 8.

WEBB, B. H., and WHITTIER, E. O. 1970. Byproducts From Milk, 2nd Edition. Avi Publishing Co., Westport, Conn.

Cross-reference: *Bioassay*.

NUTRITIONAL LABELING[1]

The safety, quality, and honest representation of the U.S. food supply, always subject to scrutiny, criticism, and improvement, has come under especially heavy attack in recent years. In addition to the wide range of difficult and often controversial questions discussed today, safety, quality, and honest representation extend to the nutritional attributes of foods. At the time of this writing it is fair to say that no food-related issue is receiving more attention than the question of the nutritional quality of the U.S. food supply especially with respect to products that have been highly processed. Since the 1969 and 1971 White House Conferences on Food, Nutrition and Health, there has been a kind of nutritional awareness revolution in the making; and along with this an unprecedented amount of energy is being directed toward means of communicating meaningful nutritional information to increasingly sensitized consumers. Terms such as "empty calories" charged against breakfast cereals, and "bellywash" directed against juiceless fruit-type drinks have strongly aroused consumers. There is now increasing demand for nutritional product improvement and nutritional labeling, and in some cases this is strongly justified.

The complexities inherent in nutritional product improvement and nutritional labeling are remarkably diverse. It therefore is not surprising that

opinions and recommendations currently being advanced by consumerists, consumers, food manufacturers and distributors, nutritionists, and governmental agencies frequently are not in agreement. In a sense the issue of nutritional product improvement and nutritional labeling is like the proverbial iceberg. What lies above the surface is readily apparent. The consumer has a right to the best nutritional quality that science and technology can economically provide, and a right to *know* the nutritional attributes of her food purchases. But hidden beneath these obvious rights are innumerable problems in providing substantive nutritional improvements and relevant consumer information that is accurate, comprehensible, and not misleading. Further, from the standpoint of the food industry, nutritional guidelines now being developed by government must be such as to prohibit unethical competitive merchandising practices, yet retain a climate conducive to nutritional product improvement through reformulation, enrichment, or fortification where real advantages can be gained.

Current efforts by governmental agencies to draft meaningful guidelines are being frustrated by many factors. In addition to numerous gaps in the state of present nutritional knowledge, these include political and economic considerations as well as the problems of educating the public in matters of nutritional relevance. Problems that must be faced by food processors with regard to raw material selection, manufacturing operations, and overall quality control to assure validity of nutritional label declarations are no less formidable. The nature of these problems must be understood by today's food scientist.

Foods Are Changing

One might ask, why has there developed an intensification of interest in nutrition in recent years? Have foods become less nutritious? Has the food industry become less ethical? Some answers can be given. If one refers back to how food was marketed in the early 1900's, and this still is essentially the way food is sold in many less technologically developed countries, it is clear that commodities were easily recognizable, and those consumers who understood that a varied diet of plant and animal products provided the necessities for health did not have difficulty in identifying such products when they were available. While this early type of marketing certainly did not guarantee a nutritionally adequate diet, it stood in sharp contrast to today's supermarket with its thousands of different items, most of which are highly processed convenience foods often obscured in terms of their component ingredients.

---

[1] Reprinted from *Food Science, 2nd Edition* (1973) by Norman N. Potter, published by Avi Publishing Co., Westport, Conn.

Today more food preparations are appearing that contain meat analogues or meat substitutes. Fabricated meat structures from soybean and other proteins can be interlaced with fats and other ingredients to provide the widest spectrum of nutrient composition. Without some kind of nutritional information or minimum standard that such products should meet, the consumer can't possibly know the nutritional attributes of the many products possible using this new technology.

An example from products belonging to the group sometimes designated as nondairy imitation milks is further informative. A large number of such products, generally formulated from vegetable oils, sugars, and proteins of dairy and other origin have appeared in recent years. While some of these products have been formulated to resemble milk in terms of amounts of protein, carbohydrate, and fat, others do not come close to milk's gross composition, and few even approach milk in terms of vitamin and mineral content. Thus, in one recent comprehensive study of 13 commercial nondairy imitation milks it was found that several of the samples contained less than 20% and some less than 10% of the riboflavin or thiamin content of cow's milk. The study further revealed gross deficiencies in levels of total protein, essential amino acids, calcium, and other nutrients for which milk is generally consumed. Alarmingly, 4 of the 13 samples contained less than 5% of the calcium present in cow's milk. Here certainly is a case for informative nutritional labeling, or some minimum standard of nutritional quality, since such products used in place of milk could lead to serious problems, especially among the young.

There presently are marketed numerous drinks that may or may not contain natural fruit juices in their formulation. The FDA and various states have set standards that include minimum contents of natural juices required in such products. Classifications of the FDA for orange juices and drinks have specified the following percentages of single-strength juice in the different products: orange juice—100%, orange juice drink—not less than 50% of orange juice present, orangeade—not less than 25%, orange drink—not less than 10%, orange soda—no juice required, imitation orange—no juice required. These classifications have been the target of much criticism on the grounds that they are not understood by the consumer and tend to misrepresent the real value of the products. Alternate designations for such products are being considered. Since orange juice commonly is consumed for its vitamin C content many believe that such products (as well as orange juice) should be required to display accurate information with respect to this vitamin on their labels.

One could cite numerous additional examples of foods that no longer resemble their generic counterparts in terms of nutritional attributes. This alone explains much of the current interest in nutrition and makes opposition to some form of nutritional labeling a very difficult position to defend.

Information Needed

The Food and Drug Administration, in cooperation with the National Research Council's Food and Nutrition Board and the food industry, has been gathering information as the basis for guidelines on nutritional labeling and fortification or enrichment practices for various classes of foods. These classes include minimally processed commodities, prepared meals, fabricated foods and analogs, breakfast cereals, and other important groups. Problems that are being given consideration include the following. What kinds of information should labels provide? Suggestions have ranged from mandatory fortification and complete listing of kinds and amounts of all essential nutrients in a given food, including trace minerals, to optional declaration of only the most important nutrients for which a food is a recognized major source. Should enrichment or fortification of major commodities be encouraged, and if so how much of which nutrients should be permitted in what commodity? Should fabricated foods be made nutritionally complete, and if so on what basis should vitamins and minerals be permitted? Obviously if a large number of foods are enriched to provide a substantial percentage of a nutrient's Recommended Dietary Allowance per serving, persons are likely to receive the nutrient in excess, which at best is wasteful, but more serious, may be physiologically harmful as with vitamin D, vitamin A, and iron. Some have suggested a food's caloric content as the base for nutrient supplementation levels on the logic that daily caloric intake is rather constant for an individual. Such a scheme would tend to promote balanced nutrition in proportion to the quantity of food consumed, but independent of dietary selection. Others have suggested that protein content of a food be included along with calories as a basis for permitted levels of added vitamins and minerals.

If protein is to be declared on labels as most agree it should, should the listing ultimately be of gross quantity, amino acid composition, or some other measure of protein quality? The consumer will draw confidence from figures designating gross quantity, but then will she appreciate the nutritional differences between various proteins, including animal and vegetable proteins in formulated products? Most will not. Nor will extensive lists of amino acids be readily comprehensible to her. Should iron be listed in terms of amount or physiological availability? In any event what analytical methods shall be deemed officially acceptable for purposes of quality control and inspection? What about changes in food standards of identity to allow nutrient additions where they are not presently permitted?

Communication and Consumer Education

As important as any of the above are the questions of communication and consumer education. Imposing lists of nutrients by themselves will prove confusing even to the moderately informed. It is becoming generally agreed that the purpose of nutritional labeling is to help the homemaker toward informed selection of nutritionally sound foods for balanced meal planning. Simplicity is to be favored over more specific data that would be required by a dietitian, and would be available to the dietitian from the manufacturer upon request. But then what is simple?

One possible kind of informative labeling wouldn't list nutrients but would simply list ingredients in the food. An example would be the listing of major ingredients and their percentages in a frozen or canned beef and vegetable stew. Brand X might then differ from Brand Y in containing 2% more beef, 3% more carrots, 6% less peas, 10% less potatoes, and 11% more water. But is the information really informative? The higher levels of beef and carrots, and the lower level of starchy potatoes in Brand X might be considered favorably by the consumer. But Brand X also has less protein-containing peas and more water. How should these be balanced? Such labeling would not only leave the average consumer in doubt but would give a trained nutritionist difficulty in deciding between the two products on nutritional grounds.

Additional simplified labeling schemes have been suggested and three have received thorough study to determine which would be most meaningful to all segments of the population.

The first of the three labeling schemes used percentages of the Recommended Dietary Allowances of the major nutrients actually present in a typical portion of a given food product. Here, still unresolved are questions arising from the fact that the Recommended Dietary Allowance values for various nutrients differ for children and adults.

The second system was similar to the first, but percentages were replaced by units. Thus, for example, a food portion containing 50% of a nutrient's Recommended Dietary Allowance listed 5 units, while another food containing 100% would list 10 units for that particular nutrient.

The third system used descriptive terms such as "fair," "good," "very good," or "excellent" corresponding to a list of important nutrients present in a serving of the food. Such a system would require FDA establishment of quantitative ranges for the important nutrients that correspond to the descriptive terms to prevent nonuniform use of terms by different manufacturers.

These labeling systems also included data on the actual amounts in grams of protein, carbohydrate, fat, and calories present in a portion of the food, and a general statement of the type "If you want more detailed information on the nutritional composition of the product write to . . ." and the address of the manufacturer.

These system proposals were considered for relative merits by food manufacturers, trade associations, advertising agencies, and were consumer tested. The study showed that some form of nutritional labeling was favored by the majority of consumers involved and that most consumers preferred a labeling scheme that utilized percentages of the Recommended Dietary Allowance for nutrients plus amount data for protein, carbohydrate, fat, and calories. These findings were incorporated into proposed rules for nutritional labeling that were published in the Federal Register on March 30, 1972. More will be said about these proposed rules shortly.

Knowledge Gaps

Quite apart from the problems of communication, a move to nutritional supplementation of foods and nutritional labeling immediately focuses attention upon present gaps in knowledge. The acquisition of nutritional data has not kept up with the rate of technological development of new food products and processes in recent years, and so a knowledge gap will have to be closed before there can be a major shift to nutritional product improvement and labeling.

Reference guides to food compositions, such as *Handbook 8* of the U.S. Dept. of Agr., will not be adequate for calculation of nutrient levels in a great many food products currently marketed. In many instances handbook values do not apply to new varieties of fruits and vegetables, or to changing geographic growing regions, harvest times, and degrees of maturity—all being influenced more and more by mechanical harvesting and special processing requirements. Nor do classical handbook values necessarily reflect nutrient changes from advanced storage methods, processing conditions, or reconstitution techniques. They do not contain data on manufactured proprietary products such as complex mixtures of ingredients, ethnic and snack foods, or food analogs. It may surprise some that one cannot now look up the nutrient composition of frozen pizza, fried egg rolls, canned soups, or various cake mixes and come away with reliable information. To be sure, nutrient compositions of many canned soups are listed in *Handbook 8* of the U.S. Dept. of Agr., but new formulations and changes in ingredients since its publication in 1963 limit accuracy. Further, many of the ethnic and regional foods for which data do not now exist are important items in the diets of poorly nourished poverty groups. Thus, the eating habits of American Indians, Mexican Americans, and certain Black American groups will have to receive special attention.

Handbook data also frequently fail to account for the food in the final form in which it will be eaten. Nutrient values for pork, chicken, or most other foods depend upon the cut, degree of trim, and extent of processing, including whether cooked at home or precooked and held on steam tables, as done with many institutional products.

The list of products for which nutritional data is presently inadequate is really quite formidable. An indication was given by Watt and Murphy in the June 1970 issue of *Food Technology*. Watt is the senior author of *Handbook 8* of the U.S. Dept. of Agr., entitled *Composition of Foods—Raw, Processed, Prepared*. Among various food groups inadequate nutritional data were cited in numerous specific areas.

Thus, in the past, the food industry generally was not concerned with quantitative data on the vitamin and mineral contents of raw or processed meat, poultry, or fish, and so new data will be required. This is especially true of meats other than beef, and for turkey in all its forms.

With regard to bread and other wheat products, data must be extended to cover breads made by the continuous mix method. Still less is known about the nutrient contents of sweet rolls, raised doughnuts, bagels, pretzels, pizzas and farina. What losses are to be expected when different types of macaroni, spaghetti, and noodles are cooked and drained? Ingredients differ in cake, cookie, pie crust, muffin, and other convenience mixes. This includes differences in kinds and amounts of fats for shortening. Adequate data also are lacking on different kinds and forms of rice.

Among fruits and vegetables, data are needed on new varieties of citrus fruits. Little is now available on the nutrient contents of varieties of avocados. Sweet potato varieties differ in vitamin A content, and are affected differently by storage. This also is true of carrots. New varieties of tomatoes have been introduced that are especially suited to mechanical harvesting. Their contents of vitamins C and A, and their sensitivities to processing losses need more study. New white potato varieties with high solids and nitrogen contents are being developed and will require investigation to determine nutrient changes during storage and processing. With regard to the considerable number of canned fruit and vegetable products, much of the nutritional data in the literature is based on intensive studies of the early 1940's. How have processing changes affected current products?

We know still less about a number of new products that have gained wide acceptance. Among these are coffee whiteners in liquid, powder, and frozen forms; dessert toppings; frozen desserts; canned puddings; dry roasted nuts; products containing soybean derivatives or freeze-dried components; snack foods; etc. The FDA already has indicated that for purposes of nutritional labeling not handbook values but direct analyses on specific products will generally be required. Certainly no less would be adequate where raw materials, formulations, and processing conditions rarely remain static.

Gaps in our knowledge go far beyond compositional data. We do not know enough about the influences of functional food additives on important nutrients. For example, what effects do chelating agents have on trace minerals, or phosphates upon calcium in processed foods? Methods of analysis will have to be improved or devised to yield rapid and accurate results despite interfering substances in complex formulations. If amino acid compositions are ever to be listed on labels then much research will be required on more reliable protein hydrolysis techniques, which yield variable results depending upon degree of completeness and severity. Basic studies involving animal feeding tests will be required if nutrient utilization information is ever to become part of nutritional labeling.

New Responsibilities

Certainly nutritional labeling will place a whole new set of responsibilities upon industry. When a manufacturer lists a nutrient and its concentration on a product label he will be responsible for the accuracy of the declaration. Further, to be meaningful, the declaration surely will have to describe the food as close to the time of consumption as feasible, rather than the product's nutrient content as manufactured. Some tolerance with respect to amount will have to be allowed, but it is doubtful that more than a 20% discrepancy on the low side of a stated nutrient level can be justified. Thus, nutrient labelers will have to maintain an active testing and quality control program to ensure nutritional values on final products in the marketplace.

Quality assurance programs will have to include controls over nutritional specifications of purchased ingredients, ingredient storage, all phases of processing, and product storage including warehousing, supermarket turnover and expected holding time by the customer where feasible. Where a product is manufactured for wide range distribution, the possible effects of climate on storage stability of nutrients will have to be taken into account. These problems are not new to manufacturers of breakfast cereals and dietetic foods, but can add significantly to the production rigors of canners, freezers, and others choosing to use nutritional labeling.

Today readily available components of manufactured foods often are purchased on short notice to take advantage of changing prices. Functionally interchangeable ingredients also are substituted for one another as availability changes with season of the year. It also is common for a manufacturer to adjust processing temperatures and times to compensate for varying raw materials. Such practices will be more difficult with nutritional labeling, as will be application of any processing innovation that may affect the validity of label statements.

Manufacturers wishing to declare nutrient composition will face additional difficulties with regard to physical space on labels. This can be a greater problem with bottles and cans than with flat packages. Products that have standards of identity need not now list ingredient composition, which simplifies labeling. A separate question, but one that is directly related to label space, is whether food standards of identity ultimately will be changed to incorporate nutritional limits. Would nutritional labeling of standardized products for consumer information then become a subsequent requirement?

Certainly nutritional labeling will become a powerful factor in the competitive marketing of foods. This will force government to carefully consider equity in the granting of enrichment or fortification rights to various classes of products. For example, today certain vitamins can legally be added to margarine but not to butter. The butter industry considers this unfair, and there are many similar examples with other products. This type of inequity will become more important as consumers increasingly seek out the nutritional attributes of different products.

The nutritional value of certain foods has been subject to adjustment for many years. Vitamin D is added to milk, iodine to salt, and flour is enriched with thiamin, riboflavin, niacin, and iron for the making of bread. More recently some major manufacturers of crackers and snack foods have begun using enriched flour in their cookie, cracker, and snack food items. Several breakfast cereals have provided substantial quantities of vitamins and iron for years. But a great deal more is coming and research and development laboratories of major food companies are intensively working at nutrition. In fact, one of their current problems is to restrain their marketing divisions, many of which are pressing for the widest variety of nutritionally adjusted new products.

Government's role in providing and enforcing nutritional guidelines will not be an easy one. Government will be caught between various interest groups. Some of the current activities related to improving the nutritional quality of meals fed to school children illustrate this.

Public demands for nutritionally adequate breakfasts and lunches in federally subsidized school feeding programs have been intensified, especially since the White House Conferences on Food, Nutrition, and Health. The U.S. Dept. of Agr. has set criteria for fortified and extended foods that can be used in its school feeding programs. Criteria have been developed for three kinds of new products. One is a fortified baked product with a cream filling that should appeal to children. It can serve as a replacement for fruit or juice and bread or cereal in school breakfasts. This product with $1/2$ pt of milk will supply $1/4$ to $1/3$ of the Recommended Dietary Allowance for a 10- to 12-yr old child. Obviously fruit, juice, and cereal interests can be affected. A second product for school lunches is a protein-fortified, enriched, macaroni-type product that can nutritionally replace $1/2$ of the present 2-oz requirement for meat, poultry, cheese, or fish. The third type of product is meat extended with texturized vegetable protein up to a level of 30% of the product by weight. These will help schools provide nutrition at a cost that might otherwise be limiting. The meat and related industries can be affected in these latter two cases.

A large number of food companies already are supplying texturized soy protein or soy-extended meat products to schools. At least one major baking company has developed cream-filled fortified baked products that meet U.S. Dept. of Agr. criteria. At least two fortified macaroni-type products also have been developed for school feeding purposes. Here standards of identity were an obstacle to approval of this kind of product. Standards of identity for macaroni define ingredients that may be used in products recognized as macaroni. A new standard of identity was proposed for fortified macaroni by the Food and Drug Administration but it was met by objections from various interests in the macaroni industry. A similar situation has existed with fortified peanut butter, and many new and nutritionally exciting products will undoubtedly have to fight their way into commercial existence against regulations that were originally adopted to ensure food quality of another kind, as well as to protect specific commodity and food industry interests.

But a more general problem that government faces in this complex area of fortification, enrichment, and nutritional labeling is to devise rules to regulate what product claims a manufacturer may properly make on labels and in advertising. Here a special set of guidelines will be required. Today relatively few food products are promoted on the basis of nutrition. Along with fortification and nutritional labeling will come an increasing motivation to use statements such as "a balanced meal in a can," or "nutritionally equivalent to a steak dinner," or "complete nourishment for the athlete," and the like. Such statements, and still more subtle ones, will require much wisdom on the part of the FDA and the Federal Trade Commission for their regulation.

As stated earlier, on March 30, 1972 the FDA published its proposed nutritional labeling rules in the Federal Register for reaction and comment. These guidelines and criteria presently are undergoing modification but continue to provide the basis for nutritional labeling regulation. Sections from these proposed rules are reproduced below:

> The Commissioner has concluded, on the basis of the information available at the present time, that nutritional labeling should be based on the following general criteria:
> 1. Vitamins and minerals should be expressed as a proportion of the Recommended Daily Allowances (RDA) modified to provide a single RDA level for all ages and sexes.
> 2. The labeling should indicate the caloric content and the amounts of protein, carbohydrate, and fat in the product.
> 3. The nutrition content should be related to a portion or serving of the food expressed in common household terms or in easily identified units.
> 4. A complete listing of the seven important vitamins and minerals should appear on all products unless the product contains essentially none of these vitamins or minerals.
> 5. A listing of protein content should appear on all products unless the product contains no protein.
> Listing protein in terms of both the amount present in the product and a percentage of the RDA offers consumers maximum information. Concern has been expressed that protein quality should be incorporated into this statement. Such a protein quality factor could be established by requiring that any protein with a quality less than that of casein must reduce the claimed contribution by the factor obtained by dividing 100 into the protein quality of the protein expressed as a percentage of the quality

of casein as determined in standard protein evaluation tests and then multiplying the actual protein content by this factor. This calculation would give the amount of protein to be used in determining the percentage of RDA for the protein. A lower limit could also be set for any statement relating to protein quality; for example, no protein with a quality less than 50% of casein could be stated on the label in terms of the percentage of RDA. This approach offers maximum information but is complicated both for the manufacturer and for the consumer. Comment is particularly requested on this question.

The Commissioner also requests that comments be provided by interested groups and individuals on whether it would be most useful to consumers for protein, carbohydrate, and fat content to be stated by percentage, by weight, or by grams per portion.

The Commissioner is aware that there is variation in the natural nutrient content of food products. In developing a nutrition labeling system, it is therefore important that the manufacturer be permitted a sufficient tolerance so that he may provide useful nutrition information on the label without incurring excess costs for quality control which will result in a significant increase in prices to the consumer. However, consumers will expect that the nutrition labels will honestly represent the product. By using a precentage of the RDA expressed in increments of 5 to 10%, some of the variation in products can be accommodated. In addition, for the purposes of nutrition labeling, the statement will be considered in compliance if at least 80% of the product in the package meets or exceeds the claimed nutrient levels, and if no sample of the product will have a nutrient content less than 80% of the nutrient claim.

Finally, manufacturers frequently ask where to print nutrition labeling and other related information which is not required on the principal display panel. It is important that such information appear in a uniform location so that consumers will have it readily available. Uniformity in displaying such information will make it more easily found and read by consumers under normal conditions of purchase and use. For a number of years canners have utilized an information panel for serving sizes and other pertinent information concerning the contents of a can. Breakfast cereal manufacturers have primarily utilized one panel for nutrition information. An information panel, as well as the principal display panel, is a suitable location for nutrition information. The Commissioner therefore proposes to define the information panel as that part of the label immediately to the right of the principal display panel. If the package has alternate display panels the information panel may appear to the right of either. If the top of the container is the principal display panel, and there is no alternate principal display panel, the information panel is any part of the label adjacent to the top.

§1.16 Food; nutrition labeling.

(a) Nutrition information relating to a packaged food may be included on the label of the product provided that it conforms to the requirements of this section.

(b) All nutrient quantities including vitamins, minerals, calories, protein, fats, and carbohydrates shall be declared in relation to the average or usual serving expressed in common household measurements or in terms of a unit which is easily identified as an average or usual serving. The weight of the serving may also be expressed in grams. The declaration shall contain the following items:

(1) The heading shall be "Nutrition Information."

(2) A statement of the serving size shall be given.

(3) A statement of the caloric content per serving shall be expressed to the nearest 5-calorie increment.

(4) A statement of the number of grams of protein, fat, and available carbohydrates per serving shall be expressed to the nearest gram.

(5) A statement of the amounts per serving of the vitamins and minerals listed in paragraph (c) of this section shall be expressed in percentages of the Recommended Dietary Allowances (RDA) as stated in paragraph (d) of this section. The percentages are expressed in 10-percent increments, except that 5-percent increments may be used up to the 20-percent level. Nutrients present in an amount comprising less than 5 percent of the RDA shall be considered insignificant and will be so listed under the RDA percentage. However, if a product does not contain at least 5 percent of the RDA for any of the vitamins or minerals listed in paragraph (c), the statement, "Contains no significant quantities of vitamins and minerals," may be used in place of the complete listing of the vitamins and minerals required in paragraph (c). The listing shall follow the order given in paragraph (c).

(6) A statement of the amount of protein present per serving shall be expressed as a percentage of the 65-gram RDA. The percentages are expressed in 10-percent increments, except that 5-percent increments may be used up to the 20-percent level. Protein present in an amount less than 5 percent of the RDA shall be considered insignificant. In such cases, the amount of protein will be represented either as 0 percent of the RDA or by the words "none" or "insignificant," whichever is appropriate. However, if a product contains no protein, the protein expressed as a percent of the RDA need not be listed.

(c) In the case of vitamins and minerals, the label declaration must contain information on vitamin A, vitamin C, thiamin, riboflavin, niacin, calcium, and iron and may contain information on any of the other vitamins and minerals listed in paragraph (d) of this section.

(d) For the purposes of nutrition labeling, the following daily amounts of vitamins and minerals are the standard Recommended Daily Allowances (RDA):

	(International Units)
Vitamin A	5,000
Vitamin D	400
Vitamin E	30
	(Milligrams)
Ascorbic acid (vitamin C)	60
Thiamin (vitamin B_1)	1.5
Riboflavin (vitamin B_2)	1.7
Niacin	20
Vitamin B_6	2
Folacin (folic acid)	0.4
Vitamin B_{12}	0.006
Biotin	0.3
Pantothenic acid	10
Calcium	1,000
Phosphorus	1,000
Iron	18
Iodine	0.15
Zinc	15
Magnesium	400
Copper	2

These nutrient levels have been adopted by the Food and Drug Administration from information in a report of the Food and Nutrition Board, National Academy of Sciences—National Research Council. *Recommended Dietary Allowances, Seventh Edition, 1968.*

(e) A statement may be included offering additional information upon written request to a specified address. Any such additional labeling shall comply with all the requirements of Part 1 and, if applicable, Part 125 of this chapter.

(f) The location of the nutrition information on the label shall be in compliance with §1.8d.

Refinements and additions to the above guidelines, based on over 3000 responses from consumers, manufacturers, scientists, and trade associations were reported in the Jan. 19, 1973 and Mar. 14, 1973 issues of the Federal Register. Reference to subsequent issues of the Federal Register will be necessary to keep abreast of official regulations governing nutritional labeling.

At the present time the decision by a manufacturer to adopt nutritional labeling is voluntary, but there is pressure to ultimately make it mandatory for at least certain foods. The FDA also has stated that where manufacturers elect to use nutritional labeling they will have to conform to a single approved system. Nonuniform nutritional labeling that would result in consumer confusion will not be permitted. Guidelines to regulate nutrient additions to various classes of foods also will be forthcoming.

The consumer does indeed have a right to improved nutrition and the right to know. But to secure these rights added costs will have to be borne by the consumer. The benefits that can be derived from nutritional upgrading and nutritional labeling intelligently applied can outweigh the costs. It is doubtful that all foods warrant nutritional supplementation or nutritional labeling, and those that do surely do so to different extents.

In the years ahead the food manufacturer will have to become increasingly concerned about nutrition. What must not be permitted, however, is a nutritional arms race encouraged by overzealous consumerists and waged by insufficiently informed and prepared manufacturers eyeing a lucrative market. This would only serve to penalize the consumer and discredit the food industry.

NORMAN N. POTTER

References

ANON. 1970. White House Conference on Food, Nutrition and Health—Final Report. U.S. Govt. Printing Office, Washington, D.C.

ANON. 1971. Philosophy and guidelines for nutritional standards for processed foods. Food Technol. 25, 36, 38.

BABCOCK, M. J. 1971. A proposed system for nutritive labeling. Food Technol. 25, 1160–1161.

CALL, D. L., and HAYES, M. G. 1970. Reactions of nutritionists to nutrient labeling of foods. Am. J. Clin. Nutr. 23, 1347–1352.

DEUTSCH, R. M. 1971. The Family Guide to Better Food and Better Health. Meredith Corp., Des Moines, Iowa.

FLECK, H., and MUNVES, E. 1969. Introduction to Nutrition. Macmillan Co., New York.

FOOD AND DRUG ADMINISTRATION, DEPT. OF HEALTH, EDUCATION AND WELFARE. 1972. Nutrition labeling—proposed criteria for food label information panel. Federal Register 37, No. 62, 6493–6497.

FOOD AND DRUG ADMINISTRATION, DEPT. OF HEALTH, EDUCATION AND WELFARE. 1973. Food Labeling. Federal Register 38, No. 13, 2124–2164.

FOOD AND DRUG ADMINISTRATION, DEPT. OF HEALTH, EDUCATION AND WELFARE. 1973. Food Labeling. Federal Register 38, No. 49, 6950–6975.

HARRIS, R. S., and VON LOESECKE, H. (Editors) 1960. Nutritional Evaluation of Food Processing. Reprinted in 1971 by Avi Publishing Co., Westport, Conn.

HOWARD, H. W. 1971. What useful purpose is served by quantitative ingredient labeling? Food Prod. Develop. 5, No. 4, 34, 36, 38.

KOSIKOWSKI, F. V. 1971. Nutritive and organoleptic characteristics of nondairy imitation milks. J. Food Sci. 36, 1021–1025.

LACHANCE, P. A. 1970. Nutrification, a new nutritional concept for new types of foods. Food Technol. 24, 724.

LACHANCE, P. A. 1971. Innovation vs. nutrition as the criterion for product development. Food Technol. 25, 615–617.

McINTIRE, J. M. 1972. Proposes nutritional guidelines for formulated meals—foods of the future. Food Technol. 26, No. 4, 34, 36, 39, 42.

NAT. ACAD. SCI.—NAT. RES. COUNCIL. 1968. Recommended Dietary Allowances. Natl. Res. Council Publ. 1694.

POTTER, N. N. 1972. Problems related to the nutritional labeling of food products. J. Milk Food Technol. 35, No. 2, 107–111.

ROBINSON, C. H. 1967. Proudfit-Robinson's Normal and Therapeutic Nutrition. Macmillan Co., New York.

U.S. DEPT. AGR. 1969. Food for Us All, The Yearbook of Agriculture. U.S. Dept. Agr.

WATT, B. K., and MERRILL, A. L. 1963. Composition of Foods—Raw, Processed, Prepared. U.S. Dept. Agr., Agr. Handbook 8.

WATT, B. K., and MURPHY, E. W. 1970. Tables of food composition: scope and needed research. Food Technol. 24, 674–676, 678, 682–684.

O

OATS

Archaeological findings demonstrate that oats were known many years B.C.; however, little is known about their use as a food crop. The widespread use of this crop as a food developed in Scotland, Germany, and Russia. However, its use as a food appears to be much later than that of wheat, rye, or barley. Ferdinand Schumacher was the first large oat miller in America.

The milling process as a food has also undergone a great deal of change and now incorporates modern methods and equipment to produce hot cereals, low in cost, but high in quality and nutritious value. Only about 5% of the American oat crop is milled for food. Approximately 85% of the crop remains on the farms as feed.

Oats of good quality are specially selected and arrive at the mill by truck and railroad car where they are unloaded and held in large storage bins.

The milling of oats involves a six-step process, the first being cleaning. Here undesirable materials such as chaff, weed seeds, and other grains, including corn, wheat, and barley, are removed. During the cleaning step, oats not suitable for milling are also extracted and sold as by-product.

The second step is usually drying, where the oats are slowly heated to reduce their moisture in preparation for hulling and to develop the distinctive roasted flavor common only to rolled oats. However, with modern impact hulling methods, it is possible to dehull "green" or undried oats.

After drying, the oats are cooled with air and then fed into the hulling machine (step 3) which utilizes centrifugal force to impact the grain against a rubber liner. This action separates the groat or kernel from the surrounding hull. The hulls can then be removed with air since their density is much lower than the hulled kernels. The hulls are ground with hammer mills and used for animal feeds and industrial applications.

The fourth step involves sizing or grading of the grain by length. Normally the huller does not remove the hull from 100% of the kernels. It is necessary to separate the unhulled kernels from the hulled so that they can be returned for another pass.

The clean groats then go to the fifth step which is cutting. The cutters convert the kernels into 2–4 uniform pieces with a minimum of fine granules or flour. The remaining portion of the cutting system is used to separate the fine, floury material and any hull slivers. Improperly cut kernels are also removed for return to the cutters.

The final step in the milling process is flaking. The cut groats are first steamed in order to condition them for flaking and to inactivate enzymes that might otherwise cause shelf-life problems. From the steamers, the cut material drops directly through two large flaking rolls which flatten them to a specific thickness. These flakes so produced become "quick cooking" or "1-minute" oat flakes.

A portion of the whole kernel stream prior to cutting can bypass the cutting system. These kernels are then steamed and flaked to a slightly larger thickness and become the "old fashioned" or "5-minute" oat flakes.

The other important product from the oat mill is oat flour. This is produced by grinding and screening the oat flakes from the rolls. The major uses for oat flour are in ready-to-eat cereals and baby foods.

The most important varieties of oats are divided into red oat (*Avena byzantina*) and white oat (*Avena sativa*). In general, the red oat has a lower protein and higher fat content than the white oat although subgroup differences may be greater than the differences between the major classes.

If oat groats (dehulled oats) are further processed in their "green" state, one will find that enzymatic (hydrolytic) rancidity will be a problem. On the other hand, if they are overprocessed, oxidative rancidity will occur very quickly. This oxidative rancidity can be avoided by using very harsh overprocessing conditions. The properly processed oatmeal is extremely stable and can be maintained in good quality in closed containers over many years. This is probably due to the fact that this grain contains caffeic acid derivatives which act as strong antioxidants. In fact, oat flour and its derivatives were used as antioxidants before the introduction of such chemicals as BHT and BHA.

The protein content of oat groats may run from 13% to as high as 22%, depending on the variety grown and fertilization practices used as well as climatic conditions during the crop year. In any event, oat groats contain the highest protein of any of the major cereal crops.

The majority of oat protein is of the glutelin type, comprising about 65–70% of the total protein. The portion of oat protein soluble in 70% ethanol is less than 5% of the total protein. Therefore oats contain substantially less prolamine than the other cereal grains. The remainder of the oat protein consists of approximately 15% albumins and 15% globulins. The electrophoretic patterns of oat protein show at least nine distinct bands and possibly more.

Oat groats have not only the highest protein content as compared to other cereals but also the highest quality protein. The quality of the protein is such that the normal protein efficiency ratio (PER) values are on the order of 2.2 over the complete range of total protein values observed. The amino acids that will be limiting for growth or food efficiency are lysine, methionine, and threonine. Appropriate supplementation of a diet where oats are the sole source of protein with these three amino acids can make the dietary protein value equal to that of egg, or, in other words, a PER approximating 4, which is the best value known.

The starch in oats is very difficult to prepare by normal methods. The granules are small and do not readily pass from the slightly viscous starch slurry. Yields of 65–86% of good quality starch have been obtained. Preparations of starch may be made by other means, but none have been found that have not had a major problem in damage to the starch granules.

The dehulled oats are consumed as whole grain rather than being degerminated as are the other cereals. There has been some confusion in the past as to the distribution of the oil content of the oat. Hand dissection of the germ from endosperm indicated an even distribution of lipid between endosperm and germ fractions. Other unpublished data indicate that the germinal fraction of oats contains a major portion of the lipid material, as is the situation in other cereal grains.

Oats are grown in spring- and winter-sown varieties with the spring-sown the predominant type. The lipids of both varieties are very similar in that linoleic acid will constitute 40–45% of the total fatty acids, followed by oleic at 25–30%, and palmitic at 15–18%, with stearic, linolenic, and lauric acids comprising the remainder of the fatty acid content.

TABLE O-1

APPROXIMATE COMPOSITION OF ROLLED OATS

Calories (per 100 gm)	385.0
	(%)
Moisture	8.1
Protein (N × 6.25)	16.7
Fat (ether extract)	6.9
Crude Fiber	1.5
Ash	1.8
Carbohydrate (by difference)	65.0
Vitamins	(Mg/100 Gm)
Thiamin	0.66
Riboflavin	0.13
Niacin	1.0
Pyridoxine	0.13
Pantothenic acid	1.48
Choline	151.0
Total Tocopherol	2.1
Alpha-tocopherol	1.9
Para-aminobenzoic acid	0.03
Folic acid	0.06
Biotin	Present
Mineral Constituents	(Mg/100 Gm)
Calcium	49.0
Magnesium	110.0
Sodium	2.3
Potassium	340.0
Chlorine	69.0
Sulfur	202.0
Phosphorus	457.0
Iron	4.3
Copper	0.9
Cobalt	0.04
Manganese	4.2
Zinc	3.3
Fluorine	Trace
Iodine	Trace, variable

Percentage Amino Acid of Total Protein

	(Wt Basis %)
Lysine	3.91
Histidine	2.34
Arginine	6.98
Aspartic	8.33
Threonine	3.35
Serine	4.62
Glutamic	22.69
Proline	5.79
Glycine	5.04
Alanine	4.47
Cystine	2.41
Valine	5.83
Methionine	1.62
Isoleucine	4.32
Leucine	8.04
Tyrosine	3.45
Phenylalanine	5.74
Tryptophan	1.07
	100.00

The content of lipid material is a varietial characteristic and is not influenced to any extent by climatic conditions or agricultural practices. As a rule of thumb, the spring oats usually contain less lipid and more protein than the winter oats but the differences between these types is often less than the differences between varieties of a given type. The range of lipid content for spring oats ranges from 5–10% while winter oats can range from 7–10%, determined as ether extract.

The ether extract obtained from oat groats that have not been heat-treated has a turbid green color while the extract from dried and steamed oats is quite clear and yellow in color. Approximately 15–20% of the ether extract from nonheat-treated oats is insoluble in cold acetone. A major portion of this acetone-insoluble material is particulate material primarily starch, while the remainder is composed of phosphotides. The phosphotides of oat lipid are primarily of the lecithin type with minor amounts of cephalin and other phosphotidic acids.

As is true of the oil from other cereals, the nonsaponifiable content of oat oil is low and very seldom exceeds 0.5% of the ether extract. The nonsaponifiable material is composed of about equal amounts of phytosterols and the fat-soluble vitamins, tocopherol and vitamin A and precursors.

When an oat flour is cooked at $100°C$, the paste viscosity does not reach a maximum over many hours of cooking, whereas if the oil is hydrolyzed enzymatically or extracted, the paste viscosity under these conditions reaches its maximum in minutes. Oat oil added to other starches will produce the same effect as described for oat flour.

Oats, like other cereal grains, are known to contain pentosans. In addition, oats contain a polyglucosan. The polyglucosan is readily soluble in hot water and yields a viscous solution. At least part of the gelatinous properties of cooked oatmeal are due to this fraction. Structural studies have shown that the oat glucosan is very similar to lichenin from Iceland moss and to a polyglucosan isolated from barley. The oat gums are concentrated in the bran layers of the oat.

W. R. GRAHAM, JR.

OLIVES

The olive tree (*Olea europeae* L.) is one of the oldest known fruit crops. It has been grown, according to earliest references, by the Semitic peoples for over 3500 yr. Since the fruit is inedible in the natural state, due to the presence of a bitter principle, it is also one of the earliest crops which mankind learned to adapt to its needs by developing special techniques for making the fruit edible and for the extraction of its oil.

The slow-growing but long-lived subtropical, evergreen olive tree thrives well in warm, arid climatic zones and can grow even on calcareous slopes and on saline soils not suitable for most other crops. It is resistant to drought and cold, requires winter chilling for blossoming, a large number of heat units to mature its fruit, and has a strong tendency to alternate bearing.

Olive culture has spread from the Mediterranean Basin, where its picturesque trunk and silvery foliage represent a characteristic landmark, to regions with similar climates in all other continents. It is now being grown commercially in some 29 countries, located mainly between $30°$ and $45°$ latitude. The world production of olives and of the major producing countries are listed in Table O-2 which shows that olive production in the world exceeds 7.4 million metric tons, with more than $3/4$ of the orchards located in the Mediterranean Basin. Production has increased, within less than 2 decades, by nearly 50%. This increase is even higher than the figures indicate since a considerable area of young groves has not yet come into bearing. In North America the olive-growing area is concentrated mainly in California, with a small, increasing production in Mexico. Limited areas of olive orchards are also found in Australia and the Far East.

The oval olive fruit is a drupe with a large, hardshelled pit. Its size and composition differ widely according to variety, climatic conditions, water supply, and size of the yield. The olive fruit reaches its maximum weight 6–8 months after blossoming late in spring and darkens progressively during ripening to a purplish black color at full maturity. The ripe fruit will weigh from 1.5 to 13 gm. The pit, with its hard shell (endocarp), takes up between 15–30% of the weight of the fruit. At full maturity the fruit meat (mesocarp) contains 6–10% soluble solids (with mannite as the major sugar) and anywhere between 15–35% oil. The seed kernel contains only about 5% oil. The characteristic bitter glycoside, oleuropein, is more concentrated close to the peal (exocarp). The nutrient value varies, according to the oil content, between 140–190 cal per 100 gm meat.

The major fruit pest of the olive, the olive fly (*Dacus oleae* Gmel.) occurs only in the Mediterranean Basin. The fly attacks the fruit at the beginning of maturation, and, since the larvae cause fermentation and abscission of the fruit, it may reduce conspicuously both the quantity and quality of the crop. The use of green, immature olives for pickling has become popular in Spain as an escape measure from the olive fly.

TABLE O-2

TOTAL WORLD PRODUCTION OF OLIVES (IN 1000 METRIC TONS)

	Avg 1948/52	Avg 1968/69	Increase (%)
By continent			
S. Europe	3889	5656	45.4
N. Africa	517	672	30.0
W. Asia	451	905	100.7
N. America	47	71	51.0
S. America	38	98	157.9
Others	3	4	33.3
Total world production	4943	7406	49.8
By major producing countries			
Spain	1602	2024	26.4
Italy	1218	2169	78.0
Greece	515	1019	97.9
Turkey	268	557	107.8
Portugal	490	462	5.7
Others	850	1175	38.2

SOURCE: Production Yearbook, Vol. 24 (1970), FAO, Rome.

Harvesting requires by far the largest amount of labor in olive production. Therefore, considerable effort is being made to develop improved mechanical procedures. For the production of high quality table olives which requires uniformly ripe fruit free of blemishes, the fruit is picked by hand. This is least injurious both to the tree and its fruit and enables, moreover, production of the highest quality oil. But conventional methods of harvesting olives for the oil industry consist of either knocking the fruit from the tree with slender poles, or in combing or shaking the fruit off the branches and collecting it from the ground. Mechanical shakers are now being introduced together with preparatory sprays designed to loosen the attachment of the fruit pedicel from the branch.

The olive, which in the past was primarily grown for its oil, is now used more and more for the production of table olives. Different by-products are manufactured from the pomace and seeds. Olive wood is highly valued for its hardness and beautiful design.

Olive Oil

Olive oil is by far the most important product obtained from the olive. Pure olive oil is produced by mechanical extraction from the ground fruit and by separating it from the oleaginous liquor. Oil prepared from properly matured, harvested, and stored fruit is consumed, unlike most other vegetable oils, without any refining treatment. It is highly esteemed by the gourmet and by those who have become used to it from infancy. Olive oil is also utilized for medicinal purposes in the pharmaceutical industry, and for cosmetic and toilet preparations. Olive oil production is concentrated mainly in six countries, as is evident from Table O-3.

The yield of olive oil varies considerably according to variety, climatic conditions, and agrotechnical practice, averaging about 200 kg of oil per ton of olives. During maturation of the fruit the size of the oil droplets within the olive increases, raising the extractability of the oil from about 20% in the early fall to as much as 90% in the fully mature fruit in midwinter.

Handling the olives—transport, storage, and washing—should be carried out rapidly and with care in order to avoid pressure and heating. In practice, it is difficult to synchronize harvesting and pro-

TABLE O-3

TOTAL PRODUCTION OF OLIVE OIL (IN 1000 METRIC TONS)

Major Producing Countries	Avg 1948/52	Avg 1968/69	Differences (%)
Italy	241	476	97.5
Spain	334	430	28.8
Greece	115	174	51.0
Turkey	47	107	127.0
Portugal	65	63	-3.1
Tunisia	60	42	-30.0
Others	78	86	10.3
World total	940	1378	46.6

cessing, and the olives are then stored in large heaps for long periods before pressing, causing fermentation, heating and deterioration of the fruit and subsequently a reduction in the quality of the oil.

Technology of Production.—Olive oil is extracted traditionally by simple equipment in essentially three steps: (1) crushing the fruit, (2) pressing the paste, and (3) separation of the oil from the liquor. Modern mechanical equipment of widely varying design is used increasingly for each of these steps, either as separate units or combined as a single-stage process. Crushing the fruit has been carried out since biblical times with revolving stone mills, operated by man or animal. The crushed paste is filled into porous baskets which are pressed in a screw press. The separation of the oil from the mother liquor and the solid tissue fragments is carried out by floating and decanting the lower density oil and/or by centrifugal separators.

But these classic, primitive, ancient techniques are being replaced more and more by modern, high-speed mills in conjunction with mixing machines, and with high capacity, high powered hydraulic presses, or continuous screw presses. Heavy duty centrifuges have also been introduced. Other new methods, including those which avoid pressing the fruit, are being constantly studied and developed, but their use is as yet limited.

The quality of the oil is impaired upon prolonged contact with the readily fermenting liquor, and cleanliness of equipment and rapidity of filtration and clarification are, therefore, particularly important.

After the first pressing, the olive residue is still rich in oil and is usually recrushed and repressed with or without the addition of warm water. Oil from the second pressing by means of more powerful presses tends to have a more intense color and a higher acid content, as well as a weaker aroma.

The remaining press cake still retains about 4–5% oil. It may be dried from about 25% to less than 10% moisture, and the oil extracted by means of a volatile solvent, such as carbon disulfate, benzine, trichlorethylene, etc. The resulting "sulfur" oil is then repeatedly rectified. The remaining press residue may be used as fuel or fertilizer, or for the production of charcoal, or, after removal of the pieces of the pit, as stock feed.

Composition and Quality.—Olive oil consists predominantly of glycerides formed by a mixture of unsaturated and saturated fatty acids; unsaturation is due primarily to oleic acid (67–83%) and only about 2% is fully unsaturated. Olive oil is characterized by a saponification value of between 187–191° and an iodine value of between 78–90. The desired color of the oil is pale yellow and its flavor is sweet and fruity. One of the major indicators of olive oil quality is the free fatty acid content.

According to the *Pharmacopeia*, edible olive oil must not contain more than 1.41% free fatty acids. Oil with a higher acid content should be refined by neutralization and removal of unsatisfactory odors, flavor, and color. But such refinement impairs its fragrance, resulting in a bland, rather tasteless oil. In olive oil producing countries the local population frequently prefers the "sharpness" of the oil with a higher acid content.

The terminology of commercial labeling, approved by the United Nations conference on olive oil in Geneva in 1961, classifies the oils into four groups according to the method of preparation as well as according to acidity:

Virgin Olive Oil.—Oil extracted by pressing, free of admixtures, called "extra" when the oleic acid does not exceed 1 gm per 100 and "fine" if the acid content does not exceed 1.5 gm per 100 gm and the flavor is perfect; "ordinary" olive oil may contain up to 3.0 gm acid per 100 gm and have a slight off-flavor; if the oil has a definite off-flavor it is classified as "lampante" (lamp oil).

Refined Olive Oil.—This oil may be called "pure" when it is refined from virgin oil and "second quality" when it is refined from solvent extracted oil.

Blended Olive Oil.—Blended oil can be called "pure" when it consists of a blend of virgin and refined oil and "blended" when it contains a blend of virgin and second quality refined oil.

Industrial Oils.—These oils are obtained by extraction of olive residues with solvents.

There exists a strong inducement to adulterate olive oil by mixing it with cheaper vegetable oil. Such practice is regarded in some countries as fraudulent and so treated.

The best storage conditions for olive oil are at a temperature close to 14°C in tightly closed containers which prevent contact with light, air, water, and harmful metals, such as Fe and Cu. Deterioration of the oil during storage will cause (a) an increase in acidity due to the action of lipases and (b) the development of rancidity due to oxidation involving changes in the aroma and taste of the oil.

Table Olives

Many different methods of converting olives into an edible product are in existence, with the different olive-growing countries and districts developing their own techniques. They differ widely in many respects, such as in the stage of harvesting the fruit, the method of removing its bitter phenolic principle, the concentration of salt and acid in the final product, etc.

The three major commercial methods are known according to their countries of origin as: (1) the Spanish method, which ferments unripe yellowish-green olives, (2) the American method which uses half-ripe, reddish fruit, and (3) the Greek method which preserves the fruit after it has become fully ripe and dark purple in color. Furthermore, there exists a very wide range of local methods which are destined mainly for the home market; and there are different experimental methods which have not, as yet, reached commercial scope.

Green Fermented Olives (Spanish Method).—The olives are harvested when they reach their full size and are still firm and light green in color. The fruit is mostly hand picked with repeated pickings, so as to obtain uniform maturity, size, and texture. The main varieties in Spain are the Sevillano (Queen) and the Manzanillo. The fruit is transferred rapidly from the grove to the pickling shed and covered in vats with a weak lye solution. The lye will penetrate into the olives and hydrolyze the bitter phenolic glycoside, oleuropein. A penetration to a depth of $1/2$-$3/4$ of the thickness of the pericarp is desired so that part of the bitterness is retained (imparting a pleasing taste) and sufficient carbohydrates are retained for subsequent fermentation. The progress of the lye is observed by means of phenolphthalein applied to the surface of the cut olives. A solution of 1.8% NaOH (3° Baumé) will penetrate the fruit to the desired depth within 4–8 hr at room temperature; the time will depend upon the maturity, size, and texture of the olives. The rate of penetration will increase with temperature; temperatures above about 28°C tend to blister and soften the olives. This can be avoided by the addition of salt to the lye solution. The lye-treated olives are immediately rinsed and soaked in water with frequent changes during 24–36 hr in order to remove the lye. The process has been shortened in Israel to 5–6 hr by neutralization with dilute acid to reduce the loss of fermentable materials. Air exposure has to be avoided, so as to prevent an oxidative darkening of the fruit.

The washed olives are placed into fermentation tanks or barrels, and covered with brine. Olives from unirrigated groves and those with a high oil content tolerate higher salt concentrations than irrigated, large, loose-textured fruit. Such fruit tends to shrink at higher brine concentrations and therefore the salt content should only be increased gradually. After equilibrium is reached, the product will contain close to 6–8% NaCl; spices are added at times according to the consumer's preference.

Since the semipermeability of the olive peel, as well as the natural lactic acid inhibitor, oleuropein, are destroyed during lye treatment, the olives will soon start to ferment when the temperature is within the range favorable for the development of lactobacilli. The domination of the lactobacilli is fostered by slight acidification of the brine, which helps to suppress competing spoilage bacteria.

FIG. O-1. THE OLIVE PICKLING SHED "HAZAIT" ("THE OLIVE") AT BETH SHEAN, ISRAEL, OWNED BY A FARMER'S COOPERATIVE

This is a modern, quite unique factory. The pickling vats, visible in the background, are filled from the upper floor. After the fermentation process has been completed, the fruit is removed by means of an adjustable hose from the base of the vats.

During fermentation the color changes from deep green to typical "olive green" shade; lactic acid content may increase up to 1.4% and the pH decrease to below 3.8. The keeping quality of the fermented olives is high, since spoilage bacteria are restricted by the high salt content and lactic acid. The fruit must be well covered by the liquid and kept in closed containers so as to prevent the development of surface yeasts and molds. Among major spoilage organisms that attack green olives in Spain there is a butyric acid-producer known as "zapatera."

Before marketing, the fermented olives are graded and sorted according to size, shape, and color. Increasingly, olives are being pitted and the pit cavity stuffed with either pimientos, onions, almonds, anchovies, or other edibles. Since the brine of the fermented fruit is turbid, it is either filtered or, more often, replaced by fresh brine. The bottled or canned products are often pasteurized.

Canned Ripe Olives (American Style).—The production of canned ripe olives is centered in California. The four leading commercial varieties are the Mission, Manzanillo, Sevillano, and Ascolano. The olives are picked when straw yellow to cherry red in color. Before the lye treatment, olives are graded according to color and size so as to ensure uniform lye penetration. Over-ripe or small fruit tends to become too soft after lye treatment; green fruit will remain too hard. Often the fresh olives are first stored in dilute brine for six weeks or longer in large wooden or concrete tanks, until the pickling tanks become available.

The salt concentration of the holding solution differs for different varieties. Mostly, the initial brine will contain 5-8% NaCl, which is gradually increased to 10%. Some lactic acid fermentation will take place which helps prevent the development of putrefactive organisms. From the holding solution the fruit is transferred into shallow pickling vats and treated repeatedly with dilute NaOH solutions, each treatment being followed by exposure to air. The olives darken progressively due to oxidation of the phenolic substances in a basic environment. The first lye solution of between 1-2% NaOH is allowed to penetrate only a short distance below the peel. Aeration is accomplished either by exposure to air with frequent stirring and turning of the lye-treated fruit, or by bubbling compressed air through the immersed fruit. The schedules of lye treatment and air exposure differ according to the variety in use, length of storage before pickling, temperature of the water, etc. In practice, some 4-8 treatments of gradually decreasing strength (3.0-0.5% NaOH) are used for a gradually deeper penetration into the fruit. The olives are aerated after each lye treatment for 1-5 days. The final lye solution is allowed to penetrate completely to the pit, destroying all the bitterness of the fruit. Then the olives are leached by frequent changes of water for 5-7 days until all traces of NaOH are removed.

At this stage the olives are often pasteurized (60°-75°C) to stop undesired fermentation and then cured in 2-3% NaCl for 2-6 days. The cured olives are graded and sorted according to color (light brown, dark brown, black) and packed into enamel-lined cans, covered with a 2.5-3.5% NaCl solution, sealed and sterilized at 116°C for about 1 hr, as required by the California State Board of Health. Pitting and stuffing of the olives is practiced more and more.

A combination of the American and the Spanish methods is also in use in California, known as "green-ripe" olives. Greener, less mature fruit is used than for the method described above. They retain their light green color, since exposure to air during processing is carefully avoided. The olives are treated with only 2 lye solutions (1.5 and 2.0%) without the use of preliminary holding solutions. They are canned and sterilized in the same manner as ripe olives.

Black (Naturally Ripe) Olives (Greek Method).— The Greek black olive industry is based on a very long tradition and experience. The varieties selected for their suitability for preservation after ripening are mainly Conservolea, Calamata, and Megaritici.

The olives are kept on the tree until fully matured and completely dark. On the farm or in nearby processing plants the olives are sorted and brined with or without previous soaking in water. The water is changed frequently in the course of 48-72 hr in order to hasten the destruction of the bitter principle. The final brine concentration is high. The salt is often added in stages, so as to prevent shriveling of the fruit. During the winter months the covering brine concentration is kept close to 10% NaCl, but during the hot summer season its concentration has to be increased up to 15-16% in order to prevent spoilage.

Brined olives ferment somewhat slowly due to the fact that the ripe olives are harvested late in the fall when most of their fermentable carbohydrates have been converted into oil. They lose their bitterness within 3-6 months. The presence of the bitter principle is partially masked in the taste by the high salt content. Pretreatment with lye solutions before brining, such as is used in the Spanish method, hastens the process of debittering and fermentation, but its use is prohibited in Greece. The lactic acid content of the fermented olives will normally not exceed 0.5% in the presence of a mixed flora of lactobacilli and coliform bacteria.

The dark purple anthocyanins of the submerged olives will turn light red. But in the preparation for marketing the bleached olives are removed from the brine and exposed to air on the sorting tables for up to three days or until the dark color of the olives is regained. For export, the fruit is carefully sorted and sized according to international size and color standards and the fruit is repacked in fresh brine containing about 8% NaCl and 0.5-0.75% lactic acid.

The spoilage organisms encountered in Greece are the butyric acid producers known as "Zapatera," anaerobic sulfate reducers known as "galazoma" spoilage, and film forming pectolytic organisms which disintegrate the fruit meat. The last mentioned is at times prevented by means of a thin layer of paraffin oil on the surface of the brine.

Other Methods of Preparing Table Olives.— A large number of different techniques of preparing olives for table use are known to exist in addition to the above three major commercial procedures. Olives are often pitted, stuffed, chopped and spiced, and packed in fancy packs. Most olive growing districts prepare special local olive products which vary widely in degree of bitterness, salt content, and the kinds and amounts of acid and spices, etc. They are usually destined for sale in bulk at nearby markets or for home use.

The use of carbonate salts or ash solutions is one of the methods of debittering. At times, the olives are brined without any pretreatment or only after soaking them in water which is changed at intervals. Such olives will ferment slowly, staying bitter for up to 1 year.

A rapid method of debittering olives consists of beating each olive lightly by hand or machine in such a manner that the peel remains intact while the inner fruit meat is injured. When such fruit is soaked in water and covered with salt brine or mixed with dry salt it will be edible within a few days. Although the blemished appearance is not attractive, such olives are in considerable demand in Mediterranean countries.

Half ripe and ripe olives are often prepared for local consumption by using dry salt rather than a salt solution. Slowly-dissolving ordinary coarse salt or rock salt is placed in alternate layers with the olives or mixed with the fruit. The salt gradually extracts the liquid from the olives, debittering and shrivelling them. The practice of adding different spices and aromatic herbs such as anise, oregano, etc., differs widely from region to region.

Producers of black olives are also familiar with techniques for the improvement of color in the finished products. Fruit harvested before it reaches full maturity and which is still yellowish to red in color can reach a color intensity similar to that of ripe olives by the addition of iron salts. Such salts are either included as accidental impurities of the rock salt or by intentional additions. This is often fortified with or followed by the addition of mordants such as gallic or tannic acid.

The Greek Calamata variety is generally prepared by cutting the fruit longitudinally and soaking it for 5–8 days in a 2% salt brine to debitter it. Then it is soaked in vinegar for 1–2 days, graded, and packed in fresh brine (6–8% NaCl) together with a top layer of a neutral oil.

Some local Greek and Turkish varieties are known to exist which lose their bitterness while still on the tree. Such olives can be preserved at low brine concentrations as sweet olives.

There also exist different, newer methods of preparing table olives, but these are, as yet, mostly still on an experimental scale. In one of these methods the bitter principle is removed from the olives rapidly by the use of hot water or hot lye solutions which cause a partial breakdown of the olive peel. Such olives can be debittered and preserved by brining, acidification, and pasteurization within hours after harvesting (Israeli patent).

Trade and Development of the Industry

As of 1969, the international trade in olive oil has grown to about 242,000 tons valued at over 155 million dollars. This quantity was exported by 35 countries to more than 100 countries in 5 continents. Spain is the largest exporter. Italy, the largest producer of olive oil, buys nearly half of the entire quantity carried by international trade. The governments of most olive-growing countries guarantee to the producer a minimum price for the oil, so as to compensate him for yearly fluctuations in yield and price.

The economic future of the olive oil industry is viewed by experts with some concern, due to the increasing competition from vegetable oils. Although olive oil production increases by about 1.4% yearly, production of vegetable oils increases on the average by about 4% per annum. Vegetable oils can be manufactured more cheaply, since growth, harvesting, and extraction techniques are highly mechanized. The olive oil industry tends to be conservative, possibly due to the venerable, time-honored traditions of the industry. The International Olive Oil Council (IOOC) located in Madrid, is making every effort to modernize and improve methods of production and to standardize quality.

Products manufactured from the whole olive have, by contrast, no competitor and the industry has been widely diversified. The development of the industry in California may perhaps be taken as an indicator of future trends. Over 90% of the California olive crop is converted into table olives and only blemished, small fruit is crushed for oil.

It appears that olive oil and, even more so, table olives, which have belonged for generations to the basic foods of the Mediterranean population, are becoming increasingly a luxury product in countries with a high standard of living.

ZDENKA SAMISH

Cross-reference: *Fermentation.*

ONIONS

The onion (*Allium cepa*), native to Asia, has been celebrated for its flavor throughout the centuries. In one of O. Henry's charming short stories, "The Priceless Ingredient," the ingredient essential to a beef stew that a group of tenants are collecting item by item is an onion. The Israelites (Numbers II) recalled with nostalgia "the leeks, and the onions, and the garlick" which they ate in Egypt. Although onion flavor is not universally liked, its popularity is attested by the U.S. per capita consumption (25 lb annually) and by the number of dishes in which it is a prized if not priceless ingredient.

Since flavor is so important a part of the appeal of onions, a brief comment on onion flavor is appropriate. The flavor of onions is the product of enzymatic development, the substrate being sulfoxide amino acids. The chief flavor compounds appear to be hydrogen sulfide, thiols, disulfides, trisulfides, and thiosulfanates. To these compounds must be added the tear-producing factor,

X, the chemistry of which has not been fully elucidated. The pungency of the onion has been ascribed to the enzymatic decomposition of S-substituted cysteine sulfoxides. Onions contain soluble sugars (the chief one being sucrose), a relatively small amount of vitamin C, some calcium, and a minute amount of iron (0.06 mg per mature onion the size of a baseball).

Onions are raised for the fresh vegetable market, for the dehydration industry, and for canning. "Spring onions" are sold in the supermarkets in small bunches in considerable volume and so, too, are "dry onions," the Bermuda and Spanish being the most common varieties. "Button onions," used for pickling, are the onions harvested just after the plant has formed a bulb.

Dry onions, the fully mature onion, keep well for several months after harvest but unless properly stored will sprout. Onions under 2 in. in diameter are sold on the fresh vegetable market, the larger onions are dehydrated. Onions are harvested mechanically. Onions to be dehydrated are inspected and graded at the dehydration plant and then allowed to cure for a few days.

The first operation in dehydrating onions is peeling. This is accomplished by a flame peeler, an oven which burns off the outer shell and the vestages of the roots. The onions are then subjected to washing under pressure, this to remove the charred skins. Next the onions are spread on a continuous stainless steel perforated belt where revolving knives slice the onions into thin slices. Hot air reaches the onions through the perforations in the belt and dries the onions down to 4% moisture. The onions are packaged in fiberboard drums lined with a foil laminate to keep out moisture.

Dehydrated onions are used in numerous products—chili sauce, relishes, ketchup, soup mixes and other mixes such as pizza, and in numerous nationality foods, e.g., Chinese egg rolls, Mexican enchiladas, and lasagne.

Onions are the principal ingredient in a number of cooked frozen food dishes, notably onion soup and French fried onions. For onion soup, the hot soup, formulated as if for canning, is filled into enamel-lined tin cans, sealed and cooled. It is frozen in airblast or in alcohol brine. French fried onion rings are prepared (using Bermuda or Spanish onions) from a standard recipe, packaged in a lined carton and then frozen. Onions are included in one form or another in many TV dinners. They freeze well and undergo no adverse changes in the process, provided that they have been properly cooked.

Canned onions are sold in volume in the United States. Varieties of onions with white skins are commonly used for canning. The first operation in canning is to remove the outer or paper skin, by hand or mechanically. Next, the onions are blanched for 4–5 min, filled into cans, brined exhausted, and then acidified. The acidification is required since a cook adequate for sterilization of this low-acid food would ruin the product. Provided it is carefully controlled, acidifying the onions makes it safe to process the product in boiling water.

Garlic (*allium saticum*) is a close relative of the onion. Allicin is the most important flavor component of garlic. The compound when isolated as an oil has a distinct garlic odor. Garlic, like onions, is sliced, dehydrated, and made into a powder. As a powder, in dehydrated flakes, or raw its only use is as a flavoring. As a flavoring it is much stronger than onion. The leek (*allium porrum*) is a meeker member of the family but it has, nevertheless, a distinctive flavor. The shallot (*allium ascolonicum*) is likewise mild and used as a flavoring; but also it is used as a pickle.

MARTIN S. PETERSON

ORGANOLEPTIC PROPERTIES OF FOOD

Organoleptic means making an impression on an organ of special sense: sight, hearing, feeling, smell and taste. The physical and chemical characteristics of foods are stimuli for the eye, ear, skin and muscles, nose, and mouth whose receptors initiate impulses that travel to the brain where perception occurs. Perception or the correlation of sensory impressions determines whether a food will be accepted or rejected.

A food need not be liked to be accepted. It need only emit sensory impressions that are perceived as affirmative responses to the questions: "Is it edible?" "Shall I eat it?"

Edibility means fit to be eaten. A first requisite of quality, it connotes absence of toxicity. Latent toxicity eludes predetection by consumers who, therefore, must rely on the quality controls of the food industry to provide edible foods. However, overt toxicity, such as from allergenic or spoiled food, can be anticipated from sensory experience and causes food to be rejected.

In general, people do not now emphasize edibility so much as the answer to "Shall I eat it?" Factors such as age, health, socio-economic status, environment, religion, attitude, personal freedom, instinct, customs, appetite, and choices form personal baselines for assessing the sensory impressions of a food. An assessment signifying dislike causes rejection; assessment signifying not disliked is passive, permitting acceptance. Acceptance is the prerequisite to liking and to true preference.

The following discussion will consider the organoleptic properties of foods and their assessment from the standpoint of the human senses. The senses are described as physical or chemical in nature depending on the nature of their stimuli.

Sight

Sight, a physical sense, enables one to judge the appearance of a food item in terms of its form, texture, and color. Appearance of a food is the first clue to its identity and often a prediction of the degree of satisfaction or pleasure to be derived from eating. To babies, it apparently is not of great importance but it becomes a prime factor in the food acceptance habits of young children. Perhaps this is because they associate the particular appearance with a food flavor liked or disliked. Whereas children refuse to taste a food because of its appearance, adults will eat it despite appearance. However, adults do make quality prejudgments on appearance. Such judgments are based on past experience, preconceived notions, or resistance to change. Decisions to buy food at the market and to eat it at the table are heavily influenced by appearance, which has implications of quality, pleasure, and aesthetics. Texture and consistency of prepared foods are usually predictable from appearance: soups, stews, salads, mashed, baked or boiled potatoes, custards, gelatin desserts, cereals, and baked goods; but not meats.

Meat flavor, sometimes, is predictable by color; for example, a rare versus a well done roast of beef or baked ham versus roast of fresh ham. Color is probably the most important of the sight factors in the acceptance or rejection of foods. Nearly all hues and shades are common. The meanings of colors are exemplified by the following: white connotes sanitation and purity and is associated with highly refined products such as salt, sugar, starch, and flour. Ripe tomatoes are red, and any off-colored spot is recognized as a source of unpleasant flavor. Ripe cucumbers appear greenskinned, and yellow coloration indicates overripeness, which will mean soft texture and loss of expected flavor. Candy colors, based in part on original colors of the natural products, forecast flavor: black for licorice, brown for chocolate, red for cherry, strawberry, anise and cinnamon, purple for grape, green for spearmint and lime, yellow for lemon and pineapple, orange for orange. Association of quality with the color of natural foods is so strong that producers take steps to add coloring—oranges, margarine, maraschino cherries, textured protein meat imitations, ice cream, and soft drinks. Depth of color frequently denotes strength or weakness of flavor; for example, dark coffee and tea are strong brews; light vinegar is expected to have "lighter" flavor than dark vinegar. Variations in depth of color may alienate a consumer by suggesting the possibility of poorly controlled processing; hence, most brands of cola beverages contain caramel coloring added to give a standard color level which implies consistency of production.

It is known that pleasing-looking food promotes the flow of digestive juices and thereby enhances the digestibility of the food. In a meal, variety of color promotes eye-appeal and implies variety of flavor and texture.

Hearing

Hearing, a physical sense, plays a minor role in food acceptance. The sound from thumping or shaking a melon may, to the practiced ear, denote ripeness. The noise of a spoon scraping ice crystals in improperly stored ice cream will merely confirm observations on appearance. A steak giving off sizzling noises is probably hot; but the sizzle will not counteract an unacceptable degree of toughness. Noise is expected to accompany the chewing of celery or the crunching of hard candy; it is missed when absent, but the kinesthetic end organs in the jaws and mouth relay information that the limp celery is old or the hard candy is soft.

Feeling

Feeling, referred to as one sense, encompasses two: the kinesthetic (muscle) sense, the nature of which is physical; and the tactile (touch) sense, a physical and chemical sense. Some of the natural chemical constituents of foods are stimuli of tactual sensations in the mouth and nose. For example, coolness of menthol in peppermint, burn of allyl isothiocyanate in mustard, the numbing effect of eugenol in cloves, bite of piperine in black and white ground pepper, tooth-coating of oxalates in rhubarb and spinach, the puckering effect of tannins in strong tea.

Mainly, however, feeling sensations from eating food are responses to texture and consistency, physical properties resulting from the way in which the food item is structured or served. Although frequently prejudged by sight, texture and consistency are respectively evaluated kinesthetically and tactually by the mouth. Both play an important role in the release of aroma and flavor factors of a food. Temperature also is a physical property. Eating-temperature of a food is tactually sensed by the mouth; it usually affects the aroma and flavor and, often, the texture and consistency.

The existence and the condition of our teeth describe the first limits of acceptance for food texture and consistency. Gruel-like and soft consistency seems to be important for acceptance by babies and toothless adults. All others can tolerate solid foods and accept them willingly as a large part of their diet; indeed, there seems to be considerable pleasure in chewing and in sensing crispness. But there also seems to be a maximum for toughness beyond which food is rejected; likewise, there are personal maximums for hardness, stringiness, tackiness, and chewiness. Irregularities of texture, as in toss salads, may be expected and desired, but the presence of an unchewable tissue in a portion of any food is displeasing. Foods containing unchewable parts, foreign matter, grit, and spicules are disturbing or alarming, and therefore unacceptable. Other generally unacceptable tactual properties are sliminess, stringiness, greasiness, and such sensations of chemical origin as astringency, tooth-coating, tongue-coating, mouth-coating, and extremes of bite, pungency, drying, and puckering.

Through experience a person learns the customary texture and consistency parameters for many food items. Deviations are judged to be indicators of lowered quality. For example, the light-colored patches of fat, called bloom, on chocolates, caused by large temperature fluctuations during storage; the toughening and extra firmness in marshmallows, ensuing from moisture loss; graininess or sandiness of lactose crystals in ice cream stored under shifting temperatures; toughening and drying of bread crumb ascribable to starch retrogradation.

Of these examples only texture-staling of bread is perhaps foretold without opening the package. Buyers customarily squeeze the loaf, kinesthetically sensing an indication of overall softness, though not of tenderness. In this connection, note that U.S. bakers assess white bread texture by manual touch.

The maximum temperature tolerable in the mouth is in the range of 150°–155°F. Above this there will be physical pain and possible temporary tissue damage, and therefore rejection. Minimum tolerable temperature is above freezing (32°F) but, actually, tolerance depends upon how quickly the food can be warmed in the mouth. For example, a large spoonful of sherbet will cause pain, but a small spoonful will melt without pain. Ordinarily, a cold food item will have a type and degree of flavor different from when it is warm or hot. There are three possible explanations of this phenomenon: (1) cold increases the density of the product making the chemical flavor factors physically less available; (2) low temperature reduces the receptivity of the sensory end organs; and (3) the volatile flavor factors are less volatile in cold products than in hot. Custom and historic use, which include climatic influences on diet, affect food-temperature selection, and the range of temperature acceptance for any particular food item is relatively wide.

Taste

Taste, a chemical sense, responds to the action of the chemical components of foods on the receptor sites of the taste buds, located mainly on the tongue. To be detected, the taste-bearing chemicals must be dissolved in the fluids of the mouth. Four primary tastes are generally conceded: sweet, sour, salty, and bitter. Common examples are sugar, vinegar, salt, and caffeine, respectively. Many other substances, as simple or more complex in their chemical constitution, produce tastes. Sensitivity of taste is thought to depend upon genetic factors as well as physiological factors of disease and age. Ability to taste the intense bitterness of phenylthiocarbamide (PTC) is transmitted genetically. However, inability to taste PTC has not as yet been shown to correlate with other taste sensitivities, including those for bitter principles. Disease and normal aging are also under scrutiny, although more needs to be known about aging. It is known that the numbers and location of taste buds change with age, and it is postulated that their physiological state also changes with age. These factors, then, may account for the differences in taste appreciation among various age groups: infants, children, youth, middle-aged, and older adults.

It is also theorized that psychic responses to the four tastes are basic and primitive in origin. For example, sweetness and saltiness are more pleasant than sourness, which, in turn, is less unpleasant than bitterness. Bitterness is typical of the vegetable alkaloids, which are toxic principles of natural origin; sourness is typical of unripe fruits and berries, which when eaten often cause digestive upsets. Both of these tastes may be warning agents, whereas sweetness and saltiness in foods are generally signs of edibility.

In addition to their qualitative aspects, tastes and their acceptance must be considered from quantitative viewpoints. In general, their order of acceptance, proceeding from high intensity (strong) to low, parallels the listing of pleasantness given above, i.e., sweetness, saltiness, sourness, and bitterness. However, high intensities of sweetness and saltiness in foods may be cloying or satiating and thirst-producing; a low level of sourness may be disappointing in sauerkraut juice; and a high level of bitterness in chocolate can be tolerated if it does not last too long.

The manner in which the taste factors interplay also affects acceptance. For example, the sourness and bitterness of grapefruit are ameliorated by the addition of sweetness (sugar, honey, table syrup). Salt, added to a level where it is barely detectable, also will counteract the grapefruit sourness and seems to relieve the bitterness. Similarly, sugar added in moderation to hot coffee, while imparting no sweetness, will reduce bitterness. This action is considered an improvement by some individuals and a degradation by others. Apparently there are personal intensity maximums for bitterness, and undoubtedly for the other tastes. However, it is fairly certain that through continued use some persons can become accustomed to and will accept foods with higher taste-intensities than formerly tolerated.

Smell

Smell or olfaction, also a chemical sense, responds to chemical components which through their inherent properties of volatility (as influenced by temperature) reach the olfactory tissue of the nose. The volatile molecules may reach this end organ by two routes: (1) through the nostrils with air inspired during normal breathing or deliberate sniffing—odor or aroma; and (2) through the region behind the palate (nasopharyngeal passage) during the acts of chewing and swallowing. In this instance the aromatic factors are regarded as the third integer of flavor (tactile feelings and tastes being the other two). It has been estimated that the human olfactory sense can differentiate 100,000–200,000 odor-bearing chemicals. Although the chemical composition of even the commonest of foods, e.g., milk, is not completely known, one can assume that a considerable number of these many odoriferous chemicals are present in foods. Since the 1950's, gas-liquid partition chromatography has been applied to naturally occurring, processed, cooked, and stored foods in order to determine their volatile constituents and, subsequently, the contributions they make to organoleptic properties. It should be noted that odoriferous chemicals may also have other organoleptic properties. For example, menthol is cool and odorous; acetic acid is sour, pungent, and odorous.

Because there is not yet a satisfactory method of classifying odors, their contribution to food acceptance or rejection must be limited to a few specific examples. As with the tastes, the aromatic factors of foods should be considered qualitatively and quantitatively. The aroma of a food, as perceived through the nose, is the second clue to its identity. Like appearance, the first clue, it often forecasts the future pleasure of eating and if pleasant it will promote salivation (mouth-watering) and thus, digestion. Also, like appearance, aroma is of prime importance to children's acceptance or rejection of food and of less importance to adults. Personal rejection may occur by identification of certain aromas with unpleasant after-effects such as after-taste, indigestion, or allergy.

Unknown, unpleasant aromas and those suggesting incipient or frank spoilage can cause adult rejection. In rejection of food by aroma two attributes may function simultaneously: unattractiveness and unfamiliarity. The following odors exemplify basically unattractive types, yet experience and historic usage have taught that such odors are inevitably present in the accepted foods cited: amine (lamb); sour (lemon juice); sulfide (poultry); earthy (mushrooms); rancid, fecal, goaty, moldy (cheeses). But rejection would occur if such odors were apparent in the following foods, for spoilage is indicated: fish (amine); raw milk (sour); eggs (sulfide); flour (earthy); lard (rancid); cream (goaty); butter (moldy). Many types of odors are seldom considered repulsive, and foods emitting the following aromas whether familiar or not usually would be considered edible: fruity, spicy, nutty, sweet-fragrant, caramel, minty.

By far the most important contribution of aromas derives from their effects when foods are eaten. Here the aromatic components of foods become part of the flavor-by-mouth. Those aromas previously classified as unattractive when smelled are not necessarily considered unattractive when released with the other sensory properties of the ingested foods: tastes, feelings, and other aromatics not evident through smelling. On the contrary, such aromatics as amine, sour, sulfide, earthy, rancid, fecal, goaty, and moldy, contribute to the identity and interest of many foods. The positiveness of their contribution seems to be dependent mainly on two factors: intensity and order of appearance, both with respect to the other components of the flavor.

Flavor

When food is taken into the mouth and prepared for swallowing, three senses are involved in assessing the food item: taste, touch, and smell. Their stimulation occurs practically simultaneously. Although their messages follow separate routes, they provide a unitary or whole impression: flavor. Except for bizarre foods, the following qualities seem to summarize the general characteristics of acceptable flavor: early impact of appropriate flavor; pleasant mouth sensation; full body of blended flavor; rapid development of full flavor in the mouth; in many cases, a rapid disappearance of flavor on swallowing; and absence of unpleasant characteristics perceived alone in early impact or in after-taste.

Assessment of Organoleptic Properties

In general, a two-step judgment seems to be involved in a consumer's acceptance or rejection of a food on the basis of its organoleptic properties: (1) quality, based on past experience; and (2) lack of displeasure. Appearance is the first attribute that can be assessed; aroma, next; but most important are the in-the-mouth properties, particularly flavor, texture, and consistency.

Components of organoleptic properties which are physical in nature are amenable to objective (by instrument) measurement. For example, color, size, temperature, viscosity, density, shear value, elasticity. Likewise, some of the chemical components can be objectively measured: moisture, headspace constituents, volatiles, pH, sugars, ash—to name a few. Wherever possible, objective measurements should be correlated with subjective observations from experienced taste or texture panels or from consumer panels. Currently, the best applications of objective measurements are control of quality and product and process research.

JEAN F. CAUL

Cross-reference: *Sensory Evaluation of Foods.*

OZONE

Ozone, chemically designated as O_3, is an unstable, blue gas of characteristic penetrating odor, its name having been derived from the Greek, ozein (to smell). It was first noted as a peculiar odor in the vicinity of electrical machines. Ozone is a potent germicide and powerful oxidizing agent in both organic and inorganic reactions. Because of the instability of the gas, it is usually produced and used *in situ* in food technological applications. Loundes (1971) has described the ozonators used in the production of ozone from air. Ozone, however, may be produced from oxygen or oxygen-gas mixtures—usually in industrial applications. Ozone is also produced from the oxygen in the atmosphere by UV energy using the sterilamp at 1850 angstroms.

In discussing ozone for water and effluent treatment, Loundes has presented comparative bactericidal data for O_3 and some commonly used disinfectants. The data of Loundes in Table O-4 show the excellent effectiveness of ozone. In connection with viruses, it was observed by Loundes that the germicidal power of O_3 was actually more pronounced against those organisms that appeared to be more resistant to conventional disinfectant techniques. Ozone is little affected by pH or ammonia.

Ozone has been more extensively used in Europe than in the United States. In France at the present time there are more than 500 installations employing O_3 for disinfection. The drinking water

TABLE O-4

CONCENTRATION OF DISINFECTANT IN MG/LITER REQUIRED TO KILL OR INACTIVATE 99% OF THE LISTED TYPES OF ORGANISM WITHIN 10 MIN AT 5°C

Disinfectant	Enteric Bacteria	Amoebic Cysts	Viruses	Bacterial Spores
O_3	0.001	1.0	0.10	0.20
HOCl as Cl_2	0.02	10	to 0.40	10
OCl as Cl_2	2	10^3	> 20	> 10^3
NH_2Cl as Cl_2	5	20	10^2	4×10
Free Cl, pH 7.5	0.04	20	0.8	20
Free Cl, pH 8	0.1	50	2	50

SOURCE: Loundes (1971).

of Nice has been ozone treated for about 65 yr Many European countries have approved the use of O_3 for water treatment; Switzerland has about 70 installations. General properties of O_3 processes and equipment for a water-treatment plant in Japan (Horie 1970) are discussed showing a cost of about 1¢ per m^3. Mehls (1971) has discussed water treatment in food plants with the possibility of selecting chlorination, UV irradiation, ozonization, oligodynamics, or ultrafiltration depending on the character of the raw water situation. Ozonized water is considered to have a characteristic "freshness," accompanied by a "blue tinge" making the water particularly palatable and visually attractive, with no evidence of odor or taste.

A few of the uses of ozone-treated water for nondrinking purposes will be cited. Fish (Salmon and LeGall 1936) preserved in ice prepared from ozonized water showed no deterioration after 8 days, whereas fish kept in ordinary ice water showed early deterioration. Similarly, edible mollusks immersed in ozonized water for 48 hr to 4 days were completely sterilized with no harmful effects and no alteration in flavor.

As production facilities for O_3 have become more economical and reliable, direct ozonization of food-plant effluents has come into use. Gardner and Montgomery (1968) have studied the treatment of sewage effluents with O_3 and measured the effects of ozonizing on chemical oxygen demand (COD), biological oxygen demand (BOD), suspended solids flocculation, organic carbon content, combined nitrogen, anionic detergents, nonionic detergents, chlorinated hydrocarbon pesticides, phenols, and nitrites. Nitrite is completely converted to nitrate and values for the other compounds substantially reduced. Ozone may still be too expensive for treating high BOD effluents. Wörner and associates (1970) have described the direct introduction of O_3 into fluid protein-containing synthetic media, purified and unpurified household effluent, and unpurified slaughter house effluent.   Comparatively small doses of O_3 had a fairly rapid antibacterial effect which was independent of pH.   *Salmonella* was eliminated after 7 min of contact time.   Dosages of 5–10 gm per m^3 were considered adequate depending on degree of contamination.   Ozone treatment of sewage may largely destroy disagreeable odors.

Ozone is also used extensively in controlling the microorganisms in cold storage rooms and in deodorizing such rooms.   Growth of microorganisms on meat, held at 55°–60°F, is inhibited by treating the meat for 2–3 days with air containing 0.5–1.0 ppm of O_3.   Kaess and Wiedermann (1968) continually treated meat held at 0.3°C and high humidities with O_3 concentration in the air ranging between 0.15 and 5 mg per m^3 and observed deleterious effects on color at O_3 levels at which the desired bacterial results were obtained.

Smock (1941) noted that in apple storage rooms the introduction of ozonized air (2–3 ppm of O_3) reduced mold growth and also destroyed box or musty odors in the room.   Degoix (1968) found that high-moisture foods could be satisfactorily stored in cold, humid air containing 2 ppm of O_3.   Similar results were observed in orange and other fruit storage rooms.   The odor substances in the atmosphere of lemon storage rooms can be destroyed, but at O_3 levels possibly dangerous to humans.   Continued human exposure to O_3 concentrations above 1 ppm by volume is considered hazardous.

A few specialized uses of O_3 deserve mention.   Ozonized air has been used to sterilize and to deodorize dry milk bottles.   Fruit brandies may be improved in flavor by introducing O_3 to promote esterification.   Rayner *et al.* (1971) describe a patented procedure by which hydrated peanut and cottonseed meals are brought into contact with O_3 gas to achieve substantial lowering of the aflatoxin content.

It has been mentioned that O_3 is a powerful oxidizing agent.   Ozone treatment of oils results in addition of three oxygens to the double bond. This reaction is utilized in the preparation of pelargonic and agelaic acids from oleic acid.   Since sunflower oil (Diamond and Fuller 1970) is high in unsaturated acids, this oil lends itself to the economical production of these two acids.   Food fats exposed even to atmospheres of low O_3 content are subject to oxidative deterioration.   Lea (1936) noted that beef fat, egg oil, and lard, treated with air containing 5 ppm of O_3 for 5 hr per day at O°C, became rancid in 12 days, while the same fats kept in air remained wholesome for 4 months.

Ozone is formed in the earth's upper atmosphere by the photochemical action of solar ultraviolet light.   It exists at the earth's surface at very low but variable concentrations, depending on season of the year, latitude, solar radiation, temperature, and related atmospheric conditions.   Kurtz and coworkers (1969) noted that whole milk powder prepared during a cold weather period when atmospheric O_3 was low (0.002 ppm) was of better flavor than when prepared in warm summer weather when the atmospheric O_3 levels were higher (0.004–0.017 ppm (mean 0.008)).   Complete removal of the O_3 from the air in the spray drying chamber by use of activated carbon yielded the best flavored whole milk powder.   It is suggested that 6-*trans*-nononal originating from trace ozonolysis of a minor lipid in the dried product is responsible for the deterioration in flavor.

ARNOLD H. JOHNSON

References

DEGOIX, P.   1968.   Use of germicidal lamps in cold chambers.   Rev. Pract. Froid. Conditionnement l'Ait *21*, No. 270, 47–49 (French)

DIAMOND, N. J., and FULLER, G. 1970. Some chemical processes utilizing oleic safflower oil. J. Am. Oil Chemists Soc. *47*, 362.

GARDINER, D. K., and MONTGOMERY, H. A. C. 1968.   The treatment of sewage effluent with ozone. Water Waste Treat. J., Sept.-Oct.

HORIE, S.   1970.   Water treatment by ozone. Food Ind. (Shokuhin Kogyo) *13*, 63. (Japanese)

KAESS, G., and WIEDERMANN, J. F.   1968. Ozone treatment of chilled beef.   J. Food Technol. *3*, 325.

KURTZ, F. E., TAMSMA, A., and PALLANSCH, M. J.   1969.   Effect of filtering ozone-polluted drier air through activated charcoal in the flavor of foam spray-dried whole milk. J. Dairy Sci. *52*, 425.

LEA, C. H.   1936.   Action of ozone on fats. H.M. Food Invest. Board, Dept. Sci. Ind., Res. Rept. 1936, 25.

LOUNDES, M. R.   1971. Ozone for water and effluent treatment. Chem. Ind. Aug. 7, 951.

MEHLS, K. F. H.   1971.   Water in food factories. Gordian *71*, 112.

RAYNER, E. T., DWARAKANATH, C. T., MANN, G. E., and DOLLEAR, F. G.   1971. Process for the reduction of aflatoxin content of oilseed meals by ozonization.   U.S. Pat. 3,592,641. July 13.

SALMON, J., and LeGALL, J.   1936.   The application of ozone to the maintenance of freshness and the prolongation of the length of time of preservation of fresh fish.   Rev. Gen. Froid. *17*, 317. (French)

SMOCK, R. M.   1941.   Recent advances in the storage of apples.   N.Y. State Hort. Soc. Proc. *86*, 175.

WORNER, R., MÜLLER, W., and STRAUCH, D. 1970.   Investigations into the application of ozone for disinfection of slaughter-house effluent.   Schlact Viehhof-Zeitung *70*, 127. (German)

P

PAPIN, DENIS (1647-1712)

Denis Papin was born at Blois, France in 1647. Early in life he became interested in mechanics, his first studies being concerned with the air pump to which he contributed a number of improvements. Of greatest interest, among his many inventions, is his "steam digester," a vessel familiar to us today as a pressure cooker. Papin's digester was fitted with a lid, tightly clamped to the vessel so that no steam could escape. High pressure inside the container was thus developed and the boiling point of water was thereby elevated. Papin was well aware of the danger of excessive pressure and invented a safety valve to relieve the pressure before it became hazardous. The pressure cooker was one of the determinants in the evolution of the modern food industry, particularly in its application to canning.

Papin's steam digester was invented in 1679. The notable inventions that followed had to do with the steam engine. He is credited with inventing the cylinder and piston steam engine, a concept that Newcomen, at a later date made practical. Papin's concept was sound in principle but his scheme, using one vessel to serve as both cylinder and boiler, was unsound. However, Papin's inventive genius and extensive scientific studies entitle him to a permanent place in the mechanization of industry, including a place in one of its most important branches, the food industry.

Denis Papin was not only an inventor but a physicist. As "temporary curator of experiments," a post created for him by the Royal Society in 1684, he carried on important investigations in hydraulics. In 1687, he was appointed a professor of mathematics at the University of Marburg. In 1690, while still at Marburg, he proposed that the condensation of steam should be used to make a vacuum under a piston, which having been raised by the expansion of steam would therefore fall.

In 1696, Papin moved to Cassel, Germany, where he resided until 1707 in which year he returned to England. He died in 1712 in London, unknown except to his associates, among whom were members of that illustrious group who brought the steam engine from uncertain beginnings to high success.

A final word should be reserved for Papin' "digester." In 1681, Papin published a monograph of some 54 pages entitled, *A New Digester o Engine for Softning* (sic) *Bones* containing the "Description of its Make and Use in these Particulars: viz. Cookery, Voyages at Sea, Confectionery, Making of Drinks, Chymistry (sic) and Dying with an Account of the Price a good bi Engine will cost, and of the Profit it will afford. The monograph contains a complete description o the digester plus reports on a number of experiments that Papin conducted. The monograph is available in Malinckrodt's collection of *Foo Classics* and is designated Volume III in tha collection.

MARTIN S. PETERSO

PASTEUR, LOUIS (1822-1895)

Before Louis Pasteur's classic investigations, prevailing conceptions of why foods spoiled were for the most part wrong and the control measure taken, though sometimes effective, were founded on some curious misconceptions. The famou chemist, Gay-Lussac, shared, for example, th view of many of his fellow chemists that th oxygen in the air promoted spoilage. It was Loui Pasteur who revealed the role of microorganism in food spoilage and opened the way to scientifi studies, first to understand and then to prevent o retard spoilage. But Pasteur's contributions to th food industry, although of chief concern to foo scientists and technologists, were rivalled by hi contributions to medicine, the most profound o which was the germ theory. It is somewhat su prising that no one saw the relationship betwee the "little beasties" that Anton Van Leeuwenhoe saw in his primitive microscope and infectiou diseases, both plant and animal. Out of Pasteur' concept, however, there quickly arose a whole new approach to the prevention of diseases in animals and food spoilage caused by bacteria. Lister's invention of an antiseptic, the introduction of vaccines, Robert Koch's development of the universally-accepted bacteriological technique are perhaps the best known of the developments.

Our concern here is with Pasteur's contributions to understanding and preventing food spoilage. The story begins with Pasteur's work with alcoholic fermentation, conducted at Lille in the 1850's. It was here that he became intensely interested in the fermentation process. Broadly stated, Pasteur's discoveries over the years can be enumerated as (1) that microorganisms have a specificity made apparent in the diseases they cause, as, for example, in the spoiling of beer or wine; (2) that these microorganisms could be destroyed by heating; (3) that the flavor of these beverages was in some degree lost by heating but that in the course of time it was restored; (4) that microorganism subsisting on an acid substrate are more quickly inactivated than when on a neutral substrate.

Pasteur's theoretics were applied to many problems in the food industry, during his lifetime and later. Pasteurization heating food to the point and only to the point where spoilage organisms and enzymes are partially destroyed, has long been applied to stabilizing wine and beer. Pasteurized milk has revolutionized the fresh milk industry during the 20th Century and it is also used to extend the shelf-life of cheese, ice cream, eggs, vinegar, caviar, packaged dried fruits, and a number of other products.

It is of interest that Pasteur was a student of superior quality, shining particularly in chemistry, physics, and mathematics. He taught physics in a preparatory school in Dijon, later joined the faculty at the University of Strassburg where he taught chemistry for 6 yr, and then successively he held posts at Lille, the Ecole Normal Superieure, the Ecole des Beux Arts, the Sorbonne, and finally at the Pasteur Institute. At Lille and his subsequent posts he was mainly engaged in research but he never relinquished his interest in his students and gave them superb training and guidance despite his concentrated application on research problems of profound importance to the food industry of France and to the world at large.

MARTIN S. PETERSON

PASTEURIZATION

The preservation of foodstuffs by the application of heat has probably been practiced by man as long as fire has been known. Sterilization is an absolute term. In the classical sense it means the complete destruction or removal of all forms of life. Substantial food preservation can, however, be achieved by treatments less than complete sterilization. Pasteurization is such a treatment and involves the destruction of susceptible non-spore-producing organisms by a mild heat or equivalent process. Accordingly, pasteurization destroys pathogens and other undesirable organisms likely to be associated with a given beverage. Pasteurization derives its name from the eminent French scientist, Louis Pasteur, who, during his studies in the years 1860–1870, found that heating liquids, especially wines, to a temperature such as 140°F improved their keeping qualities. Pasteurization came into use on a commercial scale in Denmark and in Germany shortly after 1880. In 1883 Jacobi in New York heated milk for babies momentarily to 212°F, and soon Nathan Strauss, learning of the Danish experiments, began pasteurizing small quantities of milk for distribution to poor children. About the same time, pasteurizing equipment imported from Germany began to be used in commercial pasteurizing tests. In the beginning there was much opposition to heat treatment of milk but ultimately the greatly improved health of children resulted in general acceptance of the process, so that now practically all municipal milk supplies are required to be pasteurized with intricate control and certifying devices to indicate the necessary heat treatment.

Two general methods of pasteurization are in use for milk: the holding system which consists of bringing the milk to a suitable temperature (usually 142°–143°F) and holding for 30 min; and the flash method which may be, again for milk, heating at 162°F for 15 sec. The flash method is more extensively used. In both cases, rapid cooling follows the heat treatment.

In addition to destruction of pathogens and undesirable bacteria, the purpose of pasteurization is also to extend the useful life of the product with minimum alteration of flavor and physical characteristics. Milk or cream used for such manufactured dairy products as butter, cheese, and ice cream, are subjected to heat treatments related to desired characteristics of the end product. Thus, ice cream milk is usually subjected to more vigorous time-temperature relationship than milk for the market milk industry.

Other products are often subjected to heat treatments in order to accomplish the same results as pasteurization using time-temperature relationships appropriate to the product. Thus, liquid eggs are pasteurized primarily to destroy Salmonellae, the liquid eggs being heated rapidly to

140°F and held for 3½–4 min. Higher temperatures or longer holding time may bring about a partial denaturation of the albumen. Bottled beer is usually heated for 20 min at 140°F or for 30 sec at 158°F to destroy organisms which are likely to grow: certain bacterial spores are not destroyed but do not grow under the conditions of storage. Practically all apple juice is flash-pasteurized by heating to 170°–200°F for 1–3 min. Wine may or may not be pasteurized. The heat treatment inhibits growth of organisms but also aids in stabilization and clarification of the wine. Heat treatments for wine vary considerably from flashing at 145°F (with or without rapid cooling) to holding for several days at 120°F.

Equipment has been developed to permit "no hold" heat treatment of liquids at very high temperatures for very short times, with rapid cooling. Thus, for milk such a process might involve heating the milk to 205°–207°F with a hold time of 3 sec or less. Such a milk when handled aseptically may approach sterilized milk in keeping quality. The process is generally called the ultra high temperature (UHT) treatment.

Methods other than heat exchangers have been used in pasteurizing milk. Electrical pasteurization involves passing the milk between electrodes arranged in such a manner so as to heat the milk to 161°–163°F. This procedure has been used commercially but now has little acceptance.

Radiation pasteurization is a relatively new process and not used at all in the food industry. The purpose is to use irradiation effects to destroy only a portion of the microbial contamination or to render the material free of a particular undesirable microorganism.

A. C. HERRO

Cross-reference: *Market Milk Industry*.

PATENTS

In accordance with the power granted to it by Article I, Section 8, of the U.S. Constitution, the Congress has enacted legislation (United States Code Title 35) providing for the granting of patents to inventors in the interest of promoting the progress of science and the useful arts. The patent grant secures for the inventor the right to exclude others from making, using, or selling his invention for a limited time. In patents for inventions relating to articles of manufacture, machines, processes, compositions of matter, and plants—the areas of main interest, no doubt, to food engineers, technologists, and scientists—the duration of the grant is 17 yr from the date of issuance of the patent. Patents for ornamental designs for articles of manufacture may run for 3½, 7, or 14 yr, according to the election of the patentee. During the patent term the grant permits an inventor (a) to prohibit others from profiting from his invention, (b) to profit himself by manufacturing, selling, or using the invention while enjoying a monopoly position, or by exacting payment from others who make, use, or sell the invention.

Why Does the Government Grant Patents?

The answer to this question is quite simply—for the public benefit. The founding fathers in their wisdom clearly recognized that a governmental offering of some degree of protection for inventions would motivate individuals to invent and make their inventions known, thereby giving the public the benefit of the use of their inventions and providing public access to knowledge which would, in turn, stimulate others to improve upon the disclosed ideas and thus make still further inventions. To this end, the Congress, through the enabling patent statutes, has conditioned the patent grant on the inventor's making a complete written disclosure of his invention which is sufficiently clear to teach one having skill in the particular art to which the invention pertains to make and use the invention.

Who May Acquire a Patent?

Any inventor may obtain a patent so long as the requirements of the law are satisfied. There are no restrictions as to age or sex; foreign nationals enjoy the same rights and privileges as U.S. citizens in obtaining U.S. patents.

If two or more individuals contribute to the development of an invention, the application for patent must be filed by them jointly and the patent will be issued to them as joint or co-inventors. The contribution to the invention must relate to the idea or concept of the invention, that is, an element of the development which relates to its newness or novelty. Where one person conceives the idea of an invention and another person follows his instructions in making the invention, the latter does not qualify as a joint or co-inventor. For example, a technician who builds a working model of an engineer's conception of a new device under the latter's direction does not enjoy the status of a joint inventor.

To be valid, a patent must be issued to the true inventor, that is the person who actually conceived the idea and not one who has copied the idea from another.

Employers and financial backers do not qualify as inventors for purposes of acquiring patents unless they have contributed in an intellectual sense to the novelty of the idea disclosed in the patent. While they may obtain rights to an invention through express or implied contracts with the inventor, a patent application must be filed and the patent issued only in the name of the employee or individual who furnished the idea of the invention.

Patents may, however, be granted to the personal representative, e.g., executor or administrator of a deceased inventor.

Requirements for Patentability

While the patent statutes set forth a number of standards or tests which an idea must satisfy to raise it to the level of invention entitled to patent protection, the standards which are of principal importance to the majority of inventors are as follows:

(A) The idea or subject matter must be new (novel) and useful or relate to a new and useful improvement over something previously known.

(B) The invention must not have been known or used by others in the United States, or patented or described in a printed publication in the United States or a foreign country prior to the date the invention was made by the applicant for a patent.

(C) The invention must not have been patented or described in a printed publication in the United States or a foreign country, or in use or on sale in the United States more than 1 yr prior to the date the inventor files his application for a U.S. patent.

Further, assuming standards A, B and C above are satisfied, one may not obtain a patent even though his invention is not identically disclosed in an earlier patent or printed publication, if the differences between the subject matter sought to be patented and the prior art are such that the subject matter taken as a whole would have been *obvious* at the time the invention was made to a person having ordinary skill in the art to which the subject matter pertains.

Thus, to be entitled to patent protection, an invention must contribute something to the applicable field of technology which is *new*, *useful*, and *nonobvious* when considered in the light of the teachings of the prior art in the field. In an industry as old as the food industry these requisites may at times be difficult to meet.

The standards relating to newness and usefulness are essentially objective tests which lend themselves to application with a considerable degree of accuracy and consistency. The question of whether the subject matter one seeks to patent is identical with that disclosed in a prior patent can, of course, be resolved through the precise comparison of the alleged invention with the actual disclosure of a prior patent or printed publication. However, the test of obviousness or nonobviousness is subjective in nature and the resolution of this question has always been and no doubt always will be extremely difficult for inventors, patent examiners, patent attorneys, and judges. The courts have frequently said that for invention to abide in an idea it must evidence "a flash of genius" or "be beyond the expected skill of the calling" or "be beyond the skill of the routineer," but such phrases hardly provide a clear, consistently applicable guide as to what is or is not obvious. Evidence that an idea is a commercial success and that the commercial success is directly attributable to the feature in which invention is claimed to reside, has been successfully used to establish nonobviousness. Evidence of the satisfaction of a long-felt need in the art or the solution of a problem which others have previously tried but failed to resolve has also been considered a good indication of "invention." One should not erroneously conclude, however, that commercial success is a prerequisite to the right to a patent or that it will guarantee the issuance of a patent or save an otherwise invalidly issued patent. Many ideas are patented which are never commercialized and conversely, the courts have, on perhaps all too many occasions, invalidated patents covering ideas which enjoyed tremendous success in the market place.

In short, there is no known formula or criteria which can be confidently applied in all cases to clearly establish the presence or absence of "invention." If, however, an inventor can honestly, affirmatively answer the question of whether his idea will contribute new knowledge to the art or will precipitate a reawakening of interest in old knowledge by those skilled in the art, then he can proceed with some degree of confidence that he has in fact made a patentable invention.

Transfers of Interests in Patents

A patent constitutes an intangible asset, title to which resides in the patentee(s). Consequently, an inventor may transfer his entire interest in a patent to another through a written instrument, usually a deed of assignment. Where title to a patent resides jointly in more than one inventor, any one of the inventors may transfer his interest to another without accounting to his co-inventors. In this respect, joint title holders of patents enjoy essentially the same rights of transfer as joint tenants of real estate. An inventor may license others to practice his invention under an express contract on either an exclusive or nonexclusive basis. An exclusive license limits the practice of the invention solely to *the exclusive licensee* and precludes even the inventor or patent title holder from competing with the licensee. In the case of a nonexclusive license, the inventor or title holder retains the right to practice the invention himself and he may grant as many nonexclusive licenses as he chooses. Consideration for a patent assignment or license may take many forms, but is usually either a lump sum payment in cash or a periodic cash royalty based on a percentage of the assignee's or licensee's revenue derived from the practice of the invention over a fixed period of time or throughout the remaining life of the patent.

Assistance of Counsel

While an inventor may prepare, file, and prosecute a patent application covering his own invention, and negotiate and enter into contracts for the sale or license of his invention, the preparation and prosecution of patent applications and the negotiation and documentation of transfers of interests in patents are rather highly specialized arts. Thus, it is recommended that inventors or patent holders seek the advice of patent counsel in these matters.

Usually one's general attorney can recommend local patent counsel who may be consulted. Reference may also be had to the Yellow Pages of one's local telephone directory under "Attorneys—Patent." Further, one may obtain a listing (at no charge) of local or regional attorneys or agents registered to practice before the Patent Office by writing to The Commissioner of Patents, Washington, D.C. 20231. For a detailed account of the laws relative to inventions and patents, the reader is referred to the *Encyclopedia of Patent Practice and Invention* (1964), Reinhold Publishing Co., New York. A work of specific interest to food technologists is *Commercial Food Patents, U.S., 1969*, edited by H. B. and Oliver S. North, 812 S. Ode St. Arlington, Va. 22204. Future annual additions have been proposed.

JAMES R. O'CONNOR

PEACHES

Except for citrus juices, peaches are the largest pack of all processed fruits. Most of them are canned, but there is a sizeable frozen pack and a small dried peach production. Total tonnage of all peaches has risen from 1.4 to 1.8 million tons in the last 20 yr. Of these, about $1/2$ are shipped and sold as fresh produce, most of which are freestone varieties. At one time in recent years the production of clingstone peaches in California alone was approaching the 1 million ton level, but in the last couple of years it has dropped back to 500,000–600,000 tons. At this point in history the tonnage of clingstone and freestone peaches is about equal. However, nearly all the clingstone peaches are produced in California and almost all of them are canned. A few clingstone varieties are shipped to the fresh market early in the season from the southeastern states, and in the last couple of years a small canned pack of clings has been put up in the southeast. Freestone peach production in California has been cut back drastically to about $1/2$ of the former production. They amounted to almost 200,000 tons in 1971, which was about 10% of all the peaches, both freestone and clingstone, produced in the United States. About 50% of the California production of freestone peaches is sold fresh, 25% is canned, 17% frozen, and 8% dried. The farm value of all peaches produced in the United States has been around $180,000,000 in recent years.

Varieties

There are literally hundreds of varieties of both freestone and clingstone peaches planted in various regions of the United States. The standard variety of freestones throughout the country is the Elberta, although it is being replaced as fast as new varieties can be developed and tested in the different growing areas. In California, the Fay Elberta is the most popular variety, especially for canning. The Hale varieties are suitable for the fresh market and for freezing, but unsatisfactory for canning due to excessive red pigment around the pit cavity which turns brown when heated. Kim, Alamar, Rio Oso Gem, and Kirkman Gem are other varieties which most often command premium prices in comparison to standard Elbertas. For freezing, some of these same varieties plus J. H. Hale, Halehaven, and Redhaven are used in substantial quantities. Recently, the total frozen pack in the United States has been in the 60 to 80 million pound range. Some 4000 to 6000 tons of peaches are dried each year in California, mostly by exposing them to the sun. Mrak and Perry (1948) described a method using a hot air tunnel along with blanching the fruit, which resulted in a shorter drying cycle and good, translucent color.

Clingstone varieties are available which mature from mid-July to early September in the major California growing areas. Fortuna, Dixon, Paloro, Gaume, Halford, Gomes, and Corona spread the harvest from the extra early season to the extra late season. Dixon and Halford make up a large part of the California plantings of some 80,000 acres of clings. Since 1954, Dr. L. D. Davis has introduced ten so-called "high flavor" varieties of clings, but they have not yet been planted in large quantity. These varieties should be looked at as possibilities for replants, using Everts, Youngerman, and McKune for early and late harvest, and Sweeney, Tufts, Bowen, Herrington, and Merriam for additional tests in the field. A series of new varieties of cling peaches has been introduced into the southeast, which also have high flavor and show promise for both the early fresh produce market and for canning. Over 2000 acres of these peaches have been planted in Georgia and South Carolina, mostly the Baby Gold selections from Rutgers and the Mountain Gold and Piedmont Gold from Virginia Polytechnic Institute and the Georgia Experiment Station. Fogel *et al.* (1957) and Johnson *et al.* (1962) have evaluated varieties grown in Washington and Colorado.

Harvest and Handling

It has been traditional to pick peaches from 3 to 5 times during the harvest, especially for the fresh market. However, with increasing shortage of labor and higher costs, several types of mechanical shaker harvesters have been tried. These machines work quite well on properly pruned trees for canning fruit, but are not quite acceptable yet for fresh market fruit. Many growers hydrocool their fruit in the field to remove heat, and then keep them in cold storage until shipped or processed. The cooling water usually contains a fungicide to help prevent spoilage. The most serious problem in harvesting and handling peaches, either by hand or by mechanical means, is the prevention of bruising. The only solution to this problem is very careful handling, whether by hand or by machine.

Processing

Peaches must be inspected, graded, pitted, and peeled before processing into either canned or frozen products. Size grading is essential and off-quality fruit due to shape, split pits, decay, or insect damage must be eliminated or diverted. Automatic pitters for both freestone and clingstone peaches are available from several manufacturers. The peach halves resulting from the pitting operation may be peeled by several methods. Kitson and Atkinson (1959) have described an improved lye peeling operation for both cling and freestone peaches. Their modifications include thorough wetting and preheating of fruit prior to application of low strength (2.0-2.5%) lye solutions, breaking of the softened skins by a hanging canvas sheet, and use of low pressure sprays to wash off the skins.

An alternate method of peeling consists of scalding the peach halves in steam for 1-2 min, after which the flesh is cooled by a water spray to loosen the skins. Most recently, a dry caustic peeling of peaches has been developed by Ralls *et al.* (1971), in which the skins are softened by lye and then rubbed off in a unit with revolving rubber disks without the use of large quantities of water sprays.

After these preparative steps, the peaches may be canned in the conventional way in sugar syrup as halves, slices, or dice. For freezing, the peach halves are usually sliced and packed in 40° Brix syrup containing 0.1% by weight of ascorbic acid to prevent browning. For the bakery and ice cream trade, slices are packed in syrup in 30-lb enamel-lined slip-cover cans. Freezing takes place on racks set up near cold air blasts. For details and additional literature citations on freezing of peach products see Boyle and Wolford (1968) in *Freezing Preservation of Foods, Vol. 3.*

For drying, certain varieties of peaches are halved, pitted, peeled, sulfured, and then dried in the sun or in counterflow dehydrators as described by Mrak and Perry (1948).

Certain other products such as peach juice, peach nectar, peach concentrate, peach jam and jelly, peach wine, and peach brandy are made from off-grade fruit and utilize considerable tonnage. Eisenhardt *et al.* (1958) have described the production of peach concentrate with the recovery and add-back of the volatile aroma. Woodroof *et al.* (1965) prepared a peach drink from soft-ripe peaches, but the product has not been marketed to any extent. Another method for preserving food products, especially fruits, was first described by Howard and Campbell (1946) and several other researchers at the Western Regional Research Laboratory.

FRANK P. BOYLE

References

BOYLE, F. P., and WOLFORD, E. R. 1968. The preparation for freezing and freezing of fruits. *In* The Freezing Preservation of Foods. D. K. Tressler, W. B. Van Arsdel, and M. J. Copley (Editors). Avi Publishing Company, Westport, Conn.

EISENHARDT, N. H., ACETO, N. C., CLAFFEY, J. B., and REDFIELD, C. S. 1958. Makes better peach concentrates. Food Eng. *30*, No. 1, 2.

FOGEL, H. W., CARTER, G. H., INGALSBE, D. W., and NEUBERT, A. M. 1957. Freestone peach varieties for the Pacific Northwest. Washington Agr. Expt. Sta. Bull. *576*.

HOWARD, L. B., and CAMPBELL, H. 1946. Dehydrofreezing—new way of preserving food. Food Ind. *18*, 674–676.

JOHNSON, G., JOHNSON, D. K., and KOB, C. 1962. Composition and quality characteristics of peach varieties. Colo. Agr. Expt. Sta. Gen. Ser. *794*.

KITSON, J. A., and ATKINSON, F. E. 1959. Chemical peeling of freestone peaches. Chem. Canada *19*, No. 10, 39.

MRAK, E. M., and PERRY, R. L. 1948. Dehydrating freestone peaches. Calif. Agr. Expt. Sta. Circ. *381*.

RALLS, J. W. *et al.* 1971. Dry caustic peeling of tree fruit to reduce liquid waste volume and strength. Proc. 2nd Food Wastes Symp., Natl. Symp. Food Processing.

WOODROOF, J. G. *et al.* 1965. A popular drink from surplus peaches? Canner/Packer, May.

PEANUTS

The precise origin of peanuts (*Arachis hypogaea* L.) has not been ascertained though their existence was known as early as 950 B.C. They are supposed to have been found first in Brazil or Peru, to have been carried to Africa by early explorers and missionaries, and brought to North America by slave traders. They were cheap, of high food value, did not spoil easily, and were grown in the south for home food and feed from about 1765 to 1865. Since the Civil War (1865) they have been planted, harvested, and processed in increasing amounts.

While there are several types of wild and cultivated kinds, the peanut (groundnut, earth-nut, monkey nut, pinda, Manila nut) that we know today is a legume. The flower is borne above ground and after it withers the stem elongates, bends down, and forces the ovary underground. The seed matures below the surface, and the plant favors light sandy soil. When the seed matures the inner lining of the pod, or seed coat, changes from white to brownish. The entire plant, including most of the roots, is removed from the soil during harvesting.

World Production

Peanuts are one of the leading agricultural crops of the world for the production of edible oil and plant protein. They are grown in subtropical areas of 43 countries of 6 continents. The five countries leading in production are India, China, Nigeria, Senegal, and United States. During the last 14 yr there has been an increase of 25% in world acreage and 26% in world production. Yields in any one area may fluctuate from year to year as much as 20% due to insects, diseases, or weather conditions, but world production fluctuates less. There are indications that world production will increase.

A record world crop of 17.3 million metric tons (in-shell basis) from 1.4 million acres were harvested in 1967, and 16.7 million tons in 1970. The

Courtesy of Lilliston Corp.

FIG. P-1. WHEN PEANUTS AND WEATHER ARE RIGHT, ONE MAN AND A MACHINE LIKE THIS CAN DIG AND WINDROW 200 TONS OF PEANUTS A DAY

average yield per acre was 1743 lb. In the United States 1.23 million tons were harvested from 1.513 million acres in 1970.

The Peanut Industry

Peanuts became an agri-industry during the food shortage of World War I, about 1914. The industry covers a broad spectrum including growers, shellers, brokers, wholesalers, salters, oil millers, and manufacturers of peanut butter, candy, bakery goods, and other food products. The hay and meal (ground oil-extracted cake) have been used for livestock feed the world over, until recently when it was banned on account of pesticides on the hay and aflatoxin in the meal.

The per capita consumption of peanuts is higher in the United States than anywhere else in the world. It has been increasing since about 1905 when peanut butter was first made commercially. A real jump in consumption occurred about 1940 when peanut butter was first stabilized to prevent oil separation.

In the United States, harvesting begins in Texas in July and lasts into November in the Virginia-

Carolina area. August and September are the biggest harvest months in the southeast and southwest areas. The small Spanish peanuts, grown mostly in the southwest and southeast, are used in making peanut butter, candy, and for salting; the large-kernel runner-type, used in making peanut butter, is grown in the southeast; the large-shell Virginia-type, used for salting and roasting in the shell as "ball park" peanuts, are grown in the Virginia-Carolina area; while the three-seeded Valencia-type is grown in New Mexico.

Most of the African peanuts are of the small Spanish-type, with a few large Virginia type. Peanuts grown in the Philippines are three-seeded Valencia-type.

Peanut Butter

Peanut butter is a cohesive, comminuted food product prepared from dry roasted, clean, sound, mature peanuts from which the seed coat and "hearts" are removed, and to which salt, hydrogenated fat and (optional) sugars, antioxidants and flavors are added. The manufacture is relatively simple, consisting of shelling, dry-roasting, and blanching the peanuts, followed by two stages of fine grinding and packing in hermetically sealed glass or tin containers. Due to the low moisture content and package protection, it is stable for three months against microorganisms and rancidity. Under storage at 38°F peanut butter is stable against rancidity for 3 yr and against microorganisms indefinitely.

Peanut butter contains about 1.8% moisture, 27% protein, 49% fat, 17% carbohydrates, 2% fiber, 3.8% ash, 0.63% calcium, 4.07% phosphorous, 0.02% iron, 6.07% sodium, 6.7% potassium, 0.0013% thiamin, 0.0013% riboflavin, 0.157% niacin, and (added) traces of ascorbic acid and Vitamin A; it contains 581 cal per 100 gm. It is highly flavored and is used in sandwiches, salads, desserts, ice cream, custards, confections, and baked goods in more than 400 ways.

Peanut butter is by far the most important product made from peanuts in the United States, reaching about 460 million pounds annually. Consumption in European countries is very low, and most of it is imported.

Until about 1940, peanut butter was made in small, back room plants; but far more efficient and labor-saving operations have taken over. Economically operated plants are now turning out peanut butter at a rate of five tons per hour and more. While more than 90% of the peanut butter is stabilized with hydrogenated oil and antioxidants, and consumed in homes or school lunch rooms, the remainder is unstabilized (and more flavorsome) and is used commercially in confec-

tions, bakery goods, ice cream, breakfast cereals, and other minor ways.

Peanut Candies

About 1/4 of all edible peanuts in the United States find their way into candies. The pronounced flavor, crunchy texture, and high protein content render roasted peanuts especially suitable for use in candies. About 150 million pounds of peanuts are used in more than 50 varieties of candies, and others are added constantly. Some of the most flavorsome, nutritious, and popular candies with the most pleasing texture contain peanuts. Peanut candies are mostly bars and brittle. The increased use of vending machines is stimulating the use of peanut candies.

Peanut candies are relatively high in fats which tend to shorten the shelf-life. To meet this condition peanut candies are (a) usually made as needed and seldom stored for more than three months, (b) shipped and sold under refrigeration, (c) stabilized with antioxidants which double the shelf-life, and (d) packed under vacuum, which further doubles the shelf-life.

Since peanut candies contain sugars, and possibly eggs, milk and other flavoring and coloring ingredients, the size, shape and variety of the peanuts is not of major importance. However, the flavor and texture are very important.

Peanut Oil

About 2/3 of the world's peanut crop is crushed for oil, and the ground pressed cake is used for livestock feed. Peanuts supply about 1/5 of the world's edible oil production, and about 70% of oilseed crops in India. The use of peanut oil in both India and China is increasing in parallel with the improved standard of living. Peanut oil in the United States is made from off-grade, rejected, or surplus peanuts. Production reaches about 5.25 million tons annually. Hydraulic presses for oil extraction predominated until about 1945, since then use of expellers has increased.

Peanuts naturally contain from 47 to 50% oil. It is fairly stable in that the iodine number, saponification number, acetyl number, and free-fatty acids do not change during heat treatments involved in the manufacture of peanut butter and salted peanuts. Peanut oil contains at least 8 nutritionally essential fatty acids and 76-82% unsaturated fatty acids, of which 40-45% is unsaturated oleic acid and 30-35% polyunsaturated linoleic acid. There is no apparent relation between polyunsaturated fatty acids and methods of harvesting and curing or types of damage.

The major portion of the characteristic peanut aroma and flavor is in the oil, concentrated in extremely minute quantities (1.8 gm per ton) of higher hydrocarbons ($C_{15}H_{30}$ and $C_{19}H_{38}$), both of which are in concentrated form and have an acrid nauseous taste. Of about 90 million pounds of peanut oil used in the United States, 10 million are for nonfood uses, and 80 million are for food uses as follows: cooking and salad oil, 63; shortening, 4; margarine, 4; and other uses, 9 million pounds.

Salted Peanuts

Among the peanut eating peoples of the world, salting is the most preferred way of eating them; however, in the United States about twice as many peanuts go into peanut butter as are salted. The term salted peanuts refers to those that are shelled, roasted, and salted to taste. They may or may not be blanched. While usually eaten directly from the container, they may be used in candies, salads, desserts, and other ways. While any variety of peanuts with good flavor and texture may be salted, there is a preference for larger nuts. No other form of eating peanuts imparts as much flavor as with salting, since both roasting and salting enhances the peanut flavor.

Approximately 200 million pounds of peanuts are salted in the United States by 170 firms in 32 states. This indicates that salting is done on a week to week basis, close to the areas of consumption. It is not recommended that roasted peanuts be held for more than a few weeks, even under refrigeration. Peanuts are frequently used in "mixed salted nuts," since they are cheaper than most other nuts. Salted peanuts are popular the year round, but tend to give way during December to sweet snacks.

Other Uses of Peanuts

Peanuts have much to contribute to the world of food supply, whether the need be for calories, proteins, fats, or certain vitamins. It is a paradox that some of the highest peanut producing countries are in greatest need of their food value. The biggest problem in these countries is to protect the peanuts from mold, rodents, insects, and rancidity. Otherwise they become a seasonal crop. Improvements in curing, storage, and transportation facilities make it possible to deliver peanuts and peanut products to any place in the world, at any time. The years ahead may witness new food peanut products not even dreamed-of at the present time.

Among the products that have not yet reached wide distribution are peanut protein, peanut milk, peanut cheese, boiled fresh peanuts, canned boiled peanuts shelled and unshelled, frozen boiled peanuts, partially defatted peanuts, peanut bread, peanut cereals, and dozens of products that may be developed from these.

Aflatoxin

Aflatoxin, a poison deadly to poultry and other animals, though not proven so to humans, is produced by *Aspergillus flavus* mold on peanuts. The problem was virtually unnoticed until about 1960 when meal from moldy peanuts was found to kill turkeys. Peanuts with traces of toxin as low as 30 ppb (parts per billion) are rejected for food and feed; and peanut growers, cleaners, shellers, storers, and processors the world over, are using every known means of avoiding the toxin.

Research is being directed (a) toward producing and delivering to end-users peanuts free of toxin-producing mold; (b) toward a means of destroying the toxin by the use of alkalies, as is the case in refining peanut oil, or by other means; and (c) toward investigating the role of bacteria (particularly *Bacillus subtilis*), as a biological counter-opponent to the toxin-producing mold.

The mold is progressively eliminated in peanuts by cleaning, shelling, blanching, color grading by electric eye, and by hand grading; but not by freezing, boiling, dry roasting, oil roasting, grinding into peanut butter, salting, mixing into confections, or using in bakery products.

JASPER G. WOODROOF

References

WOODROOF, J. G. 1966. Peanuts: Production, Processing, Products. Avi Publishing Co., Westport, Conn.

WOODROOF, J. G. 1969. Composition and use of peanuts in the diet. World Rev. Nutri. Dietet. *11*, 142-169.

Cross-references: *Aflatoxin, Fats and Oils.*

PECTIN

Pectic substances are a group of polysaccharides, which occur in land plants and which have partially methoxylated polygalacturonic acid as their main constituent. The present article is limited in scope to pectin, a subgroup among the pectic substances, characterized as being an industrially isolated, water-soluble, partially methoxylated polygalacturonan which is used as a food ingredient and is capable of forming gels under suitable conditions.

Raw Materials For Pectin Production

Many plant materials contain sufficient quantities of pectin to be considered as potential sources for pectin production but only apple pomace, containing 10-15% pectin and citrus peel (lemon, lime, orange, and grape fruit), containing 20-30% pectin, are being utilized at present.

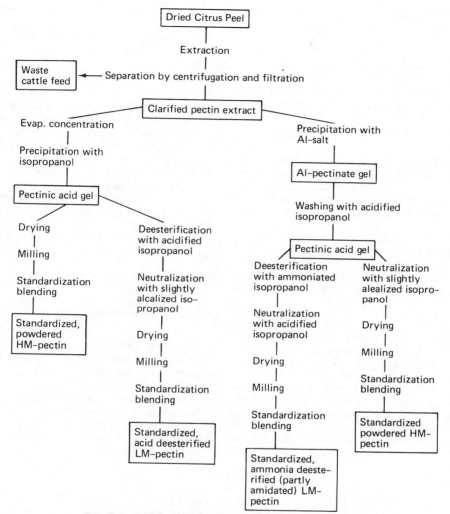

FIG. P-2. TYPICAL PECTIN PRODUCTION PROCESSES

These materials qualify as pectin raw material for a number of reasons: their high pectin substance content capable of being converted to pectin with desirable gelling properties; their availability as dried products from geographical areas where substantial fruit juice production justifies a drying plant for the by-product; their contained pectin existing in a form that makes relatively easy its isolation by industrial process from associated cellulosic and starchy materials and color.

Manufacturing Process

The objective of any industrial production of pectin is a purified pectin with uniform gelling properties or other desirable rheological properties in specific food applications.

Ideally the well-organized pectin production starts with a controlled selection of wet apple pomace or citrus peel and an immediate and careful drying to preserve the quality as a pectin source. Manufacturing processes are, in principle, simple unit operations, but much know-how is accumulated in the practical execution of the processes. Figure P-2 shows various production paths for powdered pectin from citrus peel.

Extraction of pectin is carried out at temperatures from 60° to 95°C, the extraction time varying accordingly from many hours to 30 min. Acidified soft water is used as extraction medium, a typical extraction-pH being 2.5. Not only quantity, but also quality of the pectin depends on a proper selection and control of the extraction conditions.

Precipitation of pectin from solution may either be done with alcohol from a concentrated (2-4%) pectin solution or with a aluminium salt from a dilute (0.3-0.5%) pectin solution. When pectin is isolated as aluminium pectinate, precipitation must be followed by washing with acidified alcohol to convert the aluminium pectinate to the acid form and subsequent neutralization with slightly alkaline alcohol.

Structure

As techniques of investigation of the structure of natural polymers have improved it has become increasingly clear that pectin is not a homopolymer, but a complex polysaccharide, the composition of which varies with the source and conditions used in its isolation.

D-galacturonic acid is always the principal sugar component but also present are various amounts of D-xylose, D-galactose, L-arabinose, and L-rhamnose. The D-galacturonic acid residues in pectin make up a polyuronide, which has been shown to be a linear $a(1 \rightarrow 4)$-D-galacturonan.

L-rhamnose units have been found to be an integral part of the polyuronide chain, D-xylose occurs in single unit side chains, while D-galactose and L-arabinose are probably present in pectin as constituents of galactan and arabinan molecules.

Average molecular weight of commercial pectins is in the region 60-150.000, corresponding to about 300-800 D-galacturonic acid units per molecule.

The galacturonic acid units are esterified with methanol to varying degree. The ratio of methoxylated galacturonic acid groups to total galacturonic acid groups is termed the degree of methylation (DM).

Small amounts of acetyl groups may be present, linked at C-2 and C-3 positions of galacturonic acid units.

Gelation

Considering the complexity of the pectin molecule, the kind, proportion, and distribution of substituents on the polygalacturonic acid chain, it is understandable that only a qualitative theory of gelation has been proposed as yet.

Rees (1967) suggests that segments of the pectin molecules are joined up in a 3-dimensional gel network by local limited crystallization brought about by changes in the solute. For high methoxyl (HM)-pectin (DM > 50) the required changes are addition of sugar and hydrogen ions. Addition of sugar decreases the solubility of pectin and hydrogen ions reduce the repulsion between negatively charged carboxyl groups which otherwise keep the pectin chains apart.

Addition of calcium ions is sufficient to induce gelation in low-methoxyl (LM) pectin.

Pectin Standardization

The degree of methoxylation governs the gelling mechanism of commercial pectins and serves as a criterion for division into HM-pectins and LM-pectins. The border-line DM is 45-50% depending on the method used in de-esterification.

Commercial HM-pectins are characterized by and standardized to uniform jelly grade and gelling

TABLE P-1

HM-PECTIN TYPES

Type	Gelling Time[1] (sec)	Gelling[2] Temp (°C)	Degree of Methoxylation	Typical Application
Extra rapid set	—	—	80-85	Household pectin powders, liquid household pectin.
Rapid set	< 60	> 90	72-75	Jams filled into glass jars at high temperatures (> 80°C).
Medium rapid set	100-135	80-85	68-70	Jams filled at intermediate temperatures (60°-80°C).
Slow set	150-220	60-75	62-66	Jellies, jams filled into large packages at low temperatures (< 60°C). Confectioner's jellies.

[1] Joseph and Baier (1949) method—Soluble solids: 65.0%
    pH: 2.20-2.40
    Cooling rate: in standard jelly glass in 30°C water bath
[2] Conditions
    Standard gell—Soluble solids: 70.0%
    pH: 3.15-3.20
    Cooling rate: in standard test tube in water bath allowed to cool from boiling temperature in air

velocity. Jelly grade methods all express the amount of sugar that can be gelled in a standard gel (standard composition and standard gel strength).

Various methods are used in measuring gel strength, the most common method being the SAG-method where deformation within the elasticity limit of the gel is measured. In other methods, breaking strength of the gel is determined. For specific applications the ratio between strength based on SAG-grade and strength based on breaking strength grade is of importance. In jellies, specifically confectioner's jellies, a high breaking strength is required; whereas in jams, the need for spreadability favors a pectin with a low breaking strength. International trade gives preference to the SAG-method developed by the U.S. Institute of Food Technologists' Committee on Pectin Standardization in 1959.

Methods used in standardization of LM-pectin differ even more than for HM-pectin standardization methods. Generally, LM-pectin requires calcium ions for gelation, but the optimum amount depends on many factors as DM, methods used in de-esterification, soluble solids, and pH in the test gel. Also, LM-pectin has many more and varied uses than HM-pectin. Performance tests may therefore often be preferred as evaluation methods for LM-pectin.

LM-pectin gels at fixed temperatures independent of cooling rate; gelling temperature depends on the same factors as gel strength; and gelling temperature can, therefore, not be specified without describing the system intensively in which the gelling temperature is determined.

Besides the gelling characteristics, a number of other quality criteria of pectin are of importance to the user: (1) Color of pectin powder and solution. (2) Flow of powder. (3) Dispersability. (4) Viscosity in solution. (5) Clarity in gelled state. (6) Absence of own taste and odor. (7) Purity expressed as acid insoluble residue, heavy metals content, etc.

General Properties

Commercial pectins are all water-soluble. HM-pectins are soluble in cold water if sufficient agitation is provided; LM-pectins require heat to dissolve in hard water.

Pectin solutions may be made to concentrations of 4–8% depending on the pectin type, the equipment available to dissolve the pectin, the temperature of the water, calcium content of the water, and other factors. The best equipment for making pectin solution are mixing devices where the pectin powder is introduced into water at the point of highest shear. Thereby the formation of difficult-to-disperse lumps is avoided.

Pectin, although less thermo-stable than other gelling agents at neutral pH, is more stable than gelling agents at pH of 2-4. This property makes pectin ideally suited for use in fruit products.

At its pH of optimum stability (3-4), pectin solutions may be held at $60°C$ for 8 hr without any noticeable change, whereas at $100°C$ the gelling power of pectin is reduced by 10% after 30 min. Processing times at high temperatures should therefore be minimized.

The degradation of pectin at a pH of 3 is by two processes: (1) Hydrolysis of glycosidic linkages, which reduces the molecular weight of pectin. (2) De-esterification, the practical effect of which is a prolonged gelling time/lower gelling temperature.

At pH value higher than 4, another degradation process, the so-called β-elimination becomes increasingly more pronounced; this reaction reduces the molecular weight of pectin and thereby the gelling power.

HM-Pectin Application

The importance of pectin to the food industry lies in the unique ability of its solution to produce a gel under suitable conditions.

HM-pectin requires 55-85% sugar and pH of 2.5-3.8 in order to gel. These requirements limit the possible uses of HM-pectin as a gelling agent to sweetened fruit products. About 80% of the world production of HM-pectin is used in manufacture of jams and jellies, the pectin being added to make up for a deficiency of natural pectins.

The role of pectin is to impart a texture to the jam or jelly, that allows transportation without changes, gives a good flavor release, and minimizes syneresis. In jams, a good spreadability may be a requirement, whereas in confectioners' jellies, a high breaking strength is required.

The use concentrations for pectin vary from 0.1-0.4% in jams and jellies, to 0.8-1.5% in confectioners' jellies calculated as $150°$ USA-SAG pectin.

Production of pectin in United States and Western Europe is estimated for the year 1970 to be approximately 11,000 tons of HM-pectin ($150°$ SAG) and 1000 tons of LM-pectin.

Pectin is also produced in South America and in Eastern Europe, but no production figures are available.

Pectin prices in 1971 were $1.50 per lb for HM-pectin $150°$SAG and approximately $2.00 per lb for LM-pectin.

LM-pectin Applications

LM-pectin requires no sugar or acid for gelation and is therefore used as a gelling agent especially in fruit products with a low sugar content or in products containing no added sugar.

The gelling mechanism requiring the presence of calcium ions places LM-pectin in the group with alginate as distinguished from other gelling agents, such as gelatine, agar, and carrageenan, which are independent of sugar + acid as well as of calcium concentrations.

A typical application of LM-pectin is in reversible bakers' jelly, where a LM-pectin jelly is melted by heating before being applied to the pastry surface.

Another application of LM-pectin is in canned, liquid fruit preparations intended to be mixed with cold milk to make fruit-flavored instant milk puddings. LM-pectin is especially well suited in this application since it gels only after mixing with milk, the milk providing the necessary calcium-ions for gelation.

Safe as Food Additive

Codex Alimentarius defines a food additive as a substance not normally consumed as a food by itself, but which by its use becomes a component of a food. Following this definition pectin is a food additive.

Pectin, as found naturally in plant material, has been part of the human diet since the emergence of man. The long testing time it has had suggests that pectin is a safe food additive; and controlled feeding tests where large doses of pectin were fed to test animals have shown no toxic effects.

On the basis of all available evidence, the joint FAO/WHO Expert Committee on Food Additives ascribed an "unlimited" ADI (Acceptable Daily Intake) to pectin. This places pectin in a different position from other food gums and may determine the use of pectin in applications where pectin is not economically competitive with other gelling agents, stabilizers, or thickeners.

JENS K. PEDERSEN

References

JOSEPH, G. H., and BAIER, W. E. 1949. Method of determining the firmness and setting time of pectin test jellies. Food Technol. *3*, 18.
REES, D. A. 1967. The Shapes of Molecules—Carbohydrate Polymers. Oliver & Boyd, Edingburg and London.

PEMMICAN

Pemmican is the name of a packaged food used by the North American Indians to sustain them during their nomadic journeys and during seasons when food was hard to come by. The name, pemmican, comes from the Cree word, *pimikan*, *pime* in that language meaning *fat*.

Briefly defined, pemmican consists of slices of lean venison or buffalo meat, sundried, and beaten to a powder. Melted fat was mixed with the powdered meat and, on some occasions, particularly for use on festive occasions, dried currants or chokecherries. The pemmican was then pressed into cakes, packed in rawhide sacks lined with grease, and sealed at the seams with tallow. The Pacific Coast Indians developed a similar type of pemmican using fish as a basic ingredient.

The keeping quality of pemmican was excellent, the reason being that it was dehydrated product and packaged in a virtually air- and moistureproof rawhide sack.

Pemmican has a most interesting history, much of it recorded in Steffanson's *Not by Bread Alone*. Its use by Hudson's Bay Company trappers, by the Mountain Men of the early West, by men engaged in Arctic explorations, and on occasion by the military has adequately proved its merit. It was, when properly made, a palatable preserved food, a food for all seasons.

MARTIN S. PETERSON

References

STEFFANSON, V. 1946. Not by Bread Alone. Macmillan Co., New York.

Cross-reference: *Foods of Primitive Man.*

MARY ENGEL PENNINGTON (1872–1952)

Mary Engel Pennington, born in Nashville, Tennessee in 1872, was the first woman to attain prominence in food science and technology. She received her Ph.D. in 1895 from the University of Pennsylvania where she was a Fellow until 1897. She taught at Yale University in 1897 and 1898, and then became Director of the Chemistry Laboratory of the Women's College of Medicine of Pennsylvania in 1898, which position she held until 1906. She also served as chief of the Philadelphia Municipal Chemical Laboratory and continued on there until 1907 when she was appointed Chief of the Food Research Laboratory of the U.S. Bureau of Chemistry (USDA) in Philadelphia, a post she held from 1908 to 1919.

Later she became a consultant specializing in the determination of quality of perishable foods and the freezing of foods, particularly poultry.

During World War II she was retained by the Quartermaster General as a consultant, specializing in refrigeration and refrigerated foods.

She received many honors including the Garvan Gold Medal. These honors were accorded her because of her firm stand for purity and quality in foods. Perhaps she is best known for her work on improvement of processes used in freezing poultry.

DONALD K. TRESSLER

PERSIMMONS

Although there are 190 known species in the *Diospyros* genus, only two species are grown for their edible fruit. *D. kaki* L., the Japanese persimmon of China, Japan, and Korea, is a very important fruit in these countries. The native North American species, *D. virginiana* L., is edible but is not eaten to any great extent. It has been used to flavor puddings and breads, but has not been popular due to its extreme astringency before reaching full ripeness. The wood of this tree, being a member of the ebony family, has been used in quantities of several million board feet to manufacture golf club heads and shuttles for the textile industry (Fletcher 1942).

The Japanese persimmon, "kaki," is produced in quantities in Japan, third only to Mandarin oranges and apples. Ito (1971) indicates that there are at least 1000 varieties of *D. kaki* grown in Japan on 40,000 hectares (100,000 acres) and producing nearly 500,000 metric tons of fruit. Two nonastringent varieties, Fuyu and Jiro, make up about $1/2$ of the total production in Japan. Of the many astringent varieties, Hachiya is best known in the United States and has been planted extensively in California and Hawaii. The production in California has stabilized at 460 acres yielding around 2000 tons of fruit per year, worth $300,000.

The astringent fruits must be treated in some way to remove the undesirable flavor. The most successful treatments according to Fletcher (1942) and Ito (1971) consist of holding in warm water or storage under CO_2. Contrary to popular belief, the astringency is not removed completely by freezing the fruit. Bloch and Binder (1960) made some processing studies on Hachiya persimmons in which they worked out methods for peeling, slicing, and puréeing the fruit prior to freezing, drying, and concentrating. Some of the products were successful, but have not been marketed. An extensive study of the pigments in the fruit was made by Curl (1960) in which he identified 26 different carotenoids in the Hachiya variety. The fruit is considered to be a good source of provitamin A and of vitamin C.

FRANK P. BOYLE

References

BLOCH, F., and BINDER, R. J. 1960. Report on processing trials with fruit and nuts not common in U.S. Chemurgic Dig. Oct.

CURL, A. L. 1960. The carotenoids of Japanese persimmons. Food Res. *25*, 670–674.

FLETCHER, W. F. 1942. The native persimmon. USDA Farmers' Bull. *685*.

ITO, S. 1971. The persimmon. *In* The Biochemistry of Fruits and Their Products, Vol. 2. A. C. Hulme (Editor). Academic Press, New York.

PHOTOSYNTHESIS

Photosynthesis, by transforming light energy into chemical energy, is the fundamental process upon which virtually all life on earth depends. Man is dependent on it for the oxygen he breathes, for virtually all his food, for almost all his fuel, and for much of his clothing. With the quantitatively minor exception of some bacterial photosynthesis, the process may be described as one in which green plants and algae, employing the energy of light and utilizing water as a source of hydrogen, convert carbon dioxide into carbohydrates and other complex substances. The general form of the overall equation may be written:

$$CO_2 + H_2O + \text{light energy} \longrightarrow (CH_2O) + O_2$$

where (CH_2O) stands for a basic unit of carbohydrate.

In most algae and in higher plants the photosynthetic process occurs in disc-shaped subcellular units called chloroplasts. In vascular plants these units are chiefly in the leaves. Carbon dioxide reaches the chloroplasts by diffusion from the air, and water is generally absorbed by the roots and translocated to the leaves. The oxygen produced, except for a small portion used in respiration, diffuses into the atmosphere. Radiant energy serves two principal functions: first, less than 1% is trapped by the photosynthetic apparatus, and second, about 40% is used to evaporate transpired water. The remaining energy reaching the plant area is reflected or absorbed and subsequently radiated as heat.

According to a widely accepted hypothesis, the entire photosynthetic process may be viewed as comprising five phases, each consisting of many steps, some of which differ between plant species. The first, is the light absorption phase. A light quantum of an appropriate wavelength is absorbed by one of the pigments (carotenoid, chlorophyll, or other) causing an electron in the molecule of that pigment to be raised to a higher energy level. This absorbed energy is then transferred to chlorophyll

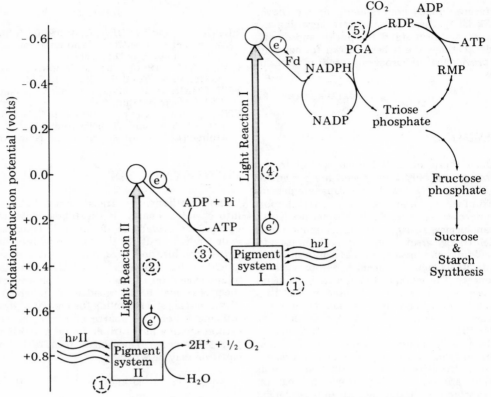

FIG. P-3. A SCHEMATIC OF THE PHOTOSYNTHETIC PROCESS

Legend:
The five phases of the process are indicated by the large numerals 1, 2, etc.
Light energy absorbed is presented by hνI and hνII.

ADP   = adenosine diphosphate
ATP   = adenosine triphosphate
Fd   = ferrodoxin
NADP   = nicotine adenine dinucleotide phosphate
NADPH = reduced form of NADP
PGA   = 3-phosphoglyceric acid
Pi   = inorganic phosphate
RMP   = ribulose monophosphate
RDP   = ribulose diphosphate

a for use in the photosynthetic process. Energy not used in photosynthesis is dissipated as fluorescent light and as heat.

The second phase is the photolysis of water. This occurs in "Light Reaction II" using absorbed light energy of about 650 nanometers. It results in the removal, from water, of four hydrogen atoms as electrons and protons, with the concomitant evolution of a molecule of oxygen. The electrons are raised against an electrochemical gradient from a redox potential of +0.8 volt to a potential of approximately 0.0.

In the third phase, electrons are transported "down" the electrochemical gradient to a potential

of about +0.4, with the released energy being used for the formation of adenosine triphosphate (ATP).

The fourth phase consists of "Light Reaction I," which uses absorbed light energy of about 680 nanometers and results in electrons being raised against an electrochemical gradient from +0.4 to a potential of about −0.6 volt. These electrons are transferred via ferredoxin to form reduced molecules of nicotine adenine dinucleotide phosphate (NADPH).

In the fifth, or carbon fixation phase, the reducing ability of NADPH, and the energy stored in ATP, are used for the reduction of carbon dioxide by appropriate enzyme systems. Two different carbon dioxide fixation routes have been proposed. In one, known as the Calvin cycle, carbon dioxide adds to ribulose diphosphate. The resulting 6-carbon intermediate splits to yield 2 molecules of the 3-carbon compound 3-phosphoglyceric acid (PGA), which can be converted to fructose phosphate for sucrose and starch synthesis. In the other, carbon dioxide adds to a 3-carbon compound, phosphoenolpyruvic acid, to give 4-carbon compounds, such as oxalacetic, malic, and aspartic acids, which are converted to PGA so that the synthesis can continue on the normal Calvin pathway.

Although carbohydrates and 4-carbon carboxylic acids represent the principal early products of photosynthesis, it has been observed in tracer experiments that radioactive carbon-14 in carbon dioxide quickly finds its way into a variety of other products in the photosynthetizing plant. Certain amino acids and some fatty acids are formed from Calvin cycle intermediates and must therefore be regarded as true products of photosynthesis.

The annual production of dry matter through photosynthetic activity is estimated at between 150 and 200 billion tons. Forests account for about $1/2$ and oceans for about $1/3$ of this total. However, because only a small proportion of the incident radiation is absorbed, the net rates of energy fixation are low. The following are some estimates of the efficiency of conversion of photosynthetically useful radiation into dry matter: laboratory experiments on leaf discs—up to 20%; sugar beet in a field, mid-growing season—8–9%; productive woodlands—up to 4%; agricultural yields for the entire growing season—up to 2%; global average for all land vegetation—0.27%.

Differences in efficiency of light utilization for carbon dioxide fixation exist between plants and, in general, the efficiency is about 30–40% higher in plants using the C_4-dicarboxylic acid pathway as the dominant route of carbon fixation.

Variations in carbon dioxide concentration are also known to affect photosynthetic rates, and greenhouse operators may artificially increase the concentration of carbon dioxide to stimulate plant growth. A worldwide increase in carbon fixation rates appears possible as a result of increased atmospheric carbon dioxide concentrations caused by our large and increasing consumption of fossil fuels. The effect to date is small because, in the past 150 yr, the atmospheric carbon dioxide content has risen only from about 290 to 320 ppm (about 10%). But greater effects may be observed if, as forecast, carbon dioxide levels rise to 400–500 ppm early in the next century.

Daytime light intensities do not generally limit photosynthetic production except in the lower, shaded, leaves of plants. Relatively low light intensities are sufficient to bring photosynthetic rates to the compensation point where the amount of carbon dioxide fixed equals the amount lost in respiration, and complete light saturation is reached far below maximum daylight intensities.

Water and other inorganic substances often limit photosynthetic rates. Water serves not only as the source of hydrogen to reduce carbon dioxide, but in vascular plants, it provides the main transpiration stream which is responsible for the transport of minerals and other substances. Its lack is often the factor that limits growth. Under conditions of good water supply photosynthetic productivity reaches maximum levels, and may, in some cases, have undesirable consequences as when drainage ditches and irrigation canals become choked by plant growth. In the oceans and in most fresh waters, the usual limitation on photosynthetic productivity is the availability of inorganic substances: nitrogen, phosphorous, iron, and other metals. Generally, these are abundant only where they are resupplied from deeper layers of the ocean or from wastes of human activities. Mineral supplies in moderate concentrations permit the growth of phytoplankton that support fish populations, but with increased concentrations, eutrophication (literally, making nutritionally complete) may lead to excessive growths of algae; thus, the addition of phosphates is often considered "pollution."

Temperature also affects photosynthetic rates and, although mean world temperatures appear to be changing little, man has caused marked changes in some localities. Warming has occurred in a number of streams and estuaries receiving water that is used to carry heat from nuclear reactors and other installations. This warming has resulted in increased and usually undesirable growths of plants.

Much attention is being given to means of increasing world food production, and always the means basically involve the sun's energy. Most predictions for the immediately-foreseeable future suggest that man's food will continue to be produced by conventional land-based agriculture, but with improved plants and increased yields reaching; for example, 500 bu of corn per acre. Further possibilities are seen through changes in the basic metabolic process of photosynthesis and in nonconventional agriculture, particularly algal culture. Opportunities for increased production from the oceans are limited because of the prohibitively large quantities of minerals needed to keep large volumes of water in a nutritionally productive state. Plant leaves, now fed to animals, might, by mechanical means, be converted directly to food with approximately a ten-fold saving in energy content; but unfortunately, the product, like that of algal culture, still lacks satisfactory palatability.

Estimates of the number of people who could live on this planet if photosynthesis were the only limiting factor (water and minerals being amply supplied) are very high indeed; e.g., 1000 billion persons. With 15% of the land surface of the world used efficiently for agricultural purposes, a population of 146 billion persons could be fed, or 7% of the land surface could maintain a population of 79 billion. A fundamentally more important question for future populations may be the amount of space a person needs for reasonably comfortable living.

J. G. ARMSTRONG

References

BOARDMAN, N. K. 1968. The photochemical systems of photosynthesis. Advan. Enzymol. *30*, 1–79.

BOLIN, B. 1970. The carbon cycle. Scientific Am. *223*, No. 3, 125–132.

HATCH, M. D., and SLACK, C. R. 1970. Photosynthetic CO_2-fixation pathways. Ann. Rev. Plant Physiol. *21*, 141–162.

LEVIN, R. P. 1969. The mechanism of photosynthesis. Scientific Am. *221*, No. 6, 58–70.

SAN PIETRO, A., GREER, F. A., and ARMY, T. J. (Editors). 1967. Harvesting the Sun. Academic Press, New York.

WALKER, D. A. 1970. Three phases of chloroplast research. Nature *226*, 1204–1208.

Cross-reference: *Carbohydrates.*

PICKLES

Pickling of plant and animal foods is an ancient mode of food preservation. Fermentation was known to the early Egyptians; sauerkraut was manufactured in ancient China; and fish appear to have been preserved by brining in prehistoric times.

Numerous vegetables and fruits can be pickled with benefit not only to their keeping quality but to their flavor as well. The categories of pickled products are many, the most common being cucumber pickles and other vegetable pickles; pickled fruits, particularly pears, peaches, and plums; pickled nuts, for example, walnuts; relishes of all kinds; cured meats, fish and poultry; and such specialty products as pickled mushrooms and pickled cherries, popular in British Columbia. Pickling, broadly defined, is the use of brine, vinegar or a spicy solution to preserve and give a unique flavor to a food adaptable to the process. The process, for example the manufacture of cucumber pickles, consists of a cure in a 10% salt solution, during which fermentation by halophyllic (salt-tolerant) bacteria takes place. The cure takes from 28 to 42 days. The salt prevents growth of spoilage organisms. Carbon dioxide, which develops in the early stages of the cure, must be released lest adverse effects occur.

When the cure is completed, the product is placed in a more concentrated salt solution and stored until final processing can be accomplished. Final processing includes immersion in water to remove the salt, the addition of vinegar, and a final bath in water that contains calcium chloride, a firming agent, and tumeric to enhance color.

Pickles are usually pasteurized in order to extend shelf-life.

The foregoing description applies to the manufacture of sour pickles. To make sweet pickles a spiced sweet vinegar is added to the final soak. For dill pickles, the dill plant or its seeds are used to give flavor to the product.

In meat cures, salt, sugar, sodium nitrate and sodium nitrite are used. The cure can be added in the dry state, as in sausages, or made up into a solution in which the meat product can be immersed. When pickled fish is mentioned, one is likely to think first of pickled herring. Salted herring are often used in the pickling process but must be desalted down to 6% before being placed in the vinegar solution. Spices are included in the vinegar solution.

The shelf-life of pickles is dependent upon the preservative agents and, where employed, on pasteurization. Vinegar, the most commonly-used of these agents, contains about 4% acetic acid. It has considerable preservative effect but its efficiency is by no means total. However, it is nontoxic, adds an appealing flavor to a food, and it has no rival under these terms as a preservative. Since the bacteria that cause food poisoning do not tolerate acetic acid, pickled foods are not likely to be suspect in a poisoning incident—at least not in those cases where vinegar is used in sufficient amount.

Pickled vegetables are packed for the most part in sealed glass jars and usually under vacuum. Lacquered cans, plastic bottles, and pouches are also used. Relishes are packaged similarly. Cured meats do not require a perfect barrier against contamination since the cure reduces the bacterial count but packaging material should be impervious to light, which impairs the color of a product, and it should also retard the loss of oxygen and moisture.

The processing and packaging of sauerkraut is treated elsewhere in this Encyclopedia, but it might be mentioned that sauerkraut is being increasingly packaged in plastic bags and marketed refrigerated.

MARTIN S. PETERSON

References

BINSTED, R., DEVY, J. D., and DAKIN, J. C. 1971. Pickle and Sauce Making, 3rd Edition. Food Trade Press, London, England.

SACHAROW, S., and GRIFFIN, R. C. 1970. Food Packaging. Avi Publishing Co., Westport, Conn.

Cross-reference: *Fermentation.*

PIES

See Baking Industry: Cakes and Pies.

PINEAPPLE

The pineapple, a native of South America, has now spread throughout the tropical world. The main sources of pineapple are Hawaii, the Philippines, Taiwan, Malaysia, South Africa, Australia, the Ryukus, and the Ivory Coast. Other important centers of production are in Mexico, Puerto Rico, Kenya, Swaziland, and Thailand.

The pineapple is an herbaceous monocot which matures fruit from 18 to 22 months following planting. Each plant produces a single compound fruit on a central stem. About 1 yr later the plant will produce a ratoon crop on one or more axillary suckers.

Pineapple is grown vegetatively from slips, crowns, or suckers. In areas which have been under pineapple cultivation for a long period of of time, the soil must be treated to reduce pests, particularly nematodes, if a satisfactory crop is to be produced. Pineapple grows best in a well-drained soil. Abundant sunshine is required for top-quality fruit production. Quality is influenced also by other climatic conditions. Excessively high temperatures yield fruit with low levels of flavor; on the other hand, excessively low temperatures will produce fruit that is too acid for optimum quality.

Although pineapple is grown and sold as fresh fruit, by far the largest portion of the world crop is processed into canned products. The processing of pineapple is unique in that special machines are used which cut it into shape to fit efficiently into cans. Pineapple is processed by first cutting out a cylinder, which, after trimming, is cut into slices, chunks, tidbits, or crushed products. These items are packed in syrup or in juice. Pineapple juice is produced from the edible portions of the fruit that are unsuitable for the production of solid pack pieces. The juice is canned as a single-strength product or converted into concentrate which may be marketed in consumer size cans or

TABLE P-2

WORLD PRODUCTION OF CANNED PINEAPPLE
(Millions of 2½ Standardized Cases)

Year	Hawaii	World	Hawaiian Percentage of World Production
1950	11.3	15.8	71.7
1955	13.7	21.6	63.7
1960	13.2	25.3	52.2
1965	12.6	30.1	41.9
1969	11.6	32.3	36.0

in bulk containers. Bulk concentrate is used primarily for the production of blended juice or drink products.

World production of canned pineapple has doubled in the last 20 yr. During this period there has not been a significant change in Hawaiian production and its market share has been considerably reduced. Figures compiled by the Pineapple Growers Association of Hawaii show that total world production of canned pineapple is now more than 30 million standardized 24/2 ½ (45 lb) cases.

By-products from canning of pineapple are sugar and cattle feed. The sugar is usually recovered by ion exchange purification of the juice pressed from the cannery waste materials. The pulp residue is dried and used as feed for cattle. Pineapple alcohol and vinegar instead of sugar may be produced from the by-product pineapple juice. These by-products are of considerable importance as an economic means of disposing of the cannery waste material.

The enzyme, bromelain, is produced on a commercial scale in some areas from pineapple stems. This enzyme has found extensive uses in the food and pharmaceutical industries.

GEORGE E. FELTON

Cross-reference: *Tropical Fruits.*

PLANT LOCATION

From an economic standpoint the suitability of a location for a food plant is determined by the availability of the raw materials to be processed, the water supply, the availability of labor, and shipping facilities. These are self-evident determinants. Not so evident is the fact that each of these factors is not likely to be optimal, that is to say, the raw materials may be abundant in a given area but the labor supply is miles away or the water supply may be ample but its quality unsuited to use in processing.

The criteria for locating a food processing operation, formerly so simple, have become complicated in recent years. Legal restraints have been placed on waste disposal and other types of pollution. Shipping facilities have been greatly expanded in this century, but costs have increased. Taxation has become an increasing burden and are greatest in areas that are highly developed—the areas, as a matter of fact, that are best suited for the location of a food plant.

A large number of criteria enter into determining the best site for locating a food plant so that the choice in the final analysis must be made on a system of trade-offs. In full recognition of the fact that the choice will be influenced by the type of food processing operation being conducted or about to be attempted, the ten factors listed are of concern in selecting a site for food processing:

Criteria for Location with Regard to Operations

Availability of raw materials	Shipping facilities
Availability of labor	Accessability of markets
Water supply and quality	Waste disposal requirements
Tax level	Availability and cost of power
Location of competitors	Cost of real estate

If these 10 factors were each given a range of values of 1 to 10, with 10 the top value and 1 the lowest possible rating, the appraisal of a given site might be measurable in terms of the percentage of desirability of that site as opposed to another. It would be necessary of course to establish a cut-off point with regard to low values. If water supply and quality were downgraded to 4, meaning poor quality and uncertain supply, the other ratings, no matter how high, could not counterbalance the deficiency with regard to the water factor. The point to be made, of course, is that once a balance of those features deemed of major importance has been reached it should be possible by cross comparison to arrive at a decision as to the best location from an operational point of view.

Assuming that operating factors are of primary concern but that socio-economic factors cannot be ignored, the following list of factors will contribute to a stable operation from the point of view of employees:

Socio-economic Factors of Concern in Plant Location

Housing (availability)	Cultural and religious resources
Recreational facilities	Schools
Climate	Real estate costs
Police and fire protection	Tax rate
Appearance of the municipal area	Medical services

Here again, giving these factors a range of values from 1 to 10, some conclusion as to the desirability of the area with regard to living conditions can be arrived at and how the rating of one municipality may compare with that of other possible locations.

The tendency of many industries to migrate from cities to smaller communities has become pronounced in recent years.

MARTIN S. PETERSON

PLANT PIGMENTS

The development of knowledge of the plant pigments has proceeded in many ways with an impetus from several directions. It is interesting to trace how and why some areas of research develop at a faster rate than others. This is true of many areas of natural product research and may be due to a combination of research interest, available tools, and possible economic payoffs. Progress in natural pigment chemistry can be attributed to all three.

Natural pigment chemistry is a branch of natural product chemistry which itself is a portion of the much bigger areas of organic chemistry and biochemistry. It has been of interest for centuries, but real progress dates back only 100 yr or so to the work of Graeber and Liebernon on the anthraquinone dyes from studies on alizarin in madder root. Perkin's famous mauve dye came from attempts to synthesize quinine. Studies on medicinal products from natural drugs, such as extracts of *Digitalis* and *Cinchona* provided a very great stimulus to this type of work in the second half of the 19th Century. The work on natural pigments led to the amazing development of the synthetic dyestuff industry, particularly in Germany towards the end of the 19th Century.

The 20th Century saw the development of a very large body of chemical knowledge in natural pigments. This was due primarily to the work of real giants of research, such as Perkin, Willstätter, and Fischer. One never ceases to marvel at the work of these men, when one considers the tools available to them. The work of Perkin on dyes, Willstätter on chlorophylls and enzymes, Emil Fischer on proteins and carbohydrates, and Robinson on anthocyanins are examples that may well serve as inspirations to modern day students.

Willstätter and his school, with displays of true chemical genius, were able to utilize the existing tools of organic chemistry to elucidate the structures of the chlorophylls and the flavonoid compounds. But others were ahead of their time. Hans Fischer had to postpone his work on proteins after a brilliant start, due to a lack of the tools of research. These were to be developed in more recent times. The first major advance came in the development of microanalytical techniques by Pregl. It was followed by column chromatography, introduced by Twsett and developed by Kuhn and Brockman on alumina. Later ion-exchange, thin layer and paper chromatography, vapor phase or gas chromatography, and electrophoretic methods, all played their role in natural pigment chemistry. The use of paper chromatography, in particular, in the 1940's made it possible to separate and identify many closely related flavonoids. Column chromatography combined with countercurrent chromatography has had similar importance in the carotenoid area.

The rate of development of chemical tools has speeded up immeasurably in the past decades, and this is particularly true in the case of the physical methods for both separation and analysis. First came the application of ultraviolet spectroscopy for structure determination. It was followed by infrared, nuclear magnetic resonance, and more recently by mass spectrometry. All are important in the determination of structure of natural pigments, and have led to the structural identification of thousands of compounds. Structural studies are still very important, but the trends of research are changing. Today the impetus is on the utilization of the very powerful tools of research towards an understanding of the role of the pigments in the whole sphere of natural products. Food science and technology is one of many areas in which the pigments are important.

The natural pigments used to be considered as primarily the greens of the chlorophylls, the oranges of the carotenoids, the yellow of the flavonoids, and the reds and blues of the anthocyanins. This concept is much too narrow today. The following passages describe some of the pigment classes and their importance to the field of food science. No attempt is made to describe each class definitely, since this will be done in other sections. Also, the anthocyanins are treated separately from the flavonoids, even though they are closely related chemically. They are very different in appearance.

Anthocyanins

Chemical research on the anthocyanins began over 100 yr ago, but real progress can be dated from the identification of cyanidin-3,5-diglucoside in roses by Willstätter in 1913. The methods in vogue at that time worked well when the pigments were available in large quantities but failed completely when minor quantities or complex mixtures were encountered. These problems were solved by a milestone in anthocyanin chemistry, namely, the introduction of paper chromatographic methods by Bate-Smith in 1948. This made it possible, for the first time, to isolate very small amounts of pigments in a short time. When paper chromatographic rf data were combined with simple spectrophotometric methods, research in anthocyanin chemistry entered a new phase. The real leaders in this field such as Bate-Smith, Harborne, Swain, Geissman, and Hayashi combined a chemical background with an interest in the new techniques and progress was rapid indeed.

The anthocyanins are all based on a single aromatic structure—the $3,5,7,3',4'$ pentahydroxy-

Anthocyanin basic structure

flavylium cation. The above compound is termed an aglycone and 16 variations are known ranging from the yellow apigeninidin to the blue delphinidin. The aglycones probably never appear in the free state in plant tissue; they are always esterified with a sugar. Glucose is the most common followed by rhamnose, galactose, xylose, and arabinose. An aglycone may have 1, 2, or 3 sugar residues. The sugars may also be esterified to an acyl component such as coumaric, caffeic, ferulic, or acetic acid. The permutations involved in the aglycones, sugars, and acyl components have resulted in approximately 120 known anthocyanins.

The discovery of many of the recently identified anthocyanins is due to the impetus of the biochemical workers in plant taxonomy. The work of Harborne, particularly, has resulted in many new compounds. The taxonomists have developed anthocyanin content as a unique tool to aid the classical morphological studies in plant taxonomy.

The new anthocyanins discovered in food products have resulted mainly from chemical studies in attempts to understand the mechanism of quality deterioration due to pigment degradation. Anthocyanins degrade slowly and continuously upon storage of heat-processed fruit and vegetable products, and, despite considerable research, the mechanisms are still incompletely understood. The role of oxygen, ascorbic acid, and metal ions in pigment degradation have been documented often but not really explained. Current research is devoted partially to relative stability of the various anthocyanins and the structures of the complexes in which the pigments occur in the natural state.

The recent action of the FDA in removing synthetic food colors from food usage has also stimulated current interest in possible greater utilization of anthocyanins as food colorants. For example, Jurd has patented a whole series of compounds similar to the anthocyanins, except that position three has a hydrogen instead of a hydroxy group. These compounds are stable and have a high tinctorial power but will have to go through extensive toxicological studies prior to usage as food colorants.

The Yellow Flavonoids

This class comprises a diverse, almost ubiquitous, group of pigments. Approximately 400 flavonoid pigments are known, and the number is increasing rapidly. Two major groups are based on the flavone and flavonol structure. Their similarity to the basic anthocyanin structure is obvious. Two

Flavone   Flavonol

minor groups are based on the chalcone and aurone structures. Earlier workers termed them the "an-

Aurone

Chalcone

thochlor" pigments because the tissue turned red or orange when fumed with ammonia, but this term is obsolete today. Two other minor groups are based on the flavanone and isoflavanone structures.

Flavanone   Isoflavanone

The above structures illustrate only the basic aglycone structure, and a number are known based

on different hydroxylation and esterification patterns in the basic structures. They are usually found esterified to sugars and also occur with acyl groups in a manner similar to the anthocyanins.

The plant taxonomists have a veritable gold mine in the flavonoid pigments, and this impetus has resulted in the large number of known compounds. Relatively little is known of their relative individual stability in foods, probably because of the lack of good quantitative methods of analysis. One flavonoid, rutin, was studied years ago, when it became apparent that a complex of iron from a tin can complexed with rutin to form a dark discoloration in asparagus. A tin complex, on the other hand, produced a desirable yellow color. One minor group of flavonoids, the flavonones which are found mainly in citrus plants, are much in the news currently, because of their possibilities as synthetic sweeteners. Naringin, a flavanone with neohesperidose in the 7 position, is an intensely bitter substance, whereas an isomer of the above compound with rutin in the 7 position is tasteless. Neohesperidose has rhamnose and glucose in an alpha $1 \longrightarrow 2$ linkage, whereas rutinose has an alpha $1 \longrightarrow 6$ linkage. This difference has been accentuated by opening the ring structure to produce chalcone structures with the neohesperidose sugar. One derivative, neohesperidine dihydrochalcone synthesized from naringin, has a sweetness nearly 2000 times that of sucrose. In 1970, 1000 lb of this compound were synthesized for toxicity studies, and preliminary reports look promising. With current problems with the cyclamates, amino acid derivatives, and saccharin, a new artificial sweetener would be very welcome.

The isoflavones have also received attention lately for their weak oestrogenic activity. Three isoflavones, isolated from clover, have produced problems in agriculture, due to the lowered fertility of sheep pastured on certain types of clover. There are possible benefits also, because possibly the flush of milk in cows in spring pasture may be due to oestrogenic isoflavones. Other effects of isoflavones such as the well-known fish toxicant, rotenone, and the glycosuria-producing phloridzin are well documented.

Another subgroup of the flavonoids which has received considerable attention recently is the biflavonyls. They are dimers of apigenin through a carbon-carbon or carbon-oxygen bond. Two compounds in this class were isolated from the ginkgo tree, the "living fossil" which appeared over 250,000,000 yr ago.

Another group, chemically related to the flavonols, has been termed leucoanthocyanins, proanthocyanins, or anthoxanthins. I prefer the last name, since it occurs after anthocyanins in the abstract journals. They are a widespread, chemically complex group of pigments responsible for astringency and sometimes haze in foods.

The Betalains

The betalains are a group of red and yellow pigments formerly called "nitrogenous anthocyanins." The pioneer efforts of Mabry in Texas and Minale in Italy and their co-workers have established this group as being chemically quite distinct from the anthocyanins.

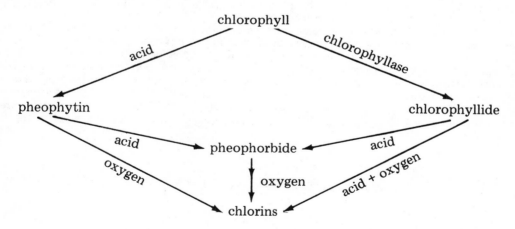

Betalain basic structure

If the R′ and R substitutes (alkyl or benzyl) extend the resonance of the double bonds above, the compound is red and is termed a betacyanin. If the resonance is not extended, the compound is a yellow betazanthin. Both red and yellow compounds have sugar and acyl components. Fifty-two betacyanins and approximately 17 betazanthins have been reported. The red and yellow

brief claim to fame as adulterants for wine when a pokeberry plant in the corner of a vineyard was insurance against a crop of grapes low in pigment content. Nowadays, it is relatively easy to distinguish betacyanins from anthocyanins. The addition of pokeberry juice to wine was outlawed in France in 1892, and the fact that is contains a purgative and emetic substance may also have had something to do with it.

The Chlorophylls

The green chlorophylls in plants have been the object of more research than all the other plant pigments combined. This is probably due to its close association with oxygen fixation in the photosynthetic process. Chlorophyll is indeed vital to plant life itself. The basic structure of chlorophyll (see Fig. P-4) was studied by Willstätter, Stoll, Grant, etc., and finally completed by Hans Fischer in 1940. Woodward confirmed the structures by total synthesis in 1960. Two forms of chlorophyll (a and b) occur in plants with three other forms (c, d, e) occurring in bacteria and algae. In green leaves, chlorophyll a and b are found in approximately a 2:1 ratio.

With chlorophylls, major research emphasis in the food field has been to retard the degradation of chlorophyll in processed foods. The major pathways of degradation in aqueous, thermally-processed foods are as follows

compounds usually occur together in a manner similar to the anthocyanins and yellow flavonoids. Anthocyanins and betacyanins do not occur together, and the latter is confined to only 10 families of the Centrospermae. The most important members in the edible food category are the pigments in red beets, but they are also found in cactus fruit, chard, etc. Many years ago, members of the Phytolacca family (American pokeberry) had a

The change from chlorophyll to pheophytin and chlorophyllide to pheophorbide involves the loss of the magnesium molecule. The change from chlorophyll to chlorophyllide involves the loss of the phytyl group by the action of the enzyme chlorophyllase.

The addition of alkali salts to green vegetables to prevent the drop in pH has been suggested as a means of retaining the green color, but this process

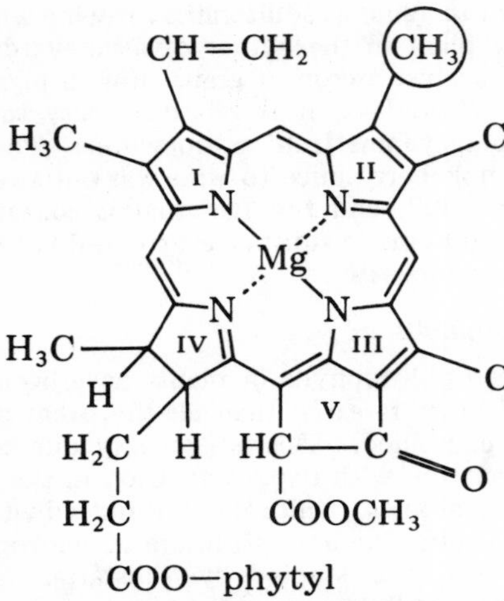

FIG. P-4. CHLOROPHYLL a

Chlorophyll b has a formyl (CHO) group instead of the methyl group encircled above.

has never been successful. A combination of alkali treatment with high temperature-short time processing is more effective, but it is still not commercially accepted.

The Carotenoids

The carotenoids have interested chemists for well over 100 yr, but real progress in their chemistry began in the 1920's, through the classic work of Karrer, Zechmeister, Kuhn, Heilbron, and their collaborators. The formulas for beta-carotene and lycopene were proposed by Karrer in the early 1930's and confirmed by total synthesis by Isler in 1950. The structures of approximately 120 compounds are known today.

The basic structure of the carotenoids has been that of beta carotene. Most carotenoids have a

centered around the provitamin activity of beta-carotene and several similar compounds. Many papers have been concerned with the stability of provitamin A in foodstuffs under a variety of conditions. Nearly all carotenoids, except crocin and some protein complexes such as ovoverdin, are oil soluble, thus the chemistry of degradation is closely connected with the oxidation of oils.

Several of the synthetic carotenoids such as canthazanthin, apo-carotenal and even beta-carotene itself, have commanded more attention lately, as food colorants.

Quinones and Xanthones

The quinones are a large group of yellowish pigments found in flowering plants, fungi, lichens, bacteria, and algae. Over 200 are known ranging in color from pale yellow to almost black. The largest subgroup is the anthraquinones, of which some members have been used as natural dyestuffs and purgatives for centuries. A small subgroup, composed of about 20 pigments, are the naptho-

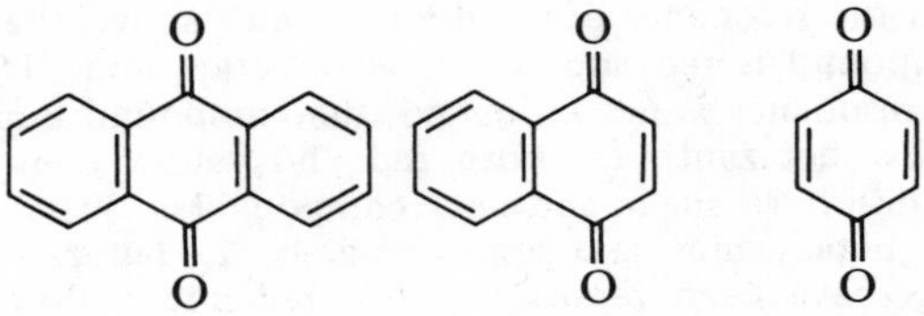

Anthraquinone   Napthaquinone   Benzoquinone

quinones. Several members of this group are ancient dyes, e.g., henna. The anthraquinones usually occur as glycosides, but the napthaquinones do not. Another larger subgroup is the benzoquinones, which occur mainly in the fungi and some flowering plants. Another subgroup of unique red pigments, confined to the actinomycetales, are the napthacenequinones, closely related to the tetra-

Beta carotene

C40 carbon skeleton, but recent research has discovered carotenoids with less than 40 carbons (e.g., crocetin with 20 carbons) and some with as many as 50 carbons (from bacteria). The diversity of the carotenoids is due to different end groups on the hydrocarbon chain. To date, 54 different end groups have been reported.

Interest in the carotenoids in the food area has

cycline antibiotics. There are many other subgroups such as the phenanthraquinones, isoprenoid quinones and a number with more complex structures.

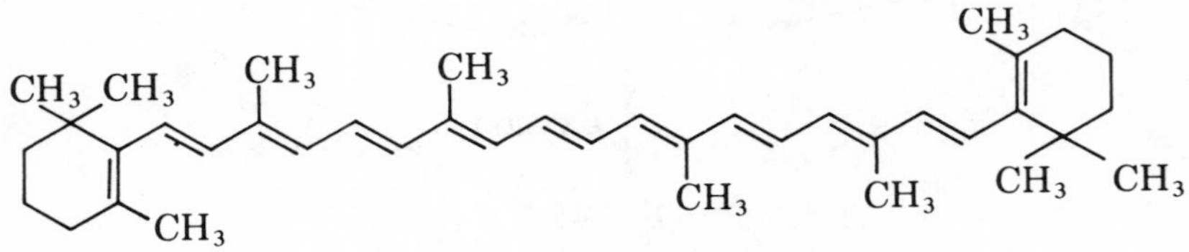

The xanthones are a group of almost 20 yellow pigments which have been confused with the quinones and the flavones. One well-known member is mangiferin which occurs as the glucoside in mangoes. They can be easily distinguished from flavones and quinones by spectral data.

Xanthone structure

Miscellaneous Pigments

There are a number of groups of compounds whose structures differ from the usual carotenoid-flavonoid-quinonoid-porphyrin concept of color. The appearance of a colored molecule may be incidental, resulting from a relatively minor structural variation which shifts the absorption of light into the visible area. One example may be taken from the aromatic ketones, where the simple compounds are colorless and complex derivatives such as gossypol are yellow. Gossypol has received much attention lately in view of the importance of cottonseed meal as a protein supplement. Many aromatic dienone compounds are found in the molds. One cyclic dienone group resembles the flavonoids and one more complex member (dracorubin) is the pigment of "dragons blood," a resin exuded from some palm trees. There are a number of other examples, such as the perinaphthenones, gamma-pyrones, sclerotiorins, vulpinic acid pigments, pyrroles, phenazines, phenoxazone, antibiotics, melanins, and compounds similar to riboflavin.

One should not leave this subject without mention of the pigment phytochrome, which is so important to overall plant growth. It controls elongation, flowering, germination, induction of dormancy, and production of anthocyanins and carotenoids. Its structure is unknown at this time.

F. J. FRANCIS

References

GOODWIN, T. W. 1954. Carotenoids—Their Cooperative Biochemistry. Chemical Publishing Co., New York.

GOODWIN, T. W. (Editor) 1965. Chemistry and Biochemistry of Plant Pigments. Academic Press, New York.

HARBORNE, J. B. 1964. Biochemistry of Phenolic Compounds. Academic Press, New York.

HARBORNE, J. B. 1967. Comparative Biochemistry of the Flavonoids. Academic Press, New York.

MABRY, T. A., ALSTON, R. E., and RUNECKLES, V. C. (Editors) 1969. Recent Advances in Phytochemistry. Appleton-Century-Crofts, New York.

VERNON, L. P., and SEELY, G. R. 1966. The Chlorophylls. Academic Press, New York.

Cross-reference: *Anthocyanins.*

PLUMS

The plum tree is the most widely distributed of all the tree fruits. Although it is native to the north temperate zones of Europe, Asia, and North America, it has been planted in many areas of the Southern Hemisphere. Like many of the world's tree fruits, the plum belongs to the Rosaceae (Rose) family. This most prolific family of plants includes such commercial fruits as apples, pears, apricots, peaches, almonds, cherries, quinces, blackberries, and raspberries, as well as plums. Hedrick (1911) lists 24 species of plums which have some commercial production, but only about 4 of them account for most of the plantings. *Prunus domestica* L. is the Old World or European species which originated more than 2000 yr ago in the Caucasus region. It accounts for most of the European and the largest segment of American production, including the prune types. Principal varieties are Agen, Imperial Epineuse, Italian Prune, and Tragedy. *Prunus insititia* L. was domesticated in Eurasia also and gave rise to the Bullace and Damson type plums. *Prunus triflora* Roxburgh is commonly known as the Japanese plum, but it originated in China and eventually was brought to the Western world. Favorite fresh fruit varieties such as Burbank, Gaviota, Kelsey, Santa Rosa, and Wickson are listed by Kinman (1943) as belonging to this species. The principal native American species, *Prunus americana* Marshall, has been developed into about 300 named varieties.

The plum and prune industry in the United States has a farm value of over $70,000,000. Although extremely variable from year to year, an average of around 500,000 tons per year of plums and prunes is produced. The major portion of this production is prunes grown in California, averaging over 400,000 tons fresh and 150,000 tons dried (see discussion of prunes under subject of Dried Fruit).

Prune juice is an important by-product of the prune dehydration business. It may be made by leaching the dried prunes with water at relatively low temperatures (175°–180°F) through a series of tanks for about 12 hr or by heating to boiling and then disintegrating the fruit in a pulper (Anon. 1964). Recently, Bolin and Salunkhe (1972) developed a rapid, continuous process for prune juice by using pectic enzymes on a slurry of whole ground prunes. Another process by Bolin and Porter (1967) helped to retain the natural fresh color and flavor of prune plums by the use of SO_2 or polyvinylpyrrolidone (PVP). The total pack of prune juice in the United States has been quite stable at around 7,000,000 cases (24/No. 2 equivalent) annually for the past decade.

Canned plums and prunes make up a pack of just under 2,000,000 cases (24/2½) each year. From 5,000,000 to 10,000,000 lb of plums are frozen yearly, mostly in large containers for remanufacture into jams and preserves. At present no fermented plum products are produced in the United States. Slivovitz, or plum brandy, has been popular in Eastern Europe for a long time. At present, the trend toward "pop" and fruit wines may make it feasible to develop a plum wine which would be acceptable. Many novel prune products have been tested by Mrak and Cruess (1929) and might be worth looking at again.

FRANK P. BOYLE

References

ANON. 1964. California packer automates prune concentrate process. Canner/Packer *133*, No. 2, 28–29.

BOLIN, H. R., and PORTER, S. L. 1967. Stabilizes color of fresh prune juice. Food Process. *28*, No. 7, 50.

BOLIN, H. R., and SALUNKHE, D. K. 1972. Develops continuous process for prune juice. Food Eng. *44*, No. 4, 129–133.

HEDRICK, U. P. 1911. The plums of New York. N.Y. State Agr. Expt. Sta. Ann. Rept. for 1910. J. B. Lyon Co., Albany, N.Y.

KINMAN, C. F. 1943. Plum and prune growing in the Pacific States. USDA Farmers' Bull. *1372*.

MRAK, E. M., and CRUESS, W. V. 1929. Utilization of surplus prunes. Univ. Calif. Bull. *483*.

Cross-reference: *Dried Fruit.*

POISONOUS PLANTS

Poisonous plants are shunned as food but they merit a brief treatment since they sometimes get into wholesome foods by accident or, as in the case of toxic mushrooms, are not recognized.

Mushrooms gathered in fields or woods by people ignorant of the botany of the various species are often the source of severe poisoning incidents. The substances responsible for the poisoning are alkaloids, the nitrogen-containing bases found in plants that often have a pronounced physiologic effect and sometimes a fatal one. Most of the cases of mushroom poisoning (myce-

tismus) come from *Amanita phalloides* and *Amanita muscaria*, the former being responsible for most of the fatalities. The toxins in *A. phalloides* are largely unidentified. The alkaloid muscarine is the toxin present in *A. muscaria*. The symptoms that mark the onset of poisoning are well known— abdominal pain, nausea, vomiting and diarrhea. Poisoning for which *A. phalloides* is responsible comes on rather slowly—unfortunately, since by the time the symptoms occur the toxins have been absorbed into the blood stream. Mortality is high. Poisoning from *A. muscaria* can be recognized earlier since the symptoms appear within 1–2 hr and the poisoning can be neutralized by atropine. Commercial mushrooms, of course, are nontoxic and completely safe.

Two edible plants contain poisons inherent in their composition—manioc from which cassava starch is made and fava beans. Manioc in the raw state contains the deadly poison, hydrocyanic acid, but happily the acid disappears on processing. Fava bean poisoning afflicts only people who are sensitive to the bean.

Some toxins in plants reach the human consumer by indirect means, an example being milk from cows that have pastured in areas where the white snakeroot abounds. Milk sold commercially is rarely if ever suspect in this regard since commercial milks are not from one but from many farms and when pooled at a central station the concentration of the toxin would be very low. Moreover, inspection of dairy farms would quickly weed out the milk from a culprit farm.

Poisonous plants pose no great threat to the consumer. Over the centuries man has learned to exclude them from his diet or, as in the case of manioc, to get rid of the toxin by processing. Something of a problem exists where, as in the case of selenium, toxic concentrations of an element can be picked up by the plant. This problem occurs only in a few areas over the world, all of which are known to soil chemists.

MARTIN S. PETERSON

Cross-reference: *Mycotoxins.*

POLLUTION

See Waste Disposal—Liquids; Waste Handling—Solids, Waste Treatment— Liquid.

POLYHYDRIC ALCOHOLS

See Humectants.

POLYOLS

See Glycerin.

PORK

Pork is the flesh of the pig (family Suidae) used as food. Hogs have been domesticated for food since prehistoric time. Pork is recorded as food as early as 3400 B.C. in Egypt and 2900 B.C. in China.

The eating of pork has been forbidden in several religions. The Jews do not accept pork as being kosher. These religious restrictions may have been derived from the habit of domestic hogs of eating garbage and other household refuse. The hog is a true omnivore, that is, his diet consists of both animal and vegetable products. As a dooryard domestic animal, the hogs serve as the village garbage disposal machine in primitive Central American communities.

The origin of pork production in the Americas may be the hogs that were brought to North America by the Norseman about 1000. It is recorded that Columbus brought eight pigs to Haiti on his second voyage in 1493. DeSota landed hogs on the mainland at Charlotte Harbor, Florida on May 25, 1539.

The first American meat packer, William Pynchon, had pork packing as his chief business. An early center of pork packing was Worcester, Mass., which enjoyed a flourishing export trade prior to 1700. Pork production pushed westward with settlement. By the mid 1800's, Cincinnati was the world center of pork packing, later to be replaced by Chicago. In more recent years, the industry has become decentralized with no one city able to claim the title of "Hog Butcher to the World" as the poet Sandburg called Chicago.

Pork is one of the most popular meats in the American diet. Per capita consumption in 1973 was estimated to be 62 lb, 36% of all red meats. Of the world's meat supply, 30% is pork. The consumption of pork excluding lard reached an all-time high of 79 lb in the United States per person in 1943 and 1944, but has tended downward slowly, averaging 71 in the 1940's, 66 in the 1950's, 63 in the 1960's and 64 in the 1970's through 1973. Pork consumption exceeded beef and other meats until 1953 when beef skyrocketed ahead to a current level 70% greater.

Consumption of lard, the fat rendered for food use from pork fatty tissue, has decreased from over 14 lb per person in 1940 to less than 8 in 1970.

In 1972 the average person used 1.4% of his disposable income to purchase $52.17 worth of pork and pork products. In 1973 the per capita purchase was $62.92. Pork prices reached their highest in 1973 when live hogs sold for a peak price of $62.25 per cwt. The lowest price recorded for top quality hogs was $5.40 per cwt in 1933. Commercial production of pork and lard in the United States in 1973 was 14 billion pounds.

Pork is often considered to be the red meat source for the less affluent portion of our society since it is traditionally less expensive than the other meats. In point of fact, pork is one of the most versatile meats, appearing in many ways as fresh, cured, smoked, canned, and in a wide variety of sausages and other meat food products. According to the most recent census of manufacturers (1969 reported in 1971), 38% of the meat used in the manufacture of sausage and other processed meat foods was derived from pork.

The lean of pork is a good source of high quality protein, phosphorus, and dietary iron. It is rich in thiamin and contains substantial quantities of riboflavin and niacin. Pork liver is one of the best sources of food iron. Contrary to a widely-held notion, pork is as digestible as any other red meat and is one of the most digestible of all foods, ranking about 98% in digestibility.

Hogs are generally finished for market at about 6 months of age and at weights ranging from 180 to 240 lb. Ideal butcher weight is close to 200 lb. Most hogs are dressed "packer style," i.e., head off, leaf lard out, ham facings off, and center split. A typical yield of chilled, packer style carcass is 70% of live weight, a greater yield than is obtainable from any of the other common meat animals.

In a typical hog dressing operation the hogs are first anesthetized, then hoisted to hang head down and killed by bleeding from the major vessels in the neck. The hair is then removed by machine following a soaking period in hot water. The carcass is then hung head down from a moving conveyor for the various dressing operations.

Various by-products and variety meats are recovered from the dressing operations. From the heads, the main meat items are the tongue, ears, snouts, cheek meat, giblet meat, and brains. The pituitary gland is often removed for pharmaceutical use. The fat trimmed off the head goes to rendering as do the bones. Other dressing operation recoveries include the variety meats such as liver, kidney, and heart, the leaf lard, ham facings, and the casings. The lungs are seldom recovered for edible use. These, together with the floor scraps, defective parts removed, and the portions of the other internal organs not used for meat or casings go to inedible rendering. The total weight, wet basis, accounted for edible items from dressing operations is about 5%, of nonedible items about 5%, leaving about 20% shrinkage and a carcass yield of 70% of live weight.

After chilling, usually about 24 hr later, the carcasses are cut into the primal and other wholesale pork cuts. The main cuts are the hams, bacon bellies, loins, picnics, butts, and spare ribs. In addition there are the fatty cuts: fat backs, clear plates, and jowls; and also, feet, neckbones, tails, and sausage trimmings.

Yields of pork cuts typical of a 140-lb carcass as a percentage of the chilled carcass weight are: hams, 20; loins, 16; bellies, 14; picnics, 7; butts, 6; ribs, 2; jowls, 3; fat, 19; sausage trimmings, 3; and miscellaneous other items, 10.

In a federally inspected packinghouse, government inspectors examine the animals alive and throughout the dressing procedure; and they supervise the maintenance of hygenic conditions throughout the establishment. About 90% of all pork production in the United States is under the direct supervision of the USDA. Most of the balance is produced under the inspection of a state or local authority. There is some pork production directly on farms which is exempt from formal inspection.

Under the Wholesome Meat Act of 1969, the individual states are required to provide meat inspection equivalent to the federal inspection standards, or federal meat inspection will be imposed within the states failing to comply. As a result, packers in these states as well as packers not federally inspected in other states will probably seek federal inspection because of its better public image and because of the privilege of entering interstate commerce with the meat products where the company is federally inspected. Within a few years, it's safe to predict that virtually all pork production will be under federal inspection or equivalent standards.

The hams from most hogs are processed by curing with salt, sugar, and sodium nitrate and are smoked to produce the product most commonly seen by the consumer. Within recent years, the vast majority of all hams are partly cooked in the process of smoking. Federal regulations require that internal temperature of the ham be brought up to 137°F or higher to qualify for the precooked designation. Curing ingredients, including water, may be added only to the degree that the finished smoked hams equal or weigh less than the weight of the fresh or "green" cut from which they were prepared, unless the ham is designated as "water added" in which case the final weight may approach 110% of green weight.

Curing of hams may be as short as a few hours, or as long as 90 days for some specialized country-cured style hams. The curing ingredients are generally injected as a water solution through the femoral artery of the ham. This gives a uniform general distribution of the curing ingredient throughout the entire piece almost instantaneously.

Historically, the curing of ham, bacon, and other pork cuts with salt or brine was primarily a preserving technique. The further process of smoking not only enhanced the flavor, but also reinforced the resistance of the meat to spoilage and insect attack. Curing and smoking in modern technology is primarily for its flavor-enhancing modification of the fresh meat. As a result, cures tend to be less salty and the application of smoke much lighter than in the days prior to universally available refrigeration.

J. E. THOMPSON

POTASSIUM SORBATE

See Sorbic Acid.

POTATOES

Potatoes are grown extensively in most parts of the world where the climate is conducive to production. Potato production in the major producing countries of the world totaled 5688 million hundredweight in 1968. The crop was grown on 42.5 million acres (Table P-3). West Germany is the leading country in production in Western Europe. Russia leads all countries in the world in production with Poland, West Germany, the United States, and France following in that order.

Potatoes are produced in every State in the United States. Potato production ranks about eighth in value of all field crops and fifth of field crops grown directly or indirectly for food. Value of sales for potatoes in 1968 was about $590 million.

The number of farms on which potatoes were planted in the United States decreased from 1,432,366 in 1954 to 310,008 in 1964, a decline of almost 4/5 in numbers. The size of the farms increased: 14,646 farms reported in 1964 planting 25 acres or more. This was 90% of the acreage and 93% of the production.

Although potatoes are grown in every State, most of the crop is concentrated in about 16 States. The leading States in order are: Idaho, Maine, Washington, California, New York, Minnesota, and North Dakota.

Late or main crop production has shifted strikingly from the Eastern and Central states to the Western states. Over 50% of the late crop is now grown in the Western states. Much of this shift in area of production is a result of the marked increase in potato processing in the states of Idaho, Washington, and Oregon.

TABLE P-3

POTATOES: ACREAGE AND PRODUCTION IN SPECIFIED COUNTRIES, ANNUALLY 1968–1969

Continent and Country	Acreage		Production			
	1968	1969[1]	1968	1969[1]	1968	1969[1]
	(1000 Acres)		(1000 Metric Tons)		(Million Hundredweight)	
North America						
Canada	303	306	2,399	2,278	52.9	50.2
Mexico	99	119	400	576	8.8	12.7
United States	1,378	1,404	13,344	13,936	294.2	307.2
Total	1,780	1,829	16,143	16,790	355.9	370.1
Europe						
Austria	321	279	3,473	2,941	76.6	64.8
Belgium-Luxembourg	143	131	1,625	1,528	35.8	33.7
Denmark	86	82	863	592	19.0	13.1
Finland	158	166	908	977	20.0	21.5
France[2]	1,134	1,023	10,033	8,811	221.2	194.2
Germany, West	1,629	1,455	19,196	15,985	423.2	352.4
Greece	116	119	620	671	13.7	14.8
Ireland	146	136	1,624	1,485	35.8	32.7
Italy	788	791	3,960	3,845	87.3	84.8
Netherlands	363	358	5,045	4,067	111.2	101.6
Norway	86	79	912	773	20.1	17.0
Portugal	259	235	1,083	1,079	23.9	23.8
Spain	927	954	4,431	4,717	97.7	104.0
Sweden	136	121	1,424	849	31.4	18.7
Switzerland	90	84	1,270	1,210	28.0	26.7
United Kingdom	692	615	6,858	6,160	151.2	135.8
Total Western Europe	7,074	6,628	63,325	56,230	1,396.1	1,239.6
Czechoslovakia	919	803	6,526	5,010	143.9	110.5
Germany, East	1,661	1,557	12,639	9,000	278.6	198.4
Poland	6,788	6,795	50,817	45,400	1,120.3	1,000.9
Yugoslavia	820	791	2,890	3,144	63.7	69.3
Other Eastern Europe[3]	1,226	1,181	5,401	4,170	119.1	91.9
Total Europe[4]	18,488	17,755	141,598	122,954	3,121.7	2,710.6
U.S.S.R.	20,512	20,509	91,966	82,500	2,027.5	1,818.8
Asia						
Japan[5]	442	413	3,870	3,404	85.3	75.0
South America						
Argentina	494	502	1,967	2,340	43.4	51.6
Brazil	561	400	1,606	1,300	35.4	28.7
Chile	198	188	725	603	16.0	13.3
Venezuela	44	44	159	143	3.5	3.2
Total	1,297	1,134	4,457	4,386	98.3	96.8
Grand Total	42,519	41,640	258,034	230,034	5,688.7	5,071.3

SOURCE: USDA Foreign Agr. Serv. Prepared or estimated on the basis of official statistics of foreign governments, other foreign source materials, reports of U.S. Agricultural Attaches and Foreign Service Officers, results of office research, and related information.

[1] Preliminary.
[2] Excluding home gardens.
[3] Bulgaria, Romania, and Hungary.
[4] Excluding U.S.S.R.
[5] Excluding autumn crop.

Since 1951, total potato acreage in the United States has been relatively stable within the limits of 1.29-1.54 million acres. Yield per acre, however, has shown an upward trend from approximately 150 cwt per acre in the early 1950's to 227 cwt in 1970.

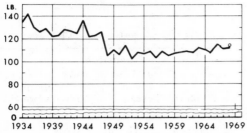

USDA Consumer and Marketing Serv.

FIG. P-5. CIVILIAN PER CAPITA CONSUMPTION OF
POTATOES IN THE UNITED STATES, 1934–1968

Includes fresh weight equivalent of processed potatoes.

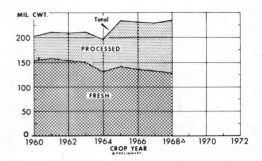

USDA Consumer and Marketing Serv.

FIG. P-6. POTATOES USED FOR FOOD, FRESH AND
PROCESSED, IN THE UNITED STATES, 1960–1968

Production attained a peak of 244 million hundredweight in 1934, declined, and then during World War II rose to 292 million hundredweight in 1946 and dropped to 195 million hundredweight in 1951. Since 1951, production has increased reaching a level of slightly over 300 million hundredweight in 4 of the last 5 yr (1966–1970).

Per capita consumption of potatoes in the United States declined since 1900 from 198 lb to about 102 lb in 1952. This downward trend was reversed by the potato processing industry and the present per capita consumption is now about 114 lb (Fig. P-5). Per capita consumption of potatoes in processed form, mostly potato chips, amounted to about 3 lb before World War II. Since that time it has steadily increased and is now over 50 lb. The per capita consumption of fresh potatoes has gradually decreased to an estimated 63 lb in 1968 (Fig. P-6).

Nutritional Value

Although the potato contains approximately only 14% starch, it is known, unfortunately, to most laymen as a "fattening food." According to the Food and Nutrition Board, National Research Council—National Academy of Sciences, the recommended daily dietary allowances designed for the maintenance of good nutrition of practically all healthy people in the United States, men 35 to 55 yr of age should consume food daily containing 2600 cal. According to data of the USDA Agricultural Research Service (1963) a 3½-oz serving of a peeled boiled potato or mashed potato with milk added would contain 65 cal.

The adult male would need to consume about 9 lb of potatoes prepared as boiled or mashed to obtain the 2600 cal needed daily for energy. More than 9 lb would be necessary for fat accumulation. Obviously, potatoes, as such, should not be classified as a fattening food.

In addition to energy, potatoes also supply liberal quantities of essential nutrients for good health, especially ascorbic acid, as well as several minerals such as calcium, iron, phosphorus, and potassium, also protein and vitamins such as thiamin, riboflavin, and niacin (Table P-4).

Processing

The growth of the processing phase of the potato industry in the United States continues at a very rapid rate. One of the factors upon which this increase is dependent, is the availability of ample quantities of potatoes from which the processing stock is selected. Most of the processed potatoes are grown as a fall crop in the United States and are comprised largely of potatoes of fair to well-mature stages and those varieties of high specific gravity or dry matter content. Figure P-7 shows that most of the increase in production during the period 1956–1969 is in the fall or late crop grown in the northern states. During the 6-yr period 1965–1970, the fall crop increased from 216 to 252 million hundredweight.

In the United States potatoes are grown primarily for food use; essentially, none is grown specifically for any use other than food and seed. Depending upon the quantity and the quality of the crop, however, varying amounts also are used for starch manufacture and for animal feed. The proportions of each which have been utilized for food and other uses in 1960–1968 are shown in Fig. P-8. The amount used for food has been increasing in recent years.

The most spectacular development has been in the growth of the processing phase of the potato industry. The amount of potatoes used for processing has increased from 24.7 million hundredweight in 1956 to over 116 million hundredweight in 1969. During the same period, the amount of potatoes used fresh as food decreased from 155 to 127 million hundredweight. The percentages of

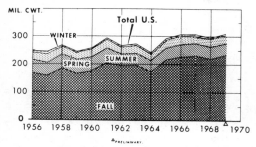

USDA Consumer and Marketing Serv.

FIG. P-7. SEASONAL PRODUCTION OF POTATOES IN THE UNITED STATES, 1956-1969

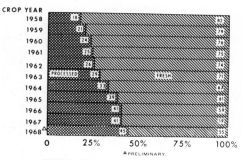

USDA Consumer and Marketing Serv.

FIG. P-9. POTATOES USED FOR FOOD, FRESH AND PROCESSED, IN THE UNITED STATES, 1958-1968

potatoes used in fresh and processed forms for the period 1958 to 1968 are shown in Fig. P-9. In 1969, 47.5% of the potatoes used for food was processed. It is estimated that in 1970 slightly more than ½ of the food use crop will be in processed form. If the trend during the past 10-12 yr continues at the same rate, by 1980 the processed forms of potatoes will constitute over 70% of the potato consumption in the United States (Fig. P-10). For many years the per capita consumption of potatoes in the United States was on a downward trend. However, since 1952 when the per capita consumption was 102 lb per person, the trend has been levelled off and actually turned slightly upward. In 1969, the per capita consumption of potatoes was about 114 lb per person. Most of this recovery in consumption of potatoes is attributed to the availability of many processed forms of potatoes which are so easily, quickly, and conveniently prepared for the table.

The principal processed forms of potatoes are frozen (mostly French fries), chips, dehydrated, and canned. Smaller quantities are made into potato salad, soups, stews, pancakes, and other items.

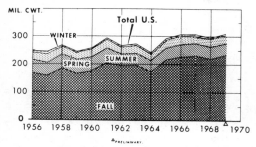

MIL. CWT.

USDA Consumer and Marketing Serv.

FIG. P-8. POTATOES USED FOR FOOD AND OTHER USES IN THE UNITED STATES, 1960-1968

From the beginning of potato processing up to 1965, potato chips utilized more potatoes than any other form. During 1965 and since that time, frozen potato products have taken the lead. In 1969, frozen products utilized 44% of the total processed and now have the greatest rate of growth of any of the products. In 1956, only 4.7 million hundredweight of potatoes were processed into French fries and related frozen products. The increases since that time have been quite phenomenal, reaching 51.5 million hundredweight in 1969. Judging from the frozen French fried potatoes in cold storage, the trend is still at a rapid rate of increase. On April 1, 1970 there were over 550 million pounds of frozen French fries in cold storage ready for consumption.

Potato chip processing growth also continues at a rapid rate. During the 10-yr period from 1958 to 1968, the chip industry doubled its output, utilizing 17 million hundredweight in 1958 and 34 million hundredweight in 1968. Growth is still at the rate of over one million hundredweight of potatoes per year and per capita consumption also is increasing. In 1969, potato chips utilized 31% of the total potatoes processed.

There also has been a rapid rate of growth in dehydrated forms of potatoes. Potatoes processed into dehydrated forms increased from 3.2 million hundredweight in 1956 to 25.5 million hundredweight in 1969. Per capita consumption also has increased from 1.7 to 12.7 lb raw potatoes in dehydrated form. In 1969, dehydrated products utilized 22% of the total potatoes processed. The most widely processed forms are flakes and granules with lesser quantities of dehydrated slices, cubes, and julienne strips.

Canned potatoes and other canned products do not comprise a very large segment of the total amount processed. The increase during the past 12 yr also has been slight, rising from 2.5 million hundredweight in 1957 to 3.8 million hundred-

TABLE P-4

COMPOSITION OF FOODS, 100 GRAMS, EDIBLE PORTION

Food and Description	Water %	Food Energy Cal	Protein Gm	Fat Gm	Carbohydrate Total Gm	Carbohydrate Fiber Gm	Ash Gm	Calcium Mg	Phosphorus Mg	Iron Mg	Sodium Mg	Potassium Mg	Vitamin A Value IU	Thiamin Mg	Riboflavin Mg	Niacin Mg	Ascorbic Acid Mg
Potatoes																	
Raw	79.8	76	2.1	0.1	17.1	0.5	0.9	7	53	0.6	3	407	Tr	0.10	0.04	1.5	20[1]
Cooked																	
Baked in skin	75.1	93	2.6	0.1	21.1	0.6	1.1	9	65	0.7	4[2]	503	Tr	0.10	0.04	1.7	20
Boiled in skin	79.8	76	2.1	0.1	17.1	0.5	0.9	7	53	0.6	3[2]	407	Tr	0.09	0.04	1.5	16
Boiled, pared before cooking	82.8	65	1.9	0.1	14.5	0.5	0.7	6	42	0.5	2[2]	285	Tr	0.09	0.03	1.2	16
French-fried	44.7	274	4.3	13.2	36.0	1.0	1.8	15	111	1.3	6[2]	853	Tr	0.13	0.08	3.1	21
Fried from raw	46.9	268	4.0	14.2	32.6	1.0	2.3	15	101	1.1	223	775	Tr	0.12	0.07	2.8	19
Hash-browned after holding overnight	54.2	229	3.1	11.7	29.1	0.8	1.9	12	79	0.9	288	475	Tr	0.08	0.05	2.1	9
Mashed, milk added	82.8	65	2.1	0.7	13.0	0.4	1.4	24	49	0.4	301	261	20	0.08	0.05	1.0	10
Mashed, milk and table fat added	79.8	94	2.1	4.3	12.3	0.4	1.5	24	48	0.4	331	250	170	0.08	0.05	1.0	9
Scalloped and au gratin																	
With cheese	71.1	145	5.3	7.9	13.6	0.3	2.1	127	122	0.5	447	306	320	0.06	0.12	0.9	10
Without cheese	76.7	104	3.0	3.9	14.7	0.3	1.7	54	74	0.4	355	327	160	0.06	0.09	1.0	11
Canned, solids and liquid	88.5	44	1.1	0.2	9.8	0.2	0.4	(4)[3]	(30)	(0.3)	1[2]	250	Tr	0.04	0.02	0.6	13
Dehydrated mashed																	
Flakes without milk																	
Dry form	5.2	364	7.2	0.6	84.0	(1.6)	3.0	35	(173)	1.7	89	(1600)	Tr	0.23	0.06	5.4	32[4]
Prepared, water, milk, table fat added	79.3	93	1.9	3.2	14.5	0.3	1.1	31	47	0.3	231	286	130	0.04	0.04	0.9	5[4]
Granules without milk																	
Dry form	7.1	352	8.3	0.6	80.4	1.4	3.6	44	203	2.4	84	(1600)	Tr	0.16	0.11	4.9	19[4]
Prepared, water, milk, table fat added	78.6	96	2.0	3.6	14.4	0.2	1.4	32	52	0.5	256	290	110	0.04	0.05	0.7	3[4]
Granules with milk																	
Dry form	6.3	358	10.9	1.1	77.7	1.5	4.0	142	237	3.5	82	1848	60	0.19	0.30	4.2	16[4]
Prepared, water, table fat added	81.4	79	2.0	2.2	13.1	0.3	1.3	31	44	0.6	234	335	90	0.03	0.05	0.8	3[4]

Food	Water	Food energy	Protein	Fat	Carbohydrate	Fiber	Ash	Calcium	Phosphorus	Iron	Sodium	Potassium	Vitamin A	Thiamine	Riboflavin	Niacin	Ascorbic acid
Frozen																	
Diced, for hash-browning																	
Not thawed	81.0	73	1.2	Tr	17.4	0.4	0.4	10	30	0.7	8	170	Tr	0.07	0.01	0.6	9
Cooked, hash-browned	56.1	224	2.0	11.5	29.0	0.7	1.4	18	50	1.2	299	283	Tr	0.07	0.02	1.0	8
French-fried																	
Not thawed	63.5	170	2.8	6.5	26.1	0.6	1.1	7	67	1.4	32[2]	506	Tr	0.14	0.02	2.1	20
Heated	52.9	220	3.6	8.4	33.7	0.7	1.4	9	86	1.8	42[2]	652	Tr	0.14	0.02	2.6	21
Mashed																	
Not thawed	80.4	75	1.7	0.1	17.1	0.4	0.7	16	39	0.7	79	229	30	0.07	0.03	0.8	6
Heated	78.3	93	1.8	2.8	15.7	0.4	1.4	25	42	0.6	359	215	140	0.06	0.04	0.7	4
Potato chips	1.8	568	5.3	39.8	50.0	(1.6)	3.1	40	139	1.8	—[5]	1130	Tr	0.21	0.07	4.8	16
Potato flour	7.6	351	8.0	0.8	79.9	1.6	3.7	33	178	17.2	34	1588	Tr	0.42	0.14	3.4	(19)
Potato salad, from home recipe, made with:																	
Cooked salad dressing, seasonings	76.0	99	2.7	2.8	16.3	0.4	2.2	32	64	0.6	528	319	140	0.08	0.07	1.1	11
Mayonnaise and French dressing, hard-cooked eggs, seasonings	72.4	145	3.0	9.2	13.4	0.4	2.0	19	63	0.8	480	296	180	0.07	0.06	0.9	11
Potato sticks	1.5	544	6.4	36.4	50.8	1.5	4.9	44	139	1.8	—[5]	1130	Tr	0.21	0.07	4.8	40

SOURCE: Watt and Merrill (1963).

NOTE: Numbers in parentheses denote values imputed—usually from another form of the food or from a similar food. Zero in parentheses indicates that the amount of a constituent probably is none or is too small to measure. Dashes denote lack of reliable data for a constituent believed to be present in measurable amount. Calculated values, as those based on a recipe, are not in parentheses.

[1] Year-round average. Recently dug potatoes contain about 26 mg ascorbic acid per 100 gm. After 3 months' storage the value is only 1/2 as high, after 6 months', about 1/3 as high.

[2] Applies to product without added salt. If salt is added, an estimated average value for sodium is 236 mg per 100 gm.

[3] Federal standards provide for addition of certain calcium salts as firming agents; if used, these salts may add calcium not to exceed 200 mg per 100 gm of finished product.

[4] Value varies widely. It is dependent on content of ascorbic acid in raw potatoes, method of processing, and length of storage of dehydrated product. Present values for dehydrated forms range from 10 to 35 mg per 100 gm.

[5] Sodium content is variable and may be as high as 1000 mg per 100 gm.

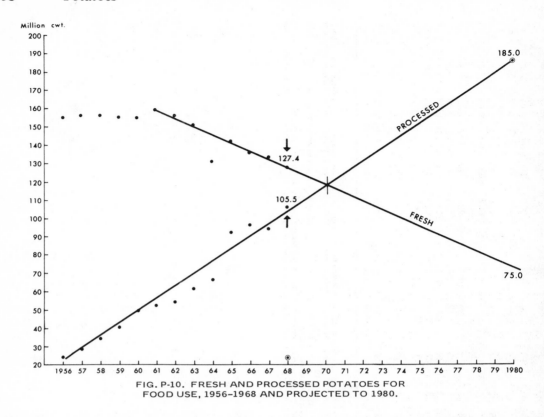

FIG. P-10. FRESH AND PROCESSED POTATOES FOR
FOOD USE, 1956-1968 AND PROJECTED TO 1980.

weight in 1969. Usually, only small potatoes from other operations are used. No potatoes in the United States are grown specifically for canning. Less than 4% of all processed potatoes are used for canning.

Processed forms of potatoes maintain a rather constant price level to the consumer not only within any one year, but from one year to another. Size of crop and abundance of the raw product are not usually reflected in the prices of processed forms of potatoes offered the consumer.

The frozen and dehydrated products are processed in or near the areas of late potato production. Expansion in this phase of the industry is occurring by additions to processing plants already in existence as well as by new processing plants in older areas and also in new areas. Expansion has been very rapid in Washington and Idaho. Other important areas of growth are North Dakota and Minnesota in the Red River Valley, Maine, Michigan, Colorado, and Oregon. Potato chips, on the other hand, are processed in essentially every State in the country; usually in or near high concentrations of population. In most instances, this means that potatoes for chipping are transported rather long distances from points of production of the raw stock. This often increases the hazards of

holding potatoes under satisfactory temperature and humidity conditions during transit for best end products. Chip processors, however, prefer to ship the raw stock for long distances rather than the finished chips.

Varieties

Over 75 varieties of potatoes are grown commercially in the United States. Only 10-15 of these varieties, however, account for the greater portion of the annual production. Some varieties, because of their particular quality characteristics or typical place of production, are used mainly for 1 or 2 methods of preparation for consumption. Varieties grown most extensively in the United States are: Russet Burbank, Katahdin, Kennebec, Red Pontiac, Norgold Russet, Irish Cobbler, Norland, Red LaSoda, White Rose, Chippewa, and Sebago. Acreages are increasing rapidly in a number of newer varieties, several of which are especially adapted to processing. Some of the above-mentioned varieties are essentially never utilized for processing. For most forms of processed product, potatoes of high total solids or specific gravity are desired. High specific gravity of the raw potatoes is directly related to the yield of processed products such as chips, French fries, and dehydrated forms of potatoes. High specific gravity also is directly related to quality of processed products such as crispness and internal texture of French fried potatoes, mealiness texture of reconstituted forms of dehydrated potatoes, and low oil content of potato chips. For some products such as whole peeled boiled potatoes and potato salad, low specific gravity potatoes are desirable because they remain firm and do not slough during cooking or preparation for the table. Some varieties are consistently higher in specific gravity than others when grown under similar conditions. On the basis of quality of finished product, it is possible, therefore, to select varieties for certain methods of cooking and forms of processed product.

Another important difference between varieties is the rate and extent of sugar accumulation in the raw stock, especially during the storage period. This characteristic of a variety is extremely important to processors of most forms of potatoes. Varieties which accumulate reducing sugars to a fairly high degree in storage are not desirable for potato chips and French fries. Somewhat higher sugar content may be acceptable for dehydrated forms of potatoes. High reducing sugar content of raw potatoes results in browned or discolored products during processing or in subsequent storage and shipping.

Therefore, characteristics of a variety which are evaluated highly for best processing quality are total solids content and reducing sugar content. Some additional desirable characteristics to the grower or the consumer and processor are: high yielding ability, disease resistance, desirable size, attractiveness, and marketability.

Factors Influencing Color and Quality of Processed Product

The most important problem in the potato chip and French fry industry is the maintenance of desirable color of product throughout the year. Control of color, which is necessary for a standard product, is difficult because color is determined by chemical composition of the tubers. Chemical composition of tubers is dependent upon many uncontrollable environmental factors in the field and also upon conditions often difficult to control during transit and storage.

Although it has been mentioned in the literature that the color of potato chips is a result of caramelization of the sugars in potatoes, it is now well-known that potato chip color is the result of a series of chemical reactions between amino acids and reducing sugars and known as the "browning reaction" or the Maillard reaction. Sugars participate in the browning reaction, but other constituents of the potato such as amino acids, ascorbic acid, or other organic components must be present before color formation occurs during frying at high temperatures. These other compounds always are present in potatoes regardless of the variety, maturity, culture, or storage. Therefore, the problem is to hold the reducing sugar content of potatoes to a low level to be assured of acceptably light color chips and French fries.

Potatoes also contain sucrose in addition to the more simple reducing sugars, glucose and fructose. When 1 molecule of sucrose is hydrolyzed or broken down, it forms 2 molecules of reducing sugars. Some of the older literature tended to be confusing because often it was shown that there was very little relationship between the total sugar content of a potato and its resultant processed color. This can now be explained on the basis that only the reducing sugars participate in the browning reaction and sucrose indirectly may affect chip and French fry color only after it has been broken down to reducing sugars. The extent to which sucrose hydrolyzes to the reducing sugars and the consequent browning is partially dependent on the degree of acidity present in the frying fat and in the potatoes.

Although sucrose does not participate directly in the browning reaction, the amount present in a potato is potentially important in determining processed color because of its ability and tendency to break down to the reactive reducing sugars. Potatoes harvested immature, such as the spring and summer crops, are usually low in reducing sugars, but relatively high in sucrose. Immature potatoes from the south which fry to excellent light color on arrival may fry too dark after several days at room temperature. The explanation is that at 70°F the sucrose, which is present in large quantity, is hydrolyzed to the reducing sugars which then result in dark chips. At low temperatures starch in the potato is rather slowly converted to glucose. Some of the reducing sugars are depleted in the process of respiration and the remainder accumulates in the tubers resulting in dark chips when they are fried.

Some of the factors which influence potato chip and French fry color are the following: varieties and growing conditions which affect sugar content of potatoes, methods of storing or handling potatoes to maintain sugars at a low level and the several methods of treating potatoes or the slices in hot water and various chemical solutions to deplete the supply of reactive sugars, and the frying and drying techniques such as hot air and microwave drying after partial frying, and vacuum frying.

Effect of Cultural Methods and Environment

Cultural and environmental factors that result in potatoes of high specific gravity generally tend to produce potatoes which, after storage, process into light color chips and French fries. The most important factors which affect color of these products are those which influence the maturity of the potato at time of harvest. Maturity is influenced by time of planting, location, soil moisture and soil type, amount and kind of fertilizers applied, temperature during the growing season, time of vine killing and time of harvest.

It is generally accepted that the more mature potatoes are when harvested the easier they are to handle, store, and recondition to light color chips and French fries. Immature tubers not only lose more weight and shrivel in storage but their chemical composition is different from those more mature. This change in composition usually makes them more difficult to store so that light color products will be produced after reconditioning. For instance, the reducing sugar content of immature potatoes stored at 50°F or lower, generally is higher than those potatoes which are more mature.

Date of Planting.—More mature potatoes as a result of earlier planting have an effect on chip and French fry color. Other factors remaining the same, the earliest planted potatoes result in lightest color products. Obtaining a greater degree of maturity by delaying harvest often increases specific gravity of tubers and results in lighter color chips and French fries.

Fields should be planted first with potatoes which are to be utilized for chips and French fries and those for seed or market should be planted later. Also, potatoes should be allowed to mature as much as possible before harvest providing the delayed harvest does not subject the potatoes to temperatures below 40°F in the field before or during harvest.

Irrigation and Soil Moisture.—Whether finished product color will be influenced by increasing the soil moisture by irrigation will depend on the rainfall, soil type, time when moisture was applied and amount added. If rainfall or rainfall plus irrigation amounts to more moisture than plants can utilize for maximum growth, it may result in potatoes of low specific gravity and processed products of dark color. Unirrigated potatoes in some seasons result in products considerably lighter in color than those which were irrigated. In other seasons, particularly if they are hot and dry, there are no consistent differences in color of products from potatoes which had been irrigated compared with those which received no additional water. Records of soil temperatures during these

latter seasons show that irrigated areas are several degrees cooler than those not irrigated. The lower soil temperature probably has a counteracting effect on the greater absorption of water, resulting in tubers of about the same specific gravity and products of similar color. Potatoes with heavy rainfall or excessive irrigation late in the growing season produce darker chips and French fries than those with less rainfall or less irrigation water. It can be rather safely predicted that in areas and in seasons where rainfall is excessive shortly before and during the harvest period that potatoes will be very difficult if not impossible to store so that they will process to light color products during the winter and spring months. During seasons such as that it is suggested that processors begin early to look elsewhere for the bulk of the crop to be stored.

Effect of Fertilizers.—Potatoes from fields of low yields usually produce the lightest color chips and French fries. This may be a result of early death of vines and greater maturity of the tubers.

Application of fertilizers often influences chip and French fry color. In most potato growing areas greatest yield response is obtained from application of nitrogen in complete fertilizers rather than from the phosphate and potash portions. Nitrogen promotes extensive vine growth and prolongs the season of active growth. As a result, potatoes are not mature at harvest and, therefore, are likely to produce dark processed products after storage and also they are more difficult to recondition at higher temperatures. In general, it can be said that as rate of nitrogen applied increases, color of chips and French fries becomes progressively darker. Nitrogen applications also result in potatoes of lower specific gravity; therefore, it is suggested that in growing potatoes for processing, the amount of nitrogen applied should be kept as low as possible, but yet sufficient to assure the grower of a good yield.

Apparently the amount or kind of phosphorus used in the fertilizer for potatoes has very little effect on color of processed products made from them.

There are some controversial results concerning the effect of potash in the fertilizer on chip color. The evidence leans slightly in favor of high applications of potash for improving chip color. Similarly, although source of potash has a definite effect on specific gravity of tubers, the effect on chip color is slight and questionable.

Killing Potato Vines.—Killing potato vines also may affect color of potato chips and French fries. Lightest color products usually result from potatoes, the vines of which were not killed. The more rapid the kill, the darker the chip color. For instance, potatoes from vines which were killed mechanically, such as with a rotobeater, usually fry darker than those from similar potatoes, the vines of which were killed with a chemical spray application. Sometimes late killing of vines or late harvesting of potatoes results in darker color chips than those killed or harvested earlier. This darkening of chips from late harvests probably is due to lower temperatures prevailing late in the season.

It is very important to harvest potatoes for chips and French fries before low soil temperatures prevail. When the average soil temperature and the lowest soil temperature are much below 48°F for 1 week before harvest or below 40°F for several days or nights, chips are likely to be too dark to be acceptable by the trade. The greater the cumulative number of degree-days the soil temperature is below 50°F the darker the color of chips will be at harvest.

Effect of Storage Temperature

It has long been known that potatoes stored at low temperatures accumulate sugars, including the reducing sugars glucose and fructose, and that the sugar content decreases when the tubers are reconditioned at a higher temperature.

Potatoes are classified as a starchy food, usually containing from 12 to 18% starch. Reducing sugars are formed from starch in the tubers. This process involves the action of the enzyme invertase. The changes in invertase generally occur parallel to the changes in reducing sugars. Invertase increases at low temperatures and decreases at higher temperatures; reducing sugars also follow this pattern.

Unless freshly harvested potatoes have been exposed to low temperatures before harvest they contain very little reducing sugars. Freshly harvested immature potatoes contain appreciable amounts of sucrose. As the tuber matures, the sucrose percentage decreases and starch increases. Immature tubers stored at 77°F lose sucrose and increase in reducing sugars. During storage at low temperatures, reducing sugars accumulate more rapidly than sucrose. At 50°F reducing sugars increase for about 15 weeks in storage; in fact they may increase from 0.2 to 1.0% within 3 days.

For lowest reducing sugar accumulation and, therefore, for light color processed products, potatoes should be stored at about 55°F followed by reconditioning at 70°F for as long as is necessary to obtain desirable light color chips. Temperatures higher than 70°F are not recommended for reconditioning because disappearance of reducing sugars is not hastened appreciably above this temperature. On the other hand, if potatoes are held at 80°F or higher, reducing sugar content actually may increase and result in dark chips and French fries.

Obviously at the above recommended temperatures potatoes will start to sprout extensively 3–4 months after harvest. Therefore, for winter and spring use, the potatoes should be treated with a sprout inhibitor. The grower and processor have a choice of applying an inhibitor to plants in the field or later applying an inhibitor to potatoes as they go into storage or after they are in place in storage.

A relationship between sprout growth of potatoes and their reducing sugar content is still claimed by some. At one time, before the advent of the use of sprout inhibitors, this probably was true. At least it was a good indication to the processor, as he received the well-sprouted potatoes, that they had been stored at a fairly high temperature and, therefore, should fry to light color. However, when sprouts are suppressed by the use of a sprout inhibitor, this relationship is not shown. Potatoes held at a warm temperature but with no sprouts due to the application of a sprout inhibitor may, of course, fry to an attractive light color. A number of workers have shown that spraying maleic hydrazide on plants in the field has no influence on reducing sugar content of tubers during subsequent storage. This is generally true also with other sprout inhibitors although some workers in Holland found higher reducing sugar content in tubers treated with CIPC after 6 months' storage at 50°F than in untreated sprouting potatoes. At 60°F storage, however, this did not appear to be true. There are two other sprout inhibiting treatments, however, which apparently do have an effect on sugar accumulation in stored potatoes. Nonanol, an alcohol, is used in several European countries, but not in the United States, for controlling sprout growth of potatoes. It is applied as an atomized liquid or a fine vapor to potato storages after the potatoes have sprouted. This treatment kills the sprouts already formed rather than preventing their original appearance. Potatoes stored at 50°F for 40 weeks had lower reducing sugar content in those untreated than in those which had been treated with nonanol.

Irradiation of potatoes for the purpose of inhibiting sprout growth is permissable in the United States and Canada, but for various reasons it is used little or not at all commercially. Experiments conducted in the United States, Canada, and in Europe show that potatoes that have been irradiated are higher in reducing sugars at least during a portion of the storage period. Some workers report a rather marked increase in reducing sugars for the first 10–12 weeks after irradiation when the potatoes are held at 48–50°F. After this time, the treated and untreated potatoes have about equal sugar content. Other workers, however, report that after six months or more storage, high sugar content rendered irradiated potatoes unsuitable for chip production. Recommendations for growers and processors in the United States who wish to use a sprout inhibitor are (1) apply maleic hydrazide to plants in the field or (2) apply CIPC to potatoes as they are placed in storage or after they are stored.

Methods of Frying and Drying Chips

There are three recently developed methods of frying potato chips in addition to the standard method which has been used for many years. These are (1) microwave finish drying of partially fried chips, (2) air drying of partially fried chips and (3) vacuum finish frying of chips. The first of these is in use in a number of plants in the United States and several in Europe. The air drying method of partially fried chips has not been developed on a commercial scale. Vacuum finish frying of chips is used in several plants in Europe, South Africa, and one plant in the United States.

Processing with Microwave Energy.—Experiments conducted with the use of microwave energy show conclusively that many of the potatoes which do not make an acceptably-colored chip, and which would be abandoned, can be processed to a saleable color by utilizing microwave drying of partially fried slices. Still more important, this process now enables potato growers and chippers to utilize considerably simpler storage buildings and techniques. The chipper also may be able to change his methods and ideals into potato procurement. The objectives of potato breeders may now take wider latitude in developing future varieties for use of the industry. The characteristics to look for may now be simpler in newer varieties which will make the microwave finished product high in quality and most economical to produce. Potato breeders may now be able to concentrate on other important characteristics such as specific gravity, starch content, cell structure, proportion of amylose and amylopectin in potato starch, yield, size, shape, depth of eyes, and disease and insect resistance.

Air Drying Partially Fried Chips.—Potatoes of high reducing sugar content have been partially fried and then subjected to dry heat from several sources such as a hot air tunnel or infrared heat.

In the hot air tunnel at 220°F or less, moisture may be removed from partially fried chips without increasing browning. Temperatures higher than 220°F induce browning and the degree of darkening increases with time. Time of frying is critical because sufficient moisture must be removed so that the chips can be finished in the hot air tunnel in 3–4 min. A moisture content of 7% or less makes it possible for the drying to be completed in a few minutes. Air movement around and through the chips is essential for removal of the moisture.

Raw slices of different reducing sugar content when fried to doneness result in chips of varying degrees of browning. When similar slices are fried only until browning begins in the areas high in reducing sugars, they are not sufficiently cooked to be dried quickly.

Infrared heat produces similar results as those obtained in the heat tunnel. Air movement is essential for moisture removal and a decrease in air movement prolongs the drying time. Drying periods of 10 min or longer result in marked textural changes in chips. The texture becomes harsh or exceedingly hard and brittle. Oil content of partially fried and dried chips is lower than that of chips fried in the conventional manner.

Conventional hot air drying techniques have not been developed to the point of commercial application.

Vacuum Finish Frying of Chips.—A vacuum fryer has been developed in Holland in which the last portion of the frying is done under partial vacuum.

The machine has a capacity of 1500–2000 lb finished chips per hour with an input of slices fried in the conventional manner to approximately 6–10% moisture. The temperature of the oil is maintained at 212°F and is heated in a heat exchanger.

This fryer also may be used for frying potato sticks or shoestrings. To get sticks of good finish color the moisture content of the sticks should be considerably higher before the vacuum process than that for chips; a moisture content of about 20% is preferred.

The color of both chips and sticks is considerably lighter when finish processed in the vacuum fryer than the same potatoes processed entirely in the conventional oven.

Thorough discussion of potato production, storing, and processing of all forms of potatoes is contained in the books by Talburt and Smith (1967) and Smith (1968).

ORA SMITH

References

SMITH, O. 1968. Potatoes: Production, Storing, Processing. Avi Publishing Co., Westport, Conn.

TALBURT, W. F., and SMITH, O. 1967. Potato Processing, 2nd Edition. Avi Publishing Co., Westport, Conn.

WATT, B. K., and MERRILL, A. L. 1963. Composition of Foods: Raw, Processed, Prepared. USDA Agr. Res. Serv., Agr. Handbook 8.

POULTRY INDUSTRY IN THE UNITED STATES

During the last two decades the U.S. Poultry Industry has become the most efficient producer of animal protein in the entire history of agriculture. In 1961, Blaxter, a noted English scientist described the industry as "... one of the most amazing pieces of integrated work that has ever been done." Poultry research has played a major role in this development.

The following examples document the rapid rate of growth and magnitude of the industry. Peterson (1967), in an economic study of the industry, concluded that past investment in poultry research had been yielding a return of about 20–30% annually.

Jasper (1962), reported that in the interval between 1910 and 1960, per capita consumption of poultry products increased from 306 to 334 eggs and from 15.5 to 28.0 lb of chicken. In the next 10-yr period, 1960–1970, egg consumption decreased to 318 and chicken and turkey consumption increased to 41.8 lb and 8.1 lb, up from 6.1 lb in 1960. Another way of illustrating the gains made by the industry are the percentage increases from 1939–1960, which amounted to an increase of 421% in gross income from broilers and 247.6% for all poultry. Changes in per capita consumption

of livestock products and projections of future requirements are illustrated in Fig. P-11 and Table P-5.

Poultry operations can be measured in annual terms of millions of pounds and dollars. In 1970, 2 companies handled 470 and 400 million pounds of dressed broilers, respectively. Another company reported that their poultry operations amounted to 100 million dollars, and still another company reported that they did 5 million dollars worth of business in canned poultry products alone. One company, whose business is built almost entirely on selling fried chicken, became the second largest food handler in the world in 1970. Franchisees of this organization alone purchase 6–8% of the entire broiler production in the United States.

As a result of these advances in poultry production in the United States, it takes 14 min work to buy 1 lb of chicken and 17 min for a dozen eggs, compared to France where 104 and 49 min are required, and Russia where 241 and 162 min are required.

Despite these optimistic statistics, in 1969, the president of one of the nation's largest poultry combines was quoted as saying (Anon. 1969) that "The industry has relied in the past on dramatic breakthroughs in technology. However, the industry has now run the gamit of nutritional and genetic and disease control breakthroughs. Improvement in production will come more slowly now. It will be necessary in the future to raise selling prices to cover the higher costs." Another industry leader was also of the opinion that the broiler industry could not hope to obtain increases in technology in the 1970's equivalent to those made in previous years.

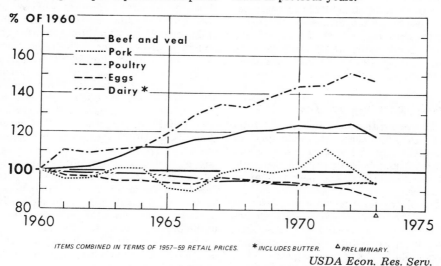

ITEMS COMBINED IN TERMS OF 1957–59 RETAIL PRICES.   *INCLUDES BUTTER.   △ PRELIMINARY.

USDA Econ. Res. Serv.

FIG. P-11. PER CAPITA CONSUMPTION OF SELECTED LIVESTOCK PRODUCTS

TABLE P-5

PROJECTED ANIMAL REQUIREMENTS IN THE YEAR 2000 FOR A POPULATION OF 300 MILLION PEOPLE

Product	Probable per Capita Consumption (Lb)	Numbers Required	Increase or Decrease over 1968 (%)
Beef	105	53.5 million to slaughter	+ 51
Veal	9	19 million to slaughter	+244
Lamb and mutton	6	36.5 million to slaughter	+301
Pork	75	131.5 million to slaughter	+ 52
Broiler meat	40	4.6 billion to slaughter	+ 78
Turkey meat	9	180 million to slaughter	+ 69
Eggs	360 (No.)	394 million laying hens	+ 25
Milk	610	11 million milking cows	– 22

SOURCE: Hodgson and Warwick (1971).

These predictions do not imply that there will be no future gains or that consumption and efficiency of production of poultry and poultry products will not increase. For example, already in 1971, it was finally possible to develop a satisfactory vaccine for Marek's disease, a disease which caused heavy condemnation rates in broilers and losses in older hens. It has been estimated that shortly, when and if it becomes economical to vaccinate all broilers, the use of this one practice alone will result in adding as much as 5% more broilers to our total meat supply, simply by reducing mortality rates and condemnations.

Jukes (1971), summarized the present status of poultry as food in the United States when he reported that "As a result of scientific agriculture, in 1971 a broiler chicken costs less in actual inflated cents per pound than it did in cents per pound in the depth of the depression." In the mid-1930's producers received an average of 20¢ per lb for live broilers; by 1939 they were receiving 17¢ per lb; by 1948, 36¢ per lb; and by 1970 the price had again declined to 13.3¢ per lb.

Factors Responsible for the Rapid Growth

Biological Characteristics of Chickens.—A brief discussion of the biological characteristics of chickens and other types of poultry and a history of the industry should help to explain the rapid growth achieved in the past and help in making future projections.

There are few places in the world where chickens and other poultry cannot grow and survive. Poultry can be easily transported by plane, ship, car or wagon train as mature breeding stock in small coops, day-old chicks or hatching eggs. They grow and thrive in close confinement and they can survive and multiply under the most primitive conditions with the only care being a crude shelter, some protection from predators, and a handful of grain. Poultry also have a low economic value per animal unit, a short generation time, and serve as a rich source of nutrients for human food. Their size is such that 1 bird supplies the meat portion for 1-2 family meals. If necessary, they can be held live until needed for food, thus eliminating the need for perishable food storage facilities which are required when large animals such as beef are slaughtered. In addition, chicken hens produce eggs year round, regardless of the season. These same characteristics make poultry especially desirable for a beginning animal agriculture in underdeveloped countries.

Chickens make ideal research animals, not only for improving the poultry industry, but also as pilot organisms for improving other animal production practices and controlling human diseases. Embryonated eggs are important for the production of many vaccines. The same characteristics which make them important to agriculture, in addition to their sensitivity to nutritional deficiencies and the fact that the embryos themselves make ideal research tools, also make them ideal laboratory animals. Chickens also have a very rapid growth rate. At 8 weeks of age chickens weigh 43.7 times their original hatching weight. If other farm animals grew at the same rate by 8 weeks of age, pigs would weigh 118 lb; calves, 3055 lb; and human beings would weigh 349 lb. As a result of these characteristics, some of the experimentation often aided the poultry industry when chickens were used to help solve problems unrelated to the industry. As one scientist observed, "The young chicken may well be the most researched animal in this much-researched world."

Poultry Breeders' Contributions.—Poultry were

first selected and bred for exhibition. In the United States the show bird era of the poultry industry lasted roughly from the late 19th to the early 20th Century. Birds were selected and bred almost entirely for their show characteristics such as plumage color and patterns, stance, and conformation. Economic characteristics such as feed efficiency, egg production, hatchability, and increased meat production efficiency were neglected.

Gradually, some breeders began selecting and breeding almost entirely for economic characteristics. At first, chickens were selected for general purpose use to supply both meat and eggs. Then breeds began to be selected and bred specifically for meat or egg production and finally breeds, varieties, and strains were crossed to improve their ability to produce either meat or eggs.

Breeding for Egg Production.—An important development in the field of poultry genetics was the recognition that like birds do not necessarily create like offspring but that if the genetic makeup of the birds could be determined by producing some offspring then rapid improvement could be made by selecting breeding stock on the basis of performance of offspring. This was known as progeny testing. To capitalize on this knowledge, the National Poultry Improvement Plan was developed in the 1930's. A principal feature of this Federal-State cooperative plan was that birds were selected for breeding on the basis of their offspring's performance.

Desirable traits for which breeder stock are selected to produce offspring for egg production are number, size, shape, and interior and shell quality of eggs produced as well as vigor of the birds, feed efficiency, and body size.

To test stocks developed by commercial breeders, random sample laying tests were set up by State agencies. In these tests, commercial breeding stocks are compared with each other under a standard, carefully controlled set of conditions. Nordskog (1966) reported that such tests stimulate breeders to improve their stock, provide poultrymen with a basis of comparison for purchasing stock, and provide useful information on the best way to test birds for performance.

In the late 1930's, the breeding systems used to produce hybrid corn were successfully utilized by the poultry industry. Two separate lines of birds, often of different breeds, were inbred and offspring selected intensively for desired characteristics for several generations. Then to overcome the effects of inbreeding, the two lines were crossed to achieve hybrid vigor and intensify the desirable genes from the parent stock. Two major breeders in the industry today still use this system. Another breeding system in current use is known

as reciprocal recurrent selection. Under this system, the nonrelated strains are crossed and the parent lines of the strains that show good "combining ability" are kept. Then individuals are selected from each of these strains to improve combining ability further.

Breeding for Broiler Production.—Broiler breeding stock must have the ability to produce offspring with rapid growth, efficient feed conversion, early rapid feathering with white feathers and yellow skin, low mortality and morbidity, high dressing yields, a reasonable number of hatching eggs and, most important, produce carcasses with thick meaty breasts and thighs. To achieve this, breeders specialize in providing either Cornish males or White Rock females as parent or foundation stock for multipliers who provide chicks for the industry. The Cornish stock provides firm, meaty flesh and dominant white feathers while the White Rock females provide rapid growth, yellow skin, fast feathering, and good egg production and hatchability to produce large quantities of offspring. The hybrid vigor resulting from such crosses produces vigorous, rapid growing, healthy chicks.

Poultry Nutrition

A very important segment of the poultry "success story" can be illustrated by the contributions to poultry nutrition made by State agricultural experiment stations, the USDA, and the feed industry. Since feed amounts to about $2/3$ of the cost of rearing broilers, any substantial improvement in feeding knowledge has been quickly adapted by the industry and has resulted in lowering the costs of production. In fact, the field of poultry nutrition research has produced such high "payoffs" that the nutrient requirements for poultry at the present time are better known than for any other animal including humans. Schiable (1970) reported that it is now possible to produce broiler chickens with average weights of 3 lb in 53 days with 2.2 lb of feed per pound of gain. The principal discoveries in the field of nutrition which, when applied to poultry feeding, made this phenomenal growth record possible were cataloged by Schiable (1970). They are:

1913	Fat-soluble vitamin A recognized
1920–1925	Importance of calcium and phosphorus recognized
1922	Role of vitamin D in rickets making confinement rearing of poultry possible
1925	Essential trace minerals were recognized; nutritional anemia prevented by iron and copper
1928	Multiple nature of vitamin B discovered

1929	Effect of hen's diet on egg hatchability
1931	Alfalfa dehydrated to supply forage nutrients
1933	Vitamin A and carotene identified
1933	Vitamin K demonstrated as essential for blood clotting
1933	Riboflavin (B_2) isolated
1934	Importance of ratio of calcium to phosphorus established
1936	Vitamin D_3 most efficient form for poultry
1936	Thiamin was isolated
1936	Improved method for producing soybean meal
1937	Manganese found to prevent perosis
1938	Choline recognized as an essential nutrient
1939	Vitamin B_6 synthesized; vitamin E identified; riboflavin and niacin marketed commercially
1940	Vitamin E offered commercially
1941	Fermentation products discovered to be source of vitamin B-complex and UGF (unidentified growth factors)
1944	Animal protein factor demonstrated
1946	Folic acid discovered
1947	High energy feeds became practical
1948	Vitamin B_{12} isolated in pure form (animal protein factor)
1949	Vitamin B_{12} was offered commercially
1950	Antibiotics, nonnutrient growth stimulants were found to increase growth
1951	Methionine produced commercially
1952	Animal fats used in feeds for energy
1953	Antioxidants first used in fats to control rancidity
1955	Whey and fishmeal practical sources of unidentified growth factors
1956	Importance of calorie to protein ratio demonstrated
1957	Importance of zinc and selenium in nutrition discovered
1957	Linear programming and "least cost" formulation

Other later developments include:

1958	Marketing of lysine and glycine in commercial quantities
1959	Use of tranquilizers for stress and aortic rupture
1960	Introduction of new and improved coccidiostats
1965	Development of the 2-days-in-1 feeding system for broilers
1965	Use of blood plasma amino acid assays to measure nutrient levels
1966	Restricted feeding of replacement pullets

These discoveries can be classified into three general categories: The identification of necessary vitamins and trace minerals and the optimum amounts required; the importance of rations with balanced nutrients; and the utilization of this knowledge for the practical purpose of obtaining the most pounds of meat or eggs with the fewest pounds of feed possible.

Poultry Diseases

Many segments of today's modern poultry industry could not be put together until some poultry diseases were controlled. A problem peculiar to the poultry industry is the fact that individual birds have such a low economic value per unit that it is necessary to treat birds as a flock or unit rather than individual birds.

Pullorum disease has been one of the most troublesome diseases for the industry. Although controlled for a number of years, it is still a problem in the industry today. Control is brought about mainly by blood testing breeding stock to eliminate positive reactors and by strict hatchery sanitation.

Another prevalent disease which can cause high mortality and excessive condemnations of broilers in processing plants is coccidiosis. This disease, caused by a group of protozoan organisms, is now controlled by use of medication in the feed of young chickens.

Blackhead or infectious enterohepatitis is another protozoan disease which causes high mortality in turkeys and to a much lesser extent in chickens. Control of this disease has aided the rapid development of the turkey industry in recent years.

Marek's disease, first characterized by Marek in 1907, is still a disease of major economic importance. During the past few years there has been outstanding progress which should lead to control of this disease. The first major development in a number of years which led to partial control of the disease occurred in 1962 when it became possible to transmit the disease experimentally. By 1967 the causative agent, a herpesvirus, was isolated and by 1969 the fact that feather follicles were the site where viral replication proceeded to completion was established. These findings led, in turn, to establishment of evidence that chickens could be immunized against Marek's disease and to the development of vaccines.

Whether costs will permit widespread use of such vaccines must be established by further testing and refinements.

Chronic respiratory disease, caused by a rickettsia-like organism, *Mycoplasma gallisepticum*, has been controlled but still remains an important cause of condemnation of broiler carcasses.

Newcastle disease, first isolated at Newcastle, England, has been a major threat to the American poultry industry from time to time. It is a viral, respiratory-nervous disorder which can cause not only high losses in young stock but also heavy loss of egg production and egg quality in mature hens. Control has been by vaccination of chicks. In 1972, a new virulent strain from foreign countries was transmitted by diseased birds to some flocks in the United States. As a result, there were strict quarantine regulations and surveillance on imported poultry.

Processing Poultry

Complete automation of poultry processing has not been achieved as yet, although improvements are still being made. Brant (1962) described the improvements which helped increase the efficiency of the processing segment of the industry. These include the use of power driven conveyor lines, agitated water for scalding, and development of automatic rubber fingered pickers. The major development in this segment of the industry occurred after World War II when plants began eviscerating poultry carcasses at the processing plant instead of after delivery to the grocery store. Agitated, in-line, quick-chilling of poultry in ice water is a development which was perfected in the 1960's and automatic on-the-line eviscerating machines were developed in the early 1970's. Mandatory inspection of poultry according to USDA standards in all plants operating in the United States was completed in the first half of the 1970's. Cutting up poultry carcasses; packaging them in the processing plant; and then "deep chilling" them by lightly freezing the surface to reduce spoilage, dehydration, and drip occurred in the 1960's.

Poultry are transported in trucks with coops or cages to the dock of the processing plant. There they are removed from the coop, hung on shackles attached to a conveyor line, and slaughtered by cutting the jugular vein. In some cases, especially with turkeys, they may be electrically stunned before bleeding to reduce struggling and injury. After slaughter, the carcasses continue on the conveyor line through a controlled temperature scalder where they are immersed from 30 to 120 sec in circulating water in the range of $122°$–$128°F$ or $138°$–$140°F$. The higher temperature scalding which is generally used for turkeys causes the outer skin to blister and rub off when the carcasses are defeathered.

Next, the carcasses are defeathered by automatic rubber fingered pickers, then the hocks and necks are scalded, generally at about $165°F$, and the carcasses are run through special pickers to remove feathers in these areas. Finally the wing feathers are removed by a special picker. Defeathered carcasses are scrubbed with rubber fingers at the same time they are washed with water, the feet are removed and the carcass is transferred to an eviscerating line.

For evisceration, the carcasses are suspended on a shackle by the feet and neck, and opened at the vent. The viscera are removed and suspended from the vent opening for examination by an inspector. Then the liver, heart, and gizzard are removed and cleaned while the remaining viscera are detached at which time the carcass is thoroughly washed inside and outside. Finally, the carcass is chilled in an agitated ice water bath before being packaged or cut-up for storage and shipment.

When turkeys are processed they are packaged in moisture- and vapor-proof, transparent, plastic film bags; the bags are heat shrunk; and then the package is immersed in a supercooled ethylene glycol or calcium chloride solution so the outer surface of the carcass is frozen to give it a pleasant, clean, white appearance. Freezing is then completed in a blast freezer.

For additional processing instead of whole or cut-up chilled or frozen poultry, meat is removed from uncooked carcasses by machines or cooked and then the meat is removed by machine or by hand. The cooked meat can be diced and the broth discarded or reused to make chicken pies, soups or other products. In some cases, poultry parts are fried to be sold as packaged, frozen, precooked, heat-and-serve dinners. Uncooked deboned poultry meat, usually from necks, backs, and wings, is used with red meats to make hot dogs and bologna products.

Processing Eggs

Shell eggs are gathered by hand or by automatic conveyers from hens kept in individual wire cages. After collection, the shells are sprayed with a thin odorless coating of mineral oil to prevent carbon dioxide loss from the shell. Then the eggs are packed in 30-doz cases, chilled and held at $55°F$ at about 70% RH until picked up in refrigerated trucks, usually twice a week, for sorting, washing, grading, and packing at a central processing plant.

At the processing plant eggs are removed from the cases by a vacuum lifter which handles 30 eggs at a time. Then they are placed on a conveyer belt which rotates the eggs and handles six rows of eggs at a time. The conveyer belt carries the eggs through a detergent, sanitizer, water wash, then a hot water rinse, and finally through a hot air dryer. At this point, in some plants, the eggs are lightly sprayed with oil again. Then the washed eggs, still rotating, are conveyed past an ultraviolet light candler where cracked and defective eggs are removed. Finally the eggs are automatically transferred to another conveyer line where they are classified according to size and automatically packaged and sealed in 1-doz-egg cartons. The cartons are then assembled in 30-doz size cardboard egg cases and held refrigerated for distribution.

Some eggs are broken on an automatic egg breaking machine which separates yolks and whites and are frozen for future use while other eggs are dried by spray dryers. Eggs processed by these methods are available as whole eggs and yolks and whites or with different proportions of yolk and other additives such as salt, sugar, or other ingredients to improve their functional properties, depending on their ultimate use.

Marketing

Poultry.—Once large numbers of high quality uniform birds and eggs could be produced in one area it was also possible to reduce the costs of marketing these products. To produce broilers, hatching eggs are now set in incubators according to the anticipated demand 11–12 weeks later. It takes 3 weeks to hatch the chicks and 8–9 weeks to produce broilers to market age. At that time, birds are picked up at the farm to allow just enough time to drive directly to the processing plant where they can be slaughtered immediately. The entire process is coordinated by telephone and two-way radio. Often, that same night the chilled carcasses are already on their way in refrigerated trucks to a supermarket distribution point. The carcasses are not only cut up but also individually packaged in unitized packages for fork lift handling as well as sorted into different weight classes.

The main developments required to achieve this high degree of efficiency were the eviscerating of poultry and, more recently, the cutting up of whole carcasses in the processing plant instead of the store and the development of better sanitary processing and refrigeration practices. Improvements in sanitation and refrigeration facilities have made it possible to ship poultry longer distances and to store them for longer periods. Trade areas have been extended over 1000 miles by super highways and modern refrigerated motor trucks.

In addition to the above advancements, improved grading and standardization along with compulsory inspection for wholesomeness have resulted in increased confidence on the part of the consumer in purchasing poultry despite temporary credibility gaps.

Eggs.—The practice of direct marketing of eggs by producers to consumers has almost disappeared because eggs obtained at food stores are now of uniformly high quality and the cost of labor for direct marketing is too expensive for the returns one can expect. Quality control consists mainly of rapid handling, keeping eggs refrigerated at all times, and performing certain functions such as egg washing in the processing plant where the operations can be closely supervised rather than on the poultry farm. Eggs offered for sale to the consumer are generally U.S. Grade AA or A grade or their equivalent in either extra large, large, medium or pullet sizes packaged in sealed 1-doz cartons with a pull date. If eggs are not sold by the pull date the seal is broken and they must be sold at a lower grade. Most states have fresh egg laws to ensure truthful labeling.

Management

Management involves taking all of the factors involved with production, processing, and marketing and developing a tightly coordinated, systematic, smooth running organization. To achieve this requires millions of dollars worth of capital and a national organization. As a result of these needs the organization of the industry is still moving toward fewer owners with larger organizations, each controlling larger portions of the market. Both vertical and horizontal integration are widely practiced in the industry.

To extend the use of capital, the parent corporation usually obtains at least a controlling interest in each segment of the system. For example, in the production of broilers: feed, chicks, litter, and medicinals are supplied by the company; while labor, land, and buildings are supplied by the grower. Contracts spell out the obligations of each party. Since the company has controlling interest, the operation is carefully supervised by their representative, a flock service man. The company decides when and where to market the mature birds and when to start a new batch of chicks. The performance of individual flocks of broilers are measured at weekly intervals or less. Often, problems can be identified several days before they occur by abrupt changes in feed and water consumption, behavior of the birds, or failure to gain as expected. Parkhurst (1967) listed the following standards for managing a broiler production operation:

Family Unit Size—45,000 broilers.
Labor—With automatic feeders, not over 18 min per 1000 per day; without automatic equipment, not to exceed 31 min.

House-Unit Size—7200 to 20,000 per house; desirable size is 15,000 in 40- by 300-ft house.

Pen Size—1200 to 2500 per pen.

Floor Space—0.8 sq ft per 3- to 3.75-lb broiler; 1 sq ft for summer-reared and per 4-lb bird and over.

Brooder Space—750 to 1000 chicks per 1000-chick size hover; varies with season, insulation, and mechanical ventilation.

Litter—2 to 4 in.—less in hot weather.

Fountains—1-gal. fountain per 100 chicks to 2 weeks old.

Water Space—Three 8-ft automatic waterers per 1000; add 1 more per 1000 birds when temperature is 90°F or higher.

Feeder Lids—One feeder lid per 100 chicks.

Feeder Space—Allow fifteen 15-in. diameter 30-lb capacity hanging feeders per 1000; allow 1 linear foot per 12 broilers for mechanical feeders.

Feedings—Follow directions of feed manufacturer or formulator.

Lights—After 2 weeks, use all-night lights; one 25-watt bulb per 100-sq ft floor space.

Security Management—Follow good management practices as far as is economically feasible.

The Future

Several industry leaders have attempted to predict some of the future developments in the industry. One predicted that by 1990 the cholesterol problem will be resolved, poultry will be produced in clusters of 5 to 20 farms, each with at least 120,000 layers with about 100 such clusters needed to supply all eggs needed in the United States. Broilers will be produced in cages by an assembly line automated system.

Another industry spokesman predicted that future complexes will handle a million birds a week. The breeding farm, hatchery, feed mill, and processing plant will be on the same site. Broilers will be produced and marketed at seven weeks of age in the same cage they started out in as baby chicks. Such birds will be under human surveillance 24 hr a day by employees who will wear sterile clothes and be required to shower before going to work in the house.

Lloyd (1969) predicts that when cage production of broilers becomes practical, a 36 × 200 ft conventional broiler house will hold 1140 2 × 3-ft plastic cages with a production capacity of 123,120 broilers a year compared with the present system which can handle 40,500 birds a year.

GEORGE J. MOUNTNEY

References

ANON. 1969. Future shape of poultry industry outlined for agricultural marketers. Feedstuffs *41*, No. 47, 12–14, 50–52.

BLAXTER, K. L. 1961. Efficiency of feed conversion by different classes of live stock in relation to food production. Federation Am. Soc. Exptl. Biol. Med. *20*, No. 1, 268–274.

BRANT, A. W. 1962. Technological changes in poultry processing affecting quality and costs. Mimeo, Proc. World's Poultry Sci. Assoc.

HODGSON, R. E., and WARWICK, E. J. 1971. Animal product needs and how to meet them. *In* A Good Life for More People. USDA AGR. Yearbook *320*.

JASPER, A. W. 1962. A rapidly changing poultry industry in the United States. Proc. 12th World's Poultry Congr., Sydney, Australia.

JUKES, T. H. 1971. Fact and fancy in nutrition and food science. J. Am. Dietet. Assoc. *59*, No. 3, 203–211.

LLOYD, R. 1969. Broiler production in the future. Feedstuffs *15*, No. 27, 27, 41.

MOUNTNEY, G. J. 1966. Poultry Products Technology. Avi Publishing Company, Westport, Conn.

NORDSKOG, A. W. 1966. Poultry random sample testing in the U.S.—trends and accomplishments. Proc. 13th World's Poultry Congr., Kiev, USSR.

PARKHURST, R. T. 1967. Commercial broiler production. USDA Agr. Res. Serv., Agr. Handbook *320*.

PETERSON, W. L. 1967. Return to poultry research in the United States. J. Farm Econ. *49*, No. 3, 656–689.

SCHIABLE, P. J. 1970. Poultry: Feeds and Nutrition. Avi Publishing Co., Westport, Conn.

Cross-reference: *Eggs and Egg Products.*

PRESCOTT, SAMUEL CATE (1872-1962)

Dr. Samuel Cate Prescott was born on a small farm in South Hampton, New Hampshire, on April 5, 1872. He was educated at the Massachusetts Institute of Technology where he graduated in 1894 with the degree of Bachelor of Science in Chemistry with specialization in the field of Sanitary and Food Chemistry and Bacteriology.

After serving as a bacteriologist and assistant chemist at the Sewage Purification Works of Worcester, Mass., he returned to M.I.T. where he became the private research assistant to Professor William T. Sedgwick, the distinguished sanitarian and head of the Department of Biology.

In 1895, he was appointed assistant in the Department of Biology, and this was the beginning of a long and distinguished career at M.I.T. where he rose to become head of the Department of Biology and Public Health and later the first dean of the School of Science at M.I.T. He retired in 1942 but continued his affiliations with M.I.T. until his death in 1962.

Through Professor Sedgwick he met William Lyman Underwood with whom he began his pioneering researches on bacteriology and sterilization processes in the canning industry which have been generally recognized as being of outstanding fundamental significance in the development of the science of canning technology and which form the scientific basis of our modern canning industry.

In addition to his work on thermal processing, Dr. Prescott, early in his career, studied mycology and fermentation in Berlin and Copenhagen, and while in Europe, he met Dr. Jean Effront whose book he translated in 1902, *Enzymes and Their Applications*. This volume became of great industrial significance.

Dr. Prescott carried out important researches in various other food processing areas including refrigeration and dehydration. He gave a great deal of attention to pasteurization and sanitary control of public milk supplies.

His books include *Water Bacteriology* with C. E. A. Winslow and M. H. McGrady, *Industrial Microbiology* with C. G. Dunn, and *Food Technology* with B. E. Proctor.

Dr. Prescott spent significant amounts of time in Central America working on the diseases of the banana. He established a laboratory there for the United Fruit Company.

During World War I, he served in the U.S. Army as a Major in the Sanitary Corps and was in charge of research on dehydration of foods.

In addition to his catholicity of research interests and writings, Dean Prescott organized the first Food Technology Conference which was held at M.I.T. in 1937 and a similar conference, also at M.I.T., in 1939. From these, in 1939, arose the Institute of Food Technologists of which he is considered the founding father.

He served as the founding chairman of the Board of Governors of The Refrigeration Research Foundation from its beginnings in 1943 until his death.

Dr. Prescott received many awards and honors for his pioneering work in Food Technology including two Honorary Doctorate degrees, one from Bates College and the other from Lehigh University. He received the Nicholas Appert Award and the Babcock-Hart Award of the Institute of Food Technologists and served as president of the Institute of Food Technologists and the American Society of Bacteriologists.

In addition to the books mentioned earlier, he wrote a history of M.I.T., *When M.I.T. Was Boston Tech*, and served as one of the editors of *Food Research* from its establishment in 1935 until 1952.

SAMUEL A. GOLDBLITH

PRESCOTT AWARD FOR RESEARCH

See Awards.

PRETZELS

Pretzels or Bretzels are a traditional German snack food generally consumed with beer. Today, pretzels are eaten by themselves or with beer, wine, soft drinks, cheese, or other foods. The name "pretzel" is derived from the diminutive of the Latin "brachium," arm (bracelet).

Pretzels are characterized by a crisp, brittle texture; a pleasant, cracker-like taste which is modified by the glutinous lye-treated crust; and by a brown, glossy surface color. As with soda crackers, salt is sprinkled onto the dough just prior to baking; and salt particles protrude from the surface of the pretzels.

Pretzels are produced in the well-known shape of a twisted (two looped) ring. The most common dimensions are: overall length—7 cm; width—5 cm; height—0.5 cm; diameter of the rounded strands forming the loops—4 mm. The weight of a pretzel is about 5.4 gm for the most common size and 3.3 gm for the "very thins." Pretzels are also made in the form of rings and in the form of thin or thick rods. The typical pretzel with a moisture content of about 4% is rather hard, and a method for the production of such hard pretzels is described below. However, soft pretzels, much larger than the hard pretzels and with a higher moisture content, are also available. Hard pretzels have a shelf-life as long as that of crackers or cookies, while soft pretzels are as perishable as rolls.

Production

The most important ingredient is flour. A soft wheat flour with a protein content of 8.5-9.5% and an ash content of 0.35-0.45% is suitable.

A basic formula for pretzel doughs is as follows:

	(Lb)
Flour	100
Shortening, vegetable	2-3
Corn syrup	3-4
Yeast, compressed	0.5
Water	variable

Pretzel doughs are usually mixed in horizontal, high speed mixers as they are common in the baking industry. However, absorption is kept low (about 40-45%) so that the doughs are quite stiff; and they are undermixed compared to a well-developed bread dough. A desirable dough temperature out of the mixer is 80°-90°F, but temperatures up to 95°F can readily be tolerated because the small size of the pretzels prevents heat retention and heat buildup. The doughs are immediately transferred to the hoppers of the forming or die cutting equipment.

Traditionally, all pretzels were made by rolling and tying of the twisted dough piece. But today most pretzels are made by (wire cutting) extrusion machines. From the cutting or forming equipment, the pretzels travel on a wire mesh belt to the cooker. The time spent on the belt (a short fermentation or rest period) may vary considerably. Generally, it is of the order of several minutes. The pretzels pass a hot alkaline bath on the wire mesh belt. The alkaline solution may be prepared with sodium carbonate, but sodium hydroxide is commonly used. The hot solution has a concentration of 0.5-1% NaOH. The dimensions of the bath are such that a cooking time from 10 to 20 sec (usually about 15 sec) results. Following the cook and before the pretzels enter the baking oven, coarse salt is sprinkled over the surface of the pretzels where it adheres to the tacky surface.

The pretzels are baked in gas fired ovens at 350°-550°F for 4-8 min to a moisture content of 12-18%, and then kiln dried or oven dried for 20-40 min at 200°-300°F. Pretzels may be packaged in trays, boxes, or bags protected with glassine, cellophane, or polyethylene combinations.

Composition

The chemical composition of pretzels from six American manufacturers was as follows:

	(%)	(Median)
Moisture	3.5-4.8	4.1
Nitrogen (dry basis)	1.7-2.1	1.8
Salt (dry basis)	2.8-6.7	4.5

GERALD REED

Reference

REISMAN, H. 1969. Modern methods of pretzel production. Proc. 44th Ann. Conf. Biscuit Cracker Manufacturers Assoc.

Cross-reference: *Biscuit and Cracker Technology.*

PROTEIN, NEW SOURCES

Of all the essential nutrients required by man, protein is without a doubt the most precious. First, because it is required in the largest quantity (calories are not a specific nutrient in terms of unique chemical structure). Secondly, protein is invariably the most expensive nutrient because it can be and often is the most limiting nutrient, either in terms of human requirements or "commercial" availability or both. Protein malnutrition or protein-calorie malnutrition in varying degrees, affects $2/3$ of the world's population.

Protein is common to all living cells and therefore there are many actual and potential sources of protein. Cultural factors have caused certain protein sources to be favored as food in different parts of the world and, whereas technological progress has sophisticated the production and marketing of these protein sources, it has also fostered the exploration and exploitation of new (not formerly used by man as food) protein sources. The new proteins are really not new; they were a part of nature all the while. Some of the proteins are considered "unconventional" simply because there is no recorded history of extensive prior use by man. The irony is that there are many existing uses by man of analogous protein sources which we often overlook. Single-cell protein in the form of bacteria is certainly not dissimilar from the bacterial protein of fermented dairy products such as yogurt, rich in a particular strain of lactobacillus. Fish protein meal or concentrate is certainly not dissimilar from the protein of whole sun-dried fish, as eaten by early man and by man today in Asia, or from the protein of sardines found in developed countries.

What is really new is the opportunity to economically manipulate the quantity, quality, and wholesomeness of the emerging protein sources.

New Proteins: Priority for Development Based on Closing the Protein Gap

The report of the Advisory Committee on the Application of Science and Technology to Development (1968) made to the Economic and Social Council of the United Nations identified as new sources of protein (primarily as supplementary sources of high quality protein): (a) oilseeds and oilseed protein concentrates, (b) fish protein concentrate, (c) synthetic amino acids and other nutrients, and (d) single-cell protein and leaf protein.

The report recognized the potential of each of the above categories of new protein and urged research emphasis in the above listed order of priority. These priorities were based upon (a) the relative availability of the new protein, and (b) the conceivable lag time needed to evolve an economically feasible processing technology—for example, the shifting and upgrading of oilseed meals and fish meals from animal feed to human food applications; and the continuous production of protein without necessarily resorting to agricultural land as is possible with single-cell protein and amino acid production.

What also must not be overlooked is the continued improvement in nutritional quality and/or yield provided by breeding. The new variations of human grade protein includes (a) high lysine corn, (b) I-R-8 rice, and (c) glandless cottonseed.

TABLE P-6

NUTRITIONAL SCORE SHEET OF SELECTED PROTEINS

	Protein (Gm/100)	Chemical Score	Limiting Amino Acid	Physiological Problem
Maize	9.5	41	Lysine	
Opaque 2	11.6	48	Isoleucine (?)[1]	None
Millet	9.7	53	Lysine	Fiber
Rice				None
IR-8	7.3	56	Isoleucine (?)	
(Milled polished)	6.7	56	Lysine	
Sorghum	10.1	31	Lysine	Fiber
Wheat (whole)	12.2	44	Lysine	
Potato	2.0	34	S–c[2]	
Groundnut (peanut)	25.6	43	S–c	Aflatoxin
Soybean (seed)	38.0	47	S–c	Flatulence
Coconut	6.6	55	Lysine	Fiber
Cottonseed	20.2	50	Isoleucine (?)	Gossypol
Palm kernel	6.6	58	Isoleucine	?
Safflower	12.6	42	S–c	
Sesame	18.1	42	Lysine	Fiber and oxalate
Sunflower (seed)	12.6	56	Lysine	Fiber
Whole egg	12.4	100	none	
Cow's milk (whole)	3.5	60	S–c	
Casein	13.3	58	S–c	
Human milk	1.2	53	S–c	
Brewers' yeast	38.8	45	S–c	Nucleic acid
Yeast algae:				
(gqs process)	70.5	45	S–c	Nucleic acid
(paraffin process)	65.0	53	S–c	Nucleic acid
Spirulina maxima				
dried	62.0	32	S–c	Chitin
Chlorella	?	49	S–c	Chitin

SOURCE: FAO Report *24* (1970).

[1] Actual investigations show lysine to be limiting.
[2] S–c indicates sulphur-containing amino acids, methionine, cystine, cysteine.

New Protein Based on Nutrition and Food Science Principles

What should not escape us is that there is no protein which can be considered a panacea. The goal must be "optimized" protein sources in terms of nutritional quality, functional properties, and cost capable of being utilized in acceptable and familiar, as well as convenient, food forms. The greatest potential results in ascertaining suitable protein combinations to meet a given nutritional and organoleptic objective. It is becoming increasingly evident that nutritional factors will be the first criteria for consideration because nutritional considerations will more often than not be the purpose for developing an interest in the proteins in question. If found acceptable in terms of functional and organoleptic properties, nutritional factors will affect labelling consideration, and nutritional deterioration may often override organoleptic deterioration in determining packaging as well as shelf-life.

A review of 164 patents issued in the field of Protein Food Supplements (Noyes 1969) reveals that the technology is available to evolve wholesome functional and organoleptically practical approaches for enhancing the utilization of low cost protein sources in nutritionally balanced protein foods.

It is not the intent here to de-emphasize the importance of particular functional properties such as solubility, in product development. However, until a uniform set of procedures are established for the functional properties of proteins, the use of selected proteins will somewhat depend on art, ingenuity, and serendipity. Meanwhile, a greater understanding of the nature of proteins at the molecular level is emerging that should permit the necessary undertaking to important breakthroughs in this area.

Table P-6 is a Nutritional Score Sheet for a cross-section of the new proteins and sources as compared to several accepted food protein sources.

In general, a protein content below 10% limits the use of that protein as an adequate single source of protein in the diet.

But, there are advantages to the blending of higher protein content foods with lower protein content foods differing in their limiting amino acids (as we unconsciously do in our everyday diet) to obtain higher protein quantity and quality. This "complementation" is the principle of Incaparina, a blend of cereal corn (58%) with oilseed cottonseed (38%) and Torula yeast (3%) with additional lysine, calcium carbonate, and vitamins (1%); or the protein mixture CSM that is gelatinized, processed corn meal (68%); toasted, defatted soy flour (25%) regular; and nonfat dry milk (5%); plus minerals and vitamins.

Very interesting products can be made from these mixtures and such products are currently emerging in the market place.

The chemical (protein) score is a relative (calculated) guide to the quality of the new protein sources. Since casein is most often used as the reference protein in biological evaluations, it can be used to qualitatively judge the potential of the other protein sources listed in Table P-6.

The limiting amino acid (relative to the profile of whole egg) dictates the chemical score. However, knowing the limiting amino acid can assist a food technologist to make the proper choices amongst the new proteins for purposes of complementation or for purposes of fortification with amino acid(s). A. E. Bender (1968) provides an example formulation of a protein mix and the calculation of the resultant chemical score.

The listing of the limiting amino acids also provides an additional piece of information and that is that certain particular essential amino acids are invariably the limiting amino acids. It would seem that a fingerprint of the values for the amino acids, lysine, threonine, methionine plus cystine and tryptophan would be sufficient to predict chemical score without knowing the remainder of the profile. This observation has not been verified but nevertheless the food technologist should be on the lookout for these five amino acids.

Finally, Table P-6 provides a column indicating the single most pressing problem hampering processing and/or extensive use of the protein in product development. Some of the factors can be controlled by breeding or processing or good sanitary practices. Obviously, once the limiting problem is controlled, the second limiting problem will become evident. In many instances this problem will be one of flavor and/or solubility. Frequently the isolation of the protein in purer form results in a blander product; however, solubility and other physical properties may remain the same. A better understanding of the structure of the protein as well as its water-protein relationship (Karmas and DiMarco 1970) can provide insight as to whether the functional properties of the protein should be further modified or whether further processing, such as spinning, capitalizing on the structure, should be attempted. These trade-offs are not simple to make and cost, in view of the projected application as well as the intended market, may often be the deciding factor at this stage.

The New Protein in Review

Cereals.—For an overall review of this topic the reader is urged to consult the proceedings of a symposium sponsored by The American Association of Cereal Chemists on protein enriched cereal foods held in 1958.

Wheat is a staple but its fortification with synthetic lysine or its complementation with low levels (circa 5%) of fish protein concentrate or other lysine-rich protein is now occurring and the scale of this approach will very likely increase.

Rice has benefited substantially from breeding. The new IR-8 strain has increased yield substantially because of a hardier stalk. Breeding for nutritional improvements is still being attempted. Meanwhile, fortification of rice with lysine and threonine is being attempted in Thailand (Rosenfield 1971). The fortification vehicle is a synthetic rice kernel produced by the Ajinomoto Company of Japan. The wheat and rice utilized in school feeding programs in Japan is fortified with lysine.

Corn fortification by means of complementation has been underway in Central America since 1957 in the form of Incaparina. The technology for the fortification of corn masa with lysine and tryptophan or a protein source of tryptophan has recently been completed (Bressani and Lachance 1970) and a model demonstration at the community level in Guatemala was initiated in the spring of 1972.

Continued progress is being made in the breeding of sorghum and millet for increased yield; however, no fortification of these grains has been undertaken. Barley and oats have not been, as yet, considered in the search for "new" protein sources.

Oilseeds.—Soybeans and particularly the soybean flours are protein rich (average protein content of 42%) and are the oilseed produced in the largest quantity. However, the production is limited, for the most part, to the United States and China. It is increasingly difficult, if not erroneous, to consider soy protein unconventional. With over 15 million pounds of soy protein isolate being used annually in the United States for food use, this protein is established. Its use as an extender of animal protein is increasing and will continue to do so. The use of soy flour to complement other cereal proteins has been mentioned previously. For an excellent review, see DeMeyer (1970). This application is promising, particularly for the nutritional enhancement of snack foods.

Cottonseed is second only to soybean in world production and has the distinct advantage of being native to several less developed countries as well as the United States and USSR. Breeding research has resulted in an excellent glandless cottonseed, the flour of which is nearly white and easily incorporated into puddings, soups, and gravies. Glandless cottonseed is being grown only in the United States and is not as resistant to insect pests as the glanded variety containing the polyphenol gossypol which is a natural insecticide. New air classification (liquid cyclone) (Martinez 1969) methods have recently evolved which permits a low gossypol product to be produced at a lower cost from glanded cottonseed as compared to the cost of changeover to glandless cottonseed. Although the flour from this new process is off-white, it reverts in color with heating and its use at high levels in food systems may be thwarted. There probably is room for both products since they are nutritionally equal and good complementation products with cereals such as corn especially if additional lysine is provided. Extensive experience exists with the nutritional virtues of cottonseed in Incaparina and what is needed is the application of a sophisticated food technology to this type of ingredient for fine products to evolve. For a further discussion of this topic, see Fisher (1969).

Peanut protein is deficient in three amino acids—lysine, methionine and threonine—as compared to soybean which is deficient principally in methionine and is a good source of lysine. Peanut protein cannot be recommended unless it is supplemented with amino acids and/or other quality sources of protein (Altschul 1967). A peanut butter sandwich is limiting in lysine unless the bread has been fortified with lysine or additional milk protein such as lactalbumin.

The remaining oilseeds of significance are sunflower, coconut, and sesame. Each is pretty much indigenous to a different part of the world (Milner 1966) and meals or protein concentrates from these sources are compromised by the high level of concomitant indigestible fiber which exerts a cathartic effect, in vivo, limiting the benefits of the quality protein. A combined chemical and enzymatic process evolved at Rutgers (Molina and Lachance 1973) for coconut may also be applicable to the other two oilseeds. What effect the process would also have on lowering the oxalate levels of sesame is completely unknown and cannot be speculated.

Fish Protein.—The state of the art of fish protein concentrate (FPC) has been discussed in a series of publications in Food Technology beginning in July 1967.[1] The Viobin process is well described by Robert Noyes (1969) and the overall status of FPC was the topic of a conference held in Ottawa, Canada in 1967 and published as Canadian Fisheries Report 10, Department of Fisheries.

A significant and recent entry into the field of new protein from fish is the ASTRA product labelled "Eviscerated Fish Protein" which is processed at sea by ASTRA, a Swedish concern, on a modified whaler. The fact that the fish is eviscerated does not restrict its sale in the United States to specific limits which have been established by the FDA for human grade FPC. Eviscerated Fish Protein is a high quality product which is being incorporated into cereal-based foods as a source of lysine to upgrade protein quality. This work is being conducted by the Nabisco Co. under the auspices of a joint venture with ASTRA of Sweden. Should Eviscerated Fish Protein prove successful on an experimental basis, its availability will be limited by the production capacity of the existing manufacturing ship. For extensive details concerning process, nutritive value, cost, and toxicity, the reader is urged to consult Finch (1970).

Single-Cell Protein.—The principle new protein sources, under the label SCP, are yeast, fungi, algae, and bacteria. For an extensive discussion of this topic, the reader is referred to Mateles and Tannenbaum (1968). The hydrocarbon fermentation of bacteria by the Esso process and yeast by the British Petroleum process are described in considerable detail by Robert Noyes (1969). Shacklady (1970) of British Petroleum described the animal nutrition experiments with hydrocarbon-grown yeast at a 1969 symposium. Meanwhile, it is known that the Esso/Nestlé bacterial product has been evaluated as a human food in children; however, the results have not been published.

Algae, bacteria, and yeasts as food or feed is the subject of a 1970 review by Lipinsky and Litchfield (1970).

For a treatise on the use of fungi, especially its potential in the conversion of food plant waste to new protein, the reader is urged to read The Use of Fungi as Food in Food Processing (Gray 1970). The use of fungi as human food is very old but the human use of fungi imperfecti fermented on food plant waste will require extensive toxicological and nutritional studies. In any event, the very promising qualities of the new protein source is such that

---

[1] The articles appeared in Food Technology as follows: Parts 1-3, July 1967; Part 4, August 1967; Part 5, September 1967; Part 6, December 1967; Part 7, June 1968; Part 8, February 1969; Part 9, January 1970; Part 10, August 1970; Part 11, October 1970.

its use in human food applications may be realized in less than a decade.

Attention should also be given to single-cell protein from cellulosic wastes as described by Han *et al.* (1971).

Leaf Protein.—Few investigators other than Pirie (1966, 1970) at Rothamsted Experimental Station in England have prepared protein concentrates by pulping young leaves and separating a liquid fraction containing protein by filtering or centrifuging out of the residue. The protein concentrate is then dried by spray drying or freeze drying. The potential of this protein has often been criticized but Pirie (1970) defends the potential of this source of protein. It has been fed to infants and children and found to approach soy protein in quality. It is important to realize that these materials flourish in wet tropics and that the extraction procedure is feasible at the village level.

Synthetic Proteins.—In 1963, it was suggested (Lachance and Vanderveen 1963) that a space exploration ration might be fabricated to meet the nutritional requirements of individual astronauts, wherein the protein would be a polymerized profile of essential amino acids, the dispensable nitrogen being derived from amide fats and other sources. In the search for edible food coatings, a contract with Southwest Research Laboratories was initiated and monitored by the author which resulted in prototype films derived from polymerized amino acids (Martin 1965). This new protein is now being evaluated as a nonallergenic synthetic skin in burn situations. The aforementioned concept for synthetic protein is somewhat different from the synthesis of protenoids (Fox and Krampitz 1964; Mathews and Moser 1967) in studies pertaining to the origin of life. More recently, complete enzymes and hormones have been synthesized (Moore *et al.* 1968; Gutte and Merrifield 1969; Denkewalter and Hirschmann 1969).

Meanwhile, innumerable investigators have fed amino acid mixtures to many species of animals as well as to humans in both normal and clinical situations.

As McPherson (1970) states, the most efficient route to high quality protein is the route of total synthesis and he believes it may become a reality in a generation.

Conclusion

In the final analysis, a "new protein" can be a fortified natural protein, a combination of different protein sources which complement each other nutritionally, or protein synthesized to match the nutritional individuality of man. The "new protein" then, is the old protein of whatever origin, optimized to guarantee better health and to conserve the most critical and expensive resource (Lachance 1970).

PAUL A. LACHANCE

References

ADVISORY COMMITTEE ON APPLICATIONS OF SCIENCE AND TECHNOLOGY TO DEVELOPMENT. 1968. Feeding the Expanding World Population: International Action to Avert the Impending Protein Crisis. Economic and Social Council, United Nations, New York.

ALTSCHUL, A. M. 1967. Food proteins: New sources from seeds. Science *158*, 221–226.

BENDER, A. E. 1973. Nutrition and Dietetic Foods. Chemical Publishing Co., New York.

BRESSANI, R., and LACHANCE, P. A. 1970. A practical approach to the lysine and tryptophan supplementation of lime-treated corn. AID/csd 2500.

DeMEYER, E. W. 1970. Soya protein isolates for food. *In* Proteins as Human Foods. R. A. Laurie (Editor). Avi Publishing Co., Westport, Conn.

DENKEWALTER, R. G., and HIRSCHMANN, R. 1969. Studies on the total synthesis of an enzyme. J. Am. Chem. Soc. *91*, 502–508.

FINCH, R. 1970. Fish protein in human foods. *In* CRC Critical Reviews in Food Technology, Vol. 1, No. 4. T. E. Furia (Editor). Chemical Rubber Co., Cleveland.

FISHER, C. H. 1969. Proceedings of the Conference on Protein-Rich Food Products from Oilseeds. USDA Agr. Res. Serv. Rept. *72-71*.

FOX, S. W., and KRAMPITZ, G. 1964. Catalytic decomposition of glucose in aqueous solution by thermal protenoids. Nature *203*, 1362–1364.

GRAY, W. D. 1970. The use of fungi as food in food processing. *In* CRC Critical Reviews in Food Technology, Vol. 1, No. 2. T. E. Furia (Editor). Chemical Rubber Co., Cleveland.

GUTTE, B., and MERRIFIELD, R. B. 1969. The total synthesis of an enzyme with ribonucleose A activity. J. Am. Chem. Soc. *91*, 501–502.

HAN, Y. W., DUNLAP, C. E., and CALLIHAN, C. D. 1971. Single cell protein from cellulose wastes. Food Technol. *25*, 31–32.

KARMAS, E., and DiMARCO, G. R. 1970. Dehydration thermophiles of amino acids and proteins. J. Food Sci. *35*, 615.

LACHANCE, P. A. 1970. The new proteins. Food Technol. *24*, 33–34.

LACHANCE, P. A., and VANDERVEEN, J. E. 1963. Problems in space foods and nutrition: Foods for extended space travel and habitation. Food Technol. *17*, 59–62.

LIPINSKI, E. W., and LITCHFIELD, J. H. 1970. Bacteria and yeasts as food or feed. *In* CRC Critical Reviews in Food Technology, Vol. 1, No. 4. T. E. Furia (Editor). Chemical Rubber Co., Cleveland.

MARTIN, E. C. 1965. Production of edible polymers from food monomers for use in packaging space rations.   Final Rept. NASA Contract *NAS-9-3162*, Southeast Research Institute, San Antonio, Texas.

MARTINEZ, W. H.   1969.   Personal communication.   USDA Southern Regional Res. Develop. Div., New Orleans.

McPHERSON, A. T.   1970.   Protein from synthetic ammonia—routes for producing high quality protein for human consumption.   Indian J. Nutr. Dietet. 7, 171–195.

MATELES, R. I., and TANNENBAUM, S. R. 1968.   Single Cell Protein.   MIT Press, Cambridge, Mass.

MATHEWS, C. N., and MOSER, R. E.   1967.   Peptide synthesis from hydrogen cyanide and water. Nature *215*, 1230–1234.

MILNER, M.   1966.   General outlook for seed protein concentrates.   Advan. Chem. No. 57, 57–62.

MOLINA, M., and LACHANCE, P. A.   1973. Protein extraction of defatted coconut flour. J. Food Sci. *38*, 607.

MOORE, G. E., HOSENBUSCH, P., GARNER, R. E., and BURNS, A. A.   1968.   A pilot plant for mammalian cell culture.   Biotechnol. Bioeng. *10*, 625–640.

NOYES, R.   1969.   Protein food supplements. *In* Food Processing Review No. 3.   Noyes Development Corp., Park Ridge, N.J.

PIRIE, N. W.   1966.   Leaf protein as food.   Science *152*, 1701–1705.

PIRIE, N. W.   1970.   Ways of meeting the world's protein needs.   *In* Proteins as Human Food. R. A. Laurie (Editor).   Avi Publishing Co., Westport, Conn.

PRESIDENT'S SCIENCE ADVISORY COMMITTEE.   1967.   The World Food Problem, Vol. II. Government Printing Office, Washington, D.C.

ROSENFIELD, D.   1971.   Current amino acid fortification program.   *In* Amino Acid Fortification of Protein Foods.   N. Scrimshaw and A. Altschul (Editors).   MIT Press, Cambridge, Mass.

SHACKLADY, C. A.   1970.   Hydrocarbon-grown yeast in nutrition.   *In* Proteins as Human Food. R. A. Laurie (Editor).   Avi Publishing Company, Westport, Conn.

PAUL A. LACHANCE

Cross-references: *Protein   Foods   from   Plant Sources; Yeasts.*

PROTEIN FOODS FROM PLANT SOURCES

Background

Plant proteins commonly utilized as food are derived from cereals that contain from 7 to 15% protein and from seeds, often the so-called oilseeds, that may contain up to 42% protein, as in soybeans. Most legumes and oilseeds contain less than 40% protein with the protein usually, but not always, in the 20–30% range.

Proteins are composed of combinations of 20–25 different amino acids.   Not all of these can be synthesized *in vivo* by man.   These that cannot, the so-called "essential" amino acids, must be supplied by the diet.   For man, the essential amino acids are isoleucine, leucine, lysine, methionine, phenylalanine, threonine, and tryptophan.   Valine and histidine are essential amino acids for the infant, but not the adult.   Cystine a nonessential amino acid can replace about 80–90% of the requirement for methionine.

The requirements for essential amino acids are not constant throughout life, but vary from infancy through adulthood.   These requirements are dependent upon the changing demand for protein. It has been estimated that the lysine requirement for an infant is 1350 mg per day.   This compares with an estimated requirement of 1600 mg per day for a 9–12 yr-old boy and with 800 mg per day for an average male adult.   The demand for lysine (i.e., protein) is greatest during the growth stage and the infant who needs almost 70% more lysine than an adult must obtain this from less than a 1000 cal per day dietary intake. This illustrates the importance for infants of protein containing adequate amounts of all the essential amino acids.

Since proteins vary in their amino acid composition, some dietary proteins will meet man's requirements to a greater degree than others.   Animal protein—i.e., meat, fish, eggs, milk—are particularly well utilized since their essential amino acid composition conforms closely to the needs of man. On the other hand, cereal proteins are low in some of the essential amino acids.   Wheat is low in lysine; corn in lysine and tryptophan; rice in lysine and possibly threonine.   Seed proteins are low in the sulfur-containing amino acids methionine and cystine but usually contain satisfactory concentrations of lysine.

Although the biological value (i.e., utilizability) of animal protein is greater than that of plant protein, plant sources contribute about 70% of the world's protein supply.   Grains alone account for 50% of the world's protein production.

Some 2,000,000,000 people world-wide depend on cereal grains for most of their calories and protein.   The *Third World Food Survey*, FAO, Rome, reported that approximately 900,000,000 people whose daily dietary intake averaged about 3000 cal consumed 90 gm of total protein, 44 gm of which were animal protein.   In contrast, more than 2 billion people whose daily dietary intake averaged less than 2200 cal consumed 58 gm of total protein, only 9 gm of which are derived from animal sources.   Although, the total protein intake on a 2200-cal diet may be generally sufficient for a healthy adult, the utilizable amounts of this plant protein leaves much to be desired, particularly if it is destined to meet the needs of the most vulnerable groups—infants, preschoolers, and women during pregnancy and lactation.

Table P-7 lists the amino acid scores for a number of proteins present in cereals, legumes, and oilseeds. Each score is a comparison of the amount of that amino acid in the plant protein with the amount of that same amino acid in a whole hen's egg which serves as the reference protein. The units of comparison are milligrams of essential amino acid per gram of total essential amino acids. Each score is expressed as a percentage. The use of whole hen's egg as a reference protein is based on FAO recommendations. Egg protein has an essential amino acid pattern that makes the protein completely utilizable.

Increasing Protein Impact of Plant Foods

From the data in Table P-7, it can be seen that for diets where cereals are the predominant source of calories some of the essential amino acid concentrations are low. The utilizability of the protein in these diets is therefore limited by the essential amino acid in least supply. One method of improving the utilizability of the protein in the cereal is to increase the concentration of the deficient amino acid(s) by adding the amino acid(s) in pure form or a protein concentrate that has an excess of the desired amino acid(s). A further possibility is to breed new cereal varieties whose proteins may have a more desirable amino acid pattern. These approaches are being tried with varying degrees of success.

Fortification with Amino Acids.—Fortification with the synthetic amino acids that are commonly low in cereals—lysine, tryptophan, threonine, and methionine—presupposes that the free amino acids are available at competitive prices. Costs of synthetic amino acids have been dropping and as the use of fortification spreads, even lower prices can be expected. Currently, lysine is available at approximately $1.00 per lb. At this price, the cost of wheat flour fortification with lysine is about 6% of the cost of the flour. Food grade methionine costs about the same as lysine. Tryptophan and threonine are considerably more expensive. However, because of the small amounts needed, threonine and tryptophan fortification would be feasible if their respective prices dropped to $3.00 and $5.00 per lb.

Fortification with amino acids must be carried out during processing or milling. This limits, to a degree, the number of people that can benefit from fortification. Amino acid fortification of home-grown crops by a subsistence farmer is most unlikely since the concept of fortification and its value is so abstract. It would require an extraordinarily effective nutrition education campaign to establish the rationale for fortification.

Fortification of cereals with synthetic amino acids is currently being evaluated under sponsorship of the Agency for International Development (a) in Tunisia where lysine plus minerals and vitamins are being added to wheat flour, (b) in Thailand where synthetic rice granules containing lysine and threonine as well as minerals and vitamins are being added to rice during the milling process at local village mills; and (c) in Guatemala where lysine, a mineral-vitamin mix, and soy flour (which serves as a source of lysine and tryptophan) are added to corn during the preparation of corn meal from whole corn, again at the local village mill.

Fortification with amino acids on a larger scale is also being carried out. Bread made from lysine-fortified wheat flour has been produced in government-owned bakeries in India (lysine has recently been replaced by protein concentrates). U.S. relief shipments of bulgur, a whole kernel form of wheat, to Nigeria have been fortified with lysine and a similarly fortified bulgur has been sent to India for incorporation into BalAhar, a wheat-based food mixture used for child feeding and distributed to school children. Fortification with amino acids is widespread in Japan where lysine-fortified foods are marketed and where lysine-fortified bread is distributed through the school lunch program.

Fortification with Protein Concentrates.—A second approach to improving cereal protein value is to supplement wheat, corn or rice with oilseed proteins. Incaparina, a mixture of corn and cottonseed protein containing 26% protein, was developed and distributed in Guatemala and other Latin American countries by INCAP. In Colombia, Quaker Oats is marketing a new Incaparina whose composition is approximately 70% rice flour and 30% soy flour and contains an appropriate mix of minerals and vitamins. This "Incaparina Blanca" follows in the footsteps of another product, Colombhirina, produced by Molimos Santa Rita Ltd., Cali, Columbia of almost identical composition. Both contain about 18% protein. "Duryea" is another protein-fortified product sold in Columbia. It contains 28% protein derived from corn, soy, opaque-2 corn, and nonfat dried milk solids plus a vitamin and mineral mix.

The U.S. Government has supplied food relief shipments that are essentially high protein-vegetable mixtures. CSM, a 20% protein mixture containing 70% gelatinized corn, 25% soy, and 5% nonfat dry milk solids plus vitamins and minerals has been

TABLE P-7

AMINO ACID SCORES

	Isoleu-cine	Leu-cine	Ly-sine	Methi-onine	Methi-onine and Cystine	Phenyl-alanine	Tyro-sine	Thre-onine	Tryp-tophan	Valine	% Protein
Wheat	78	115	68	73	113	116	110	87	104	93	12.2
Rice	77	123	80	99	82	117	112	100	104	101	7.5
Corn	71	182	53	78	80	105	108	90	56	85	9.5
Corn (Opaque-2)	68	133	91	63	79	105	107	90	113	94	11.6
Sorghum	78	198	42	58	70	108	85	73	100	92	10.1
Millet	78	135	67	98	110	102	98	93	153	95	9.7
Rye	85	113	86	75	99	121	75	106	75	108	11.0
Barley	78	108	78	78	101	126	107	93	137	100	11.0
Oats	79	114	80	75	110	117	108	89	110	98	13.0
Soy (cake)	91	109	117	56	69	105	113	102	119	89	46.0
Cottonseed (cake)	73	102	100	69	82	135	110	99	139	103	27.4
Sunflower (cake)	92	103	89	95	109	119	89	107	109	100	40.3
Sesame (full fat)	81	113	62	133	124	112	111	102	126	94	10.9
Safflower (full fat)	105	117	82	50	71	103	97	100	100	114	12.6
Mung Bean (full fat)	79	114	187	25	33	120	87	94	71	82	23.9
Peanut (full fat)	81	114	87	59	69	134	148	80	103	92	25.6

widely distributed. Over 2.6 billion pounds have been supplied worldwide. The use of bread and bread-like products as a vehicle for incorporating high-protein flours derived from soy, chick-pea, broad bean, etc., is receiving increasing attention. Wheat is unique among the cereals in that it yields a dough that can expand when leavening agents are added. The unique properties of wheat gluten proteins are responsible for this feature of wheat flour. The wheat gluten provides the structure responsible for gas retention and makes production of light leavened products of desirable texture possible. When high-protein flours derived by adding legumes or oilseeds at more than the 5% level to wheat flour, the dough-making properties characteristic of such flour are altered and loaf volume, texture, and appearance of the final bread product are inferior.

It has recently been shown that in the presence of dough conditioners such as sodium stearoyl-2-lactylate, 10–20% of these high-protein sources can be incorporated into wheat flour to produce high-protein breads of good acceptability with little if any modification of baking techniques. A particularly useful blend is a wheat flour that contains about 10–15% fat-free soy flour (50% protein).

Such high protein breads can contribute significantly to the daily protein intake and protein utilizability in the urban areas in developing countries.

Seed Proteins in Protein Foods

To date, seed proteins, after oil extraction, have been used primarily as animal feed. A more efficient utilization of this protein is to by-pass the animal converter and utilize these seed proteins directly. A barrier to acceptability has been poor flavor, poor digestibility, and in some instances excess fiber. These characteristics can be overcome.

Soybeans have received the most study and a wide range of soy-derived products have become available for human consumption. Defatted soy flour (50% protein) remaining after solvent extraction of the oil can be heat-treated to destroy toxic factors such as trypsin inhibitors and hemaglutinins and can then be incorporated into breads, meats, and cereal products as described. A more desirable additive is a 70% soy protein concentrate that can be prepared by extraction of soluble carbohydrates in addition to the oil. The soybean concentrate is rather bland in flavor and free of flatulence-producing carbohydrates such as stachyose. A soy protein isolate containing over 90% protein is also available. This latter product can be spun into edible fibers and used to prepare textured meat-like products that can be appropriately flavored to resemble products derived from beef, pork, chicken, etc.

Attempts have also been made to introduce "soy milk" as a substitute for cow's milk. This product can be produced by soaking soybeans, then grinding to a desired mesh size at a slightly alkaline pH with boiling water. The slurry can then be filtered to yield a soy milk. Soy milk is not a popular beverage per se but it has been used in the production of other soy-based drinks. These beverages are an example of a new class of protein foods, still in the evolutionary stage, that eventually may combine the enjoyment of a flavorful, refreshing soft drink with the nutritive value of a glass of milk. The goal of protein beverage research is to produce a clear, carbonated protein beverage that will be readily accepted as a "soft" drink.

Cottonseed is an alternate protein source that has received some attention. However, cottonseeds possess pigment glands that contain gossypol, a naturally-occurring toxicant. Recently, an extraction process has been developed to remove gossypol without adversely affecting flavor or otherwise creating a nonacceptable product when protein concentrates derived from cottonseed are incorporated into foods. Perhaps more promising is the discovery of a glandless variety of cottonseed which is gossypol-free and requires relatively little processing prior to utilization as a food additive. Before the glandless cotton variety is accepted, problems of yield and quality of cotton lint must be overcome. Expert opinion estimates that within a decade glandless cotton will be in world-wide use.

There is little doubt that protein derived from sunflower, rapeseed, coconut, peanut, safflower, and sesame will eventually find a place in providing protein for human consumption. Which of these protein sources will prove most useful in any given circumstance will be a function of the regional agricultural practices and food habits.

Problems and Potential of Plant Breeding

Breeding nutritionally improved varieties of cereals offers an exciting prospect for enhancing the protein quality of diets. Research is underway to develop wheat, rice, corn, sorghum, and millet varieties that have an increased protein content and/or an improved balance of essential amino acids. To achieve widespread use of improved varieties, yield, acceptability, and processing qualities must be maintained. This approach, if suc-

cessful, can reach those hardest to reach—these are the very poor in rural areas who may exist outside of a money economy and a marketing system, who cannot purchase processed foods, but perhaps grow improved varieties of better protein quality if seeds are made available.

Corn is a prime example of what may be accomplished by plant breeders. In 1964, Mertz and associates (1966) at Purdue reported that a previously identified corn mutant designated as opaque-2 had a vastly superior essential amino acid profile as compared to ordinary corn (Table P-7). Ordinary corn is deficient in lysine and tryptophan; opaque-2 corn approaches egg protein in both these categories. However, the varieties of opaque-2 corn currently available have several undesirable features. The yield compared to other corn hybrids is low and the kernels are soft (floury) rather than hard (vitreous). The kernels are also susceptible to insect damage and their appearnace is poor. On-going research promises to correct these faults, and opaque-2 varieties have been reported that apparently have few of these difficulties. Acceptable vitreous varieties of opaque-2 corn are expected to be available within the next 5-10 yr.

The breeding of rice for high protein content is an on-going research activity. The new high-yielding varieties do not appear to be genetically higher in protein quality. However, since the new varieties utilize higher rates of nitrogen fertilizer, the higher yield is accompanied by a higher protein content. The nutritional value of rice is therefore improved simply because of this latter factor. To date there is no positive indication that genetically higher quality (or quantity) protein varieties have been identified.

Wheats that yield 20-25% more protein than current varieties have been identified. This may mean an increase in protein content from about 12% in present varieties to about 15% in the wheats of tomorrow. This increase in quantity is accomplished with little change in the amino acid profile.

High-protein varieties of sorghum and millet have also been identified but changes in protein value have not been documented.

Progress in development of improved cereal varieties is a relatively slow process. The first step is to identify high-protein varieties that hopefully exhibit an improved amino acid profile. These must then be crossed with indigenous varieties that have adapted to local conditions in different world regions. Selected types which combine improved protein quantity and/or biologic value and the characteristics that make for local acceptance in terms of yield, insect and disease resistance, flavor, texture, processing qualities, etc., must be identified. This process of selection must be repeated over and over again until the ideal combination is found. The procedure is slow but the rewards can obviously be great.

The Future

Blended foods such as mixtures of rice and soy flour or corn, soy, and nonfat dried milk are being used today in the developing countries. The use of synthetic amino acids to improve cereal protein quality is gaining acceptability. Cereal varieties combining improved protein quantity and amino acid patterns are emerging as a result of the plant breeders research. The innate deficiencies of plant proteins are disappearing before man's ingenuity. There is every indication that if population growth can be stabilized, man's protein needs will be met by a proper blend of amino acid fortification, seed protein utilization, and the introduction of new cereal varieties with improved protein impact.

DANIEL ROSENFIELD
IRWIN HORNSTEIN

References

AGENCY FOR INTERNATIONAL DEVELOPMENT. 1970. Improving the Nutrient Quality of Cereals. Rept. Workshop on Breeding and Fortification. Agency Intern. Develop., Washington, D.C.

ALTSCHUL, A. M. 1969. Food: proteins for humans. Chem. Eng. News 47, Nov. 24, 68–81.

ALTSCHUL, A. M. 1974. Fortification of foods with amino acids. Nature, 248, 643–646.

ALTSCHUL, A. M., and ROSENFIELD, D. 1970. Protein supplementation: satisfying man's food needs. Progress (Unilever Quar., London) 54, No. 305, 76–84.

LAWRIE, R. A. (Editor). 1970. Proteins as Human Food. Avi Publishing Co., Westport, Conn.

MERTZ, E. T., NELSON, D. E., BATES, L. S., and VERON A. 1966. Better protein Quality in maize. *In* World Protein Resources. A. M. Altschul (Editor). American Chemical Society, Washington, D.C.

MILNER, M. (Editor) 1969. Protein-Enriched Cereal Foods for World Needs. American Association of Cereal Chemists, St. Paul.

ROSENFIELD, D., and STARE, F. J. 1970. The short-term solution to protein malnutrition. Mod. Gov. 11, No. 5, 47–61.

Cross-references: *Proteins, New Sources; Beans; Soybeans.*

Q

QUALITY CONTROL AND STATISTICS

Definition of Quality

In order to control quality one must first be reasonably certain what quality is, in other words what must be controlled. Juran (1962) lists 13 definitions of the word quality. The definition which seems most pertinent is the one called "market place quality." This is: "the degree to which a specific product satisfies the wants of a specific consumer."

Another definition which has some pertinence to the operation of a quality control department in the food industry is "the degree to which a class of product possesses potential satisfaction for people generally." This is frequently called "quality of design."

The third type of quality which is important in this context is "quality of conformance." This is the property of conforming to predetermined specifications. If quality of design is adequate and a product conforms to the specification, then quality itself will be assured.

Scope of Quality Control

In the light of the above definitions, it is evident that the responsibility for quality is a very broad one and all of its aspects are rarely under the control of a single department. Most of these responsibilities have been listed by Kramer and Twigg (1970). Some of these are treated below but for a complete list one should consult the reference.

Specifications

These are generally written by those who developed the product who are rarely in the quality control department. They are usually in research, development, new products department, or the like. Nevertheless, the quality of design is inherent in the specifications, and quality personnel will have a great interest in seeing that these are adequate to ensure a quality product.

Test Procedures

This is another item that comes to the quality department from outside, either a research laboratory or handbooks published by industrial or professional organizations. In any case it will be the responsibility of quality personnel to ensure that a given test is adequate to determine the property desired.

Bacteriological tests require special mention. Statistical methods useful in other types of measurements have been difficult to apply to this area. A complete treatment of those which are applicable as well as techniques of special usefulness in bacteriology is given by Eisenhart and Wilson (1943).

Sampling Procedures

It is the responsibility of any quality department to assure that adequate samples are obtained to represent the lot or batch being tested and to assure that necessary accuracy is obtained in the result. This is covered in some detail by Juran (1962) in Chap. 8, 13, 17, and 18; by Kramer and Twigg (1970) in Chap 14; and by Crow *et al.* (1960).

An efficient way to specify the properties of a sampling plan is to plot the probability of acceptance of a lot against the quality of that lot. Such a graph is called an operating characteristic (OC) curve and a typical example is shown in Fig. Q-1. (Kramer and Twigg 1970).

This figure also shows the vendor's risk, i.e., the risk that a lot of a specified (good)* quality will be rejected; and the consumers risk, i.e., the risk that a lot of a specified (poor) quality will be accepted.

Recording and Reporting

This subject is covered in some detail in Chap. 21 and 22 by Juran (1962) and in Chap. 15 by Kramer and Twigg (1970).

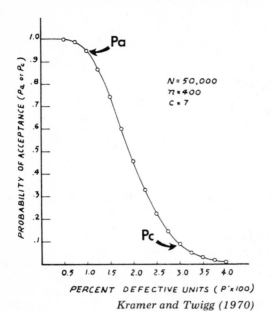

Kramer and Twigg (1970)

FIG. Q-1. OPERATING CHARACTERISTICS (OC) CURVE CHARACTERIZING AN ATTRIBUTES SAMPLING PLAN

The vendor's risk is set for minimum of 95% acceptance (P_a) for lots containing 1% defects ($P' = 0.01$), and consumer's risk is set for maximum of 9% acceptance (P_c) for lots containing 3% defects ($P' = 0.03$).

Of special note in this connection is the use of control charts, one of the primary tools of quality control in American industry. The purpose and value of this tool is well expressed by F. M. Gryna, Jr. in Chap. 13 of Juran (1962) as follows:

"The prime consideration in regulating a process is that a product meet specifications. To achieve this, it is often necessary that the process be uniform. This means that the variability of a product should be due to numerous small chance causes of variation rather than to a few large assignable causes of variation (the distinction between chance and assignable causes of variation is shown in Fig. Q-2). In controlling a process, the objective is to restrict the causes of variation to the chance causes. Assignable causes must be detected and eliminated.

"The key purpose of a control chart is to detect the presence of assignable causes of variation. This is done by taking a series of samples from the process and testing these samples for significant differences from the aggregate of all the samples.

"While this significance testing can be conducted by repeated calculations, in 1924 Dr. W. A. Shewhart devised a graphic method for doing the testing continuously. This

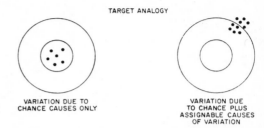

FIG. Q-2. DISTINCTION BETWEEN CHANCE AND ASSIGNABLE CAUSES OF VARIATION

method, known as the Shewhart control chart, or simply as control chart, is thus a graphic continuous test of significance."

Figure Q-3 (Kramer and Twigg 1970) shows an example of a control chart together with its relationship to the normal distribution.

Troubleshooting

Quality personnel are frequently intensely involved in troubleshooting in plants, primarily for the reason they are the first to detect the trouble. In addition, they have at their command tools to detect significant changes when attempts are made to get out of the trouble. Among the tools which may be involved in such troubleshooting are statistical design of experiments, analysis of variance, regression analysis, and other statistical means. These are covered in some detail in Chaps. 13 to 15 of Juran (1962) and in Kramer and Twigg (1970) and Davies (1967).

Regulatory Agencies

Increasing attention is being focused by regulatory agencies of government on such items as food safety, hazards to the consumer, nutrition, and advertising claims. Pressure will be felt throughout the food industry to ensure that testing of products is consistent with the requirements of these agencies. Those who are responsible for quality control will be directly involved. One development which should be especially noted is the program of the FDA to set up cooperative arrangements with food producers which involve satisfying the agency that the producer is doing an adequate job of self-control. Adequate statistical techniques play a large part in the systems required to do this.

Other Responsibilities of Quality Personnel

Because of their unique position in the organization, quality personnel are frequently involved in

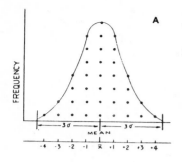

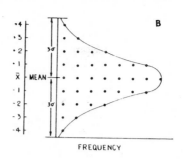

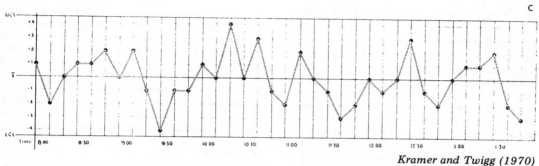

Kramer and Twigg (1970)

FIG. Q-3. RELATION OF THE X CONTROL CHART TO A NORMAL FREQUENCY DISTRIBUTION

(A)—Frequency distribution with frequency scale vertical.   (B)—Frequency distribution with frequency scale horizontal.   (C)—Control chart; frequency distribution extended into a time series.

motivational programs such as "Zero Defects," or other such quality motivation programs. In addition they may be involved in cost or quality improvement programs such as evolutionary operation (EVOP).

The advantages of statistics in the design of experiments and surveys and the analysis of data are so great that the larger food producers have staff departments devoted to this function. Techniques such as these are used extensively in product development and improvement. In addition, in consumer or market research, factor analysis and other multivariate statistical techniques are frequently found. An introduction to many of these techniques and their applications may be found in Tanur *et al.* (1972).

BRUCE A. DREW

References

CROW, E. L. *et al.* 1960. Statistics Manual. Dover Publications, New York.

DAVIES, O. L. (Editor) 1967. The Design and Analysis of Industrial Experiments, 2nd Edition. Hafner Publishing Co., New York.

EISENHART, C., and WILSON, P. W. 1943. Statistical Methods and Control in Bacteriology. Bacteriol. Rev. 7, 57–137.

JURAN, J. M. (Editor) 1962. Quality Control Handbook. McGraw-Hill Book Co., New York.

KRAMER, A., and TWIGG, B. A. 1970. Quality Control for the Food Industry, 3rd Edition, Vol. 1. Avi Publishing Co., Westport, Conn.

TANUR, J. M. *et al.* (Editors) 1972. Statistics: A Guide to the Unknown. Holden-Day, San Francisco.

Cross-reference: *Stability.*

R

RADIATION PROCESSING OF FOODS

Fast-moving subatomic particles or electromagnetic waves which are energetic enough to strip electrons from atoms or molecules of matter constitute ionizing radiation. Although there are a number of different classes of such radiation, only beta (electron), gamma, and X-ray radiations are of interest in food processing. Alpha particles do not have sufficient penetrating ability; neutrons cannot be used because they induce radioactivity in food.

The way in which ionizing radiations act is not clearly defined. There are theories calling for direct hits, and those calling for indirect hits. Both of these types probably contribute to achieving the desired effect, which may be to inhibit sprouting of tubers during storage, to slow down the ripening of fruits, or to destroy organisms causing food spoilage or disease. The direct-hit theory suggests that the nuclear rays (or high-speed electrons) strike the vital spot much in the same manner as a fast-moving projectile strikes its target. The indirect-hit theory suggests that the highly energetic particle subjects the molecule(s) near which it passes to an intense, transient electrical force. The organization of electrons within each molecule is disturbed and many molecules along the path of the particle become "excited" or ionized. In their highly reactive state, free ionized molecules enter almost instantly into reactions with one another and with neighboring molecules, producing as their end products new substances strange to the chemistry of the cell. The unstable secondary products, notably free radicals and peroxides, relay the disturbance in turn to other molecules in the cell, thus enlarging the area and scope of injury.

The choice of the food irradiation source is limited by the requirement that radiation must not be induced in the food or in any food-contacting packaging material. This limits isotope sources to Cobalt 60 and Cesium 137 because the maximum energies of their gamma rays at doses high enough to achieve sterilization in prepackaged food are well below the threshhold for inducing measurable radioactivity in elements usually present in food.

For electron irradiation, 10 MeV is the maximum energy permitted by most countries to preclude inducing radioactivity, the notable exception being the United Kingdom where the maximum energy recommended is 5 MeV. When X-rays are used, the maximum energy permitted in the United States is 5 MeV. No information is available from other countries on the maximum energy permitted for X-ray irradiation except that it must be below the threshhold for inducing measurable radioactivity.

Dosimetry

The primary standard for measuring absorbed dose is based on calorimetry where the temperature rise is directly proportional to the absorbed dose. Because this method is cumbersome, the Fricke Dosimeter using a ferrous sulfate system is routinely used as a working standard. The color change in the ferrous sulfate solution is measured as a function of the radiation dose which converts Fe^{++} to Fe^{+++}. Dosimeters used in food preservation and their effective dose measurement ranges are listed in Table R-1.

Definitions

Beta Particle   A high-speed electron ejected from an atomic nucleus in certain types of radioactive disintegration. These electrons were described as beta particles before their identity as electrons had been established.

Curie   The unit of radioactivity. A curie was originally defined as the number of nuclear disintegrations occurring each second in 1 g of radium. It is now defined as that amount of radioactivity which involves the disintegration of 3.7×10^{10} atomic nuclei in 1 sec.

Electron   A particle possessing a negative electric charge which is an integral part of every neutral atom. It has a mass of 1/1840th of that of the hydrogen atom. Free electrons can be produced in various ways, collected into beams in a vacuum and accelerated in electrical machines to a high energy potential. Electrons and beta particles are identical in nature, the term beta

DOSIMETERS AND THEIR EFFECTIVE RANGES
(RADS)

Dosimeter	Effective Range (Rads)
Ferrous sulfate (Fricke Dosimeter)	3×10^3 –4×10^4
Super Fricke (oxygen–saturated)	3×10^3 –2×10^5
Benzene–water	5×10^3 –7×10^4
Radiochromic dyes	1×10^2 –1×10^7
Photographic films	2×10^{-2}–1×10^7
Thermoluminescence dosimetry	2×10^{-2}–1×10^5
(a) Calcium fluoride	
(b) Lithium fluoride	
Glass dosimetry	
(a) Cobalt glass	1×10^4 –5×10^6
(b) Silver activated glass	
Ferrous–cupric	6×10^4 –8×10^5
High dose ferrous–cupric	
(6 times normal concentrations)	8×10^5 –8×10^6
Ceric sulfate	1×10^4 –2×10^7
Oxalic acid	7×10^5 –5×10^7
Polymethylmethacrylate	
(a) Perspex HX	1×10^5 –1×10^7
(b) Red perspex	1×10^5 –5×10^6
Polyvinylchloride	5×10^5 –7×10^6
Cinemoid films	5×10^5 –5×10^7
Cellophane (blue)	5×10^5 –1×10^7

SOURCE: Compiled by Robert D. Jarrett, Sr., U.S. Army Natick Laboratories.

particle being reserved to describe electrons originating from a disintegrating nucleus in radioactive decay.

Electron Volt (eV)   A unit of energy equivalent to the amount of energy gained by an electron when accelerated by a potential of one volt. One electron volt = 1.6×10^{12} erg.   Larger multiple units are used to describe the energy level of electrons and X-rays from electrical machine sources, or beta particles and gamma rays from radioactive sources, viz: KeV = 1000 eV; MeV = 1 million eV.

Gamma Radiation   Electromagnetic radiation of a very short wavelength produced by the spontaneous disintegration of the atomic nucleus of certain radioactive nuclides. Gamma rays are of the same nature as X-rays of short wavelengths.

Rad   The unit of energy absorbed from ionizing radiation by the matter through which the radiation passes. A radiation dose of 1 rad involves the liberation of 100 erg of energy into each gram of matter through which the radiation passes.   Larger multiple units are frequently used to express the radiation dose in food irradiation, viz: Krad = 1000 rad; Mrad = 1 million rad.

X-rays   Electromagnetic radiation of a wide variety of short wavelengths usually produced by

a machine in which a beam of fast electrons in a high vacuum bombards a metallic target. X-rays of short wavelengths are of the same nature as gamma rays except for their origin. X-rays are sometimes termed Roentgen rays.

Applications to Food Preservation

Some of the more promising applications of ionizing radiation to the treatment of food are shown in Table R-2. At the highest irradiation doses, all food spoilage organisms and pathogens transmitted by food are killed; prepackaged meats, poultry, and seafood can keep for years without refrigeration and on the plate of the consumer will still have a degree of acceptance approximating that of fresh food freshly cooked. At the lowest irradiation doses, certain physiological functions associated with sprouting in tubers such as white potatoes and in bulbs such as onions will be disrupted; these foods will not spoil during storage for as long as 1 yr because of sprouting. Exposure of fruits such as tomatoes, bananas, mangoes, and papayas to intermediate doses of ionizing radiation will slow down ripening, and give these foods an extended shelf-life ranging from a few days to several weeks. One application not included in Table R-2 is the use of irradiation to shorten rehydration and cooking time of dehydrated vegetables. For example, with diced potatoes an irradiation dose of 8 megarads can shorten cooking time from approximately 20 min to less than 4 min.

Advantages

The irradiation process is attractive because there is only a slight temperature rise in the foods during the course of the treatment. It is considered a "cold process." The irradiated foods undergo minimal changes in texture, flavor, odor, and color so that on the plate of the consumer the irradiation-preserved food is almost indistinguishable from fresh food freshly prepared.

Another advantage of the process is its flexibility; that is, the process can be used to preserve a wide variety of foods in a range of sizes and shapes ranging from crates of potatoes or fruit to prepackaged flour in 50- or 100-lb sacks, to large roasts (beef, lamb, pork), turkeys, and hams, to sandwiches of sliced meat, fish, and chicken. The variety and dimensions of products that can be preserved by ionizing radiation fit in very well with present and anticipated future processing methods of the food industry. Consumers can have their meals and snacks in ready-to-eat form, in the form of slices or sandwiches, or as warm-and-serve or cook-and-serve items. Foods processed by ionizing radiation are compatible with the trend for greater

TABLE R-2

SOME POSSIBLE APPLICATIONS OF IONIZING RADIATION TO TREATMENT OF FOOD

Food	Main Objective	Means of Attaining Objective	Dosage (Mrad)
Meat, poultry, fish and many other highly perishable foods.	Safe long-term preservation without refrigerated storage.	Destruction of spoilage organisms and any pathogens present, particularly *Cl. botulinum*.	4–6[1]
Meat, poultry, fish and many other highly perishable foods.	Extension of refrigerated storage below 3°C.	Reduction of population of microorganisms capable of growth at these temperatures.	0.05–1.0
Frozen meat, poultry, eggs, and other foods, including animal feeds, liable to contamination with pathogens.	Prevention of food poisoning.	Destruction of Salmonellae.	0.3–1.0[2]
Meat and other foods carrying pathogenic parasites.	Prevention of parasitic disease transmitted through food.	Destruction of parasites such as *Trichinella spiralis* and *Taenia saginata*.	0.01–0.03
Cereals, flour, fresh and dried fruit, and other products liable to infestation.	Prevention of loss of stored food or spread of pests.	Killing or sexual sterilization of insects.	0.01–0.05
Fruit and certain vegetables.	Improvement of keeping properties.	Reduction of population of molds and yeasts and/or in some instances delay of maturation.	0.1–0.5
Tubers (e.g., potatoes), bulbs (e.g., onions), and other underground organs of plants.	Extension of storage life.	Inhibition of sprouting	0.005–0.015
Spices and other special food ingredients.	Minimization of contamination of food to which the ingredients are added.	Reduction of population of microbes in special ingredient.	1–3

[1] There is evidence that a lower dose might suffice for certain cured products.
[2] A higher dose may be needed if pathogens with greater resistance to radiation are present.

convenience, simplicity in preparation, and reduction of labor in the kitchen. The shelf-life extensions without refrigeration are measured in days or weeks for certain fruits and vegetables and are from 3 to 5 yr and possibly even longer in the case of meat, poultry, finfish, and shellfish.

Description of the Process

For most applications it is important to use good quality ultrafresh food as starting material. Radiation cannot reverse deterioration and spoilage of food once it has begun; it can only arrest or prevent these conditions. Nor should radiation be used as an excuse for poor sanitation practices; its intended use is for ensurance against contamination which might occur in spite of all reasonable precautions.

Fruits and vegetables are irradiated in boxes or crates to minimize excessive and extraneous handling and to keep processing costs to a minimum. Meats, poultry, and fish fillets to be given pasteurizing doses to extend refrigerated shelf-life should be wrapped and chilled without delay prior to irradiation.

For prepackaged meats, poultry, and seafood which are to be given sterilizing doses to promote long-term shelf stability without refrigeration, the first step is to remove as much of the inedible material as possible by deboning and trimming off gristle and excess fat. The next step is to inactivate the proteolytic enzymes in these foods. This is done by heating (blanching) to an internal temperature between 65° and 75°C. The foods are then vacuum packaged and sealed while still hot in rigid metal cans or flexible packaging materials. The foods are then frozen without delay by blast freezer or liquid nitrogen to a temperature of −30°C and are exposed while held at −30°C ± 10°C either to gamma rays (from Cobalt-60 or

TABLE R-3

APPROVALS BY THE U.S. FOOD AND DRUG ADMINISTRATION FOR RADIATION PRESERVATION OF FOOD PACKAGING MATERIALS (JULY 1971)

Packaging Material	Petitioner	Source	Dose	Food Additive Petition No.	Filing[1] Date	Filing[1] Vol.	Filing[1] Page	Regulation[1] Date	Regulation[1] Vol.	Regulation[1] Page
Nitrocellulose coated Cellophane	AEC	Gamma	1 megarad	1297	2-8-64	29	2318	8-14-64	29	11651
Glassine paper	AEC	Gamma	1 megarad	1297	2-8-64	29	2318	8-14-64	29	11651
Wax coated paperboard	AEC	Gamma	1 megarad	1297	2-8-64	29	2318	8-14-64	29	11651
Polypropylene film with or without adjuvants	AEC	Gamma	1 megarad	1297	2-8-64	29	2318	8-14-64	29	11651
Ethylene-alkene-1-copolymer	AEC	Gamma	1 megarad	1297	2-8-64	29	2318	8-14-64	29	11651
Polyethylene film	AEC	Gamma	1 megarad	1297	2-8-64	29	2318	8-14-64	29	11651
Polystyrene film with or without adjuvant substances	AEC	Gamma	1 megarad	1297	2-8-64	29	2318	8-14-64	29	11651
Rubber hydrochloride with or without adjuvant substances	AEC	Gamma	1 megarad	1297	2-8-64	29	2318	8-14-64	29	11651
Vinylidene chloride-vinyl-chloride copolymer film (Saran wrap)	AEC	Gamma	1 megarad	1297	2-8-64	29	2318	8-14-64	29	11651
Polyolefin film with or without adjuvant substances or vinylidene chloride coatings (Saran)	AEC	Gamma	1 megarad	1297	2-8-64	29	2318	8-14-64	29	11651
Polyethylene terephthalate with or without adjuvant substances or vinylidene chloride coatings (Saran) or polyethylene coatings	AEC	Gamma	1 megarad	5M1674	7-30-65	30	9551	3-19-68	33	4659
Nylon 11	AEC	Gamma	1 megarad	5M1675	7-30-65	30	9551	3-19-68	33	4659
Vinylidene chloride copolymer (Saran) coated Cellophane	AEC	Gamma	1 megarad	6M1820	9-8-65	30	11400	3-19-68	33	4659
Vegetable parchment	AEC	Gamma	1 megarad	5B1670	2-18-65	30	9116	6-11-65	30	7599
Polyethylene film with or without adjuvants	U.S. Army	Gamma	6 megarad	5M1622	1-15-65	30	547	3-12-65	30	3354
Polyethylene terephthalate with or without adjuvants	U.S. Army	Gamma	6 megarad	5M1645	7-21-65	30	9116	6-10-67	32	8360
Nylon 6 films with or without adjuvants	U.S. Army	Gamma	6 megarad	5M1645	7-21-65	30	9116	6-10-67	32	8360
Vinyl chloride-vinyl acetate copolymer films with or without adjuvant	U.S. Army	Gamma	6 megarad	5M1645	7-21-65	30	9116	6-10-67	32	8360
Kraft paper	U.S. Army	Gamma	6 megarad	5M1645	7-21-65	30	9116	6-10-67	32	8360
	U.S. Army	Gamma	50,000 rads	7M2172	5-23-67	32	7877	7-19-67	32	10567

SOURCE: Compiled by Frank Leone, U.S. Atomic Energy Commission.

[1] Date, volume and page number of *Federal Register* publication.

TABLE R-4

GENERAL SURVEY OF IRRADIATED FOOD PRODUCTS CLEARED FOR HUMAN CONSUMPTION IN DIFFERENT COUNTRIES
(DEC. 1973)
(Grouped According to Product)

Product	Country	Purpose of Irradiation	Source of Radiation	Dose (Krad)	Date of Approval
Fruits and vegetables					
Potatoes	USSR	Sprout inhibition	^{60}Co	10	14 Mar. 1958
	Canada	Sprout inhibition	^{60}Co	10 max	9 Nov. 1960
	USA (white potatoes)	Sprout inhibition	^{60}Co	15 max	14 June 1963
			^{60}Co	5–10	30 June 1964
			^{137}Cs	5–10	2 Oct. 1964
			^{60}Co + ^{137}Cs	5–15	1 Nov. 1965
	Israel	Sprout inhibition	^{60}Co	15 max	5 July 1967
	Japan	Sprout inhibition	^{60}Co	15 max	30 Aug. 1972
	WHO[2]	Sprout inhibition	^{60}Co or ^{137}Cs	15 max	12 Apr. 1969
	Spain	Sprout inhibition	^{60}Co	5–15	4 Nov. 1969
	Hungary[1]	Sprout inhibition	^{60}Co	10	23 Dec. 1969
			^{60}Co	15 max	10 Jan. 1972
	Denmark	Sprout inhibition	10 MeV electrons	15 max	27 Jan. 1970
	Netherlands	Sprout inhibition	^{60}Co	15 max	23 Mar. 1970
			4 MeV electrons	15 max	23 Mar. 1970
	Bulgaria[1]	Sprout inhibition	^{60}Co		1971
	Uruguay[1]	Sprout inhibition	^{60}Co		1971
	Philippines[2]	Sprout inhibition	^{60}Co	15 max	13 Sept. 1972
	France[2]	Sprout inhibition	^{60}Co	7,5–15	8 Nov. 1972
	Italy	Sprout inhibition	^{60}Co or ^{137}Cs	7,5–15	30 Aug. 1973
Onions	Canada	Sprout inhibition	^{60}Co	15 max	25 Mar. 1965
	USSR[1]	Sprout inhibition	^{60}Co	6	25 Febr. 1967
	Israel	Sprout inhibition	^{60}Co	10 max	25 July 1968
	Netherlands[1]	Sprout inhibition	^{60}Co	15 max	5 Febr. 1971
			4 MeV electrons	15 max	5 Febr. 1971
Garlic	Thailand	Sprout inhibition	^{60}Co	10 max	20 Mar. 1973
	Italy	Sprout inhibition	^{60}Co or ^{137}Cs	7,5–15	30 Aug. 1973
	Italy	Sprout inhibition	^{60}Co or ^{137}Cs	7,5–15	30 Aug. 1973

Product	Country	Radiation source	Treatment	Dose (krad)	Date
Dried fruits					
Fresh fruits and vegetables	USSR	^{60}Co	Insect disinfestation	100	15 Febr. 1966
	USSR[1]	^{60}Co	Radurization	200–400 max	11 July 1964
Mushrooms	Netherlands	^{60}Co	Growth inhibition	250 max	23 Oct. 1969
Asparagus	Netherlands[1]	4 MeV electrons	Radurization	250 max	23 Oct. 1969
Strawberries	Netherlands[1]	^{60}Co	Radurization	200 max	7 May 1969
		^{60}Co		250 max	7 May 1969
Cocoabeans	Netherlands[1]	4 MeV electrons	Insect disinfestation	250 max	7 May 1969
		^{60}Co		70 max	7 May 1969
Spices and condiments	Netherlands[1]	4 MeV electrons	Radicidation	70 max	7 May 1969
Grain and grain products					
Grain	USSR	^{60}Co	Insect disinfestation	800–1000	13 Sept. 1971
		4 MeV electrons		800–1000	13 Sept. 1971
Wheat and wheat flour (changed on 4 Mar. 1966 from wheat products)	USA	^{60}Co	Insect disinfestation	30	21 Aug. 1959
		^{60}Co	Insect disinfestation	20–50	2 Oct. 1963
		^{137}Cs		20–50	26 Febr. 1964
Wheat, flour, whole wheat flour	Canada	5 MeV electrons	Insect disinfestation	20–50	25 Febr. 1966
Wheat and ground wheat products	WHO[2]	^{60}Co	Insect disinfestation	75 max	12 Apr. 1969
		^{60}Co		75 max	11 July 1964
Meat and fish					
Semiprepared raw beef, pork and rabbit products (in plastic bags)	USSR[1]	^{60}Co	Radurization	600–800	4 July 1966
Poultry, eviscerated (in plastic bags)	USSR[1]	^{60}Co	Radurization	600	31 Dec. 1971
Culinary prepared meat products (Fried meat, entrecote) (in plastic bags)	Netherlands[1]	^{60}Co	Radurization	300 max	1 Febr. 1967
	USSR[1]	^{60}Co	Radurization	800	13 Nov. 1970
Shrimps	Netherlands[1]	4 MeV electrons	Radurization	50–100	13 Nov. 1970
Other products					
Dry food concentrates	USSR	^{60}Co	Insect disinfestation	50–100	6 June 1966
Any food for consumption by patients who require a sterile diet as an essential factor in their treatment	UK	^{60}Co	Radappertization	70	1 Dec. 1969
Deep-frozen meals	Netherlands[3]	^{60}Co	Radappertization	2500 min	27 Nov. 1969
Fresh, tinned and liquid foodstuffs	Netherlands[3]	^{60}Co	Radappertization	2500 min	8 Mar. 1972

SOURCE: Compiled by Dr. K. Vas, International Atomic Energy Agency.

[1] Experimental batches.
[2] Temporary acceptance for 5 yr.
[3] For hospital patients in reversed barrier isolation.

Cesium-137), X-rays, or electrons from an electron linear accelerator. Irradiation in the frozen state minimizes adverse chemical and physical changes which may occur so that the quality of the product (taste, color, odor, texture, and vitamins) is maintained.

Clostridium botulinum is the most radiation-resistant of all the microorganisms of concern in food preservation. A dose high enough to destroy the most radiation-resistant strain of this bacterium will automatically destroy all other organisms in food which are of food spoilage or public health importance. In determining the minimum radiation dose (MRD) for sterilization, we aim for a dose high enough to reduce in number by a factor of 1×10^{12} the most highly resistant strain of *Cl. botulinum* spores. This dose is different for each food and must be determined in every case by laboratory experiments.

Problems

Not all foods can be successfully preserved by exposure to ionizing radiation. For example, dairy products and leafy vegetables may develop undesirable off-flavors or demonstrate accelerated spoilage.

Prepackaged meat, poultry, finfish, and shell fish respond very well to irradiation doses sufficiently high to achieve "commercial sterility." When prepackaged food products are exposed to sub-sterilizing irradiation doses, caution must be taken to assure that the absorbed dose is not too high so as to destroy all competitors to *Cl. botulinum* and yet be high enough to reduce the numbers of food spoilage organisms to achieve the desired shelf-life extension. If all competitors of *Cl. botulinum* are killed, this organism under the longer storage periods made possible by irradiation could germinate and produce toxin before off-odors and other conventional spoilage indices develop to warn the consumer of danger. A problem which occurs with bulbs and tubers (exposed to radiation for sprout inhibition) and other produce (fruits and vegetables) is the increased susceptibility to spoilage when damaged or bruised or when subjected to shock and vibration during transport.

The greatest single problem by far is to obtain evidence convincing to health regulating bodies at national levels that foods processed by ionizing radiation are wholesome, i.e., safe for consumption. Collection of required scientific evidence involves long-time feeding of animals to demonstrate the absence of chronic toxicity or carcinogenicity. Additional studies are necessary to demonstrate the absence of mutagens and teratogens. These studies are expensive and time consuming.

Packaging

Packaging is an important aspect of radiation sterilization. Most of the earlier work was done with the rigid metal can with an oleoresinous or epoxy-phenolic enamel because of its reliability as an impermeable and rugged container. Flexible packaging materials approved in the United States as food contactants in the radiation processing of food are listed in Table R-3.

In radiation sterilization the need is for flexible materials which can withstand the stress of high radiation doses and low temperatures down to $-40°C$ without loss of flexibility or impairment in functioning as an impermeable barrier to moisture, gases, and microorganisms. These materials must be sufficiently stable during irradiation processing so that they do not impart off-odors, off-flavors, or products toxic to the food. Their all-around reliability must equal that of the rigid metal can. In order to reinforce strength of the material and keep out light that can accelerate adverse color changes, the food contactant materials are laminated to aluminum foil and other barrier materials. Two of the more promising laminates are described here:

Food- contacting Film (inside layer)	Middle Layer	Outside Layer
High density Polyethylene (0.0051 cm)	Aluminum foil (0.0009 cm)	Polyethylene terephthalate (0.0013 cm)
Chemically bonded polyethylene terephthalate— medium density polyethylene (0.0051 cm)	Aluminum foil (0.0009 cm)	Polyimino-caproyl (nylon 6) (0.0025 cm)

Legislation

Since the process for food preservation by ionizing radiation is so new, the human race has not had the benefit of millenia of experience to vouch for the safety to the consumer of foods preserved by this method. In many countries legislation has been adopted requiring scientific proof that the foods preserved by ionizing radiation are indeed safe. Generally, the responsibility for granting approvals for this process has been vested in Ministries of Health; and, in the United States, primarily in the FDA of the Department of Health, Education and Welfare. The basic statute governing ionizing radiation in the United States is the Food, Drug, and Cosmetic Act as amended in 1958. Under this law ionizing radiation is legally defined as a food additive. The Federal Meat Inspection Act and the Poultry Products Inspection Act have been on the books for a long time. In recent years, with the great interest in consumer affairs, we have seen passage in 1966 of the Fair Packaging and Labeling Act; in 1967, of the Wholesome Meat Act; and, in 1968, of the Wholesome Poultry Act.

The impact of the Food, Drug, and Cosmetic Act of 1958 is to outlaw all new food additives, including ionizing radiation, from commercial application. The law provides for exemption from this universal ban by petitioning the FDA for approval of new food additives. For food preservation by ionizing radiation, FDA's approval is required for each food processed in this fashion. The law also requires approval by FDA of packaging materials in contact with food during radiation processing.

A listing of all foods approved for human consumption by country appears in Table R-4.

Health Physics and Licensing Aspects

Use of facilities containing radiation sources is controlled by the mechanism of licensing with periodic inspections. In order to obtain a license it is necessary to show that the operation is radiologically safe. Licensing agencies and requirements vary from country to country. In the United States, licenses for radioisotope facilities are granted and inspected either by the U.S. Atomic Energy Commission (USAEC) or by a State which has established an agreement with the USAEC. In addition, many States now require licensing or at least registration of machine sources as well.

To be radiologically safe for operating personnel, visitors, and neighbors, it is necessary not only to shield occupied areas from the radiation emitted by the source but also to limit access to the irradiation chamber in such a way that accidental entrance is impossible and intentional entrance is carefully controlled.

Routine monitoring of radiation exposure of personnel should be performed using integrating dosimeters (film badges, thermoluminescent or pocket dosimeters). Areas of potential high levels of radiation should also be monitored in such a way as to ensure that entering personnel will be aware of the radiation levels.

Radioisotope sources also require periodic testing of the encapsulation to ensure early detection if a leak should occur.

EDWARD S. JOSEPHSON

Cross-reference: Food Preservation.

RAISINS

Raisins are the dried fruit of several varieties of grapes, produced mostly, even at the present time, by sun drying, although minor quantities are mechanically dehydrated in forced draft heating chambers.

Prehistoric drawings indicate that raisins were in use at that early date. Numerous references are made in the first literary records, including the Old Testament, to the use of raisins in paying taxes, treating illness, and satiating the human appetite. The extraordinary "natural keeping qualities" of raisins (low moisture and low pH) have certainly played a big part in their utility throughout many centuries.

Raisins were formerly produced only in the Mediterranean region, but have now for some years been a leading agricultural product in California. World production of raisins by area for 1970 are approximately as follows (calculated from USDA figures):

Producing Area	Produced Weight (1000 Short Tons)	Total World Production (%)
United States	195.0	32.3
Turkey	140.0	23.2
Australia	94.9	15.8
Greece	85.0	14.1
Iran	66.0	11.0
South African Republic	13.8	2.3
Spain	7.7	1.3
Total	602.4	100.0

Egypt produces about 2000 tons of seedless variety for local consumption. Israel has had a small raisin industry since 1957, and produces both sundried and mechanically dehydrated raisins, mostly from the Thompson Seedless variety of grapes.

Minor quantities are produced in other areas, but accurate figures are not readily available.

U.S. Raisin Industry

United States raisins are produced exclusively in the San Joaquin Valley of Central California, where climate is highly suitable for drying the fruit. The raisin crop contributes significantly to the general economy of California's agricultural operation. The 1968 raisin crop, as shown by the California Crop and Livestock Reporting Service, was indicated to be 264,000 tons (14% higher than average years) at an average value of $267 per ton at farm level, thus yielding a crop return of $70,488,000. Over the five-year period: 1965 to 1970, the U.S. has exported an average of 31% of its raisin crop.

Raisin production is largely from the Thompson Seedless variety grape, with Sultanas, Muscats, and Zante "Currants" providing small quantities. Harvesting operations usually start in late August.

Clusters of ripe grapes are hand-picked and spread on paper trays to dry on the ground between the rows of vines. Depending on weather, 2–4 weeks are required to dry the grapes into raisins. Fruit color changes from a greenish yellow to a brownish purple. Moisture is reduced from 75 to 16% or less. Some farmers turn the bunches on the trays once during the period to facilitate drying, but most do not. When the fruit is dry, the paper tray is folded around the raisins to form a package or "roll." The rolls are collected and taken to a central location in the vineyard, where they are emptied onto screens and shaken to remove sand and other small debris. They are stored in boxes or bins for transportation to the processing plant. In past years, storage at the producing farm for some months was common, but in recent years storage on the farm is of short duration only.

Raisin harvesting is generally complete in late September except for the Muscat variety, which is late maturing.

Storage Before Processing.—Upon receipt by the processing plant, the fruit is examined for quality, using criteria such as percentage of moisture, berry maturity, moldy berries, insect fragments, sand, and other foreign materials. If the fruit is not to be processed immediately, the boxes or bins of fruit are stored in warehouses, or in "stacks." Stacks are large, temporary storage enclosures made by fastening special sisalkraft paper to wood framing. Construction is sufficiently tight to ensure the retention of fumigant gases, which are applied at intervals to prevent the development of insect activity. Methyl bromide is the most commonly used fumigant, applied at the rate of $1\frac{1}{2}$ lb of methyl bromide vapor per 1000 cu ft of storage volume. Recent years have seen increasing use of phosphine gas as a fumigant.

Processing.—Processing procedure is the mechanical removal of large stems by coarse screening, the removal of sand and chaff by fine screening, and blowing with air. Cap stems (the small, individual stem on each berry) are removed by passing the raisins between two rotating, symmetrically aligned, conical surfaces. The cap stem is removed by friction. Immature fruit of low quality (and low density) is removed by suction devices. The raisins may be size graded at this point with vibrating screens of various mesh sizes. The fruit is then rinsed to remove loose surface soil and washed by short-time immersion in water at approximately 100°F, with strong agitation. This is followed by hydraulic transit to riffles, where violent agitation of the raisins in water removes the remaining soil. The fruit drops to a vibrating screen, where it is rinsed with high velocity jets of clean water, sometimes chlorinated to 10 ppm. Excess surface water is removed by passing through a centrifugal device.

The raisins are inspected several times, then conveyed to packaging equipment and filled into containers, which range in size from $\frac{1}{2}$ oz to fiberboard bins holding 1500 lb or more. The various packaging materials include laminated plastic film bags and fiberboard boxes of many types and finishes.

Golden Seedless Raisins.—These differ in that the fresh Thompson Seedless grapes are picked, washed, soda dipped (generally a dilute solution of sodium hydroxide) to "check" the skin and accelerate drying; then graded and placed on trays in a closed chamber exposed to the fumes of burning sulphur. Following this, the raisins are dehydrated in forced draft heating chambers. The color of the finished raisins will vary from pale green through golden yellows to amber.

The sulphur dioxide produced by the burning sulphur is said to "bleach" the fruit. The sulphur dioxide prevents the oxidative darkening that occurs with the sun drying of fruit. After dehydration, the golden raisins retain some 1500–2500 ppm of sulphur dioxide. This excess may be slowly lost during long-term storage, with eventual darkening of the fruit.

Composition

As a food, raisins are high in sugar, of moderate acid level, and are outstandingly high in potassium content. The composition of California Thompson Seedless Raisins as shown below is taken from unpublished data of the research sponsored by C.R.A.B. at University of California and other agencies, except the fat and caloric values which are taken from USDA Agriculture Handbook 8. Data is reported on 17.0% by weight raisin moisture basis.

Component	Avg per 100 gm (Gm)
Total solids	83.0
Moisture	17.0
Sugar (total as invert)	70.2
Ash	2.1
Acid (total as tartaric)	2.12
Carbohydrates	77.2
Protein (N × 6.25)	2.77
Crude fiber	0.97
Fat	0.50
Sodium	0.013
Potassium	0.71
Calcium	0.066
Magnesium	0.033
Phosphorus	0.094
Iron	0.0032 (3.2 mg)
Copper	0.00053 (0.53 mg)
Zinc	0.00022 (0.22 mg)
Vitamin B_6 (pyridoxine)	0.00023 (0.23 mg)

Niacin	0.00060 (0.60 mg)
Riboflavin	0.000025 (0.025 mg)
Pantothenic acid	0.000055 (0.055 mg)
Thiamin	0.000100 (0.100 mg)
Biotin	0.0000045 (4.5 μg)
Caloric value	268

Future U.S. Developments

Farming to make raisins, as in producing most crops, is beset by economic risks. The greatest risk by far is that of rainfall during the drying period. The cost of mechanical dehydration as a substitute for sun drying is considered prohibitive at the present time. However, experiments are being made with partial predrying on the cut cane of the vine prior to harvest and with various types of alkaline emulsion dips prior to dehydration. Drying on the cut cane should reduce in-going moisture levels to the dehydrator; and the dipping baths, it is believed, will alter the skin of the grape to increase dehydration rates.

Labor shortages have created serious problems at harvest time and, as a result, several types of mechanical harvesters are in the process of development. Results are promising and it appears that within a few years some modification of mechanical harvesting may be in general use.

By-Products

The raisin industry has sponsored limited research in the by-product field, but presently the results are confined to raisin paste and small quantities of raisin juice concentrate. A minor amount of off-grade raisins are used for animal feed, while most "wet waste" raisins from processing are sent to the distillery for conversion to alcohol.

Uses

The consumer market for raisins has been largely by way of 1- or 2-lb containers to be used in home baking and for salads or puddings. Emphasis has been given recently to the smaller packages for "eating out of hand," particularly for the younger age groups.

Sizeable quantities are used by the baking industry in bread, cake, etc.

Large amounts of raisins are used by cereal food manufacturers for incorporation into a number of their consumer products.

Chocolate coated raisins have gained a limited market in the confectionery field.

Production in Other Countries

It is not within the province of this limited summary to discuss in detail production in countries other than the United States. Two prominent differences from U.S. methods are encountered in most other countries.

(1) The raisins (mostly Sultanas) are generally dried in well-ventilated shade on elevated wire rack shelves, as opposed to drying on paper trays on the ground in direct sunlight.

(2) The grapes are mostly dipped in and/or sprayed with dilute alkaline solutions or alkaline oil emulsions before being placed to dry.

More specifically, Australian methods, as an example, are: hand picking, carriage to a drying area on the producing farm, a quick dip (hot or cold) in one of a number of alkaline fatty acid ester dipping solutions, and placement on wire racks to dry. The rack area is roofed to prevent direct radiant exposure and to give some protection in the event of rainfall. Equipment is available in some areas to convert the drying racks into effective dehydrators when weather conditions are not conducive to drying. Processing is quite similar to that in the United States, except that the processed raisins are frequently coated with a thin film of oil so that the raisins do not clump together from surface stickiness.

S. D. POULSEN

Cross-reference: *Dried Fruit.*

RAPE AND MUSTARD IN INDIA

India is one of the largest and important producers of rape and mustard seeds. Rape is a general term for seeds of oleiferous brassicas cultivated in many parts of the world as an oilseed crop. In India, the edible oil derived from cultivated brassicas is called mustard oil, a term which in Europe and America is applied to the volatile oil of mustard seeds. In India, the principal varieties are Yellow Sarson, Brown Sarson, Toria, and Rai. Table R-5 gives an idea of the distribution of the above varieties.

The quantity of seed obtained from rape and mustard occupies the fifth position in the world for oil yielding plants following soya, peanuts, cotton, and sunflower (Table R-6).

It can be seen that the crop of rape and mustard reached almost 5 million metric tons per year. Production is especially increasing in Sweden and Canada.

Composition

Oils from the pure varieties of the different varieties of seeds of rape and mustard are very similar to each other and have only slight differences in their physical and chemical characteristics. The mustard seed of commerce available for

TABLE R-5

NOMENCLATURE OF INDIAN MUSTARD SEED

Common Name	Species	Distribution	Oil Content (%)	Volatile Oil (%)
Yellow Sarson or Indian Colza	*Brassica compestris* Linn. Var. Sarson Prain	U.P., Punjab, Bihar, and Bengal	35–48	0.27
Brown Sarson	*Brassica compestris* Linn. Var. dichotoma Watt.	Punjab	35–48	0.35
Toria, Indian rape	*Brassica compestris* Linn. Var. Toria, Fuller & Duthie	Punjab, U.P., Bengal, and Assam	33–46	0.14
Rai, Indian mustard	*Brassica juncea coss*	Bihar, Bangal, and U.P.	30–38	0.45

SOURCE: *Wealth of India, Vol. 1.*

crushing is generally a mixture of different species in varying proportions. This is due to the fact that the seed itself which is used for sowing purposes consists of a mixture of various species.

The seeds of oleiferous brassicas contain 35–50% oil and about 20% protein. They also contain a small proportion of glucosides which on hydrolysis yield volatile mustard oils.

The average fatty acid composition of rapeseed and Rai are given in Table R-7. It is seen that almost 50% of $C_{22:1}$ is present in these oils. The presence of this acid is considered as favorable or unfavorable according to the purpose for which the oil is to be used.

Extraction of Fat from Seeds

In Western countries most of the oil is obtained by screw pressing and the remainder is extracted by solvent.

In India, of the total mustard seed produced, 90% is crushed for oil production. This oil is almost exclusively used for edible purposes, being a favorite oil in Bengal, Assam, Bihar, and Orissa.

Extracted Meal

The occurrence of thioglucosides in mustard seed is an unfavorable feature. These compounds are involved in the development of goiter, the cause of thyroid disease. Therefore, the presence of thioglucosides in the mustard seed makes the use of the extracted meal for fodder difficult. It is essential that these factors be removed entirely before the meal can be used.

Results have been recently published on the use

TABLE R-6

PRODUCTION OF RAPE AND MUSTARD SEEDS

Year	World Production[1] (1000 Metric Tons)	Production in India[2] (1000 Metric Tons)
1960–61	3845	1380
1961–62	4015	1337
1962–63	4130	1294
1963–64	4390	909
1964–65	4465	1466
1965–66	4935	1268
1966–67	4744	1245
1967–68	4970	1482

[1] SOURCE: *Chemistry & Industry*, Vol. 27, p. 883 (1970).
[2] SOURCE: Eastern India Oil Millers Association (1970).

TABLE R-7

FATTY ACID COMPOSITION OF RAPE AND RAI

Fatty Acid	Rapeseed	Rai (Indian mustard)
16:0	2–4	2.2
18:0	1–2	1.1
18:1	9–24	12.9
18:2	13–16	15.0
18:3	5–12	9.9
20:0	—	0.9
20:1	7–15	8.2
22:1	36–54	49.8

SOURCE: Unpublished data, Research and Development Laboratories, Tata Oil Mills Co., Bombay.

of rapeseed protein for edible purposes. The proposed method comprises inactivation of the enzymes by the action of boiling water, draining the water, wet grinding the meal, then extracting with water to remove thioglucosides and then drying.

The dried meal is subjected to flaking, hexane extraction, and air classification to produce an edible flour. The edible meal is a white bland powder containing 60% protein.

Economic Outlook

Although much work is being done elsewhere, in India mustard oil is used mainly for edible purposes as raw oil with the cake being used as fertilizer.

In Western countries, it has been possible to produce rapeseed containing a fatty oil with no erucic acid ($C_{22:1}$) and also to produce an oil containing over 60% oleic acid, 20% linoleic acid, and 10% linolenic acid, with saturated acids of palmitic and stearic making up the rest. This oil is used as salad oil and for shortenings and margarines. While the erucic acid—($C_{22:1}$)—free oil is used for edible purposes, oils containing high erucic acid are used for industrial purposes. The major use is the brassylic acid which is obtained by the ozonolysis of erucic acid and used in the manufacture of nylons 13 and 1313.

In India no effort is being made to produce an oil with low erucic acid content. It is essential that we initiate work in these lines to produce low erucic acid-containing oil, and utilization of the meal for edible purposes. Also, it will be of interest to see whether the lecithin from this can be used.

It can be expected that the results will permit better use of this important oil-yielding raw material.

B. P. BALIGA

Cross-reference: *Fats and Oils.*

RAPESEED TECHNOLOGY

Rape is a member of the economically important Cruciferae family, which includes mustard, cabbage, turnip, cauliflower, and kale; it belongs to the genus *Brassica*. The origin of rape is difficult to determine due to the wide distribution of *Brassica* species; however, it is probable that the primary types of rape came from Asia, the Mediterranean, and western European regions. Rape has a long history, with earliest references found in Indian Sanskrit writings of 2000 to 1500 B.C.

The two basic species are *Brassica napus* and *Brassica campestris*, sometimes called Argentine and Polish rapes, respectively. Both species have winter and summer forms. *B.napus* has a greater yield potential of seed and oil than *B.campestris*. Winter forms are more productive than summer types. Europe and Japan grow winter types almost exclusively; Chile grows winter and summer types; while Canada uses only the summer types.

The rapes are adapted to temperate regions, but also thrive in subtropical areas such as northern India, Japan, and Mexico where they are used as cool season or winter crops. They grow well on a wide variety of soils. The seed is small in size, being only a few millimeters in diameter. Seed coat color is black to reddish brown. Excellent sources of information on rapeseed botany, production, processing and utilization are Bowland *et al.* (1965) and Appelquist and Ohlson (1971).

Production and Utilization

World rapeseed production is about 5 million metric tons annually, of which approximately 75% is produced and consumed in Asia. Rapeseed stands fifth in total world production among oilseed crops, following soybeans, cottonseed, groundnuts, and sunflower seed.

Canada exports more seed than all other countries combined, while Sweden and France are the main exporters of rapeseed oil. Extraction in modern mills gives 40% oil and 50% meal, the remainder being moisture. Most of the oil is used in edible products, such as margarines, shortenings, and salad and cooking oils. The oil is also used as an industrial lubricant. The meal is mainly used as a high protein feedstuff for animals, although in Japan the primary use is as a fertilizer for tobacco. Some varieties of rape are important as fodder crops in Europe, New Zealand, and to a lesser extent in North America.

Processing to Oil and Meal

The processing of rapeseed to obtain oil and meal is similar to that for other oilseeds. The demand for high quality oil and meal for food and feed uses has brought about a changeover from mechanical pressing to either straight solvent extraction or a combination of pressing and solvent extraction. In this latter process, called prepress-solvent extraction, a large portion of the oil is removed from the seeds by mechanical presses (expellers), while the remaining oil is extracted using the organic solvent n-hexane.

Prepress-Solvent Method.—Stored seed is cleaned and conveyed to the flaking or crushing rolls. These rolls flatten the seed and rupture many of the oil-containing cells. The flaking also allows the seed to be heated quickly and uniformly in a series of cooking kettles. The cooker consists of 4–5 cylindrical steam-jacketed kettles stacked one above the other. The flaked seed enters the top kettle and is kept agitated with a sweep-type stirrer. Automatic trap doors keep the seed moving down through the kettles. After 30 min the seed is discharged from the bottom kettle at approximately 100°C.

Heating conditions the seed for oil extraction and inactivates the native myrosinase. The flaked, cooked seed then passes to the expeller or screw press where about 80% of the oil is removed and the oil cake is discharged out of the end of the expeller. The crude oil is then filtered and stored or refined. The oil cake with 15-20% oil is reground and conveyed to a solvent extractor. The seed, oil, and solvent are intermixed by moving the seed mass in one direction and the solvent plus oil in the opposite direction. The solvent-saturated meal discharged from the extractor contains about 1% oil. The meal is stripped of its solvent in equipment very similar to the stack cookers. The meal is dried to about 10% moisture, cooled, and placed in storage. Similarly, a series of evaporators and separators remove most of the solvent from the mixture of oil and solvent coming from the extractor. The crude oil is then stored and shipped or refined.

Composition of Oil and Meal

Rapeseed meal, the residue remaining after the removal of oil from the seed, contains 35-40% protein, 20-25% carbohydrate, 12-16% crude fiber, and 5-7% ash. The amino acid composition of rapeseed meal from modern extraction mills compares favorably with other oilseed meals. Lysine content in meals from prepress-solvent, or straight solvent extraction plants is much higher than in meals from expeller extraction plants. Expeller extraction of oil results in protein damage, as indicated by a decrease in lysine content of the meal.

Rapeseed contains thioglucosides which under moist conditions are hydrolyzed by the native enzyme myrosinase to goitrogenic mustard oils (isothiocyanates and oxazolidinethiones). The oxazolidinethiones are primarily responsible for the enlargement of the thyroid. *B.napus* varieties have a thioglucoside content equivalent to 0.5-1.0% oxazolidinethione on an oil free basis, while *B.campestris* varieties contain only 0.2-0.3%. Thioglucosides equivalent to 0.5% isothiocyanates are present in both. Animal feeding studies over many years have indicated that intact thioglucosides are not harmful, but it is their hydrolytic products, the mustard oils, that are toxic. The thioglucoside content of rapeseed meal varies with species and variety of rape, soil, and climatic conditions, and method of processing rapeseed to oil and meal. Current methods of processing rapeseed result in

the production of myrosinase-free meal containing unhydrolyzed thioglucosides. This meal is a useful protein supplement for most animal rations if active myrosinase is not reintroduced by other ingredients or by coliform bacteria in the intestine.

Characteristic of rapeseed oil is erucic acid. Canadian varieties of *B.napus* contain 36-45% erucic acid, whereas *B.campestris* varieties contain 22-33%. In Europe, rapeseed oil contains up to 50% erucic acid. Extreme erucic acid values of 57-61% have been reported in the Indian Sarson varieties. Due to the presence of significant quantities of this long chain fatty acid, rapeseed oil or its erucic acid fraction has been used industrially as an engine lubricant, grease, lubricant for cold rolling steel, and a mold release agent. Its primary use, however, is as an edible oil, in that its relatively low linolenic acid content permits it to compete with other vegetable oils in shortenings, margarines, salad oils, frying, and household uses. Its linolenic acid content of 10% is similar to that in soybean oil, while its linoleic acid content of 13-18% is approximately $1/3$ of that in soybean oil.

Nutritional considerations led to a Canadian breeding program in the 1950's which resulted in varieties free of erucic acid (Downey 1966). The long chain fatty acids were removed almost completely, while the oleic acid content was increased significantly. Except for the presence of linolenic acid the composition of this new oil, called Canbra, greatly resembles olive oil.

Rapeseed Protein

At present, rapeseed meal is used solely as a protein supplement in a number of animal rations. Rapeseed protein has not been commercially concentrated or isolated from the meal for use in special animal feeds or human foods. Research work is being conducted in this area, however. Research programs in Canada, Sweden, and Poland are aimed at removal of thioglucosides (either by breeding or processing), improved palatability, increased protein content, and reduced fiber content. Significant strides are being made. Poland has developed the Bronowski variety (*B.napus*) which is free of thioglucosides. A process has been developed in Canada which yields a bland, light colored, thioglucoside-free, 60% protein flour (Tape *et al*. 1970). The protein in this flour is equal to or better than milk protein in promoting the growth of rats. If rapeseed protein from such a process is found to have useful properties in the manufacture of human foods, it will permit rapeseed to join soybean protein as the functional ingredient in meat analogs, meat extenders, dairy products, bakery goods, and other processed foods.

Potential expansion of rapeseed production, processing, and use by food and feed manufacturers is great. Plant breeding and processing studies have improved the usefulness of the oil and meal greatly in the past decade, and current research effort indicates further improvements. Expanded production and utilization of rapeseed, a cool climate oilseed, will have a significant economic impact on producer countries such as Canada, Sweden, Poland, France, India, and China; thereby lessening their dependence on soybeans, sunflowers, groundnuts or cottonseed.

NORMAN W. TAPE

References

APPELQUIST, L. A., and OHLSON, R. 1971. Rapeseed. Elsevier Publishing Co., New York and London.

BOWLAND, J. P., CLANDININ, D. R., and WETTER, L. R. 1965. Rapeseed meal for livestock and poultry—A review. Can. Dept. Agr. Publ. *1257*.

DOWNEY, R. K. 1966. Towards an improved rapeseed. Can. Agr. Inst. Rev. *21*, 16–18.

TAPE, N. W., SABRY, Z. I., and EAPEN, K. E. 1970. Production of rapeseed flour for human consumption. Can. Inst. Food Technol. J. *3*, No. 3, 78–81.

Cross-Reference: *Fats and Oils.*

REFINING OF CORN

See Corn and Corn Products.

REFRIGERATED STORAGE

The knowledge that food keeps better in cool than in warm places is older than history. At first, man depended on the cooler air in such places as caves, root cellars, and spring houses. These, however, provided only a moderate reduction in temperature. It is only in comparatively recent times that real refrigeration has been used.

Fish, being very perishable, was one of the first foods to benefit from refrigeration. In 1838, the captain of a Gloucester, Mass., fishing smack used ice to preserve a catch of halibut until it could reach port and be marketed. By 1858, fish were shipped in iced containers from New England to New York City.

Natural ice, harvested from frozen rivers and ponds in the winter and stored under sawdust in icehouses, was used for refrigeration at first. Development of the modern commercial ice making plant began about 1876, and ice made from

potable waters gradually replaced natural ice, which was often of questionable sanitary quality.

Mechanical warehouse refrigeration first became of practical importance around 1890, but the construction of refrigerated warehouses on a large scale did not begin until about 1915. These were mostly for meat packing plants and by 1921 comprised about 294 million cubic feet. Public and private refrigerated warehouses came into prominence about 1920. There were about 850 of them then, with a total of 250 million cubic feet of space. By 1969, refrigerated space for meat packing establishments had decreased to about 36 million cubic feet, but space in public and private cold storages had increased to about 1.3 billion cubic feet.

The development of mechanical refrigeration made it practical for large-scale preservation of food by freezing. In 1930, the list of commercial frozen foods consisted mainly of fish, small fruits, poultry, meats, eggs, and a few vegetables. The quantity and variety increased gradually through the 1930's as the home mechanical refrigerator became a standard household appliance and the frozen products were improved. The expansion of the frozen food industry was facilitated further in the 1950's by the development of the household freezer.

By 1969, the commercial frozen pack of fruits and vegetables amounted to nearly 6 billion pounds and consisted of more than 21 kinds of fruits and 34 kinds of vegetables.

Nonfreezing cold temperatures are used to preserve foods in their natural state as long as possible. The temperature used depends on the product. Some keep best at temperatures near 32°F. Others are injured by chilling even at temperatures considerably above the freezing point. For instance, fresh beef, milk, cabbage, and lettuce keep best at near 32°F, whereas sweet potatoes and mature green tomatoes are injured in temperatures lower than 55°F. For optimum storage life, the refrigeration temperature should be tailored to the requirements of the commodity.

Foods can be kept for longer periods if frozen and stored at temperatures below 0°F provided they have been properly prepared, processed, and packaged. Vegetables, after grading, washing, and trimming, are blanched with hot water or steam to reduce enzymatic action and to destroy most of the yeasts, molds, and bacteria; they are then cooled rapidly to about 50°F and packaged. Enzymes that cause browning of fruits are inhibited by added citric or ascorbic acid, treatment with sulfur dioxide, or packing in sugar syrup. Meats are often cut into portions or molded or shaped into desired forms. Economy grades of meat may be dipped in approved tenderizing solutions before freezing. Meats may be frozen raw or precooked.

Frozen products are packaged in plastic bags, plastic lined boxes, cans, glass jars, and metal foil trays. The purpose of the package is to hold the product and protect it from moisture loss and exposure to air during freezing and storage. The packaging material should be relatively impermeable to moisture to prevent desiccation; have a low gas transmission rate to retard oxidation and discoloration of the product; be free of any odor, flavor, or toxic substance that may be absorbed by the product; and have sufficient strength to resist rupture, deformation, or other physical damage.

Food products should be stacked in storage in a manner that allows adequate air circulation to maintain a uniform temperature throughout the room. This is especially important for nonfrozen foods that continue to respire and generate heat.

Modern transportation vehicles are equipped to maintain recommended temperatures while the food products are being transported to the terminal market and are being distributed to the retail stores. Refrigerated railway cars are being rapidly equipped with mechanical refrigeration units that can provide subzero temperatures for frozen foods or a range of nonfreezing temperatures for chilled foods. Trucks, trailers, and piggyback containers also are equipped with mechanical refrigeration units that are powered by the truck engine, independent gas engines, or electric units that can be plugged into electric outlets at the packing shed, warehouse, piggyback train, or container ship. Some trucks use cryogenic or bottled liquid gas refrigerating systems. For this purpose, liquid nitrogen or liquid carbon dioxide is released from pressurized tanks through a spray nozzle or nozzles at the ceiling of the truck when the need is indicated by a temperature sensing element.

Refrigeration is sometimes supplemented by modifying the atmosphere of the storage room or transportation container by chemical treatments and by irradiation.

Atmospheres containing higher than normal concentrations of carbon dioxide and less than normal concentrations of oxygen have been found useful for retarding deterioration of meat, fish, eggs, fruits, and vegetables. These modified atmospheres inhibit the development of some kinds of yeasts, bacteria, and fungi and retard physiological and compositional changes in fruits and vegetables by suppressing respiration. Modified atmospheres are especially useful for products that cannot be stored at low temperatures because of their susceptibility to chilling injury.

Modified atmospheres may be created by respiration of fruits or vegetables in a gas-tight storage room. The desired oxygen-carbon dioxide ratio is maintained by using various types of scrubbers to remove the excess carbon dioxide and ventilating with outside air when the oxygen level is too low. Modified atmospheres also may be provided by commercial generators of various types that remove most of the oxygen in the air by controlled combustion. The composition of the resulting atmosphere is adjusted by means of scrubbers and the addition of oxygen to provide an atmosphere of the desired composition. Since the generated atmosphere is continually supplied to the storage room, a positive inside pressure is maintained and the storage room need not be completely gas tight. Modified atmospheres also may be obtained by the use of Dry Ice and the release of liquified carbon dioxide or nitrogen in the storage room.

Chemical treatments that are used to supplement refrigeration are: antioxidants to retard development of rancidity in frozen poultry, fats, oils, and fat-containing foods; sprout inhibitors to retard sprouting of seed potatoes and onions; fumigation with sulfur dioxide to reduce decay and preserve the color of the stem and cap stems of California grapes; and chlorine, thiabendazole, sodium orthophenylphenate, and other chemical washes to reduce spoilage. Gamma radiation and ultraviolet light are used to a limited extent to reduce spoilage.

For maximum storage life and the highest quality, it is important that the products put in storage be of high quality. Animals should be protected from fatigue and physical damage prior to slaughter, and the carcass should be handled under sanitary conditions after slaughter. Fruits and vegatables should be as free as possible from skin breaks, bruises, decay, and other deterioration; they should be harvested at an optimum stage of maturity, and should be stored as soon as possible after harvest.

Storage rooms and transportation vehicles usually do not have sufficient refrigeration capacity and air circulation for the rapid cooling that is essential for good storage and market life. The temperature of a beef animal is about 102°F at slaughter, and chemical changes that occur for about 30 hr raise the temperature even higher. To keep spoilage to a minimum, the carcass temperature should be lowered to about 35°F as rapidly as possible. The internal temperature of hog carcasses when put in the chilling room, ranges from 100° to 106°F. The present practice is to chill and temper the carcass to an internal ham temperature of 37°-39°F in 16-22 hr. The temperature of fruits and vegetables is often 80°-90°F when they are harvested. Since fruits and vegetables are living, they continue to respire and generate heat. Rapid cooling is necessary to remove the field heat and to slow down respiration and the ripening process and decay.

Beef, pork, and lamb are precooled by hanging the carcasses or carcass halves on rails in chilling rooms in which the temperature is about 32°F. Adequate space is allowed between the carcasses for good air circulation. Variety meats (livers, hearts, kidneys, tongues, etc.) may be chilled overnight in trays in chilling rooms in which the air temperature is 30°–32°F or quick chilled by using an air temperature of approximately –5°F and higher air velocities which bring the meat temperature to 32°–34°F in 1/2–4 hr.

Fruits and vegetables may be cooled by rapidly moving refrigerated air, hydrocooled with icewater, or cooled with crushed ice in the package and on top of the load.

Air cooling may be accomplished by stacking the packed containers in a refrigerated room with adequate spacing for good air circulation. Accelerating the air circulation by fans speeds the precooling. Air cooling also may be accomplished by passing the packed unlidded containers on conveyors through a tunnel in which they are exposed to high velocity refrigerated air from overhead jets. A comparatively recent development is pressure cooling, in which the packed containers are tightly stacked in rows and the refrigerated air is forced through the containers. For this method of cooling, the containers must be constructed in such a way to permit free passage of air.

Hydrocooling may be accomplished by immersing the product, either before or after packaging, in ice water or by passing the product on conveyors through tunnels in which it is either sprayed or flooded with ice water.

Top ice and package ice are used mostly to precool products in transit. For top icing, the ice is finely crushed and blown over the load in the car or trailer. Part of the ice also falls down into the channels between the packages. For package icing, the crushed ice is usually placed in the middle of the container as it is being packed.

Vacuum cooling is cooling by rapid evaporation of water from the product. It is most effective for leafy vegetables because of their large surface area. Almost all of the California and Arizona lettuce and some eastern lettuce is vacuum cooled. There is increasing use of vacuum cooling for celery, cauliflower, green peas, and sweet corn. In vacuum cooling, the packed product is placed in a chamber that can be hermetically sealed and the air is rapidly evacuated to an atmospheric pressure of about 4.6 mm of mercury, the pressure at which water boils at 32°F. The water evaporating from the plant tissues at this reduced pressure cools the product to about 32°F in 15–20 min. Moisture loss from leafy vegetables during vacuum

cooling ranges from 1.5 to 4.7% and is not sufficient to cause noticeable wilting.

Refrigeration is the process of removing heat from a substance. Heat is commonly measured in British thermal units (Btu). A Btu is the quantity of heat required to raise the temperature of 1 lb of water 1°F. The ratio of heat required to cause an equivalent rise in the temperature of the same weight of any other material is called its specific heat. It varies with the water content and is usually calculated by the formula:

$$\text{Specific heat} = 0.008 \times \% \text{ water} + 0.20$$

The amount of refrigeration is commonly stated in "tons of refrigeration," a term that originated when ice was used. The standard ton of refrigeration is the amount of heat absorbed by a ton of ice melting in 24 hr at 32°F. This is equal to 288,000 Btu. The amount of refrigeration required to cool products and to maintain the desired storage temperature depends on the heat load. The heat load consists of (1) the field or body heat of the product and its container, (2) the heat of respiration of fruits and vegetables, (3) heat leakage of the storage chamber, and (4) heat generated by fan motors, lights, etc. The heat load due to field or body heat may be calculated by the formula:

$$\text{Heat load} = \text{specific heat of product} \times \text{weight} \times \text{temperature difference} = \text{Btu}$$

The heat load due to respiration of fruits and vegetables varies with the different kinds and the temperature. Heat of respiration rates have been calculated for various kinds of fruits and vegetables at temperatures ranging from 32° to 80°F.

Commodities Storage Conditions

Bakery Products.—Bread may be stored several weeks if frozen quickly and held at temperatures below 0°F. Slow freezing increases the rate of staling. Cakes, dinner rolls, and doughnuts keep satisfactorily for 8 weeks at 0°F. Frozen baked pies become soggy, but unbaked fruit pies keep well if stored at 0°F or lower.

Dairy Products.—Pasteurized Grade A milk has an approximate storage life of 7 days at 33°F. Evaporated milk will keep 1 yr or longer at room temperature, but it should be turned periodically to prevent separation. Dried whole milk and dried nonfat milk will keep several months at 45°–55°F. The storage life of whole dried milk is somewhat less than that of nonfat dried milk. Butter will keep for 2 months at 32°–40°F, but for longer storage it should be held at 0° to –10°F. The ideal storage temperature for cheddar cheese, after curing, is 30°–34°F. At this temperature it may

TABLE R-8

RECOMMENDED STORAGE LIFE AND TEMPERATURE FOR APPLE VARIETIES

Variety	Temp (°F)	Storage Life (Months) Norm	Storage Life (Months) Max
Baldwin	30–32	4–5	6–7
Cortland	38[1]	3–4	5–6
Delicious	30–32	3–4	8
Golden Delicious	30–32	3–4	6–8
Gravenstein	30–32	0–2	3
Grimes Golden	30–32	2–3	4
Johnathan	32[1]	2–3	5–6
McIntosh	38[1]	2–4	6–8
Northern Spy	30–32[2]	4–5	8
Rhode Island Greening	30–32	3–4	6–7
Rome Beauty	30–32[2]	4–5	6–8
Stayman	30–32	4–5	6–8
Wealthy	30–32	0–2	3
Winesap	30–32	5–6	8
Yellow Newtown	38–40[3]	5–6	8
York Imperial	30–32	4–5	6–7

[1]With modified atmosphere of 2–5% carbon dioxide and 3% oxygen.
[2]A modified atmosphere of 1–3% carbon dioxide and 2–3% oxygen results in better quality and longer storage life of these varieties.
[3]With modified atmosphere of 7–8% carbon dioxide and 2–3% oxygen.

be kept for 12–18 months. At from 45° to 70°F the storage life is only about 2 months. The relative humidity should be about 70%. Swiss cheese may be held for 2–6 months at 35°–40°F. Blue cheese may be held for 1–6 months at 40°–45°F. Cottage cheese should be stored at 35°F.

Eggs.—Shell eggs should be kept at 29°–31°F if stored for 6–9 months. Coating the shell with oil before the eggs are 24 hr old prevents escape of the carbon dioxide that is naturally present and retards loss of quality and moisture. Frozen whole eggs, yolks, and whites will keep more than a year at 0°F or below.

Fish.—Fresh fish, packed in crushed ice, can be held for 5–15 days in storage rooms with an air temperature of 33°–35°F. Fresh shell fish will keep for only 3–7 days at 33°F.

Fruits.—Apples.—The optimum storage temperature for most varieties of apples is 30°–32°F, but some, such as McIntosh and California-grown Yellow Newtown are affected by physiological disorders at these temperatures. Higher temperatures and modified atmospheres are recommended for them. The storage life varies widely depending on the variety, production area, cultural practices, climatic conditions during the growing season, maturity when picked, and storage practices. The storage life and recommended storage temperature for commonly-grown American varieties are shown in Table R-8.

Scald, a serious physiological disorder, can be controlled by diphenylamine or ethoxyquin applied as a dip or spray or impregnated on paper wrappers.

Apricots.—The optimum storage temperature is 31°–32°F. Storage life at this temperature is about 1–2 weeks.

Avocados.—Cold-tolerant varieties such as Lulu and Booth 8 can be stored at 40°F for a month or longer. Fuerte keeps best at 45°F. Fuchs, Pollock, and Waldin keep best at 55°F, and their storage life is only about 2 weeks.

Bananas.—Bananas are shipped green and ripened either in transit or in ripening rooms at the terminal markets. The shipping and holding temperature for green bananas is 58°F. Bananas will ripen in about 8–10 days at 58°F and in 4 days at 68°F. The ripe bananas can be held for 2–4 days at 56°–58°F.

Berries (Except Cranberries).—The optimum storage temperature for blackberries, blueberries, currants, gooseberries, raspberries, and strawberries is 32°F. The storage life at this temperature is shown in Table R-9.

Cranberries.—Cranberries can be stored for 3–4 months at 36°–40°F. Poorly colored fruit is sometimes held at 45°–50°F for a few weeks to improve the color.

Cherries.—Sweet cherries can be kept 2–3 weeks at 30°–31°F. The use of sealed polyethylene liners in the containers that permit the cherries to develop package atmospheres of 7–9% carbon dioxide and 3–5% oxygen by respiration will extend the storage life by at least 1 week.

Dates.—Deglet Noor and similar varieties retain flavor, texture, color, and aroma satisfactorily for 1 yr at 32°F and somewhat longer at 0°F. The

TABLE R-9

STORAGE LIFE OF BERRIES AT 32°F

Kind of Berry	Storage Life
Blackberries	2–3 days
Blueberries	2 weeks
Currants	1–2 weeks
Gooseberries	3–4 weeks
Raspberries	2–3 days[1]
Strawberries	5–7 days[1]

[1]Further ripening in the storage or shipping container and development of decay can be delayed by use of Dry Ice to produce atmospheres of up to 25% carbon dioxide.

soft, invert sugar type of dates should be stored at 0°F or lower.

Figs (Fresh).—Fresh figs are extremely perishable, but they can be kept satisfactorily for 7–10 days at 31°–32°F.

Grapefruit.—Grapefruit that is sound and has been handled carefully can be stored 4–6 weeks, but the optimum temperature for grapefruit varies with the variety and growing area. A temperature of 58°–60°F is recommended for California and Arizona grapefruit, but 50°F is recommended for Florida and Texas grapefruit. However, Florida-grown Marsh and Ruby Red grapefruit picked before January should be stored at 60°F to avoid skin pitting.

Grapes.—The *V. vinifera* table grapes grown in California can be stored for up to 6 months at 30°–31°F. For longest storage life they should be fumigated with sulfur dioxide when put in storage and at 10-day intervals during the storage period. The American varieties, which are grown in the east, have a shorter storage life and can be held for only 2–8 weeks at 31°–32°F. They should not be fumigated with sulfur dioxide.

Lemons.—Lemons are stored for 1–6 months at 58°–60°F in the production areas. Temperatures below 58°F cause pitting of the peel, staining of the membranes, and red blotches to develop. At the terminal markets, the lemons may be held for up to 4 weeks at 32°–55°F but 52°–55°F is recommended for longer periods.

Limes.—Limes, if picked while still green but after the skin has become smooth, can be stored satisfactorily for 6–8 weeks at 48°–50°F.

Mangos.—Mangos keep satisfactorily for 2–3 weeks at 55°F. Most varieties develop chilling injury at lower temperatures. The best ripening temperature is 70°–75°F. Higher temperatures often cause abnormal flavors.

Oranges.—Oranges usually go directly to the fresh market or to processing plants. However, the Valencia, a late variety, is sometimes stored to extend the marketing season. Florida and Texas Valencia oranges can be stored with a minimum of decay and rind pitting for 8–12 weeks at 32°F. California and Arizona oranges must be stored at higher temperatures to avoid rind disorders. Most California oranges should be stored at 40°–44°F, but desert-grown California Valencias may be injured at these temperatures and should be stored at 48°F. Arizona oranges harvested in March should be stored at 48°F, but those harvested in June may be stored at 38°F. The storage life is 6–8 weeks at 38°F, 4–6 weeks at 40°–44°F, and 3–4 weeks at 48°F.

Papayas.—Hawaiian papayas for shipping, are harvested at the ³/₄ ripe color stage and treated to control insects and decay. Papayas are subject to chilling injury at temperatures below 45°F. They keep satisfactorily for 7–21 days at 45°F. The should be ripened at 70°–80°F.

Peaches and Nectarines.—Peaches and nectarines do not keep well in storage but can be stored for 2–3 weeks at 31°–32°F. Peaches stored at 36°–50°F have poorer flavor and more internal breakdown after ripening than those stored at 31°–32°F.

Pears.—Most pears are stored at 29°–31°F. The temperature of the storage must be carefully controlled to prevent freezing since some pears may freeze at temperatures as high as 29.2°F. Since pears lose moisture rapidly, the relative humidity of the storage should be 90–95%. Polyethylene box liners are useful for preventing moisture loss and ripening. The best ripening temperature after storage is 65°F. The storage life of pears varies with different varieties. The safe length of storage at 30°F is shown in the Table R-10.

Scald, a physiological disease, can be controlled on Anjou pears by ethoxyquin applied as a dip or spray or impregnated in paper wrappers.

Pineapples.—The usual storage life for pineapples is 2–4 weeks. Fruit harvested at the ¹/₂ ripe stage can be stored about 2 weeks at 45°–55°F and still have about 1 week of market life. Mature green fruit is especially subject to chilling injury and should not be held at temperatures below 50°F.

Plums and Fresh Prunes.—Well-matured plums and prunes can be stored satisfactorily for 2–4 weeks at 31°–32°F. Those with high soluble solids content keep better than those with low solids. Most varieties ripen best at about 65°F. Some fail to ripen properly at 80°F or above.

Frozen Fruits.—The approximate storage life of frozen fruits is 6–12 months at temperatures of 0° to -10°F. Exposure to temperatures higher than

TABLE R-10

SAFE LENGTH OF STORAGE FOR
PEARS AT 30°F

Variety	Storage Life (Months)
Bartlett[1]	2¹/₂–3
Hardy	2–3
Comice[1]	2¹/₂–3
Kiefer	2¹/₂–3
Bosc[1]	3–3¹/₂
Seckel	3–3¹/₂
Anjou[1]	4–6
Packham	5–6
Winter Nelis	6–7

[1] Storage life of Anjou, Bartlett, Comice, and Bosc can be extended 4–8 weeks by using polyethylene liners in the boxes.

0°F, even for short periods, hastens deterioration such as flavor changes, browning, leaching of color into the syrup, and loss of vitamin C.

Meat.—Fresh beef, veal, lamb, and pork may be stored at 32°-34°F. At this temperature range the storage life is 1-6 weeks for beef, 5-10 days for veal, 5-12 days for lamb, and 7-12 days for pork. A modified atmosphere containing 10-20% carbon dioxide will extend the storage life by inhibiting the development of microorganisms that cause rapid deterioration. The storage life of meat can be greatly extended by freezing. The average freezing point for fresh meat is 28°-29°F, but for maximum storage life, the temperature should be 0° to -10°F. At -10°F, beef will keep 12-24 months, veal 8 months, lamb 12-18 months, and pork 8-15 months.

Vegetables.—The optimum relative humidity for the storage of most vegetables is 90-95%. However, 85-90% RH is better for melons and 65-70% RH is best for onions.

Asparagus.—Fresh asparagus usually goes directly to market, but it can be stored for up to 3 weeks if there is a temporary oversupply. It can be stored for 10 days at 32°F, but if it is to be stored longer, the temperature should be 36°F to avoid chilling injury.

Beans.—Green or snap beans have a storage life of only about one week. They keep best at 45°F. If kept at lower temperatures they develop surface pitting and russet discoloration 1-2 days after they are removed from storage. Unshelled lima beans can be stored for about 1 week at 32°-40°F, but the pods discolor rapidly after they are removed to room temperature. Shelled lima beans in quart baskets or perforated polyethylene bags keep in satisfactory condition for about 10-14 days at 32°F; 8 days at 36°F; and 4-7 days at 40°F.

Beets.—Topped beets keep satisfactorily for 3-5 months when stored at 32°F provided the relative humidity is high enough to prevent wilting.

Broccoli.—Broccoli is usually stored only as long as necessary for orderly marketing. If good air circulation is provided to prevent heating, it can be kept for 10-14 days at 32°F.

Brussels Sprouts.—Brussels sprouts keep in good condition for 3-5 weeks when stored at 32°F. Black specking on the leaves, loss of fresh bright-green color, decay, wilting, and discoloration of the cut stems occurs if they are stored longer.

Cabbage.—The optimum storage temperature for cabbage is 32°F. Storage life is 3-4 months for the late crop and 3-6 weeks for the early crop varieties.

Carrots.—Mature carrots keep well in storage for 4-5 months at 32°F. They are stored in large quantities for use in processing during the winter.

Cauliflower.—Cauliflower is usually not stored, but if it is in good condition, it can be held for 2-4 weeks at 32°F. Packing in crushed ice will aid in keeping it fresh. Slightly immature heads keep better than mature ones.

Celery.—Celery can be stored successfully for 2-3 months at 32°F. The relative humidity must be kept up to 90-95% to prevent wilting. Perforated polyethylene film liners in the crates or cartons aid in retarding moisture loss.

Sweet Corn.—Sweet corn is seldom stored. However, it can be held for 8 days at 32°F if it is precooled immediately after harvest and top iced.

Eggplant.—Eggplant is subject to chilling injury at temperatures below 45°F. They can be held for only about 1 week at 45°-50°F.

Endive and Escarole.—These leafy vegetables can be kept 2-3 weeks in storage at 32°F. They keep better if stored with cracked ice in or around the package.

Garlic.—Well-cured garlic, if in good condition, can be stored for 6-7 months at 32°F. The relative humidity should not be above 65-70%.

Leafy Greens.—Leafy greens (collards, kale, rape, Swiss chard, and beet and turnip greens) are very perishable. They can be held for 10-14 days at 32°F. Vitamin content is reduced if they are allowed to wilt. This can be prevented by the use of package and top ice.

Lettuce.—If in good condition, lettuce can be stored 2-3 weeks at 32°F and 95% RH. The temperature must be controlled precisely to prevent freezing damage which may occur at temperatures as high as 31.7°F. It deteriorates rapidly at higher temperatures. The use of individual plastic film head wrappers or carton liners reduces moisture loss and creates a modified atmosphere that aids in maintaining quality during storage.

Melons.—Watermelons are not suited to long storage. They are subject to chilling injury below 40°F and to decay at high temperatures. The red color fades even at 50°F. They may be kept in reasonably good condition for only about 2 weeks at 40°-50°F.

Cantaloups harvested at the hard ripe stage ($^3/_4$ to full slip) will keep for about 15 days at 36°-48°F but are injured by lower temperatures. Riper melons, harvested at the full slip stage, can be held for 5-14 days at 32°-35°F.

Honey Dew, Casaba, Crenshaw, and Persian melons are subject to chilling injury at temperatures below 45°-50°F. The storage life in this temperature range is:

	Storage Life (Weeks)
Honey Dew	3-4
Casaba	4-6
Crenshaw	2
Persian	2

Partially ripe melons should be stored at 50°F or slightly above; otherwise they will not ripen satisfactorily.

Mushrooms (Cultivated).—Fresh mushrooms do not keep well in storage. Their storage life is only 5 days at 32°F; 2 days at 40°F; and 1 day at 50°F.

Okra.—If in good condition, okra can be kept satisfactorily for 7-10 days at 45°-50°F. It is injured by lower temperatures.

Onions, Dry.—Well-cured globe onions can be stored satisfactorily for 6-8 months at 32°F. The mild, or Bermuda, types have a shorter storage life and will keep only 1-2 months. A low relative humidity (65-70%) is important. Higher humidities promote decay and root growth.

Onions, Green.—Green onions are very perishable and will keep only a few days at 32°F.

Parsley.—Parsley can be stored for 1-2 months at 32°F. Package icing is beneficial.

Parsnips.—Parsnips, if in good condition, can be stored for 2-6 months at 32°F. Parsnips lose moisture rapidly; therefore, 90-95% RH is important. Ventilated box liners are useful for retarding moisture loss.

Peas, Green.—Green peas can be stored for 1-2 weeks at 32°F if they are precooled promptly after picking. Top icing will extend the storage life a few days.

Peppers, Sweet.—Peppers can be stored 2-3 weeks at 45°-50°F. They are subject to chilling injury at lower temperatures and higher temperatures promote ripening and decay. Packaging in perforated polyethylene film retards moisture loss and may extend storage life for about one week.

Potatoes.—Early crop potatoes are only stored for relatively short periods. If they are free from serious bruising, heat injury, and decay they can be held for 4-5 months at 40°F. If cured for at least 4 days at 60°-70°F, they can be stored for 2-3 months at 50°F. The late crop potatoes produced in the northern part of the United States may be stored in nonrefrigerated or refrigerated warehouses. They should be kept at 45°-65°F and at a high relative humidity for 10-14 days to allow healing of cut and skinned areas. Then the temperature should be lowered to 38°-40°F. Lower temperatures cause the potatoes to become undesirably sweet. Most varieties can be stored for 5-8 months at 40°F. A temperature of 50°-55°F is recommended for potatoes that are to be used for making potato chips. Temperatures of 45°-50°F are satisfactory for potatoes to be used for frozen french fries. Chemical sprout inhibitors, such as CIPC, TCNB, and maleic hydrazide are often used to prevent sprouting of potatoes for processing that are stored at higher temperatures.

Pumpkins and Squashes.—Pumpkins and squashes are subject to chilling injury if stored at tempera-

tures below 50°F. In a temperature range of 50°-55°F, Connecticut Field and Cushaw pumpkins will keep about 2-3 months; Hubbard squash for 6 months; and Acorn type squashes for 8 weeks. Summer squashes, such as Yellow Crookneck, Banana, Zucchini, and other soft types that are harvested at the immature stage can be held only a few days at 32°-42°F. If held longer at this temperature they suffer chilling injury. At 45°-50°F they have a storage life of 2 weeks or less.

Radishes.—Topped radishes that have been cooled quickly and packaged in polyethylene bags have a storage life of approximately 3-4 weeks at 32°F.

Rhubarb.—Fresh rhubarb stalks with about 1/4 in. of leaf attached can be stored for about 2-4 weeks at 32°F.

Rutabagas.—Rutabagas should keep satisfactorily for 2-4 months at 32°F. Coating the roots with hot paraffin wax is effective in preventing wilting and loss of weight.

Spinach.—Spinach can be stored not more than 10-14 days at 32°F. It deteriorates rapidly at higher temperatures. Package ice and top ice is beneficial.

Sweet Potatoes.—Refrigerated storage is seldom used for sweet potatoes. Sweet potatoes are cured for 4-7 days at 85°F and about 90% RH immediately after harvesting, and then held at 55°-60°F. Temperatures of 50°F or lower will cause chilling injury. If not disturbed during storage, sweet potatoes will keep satisfactorily for 4-6 months. After removal from storage, they must be marketed quickly to avoid high losses from decay.

Tomatoes.—Mature green tomatoes are very subject to chilling injury which prevents normal ripening and development of decay. The optimum temperature range for mature green tomatoes is about 57°-60°F. At this temperature the fruit will ripen in 7-14 days. Firm ripe tomatoes can be held in satisfactory condition for approximately 1 week at 50°F.

Turnips.—Topped turnips can be held satisfactorily for 4-5 months at 32°F if they are free from injuries and bruises.

Frozen Vegetables.—The approximate storage life of frozen vegetables is 6-12 months at temperatures of 0° to -10°F. Exposure to temperatures higher than 0°F, even for short periods, hastens deterioration such as changes in color and flavor.

Dried Fruits and Vegetables.—Deterioration of dried fruits can be reduced by storage at 32°-45°F and low (55-60%) relative humidity. They will keep about 1 year at 32°F and 6-8 months at 40°F. These low temperatures also retard insect infestation. Refrigeration at 45°F or lower is needed for long storage of dried vegetables, but most of them can be kept for several months to 1 yr at 70°F.

HAROLD T. COOK

Reference

LUTZ, J. M., and HARDENBURG, R. E. 1968. The commercial storage of fruits, vegetables and florist and nursery stocks. USDA Agr. Handbook 66.

RESEARCH EVOP—EVOLUTIONARY OPERATIONS

The underlying philosophy of EVOP is to continuously probe for the opportunity for change which would result in an improvement. This is directly opposite but complementary to the control-chart approach which attempts to maintain a given process within certain limits. This objective of optimizing a process to accommodate ever-changing or evolutionary conditions was developed by Box (1957) on the assumption that it is seldom efficient to operate an industrial process to produce product alone, but rather it should be performed so as to generate product plus information on how to improve the product and reduce cost.

The search for an improved product or process by EVOP is accomplished by slightly varying each of the variables under study from the normal standard operating level, first higher then lower according to a fixed pattern. Variables under study are changed each time so slightly that even if the test did not produce a better product or process the resulting product would not be unsalable. Thus, the risk of making large quantities of a nonconforming product is minimized. The major advantage of EVOP is that it can be performed on the production line with a minimum of interruption. Other advantages are that it does not require a thorough knowledge of mathematics and that the results are available immediately to people who can use and analyze them, the line personnel. As with control charts, EVOP can be applied readily to a 1- or 2-variable situation although the statistical procedure on which it is based, mapping of response surfaces, can be applied to situations of any degree of complexity involving more than 2 variables (Duncan 1959). For "production line" use, it is recommended that studies be limited to not more than two variables. More elaborate studies, where the experimental design is saturated with all possible variables, should be limited to the laboratory.

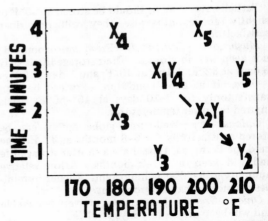

FIG. R-1. GRAPHIC PRESENTATION OF FIVE EVOP TREATMENTS ILLUSTRATING THE EMERGENCE OF A SLOPE OF STEEPEST ASCENT

For in-plant studies, we may conveniently consider two factors simultaneously, such as the effects of time and temperature on yield (Fig. R-1). The present time and temperature may be considered as treatment 1, or the central point, with 4 variations in all directions: X_1—current procedures; X_2—higher temperature and shorter time; X_3—lower temperature and shorter time; X_4—lower temperature and longer time; X_5—higher temperature and longer time. The deviations from the central point should, at least in the beginning, be small enough so that they do not affect the end product to the extent that it might become unsalable. Since variations among these treatments are small, it is not likely that an obvious difference can be demonstrated after running through these 5 treatments once only (1 cycle). If, after these 5 treatments are replicated, say 5–6 cycles, and there is still no significant difference in response in terms of yield or quality, it would then be appropriate to increase the size of the increment in one or both directions. The process would then be repeated until a significant difference emerges. Each time enough cycles are completed to justify changing the treatments, a *phase* of the EVOP procedure ends.

If it should be found that treatment X_1 (the current process) is significantly better than any variation in any direction, then the EVOP study could still be continued, but less frequently. If, however, one of the peripheral treatments (X_2, X_3, X_4, or X_5) should be found to be significantly superior to the central treatment (X_1), then the adjustments would be made in the equipment to proceed with the new "best" time and temperature as the central treatment (e.g., X_2, Y_1, in Fig. R-1), and with the previous central treatment (X_1, Y_4) serving as 1 of the 4 new peripheral treatments

(Y_2, Y_3, Y_5). In this way there could be continuous evolutionary probing in all directions for a best treatment under continuously changing conditions.

The stream of information concerning the products from the various manufacturing conditions is summarized on an information board prominently displayed in the plant so that interested personnel can follow the progress of the operation. The entries shown on the information board are: (1) The number of the present phase. (2) The number of the last cycle completed. (3) The average response observed at each set of conditions to the conclusion of the last cycle, and "error limits," "least significant difference," or "rank sum" required for a statistically significant difference. The entries on the information board are changed at the end of each cycle. The calculations required to develop these data are based on simple statistical procedures as suggested by Box (1957). Kramer (1964) has further simplified the statistical calculations by using ranks instead of actual values, thereby eliminating the calculations necessary to determine the standard deviations.

AMIHUD KRAMER

References

BOX, G. E. P. 1957. Evolutionary operation: A method for increasing industrial productivity. Appl. Statistics 6, No. 2, 3–23.
DUNCAN, A. J. 1959. Mapping response surfaces and determination of optimum conditions. *In* Quality Control and Industrial Statistics. Richard D. Irwin, Homewood, Illinois.
KRAMER, A. 1964. The effective use of operations Research and EVOP in quality control. Food Technol. *19*, No. 1, 37–39.

RHUBARB

This delicious vegetable stem can be made into a variety of jams and jellies, sauce, pie filling, juice, and confections. It was described as a drug as early as 2700 B.C. in the Chinese herbal Pen-King (Wiebe and Zubeckis 1967). Rhubarb belongs to the family Polygonaceae, genus *Rheum* which has about 50 species, 9 of which are considered to have edible stalks. Most of our modern varieties have been developed from three species, *R. hybridum Murr.*, *R. rhaponticum L.*, and *R. undulatum L.* Varieties such as Cherry, Crimson Wine, German Wine, Jersey, MacDonald, Strawberry, Sunrise, Sutton's, Valentine, and Victoria are grown for fresh market, freezing, and heat preservation. Victoria is by far the most universally grown variety in North America. The

production in the United States for freezing has been between 3000 and 4000 tons over the past 20 yr, mostly in the western states. In recent years, some 500 to 1000 tons of rhubarb have been grown in hothouses for freezing in the off-season, mostly in Washington and Michigan (Hilliker 1967; Wolford 1966). The usual procedure for freezing consists of cutting the stems into 1-in. lengths after trimming, washing, sorting, blanching for 2 min in steam, cooling, then filling into retail or institutional containers with sugar in the ratio of 6 parts fruit to 1 part sugar. The packages are frozen in the usual manner in an air blast or in still cold air.

Although rhubarb products can be packed in cans and preserved by heating, the corrosion problem even with enamel cans is too great. Blundstone and Dickinson (1964) investigated this problem of corrosion and concluded that components other than acid may be responsible. In spite of the problem, some 9000 tons of rhubarb are canned in England annually, mostly in large containers for restaurants and bakeries. A more suitable container for retail sizes would be glass. Other products such as sauce, jam, juice, and jelly may be packed in glass also as discussed by Wiebe and Zubeckis (1967). Most varieties of rhubarb contain about 10 mg per 100 gm of vitamin C and fair amounts of several mineral nutrients such as potassium, calcium, and phosphorus.

The stalks contain about the same amount of oxalic acid as spinach and other greens. These quantities are not harmful, but may combine with calcium into insoluble salts, thus depriving the body of an essential element.

FRANK P. BOYLE

References

BLUNDSTONE, H. A. W., and DICKINSON, D. 1964. The chemistry of edible rhubarb. J. Sc. Food Agr. *15*, 94–101.
HILLIKER, F. 1967. Co-op freezer keeps farmers busy with Michigan winter rhubarb crop. Canner/Packer Western Edition *136*, No. 9, 20–21.
WIEBE, J., and ZUBECKIS, E. 1967. Rhubarb. Culture and Physiology. Chemistry and Technology. Ontario Dept. Agr. Food, Toronto, Canada.
WOLFORD, E. R. 1966. Varieties of hot-house rhubarb for freezing. Private communication. Puyallup, Wash.

RICE AND RICE BY-PRODUCTS

Rice, *Oryza Sativa* L., has been one of the most commonly-used grain products since ancient times.

It is the staple food of the greatest number of people, and over $1/2$ the world's population eats rice as the main article of diet. No historian can be accurate about the first appearance of rice because rice cultivation is older than recorded events. Though a lack of historical records prevents accurate determination, botanical evidence suggests strongly that rice originated in southeast continental Asia.

The many varieties of rice reflect the wide variation of conditions of growth. Though usually thought of as a tropical lowland crop, rice is grown from $43°$ N. Latitude to $39°$ S. Latitude and at elevations of 8000 ft or more in India. The best yields are found in subtropical or warm temperature climates. Usually grown on heavy water-retaining soils under flooded conditions, rice can be and is, to some extent, grown under upland conditions as are other cereals. Rice is grown in all tropical countries in eastern and southeastern Asia including the larger nearby islands, especially Japan. The total annual world production is approximately 5 billion hundredweight. The principal rice-producing countries are China, India, Pakistan, Japan, and Indonesia. Thailand, Indochina, Burma, and the Philippines also produce large quantities of rice. These 9 countries account for more than 90% of the total world production. The important areas of production other than Asia are the United States, Spain, Italy, Egypt, and Brazil.

Rice was first produced commercially in this country in South Carolina about 1685, and its cultivation gradually spread into North Carolina, Georgia, Alabama, Mississippi, and Florida. After the Civil War, this situation changed abruptly. By about 1887, the important rice-producing area had shifted from the Atlantic seaboard to the Southern States, with a rapid increase in acreage along the Mississippi River in Louisiana. Rice growing extended to the prairies of southeastern Texas in about 1900 and to the prairies of Arkansas in 1905. In California, commercial production of rice was begun in 1912 in the vicinity of Biggs. In recent years, rice production has begun again in Mississippi. Although the United States produces only 80 million hundredweight, slightly less than 2% of the world total, approximately 60% of the domestic production is exported.

U.S. Rice Culture

The primitive, laborious rice cultivation methods of the Orient have been replaced in the United States with tractor farming, seed-planting by airplane, modern irrigation systems, power-combine harvesting, and modern drying and milling methods.

Rice does not have to be grown in water; but since it is a water-tolerant plant, flooding rice fields is the most efficient and desirable method of weed and insect control. Consequently, rice is grown in water in the United States and in most of the important rice-producing areas. The rice farmer prepares his soil in much the same way as for a wheat or barley crop by plowing, harrowing, and preparing the proper seed bed. Since rice fields must be kept evenly flooded, the grower must also level his land and prepare it for flooding. Rice is sown by broadcasting from airplanes or by using mechanical seeding machines. Fields are flooded with water about 4 in. deep. They are kept flooded for a period of about 75–100 days or until just before the rice is ready to harvest. When the rice is mature for harvesting, the fields are drained so that harvesting machinery can move into the fields. Large combines thresh the rice and unload it into spouted auger wagons that convey it to the dryer. Rice is harvested by combines when the moisture content of the grain is approximately 20%. As rice cannot be processed or stored at this moisture level, it is necessary to remove water from the grain until the moisture content is 12–13% or less. This operation is carried out in rice dryers that force heated air through a moving column of rice. Drying cannot be too rapid because excessive temperature or too rapid removal of water from the grain will result in cracking or "checking." Rice with a moisture content of 20% usually requires 3 dryings at intervals to reduce the moisture content to a level at which it can be safely stored. After rice is dried, it is sold directly to a mill for processing, stored in commercial warehouses or elevators, or stored in warehouses or bins on the farm. The market conditions at the time of harvest usually determines whether a farmer sells or stores his crop.

Varieties

Many varieties of rice are produced throughout the world. It has been estimated that there are approximately 7000 known varieties of rice. The U.S. government, in cooperation with states in which rice is grown, maintains rice experiment stations. One important function of these stations is to work with farmers toward improving varieties of rice by combining the best domestic hybrids with the most promising foreign types. The objectives of the program are higher field yields, earlier maturation, better milling qualities, disease and insect resistance, and improved cooking and processing qualities.

The physical and chemical characteristics of the rice kernel that are associated with how rice cooks and its suitability for processed rice products are: (1) amylose content; (2) alkali reaction time and value, and the gelatinization temperature de-

TABLE R-11

COMPOSITION OF RICE

100 GM (30 gm to 1 oz)

	Brown		Regular White (Unenriched)		Regular White (Enriched)		Parboiled (Enriched)		Precooked (Enriched)	
	Raw	Cooked	Raw	Cooked	Raw	Cooked	Dry Form	Cooked	Dry Form	Ready-To-Serve
Water (%)	12.0	70.3	12.0	72.6	12.0	72.6	10.3	73.4	9.6	72.9
Food energy (cal)	360	119	363	109	363	109	369	106	374	109
Protein (gm)	7.5	2.5	6.7	2.0	6.7	2.0	7.4	2.1	7.5	2.2
Fat (gm)	1.9	0.6	0.4	0.1	0.4	0.1	0.3	0.1	0.2	Trace
Carbohydrate:										
Total (gm)	77.4	25.5	80.4	24.2	80.4	24.2	81.3	23.3	82.5	24.2
Fiber (gm)	0.9	0.3	0.3	0.1	0.3	0.1	0.2	0.1	0.4	0.1
Ash (gm)	1.2	1.1	0.5	1.1	0.5	1.1	0.7	1.1	0.2	0.7
Calcium (mg)	32	12	24	10	24	10	60	19	5	3
Phosphorus (mg)	221	73	94	28	94	28	200	57	65	19
Iron (mg)	1.6	0.5	0.8	0.2	2.9[1]	0.9[1]	2.9[1]	0.8[1]	2.9[1]	0.8[1]
Sodium (mg)	9	282	5	374	5	374	9	358	1	273
Potassium (mg)	214	70	92	28	92	28	150	43	—	Trace
Thiamin (mg)	0.34	0.09	0.07	0.02	0.44[1]	0.11[1]	0.44[1]	0.11[1]	0.44[1]	0.13[1]
Riboflavin (mg)	0.05	0.02	0.03	0.01	[2]	[2]	[2]	[2]	[2]	[2]
Niacin (mg)	4.7	1.4	1.6	0.4	3.5[1]	1.0[1]	3.5	1.2[1]	3.5[1]	1.0[1]

SOURCE: Agriculture Handbook 8, Agr. Res. Serv., USDA (1963).

[1] Values for iron, thiamin, and niacin are based on the minimum levels of enrichment specified by the U.S. Government.

[2] Minimum and maximum requirements for riboflavin have not been specified as yet by the U.S. Government.

termined by the birefringence-end-point-temperature method; (3) water uptake at 77°C; (4) amylographic paste viscosity (Brabender units) at peak, when cooked 10 min at 95°C, and when cooled to 50°C; (5) cookability with malt: viscosity flow time (seconds per 150 ml); (6) parboil-canning stability: dry matter (percentage of solids loss).

Rice varieties are classified as short, medium, and long, depending on the length and shape of the grain. Both medium- and long-grain varieties are grown in the southern states. Calrose, Nato, Saturn, and Vista are popular medium-grain varieties. Belle Patna, Bluebelle, Bluebonnet 50, and Starbonnet are commonly grown long-grain varieties. Short-grain rice production is confined to the California rice-producing areas, and Caloro and Colusa are the popularly-grown varieties. The medium-grain varieties tend to be slightly sticky or moist when cooked. The short-grain rices are even stickier. The long-grain varieties are easier to cook so that the grains are separated and flaky when ready for table consumption. Personal preference determines which type of rice is used. Rice varieties are also classified from the growers' standpoint as early, midseason, and late maturing. Growers of large acreages may wish to sow 2 or 3 varieties that differ in date of maturity and grain type in order to extend the harvesting period and to provide rice of different types for the market.

Milling

The rice grain is made up of the hull (husk), the seed coat (pericarp), the embryo (germ), and the starchy endosperm. The seed coat consists of six layers of differentiated types of cells, the last nearest to the endosperm being the aleurone layer, which is rich in proteins, lipids, minerals, and B-complex vitamins (Fig. R-2). Proteins and mineral salts are present in the aleurone cells and also in the outer starch-containing cells.

Unhulled dried rice grain is called "paddy" or "rough" rice. It arrives at the mills in large sacks or in bulk. Different varieties and different grades of rice must be segregated and kept in separate lots. The first step in milling rice is to remove the hull or husk and yet preserve most of the kernels as whole or unbroken grains. In the milling process, the rough rice is dumped into large bins from which it is conveyed through a series of machines in which it is clipped, screened, and fanned to remove stones, dirt, straw, and other foreign matter.

The cleaned rough rice is passed into a rubber roll sheller or "huller." The rough rice flows down between rubber-surfaced rolls that are turning in opposite directions and each at a different rpm. The pressure between the two rolls is adjustable, being regulated pneumatically, because different varieties of rice require different shelling pressures. Some mills use the hulls for fuel to generate power; but in most mills they are dumped as waste. Other uses for rice hulls are given in another section.

Although each variety of rice has a characteristic length and breadth of kernel, the individual variations that naturally occur within each variety cause some of the grains to be unhulled on the first shelling; these grains must be returned to a second, and sometimes a third pair of shellers set more closely in clearance to shell the grains completely.

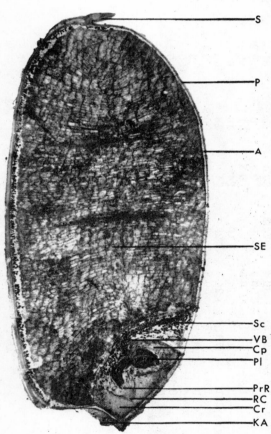

FIG. R-2. LONGISECTION THROUGH THE MIDDLE OF A KERNEL OF ZENITH VARIETY RICE

Shown are the outer structures (S) style, (P) pericarp, and (KA) kernel attachment. The endosperm is composed of (A) the aleurone layer and (SE) the main starchy storage tissue. The germ consists of (Sc) the scutellum, (Cp) the coleoptile, (Pl) the plumule, (VB) the vascular bundle, (Cr) the coleorhiza, (PrR) the primary root, and (RC) the root cap.

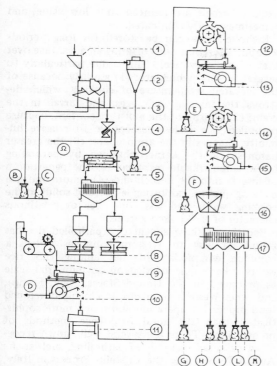

FIG. R-3. FLOW PLAN OF RICE MILLING OPERATIONS

1. Hopper. 2. Cyclone. 3. Fan and screen separator. 4. Magnetic separator. 5. Awning machine. 6. Indented disc separator. 7. Bin. 8. Disc sheller. 9. Rubber belt sheller. 10. Hull separator. 11. Paddy machine. 12. Huller. 13. Hull separator. 14. Huller. 15. Hull separator. 16. Brush. 17. Indented disc separator. A. Dust. B. Straw. C. Foreign seeds. D. Hulls. E. Bran. F. Polishings. H. Brewer's rice. I. Screenings. L. Second heads. M. Head rice.

From the shelling machines, the rice is conveyed to a device called the "paddy" machine or separator, which separates the hulled from the unhulled grains. This separator rocks back and forth continuously, shaking the grains over the surface of an inclined shaker box, the surface of which is covered with diagonally staggered metallic plates that form zigzags. The unhulled grains leave the box at the higher end, while the hulled grains leave the box at the lower end, because of the difference in the specific gravity and coefficient of surface friction of the hulled and unhulled grains.

The hulled rice at this stage of milling is known as "brown" rice; its color ranges from brown to green. In the next milling step, the brown rice is conveyed to the "hullers," which scour off the outer bran coats and germ from the rice kernels. The term "hullers" is a misnomer because these machines remove the bran, not hulls, from the rice

kernel. The huller is the most important machine in any rice mill. It removes the bran and in the process causes most of the kernel breakage, even when properly adjusted. The huller causes the bran to be abraded off mostly because of the pressure between the kernels, and also because of friction between the kernels and the rough steel screen with which the huller is provided. Loosened bran and smaller kernel pieces pass through the huller screen and are later separated by aspiration and screening.

The bran is a powdery, brown product of slightly sweet taste. Although it is palatable when fresh and rich in lipids, minerals, and B-complex vitamins, practically all rice bran is sold as a by-product for animal feeding.

The milled rice kernel has a creamy tinge and is known as undermilled rice. This rice is passed onto the brush which removes most of the inner bran coat or polish. Polish is a powder of definite sweet flavor and contains a relatively larger proportion of carbohydrates and less fat and crude fiber than the bran. It, too, is sold as a by-product for animal feed, and sometimes as an ingredient of baby foods. The rice resulting from this operation is termed polished rice.

At this stage the rice kernel consists of the white, starchy endosperm, together with fragments of the aleurone layer. Rice may be sold in this form as polished, uncoated rice; or, it may be conveyed to machines known as trumbles, in which it is coated with talc and glucose. This inert, harmless coating is used to give the rice a high gloss or sheen, which is desired in the Puerto Rican market.

Even with care, some of the kernels are broken during milling. A series of machines or classifiers separate the different size kernels. The whole and three-quarter kernels are screened into a fraction and designated as "head" rice; the one-third to three-quarter size grains are classed as "second-heads"; the one-third to one-quarter length of grains are known as "screenings"; and the still smaller fragments are termed "brewers" since they form a useful brewing adjunct. The yields of products and by-products obtained from rough rice in the milling process are as follows:

	(%)
Hulls	17.0–21.0
Bran	8.0–14.0
Polish	1.8–4.0
Head rice	37.0–65.0
Second heads	2.6–11.7
Screenings	3.1–11.0
Brewer's rice	2.0–4.9
Loss and trash	1.2–3.0

Rice is further graded according to its degree of freedom from red rice, speck, foreign grains and seeds, chalky kernels, moisture, soil, weevils, and mustiness. Purity standards have been set by the United States Department of Agriculture.

Uses of Milled Rice

Of all cereals, rice alone is eaten predominantly as milled whole grain. The largest share of the world's rice is consumed in the boiled form. Methods of cooking differ widely depending upon heating facilities in a community and upon ethnic origins and national tradition. Milled rice is the major rice product of the continental United States with consumption averaging about 8.3 lb annually per capita.

The brewing industry uses practically all the broken grades of rice, 0.5 billion pounds (rough rice equivalent), amounting to nearly $1/5$ of the total domestic consumption. This rice is used as a source of starch in brewing and is competitive with corn, although some brewers claim rice starch has some peculiar advantages not obtained from other starches in making premium beers. Broken milled rice serves as a raw material for the manufacture of rice starch on a very limited scale. Rice starch is not manufactured in the United States and several million pounds are annually imported for use in cosmetics and artists' and drawing papers.

Processed Rice Products

Parboiled Rice.—The practice of parboiling rice has been in existence for many centuries in India, Pakistan, and Burma. Approximately 20% of the world's rice crop is parboiled. Primarily, the ancient process of parboiling rice essentially consists of soaking dry rough or paddy rice (in the hull) in an excess of water to bring its moisture content to approximately 30–35%. The reconstituted rice is boiled in order to gelatinize the starch, the water drained or decanted off, and the "parboiled" rice spread out in the sun to dry. Several factors contribute to the practice of parboiling in far eastern countries. Gelatinization of the kernel effected during the cooking and subsequent restoration of the rice kernel to its normal state by drying cements the interior fissures or fractures, unifies the kernel, and leads to the disappearance of the interior white zones and natural deformities of the kernel. As a result of these structural transformations, the kernel assumes a better consistency, greater hardness, and also a better vitreousness. An augmentation in nutritive value also takes place due to the enrichment in soluble vitamins, which diffuse from the exterior to the interior of the grain during soaking and heating. The presence of vitamin E is noteworthy.

As a result of the processing a greater resistance to mechanical breakage during milling is attained, especially during the removal of the bran. The broken kernels are reduced to a low value, and sometimes nearly eliminated.

Parboiled rice can be stored for long periods without alteration, thus offering an advantage over that of ordinary rice. This is due particularly to several factors, which are: (1) sterility because of the elevated temperature of cooking, which destroys the insects, their eggs, and larvae in the grain; (2) control of the moisture content, because parboiled rice is less susceptible to relative humidity changes in the atmosphere; (3) the greater hardness of the kernel obtained by parboiling offers a remarkable resistance to the penetration of insects into the kernel; and (4) a more uniform cooking quality, exhibiting less loss of solids to the cooking water and less coherence or gelatinous character of the cooked kernels.

Because of these advantages, parboiled rice has found its way to Western countries and is a common commodity of diet among U.S. rice eaters. Parboiling of rice on an industrial scale as practiced in the United States, Italy, France, and other Western countries, is a highly-developed food processing operation and much more sophisticated than the rural or village methods of preparation. There are several well-known recognized patented methods of parboiling, such as the Avorio Process and the Cristallo Process in Italy, the Malek Process, the "Converted" Process in the United States, and the Fernandes Process in Surinam. In brief, the "Converted" Process consists of the following steps: (1) rough rice is subjected to a high vacuum to pull air from the hulls and from the deep microscopic pores of the rice kernels; (2) without releasing the vacuum, hot water is run into the tank, then maintained at high pressure to dissolve water-soluble B-vitamins and other grain constituents from the bran, hull, and germ, and force them into the grain itself; (3) then the tank is drained and the rough rice is subjected to live steam. Vacuum is applied again to partly dry the wet rice; and (4) further drying is accomplished by use of conventional drying apparatus. After 8 hr in tempering bins all rice reaches the same dryness of approximately 12–13% moisture content. Parboiled rice is milled in the conventional manner. The polished, milled rice is a rich cream color but cooks to the snowy whiteness as untreated rice does.

Quick-Cooking Rice.—In keeping with the modern trend of living and present consumer preference, convenience food items have been almost universally accepted by the American public. Quick-cooking rice is one such item. In contrast to parboiled rice, which is more dense and requires a longer cooking time than raw milled rice, quick-cooking rices are light, porous, take up water readily, and can be prepared for the table in roughly 5-6 min. There are many approaches to the methods of rendering raw milled rice into a quick-cooking product. Essentially the process consists of soaking premium grade and selected rice varieties in water to attain a moisture content of approximately 35%. The rice is then cooked, sometimes under pressure, and subsequently dried under controlled conditions of temperature in an air stream. Frequently, prior to reconstituting in water, a hot-air blast is employed to effect fissuring of the rice kernel to promote porosity as an aid in speed of water absorption. Other methods employ pressure cooking followed by release into a vacuum to effect increased porous structure of the kernel. More recently, approaches to effecting quick-cooking properties employ soaking and cooking of the rice, then freezing, thawing, and dehydrating or drying. The final dehydrated product can be prepared for consumption in approximately 5 min or less with the addition of the recommended quantity of hot boiling water. Several other processes, using the puffing-gun and pressure-vacuum methods are responsible for quick-cooking products.

Canned Rice.—Under another form, canned rice may be considered a type of quick-cooking or convenience product. Parboiled rice was formerly used as the raw material for preparation of canned rice because of the stability of the kernel and retention of its shape without disintegration under rigid retorting and heating conditions. Limiting the moisture content of the canned product to approximately 55% overcomes many of the difficulties of employing raw milled rice as the raw material. In brief, the canning process consists of: (1) soaking the rice to its equilibrium moisture content of about 30–35%; (2) cooking it 4–5 min in excess water; (3) draining and packing the rice into cans; and (4) vacuum sealing and retorting. An inherent disadvantage of canned rice is the "clumping" of the kernels so as to prevent ease of emptying the contents of the can. This difficulty has been overcome by use of surface active agents, which reduce the surface tension between cooked kernels, thereby permitting the contents to exit as discrete, individually separated kernels, more or less free-flowing. Freeze-processing is also used for alleviating the "clumping" of the canned rice. In this case the processed rice is frozen in the can and then thawed prior to labeling and release for use.

Breakfast Foods.—Ready-to-eat cereals, in general, are precooked, dried, flaked, formed and/or puffed or expanded, and toasted breakfast foods. The differences of preparation are the cooking time, steam pressure, temperature, and the addition of malt and nutrients. Rice flakes and puffed rice are prepared from quality raw milled rice, usually of the short-grain type. Cooking rice for making flakes requires about 18–19 lb steam pres-

sure. The duration of cooking is about 20 min, bleeding for 5–10 sec, and additionally cooking for 1½ hrs. Ingredients are polished rice, malt syrup, ground wheat bran, white sugar, corn sugar, salt, and vitamins for enrichment are also added. In the caes of puffed rice, frequently the rice is parboiled, and sugar syrup with salt is added and the mixture cooked for approximately 5 hr under 15 lb steam pressure. Nondiastatic malt syrup and enriching ingredients are added before cooking. The lumps of cooked rice are broken up, dried to 25–30% moisture content, and tempered. The grain mass is given an additional heating with radiant heaters to plasticize the kernel surfaces. The rice kernels are then passed through flaking rolls and subsequently put through toasting ovens to secure the puffed effect. A cereal called "Special K," manufactured by the Kellogg Co., is basically a cooked rice kernel, which is coated while moist with wheat gluten, wheat germ meal, dried skim milk, debittered brewer's yeast, and other nutritional adjuncts. Finally the material is oven-puffed. Gun-puffing may be used instead of oven-puffing to attain expansion of the product.

Rice Baby Foods.—Generally, rice baby foods are prepared by cooking ground broken rice kernels and polish, adding nutrients, and drum drying the rice slurry. The dried rice is then broken up into flakes and the mixture packaged.

Rice Flour.—The presently available rice flour of commerce in the United States is of two types. The first is produced from the waxy or glutinous rice, which is commercially grown in rather limited quantity in California. This waxy rice flour has superior qualities for use as a thickening agent for white sauces, gravies, puddings, etc., in preventing liquid separation (syneresis) when these products are frozen, stored, and subsequently thawed. A characteristic of waxy rice starch is that it has little or no amylose. Since the waxy rice starch is essentially amylopectin, flour prepared from it has this unique food use property. The other type of rice flour is prepared from the broken grains of ordinary raw or parboiled rice. When prepared from parboiled rice, the resulting flour is essentially a precooked flour. Because rice protein does not contain gluten, the use of rice flour is rather limited for confectionary and baking purposes. Instead, it is employed usually as a thickening agent in gravies, sauces, and as a dusting powder in the preparation and packaging of refrigerated bakery products.

Rice By-Products.

Rice hulls are an excellent abrasive. Their high silica content makes them desirable in the polishing of castings. Rice hulls are one of the best conditioners for commercial fertilizers, and thousands of tons are used annually for that purpose. Rice hulls are used in the manufacture of hand soaps. The finely ground hulls may be used in the manufacture of furfural. A recent development is the ammoniation of rice hulls for cattle feeding and soil fertilizer.

Until recently, when it was found to be rich in lipids, rice bran had been used exclusively as a livestock feed. By extracting fresh rice bran with commercial hexane, a crude oil of low free fatty acids content is obtained. This oil can be refined and bleached by standard methods to give a high-grade edible oil. Its smoke, flash, and fire points compare favorably with other edible oils. Its resistance to oxidative rancidity makes it superior for shelf storage. It can be winterized; and the storing quality of the hydrogenated product is superior to that of cottonseed and peanut oils.

Rice polishings, consisting of the peripheral layers of the rice endosperm, are composed of approximately 94% digestible nutrients and are high in vitamin and mineral content. As such, rice polishings have largely been used for livestock feeding and on a more limited scale for incorporation in baby foods.

J. T. HOGAN

References

BORASIO, L., and GARIBOLDI, F. 1965. Parboiled rice—production and use. Rice J. *68* No. 5, 32–35, 41; *68*, No. 8, 23–27.

ESKEW, R. K., CORDING, J., and SULLIVAN, J. F. 1963. Explosive puffing. Food Eng. *35*, No. 4, 91–92.

GATES, W. C. 1958. Puffing method and apparatus. U.S. Pat. 2,838,401, June 10.

GEHRIG, E. J. 1964. The manufacture of cereal flakes. Am. Miller Processor *92*, No. 4, 21–23; *92*, No. 5, 16–18; *92*, No. 7, 30–34.

KENEASTER, K. K., and NEWLIN, H. E. 1957. Process for production of a quick-cooking product of rice or other starchy vegetable. U.S. Pat. 2,813,769, Nov. 18.

ROBERTS, R. L., HOUSTON, D. F., and KESTER, E. B. 1953. Process for canning white rice. Food Technol. 7, 72–80.

VERITY, N. S., and ALLEN, R. C. 1964. Method of canning rice. U.S. Pat. 3,132,030, May 5.

ROTHAMSTED EXPERIMENTAL STATION

Rothamsted Experimental Station, the oldest agricultural research station in the world, was founded by John Bennet Lawes in 1843. Lawes had been experimenting on crop nutrition before this and had already invented and patented superphosphate; but 1843 is taken as the foundation date because it was then that he employed Joseph Henry Gilbert, a chemist, to collaborate with him and the first two of their systematic field experiments on crop nutrition were laid down. These experiments, made with all the main agricultural crops, were of the same general pattern. The same crop was grown year after year, and each plot was given the same treatment each year. The main treatments were no manure; farmyard manure; nitrogen only; minerals only; minerals plus nitrogen. Minerals were the constituents of the ash of crops, mostly compounds of phosphorus, potassium, sodium, and magnesium. The main question Lawes and Gilbert set themselves was the relative importance of minerals and nitrogen, not only because of its practical importance, but because Liebig asserted that crops could get all the nitrogen they needed from the air. The Rothamsted experiments soon showed the fallacy of Liebig's mineral theory; yields, except for legumes, were small without organic or inorganic nitrogen and minerals, especially with cereals. They also showed differences in the nutrient needs of different crops: potash was needed more by potatoes, and phosphate by turnips, than these were needed by cereals. Three of their original experiments, with wheat on Broadbalk, with barley on Hoos Field, and pasture on Park Grass, still continue and provide unique information on factors affecting soil fertility.

In 1848, Lawes and Gilbert also started work on animal nutrition, first by measuring the ratio of food eaten to live weight gain in different breeds of sheep, and later extending it to pigs and oxen. The relative importance and roles of different constituents of fodder were then unknown and matters of controversy; but it was widely accepted that nitrogenous substances were the most important and there was need only to know the amount of these to assess the value of the fodder. Fat in the animal was assumed to come only from fat or nitrogenous compounds in the fodder, but Lawes and Gilbert showed it could come from carbohydrate. They also showed, contrary to general opinion, that energy for muscular effort came from materials other than nitrogenous compounds, that different proteins differed in their nutritional value, and that, whereas the carbohydrate content of fodder was the more important for fattening cattle, the nitrogen content determined the value of the manure from the cattle in increasing crop yields. The work with animals ended after about 20 yr and since then the work at Rothamsted has dealt only with crops.

In 1889, Lawes set up a trust fund to continue

the Rothamsted Experiments and under his trust deed the governing body of the Station was to be appointed by the Royal Society of London, the Royal Agricultural Society of England, the Chemical Society, and the Linnean Society. This still continues, although since early in this century the work has been increasingly paid for by government funds and now is largely financed by the Agricultural Research Council.

Until 1919, the work was mainly on crop nutrition, soil fertility, and weeds, but increasingly since then it has dealt with the control of pests and diseases, with meteorology and crop growth, with the physiology and biochemistry of plants, and with statistics, especially the design and analysis of experiments. It is now concerned with all aspects of arable agriculture, except plant breeding. A good deal of work has been done on such various problems as factors affecting the malting quality of barley and the cooking quality of potatoes, the spoilage of hay and grain, and the production from leaves of a protein suitable for human consumption. However, most work lies in attempting to produce more food, rather than in food processing. It can be summarized by saying it aims to identify and overcome the factors that limit crop yields.

F. C. BAWDEN

RYE

Production

In almost all countries of the world rye is regarded as feedstuff and used as such. The exceptions are some Central and Eastern European countries where bread is produced mainly from rye or rye-wheat mixtures. For example, rye and rye-containing breads constitute over 60% of the bread produced in West Germany as compared to under 1% in the other ECM countries.

Rye acreage decreases steadily; however, increased yields per acre have kept the total amount harvested at an almost constant level of about 1.5 billion bushels. Only 4% of the world cereal production consists of rye.

Compared to wheat, very little statistical data for rye production is available, except in countries where rye is considered a bread cereal. Rye production figures for West Germany are:

	(Million Tons)
1965–1966	2.96
1967–1968	3.32
1969–1970	3.02

Rye for bread production is available in sufficient quantity with about 1.0 million tons being used

for bread. The other European Common Market countries produce considerably less rye:

	(Approx Tons)
Belgium/Luxembourg	80,000
France	380,000
Italy	80,000
Holland	190,000

Milling

The milling system used for rye is similar to that in milling of wheat. Rye requires more cleaning. It is usually washed to remove stones and needs more bolting surface since it is tougher than wheat. Smooth roll surfaces cause rye middlings to flatten, therefore corrugated rolls are used. Normal extraction ranges from 74 to 85% with corresponding flour ashes of 0.9–1.2% (dry basis). Whole rye meal is also used in the production of bread.

Milling behavior of rye is influenced by the amounts of swelling substances and by the more or less tough viscous properties which these substances (proteins, pentosans, hemicelluloses and their compounds) acquire during the tempering process. A moisture content of approximately 14.5% is desirable before the first break. Normally, the extraction and the ash content of straight run flours are lowered by high protein rye and by rye rich in pentosans. Usually, high levels of swelling substances result in a lower 1000-kernel weight. In cases where high levels of swelling substances run parallel with a lower rate of water uptake or of moisture distribution, milling tests tend to give higher extracted flours high in ash content. Since the properties of swelling substances are changed in the drying process this effect can also be encountered in rye dried at temperatures which exceed 50°C or in steam treated rye.

Using the Brabender-Quadrumat-Senior Experiment mill, tests were performed at a constant moisture of rye of 14% on the first break with rye samples of different origin (Table R-12).

Tests made with the same German rye varieties grown at different locations show that the location where grown had a great influence on the milling behavior on account of differences in the viscous properties of the swelling substances. Varieties cultivated at the same station yielded less flour if the protein content was high (Fig. R-4).

In Fig. R-5 the same trend is shown for rye of different origin.

Simultaneously, Fig. R-6 shows that low extraction rate in high protein rye is associated with comparably high flour ash.

$$\text{ash number} = \frac{\text{ash \% dry m.} \times 1000}{\text{extraction rate}}$$

TABLE R-12
MILLABILITY OF RYE GRAIN

Rye Varieties or Classes	1000-Kernel Weight Gm/Dry Basis	Ash Dry Basis (%)	Protein (N × 6.25) Dry Basis	Pentosans Dry Basis (%)	Flour Yield (%)	Flour Ash Dry Basis (%)
U.S. I	18.9	1.80	13.7	8.3	63.9	0.75
(n = 10)	16.9–21.6	1.70–1.90	13.0–14.3	7.0–9.1	59.6–66.6	0.70–0.81
U.S. II	18.9	1.78	13.9	8.2	61.5	0.77
(n = 10)	15.7–24.1	1.62–1.87	13.3–14.7	7.5–9.6	58.3–65.1	0.69–0.81
Canadian Western II	19.8	1.77	13.3	8.2	62.6	0.65
(n = 12)	18.2–22.1	1.61–1.86	12.4–14.0	7.6–8.8	56.3–65.0	0.59–0.71
UdSSR	17.9	1.74	13.4	8.1	63.2	0.71
(n = 7)	15.6–20.1	1.67–1.87	12.3–15.4	7.8–8.5	57.1–69.7	0.66–0.75
La Plata	12.0	2.16	15.0	10.0	62.2	1.11
(n = 1)						
German varieties (5 yr, 3 locations)						
Petkuser Normalstroh	16.4	1.76	9.1	7.4	69.3	0.71
(n = 14)	22.0–29.6	1.63–1.95	7.7–11.5	6.8–7.9	62.9–76.6	0.53–0.78
Petkuser Kurzstroh	24.3	1.78	9.0	8.3	68.2	0.72
(n = 14)	20.2–27.6	1.67–1.95	7.3–10.9	7.4–8.8	62.0–76.4	0.51–0.84
Carsten's rye	23.0	1.74	8.6	8.5	67.2	0.69
	18.0–26.8	1.64–1.91	6.8–10.7	7.9–9.0	61.1–75.2	0.54–0.84

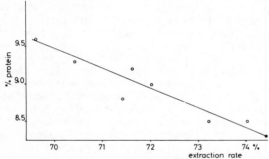

FIG. R-4. RELATION BETWEEN PROTEIN CONTENT AND EXTRACTION RATE OF GERMAN RYE

The flour yield in tetraploid rye varieties is lower than that of diploid rye on account of the higher protein content.

Baking

From the baking-technological point of view the quality of rye is closely related to the quantity and condition of starch and swelling substances. Rye starch gels at a lower temperature than wheat starch, swells more readily, and is more susceptible to enzymatic splitting by amylases. Also, the swelling substances as well as proteins and pentosans are 2–3 times more soluble than in wheat. This makes them more receptive to enzymatic hydrolysis by cellulases, hemicellulases, and pentosanases than wheat swelling substances and particularly wheat gluten.

The enzyme action causes drastic changes in the solubility, viscosity, and water-binding property of the swelling substances. The nature of the latter has not yet been adequately researched, mainly due to the difficulties encountered in trying to isolate them.

In contrast to wheat, gluten cannot be washed from rye flour. However, small quantities with properties similar to that of wheat gluten, have been isolated from the "wedge-protein" of rye. The high water-holding capacity of rye flour is

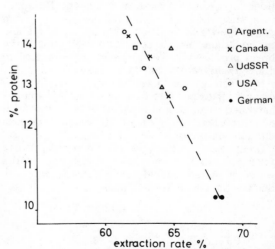

FIG. R-5. RELATION BETWEEN PROTEIN CONTENT AND EXTRACTION RATE OF RYE OF DIFFERENT ORIGIN

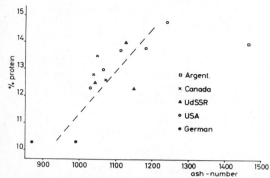

FIG. R-6. RELATION BETWEEN PROTEIN CONTENT AND ASH NUMBER OF RYE OF DIFFERENT ORIGIN

caused by the swelling substances. Compared to protein, the swelling substances, insoluble pentosans, and hemicelluloses are capable of binding several times their weight of water.

The baking quality of rye is primarily an enzymatic problem and closely connected with the enzymatic fermentation of starch and swelling substances. The enzymolysis, in turn, is governed by the intensity of the enzyme activity and the condition of the substrata. The latter is influenced by the environmental condition that exists throughout the whole growing period, while the enzymolysis is affected by the prevailing weather at the time of harvest. The properties of starch and swelling substances are affected by the conditions under which rye is grown. Central European rye contains substances which swell more readily than those of rye produced in hotter, dryer climates. Starch contained in rye from hot, dry climates tends to gel at a somewhat higher temperature and more slowly. Assuming equal alpha-amylase activity, such rye will give relatively low amylogram maxima, but higher falling number values. Also, the solubility of pentosans and their fermentation by enzymes is reduced. This lowers the portions of reducing sugars. A comparison of analytical data of rye from different countries substantiate these observations (see Table R-13).

Protein rich rye contains no more soluble substances than rye of Central European origin which indicates a higher degree of polymerization of the first mentioned. Figure R-7 shows swelling amylograms of whole rye meal of different origin as well as German varieties.

The ease with which the German rye swells and the relatively fast reduction of viscosity make an inhibition of the enzymatic activity during the baking process necessary. This is accomplished by the use of sour dough or dry acidifying agents. Even in flour from germinated cereal the alpha-amylase activity can be inhibited, if, in conjunction with the addition of salt, a pH value of about 4.2 in the dough is reached. Germination damage influences the quality of the less acidified rye-wheat bread more than that of whole rye bread. The quality of yeast-developed bread is negatively affected to an even larger extent.

High viscosity flours produce a tight dough. They are suitable for the production of loaf pan bread which allow a higher addition of water to improve the texture. The viscosity of the mucoid substances and their changes during the dough fermentation determine the amount of water to be added (Zuguß) and the dough condition. At pH

TABLE R-13
CHEMICAL COMPOSITION OR RYE GRAIN

Rye Varieties or Classes	Falling Number 7/25	Amylogram Brabender Units 90 Gm Whole Meal	Maltose Dry Basis (%)	α-amylase activity ICC-units	Soluble Pentosans Dry Basis (%)	% of Total Pentosans	Water Absorption of Centrifuged Residue Gm/100 Dry Flour
U.S. I			2.0		1.45	17.5	106
(n = 10)	130–261	330–820	1.7–2.3	0.93–3.8	1.33–1.61		95–116
U.S. II			2.1		1.36	16.6	106
(n = 10)	94–265	320–740	1.5–2.7	0.65–5.6	1.16–1.55		99–113
Canadian Western II			2.1		1.41	16.4	107
(n = 12)	135–239	415–770	1.6–2.2	1.00–3.4	1.35–1.52		100–112
UdSSR			2.0		1.39	17.2	104
(n = 7)	80–306	370–810	1.5–2.3	0.39–4.7	1.14–1.55		103–106
La Plata	355	790	2.3	0.54	1.75	17.5	115
(n = 1)							
German Varieties (5 ys, 3 locations)							
Petkuser Normalstroh			3.0		1.44	19.5	103
(n = 14)	60–300	140–1000	2.2–4.2	0.4–31.0	1.22–1.78		95–112
Petkuser Kurzstroh			3.1		1.61	19.4	106
(n = 14)	60–262	140–1000	2.2–4.7	0.4–31.0	1.28–2.10		98–115
Carsten's Rye			3.2		1.54	18.1	108
(n = 14)	60–273	110–800	2.2–4.9	0.6–35.0	1.30–2.00		101–121

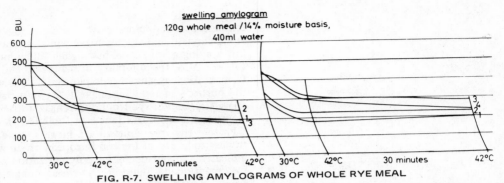

FIG. R-7. SWELLING AMYLOGRAMS OF WHOLE RYE MEAL

German varieties (left): 1—Petkuser Normalstroh; 2—Petkuser Kurzstroh; 3—Carsten's Roggen; and (right) 1—U.S. Plumb; 2—U.S. II; 3—Canadian Western II; 4—USSR.

6.3, the lowest viscosity of the mucoid substances is measured at 45°C while at 20°C a pH of 3.2 produces the lowest viscosity.

The sour dough process leads to a considerable viscosity reduction by the enzymes of microorganisms. Yeast-developed doughs retain a more stable viscosity. Germination damage and viscosity reduction of the previously mentioned swelling substances do not run parallel.

High-speed mixers are not used in the production of rye dough for two reasons: (1) In a dough with good swelling substance properties, the viscosity would be raised too high by the increased solubility of its mucoid substances. (2) In a dough with poor swelling substance properties, large portions of mucoid matter would be opened to enzymatic attacks resulting in very slack dough conditions.

Doughs from tetraploid rye are usually of poor quality. They contain few viscous mucoid substances and are susceptible to increased alpha-amylase activity.

The use of rye flour makes the production of a larger variety of bread possible and by offering the consumer greater choice presumably counteracts the presently-decreasing per capita consumption of bread. Furthermore, whole rye and rye-containing breads have a longer shelf-life than wheat bread as well as a more pronounced bread flavor.

W. SEIBEL
E. DREWS

S

SAFFLOWER

Safflower (*Carthamus tinctorius*), a member of the composite family, is indigenous to Southeastern Asia, but has long been cultivated in India, the near East, and Northern Africa. Although grown originally for its florets which were used as an adulterant for saffron and from which the rouge dye carthamine was extracted, the plant is now almost entirely raised for its seed which is a source of polyunsaturated oil and protein feed.

Climatically, safflower is adapted to the arid and semiarid regions of the world which has a frost-free growing period of 125–130 days. A minimum of 26 in. of stored moisture is required to produce reasonable yields. Under dry land farming conditions, yields will range from 350 to 1200 lb of seed per acre. As high as 4000 lb per acre can be attained with irrigation. In the United States, planting is conducted in early spring; and 5–20 days are required for emergence. Within 6 weeks branching occurs and a height of 18–40 in. is attained; 1–5 flower buds containing from 20 to 100 florets form on each branch, with each floret bearing 1 seed similar in appearance to a sunflower seed but about the size of barley seed. Harvesting is accomplished with an ordinary wheat combine in late summer.

The United States and Mexico are the major safflower seed producers. Lesser quantities are cultivated in India, Spain, Australia, Portugal, and the near East. Although introduced into the United States in the early 1940's, the crop was not considered established until the late 1950's. Total seed production in the United States, primarily in California and Arizona, reached a high of 350,000 tons in 1967 but was reduced to about 200,000 tons in 1970.

Mexican production is expected to surpass that of the United States in 1971, as it did in 1970. Total current world production is estimated at over 5000,000 tons.

The safflower seed is composed of a thick fibrous white hull encasing a yellow kernel. Commercial varieties grown in the United States average 35–40% hull and yield 39–40% oil and 15% protein. Experimental thin hull varieties have oil contents as high as 49%. Safflower hulls consist primarily of fiber and lignin and contain less than 1% oil and only 4% protein. The oil-free kernel yields a protein of good quality but somewhat deficient in lysine and methionine.

A conventional continuous screw press-solvent extraction method is used to remove the oil from safflower seed. After elimination of extraneous matter by screening and aspiration, the seed is ground, cooked under steam pressure, and mechanically pressed. Approximately $2/3$ of the oil is removed in this manner. The resultant cake containing 10–20% oil is extracted with hexane to a residual oil content of about 1%.

The extracted cake is ground and screened to yield 20 and 42% protein meal fractions which are used in cattle and poultry feeds. The higher protein fraction has recently been considered as a protein source for human consumption.

The combined crude oils from pressing and extracting are refined by washing with hot dilute caustic soda which removes free fatty acid, phosphatides, and other mucilaginous impurities. Continuous centrifugation separates the washings from the lighter oil phase. After a second wash with hot water, the oil is dried and treated with activated clay to adsorb residual soap. Some color reduction occurs at this stage but is not essential as the major color bodies are destroyed during subsequent heat treatment. The final stage of refining, deodorization, involves steam distillation under vacuum at temperatures between $450°$ and $470°F$. Residual free fatty acids and oxidative degradation products (aldehydes, ketones, etc.) are reduced to organoleptically undetectable levels yielding a bland, almost colorless product. Due to its susceptibility to oxidation, care is taken to completely exclude air during storage, transport, and packaging. This is usually accomplished by the use of an inert gas such as nitrogen.

Safflower oil is characterized by its simplicity in

ANALYTICAL CHARACTERISTICS OF
SAFFLOWER OILS

Characteristic	High Linoleic	High Oleic
Density, 25°C	0.92	0.92
Iodine Value, Wijs	144	92
Saponification Value	192	192
Viscosity, cp 25°C	42	70
Flow point, °F	0	13

composition. Linoleic acid is the chief constituent amounting to 78% of the total fatty acids. Oleic acid comprises 13% with stearic and palmitic acids contributing 3 and 6% respectively. Although traces of eicosenoic acid have been reported, linolenic acid is absent. The fatty acids are randomly distributed in the glyceryl moiety. Genetically modified varieties of safflower seed have recently been introduced with fatty acid compositions approximating 80% oleic, 15% linoleic, and 5% saturated fatty acids. (The higher concentration of oleic acid esters results in a liquid oil with far greater resistance towards rancidity.) All other compositional aspects of the oil and meal fractions appear to be identical to the high linoleic acid variety. Analytical characteristics of the two varieties are shown in Table S-1.

The initial application of safflower oil produced in the United States was in protective coatings. Due to its excellent heat bleachability, color stability, drying qualities, and uniformity of polymer structure, it is considered to be an ideal alkyd oil. Interest as a food ingredient increased rapidly as a result of studies relating fats in the diet to atherosclerotic heart disease. Its unique fatty acid composition places it highest in polyunsaturates and lowest in saturates of all commercial fats and oils. Safflower has been successfully incorporated into food products such as margarine and salad dressings and is used extensively as a retail salad and cooking oil. Its high content of polyunsaturates has limited its use in commercial frying operations which require fats with a strong resistance against oxidative deterioration at high temperatures. The new high oleic acid variety has demonstrated efficacy in such commercial applications.

R. H. PURDY

SAGO AND SAGO PRODUCTS

Sago is a processed edible starch marketed in the form of small globules or pearls. The name "sago"

originated from Malaya and East Indies where the starch was obtained from the pith of the palms, especially the sago palm (*Metroxylon sagus* or *Metroxylon rumphii*) and palm fern (*Cycas circinalis*) (Brautlecht 1953). Other sources of sago include *Cycas rovoluta*, *Sagus farinifera*, *Sagus rumphii*, *Convovolus batalas*, and *Areca oleracea*. More recently, sago globules are being manufactured in various countries from starches of tapioca, potato, sweet potato, and maize. In India, the sago of commerce is being manufactured mainly from tapioca starch. According to the standards for sago laid down by the Indian Standards Institution in 1956, sago means "the small globules or pearls made from either the starch of the sago palm or the tubers of tapioca (*Manihot utilissima*)."

The palm fern is a tree about 30 ft tall, and 2–3 ft in diameter, abundantly found in the marshy lowlands of Southeastern Asia. It yields flower spikes and fruits only once between 10 and 15 yr and then dies. Immediately before fruiting, the trunks of palm ferns and sago palms are gorged with a very loose, starchy pith which disappears on fruiting, leaving a dead hollow-trunked tree. The trees are felled and the trunks stripped of leaves and cut into lengths of 3 ft for ease of handling. The 2-in. thick outer woody rind is slit lengthway, the pith removed with a wooden hoe and beaten with water. The milky starch suspension is filtered through a coarse sieve made from mats of palm leaf stems to remove fibrous materials of the pith. The pith is washed several times, then strained and the starch milk transferred into troughs for settling and subsequent decantation. The moist starch is sun dried on mats, bagged, and shipped as "sago flour" or converted into pearl sago.

Sago Globules from Tapioca

Tapioca (*Cassava Manihot utilissima*), a low shrubby plant 2–5 m high with a cluster of tuberous roots, is a native of South America, from where it has been introduced into Africa, India, and other Far Eastern countries. It is usually propagated by cuttings of the stem. Planting at the beginning of the monsoon is preferred if the tubers are required for sago manufacture. The crop is ready for harvesting from the eighth month onwards. For harvesting, the plants are pulled out and tubers separated. Each plant yields 5–10 tubers, usually 10–20 in. long, sometimes even as long as 2–3 ft. Each tuber weighs about 2–5 lb and roots weighing as much as 25–30 lb have been reported.

The outer skin of the tapioca tuber is removed by scraping with small knives leaving a white tuber containing starch. The tubers are crushed finely in mechanically operated grinders in which water is allowed to trickle down through a perforated pipe. The starch slurry is passed through a cloth screen whereby the starch milk is separated from the fibrous material. The fibrous waste so obtained is taken out, dried, and powdered for use in the match and textile industries. The pure starch slurry is conveyed to settling tanks and the starch scraped out after draining the water.

To prepare pearl sago, the moist starch is pressed through a perforated sheet of iron or coarse screen. The pellets of starch are put into a shallow hammock-shaped cloth to which a circular swinging motion can be imparted. Swinging this contraption in the correct posture imparts a rotary motion to the pellets which, provided the moisture content is correct, become roughly spherical in shape. The pellets are compact enough for screening to remove fine particles and large aggregates. The sieved pearls are then roasted in shallow metal pans for partial gelatinization and drying as sago pearls.

Sago Starch from Sago Palm

The following flow of processing steps depicts the manner in which starch is made from the sago palm:

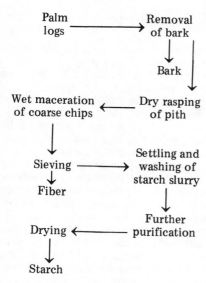

In modern starch factories, the starch slurry is centrifuged and the wet starch which is partially dried in hot air driers, is finely powdered and converted into granules in mechanically operated granulators. The granules are size graded by sieving and then roasted on hot trays with a thin coat of oil for about 10 min. The surface of the granules gets gelatinized and hardened. The grains are dried in the sun, or in driers, at a low temperature (50–60°C), separated mechanically into individual pearls, sorted, and then packed in bags for market-

ing. The yield of sago is about 25% of the weight of fresh tubers.

A product similar to sago, but somewhat coarse, is produced and marketed in Indonesia as "tapioca flakes." It is produced by rubbing moist starch (about 50% moisture) against a screen (20 mesh per in.) and baking the grains in shallow pans.

Composition of Sago and Sago Starch

The quality of tapioca sago globules depends largely on the quality of starch from which it is derived. Analysis of 21 samples collected from different factories in Salem (Tamil Nadu State of India) gave the following average values (grams per 100 gm): moisture, 12.2; nitrogen, 0.02; total ash, 0.25; acid insoluble ash, 0.06; fiber, 5.6; and loss of solids during cooking, 21.3. The pH of aqueous extract was 4.2–5.2 and color of gelatinized alkaline paste (Lovibond units) 1R + 2.1Y.

Properties of Sago Starch

Sago starch has the following properties (Knight 1969):

Granule size	Variable 20–60 μ
Granule shape	Egg shape with truncated forms
Pattern under polarized light	Irregular black
Approximate amylose/amylopectin content	27 to 73%
Gelatinization temperature range	60°–72°C
Total lipid content	Very low
Paste clarity	Translucent
Paste structure	Long, stringy fluid body
Paste strength under mechanical shear and prolonged heat	Medium/low
Paste viscosity	Medium/high, moderate setback
Taste and odor	Low

Specifications

The Indian Standards Institution has laid down the following specifications for sago (1958). The maximum permissible values (grams per 100 gm) are: moisture, 12.0; total ash (dry basis), 0.4; acid insoluble ash (dry basis), 0.075. The pH of aqueous extract should be 4.5–7.0. Not less than 95% shall pass through IS sieve 170 but retained on IS sieve 85.

Grading

Sago globules are classified according to size, color and degree of roasting: Grade I, milky white globules, well roasted; Grade II, color slightly dull, but well roasted; Grade III, color dull but containing a small percentage of half-roasted globules; and Grade IV, other than those specified above. Sago is packed in gunny bags (202 lb per bag) for the market.

Beverages from Sago Palm

There are about 50 million sugar-yielding palm trees in India. They are mostly date (*Phoenix sylvestris*), palmyra (*Borassus flabellifer*) and sago (*Caryotaurens*). The unfermented sweet juice obtained from the inflorescence of coconut palm (*Cocos nucifera*) and sago palm is called "neera." The tapping of neera for consumption as a beverage or for conversion to gur (jaggery) or sugar is a traditional small-scale industry in India. Though gur or jaggery is one of the most important by-products from neera, it is not usually manufactured on a large scale since the juices of the palms are mostly converted into "toddy," a fermented liquor (alcohol content 3–8%). During the early stages of fermentation, the smell of toddy is quite pleasant, but becomes disagreeable later due to the action of bacteria.

Neera tapped from the flowering spadix of sago palm is mildly acidic and rich in sugars as well as vitamins. It is highly susceptible to microbial spoilage, particularly by yeasts and bacteria present in the atmosphere and in the tapping vessels. Traditionally, tapped neera ferments to toddy within 8–9 hr, mainly due to the activity of yeast (production of alcohol) and bacteria (production of acids). The pots used for collecting neera are coated with lime to arrest fermentation, but the effect lasts only for a short time; it also destroys vitamin C. The removal of lime by superphosphate treatment prior to conversion to high quality gur or sugar is laborious and expensive.

It has been reported that neera could be preserved for 48 hr without any fermentation by using a mixture of 0.2% citric acid and 0.02% sodium benzoate, or the addition of Paludrine at 75–100 mg levels. The use and recommended dosage of 40 mg sulphanilamide for 4.5 litres of neera also has been reported. Freeze drying of neera would be possible but not economically feasible.

Other Uses of Sago

Sago is used as an infant and invalid food and in the preparation of puddings. It is commonly eaten as a porridge, mixed with milk and sugar; or, after soaking in curd or butter milk, with salt and spices. *In vitro* digestibility studies have shown that the digestibility of cooked sago is greater and faster than raw starch.

Production and Trade

Although statistical figures regarding production of sago in India are not available, it is reported that about 80,000 tons of tapioca sago were produced in Tamil Nadu State of India in 1965. The current annual production ranges between 125,000 and 215,000 tons, of which 60% constitutes sago and the rest starch. India is not importing sago and only small quantities of tapioca and sago products are exported according to data published by the Department of Industries and Commerce, Government of Tamil Nadu, India, in 1966.

G. RAMA RAO

REFERENCES

BRAUTLECHT, C. A. 1953. Starch, Its Sources, Production, and Uses. Reinhold Publishing Corp., New York.
KNIGHT, J. W. 1969. The Starch Industry. Pergamon Press, Elmsford, N.Y., and Oxford, England.

SALAD DRESSINGS

Salad dressings can be considered those products added to and eaten with vegetable, fruit, meat, fish, and seafood salads although their consumption is not restricted to this application. Major other uses include spreading on bread for sandwiches or simply as a bread spread. Also, various cold and hot recipes including baking contain salad dressings as ingredients. Mayonnaise has been used even for cosmetic purposes.

More specifically (excepting certain low calorie or diet types), salad dressings essentially contain oil and vinegar which are used together with eggs (yolks or whole), sugar, salt, spices, and other food ingredients to develop the desired identity. They can be spoon-type or liquid, homogenized or multiphased. In the United States, three have been defined by Standards of Identity. Products outside of the prescribed standards may not carry the description Mayonnaise, French, or Salad Dressing. Instead, they are designated as a particular dressing and must declare ingredients on the label. Currently, standardized products are declaring ingredients at the option of some manufacturers. Similar standards legislation, with modification, has been enacted in many other countries. The volume of salad dressings produced in the United States is in excess of 200 million gallons per year. Mayonnaise and Salad Dressing account for more than 85 and 70 million gallons, respectively.

Mayonnaise

Mayonnaise product is said to have been developed in 1756 on the Mediterranean Island of Mahon when the Duke of Richelieu's food supplies ran low as he laid seige to the Fort of San Felipe.

Mayonnaise is a semisolid food emulsion of edible vegetable oil, egg yolk or whole egg, a vinegar, lemon and/or lime juice, with one or more of the following: salt, a sweetener, mustard, paprika or other spice, monosodium glutamate, and other suitable food seasonings. The U.S. product contains not less than 65% of edible vegetable oil. Standards of Identity or particular regulations, depending on the country, may provide additional restrictions or definitions.

A mayonnaise emulsion is an oil-in-water type. Egg is the emulsifying agent. Vinegar and salt are the principal bacteriological preservatives.

A prototype formula could contain:

	%
Vegetable oil (liquid)	80.00
Egg yolk	7.00
Vinegar (4$\frac{1}{2}$% acid)	9.40
Sugar	1.50
Salt	1.50
Mustard	0.50
White pepper	0.10
	100.00

Mayonnaise can be manufactured a number of ways, but all consist of using beating or dispersing equipment in some stage of the process to disperse the oil. For many years, production of mayonnaise was with the planetary mixer. This was a mechanical adaptation and elaboration of the chef's wire wisk and bowl: (1) Add water, egg, and dry ingredients to bowl and agitate to mix and disperse. (2) Agitate rapidly and slowly pour in oil. (Rate of addition should be no greater than the capacity of the machine to disperse.) (3) On completion of addition of oil, gently pour in vinegar under intermediate agitation. (4) On complete mixing of all ingredients, fill into jars and cap.

Manufacturers have refined the foregoing method to improve the texture and uniformity of their finished product. This is accomplished by the employment from a selection of available colloidalizing or homogenizing machines and systems for the semicontinuous and continuous production of mayonnaise.

Mayonnaise is packaged in glass and in plastic wide-mouth jars, tubes, sachets, and individual portion cups. Jar closures are either screw cap or vacuum.

Salad Dressing

Salad dressing is a semisolid combination of mayonnaise and a cooked (or partially cooked) starch paste base. In the United States, the Standards of Identity limit a salad dressing to contain not less than 30% by weight of vegetable oil nor an egg yolk solids content less than the equivalent provided by 4% by weight of liquid egg yolks. Food starches, tapioca, and wheat and rye flours may be used singly or in combination. Optional ingredients include citric acid and emulsifiers of the vegetable gum, pectin, Irish moss, and methyl cellulose variety. As with other food products, each manufacturer has developed a formula and process to suit his requirements.

Starch base may be prepared by combining starch or a blend of starches with water, vinegar, and one or more of the following optional ingredients: sugar, dextrose, corn syrup, honey, other approved sweeteners, mustard, paprika, salt, monosodium glutamate, spices and/or citric acid, plus optional emulsifiers within the defined limits.

The mixture of slurry is then cooked by any of various methods to a desired consistency.

Mayonnaise and starch base can be combined in a planetary mixer or other suitable device. Filling and capping are as for mayonnaise.

Liquid Dressings

The liquid or pourable dressings include the French Dressings. They may be separable or homogenized. Oil content of French Dressings according to U.S. Standards of Identity may be no less than 35% by weight. If they contain egg or any of a number of listed emulsifiers (vegetable gum, propylene glycol esters of alginic acid, methyl cellulose, pectin, xanthan gum, etc.), the total content can be no more than 0.75% by weight. French Dressings may contain catsup, tomato paste, sherry wine, sugar, salt, spices, monosodium glutamate, and other natural ingredients.

Separable liquid dressings are merchandised as products with distinct proportions of oil and aqueous phases or as very "home-made" appearing. Homogenized dressings are produced by passing the mixture through a homogenizer or other colloidalizing machine. Nonseparability is generally obtained by employing a combination of mechanical and ingredient (stabilizer-emulsifier) techniques.

Specialty Dressings

There are specialty semisolid or liquid dressings not covered by Standards of Identity. Among them will be Sandwich Spread, Tartar Sauce, Thousand Island, Blue and other cheese, Green

Goddess, Russian, Italian, Low Calorie, Diet, and others. Specialty dressings may also be merchandised refrigerated or nonrefrigerated.

Ingredients

General.—For those salad products covered by Standards of Identity or similar legislation, the allowable ingredients are specifically listed by the particular governmental agency. Some ingredients, such as spices, may be grouped under one heading in the ingredient clause. Antioxidants or sequestering agents may be used in some countries and not in others. It is not the purpose here to list all of the possibilities, but merely to provide an overview of major ingredients used.

Oils.—The choice of oil is governed by quality, local preference, and the economics of availability. Among these are soy bean, cottonseed, sunflower, and corn. As the technology of refining and deodorization improves, the number of oils used grows. Oils can be used singly or in combination. In certain cases and applications, winterization of the oil is necessary to protect emulsion stability in fluctuating temperatures.

Eggs.—Eggs are used as whole, yolk, or a blend of the two. They may be stored frozen prior to use or used in dried form. Salted or unsalted eggs may be used. Legislation requiring pasteurization of eggs for Salmonella control has been enacted in a number of countries. In products such as mayonnaise where egg is a prominent ingredient, some countries specify minimum requirements.

Vinegar.—Flavored and "spirit" vinegars are used singly or in combinations. The primary function of vinegar is preservation. The secondary is flavor. In the United States, vinegars can be diluted to no less than $2^1/_2$% acidity before being used in mayonnaise.

Citric Acid.—As an "optional" acidifier, citric acid can be used at no greater concentration than 25% (as acetic) of the total weight of acid in U.S. mayonnaise.

Lemon and Lime Juice.—Similar dilution requirements of no less than $2^1/_2$% acidity apply to these juices when used in U.S. mayonnaises. The base material may be fresh juice, canned, concentrated, frozen, or dried.

Others.—Sugar, honey, dextrose, corn syrup, invert sugar, nondiastatic maltose syrup, and glucose are used as sweeteners.

Salt.

Mustard, paprika, spices, spice oils, and spice extracts.

Monosodium glutamate.

Food starches, tapioca flour, wheat flour, and rye flour for U.S. Standards of Identity Salad Dressings.

In the manufacture of specialty dressings, many approved food ingredients not listed for the standardized products are used. These include pickle relishes, cheeses, other emulsifiers and stabilizers, flavors, and colors.

Details of the U.S. Mayonnaise, Salad Dressing, and French Dressing Standards of Identity are published by the U.S. Department of Health, Education and Welfare in the *Federal Register:* CFR 21, Part 25, Dressings for Foods, July 1962, Oct. 1973.

GEORGE C. RIMNAC

Reference

SWERN, D. 1964. Bailey's Industrial Oil and Fat Products, 3rd Edition. Interscience Publishers, New York.

SALAD OIL

Salad oil is defined as an edible triglyceride oil that will not solidify at temperatures of 40°-50°F, but remains unclouded and pourable.

Although salad oil has no U.S. Government definition or Standard of Identity, the edible oil industry has defined salad oil as oil that will remain clear for 5.5 hr when held at 32°F in melting ice. This test is defined in the Standard Methods of Analysis of the American Oil Chemists' Society.

Salad oil is usually a vegetable oil made from "cooking oil" by removal of the fraction that crystallizes out at low temperature. The widespread use of mechanical refrigeration for home food storage made necessary the production of salad oil. Cooking oils (for example, refined, bleached, and deodorized cottonseed oil), if stored in a refrigerator will slowly solidify and will not pour from the bottle. If used to make mayonnaise, which is an emulsion made from eggs, vinegar, flavor, and oil, the emulsion will break if stored in the refrigerator. Salad oil, however, will remain clear and pourable for several weeks when stored in a refrigerator and mayonnaise made from salad oil will retain its consistency under refrigeration.

Salad oil is manufactured by the process of "winterization." This is the process of removal of the higher melting fraction from the oil. The term is derived from the original preparation of "winter oil" or salad oil by allowing oil in outdoor storage tanks to partially solidify in winter. As the high melting fraction solidified into crystals, they slowly settled to the bottom of the tank. The oil from the top of the tank was pumped off and could be stored at cold temperatures without clouding or becoming solid. The fat in the bottom of the tank was used for low grade shortening. Thus the term "winterization" is applied to the process although salad oil is now prepared all year.

The oil to be winterized for use as salad oil is refined to remove free fatty acids, gums, color pigments, etc., and then bleached with an absorptive clay or carbon to remove more color. The warm oil from bleaching is pumped into large narrow rectangular tanks in a refrigerated room. Each tank may hold 40,000 lb or more oil. The warm oil then slowly cools and, under very gentle agitation, starts to deposit crystals of high melting fat when the oil reaches a temperature of about 55°F in 8-12 hr. After another 12-18 hr, the temperature has dropped to about 45°F and the rate of crystallization is rapid enough to cause a slight rise in temperature from the heat of crystallization. The rise may be only 2°-3°F and then the temperature gradually decreases until about 43°-42°F is reached. The oil now is a very viscous semisolid mass so it is allowed to stand for some hours to allow more crystallization and the crystals to grow.

Filtration of the viscous mass is difficult although slow cooling and gentle agitation ensure formation of large crystals. Filtration is usually carried out in plate and frame presses although some nylon dressed cylindrical filters are used. Low pressure must be used or the fragile crystals will break and stop up the filter cloth and stop the flow of oil. Also, slow speed pumps or air pressure is used to transfer the oil to the filter. Filtration may require several days so the entire cycle of cooling and filtration may be 4-6 days.

After filtration is complete the filter cake is removed from the filter and the residual material in the cloth removed by circulation of warm oil. This crystalline material or stearine may be used in shortenings but it contains traces of wax, gums, soaps, etc., as well as considerable salad oil that is retained on the crystals.

The yield of salad oil when 108-109 IV cottonseed is used may be 75-85% with an iodine value of 110-115.

The salad oil is tested by the Standard cold test of the American Oil Chemists' Society (Cc 11-42). A 200-300 ml sample of oil is filtered and heated to 130°C to dry the oil and destroy any crystal nuclei. A clean dry 4-oz oil sample bottle is filled with the oil, and corked. The sample is cooled to 25°C in a water bath and the cork and the bottle top covered with paraffin. The bottle containing the sample is immersed in ice and water and the ice is replenished to keep the bath solidly packed. After 5½ hr the bottle is removed from the ice bath and examined for fat crystals or cloudiness. To pass the test the oil must be clear, limpid, and brilliant. The sample may be returned to the ice bath and examined at hourly intervals until crystals or cloudiness is detected. A good quality salad oil will have a cold test of 20 hr or more.

Because of the long time cycle required to produce salad oil and low yields of the conventional winterization, attempts to decrease the time and increase the yields have been made. Eckey (1940) supercooled cottonseed oil to 40°F in a heat exchanger and then allowed the oil to warm slowly to 42°F. Also, the addition of 5-10% stearine to the oil to be winterized supposedly increases the crystal size and makes filtration easier. Centrifugation to separate the stearine from the oil has been described by Little (1965) and Kirkpatrick (1965).

While most salad oil is produced by conventional winterization, the use of solvents to decrease the viscosity of cold oils and allow better crystallization and faster filtration is possible. Boucher and Skau (1951, 1952, 1955) studied hexane, acetone, and hexane-acetone solutions of oil for production of salad oil.

However, a continuous system now in use is described by Cavanagh (1959). Cottonseed oil in hexane at about 50% conc at a temperature of about 115°F is pumped through a heat exchanger where the solution temperature is decreased to about 38°F. It is then cooled to 20°-26°F or 8°-12°F at 3°-6°F per min in vertical compartments, then pumped to a tank where the temperature is decreased to 0°-5°F at about 0.5°F per min while stirring to facilitate stearin crystal agglomeration. The two phases are separated by centrifugation, the solvent removed to give a salad oil in high yield and a low iodine value stearine.

The total winterization time is about 5 hr compared to 3-6 days for conventional winterization. Table S-2 shows the characteristics of cottonseed oils and stearine produced by winterization with and without solvent.

TABLE S-2

FATTY ACID COMPOSITION OF TYPICAL COTTONSEED OIL WINTERIZATION PRODUCTS

Fatty Acid	Cooking Oil	Salad Oil	Stearine from Oil	Stearine from Solvent
Myristic (%)	0.8	0.7	0.6	0.4
Palmitic (%)	25.1	22.6	32.4	52.0
Palmitoleic (%)	0.8	0.4	0.3	0.0
Stearic (%)	2.5	2.8	2.4	1.6
Oleic (%)	19.7	19.8	17.2	12.0
Linoleic (%)	50.5	53.7	47.1	34.0
Iodine value	107.8	111.4	98.0	71.1

Some vegetable oils such as safflower, soybean, sunflower, corn, and olive oils do not require winterization but are natural salad oils. However, corn, soybean and sunflower oils contain small amounts of waxes that cause the oil to be cloudy, so they are winterized to remove these. Peanut oil cannot be winterized because it will not form crystals but sets to a gel that is unfilterable. Therefore, peanut oil is sold only as cooking oil. Cottonseed oil was the oil of choice for salad oil for many years. The oil winterized well, gave a light colored salad oil with good flavor stability.

However, the price of soybean oil is usually a few cents per pound under cottonseed oil and so has become the most popular vegetable oil in most of the world. Although soybean oil is a natural salad oil, very little untreated oil is sold for salad oil because of the flavor "reversion" of the oil.

Soybean oil can be processed to yield a light colored oil with a bland flavor. However, when exposed to air and/or light (in clear glass bottles) the flavor reverts to the original "beany flavor" which is unpleasant especially if the oil is heated and used for frying.

The cause of the reversion has been traced to the 6–8% linolenic acid in the glycerides. This triple unsaturated fatty acid is believed to oxidize very rapidly and produce off flavors. Therefore to prepare a good flavor-stable salad oil, most of the linolenic must be removed by hydrogenation.

It was found (Evans et al. 1964) if soybean oil was hydrogenated to about 110 IV under selective conditions, only about 2.5% linolenic ester remained in the glyceride and the flavor was stable. Although very selective hydrogenation forms very little saturated esters, the lightly hydrogenated oil must be winterized to make a soybean salad oil. At present, most of the salad oil is hydrogenated winterized soybean oil. Table S-3 shows the composition of this type of oil. Some is sold mixed with cottonseed salad oil.

The use of crystal inhibitors to prevent the formation of visible crystals in salad oil is a common practice. Lecithin, 0.05%, in cottonseed salad oil will extend the cold test time (Swern 1964). Polyglycerol esters (Eckey and Lutton 1941) and polysacchride fatty acid esters when added at 0.02–05%, (Bauer 1964) are reported to extend the cold test by 5–10 times the original cold test.

Oxystearin, prepared by heating saturated fat to $200°C$ and blowing with air, has been approved by the FDA (Federal Register, July 29, 1960) for use as a crystallization inhibitor. It may be added to cottonseed or soybean salad oil at levels up to 0.125%.

All crystallization inhibitors seem to prevent the growth of crystals by interfering with the deposi-

TABLE S-3

COMPOSITION OF SOYBEAN SALAD OIL

Fatty Acid	Soybean Oil	Hydrogenated Soybean Oil	Hydrogenated Winterized Soybean Oil
Myristic (%)	0.1	0.1	0.1
Palmitic (%)	11.2	11.1	10.6
Stearic (%)	4.0	5.1	4.2
Oleic (%)	24.0	42.4	42.0
Linoleic (%)	53.9	38.8	40.4
Linolenic (%)	6.9	2.5	2.7
Trans	0	18.2	16.5

tion of molecules of substrate on the crystal surface. Thus, although crystals are present, they grow very slowly so they are not visible for a long period.

The per capita use of salad oils is increasing in the United States because of the change of our diet to more salads. Also, less home baking is done so semisolid shortening is not necessary and salad oil is used for frying. Also, the indication that polyunsaturated fats prevent the onset of atherosclerois has contributed to the use of more unsaturated salad oil in the diet.

R. R. ALLEN

References

BAUER, F. J. 1964. Salad oil and methods for making them. U.S. Pat. 3,158,489, Nov. 24.

BOUCHER, R. E., and SKAU, E. L. 1951. Phase relations pertaining to the solvent winterizing of cottonseed oil in hexane and in acetone-hexane mixtures. J. Am. Oil Chemists' Soc. 28, 483.

BOUCHER, R. E., and SKAU, E. L. 1952. Phase relations in the solvent winterization of molecularly rearranged peanut oil and cottonseed oil. J. Am. Oil Chemists' Soc. 29, 382–385.

BOUCHER, R. E., and SKAU, E. L. 1955. Phase behavior in the solvent winterization of crude cottonseed oil in 85–15 acetone-hexane mixture as related to reduction in refining loss and color. J. Am. Oil Chemists' Soc. 32, 497–501.

CAVANAGH, G. C. 1959. Fractional crystallization of cottonseed oil. U.S. Pat. 2,883,405, Apr. 21.

ECKEY, E. W., and FOLZENLOGEN, R. G. 1940. "Winter" oil from cottonseed oil. U.S. Pat. 2,205,381.

ECKEY, E. W., and LUTTON, E. S. 1941. Retarding the deposition of stearin from salad oils. U.S. Pat. 2,266,591, Dec. 19.

EVANS, C. D. et al. 1964. Partial hydrogenation

and winterization of soybean oil. J. Am. Oil Chemists' Soc. *41*, 260.

FOOD AND DRUG ADMINISTRATION. 1960. Oxystearin as a crystallization inhibitor in salad oil. Federal Register, July 29, 7184.

KIRKPATRICK, W. J. 1965. Winterizing glyceride oils. U.S. Pat. 3,173,936, Mar. 16.

LITTLE, T. H. 1965. Winterizing glyceride oils. U.S. Pat. 3,145,223, Aug. 18.

SWERN, D. (Editor) 1964. Bailey's Industrial Oil and Fat Products, 3rd Edition. Interscience Publishers, New York.

WEISS, T. J. 1967. Salad oil: manufacture and control. J. Am. Oil. Chemists' Soc. *44*, 146A.

Cross-reference: *Fats and Oils*.

SALMON, PACIFIC

Salmon belong to the family Salmonidae which includes all members of the genus *Salmo* (Atlantic salmon, Pacific steelhead, Arctic char, and several species of trout) and the true Pacific salmon of the genus *Oncorynchus*.   This genus embraces six distinct species and is of considerable commercial importance to the North Pacific rim countries. The genus and species names result from the work of Pennat and Kraschennikow (1768), Günther (1866), and Walbaum (1772). Pacific salmon are anadromous fish that spend their adult lives at sea and migrate to fresh water streams, there to spawn and die. They all have similar life histories in that they return in late summer or late autumn to their parent streams where, sometimes after migrating hundreds of miles, the female digs a deep redd in the gravel bed in which she deposits her eggs.   These are fertilized by the male and covered.   The eggs develop slowly, the yolk sacs are absorbed and the young fry emerge from the gravel in the very early spring While the young fry of some species proceed downstream to the sea almost immediately, others live 1-2 yr in the lakes or streams before setting out on their downstream migration. The survival rate from the eggs to the returning adult salmon is only 0.1-0.3%. Some 500,000 metric tons of salmon are caught annually by (in order of size of catch) Japan, United States, Russia, and Canada.

The following list records the names of the 6 species of Pacific salmon together with their average and extreme weights and the length of their life cycles in years. Sockeye (*O. nerka*): 5-7 and up to 15 lb; 4-5, occasionally 3, 6 or 7 yr. Pink (*O. gorbuscha*): 3-5 and up to 10 lb; 2 yr. Coho (*O. kisutch*): 6-12 and up to 32 lb; 3 and occasionally 2 and 4 yr. Chinook or Spring (*O. tschawytscha*): 10-50 and up to 126 lb; 4-5 and occasionally 2, 6 or 7 yr. Chum (*O. keta*):

8-18 and up to 33 lb; 3-4 yr. *O. masu* (occurs only in Japan): avg 10 and up to 20 lb.

Salmon are fished commercially by trolling, gill netting, purse seining and, where permitted, by use of traps.   The method of fishing depends on species, type of market, and season. Sports fishermen catch comparatively large numbers of salmon by trolling using various lures and by mooching. They usually fish for coho or chinook salmon but on occasion catch sockeye or pink salmon.

Oncorynchus species in some cases complete their life cycle in fresh water. Thus small sockeye salmon which are usually only $1/2$-2 lb in weight, and are called kokanee, spawn in streams and complete their adult life in lakes. About 6 yr ago yearling coho and chinook salmon were planted in Lake Michigan and Lake Superior and adult fish returned for spawning, particularly in Lake Michigan. The survival rate of the planted fish was quite high. In 1968, about 91,000 coho were caught in Lake Michigan and 12,000 in Lake Superior. It is unfortunate that these fish have been exposed to quite high concentrations of DDT.

In order to maintain and if possible increase salmon stocks, active research has been conducted for many decades by such agencies as the International Pacific Fisheries Salmon Commission, the U.S. Bureau of Commercial Fisheries, The Canadian Department of Fisheries, the Fisheries Research Board of Canada, Pacific Northwest universities, the International North Pacific Fisheries Commission, and comparable organizations in Japan and Russia.   Among them, these organizations carry out important work such as regulating the harvesting of salmon on the high seas, in coastal waters, and in rivers. They also study the distribution of salmon stocks in the ocean, the maintenance of natural spawning grounds, and the establishment of artificial spawning channels.   They have played a prominent role in investigations that have been made on the effect of power dams on river migrations and on spawning grounds. The conclusion has been that power dams and good stocks of salmon are incompatible. Without the dedicated efforts of these organizations salmon stocks might long ago have been decimated. It is hoped that this great fish resource will be maintained and even expanded.

The migrations of salmon are fascinating and are, as yet, largely unsolved problems. The downstream migration involves, depending on the species, newly emerged fry, 3-in. yearlings, or large 2-yr-old fish.   They swim downstream, usually in schools, resting on occasion until they reach salt water and the active search for food commences. What triggers these migrations is not known though a rise in water temperature to about 40°F is definitely stimulatory. The means by which adult salmon, often hundreds of miles from shore, are attracted to their parent streams are still not clear, though some investigators believe that visual stimuli are responsible. On the other hand, salmon possess very sensitive olfactory senses and chemical stimuli may well be involved. Once the fish reach the immediate location of their home stream, research has shown that olfactory stimuli are all-important. As yet, attempts to identify the substance that exerts the attractant effect have met with only limited success. It would appear probable that a number of chemical attractants are involved since within one river system there usually exist different spawning grounds each with its race of fish which arrives at its destination with chronological regularity.

The transportation, preservation, processing, storage, and distribution of salmon is complex. Where processing plants are near fishing grounds and the fish are intended for canning they are rarely eviscerated or iced and are processed soon after they reach the plant. Since fish used for canning are not eviscerated they must be chilled if there is an interval of some days between capture and processing. For this reason fish collected from gill net boats, and those fished by purse seiners, were frequently iced. However, due to the quantities of fish involved the icing was often inadequate and the visceral cavities and surrounding tissues were attacked by digestive enzymes with resulting discoloration and softening. There has been much improvement in quality of landed salmon as a result of the application of the refrigerated sea water procedure whereby the fish are promptly placed in sea water chilled by mechanical means or by ice and held at about 30°F until they are unloaded. Where salmon were at one time unloaded by forking (pughing) or perhaps by brailing there is an increasing tendency to use sophisticated mechanical unloaders which convey the fish from vessel to fish plant in a stream of water at the rate of perhaps 1-2 thousand pounds per minute without damage. Refrigerated sea water transportation of salmon has enabled processors to divert more fish to outlets such as the fresh fish market where the financial rewards are greater. Troll-caught salmon, which are usually coho and chinook, are almost invariably eviscerated and iced since they command comparatively high prices.

A considerable quantity of salmon is frozen and, due to the oily nature of the fish, development of oxidative rancidity may be a serious problem. Salmon are usually frozen whole and glazed with ice which may contain an antioxidant or substances which prevent cracking. Frozen salmon steaks or fillets should not be stored except for short periods at very low temperatures (e.g., -28° to -30°F) and preferably under conditions which minimize the contact of oxygen with the fish.

The canning of salmon is a procedure which has not altered radically since its inception about 1864-1867. Most sockeye, pink, and chum salmon are canned, and coho and chinook much less frequently. Since the early days, the process has been simplified by the introduction of a number of machines. These include the iron chink which rapidly removes heads, tails, fins, and viscera. Automatic filling machines are used as well as devices for salt addition. Color sorting can now be carried out. After checks for appearance and weight, the cans are sealed using a vacuum closing machine, are retorted at about 245°F, and cooled.

H. L. A. TARR

Cross-reference: *Fish and Fishery Products.*

SALMONELLA CONTAMINATION

The incidence of salmonellosis in the United States in 1971 has been estimated at two million cases of clinical illnesses. These cases have resulted almost entirely from eating contaminated foods. The salmonellae, a group of diarrhea-causing pathogens with about 1500 recognizably different serotypes, are among the most versatile of the microorganisms producing food-borne infections. They cause a variety of illnesses ranging from typhoid and paratyphoid fevers to meningitis, endocarditis, septicemia, osteomyelitis, and arthritis in addition to their most frequent manifestation, gastroenteritis. That the reported cases of salmonellosis are increasing on a worldwide basis when many other bacterial diseases are receding in the face of technology is an anachronism. Salmonellosis, in fact, has become largely a man-made disease resulting from an ever-increasing variety of host products (Hardy and Galton 1955).

Sources of Salmonellae

Poultry Products.—Poultry, eggs, and poultry offal, which is used as animal feed, are the most common sources of salmonellae. Poultry flocks are infected both by contaminated feed, much of which is animal offal or rodent-contaminated grains, and by mingling with *Salmonella*-infected wild birds, sparrows, starlings, and pigeons. Young birds, highly disease-susceptible, may have a high mortality shortly after hatching. Survivors become infected mature birds which lay eggs that are either infected or contaminated with salmonellae. Uncontaminated fresh, Acronized (packed in slush-ice containing an antibiotic), and frozen poultry are frequently contaminated during evisceration and chilling in the processing plant (Wilder and MacCready 1966) and subsequently introduce salmonellae onto the cutting boards and utensils in the market, the home, and food-service establishments.

Egg products, frozen or dried whole eggs, yolks, or albumin which have not been pasteurized have been a major *Salmonella* source since World War II (Schneider 1946). Their inclusion as supplements in other food products such as cake or cookie dry mixes or noodles have widened their impact on the consumer. This eventually resulted in FDA regulations requiring that egg products be *Salmonella*-free. While pasteurization has greatly reduced the problem, recontamination of these products often occurs.

Pigs.—Pigs are readily infected with salmonellosis which they contract from contaminated processed offal feeds, poultry and wild bird droppings, or rodent-infested grains. Pigs raised on clean farms may become infected in the holding pens at the abattoir or subsequently on the pork assembly line. The hog-scald water may become so *Salmonella*-laden that every carcass passing through it contaminates every piece of plant equipment that it touches thereafter. (Galton *et al.* 1954).

Pests.—Pests include rodents and insects. Salmonellosis is a rodent disease (Welch *et al.* 1941). Rodent droppings contaminate raw products such as grains in the silos or box cars, the feed of animals and poultry, and the food handling equipment in the processing plants, some of which are impossible to sterilize. Roaches may be either infected, and spread salmonellae in their droppings, or infested and physically transport them on their bodies from filth to clean food. Thus, every product which contains "filth, rodent-droppings, and insect fragments" must be viewed as potentially *Salmonella*-infested.

Pets.—Pets, chiefly dogs and cats, are salmonellosis prone when young, but can be asymptomatic carriers when mature. Animal offal or by-products used as protein supplements in their foods infect pets. Members of the parrot family are so frequently infected as to have to pass quarantine in many States; turtles, recently found to be responsible for an estimated 300,000 cases of human salmonellosis in 1971, are currently the subjects of legislative control. Turtles are frequently fed carrion in the swamps in which they are raised (Lowenstein *et al.* 1971).

People.—People carry salmonellae. The under-20 age group has more than $2/3$ of the clinical illness; the mature adult will more often be a subclinical case with little or no diarrhea or vomiting, but will pass salmonellae in their stools for days or weeks. Some may become chronic carriers due to infected gallbladders and void them for a year or a life-time. Typhoid Mary was such a person. Less obvious, but perhaps an even greater danger, because he is a transient carrier, is the worker who has or has had an unreported diarrheal episode and who continues to work in a food-service or food-processing establishment during that time.

Processed Foods.—Processed foods may receive salmonellae from any or all of the aforementioned sources. In addition they may contain chocolate, coconut, spices, and food coloring, all of which come from tropical, less technologically developed countries where sanitary habits are far below our standards (Lang *et al.* 1971). Excreta from people, rodents, birds, and animals may contaminate them either at their source or during transit. Incorporation of such plant and animal by-products into an assembly line may infest both the final product and the plant equipment.

Beef and Dairy Products.—These are less frequent sources of salmonellae than the others cited. While cattle may have herd infections caused by contaminated feed, or may become infected in the holding pens, the major source of contamination of fresh beef seems to occur from plant equipment and/or at the retail butcher shop. There seems to be more infected cattle herds in Great Britain (Hobbs 1961) than in the United States, but it may be that they are only reporting the infections better. Dairy products, however, are less subject to contamination because of almost universal pasteurization of milk, whatever the final product is to be, whereas in England both pasteurized and raw milk are available at the consumer's option.

Other food products incriminated in salmonellosis are yeasts used in breweries and in dry mixes, spaghetti and noodles, nonfat dry milk (Collins *et al.* 1968), and smoked fish. Drug products of animal origin, pancreatin and thyroid extract, and carmine dye used in the hospital (Lang *et al.* 1971) may be contaminated. Finally, even modern sewage treatment plants often discharge more *Salmonella*-laden effluent into our waterways than industrial waste and raw sewage outlets do.

Control

As firmly as salmonellae are established in the American ecology, eradication of them is probably unattainable at present. However, just as botulism was so well-controlled by the food industry that commercial food products were botulism-free for four decades, a similar potential exists for salmonella control.

The first of two major obstacles is the contamination of meat animals and poultry resulting from *Salmonella*-infested feeds (Clis and Swecker 1965). The cycle of contamination from animal feeds to animals, to abattoirs, to plant equipment, to consumer must be interrupted. Towards that end, in 1967 FDA declared such infested feeds to be adulterated and liable to seizure in interstate commerce. Bone meal, blood meal, fish meal (Morris *et al.* 1970) crab meal, feather meal, and tankage were among the products designated. If the raw material is received in an uncontaminated state, the magnitude of the problem will be greatly reduced.

The second obstacle is the failure of some food processing plants to avail themselves of the knowledge of and the need for plant sanitation of the calibre necessary to produce a wholesome and hygienic product. The knowledge already exists in the institutes dealing with the specific industries in food technology. Quality control must become a way of life from the entry of the raw materials into the plant until the packaged product reaches the consumer.

Many States and municipalities are passing legislation, in some cases exceeding those of the FDA, in standards of quality and purity in foods. It will be ever more difficult to rationalize away unsanitary or adulterated foods as consumer protection committees expose undesirable practices and products to an aware public (Eickhoff 1967). Salmonellae are presently a major cause of recall, confiscation, and destruction of products with the ensuing financial losses. The present attitude of zero-tolerance of salmonellae in man's foods indicates that these economic sanctions will continue and the production of ever higher quality food products will thereby be enforced.

WELTON I. TAYLOR

References

CLISE, J. D., and SWECKER, E. E. 1965. Salmonellae from animal byproducts. Public Health Repts. *80*, 899–905.

COLLINS, R. N. *et al.* 1968. Interstate outbreak of *Salmonella newbrunswick* infection traced to powdered milk. J. Am. Med. Assoc. *203*, 838–844.

EICKHOFF, T. C. 1967. Editorial. Salmonellae on the grocery shelf. Ann. Internal Med. *66*, 1279–1283.

GALTON, M. M., SMITH, W. V., McELRATH, H. B., and HARDY, A. V. 1954. *Salmonella* in swine, cattle and the environment of abattoirs. J. Infect. Diseases *95*, 236–245.

HARDY, A. V., and GALTON, M. M. 1955. Salmonellosis. The role of food processing plants in the dissemination of *Salmonella*. Am. J. Trop. Med. Hyg. *4*, 725–730.

HOBBS, BETTY C. 1961. Public health significance of *Salmonella* carriers in livestock and birds. J. App. Bacteriol. *24*, 340–352.

LANG, D. J. *et al.* 1971. Salmonella-contaminated carmine dye. Another example of in-plant contamination during processing. Am. J. Public Health *61*, 1615–1619.

LOWENSTEIN, M. H., LAMM, S. H., GANGAROSA, E. J., and ANDERSON, H. W. 1971. Salmonellosis associated with turtles. J. Infect. Diseases *124*, 433.

MORRIS, G. K. *et al.* 1970. Salmonellae in fish meal plants: relative amounts of contamination at various stages of processing and a method of control. Appl. Microbiol. *19*, 401–408.

SCHNEIDER, M. D. 1946. Investigation of *Salmonella* content of powdered whole egg with not more than two per cent moisture content. II. General survey on occurrence of species of *Salmonella* in high-quality egg powder. Food Res. *11*, 313–318.

WELCH, H., OSTROLENK, M., and BARTRAM, M. T. 1941. Role of rats in the spread of food poisoning bacteria of the *Salmonella* group. Am. J. Public Health *31*, 332–340.

WILDER, A. N. and MacCREADY, R. A. 1966. Isolation of *Salmonella* from poultry, poultry products and poultry processing plants in Massachusetts. New Engl. J. Med. *274*, 1453–1460.

SALT: ITS USE IN THE FOOD INDUSTRY

"Salt is *not* salt," as we are so often told. Every food processor should test each product to determine which grade and screen size of salt will result in his product being of the highest quality at the lowest cost.

In the food industry, the primary function of salt should be as a flavor enhancer. Salt should not dominate the taste in a food product, but should be used only to the extent that it brings out the natural flavor of the product. An exception is pretzels. Other food products should be salted to the maximum without the salt taste being noticeable. Salt costs far less than any of the food ingredients in which it is used. Therefore, proper salting to bring out the maximum levels of taste can effect savings in ingredient costs.

Studies have shown that sodium chloride reduces the sourness of acid, and increases the sweetness of sugar. Acids, with the exception of hydrochloric acid, increase the saltiness of sodium chloride. Sugar reduces the saltiness of sodium chloride.

Small amounts of salt will increase the sweetness in food products and beverages, thereby enabling a cost savings on sugar. By the same token, an extremely sharp sugar taste may be cut by adding a small amount of salt.

In the curing of meats, salt is the main curing ingredient. The sugars, nitrate, and nitrite are used for color and flavor, and to enable the maximum amount of salt to be used without the product being too salty.

The purity of salt in food processing is of significance. As an example, small amounts of calcium will toughen the skins of beans, peas, corn, and other similar vegetables. Since these products are graded on their tenderness, canners are anxious to produce as tender a product as possible. These vegetable skins contain pectin. When the calcium content of salt is too high, the calcium combines with the pectin and toughens the normally tender skins, thereby downgrading their quality. It has been pointed out that 200 ppm of calcium is sufficient to toughen canned vegetables. This characteristic of calcium in certain salt products is utilized to firm up vegetables which tend to be soft and pulpy, such as tomatoes.

Shelf-life of fish products may be extended through the use of high purity salt. Calcium and magnesium in a lower purity salt will retard the penetration of salt into the fish, causing the fish to spoil during salting at lower temperatures.

Orange juice, lemon juice, and grapefruit juice, along with canned tomatoes, sauerkraut, and spinach, are valuable because of their vitamin content. Vitamin C, one of the most valuable, is very unstable and breaks down at the slightest cause. Copper and iron (found in salt) cause this costly vitamin to break down. Therefore, evaporated salt with the lowest content of copper and iron is needed. Salt with less than 1.5 ppm of iron and less than 1.5 ppm of copper should be used where Vitamin C is to be protected.

Copper and iron, even in small amounts, accelerate the development of rancidity in foods high in fat or oil. Therefore, we should be concerned with low copper and iron, and low calcium and magnesium content, when determining the proper salt to be used in the various food products.

Evaporated granulated salt has been improved and purified over recent years to the point that several different screen sizes are now available with the highest purity needed for the various requirements. Evaporated granulated salt is now produced with 99.99% sodium chloride content. Density and solubility will vary according to the granular size of the salt particle, with flour salt having a density of approximately 65 lb per cu ft, compared to normal pan-run evaporated granulated salt density of 75 lb per cu ft. The comparison in solubility of these 2 grades are 5 sec at 70°F for flour salt and approximately 18 sec at 70°F for the pan-run granulated salt, using the Dunn Method of test.

Salt will cake when subjected to moisture followed by drying periods. When the relative humidity is above 75%, salt will take on moisture which dissolves some of the salt. When the humidity drops, the dissolved water will evaporate and cause the salt to cake. Calcium and magnesium increase the hygroscopicity of the salt, which tends to make the salt retain absorbed moisture and retard free flowing.

However, the natural trait of sodium chloride is to be hygroscopic, so we counteract the natural caking of salt by adding tricalcium phosphate, calcium stearate, or magnesium stearate. Since these anticaking agents will cause milkiness if the salt is to be made into a brine, they cannot be used in such cases. The finer the screen size, the more likely the salt will cake. Therefore, storage of salt in dry areas, away from damp or hot areas, off the floor (on pallets), and away from walls or open doors, is desirable.

With the introduction in recent years of Yellow Prussiate of Soda (sodium ferrocyanide) as a free-flowing agent, there have been far less problems of salt becoming caked and hard. YPS is approved for food use and most salt companies are using YPS in quantities of approximately 5-13 ppm in all food grade salt. This process allows or causes small tentacles to form on each grain of salt, which break easily, yet keep the salt granules from sticking together.

To summarize, food processors must determine the proper salt needed for each product they process. Consideration must be given to screen size, purity, low calcium and magneisum content, low copper and iron content, density, solubility, and proper storage to prevent caking of the salt.

PACKIE McFARLAND

SAMUEL CATE PRESCOTT AWARD

See Awards.

SANITATION

The food industries are well aware of the values of sanitation. A sanitation program saves money, increases the efficiency of operations, and lifts the morale of plant personnel. The chance visitor who sees a clean, orderly food plant, well lighted, with spotless equipment, and well-groomed personnel comes away with the impression that the products of the company are wholesome and of high quality.

Sanitation programs may be said to begin with standards of cleanliness in three categories: chemical, physical, and microorganic. The areas of concern are buildings, equipment, personnel, waste disposal, water supply, and the areas around the plant. Procedures for systematically inspecting these various components of the plant to see that the sanitation program is being maintained are essential.

Inspection is the heart of the sanitation program. Daily inspections are indicated for the product, both the raw and the finished product, for equipment and buildings, and for lunch rooms, rest rooms, and locker rooms. These daily inspections are made for the purpose of seeing that cleaning services are being maintained at a high level of sanitation. In addition to such inspections, inspections in depth of areas where contamination is likely to occur are made. Receiving stations for raw materials, sewerages and sewage disposals, the surfaces of processing equipment, especially those that come in contact with food, and all areas used by personnel are perhaps of greatest concern.

Sanitation programs are necessary for legal reasons. The Food, Drug, and Cosmetic Act defines adulteration in terms of poisonous or deleterious substances (except substances for which tolerances have been stated, e.g., food additives) contained in a food, the presence of filthy, putrid or decomposed substances, and foods prepared or packed under sanitary conditions. This law is strict and is strictly enforced.

One of the best-known methods of sanitation is in-plant chlorination, the continuous addition of germicidal concentrations of chlorine to all processing waters. This inhibits microbial growth on equipment, reduces counts on products, and extends the period of plant operation, this last because the time required for cleaning is reduced. Chlorine has a remarkable germicidal effect but its use as a sanitizing agent requires accurate methods of control and application. A number of products, fruits, for example, take on a chlorine flavor if the concentration is too high. Metals corrode unless the chlorination level is low (2–5 ppm). In other words, chlorine must be used judiciously. It is, however, an effective agent in maintaining sanitation.

Physical methods of sanitation are chiefly two— heat and radiant energy. The use of hot water in cleaning equipment and processing areas is common in a number of branches of the food industry, particularly in the manufacture of dairy products. Radiant energy has found some application in sanitizing storages, but its use is not extensive.

MARTIN S. PETERSON

Cross-references: *Chlorine; Detergents.*

SARDINES OF NORWAY

The term "sardine" refers to various small saltwater food fish found in oceans all over the world, prized for their rich flesh and soft bones. Commonly it is the canned product, refined in a special way, that is called "sardines."

The sardine canned in Norway is refined in a unique way, unlike any other. Before canning, it is carefully smoked over slow-burning oak fires, a preserving process used by Norsemen for centuries before canning methods were perfected by Stavanger Hermetiske Fabrik in 1879. Only the Norwegian sardine has this delicious smoky-savory flavor which makes it a prized delicacy the world over.

Norway Sardine Varieties

The sardine caught and canned in Norway is of two varieties: The brisling, sometimes called the sprat (*Clupea sprattus*) and the sild (*Clupea harengus*). These two distinct species are caught within the fjords or off the coast, where the sparkling, clear sea waters are teeming with minerals, washed down by rushing mountain streams.

The Norwegian brisling is a very tender-fleshed fish, juicy and plump. When canned, it ranges in size from $3^1/_2$ to $4^3/_4$ in. long, and is usually packed in pure virgin olive oil. The Norwegian sild is firm in flesh and texture, and when canned, ranges from $3^3/_4$ to $6^3/_4$ in. long. It is usually packed in light natural oil from the fish itself. Some are packed in tomato sauce and mustard sauce.

The most common size can packed is the $^1/_4$ dingley can, net weight $3^1/_2$–$3^3/_4$ oz, with the sardines packed in 2 layers, one layer, and crosspacked. The 2-layer tin contains 14–26 sardines; the one layer, 6–12 sardines; the crosspacked, 30–38 sardines; and the mustard sauce, 6–12 sardines.

Fishing and Canning Regulated by Law

Every aspect of the Norwegian sardine processing is subjected to stringent industry and government regulations. The Norwegian Directorate of Fisheries sets the fishing season and checks the soundness, size, and fat content of each sardine catch. In addition, a Norwegian law insists that sardines must be kept alive, tightly netted, in the water, for at least three days before they are taken to the cannery. This is called "thronging" and permits the purging of any undigested food before canning.

A special Norwegian control board supervises the canning of sardines. The Norwegian Quality Control Institute, set up in 1953 to maintain the high quality of the world-famous smoked Norwegian sardines, checks every step of the canning process, from the amount of salt to the label. The Institute's headquarters and laboratory are located in Norway's sardine center, Stavanger, and its inspectors oversee the canning process, even to the purity of oils and sauces and labeling data. The Institute also approves the purity of the final product and grants export licenses.

Each can of sardines from Norway is required by Norwegian law to be labeled with a thorough description of contents, kind of oil, weight, packer, and country of origin.

Catching the Norway Sardine

The large-scale sardine fishing is done off the west coast of Norway and in the excellent fishing harbors of the fjords, which offer a natural protection for fishing boats and packing plants.

The sardine fishing season in Norway may vary slightly year to year but it is best in the summer months from May to October when waters are smooth and feeding is best. The packing season is year round, made possible by freezing the raw product.

Sardines are netted from boats when the little fish rise to feed on plankton. Called the "silver harvest" from their churning and splashing through the upper open waters, sardines are often sighted by the presence of gulls and other seabirds. In Norway, fishermen use the traditional drag line plus new methods of echo sounds to locate the shoal (school) which is then encircled by purse-seines.

The purse-seines used are generally 360 ft deep and 900–1200 ft long, and are made to stand vertically in the water by means of cork floats or air-filled glass or plastic balls at the upper edge and by lead sinkers at the bottom. A rope pulled through brass rings at the bottom forms a pocket or purse, which traps the fish.

Practically all brisling fishing is carried on today by purse-seine fishing vessels. Some of the Norwegian fishermen, however, are still using the old-fashioned methods by fishing from the shore with what are called beach seines, encircling a shoal which has come into a bay.

Sardines caught in purse-seines from boats are towed to shallow fjord waters so the fish can throng for 3 days before canning. This natural cleansing process is possible in such calm, sheltered bays as Norwegian fjords. After thronging, sardines are put into open wooden or plastic tubs, covered with cracked ice, and rushed to packing plants which are near at hand along the coast.

Sardine Canning

The expression in Norway is: "Caught and canned in a day." Inside the canning factory, machines quickly and efficiently handle everything except the hand packing. First, sardines are given a brine bath to take off their scales; this makes them more receptive to the smoking. Then they are graded to size automatically and moved along conveyor belts to a machine which threads them through the head onto thin steel rods. Suspended thus individually, they are conveyed into ovens

and lightly smoked for 1 hr over slowly-burning selected oak wood. After smoking, mechanized knives cut off the heads.

Along conveyor belts, trained packers carefully hand-layer the smoked fish into cans and inspectors check for uniform filling. Cans, incidentally, must be approved quality tinplate or aluminum, internally lacquered with approved finish.

Pure oil (either olive oil or natural sardine oil) or a sauce (tomato or mustard) is added automatically by machine. Then the lids are put on and the can is sealed hermetically, washed and placed in a steamer to cook and to thoroughly sterilize contents. Minimum sterilization time depends upon tin size; for standard tins, 112°C for 1 hr. The finished pack is taken to a storage room where it is allowed to age, like good wine. A can of Norwegian sardines, according to its packers, will last indefinitely.

Nutritional Value

Sardines are one of the best and least expensive sources of protein. They are rich in vitamins A and D and also in minerals. According to the Research Laboratory of the Norwegian Canning Industry, a can of Norway sardines contains more calcium than a cup of milk. They are also an excellent source of phosphorus. Sardines have valuable amounts of magnesium, iron, copper, ash, iodine, riboflavin, and niacin.

Serving Suggestions

Like caviar, the delectable smoked Norway sardine is prized for making canapes and hors d'oeuvres. Although it is very reasonable in price, this sardine delicacy is served by the most discriminating chefs and hostesses the world over. It is also used in salads and main dishes, such as rarebits, crepes, croquettes, shirred or scrambled eggs. Norway sardines, packed in handy, easy-opening cans, are also energy-boosting favorites with fishermen, campers, boaters, and hikers all over the world.

Industry History

The Norwegian Canning Industry was founded in 1842. During the first period mainly meats, various kinds of vegetables, and fishballs were packed, but from 1878, however, beginning with the canning of sardines in olive oil, canned fish goods became more important.

The industry works in close contact with science. The Research Laboratory of the Norwegian Canning Industry—the largest of its kind in Europe—was founded in 1931 at Stavanger to assist in the developing of new products and new machinery and to maintain control over raw materials. The Laboratory maintains chemical, bacteriological, and technical departments. It is a semiofficial body, its expenditures coming from special fees paid by the canning industry itself.

Another quasi-governmental agency aiding the industry is the Quality Control Institute, also founded at Stavanger. It maintains a strict quality control of all conserved and semiconserved fish goods, both on export goods and on commodities for the home market. No commodity may be exported without first being approved by the Control Institute.

A further manifestation of the high standards that the industry has set up for itself is a technical school which was established at Stavanger in 1952, providing a 1-1$\frac{1}{2}$ yr course to train young men and women for responsible positions in canning. The Norwegian Canning School is the only one of its kind in the world; its costs defrayed by the factories, it represents one of the most recent advances in industrial thinking.

This stressing of quality in its production has made the savory, smoked Norway sardine a favorite the world over. Some 35,000 tons were shipped in 1970 to 60 countries, with the United States its main market. There are 65 plants in Norway and they employ 4000–5000 persons.

Norway is the fifth largest producer of fish products in the world and some 50,000 Norwegians are fishermen.

CAROL LEE ASHIMINE

SAUERKRAUT

Sauerkraut is salted sliced cabbage that has undergone fermentation by lactic acid bacteria. The typical characteristics of sauerkraut can be attained only by means of the complex changes that occur during fermentation. The mellow flavor produced during fermentation is difficult to analyze and has not been duplicated artificially. Primarily, the sugars of the cabbage are converted to lactic and acetic acids, ethyl alcohol, and carbon dioxide.

Successful preservation of many foods depends upon the acids and other substances produced by the lactic acid bacteria during fermentation. These acids restrict or inhibit the growth of the various undesirable organisms capable of spoiling food if allowed to develop. While the acids and other substances are produced primarily from carbohydrates, there are also concomitant changes in other constituents. Nutritional values undergo little change, since well-controlled fermentations produce only minor alteration in caloric values, minerals, and vitamins. Fermentation also contributes certain desirable flavorsome, aromatic, and physical characteristics to many food products.

Fermentation is an ancient method of preparing and storing food to retain its wholesome characteristics and nutritive values. Practices antedate recorded history. A large number of vegetable substances are subject to fermentation by lactic bacteria and the products may be preserved for extensive time periods. The fermented mixtures of vegetables used in the Orient are very important in the diets of the peoples. These products are the forerunners of sauerkraut as it is produced in Europe and the United States. When the practices were introduced to Europe, cabbage, because of its availability and its desirable characteristics, became the primary vegetable. Cabbage is uniquely suited to fermentation because the resulting blend of flavors, the appearance, and the texture of sauerkraut are appealing to many consumers.

Present-day practices in sauerkraut technology have evolved from an ever-increasing knowledge of underlying facts. Very little is known about the ancient practices used in the Orient, but they were, without doubt, developed and improved by trial and error. The first description of sauerkraut manufacture, comparable to the methods used commercially today, is the description of the Dutch "zoorkool" given by James Lind in 1772, in his treatise on scurvy. Barrels, kegs and stone crocks were the common containers. Wooden vats were introduced in the United States about 1885. Concrete vats when first used were subject to pitting and cracking. Recently, reinforced concrete with plastic coatings and glazed tile vats have been introduced. Revolving slicers, automatic corers, revolving brushes for cleaning, and other innovations are fairly recent.

Improvements of the past 30 yr are probably, in part, the direct result of increased knowledge of the microbiological and chemical changes that occur, including better sanitary practices, control of salting, the determination and recording of acidity development, better covering of kraut in vats, and more efficient methods of canning.

The modern sauerkraut factory is well planned. The plant arrangement ensures economical handling of the product. Particular attention has been given to floors, so constructing them as to provide easy cleaning, e.g., to provide sufficient slope so that brine and water may drain off readily. Less difficulty is thereby encountered with mold growth, and the tanks themselves have a longer life. The cabbage trimming, coring, and slicing rooms are usually separated from the tank rooms so that each area may be individually heated or cooled as needed. Some factories have several tank rooms, which can be closed from each other when necessary.

Major Advances

Major advances made in the sauerkraut industry, advances which have resulted in improvement of quality and greater uniformity, are many. Salting techniques, to cite one, have been improved to give uniform distribution and concentration.

Considerable attention has been given to more efficient salting programs. In most factories, salt is weighed and applied at a 2.25% level to the shredded cabbage. Some factories are equipped to weigh each cart of shredded cabbage. In other factories, only occasional carts are weighed to check their capacity and salt is added proportionately. In some factories, cabbage is weighed on belt lines and, by means of a suitable proportioner, salt is added in the desired amount.

Processors have become increasingly aware of the influence of temperature upon the rate of fermentation. The rate and extent of fermentation will be influenced by the temperature of the cabbage at the time of filling the vat.

The use of a plastic cover is a major development in sanitation and improvement of quality. When properly weighted with water, the sauerkraut brine is kept level with the surface of the sauerkraut providing an essential, anaerobic condition preventing development of spoilage organisms.

Sauerkraut is ordinarily left in the vats until completely fermented. Since the rate of fermentation is partly dependent upon the temperature of the shredded cabbage at the time it is packed in the vat it is essential to measure the acidity in each tank at regular intervals to determine the order in which vats should be opened for canning.

Most kraut factories now practice some form of acidity determinations. Some keep an accurate record of the development of acidity in each tank comparing the rate of fermentation with temperature at the time of packing the vats.

Most of the sauerkraut produced in the United States is retailed as a canned product. Efficient methods of canning have been adopted.

In the majority of factories, cans are filled at 165°F (73.9°C), passed through an exhaust box, sealed, and cooled. This is accomplished by heating kraut in large, stainless-steel vats, using mechanical equipment to move the kraut forward to a suitably-fingered drum. The drum then places the kraut on the filling table for hand filling. Recently, a screw-type pasteurizer has been developed in which the kraut is heated by injecting steam into the kraut during passage to the filler. An automatic filler has now been perfected to replace hand filling. It will fill cans with the desired weight of kraut with very little fluctuation in drained weight.

Cooling is partially effected by rolling cans in water, followed by casing and stacking cases with sufficient air space to ensure continued cooling.

It has been shown that quality is retained better in properly cooled kraut.

Attention is given to proper cooling and storing of kraut packed in final containers. Packers have become quality conscious and are grading their own packs according to U.S. Standards.

Very little kraut is retailed as bulk kraut today. Although most kraut is retailed as a canned product, sales of kraut in plastic and glass are increasing. Further improvement in containers, particularly in the use of plastic materials and glass may be effected in the near future.

A major contribution to the elucidation of the microbiology and chemistry of vegetable fermentations was made when Pederson in 1930, showed that the sauerkraut fermentation was initiated by the bacterial species, *Leuconostoc mesenteroides* and completed in sequence by the species *Lactobacillus brevis* and *Lactobacillus plantarium*. The significance of this observation concerning the activity of *Leuconostoc mesenteroides* was not fully appreciated until further study revealed its complete role.

Leuconostoc mesenteroides initiates growth in vegetables because it grows more rapidly than any other lactic acid bacterium and over a wide range of temperatures and salt concentrations. It produces carbon dioxide and acids quickly to lower the pH, thereby inhibiting the development of undesirable microorganisms and the activity of their enzymes which may soften vegetables. The carbon dioxide produced replaces air and provides an anaerobic condition favorable to stabilizing the ascorbic acid and the natural color of the vegetable. The growth of this species apparently changes the environment making it more favorable for the growth of other lactic acid bacteria in the bacterial sequence. The combination of acids, alcohol, esters, and other growth products imparts a unique and desirable flavor. The species converts excess sugars to mannitol and dextran, which are generally nonfermentable, to organisms other than lactic acid bacteria. Mannitol and dextran, unlike sugars, do not have free aldehyde or ketone groups to combine with amino acids to initiate darkening of the food. The species produces a higher pH for any given level of acid than the homofermentative bacteria. Elucidation of the role of the species *Leuconostoc mesenteroides* has changed and standardized certain practices in the sauerkraut industry. *Leuconostoc mesenteroides* is truly a very valuable species whose role should be studied and appreciated in many food fermentations.

Use of Sauerkraut with Other Foods

The feasibility of using sauerkraut or its juice in blends with other food products has many possibilities which have never been fully exploited.

Three primary methods of utilization may be considered: the possibility of fermenting the cabbage with other foods; the use of sufficient kraut or juice in combination with other foods to lower the pH of the blend sufficiently for low temperature processing; and the preparation of foods other than meats with sauerkraut. The chopped kraut now produced in sizeable quantities in some sections of the country is attractive. Fermentation methods are applicable not only to cabbage, but to other vegetables and fruits, cereals, milk, and meat products blended with cabbage. A mixture of several vegetables will often yield a balanced composition of desirable characteristics in the fermented product.

Sauerkraut is often eaten as an adjunct to other foods, thereby making them more appetizing and digestible. It is generally recognized that when sauerkraut is cooked with other foods, particularly meats, it enhances their palatability.

CARL S. PEDERSON

Cross-reference: *Fermentation.*

SAUSAGE

Sausage is one of the oldest forms of processed meat products. Where, how, and when it was developed is not known. Reference to some type of sausage shows up from time to time in ancient records. Homer in his *Odyssey* mentions sausage as one of the favorite foods of the Greeks.

The Romans had high regard for sausages and used them for many festive occasions. The word "sausage" is derived from the Latin "salsus" denoting salted or preserved. Epicurus writing on cookery lists a number of sausage products. Some of these products were produced from pork and spices and stuffed into casings and smoked or cooked in wine.

In Europe during the middle ages many of the sausages acquired the name of the area or city in which they were prepared. For example, Frankfort, Bologna, Braunschweig, Genoa, Gothenborg, Lyons, and Arles gave rise to sausage products that have carried these descriptive names through the centuries. In the United States, sausage has acquired a distinctive status as a convenience food and the frankfurter or weiner is affectionately called the "hot dog."

Sausage classifications can be made in a variety of manners with no single classification entirely satisfactory. The most useful classification separates into (1) coarse ground and (2) emulsified products.

The coarse ground products are prepared by grinding the meat items and mingling the fat and lean particles in a uniform mix. The emulsified products are prepared by mixing, chopping, and emulsifying the ground meats with ice, salt, spices, and curing salts in such a manner as to produce an emulsion. This emulsion contains fine fat particles coated with protein dissolved from the lean meat. In heating in the smokehouse, the protein coagulates or sets solid and entraps the fat particles in the protein matrix.

The coarse ground or the emulsified products can be stuffed into suitable sized casings and utilized fresh or then can be further processed by fermenting, smoking, cooking or drying, or by using various combinations of these operations.

A frankfurter or bologna may be prepared in an identical manner, using the same ingredients, and vary only in size. Sausages are normally cylindrical in shape and this shape is one of the regulatory requirements for sausage, i.e., a cylindrically shaped meat item must meet the composition requirements for sausage if it is to be labeled "sausage."

Frankfurters and bologna represent approximately 70% of the sausage prepared in the United States and are characteristic of the comminuted, emulsified, stuffed, linked, smoked, and cooked meat products. Frankfurters are unit packed usually 8–10 to the pound and bologna is sliced and unit packed at the sausage plants for sale in our modern merchandising systems.

While animal casings were used exclusively in the past, the modern usage is predominantly cellulosic casings for sausage products. Animal casings limited the amounts of sausage in the past; however, since the advent of cellulosic and regenerated collagen casings, the available meat supply is the limiting factor for sausage production. The "skinless frankfurter," the largest volume sausage in the United States, is prepared in the manner mentioned above and after processing the cellulosic casing is removed by stripping or peeling the casing from the sausage and the skinless frankfurter results.

The semidry or dry sausage process is the most ancient of the sausage arts and involves grinding the meats and mixing them with salt, spices, curing salts such as sodium or potassium nitrate, and, in some instances, small amounts of sodium nitrite. The mixture is held under refrigerated conditions for an extended period of time to develop a fermentation system within the mixture. This is comparable to the fermentation of wine, cheese, or bread. The modern tendency is to use a starter culture such as *Pediococcus cervisiae* in the semidry or dry sausage. The sausage mixture is stuffed into casings, held at a temperature suitable for acquiring the proper growth of the acid-producing organisms and finally smoked and dried. The drying time and temperature cycle may require from 20 to 90 days depending on the type and the diameter of the sausage.

Other types of dry or semidry sausages are Genoa, Milano, and Apennino (dried, not smoked); Pepperoni and Salami (smoked and dried); Lebannon (smoked, not cooked). Lebannon is a beef product produced initially in Pennsylvania with a distinctive flavor and of excellent keeping quality.

Liver sausage or braunschweiger is an emulsified liver and pork fat product that is water cooked. This sausage may be prepared with or without curing salts although the trend is to use some cure.

Approximately four billion pounds of sausage were produced in the United States in 1971. Sausage is one of the most economic uses of meat and the industry will continue to grow. Sausage acceptance by the consumer is often based on color, texture, and flavor. The flavor results from the meat and spice combinations, the processing conditions, and the ratio of moisture and fat in the product. Spicing is one of the most guarded secrets of each processor. The processed meat industry is the largest single user of pepper, while mace, nutmeg, coriander, sage, allspice, clove, cinnamon, basil, and many other spices are used in varying degrees.

Some specialty sausages use various meat tissues other than muscle and blends of milk, cereal, and vegetable products such as potatoes and soy meal.

Sausage compositions may vary to a degree; however, the government regulatory requirements for moisture, protein, and fat assure a reasonably uniform composition for each product type. Nutritionally, sausage reflects the nutritive value of the beef, pork, mutton, and poultry meats used in our modern sausage. Sausage is versatile; and muscle from fish, goats, whales, donkeys, and in some areas of the mid-east muscle from camels is used in sausage. Basically, any lean muscle would be suitable for sausage when blended with the proper type and quantity of fat. The quality of the meat and the additives are carefully checked prior to use. The processing conditions and the hygienic handling are highly controlled in order to produce wholesome sausage products.

Liver sausage and some of the smoked sausage prepared in the southern part of the United States are especially nutritious based on the proportion of meat specialty tissues used in the product.

Since sausage can be varied to meet requirements for either high or low calorie levels and yet meet the essential protein requirements, it should have a commanding place in our dietary and in the dietary of the world population.

F. WARREN TAUBER

Cross-reference: *Meat Curing and Smoking.*

SCALLOPS

There are at least a dozen species of scallops of commercial importance in world trade. Of these, three are of particular interest to the U.S. fisherman—the sea scallop (*Placopecten magellanicus*), calico scallop (*Argopecten gibbus*), and bay scallop (*Aequipecten irradians*).

The sea scallop is by far the most important of these species, but landings by the U.S. fishing fleet have been decreasing greatly over the past years. In 1970, only 7.4 million pounds of meats were landed, less than $1/2$ the 1964–1968 average of 15.4 million pounds. Demand is, however, so great that although landings decreased by 2.3 million pounds in 1970 as compared with 1969, the value to the fisherman decreased only $0.5 million from the $9.8 million earned in 1969.

It is possible that with the recent development of automated shucking methods adapted to use aboard the vessels, the calico and, to some extent, the bay scallop will increase in importance. The bay scallop fishery, however, is particularly susceptible to pollution problems and, despite intensive management efforts, may have to depend on new developments in mariculture as well as the automated shucking processes to achieve a position of major importance in the scallop industry.

Although its range extends from the Gulf of St. Lawrence to Cape Hatteras, Georges Bank off Cape Cod, Mass., is the most important fishing ground for sea scallops. Second in importance to Georges Bank is the area off the Virginia Capes which supplied a large part of the landings during the mid-1960's.

Fluctuations in abundance of sea scallop stocks appear to result mainly from fishing pressures. In the larval stages, plankton eaters will take their toll; and after the scallops become bottom dwellers, boring sponges, snails, starfishes, and bottom feeders such as cod will weaken or consume the young scallops. There does not appear to be any particular organism causing losses from disease. Where mass mortalities do occur, they most likely are caused by an adverse change in the environment, particularly with an increase in water temperature since scallops are very intolerant of temperatures above 20°C (Merrill 1971).

The calico and bay scallops appear to be subject to predation similar to the sea scallop; but in addition, as noted above, the bay scallop is subject to pollution problems and possibly even more devastating is destruction of its natural habitat by eel grass disease (Hanks 1971).

Harvesting

Sea scallops are caught by vessels up to 100-ft long towing 2 dredges simultaneously—1 from each side of the vessel (Peters 1968B). For calico scallops, tumbler dredges (which will fish either side up) have been the gear of choice; but, recently, scallop trawls capable of producing 60 bu per 5-min tow have become increasingly popular for use on hard, sandy bottoms where they will often outfish the dredges by as much as 6 to 1 (Cummins 1971; Rivers 1962). Bay scallops may be caught with dredges similar to those used with the other species; or in the shallow tidal flats they may be taken with dip nets, rakes, or even picked by hand.

Processing at Sea

Sea Scallops.—Considerable trash ranging from undersized scallops and unmarketable species of fish to large boulders are picked up in each tow of the dredge and must be disposed of—scallops measuring $3\frac{1}{4}$ in. and over in shell height are saved, and the trash is shoveled overboard.

A special knife is used to separate the shells and cut the adductor muscle (which is the only part saved by U.S. fishermen) free from the shell. In Europe, the gonads are also saved and are highly esteemed as a delicacy exceeding that of the adductor muscle itself.

The meats are then washed and put in muslin bags which hold about 35 lb. The filled bags are carefully iced in the hold to keep the scallops from spoiling.

Calico and Bay Scallops.—The small size of these scallops makes it impossible economically to shuck them by hand aboard the vessel. However, machines based on the "shock-heat-shock" method have been developed and installed aboard some of the larger vessels (Webb and Thomas 1971; Cummins and Rivers 1970). After shucking, the meats are washed in sea water, packed in plastic tubs holding about 10 lb, then iced down in the vessel's hold.

Processing Ashore

Sea Scallops.—As the catch is unloaded, the meats may be processed immediately, or sometimes the bags of meats are packed with ice in boxes or barrels and held overnight, or occasionally longer before processing.

At the processing line, the meats are dumped into a washing tank containing a 6°–8° salometer brine (about 1.5–2.0% salt by weight) and given a brief rinse. The meats are then conveyed to the packing table. Large meats are cut into "bite-size" pieces before packing into waxed cartons or plastic pouches. Quick freezing the meats individually in air-blast, liquid nitrogen, liquid carbon dioxide, or liquid refrigerant (Freon 12) before packing is also practiced; and very often, the meats will be coated with batter and breading, deep-fat fried, then frozen and packaged (Peters 1968 A, B).

Calico and Bay Scallops.—As the shell stock is unloaded, it is packed into boxes or baskets and held overnight. Much of the shucking is still done by hand at a rate of 1 gal. (8 lbs) of meats per hour. As it takes about 1.75 bu to produce 1 gal. of meats and as average daily landings are about 500 bu per vessel (Cummins 1971), then during an 8-hr day, each shucker will process 14 bu of shell stock, and 35–40 shuckers will be required per vessel! It is obvious that before these resources can be fully and economically utilized, automated shucking processes must be adopted; and for maximum quality, the equipment should be installed on the vessel as described by Cummins and Rivers (1970). In any case, the shucked meats are washed and frozen, very often individually in liquid-nitrogen freezers, then packed in 5-lb plastic bags (Cummins 1971).

Quality Considerations

Washing Shucked Meats.—In the sea scallop fishery, the washing process may range from a brief rinse to a 6-hr soak in sea water at temperatures as high as 16°C in the summer. Quality deteriorates both from rapid start of bacteria growth, and the ineffectiveness of soaking as a means of removing sand from the meats (Peters 1968 A).

Cooling Rate in Ice.—The time needed to cool a 35-40-lb bag of sea scallop meats to 0°C at the center may be as long as 48 hr, depending on time and temperature of soaking. Varga and Blackwood (1969) report on tests comparing the quality of sea scallop meats cooled in the conventional manner with the quality of those cooled rapidly in refrigerated sea water prior to storage in ice. The results show conclusively that rapid cooling of scallop meats prior to bagging and icing yields a product of significantly higher quality.

It is expected that similar results would be obtained with calico and bay scallops.

Freezing Scallops Aboard the Vessel.—Only limited tests have been conducted on freezing scallop meats aboard the vessel, but the results show that even slowly frozen sea scallop meats (approximately 24 hr to reach -15°C) are superior in quality to scallop meats held 48 hr in ice then plate frozen ashore (Peters et al. 1958).

The scallop industry is one of considerable value to the economy of the U.S. fishing industry; and with further development of automated shucking equipment, rapid chilling and freezing aboard the vessel, and better quality control in general, it should continue to increase in importance.

JOHN A. PETERS

References

CUMMINS, R., JR. 1971. Calico scallops of the Southeastern United States, 1959-1969. Spec. Sci. Rept.—Fisheries *627*. Natl. Marine Fisheries Serv., Seattle, Wash.

CUMMINS, R., JR., and RIVERS, J. B. 1970. Calico scallop fishery of Southeastern United States. A photo review of latest developments. Com. Fisheries Rev. *32*, No. 3, 38-43.

HANKS, R. W. 1971. Minor species—bay scallops, razor clams, and mussels. Proc. Symp. Commercial Marine Mollusks of the United States. American Malacalogical Union, Febr.

MERRILL, A. S. 1971. The sea scallop. Proc. Symp. Commercial Marine Mollusks of the United States. American Malacological Union, Febr.

PETERS, J. A. 1968A. Characteristics of frozen shellfish: Factors affecting quality change during freezing and storage. Chap. 9, Part 3, Scallops, Clams, and Abalone. *In* The Freezing Preservation of Foods, 4th Edition, Vol. 2. D. K. Tressler, W. B. Van Arsdel, and M. J. Copley (Editors). Avi Publishing Co., Westport, Conn.

PETERS, J. A. 1968B. Preparation for freezing and freezing of shellfish. Chap. 9, Part 3, Oysters, Scallops, Clams, and Abalone. *In* The Freezing Preservation of Foods, 4th Edition, Vol. 3. D. K. Tressler, W. B. Van Arsdel, and M. J. Copley (Editors) Avi Publishing Co., Westport, Conn.

PETERS, J. A., McLANE, D. T., LUKSHIN, D. A., and SLAVIN, J. W. 1958. Tests on freezing and storage of scallop meats. Unpublished data. Natl. Marine Fisheries Serv., Atlantic Fishery Prod. Technol. Center, Gloucester, Mass.

RILEY, F. 1971. Fisheries of the United States, 1970. Natl. Marine Fisheries Serv. Current Fishery Statist. *5600*.

RIVERS, J. B. 1962. Fishing vessels and gear developments. Equipment Note No. 12—A new scallop trawl for North Carolina. Com. Fisheries Rev. *24*, No. 5, 11-14.

VARGA, S., and BLACKWOOD, C. M. 1969. Effect of seawater chilling on landed quality of scallop meat. J. Fisheries Res. Board Canada *26*, No. 9, 2523-2526.

WEBB, N. B., and THOMAS, F. B. 1971. Influence of mechanical processing on the quality and yield of bay scallop meats. Spec. Sci. Rept.—Fisheries *624*, Natl. Marine Fisheries Serv., Seattle, Wash.

Cross-reference: *Shellfish.*

SENSORY EVALUATION

Sensory evaluation is a valuable tool in solving problems involving food acceptability. It is useful in product improvement, quality maintenance, new product development, and market research.

Sensory evaluation panels can be grouped into three types: (1) highly trained experts, (2) laboratory panels, and (3) large consumer panels. Highly trained experts evaluate quality and large consumer panels are used to determine consumer reaction to products. Evaluations by trained laboratory panels are useful in quality control, in product development, and product improvement.

Control of Conditions

In any type of analytical work there must be standardization and control of conditions. This is especially so with sensory evaluation. Standardized procedures have been developed in an effort to control or minimize the effect that psychological and physical conditions can have on human judgement.

It is generally recommended that testing be conducted in a special room where as many variables as possible are controlled. This room should be separate from, though adjacent to, the sample preparation area. It should be air-conditioned and free from cooking odors, noise, and distractions.

Panelists can be easily influenced by the reactions of other panelists. Because of this the panelists usually work independently in separate booths. Conversation and discussion are not permitted during testing so that judgements will not be swayed.

The testing booths should be well lighted. They are often equipped with colored lights which, when used in a darkened room, will mask color differences. A very low level of illumination can also be used to mask color differences.

The testing conditions for any particular product should be exactly the same each time that product is tested.

The time of day when tests are conducted might influence results. Although this cannot be controlled if there are many tests, late morning and mid-afternoon have been found the best times for testing.

The questionnaires on which the panelists record their responses should be as simple as possible. New questionnaires should be prepared if the testing method is changed. The experimenter should use separate summary sheets for tabulating results rather than including provision for this on the questionnaire. When computers are used to analyze data, computer cards can sometimes be used by the panelists for recording responses. The panelists must be carefully instructed in this method so that needless errors are avoided.

Samples

The panelists are influenced by all the characteristics of the test material. Information which they are given about the test will affect the results. Because of this, panelists should not be given detailed information relevant to the test, and those persons who are directly involved with the experiment should not be included on the panel.

In his desire to be "right" the panelist's judgement may be influenced by irrelevant characteristics of the samples. All samples should be as uniform as possible. The only differences should be in the characteristic being studied. If unwanted differences occur between samples they should be masked whenever possible. In order to obtain a representative sample several cans or packages from one lot should be thoroughly mixed or blended.

Samples are generally served at the temperature at which the food is usually eaten. However, the taste buds are less sensitive at very high or very low temperatures and it is recommended that cold drinks should not be cooler than about 45°F and hot foods not above 170°F. There should be refrigerators and waterbaths or warming trays for keeping samples at constant temperatures until they are presented to the panelists. The sample should be at the same temperature each time it is tested.

Samples should be coded so that the panelists cannot identify them. The code itself should not introduce any bias. Since people generally associate "1" or "A" with "best" it is recommended that three-digit numbers from tables of random numbers be used for coding.

The quantity of each sample given to each panelist should be controlled. This is especially true when testing spices where the amount will influence the intensity of the sensation.

The samples should be presented to the panelists in clean, odorless, and tasteless containers.

Comparisons between samples served at the same session to each panelist are more reliable than comparisons between samples served at different sessions or to different panelists. However, it is not always possible to serve all the samples at each session. In this case an incomplete block design can be used in which each sample is tested at the same session as every other sample at least once.

The number of samples that can be evaluated in one session without fatigue should be determined by preliminary testing. The type of product being tested, and the experience of the judges must be considered when deciding upon the number of samples to test at one session. Motivation is an important factor in this regard. Panelists often lose their desire to discriminate before they lose their capability.

When a test involves more than one sample the order in which the samples are tested must be controlled. The presentation of a sample of "good" quality just before one of "poor" quality

results in the rating of the second sample being lower than it would normally be. Similarly if a "good" sample follows a "poor" one it will be given a higher rating. This phenomenon is called "contrast effect." In some tests a positional bias has been demonstrated. In a triangle test if the differences are very small there is a tendency to choose the middle sample as odd. In order to neutralize errors associated with the order of samples, the American Society for Testing and Materials (1968) recommends that the order of presentation of the samples be balanced so that over the entire test each sample will have preceded and followed each other sample an equal number of times. In a large experiment the order of presentation could be randomized.

Only one characteristic should be evaluated at a time. When a sample is evaluated for more than one characteristic, a "halo effect" may be produced. The panelist often forms a general impression of a product and if asked to evaluate it for texture, color, and flavor at the same time, the results might be different than if each characteristic were rated individually.

It is generally agreed that, except with certain products, the results are not affected whether a panelist swallows the sample or not. However he should use the same method with each sample in the test.

Water can be used to rinse the mouth between tasting samples. The rinse water should be at room temperature. With certain foods, crackers, white bread, or celery may be more effective than water. Once again the panelist should be consistent.

Panelists

The panel is the analytical tool in sensory evaluation. The value of this tool depends upon the objectivity, precision, and reproducibility of the judgements of the panelists. Before a panel can be used with confidence, the ability of the panelists to reproduce judgements must be determined. Interest, motivation, general attitude, and emotional state of the panelists may be responsible for inconsistent judgements.

Panelists are usually office, plant, or research staff. It should be considered a part of work routine for personnel to serve as panelists. It is necessary to have full cooperation of the supervisors of persons who serve as panelists. No person should be required to evaluate foods to which he objects.

The greater the number of persons on a semitrained panel the more likely it is that individual variations will balance out. However, a small highly trained panel will give more reliable results than a large untrained panel. The minimum number of panelists should be 4–5. A laboratory panel is usually composed of 10–20 persons with 3–4 replications per judge per treatment.

Persons who serve as panelists should be in good health and should absent themselves when suffering from conditions that might interfere with normal functions of taste and smell. Emotional factors, interest, and motivation appear to be more important than the age or sex of a panelist. It is generally recommended that panelists refrain from smoking, chewing gum, eating, or drinking for some time before testing; 30 min is probably sufficient.

The motivation of the panelist affects his response. An interested panelist is always more efficient. The panelists should be made to feel that panels are an important activity and should realize the importance of their contribution. The importance of panels can be demonstrated by running the tests in a controlled, efficient manner.

The interest of the panelists may be maintained by publishing test results. However, the panelists should feel that you are pleased to have them test and that you will be pleased no matter what the results.

Amerine *et al.* (1965) believe that by selecting the most stable and sensitive panelists and training them, a small but efficient panel can be obtained. Threshold tests are probably not of much value in selecting panelists. Sensitivity to the primary tastes may not be related to ability to detect differences in food. A more realistic approach is to select panelists on the basis of their ability to detect differences in the food to be tasted. Start with as large a group as possible and rank them according to their ability to discriminate among samples prepared so as to obtain variations similar to those which will be met in the actual experiment. The selected panelists should have an inherent sensitivity to the characteristic being evaluated, and should be able to duplicate judgements. A new panel should be selected for each product. Persons who do well on some products often do poorly on others.

In order to make objective decisions, panelists must be trained to disregard their personal preferences. They must be familiar with the product being tested and must know what constitutes good quality in the product being tested. The panelists must become familiar with the testing method with which they will be concerned. All panel members must know and agree upon the exact connotation of each descriptive term used. The use of physical standards during training sessions will help the panelists become more stable in their judgements. During the training period the method of handling and testing the samples should be discussed and a common procedure agreed upon.

Methods

Several different test methods have been developed and some of the more commonly-used ones are described below. The experimenter should be thoroughly familiar with each method, its advantages and limitations. He should be sure that the method he selects for a particular situation is the most practical and efficient one. No one method can be used universally. The experimenter must precisely define the purpose of the test and what information he wants to acquire.

Some of the methods described below will merely determine whether there is a difference or not, some methods can be used to measure the intensity and direction of the difference, and others indicate the quality of the products.

Paired Comparisons.—A pair of coded samples, one representing the standard or control and the other an experimental treatment, is presented for comparison on the basis of some specified characteristic, such as sweetness or hardness.

The task of the panelist is straightforward. In certain cases, the panelists may want to declare a tie rather than select one sample. Some workers feel that ties should not be allowed since the panelists may take the easy way out when faced with a difficult decision. Others feel that the panelists should be able to declare a tie when they cannot detect a difference.

The method becomes cumbersome when there are several treatments since each treatment should be compared with every other treatment.

Results of paired comparisons do not indicate the quality of the samples but only if there is a difference. The panelists can be asked to indicate the magnitude of the difference they detect. This method yields more information than simple paired comparisons.

Statistical Tables are available for determining if the results of paired comparisons tests are significant (Bengtsson 1953; Bradley 1954). Computer programs have been developed for analysis of paired comparisons data.

Triangle Test.—Three coded samples are presented to the panelist. He is told that 2 are the same and 1 is different and is asked to identify the odd sample.

This method is useful in quality control work and for selecting panelists. It should not be used when there are more than two treatments or when homogeneity of samples is difficult to obtain.

The triangle test has been thoroughly studied by many investigators and many biases have been demonstrated.

Statistical Tables are availalbe for the analysis of data from triangle tests.

Duo-Trio Test.—In the duo-trio test, three samples are presented to the panelist. One is labeled R (reference) and the other two are coded. One coded sample is identical with R and the other is different. The panelist is asked to identify the odd sample.

This test is more efficient when R is always the control sample. This method should not be used when there are more than two treatments. Statistical Tables can be used to determine the significance of results.

Ranking.—The panelist is asked to rank several coded samples according to the intensity of some particular characteristic.

The ranking method is generally used for screening 1 or 2 of the best samples from a group of samples rather than to test all samples thoroughly. This method is rapid and allows for testing of several samples, but no more than six samples of any product should be ranked at a time. Ranking gives no indication of the amount of difference between the samples since samples are evaluated only in relation to each other; results from one set of ranks cannot be compared directly with results from another. Tables for rapid determination of significant differences are available (Kramer 1963).

Multiple Comparisons.—A reference or standard sample is labeled R and presented to the panelist with two or more coded samples. The panelist is asked to compare each coded sample with R. He decides whether it is better than, equal to, or inferior to the reference and indicates the size of the difference.

A coded reference sample is often included with the other coded samples to serve as a check on the panelists.

Multiple comparisons can be used very efficiently to evaluate 4–5 samples at a time. Information regarding the direction and the magnitude of the difference is obtained.

In order to analyze the results of paired comparison tests, numerical values are assigned to the responses of the panelists. Analysis of variance is then calculated.

Scoring.—Coded samples are evaluated for some specified characteristic by the panelist who records his evaluation on a descriptive graduated scale.

Scoring gives an indication of the size and the direction of the differences among samples. It has broad application and can be used to evaluate different characteristics by modifying the wording of the questionnaire. A great variety of scales has been developed. The scale should have at least 5 categories but not more than 9. The number of categories should not exceed the number of degrees of the characteristic that can be perceived. There is a tendency for the panelists to refrain from using the extreme ends of the scale.

The characteristic being measured must be under-

stood by the panelists and the different degrees of quality recognized.

There is a tendency for the scales to drift in meaning with time. This instability is a marked disadvantage when scoring is used in storage stability studies over an extended period. Standard products to represent different points in the scale will act as anchors and will help minimize panel variability.

Scoring yields more information than ranking and is more efficient than paired comparisons.

A numerical scale can be used rather than a verbal scale; however, descriptive terms are usually more meaningful to the panelists unless they are very well trained. Descriptive terms are a help to the panelists but the descriptive words must be carefully chosen if the scale is to be meaningful.

The categories on the scale are assigned numerical values and results are analyzed by analysis of variance.

A particular type of scoring system is the hedonic scale which measures the degree of like or dislike for a product. It is simple and requires no experience by the panelists. The verbal categories can be replaced by caricatures (Ellis 1961).

Descriptive Sensory Analysis.—One of the best-known descriptive methods is the "flavor profile" developed at Arthur D. Little, Inc. (Caul 1957). This method requires a panel of 4–6 trained persons who function as a unit under the direction of a panel leader to produce a verbal description of a product. The flavor complex is described in terms of character notes, intensity, order of appearance, after-taste, and amplitude. The panelists evaluate the product independently and then discuss results in order to arrive at a common opinion.

The selection and training of a profile panel is a lengthy process usually taking 6–12 months. However, once trained it is very efficient since several factors can be evaluated in one session. Profile panels have been found to very reliable.

A descriptive method of analyzing texture was developed using Szczesniak's (1963) texture classification system and standard rating scales developed by General Foods, Inc. This method, called the "texture profile" method, is defined as the organoleptic analysis of the texture complex of a food in terms of its mechanical, geometrical, fat, and moisture characteristics, the degree of each present, and the order in which they appear from first bite through to complete mastication (Brandt *et al.* 1963). The panel must be intensively trained in order to use this method reliably.

Design of Experiments and Analysis of Data

When planning an experiment involving sensory evaluation the most appropriate method should be selected, the number of samples that can be tested in one session should be determined, and the number of testing sessions should be estimated. With this information the amount of experimental material required can be calculated and sufficient material can be prepared in advance.

The advice of a statistician is valuable in planning experiments since the method of analysis must be decided upon before the testing is done.

The use of experimental "designs" such as those described by Cochran and Cox (1957) makes the test more efficient and saves time and material. Replication will strengthen results.

Because of the quantity of data obtained from sensory evaluation and its variability, results cannot usually be interpreted by direct examination. The data must be summarized and analyzed statistically. There are several techniques available and special treatments have been developed for use in particular situations. For some types of tests, statistical Tables have been developed for rapid analysis of the data, e.g., paired comparison, triangle, and duo-trio tests. For most other methods a t-test or analysis of variance can be used to analyze results. Procedures for analyzing data obtained by various testing methods have been described by Larmond (1970). By following the examples a worker who is not familiar with statistics can readily analyze panel results.

Statistical analysis is used to determine the probability that the results obtained in the experiment would occur if chance alone were operating. The probability is commonly expressed in degrees of significance.

In the paired comparison, triangle, and duo-trio tests, a greater degree of significance of results does not mean a greater degree of difference between the samples. The significance is related to the number of evaluations. In order to measure the amount of difference in these tests the percentage of correct responses should be calculated.

Although statistical analyses are essential for interpretation of results they will not correct erroneous data, improve a poor method, or compensate for inadequate control of experimental variables. The results of statistical procedures are no more reliable than the data on which they are based.

Example of a Typical Questionnaire and Analysis of Data

The following is an example of a questionnaire used to measure the firmness of four different samples of baked beans.

Scoring

Name _____

Date _____

Please evaluate these samples of baked beans for firmness. Check the point on the scale that best describes your evaluation of the sample.

Code	Code	Code	Code
_____ extremely soft	_____ extremely soft	_____ extremely soft	_____ extremely soft
_____ very soft	_____ very soft	_____ very soft	_____ very soft
_____ moderately soft	_____ moderately soft	_____ moderately soft	_____ moderately soft
_____ slightly soft	_____ slightly soft	_____ slightly soft	_____ slightly soft
_____ slightly firm	_____ slightly firm	_____ slightly firm	_____ slightly firm
_____ moderately firm	_____ moderately firm	_____ moderately firm	_____ moderately firm
_____ very firm	_____ very firm	_____ very firm	_____ very firm
_____ extremely firm	_____ extremely firm	_____ extremely firm	_____ extremely firm

Comments:

Ten panelists rated the coded samples using the above questionnaire. The order of presentation of the samples was randomized for each panelist. The ratings were then given numerical values with extremely soft = 1, and extremely firm = 8. The data was analyzed by analysis of variance and Tukey's test (Snedecor 1956) was used to determine which samples were significantly different.

Panelists	S_1	S_2	S_3	S_4	Total
1	6	5	6	4	21
2	6	4	5	6	21
3	4	4	5	3	16
4	7	6	7	3	23
5	5	4	4	3	16
6	5	5	5	5	20
7	4	5	7	4	20
8	6	4	7	6	23
9	6	6	6	4	22
10	5	6	6	5	22
Total	54	49	58	43	204

$$\text{Correction Factor} = \frac{204^2}{40} = 1040.4$$

$$\text{Sum of squares, samples} = \frac{54^2 + 49^2 + 58^2 + 43^2}{10} - CF$$

$$= 1053.0 - 1040.4 = 12.6$$

$$\text{Sum of squares, panelists} = \frac{21^2 + 21^2 + 16^2 + \cdots + 22^2}{4} - CF$$

$$= 1055.0 - 1040.4$$

$$= 14.6$$

$$\text{Total sum of squares} = 6^2 + 6^2 + 4^2 + \cdots + 5^2 - CF$$

$$= 1090.0 - 1040.4$$

$$= 49.6$$

Analysis of Variance

Source of Variance	df	SS	MS	F
Samples	3	12.6	4.2	5.25**
Panelists	9	14.6	1.6	2.00 MSD
Error	27	22.4	0.8	
Total	39	49.6		

**There is a significant difference among samples at the 1% level.

Sample Score	S_1	S_2	S_3	S_4
	54	49	58	43

Sample Mean	5.4	4.9	5.8	4.3

Ordered Sample Means:	S_3	S_1	S_2	S_4
	5.8	5.4	4.9	4.3

Standard Error of the Sample Mean:

$$SE = MS \text{ for Error/number of judgements for each sample}$$

$$= \sqrt{(0.8/10)} = \sqrt{0.08} = 0.28$$

In order to be significantly different the difference between two sample means must exceed S E X Q factor (Snedecor P252).

$$= 0.28 \times 3.87 = 1.1$$

$$S_3 - S_4 = 5.8 - 4.3 = 1.5 > 1.1 \text{ (}S_3 \text{ significantly different from } S_4\text{)}$$

$$S_3 - S_2 = 5.8 - 4.9 = 0.9 < 1.1 \text{ (}S_3 \text{ is not different from } S_2\text{)}$$

$$S_1 - S_4 = 5.4 - 4.3 = 1.1 = 1.1 \text{ (}S_1 \text{ is not different from } S_4\text{)}$$

$$S_3 \quad S_1 \quad S_2 \quad S_4$$

Conclusion: S_3 is significantly more firm than S_4.

ELIZABETH LARMOND

References

ASTM. 1968. Manual on Sensory Testing Methods. ASTM Spec. Tech. Publ. *434*. Am. Soc. Testing Materials, Philadelphia.

AMERINE, M. A., PANGBORN, R. M., and ROESSLER, E. B. 1965. Principles of Sensory Evaluation of Food. Academic Press, New York.

BENGTSSON, K. 1953. Taste testing as an analytical method: Statistical treatment of the data. Wallerstein Lab. Commun. *16*, No. 54, 231–251.

BRADLEY, R. A. 1954. Rank analysis of incomplete block designs. II. Additional tables for the method of paired comparisons. Biometrika *41*, 502–537.

BRANDT, M. A., SKINNER, E. B., and COLEMAN, J. A. 1963. Texture profile method. J. Food Sci. *28*, 404–409.

CAUL, J. F. 1957. The profile method of flavor analysis. Advan. Food Res. 7, 1–37.

COCHRAN, W. G. and COX, G. M. 1957. Experimental Designs. John Wiley & Sons, New York.

ELLIS, B. H. 1961. A Guide Book for Sensory Testing. Continental Can. Co., Chicago.

KRAMER, A. 1963. Revised tables for determining significance of differences. Food Technol. *17*, 124–125.

LARMOND, E. 1970. Methods for sensory evaluation of foods. Canada Dept. Agr. Publ. *1284*.

SZCZESNIAK, A. S. 1963. Classification of textural characteristics. J. Food Sci. *28*, 385–389.

SNEDECOR, G. W. 1956. Statistical Methods, 5th Edition. Iowa State University Press, Ames, Iowa.

Cross-reference: *Organoleptic Properties of Food.*

SESAME

Sesame is one of the oldest vegetable crops cultivated by man. Among oilseeds it ranks 9th among the 13 commercial oilseeds grown. The sesame plant providing this seed grows in height anywhere from 2 to 6 ft, has a white or pink flower. The magic words "Open Sesame" found in the Arabian Nights were probably inspired by the characteristic dehiscence of the sesame pods. This characteristic of the pod opening at harvest time has necessitated the hand harvesting of the crop. Research has been carried on to develop a strain of seed which would lend itself to commercial harvesting, but at this time the results have not been successful enough for commercial growing to be carried on in the United States.

For centuries sesame seed and the products made from sesame have found immediate acceptance. A series of Tablets now in the British Museum give the Assyrian account of the creation of the world. A meeting of the gods was held in their council chambers, where they "had bread and drank sesame wine." In latter years the seed was often the subject of contracts and accounting as shown by the references to sesame on the Tablets and deeds now in the Babylonian Room of the British Museum.

Geographical Occurrence

The origin of sesame is unknown. However, according to some references sesame seed was brought from the Sundae Islands to India several thousand years ago and then migrated to Egypt. Today, sesame is cultivated in China, India, Africa, South America, Central America, and Mexico. Sesame was introduced into the western hemisphere in the late 17th Century by slaves who brought the seed from Africa to the plantations along what is now the South Carolina coast.

Since the introduction of sesame seed in the United States, there have been numerous attempts to develop sesame as a crop but, due to its shattering characteristics, little success was achieved. In the 1950's a significant attempt was made in Texas, New Mexico, and Arizona, but the economic conditions were such that the crop was discontinued in 1960.

World production of sesame is estimated to be in excess of 1,500,000 metric tons. Approximately 90% of this amount is retained in the growing countries for their domestic consumption, pri-

TABLE S-4

AMINO ACID ANALYSIS OF
SESAME PROTEIN

Grams per 16 Gm of Nitrogen—Nx 6.25		
	Mg/Gm	%
Methionine	13.2	2.5
Cystine	12.1	2.3
Lysine	13.3	2.5
Tryptophan	7.7	1.5
Threonine	21.3	4.1
Leucine	41.7	7.9
Isoleucine	23.6	4.5
Valine	29.5	5.6
Phenylalanine	27.4	5.2
Tyrosine	21.6	4.1

SOURCE: John Kraft Sesame Corp.

TABLE S-6

ANALYSIS OF CRUDE SESAME OIL
(AVERAGE)

Free fatty acid (as oleic)	1.3%
Color	35y/1.2r
Iodine Value	110
Peroxide Value	13
AOM	24 hr
Percent unsaponifiable	2.3%
Smoke point	330°F
Specific gravity @ 25°C	0.918
Saponification Value	185.8
Fatty acids (natural oil)	(%)
Oleic	40
Linoleic	44
Other unsaturates	1
Palmitic	9
Stearic	5
Other saturates	

SOURCE: USDA Southern Regional Laboratories.

marily in the form of oil. The remaining 10% finds its way into world trade, most of which finds its way to Italy and Belgium. Imports to the United States are approximately 20,000 tons. This represents an increase in excess of 100% since 1954. The major sources of supply of seed consumed in the United States are Ethiopia and Sudan, Mexico and the Central American countries of Nicaragua, Honduras, and El Salvador. Smaller quantities are being imported from Brazil, Venezuela, and Colombia. The annual production of sesame in India in 1964 was 410,000 metric tons as produced on 18,744,000 hectares. In the same year, Mexico produced 150,000 metric tons on 1,920,000 hectares. Other production data are given in the FAO Yearbook for 1964.

Sesame Today

By far the most important use for sesame internationally is to provide oil. The meal resulting from the production of oil is used as stock food. In the Middle Eastern countries sesame is used in the production of "tahini," which is a spread made from the whole seed, to which has been added honey. These countries also consume significant quantities of a confection called "halvah," which is approximately 70% sesame seed. In the United States sesame enjoys a unique position, that of a spice and an oilseed. The prime use in the United States is in the bakery industry, where sesame is used as a decoration on bread and rolls. A significant quantity of oil is used by the cosmetic and pharmaceutical industries as an emollient or a carrier for medicines.

With the new emphasis being placed on nutrition, the protein of the sesame seed has become increasingly important. The unique quality of

TABLE S-5

COMPOSITION OF SESAME SEED AND MEAL

	Seed		Meal—Screw-Pressed		Solvent Extracted	
	Unhulled	Hulled	Feed Grade	Food Grade	Feed Grade	Food Grade
Crude protein (%)	20	25	49	53	52	60
Ether extract (fat)(%)	49	54	8	15	1	1
Crude fibre (%)	6	2.5	8	5	8	5
Ash (%)	5	5	10	6	11	6
Carbohydrates (%)	15.8	13.5	19	15	24	24
Moisture (%)	5	5	6	6	5	5
Phosphorus (%)	0.7	0.7				
Calcium (%)	1.0	0.5				
Manganese (mg/lb)			19.4			
Riboflavin (mg/lb)			2.1			
Niacin (mg/lb)			50.4			
Pantothenic (mg/lb)			4.1			

TABLE S-7

EFFECT OF SESAMOL ON STABILITY OF
SESAME OIL

	AOM (Hr)	Sesamol (%)	Sesamolin (%)
Crude sesame oil	19	0.003	0.133
Alkali refined	9.5	0.001	0.139
Bleached (neutral dry)	56	0.089	0.015

SOURCE: USDA Southern Regional Laboratories.

sesame protein is traced to the presence of a high level of the sulphur-containing amino acids, methionine and cystine. Its limiting amino acid is lysine (see Table S-4). Because of these unique properties, sesame protein has been used in conjunction with other vegetable proteins to increase their nutritive qualities. Sesame protein does not contain some of the objectionable characteristics found in soy protein, particularly with regard to the trypsin inhibiting factor. The most obvious advantage enjoyed by sesame protein is its pleasant flavor. Until recently the bulk of sesame meal was used in animal feed. The feed had not been considered fit for human consumption in that it was made from natural unhulled sesame seed. Human grade sesame protein is now being offered in the United States by one company. Properties of the sesame seed and sesame meal are described in Table S-5.

Sesame oil has achieved a unique status in that it is the most stable naturally-occurring liquid vegetable oil. The stability is traced to the presence of natural antioxidants present in the crude oil. Sesame oil is considered a polyunsaturated oil containing approximately 44% linoleic acid (Table S-6). Its mono-unsaturated fatty acid percentage (as oleic) is approximately 40%. Table S-7 describes the effect of the natural oxidants sesamol and bound sesamol (sesamolin) on the stability of the oil. The variation in the stability of sesame oil at different stages of processing has been found to

TABLE S-8

EFFECT OF HYDROGENATION ON
SESAME OIL

	Iodine Value	AOM (Hr) Stability
1	112.1	19
2	98.2	43
3	88.8	96
4	71.5	159
5	68.7	682

SOURCE: USDA Southern Regional Laboratories.

be correlated with its content of sesamol. Sesamol is removed from the oil by alkali refining but regenerated from sesamolin by bleaching with certain clays. Hydrogenated sesame oil will result in a shortening of exceptional stability in excess of 500 hr (Table S-8).

Sesame in many forms is now offered for human consumption to the food industry. Some of those forms are as follows:

> Dry cleaned, unhulled sesame seed
> White hulled sesame seed
> Toasted sesame seed
> Toasted flaked sesame seed
> Partially defatted sesame flour
> Solvent extracted sesame flour
> Sesame butter made from toasted sesame seed

Aside from the uses of the seed as a decoration for bakery products, sesame is being used to enhance the flavor of breading mixes, for incorporation into fried or baked snacks, high protein beverages, cereals, candies, cookies, seasoning blends, as a garnish for vegetables, high protein breads, and pies.

H. S. VILLARS

SHELLFISH

Since shellfish are discussed in detail under their species names, they will be described here in terms of their classification, areas where grown or caught, types of processing, and nutritive values. Shellfish are found along seacoasts, in bays, and in lakes and rivers. By far the greatest volume of shellfish comes from saltwater sources.

Shellfish, as the name indicates, are distinguished from finfish by their shells. There are two major classes: mollusks, with hinged shells, and crustaceans with segmented shells and jointed appendages. Clams, mussels, oysters and scallops are members of the mollusk class; crayfish, crab, lobster, and shrimp are the chief species of the crustacean group. The crustaceans are higher up on the evolutionary ladder than the mollusks since they have gills, sensory organs, and a means of locomotion.

Oysters are grown, farmed one might say, on the east coast of the United States, the Gulf of Mexico, and off the Louisiana coast. A different species of oyster, the Japanese oyster, is grown on the Pacific coast. Clams are widely distributed but the chief areas are the coasts of New England, the Middle Atlantic and the Pacific Northwest. Scallops are almost exclusively taken along the coasts of New England, New York, and New Jersey. Mussels are found along the Atlantic coast, principally in rocky areas.

Members of the crustacean classification are found on both coasts, the one exception being lobster which is trapped for the most part on the New England coast and the maritimes. Crabs are taken along the coast of New England, the mid-Atlantic coastal waters, Louisiana, and the Pacific Coast states. The blue crab is the dominant species on the Atlantic side of the United States, the Dungeness and Alaska king on the Pacific Dungeness side. Shrimps are caught on both coasts but the principal source is the Gulf of Mexico.

Although shellfish are preserved by canning (lobster, crab, shrimp, oysters, and mussels, for the most part) and by dehydration (notably shrimp) and by smoking (oysters), they are more usually bought fresh or in the frozen form. Large quantities of shellfish are frozen in the United States. In fact, every form of shellfish mentioned in this brief article is available in frozen form. Freezing promises to be the dominant method of preserving shellfish in the future not only in the United States but in the world at large.

Shellfish have excellent nutritional qualities. Shrimp has as high a percentage of protein per gram as beef, a low fat content and no carbohydrate. All shellfish have a relatively high mineral content, including iodine, one of the essential minerals.

The foregoing aspects of shellfish plus many others are discussed in depth in the articles devoted to particular species.

MARTIN S. PETERSON

SHORTENINGS

Shortenings, used to shorten or tenderize foods, usually are plastic fats, workable at room temperatures; however, they may also be liquid oils which likewise provide tenderness, richness, or palatability. Rendered meat fats and butter are shortening agents, but generally "shortening" refers to fats that have undergone special processing. The use of fluid shortenings is increasing. They usually are limpid, but may be opaque due to the addition of suspended high-melting fats and/or emulsifying agents. The term "liquid" is often misused to describe normally plastic fats which are handled in melted condition.

Shortenings tenderize foods because films or clumps of fat throughout the food prevent the protein and carbohydrate components from cooking to a continuous hardened mass. Cake batters and icings often contain tiny air bubbles trapped in shortening, that help to develop a fine delicate structure.

Shortenings used in frying serve primarily as heat-transfer media and antisticking agents, but the absorbed fat also provides tenderness and richness of flavor.

Commercial processes were developed during this century for refining, hydrogenation, and deodorization, making possible the use of vegetable oils not previously considered edible. Within a few years hydrogenated vegetable shortening, rather than lard or beef fat (tallow), became the quality standard for home and industrial use. The U.S. vegetable-margarine industry, made possible by the same technical progress, has largely replaced butter for most uses. The development of effective, safe chemical antioxidants has made possible the production of excellent animal fat shortenings, thus removing much of the onus associated with these raw fats. Animal fats are devoid of natural antioxidants. Antioxidants also benefit vegetable fat products, but to a much lesser degree, because the seed oils contain natural antioxidant materials.

Chemical and Physical Characteristics

Shortenings are an intimate mixture of microscopic solid crystals and liquid fat. The hardness of the shortening generally can be correlated with the Solid Fat Index (AOCS methods), which is usually estimated dilatometrically over a range of temperatures. Melting and Congeal Points (AOCS methods) also are frequently specified as guidelines to control firmness.

Plastic shortenings usually contain 8–14% by volume of finely dispersed air or nitrogen. The melted fat will have a light yellow color with varying shades of reddish tint, usually measured by Lovibond Color (AOCS methods).

Each raw fat or oil has a strong characteristic odor and flavor which, though very largely removed by processing, can still be identified by discriminating experts. Some of these flavors and odors may reappear on aging, heating, or exposure to light, (perhaps somewhat altered in the process) and again may become objectionable. This phenomenon, usually called "flavor reversion," is most noticeable in shortenings made from oils that contain linolenic acid, $C_{17}H_{29}COOH$ (three double bonds), or other highly unsaturated fatty acids. Great progress has been made in overcoming this difficulty in soybean oil, so much so that since 1950 this has constituted the chief raw material for vegetable shortening. Coconut oil has an extremely bland flavor but is susceptible to the development of a soapy taste, especially in foods containing moisture and inorganic salts, because hydrolysis of the oil tends to occur; it is quite hard at cool temperatures and is not generally considered a shortening component, being used primarily in candies, coatings, and the like.

Butter, lard, and to some extent tallow (beef fat), were the only food fats commonly available in the United States until the early part of this century. Although the proportion is declining, these fats still account for over 25% of the U.S. domestic fat consumption. Moreover, approximately $2/3$ of the lard is still used as the naturally rendered product; the balance is treated as a raw fat and subjected to refining and other processing. All meat fats sold in interstate commerce must be processed under supervision of USDA; container labels bear an inspection certification.

Virtually all other fats are of vegetable origin and require refining and other treatment as outlined below to make them suitable for human food. Relatively insignificant quantities of crude olive (see below) and other oils are sold without processing as "natural" products. Cottonseed oil was and still is the preferred raw material for most shortening uses because of its availability, chemical stability, and relatively bland flavor. However, in the past 20 yr the production and use of soybean oil has far outpaced all other oils in spite of its relatively poor stability and rather unpleasant characteristic flavor and odor. Corn, olive and safflower oils are used primarily as salad oils (see Winterization described below).

The smoke point is directly related to the free fatty acids content and is usually above about 450°F with well-processed deodorized shortenings, except those containing emulsifiers. It is probably a less important characteristic of frying shortenings than is generally believed, since all shortenings undergo sufficient hydrolysis or contamination with nonfat materials after continued use to lower the original smoke point materially. Other physical characteristics, such as viscosity, refractive index, flash point, and fire point, are not usually considered important in evaluating shortenings.

Raw Materials and Manufacture

Table S-9 shows the continuation of many longstanding trends. Butter usage declined, but was accompanied by an increased consumption of margarine so that the per capita consumption of the 2 table spreads decreased only to 12.0 (1971) from 13.5 lb (fat basis). During the same period (1963–1971), the total per capita use of fats increased markedly to 52.7 from 48.8 lb. Cottonseed oil usage dropped, primarily because of declining production, but soybean oil usage continued to increase. The notable recent increase in palm oil probably indicates the start of a trend as tremendous new plantations in Southeast Asia reach productivity; the total world production is estimated to more than triple from 1972 to 1980. The increase in use of peanut oil parallels the increasing tonnage of domestic production crushed

TABLE S-9

DOMESTIC USE OF FOOD FATS AND OILS IN THE UNITED STATES

	1963–64	1972–73[1]
	(In Million Pounds)	
Butter	1,399	1,050
Lard	1,786	1,450
Tallow	578	550
Corn oil	416	450
Cottonseed oil	1,407	1,100
Soybean oil	4,058	6,450
Olive oil	66	65
Palm oil	23	300
Peanut oil	69	200
Safflower oil (est)	160	100
Sesame oil	1	2
Less processed foods and exports	- 111	- 65
	9,852	11,652

SOURCE: USDA *Fats and Oils Situation*, Nov. 1972.
[1] Estimated.

for oil. The per capita use of salad and cooking oils increased to 16.9 lb in 1971 from 6.5 lb (1935–1939 avg).

Raw food fats and oils are normally subjected to several processing steps as follows (Swern 1964):

Refining.—Most fats contain foreign matter which is agglomerated and removed by treatment with a small percentage of sodium hydroxide at temperatures under 100°C plus centrifuging, followed by water washing and vacuum drying.

Bleaching.—Most fats are somewhat dark in color, part of which can be removed by adsorption onto unique mineral clays.

Winterization.—Liquid shortenings comprise almost entirely what is called "salad oil," liquid vegetable oils that will remain clear when chilled to refrigerator temperature of about 40°F. Soybean, safflower, and a few other oils are naturally winterized. Corn oil contains a small amount of waxy material which must be removed by chilling and filtration. Cottonseed oil must undergo a more extensive chilling and filtration process to remove approximately 10% fat which crystallizes at about 42°–45°F. In recent years, most large shortening companies make a lightly hydrogenated winterized soybean oil, having found that this provides an oil with improved flavor and resistance to oxidation; such a product has an iodine value of about 110 compared to about 130 for natural soybean oil. Winterization customarily precedes deodorization.

Hydrogenation.—Most vegetable shortening fats have been altered by chemical hydrogenation, done prior to deodorization, converting naturally liquid fats to analogs that have the physical properties of plastic solids at room temperature. In order to achieve specific physical, chemical, and biological properties, it is common to blend three or more such different shortening fats.

Deodorization.—The characteristic flavor and odor of fats is due to relatively minor quantities of organics that are fat-soluble and cannot be removed except by steam distillation at elevated temperature under a high vacuum. Typical conditions approximate 250°C at 2.0 mm absolute pressure (Hg) for 1-4 hr with strong steam sparging. Flavor and odor are virtually removed, free fatty acids can be less than 0.02%, unsaponifiable matter is markedly reduced.

Additives.—Fat-soluble surface active agents (emulsifiers) may be added, usually after deodorizing, to provide ease of mixing, or more stable emulsions. Frying fats may contain material(s) to reduce the tendency toward foaming. Several antioxidant additives may be used to help protect fats from oxidative rancidity. All such agents and additives are subject to FDA limitations. New labeling regulations, intended to clarify the nutritional properties of all food fats, are in preparation by FDA at this writing; hence discussion of fat labeling is inappropriate.

Uses

General Purpose Shortening Fats.—These are plastic solids at temperatures between about 60°-90°F (ca 16°-32°C) which may be used for a variety of uses not requiring high specific functionality. They may be used in preparing foods such as biscuits, cookies, pie crusts, bread, rolls, pancakes, and pan frying. Household shortenings available in food stores in metal containers usually contain monoglyceride type emulsifiers so that they may also be used for cakes, icings, frostings, and the like wherein relatively large amounts of fat and water must be mixed together without danger of phase separation.

Frying Fats.—Usually these are specially hydrogenated to have a relatively low iodine value (unsaturation) so that they resist oxidation at high temperatures. Such oxidation causes the fat to darken, become more viscous, foam during frying, and develop unpleasant flavors and odors. The addition of antioxidants and antifoam agents can be quite beneficial. Short chain length fats such as coconut oil or palm kernel oil are not suitable for deep fat frying of high moisture foods because they are very subject to foaming due to hydrolysis; as little as 5% of such fats is known to create extreme foaming almost immediately.

Special Emulsifying Shortenings.—These are often formulated to provide special properties in prepared baking mixes, whipped toppings, icings, fillings, and the like. These shortenings often contain four or more surface active agents which complement each other, each providing some particular characteristic.

Liquid Vegetable Oils.—Liquid oils are required in mayonnaise and salad dressings, but may be used in other products for diverse reasons. They provide notable convenience in the kitchen, can be high in polyunsaturated fats and low in cholesterol (which have purported nutritional value) and the mouth feel of foods cooked in oil can be more pleasing.

W. F. SCHROEDER

References

AOCS. 1973. Official and Tentative Methods of the American Oil Chemists Society Including Additions and Revisions, 3rd Edition. Assoc. Offic. Oil. Chemists, Champaign, Ill.

SWERN, D. (Editor). 1964. Bailey's Industrial Oil and Fat Products, 3rd Edition. John Wiley & Sons, New York.

Cross-reference: *Fats and Oils.*

SHRIMP: HANDLING AND PROCESSING

The harvesting of shrimp is confined almost entirely to night fishing on bottoms ranging from sandy to very muddy. The type of bottom from which shrimp are taken to a large degree determines the subsequent quality, all other factors being equal. Shrimp harvested from muddy bottoms may contain up to 30 million bacteria per gram while those from sandy bottoms contain far less.

The quality of the shrimp starts in the trawl, varying with the time in which the trawl is towed. Shrimp trawls are towed slowly along the ocean floor from 1½-5 hr (Osborn *et al.* 1969) depending on the concentration of shrimp. Shrimp caught early in trawling may die and start to deteriorate long before the catch is dumped on the deck. The high temperature of the Gulf of Mexico waters during the shrimping season contributes to the degradation process while shrimp are in the trawl.

Shrimp are taken for the most part in otter trawls ranging in size from 12 to 110 ft (measured as the width along the headrope) depending on the size and power of the individual boat. Once the trawl is hauled in, the catch is dumped on deck where the shrimp are separated from the rest of the catch. In addition to shrimp, the catch may consist of crabs, fish, sponges, and a variety of sea animals, plus stones, shells, and other debris. Sorting out the shrimp may take several hours, thus adding to the time in which deterioration can take place. The shrimp are then deheaded, thoroughly washed, and placed in the hold of the vessel. Sufficient ice is mixed with the shrimp tails (hereafter referred to as shrimp) to maintain the quality of the catch until arrival at the dock.

The time is critical from death of the shrimp until they are placed on ice. Immediately after death, autolytic and bacterial enzymes begin breaking down the proteins, lipids, carbohydrates, etc. It is imperative that the shrimp be thoroughly washed to remove as much bacteria as possible and then reduce the ambient temperature well below that of its natural environment. The bacterial flora associated with shrimp are confined mainly to the genera *Flavobacter, Achromobacter, Bacillus*, and *Micrococcus*. The predominance of each genus changes considerably during storage (Carroll *et al.* 1968). For example, the first major change occurs between the 4th and 5th day of iced storage, the second change between the 10th and 11th day, the third and last major change takes place between the 12th and 15th day of storage. The maximum storage time of shrimp on ice varies up to three weeks depending on thoroughness of washing and efficiency of icing after washing. Generally, the shrimp are layered with ice, i.e., a layer of ice and a layer of shrimp with the ratio of ice to shrimp 2:1. It is essential that the hold be held at a temperature just above freezing to allow the ice to melt thereby washing away bacteria and enzymes which may accumulate on the surface of the shrimp. The holds of the boats are constructed so that the melted ice and shrimp juices can be removed during storage.

In a few instances shrimp boats are equipped with refrigerated sea water (RSW) in which the shrimp are held at 35°–40°F. There are several drawbacks to this method: (1) the boat must be equipped with refrigeration equipment; (2) the RSW shifts in the boat during rough seas increasing the likelihood of capsizing the boat; (3) the RSW must be changed frequently, probably increasing the cost over ice-held shrimp; (4) shrimp are in contact with the RSW for long periods of time thereby reducing the storage life; (5) holding in RSW tends to increase the sodium content of the shrimp; and (6) possibility of a refrigerant leak endangering the lives of the crew and contaminating the catch with the refrigerant.

A few shrimp boats have installed a sugar-brine freezing solution on an experimental basis. Washed shrimp (50 lb) are placed in a mesh bag and immersed in the solution until the shrimp are frozen. This method provides individually frozen shrimp which are then glazed and packed in cartons for subsequent storage.

The installation of mechanical freezing equipment on boats is becoming more prevalent. This equipment allows the shrimp to be frozen on the spot. This is a most ideal system and shrimp handled in this manner are always of prime quality. Graders and plate freezers are part of the system.

Once in port, iced shrimp are unloaded by a hoist and a large basket and then placed in a deicing tank. A conveyor moves the shrimp to an inspection station where inspectors further remove trash, ice, and decomposed shrimp; shrimp are then conveyed into the processing plant. Subsequently the shrimp are moved to a mechanical grader and sized in increments of 5, i.e., 21-25, 26-30, 31-35, etc., shrimp per pound. The shrimp are weighed into 5-lb cartons to be frozen or placed in 100-lb boxes and mixed with ice to await further processing. The 5-lb cartons are frozen in a plate or blast freezer at −40°F, glazed with ice water, packed in 50-lb master cartons, and stored at −10°F.

Shrimp frozen and packaged at sea are unloaded at dock side and placed directly in a holding freezer.

Shrimp are processed in many ways and utilized in various products. The majority of shrimp are peeled, breaded, and frozen, or peeled and frozen. Breaded shrimp are marketed as "frozen raw breaded" or "breaded precooked" shrimp. The peeled shrimp are sold as raw "peeled and deveined" (P&D) or "cooked peeled" shrimp. Shrimp may also be sold in the shell frozen or iced. Small peeled shrimp are utilized in specialty items such as gumbo, shrimp creole, cocktails, smoked shrimp, pickled shrimp, shrimp soups, and paste.

Shrimp are mechanically peeled for the most part although some hand peeling still exists. The manner in which shrimp are peeled is determined by the end product. For breaded shrimp, all segments of shell are removed down to, but not including, the last (or sixth) segment. The entire shrimp is then covered with breading. All shell segments and the fantail are removed from shrimp to be used in speciality items, cooked peeled, P&D, and canned shrimp. After processing, the product is again frozen or canned ready to be offered for sale.

Shrimp used for canning purposes are handled somewhat differently from those to be frozen or utilized in gourmet items. Small shrimp are taken from the inside waters at certain times of the year and brought in on small boats (25–30 ft in length). These shrimp are brought in overnight to the canneries and generally are not deheaded. Very little ice is used. The shrimp are conveyed to a mechanical peeler which removes the heads and shells leaving only the meats. The peeled shrimp are blanched in a salt solution, graded, and placed in cans. Hot brine is added, the cans are sealed and heat processed. Additives, such as citric acid or lemon juice, may be added to the cans before sealing to prevent chemical changes in the product during storage.

Spoiled shrimp are characterized by a strong ammonia odor and in advanced stages of spoilage will discolor and contain a heavy slime. Shrimp that are not handled properly will develop "black spots" on shell segments particularly in the area where the head is removed. Delayed deheading or poor icing techniques will enhance this development which will eventually spread to the meats. Sodium bisulfite is used as a dipping solution (1.25%) to prevent the formation of black spot (Camber *et al.* 1957). Proliferating enzymes in the head are responsible for this spoilage which is referred to as "melanosis."

In 1961, at least one plant on the Gulf was freeze-drying shrimp. Due to difficulty in rehydrating the product the process has not been widely accepted.

Shrimp heads and waste products are ground up and dried to produce shrimp meal. This product is used in animal feeds where high concentrations of protein are desired.

MELVIN E. WATERS

References

CAMBER, C. I., VANCE, MARY H., and ALEXANDER, J. E. 1957. The use of sodium bisulfite for the control of black spot in shrimp. State of Florida Board of Conservation Tech. Ser. *20*, Marine Laboratory, Virginia Key, Univ. Miami.

CARROLL, B. J., REESE, G. B., and WARD, B. Q. 1968. Microbiological study of iced shrimp. Excerpts from the Iced Shrimp Symposium. U.S. Fish Wildlife Serv. Circ. *284*, U.S. Dept. Interior, Washington, D.C.

OSBORN, K. W., MAGHAN, B. W., and DRUMMOND, S. B. 1969. Gulf of Mexico shrimp atlas. U.S. Fish Wildlife Serv. Circ. *312*, U.S. Dept. Interior, Washington, D.C.

Cross-reference: *Shellfish.*

SMELT

The smelt is a small and slender fish with a silvery sheen on its side. The flesh is delicate and very flavorful and when fresh has a characteristic cucumber smell. The smelt is abundant in the northern sections of both coasts of North America, in the Great Lakes, and in the northern waters of

Europe and Asia. The American smelt (*Osmerus mordax*) ranges from Labrador to New Jersey on the Atlantic coast, and throughout the Great Lakes. The eulachon or candlefish (*Thaleichtys pacificus*) ranges from Oregon to Alaska on the Pacific coast. The American smelt is a lean fish with a fat content no greater than 5% (whole fish). The eulachon of the Pacific coast is a fat fish with a fat content of about 10%; in fact, it is so fat that Amerinds used to dry it in the sun and use it as a candle. That is why it is also called the candlefish.

Commercial Fisheries

The marine species migrates to streams for spawning, and the commercial fishery is based on that migration. On the Atlantic coast, the migration takes place in the fall when smelts invade bays and estuaries previous to the spawning run the following spring. The fishery lasts from late fall to late winter. On the Pacific coast, the fishery precedes the spring run. In the Great Lakes, the fishery is also connected with the spring run, except in Lake Erie where the fishery lasts all year round in addition to a major fishery at spawning time and in Lake Michigan where a winter fishery under the ice is the major fishery.

The East Coast Fishery.—Scattered operations take place all along the coast, but the main fishery is in the Gulf of St. Lawrence on the New Brunswick coast. Small catches are made by means of gill nets and beach seines in early fall; major catches are made in late fall and throughout the winter by means of box nets and bag nets set under the ice in streams and bays. The mesh size is usually $1^1/_8$ in.

Smelts on the east coast attain sexual maturity at the end of their second year of life; the immature fish (male and female) make up about 65% of the catch; mature fish to the age of 3 yr make up another 30% of the catch; fish of 4-5 yr make up only 5%. The market recognizes 4 grades: shorter than 4 in., classified as small; fish up to $5^1/_2$ in., called mediums; fish up to 7 in., called number ones; and larger fish rated as extras.

After grading, fish graded as extras are made up 58% of age 3 and 35% of age 4 fish; those graded as "number ones" are made up 59% of age 2 and 40% of age 3 fish.

The annual catch in the Maritime provinces used to average 7 million pounds with a landed value of about $800,000. Recent competition from the Great Lakes caused it to decrease to about 3 million pounds a year with a value of $300,000.

The West Coast Fishery

This fishery is based on the spawning migration in the winter months, and mainly in the Columbia

FIG. S-1. BRINGING UP A PURSE SEINE WITH A CATCH OF SMELT

FIG. S-2. ICING THE SMELT IN CRATES ABOARD SHIP

River and its tributaries. In the Columbia River the catch is by means of gill nets, in the tributaries by means of dip nets. The fishery is exclusively for human consumption and varies between 1 million and 2 million pounds a year. Apparently, the catch is limited by market demand. Recent reports indicate that a trawl fishery for eulachon in the Columbia River is possible and could lead to improved quality.

The Great Lakes Fishery

Smelt is an introduced species in the Great Lakes; earliest plantings were in the St. Mary's River in 1905–1906 where smelt eggs from the Atlantic coast were deposited. Plantings were continued at different locations during succeeding years and apparently one of the most successful plantings was in Crystal Lake on the east shore of Lake Michigan. The smelt became established and started spreading out to different parts of Lake Michigan and eventually to the other Great Lakes. Lake Michigan and Lake Erie now have large, well-established populations of smelt that support commercial fishing operations. However, the two fisheries are entirely different in types of gear used and time of year. In Green Bay of Lake Michigan, production is by means of pound nets set under the ice during the winter months. In Lake Erie, production used to be based on the spawning run taking place mainly on the north shore of the lake in late April and early May. Pound nets were used and are still used for that type of fishery located mainly around the Wheatley area near the western end of the lake. At other times of the year the fishery is by means of trawls in the Eastern Basin of the lake where smelt congregate and where practically year-round fishing takes place.

An unknown factor affects smelt reproduction on alternating years in Lake Erie; one year the catch consists of equal amounts of 2- and 3-yr-old fish, and the following year the catch consists of mostly 2-yr-old fish. This causes marketing problems on alternate years (Hart and Ferguson 1966).

The value of the fishery increased considerably in Lake Erie with the introduction of trawling gear around 1960, causing a corresponding decrease in the value of the marine fishery on the east coast.

The annual catch appears to be stabilized at about 12 million pounds per year and indications are that the fishery could sustain a higher volume of production. Landed value on Lake Erie is approximately $500,000 per year.

Research

The Canadian Federal Government carries out biological research on smelt on the east coast while the Ontario Government carries out biological research on smelt in Lake Erie. Starting in 1957, these two governments cooperated in a gear development program to improve the smelt fishery in Lake Erie. Up to then the fishery had been a seasonal operation limited to about six weeks which produced a glut on the market. Freezing part of the catch was used to spread the availability of smelt over a few more months; but the real need was for continuous production over the months to maintain processing operations and marketing at a more stable level. Echo sounding and trawling gear were used to locate smelt concentrations and to determine the type of gear which could economically be used. Trawling for smelt is now a well-established operation on Lake Erie, leading to better processing continuity, better quality, and adjustable production in response to market demands.

One of the problems of this fishery is the variation in size of fish within a catch and from year to year caused by a factor related to reproduction. Initial sorting as to size is done on board the fishing boat at the batch level; if a trawl load appears to be mainly very small fish it is immediately rejected. Sorting by means of mechanical sorters is carried out at the processing plant. Smelts acquire distorted shapes when stored in ice previous to processing, making it difficult to sort out and to process by automatic machinery. A method which prevents these problems has been proposed and has been successfully tested by the Fisheries Research Board of Canada. Smelts, as soon as caught, are transferred to holding tanks aboard the fishing vessel; the holding tanks contain slush ice, a medium that not only cools the fish rapidly but in which smelts maintain their symmetrical elongated form. Holding under similar conditions during transport and during holding before processing allow optimum processing quality and efficiency. The Division of Fish and Wildlife of Ontario developed specially designed toteboxes with removable polyethylene liners for holding smelt.

Utilization

Research directed towards greater product diversification and total use of the smelt harvest has been undertaken by government agencies and to a limited degree by the industry.

Government workers have directed investigations in areas of product development such as examining methods of utilizing the smaller, less readily marketable smelts which are caught incidentally during fishing operations, and new products in line with modern marketing philosophy with the intent to increasing the resource value. This type of research has been undertaken in large part by the Fisheries Research Board of Canada and has included examining the nutrient constituents of smelt; the potential of smelt processed as a canned sardine-style product, smoked, packed with oil, and packed with various sauce mediums; and experimental processing of sausage and wiener products using smelt flesh as the primary raw ingredient. Problems were encountered with this latter type of product because of the uncohesive characteristics of the flesh and a grey unappealing discoloration taking place when minced, due to the homogenization of the dark pigments present in various areas of the fish. It was found, however, that smelt flesh combined with the flesh of other, more suitable fish would produce a product with acceptable texture and color characteristics.

Industry has concentrated largely on developing and marketing processed products in the fresh or frozen dressed form and the fresh or frozen breaded and precooked form.

General Biology

Studies have been conducted by the Department of Lands & Forests of the Province of Ontario towards determining: distribution patterns in Lake Erie according to various age groups throughout the year and evaluation of the significance of the movement of smelt concentrations and dispersions; the relationships between water depth, temperatures, and oxygen concentrations; spawning habits and locations and the effect of fluctuating water levels and rainfall on mortality; the phenomenon of successful reproduction on alternate years; diseases that may affect spawning, growth, and mortality.

Sport Fishery

Wherever smelt are present, sport fishermen are there to exploit them. The fishery is varied. On the east coast, sport fishermen line wharves and jetties in the fall to catch smelt with baited hooks. In the winter time, huts are moved on to the ice and smelt are caught again with baited hook through holes in the ice. A famous area for such ice fishing is Little Bay de Noc of Lake Michigan.

The sport fishery on Lake Erie is in connection with the spring run, usually in April. Thousands and thousands of ardent fishermen, groups, and families invade the beaches in the evening, harvesting smelt with beach seines, dip nets, and any type of gear that can hold small fish. Smelt are so abundant at times that they simply roll to the beach. It is a time of festivities that can go on well into the night. But as soon as the water starts warming up, the spring run is over and the fans put their gear away for another year. The same spectacle is re-enacted on the shores of Lake Michigan and on the shores of the Columbia River on the West coast. The smelt is a species which definitely adds to the pleasures of sport fishing.

L. C. DUGAL
DAVID G. IREDALE

Reference

HART, J. L., and FERGUSON, R. G. 1966. The American smelt. Trade News *18*, No. 9, 22–23.

Cross-reference: *Fish and Fishery Products*.

SMOKING PROCESS

The practice of smoking meat and fish over open fires comes down to us from prehistoric ancestors. The food could be both cooked and preserved by this simple treatment. In spite of the fact that refrigeration and canning have removed the necessity of heavy smoking as a preservative, lightly smoked foods are still highly popular, mainly because of their flavor.

As with many other ancient practices, the art of smoking is evolving rather slowly into a science. The slowness is perhaps not too surprising, considering the complexity of smoke. Within the smoldering mass, the celluloses, hemicelluloses and lignins of the hardwoods thermally decompose. The resulting clouds of smoke consist of invisible vapors within which float visible particles and droplets. Literally hundreds of chemical degradation products are distributed in the vapor, dissolved in the water droplets, or condensed on solid particles. The physical distribution is constantly changing; compounds continue to distill from particle to vapor phase or vice versa. Many of the physical parameters of the system (type of wood, temperature, moisture, oxygen supply, etc.) can affect not only the total amount of smoke but also the relative concentrations and distribution of components.

The actual treatment of foods with natural smoke has not changed drastically from olden times. In many places to-day the meat or fish is simply exposed in a smoke house over smoldering sawdust, chips, or excelsior. More advanced technologies use smoke generators or kilns in which burning conditions can be at least partially controlled and the smoke led through ducts to a chamber containing the exposed foods. Continuous operations may supplant the batch type smoke house. Other innovations include generation of smoke from logs by friction, electrostatic deposition of smoke, and the experimental use of inert gas to fluidize the sawdust, followed by a controlled oxidation.

The most promising departure from conventional procedures appears to be the development of "liquid smokes," i.e., solutions of smoke constituents in water or oil. Water-based preparations have been available for more than 20 yr, but recent offerings are great improvements over the older, acrid, tarry "pyroligenous acid" derivatives. Smoke from a controlled generator is led through water to give "natural smoke flavorings" which may be further modified to remove tarry residues, traces of hydrocarbons, etc. Oil-based smokes, described in a 1969 patent to C. M. Hollenbeck and now available commercially, are prepared by extracting the water solutions with a vegetable oil. These bottled smokes should allow much more rapid progress in identifying, measuring, and controlling desirable and undesirable components of smoke and in simplifying the process of smoking foods. Properly labeled, i.e., "smoke flavoring added," foods treated with approved liquid smokes in lieu

of, or in addition to, the natural smoking process, are acceptable to government regulatory agencies.

The most dangerous known components of natural smokes are polycyclic hydrocarbons, several of which have been implicated as carcinogens. The main carcinogen found in smoke and smoked foods is benzo(a)pyrene (3,4,benzopyrene), present in whole smoke from smoldering wood and in lesser quantities in the vapor phase. The amount present in smoked foods varies from essentially zero to values of 50–60 μg per kg. Cold-smoked products have less than hot-smoked products, and in the newer (largely experimental) processes involving heated gas followed by controlled oxidation, the smoke is practically free of this carcinogen. Cellulose casings, used, for example, during processing of skinless frankfurters and later peeled off, have been found to restrict entrance of hydrocarbons while allowing the passage of other smoke constituents. All polycyclic hydrocarbons are removed from approved liquid smokes.

The possible consequences to health of carcinogens in smoked food are difficult to evaluate. In regions where heavily smoked fish and meat are a major component of the diet (Iceland has been most thoroughly investigated), a corresponding high incidence of stomach cancer has been observed. In the United States, on the other hand, stomach cancer has been decreasing for several decades, as contrasted to large increases in lung cancer attributed to cigarette smoking and air pollution. Toxic hydrocarbons are rather widespread in the environment. Shellfish from waters polluted with petroleum oils concentrate these carcinogens to values many times those of smoked meat and fish. Vegetables grown near urban areas can be heavily contaminated from polluted air. Thermal decomposition of any food is likely to generate these hydrocarbons; charcoal broiled steaks and even roasted coffee have been shown to contain them in variable amounts. The setting of an upper limit for safety is complicated by the fact that their carcinogenic effect can be greatly increased by other components of the diet, including phenols and certain metals.

Attributes of Wood Smoke

The desirable attributes of wood smoke, i.e., flavor, antioxidant activity, and bactericidal effect, seem to be associated with phenolic fractions of the smoke. Flavor is of paramount importance; this is the main reason for smoking in modern times. Researchers at Michigan State University have found a good correlation between the phenolic content and smoke odor in successive layers of smoked bologna, wheras carbonyls and acids in the smoked meat were no higher than in the unsmoked. USDA workers demonstrated that a smoke fraction responsible for most of the aroma contained most of the phenolics, but such fractions are still complex and not limited to phenolic compounds. Further attempts by this and other groups to duplicate natural smoke aroma by combining a number of pure phenolic derivatives having low odor thresholds and known to be present in smoke have not been highly successful. It may be that many compounds, including carbonyls and acids as well as phenols, may contribute to the flavor and aroma.

Liquid smokes as well as the natural smoking process, retard the development of rancidity and inhibit microorganisms. Again, phenolic fractions are known to be involved, but there has been very little work on the evaluation of individual smoke components. Guaiacol (2-methoxyphenol), present in fairly large concentrations in smoke, has bactericidal and antioxidant effects, as well as a pronounced odor. But this compound alone can account for only a fraction of the overall activity of wood smoke.

It should be emphasized that the mild smoke treatment usually given meats or fish in this country is not sufficient to preserve them at ordinary temperatures or to decrease significantly heat or cold treatments required for preservation. Marketing of smoked fish in vacuum packed bags without refrigeration resulted in several deaths and a number of cases of illness from Type E botulism in 1963. Mold growth and bacterial spoilage occur quite readily on such products when exposed to air.

A true picture of the effect of smoke is further complicated by the fact that many smoke constituents can react with each other and with food components. Extensive formation of esters from reactions of methanol with formic and acetic acids in smoke condensates has been observed by USDA scientists. Studies at Wageningen, Holland, related the typical reddish brown color of smoked foods to interactions between smoke aldehydes and food amino acids and proteins. Glyoxal, methyl glyoxal and glycolic aldehyde were markedly active in color development with glycine, and the concentration of these aldehydes in water decreased rapidly upon addition of amino compounds. Other reactions, for example between phenols and sulfhydryl groups, or Strecker type degradations of amino acids to aldehydes and other decomposition products, might also be expected. The extent of such secondary smoke reactions and their contribution to important smoke attributes, remain almost unexplored.

BETTY M. WATTS

Cross-reference: *Meat Curing and Smoking.*

SOLID FOOD WASTE

See Waste Handling—Solids.

SORBIC ACID

Sorbic Acid was first isolated in 1859 by A. W. Hofmann from mountain ash berries, the fruit of the rowanberry tree (*Sorbus aucuparia* L.). The antimicrobial activity was discovered in 1939 by E. Müller (German Pat. 881,299) and in 1940 by C. M. Gooding (U.S. Pat. 2,379,294).

Physical and Chemical Properties

Sorbic acid is *trans*, *trans*-2,4-hexadianoic acid: $CH_3-CH=CH-CH=CH-COOH$; molecular weight: 112.12; melting point: 133°C. It is sparingly soluble in cold water (0.16%), more easily soluble in alcohols (ethanol, 12.9%; propylene glycol, 5.5%) and in glacial acetic acid (11.5%). Potassium sorbate is easily soluble in cold water (58.2%).

Synthesis

The technical synthesis starts from ketene and crotonaldehyde which form a polymeric ester. This is isomerized by acids or heat into sorbic acid (Moline *et al.* 1969).

Analytics

After isolation by steam distillation sorbic acid can be detected by paper, thin-layer, or gas chromatography. Best methods for quantitative determination are spectrophotometry in UV (Melnick and Luckmann 1954) or color reaction with 2-thiobarbituric acid (Schmidt 1960).

Toxicology

Sorbic acid is metabolized like other fatty acids (Fingerhut *et al.* 1962). The LD_{50} is about 10 gm per kg (rat) (Deuel *et al.* 1954). In chronic feeding tests diets containing 5–10% sorbic acid were without adverse effect (Lang 1960).

Microbiology

Sorbic acid acts primarily against fungi (yeasts and molds), but the growth of certain bacteria is also inhibited. Against lactobacilli and clostridia sorbic acid is rather inactive (Emard and Vaughn 1952). Some fungi can degrade sorbic acid when the organism count is too high. Sorbic acid therefore can be used only for the preservation of foods which are manufactured under good hygienic conditions.

The activity of sorbic acid depends on the pH because only the undissociated acid is fungistat ically active. From a limit of about pH 6.5 sorbic acid is the more active the lower the pH of the culture medium.

Fields of Application

The main application of sorbic acid, potassium sorbate, and calcium sorbate is the preservation of food and feedstuffs. When used in correct concentrations (1000–3000 ppm, dependent on the type of foods) sorbic acid alters neither the taste nor the aroma or color of the foodstuffs.

Fat Products.—In fat emulsions like margarine, mayonnaise and dressings sorbic acid inhibits in concentrations of 1000–1500 ppm yeasts, molds, and microbial rancidity. Butter can be protected by additions of about 500 ppm or with fungistatic wrappers.

Cheese.—For the preservation of cheese against molds, including aflatoxin-producing species, sorbic acid can be used in different ways: addition of sorbic acid to the cheese (processed cheese, cottage cheese), addition of potassium sorbate to the salt brine (hard cheese), surface treatment with aqueous solutions of potassium sorbate (hard cheese, processed cheese), dusting the surface with sorbic acid or calcium sorbate in powder form (hard cheese), or use of fungistatic wrappers with sorbic acid, potassium sorbate, or calcium sorbate as active components (soft cheese, hard cheese, processed cheese) (Geminder 1959). For long ripening types of hard cheese suspensions of calcium sorbate are advisable (E. Lück, U.S. Pat. 3,486,909). Application concentrations are 1000–2000 ppm in hard cheese, 500–1000 ppm in soft cheese and processed cheese and 500–700 ppm in cottage cheese.

Meat and Fish Products.—The use of sorbic acid for high-protein foods of animal origin is somewhat restricted because of the limited activity against bacteria. Its greatest technical value is for the surface preservation of sausages and of smoked and dried fish products against molds and yeasts.

Vegetable Products.—Sorbic acid does not harm the lactic acid fermentation which is necessary for the production of pickled cucumbers, pickled olives, and sauerkraut. Therefore, it is possible to add potassium sorbate to the brine before fermentation to inhibit deleterious molds and yeasts. By using potassium sorbate, quality and yield of pickled products are increased (Courtial 1968). The application concentrations depend on the salt concentration of the brine. Normally they are in the range of 1000–3000 ppm, calculated on the weight of the brine.

Dried Fruit.—In ready-to-eat "tenderized fruit" of high water content potassium sorbate is used in concentrations of 500 ppm against mold attack.

Jams, Marmalades and Their Raw Materials.—Fruit pulp can be protected from molds and fermentation by admixing 1000–2000 ppm potassium sorbate. Since sorbic acid does not prevent oxidative browning, the additional use of 200–400 ppm SO_2 is advisable. In jams, jellies and marmalades sorbic acid is useful as an antimold agent. The preservative can be added during the manufacturing process or may be sprayed on the surface.

Fruit Juices and Soft Drinks.—Potassium sorbate is used in concentrations of 500–1000 ppm to prevent mold attack and alcoholic fermentation, mainly in bulk products. It protects pasteurized products after opening the containers. In soft drinks 300–500 ppm are an additional safeguard against decay.

Wine.—Wine with a residual content of sugar becomes increasingly popular. To inhibit after-fermentation, potassium sorbate can be added in concentrations of 200–400 ppm, depending on the alcohol content. Potassium sorbate is by far more active against wine-spoiling yeasts than sulfur dioxide. So by using sorbic acid, wine with a lower SO_2 content can be produced. However some SO_2 is still necessary, because sorbic acid does not act against bacterial fermentation or oxidation nor does it combine with acetaldehyde. Taste and aroma of the wine are not effected by sorbic acid.

Confectionery.—Fillings, marzipan and other confectionery products can be preserved against molds and yeast attack by adding 1000–2000 ppm sorbic acid. The preservative is particularly advisable for goods with a high water and a low sugar content. The main advantage of sorbic acid in this type of foodstuffs is its high effectiveness in the upper pH range and its good organoleptic properties.

Bakery Products.—For the protection of cakes, tarts including their fillings, and toppings and similar products, sorbic acid can be used as protection against mold decay. It is added to the dough. The application concentration is about 1000–1500 ppm.

In yeast-raised bakery goods, e.g., bread, sorbic acid can disturb the yeast fermentation. So it can be used only in limited concentrations, depending on the type of the bread. Sour dough fermentation is less disturbed than a pure yeast fermentation.

The mixed anhydride of sorbic acid and palmitic acid, called sorboyl palmitate, does not inhibit the growth of the yeasts. During the baking process it is quantitatively split into palmitic and sorbic acids, the latter giving the desired protection. (H. Fernholz, E. Lück, and H. Neu, U.S. Pat. 3,510,317). The application concentration of

TABLE S-10
LEGAL STATUS OF SORBIC ACID BY COUNTRY

	Australia	Austria	Belgium	Canada	Denmark	East Germany	Finland	France	Germany	Great Britain	Italy	Latin America	Netherlands	South Africa	Sweden	Switzerland	United States
Margarine		x	x	x	x	x	x	x	x		x	x	x		x		x
Cheese	x		x	x	x		x	x	x		x	x		x	x		x
Pickles	x	x	x	x	x	x	x	(x)	x	x	(x)	x	x	x	x	x	x
Dried fruits	x	x	x	x	x		x	x	x	x	x	x	x	x	x	x	x
Fruit pulps, jams, etc.	x	x	x	x	x	x	x		x			x	x	x	x	x	x
Fruit juices, soft drinks	x	x	x	x	(x)	x	x	(x)	(x)		(x)	x	x	x	x	x	x
Wine	x	x	x	x	x	x	x	x	x	x	x	x	x	x	x	(x)	x
Cakes	x	x	x	x	x	x	x				x	x	(x)	x	x		x
Bread	(x)	(x)	(x)				(x)	(x)	(x)			x			x		

x—Permitted.
(x)—Permitted only in certain types.

---

sorboyl palmitate is 4000–6000 ppm, calculated on the flour weight.

Packaging Materials.—Sorbic acid, potassium sorbate, and calcium sorbate are valuable agents for the manufacture of fungistatic wrappers, mainly for cheese and margarine. The preservatives are fixed on the wrappers (paper, cellophane, plastic films) with binding agents. Wrappers most stable against oxidation can be obtained by using calcium sorbate as active agent. The application concentration is about 2–6 gm per sq m.

Pharmaceuticals and Cosmetics.—Sorbic acid and potassium sorbate are useful in pharmaceuticals and cosmetics if the pH of the product is below 6.5. Nonionic emulsifiers do not inactivate sorbic acid.

Feedstuffs.—High-moisture pet food products are protected against mold attack by the addition of about 3000 ppm potassium sorbate. Sorbic acid is used for the prevention of mold on damp wheat.

Other Applications.—Sorbic acid and its salts are furthermore used for the preservation of other foodstuffs, tobacco, articles in contact with foodstuffs or the human body. For economic reasons its applications in other fields are only limited, e.g., for improving the characteristics of drying oils or the milling properties of cold rubber.

Legal Aspects.—Due to its harmlessness the FAO/WHO expert committee has assessed the acceptable daily intake (ADI) as 25 mg per kg body weight. Sorbic acid and its sodium, potassium, and calcium salts are permitted in practically all countries as food additives. In the United States, they are considered as "generally recognized as safe" (GRAS). A rough survey of the legal situation in some important countries is given in Table S-10 (Lishmund 1969).

E. LÜCK

References

COURTIAL. W. 1968. Ind. Obst. Gemuseverwartung *53*, 381.

DEUEL, H. J., ALFIN-SLATER, R., WEIL, C. S., and SMYTH, H. F. 1954. Food Res. *19*, 1.

EMARD, L. O., and VAUGHN, R. H. 1952. J. Bacteriol. *63*, 487.

FINGERHUT, M., SCHMIDT, B., and LANG, K. 1962. Biochem. Z. *336*, 118.

GEMINDER, J. 1959. Milk Dealer *48*, 4, 44, 153.

LANG, K. 1960. Arzneimittel-Forsch. *10*, 997.

LISHMUND, R. E. J. 1969. Food Process. Ind. *38*, 51–53, 458.

LÜCK, E. Sorbic Acid. Monography in 4 volumes. B. Behr's Verlag, Hamburg, Germany. (German)

MELNICK, D., and LUCKMANN, F. H. 1954. Food Res. *19*, 20.

MOLINE, S. W., COLWELL, C. E., and SIMERAL, J. E. 1969. Sorbic acid. *In* Encyclopedia of Chemical Technology, Vol. 18. R. E. Kirk and D. F. Othmer (Editors). John Wiley & Sons, New York.

SCHMIDT, H. 1960. Z. Anal. Chem. *178*, 173.

SORGHUM[1]

Sorghum is a member of the Gramineae family and the tribe Andropogoneae. The sorghums of commercial importance are *Sorghum bicolor* L. Moench.

Sorghum grain is the term used to refer to the kernels or caryopsis produced by sorghum. "Milo" and "Grain Sorghum" are popular terms used to refer to sorghum grain in the United States. Other terms still used to refer to sorghum grain in the United States are: milo maize, gyp corn, grain, higear, and kafir corn. These terms originated from the sorghum varieties introduced into the United States which included kafir, milo, durra, shallu, and many others. The term "cane" is used to refer to tall sorghums which are grown for forage, syrup, or sugar.

Jowar, Juar, and Cholam are common names for sorghum in India. The guinea corn of West Africa, kafir corn of South Africa, durra of Sudan, and mtama of East Africa all mean sorghum. The Chinese use kaoliang while English publications often call sorghum the great millet.

The cultivated sorghums have been divided into four major categories based on agronomic, plant, and major uses: (1) grain sorghum, (2) forage or sweet sorghums, (3) grassy sorghums, and (4) broomcorn. Grain sorghum refers to dwarf sorghums bred specifically for grain production. Grain sorghums are usually 2-5 ft high. The sweet sorghums (sorgos) have tall, sweet, juicy stalks that are used for forage, syrup, and sugar production. Grassy types of sorghum have thin stems, narrow leaves, and numerous tillers which make them useful for hay or grazing of livestock. The broomcorns have long panicle branches which were useful for production of brooms.

Sorghum ranks as the third largest U.S. cereal crop in terms of total pounds produced. Between 700-950 million bushels (56 lb per bu) have been produced in each of the last 5 crop years. The U.S. production of sorghum has grown dramatically during the last three decades. In 1930, 49 million bushels of sorghum were harvested from 3.4 mil-

lion acres: in 1973, 937 million bushels were harvested on 15.9 million acres. The current sorghum crop is approximately 12-18 times the size of the 1930's crops.

Production

The U.S. sorghum belt is the Southern Great Plains. This belt which consists of Texas, Oklahoma, Kansas, Nebraska, and portions of Colorado, Missouri, and New Mexico produced 89% of the U.S. sorghum grain crop in 1973. Texas produced 42% of the 1973 crop. California and Arizona produce significant quantities of sorghum grain and some sorghum is produced in many other states especially in the Southeast and corn belt areas.

Sorghum is the fourth ranking cereal food crop in the world. The estimated world sorghum crop was 56 million metric tons or 2.2 billion bushels in 1966. Major producing countries were: United States, India, Red China, Nigeria, Ethiopia, Argentina, Sudan, Upper Volta, South Africa, United Arab Republic, and Mexico. Australia and Thailand have recently expanded sorghum production. The United States, Africa, Latin America, and Asia produced approximately 30, 25, 7 and 40%, respectively, of total world production of sorghum. Red China and India account for 96% of Asian sorghum production. Argentina and Mexico produce more than 90% of sorghum in Latin America.

Adaptation and Culture

Sorghum is grown mainly in dry, hot regions where corn cannot be produced successfully. It is a tropical or subtropical plant; but, it can be grown successfully in temperate regions where the mean summer temperatures are 65°F with more than 120 frost-free days. Although well adapted to semiarid conditions, sorghum makes efficient use of fertilizer and irrigation. Grain yields of 8-10 thousand pounds per acre are common in the Southwest. Some grain yields have exceeded 12,000 pounds per acre. The average yield of sorghum grain in the United States has exceeded 50 bu per acre each of the past 5 yr.

The sorghum plant withstands drought and heat better than other crops; but yields are reduced. The mechanism is not understood, but some sorghums become partially dormant during short drought periods and resume growth when moisture becomes available. Sorghum has more roots and a smaller leaf area than corn. The leaves tend to inroll and have a waxy cuticle that apparently conserves moisture.

Sorghum is an annual although it can be a perennial under tropical conditions where old stalks are removed and a rattan crop is obtained.

---

[1] Contribution from the Cereal Quality Laboratory, Soil and Crop Science Department, Texas A&M University, College Station, Texas.

FIG. S-3. A FIELD OF IRRIGATED GRAIN SORGHUM
IN THE TEXAS PANHANDLE

FIG. S-4. SORGHUM PANICLE SIZE AND SHAPE
VARIES FROM GRASSY TYPES (LEFT) TO COMPACT
CROOKED NECK DURRAS (RIGHT)

Sorghum production during the dry season may offer potential for increased grain production in rice growing areas of Asia.

Diseases and insects have generally been controlled in U.S. sorghum production although they are constantly changing. For instance, presently maize dwarf mosaic virus (MDMV) and greenbugs are serious problems in sorghum production. But they were not of economic importance 5 yr ago. Perconia root rot, head smut, downy mildew, anthracnose, and stalk rots are significant economic diseases of sorghum. Generally, major losses due to diseases have been avoided by prompt action of plant breeders and pathologists in release of resistant varieties.

Insects have been controlled by management techniques or by insecticides for greenbugs. Resistant varieties of sorghum are being developed. The sorghum shootfly and witch weed are serious pests of sorghum in Asia and Africa.

Sorghum Plant

The sorghum plant is a coarse annual with culms or stems 2–15 ft or higher. The vegetative structure of the sorghum plant is similar to corn. The culms or stalks are made up of 7–18 or more nodes and internodes. The diameter of the stalk at the base varies from a fraction of an inch to 2 in. The stalks may be juicy or dry, sweet or nonsweet. A leaf occurs at each node; and nodes are alternate and on opposite sides of the culm. The surface of the culms, sheaths, and leaves is glaucous. The leaf sheaths are long and overlap in dwarf varieties (grain sorghum types).

The inflorescence or "head" of sorghum is a panicle ranging from 3–20 in. in length and 1.5–8 inches in width. Shape of the sorghum panicle varies from loose grassy types to compact types. Each flower has female and male organs and is self pollinated. Each panicle contains from 800 to 3000 kernels. The kernels are enclosed in floral tracts (lemma and palea) which usually thresh free of the kernel during harvesting. It remains attached in many sorgos, grassy types, and broomcorn. The sorghum kernel and floral tracts are inside the glumes. Color of the glumes vary from light brown, red, purple, etc., and the phenolic pigments migrate from the glume and discolor the kernel.

The Sorghum Kernel

The sorghum of commerce is a kernel or caryopsis. The commercial sorghum caryopsis ranges in size from 8 to 35 mm; 12–30 thousand kernels comprise 1 lb of most commercial varieties. The shape varies from obovoid to ellipsoid. The kernels are flattened spheres 4.0 mm long by 3.5 mm wide by 2.5 mm thick. An individual kernel of common sorghum varieties weighs 20–32 mg.

Botanically, the sorghum kernel or caryopsis is a dry, indehiscent single-seeded fruit. The caryopsis is composed of three major portions, the outer covering (pericarp), the storage tissue (endosperm), and the germ. The pericarp consists of four distinct layers. The outside layer is the epicarp which contains pigments and wax. The middle layer, or mesocarp, contains small starch granules.

FIG. S-5. KERNELS OF A COMMON, COMMERCIAL
SORGHUM HYBRID

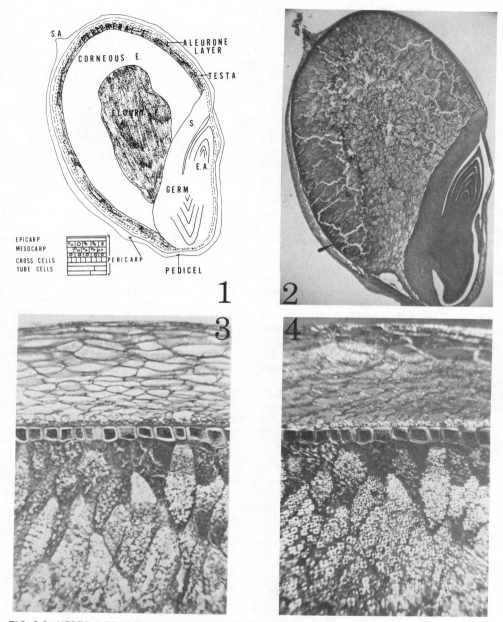

FIG. S-6. UPPER LEFT (1) IS A DIAGRAM OF THE SORGHUM KERNEL; UPPER RIGHT (2) IS A PHOTOMICROGRAPH OF A LONGITUDINAL SECTION; LOWER LEFT AND RIGHT (3 and 4) ARE MORE DETAILED VIEWS FROM THE PERICARP TO THE FLOURY ENDOSPERM UNDER NORMAL AND PLANE POLARIZED LIGHT

The inner portion of the pericarp (endocarp) is composed of cross and tube cells. The testa, sometimes referred to as the seedcoat, undercoat or subcoat, contains pigments and is not present in many sorghum varieties.

The endosperm is composed of an aleurone layer and peripheral, corneous, and floury endosperm portions. The aleurone layer is one cell layer thick composed of small, blocklike cells that are high in protein, fat, ash, vitamins, and enzymes.

TABLE S-11

MEAN CONTENT OF THE MAJOR STRUCTURAL PORTIONS OF THE
SORGHUM KERNEL AND THE COMPOSITION OF EACH PORTION[1]

	Percentage of Kernel	Starch (%)	Protein (%)	Fat (%)	Ash (%)
Whole kernel	100	73.8	12.3	3.6[2]	1.65
Endosperm	82.3	82.5	12.3	0.6	0.37
Bran	7.9	34.6[2]	6.7	4.9	2.02[2]
Germ	9.8	13.4[2]	18.9	28.1	10.36[1]

SOURCE: Data adapted from Wall and Ross (1970).

[1] All values are on oven dry weight basis.
[2] Includes wax—0.29–0.44%, mean 0.32%.

The starchy endosperm is the peripheral, corneous, and floury portions.

The peripheral endosperm is beneath the aleurone layer and consists of several cell layers which are distinguishable from the remainder of the endosperm because the cells are small and contain small starch granules which are enmeshed in a thick, proteinaceous matrix. The floury endosperm is in the center of the kernel whereas the corneous endosperm is to the outside of the kernel. Lines of sorghum which genetically produce floury and all-corneous endosperm textures are available. Environment influences the proportion of corneous to floury endosperm, also.

The starchy endosperm consists of cells in which starch granules are encapsulated in a matrix composed of protein. Some protein is stored in the form of small spherical structures called protein bodies that are scattered throughout the endosperm.

The germ is firmly embedded in the kernel and is difficult to remove during processing.

The starchy endosperm is the major portion of the sorghum kernel (Table S-11). The bran consists mainly of the pericarp and aleurone layer. Nearly 80% of the total protein is located in the endosperm whereas the germ contains 75% of the fat in the kernel. A carnauba-like wax is the major component of the ether extract of the bran. The protein and fat content of the endosperm are highest in the peripheral area and lowest in the center of the floury area. Approximately 95% of the starch is in the starchy endosperm. The mesocarp contains the remaining starch granules. The highest concentration of starch is located in the center of the floury area.

TABLE S-12

PROXIMATE ANALYSIS OF SORGHUM GRAIN AND CORN[1]

	Sorghum		Corn	
	Range (%)	Mean (%)	Range (%)	Mean (%)
Moisture	8–20	15.5	7–23.0	16.7
Starch	60–77	74.1	64–78	71.5
Protein ($N \times 6.25$)	6.6–16.0	11.2	8.0–14.0	9.9
Fat	1.4–6.1	3.7	3.1–5.7	4.8
Ash	1.2–7.1	1.5	1.1–3.9	1.4
Crude fiber	0.4–13.4	2.6	1.8–3.5	2.7
Sugars (dextrose)	0.4–2.5	1.8	1.0–3.0	2.6
Tannin	0.003–0.17	0.1	—	—
Wax	0.2–0.5	0.3	—	—
NFE	65.3–85.3	—	77.9–82.1	—
Pentosans	1.8–4.9	2.5	5.9–6.6	—
Total Carotenoids (mg/kg)	1.5–10.0	1.5	5–40	30

SOURCE: Data for range and mean were taken from Miller (1958) and Watson (1967) respectively.

[1] Expressed on a dry weight basis.

Composition

The composition of corn and sorghum is compared in Table S-12. Compositional data only provide an approximate comparison because the influence of environment is very striking. Sorghum grain has slightly more starch and protein than corn which is approximately 1% higher in fat content. Corn contains yellow carotenoid pigments while sorghum is lacking in pigments even though certain new yellow endosperm types have additional carotenoid pigments. Otherwise, sorghum grain is comparable to corn in vitamin and mineral content. Sorghum contains 0.1-0.3% waxes which is 50 times the quantity of wax in corn. Polyphenolic compounds sometimes referred to as tannins are present in the pericarp and testa of sorghums especially those that are bird resistant.

Environment and cultural practices used in producing sorghum grain cause widespread variation in physical and chemical properties of the grain. Generally, high yields of grain are inversely related to protein content of the grain. Sorghum is produced under more variable environmental conditions than corn which explains why the composition of sorghum varies more than corn.

Carbohydrates.—Starch, cellulose, simple sugars, and pentosans comprise 80–85% of the dry weight of the sorghum kernel. Corn and sorghum starches have the same properties and for most purposes can be used interchangeably. Starch granules are the same shape. Sorghum starch granules are slightly larger and have a higher gelatinization temperature range than corn. Sorghum starches contain 20–30% amylose and 70–80% of the starch is amylopectin. Waxy type sorghums produce nearly all amylopectin type starch which is used in many food applications. Sorghum starch has a bland taste and an off-white color. The pigments of sorghum are removed from starch by a bleaching procedure. Waxy sorghum starch gives higher viscosity curves upon cooking than corn starch does. The gelatinization temperature range of sorghum starch is 67°-77°C compared to 62°-72°C for corn starch.

Sucrose, glucose, fructose, and raffinose are the major sugars present in sorghum grain.

Proteins and Amino Acids.—The amino acid composition of sorghum grain protein is similar to corn. The first limiting amino acid is lysine followed by threonine, tryptophan, and methionine. Increasing the protein content of sorghum grain tends to cause a decrease in the distribution of lysine in the protein even though total quantity of lysine increases. Kafirin, which is the endosperm protein soluble in 70% alcohol, is exceptionally low in lysine, threonine, tryptophan, and

TABLE S-13

COMPARISON OF AMINO ACID ANALYSIS OF
SORGHUM GRAIN AND CORN
(PERCENTAGE OF PROTEIN)

Amino Acid	Sorghum Grain	Corn
Lysine	2.1	2.7
Histidine	2.2	3.0
Arginine	2.8	5.2
Aspartic acid	6.6	6.8
Threonine	3.2	3.6
Leucine	4.4	5.2
Glutamic acid	21.5	21.3
Proline	8.1	10.0
Glycine	3.3	4.0
Alanine	9.5	8.1
Half cystine	1.1	1.6
Valine	5.2	4.7
Methionine	1.5	1.7
Isoleucine	3.9	3.5
Leucine	13.3	12.4
Tyrosine	1.6	4.4
Phenylalanine	5.0	5.0
Tryptophan	1.0	1.0
Protein (%)	10.0	10.0

SOURCE: Adapted from Wall and Ross (1970).

methionine. The content of kafirin increases when the protein content of the grain is increased by fertility treatments or cultural practices which accounts for the decreased nutritional value of the protein, at least for nonruminants.

Screening for amino acid content of the world collection of sorghums has indicated considerable variability in protein content and lysine distribution; but, the differences appear related to environmental factors or are in grassy sorghums that produce small, shrunken kernels.

Lipids.—The lipids of sorghum are important nutritionally and influence flavor and acceptability or sorghum products. The fatty acid composition or sorghum germ oil is similar to corn oil and is used for similar purposes. Ether extract of sorghum bran is composed mainly of long chain alcohols and esters with some long chain hydrocarbons.

Utilization of Sorghum in the United States

The major use of sorghum grain is livestock feed for cattle, sheep, goats, poultry, and swine. Less than 1% of U.S. production is used for food and industrial purposes. Dry and wet milling and distillation industries consume approximately 15-20 million bushels annually.

Wet Milling.—Approximately 6-8 million bushels were wet milled into starch, oil, and feed by-products annually; but recently, wet milling of sorghum other than small quantities of waxy types has ceased. Apparently, it is more economical to mill corn than sorghum. Sorghum is more difficult to wet mill than corn because (1) the starch and protein are difficult to separate, (2) sorghum germ is more difficult to extract from the kernel, (3) pigments discolor the starch and must be removed by bleaching, and (4) recovery of starch is lower than with corn. New hybrids have been developed which have improved wet milling characteristics and substantial progress could be made in selection of sorghum varieties for wet milling characteristics.

Dry Milling.—Approximately 3–6 million bushels of sorghum are dry milled into various products which range from highly refined grits and flours to less refined products. The applications of sorghum products overlap those of corn dry milled products. The lower cost of sorghum affords an advantage for many of the markets. Major markets for sorghum products are brewers' grits, aluminum ore refining, building products, dog food grits, paper making, mineral processing, charcoal briquets, oil well drilling, and foundry binders. Only limited quantities are used in food applications although sorghum has many potential uses in food products.

The dry milling processes for sorghum grain consist of roller milling and pearling or decortication procedures. The roller milling process was modified from wheat milling procedures and produces semirefined products. The yield, degree of refinement, and separations are deficient for many applications.

A combination of pearling followed by impact degermination produces highly refined sorghum products. The pericarp or bran can be removed completely by proper abrasive milling. This eliminates much of the wax, tannins, and crude fiber which are generally undesirable for many uses. Barley pearlers and rice pearling equipment satisfactorily remove the bran. Most of these contain carborundum-coated discs that revolve rapidly within a perforated cylinder. The abrasive action of the kernel on the surface of the cylinder, disc, or other kernels removes the pericarp without breaking the kernel. The fines are removed by aspiration.

The debranned kernel is degermed by impact or attrition-type equipment. The germ and endosperm particles are classified by sieving and specific gravity separators. Major products are grits, bran, germ, and fines. Grits are 0.6% oil, light in color and produce an off-white flour with excellent properties. The germ contains 20% oil. The composition of typical dry milled sorghum grain products is presented in the Table S-14. Many different products can be made by blending the various mill streams. Pregelatinized and chemically modified sorghum flours are available.

TABLE S-14

ANALYSIS OF DRY-MILLED SORGHUM PRODUCTS

Product	% (Moisture-free Basis)				
	Mois-ture	Pro-tein	Oil	Fiber	Ash
Whole grain sorghum	13.3	9.6	3.4	2.2	1.5
Pearled grain sorghum	12.5	9.5	3.0	1.3	1.2
Sorghum flour, crude	12.0	9.5	2.5	1.2	1.0
Sorghum flour, refined	11.5	9.5	1.5	1.0	0.8
Sorghum brewers' grits	11.7	9.5	0.7	0.8	0.4
Grain sorghum bran	12.0	8.9	5.5	8.6	2.4
Grain sorghum germ	12.0	15.1	20.0	2.6	8.2
Sorghum hominy feed	11.0	11.2	6.5	3.8	2.7

SOURCE: Adapted from Hahn (1969).

The sorghum grain is conditioned prior to milling by tempering with water which facilitates the milling operations.

Fermentation Industry.—Approximately 2.5 million bushels of sorghum grain are used for production of alcohol annually. The whole grain is ground to produce a 12–60 mesh meal. The grain is cooked and the mash is hydrolyzed by enzymes or acid hydrolysis. The liquid is cooled and inoculated with yeast. After yeast fermentation, the alcohol is recovered by distillation. Beverage alcohol follows a similar procedure except malt enzymes are preferred for hydrolysis. The distillate which is approximately 95% alcohol by volume is filtered through charcoal, blended, and aged. Sorghum has been used to produce lactic acid, riboflavin, microbial polysaccharides, antibiotics, and citric acid. Use of sorghum depends on its price relative to other grains.

Syrup and Sugar From Sorghum.—Sweet sorghum stalks are crushed and the juice is condensed to produce a distinctively flavored, mild, sweet, light amber-colored syrup. Good quality syrup has little or no after-taste, no crystallization tendencies, high viscosity, and does not gel during storage. Quality varies considerably and local preferences differ. Syrup is primarily a speciality product especially of the Southeastern States.

New methods of eliminating starch and solving other problems make the future look bright for at least limited processing of sweet sorghums into sugar on a commercial basis. Sweet sorghum could serve as a supplementary sugar crop for the sugar cane and sugar beet industries.

Feed for Ruminants.—The sorghum belt has been the scene for steady growth in livestock feeding. Recently, rapid expansion of cattle feeding has occurred in the sorghum belt especially in the Texas panhandle. Texas ranks first or second in number of feedlot cattle. Swine and poultry production is increasing. This gigantic industry is based upon sorghum grain as the principle energy source.

Sorghum grain has been considered to have 90–95% the value of corn for livestock. Sorghum grain must be processed to obtain maximum feed efficiency by cattle. Numerous methods of processing the grain have been devised. They include grinding, rolling, steam rolling, pressure cooking and flaking, popping, extruding, micronizing, reconstitution, and early harvesting and exploding. One of the more popular methods in the large feedlots is pressure cooking and flaking. The grain is treated with steam under pressure and flaked through large steel rolls which are adjusted to produce a thin flake. This method improves feed efficiency by approximately 5–10% over dry, ground grain. The processes cause disruption of the subcellular structure of the sorghum kernel and facilitate movement of digestive enzymes and juices into contact with the starch, protein, and other constituents.

Feed for Nonruminants.—Sorghum grain is an excellent feed for swine and poultry when properly supplemented and compares favorably with corn. Sorghum grain-fed hogs gain as rapidly, but usually require 5–10% more feed to produce 100 lb of gain as compared to corn. Gross energy for corn and sorghum is similar; but digestible energy is higher in corn as compared to sorghum. Combination of sorghum grain with a high quality protein supplement such as toasted, defatted soybean meal along with synthetic DL-methionine provides a satisfactory feed.

Sorghum can be used satisfactorily for production of broilers and maintenance of layers; however, it lacks the yellow pigments needed to produce yellow-meated broilers and colored yolks. However, it is an advantage in some countries where white-meated broilers and less pigmentation of the yolk is desired.

World Use of Sorghum

Sorghum is the staple food in parts of Asia and Africa. Preparation of sorghum for food is simple. It is usually consumed as a porridge or stiff paste prepared by adding pounded flour to hot water. Sometimes a flat cake is prepared and the grain may be parched, popped, or boiled whole.

A common Nigerian food is "tuwo" prepared by stirring flour into hot water and allowing the thick paste to cool and gel. Pieces of the cooled gel are eaten with soup. Occasionally, unripe sorghum panicles are roasted similar to U.S. sweet corn. Pop sorghum varieties are grown and popped similar to popcorn.

Bantu or kafir beer is a popular beverage consumed in parts of Africa. It differs from beer made from barley malt in that it is an opaque reddish-colored fluid with good body which contains 5–6% solids, has a yeasty sour taste, low alcohol content, and high nutritional value. Red sorghum grains are preferred for malting and brewing.

In India, sorghum grain is ground or cracked, prepared into a dough and baked as flat, unleavened bread (rotti) or cooked like rice. White, pearly grains are preferred for bread. Whole grain is parched or "fried" in a hot pan and then ground and mixed with salt, buttermilk, or molasses. Special sorghums for popping, roasting or other uses are frequently grown in small quantities. "Vani" jowars are harvested in the dough stage, roasted, and consumed with a spicy noodle. A major use of sorghum in China is for wine production. In addition, red glumes are steeped in water to make a dye used for reddening wine.

Japan and Israel import large quantities of sorghum grain for use as feed grain in poultry, swine, and cattle production. Israel obtains most of its sorghum from the United States. Japan imports sorghum grain from the United States, Argentina, Australia, and Thailand.

U.S. Market Classes of Sorghum

The USDA recognizes four classes of grain sorghums: yellow, white, brown, and mixed. Visual appearance of the kernel is the basis for classifying sorghums. Visual appearance of grain (hence market class) is influenced by combinations of pericarp color, thickness of the pericarp (translucent or opaque), types of endosperm, and the testa (Table S-15).

The yellow grain sorghum class is the major commercial sorghum in the United States. Red, white, yellow, brownish red, or variations of red grain without an undercoat or testa comprise the yellow class. Yellow endosperm hybrids fall into the yellow class unless they have a brown pericarp and/or testa. The white grain sorghum class is composed of white grain without a testa. Little white grain sorghum is produced although recently new white grain hybrids have been developed which have excellent properties for food and industrial applications. The brown grain sorghum class has a brown pericarp and testa and is produced mainly in areas where birds and sprouting in the field prior to harvest are problems. The immature grain of the "bird resistant" sorghums has an astringent characteristic which makes it less attractive to

TABLE S-15

INFLUENCE OF PERICARP, UNDERCOAT, AND ENDOSPERM CHARACTERISTICS ON APPEARANCE
AND U.S. MARKET CLASS OF GRAIN SORGHUMS

Market Class	Pericarp	Undercoat	Endosperm	Appearance
Yellow	Variations of red, translucent or opaque[1]	Absent[2]	Nonyellow	Variations of red, salmon pink, brownish-red
White	White, translucent	Absent	Nonyellow	Glossy white, pearly
White	White, opaque	Absent	Nonyellow	Chalky, dull white
Brown	White, translucent	Present	Nonyellow	Brown, bluish-white, black, purple, tan, bluish-silver
Brown	White, opaque	Present	Nonyellow	Chalky bluish-white
Brown	Brown	Present	Nonyellow	Brown
Yellow[3]	White, translucent	Absent	Yellow	Yellow
White	White, opaque	Absent	Yellow	Chalky white
Yellow	Red, translucent	Absent	Yellow	Bronze
Yellow	Red, opaque	Absent	Yellow	Red, slightly bronze
Brown	Brown	Present	Yellow	Brown
Brown	White, translucent	Present	Yellow	Brown, black, purple, blue-silver
Brown	White, opaque	Present	Yellow	Chalky, bluish white

[1] A thick mesocarp (middle layer of the pericarp) makes the pericarp opaque while a mesocarp that is thin or absent gives the pericarp a translucent appearance.
[2] In some varieties, remnants of the undercoat are present.
[3] Class the grain would probably be in under present standards.

birds. Brown grain sorghums are produced mainly in the Southeastern United States.

Genetic Diversity and Variety Improvement

Ten to 12,000 lines of sorghum from over the world have been placed in a world collection. These sorghum lines contain genes for disease resistance, insect resistance, yield, drought resistance, kernel structure, size, shape, color, composition, and other traits. This bank of genes is continuously being expanded to provide plant breeders with the opportunity of isolating and transferring desirable genes to improve commercial sorghum hybrids. For instance, resistance to greenbugs is being developed through use of this germ plasm.

The collection is composed mainly of tall, late maturing types that are not useful under temperate zone conditions. Therefore, many of these lines are converted to short, early maturing lines which are useful in breeding programs in the United States and other countries. This conversion project is a joint effort of the Texas Agricultural Experiment Station and USDA.

Sorghum grain from the world collection varies from 50.2 to 62.0 lb per bu test weight, 5.6 to 72.0 gm per 1000 kernels, 1.212 to 1.402 gm per cc kernel density. The kernel shape and gross structure range from sea shell shape to buck shot shape, from all floury to all corneous endosperm

texture. Color varies from white or clear, reds, yellows, purples, and browns. Sorghum with waxy, yellow, and sugary type endosperms are available. Waxy endosperm sorghums were processed during World War II as a substitute for tapioca starch. The yellow endosperm type is used in many hybrids and increases carotenoid content somewhat. Sorghum lines with improved nutritional value similar to *opaque* 2 and *floury* 2 corn have been found, but they are not currently practical for U.S. production. Processing characteristics such as dry milling properties of many of the sorghum lines are much improved over existing commercial sorghums.

L. W. ROONEY

References

ANON. 1971. Grain sorghum research in Texas— 1970. Texas Agr. Expt. Sta. Consolidated Progr. Repts. *2938-2949.*

DOGGETT, H. 1970. Sorghum. Longmans, Green and Co., London, England.

HAHN, R. R. 1969. Dry milling of grain sorghum. Cereal Sci. Today *14*, 234–237.

MARTIN, J. H., and LEONARD, W. H. 1967. Cereal Crops, 2nd Printing. Macmillan Co., New York.

MILLER, D. F. (Editor) 1958. Composition of cereal grains and forages. Natl. Acad. Sci.— Natl. Res. Council Publ. *585.*

ROONEY, L. W., and CLARK, L. E. 1968. The chemistry and processing of sorghum grain. Cereal Sci. Today *13*, 258.

ROONEY, L. W., JOHNSON, J. W., and ROSE-NOW, D. T. 1970. Sorghum quality improvement: types for food. Cereal Sci. Today *15*, 240–243.

WALL, J. S., and ROSS, W. M. (Editors) 1970. Sorghum Production and Utilization. Avi Publishing Co., Westport, Conn.

WATSON, S. A. 1967. Manufacture of corn and milo starches. *In* Starch Chemistry and Technology, Vol. II Industrial Aspects. R. L. Whistler and E. F. Paschall (Editors). Academic Press, New York.

Cross-reference: *Sugars and Sweeteners.*

SOUL FOOD

"The origin of soul cookery is a study of the lineage of the Afro-American rocked from a troubled birth in the cradle of the South. The birthplace, in speech and lifestyle, in rhythm and folklore, is indelibly imprinted with the traces of its black progeny—a bondaged people with a soaring spirit, a soul which no fetters could seize upon and wrestle to obedience" (Pamela 1969).

As in any culture, creative forces on all levels of endeavor are inspired by necessity. This is particularly true of the black man and his efforts to survive the perils of slavery in the deep South. Not only was spiritual singing a form of self-expression for the black man, but also a method by which he could communicate with the underground railroad in an effort to gain freedom.

Since slaves enjoyed so few pleasures, the meal, when not eaten while working in the fields, became an event of great joy—a soulful event. The cooking was always left to those most skillful at the art. Hence, soul food has come to mean more than just the chitlins on the table; it has come to mean the care and love taken in its preparation and the fellowship with those present at meal time.

The influence of the black man on the culinary patterns of America and especially the South is great. It is difficult to understand how, for so long, the white man held that the black man contributed nothing, by way of his African heritage, to American life. Maybe this ignorance is partly due to those social and economic forces that shaped our developing nation; and more directly to the institution of slavery, where blacks were set apart not only by social status but also by the color of their skin. Hence, to recognize contributions (which are most often subtle) of the black man would have been difficult for the white man and even when he did, to admit it was certainly

not in vogue. Many cases can be found where, for some reason or other, newly arrived slaves from Africa were put in the kitchen and, to their master's surprise, performed very well. It is interesting that the masters never once considered the implications of his newly arrived slave's ability to satisfy his "unique and sophisticated" tastes.

Today, when one compares the cooking patterns of the northern and southern sections of the United States, one can find great differences. Since both of these areas were originally settled by white people of British and French descent, one could easily theorize that maybe the slaves, because they did most of the cooking, changed the cooking styles and tastes of the southern white man for all time. For example, the extensive use in the South of okra—fried or in gumboes (gumbo comes from an African word for okra), the many ways of making stews from pork and fish in an effort to extend the use of meat, the combination of such dishes as rice and beans, the common practice of using hot peppers or hot sauce, the many ways of preparing greens and yams (another African word) are all recognizably African and were surely part of the culinary art employed by Africans prior to the first slave's arrival in Virginia in 1619.

The slaves brought to America came almost exclusively from the west coast of Africa. The English brought captives from the Senegal and Gambia rivers, and even as far south as Angola—a coast of about 4000 miles. The Dutch brought slaves from the Gold Coast and later from Angola after overrunning the Portuguese forts located there. The French brought slaves from the Senegal River area and from other areas located along the west coast of Africa. The heart of the trade, however, was the Slave Coast and the Gold Coast, and behind this a territory extending into central Africa where many different tribes were located and from which many slaves were gathered.

From this brief historical sketch, it is easy to visualize the varied backgrounds the slaves must have brought to America including many different tongues. One very common factor shared by most slaves, however, was their choice of food. Although slaves were gathered from several points along the West African Coast, the food and methods of preparation, because of the similar environment, were very much the same.

Choosing foods that would accompany the slaves to America must have been of concern to the slave traders; for no doubt, keeping the slaves alive on the long voyage to America was of paramount financial importance. For this reason, several foodstuffs were chosen for pragmatic reasons and in no way were these foods chosen to reflect the desire or preference of the slaves. Of these foods, the peanut, the okra, the black eye pea, and the

TABLE S-16

AVERAGE COMPOSITION OF SELECTED SOUL FOODS
(100 Gm, Edible Portion)

Food Item	Water (%)	Food Energy (Cal)	Protein (Gm)	Fat (Gm)	Total Carbohydrate (Gm)	Ash (Gm)	Calcium (Mg)	Phosphorus (Mg)	Iron (Mg)	Sodium (Mg)	Potassium (Mg)	Vitamin A IU	Thiamin (Mg)	Riboflavin (Mg)	Niacin (Mg)	Vitamin C (Mg)	Magnesium (Mg)
Peanuts	5.6	564	26.0	47.5	18.6	2.3	69	401	2.1	5.0	674	—	1.14	0.13	17.2	0	35
Okra	91.1	29	2.0	0.3	6.0	0.6	92	41	0.5	2.0	174	490	0.13	0.18	0.9	20	41
Blackeye peas	71.8	108	8.1	0.8	18.1	1.2	24	146	2.1	1.0	379	350	0.30	0.11	1.4	17	230
Sesame seeds	5.4	563	18.6	49.1	21.6	5.3	1160	616	10.5	60.0	725	30	0.98	0.24	5.4	0	181
Collard greens	89.6	33	3.6	0.7	5.1	1.0	188	52	0.8	—	262	7800	0.11	0.20	1.2	76	57
Pokeberry	92.9	20	2.3	0.4	3.1	1.3	53	33	1.2	—	9	8700	0.07	0.25	1.1	82	—
Tripe	79.1	100	19.1	2.0	0	0.4	127	86	1.6	72.0	—	—	—	0.15	1.6	—	70
Tongue	56.6	267	19.3	20.3	0.3	3.5	—	—	—	72.0	—	—	—	—	—	—	70

SOURCE: *Composition of Foods*, Agriculture Handbook 8, USDA.

It should be noted that: The peanut is a good source for energy, protein, iron, thiamin, and niacin. Okra is high in vitamins A and C. Blackeye peas are a good source for protein, vitamins A and C, niacin, and magnesium. Sesame seeds are a good source for energy, protein, calcium, iron, riboflavin, niacin, calcium, and magnesium. Collard greens have large quantities of vitamins A and C and provide a good source of calcium and riboflavin. Both tripe and tongue are good sources of protein. Pokeberry provides a good source for vitamins A and C and riboflavin.

sesame seed were in greatest supply. Aside from being familiar to the slave, these foods shared the unique ability of remaining palatable for long periods of time, a must for the long ocean voyage. These foods were also thought to be capable of adapting to the climate and soil conditions of the South, the destination of the slaves, as southern growing conditions are similar to those of Africa.

After landing in America, the slaves were put to work in the fields (field niggers) and in the "big house" (house niggers). Except in cases where some of the "house niggers" were given the privilege of eating the master's scraps, both field and house niggers ate essentially the same foods. (Where house niggers extended the table scrap privilege by taking food from the kitchen for others, a good beating was certainly in order if caught.) Of course, the slave's food included the peanut, okra, black eye pea, and sesame seed brought from Africa and grown in slave gardens and around the edge of cotton fields. Also used as regular dietary items were the scraps of the pig: chitlins, from the small intestines; pig's feet, also called trotters; and pig ears; from the cow: neckbones, tongue, and tripe (stomach). In addition to these foods, the slaves found many opportunities to give expression to their African heritage by making use of many weeds of the woods. Many of these weeds were used both for eating and medicinal purposes. A few examples are:

Pursley (purslane) (*Portulaca oleracea*) and pokeweed (*Phytolacca*) were parboiled and cooked with wild onions and salted meat and served with corn pone. Pursley was also used to cure dysentery and diarrhea.

Mullein (*Verbascum*), "pinetop," and salt were used as a bath to remedy the swelling of feet and to cure dropsy. Mullein was also taken internally as a tea.

Mayapple (*Podophyllum peltatum*) root was used as a laxative and cherry root was made into a tea to improve the appetite.

Elderberry (*Sambucus conadensis*) and pokeberry (*Phytolacca*) were always good for making wine and jelly.

It was rather fortunate for the slave that he ate some of the foods he did. Examination of the average composition of some of these foods will show them to be high in protein and other essential nutrients that are now part of our recommended dietary allowances. Some average composition profiles of some of these food items are shown in Table S-16.

As slavery progressed in Southern America to meet the needs of the rapidly growing economy, so did the assimilation of the slave's food onto the white man's table and eventually into the first Southern cookbook. While at first, slave's food was considered unfit for the master's table, many events were to occur to change this notion. Mary Tolford Wilson (1964) referred to this process of the plantation owner's adoption of his slave's food as "peaceful integration."

Sesame seed was first recognized commercially and used for its high quality oil, although the blacks had eaten it raw, toasted, in soups and greens, and baked in bread for some time. The black eye pea is said to have been planted and eaten by Thomas Jefferson and okra became a staple in Southern gumboes. The peanut (also called "ground pea," "ground nut," "earth nut," and by two African words "pindar" and "goober") because of its oil content and value as a food for livestock, became the most popular (and economically important) of the original slave foods.

It would seem so fitting then that the great food scientist, Dr. George Washington Carver, son of slaves, would be destined to develop so many products from the peanut such as cheese, milk, coffee, flour, ink, dyes, soap, and wood stains, to list but a few of his 300 or more products.

As education was denied the slaves, reading and writing was learned by only a few; therefore, recipes of the early foods prepared by slaves were never written down. A young girl, eager to learn the art of soulful cooking, had to do so through experience by watching her mother and other women of the kitchen. As she grew in the art, she instinctively added her own ideas and new ingredients from whatever sources were made available.

This is the key to soulful cooking—the desire to please: the ingenuity of knowing how to prepare mouth-watering dishes from whatever is available.

Today, with the new awakening on all levels of black culture, "soul food" is definitely in vogue. Such dishes as fried chicken; spareribs; blackeye peas; candied yams; mustard, turnip, and collard greens; along with the ever-popular chitlins; pig's feet, ears, tail, and neckbones will almost always be found on the menu at any number of soul food restaurants in America. A popular meal in the New York City area is chitlins and champagne served at "tie only" restaurants. Soul food meals of this type are popular with whites and blacks alike.

To meet the new demands for soul food cookery, several soul food cookbooks have been written which give recipes of soul food from sandwiches to full course dinners. It is not unlikely to be invited to a soul food party where the host is serving chitlins (marinated then smothered with hot sauce), turnip greens, and potato salad with a side dish of hot buttered cornbread. The dessert for such a meal is often sweet potato pie.

If you are interested in a soulful feast, try these recipes for a delightful meal and experiment in true black culinary art.

Chitlins

Frozen chitterlings (chitlins)	5	lb
Water	1/4	cup
Onion	1	medium
Celery, sliced	1	stalk

Allow the chitlins to thaw overnight in a pan. When completely thawed, soak in cold water and remove as much fat as possible. This step will take about 1 hr. It should be emphasized that cleaning the fat from the chitlins is very important to the eventual flavor of the food.

Drain the cleaning water and rinse several times with cold water. Put the chitlins in an appropriate size pot and add water, onion, and celery. Cover and cook over medium heat until the chitlins are tender—about 4 hr. Season with salt and pepper. Serve hot with vinegar and hot sauce. Makes 4 servings.

Collard Greens

Collard greens	4-5	bunches
Ham hocks or fat back	1-2	lb
Red pepper	1	
Monosodium glutamate	1/4	tsp
Onions, chopped	optional	

Remove damaged leaves and large stems from collards. Wash well in water to which 6 tbsp of salt has been added. Parboil meat until tender (this step can be done while greens are being washed). Remove meat from pot and add collards to liquid. Place meat on top. Cover pot and cook over low-medium flame until collards have cooked down. Add red pepper and monosodium glutamate. Cook again under low flame until collards are tender. Add water when necessary to avoid greens cooking dry. Add salt and pepper to taste. Serve with vinegar, hot sauce, and chopped onions. This recipe is also good for use with turnip and mustard greens. Makes 8 servings.

Yams

Sweet potatoes	6	medium
Brown sugar	1/2	cup
Butter	4	tbsp

Wash and pare the sweet potatoes. Boil for 10 min in salted water. Drain and cut lengthwise in halves. Place potatoes in a baking dish with butter and bake in a moderate oven (350°F). Make a syrup by boiling 1/2 cup brown sugar with 3 tbsp water. During baking, baste the potatoes with the syrup and bake until tender. Makes 6 servings.

Okra

Okra pods	1–1½ lb
Butter, melted	4 tbsp
Monosodium glutamate	Pinch
Black pepper	Pinch

Cut stem ends off okra pods and wash well. Place in sauce pan and boil in salted water for about 20 min over low heat until tender. Drain water and add melted butter, monosodium glutamate, and black pepper. Makes 5–6 servings.

Cornbread

Yellow corn meal	2 cups
Whole milk	2 cups
Eggs	2
Sugar	2 tbsp
Baking powder	1 tbsp
Salt	½ tsp
Bacon fat	2 tbsp

Preheat oven to 425°F. Mix the corn meal, sugar, baking powder and salt together. Beat together the milk, eggs, and bacon fat. Add the dry mixed ingredients to the liquid ingredients with light beating. Pour into a buttered baking pan and bake for about 20 min. Serve hot with butter and strawberry preserves. Makes 5–6 servings.

Rice Pudding

Rice, cooked	2 cups
Eggs	2
Sugar	1 cup
Salt	¼ tsp
Vanilla	½ tbsp
Raisins	1 cup
Butter	2 tbsp
Nutmeg	½ tsp

Beat eggs in a large bowl. Add all other ingredients except butter and nutmeg. Pour into greased casserole dish. Dot with butter and nutmeg. Bake at 350°F for about 45 min. Serve hot or chilled. Makes 4–6 servings.

The following beverages are fitting accompaniments: buttermilk; cornbread buttermilk (crumbled cornbread added to buttermilk and served with a spoon); sassafras tea; dandelion or elderberry wine.

FELIX A. BURROWS, JR.

References

PAMELA, PRINCESS. 1969. Princess Pamela's Soul Food Cookbook. New American Library, New York.

WILSON, MARY TOLFORD. 1964. Peaceful Intergration: The Owner's Adoption of His Slaves' Food. J. Negro Hist. *49*, No. 2, 116.

Cross-reference: *Food: What Man Eats.*

SOYBEANS

Soybeans are native to eastern Asia. Although introduced into the United States during the 19th Century, soybeans received little commercial attention until the 1920's and 1930's. Soybeans became an important source of food fat and were a large farm crop in the United States during World War II. *Glycine max.* (L) Merrill, known variously as soybean, soya bean, soja bean, Chinese pea, or Manchurian bean, is grown extensively throughout most of the Mississippi Valley and the Southeastern states. It thrives throughout the Temperate Zones and where varieties have been developed for specific localities. Plant breeders continually develop new and improved varieties for the midwest—Corsoy, Hark, and Wayne; for the south—Bragg, Hill, and Lee; and for the north (Minnesota)—Merit and Portage; or improved edible varieties for the east like Verde. In Table S-17, soybean production for seven leading states is shown as well as the U.S. totals for 1930 to 1973 (Kromer 1973).

Short hairy pods containing from 2 to 3 seeds are attached to the plant. Shape and size vary from small, round pea-sized to larger, elongated beans. Colors vary from yellow, brown, green, to black. The bean consists primarily of a hull, hypocotyl, and two cotyledons. Most soybeans used for food products are No. 2 yellow beans that have a yellow hilum or seed scar. The grades of soybeans for trading are determined in accordance with U.S. Grain Standards administered by USDA. Requirements for the numerical grades are given in Table S-18. Soybeans not equal to these grades, or which are musty, sour, or heating, are called sample grade (USDA 1970). The composition of soybeans varies as a result of varietal and climatic differences, but overall they will have the composition listed in Table S-19 (Kawamura 1967).

Handling and Storage

Beans are generally harvested from September in Minnesota to late November in the Gulf States and South Carolina. They are unique among grains in the United States because most of them flow to market for processing and exporting. Livestock and poultry do not thrive on whole soybeans because they contain antinutritional factors that must be destroyed by processing before their maximum food or feed value is realized. Large amounts of soybeans must be stored just after harvest to allow for an orderly processing. Huge storage bins are adjacent to most processing plants and at marketing areas; there is also storage on the farm in smaller steel or wooden bins. Large commercial concrete bins have diameters of 20–40

TABLE S-17

U.S. SOYBEAN PRODUCTION FOR 44 YEARS

Year	Millions of Acres	Yield in Bu[1] per Acre	Total Yield, Millions of Bushels
1930	1.07	13.0	13.9
1940	4.81	16.2	78.0
1950	13.81	21.7	299.2
1960	23.66	23.5	555.1
1970	42.45	26.7	1127.1
1973	56.17	28.0	1574.6
Production in 1973 for Leading States			
Arkansas	4.6	22.0	101.6
Ohio	3.6	26.0	92.5
Indiana	4.3	33.0	140.9
Illinois	9.2	32.0	295.4
Iowa	7.9	35.0	274.8
Missouri	4.8	28.0	133.0
Minnesota	4.4	29.0	127.6

[1] Bushel is 60 lb.

ft and heights over 150 ft; some are cone-shaped structures and hold as much as 2 million bushels.

Proper storage requires that beans have 12% moisture or less when held for 1 yr or more. Under these or slightly higher moisture conditions, mixing of the beans is sometimes necessary because of seasonal flow of moisture to cold walls. Such flow creates areas of high moisture that stimulate mold growth. With 13–15% moisture, beans can be stored successfully during much of the processing year in cooler parts of the country. Molds grow rapidly at 18% moisture and 78°F. Hot spots develop that must be broken up and mixed to avoid charring or complete loss of the stored beans by fire. Long-term storage of soybeans (3 yr) can lower nutritive value of protein products, whereas storage of the meal products does not (Mitchell and Beadles 1949).

Processing

Because soybeans store easily and have a high bulk density of 45 lb per cu ft, they may be processed far from the area in which they were grown. Although many U.S. soybeans are exported to oil-poor or meal-poor countries, much of the crop is processed domestically. Solvent extraction is the major processing method for soybeans because it efficiently separates the higher priced oil from the lower priced meal. Some continuous screw press and extruder-cooker operations are used for special products.

TABLE S-18

REQUIREMENTS OF GRADES

Condition	Grade			
	No. 1	No. 2	No. 3	No. 4
Minimum test (wt lb/bu[1])	56	54	52	49
Moisture (%)	13	14	16	18
Maximum limits (%)				
Splits	10	20	30	40
Damaged kernels	2	3	5	8
Foreign material	1	2	3	5
Colored beans[2]	1	2	5	10

[1] Legal weight for trading purpose is 60 lb.
[2] In yellow soybeans, beans that are not yellow or pale green.

TABLE S-19

COMPOSITION OF THE SOYBEAN AND ITS PARTS

Fraction or Part	Protein (N × 6.25) (%)	Carbohydrate (%)	Fat (%)	Ash (%)
Hull (8%)	8.8	86	1	4.3
Cotyledon (90%)	43	29	23	5.0
Hypocotyl (2%)	41	43	11	4.4
Whole bean	40	34	21	4.9

About 95% of the beans processed flow through large (400 or more tons per day) plants that extract the oil with hexane. Figure S-7 depicts the various processing steps and final products. Sound beans flow through a magnetic separator to remove iron and steel objects and a scalper to remove small seeds and larger objects by screening in order to clean the beans. The beans are cracked by rolls into about 5 parts, 4 of which come from splitting the 2 cotyledons and the fifth is the hull and hypocotyl (part of the bean that often becomes separated from the hull and where sprouting starts). By screening and aspirating, the cracked cotyledons are separated from the hull and hypocotyl for making 49%-protein meal, defatted soy flour, and derived high-protein products. The hulls go to special feed products called mill feed (13% protein) and mill run (11% protein). After conditioning to 10.5% moisture, the cracked beans are flaked and the flakes extracted with hexane.

Extraction

In the United States, the petroleum hydrocarbon mixture called hexane (bp 66°–69°C) is widely used to extract oil. Other solvents used commercially are heptane and cyclohexane (Europe). Ethanol and trichloroethylene have been used; alcohol improves flavor but lowers functionality of the meal proteins. The chloro compound reacts with the meal to give products toxic to cattle. The hexane solvent tests negatively for carcinogenic hydrocarbons.

Extraction is carried out in a variety of ways, including a presoaking period to remove most of the oil and a countercurrent flow of flakes and solvent. Details of such operations or references thereto can be found elsewhere (Norris 1964). For feed purposes, a desolventizer-toaster removes the solvent by injecting steam into the flakes and heating the moist meal for 30–45 min at about 110°C. Soy flakes for flour, protein concentrate, and protein isolate are described later.

The solvent-oil mixture called miscella is filtered or otherwise treated to remove fines, and the solvent removed by rising film evaporators and

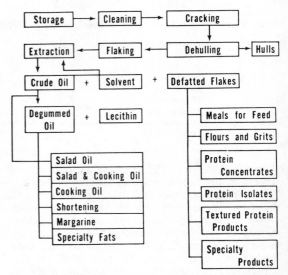

FIG. S-7. FLOW OF SOYBEANS THROUGH A MODERN PROCESSING PLANT

stripping columns. Steam is passed countercurrently through the oil in packed columns under diminished pressure to remove the last of the hexane. Crude oil from the stripping columns is mixed with 1% of water to hydrate the phosphatides, sometimes called gums or lecithin. The hydrated gums are continuously separated in centrifuges under pressure to degummed oil and crude phosphatides (25% water and 75% phosphatides plus oil). After drying under reduced pressure to 0.5% moisture, a thick viscous fluid or oily solid is obtained and is known as soybean lecithin. Acetic anhydride may also be used to separate oil from phosphatides (Hayes and Wolff 1956).

Oil Products for Food

Degummed or crude soybean oil refines readily with alkali to a neutral oil suitable for bleaching, hydrogenating, and deodorizing to consumer products (Norris 1964). Oil containing from 0.5 to

0.75% fatty acid is mixed mechanically with a slight excess of alkali to react with fatty acids present to form soaps. The mixture is warmed to 60°-70°C and then centrifuged to separate oil from soapstock. After washing with 0.1 part of water at 71°-80°C, the water is separated from the oil in a second centrifuge. About 3 min are required for alkali treatments and 10 min for water washing. Some plants use dilute phosphoric or citric acid in the water-washing step. Oil is sprayed into a vacuum dryer at about 5 mm to lower moisture from about 0.5 to 0.05%.

Most alkali-refined oils are bleached by the use of a natural earth, such as Fuller's earth (hydrated aluminum silicate), an acid-activated clay containing bentonite or montmorillonite, or activated carbon. About 1% of a high-grade bleaching earth is mixed with a dried and deaerated oil. The slurry is passed into an evacuated chamber to spray the oil-clay mixture and to remove water and oil from the clay. Mixture is warmed to about 110°C and sprayed into the chamber again to release bonded moisture. The oil is pumped through a closed filter to remove clay and the bleached oil is ready for hydrogenation, winterization, or deodorization (Mattil 1964; Norris 1964).

Soybean oil is mixed usually with 10–20% cottonseed oil and hydrogenated for all-purpose shortening and a standard type of margarine. One type of hydrogenated product is worth more description here since the final product is a cooking and salad oil. It is partially hydrogenated-winterized soybean oil. A bleached oil is hydrogenated with nickel catalyst to an iodine value (IV) of about 107 and winterized to give a final product with an IV of 110 (Evans et al. 1964). Winterization may be achieved by cooling oil to about 55°F over 12 hr until the first solid fat crystals appear. The cooling rate is slowed for the next 18 hr when it is cooled to 40°–42°F and held there about 12 to 72 hr more at 40°F; about 12 hr are usually required in order to have the oil pass the 20-hr cold test at 32°F. Oil is then filtered through a plate and frame press or crystals are separated from liquid oil by other means. (For a discussion of hydrogenation see this subject in Section H.)

Deodorization (Mattil 1964) removes most of the volatile compounds affecting the initial taste and odor of the oil by passing steam through the heated oil under diminished pressure. An increase from 177° to 232°C will increase the rate of removal about 9 times. Some deodorizers operate as high as 275°C. Many modern deodorizers operate at 6 mm (mercury) and others go as low as 1–3 mm through the use of multiple steam-jet ejectors. About 5% by weight of steam throughput is considered normal.

Although both continuous and semicontinuous deodorizers are available today, the latter are probably more popular since the vacuum is the same on the finished oil as on the entering oil. Older multitray-type deodorizers require about 60 min for deodorization (Wolf and Cowan 1971). Recent models claim deodorization times as low as 15 min. Time and temperature are important variables, and the initial quality of an oil treated at 270°C for 0.5 hr is superior to one treated for 2 hr in which oxidative and flavor stabilities are lowered. In the last stages or final tray of the deodorizer, metal-inactivating agents, antioxidants, antifoam agents, and crystal inhibitors are added when desired. Citric or phosphoric acid inactivates trace metals in the oil. About 0.005% of citric acid is a desirable amount. Phosphoric and citric acids are sometimes used in the deodorizer, but care is needed to avoid too much phosphoric acid since it leads to "cucumber" flavors and odors. Methyl silicone acts as an antifoam agent and is particularly desirable for oils for deep fat frying. Such antioxidants as t-butyl hydroxyanisole and t-butyl hydroxytoluene improve stability of derived baked goods; propyl gallate improves oxidative stability as measured by the active oxygen method. Oxystearin is sometimes added as a crystal inhibitor. Total amounts of these additives must not exceed 0.02%.

Food Uses of Soybean Oil

Specifications (Wolf and Cowan 1971) for soybean salad oils, salad and cooking oils and cooking oil are shown in Table S-20. These products are to some extent interchangeable but usually are not for economic reasons. Properly deodorized, unhydrogenated soybean oil is usually completely liquid at 0°C for extended periods of time but may develop a little haze from crystallization of a wax in the oil. Partially hydrogenated-winterized soybean oil serves as both a salad and cooking oil, but it is more expensive than either soybean salad oil or cooking oil (prepared by hydrogenating to IV of 95–105). The hydrogenated oil finds much use in restaurant chains and institutions for deep fat frying of foods.

Soybean oil presents certain problems to the food manufacturer or related industry. Unhydrogenated oil contains from 6 to 9% of linolenate ester. Oxidation of this linolenate gives odors and flavors different from linoleate in cottonseed, safflower, or corn oil. These odors and flavors arise particularly when the oil is heated or allowed to oxidize at room temperature. These off-flavors are characterized as beany, grassy, fishy, and painty and sometimes appear at low levels of oxidation. Metallic impurities accelerate the

TABLE S-20

SPECIFICATIONS FOR EDIBLE SOYBEAN OIL

Condition	Fully Refined Salad Oils		Partially Hydrogenated-winterized Salad and Cooking Oils		Cooking Oil
	ASCS[1]	NSPA[2]	ASCS[1]	Fed. Spec. JJJ-S-30F	
Appearance	Clear and brilliant at 70°-85°F				
Settlings	None and no foreign matter				
Odor and flavor	Bland and free of rancid and other odors				
Moisture and volatiles (min %)	0.1	0.1	0.06	0.05	0.0
Flash point (°F)	550	550	550	550	550
Refined bleach color					
Lovibond red	2.0	2.0	2.0	2.0	1.5
Lovibond yellow	20.0	20.0	20.0	20.0	15.0
Peroxide value Meq/kg max	0.5	2.0	0.6	0.20	0.5
Peroxide value Meq/kg in 8 hr AOM[3] test max	35	35	8.0	25[4]	25[4]
Linolenic (Max %)			3.0	3.0	2.8

[1] Agricultural Stabilization and Commodity Service.
[2] National Soybean Processors Association.
[3] Active oxygen method.
[4] Peroxide value < 100 after 25 hr.

appearance of these off-flavors, but they can be inactivated by proper use of citric or phosphoric acid or sorbitol. Although many compounds have been suggested as a precursor or constituent of the odors and flavors, inactivation of metals and removal of linolenate appear to be key factors in the flavor stability of soybean oil. Linolenate appears to be a precursor of these odors and flavors produced when the oil oxidizes (Wolf and Cowan 1971). Traces of iron and copper accelerate this oxidation.

Lecithin

Since the industry processes more than 700 million bushels (60 lb each or 42 billion pounds) by methods that extract about 0.2–0.6% of soybean flakes as the phosphatides or lecithin, large amounts of it are available. There is a variety of

TABLE S-21

DIFFERENT GRADES OF COMMERCIAL LECITHIN—BLEACHED

Characteristics	Properties of Different Grades[1]			
	A	B	C	D
Consistency	Plastic	Fluid	Fluid	Fluid
Acetone insoluble (%)[2]	67–72	62–64	54–60	62–64
Moisture (%)	1.1	0.75	0.75	0.75
Benzene insoluble (max %)	0.1	0.1	0.1	0.05
Acid value	25	32	40	32
Centipoises at 80°F	—	15,000	7,000	15,000

SOURCE: Lecithins, Technical Sales Manual, Central Soya, Inc., Chicago, Ill.

[1] Grades with A, B, C, and D can result from different amounts of bleaching with hydrogen peroxide.
[2] Actual percentage of phosphatides—remainder primarily oil or additives like fatty acids.

TABLE S-22

COMPOSITION AND PROPERTIES OF COMMERCIAL LECITHIN FRACTIONS

Property	Oil-free Lecithin	Phosphatidyl Choline Fraction	Phosphatidyl Inositol Fraction
Solubility in:			
Alcohol	Dispersible	Soluble	Insoluble
Water	Dispersible	Dispersible	Dispersible
Oil	Soluble	Soluble	Soluble
Choline fraction (%)	30	60	4
Cephalin fraction (%)	30	30	29
Inositol fraction (%)	32	2	55
Oil (%)	3	4	4
Type of emulsifier	O/W[1] or W/O[2]	O/W	W/O

SOURCE: Lecithins, Technical Sales Manual, Central Soya, Inc., Chicago, Ill.

[1] Oil in water.
[2] Water in oil.

grades of lecithin available that results from the addition of bleaching agent and fatty acid, removal of oil, and separation of oil-free lecithin into alcohol-soluble and -insoluble fractions. Lecithins find wide usage in foods, as well as in nonfood products, that depend on their emulsifying or related properties. The lecithins are minor components of many foods where they serve as foam stabilizers, suspending agents, release agents, wetting agents, nutritive supplements, and antispattering agents (Iveson 1961; Wolf and Cowan 1971; Puski and Szuhaj 1971).

The crude dried product containing 28–33% of oil is usually bleached with H_2O_2 to lighten the tan-to-brown color and is often mixed with fatty acids to improve fluidity. Table S-21 shows some of the characteristics of the different grades of lecithin. Separation of acetone-solubles from acetone-insolubles results in a purified lecithin containing less triglycerides. Further fractionation of lecithin gives two additional kinds of phosphatides: the alcohol-soluble fraction consists of phosphatidyl choline and cephalin and the alcohol-insoluble portion is comprised primarily of inositol phosphatides. Table S-22 shows some of the differences between the purified lecithins. Both bleached plastic and fluid lecithins find use in baked goods, cake mixes, instant foods to improve and speed the dispersion of the fat, and in candies to improve their texture, smoothness, brittleness, and clarity (Iveson 1961). The alcohol-soluble fraction gives more stable oil-in-water emulsions and is useful in preparation of emulsion for intravenous feeding. The alcohol-insoluble fraction gives more stable water-in-oil emulsions and serves as an antispattering agent and a pan grease. Hydrogen peroxide can hydroxylate, as well as

bleach, lecithins. Such a reaction improves hydrophilic products by improving moisture retention and effectiveness in making stable oil-in-water emulsions.

Protein Products

Whole Soybeans.—Although whole soybeans contain about 40% protein, they are consumed in very small amounts in U.S. foods, which include canned soybeans in tomato sauce and canned green soybeans. Soy milk-based infant formulas and beverages, made by extracting the proteins, oil, and water-soluble compounds from whole soybeans, are also available. These products are eaten primarily by vegetarians. Roasted soybeans have been available for several years as snack foods. In 1971, a new product similar to lightly roasted peanut halves was introduced. It is prepared by soaking and leaching soybeans followed by removal of the seed coat and an undisclosed drying process which minimizes shrinkage of the expanded cotyledons. This product is available in halves, in diced form, and as a flour; it is intended for the bakery, candy, confectionery, ice cream, and salted nut trades.

Small amounts of whole beans are also converted to Oriental foods in Pacific Coast cities. The largest use of whole soybeans is in the Orient where they are converted into soy sauce, soybean milk, tofu, miso, and tempeh (Hesseltine and Wang 1972). Sizeable quantities of U.S. soybeans are exported to Japan for food uses.

Flours and Grits.—Flours are differentiated from grits on the basis of particle size. Coarse, medium, and fine grits have respective mesh (U.S. screen) sizes of 10–20, 20–40, and 40–80. Flours are 100

TABLE S-23

PROXIMATE ANALYSES OF COMMERCIAL SOYBEAN FLOURS AND GRITS[1]

Flour or Grit Type	Moisture (%)	Protein (N × 6.25) (%)	Fat (%)	Crude Fiber (%)	Ash (%)
Full fat	5.0	41.5	21.0	2.1	5.2
Low fat	5.5	46.0	6.5	3.0	5.5
Defatted[2]	5.0	53.0	0.9	2.9	6.0
Lecithinated[3]	5.5	45.2	16.4	2.4	5.3

[1] These analyses are not product standards but are values typical for product (Meyer 1970).
[2] Available in a variety of moist-heat treatments.
[3] Available with lower lecithin contents.

mesh or finer. Flours and grits are available with varying fat and protein contents (Table S-23). Amino acid content of a defatted meal (equivalent in composition to flours or grits) is given in Table S-24. Flours and grits also vary in the amount of heat treatment they receive during processing to provide a range of physical and functional properties. For optimum nutritive value, soy protein products should be heated either during manufacture or during some stage of food processing, such as sterilizing or cooking the

TABLE S-24

AMINO ACID COMPOSITION OF SOYBEAN PROTEIN PRODUCTS

Amino Acid	Grams Amino Acid per 16 Gm Nitrogen		
	Meal	Concentrate	Isolate
Essential			
Lysine	6.9	6.3	6.1
Methionine	1.6	1.4	1.1
Cystine	1.6	1.6	1.0
Tryptophan	1.3	1.5	1.4
Threonine	4.3	4.2	3.7
Isoleucine	5.1	4.8	4.9
Leucine	7.7	7.8	7.7
Phenylalanine	5.0	5.2	5.4
Valine	5.4	4.9	4.8
Nonessential			
Arginine	8.4	7.5	7.8
Histidine	2.6	2.7	2.5
Tyrosine	3.9	3.9	3.7
Serine	5.6	5.7	5.5
Glutamic acid	21.0	19.8	20.5
Aspartic acid	12.0	12.0	11.9
Glycine	4.5	4.4	4.0
Alanine	4.5	4.4	3.9
Proline	6.3	5.2	5.3
Ammonia	2.1	1.9	2.0

SOURCE: Wolf and Cowan (1971).

final product. Heat treatment of flours and grits denatures the proteins; hence, protein solubility measurements are used to determine extent of heat treatment. Nitrogen solubility index (NSI) and protein dispersibility index (PDI) are the two most commonly-used measurements. The first method measures the percentage of total Kjeldahl nitrogen of the sample that is soluble in water, whereas the second method measures the percentage of total protein (N × 6.25) dispersible in water under specified conditions (American Oil Chemists' Society 1970). Differences in extraction conditions between the two methods may result in dissimilar numerical values for a given sample.

The extent of heat treatment given defatted flours and grits is determined primarily by controlling time, temperature, and moisture content during removal of residual hexane after soybean flakes leave the extractor (Becker 1971). One of three desolventizing processes may be selected to prepare edible-grade flakes: (a) The Schneckens system, (b) flash desolventizer, and (c) vapor desolventizer-deodorizer. The Schneckens system, the oldest of the three, produces flakes with maximum PDI values of 65–70 but normally PDI values range from 40 to 50. With the flash desolventizer, PDI values of 90 or higher are attainable. The vapor desolventizer-deodorizer, however, is readily adaptable to producing products ranging from raw (PDI ≥ 90) to completely cooked (PDI 10–15).

Edible flours and grits are manufactured from No. 1 or 2 yellow soybeans under sanitary conditions to yield products free of pathogenic organisms and having standard plate counts of less than 50,000 (Horan 1967). Full-fat flours and grits are prepared by steaming soybeans to inactivate enzymes, cracking, dehulling, and grinding. Alternatively, full-fat flours can be made from dehulled beans by extrusion-cooking (Mustakas et al. 1970). Other flours and grits are usually produced from defatted flakes; oil or lecithin may be added back

TABLE S-25

ANALYSES AND PROPERTIES OF SOY PROTEIN CONCENTRATES

Property	Alcohol Leached	Acid Leached	Moist Heat-water Leached
Protein ($N \times 6.25$) (%)	66	67	70
Moisture (%)	6.7	5.2	3.1
Fat (petroleum ether extractable) (%)	0.3	0.3	1.2
Crude fiber (%)	3.5	3.4	4.4
Ash (%)	5.6	4.8	3.7
Nitrogen solubility index	5	69	3
pH of 1:10 water dispersion	6.9	6.6	6.9

SOURCE: Meyer (1967).

to defatted products to desired fat or lecithin contents.

Protein Concentrates.—Soybean protein products containing a minimum of 70% protein are termed protein concentrates. They are prepared from defatted flakes or flours by removing water-soluble sugars, ash, and other minor constituents including compounds giving raw soy, beany, and bitter flavors. Concentrates consist of the major proteins plus the polysaccharides, and are made by three methods that insolubilize the major proteins while the low-molecular compounds are removed. One process consists of extraction with aqueous alcohol (Mustakas *et al.* 1962; O'Hara and Schoepfer 1965), whereas a second (Sair 1959) involves extraction with dilute acid at pH 4.5 (the isoelectric point and region of insolubility of the major proteins). The acid-leached concentrate is neutralized before drying. In a third process the proteins are insolubilized by heat denaturing them; the low-molecular weight constituents are then washed out with water (McAnelly 1964). The three types of concentrates are similar in chemical composition but differ mainly in water solubility of proteins (Table S-25). The acid-leached concen-

trate has a high-protein solubility, whereas the proteins in the other two products are extensively denatured and insoluble. Amino acid composition for a concentrate made by alcohol extraction is given in Table S-24.

Isolates.—These are the most refined soy proteins available. They are prepared by removing all water-insoluble polysaccharides, as well as water-soluble sugars and other minor constituents. Defatted flakes or flours of high-protein solubility are extracted with dilute alkali (pH 7–9) at 50°–55°C. After the insoluble residue (water-insoluble polysaccharides plus residual protein) is separated by screening, filtering, and centrifuging, the extract is adjusted to pH 4.5 with food-grade acid. Of course, when the major proteins are brought to their isoelectric point, they precipitate. This protein curd is filtered or centrifuged from the solubles (soy whey) and washed. The curd may be spray dried to yield the isoelectric form of the protein, but more commonly, it is neutralized and spray dried to give the proteinate form, which is water-dispersible. Sodium proteinates are the major type sold although potassium and calcium proteinates are also manufactured.

TABLE S-26

PROXIMATE ANALYSES OF COMMERCIAL SOY PROTEIN ISOLATES

Property	A	B	C	D
Protein (%)	92.8	92.2	92.9	94.7
Moisture (%)	4.7	6.4	7.6	3.7
Crude fiber (%)	0.2	0.1	0.1	0.2
Ash (%)	3.8	3.5	2.0	2.7
Nitrogen solubility index	85	95	—	—
pH of 1:10 water dispersion	7.1	6.8	5.2	5.5

SOURCE: Meyer (1967).

Compositions and properties of commercial protein isolates are summarized in Table S-26. Samples A and B are sodium proteinates, whereas C and D are isoelectric forms typified by their low pH, low ash, and insolubility in water. Although protein contents of commercial isolates may be similar, their physical properties, including solubility and molecular-weight distribution, can be appreciably different when similar types are compared because processing varies between manufacturers (Nash and Wolf 1967). Amino acid composition of a typical isolate is given in Table S-24. Detailed discussions of physical and chemical properties of soybean proteins are available (Wolf and Cowan 1971; Wolf 1972).

Protein Hydrolysates.—Two types of soy protein hydrolysates are produced commercially. One, obtained by pepsin hydrolysis, serves as a foaming agent in mixtures with syrups for nougat, creams, and fudge-like candies; in chiffon mixes; and in whipped cake mixes (Burnett 1951). Secondly, acid hydrolysis of soy proteins gives products having meat-like flavors (also referred to as hydrolyzed vegetable proteins). A process recently described starts with soy protein concentrate and hydrolyzes until 54–89% of the peptide bonds are cleaved (Sair 1968).

Uses of Soy Proteins

Even though the volume of soy protein usage is still small, it is growing. Until about 1970, its major application was as functional additives at low levels to improve such properties as handling during processing, texture, and appearance of processed foods. Functional properties of soy proteins are discussed in detail by Wolf and Cowan (1971). The use of soy proteins for nutritional purposes is now becoming more important; supplementation of cereals, meat extenders, and simulated meats are examples of this application.

Selling prices (1974) and production estimates for soy protein products (1973) are listed in Table S-27. Flours and grits production estimates are for total edible grades, which are also used extensively in pet foods and calf starters. In 1970, 11 concerns manufactured flours and grits, 4 produced concentrates, and 3 made isolates (Manley and Gallimore 1971). Soy flours and grits, used largely because of their low cost, are added to a variety of foods (Table S-28). The major consumption of flours and grits is in baked goods followed by meat products, breakfast cereals, and infant foods.

Concentrates are added primarily to meat products for their functional properties (fat emulsification and binding) and as meat extenders; other uses include breakfast cereals and infant foods. Consumption of concentrates expanded significantly in the early 1970's; several additional companies were considering entry into the market in 1971–1972. One company in 1971 introduced a concentrate fortified with vitamins and minerals to meet requirements as a meat extender in type A school lunch programs as allowed by the Food and Nutrition Service of USDA (1971).

Isolates are the basic ingredient of spun fiber types of meat analogs and are also added to comminuted meat products to emulsify and stabilize the fat. Other applications are infant foods and as binders for chopped meat fibers in casserole mixes.

Production of meat analogs either by extruding soy flour or by spinning protein isolate into fibers is estimated to be about 110 million pounds

TABLE S-27

SELLING PRICES AND PRODUCTION ESTIMATES FOR SOYBEAN PROTEIN PRODUCTS

Product	Protein Content[1] (%)	Price per Pound[2] ($)	Price per Pound of Protein ($)	Annual Production for Foods[3] (Million Pounds)
Flours and grits (defatted)	50	0.14–0.17	0.28–0.34	450–600
Concentrates	70	0.30	0.43	55
Isolates	97	0.55–0.56	0.57–0.58	50
Meat analogs:				
Extruded	50–55	0.27 and up[4]	0.54 and up[1]	110
Spun fiber	90+	0.50 and up[4]	0.93 and up[1]	

[1] Dry basis.
[2] March 1974.
[3] Estimates for 1973 from Lockmiller (1974).
[4] Frozen, 60–65% moisture.

TABLE S-28

USES OF SOYBEAN PROTEIN PRODUCTS

Flours and Grits	Concentrates	Isolates
Baked goods	Meat products	Meat analogs
Breads, rolls, buns	Cooked sausages	Cooked sausages
Doughnuts	Luncheon loaves	Luncheon loaves
Sweet goods	Ground meats	Infant foods
Cakes and cake mixes	Breakfast cereals	Casserole mixes
Waffle and pancake mixes	Infant foods	
Cookies and specialty crackers		
Meat products		
Cooked sausages		
Luncheon loaves		
Patties		
Ground meats (chilli, etc.)		
Meat analogs (extruded)		
Breakfast cereals		
Infant and junior foods		
Confectionery items		
Dietary foods		

annually (Table S-27). These products are available in flavored and unflavored forms and are priced accordingly. The unflavored items are priced lowest. Meat analogs are discussed in detail by Wolf and Cowan (1971).

J. C. COWAN
W. J. WOLF

References

AMERICAN OIL CHEMISTS' SOCIETY. 1970. Official and Tentative Methods, 3rd Edition. Methods Ba 10-65 and Ba 11-65.

BECKER, K. W. 1971. Processing of oilseeds to meal and protein flakes. J. Am. Oil Chemists' Soc. 48, 299.

BURNETT, R. S. 1951. Soybean food products. In Soybeans and Soybean Products, Vol. II. K. Markley (Editor). Interscience Publishers, New York.

EVANS, C. D. et al. 1964. Partial hydrogenation and winterization of soybean oil. J. Am. Oil Chemists' Soc. 41, 260.

FOOD AND NUTRITION SERVICE, USDA. 1971. Textured vegetable protein products (B-1) to be used in combination with meat for use in lunches and suppers served under child feeding programs. FNS Notice 219, U.S. Dept. Agr., Febr. 22.

HAYES, L. P., and WOLFF, H. 1956. Novel method for refining soybean oil. J. Am. Oil Chemists' Soc. 33, 440.

HESSELTINE, C. W., and WANG, H. L. 1972. Fermented soybean food products. In Soybeans: Chemistry and Technology, Vol. 1. Proteins. A. K. Smith and S. J. Circle (Editors). Avi Publishing Co., Westport, Conn.

HORAN, F. E. 1967. Defatted and full-fat flour by conventional processes. Proc. Intern. Conf. Soybean Protein Foods. U.S. Dept. Agr. ARS-71-35.

IVESON, H. T. 1961. Soybean lecithin. Soybean Dig. 21, No. 8, 18.

KAWAMURA, S. 1967. Quantitative paper chromatography of sugars of the cotyledon, hull, and hypocotyl of soybeans of selected varieties. Kagawa Univ. Fac. Agr. Tech. Bull. 18, No. 2, 117.

KROMER, G. W. 1973. Fats and Oil Situation. U.S. Dept. Agr. FOS-270 (Nov.). See also Soybean Dig., Blue Book Issue, 34, No. 6, 1974.

LOCKMILLER, R. N. 1974. Marketing of fabricated foods and their ingredients. Presented at Fabricated Foods Short Course, Div. Agr. Food Chem., Am. Chem. Soc., Las Vegas, Nevada, Mar. 27–29.

McANELLY, J. K. 1964. Method for producing a soybean protein product and the resulting product. U.S. Pat. 3,142,571, assigned to Swift & Co.

MANLEY, W. T., and GALLIMORE, W. W. 1971. Emerging Product Inroads into Agriculture: Synthetics and Substitutes. USDA Outlook 1971.

MATTIL, K. 1964. Plastic shortening agents. In Bailey's Industrial Fats and Oils. D. Swern (Editor). Interscience Publishers, New York.

MEYER, E. W. 1967. Soy protein concentrates and isolates. Proc. Intern. Conf. Soybean Protein Foods. U.S. Dept. Agr. ARS-71-35.

MEYER, E. W. 1970. Soybean flours and grits. Proc. SOS/70, 3rd Intern. Congr. Food Sci. Technol., Inst. Food Technol., Chicago.

MITCHELL, H. H., and BEADLES, J. R. 1949. The effect of storage on nutritional qualities of proteins of wheat, corn and soybeans. J. Nutr. *39*, 463.

MUSTAKAS, G. C., KIRK, L. D., and GRIFFIN, E. L., JR. 1962. Flash desolventizing defatted soybean meals washed with aqueous alcohol. J. Am. Oil Chemists' Soc. *39*, 222.

MUSTAKAS, G. C. *et al.* 1970. Extruder-processing to improve nutritional quality, flavor and keeping quality of full-fat soy flour. Food Technol. *24*, 1290.

NASH, A. M., and WOLF, W. J. 1967. Solubility and ultracentrifugal studies on soybean globulins. Cereal Chem. *44*, 183.

NORRIS, F. 1964. Extraction of fats and oils. *Also* Refining and bleaching. *In* Bailey's Industrial Fats and Oils. D. Swern (Editor). Interscience Publishers, New York.

O'HARA, J. B., and SCHOEPFER, A. E. 1965. Countercurrent extraction of vegetable material by a split-solvent process. U.S. Pat. 3,207,744, assigned to A. E. Staley Mfg. Co.

PUSKI, G., and SZUHAJ, B. F. 1971. Soybean lecithins and proteins as emulsifiers. Proc. Symp. Soy—The Wonder Bean, Southern Calif. Sect. Am. Assoc. Cereal Chemists.

SAIR, L. 1959. Proteinaceous soy composition and method of preparing. U.S. Pat. 2,881,076, assigned to Griffith Laboratories, Inc.

SAIR, L. 1968. Production of flavorful protein hydrolysate. U.S. Pat. 3,391,001, assigned to Griffith Laboratories, Inc.

U.S. DEPT. OF AGR. 1970. Official Grain Standards of the United States. USDA Consumer Marketing Serv.

WOLF, W. J. 1972. Purification and properties of proteins. *In* Soybeans: Chemistry and Technology, Vol. I, Proteins. A. K. Smith and S. J. Circle (Editors). Avi Publishing Co., Westport, Conn.

WOLF, W. J., and COWAN, J. C. 1971. Soybeans as a food source. Critical Rev. Food Technol. *2*, 81–158.

Cross-references: *Fabricated Foods; Protein Foods from Plant Sources.*

SPACE FOODS AND THEIR DEVELOPMENT

Until 1960, man's preoccupation with reaching the moon was centered primarily on the hardware necessary to make the trip. The development of the rocket systems necessary for space exploration was an accomplished fact before serious consideration was given to the development of a feeding system capable of maintaining him in space. As a result of experience gained in the development of advanced systems for feeding both the Army and the Air Force under stress, the food research and development organization of the U.S. Army Natick

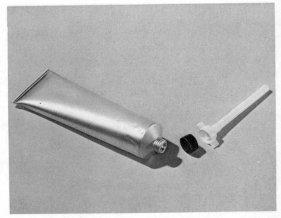

FIG. S-8. SEMISOLID, THERMOSTABILIZED MEAT COMBINATIONS AND FRUITS FOR FIRST MERCURY FLIGHTS WERE PACKAGED IN COLLAPSIBLE ALUMINUM TUBES

Laboratories was called upon to design and implement the feeding requirements for the Project Mercury flights of 1961–1963 and to continue developing foods for subsequent Gemini and Apollo flights. The hardware experts had a 20-yr head start.

Designing space food involved more than developing acceptable nutritious food. Consideration had to be given to weight and volume, the nonavailability of refrigeration requirements for short-term exposure to temperatures exceeding 55°C, the lack of cooking facilities and concomitant need for ready-to-eat or simple-to-prepare foods, and the fact that the food was to be consumed in a weightless environment. These requirements indicated a need for highly stable "convenience" foods.

Toward this end five categories of food have been developed, namely: semisolid foods, bite-sized dehydrated foods to be eaten dry; precooked dehydrated foods to be reconstituted before consumption; wet foods thermally stabilized in flexible packages; and intermediate moisture foods.

Semisolid Foods

Although some of the apprehension regarding the effects of weightlessness on man's ability to eat and drink had been alleviated by the 40-sec weightlessness experiments conducted in aircraft flying a parabolic trajectory, extreme caution was exercised in the selection of food for the first space diets.

The introductory feeding system for Project Mercury was an expediency based on feeding pilots operating under conditions requiring pressurized head gear. Semisolid, thermostabilized meat combinations and fruits developed for high altitude flight use were adapted to Project Mercury use (Fig. S-8). These products were heat-sterilized compositions of the consistency of junior baby foods and were packaged in collapsible aluminum tubes (approximately 140-gm capacity). A polystyrene extension tube, called a "pontube," replaced the screw cap of the aluminum tube and carried the comminuted food into the astronaut's mouth.

Two meat items (beef and vegetables and beef and gravy) and two fruits (applesauce and peaches) were made available to Astronauts Glenn, Carpenter, and Schirra.

The technological problems associated with the successful development of these semisolid foods included: developing formulations which would remain acceptable and maintain the desired viscosity after heat sterilization and subsequent storage for 6 months at 4°, 21°, and 38°C; attain-

ing required caloric densities; achieving desired salt levels without breaking emulsions; selecting appropriate internal coating for the aluminum tubes, particularly the tubes containing applesauce; finding reliable sealing compounds and modifying tube closing equipment to eliminate trapped air. Most of these problems had been resolved prior to NASA's requirement for semisolid foods to be used on Project Mercury flights.

Experience from the early Project Mercury flights demonstrated that semisolid foods, although convenient, are not well accepted for routine use, are low in calories, and costly in terms of weight and cube. The demonstration that the water produced as a by-product of fuel cell operation could be made potable, favored the use of dehydrated foods as a replacement for semisolid food.

NASA supported simulator studies, conducted at Wright Patterson Air Force Base and several major aircraft companies (e.g., North American, Re-

FIG. S-9. BITE-SIZED FOODS AND REHYDRATABLE FOOD ITEMS WERE DEVELOPED FOR LATER MERCURY FLIGHTS

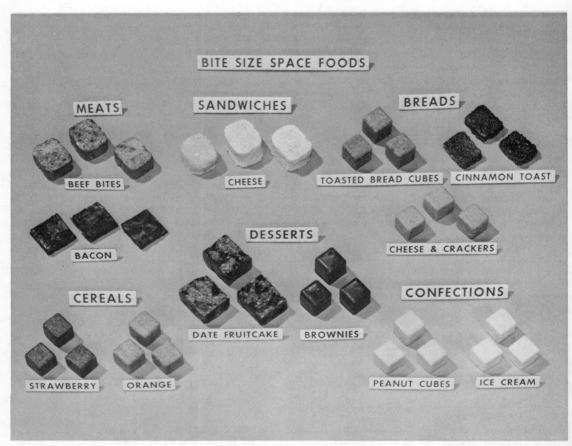

FIG. S-10. BITE-SIZED FOODS WERE EITHER CUBES COMPRESSED FROM DRY MIXTURES OR REC
TANGLES FREEZE-DRIED WITHOUT COMPRESSION

public, Boeing), in which the diet was comprised solely of dehydrated foods. These provided the preflight experience required to assure the acceptance of dehydrated diets by the astronauts.

Dehydrated Bite-Sized Foods

Two approaches to dehydrated foods were pursued, bite-sized foods and rehydratable items. The availability of acceptable prototypes of bite-sized and rehydratable foods permitted the elimination of semisolid foods from the final Mercury flight menu (Fig. S-9). This menu included four products (two meat items and two beverages) to be rehydrated in and consumed from a special package. In addition, a variety of bite-sized pieces, to be consumed by placing directly in the mouth, were added to the menu.

The simplest, most convenient approach to space feeding is the use of bite-sized units since these require no preparation by the astronaut (Fig. S-10). In the form of cubes or rectangles, they pack efficiently with a favorable ratio between food and packaging material. Special formulation and dehydration in conjunction with compression permit high nutrient content per unit of weight and cube, and improve stability after packaging. In general, bite-sized foods are either cubes compressed from dry mixtures, or rectangles freeze-dried without compression. Freeze drying is the preferred method for dehydrating meats, fruits, sandwiches, and desserts, since few deleterious changes occur during drying, and the resulting products are capable of rapid rehydration in the mouth.

Beginning with Astronaut John Glenn, all American astronauts have carried bite-sized portions of food. The compressed chocolate malted milk tablets furnished Astronaut Glenn were chosen because they were simple to eat, acceptable to him, and not likely to cause digestive problems. Once

TABLE S-29

CRITERIA FOR SPACE FOOD

Acceptability
    Liked by astronauts
    Familiar flavor and texture
    Assure consumption
Physiologic
    Nutritious
    Digestible
    Low residue
    Nongas-producing
    Wholesome[1]
    Cause no physical or mental disturbance
Stability
    Biologically, chemically, and physically stable
        without refrigeration
    Withstand flexible packaging at 25 torr pressure
        (i.e., 29 in. vacuum)
    Withstand storage at:
        Gemini
            58°C for 3 hr
            38°C for 2 weeks
        Apollo
            0–54°C for 100 hr
            24° for 400 hr
Utility
    Crumb-free at time of consumption
    Reconstitute in 27°C water (Gemini)
    Reconstitute in 7°C and/or 68°C water (Apollo)
    Meet quality assurance provisions
    Small volume
    Lightweight

[1] Microbiological requirements for dehydrated foods are:

Total aerobic plate count	Not greater than 10,000/gm
Total coliform count	Not greater than 10/gm
Fecal coliform count	Negative in 1 gm
Fecal *Streptococci* count	Not greater than 20/gm
Coagulase positive *Staphylococci*	Negative in 5 gm
Salmonella	Negative in 10 gm

it became apparent that swallowing and digesting food in zero gravity are not problems, development of bite-sized foods was accelerated. This permitted the inclusion of increasingly sophisticated bite-sized foods on each subsequent Mercury flight. Need for two areas of product modification and improvement became apparent as a result of Project Mercury feeding experiences: (1) to control crumbliness and fragmentation of bite-sized foods and (2) to enable the pieces to withstand temperatures in excess of 43°C for short periods of time without undesirable physical and chemical changes such as melting, hardening, and fusing.

To assure flight qualifiable foods for Gemini and Apollo use, more rigid stability requirements were established for the packaged foods (Table S-29). Not only must the food be crumb-free at the time of consumption but it must also withstand being

sealed in a flexible package under vacuum, and remain stable both for 3 hr at 58°C and for 2 weeks at 38°C. Control of crumbs has been accomplished in several ways, primarily through careful product formulation. Binders in compressed food, gelatin in molded freeze-dried products, and careful control of fat content have aided in the control of crumbling. A practical expedient has been the application of edible protective coatings. These are applied to all bite-sized foods except bacon. After compression the bacon squares are immediately packaged under vacuum in a flexible package. This prevents relaxation and results in a crumb-free, smooth, hardened surface.

Coatings for Bite-Sized Foods

Most bite-sized foods are now coated with one of three basic coatings. Compressed cereal and bread cubes and fruitcake pieces are compatible with a simple gelatin solution. For the high fat confection products a zein-in-alcohol solution has proved most satisfactory. Other products are coated with an emulsion composed of sodium caseinate, lipid, glycerine, gelatin, and water. All coatings are applied as solutions and the excess moisture or solvent is removed by drying, usually freeze drying. After drying, the coating becomes firm and protects the food from damage in subsequent handling. Table S-30 illustrates the main areas of research and development on coating bite-sized foods.

Coating problems were intensified by the requirement that all space food be sealed in nonrigid containers evacuated to approximately 25 torr and withstand storage at 38°C under atmospheric pressure. The result of exposing food so packaged to atmospheric pressure produced undesirable changes. For example, compressed gingerbread, brownies, and fruitcake exuded oily fluids. To correct this problem, it was necessary to change both the ingredients and the coatings and to lower the moisture level. Freeze drying the fruitcake pieces corrected their exudation problem. Baked items such as pound cake and fresh bread collapse when packaged in a flexible pouch under vacuum. Their resultant textures are gummy and unappetizing. Until fresh bread was approved for flight use (Apollo 10) the only normal baked product used was fruitcake; all bread items used were either compressed (i.e., toasted bread cubes) or freeze dried (i.e., sandwiches, cinnamon toast).

Common problems which have been met in bite-sized compressed foods are fragility, splitting, lack of cohesion, relaxation after compression, variable density, nonuniformity in size and shape, loss of palatability, and extreme variability in texture between lots.

TABLE S-30

EVOLUTION OF COATINGS FOR SANDWICHES[1] AND MEAT BITES

Where Used	Coatings Used	Reason Discontinued
Mercury 9	Acetylated monoglycerides (mp 43°C)	Flight cabin temperature exceeded 43°C; coating melted
Gemini 3	Hydrogenated palm kernel oil (mp 58°C) plus a high amylose starch film overcoat	Coatings were incompatible; starch film flaked badly and turned bitter on storage
Gemini 4–8	Hydrogenated palm kernel oil (mp 58°C); 2 coats	Unacceptable to astronauts (inhibited hydration in mouth and covered roof of mouth); poor digestibility, steatorrhea
Gemini 9–12	Sodium caseinate-fat-sugar emulsion	Sweetness not liked on non-sweet products
Apollo	Sodium caseinate-fat emulsion (standard coating)	(Still in use)

[1] All sandwiches are coated with gelatin during manufacture.

Throughout Project Gemini, volume constraints were influential factors in meal design. Their effect was most noticeable on the longest Gemini flight, Gemini 7. Difficulties encountered in stowing the planned 14-day food supply in the allotted compartments led to an unplanned reduction in the amount of food and consequently the calories supplied Borman and Lovell. Thirty-seven percent of the total number of servings stowed aboard the ten manned Gemini flights were provided in the form of bite-sized food units. These foods made a variable but significant contribution to the nutrient content of each Gemini menu. They contributed from 35 to 62% of the total amount of protein furnished.

For Apollo 7, Cunningham, Schirra, and Eisle received 50%, 47% and 39%, respectively, of their calories in the form of bit-sized foods; on Apollo 8 and 9, a variety of 9 bite-sized foods furnished at least 40% of the total calories plus 45% of the total protein. On the Command Module menus of Apollo 10 and 11 their contribution dropped to approximately 29% of total calories and 26% of the total protein. The availability of thermostabilized wet meats and fresh bread and sandwich fillings on Apollo 10 and subsequent flights has resulted in a decrease in the number of bite-sized foods (e.g., sandwiches and meat bites) selected by the astronauts. Notwithstanding the availability of fresh bread and sandwich fillings the bite-sized sandwiches have not been completely eliminated from the flight menus. Bite-sized beef, chicken, and cheese sandwiches were selected for individual menus on Apollo 11 and 14 flights.

Rehydratable Foods

For almost a decade before man's first flight into space, a variety of freeze-dried foods, both raw and cooked, were under development as operational rations for the U.S. Armed Forces. Precooked, freeze-dried foods are prepared for consumption simply by the addition of water. These products (soups, meats, salads, vegetables, fruits, puddings, cereals, and beverages) were adapted to the exacting requirements of NASA (Table S-29) and have subsequently been improved. Figure S-11 depicts these foods packaged in the special reconstitution package and feeder as utilized throughout Project Gemini. Apollo has utilized a similar package (Fig. S-12). The attached tablet is an antiseptic to stabilize whatever food remained in the pouch after the astronaut had finished eating. A major problem was the attainment of acceptable meats, soups, and vegetables with only 27°C water for reconstitution. The availability of 68°C water on Apollo has improved acceptability. In addition, new classes of freeze-dried products, such as meat salads, have been developed and qualified for space feeding. To improve the texture and chewability of meat and gravy, meat and vegetables, and chicken salad entrees for Apollo flight menus, the meat constituents are being "textured" prior to cooking and

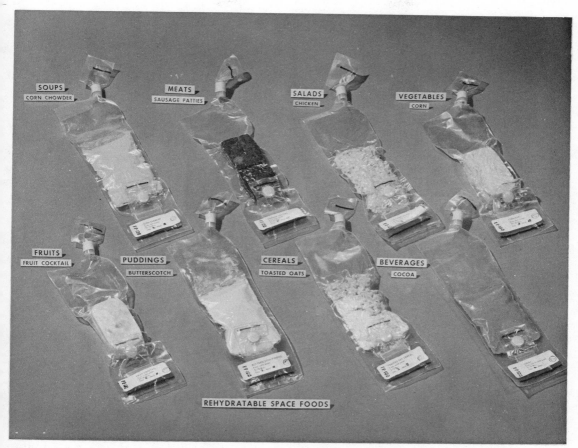

FIG. S-11. REHYDRATABLE FOODS IN THESE SPECIAL FEEDER PACKAGES WERE EITHER PRECOOKED AND FREEZE DRIED OR DRY MIXES; AFTER RECONSTITUTION IN FLIGHT, THEY WERE CONSUMED DIRECTLY FROM THE PACKAGE

dicing by a special process.[2] In addition, the size of the meat dice has been increased from $1/4$ in. to $3/8$ in.

High caloric soups were formulated by using a coffee whitener as a creaming agent. Experience has shown that high sugar levels in fruits potentiate the problem of foaming and thawing during freeze drying. Therefore a reduction in the sucrose content of sweetened fruits was found necessary. Compaction of the fruit before freeze drying resulted in better control of bulk density. Rehydratable fruits and natural fruit juices packaged in flexible pouches under high vacuum caked and fused when held at 38°C for 2 weeks. For

applesauce this problem was resolved by starting with freshly peeled, cored and cooked apples; pressing out and discarding 50–60% of their juices; freeze drying the pressed apple pulp; comminuting it; and adding sufficient sucrose and malic acid to replace the fruit sugars and flavor lost in the juice extraction step. No means have been found to prevent natural fruit juices from hardening under high vacuum conditions. As an expedient, the astronauts have been furnished commercial formulated fruit flavored drinks as a substitute for natural citrus and other juices. For Apollo 12 and subsequent flights, however, NASA relaxed the vacuum packaging requirement to permit dehydrated natural orange juice to be packaged at a slight positive pressure under nitrogen. Fresh bread has been similarly packaged since Apollo 10.

As the result of improvements in the precooked, dehydrated entrées of the Food Packet, Long

---

[2] Developed by Swift & Company, subcontractor to the Whirlpool Corporation, St. Joseph, Michigan (NASA Contract NAS9-9032).

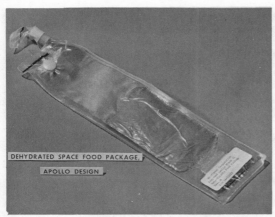

FIG. S-12. A CLOSEUP OF THE REHYDRATABLE FEEDER PACKAGE—USED ON THE APOLLO PROJECT—SHOWING THE ATTACHED ANTISEPTIC TABLET TO STABILIZE WHATEVER FOOD REMAINED IN THE POUCH UNEATEN

FIG. S-13. THE "SPOON AND BOWL" ZERO GRAVITY FEEDER USED ON APOLLO FLIGHTS

Feeder was provided with a valve to facilitate rehydration with the standard hot water probe provided on the Apollo vehicle; then could be opened at opposite end for feeding (see Fig. S-14).

Range Patrol, the following freeze-dried items were adopted for space flight beginning with Apollo 10: spaghetti with meat sauce, beef stew, chicken stew, and pork with escalloped potatoes. NASA introduced these products in a new package, the "spoon and bowl" zero gravity feeder[3] (Fig. S-13). The feeder has a valve to facilitate rehydration of the food with the standard hot water probe provided on the Apollo vehicle. After reconstitution food is consumed with a spoon. As shown in Fig. S-14, the lower zipper, in the open mode, serves as a scraper to prevent contamination of the top zipper which serves as a closure system. After food contents have been removed and the antimicrobial agent added, the zippers are closed and the package stored in the waste area. This spoon and bowl feeder has replaced the standard Apollo feeder for all rehydratables, excepting beverages. Beverages are still packaged as shown in Fig. S-12.

Microbiological standards were developed for dehydrated foods to safeguard their microbiological wholesomeness. Table S-29 presents the current microbiological standards. All bite-sized and rehydratable foods produced for space flight use are tested against these standards.

Thermostabilized Wet Products

Early in Project Gemini, it was postulated that astronauts would someday eat normally in space. As early as 1966, plans were made for testing concepts of utensils for eating and preparation of sandwiches. At that time it was believed that

products to be eaten with a spoon would have to be quite viscous. Subsequently the Air Force, using aircraft flying parabolic paths, proved the feasibility of eating all types of food, except liquids, with a spoon under zero gravity conditions.

These experiments enabled NASA to introduce a fourth category of food into space flight menus—normally moist heat-sterilized meat items processed in a flexible pouch. The most popular items are shown in Fig. S-15. A fourth item, turkey and gravy, was furnished each member of the Apollo 8 crew in a special Christmas meal pack. This menu included three rehydratables (cranberry applesauce, grape drink, and coffee) and a spoon. The

FIG. S-14. FOOD IS CONSUMED WITH A SPOON WHEN FEEDER IS OPEN

[3] NASA Contract NAS 9-9032, Whirlpool Corporation, St. Joseph, Michigan.

FIG. S-15. THIS NEW CATEGORY OF SPACE FOOD WAS INTRODUCED ON THE APOLLO PROJECT AND CONSISTED OF NORMALLY MOIST HEAT-STERILIZED MEAT ITEMS SUCH AS FRANKFURTERS, MEAT BALLS, BEEF AND GRAVY

turkey and gravy was provided in bite-sized pieces ($^3/_4 \times {}^3/_4 \times {}^5/_8$ in.) with a normal moisture content, and was consumed with the spoon. Actually, the gravy was quite viscous at ambient temperature. However, since a heater is to be provided on future

Apollo spacecraft, no attempt has been made to modify the consistency of the gravy, which thins down when heated. The turkey and gravy were highly acceptable even when eaten unheated.

The frankfurters, offered for the first time on Apollo 11, were developed for a military combat ration. Since commercial frankfurters burst and became mushy after heat processing when packaged under a partial vacuum in a flexible pouch, the use of a specially formulated, all meat, skinless frankfurter was deemed essential. The frankfurters which proved satisfactory were made by Oscar Mayer Company. This product has shown excellent storage stability—no significant difference in preference was found by a panel of 26 consumers between products stored for 1 yr at 4°C or at 38°C.

The formula and procedure for meat balls for Apollo 13 is the same as prescribed in the military specification (MIL-M-43506) for precooked, dehydrated meat balls for operational ration use, except that the freezing and freeze drying steps are omitted. The deep fat fried meat balls are mixed with a sauce containing tomato paste, water, oil, seasonings, and spices. Each pouch contains 20–21 meat balls (78 gm) and 50 gm of tomato sauce.

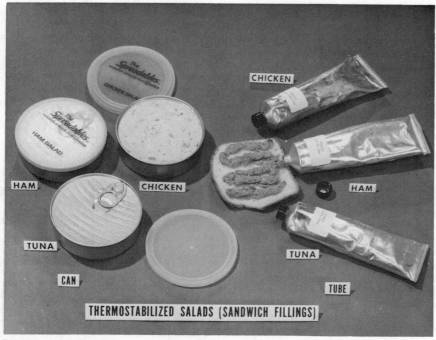

FIG. S-16. ANOTHER PROTOTYPE FOOD USED ON THE APOLLO PROJECT WAS THERMOSTABILIZED SEMISOLID TYPE SANDWICH FILLINGS PROCESSED IN ALUMINUM TUBES WHICH LATER APPEARED AS A COMMERCIAL PRODUCT CALLED "SPREADABLES"

The technological problems associated with processing wet products in flexible containers was solved in earlier work on Armed Forces ration components. These products are thermally processed in a retort equipped with racks and dividers which provide physical separation of the pouches to ensure uniform heat penetration into each package. Sufficient and closely controlled overriding air pressure is maintained to prevent straining of pouch seals during processing. A thermoprocessing F_0 value of 8 is attained.

All thermostabilized meat products used to date by NASA have been prepared at the U.S. Army Natick Laboratories. A space food prototype production guide for Meat Products, Thermostabilized, has been prepared for in-flight-food certification documentations in accordance with operational requirements of NASA. Since these are experimental items and not in routine production precautions are being taken to assure their wholesomeness. In current production, the reliability of the heat treatment was assured by incubating $1/6$ of the production lot at $32°C$ and $1/6$ at $55°C$ for 20 days and then applying a sterility test to $1/2$ of each group of incubated samples. This involved further incubation in tryptic soy broth for 5–7 days at $32°C$ and at $55°C$. The performance of the foil laminated material used for the package was established by a thorough testing program. However, the integrity of the container seals when subjected to pressures to 10^{-6} torr had to be determined. Six pouches from each lot were subjected to pressures of 10^{-6} torr for 6 cycles. There has been no evidence of product leakage, bursting of the package, or delamination as a result of these tests. To complete the flight qualification test requirements, product from each lot is rated for preference on a 9-point hedonic scale by a consumer panel of at least 36 testers. Thermostabilized, semisolid type sandwich fillings (ham, chicken, and tuna salads) were specially formulated (Trenton Foods Division of Carnation Company) at approximately 60% moisture content. They were processed in aluminum tubes (and later as a commercial item in aluminum cans) in a hyperbaric chamber to minimize texture and flavor changes normally occurring in heat processed foods. Ham salad, packaged in an aluminum tube, was the first such item to be used (Apollo 10) (Fig. S-16). Subsequently, commercial counterparts of these salads packaged in an aluminum can with an easy-open type top were utilized on the Command Module menus. The aluminum tubes are still used on all Lunar Module menus. NASA added two thermostabilized puddings (lemon and vanilla) and two fruits (peaches and mixed fruit) packaged in aluminum easy-open type cans to the Apollo 14 menu. All products are

from commercial production. Three additional flexibly packaged sandwich fillings have been included on later Apollo flight menus—peanut butter, cheese spread, and jelly. These products were thermostabilized immediately before packaging (hot fill) into foil laminate pouches.

Intermediate Moisture Foods

Commercially produced dried apricots, peaches and pears, approximately 27% moisture by weight, were packaged under a partial vacuum and included on Apollo 10 and all subsequent Apollo flight menus. Foods such as these fruits fall into the intermediate moisture food category. They owe their microbiological stability to a reduced water activity but contain too much water to be classified as dry.

Jellied fruit candy, long popular as a military ration component, is classed as an intermediate moisture Apollo confection. After being vacuum packaged the product is placed in a $57°C$ oven for 30 min. This fuses the sugar coating applied to prevent stickiness so that it will not pose a crumb hazard in the spacecraft. Bacon squares, the most popular of the bite-sized meat items, is an intermediate moisture food. This item has been on every space flight menu since Gemini 3.

Intermediate moisture foods are potentially advantageous for special military and space feeding situations. Being low in moisture content they provide a concentrated source of calories. Being plastic they can be molded to any desired form. Being moist they are suitable for direct consumption without giving rise to the sensation of harsh dryness usually associated with the direct consumption of freeze-dried foods. Furthermore, the texture of intermediate moisture foods is much

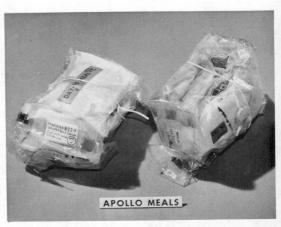

FIG. S-17. SPACE FOOD MEALS WERE ASSEMBLED AND OVERWRAPPED IN FLAME-PROOF FLUOROHALOCARBON FILM FOR THE APOLLO FLIGHTS

TABLE S-31

DAY 2 MENUS OF GEMINI AND APOLLO FLIGHTS 7 AND 12

Gemini 7		Gemini 12		Apollo 7 (Cunningham)		Apollo 12 (Conrad, CDR)	
Meal A		**Meal A**		**Meal A**		**Meal A**	
Chicken and gravy	R	Applesauce	R	Applesauce	R	Apricots	IMB
Beef sandwiches (6)	DB	Sugar frosted flakes	DB	Beef hash	R	Sausage patties	R
Applesauce	R	Bacon squares (8)	R	Cinnamon toast (8)	IMB	Scrambled eggs	RSB
Peanut cubes (6)	DB	Cinnamon toast (6)	DB	Apricot cereal cubes (8)	DB	Grapefruit drink	R
		Cocoa	R	Grapefruit drink	R	Coffee w/sugar	R
		Orange drink	R				
Meal B		**Meal B**		**Meal B**		**Meal B**	
Orange-grapefruit drink	R	Beef w/vegetables	R	Tuna salad	R	Turkey and gravy	WP
Beef pot roast	R	Meat and spaghetti	R	Beef sandwiches (8)	DB	Cheese crackers (4)	DB
Bacon and egg bites (6)	DB	Chicken sandwiches (6)	DB	Cinnamon toast (8)	DB	Chocolate pudding	RSB
Chocolate pudding	R	Apricot pudding	R	Butterscotch pudding	R	Orange-grapefruit drink	R
		Gingerbread (6)	DB	Pineapple-grapefruit drink	R		
		Grapefruit drink	R				
Meal C		**Meal C**		**Meal C**		**Meal C**	
Potato soup	R	Pea soup	R	Beef and vegetables	R	Pork and scalloped potatoes	RSB
Shrimp cocktail	R	Tuna salad	R	Barbecued beef bites (8)	R	Bread slice	DB
Date fruitcake (4)	DB	Cinnamon toast (6)	DB	Cinnamon toasted bread cubes (8)	DB	sandwich spread	WP
Orange drink	R	Date fruitcake (4)	R	Banana pudding	DB	Jellied candy	IMB
		Pineapple-grapefruit drink	R	Orange drink	R	Cocoa	R
						Orange drink	R
Day's total calories 2304		Day's total calories 2514		Day's total calories 2503		Day's total calories 2346	

Legend:

IMB—Intermediate Moisture Bite
R—Rehydratable
RSB—Rehydratable Spoon-Bowl
WP—Wet Pack
DB—Dry Bite

TABLE S-32

SKYLAB BASELINE FOOD LIST

(1) Ham sandwich spread (T)[1]	(37) Pea soup (R)
(2) Butterscotch pudding (T)	(38) Pineapple (T)
(3) Tuna sandwich spread (T)	(39) Lobster Newburg (F)
(4) Lemon pudding (T)	(40) Turkey and gravy (T)
(5) Dry roasted peanuts (W)	(41) Hard candy (W)
(6) Vanilla ice cream (F)	(42) Grape drink (B)
(7) Dried apricots (W)	(43) Applesauce (T)
(8) Orange crystals (B)	(44) Hot dogs (T)
(9) Sugar cookie wafers (W)	(45) Potato salad (R)
(10) Grapefruit crystals (B)	(46) Peaches (T)
(11) Cheddar cheese cracker (W)	(47) Pears (T)
(12) Mints (W)	(48) Biscuit (W)
(13) Sausage patties (R)	(49) German potato salad (R)
(14) Ham and cheese cracker (W)	(50) Cocoa-flavored instant breakfast (B)
(15) Sugar-coated cornflakes (R)	(51) Shrimp cocktail (R)
(16) Scrambled eggs (R)	(52) Cheddar cheese sandwich spread (T)
(17) Bacon wafers (W)	(53) Turkey rice soup (R)
(18) Mustard (T)	(54) Rice Krispies (R)
(19) White bread (F) or (I)	(55) Chicken and rice (R)
(20) Catsup (T)	(56) Creamed peas (R)
(21) Filet mignon (F)	(57) Chicken and gravy (R)
(22) Asparagus (R)	(58) Cocoa (B)
(23) Lemonade (B)	(59) Pork and scalloped potatoes (R)
(24) Prebuttered roll (F)	(60) Orange drink (B)
(25) Salmon salad (R)	(61) Mashed sweet potatoes (R)
(26) Pork loin w/dressing and gravy (F)	(62) Black coffee (B)
(27) Strawberries (R)	(63) Beef hash (R)
(28) Vanilla wafer (commercial cookie) (W)	(64) Stewed tomatoes (T)
(29) Ham (T)	(65) Cream style corn (R)
(30) Canadian bacon and applesauce (R)	(66) Tea with lemon and sugar (B)
(31) Coffee cake (F)	(67) Sliced dried beef (W)
(32) Mashed potato (R)	(68) Prime rib of beef (F)
(33) Peanut butter (T)	(69) Peach Ambrosia with pecans (R)
(34) Chili with meat (T)	(70) Fruit beverage (B)
(35) Cream of tomato soup (R)	(71) Veal and barbecue sauce (R)
(36) Fruit jam (T)	(72) Spaghetti and meat sauce (R)

[1] Interpretation of symbols: (T)—Thermostabilized; (W)—Wafer or Bite-Sized or Natural State; (F)—Frozen; (R)—Rehydratable; (B)—Beverage; (I)—Irradiated.

closer to normal food than the crisp or rigid structure of freeze-dried and other fully dehydrated foods.

Current research is directed toward the attainment of a wide variety of intermediate moisture foods of high acceptability. The desirability of such foods for space flight use was reported at the 29th National Meeting of the Institute of Food Technologists, Chicago, Illinois, May 1969.

Packaging

A clear, 4-ply flexible laminate comprised of an inner and outer layer of polyethylene with fluorohalocarbon and polyester layers between is used for packaging of all dehydrated and intermediate moisture foods. A heat processable, laminated packaging material (modified polyolefin-aluminum foil-polyester) is used for all wet foods. A flameproof fluorohalocarbon film is employed as a meal overwrap material (Fig. S-17), and as a package for fresh bread. Throughout Project Gemini and until Apollo 11 flight food was always packaged and supplied as meals, three per man per day. To give the Apollo 11 and all subsequent Apollo crews the option of planning their own menu in flight, NASA authorized stowage of approximately $1/2$ of the food items loose in one of the stowage compartments; 5 days of food continues to be supplied as prepacked overwrapped meals.

Menus

Menus are planned for each flight. The 3-meal schedule adopted since the Gemini 5 flight is acceptable to the astronauts; a 4-day menu cycle is

FIG. S-18. THE NEW COLLAPSIBLE BEVERAGE DIS-
PENSER DEVELOPED FOR SKYLAB

stabilized wet products and intermediate moisture foods to the Apollo diet is most evident in the reduction in the number of bite-sized foods used in these Apollo menus.

Skylab[4]

The scope of the Skylab foods is revealed by the list of 72 Skylab foods (Table S-32). The Skylab was launched early in 1973. Each manned phase of the Skylab program had a crew of three astronauts. The 1st Skylab mission had a scheduled duration of 28 days, followed by 2 more flights of 56 days each.[5] Each crewmember had an individualized menu. The Skylab flight menus were computer calculated and adjusted in real time as a function of crew selection in order to carefully control nutrient intake during the mission. Skylab foods were packaged in drawn aluminum cans with full-panel pull-out lids. At meal time, the astronaut assembled these cans into meals in the Skylab food warmer/retainer tray. Skylab foods, other than beverages, were consumed in flight from the opened cans, using tableware. Skylab beverages

used with repetition as dictated by the flight schedule.

Table S-31 compares the Day 2 menu for the Gemini 7, Gemini 12, Apollo 7 and Apollo 12 flights. Two-day menus similar to those for Apollo 12 are also provided on the Lunar Module.

The impact of adding fresh bread, thermo-

[4] The Section on Skylab foods and the Shuttle Food System following are adapted from Space Foods (in mimeo) by C. S. Huber, N. D. Heidelbaugh, M. C. Smith, NASA, and Mary Klicka of U.S. Army Natick Laboratories, Natick, Mass.

[5] Actually, these flights were extended to 59 and 84 days, respectively.

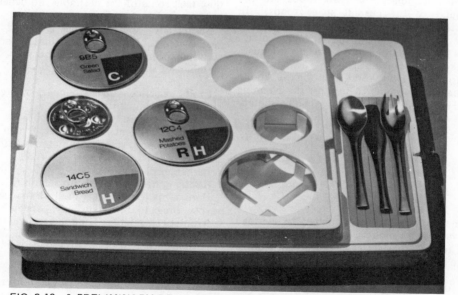

FIG. S-19. A PRELIMINARY DESIGN FOR A SHUTTLE FOOD TRAY WHICH MIGHT ATTACH TO THE CREW COUCH AND WHERE HOT AND COLD TEMPERATURE CONTROL COULD BE SUPPLIED TO DIFFERENT TYPES OF FOODS REQUIRING DIFFERENT EATING TEMPERATURES

were packaged in a new collapsible dispenser (Fig. S-18) that improved the convenience of consumption of liquid food in null-gravity.

Shuttle

The Shuttle Food System design studies are making maximum utilization of techniques of food processing, packaging, and in-flight handling learned from other space programs. Initial shuttle launches are planned for the late 1970's. The Shuttle Food System is designed for minimal overall weight and volume, maximal product quality and stability. In previous systems, such requirements favored the use of rehydratable and dehydrated foods. A preliminary design for the shuttle food tray as it might attach to the crew couch at meal time is given (Fig. S-19). This food tray configuration closely resembles the Skylab tray. For the Shuttle tray, however, initial studies favor food temperature control by circulating hot and cold water as opposed to the resistance heaters that were built for Skylab.

The Shuttle Food System design studies are an example of the analytical procedures used to identify space food system characteristics and optimal benefit-penalty ratios in process and standard selection. A Shuttle Food System analysis tree was developed with each segment of the tree undergoing interface definition and trade-off analyses to identify optimal criteria for each system element.

Dry and unfamiliar, bite-sized foods are the least popular of the current space foods. In planning the Apollo menus, NASA was most concerned with encouraging the astronaut to eat. This is NASA's approach to assuring adequate food intake and good nutrition. The new categories of food which were added during the Apollo program have done much to support the planning of menus better aligned to the individual dietary preferences of the astronauts.

MARY V. KLICKA

SPICES

The term "spices" can be applied to a broad range of vegetable products used for the flavoring of foods and pharmaceuticals. Although applied to some extent in perfumery, they should not be confused with the vegetable extracts used exclusively for their aromatic properties. As applied to foods, spices perform the dual role of flavor amelioration and excitement of the taste buds which, in turn, may have a beneficial effect on appetite and stimulation of the gastrointestinal function by increased salivation and gastric flow. So broad is the application of spices in food preparation that it may be said that there are few food items which do not contain one or more of the common spices. Many and varied food products marketed under well-known brand names derive much of their quality from the spice additives used, the formulas for which are, in many cases, carefully guarded secrets of their manufacturers. Since these formulas may stipulate not only the varieties of the combined spices but also their origin or place of growth, it will be seen that the spice traders operate in a field filled with the complexities of harvests, seasonal quality variables, cost fluctuations, product uniformity and trends in the food trade itself where these trends concern new food forms and consumer taste preferences.

End-product uniformity being the essential of successful national distribution, the attainment of absolute flavor uniformity in pure spices is sometimes impossible to obtain and, for this reason, the use of extractives is now widely practiced. Essential oils and oleoresins can be used "as is" or combined with a carrier such as salt or sugar to obtain the laboratory controlled uniformity in flavor intensity and character necessary for many processed or manufactured products. Extractives, however, cannot replace the pure or whole spices in all product categories for the reason that they do not withstand high temperature and fermentation process treatments; for certain applications they lack some of the desirable and delicate flavor notes.

Botanically, spices can be classified in seven groups—fruits, flowers, seeds, barks, roots, herbs and the aromatic vegetables, the most common members of which are:

Fruits: allspice, black pepper, white pepper, chilies, nutmeg, paprika, vanilla.
Flowers: cloves.
Seeds: anise, fennel, coriander, fenugreek, caraway, dill, poppy, sesame, cardamom, cumin, mustard.
Barks: cassia, cinnamon.
Roots: ginger, turmeric, horseradish.
Herbs: marjoram, sweet basil, thyme, sage, mint, savory, oregano, rosemary, bay, parsley.
Aromatic vegetables: onion, garlic, chives.

If spices were to be classified according to their properties, the list, in brief, would be:

Stimulating: peppers, mustard, horseradish, garlic.
Aromatic: anise, cardamom, cinnamon, cloves, ginger.

Herbals (sweet): marjoram, rosemary, basil, thyme, sage, etc.

The majority of mixed spice formulations are a blend of these three property types with greater or less accent on one of the particular properties or flavors. Many food products are characterized by the dominant spice such as oregano in pizza, pepper or garlic in some sausage varieties.

Correct flavor notes imparted by spices are to quite an extent dependent upon the freshness of the spice. As in all products of nature, deterioration can occur in storage and, to minimize this, the spice dealer must store his inventory under suitable conditions of temperature and atmospheric humidity. He must also protect his products from insect infestation and flavor cross-contamination. While the less volatile types may be stored in bags or sacks, others require moisture vapor and molecular barriers. Optimum storage facilities are, of course, most adequately provided by the supplier; and the user, except in the case of "hedge" buying, purchases in minimal economical quantities to ensure rapid inventory turnover and full flavor. Extractives are far more storage-stable.

While the greater percentage of spices is used by the processed food industry, a considerable volume finds its way into the home and restaurant kitchens. The herb garden of old has been replaced by the small jars and cans of whole and ground spices and few kitchens are without a spice rack. The availability of a wide range of spices in ready-to-use form has encouraged the interest in, and the making of, gourmet type dishes, and an outstanding job has been done through the public relations programs of the American Spice Trade Association which provide a steady flow of recipes and information through newspapers, magazines, radio, and television. Whereas 50 yr ago no more than about 6 spices were known to the average housewife, she is familiar today with about 4 times this number. It is perhaps unfortunate that spices in the home are usually stored on the shelves of the spice racks where they are subject to fluctuating temperatures, high humidity, and, in many cases, to the adverse effects of radiation from fluorescent lights. Under such conditions many spices, and particularly the leaf herbs, may lose much of their quality and fail to contribute their full flavor effect to the foods in which they are used. With the exception of the stronger aromatic and stimulating types, prepared spices on the home shelves should be replaced with new stock at least once per year.

Food Industry Spices

Prepared meats and convenience foods constitute some of the outstanding food industry developments of recent years. Their vast volume accounts for the great tonnages of spices of all kinds required today. The popularity of these foods can be credited to a great extent to the careful selection and blending of their flavor ingredients so as to appeal to the taste preferences of the majority of people. The great variety of sausage meats derive their individuality from the spice blends used. These are usually supplied as "seasoning mixes," the spice house being responsible for the maintenance of the standards that are of vital importance to the processor. In such seasoning mixes there may be as many as 12 or more spices in pure form, as extractives, or as a combination of pure and extractive. Such mixes are evaluated organoleptically and colorimetrically both in their raw state and following the preparation and cooking of the end product. The spice supplier's responsibility is an onerous one and to a great extent his customers are dependent upon him for the quality standards of their products.

Another spice application of major importance is in the snack food field. Items such as potato chips, crackers, biscuits, cookies, and puffed starch products come in a wide variety of flavors, nearly all of which derive from individual or blended spices. Meat-like flavors are obtained from blends of hydrolyzed proteins, autolyzed yeasts, protein derivatives, and spices. Such compounded flavorings find applications not only in snack foods but also in soup and sauce mixes, casserole bases, and prepared meat items.

That the United States is a major importer of spices is shown in the following table for the year 1968:

	Avg Price per Lb[1]	Imports (1000 Lb)	Value ($1000)
Allspice	0.69	1,022	708
Anise seed	0.24	369	88
Basil	0.30	133	40
Bay (laurel) leaves	0.19	662	123
Capsicum peppers (chilies)	0.26	15,063	3,898
Caraway seed	0.16	7,669	1,222
Cardamom seed	2.63	118	310
Cassia	0.60	8,966	5,422
Celery seed	0.22	3,790	835
Cinnamon	0.33	5,202	1,691
Cloves	0.39	3,919	1,525
Coriander seed	0.08	3,553	288
Cumin seed	0.14	3,952	559
Dill	0.12	711	84
Fennel seed	0.17	974	168
Ginger root	0.19	3,592	675
Mace	0.53	503	265
Marjoram	0.27	837	222
Mint leaves	0.62	100	62
Mustard seed	0.08	62,151	4,766

Nutmegs	0.40	4,107	1,625
Origanum leaves	0.24	3,279	782
Paprika	0.32	12,863	4,153
Parsley (manu-factured)	0.55	49	27
Pepper, black	0.27	48,827	13,000
Pepper, white	0.32	4,239	1,345
Poppy seed	0.19	8,074	1,528
Rosemary	0.07	832	57
Saffron (est)	100.00	NA	NA
Sage	0.25	2,687	674
Savory	0.16	4.4	0.7
Sesame seed	0.14	33,993	4,799
Tarragon	0.55	3.3	1.8
Thyme	0.16	618	101
Turmeric	0.16	3,384	556
Vanilla beans	4.55	2,160	9,835

[1] Price per pound in country of origin, exclusive of import duty, freight, and insurance charges; given in U.S. dollars.

These import totals represent approximately 25% of the estimated world production.

The common spices of the food trade comprise about 36 varieties some of the more important of which are described here.

Black Pepper (*Piper nigrum* L.)

Black pepper is the most important of all spices and amounts to about 25% of the spice trade.

The plant grows in tropical countries, native to the East Indies, India, Thailand, Vietnam, Cambodia, Indonesia, Ceylon, and Brazil. Black pepper is always sold by terms indicating origin, such as Malabar for Indian, Lampong for Indonesian, Saigon for Vietnamese and Cambodian, Ceylon, Sarawak, and Brazilian. Brazil is the only country in the Western Hemisphere growing pepper; it has been producing it in increasing quantities since World War II, during which period most of the pepper-growing countries were occupied by the Japanese.

The difference between peppers originating in different parts of the world is immense; not only in flavor and oil content, but also in appearance after grinding. The color may vary from a deep black to brown, grey or greenish.

Oil Content.—According to U.S. Government Standards, pepper must have a minimum of 6.75% nonvolatile ether extract.

Uses.—It is an essential for the housewife and in the manufacture of food products, such as pickles, soups, meat dishes, and sausages. It is the most important ingredient in frankfurters, bologna, hamburger, salami, pepperoni, mortadello, and fresh pork sausage. It is also an important in-gredient in pickling spice, curry powder, and poultry dressing. Pepper is frequently used in salt-free diets due to its pleasant tanginess.

White Pepper

White pepper is produced from fully-ripened black pepper berries. After being soaked in slow-flowing water for about a week, the outer black hull is removed, and the inner pepper-corns are then sun bleached.

The odor and taste are similar to that of black pepper, but less aromatic. The black shell of the pepper contains a fine flavor which is characteristic of natural black pepper only. This flavor is lost during the process of manufacture of white pepper.

Uses.—White pepper is used in products where the black color is objectionable, particularly in thin sausage such as frankfurters. White pepper is usually more expensive than the black, due to the extra cost of processing.

Red Peppers (*Capsicum* L.)

While as many as 90 species have been described it is probable that no more than 5–6 comprise the bulk of the cultivated ones. All are marketed as the dried pods or fruits under the common name of chilies and for practical purposes may be divided into two categories—sweet and hot.

Sweet Peppers.—The sweet varieties, after dehydrating and grinding, make a powder known as paprika. They are grown in California, Spain, Portugal, Hungary, Bulgaria, and Roumania.

There is a great difference in taste and color of paprikas. While paprikas from California, Hungary, Bulgaria, and Roumania have a pleasant flavor characteristic, the Spanish and Portugese can only be used as coloring agents in food products as they have little flavor. Paprika is the only item permitted by U.S. and Canadian food regulations to be used in meat dishes and sausages as a coloring agent, due to the high vitamin C content. The varieties containing flavor are used in garnishing fish, meat dishes, salad dressings, and in the manufacture of sauces, catsup, and Mexican chili powder. In diced form they are used for eye-appeal in potato salad, cole slaw, and similar products.

Hot Peppers (Cayenne).—The hot varieties are grown in Japan, Nigeria, China, Central America, and in the southern part of the United States. Cayenne contains more pungency than black pepper and was used during World War II as an additive to imitation black and white pepper.

Uses.—Cayenne is used for flavoring of meats, sauces, and fish dishes. It is an important ingredient in sausages, particularly the Italian varieties which are hot in character such as pepperoni and mortadella. It is a necessary component of curry powder and pickling spice.

Oil Content.—According to U.S. Government Standards, cayenne, red or paprika should contain a minimum of 15% of nonvolatile ether extract.

Allspice (*Pimenta dioica* L.)

This spice is native to Jamaica, Central America, and Mexico. According to U.S. regulations labeling as pure allspice is allowed for Jamaica material only, which indeed contains the most characteristic fragrance of allspice.

The name "allspice" was given to the pimento berry because its flavor contains a resemblance to a combination of spice, cloves, cinnamon, and nutmeg. The marketing of allspice is now a monopoly of the Jamaica government which controls the quality and the pricing.

Oil Content.—Jamaica allspice will yield 3–4$\frac{1}{2}$% volatile oil.

Uses.—Allspice is an important flavoring agent in smoked meats, sausages, gravies, relishes, pies, puddings, pickles, catsup, and fish dishes. It is also an important ingredient in the formulation of pastry spice, curry powder, and poultry dressing.

Nutmeg and Mace (*Myristica fragrans* L.)

These are native to Grenada and Indonesia. In the trade they are distinguished by the names of West Indian and East Indian nutmeg. There is a substantial difference between the flavor of the two. West Indian nutmeg will yield a higher oil content, but the East Indian contains more fragrance and subtle aroma. While in the United States both varieties are popular, in Canada only West Indian (Grenada) is being imported, due to the fact that there is no custom duty applied to materials from the West Indies.

The membrane covering the seed shell of the nutmeg is separated and is known as mace. It is somewhat less "sweet" than nutmeg and has an orange color whereas nutmeg powder is brownish.

Oil Content.—Nutmeg will yield 7–15% of volatile oil. The grinding process of nutmeg is a complicated one if the volatile oils are to be preserved.

Uses.—Nutmeg and mace are used in puddings, sauces, pies, sausages, mincemeat, cake mixes, and the manufacture of pastry spice and apple seasoning.

Cinnamon and Cassia (*Cinnamomum* L.)

Native to China, Burma, Indonesia, Vietnam, Ceylon. While originally the word cinnamon was applied to the Ceylon quills (rolled bark), today all ground cinnamon sold on the North American continent is made from cassia. The difference is in the bark; while the cinnamon is a delicate thin bark of a yellowish brown color, cassia is a thicker and coarser bark of reddish brown, sometimes grayish cast. There is also a difference in flavor: cinnamon has a fine, delicate aroma; cassia has a more pungent, sweet, and astringent taste. The best cassia is grown in Vietnam, and called Saigon. Next in quality is Chinese. Indonesia cassia is graded as A, B, and C.

Oil Content.—Cinnamon will yield 0.5–1% volatile oil. Cassia will yield 0.5–4% volatile oil.

Uses.—A very important spice in the baking industry for flavoring of buns, cakes, pies, puddings, and toasts. It is used by fruit canners and confectioners. It is a constituent of pastry spice, pickling spice, and mincemeat spice.

Ginger (*Zingiber officinale* L.)

This root is native to tropical Asia and is cultivated in the West Indies, India, Africa, China, Japan, and Indonesia. The best ginger is of Jamaican origin, which is classified as No. 1, No. 2, No. 3, and Ratoon. All Jamaican ginger has a fine aroma. Cochin ginger from India is next in quality. Cheaper goods come from Nigeria, Sierra Leone, Japan, Indonesia, and China. The annual world production is about 25,000 tons.

Oil Content.—Ginger will yield 1–3% volatile oil.

Uses.—Ginger is used for flavoring of pies, cookies, cakes, biscuits, gingerbread. It is included in formulas for sausage seasoning, mincemeat, curry powder, pastry spice. Huge quantities of ginger extractives are used in the manufacture of soft drinks and beverages. It is the essential ingredient in ginger ale.

Cloves (*Syzygium aromaticum* L.)

These are flower buds from an evergreen tree, native to Zanzibar, Madagascar, Indonesia, India, Ceylon, and Malaysia. Cloves have a very strong, aromatic, and pungent odor. They are graded according to appearance and impurities as No. 1, No. 2, and No. 3. According to the U.S. regulations, pure cloves shall not contain more than 5% of clove stems. Prices went up drastically from 33¢ per lb in 1967 to $2.00 in 1969.

Oil Content.—Cloves yield 14–21% volatile oil.

Uses.—Cloves are used for flavoring of hams, sausages, hamburger, soups, stews, pickles, catsup, cakes, puddings. Also it is a constituent of pickling spice, pastry spice, and poultry dressing.

Herbs (Sweet)

Described as "sweet" because they have no heat or "pepper bite." This group, for the most part, belongs to the mint family of plants. These include marjoram (*Majorum hortensis* L.), oregano (*Oreganum vulgare* L.), basil (*Ocimum basilicum* L.), thyme (*Thyme vulgaris* L.), sage (*Salvia officinalis* L.), peppermint (*Mentha piperita* L.), spearmint (*Mentha spicata* L.), savory (*Satureja hortensis* L.) and rosemary (*Rosemarinus officinalis* L.). While there is some confusion between marjoram and oregano, it is generally recognized that the so-called Mexican oregano is *Lippia graveoleus*, a member of the verbena family. Bay leaves (*Laurus nobilis*), used as a spice herb, should not be confused with the West Indian bay (*Pimenta acris* L.) the leaves of which are used to make bay rum.

The sweet herbs are used individually, or in combination, for the flavoring of a great number of foods of all kinds; and the mints, as extracted oils, are used in confectionery, toothpaste, and other products.

Celery Seed (*Apium graveolens* L.)

This seed is native to Southern Europe and is now cultivated in large quantities in India and France. While the Indian variety is a light brown seed, the French is darker in appearance. The flavor of the French variety is mellow and pleasant and is of better value than the Indian. During 1969-1970, the price went up from 30¢ to $2.00 per lb.

Oil Content.—Celery seed will yield 2.5-3% essential oil.

Uses.—Celery in ground or extracted form is an important ingredient in soups, sauces, and chicken loaf. It is used in pickling spices and celery salt.

Fennel Seed (*Foeniculum vulgare millar* L.)

A member of the parsley family, native to Europe. It is cultivated in India, Italy, France, Syria, Japan, and Russia. While the Indian variety is of a bright green color the others are darker in appearance.

Oil Content.—Fennel seed will yield 4-6% essential oil.

Uses.—Popular in Italian and Spanish dishes for cooking and baking. It is also used in fish dishes, sauces, and pastry spice.

Anise Seed (*Pimpinella anisum* L.)

A member of the parsley family, native to Egypt and cultivated in countries of warm climates, such as Spain, Mexico, and the Middle East countries. While the Spanish and Mexican seeds are greenish-gray and larger in size, those from the Middle East are grayish-brown and small. Another variety called Star Anise is derived from a small tree of the Mongolia family. This seed has a more pungent flavor and is widely used in the Far East.

Oil Content.—Anise seed will yield 2-3% essential oil.

Uses.—In the confectionery trade to flavor licorice and other candies. In the baking trade to flavor cakes, cookies, and biscuits. In the liqueur industry for flavoring Anisette.

Caraway Seed (*Carum carvi* L.)

A member of the parsley family, native to temperate climate areas of Europe such as Holland, Poland, and Russia, as well as North America.

Oil Content.—Caraway will yield 3-7% volatile oil.

Uses.—It is the principal flavoring in rye bread. In Europe it is used in cakes, biscuits, cheeses, sauerkraut, and as a flavoring for Kümmel liqueur.

Cardamom (*Elettaria cardamomum matom* L.)

A member of the ginger family of plants native to India and cultivated in Central America. They are sold in three forms: green, bleached, and decorticated.

Oil Content.—Cardamom will yield 3-8% essential oil.

Uses.—It is a flavoring ingredient of cookies, cakes and Danish pastries. It is also used in pork sausage, liver sausage, and hamburger.

Mustard Seed (*Sinapis alba* L.)

Native to Europe and Southwest Asia and cultivated in Holland, England, Germany, North Africa, and North America. There are two varieties: the yellow or white mustard and the black mustard seed. The black mustard when used in vinegar will give an irritating odor.

Oil Content.—Mustard seeds will yield 0.5-1% of volatile oil.

Uses.—Ground mustard is used with meats of all kinds, in salad dressings, sauces, and in the manufacture of prepared mustard.

Turmeric (*Curcuma longa* L.)

Native to Southeast Asia and cultivated in India, China, and the West Indies. The Indian turmeric is classified into Alleppey and Madras varieties. When ground, the Alleppey gives an orange-yellow color, while the Madras gives a lemon-yellow color.

Oil Content.—Turmeric will yield 5% of volatile oil.

Uses.—It is employed for coloring and flavoring of meat and egg dishes, prepared mustard, and in the composition of curry powder.

Future Spice Trends

Although, for the most part, spice flavorings derive from plants, there are also some synthetics or imitations. Vanillin has largely displaced pure vanilla in many products due to its lower cost and, though it lacks the subtle flavor notes and bouquet of pure vanilla, the consuming public is seldom capable of recognizing this. There are several other synthetics such as pepper, celery, and cloves, that are in limited use or in the development stage.

With developing affluence and changing attitudes in many parts of today's world there is a constant demand for new food forms with appealing flavors and greater convenience in preparation. Food technologists and scientists in ever-increasing numbers are continually developing new and better products tailored to the needs, tastes, and demands of the consumer. Prepared meals and meal items in cooked or ready-to-cook forms constitute one of the major developments of recent years and good flavor is imperative in these and other processed food products. It is sophisticated spicing that adds the gourmet touch and creates the true character of traditional dishes.

The trend to better eating is worldwide and this has led to so much demand for spices that shortages and market upheavals have occurred, with resulting prices in some cases soaring to as much as six times their previous level.

Increasing production costs, the requirement of land for food production, and the unattractive labor characteristics involved in spice growing and harvesting, make it reasonable to suppose that synthetics may eventually replace pure spices almost entirely. It is an exciting possibility that flavor chemistry may be able to create new and attractive spice-like flavors quite unknown today.

ARTHUR WOHL

Cross-reference: *Flavorings and Essences.*

STABILITY

The term stability is very broad and difficult to define in an uncomplicated way, even when restricted solely to foods. With food raw materials, raw materials undergoing processing, products undergoing storage, utilization, and subsequent nutritional and metabolic events, the term in general usually refers to resistance, qualitatively and kinetically, to one or more forms of undesirable changes.

Examples that will receive primary attention are not listed necessarily in the order of their economic, chemical or biological importance since the undesirable deterioration varies greatly in different food materials. The main changes include loss of organoleptic acceptability; unwanted changes in physical characteristics such as texture, color and appearance; development of toxic substances; and loss of nutritive value.

Before referring specifically to the nature of some of the more common forms of undesirable instability, several examples of changes that make it difficult to define food stability precisely should be cited. In a sense, the tenderizing of meats at temperatures slightly above freezing involves degradative changes from a chemical standpoint that are considered desirable. As a somewhat similar example, some cheeses are stored under controlled conditions to permit them to undergo desired changes in texture, odor, and flavor. In both of these types of products, physical, chemical, and biological changes occur, but are not considered to represent instability; instead they are regarded as normal processing.

In a somewhat different type of situation, certain foods during storage under abnormal temperatures, pressures, and other environmental conditions undergo changes, but when restored to normal conditions for greater or lesser periods of time, reacquire their original acceptability through reversal of the changes they have undergone or otherwise. They are not regarded as having been unstable, even when some permanent changes may have occurred.

Although many examples can be given that illustrate why a generalized definition of food stability is difficult, the third and last to be cited is somewhat more complex than the two previous examples. In many parts of India where ghee, the butter derived from Indian buffalo milk is consumed, refrigeration is not available generally. Under hot climatic conditions, ghee quite rapidly undergoes oxidative and other changes that produce odors and flavors characterized in other parts of the world as "rancid." In these regions of India, the product is not considered normal or desirable organoleptically until the rancid state has been attained, even though the rancidification reactions very likely reduce to some extent the nutritive value. Thus, in this case, rancidification appears to be regarded as normal processing.

The foregoing indicates that psychological, as well as physical, chemical, and biological factors are involved in evaluating food quality and stability. More specific definition requires different criteria for each food or class of food substances. All that can be said in general is that stability involves resistance to undesirable change in one or more of many properties.

Factors Involved in Food Stability

Stability, that is, the resistance of individual food materials to undesirable changes of various kinds, is dependent on an almost limitless number of factors. Only a summation, with almost no precise description of pathways and mechanisms, can be given in most cases.

Composition and Changes in Natural Components During Processing.—In addition to the three major quantitative classes of biological substances that are contained in food materials, i.e., proteins, carbohydrates, and fats, there are numerous naturally-occurring minor components whose stability, and effects on other components, may be important to acceptability and nutritive quality. Also, proportions and structures of the original components may be changed during processing. The stability of a food product may be enhanced or decreased by naturally-occurring minor components such as enzymes, vitamins, antioxidants, nonmetallic pigments, and naturally-occurring metallic complexes such as chlorophyll and hematin compounds, among others. Interactions between the naturally-occurring components (including also derivatives of natural components developed during processing) may be involved in undesirable changes.

External Factors.—Besides natural minor components, deliberately or adventitiously added minor components play important roles in stability in many cases. Deliberately added substances such as antioxidants to prevent damage by oxidation, and preservatives such as sodium benzoate, sodium chloride, and other additives to prevent damage by microorganisms are present in many foods. Alternatively, contamination by metallic compounds or microorganisms during processing or storage of food materials are often damaging.

Environmental oxygen and moisture are particularly notorious in reacting unfavorably with components on the surface of food substances, or by penetrating and reacting detrimentally within food materials. Other environmental conditions such as temperature, pressure, and light frequently play roles in reducing stability. In cases of exposure to visible or ultraviolet light, interactions with photochemical pigments or other light-sensitive substances sometimes produce undesirable products directly, or catalyze other reactions, notably oxidation, that produce undesirable changes.

Major Stability Problems and Preventative Measures

Obviously, the stability of food materials is a very complex subject because of many variations in content of major food components, effects of minor natural or added components that enhance or retard stability, and environmental factors.

Stability, in general, is an individual or unique problem with each raw food material or type of food product, and only a few more important examples are described. The selection of examples is based, in most cases, on factors that are common to stability in more than one type of food.

Proteins and Protein-Containing Products.—Perhaps some of the longest known and best understood forms of instability and deterioration are those in foods consisting mainly of protein.

The two principal forms of spoilage in uncooked meats and meat products involve breakdown caused by proteolytic enzymes that are present naturally in raw meat, and by contaminating microorganisms. Well-known methods for prolonging the stability of meat proteins involve storage at low or freezing temperatures, freeze dehydration, avoidance of microbial contamination, and addition of sodium chloride and other sodium salts with nitrogen-containing anions that assist not only in "curing" meats, but also inhibit to a considerable extent both enzymic and microbial deteriorative reactions.

Some meat products such as pork sausage are prone to becoming "sour," but this breakdown of fat as well as protein is caused largely by hydrolytic enzymes in the major components of the product and by microbial contaminants. Storage at low temperature and avoidance of microbial and other catalytic environmental factors are helpful, but generally not as effective as with unground meats.

Another important protein-containing food of animal origin, bovine milk, is subject to several deteriorative changes involving not only major components such as the casein and milkfat, but also minor components. The long-known process of pasteurization is still relied on as the major deterrent to the spoilage of whole milk by enzymes and microbial contaminants.

Precautions against introduction of microbial and metallic contaminants from the environment and processing equipment assist in retarding protein spoilage, hydrolytic rancidity, and the development of "oxidized" flavor.

However, none of the above precautions or treatments can preserve the quality of liquid forms of milk or important milk products such as butter for prolonged periods, even though stored at refrigerator temperatures. Some cheeses, however, maintain acceptable flavors for relatively long periods because induced microbial changes, which sometimes also apparently retard other undesired changes, are a part of their processing. In general, however, cheeses must also be protected from undue exposure to air and to conditions that lead to dehydration if they are to maintain acceptable quality for any appreciable time.

For prolonged storage of whole milk, skim milk, milkfat, and other milk derivatives, the most effective measures are dehydration, then storage under vacuum or inert gas, and storage at low temperatures. Most of these products, when used without further treatment, or after being reconstituted with water in the preparation of other products, can usually be made quite acceptable.

In general, aquatic food products, especially important varieties of edible fish, offer many stability problems similar to but more pronounced than those of terrestrial meat animals in that most of them consist primarily of major components that are more readily susceptible to spoilage. Some of the same precautions used with meats of land animals are successfully used to prolong their acceptability. However, there are two major complications in the preservation of fish and some other aquatic food products. First, fish contain fatty oils that are far more unsaturated in general than those of land animals and therefore are more susceptible to oxidative deterioration. Second, fish contain minor components that are derivatives chemically of quite simple amines, such as trimethyl amine; these amines are released quite readily if the fish or fish product is not preserved properly and are largely responsible for the principal offensive odors of spoiled fish.

Combating spoilage of fish and fish products as well as other marine products for relatively long periods involves storage of the whole product in a frozen state, or processing by heat treatment and packaging in sealed containers under conditions involving a maximal exclusion of oxygen. Also, salting or smoking or both, in some cases, produce products that, although differing greatly from the taste of the original fresh produce, are acceptable and nutritious and, at the same time, more stable.

In recent years a more serious problem, that may be regarded as a stability problem in a broad sense, has been found in vegetable sources of food proteins (some of which are important also as carbohydrate and oil sources). Under some conditions when some grains or seeds (soybeans, although frequently cited, are only one of a number of species) are stored after having become contaminated with certain molds, substances known as aflatoxins are produced, some of which are highly toxic to animals and man. The principal controls that are practiced at present are avoidance or elimination of the contaminant molds insofar as possible, and storage of the beans or seeds at low moisture levels and under other conditions that are unfavorable to mold growth and their production of the toxic materials.

Carbohydrate Foods.—In solid form, carbohydrate foods offer relatively few stability problems insofar as the carbohydrate is concerned. However, when an appreciable amount of moisture is present together with enzymes in some of the other food components, or together with inadvertent contamination by microorganisms, carbohydrate foods may sour or undergo a variety of other undesirable odor and flavor changes. The principal preventatives are elimination of contamination, application of heat, and control of moisture content. Also, preservatives such as sodium benzoate are helpful in some foods containing appreciable amounts of sugar.

Many food products that are not protected by proper packaging undergo undesirable changes in texture and flavor because of adding or losing moisture. Bakery products are particularly susceptible to such changes at ordinary temperatures.

If properly handled, the more common forms of food that contain vegetable protein can usually be stored for considerable periods before or after being processed, even at ambient temperatures. However, in certain food products that contain proteins in mixture with carbohydrates, the nitrogen-containing moieties of the protein may react with the aldehyde moieties of the carbohydrate in the well-known Maillard reaction to produce a brownish color that is unsightly, but is not known to be seriously damaging to the nutritional qualities of the foods. The rates of the Maillard or "browning" reactions are usually low, and can be made lower by storage under proper conditions of temperature and moisture. However, in a few cases, no highly effective method to eliminate this reaction economically has been found in food products where this is a pronounced problem.

Fats and Fat-Containing Products.—Foods that consist almost wholly or largely of triglyceride fats and oils are subject to two major types of deterioration: first, there are various oxidative reactions involving atmospheric oxygen, that at low levels produce various types of usually undesired odors and flavors; and second, hydrolytic reactions that involve contact of the fat or oil with moisture alone, or with moisture in the presence of microorganisms and lipolytic enzymes that catalyze hydrolytic reactions.

With all unsaturated fats and oils, but especially in those containing higher proportions of more unsaturated acyl moieties, highly undesirable odors and flavors are produced. In products derived from more saturated fats such as animal fats, the development of these forms of deterioration are retarded for quite long periods by addition of various antioxidants. With more highly unsaturated oils such as cottonseed, corn, and soybean oils, the problems are further alleviated in many products by partial hydrogenation.

The oxidative reactions are relatively complex chemically and are influenced by many positive and negative catalytic factors. The principal undesirable products that are formed include various short chain aldehydes, ketones, and acids. These are considered undesirable not only from the standpoint of flavors and odors, variously described by such terms as "rancidity," "reversion," and "oxidized flavor," but in addition the oxidation products are alleged, sometimes on the basis of doubtful evidence, to be toxic in various ways. However, it is well established that during the oxidative reactions, other valuable nutrients such as certain fat-soluble vitamins are destroyed.

The many factors that influence the course and kinetics of oxidation reactions of fats and oils include degree of unsaturation, presence of antioxidants or prooxidants (including natural biological antioxidants such as vitamin E and citric acid and also natural prooxidants such as hematin compounds), and environmental factors such as heat, light, and light in combination with photochemical pigments.

Among the more common synthetic antioxidants that are now employed in the preservation of fat-containing food products are propyl gallate, butylated hydroxyanisole, butylated hydroxytoluene, citric acid, tocopherol or vitamin E concentrates, or combinations of these at low concentrations.

Hydrolysis reactions may also produce unwanted sour odors and flavors in some fat and oil food products. In some products however, for example different types of dry sausage, a high level of free acidity may develop without impairing organoleptic acceptability or imparting any toxic or destructive nutritional effects. Unwanted hydrolytic reactions may be retarded or controlled by various means among which the more important are control of moisture content, avoidance of microbial and other types of contaminants that promote hydrolysis, destruction of enzymes by heat or suppressive additives, and storage at low temperature.

Summary

Most food substances consist of portions of at least 2 and usually 3 of the major components of food materials, that is, proteins, lipids, and carbohydrates. Consequently, stability problems are complicated in that deterioration of 1 of these 3 components will lead to products that will react with either or both of the other 2 components, and in many cases these forms of instability lead to unsuitable products for human consumption. Moreover, many minor constituents of food materials play very important roles in various aspects of the stability of foods, either because of undesirable organoleptic or nutritional influences that they may themselves exert directly because of their own changes under some conditions, but also because of positive or negative influences that

they may exert on the stability of major food components.

WALTER O. LUNDBERG

Cross-references: *Food Preservation; Quality Control and Statistics.*

STALING: BAKERY PRODUCTS

Bread starts to stale the minute it leaves the oven and the following changes take place: Moisture moves from the crumb, which has an initial moisture content of about 45% to the crust, which has a low moisture content of around 6%. Thus, the crumb becomes drier and the crust, originally dry and crisp, becomes moist, soggy and tough. Flavor changes occur either due to loss of flavor components to the atmosphere, absorption by the solid components of the bread, or chemical change due to oxidation or inter-reactions. The crumb becomes firm, harsh, opaque, more crumbly, and its ability to swell in water diminishes.

Thus, staling of bread is a complex combination of many changes, the total results of which can be determined only by a panel that has been selected because of the ability of its members to detect small differences in the age of bread. The development and use of such a panel have been described by Bechtel and Meisner (1954).

Methods have been developed to determine each of the individual changes (such as the approved Methods of the American Association of Cereal Chemists) but the method most commonly used to study staling is one to detect changes in compressibility or firmness of the loaf. There are several reasons for this. The most important of these is that this method is easy to use, and second, the compressibility of the loaf is the factor most usually employed by the housewife in selecting bread from the market place. She squeezes the loaf in the belief that the softer it is the fresher it is, and since industry is particularly interested that the bread move from the grocer's shelf, softness is an extremely important factor.

Softness, however, depends upon a number of factors other than age. A compact loaf fresh from the oven is always firmer than the blown-up loaves typical of commercial baking. Bakers employ certain surface active agents which tend to retard the swelling of the starch granule and, therefore, produce starch pastes within the loaf that are less firm than those produced without the use of the surface active agents. The most commonly-used softeners are monoglycerides of fat-forming fatty acids or combinations of mono- and digly-cerides of the same fat-forming acids. It is the monoglyceride fraction that is the active agent, however. These agents do not retard staling but, because they produce a softer loaf of bread, their use gives the impression of freshness.

The increase in the firmness of bread is due to the retrogradation of the starch which, of course, is the main component of bread flour. As starch retrogrades it becomes more crystalline and the starch paste, therefore, becomes firmer. Attempts have been made to use bacterial amylases (Herz 1965) as a means of keeping bread from firming. Under controlled temperature, just the right amount of bacterial amylase may be added to the dough so that enough of this heat-stable enzyme will remain in the bread to digest starch at the same rate it retrogrades so that starch paste doesn't become firm. Commercially, however, the baker has no control of the temperature of the bread in the retail outlet or the home. If the temperature is too low no starch is digested. If the temperature is too high, too much digestion results in a soggy mess.

The rate of retrogradation of starch is a function of temperature. Starch retrogrades faster at lower temperature than it does at higher temperatures. Thus, storing of bread in the refrigerator hastens the staling process. On the other hand, if the temperature is lowered to the point where bread freezes, retrogradation of starch and, therefore, the firming of the loaf is retarded. Bread can be maintained for long periods of time at $0°F$ without any detectible evidence of staleness after the bread has been properly thawed.

Of more importance than the firming of the crumb in the evaluation of staleness by the taste testing panel, is the migration of water from the crumb to the crust. This was studied by Bechtel, et al. (1953) who compared the sensory perception judgement of the freshness of bread stored with and without crust. Moisture, compressibility, crumbliness, and swelling power of the same bread were also determined. They found that the moisture content of the crumb from which the crust had been removed as soon as the bread had cooled, remained constant over a 140-hr period, whereas the moisture content of the crumb from the intact bread was reduced from 43.4 to 39.8% over the same period. The changes in the compressibility, crumbliness, and swelling power of the crustless crumb and crumb from the intact loaf, were identical at the end of 140 hr but the taste test panel judged that the crumb from the intact bread had retained only 14% of its original freshness, whereas the crumb from the crustless bread had retained

63% of its original freshness. These differences were significant below the 0.1% level. This undoubtedly is the reason that hearth breads stale at a much more rapid rate than breads baked in pans. Hearth breads have much more crust in proportion to crumb than the usual round-top of commerce and, therefore, there is a more rapid transfer of moisture from the crumb to the crust. The underbaking of bread, which is a common practice, probably actually slows the staling process by producing less crust to which the crumb moisture can migrate.

Bread can be refreshened by heating and, it is for this reason, that stale bread makes as good toast as does fresh bread, because in the toasting process the heat has reversed the staling phenomenon. Intact loaves of hearth bread, moistened with water and placed in the oven until the crust is dry, will be found to be fresh bread; a trick which is frequently used in Italian restaurants where good, fresh Italian bread is on the table.

No bakery products stale as rapidly as bread but even the richer bakery foods, such as cake, do stale if kept long enough. Frozen cakes are available on the market which after being "thawed" have all the characteristics of fresh cake. The reason for qualifying the word "thawed" is that the body of a cake contains so much sugar in relation to water that it really never freezes. Apparently, the starch component is deprived of sufficient moisture during the storage at $0°F$ so that it does not retrograde.

Dry bakery foods, such as crackers, also stale. They stale because they pick up moisture from humid air, providing sufficient moisture for the retrogradation of the starch in the cracker. They, like bread, can be refreshened by heating but here it is desired that the heat drive the moisture out of the product rather than drive the moisture from the surface of the product to the center.

Bread can deteriorate also through the action of microorganisms. Many different molds are capable of infecting bread. Bread, of course, is free of any viable mold when it leaves the oven but can become air contaminated during the cooling process before it is protected by the wrapper. Molding of bread is more troublesome during the hot weather than during the winter time. The best method of controlling mold is good sanitation in the bakery and the use of calcium propionate in the dough. The short chain propionic acid effectively retards but does not stop mold growth. The Standards of Identity for enriched bread provide for the use of calcium propionate up to a level of 0.32% of the weight of the flour used.

A much less frequently observed form of spoilage

is rope which is caused by a spore-forming organism, a strain of *Bacillus subtilis*. All flour contains some rope spores and if the conditions in a bakery are sufficiently unsanitary, there are moist doughs left in the equipment. This permits the organism to multiply to the point that some of the spores live through the baking process. Ropy bread develops an odor similar to that of an overripe cantaloupe and if one breaks a slice of this bread and pulls it apart, it will string out like taffy. This stringiness is due to the formation of polysaccharides by the rope organism. Rope can be prevented by good sanitation in the bakery. Should it develop, the baker not only needs to apply sanitary measures but needs to reduce the pH of his doughs and increase the amount of calcium propionate employed.

WILLIAM B. BRADLEY

References

BECHTEL, W. G., and MEISNER, D. F. 1951. Present status of the theory of bread staling. Food Technol. *5*, 503.

BECHTEL, W. G., and MEISNER, D. F. 1954. Staling studies of bread made with flour fractions. II. Selection of the sensory test panel. Cereal Chem. *31*, 171.

BECHTEL, W. G., MEISNER, D. F., and BRADLEY, W. B. 1953. The effect of the crust on the staling of bread. Cereal Chem. *30*, 160.

BRADLEY, W. B., and THOMPSON, J. B. 1950. The effect of crust on changes in crumbliness and compressibility of bread crumb during staling. Cereal Chem. *27*, 331.

HERZ, K. O. 1965. Staling of bread—a review. Food Technol. *19*, 1836.

SHOCH, T. J., and FRENCH, D. 1947. Studies on bread staling. I. The role of starch. Cereal Chem. *24*, 231.

STANDARDS, FOOD

See USDA Grade Standards for Food.

STARCHES

Occurrence, Structure and Properties

Starch is a reserve carbohydrate found principally in the seeds, roots, tubers, fruits, and sometimes in the pith of plants. It occurs as very small water-insoluble granules, usually associated with proteins, fats, and inorganic salts. The granules vary in shape and size ranging from about 1 to 100 μ in diameter depending on the source. With the aid of a microscope the granules can be seen easily and the starch type can sometimes be identified by physical appearance.

Granules are composed of linear and branched molecules, i.e., amylose and amylopectin, respectively. These molecules are deposited within the granules in regions of high and low density that are held together by hydrogen bonds. The high density regions are crystalline as evidenced by X-ray and microscopic data. When heated in water, the crystalline regions are destroyed and the granules progressively swell and finally rupture with release of amylose, amylopectin, but generally with some small fragments of the swollen granule remaining. The temperature at which granule swelling occurs varies with different starches, but usually this occurs between 60° and 73°C. Also, all granules of a given starch do not swell at the same temperature, but generally over a 10°–15°C temperature range. Root and tuber starches often swell at lower temperature than cereal starches. The recently-developed high amylose starch requires temperatures well above 100°C to effect complete swelling.

The temperature at which maximum swelling occurs is called the pasting or gelatinization temperature. This is also the temperature at which maximum viscosity develops. Prolonged heating and high shearing forces introduced by stirring reduce viscosity by disintegration of the swollen granules. The pasting temperature of starch can be lowered by derivatization, or by addition of chemicals such as urea, ammonium thiocyanate, sodium hydroxide, and chloral hydrate to cite only a few. Conversely, gelatinization temperature can be increased by addition of inorganic salts to the starch slurry; sodium sulfate is a particularly effective agent.

Chemically, starch is a homopolymer of glucose. Glucose, in the form of anhydroglucose units, is joined through α-1,4 and α-1,6 glucosidic bonds to form the amylose and amylopectin molecules. Amylose, the linear molecule, consists entirely of α-1,4 glucosidic bonds. Average molecular weights range from about 200,000 to 1,000,000 within the different starches. Amylopectin consists of α-1,4 linked backbone segments which are branched through α-1,6 bonds to give a highly ramified bush-like structure. Molecular weight of amylopectin is now considered to be in excess of 50 million.

Starch properties are greatly influenced by the ratio of amylose to amylopectin. This ratio varies according to the type of starch and the fractions may range from 70% amylose and 30% amylopectin, in recently developed high amylose starches, to practically 100% amylopectin in the so-called waxy starches. Common starches, however, such as corn, wheat, rice, barley, tapioca, sago, and potato, contain 17–27% amylose and 73–83% amylopectin. For any one species of starch, the ratio is constant.

Starch chemists have separated the amylose and amylopectin components and have studied their properties in great detail. The amylose molecules readily associate in water by hydrogen bonding to form precipitates in dilute solutions and rigid, turbid gels in concentrated solutions. This molecular association phenomena is called retrogradation and the precipitates are generally crystalline. The degree of association is to some extent a function of the molecular weight. Large amylose molecules, such as are obtained from the root and tuber starches, show less tendency to retrograde because of their lower mobility and reduced tendency for alignment. Since amylopectin is highly branched, it does not readily associate in dilute solutions. Solutions of amylopectin remain relatively clear and do not form gels except at high concentrations. Then the gels are soft rather than stiff as in the case of amylose gels at the same concentration. The amylopectin gels also can be reversed at 100°C while retrograded amylose gels require autoclave (121°C) temperatures.

Manufacturing Processes

Methods for manufacture of starches differ according to the type of starch. In general, starches from cereal grains require a pretreatment process in which the kernels are steeped with dilute solutions of sulfur dioxide or sodium hydroxide. Steeping swells the kernels and loosens internal bonding forces holding together the matrix of starch and protein in the endosperm as well as loosening the germ and fiber components of the kernel. In the case of the corn starch, steeping is followed by (1) grinding, (2) flotation to remove germ, (3) screening to remove fiber, and (4) centrifugation to separate protein from starch. Rice is generally steeped in sodium hydroxide prior to grinding and recovery of starch. An older process for manufacture of wheat starch also involved steeping in sodium hydroxide. Newer process, however, involves mixing flour with water, washing the starch from the vital gluten dough, and recovery of the starch and gluten.

Manufacture of tuber and root starches (potato, tapioca, and arrowroot) is a relatively simple operation that involves grinding of the tubers or roots to disintegrate the cells and free the starch granules, removing the skin and fiber by screening, followed by separating the starch from water-soluble materials either by settling the starch or by centrifugation. Sago starch obtained from the pith of certain palm trees is grated into small pieces, kneaded with water to free the starch, and the starch separated from the pulp by screening.

Industrially Important Food Starches

Corn starches, including recent genetically modified waxy and high amylose starches, are the dominant starches in the U.S. food industry today. They are low in cost, readily available, and can be easily manufactured in pure form. By selection of the base starch, chemists have developed a range of properties, through selected chemical modification, that meet the rigorous processing conditions and product performance demanded in today's high-speed, automated food processing equipment. Other cereal starches, such as wheat, milo, and rice starch are used in lesser volume, generally in applications where some specific property is sought. Rice starch, for example, is used in Europe in laundering and in dusting powders where the small granule size is desired. Waxy rice starch is reported to give excellent freeze-thaw stability in food-thickening uses. Wheat starch is used in soups where presumably the lower gelatinization temperature and shorter gel temperature range is an advantage.

Root and tuber starches are manufactured in large quantities in those parts of the world where corn starch is not readily available. Today, large tonages of tapioca starch are shipped into the United States. Manufacturers of specialty starches sometimes use tapioca starch as a base for further modification because of its textural qualities and superior freeze-thaw stability. A major food use for tapioca starch is in the well-known tapioca puddings. Potato starch is manufactured in the United States and to greater extent in Europe where it competes in price with corn starch. Food uses for potato starch in the United States are minor with the bulk being sold for nonfood uses. Sago and arrowroot starches are used in minor quantities in specialty applications where a specific property is desired.

Food Starches: Properties, Modifications, Uses

Native starches may be classified according to their cooked paste properties. Grouped below are starches that have similar paste properties.

(1) Cereal starches (corn, grain sorghum, wheat, and rice). These form viscous, short-bodied pastes that set to opaque gels upon cooling.

(2) Root and tuber starches (potato and tapioca). These form highly viscous pastes that are long-bodied, relatively clear, and develop a weak gel structure upon cooling. Viscosity is significantly reduced under shear condition.

(3) Waxy starches (corn, grain sorghum, and rice). Generally, these starches form heavy-bodied,

somewhat stringy pastes that are sensitive to shear. The most important properties are high paste clarity and reduced gelation tendency.

(4) High amylose starch (corn). This starch requires high temperatures for cooking. The cooked pastes are short-bodied, and form very rigid opaque gels upon cooling.

Many of the above properties are undesirable for food applications and must be modified to make the starch acceptable for use. Below is a list of physical and chemical treatments employed by starch manufacturers along with property changes and major food use.

(1) Acid-Modified Starches: Starch in aqueous suspension is treated with dilute acid, neutralized, dewatered, and dried. This treatment reduces paste viscosity. The major food use is in gum confections.

(2) Dextrins: Dry starch is roasted, usually in the presence of acid catalysts, to form a range of products classified as British gums, and canary and white dextrins. Dextrinization reduces viscosity and increases solubility in cold water. Paste clarity is also increased if the roasting is carried out under neutral or slightly alkaline conditions because of repolymerization to produce branching. Dextrins are used to a limited extent in foods primarily as carriers for food flavors. Major use is in adhesive applications for packaging.

(3) Oxidized Starches: Aqueous starch suspensions are treated with oxidizing agents, usually sodium hypochlorite, followed by removal of excess hypochlorite, dewatering, and drying. Viscosity is reduced and paste clarity increased. Products are used to a limited extent in foods as thickeners and emulsion stabilizers. Major use is in textile and paper coatings.

(4) Crossbonded Starch: A suspension of starch is treated with a small amount of difunctional chemical, such as epichlorohydrin, phosphorus oxychloride or sodium trimetaphosphate, and an alkaline catalyst. The treated slurry is neutralized, dewatered, washed, and dried. Crossbonding inhibits disintegration of the cooked swollen granules and maintains high viscosity in the presence of acids and shear. Major use is for food thickeners in pies, gravies, baby foods, and salad dressings.

(5) Starch Derivatives: Starch is treated with monofunctional reagents as described above for difunctional reagents to form monoesters and ethers. Typical derivatives include starch acetate, starch phosphate, starch succinate, and hydroxypropyl starch. These have improved freeze-thaw stability and paste clarity compared to the base starch. Derivatives made from waxy corn starch are used broadly as food thickeners, particularly when they are also crossbonded.

(6) Pregelatinized Starches: Any of the starches described above may be converted to a dry cold water dispersible form by precooking and roll or spray-drying. These are used in relatively low volumes in applications where convenience is desired or when cooking facilities are not available.

Production of Food Starches

The following 1971 production data for food starches were obtained from the Corn Refiners Association, Washington, D.C.

In 1971, slightly over 8 billion pounds of corn starch was produced by the wet milling industry; about 5 billion pounds was converted internally to dextrose and corn syrup for food uses; the remaining 3 billion pounds was sold for food and nonfood uses. Nearly $\frac{1}{2}$ billion pounds of corn starch was sold for food use. The breakdown of sales of corn starch (raw and modified) to the various segments of the food industry in 1971 is as follows:

Use	Millions of Pounds
Bakers	49
Baking Powder	40
Brewers	95
Candy, chewing gum	45
Packaged (grocers)	160
Miscellaneous	100

Approximately 200 million pounds of wheat starch was manufactured in the United States in 1971. About 78 million pounds of this was consumed in foods with the remainder being sold for industrial nonfood uses.

Imports of tapioca starch and flour in 1971 totaled 182 million pounds. No figures were available for a breakdown into food and nonfood uses.

Potato starch is manufactured from cull potatoes and the volume produced in the United States fluctuates from year to year depending on potato prices and availability. Current information indicates an average yearly production of refined potato starch of about 200 million pounds with 5 million pounds imported. Only a small fraction of this production is used in food. Potato flour, however, is used to much larger extent in dehydrated potato-based products. Approximately 700 million pounds of potato flour was produced in 1971.

Imports of arrowroot and sago starches and flours in 1971 were only 3.2 million pounds. No further breakdown is available from published literature.

EUGENE F. PASCHALL

References

KERR, R. W. 1968. Chemistry and Industry of Starch. Academic Press, New York.

WHISTLER, R. L., and PASCHALL, E. F. 1965, 1967. Starch: Chemistry and Technology, Vol. 1 Fundamental Aspects, Vol. 2 Industrial Aspects. Academic Press, New York.

STERILIZATION OF CANNED FOOD BY HEAT

In commercial canning, when a food is put into a container, it always contains microorganisms that would cause the food to spoil if they were not subsequently destroyed. Some microorganisms will not cause spoilage when subjected only to ordinary temperature and such organisms it may not be considered necessary to destroy. When the destruction of the spores of a certain organism has reached a certain pre-established point, the food is said to be sterile in respect to that organism. The object in heat processing canned foods is the attainment of sterility in respect to the most heat-resistant microorganism present that would bring about spoilage.

Dictionary definitions of sterilization do not apply when foods in general are being considered. Tanner (1944) had this to say in regard to a definition: "Some canning technologists have modified the term 'sterilization' to indicate the bacteriological condition attained in some foods by processing. Since the term 'sterilization' implies the absolute destruction of all living organisms, and since this condition may not be attained in some processed foods, the term 'commercial sterilization' has been introduced." In the following discussion, sterilization refers to this condition.

The key to successful canning is sterilization followed by protection of the food from contamination with viable microorganisms. The possibility of accomplishing sterilization by heating was discovered by a Frenchman, Nicolas Appert, at the close of the 18th Century. For almost a century and a half, heat was the only medium that received consideration as a preserving agent aside from the preservation means which developed during past centuries, primarily as a result of natural phenomena—largely without voluntary human participation. These are asepsis, fermentation, dehydration, addition of chemical substances, and low temperature.

Asepsis, particularly, was almost solely the result of natural phenomena, as exhibited, for example, by the impervious covering of an orange or an apple. Asepsis implies the absence of viable microorganisms in a food and a continued protection of the food from contamination by microorganisms. Asepsis also prevents passage of extraneous solid, liqueform, or vaporous substances to or from the food material.

Requirements of a Satisfactory Process

In evaluating the merits of a process, one must examine it from the standpoints of four factors: (1) economy, (2) quality of product, (3) uniformity of product, and (4) sterilization of the product. It may at first appear that we should be interested only in the fourth factor. In studying processing, however, we quickly learn that the four factors are inseparable.

During the last third of a century, extensive research has been carried on in two systems for sterilizing food, involving the use of electrical energy as the sterilizing agent. The greater part of this research has been applied to employing irradiation energy as the sole sterilizing agent. Sterilization is accomplished through the application of ionizing radiation, which produces substantial chemical changes in most foods; because of this, while the food is sterilized, the returns from the research have been all but sterile when low-acid foods are involved, which require a heavy treatment. The other system is primarily a heat process, the energy for which is provided by microwave treatment. There is said to be slight radiation produced by the microwave treatment but, as indicated above, this is regarded as a heat process. Since, because of cost, as well as of functional defects, these systems which rely upon electrical energy have not attained an appreciable volume of use, this discussion will be concerned almost entirely with the processing systems in which heat is supplied by either steam or hot water, depending upon the pressure under which the process is conducted.

Salt Bath Processing

In the early days of canned foods sterilization, owing to difficulties encountered in controlling the operation of the autoclave and the attendant danger of explosion, the autoclave (pressure vessel) did not grow rapidly in favor. Numerous canners, recognizing the economic advantage of processing low-acid foods at temperatures above 212°F, processed in a bath of salt solution (either sodium or calcium chloride) at atmospheric pressure. Inasmuch as a temperature of 240°F was easily obtained in a bath of calcium chloride, the length of process was greatly reduced from the 5–6 hr which were necessary at boiling water temperature. Because of two weighty disadvantages of the salt bath procedure, namely, corrosion of metal containers and danger of bursting of cans because of no overriding external pressure, the salt bath was gradually abandoned in favor of the steam and water pressure retort.

Changing Ideas of How Process Operates

Processes for canned foods have always been designated in terms of time and temperature, with attention to the rate of heat transfer of the heating medium to the food in the can.

For a simple process, the temperature named is the temperature held uniformly in the heating medium during the part of the process that exerts the major sterilizing effect on the food in the container. The time named designates the period during which the temperature is held; for example, a process of 15 min at 240°F is one in which the medium surrounding the container is held at 240°F for 15 min.

Appert's description of his processes shows him to have been a scientist. His careful specifications of the procedure to be followed show that he appreciated the fact that coming-up time and cooling time are important in the process. Later, however, most canners lost sight of the importance of these steps. The factors of coming-up time and cooling time increased in importance when high temperature processing of foods came into vogue; nevertheless, except in rare instances, canners of 50 yr ago discounted effects of coming-up time and cooling time upon the food. Moreover, since the process was described merely as a process of x minutes at y°F, the conception generally accepted was that every particle of the food was subjected to a temperature of y°F for x minutes.

Scientists of the canning industry almost 70 yr ago began to realize that, to understand processing, they must know the rate at which temperature rises at the point in the container last reached by the heat traveling into the container during the process. Thus, the line of investigation known as heat penetration study was born.

The earliest scientific reference to this subject found in the literature is by Prescott and Underwood (1902). By the use of maximum registering thermometers, they found that at the center of a can of creamed corn being processed in a retort at 246°F, a temperature of 227°F was reached in 30 min when the temperature of the corn at the beginning of the process was between 180° and 190°F. Temperatures of 237.2° and 246°F were registered at the end of 45 and 55 min, respectively. The following year Underwood (1937) said that in a large number of cases of spoilage, especially in its first stages, the souring may be found only at the center of the container. He stated "The corn may be sweet at the top of the

can, but on taking a sample from the center, souring will be found. Should these cans stand at a favorable temperature for some time, the infection will become general throughout the whole contents. This proves that the heat sufficient for complete sterilization has not penetrated through the central portion on account of the low conducting power of creamed corn."

Food sterilization, as widely practiced, is accomplished by heating the food in sealed containers. Under certain circumstances, however, food is either sterilized or pasteurized while flowing through a heat exchanger of tubular, plate, or other design. Or, it may be sterilized in batchwise procedure by being held in bulk, with stirring, in a vessel which either has a jacket, through the chamber of which either steam or hot water may flow to heat the food indirectly, or has a means of releasing steam directly into the food. The former procedure is called indirect, the latter, direct heating by steam. Direct heating may be effected also while the food flows through a heat exchanger, in which either steam is injected into the food or the food in a layer of small thickness passes through an atmosphere of steam or of other hot vapor.

Batchwise heat application is that in which the application of heat is sporadic or discontinuous. In the system which has been predominant in use through the years, the food, in consumer packages is treated in retorts or autoclaves (Fig. S-20) in separate portions and each portion receives the required amount of lethal heat to accomplish the intended purpose, after which the advent of heat is stopped. Continuous processing, on the contrary, is processing in which the supplying of a heating medium is continuous in a certain region or loca-

Courtesy of A. K. Robins & Co.

FIG. S-20. BATTERY OF RETORTS WITH UNIVERSAL CONTROL SYSTEM FOR PROCESSING VEGETABLES BY CONVENTIONAL PROCEDURE

Courtesy of FMC Corp.

FIG. S-21. CUTAWAY VIEW OF SPIRAL TYPE OF CONTINUOUS PRESSURE COOKER (STERILMATIC) AND CAN ENTRANCE VALVE

Shows spiral flange which guides cans in their movement from entrance point to exit point. The smaller tank is a continuous pressure cooler. Control instrument panel is mounted alongside the cooker.

tion and the food is moved continuously into and out of the influence of the heating medium within the given region. During this cycle of movement of the food, each particle of food receives the

amount of heat energy required to accomplish sterilization, provided the system is properly designed and operated.

Commercial processing techniques are changing gradually from batchwise to continuous types. Continuous processes are more economical in the use of heat energy, labor, and time than are batchwise processes but cost of equipment for continuous processing generally is greater (Parker *et al.* 1954; Charm 1971). The efficient continuous food sterilizing systems operate on about 50% as much steam and from 15 to 40% as much labor per unit of food processed as conventional batchwise systems.

In Europe three continuous systems, known respectively as hydrostatic sterilization, high velocity air sterilization, and Steriflamme sterilization, attained considerable prominence before the first and third systems named above were introduced to the United States during the last 10 yr because, primarily, of their economic advantages over the Sterilmatic cooker, which has had extensive use for 75 yr (Fig. S-21). This sterilizer, formerly known under the name of Anderson-Barngrover, will be further discussed later.

The Hydrostatic Sterilizer

For more than 15 yr, canners in the United States watched their counterparts in Europe expand the use of the hydrostatic continuous sterilizer without being impressed. They were unim-

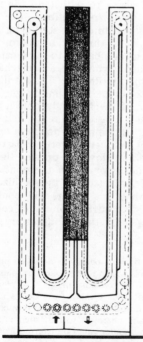

Courtesy of Chemetron Corp.

FIG. S-22. DIAGRAM OF HYDROSTATIC COOKER WITH CONTINUOUS POSITIVE ADJUSTABLE AGITATION

The broken lines represent chains—the shorter one to propel the containers through the cooker, the longer one to rotate the carriers holding the containers.

Courtesy of Chemetron Corp.

FIG. S-23. CONTAINER CARRIER OF HYDROSTATIC COOKER FOR EITHER END-OVER-END OR AXIAL ROTATION OF THE CONTAINERS

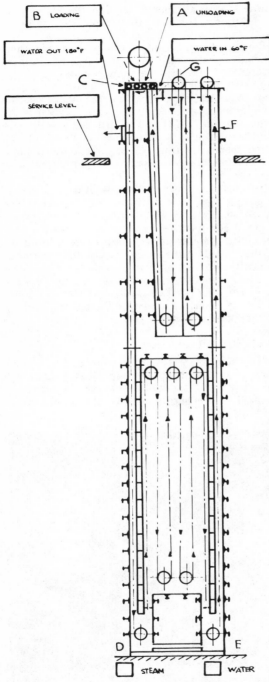

FIG. S-24. DIAGRAM OF HYDROSTATIC COOKER OF STANDARD TYPE FOR STERILIZING PRODUCTS SUCH AS BRINE-PACKED GREEN PEAS OR GREEN BEANS WHICH REQUIRE ONLY SHORT EXPOSURE

pressed by the recital by the manufacturers and users of the hydrostatic sterilizers of the advantages in the form of economy and simplicity which were claimed for these sterilizers over the spiral type sterilizer (Sterilmatic) with rotary pressure valves for feeding cans into and for discharging them from the sterilizing chamber, the use of which had increased rapidly. Some of the supposed advantages of the rotary type continuous sterilizer began to appear to be disadvantages.

In 1963, only a very short period of operation of the first hydrostatic sterilizer in the United States, processing 300 cans per minute of pork and beans for 75 min at 250°F was necessary to initiate an order for 3 more machines. From that momentum, the number of hydrostatics in the United States multiplied rapidly and within 8 yr, 50 hydrostatics were operating in U.S. canneries and a prominent canning machinery manufacturer was manufacturing hydrostatic sterilizers.

This system in its standard form, conveys the sealed containers of food, with virtually no agitation, continuously to an elevated position, where they enter a "preheating leg" containing a sufficient head of water to withstand the pressure of steam in the sterilizing section. The containers thus are conveyed into the sterilizing section by moving downward through a column of water, which functions as a barrier to the escape of steam from the sterilizing chamber, as a mechanical valve functions in the Sterilmatic. The sterilizing chamber extends to about the same height as the preheating leg or, if mechanically convenient, could extend to either a lesser or greater height than the preheating leg, and is large enough in cross section to permit any number of vertical passages of the containers up and down to provide the necessary processing time, after which the containers enter water again at the bottom of the sterilizing section.

After entering this water, the containers are carried upward through a column of cooling water in a "cooling leg," then if necessary, through a

The sterilizing chamber occupies the lower portion of the tower while the cooling chamber occupies the upper portion.

Definitions of label symbols: A—Container exit port. B—Container entrance port. C—Position of container as it enters continuous chain at top of preheating chamber. D—Position of container when transferred from preheating chamber to sterilizing chamber. E—Position of container when transferred from sterilizing chamber to precooling chamber. F—Position of container when transferred from precooling chamber to intermediate spray cooling sub-chamber at atmospheric pressure if additional cooling is required. G—Position of container when transferred from intermediate spray cooling sub-chamber to final spray cooling sub-chamber.

descending and an ascending spray cooling leg, and finally through a descending "drying leg," where the containers are sufficiently dried before being discharged at the bottom of the structure.

The advantages of the hydrostatic system are said to be: (1) economy of floor space (the unit is installed outside the building), (2) economy in steam and water, (3) economy in labor, (4) gentle handling of containers, and (5) high capacity.

A hydrostatic sterilizer in which the container is rotated continuously either axially or end-over-end at any of a wide range of speeds (Fig. S-22, S-23, S-24) agitates the container during processing. The agitating sterilizer is used in processing food substances, the quality of which is not impaired by the agitation, to accelerate the passage of heat through the product making it possible to sterilize the food by a shorter process than that required when there is no agitation.

The hydrostatic cooker is also designed for operation with overriding pressure to a maximum of almost 30 psig in the sterilizing and cooling chambers (Fig. S-25). Overriding pressure, produced by introducing air into the sterilizing section at higher pressure than that of the steam, is required in processing food in glass containers with caps that could be dislodged by internal pressure or in processing flexible containers, which might burst from internal pressure. Figure S-26 shows various designs of carriers for cylindrical containers in both standard and rotating type machines.

The Steriflamme System

The Steriflamme sterilization system (Fig. S-27) originated in France. It is a continuous system for heat processing brine-packed vegetables, with the possibility of being in the high temperature-short time processing area. High temperature-short time processing is a rapidly growing type of processing with proven potential for yielding sterile low-acid products of improved quality. It will be discussed more fully later.

Five Steriflamme installations that are operating commercially in the United States are applied to mushrooms in cans varying from 2 to 3 oz in capacity. Rates of cooking vary from 100 to 500 cans per minute.

In Europe, 7 plants use the Steriflamme System to sterilize mushrooms in cans of 0.125, 0.25, 0.50, and 1 kg capacity at production rates varying from 36 to 140 cans per minute and 12 plants sterilize green beans in cans of 0.50 or 1 kg capacity at production rates varying from 180 to 500 cans per minute.

Mushrooms in clear brine are particularly well adapted to flame treatment because of the size of the solid pieces in the product, coupled with the

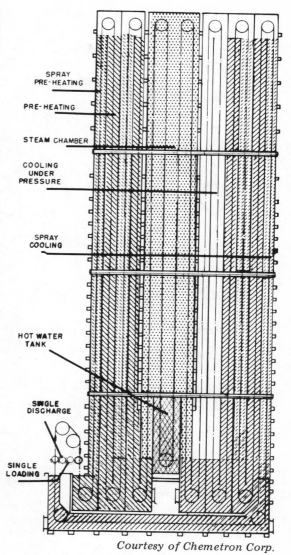

SPRAY PRE-HEATING

PRE-HEATING

STEAM CHAMBER

COOLING UNDER PRESSURE

SPRAY COOLING

HOT WATER TANK

SINGLE DISCHARGE

SINGLE LOADING

Courtesy of Chemetron Corp.

FIG. S-25. DIAGRAM OF HYDROSTATIC COOKER DESIGNED FOR OPERATION WITH OVERRIDING PRESSURE IN THE STERILIZING CHAMBER

This diagram indicates the pressure in the sterilizing chamber to be (a + 2b) psig, where a is atmospheric pressure and b is the pressure that is contained by one column of water.

possibility of utilizing an intermittent application of heat in such a pattern that the rise of temperature in the can contents can be ideally related to the amount of heat applied. An opinion, formulated in a complete lack of experience with Steriflamme sterilization, perhaps should be ventured here that, a product which is wholly or in part liquid, con-

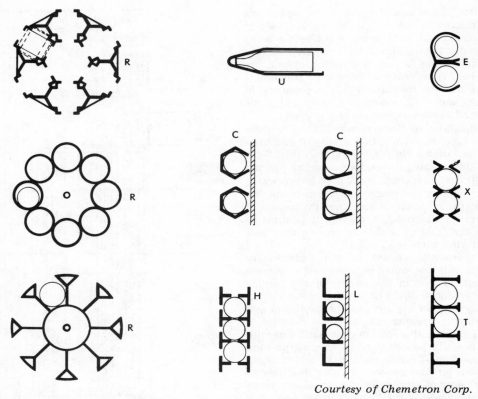

Courtesy of Chemetron Corp.

FIG. S-26. DIAGRAM SHOWING DESIGNS OF THE TYPES OF CONTAINER CARRIERS
AVAILABLE IN HYDROSTATIC COOKERS

C and E types for glass and metal containers in large diameter range. L, T, H, and X types for
cans. R type for agitating cans, bottles, and jars. U type for bottles.

taining minute solid particles, such as milk, may
not be a suitable product for sterilization in the
Steriflamme system because, through the "burn-
on" process, the particles would form a stubborn
coating on the inside surfaces of the metal, where
the metal is touched on the outside by the flame.

The successive steps in the Steriflamme procedure for mushrooms are the following: (1) after
filling, a steam exhaust brings the product in the
unsealed containers to a temperature of 180°F,
(2) the containers are sealed, (3) in a preheating
chamber atop the Steriflamme cooker, the liquid
portion of the product in the sealed container is
heated to about 204°F, (4) in the Steriflamme
cooker, cans, while being rolled on tracks over gas
burners for 2 min, allow the liquid contents to be
heated to approximately 258°F, (5) temperature
of the liquid contents is held at approximately
258°F for 4 min while the cans are rolled above a
second series of gas burners, and (6) the cans are
rolled through a water spray which cools the

product to 212°F in 20 sec and to 90°F in several
minutes. This completes the process in which the
time-temperature heating curves of the liquid and
of the critical points in the mushrooms are shown
in Fig. S-28, which shows the intermittent nature
of the temperature rise of the liquid. This intermittent heating of the liquid, as stated above, is
one of the advantages of Steriflamme treatment.
It provides proper control of the relationship
existing between temperature of liquid and temperature of solid throughout the process.

The functional effects on the product, enumerated in the above 6 steps, are common in all heat
processing except that step 3 is unique to the
Steriflamme method and step 5 is included in less
than half of the systems as a voluntary distinct
step. Also, the Steriflamme system is the only
system having the controlled intermittent heating
effect shown in Fig. S-28.

A limit to the temperature that can be put into
the can in Steriflamme processing is established by

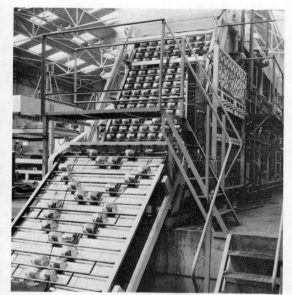

Courtesy of A. K. Robins & Co.

FIG. S-27. STERIFLAMME CONTINUOUS STERIL-
IZER AND COOLER

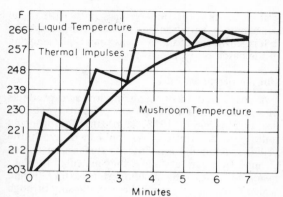

Courtesy of A. K. Robins & Co.

FIG. S-28. CURVES SHOWING RISE OF TEMPERA-
TURE IN LIQUID AND IN CENTER OF A MUSHROOM
IN A STERIFLAMME COOKER

the pressure imposed by that temperature, the gauge of the steel of which the can ends are made, the amount of noncondensable gas (air) in the can, and the diameter of the can. It is customary to regard 130°C (266°F) as the maximum temperature to be attained in the can. The criterion is buckling of the can ends by internal pressure. Buckling is not permissible. If that temperature is to be exceeded, one of the following two compensating factors must be brought into play: (1) the can diameter must be smaller than 3 in. or (2) the thickness of the ends must be greater than standard for the diameter being used.

Two steps in procedure by the canner to control the amount of air in the can are the heating (exhaust) of the can contents to 82.2°C (180°F) immediately before the can is sealed and controlling the volume of the headspace (space in the sealed can not occupied by food) in the filling operation.

An important disadvantage of the Steriflamme

Courtesy of Food

FIG. S-29. HOT AIR STERILIZING SYSTEM SHOWING CLOSEUP VIEW OF
STERILIZER AT RIGHT

system is its limitation to uses only with metal containers. An advantage claimed for the system is less shrinkage of mushrooms than that occurring in the batch retort process.

Hot Air Sterilizer

A novel method of sterilizing low-acid products in hot air under atmospheric pressure went into use in Sweden in 1955, sterilizing homogenized milk. A description was published by Sporle (1955). After the cans interior surfaces have been cleaned by steam at 212°F they are filled to slight headspace with milk at temperature 161.6°F and sealed with a double-seamed cover. Passing through a second water wash at 176°F, they are conveyed into the top section of the hot-air continuous sterilizer, which is approved for use by the Swedish Farmers' Association (Fig. S-29).

The conveyors within the sterilizer consist of 9 horizontal sections 25 m in length, stationed in vertical alignment so that the cans pass by gravity from the uppermost conveyor to that next below and from that to the other 7 lower conveyors successively in each of 3 separate lanes.

The cans are said to enter the sterilizer at 158°F and, after a 15-min exposure to circulating air at 293°F are released from the sterilizer at a temperature of approximately 253°F and are continuously cooled immediately to about 86°F.

Sterilmatic Sterilizer

The continuous processor of the Anderson-Barngrover type, now called the Sterilmatic cooker, which rotates the container about the container's principal axis during about $1/3$ of each rotation of the can-carrying reel, has made phenomenal advances in the high temperature-short time (HTST) sterilization of evaporated milk. This processor has for many years been a growing factor in evaporated milk sterilization and, as knowledge increased at an accelerated pace on the control of the physical stability of milk, both in processing and in storage, the speed of the passage of cans through the cooker has attained the high rate of 500 cans per minute to reduce the length of process from 15–18 min at 245°F to from 2–3 min at from 260° to 265°F. This process became commercial in 1960. There are now in commercial use, on the short process of evaporated milk and other milk products in 14-oz or smaller cans, about 50 installations.

Unfortunately, we have here the interplay of counterbalancing factors that complicate the problems. The moderately heavy heat treatment that must be used to give physical stability to evaporated milk largely neutralizes the benefit of improved color and flavor which one might legitimately expect to realize from conversion to an HTST process. The net improvement in quality is disappointing. The process could be further shortened by using end-over-end rotation and still further reduced by using reciprocating agitation, or the Heat-Cool-Fill (HCF) or Pressure Filling and Closing (PFC) methods. The chances are, however, that little additional improvement in color and flavor would be realized because of the retrograding effect of the stabilizing treatment when this constitutes a heat treatment of the raw materials. Shortening the process adds to the intensity of the stabilizing treatment required.

For at least 40 yr, this problem of physical stability of HTST processed evaporated milk has claimed the attention of organic and physical chemists in industrial and university laboratories. Many announcements of success have been made but, somehow, in the face of these "successes," the problem refused to be solved to the satisfaction of the processor.

Rigidly controlled timing in distribution to the consumer would permit the use of a process yielding quality greatly superior to that of the product that is physically stabilized by the sterilizing process. Also, refrigeration during storage substantially increases the length of stability. Points of interest in regard to the Sterilmatic processor, as enumerated by the FMC Corp: "The first mechanical effect of interest results from rolling of the cans around the bottom of the shell. As the cans roll, thin products are agitated, mixing the contents and heating the product at a much higher rate than in a still retort. Thus, this 'induced convection' results in reduced process times as compared to those of a still retort. Neither highly viscous nor solid products flow under mild agitation; hence their heat transfer rates are similar to those in still processing, as in a still retort or in standard hydrostatic sterilizer.

"The rotary valves provide instantaneous introduction of the cans to the full steam temperature and pressure in the retort. The ends of the cans, acting like diaphragms, are forced in, decreasing the headspace in the can. Since induced convection results from movement of the headspace bubble in the product, agitation is impeded during the first stages of the process. As heating continues, the internal pressure of the can increases, the ends are forced outward, and induced convection of the product becomes fully effective. Because the can ends are fully distended at the termination of the heating phase of the process, products heating by induced convection as well as products heating by natural convection are subjected to maximum agitation during the first portion of the cooling phase, resulting in rapid cooling."

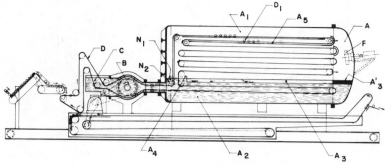

Courtesy of A. K. Robins & Co.

FIG. S-30. VERTICAL CROSS SECTION DIAGRAM OF HYDROLOCK CONTINUOUS STERILIZER AND COOLER

A—Sterilizing chamber which, for glass or flexible pouch containers, carries a mixture of steam and air to maintain an overriding pressure; steam-air mixture is kept in violent circulation by the powerful fan F. A_2—Water in precooling section. A_3—Hollow insulating partition between the heating vaporous medium and the precooling water. B—Hydrolock. C—Sump tank for recovery of water to ambient temperature. D—Chain conveyor of containers to be sterilized, entering the hydrolock. N_1 and N_2—Maximum and minimum levels, respectively, of surface of water in precooler. A_3—Extension of insulating partition A_3—surface in contact with steam-air mixture. A_1—Steam and air mixture in sterilizing chamber. A_4—Chain conveyor of containers entering cooling water. A_5 and D_1—Chain conveyor of containers in early part of sterilizing exposure.

Hydrolock Sterilizer

Another sterilizer of French origin is the Hydrolock. This sterilizer functions similarly to the hydrostatic except that the travel of the containers is on a horizontal track instead of in vertical movement; also, since the sterilizing chamber does not have sufficient height to accommodate a preheating leg containing a sufficiently long column of water to serve as a pressure-retaining valve for the sterilizing chamber, the packages enter the sterilizing chamber and leave the precooling chamber via a mechanical valve, called the Hydrolock. This valve operates under water which accomplishes a short preheating of the packages and, being in direct communication with water which fills a precooling compartment in the bottom of the horizontal retort, accomplishes the final portion of the precooling of the packages under the pressure maintained in the sterilizing chamber. In a vertical cross-sectional diagram, (Fig. S-30), the various components of the Hydrolock sterilizer and cooler are designated symbolically. The machine is designed so that cylindrical containers may either rotate or not rotate while traveling through the sterilizing and precooling sections but differs in this respect from the hydrostatic system in that, in the Hydrolock, rotation is produced by rolling the container on a solid track, whereas in the hydrostatic, rotation is produced by confining the

containers in specially designed carriers, which, by themselves rotating, rotate the food containers, thus making it possible to rotate containers of any shape which can be held in the carriers. On the other hand, the Hydrolock is adaptable to the use of overriding pressure in the sterilizing and precooling chambers more economically than the hydrostatic machine. Figure S-30 shows the outline of a powerful fan in the end of the retort for thoroughly mixing and circulating the steam and air and maintaining uniform temperature throughout the chamber.

Agitation by Rotation

The low rate of heat penetration of cream-style corn makes a prolonged heat treatment under superatmospheric steam pressure necessary in order to sterilize the product by conventional still-cook method. Work by the National Canners Association before 1920 established the fact that agitation of cream-style corn during heat processing for sterilization produces coagulation of the creamy portion of the product.

Initiated in 1920, attempts were made to produce a practical continuous cooker in which cream-style corn could be sterilized without curdling. Success with the Anderson-Barngrover cooker, based upon the use of a special starch in the product, was an-

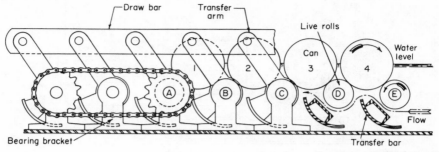

Courtesy of FMC Corp.

FIG. S-31. DIAGRAMMATIC VIEW FROM SIDE OF THERMO-ROTO MACHINE, AN AGITATING ATMOSPHERIC PRESSURE PROCESS

View shows end bearings for a series of rollers, transfer bars at rest during rolling period, and draw bar by means of which transfer bars are operated.

nounced in 1950. At this time the name of the cooker was changed to Sterilmatic.

The cost of the Sterilmatic process in seasonal operation on cream-style corn alone may present a difficult situation for the average canner, the difficulty of which is augmented materially by the required strict control of the consistency of the product and of the amount of headspace in the can to ensure success of the Sterilmatic process.

End-Over-End Rotation

End-over-end rotation is effective in accelerating the rise of temperature of the entire contents of the containers to a greater degree than any other type of container movement. When the axis of rotation is located externally to the containers, however, the speed of rotation must be so controlled as to be held at a lower maximum than is required when the rotation is about an axis passing through the center of the container because under the latter condition the composite force of the centrifugal and gravity effects will not produce stagnation in the product sufficient to increase the time required to raise the temperature of the entire contents at as low a speed as when the axis is external to the package.

Studies indicate that in end-over-end rotation the maximum rate of heating of liqueform products occurs when the speeds of rotation are such that the headspace bubble passes through the product at various levels in the container, the location of which level depends upon both the speed of rotation and the viscosity of the product. The attainment of the maximum rate of heating obviously occurs when the net centrifugal force in the interior region of the container which is the furthest, vertically upward, from the axis of rotation equals the net force of gravity.

Axial Rotation

The kind of agitation that appears to offer the greatest promise of growing use now is the least effective kind, viz., rotation of the container on its horizontal (usually the long) axis. Engineering and economy are the deciding factors.

Casimir (1962) reviewed the literature on can rotation during thermal processing and presented results of his own studies in this sphere. His data showed that, depending upon the viscosity of the product, the dimensions of the container, and the volume of the headspace, the rate of heating of a product increases as the rate of rotation increases to from 100 to 200 rpm.

The limiting factor, of course, is conflict between centrifugal force, the force of gravity, and resistance to shear in producing or inhibiting forced convection currents in the product. A rate of rotation greater than that at which the maximum rate of heating first occurs may produce either the maximum rate of heating or a rate somewhat lower than the maximum.

The maximum rate of heating, as increased by high speed rotation of the container on its axis in horizontal position, puts the process into the category of an HTST process for products up to a medium level of viscosity and in containers of diameter up to about 4 in.

Casimir's data can be interpreted as confirming the principle that, as the rate of rotation increases, gravity effect is overcome by centrifugal effect and resistance to shear progressively from periphery to the axis. Based upon the definition of centrifugal force, this condition in a can of any size, containing a given food, at a given rotation speed, presumably occurs at a given distance from the axis. Until this condition is reached at a distance from the axis equal to the radius of a cylinder

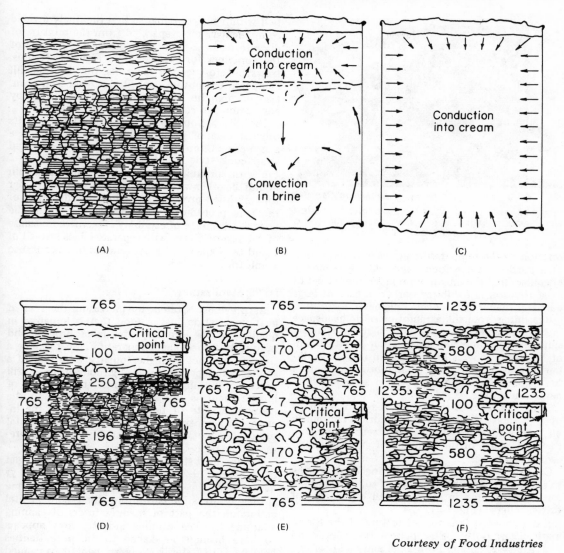

Courtesy of Food Industries

FIG. S-32. STRATA-COOK PATTERNS OF HEAT FLOW AND OF DISTRIBUTION OF LETHAL VALUES IN VERTICAL PLACES PASSING THROUGH CENTERS OF NO. 2 CANS OF STRATA-COOK CORN AND PREMIXED CREAM-STYLE CORN

(A) Sealed can is inverted for processing (desirable but not necessary). (B) Heat flows into product by convection and conduction. (C) In premixed corn, there is no convection. (D) In No. 2 cans, Strata-Cook corn is sterilized in 46 min at 250°F. Numerals indicate percentage of lethal heat reaching different points. (E) But after 46 min at 250°F, only 7% of lethal heat has reached center of No. 2 can of premixed cream-style corn. (F) So it takes 74 min at 250°F to bring center of premixed cream-style corn to 100% lethal heat, overprocessing other parts.

which has approximately the length of the container, and has the same volume as the headspace (void space) in the container, there is no agitation of the contents because of the effect of gravity upon the contents of the rotating container and because of the headspace within the container.

Thus, except for the agitating effect of shear in surfaces approximately concentric to the container wall, the greater the volume of the headspace, the sooner should the condition of nil agitation of the contents be attained. Also, the larger the diameter of the container, the sooner, in respect to speed of

Courtesy of American Can Co.

FIG. S-33. HCF UNIT: ASEPTIC CANNING CHAMBER WITH ACCESSORIES, KNOWN AS CANCO 300 SFC-G ASEPTIC UNIT

rotation, is the temperature effect of nonagitation of a portion of the food exhibited. This means, of course, that the maximum temperature effect of axial rotation is exhibited earlier in cans of large diameter than in cans of small diameter.

Reasoning from the assumption of no headspace in the container, one concludes that the relationship between time and the position of attainment of "no agitation" is logarithmic in respect to distance from the periphery (representing position 1) to the axis (representing position zero, which is never reached).

These concepts of the nature of agitation effects of high rates of rotation of cylindrical containers on their central longitudinal axes seem to explain the significance of the blending of gravitation and centrifugal forces.

Casimir states "The first agitating cooker using this principle was the 'Thermo-Roto' in which the cans were rotated in a water bath on a series of driven rollers" (Fig. S-31).

Axial rotation is a normal feature of the Sterilmatic, Thermo-Roto, Steriflamme, Hydrolock, and Hot Air systems and both axial and end-over-end rotation are available features in the hydrostatic system, all of which systems have been described herein.

Strata-Cook Process

A method of speeding up the sterilization in still retort processing of products of slurry type, consisting of a mixture of discrete particles and a finely divided component in a liquid such as water or brine, which was developed and put into commercial use since 1950, is the Strata-Cook process.

This process is applicable provided the product can be formulated by assembling the three components of the product in the container in a specified manner so that the components can be strati-

fied within the container so that the finely divided component is kept separated from the mixture of discrete particles and brine during the heating of the container for sterilization. Figure S-32 illustrates by cross-section diagrams, the stratified fill compared to conventional fill of cream-style corn, also diagramatic representation of heat flow by convection and conduction into the product.

The Strata-Cook procedure has outgrown its original plan of packing the entire product in a single can. Chop suey and chow mein are packed strata-cook style by using 2 cans instead of 1—1 can with sprouts, other vegetable solids, and thin liquid; the other with a highly viscous sauce. Under this modified procedure, the quality advantage of the true procedure is retained but much of the normal advantage of economy is sacrificed because of the use of 2 cans with separate labels instead of 1 and the expense of incorporating the 2 cans into 1 unit for marketing.

HTST Sterilization

As previously stated, by increasing the rate of heat penetration into a food that is impaired in quality by the ordinary sterilizing process and raising the processing temperature, we produce a finished product of higher quality than that of a similar product produced by conventional still process. Within practical limits, the amount of improvement is nonlinearly proportional to the increase in rate of heat penetration and the increase in temperature. This is the fundamental principle upon which so-called high temperature-short time processing operates.

Development studies of HTST sterilization began in the early 1920s but only within the last 30 yr has interest in commercial application become sufficient to stimulate more than coincidental action on the part of manufacturers of canning equipment. The canning industry now appears to have become awakened to the potentialities held by HTST sterilization for benefit to canned foods.

Foremost among the specific procedures in this category is that of aseptic canning, known in the early development period as the Heat-Cool-Fill (HFC) system. Figure S-33 shows the first HCF unit that operated successfully in the United States. It was installed in 1938 and operated over a period of 22 yr sterilizing 300 cans of chocolate-flavored milk beverage per minute. Dole Engineering Co. first marketed an aseptic canning process for liqueform products in 1950.

Between 40 and 50 yr ago, the food processing terms "Heat-Cool-Fill" (HCF) and "Pressure Filling and Closing" (PFC) began to gain the status of well-known terms in the canning industry—each

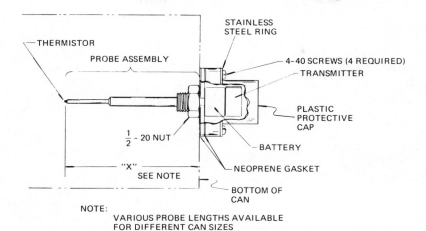

NOTE:
VARIOUS PROBE LENGTHS AVAILABLE
FOR DIFFERENT CAN SIZES

Courtesy of Aerotherm Corp.

FIG. S-34. TRANSMITTER AND PROBE ASSEMBLY FOR MEASURING
TEMPERATURE WITHIN A SEALED CONTAINER BY TELEMETRY

designating a mode of processing canned foods for sterilization by heat in one of the high temperature processes which have attained widespread use by the industry. These procedures constitute a manner of producing improved quality of the foods over the quality obtained by using the traditional processing methods.

Commercial names of the other HTST systems are Avoset, Flash 18 or Super IT, Steriflamme, and Smith-Ball process.

Measurement of Temperature (Heat Penetration)

The term "heat penetration," a loosely-used term to convey the general idea of heat flow into, or out of, a food material under heat process, has,

Courtesy of Aerotherm Corp.

FIG. S-35. TEMPERATURE TELEMETRY SYSTEM COMPONENTS: (LEFT TO RIGHT) PROBE AND MOUNTING PLATE, BATTERY, TRANSMITTER, AND PROTECTIVE CAP

during its more than 50 yr of use, become a fixed part of canning technology. A heat penetration curve is a time-temperature curve for a given point in a food at which changes in the quantity of heat energy are produced by transmission of heat energy through the medium surrounding the point, which medium offers resistance to the flow of heat energy. We venture to define the expression "rate of heat penetration" as the rate of change of temperature at the point being considered, brought about by changes in the quantity of heat energy possessed by the molecules of the material at the point when the changes are produced by transmission of heat energy through the material surrounding the point.

There are many things about heat penetration and heat penetration curves that must be understood by food technologists but which cannot be discussed here for lack of space. Either a thermometer or a thermocouple, passed through a sealed fitting in the wall of the food container and so fixed in position that the thermometer bulb or the thermocouple junction is held rigidly at the critical point, serves to measure the temperature at that point during a heat process. Figure S-34 shows, in cut-away cans, these instruments in fixed positions for heat penetration tests. The results of these tests, depicted as time-temperature curves, provide running records of temperature at the critical point in food during the heating and cooling phases of a heat sterilization process. In tests by thermocouple, the temperature is displayed by a potentiometer, to which are attached two wires leading to the thermocouple. In a test by thermometer, involving temperature above that of boiling, the thermometer passes through a steam-tight packing gland in the top wall of the retort

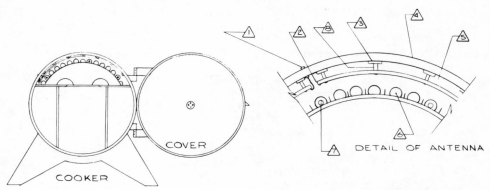

FIG. S-36. ANTENNA   INSTALLATION   OF   TEMPERATURE   TELEMETRY   SYSTEM   IN
STERITORT COOKER

(1) Amphenol coax connector.   (2) Antenna termination (open).   (3) Steel weld tab antenna support.
(4) Cooker outer wall.   (5) Antenna ($1/8 \times 1/2$ in. bar).   (6) Cans.   (7) Transmitter on a can.   (8) Ceramic spacer.

so that it can be read while the test is in progress. Heat penetration curves are essential to serve as bases for determining the required time and temperature of the sterilizing process.

There is now available an instrument assembly that yields data for heat penetration curves on a container being processed in a continuous sterilizer, for example, in Sterilmatic, hydrostatic, Hydrolock, Steriflamme, and hot air sterilizer.   The assembly, constituting a telemetry system, consists of a temperature sensing probe, a miniature radio transmitter, and a protective cap assembly in and on the can, plus a receiver and a digital temperature display located externally to the container.

The probe (in the can) consists of a body of low thermal conductivity material, a thermistor on the tip of the probe, which, in use, is located at the critical point in the food, and a mounting plate. A transmitter and battery, plugged together, plug into the mounting plate (Fig. S-35). The function of the protective cap assembly is to keep the transmitter and battery free of moisture.

Sterilmatic was the first sterilizer to be equipped with the Aerotherm telemetry system.   Figure S-36 shows a typical Sterilmatic antenna installation.   One antenna is mounted in the entire length of one of the can channels in the center of the open slot in the bottom of the channel. Thus, the test can is always in proximity to the receiving antenna as it travels through the retort. By selecting the proper time to insert the test can into the cooker, it will always fall in the can channel with the receiving antenna.

The receiving antenna is connected to an insulat-

ing commutator mounted on the cooker shaft, from which the signal is fed through the cooker wall to the receiver display and recording unit. A Conax Power Load Pressure Seal is used to feed the signal through the cooker wall. This connector has a pressure seal sufficient to withstand the maximum pressure used in a Sterilmatic cooker.

C. OLIN BALL

References

CASIMIR, D. J. 1962. New methods of sterilizing by heat. Can rotation during thermal processing. Fourth International Congress of Canned Foods, Rome, Italy.

CHARM, S. E. 1971. The Fundamentals of Food Engineering, 2nd Edition. Avi Publishing Co., Westport, Conn.

PARKER, M. E., HARVEY, E. H., and STATELER, E. S. 1954. Elements of Food Engineering, Vol. 3. The Fundamentals of Food Engineering. Reinhold Publishing Corp., New York.

PRESCOTT, S. C., and UNDERWOOD, W. L. 1902.   Sterilizing processes in the canning industry; the packing of sweet corn. *In* Science and Experiment as Applied to Canning. Sprague Canning Machinery Co., Hoopeston, Ill.

SPORLE, C. H. 1955. Sterilizing milk by hot air. Food, July, 1955.

TANNER, F. W. 1944. The Microbiology of Foods. Garrard Press, Champaign, Ill.

UNDERWOOD, W. L. 1937. The cause and prevention of sour corn. *In* Appertizing. The Trade Pressroom, San Francisco.

Cross-references: *Canning; Heat Exchange.*

SUGARS AND SWEETENERS

The sophisticated carbohydrate sciences that today produce our many sweeteners have developed slowly over many thousands of years. Curiously, the growth of sweetener consumption and development of technology are closely related to two influences: progress and war. Progress in the form of opening new countries and developing older ones has provided a steady pressure on the increasing use of sweeteners. When a backward area begins to emerge, one of the first commodities to increase in use is sugar. War has been the other major influence on the carbohydrate sciences. For instance, if Napoleon's France had not been under naval blockade and unable to import cane sugar, the important development of sweeteners from vegetable products might have come later than it did. World Wars I and II also spurred the technology that is now producing our many grain-derived sweeteners.

It has taken these many thousands of years, much scientific study, and the influence of several world catastrophes to enable us to emulate what the age-old honey bee has done by simple instinct —make pure sugars from nature's bounty.

Sweetener Types

The types of sweeteners commercially available today are numerous and within these types there are many more variations. The general types are:

Sucrose—a compound sugar consisting of levulose and dextrose

Invert—a mixture of simple sugars, levulose, dextrose, and sucrose

Dextrose—a simple sugar

Lactose—a compound sugar of dextrose and galactose

Corn syrup—a mixture of dextrose and its polymers

Maltose—a compound sugar of two dextrose units

Dextrose-levulose syrups—a dextrose solution rich in levulose

Molasses—a mixture of levulose, dextrose, and sucrose

Maple—composed of levulose, dextrose, and sucrose

Honey—composed of levulose, dextrose, sucrose, and invert

Non-nutritive—sweeteners not composed of carbohydrates

The major food industries using the largest quantities of sweeteners in order of volume are: soft drinks, baking, confectionery, canning, dairy, brewing.

Sucrose[6]

The development and use of sucrose as a sweetener probably began in the South Pacific approximately 8000 yr ago. Sugar cane may have first grown in New Guinea—nobody seems to know for sure—and moved on—nobody seems to know how —to Southeast Asia and India. It was mentioned first in history in 325 B.C. by an officer of Alexander the Great's army while in India.

Military adventurers, army movements, the Crusades, and traders moved sucrose in ever-widening circles until by 1300 A.D. Venice was the sugar center of the world.

The further movement of the product of sugar cane can be traced in succession to Portugal, Africa, Brazil, and the Canary Islands.

Columbus brought sugar to this country on his second voyage. From that small introduction the United States has become the second largest sugar user in the world, with U.S.S.R. the largest user.

Another important source of sucrose is the sugar beet. Its history goes back to ancient times, but it was not until 1744 that a German chemist proved that sugar from the white beet was the same sucrose obtained from sugar cane.

Once a practical method for extracting the sucrose had been developed, manufacture of beet sugar spread from Germany to France, Austria and Russia. By 1813, France, under blockade by England and unable to import cane, had 334 beet sugar factories producing 35,000 tons.

Sugar from beets today accounts for about 40% of the world's sugar. The United States is the second largest producer in the world, with sugar beets being raised in 25 states.

Cane Sugar.—Although in the modern sugar refineries of today there are many improvements on the ancient methods, the process is still one of crushing the cane to extract the juice, purifying, and drying raw sucrose. Cane is still cut by hand— or mechanically in some instances where topography and acreage permit, and the juices are squeezed out between pressure rolls. The juices are centrifuged; then partially boiled off under vacuum until the raws are dry enough to ship to the refineries of the world. The major producers of cane sugar raws are Argentina, Australia, Brazil, China,

[6] For specific information write to Sugar Information, General Post Office Box 94, New York, N.Y. 10001.

TABLE S-33

SUGAR DELIVERIES, BY TYPE OF PRODUCT OR BUSINESS OF BUYER AND BY TYPE OF SUGAR,
CALENDAR YEAR 1972

Product or Business of Buyer	Beet (Total)	Cane (Total)	Imported D.C. (Total)	Total All Sugar	Liquid Sugar Included in Totals	
					Beet	Cane
	(Deliveries in Hundredweights[1])					
Industrial						
Bakery, cereal and allied products	11,236,889	17,533,797	216,687	28,987,373	298,908	2,039,944
Confectionery and related products	6,979,988	1,402,875	131,201	21,139,064	195,072	3,155,042
Ice cream and dairy products	4,603,347	7,353,141	29,005	11,985,493	2,085,208	5,321,833
Beverages	11,940,071	36,767,372	32,080	48,739,523	6,149,216	23,003,001
Canned, bottled, frozen foods, jams, jellies and preserves	8,845,642	10,806,433	87,062	19,739,137	2,875,535	5,489,181
Multiple and all other food uses	3,712,333	6,332,092	113,402	10,157,827	224,373	1,544,970
Nonfood products	359,999	1,430,372	20,701	1,811,072	60,056	654,593
Subtotal	47,678,269	94,251,082	630,138	142,559,489	11,888,368	41,208,564
Nonindustrial						
Hotels, restaurants, institutions	121,463	1,533,196	38,000	1,692,659	15,618	92,702
Wholesale grocers, jobbers, sugar dealers	12,413,962	29,205,937	436,755	42,056,654	178,506	333,997
Retail grocers, chain stores, supermarkets	4,792,296	21,237,573	294,111	26,323,980	131,819	189,393
All other deliveries, including deliveries to government agencies	673,547	1,041,341	42,385	1,757,273	33,217	106,074
Subtotal	18,001,268	53,018,047	811,251	71,830,566	359,160	722,166
Total Deliveries	65,679,537	147,269,129	1,441,389	214,390,055	12,247,528	41,930,730
Deliveries in consumer-size packages (less than 50 lb)	9,690,019	41,170,595	275,362	51,135,976		
Deliveries in bulk (unpackaged)	30,179,160	35,624,011	3,482	65,806,653		

SOURCE: USDA Sugar Reports 250, Mar. 1973.

[1] Reported as produced or imported and delivered except liquid sugar which is on a sugar solids content basis.

Cuba, Dominican Republic, Hawaii, India, Mexico, Philippines, Republic of South Africa, and the United States. Production in the latter area is still relatively small and will probably remain so because of high land and labor costs and low profit yields from sugar manufacture.

The washed and decolorized raws, as unrefined sucrose is referred to in the industry, is sticky and brownish in color. In the refinery, the familiar dry white sucrose is separated from the brown sugars and molasses. When fully refined, the white crystalline sucrose is packed either in small sacks and 100-lb bags or offered to industry in bulk in standard, medium, fine, extra fine, bakers SP, and powdered 4X, 6X, and 10X. Some of the refined cane is also made into icing-type sucrose at the refinery. (Brown sugar is produced in three color-graded types—dark, medium, and light.) Some is destined to become liquid and sold as straight sucrose, invert, or blended with other sweeteners

TABLE S-34

CORN REFINERS' SHIPMENTS OF CORN SYRUP AND DEXTROSE, BY TYPE OF BUYER, CALENDAR YEAR 1972 AND 1971[1]

Type of Buyer	Corn Syrup, Unmixed		Dextrose		All Corn Sweetners	
	1972	1971	1972	1971	1972	1971
	(Shipments in Hundredweights, Dry Basis)[2]					
Bakery, cereal and related products	5,740,326	4,666,603[5]	3,273,525	3,745,578[5]	9,013,851	8,412,181[5]
Confectionery and related products	8,768,286	8,169,193	1,205,053	1,145,979	9,973,339	9,315,172
Ice cream and dairy products	4,421,012	4,136,294	140,538	151,699	4,561,550	4,287,993
Beverages	1,812,724	1,523,203[5]	181,903	186,245[5]	1,994,627	1,709,448[5]
Canners and packers, jams jellies and preserves	3,728,177	3,271,639	633,963	704,150	4,362,140	3,975,789
Multiple and all other food uses	6,298,434	5,578,721[5]	3,664,157	3,914,407[5]	9,962,591	9,493,128[5]
Nonfood uses[3]	1,227,224	1,012,495[5]	1,803,770	1,814,626[5]	3,030,994	2,827,121[5]
Total shipments[4]	31,996,186	28,358,149[5]	10,902,910	11,662,684[5]	42,899,096	40,020,833[5]

SOURCE: USDA Sugar Reports 250, Mar. 1973.

NOTE: Through last half of 1972 and first quarter of 1973 quarterly increases of use of corn sweeteners averaged better than 50% per quarter. Data in the Table are the last published by USDA because of this rapid increased use.

[1] Domestic shipments of members of Corn Refiners Association, Inc.
[2] Assumes a solids content of 80.3% for corn syrup and 92% for dextrose thus, dry weight basis is reported weight shipped multiplied by 0.803 for corn syrup and 92 for dextrose.
[3] Includes shipments to jobbers (wholesalers).
[4] Due to rounding totals may not be exact sums of individual items.
[5] Revised.

Liquid sugar is one of the newest products of the sucrose industry. Far from being a simple addition of water to dry sucrose to produce a liquid, the manufacture of liquid sucrose is a complex and precise process. This development will be covered below in greater detail, and since the basic refining steps are similar they will be described in that section.

Beet Sugar.—Removing sucrose from sugar beets requires a process quite different from that of cane. The beets—each 1 weighing about 2 lb and containing approximately 14 tsp of sugar in its root—are washed upon arrival at the factory from the farm. They are sliced into shoestring-like strips. are placed in large tanks of hot water where the sweet juice is soaked out.

The juice is next purified, filtered, and concentrated in much the same way as cane juice is treated. Unlike cane, beet sugar processed in the United States is not shipped from one point to another in its raw state. Complete processing from receiving beets to the production of granulated sugar, ready for market, is carried out within the same factory.

Corn Sweeteners—Dextrose and Corn Syrup[7,8]

From an anonymous German chemist, who lived in the time of Napoleon I, to a Russian named Kirchoff (who accidentally produced starch syrup while searching for a binder for porcelain), to a French chemist named de Saussure, the early development of sweeteners from starch was rather roundabout.

Once the starch syrup—as it was first called—was developed, its first applications were in brewing and the manufacture of spiritous liquors. This use continued until 1814 when Napoleon's blockade was lifted and cane sugar returned to general use.

---

[7] For more complete information on corn sweeteners, their properties, and use, write to Corn Refiners Association, 1001 Connecticut Ave., N.W., Washington, D.C. 20036.
[8] Available from CPC International, Industrial Division, Englewood Cliffs, N.J. 07632, are the following which give comprehensive treatment of the subject of sweeteners: The Key to Carbohydrates; Cerelose Dextrose, A Highly Versatile Food Ingredient; and This Is Liquid Sugar.

The starch-derived sweeteners, however, had proved their practicality and usefulness.

By 1857, the demand for starch syrups in the United States was significant, the future looked promising, and the real study of its production and use began in earnest.

William B. Newkirk of Corn Products Refining Company, now CPC International, Inc., was the first to develop a commercial and practical process for the manufacture of pure dextrose from starch. Today, corn is the largest U.S. grain crop being converted to starch, thence to corn syrup and dextrose. Of all the starch made in the United States, 60% is converted into sweeteners and of this amount $2\frac{1}{2}$ billion pounds become corn syrup and well over a billion pounds are made into dextrose. Though the total corn grind is in the area of 200 million bushels, this figure represents only about $4\frac{1}{2}\%$ of the annual U.S. corn crop. Raw material is plentiful. In certain areas of the world, not corn but potatoes and tapioca provide the raw material for sweeteners.

Briefly, the corn starch conversion process is this: first a thoroughly agitated starch slurry is heated in the presence of dilute hydrochloric acid (more dilute than is found in the human stomach). As the reaction continues, the starch is converted into polysaccharides of lower and lower molecular weight. If the process is halted at any given point a corn syrup of a certain Dextrose Equivalent (DE) is produced. The longer the process continues the higher the DE and the sweeter the product until, with complete conversion, the end result is dextrose.

DE is an expression of the reducing sugar content calculated as anhydrous dextrose and expressed as a percentage of the total dry substance. Pure dextrose has a DE of 100.

One of the new developments in production of corn syrup and dextrose is enzyme conversion wherein a purified diastatic enzyme is introduced after partial acid conversion. Use of different enzymes will produce syrups with different saccharide compositions. In fact, the individual saccharides of an acid-converted corn syrup and syrup made by acid-enzyme conversion can be quite different. For this reason corn syrups with the same DE may have very different saccharide profiles (Fig. S-37). Table S-35 shows the carbohydrate composition of several commercially available corn syrups. Table S-36 lists typical grades of dextrose that are commercially available. There are also a number of other grades available for specific applications.

Recently, due to technical developments which permit enzymatic conversion of starch to dextrose, a clear, sweet liquid product has come into widespread use. It has a dextrose equivalent of 95% min. and is 95% fermentable. Because of its high fermentability, it is especially applicable to bread baking and the manufacture of fermentation chemicals. It produces high osmotic pressure in solution which makes it useful in preserved fruits. Its iso-sweet sucrose characteristics make this product acceptable in flavored carbonated beverages.

Corn syrups are used in so many food products, it is impossible to list them all. But the list below gives some idea of their broad popularity:

Baby foods	Frozen fruits
Bakery products	Fruit juice drinks
Beer and ale	Fruit wines
Canned fruits	Ice cream and frozen
Carbonated beverages	desserts
Confections and	Jams, jellies and
chewing gum	preserves
Cordials and liqueurs	Meat products
Dressings and	Pickles and condiments
seasoning sauces	Sweetened condensed
Dry bakery mixes	milk
Fountain syrups and	Table syrups
toppings	

Dextrose, a monosaccharide simple sugar, is commercially obtained by the complete hydrolysis of starch, then purified by crystallization. There are two basic types, monohydrate containing one molecule of water for each molecule of dextrose; and anhydrous dextrose containing no combined water.

Dextrose is sweet and is known to produce a synergistic effect with other sweeteners. Dextrose, in liquid or dry form, is used in many food products and in large volumes. The properties and uses of dextrose are indicated by the following:

Browning reaction	Nutritive solids
Fermentability	Osmotic pressure
Flavor enhancement	Sweetness

Dextrose Equivalent	36 (Acid)	42 (Acid)	42 (Acid/Enzyme)
Dextrose	13.7	18.6	5.9
Disaccharide	11.5	13.9	44.4
Trisaccharide	10.1	11.6	12.7
Tetrasaccharide	9.2	9.9	3.3
Pentasaccharide	7.9	8.3	1.8
Hexasaccharide	6.5	6.6	1.5
Heptasaccharide & Higher	41.1	31.1	30.4

Courtesy of CPC International, Industrial Div.

FIG. S-37. COMPOSITION OF SEVERAL CORN SYRUPS

TABLE S-35

EXAMPLES OF CARBOHYDRATE COMPOSITION OF COMMERCIALLY AVAILABLE CORN SYRUPS

Type of Conversion	DE	Percent Saccharides							
		Mono-	Di-	Tri-	Tetra-	Penta-	Hexa-	Hepta-	Higher
Acid	30	10.4	9.3	8.6	8.2	7.2	6.0	5.2	45.1
Acid	42	18.5	13.9	11.6	9.9	8.4	6.6	5.7	25.4
Acid-enzyme[1]	43	5.5	46.2	12.3	3.2	1.8	1.5	—	29.5[2]
Acid	54	29.7	17.8	13.2	9.6	7.3	5.3	4.3	12.8
Acid	60	36.2	19.5	13.2	8.7	6.3	4.4	3.2	8.5
Acid-enzyme[1]	63	38.8	28.1	13.7	4.1	4.5	2.6	—	8.2[2]
Acid-enzyme[1]	71	43.7	36.7	3.7	3.2	0.8	4.3	—	7.6[2]

SOURCE: Corn Refiners Association.

[1] The carbohydrate composition of acid-enzyme syrups will vary as a result of different processes used. The values given in the Table are to be considered only as examples of ranges of values that are available commercially.
[2] Includes heptasaccharides.

Humectancy Viscosity
Hygroscopicity Reactivity

Another type of corn sweetener is corn syrup solids. This product results from the drying of regular or low conversion corn syrup until it contains less than $3\frac{1}{2}\%$ moisture. It is a powdery product, colorless, mildly sweet, and hygroscopic. It is used in soups, puddings, ice cream, and dessicated foods.

Corn sweeteners have certain specific characteristics which account for their usefulness in many food applications. Here are some of them: They are readily soluble. Dextrose cools as it dissolves, making it more attractive to bakers who wish to cool doughs. Because they are generally hygroscopic, corn sweeteners are good humectants. They control crystallization of sucrose and other sugars, making them useful in confections, ice cream, frozen desserts, jams, jellies, and preserves. Used in canning, corn sweeteners produce glossy-looking

TABLE S-36

DEXTROSE: TYPICAL GRADES
AND SPECIFICATIONS

Type	Solids (%)	DE
Dextrose hydrate[1]	91.5	99.5+
USP[2]	91.5	99.8+
USP anhydrous[2]	99.8	99.8+
Anhydrous	99.9	99.8+
Liquid	68.0–69.0	99.5

SOURCE: CPC International, Inc.

[1] Dextrose hydrate is produced in a variety of particle sizes. Granular, powdered and pulverized forms are available in addition to the standard grade.
[2] Conforms to specifications of United States Pharmacopoeia.

fruits. The high osmotic pressure of dextrose is effective in inhibiting microbial spoilage in preserves and in improving the texture of canned fruits and pickles.

Syrups made from corn, but with controlled amounts and types of saccharides, are among the latest developments to come upon the corn sweetener scene. Several manufacturers are studying the potential of these syrups, which are produced by a special enzyme process. The unfinished syrups are composed of levulose, dextrose, and maltose. The ratio of one sugar to another—theoretically—can be regulated to make a syrup with a profile to fit a particular application. Their main markets would seem to be in the baking and beverage industries. Technical and production problems at present limit use of these syrups; but they are being subjected to research to solve these problems. It is too soon to place them in proper perspective in relation to all the other available nutritive sweeteners.

Production of Liquid Sugar and Blends

The first manufacture and distribution of liquid sugar began in a 50-yr-old warehouse in New York City where total daily capacity was only 25 tons. Development of production and application technology began there; and during the early 1930's, the liquid products gained acceptance. They have continued to grow each year. Their main attraction is that they lend themselves readily to liquid systems and are easy to store and transfer.

Since 1957 commercial blends of sucrose, invert sugar, dextrose and corn syrup have also appeared in the industry.

Liquid sugar (sucrose) is made commercially from either cane or beet sugar. The production process includes not only the standard basic refinery procedures of affination, defecation, clarification, and char treatment, but also granular and powdered carbon filtration and sometimes ion exchange.

When made from cane, liquid sugar can be obtained by remelting (redissolving) granulated sugar refined in the conventional way, or by producing it directly from raws as a liquid in refineries designed and equipped for this process. When made from beet, liquid sugar is obtained only by remelting granulated sugar and filtering through carbon as the beet process still requires final crystallization before a pure sucrose is obtained.

Invert, a mixture of dextrose and levulose, is made by enzyme or acid hydrolysis of sucrose in solution. An exceptionally high quality invert sugar is made by passing a sucrose solution through a column of cation exchange resin. The sucrose solution is not only inverted but it is also demineralized.

Refining and blending of liquid sweeteners calls for modern technology, scientific knowledge, and quality control during manufacturing.

Manufacture is, briefly, as follows: raw sugar (a mixture of crystals of sucrose surrounded by a film of molasses) undergoes affination, the process which softens and removes the molasses film with a saturated sugar liquor. The next steps are defecation and clarification, which remove impurities such as pectins, gums, starches, and albumins. The liquor is next passed through either char and/or vegetable or granular carbon filtration, removing color bodies.

An additional operation in the production of premium sucrose liquid sugars is the use of the single unit ion exchange process, commonly referred to as the monobed, which removes remaining traces of color and ash, or mineral content, and yields a water-white, essentially ash-free liquor.

Finally, sucrose solution is heat-sterilized and then concentrated in an evaporator to 67% solids. The finished product is then cooled and pumped to storage tanks.

Char liquor is similarly treated with activated carbon, passed through filters, polished and inverted by percolation through the acidic cation exchange resin at elevated temperatures in tanks. The liquor, inverted to any desired degree, is heat sterilized and evaporated to solids specifications, cooled, and stored.

Char liquor is used for the manufacture of dry sugar through successive stages of evaporation, crystallization, centrifuging, drying, cooling, and screening. Golden syrups are produced from the liquor remaining after several strikes of granulated sugar have been separated. This liquor is filtered through activated carbon, concentrated by evaporation, inverted if desired, and polished to yield either golden sucrose or golden invert syrups.

Many types of sweetener blends are produced by the liquid sugar refiner and others equipped with appropriate facilities. In addition to all-sugar blends such as sucrose/dextrose and invert/dextrose, various combinations of corn syrups with sucrose and invert are manufactured and are generally available.

By mid-June 1974, sugar prices hit an all-time high of 32¢ per lb. Corn-derived syrups and dextrose prices are $1/2$ of the 32¢ price and therefore are being readily substituted in most commercial formulations. Also, because of recent enzymatic conversion of dextrose to dextrose-levulose isomer, virtually equal to invert, the use of up to 75% of this product is permitted in beverages, baking, bottled goods, etc. Actually, corn syrups and dextrose are on allocation based on previous record of use—in other words, these products are rationed to the trade because corn refiners are in an oversold position despite full capacity operations and expanded production.

Other Sugars

Lactose, or milk sugar, is manufactured from whey and skimmed milk. It is less sweet than sucrose and considerably less soluble in water. Its primary use is in pharmaceuticals and specialty products as a bulking agent.

Multose, malt sugar, is made from starch by a yeast process. It is less sweet than sucrose. Mixed with dextrose it is used in bread baking and infant foods.

Molasses, a by-product of cane refining, is used mostly in table sugars and in certain baked products. There are two main types: edible, the highest grade; and blackstrap, the last grade in the refining process. The latter is most often used in industrial fermentation.

Honey is used in limited quantities in certain types of foods. It is an invert type sugar, composed of levulose, dextrose, sucrose, water, and a small amount of acid and ash. Its composition varies with the source of nectar, i.e., the type of flower it came from.

Maple sugar and maple syrup come from maple tree sap. American Indians taught early settlers how to reduce the sap to syrup and sugar through a long boiling process. To make 1 gal. of maple syrup, 4 40-yr-old maple trees must first produce 40 gal. of maple sap. The liquid product is used mostly for table syrup and the sugar mostly for confections. Its composition is sucrose, invert, and a small amount of ash.

Non-Nutritive Sweeteners

Man-made sweeteners have been referred to as artificial, synthetic, or non-nutritive. Non-nutritive is a term that has been applied to these products by industry and government. Wherever Standards of Identity have been established, especially for dietetic foods, they permit the use of non-nutrient sweeteners in the place of carbohydrates.

The development of saccharin, one of the earliest synthetic sweeteners, dates back to Ira Remsen of John Hopkins University in 1879. This commercially available product is 300 times as sweet as sucrose. Until dieting to control weight became as widespread as it is at the present time, saccharin's use was primarily as a sugar replacement for those who must restrict their intake of natural sugars. It is also used in toothpaste, pharmaceuticals, and tobacco curing.

Since the cyclamates were removed from the market, saccharin has been the principal sweetening agent in beverages with lowered caloric content. It is also used in considerable quantities in canned and frozen fruits. Its bitter after taste has generally been a barrier to more widespread use.

The use of non-nutritive sweeteners in soft drinks seems, from most statistics, to be a new market, jumping from 500 cases in 1950 to 250,000,000 cases in 1965. The 1954 and 1964 figures for consumption of beverages sweetened with nutritive sweeteners also show a per-capita increase.

Other non-nutritive sweeteners are being developed by industry researchers. Products such as the dihydrochalones and aspartylphenylalanine show some promise as substitutes for nutritive sweeteners in some applications; but, as is true with any product whose use is intended for food, much testing and approval by FDA must precede acceptance. Traditionally, new sweeteners—nutritive or non-nutritive—have found adoption by the food industry a slow process. It's safe to assume that any new sweeteners will probably face the same challenge.

There are 3 dihydrochalones; 2 of them are 150 times sweeter than sucrose; a third, neohesperidine, is 2000 times sweeter than sucrose. At this writing, none have gained FDA approval and because they are made from citrus wastes, raw material supply may be limited.

Aspartylphenylalanine is approximately 250 times sweeter than sucrose. The experimental product has no after taste, no flavor other than sweetness, and toxicity should not be a problem since it is a dipeptide and degrades to a simple amino acid, easily metabolized. The production process is complex, which will affect cost, assuming testing gives favorable results and the FDA gives its approval.

Two other products warrant mention in this section: malted and ammoniated glycyrrhizin found in licorice. Rather than sweeteners, as such, these are flavor enhancers which emphasize the sweetness of caloric sweeteners. They are approved and commercially available, although at this time they are not enjoying widespread application.

PETER X. HOYNAK

Cross-references: *Carbohydrates; Molasses.*

SUNFLOWER SEED

The sunflower (*Helianthus annuus*) originated in North America, but, until recently, has not been of commercial importance there. The only areas where its cultivation has become important are the Soviet Union, Argentina, Eastern Europe, and South Africa. Increasing importance in South Africa has been due in large part to official encouragement. Argentina started encouraging the expansion of the cultivation of sunflowers in the middle 1930's with substantial results toward the end of the 1940's. In the Soviet Union, the most important developments are recent. Scientific research has brought about spectacular improvements in yield and in oil content. These improvements have contributed to the expansion of production which, in the 1960's, has permitted exports of considerable importance to Eastern Europe, themselves large producers, and to other countries.

Basic Data

Yields of seed:

	1966	1967	1968
		(Lbs per Acre)	
Soviet Union	1097	1230	—
Europe	1295	—	—
France	1525	1550	1893
Italy	1878	—	—

Yield of crude oil from the seed in 1967:

	(%)
Soviet Union	44.2
France	42
Latin America	40

Yield of oil-cake (also designated as press-cake): 37%.

Protein in oil-cake:

	(%)
Soviet Union	44
France	40–42
Argentina	39–40

TABLE S-37

COMPOSITION OF SUNFLOWER SEED

| | Entire Seed | | Hulled Seed | | Hulls (Dry Basis) |
	Dry Basis (%)	Dry and Oil-Free (%)	Dry Basis (%)	Dry and Oil-Free (%)	(%)
Organic material	97.24	95.56	96.59	94.78	98.06
Protein	19.34	24.08	31.05	47.49	4.96
Lipids	19.67	—	34.62	—	1.13
Fiber	30.48	37.93	3.07	4.70	64.35
Non-nitrogenous material	27.75	34.55	27.87	42.63	27.62
Ash	2.76	3.44	3.41	5.22	1.94
Coefficient of digestibility of proteins			83.80		39.00
Crude protein assimilability			25.95		1.93

Characteristics of the oil:

Consistency	Liquid
Color	Pale Yellow
Odor	None
Flavor	None
Solidification Point	$-16°$–$18.5°C$
Maumené	$67.5°$–$75°C$
Sp Gr at $15°C$	0.912–0.936
Index of Refraction ($20°C$)	1.4736
Saponification Value	186–194
Iodine Value	115–135
Hehner Value	95
Reichert-Meissel Value	0.25
Polenske Value	0.25
Acetyl value	14.5
Solidification Point of fatty acids	$17°$–$18°C$
Titer	$22°$–$24°C$
Unsaponifiable matter	0.3–1%
Slowly drying oil	

Composition of sunflower seed: See Table S-37.
Composition of sunflower seed oil:

	(%)
Palmitic acid	7–10
Stearic acid	4–8
Oleic acid	17–22
Linoleic acid	60–75
Arachidic acid	Tr
Phospholipids	0.30
Sterols (rich in stigmasterol)	0.25
Tocopherols (About 70 mg %/gm)	

Varieties and Oil Yields

The varieties cultivated until 1960 in France (Nain Noir, Gris Strié de Provence, Rudorf, and Jupiter) are now being discontinued and are being replaced by Soviet varieties which have an oil content of 39–45% (Table S-38). In 1969 two new French varieties were added to the "list of certified varieties": Issanka; Obtainer: INRA.

The yield of seed as well as the oil content will be greater than those hitherto recorded from early commercial varieties.

INRA 6501 will be characterized by its short stem and regularity, having a great resistance to "beating down." It will also be resistant to spoilage due to botrytis, and will have a flowering and a very homogeneous maturity.

The oil content of this variety will be somewhat inferior to that of Peredovik, but will have a greater yield of seed.

Production of Sunflower Seed

From 1957 to 1967, the world production of sunflower seed has climbed from 4,520,000 to 9,870,000 metric tons (Table S-39).

It is the Soviet Union which has contributed the greatest to this increase: in terms of oil, its production since 1952–1956 has almost tripled. That of

TABLE S-38

SUNFLOWER VARIETIES AND OIL YIELDS

	Iénissei	Armavir 93–45	Peredovik
Maturity	Early	Semiearly	Semilate
Height (meters)	1–1.4	1.4–1.6	1.4–1.75
Oil at 9% moisture (%)	39–41	42–44	43–45
Resistance to "beating down"	Good	Moderate	Rather good

TABLE S-39

WORLD PRODUCTION OF SUNFLOWER SEED

	1957	1962	1967
	(In 1000 Metric Tons)		
Soviet Union	2,801	4,795	6,589
Argentina	625	860	1,120
Romania	255	450	720
Bulgaria	209	357	478
Yugoslavia	93	161	250
Turkey	95	60	215
South Africa	75	97	101
Hungary	90	131	79
France	3	18	13
Italy	4	4	2
World total	4,520	7,190	9,870

Argentina has doubled, that of Romania has more than tripled (360%).

Soviet Union Production.—The sunflower has been cultivated for many years in Russia. In 1911–1913, production was already at 660,000 metric tons. There were two definite uses for the seed: oil production and direct human consumption in the form of roasted seed.

The quantities ground are now of the order of 5,500,000 metric tons, giving a yield of oil of 2,400,000 metric tons.

The tonnage of 1967 was produced on 1,180,000 acres. The yield has been 1230 lb per acre against 535 in 1952.

In the Ukraine 3,700,000 acres were seeded and almost 4,940,000 acres in the northern Caucasus, the delta of the Volga and the Central Territories; the remainder was divided among Moldavia, Georgia, Azerbaïdjan, etc.

Argentina Production.—The production of sunflower seed in Argentina is extensive. About 2,640,000 acres are planted. The yield reaches 800 lb per acre.

Romania Production.—Land in cultivation with sunflowers reached 1,185,000 acres in 1967. The yields have been 1340 lb per acre.

Bulgaria Production.—Land cultivated in 1967 reached 662,000 acres, and the yields have been 1590 lb per acre; 100,000 metric tons have been exported.

Yugoslavia Production.—Land in cultivation in 1967 attained 363,500 acres. The yields run 1520 lb per acre.

Production of Sunflower Oil

In 1967 the largest producers of oil were in the same order of importance as the producers of seed:

	Metric Tons
Soviet Union	2,200,000
Argentina	325,000
Romania	242,000
Bulgaria	131,000
Yugoslavia	101,000

In 1957 the Soviet Union accounted for 72% of the world production of oil, but this percentage returned to 66% in 1967.

International Commerce

In 1967, 450,000 metric tons of seed were exported; 225,000 by the Soviet Union, 100,000 by Bulgaria, 64,000 by Romania, and 6000 by France.

The importers of seed were primarily members of the European Common Market (219,000 metric tons), and, in order of importance, Japan (96,000 metric tons), East Germany (88,000 metric tons), and Czechoslovakia (47,000 metric tons).

In 1967, 896,000 metric tons of oil were exported of which 670,000 metric tons were by the Soviet Union, 100,000 metric tons by Romania, 81,000 metric tons by Argentina, and 13,000 metric tons by Hungary.

The importing countries in order of importance are as follows:

	Metric Tons
West Germany	141,600
East Germany	105,000
Iran	55,800
Cuba	50,000
Holland	49,300
Czechoslovakia	45,000
Poland	44,800
Morocco	41,000
Italy	22,900
Economic Union of Belgium and Luxembourg	16,200
France	5,000
World total	791,000

Utilization

The sunflower is utilized principally for human food and for animal feeding.

The sunflower furnishes one of the best food oils. The cold-pressed oil is even considered a dietetic product especially valuable for its anti-cholesterol activity. Its appealing flavor and its food value have made it a product of choice.

Sunflower seed oil may be utilized in the manufacture of margarine, such as the following examples.

Formula based on a single oil:

	(%)
Hydrogenated sunflower seed oil (MP 44°C)	20
Hydrogenated sunflower seed oil (MP 32°C)	60
Liquid sunflower seed oil	20

TABLE S-40

COMPOSITION OF SUNFLOWER SEED PRESS-CAKE

	Straw A[1]		B[2]	50% Dehulled NF[3]		C[4]	Dehulled A[1] Pressed		Extracted		NF[3] Extracted	
	Avg	Extreme		Min	Max		Avg	Extreme	Avg	Extreme	Min	Max
Moisture	8.2	4–14	10–12	12		6.5	8.5	3–19	10	0.7–16		12
Protein (N × 6.5)	18.8	12–22	20–32	30		16.9	35.6	29–43	38.4	29–43	40	
Lipids	2.6	1.5–3.6	9–15			23.9	7.1	4–15	3.6	2–6	0.5	
Non-nitrogenous material	22.1		26–32			21.9	26.5		26.6			
Crude cellulose	44.7	39–43	18–20	18		27.9	16.1	7–23	14.5	9–18		10
Ash	3.6	2.6–4.2	5–6			3.2	6.2	5–11	6.9	4–8		

[1] Leroy *et al.* (1949).
[2] Bussard *et al.* (1925).
[3] French Standard (1950).
[4] Quiros (1945).

Recent formulas for products with special characteristics:

Margarine Rich in Essential Fatty Acids

	(%)
Coconut oil	30
Palm oil	10
Palm kernel oil	15
Hydrogenated palm oil (MP 42°C)	10
Liquid sunflower oil	35

Margarine Rich in Polyunsaturated Fatty Acids

	(%)
Liquid sunflower oil	88
Hydrogenated palm kernel oil	6
Hydrogenated palm oil	6

Margarine Prepared from a Mixture of Interesterified Oils

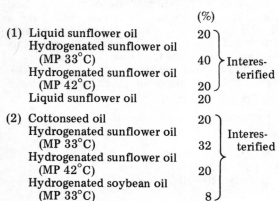

(%)

(1) Liquid sunflower oil   20 ⎤
    Hydrogenated sunflower oil (MP 33°C)   40 ⎬ Interesterified
    Hydrogenated sunflower oil (MP 42°C)   20 ⎦
    Liquid sunflower oil   20

(2) Cottonseed oil   20 ⎤
    Hydrogenated sunflower oil (MP 33°C)   32 ⎬ Interesterified
    Hydrogenated sunflower oil (MP 42°C)   20 ⎪
    Hydrogenated soybean oil (MP 33°C)   8 ⎦
    Liquid sunflower oil   20

Sunflower seed of certain varieties is eaten roasted, especially in the Soviet Union.

The sunflower is well utilized by animals with the precaution that the percentage of cellulose of the oil-cake does not exceed 10%.

In 1967, Argentina exported 394,000 metric tons of oil-cake, the Soviet Union 139,000 metric tons, Turkey 104,000 metric tons, and Uruguay 29,000 metric tons.

The importing countries were Holland (175,000 metric tons), Great Britain (81,000 metric tons), East Germany (62,000 metric tons), and the Economic Union of Belgium and Luxembourg (58,000 metric tons).

The composition of sunflower seed press-cake is given in Table S-40. Protein quality is characterized by a low lysine level. Amino acid levels are as follows: arginine 8.2; histidine 1.7; lysine 3.8; tyrosine 2.6; tryptophan 1.3; phenylalanine 5.7; cystine 1.5; methionine 3.4; threonine 4.0; leucine 6.2; isoleucine 5.2; valine 5.2; alanine 3.2; serine plus aspartic acid 2.5.

The vitamin B complex content of defatted sunflower seed flour is superior to the products prepared from wheat germ, corn germ, and soya.

Nondehulled sunflower seed oil-cake is a food product of poor digestibility, and is low in glucides and proteins. On the contrary, the oil-cake prepared from dehulled seed is an excellent feed, easily digestible, and of a very acceptable richness of assimilable protein and glucides.

Treatment of Sunflower Seed

Cleaning.—The efficiency of cleaning of sunflower seed is a function of the rate of flow, the initial concentration of impurities, and the angle of inclination of the sieve. An increase in the rate of flow causes an important increase in the percentage of impurities. A higher initial degree of contamination will show a greater absolute quantity of impurities removed, but the relative degree of impurities removed is not greatly increased.

Concerning the inclination of the sieve, the optimum angle is 10°, and that of the bolting machine 10°-12°.

Dehulling.—The treatment of sunflower seed with separation of the hull responds to fundamental requirements; 6-8% hull may be taken as optimum.

Economically, it is rational to treat the seed, rich in oil, so that the amount of oil in the shell which is contained in the oil-cake is not greater than that in the separated shell or hull.

The hulls from seed rich in oil contain up to 3.1% of extractable lipids using petroleum and up to 3.8% lipids extractable with ethyl ether (calculated on the dry basis). More than 60% of these lipids are wax-like.

Grinding.—To characterize the comminution of oily materials, it is convenient to use the method of determination of specific surfaces. That will give an index, not only of the initial state of the material but equally of its modification in the process of technological treatment.

In the process of double pressings on screw presses FP-EP, the optimum specific surface of the meats (at 3-4% shell and 5-6% moisture), coming from seed containing 43-44% oil (from material completely dry), represents 4.6-4.8 sq m per gm. The optimum specific surface of the prepress cake obtained from such meats and ground represents 1.1-1.6 sq m per gm.

Pressing.—The technology of pressing sunflower seed does not differ much from that of pressing peanuts. In the heating and hydration chambers of the preliminary press, a moisture percentage of 8-8.5% is obtained. The parameters of the pulp entering into these presses are as follows:

Temperature	107-112°C
Moisture	4.2-4.8%

The cake of the first pressing should be less thick than that of the second pressing and should have a thickness of 5-7 mm.

The maintenance of the pulp in the 6-part cooker for 55-60 min with an addition of 10-12% dry defatted product permits an extraction of oil of 87-92% on the preliminary presses based on the total quantity in the seed.

The operation of the preliminary presses should be maintained to assure that the flake contains 10-13% oil.

The addition of oil-rich residues such as filter-press residues and foots should be made only to the top chamber of the cookers of the preliminary presses.

The grinding of the material from the first pressing should assure a flour which will pass through a screen with 1-mm openings at the rate of 92-94%.

Before the screw presses of the second pressing, the meats should be retreated in the first stack of the cookers of the screw presses to give a moisture of 5-6%. If this is not obtained, direct water vapor is introduced into the second stack.

It is recommended to introduce the pulp for the second pressing with a moisture of 3.7-4.2%, and a temperature of 121°-125°C.

With a flake thickness of at least 6-8 mm, a press cake which runs 4.2-4.6% oil will be obtained.

For the second pressing, the prepared pulp is normal in humidity, plasticity, and porosity when the Ammeter of the press motor shows 22 A. Lower amperage readings indicate a pulp perhaps raw or in insufficient quantity; superior to 22 A, the pulp may be too dry or in excessive quantity.

Soluble protein content (based on material dry, defatted, and dehulled) of the press cake from the screw presses runs 40%, and that of the cake from prepressing 48%, which is an indication of high nutritive value. It has been established that the content of soluble protein is mostly lowered during the grinding of the kernel, during the treatment in the hydration chambers, and during the final pressing. It follows then that it would be rational to replace this latter method by extraction.

Extraction.—A study of the solid phase of the miscella has made it possible to establish that the dimensions of the particles were varying from 0.004-0.2 mm, as follows:

	(%)
ϕ of particles > 0.16 mm	74
From 0.10 to 0.16 mm	16
From 0.05 to 0.10 mm	5
< 0.05 mm	5

The installation at the first stage of purification of a hydrocyclone of ϕ mm, having a delivery rate of 5-10 cu m per hr, at an operation pressure of 1-6 atm will increase the intervals between cleanings of the filters by 80%.

The best quality of filtrate is obtained by employing a filter cloth of belting and of "kapron." In this case, one obtains also the most rapid rate of flow.

The speed of filtration of the miscella depends on the amount of impurities in suspension. For example, at a pressure of 1500 kg per sq m, the filtration rate with 0.2% and 2.5% sediment by weight is 0.00034 and 0.00010 m^3 (m^2 s) respectively.

During the course of a graded extraction and with a countercurrent flow of the prepressed cake, the principal characteristics of the oil (acid value, color, unsaponifiable matter) deteriorate with an increase in degree of extraction; the same result is obtained when the extraction rate is reduced. A separate collection of the various fractions, corresponding to different degrees of extraction, might give a means of improvement in the nutritional value of the extracted oils with consideration given to the economics involved.

B. SOLOMON

References

ANON. 1950. Composition and standards of oilcakes. N.F. (French Standard). Tech. Committee Oil Milling Mem. (French)

ANON. 1969. The sunflower: technical and statistical data, 1957–67. Soc. Interprofessionelle Oleagineaux Fluides Alimentaire, Paris. (French)

BUSSARD, L. *et al.* 1925. Edible Oil-Cakes. Beranger, Paris. (French)

DAY, H. G., and LEVINE, E. 1945. The nutritional value of sunflower seed meal. Science *10*, 438–439.

FERON, R. 1969. *In* Margarine: An Economic, Social and Scientific History, 1869–1969. J. H. Van Stuijvenberg (Editor). Dunod, Paris; Liverpool University Press.

GOASCOZ, R. 1965. Special problems in obtaining and refining sunflower oil. Inst. Corps gras, Paris. (French)

HUNT, K. H. 1969. *In* Margarine: An Economic, Social and Scientific History, 1869–1969. J. H. Van Stuijvenberg (Editor). Dunod, Paris; Liverpool University Press.

LEROY, A. M. *et al.* 1949. The chemical composition and nutritive value of animal feeds. Ann. Agron. *19*, 791.

MASSON, C. 1968. The sunflower and some other oil-bearing materials: Production and conversion of seeds in Roumania, Russia and Yugoslavia. Cetion, Paris. (French)

QUIROS, M. A. 1945. The sunflower: Importance of its cultivation in Costa Rica. Costa Rica Dept. Nacl. Agr. Tech. Bull. *50*.

ROMBAUTS, P. 1951. Press cake from sunflower seeds. I. Composition, nutritive value and protein efficiency. Oleagineaux *6*, 203–210, 273–281. (French)

SOLOMON, B. 1970. Soviet technology of sunflower. Rev. Franc. Corps gras *17*, No. 1, 23–35. (French)

SURFACE TENSION

Definition

Molecules, within the body of a liquid, are subjected to molecular attractions which are evenly distributed and symmetrical to all directions. This is because they are completely surrounded by other molecules of the liquid. However, those molecules at or near the surface are only partially surrounded by other molecules, namely, those underneath. Because of this, these surface molecules are being "pulled" more firmly toward the body of the liquid thus resulting in a molecular cohesion and orientation resembling the appearance of "an invisible stretched, elastic membrane." This behavior of the surface is called "surface tension" and is the effect responsible for the "resistance a liquid exhibits to surface penetration." It is, in other words, a downward and also lateral force that pulls the molecules in the surface. By doing this, this force represents the tendency of a liquid to reduce its surface or, rather, to assume the shape of the smallest possible surface. Surface tension is usually symbolized by γ and is considered as the force in dynes acting along 1 cm length of surface. Phenomena such as the nearly spherical shape of falling water droplets, the spherical mercury particles sliding on a flat surface, and the rise of liquid in capillary tubes, are all attributed to the existence of surface tension.

In food technology, a complete understanding of the importance of this property may sometimes mean how pure a product may be or how efficiently it can be dried in a spray dryer.

Measurement or Prediction of Surface Tension

Surface tension is a characteristic property of each liquid and varies greatly in magnitude for different liquids or same liquids but of different purity or at different temperatures. Therefore, a measurement or a theoretical prediction of a liquid's surface tension is quite often required. In measuring, there are three general methods: the capillary tube method, the stalagmometer ("drop weight") method, and the ring method.

The capillary tube method measures γ, as the total lifting force in a capillary tube, by determining the height of the liquid column in the tube:

$$\gamma = r \times h \times d \times g/2 \qquad (1)$$

where

r = radius of capillary tube
h = height of liquid column
d = density of liquid
g = gravity constant

(If all units are metric the result is expressed in dynes/cm.)

In the stalagmometer method the liquid is allowed to pass very slowly through a calibrated tip of a special glass bulb holding the liquid. The resulting number of drops falling through this tip for a definite liquid volume is a measure of the liquid's surface tension.

Finally, in the ring method (DuNoüy's Method) the downward pull exerted on a ring of platinum wire, immersed in a liquid and in contact with its surface is determined. The force required to break this wire ring loose is measured and expressed in dynes/cm^2.

DuNoüy's method is usually employed for determining the surface tension of colloidal solutions. If direct measurement of γ is not feasible or available, then a more-or-less accurate prediction can be made (Perry 1963) either by the liquids refractive index or its liquid and vapor densities by Equations (2) and (3) respectively.

$$\gamma = \left[\frac{Pn^2 - 1}{R_d n^2 + 2} \right]^4 \quad (2)$$

where

P = liquid's parachor
R_d = liquid's molar refraction
n = refraction index

$$\gamma = \left[\frac{P(P_e - P_v)}{M} \right]^4 \quad (3)$$

where

P = liquid's parachor
P_e = density of the liquid
P_v = density of the vapor
M = molecular weight

Data on how to predict surface tension are given in the literature (Perry 1963). Table S-41 presents surface tension values for some common foodstuffs.

Surface Tension Applications

Since surface tension is a characteristic property of a liquid, it can be used as a criterion of purity.

The presence of colloids, proteins, or fats may influence the surface tension of a liquid. Thus, its purity may be measured indirectly by a measurement of the liquid's surface tension. In beet sugar, for example, as the colloidal impurities increase a decided decrease in γ is observed until a minimum is reached at about 25° Brix (Jacobs 1951). Also, increased fat or acidity may have an effect on surface tension and therefore on the liquid's purity. For example, see values of γ in Table S-41 for whole milk and skim milk. For the same reason, a high-ratio shortening can, reportedly, be differentiated from ordinary fats by its low surface tension (Jacobs 1951) (see Table S-41).

In evaporation, the surface tension of a liquid is also a critical factor. It should be remembered that it is a measurement of the ease by which a liquid may be vaporized. For instance, from the 540 cal of latent heat of vaporization of water, only 40 cal are really needed to overcome the

TABLE S-41

SURFACE TENSION OF SOME COMMON FOODSTUFFS

Liquid	Surface Tension[1] dynes/cm^2
Water	73
Whole milk	50
Skim milk	55
Ordinary fats	26–28
High-ratio shortening	3–48

[1] Measured by the DuNoüy's Method.

vapor density and atmospheric pressure; 500 cal are approximately being consumed to overcome the 73 dynes/cm of surface tension of water.

Surface tension is most critical in present-day spray drying of foodstuffs. Atomization of the liquid to be spray dried is very critical to the economy of drying as well as the physical properties of the dried product (particle shape, absorbicity, etc.). It is reported (Marshall 1954) that the energy of atomization is directly proportional to the liquid's surface tension. Similarly, the atomization efficiency of a spray dryer is directly related to the liquid's surface tension. In some cases, the liquid's surface tension, through its capillary action, may be responsible for the production of hollow or porous particles in spray drying.

Finally, the use of reagents known as "surface active agents" can increase or decrease the surface tension of a liquid and create various conditions of foaming or defoaming. (See Foam Phenomena in Section F.)

A. P. KOULOHERIS

References

JACOBS, M. B. 1951. The Chemistry and Technology of Food and Food Products, 2nd Edition, Vol. 1. Interscience Publishers, New York.
MARSHALL, W. R., JR. 1954. Atomization and spray dyring. Chem. Engr. Progr. Monograph Ser. 2, Vol. 50, A.I.Ch.E.
PERRY, T. H. 1963. Chemical Engineer's Handbook, 4th Edition. McGraw-Hill Book Co., New York.
PRUTTON, C. F., and MARON, S. H. 1951. Fundamental Principles of Physical Chemistry, Revised Edition. Macmillan Co., New York.

SWEETENED CONDENSED MILK

The father of Sweetened Condensed Milk was Gail Borden, school teacher, newspaper publisher, surveyor, port authority, and inventor. During a return voyage to the United States from the International Exhibition in London in 1851, Gail saw many babies dying as a result of the lack of pure, fresh milk. As a result, he resolved not only to find a way to preserve milk, but to keep its good taste and quality. After many unsuccessful attempts, he finally perfected his process and received a British patent on Feb. 28, 1856. Shortly thereafter, he received a U.S. patent covering the same process on Aug. 19, 1856. That same year, efforts were made to establish the first factory to produce the product in Wolcottville, Conn.; however, with meager resources at hand, he finally ran out of funds and the venture was a failure. The next year, in 1857, a second effort was made to establish a factory to produce the product in Burville, Conn.; however, the depression interfered with this effort. Finally, in 1858, with the backing of Jeremiah Millbank, a private banker in New York City, a successful business was established to produce and market Sweetened Condensed Milk.

The first product was peddled in the streets of New York City using a ladle out of a hand cart. In view of the fact that this was the first source of germ-free, wholesome milk, the demand increased rapidly. The name was changed from Gail Borden and Company to the New York Condensed Milk Company, and another plant was established in 1861. Shortly thereafter, with the advent of the Civil War, the Union Army commandeered all Sweetened Condensed Milk production for use by Union troops. Several more factories were built to keep up with the demand, and the military spread the product across the face of the United States during the Civil War. This was the beginning of the company, Borden, Inc., as we know it today.

Infant feeding instructions appeared on the label of the product from the early 1900's until 1938 when doctors started prescribing infant feeding formulas. The consumption of the product hit a peak during World War I when almost seven million cases were consumed during the year of 1919. The consumption of the product gradually declined after World War I and then again hit a peak shortly after World War II when sugar was very scarce to the consumer. Consumers were using the product in the preparation of desserts because of its high sugar content. Today, due to its unique physical properties, the product is used mainly in the preparation of fancy desserts.

Definition

Sweetened Condensed Milk is a mixture of pure, whole cow's milk and sugar with 60% of the water removed before it is packed in hermetically sealed cans. An approximate analysis of the product is as follows:

	(%)
Milk fat	8.5
Milk-solids-not-fat (MSNF)	20.5
Sugar	44.0
Moisture	27.0
Total	100.0

Sweetened Condensed Milk is actually very similar to homemade jelly, except that sugar is being used to preserve milk solids rather than the juice of fruits or berries, as is the case with jelly.

Manufacturing Process

Raw milk arrives fresh from the farm at the condensory's receiving platform where it is checked for quality and temperature. The milk is tested for fat and total solids and then standardized. This standardized milk is blended with sugar and pumped into large stainless steel tanks called "hot wells" to pasteurize the milk and destroy any pathogenic bacteria that might be present. The heat treatment in the hot well is varied with the seasons of the year to control physical instability which otherwise might occur in the product.

The blend of heated, standardized whole milk and sugar is then drawn into a vacuum condensing pan to reduce it to the required consistency and total solids content. To preserve the original flavor and color, the milk is boiled at a low temperature of approximately 130°F under vacuum. When the correct concentration is reached, the milk is drawn quickly from the vacuum pan to the vacuum cooling tank where the temperature is rapidly lowered to approximately 70°F. During this cooling procedure, a predetermined amount of finely ground milk sugar (lactose) is added to the product to control the crystallization of the sugar present. At this point, the preparation of the product is completed. It is now thick, smooth in texture, and creamy in color. Until canned, the milk is held in insulated storage tanks that are sealed and sterile.

Before filling, the consumer size cans are washed and sterilized inside and out by live steam and then fed automatically into a filling machine that is protected to prevent bacterial, yeast, and mold contamination to the product. The milk flows from the storage tank to a continuous filling machine where the filled cans are immediately sealed. Unlike most canned foods, the container is completely filled to prevent the presence of air which could result in the growth of yeast and/or mold in the product. After the cans are coded with the factory date of manufacture, they are then labeled and finally packed for shipping, 24 cans to a case. When final approvals for bacteriological, chemical, and physical analyses are given, the milk is shipped out to supermarkets across the United States and around the world.

Today, most of the Sweetened Condensed Milk in the United States is still produced by Borden, Inc., and the product is still essentially the same as that produced by Gail Borden back in 1856. The product is packed in 14-oz cans and is used in the preparation of fancy desserts. Also, a considerable amount of bulk product is produced for use in the baking and confectionery industries.

JOHN A. JAYNES

Cross-references: *Borden, Gail (1801–1874); Evaporated Milk History.*

SYNTHETIC SWEETENERS

Sweet substances are present in nature or are synthesized by man. The man-made sweeteners can be identical with those present in nature or different chemically. By misuse, the term "synthetic sweeteners" has been limited to designate those man-made sweeteners that are not natural products. The terms "non-nutritive sweeteners" and "artificial sweeteners" have also been used as synonyms to synthetic sweeteners.

Among the many sweet substances synthesized in the laboratory two, the cyclamates (up to the year 1969) and the saccharins, found extensive use in the United States, and a third one, dulcin, elsewhere. Originally intended to be used as pharmaceuticals, the synthetic sweeteners enjoyed a great popularity during the past 10–15 yr as no-calorie sugar substitutes by people of excessive weight and others trying to prevent it. In October 1969, the U.S. Department of Health, Education and Welfare prohibited the addition of cyclamates to soft drinks and subsequently to all other foods. Cyclamates, however, are still available as drugs. The safety of saccharins is being reviewed at the time of this writing.

Relative Sweetness

The sweet taste of a substance is quantitatively expressed as relative sweetness; that is the grams of sucrose dissolved in a certain volume of water which results in the same sweetness as 1 gm of sweetener dissolved in equal volume of water.

The relative sweetness changes with concentration as shown in the data below of the relative sweetness of saccharin, cyclamate, and dulcin at various levels of sweetness:

Level of Sweetness as % Sucrose in Solution	Saccharin	Cyclamate	Dulcin
2	550	40	380
5	360	36	110
10	330	33	70
15	300	27	—
20	200	24	—

At levels of sweetness greater than that corresponding to 10% sucrose it is difficult to establish accurate relative sweetness factors, probably because after-taste effects become very pronounced. It must be noted that the taste sensation of sweetness generated by synthetic sweeteners is not identical with that of sucrose. Synthetic sweeteners build up their sweetness impact more slowly than sucrose and the sensation they cause lingers on while that of sucrose has a sharp, clean end. Also an after-taste, sometimes described as metallic, astringent, drying, or bitter, and varying with the sweetener, the taster, the concentration of the sweetener and the type of the food, is associated with synthetic sweeteners. In food formulation, replacement equivalents for sucrose by sweeteners, synthetic as well as natural (e.g., glucose), should be established by taste panels. In substituting a synthetic sweetener for sucrose in a product it may be necessary to change the pH, the acidulant, the visosity, the type of other flavorings which may be incompatible with the sweetener, or use two or more sweeteners, eventually mixing synthetic and natural ones, in order to avoid the shortcomings of the synthetic sweeteners. The mouth feel and body character imparted to a food by sucrose must be compensated for if synthetic sweeteners are used. Duplication of a sugar-sweetened product may be impossible, but similar acceptability of a synthetically-sweetened food analog may be the aim in new product development.

Saccharin

Chemically, saccharin is *o*-benzosulfimide (I). It is a fairly strong acid due to the ionization of the imide hydrogen. In the food industry the sodium (II) and calcium (III) salts of saccharin, also referred to as saccharins, are preferably used as more water-soluble than saccharin proper. At 25°C, 1 gm of I is soluble in 290 ml of water, while 1 gm

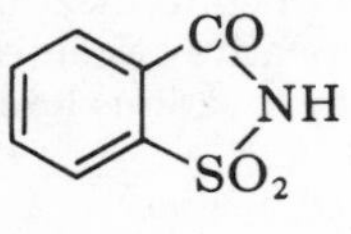

I

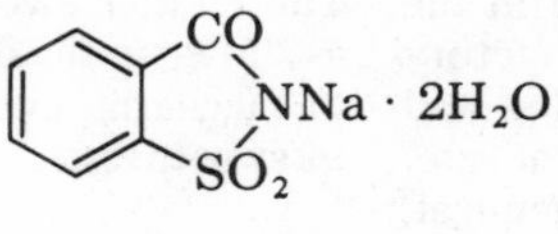

II

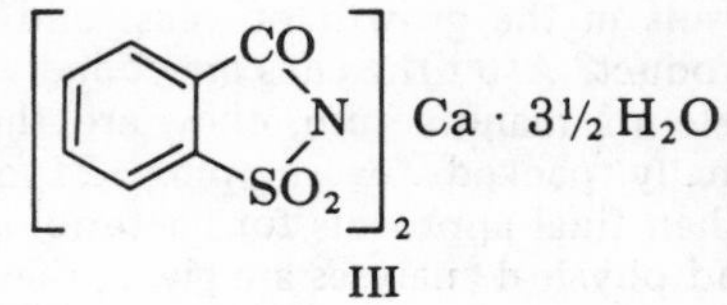

III

of II or III is soluble in approximately 1.2 ml or 2.0 ml of water, respectively. In ethanol, saccharin is more soluble than its salts. All saccharins are marketed as white crystals or crystalline powders, as tablets, or as solutions. The effervescent tablets are a mixture of saccharin and sodium carbonate or bicarbonate. The saccharins are also incorporated into a number of food products, such as soft drinks, jams, jellies and preserves, gelatin desserts, instant puddings, salad dressings, etc. Following the ban of cyclamates, the saccharins, being the only synthetic sweetener allowed to be used in foods in the United States, have found increasing application by the food industry. The saccharins are generally resistant to processing temperatures; at pH 7.0, heating in an autoclave for 1 hr at 125°C will result in 0.3% of decomposition and at pH 3.3, the same heating will cause 1.0% decomposition of saccharin. The Food Chemicals Codex contains specifications and tests for the saccharins. According to the Federal Dietary Food Regulations, Section 125.7, the label of a food containing saccharins shall bear the statement, "Contains ... saccharin (or saccharin salt), a nonnutritive artificial sweetener which should be used only by persons who must restrict their intake of ordinary sweets," the blank to be filled in with the percentage by weight of saccharin or saccharin salt in such foods.

Cyclamates

The sodium (I) and the calcium (II) salts of cyclohexyl-sulfamic acid, are commonly called cyclamates. These are white crystalline substances,

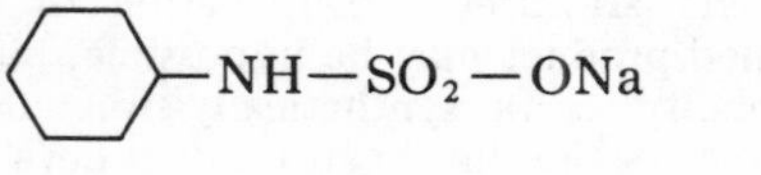

I

II

soluble in water (1 gm dissolved in 4–5 ml of water), which were used extensively in the 1960's until they were found to cause cancer in the bladder of experimental animals and were withdrawn from the list of approved food chemicals.

Dulcin

Chemically, dulcin is 4-ethoxyphenylurea. It has not been approved as a food additive in the United

States, although it has found use elsewhere (Germany).

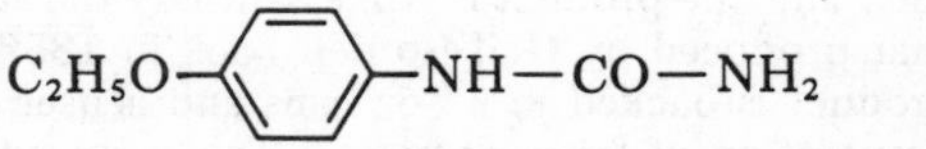

As this article was going to print a new sweetener was approved by the Food and Drug Administration (Federal Register, July 26, 1974). In the trade it is known as asparatame and its chemical name is 1-methyl N-L-α-aspartyl-L-phenylaline ($C_{14}H_{18}N_2O_5$). This ester of a dipeptide is about 180 times as sweet as sucrose. Asparatame is metabolized in the body as a protein rather than a carbohydrate and provides 4 kcal per gm. Used to sweeten other foods it will provide only 1/180th of the calories of ordinary sugar and therefore its caloric contribution will be minute. Prolonged cooking or exposure to high temperatures, as encountered in frying or baking, can cause significant breakdown of asparatame to diketopiperazine, with a consequent loss of sweetness. The FDA order, therefore, does not approve any use which would result in appreciable breakdown of asparatame; it does approve the following: (a) use in dry, free-flowing sugar substitutes for table use (not to include use in cooking) in package units not to exceed the sweetening equivalent of 2 teaspoonfuls of sugar; (b) use in sugar substitute tablets for sweetening hot beverages, including coffee and tea; (c) use in cold breakfast cereals; (d) use in chewing gum; (e) use in dry bases for beverages, instant coffee and tea, gelatins, puddings, fillings, and dairy product analog toppings. Its use as a flavor enhancer in chewing gum is also approved.

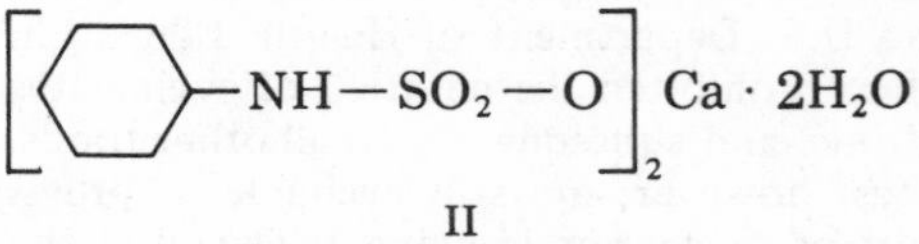

Other Sweeteners

Some of the other synthetic sweeteners which have been proposed as sugar substitutes are the following: Perillaldehyde-anti-aldoxim; 4-nitro-2-aminophenol-n-propylether; 1-ethoxy-2-amino-4-nitro-benzol; and sodium 4-methoxy-2-benzoyl-benzoate.   Recently the dihydrochalcones of naringin and neohesperidin, which are derivatives of the natural flavanones, naringin and neohesperidin, have been considered as artificial sweeteners. Also the berries of *Dioscoreophyllum cummimsii* were found to contain a very sweet principle. Previously, the leaves of *Stevia rebaudiana* were reported to contain a sweet glycoside. Glycyrrhizin, the sweet constituent of licorice has been used by pharmacists for a long time.

PERICLES MARKAKIS

Cross-reference: *Additives*.

T

TABASCO (HOT PEPPER) SAUCE

Hot sauce or pepper sauce is the generic name for a large family of bottled condiments produced by many manufacturers in the United States and through the world. The hot peppers, usually varieties of *Capsicum annum* and *C. frutescens*, give the products their heat and flavor characteristics and the vinegar is the liquid medium. Oil of Capsaicin in these peppers is the active ingredient.

Manufacturing processes vary, however; in most, the hot peppers are either ground and used fresh or stored whole in brine for several months until needed. Salt and vinegar are added to the ground peppers and the mixture is run through processing machines to remove the seeds. The end-product, a stable suspension, is then bottled. The red color of the products usually comes from the red peppers themselves; however, in some instances, artificial coloring is added. Individual products vary widely in specifications, however, most products fall in the following ranges:

Total solids	4.0–10.0
Salt as NaCl	1.0– 6.0
Acidity as acetic acid	4.0– 9.0
pH	3.0– 3.2

Hot peppers may be grown in most of the southern United States. Most commercial production is from the states of Louisiana, Texas, and California. Perhaps the best known product in this category is Tabasco pepper sauce, made by McIlhenny Company of Avery Island, Louisiana and marketed internationally. In the Tabasco pepper sauce process, the fresh red peppers are selected by hand by harvest workers and ground the same day. A small amount of salt is added to the ground peppers which are then packed into oak barrels. The barrels are placed in aging warehouses for a minimum of 3 yr. After the aging period has been completed, the ground peppers are mixed with 100-grain distilled vinegar and the mixture stirred for 4 weeks. The seeds and pepper skins are then removed mechanically and the end-product bottled. No artificial coloring is added to Tabasco pepper sauce.

EDWARD M. SIMMONS

Cross-reference: *Flavorings and Essences.*

TABOOS AND FOOD PREJUDICES

When Captain Cook discovered Polynesia he also discovered a new word that focused in on centuries of mankind's eating habits. He found that a system existed among the natives by which certain objects are set aside as sacred or accursed. The word used in Polynesian was "tapu," meaning consecrated. Its meaning relates to a political, social, or religious prohibition. In our language this word is spelled "taboo." Taboos play a vital part in the menu of all human beings—from the Yoruba of western Nigeria to the modern orthodox Jew.

Prejudices are quite different from taboos. Prejudices are opinions formed by people on the basis of preconceptions or unreasonable judgments. They lack the symbolic value inherent in a taboo and yet, prejudices like taboos, strongly influence how and what men eat. The middle American *prejudice* against "chitterlings" (pig intestines) probably relates to their original use by black slaves eating the discards of white plantation owners. The orthodox Jewish *taboo* against the consumption of pig products is even more deeply entwined in history. Perhaps it was because swine are unclean, or that undercooked pork yields tapeworms (trichina). No one really knows the actual source of the taboo. However, there appears to be many valid political, social, and religious reasons for this taboo.

Political Taboos and Prejudices

The division of food taboos and prejudices into political, social, and religious groups simplifies their categorization. In essence, most taboos, whatever their outward trend, are based on religion. To ancient man and even to modern man, religion was and is the basic source of the vast majority of taboos and prejudices. Yet, exceptions exist.

Snails as food were first mentioned by Moses as being a forbidden food. The Romans, by contrast, started snail parks where snails were fattened with wheat flour and aromatic plants. Eaten by monks and nuns during the Middle Ages, they were regarded as a religious food. Today, in midwestern Nigeria, a deeply entrenched political taboo prevents the eating of snails. A legend exists that ancient warriors who had eaten snails became sick and were easily caught and killed by their enemies. Today, natives do not eat snails because they believe that wars will be lost should the warriors eat snails. This taboo appears to have some degree of truth in its origin. Snails, if not carefully processed before eating, can be highly dangerous. Even though the snail is not poisonous, it eats a wide variety of foods harmful to man. Wartwort, henbane, and nightshade, for example, are eaten by snails. The consumption of such snails can lead to death or, in any event, to severe pain. It appears logical to assume that the ancient Nigerian warriors ate poisoned snails and the present-day taboo in Nigeria may be based on a rational premise.

Other food taboos based on political origins exist. Until recently, Roman Catholics could not eat meat on Friday. Fish was the substitute protein and large quantities of fish were consumed by Catholics on Friday. As a "church law," this prohibition appears to be based on the lobbying activity of the fishing industry during the Middle Ages. In order to support the fishing trade, many subtle pressures were brought to bear on the church. It appears reasonable to suppose that a meatless Friday was the result of this effort. In England, during the 16th Century, attempts to enforce the observance of fish days during Lent were probably due to meat shortages. The English navy was battling Spain in that century and the demands for meat were severe. Various other fish days were tried over the years. The English Parliament in 1548 made Saturday a fish day—but unsuccessfully. Wednesday was also tried. This type of political taboo carried over to World War II where the closing of delicatessan stores on Tuesday was based on a hoped-for decrease in meat consumption and the substitution of fish or poultry.

Chinese cuisine, whether it be from Canton, Shanghai, Fukien, Szechuen, or Peking, is almost totally devoid of dairy products. Bean curd and other soybean products play a vital part in a Chinese menu, but not milk, cow cheese, yogurt, etc. This food prohibition probably originated in ancient China and today, even though few recognize it, it is based on a political prejudice. The ancient Chinese were farmers and their enemies were the Tartars and Mongols. Large herds of cattle were common to these tribes but not to the Chinese. The association of dairy cattle with an enemy may be responsible for the attitude of Chinese toward dairy products.

An analogous situation appears to be one of the reasons behind the pork prohibition of orthodox Jews. The early Hebrews were herdsmen and their enemies were farmers and swineherds. Can we conjecture that the prohibition against pork by Jews is based on a political prejudice against using the food of the enemy?

Social Taboos and Prejudices

Few Americans like kidneys, hearts, or lungs, yet the French find them delicious. Scottish haggis is thought of as a barbarian dish in the United States. When one speaks of "fat back," poor Southerners come to mind. "Incaparina," a protein-enriched food supplement introduced to the starving masses of Central America encountered resistance at first because of social prejudices. Yet, all these foods have nutritional value in an integrated menu (with the possible exception of fat back).

The organ meats—kidneys, tripe, lungs, hearts and liver—are not generally consumed by affluent Americans simply because of social taboos. They are thought of as foods for the poor or for dogs and cats. In contrast, in England, kidney pie is a great favorite and the French work wonders with "tripe à la mode Caen" and kidney stews. No unfavorable connotation or taboo exists in Europe regarding these foods. Actually, these taboos may be slowly disappearing in the United States. The acceptance of liver (discarded by butchers as worthless several years ago) may be a sign of changing trends.

Most people, other than Scotsmen, find haggis repulsive and not worthy of human consumption. It is a strange food and social mores prohibit its use, probably because of its unique character. A haggis is made from the stomach of a sheep. The stomach is thoroughly cooked and then turned inside out. It is then stuffed with a minced mixture of boiled heart, liver, and lungs spiced with salt, pepper, nutmeg, and onion. Oatmeal is added and also beef suet. The stomach is then wrapped around the mixture, sewed up, and boiled in water. Served with Scotch whiskey, it actually is quite delicious and nutritious. In an effort to "dress up" this dish, the Scotch serve haggis with an escort of bagpipes and it is eaten as a ritual on St. Andrew's Day.

Fat back used now by many Southerners to flavor vegetables is composed mostly of fat and a little meat. It is still used as the basic source of protein by many poor Southerners, but its connotation as a dish for the lower social strata prevents its widespread use by the other classes.

Incaparina was introduced to the people of Central America several years ago. Based on modern food technology, it is a protein-enriched food supplement designed to increase the protein content of the diet of undernourished people. Because the peasants believed that people only poorer than themselves could eat Incaparina, it was slow in gaining acceptance even though sorely needed.

Religious Taboos and Prejudices

There are Christians who will not eat pork as well as Jews and Moslems. Some Hindus eat fish; others will not. Fish without scales are prohibited for consumption by Mosaic law; the ancient Indians and natives of Tasmania also will not eat fish without scales.

Religious taboos and prejudices predate the recorded era. Usually based on a seemingly plausible fact, there are many inconsistencies that are inexplicable. Why do both orthodox Jews and Navaho Indians not eat pork? Moslems are not permitted to eat pork and this appears logical because Islam is derived from Judaic principles. But the camel (nonkosher due to its not having cloven hooves) is a Moslem food served as camel couscous, camel paunch à la Marocaine, and camel pilaf.

Most major religions have some type of dietary laws in the form of religious taboos. The orthodox Jew and Hindu have some of the most highly formalized laws of all religions. For orthodox Jews, these dietary laws are found in the Books of Genesis, Exodus, Leviticus, and Deuteronomy. Only cud-chewing and cloven-hooved animals may be eaten. Birds of prey are forbidden food as well as fish without scales and all types of shell fish. Meat dishes may not be mixed with dairy dishes and even the hindquarter of kosher animals is forbidden. Certain foods such as vegetables and fish are neutral and they may be eaten with milk or dairy foods.

The word used in Hebrew (or Aramaic) to describe the formal dietary laws of orthodox Jews is "kosher." Why and how these food taboos originated is long lost in history. Modern man can only guess and speculate as to their derivations. The prohibition against mixing meat and milk is found in Deuteronomy, "thou shalt not seethe a kid in its mother's milk." This food taboo was probably practiced long before it became written in the Torah (Jewish book of laws) and the rabbis merely sought to support a practice inherent in ancient Hebrew cookery. In Canaan, a kid was cooked in its mothers milk as part of various ancient fertility rites. The Hebrews, originators of Monotheism, despised pagan practices and a Canaanite ritual was considered taboo to the ancient Hebrews.

The prohibition against eating fish without scales and fins may have originated because such fish bear a close resemblance to reptiles. Since eating fish was held in great esteem by the ancient Hebrews, this taboo appears logical. But the ancient Indians, Tasmanian natives, Iranians also do not eat scaleless fish. It appears that the "reptilian" explanation is a valid observation since it runs through various and diverse cultures. Although there are other possible explanations for the many food rules of orthodox Jews, there is one that is of particular interest. A taboo is a means of conditioning a person to a pattern that allows him a certain degree of self-sanctification. This is also true of Hinduism and Christianity.

The Hindu religion contains a highly ritualized system of food taboos. Cows are considered sacred to Hindus, but milk and milk products may be eaten. Vegetarianism runs strong in Hindu culture and the higher caste Hindus are almost all strictly vegetarians. Perhaps the deprivation of meat which others eat makes them feel holier. This sense of sacrifice is inherent in other religions. Christianity has its cloistered orders and it was Paul of Tarsus who said, "Tis better to marry than burn." A religious person of high dedication can do without the temptations of the flesh and thus can better concentrate on being a son of God.

The Hindu caste system is a complex one. Not all Hindus are vegetarians. Some eat fish and not meat. Others will not eat seeds or nuts. Some will not kill insects, even flies (even though they are annoying or a health hazard). Food for a high caste Brahman cannot be cooked by a lower caste Untouchable. Modern India is attempting to break down these cumbersome regulations and is having some degree of success in cities. But in the rural areas, the caste system still is strong.

The Islamic prohibition against the consumption of pork and pig products is strong. Even though the Israelis and Arabs are at war in the Middle East, Arabs in Western nations will only buy their meat from kosher butchers. This is verification that the meat is ritually proper, and it displays again the closeness of Judaism to the Islamic faith. The Sepoy Mutiny in India started because hired Moslem soldiers would not put lard-covered bullets in their mouths. These soldiers were hired by the British to fight the Hindus and the taboo against pork prevented the capture of Calcutta.

Canned products exported from Western nations to Arab lands must have a certification that the food was killed according to Islamic ritual. This must appear on the label and is a mandatory requirement for export. Islamic ritual is quite similar to Judaic ritual and if enough Moslems migrate to Western lands, it is safe to assume that a formalized set of rules, similar to kosher regulations, would be instituted for their protection.

Christian groups such as the Seventh Day Adventists are vegetarians and even operate canneries and food co-ops for the purpose of manufacturing accepted foods. Seventh Day Baptists will not eat pork. Certain provincial liquor stores in Quebec sell only "sacremental wines" for use in the Catholic Mass. Fish only may be consumed during the Lent season for Roman Catholics and meat is prohibited. Fast days abound in Catholicism and other Christian denominations.

Certain groups follow food taboos influenced by several religions. In the interior of Ethiopia live the Falashas who follow ancient Hebrew laws. Believed to be descendants of the Queen of Sheba's marriage to King Soloman, their bible is printed in Geez. Unknown to them are Western Jewish food habits, but kosher regulations are strictly observed. And integrated in their foods are taboos associated with the neighboring Coptic Christians and pagans.

Religious prejudice exhibited in food taboos appears to be breaking down and possibly will soon be nonexistant in modern nations. However, Jewish sacremental wine is a large seller in the Baptist South (its sweet flavor appears to be the attraction). Israelis from Europe consume large amounts of the Arab "hummous" eaten by their enemies.

Some food taboos and prejudices will probably persist but which ones and why cannot be predicted. The origin, change, and disappearance of taboos and prejudices run parallel with other phases of human culture. Cultural habits develop in response to some need, change with a changing need or needs, and slowly disappear after the disappearance of that need.

STANLEY SACHAROW

TAMALE

Tamale (Mexican *tamalli*) is a native Mexican food consisting of minced meat and red peppers rolled in corn and wrapped in cornhusks. It is cooked either by steaming or baking.

There are many variations of this basic recipe. The true Mexican tamales are made from hominy meal prepared with lye, that is, parched corn, as opposed to corn meal.

A typical formula insofar as the tamale is made in the United States is concerned would be:

Ingredients:

Corn meal	Onions
Beef	Garlic
Chili pepper	Salt
Tomatoes	Wheat flour

Procedures:

Grind the beef together with the onions, garlic and tomatoes.

Make a paste of the cornmeal and wheat flour using the beef broth.

Add salt.

Roll the paste into a thin sheet and wrap the meat in it.

Wrap the tamales in corn shucks that have been steamed for a few minutes.

In canning tamales a salt brine is used. The process is 70–100 min at 240°F, depending on can size.

MARTIN S. PETERSON

Cross-reference: *Nationality Foods*.

TAPIOCA

Tapioca is derived from the roots of a tropical shrub known as cassava, manioc, and yucca. There are over 2000 varieties of the plant (*Manihot utilissima*, the bitter type, and *Manihot palmata*, the sweet) which is a member of the family of Euphorbiaceae. Though they are not clearly defined morphologically, these two types, bitter and sweet, contain relatively greater or lesser amounts of prussic acid throughout the plant. The presence of this bitter component comes about through the action of a glucoside contained in the plant juices. The so-called bitter varieties are cultivated for commercial tapioca starch manufactured because of the higher yield. The sweet varieties are raised for table use in the same manner as potatoes. All of the prussic acid disappears in the starch extraction process. The names "tapioca," "manioc," and "cassava" all refer to the same thing.

Tapioca, a native of central Brazil, was transported at the turn of the 19th Century by Spanish and Portuguese explorers to the East Indies from whence it spread throughout Asia and Africa. The plant thrives well in relatively poor soil throughout the equatorial region. The sweet variety serves as a staple food item in many countries in this region between the Tropics of Capricorn and Cancer. The roots may be used, as are potatoes, by boiling or baking. Many other edible products are made that are essentially dried or toasted manioc root meal. These are known by several names such as raspa, gaplek, gari, and farofa.

Dried root chips, produced in Angola, were processed into starch in French potato starch factories a few years ago but this industry has largely disappeared because of high manufacturing costs and unavailability of prime raw material. The roots were from the indigenous sweet variety commonly cultivated for food by the native population.

At one time, Brazilian law required the partial substitution of wheat flour with manioc meal in bread making when wheat was in short supply. The result was a darker, tougher bread not favored by Brazilians and thus the requirement was eventually abandoned. Tapioca root chips are produced in large quantities in both Thailand and West Malaysia. These are converted into pellets for shipment to Western Europe where they are used as an animal food adjunct.

Tapioca starch, frequently called tapioca flour (although it has little or no protein), is by far the most important product, economically, that comes from the manioc plant. The focus of the prime producing and exporting countries has shifted considerably in the last 70 yr as a result of war and economic factors. Java, until approximately 1940, supplied the world and primarily the United States with nearly 200 thousand tons of high quality starch. Since World War II brought about the destruction of the Java plantations and tapioca factories, the world supply was cut off. Brazil, during the next 10-12 yr, became the main source of tapioca. However, Thailand is now the major producer and exporter of tapioca starch with the U.S. consumption totalling 143 thousand metric tons annually. Japan purchases 55 thousand tons. As for the other countries where tapioca is produced, the exports of starch for 1970 were:

	Tons
Brazil	12,000
Madagascar	5-10,000
Togoland	3- 8,000
Malaysia	5,000
Indonesia	None

The tapioca plant is propagated by placing short stalk cuttings into the ground. It requires 10-18 months for the development of mature roots de-

pending upon the climate and soil conditions. A good yield on a carefully run plantation will amount to 15 tons per acre but some localities give only 4-5 tons per acre.

At harvest time, the field workers cut down the stalks that may have grown to 8-10 ft in height. Some of these stalks are reserved for future planting. The roots, resembling very large sweet potatoes, are then dug by hand, collected in piles, and transported to wagons or trucks for shipment to the starch factory. Roots must be fresh to produce the best starch as they deteriorate rapidly once they are dug. It requires approximately 5 tons of roots to produce 1 ton of tapioca starch in the more efficient extraction process.

Starch extraction is relatively simple wherein the roots are washed, peeled, and ground to a fine pulp which is passed over a series of screens to remove both coarse and fine root fibers. Further refinement is achieved by the use of settling basins or centrifuges. Drying of the starch is carried out in continuous belt- or flash-dryers. Starch factories range from relatively crude cottage industries using homemade wooden equipment yielding a few bags a day, to specially constructed installations using stainless steel equipment and machinery capable of producing upwards of 50 tons of prime quality starch per day.

The uses for tapioca starch are varied but the principal application is in the manufacture of conversion products such as dextrins and glues for corrugated paper, postage stamp adhesives, and textile sizing. Tapioca starch is used in food manufacture both in its natural state as well as modified and pregelatinized versions for special applications.

High grade tapioca starch for food purposes will have a brilliant white color; be free of fine dirt and specks; have a low bacteria, yeast, and mold count; and a strong viscosity when cooked yielding a nearly clear, tasteless gel. The criteria for an acceptable cooked viscosity depend upon the specific application and method of measurement.

Granulated tapioca used to make the popular pudding containing the small lumps or granules is made by special cooking, grinding, and screening methods. In addition to this quick-cooking granulated tapioca, pearl tapioca that requires prior soaking and gives much larger lumps in puddings, is also marketed in the United States in limited quantities; all of the pearl type is imported.

LEE SHIPMAN

References

BAUTLECHT, C. A. 1953. Starch. Reinhold Publishing Co., New York.

HOLLEMAN, L. W. J., and ATEN, A. 1956. Processing of cassava and cassava products in rural industries. FAO, Rome, Italy.

SHIPMAN, L. 1967. Tapioca, arrowroot, and sago starch manufacture. *In* Starch: Chemistry and Technology, Vol. 2. R. L. Whistler and E. F. Paschall (Editors). Academic Press, New York.

SHIPMAN, L., and VAN BIEMA, G. 1952. Making top grade tapioca flour. Food Eng. *24*, No. 3, 56, 132, 182, 184.

TEA

The tea plant, classified by Linnaeus as *Thea sinensis*, is an evergreen tree, which is pruned down to a height of 3-5 ft for purposes of harvest. If left unpruned the tree would grow to a height of 15-30 ft. The leaves of the tea plant vary from 2 to 10 in. in length and from 1 to 4 in. in width. The plant grows best at a fairly high altitude in a warm climate where the rainfall is abundant. It is distinctly a tropical plant and tea plantations or gardens are often found in mountainous areas bordering the equator. Tea can be grown in the temperate zone but not as profitably as in the equatorial areas of the world. The chief sources of supply are China, Taiwan, Japan, Pakistan, Ceylon, India, Indonesia, and several African countries.

Chemically, tea is composed of caffeine, tannin, protein, sugar, and, after the fermentation period, the essential oil that contributes to the flavor. Caffeine adds zest to tea and tannin the pungency, slight astringency, and color. A cup of tea contains about 100 mg of caffeine.

The history of the tea trade is of much interest but can only be touched upon here. Legend has it that tea as a beverage originated in China 2500 yr ago; but the earliest mention clearly referring to tea occurred in 350 A.D. Tea was brought to Europe by the Dutch in the 17th Century. It gained favor somewhat slowly but by the middle of the 18th Century was well established, particularly in England and America. In the 19th Century it was a thriving industry in both hemispheres as it continues to be in this century.

Consumption is perhaps the greatest in Communist China with Great Britain, Ireland, and the Commonwealth nations next. In the USSR, tea is drunk at all meals accounting for the very large

TABLE T-1

CHIEF CHARACTERISTICS OF THE THREE TYPES OF TEAS

Type	Production Areas	Classifications and Characteristics
Black	India, Ceylon, Java, Sumatra, Pakistan, Japan, Taiwan, Malawi, Kenya	Orange pekoe and pekoe: Three young shoots at the top of the plant are used for this class of tea. These tips produce the finest quality of black tea. Souchong: The leaves immediately below the Pekoe are used. This class of tea is of lesser quality and, by consequence, of lesser cost. In Ceylon there are three classifications, viz, high grown, medium grown, and low grown and a further designation by tea-growing districts.
Green	Japan, China, India, Indonesia	Basket-fired: Long leaves are used in the production of this type of tea. Pan-fired: Short leaves are used. Gunpowder: Small, round, rolled leaves characterize this type of green tea. Imperials: Large round rolled leaves. Young hysons: Long rolled leaves.
Oolong	Taiwan and Foochow	Partially fermented before being dried.

consumption there. Tea is not a major beverage in the United States.

Tea has been at the center of a number of historic events, the Boston Tea Party, for one, and the great tea race of 1866, another. The Boston Tea Party was one of the acts of defiance that contributed to the American Revolution. The tea race of 1866 was a bloodless conflict that involved the clipper ships. Eleven clippers started from Foochow and finished either at the London Docks and or at Downs. The Taeping finished first at the London Docks and the Ariel was the winner at the Downs. The time was 99 days and the distance 16,000 miles.

With regard to cultivation, the tea plant is produced from seed. When the plants are from 6 to 8 in. tall, they are set out in a number of patterns. In some growing areas they are set in straight-line rows 4–6 ft apart; in hilly country the rows are contoured; on flat lands they are usually set out in squares or triangles, or, as in India, in equilateral rectangles. The bushes are ready for harvesting in 3 yr but do not come into full bearing until 10 yr old. The yield when fully mature is about $1/4$-lb per bush. The tea plant has its enemies, both diseases and insects, but modern means of control and vigilance on the part of the growers hold the attacks down and the damage done to the crop is minimal in most of the major growing areas. Tea is harvested continuously, the crops or flushes maturing about every 40 days. The harvested leaf is classified as fine, medium, or coarse, these designations relating to the time when the leaf was plucked.

Processing tea is best described in terms of the methods used in the three main types of tea—black, green, and oolong.

In processing black tea (the major type consumed in the United States) there are four major unit operations:

Withering: Withering methods differ in the different tea-growing nations but the leaf is usually wilted on racks for 18–24 hr. When the leaf has lost slightly over $1/2$ its moisture, it is considered to be ready for rolling.

Rolling: The withered leaf is fed to a roller where the leaf cells are broken to release the juices and the enzymes. This operation starts the fermentation process. Also, in the rolling process the leaf is given its characteristic twist. The next operation is fermentation.

Fermenting: In this phase of processing the leaf is spread, 3–4 in. thick on a flat surface in the fermentation room where the humidity is just slightly short of the saturation point. During fermentation oxidation occurs. Oxidation engenders changes that produce the flavor and color

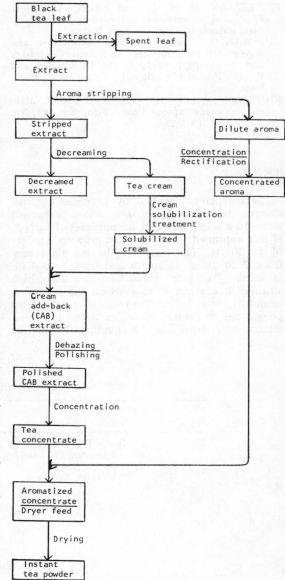

Courtesy of World Coffee & Tea

FIG. T-1. FLOW CHART FOR GENERALIZED IN-STANT TEA MANUFACTURING PROCESS

The flavor of tea derives from the volatile compounds in the tea leaf. Over 140 compounds contributing to tea flavor have been identified. Capturing these volatile compounds, concentrating them, and incorporating them into the instant tea product is a complicated process.

of the infused leaves. Fermentation is stopped when the aroma and color are at their peak.

Firing: The purpose of firing is to stop fermentation. Firing can be achieved by exposure to the sun, by oven heat, or by applying currents of hot air to the fermented leaf.

In processing green tea, which incidentally is not fermented, only three operations are required:

Steaming: The leaf for green tea is steamed rather than withered. Steaming makes the leaf more pliable and also prevents fermentation.

Rolling: Rolling, as is true of rolling to produce black mechanized tea, is accomplished by machinery. In Japan the mechanized rolling process duplicates in some degree the hand rolling process. The rolls are usually of brass.

Firing: Firing in processing green tea serves the purpose of killing organisms that might cause discoloration of the leaf or, conceivably, start the fermentation process anew.

Oolong tea is slightly withered, partly fermented, dried, rolled and fired, the degree of processing being midway between the processes used for black and green tea.

Packaging tea has undergone a number of changes in recent years. Although loose tea is still packed in chests (holding 100 lb each and lined with aluminum foil) when exported from factories in the growing areas, retail packages have been modified in accord with innovations in the merchandizing of tea. Tea bags, a response to the convenience trend, account for the packaging of roughly $\frac{1}{2}$ of the tea packaged in the United States. Iced tea mix and instant tea are largely packaged in glass jars. Iced tea mix is also packaged in metal cans. Shipping containers for tea have not changed materially over recent years but it is of interest that tea chests are now increasingly being palletized into unit loads.

What has changed—and quite remarkably so—is consumer use patterns as revealed by the following data comparing 1950 and 1970 production of tea products:

Product	1950	1970
	(In 1000 Lb)	
Iced tea mix	0	11,600
Instant tea	410	37,800
Tea bags	27,880	62,600
Loose tea	41,000	14,000
Total	64,700	130,000

A considerable factor in this change, as mentioned, is the general trend toward convenience foods and packaging. Also, youthful consumers have been a factor, particularly with regard to their increased consumption of iced tea. Worldwide consumption of tea amounts to over 2 billion pounds annually, with better than 1 billion pounds being consumed in the growing areas.

MARTIN S. PETERSON

Cross-reference: *Caffeine.*

TOCOPHEROLS

Tocopherols are pale yellow or yellow-tan viscous liquids at room temperature (75°F or 23°C) some of which can be made to crystallize, and more readily so at lower temperatures. At high purity they are relatively odorless and colorless. They are oil soluble and hence, fully soluble in lipoidal solvents and insoluble in water. The name tocopherol is derived from the Greek words "tokos" (offspring), "pherein" (to bear), and "ol" (alcohol) as the first isolated member of the series was found to have antisterility properties.

Eight compounds are known in the tocopherol series, occurring in nature, all of which are derivatives of 6-chromanol. This series is made up of 4 compounds with a tocol structure which bear a saturated isoprenoid C_{16}-side chain and 4 compounds with a tocotrienol structure bearing 3 double bonds in the C_{16}-side chain.

The structural formulae of the eight tocopherols are

Tocol Structure

Tocotrienol Structure

Position of Methyls	Trivial Name (Abbreviations)	
	Tocol Structure	Tocotrienol Structure
5,7,8	α-tocopherol (α-T)	α-tocotrienol (α-T-3)
5,8	β-tocopherol (β-T)	β-tocotrienol (β-T-3)
7,8	γ-tocopherol (γ-T)	γ-tocotrienol (γ-T-3)
8	δ-tocopherol (δ-T)	δ-tocotrienol (δ-T-3)

TABLE T-2

TOCOPHEROLS IN FOOD (MG/100 GM)

Food	No. of Values Averaged	α-T	α-T-3	β-T	β-T-3	γ-T	γ-T-3	δ-T	δ-T-3
Nuts and grains									
Almond	2	27.4	0.5[1]	0.3[1]	—	0.9[1]	—	—	—
Barley	5	0.4	1.3	0.3	0.7[5]	0.05[4]	0.2[3]	0.01[1]	—
Corn	11	0.6	0.2[6]	—	0.4[1]	3.8	0.5[6]	tr	—
Millet	1	0.05	—	tr	—	1.3	—	0.4	—
Oats	6	0.7	0.7	0.2[4]	0.1[4]	0.3[4]	—	—	—
Peanuts	1	9.7	—	—	—	6.6	—	—	—
Peas	3	0.5	—	—	—	6.4[3]	—	0.6[1]	—
Pecans	1	1.2	—	—	—	19.1	—	—	—
Poppy seed	1	1.8	—	—	—	9.2	—	—	—
Rice	5	0.3	tr	—	—	0.3[4]	0.5[3]	0.04[5]	—
Rye	4	0.8	1.3[4]	0.4[4]	0.9	0.6[1]	—	—	—
Walnut, English	1	0.4	—	—	—	15.8	—	1.3	—
Wheat	9	1.0	0.4[8]	0.9	2.5[7]	—	—	0.08[1]	—
Vegetable oils									
Coconut	1	0.5	0.5	—	0.1	—	1.9	0.6	—
Corn	8	11.2	—	5.0[1]	—	60.2	—	1.8[3]	—
Cottonseed	9	38.9	—	—	—	38.7	—	—	—
Neem	1	—	—	—	—	58.0	—	59.0	—
Olive	4	5.1	—	—	—	—	—	—	—
Palm	4	25.6	14.3[1]	—	3.2[1]	31.6[2]	28.6[1]	7.0[1]	6.9[1]
Peanut	11	13.0	—	—	—	21.4	—	2.1[3]	—
Rapeseed	5	18.4	—	—	—	38.0	—	1.2[1]	—
Safflower	3	38.7	—	—	—	17.4	—	24.0[1]	—
Sesame	2	13.6	—	—	—	29.0	—	—	—
Soybean	14	10.1	—	—	—	59.3	—	26.4[9]	—
Sunflower	10	48.7	—	—	—	5.1	—	0.8[3]	—
Walnut	1	56.3	—	—	—	59.5	—	45.0	—
Wheat germ	3	133.0	2.6[1]	71.0	18.1[3]	26.0[1]	—	27.1[1]	—
Mustard seed	1	8.6	—	—	—	17.6	—	5.8	—
Asparagus (fresh weight)	—	1.8	—	0.05	—	0.07	—	—	—
Carrots (fresh weight)	—	0.51	0.04	0.01	0.08	—	—	—	—
Cucumber	—	8.4	—	—	—	—	—	—	—
Mango, flesh, green	—	0.26	—	—	—	—	—	0.27	—
Mango, flesh, ripe	—	0.98	—	—	—	—	—	—	—
Muskmelon	—	10.1	—	—	—	—	—	—	—
Tomato	—	18.2	—	—	—	—	—	—	—

[1] One value reported.
[2] Slover, unpublished data.
[3] Average of two values.
[4] Average of three values.
[5] Average of four values.
[6] Average of six values.
[7] Average of seven values.
[8] Average of eight values.
[9] Average of twelve values.

Full chemical name of α-tocopherol would be 2,5,
7,8-tetramethyl-2-(4′,8′,12′-trimethyltridecyl)-6-
chromanol and for α-tocotrienol it would be 2,5,7,
8-tetramethyl-2-(4′-8′-12′-trimethyltrideca-3′,7′,
11′-trienyl)-6-chromanol.

The tocopherols are subject to oxidation to
form quinones, dimers, and trimers; oxidation is
accelerated by exposure to light, heat, alkali, and
in the presence of certain trace minerals such as
iron (Fe^{+++}) and copper (Cu^{++}). The tocopherols
are more stable in acid than in alkali to oxidation.

In the absence of oxygen they are relatively heat
and light stable and relatively stable to alkali.
Esters prepared by acylation of the free phenolic
hydroxy increase the oxygen stability of the
compounds.

Source and Biogenesis

The tocopherols came into prominence about 50
yr ago when a factor present in plant sources was
recognized by Evans and coworkers (1936) as essential for normal reproduction in the rat. α and β-
Tocopherol were isolated from wheat germ followed by γ-tocopherol from cotton seed oil and
δ-tocopherol from soybean oil. Subsequent investigations, finding the 4 tocotrienols in several
vegetable oils, bring to date the existence of the 8
structures occurring almost exclusively in plant
life. That they occur in animal tissue is primarily
the result of animal consumption of plant food or
from synthetic tocopherols added to their diet.

Caution must be exercised when examining the
many values in the past literature for these compounds. Most determinations have been based on
the reducing properties of the tocopherols without
prior separation of the different molecular forms
and, at times, without the elimination of non-
tocopherol reducing substances; thus, the earlier
data tend to overestimate true content. Only
recently have methods been developed for the
separation and measurement of the individual
tocopherols. Bunnell (1971) and Govind Rao and
Perkins (1971) have considered the assay aspects of the tocopherols. The most recent compilation of tocopherol values in foods is that of
Slover (1971) (Table T-2).

The tocopherols occur mainly in the free alcohol
form in a variety of plant life such as nuts, seeds,
oils, fruits and vegetables (Table T-2). Seeds,
grains, and vegetable oils are superior sources to
fruits and vegetables. Their distributional pattern
is modified by species, variety, stage of maturity,
harvesting, and processing procedures. The action
of oxidative enzymes in abraded fresh plant tissues

and food refining techniques are quite destructive
to tocopherol content. Animal tissue and animal
products are usually low to poor sources. Exposure of tocopherols to peroxides formed in
developing oxidative rancidity in fats also lowers
tocopherol content. Refined and processed foods
are thus variable and less predictable sources than
fresh foods.

Based on fragmentary data the biogenesis of the
tocopherols in plant life is judged to be through
the intermediate of the tocotrienol structure. The
α- form, as an alternate route, can arise as successive methylations of mono- and di-substituted
tocols or transmethylations. These hypotheses
arise from the change in concentration of the tocol
and tocotrienol structures during the developing
stages of the plant life. The tocopherols play a
developmental role in the life of the plant and are
not merely exogenous substances.

Synthesis

The commercially most important and the most
biologically active form from a nutritional viewpoint is α-tocopherol. It was first synthesized in
1938. Since that time, synthetic methods have
gained extensive applications in the structural and
stereochemical elucidation of the tocopherols and
tocotrienols and have been useful for the commercial production of the tocopherols. The tocols
contain 3 asymmetric carbons including 1 at C-2 in
the ring and 2 in the side chain at the 4′ and 8′
position thus making possible a total of 8 optical
isomers. The epimeric configuration at the 2- position is apparently dominant in determining biological activity. Using the nomenclature proposed
by the IUPAC-IUB Commission and the rules for
the specification of asymmetric centers, examples
of the tocopherols can be indicated as follows:

Isomer Name	Compound and Trivial Name
2R, 4′R, 8′R-α-tocopherol	d,α-tocopherol (RRR-α-tocopherol)
2RS, 4′RS, 8′RS-α-tocopherol	dl,α-tocopherol (all-rac-α-tocopherol)

In the synthesis of tocopherols and tocotrienols,
an appropriate terpene alcohol is required as an intermediate. For the manufacture of dl,α-tocoph-
erol, isophytol is employed in the synthesis according to the following scheme:

TRIMETHYLHYDROQUINONE   ISOPHYTOL

The syntheses of the tocopherols are discussed in detail in the reviews of Mayer *et al.* (1971) and Schudel *et al.* (1972). The largest commercial production of any tocopherol series to date is that of *dl*,α-tocopherol and *dl*,α-tocopheryl esters by chemical synthesis.

Tocopherols as a Nutrient

Not all tocopherols possess biological or vitamin E value. The term vitamin E refers to tocopherol structures possessing vitamin E activity. α-Tocopherol, the fully methylated α-tocol, predominates in many species and is significantly more potent than any other tocopherol. Usually a determination of α-tocopherol content is a good approximation of the total vitamin E activity of the food or feed source under examination. The main criteria used in the biological evaluation of the tocopherols have been the resorption gestation assay, the muscular dystrophy assay, the erythrocyte hemolysis test, and determination of tocopherol levels in liver and plasma. A summary of the biopotency of

TABLE T-3

VITAMIN E ACTIVITY OF TOCOPHEROLS (BIOASSAY METHOD)

Structure	Resorption-gestation (%)	Hemolysis (%)
α-tocopherol	100	100
β-tocopherol	25–40	15–27
γ-tocopherol	8–19	3–20
δ-tocopherol	0.1–1	0.3–2
α-tocotrienol	21	17–25
β-tocotrienol	4	1–5

TABLE T-4

PATHOLOGY OF VITAMIN E DEFICIENCY

Condition	Animal	Tissue Affected
Reproductive Failure		
Embryonic degeneration	Female: rat, hen, turkey Ewe	Vascular system of embryo
Sterility	Male: rat, guinea pig, hamster, dog, cock	Male gonads
Liver, Blood, Brain, Capillaries, etc.		
Liver necrosis	Rat, pig	Liver
Erythrocyte destruction	Rat, chick	Blood (RBC hemolysis)
Blood protein loss	Chick, turkey	Serum albumin
Encephalomalacia	Chick	Cerebellum (Purkinjee cells)
Exudative diathesis	Chick, turkey	Capillary walls
Kidney degeneration	Rat, monkey, mink	Tabular epithelium
Steatitis	Mink, pig, chick	Depot fat
Nutritional Myopathies		
Nutritional muscular dystrophy	Rabbit, guinea pig, monkey, duck, chick, turkey	Skeletal muscle
Stiff lamb	Lamb, kid	Skeletal muscle
White muscle disease	Calf, sheep, mouse, mink	Skeletal and heart muscle
Myopathy of gizzard and heart	Turkey poult	Gizzard, heart, skeletal muscle

TABLE T-5

BIOCHEMICAL AND PHYSIOLOGICAL VITAMIN E FUNCTIONS AND
DEFICIENCY EFFECTS

Necessary for synthesis of heme compounds	Effect on:
(1) Hemoglobin	Life span of erythrocytes and respiration
(2) Cytochromes	Electron carriers in transport system Adrenal steroidogenesis
(3) Catalase	H_2O_2 decomposition

Inhibits fatty acid peroxide formation and resulting peroxide damage to:
(1) Proteins such as enzymes (all SH enzymes).
(2) Amino acids (methionine, histidine, serine, cystine).
(3) Erythrocytes in premature infants, infants with malabsorption.
(4) Lysosomal membranes—release of enzymes causing tissue damage.
(5) Liver mitochondria.
(6) Liver microsomes—interference in NADPH-dependent oxidations, drug metabolizing system, etc.

Modifies enzyme activity
(1) Reverses inhibition of β-glucuronidase by peroxidized linoleic acid.
(2) Necessary for glutathione peroxidase. Keeps selenium in reduced form.
(3) Required for activity of tryptophan oxygenase and NAD synthesis.
(4) Deficiency increases activity of aspartate aminotransferase, of all the LDH isoenzymes (especially LDH_5) and of alanine aminotransferase.

Required for normal function of the pituitary-thyroid axis.
Protects unsaturated side chain of Coenzyme Q_{10} from oxidative damage.
Decreases malondialdehyde formation and subsequent ceroid pigment formation.

the various tocopherols is shown in Table T-3. A deficiency of vitamin E results in a variety of symptoms in animals as cited by Scott (1969) in Table T-4. The subject of vitamin E is further reviewed by Draper (1970) and by Brubacher and Weiser (1967).

Vitamin E was used in animal nutrition long before its functions were elucidated for humans. Erythrocyte hemolysis in premature babies and in infants with diarrhea was one of the first indications of vitamin E requirement. The hemolysis could be inhibited in vitro as well as in the body with the addition of α-tocopherol. Subsequent plasma and liver assays indicated a dire need for supplementary vitamin E in these infants. Table T-5 is a partial list of the variety of vitamin E functions. This list continues to grow as we learn more about cellular biochemistry, membrane lipids, and heme synthesis. Vitamin E deficiency involved in failure to maintain heme synthesis is multidirectional since there is a decrease in δ-aminolevulinic acid synthase in bone marrow which controls the reaction of glycine and succinyl coenzyme A to form δ-aminolevulinic acid. There is also a decrease in liver δ-aminolevulinic acid dehydratase

which regulates the reaction of δ-aminolevulinic acid to porphobilinogen which ultimately goes to protoporphyrin IX. Thus, heme protein synthesis is decreased, not only hemoglobin but also cytochrome 450 and catalase. Furthermore, vitamin E deficiency increases the susceptibility of the individual to iron toxicity.

Free radical lipid peroxidation is a dynamic biological phenomenon which damages cellular and intercellular structures and destroys enzyme and other labile compounds. The fact that the membranes in subcellular particles are susceptible to lipid peroxidation has been well established. McCay et al. (1971) are convinced that the enzymes in the microsomal membranes such as NADPH oxidase initiate peroxidation in microsomal lipids, a reaction which occurs at a more rapid rate in microsomes of tocopherol-deficient animals. Protection of membranes from damage by peroxidized lipids is indeed one of the primary functions of α-tocopherol. The most striking example has been red blood cell (RBC) hemolysis when the plasma levels are below 0.5 mg% tocopherol. Although the tocopherol content of the RBC is lower than plasma, it is in proportion to plasma levels. Lucy

(1971) has hypothesized that the tocopherol is bound onto the membrane by the phytol side chain to arachadonic acid in the lipid layer of membranes. The antioxidant is thus available to compounds passing in and out as well as compounds in the membrane itself. Similar to RBC, lysosomes break in the presence of lipid peroxides, a process which releases their enzymes which, in turn, cause tissue damage. It is probably this free radical damage that results in the severe cellular damage seen in rabbit muscle, in chick cerebella, and in rat testes in vitamin E deficiency. The lipid products such as malondialdehyde react with amino acids to produce fluorescent pigments, resembling age pigments. It also has been shown to inhibit DNA replication, protein synthesis, and cell division and both malondialdehyde and peroxidized linolenate cause inactivation of ribonuclease A and other enzymes especially SH-containing ones.

Synthetic dl,α-tocopherol, dl,α-tocopheryl acetate and d,α-tocopheryl acetate have been produced commercially for the past 30 yr and have been used in the food, feed, and pharmaceutical industries as a source of vitamin E. The only natural form, d,α-tocopherol, is concentrated from natural sources. A listing of the vitamin E activity of the various α-tocopheryl forms available commercially are as follows:

(1 Mg)	(IU)
dl,α-tocopheryl acetate	= 1
dl,α-tocopherol	= 1.10
d,α-tocopheryl acetate	= 1.36
d,α-tocopherol	= 1.49
dl,α-tocopheryl acid succinate	= 0.89
d,α-tocopheryl acid succinate	= 1.21

The recommended daily allowance (US-RDA) for vitamin E lists 5 IU per day for infants below 1 yr, 10 IU per day for children between 1 and 4 yr, and 30 IU per day for individuals over 4 yr of age.

Although tocopherol, the acetate, and the succinate esters are water-insoluble, a variety of marketable forms have been developed for food, feed, and pharmaceutical applications. Dry powder preparations mix readily into food products and some are water-dispersible. Tocopherol and the acetate ester are soluble in polysorb 80 and result in clear water dispersions; each gram of tocopherol requires 15 gm of polysorb 80 whereas each gram of tocopheryl acetate requires 6 gm of the emulsifier.

Whole cereal grains and vegetable oils have been the richest sources of vitamin E in our diet. Food processing removes considerable vitamin E. White flour is very low in vitamin E and a recent study of breakfast cereals by Herting and Drury (1969) shows a drastic loss of vitamin E in processing. Refined vegetable oils, although containing fair

amounts of vitamin E, contain considerably less than the crude oil. Losses of vitamin E due to the oxidative destruction of free tocopherol can also occur in cooking in vegetable oils and margarines. Furthermore, losses of vitamin E in foods during frozen storage can be considerable. The vitamin E intake provided by the present average diet is, therefore, not over-abundant as demonstrated by the work of Bunnell et al. (1965). An increase in the vitamin E requirement with increased intake of polyunsaturated fatty acids (PUFA) has been indicated both for adults and infants. The total effect of these factors has caused some concern for the need of supplementary vitamin E addition to food products. In Europe, some manufacturers are adding α-tocopheryl acetate to margarine. Salad oils with high PUFA content would be another suitable carrier. Formulated infant diets also rate highly as a food to be nutrified with α-tocopheryl acetate.

Tocopherols as Antioxidants

Fatty components of foods, particularly if they contain double bonds or unsaturated fatty acids or esters undergo deteriorative changes usually resulting in undesirable odors and flavors or loss of nutrient potency. Fatty components subject to these changes are the edible fats and oils, lipoproteins, phospholipids, sterol esters, vitamin A and D esters, carotenes, and oxycarotenoids. These changes are predominantly caused by oxygen involving direct oxidative reactions; however, they may be catalyzed by heme compounds, metals, and enzymes of food of microbial origin. The action of oxygen and oxidases is inhibited by antioxidants which retard the autoxidation of primary and secondary substrates. Antioxidants also retard the nonenzymic changes by oxygen and and air catalyzed by trace minerals and heme compounds, in which a chain of reactions occurs, producing first peroxide, hydroperoxides, more peroxides, and then volatile carbonyl compounds bringing odors and flavors characteristic of oxidative rancidity.

For many years, tocopherols have been proposed as additives to fats and oils for their antioxidant properties. In fact, tocopherols, concentrated from vegetable oils, were initially called "inhibitors" and recognized as antioxidants before their identification with vitamin E activity. Chipault (1962) and Aaes-Jorgensen (1962) cover some of the early work on tocopherols as antioxidants. Levels of 0.01% were proposed to protect β-carotene in mineral oil, lard, methyl linoleate, butter oil, cottonseed oil, and vitamin A. Unfortunately, at that time, clear, tasteless tocopherols prepared by molecular distillation or by chemical synthesis were not readily available.

In vitro animal fat oxidation studies, such as AOM, Schaal Oven, and oxygen absorption tests, show that tocopherols have antioxidant activity. Levels as low as 0.008% in animal fat have demonstrable activity against peroxide formation (rancidity); in fact, mixed with ascorbyl palmitate and citric acid, tocopherols are as efficient as BHA, BHT, and combinations in lard in Schaal Oven tests. In orange oil, *dl*,α-tocopherol at 0.1 and 0.05% has shown protection against off-odor and color formation as well as protection against oxygen absorption as measured in the Warburg apparatus and is judged one of the most efficient antioxidants.

Many of the vegetable oils contain sufficient tocopherols and, as a result, it is difficult to demonstrate antioxidant activity by adding more. In vegetable oils, "stripped" of tocopherols on a molecular still, it is possible to demonstrate antioxidant activity of alpha, gamma, delta, and mixed monomethyl tocopherols.

Tocopherols can be readily added to fats and oils since they are freely soluble in oil. In addition, they are soluble as high as 50% in alcohol. α-Tocopherol should be added at the level of 0.02% in animal fats since it has the same or slightly less activity at 0.05 and 0.2%. On the other hand, γ-tocopherol displays increased activity at 0.05% over the 0.02% level and only slightly increased antioxidant activity at 0.2% in animal fats. As antioxidants, both tocopherols function similar to other known hindered phenolic antioxidants by scavenging free radicals formed at the double bonds in unsaturated fatty acids and, therefore, interrupting free radical chain reactions.

Many vitamin A marketed products contain at least 10 mg tocopherol per 1 million units and as high as 100 mg per MU vitamin A both in dry beadlet and water-dispersible preparations. They also function in the protection of β-carotene. Furthermore, the tocopherols are considered to function as protective antioxidants during both storage and absorption in the GI tract.

Comparative studies on alpha, gamma, delta, and mixed monomethyl tocopherols both in our laboratories and as far back as Chipault have shown that in tocopherols, unsubstituted in the 5 position, namely γ and δ tocopherols, were more effective in protection of carotene in oil, lard esters at 90°C, of methyl linoleate at 50°C, of lard in AOM at 0.01% tocopherol concentration at 100°C, of cottonseed and butter oil. Olcott and Van Der Veen (1968) have shown that γ-tocopherol is a better antioxidant than α at any temperature in menhaden oil and squalene.

Comparative studies, on α- and γ-tocopherols have been made in the Roche laboratories and an average of six separate experiments appear in Table T-6. These were run in 0.2 ml of fat in a watch glass in an oven at 45°C. Samples were assayed daily for peroxides and the days to reach 20 meq gives the comparative antioxidant activity. *dl*,α-Tocopherol by itself is not particularly efficient but in combination with ascorbyl palmitate, it is as good as most commercial antioxidants. γ-Tocopherol at 0.02% in pork, chicken, and beef fat is, at

TABLE T-6

COMPARATIVE ANTIOXIDANT ACTIVITY

Additive	(%)	Schaal Oven, Thin Layer, 45°C Chicken Fat Pork Fat (Days to Reach 20 Meq Peroxides)	
None		8	3
BHA	0.01	14	14
BHA	0.02	20	28
BHT	0.02	15	18
Tenox 2	0.05	28	32
α-Tocopherol	0.02	13	15
α-Tocopherol	0.05	13	15
α-Tocopherol	0.2	10	15
α-Tocopherol	0.02	28	28
Ascorbyl Palmitate	0.02		
γ-Tocopherol	0.02	29	37
γ-Tocopherol	0.05	40	58
γ-Tocopherol	0.2	46	61
γ-Tocopherol	0.02	53	67
Ascorbyl Palmitate	0.02		
Ascorbyl Palmitate	0.02	10	9

least, twice as active as α and in combination with ascorbyl palmitate, at least twice as active as any of the commercial antioxidants studied.

Generally speaking, in phenolic antioxidants, substitution on the ring in the two positions adjacent to the OH increases antioxidant activity such as in BHT. However, it has been shown by many workers that substitution in the 5 position in the 6-chromanols does just the opposite; it decreases antioxidant activity. Thus, 6-chromanols function differently from phenols. Skinner and Parkhurst (1970) claim that a lack of substitution in the 5 position results in formation of a quinone which increases the scavenging of free radicals and interruption of the free radical chain reaction of the unsaturated fatty acids. In any event, these workers have shown in many previous publications as other workers throughout the last ten years have also shown, that gamma and delta tocopherol are better antioxidants than alpha.

Current research demonstrates that low tocopherol tissue levels in animal products result in oxidative deterioration during storage as revealed by high TBA values. Feeding supplementary α-tocopherol or the acetate ester to poultry and swine increases the stability of tissues to flavor changes during storage. Dairy cows fed supplementary α-tocopherol or tocopheryl acetate can improve the oxidative stability of secreted fluid milk processed and held in refrigerated storage. These are examples of indirect addition of tocopherols to foods for improved stability. Direct addition of tocopherols to the milk in aqueous form directly after milking can also be shown to retard the development of oxidized flavor.

In the United States in the past, tocopherols have not been widely used as antioxidants because of the ready availability and low price of BHT and BHA. However, antioxidants which do not appear in nature, such as BHT, may not be preferred as the compound of choice; tocopherols may have increased usage in the future. Tocopherols are used widely in Europe particularly in countries which do not permit the use of BHT. Combinations of tocopherol, ascorbyl palmitate, colamine, citric acid, etc., have been found to be extremely effective.

Tocopherols are listed in the Code of Federal Regulations, Title 21; 121.101, with the other antioxidants as chemical preservatives. Ascorbic acid, ascorbyl palmitate, and tocopherols do not have a quantitative tolerance limit in 121.101 whereas other antioxidants (BHA, BHT, PG, TBP, TDP, DLTDP) are limited to total content of 0.02% of fat or oil either alone or in combination.

J. C. BAUERNFEIND
W. M. CORT

References

AAES-JORGENSON, E. 1962. Autoxidation of fatty compounds in living tissue, biological antioxidants, Vol. 2. W. O. Lundberg (Editor). Interscience Publishers, John Wiley & Sons, New York.

BAUERNFEIND, J. C. 1970. Food processing with added ascorbic acid. Advan. Food Res. 18, 219.

BIERI, J. G., PEAKE, I. R., and WINDMUELLER, H. G. 1962. Comparative intestinal absorption lymph and plasma transport and tissue uptake of alpha and gamma tocopherols. Federation Proc. 31, No.2, A2697.

BRUBACHER, G., and WEISER, H. 1967. Biological activity of tocopherol and antioxidants. Wiss. Veroeffentl. Deut. Ges. Ernaehrung 16, 50-66.

BUNNELL, R. H. 1971. Modern procedures for the analysis of tocopherols. Lipids 6, 245.

BUNNELL, R. H., BORENSTEIN, B., and SCHUTT, G. W. 1971. Future considerations in margarine fortification. J. Am. Oil Chemists' Soc. 48, No. 4, 175A.

BUNNELL, R. H., KEATING, J., QUARESIMO, A., and PARMAN, G. K. 1965. Alpha-tocopherol content of foods. Am. J. Clin. Nutr. 17, 1.

CHIPAULT, J. R. 1962. Antioxidants for use in foods. In Autoxidation and Antioxidants, Vol. 2. W. O. Lundberg (Editor). Interscience Publishers, John Wiley & Sons, New York.

CORT, W. M. 1974. Antioxidant activity of tocopherols, ascorbyl palmitate, and ascorbic acid and their mode of action. J. Am. Oil Chemists' Soc. (in press).

DRAPER, H. H. 1970. The tocopherols. Fat soluble vitamins. In International Encyclopedia of Food and Nutrition, Vol. 9. R. A. Morton (Editor). Pergamon Press.

EVANS, H. M., EMERSON, O. H., and EMERSON, G. A. 1936. The isolation from wheat germ oil of an alcohol, alpha tocopherol, having the properties of vitamin E. J. Biol. Chem. 113, 319.

GOLUMBIC, C., and MATTILL, H. A. 1941. Antioxidants and the autoxidation of fats. XII. The antioxygenic action of ascorbic acid in association with the tocopherols, hydroquinones and related compounds. J. Am. Chemists' Soc. 63, 1279.

GOVIND RAO, M. K., and PERKINS, E. G. 1971. Identification and estimation of tocopherols and tocotrienols in vegetable oils using gas chromatography—mass spectrometry. J. Agr. Food Chem. 20, 240.

GRAU, R., and FLIECHMANN, O. 1966. Effect of feeding vitamin E hogs on the stability of lard—and pork—fat—containing products. Z. Lebensm. Untersuch. Forsch. 130, No. 5, 277-291.

HARRIS, P. L., and EMBREE, N. D. 1963. Quantitative consideration of the effect of polyunsaturated fatty acid content of the diet upon the requirements for vitamin E. Am. J. Clin. Nutr. *13*, 385.

HARRIS, R. S. 1962. Influences of storage and processing on the retention of vitamin E in foods. Vitamin Hormone *20*, 603.

HERTING, D. C., and DRURY, E. J. E. 1963. Vitamin E content of vegetable oils and fats. J. Nutr. *81*, 335.

HERTING, D. C., and DRURY, E. J. E. 1969. Alpha-tocopherol content of cereal grains and processed cereals. J. Agr. Food Chem. *17*, 785.

HERTING, D. C., and DRURY, E. J. E. 1969B. Vitamin E content of milk, milk products, and simulated milks: Relevance to infant nutrition. Am. J. Clin. Nutr. *22*, 147.

KENYON, E. M., and PROCTOR, B. E. 1951. Effect of antioxidants on orange oil. Food Res. *16*, 365.

KESTERSON, J. W., and McDUFF, O. R. 1949. Antioxidant studies. Am. Perfumer Essential Oil Rev. *285*, Oct.

KING, R. L. 1968. Direct addition of tocopherols to milk for control of oxidized flavor. J. Dairy Sci. *51*, 1705.

KLAÜI, H. 1971. The functional (technical) uses of vitamins. Proc. University of Nottingham Residential Seminar on Vitamins. M. Stein (Editor). Churchill Livingston, London.

LUCY, J. A. 1971. Functional and structural aspects of biological membranes. Abstr. Proc. Conf. Vitamin E and its Role in Cellular Metabolism, New York City, Dec. 6–7.

MARUSICH, W. L. *et al.* 1974. Effect of supplemental vitamin E in control of rancidity in poultry meat. Presentation at 63rd Poultry Science Assoc. Meeting, Morgantown, W. Va., Aug. 5–9.

MAYER, H., and ISLER, O. 1971. Synthesis of vitamin E. *In* Methods of Enzymology, Vol. 18. Academic Press, New York.

McCAY, P. B. *et al.* 1971. A function of alpha-tocopherol. Stabilization of the microsomal membrane from radial attack during TPNH-dependent oxidation. Lipids *6*, 297.

OLCOTT, H. S., and VAN DER VEEN, J. 1968. Comparative antioxidant activities of tocol and its methyl derivatives. Lipids *3*, 331.

ROTRUCK, J. T. *et al.* 1973. Selenium: Biochemical role as a component of glutathione peroxidase. Science *179*, 588.

SCHUDEL, P., MAYER, H., and ISLER, O. 1972. Chemistry of tocopherols. *In* The Vitamins, Vol. 5. W. H. Sebrell, Jr., and B. S. Harris (Editors) Academic Press, New York.

SCOTT, M. L. 1969. Nutritional value of vitamin E: Animal studies. Proc. Symp. Biochemistry, Assay and Nutritive Value of Vitamin E. Assoc. Vitamin Chemists, Chicago, May 27.

SKINNER, W. A., and PARKHURST, R. M. 1970. Antioxidant properties of alpha-tocopherol derivatives and relationship of antioxidant activity to biological activity. Lipids *5*, 184.

SKINNER, W. A., JOHNSON, H. L., ELLIS, M.,

and PARKHURST, R. M. 1971. Relationship between antioxidants and antihemolytic activities of vitamin E derivatives "in vitro." J. Pharm. Sci. *60*, 643.

SLOVER, H. T. 1971. Tocopherols in foods and fats. Lipids *6*, 291.

WEBB, J. E., BRUNSON, C. C., and YATES, J. D. 1971. Effect of feeding antioxidants on rancidity development in pre-cooked, frozen broiler parts. Poultry Sci., *50*, No. 5, 1601.

TOMATOES

The tomato plant (*Lycopersicon esculentum*) is a native of South America. The name derives from the Nahuatl word, *tomatl*, on which word both the Spanish *tomate* and the English *tomato* are based. The tomato plant was brought to Europe by the Spaniards in 1596 and in the course of time was cultivated in all parts of the world except the arctic and antarctic. There are numerous varieties of tomatoes and much research has been expended on determining their values as processed products, e.g., as juice, canned, dehydrated, or frozen products. Plant geneticists have contributed in major degree to the improvement of tomatoes, the qualities of interest being color, shape, flavor, and size. Juice yield, total solids, viscosity, and pH are other factors of concern to plant breeders. Field yield, of primary interest to growers, has been greatly increased over the years as a result of breeding experiments.

Tomatoes for the fresh vegetable market vary in quality, the best being bright red or a golden yellow, round or oval in shape, ripe, and neither too acid nor too sweet. Yellow tomatoes are equal in flavor to the red but the color does not appeal to all consumers and for processing are graded low.

Tomatoes are processed in a variety of ways—by canning, dehydrating, freezing, and green tomatoes are pickled. Canned tomatoes are available to the consumer in the form of tomato pulp (purée), canned whole tomatoes (perhaps the most familiar form), ketchup, tomato paste, tomato juice, and tomato soup. Although the canning process differs for each of these products, the generic process, if it may be so labeled, begins with inspection to determine the percentage of unuseable fruit, then proceeds to washing, scalding, peeling, filling, exhausting, and processing. Washing tomatoes is required no matter what the end product since soil or other contaminants may cling to the skin. Washing is accomplished mechanically. The operation usually begins with soaking after which spraying is used to effect a thorough cleaning. The scalding operation has a single purpose, loosening the skin so that peeling is more easily and less wastefully accomplished. Hand peeling prevails in the tomato canning industry. One reason for this is that mechanical peelers have not yet been perfected. The filling operation is accomplished mechanically for the most part, the chief exception being the hand filling of fancy whole tomatoes packed in tomato juice. Tomatoes are easily bruised or crushed and to minimize this calcium chloride up to 0.07% (the legal limit) is added. Exhausting is required since tomatoes are filled somewhat colder than for other products. Process times run from 35 to 80 min at a temperature of 212°F. Ketchup, tomato paste, and tomato purée have an additional unit operation to those just mentioned—pulping. The tomatoes are passed to the pulper after having been washed either cold (the cold break process) or after having been steamed (the hot break process). Evaporation to the desired degree of concentration is accomplished in the pulp tank.

Many new technologies for food preservation have been developed in recent years, in the main these are new types of dehydration and the freezing preservation of food. Vacuum puff drying, one of the comparatively recent dehydration methods, has been shown to be capable of producing a tomato powder of good quality at a reasonably low cost. The process utilizes a high vacuum which puffs the juice up to many times its initial volume. The sponge thus created is then crushed and the resultant powder has been shown to have good rehydrating properties.

Tomato juice can be dehydrated successfully by freeze drying, a dehydration method that was in the experimental stage in the 1950's but is now a considerable commercial enterprise. It is a comparatively expensive form of preservation and is best applied to the more expensive foods with which tomatoes cannot be classified.

Foam-mat drying has been demonstrated to be an excellent method for producing tomato powder for tomato juice. The powder reconstitutes in a few seconds and the quality of the juice is equal to the freeze-dried product and not so costly to produce. Foam-mat drying has received wide industrial recognition in a very short time and is applied to many products. Tomato powder is used in dry soup mixes and in a number of other mixes, e.g., pizza pie mix. Dehydrofreezing, a technology that came into being at the close of World War II, has been applied to the preservation of numerous products including tomatoes. As the name indicates, dehydrofreezing combines dehydration with freezing. The process can be applied to tomatoes and a considerable reduction in weight and volume results, a factor that has made dehydrofrozen products of much appeal to institutions which store large quantities of foods under refrigeration.

Although tomatoes can be frozen successfully, one of the limiting factors is that freezing causes the fruit to collapse. The cause of the collapse is associated with cell rupture and changes in the pectin and cellulose structures. As in canning, calcium salts help in some degree to forestall the breakdown but it is only partially effective. The calcium salts are added prior to freezing. Frozen tomatoes are produced in some volume in Europe but have only a modest share of the market for tomatoes in the United States.

Frozen tomato juice has good quality but it, too, is somewhat impaired by freezing. When the product is thawed the pulp tends to disengage from the liquid, not a major problem to be sure but nevertheless a blemish. In preparing frozen tomato juice, the tomatoes are washed, scalded, peeled, and then chopped into small pieces. After passing through a flash heater and heated to 185°–195°F for pasteurization purposes, the juice is extracted and cooled.

Fresh tomatoes cannot withstand low temperatures. If picked before they are ripe, they can be stored at 50°F and held for several weeks, during which time they ripen. The flavor, however, is not up to that of vine-ripened fruit.

Tomatoes are comparatively high in vitamins A B, and C and in the minerals, particularly iron sodium, and potassium.

MARTIN S. PETERSON

TROPICAL FRUITS

Acerola (*Malphigia glabra* L.)

The acerola cherry, also known as the West Indian cherry and the Barbados cherry, is reported to be one of the highest-known fruit sources of ascorbic acid (vitamin C). Values of 2000–3000 mg per 100 gm of fruit have been determined. This single characteristic accounts for most of the interest in processing acerola. Purée and clear juice have been used as additives to other fruit purées and juices to enhance their ascorbic acid level.

To produce a purée, the washed fruit is comminuted in a cutting or grinding mill, then passed through a paddle finisher. The purée product can be stored frozen at 0°F or pasteurized and packaged in a hermetically sealed enamelled can. Separation of a considerable amount of sediment will be seen in the heat-processed purée.

A clear juice can be produced by centrifuging the purée or by pressing the milled fruit in a hydraulic press. The cloudy juice from the press is then filtered in a plate and frame filter press with the aid of diatomaceous earth. The clear, red juice at pH 3.0–3.5 can then be frozen or can be pasteurized at 190°F for about 45 sec. It is filled hot into enamelled cans, sealed in vacuum, and the cans cooled rapidly in a spray cooler. Stored at room temperature, cans of pasteurized acerola juice show swelling in a few weeks, with no signs of microbial spoilage. This swelling has been shown to be due to evolution of carbon dioxide from the decomposition of ascorbic acid. Pasteurized juice held 1 yr at room temperature may lose well over 50% of its ascorbic acid. Retention of ascorbic acid, in frozen acerola juice has been reported to be over 90% after 1 yr of storage.

Commercial production of ascorbic acid from acerola fruit involves low-temperature, vacuum evaporation of the juice. The concentrated juice, containing 50% solids or more, can be dried in a vacuum shelf drier to a powder rich in vitamin C. More sophisticated separation and crystallization techniques will yield crystalline ascorbic acid from the concentrate.

Avocado (*Persia americana*)

The avocado tree is native to Central America. Three types of avocado are generally recognized: Guatemalan, West Indian, and Mexican. An outstanding characteristic of the avocado fruit is its high oil content; values of up to 30% by weight of the edible portion have been reported.

Avocado oil has been an article of commerce for some years, most of it being used in soaps and cosmetics. It is classed as a semidrying oil; iodine values of oils from different varieties range from 70 to 95. The oil can be separated from the pulp by a number of processes. In one, the pulp is heated to about 190°F, 3–4% by weight of diatomaceous earth is mixed with the heated pulp, and the mass is pressed in a hydraulic rack and cloth press. A mixture of oil and water is expressed and the oil is separated by decantation. Solvent extraction of dried slices or pieces of avocado has been used to separate the oil. The so-called "Acapulco Process" made use of a fine screen to separate oil from a purée of avocado pulp and water. Once the oil is separated from the pulp, by whatever means, it can be refined by alkali treatment, bleaching, and filtration. The flavor is bland and it resembles olive oil in chemical composition.

Attempts to heat-process avocado slices or purée have met with very little success. An unpleasant, bitter flavor develops in avocado tissue upon heating.

A patented process for freezing avocado halves or slices involves dipping in an antioxidant solution, partial freezing in a liquified gas at about −100°F, completing the freezing at about 0°F, glazing with antioxidant solution, then packaging in a container devoid of oxygen. The claim is that upon thawing, the pieces retain normal avocado flavor and satisfactory color and texture.

A frozen avocado product with keeping qualities suitable for commercial handling and distribution in frozen food lockers and cabinets has been developed by modification of recipes for preparing an avocado spread called gaucamole. The acidity is increased to about pH 4.5 by the addition of lemon or lime juice, and salt is added to enhance the flavor. This relatively acid product retains an appealing light green color and desirable avocado flavor in frozen storage (0°––10°F) for at least 1 yr. A convenient container for marketing and use of the frozen product has been found to be collapsible metal tubes, although cans, jars, and waxed fiber cups can also be used.

A mechanical device for separating avocado pulp from the peel has been developed by USDA food technologists. The machine consists of 2 drums, 1 with a solid surface and the other with a perforated surface, which revolve toward each other. After the pit is removed, the avocado halves or pieces are placed pulp side down on the perforated drum. As the drums revolve, the fruit is passed between them, the pulp is forced through the perforations, and the peel passes on between the drums for discard.

Avocado powder has been produced by freeze-drying the pulp at a temperature of −40°–50°C. Dried to about 4.2% moisture, the pulp is screened to give a fine powder. Quality retention was satisfactory when stored at 32% RH or lower, and at room temperature.

Banana (*Musa* spp.)

More bananas are marketed in world trade than any other tropical fruit. Fresh bananas are so widely available that the demand for processed banana products has not developed as rapidly as it has for other fruits. The bananas most familiar to consumers in the United States are the dessert type which are generally eaten fresh. Cooking type bananas, often referred to as plantains and generally cooked, are more familiar to consumers in other parts of the world. Processed dessert bananas include purée, flour, flakes or powder, air-dried slices or figs, freeze-dried slices, oil cooked chips, and canned slices.

Banana purée is frozen, heat processed, aseptically canned, or preserved refrigerated. It is used in bakery goods, baby foods, some dairy products, and other specialty items. Peeled bananas are mashed to yield a purée. The enzyme systems which cause browning and gelation must then be inhibited by addition of a small amount of bisulfite (100–200 ppm) or other permissible chemical additive (citric acid and ascorbic acid), or by heat inactivation. The purée to be handled as a frozen product is passed through a heat exchanger in which it is held at about 195°–200°F for approximately 2 min, and then cooled. The cooled purée is put through a paddle pulper fitted with a fine screen (0.033-in. perforations) to remove the tiny dark seeds and fibrous material. It is packaged in suitable containers and frozen rapidly.

A stable banana purée for long-term refrigerated storage is prepared in the same fashion as for frozen storage; citric acid to adjust to pH 4.2, and then 200 ppm of potassium sorbate are mixed in thoroughly. This purée product is stable for at least 6 months' storage at 45°F.

Purée to be preserved by heat processing is passed through a pulper before the heat exchanger. It is acidified to pH 4.1–4.2, and then pumped to the heat exchanger. The purée is taken directly from the hot side of the heat exchanger to a filling machine and cans are filled at 200°–205°F. The sealed cans are inverted and held for about 10 min. They are then cooled rapidly in a water spray to about 100°F before casing. Aseptic canning is done in specially designed equipment in a closed system. The purée is raised to sterilizing temperature, cooled, filled into sterilized cans or drums, and sealed, after which the containers emerge from the closed system.

Banana slices or chunks are canned in acidified syrup by conventional canning methods. The slices are packed into cans, covered with acidified syrup (30° Brix, 0.5% citric acid, 0.1–0.2% calcium chloride) near the boiling point to give a headspace of $5/16$ in. The open cans are exhausted to a center temperature of 160°F then sealed and processed in water at 212°F for 10–12 min (200°F center temperature), and then cooled to 100°F.

Dried banana products in several forms have been available for many years. So-called banana "figs" are dried whole or halved bananas, and have been known in some parts of the world since the 11th Century. Traditionally, banana figs were dried in the sun; in recent years, more modern dehydration methods have been used. Halved or sliced bananas are dipped in a 1% solution of sodium bisulfite for about 2 min. They are dried on trays in a forced draft oven (air velocity 2000 fpm or greater) or tunnel drier at 180°F for 2 hr, and at 140°F for the rest of the time required (6–9 hr) to yield a product containing 17–20% moisture. Total drying time depends on tray loading, rate of air movement, temperature, and humidity of the air. A residue of sulfur dioxide (>50 ppm) in the dried product enhances its stability.

Piece-form dried bananas can also be produced by freeze drying and by osmo-vac drying. In the former method, slices or halves are frozen rapidly on trays at 0°F or colder. The frozen fruit is then placed in a freeze-dryer or sublimator and dried under high vacuum (0.005 mm Hg P). Drying is continued until the product is at about 3% moisture or below. Osmo-vac drying combines osmotic withdrawal of water from banana slices or halves and subsequent vacuum oven drying. Banana pieces are submerged in 67°–70° Brix syrup for several (8–12) hr. They are then drained, rinsed, and dried in vacuo (10 mm Hg P) at 150°–160°F. The pieces puff up during the vacuum drying and are crisp and porous after drying to about 2.5% moisture. These low moisture banana products are hygroscopic and must be packaged in moisture-proof containers to retain their quality.

Finely divided dried banana products are generally classified as either flour or powder. Flour is commonly known as the dried product from green bananas or from plantains; it is high in starch and relatively low in sugars. Powder is made from fully ripe bananas and contains upwards of 65% sugars (soluble solids). Banana flakes are also made from ripe fruit and are simply not as finely divided as powder. Spray drying is also used to produce flour and powder. The peeled bananas are mashed and screened to form a fine purée devoid of seeds and large fiber particles. Such ingredients as sodium bisulfite (200–500 ppm), dry milk solids, or isolated soybean protein are added and sufficient water to permit atomization in the spray drier. The banana slurry is sprayed into the drying tower where it is dried rapidly in a current of heated air; product temperature should not exceed 95°F and it should contain no more than 3% moisture. Flour (from green fruit) is less hygroscopic than powder (from ripe fruit), but both products must be packaged in moisture-proof containers.

Banana flakes are made by drum drying banana purée. The purée is fed onto the outside surface of steam-heated drums in a layer of uniform thickness (i.e., 0.01 in.). Proper adjustment of speed of rotation and steam pressure in the drums should be made to give a dried product at less than 3% moisture as it is removed from the drum surface by doctor blades. Additives such as bisulfite or EDTA in the purée help to preserve and stabilize the color of the dried flakes. Flakes at 3.5% moisture tend to cake; those below 3% remain free flowing if packaged in a hermetically sealed container.

Fried, salted banana chips have appeared on the market from time to time. Slices of unripe bananas are deep fat fried, then the cooled slices are sprinkled with salt. Some chips are treated with artificial banana flavor to impart this flavor into the otherwise bland product. Antioxidant (BHT or BHA) incorporated in the oil-fry bath increases the stability of the chips.

Guava (*Psidium guajava*)

The fruit of the guava tree has a rough-textured yellow skin and varies in shape from round to pear-shaped. The color of the inner flesh may be white, yellow, deep pink, or salmon-red depending upon the variety. The central seed cavity contains many hard seeds that are inedible and are removed during processing. The flesh or pulp contains numerous small stone cells, the larger of which are removed by a screening operation. Guava fruit is an excellent source of vitamin C. Products made from guava include purée, clear juice, nectar and other beverages, jam and jelly, paste, syrup, canned halves or whole fruit, and concentrated purée and juice.

Canned guava shells (halves with seeds scooped out) and whole fruit account for a very small portion of the volume of processed guava products. Standard canning procedures are employed. Washed and sorted fruit is packed into cans, covered with hot syrup, exhausted to 160°F center temperature, sealed and processed 8-10 min in a boiling water bath. The cans are cooled in a water spray to about 100°F. For canned shells, the fruit is cut in two and the seeds are scooped out by hand. The deseeded halves (shells) are then canned and processed as above.

By far the larger proportion of guava that is processed is made into purée; from this form, many other products are made. Whole guava fruit is sorted, washed and conveyed to a paddle pulper. This machine breaks up the fruit, forces the pulp or purée out through a cylindrical screen (0.033–0.045-in. perforations) and ejects the seeds through a separate port. The pulp is moved by gravity or by pump to a paddle finisher. The finisher is identical to the pulper but fitted with a finer cylindrical screen (0.017–0.020-in. perforations). The larger stone cells are separated from the purée by the finisher. The purée is then packaged and frozen, or is preserved by heat processing. For freezing, the purée can be packaged in 30-lb tins with plastic bag liners, in paper boxes with plastic bag liners, or other suitable container which will permit rapid freezing. Slush freezing in a heat exchanger before packaging is recommended to preserve quality.

The purée can be pasteurized or heat processed for storage at ambient temperature. Finished purée is heated rapidly to 200°F in a heat exchanger, filled hot into No. 10 cans (or other suitable container), hermetically sealed, inverted and held for 8-10 min, then cooled rapidly to 100°F in a spray cooler.

Guava purée is used in production of nectar or other types of guava beverages. The purée is mixed with water, sugar, and citric acid to yield a beverage which can be preserved by freezing or heat processing. Standards of Identity for guava beverages have not been formulated. A beverage containing 20% guava purée, sugar, and water to give a product at about 14° Brix and about pH 3.2 has been widely accepted.

Purée is used in making guava jam, which product must conform to Standards of Identity under the Federal Food, Drug and Cosmetic Act. Nine parts of guava purée is mixed with 11 parts of sugar by weight, and the mixture is boiled to the desired end point. The jam must contain 65% soluble solids. It is filled hot into suitable containers, then cooled rapidly.

A clear juice is produced from purée by treating the purée for a few hours at room temperature with a pectin-degrading enzyme, mixing with a filter aid, and expressing juice by means of a hydraulic rack and cloth press or a bag press. The juice is further clarified by centrifugation or by a filter press operation. Beverages or jelly can be made from the clear juice. Juice or purée can be used in preparation of syrups to impart natural flavors and colors to these products. The syrups can be used as ice cream toppings, table syrups, or dessert ingredients. To enhance their stability, it is common practice to add antimicrobial agents such as sodium benzoate, sorbic acid, or combinations of preservatives. This prevents spoilage after the container is opened. Guava purée has a tendency to separate into clear and cloudy layers which detracts from the appearance of a syrup. This is prevented by adding a small amount of a colloidal stabilizer such as a gum, alginate, or cellulose derivative.

In some tropical countries, a paste is made from guava purée by merely boiling it down to a pasty consistency. This is sometimes further dried in the sun as a thin sheet spread on trays. The resulting dried sheet or "leather" is consumed as a confection.

High quality concentrates of guava purée and juice can be made by evaporation at low pressure and temperature. Enzymatic depectinization is a desirable pretreatment for purée to be concentrated. Purée thus pretreated can be concentrated 3.5- to 4-fold; purée that has not been depectinized is very difficult to concentrate to 2.5-fold in the same equipment. Several types of evaporators are satisfactory; recovery of volatile flavors for restoration to the concentrate is desirable. Concentration of the depectinized clear juice can be carried to 8-fold or higher. Recovery and restoration of volatile flavors is desirable for juice concentrate as well.

Lychee (*Letchi chinensis* Sonn.)

The lychee is a subtropical tree native to south China that also thrives in tropical areas. Lychee fruits are round to oval and 1-1½ in. in diameter.

The pericarp is bright red or brownish red, leathery, and with many small pyramidal protuberances. The edible portion, the aril, is white-to-cream in color and in consistency resembles fresh grapes. A single seed occupies $1/5$-$1/2$ the volume of the fruit, depending on the variety. The earliest known publication on lychee was written by Ts'ai Haiang in 1059 A.D. Sun-dried lychee, so-called "lychee nut," has been available from the Orient for many years. They are of acceptable quality, but recent work on dehydration of lychee has shown that a high quality dried lychee can be produced by tunnel or cabinet drying. The whole fruits are dried in a forced draft tunnel or cabinet drier at 160°F and an air flow rate of about 35 cfm for 30 hr. The dried product contains 26% moisture or less and is stable in storage at 75–80% RH for several months.

Lychee are canned by standard procedures after removing the peel. The peels have been removed by hand traditionally. However, recent work has shown that 20% NaOH at 90°C disintegrates the pericarp in a period of 3 min. It is sufficiently disrupted that it can then be removed by an opposing-belt scraper device followed by a rotary rod washer with water sprays. The peeled whole fruit, or halves with the pit removed, are filled into cans, covered with hot, acidified syrup (50° Brix), exhausted in a steam chest to a temperature of 170°F, sealed, and processed in a boiling water bath for 10–12 min.

Lychee frozen in syrup make an attractive dessert product. The peeled fruits are covered with 25°–30° Brix syrup in a suitable container and frozen rapidly at -20°F or below. The frozen product should be held at 0°F or below.

Mango (*Mangifera indica*)

The mango is indigenous to southern Asia, probably originating in the Indo-Burma area thousands of years ago. It is said that more people eat mango than any other fruit in the world as it grows profusely in those parts of the world most heavily populated. Commercial production of mango is greatest in India where 2 million acres yield about 5 million tons of fruit annually.

The ovate-oblong mango fruit varies in size among varieties, some fruits weighing as much as 1 lb. The flat, oval seed may be clingstone or freestone in nature and comprises 7–20% of the weight of the whole fruit. Skin or peel color varies from green to yellow and red in ripe fruit. The peel portion of most varieties appears to consist of three types of tissue. The outermost layer is a very thin waxy cuticle beneath which is a thin (0.1 mm), tough, highly pigmented pellicle; beneath this is a layer (1–2 mm) of fibrous, firm tissue. These three layers are generally referred to as the peel or exocarp. It is desirable to remove the peel in preparing cheeks and slices for freezing or canning.

An important characteristic for processing is the pH of the edible portion, the flesh or pulp. pH values of 4.5 or slightly higher have been recorded for some varieties of mangoes, although most varieties are slightly below pH 4.5. It is important that mango products for heat processing be acidified sufficiently to render the pH well below 4.5. Slices for canning must be covered with acidified syrup to lower the pH of the product.

Preparing mango slices for canning or freezing involves removal of the peel. This is done by hand or can be done by means of steam or hot lye treatment. Whole mangoes are steamed for 2–2½ min, a tiny slit is cut in the peel and it is readily slipped off by hand. Lye treatment in 20% NaOH at 90°C for 6–7 min removes the outer layers of the exocarp, the cuticle, and pellicle. The peeled fruit is sliced and the seed removed. The slices are filled into a plain tin can, covered with acidified syrup (40° Brix with 0.25% citric acid) close to the boiling point, then held 2–3 min in flowing steam in an exhaust box. The cans are sealed and immersed in boiling water for 8–10 min to raise the center temperature to 195°F. The cans are then cooled rapidly to 100°F center temperature in a spray cooler.

Slices for freezing are packed into a suitable container and covered with syrup (25°–30° Brix). Freezing is done as rapidly as possible at subzero temperatures and the frozen product is stored at 0°F or below.

A high quality mango purée is used for preparation of nectars or other beverages, for table syrups, for bakery and dairy products, and can be drum dried to yield dried flakes. Whole, ripe mangoes are washed, steamed for 2–2½ min, spray cooled, and transferred to a stainless steel tank. Steam treatment softens the peel sufficiently that the fruits are broken and pulped by a power stirrer fitted with a saw-toothed propellor blade. The fruit tissue is removed from the pits without cutting or breaking them. The pulp is separated from the seeds and peels by a centrifugal basket separator. The pulp is passed through a paddle pulper fitted with a 0.033-in. screen to remove fiber and small pieces of peel. The purée is pumped through a heat exchanger to heat-inactivate enzymes (200°F for 2 min), then the product is cooled. The finished purée, about 70% of the weight of in-going fruit, is packaged in a suitable container for rapid freezing.

A typical, acceptable nectar is made with 25% mango purée; water, sugar, and citric acid (50% solution) are added to give a nectar product at about 14° Brix and pH 3.5. The ingredients are thoroughly mixed, heated rapidly to 190°F, filled hot into cans, (plain tin or enamel-lined), sealed, and processed in a boiling water bath to give a center temperature of 195°F. The cans are then cooled in a water spray to a center temperature of 100°F.

The canned nectar may also be preserved by spin processing, a method of heat processing in which the cans are rotated on their long axis in a steam chamber. The fill of the container must be carefully controlled to give optimum headspace for each can size. For a No. 2 can (307 × 409), a $5/16$-in. headspace after sealing is satisfactory. The nectar at room temperature is poured into the can; the can is sealed at a vacuum of 15–20 in. and placed in the spin cooker. A generous flow of steam into the cooker is necessary to prevent cold spots. The cans are spin-cooked for 3 min at 125 rpm, then immediately spin-cooled in a water spray for 3 min. to reduce the temperature of the contents to 100°F.

Dried mango flakes and powder are prepared by means of a drum dryer. Material to be dried is fed into the trough formed by the two counter-rotating drums. Spacing between drums can be adjusted to maintain the desired layer thickness of material deposited on the surfaces. As the drums rotate, water is evaporated from the thin layer of material on the surface of the internally heated (steam) drums. A scraping blade is positioned to remove the dried material from the surface of each drum. A drum spacing of 0.010 in., steam pressure of 45 psig in the drums, and drying time on the surface of about 25 sec can be expected to give a satisfactory product. The dried purée is removed from the drum as a thin sheet, bright yellow in color, and with the flavor of cooked mango. It should be at 3% moisture content or below in order to be easily handled in powder or flake form.

Papaya (*Carica papaya*)

The papaya tree is indigenous to the tropics of Mexico and Central America but is now grown widely throughout the tropical world. Growing straight without branches like the palm, the papaya tree is crowned by large deep-lobed leaves, and bears fruit before the end of the first year. The Solo variety selected and developed in Hawaii is widely accepted as superior in quality and flavor to most varieties. Most of the papaya consumed in the world is as fresh fruit. Some processed products have been marketed: canned slices, canned nectar or other beverage, frozen or canned purée, papain, and papaya jams and jellies.

The edible portion of papaya, the flesh or pulp, is in the nonacid category of plant tissues, having a pH of 5 or above. Thus, for papaya products preserved by heat processing the pH must be adjusted to well below 4.5. It is an excellent source of vitamin C.

In preparing slices for canning, the papaya is first peeled by hand. No mechanical means of removing the peel from whole papaya has been described. The seeds are removed and the slices cut to the desired size. They are packed in a plain tin can, covered with acidified syrup (50° Brix, 0.5% citric acid) near the boiling point, the can and contents are heated in an exhaust box to a temperature of 170°F, sealed, then processed in a boiling water bath for 10–12 min. The cans are then cooled in a water spray to a temperature of 100°F.

Purée is prepared from fruit that is not of fresh market quality, but that is fully ripe and free from rot. The fruit is steamed for $1^1/_2$ min in a steam chamber on a conveyor belt, then spray cooled with water. The cooled fruit is sliced by a mechanical slicer, then passed to a crusher-scraper device within which the flesh and seeds are loosened and removed from the peel. Citric acid (1.0%) is mixed into the macerate of skins, pulp, and seeds; this inhibits gelation and development of undesirable flavors. The macerate is fed to a centrifugal separator and the peels are separated from the pulp and seeds. The seeds are separated from the pulp in a mechanical paddle pulper. The pulp (purée) is then passed through a heat exchanger. The temperature of the pulp is raised to 205°F, held at that temperature for 2 min, then cooled to 85°F in a continuous flow. This heating inactivates enzymes in the purée. The cooled purée is passed through a paddle finisher fitted with a 0.020-in. screen which removes coarse fiber and specks to yield a smooth purée. The purée is then packaged and frozen.

For a heat-processed or pasteurized purée, the finisher is placed before the heat exchanger. Then the finished purée is pumped to the heat exchanger, and the purée is taken hot from the exchanger to a filler. It is filled hot into cans, hermetically sealed, and held for several minutes before cooling.

Purée is used in preparation of nectars, jams, bakery and dairy products, and other specialty products. Nectar or similar beverage products can be prepared by mixing purée with water, sugar, and citric acid to adjust the pH. No Standards of Identity have been established for papaya beverages. A nectar containing 20% papaya purée by weight and at about 13° Brix and pH 3.5 has been judged to be an attractive product. The composition of jams are specified in the FDA Standards of Identity; likewise, there are Standards of Identity for jellies. Papaya jelly can be made from the clear juice expressed from papaya purée which has been treated with a pectinolytic enzyme. The depectinized purée is mixed with about 2% by weight of diatomaceous earth or other pressing aid and pressed in a bag press or similar equipment. The expressed juice is further clarified by means of a filter press.

Papaya purée and papaya juice concentrates are prepared with a low-temperature, low-pressure evaporator. The depectinized purée can be concentrated to about 3.0-fold, whereas the clarified juice can be concentrated about 5-fold. The concentrates offer advantages in shipping, handling, and storage space requirements.

Papain, a proteolytic enzyme, is found in papaya fruit and leaves. The latex from the skin of green papayas is the richest source of papain. In some tropical countries, usually in a low labor cost area, workers scratch the surfaces of green papaya while still on the trees, then gather the latex that exudes from the scratch marks on the fruits. The latex is dried with mild heat to give a crude material rich in proteolytic activity. This is shipped to processors who further refine the material to give a product with greater proteolytic activity. Papain is used as a meat tenderizer and if sufficiently purified is used in pharmaceutical preparations.

Passion Fruit (*Passiflora* spp.)

Two types of passion fruit are preferred for processing: the purple (*Passiflora edulis* Sims) and the yellow (*Passiflora edulis* f. *flavicarpa* Degener). The latter is cultivated as a commercial crop in Hawaii. It is a vigorous, woody, perennial vine which under most conditions is more robust than the purple variety. The fruit of the yellow variety is usually larger and the juice is more acid than the purple variety, but is considered by some to have less aromatic passion fruit flavor. The fruit is round or oval in shape and varies from $1\frac{1}{2}$ to $2\frac{1}{2}$ in. in diameter, and from $2\frac{1}{2}$ to 4 in. in length. It has a tough rind with a smooth glossy surface and an inner white layer similar to the albedo of citrus fruits. Within this hard, brittle rind are numerous small black seeds each enclosed in a sac containing a yellowish, aromatic juice with a pleasant but rather acid flavor. Passion fruit juice is a fair source of vitamins A and C. It contains significant amounts of starch, estimated at 2–5% for the purple type and lesser quantities in the yellow. The main consideration in passion fruit processing is separation of the juice from rind and seeds.

In the method commonly used in Hawaii, the fruit is washed, then passed through a mechanical slicer with rotary blades about $\frac{3}{4}$ in. apart. The cut fruit drops into a centrifugal separator consisting of a stainless steel basket with 16° inclined perforated walls punched with $\frac{1}{4}$-in. holes on $\frac{5}{8}$-in. centers. As the basket rotates, the seeds

and juice are moved out through the wall perforations and the rinds move up over the rim of the basket to a discharge port. The juice and seeds mixture flows from a separate port into a paddle pulper fitted with a screen with 0.033-in. perforations; this ejects the seeds and the juice is then passed through a paddle finisher fitted with a 0.0177- or 0.020-in. screen to remove broken seeds and specks.

In Australia, two different extraction methods are used. One utilizes a machine in which the fruit falls into rows of hemispherical pockets where they are held and pierced from below to give a cross-shaped cut through the rind. A plunger then descends on the fruit and ejects the seed and juice through a hole in the bottom of the pocket. The plunger virtually turns the fruit inside out. This procedure minimizes contact of juice with cut rind, an important consideration when handling the purple-pigmented fruit. In another method, the fruit is squeezed between rotating rollers which bursts the rind and juice and seeds are ejected. Juice is then separated by means of a pulper and finisher as above.

The juice can be frozen or pasteurized for storage. For pasteurization, the juice is filled into an enamel-lined can, vacuum sealed, spin processed in flowing steam to a center temperature of 190°F, then cooled in a water spray to 100°F.

The juice is used in preparation of nectar bases by addition of sugar equal to 60% of the weight of the juice. This high solids base is stored frozen. One part of the thawed base is diluted with $4–4\frac{1}{2}$ parts of water to prepare a nectar. The same proportions of juice, sugar, and water are mixed to prepare a nectar for canning. The nectar is filled cold into cans, vacuum sealed, and spin processed to a center temperature of 190°F. The cans are then rapidly cooled before storage. Passion fruit juice is used in blends with other juices or purées; some of the more popular are passion fruit-orange, passion fruit-guava, and passion fruit-papaya. Due to its strong flavor, passion fruit is particularly useful in blends and punch products.

Passion fruit is too acidic to be easily used in ice cream, but this characteristic is an advantage in preparation of sherbet. The addition of 10–15% of passion fruit juice to a basic sherbet mix yields a full-flavored product. The juice is used in making jellies and jams alone or in combination with other fruits.

A passion fruit table syrup contains about 20% passion fruit juice, water, and sugar sufficient to give a product at 65° Brix. Passion fruit juice and its products tend to separate into clear and cloudy layers. To prevent this in the syrup product, 0.5% of gum tragacanth is added. The syrup is filled hot (190°F) into bottles or cans and cooled at once in a water spray.

Soursop (*Annona muricata*, L.)

The fruit of the soursop tree is large (3–8 lb), unsymmetrical, often kidney-shaped, rough-skinned, green, and soft when ripe. The inner portion of the fruit is a white, soft, somewhat fibrous mass in which are imbedded many large dark-colored seeds. The pulpy inner portion has a pleasing, winey, rich flavor.

The fruit is peeled by hand. The pulp is separated from the seeds in a paddle pulper fitted with a 0.060- or 0.045-in. screen. It is then passed through a paddle finisher fitted with a 0.020-in. screen. A yield of about 50% of the weight of in-going fruit is recovered as a white purée. The Brix is usually about 15°–20° and typically the purée is at pH 3.5–3.7. The purée can be heat-processed in plain tin cans or can be frozen in suitable containers. Before freezing, the purée is passed through a heat exchanger in which the temperature is raised to 185°F, it is held at that temperature for 2 min, then cooled at once to room temperature. This inactivates peroxidase and prevents the development of pink discoloration and undesirable flavors during frozen storage.

The purée is used in ice creams, sherbets, and in beverage products. A highly acceptable nectar contains about 25% soursop purée, sugar, and water to give a final product at about 15° Brix. The nectar is heat processed in bottles or cans.

JOHN BREKKE

Cross-references: *Citrus Industry; Pineapples.*

U

ULTRAFILTRATION AND REVERSE OSMOSIS

Within the past 5 yr, 2 new membrane separation processes, ultrafiltration and reverse osmosis, have emerged from the laboratory to take their place among the commercial techniques used for processing dairy and food products and waste streams. Unlike the third membrane process, electrodialysis, ultrafiltration and reverse osmosis are driven by pressure only. Another main inherent feature is operation at moderate temperatures (5°–50°C). To better understand the potential place of ultrafiltration and reverse osmosis in the dairy and food industries, a closer look at specific features is required.

Reverse osmosis has been worked on for over 10 yr as a means of producing pure water from brack-ish and sea waters. The process got its name from reversing the normal osmotic process which takes place in the cells in our bodies, in plants, and other organisms where water and a solution are separated by a membrane and water passes naturally through the membrane to dilute the solution. In reverse osmosis, the natural behavior is turned around, as shown in Fig. U-1. The membrane in reverse osmosis is a synthetic polymer made of a cellulose derivative or other material; it can be considered a filter which is capable of working on dissolved solids of molecular size.

Ultrafiltration membranes were developed soon after reverse osmosis membranes. They are usually quite similar in construction, with the main difference being the size of the pores. Figure U-2 shows the difference in behavior between ultrafiltration and reverse osmosis membranes. In ultrafiltration, the large molecules being retained exhibit negligi-

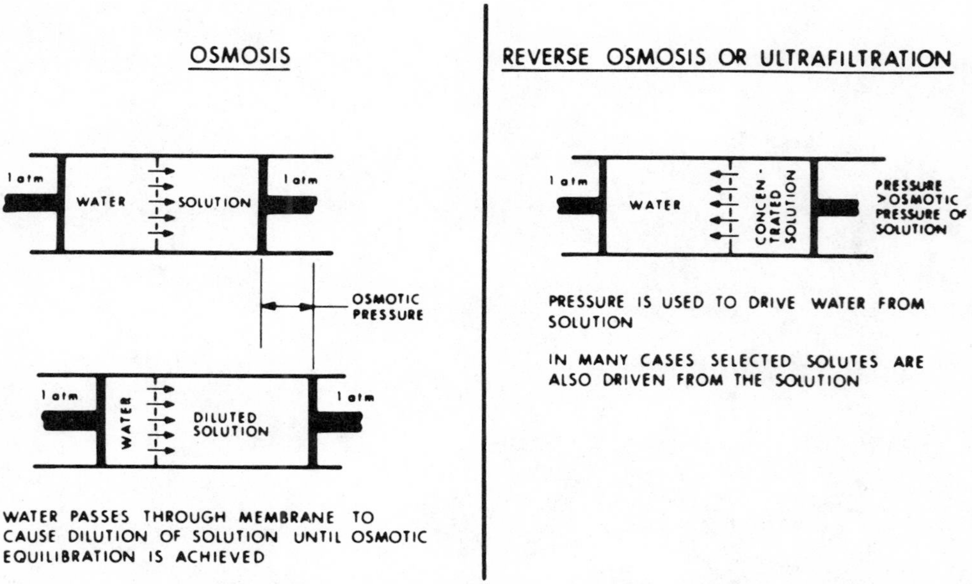

FIG. U-1. NATURAL BEHAVIOR OF OSMOSIS IS TURNED AROUND IN REVERSE OSMOSIS OR ULTRAFILTRATION

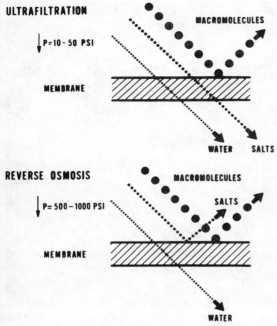

ULTRAFILTRATION

P=10 - 50 PSI

MACROMOLECULES

MEMBRANE

WATER   SALTS

REVERSE OSMOSIS

P= 500 – 1000 PSI

MACROMOLECULES

SALTS

MEMBRANE

WATER

FIG. U-2. DIAGRAM DEPICTING THE DIFFERENCE IN BEHAVIOR BETWEEN MEMBRANES OF ULTRA-FILTRATION AND REVERSE OSMOSIS

trating food solutions, equipment design is an essential key to successful application. The membranes can be used in the following forms: (1) tubular, with the membranes cast or inserted in $1/2$-in. diameter tubes (for reverse osmosis) or 1-in. diameter tubes (for low-pressure ultrafiltration), (2) flat leaf, with flat sheet membranes incorporated in cartridges containing a series of square leaves, (3) spiral wound, with flat sheet membranes wound up into a configuration similar to a music roll, (4) thin channel, with flat sheet membranes in stacks or other arrangements, (5) hollow fibers, with flow on the interior or exterior surfaces.

Generally, the tubular configuration appears the most practical when building systems which will be easy to clean and sanitize in keeping with current practices in the dairy and food industries.

Commercial Status

The application which has brought ultrafiltration and reverse osmosis into commercial reality, where sanitary, CIP (clean-in-place) systems are mandatory, is the processing of cheese whey. An illustration of a flow schematic showing ultrafiltration used to separate and concentrate undenatured whey proteins followed by reverse osmosis to concentrate the lactose solution (which is the effluent from ultrafiltration) is given in Fig. U-3. Direct concentration of whole whey by reverse osmosis is an alternative. When reverse osmosis is applied to either whole whey or the lactose solution, the water pollution control benefits of the process are realized by the use of a very tight membrane which leaves a low BOD (biological oxygen demand) ef-

ble osmotic pressures so that one is not overcoming these pressures to create reverse osmosis. Hence, the different terminology for these two pressure-driven processes.

Regardless of the membrane material chosen and its specific properties for separating and concen-

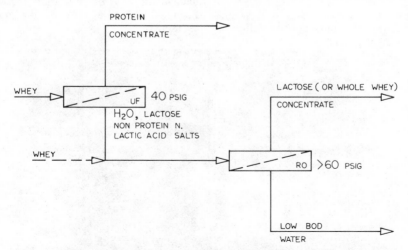

PROTEIN
CONCENTRATE

WHEY

UF   40 PSIG
H2O, LACTOSE
NON PROTEIN N.
LACTIC ACID SALTS

LACTOSE (OR WHOLE WHEY)
CONCENTRATE

WHEY

RO >60 PSIG

LOW BOD
WATER

FIG. U-3. SCHEMATIC SHOWING ULTRAFILTRATION USED TO SEPARATE AND CONCENTRATE UNDENATURED WHEY PROTEINS FOLLOWED BY REVERSE OSMOSIS TO CONCENTRATE THE LACTOSE SOLUTION fluent for discharge or possible reuse within the plant.

Reverse osmosis is finding the following three specific roles in whey processing:

(1) For plants with existing evaporator capacity and increasing cheese production, reverse osmosis is a very economical approach to preconcentration. This means the removal of 30–50% of the water, which effectively increases the capacity of the evaporation equipment by 30–50%. In this application reverse osmosis would be used to raise the solids level from 6 to between 9 and 12%.

(2) For concentrating whole whey prior to hauling to a centralized processing plant, reverse osmosis would be used to bring the solids up from 6% to approximately 25%.

(3) In processing the lactose solution coming from ultrafiltration, reverse osmosis can be used to concentrate to 25% total solids prior to further lactose processing, such as the production of crystalline products of varying purity.

If water effluent quality is not a critical issue, reverse osmosis membranes are now available which will pass some of the mineral salts during the concentration process. The exact extent of demineralization which can be obtained without losing lactose is being studied in a number of different laboratories. Possibilities appear good for producing partially demineralized whole whey concentrates and for improving recovery of high purity lactose products.

A commercial whey protein ultrafiltration plant has been in operation in New Zealand for over seven months at the time of the writing of this article (Zall et al. 1971). In the United States, a 300,000-lb-per-day ultrafiltration and reverse osmosis plant is now going into operation at

FIG. U-4. COMMERCIAL ABCOR WHEY PROTEIN ULTRAFILTRATION PLANT IN NEW ZEALAND

View shows portion of sanitary UF cabinets, permeate collection tank, and control panel.

Crowley Foods, in La Fargeville, N.Y., under a water pollution control demonstration grant partially funded by the Environmental Protection Agency (Amundson 1970; Goldsmith et al. 1971, 1972; Zall et al. 1971). Figure U-5 shows a view of the ultrafiltration section and control panels for the plant during installation, while Fig. U-6 shows a view of the reverse osmosis section.

FIG. U-5. UF/RO WHEY PROCESSING PLANT AT CROWLEY FOODS SHOWING ULTRAFILTRATION SECTION AND COMPLETE CONTROL PANEL

FIG. U-6. VIEW OF THE REVERSE OSMOSIS SECTION OF THE CROWLEY WHEY PROCESSING PLANT HAVING A CAPACITY OF 300,000 LB (140,000 LITERS) PER DAY

The preponderance of normal dairy pumps, piping, and fittings is a feature of ultrafiltration and reverse osmosis equipment designed for dairy and food applications.   Wherever possible, 3-A Standards are used for the selection of the components surrounding the tubular ultrafiltration membranes and tubular reverse osmosis modules. An example, as shown in Fig. U-6, is the selection of homogenizer pumps for operation of reverse osmosis at 800 psig.

Other Dairy Applications

In addition to helping convert cheese and casein wheys into a profitable material, ultrafiltration is now receiving a great deal of attention in Europe for processing skim milk prior to cheese making. Evaluations of the process in France and Italy indicate that very significant increases in yield are attained and that this application is ready for wide-spread pilot testing and commercial application. In this country, ultrafiltration can be used to improve the economics of the manufacture of cottage and ricotta cheese as well as to produce milk protein concentrates for a wide range of end uses. Ultrafiltration could prove useful in concentrating whey proteins for the manufacture of ricotta or ricotone from whey. Early work on ultrafiltration of whole milk is also promising, so further application to ricotta cheese manufacture is possible.

Other Food Applications

The U.S. Environmental Protection Agency and Central Soya are presently evaluating ultrafiltration and reverse osmosis for the treatment of soy whey.   The volumes to be treated in full-scale plants are considerably larger than those encountered in the case of cheese whey, though the numbers of plants with the soy whey pollution prob-

FIG. U-7. OVERALL VIEW OF ULTRAFILTRATION (AT LEFT) AND REVERSE OSMOSIS PILOT PLANT FOR PROCESSING SOY WHEY AT CENTRAL SOYA, CHICAGO

lem is much smaller. A view of the Central Soya pilot installation is shown in Fig. U-7 (De Filippi *et al.* 1971; Goldsmith *et al.* 1972).

In addition to cheese, soy whey and milk, any solution containing macromolecules such as proteins and polysaccharides can be concentrated by ultrafiltration. Specific applications include: concentrating and desalting enzymes, treating vegetable protein wastes other than soy proteins, concentrating and fractionating corn and other grain steep liquor, concentrating and fractionating beverage still bottoms, concentrating packing house blood, concentrating egg albumin, and concentrating and purifying soluble fish protein.

Solutions with lower molecular weight materials such as sugars, salts, and flavor compounds can be concentrated by reverse osmosis. Presently, the number of applications for reverse osmosis is limited by lifetime of the membranes and modules, at pressures required to give economical flux rates. Sanitary considerations currently prevent using anything other than the tubular membrane configuration. Also, certain flavor compounds cannot, at this time, be retained. However, the "state-of-the-art" is improving rapidly. Several applications which appear most promising are: concentrating fruit juices and selected juice plant wastes, concentrating various sugar solutions from grain and other vegetable processing operations, and concentrating coffee and tea.

BERNARD S. HORTON

References

AMUNDSON, C. H. *et al.* 1970. Membrane separation processes for the abatement of pollution from whey. Proc. 18th Intern. Dairy Congr., Sydney, Australia, Oct. 12-16.

DEFILIPPI, R. P., GOLDSMITH, R. L., and HOSSAIN, S. 1971. New membrane process applications. Proc. AICHE Meeting, Aug. 1971.

GOLDSMITH, R. L. *et al.* 1971. Membrane processing of cottage cheese whey for pollution abatement. Proc. 2nd Natl. Symp. Food Processing Wastes, Denver, Mar. 23-26.

GOLDSMITH, R. L., HORTON, B. S., HOSSAIN, S., and ZALL, R. R. 1970. Membrane separation processes for the abatement of pollution from cottage cheese whey. Proc. Cottage Cheese and Cultured Milk Prod. Symp., Univ. Maryland, Mar. 11.

GOLDSMITH, R. L., HORTON, B. S., and ZALL, R. R. 1972. Membrane processing of cheese whey reaches commercial scale. Food Technol. *26*, No. 2, 30-35.

GOLDSMITH, R. L., KEELER, G., STAWIARSKI, M., and WILHELM, E. 1972. Treatment of soy whey by membrane processing. Proc. 3rd Natl. Symp. Food Processing Wastes, New Orleans, Mar. 28.

ZALL, R. R. *et al.* 1971. Membrane processing of 300,000 lbs/day cottage cheese whey for pollution abatement, phase II. Proc. 64th Ann. Meeting, AICHE, San Francisco, Nov. 28-Dec. 2.

Cross-reference: *Filtration.*

ULTRASONIC ENERGY

Among the various forms of energy that react with different types of matter are sound waves, mechanical vibratory energy. Sound waves are generally audible to the human ear if the vibratory frequency is in the range of from 20 to 20,000 cycles per second. The unit of frequency is the Hertz (Hz) equivalent to one cycle per second. The frequency range below 20 Hz is designated as infrasonic and that above 20,000 Hz as ultrasonic. Much of the application of sound energy to technology occurs in the ultrasonic range; i.e., over 20 KHz (over 20,000 Hz) up to several thousand MHz (million Hz).

Ultrasonic phenomena have found many and varied applications in food technology. Brennan (see cross-reference below) has discussed equipment for producing ultrasound frequencies, bases for their effects, and their application to emulsification and cleaning of equipment. The velocity of sound in liquids depends on the compressibility and density of the medium and accordingly is characteristic of a particular medium. This means that when a sound wave passes from one medium to another, only the wavelength will change if the adjoining media differ from one another as regards velocity of sound in them. The frequency of the sound waves is determined by the source of the acoustic vibrations. The scope of this discussion deals primarily with the consideration of ultrasonic effects in food technology and not the physical phenomenon.

White (1972) and others have pointed out applications of ultrasonics to the food industry. These include emulsification and equipment cleaning (already mentioned); bacterial destruction; yeast cell disintegration for release of enzymes; increase in number of nuclei in crystallizing systems; analysis of milk and ice cream for fat and solids-not-fat content; analysis of wine for alcohol and Brix value; fat crystallization phenomena; characteristics of fat mixtures; detection of adulteration of butter oil with other fats; accelerating the maturing of wines; determination of carcass characteristics of cattle, swine, and sheep; aging of meat; boiler scale prevention; sterilization of liquid foods; and many others. The more significant of these applications will be discussed under this subject. Many of the situations mentioned require development of devices or equipment adapted to the individual product.

Ultrasonic experimentation with dairy products, especially with milk, has been extensive. By comminuting the fat globule, a soft-curd milk can be produced. Homogenization of milk, however, effects the same result and has become general practice. Destruction of bacterial cells in milk by ultrasonic treatment was viewed hopefully as a means of sterilization without the use of heat. Substantial numbers of bacteria were destroyed but earlier results did not result in commercialization. A recent British patent (Brit. Pat. 1,179,827, 1970), however, described ultrasonic equipment for sterilizing milk. The Darison, an instrument based on the ultrasonic characteristics of milk constituents, has been claimed as an accurate and rapid method for determining fat and solids-not-fat in milk and in ice cream. The basis for the procedure is described by Fitzgerald et al. (1961). In a later publication, Moy and Winder (1971) describe adaptation of the Darison Solution Analyser to the continuous determination of fat and solids-not-fat in milk as it flows through the instrument. Similarly, Winder and associates (1970) have adapted the Solution Analyser to the determination of alcohol and extract (Brix) in wines. In general, the Solution Analyser can be adapted to the analysis of the following mixtures of two liquids: concentration of alcohol in liquids, concentration of solids in liquids, acid content of water, aqueous sugar concentration, suspensions of protein in water, concentration of oils suspended in water, and aqueous solutions of salts.

Extensive investigations have been conducted on the ultrasonic characteristics of animal tissues before slaughter. Results are based on different acoustic effects through fatty and muscular tissue as related to eventual yield and quality of hog, cattle, and lamb carcasses. When the Branson Model 12 Ultrasonic Animal Tissue Tester was used by Anderson and Wahlstrom (1969) to predict percentage of ham and loin, percentage of lean cuts, and kilograms of lean cuts, the greatest accuracy of prediction was achieved with the latter. Aulstad (1969) reported that evaluation of ultrasonic back-fat measures were highly correlated with carcass quality. McReynolds and Arthaud (1970) found significant correlation between ultrasonic measurements on the longissimus muscle of beef cattle and the muscle on slaughter. German experiments with farm animals using the "Vidoson" (Siemen's equipment) report similar results. Zayas et al. (1972) noted conditions of ultrasonic treatment of meat which brought about a tenderizing effect comparable to natural maturing.

Chkaidze and co-workers (1970) have noted the conditions by which ultrasonic treatment of fluid dough brought about more intensive fermentation. Other investigators observed improved gas retention in dough and bread systems on processes involving ultrasonic treatment. In a related situation, yeasts treated by a combination of ultrasound and temperature in a special pasteurizer achieved lethality of bacteria but permitted preservation of the yeast. Bread produced from the yeast had superior crust color and crumb aroma, while requiring less sugar in the dough process. Verkhovskii (1971) describes an impulse generator and magnetostrictive transducer which keeps the boiler in ultrasonic vibration, thereby preventing the deposition of scale. Volkov and associates (1970) give detailed information with diagrams on the UPT-14 ultrasonic sealer and its application to packaging processed cheese in low-density polyethylene tubes.

Adams and Lane (1970) hold a patent for cleaning eggs by passing them through an ultrasonically cavitating alkaline cleaning solution. It was observed by others, however, that ultrasonic treatment of eggs may have deleterious effects on the egg and may impair keeping quality. Others have observed that, in the case of fruits and vegetables treated with Bordeaux mixture, the Cu is much more completely removed by ultrasonic washing than by the usual washing procedures.

Khadzhiiski (1970) used ultrasonics in the wine industry to accelerate maturation. Red wines were also improved in flavor and color. Ultrasonic treatment was used to clarify wines and cider as well. Bentonite used for wine clarification must be activated. Application of ultrasonic energy shortened activation time and permitted reduction of bentonite addition. Experimental procedures with ultrasonic energy indicate that wine can be sterilized.

Ultrasonic mixers (Anon. 1970) have been developed for the preparation of stable emulsions of flavor concentrates or fruit juices. Such a device is the Rapisonic 8B using the jet-edge tone phenomenon to produce shock waves of 10 million pounds per square inch. The particle size of the emulsion in the case of a fruit juice product was reduced from 1–20 μm to 1–2 μm.

Ultrasonic devices have been used to liberate enzymes from mold and yeast. Heyse and Piendl (1971) have described such a device for yeast. Other workers report an increase in enzyme activity by 6–7 times in mold suspensions subjected to ultrasonic treatment. A related phenomenon is the liberation of the bitter substance from hops for use in the brewing industry.

A Canadian patent (Hass and Bauer 1970) describes an ultrasonic process for the impregnation of fibrous protein foods with binders, coloring agents, and flavors. By immersing hams and pieces of meat in an aqueous seasoning liquid, ultrasonic treatment brings about complete diffusion of the spice into the meat. Gas may be more readily impregnated into an aqueous medium by ultrasonic phenomena.

Ultrasonic treatment superimposed on corn and wheat being dried accelerates the rate of moisture loss. Ultrasonic treatment of barley being steeped for malt production (Segal and Groger 1971) had a favorable effect on germination and produced a considerable activation of amylolytic enzymes.

Winder and Swanson (1969) have reported that ultrasonic compression waves with 100 to 100,000 cycles per second and energy output of 0.5 watt hours per pound accelerate the ripening process in cheese. The process may be applied to curd in the vat or in the press, or immediately after pressing. It is claimed that day-old cheddar cheese treated in this way reached desirable body and flavor characteristics in 6 weeks instead of the usual 4–5 months. Recent work showed a more rapid proteolytic breakdown of protein as a result of ultrasonic treatment.

Haevecker (1970) describes the application of ultrasonics to the fruit industry including bactericidal, emulsifying, or dispersing effects; acceleration of cleaning or crystallization; and treatment of pulp to increase press yield. Duration and frequency of the sound is related to the results desired.

The selected applications of ultrasonic energy to food technology are illustrative of the usefulness of this phenomenon.

ARNOLD H. JOHNSON

References

ADAMS, L., and LANE. 1970. Ultrasonic egg cleaning. Can. Pat. 835,141.

ANDERSON, L. M., and WAHLSTROM, R. C. 1969. Ultrasonic prediction of swine carcass composition. J. Animal Sci. *28*, 563.

ANON. 1970. Reynolds foods adds punch to concentrate. Citrus Vegetable Mag. *21*, No. 3, 153.

AULSTAD, D. 1969. *In vivo* estimation of carcass composition of young boars. II. The use of ultrasonic measurements of backfat thickness. Acta Agr. Scand. *19*, 189.

CHKHAIDZE, R. E. *et al.* 1970. More intensive fermentations of liquid dough by means of ultrasonics. Khlebopekarnaya Konditerskaya Prom. *13*, No. 9, 7 (1969). Cited in Food Sci. Technol. Abstr. *2*, 4M291.

FITZGERALD, J. W., RINGO, G. R., and WINDER, W. C. 1961. An ultrasonic method for the measurement of solids-not-fat and milkfat in fluid milk. I. Acoustic properties. Univ. Wisconsin Preprint, June 13. Also J. Dairy Sci. *44*, 1165.

HAEVECKER, E. 1970. Patented applications of ultrasonics in the fruit processing industry. Lebensmittel Industrie *17*, No. 2, 63. (German)

HASS, P. D., and BAUER, W. G. 1970. Fiber impregnation process. Can. Pat, 850,599.

HEYSE, K., and PIENDL, A. 1971. Breakdown of brewers yeast by ultrasonics. Brauwissenschaft *24*, 231. (German)

KHADZHIISKI, D. 1970. Use of ultrasonics in wine production. Logarstvo Vinarstvo *18*, No. 5, 30. Cited in Food Sci. Technol. Abstr. *2*, 5H545.

McREYNOLDS, W. E., and ARTHAUD, V. H. 1970. Ultrasonic application for estimating fat thickness in beef cattle. J. Animal Sci. *30*, 503.

MOY, C. F., and WINDER, W. C. 1971. Development of an ultrasonic method for continuously monitoring the fat and solids-not-fat content of fluid milk. J. Dairy Sci. *54*, 757.

SEGAL, B., DAN, V., and GROGER, W. 1971. Effect of ultrasonics in the germinating capacity of barley. Brauwissenschaft *24*, 241. (German)

VERKHOVSKII, B. S. 1971. Molochnaya Prom. *31*, No. 2, 16 (1970). Cited in Food Sci. Technol. Abstr. *3*, 7P1024.

VOLKOV, S. S., ASTAKHOVA, R. N., and KIDESHOVA, M. F. 1970. Ultrasonic sealing of polyethylene tubes containing processed cheese. Molochnaya Prom. *30*, No. 8, 15 (1969). Cited in Food Sci. Technol. Abstr. *2*, 2P232.

WHITE, G. W. 1972. Physics in the food laboratory. Lab. Pract. *21*, No. 1, 20.

WINDER, W. C., RICE, D. J., and RICE, A. C. 1970. An ultrasonic method for the direct and simultaneous determination of alcohol and extract content of wines. Am. J. Enol. Vitacult. *21*, 1.

WINDER, W. C., and SWANSON, A. M. 1969. Method for ripening cheese. U.S. Pat. 2,882,164, Apr. 14.

ZAYAS, J. F. *et al.* 1972. Tr. Vses. Nauchni-Issled, Institut Myasnoi Prom. *22*, 43 (1969). Cited in Food Sci. Techno. Abstr. *4*, 4S374.

Cross-reference: *Emulsification, Mechanical Procedures.*

ULTRAVIOLET RADIATION

Ultraviolet (UV) radiation constitutes that part of the electromagnetic spectrum which extends from the extreme violet end of the visible spectrum to the boundary of the X-ray region. The wavelength is therefore between 4000 Å to 200 Å. An angstrom (Å) is 1/10,000,000 mm. Wavelengths are also expressed as nanometers (nm); that is, in billionths of a meter. It has been known for nearly 200 yr that such radiations were able to promote a special type of reaction. Many molecules are able to absorb radiation of specific frequencies, such selective absorption being a characteristic of the molecular structure. Absorption of energy from the radiation involves the transfer of discrete quantities of energy from the radiation to individual molecules, and if the energy content is sufficiently high, the effected molecule undergoes change. The energy increases with decreasing wavelength and in the violet and UV regions it is sufficient to excite photochemical action in substances having absorption spectra in these regions.

In food technology, UV radiation phenomena have many and variable applications. About 10% of the sun's energy is in the UV frequency but due to absorption by ozone in the upper atmosphere and to the effects of clouds, dust, fog, smoke, and season of the year, much lower UV energies exist at the earth's surface. The shortest measured wavelength at the earth's surface was found to be 286.3 nm at an elevation of 1600 m in the Alps. It was observed many years ago that sunlight had bactericidal action. This led to the development of light sources in the UV range. It is now possible to match any limited area of the solar spectrum, although no single type of lamp or arc is known which has the same energy distribution as the sun's spectrum over the entire range. Stiff (1969) has discussed the increasing use of UV lamps for disinfection. Using a variety of UV sources it has been possible to fix the wavelength having specific effects. Thus the wavelength having the most lethal effects has been found to be at about 2600 Å, the lethality falling off sharply to about 10% of the maximum at 2000 and 3000 Å.

Much investigation has been made of the bactericidal effect of UV radiation. Burton (1951) has reviewed the results with milk. While it is claimed that 99% of the bacteria in milk may be destroyed, no commercialization of the process has been made, due to the poor keeping quality of the treated milk, probably related to the type of surviving organisms. However, a recent German patent (1970) proposes successive treatments with UV and IR (infrared) radiation respectively, the milk being irradiated at 37°C for 3–10 sec with 253.7 nm UV and for 2–10 sec with IR of 1400–3000 nm wavelengths. During the process, the milk attains a temperature of about 85°C. An Australian patent (Aquitron Corp. 1969) describes transferring the milk or other liquid into a plant in which pipelines, containers, etc., be made of UV permeable material with processing being conducted continuously in rooms irradiated with UV light. The UV light is directed to the pipelines so that the desired bactericidal effect is obtained.

Ueberall (1969) discusses the present state of UV sterilization with special reference to drinking water. The operating details of a plant with radiation at 253.7 nm and capacity of 9 m^3 per hr is described. Among the many other bactericidal or sterilizing effects of UV radiation are the following: treatment of cider to improve keeping quality; treatment of maple sap so that it can be held safely awaiting further processing; treatment of brines in cheese making to control growth of microorganisms; use in sugar-refining plants to control microorganisms; use in Emmental cheese ripening rooms to prevent surface molding; use to control fungi and bacteria in cold store rooms, and in tanks and in laboratories, particularly with the fermentation industries.

UV radiation also finds extensive application in treating packaging material or containers, such as plastic film, sausage casings, cans, and milk bottles. Food packed in containers irradiated prior to filling show lower bacterial values and improved keeping quality.

In addition to the germicidal effects of UV lamps, such lamps may also produce ozone. Thus the hydrogen arc sterilamp radiates in the 2537 Å region as well as in the 1850 Å region (Knowles and Reuter 1940). The longer waves have strong germicidal effects and the shorter waves produce ozone from atmospheric oxygen. The sterilamp has found special use in meat tenderizing which process involves aging the meat at higher than the usual refrigerator temperatures. Ewell (1939) reported that a sterilamp supplying ozone to the atmosphere at levels of 0.001 ppm as well as UV irradiation inhibited mold and bacterial growth on meat surfaces, whereas ozone by itself at 1.0 ppm was required to attain this result. The high levels of ozone may also cause development of rancidity in the treated product.

As stated earlier, many molecules are able to absorb radiation of specific frequencies. This makes it possible to obtain absorption spectra which are characteristic of the molecule and which serve to identify the molecule for analytical purposes. It is first necessary to isolate the particular molecule so that it can be submitted to UV spectral analysis. Thus UV and IR spectra have been published for 76 pesticides (Gore *et al.* 1971). Tabulation of similar data exists for many types of chemical compounds. In a specific instance, pure all-*trans* vitamin A alcohol (Strohecker and Henning 1965) in isopropanol has an absorption maximum at 325 nm. The extinction at this wavelength is proportional to the vitamin A concentration so that the total amount of vitamin A can be calculated in International Units from the measured extinction (E_1), the concentration (c) (1 gm sample in 100 ml isopropanol solution), the cell thickness (d), and a factor (F). Further instances where UV spectra have been used in analysis are the following: antioxidants in oils; organic preservatives in foods; migration of plastics into foods; identifying source of citrus oils; chemical composition of rosaceae, solanaceae, and oleaceae oils; identifying organoleptic constituents in foods (Reymond 1971); establishing a ripeness index for berries (e.g., raspberries); and determining hydroxy cinnamic acid in vegetables, just to name a few instances.

Extensive use of UV spectral analysis has been made by measuring changes in spectra during storage. This phenomenon has been especially useful for fats and oils. Thus Sedlacek and Bohuslar (1970A) determined various properties of fats in relation to the first maximum extinction (E_1) according to the direct UV method. Sunflower, rapeseed, peanut, soybean, and corn oils; lard butter; beef tallow; and hardened edible fat were investigated in this study. An enhanced peroxide value was found when E_1 increased, the value depending on the unsaturated fatty acid content. Sedlacek and Bohuslar (1970B) also further studied the UV spectra of oxidized and polymerized fats. Other UV spectral studies have been made on various oils, including olive and coconut, to ascertain their status in regard to oxidation, how best to hold them in storage, and how to handle them in subsequent processing.

In order to protect packaged food from deterioration by light, especially UV light, various absorbers are used. An epoxy resin, designated as Color Guard (Anon. 1969), is described for application to glass containers which will protect the contents from UV deterioration. *Modern Plastics Encyclopedia* lists a considerable number of UV absorbers with recommendation for use on plastic film packaging material.

Cook (1963) has reviewed radiation for the dairy industry. In addition to some effects already noted, he reports on the increase in the vitamin D content of milk by UV irradiation at 2400–3000 Å. This is the result of conversion of 7-dehydrocholesterol to vitamin D_3. The vitamin D content can be increased by this process to 300 IU per liter of milk (8 times its natural level). This process of increasing the vitamin D content of milk has been largely replaced by direct addition of the vitamin to milk. Cook also noted patented procedures whereby the enzymic process in cheese ripening may be accelerated by exposure for 6 hr daily to irradiation with carbon arc lamps; cheddar and brick cheese could be ripened in 4 weeks.

A few somewhat nontypical effects of UV deserve mention.

(1) Dyed pork samples are tested for trichina contamination by UV microscopy. The parasites become more visible through their strong absorption of UV radiation of 250–300 nm wavelength.

(2) Wine or other drinks (Stoutz 1970) flowing through a pipe system is subjected to UV radiation predominantly of 253.7 nm at 230 μW per cm^2 and to IR radiation of 2000–3500 nm at 2–10 μW per cm^2 in order to prevent tartar sediment.

(3) Ethylene and 7 other hydrocarbon gases were substantially reduced by operation of a 4-watt UV lamp in a banana storage room. The ethylene content was reduced from 0.3 to <0.003 μg per liter in 2 hr.

(4) Mutants of *Saccharomyces cereviciae* could be prepared by irradiation of the yeast cells.

(5) The activity of trypsin could be reduced or inhibited by UV radiation.

(6) Wheat grains irradiated with UV in the green glume stage effected an increase in α-amylase activity, but the UV treatment has a harmful effect on the more mature wheat kernel and on the mature grain.

(7) Off-flavor in UV irradiated casein is related primarily to the formation of indole and skatole.

The above instances selected from many show the application of UV in food technology. Selected references for some of the cited applications have been given.

A. H. JOHNSON

References

ANON. 1969. Glass-maker claims breakthrough (Color Guard). Good Packaging *30*, No. 5, 8.

AQUITRON CORP. 1969. Sterilizing. Australian Pat. 292,563.

BURTON, H. 1951. Ultraviolet irradiation of milk. Dairy Sci. Abstr. *13*, 229-244.

COOK, D. J. 1963. Radiations for the dairy industry. Dairy Ind. *28*, 465,536.

EWELL, W. 1939. New developments in the use of ultraviolet light in food storage. Refrig. Eng. *37*, 27.

GORE, R. C., HANNAH, R. W., PATTACINI, S. C., and PARRO, T. J. 1971. Infrared and ultraviolet spectra of 76 pesticides. J. Assoc. Offic. Anal. Chemists *54*, 1040.

KNOWLES, D. D., and REUTER, E. 1940. Sterilamp. Trans. Electrochem. Soc. *78*, 12-page preprint.

REYMOND, D. 1971. Analytical evaluation of food quality. Food Technol. *25*, 1152.

SEDLACEK, B. A., and BOHUSLAR, A. J. 1970A. UV spectra of autolyzed fats. Fette, Seifen, Anstrichmittel *72*, No. 6, 488. (German)

SEDLACEK, B. A., and BOHUSLAR, A. J. 1970B. UV spectra of oxidized and polymerized fats. J. Nahrung *14*, 241. (German)

STIFF, F. R. 1969. UV lamps for disinfection. Process. Biochem. *4*, No. 11, 27.

STOUTZ, W. P. de. 1969. Process for preserving milk. West Ger. Pat. 1,300,813. (German)

STOUTZ, W. P. de. 1970. Process for treating alcoholic drinks, in particular wine. West Ger. Pat. 1,442,344. (German)

STROHECKER, R., and HENNING, H. M. 1965. Vitamin Assay Testing Methods. Verlag Chemie GMBH, Weinheim/Bergstr., Germany.

UEBERALL, P. 1969. Nonchemical sterilization of drinking and industrial waters by UV irradiation. Stärke *21*, 321. (German)

Cross-reference: *Sanitation.*

USDA GRADE STANDARDS FOR FOOD

U.S. Department of Agriculture grade standards for food, along with standards for other agricultural products, have been developed to identify the degrees of quality in the various products, and thereby aid in establishing their usability or value.

The first U.S. grade standards established by the U.S. Department of Agriculture (USDA) for a food product were for potatoes in 1917. Since that time, grade standards have been established for many other food products. The dates in parenthesis indicate the date of first establishment of official U.S. grade standards for the commodity or the commodity group:

Fresh fruits, vegetables, and nuts (1917); butter, cheddar cheese, nonfat dry milk, and certain other dairy products (1919); rice, dry beans, peas, and related products (1926); eggs (1925); poultry (1930); beef, veal and calf, and lamb and mutton carcasses (1926); canned, frozen, and dried fruits and vegetables, and other related products such as preserves (1928).

U.S. grade standards are also available for various grains, but not for the food products, such as flour or cereals, into which grain is processed.

A complete list of the food products for which U.S. grade standards are in effect is in Agriculture Handbook *341*, USDA Standards for Food and Farm Products.

USDA provides grading and inspection services—official certification of the grade of products—for each commodity group. Grading is voluntary, except in certain instances, and is provided on a fee-for-service basis.

Early Federal work on grade standardization of food products was done under Congressional authorization for studies on the marketing of farm products (1913) and the U.S. Grain Standards Act (1916). Standardization and voluntary grading and inspection services are now conducted by the authority of the Agricultural Marketing Act of 1946 and the U.S. Grain Standards Act of 1968.

Purpose of the Standards

Although grade standards for each commodity group were developed independently of each other, the original purpose of the standards was basically the same: To aid in the marketing of farm products by providing a common language for wholesale trading and a means of measuring value or a basis for establishing prices. State and local standards and trade terms had existed for some products for some time before establishment of official U.S. grade standards. The need for standards which would be applicable nationwide, brought on especially by the growth of long-distance trading, gave impetus to development of the U.S. grade standards.

The express purpose of the meat carcass standards was to reflect back to producers, primarily through the prices obtained for different grades, the qualities most desired by consumers.

Other early purposes for developing grade standards were to help establish loan values for products in storage and to assure that products purchased by the Government (for example, by the military services) were of acceptable quality.

These original purposes are still served by the grade standards, but the standards have found many other uses. Private procurement agencies—restaurants, shipping lines, and other feeding establishments—as well as Federal and State government agencies, use the grade standards as specifications in purchasing foods. Contracts between packers or processors and producers are often based on the grade of the product as delivered to the processing plant, and processors use the standards as aids in quality control. Trading of food products on the futures market is also often based on official grades.

In recent years, consumers have come to depend on the USDA grades in buying foods.

Criteria for Grade Standards

The U.S. grade standards provide a means of classifying the entire range of quality of a product. Because some products are naturally more variable than others, it is necessary to have more grades for some products than for others. Quality in general refers to the usefulness, desirability, and value of a product—its marketability—but the precise definition of quality depends on the commodity. The standards define the quality requirements of each grade of a product. Criteria for grade standards for the various commodity groups are as follows.

Beef, Veal and Calf, Lamb and Mutton.—Quality grades predict the "eating quality" of meat. Eating quality is indicated by the color, firmness, texture, and marbling of the meat in relation to its maturity or age. The range of quality in beef requires 8 grades; in veal and calf, 6; in lamb and mutton, 5. The three top grades for all are U.S. Prime, U.S. Choice, and U.S. Good.

In addition to quality grades for beef and lamb, there are also U.S. yield grades, which are used to indicate the differences in yield of trimmed retail cuts from carcasses. The yield grades are described in Marketing Bulletin *45*, USDA Yield Grades for Beef, and Marketing Bulletin *52*, USDA Yield Grades for Lamb.

Poultry.—Standards measure "table quality" in terms of the proportion of edible meat in relation to bone, the "finish" of the bird, and freedom from defects such as cuts, tears, and bruises. Tenderness is not a grade factor, as it relates chiefly to the age difference between young and older birds and is indicated separately in labeling (for example, "fryers"). Turkey, chicken, duck, goose, guinea, and squab may be graded U.S. Grade A, B, or C.

Eggs.—Standards provide for quality grades and for weight classes (size). Standards for quality relate to the appearance of the egg and its suitability to various methods of cooking. They define such factors as thickness of the albumen, and condition of the yolk and shell. Standards for size are based on the weight of a dozen eggs—a 3-oz weight difference is provided between sizes. Eggs are graded U.S. Grade AA or Fresh Fancy, Grade A, and Grade B. Sizes are U.S. Jumbo, Extra Large, Large, Medium, Small, and Peewee. One dozen Large size weighs at least 24 oz.

Butter and Cheddar Cheese.—Standards define levels of eating quality, based on flavor, texture, and body. Age or degree of cure is also a factor in cheddar cheese. U.S. grade names are U.S. Grades AA, A, and B.

Instant Nonfat Dry Milk.—Quality factors are flavor, color uniformity, bacterial count, dispersibility, solubility index, and moisture and milkfat content. The U.S. grade name is U.S. Extra.

Fresh and Processed Fruits and Vegetables.—Standards for both fresh and processed fruit and vegetables vary with the individual product. They usually define such factors as color, shape, size, maturity, and number and degree of defects. For some products, especially those that are processed, flavor and tenderness are also rated. The typical range of grades for fresh fruits and vegetables include U.S. Fancy, U.S. No. 1, and U.S. No. 2. U.S. No. 1 is the chief trading grade for most products. Grade names for processed fruits, vegetables, and related products are U.S. Grades A, B, and C.

Rice, Dry Beans, and Peas.—Standards measure uniformity of shape, size, color, moisture content, damage, and foreign material. Moisture measurement is significant because it determines the amount of dry matter of the commodity, and more important, its storability. Grades range from U.S. No. 1 to U.S. No. 6 for rice; U.S. No. 1 to

Courtesy of U.S. Dept. of Agriculture

FIG. U-8. A USDA GRADER MARKS RETAIL BEEF CARCASS WITH GRADE

Starting high on the top of a USDA Choice grade beef carcass, a long row of purple grade marks will distinguish this carcass from its lower quality counterparts. The mark is placed on the carcass in such a way that it will appear on most cuts of beef made from the carcass—unless the butcher cuts off the grade mark with some of the fat trim. The purple color is a harmless food dye and need not be trimmed before cooking.

U.S. No. 3 for dry peas; and U.S. No. 1 to U.S. No. 3 and U.S. Substandard for dry beans, except that the highest grade for dry lima beans is U.S. Extra No. 1. In addition, the lowest grade for each commodity is U.S. Sample Grade.

Consumer Grades

Many of the U.S. grade standards are used to identify grades on consumer packages. Some standards have been developed specifically as consumer standards.

USDA grades for butter were first used on consumer packages in 1924.

The USDA grade specifications have been used on retail cuts of beef, veal, and lamb since the

Courtesy of U.S. Dept. of Agriculture

FIG. U-9. GRADING FRESH TABLE GRAPES IN THE VINEYARD

Fresh table grapes are sometimes graded in the vineyard just after they've been picked. The Federal-State inspector measures the sugar content of grapes with a refractometer. Sugar content indicates maturity, one factor in determining the U.S. grade.

standards for these meats were established. The grade mark is applied to the carcass or to wholesale cuts in a long, ribbon-like imprint, so the grade stamp carries through on most cuts.

Consumer grades were developed for shell eggs, turkeys, and chickens 25 yr ago and have found extensive use in the last 10 yr. These consumer grades are sometimes used by the wholesale trade, rather than the wholesale grades.

Grades for canned and frozen fruits and vegetables were first developed during the 1930's and most of them are designed to classify the quality of the product after it has been packed into consumer-size packages for sale at retail.

Grade labeling of fresh fruits and vegetables dates from about 1930, when shippers began to pack these products in packages for consumers. Special consumer grades were developed for some products, but they are seldom used. The wholesale grade standards for most fresh fruits and vegetables have been revised in recent years to provide for grading products in consumer packages.

U.S. grades for rice, dry beans, peas and related products are seldom used on consumer packages.

Grade labeling is not required by law, even though the product has been officially graded or inspected. For most commodities, if an official U.S. grade name or grade shield is used, however, the product must have been officially graded or inspected. The only exception is for fresh fruits, vegetables, and a few other products, where the practice of grade labeling without official inspection has existed through the years.

Inspection and Grading Services

Concomitant with development of U.S. grade standards, and in some instances preceding them, USDA began to establish an official system of inspection and grading. Originally limited in scope, it has become nationwide and now is available in practically all major production areas and major destination markets in all States.

From the outset, USDA has encouraged cooperative activity with State and market agencies in the inspection and grading services. Commodities may therefore be officially graded by Federal graders or by State personnel licensed and supervised by Federal graders.

Various types of inspection or grading services are available; for example, in-plant or continuous inspection during processing; lot inspection; sample inspection; and inspection of raw products for processing. (See: Marketing Bull. *48*, Dairy Inspection and Grading Services; *PA-675*, Food Acceptance Service; *AMS-520*, Official Grade Standards and Inspection for Fresh Fruits and Vegetables; *PA-803*, Processed Fruit and Vegetable Inspection At Your Service; Marketing Bull. *47*, USDA's Acceptance Service for Meat and Meat Products; Marketing Bull. *46*, USDA's Acceptance Service for Poultry and Eggs; *AMS-366*, Dairy Products Inspection Service Aid for Quality Buyers.

Development of Grade Standards

Three basic principles are followed in developing grade standards. First of all, there must be a need for the standards. Second, because use of the standards and grading is voluntary, there must be interest and support from the industry. And third, the standards must be practical to use.

Requests for standards may come from trade or consumer groups, State Departments of Agriculture, or others. USDA standardization specialists, who develop the standards, may initiate standards to more accurately reflect the type of product being produced. New standards are developed as new products come on the market or increase in consumer use. Recent examples are the grade standards for boneless poultry breasts and thighs and canned leafy greens.

The first step in developing standards is study of the product to determine the quality factors involved and the range of quality produced. Standardization specialists investigate cultural or production practices in major producing areas; varieties or types; harvesting, slaughtering, packing, and processing techniques; and consumer buying practices. They may call upon statisticians for aid in drawing up plans for taking samples of the product in various parts of the country, criteria for evaluating quality, and a mathematical means of evaluating the information collected.

They interview producers, packers, processors, shippers, receivers, consumers, scientists and marketing specialists at experiment stations and universities, and others. Economic studies may be made to determine the attributes that are important to sellers and buyers, including the final consumers. Where possible, laboratory studies are made to find ways of measuring the physical differences in quality.

Extensive data are collected on all quality factors and on defects that occur in the product. For most commodities (except meat carcasses, which are graded individually), an allowance must be made within each grade for a certain percentage of individual units within a lot that do not meet the standards. This is done because of practical limitations in packing and grading. The speed necessary in handling perishable products makes it almost impossible to remove all defective units. The "tolerance" (number of defective units or types of defects allowed) is more restrictive, of course, in the higher grades than in the lower grades.

Studies are made in processing or packing plants, or wherever the product may be graded, to determine if the standards are practical to use. Statistical methods are used to help ensure the validity of the testing procedures. For example, the capability of processing equipment to size a product within certain limits must be determined. Standards must be adjusted to processing methods —what is capable of being produced—within the limits of what the public is willing to pay for a product.

Standardization specialists then draw up proposed standards. For products for which FDA minimum standards of quality have been established, USDA adopts, as the minimum level for the lowest U.S. grade, specifications that are at least as high as these mandatory requirements. In establishing U.S. grade standards, it is customary to have one or more levels of quality above the lowest grade.

The proposed standards are published in the Federal Register as a Notice of Proposed Rule Making, and a specified time period is set to allow interested persons to study and comment on the proposal.

A press release is issued at the same time to notify industry members, consumer groups, trade organizations, State Departments of Agriculture, and anyone concerned. Copies of the proposed standards are sent to those who request them.

All comments are taken into account in considering whether the standards should be issued as proposed, with amendments, or withdrawn.

If it is decided to promulgate the standards, they are issued in final form in the Federal Register, with a specified date on which they are effective. A press release is again issued.

A revision of grade standards follows the same process. Revisions are often based on changes in marketing practices or improvements in production or processing methods that bring about improvements in the quality of a product. With the recent increase in use of pink- and red-fleshed varieties of grapefruit to make frozen concentrated grapefruit juice, for example, the grade standards for this product were revised to provide for grading of pink juice. A revision of the standards for canned cherries was made after a 5-yr study by USDA standardization specialists showed the capability of processing equipment to remove pits without damaging the cherries could be improved, without excessive cost. (See the following USDA *Agricultural Marketing* issues: A Statistician Looks at Standardization, Jan. 1970; A Statistician Looks at Grading by Attributes, Febr. 1970; and A Statistician Looks at Sampling Plans, June 1970).

Plant Sanitation

Official grading of meat, poultry and egg products is done only in plants under Federal or federally-approved inspection for wholesomeness. Wholesomeness of other food products is regulated by FDA. USDA, however, has its own sanitation requirements for certain types of plants and grading of certain products. Official grading of a manufactured dairy product is done only after a plant has been surveyed by USDA dairy inspectors and the quality of raw material, sanitation, condition of the plant and equipment, and processing procedures have been approved. In shell egg packing plants, the official inspector is responsible for checking the sanitation of the plant, seeing that the eggs are washed properly and held under proper conditions, and checking all packing equipment and procedures. In fruit and vegetable processing plants using the USDA continuous inspection program, the USDA inspector checks the plant sanitation, the raw material used, and sees that the product is properly handled through all processing.

Applying the Standards

The standards must be prepared in terms that can be easily understood and uniformly applied, because much grading is a subjective process. Standardization specialists prescribe specific physical and chemical tests for certain products and prepare handbooks for the official graders and inspectors to use in interpreting the standards. They also prepare models, color slides and photographs, and such other materials as will aid in uniform interpretation of the grade standards. Training of graders and inspectors is also an important part of maintaining uniformity.

The method of officially inspecting or grading a product depends on the nature of the product, the degree of quality variation in the product, how it is processed or packed, and the techniques available to objectively measure quality factors. For poultry, eggs, and fresh and processed fruits and vegetables, the official graders or inspectors certify the grade of a quantity or lot of the product by inspecting or "check-grading" a representative sample of the lot, usually after it has been sorted into grades by plant workers. Meat carcasses are individually graded by the USDA grader.

Sampling plans are developed to assure the sample adequately represents the lot being graded, whether inspection is done during processing of the product, at a terminal market or warehouse, or elsewhere. USDA statisticians, working with standardization specialists, have developed sampling plans based on acceptable quality level (AQL) and sampling risk or error.

AQL refers to the maximum number of defects or defective units acceptable per hundred units. AQL's can be written into the standards themselves —as the "tolerance" for defective units or defects allowed within a grade. When AQL's are used, the grading technique involves counting the number and type of defects or defective units in a sample, rather than computing percentages.

Techniques of Inspecting and Grading

Meat.—Meat carcasses are graded individually and the official grade stamp is applied to each carcass. For quality determination, graders examine carcasses visually, and no objective measurements are used. Pictures showing degrees of marbling of beef are provided as aids in determining quality. Since 1965, USDA has required that carcasses be partially separated into hindquarters and forequarters so that the grader can see a section of the rib eye muscle, an important factor in determining grade.

For determining yield grades of beef carcasses, graders may use a clear plastic grid to measure the area of the rib-eye and a ruler to measure thickness of fat. In normal grading practice, these factors are estimated. A mathematical aid, the Yield Grade Finder, which operates somewhat like a slide rule, is used to put together the yield factors to obtain the yield grade. A similar device is available for determining yield grades of lamb.

Poultry.—Chickens, turkeys, other poultry, and poultry parts are sorted into grades individually by plant workers and then check-graded by official graders. Official grading is based on AQL's and specified sample sizes. Grading is visual.

Raw, ready-to-cook poultry rolls, roasts, bars, or logs have been graded since 1965. The grader examines the whole birds from which the roasts are made and checks during processing for removal of blood vessels, bone chips, and the like.

Eggs.—Eggs are graded by plant workers, and the official grader spot checks the eggs as they are being packed and after packing. Mass scanning techniques now available have eliminated the older method of hand-candling eggs to check for interior quality—depth of air cell, condition of albumen and yolk, and presence of blood spots. In mass scanning, large numbers of eggs are moved across a lighted area at the same time, and plant workers remove undergrades. The eggs are automatically sized. Color charts, showing candled appearance of eggs, broken-out appearance of eggs, and types of shell condition and cleanliness, are available for graders as visual aids.

Butter and Cheddar Cheese.—Both products are graded after manufacture by official graders. The grader takes samples of each batch or segment of a continuous production run and examines them organoleptically. Flavor, uniformity of color, body, and texture are considered. Color guides are available to check the color of butter.

Instant Nonfat Dry Milk.—The official grader takes a sample of the product after manufacture and certifies its quality. He makes organoleptic checks for lumps, color uniformity, and specks in the powdered milk, and flavor and odor of the reconstituted milk. A number of laboratory tests are performed: analyses for dispersibility, by the modified Moates-Dabbah method; determination of moisture content by the toluol or vacuum oven method; determination of fat, solubility index, titratable acidity, and scorched particles; bacterial estimates by standard plate count and direct microscopic clump count.

Fresh Fruits and Vegetables.—Fresh fruits and vegetables are sorted into grades by plant workers during packing. Federal or Federal-State inspectors certify the quality of products on a sample basis. Most inspection is visual. Internal as well as external quality of many products is examined. Models, color guides, and color photographs are available for inspectors to check samples for shape, degree of coloring, and degree of defects or damage. AQL's are part of the standards for some citrus products.

As increasing amounts of fruits and vegetables move into processing channels, new methods are developed to inspect the raw product before processing. Mechanically harvested grapes, for example, are inspected on the vine before harvest, to determine sugar content and grade. Special sampling plans were developed for vineyard inspection. Two methods of automatically sampling tomatoes harvested into bulk bins have been developed.

Refractometers are used to determine sugar content of both grapes and citrus products before processing. Potatoes to be used for french frying and chipping are tested for amount of bruising, fry color, or chipping quality. Specific gravity tests are made of potatoes for processing to determine yield.

Mechanical equipment to aid in sampling and inspecting peanuts is highly developed; it includes pneumatic samplers, an automatic sheller, and a machine that splits kernels. Peanuts are also examined microscopically for aflatoxin before they are allowed to move into food channels.

Processed Fruits and Vegetables.—These products are sorted into grades by plant workers during processing, and checked by USDA inspectors on a sample basis. Grading is generally based on a scoring system of four quality factors: color, uniformity of size, absence of defects, and character (tenderness, texture, and maturity).

Chemical and physical tests are performed wherever possible. Subjective measurements are also used. Acid and sweetness measurements are made of citrus juices and other fruit products; specific gravity tests are made to determine maturity of peas. Gas chromatography is used to test for aflatoxin in peanut butter.

Special equipment has been developed to measure flowing quality of such products as catsup and consistency of applesauce. Sizing devices, color guides, and models are available to inspectors.

AQL's are part of the standards for some products.

Rice, Dry Beans, and Peas.—The official inspector grades rice on the basis of a sample he has taken. The amount of broken kernels is determined by sieving. Type samples showing the degree of milling of rice and type samples for certain defects, such as heat damage, are provided for the inspector to aid him in grading.

Dry beans, peas, and like products are also inspected on the basis of a sample taken by the inspector. Inspection is mainly visual, except that electric moisture meters are used to determine moisture content of dry beans and peas, as well as rice.

Quality Control

The grade standards are often used by packers and processors as a means of quality control. When official grading and inspection is done in a plant, the inspector aids in quality control because he can advise plant management, during processing and packing, when the product is not meeting the standards. Quality control charts are a part of some of the grade standards in which AQL's are used. With these standards, the inspector keeps a running chart of quality during processing, and management can begin to regrade or take corrective measures immediately when the product falls below the quality they wish to meet.

Quality control in meat production goes back to production of the live animal. Standards for feeder and slaughter animals are designed to be correlated with the carcass standards. Thus, a Choice feeder steer has the potential to develop into a Choice grade slaughter steer, which, in turn, can be expected to produce a U.S. Choice beef carcass.

USDA Standards of Identity and Minimum Content

Over the past 60 yr, USDA has established minimum content requirements for Federally-inspected meat and poultry products. To be labeled with a particular name—such as "All Beef Franks" or "Chicken Soup"—a Federally-inspected meat or poultry product must meet these specific requirements: "All Beef Franks," for instance may contain only the meat of beef animals, and no more than 30% fat, 10% added water, and 2% corn syrup. "Chicken Soup" must contain at least 2% chicken meat on a ready-to-serve basis. In "Breaded Steaks" or "Breaded Chops," the breading cannot exceed 30% of the finished product weight. A "Turkey Pot Pie" must contain at least 14% turkey meat.

USDA has also established complete Standards of Identity for three products: chopped ham, corned beef hash, and oleomargarine. These standards are explicit about each ingredient that must go into a product bearing one of these three names, and about additional ingredients, such as artificial coloring and vitamin additives, that may be included under Federal law. The goal of both product composition standards and standards of identity is to help assure that product names are properly used to denote what's inside cans and packages of Federally-inspected meat and poultry.

GEORGE R. GRANGE

U.S. PHARMACOPEIA

The *Pharmacopeia of the United States*, 18th Revision, 1970, is chiefly useful to physicians and pharmacists, somewhat less so to their colleagues in related professions which would include food science.

The preface to the first volume (1820) reads: "It is the object of the Pharmacopeia to select among substances which possess medicinal power, those the utility of which is most fully established and best understood; and to form from them preparations and compositions, in which their powers may be exerted to the greatest advantage." "The value of a Pharmacopeia," the preface goes on to state, "depends upon the fidelity with which it conforms to the best of the medical knowledge of the day." From that remote day to the present the *Pharmacopeia* has had the approval of the medical community and all scientists specialized in the fields which it serves. A century and a half after the first edition was issued, it can be reiterated that the value of the *Pharmacopeia* lies in its faithful reflection of the best medical and pharmacological knowledge of the day. It is an authoritative book, recognized as a standard reference the world over.

The food technologist will find useful information on humectants, reactants, flavor aids, the vitamins, and many other topics. Detailed accounts of biological tests and assays are provided.

Revision and publication of the *Pharmacopeia* are accomplished privately by a nonprofit organization. The cost of publication is defrayed by sales of the volume and fees derived from USP reference standards.

MARTIN S. PETERSON

V

VANILLA EXTRACT AND SYNTHETIC VANILLIN

Vanilla Extract

In 1492, Columbus tried to find a direct route to the fabulous silks and spices of the Orient. Instead, he found a "new" world in which, for untold centuries, men had built great cities and pyramids. More important, however, were the new-world foods which were to revolutionize the diets of people everywhere.

Central and South American Indians, in addition to being fine architects and astronomers, were advanced agriculturists in many respects. They had developed corn as a hybrid from wild grasses by methods which would do credit to a modern Burbank. They gave us the white and sweet potatoes, yams, lima beans, tomato, pumpkin, papaya, avocado, kidney bean, peanut, and rubber to mention only a portion of their staples. Tobacco first came from these people and likewise quinine, cascara segrada, balsam of Peru, and henequen. The finest strains of long-staple cotton originated in the Western Hemisphere.

The food industry is also indebted to these people for chocolate, pineapple, and vanilla. Native to their forests and growing in no other part of the world at that time, the Indians found a fruit pod which became deliciously aromatic when ripened, fermented, and cured in their bountiful sunshine. This was the vanilla bean—fruit of a true tropical orchid vine.

It is likely that vanilla was used for many centuries in that area by the Aztecs and their predecessors, whose origins are presently unknown and whose records were almost entirely destroyed by the Spanish invaders, who found the Aztecs using these slick, black vanilla pods in many of their foods, but particularly to enrich their favorite, chocolate. The Mayas of Yucatan, called the vanilla plant "zizbic." The Totonacs named the pods "tlilxochitl"—a compound word derived from "tlil" meaning black, and from "xochitl" meaning flower. Vanilla constituted one of the tributes paid to the Aztec overlords by certain of their subject tribes including the Totonacs of El Tajin, the urban center near present-day Papantla, State of Vera Cruz. The Spaniards had great difficulty with the Aztec words. Some were easily adapted—chocolatl, for instance, becoming chocolate—but tlilxochitl was much too difficult and had to become something different. It came to be called "Vaynilla" meaning little scissor sheath, due no doubt to the appearance of the fruits when they had partially opened after ripening upon the vine, but it was not until 1658 that there was a written reference in a Spanish publication to this commonly-used term.

The exact year in which the vanilla fruits may have been taken to Europe is not known. It may be assumed that there was little opportunity for this prior to 1519, when Cortez dispatched Emperor Montezuma's opulent gifts of golden handicrafts, textiles, and other products back to the astounded court of Madrid. Soon after the conquest, vanilla pods became an article of commerce and their use spread to many parts of Europe.

The exact date of the first successful attempt to transplant the vine itself to European gardens is also shrouded in doubt. Cuttings of the cultivated variety were forwarded from Campeche by Robert Millar to Philip Miller, of England, who successfully germinated them some time between 1750 and 1775. From England, it is thought that cuttings were taken to the Netherlands and to the Royal Botanical Gardens in France. From Antwerp, in 1819, vanilla was introduced into Java and in 1822, cuttings from France arrived in Réunion. The modern vanilla industry dates from that time. The plant was then taken to Tahiti in 1848, to the Seychelles in 1866, to Nossi-Bé (off the N.W. coast of Madagascar) in 1870, to the Comores in 1873, to Mauritius in 1880 and to Madagascar (now the Malagasy Republic) in 1891. Other plantings have been made in East Africa, Malaya, and Ceylon.

In the Western Hemisphere, vanilla is found in virtually all tropical countries, the most important producers being Mexico, Guadeloupe, and Dominica. The plant was introduced into Puerto Rico in 1909 by the United States Department of Agriculture.

There are 110 known varieties of the vanilla orchid, but only 1 that produced fruits which were commercially acceptable for fine flavoring. This variety was known until recently as *Vanilla planifolia*, but in accordance with international conventions in this field of science, the name was recently changed to *Vanilla fragrans* when it was found that the *fragrans* designation had been used in 1807, a year prior to the use of the *V. planifolia* name. There may be some confusion because of this change but the plant is one and the same.

The vanilla plant is a vine which attaches itself to a support by means of tendrils. Terrestrial roots obtain the vital nourishment from the soil in which the plant grows. Secondary roots trail down the support from the vine's joints, or nodes, and assist in maintaining the health of the plant. Propagation is achieved by means of cuttings taken from healthy vines which have never borne fruit. A seed piece contains from 8 to 12 nodes, 2 of which are attached to the support tree by means of a bit of banana leaf with the other nodes trailing off from the base of the support and being covered with decaying vegetable matter.

Upon germination, the vine grows upward in a characteristic zig-zag pattern and, if not trained around the lower branches of the support, it would grow to the very top of the tree. In order to make the flowers and fruits grow within reach of the field workers, the support trees are pruned to form a living trellis and the growing vine is trained from branch to branch in loops that may readily be reached.

In Mexico, the original home of the plant, certain birds and insects performed the necessary pollination but even this was haphazard and did not result in satisfactory commercial quantities of vanilla fruits. In 1780, more than 200 yr after an export demand had been created for this subtle flavoring, Abbé Raynal reports that Mexico exported only 2½ tons of cured vanilla beans at a price equivalent to $17 per lb. The greatest problem in the various new locations to which vanilla was transplanted was to find some means for bringing about a great production through a satisfactory pollination.

The first artificial pollination was accomplished in Liege, Belgium in 1836, and the experiment was repeated successfully again in Paris in 1838 but the methods used were not satisfactory for use in the field. It remained for a 12-yr-old black slave, named Edmond Albium, in 1841 to develop a simplified procedure through his own practical observations on the plantation Sainte-Suzanne in

FIG. V-1. THE MADAGASCAR VANILLA FLOWER

Réunion. This ingenious transfer of the pollen within the same blossom revolutionized vanilla production and is the method still used wherever vanilla is grown.

Réunion's first exports were in the grand total of 110 lb in 1848. Fifty years later, that source exported 200 tons, so that we see how a humble young man proved to be the real father of the vanilla industry.

The blossoms are generally not pollinated until the plant gathers strength and reaches its second or third year. In early spring, a flower spike appears and a raceme of flowers develops with as many as 24 blossoms, which open 1 by 1 over a period of almost 8 weeks. The vital organs of the flower resemble the English letter "F" with the pollen being carried on the lower side of the topmost member and having to reach the lower side of the inferior member in order to achieve a successful result.

The stem, by which the blossom is attached to the raceme, is the ovary of the flower. If the pollination is successful, the blossom withers and remains while the stem enlarges and becomes a full sized fruit within 6 weeks; another 7–8 months are required for complete maturation. If the pollination is unsuccessful, the blossom falls away

FIG. V-2. VANILLA BEANS CURING IN THE SUN IN MADAGASCAR

FIG. V-3. DEPENDING UPON STAGE OF FERMENTATION DEVELOPMENT, FULL SUN CURING IS SOMETIMES ALTERED BY CURING UNDER COVER OF BLANKETS

and the stem also drops a little later during the summer.

When mature, the fruits show a yellowish color at the blossom end and this is the signal for their harvesting.   The mature pods resemble small bananas or large string beans. They have a somewhat triangular cross section with a central canal running from the blossom end to the stem end and this canal is lined with thousands of tiny black seeds. If the mature fruits are allowed to remain upon the vine, the fruits begin to split open in order to perform the natural function of broadcasting the seeds for the propagation of the species. At this stage, fermentation begins and the pods begin to turn black.

The mature pods have no flavor and no aroma. These must be developed by a process of artificial curing. The fruits are collected and sorted as to size and condition. They run from 4 in. in length up to 9–12 in., depending upon the number of fruits allowed to develop upon the plant. After sorting, the fruits are ready for the curing procedures. In Mexico, the ancient procedure of sunning provides the heat necessary to stimulate the fermentation; but in Madagascar, the fruits are dipped into hot water in order to stimulate the enzymatic reactions which eventually develop the characteristic vanilla aromas.

The fruits are placed in insulated boxes as often as required during the initial stages in order to accelerate the fermentation and this close confinement at night is alternated with exposure to the full sun during the day, sometimes under cover of blankets and sometimes without, depending upon the stage of development as judged by the expert master curer. The original yellow and green color of the fruit rapidly turns to light brown, then dark brown, and finally to a deep black brown. The juices of the fruit resinify within the first few

days of this procedure. The fats exude from the seeds and are taken up by the resins, helping to provide the basis for the future compounds which are peculiar to vanilla and not found in other sources in nature. Vanillin also develops at a very early stage and eventually becomes the backbone of the vanilla aroma and flavor, modified by many other organic compounds which contribute the typical fruity nature to a fine vanilla flavoring.

When the sweating and sunning period has come to an end, which generally encompasses a period of from 9–12 weeks, the cured beans are then placed in racks in a well-ventilated room and allowed to mature further. As with other fermented products, newly cured vanilla beans lack the subtlety and sweetness of aroma which can only result from further oxidation and aging. A further period of storing in conditioning boxes permits the curer to have a uniform moisture content within his various lots and the fully-cured fruits are then ready for packaging for shipment to the consuming markets.

From the moment of harvesting to the time of shipping, a minimum period of 6–7 months is required in order to have a fine product. One of the problems of this industry is this time factor. There is an investment in labor for 3 yr prior to the possibility of a first harvest and then almost another year before the cured product reaches the market. This time lag makes the production and curing of vanilla a financial gamble because of interest expenses and possible vanilla price fluctuations. Also, because production is, of necessity, confined to somewhat primitive areas where virgin forest lands are plentiful there seems to be an almost complete lack of sensitivity to the needs of the consuming markets.

There have been attempts to produce vanilla

FIG. V-4. PACKAGES OF FULLY-CURED VANILLA BEANS READY FOR MARKETING

beans upon a modern basis, with increased yields per acre. Unfortunately, the plant is a gross feeder and is not at home under neat plantation conditions and becomes subject to the invasion of a fungus which weakens the plants and shortens their producing life. This disease attacks the terrestrial roots, without which the plant soon dies. A concentrated research project in Puerto Rico tried to find the solution for the ravages of this disease but was abandoned after almost 20 yr when the effort met with little success. The Federal Experiment Station there and the Agricultural Research Station near Antalaha, Malagasy Republic are both working upon the development of hybrids which may prove to be disease-resistant and whose fruits may have the subtle qualities of the cultivated *Vanilla fragrans*. These experiments show some sign of promise but since each hybrid cycle takes almost 8 yr before its new fruits may be flavor tested, this approach may not have commercially interesting results for many years to come.

As with any other fruits, vanilla beans from each producing area have their own peculiar characteristics, due to the differences in climate and soil and to the curing techniques. The original Mexican source produces a product that has a somewhat greater depth than vanillas from other areas. The beans from the Indian Ocean areas are generally richer in top aromatics and somewhat lacking in the deeper notes. West Indian beans lie somewhere in between the two others. The beans from Tahiti are, in most part, the fruits of a variety of vanilla known as *Vanilla Tahitensis* and entirely different in aromatic character from those of *Vanilla fragrans*. The Tahiti product has the sweetness which comes from the heliotropine-like compounds developed in its cure and which are not found in the fruits from the Mexican and other areas.

Until recently, very little was known about the

constitutents which give vanilla its unique aroma and flavor. Quantitatively, vanillin is present in greater quantities than any other aromatic material, but vanillin alone does not impart a complete vanilla flavor in the finished food product. The final aroma results from a combination of aldehydes, esters, organic acids, etc. Most of these compounds are present only in parts per million and lesser quantities; all of them modify each other and are modified, in turn, by the fats and resins with which the cured fruits become saturated.

In 1963, the federal government published Standards of Identity for vanilla products. These standards specify the quantity of vanilla constituent that must be present in a vanilla extract, flavor, or sugar. Permissible solvents and optional ingredients are also specified. A vanilla extract must contain all the sapid and odorous principles extractable from one unit of vanilla constituent per gallon of extract or 8 lb of sugar. A unit of vanilla constituent is defined as 13.35 oz of vanilla beans of not more than 25% moisture content (or 10 oz of vanilla bean solids). If the moisture exceeds 25%, correspondingly more vanilla beans must be used. A higher strength vanilla product must be made from a corresponding quantity of vanilla constituent. Thus, for example, a 3-fold vanilla extract would be made from 3 units of vanilla constituent. The Standards of Identity also provide for vanilla-vanillin products. In this category, it is permissable to add 1 oz of vanillin for each unit of vanilla constituent. Thus a 4-fold vanilla-vanillin extract would be a 2-fold vanilla extract with 2 oz of added vanillin per gallon. A vanilla extract must contain not less than 35% alcohol. Most commercial extracts contain from 35–45% alcohol. A vanilla flavor contains less than 35% alcohol and may, in fact, be nonalcoholic. Of course, there are no standards of identity for imitation vanilla flavors.

With the promulgation of vanilla standards, it became essential to develop analytical methods which would assure that vanilla products meet the requirements of the standards. The research committee of the Flavor and Extract Manufacturers Association with the help and cooperation of the member companies and of FDA was instrumental in developing a large number of new analytical methods. These methods very quickly improved the quality of the vanillas found in the marketplace. These methods are official and are published by AOAC. They include an organic acid determination by gas liquid chromatography; 1- and 2-dimensional fluoresence chromatograms; improved vanillin analysis; TLC method for detection of foreign aromatics; nonvanillin, vanilla aromatics method, utilizing gas liquid chromatography (which is still undergoing further study). Currently, other methods are being studied for future inclusion in the official methods, these include an improved amino acid determination, and possible application of liquid chromatography to vanilla analysis.

Despite the many excellent analytical methods, the interpretation of analytical results requires much experience. Vanilla, being a product of nature, will vary in composition. Extraction techniques, variations in solvent composition, etc., will also effect the analytical constants.

Synthetic Vanillin

Vanillin is a substance which is used primarily in food flavoring, as an intermediary in the manufacture of drugs, and to some extent in perfumes.

The commercially pure compound is a solid formed in colorless, monoclinic needles; it has a melting point at $81°$-$82°C$ and a boiling point of $285°C$. The material is somewhat soluble in hot water, very soluble in alcohols, ethers, and a number of other organic solvents.

Vanillin is available to the trade in synthetic form or as a natural extract of vanilla, the latter derived from the vanilla bean. The two grades differ in that the natural product contains a number of additional constituents which provide flavor sensations supplementing the basic note of vanillin. No such supplementary components at present appear in the pure synthetic vanillin.

The synthetic product is obtained by three different routes starting from eugenol, guaiacol, and lignin respectively. The products obtained by these three routes are identical in terms of chemical analysis but they differ slightly in flavor due to the presence of trace contaminants introduced by the raw material and some of its derivatives. The contaminant flavor in the eugenol-derived product is considered least objectionable. Accordingly, synthetic vanillin based on eugenol has retained some importance, although it is the most costly route and its product carries a premium price.

Despite the outstanding importance of synthetic vanillin in the perfuming and flavoring field, surprisingly little information has been published on techniques employed in its production.

Production from Eugenol.—Eugenol is obtained from oil of cloves. It is converted to vanillin by a series of reactions.

Conversion to isoeugenol is carried out in dilute caustic solution under pressure at $160°C$. Upon completion of this reaction an equimolar amount of nitrobenzine is introduced slowly into the autoclave. When the resulting oxidation to sodium vanillate is complete, the batch is cooled and the permanent gases are blown off. By solidification

of the batch, vanillin is precipitated from solution and recovered by filtration. The vanillin yield is approximately 80% of theory on eugenol.

Production from Guaiacol.—Several routes permit the synthesis of vanillin from guaiacol. In one such process, sodium guaiacolate is reacted with glyoxylic acid and the product oxidized to yield vanillin.

A 2–2.5% aqueous solution of glyoxylic acid is neutralized with caustic soda and this is then condensed with guaiacol in the presence of excess caustic soda at 30–33%. Reaction time is about 8 hr. Unreacted guaiacol is extracted by dichlorethane.

m-Nitrobenzene sulphonic acid is mixed with the reaction medium and the oxidation step is allowed to proceed at $100°C$ for 7 hr. The mass is then cooled, and the vanillin, precipitated upon acidification with sulphuric acid, is extracted with dichlorethane and purified by vacuum distillation and recrystallization.

Yield is reported to be 80% based on guaiacol.

A key intermediate in this synthesis is glyoxylic acid. For its formation, various routes are at hand. Yields of 75–80% are reported in the electrolysis of oxalic acid. Following neutralization, the aqueous solution of glyoxylic acid may serve directly. In an alternative method, glyoxylic acid is obtained by hydrolysis of dichloroacetic acid but this route requires subsequent purification before the acid may function in the vanillin synthesis.

Another method which has been employed commercially, involves the reaction of guaiacol with formaldehyde and m-phenylhydroxyl-amino-sulphonic acid. The latter is formed *in situ* from m-nitrobenzene-sulphonic acid. In a more recent variant of this reaction, guaiacol is reacted with formaldehyde and p-nitrosodimethylaniline. Yield has been reported at 45–55% on guaiacol.

One more route from guaiacol to vanillin involves guaiacol's reaction with chloral. The resulting acylation derivative is oxidized to vanillin. Using air as an oxidizing agent in caustic medium and in the presence of potassium permanganate as a catalyst, a 50–55% yield is reported.

Production from Lignin-Containing Materials.—Since its introduction in 1937, this method has become the leading commercial source of vanillin. The starting material is generally waste sulphite liquor which contains some 15% lignosulphonic acid. Several versions exist of these processes, their underlying reaction being the air oxidation of the lignin structure in a ligninsulphonate salt to yield the corresponding vanillate which is then acidified to vanillin.

In a typical process for the production of vanillin from spent sulphite liquor, the raw sulphite liquor is treated with milk of lime in 2–3 successive stages operating at increasing pH, to precipitate calcium lignosulphonate. The solids are filtered off and are treated with excess sodium sulphate in aqueous solution. The resulting calcium sulphate is filtered off. Sodium lignosulphate solution passes through as filtrate. To this is added 25 wt % sodium hydroxide (based on lignin content). The resulting solution is autoclaved where it is heated to 160°C for 1-2 hr, air being injected into the reaction mass.

In the process, sodium vanillate is formed in 5% concentration which, after cooling to 25°C, is extracted from the aqueous phase with butanol. In a second extraction state, the vanillate is water-washed from the butanol solution and the organic solvent is recirculated.

At this stage the vanillate solution is treated with sulphur dioxide. This will result in precipitation of the undesired phenolic compounds. At the same time vanillin bisulphite is formed which remains in aqueous solution. Treatment with sulphuric acid precipitates vanillin which is filtered and purified by vacuum distillation and recrystallization. Overall yield is reported at 15% based on dry lignin solids.

The Ontario Paper Company of Thorold, Ontario, had been interested for many years in finding commercial uses for the huge quantities of sulphite liquor which were being produced and had to be disposed of. The interest was two-fold. First, it wished to make as much use of the raw material as possible to meet continually rising costs of newsprint production; and, second, it was looking for ways to ease its water pollution problem.

At Marathon Corporation in Wisconsin and Howard Smith Paper Mills at Cornwall, Ontario, sulphite liquors were used for this purpose for some years before studies began at Thorold, but The Ontario Paper Company sought a different and more economical process.

In 1943 the initial step was taken by establishing the first successful plant in North America for making industrial alcohol by fermenting the sugars in the sulphite liquors. The next step was finding a use for the alcohol plant effluent which contained lignin, the glue that binds the wood fibers together. Vanillin was the company's choice.

More than 8 yr after experiments began and after considerable investment in a pilot plant and the original vanillin plant, the first commercially acceptable product was turned out late in 1952. Total investment in plant and equipment, counting the original plant and subsequent additions and improvements, is estimated at more than 3 million dollars.

The same basic process has been used in the plant since it opened. There have been modifications over the years; a major improvement in 1958

increased the yield $2^{1}/_{2}$ times, using relatively the same amount of liquor. The development of the original process was headed by three men, Dr. Charles A. Sankey, the Research Director, Dr. J. H. Fisher, now with MacMillan Bloedel & Powell River Company, and Dr. H. B. Marshall of The Ontario Research Foundation.

The liquor, after going through the alcohol plant where sugar is removed, is treated with lime and air in a reactor under high temperature and pressure. A liquid and a sludge are formed with vanillin salt present in both parts of the mixture. The liquid is separated and carbon dioxide is added to free the vanillin. This process differs from the Marathon and Howard Smith methods previously described, in that lime, instead of the more expensive caustic soda, is used to treat the liquor.

The development of the vanillin and alcohol processes are two examples of how newsprint companies can make commercial use of materials that are by-products of newsprint operations. However, these processes may not be economically feasible for some newsprint producers, particularly vanillin production which has three distinct limitations.

Thus, there is the know-how required to develop the process and the large capital investment in setting up the plant. There is also the fact that soft woods, which are required for vanillin production, are used in sulphite pulping, these being found in quantity in Canada and the United States. More important, however, is the limited market for vanillin.

The following companies produce adequate vanillin requirements: Ontario Paper Company and Howard Smith Paper Co. in Canada; Monsanto Chemical Company and Sterwin Chemicals Inc. in the United States; and Borregaard Paper Mill in Norway. Quantities are also produced in the USSR and the Chinese People's Republic. While vanillin is sold in all parts of the world, the plant at Thorold has the capacity to supply the vanillin needs of the entire North American Continent. Therefore, if other newsprint manufacturers were to undertake vanillin production, new uses for it, particularly as an industrial chemical, would have to be found. Recently, there have been such developments in the pharmaceutical field which may require large quantities of vanillin.

At an installed world capacity of approximately 13 million pounds per year, there is a shortage of 2-3 million pounds due to nonavailability of caustic soda and other raw materials.

In addition to Vanillin USP, there is a technical grade of vanillin which consists of approximately $98^{1}/_{2}\%$ pure material, plus impurities. These impurities are acetonvanillome, parahydroxybenzaldehyde, and 5-formyl-vanillin. Before commercial production of Vanillin USP, Technical Grade Vanillin was a product which could not be purchased. No one sold it. Today, it receives growing recognition as a basic chemical of value in the manufacture of a wide variety of products. It is used in metallurgical processing, in pharmaceutical products, and in dyes and perfumes. Vanillin is used in zinc plating baths, and chemicals used in tanning can be made from it. Vanillin added to lubricating oils prevents foaming. Other chemicals produced from vanillin have an action like 2,4-D in killing weeds and in other products which are potential disinfectants.

The vanillin molecule, which is receiving a great deal of attention in research laboratories at present, should ultimately attain as significant a position as a chemical intermediate as it has as a flavoring compound. L-dopa, the anti-Parkinsonism compound, is prepared from vanillin as is carba-dopa.

Another pharmaceutical application is in methyl dopa. Vanillin is used as an intermediate for this product. Methyl dopa is marketed as "Aldomet" and possesses antihypertensive and tranquilizing properties.

Among future chemical applications is isovanillin prepared from vanillin and used in the manufacture of a class of synthetic sweeteners known as dihydrochalcones. FDA approval of these sweeteners has not yet been granted and their future impact on vanillin production is difficult to estimate.

Acknowledgment

The author wishes to thank Morris R. Jones, Manager of Chemical Sales, The Ontario Paper Co., Thorold, Ontario for providing essential background material for much of the discussion on synthetic vanillin and Kurt L. Schoen, Vice President, Research and Development, David Michael & Co., Inc., Philadelphia for his review of vanilla analysis.

EDWARD W. ROSENBAUM

Cross-reference: *Flavorings and Essences.*

VINEGAR

Vinegar has been known and appreciated as an important food adjunct (condiment and preservative) for as long as man has been able to practice the arts of brewing and wine making. Back to almost prehistoric times, vinegar, salt, smoking, and herbs were recognized as materials or methods for preserving food. Vinegar is mentioned in the Bible and Hippocrates used it as a medicine.

Vinegar is defined as "a sour liquid consisting of dilute and impure acetic acid obtained by acetous fermentation from wine, cider, beer, ale, or the like." The word "vinegar" is derived from the French "vinaigre" meaning literally sour or sharp wine. In addition, it may be defined as the product resulting from the acetification of alcoholic solutions derived from sugary or starchy materials. By the 16th Century, wine vinegar was being produced in France for home use and export. In England, vinegar was first made from malt liquors as a method of disposing of ale or beer which had soured. Today, standard table vinegars of France, the British Isles, and the United States are made from grapes, malt, and apples, respectively.

Vinegar may be produced from a wide variety of substances, the main requirement being sufficient alcohol or sugar from which alcohol can be derived with a satisfactory flavoring substance. Thus oranges, pineapple, and honey have been used in vinegar production; also, whey in the United States and Russia.

White distilled vinegar or vinegar made from pure alcohol diluted with water to which certain nutrients have been added, is the vinegar most commonly used in industry. This is the vinegar used (sometimes in a mixture with condiment vinegar) in commerical salad dressing, ketchups, pickles, and other similar products.

Two entirely different microbial processes are required to produce vinegar. According to the Gay-Lussac equation, the conversion of sugar in the substrate to alcohol by a particular strain of yeast is

$$C_6H_{12}O_6 \longrightarrow 2CH_3CH_2OH + 2CO_2$$

Hexose   Alcohol + Carbon Dioxide

The strain of yeast used will depend upon the sugar to be fermented. The resultant alcohol-containing material now becomes the raw material for the second step, the conversion of the alcohol to acetic acid:

$$2CH_3CH_2OH + 2O_2 \longrightarrow 2CH_3COOH + 2H_2O$$

Alcohol + Oxygen   Acetic Acid + Water

The organism used here is the acetobacter which in the presence of air will convert ethyl alcohol to acetic acid and water. It is an absolute necessity to have air (oxygen) for the vinegar-making process.

The yeast fermentation theoretically produces an amount of alcohol equal to about $1/2$ the amount of sugar fermented, 85-90% of theoretical usually being attained. Theoretically, conversion of alcohol to acetic acid should yield more acetic acid than substrate alcohol. In practice, the yield is about the same; some alcohol is used by the acetobacter and some may be lost by evaporation.

The alcoholic fermentation is usually conducted at 75°-80°F using a starter which is a selected strain of *Saccharomyces cereviciae* which has been grown in the presence of a minimum amount of sulfur dioxide.

The fermentable sugar content of the substrate is adjusted to a level not below 8% nor more than 20%. A primary fermentation stage of 3-7 days, conducted in open vats with cooling facilities to control temperature, results in conversion of the bulk of the sugar to alcohol. The secondary fermentation, lasting for a week or more, is conducted in closed vats. In the course of the fermentation it may be necessary to add potassium or ammonium phosphate as yeast nutrients and sulphites to control bacterial contamination. Sulphur dioxide as liquid sulphur dioxide or as sodium or potassium metabisulfite is usually added (particularly to apple juice or other sugar-containing media) before the addition of the yeast starter in order to prevent the activity of undesirable yeast and bacteria, an initial level of 50-100 mg per liter being sufficient. On completion of the alcoholic fermentation the yeast cells are removed by sedimentation. The resulting sugar content should be low—preferably below 0.3%.

There are basically two commerical methods of manufacturing vinegar from an alcohol-containing substrate: the packed generator system and the submerged fermentation system. The packed generator system depends upon a vessel packed full of inert coarse material which acts as a physical support for the acetobacter organisms and allows the air to be distributed upwards from a small blower in the bottom. The most common carrier is beechwood shavings, but coke, porcelain chips, glass beads, and corn cobs have been used either in research or commercially.

The generator system consists of a batch tank to hold the substrate and a pump to circulate the substrate across the generators which have been inoculated with acetobacter. Air is introduced at the bottom of the generator. The substrate liquid is allowed to trickle down across the beechwood shavings and into a false bottom in the generator. It is then removed, cooled, and recirculated across the generator until all of the alcohol is converted to acetic acid.

The Frings generator consists of an air-tight tank usually 14 ft in diameter and 15 ft high, with wooden gratings near the bottom and distributary spraying arm near the top. A 4-in. vent with proper appertinances serves to control the air supply. Filtered air enters the generator through 10 holes located just above the wooden grating. Tubular cooling coils are located in the collector below the grating and these are connected by a centrifugal pump to a feed line supplying the sprayer. The vinegar stock or mix is allowed to circulate through the packed column until vinegar of the desired strength is obtained. It is often necessary to add nutrients to the mix, the composition of which may vary with the type of generator packing material. In a larger Frings generator, with a good operation, a 2500-gal. batch of mix containing 10.5% alcohol and 7 lb of Aceto-pep nutrient requires 3-5 days cycle time to reach 10.5% acetic acid.

The submerged system depends on heavy stirring and aeration in a tank containing the alcohol substrate. An inoculum of acetobacter is introduced, or some finished vinegar from a previous batch is allowed to remain as inoculum. The stirring and aeration are started and do not stop until the entire batch of substrate is converted to acetic acid.

At present, three methods of submerged acidification are known: the "acetator" developed in Austria, the "Cavitator" based on a procedure for the biological oxidation of domestic sewage, and the "aspirator." These procedures differ in their methods of introducing and distributing air. The procedures for the production of vinegar by submerged fermentation were given impetus by the success of antibiotic production by such procedures.

Vinegar eels (*anguilla aceti*) frequently infect vinegar and are usually considered undesirable. These eels are nematodes of about $1/16$ in. in length. Some investigators have, however, observed higher acid production in vats infected with the eels and have suggested that they act as scavengers to keep the beechwood shavings free of dead bacteria and also to supply the viable bacteria with more readily available nutrients. Ultimately, eels are removed from the vinegar in the final steps of vinegar manufacture which include clarification, filtration, and pasteurization in preparation for packaging.

Production figures for the main types of vinegars produced in the United States in 1969 are

	Rounded to Units of 1000 Gal.	% of Total
White	93,303	75.30
Cider	25,692	20.73
Wine	3,279	2.65
Malt	924	0.75
Others	711	0.57
Total	123,909	

Other vinegars include amber distilled, corn syrup, flavored, malt, pear cider, rex amber, salad, sweet cider.

Primary disposition of the annual production of vinegar is indicated by the following figures:

Disposition	Rounded to Units of 1000 Gal.	% of Total
Shelf pack	29,733	24.00
Pickle industry	25,013	20.19
Other processed foods	19,017	15.34
Salad dressings	14,574	11.76
Tomato products	11,252	9.08
Mustard industry	9,549	7.71
Nonmanufacturing bottlers	7,741	6.25
Other vinegar manufacturers	4,310	3.48
Carry-over (storage)	2,493	2.01
Nonfood use	215	0.17
To export	12	0.01

Of the shelf-packed classification, more than 80% was made up of cider and white vinegar, with cider vinegar predominating. While shelf-pack vinegar is available in many sized glass containers from 8 oz to 1 gal., cider and white vinegars are predominately packaged in the 1 qt and 1 gal. sizes.

By federal standards vinegar shall not contain less than 4 gm of acetic acid in 100 ml of solution. A concentrated vinegar up to 100–125 grain strength (10–12.5% acetic acid) can be obtained in the production of distilled vinegar by suitable adjustment of the alcohol and acid content of a denatured vinegar stock. Wine vinegar and cider vinegar of this strength can be made by concentrating the respective juices before fermentation.

Herb- and spice-flavored vinegars are produced by careful compounding, blending, and aging to yield especially desired flavors. Taragon vinegar is probably the best known vinegar of this class.

HAROLD YOUNG

VITAMINS

Vitamins are organic compounds required in small amounts to promote normal growth, to help regulate body processes, and to maintain good health. Some vitamins are essential for all animals, but not all the vitamins now known are needed for all animals. Most higher plants manufacture whatever vitamins they require, but animals, by contrast, must have most of their vitamins supplied in food. Differences exist between man and lower animals as to their vitamin requirements but there are more similarities than differences. Discovery of the vitamins, a 20th Century achievement, has had a profound effect on dietetics and modern medicine.

Vitamins are divided into two groups—the fat soluble and the water soluble. Fat-soluble vitamins (A, D, E, and K) are found in foods in association with lipids, and are absorbed along with dietary fat. Fat-soluble vitamins are stored by the body in moderate quantities, and as a result animals are not dependent on a daily supply in the diet. In contrast, water-soluble vitamins are not associated with lipids and are excreted in small amounts in the urine. They are not stored by the body in appreciable quantities and a constant dietary supply is desirable if depletion and disturbance of function are to be avoided.

Prolonged lack of vitamins in the diet causes characteristic deficiency diseases. This century has seen the isolation of vitamins in pure, crystalline form, their chemical identification and synthesis[1] and the determination of their metabolic role and the amounts required by man. Table V-1 summarizes vitamin sources, functions, and stability under processing and storage.

The Fat-Soluble Vitamins

The physiology of vitamins is related to their solubility. Thus, the fat-soluble vitamins are associated with lipid-rich foods and are absorbed with the dietary fats. When conditions are favorable to normal fat uptake, the fat-soluble vitamins are absorbed and not excreted in the urine. They are retained in moderate quantities, in the body. Their storage thus frees man from the need for a daily dietary supply.

Vitamin A.—Both McCollum and Davis, and Osborne and Mendel noted that a factor occurring in certain fats was indispensable for growing rats. It has been since demonstrated that all vertebrates require vitamin A. A deficiency of the vitamin can result in night blindness, poor growth, atrophy of epithelial tissues and tissues of the eye as well as poor resistance to infection. It occurs naturally only in animals. It can be isolated from the unsaponifiable fraction of their fats. It is present in highest concentrations in the liver, and a most important natural source of the vitamin is fish liver oils. In plant material, vitamin A activity is due to

---

[1] The molecular structures of the various vitamins are not supplied in this article since they can be readily found elsewhere; for example, in the excellent chapter on the vitamins in the *Heinz Handbook of Nutrition*, pp 72–105, (1959).

certain carotenoids that are precursors or pro-vitamins A.

Vitamin A, a pale, viscous, fat-soluble alcohol, has two closely related forms: Vitamin A_1, found in mammals and salt-water fish, and vitamin A_2, found in fresh-water fish. They both possess similar biologic activity, but vitamin A_1 is the substance of primary importance in human physiology.

Vitamin A is relatively stable to heat, but not in the presence of oxygen. Since vitamin A is stored in the body, it is a good practice to eat liberal portions of foods rich in this vitamin during the season when these foods are plentiful. The reserve thus built up may be used when these foods are not available. Vitamin A is labile to oxidation and destruction when fats that contain it turn rancid. It is also destroyed by exposure to sunlight.

Vitamin A requirements are expressed in International Units (IU) rather than in milligrams or micrograms. One IU is equal to 0.344 µg of crystalline vitamin A acetate which in turn is equivalent to 0.300 µg of vitamin A alcohol or 0.600 µg of beta-carotene. These standards are based on experiments with rats and it should be noted that in man the conversion from carotene is not as complete as in the rat. The amount of dietary vitamin A available to humans varies depending upon whether the major part of the dietary intake is in the form of vitamin A or in its less potent provitamin. One-third of the average diet contains vitamin A in the active form. On this basis, the recommended daily allowance[2] of the National Research Council Food and Nutrition Board is 5000 IU per day for the adult. The requirements are higher in periods of rapid growth, in pregnancy, and in lactation.

If one follows the rules for the selection of an adequate diet, one may easily attain the recommended allowance of vitamin A. However, the ubiquitous vitamin capsules and vitamin A concentrates make it easy to take large amounts of vitamin A and hence restraint should be exercised since an excess of vitamin A has a toxic effect.

---

[2] The recommended daily allowances (RDA) are intended for the maintenance of good nutrition for most normal persons as they live in the United States under usual environmental stresses. For this reason, they allow for a considerable margin of safety to allow for individual variations. The minimum daily requirements (MDR) of nutrients represents levels established by USDA and are used primarily in connection with legal label requirements for foods, vitamin preparations, etc. Nutrient intakes below the MDR would probably produce clinical deficiency signs.

Toxic symptoms include loss of appetite, skeletal pain, patchy loss of hair, dry skin with ulcerated areas, fissures of the lips, tenderness and swelling in the extremities.

For many years the rat-curative bioassay was the only official method available for the determination of vitamin A. Unfortunately, this procedure is impractical for routine analyses because it is time-consuming and expensive. Today, liver assay methods are preferred since while retaining the advantage of measuring biological activity they are much less time-consuming.

The most widely used chemical method is the Carr-Price reaction adapted for photoelectric measurement of the blue color formed when vitamin A is treated with antimony trichloride. Though less precise than ultraviolet absorption methods, this assay is more specific and more sensitive, and therefore has wider applicability. The reproducibility of the method is from 3 to 10% depending upon the product.

Carotene.—The provitamins of vitamin A are designated alpha, beta, and gamma carotene and cryptoxanthin. When taken into the body, they split in half and are converted to vitamin A. The conversion in man takes place in the intestinal wall during absorption into the body and liver. The site as well as the capability of conversion differs with the animal species. Theoretically, beta-carotene may be split to give two molecules of vitamin A, but this conversion in man is incomplete.

The provitamins are extremely sensitive to oxidation, autooxidation, and light. They are stable to heat in inert atmospheres and soluble in fats. The best sources of carotene are yellow and green vegetables and fruits. The carotene content of foods is measured by bioassay, by the solvent partition method, and by the chromatographic technique. The biologic assay is regarded, however, as the only one that indicates the actual vitamin A activity of foods and feeds.

Vitamin D.—Nutritionally, the most important forms of vitamin D are activated ergosterol, vitamin D_2 or calciferol, and activated 7-dehydrocholesterol, vitamin D_3. Vitamin D occurs in nature only in small amounts although in the livers and viscera of some fish it is present in considerable quantities. Except for whole egg, egg yolks, butter, cheese, milk, and vitaminized margarine, and plant foods supplying ergosterol, other foods are relatively poor sources of vitamin D.

Vitamin D is essential for strong bones and teeth and thus babies and young children particularly need the vitamin. Deformities of the skeleton such as rickets, characterized by knock-knees, enlargement of the ends of the long bones, curvature of the spine and deformities of the pelvis and

TABLE V-1

VITAMIN SOURCES, FUNCTIONS, AND STABILITY

	Food Sources	Functions	Effects of Processing[1]	Effects of Storage[2]
Fat-soluble vitamins				
Vitamin A and carotene	Liver, kidney, eggs, butter, whole milk, fortified skim milk, cream, cheese, dark green and deep yellow vegetables and deep yellow fruit.	Essential for healthy skin, eyes and hair; keeps mucous membranes firm and resistant to infection; prevents night blindness, and controls bone growth.	No appreciable loss by heating, freezing, preserving, or canning.	In the absence of air, stable. High storage temperatures in the presence of air result in loss.
Vitamin D (the sunshine vitamin)	Fish liver oils, sunshine on skin, vitamin D milk, egg yolk, margarine, mackerel, sardines, salmon, tuna, cod liver oil.	Necessary for teeth and bones, and normal utilization of calcium and phosphorus; prevents bone deformities.	Little or no loss unless oxidized.	Little or no loss unless oxidized.
Vitamin E	Whole grain cereal, pulses, wheat germ, soybean, cottonseed, peanut and corn oils, eggs, liver, butter, margarine.	Essential for normal muscle; antioxidant, preserving vitamins and unsaturated fatty acids in foods or the body; required for integrity of red blood cells.	Little or no loss unless food becomes rancid.	Little or no loss unless food becomes rancid.
Vitamin K	Cabbage, cauliflower, pork liver, soybean, spinach, wheat bran.	Essential for normal blood clotting.	Destroyed by irradiation.	No appreciable loss.
Water-soluble vitamins				
Vitamin B_1 (thiamin)	Liver, pork, poultry, fish, eggs, beans and peas, whole grain cereal, enriched bread, lean meat, potatoes, broccoli, collards, yeast.	Necessary for growth, fertility and lactation; promotes normal appetite; aids metabolic processes, releasing energy from food; keeps nervous system healthy and prevents irritability.	The higher and longer the heating period, the greater the loss. Loss is decreased in presence of acid and small amounts of water.	Refrigeration lessens destruction.
Vitamin B_2 (riboflavin)	Milk, cheese, ice cream, liver, meat, fish, poultry, eggs, yeast.	Assists in conversion of tryptophan to nicotinic acid; necessary for healthy skin; essential for build-	Stable to heat but may be dissolved and discarded in cooking water. Open vessels (or light) and use of	Relatively stable.

	Sources	Function	Stability in Processing and Cooking	Stability in Storage
Niacin	Liver, lean meats, eggs, peas, beans, nuts, peanut butter, enriched bread, whole grain cereal, yeast.	...ing and maintaining body tissues and the use of oxygen by cells. Prevents pellagra; necessary for growth and health of tissues; promotes appetite and good utilization of food in the body.	sodium bicarbonate in cooking water will destroy riboflavin. No loss during ordinary cooking processes, but may lose some in cooking water.	Relatively stable.
Pyridoxine hydrochloride	Barley, meat, cabbage, carrots, corn, cottonseed meal, milk, peanuts, peas, rice, wheat, brewers' yeast, lima beans.	Coenzyme, necessary for protein, tryptophan and fat metabolism; promotes normal red blood cell formation.	Loss occurs due to leaching of vitamin in cooking water (30%). Destroyed by high temperature, high irradiation dose, and exposure to light.	Loss increases with temperature and time of storage.
Pantothenic acid	Wheat, eggs, milk, meat, fish, yeast, molasses, oatmeal, broccoli, cabbage, cucumbers, corn, tomatoes, potatoes, peas, liver, nuts.	Essential for metabolism of carbohydrates and fats.	Fairly stable in moist heat, particularly in neutral solution; readily destroyed by prolonged dry heat in alkaline environment. Can be leached by water.	Relatively stable.
Biotin	Yeast, liver, peanuts, beans, eggs, kidney.	Important to intermediary metabolism-energy release mechanisms.	Stable to heat, but can be dissolved in cooking water.	Relatively stable.
Folic acid	Liver, dark green leafy vegetables; cauliflower, kidney, beef, veal, wheat breakfast foods, bran, blackeyed peas.	Prevents certain anemias; with vitamin C aids tyrosine metabolism in energy conversion cycles; aids in red blood cell formation.	High temperature processing is detrimental to folic acid stability.	Low temperatures of storage are preferred to room temperature to enhance stability.
Vitamin B$_{12}$	Liver, beef extract, dry milk, oysters, lean meat.	Prevents certain anemias and promotes good general nutrition by contributing to health of nervous system.	Very stable in neutral solutions, but loses potency in either acid or alkaline solutions. Cooking losses range from 24-90%.	More stable to storage than to processing; affected by presence of thiamin and nicotinamide in aqueous pharmaceutical preparations.
Ascorbic acid	Fresh fruits and vegetables, particularly citrus fruits and leafy vegetables.	Essential for healthy bones and strong teeth; helps to maintain body's resistance to infection; prevents capillary fragility; essential for growth and wound healing.	Most easily destroyed of all vitamins and should be processed in stainless steel or glass as a protective measure.	Foods can lose as much as 50% and more depending upon storage time and temperature. Storage at 0°F (−18°C) or below recommended for good retention.

[1] Loss of water-soluble vitamins may be large or small depending upon the processing and cooking techniques and methods that are employed.
[2] Vitamin losses in storage may be large or small depending on storage time and conditions, the product involved, and the vitamin in question.

thorax can be caused by an insufficient amount of vitamin D. If the vitamin is supplied after these deformities have developed it will prevent further impairment but it cannot restore bones to their normal shape and structure. Vitamin D increases the utilization in the body of calcium and phosphorus. It also increases the absorption of dietary calcium and phosphorus from the intestine.

Vitamin D is produced by the action of the sunlight (ultraviolet light) on ergosterol in the skin; when formed in this manner it is readily taken into the local circulation and carried by the blood to all parts of the body. The excess formed can be stored in considerable amounts in the liver and may be found in the fatty tissues, lungs, spleen, and brain. Vitamin D is one of the most potent vitamins known. A daily intake of 2.5–10 μg—equivalent to 100–400 IU—will prevent rickets in children, but a daily intake of 1–2 mg can be toxic if continued for long periods. The toxicity syndrome resembles that of overactive parathyroid glands. It is characterized by loss of appetite, vomiting, headache, drowsiness, and diarrhea. Excessive and painful urination as well as extreme thirst may occur. Serum calcium and phosphorus levels are increased, and misplaced calcium deposits may be found in the heart, large vessels, renal tubules, and other soft tissues. Fortunately, the effects of this excessive vitamin condition are reversible if the administration of vitamin D is stopped and low calcium diet is consumed during the adjustment period.

Vitamin E.—There are four closely related compounds that possess vitamin E activity: alpha, beta, gamma, and delta tocopherol. Each is a viscous oil, soluble in fat solvents, stable to heat and acids, and unstable to alkalies, ultraviolet light, and oxygen. The tocopherols are excellent antioxidants and protect both vitamin A and carotene. Of the four forms of tocopherol, alpha-tocopherol is the most active, biologically.

The tocopherols are present in many foodstuffs; the fats of vegetable origin (particularly those derived from corn, soybean, peanut, coconut or cottonseed), cereal products, and eggs are the richest sources. The U.S. diet varies widely in vitamin E content (2 to 66 IU).

Although vitamin E is an essential factor for a number of animals, so far there is little evidence that vitamin E deficiency occurs in man. It is clear, however, that the vitamin is present in human tissues and that it is necessary for normal metabolism.

The intake of polyunsaturated fatty acids will increase the requirement of vitamin E. Additional factors such as the presence of selenium and other nutrients affect the requirements for vitamin E, but its role in nutrition has not yet been as clearly assessed for man as for animals. Its distribution in foods is such, fortunately, that there is relatively little chance of deficiency in the normal human dietary. There is no evidence that the vitamin is toxic, even in high above-physiological levels. This is in marked contrast to other fat-soluble vitamins.

Vitamin K.—The two major natural sources of vitamin K are plant food sources such as green, leafy vegetables (K_1) and that which is synthesized by the bacterial flora of the human intestinal tract (K_2). Vitamin K_3, menadione, is the synthetic form of the vitamin and biologically is the most potent.

All forms of the vitamin are yellow and quite stable to heat, air, and moisture but not to light. Vitamin K is essential for synthesis of prothrombin (precursor for enzyme thrombin which causes blood to clot) formation by the liver and the coagulability of the blood. Much remains to be known as to the precise mode of action of vitamin K in prothrombin formation by the liver. It may be concerned in stimulating oxidative phosphorylation.

The effects of vitamin K deficiency can be detected by determining the time it takes the blood to clot—the prothrombin time. Excessive doses of the synthetic vitamin K result in the breakdown of red blood cells in the rat and jaundice, hemolysis, and hemoglobinuria in human infants.

Water-Soluble Vitamins

Vitamin C and the B group of vitamins are water soluble and, in general, cannot be stored in the body. Amounts above what are used are rapidly excreted in the urine. Hence, the requirements must be supplied daily.

Vitamin C (Ascorbic Acid).—Ascorbic acid is a white, crystalline substance, stable, when dry, in light and air. Highly soluble in water, it is easily oxidized particularly in an alkaline medium and on exposure to heat, and in contact with traces of metal, especially copper. It is the most active reducing agent known to exist naturally in living tissues. The first oxidized step of ascorbic acid to dehydroascorbic acid is reversible; the next step to diketogluconic acid is not reversible. Therefore, dehydroascorbic acid is biologically active; diketogluconic acid is not.

Ascorbic acid is essential in the formation of the intracellular substance of collagenous and fibrous tissue in animals. It is required in the development of normal teeth, bone, cartilage, connective tissue, and skin as well as for the structural integrity of the capillary walls. Its importance in healing of wounds and burns is well known. Ascorbic acid requirement is increased during periods of stress due to infections and bacterial toxins.

Ascorbic acid has an important role in the oxidation of phenylalanine and tyrosine, in conversion of folic to folinic acid and in the regulation of the oxidation-reduction potentials within the cells. It exerts a sparing action on the requirements of members of the vitamin B complex, and is involved in the utilization of certain minerals such as calcium, phosphorus, iron, and copper. It is involved, in short, in numerous metabolic processes.

Ascorbic acid is absorbed from the small intestine and is stored by way of tissue saturation. Vitamin C that is not needed for metabolic requirements and tissue storage is excreted in the urine. It is of interest that high concentrations of the vitamin are found in the adrenals, pituitary gland, thymus, and in the corpus luteum.

Animal species as a rule are capable of synthesizing their requirement for ascorbic acid. A few known exceptions are man, monkey, guinea pig, the Indian fruit-eating bat, and the bulbul bird. Vitamin C deficiency in man leads to scurvy, a disease characterized by weakness, swollen tender joints, delayed wound healing, spongy gums, loose teeth, and hemorrhages. The daily allowance recommended by the Food and Nutrition Board of the NRC is 45 mg per day.

Foods richest in vitamin C are citrus fruits and their juices, strawberries, cantaloupes, raw or minimally cooked vegetables, especially peppers, broccoli, cauliflower, kale, Brussel sprouts, turnip greens, cabbage, tomatoes and potatoes. Synthetic vitamin C is inexpensive and harmless in doses up to at least 1 gm a day. Excessive amounts are rapidly lost in the urine.

The Vitamin B-Group.—*Thiamin (Vitamin B$_1$).*— Thiamin, a white crystalline powder with a yeasty odor and a salty nut-like taste, is sometimes referred to as vitamin B$_1$, thiamin hydrochloride, aneurin, antineuritic vitamin, or more colloquially, as the antiberiberi vitamin. It is water soluble, relatively stable to heat and labile to alkali (baking soda) and oxidation. It occurs in natural foods and other biological materials, either in the free or combined form—protein complex, or as a phosphorus-protein complex, or as the pyrophosphoric acid ester, cocarboxylase.

Clinical signs of thiamin deficiency are evident as beriberi in the following forms: "dry" type— multiple peripheral neuritis with subsequent muscular atrophy; "wet" type—generalized edema, combination dry and wet beriberi, and infantile beriberi.

Food sources of thiamin are numerous. Pork, organ meats, yeast, lean meats, eggs, green leafy vegetables, whole grain or enriched cereals, nuts, and legumes are the richest sources. This vitamin is also synthesized by the bacterial flora of the human intestinal tract but not in sufficient quantity to cover man's requirement. Thiamin is lost in the cooking water of vegetables when the water is discarded. In meats, roasting causes more destruction of thiamin than either broiling or frying. Dehydration has less effect on the thiamin content of food than irradiation. Frozen food should be stored at 0°F (-18°C) or below to minimize thiamin loss.

The thiamin requirement is related to calories derived primarily from carbohydrate and is usually stated in terms of caloric intake (0.5 mg per 1000 Kcal for adults). The minimum daily intake recommended for adults is 1.0 mg even if calories consumed are less than 2000.

Riboflavin (Vitamin B$_2$).—Riboflavin, lactoflavin, vitamin G, or vitamin B$_2$ is a yellow-green, fluorescent, water-soluble pigment, widely distributed in animal and plant cells. It is slightly soluble in water and very soluble in alkaline solutions. Crystalline riboflavin, when protected against light, is stable. In solution, it is unstable and its decomposition is greatly influenced by light, temperature, and pH of the solution. Only slight destruction occurs by heating.

Ariboflavinosis is riboflavin deficiency in human beings and is characterized by cracking of the skin at the corners of the mouth and an oily dermatitis around the folds of the nostrils. Another symptom of riboflavin deficiency is an abnormally smooth condition of the tongue accompanied by a change in its color to purplish-red.

Riboflavin is necessary for growth and general health at all ages. Before it can be absorbed in the body, riboflavin must be phosphorylated in the intestinal tract. Its chief role is in oxidation-reduction reactions centering around two important riboflavin coenzymes—flavin mononucleotide and flavin adenine dinucleotide.

Riboflavin is found in significant amounts in organ meats, liver, sausage, milk, cheese, meat, eggs, green leafy vegetables, whole grains, and legumes. The Food and Nutrition Board has recommended a daily allowance of 0.6 mg riboflavin per 1000 Kcal consumed by the adult.

Niacin (Nicotinic Acid).—Niacin, another member of the vitamin B-group is also known as nicotinic acid or the antipellagra vitamin. Niacinamide is the biologically active form predominantly found in animal tissues. Both forms are stable in the dry form and in aqueous solutions and are unaffected by heat, light, or pH.

Niacin is a mild vasodilator and therefore, the amide, which is not a vasodilator, is used in pharmaceutical preparations. Niacin constitutes part of two known coenzymes, coenzyme I and coenzyme II, which are essential for the operation of a large number of enzyme systems. Coenzymes I and II (DPN and TPN) are the functional groups in important intracellular oxidation-reduction enzyme systems which are necessary for the utilization of all major nutrients. Pellagra is the clinical sign of niacin deficiency. With pellagra, one may have symptoms of dermatitis, diarrhea, soreness and a burning sensation in the mouth, and smooth, red, painful tongue, accompanied by mental. changes.

In man, niacin can be synthesized from tryptophan in the presence of vitamin B_6 (approximately 60 mg of tryptophan is required to furnish 1 mg of niacin). The recommended allowance for adults in niacin equivalents is 6.6 mg per 1000 Kcal.

Liver, meats, fish, enriched breads, whole grain cereals, peas and beans, nuts, and peanut butter are excellent sources of niacin. It is quite possible that this vitamin may also be produced by the bacterial flora in human intestine.

Pyridoxine (Vitamin B_6).—Vitamin B_6, also called antiacrodynia rat factor, or the rat antidermatitis factor, is known to exist in three forms: pyridoxine, pyridoxal, pyridoxamine. The term "vitamin B_6" is used as a collective term for the group. All three forms are white solids and have equal activity when fed to laboratory animals. Pyridoxine is much more stable to heat than the other two compounds, but all are stable to acid and alkali. The "amine" and "al" forms are labile when in dilute solutions and rapidly destroyed by exposure to heat and air. Processing or cooking may destroy up to 50% of the vitamin B_6 in foods. Best retention during frozen storage is obtained at $0°F (-18°C)$ or below.

Vitamin B_6 is essential for animals and man but deficiency signs vary with the species. Deoxypyridine, a chemical analogue of pyridoxine, an antivitamin, inhibits the activity of pyridoxine. Symptoms of B_6 deficiency are similar to those for riboflavin and niacin. Vitamin B_6 is involved in the metabolism of amino acids, fats, and carbohydrate. As mentioned earlier, it plays a specific role in the metabolism of tryptophan. There are many enzymes which require pyridoxal phosphate as coenzyme.

Recently, the Food and Nutrition Board established 2 mg as the recommended daily allowance for vitamin B_6. This vitamin occurs widely in both animal and plant products. Liver, yeast, bran, milk, whole grain cereals, legumes, meats, and fresh vegetables are good sources of the vitamin.

Pantothenic Acid.—Pantothenic acid occurs in all types of animal and plant tissues. It is most stable as its calcium or sodium salt and is commercially available in these forms. It has been identified with the chick antidermatitis factor, the chick antipellagra factor, and others.

Pantothenic acid deficiency in man has not been shown but it has been observed that in humans deficient in other vitamins of the B complex the level of pantothenic acid in the blood is about 25% below normal. It is synthesized by microorganisms in the intestine. Pantothenic acid is a constituent of coenzyme A, an essential coenzyme involved in many reversible acetylation reactions in carbohydrate, fat, and amino acid metabolism. As the key constituent of the coenzyme, pantothenic acid is of prime importance in cellular metabolism. Deficiency symptoms can be induced either with methylpantothenic acid or a pantothenic acid deficient diet. They include torpor, apathy, abdominal pains, increased susceptibility to infection, depression, cardiovascular instability, impaired adrenal function, and a neuromotor disorder causing a burning sensation of the skin (paresthesia) and muscle weakness.

Folic Acid.—Folic acid, folate, folacin, vitamin B_c, liver *L. Casei* factor, pteroylglutamic acid, or "vitamin M" is a water soluble, yellow, crystalline compound, labile to heat in acid media, and, when in solution, labile to sunlight.

Folic acid and its closely related, biologically active compound, folinic acid, occur as conjugates with glutamic acid. The presence of ascorbic acid assists in the conversion of folic acid to the more active form folinic acid. Folic acid is required for normal growth and blood formation in the chick, fox, mink, and monkey but not in rats and dogs under conditions of normal activity of intestinal bacteria. Persons with scurvy and infants on a milk diet may develop macrocytic anemia because of folic acid and ascorbic acid deficiency. The coenzymes formed from folic acid are necessary in intermediary metabolism. Vitamin B_{12} is necessary for the activity of the folic acid coenzymes.

Vitamin B_{12}.—Vitamin B_{12} and its most common form, cyanocobalamin, is a red, odorless, tasteless powder. Vitamin B_{12} is soluble in water and extremely hygroscopic. It is labile to acids, alkalies, and light. It is the only vitamin that contains an essential mineral (cobalt). Vitamin B_{12} usually occurs in combination with protein.

Pernicious anemia typifies vitamin B_{12} deficiency. It is due to stomach secretions which cause poor absorption of the vitamin. Individuals with this deficiency may develop sore tongue, paresthesia, and may show signs of degeneration of the spinal cord. The deficiency may be hereditary. Vitamin B_{12} plays a part, as do choline and folic acid, in the metabolism of methionine. It is necessary for normal function of all types of cells, especially those in bone marrow, the nervous system, and the gastrointestinal tract. Vitamin B_{12} is of major importance in nucleic acid and folic acid metabolism.

The best sources of vitamin B_{12} are eggs, liver,

kidney, milk, and muscle meats. A diet providing 3-5 μg of vitamin B_{12} per day will satisfy the requirement. The average American diet satisfies these requirements.

Biotin.—Biotin forms a stable complex with avidin from raw egg white which is unaffected by proteolytic digestion and in this form is unavailable biologically. Biotin acts, presumably, as a coenzyme involved in the carboxylation and decarboxylation of oxaloacetate, succinate, aspartate, and malate. Biotin has also been related to the biosynthesis of aspartate, citrulline, unsaturated fatty acids, and the oxidation of pyruvate.

There is no definite human disease ascribable to biotin deficiency. However, experimental biotin deficiency in man results in scale dermatitis, loss of appetite, muscle pains, insomnia, slight anemia, grayish pallor, and extreme lassitude.

Choline.—Although a dietary deficiency of choline in man has not been obtained under experimental conditions, it meets the requirements for being termed a vitamin. It is an essential component of the body tissues. It is a component part of phospholipids (lecithin, sphingomyelin) and acetylcholine.

Choline serves as a methyl donor for transmethylation in the body. As a constituent of several phospholipids it aids in the transport and metabolism of fats and as a constituent of acetylcholine it plays a role in the normal functioning of nerves. Betaine, with three methyl groups, may be considered a sparing agent, but is not fully equivalent to choline.

Symptoms of choline deficiency in animals vary with the species and are dependent in part on other essential factors. Choline deficiency in the rat leads to fatty liver, hemorrhagic degeneration of the kidney, and cardiovascular lesions. In the chick, poor growth and defective bone formation are caused by choline deficiency. Choline deficiency in the dog results in weight loss, anemia, dermal and peptic ulcers, and a fatty cirrhotic liver. The choline-deficient pig has poor locomotor coordination and reproduces poorly. In man, further studies of the role of choline and methionine in the pathogenesis and therapy of fatty liver disease are required.

Choline is present in egg yolk, whole grains, legumes, wheat germ, and meats of all types. In foods it is heat stable and little or no loss occurs in dried foods when stored for long periods. The average American diet for an adult contains 300–600 mg of choline. The human requirement is estimated to vary between 0.5 and 1.0 gm per day.

MIRIAM H. THOMAS

Cross-reference: *Enrichment, Restoration, and Fortification.*

W

WASTE DISPOSAL—LIQUIDS

Waste disposal for the food industry is becoming increasingly important and is a costly part of its operations. Formerly, it was possible to discharge liquid wastes untreated into receiving waters and to dump solid wastes on vacant land with little attention to subsequent putrefactive odors or runoff. Over the years regulations have properly become increasingly restrictive.

The Federal Water Pollution Control Act Amendments of 1972, PL 92-500 (Oct. 18, 1972) replaces all previous federal water laws, establishes much more stringent effluent standards, and defines penalties of up to $25,000 per day or 6 months' imprisonment, or both, for the first convicted violation of certain sections of the law and up to double these penalties for conviction of a second violation. Effluent limitations for industry are to be consistent with the "best practical" control technology by June 1, 1977, and with the "best available" technology by June 1, 1983.

Primary treatment normally refers to the processes using raw waste as the influent and includes skimming to remove floating oil, grease, and other matter, sometimes with air flotation; screening to separate coarse suspended solids, which then may be ground and added back for subsequent treatment; collection of grit in grit chambers; and removal of coarse and fine suspended solids by fine screens or sedimentation, possibly aided by chemical agglomerating agents. Grit may go to land fill, organic solids to digesters, and residual liquid to secondary treatment.

Secondary treatment, usually but not always, is preceded by primary treatment and is mainly for reducing the biochemical oxygen demand (BOD) in the waste water. The dissolved and suspended organic matter in the waste promotes the growth of microorganisms which utilize dissolved oxygen (DO) for assimilation and growth. Game fish, such as trout and bass, require a higher DO for optimum activity and survival than do scavengers, such as

carp. Facultative organisms continue to grow after all DO has been utilized and they as well as anaerobic organisms then utilize combined oxygen from sulfates and so create septic conditions with the liberation of sulfides.

Biochemical oxygen demand (BOD) varies with the number and kind of microorganisms present, the temperature, and the elapsed time. The standard test (BOD_5) is run at 20°C (68°F) for 5 days (120 hr) in the presence of suitable seed and suitable inorganic salts. For domestic wastes and for milk, and some other food wastes, the BOD_5 is about 68% of the ultimate BOD and for these wastes the ultimate BOD is usually about 99% complete in 20 days at 20°C. In order to avoid a 5-day wait, the BOD test has been run for shorter times and an attempt made to extrapolate to the 5-day results. Also, for estimating the BOD there are various chemical oxygen demand (COD) methods and use of the Warburg respirometer.

Since the BOD in raw waste is due both to soluble and to suspended organic matter in the liquid, physical removal of suspended matter for separate treatment will reduce the residual BOD in the liquid. In aerobic (oxidative) treatment, the living organisms metabolize dissolved and finely suspended organic matter and oxygen from the waste, convert the BOD into new protoplasm and energy, and discharge carbon dioxide and other products of oxidation. Autolysis of dead cells provides food for new cells. Of the total or ultimate BOD removed at 20°C about ⅝ is assimilated and either stored or used to form new cells and ⅜ is oxidized to carbon dioxide. The cell material is subsequently oxidized at the rate of about 1% per hr at 20°C. The rate of purification is temperature-dependent, higher at higher temperatures within the growth range of the organisms. Some organisms apparently can carry on purification at temperatures as low as 1°-4°C.

Various methods have been used to provide oxygen for aerobic growth. The liquid waste can be circulated or recirculated in a thin layer over a solid surface which is covered with a relatively thin layer of microbial growth exposed to the air. In the trickling filter, first developed about 1892, the waste is applied by spray or rotating distributor to the top of a 3- to 12-ft deep bed of coarse (1½ to 4 in.) rock, slag, or anthracite with large voids and a large surface area. The waste flows in a thin film over a surface film of living and dead organisms, collects in underdrains and may be recirculated over the filter before separation of suspended solids and discharge of the treated liquid. Many variations of this process have been developed: low rate, high rate, single-stage, two-stage, alternating two-stage, and with no recirculation or with recirculation ratios of up to 10 to 1 or more, and with no clarification of the raw and recirculated waste or with clarification of the raw and/or recirculation.

Ceramic contact surfaces are little used. However, light weight molded organic sheet contact media is being used increasingly with bed depths of 20–40 ft or more. With recirculation, these media permit much greater BOD and hydraulic loadings per cross-sectional area than do the rock media. A high BOD load combined with low hydraulic load may promote film growth sufficient to fill the voids in the filter, cause ponding, and even require replacement of the fouled media.

An intermittent sand filter may be used for polishing wastes after pretreatment to remove most of the BOD and suspended matter. The bed of uniform coarse sand, 2–3 ft deep, is layered over graded gravel and drain tile. In operation the bed is flooded quickly to a depth of about 6 in., the flow diverted to another bed, and the treated waste allowed to drain completely leaving the bed remain idle for possibly two days. The biological film on the sand grains traps suspended solids and organic matter, exposure to air causes oxidation, and the percolate is usually very low in BOD and suspended matter. Gradually the pores become filled and the upper few inches of sand are removed for separate disposal. After several such removals, fresh sand is added to bring the bed to the original depth.

When properly operated, spray irrigation of liquid waste on growing vegetation functions as aerobic treatment. Here the temporary heavy application saturates the soil surface, organic matter in the waste is taken up by the biologic film on vegetation and top layer of the soil, and most of the applied volume discharges to the air by evapotranspiration so that there is no runoff and little percolation to the ground water table. Oxidation in the biologic film occurs on exposure to air during the periods, often of 5–7 days, between repetitive liquid applications. Excessive loadings of BOD and suspended solids as well as high hydraulic loading result in plugging the voids in the soil, ponding, septic conditions, odors, and runoff.

In practice, due to failure to expand the area under spray irrigation as required by increased BOD and hydraulic loads and the decrease in percolation ability of the soil, some spray irrigation installations have experienced severe problems with odor and runoff and even killing of vegetation by lack of oxygen in the soil and by the toxic effect of hydrogen sulfide.

Spray irrigation has been used the year around, even in the Midwest. However, winter maintenance problems and the high BOD in the spring melt of the heavy ice layer have led to the winter use of ridge-and-furrow irrigation or of seepage trenches. Here the aim is to use several areas of percolation in sequence, one day at a time, so that the heavy liquid application completely seeps into the ground before the succeeding application is made. This system has been used the year around with vegetative growth on the ridges and adjoining the trenches, transpiring much of the applied water to the air. In winter the maximum rate of application is much lower. An ice layer bridges the furrow or trench and protects the liquid below from freezing. Here soil percolation determines the liquid removal. Organic growth in the liquid contact area may require removal along with some of the soil each year or so. With unfavorable soil conditions there has been contamination of the ground water with BOD.

Land disposal of waste waters has been used for at least 4 centuries and the methods used fall into three groups: infiltration, crop irrigation, or spray-runoff. In infiltration systems the loading rate may be high (up to 90 m per yr), runoff is nil, evaporation losses are insignificant, and up to 99% of the applied volume appears as recharge to the ground water. In crop irrigation, the loading rate is low (0.5–2.5 m per yr), runoff may or may not be controlled, much of the applied volume is lost through evapotranspiration (50–99%), and the residual goes to the ground water. The spray-runoff (grass filtration) method has been used continuously for 80 yr at Melbourne, Australia in the winter season with low operating costs and excellent removal of BOD and suspended solids.

While land management can be successful in disposing of liquid waste with no nuisance created at the application site, recent attention has been focused on problems of the accumulation in the soil of toxic chemicals and of ground water contamination, particularly with surfactants and nitrogen compounds (nitrates). New standards being developed for drinking water, if applied to ground water, will further complicate use of land for waste disposal.

Aeration methods using a biologic floc suspended in the liquid include conventional activated sludge (introduced in 1914) with a relatively short time of contact between the raw waste and the sludge (up to 6 hr) before separation of sludge and its recycle or partial removal to digesters or to separate disposal such as application to land. In variants of the activated sludge process, air under pressure may be supplied as bubbles from diffusers of various types in the lower part of the aeration tank or from agitation of the surface by mechanical means so as to assure intimate mixing of the waste, sludge, and air. For food plant wastes the aeration period may be extended for several days. The shape and size of the aeration compartment may vary greatly and include (a) relatively narrow channels with 10 ft or more water depth and volume equal to less than 6 hr raw flow; (b) oval oxidation ditches with about 5-ft water depth, 1-2 days waste volume, and aeration and mixing from brush rotors; (c) large shallow earthen basins channeled so that the waste is recirculated and aerated by a large air lift installation across the channel; (d) large shallow earthen basins with mechanical surface aerators and having 1-2 days retention and either having some sludge settling area in the basin or followed by a second aeration basin allowing for more complete solids separation; and (e) relatively deep earthen basins in which aeration maintains aerobic conditions in the upper portion with the lower portion allowed to go anaerobic and the aeration adequate to handle reduction products rising from the sludge on the bottom. Usually, agitation in the aeration basin keeps the sludge in suspension and suspended solids in the effluent require removal and treatment or disposal, as in a digester or direct application to land by a spray system or tank truck.

Shallow lagoons, 4-6 ft deep, have been used since 1948 in increasing numbers in the Missouri Basin for treatment of sewage from small towns. BOD loadings for satisfactory operation are less than a 20-lb BOD_5 per acre per day for a 12-month operation with ice cover in the winter and possibly up to 160 lb BOD_5 per acre per day in warm weather. Several installations for food plant wastes have given unsatisfactory results, apparently due to excessively high BOD loadings and inadequate retention times.

In the anaerobic digestion of practically all carbonaceous substances except hydrocarbons, there is molecular rearrangement with the formation of a humus-like solid and small quantities of hydrogen with 95% of the gas being methane and carbon dioxide. Anaerobic treatment appears practical only as pretreatment of concentrated wastes since the effluent typically is dark colored, foul smelling, and may contain 100 ppm BOD_5 or more.

At one time concentrated food plant wastes were discharged to large earthen lagoons for storage, particularly over winter, where sedimentation and some 30-50% reduction in BOD_5 occurred. In early spring at the time of ice melting and high water, the lagoon contents were discharged directly to the stream without causing serious depletion of dissolved oxygen, or in other cases were sprayed on land. Odors from such anaerobic digestion have been reported to carry a considerable distance in the air—many hundred feet to several miles—and so have led to nuisance complaints.

Anaerobic digestion of wastes in septic tanks with effluent disposal in drain fields has been used for small food plants but appears to have been abandoned except for treatment of domestic wastes.

The types of wastes originating from the food industries are many and varied, each often lending itself to specific methods of treatment. For more detailed information the proceedings of the various Industrial Waste Conferences held at Purdue University, Lafayette, Indiana, can be recommended. Also, the following aspects of waste disposal are reported in the Proceedings of the 2nd Annual National Symposium on Food Processing Wastes:[1] pollution abatement and by-product recovery in the shellfish industry, reduction or reclamation of salt from processing brines, disposal practices for liquid wastes in the canning and frozen fruits and vegetables industry, dry caustic versus conventional caustic peeling of fruit in relation to liquid waste handling, methods for processing potato starch plant effluents, continuous treatment of corn and pea processing waste water with fungi imperfecti, cannery treatment with the Rotating Biological Contactor and extended aeration, cannery waste treatment by lagoons and oxidation ditch in Australia, biological treatment of citrus processing water wastes, treatment of meat-packing waste using PVC trickling filters, dehydration of cattle rumen and whole blood, waste treatment in poultry processing, recovery of fatty materials from edible oil and fat refinery effluents, biological treatment of high BOD yeast wastes, membrane processing of cottage cheese whey, activated sludge and trickling filtration treatment of whey effluents, methane fermentation of whey, state of the art for

---

[1] Water Pollution Control Res. Ser. *12060-03/71* available from Superintendent of Documents, U.S. Government Printing Office, Washington, D.C., Stock No. 5501-0167.

treating dairy food plant wastes, anaerobic-aerobic ponds for treatment of beet sugar wastes, and oxidation ditch treatment of meat-packing wastes. These treatment procedures for waste waters originating from the processing of some important foods are illustrative of the procedures used for pollution abatement in the food industry.

For food plant waste disposal, consideration should be given to the following.

(1) Reduction in waste volume and strength as much as economically possible, resulting in increases of saleable products. This involves elimination of spillage, leaks, and drips, and handling scrap in a sanitary manner. Recycling of product and water should be practiced if allowable.

(2) Utilization of by-products, such as skim milk, buttermilk, whey, cheese trimmings, and corresponding by-products from other food industries in human food or animal feeds. In some cases, conversion by microbial fermentation to end-products of higher economic value, such as delactosed whey, alcohol, vinegar, etc., may be practical.

(3) Disposal of solid organic wastes directly as animal feed, or by fermenting, by composting, by land fill, by recovery, or by heat value as by incineration.

(4) Recycling of glass, metal, and paper if economically practical, otherwise incinerating or using it as land fill.

(5) Utilization of municipal sewers for liquids where practical. Usually domestic wastes from toilets and washrooms can be discharged directly to the sanitary sewer. Cooling waters should be segregated and may require temperature adjustment before discharge to the storm water sewer or to a water course. Plant floor wastes probably will require pretreatment to meet local requirements for pH, BOD, suspended solids, temperature, grease content, etc., before discharge to the sanitary sewer.

(6) Tertiary treatment before discharge to a water course if municipal sewers are not available. Local requirements may require lower BOD and suspended solids than given by usual secondary treatment and may require reduction in phosphates, etc.

(7) Utilization of processes and equipment developed for desalination which offer interesting possible applications for waste treatment by reverse osmosis-ultrafiltration, electrodialysis, multistage evaporation, vacuum freezing-vapor compression, or secondary refrigerant freezing. By employing a two-step ultrafiltration-reverse osmosis process, cheese whey can be processed into protein and lactose concentrates for food use.

H. GORDON HARDING

Reference

CANALE, R. P. 1971. Biological waste treatment. *In* Biotechnology and Bioengineering Symposium. Interscience Publishers, New York.

Cross-references: *Ultrafiltration and Reverse Osmosis; Waste Handling—Solids; Waste Treatment—Liquids.*

WASTE HANDLING—SOLIDS

The collection, processing, and disposal of solid wastes from the food industry generally follow procedures and practices employed in handling other types of solid wastes. The waste systems industry as a whole has become increasingly sophisticated during recent years through the development and use of more efficient collection equipment and processing and disposal practices and, as a consequence, is positioned to provide more environmentally acceptable and—in most cases—more economical services.

Industrial-commercial collection practices among the larger companies now employ on-site containers for waste storage, ranging in size from small "detachable" containers, which can be hoisted and emptied into the compaction body of a front-end loader truck by one man who never has to leave his driver's seat, to large 50-cu-yd "roll-off" containers which are placed empty at large-volume refuse generation points and removed when filled for transportation to disposal sites. All sizes of on-site containers can be either open or enclosed, depending upon the nature of the waste material deposited in them. Collections are made either on a predetermined schedule or on an "as needed" basis, depending upon the rate of refuse generation.

The annual rate of solid waste generation in the United States is currently estimated by industry and governmental sources to be on the order of four billion tons and is increasing. Of that total, animal wastes accounted for about 2 billion tons; mineral wastes for more than 1 billion tons; agricultural wastes for about 650 million tons; household, commercial, and other municipal waste for about 300 million tons; and industrial waste for nearly 130 million tons.

In addition to increases due to population growth, changes in packaging practices, including food packaging, have been suggested as significant contributing factors to the increasing volume of solid waste generation in this country. The growing use of plastics and other nonbiodegradable materials in food packaging have also been suggested as factors contributing to the complexity of present-day solid waste disposal. Convenience packaging, for example, has mushroomed in popularity in the food industry, adding such new, increased, and different ingredients to the waste stream as paper, metals, glass, and plastics. While some of these elements—such as paper and ferrous and aluminum metal cans—appear to hold economic potential for recovery and recycling, many others are not economically viable at this time and, being nonbiodegradable, pose disposal problems of significant concern.

In the area of solid waste disposal, properly designed and operated sanitary landfills provide the most environmentally-compatible and economical method available today. Spurred by federal environmental programs, many communities are closing antiquated, hazardous, open-burning dumps and turning to sanitary landfills.

Properly-sited, well-designed and -operated sanitary landfills involve extensive analyses of topography, climate, land use, accessibility, drainage, availability of cover material, proximity to homes and industrial/commercial facilities, ground and/or surface water contamination potential, zoning restrictions, and public acceptance for the site.

At a sanitary landfill, incoming refuse is spread, compacted, and covered as quickly as possible to prevent the development of odor problems, blowing paper, and the attraction of birds, rodents, vermin, flies, and other disease vectors. At the end of each working day, all refuse is completely covered, giving the landfill the appearance of a large construction site where site preparation is in progress. No open burning is permitted, and the landfills are properly vented to prevent the build-up or uncontrolled release of gases (some of which are flammable) generated in the decomposition of putrescible materials. Proper site engineering and preparation prevents the leaching of noxious, polluting materials into subsurface aquafiers.

Virtually all properly operated sanitary landfills maintain a special trench for animal carcasses and other highly-putrescible materials so they can be immediately covered as soon as they are deposited at the site.

Composting, a common form of disposal for organic wastes in other parts of the world, is an acceptable disposal method, but to date has proven economically unsuccessful in this country when attempted on any significant scale. Compost is produced as a result of biological decomposition under carefully-controlled conditions of aeration, temperature, and moisture. It is an inert, humus-like material suitable for use as a soil-conditioner or for disposal in a sanitary landfill.

In addition to its attractiveness as a means of volume reduction of solid wastes, composting also offers the advantages of resource recovery since the organic wastes can be reused for socially-beneficial purposes. Unfortunately, present production and distribution costs of refuse compost preclude its competition with commercial soil conditioners.

Courtesy of Browning-Ferris Ind.

FIG. W-1. COMPACTED WASTE IS COVERED WITH A LAYER OF EARTH IN A TYPICAL SANITARY LANDFILL

Some food industry wastes lend themselves to ensiling. This is particularly true of wastes from pea and corn canneries. The ensiled material is used in feeding livestock, particularly dairy and beef cattle. Solid wastes from the orange juice industry may be dried and used as cattle feed. Liquid waste may be fermented to yield a vinegar. Liquid waste from distilleries, sometimes called stillage, is also used "as is" or when dried in livestock feeding. Other food industries may also resort to specific waste handling characteristic to the industry.

Yet another disposal method available today is incineration in which refuse is burned at temperatures ranging from 1300° to 2000°F. This technique produces a volume reduction of 80% or more, reducing the amount of material which must be landfilled and, thus, prolonging the useful lives of landfill disposal sites. Offensive qualities of refuse are also eliminated, increasing the degree of community acceptance.

However, incineration, unless practiced properly, trades one problem for another: air pollution. Proper, environmentally-acceptable incineration, therefore, is a costly procedure and does not appear, at present, to be a generally attractive alternative to sanitary landfilling of wastes.

It should be noted, however, that projects are underway which will involve the marketing of the heat produced by large-volume incineration to help defray disposal costs. At this time, it would be premature to attempt to evaluate the success of these programs since most are only in design or early operation stage.

Akin to incineration as a disposal method for solid wastes is the technique of pyrolysis, or the breaking down of compounds into simpler compounds and elements through the application of heat in the absence of oxygen. Since the pyrolysis process is fully contained, no air pollution results and volume reductions of up to 90% may be achieved.

Pyrolysis requires higher capital investment than landfill or composting and is still in the research and development stages. It does, however, appear promising as an alternative to incineration.

One of the more attractive aspects of pyrolysis is its potential for resource recovery. According to a report from the U.S. Bureau of Mines, Department of Interior, which has been researching pyrolysis as a resource recovery method since 1929, 1 ton of municipal solid waste pyrolyzed at approximately 1600°F will produce nearly 18,000 cu ft of gas, 114 gal. of liquid, 25 lb of ammonium sulfate, 0.5 gal. of tar, and 154 lb of solid residue. Changes in pyrolysis temperature will vary the proportions of the products produced.

Gases produced include hydrogen, carbon monoxide, methane, and ethylene, with the mixture being a low-sulphur fuel possessing between 5 and 8 million BTU of available heat.

The resulting liquid is a highly-complex mixture of water and organic compounds whose only use presently appears to be possibly as a wood preservative or insecticide.

According to statistics compiled by Browning-Ferris Industries, Inc., the nation's largest waste systems company, and published in its 1972 Annual Report, among manufacturing industries food and kindred products rank third in total annual volume of solid wastes produced for disposal with 19,130,000,000 lb estimated by 1975. Only printing, publishing, and allied industries and lumber and wood products are expected to produce more.

The same BFI study disclosed that, of 14 food manufacturing companies sampled and which produced 11.5 billion pounds of known scrap and waste in 1965, only 0.08% of that volume was utilized in some manner and was not waste for disposal.

It may also be significant to note that of the contents of typical residential, commercial, and institutional refuse received at disposal facilities in 1969, food wastes accounted for 18.2% by weight (second only to paper) of all types of refuse received.

The general reference cited below gives useful information on solid waste disposal programs and concepts.

BEN GILLESPIE

Reference

ANON. 1971. Proc. 2nd Natl. Symp. Food Process. Wastes, Water Pollution Control Res. Ser. 12060-03/71. U.S. Government Printing Office, Washington, D.C. Stock order No. 5501-0167.

Cross-references: *Waste Disposal—Liquids; Waste Treatment—Liquids.*

WASTE TREATMENT—LIQUID

The large volumes of water used in various food processing operations (product washing, hydraulic conveying, equipment washing, product processing, cooling, etc.) present the industry with a disposal and pollution abatement problem when wastes cannot be discharged to the municipal treatment plant. The extent of these waste volumes can be appreciated from the data shown below:

Type of Plant	Volume of Waste
Beet sugar	5000 gal./ton of beets (no recycle)
Vegetable canning	1200-6000 gal./ton
Fruit canning	1500-10,000 gal./ton
Creamery	In excess of milk processed
Brewing	5-10 times volume of beer produced
Soft drinks	5-20,000 gal./1000 standard cases

Wastes from most food plants are characterized by a high BOD content and, therefore, usually require biological methods as employed for sewage treatment (e.g., activated sludge or some modification). Flocculents such as lime and ferric chloride or polyelectrolytes are generally used to condition the sludge from the primary and secondary clarifiers so it may be adequately dewatered by filtration or centrifugation for disposal as a relatively dry sludge. Otherwise, such sludges may be disposed of by hauling to a disposal area, lagooning, or pumping to a land fill.

Other types of wastes, especially those resulting from washing operations, usually require removal of suspended solids to either permit reuse or disposal through available means whether a stream, lagoon, or irrigation area. Such treatment usually requires only some type of flocculation either with lime and alum or a polyelectrolyte or coagulant aids such as sodium aluminate. Some typical examples are given below.

Beet Sugar Factory (Flume Water)

This is primarily the water used for sluicing, fluming and washing the beets but may also include other miscellaneous plant waste streams (e.g., excess condensate, cooling water, spills, etc.). The amount of solids carried by the flume water depends upon the cleanliness of the beets. With mechanical harvesting, the amount of soil and trash fluctuates considerably, especially from dry to wet soil conditions. Some sugar is also leached from the beets along with organic matter, especially from frozen or deteriorated beets.

Recycling the flume water requires removal of solids. Coarse material such as beet tops, trash, and other matter can be removed by screening (e.g., a curved screen with 3-mm openings such as the DSM®[2]). Following screening, milk of lime is added to flocculate the soil and suspended solids so the flume water can be readily clarified in a Dorr type thickener, the underflow being

---

[2] Registered trademark Dorr-Oliver Inc.

pumped to a mud pond or otherwise disposed of. With liming to a pH of 10 or above, 90% removal of the settleable solids is possible as long as the water temperature does not exceed about 20°C (Beck and Weckel 1971). Settling ponds may also be employed but require periodic excavation of the mud. In place of lime, polyelectrolyte flocculents may also be used. The substantially increased settling rates indicate that smaller thickeners may be feasible.

Cane Washing

To lessen the mud load on the clarifiers and filters in the juice clarification process, a number of mills have installed cane washing facilities ahead of the crushing, cutting, and shredding operations. Such practice is widely in use when mechanical harvesting is practiced (as in Hawaii) due to the greater volume of field soil accompanying the cane. In some mills, spent water is simply pumped through a battery of cyclones to remove heavy solids while the overflow along with other mill wastes is pumped to the fields for irrigation. However, this practice creates problems in the field due to the clogging of ditches and the presence of nutrients that hinders harvesting.

In order to avoid this problem and reuse the cane wash water, a continuous solids removal process is necessary. This can be accomplished by flocculating with lime at dosages on the order of 150 ppm to a pH around 10. Mud sedimentation rates are substantially increased so that a moderate size clarifier (or a settling pond) can provide an adequately clarified wash water for reuse or diversion to the fields for irrigation purposes (Schantz and Kemmer undated).

Fruits and Vegetables (Washing)

Washing of these raw products prior to processing is commonplace in the industry. Where disposal presents a pollution problem, reuse of these wash waters is mandatory in many instances. Flocculation of the suspended solids is probably best accomplished with polyelectrolyte polymers. Dosages of 5-10 ppm are usually recommended.

Brewery Wastes

The high volume of brewery wastes largely arise from the numerous washing operations. Organic matter content is high (the waste from a 2500 barrel per day brewery equivalent in BOD loading to a domestic population of 40,000). While many breweries discharge their wastes to the municipal sewage treatment plant, others must provide an adequate biological treating process. In the primary treatment of these wastes where spent grains, hops, and yeast are present, sedimentation times must not be excessive as putrefaction can occur. To hasten sedimentation, chemical flocculents may be employed, either lime and alum or polyelectrolytes along with coagulant aids where applicable (Mulligan 1967).

In the lautering process, dewatering of the spent grain in a screw press produces a press filtrate with considerable protein material (2–3%). Since it exhibits a marked flocculating tendency, the protein solids can readily be settled and removed by filtration as a valuable by-product, thus reducing the waste load to the municipal plant or waste treating facility.

Meat Packing Waste

These wastes are high in organic matter content and do not lend themselves readily to the conventional activated sludge type of biological treatment. Experience has shown that anaerobic organisms are especially suited for the destruction of the organic matter. Field trials with polyelectrolyte flocculents for the purpose of increasing settling rates and sludge concentration in sedimentation units and subsequently in the digesters has not proved to be an economical solution compared to process modifications. However, it has been demonstrated (Schaffer 1964) that polyelectrolytes can be advantageous for overload or plant upset conditions by maintaining the mixed liquor suspended solids at a high enough level. With a decreasing solids level, final effluent BOD removal is seriously affected. The optimum polymer dosage appears to be in the 10–15 ppm range.

Fish Wastes

Methods for handling fish wastes have been reported by Sonderquist (1970). Salmon wastes are first screened to remove at least $1/2$ of the solids. Fats and grease can then be removed by sedimentation or flotation after chemical precipitation with clay, lime, and ferric chloride. The most promising coagulant was said to be alum.

Potato Waste

Potato processing water contains suspended solids (500 to 3000 ppm or more) and BOD levels on the order of 1500–2000 ppm. Activated sludge treatment of this waste has generally not been too successful due to difficulties in maintaining optimum conditions for adequate BOD reduction. Sludge bulking usually develops followed by deterioration in performance. One solution (Allen 1971) has been to combine a trickling filter with activated sludge to provide for handling shock loads and more rapid bacterial growth. In another case (ANON. 1970) waste silt water was combined with the light sludge from the secondary clarifier of the activated sludge system and further settled in a clarifier-thickener followed by dewatering on a vacuum filter. Sludge bulking was also a problem but attributed to aeration failures (higher DO levels required). It was found that the performance of the clarifier-thickener could be materially improved by employing an anionic polyelectrolyte flocculent. Overall COD and BOD removal efficiencies of 80% were obtained and TSS removed exceeded 90% (with silt water only through the clarifier-thickener).

Bakery Waste

Clean-up waste water contains suspended solids, fats, and other solubles. When the pH is high, sulfuric acid may be added for pH reduction followed by flocculation with lime, alum, and special agents for precipitating fats and other solubles. Filtration on rotary drum vacuum precoat unit produces a filtrate with substantially lower solubles for discharge to waste. With a 4-in. thick precoat, operating cycles up to 6 days are sometimes obtained before re-precoating is required.

H. V. MILES

References

ALLEN, T. R. 1971. Water re-use in the food processing industry. Proc. Engineering Found. Res. Conf., Pacific Grove, Calif., Febr. 21–26.

ANON. 1970. Cleaning up waste water. Probes treatment of potato wastes. Proc. Natl. Symp. Food Process. Wastes, Portland, Oregon, Apr. 6–8 appearing in Food Eng. July, 42, No. 2, 72.

BECK, E. W., JR., and WECKEL, W. O. 1971. Sugar factory wastewater treatment. Proc. Engineering Found. Res. Conf., Pacific Grove, Calif., Febr. 21–26.

HART, S. A., and McGAUHEY, P. H. 1964. The management of wastes. Food Technol. 30, 30–36.

MULLIGAN, T. J. 1967. Characteristics and treatment of brewery waste. Brewers Dig. Aug. 82–88.

OPILA, R. L., and NEELUND, H. E. 1969. Pollution control in the food industries. Vol. 2 Proc. Am. Inst. Chem. Engrs. Workshop, Water Committee, Houston, Apr. 24–25.

PORGES, R., and STRUZESKI, E. J., JR. 1961. Wastes from the soft drink bottling industry. J. Water Pollution Control Federation 33, No. 2, 167–175.

SCHAFFER, R. B. 1964. Polyelectrolytes in industrial waste treatment. Water Sewage Works Ref. R-300-305.

SCHANTZ, J. C., and KEMMER, F. N. Undated. Some aspects of water pollution by the Hawaiian sugar industry. Nalco Chemical Co. Rept.

SONDERQUIST, M. R. 1970. Advanced ways to treat fish wastes. Proc. Natl. Symp. Food Process. Wastes, Portland, Oregon, Apr. 6-8 appearing in Food Eng. July, 70.

WATER ACTIVITY IN FOODSTUFFS

Water is an all-present agent in our foodstuffs; in rough food materials it is the constituent with the highest concentration.

The presence of water in foodstuffs and its concentration determine to a high degree the palatability and digestability, and the physical structure and technical handling ability of the food material. Most important, however, practically all deteriorative processes which take place in foodstuffs are influenced in one way or the other by the concentration and mobility of the water in foodstuff. As a rough orientation, it can be said that, independent of the composition of food materials at high water concentrations, spoilage is caused by the growth and development of bacteria and molds on the foods and by enzymatic or nonenzymatic reactions; at low water concentrations quality losses are caused mainly by autoxidative reactions and physical deterioration.

The intensity and rate of the various deteriorative processes are different at different water concentrations in general; however, food material is more stable at low water concentrations than at high concentrations. The potential of the water to take part in deteriorative processes in a food product is characterized by the activity of the water in the product, which is, according to the generalized Raoult's law, the relationship between the water vapor pressure of the product at a temperature t_p and the saturation pressure of water at the same temperature

$$a = (p_{\text{product}}/p_0)$$

where

$$t = \text{constant}$$

The water activity of any product depends on the chemical composition of the product, the state of aggregation of its constituents, the water content, and the temperature of the product. A plot of the water content of a product versus its water activity at a given temperature is called a sorption isotherm. Through the sorption isotherm the thermodynamic state of the water in a food product is sufficiently characterized; materials which bind relatively high amounts of water at low activity values are characterized as highly hygroscopic (Heiss 1968).

The Sorption Isotherm

Description, Theory and Measurement.—The sorption isotherms of most food products are usually of sigmoid shape whereas different types of the shape are possible. Since the water sorption behavior of food products is determined by the chemical composition and the physicochemical state of the constituents, the sorption isotherms of the various food products differ in their shape considerably. Even similar products may show deviations in the shape of their sorption isotherm when they are of different origin (Fig. W-2).

Starchy products including grains absorb more water at low activities than protein-rich materials like meat.

Sugars, in general, represent a group of materials which exhibit two types of sorption behavior. In the amorphous state they are rather hygroscopic, whereas in the crystalline state they are little hygroscopic. Problems can be caused by a change from the amorphous state to the crystalline, because water is released during this changeover. If the sugar is part of a mixture, the other materials present in the mixture pick up the water and are thereby usually subject to chemical and physical changes (Reidel 1965).

The effect of a thermal or any other (pre)treatment of a product on its sorption behavior and thereby on the shape of its sorption isotherm can be more pronounced than the addition of a con-

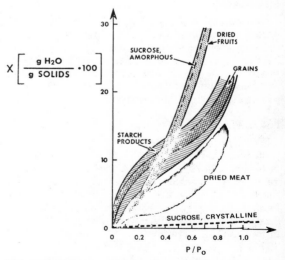

FIG. W-2. TYPICAL SORPTION ISOTHERMS FOR DEHYDRATED FOODS

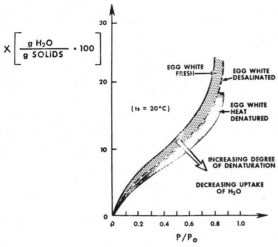

FIG. W-3. ADSORPTION ISOTHERMS FOR EGG WHITE

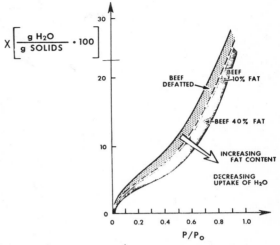

FIG. W-4. ADSORPTION ISOTHERM FOR BEEF

stituent of lower or higher water binding ability. In general, the water binding of a product is reduced by a pretreatment since the number of active sites which are capable of binding water are reduced usually by denaturative processes like heating, desalting, pH changes, etc. (Fig. W-3). A reduction of the water binding capability of foodstuffs is also obtained by coating hygroscopic materials using materials that are only slightly hygroscopic such as fat (Fig. W-4) (Labuza and Rutman 1967; Makower and Dye 1956).

Theory of Water Sorption

The phenomena of water sorption by foodstuffs have attracted the interest of numerous research workers since until the present time a consistent theory on this particular matter is still lacking. The reason for the failure of most of the theoretical models is that foodstuffs are products and materials which have rather complicated chemical compositions and also very complex physical structures.

The sorption of water by foodstuffs can be classified into three main categories (Adamson 1963; Freundlich 1926): (a) sorption without structural changes of the sorbens, e.g., surface sorption in the case of crystalline sugar; (b) sorption accompanied by structural changes of the sorbens, e.g., milk, egg white; (c) sorption under formation of a solution, e.g., sugar solutions.

Theoretical approaches made on the basis of this and similar classifications include:

1. The Langmuir and BET (S. Brunauer, P. H. Emmet, and E. Teller) equations which were de-

rived from kinetic considerations (Brunauer et al. 1938; Sharp 1962).

2. The theory by Harkins and Jura and others which is based on considerations about the force field caused by the surface of a solid material.

3. The theory of capillary condensation which takes into account the porous structure of food materials (Henderson 1952).

4. Theoretical considerations based on physical laws concerning vapor pressures in solutions.

5. Theoretical considerations taking into account the heterogeneous structure of food products, like the sorption isotherm equation by Riedel (Fig. W-5).

The most popular approach to the problem of water sorption by foodstuffs is the BET approach. Despite the fact that most of the assumptions on which the theory is based are not acceptable for food material, a discussion seems valuable for the understanding of some of the problems involved.

The BET theory was derived from observations of the adsorption of nonpolar gases at the surface of catalytic agents; the basic assumptions are:

(A) Sorption occurs only at specific sites at the product surface.

(B) The heat of sorption for the first layer (called monolayer) is constant and equal to the heat of vaporization plus the heat of site interactions.

(C) The heat of sorption for the second and any other layer above the first layer is equal to the heat of vaporization.

The general equation for the BET isotherm can be derived from kinetic, thermodynamic, and sta-

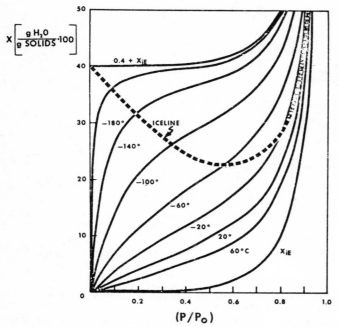

$$X\left[\frac{g\ H_2O}{g\ SOLIDS}\cdot 100\right]$$

$$X = X_{iA} + X_{iE} = \frac{\varepsilon\ (P/P_0)}{K + P/P_0} + \frac{\lambda\ (P/P_0)^3}{1 - P/P_0}$$

X_{iA} = INTRA MOLECULAR BOUND WATER
X_{iE} = INTER MOLECULAR BOUND WATER

ε = FRACT. OF AMOUNT OF
　　WATER WHICH CAN BE BOUND
　　INTRA MOLECULARLY

K = EQUILIBRIUM CONSTANT

λ = EMPIR. COEFFICIENT

FIG. W-5. THEORETICAL SORPTION ISOTHERM FOR BEEF

tistical mechanics considerations:

$$\frac{a}{(1-a)\,v} = \frac{1}{v_m\,C} + \left[\frac{(C-1)}{V_m\,C}\right] a$$

where

v = volume adsorbed per gram solid
v_m = volume adsorbed by first layer per gram solid
a = activity $\dfrac{p}{p_s}$ product
$C = k \exp (Q_s/RT)$
k = coefficient $\simeq 1$
Q_s = heat of adsorption on homogenous sites
R = gas constant
T = absolute temperature

The equation includes only the first layer adsorption which is considered the isotherm of Langmuir. A plot of the left hand term of the equations versus a results in a straight line.

If the monolayer coverage value for water is calculated from the slope and intercept of experimentally obtained sorption isotherms, the monolayer value for water as a polar gas is usually more than 100 times larger than for nitrogen or other nonpolar gases. The reason for this observation is that foodstuffs are very likely to be solutions of varying degrees with receptive sites for the water not only at the surface but also inside the material.

As it is clear from the classification of sorption processes in foods, as a further difference to the BET theory the energy levels of the available sites vary considerably in a given product. In general, we have to deal with molecular groups like ionic groups with highest affinity to water, with non-ionized hydrogen binding sites as a type of binding energy with medium affinity, and in the range of high activity values with binding energies caused by capillary forces and the dissolution of soluble constituents (Sharp 1962; Spieb et al. 1969).

According to Nemitz and other authors, in the case of the water sorption by dry proteins, in a first step, the polar amino acid groups are saturated with water molecules. In a second step, water molecules are bound by hydrogen bindings of the amide and carbonyl groups of polypeptide chains, in this way building up the structural matrix and exposing other interior sites with a lower energy level to additional adsorption processes of different character.

The gradual saturation of energy sites at different energy levels is also illustrated if the heat of adsorption or desorption, respectively, is calculated from sorption data obtained at different temperatures according to the Clausius-Clapeyron relationship. The actual amount of heat of sorption decreases gradually with increasing water content, that means with growing activity values; in general,

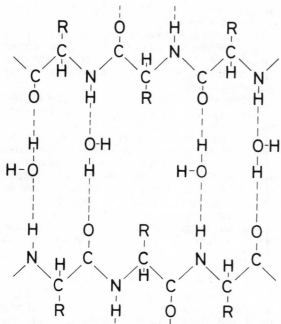

FIG. W-6. SCHEME OF THE BINDING OF WATER BE-
TWEEN POLYPEPTIDE CHAINS

it equals the heat of vaporization at water contents of approximately 25–35% [(kg H_2O/kg solids) · 100]. If the heat of sorption is calculated on the basis of the BET equation it has a constant value at water contents less than the hypothetical mono-layer value and it equals the heat of sorption at water contents higher than this value (Fig. W-7). The amount of heat calculated on the basis of the BET equation is also smaller than the actual amount (Kuprianoff 1958; Nemitz 1961).

Hysteresis

If the adsorption and desorption data are plotted together, the adsorption curve shows, with the exception of very low and very high activities values, always lower values for the water content than the desorption shows in presence of the same water activities. This hysteresis phenomenon is another expression of the complicated binding situation of the water in the various food materials. As explanation for the hysteresis effect, several types of theories have been proposed:

(1) For porous material, the hysteresis can be explained by a change in the contact angle between adsorption and desorption during capillary conden-sation in pores or evaporation out of pores, respec-

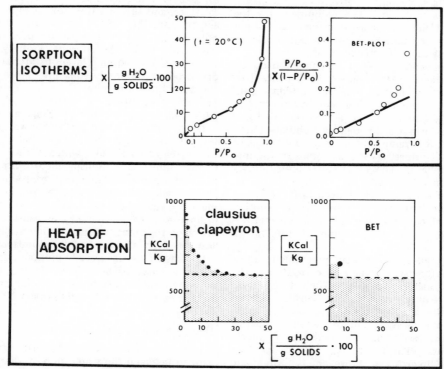

FIG. W-7. SORPTION OF WATER BY EGG WHITE

tively. The basis for these theories is the Kelvin equation concerning the vapor pressure depression in pores.

(2) In the case of nonporous materials, the hysteresis can be explained by energy consuming processes in the interior of a product like swelling, relaxation processes, etc.

(3) For porous and nonporous materials, further theories have been offered to explain hysteresis, like the theory of phase changes (Heiss 1968).

Determination of Sorption Isotherms

The precise determination of the relationship between water activity of a foodstuff and its equilibrium moisture content is a rather simple procedure which requires, however, experience and experimental skill.

The sorption behavior of a foodstuff is usually analyzed by gravimetrical or manometrical methods. Both methods can be carried through batchwise or as a continuous process; furthermore, in both methods the equilibrium weight adjustment can be done by means of static or dynamic procedures.

The gravimetrical method is the most frequently used method for measuring the sorption properties of foodstuffs since only relatively easily available equipment is required. The equipment for the gravimetrical method mainly consists of a gas-tight container for setting a constant RH and a balance for measuring the weight changes of the sample.

The gravimetrical method is characterized by exposure of a sample of known water content to environments of known relative humidity until equilibrium is reached. The equilibrium weight gain or weight loss, respectively, is recorded and assigned to the respective relative humidity (RH). The desired RH values are obtained by means of saturated salt brines, H_2SO_4 solutions or thermostatic water bath. The water vapor pressure over those agents is tabulated in dependence of the constituents (salt brines), concentration (H_2SO_4 solution) and temperature (water bath). Another possibility of adjusting the RH in atmospheres is the mixing of dry and humid air of known concentrations.

Practically all types of high precision balances are possible for use. In the case of routine work, analytical balances provide sufficient accuracy. Since such equipment is usually sensitive against high RH, the samples to be weighed have to be removed from the hygrostat and weighed in a low RH; for this reason the procedure may implicate certain errors. The use of one balance together with many hygrostats, however, is faster and cheaper than the installation of highly sensitive

balances in single hygrostats like a quartz spring or an electric balance.

The manometric methods are, in general, applied to measure the water activity of a given sample; for instance, to evaluate the water content of a material, making use of the sorption isotherm, for purposes of quality control.

In most cases, the manometric methods are too cumbersome for the determination of complete sorption isotherms.

The vapor pressure over a sample can be measured either directly by measuring the water vapor pressure manometrically after removing the noncondensible gases like nitrogen and oxygen by exposing the sample to a vacuum system, or it can be measured indirectly by alterations occurring in materials exposed to the sample, for instance, the electrical resistance of moisture-sensitive electrical conductors (Gál 1967; Van Arsdel *et al.* 1973).

Food Deterioration and Water Activity

It has been outlined that water activity has a prominent influence on the deterioration of products and thereby on the shelf-life. Since the reduction of the water activity of a food product by dehydration not only improves its capability for storage but may also affect its physicochemical state, and through this, for example, its palatability and the cost load of the dehydration process, the water activity of products to be stored has to be chosen very carefully. Factors influencing the required level of water activity of a dry product before it goes into storage are the turnover time; the rate of quality deterioration; and the cost situation of the dehydration and packaging process including packaging material.

The water activities values which will result from these considerations are, in general, higher than the water activity value which allows the longest storage time. The limiting factor, in any case, is the consumer acceptance of the product which is reached when the quality of the product does not meet consumers' expectations.

Since a deterioration may be caused by various types of reactions, a general relationship between water activity and kind of deterioration cannot be established. As was already pointed out, ranges of water activity can be defined where certain types of deteriorative reactions are dominant (Table W-1) (Lea 1958; Salwin and Slawson 1959).

Deterioration by Microorganisms

The range where microorganisms grow is expanded between the water activity values of 1 and 0.65 whereas at water activity values of 0.75 and

TABLE W-1

RANGE OF WATER ACTIVITIES AND THEIR DETERIORATIVE REACTIONS

Range of Water Activity	Type of Dominant Deteriorative Reaction	Type of Possible Deteriorative Reaction
1–0.8 0.91 0.88 0.8	Microorganism growth Bacteria Yeasts Molds	Enzymatic reactions
0.8–0.65 0.75 0.7 0.65	Enzymatic reactions (fat decomposition and browning reactions)	Nonenzymatic browning Microorganism growth, halophylic bacteria Osmophylic yeast Xerophylic molds
0.65–0.3	Nonenzymatic browning reactions (Maillard reaction)	Enzymatic reactions, autoxidation
0.3–0.0	Autoxidation, physical changes	Nonenzymatic browning reactions, enzymatic reactions

0.65 only very specialized types of microorganisms like osmophilic yeast can grow.

In the case of deterioration by microorganisms, the time factor is of rather high importance since, after an initiation time of 3–4 days, a microorganism growth can be observed on food products with a high water activity. At water activities at a level of $a = 0.8$ it takes usually 4–5 weeks until the product is spoiled by microorganisms and in the area of $a = 0.7$ and lower the time in question is in the magnitude of months (Christian 1963; Mossel and Ingram 1955).

Chemical Deteriorative Reactions

Enzymatic Reactions.—Enzymatic reactions occur practically at any water activity values; they are, however, prominent at water activity values above 0.3. The enzymes which cause the enzymatic reactions are either intrinsic enzymes of the product or foreign enzymes from microorganisms, for example. The most important enzymatic reactions are the fat decomposition through the action of lipases, phospholipases and lipoxidases in fat-containing materials; and the enzymatic browning reactions in fruits and vegetables through peroxidases and phenoloxidases.

The action of enzymes during storage can be prevented or diminished by a blanching process to which the material is exposed in general before the dehydration process (Acker 1962; Purr 1970).

Nonenzymatic Reactions.—The nonenzymatic browning reactions which are also called Maillard reactions occur also practically at any water activity values; they have, however, a pronounced maximum at medium water activity values, 0.4 $\leqslant a \leqslant 0.6$. Characteristic for the reaction is a brown discoloration of the product which usually is connected with the occurrance of a bitter off-flavor. The changes are due to the reaction of carbohydrates with the amino groups of amino acids and proteins. Foods sensitive to the Maillard reaction should be kept at water activity levels lower than the described dangerous range (Karel and Nickerson 1964).

Autoxidation.—At low water activity values the most important type of deterioration is the autoxidation of lipids which arises from free radical reactions between oxygen and unsaturated lipids. Since the human senses are very sensitive against the rancid products of the autoxidative reactions, even traces of oxidized fats may lead to a rejection of a product. The protection of a fat-containing dry material against the attack of oxygen is therefore in many cases more important than the protection against water.

The effects of the autoxidation decrease steadily with increasing water content, so that a protecting effect of the water can be assumed. The hypothesis that the autoxidation will disappear in case a monolayer of water on the product is formed is not correct, however. A detailed explanation how the water protection works is yet not available. It seems, however, that the protective effect is linked with a stabilization of constituents which tend to form free radicals.

Physical and Physicochemical Deterioration

If protein- and starch-containing materials are dried to extremely low water activity values an irreversible denaturation of those materials will occur. The denaturation is caused by an interaction of reactive sites and results in changes of the texture mainly in protein-rich foods (Heiss 1968).

W. E. L. SPIESS

References

ACKER, L. 1962. Enzymic reactions in foods of low moisture content. Advan. Food Res. 11, 263–330.

ADAMSON, A. W. 1963. Physical Chemistry of Surfaces. Interscience Publishers, New York.

BRUNAUER, S., EMMETT, Ph., and TELLER, E. 1938. The adsorption of gases in multimolecular layers. J. Am. Chem Soc. 60, 309–319.

CHRISTIAN, J. H. B. 1963. Water activity and the growth of microorganisms. In Recent Advances in Food Science, Vol. 3. J. M. Leitch and D. N. Rhodes (Editors). Butterworths, London, England.

FREUNDLICH, H. 1926. Colloid and Capillary Chemistry. Methuen & Co., London, England.

GAL, S. 1967. Methodology of Water-Vapor Sorption Determinations. Springer-Verlag, Berlin and Heidelberg, Germany; New York. (German)

HEISS, R. 1968. Shelf-life and Water Sorption Properties of Low Moisture Products. Springer-Verlag, Berlin and Heidelberg, Germany; New York. (German)

HENDERSON, S. M. 1952. A basic conception of equilibrium moisture. Agr. Eng. 33, 24.

KAREL, M., and NICKERSON, J. R. R. 1964. Effects of relative humidity, air, and vacuum on browning of dehydrated orange juice. Food Technol. 18, 104.

KUPRIANOFF, J. 1958. "Bound water" in foods. In Fundamental Aspects of the Dehydration of Foodstuffs. Soc. Chem. Ind. (London).

LABUZA, T. P., and RUTMAN, M. 1967. The effect of surface active agents on sorption isotherms of model systems. Proc. 17th Ann. Can. Chem. Engrs. Conf., Oct. 18.

LEA, C. H. 1958. Chemical changes in the preparation and storage of dehydrated foods. In Fundamental Aspects of the Dehydration of Foodstuffs. Soc. Chem. Ind. (London).

MAKOWER, B., and DYE, W. 1956. Equilibrium moisture content and crystallization of amorphous sucrose and glucose. J. Agr. Food Chem. 4, 72.

MOSSEL, A. A., and INGRAM, H. 1955. The physiology of the microbial spoilage of foods. J. Appl. Bacteriol. 18, 232.

NEMITZ, G. 1961. Water-binding capability of proteins and their behavior during drying. Diss. Univ. Karlsruhe, Germany. (German)

PURR, A. 1970. Description of the chemical changes in low-moisture foods. II Experiments with lipoxygenase and other mixed enzymes and their effect on autoxidative fat deterioration in dry products in respect to their equilibrium moisture content. Fette, Seifen, Anstrichmittel 27, No. 8, 725. (German)

REIDEL, L. 1965. Wasser Handbuch der Lebensmittelchemie, Vol. 1. Springer-Verlag, Berlin and Heidelberg, Germany.

SALWIN, H., and SLAWSON, V. 1959. Moisture transfer in combinations of dehydrated foods. Food Technol. 13, 715.

SHARP, J. G. 1962. Non-enzymatic browning deterioration in dehydrated meat. In Recent Advances in Food Science, Vol. 2. Butterworths, London, England.

SPIEB, W. E. L., SOLE, C. P., and PRITZWALD-STEGMANN, B. F. 1969. Water-vapor sorption isotherms and their correlation to the specific surface of certain important food stuff. Deutsche Lebensm.-Rundschau 65, 115–120. (German)

VAN ARSDEL, W. B., COPLEY, M. J., and MORGAN, A. I., JR. 1973. Food Dehydration, 2nd Edition, Vol. 1, Drying Methods and Phenomena. Avi Publishing Co., Westport, Conn.

WATER TREATMENT—FOOD PLANTS

The water for a food plant should preferably be "soft," cold and free from impurities. Such a supply is seldom available in sufficient quantity and the best available water usually requires treatment to meet plant requirements.

Water dissolves nearly all matter to a certain extent and tends to collect foreign matter from the time of formation as precipitation and continuing during run-off and seepage into the ground. Gases from the air and carbon dioxide from decomposing vegetation aid in dissolving minerals, particularly limestone to form calcium bicarbonate which is a major source of water hardness.

The total dissolved solids in natural waters varies greatly, from about 20 ppm in mountain streams over granite to more than 1000 ppm in deep well waters in a limestone region and in mineral springs. Ground water, which reaches the surface from wells and springs, may increase the hardness in surface waters. Surface waters collect particulate matter from run-off and pollution from sewers of municipalities and industry.

If available, the best water supply for the food industry is usually the municipal supply which should be safe and potable. If its source is a large lake, the mineral content may be relatively low and constant and, when filtered, require less treatment than any well water. If the city supply is a stream or small body of water, the mineral content may vary widely with the seasons, and if from wells the mineral content may be very high.

Water conservation is important due to the impending shortage of water supply, the increasing cost of water, the cost of liquid waste water disposal. Often, water first used for "once-through" cooling can then be used for boiler feed or cleaning. Cooling water can be recycled through spray towers or cooling ponds. Final rinse water in cleaning can be picked up and used as a second rinse, then as first rinse, and finally as make-up for recirculated reused cleaning solutions.

The results of a complete analysis of the water supplies to a food plant should be used in planning water treatment for boiler feed, heating, cooling, cleaning, and other uses. Complete analysis for public water supplies usually are available from local or state agencies. Boiler insurance companies usually make water analyses and reliable recommendations for boiler water treatment for their insured clients. The U.S. Geological Survey has bulletins giving analyses of water supplies for hundreds of cities and areas in the United States.

Of prime importance to the food plant are the sanitary quality and the taste, odor, and color of the water supply. Impurities in the water which affect its use include suspended matter, total dissolved solids, alkalinity and pH, sulfides, chlorides, silica, dissolved gases, hardness, iron, and manganese.

Water for cleaning purposes should meet local, state, and federal standards for potable water used in the manufacture and processing of food products. This potable water must be free from pollution at the source and protected from subsequent pollution. Properly treated municipal supplies are usually satisfactory, as are most deep well supplies. Shallow well and surface supplies often are contaminated. If permitted by supervising health authorities, an unsafe water may be made safe by suitable changes in the collecting and distribution system together with proper treatment.

Surface waters may have objectionable tastes, odors and/or color from rotting vegetation, algae growths, or wastes entering the supply. Often, gaseous impurities can be removed by aeration in a spray pond or tower. Overtreatment with chlorine to remove odor may leave excess chlorine and chlorophenols which can be removed with carbon filtration. Activated carbon filters can be used to remove fixed odors and colors.

Suspended matter (such as clay, silt, and organic matter in surface waters), or fine sand in well water, or insoluble ferric iron oxide or insoluble manganese dioxide (formed by chlorination of waters containing soluble ferrous iron or manganous manganese) may be present in objection-

able amounts and are usually removed with gravity- or pressure-type sand and gravel filters which are backwashed as required, usually daily. Flow rates are controlled, usually at 2–3 gal. per min per sq ft of filter area for maximum operation and at about 12 gal. per min per sq ft for long enough in backwashing to remove all collected sediment.

Periodic examination of the filter bed may show fouling. If backwashing at a higher rate does not correct the problem, replace the sand bed. The filter may be sterilized by filling with a 50 ppm available chlorine solution and holding for 24 hr.

The water prior to filtration may be treated with flocculating agents which at very low concentrations assist in agglomeration and so give a better effluent from the filter. For potable waters the maximum allowable polymer content is usually 1 ppm. (See Flocculation in Section F.)

Water containing considerable suspended matter is usually satisfactory for cooling or for boiler feed.

High dissolved solids is not a problem in water used for cleaning purposes unless it results in water spots or is associated with high hardness. For cooling purposes, water with high dissolved solids associated with excessive bicarbonate hardness may result in scale deposits; and water with low solids associated with high free carbon dioxide tends to be corrosive. For boiler feed water, a low solids content is desirable since it means less blowdown.

For some food plant uses it will be desirable to reduce the pH and alkalinity of the water. Wash water for cottage cheese preferably should be in the range of pH 6.0–6.5. The addition of food grade lactic or phosphoric acid can be metered into an alkaline supply. Alkalinity and pH have little effect on water used for cleaning purposes unless they lead to corrosion or scale formation. A high calcium and magnesium content together with high bicarbonate alkalinity in a water indicate a tendency to form scale by loss of carbon dioxide through aeration, heating, or addition of alkaline salts. The addition of food grade acid to rinse water can control scale formation.

In boiler waters, low alkalinities and low free carbon dioxide are desirable. Most of the free carbon dioxide and part of that from the bicarbonate may be removed in an open deaerating preheater with greater carbon dioxide removals at high preheating temperatures.

Sulfide compounds in water are undesirable because of odor, color, flavor, and tendency to discolor and corrode metals. Such a water should be avoided if possible. Sufides may be greatly reduced by acidification followed by aeration, preferably with heating, cooling, and ion exchange. This procedure is complicated and expensive.

High chlorides (over 40 ppm) have no effect in

alkaline cleaning solutions; however, if the pH is below 7, the water may be corrosive. High chlorides in boiler drum water, especially in combination with magnesium, at pH less than 10.5, are often very corrosive. Here the treatment is (1) to raise the pH with caustic to precipitate magnesium hydroxide, and (2) to reduce dissolved oxygen by proper pretreatment or by reducing chemicals such as sodium sulfite added to the drum water. Chlorides can be removed by deionization which is also complicated and expensive.

Silica does not matter in waters used for cooling or cleaning. However, in boiler waters where the ratio of silica to total dissolved solids is relatively high, the concentration in the boiler due to evaporation, will make it necessary to increase the blowdown or to remove silica from the boiler make-up water. Silica can be removed (1) by hot process precipitation in which calcium, magnesium, and silica are precipitated at high alkalinity, (2) by demineralization, or (3) by salt-splitting in which sodium-cycle cation exchanger effluent is passed through a caustic regenerated anion exchanger. Salt-splitting gives a caustic soda solution with extremely low chloride, sulfate, and silica, and is applicable to low solids waters where extremely low silica is needed but has no application in low pressure boilers.

Dissolved gases, such as oxygen, carbon dioxide, hydrogen sulfide, and sulfur dioxide can cause a water to be corrosive, particularly in recirculated cooling water. In some cases, "threshold" treatment and pH adjustment may be adequate. Treatments which deposit on the metal surface of the cooling system a protective film from sodium silicate (water glass), organic amines, etc., or heavier, egg-shell films of calcium carbonate may control corrosion. Dissolved gases may cause severe corrosion in hot water systems and in boilers and condensate lines, then corrective treatment becomes necessary.

Methods used to control corrosion from dissolved gases include: (1) Cold aeration to remove most of the free carbon dioxide and reduce the hydrogen sulfide although dissolved oxygen is usually increased. (2) Hot aeration to remove dissolved oxygen as well as carbon dioxide and hydrogen sulfide. (3) pH adjustment with caustic soda to inactivate carbon dioxide, sulfur dioxide, and hydrogen sulfide. (4) The addition of reducing compounds, such as sodium sulfite or hydrazine to remove oxygen. Hydrazine is not approved for culinary steam. (5) Passage of water through a closed contact bed of iron scrap, to remove dissolved oxygen or hydrogen sulfide.

Methods for the formation of protective films include:

(1) Leaving in the softened water or adding to it sufficient hardness to form an eggshell thickness scale on the boiler or pipe surfaces. Formerly, this was widely advocated but in practice is difficult to control and usually the film is either incomplete with consequent pitting or is too thick with reduction in heat transfer and in carrying capacity of the pipe.

(2) Feeding water-glass type sodium silicates into the water at a rate of 8–16 ppm as SiO_2 for once-through systems and up to 60 ppm as SiO_2 for recirculated ice waters and tower waters. Avoid silicates for boiler feed waters.

(3) Using "threshold" treatment, the addition of sodium hexametaphosphate, usually 2–16 ppm, to the water. At room temperature or lower, this treatment may greatly reduce scale formation and corrosion in pipe lines and equipment.

(4) Feeding beta-glucoside and its salts reportedly is effective if adequate amounts are used.

(5) The use of two inhibitors, orthophosphate and chromate, to control corrosion in circulating water cooling systems is named the "dianodic" method and is patented. Used at concentrations of 40 ppm of orthophosphate and 20 ppm of chromate at a controlled pH of 6.0–7.0, many corrosion problems are controlled.

Total water hardness is due to dissolved calcium, magnesium, iron, and aluminum and is expressed as equivalent calcium. The U.S. Geological Survey classification of waters for hardness expressed as calcium carbonate is: soft water, 0–60 ppm; moderately hard water 60–120 ppm; hard water, 120–180 ppm; and very hard water, over 180 ppm. Hardness may be expressed as milligrams per liter (which is essentially the same numerically as ppm) or expressed as grains per gallon (gpg) (1 gpg is equal to 17.1 mg/per liter or approximately 17.1 ppm). Usually, the hardness contributed by iron and aluminum is insignificant and is disregarded. Hardness may be approximated by the soap method. The EDTA (ethylene diamine tetraacetate) test is much more accurate, rapid, and reproducible. An indicator, such as Eriochrome Black T, shows a sharp color change from the presence of free calcium ions to their absence.

Temporary hardness consists of the calcium and magnesium present in the water as bicarbonates which on loss of carbon dioxide, as by heating, are converted to insoluble carbonates which tend to form objectionable deposits. Noncarbonate, also called permanent hardness from sulfates and chlorides, does not precipitate or form deposits at as low concentrations as carbonate hardness. However, in boilers, evaporation may concentrate the calcium sulfate above its solubility limit and very hard, insoluble sulfate scale may be deposited. Unfortunately the solubility of calcium sulfate decreases with a rise in temperature and is 1250 ppm at 212°F, 100 ppm at 338°F (100 psi), and 55 ppm at 392°F (210 psi).

Water composition and usage will determine the most economical type of treatment for the control or removal of hardness. Threshold treatment often will be adequate for cooling purposes. For use in cleaning with waters of more than 85 ppm hardness, ion-exchange (zeolite) softening is most satisfactory. Often, internal treatment may be adequate for boiler feed waters. With hard waters and with large boilers, external softening with either zeolite or the hot lime-soda process may be desirable.

Ion exchange materials are very porous solids which are able to take a "charge" of cations or anions from liquid and exchange them for different ions of the same polarity. Cations are positively charged ions such as aluminum, calcium, iron, magnesium, hydrogen, potassium, and sodium. Anions are negatively charged ions such as bicarbonate, carbonate, chloride, sulfate, and sulfide.

For instance, sulfonated polystyrene resin, a cation exchanger, when operated on the "sodium cycle" is charged with sodium ions and will pick up from the liquid flowing over it cations such as calcium, magnesium, iron, etc., and release equivalent sodium ions. When exhausted, the resin is regenerated by backwashing to remove suspended matter from the top of the bed, contacted with a sodium chloride brine to recharge the resin with sodium ions and release the picked-up calcium and other ions to the spent brine which is then rinsed to waste.

Various cation exchange materials have been used commercially. Natural greensand, a sodium aluminum silicate, has a low exchange capacity of about 3000 grains (as calcium carbonate) per cubic foot. High capacity greensand has an exchange capacity of about 5000–8500 gr per cu ft and synthetic alumina-silicate gel type zeolite has a capacity of about 5000–12,000 gr per cu ft. These are no longer popular and have been superseded by sulfonated organic coal derivatives, sulfonated polystyrene, and other synthetic organic resins which can be used over a much wider range of pH and temperature and can be obtained with exchange capacities of more than 50,000 gr per cu ft.

Many cation exchange resins can be operated on the "hydrogen cycle." During regeneration they are charged with hydrogen ions from an acid such as hydrochloric or sulfuric acid and in use release hydrogen ions equivalent to the picked-up calcium, magnesium, and other cations. The effluent then contains carbonic acid, hydrochloric acid, sulfuric acid, etc., equivalent to the bicarbonates, chlorides, and sulfates in the water being treated.

Certain resinous materials, anion exchange resins, when regenerated with alkalies such as sodium carbonate, will exchange the carbonate ion from the resin for chloride, sulfate, and other negative ions in the water. Thus, a natural water first passed through a hydrogen-cycle cation exchanger and then through a carbonate-cycle anion exchanger will contain only carbonic acid which can be removed by aeration and leave a demineralized (deionized) water with about the same low solids as commercial distilled water. More strongly basic anion exchangers regenerated with sodium hydroxide and used with a hydrogen-cycle exchanger can give an effluent with extremely low solids.

Sodium-cycle cation exchangers increase the total solids of the treated water and leave anions unchanged. With waters with high bicarbonate hardness the total solids can be reduced by chemical precipitation treatment, hot process lime-soda treatment. Hydrated lime and soda ash are added to the exact requirements of the heated water, mixed, settled, and the clear softened water passed through a filter bed of fine, graded anthracite coal before use in the boiler. Very careful control is necessary to obtain less than 1 gpg hardness in the effluent and careful internal treatment is required. Control difficulties lead to precipitation in the filter itself and have caused many food plants to abandon the hot lime-soda treatment.

The cold lime-soda process treatment is similar to the hot process but requires a longer processing time, larger equipment, and gives an effluent with about 5 gpg hardness which is too high for satisfactory use in cleaning.

For reduction in dissolved solids, the reverse osmosis (RO) process may be used. The water to be treated is applied at high pressure, often several hundred psi, to one side of a semipermeable membrane which permits water and a certain proportion of the dissolved solids to pass through while retaining much of the dissolved solids on the high pressure side. Membranes with various selectivities are available. It is proposed to use this process for reduction in the salinity of the Colorado River water for irrigation in Mexico.

Most treatments for the disinfection of water use chlorine because of low cost, availability, and ease of application. In chlorination of water, a chlorine compound, such as chlorine gas, or sodium or calcium hypochlorite solution, is added in such concentration that in the time of contact at the prevailing temperature and pH, there will be more than adequate germicidal action. Under average conditions a concentration of 0.2–0.4 ppm of free available chlorine residual will disinfect water in 10 min. To achieve this residual in water free of color, turbidity, and dissolved organic matter, a dosage of 2.0 ppm may be adequate. For some polluted waters 30 ppm or more of available chlorine must be applied. The exact amount to be applied depends upon water quality and must be determined for each water supply.

The "Western Besi" (bacterial elimination by sterilizing instantly) unit is based on the greatly increased germicidal action of chlorine at low pH and effects excellent bacterial reductions with a low chlorine concentration by acidification, addition of chlorine, and after a very short contact time raising the pH to the desired level by addition of alkali. Equivalent kills are obtained with about $1/20$ of the chlorine applied in about 6 ft of corrosion-resistant line at flows of 400 gal. per min.

Many tastes and odors in water can be removed by chlorination. Hydrogen sulfide in water is oxidized to sulfate at pH 6.4 or lower and also to free sulfur at higher pH values. Chlorine will remove some color from water and will oxidize iron and manganese for removal. Chlorine can react with phenols to form chlorophenols which have a very low taste threshold and, if formed, can be removed by activated carbon filtration.

H. GORDON HARDING

Cross-reference: *Flocculation; Ion Exchange.*

WHEY

Whey, the fluid portion of milk drained from the curd in cheese or casein manufacture may be sweet or acid. Of the 23 billion pounds of whey produced annually in the United States, about 25% is acid whey (pH 4.7) resulting from cottage cheese production. The remainder is sweet rennet whey (pH 6.2) from cheddar, Swiss and specialty cheeses. Casein whey, the U.S. production of which is small, contains the precipitating acid, either hydrochloric, sulfuric, or naturally-formed lactic. Billions of pounds of whey are produced in other countries notably in Europe, Australia, and New Zealand. In every whey producing area the problem of utilization vs. disposal into streams or sewers is being met by a vigorous search for new and profitable uses.

One hundred pounds of whole milk will produce about 10 lb of cheddar cheese and 90 lb of whey; 100 lb of skim milk will produce 16 lb of cottage cheese and 84 lb of whey or 2.8 lb of casein and 91 lb of whey.

Composition

Whey contains $1/2$ the solids of the original milk; the fat and much of the protein are removed in cheese making. The composition of whey is shown in Table W-2. Whey is actually a 5% solution of lactose containing 2% of other milk components. It contains almost as much riboflavin as does milk. Acid whey contains more calcium and phosphate than sweet whey because of the solvent action of the acid used to precipitate the casein. The residual fat (0.3%) in sweet cheese whey is recovered by centrifugal separation. The protein is calculated from the nitrogen content of the whey or fractions

TABLE W-2

THE COMPOSITION OF WHEY

	Sweet Cheese Whey[1]	Cottage Cheese Whey	Casein Whey[1]
Lactose	4.9	4.6	5.1
Heat-coagulable protein	0.5	0.5	0.6
Nonheat-coagulable nitrogenous matter	0.4	0.4	0.4
Ash	0.6	0.7	0.7
Fat	0.3	0.1	0.1
Lactic acid	0.2	0.6	—
Total Solids	7.0	7.0	7.0
Water	93.0	93.0	93.0

[1] SOURCE: Nutting (1970).

separated from it. Whey, not treated to separate its proteins, contains β-lactoglobulin, α-lactalbumin, serum albumin, serum globulins, and other heat-denaturable proteins. Rennet treatment of the milk leaves a macropeptide in the whey which has a molecular weight of 8000; this macropeptide is split from κ-casein in the initial step of the clotting process. The proteins of whey may be separated by heat or heat plus acid and used in food preparation.

The composition of a commercial, edible, dried, sweet whey is shown in Table W-3. This composition is typical of the products prepared for food manufacture. Products of similar composition, but usually containing more lactic acid and correspondingly less lactose, are dried for animal feed. At present more than $1/2$ the dried whey produced in the United States is sold for animal feed at a price that barely covers production costs. A high protein whey feed is made by delactosing whey with a lactose fermenting yeast thereby replacing the lactose with yeast cells.

Nutritive Value

The nutritive value of whey is high in some respects but low in others. The fat and most of the protein have been diverted to cheese. However, the biological value of the remaining whey proteins is higher than that of casein but their concentration is low. Excessive heat during processing, especially during the roller drying of whey, may lower its amino acid values by rendering them, especially the lysine, biologically unavailable. Most of the lactose and minerals remain in sweet whey, less in acid (fermented) whey. A lactose intolerance exists in some people who lack ability to hydrolyze the sugar; this gives rise to temporary abdominal discomfort. Since 73% of whey solids is lactose, the amount of whey that can be consumed by

TABLE W-3

COMPOSITION OF
COMMERCIAL DRIED
SWEET CHEESE WHEY

Component	(%)
Chemical Composition[1]	
Protein	12.0
Fat	0.9
Ash	8.0
Lactose	71.0
Lactic acid	2.2
Calcium	0.6
Phosphorus	0.6
Sodium	0.7
Moisture	4.3
Amino Acid Composition	
Arginine	0.32
Methionine	0.25
Lysine	1.07
Tryptophan	0.22
Histidine	0.20
Isoleucine	0.74
Leucine	1.14
Phenylalanine	0.36
Valine	0.73
Threonine	0.83

[1] Values based on published figures from brochure *Whey Products from Kraft*, Kraft Foods, 1970.

lactose-intolerant persons is limited. Whey solids can make a positive nutritional contribution to foods when used at a 3–10% solids level.

TABLE W-4

VITAMIN CONTENT OF WHEY[1]

	Fluid	Dried
A (IU/100 gm)	11.0	50.0
	(Mg/Liter)	(Mg/Kg)
Thiamin	0.4	3.7
Riboflavin	1.2	23.4
Nicotinic acid	0.85	9.6
Pantothenic acid	3.4	47.3
Vitamin B_6	0.42	4.0
Biotin	0.14	0.37
Folic acid	—	0.89
Vitamin B_{12}	0.0020	0.021
Choline	—	1356.0
Vitamin C	13.0	—

[1] Many unidentified growth factors have been attributed to dried whey when used as an animal feed. See Hartman and Dryden (1965) from which the values in this Table were taken.

TABLE W-5

DRIED WHEY STANDARD FOR
U.S. EXTRA GRADE

	Not More Than
Bacterial estimate	50,000/gm
Butterfat	1.25%
Moisture	5.0%
Scorched particle content	15 mg
Solubility Index	1.25%
Titratable acidity	0.16%

NOTE: Flavor, odor, and physical appearance must be normal as given in the standard.

The vitamin content of whey is given in Table W-4. When whey is concentrated and dried there is approximately an 11-fold increase in solids and this concentration increase is reflected by an increase in most of the vitamins as shown in Table W-4. Other properties of food grade dried whey are given in Table W-5.

Processing

Sweet whey must be processed within hours of its removal from the cheese curd to preserve its quality. Acid whey produced from casein or cottage cheese is more stable since lactic acid bacteria and many other organisms are inhibited in their growth at acidities below about pH 4.7.

The first step in processing is pasteurization which is usually followed by concentration and drying. Pasteurization is done at 180°–205°F. If denaturation of the whey protein is to be avoided temperatures below 165°F are used. The whey is concentrated under vacuum to 40–50% solids except in new reverse osmosis (RO) procedures. RO can be used to concentrate small quantities of whey (up to 100,000 lb per day) to 25% solids. This reduction in bulk facilities shipment to a central processing or drying plant where large scale vacuum evaporating and drying equipment is available. There should be at least 100,000 and 750,000 lb whey per day available, respectively, to justify installation of a vacuum evaporator or spray dryer. Large whey drying operations will handle from one to several million pounds of whey daily.

Most of the whey that is processed is dried to preserve it for shipment, storage, and handling as a food or feed ingredient. For this purpose a non-hygroscopic product is desirable. Since 70% of dried whey is lactose, which normally dries as a hygroscopic glass, the lactose is generally crystallized in the concentrate (50% TS) and during the drying process. Whey dried from this concentrate yields a stable, crystalline sugar which will not absorb moisture as will the syrup form. The powder is packaged in multiwall bags of 50–100 lb capacity.

Utilization of Whey

Sound factory and environmental practices demand that whey be salvaged for constructive purposes. Federal and state water quality standards have practically eliminated the practice of whey disposal into rivers and streams. Most municipalities are charging on a BOD basis for disposal into city sewers. Whey contains 6.3% organic solids. Its Biological Oxygen Demand (BOD) is the amount of dissolved oxygen taken up by the sample expressed in parts per million (ppm). The BOD measured over a 5-day period is expressed as BOD_5. The BOD_5 of 100 lb of cheddar cheese whey is 3.5 and the population equivalent is 21. Thus, 5 lb of whey is considered to cause pollution equal to that of the waste from an average individual. A cheese plant discarding 100,000 lb of whey per day would then require sewage disposal facilities the size of a town of 20,000 people. The importance of processing whey into useful feed or food products is clearly indicated.

Whey has long been fed to swine and other farm animals but part of the supply is now bringing better prices as a food ingredient. Lactic acid, alcohol, and vinegar were whey products for many years. Recently, however, whey has been largely displaced by less expensive fermentable materials. Whey is the raw material for lactose production and the amount of lactose manufactured is limited only by the uses that can be found for this unique carbohydrate. Small quantities of whey solids can be used in cheese spreads and in process cheese, and have been gradually displacing part of the nonfat milk used in bakery goods, confections, and ice cream. It is especially adaptable to sweet baked goods because it produces a soft cake-like texture. In ice cream, the addition of whey is permitted in an amount not to exceed 25% replacement of the nonfat milk solids. When it is used to increase rather than replace milk solids, an improvement in body and flavor results. Ten to 15% of fudge or caramel solids can consist of whey solids to the improvement of both body and flavor of these candies. Nutritionally, whey could be an important ingredient in fruit-flavored beverages and soft drinks but this market is still undeveloped.

Whey protein and lactose fractions are prepared for food manufacture by several fractionation or concentration processes. A high degree of purity often is not necessary when the whey product is to be used directly in food. Electrodialysis will take out part of the salts from which some of the lactose may have been already removed. Fractiona-

tion by ultra filtration (UF membranes, a form of reverse osmosis), is a newly developed procedure which has been made possible through the availability of improved long-lasting membranes. Typically, a fractionation membrane can remove 90% of the cottage cheese whey volume as permeate containing 80% of the lactose and more than 90% of the ash. The remaining high protein fraction resembles skim milk in its proportions of lactose, protein, and salts. Thus, on a dry weight basis, if the original cottage cheese whey contained 68% lactose and 8% protein, a dry protein concentrate could be produced containing 33% protein and 52% lactose.

Gel permeation can be used to obtain high protein fractions by flowing the whey over a column packed with a suitable gel (Sephadex) which retains the smaller molecules of salts and lactose. The separation can be made more effective by first making an ultra filtration membrane separation. Such a concentrate may contain up to 80% of its solids as protein. Protein concentrations of 60–75% of solids can also be produced by diluting the first UF concentrate with water and refiltering it.

The economic aspects of whey utilization largely govern its final disposition. Whey has many possible uses but the cost of preparing it for special purposes must not cause it to lose its competitive position with alternate materials. It costs almost as much to dry and bag as it will bring as a feed ingredient (about 4¢ per lb). In unprocessed liquid form it can be fed to swine or recycled back to the cows, but again handling costs are scarcely recovered as available nutrients for the animal. Nevertheless, processing as feed at a break-even price is better than paying a BOD charge for waste disposal. Whey solids are most valuable as human food, especially when high protein preparations are made from it. These too must be competitive with casein, vegetable protein, and egg white.

BYRON H. WEBB

References

HARTMAN, A. M., and DRYDEN, L. P. 1965. Vitamins in Milk and Milk Products. American Dairy Science Association, Champaign, Illinois.

INTERNATIONAL DAIRY FEDERATION. 1969. IDF Seminar on Whey Processing and Utilization in Weihenstephan, Germany.

MANN, E. J. 1969. Whey Processing and Utilization. Dairy Ind. *34:* No. 8 and 9, 507–508, 571–572.

NUTTING, G. C. 1970. The byproducts of milk. *In* Byproducts from Milk, 2nd Edition. B. H.

Webb and E. O. Whittier (Editors). Avi Publishing Co., Westport, Conn.

U.S. DEPT. OF AGR. 1970. Proceedings—Whey Utilization Conference. University of Maryland, College Park, Maryland. USDA Agr. Res. Serv. ARS-73-69.

WEBB, B. H., and JOHNSON, A. H., and ALFORD, J. A. 1974. Fundamentals of Dairy Chemistry, 2nd Edition. Avi Publishing Co., Westport, Conn.

WEBB, B. H., and WHITTIER, E. O. 1970. Byproducts From Milk, 2nd Edition. Avi Publishing Co., Westport, Conn.

WEBB, B. H., and WHITTIER, E. O. 1948. Utilization of Whey: A Review. J. Dairy Sci. 31, 139–164.

WINGERD, W. H., SAPERSTEIN, S., and LUTWAK, L. 1970. Whey protein concentrate. Food Technol. 24, 758.

Cross-references: *Market Milk Industry; Ultrafiltration and Reverse Osmosis.*

WINE

Fermented beverages have been produced since the Paleolithic period—probably at first by accident from honey. Later, cereals were used, and then grapes and various fruits. Soma and other early beverages were probably produced from honey or honey-cereal-fruit mixtures. During the Neolithic period beer from fermented cereals was most popular in the Middle East and Egypt. Wines from fruits, and especially from grapes, were more popular in Greek and Roman territory.

Artifacts of the manufacture of wines begin to appear about 3000–4000 B.C. in the Middle East. The culture of the vine, which made this possible, spread from the Middle East to the Mediterranean where it achieved and still maintains its largest culture. The date and fig were also fermented during the neolithic period. Other fruits, such as the peach, pear, apricot, and berries, were fermented as they were domesticated, but never in quantities approaching grapes. Since the sugar content of fruits is low (except for the date and fig) they produced a low-alcohol, easily-spoilable beverage. They were, therefore, not popular. Except as a minor household industry and in cold regions where grapes do not grow, wines from fruits were and remain of relatively minor importance. Apple cider and perry (from pears) are local exceptions. More popular are liqueurs distilled from these fruit wines: Kirschwasser (from cherries), slivovitz (from plums), framboise (from raspberries), etc.

Earthenware jars (called amphora by the Greeks and Romans) were used to store and transport the wine during and after the Neolithic period. During the period of Greek expansion throughout the Mediterranean, a lively trade in wines between Greece and her far-flung colonies and other nations developed. Later, vines were planted by the colonists and wines were produced in the colonies. Gradually, the vine was introduced to all the countries around the Mediterranean and Black Sea basins, and from them to adjacent regions (Germany, Hungary, Rumania, etc.). Still later, culture of the vine spread throughout the temperate zone as the following 1972 acreage and production figures show, reported by the Office International de la Vigne et du Vin Bull. *46* (1973):

	Acreage (1000 A)	Production (1000 Gal.)
Europe	15,793	5,915,770
Asia	2,601	52,980
South America	1,212	710,490
Africa	1,133	349,945
North America	546	267,551
Oceania	144	72,484
Total	21,429	7,369,220

Obviously the greatest acreage and most of the wine production is in Europe. Italy, France, and Spain are the largest producers.

Influence of the Raw Material

Varieties of the European grape, *Vitis vinifera*, proved to be an almost ideal media for alcoholic fermentation. As wild types normally ripen they contain 10–20% sugar and have 1–2.5% acidity (as tartaric). As varieties were domesticated those of higher sugar and lower acidity were selected. Under favorable climatic conditions grapes of *V. vinifera* easily reach 18–24% sugar with only 0.5–1.5% acidity.

In the Western Hemisphere, and specifically in Eastern United States, other species of *Vitis* grow wild. During the first half of the 19th Century a number of these were domesticated—primarily varieties of *Vitis labrusca*. Some of the seedlings that were propagated were probably chance *V. labrusca* × *V. vinifera* hybrids. The domesticated native varieties and the hybrids withstood the cold winters of this region and were more resistant to fungus, virus, and insect diseases than *V. vinifera* varieties. About 10–15% of U.S. wine production is from these varieties: Catawba, Concord, Delaware, Ives Seedling, Niagara, French hybrids, etc.

Production.—Even before the Greek period viticulturists had learned to curtail overproduction by pruning. Wine grapes of 18–22% sugar and no more than 0.6–1.5% acidity (as tartaric) could be produced not only in the Mediterranean region but also in cooler areas.

Climate.—The most important differences in the composition of grapes are due to climatic conditions. In the coolest regions grapes often do not mature. The present northern limit in Europe where grape culture is possible runs from Normandy to Champagne, along the Moselle and Rhine and from the Danube to Moldavia and the lower Don in the USSR. It is generally agreed by viticulturists that the grape does not grow unless the average daily temperature reaches 50°F (10°C). The greater the accumulation of heat above this temperature the faster grapes mature. At the same time, in the warmest regions the grapes achieve a given level of sugar at a lower total acidity and, for red colored varieties, with less color. The fruit also ripens earlier and during the warmest period of the season—thus compounding these effects. In cooler regions, or in cooler years, the opposite is true: grapes mature later, have higher total acidity and more color, but also they may lack sufficient sugar to produce enough alcohol for a stable wine—especially in cool seasons.

Varietal Influence.—More than 5,000 varieties of *Vitis vinifera* are believed to exist. These occur in a bewildering range of color, shape, size, composition, time required to mature, sensitivity to fungus diseases and insect pests, flavor, susceptibility to excessive temperature, production, etc. In general, the best varieties for table wines are those which mature with moderate sugar content and acidity. The preferred varieties for dessert wines have a high sugar content and a lower acidity.

Fermentation

Alcoholic fermentation occurs through the intermediary of enzymes produced by yeasts. The primary yeast responsible is *Saccharomyces cerevisia*. This yeast occurs widely in nature: on soils, on grapes, and in wineries. Unless unfavorable climatic conditions occur during ripening sufficient numbers of desired yeasts occur on the grapes to start fermentation as soon as the grapes are crushed. However, since Pasteur's research revealed the importance and necessity of yeasts for alcoholic fermentation, wine makers usually add pure cultures of a desired strain of yeasts in order to be sure that alcoholic fermentation will start immediately, and will proceed to completion. This is particularly important when the grapes ripen under unfavorable climatic conditions which lead to invasion of fungus diseases and a deficient or defective yeast flora. To inhibit growth of undesirable microorganisms small amounts of sulfur dioxide (100–150 mg per liter) are added immediately after crushing.

The process of alcoholic fermentation has been clearly elucidated by modern biochemists. It proceeds with at least 20 enzyme proteins, 3 to 8

dissociable organic cofactors and several inorganic cofactors. Moreover, the supporting systems to produce these enzymes and organic cofactors require a large number of reactions.

Effect of composition.—The primary sugars present in grapes are glucose and fructose. At full maturity grapes contain about equal proportions of these two sugars, though the ratio varies with variety of grape, climatic conditions, and time when harvested. At the usual total sugar content of 19–23% alcoholic fermentation proceeds rapidly and, with alcohol-tolerant strains of yeast, to completion—producing about 10–12.5% alcohol (by volume). If the sugar content is greater than 23% the high sugar content may inhibit fermentation and the rate of fermentation will be slower and may be incomplete. Under special conditions of stimulation, 16–18% alcohol can be reached, but normally in commercial operations 13–15% is the maximum.

Where insufficient sugar is present in the grapes to produce sufficient alcohol (at least 10%) sugar may be added to the must.[3] This occurs frequently in the grape-growing areas of Germany, in the Burgundy region of France, in eastern United States, and in cool regions elsewhere. In each case, the amount which may be added is strictly controlled by the government.

The two main acids of grapes are tartaric and malic acids, with small amounts of citric. At total acidities of less than 1% (and a pH of over 3) alcoholic fermentation is not inhibited. In some cases, the acidity may be too low to produce a balanced wine. In this case the acidity may need to be augmented, usually with tartaric acid. Contrariwise, in the coolest regions reduction of acidity will be needed in order to promote fermentation and to reduce the overtartness of the resulting wine. The methods used for this are addition of calcium carbonate, ion-exchange, and addition of water (followed by addition of sugar to make up for the dilution).

Yeasts require a number of amino acids for growth. Fortunately, most varieties of grapes contain adequate amounts to promote yeast growth. This is the main difference between grapes and other fruits which often contain insufficient nitrogenous constituents to promote active yeast growth. In these cases, supplementary addition of nitrogenous materials may be necessary. Among the amino acids found in grapes are α-alanine, γ-aminobutyric acid, arginine, aspartic acid, citruline, cystine, glutamic acid, glutamine, glycine, histidine, isoleucine, leucine, lysine, methionine, ornithine,

---

[3] Must refers to the crushed grapes (juice, seeds, and skins) or to the juice from pressed grapes.

phenylalanine, proline, serine, threonine, tryptophan, tyrosine, valine, and others.

Crushing and Stemming

In ancient times, and in some areas where labor
was cheap until the 20th Century, grapes were
crushed by stomping on them with the human
foot. Increasing cost of labor, the large scale of
operations, and aesthetic considerations have resulted in the nearly universal use of mechanical
crushers.

The modern winery uses a combined crusher-
stemmer. The grape clusters fall into a perforated
cylinder inside of which paddles revolve at 600–
1200 rpm. This crushes the berries and juice drops
through the perforations. The stems are ejected
from the end of the cylinder.

The process for making different types of wines
varies from this point on.

White Wine Production

If white wines are to be produced the skins and
juice are immediately separated from each other
by draining or pressing, or both. Hydraulically
operated basket presses were most popular until
recently. Now horizontal presses with pressure
from both ends are often used. The Willmes' press
with an inflatable bag in the center is also common.
When the juice is separated continuous presses may
be used.

Any necessary corrections of acidity or sugar are
then made and the requisite amounts of sulfur dioxide and yeast culture (or pressed yeast) added.
In eastern United States, water and sugar may be
used simultaneously providing the volume is not
increased more than 35%. Similar corrections of
sugar are made in some parts of France and in Germany and other northern European countries. The
acidity, however, is not lowered with water
but is reduced with calcium carbonate, with ion-
exchange, or by a malo-lactic fermentation during
or after the alcoholic fermentation.

Enologists generally agree that the best white
wine is produced by fermenting at very moderate
temperatures, 50°–60°F (10°–15.6°C). The fermentation will be slower at these temperatures but
the finished wine will retain a more desirable
aroma. At these temperatures 3–6 weeks may be
required to complete the fermentation. With large
tanks, 50,000–100,000 gal., control of temperature
is a major problem since there is less heat loss from
these tanks than there is with small tanks.

When small (50–500 gal.) fermenters are used
fermentation traps to prevent ingress of air may be
necessary. When large fermenters (over 1000 gal.)
are employed this is unnecessary as the volume of
carbon dioxide given off prevents entry of air.

Rosé (or Pink) Wine Production

If low-colored varieties of grapes are used the
skins need not be separated from the juice for 1–3
days after crushing. With full-colored grapes the
must from the crusher-stemmer may contain sufficient color to permit immediate separation of the
skins and juice, i.e., draining and pressing. Usually,
however, the crushed grapes are pumped to a fermenter and after 12–48 hr the free-run juice is removed and used for rosé wine production.

Otherwise the production of rosé wines proceeds
as for white wines—lower temperatures of fermentation are required.

Red Wine Production

Most red-colored varieties of grapes have their
red-colored pigments (anthocyans) only in the
skins. In order to produce a full red-colored wine
it is necessary to ferment the skins and juice in
contact with each other (usually for 12–14 days.)

The optimum temperature for fermentation of
red wines is higher than that of whites and rosés in
order to favor this extraction of color (and flavor)
from the skins. The optimum temperature is believed to be 70°–80°F (21.1°–27.4°C).

Red wines also differ from whites because of the
floating cap of skins which develops early in the
fermentation period. Unless the cap is placed in
contact with the liquid little color extraction will
occur. To achieve this the cap in small fermenters
is periodically punched down (i.e., submerged).
This is not possible with large containers and the
juice is pumped out from below the cap and
pumped or sprayed over the cap.

If the harvested grapes (red, rosé or white) are too
warm the fermentation temperature may exceed
the optimum range. In this case, external cooling
must be applied, and, as with white musts, with
large tanks this is a major problem.

Dessert Wines

Dessert wines are wines to which distilled spirits
(usually distilled from wine) are added during or
after fermentation.

When the spirits are added after fermentation is
nearly completed, it is to produce wines of the dry
sherry or dry Madeira type. When added during
fermentation, the purpose is to add sufficient alcohol to stop fermentation—17-20% being sufficient—and to leave more or less sugar in the wine.
This results in the production of sweet wines which
are no longer subject to fermentation—port, sweet
sherry, angelica, muscatel, etc.

Special Types

Under conditions of high humidity during ripening (above 98% RH) grapes may be attacked by

the fungus *Botrytis cinerea*. The result of the attack is to loosen the skin from the flesh. If a period of lower humidity follows, water will be lost from the berries and the fruit will shrink. This results in a special flavor and in a high sugar and glycerin content in the fruit. In the Sauternes district of France and in Germany this process is used to produce wines of high sugar but only moderate alcohol. Filtration, aging, and the use of sulfur dioxide results in stable wines which do not referment after bottling. The process can also be accomplished on a pilot plant scale following harvesting of the grapes by raising the humidity and inoculating with *Botrytis* spores. After 1-2 days the humidity is lowered, loss of moisture occurs, and high sugar musts are produced.

In the making of Spanish flor-type sherries, the flavor is produced by a film stage of the yeast. Certain alcohol-tolerant strains of yeast will grow on the surface of wines in the presence of air and produce acetaldehyde. If the alcohol is 14.5-16%, acetic acid bacteria will not grow. In Spain such wines are aged in a fractional blending system which tends to produce wines of standard flavor and age. A similar process is commercially used in the Soviet Union, South Africa, and Australia.

It has also been shown in California that under oxidative conditions with agitation a number of yeast strains will grow in submerged culture to produce wines with flor flavor. The process is being used commercially in California.

Heating wines to produce a carmelized or baked odor was known in the Roman period. In the 19th Century, it was first used in the Madeira Islands. Wines were held at 120°-140°F (48°-60°C) for 2-3 months. The same process is now widely used in California to produce a type known as California sherry.

The production of sparkling wines is covered below in this review of wines and their production.

Clarification

As musts finish their fermentation the new wine is cloudy—primarily with yeast cells. Under favorable circumstances—dry table wines of relatively low pH and high acidity, small wood containers, and low temperatures—the suspended cells settle out rapidly. This clarification seems to be aided by the simultaneous precipitation of the excess potassium acid tartrate (cream of tartar).

In the opposite case—sweet dessert wines of high pH and low acidity stored at high temperatures—clarification may be very much delayed.

Under either circumstance clarification is seldom sufficiently complete within a reasonable period for commercial bottling. The wine maker may aid the clarification by early racking. This separates the clearer wine from the yeast cells. The effects of yeast autolysis is thus reduced. Simultaneous addition of sulfur dioxide further favors clarification and suppresses bacterial and yeast growth. Of course, where it is necessary to stimulate a malo-lactic fermentation one delays the first racking, maintains the temperature, and adds no sulfur dioxide. The malo-lactic fermentation is carried on by lactic acid bacteria and results in the decarboxylation of malic acid to produce lactic acid and carbon dioxide. The progress of the malo-lactic fermentation must be carefully controlled by analysis for total acid, pH, disappearance of malic acid (by paper chromatography), and by sensory evaluation.

Even with racking and temperature control wines seldom clarify themselves sufficiently for aging and bottles. Fining and filtration are almost always necessary.

Fining.—This is a very ancient clarification practice, already in use by the Romans. It consists of adding materials to the wine which precipitate in the wine and as they settle out clarify the wine. The actual clarification may be purely mechanical, or there may be adsorption of suspended material on the fining agent, or there can be chemical reactions between the suspended material and the fining agent. The mechanical effect occurs with all types of fining agents to a greater or lesser extent. Adsorption is the primary effect of bentonite, the most-used fining agent. Bentonite is a montmorillonite clay. It has tremendous swelling properties. It removes some protein which is particularly important with wines subject to copper-protein cloudiness. It is effective with many wines that are difficult to clarify by other methods. Calcium and sodium forms are available, the former generally being preferred. About 3-9 lb per 1000 gal. are the amounts usually used. Only the minimum quantity needed should be employed as bentonite forms a voluminous sediment in wine. The effect of bentonite is fairly rapid so the clear supernatant liquid can be racked off or filtered within a week. Some wineries use gelatin followed by bentonite.

Gelatin has been used for a long time by wine makers. In the wine it combines with tannins and a precipitate forms. Only gelatins that are free of off-odors should be used. Since red wines contain enough tannin to cause gelatin precipitation, no extra tannin need be used. But in the case of white wines it is customary to add a small amount of tannin before the gelatin.

Casein solutions have also been used for fining. The casein must be odorless and tasteless. It also removes some color.

Polyvinylpyrrolidon (PVPP) and modifications of it, have found some use for clarifying red wines but does not appear to have much, if any, advantage over gelatin for this purpose. Use of PVPP to remove color from white wines has been reported. Polyamide esters, nylons, have been used on some wines with moderate success.

Fining agents have also been employed to remove excess metals. "Blue" fining has been recommended in Germany since 1911. It involves the use of potassium ferrocyanide which removes copper, iron, etc. It may now be employed under governmental control in a number of countries. "Cufex," a proprietary product containing potassium ferrocyanide, is approved for use in this country for removal of iron when needed (now rare).

Filtration.—This is another ancient practice. Originally it involved pouring the wine through cloth. Gradually, filter pads of small pore size were developed. Filters can be made to remove larger sized particles, smaller particles such as yeast cells, or to remove organisms as small as bacteria. Modern filters remove some material by adsorption and some solely on the basis of particle size.

The pad filters are most common. They are produced with pores of various size. Very large filters are employed for rough filtration of young wines.

In order to increase filter life, diatomaceous earths are added to wines during filtration. These mix with the mucilaginous materials and maintain the capacity of the filter for longer times, i.e., increase filter capacity.

Smaller filters using pads of small pore size are used for filtering finished wines preparatory to bottling. It is possible to use pad filters with a pore size small enough to "germ-proof" the wine. This does not mean that all viable microorganisms are removed—only those which might develop in the wine.

Recently, membrane filters have been widely employed for wines. These have uniform but small pore size so that a very large percentage of the filter surface is available for filtration. They will effectively produce yeast-free wines when properly used. They also greatly reduce the number of bacteria.

Tartrate Stabilization.—New wines are supersaturated with respect to potassium acid tartrate. The rate of deposition of the excess tartrate varies with different types of wines depending on their composition. The rate of deposition not only depends on the composition of the wine but on temperature, size of container, smoothness of the walls of the container, agitation of the wine, and other factors.

The traditional, and still the most widely employed procedure, is to reduce the temperature of the wine for a period of time. In cool regions where wines are stored in small containers adequate tartrate stabilization can be achieved in 1–2 yr. To facilitate this, the cellar may be opened to winter temperatures or the casks containing wine may be placed out in the open.

For large scale operations this is obviously not possible. Refrigeration is necessary in such cases. Various procedures are possible: cooling coils in the tank, tanks in cold rooms, etc. Holding table wines at 25°F (–3.9°C) or dessert wines at 21°F (–5°C) for 1 week will usually produce tartrate-stable wines. If the potassium content is reduced to less than 600–700 mg per liter the wines will normally be tartrate-stable. However, wines differ greatly in the potassium level necessary for complete tartrate-stability. Enologists have developed equations for predicting tartrate-stability.

Another procedure for achieving tartrate-stability is ion-exchange resins. Passing the wine through sodium ion-exchange resins will reduce the potassium content. Since sodium acid tartrate is much more soluble than potassium acid tartrate the resulting wines will be free of tartrate instability. However, excessive use of ion-exchange resins is undesirable. Too much sodium yields wines of undesirable taste, removes too much vitamins and amino acids, and gives wines which are less desirable from the public health point of view. Most wineries using ion-exchange are quite aware of these dangers and control the process. European countries generally limit the maximum sodium content for this reason.

Pasteurization.—In the 1860's Pasteur proposed heating wines as a protection against spoilage. Spoilage from bacterial spoilage was a major problem at that time. As the rational use of sulfur dioxide and pure yeast cultures were introduced along with recognition of the danger of aerobic conditions, wine spoilage became more rare. Therefore, pasteurization of wines as a method of preventing spoilage is rarely employed today.

Heating is occasionally employed as a method of achieving clarification. High-protein table wines which cloud after bottling respond favorably to heat treatment. However, use of bentonite has made even this of less importance. At present, the only case where heat treatment of table wines is employed is where young, sweet wines are being bottled. Hot-bottling, a form of pasteurization, is an effective means of securing stability of such wines. Even in this case, close filtration is considered a better procedure.

Centrifugation.—Cloudy white musts are sometimes centrifuged in order to produce a clear must. Such musts are less subject to enzymatic darkening. Wines are sometimes centrifuged in preference to filtration.

Aging.—Wines are aged in barrels (50 gal.), puncheons (100–500 gal.) or tanks (500–500,000 gal.). The tanks may be of wood, concrete, or metal. The aging may last from a few months to several years. White table wines nowadays are seldom aged more than 1–2 yr before bottling. Red table and dessert wines profit by longer aging. However, for ordinary quality wines the small improvement in quality during aging frequently does not justify the longer aging.

Wine Disorders

Wines are subject to undesirable cloudiness and chemical and flavor changes. These may be caused by microbial growth, by enzymatic action, and from chemical reactions.

Undesirable microbial growth is no longer a major problem of the wine industry except in areas of primitive winemaking procedures. When wines are not protected from air aerobic microorganisms may grow on and in the wine. The most common is *Acetobacter* sp. which results in production of acetic acid and ethyl acetate. For this reason, limits on the amount of acetic acid are legally imposed—0.120 gm per ml (exclusive of sulfur dioxide) of acetic acid for white table and dessert wines and 0.140 gm per ml for red table wines in this country. Other states and countries have similar limitations.

Various species of yeast will also grow on the surface of wines exposed to the air: *Pichia* sp., *Hansenula* sp., *Kloeckera* sp., and *Saccharomyces* sp. Keeping containers full will protect wines from these disorders.

Sweet table wines may also become cloudy from yeast growth. Careful clarification, including close filtration, and maintaining a free sulfur dioxide content of over 30 mg per liter usually are adequate control. Recently, the antiseptic agent diethylpyrocarbonate (DEPC) has been used for this purpose but it has been prohibited in several countries, including the United States. Current research indicates that it is not toxic and its use may again be approved.

Various heterofermentative and homofermentative lactic acid bacteria will grow in wines under anaerobic conditions. These induce cloudiness and some produce carbon dioxide resulting in undesirable odors. Fortunately, these microorganisms are rather sensitive to sulfur dioxide. A total sulfur dioxide of 100–125 mg per liter is usually sufficient.

When grapes are attacked by molds before harvesting the resulting musts and wines may contain the enzyme polyphenol oxidase. When these musts or their wines are exposed to the air rapid darkening of color will occur. Settling the musts and using only the clear supernatant liquid for fermentation reduces the amount of polyphenol oxidase and hence the tendency to darken. Centrifugation has also been employed. Pasteurization inactivates the enzyme but injures the quality.

The most common chemical reaction resulting in clouding formerly was excess tartrate precipitation. Cooling or ion-exchange has made this rare. Excess iron or copper will also yield wines which easily cloud. Use of stainless steel equipment has greatly reduced iron contamination. In some countries the wines can be fined with small amounts of potassium ferrocyanide to remove the excess iron, as previously mentioned.

Excess copper results in copper-protein clouding. Fining with bentonite, particularly if the wine is warm, removes sufficient protein to reduce the tendency to copper-protein clouding.

A few cases of calcium tartrate precipitation have been reported. The excess calcium often results from storage in concrete tanks.

Chemical and Sensory Analysis

Wines need to be analyzed for a number of reasons. Legal restrictions on alcohol, volatile acidity, sulfur dioxide, etc., require careful analyses. Wines also need to be analyzed for sugar content, total acidity, tartrate, iron, copper, tannin, pH, and other components as an aid to winery operations.

Sensory analyses of wines is also necessary—to separate good and poor wines, to select wines for special purposes, or to guide operations. Score cards, descriptive analysis, paired and triangle tests, and ranking are the procedures most used.

Bottling and Labeling

Considerable amounts of wine are still distributed in bulk in Europe to restaurants, to grocery stores, or to wine merchants. In this country, practically all wines are bottled for sale.

The label requirements are myriad and vary from country to country. In this country, wines are labeled with generic names (burgundy, chablis, claret, port, rhine, sherry, etc.) or with varietal appellations (Cabernet Sauvignon, muscatel, Pinot noir, Sémillon, Zinfandel, etc.). In addition, if at least 75% of the wine comes from a district the regional name may be used: California, Napa Valley, New York, etc.

In Europe, many wines carry the regional name (Bordeaux, Burgundy, Moselle, etc.), or the name of some specific area (St. Emilion, Pommard, Medoc, etc.), or even the vineyard name (Schloss Johannisberg, Château Margaux, Chambertin, etc.).

Sparkling Wines

Sparkling wines were produced in very limited quantities in the 17th and 18th Centuries. But it was not until about 1840 that the present highly-organized sparkling wine industry began its great expansion. This was directly related to the development of chemistry and an understanding of how to measure the sugar content of the base wine. The major seat of the industry was the Champagne district in northern France. However, before the end of the 19th Century sparkling wines were being produced on a large scale in other regions of France as well as in many other countries, including the United States.

Sparkling wines are defined as wines which contain an excess of carbon dioxide. Specifically, in the United States it refers to wines with more than 0.277 gm per 100 ml of carbon dioxide. The traditional sparkling wines had 2–4 atm of pressure of carbon dioxide when they reached the market. In recent years a number of wines of 0.5–1 atm of pressure (just under and over the 0.277 limit) have been produced in Germany, Portugal, Australia, and elsewhere. These have been known as "pearl" or "crackling" wines.

In France, champagne can only be produced in the region of that name. Sparkling wine produced in other parts of France are labeled "mousseau." In Germany, sparkling wines are called "Sekt," in the Soviet Union, "shampanski," in Italy, "spumante," in Spain, "espumante." In the United States, sparkling wines produced by the bottle process are called "champagne." If produced by the tank process they must be labeled "champagne—tank (or bulk) process" or "champagne—Charmat process."

To obtain the excess carbon dioxide a variety of techniques may be used. The original French procedure was to place clarified wine in a bottle with the appropriate amount of sugar, to produce 6 atm of pressure when the sugar was completely fermented, and some yeast. A cork was tied or clamped on and the wine allowed to ferment. Later, the secondary fermentation was often carried on in a closed metal tank and, after the fermentation, filtered under pressure into the bottle. Direct carbonation of wine has also been practiced.

Wines Produced by Secondary Fermentation

Base Material.—The selection and preparation of the base wine is of critical importance for sparkling wines to be produced by a secondary fermentation. If the alcohol content is too high, over 12.5% (vol) alcohol, the secondary fermentation will be slow or may not occur. If the alcohol content is too low, below 10%, the resulting wine will taste thin and will not have a good carbon dioxide holding power. An alcohol content of 10.5–11.5% is preferred.

The wine must not have the least strange or off-odor. Therefore, it must be made from varieties of grapes which do not have too strong a character. The exception would be where a muscat- or Concord-flavored wine is to be produced. In these cases, of course, wines made from muscat- or Concord-type varieties would be used. Generally, the base wine, called the "cuvée," is made up by blending a number of wines until the desired balance of flavor is achieved.

The base wine should have a low pH and high total acidity. In general, enologists prefer the pH to be below 3.3 and the acidity above 0.75% (as tartaric). The reason for this is that the fermentation is more likely to be free of undesirable secondary fermentation odors if fermented under these conditions.

Finally, the wine must be completely free of suspended material, i.e., brilliant. In addition, it should be tartrate-stable. These objectives are achieved by chilling the wine to $21°$–$25°$F $(-5°$–$-3.9°$C) for 1–2 weeks and close-filtering off the precipitated tartrates. The wine is usually clarified with bentonite or isinglass or some other fining agent.

Secondary Fermentation.—In the bottle process the wine is assembled in a blending tank and the necessary yeast culture (1–3%) and sugar (2.0–2.3%) are added. Producers of sparkling wines select the strain of yeast with care. They should be alcohol-tolerant, nonsulfide-producing, capable of fermenting easily at $50°$–$60°$F $(10°$–$15.6°$C) and have good settling properties. The so-called "champagne" strain of Saccharomyces cerevisia is popular but other strains seem to give equally good results. It is wise to acclimatize yeasts to grow in wines to avoid slow growth when first introduced into the cuvée. This can be done by several transfers of yeast cells growing under these conditions.

The amount of sugar required to produce 1 atm of pressure varies slightly depending on the alcohol content. Tables showing the exact amount required at various alcohol contents are available in the standard enology texts. Trial fermentations may also be conducted and the pressure produced measured.

While stirring, the wine from the blending tank is bottled. Nowadays, the bottle is usually closed with a crown cap. Previously a cork was used and was held in with a steel clamp ("agrafe"). The bottles are then stacked and held at about $50°$–$60°$F $(10°$–$15.6°$C). At the lower temperature the secondary fermentation may take 1–2 months. At $60°$–$65°$F $(15.6°$–$18.3°$C) the fermentation may be completed in as little as 2–3 weeks.

In the tank process, the base wine is pumped into tanks, usually stainless steel and capable of withstanding over 150 psi pressure. Tanks of 500–20,000 gal. capacity have been used. These tanks are double walled so that cooling solutions may be used. In addition the whole tank may be insulated.

The necessary sugar solution and yeast are then added. Many wineries add sufficient sugar to produce 5–6 atm of pressure and still retain whatever sugar content is desired in the final product. The fermentation is stopped at the desired stage by cooling the tank to 32°F (0°C). Yeast starters or pressed yeast of the desired strain are used (1–3%). The temperature of fermentation is usually 60°–70°F (15.6°–21.1°C). The fermentation is completed in 1–3 weeks. Some fermentation tanks are equipped with stirrers. These are said to speed up the fermentation and improve the flavor.

Finishing

In the original process of bottle fermentation the best quality wines were and are held on the yeast for one or more years after the completion of the secondary fermentation. This is believed to improve the bouquet of the wine, possibly due to slow yeast autolysis. However, many producers leave the wine in the bottle for only 6 months to 1 yr.

The traditional method of finishing the wine was to turn the bottles on end, place them in racks at about a 45° angle and turn them to the left and right daily to get the yeast deposit into the neck of the bottle and onto the cork. The process is called riddling ("remuage"). The temperature of the whole bottle is then reduced to about 30°–40°F (−1.1°–5.5°C). The neck of the bottle, containing the yeast deposit is then frozen (by placing in brine or other freezing solution). When the cork is removed the solid plug containing the yeast is ejected. This is called disgorging. When skillfully done only 1–3% of the wine is lost.

The bottle is immediately filled. Occasionally, it is filled with wine of the same type but many consumers find such a wine too dry. Normally, the driest wine commercially produced contains about 1–1½% sugar ("brut"). A 50% sugar solution in wine or wine plus brandy is used to adjust the sweetness. Sweeter types, "sec," "demi-sec," and "demi-doux," contain about 2.5, 5, and 7.5% sugar. Different companies may vary these amounts. The wine is immediately stoppered, either with a cork or polyethylene stopper, and the closure held on with a wire netting. It is generally believed that if the sparkling wine is to be kept for sometime before use that cork stoppers are best. Polyethylene stoppers are more permeable to oxygen than cork stoppers. The sugar added to the wine doesn't ferment because yeasts do not multiply easily under the conditions of 11.5–12.5% alcohol and 30 psi or more pressure of carbon dioxide. The wine also contains less nitrogenous constituents at this stage. Therefore, even if some viable yeast cells remain in the bottle after disgorging there is little chance of their multiplying.

The riddling-disgorging process requires considerable hand labor and time and hence is expensive.

As a substitute for this, the contents of the bottles may be transferred under pressure into a tank. The necessary sugar solution is then added, depending on the type, and the wine filtered into bottles and stoppered, usually with polyethylene stoppers. This is called the transfer system. It is obviously much simpler and cheaper than the riddling-disgorging system. Because some air may be introduced during disgorging into the tank or in filtering, or in bottling, some sulfur dioxide is often added.

In the tank process, the finished wine is filtered under iso-barometric pressure into a bottling tank and thence through a membrane filter into the bottle. Because some air is usually introduced during the pumping from tank to tank, and tank to bottle, some sulfur dioxide may be added to prevent oxidation and darkening of the wine. Polyethylene stoppers are normally used.

Carbonated Wines

Very few carbonated wines are produced in this country. This may be because of the prestige of noncarbonated wines which can be called champagne, which carbonated wines cannot. Nevertheless, when the base wine is properly selected and the carbonation carefully performed a creditable product can be produced.

Since no fermentation is required, wines of higher alcohol content are used, 11.5–12.5%. Wines which are fully mature are also preferred. The desired sugar is added to the wine before carbonation. The wine must be brilliant. Some sulfur dioxide (100–150 mg per liter) is added to prevent refermentation. The wine could also be sterile-filtered through a membrane filter prior to carbonation.

For best carbonation it has been shown that deaerated wine should be used. When carefully done, good carbon dioxide retention can be achieved. Cork, polyethylene, or crown cap closurers are used.

M. A. AMERINE

Cross-reference: *Distilled Beverage Spirits.*

WORCESTERSHIRE SAUCE

"Worcestershire Sauce," now a generic term for a type of food condiment, was originally coined in the early 1830's by John Wheeley Lea and William Perrins, partners in a small chain of drug stores in the West Midlands of England, who formulated the original product. Folklore has it that the basic idea for such a sauce originally came from India and was brought back to England by a retiring Governor General.

To be the genuine article it should include vinegar, molasses, sugar, soy, anchovies, tamarinds, eschalots, garlic, onions, and salt. Spices and flavoring are added (type not divulged), and water is added to bring the whole to a specific gravity in the range of 1.130 with total solids of approximately 30% by weight.

The ingredients are then allowed to mature and ferment over a long period of time, with occasional agitation for proper blending. Unless this time element is followed the product will never attain the proper bouquet and flavor.

Once the ingredients have been allowed to mature they are processed by pressing and straining through a mesh screen which allows some of the insoluble solid to pass through. The presence of such insoluble solids is essential to the product although they precipitate and must be redispersed into the liquid by shaking before using. The final product must be pasteurized to stop further fermentation. If this is not done the flavor will deteriorate and become rancid although the sauce itself will not prove harmful.

Properly prepared worcestershire sauce will appear as a very dark, almost black, liquid with about 25% visible sediment of slightly lighter color. When these solids are dispersed throughout the liquid the sauce has a dark brown opaque appearance. The volatile oils of the sauce give off a very aromatic, appetizing scent, and to the taste it is tangy, spicy, and with a slight indication of bitter/sweetness.

Made from all natural products without artificial sweeteners, coloring or other additives, it is a sauce for all seasons and practically all foods. While generally associated with meats and gravies, it is added as a seasoning very effectively to tomato products, soft cheeses, egg dishes, soups, and salad dressing.

W. WALLACE RYAN

Cross-reference: *Flavorings and Essences.*

X

XANTHOPHYLL

Xanthophyll ($C_{40}H_{56}O_2$) which, translated from the Greek, means "yellow leaf" is a yellow crystalline pigment found in green leaves together with chlorophyll. It is related to carotene but has no vitamin A activity. Although xanthophyll is present in green leaves, the yellow color is masked by the chlorophyll. In the autumn, however, the yellow is fully manifested. Xanthophyll occurs in the yolks of eggs, contributing to their color, and is also one of the pigments found in algae.

MARTIN S. PETERSON

Cross-reference: *Carotenoids and Food Technology*.

Y

YEASTS—INDUSTRIAL APPLICATIONS

Yeast, a single-celled plant, is widely distributed over the world. It has been useful to man since prehistoric times, the more familiar uses being as a fermentative agent in beer, ale, and wine and as the leavening agent in bread making.

There is evidence to show that yeast was present in nature 400 million years ago, this on the basis of imprints on fossilized plants dating from the Devonian age. In historic times, there is ample evidence to show that yeast was known and used by the ancient Egyptians, the Greeks, the Romans, and by the Germanic branch of the Indo-European family. The term "yeast," according to the Oxford Dictionary, derives from the Sanskrit word, yás(y) ati, meaning to bubble, boil, or seethe—a reflection, no doubt, of the action of yeast during the fermentation process.

Industrial Applications

The applications of yeast in the food industry are numerous.

Baker's Yeast.—The role of yeast in the baking industry is to leaven bread and related products. Two types of baker's yeast are on the market—compressed, with a moisture content of 70%, and activated dry yeast, containing 7.5% moisture. In the dry form, yeast is not active and must be rehydrated in warm water before the yeast plants will grow. Dry yeast is more stable than compressed and as a consequence found special applicability in World War II in the tropics where bread making with compressed yeast was difficult to control.

Yeast growth in dough produces carbon dioxide gas, a key factor in the development of a light porous texture in baked products. The amount of CO_2 produced is directly proportional to the amount of yeast used.

The baker's yeast industry of today uses molasses as a substrate, an inorganic source of nitrogen, and aeration to prevent the production of alcohol.

Harvesting methods are greatly improved over those used in the last century.

Brewers' Yeast.—This yeast, a by-product of the brewing industry, is high in amino acids and vitamins and in addition to its primary usefulness in the brewing of beer, it has importance in human nutrition and as a source of protein and vitamins in animal feeds. Brewers' yeast derives from strains of *Saccharomyces carlsbergensis*, the strains used in brewing lager beer. Unless debittered, brewers' yeast is bitter to the taste, the source of the bitterness being the hops contained in the wort.

Wine Yeasts.—Strains of *Saccharomyces cerevisiae* are used in making wine. Wines are made from the juices of fruits and berries, and the function of yeast is to convert the sugars of these products into alcohol.

Yeast Production of Alcohol.—Yeast is used in the production of alcohol, molasses and the cereal grains being the substrates commonly employed. Glycerol is also a product of the wine yeasts.

Food and Feed Yeasts.—Torula yeast, more precisely identified as *Candida utilis* (*Torulopsis utilis*) has had some success in human feeding but is produced mainly for inclusion in animal feeds. One limitation of yeast for human feeding is that the sulfur-containing amino acids are present only in low amounts. *Candida utilis* grows well on sulfite waste liquor (which provides a disposal problem for paper mills) and since the yeast is of good quality, a double benefit occurs.

Yeasts in Vitamin Production.—A number of yeasts—brewers' yeast, baker's yeast, and *Candida utilis*—are rich in biotin, choline, folic acid, inositol, nicotinic acid, para-aminobenzoic acid, pantothenic acid, pyroxidine, riboflavin, and thiamin. By irradiation with ultraviolet, the sterols produced by yeast can be converted to calciferol (vitamin D_2).

There are other industrial applications of yeasts, for example yeasts as a source of enzymes (invertase and lactase).

MARTIN S. PETERSON

Reference

PHAFF, H. J., MILLER, M. W., and MRAK, E. M. 1966. The Life of Yeasts. Harvard University Press, Cambridge, Mass.

Cross-reference: *Leaveners and Leavening.*

YEASTS—PRODUCTION TECHNOLOGY, NUTRITIONAL QUALITY, MARKETS[1]

Yeasts Grown on Carbohydrates

Apart from mushrooms the only cells produced as food in significant quantities are yeasts grown on carbohydrates. Cheap carbohydrate sources vary from country to country: In the United States and the United Kingdom they are brewers' wort; in Germany and Central Europe waste sulphite liquors; in France and Spain spent grapes and distillers' solubles; and in South Africa and Taiwan, cane molasses.

The choice of yeast species for a particular substrate depends on the composition of the substrate. *S. cerevisia* grows better than *S. carlsbergensis* at high temperatures and thus can be made to produce cells more rapidly than the other brewing strain. *Saccharomyces fragilis* is utilized where whey is the substrate. *Saccharomyces* strains readily undergo spontaneous mutation during use and it is necessary to maintain a good strain in an unchanged condition by reselecting cells and testing from time to time. The most versatile of these yeasts for general substrates is *Candida utilis* (which was formerly known as Torula and this name is still widely used).

For the production of 100 lb dry yeast substance having 8% nitrogen content the following ingredients are required:

	(Lb)
Molasses	400
Aqueous ammonia	25
Ammonium sulphate	15
Ammonium dihydrogen phosphate	7
Air	75 (cu ft/hr)

The introduction of air into the medium and its control during yeast growth are extremely important in obtaining maximum efficiency. The air must first be sterilized. The actual quantity of oxygen which will be required by the yeast as it grows is fairly closely related to the consumption of the substrate, so that the introduction of air

[1] Reprinted with permission from *Activities Report* Vol. 24, No. 2, 1972.

can be programmed in essentially the same way as the feed of molasses. During the latter part of a feed batch operation the demand of oxygen becomes very high, and its adequate supply, which is governed by the rate of solution of oxygen in the medium, depends on obtaining a very large flow of air bubbles through the liquid. On the other hand, passing very large volumes of air through a liquid demands a high power input and it is therefore highly important to ensure that the largest possible proportion of the oxygen in the bubbles is actually dissolved. In the most commonly used aeration system, perforated pipes placed at the bottom of the vessel introduce the air into the vessel and the motion of the bubbles serves also to agitate and mix the suspension.

European Processing Developments

The following interesting processes for the production of microbial cells (other than yeasts) are currently being developed in Europe.

For the past 4 yr, Rank, Hovis and McDougall have been carrying out a single-cell protein development using a Fusarium mold which is grown on field bean starch. As with yeast production, the fermentation is aerobic and after the fermentation cycle the mold is harvested by centrifuging and is then either extruded as a paste or dried. This mold has some texture, unlike yeast. Its protein content is 65% of which 52% is amino nitrogen. Since Rank, Hovis and McDougall plan to market this as a food protein, the 4% nucleotide content has to be removed by solvent extraction. Estimated production costs are $168 per ton for the product containing the nucleotides and $240 per ton for the product with nucleotides removed. So far, the protein has only been marketed successfully as a meat simulant in pet foods and probably this product will be used mainly in pet foods provided the price level can be reduced.

Tate & Lyle are trying to develop a protein-enriched starch suitable as animal feed. Their starch source is carob bean, indigenous to many Middle Eastern countries. After extraction of the gum Tragacanth, the beans are dehulled, macerated with water, the slurry forming the fermentation medium. The mold *Aspergillus oryzae* is grown on this medium. At the end of the fermentation the entire medium is dried to produce a 3% protein-enriched carob starch. Tate & Lyle intend to construct a 150 ton per year pilot plant for the production of this product in Cyprus.

The Symba process is now under development by the Swedish Sugar Corporation. This involves the two-stage production of yeast on waste potato starch effluent. In the first stage, the starch is hydrolyzed to sugars with amylase enzymes. The

TABLE Y-1

ANNUAL PRODUCTION AND MARKET VALUE OF YEASTS WORLD-WIDE (1971)
(Ton Dry Weight)

	Baker's *Saccharomyces* Yeast	Brewers' *Saccharomyces* Yeast	*Candida* Yeast	*Saccharomyces fragilis* Yeast
United Kingdom	23,000	15,000	—	—
France	21,000	5,000	8,000	800
Germany	20,000	4,000	15,000	—
Hungary	—	—	10,000	—
Rumania	—	—	12,000	—
USSR	—	—	250,000	—
Scandinavia	—	—	10,000	—
Other	Balance	Balance	Balance	
Europe	85,000	40,000	335,000	
United States	60,000	20,000	3,000	
Cuba	—	—	9,000	
South America	6,500	3,000	9,000	
Asia	10,000			
Taiwan			13,500	
Australasia	3,000	3,000		500
South Africa	2,500	1,000	2,000	
Total	167,000	67,000	360,000–400,000	1,300
	of which 100% is for baking	of which 80% is for animal feed and 20% for food	of which 95% is for animal feed and 5% is for food	of which 50% is for animal feed and 50% for food
Avg price per ton	$700	$200 for animal feed / $350 for human food	$200 for animal feed / $350 for human food	$200 for animal feed / $350 for human food
Price volume	$116,900,000	$15,410,000	$83,000,000	$357,000

Total price volume for 635,300 ton yeast: $215,667,000.
Total price volume for approximately 468,300 ton food and feed yeasts (excluding baker's yeast): $98,767,000.

sugars produced then serve as growth medium for *Candida* yeast. The Symba process is an excellent example of effluent treatment combined with producing animal food. In this case, the cost of the starch source is actually a negative value since it is an effluent and its high BOD content would have to be removed prior to disposal. About ½ ton per week of yeast is produced and the Swedish Sugar Corporation is evaluating process economics.

Markets

The total production of yeasts worldwide (1971) is shown in Table Y-1. It is significant to note that major producers of *Candida* yeast are USSR (from wood hydrolysate), Taiwan (from cane molasses), Cuba (from cane molasses), and Rumania (from spent sulphite liquor). In these countries, *Candida* production plants were built during or after World War II in order to supplement the shortage of indigenous protein animal food. The United States

had a much larger production capacity of *Candida* pre-World War II but this has now diminished due to the availability and cheapness of soy meal as protein animal food.

With the increasing legislation against the discharge of whey into streams, it is likely that the production of yeast from these sources will increase in the near future.

Production Costs

At the present (1971) the price for food and feed yeasts from carbohydrate sources appears to be dominated by the availability of large amounts of surplus yeast from breweries. This is available from $200 per ton for feed and $350 per ton for food yeast.

It is rather significant that, in general, *Candida* yeast (from waste sulphite liquor) is sold at the same price range as spent brewer's yeast, i.e., $200 per ton. The production cost of *Candida* yeast can be broken down into the following categories:

	($) per ton
Carbohydrate source	0–30
Other nutrients	53–67
Energy	13–27
Steam	3– 5
Fuel	17–18
Labor	27–33

It should be noted that the cost of the carbohydrate source is the most variable factor—if this is a waste product it can, and often is, costed at zero. In addition, the price fluctuates depending on the size of the plant. The lower price limit applies to a 50 ton per day plant and the upper limit to a 5 ton per day plant.

As mentioned previously, the cheapness and availability of soy meal protein in the United States gives no incentive to produce feed yeast there. On the other hand, the substantial yeast production in Eastern Europe is the result of shortages of other sources of animal food protein such as fish meal. As we shall point out in the next section, yeasts grown on hydrocarbons will be subjected to exactly the same market restrictions.

In summary, profitable production of yeasts for animal feed can be developed using such waste sources as spent sulphite liquor, spent grapes, distillers' solubles, etc., where the cost of the carbohydrate is very low, and provided the plant has a production capacity in excess of 50 tons per day. One major reason why many animal feed yeast plants are unprofitable is due to their inefficient design and small production capacity. Obviously, the petroleum companies who are now producing yeast on hydrocarbons are very conscious of the cost advantages inherent in large production plants.

Yeasts Grown on Hydrocarbons

The production of microbial cells on hydrocarbons has undoubtedly been one of the most important developments in industrial microbiology during the past decade. During the 1960's extensive research and development programs were initiated by many large petroleum companies in the world who were firmly convinced that large-scale production of single-cell protein could be designed and engineered without too many difficulties. However, they generally underestimated the many difficulties involved in this novel interdisciplinary subject. Many basic problems concerning the biochemistry and physiology of microbial reproduction on hydrocarbons were virtually unknown and, as a result, the design of fermentation systems using either crude oils, gas

oil, refined alkanes, or methane, led to many unforeseen complications.

It was soon realized that the real costs for production of yeast on hydrocarbons were not substantially lower than those for yeasts on cheap carbohydrates. Many companies subsequently ceased working in this area so that at present only a relatively small number of successful processes have been developed—notably those of British Petroleum.

Technology.—For the production of yeasts on hydrocarbons, substrates can be either waxy crude oils, gas oils or n-alkanes, usually in the C_{12}–C_{18} range.

One of the major differences between carbohydrate and hydrocarbon fermentations is the relatively low solubility of hydrocarbons in water. Compared with carbohydrate fermentation, three times the volumetric oxygen rate is required to grow yeast on hydrocarbons. Thus, for a given production of yeast the increase in oxygen requirement reduces the output of cells which can be produced per unit time, and this effectually reduces the capacity of the fermenter.

The difference in oxygen requirements in the production of 1 gm of dry cells can be demonstrated by the following:

Carbohydrate $(CH_2O)_n$	2.0 + gm
Oxygen	0.34 gm

compared with

Hydrocarbon (CH_2)	1.00 + gm
Oxygen	0.98 gm

Thus hydrocarbon fermentation will produce $1/3$ as much cells (based on O_2 limitation) than carbohydrate fermentation, and $1/2$ as much hydrocarbon as carbohydrate is required for fermentation.

Hydrocarbon fermentations must operate so as to entrain and disperse the oil phase continually. This has been described as a 3-phase fermentation by some research workers.

At least a 2-stage continuous-fermentation system is required—and some claim the advantages for a 3-stage system. In the 2-stage system, the first stage serves to optimize cell productivity; the second stage serves to optimize substrate utilization and prepare the cells for optimal recovery by minimizing the residual oil content and by concentrating the cells. For the second stage, a more traditional type of fermenter could be used. Hydrocarbon fermentations generate more heat than carbohydrate fermentations and this must be taken into consideration. Recovery costs, which are related to concentration and residual oil content of the two cells, as well as cell productivity and substrate utilization costs, are also important factors.

At the end of the fermentation cycle, the cells (hydrocarbon water emulsions) have to be broken in order to achieve maximum cell recovery. Usually this is carried out in high-speed centrifuges of a nozzle-discharge type. Finally the cells are spray dried.

A wide variety of microorganisms can grow on liquid n-alkanes as the sole carbon and energy source; for example, bacteria such as *Mycobacteria*, *Pseudomonas*, *Nocardia*, *Corynobacterium*, and *Micrococcus*; and yeasts such as *Candida*, *Torulopsis*, *Rhodotorula*, *Pichia*, and *Debaromyces* as well as a wide variety of filamentous fungi.

Methane is an even more difficult medium than liquid hydrocarbon.

During methane fermentations, there is a considerable explosion hazard. This can be reduced, though not eliminated completely, by carefully adjusting certain air/methane gas mixture ratios and incorporation of sophisticated control instrumentation as well as the use of fine emulsions and mechanical foam separation.

Bacteria are the only microorganisms that can utilize methane as a fermentation medium. The mechanism of methane oxidation is not yet understood and experimental results available tend to give conflicting interpretations, particularly in regard to the relation of methane oxidation to other n-alkane oxidation pathways.

Yields and Amino Acid Contents.—In yeasts, lysine and threonine are produced in adequate amounts, whereas methionine and tryptophan are not produced in adequate amounts. In bacteria, on the other hand, lysine and threonine are produced in adequate amounts whereas methionine and tryptophan are not quite at the FAO minimum standards, although the values are better than those obtained with yeasts.

The essential amino acid contents of microbial cell protein is significantly higher than common food proteins with the exception of fish meal.

Microbial Hydrocarbon Projects Worldwide.—Three main hydrocarbon substrates can be used for production of microbial cells: waxy oils, gas oils (1-2 ¢ per lb) and refined n-alkanes (2-4 ¢ per lb). Most companies who are currently involved in development products prefer n-alkanes. However, gas oils due to their cheapness still have an economic attraction. Only one process in Europe uses gas oil as substrate—BP at Lavera, France, who are currently constructing a 16,000 ton per year plant using 10% paraffin containing alkane. The fermenters are of the air-lift type. The

medium requires no sterilization before fermentation. It is claimed that the paraffins are entirely consumed at the end of the fermentation cycle. However, to remove entrained hydrocarbons from the yeast cells, several stages of solvent extraction are necessary.

On the other hand, British Petroleum's (BP) Grangemouth plant which has just been commissioned, produces 4000 tons per year of yeast on n-alkanes. Sterilization of the medium prior to fermentation is necessary, and after the fermentation the yeast is separated from the medium by centrifuging and subsequently dried.

Although originally most interest was shown by companies in producing yeast on waxy crude oils, the pour point improvement of the treated oil achieved by metabolising straight chain compounds has been overrated and increased difficulties have arisen during fermentation and recovery.

Below is a list of worldwide development projects for microbial cells on hydrocarbons.

Czechoslovakia
Czechoslovak Academy of Science, Institute of Microbiology, Prague
> Organism: *Candida* yeast.
> C Substrate: n-alkanes.
> Scale: development plant up to 10,000 liter chemostat.
> Status: process is being evaluated and the yeast tested as feed for chicken and swine. According to latest information problems have been encountered with regard to digestability and protein conversion of feed.

France
Institute Francaise du Petrole, Falaise, France
> Organism: *Candida* yeast.
> C Substrate: gas, oil, and n-alkanes.
> Scale: 7.5 ton per year development plant.
> Status: Still trying to obtain a feasible process.

British Petroleum (BP), Lavera, France
> Organism: *Candida* yeast.
> C Substrate: gas and oil.
> Scale: 16,000 ton per year plant.
> Status: plant now under construction. Eventually the process economics and product will be compared with BP Grangemouth to determine whether to build a large yeast plant using gas, oil, or n-alkanes.

India
Institute Francais du Petrole and Regional Research Laboratory, Assam, India
> Organism: *Candida* yeast.
> C Substrate: n-alkanes.
> Scale: 15 tons per year development.

Status: the product is being test marketed as animal feed.

Japan
  Dainippon Chemical, Tokyo, Japan
    Organism: *Candida* yeast.
    C Substrate: n-alkanes.
    Scale: 20,000 ton per year production plant.
    Status: planning stage at present.
  Kanegafuchi, Kobe, Japan
    Organism: *Candida* yeast.
    C Substrate: n-alkanes.
    Scale: production plant 60,000 tons per year.
    Status: plant under construction and will be on-stream by 1972.
  Kyowa Hakko, Tokyo, Japan
    Organism: *Candida* Yeast.
    C Substrate: n-alkane.
    Scale: 20,000–50,000 ton per year production plant.
    Status: have obtained license for the BP process and their plant is now under construction.
  Mitsui Toatsu, Hokaido, Japan
    Organism: *Candida* yeast.
    C Substrate: n-alkanes.
    Scale: pilot plant.
    Status: large-scale plant is being planned.
    Note: All Japanese hydrocarbon single-cell protein plants are being held in abeyance until government approval has been obtained.

Switzerland
  Nestlé Alimenta, Vevey, Switzerland
    Organism: *Candida* yeasts and bacteria.
    C Substrate: n-alkanes and methane.
    Scale: laboratory fermenters.
    Status: in view of cessation of Esso-Nestlé project in United States, the future of Nestlé's interest in microbial cell production is doubtful.

Taiwan
  Chinese Petroleum Corporation, Taiwan
    Organism: *Pseudomonas*.
    C Substrate: gas and oil.
    Scale: pilot plant—50 Kl chemostat.
    Status: product test marketed as animal feed.

United Kingdom
  British Petroleum (BP), Grangemouth, Scotland
    Organism: *Candida* yeast.
    C Substrate: n-alkanes.
    Scale: 4,000 ton per year development plant using continuous fermentation.
    Status: plant recently commissioned. Product is being test marketed as a feed-grade protein.
  ICI Agricultural Division, Billingham, England
    Organism: *Pseudomonas*.
    C Substrate: originally methane, now methanol since ICI have their proprietary methanol process.
    Scale: laboratory plant using fermenter linked to computer.
    Status: similar difficulties encountered as Shell.
  Shell Research, Sittingbourne, England
    Organism: *Pseudomonas* and *Candida* yeast.
    C Substrate: methane, methanol, hexane, and heptane.
    Scale: pilot plant using 2000-liter continuous fermenters.
    Status: many difficulties have been encountered due to poor strain and low cell density.

United States
  Allied Chemical Corporation, Morristown, New Jersey
    Organism: unknown.
    C Substrate: propane and n-alkanes.
    Scale: laboratory.
    Status: practically abandoned.
  American Oil Company, Whiting, Indiana
    Organism: *Candida* yeast.
    C Substrate: n-alkanes.
    Scale: pilot plant.
    Status: very active, looking to food use for their yeast.
  Esso, New Jersey & Nestlé, New Jersey
    Organism: bacteria and yeasts.
    C Substrate: n-alkanes.
    Scale: large pilot plant.
    Status: latest information is that Esso will withdraw from this project due to unfavorable economics.
  Gulf Oil Corporation, Houston, Texas and Wasco, California
    Organism: *Candida* yeast.
    C Substrate: n-alkanes.
    Scale: 10,000-gal. fermenters.
    Status: maintained at former IMC plant. Abandoned 1970 because of poor economics. Process and plant available for purchase.
  Mobil Oil Company
    Organism: bacteria and yeasts.
    C Substrates: n-alkanes.
    Scale: laboratory.
    Status: not active, interested in selling process.
  Standard Oil of California, Chevron Research, San Francisco
    Organism: *Corynebacterium* species.
    C Substrate: n-alkanes.
    Scale: pilot plant.
    Status: active in 1966, now abandoned.

USSR
  Academy of Sciences, Institute of Microbiology, Moscow
    Organism: *Candida* yeast.

C Substrate: gas, oil, and n-alkanes.

Scale: pilot plant.

Status: many difficulties encountered due to poor strain and inability to achieve proper separation of yeast from hydrocarbons.

Production Costs for Yeast on n-Alkanes

The following is an estimation for a plant producing yeast on n-alkanes in which the fermentation is carried out on a continuous basis in a 1000-gal. continuous fermenter to produce 200 tons per year of yeast. For reasons of efficiency, practically all hydrocarbon fermentation plants at present are continuous and it is reasonable, therefore, to use a continuous system as model. It should be borne in mind that this is really a pilot plant and for the sake of comparison we have made a brief assessment of a 50-ton per day yeast plant.

	$/Ton	Depreciation 20% PA $/Ton	
Capital costs			
Prime cost	134,520	128.2	
Piping, etc.	72,480	68.6	
Instruments	24,000	22.8	
Electricals	9,416	8.9	
			228.5
Operating costs			
Substrate		108.0	
Minerals		48.0	
Vitamins		2.4	
Antifoam		36.0	
Labor		204.0	
Electricity		76.0	
Fuel oil		22.8	
Water		5.0	
Packaging		15.0	
Maintenance		10.0	527.2
			$755.7

This figure is clearly far too high from a production point of view. If we decimate the capital by operating on a 50-ton per day basis, capital costs will be $22.8 per ton and labor costs will be $20.4 per ton, thus giving the following production costs:

	$/Ton
Prime cost	22.8
Medium	194.4
Labor	20.4
Electricity	76.0

Fuel oil	9.6
Water	5.0
Packaging	15.0
	$343.2

These estimated costs for a model plant indicate that yeast can only be produced economically in a large-scale plant of minimum capacity of 50 tons per day and which costs $343 per ton. This is obviously the major reason why the petroleum companies are only operating very large-scale yeast production units. At present, the production costs of yeast on hydrocarbons are considerably higher than $343 per ton. Thus all BP's efforts are now devoted to test marketing of the yeasts from Grangemouth and Lavera to establish that feed compounders are satisfied with the protein quality and consistency. It is interesting to note that these yeasts are deficient in methionine which is, therefore, added as a supplement. The present selling price of BP's yeast is $260 per ton, which is considerably lower than their production cost. Once they have gained consumer acceptance from animal food compounders, BP plans to build a 100,000-ton per year yeast plant. This should enable them to reduce production costs to a sufficient level so that they are able to sell their yeast at $260 per ton and make a reasonable profit.

It is not likely that this large BP plant will be operational before 1976. At that time, however, this novel form of animal feed protein should prove to be a commercial threat to fish meal but not to soybean cake in Europe.

BERNARD WOLNAK

Cross-reference: *Protein Foods from Plant Sources.*

YOGURT

Whether you spell it yogurt, yoghurt, yogourt, or yoghourt, this food is a nutritious fermented milk product consumed in ever-increasing quantities in the United States and Europe.

Generally considered to have been originated by early nomadic herdsman, especially in Asia and Southern and Eastern Europe, the present-day cultured yogurt is related to other fermented products such as acidophilus milk, cultured buttermilk, koumiss, and kefir.

Today, yogurt is available in a number of different styles, with or without added flavors, and in a number of different size packages. Most workers in the field agree yogurt is the product produced by the fermentation of milk by the microorganisms, *Streptococcus thermophilus* and *Lactobacillus Bulgaricus*. Milk, usually cow's milk, is the principal ingredient. The first step is to prepare a mix from milk and other ingredients. It is common practice to partially skim this milk to a butterfat content of from 1-2% by weight, although a limited quantity of whole milk yogurt is offered for sale. Additional solids may be added to the mix in the form of nonfat dry milk, lactose, sodium caseinate, etc., to produce a solids-non-fat content of approximately 10-15%. These added solids build body and improve consumer acceptance.

The milk must be of a particularly high quality. Screening tests must be used by the manufacturer to prevent the use of milk and or other ingredients which may contain residual antibiotics or other bacteriostatic materials to which the yogurt cultures are extremely sensitive. Good finished product quality demands close control of the composition of the mix. Where legislation permits, stabilizers, rennet, gelatin, calcium (in the form of caseinates, lactates, gluconates, etc.), carrageenan, and other edible materials may also be used to build body. Their use is also dependent upon the style of yogurt to be produced. Although sucrose is not normally used in plain yogurt, it is used in flavored yogurts as a sweetening agent (4-6%). Preserved or cooked fruit is the most frequently-used flavoring.

After the composition of the mix has been standardized, it is clarified, pasteurized, and homogenized. Clarification removes unwanted sediment, undissolved powder, leucocytes, and epithelial cells. Pasteurization is usually batch style at between 70°-90°C for holding times of between 5 and 45 min. Some success has been achieved with continuous pasteurization, particularly where stabilizers and/or binding agents may be used.

The methods of addition of the culture to the mix and the type of processing after innoculation determine the style of yogurt to be produced. Frozen yogurt cultures which can be added directly to the mix without elaborate transfer procedures are becoming increasingly popular. Their use eliminates a number of microbiological problems associated with conventional culture transfer procedures.

There are two basic types of finished yogurt.

(1) "Set-type," sometimes called sundae style or fruit-on-the-bottom. This type is produced by adding the yogurt culture (level of inoculation is dependent upon a number of factors but is usually 4-6%) to the pasteurized, homogenized mix which has been cooled to the correct incubation temperature (43°-49°C), immediately filling this mixture into the container in which the yogurt is to be sold (with the fruit already on the bottom if required), holding these containers in hot rooms or

tunnels to develop the coagulum, and cooling rapidly to control the final titratable acidity (1.2-1.5%, depending upon total solids of mix).

(2) "Stirred-type," sometimes called Swiss style or parfait style. This type is produced by adding the yogurt culture to the pasteurized, homogenized mix which has been cooled to the correct incubation temperature, holding this mix in a suitable vat to allow the coagulum to develop (1.5-2.5 hr), breaking the coagulum, and cooling through a plate or other suitable device to reduce the temperature and control the acidity, adding fruit if required, and blending together to produce a relatively homogeneous product.

Variations of the set-type yogurt include plain, fruit-on-the-bottom with plain on top, and fruit-on-the-bottom with colored and/or flavored yogurt on top (so-called California style). Variations of the stirred-type include plain, flavored with fruit particles suspended in the coagulum, and fruit-on-the-bottom with stirred type plain and/or flavored yogurt on top.

A recent survey of a large U.S. food market indicated 15 different flavors offered for sale. Fruit flavors predominated with strawberry, raspberry, blueberry, and cherry among the more popular varieties. Distribution from the factories to stores is usually in refrigerated vehicles at temperatures not above 10°C. Shelf-life varies from 14 to 28 days depending upon plant sanitation, processing techniques, type of package, distribution temperatures, and the use of preservatives, if allowed.

Glass, waxed paperboard, plastic-coated paperboard, and plastic are the principal packaging materials used. Choice of material is dependent upon consumer acceptance, anticipated shelf-life, and cost factors. Principal size in the United States are 5- and 8-oz units. A limited number of 16- and 32-oz units are also produced. In Europe, the principal sizes are 100, 150, 180, and 500 gm packages.

Careful examination of the finished product is the basis for consistent quality. Firmness, consistency, flavor and aroma are generally considered to be the most important characteristics.

Firmness and Consistency.—The texture should be smooth and fine without lumpiness or powderiness. No whey seperations should be evident. The body should be firm but not gelatinous.

Flavor and Aroma.—The aroma and flavor of yogurt are distinctive and unique. No bitter or unclean flavors should be present. The acid levels should not be overpowering. It is felt that a balance of 1:1 of rods and cocci bacteria will promote optimum flavor at proper acid levels.

Although no theraputic claims can be made for

food products, a number of researchers have maintained that health-promoting properties of yogurt cannot be disregarded. The organisms in yogurt allegedly establish themselves in the lower portion of the gastro-intestinal tract to the exclusion of certain putrifactive bacteria. Others have discussed the importance of yogurt after antibiotic therapy in helping re-establish intestinal flora. A number of factors have contributed to a substantial increase in yogurt consumption in the last decade. Probably foremost was the introduction of flavors. Also important were improved methods of production, better packages, and improved distribution methods.

Using the production figures of the States of California and New York as a basis for growth comparison, sales increased from 23,000,000 lb in 1959 to 112,000,000 lb in 1969.

Other information on yogurt properties and manufacturing are given in the references.

ROBERT G. CHRISTIE

References

HUMPHREYS, C. L., and PLUNKETT, M. 1969. Dairy Sci. Abstr. *31*, 609.
KURMAN, J. A. 1967. Le Lait *47*, 267, 415.

Cross-reference: *Market Milk Industry*.

Z

ZERO MILK

Zero milk is the term used to designate milk produced on synthetic, protein-free feed, using urea and ammonium salts as the nitrogen source. This is a development for which Arrturi I. Virtanen, Director of the Biochemical Research Institute, Helsinki, Finland, received the Nobel Prize. Zero milk has much the same composition as milk produced on normal feed. The average fat content varies from 4.5 to 6.3% and the protein content from 3.2 to 4.3%. The sugar content varies from 4.4 to 4.7%. The fat and protein content of milk from normal feed is somewhat lower than that of zero milk, and the sugar content (lactose) somewhat higher. The amino acid content of zero milk is not essentially different from that of the milk proteins in milk derived from normal feeds.

The value of zero milk lies in the fact that in many regions of the earth proteins come almost exclusively from cereals, proteins that unfortunately may lack one or more of the essential amino acids; zero milk produced from a protein-free synthetic diet (for example, feeds containing dried sugar beet pulp, hydrolyzed hemicellulose from wood wastes) contains all of the essential amino acids, thus offering the possibility that a protein of high quality can be made available anywhere in the world.

MARTIN S. PETERSON

Reference

VIRTANEN, A. I. 1967. Milk production on a protein-free and protein-poor feed. Neth. Milk Dairy J. *21*, 223–244. Eng.

Index

NOTES

NOTES

NOTES